A DICTIONARY OF TURKISH VERBS
In Context and by Theme

Örnekli ve Tematik
Türkçe Fiiller Sözlüğü

A DICTIONARY OF TURKISH VERBS
In Context and by Theme

Örnekli ve Tematik
Türkçe Fiiller Sözlüğü

by

Ralph Jaeckel and Gülnur Doğanata Erciyeş
With the collaboration of Mehmet Süreyya Er

Georgetown University Press
Washington, D.C.

In memory of my mother
Hilde Jaeckel 1905-1992

As of January 1, 2007, 13-digit ISBN numbers will replace the current 10-digit system.
Paperback: 978-1-58901-057-4

Georgetown University Press, Washington, D.C.

Selected category & subcategory names and numbers from Synopsis of Categories from *Roget's International Thesaurus,* 5th Edition by Peter Mark Roget and edited by Robert L. Chapman.

Library of Congress Cataloging-in-Publication Data

Jaeckel, Ralph.
  A dictionary of Turkish verbs : in context and by theme / Ralph Jaeckel and Gulna Doæganata Erciyes ; with the collaboration of Mehmet Süreyya Er.
      p. cm.
   ISBN 1-58901-057-4 (alk. paper)
  1. Turkish language--Verb--Dictionaries--English. I. Erciyes, Gulna Doæganata. II. Title.
  PL161.J34 2005
  494'.35321--dc22
                                2004061778

13 12 11 10 09 08 07 06   9 8 7 6 5 4 3 2
First printing

Printed in the United States of America

Here is the key.
It is for you to turn.
Take up the challenge
and
Open the door.

CONTENTS

ACKNOWLEDGMENTS

In the late 1980s and early 1990s a committee of the American Association of Teachers of Turkic Languages [AATT] held a series of meetings that produced the Provisional Guidelines for Turkish [1995] and the corresponding Language Learning Framework [1995]. The issues raised and the calls for instructional materials that emerged from those stimulating sessions largely inspired the creation of this dictionary. We are indebted to the agencies that sponsored the meetings.

For his thorough revision of the Turkish examples of the **Turkish-English Dictionary of Verbs** and for providing many additional examples, we especially wish to thank our collaborator M. Süreyya Er, a Ph.D. candidate at UCLA and lecturer in modern Turkish at the University of Michigan, who has also served as our Turkish language editor.

For checking a late draft of the Turkish of Part 1, we thank Ismail Acar, assistant professor of Islamic law, Dokuz Eylül University, Izmir; Derya Er, English instructor, Özel Mavigün Anadolu Lisesi, Istanbul; and Çiğdem Atakuman Eissenstat. For editorial consultation on the English of the entries and on various aspects of the structure of this book, we are indebted to Leyla Ezdinli. For many helpful suggestions we are grateful to William C. Hickman.

For his assistance in the early stages of preparing this volume, we are indebted most of all to Abdurrahman Tanrıöğen, Pamukkale University, Department of Education [Pamukkale Üniversitesi Eğitim Fakültesi], Denizli, Turkey. For many helpful comments, numerous corrections, and suggestions for additional entries in an early draft, we also wish to thank Kurtuluş Öztopçu, University of California, Berkeley and Los Angeles; Robert Dankoff, University of Chicago; and Tuba Zafer, at that time of Los Angeles, now of Istanbul; and Çiğdem Atakuman Eissenstat. For correcting our English and tracking down inconsistencies in an earlier version, we are in debt to Ada Shissler, University of Chicago. For valuable suggestions on the introduction, we thank Jala Garibova, Western University, Baku, Azerbaijan. For his assistance with computer matters and questions of format, we owe a special debt of gratitude to James T. Maccaferri, Clarion University of Pennsylvania.

The authors, of course, assume the responsibility for all decisions regarding method of presentation, entry selection, entry content, translations, and for the errors that invariably remain in such a complex work. We invite suggestions for corrections and improvements in all these areas.

For encouraging us to produce instructional materials to support Turkish studies in the United States, we wish to express our appreciation to András J. E. Bodrogligeti, UCLA. For providing certain facilities, we owe a debt of gratitude to Antonio Loprieno, former chair, Department of Near Eastern Languages and Cultures, UCLA, and to William M. Schniedewind, current chair. We are also indebted to Irene Bierman and the late Georges Sabah, past directors of the Gustave E. von Grunebaum Center for Near Eastern Studies, and to the late Russell N. Campbell, past director of the Language Resource Program. Their efforts to promote innovative language teaching at UCLA inspired us throughout the course of our work. We also wish to thank the Institute of Turkish Studies for a travel grant that permitted preliminary consultations in Turkey in 1989. For access to instructional materials, we thank Ray Clifford, chancellor, Defense Language Institute. The funding for this project, however, was provided primarily by Ralph Jaeckel.

INTRODUCTION

A General Description of This Book

A Dictionary of Turkish Verbs: In Context and by Theme is designed for all students of Turkish, but particularly for those whose native language is English. Its main purpose is to help students express themselves in Turkish rather than to serve as a reference tool for Turkish to English translation. We hope this book will meet an urgent need for a basic reference tool geared to the requirements of beginning, intermediate, and advanced students. We hope that it will serve as an effective self-teaching tool, increase student exposure to Turkish outside the classroom, and further the goals of proficiency-based instruction. It is also intended to facilitate the work of teachers of Turkish and of anyone preparing materials for teaching this intriguing language.

A Turkish verb stem with its various suffixes of mode, tense, person, and so on, may be the equivalent of a whole English sentence. Additional elements such as subjects and objects are usually placed in front of this basic unit. Thus, one may regard the Turkish verb as the core of the Turkish utterance and as a starting point for its study. For students of Turkish, the correct use of Turkish verbs is the greatest hurdle to linguistic and cultural mastery, but standard dictionaries don't usually provide enough practical, contextualized examples to help them. This dictionary seeks to fill that void in practical, instructional tools.

In selecting approximately 1000 key verbs considered critical to social interaction and cultural understanding, we adopted the "communicative" or "functional-notional" approach, broadly conceived. This means that we attempted to determine the situations that students of Turkish would want to participate in, the different functions that they would want to perform in them, and the ideas that they would want to express. We focused first on situations closest to their personal lives and then extended our net outward to the world beyond. We selected the verbs essential for dealing with these situations at a relatively high level of proficiency and compiled the related grammatical and cultural information required to use the verbs effectively. Just as we limited the number of entry verbs, we also restricted the number of definitions under each entry to those we felt were most important. Each definition is illustrated with examples whose main purpose is to serve as useful pattern sentences rather than as mere illustrations of meaning. In addition to the approximately 1000 entry verbs, the Turkish examples contain additional Turkish verbs and many other forms of speech, making the total Turkish word count of this dictionary well beyond 1000.

This book emphasizes colloquial, everyday speech and provides up-to-date Turkish vocabulary in a form that expresses basic needs and wishes in the most common situations in any Turkish-speaking environment. It includes considerably more verbs than students would learn to use actively in the first two years of regular university study.

A unique feature of this book is that it contrasts English and Turkish means of expression wherever our teaching experience has shown that confusion and errors arise. It also steers students away from modes of expression that are unnatural to a Turk but that are likely to be produced by an English speaker proceeding by analogy to English. Another distinctive feature of this work is that most verbs are cross-referenced to synonyms, antonyms, related verbs, and even to broader themes or categories of meaning. In this way this book is a vocabulary builder and introduces students to the fascinating, complex web of the Turkish linguistic imagination.

How to Use This Book

• To find the common uses of a Turkish verb, use this book exactly as you would any Turkish-English dictionary.

• To find the most suitable Turkish equivalent of an English verb, locate the English verb in the **English-Turkish Index**, select the appropriate Turkish verb, and then, for more extensive information on its use, look it up in the **Turkish-English Dictionary of Verbs**.

• To find different Turkish verbs that express a concept or theme, either:

> • go to the **English-Turkish Index**, find the English verb that most closely expresses that concept, note the theme numbers at the end of the index entry, and then locate those numbers in **3.3, Turkish Verbs Classified by Theme**,

> OR

> • go to **3.1, Theme Names in Alphabetical Order**, find the theme name, note the number following the name, and then locate that number in **3.3, Turkish Verbs Classified by Theme**.

• To find a proverb included in the dictionary, look it up by the first word of the proverb in **Proverbs in the Turkish-English Dictionary of Verbs**.

> • To find other examples for the verbs in a proverb, look up the verbs underlined in the proverb as it appears in **Proverbs in the Turkish-English Dictionary of Verbs**.

The following provides detailed information on each section of this book.

A Description of the Main Sections of This Book

PART 1. TURKISH-ENGLISH DICTIONARY OF VERBS

How the Entries Are Presented

This dictionary shows verbs as they function with their collocations and in the extended structures in which they commonly occur. Since correct use of a verb involves knowledge of its meaning, of its relationship to other words, and of the setting in which it is used, entries always include information in the areas of lexicography, grammar, and usage.

The grammatical and structural information will help native speakers of English overcome the difficulties they are likely to encounter when learning Turkish. To natural translations, we have often added not entirely natural literal ones to clarify Turkish grammar. This information will serve to aid memory and will encourage users to go beyond understanding to produce similar sentences of their own. When the examples with their translations alone may not suffice to draw attention to the difficulties involved, we have added comments and explanations.

Sample Entry

{tekrar et- [eDer]/<u>tekrarla-</u> [r]} '- repeat' [A. tekrar (. -) 'repetition, repeating' + verb-forming suf. -lA]: * **Anla.YAMA.dım.** * **Lütfen {tekrar eder misiniz/tekrarlar mısınız}?** 'I didn't [lit., COULDN'T] understand. * Would you please repeat what you said?' • In the situation above, the negative potential, i.e., **Anla.YAMA.dım**, is usually preferred to the simple negative past, i.e., **AnlaMADIM.** 'I DIDN'T understand.' The former indicates that an effort to understand has been made. • The English verb '- repeat' usually requires an object, i.e., what you said. **Söylediklerinizi duy.AMA.dım. Tekrar eder misiniz lütfen?** 'I didn't [lit., COULDN'T] hear what you said. Would you please repeat?' * **Ne söylediğ.iniz.i kaçırdım.** * **Lütfen tekrar eder misiniz?** 'I {missed/couldn't catch} what you said. Would you please repeat {it?/what you said?}' *848:7.* repetition: - repeat.

1. The Headword Unit
The headword unit is all the elements of an entry preceding the examples of the entry verb.

1.1 The Form of Entry Verbs
Verb stems followed by an attached hyphen [**aldat**-] rather than complete infinitives [**aldatmak**] appear as entries and are alphabetized accordingly. Thus, **aldat**- precedes rather than follows **aldatıl**-. This arrangement focuses attention on the essence of the verb, keeps closely related forms grouped alphabetically, and saves space. In definitions, a hyphen substitutes for 'to.' Thus, 'to go' is shown as '- go.'

1.2 Verb Entries Consisting of More than One Verb
Some entries consist of two or more verbs enclosed in curly parentheses and separated by a slash:

> {tekrar et- [eDer]/<u>tekrarla- [r]</u>} '- repeat.'

These verbs are such close synonyms in current Turkish that we present them as a single entry. Sometimes, as in the case above, both verbs are based on the same form. Sometimes their forms differ:

> {ertelen- [ir]/**tehir edil**- [ir]} '- be postponed, delayed, put off.'

In multiple entries, the first verb is usually the most common. Those that follow, if based on an Arabic noun, are also more formal, as in the case of **tehir edil**- here. All the verbs in the multiple-entry unit are usually appropriate in all the examples that follow. When they are not, as in the case of certain proverbs and set expressions, only the appropriate verb appears in the example.

1.3 The Placement of Entry Verbs and Subentries
To highlight structural similarities, entry verbs appear in alphabetical order word-by-word rather than letter-by-letter. Thus, the entry **ad koy**- is followed in sequence by **ad tak**-, **adlandır**-, and **adlandırıl**- rather than by **adlandır**-, **adlandırıl**-, **ad tak**-.

A Turkish verb consisting of several parts [**perhiz yap**-] or a longer collocation [**Allah rahatlık versin**] is defined under the last element, that is, under the verb. This means that **perhiz yap**- is defined under **yap**- and **Allah rahatlık versin** under **ver**-. However, when that final element is **et**- [**teşekkür et**-], **eyle**- [**rahmet eyle**-], or **kıl**- [**namaz kıl**-], the construction is defined under the next-to-last part [i.e., under **teşekkür, rahmet, namaz**].

A phrase or collocation that appears within an entry [e.g., **akıl al**-, which is defined within the entry **al**- 1] also appears in the main alphabetical listing by first word [i.e., **akıl al**- also appears flush left after the main entry **ak**-]. In the main alphabetical listing it is not defined but is cross-referenced to the meaning of the verb under which it is defined (i.e., to **al**- 1). Thus, following the main entry **ak**-, one under the other, are **akıl al**-. → **al**- 1, **akıl ver**-. → **ver**- 1, **akılda kal**-. → **kal**- 1, and **akıldan çık**-. → **çık**- 1. Such a listing places all such elements beginning with the same letter together and enables students to find any phrase or collocation by first word.

1.4 Elementary-Level Verbs Underlined

An underlined entry verb represents one of the 176 verbs on the Provisional Elementary Level Turkish Vocabulary List of the American Association of Teachers of Turkic Languages [AATT], version 0.2, 1995. The AATT list was compiled from word lists that teachers of Turkish used in their introductory courses.

1.5 The Aorist Form of Entry Verbs

The entry verb is followed, in brackets, by the third-person singular form of the aorist tense. This means that a verb stem ending in a vowel is always followed by a bracketed **r**: **oku-** [r], indicating that the third-person singular aorist form of **oku-** is **okur**.

A verb stem ending in a consonant is followed by the aorist third-person singular suffix formed according to the following rules: Monosyllabic verb stems usually take **-Er**: **bak-** [ar]. The exceptions are thirteen monosyllabic stems that take **-Ir**: **al-** [IR]. Polysyllabic and all derived stems take **-Ir**: **çalış-** [Ir]. The irregular forms are shown in uppercase letters. Such marking will serve as a reminder to students and help them produce the correct forms automatically.

In the entry **git-** [giDer] and in all entries involving **et-** [eDer]: **teşekkür et-** [eDer], uppercase letters remind students of the **t** to **d** change these verbs require.

1.6 Cases Entry Verbs Require

The aorist form is followed, within slashes, by letters indicating the case suffixes the verb requires. The case suffixes appear as shown below, where the use of each suffix is briefly described. For more detailed information on the cases, see a standard grammar such as Göksel and Kerslake [2005] or Lewis [2000]. As is standard practice in some Turkish grammars, in this book uppercase letters represent sounds that vary according to the rules of vowel or consonant harmony, lowercase letters represent those that do not:

A represents the dative case, that is, the letters {[y]a/[y]e}, the **y** being used after a vowel. This suffix occurs on a noun indicating destination, goal, or purpose and is usually translated with 'to', sometimes with 'for': **Ankara'yA gitti.** 'He went TO Ankara.'; **Sizi görmey.E geldik.** 'We came TO see you.'; **Yangında ölen insanlar.A çok acıdım.** 'I felt very sorry FOR the people that perished in the fire.' Other translations of this suffix may also be appropriate.

DA represents the locative case, that is, the letters {da/de/ta/te}. This suffix occurs on a noun indicating position and is usually translated with 'at', 'in', or 'on': **Şimdi Ankara'DA.** 'He is IN Ankara now.'

DAn represents the ablative case, that is, the letters {dan/den/tan/ten}. This suffix occurs on a noun indicating source, origin, or cause and is usually translated with 'from': **Ankara'DAN dönüyor.** 'He is returning FROM Ankara.' Other translations of this suffix may also be appropriate.

I represents the accusative case, that is, the letters {[y]ı/[y]i/[y]u/[y]ü}, the **y** being used after a vowel. This suffix marks a direct noun object as definite, generic, or specific and is often translated with 'the': **Kitab.I masadan aldı.** 'He took THE book from the table.' Sometimes it is not translated: **Ankara'yI gezdi.** 'He toured θ Ankara.' In the English of the last sentence, the symbol θ calls attention to the fact that the English has no separate element corresponding to the Turkish accusative suffix **-yI**.

In this dictionary the accusative case suffix is shown in a headword unit after an entry verb only where students might have difficulty with its use. It is shown, for example, with the verb **bekle-** '- wait', since students expect the dative case to match the English preposition 'for'. The accusative case may also be shown after an entry verb that may take more than one case.

In most of the example sentences above, there are fairly clear, one-to-one correspondences between the case suffixes and English prepositions and articles. However some Turkish verbs require case suffixes different from what those correspondences might suggest, causing students difficulty. The following example of an entry verb shows how this dictionary can help them.

<u>gir-</u> [er] /**A**, **DAn**/ '- enter /θ, {THROUGH/BY WAY OF}/, - go /{IN/INTO}, {THROUGH/BY WAY OF}/'

In the example above, note the Turkish case suffixes in slashes following the aorist suffix; note also the English corresponding to these case suffxes, also in slashes, in the definition. A comma separates the Turkish suffixes and also the corresponding elements in the English. Curley brackets enclose possible choices. In the example, the dative case suffix **A**, the first suffix in slashes, either a) has no separate English equivalent, no preposition, i.e., is θ, with the verb '- enter' or b) is translated with the prepositions 'in' or 'into' with the verb '- go.' The ablative case suffix **DAn**, the second suffix in slashes, has the English equivalent preposition 'through' or the prepositional phrase 'by way of' rather than 'from' with both verbs. These correspondences are important for students to note when translating from English into Turkish.

In this dictionary, both at the beginning of the entry and in the examples, potential problems are highlighted. Case suffixes that a native English speaker might omit or get wrong are indicated as follows: The Turkish suffix, in slashes, is in bold; the corresponding English translation of the case suffix, also in slashes, is in uppercase letters; the symbol θ indicates that the English has no separate element to correspond to the Turkish.

1.7 Postpositions and Other Elements Associated with Entry Verbs
Also within slashes after the entry verb are some of the main postpositions, phrases, and so on, that commonly occur with the verb, such as **lA**, **A dair**, **diye**, **DAn dolayı**, **DIğI için**, **nedeniyle**, **olarak**, **için**, **yüzünden**, etc.

1.8 Definitions of Entry Verbs
Each verb is followed by its most common conversational meanings, which are usually given in order from most to least common. The numbers of definitions of main entry verbs appear without parentheses: **1**. The numbers of definitions of subentries appear within parentheses: **(1)**.

1.9 Composition of Entry Verbs
Many entries include, in brackets, brief notes on how the entry verbs are formed. Components of verb phrases are presented and defined in brackets. Nouns of Turkish origin in verb phrases are left unmarked. Below, for example, the noun **yardım** is of Turkish origin.

yardım et- [eDer] /**A**/ '- help /θ/, - assist /θ/' [**yardım** 'help, assistance']

Nouns of non-Turkish origin are preceded by an abbreviation indicating the language of origin. Below, the uppercase letter 'A' indicates that **acele** comes from the Arabic.

acele et- [eDer] /için/ '- hurry /in order to/' [A. **acele** 'haste']

An adjective may also be a component of an entry verb:

acık- [ır] '- be or - become hungry' [**aç** 'hungry' + verb-forming suf. **-Ik**]

Notes on the suffixes used to form the verb are also found in brackets, as in the following example:

açıkla- [r] [açık 'open, clear' + verb-forming suf. -lA] 1 /A/ '- explain sth /to/ sb, - clarify sth /FOR/ sb'

The passive, reflexive, reciprocal, or causative form of a verb is always shown as deriving from a simpler form:

acıt- [ır] '- hurt, - cause pain to' [acı- + caus. suf. -t]

The symbol -θ indicates that the verb is formed without the addition of any suffix:

acı- [r] [acı 'pain, ache' + verb-forming suf. -θ] 1 '- hurt, - feel sore'

Because the same suffixes recur with different verbs, after using this dictionary for only a short time, students will often be able to guess the meaning of a verb they have never encountered. For more information on such suffixes and additional examples of each suffix, see **Part 5: Turkish Verb-Forming Suffixes**.

1.10 Pronunciation of Entry Verbs
Some entry verbs include a noun of non-Turkish, usually of Arabic or Persian origin, the standard Turkish pronunciation of which is not reflected in standard Turkish orthography [e.g., **tarif et-** '- describe sb or sth /to/']. To help readers pronounce these verbs correctly, the standard Turkish pronunciation of the noun is indicated in parentheses, with dots for short vowels and hyphens for long ones. For example: A. **tarif** (- .) 'description'.

Again, the letter 'A' indicates that the noun is Arabic. The following noun is in the form it has in Turkish. The hyphen and dot in parentheses show the standard Turkish pronunciation as **târif**, with the long 'a', not **tarif** as the Turkish orthography would suggest, nor **ta'riif**, its Arabic pronunciation. Note that the originally non-Turkish noun is followed by its standard Turkish pronuncaition, not by its pronunciation in its language of origin. Our source for modern Turkish pronunciation is *Türkçe Sözlük* [1988].

Indication of Spoken Forms that Differ from Written Ones
This dictionary indicates certain standard written forms together with their usual spoken forms. Thus, with **sıhhatler olsun** ['May you enjoy good health., Good health to you.'], we give the common pronunciation **sâtler olsun**, the translation of which, i.e., 'Let hours be', is however completely irrelevant in this context. With **Allaha ısmarladık** ['Goodbye.'], we give the common pronunciation **Alâısmarladık**.

1.11 Adjectives Associated with Entry Verbs
Frequently the last item in the headword unit, the item preceding the examples, is the adjective related semantically, and usually structurally, to the verb:

evlen- [ir] /lA/ '- get married /TO/, - marry /θ/' [ev 'house' + verb-forming suf. -lAn. ADJ. **evli** 'married']

2. The Examples

2.1 Various Forms of Entry Verbs
An entry often includes noun and participle forms of the verb as well as the infinitive and the finite form. Thus, the entry for the verb **gül-** ['- laugh'] includes the participle **gülen**: Çok gülen çok ağlar. 'He who laughs much weeps much.'

2.2 Basic Sentence Patterns Included
Each entry contains enough basic sentence patterns to permit readers to find examples of sentences expressing thoughts we think they are likely to want to express with the verb. A particularly difficult pattern usually has more than one example. We have provided only

examples useful to memorize, athough an entry may include both simple and complex examples.

We assume readers have a basic knowledge of Turkish grammar. Teaching experience tells us, however, that intermediate and even advanced students still have difficulty with certain sentence patterns such as those involving the Turkish equivalents of English noun clauses. In such sentences we therefore frequently separate basic units of meaning [morphemes] from base words with a period. Under **söyle-** ['- say, tell'], the example appears as follows: **Şimdi size ne yapma.nız gerektiğ.i.ni söyleyeceğim.** 'Now I am going to tell you what you have to do.' The periods separate the suffixes required on the verbal forms in the Turkish equivalent [**ne yapma.nız gerektiğ.i.ni**] of the English noun clause ['what you have to do'].

In spoken Turkish, as in spoken English, the passive is not uncommon, but it is not used frequently with an agent noun. For this reason, in examples with the passive, we often put the agent noun together with {**tarafından/CA**} ['by'] in brackets. Thus, the entry **aldatıl-** has the following example: **Eyvah, bu yüzük altın değilmiş. [Kuyumcu tarafından] Aldatıldım.** 'O dear, it seems this ring is not gold. I've been cheated [by the jeweler].' In some cases {**tarafından/CA**} appears after the passive entry verb to indicate possible use but does not appear in the examples at all. **Tarafından** is usually used with an animate agent; the suffix **CA** occurs in more formal contexts with an offical agent: a government office, a ministry, or other organization.

2.3 Examples in Context

When possible, entry verbs are embedded in longer examples, from phrases to dialogues with enough exchanges to complete the conversation naturally. In dialogues in question-answer form, **S** stands for **soru** 'question', **C**, for **cevap** 'answer'. Multiple responses to a single question are numbered **C1, C2**, where **C1** is the first response, **C2**, the second, and so on. In the corresponding English, Q stands for question, A for answer. The entry **acık-** has:

> **S: Karn.IN acıktı mı?** 'Q: Are YOU hungry?' **C1: Evet, [karn.IM] acıktı.** 'A1: Yes, I am.' **C2: Hayır, [karn.IM] acıkmadı.** 'A2: No, I'm not.'

In dialogues not in question-answer form, **A** indicates the first speaker, **B**, the second, and so on. In the corresponding English, A and B play the same role. The entry **eksik ol-** has:

> **A: Annem aniden hastalanıp öldü.** 'A: My mother suddenly became ill and died.' **B: Başınız sağ olsun.** 'B: My sincere condolences.' **A1: Siz de sağolun, eksik olmayın.** 'A1: May you too be healthy! Thank you.' or **A2: Eksik olmayın, dostlar sağ olsun.** 'A2: Thank you. May [our] friends be healthy.'

Above, the first **A**, with no following number, marks the first entrance of the speaker; **A1** and **A2** mark his return with two possible responses to **B**.

Sometimes an example appears in a short set of sentences depicting states or activities likely to occur together. The entry **uzan-** has:

> **Engin eve geldiğinde çok yorgundu. Üzerini değiştirmeden yatağına uzandı.** 'When Engin came home, he was very tired. He stretched out on his bed without changing his clothes.'

Sometimes a short descriptive phrase provides the setting for an example. Under **benze-**, the example is briefly introduced:

In an ad for a product: * **Benzerler.İ.nE benzemez.** 'There is nothing else like it [lit., It doesn't resemble those similar to it].'

In each example we have attempted to use only the most common, useful Turkish words.

2.4 Notes on Grammar Where Required

Occasionally grammar notes clarify examples. The entry **gör-** ['- see'] has the following dialogue: **S: Görüyor musun? Benzinci tam köşede.** 'Q: Do you see [it]? The gas station is right [there] on the corner.' **C: Evet, görüyorum.** 'A: Yes, I see it.' A note on the tenses in the Turkish and the English follows: • For present time, with verbs of thinking, perception, feeling, etc., Turkish usually has the present continuous tense, i.e., **-iyor**, while English usually has the simple present tense, as above. In such notes we usually employ the grammatical terminology traditionally used for Turkish grammar in such grammars as Göksel and Kerslake [2005] or Lewis [2000].

2.5 Common Collocations

Examples include the nouns or other parts of speech commonly associated with a verb, particularly when they are limited. Under **din-** ['- cease, - stop'], for example, we note that this verb is used with a rather limited set of subjects and provide the appropriate choices between curly parentheses: Nouns of weather: **{a: Rüzgâr/b: Yağmur/c: Kar/d: Dolu/e: Fırtına} dindi.** 'The {a: wind/b: rain/c: snow/d: hail/e: storm} has stopped.' Nouns of physical or mental pain: **Kocası öldüğünden beri {a: acı.sı/b: gözyaşlar.ı} dinmiyor.** '{a: She hasn't stopped grieving [lit., her sorrow hasn't ceased]/b: She hasn't stopped weeping [lit., her tears haven't stopped]} since her husband died.'

2.6 Useful Substitutions

Sometimes curly parentheses enclose a set of common, useful substitutions. In the entry **tanıştır-** ['- introduce'], the example includes several nouns designating people that readers may be called upon to introduce:

Tanıştırayım: {a: annem/b: babam/c: kardeşim Nur/d: öğretmenim Aysel hanım [family name: **Çelik]/e: eşim Selma/f: patronum Selim bey** [family name: **Şimşek]}.** 'A: Let me introduce: {a: my mother/b: my father/c: my younger brother Nur/d: my teacher Miss [or {Mrs./Ms.}] Çelik/e: my wife Selma/f: my boss Selim Şimşek}.'

2.7 Common Equivalent Expressions

Occasionally we indicate how a notion expressed with one verb is also commonly expressed with another or in another way. Under the verb **bil-** ['- know'], following the sentence **Türkçe biliyor.** 'He knows Turkish.', is the very common equivalent **Türkçe'si var.**

2.8 Attention to Corresponding Elements

Sometimes curly parentheses simply call attention to the relationship between the Turkish and the corresponding English. The following example shows that the Turkish **affedersiniz** has two English equivalents: **A: {Affedersiniz}. Bir şey sorabilir miyim?** 'A: {Pardon/Excuse} me. Could I ask [you] something?'

2.9 Common Idioms and Proverbs

To help students remember the verbs, dictionary entries include common idioms and proverbs. The proverbs, in particular, will engage student interest: they reflect important facets of Turkish culture, cover essential vocabulary related to the entry verb -- such as synonyms, antonyms, and useful collocations -- and exemplify important points of grammar. Being short, they are easy to memorize. All are from well-known collections, and all Turks know their constituent vocabulary. The same proverb may appear under several entries when it has more than one useful verb. The proverbs in the dictionary are also listed together in **Part 4: Proverbs in the Turkish-English Dictionary of Verbs**.

2.10 Annotations on Register
When the example does not suffice to indicate the register of the utterance, we have provided further annotation in italics, such as *colloq[uial], formal, informal*.

2.11 Translations of Examples
The first translation of an example is usually idiomatic. It may be followed by a literal translation if it is helpful. Sentences or sentence segments preceded by an asterisk [*] harbor special difficulties and will require extra attention to understand and to use. They are entirely correct and idiomatic but, because of their structure and the corresponding English, they may strike a native English speaker as strange. They are usually followed, in brackets, by a word-for-word literal translation. We have made a concerted effort to include common sentences of this type. For example:

> * **Türkçe'm.E yardım et.** 'Help me WITH my Turkish [lit., ** Help TO my Turkish].'

Such literal translations highlight the structural differences between Turkish and English without recourse to grammatical terminology, clarify Turkish thought processes, help the student make sense of the Turkish, and thus help him learn it.

A literal translation that is not acceptable in standard English is marked by double asterisks, as above. There it shows that while the most common translation of the dative case **A** is 'to', in this example it is 'with', and that the natural English sentence has a different structure. While a native English speaker will usually know if a literal translation is natural English, a native Turkish speaker teaching Turkish to native English speakers may appreciate having potential problems of his students highlighted. If the pattern is typical, as here, we provide more than one example. This marking of sentences troublesome to native English speakers is a unique feature of this dictionary.

2.12 Turkish Personal Names in the Translations of the Examples
Turkish personal names appear in English in the same form as in Turkish. When the gender of a personal name is not clear from the context, women's names are followed by [f.], men's names by nothing, names used for both genders by [f., m.].

2.13 Warnings against Likely Mistranslations
A literal English translation of a Turkish utterance may mislead an English speaker. For example, the expression **başına gel-** means '- happen to'. However, its literal translation is '- come to one's head.' This may suggest the INCORRECT translation '- occur to'. In such instances this dictionary warns against the incorrect meaning and refers students to the correct Turkish for what the literal translation suggests, in this case to **aklına gel-** '- occur to'.

2.14 Indications of a Lack of Turkish Equivalents
This dictionary calls attention to cases where Turkish lacks a close equivalent for a common English expression. Thus, under **alkışla-** ['- applaud'], it notes that Turkish can express the idea 'The audience applauded HIM' but has no equivalent for 'The audience applauded HIS PERFORMANCE', both possible in English. Here again teaching experience helps us anticipate student difficulty, in this case an inappropriate extension suggested by possibilities in English.

2.15 Explanations of Cultural Matters
Some entries explain cultural contexts where ignorance might lead to misunderstanding or bad feelings. Thus, under the entry **anla-** ['- understand'], this dictionary points out that the question **Anlatabildim mi?** ['HAVE I BEEN ABLE to explain it?'] is often

preferred to **Anladınız mı?** ['DID YOU understand?'] because the former is regarded as more polite, although the latter would seem more natural to a native English speaker.

Students of Turkish should be able to talk about their own lives, beliefs, and ideas even if there is no direct counterpart in Turkish culture. This dictionary gives them the means to do so but also explains how a Turkish audience might react. For example, under **öde-** ['- pay'], this dictionary shows readers how to express the idea of '- go dutch', but notes that this is not common practice in Turkey today, that in a small group of associates one person usually pays for everyone and that, in time, everyone is expected to take a turn. This dictionary applies the principles of contrastive analysis in its treatment of culture, as reflected in practices and attitudes, just as it does in its treatment of grammar. Of course, readers should realize that culture differs from place to place within Turkey and that these observations are based largely on likely experiences in major cities such as Istanbul, Izmir, and Ankara. Then, too, any culture, like the language that expresses it, is always changing, but not so rapidly as to make all observations invalid. Our remarks naturally focus on differences but they are meant as general guides against misunderstandings and offensive and unacceptable behavior, not as iron-clad rules.

3. Classification of Each Meaning of an Entry Verb by Theme
Each definition of an entry verb is followed by a theme marker designating a category of meaning. For example, at the end of the entry **benze-** ['- look /LIKE/, - resemble'], readers will find: *783:7.* similarity: - resemble. Here *783* is the number assigned to the main theme, that is, 'similarity', and the final *7,* the number assigned to the subtheme, that is, '- resemble.' These numbers appear in italics. Theme and subtheme numbers are written together but separated by a colon rather than by theme names. Since a given meaning of a verb may fall under different themes, one meaning may be followed by more than one theme marker. For example, the verb **abart-** ['- exaggerate, - overstate, - make too much of, - exaggerate the importance of'], falls under two themes: *355:3.* exaggeration: - exaggerate AND under *992:10.* excess: - overdo. These numbers allow readers to find all instances of a given theme anywhere in the dictionary. To find all the items in this dictionary that fall under a particular theme, refer to **Part 3: Turkish Verbs by Theme**.

The system of themes is taken from *Roget's International Thesaurus* [1992] and is used with the publisher's permission. Like most such works, Roget's includes all the themes employed by authorities in the functional-notional approach to language teaching. We have designated themes according to the English meaning of the Turkish verb. On occasion we have added themes not in Roget's. We have marked them with an asterisk preceding the added part [e.g., **131: * 16**] or with letters beginning with the letter **b** [e.g., **54:8b**]. In the latter case, the Roget reference is the theme number without the lowercase letter [i.e., **54:8**].

4. Cross-References to Synonyms, Antonyms, and Otherwise Related Verbs
An arrow [→] meaning 'see' follows many examples and most theme numbers and points to another entry in this dictionary. If the symbol '=' follows the arrow, the following verb is a synonym. Thus, at the end of the first meaning of the entry **takdim et-** '- introduce', readers will find: → = **tanıştır-**.

If the symbol '≠' follows the arrow, the following verb is an antonym. Thus, at the end of the entry **kalk** '- get up, - rise', readers will find: → ≠ **otur- 1**. The number following **otur-** indicates that the antonym of **kalk-** is the first meaning of **otur-** as it appears in this dictionary.

For more precise differentiation, definitions or other comments in brackets follow some synonyms and antonyms. Thus, at the end of the entry **ayağa kalk-** '- stand up, - get /to/ one's feet', the reader will find: → ≠ **otur- 1** ['- sit down /IN/', i.e., - move INTO a sitting position], ≠ **çök- 2** ['- sit down suddenly, heavily /IN/, - collapse /INTO/', chair]. Here **otur-** is the standard verb for the action of sitting down, whereas **çök-** indicates sitting down in a particular way.

If neither '=' nor '≠' follows the arrrow, the following verb is neither a synonym nor an antonym but is related in some other way that students might find useful to know at that point. Thus, at the end of the entry **acık-** '- be or - become hungry', students will find: → **susa-** ['- be thirsty'], a cross-reference to a verb students might wish to learn together with the verb **acık-**.

These cross-references respond to frequent student requests for this information.

5. Parallel Structure in Synonym and Antonym Entries
Entries related to one another as synonyms or antonyms are often parallel in structure to bring out the relationship between them.

6. The Same Basic Vocabulary and Sentence Patterns Repeated in Different Entries
The same basic vocabulary and sentence patterns often appear in different entries to emphasize the basics.

7. Punctuation and Capitalization
In this book we replicate the Turkish punctuation and capitalization of our examples. At present there are few generally accepted standards in this area, the most widely known being those of the Turkish Language Society [Türk Dil Kurumu], which can be accessed from the Internet.

7.1 Punctuation [Noktalama]
Turkish uses the same punctuation marks currently used in English but applies them somewhat differently. Here are some of the major differences:

Comma [Virgül] In Turkish a comma does not usually follow phrases and subordinate clauses as it does in English. In the Turkish sentences below we show in uppercase letters the Turkish forms that come at the end of such elements and set them off from the rest of the sentence. This is not traditional practice in Turkish. In the translations, we show the corresponding elements in uppercase letters. Note the absence of the comma in the Turkish (underlined) and its presence (underlined) in the English.

> **Yağmurdan SONRA_ hava açtı.** 'AFTER the rain, {the weather/it} cleared up.'

> **Otobüs kazasında babaları öl.ÜNCE_ üç kardeş yetim kaldı.** 'WHEN their father died in a car accident,_ the three {brothers/sisters/siblings} were orphaned.'

> **Allah gümüş kapıyı kapar.SA_ altın kapıyı açar.** 'IF God closes the silver door, He opens the golden door.'

In Turkish, a comma often follows the subject of a sentence, especially in long sentences or when its absence might lead to a misreading. The English has no comma:

> **Bankayı soyan, adam hapse girdikten sonra pişman oldu.** 'The one who robbed the bank was sorry after the man [i.e., sb who was not guilty] went to prison.'

Contrast the above with the following sentence with no comma after **soyan**:

> **Bankayı soyan adam_ hapse girdikten sonra pişman oldu.** 'The man who robbed the bank was sorry after he [i.e., he himself] went to prison.'

A comma often separates coordinate clauses in Turkish, where standard English would have a semicolon or a period:

> **Kediyi yavaş sev͟, sakın can.I.nı acıtma͟, seni tırmalayabilir.** 'Pet the cat gently͟. Be careful; don't hurt it͟. It may scratch you.'

> **Ben meşgulü͟m,͟ telefon.U sen açar mısın?** 'I'm bus͟y. Would you get the phone?'

Exclamation point [Ünlem işareti] Turkish uses the exclamation point much less frequently than English.

Period [Nokta] In Turkish the period is used to form ordinal numbers: **15** i.e., **on beş** 'fifteen', **15͟.** i.e., **on be͟şinci** 'fifteen͟th'. It is also used to divide digits in numbers into groups of three: **20͟.000͟.000** '20,000,000'

A period frequently occurs before the word **çünkü** 'because' when it introduces an explanation of a preceding comment:

> **Artık doktor gelse de farketmez͟. Çünkü hasta öldü.** 'Now even if the doctor comes, it won't make any difference͟, because the patient has died.'

But the following also occurs:

> **Müge bugün gelemeyece͟k,͟ çünkü odadan çık.ma.ma ceza.sı yedi.** 'Müge isn't going to be able to come today because she is being punished by not being permitted to leave her [lit., the] room.'

Colon [İki nokta] In Turkish the colon is more often followed by an uppercase letter than it is in English.

Apostrophe [Kesme işareti] In Turkish the apostrophe separates a proper name from a suffix:

> **Ahmet'e verdim.** 'I gave it to Ahmet.'

When, however, a title follows a proper name, the apostrophe does not follow the title: **Ahmet beye verdim.** 'I gave it to Ahmet bey.'

Hyphen [Tire] In Turkish hyphenation is by syllable, thus much simpler than in English.

Semicolon [Noktalı virgül] The semicolon is less common in Turkish than it is in English. Turkish more frequently has a comma where English would have a semicolon. Sometimes Turkish has a semicolon where English would have a period:

> **Arkadaşım evden çıkarken cüzdanını bizde unuttu; arkasından bağırdım ama beni duymadı.** 'When my friend left the house, he left [lit., ** forgot] his wallet behind [with us]. I shouted after him, but he didn't hear [me].'

The semicolon is sometimes used where the English would have a comma:

> **Her yer.İ aradım; fakat gözlüğümü bulamadım.** 'I looked θ everywhere, but I couldn't find my glasses.'

7.2 Capitalization [Küçük ve Büyük Harfler]

Names of days of the week are not capitalized except at the beginning of a sentence. Names of the months are capitalized according to some sources but not according to others. In this work we capitalize the names of months within a sentence when they are part of a definte date but not otherwise: **Otuz bir Mayıs'ta tatile gireceğim.** 'I'm going ON vacation May 31.' **Yargılanma kararı haziran.a kaldı.** 'The decision regarding a [court] hearing has been put off to June [lit., ** remained to June].'

Current written Turkish has no consistently applied standard governing the capitalization of conventional titles such as **bey** 'Mr.', **hanım** '{Miss/Mrs./Ms.},' and **efendi**, a title today reserved mostly for persons of humble station, such as doormen, gardeners, and domestic servants. These titles will be found with both uppercase and lowercase letters: **Ahmet Çelik Bey, Ahmet Çelik bey, Ahmet Bey, Ahmet bey.** In this work we use the lower case form for such titles as well as for kinship names such as **abla** 'older sister', **amca** 'paternal uncle', **teyze** 'maternal aunt' when they follow a name: **Sibel abla** 'Older sister Sibel'. However, when a famous person is widely known by his first name and a title, the title is usually capitalized, perhaps because it has become regarded as part of the name: **Mustafa Kemal Paşa**, or a famous Ottoman composer: Dede Efendi.

PART 2. ENGLISH-TURKISH INDEX

The **Index** is a guide to **Part 1. Turkish-English Dictionary of Verbs**. It provides Turkish equivalents, often with the associated elements [cases, postpositions, and other words], but it has no Turkish example sentences. We decided on an index rather than on a full English-Turkish dictionary partly to save space but mostly to get students to refer to **Part 1**, where they would see Turkish elements in a broader Turkish context rather than simply as Turkish equivalents of English.

Examples of Different Types of Index Entries

Verb Entry

- BURN, - be on fire, - be burning [The building is burning.]: **yan-** 1. *1019:24.* heating: - burn.
- burn or - ignite, - light, - set /ON/ fire, - set fire /TO/: **yak-** 1. *1019:22.* heating: - ignite.
- burn, - make smart, - ache [Hot pepper burns one's mouth.]: **yak-** 2. *26:7.* pain: - inflict pain.
- burn DOWN, UP: **yan-** 1. *1019:24.* heating: - burn.
- burn or - scald ONESELF with a hot liquid, - get scalded /{BY/from}/: **/DAn/ haşlan-** 2. *393:13.* impairment: - inflict an injury.
- burn OUT [subj: light bulb]: **yan-** 2. *1021:8.* incombustibility: - burn out.
- burn TO DEATH: **yanarak öl-.** → yan- 1. *1019:24.* heating: - burn.

Most index entries are verbs and begin with a hyphen representing the English preposition 'to'.

An entry word in uppercase letters, like '- BURN' above, introduces a set of entries beginning with the same word but differing in meaning or use.

To guide students rapidly to the exact Turkish they need, members of the set are differentiated in several ways: by uppercase letters marking words closely associated with the verb; by additional definitions; and by comments or examples in brackets. The bracketed nouns, see '- burn out' above, are only a representative sample and should be understood as being followed by 'etc.'

Each English entry is followed by one or more Turkish equivalents. They may not, however, be interchangeable, as synonyms usually differ in meaning and use. To determine their precise use, consult our dictionary.

Each Turkish equivalent is followed by one or more English theme markers. Since the theme names are often very general, a particular theme name may not exactly match the Turkish meaning. To find the other items in our dictionary that belong to the same theme, see **Part 3: Turkish Verbs by Theme**.

Parts of Speech Other than Verbs

Certain entries are not verbs but other parts of speech, expressions, or idioms, the Turkish of which is derived from verbs in our dictionary:

AT [a certain TIME] TO [the hour] [in telling time: 'at a quarter to five']: **/A/ kala 1** → kal- 3. *833:7.* previousness: prior to.
at a specific DISTANCE FROM [always following a specific measure of distance: 'at a distance of two kilometers from the school']: **/A/ kala 3** → kal- 3. *261:14.* distance, remoteness: at a distance.
at LEAST: **hiç olmazsa** → ol- 11 → olmaz, **olsun 3** → ol- 11. *248:10.* insignificance: in a certain or limited degree.

BEFORE, prior /to/ [always following a specific time expression: 'five days before the meeting']: **/A/ kala 2** → kal- 3. *833:7.* previousness: - prior to.

Expressions or Idioms

Thank goodness, Fortunately: **Bereket versin [ki]** → ver- 1. *1009:16.* prosperity: fortunately.
Thank you!, Thanks.: **Teşekkür ederim.** → teşekkür et-, **Sağol!** → sağ ol- → ol- 12, **Eksik olmayın.** → eksik ol- → ol- 12. *150:6.* gratitude: INTERJ. thanks!
Thanks be to God that: **/A/ Şükürler olsun [ki]** → ol- 11 → olsun. *150:6.* gratitude: INTERJ. Thanks!; *509:22.* approval: INTERJ. bravo!

PART 3. TURKISH VERBS BY THEME [THESAURUS]

One purpose of this book is to provide multiple points of access to a selection of Turkish verbs and their meanings. In the first part, the **Turkish-English Dictionary of Verbs**, access is provided through the verbs themselves. In the second part, the **English-Turkish Index**, it is provided through the English equivalents of these verbs. In this thesaurus it is provided through the themes or categories of meaning that the verbs express. Each theme may be regarded as a window and each verb as an object possible to view from one or more of these windows. For this reason one verb often appears under different themes. The perspective afforded by this thesaurus goes beyond providing access to a verb to providing insights on the Turkish language and its resources for expression.

3.1 Theme Names in Alphabetical Order provides the most rapid access to a theme. Each theme name is followed by a theme number indicating the numerical sequence in which that theme name appears in part 3.3:

ABANDONMENT 370
ABNORMALITY 869
ABRIDGMENT 557
ABSENCE 222
ACCOMPANIMENT 768

3.2 Bird's Eye View of Themes reveals the nature of Roget's theme system: the order of the theme names as they appear in part 3.3 and the relationship of the themes to each other. Gaps in the numerical sequence indicate themes present in Roget's but not represented among the verbs in this dictionary:

CLASS 1: THE BODY AND THE SENSES

1 BIRTH
3 HAIR
5 CLOTHING
6 UNCLOTHING

3.3 Turkish Verbs Classified by Theme includes all the verbs in our dictionary together with their English definitions. The Turkish items under each theme name are given in alphabetical order by the first element in the verb or the verbal phrase rather than by the scheme used in Roget's work:

CLASS 1: THE BODY AND THE SENSES

0-100

1 BIRTH
1:2 - be born doğ- 1 '- be born'; dünyaya gel- '- be born', lit., '- come /INTO/ the world' → gel- 1.

1:3 - give birth /DAn/ çocuğu ol- '- have {children/a child} /from/, - give birth to a child' → ol- 6; doğur- '- give birth /TO/, - bear'; dünyaya getir- '- bring /INTO/ the world, - give birth /TO/, - bear'.

As we noted above, one verb may appear under different theme names. For example, the verb **abart-** ['- exaggerate, overstate, make too much of, exaggerate the importance of'] falls under two themes: *355:3.* exaggeration: - exaggerate and also under *992:10.* excess: - overdo. Such multiple categorization may occur because of an associated element. For example, the verb **çık-** [3 '- appear /from/, - come out /OF/, - emerge /from/'] appears under theme 33:8 - appear and also under 1018:23 - smoke, fume in the phrase **duman çık-** ['for smoke - rise /from/, for sth - smoke'].

Definitions are numbered only if there is more than one meaning of a verb for the same theme. The numbering is the same as that under the entry for that verb in our dictionary.

A phrase not followed by a cross-reference indication [→] appears in our dictionary under the final verb. Thus, **haber getir-** will be found under **getir-**.

Passive forms usually appear under the active theme name unless Roget's has the passive theme as a separate category. Themes that we have added, which are not present in Roget's, are indicated with an asterisk preceding the added part [e.g., **131:** * **16**] or with letters beginning with the letter **b** [e.g., **54:8b**]. In the latter case, the Roget reference is the theme number without the lowercase letter, i.e., **54:8**.

To help readers select the appropriate verb, definitions in **Turkish Verbs Classified by Theme** are often followed in brackets by comments or a representative sample of subjects or objects of the verb: **analiz et-** '- analyze [blood, historical event].'

PART 4. PROVERBS IN THE TURKISH-ENGLISH DICTIONARY OF VERBS

Proverbs play an important role in Turkish culture and can serve as an effective instructional tool. In this section of this book, the approximately 250 proverbs scattered throughout our dictionary are listed together in alphabetical order by first word. With it, users can determine what proverbs occur in the dictionary, under which entries they appear and, in those entries, they can find other, useful examples of the verbs in the proverb.

PART 5. TURKISH VERB-FORMING SUFFIXES

Above, under **Composition of the Entry Verb**, we noted that many entries in our dictionary show the suffixes used in verb formation. This index assembles all these suffixes alphabetically under two main headings:

      1. Suffixes that form verb stems from parts of speech other than verbs [i.e., adjectives or nouns]

      2. Suffixes that form verb stems from verbs.

Each suffix is followed by the verbs from our dictionary that include the suffix.

With this index, students can review their knowledge of suffix use and find many examples of each suffix. This index will also serve as a resource for teachers and for writers of instructional materials .

How the Turkish-English Dictionary of Verbs Was Compiled

The authors selected the core verbs from various sources, including textbooks for teaching Turkish; several lists; materials prepared for tourists to Turkey, such as tourist guides and conversation manuals; and the 176 verbs on the Provisional Elementary-Level Turkish Vocabulary List of the American Association of Teachers of Turkic Languages [AATT], version 0.2, 1995. We also consulted written records of natural speech, including Turkish comic books and books of idioms, phrases, and set expressions. Finally, we consulted educated native speakers on our selection.

We evaluated the resulting list according to the situational and notional categories drawn up by authorities in the communicative approach to language teaching, such as Alexander, Brumfit, Ek, Finocchiaro, and Omaggio Hadley. For such categories we also consulted works prepared for the learners of more commonly taught foreign languages such as Spanish and French. We aimed to include all the essential verbs that students would require to communicate in categories widely regarded as essential. Naturally, we also considered the immediate needs of our own students in the classroom and, beyond that, whatever else common sense would suggest.

We collected examples from the relevant areas of experience, always seeking a natural Turkish context, often in the form of a brief dialogue. To find examples that would occur automatically to a native Turkish speaker, we asked native informants to free associate with the selected verbs. Our purpose was to give more weight to the vocabulary on the tip of the native speaker's tongue than to the written language. Whenever possible, we included sentences that met this criteria but that, while entirely natural to a Turk, would not occur to a native speaker of English with only a basic knowledge of Turkish grammar. Finally, we submitted our work to educated native speakers for review. We hope we have met the needs of our students and their teachers.

A Call for Help

The authors invite detailed suggestions for corrections and improvements. Send your comments to Ralph Jaeckel, Department of Near Eastern Languages and Cultures, University of California, Los Angeles, 405 Hilgard Avenue, Los Angeles, California 90024; e-mail: Jaeckel@humnet.ucla.edu.

Bibliography

Frequency Word Lists

Pierce, Joe. 1964. *A Frequency Count of Turkish Words.* Manuscript.

Provisional Elementary Level Turkish Vocabulary List of the American Association of Teachers of Turkic Languages [AATT], version 0.2, 1995.

Turkish Reference Grammars

Göksel, Aslı, and Celia Kerslake. 2005. *Turkish: A Comprehensive Grammar.* London and New York: Routledge.

Kornfildt, Jaklin. 1997. *Turkish.* New York: Routledge.

Lewis, G. L. 2000. *Turkish Grammar.* 2nd ed. Oxford: Clarendon Press.

Turkish Language Teaching Materials

Halman, Talat Sait. 1981. *201 Turkish Verbs Fully Conjugated in All Tenses.* Woodbury, N.Y.: Barron's Educational Series, Inc.

Hengirmen, Mehmet, and Nurettin Koç. 1983. *Türkçe Öğreniyoruz.* I. Ankara: Engin Yayınevi.

Hengirmen, Mehmet. 1983. *Türkçe Öğreniyoruz.* III. Ankara: Engin Yayınevi.

Koç, Nurettin, and Mehmet Hengirmen. 1983. *Türkçe Öğreniyoruz.* II. Ankara: Engin Yayınevi.

Özel, Suzan. 1997. *Turkish: A Communicative Approach.* Bloomington: Indiana University.

Sezer, Engin. 1994. *Yaşayan Türkçe.* Version 1.1. Harvard University.

Tornow, Ute. 1994. *Das Verb im Türkischen.* Wiesbaden: Harrossowitz.

Tunç, İsmet, and Ali Tunç. 1973. *Türkçemiz.* Istanbul: Millî Eğitim Basımevi.

Turkish Basic Course. Units 1-30. 1974. Washington: Foreign Service Institute.

Turkish Basic Course. Units 31-50. 1968. Washington: Foreign Service Institute.

Turkish Basic Course. Vols. 1-14. 1965, all volumes revised between 1980 and 1981. Presidio of Monterey, CA: Defense Language Institute, Foreign Language Center.

Turkish Basic Course. March 1990. Validation Edition. Lessons 1-30. Presidio of Monterey, CA: Defense Language Institute, Foreign Language Center. This text supersedes the one above.

Turkish Headstart. 1982. Presidio of Monterey, CA: Defense Language Institute.

Underhill, Robert. 1976. *Turkish Grammar.* Cambridge, MA: MIT Press.

West, Steven, and Eser Erguvanlı. 1976. Unpublished manuscript of corrections of Underhill [1976 edition].

Works on Idioms and Proverbs

Aksoy, Ömer Asım. 1989. *Atasözleri ve deyimler sözlüğü.* Istanbul: İnkilâp Kitabevi.

Atsız, Bedriye, and Hans-Joachim Kissling. 1974. *Sammlung Türkischer Redensarten.* Wiesbaden: Otto Harrassowitz.

Gözler, H. Fethi, and M. Ziya Gözler. 1982. *Açıklamalı Türk Atasözleri Sözlüğü.* Istanbul: İnkilâp ve Aka Kitabevleri.

Karlı, Gülten. 1999. *Atasözleri Sözlüğü.* Istanbul: Assos Yayınları.

Yurtbaşı, Metin. 1993. *A Dictionary of Turkish Proverbs.* Ankara: Turkish Daily News.

Works on Methodology

Finocchiaro, Mary, and Christopher Brumfit. 1983. *The Functional-Notional Approach: From Theory to Practice.* New York: Oxford University Press.

Omaggio Hadley, Alice. 2001. *Teaching Language in Context.* Third edition. Boston: Heinle and Heinle.

Van Ek, J. A., and L.G. Alexander. 1975. *Threshold Level English.* Oxford: Pergamon Press.

Dictionaries and Thesauri

English-English

Longman Dictionary of Contemporary English. New Edition. 1987. Longman: Harlow, [Essex], England.

Longman Dictionary of American English. A Dictionary for Learners of English. 1983. White Plains, N.Y.: Longman Inc.

McArthur, Tom. 1981. *Longman Lexicon of Contemporary English.* Longman: Harlow [Essex], England.

Oxford Advanced Learner's Dictionary of Current English. Fourth edition. 1989. Oxford: Oxford University Press.

Roget's International Thesaurus. 1992. Fifth edition. Edited by Robert L. Chapman. New York: HarperCollins.

English-Turkish

Longman-Metro Büyük İngilizce Türkçe-Türkçe Sözlük. 1993. This is a Turkish adaptation of the *Longman Dictionary of Contemporary English* cited above under English-English dictionaries. It is not clear which edition. The following information appears in this Turkish adaptation: For the English original: Longman Group UK Limited, Longman House, Burnt Mill, Harlow, Essex CM20 2JE, England. For the Turkish adaptation: Metro Kitap Yayın Pazarlama A.Ş., Nuruosmaniye Cad. Kardeşler Han No: 3 Kat: 1, 34410 Cağaloğlu, Istanbul, Turkey.

Turkish-English

Cete, Hayrettin. 2000. *Türkçe-İngilizce Fiiller Sözlüğü.* İstanbul: Pastel Matbaacılık.

Moran, A. Vahid. 1985. *Büyük Türkçe İngilizce Sözlük*. Istanbul: Adam Yayınları.

New Redhouse Turkish-English Dictionary. 1981. Istanbul: Redhouse Yayınevi.
Redhouse Contemporary Turkish-English Dictionary. 1983. Istanbul: Redhouse Yayınevi.

Redhouse Portable Dictionary. English-Turkish/Turkish-English. 1975 [1989, 13th printing]. Istanbul: Redhouse Yayınevi.

Turkish-German

Tezcan, Nuran. 1988. *Elementarwortschatz Türkisch-Deutsch. Turkologie und Türkeikunde*. Vol. 1. Wiesbaden: Otto Harrassowitz. A Turkish-German learner's dictionary.

Abdülhayoğlu, Suphi. 1990. *Türkisch-Deutsches Valenzlexikon*. Hohengehren: Schneider Verlag.

Turkish-Russian

Turetsko-Russkii Slovar. 1977. Moscow: Russian Language Publishing House.

Turkish-Turkish

Örnekleriyle Türkçe Sözlük. 1995-1996. 4 vols. Ankara: Millî Eğitim Bakanlığı.

Püsküllüoğlu, Ali. 1988. *İlkokullar için örnekli-resimli Türkçe Sözlük*. Istanbul: ABD Kitabevi.

Türkçe Sözlük. 1983. Seventh edition. 2 vols. Ankara: Türk Tarih Kurumu Basımevi.

Türkçe Sözlük. 1988. 2 vols. Ankara: Türk Tarih Kurumu Basımevi.

SYNOPSIS OF ABBREVIATIONS AND SYMBOLS

[^] A circumflex indicates the palatalization of a preceding **g**, **k**, or **l** with the vowel **a** [as in **rüzgâr** 'wind', **kâbus** 'nightmare', **evlât** 'child'] and with the vowel **u** [as in **mahkûm** 'doomed, sentenced'].

It also marks a long vowel in foreign borrowings. In current Turkish orthography: **â** [as in **âlet** 'instrument'], **î** [as in **ciddî** 'serious']. Our source for modern Turkish pronunciation and standard orthography is *Türkçe Sözlük* 1988.

In a few instances a circumflex indicates a pronunciation not reflected in standard Turkish orthography: **Ağabeyim** [usually pronounced **âbim**], **Sıhhatler olsun.** [usually pronounced **sâtler olsun**], **Allahaısmarladık.** [usually pronounced **Alâsmarladık**].

[θ] This symbol indicates the absence of an element. In the following example it indicates that the noun **ağrı** is used as a verb stem without the addition of a verb-forming suffix: **ağrı-** '- ache, - hurt, - throb with pain' [n. **ağrı** 'ache' + verb-forming suf. -θ].

In an English translation it often warns the English-speaking user of a potential pitfall. In the following entry, it warns him that, although English does not use a preposition with the verb '- avoid', the corresponding Turkish requires the case suffix **DAn**: **kaçın-** [ır] /DAn/ '- avoid /θ/, - refrain /from/'.

[→] An arrow means 'see' and refers the user to the element indicated.

[-] A hyphen indicates the infinitive in Turkish and in English: In Turkish, directly attached, it takes the place of the suffix **mAk**: **git-** for **gitmek**. In English, followed by a space, it takes the place of 'to': '- go' for 'to go'.

In brackets that enclose comments on composition, a hyphen is used before a suffix that is normally attached to an element to form a verb. In the following example it shows that the verb **anla-** is formed by adding the suffix -**lA** to the noun **an**: **anla-** '- understand, realize' [**an** 'mind, perception' + verb-forming suf. -**lA**].

[.] A period is used to form ordinal numbers: **15** i.e., **on beş** 'fifteen', **15.** i.e., **on beşinci** 'fifteen<u>th.</u>'

It is also used to divide digits in numbers into groups of three: **20.000.000** '20,000,000.'

In this dictionary, but not elsewhere, a period is used to separate Turkish morphemes [units of meaning] from base words and from each other to clarify grammatical structure for students of Turkish: **İste.diğ.i.ni söyle.yen isteme.diğ.i.ni işitir.** 'He who says what [ever] he likes [lit., wants] will hear what he doesn't like.'

[•] A raised dot marks a note on grammar or usage. Under the entry **bak- 2**: • In a store **bak-** '- look for, - want' is used for all items EXCEPT food:...

| : | A colon separates a main theme number from a subtheme number and a main theme name from a subtheme name: *449:11.* aid: - aid.

| '...' | Single quotation marks enclose English translations and thus often separate translations from following comments: **Bu kalem.in uc.u körelmiş açmak lâzım.** 'This pencil [lit., the point of this pencil] has gotten dull. It should be sharpened.' Also, but not so common: **Bu kalem körelmiş...** 'This pencil has gotten dull....'

| "..." | Double quotation marks enclose quotes within the Turkish and within the English translation: **Annem ban.A "Ayşe buraya gel!" diye bağırdı.** 'My mother shouted AT me saying, "Ayşe, come here!"'

| = | An equal sign means synonym.

| ≠ | An unequal sign means antonym.

| + | A plus sign marks the addition of an element in verbal composition: **acıt-** [ır] '- hurt, - cause physical pain to' [**acı-** + caus. suf. **-t**]

| (+) | A plus sign in parentheses marks a sentence as affirmative: (+) **Ahmet hasta[dır].** 'Ahmet [is] ill.'

| (-) | A minus sign in parentheses marks a sentence as negative: (-) **Ahmet hasta değil[dir].** 'Ahmet [is] not ill.'

| / | A slash within curly brackets separates possible choices: **telefon {et-/aç-}.**

| // | Double slashes within curly brackets separate possible choices already separated by a single slash. In the English translation below, double slashes separate two sets of alternatives: **İyi bir {okçu/atıcı} sayılmam, on atış.TAN sadece altısında isabet kaydettim, * gerisi karavan.a.** 'I'm not [lit., I'm not considered] a good {archer/bowman//marksman/shot}. OUT OF ten attempts [lit., shots] I hit the target only six times. * The rest missed the target entirely [lit., ** the rest of it to the cauldron].'

| /... / | A pair of slashes enclose complements [case suffixes, postpositions, etc.] that appear after the entry verb. They also enclose the English equivalents of those complements: **ak-** [ar] /DAn, A/ '- flow /from, {to/INTO}/, - pour /from, INTO/'

| # | A pound sign separates Turkish elements that might otherwise be read together. It usually separates an example from a preceding cross-reference: → ≠ **koy-** 1. # **Türkçe kitabını Kenan'dan alır mısınız?** 'Would you [please] take the Turkish book from Kemâl?'

[ ] Square brackets enclose the aorist tense of a verb [directly after the headword] as well as explanatory information: **acıt-** [ır] '- hurt, - cause physical pain to' [**acı-** + caus. suf. **-t**].

Within entries, square brackets enclose definitions of verbs related to the entry verb, sometimes of synonyms and antonyms but mostly of otherwise semantically related verbs. These definitions clarify the relationship between the entry verb and the related verbs. At the end of the entry **acık-**: → **karnı zil çal-** ['for one's stomach - growl from hunger'].

Square brackets may also enclose descriptive comments. At the end of the entry **aç- 2**: → = **yak- 3** [with all items above except radio, TV, computer].

( ) Parentheses within brackets function like ordinary brackets: [**karın** (kaRNı) 'stomach'].

Parentheses also enclose the numbers of subentry definitions. Under the entry **aç- 2**, is the following subentry: **yol aç-** /A/ [**yol** 'road, way'] **(1)** '- clear a way /to/, - open a road /to/'.

{ } Curly brackets enclose possible choices. Slashes [/] within curley brackets separate the choices. In a headword unit consisting of more than one verb, e.g., {**tekrar et-** [eDer]/**tekrarla-**}, curly brackets enclose synonyms that are appropriate in all the examples provided below it.

In the examples, curly brackets in one language may not appear in the corresponding part in the other: **Ağlamayın. Her şey düzelecek.** 'Don't cry. Everything {will be OK/will turn out all right/lit., will straighten out}.'

---

* An asterisk precedes a Turkish sentence or phrase that is difficult for most native English speakers.

An asterisk also precedes the number of a subcategory that we have added to those used in Roget's. In both of the following, the asterisk precedes the subcategory number, indicating that 'gestures of' has been added to both categories: *131: * 17.* inexpectation: gestures of; *441:3. * 1.* consent: gestures of.

** Double asterisks mark a literal translation that is unacceptable in standard English. They alert Turkish teachers to the possible problems of their English-speaking students: * **Kendimi iyi hissetmiyorum.** 'I don't feel well [lit., ** I don't feel MYSELF well].'

< > In **Part 3: Turkish Verbs by Theme**, these brackets enclose additional qualifying statements: 58 STRIDENCY <HARSH AND SHRILL SOUNDS>

Strike-throughs. A crossed-out item, usually preceded by 'NOT', is incorrect or inappropriate in a particular context where it might be anticipated. In the following example, it indicates that, although in other parts of the entry {**kaybet-**/**yitir-**} ['- lose'] the verbs **kaybet-** and **yitir-** are both used with all subentries, in this one [with **kendini**], **yitir-** is not: **kendini** {**kaybet-**/NOT ~~**yitir-**~~}.

---

a: A lowercase letter followed by a colon helps readers match the Turkish with the English translation: **Doktorlar hasta.nın {a: AİDS'TEN/b: verem.DEN/c: kalp kriz.i.nDEN} öldüğ.ü.nü açıkladı.** 'The doctors disclosed that the patient had died {a: OF AIDS/b: OF TB/c: OF a heart attack}.'

---

a) A lowercase letter followed by a parenthesis distinguishes a grammatical structure or pattern from others: **a) Bizim çocuk hasta ama doktora git.me.mek.te direniyor.** 'Our child is ill, but he refuses to go to the doctor [lit., ** he insists on not going to the doctor].'
b) Bizim çocuk hasta ama {doktora git.mem diye direniyor}. 'Our child is sick but he refuses to go to the doctor [lit., ** he insists saying "I won't go to the doctor."]'

It also marks different uses of the same structure, often when it has the same English equivalent: **Rica ederim. (1)** 'Please' **a)** In a simple request: **Rica ederim, konuşmayın.** 'Please, don't.'

A. Arabic: [A. **miras** 'inheritance']

A: A: marks the first speaker in a non-question-answer dialogue: **A: Hoş geldiniz.** 'A: Welcome.' **B: Hoş bulduk.** 'B: Glad to be here.'

A: is also used in the English translation of dialogues to mean 'Answer'.

In dialogues, an uppercase letter other than 'A' followed by a number, i.e., B1, C2, indicates another possible response: **A: Geceyarısı oldu, Murat hâlâ ortada yok. Çok endişe ediyorum.** 'A: It's midnight. Murat still hasn't turned up [lit., isn't anywhere about]. I'm very {worried/concerned}.' **B1: Endişe etmek.TE haklısın.** 'B1: You're right to be worried.' **B2: Endişe etmey.e gerek yok.** 'B2: There's no need to worry.'

ADV. adverb

ADJ. adjective

B: B: marks the second speaker in a non-question-answer dialogue.

C: In a question-answer dialogue C stands for **cevap** 'answer'.

caus. causative
colloq. colloquial
CONJ. conjunction
fig. figurative
Gk. Greek
[i.] intransitive. Indicated only when this is not clear from the verb as presented.
INTERJ. interjection
i.o. indirect object
irr. irregular
It. Italian

lit. literal, literal translation, literally.
n. noun
obj. grammatical object
P. Persian
pass. passive
PHR. phrase
PREP. preposition
prov. provincial
Q: 'question'
subj. grammatical subject
S: Turkish for **soru** 'question'
sb somebody
Sl. slavic
sth something
suf. suffix
[t.] transitive. Indicated only when this is not clear from the verb as presented.

PART 1.
TURKISH-ENGLISH DICTIONARY
OF VERBS

PART 1. TURKISH-ENGLISH DICTIONARY OF VERBS

Below the hyphen attached to the Turkish verb stem represents the suffix **mAk**, i.e., {mak/mek}: abart- = abartmak. The separate hyphen preceding the English verb represents the word 'to': - exaggerate = to exaggerate.

- A -

abart- [ır] '- exaggerate, - overstate, - make too much of, - exaggerate the importance of': **Gerçekleri abartmayalım.** 'Let's not exaggerate the facts.' **Bu işi fazla abartmak doğru değildir.** 'It's not right to make too much of this matter.' **Lütfen olayı bu kadar abartmayın. Bu sadece bir şakaydı.** 'Don't make so much of {the incident/the event}. It was only a joke.' **Hiç abartmıyorum,** * **olay öyle oldu.** 'I'm not exaggerating at all. * That's the way it happened [lit., The event happened that way].' * **Aslına bakarsan[ız] olay onun anlattığı gibi değil, abartıyor.** 'To tell the truth [lit., ** If you look at the truth of it], the event did not happen the way he said it did. He's exaggerating.' **{a: Tehditleri/b: Tehlikeleri/c: Zorlukları/d: Engelleri} ne küçümsemek ne de abartmak doğrudur.** 'It is correct neither to minimize nor to exaggerate {a: [the] threats/b: [the] dangers/c: [the] difficulties/d: [the] obstacles}.' **O tatil köy.ü.nü anlatırken biraz abarttığımı düşünebilirsiniz ama** * **orası gerçekten dediğim gibi;** * **eksiği yok, fazlası var.** 'When I describe that holiday village you may think that I'm exaggerating a bit, but * it's really as I say. * It's even better than that [lit., ** It has more, not less].' *355:3.* exaggeration: - exaggerate; *992:10.* excess: - overdo. → = **büyüt-** 2, ≠ **küçümse-** 2.

abdest al-. → **aptes al-.** → **al-** 1.

{abuk sabuk/saçma sapan} konuş-. → **konuş-.**

abur cubur ye-. → **ye-** 1.

{acayibine/garibine/tuhafına} git-. → **git-** 1b.

acele et- [eDer] /için/ '- hurry /[IN ORDER] TO/' [A. acele 'haste']: **Acele edin!** [= **Çabuk olun!**] **Otobüs geliyor.** 'Hurry! The bus is coming!' **Daha bir saatimiz var,** * **niçin acele ediyorsunuz?** 'We still have an hour. * What's the hurry? [lit., Why are you hurrying?]' **Tatil.E çık.mak İÇİN acele ediyor.** 'He is hurrying [IN ORDER] TO leave FOR vacation.' • Note also the following where **acele** occurs without **et-:** * **Acele.m var.** 'I'm in a hurry [lit., ** My hurry (is) existent].' **Acele acele nere.ye gidiyorsun?** 'θ Where are you going in such a hurry?' *401:5.* haste: - make haste. → = **çabuk ol-** → **ol-** 12, ≠ **yavaşla-.**

acı- [r] [acı 'pain, ache' + verb-forming suf. -θ] 1 '- hurt, - feel sore': S: * **Nere.si acıyor?** 'Q: * Where does it hurt? [lit., ** Its where hurts?]' * **Bura.sı acıyor mu?** 'Does it hurt here? [lit., ** Does its here hurt?]' C: * **Bura.sı acıyor.** 'A: It hurts here [lit., ** Its here hurts].' **Dün kesilen parmağım çok acıyor.** 'The finger that I cut [lit., ** My finger that {got/was} cut] yesterday hurts a lot.' → = **ağrı-.** *26:8.* pain: - suffer pain.

canı acı- '- hurt, - feel pain' [P. **can** (-) 'soul'], lit., ** 'for one's soul - hurt': **Elimi kestim** * **çok can.IM acıyor.** 'I cut my hand. * It really hurts [lit., ** MY soul hurts a lot].' **Lütfen saçlarımı yavaş tara,** * **can.IM çok acıyor.** 'Please comb my hair gently, * it really hurts.' * **Kedi.NİN can.I acıyınca çocuğun elini tırmaladı.** 'When the cat was hurt, it scratched the child's hand.' *26:8.* pain: - suffer pain. → = **canı yan-** → **yan-** 1.

2 /A/ '- pity /θ/, - feel sorry /FOR/': **Yangında ölen insanlar.A çok acıdım.** 'I felt very sorry FOR the people that perished in the fire.'

3

145:3. pity: - pity. → = üzül-, = yüreği parçalan- → parçalan- 2.

acı çek-. → çek- 5.

acık- [ɪr] '- be or - become hungry' [aç 'hungry' + verb-forming suf. -Ik]: Dün kahvaltı etmedim. Öğleye doğru çok acıktım. 'I didn't have breakfast yesterday. Toward noon I {was/got/became} very hungry.' At noon TODAY in reference to his PRESENT hunger a person may say: * Bugün kahvaltı etmedim. Çok acık.TIM. 'Today I didn't have breakfast. I'M very hungry.' In this example the PAST tense acıktım refers to a state in effect at PRESENT, i.e., the time of speaking, so the translation is PRESENT tense. • In reference to a PRESENT condition, certain common Turkish verbs designating a state, i.e., a feeling, emotion, or sensation, often have the simple PAST tense, but the equivalent English has the simple PRESENT tense. Kedi miyavlıyor, herhalde acıktı. 'The cat is meowing. It's probably hungry.' Two other, but somewhat less common, ways of indicating present hunger employ the ADJECTIVE aç: a) Ahmet aç. 'Ahmet is hungry.' Açım. 'I'm hungry.' b) Ahmet'in karnı aç. 'Ahmet is hungry [lit., ** Ahmet's stomach kaRNı (from karın) is hungry].' Sabahtan beri bir şey yemedim. Karnım aç. 'I haven't eaten anything since this morning. I'm hungry.' *100:19.* desire: - hunger. → karnı zil çal- ['for one's stomach - growl from hunger'] → çal- 3, ≠ doy- ['- have enough /OF/, - be satisfied /WITH/, - eat one's fill, - be full'], susa- ['- be thirsty'].

karnı acık- '- be or - become hungry' [karın (kaRNı) 'stomach']: Karn.IM çok acıktı, yemek yiyelim. 'I'M very hungry. Let's eat.' S: Karn.IN acık.TI mı? 'Q: ARE YOU hungry?' C1: Evet, [karn.IM] acıktı. 'A1: Yes, I AM.' C2: Hayır, [karn.IM] acıkmadı. 'A2: No, I'm not.' Sabahtan beri bir şey yemedim. Karnım acıktı. 'I haven't eaten anything since [this] morning. I'm hungry.' *100:19.* desire: - hunger. → ≠ karnı doy-.

acıt- [ɪr] '- hurt, - cause physical pain to' [acı- + caus. suf. -t]: canını acıt- '- hurt sb' [P. can (-) 'soul'], lit., ** '- hurt sb's soul': Can.IM.ı çok acıtıyorsun, lütfen saçlarımı yavaş tara. 'You're really hurting me [lit., ** hurting MY soul]. Please comb my hair [more] gently.' Şu küçücük sivilce can.IM.ı çok acıtıyor. 'This tiny pimple really hurts me.' Dişçide: Birazcık acıtacak. 'At the dentist: This will hurt a little.' Kediyi yavaş sev, sakın can.I.nı acıtma, seni tırmalayabilir. 'Pet the cat gently. Be careful; don't hurt it. It may scratch you.' *26:7.* pain: - inflict pain. → = canını yak- → yak- 2.

aç- [ar] 1 '- open sth' [ADJ. açık 'open']: Lütfen {paketi/meyva sularını/su şişesini} açar mısın? 'Would you please open {the package/the fruit juices/the water bottle}?' {Sınav/İmtihan} bitti, kitapları açabilirsiniz. '{The examination} {is over./lit., ** finished.} You may open the [i.e., your] books.' Zil çaldı, kapıyı aç. 'The [door] bell rang. Open the door.' Proverbs: Allah gümüş kapıyı kaparsa altın kapıyı açar. 'If God closes the silver door, He opens the golden door.', i.e., Don't be discouraged: a better opportunity may follow one lost. *130: * 16.* expectation: proverbs. Tatlı dil bin kapı açar. 'A sweet tongue opens a thousand doors.' *524: * 35.* speech: proverbs. → ≠ {kapa-/kapat-} 1, ≠ ört- 2. # Yatmadan önce ellerimi açıp Allah'a dua ettim. 'Before going to bed, I opened my hands [to God's grace] and prayed to God.' The gesture of holding one's hand's palms up open in front of oneself is a part of the sequence of prayer acts. Gözlerinizi açın! 'Open your eyes.' → ≠ gözlerinizi {kapa-/kapat-} → {kapa-/kapat-} 1, ≠ gözlerinizi yum-. # Hediye paketlerini açtım. 'I opened the gifts [lit., gift packages].' → ≠ sar- 1 ['- wrap one thing /{IN/AROUND}, with/ another']. *292:11.* opening: - open.

bavulunu aç- '- unpack', or just '- open one's bags' [It. bavul 'bags, luggage']: Otele geleli üç saat oldu ama hâlâ {bavulunu/ valizini} açmamışsın, bir sorun mu var? 'It's been three hours since you got to the hotel, but [it seems]

4

you still haven't unpacked {your bag[s]/your suitcase[s]}. Is there a problem?' *292:11.* opening: - open; *908:23.* ejection: - unload. → ≠ **bavulunu hazırla-** ['- pack, - pack up' or just '- prepare one's bags'].

yol aç- [**yol** 'road, way'] (1) /A/ '- clear a way /to/, - open a road /to/': **Araba geliyor, yolu açın.** 'A car is coming. Clear the way.' **Kardan kapanan köy yolunu buldozerler açtı.** 'The bulldozers {cleared the way/opened the road} to the village that had been closed off because of [the] snow.' *292:13.* opening: - make an opening.
(2) *fig.* /A/ '- cause /θ/, - bring about /θ/, - lead /to/': **Hükümetin yanlış ekonomi politikası enflasyon.A yol açtı.** 'The government's mistaken economic policy {caused θ/led to} inflation.' **GAP [Güney-Doğu Anadolu Projesi] projesi bu bölge.nin kalkınma.sı.nA yol açacak.** 'The GAP [South-East Anatolia Project] Project will bring about θ the development of this region.' *885:10.* cause: - cause. → = {**sebep/neden**} **ol-**. → **ol-** 12.

2 '- turn or - switch on', electricity, light, radio, TV: **Işığı açar mısınız?** 'Would you please switch on the light?' **Radyoyu açtığım zaman başbakan konuşuyordu.** 'When I turned on the radio, the prime minister was speaking.' {a: **Elektriği**/b: **Işığı**/c: **Lâmbaları**/d: **Radyoyu**/e: **Televizyonu**/f: **Ocağı**/g: **Fırını**/h: **Bilgisayarı**} **açayım mı?** 'Should I turn on {a: the lights [lit., electricity]/b: the light(s)/c: the lamps/d: the radio/e: the TV/f: the gas-burner [i.e., on the stove top, not the stove]/g: the oven/h: the computer}?' *1031:25.* electricity: - electrify. → = **yak-** 3 [with all items above except radio, TV, computer], ≠ {**kapa-/kapat-**} 2, ≠ **söndür-** 2 [with all items above except radio, TV, computer].

'- turn on', water, the faucet: **Çiçekleri sulamak için** {**suyu/musluğu/çeşmeyi**} **aç-mıştım ama kapayıp kapa-madığımı hatırlamıyorum.** 'To water the flowers I turned on {the water/the faucet/the fountain}, but I don't remember whether I turned it off or not.' *292:11.* opening: - open;

817:11. beginning: - inaugurate. → ≠ {**kapa-/kapat-**} 2.

3 /I/ '- turn /TO/ [page 5, TV channel], - open /TO/ [page 5], - tune /{TO/INTO}/ [radio station], - put on or - turn on [TV channel, radio station]': S: * **Hangi sayfa.yI açayım?** 'Q: * Which page should I {turn/open} TO [lit., ** Which page should I open]?' C: * **İkinci sayfa.yI açın.** 'A: * {Turn/Open} TO page 2 [lit., the second page].' S: * **Hangi kanal.I açayım?** 'Q: * Which [TV] channel should I {put on/turn TO}?' C: * **Üçüncü kanalı aç.** 'A: * {Put on/Turn TO} channel 3 [lit., the third channel].' *371:14.* choice: - select; *914:9.* rotation: - rotate. → = **çevir-** 4 [If the instrument is already on and you want to make a change.]

4 /A/ '- telephone, - phone, - ring up sb': * **telefon aç-**. → **telefon** {**et-/aç-**}.

5 '- answer, - get, pick up': **telefon.U aç-** '- get, - pick up, or - answer the phone': **Ben meşgulüm, telefon.U sen açar mısın?** 'I'm busy. Would you get the phone?' *347:18.* communications: - telephone; *982:5.* attention: - attend to. → = **telefon.A** {**bak-/cevap ver-**} → **bak-** 3, **ver-** 1, ≠ **telefon kapan-** ['for the phone - be hung up'] → **kapan-** 1; ≠ **telefon.U kapat-** ['- hang up'] → **kapat-**.

6 '- sharpen': * **kalem aç-** '- sharpen a pencil': **Kalemtıraşınız var mı? Kalemimi açmak istiyorum.** 'Do you have a pencil sharpener? I want to sharpen my pencil.' * **Bu kalem.in uc.u körelmiş, açmak lâzım.** 'This pencil [lit., the POINT of this pencil] is [lit., has gotten] dull. It should be sharpened.' Also, but not so common: **Bu kalem körelmiş...** 'This PENCIL is dull...' *285:7.* sharpness: - sharpen. → **bile-** [for '- sharpen' implements other than a pencil, such as a knife].

7 '- clear up, - become nice, pleasant, good [weather]': * **hava aç-** 'for weather - clear up, - become nice, pleasant, good' [A. **hava** 1 'air'. 2 'weather']: **Hava ne zaman açacak?** 'When will {the

weather/it} clear up?' **Bugün hava açacak mı?** 'Will {the weather/it} clear up today?' **Yağmurdan sonra hava açtı.** 'After the rain, {the weather/it} cleared up.' *392:7.* improvement: - get better. → = **hava açıl-** → açıl- 7, ≠ **hava boz-** → boz- 4, ≠ **hava bozul-**, ≠ **hava kapan-** ['- cloud over, - become cloudy, overcast'] → kapan- 4.

8 '- come out, - appear, - reveal itself': * **güneş aç-** 'for the sun - come out, appear': **Yağmur dindi, güneş açtı. Biraz dışarı çıkalım mı?** 'The rain has stopped, and the sun has come out. Shall we go out for a bit?' *33:8.* appearance; - appear; *190:11.* emergence: - emerge. → = **güneş çık-** → çık- 3, = **güneş doğ-** → doğ- 2, ≠ **güneş bat-** → bat- 1.

9 '- open, - blossom, - bloom, - flower': **Bahar geldi, çiçekler açtı.** 'Spring has come, the flowers have bloomed.' **Geçen sene diktiğimiz fidanlar bu sene çiçek açtı.** 'The saplings [that] we planted last year bloomed this year.' *310:32.* plants: - flower.

10 '- bring up or - open a subject': **konu aç-** '- bring up or - raise a subject, - move on to a new subject, topic': **Bu konuyu yeteri kadar tartıştık, izninizle ben yeni bir konu açmak istiyorum.** 'We've discussed this topic enough. With your permission I want to go on to [lit., ** open] a new subject.' **A: Zam istediğimi patrona söyledim.** 'A: I told the boss that I wanted a raise.' **B: Yaa, konuyu nasıl açtın?** 'B: Oh really, how did you bring up the subject?' *817:12.* beginning: - open. → ≠ **konu {kapa-/kapat-}** → {kapa-/kapat-} 6.

11 '- establish, - found, - open': **Millî Eğitim Bakanı on tane yeni ilkokul açtı.** 'The Minister of Education opened ten new primary schools.' *817:11.* beginning: - inaugurate; *891:10.* production: - establish. → ≠ **{kapa-/kapat-}** 1.

12 '- bring or - file a court case': **dava aç-** /aleyhine, için/ '- bring or - file a suit or charges /against [sb], for [a misdeed]/, - file a complaint or

claim /against/ sb, - sue sb' [A. **dava** (- -) 1 'suit, lawsuit, action'. 2 'claim']: * **Miras hakkımı almak için dava açacağım.** 'I'm going to sue for my rights of inheritance.' **Kiracıları evden çıkart.abil.mek için dava açacağım.** 'I'm going to sue to evict [lit., to be able to evict] the tenants from the house.' **Başıma gelen bu kaza.nın çalışma koşullar.ı.nın yeter-sizliğ.i.nden kaynaklandığ.ı iddia.sı.yla tazminat davası açabilir miyim?** 'Can I file for damages, claiming that the accident [that] I was involved in [lit., '{that happened to me/** that came to my head}'] resulted from lack of the proper working conditions?' Here **baş** 'head' represents the whole person. **Duydun mu, Selma boşanma davası açmış.** 'Have you heard? Selma [f.] has sued for divorce.' **Müdür bey, "sekreteriyle aşk yaşadığı" yönünde haber yayınlayan bir gazetenin aleyhine 50 bin liralık maddi ve manevi tazminat davası açtı.** 'The director filed a 50,000 lira libel suit for compensation for material loss and mental anguish against the newspaper that had published an item to the effect that he had carried on an affair with his secretary.' *598:12.* legal action: - sue. → = /I/ **dava et-** ['- bring a suit or charges /AGAINST/, - sue'], **mahkemeye ver-** ['- sue, - take to court'] → ver- 1.

{açık/açıkça} konuş-. → konuş-.

{açık/açıkça} söyle-. → söyle- 1.

açıkla- [r] [**açık** 'open, clear' + verb-forming suf. -lA] 1 /A/ '- explain sth /to/ sb, - clarify sth /FOR/ sb': **Öğretmen biz.e anlamadığ.ımız bölümleri açıkladı.** 'The teacher explained to us the sections we did not understand.' *521:6.* intelligibility: - make clear. → = **anlat-** 1, = **izah et-**.

2 /A/ '- disclose, - make public, - reveal /to/': **Doktorlar hasta.nın {AİDS'TEN/verem.DEN/kalp kriz.i.nDEN} öldüğ.ü.nü açıkladı.** 'The doctors disclosed that the patient had died {OF AIDS/OF TB/OF a heart attack}.' **Basın sözcüsü işçi maaşlarına zam {a: yapılmış olduğ.u.nu/b:**

yapıldığ.ı.nı/c: yapılacağ.ı.nı/
d: yapıl.abil.eceğ.i.ni} açıkladı. 'The press secretary disclosed
that workers' wages {a: had been
increased/b: have been increased/c:
would be increased/d: might be
increased}.' Basın sözcüsü
Başbakan.nın {a: ne zaman/b:
niçin/c: nasıl/d: kim.LER.le}
Avrupa'ya gittiğ.i.ni açıkladı.
'The press secretary disclosed {a:
when/b: why/c: how/d: with whom
[i.e., with which individuals]} the
prime minister had gone to Europe.'
351:4. disclosure: - disclose; 352:12.
publication: - announce. → = duyur-
, ≠ sakla- 1.

açıl- [ır] [aç- + {pass./refl.} suf. -Il] 1
/{tarafından/CA}/ '- be opened /by/':
Bankanın kapısı bekçi
tarafından açıldı. 'The door to the
bank was opened by {the guard/the
watchman}.' 292:11. opening: - open.
→ ≠ kapatıl- 1.

2 /{kendi kendine/kendiliğinden}/ '-
come open, - open /of its own accord
[or (all) by itself]/': Kapı açıldı ve
uzun boylu bir adam oda.yA
girdi. 'The door opened and a tall
man entered θ the room.' Bavulum
[{kendi kendine/ kendi-
liğinden}] açıldı, eşyalarım
yer.E döküldü. 'My suitcase
opened [(all) by itself] and my things
spilled out {ON/ONTO} the floor.'
Bu odanın kapısı sıkışmış, *
açılmıyor. 'The door to this room is
stuck. * It won't open.' Proverb: Bir
kapı kapanırsa bin kapı açılır.
'If one door closes, one thousand
doors will open.' 292:11. opening: -
open; 130: * 16. expectation:
proverbs. → ≠ kapan- 1.

3 '- open, - open up', temporarily or
permanently [subj.: organization,
business]: {Dükkanlar/Bankalar}
{saat kaçta/ne zaman} açılıyor?
'{At what time/When} do the
{stores/banks} open?' Bugün
postane açılmıyor. 'The post
office {isn't open/lit., isn't
open.ING} today.' Mahalle-
.miz.DE yeni bir
{pastane/lokanta/bakkal} açıldı. 'A new (pastry shop/
restaurant/grocery store) has opened
IN our neighborhood.' 292:11.
opening: - open. → ≠ kapan- 3.

4 '- open, - begin an academic year,
for a season - begin': Okullar bu

yıl {geç/erken} açıldı. 'The
schools opened {late/early} this
year.' * Okullar ay.ın kaç.ı.nda
açılıyor? '{On what date/On what
day of the month} do the schools
open?' Basketbol sezonu daha
açılmadı. 'The basketball season
hasn't begun yet.' 292:11. opening: -
open. → ≠ kapan- 1.

5 /{tarafından/CA}/ '- be turned or
switched on /by/': Evin bütün
{ışıkları/lâmbaları} ev sahibi
tarafından açıldı. 'All {the
lights/the lamps} in [lit., ** of] the
house were turned on by the
proprietor.' 817:11. beginning: -
inaugurate; 1031:25. electricity: -
electrify. → ≠ kapatıl- 2.

6 '- go on', lights, lamps: Evin
bütün {ışıkları/lâmbaları}
açıldı. 'All {the lights/the lamps} in
the house went on.' 1024:27. light: -
grow light; 1031:25. electricity: -
electrify. → = yan- 4, ≠ kapan- 2.

7 '- clear, - clear up': hava açıl-
'for weather - clear up, - become
pleasant, good, nice' [A. hava
'weather, air']: Yağmurdan sonra
hava açıldı, güneş çıktı. 'After
the rain, the weather cleared up, the
sun came out.' 392:7. improvement: -
get better. → = hava aç- → aç- 7, ≠
hava boz- → boz- 4, ≠ hava
bozul-, ≠ hava kapan- ['- cloud
over, - become cloudy, overcast'] →
kapan- 4.

8 '- be unblocked, cleared, opened
/to/': Köprüye giden yollar
trafiğ.e açıldı. 'The roads leading
[lit., going] to the bridge were opened
to traffic.' 292:12. opening: - unclose.
→ ≠ kapan- 4, ≠ kapatıl- 4.

9 '- become more spacious, - open
up': * arası {açıl-/bozul-} /lA/ '-
have a falling out /with/, - get on bad
terms /with/' [ara 'the space between
[the parties]', bozul- '- break down,
- spoil'], lit., ** 'for the space
between the parties {- open/- spoil}':
• Note the different possessed
suffixes on ara: Nilgün dün
babasının evine geri dönmüş, *
kocası ile {ara.LARI/ara.SI}
açılmış. 'Nilgün returned to her
father's house yesterday. * She had a
falling out with her husband [lit., **
{The spaces/The space} between
THEM opened].' Kira yüzünden

7

ev sahibi ile ara.MIZ açıldı. 'Because of [the matter of] rent, WE had a falling out with the landlord.' **Ara.NIZ açıldı mı?** 'Have YOU had a falling out?' **Gürültü yüzünden komşularla {a: ara.M/b: ara.N/c: ara.SI/d: ara.MIZ/ e : ara.NIZ/f: ara.LARI} açıldı.** 'Because of the noise {a: I/b: YOU [s.]/c: HE/d: WE/e: YOU [pl.]/f: THEY} had a falling out with the neighbors.' **Araları fena açıldı.** 'They had a terrible falling out.' *379:4.* dissuasion: - disincline; *456:10.* disaccord: - fall out with. → = **bağlar kop** ['for relations between people - come to an end, - break off, - have a falling out /with/, - become estranged /FROM/'] → kop- 1, = **soğu-** 2 ['- cool /TOWARD/, - lose one's love, desire, or enthusiasm /FOR/; - cease to care /FOR/ sb, sth'], = **uzaklaş-** 2 ['- become remote or distant /from/ in feeling'], ≠ **arası düzel-** ['for things - get straightened out, patched up between people'].

10 '- be opened, taken up', a topic, subject: **Bu konu burada kapandı. * Lütfen bir daha açılmasın.** 'This topic is now [lit., here, at this point] closed. * We're not going to take it up again [lit., ** Please let it not be opened again].' *404:3.* undertaking: - undertake. → ≠ **kapan-** 5.

açtır- [ır] '- have /θ/ sb open sth, - get /θ/ sb to open sth' [aç- + caus. suf. -DIr]: **Arabanın kapısını kendim açamadım. Ahmet'E açtırdım.** 'I couldn't open the door myself. I had θ Ahmet open it.' **Kapı.yI kim.E açtırdın?** 'θ Who did you {have open/get to open} the door?' → ≠ **kapattır-**.

hesap açtır- '- open an account', [A. **hesap** (. -) 'check, bill'], lit., '- have an account opened': A customer at a bank: * **{Çek hesabı/Vadeli hesap/Tasarruf hesabı} açtırmak istiyorum.** 'I want to open {a checking account/a savings account/a savings account [lit., I want to HAVE a checking account...OPENED].' • The causative is used because the actual opening of the account is regarded as being done by the bank employee, not by the customer. **İş Banka.sı.nda bin liralık bir hesap açtırdım.** 'I opened a 1,000

lira account at the İş Bank.' *292:11* opening: - open. → ≠ **hesap {kapat-/kapa-}** → {kapa-/kapat-} 1.

{ad/isim} koy-. → koy- 1.

{ad/isim} tak-. → tak-.

{ad/isim} ver-. → ver- 1.

adam ol-. → ol- 12.

âdet gör-. → gör- 3.

{adlandır- [ır]/isimlendir- [ir]} /diye/ '- call, - name, - dub, - refer to /AS/,' [{ad/A. isim (iSMi)} 'name' + verb-forming suf. -lAn = {adlan-/isimlen-} '- be named' + caus. suf. -DIr]: **Gelişmiş ülkeler geri kalanları {gelişmemiş/az gelişmiş/gelişmekte olan} ülkeler DİYE adlandırdı.** 'Developed nations called the backward ones [*or* the other ones] {undeveloped/underdeveloped/ developing} nations [lit., called...SAYING].' **Köylüler o.nU "Deli Mehmet Ağa" DİYE adlandırdı.** 'The villagers called him θ Mad Mehmet Ağa [lit., ** called him SAYING Mad Mehmet Ağa].' *527:11.* nomenclature: - name. → = **{ad/isim} koy-** → koy- 1, = **{ad/isim} ver-** → ver- 1, = **{ad/isim} tak-**, = **de-** 4.

{adlandırıl- [ır]/isimlendiril- [ir]} /{diye/olarak}, {tarafından/CA}/ '- be called, named /θ/, referred to /AS, by/' [{adlandır-/isimlendir-} + pass. suf. -Il]: **Türkiye'nin Avrupa tarafında kalan kısm.ı "Trakya" DİYE adlandırılır.** 'The part of Turkey remaining in Europe is {called θ/referred /to/ AS} Thrace.' **Türkmenistan, Özbekistan, Kırgızistan ve Kazakistan Orta Asya Türk Cumhuriyetleri OLARAK adlandırılır.** 'Turkmenistan, Uzbekistan, Kyrgyztan and Kazakhstan are {called θ/referred to AS} the Central Asian Turkic republics.' *527:13.* nomenclature: - be called. → = **den-**.

affet- [affeDer] [A. **af** (aFFı) 'pardon' + et-]: **1** '- forgive an act': * **Babası yalan söyleme.si.ni affetti.** 'His father forgave him FOR lying [lit., ** forgave HIS lying].' **Beni**

8

aldatma.sı.nı affedemiyorum. 'I can't forgive him for deceiving me [lit., ** forgive his deceiving me].' *148:3a.* forgiveness: - forgive.

2 /DAn dolayı, DIğI için/ '- excuse, - forgive, - pardon sb /because of, because/': **Affet beni.** 'Excuse me., Pardon me., Forgive me.' = **Bağışlayın beni.** *148:3b.* forgiveness: expressions requesting forgiveness. **Top oynarken camımı kıran çocukları affettim.** 'I forgave the children who had broken my window while playing ball.' * **Baba.sı Bülent'i özür dile.DIĞ.İ İÇİN affetti.** 'Bülent's father forgave him BECAUSE he had apologized [lit., ** His father forgave Bülent...].' * **Babası Bülent'i özür dileme.si.nDEN DOLAYI affetti.** 'Bülent's father forgave him because he had apologized [lit., ** BECAUSE OF his apologizing].' * {**Hayatım boyunca/Ömrüm oldukça**} **onları affetmeye-ceğim.** 'I won't forgive them {* as long as I live}.' *148:3a.* forgiveness: - forgive. → = **bağışla-** 2.

Affedersiniz. 'I beg your pardon.': S: {**Affedersiniz**}. **Bir şey sorabilir miyim?** 'Q: {Pardon/Excuse} me. Could I ask [you] sth?' C: {**Tabii/ Estağfurullah**} **buy[u]run.** 'A: {Of course/Please}, go ahead.' A common non-verb alternative to **Affedersiniz** above is **Pardon.** *343:8.* * *1.* communication: conversation initiators. **Affedersiniz, geç kaldım.** 'Pardon me, I'M late.' *148:3a.* forgiveness: - forgive; *148:3b.* forgiveness: expressions requesting forgiveness. → = **Kusura bakma.** → **bak-** 1, = **Özür dilerim.** → **dile-** 2.

Afiyet olsun. → **ol-** 11. → **olsun.**

ağır duy-. → **duy-** 1.

ağır işit-. → **işit-** 1.

ağla- [r] '- cry, - weep': **Ağlamayın. Her şey düzelecek.** 'Don't cry. Everything {will be OK/will turn out all right/lit., will straighten out}.' **Dede.m.in öldüğ.ü.nü öğrenince çok ağladım.** 'When I learned that my grandfather had died, I cried a lot.' **Lunaparktaki küçük** **kız annesini kaybettiği için** {**hıçkıra hıçkıra ağlıyordu/hüngür hüngür ağlıyordu**}. 'The little girl at the amusement park {was sobbing} because she had lost her mother.' **İstediği hediye alınmayınca çocuk bütün gün zırıl zırıl ağladı.** 'When the child didn't get [lit., was not bought] the gift that she {had wanted/had asked for}, she wept bitterly the whole day.' Proverbs: **Ağlamayan çocuğ.a meme vermezler.** 'One doesn't [lit., They don't] {nurse /lit., give the breast to} a child that doesn't cry.', i.e., The squeaky wheel gets the oil. **Çok gülen çok ağlar.** 'He who laughs much weeps much.' *12:12.* excretion: - excrete; *115:12.* lamentation: - weep. → = **göz yaşı dök-** → **dök-1**, ≠ **gül-** 1.

ağrı- [r] '- ache, - hurt, - throb with pain' [n. **ağrı** 'ache' + verb-forming suf. -**θ**]: **Doktor:** * **Nere.NİZ ağrıyor?** 'Doctor: * Where does it hurt [lit., ** YOUR where hurts]?' **Hasta:** * {**Bura.M/Şura.M**} **ağrıyor.** 'Patient: * It hurts {here/there} [lit., ** {MY here/MY there} hurts].' {**a: Sırt.ım/b: Mid.em/c: Diş.im/ d: Baş.ım/e: Kulağ.ım**} **ağrıyor.** 'I have a {a: backache/b: stomachache/c: toothache/d: headache/ e: earache} [lit., '{a: My back/b: My stomach/c: My tooth/d: My head/e: My ear} aches].' * **Boğaz.ım ağrıyor.** 'I have a sore throat [lit., ** My throat aches].' * **Diz.im ağrıyor.** 'I have a sore knee.' **Sırt.ım** {**sürekli/arada sırada**} **ağrıyor.** 'My back hurts {all the time/from time to time}.' **S: Ne zamandan beri ağrıyor?** 'Q: Since when has it been hurting?' **C:** {**Sabah.tan beri/Dün gece.den beri/* İki saat.ten beri**} **ağrıyor.** 'A: It has been hurting {since this morning/since last night/* FOR [the last] two hours}.' **S: Ne zamandır ağrıyor?** 'Q: How long has it been hurting?' Responses indicating the beginning point of the action, i.e., the hurting: **C1:** {**Sabah.tan beri/Dün gece.den beri/İki saat.ten beri**} **ağrıyor.** 'A1: It has been hurting {since this morning./since last night./* FOR [the last] two hours.}' The response indicating the duration of the action: **C2: İki saat.tır ağrıyor.** 'A2: It has been hurting FOR 2 hours.' * **En çok ne zaman ağrıyor?** 'When

9

does it hurt most?' *26:8*. pain: - suffer pain. → = acı- 1.

ağzından [lâf] kaç-. → kaç- 1.

ağzından [lâf] kaçır-. → kaçır- 2.

ahlâkını boz-. → boz- 1.

aile kur-. → kur- 1.

ak- [ar] /DAn, A/ '- flow /from, {to/INTO}/, - pour /from, INTO/': **{Çeşme.den/Musluk.tan/Duş.- tan} su akmıyor.** 'Water is not running {from the fountain/from the faucet/from the shower}.' **Kızılırmak kuzey.E doğru akar.** 'The Kızılırmak [lit., Red River] flows θ north.' **Sultan Ahmet Çeşme.si.nin su.yu kesilmiş, artık akmıyor.** 'The water from the Sultan Ahmet fountain has been turned off. It doesn't flow anymore.' Proverb: **Akarsu çukurunu kendi kazar.** 'Running water cuts its own channel [lit., cuts its channel itself].', i.e., An enterprising person creates his own oppportunities. *190:13*. emergence: - run out; *238:16*. stream: - flow. → = dökül- 3 [for a river '- flow into' a sea].

kan ak- /DAn/ '- bleed /from/' [kan 'blood']: **Kesilen parmağ.ım.dan çok kan aktı.** 'Much blood flowed from my cut finger [lit., from my finger that {got/was} cut].' **Yara.dan oluk oluk kan akıyordu.** '[The] blood was spouting from the wound.' oluk 'spout' Proverb: **Akacak kan damarda durmaz.** 'The blood that is going to spill will not stay in the vein.' *12:17*. excretion: - bleed; *190:13*. emergence: - emerge; *963:11*. predetermination: PHR. it is fated. → = kana-, = kan gel- → gel- 1.

akıl al-. → al- 1.

akıl ver-. → ver- 1.

akılda kal-. → kal- 1.

akıldan çık-. → çık- 1.

akıllan- [ır] '- become wiser through bitter experience, - come to one's senses about a matter, - wise up' [A. **akıl** (aKLı) 'intelligence' + verb-forming suf. -lAn]: **Bankayı soyan**

hırsız, hapse girdikten sonra akıllandı. 'The thief who had robbed the bank came to his senses after going to prison.' **Bekârken çok para harcardı. Evlendikten sonra akıllandı, para biriktirmeye başladı.** 'When he was a bachelor, he used to spend a lot [of money]. After getting married, he came to his senses. He began to save [money].' *570:10*. learning: - learn by experience; *924:2*. sanity: - come to one's senses. → = **aklı başına gel-** → gel- 1, **adam ol-** ['- become morally correct, mature, responsible, - grow up, - amount to sth, - shape up'] → ol- 12, **ders al-** 2 ['- learn a [moral] lesson /from/'] → al- 1.

akla gel-. → gel- 1.

aklı alMA-. → al- 1.

aklı başına gel-. → gel- 1.

aklı karış-. → {kafası/aklı} karış-. → karış- 4.

aklı takıl-. → takıl- 2.

aklıma gelmişken. → gel- 1.

aklına takıl-. → takıl- 2.

aklını {kaybet-/yitir-}. → {kaybet- /yitir }.

Aksiliğe bakın. → bak- 1.

akşam yemeği ye-. → ye- 1.

aktar- [ır] 1 /DAn, A/ '- transfer /from [one place], to [another]/, - move /from [one container], to [another]/, - pass on, - convey': **Yumurtaları öteki sepet.e aktarırken * dikkat et, kırılmasınlar!** 'Be careful while transferring the eggs to the other basket. * Watch out [that] they don't get broken [lit., ** Let them not get broken].' **Bugün size bazı gözlemlerimi ve kulağım.a gelenleri aktaracağım.** 'Today let me [lit., I will] pass on to you some of my observations and some of the information that has come to my hearing [lit., ** the things that have come to my ears].' *176:10*. transferal, transportation: - transfer.

2 /DAn, A/ '- translate /from, INTO/', in written form or orally: **Bu**

kitabı İngilizce'den Türkçe'yE aktaran kişi belli ki çok zorlanmış. 'It is clear that the person who translated this book from English INTO Turkish had {a very hard time/great difficulty}.' *341:12.* interpretation: - translate. → = tercüme et-, = çevir- 6.

aktarma yap-. → yap- 3.

al- [IR] 1 /DAn, A/ '- take /from, to/, - pick sth up /from/': Masadan kitabı alır mısın? 'Would you [please] take the book from the table?' Kütüphaneden birkaç kitap aldım. 'I {took/checked out} several books from the library.' * Bunları yan.ım.a alabilir miyim? '{May/Can} I take these with me [lit., ** to my side]?' *480:21.* taking: - take from. → ≠ koy- 1. # Türkçe kitabını Kenan'dan alır mısınız? 'Would you [please] take the Turkish book from Kenan?' Bu ilâç.TAN günde iki defa {a: yemekler.den önce/b: aç karn.ı.nA/c: yemekler.den sonra/d: tok karn.ı.nA/e: yemekler.le beraber} alın. 'Take this medicine [lit., ** FROM this medicine] twice a day {a: before meals/b: ON an empty stomach/c: after meals/d: ON a full stomach/e: with food}.' Proverbs: Aldığını veren aradığını bulur. 'He who returns what he borrows [lit., what he takes] will find what he seeks.' Veren el alan el.DEN üstündür. 'The hand that gives is {superior TO/better THAN} the hand that takes.' It is better to give than to receive. → ≠ ver- 1.

akıl al- /DAn/ '- ask sb's advice, - take or - get advice /from/ sb, - consult /θ/ sb' [A. akıl (aKLı) 'idea, opinion']: Turgut kimseden akıl almaz, * kendi bildiğini {okur/yapar}. 'Turgut never takes advice from anyone. * He always {does} just what he wants [lit., ** what he knows].' Yeni bir araba satın almadan önce Ahmet'ten akıl alalım. 'Before purchasing a new car {we should/lit., let's} consult θ Ahmet.' *422:7.* advice: - take or - accept advice. → = fikir al- below, ≠ akıl ver- → ver- 1.

aklı alMA- 'NOT - understand, grasp, figure out, - make NO sense of', lit., 'for one's mind NOT - take, grasp' [A. akıl (aKLı) 'mind,

comprehension']: Nasıl böyle bir delilik yaptı, hâlâ aklım almıyor. 'I still can't figure out how he could have done something so stupid.' Lisedeyken fiziği bir türlü aklım almazdı. 'When I was in {high school/lycée}, I couldn't make any sense at all of physics.' *522:11.* unintelligibility: not - understand. → ≠ anla-.

* alaya al- '- make fun of, - ridicule, - laugh at' [alay 'mockery, ridicule, teasing']: Çok muzip bir çocuktur, her şey.İ alay.A almaya bayılır. 'He is a very mischievious child. He takes delight in {making fun of/ridiculing} everything.' *508:8.* ridicule: - ridicule. → = /lA/ alay et-, = /lA/ dalga geç- 2 → geç- 1, = /lA/ eğlen- 2, /A/ gül- 2 ['- laugh /AT/, - mock /θ/, - make fun /OF/'].

aptes al- '- perform the ritual ablution' [P. abdest 'the ritual ablution']: Aptes [also pronounced abtes or abdest] almak namaz.ın şartlar.ı.ndan bir.i.dir. Müslümanlar günde 5 vakit namaz kılmadan önce aptes alırlar. 'To perform the ritual ablution is one of the conditions for performing [lit., conditions of] the namaz [i.e., the Islamic prayer ritual]. [When required] Muslims perform the ritual ablution before performing the namaz daily at the 5 designated times.' These prayer times are: 1. sabah 'morning', just before sunrise; 2. öğle 'noon', actually just after noontime; 3. ikindi 'late afternoon'; 4. akşam 'evening', just after sunset; 5. yatsı 'night, two hours after sunset.'

* ayağının altına al- '- give a whipping, beating, thrashing, - beat, - thrash' [ayak 'foot', alt 'the underpart of anything'] lit. '- take θ under one's foot': A threat: Alırım ayağ.IM.ın alt.ı.nA! 'I'll give you a whipping [lit., ** I'll take you θ under MY foot]!' *514: * 5.* threat: INTERJ. specific threats; *604:12.* punishment: - slap; *901:14.* impulse, impact: - hit.

borç al- /DAn/ '- borrow [money only], - take a loan /from/' [borç (borCu) 'debt, loan']: Hiç param kalmadı. Orhan'dan 5 yüz lira borç aldım. 'I had no money left. * I borrowed 500 liras from Orhan.'

621:3. borrowing: - borrow. → = **ödünç al-** ['- borrow money or anything else /from/'], ≠ **borç ver-** ['- lend, - extend a loan /to/', money only] → ver- 1, ≠ **ödünç ver-** ['- lend', money or anything else] → ver- 1, **borçlan-** ['- get into debt /to/, - owe'].

ders al- [A. ders 'lesson'] (1) /DAn/ '- take lessons /from/': **Üniversiteye giriş sınavlarına hazırlanmak için özel ders alıyorum.** 'I'm taking private lessons to prepare myself for {the college/the university} entrance examinations.' *570:11.* learning: - be taught, - receive instruction. → ≠ **ders ver-** 1 → ver- 1.
(2) /DAn/ '- learn a [moral] lesson /from/': **Bülent başına gelen trafik kazasından iyi bir ders aldı. Artık * araba.sı.yla sürat yapmıyor.** 'Bülent learned a valuable lesson from the traffic accident he had [lit., ** that came to his head]. He no longer * {drives fast/speeds} [lit., ** He no longer makes speed with his car].' *570:6.* learning: - learn. → ≠ **ders ver-** 2 → ver- 1, **akıllan-** ['- become wiser through bitter experience, - come to one's senses about a matter, - wise up'].

* dikkate al- '- take note /OF/, - take /INTO/ consideration, - consider' [A. dikkat (dikkatİ) 'careful attention']: **Başvurunuzu dikkat.E aldık.** 'We have considered your application.' **Önerinizi dikkate alacağım.** 'I'll consider your proposal.' **Şimdi bütün {olasılıkları/ihtimallEri} dikkate alalım.** 'Now let's consider all {the possibilities}.' *930:12.* thought: - consider.

duş al- '- take a shower' [duş 'shower']: **Yatmadan önce duş almak istiyorum.** 'Before going to bed, I want to take a shower.' *79:19.* cleanness: - wash. → = **duş yap-** → yap- 3, **banyo yap-** 1 ['- take a bath, - bathe'] → yap- 3, **yıkan-** 1 ['- wash oneself /with/; - take a bath, - bathe'].

ele al- '- take up, - consider a matter' [el 'hand']: **Müdür: Bugünkü toplantıda ilk önce öğrenci disiplini ile ilgili konuları el.E almak istiyorum.**

'Principal [of a school]: At today's meeting I would like first of all to take up matters [lit., topics] having to do with student discipline.' **Daha önce değindiğimiz bu konuyu şimdi ayrıntıları.yLA el.E alacağız.** 'Now we'll take up IN detail [lit., ** with its details] this issue which we touched on earlier.' *404:3.* undertaking: - undertake.

fikir al- /a: DAn, b: hakkında, c: konusunda/ '- get an idea or advice /a: from, b: about, c: on the subject of/' [A. fikir (fiKRi) 'thought, idea, opinion']: **{Bilgisayar/Lokanta/ Dava açma} konusunda Uğur'dan fikir alalım.** 'Let's get some advice from Uğur on the subject of {computers/restaurants/bringing a law suit}.' *422:7.* advice: - take or - accept advice. → = **akıl al-** above, **danış-** ['- consult /θ/, - refer /to/'], ≠ **akıl ver-** → ver- 1.

fikrini al- '- get sb's opinion or view, - take sb's advice, - consult' [A. fikir (fiKRi) 'thought, idea, opinion']: **Yeni bir bilgisayar almak istiyorum. Karar vermeden önce fikrinizi alayım. Siz bana ne {tavsiye eder-siniz?/önerirsiniz?}** 'I want to buy a new computer. Before deciding, let me get your opinion. What do you recommend [to me]?' **S: Hafta sonu piknik yapmak istiyoruz, ne dersin?** 'Q: {During/Over} the weekend we want to have a picnic. What do you say?' **C: * İyi olur ama bir de diğer öğrenciler.in fikirler.i.ni alalım.** 'A: That's a good idea [lit., That would be good], but let's also consult the other students [lit., let's get the other students' views].' **Evlilik konusunda aile.m.in fikr.i.ni de aldım.** 'On the matter of marriage I also got my family's views.' **Ercan çok inatçıdır. Kimse.nin fikr.i.ni almaz; * [hep] kendi bildiğ.i.ni {okur/yapar}.** 'Ercan is very stubborn. He doesn't listen to anyone [lit., doesn't take anyone's advice]. * He always {does} just what he wants [lit., ** what he knows].' *422:7.* advice: - take or - accept advice. → = **akıl al-** above, **danış-** ['- consult /θ/, - refer /to/'], ≠ **fikir ver-** 2 ['- give advice /to/, - advise /θ/, - suggest a course of action /to/'] → ver- 1.

12

geri al- [geri 'back, rear, the space behind'] **(1)** /DAn/ '- take back [to oneself] /from/': **Sedat'a verdiğim kitapları [ondan] geri aldım.** 'I took back [from him] the books I had given to Sedat.' **Bozuk çıkan saati saatçi geri aldı.** 'The watchmaker took back the watch that had turned out defective.'

kararını geri al- '- withdraw or - rescind one's decision': **İşçiler grev kararını geri aldılar.** 'The workers {decided not/lit., ** withdrew their decision} to strike.' *363:6.* changing of mind: - change one's mind'; *370:7.* abandonment: - give up. → = **kararından vazgeç-.**

parasını geri al- /DAn/ '- get one's money back, - get a refund /from/': **Müşteri: Bu çantayı iade etmek istiyorum. Paramı geri alabilir miyim?** 'Customer: I want to return this {handbag/ purse/briefcase}. Can I get my money back?' **Satıcı 1: Maalesef satılan malı geri almıyoruz efendim.** 'Salesman 1: Unfortunately we don't accept returns [on merchandise] [lit., take back goods that have been sold], {sir/ma'am}.' **Satıcı 2: Tabii, alabilirsiniz.** 'Salesman 2: Of course you can.' **Satıcı 3: Paranızı geri alamazsınız ama başka bir çanta.yLA değiştirebilirsiniz.** 'Salesman 3: You can't get your money back, but you can exchange it FOR another one [lit., handbag...].' *481:6.* restitution: - recover. → ≠ **geri ver** → **ver-** 1.

sözünü geri al- '- take back or - retract one's words, - recant': **Çok sert bir tepkiyle karşılaşınca sözünü geri aldı.** 'When he was faced with a strong reaction [i.e., to what he had said], he retracted his words.' *445:2.* repeal: - repeal.

(2) '- set or - turn back [clocks]': **Bu gece saatleri bir saat geri aldık.** 'This evening we set back the clocks one hour.' *163:8a.* regression: - turn sth back. → ≠ **ileri al-** below.

görevden al- '- fire, - relieve sb of his {duties/position}' [görev 1 'duty'. 2 'office, post'], *formal*: **Başbakan Savunma Bakanını {görevden/görev.i.nden} aldı.** 'The prime minister {fired the minister of defense/relieved the minister of defense of his duties}.'

908:19. ejection: - dismiss. → *neutral*: = **işine son ver-** → **son ver-**, → **ver-** 1, *informal*: = **işten {at-/kov-}** → **at-** 1, **kov-** 2, *neutral*: = **işten çıkar-** → **çıkar-** 1, ≠ {**ata-/tayin et-**}, ≠ **görevlendir-.**

hava al- [A. hava 1 'air'. 2 'weather'] **(1)** '- breathe fresh air, - get a breath of fresh air': **Bütün gün evde oturduk, biraz çıkıp hava alalım.** 'We've sat in the house all day. Let's go out and get a breath of fresh air.' *318:21.* * *1.* wind: - breathe. → **dolaş-** 1 ['- go, - walk, - wander, or - stroll about'], **gez-** ['- go or walk about, - tour'], **yürüyüşe çık-** ['- go out /for/ a walk'] → **çık-** 2.
(2) '- absorb air, - take in air, - get air, - air out': **Şu camları aç da oda biraz hava alsın.** 'Open these windows, and let the room get a little air.' *317:10.* air, weather: - air. → **havalandır-** ['- air out a place'].

içine al- [iç 'inside'], lit., ** '- take to its inside' **(1)** '- include, - cover, - encompass': **"Kültür" çok geniş bir kavramdır. Pek çok şey.I iç.i.nE alır.** 'Culture is a very broad concept. It includes very many things.' **Demokrasi insan haklarını da içine alır.** 'Democracy also involves [i.e., includes] human rights.' {a: **Ara sınav/**b: **Dönem son.u sınav.ı/**c: **Final sınav.ı/**d: **Yıl son.u sınav.ı}** **bütün kitabı içine alıyor mu?** 'Does {a: the midterm examination/b: the quarter [*or* semester] final examination/c: the final examination/d: the year final examination} cover the whole book?' **Sağlık sigortanız bütün hastalıkları içine alıyor mu?** 'Does your health insurance cover all illnesses?' **Öğrenci: {Öğretmen.İM}, bu imtihan altıncı dersi de içine alıyor mu?** 'Student: Teacher [lit., ** 'MY teacher', the common form of address to one's teacher], does this examination also include the 6th lesson?' **Bir gecelik otel parası kahvaltıyı da içine alıyor mu?** 'Does the hotel rate for one night also include breakfast?' *771:3.* inclusion: - include. → = **içer-**, = **kapsa-**, **dahil ol-** ['- be included /IN/'] → **ol-** 12.
(2) '- hold, - contain': * **Bu bidon [içine] 15 litre benzin alır.** 'This

13

plastic jerry can holds fifteen liters of gas.' *771:3*. inclusion: - include.

ifade al- /DAn/ '- examine sb and record his testimony, - take a deposition /from/' [A. **ifade** (. - .) 1 'expression, statement'. 2 'evidence, deposition']: **Polis ifade aldı.** 'The police took depositions.' The pattern **ifade.si.ni al-** is preferred to /DAn/ ifade al-: **Polis cinayetin işlendiği evdeki herkes.in ifade.si.ni aldı.** 'The police took the deposition of everyone in the house where the murder had been committed.' **Polis, olayı gören {biri.nin/birisi.nin} ifade.si.ni almış.** 'The police [apparently] took the deposition {of sb} who had witnessed the event.' *956:9*. evidence, proof: - testify. → ≠ **ifade ver-** [*law* '- give evidence /to/, - testify, - give testimony, - give or - make a statement'] → **ver-** 1, ≠ **tanıklık et-**.

ileri al- '- set or - turn clocks ahead, forward': **Bu gece saatleri bir saat ileri aldık.** 'This evening we set the clocks ahead one hour.' *162:2*. progression: - progress. → ≠ **geri al-** 2 above.

karar al- /için/ '- make a decision /TO/, - decide /{TO/ON}/, - resolve /TO/' [A. **karar** (. -) 'decision'], lit., ** '- take a decision /for/'. The subject is usually a group, organization, or society acting in an official capacity: **Fabrika işçileri * grev için karar aldı.** 'The factory workers * decided {TO strike./ON a strike.}' **Meclis bu yıl genel af karar.ı aldı.** 'This year the Parliament decided TO grant a general amnesty [lit., ** took a general pardon decision].' **Yüksek Öğretim Kurulu [YÖK] bu yıl üniversitelerin bir ay geç kapanması karar.ı.nı aldı.** 'The Council on Higher Education decided TO close the universities a month late this year [lit., ** took a late-closing decision].' *359:7*. resolution: - resolve. → = /A/ **karar ver-** [subj.: usually individuals or a family, not in an official capacity] → **ver-** 1, = **kararlaştır-** [at least two persons reaching a decision together].

kilo al- '- put on weight, - gain weight': **Son günlerde çok kilo aldım, perhiz yapmam lâzım.** 'I've put on a lot of weight lately.

I've got to go on a diet.' **Suna çok kilo almış, * tanıyamadım.** 'Suna had put on a lot of weight. * I didn't [lit., couldn't] recognize her.' *259:8*. expansion, growth: - fatten. → = **şişmanla-**, = **topla-** 3, = **toplan-** 4, ≠ **kilo ver-** → **ver-** 1, ≠ **zayıfla-** 1.

misal al-. → {**örnek/misal**} **al-** below.

nefes al- '- breathe, - take a breath; - inhale' [A. **nefes** 'breath']: **Doktor: Derin derin nefes alıp verin.** 'Doctor: Take a deep deep breath, then {let it out/exhale}.' **Hasta.nın nefes almak.TA güçlük çektiğ.i görüldü.** 'It was observed that the patient was having trouble {θ/in} breathing.' {* **Oda.nın iç.i çok sigara dumanı oldu/Oda sigara dumanı ile doldu**}, **nefes alamıyorum.** '{The room filled with cigarette smoke./The room became full of cigarette smoke.} I can't breathe.' **Ahmet bey bir {sigara/ puro/pipo} yaktı. Derin bir nefes aldı.** 'Ahmet bey lit up a {cigarette/cigar/pipe}. He {took a deep {puff/drag}/inhaled deeply}.' *89:14*. tobacco: - use tobacco; *187:12*. reception: - draw in; *318:21*. * 1. wind: - breathe. → = **içine çek-** ['- inhale'] → **çek-** 1, = **nefes çek-** ['- take a wiff, puff, drag (of tobacco)'] → **çek-** 1, ≠ **nefes ver-** → **ver-** 1, **nefes tut-** ['- hold one's breath'] → **tut-** 4.

ödünç al- /DAn/ '- borrow /from/', money or anything else [**ödünç** 'loan, borrowed']: **Şu kitabı birkaç günlüğ.ü.nE ödünç alabilir miyim?** 'May I borrow this book FOR a few days?' **Orhan'dan {10 bin lira/bir saat} ödünç aldım.** 'I borrowed {10,000 liras/a watch} from Orhan.' *621:3*. borrowing: - borrow. → = **borç al-** [money only] above, **borçlan-** ['- get into debt /to/, - owe'], ≠ **borç ver-** ['- lend, - extend a loan /to/', money only] → **ver-** 1, ≠ **ödünç ver-** ['- lend', money or anything else] → **ver-** 1.

öne al- '- move up in time, - make earlier than originally planned' [**ön** 'the front part of anything']: **Antalya'ya gitme tarih.i.ni ön.E aldım.** 'I moved up the date of

14

departure for Antalya.' **Antalya'ya 5 Ağustos'ta gidecektik, fakat tarihi öne aldık, 25 Temmuz'da gideceğiz.** 'We were going to go to Antalya on the fifth of August, but we moved up the date. We're going to go on the 25th of July.' **Öğretmen fizik sınavını bir hafta öne aldı.** 'The teacher moved the time of the physics examination up a week.' *163:8a.* regression: - turn sth back. → ≠ **bırak-** 6, ≠ {**ertele-/tehir et-**}.

{örnek/misal} al- '- take as an example, role model /FOR/' [{**örnek/A. misal** (. -) (**misalİ**)} 'example']: **Pek çok ülke gelişmek için Japonya'yı örnek alır.** 'Many countries take Japan as an example for [their own] development.' * {**Bu konuda**} **Ahmet'i kendim.E örnek alıyorum.** '{In this matter/On this subject} I take Ahmet AS an example FOR myself.' *956:13.* evidence, proof: - cite.

para al- /A, için/ '- charge /FOR/, - take money /FOR/' [**para** 'money']: **Çileğ.in kilo.su.nA ne kadar [para] alıyorsunuz?** 'How much [money] do you charge FOR a kilo of strawberries?' The same information is more commonly elicited as follows: * **Çileğin kilosu kaç.A?** 'How much is a kilo of strawberries?' **Limon.un tane.si.nE ne alıyorsunuz?** 'What do you charge apiece FOR lemons?' Or more commonly: **Limon.un tane.si kaç.A?** 'How much for one lemon [lit., ** for one unit of lemon]?' **Müşteri: Televizyon tamir.i için ne kadar [para] alıyorsunuz?** 'Customer: How much do you charge to repair a TV set?' **Tamirci: Önce bir bakmam lâzım. Fiyatı sonra {konuşuruz/tespit ederiz/ kararlaştırırız}.** 'Repairman: First I'll have to take a look. Then {we'll talk about a price/we'll set a price/we'll decide on a price}.' *630:12.* price, fee: - charge. → = **ücret al-** below, ≠ **para ver-** ['- pay'].

fazla para al- /için/ '- overcharge /for/': **Benden fazla para aldınız.** 'You have overcharged me.' **Tamirciler ufak bir iş için bile çok fazla para alıyorlar.** 'Repairmen charge too much even for a small job.' *632:7.*

expensiveness: - overprice; *992:10.* excess: - overdo. → *formal*: **dolandır-** ['- cheat, - swindle, - rip off, - defraud']. The two following are *very common slang:* **kazık at-** ['- gyp, - rip off, - swindle, - cheat; - sell sb sth at an exorbitant, outrageous price'] → **at-** 1, **kazıkla-**. Same.

tozunu al- '- dust' [**toz** 'dust'], lit., ** '- take the dust of': * **Bu masa ne kadar tozlanmış, hiç toz.u.nu almıyor musun?** 'Look how dusty this table has gotten! Don't you ever dust it?' {a: **Televizyon.un/b: Sehpalar.ın/ c: Biblolar.ın/d: Kitaplığ.ın**} **toz.u.nu al.** 'Dust {a: the TV set/b: the small tables [i.e., end, coffee, etc.]/c: the knicknacks/d: the bookshelves}.' *79:18.* cleanness: - clean. → **sil-** 2 ['- wipe clean', usually with a wet cloth or mop], **temizle-** ['- clean'].

ücret al- /için/ '- charge /for/, - take a fee /for/' [A. **ücret** 1 'fee; wage salary'. 2 'charge']: **Müşteri: Radyonun pilleri için ayrıca ücret alıyor musunuz?** 'Customer: Do you charge {extra/separately} for the batteries [of the radio]?' **Satıcı: Hayır [ücret] almıyoruz, piller ücretsiz.** 'Salesman: No, we don't. The batteries are free.' Without the word **ücret: Ne kadar alıyorsunuz?** 'How much do you charge?' • Note also the following more common equivalent expressions: {**Kaç para?/Kaç?**} 'How much? [lit., {How much money?/How much?}]' *630:12.* price, fee: - charge. → = **para al-** above, ≠ **para ver-** ['- pay'].

{vakit/zaman} al- '- take time', often with a preceding adjective [{A. **vakit** (vaKTİ), A. **zaman** (. -)} 'time']: **Tepeye kadar çıkmak epey vakit alıyor.** 'It takes quite a while to climb to the top of the hill.' **Buradan yürü.yerek fırına gitmek pek vakit almaz.** 'It doesn't take long to walk [lit., ** to go by walk.ing] to the bakery from here.' *811:4b.* continuity: for sth - continue; *820:6.* time: - spend time. → = **sür-** 3, = **çek-** 10.

2 /DAn/ '- pick up /from/, - take on [passengers], - give a {ride/lift}': **Siparişlerimi ne zaman**

alabilirim? 'When can I pick up my purchases?' **Okula giderken beni de alabilir misiniz?** 'On the way to school can you give me a {ride/lift} too?' **Lütfen gelip beni okuldan alır mısınız?** 'Would you please [come and] pick me up from school?' **Tren yolcuları almak için istasyonda durdu.** 'The train stopped at the station to {take on/pick up} the passengers.' → ≠ **bırak-** 2, ≠ **indir-** 2 ['- let off, - discharge, - unload /at, from/ vehicle', passengers]. *176:16.* transferal, transportation: - fetch.

3 /DAn/ '- get, - receive /from/': **Dün annesinden bir mektup almış.** 'Yesterday he received a letter from his mother.' * **Şoförden para.nın üst.ü.nü aldınız mı?** 'Did you get the change [lit., the rest of the money] from the driver?' *479:6.* receiving: - receive. → ≠ **ver-** 1, ≠ **teslim et-** ['- hand sth over /to/, - turn sth over /to/, - deliver sth /to/, - turn sth in /to/'].

ceza al- /DAn/ '- receive punishment /from/, - be punished /by/' [A. **ceza** (. -) 'punishment']: **Orhan ödevlerini yap.madığ.ı için bugün öğretmenden ceza aldı.** 'Orhan was punished by the teacher today because he hadn't done his homework [lit., ** Orhan received punishment from the teacher today...].' *604:10.* punishment: - punish. → = **ceza ye-** → ye- 2, ≠ **ödüllendiril-**.

fiyat al- /DAn/ '- receive a price offer /from/, - get a bid, estimate, quote /from/' [**fiyat** or **fiat** 'price']: **Okulumuza alacağımız bilgisayarlar için birkaç firmadan fiyat aldık. En ucuz fiyatı veren firmayı tercih edeceğiz.** 'We received bids from several companies regarding computers that we're going to buy for our school. We'll choose the company that offers the lowest price.' *630:11.* price, fee: - price.

gün al- /a: DAn, b: için, c: A/ '- {make/get} an appointment [for a {date/day}] /a: from [sb], b: for [sth], c: FOR [a time]/, - set a {date/day} /b: for/' [**gün** 'day']: {**Ehliyet imtihanı/Doktora tez savunmam/Nikâh**} **için gün aldım.** 'I set a date for {the license examination/the defense of my Ph.D.

dissertation/the civil wedding service}.' **Genel bir muayene için hastane.DEN gün aldım.** 'I {made/got} an appointment for a general physical [examination] AT the hospital.' **Doktordan pazartesi.yE gün aldım.** 'I got an appointment from the doctor FOR Monday.' **Gelecek pazartesi için doktor.DAN gün aldım.** 'I {made/got} an appointment WITH the doctor for next Monday.' *964:4.* prearrangement: - prearrange. → **randevu al-** ['- get an appointment'] → al- 3, ≠ **gün ver-** ['- give a {date/day} for an appointment /to/'] → ver- 1.

haber al- /DAn/ '- get word, news /{OF/from}/, - find out /from/' [A. **haber** 'news, information']: **Metin'den hiç haber alamadık.** 'We haven't been able to get any news {OF/from} Metin.' **Ali'lere {a: gittiğ.iniz.i/b: gideceğ.iniz.i/c: gitmeniz gerektiğ.i.ni} haber aldık.** 'We received word {a: that you had gone/b: that you were going to go/c: that you had to go} to Ali's place [i.e., the residence of Ali and those people associated with him, e.g., his immediate family or his friends].' **Ali'lere {a: nasıl/b: ne zaman/c: neden/d: niye/e: niçin/f: kimlerle} gideceğ.iniz.İ haber aldık.** 'We received word as to {a: how/b: when/c, d, e: why/f: with whom [i.e., with what people]} you were going to go to Ali's place.' **Ali'lere gidip {gitmediğiniz.İN/gitmeyeceğiniz.İN} haber.İ.ni aldık.** 'We received word as to whether or not {you had gone/you were going to go} to Ali's place.' *570:6.* learning: - learn; *927:14.* knowledge: - learn. → ≠ **haber ver-** → ver- 1.

{**izin/müsaade**} **al-** /DAn, için/ '- get permission /from, to/' [{A. **izin** (iZNi)/A. **müsaade**} 'permission']: **Sinemaya gitmek için babandan izin aldın mı?** 'Did you get permission from your father to go to the movies?' *443:9.* * *1.* permission: * - get permission. → ≠ **izin ver-** ['- give /Ө/ sb permission'] → ver- 1.

müsaade al-. → {**izin/müsaade**} **al-** just above.

16

randevu al- /DAn, için/ '- make an appointment /for/, - get an appointment /from, for/' [F. **randevu** 'appointment, engagement']: **Müdür beyle görüşmek istiyorum. Yarın için bir randevu alabilir miyim?** 'I would like to speak with the director. Can I get an appointment for tomorrow?' **Saat kaç için randevu alabilirim?** 'For what time can I get an appointment?' *582:19.* sociability: - visit; *964:4.* prearrangement: - prearrange. → **gün al-** ['- {make/get} a {date/day} for an appointment'] → above, ≠ **randevu ver-** → **ver-** 1.

soğuk al- '- get a chill, - catch a chill', the early stage of a cold [**soğuk** 'cold' as opposed to heat]: **Dün yatak odamın penceresi açık kalmış, soğuk almış olmalıyım.** * **Kendimi iyi hissetmiyorum.** 'Yesterday the window of my bedroom {was left/lit., stayed} open. I must have caught a cold. I don't feel well [lit., ** I don't feel MYSELF well].' **Dün akşam soğuk almışım.** * **Nezle oldum.** 'Last night I seem to have been affected by the cold. * I have the sniffles.' **Banyo yaptıktan sonra saçlarınızı kurutmazsanız soğuk alabilirsiniz.** 'If you don't dry your hair after taking a bath, you may catch a cold.' *85:46b.* disease: - take sick in particular ways; *1022:9.* cold: - freeze. → = **üşüt-** 2, **nezle ol-** ['- catch or - get a cold'] → **ol-** 10.2.

4 /a: A, b: DAn, c: DAn, d: DAn/ '- buy, - purchase sth /a: AT [a price, total OR per unit], b: {AT [a price, PER unit], c: AT [a store], d: from [a person]}/': • Source is usually indicated with the ablative case: **S: Pazar.DAN {ne/hangisini/ hangilerini} aldınız?** 'Q: {What/Which one/Which ones} did you buy AT the market?' Sometimes '- take': **C: {a: Bunu/b: Mavi olan.ı [or Mavi.si.ni]/c: Büyüğ.ü.nü/d: Ucuz.u.nu/e: Taze.si.ni/f: Orta beden.i/g: 37 numara.yı} aldım.** 'A: I {took/bought} {a: this one/b: the blue one/c: the large one/d: the inexpensive one/e: the fresh one/f: the medium size/g: size 37}.' **Şekerci.DEN biraz şeker {al}.** '{Get/Buy} a little candy from the candy seller.'

S1: * **Karpuz.U kaç.A aldın?** 'How much did you pay for the watermelons {IN TOTAL/PER UNIT, i.e., apiece or per kilo, etc.}?' **C1: Tane.si.nİ 1 lira.yA aldım.** 'A1: I paid 1 lira apiece for them.' **C2: Kilo.su.nU 20 kuruş.A aldım.** 'A2: I paid 20 kurush a kilo for them.'

S2: * **Karpuz.un {TANE.Sİ.Nİ/KİLO.SU.NU} kaç.A aldın?** 'Q: How much did you pay for the watermelons {APIECE/PER KILO}?' Same responses as above under **S1.**

S3: * **Karpuz.U kaç.TAN aldın?** 'Q: How much did you pay for the watermelons [i.e., PER UNIT, i.e., {apiece/per kilo}, etc.]?' **C1: Tane.si.ni 35 kuruş.TAN aldım.** 'A1: I paid 35 kurush apiece for them.' **C2: Kilo.su.nu 5 kuruş.TAN aldım.** 'A2: I paid 5 kurush {a/per} kilo for them.'

Şimdi bilgisayar alman.ın tam zaman.ı. '{Now/This} is the best time to buy a computer.' **Bilgisayar almışken** * **iyi.si.ni al.** 'Since you are going to buy a computer, * buy the best [lit., ** a good one of (its kind)].' Proverbs: **Ucuz alan pahalı alır.** 'He who buys at a low price buys at a high price.', i.e., pays too much for what he gets. * **Ucuzluk.TA alır, pahalılık.TA satar.** '{a: He buys low and sells high./b: He buys when it is cheap [lit., ** IN cheapness], and he sells when it is expensive [lit., ** IN expensiveness].}' *733:7.* purchase: - purchase. → = **satın al-** below, **alışveriş yap-** ['- shop, - do shopping'] → **yap-** 3, ≠ **sat-**.

satın al- /A, DAn/. Same as above. Often used when **al-** alone might be ambiguous. **Satın** has no current independent use outside of its use with **al-**: **S:** * **Peyniri nere.DEN [satın] aldın?** 'Q: Where [lit., ** FROM where] did you [s.] buy the cheese?' • Source is usually indicated with the ablative case. **C: {a: Bakkal.DAN/b: Market.TEN/c: Pazar.DAN/d: Çarşı.DAN} aldım.** 'A: I bought it {a: AT the grocery store/b: AT the supermarket/c: AT the {market/bazaar}/d: AT the {market/bazaar}}.' **Babam yeni bir araba satın aldı.** 'My father bought a new car.'

Arabanı çok beğendim. Eğer satmak istersen, istediğin fiyat.A satın alırım. 'I like your car very much. If you want to sell it, I'll buy it AT the price you ask.' In reference to a house: Satın mı aldınız, yoksa {kira.DA/ kira.yLA} mı oturuyorsunuz? 'Did you buy it or are you renting [lit., ** living {in rent/BY MEANS OF rent}]?' *733:7.* purchase: - purchase. → = al- 4, alışveriş yap- ['- shop, - do shopping'] → yap- 3, ≠ sat-.

5 '- use habitually', almost exclusively of alcohol: * {alkol/içki} al- '- drink {alcohol/alcoholic drinks}': {Alkol/ İçki} almıyorum. 'I don't drink.' *88:24.* intoxication: - tipple. → = kullan-.

alay et- [eDer] /lA/ '- make fun /OF/, - ridicule /θ/, - mock /θ/' [alay 'mockery, ridicule, teasing']: Süleyman adını tahtaya yazamayınca bütün sınıf [onun.LA] alay etti. 'When Süleyman couldn't write his name on the blackboard, the whole class made fun OF him.' Lütfen benim.LE alay etme, pilot olmak konu.su.nda çok ciddîyim. 'Don't make fun OF me. I'm quite serious ABOUT [lit., ** on the subject of] becoming a pilot.' *508:8.* ridicule: - ridicule. → = alaya al- → al- 1, = /lA/ dalga geç- 2 → geç- 1, = /lA/ eğlen- 2, = /A/ gül- 2 ['- laugh /AT/, - mock /θ/, - make fun /OF/'].

alçal- [ır] 1 /DAn, A/ '- come down, - descend /from, to/ a lower level' [alçak 'low', final k to l + θ]: Uçak 10 bin metre yükseklik.ten hızla alçalmay.a başladı. 'The plane began to descend rapidly from an altitude of 10,000 meters.' Kuşlar alçaldı ve tarla.yA kondu. 'The birds descended and alighted IN the field.' Uçurtma alçaldı ve çatı.yA düştü. 'The kite [i.e., the toy] came down and fell ON the roof.' *194:5.* descent: - descend. → ≠ yüksel- 1.

2 *fig.* in a moral sense: '- demean oneself, - stoop to doing sth despicable, - sink to a low level in behavior': O.nun bu kadar alçal.abil.eceğ.i.ni doğrusu tahmin etmemiştim. Alçak

herif! 'I really didn't imagine that he could stoop so low! The scoundrel!' *137:7.* humility: - humble oneself.

{aldan- [ır]/kan- [ar]} /A, not with tarafından/ '- be deceived, fooled, taken in /BY/': Kuyumcudan aldığım yüzüğün altın olmadığını öğrenince aldandığ.ım.ı anladım. 'When I learned that the ring I had bought from the jeweler was not gold, I realized that I had been taken in.' Person as cause: Satıcı.yA aldandım, 10 liralık pantolonu 20 lira.yA aldım. Keşke o.nA aldanmasaydım. 'I was taken in BY the salesman. I bought a 10 lira pair of trousers FOR 20 liras. If only I had not been taken in BY him!' Thing as cause: Onun {yalanları.nA/söyledikleri.nE} aldanma! 'Don't be taken in {BY his lies!/BY what he says!}' Görünüş.E aldanma. 'Don't be deceived BY appearances.' Güneş.E aldanıp ceketsiz sokağ.a çıktım. 'Being fooled BY the sun, I went out into the street without a jacket.' Proverb: Aldatayım diyen aldanır. 'He who intends to deceive is deceived [lit., The one who says let me deceive is deceived].' *356:14.* deception: - deceive.

aldat- [ır] 1 '- cheat, - deceive': Aldığım yüzüğün altın olmadığını öğrenince kuyumcunun beni aldattığını anladım. 'When I learned that the ring that I had bought was not gold, I realized that the jeweler had cheated me.' Bütün insanları aldatmanın mümkün olduğunu mu sanıyorsun? 'Do you think you can deceive everyone [lit., all the people]?' Kendini asla aldatamazsın. 'You can never deceive yourself.' {Kendi kendimizi/Birbirimizi} aldatmayalım. 'Let's not fool {ourselves/one another}.' Proverb: Herkesi aldatamazsın. Aldatayım diyen aldanır. 'You can't deceive everyone. He who intends to deceive is deceived [lit., The one who says let me deceive is deceived].' *356:14.* deception: - deceive; *356:18.* : - cheat. → = kandır- 1.

2 /I/ '- be unfaithful /TO/, - cheat /ON/': Sibel hanım kocası.nın kendisi.nİ aldattığ.ı.nı öğrenince evi terk etti. 'When

Sibel hanım learned that her husband had been unfaithful TO her, she left {him/lit., the home} [for good].' **Kendisi.nİ aldatan kocasını bağışladı.** 'She pardoned her husband who had cheated ON her.' *356:18.* deception: - cheat; *645:12.* improbity: - be unfaithful.

aldatıl- [ır] /{tarafından/CA}/ '- be cheated, deceived /by/ [aldat- + pass. suf. -Il]: **Eyvah, bu yüzük altın değilmiş. [Kuyumcu tarafından] Aldatıldım.** 'O dear, it seems this ring is not gold. I've been cheated [by the jeweler].' **Seyahat acentesi tarafından aldatıldım.** 'I was cheated by the travel agency.' *356:14.* deception: - deceive; *356:18.* : - cheat.

aldır- [ır] /a: A, b: A, c: DAn, d: DAn/ [al- + caus. suf. -DIr]: **1** '- have /a: θ sb buy, purchase sth, b: AT [a price], c: AT [a store], d: from [a person]/': **Kapıcı.yA {bakkal-.DAN/Ahmet bey.den} beş kilo şeker aldırdım.** 'I had θ the caretaker [*or* the doorman] [go and] buy 5 kilos of sugar {AT the grocery story/from Ahmet bey}.' *733:7.* purchase: - purchase.

2 /A/ '- mind, - care /ABOUT/, - pay attention /to/' *339:6.* carefulness: - care. Usually in the negative: **aldırMA-** '- ignore, NOT - pay attention /to/, NOT - care /ABOUT/': **Hayat.ta hiçbir şey.E aldırmaz.** 'He doesn't care ABOUT anything in life.' **Ben dış görünüş.E hiç aldırmam.** 'I don't pay any attention to [external] appearances.' **Asuman sınıfta kaldı ama hiç aldırmıyor.** 'Asuman was held back in school [lit., ** 'stayed in the class', i.e., didn't pass on to the next grade], but she doesn't care at all.' **A: Şu adam hep bana bakıyor.** 'A: This man is always looking at me.' **B: Boş ver, aldırma.** 'B: Never mind; just ignore him.' *340:6.* neglect: - neglect; *997:12.* unimportance: - attach little importance to. → ≠ **aldırış etME-**, ≠ **boş ver- 1** → ver- 1.

aldırış etME- [z] 'NOT - mind, NOT - pay attention to, - disregard, - ignore' [aldırış 'care, attention']: **S: Dün Murat'ı başka bir kızla gördüm, ne yapayım?** 'Q: Yesterday I saw Murat with another girl. What should I do?' **C: Boş ver, aldırış etme. Nasılsa sana döner.** 'A: Never mind; don't pay any attention. He'll come back to you anyway.' *340:6.* neglect: - neglect; *997:12.* unimportance: - attach little importance to. → = **aldırMA-**, = **boş ver- 1** → ver- 1.

alın- [ır] [al- + pass. suf. -In] **1** /DAn/ '- be taken, received /from/': **Bu {yazı/makale} nereden alındı?** 'Where was this article taken from?' *480:21.* taking: - take from. **ele alın-** '- be taken up, considered', subject, topic [el 'hand'], lit., ** '- be taken in hand': **Toplantıda ilk önce Irak'A uygulanan ambargo konusu el.E alındı.** 'At the meeting, the subject of the embargo imposed ON Irak was taken up first.' *404:3.* undertaking: - undertake.

görevden alın- '- be fired, relieved of one's {duties/position}' [görev 1 'duty'. 2 'office, post']: **Rüşvet yiyen gümrük müdürü {görevden/görevinden} alınmış.** 'The director of customs who had taken bribes {was fired/was relieved of his duties}.' *908:19.* ejection: - dismiss. → = **işinden ol-** → ol- 7, = **görevine son veril-**, ≠ {**atan-/tayin edil-**}, ≠ **görevlendiril-**, ≠ **tayin ol-** → ol- 12.

tedavi altına alın- '- be taken in for treatment' [A. tedavi (. - .) 'treatment', alt (Tı) 'the underpart of anything'], lit., ** '- be taken under treatment': **{Ambulans.LA/ Cankurtaran.LA} en yakın hastane.ye götürülen yaralılar hemen tedavi alt.ı.na alındı.** 'The wounded who were taken to the nearest hospital {BY ambulance} were at once taken in for treatment.' *91:24.* therapy: - treat. → **taburcu ol-** ['- be {discharged/released} /from/ a hospital'] → ol- 12.

2 /{tarafından/CA}, A/ '- be bought, purchased /by, FOR/': **Millî Eğitim Bakanlığı'nA yüz tane bilgisayar alındı.** 'One hundred computers were bought FOR the Ministry of Education.' {**Millî Eğitim Bakanlığı'nca/Millî Eğitim Bakanlığı tarafından**} **yüz tane bilgisayar alındı.** 'A hundred computers were bought {by the Ministry of Education}.' *733:7.* purchase: - purchase. → ≠ **satıl-**.

3 /A, DAn dolayı/ '- be offended or hurt /BY, because of/, - take offense /AT/': * **Söylediği {iğneli} sözler.den dolayı Ahmet'E çok alındım.** 'I was very offended {by Ahmet's {biting/sharp} words./lit., BY Ahmet because of the {biting/sharp} words he said.}' **Hasan'ın bana öyle bağırma.sı.nA çok alındım. Artık onunla konuşmayacağım.** 'I was very offended BY Hasan's shouting at me like that. I'm not going to speak to him anymore.' **Konuşurken çok dikkatli ol. Ayşe çok alıngandır, * her söz.E alınır.** 'Be very careful when you speak. Ayşe is very sensitive. * She takes offense AT the slightest remark [lit., AT every word].' *152:21.* resentment, anger: - offend; *156:5.* disrespect: - offend. → = **darıl- 2,** = **kırıl- 3.**

alıntı yap-. → **yap- 3.**

alış- [ır] 1 /A/ '- get, - become, or - be accustomed /to/; - get, - become or - be used /to/' [ADJ. **alışık**]: NON-verbal noun as object: **Okul hayat.ı.na {yavaş yavaş/biraz zor/çok zor} alışıyorum.** 'I'm {slowly/having some difficulty/having great difficulty} getting used to school life.' **Şu bilgisayar.A bir türlü alışamıyorum. Program-lar.ın nasıl çalışacağ.ı.nı {hep/sürekli} unutuyorum.** 'I simply can't get used to that computer. I keep forgetting [or I'm {always} forgetting] how the programs work.' * **Bunca zamandır Amerika'dayım hâlâ kahve.ye alışamadım.** 'I've been in the States all this time, and I still haven't been able to get used to the coffee.'
VERBAL noun as object: **Amerika'ya geldikten sonra kahvaltıda kahve içmey.e alıştım.** 'After coming to the United States, I got used to drinking coffee at breakfast.' S: **Seni uyandırmamı ister misin?** 'Q: Do you want me to wake you up?' C: * **Gerek yok. {5'te/erken} kalkma.ya alıştım.** 'A: * That won't be necessary. {I got/I AM} used to getting up {at 5 o'clock/early}.' In this example the PAST tense **alıştım** may refer to a state in effect at PRESENT, i.e., the time of speaking, in which case the PRESENT tense translation is appropriate. • In reference to a PRESENT condition, certain common Turkish verbs designating a state, i.e., a feeling, emotion, or sensation, often have the simple PAST tense, but the equivalent English has the simple PRESENT tense. The ADJECTIVE **alışık** 'used to, accustomed to', plus a Turkish equivalent of '- be' is also possible: **Saat beşte kalkmaya alışığ.ım.** 'I'm used to getting up at 5 o'clock.' Although a literal equivalent of the English, it is less frequently encountered than **alıştım.** It appears to be used mostly when the emphasis is on a present state rather than on a present result. *373:12.* custom, habit: - be used to.

2 /A/ '- get, - become, or - be addicted /to/': **Mehmet {a: sigara.ya/b: içki.yE/c: kahve-.ye/d: pipo.ya/e: kumar.a/f: kumar oynamay.a} çok alıştı, * artık bırakamıyor.** 'Mehmet has gotten quite {used/addicted} {a: to cigarettes/ b: to drinking/c: to coffee/d: to pipe smoking/e: to gambling/f: to gambling}. * He's gotten to the point where he can't give it up anymore.' *373:11.* custom, habit: - become a habit.

alıştırma yap-. → **yap- 3.**

alışveriş et- [eDer] /DAn/ '- shop, - trade /AT/, - patronize /θ/ [**alış** 'buying, taking', **veriş** 'giving', **alışveriş** 'shopping']: **Bu çarşıdaki her dükkan.DAN alışveriş etmem.** 'I don't {shop AT/trade AT/patronize θ} every shop in this bazaar.' *731:16.* commerce, economics: - trade with; *733:8.* purchase: - shop. → = **alışveriş yap-.** → **yap- 3.**

/lA/ '- do business /with/ sb': **Osman çok kurnaz birisidir. Sakın onun.la alışveriş etme.** 'Osman is a very cunning fellow. Watch out, don't do business with him.' Proverb: **Dost ile ye, iç; alışveriş etme.** 'Eat and drink with a friend, but don't do business with him.', i.e., Don't mix business and friendship. *731:16.* commerce, economics: - trade with. → = /lA/ **iş yap- 2.**

alışveriş yap-. → **yap- 3.**

alışverişe çık-. → **çık- 2.**

alkışla- [r] /I/ '- applaud /θ/ sb, - applaud or - clap /FOR/ sb' [alkış 'applause' + verb-forming suf. -lA]: Konserden sonra seyirciler Sezen Aksu'yu çılgınca alkışladılar. 'After the concert, the audience applauded Sezen Aksu wildly'. • There is no natural Turkish equivalent for 'They applauded her PERFORMANCE.' 509:10. approval: - applaud. → ≠ ıslık çal- ['- whistle', as a sign of disapproval] → çal- 2, ≠ yuhala- ['- boo'].

Allah belâsını versin. → ver- 1.

Allah bilir. → Ne bileyim 1. → bil- 1.

Allah göstermesin! → göster- 1.

Allah kahretsin! → kahret-.

Allah kavuştursun! → kavuştur-.

Allah kolaylık versin. → ver- 1.

Allah korusun. → koru-.

Allah kurtarsın. → kurtar-.

Allah rahatlık versin. → ver- 1.

Allah sağlık versin. → ver- 1.

Allah saklasın. → sakla- 4.

Allah şifa versin! → şifa ver- → ver- 1.

Allah yardımcımız olsun. → ol- 3, Additional examples. a) 3. Selected examples...: olsun.

altına kaçır-. → kaçır- 2.

altını çiz-. → çiz- 1.

altını ıslat-. → ıslat-.

ameliyat geçir-. → geçir- 2.

ameliyat ol-. → ol- 10.1.

anahtarı içeride unut-. → unut-.

analiz et- [eDer] '- analyze' [F. analiz 'analysis']: Kimya dersinde suyu analiz ettik. 'In chemistry class we analyzed water.' Doktor hastanın kanını analiz etti ve * şeker hastalığı.ı teşhis.i koydu. 'The doctor analyzed the patient's blood and * diagnosed [her condition as] diabetes [lit., ** placed the sugar disease diagnosis].' Tarihteki olayları analiz edip onlardan ders almalıyız. 'We must analyze historical events [lit. events in history] and learn from [lit., take lessons] from them.' 800:6. analysis: - analyze; 934:15. reason: - reason. → = tahlil et- ['- analyze blood, historical event'].

anımsa-. → {hatırla-/anımsa-}.

anımsat-. → {hatırlat-/anımsat-}.

anla- [r] '- understand, - realize' [an 'mind, perception' + verb-forming suf. -lA]: Problemi öğretmen ile tartıştıktan sonra daha iyi anladık. 'We understood the problem better after discussing it with the teacher.' After someone has explained sth he may ask: S: Anladınız mı? 'Q: {Do/Did} you understand?' or Anladınız, değil mi? 'You understood, didn't you?' • More polite: Anlat.ABİL.dim mi? lit., 'Was I ABLE TO explain it?', implying that if the hearer didn't understand, you, the person explaining, were at fault. Anladınız mı? seems to imply a deficiency in the hearer. C1: Hayır. Anla.YAMA.dım. 'A1: No, I COULDN'T understand.' The negative potential, which indicates that an effort to understand has been made, is preferred here to the simple negative past: AnlaMADIM. 'I DIDN'T understand.' C2: Eh işte, biraz anla.DIM. 'A2: Well, I {underSTAND/understood} it a bit.' In the above, when the understanding occurred and continues in the present, translations in both the present and past tenses are possible, although the present is more likely. • In reference to a PRESENT condition, certain common Turkish verbs designating a state, i.e., a feeling, emotion, or sensation, often have the simple PAST tense, but the equivalent English has the simple PRESENT tense. # When you suddenly understand sth that has been explained: * Ha, anladım. 'Oh, {I {see/underSTAND}./Now I get it./I just got it.}' Here again the Turkish has the past tense when the result of the action of the verb is considered as extending to the present time. The

English has the present, i.e., I underSTOOD after you spoke so NOW I underSTAND. * **Bu.nun doğruluğ.u.nu anladım.** 'I understood [that] this was correct [lit., ** the correctness of this (action)].' **Ali'nin İstanbul'a {a: gittiğ.i.ni/b: gideceğ.i.ni/c: gitme.si gerektiğ.i.ni} anladım.** 'I realized [or understood] that Ali {a: had gone/b: was going to go/c: had to go} to Istanbul.' **Ali'nin İstanbul'a {a: nasıl/b: ne zaman/c: neden/d: niçin/e: niye/f: kimlerle} gittiğ.i.ni anladım.** 'I understood {a: how/b: when/c, d, e: why/f: with whom [i.e., with what people]} Ali had gone to Istanbul.' **Ne demek {istediğ.İ.ni/istediğ.İN.i} anladım.** 'I understood {what HE/what YOU [s.]} meant.' **Ayağa kalkan.a kadar konuştuğum {adam.ın/bey.in} kör olduğ.u.nu anlamadım.** 'Until he got up, I didn't realize that {the man/the gentleman} I had been speaking with was blind.' **Hiç kimse neler olduğunu anlayamıyordu.** 'No one could understand what was going on.' *521:7.* intelligibility: - understand. → **takdir et-** 2 ['- appreciate or - understand sb's situation, difficulties'], ≠ **aklı alMA-** → **al-** 1.

/DAn/ **anla-** '- understand a lot /ABOUT/, - know sth /ABOUT/', usually a field of knowledge, implies expertise: NON-verbal noun as object: S: **{a: Pul.DAN/b: Silâh.TAN/c: Resim.DEN/d: Müzik.TEN} anlar mısın?** 'Q: Do you understand anything {a: ABOUT stamps/b: ABOUT weapons/c: ABOUT pictures/d: ABOUT music}?' C: **{Evet anlarım./* Hiç anlamam.}** 'A: {Yes, I do./* No, nothing at all.}' **Pullar.DAN çok iyi anlar.** 'He knows a lot ABOUT stamps.' VERBAL noun as object: **YEMEK yapmak.TAN anlamam ama çok güzel çay demlerim.** 'I don't know a thing ABOUT cooking [lit., making food], but I can brew up some great tea.' *521:7.* intelligibility: - understand.

* **Anladığı kadarıyla** '{As far as he understands/As far as he can tell/To the best of his understanding}', very common in the first person: **Anladığ.IM kadarıyla** 'As far as I understand, etc.': **Anladığım kadarıyla siz de üniversite öğrenci.si.siniz.** 'As far as I can tell, you, too, are a {college/university} student.' **Anladığım kadarıyla bu konuda siz de benim gibi düşünüyorsunuz.** 'As far as I understand, you, too, think like I do on this issue.' *927:30.* knowledge: ADV. to one's knowledge. → **Bildiği kadarıyla** ['As far as he knows'] → **bil-** 1.

yanlış anla- '- misunderstand' [**yanlış** 'error, wrong, wrongly']: **Taksi şoförü verdiğim adresi yanlış anladı ve beni başka bir müzeye götürdü.** 'The taxi driver misunderstood the address I had given him and took me to another museum.' **Beni hep yanlış anlıyorsun, halbuki ben senin iyiliğin için çalışıyorum.** 'You always misunderstand me, but [don't you realize that] I always have your best interests in mind [lit., that I'm working for your good]?' **Yanlış anlamayın, benim amacım sizi yargılamak değil, sadece gerçeği öğrenmek.** 'Don't misunderstand. My purpose is not to {pass judgment/sit in judgment} on you, but only to find out the truth.' **Yanlış anlamayın, bu soruyu eleştirel anlamda sormuyorum.** 'Don't misunderstand. I'm not asking this question with the intention to criticize [lit., ** in a critical sense].' **Lütfen beni yanlış anlama, seni seviyorum fakat şu anda senin.LE evlenmeye hazır değilim.** 'Please don't misunderstand me. I love you, but I'm not ready to marry θ you right now.' *342:2.* misinterpretation: - misinterpret.

anlaş- [ır] [**anla-** + recip. suf. -ş] 1 '- understand one another, - get along or on with one another': **Ayşe ile Selma çok iyi anlaşıyorlar.** 'Ayşe [f.] and Selma [f.] {understand one another/get on} very well.' *409:12.* success: - manage; *521:7.* intelligibility: - understand. → = **geçin-** 1 ['- get along or on with'].

2 /a: lA, b: DA, c: üzerinde, d: konusunda, e: için/ '- agree, - come to an agreement, - reach an understanding /a: with, b: {on/upon}, c: {on/upon}, d: on the subject of/e: {to/in order to}/': **Satıcı: Sizin**

için bu kolyenin son fiyatı 2,5 lira olur. 'Salesman: For you the final price of this necklace is 2.5 liras.' **Müşteri: * Tamam anlaştık.** 'Customer: * It's a deal [lit., ** OK, we have reached an agreement].' **Her konuda anlaşıyoruz.** 'We agree {on every issue/on all matters}.' **Turhan'la bu konuda anlaştık.** '{Turhan and I reached an agreement on this subject./We reached an agreement with Turhan on this subject.}' • With the first person plural suffix on the verb [**anlaş.TIK**], the total number of subjects may be two or more. With the first person singular suffix on the verb [**anlaş.TIM**], only two subjects would be involved and the emphasis would be on the first person speaker. **Sonunda, ABD [Amerika Birleşik Devletleri] ile Rusya nükleer silahlar.ın sınırlandır.ılma.sı konu.su.nda anlaştılar.** 'Finally the United States and Russia have agreed to limitations on nuclear weapons [lit., on the subject of nuclear weapons being limited].' In the negative this verb is usually found in the inability form: **Bilim adamları konu üzerinde anlaşamadılar.** 'The scholars couldn't reach an understanding on the subject.' **Ayşe ile Fatma birçok konuda iyi anlaşmalarına rağmen, {a: tatil/b: evlilik/c: müzik/d: kürtaj} konu.su.nda hiç anlaş.amı.yorlar.** 'Although Ayşe [f.] and Fatma [f.] agree on many subjects, they can't agree at all on [the subject of] {a: {vacation/holidays}/b: marriage/c: music/d: abortion}.' **Cemil beyin işyerini kiralamak için kardeşi ile anlaştım.** 'I had come to an agreement with his brother to rent Cemil bey's {office/work place}.' Proverb: * **İnsanlar konuş.A konuş.A, hayvanlar koklaş.A koklaş.A [anlaşır].** 'People [come to understand one another] BY speak.ING, animals BY sniff.ING one another.' *332:10.* assent: - come to an agreement. → **kontrat yap-** ['- make a contract, - sign a contract or agreement /with/'] → **yap- 3.**

anlaşıl- [ır] /{tarafından/CA}/ '- be understood /by/, - be or - become clear, - be determined' [irr. pass. of **anla-**]: **Bu konu herkes tarafından anlaşıldı mı?** 'Has this topic been understood by

everyone?' **Yeni gelen Amerikalı öğrenci.nin Türkçe.si herkes tarafından anlaşılıyordu.** 'The Turkish of the newly arrived American student was understood by everyone.' **Ne kadar kötü bir insan olduğu sonunda anlaşıldı ama artık çok geçti.** 'It finally became clear what a bad person he was, but it was too late.' **Bizim karakola {gideceğ.imiz/gitme.miz gerektiğ.i} anlaşıldı.** 'It was clear {that we were going to go/that we had to go} to the police station.' **Polisler.in bize {a: nasıl/b: ne zaman/c: neden/d: niçin/e: niye/f: kimlerle} gittiğ.i anlaşıldı.** 'It became clear {a: how/b: when/c, d, e: why/f: with whom [i.e., with what people]} the police had gone to our house.' **Cinayet.in gerçek neden.i anlaşıl.ama.dı.** 'The real reason for the murder could not be {determined/understood}.' *521:5.* intelligibility: - be understood.

* **anlaşılan** 'it is clear that [lit., what is clear, understood], evidently': * **Sen.İ çok kararlı görüyorum. Anlaşılan bu yıl okul.un.u bitireceksin.** 'I see that you are very determined [lit., ** I see you very determined]. It is clear that you will graduate this year [lit., what is clear, you will finish your school this year].' **Bugün hava çok bulutlu. Anlaşılan yağmur yağacak.** 'The weather is very cloudy today. {Obviously/It's clear that} it's going to rain.' **Anlaşılan** frequently comes at the end of the sentence. *348:14.* manifestation: ADV. manifestly.

Anlaşıldı mı? 'Is that {understood/clear}?' *521:5.* intelligibility: - be understood. Often used as a warning: **Okul müdürü: Okulda sigara içmek yasak. Anlaşıldı mı?** 'Principal: In school smoking is forbidden. Is that clear?' **Öğrenci: Anlaşıldı efendim.** 'Student: [Quite] clear, {sir/ma'am}.' *399: * 9.* warning: expressions of.

yanlış anlaşıl- '- be misunderstood' [**yanlış** 'error, wrong, wrongly']: **Yanlış anlaşıldım.** 'I've been misunderstood.' Often the more common English equivalent is: 'You've misunderstood me.' The passive in the Turkish is more polite. **Yanlış anlaşılmak.TAN**

korkuyorum. 'I'm afraid OF being misunderstood.' **Yanlış anlaşıl- masın** '{Don't misunderstand/Don't get me wrong} [lit., Let it not be misunderstood]': **Öğretmen: Yanlış anlaşılmasın, dönem sonu sınavında sadece defterleriniz açık olacak, kitaplarınız değil.** 'Teacher: Don't misunderstand, during the {term/semester/quarter} [lit., period] final exam only your notebooks may be open, not your [text] books.' *342:2.* misinterpretation: - misinterpret.

anlat- [ır] [anla- + caus. suf. -t] **1** /A/ '- explain sth /to/ sb, - make sth clear /to/ sb': **Beni niçin bu kadar beklettin, anlatır mısın?** 'Why did you keep me waiting so long? Would you explain?' After giving an explanation: * **Bilmem anlatabiliyor muyum?** '{Have I made myself clear?/Have I gotten my point across?}' **Tarih profesörü Birinci Dünya Savaşına girmemiz.in nedenler.i.ni anlattı.** 'The history professor explained the reasons for our entering the First World War.'

* **Anlat.abil.dim mi?** '{DO/DID} YOU understand [lit., ** Was I able to explain it]?' *common colloq:* 'You know what I'm saying?' • This is more polite and often preferred to **Anla.DINIZ mı?** lit., 'DID you understand?', because it suggests that the explainer is at fault, whereas the latter implies a deficiency in the hearer. Also: 'you see?, you understand?': **A: Hafta sonunda vereceğim partiye mutlaka gel, bekliyorum.** 'A: Be sure to come to the party I'm giving [lit., going to give] this weekend. I'm expecting you.' **B: Çok iyi olurdu ama daha önce de söylediğim gibi büyükanneme söz verdim, gelemem, [bilmem] anlata- bildim mi?** 'B: That would have been very nice, but, as I said earlier, I promised my grandmother [that I would visit her], so I won't be able to come, you see? [lit., ** (I don't know), have I been able to explain it?]' *521:6.* intelligibility: - make clear. → = **açıkla- 1**, = **izah et-**.

* **Nasıl anlatayım?** '{How shall I put it?/How can [lit., shall] I explain it?}', a common filler phrase that gives the speaker time to think of a way of explaining sth or answering a question. = * **Nasıl anlatsam?** *362:13.* irresolution: ADV. * filler phrases and stallers. The two most common filler phrases, neither formed from a verb, are **Efendim** and **Şey.** For other filler phrases, → **Efendime söyleyeyim** → söyle- 1, **Ne bileyim ben? 2** → bil- 1.

2 /A/ '- relate sth /to/ sb, - tell /θ/ sb sth, - tell sth /to/ sb': **Bu mesele biraz karışık.** * **Nere.si.nden başlasam anlatma.ya?** 'This issue is a bit complicated. * I hardly know where to begin [lit., ** I wonder from its where I should begin to relate?]' * **Eee anlat,** * **daha ne bekliyorsun?** '{Well/So} go ahead and tell [us]. * What are you waiting for?' NON-verbal noun as object: **Bu olay ile ilgili düşüncelerinizi Türkçe anlatın.** 'Relate in Turkish your thoughts about this event.' **İsterseniz** * **konuyu detaylı bir biçimde baştan anlatayım.** 'If you like, * I'll go into detail about the matter from the beginning.' **Fikr.i.ni herkes.E anlattı fakat kimse.yİ ikna edemedi.** 'He told θ everyone his idea, but he couldn't convince anyone.' For '- tell about yourself', → **bahset-.** * **Derd.im.i anlatacak kadar Türkçe.m var.** 'I know enough Turkish to express my needs [lit., ** I have enough Turkish to relate my troubles.]' * **Kocam üç aydır işsiz, evimizin kirasını ödeyemiyoruz.** * **Çoluk çocuk perişan olduk. Derd.imiz.i kim.E anlata- cağımızı bilmiyoruz.** 'My husband has been without work for 3 months. We can't pay our rent. * Our whole family is [lit., became] distraught. We don't know who we can tell about our troubles.' * **Evet, ne oldu anlat bakalım.** 'Well, go on and tell [us] what happened [lit., Yes, what happened? Tell (us); let's see].' **Ben sorunumu hiç kimseler.e anlatamıyorum.** 'I can't tell anyone {what's bothering me/lit., my problem}.' **Ne zaman görsem, dedem ban.A askerlik anılarını anlatır.** 'Whenever I see him, my grandfather tells me his recollections of his military service.' **Ünlü sanayici Sakıp Sabancı televizyonda hayat hikâyesini anlattı.** 'The famous industrialist Sakıp Sabancı {related/told} his life story on TV.'

With certain noun objects denoting feelings, thoughts, ideas, **anlat-** may translate '- express ONESELF', the LITERAL Turkish equivalent of which, i.e., {**kendini/kendinizi**} **anlat-**, USUALLY means to '- tell ABOUT oneself', rarely '- express oneself': * {**duygularını/ düşüncelerini/fikirlerini**} **anlat-** '- express or relate {one's feelings/one's thoughts/one's ideas}.' [**duygu** 'feeling', **düşünce** 'thought', **fikir** 'idea, opinion']. *532:4.* diction: - phrase. → = **kendini ifade et-** → **ifade et-** 1. VERBAL noun as object: * **Söylemek istedikleriniz.i** {**a: Türk.ÇE/b: İngiliz.CE/c: Alman.CA/d: Fransız.CA**} **anlatın.** 'Say what you want to say {a: IN Turkish/b: IN English/c: IN German/d: IN French}.' {**İşyeri sahibi/Patron**}, **bütün işçiler.e, yani ustalar.a, kalfalar.a ve çıraklar.a, ne yapacakları.nı** {**etraflı/ ayrıntılı**} [**bir**] **şekilde anlattı.** 'The boss explained to all the workers, that is, the top people, the foremen, and the apprentices, in detail [lit., in a {thorough/detailed} way] what they were going to do.' **Çocuklar nineleri.nDEN bir** {**masal/hikâye**} **anlatması.nı istediler.** 'The children asked θ their grandmother to tell them a {fairy tale/story}.' **Turist** * **baş.ı.ndan geçenler.i ve tanık olduğu olayları** {**bir bir/uzun uzadıya**} **anlattı.** 'The tourist related {in detail [lit., one by one]/at great length} * what had happened to him [lit., ** the things that had passed through his head] and what he had witnessed.' **Baş** 'head' above represents the whole person, not merely his head. *552:11.* news: - report.

3 /I/ '- tell /ABOUT/, - describe /θ/': {**Atatürk'Ü/Kendiniz.İ**} **biz.E biraz anlatır mısınız?** 'Would you please tell us a little {ABOUT Ataturk?/ABOUT yourself?}' *349:9.* representation, description: - describe; *864:10.* particularity: - characterize.

aptes al-. → **al-** 1.

ara- [r] **1** /I/ '- look /FOR/, - search /FOR/': **Ne arıyorsun?** 'What are you looking for?' **S: Nasıl bir yer arıyorsun?** 'Q: What kind of a place are you looking for?' **C:** {**a: Ucuz**

bir otel/b: İyi bir motel/c: Sessiz bir pansiyon/d: Tek kişilik bir oda/e: Büyük bir apartman dairesi} **arıyorum.** 'A: I'm looking for {a: a cheap hotel/b: a good motel/c: a quiet pension/d: a room for one person/e: a large apartment}.' * **Her yer.İ aradım; fakat gözlüğümü bulamadım.** 'I looked θ everywhere, but I couldn't find my glasses.' **S: Acaba Ali nerede?** 'Q: I wonder where Ali is?' **C:** * **Herhalde buralarda bir yerdedir. Arayalım mı?** 'A: He's probably around here somewhere. Shall we look for [him]?' **Ahmet ile John istasyonda kim.i arıyorlar?** 'Who are Ahmet and John looking for at the station?' **Epeydir böyle bir ev arıyorduk.** 'We'd been looking for such a house for a long time.' **Aradığım mutluluğu sonunda buldum.** 'I finally found the happiness [that] I was looking for.' **Gökte ararken yerde bulduk.** 'While looking for it in the sky, we found it [right here] on earth.', i.e., We didn't have to look so far. Proverbs: **Arayan Mevlâsını da bulur, belâsını da.** 'He who seeks will find either his Lord or his calamity.', i.e., A person will find whatever he seeks. **Derdi çeken derman arar.** 'He who has troubles seeks a remedy [for them].' **Kusursuz dost arayan, dostsuz kalır.** 'He who seeks a friend without faults will remain without friends.' *937:30.* inquiry: - seek.

2 '- call on the phone': [**telefonla**] **ara-** '- call up [lit., ** - search for] [by phone], - ring up': **Kim arıyor?** 'Who's calling?' = **Kiminle görüşüyorum?** '{Who am I speaking to?/With whom am I speaking?}' → **görüş-** 1. When the caller has the wrong number: * **Hangi numara.yı** * **aradınız?** 'What [phone] number * are you calling [lit., did you call]?' **Aradığınız numara cevap vermiyor.** 'The number you are calling doesn't answer.' **Sizi yarın ararım.** 'I'll call you tomorrow.' **Yarım saat SONRA arayabilir misiniz?** 'Could you call back IN half an hour?' **Sorunuz.a şimdi** {**net/kesin**} **bir cevap veremiyorum. Siz.i yarım saat SONRA arayabilir miyim?** 'I can't give you a {definite} answer right now. Could I call you [back] IN half an hour?' **Lütfen ona Fatma**

Çiçekçi aradı der misiniz? 'Would you please tell him that Fatma Çiçekçi called [him]?' **Haber vermek için aradım.** 'I called to convey some information.' **Bu numarayı arayarak bize ulaşabilirsiniz.** 'You can reach us at [lit., by calling] this number.' **Aramanız gereken numara şu...** 'The number you should call is...' * **Ben Mehmet. İzmir'den arıyorum.** 'This is Mehmet. I'm calling from Izmir.' **Recep! Los Angeles'a gelir gelmez lütfen beni şu numara.DAN ara: Alan kodu 310, 462 85 09** [read: **üç yüz on dört yüz altmış iki seksen beş sıfır dokuz**]. 'Recep! As soon as you arrive in Los Angeles, please give me a call AT the following number: area code 310 462 8509.' **Lütfen * Can'a ben.i arama.sı.nı söyler misiniz?** 'Would you please ask [lit., tell] θ Can to call me [back]? [lit., ** tell θ Can his calling me.]' **Hasan'ın babası çok hastaymış, * telefon.LA arayıp, hal.i.ni soralım.** 'Hasan's father is very ill. * Let's call up [lit., ** look for BY phone] and ask how he is [lit., ask ABOUT his condition].'

/I/ telefondan ara- '- call ON the phone': * **Sizi telefon.DAN arıyorlar** [more common: **istiyorlar** 'they want']. '{There's a [phonc] call for you./You're wanted ON the phone./They're calling you ON [lit., ** FROM] the phone.}' = * **Siz.E telefon var.** 'There's a call FOR you.' → = **telefon {et-/aç-}.** *347:18.* communications: - telephone.

[telefonla] tekrar ara- '- call back, - call again' [**tekrar** 'again']: **Sonra tekrar ararım.** 'I'll call {back/again} later.' *347:18.* communications: - telephone.

ödemeli ara- '- call collect, - make a collect [telephone] call' [**ödemeli** 'collect']: **Sivas'tan ödemeli arıyorlar. Kabul ediyor musunuz?** 'There is a collect call from Sivas [lit., They are calling collect...]. Do you accept [the call]?' **Ahmet bey, amcanız Ankara'dan ödemeli arıyor. Kabul ediyor musunuz?** 'Ahmet bey, your [paternal] uncle is calling collect from Ankara. Do you accept [the call]?' **Sinop'U ödemeli aramak istiyorum.** 'I want to call

Sivas collect.' *3 4 7 : 1 8.* communications: - telephone.

3 /DAn/ '- call for or - pick up /AT/': **Yarın saat dokuzda beni otelim.DEN arayın.** '{Pick me up/Call for me} tomorrow at nine o'clock AT my hotel.' *176:16.* transferal, transportation: - fetch.

4 '- miss, - long /FOR/ sb or sth absent': **Beş senedir Dilek'i** [but pronounce **Dileği**] **görmüyoruz. Onu çok arıyoruz.** 'We haven't seen Dilek for five years. We miss her very much.' • Proper names are usually written in their nominative form when case suffixes are added, but they are pronounced like other nouns with suffixes, so that in the above the **k** is pronounced **ğ**. * **Çocukluk günlerimi öyle arıyorum ki!** 'How I miss my childhood days!' *100:16.* desire: - wish for; *991:7.* insufficiency: - want. → = **hasret çek-** → **çek- 5,** = **özle-.**

ara ver-. → **ver- 3.**

araba kullan-. → **kullan-.**

araba sür-. → **sür- 1.**

aran- [ır] /{tarafından/CA}/ '- be sought, looked for /by/' [**ara-** + pass. suf. **-n**]: * **{a: Beş gün önce kaybolan çocuk/b: Hırsız/c: Katil/d: Terörist} hâlâ aranıyor.** '{The search still continues/They are still searching} for {a: the child who was lost five days ago/b: the thief/c: the murderer/d: the terrorist} [lit., The child...is still being sought].' **Biraz pahalı, ama çok aranan bir kitap.** 'It is a somewhat expensive but widely sought book.' In employment ads: * **[Bayan] sekreter aranıyor.** '[Female] secretary wanted [lit., is being sought].' **Eleman aranıyor.** 'Personnel wanted.' *937:30.* inquiry: - seek. → ≠ **bulun- 1.**

arası açıl-. → **arası {açıl-/bozul-}** → **açıl- 9.**

arası düzel-. → **düzel-.**

araştır- [ır] [**ara-** + intensifying suf. **-[I]ştIr**] **1** '- search thoroughly, - search through': **Bütün {a: dosyalarımı/b: dolaplarımı}**

araştırdım fakat aradığımı bulamadım. 'I searched through all {a: my files/b: my {closets/cupboards}}, but I couldn't find what I was looking for.' *937:31.* inquiry: - search.

2 '- investigate, - explore, - research, - study, - do research on, - try to find out': **Bilim adamları yeni enerji kaynakları bulmak için denizleri araştırıyorlar.** 'The scientists are exploring the oceans to find new sources of energy.' **Polis bu {olayı/hırsızlığı/cinayeti} araştıracak.** 'The police will investigate this {incident/theft/ murder}.' **Selma'nın partiye {ne zaman/nasıl/kimlerle} geldiğ.i.ni araştırdı.** 'He tried to find out {when/how/with whom [i.e., with what people]} Selma [f.] had come to the party.' **Selma'nın partiye gelip {gelmediğ.i.ni/ gelmeyeceğ.i.ni} araştırdı.** 'He tried to find out whether or not Selma {had come/was going to come} to the party.' *937:23.* inquiry: - investigate. → **incele-** ['- examine carefully, closely, minutely, in detail, - study carefully, - inspect, - investigate, - research'], **tetkik et-.** Same., **muayene et-** ['- examine', mostly for a doctor and a patient], **kontrol et-** ['- check, - inspect, - check on, - check to see whether sth is the case or not'].

arayıp sor-. → **sor-.**

arıza yap-. → **yap- 3.**

arkasından konuş-. → **konuş-.**

arkasını çevir-. → **çevir- 3.**

arkasını dön-. → **dön- 4.**

art- [ar] 1 '- increase, - go up', prices, heat, output, risk: **Ekmeğin fiyatı arttı.** 'The price of bread has gone up.' * **Sıcaklar yine arttı.** 'Temperatures have risen again.' **Grevden sonra fabrika.nın üretim.i {giderek/yavaş yavaş} arttı.** 'After the strike, the output of the factory {gradually/slowly} increased.' **Enerji üretimi, ocak ayından bu yana, geçen yıl.a oran.LA % [read: yüzde] 70 artmış.** 'Energy output, from the month of January to the present, has risen 70 % IN comparison to last year.' **Depresyon arttıkça kalp**

krizi riski artıyor. 'As depression increases, the risk of heart attack increases.' * **Yaşlı nüfus gittikçe artıyor.** 'The number of old {folks/people} [lit., The aged population] is gradually increasing.' **Çalışabilir nüfus genel nüfus.TAN daha hızlı artıyor.** 'The able workforce is increasing more rapidly THAN the general population.' *251:6.* increase: - grow, increase [i.]. → = **çık- 6, çoğal-** ['- increase in number'], = **fırla- 2** ['- skyrocket, - increase or - rise suddenly, - soar, - jump'], = **tırman- 2,** = **yüksel- 2,** ≠ **azal-,** ≠ **eksil- 1,** ≠ **in- 4.** # **Hastanın ateşi birdenbire arttı.** 'The patient's temperature suddenly rose.' → = **çık- 6,** = **fırla- 2,** = **tırman- 2,** = **yüksel- 2,** ≠ **azal-,** ≠ **düş- 3,** ≠ **in- 4.**

2 '- be left over, - remain': * **Az [sayıda] misafir gelince yemek arttı.** 'Since few guests [lit., ** Since guests few in number] came, there was food left over.' *256:5.* remainder: - remain. → = **kal- 2.**

{artır-/arttır-} [ır] [art- + caus. suf. -Ir; art- + caus. suf. -DIr] **1** '- increase sth, - cause sth to increase': **Grevden sonra fabrikalar üretimlerini artırdı.** 'After the strike the factories increased their output.' **Patronum yaptığ.ı son zam.la maaş.ım.ı yüz.de onbeş artırmış oldu.** 'My boss, with the last increase that he made, had increased my salary fifteen percent.' **İktidar partisi yeniden seçilirse ücretleri artıracağ.ı.nı vadetti.** 'The party in power promised that, if it is reelected [lit., elected again], it would raise wages.' *251:4.* increase: - increase sth. → = **çoğalt-,** ≠ **azalt-.**

2 '- save': **para artır- /için/** '- save money [up] /for/': **Her ay yüz dolar artırıyorum.** 'I'm saving $100 every month.' *635:4.* thrift: - economize. → = **para biriktir-** → **biriktir- 2,** = **tasarruf et-, masraftan {kaç-/kaçın-}** ['- avoid /θ/ expense, economize'] → **kaç- 2,** ≠ **para {harca-/sarf et-}** ['- spend money'] → **{harca-/sarf et-} 1,** ≠ **masraf {et-/yap-},** ≠ **masraf çek-** ['- foot the bill, pay', *informal, jocular*] → **çek- 5,** ≠ **masraf gör-** ['- meet expenses, finance, pay for']

→ gör- 4, ≠ **masraf karşıla-**. Same.
→ **karşıla-** 2, ≠ **masrafa gir-** ['-spend a lot of money on sth or to get sth done, - have a lot of expenses, - incur great expense'].

arzu et- [eDer] '- want, - desire' [P. **arzu** (. -) 'wish, desire']: **Lise.yi bitirdikten sonra doktor olmay.I çok arzu ettim.** 'After finishing {high school/lycée}, I wanted very much to become a doctor.' **Ahmet, Ayla ile evlenmey.İ çok arzu ediyordu.** 'Ahmet wanted very much to marry Ayla.' At a restaurant: **Garson: Ne arzu etmiştiniz efendim?** 'Waiter: What would you like, {sir/ma'am}?' • The waiter might also say: **Ne arzu {ediyorsunuz/ edersiniz}?** o r **Ne {emredersiniz}?** lit., ** 'What do you {order/command}?' Simply **Ne istiyorsunuz?** 'What do you want?' would be impolite. * **Nasıl arzu edersen öyle olsun.** 'Let it be as you wish.' *100:14.* desire: - desire; *100:15.* - want to. → = **dile-** 1, = **iste-** 1.

Arzunuza kalmış. → **kal-** 1.

as- [ar] 1 /a: A, b: DAn, c: lA/ '- hang [up] /a: {IN/ON}, b: BY, c: with/': **El ilanlarını duvar.A raptiye ile mi astın, toplu iğne ile mi?** 'Did you hang the flyers ON the wall with thumbtacks or with pins?' **Bahçe.yE çamaşırları astın mı?** 'Have you hung the laundry up IN the garden?' → ≠ **çamaşır topla-** ['- take {in/down} the laundry'] → **topla-** 1. **{Paltonu/Ceketi/Elbiseni} şu askı.yA asabilirsin.** 'You may hang {your coat/the jacket/your suit} ON this hanger.' A threat: **Bana bak {çocuk/velet}, yaramazlık yapma, seni ayağın.DAN {tavan.A/ağac.A} asarım!** 'Look here, {kid}, behave yourself [lit., don't misbehave] [or] I'll hang you {ON the ceiling/ON the tree} BY your feet!' *202:8.* pendency: - suspend; *514: * 5.* threat: INTERJ. specific threats.

* **surat as-** '- put on a sour face, - look annoyed, angry, or unhappy; - sulk; - pout' [**surat** 1 'face, countenance'. 2 'sour face; angry look']: **S: * {Neden suratını asıyorsun/Neden suratın asık}, birşey mi oldu?** 'Q: Why are you sulking [lit., ** {Why are you

hanging your face/Why is your face hanging}]. Has sth happened?' **C: Müdür bey hafta sonunda da çalışmamı istiyor. Bu.nA çok canım sıkıldı.** 'A: The director wants me to work on the weekend too. I'm very annoyed [AT that].' *110:14.* ill humor: - sulk; *265:8.* distortion: - grimace.

2 /A, DAn, yüzünden/ '- hang /to, FOR, for/', as a form of execution: **Adamı vatan.A {a: ihanet.TEN/ b: ihanet suç.u.nDAN/ c: ihanet yüzünden} astılar.** 'They hung the man {a: FOR treason/b: FOR the crime of treason/c: FOR treason} AGAINST the fatherland.' *202:8.* pendency: - suspend; *604:18.* punishment: - hang.

asıl- [ır] [as- + {pass./refl.} suf. -Il] 1 /a: A, b: {tarafından/CA}, c: DAn, d: nedeniyle/ '- be hung /a: {ON/IN}, b: by [sb], c: BY [part of body], d: {on the occasion of/on account of}/': **Tablolar [işçiler tarafından] duvar.A asıldı.** 'The pictures were hung ON the wall [by the workers].' **23 Nisan Bayramı nedeniyle okulun bahçesi.nE bayraklar asılmıştı.** 'On the occasion of the 23 April Holiday, flags had been hung up ON the school grounds.' Proverb: **Her koyun kendi bacağı.nDAN asılır.** 'Every sheep is hung BY its own leg.', i.e., Everyone is held responsible for his own misdeeds. *202:8.* pendency: - suspend.

2 /a: A, b: lA, c: {tarafından/CA}/ '-be hanged /a: {to/ON}, b: FOR, c: by/', as a form of execution: **S: Kaç kişi asıldı?** 'Q: How many people were hanged?' **C: Üç adam asıldı.** 'A: Three men were hanged.' **Basit bir suç.LA adam asılmaz.** 'A man is not hanged FOR a simple offense.' **{Eşkiyalar tarafından/ Eşkiyalar.ca} asılan kişiler arasında çocuklar da varmış.** 'It seems there were also children among those hung {by the bandits}.' *604:19.* punishment: - be hanged.

3 /A/ '- come on /to/ sb, - make a play /FOR/ sb, - chase /AFTER/ sb', i.e., approach with sexual intent, *slang*: **O adam görgüsüz.ün tek.i.dir. Gördüğü her kadın.A asılır.** 'That man is a real {boor/cad} [lit., unmannerly person]. He chases

AFTER every woman he sees.' **Partide gördüğü sarışın kız.A asılması.na rağmen * tavlayamadı**. 'Although he chased AFTER the blond girl he saw at the party, * he couldn't get anywhere with her.' *382:8*. pursuit: - pursue; *562:21*. lovemaking, endearment: - court. → = **kur yap-** [*a more formal, polite* equivalent: '- chase /AFTER/, - court /θ/, - pay court /to/, - try to woo /θ/'] → yap- 3.

askerlik yap-. → yap- 3.

Aslına bakarsanız. → bak- 1.

âşık ol-. → ol- 12.

Aşkolsun. → ol- 11. → olsun.

<u>at-</u> [ar] 1 /A/ '- throw /{AT/ON/IN/INTO}/': **Sinan topu attı, Emre yakaladı**. 'Sinan threw the ball, and Emre caught it.' ≠ **yakala- 1** ['- catch']. **Çocuklar topu cam.A atınca cam kırıldı**. 'When the children threw the ball AT the window, the window broke.' <u>Proverbs</u>: **Deli.nin bir.i kuyu.yA bir taş atmış, kırk akıllı çıkaramamış**. 'A certain fool threw a stone INTO the well. Forty wise men couldn't get it out.' **Sırça köşkte oturan, komşu.su.nA taş atmamalı**. 'A person who lives in a crystal palace shouldn't throw stones AT his neighbor.' People who live in glasshouses shouldn't throw stones. *903:10*. pushing, throwing: - throw. → = **fırlat-**, ≠ **yakala- 1** ['- catch'], ≠ **tut- 1**.

çığlık at- /lA, DAn/ '- scream /{with/IN}, WITH/' [çığlık 'scream']: **Çocuklar palyaçoyu görünce sevinç.TEN çığlık attılar**. 'When the children saw the clown, they screamed WITH pleasure.' **Koca köpeği görünce, korku.yLA çığlık attı**. 'When he saw the huge dog, he screamed {with/IN} fear.' **Yaralanan çocuk acı.yLA çığlık atıyordu**. 'The wounded child was screaming IN pain.' *59:6*. cry, call: - cry. → = **bağır-**, = **bağırıp çağır-** → çağır- 3, = **haykır-**, **fısılda-** ['- whisper'].

göbek at- '- belly dance, - perform a belly dance' [göbek 'navel']: **Dayım oğlunun düğününde dansözle birlikte göbek attı**. 'At

his son's wedding my maternal uncle [belly] danced with the belly dancer.' *705:5*. dance: - dance. → **dans et-** ['- dance'], **oyna- 4** ['- dance, - perform a dance', used with the names of various folk dances].

göz at- /A/ '- glance /AT/, - take a look /AT/' [göz 'eye']: **İzin verirseniz gazeteniz.E bir göz atabilir miyim?** '{Would it be all right if/Would you mind if} I took a look AT your newspaper?' **Sınavdan bir gün önce tüm notlarım.A [şöyle bir] göz attım**. 'One day before the examination I {[casually] glanced AT all my notes/gave all my notes a [cursory] glance}.' *937:26*. inquiry: - examine cursorily. → **karıştır- 3** ['- rummage or search /THROUGH/, leaf, thumb, or flip /THROUGH/'], **şöyle bir bak-** ['- just look around, - browse'] → bak- 1.

işten at- '- fire, - sack, - can, - dismiss from a job' [iş 1 'work'. 2 'job'], *informal*: **Fabrika müdürü 10 işçi.yİ işten attı**. 'The director of the factory fired θ 10 workers.' *908:20*. <nonformal terms> - fire. → = *neutral*: **işine son ver-**, → son ver-, → ver- 1, *informal*: = **işten kov-** → kov- 2, *formal*: = **görevden al-** → al- 1, *neutral*: = **işten çıkar-** → çıkar- 1, ≠ { **ata-** /**tayin et-**}, ≠ **görevlendir-**.

kazık at- /A/ '- gyp, - rip off, - swindle, - cheat; - sell sb sth at an exorbitant, outrageous price', *very common slang* [kazık *slang* 'trick, swindle']: * **Tüh, biz.E kazık atmışlar**. * **İpek DİYE aldığımız bluz polyester çıktı**. 'O damn, they've really ripped us off. * The blouse that we bought THINKING it was silk [lit., ** thinking it θ silk] turned out to be polyester.' * **Ömer biz.E öyle bir kazık attı ki, ömrüm boyunca unutmayacağım**. 'Ömer cheated us so {badly/flagrantly} that I'll never forget it as long as I live.' *356:19*. deception: nonformal terms - gyp. → = /I/ **kazıkla-**, = *formal*: /I/ **dolandır-**, /DAn/ **fazla para al-** ['- overcharge'] → al- 1.

2 '- throw out, away, - discard, - get rid of': * **Evdeki gereksiz eşyaları attık**. 'We threw out the things in the house that we didn't need anymore [lit., the unnecessary

things in the house].' *390:7.* disuse: - discard. **çöp at-** /A/ '- litter, - throw trash /{ON/INTO}/' [**çöp** 'litter, trash']: **Sokaklar.A çöp atmak doğru değildir.** 'It's not right to throw trash ON the street [lit., on the streetS].' *80:15a.* uncleanness: - dirty; *810:2.* disarrangement: - disarrange. → = **çöp dök-** → **dök-** 3.

çöpe at- '- throw /{IN/INTO}/ the trash, - discard, - throw out, away': **Masadaki kâğıtlar artık lâzım değil, çöp.E atabilirsin.** 'The papers on the table are not needed anymore. You may throw them away [lit., {IN/INTO} the trash].' *390:7.* discard: - discard. → = **çöpe dök-**.

3 /A/ '- put /ON/': **Yemeğ.E tuz attın mı?** 'Did you put salt ON the food?' *159:12.* location: - place. → = **koy-** 1.

imza at- /A/ '- sign /θ/', *colloq.* '- put one's John Hancock /ON/ [obj.: check]' [A. **imza** (. -) 'signature']: **Çek.E imza.n.ı atmay.I unutma!** 'Don't forget to {sign θ the check./*colloq.* put your John Hancock ON the check.}' *546:6.* letter: - letter. → = {**imzala-/imza et-**} ['- sign', perhaps *more formal* than **imza at-**].

tarih {**at-/koy-** [ar]} /A, {üzerine/üstüne}/ '- date /θ/ sth, - put the date /{IN/ON}, on/ sth' [A. **tarih** (- .) 'date', **koy-** '- put place']: **Mektub.u.nun sağ üst köşe.si.nE tarih attı.** 'He put the date IN the upper right corner of his letter.' **Postane görevlileri zarf.ın {üzer.i.ne/üst.ü.ne} tarih atmışlar mı?** 'Did the employees of the post office put the date {on} the envelope?' *831:13.* measurement of time: - date.

4 '- mail, - post, - send off mail', *informal*, perhaps more like '- drop in the mailbox': **Mektupları attın mı?** 'Have you mailed the letters?' *176:15.* transferal, transportation: - send; *553:12.* correspondence: - mail. → = **postala-**, = *noun for item of mail* {**gönder-/yolla-**}.

5 /A/ '- beat /θ/, - hit /θ/, - kick /θ/, - slap /θ/, - strike /θ/', depending on the noun of striking preceding **at-**:

dayak at- /A/ '- beat, - give a whipping, beating, - thrash /θ/'

[**dayak** 'stick']: * **Yalan söylediğini anlayınca annesi çocuğ.A dayak attı.** 'When she realized that her child had told a lie, she gave him a whipping [lit., When his mother realized that he had told a lie, she gave θ the child a whipping].' *604:13.* punishment: - whip; *901:14.* impulse, impact: - hit. → **döv-** ['- beat, - strike'], **dayak ye-** ['- get a thrashing, beating'] → **ye-** 2.

tekme {**at-/vur-**) '- kick /θ/ sb, sth' [**tekme** 'a kick']. See under **yumruk** {**at-/vur-**) below. *901:21.* impulse, impact: - kick. ≠ → **tekme ye-** ['- get a kick, - receive a blow'] → **ye-** 2.

tokat {**at-/vur-**} /A/ '- slap /θ/ sb' [**tokat** 'a slap']. See under **yumruk** {**at-/vur-**} below. *604:12.* punishment: - slap; *901:19.* impulse, impact: - slap. → = **eliyle vur-** → **vur-** 1, **tokat ye-** ['- GET a slap, - BE slapped'] → **ye-** 2.

yumruk {**at-/vur-** [ur]} '- punch' [**yumruk** 'fist']: **Adam.A bir {tekme/tokat/yumruk} attı.** 'He {kicked/slapped/punched} θ the man.' *901:14.* impulse, impact: - hit. → **yumruk ye-** ['- GET a punch'] → **ye-** 2.

6 /A/ '- shoot /AT/': **kurşun at-** '- shoot [bullets] /AT/, - fire a gun /AT/' [**kurşun** 1 'lead'. 2 'bullet']: **Hedef.E üç kurşun attı, ama vuramadı.** 'He shot three bullets AT the target, but he couldn't hit it.' *459:22.* attack: - pull the trigger; *903:12.* pushing, throwing: - shoot. → = **ateş et-**.

7 '- beat': {**kalbi/yüreği**} **at-** 'for one's heart - beat' [{A. **kalp** [kalBİ]/**yürek**} 'heart']: * **Adam.ı öldü sandık fakat kalb.i hâlâ atıyordu.** 'We thought the man had died [lit., ** We thought the man he died], but his heart was still beating.' *916:12.* agitation: - flutter. → = {**kalbi/yüreği**} **çarp-** → **çarp-** 2.

{**kalbi/yüreği**} **hızlı hızlı at-** /DAn/ 'for one's heart - palpitate, - pound, - race /{BECAUSE OF/IN/ WITH/from}/' [**hızlı** 'rapidly']: **Dört kat merdiveni bir soluk.ta çıkınca yaşlı adam.ın kalb.i hızlı hızlı atmaya başladı.** 'When the old man climbed four flights of stairs in a single bound [lit.,

** in one breath], his heart began to beat rapidly.' **Sınava girmeden önce Ahmet'in kalb.i hızlı hızlı atıyordu.** 'Before taking the exam, Ahmet's {heart} was beating rapidly.' **Yaşlı hanım.ın kalb.i { a: h e y e c a n.DAN/b: korku.DAN/c: endişe.DEN/d: koşmak.TAN} hızlı hızlı atıyordu.** 'The old woman's heart was beating rapidly {a: {BECAUSE OF/IN} excitement/b: {BECAUSE OF/IN} fear/c: {BECAUSE OF/WITH} anxiety/d: from running}.' *916:12*. agitation: - flutter. → = **{kalbi/yüreği} hızlı hızlı çarp-** → çarp- 2.

{ata- [r]/tayin et- [eDer]} /A, olarak/ '- appoint, - assign, - name sb /to [a position], AS/' [A. **tayin** (- -) 'appointment']: **Millî Eğitim Bakanlığı ağabeyimi öğretmen OLARAK Bandırma Lisesi'nE atadı.** 'The Ministry of Education appointed my older brother TO the Bandırma {High school/Lycée} AS a teacher.' **Başbakan bugün yeni Dışişleri Bakanını atadı.** 'The prime minister today appointed the new foreign minister.' **Boş bulunan görevler.e yeni memurlar atadık.** 'We appointed new employees to the posts that were {vacant/unoccupied}.' **Bu öğretmen.in yer.i.nE bir başka.sı.nı atadılar.** 'They appointed someone else [lit., another one] IN place of this teacher.' *615:11*. commission: - appoint. → = **görevlendir-**, ≠ **görevden al-** → al- 1, ≠ **işten {at-/kov-}** → at- 1, kov- 2.

{atan- [ır]/tayin edil- [ir]} /a: A, b: olarak, c: {tarafından/CA}/ '- be appointed, assigned, named /a: to [a position or a place], b: AS, c: by/' [ata- + pass. suf. -n]: **Üniversiteyi bitirince Millî Eğitim Bakanlığı tarafından öğretmen OLARAK küçük bir kasaba.yA atandım.** 'When I had graduated from [lit., had finished] {college/[the] university}, I was appointed by the Ministry of Education AS a teacher TO a small town.' *615:11*. commission: - appoint. → = **görevlendiril-**, = **tayin ol-** → ol- 12, ≠ **görevden alın-** → alın- 1, ≠ **görevine son veril-**, ≠ **işinden ol-** → ol- 7.

ateş et- [eDer] /A/ '- fire /{ON/UPON}/, - shoot /AT/': **Avcı kuşlar.A ateş etti.** 'The hunter shot AT the birds.' **Polis kaçan katil.E ateş etti.** 'The police fired UPON the killer who was fleeing.' *459:22*. attack: - pull the trigger; *903:12*. pushing, throwing: - shoot. → = **kurşun at-** → at- 6.

ateş yak-. → yak- 1.

ateşi düş-. → düş- 3.

atıştır- [ır] [a t- + intensifying suf. - [I]ştIr] 1 '- bolt down, - gobble up, - gobble down, - wolf down [food]; - gulp down [a drink]': **Öğle yemeğ.i.ne gitmedim; kantinde bir şeyler atıştırdım, o kadar.** 'I didn't go to lunch. I just bolted down something at the {canteen/snack bar}, that's all.' **Sofranın hazırlanmasını bekleyemedim, dolmalar.DAN atıştırdım.** 'I couldn't wait for the table to be {set/prepared} [so] I just gobbled down some OF the dolmas [i.e., stuffed tomatoes, peppers, etc.].' **Abur cubur atıştıracağına doğru dürüst yemek yesene!** 'Instead of just gobbling down this and that why don't you eat properly?' *8:23*. eating: - gobble.

2 '- grab a bite, - have or - eat a snack, - snack': **Sinemaya girmeden önce * istersen şu büfede bir şeyler atıştıralım!** 'Before we go to the movie [lit., enter θ the movie house], * how about grabbing a bite from this counter? [lit., let's grab a bite from this counter if you like].' *8:26*. eating: - pick. → **abur cubur ye-** ['- have a snack, - snack, - eat food as a casual snack'] → ye- 1.

atla- [r] 1 /a: DAn, b: A, c: DAn, d: üzerinden/ '- jump, - leap /a: from, b: to, c, d: over/': **Yangın.dan kurtulmak için üçüncü kat.TAN yer.E atladı.** 'He jumped from the third floor to the ground [in order] to escape θ the fire.' * **Aşk uğruna ölüme atladı.** 'For [the sake of] love he leaped to [his] death.', i.e., He was rejected by the girl he wanted to marry. **Anahtarı unutunca bahçe {kapı.sı.nın üzer.i.nden/kapı .sı.nDAN} atladım.** 'When I forgot the key, I jumped {OVER the garden gate}.' *366:5*. leap: - leap.

2 /I/ '- omit, - skip': **Bütün sorular.A cevap vermek zorunda değilsiniz, 2.** [read: ikinci] **ve 5.** [read: beşinci] **{soruyu/ soruları} atlayabilirsiniz.** 'You don't have to answer all the questions. You may omit the second and fifth questions.' **Öğretmen dersin ikinci bölümünü atladı.** 'The teacher skipped the second section of the lesson.' *340:7.* neglect: - leave undone.

3 /A/ '- hop /INTO/ a taxi, car, bus; - catch /θ/ a plane, train': **Bu otobüs gelmeyecek galiba, ha[y]di bir taksi.yE atlayıp gidelim.** '{It looks like this bus isn't going to come/lit., This bus probably isn't going to come}. Let's hop INTO a taxi and be off [lit., let's go].' *193:12.* ascent: - mount. → = **bin-** 1, ≠ **in-** 2.

4 '- miss out on a news story, - miss a scoop': **Dün İstanbul'da önemli bir kongre yapıldı. Ama bütün gazeteler bu haberi atladı.** 'An important convention was held in Istanbul yesterday, but all the newspapers missed out on this story.' *983:2.* inattention: - be inattentive.

atlat- '- pull through, - get over or - kick an illness, - overcome or - survive a difficulty' [atla- + caus. suf. -t]: **Arkadaşım ağır bir hastalığ.A yakalandı, inşallah atlatır.** 'My friend has come down WITH a serious illness, I hope [lit., God willing] he'll pull through.' **Şükürler olsun [ki], kazayı birkaç sıyrıkla atlatmış.** 'Thank God he survived the accident with just a few scrapes.' * **Kaza.yI ucuz atlattığımız.A şükrettik.** 'We thanked God θ that we {had not been harmed/had gotten off lightly} in the accident.' *396:20.* restoration: - recover.

ayağa kalk-. → **kalk-** 1.

ayağının altına al-. → **al-** 1.

ayak bas-. → **bas-** 1.

ayaklan- [ır] /A karşı/ '- rebel, - revolt, - rise up /against/, - riot' [**ayak** 'foot' + verb-forming suf. -lAn]: II. [read: İkinci] **Mahmud zamanında Yeniçeriler sık sık ayaklandı.** 'At the time of Mahmud II the Janissaries frequently revolted.' **Maaşlarına yapılan zammı az bulan işçiler ayaklandı ve hükümet binası.nA yürüdü.** 'The workers who found the wage increases insufficient rebelled and marched ON the government building.' **Mahkumlar hapishane idaresi.ne karşı ayaklandılar.** 'The prisoners rose up against the administration.' *327:7.* disobedience: - revolt. → = **başkaldır-**.

ayakta dur-. → **dur-** 3.

ayarla- [r] [**ayar** 'guage, device for checking the accuracy of scales or of measurement' + verb-forming suf. - lA] 1 '- regulate, - fix, - set, - adjust': **Bu âlet oda sıcaklığ.ı.nı ayarlıyor.** 'This instrument regulates {the temperature in the room/lit., the room temperature}.' *573:8.* direction, management: - direct. → = **düzenle-** 3.

/A göre/ '- set /{BY/according to}/': **Saatimi radyo.yA göre ayarladım.** 'I set {my watch/my clock} BY the radio.' *787:7.* agreement: - make agree. → = **düzelt-** 4.

/A/ '- set /to/, - tune /to/': **{Televizyon.u/Radyo.yu} müzik kanal.ı.na ayarladım.** 'I sct {thc TV/thc radio} to thc music station.' **Fırını 230 derece.ye ayarlayıp ısıtın.** 'Heat the oven to a temperature of 230 degrees [lit., ** Set the oven to 230 degrees and heat].' *787:7.* agreement: - make agree.

2 '- put or - get in order, - arrange': **Eğer işlerimi ayarlayabilirsem, bu yaz Marmaris.E * tatil.E gideceğim.** 'If I can get my affairs in order, this summer * I'll go TO Marmaris ON {vacation/holiday}.' *807:8.* arrangement: - arrange. → = **düzenle-** 1

3 '- plan, - arrange': **Hafta sonu için bir piknik ayarladık. * Bütün sınıf gideceğiz.** 'We {planned/arranged} a picnic for the weekend. * We'll go all together as a class [lit., ** The whole class we will go].' **Bugün Osman beyle buluşmam lâzım. Benim için bir randevu ayarlayabilir misin?** 'I must get together with

Osman today. Could you arrange an appoinment for me [with him]?' *381:8.* plan: - plan; *405:6.* preparation: - prepare; *964:4.* prearrangement: - prearrange. → = **düzenle- 2.**

aybaşı ol-. → ol- 10.1.

ayıl- [ır] 1 '- sober up': { a: **Körkütük/b: Zilzurna} sarhoş olmuş, hâlâ ayılamadı.** 'He became {a: blind drunk/b: {soused/looped}}. He still hasn't sobered up [lit., couldn't sober up].' Words of a song: * **Öyle sarhoş olsam ki bir daha ayılmasam!** 'Let me get so drunk that I never sober up again!' *516:2.* sobriety: - sober up. → ≠ **sarhoş ol-** → ol- 12.

2 '- come to, - regain consciousness': {**Sıcak.tan/Havasızlık.tan/He-yecan.dan} bayılan kadın on dakika sonra ayıldı.** 'The woman who had fainted {from the heat/from lack of air/from excitement} came to ten minutes later.' *306:8.* life: - come to life; *396:20.* restoration: - recover. → = **kendine gel- 1** → gel- 1, ≠ **bayıl- 1,** ≠ **kendinden geç- 1** → geç- 1, ≠ **kendini kaybet- 1,** ≠ {**şuurunu/bilincini} kaybet-**[or yitir-] 1 → {kaybet-/yitir-}.

ayıp et- [eDer] /mAklA/ '- behave shamefully /BY...ing/' [A. **ayıp** (aYBı) 'shame']: **Sinan'ı ara.ma.MAKLA çok ayıp ettin. * Senden telefon bekliyordu.** 'You behaved shamefully BY not telephon.ING Sinan. * He was expecting {you to call/lit., a phone call from you}.' * **Nihal'le sinemaya gidecektik. * Nasıl da unuttum! Çok ayıp ettim.** '{I was/We were} going to go to the movies with Nihal. * How could I {forget/have forgotten}! I behaved shamefully.' *322:4.* misbehavior: - misbehave; *510:27.* disapproval: INTERJ. God forbid!

ayır- [ır] 1 /DAn/ '- separate, - take away /from/': **Hasta [olan] bebeği annesinden ayırdılar.** 'They separated the baby who was ill from its mother.' **Sevenleri ayırmayın!** 'Don't separate [the] lovers.' Proverb: **Allah doğru yoldan ayırmasın!** 'May God not lead us astray [lit., ** separate (us) from the true path].' **Yetimi giydir, açı doyur, kavgacıyı ayır.** 'Clothe the orphan,

feed the hungry, separate {those who are fighting/lit., the fighter}.' *801:8.* separation: - separate. → ≠ **kavuştur-,** ≠ **birleştir-.**

2 /için, A/ '- set aside /for, FOR/': **Annem pasta.nın bir kısm.ı.nı {benim için/ban.A/akşam.A} ayırmış.** 'My mother set aside a part of the pastry {for me/FOR me/FOR the evening}.' *386:12.* store, supply: - reserve. → = **koy- 3,** = **sakla- 3.**

3 /A/ '- divide /INTO/': **Ortaklar dükkânı iki.yE ayırdılar.** 'The partners divided the shop INTO two [sections].' *801:8.* separation: - separate. → = **böl-,** ≠ **birleştir-.**

4 '- separate, - distinguish, - differentiate': **İnsanla hayvanı ayıran sözdür.** 'What separates man and animals is language.' *801:8.* separation: - separate; *864:10.* particularity: - characterize.

ayırt- [ır] /a: için, b: DAn, c: DA, d: adına/ '- reserve [a place] /a: for, b: {IN/AT}, c: at, d: in the name of/, - set apart' [**ayır-** + caus. suf. -t]: {* **Divan oteli.nDEN/Divan oteli.nDE} {a: bir yatak.lı/b: banyo.lu/c: duş.lu/d: telefon.lu/e: televizyon.lu/f: manzaralı/g: internet bağlantı.lı** [or **bağlantı.sı olan**]} **bir oda ayırtmak istiyorum.** 'I want to reserve a room {a: with one bed/b: with a bath/c: with a shower/d: with a phone/e: with a TV/f: with a view/g: with an Internet connection [or which has an Internet connection]} {* AT the Divan hotel}.' **İki hafta önce burada bir oda ayırtmıştım.** 'I [had] reserved a room here two weeks ago.' **Bu akşam için bir masa ayırtabilir miyim?** 'Could I reserve a table for tonight?'

yer ayırt- /adına, DAn/ '- reserve a place /in the name of, IN [a place]/' [**yer** 'place']: **Cuma akşamki gösteri için Halil Çevik adına iki yer ayırtmak istiyorum.** 'I want to reserve two places for the Friday evening show in the name of Halil Çevik.' **Cuma akşamı gelecek olan grup için oteliniz.DEN yer ayırtmak istiyorum.** 'I would like to reserve a room IN your hotel for a party that will arrive Friday evening.' S: {a: **Kaç kişilik/b: Kaç gecelik/c: Hangi gece için} yer ayırtmak**

istiyorsunuz? 'Q: {a: For how many people/b: For how many nights/c: For which night} do you want to reserve a room?' C: {a: İki kişilik/b: İki gecelik/c: Salı gecesi için} yer ayırtmak istiyorum. 'A: I want to reserve a room {a: for two people/b: for two nights/c: for Tuesday night}.' Note the following examples with vehicles: Saat 12:15 [read: oniki on beş] {otobüs.ü.nE/tren.i.nE} bir yer ayırtmak istiyorum. 'I would like to reserve {a seat/a place} ON the 12:15 {bus/train}.' *477:9.* apportionment: - allot. → = rezervasyon yaptır-.

ayrıl- [ır] [ayır- + {pass./refl.} suf. -Il] 1 /DAn/ '- part, - part company, - break or - split up /WITH/, - separate /from/ one another': Ayrılmadan önce son bir defa daha birbirleri.nE sarıldılar. 'Before {parting/going their separate ways}, they embraced θ one another once more one last time.' Duydun mu, Sezen son sevgilisi.nDEN de ayrılmış! 'Have you heard? Sezen has broken up WITH his last lover too!' *801:19.* separation: - part company.

'- get or - be divorced /from/, - split up /WITH/': 25 Yıllık evlilikten sonra Ahmet ve Belma ayrıldı. 'After 25 years of marriage Ahmet and Belma [f.] split up.' Beş yıllık evlilikten sonra {kocam.dan/ karım.dan} ayrıldım. 'After five years of marriage I got divorced {from my husband/from my wife}.' * Eşim.DEN ayrıldım. '{I've split up WITH my {wife/husband}./I'm divorced [from my {wife/hus-band}].}' *566:5.* divorce, widowhood: - divorce. → = boşan-, ≠ /lA/ evlen- ['- marry sb, - get married to sb'], ≠ dünya evine gir- ['- get married, - marry'].

2 /A, {tarafından/CA}/ '- be divided, split /INTO, by/': Dükkân [ortaklar tarafından] iki.yE ayrıldı. 'The shop was divided INTO two [sections] [by the partners].' Zeytinler boyların.a göre dörd.E ayrılır. 'Olives are divided INTO four [categories] according to their size.' *801:8.* separation: - separate. → = bölün-.

'- be separated, distinguished': Yasama, yürütme ve yargının birbirinden tamamen ayrılması lâzım. 'Legislation, execution, and judgment must be completely separated from one another.'

3 /DAn/ '- leave /θ/, - depart /from/': Tren istasyon.DAN tam vaktinde ayrıldı. 'The train left θ the station right on time.' Parti.DEN ayrılırken herkes.LE {tek tek} vedalaştım. 'While leaving θ the party, I said good-bye TO everyone, {individually/one by one}.' *188:6.* departure: - depart. → = hareket et- 3 [usually by means of a land vehicle, i.e., bus, train, not a boat and not a person on foot].

/DAn/ '- check out /OF/ a hotel or motel': Otel.DEN saat 12'de ayrılmanız gerekmektedir. 'You must check out [OF the hotel] at 12 noon.' {a: Bugün/b: Yarın/c: Saat onbirde/d: Cuma günü} ayrılıyorum. 'I'm checking out {a: today/b: tomorrow/c: at 11 o'clock/d: ON Friday}. *188:13.* departure: - check out. → = çık- 1, = terk et-, = uzaklaş- 1 ['- leave /θ/, - go away /from/, - become distant /from/, - move away /from/; - quit'], ≠ gel- 1, ≠ var-, ≠ yaklaş-.

AyrılMAyın '{DoN'T hang up./Stay on the line./Hold.}', on the phone: A: Mert bey.LE görüşmek istiyorum. 'A: I would like to speak TO Mert bey.' B: [Hat.TAN] Ayrılmayın lütfen, hemen bağlıyorum. 'B: Please {don't hang up/stay on the line/hold} [lit., ** don't leave (θ the line)], I'll connect you right away.' [• Note also: Hat.ta kalın lütfen. 'Please stay on the line.' Bekleyin lütfen. 'Please wait.'] *347:18.* communications: - telephone. → = bekle- 1, ≠ kapat-, telefonu kapat- ['- hang up' in the affirmative, as in 'He hung up.'] → kapat-.

* emekliye ayrıl- /DAn/ '- retire /from/, - go into retirement' [emekli 'retired']: Matematik öğretme-nimiz bu yıl emekli.yE ayrılacak. 'Our mathematics teacher will retire this year.' Babam üç yıl önce askerlik.TEN emekli.yE ayrıldı. 'My father retired FROM the military three years ago.' *188:9.* departure: - quit; *448:2.* retirement: - resign.

görevinden ayrıl- '- resign /from/, - leave /θ/ one's post' [görev 1 'duty'. 2 'office, post']: {a: Başbakan/b: Dekan/c: Süleyman bey/d: Dışişleri Bakanı} görevinden ayrıldı. '{a: The prime minister/b: The dean/c: Süleyman bey/d: The foreign minister} resigned [from his post].' *188:9.* departure: - quit; *448:2.* resignation: - resign. → = istifa et- ['- resign /from/'], = işinden çık- ['- leave or - quit /θ/ one's job'] → çık- 1, = işinden ayrıl-. Same. → işten ayrıl- directly below.

işten ayrıl- '- leave or - quit /θ/ one's job' [iş 'work, job']: Kocam {iş.TEN/işi.nDEN} ayrıldı. 'My husband has left θ his job.' Patronum işten ayrılma isteğim.i anlayış.la karşıladı. 'My boss reacted with understanding TO my request to leave the job.' *448:2.* resignation: - resign. → = işinden çık- → çık- 1, = görevinden ayrıl-.

ayrıntıya gir-. → {ayrıntıya/ ayrıntılara/detaya/detaylara} gir-. → gir-.

az 'a few, a little', often used with verbs to render 'under': {az/eksik} tahmin et- '- underestimate'. → tahmin et- 2. → ≠ çok, ≠ fazla.

azal- [ır] '- decrease, - become less, - get or - run low on [supplies], - drop, - fall' [az 'little' + verb-forming suf. -Al]: * Bankadaki hesabım {giderek/gitgide/gittikçe} azalıyor. 'The money in my bank account [lit., My account at the bank] is {gradually} decreasing.' Doktora programındaki öğrenci sayı.sı gittikçe azalıyor. 'The number of students in the Ph.D. program is gradually decreasing.' * Benzinimiz azaldı, benzinciye gidelim. 'We're running low on gas, let's go to the gas station.' * Şekerimiz iyice azaldı. * Yeniden almak lâzım. 'We're really getting low on sugar [lit., ** Our sugar has sharply decreased]. * We must buy some more [lit., It is necessary to buy (some) again].' → = eksil- 1, ≠ art- 1, ≠ çoğal-. # Ocak ayında ihracat yüzde 19.2, ithalat ise yüzde 29.9 oranında azaldı. 'In the month of January exports decreased [at the rate

of] 19.2%, [as for] imports, 29.9%.' *252:6.* decrease: - decrease. → = eksil- 1. # Hastanın ateşi azaldı. 'The patient's temperature fell.' → = düş- 3, = in- 4, ≠ art- 1, ≠ çık- 6, ≠ yüksel- 2.

azarla- [r] /DIğI için/ '- scold, - reprimand, - rebuke /{for/because}/' [azar 'scolding, reprimand' + verb-forming suf. -lA]: Öğretmen ev ödevini yapmayan çocukları azarladı. 'The teacher scolded the students who had not done their homework.' Patron çalışmayan işçileri azarladı. 'The boss reprimanded the workers {who had not done their work./who were not working.}' Vazoyu kır.dığı için çocuğu azarladı. 'She scolded the child because he had broken the vaze.' *510:17.* disapproval: - reprove.

- B -

bağır- [ır] /A, diye/ '- shout, - scream, - yell /AT, saying/': A mother to her screaming child: Öyle bağırma! 'Don't scream like that!' Ne diye bağırıyorsun? 'Why are you shouting?' * Bağırman.A gerek yok. Ne dediğin.i anladım. 'There's no need FOR you to shout [lit., ** FOR your shouting]. I understood what you said.' Annem ban.A "Ayşe buraya gel!" diye bağırdı. 'My mother shouted AT me saying, "Ayşe, come here!"' Çocuk "Annemi isterim" diye [avaz avaz] bağırıyordu. 'The child was shouting [at the top of his lungs] [saying], "I want my mother!"' Kardeşleri dereye düşünce çocuklar hep bir ağızdan çığlık çığlığa bağırmaya başladı: Yetişin! Çabuk buraya gelin! 'When their {brother/sister} fell into the stream, the children began to shout all together at the top of their lungs: Help! Come quick!' Dünkü basketbol maçında bağırmaktan {sesim kısıldı}. 'I {lost my voice/got hoarse} from shouting at the basketball game yesterday.' Arkadaşım evden çıkarken cüzdanını bizde unuttu; arkasından bağırdım ama beni duymadı. 'When my friend left the house, he left [lit., ** forgot] his wallet behind with us. I shouted after him, but he didn't hear [me].' *59:6.*

cry, call: - cry. → = çığlık at- → at-
1, = haykır-, fısılda- ['- whisper'].

bağırıp çağır-. → çağır- 3.

bağışla- [r] [bağış 'gift, grant,
donation' + verb-forming suf. -lA] 1
/A/ '- give /to/, - donate /to/, - make a
donation /to/': **Fatma hanım bütün
mallarını Kızılay'a bağışladı.**
'Fatma hanım donated all her
property to the Red Crescent Society
[i.e., the Muslim equivalent of the
Red Cross].' *478:12.* giving: - give.
→ = ver- 1.

2 /I/ '- forgive, - pardon sb':
**Kendisi.nİ aldatan kocasını
bağışladı.** 'She forgave her husband
who had cheated ON her.'
Bağışlayın beni. 'Excuse me.,
Pardon me., Forgive me.' = **Affet
beni.** *148:3a.* forgiveness: - forgive;
148:3b. : expressions requesting
forgiveness. → = affet- 2.

3 '- spare sb's life, not - separate sb
from sb else': **Allah bağışlasın.**
'May God not separate {them/her/
him} from you': **A: Çocuğunuz
var mı?** 'A: Do you have any
children?' **B: Bir kızım var
efendim.** 'B: I have one daughter,
{sir/ma'am}.' **A: Allah
bağışlasın.** 'A: May God not
separate her from you.' *430:14.*
freedom: - exempt; *504: * 20.*
courtesy: polite expressions.

bağla- [r] 1 /A, lA/ '- tie
/{to/AROUND}, with/, - connect /to/,
- tie up /with/, - fasten, - bind' [bağ
'tie' + verb-forming suf. -lA]:
**Tezgâhtar istediğim kitapları
paketledi ve sıkıca bağladı.**
'The salesman wrapped up the books
I had asked for and {tied/bound}
them up tightly.' **Hediye paketini
kırmızı bir iple bağladı.** 'He tied
the gift [package] up with a red
ribbon.' **Başı.nA kırmızı bir
eşarp bağladı.** 'She tied a red scarf
AROUND her head.' **{Bisikletini/
Atını} direğ.e sıkıca bağladı.**
'He tied {his bicycle/his horse}
securely to the post.' * **Kravatını
{ayna.da/ayna.yA bakarak}
{dikkatle/özenle} bağladı.**
'Looking in the mirror, he tied his tie
{carefully/with care} [lit., ** He tied
his tie carefully {in the mirror/lit.,
looking IN the mirror}].' <u>Proverb</u>
[Also a Tradition 'Hadis']: **Deveni
sağlam kazığ.a bağla, ondan**

sonra Allah'a tevekkül et. 'Tie
your camel securely to a stake. Then
entrust it to God.' On a plane:
**[Emniyet] kemerlerinizi bağla-
yınız.** 'Fasten your seat belts.'
352:7. publication: poster: * specific
signs; *799:9.* joining: - bind. → ≠
çöz- 1.

2 /A/ '- put through /to/, - connect
one party /WITH/ another': On the
phone: Both parties mentioned:
**Lütfen beni Mert bey.E bağlar
mısınız?** 'Would you please {put
me through to/connect me WITH}
Mert bey?' Only one party
mentioned: * **{415 numaralı
oda.yI/Ahmet bey.İ}
bağlayabilir misiniz?** 'Could you
please put me through {TO room
number 415?/TO Ahmet bey?} [lit.,
Would you please connect {room no
415?/Ahmet bey?}]' **{Müdür
bey.İ/Tarih bölümü.nÜ} bağlar
mısınız?** 'Would you please put me
through {to the director?/to the
history department?} A possible
response to the questions above:
**Ayrılmayın lütfen, hemen
bağlıyorum.** '{Hold on
please/Don't hang up please}, I'll
{put you through/connect you} right
away.' *799:5.* joining: - put together.
→ = /lA/ **bağlantı kur-,** = /lA/
temas kur-.

bağlan- /A/ [bağla- + {pass./refl.} suf.
-n]: 1 /a: A, b: lA, c: tarafından/ '- be
tied /a: {to/AROUND}, b: with, c:
by/, - be connected, tied up, fastened,
bound /a: to, b: with, c: by/':
**Kitaplarım [tezgâhtar
tarafından] paketlendi ve sıkıca
bağlandı.** 'My books were wrapped
up and tied up tightly [by the
salesman].' **Hediye paketi kırmızı
bir iple bağlandı.** 'The gift
[package] was tied with a red ribbon.'
799:9. joining: - bind.

2 /A/ '- be connected /to/, - be put
through /to/': **İngilizce için 1'İ,
Türkçe için 2'yİ operatör.E
bağlanmak için 3'Ü tuşlayın.**
'For English press 1, for Turkish,
press 2, to * speak to [lit., be
connected to] an operator, press 3.'
799:11. joining: - be joined.

3 /A/ '- connect oneself /to/, - log on
/to/': **internete bağlan-** '- log on
/to/ the Internet': **Bilgisayarımı
açtım, internet.e bağlandım.** 'I
turned on my computer and logged on

36

to the Internet.' *617:14.* association: - join; *1041:18.* computer science: - computerize. → ≠ **internetten çık-** → **çık-** 1.

bağlantı kur-. → **kur-** 1.

bağlar kop-. → **kop-** 1.

{**bahse/iddiaya**} **gir-.** → **gir-.**

bahset- [bahseDer] /DAn/ '- talk /ABOUT/, - mention /θ/, - discuss /θ/' [A. **bahis** (baHSİ) 'topic' + **et-**]: **Biz.E biraz kendiniz.DEN bahseder misiniz?** * **Türkçe OLARAK lütfen.** 'Would you please tell us a little ABOUT yourself? * IN Turkish please.' **Kendim.DEN bahsetmey.İ hiç sevmem.** 'I don't like to talk ABOUT myself at all.' **Ülkem.DEN bahsetmey.İ çok severim.** 'I like to talk ABOUT my country a lot.' **Politika.DAN bahsetmesek iyi olur.** 'It would be better if we didn't {discuss θ/talk ABOUT/mention θ} politics.' **Önce sözünü tut sonra namus.TAN bahset.** 'First keep your word, then talk ABOUT honor.' *541:12.* conversation: - discuss; *551:8.* information: - inform. → = /DAn/ **söz et-**, = /a: I, b: hakkında.../ **konuş-** ['- speak /a, b: about.../]'.

bahşiş ver-. → **ver-** 1.

bak- [ar] 1 /DAn, A/ '- look /{from/OUT/THROUGH}, AT/': **Garson bey, bizim hesab.A bir daha bakar mısınız?** * **Bir yanlışlık** {**olsa gerek/olmalı**}. 'Waiter, would you please take a look AT our check again. * There must be some mistake.' **Fotoğraflarınız.A bakabilir miyim?** 'May I {look AT/take a look AT} your photographs?' **Yeni gelen komşumuz.A dikkatlice baktım.** 'I looked carefully AT our neighbor who had just arrived.' * **Pencere.DEN** [**dışarı.yA**] **baktım.** 'I looked OUT [OF] the window [lit., ** FROM the window (TO the outside)].' * **Pencere.DEN gökyüzü.nE baktım.** 'I looked OUT [OF] the window AT the sky.' **Sağ.ı.na sol.u.na baktı. Kimse yoktu.** 'He looked to his right, he looked to his left. There was no one there.' Proverbs: **Bir bakmak.TAN, bir tatmak yeğdir.** 'It is better to taste once THAN to look once.' * **Dost baş.A**

düşman ayağ.A bakar. 'A friend looks AT [one's] head, an enemy looks AT [one's] feet.' Some current interpretations of this well-known proverb: Always dress as well as possible because both those who know you and those who don't will judge you from your appearance. Or: A friend looks at the real nature of a person, while a person with evil intentions looks at one's shoes, the superficial aspects. Or: A friend looks one in the eye, while one's enemy averts his gaze and looks at one's feet. Or: A friend wants us to succeed, rise in the world, an enemy wants us to slip and fail. *27:13.* vision: - look.

* **Aksiliğe bakın.** '{What a nuisance!/*colloq:* What a bummer!/What a mess!}' [**aksilik** 'unforseen difficulty, untoward event, hitch'], lit., ** 'Look AT the nuisance': * **Hay Allah! Aksiliğ.E bakın. Tam yazdığım e-maili göndermek üzereyken bilgisayar dondu. Şimdi tekrar yazmam lâzım.** '* O dear! What a {nuisance/bummer}! Just as I was about to send off the e-mail I had written the computer froze. Now I have to write it again.' *98:31.* unpleasantness: INTERJ. eeyuk!

* **Aslına bakarsan[ız]** 'To tell the truth' [**asıl** (aslı) 'truth, reality'], lit., ** 'If you look AT the truth of it': **Aslına bakarsan[ız] olay onun anlattığı gibi değil, abartıyor.** 'To tell the truth, the event didn't happen as he said. He's exaggerating.' *644:22.* probity: ADV. truthfully. → = **Doğrusunu istersen[iz].** ['To tell the truth, If you want the truth (lit., ** the truth of it)]' → **iste-** 1.

Bak 'Now, Look', an emphatic, a word expressing emphasis: A: * **Ne dersin, bu akşam sinemaya gidelim mi?** 'A: {What do you say?/How about it?} How about going to the movies tonight [lit., Shall we go to the movies tonight?]' B: * **Bak, bu çok** {**iyi/güzel**} **bir fikir.** 'B: * Now that's a great idea.' *334:* * *11.* affirmation: INTERJ. I swear!

* {**bakalım/bakayım**} lit., '{let's see/let me see}' (1) 'I don't know if.../I wonder if...', to express doubt: **Önceki gün gelmedi. Dün de**

37

gelmedi. Bakalım bugün gelecek mi? 'He didn't come the day before yesterday. He didn't come yesterday either. {I wonder if/Let's see if} he'll come today.'
(2) 'come on and..., Now...', words of encouragement: Biliyoruz, oradaydın. Anlat bakalım, ne oldu? 'We know you were there. Now tell us what happened.' * Bil bakalım 'Come on, take a guess [lit., Guess, ** let's see]': Bil bakalım * bu şiir kimin? 'Come on, take a guess: * who wrote this poem [lit., whose poem is this]?'
(3) 'Well [then] you'd better...!', with an imperative to indicate a threat: Anlat bakalım, neden derse gelmedin? 'Well then explain: Why didn't you come to class?' Söyleyin bakalım çocuklar, kavgayı kim çıkardı? 'OK, {let's have it/out with it} children. Who {picked/started} the fight?'
(4) 'Let's see...', etc., to indicate a desire to know: You see sb approaching. You say: İşte Bülent. Merhaba Bülentciğim. Gel bakayım. Nasılsın? 'Well, here's Bülent. Hello, Bülent, {old friend/buddy} [NOT ʻmy dearʼ]. Come here, let me see. How are you?' Soralım bakalım, biliyor mu? 'Let's ask and see if he knows [lit., ** Let's ask, let's see, does he know]?' Bir dakika bakayım, kitapta var mı? 'Just a minute. Let me see if it's in the book [lit., Let me look. Is it in the book?].' Şimdi sorularınızı cevaplayayım. * Ha[y]di bakalım ilk soruya. 'Now let me answer your questions. * Now on to the first question.'

* bakarsın 'it might just happen that, possibly, maybe [lit., ** you'll see]': S: Turhan bey bugün gelir mi? 'Q: Will Turhan bey come in today?' C: * Hiç belli olmaz, bakarsın gelir. * Hiç gelmeyebilir de. 'A: {It's hard to say./It's impossible to say./You can never tell.} {Maybe} he will [lit., he'll come]. * He may not even come at all.' = belki. 965:9. possibility: ADV. possibly.

* {Baksana!/Baksanıza!} 'Look here!, Say', informal: 'Hey there!': Baksana bu elbise üzerimde nasıl duruyor? 'Take a look: How does this suit look on me?' Baksanıza, size söylüyorum.

Bilet almadan geçtiniz. '{Look here/Hey there}, I'm talking to you. You've gone through without buying a ticket.' 982:22. attention: INTERJ. attention!

* Bana bak! '[Now] look here! [lit., ** Look AT me]', an attention-getting formula frequent in warnings: Ban.A bak! İşin.E devam etmek istiyorsan daha hızlı çalışmalısın. '[Now] look here! If you want to keep your job [lit., continue IN your job], you'll have to work more quickly.' 982:22. attention: INTERJ. attention!

dik dik bak- /A/ '- stare angrily /AT/, - glare /AT/' [dik 'intent, fixed, penetrating look']: S: Niye ban.A öyle dik dik bakıyorsun? Bir hata mı yaptım? 'Q: Why are you glaring AT me like that? Have I made a mistake?' C: San.A çok kızıyorum * da, ondan. 'A: I'm very angry AT you. * That's why.' 27:16. vision: - glare; 152:25a. resentment, anger: gestures of.

* etrafa bak- '- look around, - have a look around' [A. etraf (. -) 'sides, surroundings'], lit., ** '- look AT the sides': S: * Etraf.a bir bakabilir miyim? 'Q: Could I have a look around?' C: Buy[u]run. 'A: [Please.] Go right ahead.' 27:13. vision: - look; 937:31. inquiry: - search.

* Kusura bakma. 'Excuse me., Pardon me., Forgive me., Sorry.' [A. kusur 'fault'], lit., ** 'DON'T look AT the fault': Kusura bakmayın, geç kaldım. 'Sorry I'm late.' Epeydir yazamadım, kusura bakmayın. 'I haven't been able to write for quite a while. Pardon me.' A friend has come up to your room. You apologize for its condition: Kusura bakmayın, odam çok dağınık. 'Excuse me please. My room is {very messy/a real mess}.' 148:3b. forgiveness: expressions requesting forgiveness. → = affet-2, = özür dile- → dile- 2.

* Önüne bak! 'Eyes front!' [ön 'the front part of anything', önün 'your front'], lit., ** 'Look AT your front': Önüne bak, düşme! 'Look where you're going, don't fall!' {Sınav/İmtihan} sırasında öğretmen Ahmet'e "Önüne bak!" diye bağırdı. 'During {the

exam} the teacher shouted at Ahmet saying "Eyes front!'"

* şöyle bir bak- '- just look around, - browse' [şöyle bir 'casually, desultorily']: Satıcı: * Yardım.A ihtiyacınız var mı? * Nasıl bir şey istiyorsunuz? 'Salesman: Do you need any help [lit., Do you have a need FOR help]? * What kind of a thing are you looking for?' Müşteri: Şöyle bir bakıyorum, teşekkür ederim. 'Customer: I'm just {looking around/browsing}. Thank you.' or Sadece bakıyorum. 'I'm just {looking around/browsing}.' 570:13. learning: - browse; 733:8. purchase: - shop; 937:26. inquiry: - examine cursorily. → = göz at- ['- glance /AT/, - take a look /AT/'] → at- 1.

* Şuna bak be! 'Just look AT that, will you!, Imagine!, [Why] the nerve!' [şu 'that']: A: Kirayı artırmazsan seni evimden çıkartacağım. 'A: If you don't pay more rent, I'll {evict you/throw you out of my house}.' B: Şuna bak be! Daha geçen ay zam yaptık, yine zam istiyor. 'B: Why the nerve! Just last month we paid more, and again he is asking for more!' 152:25b. resentment, anger: expressions of.

* tadına bak- '- taste, - have a taste, - sample a food' [tat 'taste'], lit., ** '- look AT its taste': Baklava yaptım, tad.ı.na baksana? 'I've made some baklava. Why don't you have a taste [lit., of it]?' Yemek yemeyeceğim ama dolma.nın tad.ı.na bir bakayım. 'I'm not going to eat, but just let me have a taste of the dolma [i.e., stuffed tomatoes, peppers, etc.].' Şu peynir.in tad.ı.nA bakabilir miyim? 'May I taste that cheese?' 62:7. taste: - taste; 941:8. experiment: - experiment. → = tat-.

Tesadüfe bakın. 'What a coincidence!' [A. tesadüf (. - .) 'chance event, accidental encounter, coincidence'], lit., ** 'Look AT the coincidence': Tesadüfe bakın, çocukluk arkadaşım Emre ile aynı okul.a öğretmen OLARAK atandık. 'What a coincidence! My childhood friend Emre and I {were/have been} appointed to the same school AS teachers.' 131:15. inexpectation: ADV. surprisingly;

835:7. simultaneity: ADV. simultaneously.

2 /A/ '- look /{FOR/IN}/, - search /FOR/': * İstediğiniz makale.yE baktım. Fakat bulamadım. 'I looked FOR the article you asked for, but I couldn't find it.' Adres defterim.E baktım fakat Hasan'ın adresini bulamadım. 'I looked IN my address book, but I couldn't find Hasan's address.' • In a store bak- '- look for, - want' is usually used for all items except food: Satıcı: Nasıl bir şey bakıyorsunuz? 'Salesman: What [sort of thing] are you looking for?' Müşteri: {a: Yün bir ceket/b: Kareli bir gömlek/c: 44 beden bir pantolon/d: Siyah bir kazak} bakıyorum. 'Customer: I'm looking FOR {a: a wool jacket/b: a checkered shirt/c: a pair of trousers size 44/d: a black sweater}.' → iste-1 ['- want, - want to']. • Note the two dialogue patterns in the following:
a) Satıcı: * Kim[in] için bakıyorsunuz? 'Salesman: * Who is it for? [lit., ** For whom are you looking (for the item of clothing)?]' Müşteri: {a: Kendim/b: Karım/c: Arkadaşım/d: Oğlum} için [bakıyorum]. 'Customer: [I'm looking for sth] for {a: myself/b: my wife/c: my friend/d: my son}.'
b) Satıcı: * Kim.E bakıyorsunuz? 'Salesman: Who is it for? [lit., ** 'Who are you looking AT?' In other contexts this literal meaning might apply.] Müşteri: {a: Kendim.E/b: Karım.A/c: Arkadaşım.A/d: Oğlum.A} bakıyorum. 'Customer: [I'm looking for sth] {a: FOR myself/b: FOR my wife/c: FOR my friend/d: FOR my son}.' *937:30.* inquiry: - seek. → = ara- 1, = iste- 1.

3 /A/ '- look /AFTER/, - take care /OF/, - attend /to/': A common farewell to a person departing for an extended period: Kendin.E iyi bak! 'Take good care OF yourself!' *188:22.* departure: INTERJ. farewell!; *339:9.* - look after: - be careful. * Lütfen bakar mısın[ız]? '{Sir/Ma'am} [lit., Would you please look (here)?]', i.e., Come here please. I need help, etc., the equivalent of various expressions used to call for assistance at a shop or restaurant, etc. Not a call for help in an emergency [medical, etc.]: Garson bey, bakar mısınız? 'Waiter!', the usual polite

way of summoning a waiter. A less polite English equivalent: 'Hey, waiter!' **Devlet hastanesindeki hemşireler, hastalar.A çok iyi bakıyorlar.** '[The] nurses in the state hospital {take very good care of [the] patients/look after [the] patients very well}.' **Odacımız Mehmet efendi uzun zamandan beri izinde. * Bura.yA başka bakan da yok.** 'Our janitor, Mehmet efendi, has been on leave for a long time. * And there isn't anyone else to look AFTER this place [lit., ** after here].' **Bizim {lavabo/tuvalet/küvet} tıkalı. * Bir ara uğrayıp bakmanızı rica ediyorum.** 'Our {washbasin/toilet/ sink} is clogged up. * Please [lit., I'm asking (you) to...] stop by sometime and take care of it.' Proverb: **Bakarsan bağ olur, bakmazsan dağ olur.** 'If you look after it, it will become a vineyard; if you don't, it will become a mountain [i.e., a barren area].' *339:9.* carefulness: - look after; *982:5.* attention: - attend to; *1007:19.* protection: - care for. → = /lA/ **ilgilen-** 2, = /lA/ **meşgul ol-** 2 → **ol-** 12.

***noun of pleasure* bak-** '- {amuse/enjoy} onself': * **Arkadaşlar benim hemen çıkmam lâzım, siz eğlenmeniz.E bakın.** 'Guys, {I'm off./I've got to get out of here right away.} {Have a good time./Enjoy yourselves.}' * **Keyf.in.E bak, sen kahveni yudumlarken ben valizleri hazırlarım.** 'Just {enjoy/amuse} yourself [for a bit]. While you're sipping your coffee, I'll get the baggage ready.' *743:22.* amusement: - amuse oneself.

* **kapıya bak-** '- get or - answer θ the door': * **Kapı çalıyor, bakar mısın lütfen?** 'The doorbell [lit., ** door] is ringing, would you please get it?' **A: * Kapı çalınıyor.** 'A: Someone's knocking on the door [lit., ** the door is being rung].' **B: * Ben bakarım. * Kim acaba?** 'B: I'll get it. * I wonder who it is.' **Kapı.yA baktım.** 'I answered θ the door.' → **Kapıyı aç.** ['Open the door.'] → **aç-** 1. *339:9.* carefulness: - look after; *982:5.* attention: - attend to.

* **telefona bak-** '- get, - pickup, or - answer θ the phone': **Telefon çalıyor, bakar mısın lütfen?**

'The phone is ringing, would you please {get/answer} it?' **Telefon.A baktım.** 'I answered θ the phone.' *339:9.* carefulness: - look after; *347:18.* communications: - telephone; *982:5.* attention: - attend to. → = **telefonA cevap ver-** → **ver-** 1, = **telefonU aç-** → **aç-** 5; ≠ **telefon kapan-** ['for the phone - be hung up'] → **kapan-** 1; ≠ **telefon.U kapat-** ['- hang up'] → **kapat-**.

4 /A, olarak/ '- regard /θ [sb, sth], AS/, - look /UPON [sb, sth], AS/, - consider /θ [sb, sth]': **Beşiktaş'A bu yılın şampiyonu OLARAK bakıyorum.** 'I regard θ Beşiktaş [i.e., a soccer team] AS this year's champion.' **Müdür olay.A farklı bir açıdan bakıyordu.** 'The director was looking AT the event from a different angle.' **Herkes hadise.yE kendi çıkarı açısından bakıyor.** 'Everyone {regards θ/looks AT} the event from the viewpoint of his own interests.' *952:11.* belief: - think. → = /I, olarak/ **gör-** → **gör-** 2, = **say-** 4.

balık tut-. → **tut-** 1.

Bana bak! → **bak-** 1.

Bana öyle geliyor ki... → **gel-** 1.

banyo yap-. → **yap-** 3.

barış- [ır] /lA/ '- make up /with/, - come to an understanding /with/, - make peace /with/': [**barış** 1 'peace'. 2 'reconciliation' + verb-forming suf. - θ]: **{Haftalardır/Aylardır/ Yıllardır} süren dargınlıktan sonra, bu gece kocası.yla barıştı.** 'After {weeks/months/ years} of anger [lit., anger which lasted {weeks...}], tonight she made up with her husband.' *465:10.* pacification: - make up. → = **arası düzel-**, ≠ **arası {açıl-/bozul-}** → **açıl-** 9.

bas- [ar] **1** /A/ '- step /ON/, - trample /{ON/θ} /' : **{Gaz.A/Fren.E/ Debriyaj.A} bas.** 'Step {ON the gas/ON the brake/ON the clutch}.' **Çimenler.E basmayınız.** 'Don't step ON the grass [lit., 'grassES', plural for an extended area].' Proverb: **Uyuyan yılanın kuyruğu.nA basma.** 'Don't step ON the tail of a sleeping snake.'

177:27. travel: - walk; *3 5 2 : 7.* publication: poster: * specific signs.

ayak bas- /A/ '- set foot /ON/' [ayak 'foot']: **Ay.A ilk ayak basan adam Armstrong'dur.** 'The first man to set foot [lit., The man who first set foot] ON the moon was [lit., is] Armstrong.' *177:27.* travel: - walk.

Bas git! 'Get lost!, Beat it!, Scram!, Get out!, Go away!, Be off!, Off with you!, Clear out!, Away with you!': **Baba: Bir daha kız.ım.ın yan.ı.nda dolaştığ.ın.ı görmeyeyim. * Çabuk bas git buradan!** 'The father: Don't let me see you around [lit., ** walking about at the side of] my daughter anymore. * Quick, off with you [lit., ** off with you from here]!' *908:31.* ejection: INTERJ. go away! → = **Defol!** → ol- 12, = **Güle güle 2, kov-** 1 ['- throw, - chase, or - run sb /OUT OF/, - eject sb /from/'].

* **yaşına {bas-/gir- [er]}** '- turn a certain age' [yaş 'age, year of a person's life'], lit., ** '{- step INTO/enter θ} [a certain] age': **{Dedem/Türkiye Cumhuriyeti} pazar günü seksen ikinci yaş.ı.nA bastı.** '{My grandfather/The Turkish Republic} turned 82 on Sunday [lit., ** stepped INTO {his/its} 82nd year...].** • In English this LITERAL translation would mean that the subject is 81 years old. However the Turkish means that he has completed his 82nd year, and that he is 82 years old. Thus I might also say: **Şimdi seksen iki yaşında.** 'Now he is 82 years old. The following pattern without the word **yaş** is also used: **Bugün seksen iki.yE bastı.** 'He turned 82 today.' *303:9.* age: - mature; *817:7a.* beginning: - begin sth. → = **yaşını {doldur-/tamamla-}** → doldur- 1.

2 /A/ '- press /{θ/ON}/, - push /θ/ [button, horn]': *297:11.* weight: - weigh on; *912:4.* depression: - depress. **Düğme.yE basınız.** 'Press θ the button.' *352:7.* publication: poster: * specific signs. **korna.yA bas-** '- hit /θ/ or honk /θ/ a car horn' [It. **korna** 'car horn']: **Şoför aniden karşısına çıkan çocuğu görünce korna.yA bastı.** 'When the driver saw the child that had suddenly appeared in front of him, he {hit/honked} θ the horn.' *58:8.*

stridency: - screech; *708:42.* music: - blow a horn; *912:4.* depression: - depress. → ≠ **korna çal-** → çal- 2. **zile bas-** '- ring [lit., ** - press ON] a bell': **Kapı.ya yaklaştı ve zil.E bastı.** 'He went up to the door and rang the bell.' *54:8a.* resonance: - ring sth.

* **hava bas-** /A/ [A. **hava** 'air'], lit., ** '- press air /INTO/' (1) /A/ '- fill /WITH/ air, - pump up': **Lâstikler.E hava basmak gerekiyor.** 'One must {pump up the tires/fill the tires [WITH air]}.' **Lâstikler.E hava basar mısınız?** 'Would you please put some air IN the tires?' *793:7a.* completeness: - fill sth.
(2) '- show off, - act snobbishly, - give oneself airs': **Niye hava basıp duruyorsun?** 'Why are you showing off [like that]?' **Yeni ayakkabısını giydi, hava basıyor.** 'He has put on his new shoes. He is showing off.' *501:16.* ostentation: - show off. → = **gösteriş yap-** → yap- 3, **kendini beğen-** ['- be conceited, stuck on oneself'] → beğen- 1.

3 /I/ '- print, - publish': **Üniversite matbaası gün.DE 3 bin tane kitap basıyor.** 'The university press prints 3,000 volumes θ a day.' *548:14.* printing: - print.

film bas- '- develop and print' or only '- print', photographic film: If you want a role of film developed and prints as well, you say: **Bu filmleri basar mısınız?** 'Would you develop these films?' If you have the negatives and only want prints, you say: **Bu film.DEN {a: bir.er/b: iki.şer/c: dörd.er/d: altı.şar} adet basın.** 'Print {a: one/b: two/c: four/d: six} pictures [lit., item(s)] OF each negative.' *548:14.* printing: - print; *714:15.* photography: - process. → **banyo yap-** 2 ['- develop photographic film'] → yap- 3.

4 '- set in, for a certain state - come upon, - cover': * **{Karanlık/Sis} basıyor.** '{Darkness/Fog} is setting in.' * **Her yan.ı duman bastı, yangın var galiba.** 'Smoke {has settled everywhere./is everywhere./has enveloped the whole area./lit., ** has settled (over) every side of it]}.' There must be a fire.' → = **çök-** 3. For weather only: *

{Sıcak/Soğuk} bastı. '{The weather's/It's} [common for 'The weather has/It has'] gotten {hot/cold}.' *817:7b.* beginning: for sth - begin; *1018:22.* heat: - be hot; *1022:9.* cold: - freeze. → = çök- 3.

* ter bas- /DAn/ '- break out in a sweat, - be covered in sweat /{from/BECAUSE OF}/' [ter 'sweat']: * Bu oda ne kadar sıcak, * her yanım.I ter bastı. '{It's really hot in here!/This room is really hot!/How hot this room is!} * I'm all covered with sweat.' * Matematik sözlü sınavında [heyecan.DAN] Sezen'İ ter bastı. 'During the oral mathematics examination Sezen [f.] broke out in a sweat [BECAUSE OF nervousness].' *12:16.* excretion: - sweat; *127:13.* fear, frighteningness: - flinch. → terle- ['- sweat, - perspire'].

{bastır- [ır]/tabettir- [ir]}: film {bastır-/tabettir-} '- have photographic film developed and printed or just printed' [bas- + caus. suf. -DIr; A. **tab** 'a printing' + et- '- print' + caus. suf. -DIr]: B u filmleri bastırmak istiyorum. 'I want to have these films developed and printed.' Bu film.DEN ikişer tane bastırmak istiyorum. 'I want to have two prints OF each negative printed.' Ürgüp'te çektiğimiz {filmleri/ fotoğraf- ları} bastırdın mı? 'Did you have {the films/the pictures [o r photographs]} that we took in Ürgüp {developed/printed}?' *714:15.* photography: - process. → film yıkat- ['- have photographic film developed (but not printed)'] → yıkat- 2.

baş eğ-. → eğ-.

baş kesil-. → kesil- 1.

<u>başar-</u> [ır] /I/ '- succeed /IN/, - be successful /IN/' [baş 'head' + verb-forming suf. -Ar. ADJ. başarılı 'successful']: Ahmet'in geçen ay üniversite sınav.ı.na girdiğ.i.ni duyduk. Ne oldu? Başardı mı? 'We heard that Ahmet had taken {the college/the university} entrance exams last week. What happened? Did he pass? [lit., Did he succeed?]' <u>Proverb</u>: Başaran bal yer, başaramayan yal yer. 'The one who succeeds eats honey; the one who cannot succeed eats mash.'

NON-verbal noun as object: * Dersler.i.nİ başararak sınıf.ı.nı geçti. 'When he was successful [lit., Succeeding] IN his classes, he went on to the next grade [lit., ** passed his grade].' * Zor.U başarmak bana daha fazla heyecan verir. * [The challenge of] succeeding IN something difficult is more exciting [lit., ** gives more excitement].' Sen.in bu iş.İ de başaracağ.ın{.A/.DAn} emin.im. 'I'm sure θ that you will succeed IN this job, too.' VERBAL noun as object: * Sonunda babamdan izin almay.I başardım. 'Finally I succeeded IN getting permission from my father [lit., ** succeeded θ getting...].' Hırsız içeri girmey.İ denemiş, ama [girmey.İ] başaramamış. 'The thief tried to enter, but he couldn't [lit., ** he couldn't succeed (θ entering)].' *409:7a.* success: - succeed. → = /DA/ başarı göster- → göster- 1.

başarı göster-. → göster- 1.

başarılar dile-. → dile- 1.

başı dön-. → dön- 1.

başına gel-. → gel- 1.

başından geç-. → geç- 1.

başını alıp git-. → git- 1a.

{başını/kafasını} dinle-. → 2 dinle-.

başını salla-. → salla-.

Başınız sağ olsun. → sağ ol-. → ol-12.

başkaldır- [ır] /A/ '- rebel, - revolt, - rise up /AGAINST/, - riot' [baş 'head', kaldır- '- raise']: II. Mahmud zamanında Yeniçeriler sık sık başkaldırdı. 'In the time of Mahmud II the Janissaries frequently revolted.' Okul yemeklerini beğenmeyen öğrenciler başkaldırdı. 'The students who didn't like the school food rioted.' O yıllarda Karadağlılar devlet.E başkaldırmışlar. 'In those years the Montenegrins rose up AGAINST the state.' *327:7.* disobedience: - revolt. → = ayaklan-.

başla- [r] [baş 'head' + verb-forming suf. -lA] 1 /DAn/ 'for sth - begin, - start /WITH/' [i.]: {Film/Konser/Maç} {[saat] kaçta/ne zaman} başlıyor? '{At what time/When} does {the movie/the concert/the game [i.e., soccer, basketball]} begin?' {Kış/Evimizin inşaatı} başladı. '{Winter/The construction of our house} has begun.' * Okullar bu yıl erken başladı. '{School/The schools} began early this year.' For schools as subject, → also açıl- 1. Proverb: Hırsızlık bir yumurta.DAN başlar. 'Thievery begins WITH [the theft of] a single egg.' *817:7b.* beginning: for sth - begin. → patla- 3 ['(for sth unpleasant) - break out'], ≠ bit- 1, ≠ din-, ≠ sona er- → er-.

2 /A/ 'for sb - begin or - start /θ/ sth': NON-verbal noun as object: Yeni öğrenci altıncı ders.E başladı mı? 'Has the new student begun θ the sixth lesson?' Proverbs: Bir iş.İ bitir.meden başka iş.E başlama. 'Without having finished one task, don't begin θ another [task].' Kırkın.dan sonra saz.A başlayan kıyamette çalar. 'He who begins θ the [study of the] saz after [the age of] forty, will play it on doomsday.', i.e., Don't waste time on frivolous things; life is short. *845: *21.* lateness: PHR. it's too late. VERBAL noun as object: Koltuğ.A oturup romanı okumay.A başladık. 'We sat down IN the armchair and began {TO read/readING} the novel.' *817:7a.* beginning: - begin sth. → = koyul-, ≠ bitir- 1, ≠ son ver- → ver- 1, ≠ tamamla- ['- complete, - finish'].

başlat- [ır] /I/ '- cause sth to begin, - begin sth, - start sth' [başla- + caus. suf. -t]: Hakem maç.ı hemen başlattı. 'The referee started the game [i.e., soccer, basketball] at once.' Hükümet okuma yazma kampanyası başlattı. 'The government began a literacy [lit., reading writing] campaign.' Bütün katılımcılar gelince başkan {açık oturum.U/panel.İ/tartışma.yI} başlattı. 'When all the participants had arrived, the chairman began {the open session/the panel/the discussion}.' Bütün seyirciler gelmeden makinist film.İ başlatmadı. 'The projectionist did not begin the film until the whole audience had come.'

817:7a. beginning: - begin sth. → ≠ durdur-.

başsağlığı dile-. → dile- 1.

{* başvur- [ur]/müracaat et- [eDer]} 1 /A, için/ '- consult /θ [sb or sth], for/, - refer, - resort, - turn, or - appeal /to, for/, - have recourse /to, for/, - look sth up /IN/' [baş 'head', vur- '-strike']; A. müracaat (. - . .) 'applying, application, recourse']: Reference source as object: Kelimenin anlamını çıkaramayınca sözlüğ.E başvurmak zorunda kaldım. 'When I couldn't {figure out/come up with} the meaning of the word, I had to {look it up IN/consult θ} the dictionary.' *387:14.* use: - avail oneself of; *937:30.* inquiry: - seek. → = danış-. Person as object: Param kalmayınca yine en yakın arkadaşım Ayşe'yE başvurdum. 'When I ran out of money, I again turned TO my closest friend Ayşe.' Kolumdaki yara geçmeyince bir doktor.A başvurdum. 'When the wound on my arm didn't heal [lit., ** pass], I consulted θ a doctor.' *387:14.* use: - avail oneself of. → danış- ['- consult a person or office'].

2 /A, için/ '- apply or - submit an application /to, for/': Hangi işler.E başvuruyorsun? 'Which jobs are you applying FOR?' İş İÇİN bir elektrik firması.nA başvurdum. 'I applied TO an electric company FOR work.' Hangi {okullar.A/bölümler.E/fakülteler.E} başvuruyorsun? 'Which {schools/departments/schools [e.g., medical, law] or departments [e.g., literature]} are you applying TO?' Bahar burs bulmak için birçok {kuruluş.A/vakf.A} başvurdu. 'Bahar [f.] applied TO several foundations [vakıf (A. vakfı)] [in order] to find a scholarship.' * Kayıp eşya için nere.yE başvurmalıyım? 'Where's the lost and found? [lit., θ where should I apply for lost property?]' *440:10.* request: - petition; *937:30.* inquiry: - seek.

bat- [ar] 1 /A/ '- sink /{IN/INTO}/, - set [sun, moon]': * Elim.E iğne battı, * kanıyor. 'I pricked myself [lit., ** A needle sank INTO my hand]. * I'm bleeding [lit, It (i.e., the hand) is bleeding].' Koskoca "Titanik" gemisi ilk seferinde bir buzdağı.nA çarpıp battı. 'The huge liner Titanic hit θ an iceberg on its first voyage and sank.' Güneş battı. Akşam oldu. 'The sun has set. It's evening.' *194:6.* descent: - sink; *1026:12.* darkness, dimness: - grow dark. → = hava karar-, ≠ güneş çık- → çık- 3, ≠ güneş doğ- → doğ- 2, kaybol- [for the disappearance of the moon or stars] → ol- 12.

'- sink and - get stuck /IN/': Arabam çamur.A battı. 'My car got stuck [lit., ** sank] IN the mud.' *194:6.* descent: - sink.

2 '- go bankrupt, - go under': {a: Yıldız sineması/b: Bu işyeri/c: Bülent bey/d: Dükkân} battı. '{a: The Star movie house/b: This workplace/c: Bülent bey/d: The shop} has gone {bankrupt/under}.' Arjantin batıyor Türkiye çıkıyor. 'Argentina is going bankrupt. Turkey is {emerging/ improving} [financially].' *625:7.* nonpayment: - go bankrupt. → = iflâs et- 1.

bavulunu hazırla-. → hazırla-.

bayatla- [r] '- spoil, - go bad, - go stale' [bayat 'stale, old' + verb-forming suf. -lA]: Bu ekmekler bayatlamış. 'This bread has gone stale.' Bu {yemek/balıklar} bayatlamış. Kokuyor. 'This {food/fish} has spoiled. It stinks.' *393:22.* impairment: - decay. → = bozul-, kok- 2 ['- smell (bad), - stink (subj.: food)'], ≠ dayan- 4 ['- keep, - stay edible (subj.: food)'].

bayıl- [ır] 1 '- faint, - pass out': Babasının ölüm haberini alınca bayıldı. 'When he received [the] news of his father's death, he fainted.' {Sıcak.tan/Havasızlık- .tan/Heyecan.dan} bayılan kadın on dakika sonra ayıldı. 'The woman who had fainted {from the heat/from lack of air/from excitement} came to ten minutes later.' *25:5.* insensibility: - faint. → = kendinden geç- 1 → geç- 1, = kendini kaybet- 1, = {şuurunu/bilincini} kaybet-[or yitir-] 1 → {kaybet-/yitir-}, ≠ ayıl- 2 ['- come to'], ≠ kendine gel- 1. Same. → gel- 1.

2 /A/ '- be crazy /ABOUT/ sth, - adore /θ/, - like sth a great deal, - be carried away /BY/ sth': İmam bayıldı. {'The imam was crazy about it./The imam fainted'}. Written as one word, i.e., imambayıldı, it is the name of a popular dish of stuffed eggplant cooked in olive oil. NON-verbal noun as object: Böyle kızlar.A bayılırım. 'I'm crazy ABOUT girls like that.'
VERBAL noun as object: O kızın şarkı söylemesi.nE bayıldım. 'I was just carried away BY that girl's singing.' Çok muzip bir çocuktur, her şey.İ alaya almay.A bayılır. 'He's a very mischievous child. He takes great delight IN ridiculing everything.' *101:7.* eagerness: - be enthusiastic. → beğen- 1 ['- like'], hoşuna git-. Same. → git- 1b, sev- 1 ['- love, - like; - be fond of'], ≠ nefret et-.

bayram et- [eDer] '- be overjoyed, - be in seventh heaven, - be on cloud nine, - have a ball' [bayram 'festival']: Erhan millî piyango.DAN 5 bin lira kazanınca bayram etti. 'When Erhan won 5,000 liras IN the national lottery, he was in seventh heaven.' Bütün gün durmadan kar yağınca çocuklar bayram etti. 'When it snowed nonstop [lit., without stopping] the whole day, the kids had a ball.' *95:11.* pleasure: - be pleased. = çok sevin-.

beğen- [ir] 1 '- like': NON-verbal noun as object: Uzun saçlı kızlar.I beğenirim. 'I like girls with long hair.' Apartmandaki komşular.I hiç beğenmiyorum. 'I don't like my neighbors in the apartment building at all.' S: İstanbul'U beğendin mi? 'Q: {DO/Did} you like Istanbul?' • With verbs of feeling or sensation Turkish often has the past tense where English has the simple present. S: * {a: Bura- .yI/b: Bura.sı.nI/c: Bura.lar.I} beğendin[iz] mi? 'Q: {Do/Did} you like IT here? [lit., ** Do you like θ {a: here/b: its here/c: hereS, i.e., around here, these places}?]' S: * {a: Ora.yI/b: Ora.sı.nI/c: Ora.lar.I} beğendin[iz] mi? 'Did you like IT there? [lit., ** Do you like θ {a: there/b: its there]/c: thereS, i.e., around there, those places}?]' C1: Çok beğendim. 'A1: I liked it a lot.' C2: Hiç beğenmedim. 'A2: I didn't like it at all.' En beğendiğ.im yazar Aziz

Nesin'dir. 'My favorite writer [lit., the writer I liked most] is Aziz Nesin.' **Bu halı.nın renkler.i.ni hiç beğenmedim.** 'I didn't like the colors of this rug at all.' You scold sb for sth he has done. You say: * **Beğendin mi yaptığını?** '[Now just look at what you've done!] Are you {proud of/pleased with} yourself? [lit., Do you like what you've done?]' *510:27.* disapproval: INTERJ. God forbid! **Hünkâr beğendi.** 'The Sultan liked it.' Written as one word, i.e., **Hünkârbeğendi**, it is the name of a dish of meat and puréed eggplant. Proverb: * **Herkes kendi akl.ı.nı beğenir.** 'Everyone values [lit., likes] his own opinion.'

{*verb stem.***Iş**/*verb stem.***mA.sI**} as object: S: **Allahaşkına, * o kız.ın ne.yi.ni beğeniyorsun?** 'Q: For heaven's sake, * {what do you like about that girl?/what is it you like about that girl?}' C: **O kız.ın {yürüyüş.ü.nü/gülüş.ü.nü/konuşma.sı.nı} beğeniyorum.** 'A: I like {the way that girl walks/the way that girl laughs/the way that girl talks} [lit., ** that girl's walking...].' • The *verb stem.***mAk** is not usually used as the object of **beğen-**, e.g., NOT ~~Yüzmey.i beğeniyorum. 'I like swimming.'~~ It may, however, be used with the following verbs: **sev-, hoşlan-, hoşuna git-.** *95:12.* pleasure: - enjoy. → = **hoşlan-**, = **hoşuna git-** → **git- 1b**, = **memnun kal-** → **kal- 1**, = **memnun ol-** → **ol- 12**, = **sev- 1**, /A/ **bayıl- 2** ['- be crazy /ABOUT/ sth, - like sth a great deal, - be carried away /BY/ sth'].

kendini beğen- '- be conceited, stuck up, stuck on oneself' [**kendi** 'self']: **Zerrin kendini çok beğenir, onunla arkadaşlık etmek zordur.** 'Zerrin is very {stuck up/conceited}. It's hard to be friends with her.' *140:6.* vanity: - be stuck on oneself. → **hava bas- 2** ['- show off, - act snobishly, - give oneself airs'] → **bas- 2.**
2 '- choose': * **Beğen beğendiğ.in.i.** 'Choose {the one/whichever} you like.' → = **seç- 1**, = {**tercih et-**/**yeğle-**} **2.** *371:13.* choice: - choose.

{**bekâretini/kızlığını**} **kaybet-.** → {**kaybet-/yitir-**}.

bekle- [r] [**bek** ? + verb-forming suf. -**lA**]: **1** /I/ '- wait /FOR/, - await'. NON-verbal noun as object: • Note the ACCUSATIVE case, not the dative: **Bir dakika ben.İ bekleyin, kitaplarımı alıp geleyim.** 'Wait FOR me a minute. I'll get my books and come.' **Acele etmeyin, siz.İ bekleriz.** 'Don't hurry. We'll wait FOR you.' **Burada sizi bekleyen biri[si] var.** '{There's someone here waiting for you./Someone is waiting for you here.}' **Buy[u]run efendim, {doktor/patron/müdür bey} siz.İ bekliyor.** 'Come in {sir/ma'am}, {the doctor/the boss/the director} is {expecting/waiting FOR} you.' {**Biri.nİ/Birisi.nİ**} **bekliyorum.** 'I'm waiting {FOR sb}.' S: **Kim.İ bekliyorsun?** 'Q: Who are you waiting FOR?' C: **Doktor.U bekliyorum.** 'A: I'm waiting FOR the doctor.' S: **Ne zamandan beri bekliyorsun?** 'Q: Since when have you been waiting?' C: {**Yarım saat.ten beri/Beş dakika.dan beri**} **bekliyorum.** 'A: I've been waiting {[FOR] half an hour/[FOR] five minutes}.' S: **Ne zamandır bekliyorsun?** 'Q: How long have you been waiting?' Responses indicating the beginning point of the action, i.e., the waiting: C1: {**Yarım saat.ten beri/Beş dakika.dan beri**} **bekliyorum.** 'A1: I've been waiting {[FOR] half an hour/[FOR] five minutes}.' Some responses indicating the duration of the action: C2: {**Yarım saat.tir/Beş dakika.dır/ Saatler.dir**} **bekliyorum.** 'A2: I've been waiting {[FOR] half an hour/[FOR] 5 minutes/[FOR] hours}.' * **Nerede kaldın, {sabahtan beri/öğleden beri/saat beşten beri} seni bekliyorum.** 'Where have you been [lit., ** Where have you stayed]? I've been waiting for you {since this morning/since noon/since five o'clock}.' **Neredeydin?** {a: **Akşam.A kadar**/b: **Kütüphane kapanan.A kadar**/c: **Saat yedi.yE kadar**/d: **Saatlerce**} **seni bekledim.** 'Where were you? I waited for you {a: until evening/b: until the library closed/c: until seven o'clock/d: for hours}.' S: {**Daha ne kadar/Daha ne zaman.A kadar**} **bekleyeceksin?** 'Q: {How much longer/Until what time} are you going to wait?' C: **Eşim {gel.en.E/gel.ince.yE} kadar bekleyeceğim.** 'A: I'll wait until my spouse comes.' C: {Biraz daha/Yarım saat kadar daha} bekleyeceğim. 'A: I'll wait {a little longer/about a half an hour longer}.' * Bir arkadaşım.dan telefon bekliyorum. 'I'm waiting {for a friend to call/for a call from a friend}.'

On the phone '- hold, - wait': S: Müdür beyle görüşebilir miyim? 'Q: May I speak with the director?' C: Şu anda diğer hatta, * bekleyin lütfen. 'A: He's on the other line {right now/at this moment}. * {Please hold./One moment please.}' * Beklediğ.İMİZ. E değdi doğrusu, konser çok güzeldi. 'It was really worth θ waiting for [lit., ** θ OUR waiting for]. The concert was really beautiful.' Proverb: {Bekleyen/Sabreden} derviş murad.ı.nA ermiş. 'The dervish {who waited/who was patient} reached θ his goal.' Everything comes to him who waits.

VERBAL noun as object: S: Ne.yİ bekliyorsunuz? 'Q: What are you waiting for?' C: * {Konser.in/Futbol maç.ı.nın/ Film.in} başlama.sı.nI bekliyorum. 'A: I'm waiting for {the concert/the soccer game/the movie} to begin [lit., ** for the beginning of the concert...].' C: {Otobüs.ün/Tren.in/Vapur.un} kalkma.sı.nI bekliyorum. 'A: I'm waiting for {the bus/the train/the ferry [boat]} to depart [lit., ** for the departing of the bus...].' 130:8. expectation: - await.

dörtgözle bekle- '- wait eagerly /for/, - await eagerly' [dört 'four', göz 'eye']: Ağabeyim.in askerden dönme.si.nİ dörtgözle bekliyorum; onu çok özledim. 'I'm eagerly awaiting my older brother's return from military service. {I miss/I've missed} him a lot.' 130:8. expectation: - await.

* Yine bekleriz. 'Please come again [lit., ** We await (you) again].', a formula said to departing guests. A possible response: Biz de sizi bekleriz. 'We also look forward to seeing you [again].' At the bottom of a receipt from a store: * İyi günler. * Yine bekleriz. 'Have a good day. * Please come again.' 504: * 20. courtesy: polite expressions.

2 '- expect': NON-verbal noun as object: Bugünlerde annemden bir mektup bekliyorum. 'I'm expecting a letter from my mother {any day now/lit., these days}.' * Bir arkadaşım.dan telefon bekliyorum. 'I'm expecting {a friend to call./a call from a friend.}' You turn up unexpectedly at a party. Someone is pleased to see you and says: Bu ne sürpriz! Siz.İ hiç beklemiyorduk. 'What a surprise! We weren't expecting you at all!' Selma Ağustos ayında bir bebek bekliyor. 'Selma is expecting a baby in August.' Biz.i akşam yemeğ.i.nE bekliyorlar. 'They're expecting us FOR dinner [i.e., the evening meal].'
VERBAL noun as object: * Matematik dersi.nDEN kalmay.I beklemiyordum. 'I didn't expect to fail IN [lit., ** stay FROM] mathematics.' Sözünüzü tutmanızı bekliyoruz. 'We expect you to keep your word.' Öğretmenim.in bize {geleceğ.i.ni/gelme.si.ni} beklemiyordum. 'I wasn't expecting {that my teacher would come/my teacher to come} to our house [lit., to us].' 130:8. expectation: - await. → = {ümit et-/um-} 2.

karşılık bekle- '- expect sth in return for sth given or done' [karşılık 'equivalent']: Bu işi sizi sevdiğim için yapıyorum, hiç bir karşılık beklemiyorum. 'I'm doing this [just] because I {like/love} you. I'm not expecting anything at all in return.' 130:8. expectation: - await.

beklet- '- let or make sb wait, - keep sb waiting' [bekle- + caus. suf. -t]: S: Beni niçin bu kadar beklettin, söyler misin lütfen? 'Q: Why did you keep me waiting so long? Would you please explain?' C1: Otobüs.E yetişemedim. 'A1: {I missed the bus./lit., I couldn't catch θ the bus.}' C2: Otobüs.ü kaçırdım. 'A2: I missed the bus.' C3: Otobüs geç geldi. 'A3: The bus was late [lit., The bus came late].' C4: Otobüs geç kalktı. 'A4: The bus set out late.' C5: * Trafik çok sıkışıktı. 'A5: The traffic was very heavy.' C6: * Akşam trafiğ.i.nE takıldım. 'A6: I got {caught/stuck} IN evening [i.e., probably 'rush hour'] traffic.' A: Beklettiğim için özür dilerim. 'A: Sorry for making you wait.' B: Responses to the apology: a: Rica ederim. '{That's all right./Never mind./No need to apologize.}' b: {Önemli/ Mühim} değil. 'It's not {important}.' c: {Zararı/Ziyanı} yok. 'No problem.' *845:8.* lateness: - delay.

belirt- [ir] '- state, - make clear' [belir- '- become clear, visible' + caus. suf. -t]: Açıkça belirtmek isterim ki, sizinle ortaklığımız.ın devam.ı.nA imkân yok. 'I want to make it quite clear that it is not possible for our partnership to continue [lit., ** there is no possibility FOR our partnership's continuing with you].' Maliye Bakanı işçi ücretler.i.nin yüzde otuz oranında {a: artırıldığ.ı.nı/b: artırılacağ.ı.nı/c: artırılma.sı gerektiğ.i.ni} belirtti. 'The finance minister stated that the wages of workers {a: had been increased/b: would be increased/c: {had/have} to be ' increased} 30%.' *334:5.* affirmation: - affirm; *524:24.* speech: - state. → dikkat çek- ['- call or - draw attention /to/, - refer /to/, - point out /θ/, - note /θ/'] → çek- 1, işaret et- 2 ['- point out /θ/, - indicate /θ/ a fact, - call attention /to/'].

benze- [r] 1 /A/ '- resemble /θ/, - look like': Ahmet baba.sı.nA çok benziyor. 'Ahmet looks a lot like his father.' Sezen anne.si.nDEN daha çok ninesi.nE benziyor. 'Sezen [f.] looks more like her grandmother THAN her mother.' * İkiniz birbiriniz.E çok benziyorsunuz. 'The two of you {strongly resemble θ each other/look much alike}.' Üzülme şekerim, bütün erkekler birbiri.nE benzer, * hepsi.nin göz.ü dışarda. 'Never mind, dear. All men are alike [lit., resemble θ one another]: they all have roving eyes [lit., ** the eyes of all of them are outside].' * Biz biz.E benzeriz. '{We are unique./lit., ** We resemble θ ourselves.}', a phrase Turks often use to indicate their uniqueness as a people. In adds for a product: Taklitler.i.nE benzemez. Gerçek markadır. 'It does not resemble θ imitations of it. It is the original brand.' * Benzerler.i.nE benzemez. 'There is nothing else like it [lit., ** It doesn't resemble θ those similar to it].' S: Bu CD'yi [pronounce: si di'yi] nasıl buldun? 'Q: How do

you {like/lit. find} this CD?' C: Doğruyu söylemek gerekirse beğenmedim. * Hiç bir şey.E benzemiyor. 'A: To tell the truth, I didn't like it. * It's not worth a cent [lit., ** It doesn't resemble θ anything (i.e., worth mentioning)].' Proverb: * Dert derd.E benzemez. 'One {trouble/sorrow} does not resemble θ another.' *783:7.* similarity: - resemble.

2 /A/ '- appear, - look like, - seem': NON-verbal noun as object: S: Hangi karpuzu alayım? 'Q: Which watermelon should I buy?' C: * Bu iyi.yE benziyor. 'A: This looks like a good one.' VERBAL noun as object: * ACIK.MIŞ.A benziyorsun. 'It looks like you're [lit., ** you've GOTTEN] HUNGRY.' * Annem yemeği HAZIRLA.MIŞ.A benziyor. 'It looks like my mother HAS PREPARED the food.' Yeni reklam kampanya.sı ürünlerin satışında etkili OL.MUŞ.A benziyor. 'It appears that the new ad campaign HAS BEEN effective in [increasing] sales [of the products].' * Bu yaz sıcak OL.ACAĞ.A benziyor. 'It looks like this summer IS GOING TO BE hot.' *33:10.* appearance: - appear to be. → = gibi görün- → görün- 2, gibi göster- ['- look like' in reference to a condition or type, not a particular person] → göster- 2.

benzet- [ir] [benze- + caus. suf. -t] 1 /A/ '- mistake one thing or person /FOR/ another': Karanlıkta sen.İ Ahmet'E benzettim. 'In the darkness I mistook you FOR Ahmet.' S: * Sizi bir yerden hatırlıyorum ama nereden? Geçen haftaki konferansta tanışmış mıydık? 'Q: Don't I know you from somewhere? [lit., I remember you from somewhere, but from where?] Didn't we meet at the conference last week? C: Hayır, sanmıyorum. * Karıştırdınız. * Herhalde beni birisi.nE benzettiniz. A: No, I don't think so. * {You're confusing/You've confused} me with sb else. * You've probably mistaken me for sb else.' *974:13.* error: - mistake, - make a mistake. → {san-/zannet-} ['- think, - suppose', as in 'I thought you were Ahmet.']

47

2 /A/ '- liken sb or sth /to/ sb or sth else, - note, - indicate, - see or - feel a resemblance between, - think that sb or sth is /LIKE/ sb or sth else; - compare sb or sth /to/ sb or sth else AND note the similarity; for sb or sth - remind sb of sb or sth else; - remind /OF/ [one thing or person brings another to mind]': **Amerikan basını Saddam'ı Hitler'E benzetti.** 'The U.S. press {likened/compared} Saddam to Hitler [i.e., compared and noted the similarity].' * **Küçük çocuğu rahmetli dedesi.nE benzettim.** 'I thought the little child resembled θ his deceased grandfather.' * **San Fransisko'yU İstanbul'A benzettim.** '{San Fransisco reminded me OF Istanbul./I thought that San Francisco was LIKE Istanbul.}' **Filmdeki artist.İ arkadaşım Mine'yE benzettim.** '{The movie star in the film reminded me OF my friend Mine [f.]./I thought the movie star in the film was LIKE my friend Mine.}' *942:4.* comparison: - compare; *988:20.* memory: - remind. → /1A/ {**karşılaştır-/mukayese et-**} [both verbs mean '- compare sb or sth /with/ sb or sth else', but no particular result of the comparison is implied], = {**hatırlat-/anımsat-**} 3 ['- remind'].

bereket versin [ki]. → **ver-** 1.

<u>besle-</u> [r] 1 '- feed, - nourish': **Bebeğimi dört saat.TE bir beslerim.** 'I feed my baby {every four hours/once in four hours}.' <u>Proverb</u>: **Yenilen değil, hazmedilen besler.** 'It is not what is eaten but what is digested that nourishes [the body].' *385:9.* provision: - provision.

2 '- raise [animals], - keep [animals, pets]': Pets: **Komşumuz evinde kedi, köpek besliyor.** 'Our neighbor {has/keeps} cats and dogs at his house.' Farm animals: **Çiftçi Mehmet çiftliğinde {a: tavuk/b: hindi/c: inek/d: koyun} besler.** 'Farmer Mehmet raises {a: chickens/b: turkeys/c: cows/d: sheep} on his farm.' *1068:6.* animal husbandry: - raise. → = **yetiş-** 7 ['- raise plants and animals', usually on a farm].

bestele- [r] /için/ '- compose music /for/' [**beste** 'musical composition' + verb-forming suf. -lA]: **Ünlü besteci bu {a: şarkı.yı/b: senfoni.yi/c: türkü.yü/d: oyun havası.nı/e: opera.yı} karısı için bestelemiş.** 'The famous composer composed this {a: song/b: symphony/c: **türkü** [a kind of folk song]/d: tune [which accompanies a folk dance]/e: opera} for his wife.' *708:46.* music: - compose.

beş para etME-. → **et-** 2.

beyan et- [eDer] '- declare, - announce' [A. **beyan** (. -) 'declaration']: **Gümrük memuru: Beyan edecek bir şeyiniz var mı?** 'Customs official: Do you have anything to declare?' **Yolcu 1: Hayır, beyan edecek bir şeyim yok.** 'Traveler 1: No, I have nothing to declare.' **Yolcu 2: Evet, iki dizüstü bilgisayarım ve bir kameram var.** 'Traveler 2: Yes, I have two laptop computers and a camera.' **Hükümet vergiler.in yüzde on oran.ı.nda düşürüleceğ.i.ni beyan etti.** 'The government announced that taxes would be reduced 10 percent [lit., ** in the proportion of 10 percent].' *352:12.* publication: - announce. For '- announce', but not '- declare [at customs]' → = **duyur-**, = **açıkla-** 2.

{**bık-** [ar]/**usan-** [ır]} /DAn/ '- be, - get, or - grow tired /OF/, - tire /OF/, - get bored, fed up /WITH/, - be fed up, disgusted /WITH/': {**Hergün aynı yemeği yemek.TEN/Sen.DEN} bık.TIM.** '{I'M/I got} tired {OF eating the same food every day/OF you}.' In the sentence above **bıktım** may refer to a feeling still in effect, in which case it would probably be translated with the PRESENT tense. If the feeling is no longer in effect, it would probably be translated with the PAST tense. • In reference to a PRESENT condition, certain common Turkish verbs designating a state, i.e., a feeling, emotion, or sensation, often have the simple PAST tense, but the equivalent English has the simple PRESENT tense. <u>Proverb</u>: **Can cefa.DAN da usanır, sefa.DAN da.** 'One [lit., ** the soul] grows weary OF suffering as well as OF pleasure.' **Bık-** and **usan-** are sometimes found together in two patterns

meaning '- be THOROUGHLY tired of, disgusted with':
a) With the SAME personal suffix on both verbs: **Bir insan hergün baklava yese o.nDAN da bık.AR usan.IR.** 'If a person were to eat [sth as delicious as] baklava every day, he would get tired of it too.'
b) With the -Ip suffix on the first, a personal or other suffix on the second: **Başarılı olmak için bık.IP usan.MADAN çalışmak lâzım.** 'To be successful one must work tirelessly [lit., without tiring].' *118:7b.* tedium: - get bored. → = sıkıl- 1.

bırak- [ır] 1 /DA/ '- leave [i.e., NOT to take sth from where it is], - leave sth /{on/in/at}/, - leave behind, /in/ a certain condition': The books are now on the table. You don't want them to be taken away. You say: **Kitapları masa.DA bırakın.** 'Leave [i.e., DON'T take] the books ON the table.' *256:6.* remainder: - leave. → ≠ al- 1. # **Çıkarken {kapıyı/ pencereyi/camı} açık bırakın lütfen.** 'When you go out, please leave {the door/the window/the window} open.'

sınıfta bırak- '- fail, - flunk sb [in a grade]' [A. sınıf 'class'], lit., ** '- leave in the grade': **Öğretmen iki tembel öğrenci.yI sınıf.TA bıraktı.** 'The teacher flunked {a: two/b: two of the/c: the two} lazy students.', i.e., did not allow them to advance to the next grade. *410:17.* failure: - flunk sb. → ≠ geçir- 1.

2 /A/ '- leave /{ON/IN/AT}/ [i.e., PUT sth SOMEWHERE], - leave or - drop off /AT/': The books are NOT on the table. You say: **Kitapları masa.yA bırakın.** 'Leave [i.e., PUT] the books ON the table.' **Kıymetli eşyalarımı {kasa.nız.A/bura.yA} bırakabilir miyim?** 'May I leave my valuables [lit., ** valuable things] {IN your safe-deposit box]/θ here}?' → = koy- 1, ≠ al- 1. # **Beni şehr.E bırakır mısınız?** 'Would you {leave/drop} me off IN town?' * **Sizi nere.yE bırakmamı istersiniz?** 'Where would you like me to drop you off?' **İstersen seni * arabam.LA evin.E bırakabilirim.** 'If you {like/wish}, * I can {give you a lift/drive you home}. [lit., ** leave you AT your

home WITH my car].}' **Tren, yolcuları bırakmak için istasyonda durdu.** 'The train stopped at the station to let the passengers off.' → = indir- 2, ≠ al- 2, ≠ bindir-. *159:12.* location: - place.

mesaj bırak- /{A/için}/ '- leave a message /for/': **Nurdan için bir mesaj bırakmak istiyorum.** 'I'd like to leave a message for Nurdan [f.].' S: * **Ban.A mesaj bırakan oldu mu?** 'Q: Has anyone left a message FOR me? [lit., ** Has there been anyone who has left a message for me?].' C1: **Evet, bir kişi mesaj bıraktı ve öğleden sonra tekrar arayacağ.ı.nı söyledi.** 'A1: Yes, one person left a message, and he said [that] he would call back later.' C2: **Hayır, * [siz.E mesaj bırakan] olmadı.** 'A2: No, no one has left a message FOR you [lit., ** there hasn't been anyone who has left a message for you].'

* oluruna bırak- '- let matters run or take their course without interference, - leave or - let well enough alone, - let nature take its course, - let things be': A: **Boş ver, * takma kafana, her şey.I oluruna bırak. Göreceksin, * her şey yol.u.na girecek.** 'A: Never mind; forget about it; don't let it {get to/bug} you. Let things be. You'll see that everything will turn out {all right/OK}.' B: * **İyi de, oluruna bırakırsam, işler nasıl yürüyecek, * söyler misin lütfen?** 'B: OK, but if I just let things be [and don't do anything], how are things going to get done? * Just tell me that, will you.' *430:16.* freedom: not - interfere.

3 '- stop, - drop, - quit an activity, - give up a habit; - leave, - abandon a person': NON-verbal noun as object: * **Üniversiteye başlayınca piyano derslerini bıraktım.** 'When I started {college/university}, I {stopped/dropped} [my] piano lessons.' **O dersi bırakmay.a karar vermiştim ama ev arkadaşım beni vazgeçirdi.** 'I had decided to drop that class, but {my roommate/the person I live with/lit., my housemate} talked me out of it.' **Ahmet bey 30 [read: otuz] yıl sonra * sigara.yI bıraktı.** 'Ahmet bey * quit smoking after 30 years.' * **Bir türlü

bırakamıyorum bu namussuz sigara.yI. 'I just can't seem to give up these damn cigarettes!' * Gürültü.yü bırak! 'Stop that noise!' Ne olur bırakma beni. 'Please don't leave me.' Mehmet karısını bıraktı. 'Mehmet left his wife.'

VERBAL noun as object: Yeter artık, bırak şu ağlamay.I! 'That's enough now, stop this crying!' Çene çalmay.I bırak da, dersin.E çalış! 'Stop chatting and study your lesson!' Bırak şu kitabı aramay.I. * Şimdi sırası mı? 'Come on now! Stop looking for that book. * Is this the time for that?' [i.e., it isn't] * Bırak inat etmey.İ de ha[y]di bizimle gel. 'Come on, don't be so stubborn and come with us.' Evlendikten sonra resim yapmay.I bıraktım. 'After I got married, I stopped {drawing/painting} [lit., making pictures].' 370:5. abandonment: - abandon; 856:6. cessation: - cease sth. → = durdur-, = terk et-, kes- 4 [- stop an activity as in '- stop (the crying/the noise)'].

4 '- leave sb alone, - stop bothering sb': Bırak! 'Stop it!, Knock it off!, Leave me alone!, Quit it!, Come off it!' {Bırak beni!/Beni bırak!} 'Leave me alone! [or 'Quit it!' or 'Take your hands off me!']' A: Bu işi Ahmet'le yapsak iyi olur. 'A: It would be good if we did this {job/task} with Ahmet.' B: * Bırak yahu! O adamla iş yapılmaz, sahtekâr.ın tek.i.dir. 'B: Come off it! No one can deal with that fellow! He's a swindler!' 856:6. cessation: - cease sth; 1011:13. hindrance: - stop.

rahat bırak- '- leave in peace, - leave alone' [A. rahat 'comfort, comfortable']: Beni rahat bırakın. 'Leave me in peace!' → dur- 4. # Öf bu sinekler! * Bizi rahat bırakmıyorlar! 'Oh those flies! * They just won't leave us in peace!' 390:4. disuse: - cease to use; 856:6. cessation: - cease sth.

yalnız bırak '- leave sb alone' [yalnız 'alone']: Şu an kimseyle konuşacak durumda değilim, lütfen beni yalnız bırakın. 'Right now I'm not in a state to speak with anyone. Please leave me alone!' 390:4. disuse: - cease to use; 871:6. oneness: - stand alone.

5 '- let go of, - release, - put down': Murat tuttuğu kuşu bıraktı. 'Murat {let go of/released} the bird he had caught.' * Bu kitabı mutlaka okuyun! {a: Çok eğlenceli/b: Sürükleyici}. * El.iniz.DEN bırakamıya-caksınız. 'Be sure to read this book! It is {a: very entertaining/b: {fascinating/gripping/ riveting}}. * You won't be able to put it down [lit., ** release it FROM your hands].' 159:14. location: - deposit; 431:5. liberation: - release. → ≠ tut- 1.

serbest bırak- '- release, - free, - set free, - liberate, - let go' [serbest 'free, unrestricted']: Hava korsanları iki saat pazarlıktan sonra yolcular.ın bir kısm.ı.nı serbest bıraktı. 'The hijackers released some of the passengers after two hours of negotiations.' 120:6. relief: - release; 398:3. rescue: - rescue; 431:5. liberation: - release. → = salıver-.

6 /A/ '- leave /to/ a later time, - postpone /to/, - put off /to/': Öğretmen Türkçe sınavını gelecek hafta.yA bıraktı. 'The teacher put off the Turkish examination TO next week.' Ev işini Ankara dönüşü.nden sonra.yA bıraktı. 'He left the matter of his housing UNTIL after his return from Ankara.' Proverb: {Bugünkü iş.i/Bugün.ün iş.i.ni} yarın.a bırakma. 'Don't put off to tomorrow what you can do today [lit., ** Don't leave {today's work} to tomorrow].' 845:9. lateness: - postpone. → = {ertele-/tehir et-}, ≠ öne al- ['- move up in time, - make earlier than originally planned'] → al- 1.

7 '- leave sth /to/ sb, - bequeath sth /to/ sb': Mehmet karısı.nA çok mal bıraktı. 'Mehmet left {his wife a lot of property/a lot of property to his wife}.' 478:18. giving: - bequeath.

bıyık altından gül-. → gül- 2.

biç- [er] 1 '- cut up [timber], - cut out [cloth], - cut to size in accordance with a model or measure': Terzi kumaşları yanlış biçmiş. * Şimdi elbise ban.A olmuyor. 'The tailor cut the cloth incorrectly. * Now the suit doesn't fit θ me.' 262:7. form: - form.

2 /lA/ '- reap, - mow /with/':
Eskiden çiftçiler ekinleri
{orak.la/tırpan.la} biçerlerdi. *
Artık ekinler gelişmiş
makinalar.la biçiliyor. 'Formerly
farmers reaped [the] crops {with a
sickle/with a scythe}. * Now the
reaping is done [lit., ** they are
reaped] with {advanced/modern}
machines.' Bahçedeki çimenler
çok uzamış, artık biçmemiz
lâzım. 'The grass [lit., ** grassES]
in the garden has gotten too high. We
must mow it now.' Proverbs: Arpa
eken buğday biçmez. 'He who
sows barley will not reap wheat.' Ne
ekersen onu biçersin. 'You reap
what you sow.' As you sow, so shall
you reap. Rüzgâr eken fırtına
biçer. 'He who sows the wind reaps
the storm.' 1067:19. agriculture: -
harvest. → ≠ ek-.

bil- [İR] 1 (1.1) '- know sth, a fact, a
thing, not a person': When leaving a
decision to sb else: S: Sinemaya
gidelim mi? 'Q: Shall we go to the
movies?' C: Vallahi * sen
bilirsin. İstersen gidelim. 'A:
Well, * it's really up to you [lit., **
you know]. If you like, let's go.' S:
Burada ne kadar kalacaksınız?
'Q: How long will you be staying
here?' C: * {Daha/Henüz}
bilmiyorum. 'A: * I don't know
{yet}.' * Kim.E {sor.sanız/
sor.arsanız sorun} bilir.
'Everyone you ask knows [lit., ** θ
whomever you ask knows].' *
{Bil.en/Daha iyi bir fikr.i
ol.an} varsa söylesin. 'If anyone
{knows/has a better idea}, let him
speak up.' İnsanlar.a yardımcı
olmak.LA övünme, * Allah
bilsin yeter. 'Don't boast ABOUT
being helpful to people. * It's enough
if God knows [lit., Let God know,
that's enough].' {Sevgilim/
Anneciğim} seni ne kadar
özlediğimi bir bilsen!
'{Dear/Mommy}, if you only knew
how much I miss you!' Proverbs:
Bilmediğin iş.E karışma,
bilmediğin yol.A gitme. 'Don't
get involved IN a matter you don't
understand and don't set foot UPON
a path you don't know.' Bilmemek
ayıp değil, öğrenmemek
ayıptır. 'Not knowing is not
shameful, but not learning is
[shameful].' Çok bil.en çok
yanılır. 'He who knows a lot [also]
makes lots of mistakes.' Çok
oku.yan değil, çok gez.en bilir.

'It's not the one who has read a lot,
but the one who travels a lot that
knows [a lot].' Çok yaşa.yan
bilmez, çok gez.en bilir. 'It's not
the one who has lived long, but the
one who has traveled widely that
knows [lit., The one who has lived
long does not know; the one who has
traveled a lot knows].' 570: * 19.
learning: PHR. experience is the best
teacher. Yol bilen kervan.A
katılmaz. 'The one who knows the
way doesn't join θ the caravan.'
NON-verbal noun as object: Türkçe
biliyor. 'He knows Turkish.' Often
used where the English speaker
would say 'He SPEAKS Turkish.' •
The notion of knowing a language is
frequently expressed with the name of
the language plus the possessed suffix
plus var: Türkçe.Sİ var. lit., **
'{HE HAS Turkish./HIS Turkish (is)
existent.}' Sadece birkaç kelime
Türkçe biliyorum. 'I know only a
few words of Turkish.' Bu {a:
bölgeyi/b: semti/c: mahalleyi/
d: şehri} bilmiyorum. 'I don't
know this {a: area/b: neighborhood/c:
district/d: city [şehir (şeHRi)]}.' A
phrase introducing the statement of a
fact: Bunu biliyor muydunuz?
'Did you know this?'
VERBAL noun as object: Ne
yapacağ.ım.ı bilmiyorum. 'I
don't know {what to do/lit., what I'm
going to do}.' Cemil * kendisi.nE
mektup geldiği.ni bilmeyebilir,
lütfen haber verin. 'Cemil may
not know * that he has a letter [lit.,
that a letter has come FOR him].
Please * let him know [lit., ** give
him news].' Ben.İM kim
olduğ.UM.u biliyor musunuz?
'Do you know who I am?'
Ahmet'in işinden {a:
ayrıldığ.ı.nı/b: ayrılacağ.ı.nı/c:
ayrılma.sı gerektiğ.i.ni}
biliyordum. 'I knew that Ahmet {a:
had left/b: was going to leave/c: had
to leave} his job.' Ahmet'in
işinden {a: nasıl/b: ne zaman/c:
neden/d: niçin/e: niye}
ayrıldığ.ı.nı biliyordum. 'I knew
{a: how/b: when/c, d, e: why} Ahmet
had left his job.' Ahmet'in nere.yE
taşındığ.ı.nı bilmiyorum. 'I
don't know θ where Ahmet has
moved.' Ahmet'in İstanbul'dan
dön.üp {dönmediğ.i.ni/
dönmeyeceğ.i.ni} bilmiyorum.
'I don't know whether Ahmet {has
returned/will return} from Istanbul or
not.' Bugün {haber} al.ıp
alamayacaklar.ı.nı bilmiyorlar.

'They don't know whether or not they will be able to get {word/information} today.' **Hava yağmurlu olmasına rağmen, Ahmet dışarı şemsiyesiz çıkıyor. Vallahi bu çocuk ne yaptığ.ı.nı bilmiyor!** 'In spite of the fact that it is raining [lit., ** the weather's being rainy], Ahmet is going out without an umbrella. Really this child doesn't know what he's doing!' Proverb: **Akıllı bildiğ.i.ni söyler, deli söylediğ.i.ni bilmez.** 'An intelligent person says what he knows, but a fool doesn't know what he [himself] says.' FINITE VERB FORM 'as object': * **Biz o.nU okula gid.İYOR bilirken, o** * **arkadaşlarıyla gezmeye gidiyormuş.** 'While we were under the impression [that] he was going to school [lit., ** While knowing him he is going to school], he was [actually] * {hanging out/going around/loafing around} with his friends.' *927:12.* knowledge: - know.

Allah bilir. 'God knows.': → **Ne bileyim [ben]?** below.

* **bileme-** '- have no idea, not - be able to figure out, [just] not - know, lit., ** - be unable to know, not - be able to know' [bil- + the inability suf. -AmA-]. An English translation including the notion of inability will often seem awkward or over emphatic. **Nasıl başlayacağ.ım.ı bilmiyorum.** 'I {have no idea/can't figure out} how to begin [lit., ** how I will begin].' **Ne yapacağ.ım.ı, ne.yE karar vereceğ.im.i bilmiyorum.** 'I just don't know what to do, what to decide.' **Ne yapayım bilmiyorum.** 'I {[just] don't know/have no idea} what to do.' **Ne diyeceğimi bilmiyorum.** 'I don't know what to say.' **Müdür bey sabah çıktı.** * **Ne zaman döner bilmiyorum.** 'The director stepped out this morning. * I have no idea when he'll be back [lit., ** When he'll be back, I have no idea].' **Sevinsin mi üzülsün mü, bilemedi.** 'He didn't know whether to be glad or sorry [lit., ** Should he be glad, should he be sorry, he couldn't know].' **Şaşkınlık ve heyecan.dan ne yapacağı.nı bilemedi.** 'Because of surprise and excitement he didn't know what to do.' **Bir süre ne diyeceğini**

bilemedi. 'For a moment he didn't know what to say.' **O kadar sevindi ki ne yapacağını bilemedi.** 'He was so delighted [that] he didn't know what to do.' **Seni ne kadar özlediğimi bilemezsin.** 'You just don't know how much I miss you!' * **Türkiye'deki eğitim sistemini pek bilemiyeceğim.** 'I don't really know the education system in Turkey.' * **Dersini bilemedi, demek ki yeterince çalışmamış.** 'He didn't know his lesson. That means he didn't study enough.' *19:8.* impotence: cannot.

* **Bildiği kadarıyla** '{As far as he knows/As far as he can tell/To the best of his knowledge}', very common in the first person: **Bildiğ.İM kadarıyla** 'As far as I know': S: **Ahmet'ten haber alıyor musun?** 'Q: Do you have any word of Ahmet?' C: **Bildiğim kadarıyla Antalya'da tatil yapıyor.** 'A: As far as I know, he's on {vacation/holiday} in Antalya.' *927:30.* knowledge: ADV. to one's knowledge. → **Anladığı kadarıyla** ['{As far as he understands/As far as he can tell/To the best of his understanding}'] → anla- 1.

* **Biliyor musun?** 'Guess what [lit., Do you know?]', a phrase used to call attention to following words: A: **Biliyor musun, davayı kazandık.** 'A: Guess what? We won the case!' B: * **Ne diyorsun?** * **Öyle sevindim ki, anlatamam.** 'B: {Well, what do you know [lit., say]!/You don't say!} * That's great! [lit., ** I'm so pleased (that) I can't say].' * **Baş.IM.a ne geldi, biliyor musun?** '{Guess what happened to ME [lit., ** what came to my head]./Do you know what happened to ME?'}, a phrase used to call attention to following words. *982:22.* attention: INTERJ. attention!

* **Bilmem.** 'I don't know.' Also: 'I wonder [whether]'. Sometimes better left untranslated: **Bilmem gelir mi?** 'I wonder whether he'll come [lit., I don't know, will he come?].' A common alternative is **acaba**: **Acaba gelir mi?** Same translation. * **Bilmem anlatabiliyor muyum?** '{Have I made myself clear?/Have I gotten my point across?}' *929:11.*

ignorance: not - know; *970:9.*
uncertainty: - be uncertain.

ezbere bil- '- know from memory,
by heart' [P. **ezber** 'memorization']:
Ismail çok iyi bir hafızdır,
bütün Kuran'ı ezbere bilir.
'Ismail is a very good hafiz. He
knows the whole Qur'an from
memory.' * **Her piyanist çaldığı
parçalar.ın notalar.ı.nı ezbere
bilmez.** 'Not every pianist knows by
heart the pieces he plays [lit., Every
pianist doesn't know by heart the
notes of the pieces he plays].' *988:17.*
memory: - memorize.

* **iyi bil-** '- know for sure, certain':
S: Acaba buradan oraya kaç.A
götürürler? 'Q: I wonder how much
they'll charge to take sb from here to
there? [lit., FOR how much they'll
take sb from here to there?]' C: İyi
bilmiyorum ama her halde 8
lira tutar. 'A: I'm not sure, but it'll
probably {come/amount} to 8 liras.'
969:9. certainty: - be certain. →
emin ol- ['- be or - become sure,
certain, convinced /OF/, /θ/ that'] →
ol- 12.

* **İyi bildin!** 'Right you are!',
colloq.: 'Right on! [lit., ** You know
it!]': A: Aklın sınav.A takıldı
galiba. 'A: You're probably
preoccupied WITH the examination.'
B: İyi bildin! 'B: Right you are!'
colloq.: 'Right on!' *972:25* truth:
PHR. <nonformal terms> right on!
More formal: = Haklısın.

Kim bilir? 'Who knows?': Mary
Türkiye'ye gideli 5 ay oldu.
Kim bilir şimdi neler
yapıyordur? 'It's been 5 months
since Mary went to Turkey. Who
knows what she's doing now?' S:
Ne dersin, seçimleri kim
kazanacak? 'Q: What do you
think? Who's going to win the
elections?' C: Kim bilir? 'A: Who
knows?' *929:11.* ignorance: not -
know.

* **Ne bileyim [ben]?** (1) 'How
should I know?': S: Ne olacak
şimdi? 'Q: What's going to happen
now?' C: {Ne bileyim ben? [or
Bilmem ki]/Allah bilir}. 'A:
{How should I know?/[Only] God
knows.}' *929:11.* ignorance: not -
know.
(2) 'Well, let's see', a filler phrase
for stalling for time: S: Metin'in

partisine gitmeyi hiç
istemiyorum. * Ona ne desem
acaba? 'Q: I really don't want to go
to Metin's party. * I wonder what I
should say to him?' C: Ne bileyim
ben, meselâ hasta olduğunu
söyleyebilirsin. 'A: Well, let's
see, for example, you could tell him
that you're sick.' *362:13.* irresolution:
ADV. * filler phrases and stallers.
One of the most common fillers is the
single word **efendim** used without a
verb. For other filler phrases, →
Efendime söyleyeyim → söyle- 1,
Nasıl anlatayım? → anlat- 1,
Nasıl anlatsam? → anlat- 1.

önceden bil- '- know in advance'
[**önceden** 'in advance, beforehand']:
Bu yarışta hangi atın
kazanacağını önceden bilmek
çok zor. 'It is very difficult {to
know in advance/to predict} which
horse is going to win this race.'
960:6. foresight: - foreknow. → =
kestir- 2, = **tahmin et-** 3.

(1.2) '- know the real nature of sb,
what kind of person he is, what can
be expected of him', not in the more
casual sense of '- be acquainted with
a person': Ahmet'i biliyorum. 'I
know Ahmet.', i.e., I know what kind
of a person he is., which may also be
expressed: * Ahmet'İN nasıl
biri[si] olduğ.u.nU biliyorum.
[lit., ** how a one Ahmet is].'
927:12. knowledge: - know. → =
tanı- 1.2.

2 '- know how to do sth': NON-
verbal noun as object: * İyi
{dikiş/örgü} bilir. 'She knows
HOW TO {sew/knit} well [lit., **
knows {sewing/knitting} well].'
VERBAL noun as object: *
{Yüzmey.İ/Yüzme.si.ni}
bilmiyorum. 'I don't know HOW
TO swim [lit., ** know swimming].'
927:12. knowledge: - know.

3 /I/ '- think of as, - know as': *
Ben de sen.İ dost biliyordum,
yazık ki değilmişsin. 'And here I
thought all along [that] you were my
friend [lit., ** I thought you a friend]!
Too bad you're not.' * Sen.İ dürüst
biri bilirdim ama yanılmışım.
'[Here] I thought [that] you were an
honest person [lit., ** I thought you
an honest person], but I guess I was
{mistaken/wrong}.' *952:11.* belief: -
think. → = {san-/zannet-}.

53

4 '- guess, - take a guess': **Millî maçların sonuçlarını bilin, armağanlar kazanın.** 'Guess [correctly] the results of the national championships and win prizes.' * **Bil bakalım** '[Come on,] take a guess [lit., ** Take a guess, come on (lit., let's see)]': **Bil bakalım bu şiir kimin?** 'Take a guess: who wrote this poem [lit., whose poem is this]?' **Bilin bakalım aklıma ne geliyor?** 'Guess what I'm thinking [lit., ** what is coming to my mind].' *945:9.* judgment: - estimate; *950:11.* theory, supposition: - conjecture. → = **tahmin et- 2.**

Bildiği kadarıyla. → bil- 1.

bildir- [ir] /A/ '- inform /θ/, - get information /to/, - report /to/' [bil- + caus. suf. -DIr]: NON-verbal noun as object: * **Polis.e {bir cinayet.İ/bir hırsızlığ.I/bir olay.I} bildirmek istiyorum.** 'I want to report {a murder/a theft/an incident} to the police.'
VERBAL noun as object: **Ahmet'E bu tren.LE geleceğ.im.İ bildirmiştim.** 'I had informed θ Ahmet that I was going to come ON this train.' **Dayım.ın bize {a: geldiğ.i.ni/b: geleceğ.i.ni/c: gelme.si gerektiğ.i.ni} bildirmiştim.** 'I had informed [them] that my maternal uncle {a: had visited/b: was going to visit/c: had to visit} us.' **Dayım.ın bize {a: nasıl/b: ne zaman/c: neden/d: niçin/e: niye/f: kimlerle} geldiğ.i.ni bildirmiştim.** 'I had informed [them] {a: how/b: when/c, d, e: why/f: with whom [i.e., with what people]} my maternal uncle had visited us.' *551:8.* information: - inform. → = **haber ver-** → ver- 1, = **bilgi ver-** → ver- 1, ≠ **haber al-** → al- 3.

önceden bildir- /I/ '- give advance notice /OF/, - predict', subj.: usually ordinary persons or experts, but not particularly persons divinely inspired, oracles, etc. [önceden 'in advance, beforehand']: **Buraya geleceğ.imiz.i daha önceden bildirmiştik.** 'We had already given advance notice that we were going to come here.' **Meteoroloji uzmanları fırtına çıkacağ.ı.nı önceden bildirdi.** 'The meteorologists predicted {that there would be a storm/that a storm would break out}.' *961:9.* prediction: -

predict. For '- predict' when the subject is a wise man, mystic, or soothsayer, not an ordinary man or an expert, → **kehanet et-**, **kehanette bulun-** → bulun- 3.

bile- [r] '- sharpen' a knife, razor [ADJ. keskin 'sharp']: **Bu bıçak {hiç kesmiyor/çok körelmiş}, bilemek lâzım.** 'This knife {doesn't cut at all/has gotten very dull}. It needs sharpening [lit., It's necessary to sharpen it].' **Berber usturasını dikkatlice biledikten sonra traşa başladı.** 'After carefully sharpening his razor, the barber began the shave.' **Bile-** is not used for '- sharpen a pencil', for which → **kalem aç-** → aç- 6. *285:7.* sharpness: - sharpen.

bilgi edin-. → edin-.

bilgi ver-. → ver- 1.

bilginiz olsun. → {haberiniz/ bilginiz} olsun. → ol- 11. → olsun.

bilgisine danış-. → danış-.

bilincini {kaybet-/yitir-}. → {şuurunu/bilincini} kaybet-. → {kaybet-/yitir-}.

bin pişman ol-. → pişman ol-. → ol- 12.

bin- [er] 1 /A/ '- get /ON/, - get on board, - board /θ/, - catch /θ/, - take /θ/ [a vehicle: bus, train, plane], - mount /θ/ [animal: horse, donkey]': * **Otobüs.E nere.DEN binebiliriz?** 'θ Where [lit., ** FROM where] can we {get/catch} θ the bus?' **Bebek otobüs.ü.nE nere.DEN binebilirim?** 'Where can I {get/catch} the {Bebek bus?/the bus for Bebek?} [a section of Istanbul] • The ablative case suffix -DAn is on the noun designating the point of departure. **Sirkeci'ye gitmek için hangi otobüs.E binmeliyim?** 'Which bus should I {take/catch} to get to Sirkeci [a section of Istanbul]?' **Otobüs.E nere.DEN bindiniz?** 'θ Where did you {get ON/catch θ} the bus?' *193:12.* ascent: - mount. → = **atla- 3** ['- hop /into/ a taxi, car, bus; - catch a plane, train'], ≠ **in- 2.**

2 '- ride': * **Yedi yaşı.nDAN küçükler binemez.** 'Children under the age of 7 are not allowed to ride! [lit., cannot {ride/get on}!]' *352:7.* publication: poster: * specific signs. <u>Proverb:</u> **Alçacık eşeğ.E herkes biner.** 'Everyone can ride [lit., rides] a very low donkey', i.e., Everyone takes advantage of a timid person.
* **bin-** versus **git-**. The NOUN form of **bin-**, i.e., **binmek**, is usually translated into English by 'riding': {**Bisiklet.E/At.A**} **binmey.İ çok severim.** 'I like {bicycle/horse} riding a lot.' The Turkish FINITE VERB used to express '- ride', meaning '- go in or by means of a mount or vehicle', however, is not **bin-** but **git-**: **Bisiklet.E bindim, şimdi bakkala gidiyorum.** 'I got on the bike, and now I'm riding [lit., going] to the store.' The verb **bin-** is not used for the second verb in the above sentence. *177:33.* travel: - ride.

bindir- [ir] /A/ '- put sb /ON/ a vehicle or a mount [i.e., animal]' [**bin-** + caus. suf. **-DIr**]: **Anneannem.i {a: tren.E/b: otobüs.E/c: uçağ.A/ d: vapur.A} bindirdim ve İstanbul'A uğurladım.** 'I put my [maternal] grandmother {a: ON the train/b: ON the bus/c: ON the plane/d: ON the steamship [*or* ferry]} and {saw her off/wished her a safe journey} to Istanbul.' **Lunaparkta kızım.ı atlıkarınca.yA bindirdim.** 'At the amusement park I put my [little] girl ON the merry-go-round.' *159:12.* location: - place; *193:12.* ascent: - mount. → ≠ /DAn/ **indir- 2.**

bindiril- [ir] /A/ '- be boarded, - be put /ON/ a vehicle or mount [i.e., animal]', subj.: person [**bindir-** + pass. suf. **-Il**]: **Çocuklar {a: vapur.A/b: uçağ.A/c: tren.E/d: gemi.yE/e: otobüs.E} bindirildi.** 'The children were put {a: ON the steamer [*or* ferry]/b: ON the plane/c: ON the train/d: ON the ship/e: ON the bus}.' *159:12.* location: - place; *193:12.* ascent: - mount. → ≠ /DAn/ **indiril- 2.**

binil- [ir] /DAn/ '- be boarded [vehicle], - be mounted [animal] /{AT/from}/' [**bin-** + pass. suf. **-Il**]: **Otobüsler.E ön kapı.DAN binilir, arka kapı.DAN inilir.** 'Buses are boarded {AT/from} the front [lit., from the front door] and exited {AT/from} the rear [lit., from the rear door].' • If the ACTIVE form of a verb requires the DATIVE case on the noun OBJECT [i.e., **Otobüs.E bindi.** 'He got ON the bus.'], the PASSIVE form of the same verb also requires the dative case when that object becomes the SUBJECT. Thus the DATIVE is required on the vehicle boarded, here **otobüsler**, the SUBJECT of the sentence. *193:12.* ascent: - mount; *352:7.* publication: poster: * specific signs. → ≠ **inil-.**

bir araya gel-. → **gel- 1.**

biriktir- [ir] **1** '- collect sth' [**birik-** '- come together, - gather' + caus. suf. **-DIr**]: **Dayım {10 yaşından beri} pul biriktiriyor.** 'My maternal uncle has been collecting stamps {since he was ten years old/from the age of 10}.' *769:18.* assemblage: - bring or - gather together. → = **topla- 1,** ≠ **dağıt- 1.**

2 '- save up /for/': **para biriktir- /için/** '- save [up] money /for/': **Yaz tatili için {a: uzun zamandır/b: 7 aydır/c: 7 aydan beri} para biriktiriyor.** 'He has been saving up [money] for the summer {vacation/holiday} {a: for a long time/b, c: for 7 months}.' **Seyahat etmek için biraz para biriktirdim.** 'I saved [up] a little money for traveling.' *635:4.* thrift: - economize. → = **para artır-** → {**artır-/arttır-**} **2,** = **tasarruf et-, masraftan {kaç-/kaçın-}** ['- avoid /θ/ expense, - economize'] → **kaç- 2,** ≠ **para {harca-/sarf et-}** ['- spend money'] → {**harca-/sarf et-**} **1,** ≠ **masraf {et-/yap-}, masrafa gir-** ['- spend a lot of money on sth or to get sth done, - have a lot of expenses, - incur great expense'].

birleştir- [ir] '- join, - unite, - bring together' [**birleş-** '- come together, unite' + caus. suf. **-DIr**]: **Boğaz köprüsü Asya ile Avrupa'yı birleştirdi.** 'The Bosphorus bridge joined Europe and Asia.' → = **kavuştur-,** = **ulaştır- 2,** = **yaklaştır-** ['- bring one thing /{to/NEAR/UP TO/OVER TO}/ another, join'], ≠ **ayrı- 1.** # **Garson iki masa.yI birleştirdi; hep beraber oturduk.** 'The waiter brought {a: two/b: two of the/c: the two} tables together, and we sat down altogether.' *799:5.* joining: - put together. → = **yaklaştır-**, ≠ **ayır- 1.**

bit- [er] **1** '- come to an end, - finish, - be over, finished, completed': **Ders bitti.** 'The {lesson/class} is over.' **Ev ödevlerim bitti.** 'My homework is finished.' **Konser saat kaçta bitiyor?** 'At what time does the concert end?' Proverb: * **Çalış.makla her iş biter.** 'With effort [lit., by working] every task is completed.', i.e., Success is achieved. *819:6.* end: - come to an end. → = **din-** ['- cease, - stop, - let up', with a limited set of noun subjects: nouns of weather, pain, emotion], = **kesil- 2** ['- stop, - cease of itself', with a limited set of noun subjects, most having to do with weather: rain, etc.], = **sona er-** → **er-**, ≠ **başla- 1.**

Oldu bitti. 'It's over and done with [lit., It happened., It's finished].' **Neyse, oldu bitti,** * **bu mesele.yE takılıp kalmayalım artık, ileri.ye bakalım.** 'Anyway, it's over and done with. * Let's not get hung up ON this problem now. Let's forget about it and {move on/look to the future}.' *819:14.* end: PHR. that's all.

oldubitti 'a done deal, a fait accompli'. An older and today more learned equivalent: **emrivaki:** Λrkadaşlar, bir {oldubitti/ emrivaki} karşısındayız, bence sonuçlarını iyice düşünmeden bu anlaşmayı imzalamayalım. '{Guys/Friends}, we are faced with {a done deal/a fait accompli}. {I say/I think} we shouldn't sign this agreement without considering the consequences carefully [lit., ** According to me let's not sign this agreement...]' **Oğlumuz biz.E danışmadan o kız.LA evlenmey.e karar vermiş, düğün davetiyelerini bile bastırmışlar. {Oldubitti/ Emrivaki} karşısındayız yani,** * **ne yapabiliriz ki?** 'Our son decided to marry that girl without consulting us. They even printed the wedding invitations! So we're faced with {a done deal/a fait accompli}, * what can we do?' **Ben bu tür {oldubittileri/emrivakileri} hiç sevmem.** 'I don't like such done deals at all.' *328:3.* action: NOUN act.

{olup/olan} biten 'what happened, event': **Son zamanlarda**

{olup/olan} bitenler.i pek izleyemedim, önemli bir haber var mı? 'I haven't been able to keep abreast of [the] events recently. Is there some important news?' **Sen önce bana {olup/olan} biteni bir anlat bakalım, belki bir çare bulurum.** 'First tell me in detail what happened, perhaps I can [lit., will] find a solution.' *830:2.* event: NOUN event.

2 /DAn/ '- be worn-out, exhausted, tired out /from/': **Öf, ev temizlemek.TEN bittim.** 'Oh [a sound expressing exhaustion], I really got tired out from cleaning the house.' *21:5.* fatigue: - burn out. → **yorul-** ['- get tired /from/, - be tired /from/, - tire (oneself)'].

3 '- be used up, for no more - be left, - be all gone, used up, - run out of': **{Şeker/Yağ} bitti.** 'The {sugar/oil} is all used up.' *388:4.* consumption: - be consumed. → = **tüken-.**

bitir- [ir] **1** '- finish sth, - bring sth to an end' [bit- + caus. suf. -Ir]: **Ev ödevlerim.İ bitirdim.** 'I've finished my homework.' **{İçkini/Yemeğini} bitir.** 'Finish {your drink/your food}.' Proverb: **Bir iş.İ bitir.meden başka iş.E başlama.** 'Without having finished θ one task, don't begin θ another [task].' *793:6.* completeness: - complete; *819:5.* end: - end sth. → = **son ver-** → **ver- 1,** = **tamamla-** ['- complete, finish'], ≠ **başla- 2.** Contrast with **bit- 1** [i.] above.

2 '- exhaust, - destroy, - kill, - finish off sb': **İçki, kumar, kadın onu bitirdi.** 'Drink, gambling, and women finished him off.' **Bana öyle geliyor ki bu hastalık beni bitirecek.** 'A: It seems to me that this illness is going to finish me off.' *395:10.* destruction: - destroy.

3 '- use up, - finish': **{Şekeri/Yağı} bitirdik.** 'We've used up all {the sugar/the oil}.' *387:13.* use: - spend; *388:3.* consumption: - consume.

4 '- graduate from, - finish a school or department of a university': S: * **En son hangi okul.U bitirdiniz?** 'Q: {a: {Where/Which school} did you graduate from?/b: What was the highest level of education you received?} [lit., ** Which school did you finish last?]' An equivalent, more formal, question: **Tahsiliniz nedir?** 'What is your education?' Some typical responses: C1: {a: **İlkokul.U/b: Orta okul.U/c: Lise.yİ.} bitirdim.** 'A1: I finished {a: primary school/b: secondary school/c: {high school/lycée}}.' C2: * {a: **Üniversite.yİ/b: Hukuk fakültesi.nİ} bitirdim.** A2: I have {a: {a college/a university}/b: a law} degree. C3: * **T ı p fakültesi.nI bitirdim.** 'I have an MD'. C4: * **Edebiyat fakültesi.nİ bitirdim.** 'A4: I have a degree in literature.' *409:7b.* success: - succeed in specific ways; *793:6.* completeness: - complete. → = /DAn/ **mezun ol-** ['- graduate /from/'] → ol- 12.

boğul- [ur] [boğ- 1 '- choke, - strangle'. 2 '- suffocate' + {pass./refl.} suf. -Il] The following all imply a lack of sufficient air or oxygen. 1 /DAn/ '- drown {BECAUSE OF/DUE TO}': **Denize düşen adam boğulmuş.** 'The man who had fallen into the {sea/ocean} drowned.' **Kayıp kadın boğulmuş OLARAK bulundu.** 'The woman who had been lost was found θ drowned [lit., ** {BEING/AS} drowned].' **7 çocuk boğul.ARAK öldü.** 'Seven children drowned [lit., ** died BY drown.ING].' Proverb: **Deniz.DEN geçti çay.da boğuldu.** 'He crossed {θ/OVER} the ocean but drowned in the brook.', i.e., {From/OUT OF} the frying pan into the fire. *307:24.* death: - die a natural death; *308:18.* killing: - strangle; *367:7.* plunge: - submerge; *393:48.* impairment: ADV. out of the frying pan into the fire.

2 /DAn/ '- be suffocated, - suffocate, - smother, - be stifled, - be strangled, - feel faint /{from/BECAUSE OF/DUE TO}/': **Kurtarma çalışmalar.ı sonuç vermeyince denizaltı mürettebat.ı.nın hep.si havasızlık.TAN boğuldu.** 'When rescue efforts failed [lit., ** did not give a result], the entire crew of the submarine suffocated {from/BECAUSE OF/DUE TO} lack of air.' **Kahve.nin iç.i o kadar havasızdı ki, neredeyse [havasızlık.tan] boğuluyordum.** 'The coffee house [lit., ** the inside of the coffee house] was so stifling [lit., airless] [that] I almost suffocated

[from lack of air].' *308:18.* killing: - strangle.

bombala- [r] '- bomb' [It. **bomba** 'bomb' + verb-forming suf. -lA]: **Teröristler şehr.in merkezindeki bazı binalar.I bombaladılar.** 'Terrorists bombed some buildings in the center of the city.' *459:23.* attack: - bomb.

borca gir-. → gir-.

borcunu kapa-. → {kapa-/kapat-} 8.

borcunu öde-. → öde-.

borç al-. → al- 1.

borç kapatıl-. → kapatıl- 7.

borç ver-. → ver- 1.

borçlan- [ır] /A, θ/ '- get into debt /to [sb], {θ/for} [an amount]/, - owe /θ [sb], θ [an amount]/' [**borç** 'debt' + verb-forming suf. -lAn]: **Ev almak için banka.ya 50 bin lira borçlandım. Fakat borcumu geri ödeyemedim.** 'To purchase a home I got 50,000 liras in debt to the bank, but I couldn't repay my debt.' **Aysel'E 10 bin lira borçlandım.** 'I {owe θ Aysel 10,000 liras./lit., I got 10,000 liras in debt to Aysel}.' *623:5.* debt: - owe; *623:6.* : - go into debt. → = **borca gir-**, ≠ **borcunu {kapa-/kapat-}** ['- pay up, - pay off one's debts'] → {kapa-/kapat-} 8, ≠ **borcunu öde-**. Same.

boş ver-. → ver- 1.

boşa- [r] '- divorce' [**boş** 'empty, free' + verb-forming suf. -A]: **Benİ aldattığ.ı.nı öğrenince karı.m.ı boşadım.** 'When I learned that my wife had been cheating on me, I divorced her [lit., When I learned that she had been cheating on me, I divorced my wife].' *566:5.* divorce, widowhood: - divorce.

boşa çık-. → çık- 7.

boşa git-. → git- 5.

boşal- [ır] [**boş** 'empty' + verb-forming suf. -Al]: 1 '- become empty, - empty out; - become vacant': **Öyle acıkmıştık ki, kurabiye kutusu on dakikada boşaldı.** 'We were so hungry that the cookie box was emptied out in ten minutes.' {Şeker kutusu/Su şişesi} boşaldı. 'The {candy box/water bottle} got empty.' Buzdolabı iyice boşaldı, bakkal.A gidelim. 'The refrigerator is quite empty [lit., ** has quite emptied out], let's go to the grocery story.' Ay sonu geldi, benim ceplerim yine boşaldı. 'It's the end of the month and again my pockets are empty [lit., ** have emptied out].' {Sinema/Konser/ Tiyatro} bitince bütün salon boşaldı. 'When {the movie/the concert/the theater performance} ended, the whole hall emptied out.' *190:13*. emergence: - run out. → ≠ dol- 1.

2 /DAn, A/ 'for a liquid - run, - pour, - stream /{from/OUT OF}, ONTO/; - overflow': Sular küvetten yer.E boşaldı. 'The water overflowed [i.e., ran out] from the bathtub ONTO the floor.' → = taş-. *190:13*. emergence: - run out; *238:17b*. stream: - overflow.

3 '- come, - ejaculate, - climax, - have an orgasm', more frequently for men but also for women: Cinsel birleşme sırasında erkeklerin erken boşalması eşler arasında sorunlara yol açıyor. 'During sexual intercourse, the man's premature ejaculation causes problems between the spouses.' *75:23*. sex: - climax; *908:25*. ejection: - disgorge. → = gel- 3 [for both sexes], = orgazm ol-. Same. → ol- 10.1.

boşalt- [ır] /A/ '- empty sth, - empty out /INTO/, - clear out' [boşal- + caus. suf. -t]: Oteldeki odasına girince hemen {a: bavulunu/b: dolapları/c: çekmeceleri/d: ceplerini} boşalttı. 'As soon as he entered his hotel room, he emptied out {a: his suitcase/b: the cupboards/c: the drawers/d: his pockets}.' * Suyu şişe.den sürahi.yE boşalttı. * İç.i.nE buzları doldurdu. 'He poured [lit., emptied] the water from the bottle INTO the pitcher. * He filled it with the ice [lit., ** He filled the ice into its (i.e., the pitcher's) inside].' Kapıcı apartmanın çöplerini topladı ve köşedeki çöp bidon.u.nA boşalttı. '{The caretaker/The doorman} gathered the trash from the apartment building and emptied it out INTO the trash barrel.'

{Arkadaşlar} lütfen toplantı.yı kısa kesin, binayı boşaltmak zorundayız. '[Come on], {folks/people}, please cut short the meeting. We have to clear out the building.' *908:22*. ejection: - evacuate. → ≠ doldur- 1.

boşan- [ır] /DAn/ '- get divorced /from/, - split up /WITH/' [boş 'empty, free' + verb-forming suf. -A = boşa- '- divorce sb' + refl. suf. -n]: Beş yıllık evlilikten sonra {kocam.dan/karım.dan} boşandım. 'After five years of marriage, I got divorced {from my husband/from my wife}.' S: Onlar [Cemil ile Sibel] niçin boşanmışlar, biliyor musun? 'Do you know why they [Cemil and Sibel] got divorced?' C1: Evet, şiddetli geçimsizlik yüzünden. 'A1: Yes, because of irreconcilable [lit., severe] incompatibility.' C2: Evet, Cemil eşini [başka bir kadınla] aldatıyormuş, * ondan. 'A2: Yes, Cemil cheated on his wife [with another woman]. * That's why.' <u>Proverb</u>: Boşanıp kocan.A varma, sevişip dostun.A varma. 'Don't remarry the man you divorced, and don't marry the lover for whom you abandoned your husband.' *566:5*. divorce, widowhood: - divorce. → = ayrıl- 1, ≠ evlen-, ≠ dünya evine gir-.

boya- [r] /A/ '- paint, - color /θ/ a color' [boya 'paint, color, dye' + verb-forming suf. -θ]: Hafta sonunda odamın duvarlarını boyamak istiyorum. 'I want to paint the walls of my room over the weekend.' Anneciğim, kitaptaki resimleri boyayabilir miyim? 'Mommy, may I color the pictures in the book?' * Evimiz.in duvarlar.ı.nı sarı.yA boyadım. 'I painted the walls of our house θ yellow.' *35:13*. color: - color.

boya yaptır-. → yaptır- 2.

boyat- [ır] /A/ '- have sth painted, colored, or dyed /θ/ a color; - have /θ/ sb paint, color, or dye sth /θ/ a color' [boya- + caus. suf. -t]: Saçlarımı boyatmak istiyorum. 'I want to have my hair colored.' * Arabamı mavi.yE boyatmak istiyorum. 'I want to have my car painted θ blue.' Saçlarımı eski berberim.E boyatmak istiyorum. 'I want to have θ my old [i.e., former] barber color my hair.' *35:13.* color: - color.

boyu uza-. → uza- 1.

boz- [ar] /I/ 1 '- ruin, - spoil, - break, - corrupt, - violate' [ADJ. **bozuk** 'ruined, spoiled, broken']: **Misafirin çocuğu {saati} bozdu.** 'The guest's child broke {the watch/the clock}.' **Rüzgâr kum kaleyi bozdu.** 'The breeze ruined the sand castle.' **Sami [uzun bir uğraş sonunda varılan] anlaşmayı bozdu.** 'Sami broke the agreement [that had been reached as the result of a long effort].' **İstisnalar kaideyi bozmaz.** 'Exceptions don't violate the rule.' Proverb: **Biri yapar biri bozar, dünya böyle geçer.** 'One builds; another ruins it. This is the way of the world [lit., Thus the world passes].' *393:10.* impairment: - spoil; *395:10.* destruction: - destroy. → **çiğne-** 3.

* **ahlâkını boz-** '- lead sb astray, - corrupt sb's morals' [A. **ahlâk** (. -) (ahlâkI) '(good) morals']: **Kötü arkadaşlar edinme, ahlâkını bozarlar.** 'Don't pick up bad friends. They {will lead you astray /lit., will corrupt your morals}.' *393:12.* impairment: - corrupt.

* **kafasını boz-** '- spoil sb's mood, - put or - get sb out of sorts' [A. **kafa** 1 'head'. 2 'mental state, mood']: A threat: **Kafa.M.ı bozma, yoksa * karışmam, [* ona göre]!** 'Don't spoil MY mood, or * who knows what I might do, [* so act accordingly]!' *96:13.* unpleasure: - annoy; *514: * 5.* threat: INTERJ. specific threats.

* **midesini boz-** '- make [physically] sick, sick to one's stomach', subj.: food [A. **mide** (- .) 'stomach']: **Bu yemek mide.M.i bozdu.** 'This food made ME sick.' *96:16a.* unpleasure: - distress; *393:9.* impairment: - impair; *809:9.* disorder: - disorder. → = **dokun-** 2.

moralini boz- '- spoil sb's mood, - depress sb' [F. **moral** 'mood']: **Moralinizi bozmak istemem ama bu iş olacak gibi değil.** 'I don't want to spoil your mood, but this {project/matter} doesn't look like it's going to work out.' *112:18.* sadness: - sadden.

rahatını boz- '- disturb, - annoy' [A. **rahat** 'comfort, comfortable']: * **Rahat.IM.ı bozma, başka yer.E otur!** 'Don't disturb ME [lit., ** disturb MY comfort]. Sit θ somewhere else.' *96:13.* unpleasure: - annoy. → = **rahatsız et-.**

{sırayı/kuyruğu) boz- (1) '- cut in a line' [**sıra** 1 'row, file'. 2 'order, sequence', **kuyruk** 'tail, line of people']: Ticket taker at an entrance: **Lütfen sırayı bozmayın.** 'Please don't cut in [lit., ** don't spoil the line].', i.e., the end of the line's back there. *214:5.* intrusion: - intrude.
(2) '- get out of line': **Lütfen sırayı bozmayalım, herkes teker teker içeri girecek.** 'Let's not get out of line. Everyone will [i.e., should] enter one by one.' *263:3.* formlessness: - deform; *810:2.* disarrangement: - disarrange. → ≠ **{sıraya/kuyruğa} gir-.**

2 '- change, - make change /for/, - GIVE change /for/, - break a bill', a specified amount of money into smaller units: **Şu 5 yüz doları bozar mısınız?** 'Would you please change these $ 500 [for liras]?' **Veznedar turist.in * 5 yüz dolarını bozdu.** 'The teller changed the tourist's $500 [for liras].' *857:11.* conversion: - convert.

3 '- cash', a check, '- change money from one form into another, - exchange', foreign money into local currency, - GIVE one form of money for another: **çek boz-** '- cash a check': **Veznedar seyahat çekimi bozdu.** 'The teller cashed my traveler's check.' *728:29.* money: - cash; *857:11.* conversion: - convert.

döviz boz- '- change foreign money into local currency, - exchange, - GIVE local currency for foreign currency' [F. **döviz** 'foreign exchange, money']: **Döviz bozdurmak istedim fakat veznedar kasada yeterli para olmadığı için [döviz] bozamadı.** 'I wanted to exchange some foreign money [lit., wanted to HAVE some foreign money exchanged, i.e., get the teller to exchange the money], but the teller couldn't exchange it because there wasn't enough money in the cash register.' The names of specific currencies may be substituted for the word **döviz: Veznedar {a:**

euromu/b: dolarımı/c: markımı/d: sterlinimi} bozdu. 'The teller exchanged {a: my euros/b: my dollars/c: my marks/d: my pounds}.' *857:11.* conversion: - convert.

4 '- change for the worse [weather], - turn bad': **Hava bozuyor.** 'The weather is turning bad.' *393:16.* impairment: - deteriorate. → = **hava bozul-**, ≠ **hava aç-** → aç- 7.

bozdur- [ur] /I, A/ [boz- + caus. suf. -DIr]. In all of the following sb, a customer, causes sb else, a bank teller, etc., to do the activity of the verb **boz-**. 1 '- get change /for/, - have sb break a bill, a specified unit of money, into smaller units': **Paramızı bozdurmak istiyoruz.** 'We want to get some change [lit., have our money changed].' *857:11.* conversion: - convert.

2 '- cash, - have sb cash', a check, '- change, - have sb change money from one form into another, - exchange', foreign money into local currency: **Ne bozduracaksınız?** 'What are you going to exchange?' **çek bozdur-** '- cash a check, - get a check cashed': **Seyahat çekimi nerede bozdurabilirim?** 'Where can I {cash my traveler's check?/get my traveler's check cashed?}' → = **değiştir-** 2. *728:29.* money: - cash; *857:11.* conversion: - convert.

döviz bozdur- '- change, - have sb change foreign money into local currency, - exchange' [F. **döviz** 'foreign exchange']: **Döviz bozdurmak istiyorsanız en yakın döviz bürosu Konak'ta.** 'If you want to get some foreign money changed, the nearest exchange office is in Konak [i.e., an area of the city of Izmir].' **Daha dün döviz bozdurmuştum, yine param kalmadı.** 'I changed money only yesterday, and now, again, I have no money left.' The names of specific currencies may be substituted for **döviz**: **Nerede {dolar/mark/sterlin} bozdurabilirim?** 'Where can I exchange {dollars/marks/pounds sterling}?' **Dövizini banka.yA mı bozduracaksın, yoksa döviz bürosu.nA mı?** 'Are you going to have θ the bank or θ the foreign exchange office exchange your

foreign money?' *857:11.* conversion: - convert.

3 '- sell sth for money and then buy sth else with that money': * **Altın bileziğimi bozdurup elmas yüzük alacağım.** 'I'm going to sell my gold bracelet and buy a diamond ring [with the money].' *857:11.* conversion: - convert; *862:4.* interchange: - interchange.

bozul- [ur] '- break down, - go out of order, - give out, - spoil, - get {bad/worse}, - deteriorate' [boz- + refl. suf. -Il. ADJ. **bozuk** 'broken, out of order; spoiled']: Weather: **hava bozul-**: * **Hava ne güzeldi, birden bozuldu.** 'The weather was gorgeous [lit., How nice the weather was], and then suddenly it changed for the worse [lit., got bad].' *393:16.* impairment: - deteriorate. → = **hava boz-** → boz- 4, **hava kapan-** ['- cloud over, - become cloudy, overcast'] → kapan- 4, ≠ **hava aç-** → aç- 7, ≠ **hava açıl-** ['for weather - clear up, - become pleasant'] → açıl- 7.

Equipment: **Yolda giderken arabam birdenbire bozuldu.** 'While on the road, my car suddenly broke down.' **Bir ay evvel saatim bozuldu. Hâlâ bozuk.** 'My watch broke a month ago. It is still broken.' *393:25.* impairment: - get out of order. → **arıza yap-** ['- break down' usually for large items run on energy sources such as fuel, batteries or house current, less frequently for small items such as clocks, radios, videos.] → yap- 3; **ömrünü tamamla-** ['- complete one's life, - come to the end of one's life, - die, - pass away', person; '- outlive its useful life, usefulness', machine].

Food: **Bu {yemek/meyvalar} bozulmuş, yenmez.** 'This {food/fruit [i.e., large quantity or different kinds]} has spoiled; it can't be eaten.' **Buz dolabına koymay.I unutunca süt bozuldu.** 'When they forgot to put it in the refrigerator, the milk {went bad/spoiled}.' → = **bayatla-**, **kok-** 2 ['- smell (bad), stink (subj.: food)], ≠ **dayan-** 4 ['- keep, - stay edible (subj.: food)]'. *393:22.* impairment: - decay.

An arrangement: **Bu {iş/anlaşma} bozuldu.** 'This {arrangement/ agreement} has broken down.'

An ability: **Mary'nin Türkçe'si günden güne bozuluyor.** 'Mary's Turkish is getting worse from day to day.' *393:16.* impairment: - deteriorate. → = **g e r i l e - 2,** = **zayıfla- 2,** ≠ **geliş- 2,** ≠ **ilerle- 2.**

A part of the body: * **Mide.M bozuldu.** '{MY stomach is upset./I'm having stomach trouble [*or* problems].}'
A state of mind: **morali bozul- '-** get depressed, discouraged, - lose heart' [F. **moral** 'morale'. ADJ. **morali bozuk**]: **Coğrafya sınavı.nDAN k a l d ı ğ ı m ı öğrenince moral.İM bozuldu.** 'When I heard that I had failed the geography examination, I got depressed.' *112:16.* sadness: - lose heart; *393:24.* impairment: - break down. → **kahrol-** ['- be deeply grieved or distressed, - be devastated or overcome /{WITH/BY}/ grief'] → **ol- 12, yıkıl- 3** ['- lose one's health and morale; for sb - be broken or ruined by a disaster, - be devastated'].

* **sinirleri bozul-** [**sinir** 'nerve'] (1) '- get upset, angry, - lose one's cool, temper, composure', lit., ** 'for one's nerves - go out of order', BUT here the meaning is not '- get nervous' in the sense of anxiety: **Otobüs şoförü ile kavga edince sinirlerim bozuldu.** 'When I got into a fight with the bus driver, I lost my {temper/cool}.' *96:16b.* unpleasure: - be distressed; *152:17.* resentment, anger: - become angry; *152:20.* : - fly into a rage, → = **sinirlen-, patla- 2** ['- be ready to explode, - feel like screaming /{ON ACCOUNT OF/DUE TO}/, - explode, - fly off the handle, *colloq.* lose one's cool'].
(2) '- be badly shaken up, for one's nerves - get shot': **Araba kazasından sonra sinirlerim bozuldu, titremeye başladım.** 'After the accident I was badly shaken up. I began to tremble.' *128:7.* nervousness: - lose self- control.

A relationship between people: **arası bozul-.** → **arası {açıl-/bozul-}** → **açıl- 9.**

böl- [er] /A/ '- divide [up] /INTO/': **Ali pastayı bölüp {yarı.sı.nı/bir dilim.i.ni} yedi.** 'Ali divided up the pastry and ate {half of it./a slice of it.}' **Ortaklar dükkânı iki.yE böldüler.** 'The partners divided the shop INTO two [sections].' **Teröristler ülkeyi bölmey.e çalışıyorlar.** 'Terrorists are trying to divide the country.' **Böl, parçala, yönet!** 'Divide and rule [lit., ** Divide, break up, and rule].' *801:8.* separation: - separate. → = **ayır- 3,** ≠ **birleştir-.**

'- divide one number /BY/ another': **284'ü [iki yüz seksen dörd.ü] 2'yE [iki.yE] bölersek, 142 eder.** 'If we divide 284 BY 2, 142 remains.' *1016:17.* mathematics: - calculate.

bölün- [ür] /A, {tarafından/CA}/ '- be divided, split /INTO, by/' [**böl-** + pass. suf. **-In**]: **Pasta iki dilim.E bölündü.** 'The pastry was divided INTO two slices.' **Dükkân [ortaklar tarafından] iki.yE bölündü.** 'The shop was divided INTO two [sections] [by the partners].' II. [read: İkinci] **Dünya savaşından sonra * Almanya, Doğu ve Batı OLARAK iki.yE bölündü.** 'After the Second World War, * Germany was divided INTO two [parts]: θ East and West [lit., ** {BEING/AS} East and West].' **Vatan asla bölünmez.** 'The motherland will never be divided.' *801:8.* separation: - separate. → = **ayrıl- 2.**

'- be divided /BY/': **284 [iki yüz seksen dört] 2'yE [iki.yE] bölünürse 142 eder.** 'If 284 is divided by 2, one gets 142.' *1016:17.* mathematics: - calculate.

buharlaş- [ır] '- turn into steam, - vaporize, - evaporate' [A. **buhar** (. -) 'steam, vapor' + verb-forming suf. - **lAş**]: **Ocağı kapar mısın lütfen, çaydanlıktaki su bir saattir fokur fokur kaynıyor, * neredeyse tamamen buharlaştı.** 'Turn off the stove please. The water in the teapot has been bubbling away for an hour now. * It has almost completely boiled away [lit., turned into steam].' *1065:8.* vapor, gas: - vaporize.

bul- [UR] 1 /DA, DAn/ '- find sth /{at/on/in}, ON/': **Sizin e-posta adresinizi internet.TEN buldum.** 'I found your e-mail address ON the Internet.' **Nere.de taksi bulabilirim?** 'Where can I find a taxi?' **Bir {tercüman.A/ çevirmen.E} ihtiyacım var. Nerede bulabilirim?** 'I need {θ a translator}. Where can I find one?' **Geçen hafta kaybettiğ.im saat.im.i buldum.** 'I found my watch, which I had lost last week.' **Bir saattir çantamı arıyorum, bulamıyorum. * Hah, işte buldum!** 'I've been looking for my {handbag/purse/briefcase} for an hour. I can't find it. * Oh, here it is!' **Elindeki adresi sora sora buldu.** 'She found the address she was looking for [lit., the address in her hand] by asking [lit., ** by asking asking, i.e., by persistent questioning].' **Gökte ararken yerde bulduk.** 'While looking for it in the sky, we found it [right here] on earth.', i.e., We didn't have to look so far. → ≠ kaybet-. # **Aradığım mutluluğu sonunda buldum.** 'I finally found the happiness [that] I was looking for.' Proverbs: **Arayan Mevlâsını da bulur, belâsını da.** 'He who seeks will find either his Lord or his calamity.', i.e., A person will find whatever he seeks. **Derdini söylemeyen derman bulamaz.** 'He who keeps his troubles to himself [lit., doesn't tell his troubles] won't be able to find a remedy [for them].' **İyilik eden iyilik bulur.** 'He who does good will be the recipient of acts of kindness [lit., will find goodness].' **Misafir umduğunu değil, bulduğunu yer.** 'A guest doesn't eat what he hopes for, he eats what he finds.', i.e., He can't be choosy. *940:2.* discovery: - discover.

çözüm [yolu] bul- /{için/A}/ '- find a way of solving a problem, - find a solution /{for/to}/ a problem, - find a way to do sth' [çözüm 'solution, a way of solving a problem', yol 'road, way']: **Ev taksidini ödemek için sadece üç günümüz kaldı. Ertelemek için bir çözüm [yolu] bulmalıyız.** 'We have only 3 days to make our house payment [lit., pay the house installment]. We must find a way to put it off.' **Kürtaj problem.i.ne bir çözüm [yolu] bulmak gerek.** 'It is necessary to find a solution {to/for} the problem of abortion.'

Yeni iktidar bu sorun.a mutlaka çözüm bulmalı. 'The new government in power must certainly find a solution to this problem.' *939:2.* solution: - solve. → **çöz-** 2 ['- solve a problem, - figure sth out', usually a puzzle, mathematical problem], **hallet-** ['- solve' in regard to a situation, personal problem].

Hoş bulduk. 'Glad to be here.' [P. **hoş** 'pleasant, pleasantly']: **A: Hoş geldiniz.** 'A: Welcome.' **B: Hoş bulduk.** 'B: Glad to be here.' *504: * 20.* courtesy: polite expressions; *585:14.* hospitality, welcome: INTERJ. welcome!

iş bul- '- find work, a job, employment, - become employed': **Bu zamanda iş bulmak kolay mı?** 'Is it easy to find work in these times?' Proverb: **Boş duran.A şeytan iş bulur.** 'Satan finds work FOR the idle [lit., for the one who remains unoccupied].' *724:12.* occupation: - work. → = **işe gir-**.

söz bulAMA- '- be at a loss for words, not - know what to say' [söz 'word, utterance']: **Öyle {sevinçliyim/heyecanlıyım/üzgünüm} ki söyleyecek söz bulamıyorum.** 'I'm so {happy/excited/sorry} [that] I {don't know what to say/am at a loss for words}.' **Öyle şaşırdı ki söyleyecek söz bulamıyordu.** 'He was so surprised [that] he {didn't know what to say/was at a loss for words}.' *51:8.* silence: - silence.

2 '- discover', a place, a truth, a new way of doing sth, a new invention: **Amerika kıta.sı.nı Kristof Kolomb buldu.** 'Christopher Columbus discovered the Continent of America.' **Arkeologlar yeni bir antik kent buldular.** 'Archeologists have discovered a new ancient city.' *940:2.* discovery: - discover. → = **keşfet-**.

3 '- think of, about in a certain way, - find': **S: {Bu kitabı/Bu CD'yi [pronounce: si di'yi]/Türkçe.m.i} nasıl buluyorsunuz?** 'Q: How do you find {this book/this CD/my Turkish}?' **C1: {a: Mükemmel/ b: Harika/c: Harikulade/d: Çok güzel/e: Gayet güzel/f: İyi/g: Fena değil/h: Hiç iyi değil/i: Çok fena/j: Çok kötü}.** 'A: {a: Excellent/b, c: Marvellous/d, e: Very

good/f: Good/g: Not bad/h: Not good at all/i, j: Very bad}.' C2: Doğruyu söylemek gerekirse beğenmedim. * Hiç bir şey.E benzemiyor. 'A2: To tell the truth, I didn't like it. * It's not worth a cent [lit., ** It doesn't resemble anything (worth mentioning)].' Bu {iddiaları} ne kadar {inandırıcı} buluyorsunuz? 'How {convincing/compelling} do you find these {claims/arguments}?' 945:11. judgment: - decide. → = düşün- 4.

* 4 '- remember, - have it', as in 'I have it', when one suddenly recalls sth forgotten, or in the sense of 'Oh, I know', when one suddenly discovers the solution to a problem: Suna'nın telefon numarası neydi, hatırlayamıyorum. {* Ha, tamam buldum "38-25-17"./Dur, buldum!} 'What was Suna's [f.] phone number? I can't remember it. * {Oh, OK, I have it! 38-25-17./Wait, I have it!}' 988:10. memory: - remember. → = {hatırla-/anımsa-}, ≠ unut-.

bulan- [ır] '- be upset', stomach, not feelings: mide.si bulan- '- for one's stomach - be upset, - feel sick to one's stomach, - have an upset stomach, - feel nauseated, nauseous, - get queasy': Lunaparktaki dönmedolab.a binince mide.M bulandı. 'When I got on the Ferris wheel at the amusement park, I got queasy.' Midem bulanıyor, kusacağım. 'My stomach is upset. I'm going to throw up.' Ayşe'nin mide.si bulanıyor * yediği bir şey dokunmuş olmalı. 'Ayşe has an upset stomach. * It must be something she ate [lit., something [that] she ate must have affected her].' Ayşe üşütmüş olmalı, baş.I dönüyor, mide.Sİ bulanıyor. 'Ayşe must have gotten cold. She's dizzy [lit., her head is spinning], and HER stomach is upset.' 85:46b. disease: - take sick in particular ways.

bulun- [ur] [bul- + {pass./refl.} suf. -In] 1 /a: DA, b: {tarafından/CA}, c: mAklA/ '- be found, discovered /a: {in/at} [a place], b: by [a person], c: BY...ing/': {Kayıp çocuk/Aranan katil} terkedilmiş bir evde [polis tarafından] bulundu. '{The lost child/The murderer who was being sought} was found in an abandoned house [by the police].' Kayıp kadın {ölü/boğulmuş OLARAK} bulundu. 'The woman who had been lost was found {dead/θ drowned}.' Proverbs: Sor.A sor.A Bağdat bulunur. 'BY ask.ING and ask.ING, one finds Bagdad [lit., Bagdad is found].' Seek and ye shall find. Yol sor.MAKLA bulunur. 'The [right] {road/way} is found BY ask.ING.' 940:2. discovery: - discover. → ≠ aran-.

2 /DA/ '- be, - exist, - find oneself /{in/at}/, - be situated /{in/at}/ a place': S: Buralarda içme su.yu bulunur mu? 'Q: Is there any drinking water around here?' Also possible, less formal: Buralarda içme su.yu var mı? Same. C: Maalesef bulunmaz. 'A: Unfortunately there isn't any' • The third person possessed form of su is suyu, NOT the expected su.su. # Ankara'da [hiç] bulundunuz mu? 'Have you [ever] been {to/lit., in} Ankara?' → = git- 1a. # Kaçta okulda bulunayım? 'At what time should I be at school?' Someone on the telephone asks you where you are: Şu anda nerede bulunuyorsunuz? 'Where are you right now?' less formal: Şu anda neredesiniz? Same. Burada tatilde bulunuyorum. 'I'm here ON [a] {vacation/holiday}.' Haritada nerede bulunduğ.um.u gösterir misiniz? 'Would you please show me on this map where I am?' Çok ciddî tehditler.le karşı karşıya bulunuyoruz. 'We are facing very serious threats.' Kazada uçakta bulunan 200 yolcu ve 8 mürettabat.TAN kurtulan olmadı. 'OF the 200 passengers and 8 crew members in the plane at the time of the accident, none survived.'

• Note the differences between the following three common dialogues involving bulun- with either -DAn beri or -DIr. Note that the form of the question in a) and b) is the same, but that it may be translated in two ways and answered accordingly:
a) S: Ne zaman.DAN BERİ Türkiye'de bulunuyorsunuz? 'Q: SINCE WHEN have you been in Turkey?' C: {a: Temmuz.DAN BERİ/b: 15 Eylül.DEN BERİ/c: 1985'TEN BERİ} [{burada bulunuyorum/burada.yım}]. 'A: [I've been here] {a: SINCE July/b:

SINCE the 15th of September/c: SINCE 1985}.'
b) S: Ne zaman.DAN BERİ Türkiye'de bulunuyorsunuz? 'HOW LONG have you been in Turkey?' **C: 8 ay.DAN BERİ [{burada bulunuyorum/ burada.yım}].** 'A: [I've been here] FOR 8 months.'
c) S: Ne kadar zaman.DIR Türkiye'de bulunuyorsunuz? 'Q: HOW LONG have you been in Turkey?' **C: {a: 8 gün.DÜR/b: 5 ay.DIR/c: 3 yıl.DIR/d: Temmuz.DAN BERİ} [{burada bulunuyorum/burada.yım}].** 'A: [I have been here] {a: FOR 8 days/b: FOR 5 months/c: FOR 3 years/d: SINCE June}.' *221:6.* presence: - be present; *760:8.* existence: - exist. → = **ol- 3.**

hazır bulun- /DA/ '- be present /{at/in}/', person as subject: **Sanatçının jubilesinde Başbakan da hazır bulundu.** 'The prime minister was also present at the artist's jubilee.' *221:6.* presence: - be present; *760:8.* existence: - exist. → = **var ol-** → {var/yok} ol- 2 → ol- 12.

3 /DA/ **bulun-** preceded by certain nouns denoting an activity forms a *formal* verbal phrase, literally meaning '- be in, - find oneself in, a certain activity, action'. The **bulun-** segment, like any verb, may occur in various tenses:

cinsel ilişkide bulun- /lA/ '- have sex /with/, - have sexual intercourse /with/', *formal, polite* [**cinsel** 'sexual', **ilişki** 'relation']: **Leyla Orhan ile cinsel ilişkide bulunmuş.** 'Leyla had {sex/sexual relations} with Orhan.' **Kız: Daha önce hiç cinsel ilişkide bulunmadım.** 'Girl: I have never had sex before.' **Oğlan: Bakire olduğunu bilmiyordum.** 'Boy: I didn't know [that] you were a virgin.' *75:21.* sex: - copulate. → = **seviş-** 2, = **yat-** 2 ['- go to bed /with/, - sleep /with/', i.e., - have sex /with/].

kehanette bulun- /{hakkında/A dair}/ '- make a prediction /about [*or* concerning]/, - predict /θ/', subj.: a wise man, oracle, fortune-teller, or soothsayer only [A. **kehanet** (. - .) 'soothsaying, prediction']: **16.** [read: **on altıncı**] **yüzyılda yaşayan kâhin Nostradamus, 20.** [read: **yirminci**] **yüzyılda olacak**

depremler ve önemli {olaylar hakkında/olaylar.A dair} kehanette bulunmuş. 'The oracle Nostradamus, who lived in the sixteenth century, predicted θ the earthquakes and important events that would occur in the twentieth century.' **Yaşlı adam çok yakında kıyamet.in {kopacağ.ı hakkında/kopacağ.ı.nA dair} kehanette bulundu.** 'The old man predicted θ that the end of the world [lit., that doomsday] would come very soon.' *961:9.* prediction: - predict. → = **kehanet et-, önceden bildir-** [for '- predict' when the subject is an ordinary person or expert, not a wise man or oracle].

yardımda bulun- /A/ '- help /θ/, - assist /θ/, - aid /θ/, - provide aid /to/', *formal* [**yardım** 'help, assistance']: **Hastanemiz.E bağış ve yardımda bulunan tüm kişi ve kuruluşlar.a teşekkür ederiz.** 'We thank all the people and organizations that have provided help and assistance to our hospital.' *449:11.* aid: - aid. → = **yardım et-** ['- help /θ/, - assist /θ/', a *more common, less formal* equivalent], **el ele ver-** ['- help one another'] → **ver-** 1, **yardım elini uzat-** ['- extend a helping hand /to/, - help out, - extend aid, assistance /to/'], **yardımcı ol-** ['- help /θ/, - assist /θ/, - be of assistance /to/, - be helpful /to/'] → ol- 12.

4 '- have, - be available' in a place such as in a store or a library, *formal, educated usage*: **Sizde bu kitap bulunur mu?** 'Do you have this book?' The *less formal, more common* equivalent: **Sizde bu kitap var mı?** → {var/yok} ol- → ol- 12, a) 2. *221:6.* presence: - be present.

buluş- [ur] /lA/ '- come together, - meet /θ/', usually after a previous agreement to meet. [bul- + recip. suf. -İş]: * **Ahmet'LE istasyonda buluşacaktık ama gelmedi.** '{I was/We were} supposed to [lit., going to] meet θ Ahmet at the station, but he didn't turn up [lit., come].' • With the first person plural suffix on the verb **buluş-** [buluşacak.TIK], the total number of subjects may be two or more. With the first person singular suffix on the verb [buluşacak.TIM], only two subjects would be involved and the emphasis would be on the first person speaker. **Kütüphanede buluşalım mı?** 'Shall we meet at the library?' **S: Beraber sinemaya gidelim. Nerede buluşalım?** 'Q: Let's go to the movies together. Where shall we meet?' **C: {Okulda/Öğrenci yurd.u.nda/Sinema.nın ön.ü.nde}** [buluşalım]. 'A: [Let's meet] {at school/at the dormitory/in front of the theater}.' **S: {[Saat] kaçta/Ne zaman} buluşalım?** 'Q: {At what time/When} shall we meet?' **C: Aynı yerde aynı saatte.** 'A: Same time, same place [lit., At the same time (and) at the same place].' **Baba-oğul, yıllarca süren ayrılıktan sonra buluştular.** 'After years of separation, father and son met.' *769:16.* assemblage: - come together. → = **karşılaş-** 1 ['- meet one another'], **bir araya gel-** ['- come together, - get together /with/, - meet /with/'] → gel- 1. For '- encounter by chance', see **rastla-** 1 and **tesadüf et-** 1; **kavuş-** 1 ['- be reunited /WITH/'].

bunalım geçir-. → geçir- 2.

bunalıma gir-. → gir-.

burk- [ar] '- twist, - sprain [ankle]': **{Ayağımı/Ayak bileğimi} burktum.** 'I've sprained {my foot/my ankle}.' *393:13.* impairment: - inflict an injury.

burnunu sok-. → sok- 1.

buruş- [ur] /DAn/ '- get wrinkled /from/': **Otur.mak.tan elbisem buruştu.** 'From sitting my clothes got wrinkled.' *290:3.* furrow: - furrow.

yüzü buruş- [yüz 'face'] (1) '- grimace, - scowl, - make a face', lit., ** 'for one's face - wrinkle': **Ayrıldığı kocasını görünce yüzü buruştu.** 'When she saw her ex-husband [lit., her husband from whom she had separated], she scowled.' **Yine aynı yemeği görünce yüzü buruştu.** 'Upon seeing the same food again, she grimaced.' *152:25a.* resentment, anger: gestures of; *265:8.* distortion: - grimace; *510:20.* * 1. disapproval: gestures of. → ≠ **gülümse-** ['- smile /AT/'], **kaşlarını çat-** ['- knit one's brows, - frown']. (2) 'for a person's face - become or - get wrinkled': **Teyzemi görünce**

tanıyamadım. * **Yüzü ne kadar buruşmuş!** 'When I saw my maternal aunt, I didn't [lit., couldn't] recognize her. * Her face had become so wrinkled! [lit., How wrinkled her face had become!]' *290:3.* furrow: - furrow; *303:10.* age: - age.

buruştur- [ur] '- crumple up; - wrinkle, - make sth wrinkled' [buruş- + caus. suf. -DIr]: **Masasındaki kâğıtları buruşturup çöp.e attı.** 'He crumpled up the papers on his desk and threw them in the trash.' **Kucağım.A oturma! Elbisemi buruşturacaksın.** 'Don't sit ON my lap! You'll wrinkle my clothes.' *291:6.* fold: - wrinkle.

yüzünü buruştur- '- grimace, - scowl, - make a face' [yüz 'face'], lit., ** '- wrinkle one's face': **Limon çok ekşi herhalde, yüzünü buruşturdun.** 'The lemon must be very sour. You puckered up your face.' **Ayrıldığı kocasını görünce {sıkıntı.yLA/öfke.yLE} yüzünü buruşturdu.** 'When she saw her ex-husband [lit., her husband from whom she had separated], she made a face {IN annoyance/IN anger}.' **Ayağ.ı.na iğne batınca acı.yLA yüzünü buruşturdu.** 'When a pin went into her foot, she grimaced IN pain.' *152:25a.* resentment, anger: gestures of; *265:8.* distortion: - grimace; *510:20.* * 1. disapproval: gestures of. → ≠ **gülümse-** ['- smile /AT/'].

buyur- [ur] 1 '- order to be done, - command, - decree': **Kral vergiler.in artır.ıl.ma.sı.nı buyurdu.** 'The king ordered an increase in taxes [lit., ** the taxes' being increased].' *420:8.* command: - command. → = **emret-**.

2 This verb is used in a polite mode of welcoming, offering, inviting, granting permission, etc., most commonly encountered in the imperative form: **Buy[u]run[uz].** The second u is usually not pronounced. 2.1 'Come in': You arrive at a friend's house. He meets you at the door with the words: **Buy[u]run efendim. Hoş geldiniz!** '{Won't you come in/Please come in} {sir/ma'am}. Welcome!' **İçeri buy[u]run.** '{Come inside./Come on in.}' 2.2 'Go ahead, you [go] first': You and another person both come to a

door. You politely insist that he go through first. You say: **Buy[u]run.** '{Please go ahead./After you.}'
2.3 'Here you are., Help yourself., Won't you have {a/some}...': **S: {Pasaport.unuzu/Kimliğ.inizi [or Hüviyet.inizi]} görebilir miyim?** 'Q: May I see {your passport/your ID}?' **C: Buy[u]run, {pasaportum/kimligim}.** 'A: Here you are, {my passport/my ID}.' [**Buy[u]run** may also take a noun in the accusative case, where it may have the sense of '- take': An official is speaking: **Buy[u]run {biletiniz.İ/pasaportunuz.U}.** 'Here is [i.e., Take] {your ticket/your passport}.'] You are entertaining a friend. You offer him a {cigarette/candy}, etc. You say: **Buy[u]run.** '{Please help yourself./Won't you have [e.g., {a cigarette/some candy}]?/Here you are.}' **S:** * **Bir kibrit rica edeceğim.** 'Q: {May/Could} I trouble you for a match?' **C1: Tabii, buy[u]run.** 'A1: {Sure/Of course}, here you are.' **C2:** * **Ne demek, buy[u]run.** 'A2: {Sure/Of course} [lit., ** What does that mean?, i.e., No need to ask], here you are.' **C3: Estağfurullah, buy[u]run.** 'A3: Of course, here you are.'
2.4 'Please do so, Go ahead': **S: Telefon.unuz.u kullanabilir miyim?** 'Q: Could I use your phone?' **C: Tabii, buy[u]run.** 'A: Of course, go ahead.' **S: Siz.E bir şey sorabilir miyim?** 'Q: {May/Could} I ask θ you sth?' **C: Tabii, buy[u]run efendim, sorun.** 'A: Of course, go right ahead, {sir/ma'am}, ask.' When answering the phone: **Alo...buy[u]run.** 'Hello... [Please go ahead with what you want to say.]'
2.5 /A/ 'Please come /to/ a place': When sb is guiding you to a place as, for example, in a restaurant or theater: * **Şöyle buyurun.** 'This way please.' **İçeri buyurmaz mısınız?** 'Won't you come in?' You invite your friend to come to the dining table: **Sofra.yA buy[u]run.** 'Won't you come to the table?' You have been visiting a friend. Now you are leaving. Your friend says: **A: {Gene/Yine/Tekrar} buy[u]run.** 'A: Come {again}.' **B: İnşallah geliriz,** * **siz de biz.E buy[u]run.** 'B: God willing, we will come. * You must come to our house [lit., to us], too.' *504:* * *20.* courtesy: polite expressions.

büyü- [r] '- grow, - become larger, - grow up' [ADJ. **büyük** 'large' - k = **büyü-**]: * **Aslen New Yorkluyum ama Los Angeles'ta büyüdüm.** 'I'm originally from New York, but I grew up in Los Angeles.' **İzmir'de doğdum ama İstanbul'da büyüdüm.** 'I was born in Izmir, but I grew up in Istanbul.' **Ablamın çocukları artık büyüdü.** 'My older sister's children {are grown up now/have now grown up}.' Proverb: **Çocuk düş.e kalk.a büyür.** 'A child grows up by falling and getting up [again]', i.e., through experience. **Bahçe.yE diktiğim güller iyice büyüdü.** 'The roses [that] I planted IN the garden have really grown.' *259:5.* expansion, growth: - become larger; *303:9.* age: - mature.

büyük aptes yap-. → **yap-** 3.

büyüt- [ür] [**büyü-** + caus. suf. -t]: **1** '- enlarge': **Bu resmi büyütebilir misiniz?** 'Could you enlarge this picture?' *259:4.* expansion, growth: - <make larger>.

2 '- exaggerate, - overstate, - make too much of': **Bu işi fazla büyütmek doğru değildir.** 'It's not right to give too much importance to this matter.' **Lütfen olay.ı bu kadar büyütmeyin. Bu sadece bir şakaydı.** 'Don't make too much of {the incident/the event}. It was only a joke.' *355:3.* exaggeration: - exaggerate; *992:10.* excess: - overdo. → = **abart-**, ≠ **küçümse-** 2.

3 '- raise or - bring up a child': **Annem ben küçükken ölmüş, beni teyzem büyüttü.** 'My mother died when I was a child. My [maternal] aunt raised me.' *568:13.* teaching: - train. → = **yetiştir-** 2 ['- bring up, - rear, - raise, - educate, - train', children].

- C -

canı acı-. → **acı-** 1.

canı çek-. → **çek-** 1.

canı iste-. → **iste-** 1.

canı sıkıl-. → **sıkıl-** 1.

canı yan-. → **yan-** 1.

Canın sağ olsun! → sağ ol-. → ol-12.

canına kıy-. → kıy- 2.

canından ol-. → ol- 7.

canını acıt-. → acıt-.

canını sık-. → sık- 3.

canını yak-. → yak- 2.

caydır-. → {vazgeçir-/caydır-}.

{cevap/yanıt} ver-. → ver- 1.

{cevapla- [r]/cevaplandır- [ır]/yanıtla- [r]} /I/ '- answer, - reply, - respond to' [A. cevap (. -) (cevaBı) 'answer, response' + verb-forming suf. -lA; cevapla- + pass. suf. -n [form not used] + caus. suf. -DIr; yanıt 'answer, response' + verb-forming suf. -lA]: Answer questions: Sorular.I iyice düşündükten sonra cevaplayınız. 'Answer the questions after {considering/thinking about} them carefully.' Sınavda sadece bir soru.yU cevaplayamadım. 'On the examination there was only one question I couldn't answer [lit., I couldn't answer θ only one question].' Aşağıdaki sorular.I cevaplayınız. 'Answer the questions below.' ≠ soru sor- ['- ask a question']. Answer a questionnaire: Anketi cevaplayamadım. 'I couldn't answer the questionnaire.' * {Sınav/İmtihan} kâğıdını cevaplayabildim. 'I was able to answer [the questions on] the {examination} [paper].' Answer a letter: Her gün onlarca mektup alıyorum, hepsi.nİ cevaplamam mümkün değil. 'I receive many [lit., tens of] letters every day. It isn't possible for me to answer them all.' Answer a person: Öğretmen.İ cevaplayamadım. 'I couldn't answer the teacher.' Selma biraz {tereddüt ettikten/ duraksadıktan} sonra öğretmen.İ cevapladı. 'Selma [f.] answered the teacher after hesitating [a moment].' 938:4. answer: - answer. → = karşılık ver- 1 → ver- 1, soruya cevap ver- ['- answer a question'] → ver- 1. For '- answer the phone', → cevap ver- → ver- 1.

cevaplandır-. → {cevapla-/cevaplandır-/yanıtla-} above.

ceza al-. → al- 3.

ceza çek-. → çek- 5.

ceza kes-. → kes- 5.

ceza ver-. → ver- 1.

ceza ye-. → ye- 2.

cezalandır- [ır] /I/ '- punish' [A. ceza (. -) 'punishment' + verb-forming suf. -lAn '- be punished' + caus. suf. -DIr]: Kimin suçu varsa onu cezalandıralım. 'Let's punish whoever is guilty.' Yaramazlık yapan çocukları cezalandırmak gerekir. 'One must punish [the] children who are naughty [lit., ** who do naughtiness].' 604:10. punishment: - punish. → = /A/ ceza ver- → ver- 1, /A/ ceza kes- ['- fine /θ/, - give a ticket /to/'] → kes- 5, ≠ ödüllendir-.

cezalandırıl- [ır] /lA/ [cezalandır- + pass. suf. -Il]: 1 /lA/ '- be punished /with/': Okulun camlarını kıran çocuk "uzaklaştırma" [ceza.sı] ile cezalandırıldı. 'The child who had broken the windows was expelled [lit., ** was punished with the {expulsion/sending away} (punishment)].' 604:10. punishment: - punish. → = ceza ye- → ye- 2, ≠ ödüllendiril-.

2 /lA/ '- be sentenced /TO/ a punishment': Genç bir kadın.I öldüren katil, {a: 25 yıl/b: ömür boyu/c: müebbet} hapis.LE cezalandırıldı. 'The murderer who had killed a young woman was sentenced TO {a: 25 years/b, c: life} imprisonment.' 602:3. condemnation: - condemn. → = mahkûm ol- 1 → ol- 12.

cezasını çek-. → çek- 5.

cinayet işle-. → işle- 2.

cinsel ilişkide bulun-. → bulun- 3.

- Ç -

çaba sarf et-. → {harca-/sarf et-} 1.

çabala- [r] /A/ '- strive /to/, - struggle /to/, - do one's best /to/' [çaba 'effort' + verb- forming suf. -lA]:

Denize düşen adam yüzmey.e çabaladı ama başaramadı. 'The man who had fallen into the {sea/ocean} struggled to swim, but he wasn't able to [lit., couldn't succeed].' **Vaktinde çalışmadı, {dönem} sonunda bütün ödevlerini yetiştirmey.e çabalıyor.** 'He didn't do his work on time. At the end of the {term/semester/quarter/lit., period}, he's struggling to catch up on all his homework.' * **Boş yer.E çabalıyorsunuz.** 'You're going to a lot of trouble for nothing.' **Çocuklarımızın bizim çektiğimiz acı ve sıkıntıları çekmemeleri için çok çabaladık.** 'We did our very best so that our children would not [have to] {go through/endure} the pain and troubles that we endured.' *403:13.* endeavor: - do one's best.

çalış[ıp] çabala- '- try hard, - do one's best': * **O kadar çalış çabala, yine de sonuç yok.** 'So much effort [lit., ** Try so hard] and again no result.' *403:13.* endeavor: - do one's best. → = **uğraş-** 1, = **elinden geleni yap-** ['- do all one can, - do one's level best'] → **yap-** 3.

çabuk ol-. → **ol-** 12.

çağır- [ır] /A/ 1 '- call, - send for, - summon /to/, - call sb or sth /FOR/ sb': {**Çabuk/Acele**} **bir {a: doktor/b: {ambulans/cankurtaran}} çağırın.** '{Quick}, call {a: a doctor/b: an ambulance}!' **Ban.A bir doktor çağırır mısınız?** 'Would you {call θ me a doctor/call a doctor FOR me}?' **Polis çağırın.** 'Call the police.' **Şef garsonu çağırır mısınız?** 'Would you please {call/summon} the head waiter?' **Dolmuş yoksa, telefon eder bir taksi çağırırım.** 'If there's no shared cab, I'll phone [and] call a taxi.' *420:11.* command: - summon. → **seslen-** ['- call out /to/, - call'].

2 '- invite /{to/FOR}/': **Parti.yE kimleri çağırayım?** 'Who[m] [i.e., what people] shall I invite TO the party?' **Teyzemler bizi akşam yemeğ.i.nE çağırdılar.** '[Our] maternal aunts invited us {to/FOR} dinner [i.e., the evening meal].' *440:13.* request: - invite. → *More formal:* = **davet et-**.

3 '- shout, - call out': **bağırıp çağır-** '- scream and shout, - make a big racket': * **Biraz sakin ol lütfen, bağırıp çağırmay.a gerek yok.** 'Please calm down. There's no need to scream and shout.' *59:6.* cry, call: - cry. → **çığlık at-** ['- scream'] → **at-** 1, **haykır-** ['- cry out, - shout, - scream'].

4 /diye/ '- call, - refer to /AS [lit., saying]/': **Ninem kedisi.nİ "Minnoş" diye çağırıyor.** 'My grandmother calls her cat θ Minnosh [lit., calls her cat SAYING Minnoş].' *527:11.* nomenclature: - name. → **seslen-**.

çakıl- [ır] [çak- 1 '- drive sth into sth. 2 '- land a blow on' + {pass./refl.} suf. -Il] 1 /A, {tarafından/CA}/ '- be driven or hammered /{IN/INTO}, by/ [subj.: nail, peg]; - be pegged, nailed down': **Bu çiviler bura.yA niye çakılmış anlayamadım.** 'I couldn't understand why these nails had been driven IN here.' **Bu kocaman çivilerin {çocuklar tarafından/çocuklar.ca} çakılmış olması mümkün değil.** 'It isn't possible that these big nails had been hammered in by the children.' *799:8.* joining: - hook.

2 /A/ '- crash, - nose dive /INTO/': **İniş takımları arıza yapan uçak inerken {pist.E/okyanus.A} çakıldı.** 'The plane, whose landing gear experienced a mechanical failure on descending, crashed {INTO the runway/INTO the ocean}.' **yere çakıl-** '- nose dive /INTO/ the ground, crash, crack up', plane: **Havalanırken arıza yapan uçak büyük bir gürültüyle yer.E çakıldı ve parçalandı.** 'The plane that had a mechanical failure {on takeoff/while taking off} crashed INTO the ground with a great roar [lit., noise] and broke into pieces.' *184:44.* aviation: - crash. → = **düş-** 5.

çal- [ar] 1 /DAn/ '- steal /from/': **Hırsızlar {a: cüzdanımı/b: pasaportumu/c: çantamı} çaldılar.** 'The thieves stole {a: my wallet/b: my passport/c: my {handbag/purse/briefcase}}.' **Müze.den kıymetli eserleri çalan hırsız [polis tarafından] yakalandı.** 'The thief who had stolen valuable objects from the museum was caught [by the police].' *482:13.* theft: - steal.

2 '- play a musical instrument, radio, record player, tape recorder, - honk a horn': **Piyano çalar mısınız?** 'Do you play the piano?' **Lütfen ben ders çalışırken {a: flüt/b: saz/c: piyano/d: keman/e: gitar/f: teyp/g: radyo/h: CD [pronounce: si di]} çalma! * Rahatsız oluyorum.** 'Please don't play {a: the flute/b: the saz/c: the piano/d: the violin/e: the guitar/f: the tape recorder/g: the radio/h: the {CD player/CD disk}} while I'm studying! * It disturbs me [lit., ** I become uncomfortable].' *708:39a.* music: - play sth. Proverbs: **Kırkından sonra saza başlayan kıyamette çalar.** 'He who begins the [study of the] saz after [the age of] forty, will play it on doomsday.', i.e., Don't waste time on frivolous things; life is short. *845: * 21.* lateness: PHR. it's too late. **Parayı veren düdüğü çalar.** 'He who pays the money plays the whistle.', i.e., 'He who pays the piper calls the tune.' *58:8.* stridency: - screech.

'- play, - perform a piece of music': **Konserde hangi eserleri çalıyorlar?** 'Which works are they performing during the concert?' *708:39a.* music: - play sth. → **yorumla- 2** ['- interpret, - perform', piece of music].

çene çal- /lA/ '- chat, - gossip, - chew the fat /with/' [**çene** 'jaw']: * **Bize gelsene, çay içer çene çalarız.** 'Why don't you come on over to our house [lit., come to us]. We'll have some tea and chat.' * **Orada ne çene çalıp duruyorsunuz, * gelin biraz bana yardım edin.** 'Why are you just standing over there chatting away? * Come [over here] and give me a hand for a moment.' **Çene çalmay.I bırak da, dersin.E çalış!** 'Stop chatting and study θ your lesson!' *541:10.* conversation: - chat. → **dedikodu yap-** → ['- gossip /about/'] → **yap- 3**, **arkasından konuş-** ['- speak ill of sb behind his back'].

ıslık çal- '- whistle' [**ıslık** 'whistle, whistling sound']: **Taksi.yi durdurmak için ıslık çalmalısınız.** 'You'll have to whistle to stop {a/the} taxi.' *708:38.*

music: - sing; *708:42.* music: - blow a horn. As a sign of disapproval: **Maçtan sonra seyirciler hakemi yuhalayıp ıslık çaldılar.** 'After the game [i.e., soccer, basketball], the spectators booed the referee and whistled.' *508:10.* ridicule: - boo. → **yuhala-** ['- boo'], ≠ **alkışla-** ['- applaud']. As a sign of approval: **Genç adam, sokakta yürüyen * güzel kız.ın arka.sı.nDAN ıslık çaldı.** 'The young man whistled * AT [lit., ** from behind] the beautiful girl who was walking down the street.' **Seyirciler operanın sonunda uzun uzun alkışlayıp ıslık çaldılar.** 'At the conclusion of the opera, the audience applauded long and hard and whistled.' *509:10.* approval: - applaud.

korna çal- '- hit /θ/ or - honk /θ/ a car horn' [It. **korna** 'car horn']: **Trafik sıkışınca bütün sürücüler kornalarını çaldı.** 'When the traffic started to pile up, all the drivers honked their horns.' *58:8.* stridency: - screech; *708:42.* music: - blow a horn; *912:4.* depression: - depress. → = **korna.yA bas-** → **bas- 2**.

3 'for a bell, etc. - ring, - strike': **zil çal-** 'for a bell - ring': **Kapı.nın zil.i çalıyor, * kim geldi acaba? * Açar mısınız?** 'The door bell is ringing, * I wonder who it is [lit., who came]? * Would you please answer it [lit., open it]?' **Zil çalıyor. Ders bitti.** 'The bell is ringing. The class is over.' **Telefon çalıyor, bakar mısın lütfen?** 'The phone is ringing, would you please {get/answer} it [lit., {take care of it/look after it/see to it}].' **Telefon çaldı. Ahizeyi kaldırdı. * Fatma hanım.ı telefon{.A/.DAN} istiyorlardı.** 'The phone rang. He picked up the receiver. * Fatma hanım was wanted [lit., They wanted Fatma hanım] ON the phone.' *54:8b.* resonance: - ring, make a ringing sound.

* **karnı zil çal-** 'for one's stomach - growl from hunger [lit., ** for one's stomach, **karın** (kaRNı), - ring]; - be very hungry': • Note the personal suffixes: **Öyle acık.TIM ki, karn.IM zil çalıyor.** 'I'm so hungry that MY stomach is growling.' *54:8b.* resonance: - ring, make a ringing sound; *100:19.* desire: - hunger. → **acık-** ['- be or - become

hungry'], **doy-** ['- have enough /OF/, - be satisfied /WITH/, - eat one's fill, - be full'], **susa-** ['- be thirsty'].

4 'for a clock, etc. - ring the hour': **saat saati çal-** 'for the clock - ring the hour': **Bu sabah evden çıkarken * saat tam sekiz.İ çalıyordu.** 'When I was leaving the house this morning, * it was just striking θ eight o'clock [lit., the clock was striking exactly eight].' *54:8b.* resonance: - ring, make a ringing sound.

5 /I/ '- knock /{AT/ON}/': * **Ahmet kapı.yI çaldı, ama kimse açmadı.** 'Ahmet knocked AT the door, but no one answered [lit., opened it].' **{On dakika.dan beri/On dakika.dır} kapı.yI çalıyorum.** 'I've been knocking {AT/ON} the door {for ten minutes}.' * **Uzun zaman.dır kapı.mız.ı çalan olmadı.** 'No one has knocked AT our door {for/in} a long time [lit., ** for a long time there was not a person who was knocking AT our door].' **Ahmet'in kapı.sı.nI çalıp bekledim.** 'I knocked {AT/ON} Ahmet's door and waited.' *901:16.* impulse, impact: - pound. → = **kapıyı vur-** → **vur-** 1.

çalın- [ır] [**çal-** + pass. suf. -**In**] **1** /DAn, {tarafından/CA}/ '- be stolen /from, by/': **Paris'teki müzeden çok değerli tablolar çalınmış.** 'Very valuable pictures were stolen from the museum in Paris.' **{a: Pasaportum/b: Cüzdanım/c: Çantam} [hırsızlar tarafından] çalındı.** '{a: My passport/b: My wallet/c: My {handbag/purse/ briefcase}} was stolen [by (the) thieves].' Proverb: **At çalındıktan sonra ahırın kapısını kapatmak {boşunadır/beyhudedir}.** 'After the horse has been stolen, it is useless to close the door of the barn.' To lock the barn door after the horse is gone. *482:13.* theft: - steal; *845:* * *21.* lateness: PHR. it's too late.

2 /{tarafından/CA}/ '- be played [a musical instrument, audio equipment] /by/': **Partide sadece {a: saz/b: piyano/c: gitar/d: keman/e: teyp/f: radyo/g: CD [pronounce: si di]} [ev sahibi tarafından] çalındı.** 'At the party only {a: the saz/b: the piano/c: the guitar/d: the violin/e: the tape recorder/f: the radio/g: the CD player} was played

[by the host].' *708:39a.* music: - play sth.

'- be played, performed [a piece of music] /by/': **Konserde hangi eserler [{orkestra/saz heyeti} tarafından] çalındı?** 'Which works were performed [by the {orchestra/saz ensemble}] during the concert?' *708:39a.* music: - play sth.

3 /{tarafından/CA}/ '- be rung /by/': **Zehra! Kapı çalınıyor, açıver.** 'Zehra! The door bell is ringing [lit., ** The door is being rung]. [Go and] open it!' **Kapı [çocuk tarafından] çalındı.** 'The door [bell] was rung [by the child].' *54:8a.* resonance: - ring sth.

4 'lit., ** - be knocked at': **Zehra! * Kapı çalınıyor, açıver.** 'Zehra! * Someone's knocking at the door [lit., ** The door is being knocked at]. [Go and] open it.' A: **Kapı çalınıyor.** 'A: Someone's knocking on the door.' B: * **Ben bakarım. Kim acaba?** 'B: I'll get it. I wonder who it is.' **Dün gece yarısı kapımız çalındı.** 'Someone knocked at our door [lit., ** our door was knocked at] at midnight last night.' *901:16.* impulse, impact: - pound.

çalış- [ır] /I, A/ **1** '- work, - study, -work /ON/, - practice sth' [ADJ. **çalışkan** 'hardworking, industrious']: "**Türk! Övün, çalış, güven!**" M.K. Atatürk. "'[O] Turk! Be proud, strive, have confidence!" M[ustafa] K[emal] Atatürk.' S: **Nerede çalışıyorsunuz?** 'Q: Where do you work?' C: **{a: Bir ofiste/b: Bir bankada/c: Kütüphanede/d: Evde} çalışıyorum.** 'A: I work {a: in an office/b: {at/in} a bank/c: in the library/d: at home}.' **Kocası altı aydan beri işsiz, çalışmıyor.** 'Her husband has been unemployed for six months. He isn't working.' Proverb: * **Çalış.makla her iş biter.** 'With effort [lit., by working] every task is completed.', i.e., Success is achieved. * **Bugün matematik.TEN {sınav/ imtihan} var. Çalıştın mı?** 'We're having {an exam} [lit., There is an exam] IN math today, did you study?' S: **Dersiniz.İ çalıştınız mı?** 'Q: Did you study your lesson?' C: **{a: Çok/b: Çok sıkı/c: Yoğun/d: Gece gündüz} çalıştım.** 'A: I studied {a: {a lot/very hard}/b, c: very intensely/d:

day and night}.' **Bu konu.yU henüz çalışmadım.** 'I haven't studied this {subject/topic} yet.' *570:12.* learning: - study; *724:12.* occupation: - work; *725:12.* exertion: - work. → **çabala-** ['- strive /to/, - struggle /to/, - do one's best /to/'], **emek ver-** ['- put effort /INTO/, - devote effort /to/, - work /AT/, - take pains /WITH/'] → **ver-** 1, **uğraş-** 1 ['- strive, - struggle, - endeavor /TO/, - exert oneself, - put forth an effort /for/, - work hard'].

'- practice, - work on': **Turhan gün.DE beş saat piyano çalışıyor.** 'Turhan practices the piano [for] five hours θ a day.' **Bugünlerde Semra tenis çalışıyor.** 'Semra [f.] is working on [her] tennis these days.' *328:8.* action: - practice.

ders çalış- '- study' [A. **ders** 'lesson']: S: **Ne yapıyorsunuz?** 'Q: What are you doing?' C: **Ders çalışıyorum.** 'A: I'm studying.' **Genelikle {a: sabah[ları]/b: öğleden sonra[ları]/c: akşam[ları]} ders çalışırım.** 'I usually study {a: IN the morning[s]/b: AT noon/c: IN the evening[s]}.' **Üç saattir ders çalışıyorum, sıkıldım artık, çıkıp biraz dolaşayım.** 'I've been studying for three hours now. I'm bored. [I think] I'll go out and walk around [for] a bit.' **Her gün ders çalışıyor musun[uz]?** 'Do you study every day?' **Her gün ders çalışmalısınız.** 'You must study every day.' **Ders çalışmayan çocuk çok şey öğrenemez.** 'The child who doesn't study can't learn much.' • A particular class subject may replace **ders**: **Altı aydan beri Türkçe çalışıyorlar.** 'They've been studying Turkish for six months.' → also **dersE çalış-** below. *570:12.* learning: - study. • For a MAJOR subject as the object of '- study', rather than a particular class, as in 'I'm studying ECONOMICS', → **tahsil et-, oku-** 2.

* **dersE çalış-** '- study, - work ON a particular lesson': * **Çene çalmay.I bırak da, ders.in.E çalış!** 'Stop chatting and study your lesson!' S: **Şimdi hangi ders.E çalışıyorsun?** 'Q: Which lesson are you {studying/working on} now?' C1: **Matematik çalışıyorum.** 'A1: I'm {studying/working on} math[ematics].' C2: **{Matematik ders.i.nE/Yedinci ders.E} çalışıyorum.** 'A2: I'm {studying/working on} {the math[ematics] lesson/the seventh lesson}.' **Derslerin.E iyi çalış, * ödevlerini ihmal etme.** '{Study hard/[lit., Study your lessons well]}. Don't neglect your * homework[* NOT ~~homeworkS~~].' S: **Çocuğunuz dersler.i.nE çalışıyor mu?** 'Q: Is your child studying his lessons?' C: * **Çalışıyor çalışmasına ama notları iyi değil.** 'Yes, he is studying, but his {marks/grades} are not good.' **Işıklar sönünce derslerimiz.E çalışamadık.** 'When the lights went out, we couldn't study our lessons.' *570:12.* learning: - study.

2 /A/ '- try /to/, - attempt /to/': **Elimden geleni yapmay.a çalışacağım.** 'I'll try to do my best.' **Hırsız eve girmey.e çalışmış, fakat başaramamış.** 'The thief tried to enter the house, but he couldn't [lit., couldn't succeed].' *403:6.* endeavor: - attempt. → = /I/ **dene-.**

3 '- function, - work, - run': **Bu {alet/bilgisayar} nasıl çalışıyor?** 'How does this {instrument/computer} work?' **{a: Lâmba/b: Telefon/c: Televizyon/d: Bu fotoğraf makinası} çalışmıyor.** '{a: The lamp/b: The phone/c: The television/d: This camera} doesn't work.' *888:7.* operation: - be operative. → = **işle-** 1.

çalışıp çabala-. → **çabala-.**

çalıştır- [ır] [**çalış-** + caus. suf. -DIr] 1 a) /I/ '- have or - make sb work, - work sb, - allow sb - work': **Fabrika sahibi işçileri çok çalıştırıyordu.** 'The owner of the factory was {making the workers work a lot/working the workers hard}.'
b) /A/ '- have or - make /θ/ sb work on sth; - tutor /θ/ sb': * **Komşumuzun oğlu biz.E Fransızca çalıştırıyordu.** 'Our neighbor's son was {making θ us work on French/tutoring θ us in French}.' *424:4.* compulsion: - compel; *568:11.* teaching: - tutor.

2 '- work, - run, or - operate a machine': **Klimayı çalıştırır mısınız?** 'Can you {work/run/operate/turn on} the air conditioning?' *888:5.* operation: - operate sth.

çalkala- [r] **1** '- shake': On a bottle: { a: **Aç.madan önce/b: Kullan- .madan önce/c: İç.meden önce} iyice çalkalayın.** 'Shake well {a: before opening/b: before using/c: before drinking}.' *916:10.* agitation: - agitate.

2 /1A/ '- rinse {with/IN}': **Tuzlu suyla ağzınızı iyice çalkalayın.** 'Rinse your mouth thoroughly with salt water.' **{Tabakları/Bardak- ları} iyice çalkala, deterjanlı kalmasın.** 'Rinse the {dishes/glasses} thoroughly. Let no detergent remain on them.' *79:19.* cleanness: - wash. → = **durula-** ['- rinse dishes, glasses, sheets', but not 'mouth'].

çarp- [ar] /A/ **1** '- hit /θ/, - strike /θ/, - bump /{AGAINST/INTO/ON}/, - run or - crash /INTO/': **Dün bir kamyon arabam.A çarptı.** 'Yesterday a truck {struck θ/ran INTO} my car.' **Otobüs küçük bir çocuğ.A çarptı.** 'The bus struck θ a small child.' **Biraz yavaşla, şimdi biri.nE çarpacaksın.** 'Slow down, you're going to hit θ sb.' **Yağmur damlaları pencere.nin cam.ı.nA çarpıyordu.** 'The rain drops were hitting θ the window pane [lit., the glass of the window].' → **vur-** 1. # **Ayağım.I taş.A çarptım, çok acıyor.** 'I hit my foot ON a stone. It really hurts.' **Kedi şişe.yE çarptı ve süt döküldü.** 'The cat bumped {AGAINST/INTO} the bottle, and the milk spilled.' *901:13.* impulse, impact: - collide.

güneş çarp- /A/ '- get sunstroke', lit., ** 'for the sun, **güneş**, - strike /θ/': **Güneş banyosu yaparken çok dikkatli olmalıyız, güneş çarpabilir.** 'While sunbathing, one [lit., we] must be very careful. It is possible to get a sunstroke.' * **Zerrin'E güneş çarpmış.** 'Zerrin got sunstroke.' *85:46b.* disease: - take sick in particular ways.

kapı çarp- '[for a door] - slam shut': **Lütfen kapı.yA dayanmayın, otomatik kapı çarpar.** 'Please don't lean ON the door, or the automatic door will slam shut.' *53:7.* loudness: - din; *293:6.* closure: - close; *352:7.* publication: poster: * specific signs.

kapıyı çarp- '- slam the door': **Baktım ki patronla anlaşamıyoruz, kapıyı çarptım çıktım.** 'I saw that the boss and I weren't reaching an agreement, so I slammed the door and left.' **Kapıyı çarpma.** 'Don't slam the door!' *53:7.* loudness:- din; *293:6.* closure: - close. → = **kapıyı vur-** → **vur-** 1, **kapıyı yavaş {kapa-/kapat-}** ['- close the door {gently/quietly}', i.e., Don't slam the door.] → {**kapa- /kapat-**} 1.

yıldırım çarp- /I/ 'for lightning - strike': **Jumbo uçağı.nI yıldırım çarptı.** 'Lightning struck the jumbo jet.' *901:14.* impulse, impact: - hit. = /A/ **yıldırım düş-.**

2 /DAn/ '- beat /{BECAUSE OF/IN/WITH/from}/': {**kalbi/ yüreği} çarp-** 'for one's heart - beat' [{A **kalp** [kalBİ]/**yürek**} 'heart']: * **Adam.ı öldü sandık fakat kalb.i hâlâ çarpıyordu.** 'We thought the man had died [lit., ** We thought the man he died], but his heart was still beating.' *916:12.* agitation: - flutter. → = {**kalbi/ yüreği} at-** → **at-** 7.

{**kalbi/yüreği} hızlı hızlı çarp-** 'for one's heart - palpitate, - pound, - race /{BECAUSE OF/IN/WITH/ from}/' [**hızlı** 'rapidly']: **Dört kat merdiveni bir solukta çıkınca yaşlı adam.ın kalb.i hızlı hızlı çarpmaya başladı.** 'When the old man had climbed four flights of stairs in a single bound [lit., ** in one breath], his heart began to race.' **Sınava girmeden önce Ahmet'in kalbi hızlı hızlı çarpıyordu.** 'Before taking the exam, Ahmet's heart was pounding.' **Yaşlı hanım.ın kalbi {a: heyecan.DAN/b: korku.DAN/c: endişe.DEN/d: koşmak.TAN} hızlı hızlı çarpıyordu.** 'The old woman's heart was beating rapidly {a: {BECAUSE OF/IN} excitement/b: {BECAUSE OF/IN} fear/c: {BECAUSE OF/WITH} anxiety/d: from running}.' *916:12.* agitation: - flutter. → = {**kalbi/yüreği} hızlı hızlı at-** → **at-** 7.

3 /ile/ '- multiply /BY/': * **128** [read: **yüz yirmi sekiz**] **İLE 50'yi** [read: **elliyi**] **çarparsan 6400** [read: **altı bin dört yüz**] {**olur/eder**}. 'If you multiply 128 BY 50, you get [lit., ** {it becomes/it makes}] 6400.' *1016:17.* mathematics: - calculate.
4 '- get an electrical shock': /I/ **elektrik çarp**-: * **Elimi elektrik çarptı**. 'I got a shock [lit., ** The electricity struck my hand].' *1031:25.* electricity: - electrify.

çarpıl- [ır] /lA/ [**çarp**- + pass. suf. -**Il**]: 1 '- be multiplied /BY/': * **128** [read: **yüz yirmi sekiz**] **İLE 50** [**elli**] **çarpılırsa 6400 eder**. '{128 times 50 is 6400./When you multiply 128 by 50, you get 6400/[lit., ** If 128 is multiplied BY 50, {it makes 6400/6400 will result}].' *1016:17.* mathematics: - calculate.

2 /A, not with **tarafından**/ *colloq.* '- be swept off one's feet /BY/, - fall /FOR/ sb', i.e., - fall in love /WITH/: **Şu kumral saçlı kadın.A çarpıldım**. 'I've fallen FOR that brunette [lit., that brown haired woman].' **Uzun boylu sarışın kadını görünce genç adam çarpıldı**. 'When the young man saw the tall, blond woman, he {was swept off his feet/fell FOR her}.' *104:22.* love: - fall in love. → = /A/ **âşık ol**- ['- fall in love /WITH/'] → **ol**- 12.

çarpış- [ır] '- collide, - run into each other' [**çarp**- + recip. suf. -**Iş**]: **Arabalar tam evimizin önünde çarpıştı**. 'The cars collided right in front of our house.' **Çarpışan arabalardaki iki kişi yaralan.madan kurtuldu**. 'Two people in the cars that had collided were rescued unharmed [lit., ** without being injured].' *901:13.* impulse, impact: - collide. For '- run into', i.e., for people '- meet unexpectedly', → **karşılaş**- 2, **rastla**- 1, **tesadüf et**- 1.
çarşıya çık-. → **çık**- 2.

çat pat konuş-. → **konuş**-.

çat- [ar] '- tack together': **kaşlarını çat**- '- knit one's brows, frown', lit., ** '- bring one's eyebrows, **kaş**, together': **Çamurlu ayakkabılarla eve girince annem kaşlarını çattı**. 'When I entered the house with muddy shoes, my mother frowned.' *152:25a.* resentment, anger: gestures

of; *510:20.* * *1.* disapproval: gestures of. → **yüzü buruş**- 1 ['- grimace, - scowl, - make a face'] → **buruş**-, ≠ **gülümse**- ['- smile /AT/'].

çatış- [ır] /lA/ 1 '- quarrel, - clash /with/': **Sokak çeteleri sık sık birbirleri.yle çatışırlar**. 'Street gangs frequently clash with one another.' *456:11.* disaccord: - quarrel; *457:13.* contention: - contend. → **dövüş**- ['- fight, - struggle, - engage in combat /with/ one another, in striking one another'], **kavga et**- ['- fight, - quarrel /with/', physical or just verbal].

2 '- be in conflict, - clash': * **Babamla fikirlerimiz daima çatışıyor. Hiçbir konuda anlaşamıyoruz**. 'My father's views and mine [lit., ** With my father our views] always clash. We can't agree on anything [lit., on any subject].' *779:5.* difference: - differ; *788:5.* disagreement: - disagree.

çek- [er] 1 /I, A/ '- pull, - tow, - draw; - attract': **İçeri girmek için kapıyı çekin**. 'To enter, pull [the door].' {**Arabamızı/Karavanımızı/Kamyonumuzu**} **çekebilir misiniz**? 'Can you tow {our car/our camper/our truck}?' **Arabanızı oradan çeker misiniz**? * **Orası benim park yerim**. 'Would you please {move/tow} your car away from there? * That's my parking place.' **Arabam bozuldu**, * **sizin arabayla çekebilir miyiz**? 'My car has broken down. * Could we use your car to tow it? [lit., ** Could we tow it with your car?]' **Tahta arabayı iki at çekiyordu**. 'Two horses were {pulling/towing} the wooden cart.' → ≠ **it**-, ≠ **ittir**-. # **Masa.yı pencere.nin yan.ı.na çekti**. 'He pulled the table over to [lit., the side of] the window.' *904:4.* pulling: - pull. → ≠ **it**-. Proverb: **Para para.yI çeker**. 'Money attracts θ money.'

canı çek- '- feel like doing sth, - have a craving for' [P. **can** (-) 'soul'], lit., 'for one's soul - pull, attract': **Anne: Kızım, neden yemek yemiyorsun**? 'Mother: {Dear/Child/lit., ** My girl}, why aren't you eating?' **Kız: Bugün can.IM çekmiyor**. 'Daughter: Today I don't feel like it.' NON-verbal noun as object: * **Hamileyken can.IM erik çekmişti**. 'When I was

pregnant, I {had a craving for/felt like eating} plums.' **Çocuğunuz.un iştah.ı yok galiba, can.I hiç bir şey çekmiyor.** 'It seems that your child has no appetite. He has no desire for anything.'
VERBAL noun as object: **Şimdi patlıcan yemey.I can.ım çekmiyor.** 'I don't feel like eating eggplant right now.' *100:14.* desire: - desire. → = **canı iste-** → **iste-** 1.

dikkat çek- /A/ '- call or - draw attention /to/, - refer /to/, - point out /θ/, - note /θ/' [A. **dikkat** (**dikkatİ**) 'careful attention'. ADJ. **dikkat çekici** 'attention attracting']: **Bir tehlike.ye dikkat çekmek istiyorum.** 'I {want/would like} to call attention to a danger.' **Eleştirmenler bu oyun.un özgün olmadığ.ı.nA dikkat çektiler.** 'The critics {pointed out/noted} θ that this play was not original.' **Geçen haftaki toplantıda dikkat çektiğimiz nokta hâlâ aydınlanmadı.** 'The point that we {called attention to/referred to} at last week's meeting has still not been clarified.' *982:10.* attention: - call attention to. → = **işaret et-** 2.

{dikkat/dikkati} çek- /lA/ '- attract attention, - catch the attention, - strike the eye /with/' [A. **dikkat** (**dikkatİ**) 'careful attention']: With an adverb, here **çok**, only **dikkat**, not **dikkat.İ**, otherwise both: **Zeynep yeni kırmızı elbisesi.yle çok dikkat çekti.** 'Zeynep attracted a lot of attention with her new dress.' **{Kardeşler} arasındaki benzerlik hemen {dikkat/dikkati} çekiyordu.** 'The resemblance between {the brothers/the sisters} at once {struck everyone/attracted attention}.' *982:11.* attention: - meet with attention.

dikkatini çek- '- call sb's attention to sth, for sth - attract sb's attention': **Metin'in Selma'yA olan ilgisi herkes.in dikkat.i.ni çekti.** 'Everyone noticed Metin's interest IN Selma [f.] [lit., Metin's interest IN Selma attracted everyone's attention].' **Küçük yaşlarından itibaren {güzelliğ.i.yle/{a: kıvrak/b: ince/c: keskin} zekâ.sı.yla} herkes.in dikkat.ini çekmeye başlamıştı.** 'From an early age she had began to attract everyone's attention {with her beauty/with her {a: perceptive/b: subtle/c: keen} intelligence.' *982:11.* attention: - meet with attention. → = **gözle-** 1.

* **iç çek-** '- sigh, - heave a sigh' [**iç** 'inside']: **Derin bir iç çektikten sonra konuşmaya başladı.** 'After heaving a deep sigh, he began to speak.' *52:14.* faintness of sound: - sigh.

* **içine çek-** '- inhale' [**iç** 'inside'], lit., '- pull, - draw /to/ one's inside': * **Sigara.nın duman.ı.nı derin derin içi.nE çekti.** 'He took a deep drag on his cigarette [lit., He inhaled the smoke of the cigarette deeply].' **Yağmurdan sonra toprağın kokusunu iç.İM.E çektim.** 'After the rain, I inhaled the scent of the earth.' *89:14.* tobacco: - use tobacco; *187:12.* reception: - draw in; *318:21.* * *1.* wind: - breathe. → = **nefes al-** ['- breathe, - take a breath; - inhale'] → **al-** 1, = **nefes çek-** ['- take a wiff, drag (of tobacco)'] → **çek-** 1, ≠ **nefes ver-** → **ver-** 1, **nefes tut-** ['- hold one's breath'] → **tut-** 4.

ilgi çek- '- appeal to, - interest, *colloq.:* - be into' [**ilgi** 'interest']: **Profesör.ün konferan.sı {herkes.İN/öğrenciler.İN} ilgi.Sİ.nİ çekti.** 'The professor's talk interested {everyone/the students} [lit., attracted {everyone'S/the students'} interest].' **S: {Klâsik müzik konserine/Heykel sergi-sine/Konferansa} geliyor musun?** 'Q: Are you coming {to the classical music concert/to the sculpture exhibit/to the lecture}?' **C: Hayır, hiç ilgi.M.İ çekmiyor.** 'A: No, it doesn't {appeal to/interest} ME at all [lit., ** it doesn't attract MY interest...].' *377:6.* allurement: - attract; *980:3a.* curiosity: - make curious, - interest. → = **ilgilendir-** 1 ['for sth - interest, - arouse the interest of'].

kenara çek- '- pull aside, - pull off /to/ the side' [**kenar** (. -) 'side']: **Polis aşırı sürat yapan arabanın şoförüne "Kenar.A çek" diye bağırdı.** 'The police shouted at the driver who had been driving too fast [saying], "Pull off to the side".' *164:6.* deviation: - avoid.

nefes çek- '- take a wiff, drag, puff'
[A. nefes 'breath']: Ahmet bey bir
{sigara/puro/pipo} yaktı. Derin
bir nefes çekti. 'Ahmet bey lit up a
{cigarette/cigar/pipe}. He {took a
deep drag/inhaled deeply}.' 89:14.
tobacco: - use tobacco; 187:12.
reception: - draw in; 318:21. * 1.
wind: - breathe. → = içine çek- ['-
inhale'] → çek- 1, = nefes al- ['-
breathe, - take a breath; - inhale'] →
al- 1, ≠ nefes ver- ['- breathe out, -
exhale, - let out a breath'] → ver- 1,
nefes tut- ['- hold one's breath'] →
tut- 4.

2 '- take /out of/, - withdraw, -
remove /from/, - extract': Bu dişi
çekmek gerekiyor. 'This tooth
must be {pulled/extracted} [lit., It is
necessary to {pull/extract} this
tooth].' para çek- /DAn/ '- take
money /{OUT OF/from}/, - withdraw
money /from/' [para 'money']:
Bankaya gidiyorum, para
çekmem lâzım. 'I'm going to the
bank. I have to withdraw some
money.' * Bankadaki tüm paramı
çektim. 'I withdrew all the money
[that] I had in the bank.' Banka.dan
tüm paramı çektim. 'I withdrew
all my money from the bank.' 192:10.
extraction: - extract. → ≠ para
yatır- 1 → yatır- 2.

3 /DAn/ '- take off': * Ellerini
üzeri.m.DEN çek! 'Take your
hands OFF me [lit., ** off my
surface, top]!' 176:11. transferal,
transportation: - remove. • For '-
remove clothes, - undress', → çıkar-
2, soyun-.

4 '- pull shut': * Akşam oldu,
perdeleri çekelim. 'It's evening
[lit., ** It has become evening]. Let's
{shut the curtains./pull the curtains
shut.}' 293:6. closure: - close. → =
{kapa-/kapat-} 1.

fermuar çek- '- zip up' [F.
fermuar 'zipper']: {Paltom.un/
Mont.um.un} fermuar.ı.nı
çekme.yi unutmuşum, çok
üşüdüm. 'I seem to have forgotten
to zip up {my coat/my jacket} [lit., **
pull {my coat's/my jacket's} zipper].
I'm very cold.' 293:6. closure: -
close.

5 '- endure, - suffer, - put up with, -
go through', often with nouns
indicating difficulty, trouble: * Neler

çektik neler! '[You can't imagine]
what [things] we had to put up with
[lit., ** What things we put up with,
what things]!' * Nedir bu
çektiğim Allahım! 'Oh my God,
the things [that] I've had to put up
with!' Benim çektiklerimi Allah
başka kimse.yE çektirmesin.
'May God not make θ anyone else
suffer what I have endured.' *
İnşallah o benim çektiğim
sıkıntıları çekmez. 'I hope he
won't have to go through the
difficulties I had to deal with.'
Kadıncağız çok çekti. 'The poor
woman has gone through a lot.' *
Senden çok çektim, boşanmak
istiyorum. 'I've put up with a lot
from you. I want a divorce.' Proverb:
Hekim.DEN sorma, çeken.DEN
sor. 'Don't ask θ the doctor, ask θ
the one who is suffering, i.e., the one
who has experienced the pain. Today
the term doktor is usually preferred
to the older term hekim. 134:5.
patience: - endure; 1047:3. toughness:
- toughen. → = dayan- 3, = katlan-
2, = tahammül et-, uğraş- 3 ['-
put up with a person'].

acı çek- '- suffer, - endure pain, - be
in pain', physical or mental [acı
'pain']: * Apandisit ameliyatı
olalı neredeyse onbeş gün oldu
fakat hâlâ acı çekiyorum. 'I had
my appendix removed [lit., I had an
operation for appendicitis] almost 15
days ago, but I'm still {feeling pain/in
pain}.' * Kaçırılan çocuğ.u.nun
acı.sı.nı yıllardır çekiyor. 'For
years he has been suffering the pain
resulting from the abduction of his
child [lit., suffering the pain of his
child who had been abducted].' Çok
genç yaşta evlenme.nin
acı.sı.nı çektim. 'I've endured the
pain of having married too early.'
26:8. pain: - suffer pain. → dert
çek- ['- endure troubles' rather than
physical pain].

ceza çek- '- serve a prison sentence,
- serve or - do time' [A. ceza (. -)
'punishment']: Beş yıl ceza
çektikten sonra {a:
dolandırıcı/b: hırsız/c: yan-
kesici/d: kapkaççı} artık
hapishaneden çıkıyor. 'After
serving a five-year sentence, {a: the
swindler/b: the thief/c: the
pickpocket/d: the purse-snatcher} is
finally leaving prison.' 429:18.
confinement: - be imprisoned; 824:5.

spell: - take one's turn. → **cezasını çek-** 2.

cezasını çek- [A. **ceza** (. -) 'punishment'] (1) '- suffer for a deed, - get one's just deserts or dues for a deed': A: **Rüşvet yiyen gümrük müdürü görevinden alınmış.** 'A: The director of customs who had taken bribes was fired [from his position].' B: **İyi olmuş,** * **cezasını çeksin!** 'B: Good, * that's what he deserves [lit., let him suffer punishment for it]!' Proverb: **Akılsız baş.ın ceza.sı.nı ayaklar çeker.** 'The feet will suffer punishment for an empty [i.e., brainless] head.', i.e., They will be forced to do unnecessary walking. *639:6.* dueness: - get one's deserts. (2) '- serve a prison sentence /for/, - serve or - do time /for/': **Mahkûm beş yıllık cezasını çekti. Yarın hapishaneden çıkacak.** 'The convict served his five year sentence. He {will be released from/lit., will leave} prison tomorrow.' *429:18.* confinement: - be imprisoned; *824:5.* spell: - take one's turn. → = **ceza çek-**.

dert çek- '- suffer, - endure, - put up with troubles' [P. **dert** 'trouble, care, worry']: **Hayatı boyunca çok dert çekti zavallı.** 'Throughout {her/his} life {he/she} had a lot of troubles, the poor soul.' **Babam öldüğünden beri bütün derdimizi annem çekiyor.** 'Since my father's death, my mother has put up with all our troubles.' Proverb: **Derdi çeken derman arar.** 'He who has troubles seeks a remedy [for them].' *26:8.* pain: - suffer pain. → **acı çek-** ['- suffer, - endure pain, - be in pain', physical or mental].

{güçlük/zorluk} çek- /DA/ '- have a hard time, difficulty, trouble /{θ/on/in}/, - experience adversity' [{**güçlük/zorluk**} 'difficulty']: **Savaş yıllarında bütün ülke güçlük çekti.** 'During the war years the whole country {went through/experienced} difficult times.' **Ev bulmak.TA çok güçlük çektik.** 'We had a very hard time {θ/in} finding a house.' **Hasta.nın nefes almak.ta güçlük çektiğ.i görüldü.** 'It was observed that the patient was having trouble θ breathing.' *1010:9.* adversity: - have trouble; *1012:11.* difficulty: - have difficulty. → = **zorlan-** 3 , =

{zorlukla/güçlükle} karşılaş- → karşılaş- 3.

hasret çek- '- long for, - yearn for, - miss /θ/ sb or sth absent' [A. **hasret** 'longing, yearning']: • Note the two patterns: a) **bir şey.E hasret çek-: Türkiye'ye geldiğimden beri {a: vatanım.A/b: ailem.E/c: arkadaşlarım.A/d: Amerikan yemekler.i.nE} hasret çekiyorum.** 'Since coming to Turkey I have missed {a: θ my country/b: θ my family/c: θ my friends/d: θ American food}.' b) **bir şey.İN hasret.İ.ni çek-:** lit., ** '- endure the longing OF sth': **Türkiye'ye geldiğimden beri {a: vatanım.İN/b: ailem.İN/c: arkadaşlarım.İN/d: Amerikan yemekleri.NİN} hasret.İ.ni çekiyorum.** Same translation as under a} above. • Note the following possibility without **çek-:** * **Uzun süredir Türk yemekler.i.nE hasret.İM.** '{I have missed θ/I've been longing FOR} some Turkish food for a long time.' *100:16.* desire: - wish for; *991:7.* insufficiency: - want. → = **ara-** 4, = **özle-**.

masraf çek- '- foot the bill, - pay', *informal, jocular* [A. **masraf** 'expense, outlay']: S: **Bu gece dışarda yemek yiyelim mi?** 'Q: Shall we eat out tonight?' C: **Masrafları sen çekersen olur.** 'A: Sure, if you foot the bill [lit., If you foot the bill, it's OK].' For *formal* equivalents, → = **masraf gör-** → gör- 4, = **masraf karşıla-** → karşıla- 2, = **masraf {et-/yap-}**, = **öde-**, **masrafa gir-** ['- spend a lot of money on sth or to get sth done, - have a lot of expenses, - incur great expense']. *729:15.* finance, investment: - finance.

sıkıntı çek- '- have difficulties, troubles, - suffer annoyance, inconvenience' [**sıkıntı** 'distress, trouble, difficulty, annoyance']: **Yeni doğmuş bebeğimizle İzmir'den Antalya'ya giderken otobüste çok sıkıntı çektik.** 'While going from Izmir to Antalya with our new baby, we had a lot of {problems/troubles}.' Often '- be in financial straits, difficult financial circumstances.' • Note the compound in the following: **Geçen yıldan beri para sıkıntı.sı çekiyoruz.**

'We've been having money problems since last year.' **Çocuklarımızın bizim çektiğimiz acı ve sıkıntıları çekmemeleri için çok çabaladık.** 'We did our very best so that our children would not [have to] endure the pain and troubles that we endured.' *1012:11*. difficulty: - have difficulty.

üzüntü çek- [üzüntü 'distress; unhappiness, sorrow, sadness, regret'] **(1)** '- endure sorrow, sadness, - be depressed, sad': **Ailesini bir trafik kazasında kaybetmiş, yıllardır üzüntü çekiyor.** 'He lost his family in a {car/traffic} accident. He has been depressed for years.' *112:16*. sadness: - lose heart. → **acı çek-** ['- suffer, - endure pain, - be in pain', physical or mental].
(2) /DIğI için/ '- feel regret, sorrow, - be sorry /{that/on account of/because/for}/', a past action: **Öğretmene yalan söylediğim için çok üzüntü çekiyorum.** 'I'm very sorry {that/because} I told the teacher a lie.' *113:6*. regret: - regret. → = **pişman ol-** → **ol-** 12.

vicdan azabı çek- /DIğI için/ '- feel pangs of conscience, - feel guilty /{on account of/for}/' [A. **vicdan** (. -) 'conscience', A. **azap** (. -) 'pain, torment', **vicdan azabı** 'pangs of conscience']: **Ona yalan söylediğim için vicdan azabı çekiyorum.** 'I feel pangs of conscience for having told him a lie.' *113:6*. regret: - regret.

yalnızlık çek- '- be lonely' [**yalnızlık** 'loneliness']: **Eğer yalnızlık çekiyorsan, biz.e gel.** 'If you're lonely, come on over [lit., come to us].' *584:7*. seclusion: - seclude oneself; *871:6*. oneness: - stand alone.

zorluk çek-. → **{güçlük/zorluk} çek-** above.

6 '- subject, - expose /to/' *643:4* imposition: - impose: **sorguya çek-** '- cross-examine, - question, - interrogate, - grill, - subject /to/ interrogation' [**sorgu** 'interrogation, grilling, cross-examination']: **Gazeteciler basın toplantısında Başbakan.ı sorgu.yA çektiler.** 'The reporters questioned the prime minister at the press conference.' **Polis hırsız.ı sorgu.yA çekti.** 'The police cross-examined the thief.'

Öğretmen kopya çeken çocuğ.u sorgu.yA çekti. 'The teacher questioned the child who had copied [from another student].' *937:21*. inquiry: - interrogate.

7 '- photograph, etc.': **film çek-** '- make a movie, film, - film', subj.: BOTH amateur and professional film makers [F. **film**]: **Ünlü film yönetmeni Atıf Yılmaz bu yıl üç film çekti.** 'The famous movie director Atıf Yılmaz made three movies this year.' **Bütün gün kız.ı.nın film.i.ni çekti.** 'He spent the whole day {making a movie of/filming} his daughter.' *704:28*. show business, theater: - dramatize; *714:14*. photography: - photograph. → = **film çevir-** 2 → **çevir-** 3.

{resim/fotoğraf} çek- '- take {pictures/photographs} /of/, - photograph' [A. **resim** (reSMi) 'picture']: **Tatilde ailem.in pek çok resm.i.ni çektim.** 'During the holidays I took many pictures of my family.' **S: Resim çekebilir miyim?** 'S: May I take pictures?' **C: Hayır, resim çekmek yasak.** 'A: No, it's forbidden to take pictures.' **S: Resminizi çekebilir miyim?** 'Q: May I take your picture?' **C: * Hay hay, çekin.** 'A: {Of course/Sure}, go right ahead.' *714:14*. photography: - photograph.

8 '- copy': **fotokopi çek-** '- make a photocopy of, - photocopy': **Şu.nun bir fotokopi.si.ni çeker misin lütfen?** 'Would you please make a photocopy of this?' **Bütün kitab.ın fotokopi.si.ni çektim.** 'I made a photocopy of the whole book.' *784:8*. copy: - copy.

kopya çek- [It. **kopya** 'copy']: **(1)** '- copy illegitimately', that is, - cheat, - crib: **Öğrenci kopya çektiğ.i.ni inkâr etti.** 'The student denied that he had copied [the material].' *356:18*. deception: - cheat; *784:8*. copy: - copy.
(2) * '- cheat by exchanging information ORALLY': **Öğretmen: Kopya çekmey.E utanmıyor musun?** 'Teacher: Aren't you ashamed OF cheating?' **Öğrenci: Kopya çekmiyordum öğretmenim.** 'Student: I wasn't cheating, teacher.' **Öğretmen: Yalan söyleme! Ahmet'in ikinci sorunun cevabını sana söylediğ.i.ni duydum.** 'Teacher:

Don't lie! I heard Ahmet telling you the answer to the second question.' *356:18*. deception: - cheat.

kopyasını çek- '- make a copy of': **Bütün kitab.ın kopya.sı.nı çektim.** 'I made a copy of the whole book.' *784:8*. copy: - copy. → = **kopya et-**, = **kopyasını çıkar-** → çıkar- 7.

* **temize çek-** '- recopy, - rewrite, - make a clean or fresh copy of a piece of writing' [P. **temiz** 'clean']: **Bugün derste tuttuğum notları temiz.E çekiyorum.** 'I'm {recopying/making a fresh copy of} the notes [that] I took in class today.' **Yazdıklar.ın.ı okuyamıyorum, lütfen temiz.E çeker misin?** 'I can't read what you've written. Would you please {rewrite it?/make a clean copy?}' *784:8*. copy: - copy.

9 '- send': **faks çek-** /A/ '- send a fax /to/': **Yakınlarda faks çekebileceğim bir yer var mı?** 'Is there a place nearby where I can send a fax?' **Bu dilekçem.in saat 5'e kadar okul.a yetişme.si gerekiyor. Hemen faks çekebilir misin?** 'This {application/petition} of mine must get to the school by 5 o'clock. Can you send a fax {right away/immediately}?' **Bura.dan okul.a faks çekmem mümkün mü acaba?** 'I wonder if I could send a fax to the school from here? [lit., ** Is my sending a fax to the school from here possible?]' *347:19*. communications: - telegraph. → = **faks gönder-, faksla-** ['- fax sth /to/'].

tel çek- /A/ '- send a wire /to/, - wire /θ/', today used mostly only for banking [tel 'wire']: **S: Los Angeles'daki bankam.A tel çekebilir misiniz?** 'Q: Can you wire θ my bank in Los Angeles?' **C: Elbette çekeriz, merak etmeyin.** 'A: Of course we can [lit., we will wire], don't worry.' *347:19*. communications: - telegraph.

10 '- take, - last', time: * **Gideceğimiz yer buradan taksiyle ne kadar çekiyor?** 'How long does it take to get there by taxi? [lit., ** How long does the place we are going to go to take from here?]' *811:4b*. continuity: for sth - continue;

820:6. time: - spend time. → = **sur-3**, = {**vakit/zaman**} **al-** → al- 1.

11 '- shrink, - become smaller': {**Yün kazağım/Gömleğim/ Elbisem**} **yıkandıktan sonra çekti.** '{My wool sweater/My shirt/My suit} shrank after it was washed.' *260:9*. contraction: - shrink.

çekidüzen ver-. → ver- 1.

çekin- [ir] /{A/DAn}/ '- hesitate /to/, - feel, or - be hesitant, reluctant, embarrassed /to/ do sth, not - dare /to/ do sth, *less frequently* - fear' [**çek-** + refl. suf. **-In.** ADJ. **çekingen** 'shy, reluctant']: * **Söyleyecekleriniz olduğunu hissediyorum.** * **Çekinmeyin.** 'You look like [lit., I sense that] you want to say something [lit., that you have sth to say]. * [Go ahead,] don't hesitate.' **Bu hastanede hastalar sorunlarını çekinmeden anlatabiliyorlar.** 'In this hospital patients can tell of their concerns without being embarrassed.' **Hiçbir grup.TAN çekindiğim, korktuğum yok.** 'I'm not intimidated BY or afraid OF any group.' Reluctance to carry out an action: /{A/DAn}/ on the preceding verb: **Eğer bir problemin olursa lütfen beni** {**aramay.A/ aramak.TAN**} **çekinme.** 'If you have a problem, please don't hesitate TO look me up [lit., 'seek me out', i.e., in person or by phone].' **Öğretmene aynı soruyu ikinci defa** {**sormay.A/sormak.TAN**} **çekindim.** 'I hesitated {TO ask} the teacher the same question the second time.' **Küçük çocuk köpeği** {**sevmey.E/sevmek.TEN**} **çekindi.** 'The little child hesitated TO pet the dog.' **Tanımadığım insanlardan hediye** {**almay.A/ almak.TAN**} **çekinirim.** 'I hesitate TO accept presents from people I don't know.' **Akşamları sokakta yalnız** {**yürümey.E/ yürümek.TEN**} **çekinirim.** 'I hesitate TO walk about alone [on the street] in the evenings.' **Uzattığım parayı çekin.erek aldı.** 'He hesitantly took the money I held out [to him].'

Reluctance to carry out an action in sb's presence: **a)** Person alone 'as object': /DAn/ on the noun designating the person: * **Sigara iç.me.sem iyi olur, babam.DAN çekiniyorum.** 'It would be better if I didn't smoke. I'm reluctant to do so in front of my father.', i.e., He wouldn't like it. **Hakan hiç kimse.DEN çekinmez, herkes.E karşı dobra dobra konuşur.** 'Hakan isn't afraid OF anyone. He speaks frankly {to/with} everyone.' **b)** Person and action together: The following elements, all designating presence, follow the noun designating the person: **yanında** 'in the presence of [lit., at the side of]', **huzurunda** 'in the presence of', *more frequent in formal* contexts; **varken** '{in the presence of/when sb is around}'; /{A/DAn}/ is on the verb: **Babam.I N {yan.ı.nda/ huzur.u.nda} sigara içmey.e çekiniyorum.** '{I'm reluctant/I don't dare} to smoke in front of my father [lit., {at my father's side/in my father's presence}].' **Babam varken sigara içmey.e çekiniyorum.** 'I'm reluctant to smoke when my father's around.' **Hakim.in huzur.u.nda her şey.İ anlatmay.a çekindim.** 'I was reluctant to tell the judge everything [lit., tell everything in the presence of the judge].' **Babam.IN {yan.ı.nda/huzur.u.nda} evlilik {konusunda/hakkında} konuş-may.a çekiniyorum.** '{I don't feel like talking/I'm hesitant to talk} to my father [lit., in my father's presence] about marriage.' *325:4.* unwillingness: - demur; *362:7.* irresolution: - hesitate. → = /{DA/A}/ **tereddüt et-.**

çektir- [ir] [çek- + caus. suf. -DIr] **1** /A/ '- have sth towed, - have /θ/ sb tow sth': **Bozulan arabamı en yakın tamirci.yE çektirdim.** '{I had my car, which had broken down, towed to the nearest repair shop./I had my car, which had broken down, towed BY the nearest repair shop./I had the θ nearest repair shop tow my car.}' *904:4.* pulling: - pull.

2 /A/ '- have sth pulled, extracted, - have /θ/ sb pull, extract sth': **diş çektir-** '- have teeth pulled': **İki dişimi çektirdim.** 'I had two of my teeth pulled.' **Dişini kim.E çektirdin?** 'θ Who did you have pull your tooth?' *91:24.* therapy: - treat; *904:4.* pulling: - pull.

3 /A/ '- have taken, - have /θ/ sb take', pictures, photographs: {**resim/ fotoğraf**} **çektir-** '- have {pictures/photographs} taken, - {have/let} /θ/ sb take {pictures/

photographs}': **Bu resimleri kim.E çektirdin?** 'θ Who did you have take these pictures?' **Kız.ım.ın resm.i.ni çektirip teyzesine yolladım.** 'I had my daughter's picture taken and sent it off to her maternal aunt.' **Vesikalık resim çektirmek istiyorum. * Nere.yE çektirebilirim?** 'I want to have a passport picture taken. * θ Where can I have it taken?' **Hırsız resmini çektirmek istemedi.** 'The thief didn't want to {a: have his picture taken./b: {have/let} anyone take his picture.}' *714:14.* photography: - photograph.

röntgen çektir- '- have an X-ray [taken]' [G. röntgen 'X-ray']: **Geçen sene hastanede genel bir muayene olmuş, birçok {röntgen/röntgen filmleri} çektirmiştim.** 'Last year I was given a physical [lit., ** A general examination occurred] at the hospital and had a number of {X-rays} taken.' *714:14.* photography: - photograph.

4 /A/ '- make /θ/ sb suffer, - cause /θ/ sb to suffer, - cause /θ/ sb trouble, - make trouble /FOR/': **Bu çocuk ban.A çok çektirdi.** 'This child has caused me a lot of trouble.' **Benim çektiklerimi Allah başka kimse.yE çektirmesin.** 'May God not make θ anyone else suffer what I have endured.' *96:16a.* distress: - distress; *98:15.* unpleasantness: - vex.

çektiril- [ir] /{tarafından/CA}/ '- be towed away /by/' [çektir- + pass. suf. -Il]: **Burası özel oto parktır. Yabancı araçlar çektirilecektir.** 'This is a private parking area. Unauthorized [lit., ** Foreign] vehicles will be towed away.' *352:7* publication: poster: * specific signs; *904:4.* pulling: - pull.

çeliş- [ir] /lA/ '- contradict one another [ideas, behavior], - be in conflict, - be contraditory, in contradiction /with/' [ADJ. çelişkili 'contradictory, incompatible']: **Lâboratuar sonuçları teori İLE çelişiyor.** 'The results obtained in the laboratory {contradict θ/conflict WITH} the theory.' **Konuşmacının sözleri birbiri.yLE çelişiyor.** 'The speaker's words were {contradictory/in contradiction WITH one another}.' * **Ali'nin söyledikleri İLE yaptıkları çelişiyor.** '{What Ali says AND what he does are in conflict./Ali's

words and deeds are in conflict.}'
**Hâkim, baba İLE oğlu.nun
ifadeler.i.nin çeliştiğ.i.ni
söyledi.** 'The judge said that the
testimony of the father AND his son
were contradictory.' *451:6.*
opposition: - contradict; *788:5.*
disagreement: - disagree.

çene çal-. → **çal-** 2.

çenesini tut-. → {çenesini/dilini}
tut-. → **tut-** 4.

çevir- [ir] **1** '- turn, - rotate': **Kapı.nın
tokmağ.ı.nı çevirdi fakat kapı
açılmadı.** 'She turned the handle of
the door, but the door didn't open.'
914:9. rotation: - rotate.

* **taksi çevir-** '- hail a cab, taxi':
**Kazadan sonra * üst.üm.ü
baş.ım.ı toparlayıp hemen yola
çıktım ve bir taksi çevirdim.**
'After the accident, * I tidied myself
up [lit., ** tidied up my clothes], set
out on my way, and hailed a
{cab/taxi}.' *420:11.* command: -
summon; *517:21.* signs, indicators: -
gesture.

2 /A, A doğru/ '- turn sth /to,
toward/': **Şoför kazayı önlemek
için direksiyonu {sağ.a/sol.a}
çevirdi.** 'The driver turned [the
steering wheel] {to the right/to the
left} to prevent an accident.'
**Televizyon anten.i.ni kuzey.e
çevirdi.** 'He turned the television
antenna to the north.' **Yüzünü
ban.A doğru çevir.** 'Turn your
face toward me.' **Çiçekler
yapraklarını güneş.e doğru
çevirir.** 'Plants turn their leaves
toward the sun.' *914:9.* rotation: -
rotate. → = **döndür-** 1.

3 '- turn over, - turn, - flip': **Sayfayı
çevir.** 'Turn the page.' **Omleti
çevir de yanmasın.** '{Turn/Flip}
the omelette over so [that] it doesn't
burn.' *205:5.* inversion: - invert.

arkasını çevir- [arka 'back, back
part of anything'] **(1)** [sırt 'the back
of a person or animal'] /A/ '- turn
around, - turn one's back /to/': **Beni
görünce {arka.sı.nı/sırt.ı.nı}
çevirdi ve gitti.** 'When he saw me,
he turned around [lit., turned {his
back}] and walked off.' *914:9.*
rotation: - rotate. → = {arkasını/
sırtını} **dön-** → **dön-** 4.

(2) '- turn over', lit., ** '- turn its
back', i.e., the back of an object: *
**Bütün resimler.in arka.sı.nı
çevirip imzasını attı.** 'He turned
all the pictures over [lit., ** turned
the backs of all the pictures] and
signed them.' *205:5.* inversion: -
invert.

film çevir- [F. **film** 'film, movie']
(1) '- act in a movie or film, - make
a movie [subj: actor]': **Yeşilçam'ın
meşhur film artisti Türkân
Şoray kaç film çevirdiğ.i.ni
hatırlamıyor.** 'The famous
Yeşilçam movie star Türkân Şoray
doesn't remember how many films
she has made [i.e., acted in].'
Yeşilçam [lit., 'Greenpine'] is the
Turkish equivalent of Hollywood.
704:29. show business, theater: - act.
→ = **filmde oyna-** → **oyna-** 3.
(2) '- produce, - make a movie',
subj: producer, professional film
maker: **Ünlü film yönetmeni Atıf
Yılmaz bu yıl üç film çevirdi.**
'The famous movie director Atıf
Yılmaz made three movies this year.'
704:28. show business, theater: -
dramatize; *714:14.* photography: -
photograph. → = **film çek-** → **çek-**
7.

4 /I/ '- turn /TO/ [page 5, TV
channel], - switch /TO/.' If the
instrument is already on and you want
to make a change: '- put on, - turn on
[TV channel, radio station]':
Sayfa.yI çevirin. 'Turn the page.',
i.e., Turn to the next page. * **İkinci
sayfa.yI çevirin.** 'Turn TO page 2
[lit., ** Turn the second page].' * **S:
Hangi kanal.I çevireyim?** 'Q:
Which [TV] channel should I {put
on/turn TO/switch TO}? [lit., **
Which channel should I turn?]' **C:
Üçüncü kanal.I çevir.** 'A: {Put
on/Turn to/Switch to} channel three
[lit., ** Turn the third channel].' → =
aç- 3. # **Çevir şu kanalı! Bu
{filmi/müziği} beğenmedim.**
'Switch the channel! I don't like this
{movie/music}.' → = **değiştir-** 1.
371:14. choice: - select; *914:9.*
rotation: - rotate.

5 /lA/ '- surround /with/, - place sth
/around/ sth else': **Bahçe.yİ
duvar.LA çevirdi.** 'He placed a
wall around the garden [lit., He
surrounded the garden with a wall].'
209:6. environment: - surround.

6 /DAn, A/ '- translate /from, INTO/': **Yaşar Kemal'in romanlarını [Türkçe'DEN] İngilizce'yE çevirmek kolay değildir.** 'It's not easy to translate Yaşar Kemal's novels [FROM Turkish] INTO English.' **Tercüman Amerikalı iş adamının konuşmalarını Türkçe'yE çeviriyordu.** 'The interpreter was translating the speeches of the American businessman INTO Turkish.' *341:12.* interpretation: - translate. → = **tercüme et-**, = **aktar-** 2.

7 '- dial [a phone number]': **A: Ayşe ile {görüşebilir/ konuşabilir} miyim?** 'A: May I please {speak} with Ayşe [f.]?' **Görüş-** is always appropriate, **konuş-** is perhaps *less formal.* **B: * Burada Ayşe DİYE biri yok.** 'B: There's no one here {BY THE NAME OF/CALLED} Ayşe.' **A: Özür dilerim, {yanlış numara/ yanlış numarayı} çevirmişim.** 'A: Excuse me, I seem to have dialed {a wrong number/the wrong number}.' *974:12.* error: - misdo. **Doğru numarayı çevirdiğim{.E/.DEN} eminim, fakat telefon.A {a: çıkan/* b: bakan/c: cevap veren} olmadı.** 'I'm sure θ [that] I dialed the right number, but there was no answer [lit., ** {a: the person who came to the phone/b: the one who looked after the phone/c: the one who answered the phone} did not turn up].' *347:18.* communication: - telephone; *914:9.* rotation: - rotate.

8 /A/ '- turn /INTO/, - become /θ/' [I.]: **Akşam.A doğru yağmur dolu.yA çevirdi.** 'Toward evening the rain turned INTO hail.' *851:6.* change: - be changed. → = **dön-** 6, = **dönüş-**, = **kesil-** 5, = **ol-** 1.

9 /A/ '- turn sth /INTO/ sth else, - convert sth /INTO/ sth else': **Yazın deniz kenarındaki evimiz.İ motel.E çeviririz.** 'In the summer we turn our house at the seaside INTO a motel.' **Eski pantolonu.nU şort.A çevirdi.** 'He turned his old trousers into shorts.' *857:11.* conversion: - convert. → = **döndür-** 2.

çığlık at-. → **at-** 1.

çık- [ar] /DAn, DAn/ **1** '- come out /OF, {THROUGH/BY WAY OF}/, - leave, - get /OFF/': **S: Hoca.M, * önemli bir işim var; bugün biraz erken çıkabilir miyim?** 'Q: {Professor/Teacher} [lit., ** {MY professor/MY teacher}, the common Turkish form of address to a professor or teacher], * I have an important matter to attend to. May I leave a little early today?' **C: * Rica ederim, tabii [çıkabilirsiniz].** 'A: [* This first expression is usually not translated in this situation.] Of course [you may leave (early)].' **{a: Okul.DAN/b: Ders.TEN/c: Konser.DEN/d: İş.TEN/e: Müzik kursu.nDAN} kaçta çıkıyorsunuz?** '[At] What time do you get out {a: OF school/b: OF class/c: OF the concert/d: OF work/e: OF the music class}?' **Gökhan bu tren.LE geleceğini söylemişti fakat tren.DEN çıkmadı.** 'Gökhan said that he was going to {be on/come in on [lit., come ON]} this train, but he didn't get OFF the train.' → ≠ **bin-** 1. # **Saat 1'de kapı.DAN çıktım.** 'I went OUT the door at 1 o'clock.' Proverb: **Rüşvet kapı.DAN girince insaf baca.DAN çıkar.** 'When bribery enters THROUGH the door, {justice/fairness} leaves THROUGH the chimney.' → ≠ **gir-.** In response to an untimely phone call: **Ben şimdi {çıkıyordum/çıkmak üzereydim}, * yarın konuşsak olmaz mı?** 'I {was just about to step out}. * How about if we talk tomorrow? [lit., ** If we talk tomorrow, won't that do?]' *188:6.* departure: - depart. → = **ayrıl-** 3. # **Bu kâğıt parçası şu kitap.TAN çıktı.** 'This piece of paper came {OUT OF/from} that book.' At a meeting: *** Her kafadan bir ses çıkıyordu.** 'Everyone was speaking all at once [lit., ** A sound was coming out of each head].', i.e., often implying a clash of opinions. *** Kimseden ses çıkmadı.** 'No one said a word [lit., ** a sound came from no one].' **Çıkmayan can.dan ümit kesilmez.** 'Where there's life there's hope [lit., ** Hope is not cut off from a soul that has not left the body].' **Ok yay.DAN çıktı.** 'The arrow has left θ the bow', i.e., It's too late to solve the problem. *190:11.* emergence: - emerge; *845: * 21.* lateness: PHR. it's too late.

akıldan çık- '- slip /θ/ one's mind, - forget' [A. akıl (aKLı) 'mind, memory'], lit., '- leave one's mind': **S: İstediğim kitabı getirdin mi?** 'Q: Did you bring the book I asked for?' **C: Kusura bakma akl.IM.dan çıkmış, yarın getireyim.** 'A: I'm sorry. I seem to have forgotten. I'll bring it tomorrow.' **Böyle şeyler akıldan çıkıp gidiyor.** 'Such things [easily] slip one's mind.' *989:7.* forgetfulness: - be forgotten. → = unut-, ≠ akılda kal- → kal- 1.

internetten çık- '- log off, - get off θ the Internet': **Lütfen internetten çıkar mısın, telefon açmam gerekiyor.** 'Please get off θ the Internet. I have to make a phone call.' *1041:18.* computer science: - computerize. → ≠ internete bağlan- → bağlan- 3.

* işin içinden çık- [iş 'matter', iç 'the inside of sth'], lit., ** '- emerge from the inside of the matter': (1) '- escape from a difficult situation, predicament; - get out of or - avoid doing something complicated': **Görmedim, duymadım, bilmiyorum de.mekle iş.in iç.i.nden çıkabileceğini mi sanıyorsun?** 'Do you think that by saying "I didn't see it, I didn't hear it, I don't know" you'll be able to get out of this situation?' **Bu işin içinden nasıl çıkabileceğimizi * bilemiyorum.** 'I don't see [lit., ** can't know] how we're going [lit., to be able] to get out of this predicament.' *368:7.* avoidance: - evade. = işin içinden sıyrıl-.
(2) '- work out a solution for something complicated, - resolve a difficult problem, - figure sth out': * **Bütün gece düşünüp taşındı, fakat işin içinden çıkamadı.** 'He thought and thought the whole night, but he couldn't solve the problem.' **Anlamaya çalıştım ama işin içinden çıkamadım.** 'I tried to understand it, but I just couldn't figure it out.' *939:2.* solution: - solve.
işinden çık- '- leave or - quit /θ/ one's job' [iş 'work, job']: **Atillâ geçen ay işi.nDEN çıktı.** 'Atillâ quit θ his job last month.' *188:9.* departure: - quit; *448:2.* resignation: - resign. → = görevinden ayrıl- → ayrıl- 3, istifa et- ['- resign /from/'].

komadan çık- '- come out of or - emerge from a coma': **Allaha şükür Selim koma.dan çıkmış, hızla iyileşiyormuş.** 'Thank God Selim has come out of the coma and is recovering rapidly.' *190:11.* emergence: - emerge; *392:8.* improvement: - rally, - get better. → ≠ komaya gir-.

* sözünden çık- '- disobey, not - do what sb says' [söz 'word, utterance'], lit., ** '- leave, - depart /from/ one's word': * **Maşallah çok uslu bir çocuktur, hiç söz.ÜMÜZ.den çıkmaz.** 'Good for him! He's a very well-behaved child. He always does exactly what WE tell him to do [lit., ** He never departs from OUR words].' * **Maşallah** means 'What God does [is well done]' and implies that His will should be accepted. This word is often used in the sense of 'May God protect him from evil' and therefore to ward off the evil eye. As above, it often precedes words of admiration or praise. *327:6.* disobedience: - disobey. → = the negative of the following: ≠ {lâf/söz} dinle- → 1 dinle- 2; ≠ sözünü tut- 2 → tut- 5; ≠ /A/ uy- 6.

2 '- go out to': alışverişe çık- '- go /θ/ shopping' [alışveriş 'shopping', lit., alış 'taking, buying', veriş 'giving']: **Ablamla hafta sonunda alışveriş.E çıktık.** 'On the weekend my older sister and I went θ shopping.' *733:8.* purchase: - shop. → = çarşıya çık directly below, alışveriş yap- ['- shop, - do shopping'] → yap- 3.

çarşıya çık- '- go /θ/ shopping', lit., '- go /to/ the market': **Çarşı.yA çıkıyorum. Saat 5'te dönerim. Bir şey lâzım mı?** 'I'm going θ shopping. I'll be back at 5 o'clock. Do you need anything [lit., ** Is anything necessary]?' **Yeni evimize eşya almak için [hepimiz] çarşı.yA çıktık.** 'We [all] went θ shopping to purchase furniture for our new house.' *733:8.* purchase: - shop. → = alışverişe çık-, alışveriş yap- ['- shop, - do shopping'] → yap- 3.

dışarı[yA] çık- [dışarı 'out, outside'] (1) '- go or - step {out/outside}', the place left is not indicated: **S: Hoca nerede?** 'Q: Where's the {teacher/professor}?' **C: Dışarı[.yA] çıktı.** 'A: He's gone

82

{out/outside}.' * **Herkes dışarı çıksın. Kütüphane boşaltılacak.** 'Everybody out! The library is going to be evacuated.' *190:12.* emergence: - exit. → ≠ **içeri[.ye] gir-**.

* **/DAn/ dışarı[.yA] çık-** '- leave /θ/ [a place]', lit., ** '- leave from [the place] to the outside': **Biraz sonra annem elinde boş çay tepsisiyle oda.DAN dışarı[.yA] çıktı.** 'A little later my mother left θ the room with an empty tea tray in her hand.' • Note: the noun designating the place left has the suffix **-DAn**. *190:12.* emergence: - exit. → ≠ **/DAn/ içeri[.yE] gir-**.

(2) '- have a bowel movement *or* BM, - defecate': **Doktor: Bugün hiç dışarı.[ya] çıktınız mı?** 'Doctor: Have you had a bowel movement today?' **Hasta: Hayır, hiç çıkmadım.** 'Patient: No, I haven't.' *12:13.* excretion: - defecate. → = **büyük aptes yap-** → yap- 3, **ihtiyacını gör-** ['- defecate, - urinate'] → gör- 4, **tuvalet yap-** ['- have a bowel movement *or* BM, - urinate, - do one's business, - use the facilities, the restroom; - make one's toilet, i.e., usually for a woman to dress or to arrange her hair'], **tuvalete git-** ['- go to the restroom, - use the toilet'] → git- 1a.

gezmeye çık- '- go {out for a walk/θ sight-seeing}' [**gez-** '- go or - walk about, - tour, - sightsee, - stroll']: **Ben gezmey.E çıkıyorum, gelmek isteyen var mı?** 'I'm going θ sight-seeing. Does anyone want to come? [lit., Is there anyone who wants to come?]' *177:21.* travel: - journey; *917:6.* spectator: - sightsee. → **yürüyüşe çık-** ['- go out /for/ a walk'] → çık- 2, **dolaş- 1** ['- go, - walk, - wander, or - stroll about or around, - make one's way through, - cover ground', usually on foot], **gez-** ['- go or - walk about, - tour, - sightsee, - stroll'], **hava al- 1** ['- breathe fresh air, - get a breath of fresh air'] → al- 1, **seyahat et-** ['- travel or - take a trip /to/'].

* **satışa çık-** '- go /ON/ sale', i.e., become available for purchase, not necessarily at a reduced price [**satış** 'sale']: **{a: Mevsimlik/b: Yazlık/c: Kışlık/d: Son moda} kıyafetlerimiz hafta.ya satış.A çıkıyor.** 'Our {a: spring/b: summer/c: winter/d: latest} fashions go ON sale next week.' **{Son model arabalarınız/Yeni ürünleriniz} ne zaman satış.A çıkacak?** 'When will {your latest model cars/your new products} go ON sale?' *734:10.* sale: - put up for sale.

sokağa çık- '- go out [from the house] /into/ the street' [**sokak** 'street']: **S: Baba, sokağ.A çıkabilir miyim?** 'Q: Dad, may I go out?' **C: Olur yavrum, çık.** 'A: All right {dear/my child}, go.'

tatile çık- '- go ON {vacation/holiday}, - leave FOR {vacation/the holiday[s]}, - begin a vacation' [A. **tatil** (- .) 'vacation, holiday']: **Bu yaz Ahu ile tatil.E çıkmak istemiyorum.** 'I don't want to go ON vacation with Ahu [f.] this summer.' **Tatil.E çık.mak İÇİN acele ediyor.** 'He is hurrying [IN ORDER] TO leave FOR (vacation/the holidays}.' **Burhan'la tatile çıkmanı istemiyorum.** 'I don't want you to go on vacation with Burhan.' **İlk ve orta öğretimde okuyan milyonlarca öğrenci, yarın * 3 aylık yaz tatiline çıkıyor.** 'Tomorrow millions of primary and secondary students [lit., ** students studying in primary and secondary education] * will begin a 3-month summer vacation.' *20:9.* rest, repose: - vacation. → = **tatile gir-**, = **tatile git-** → git- 1a, = **tatil yap-** → yap- 3.

yemeğe çık- '- go out {for/to} dinner, - dine out': * **Ne dersin, bu akşam yemeğ.E çıkalım mı, sonra da sinemaya gideriz istersen.** 'How about going out {for/to} dinner this evening [lit., * What do you say: Shall we go out {for/to} dinner this evening]? And afterwards we can [lit., we'll] go to a movie if you like.' For **çık-** with specific meals, **için** is used instead of the dative case: **Ahmet bey {kahvaltı/öğle yemeği/akşam yemeği} için çıktı, * birazdan gelir.** 'Ahmet bey has gone out for {breakfast/lunch/dinner [lit., the evening meal]}. * He'll be back shortly.' *8:21.* eating: - dine.

yola çık- '- start off, - set out or - leave /ON/ a {trip/journey}, - set out /ON/ the road', person on foot or vehicle [yol 'road, way']: **Erken yol.A çıkarsak zamanında erişiriz.** 'If we {leave/set out} early, we'll get there in time.' **Ne olur ne olmaz, * her ihtimal.E karşı sen iki saat önce yol.A çık.** 'Just in case, * {just to be safe/lit., against any eventuality}, set out two hours early.' **Sevgi yarım saat önce yol.A çıktı.** 'Sevgi {left/set out} half an hour ago.' **8:30 tren.i yol.A çıkmış.** 'The 8:30 train has left.' Proverb: **Deli ile çıkma yola, başına getirir bela.** 'Don't set out ON a journey with a madman, he will cause you trouble [lit., ** will bring trouble to your head].' **Baş** 'head' here represents the whole person. *188:8.* departure: - set out; *817:7a.* beginning: - begin sth. → **yola koyul-,** = **hareket et- 2** [subj.: vehicle or person in vehicle], = **kalk- 2,** ≠ **var-,** ≠ **eriş- 1.**

yürüyüşe çık- '- go out /for/ a walk' [yürüyüş 'a walk, walking']: **Hava çok güzel. * Yürüyüş.E çıkalım mı?** 'The weather's very nice. * {Why don't we/lit., Shall we} go out FOR a walk?' *177:29.* travel: - go for a walk. → **dolaş- 1** [- go, - walk, - wander, or - stroll about or around, - make one's way through, - cover ground', usually on foot], **gez-** ['- go or - walk about, - tour, - sightsee, - stroll'], **hava al- 1** ['- breathe fresh air, - get a breath of fresh air'] → **al- 1, seyahat et-** ['- travel or - take a trip /to/'], **yürü- 1** ['- walk, - take a walk'].

3 '- appear /from/, - come out /OF/, - emerge /from/': **Petrol çıktıktan sonra ülkede ekonomik durum birdenbire gelişti.** 'After oil appeared, the economic situation in the country suddenly improved.' **Güneş çıktı, yürüyüş.E çıkalım mı?** 'The sun has come out, shall we go FOR a walk?' → = **güneş aç-** → **aç- 8,** = **güneş doğ-** → **doğ- 2,** ≠ **güneş bat-** → **bat- 1,** ≠ **hava karar-** ['for it - get or - grow dark']. **Ay çıktı.** 'The moon has come out.' → ≠ **ay kaybol-** → **kaybol-** → **ol- 12. Yıldızlar çıktı.** 'The stars have come out.' → ≠ **Yıldızlar kaybol-** → **kaybol-** → **ol- 12. Bebeğin {saçları/dişleri} çıkmaya başladı.** 'The baby's {hair has/teeth have} begun to appear.' * **Anneannem.de {şeker hastalığı/yüksek tansiyon}**

çıkınca * perhiz yapmaya başladı. 'When my [maternal] grandmother first developed {diabetes/high blood pressure} [lit., When {diabetes/high blood pressure} appeared in my (maternal) grandmother], * she went on a diet [lit., began to diet].' **Adam karısına: Ayten senden ayrılmak istiyorum.** 'A man to his wife: Ayten, I want to leave you.' **Karısı: * Bu da nere.DEN çıktı?** 'His wife: What in God's name! [lit., Where did that (idea) come FROM!]' **Önümüz.e çıkan fırsatları en iyi şekilde değerlendirmeliyiz.** 'We must make the most of [lit., ** take advantage in the best way of] the opportunities that appear before us [lit., ** to our front].' Proverb: **Ummadığın yer.den yılan çıkar.** 'A snake [i.e., evil, treachery] will appear from the place where you least [lit., don't] expect it.' *190:11.* emergence: - emerge.

/A/ '- lead /to/, - come out /{AT/ON}/': **S: Bu yol nere.yE çıkıyor?** 'Q: θ Where does this road {lead?/come out?}' **C: {Atatürk Bulvar.ı.nA/Taksim meydan.ı.nA} çıkıyor.** 'A: It {leads to/comes out ON} {Atatürk Boulevard/Taksim Square}.' **Ankara'ya giden otoyol.a nasıl çıkabilirim?** 'How can I get to the highway that goes to Ankara?' * **Çıkmaz yol.** '{Dead end./No through road.} [lit., ** Road that does not come out].' *190:11.* emergence: - emerge; *352:7.* publication: poster: * specific signs.

duman çık- /DAn/ 'for smoke - rise /from/, for sth - smoke' [duman 'smoke']: **Yangın söndü fakat hâlâ duman çıkıyor.** 'The fire has gone out, but there is still smoke [lit., smoke is still emerging].' The plural indicates a large quantity of smoke: **Enkazdan dumanlar çıkıyor.** 'The ruins are smoking [lit., Smoke is rising from the ruins].' **Kış geldi, bacalardan dumanlar {çıkmaya/tütmeye} başladı.** 'Winter has arrived. Smoke has begun to rise from the chimneys.' Proverb: **Ateş olmayan yerden duman çıkmaz.** 'Smoke does not appear from a place where there is no fire.' Where there's smoke there's fire. For '- smoke' as in '- smoke cigarettes', → **iç- 2.** *1018:23.* heat: - smoke, - fume.

karşı çık- /A/ '- oppose /θ/, - come out /AGAINST/, - object /to/, - say no /to/' [karşı 'opposite, against']: Öğrenciler, üniversitedeki öğrenci dernekler.i.nin kapat.ıl.ma.sı.nA karşı çıktılar. 'The students objected to the closing [lit., ** BEING closed] of the student associations at {the university/the college}.' Bakan kürtaj.ın serbest bırak.ıl.ma.sı ile ilgili öneri.yE karşı çıktı. 'The minister {came out against/opposed θ} the proposal to lift [lit., ** on the BEING lifted of] the prohibition against abortion.' Bu akşam sinemaya gitmek istemiyordum fakat Tufan çok ısrar edince karşı çıkamadım. 'I didn't want to go to the movies this evening, but when Tufan really insisted, I just couldn't say no [lit., I couldn't oppose her].' Böyle bir karar önüme gelirse ben kesinlikle karşı çıkarım. 'If I am faced with such a decision [lit., If such a decision comes before me], I will {certainly/definitely} oppose it.' 333:5. dissent: - dissent; 451:3. opposition: - oppose; 788:5. disagreement: - disagree. → = /A/ itiraz et-, /I/ protesto et- ['- protest /{θ/AGAINST}/'], reddet- 1 ['- refuse, - reject'].

karşısına çık- '- appear suddenly in front of, - bump into' [karşı 'opposite, against']: Yolda giderken Adnan karşı.M.A çıktı. 'While I was walking along the street, I bumped into Adnan [lit., Adnan suddenly appeared in front of ME].' 131:6. inexpectation: - be unexpected; 223:11. nearness: - meet.

meydana çık-. → directly below.

* {ortaya/meydana} çık- '- appear, - turn up, - come out, - turn out, - be revealed, - come forward' [orta 'middle, center, the space around', A. meydan 'open space, public square'], lit., ** '- come out to the middle', i.e., where it is apparent: {a: {Gerçeğ.in/Hakikat.in}/b: {Gerçek.LER.in/Hakikat-.LER.in}} ortaya çıkma.sı.nı istiyorum. 'I want {a: the truth}/b: the facts} to come out.' {Ateş/Deprem/Patlama} haber.i.nin asılsız olduğ.u ortaya çıktı. 'It turned out that the news of {the fire/the earthquake/the explosion} was incorrect [lit., without foundation].' Durum.un sanıl-

dığ.ı.ndan kötü ortaya çıkmıştı. 'The situation had turned out worse than expected [lit., thought].' Çocuğu kaçıran.ın üvey babası olduğ.u ortaya çıktı. 'It was revealed that the one who had abducted the child was the stepfather.' Some words of challenge: Kendi.nE güvenen ortaya çıksın! 'Let the person {who has confidence IN himself/with confidence IN himself} come forward!' 351:8. disclosure: - be revealed.

4 '- come up, - occur, - break out': {Savaş/Fırtına} çıktı. '{A battle/A storm} broke out.' → = kop- 2, = patla- 3. # Televizyon patlayınca yangın çıktı. 'When a television set exploded, a fire broke out.' S: Siz.ce III. [read: üçüncü] Dünya savaşı çıkar mı? 'Q: In your opinion will a third world war break out?' C: * Çıktı bile! 'A: It already has!' S: Bu akşam geliyor musunuz? 'Q: Are you coming this evening?' C: Maalesef bu akşam gelemiyeceğim. * Bir işim çıktı. 'A: Unfortunately I won't be able to come tonight. * Something [lit., ** A business of mine] has come up.' 830:5. event: - occur.

5 /DAn, A/ '- go up, - ascend, - climb, - mount /BY WAY OF, to/': {Yaşlı adam/Dedem} merdivenleri {a: ağır ağır/b: yavaş yavaş/c: dinlene dinlene/d: nefes nefese/e: oflaya puflaya/f: zar zor/g: güçlükle} çıkmış. '{The old man/My grandfather} climbed the stairs {a, b: slowly/c: resting along the way/d: {breathing heavily/out of breath}/e: panting/f, g: with difficulty}.' * Bilge hanım {koşar adımlar.la/koşar adım} merdivenleri çıktı. 'Bilge hanım ran up the stairs.' 174:8. swiftness: - speed; 401:5. haste: - make haste. * Merdivenler.DEN {a: dördüncü kat.a/b: beşinci kattaki oda.sı.na/c: çatı katı.na/d: üst kat.a} çıktı. 'She went up [the] stairs {a: to the fourth floor/b: to her room on the fifth floor/c: to the roof/d: {to the next floor/to a floor above/to the top floor}}.' Dağcılar zirve.yE üç günde çıkabildiler. 'The mountain climbers were able to reach [lit., climb to] the summit [of the mountain] in three days.' * Minare.yE çıkabilir miyiz?

'May we go up θ the minaret?' **Altuğ bu merdiven.DEN [yukarı(.ya)] çıktı.** 'Altuğ went up [BY WAY OF] {these stairs/this ladder}.' **Altuğ yukarı[.yA] çıktı.** 'Altuğ went θ up.', i.e., usually by stairs, ladder. **Adam.ın peş.i sıra bahçe.nin merdivenler.i.ni çıkmaya başladı.** 'Following the man, he began to climb the stairs of the garden.' **İtfaiyeciler evin duvarı.nA merdiven dayayıp teker teker [merdivenden] üst kat.a çıktılar.** 'The firemen propped a ladder AGAINST the wall of the house and climbed up to the top floor {one step at a time/step by step}.' Proverb: * **Her çıkış.ın bir iniş.i var.** 'What goes up must come down [lit., Every ascent has a descent].', often in reference to a person's position in society. *193:11.* ascent: - climb. → ≠ /DAn, A/ in- 1.

dağa çık- '- climb mountains, - go mountain climbing' [**dağ** 'mountain']: **Dağa çıkmay.a korkuyorum.** 'I'm afraid to go mountain climbing.' *193:11.* ascent: - climb. → = **tırman-** 1, ≠ [aşağıya] in- 1.

* **Sinirim tepe.m.e çıktı.** 'I'm really pissed off.' [**sinir** 'anger, irritation', **tepe** 'hill, peak', i.e., head], lit., ** 'My anger rose to my head': **Ne[re]den hatırlattın o herifi bana ya, sinirim tepeme çıktı yine.** 'How come you reminded me of that {guy/fellow} [now]? I'm really pissed off again!' *152:25b.* resentment, anger: expressions of.

6 '- rise, - go up, - increase /to/', prices, fever: **Irak'ın Kuveyt'i işgaliyle beraber petrol fiyatları birdenbire çıktı.** '[Together] with Irak's occupation of Kuwait, oil prices suddenly increased.' * **Dolar kaç lira olacak, çıkacak mı, inecek mi?** 'How many liras will there be to a dollar? Will it [i.e., the dollar] rise or fall?' → = **art-** 1, **fırla-** 2 ['- skyrocket, - increase or - rise suddenly, soar'], **pahalan-** ['- become more expensive, - increase in price'], = **tırman-** 2, = **yüksel-** 2, ≠ **düş-** 3, ≠ **in-** 4, **ucuzla-** ['- get cheaper, - drop in price']. **Hastanın ateşi sabaha doğru 40 derece.yE çıktı.** 'The patient's temperature rose to 40 degrees [i.e., centigrade or 104 Fahrenheit] toward morning.' *251:6.* increase: - grow, increase [i.]. → = **art-** 1, = **yüksel-** 2, ≠ **düş-** 3, ≠ **in-** 4.

7 '- turn out, - come out', well, badly: **Aldığım bilgisayar bozuk çıktı, geri göndereceğim.** 'The computer I bought turned out to be defective. I'm going to send it back.' **Seçtiğim karpuz {a: iyi/b: güzel/c: ham/d: kötü} çıktı.** 'The watermelon I chose turned out to be {a: good/b: fine/c: unripe/d: bad}.' **S: İstanbul'da çektiğimiz fotoğraflar nasıl çıktı?** 'Q: How did the pictures that we took in Istanbul turn out?' **C1: {a: Şahane/b: Çok güzel/c: Biraz bulanık/d: Flu/e: Kötü} çıktı.** 'A1: They turned out {a: splendidly/b: very nice/c: a little blurred/d: blurred/e: bad}.' **C2: Maalesef filmler {çıkmadı}, çünkü yandı.** 'A2: Unfortunately they [lit., the films] {didn't turn out/didn't come out} because they got over exposed [lit., ** they burned].' * **Meteoroloji {doğru/yanlış} çıktı.** 'The weather bureau {was/turned out to be} {correct/wrong}.' **Bakalım kim haklı çıkacak.** 'Well, let's see who turns out to be right.' * **{Ben sana demedim mi?/Ben dememiştim!} Bak, yine haklı çıktım.** 'Didn't I tell you? You see? I {was right/turned out to be right} again.' **Tüh, biz.E kazık atmışlar.** * **İpek DİYE aldığımız bluz polyester çıktı.** 'O damn, they've really ripped us off! * The blouse that we bought THINKING it was silk [lit., ** thinking it θ silk] turned out to be polyester.' * **Eski polis şefi hırsız çıktı.** 'The former police chief turned out to be a thief.' *830:7.* event: - turn out; *886:4.* effect: - result.

boşa çık- '- come to naught, not - be realized, - be dashed', hopes, expectations, dreams, efforts [**boş** 'vain, useless']: **Yıllarca kızımın doktor olmasını hayal etmiştim fakat {umutlarım/ çabalarım} boş.A çıktı.** 'For years I had dreamed that my daughter would become a doctor, but {my hopes/my efforts} came to nothing.' **Bir millî piyango bileti almıştım. Fakat sonuçları öğrenince hayallerim boş.A çıktı.** 'I had bought a national lottery ticket. But when I learned the results [of the drawing], my dreams were dashed.' 395:23. destruction: - perish; 473:6. loss: - go to waste; 910:3. shortcoming: - fall through. → boşa git- ['- be in vain, of no use, for nothing'] → git- 5.

meşgul çık- 'for the phone - be busy' [A. meşgul (. -) 'busy, occupied']: Ali Rıza'yı aradım ama meşgul çıktı. Biraz sonra tekrar ararım. 'I called up Ali Rıza, but the line was busy. I'll try again a little later.' Bu numara {hep/daima} meşgul çıkıyor. * [Sakın] yanlış olmasın. 'This number is {always} busy. * I hope I haven't dialed the wrong number [lit., ** let there not be a mistake].' Bayramda * Türkiye'yi aradım fakat hatlar hep meşgul çıktı. 'Over the vacation * I tried to get through to [lit., ** I sought] Turkey, but the lines were always busy.' 330:10. activity: - be busy.

8 '- come out, - appear, - be issued', news, publication: Fransa cumhurbaşkan.ı.nın eylül ayında Ankara'ya geleceğ.i gazetelerde çıktı. 'The news that the President of France was going to come to Ankara in September appeared in the papers [lit., ** The President of France's going to come to Ankara in September appeared in the papers].' Akşam gazetesi çıktı mı? '{Is the evening paper out [yet]?/lit., Has the evening paper come out [yet]?}' "Bilim ve Teknik" dergisi ay.DA bir [defa] çıkıyor. 'The journal "Science and Technology" comes out once θ a month.' 33:8. appearance: - appear.

9 /DAn/ '- be subtracted /from/': 84'ten [read: seksen dört.ten] 15 [read: on beş] çıkarsa 69 [read: altmış dokuz] kalır. '84 minus 15 is 69 [lit., ** If 15 is subtracted from 84, 69 remains].' 255:9. subtraction: - subtract; 1016:17. mathematics: - calculate. → ≠ toplan- 5.

10 /lA/ '- go [out] on a date /with/, - go out /with/, - date, - be dating.' This practice is socially acceptable mostly in the larger cities: Meral yaklaşık iki seneden beri Bülent'le çıkıyormuş. 'Meral [f.] has been going out with Bülent for about two years.' İnan ki sen.DEN başka

bir erkekle çıkmadım. 'Believe me, I've never gone out with {another man BUT you/a man other THAN you}.' Hasan bey üç aydan beri sekreteri ile çıkıyor. 'Hasan bey has been {dating/going out with} his secretary for three months.' 562:14. lovemaking, endearment: - make love; 769:16. assemblage: - come together. → = flört et-.

11 '- go out, - come out', spot, stain: A: * Elbisem kiraz leke.si oldu. 'A: My suit got a cherry {spot/stain} ON it [lit., ** My suit has become cherry spot].' B: Üzülme yıkanınca çıkar. 'B: Don't worry, it'll come out when it is washed.' Yıkadıktan sonra pantolonumdaki şeftali lekesi çıktı. 'The peach stain on my pants came out after washing.' O kadar uğraştım ama gömleğimdeki kiraz leke.si çıkmıyor. 'I've tried so hard, but the cherry stain on my shirt just isn't coming out.' Proverb: İs kara.sı çıkar, yüz kara.sı çıkmaz. 'The blackness of soot will come out; the blackness of face [i.e., dishonor] will not [come out].' 34:2 a. disappearance: - disappear.

çıkar- [ır] [çık- + caus. suf. -Ar] 1 /DAn/ '- take sth /{OUT OF/from}/, - remove sth /from/': Ceb.i.nDEN mendilini çıkardı. 'He took his handkerchief {OUT OF/from} his pocket.' Otele gelir gelmez, bütün eşyaları bavul.DAN çıkardı. 'As soon as he arrived at the hotel, he unpacked [lit., took all the things OUT OF the suitcase].' 908:23. ejection: - unload. Paralarını çıkar! 'Hand over [lit., Take out] your money!' Proverbs: Deli.nin bir.i kuyu.yA bir taş atmış, kırk akıllı çıkaramamış. 'A certain madman threw a stone INTO the well. Forty wise men couldn't get it out.' Tatlı dil yılanı deliğ.i.nDEN çıkarır. 'A sweet tongue will get a snake to come OUT OF its hole.' 192:10. extraction: - extract; 524: * 35. speech: proverbs. → ≠ [içine] koy- 1.

'- dig up': Otopsi için cesedi çıkarmak gerekiyordu ama ailesi izin vermedi. 'It was necessary to dig up the body for an autopsy, but the family didn't grant permission.' 192:11. extraction: - disinter. → ≠ göm- .

'- evict, - throw out /of/': **Ev kirasını bu ay da ödeyemezsek * hapı yuttuk. Ev sahibi bizi mutlaka evden çıkarır.** 'If we can't pay the rent this month either, * {we're done for/we're screwed} [lit., ** we've swallowed the pill]. The landlord will certainly throw us out of the house.' *908:15.* ejection: - evict.

'- fire, - dismiss': **işten çıkar-** '- dismiss, - fire from a job', *neutral,* does not necessarily imply inappropriate behavior, may be a result of a need to reduce the work force [**iş** 1 'work'. 2 'job']: **Bugün beni işten çıkardılar.** 'They fired me today.' *908:19.* ejection: - dismiss. → *formal:* = **görevden al-** → **al-** 1, *neutral:* = **işine son ver-** → **son ver-,** → **ver-** 1, *informal:* = **işten {at-/kov-}** → **at-** 1, **kov-** 2, ≠ **{ata-/tayin et-},** ≠ **görevlendir-.**

2 '- take off, - remove': **Doktor hastaya "Elbisenizi çıkarın" dedi.** 'The doctor said to the patient "Take off your clothes".' → = **soyun-** ['- undress oneself, - take off or - remove one's clothes'], ≠ **giy-,** ≠ **giyin-.** # **Öğretmen gözlüğünü çıkardı.** 'The teacher took off his glasses.' → ≠ **tak-** ['- put sth /ON/ (oneself, usually small items, accessories: glasses, jewelry)]. *6:6.* unclothing: - take off; *176:11.* transferal, transportation: - remove. For '- take off' as in '- take your hands off me', → **çek-** 3.

'- remove a spot, stain': **Bu deterjan her türlü leke.yİ çıkarır.** 'This detergent removes all kinds of stains.' **Bu lekeyi çıkarabilir misiniz?** 'Can you remove this spot?' *192:10.* extraction: - extract.

3 '- get rid of, - dispose of, - eliminate': **yorgunluk çıkar-** '- relax, - unwind, - rest' [**yorgunluk** 'tiredness']: **Eve gelince bir duş yapıp yorgunluk çıkardım.** 'When I came home, I took a shower and {unwound/rested}.' *20:6.* rest, repose: - rest. → = **{başını/ kafasını} dinle** → 2 **dinle-,** = 1 **dinlen-,** = **istirahat et-,** ≠ **yorul-** ['- get tired'].

4 /A/ '- take sb or sth up /to/, - have sb go up /to/': **Şehr.in manzara.sı.nı göstermek için onu en üst kat.a çıkardılar.** 'To show him a view of the city, they took him up to the top floor.' Proverb: **Eşeği dam.a çıkaran yine kendi indirir.** 'He who takes a donkey up to the roof takes him down again himself.', i.e., The person who creates a difficult situation has to straighten it out himself. *911:8.* elevation: - pick up. → ≠ /DAn/ **indir-** 1.

5 /DAn/ '- subtract one number /from/ another': * **84'ten 15 çıkarırsan 69 kalır.** 'If you subtract 15 from 84, you get 69 [lit., 69 remains].' *255:9.* subtraction: - subtract; *1016:17.* mathematics: - calculate. → ≠ **topla-** 4.

6 '- vomit': * **KENDIM.İ iyi hissetmiyorum, çıkaracağım.** 'I'm not feeling well [lit., ** feeling MYSELF well]. I'm going to vomit.' *908:26.* ejection: - vomit. → = **kus-** ['- throw up'], ≠ **yut-** ['- swallow [food], - take pills; - gulp down food'].

7 /DAn/ '- cause sth to come out or appear, - create, - produce, - bring forth /from/': **Kelimenin anlamını çıkaramayınca sözlüğ.E başvurmak zorunda kaldım.** 'When I couldn't {figure out/come up with} the meaning of the word, I had to {look it up IN/consult θ} the dictionary.' At the doctor's office: **Dilinizi çıkarın lütfen.** 'Please stick out your tongue.' **Onu tanırım;** * **çok çalışkan biridir, ekmeğini taş.tan çıkarır.** 'I know him very well. * He's a very hardworking person. He {produces/will produce} his bread [even] from stone.', i.e., can produce something from nothing. *891:8.* production: - produce, - create.

'- put out, - bring out, or - issue a publication': **Öğrenciler yeni bir okul gazetesi çıkarmışlar, okudun mu?** 'The students have put out a new school newspaper. Have you read it?' *352:14.* publication: - issue.

{güçlük/zorluk} çıkar- /A, DAn dolayı/ '- make or - create difficulties /FOR, on account of/, - make trouble /FOR, because of/': **Gümrükten geçerken [yanımızdaki elektronik eşyalar.dan dolayı] biz.E çok güçlük çıkardılar.** 'They made a lot of trouble FOR us

while we were passing through customs [because of the electronic equipment (we had) with us].' **Almanya'ya gitmek istiyorduk. Fakat vize işleriyle ilgili bir sürü güçlük çıkardılar, vazgeçtik.** 'We wanted to go to Germany, but they created a whole series of difficulties with regard to visas, [so] we dropped the matter.' *1012:14*. difficulty: - cause trouble.
→ ≠ **kolaylık göster-** ['- make sth easy /FOR/, - facilitate matters /FOR/'] → **göster-** 1.

hesap çıkar- '- calculate the bill, - add up the bill, - figure up the bill' [A. **hesap** (. -) 'account, bill']: At a hotel or in a restaurant: **Müşteri: Lütfen hesabı çıkarır mısınız?** 'Customer: Would you please figure up the bill?' **Resepsiyon memuru: Tabii efendim, * buy[u]run.** 'Hotel clerk: Of course {sir/ma'am}, * here you are.' *1016:18*. mathematics: - sum up. → **hesapla-** ['- calculate, - figure up, - add up'].

kavga çıkar- /lA/ '- provoke a quarrel, - pick or - start a fight /with/' [**kavga** 'fight, quarrel']: S: * **Söyleyin bakalım çocuklar, kavgayı kim çıkardı?** 'Q: OK, {let's have it/out with it} children, who {picked/started} the fight?' C: **Ayhan çıkardı.** 'A: Ayhan did.' **Ali Ahmet'le sınıfta kavga çıkardı.** 'Ali started a fight with Ahmet in the classroom.' *375:17*. motivation: - incite; *459:14*. attack: - attack; *817:7a*. beginning: - begin sth.

kopyasını çıkar- '- make a copy /of/ or - photocopy' [It. **kopya** 'copy']: **Öğretmen.in dağıttığ.ı notlar.ın 20 kopya.sı.nı çıkardık.** 'We made 20 copies of the notes [that] the teacher handed out.' **Şu makale.nin bir kopya.sı.nı çıkarıp bana gönderin.** 'Make of copy of that article and send it to me.' *784:8*. copy: - copy. → = **kopya et-**, = **kopyasını çek-** → **çek-** 8, **temize çek-** ['- recopy, - rewrite, - make a clean or fresh copy of a piece of writing'] → **çek-** 8.

meydana çıkar-. → directly below.

{ortaya/meydana} çıkar- '- bring to light; - expose to view, - disclose, - reveal' [**orta** 'middle, center', A.

meydan 'open space, public square']: **Komiser, cinayeti kim.in işlediğ.i.ni orta.yA çıkardı.** 'The police chief disclosed who had committed the murder.' **Ünlü gazeteci, milletvekili.nin yolsuzluklar.ı.nı orta.yA çıkardı.** 'The famous journalist revealed the corrupt practices of the member of parliament.' *351:4*. disclosure: - disclose.

ses çıkar- [**ses** 'voice, sound'] (1) '- raise one's voice, - speak up': **Biraz ses.in.i çıkar, ne dediğ.in.i duyamıyorum.** 'Speak up a bit. I can't hear what you're saying.' *524:26*. speech: - utter in a certain way.
(2) '- voice one's opinions, - say sth, - speak up against sth, - say sth against, - raise one's voice against, - object': **"Ağlamayan çocuğa meme vermezler", lütfen sesinizi çıkarın!** '[You know the proverb that says] "One doesn't [lit., They don't] give the breast to a child that doesn't cry", [so] please speak up!' Quotes enclose a Turkish equivalent of the English proverb: The squeaky wheel gets the oil. *453:3*. resistance: - offer resistance.

ses çıkarMA- (1) '- keep quiet, NOT - say anything, NOT - speak up': **Yanlış anlama! Tartışmak istemediğim için sesimi çıkarmıyorum.** 'Don't {get me wrong/lit., misunderstand [me]}. I'm not saying anything because I don't want to get into an argument.' *524:22*. speech: - speak up.
(2) '- raise no objection, not - object': **Ses.im.i çıkarmadım DİYE büroda bütün işleri {üst.üm.e yıktılar./bana verdiler}.** 'BECAUSE I didn't object, in the office {they loaded (*or* dumped) all the work on me/they gave me all the work}.' *453:3*. resistance: - offer resistance.

çıkıl- [ır] /DAn, A/ 'for sb or sth - go out /{THROUGH/BY WAY OF}, to/; - go up /to/, - climb /to/', impersonal passive [**çık-** + pass. suf. -**Il**]: * **Bu sokak.TAN Taksim meydan.ı.nA çıkılır mı?** 'Does this street go through to Taksim Square [lit., Does one come out AT Taksim Square {THROUGH/BY WAY OF} this street]?' **Bu merdivenler.DEN çatıkatı.nA çıkılır.** 'These stairs go up to the attic [lit., {by way of/from} these stairs one goes up to the attic].' "Çıkılır" [also "Çıkış"] levhasını görmedin mi? Bu kapı.DAN girilmez, çıkılır. 'Didn't you see the Exit [lit., one goes out] sign? One doesn't enter THROUGH this door, one exits [through it].' 190:12. emergence: - exit; 352:7. publication: poster: * specific signs. → ≠ giril-.

çıldır- [ır] '- go crazy, mad, insane, nuts, out of one's mind, - take leave of one's senses, - lose one's mind, - have a nervous breakdown': Zavallı adam kazada bütün ailesini kaybedince çıldırdı. Şimdi tımarhanede. 'When the poor man lost his whole family in an accident, he had a nervous breakdown. He is now in a mental hospital.' fig.: {Çıldırdın mı ya?} Hiç bu havada denize girilir mi? '{Are you crazy?/Have you lost your mind?} Who would go swimming in such weather [lit., Does anyone go swimming in such weather]?' Oktay'la çıkmayı kabul ettiğin.E göre çıldırmış olmalısın. 'You must be {crazy/nuts} to agree to go out with Oktay [lit., Since you agreed to go out with Oktay you...].' 925:21. insanity, mania: - go mad. → = aklını {kaybet-/yitir-}, = delir-, = {şuurunu/bilincini} kaybet-[or yitir-] 3 → {kaybet-/yitir-}.

çırp- [ar] '- beat, - whip', a food: Yoğurt, sıvıyağ ve yumurta akını bir kasede çırpın. 'Beat the yogurt, oil, and egg whites in a bowl.' 916:10. agitation: - agitate.

çiğne- [r] 1 '- chew': Yiyecekleri iyice çiğnemelisiniz. 'You should chew {your food/lit., the food} well.' Sakız çiğnemey.İ çok severim. 'I just love chewing gum.' Proverb: Çiğnemeden ekmek yenmez. 'Bread cannot be [lit., is not] eaten without chewing it.' 8:27. eating: - chew.

2 '- run over': Araba küçük bir kedi.yİ çiğnedi. 'The car ran over a little cat.' 909:7. overrunning: - run over.

3 '- violate laws, rules, principles': {Yasayı/Ahlâk kurallarını/ Okul kurallarını} çiğnedi. 'He violated {the constitution/the moral principles/the rules of the school}.' 327:6. disobedience: - disobey; 435:4. nonobservance: - violate; 674:5. illegality: - break or - violate the law. → boz- 1, ≠ kurallara uy- → uy- 4, yerine getir- 1 ['- carry out, - perform, - execute an order, a wish'].

çimdikle- [r] '- pinch with one's fingers' [çimdik 'pinch' + verb-forming suf. -lA]: Otobüste adam bacağımı çimdikledi. 'On the bus a man pinched my leg.' Anne, Suzan beni çimdikledi. 'Mother, Suzan [f.] pinched me.' 26:7. pain: - inflict pain; 260:8. contraction: - squeeze.

çisele- [r] '- drizzle, - sprinkle, - rain lightly' [çise 'drizzle' + verb-forming suf. -lA]: * Yağmur çiseliyor, şemsiyemizi alalım. 'It's drizzling, let's take our umbrellas.' 316:9 rain: - rain.

çiş yap-. → çiş {yap-/et-}. → yap-3.

çişi gel-. → gel- 1.

çiz- [er] 1 /A, {üstüne/üzerine}/ '- draw /{ON/IN}, on/': Öğretmen tahta.yA bir harita çizdi. 'The teacher drew a map ON the [black] board.' Defter varken neden kitabın.ın {üst.ü.ne/üzer.i.ne} resim çiziyorsun? 'Since you have [lit., there is] a notebook, why are you drawing [pictures] {on} your book?' 349:9. representation, description: - describe.

altını çiz- /lA/ (1) '- underline, - underscore, - draw a line under /with, IN/' [alt [Tı] 'the underpart of anything']: Günleri bildiren kelimeler.in alt.ı.nı {a: kurşunkalem.LE/b: kırmızı kalem.LE} çiziniz. 'Underline {a: {IN pencil/with a pencil}/b: with a red pencil} the words that indicate the days.' 517:19. signs, indicators: - mark.
(2) fig. '- underline, - emphasize': Arkadaşlar, tekrar altı.nı çiz.erek belirteyim ki izinsiz yurdışı.nA çıkanlar {iş.ten ayrılmış/müstafi} sayılacaklardır. 'Friends, let me once more underline the fact [lit., indicate by underlin.ing] that those who have gone abroad without permission will be considered {to

have left their jobs}.' *996:14.*
importance: - emphasize. → =
vurgula- 1 ['- emphasize, - stress, -
lay stress on'].

resim çiz- '- draw a picture,
pictures' [A. **resim** (reSMi)
'picture']: **Mehmet üç yaşından
beri resim çiziyor.** 'Mehmet has
been drawing since the age of three.'
**Çocuk duvar.ın {üst.ü.ne/
üzer.i.ne} resim çizdi.** 'The child
drew a picture {on} the wall.' *349:9.*
representation, description: - describe.

2 /{üstünü/üzerini}/ '- cross out or
off, - scratch out': **Öğretmen
yanlış cevaplar.ın {üst.ü.nü/
üzer.i.ni} çizdi.** 'The teacher
crossed out the incorrect answers.'
395:16. destruction: - obliterate. → =
karala-.

3 '- scratch, - scarify': **Birisini
senin arabanı çizerken gördüm.**
'I saw someone scratching your car.'
290:3. furrow: - furrow; *393:13.*
impairment: - inflict an injury;
517:19. signs, indicators: - mark. →
kaşı- ['- scratch' when an itch is
scratched], **kaşın-** ['- scratch
oneself' when an itch is scratched],
tırmala- ['- scratch' as in 'The cat
scratched my arm'].

çocuğu ol-. → **ol-** 6.

çocukluk et- [eDer] '- be childish, - act
childishly' [**çocukluk**
'childishness']: **A: Mezuniyet
törenime gelmediği için Gül'E
küstüm, artık onunla
konuşmayacağım.** 'A: I'm mad
AT Gül for not coming to my
graduation ceremony. I won't speak
to her anymore.' **B: Çocukluk
etme, belki önemli bir mazereti
vardır.** 'B: Don't be childish!
Perhaps she has a {good/valid} [lit.,
important] excuse.' *921:12.*
unintelligence: - be stupid.

çoğal- [ır] '- increase in number' [**çok**
'much, a lot', **k** to **ğ**, + verb-forming
suf. **-Al**]: **Dünya nüfus.u her gün
biraz daha çoğalıyor.** 'The
population of the world is increasing
a little more every day.' **Son
yıllarda üniversiteye giden
öğrenci sayı.sı hızla çoğalıyor.**
'In recent years the number of
students going to {college/university}
has been increasing.' **İş.i
olmayanlar.ın sayı.sı günden**

güne çoğalıyor. 'The number of
{the unemployed/those without
work/lit., those who do not have
work} is increasing day by day.'
251:6. increase: - grow, increase [i.].
→ = **art-** 1, = **tırman-** 2, ≠ **azal-**, ≠
eksil- 1.

/ArAk/ '- multiply, - grow, -
proliferate, - reproduce /by...ing/',
almost exclusively for living things
[i.]: **Hücreler bölün.erek
çoğalırlar.** 'Cells multiply by
divid.ing.' *78:7.* reproduction,
procreation: - reproduce; *251:6.*
increase: - grow, increase [i.]. → =
üre-.

çok 'much, many', often used with verbs
to render 'over.' → = **fazla**, ≠ **az.**
See directly below.

çok ol-. → **ol-** 12.

çok uyu-. → **uyu-** 1.

çorap kaç-. → **kaç-** 1.

çök- [er] 1 '- collapse, - fall down':
**Erzincan depreminde çok
sayıda ev çöktü.** 'Many [lit., many
in number] houses collapsed in the
Erzincan earthquake.' *393:24.*
impairment: - break down. → =
yıkıl- 2.

2 /A/ '- sit down suddenly, heavily
/IN/, - collapse /INTO/': **Çarşıdan
eve gelince yorgunluktan
koltuğ.A çök.üverdim.** 'When I
came home from the market, I
collapsed INTO an armchair from
exhaustion.' The structure *verb
stem.*I**ver-** in **çöküverdim**
conveys the sense of 'just, quickly'.
912:10. depression: - sit down. → /A/
otur- 1 ['- sit down /IN/'], ≠ /DAn/
fırla- 1 ['- jump up /from/'].

3 /{üstüne/üzerine}/ '- come down
/upon/, - settle /on/': **Şehr.in
{üst.ü.nE/üzer.i.nE} {sis/
duman} çöktü.** '{Fog/Smoke}
settled down {ON} the city.' *194:10.*
descent: - light upon. → = **bas-** 4.

4 '- fall, - come to an end, - collapse':
**Bizans İmparatorluğu 1453
yılında çöktü.** 'The Byzantine
Empire fell in 1453.' *393:24.*
impairment: - break down.

5 '[for a system] - fail, - crash, - break down, - be down': **Bilgisayar [sistemi] çöktü.** 'The computer [system] {has crashed/is down}.' **Bütün {siyasî/ideolojik sistem} çöktü.** 'The whole {political/ideological} system has broken down.' *393:24.* impairment: - break down; *1041:18.* computer science: - computerize.

çöp at-. → at- 2.

çöp dök-. → dök- 3.

çöpe at-. → at- 2.

çöpe dök-. → dök- 3.

çöz- [er] 1 '- untie, - unfasten, - undo, - unbutton': **Ahmet eve girer girmez {gömleğ.i.nin düğmeler.i.ni/kravat.ı.nı} çözdü.** 'As soon as Ahmet entered the house, he {unbuttoned his shirt/untied his tie}.' **Kemer.im.i çözebilir miyim?** 'May I unfasten my [seat] belt?' **Paketin düğümünü bir türlü çözemedim.** 'I simply couldn't undo the knot on the package.' *801:10.* separation: - detach. → ≠ **bağla-** 1, **ilikle-** ['- button, - button up'].

2 '- solve a problem, - figure sth out', usually a puzzle, mathematical problem: **{Gazetedeki bulmacayı/Kitaptaki matematik problemlerini} {a: kolayca/b: güçlükle/c: zor/d: hemen} çözdüm.** 'I {a: easily/b, c: with difficulty/d: at once} solved {the crossword puzzle in the newspaper/the mathematics problems in the book}.' **Harita.nın yardım.ı ile Konya'ya nasıl gideceğ.im.i çözdüm.** 'With the help of the map, I figured out how I would go to Konya.' **Bu sorunu çözme.nin yol.u var mı?** 'Is there a way of solving this problem?' A maxim of murder mysteries: **{Parayı/Kadını} takip et, olayı çöz.** 'Follow {the money/the woman} and {solve the crime/figure out what happened [lit., the event]}.' *939:2.* solution: - solve. → **çözüm yolu bul-** ['- find a way of solving a problem, - find a solution /{for/to}/ a problem, - find a way to do sth'] → **bul-** 1, → **hallet-** ['- solve' in regard to a social situation, personal problem].

çözüm [yolu] bul-. → bul- 1.

- D -

dağıl- [ır] /A/ [refl. of dağıt-] 1 '- scatter, - disperse /to/' [i.]: **Güneş çıktı, bulutlar dağıldı.** 'The sun came out, and the clouds dispersed.' **Polis gelince kalabalık dağıldı.** 'When the police arrived, the crowd {dispersed/scattered}.' **Toplantıdan sonra bütün öğrenciler sınıflar.ı.na dağıldı.** 'After the meeting, all the students dispersed to their classrooms.' *770:8.* dispersion: - disband. → ≠ **bir araya gel-** [for individuals '- come together, - get together'], ≠ **buluş-** [for individuals '- come together, - meet /θ/', usually after a previous agreement to meet], ≠ **toplan-** 3.

dikkati dağıl- '- be or - get distracted' [A. dikkat (dikkatI) 'careful attention'], lit., ** 'for one's attention - disperse': **Sınıfa {aniden} müfettiş girince dikkatimiz dağıldı, ders.İ dinleyemedik.** 'When the inspector {suddenly/unexpectedly} entered the classroom, we got distracted and couldn't follow [lit., listen to] the lesson.' *984:6.* distraction, confusion: - distract. → **dikkati topla** ['- concentrate, - focus or - concentrate one's attention /ON/'] → topla- 1.

2 '- let out, - be over, - break up', always with the notion of the dispersion of the participants: **{Konser/Futbol maçı/Sinema} saat onikide dağıldı.** '{The concert/The soccer game/The movie} let out at 12 o'clock.' **Parti gece ikide dağıldı.** 'The party broke up at 2 o'clock in the morning.' *770:8.* dispersion: - disband; *819:6.* end: - come to an end [i.]. → **bit-** 1 ['- come to an end, - finish, - be over, finished, completed'], **sona er-.** Same. → er-.

3 '- break up, - fall apart, - disintegrate, - disband': **Annemin ölümü.yLE {evimiz/ailemiz/ yuvamız} dağıldı.** '{With/ AFTER} my mother's death, {our household/our family/our family [lit., our nest]} broke up.' **Sovetler Birliği kimse.nin beklemediğ.i bir anda birden dağıldı.** 'The

Soviet Union suddenly broke up at a moment no one expected.' *770:8.* dispersion: - disband; *805:3.* disintegration: - disintegrate.

4 '- get untidy, - be messed up', generally in reference to places: {a: Oda/b: Ev/c: Salon/d: Yazıhane} çok dağıldı. 'The {a: room/b: house/c: living room/d: office} was a real mess [lit., got very untidy].' Saçları çok dağılmış. 'Her hair was a real mess.' *810:2.* disarrangement: - disarrange. → = karış- 3, ≠ toplan- 2.

dağıt- [ır] [irr. caus. of dağıl-] 1 '- scatter, - disperse sth' [ADJ. dağınık 'scattered, dispersed']: Polis gösteri yapan öğrencileri dağıttı. 'The police dispersed the students who were demonstrating.' *770:4a.* dispersion: - disperse sth. → ≠ topla- 1.

2 /A/ '- distribute /to/, - hand out /to/, - serve [out] /to/, - dispense /to/': Kurban Bayramında fakirler.E et dağıttık. 'On the Feast of the Sacrifice we distributed meat to the poor.' Soru kitapçıklarını öğrenciler.E sabah 7'de [read: yedide] dağıttık. 'We distributed the examination booklets to the students at seven o'clock in the morning.' *770:4a.* dispersion: - disperse sth. → ≠ topla- 1.

3 '- mess up, - put into disorder': Rüzgâr saçlarımı dağıttı. 'The wind messed up my hair.' Dün çocuklar evi çok dağıtmışlar. * Hâlâ çok dağınık. 'The children really messed up the house yesterday. * It's still a big mess.' *810:2.* disarrangement: - disarrange. → = karıştır- 4, ≠ toparla- 3, ≠ topla- 2.

dağıtıl- [ır] /a: {tarafından/CA}, b: 1A, c: A/ '- be distributed, handed out /a: by [sb], b: by means of, c: to/' [dağıt- + pass. suf. -Il]: Saat 10'da dağıtılan {sınav/imtihan} kâğıtları saat 1'de toplandı. 'The {examination} papers that had been distributed at 10 o'clock were collected at 1 o'clock.' Savaş zamanı halk.a ekmek karne.yLE dağıtıldı. 'In wartime bread was distributed to the people BY ration card.' Köylülerin alacakları Toprak Mahsülleri Ofisi tarafından dağıtıldı. 'The

payments destined for the villagers [lit., The things (that) the villagers were to receive] were distributed by the Land Products Office.' *770:4a.* dispersion: - disperse sth. → ≠ toplan- 1.

dahil ol-. → ol- 12.

dal- [ar] 1 /A, DAn/ '- dive, - plunge /INTO, {from/OFF}/': Çocukken kardeşim.le beraber iskele.DEN deniz.E dalardık. 'When I was a child {my brother/my sister} and I used to dive INTO the ocean {from/OFF} the pier [lit.,...{with my brother/with my sister} we used to...].' *367:6.* plunge: - plunge.

2 /A/ '- enter or - be in a particular mental or physical state': {düşünce.yE/düşünce.ler.E} dal- '- get or - be lost /IN/ thought, for one's mind - wander off, - give oneself up to reverie, - reminisce' [düşünce 'thought']: Arasıra düşünce.yE dalıyor arkadaşının sesi.yLE bu düşünceler.DEN uyanıyordu. 'Every now and then he would get lost IN thought. Then he would come OUT OF his reverie [lit., ** wake up from these thoughts] AT the sound of his friend's voice.' Ahmet kapının zili.yLE daldığı düşünceler.DEN uyandı. 'Ahmet came out of his reverie [lit., ** woke up from the thoughts he had wandered off to] AT the sound of the door bell.' Ne yapacağını bilmiyordu. Kara düşünceler.E daldı. 'He didn't know what to do. He gave himself up to negative thoughts.' *984:9.* distraction, confusion: - muse; *988:11.* memory: - reminisce. → = hayale dal-, ≠ düşüncelerden uyan-.

{hayal.E/hayaller.E} dal- '- daydream, - start to daydream, - go off /INTO/ daydreams, reverie, - reminisce' [A. hayal (. -) 'image, daydream']: Nergis Nurhan'I düşünürken hayal.E daldı. 'While Nergis [f.] was thinking about Nurhan, she started to daydream.' Eski fotoğraflara bakarken hayaller.E daldı. 'While he was looking at the old photographs, he started to daydream.' *984:9.* distraction, confusion: - muse; *988:11.* memory: - reminisce. → = {düşünceye/düşüncelere} dal-.

uykuya dal- '- fall asleep; - doze off, - drop off /to/ sleep' [uyku 'sleep']: Uyku.yA dalmadan önce günlük gazeteleri okumak adetimdir. '{I usually/lit., It is my habit to} read the daily papers before dropping off to sleep.' Başını yastığ.A koyar koymaz derin bir uyku.yA daldı. '{As soon as his head hit the pillow/[lit., As soon as he placed his head ON the pillow]}, he dropped off INTO a deep sleep.' Engin eve geldiğinde çok yorgundu. * Üzerini değiştirmeden yatağına uzandı. Gözlerini yumdu. * Çok geçmeden derin bir uyku.yA daldı. 'When Engin came home, he was very tired. He stretched out on his bed * without changing [lit., without changing what he had on]. He closed his eyes. * Soon [lit., ** without much (time) passing] he fell INTO a deep sleep.' • The verb dal- without uyku is often used in the same meaning: Kanepenin üzerinde dalmışım, telefonun sesi.yLE uyandım. 'I seem to have dozed off on the sofa. I woke up AT the sound of the phone.' 22:16. sleep: - go to sleep. → = uyukla- ['- doze, - doze off'], uyu- 2 ['- go to sleep'], kendinden geç- 3 ['- pass out, - fall asleep'] → geç- 1, yat- 1 ['- go to bed, - lie down, - retire for the night'], ≠ uyan- 1.

3 /A, DAn içeri/ '- enter /θ/ a place suddenly, - dash or - rush /INTO, IN THROUGH/': Çantası çalınan kadın hızla karakol.A daldı. 'The woman whose {purse/handbag} had been stolen rushed INTO the police station.' Hırsızı yakalamak için polisler kapı.DAN içeri daldı. 'To catch the thief the police rushed IN THROUGH the door.' 189:7. entrance: - enter.

kalabalığa dal- '- plunge or - disappear /INTO/ a crowd' [kalabalık 'crowd']: Hırsız polisin elinden kurtulup kalabalığ.A daldı. 'The thief got away from the police and disappeared INTO the crowd.' 34:2a. disappearance: - disappear. → = karış- 7, kaybol- ['- be lost, - get lost; - disappear from sight'] → ol- 12.

4 /A/ '- begin suddenly, - plunge /INTO/ an activity': sohbete dal- '- get involved /IN/ or - plunge /INTO/ a friendly conversation' [A. sohbet 'friendly conversation, chat, talk']: Öyle özlemişiz ki birbirimizi, sarılıp öpüştükten sonra * hemen oracıkta uzun bir sohbet.E daldık. 'We had missed each other so much that after hugging and kissing [one another], * right then and there we plunged INTO a long, friendly conversation.' Kim.in ne dediğ.i.ni bilmeden * sohbet.E {balıklama/orta yeri.nDEN} daldı. 'Without knowing who had said what, * he jumped {headlong into/right into the middle of} the conversation.' 476:5. participation: - participate; 541:10. conversation: - chat; 817:9. beginning: - enter.

dalga geç-. → geç- 1.6.

danış- [ır] /a: A, b: I, c: konusunda/ '- consult /a: θ [sb, an office], b: {about/on}, c: {about/on the subject of}/, - refer /to [sb], regarding/': A person as object: San.A bir şey danışmak istiyorum. 'I want to consult θ you about {something/a matter}.' Klâsik müzik konusunda Özcan'ın bilgisi fazladır. Bir de o.nA danışalım. 'Özcan is very knowledgeable on the subject of classical music. Let's also consult θ him.' Kocamdan ayrılmak için avukat.A danıştım. 'I consulted θ a lawyer about getting a divorce from my husband.' Uzun zamandan beri zaten bu mesele.yİ siz.E danışmak istiyordum. 'I've been meaning to consult θ you ABOUT this problem for a long time already.' Siz.den başka sorun.um.U danışacak kimsem yok. 'I have no one but you to consult ABOUT my problem.' Proverb: Bin bilsen de bir bilen.E danış. 'Even if you know a thousand [things], still consult θ an expert [lit., sb who knows (more)].' A place or office as object, but again it is really the workers there who are being consulted: Otobüste unuttuğum çantam İÇİN kayıp bürosu.nA danıştım. 'I contacted [lit., consulted] θ the lost and found ABOUT my {handbag/purse/ briefcase}, which I had left [lit., forgotten] on the bus.' → {başvur- /müracaat et-} 1 ['- consult a reference source', i.e., dictionary, encyclopaedia]. 387:14. use: - avail oneself of; 937:30. inquiry: - seek.

* bilgisine danış- '- consult a person', lit., ** '- consult /θ/ sb's knowledge' [bilgi 'knowledge']: **Osmanlı Tarihi konusunda tarih bölümündeki profesörler.in bilgi.si.nE danıştım.** 'I consulted [lit., ** consulted θ the knowledge of] professors in the history department on the subject of Ottoman history.' *387:14.* use: - avail oneself of; *541:11.* conversation: - confer; *937:30.* inquiry: - seek. → = {**başvur-/müracaat et-**} 1, **fikir al-** ['- get an idea or advice /from/'] → **al-** 1, **akıl al-** ['- ask sb's advice, - take or - get advice /from/ sb, consult /θ/ sb'] → **al-** 1.

dans et- [eDer] '- dance': **Dans etmek ister misiniz?** 'Would you like to dance?' **Benimle dans eder misiniz?** 'Would you dance with me?' S: **Dans edelim mi?** 'Q: Shall we dance?' C1: {a: **Tabii.**/b: **Olur.**/c: **Peki.**/d: **Edelim.**/e: **Memnuniyetle.**/f: **Seve Seve.**} 'A: {a: Of course./b: All right./c: OK./d: Let's./e: With pleasure./f: Gladly.}' C2: **Teşekkür ederim, hayır.** * **Biraz rahatsızım.** 'A2: Thank you, no. * I'm not feeling very well.' * **Tatilde çok iyi vakit geçirdim. Kitap okudum, yüzdüm, dans ettim.** 'I had a very good time * {over vacation/during the holidays}. I read, swam, and danced.' *705:5.* dance: - dance. → **göbek at** ['- belly dance, - perform a belly dance'] → **at-** 1, **oyna-** 4 ['- dance, - perform a dance', used with the names of various folk dances].

darıl- [ır] 1 /A, diye/ '- be or - get mad /AT/, angry /{WITH/AT}, BECAUSE/' [ADJ. **dargın**]: **Teklifini reddettim DİYE ban.A darıldı.** 'He was angry WITH me BECAUSE I had not accepted his proposal.' **Ayla san.A çok darıl.DIM. Ahmet'e benim için "Çok cimridir" demişsin.** 'A: Ayla, {I'M/I was} very angry {WITH/AT} you. You apparently told Ahmet that I'm very stingy [lit., concerning me you said "he is very stingy"].' In this sentence if the anger is understood to continue at present, **darıldım** should be translated with the present tense. If the anger is no longer regarded as being in effect, the past tense is appropriate. • In reference to a PRESENT condition, certain common Turkish verbs designating a state, i.e., a feeling,

emotion, or sensation, often have the simple PAST tense, but the equivalent English has the simple PRESENT tense. *152:17.* resentment, anger: - become angry. → = **küs-, kız-** 1 ['- get or - be angry, cross /AT/ (sb)'].

2 /A/ '- be or - get hurt or offended /BY/; - take offense /AT/': **Bana mektup yazmadığ.ı için o.nA çok darıldım.** 'I was very hurt that he didn't write me [letters] [lit., I was very offended BY him because he didn't write me letters].' *152:21.* resentment, anger: - offend. → = **alın-** 3, = **kırıl-** 3.

dava aç-. → **aç-** 12.

dava et- [eDer] /I/ '- bring a suit or charges /AGAINST/, - sue' [A. **dava** (- -) 1 'suit, lawsuit, action'. 2 'claim']: **Üst katta oturanlar.I dava edeceğim, çok gürültü yapıyorlar.** 'I'm going to sue the people who live on the top floor. They make too much noise.' **Ünlü artist, kendisi hakkında yalan haberler yazan gazeteyi dava etti.** 'The famous artist sued the newspaper that had written lies [lit., false news] about him.' *598:12.* legal action: - sue. → = /aleyhine, için/ **dava aç-** ['- bring a suit or charges /against [sb], for [a misdeed]/, - file a complaint /against/ sb, - sue sb'] → **aç-** 12, **mahkemeye ver-** ['- sue, - take to court'] → **ver-** 1.

dava kazan-. → **kazan-** 2.

davet et- [eDer] /A/ '- invite /{to/FOR}/' [A. **davet** (- .) 'invitation, summons']: NON-verbal noun as indirect object: S: **Parti.yE kimler.İ davet ettiniz?** 'Q: Who[m] [all] did you invite to the party?' C: {**Herkes.İ/Ahmet bey.İ/Ayşe hanım.I**} **davet ettim.** 'A: I invited {everyone/Ahmet bey/Ayşe hanım}.' **Siz.İ yemeğ.E davet edebilir miyim?** 'May I invite you {to/FOR} a meal?' VERBAL noun as indirect object: **Yurdaer'i bizimle birlikte {çay içmey.E/sinemaya gitmey.E/yemek yemey.E} davet ettim.** 'I invited Yurdaer {to drink tea/to go to the movies/to eat} with us.' *440:13.* request: - invite. → *Less formal:* = **çağır-** 2.

davran- [ɪr] /A, A karşı/ '- behave /TOWARD, toward/, - deal /WITH/, - treat /θ/': O.nA karşı her zaman {a: iyi/b: kibar/c: kötü/d: kaba} davrandım. 'I always behaved {a: well/b: politely/c: badly/d: rudely} TOWARD him.' Çocuklar.A fazla {sert/ yumuşak} davranmayın. '{Don't treat θ the children too {strictly/leniently}./Don't be too {strict/lenient} WITH the children.}' Bu konuda daha hassas davransaydı iş bu noktaya gelmezdi. 'If he had behaved with greater sensitivity on this matter, things would not have come to this point.' Daha hoşgörülü ve anlayışlı davranmak zorundayız. 'We must behave more tolerantly and with greater understanding.' * Hiçbir şey olmamış gibi davranamayız. 'We can't behave as if nothing had happened.' We meet, and you act as if you don't know me, I say: * Eller gibi davranıp gör.me.mezlikten gelme. 'Don't treat me like a stranger, pretending not to have seen me.' These are also the words of a song. 321:6. behavior: - treat. → = hareket et- 4.

{daya- [r]/yasla- [r]} /A/ '- lean, - prop, - rest sth /{AGAINST/ON}/' [A D J . /A/ dayalı '{propped/leaning} /{AGAINST/ON}/']: Merdiveni duvar.A sıkıca daya, düşmesin. 'Prop the ladder firmly AGAINST the wall; don't let it fall.' İtfaiyeciler evin duvarı.nA merdiven dayayıp {teker teker} [merdivenden] üst kat.A çıktılar. 'The firemen propped a ladder AGAINST the wall of the house and climbed up to the top floor {one step at a time/step by step}.'

sırtını {daya-/yasla-) (1) /A/ '- lean /{AGAINST/ON}/', lit., '- lean one's back, sırt, /{AGAINST/ON}/': Büyükbabam yemek yedikten sonra sırtını duvar.A dayadı ve uyuklamaya başladı. 'After eating, my grandfather leaned back AGAINST the wall and began to doze off.' He is sitting on a backless sofa. 159:14. location: - deposit; 204:10. obliquity: - incline; 900:22. support: - rest on. → = dayan- 1 ['- lean [oneself] /{AGAINST/ON}/']. (2) /A/ '- rely or - depend /{ON/UPON}/ for support': * Oh ne

âlâ! Sırtını dayamış kayınpeder.i.nE çalışmadan yaşıyor. '{Oh great!/How convenient!} He has been relying ON his father-in-law [to take care of his needs]. He doesn't have to work for a living [lit., ** he is living without working].' Sırtını birileri.nE dayayarak ne kadar yükse-lebileceğini sanıyorsun? 'How far do you expect to get ahead [in life just] by relying ON other people?' 952:16. belief: - rely on. → = dayan-2.

dayak at-. → at- 5.

dayak ye-. → ye- 2.

dayan- [ɪr] [daya- + refl. suf. -n] 1 /A/ '- lean [oneself] /{AGAINST/ON}/': Two common signs above the exit door of a bus: Kapı.yA dayanmak yasak ve tehlikelidir. 'To lean AGAINST the door is forbidden and dangerous.' Lütfen kapı.yA dayanmayın, otomatik kapı çarpar. 'Please don't lean ON the door, or the automatic door will slam shut.' 352:7. publication: poster: * specific signs. Başım dönünce düşmemek için duvar.A dayandım. 'When I became dizzy [lit., ** When my head turned], I leaned AGAINST the wall so as not to fall.' 204:10. obliquity: - incline; 900:22. support: - rest on. → = sırtını {daya-/yasla-} 1 ['- lean /{AGAINST/ON}/', lit., '- lean one's back, sırt, /{AGAINST/ON}/'] → {daya-/yasla-}.

2 /A/ '- rely or - depend /{ON/UPON}/ for support': Dünyada dayanacak kimsem kalmadı. 'There is no one left in the world {for me to rely upon/that I can rely upon} for support.' Nikâh memuru: Bana verilen yetkiler.E dayanarak nikâh.INIZ.ı kıyıyor ve sizleri karı koca ilân ediyorum. 'Civil marriage official: On the basis of [lit., ** basing ON] the authority vested in me, I join YOU in marriage [lit., ** perform your marriage ceremony] and pronounce [lit., ** announce, i.e., make public] you man and wife.' Proverb: Adam.A dayanma ölür, ağac.A dayanma kurur, duvar.A dayanma yıkılır. Hakk'A dayan! 'Don't rely ON a person, he will die; don't lean AGAINST a tree, it wither; don't lean AGAINST a

wall, it will collapse. Rely UPON God!' *952:16.* belief: - rely on. → = **güven-**, = **sırtını** {**daya-**/**yasla-**} **2**.

3 /A/ '- put up /WITH/, - bear /θ/, - stand /θ/, - tolerate /θ/, - endure /θ/, - suffer /θ/, - take /θ/': **Türk hamamları çok sıcak olur. Onbeş dakika.DAN fazla dayanamazsınız.** 'Turkish baths get very hot. You can't stand more THAN fifteen minutes [in one] [i.e., in the hot steam section].' **Kızım Amerika'ya gidince çok özledim, dayanamadım ben de * arka.sı.nDAN gittim.** 'When my daughter went off to the United States, I missed her very much. I couldn't stand it and * joined her [lit., ** went from her back].' NON-verbal noun as object: **Yazın İzmir'in sıcağı.nA dayanamıyorum.** 'I can't stand θ the heat in Izmir in the summer.' **Annem ve babam ölünce her türlü zorluğ.A yalnız baş.IM.a dayan.DIM.** 'When my mother and father died, I {endured/put up with} all kinds of difficulties by myself.' • Note that the possessed suffix on **baş** agrees with the subject of the sentence. **Açlığ.A dayanırım ama susuzluğ.A dayanamam.** 'I can stand θ hunger, but I can't stand θ thirst.' **Benim hanım yalnızlığ.A dayanamaz.** 'My wife can't bear θ {lonliness/being alone}.' **Bütün bunlar.A nasıl dayanabiliyorsun?** 'How can you put up with all these things?' **Böyle bir {sorun.la/problem.le} karşılaştığında bakalım sen ne kadar dayanabileceksin?** 'When you {come up against/are faced with} such a problem, let's see how long you'll be able to {put up with it/take it}.'
VERBAL noun as object: **Bebeğin ağlama.sı.nA dayanamadım ve evden ayrıldım.** 'I couldn't stand θ the baby's crying and left the house.' *134:5.* patience: - endure; *1047:3.* toughness: - toughen. → = **katlan-2**, = **tahammül et-**, = **çek- 5**, **uğraş- 3** ['- put up with a person'].

4 '- keep, - stay edible [subj.: food]': **Bu {a: etleri/b: yemeği/c: sütü/d: tatlıyı} buzdolabına koy, dışarıda dayanmaz, bozulur.** 'Put this {a: meat/b: food/c: milk/d: sweet dessert} in the refrigerator. It won't keep outside,

it'll spoil.' *826:6.* durability: - endure. → ≠ **bozul-**, ≠ **bayatla-**, **kok- 2** ['- smell [bad], - stink'].

5 /A/ '- last, - hold out, - be enough /FOR/', subj.: supplies: **Bu kış kömürümüz iyi dayandı.** 'This winter {we had quite enough coal/lit., our coal held out quite well}.' * **Mutfak masraf.ı.nA para dayanmıyor.** 'There's not enough money FOR kitchen expenses [lit., The money FOR kitchen expenses is not holding out].' *990:4.* sufficiency: - suffice. → = **yet-** ['- suffice /FOR/, - be enough /FOR/'], = **yetiş- 6** ['- be enough /FOR/, - suffice /FOR/'].

de- [r] **1** '- say': **Pardon. Ne dediniz?** 'Excuse me, what did you say?' However the most common way of requesting a repetition is to say **Efendim?** [lit., ** 'My {sir/ma'am}?']. **Türkçe'de "hello" nasıl dersiniz?** 'How do you say "hello" in Turkish?' When you've lost your train of thought: * **Ha, ne diyordum?** 'Now, what was I saying?' Someone named **Can** is speaking, and you don't understand what he is saying. You ask sb: **Can ne diyor?** 'What is Can saying?' # You express surprise that sth I had predicted happened. I respond: 1. * **Ben demiştim.** 'I told you so [i.e., that was going to happen].' 2. **Dememiş miydim?** 'Didn't I tell you?' A response to a suggestion: **S**: * **Bu akşam dışarıda yiyelim mi?** 'Q: {How about eating out tonight?/lit., Shall we eat out tonight?} **C: Peki** {**sevgilim/hayatım**}, * **sen** {**ne/nasıl**} **dersen öyle olsun.** 'A: OK {my dear/my darling [lit., my life]}, * whatever you say [lit., ** {whatever/however} you say, let it be so].' **S: Madem o gün sınavın vardı, neden onunla buluşmayı kabul ettin?** 'Q: Since you had an exam that day, why did you agree to meet him?' **C: Maalesef, kimseye hayır diyemiyorum.** 'A: Unfortunately I can't say no to anyone.' A sentence frequently encountered on plaques hung in the homes and shops of devout Muslims: **Allah'ın dediğ.i olur.** 'What God says comes to pass.' **Derler ki...** '{They say that.../It is said that...}': **Derler ki burada büyük bir veli yatıyormuş.** 'They say that a great [Sufi] saint lies [buried] here.' Some famous words of Atatürk: * **Ne**

mutlu Türküm di.yen.E. 'How fortunate is the person who can say that he is a Turk [lit., How fortunate FOR the one who says "I am a Turk"].' * **Kim ne derse desin** '{No matter what anyone says/I don't care what anyone says}': * **Kim ne derse desin, ben bu {Maliye Bakanı'nı/sözlüğü/mevsimi} seviyorum.** 'No matter what anyone says, I like that {Minister of Economics/dictionary/season}.'
Proverbs: **Hoca.nın dediğ.i.ni yap, yaptığ.ı.nı yapma.** 'Do what the teacher says, not what he does.' Don't do as I do, do as I say. **Kaza geliyorum demez.** 'An accident doesn't announce its coming [lit., doesn't say "I'm coming"].' **Kul.un dediğ.i olmaz, Allah'ın dediğ.i olur.** 'What God's humble servant [i.e., any mortal] says does not happen, what God says, does.' **"Ne oldum" dememeli, "Ne olacağım" demeli.** 'One must not say, "This is what I have become", but rather "[Who knows] what I will become?"', i.e., One must not boast about one's present fortunate state, but keep in mind the possibility of future uncertainty. *524:23*. speech: - say. → = **söyle- 1, yaz- 2** ['- say' when a written source (e.g., a newspaper) is the subject].

• **de-** versus **söyle-**: **De-** is the only verb that may DIRECTLY follow a DIRECT quotation: **"Geliyorum" dedi.** 'He said, "I'm coming."' Other verbs of verbal expression such as saying, asking, answering, shouting, etc., MUST HAVE **diye** 'saying', a form of **de-**, BETWEEN them and the ACTUAL WORDS said: **"Geliyorum" DİYE cevap verdi.** 'He answered, "I'm coming."' [lit., ** 'I'm coming', SAYING he answered]. For details on **diye**, see **diye** below. **Söyle-** is not used after a DIRECT quotation but with the **DIk** or **AcAk** participle in INDIRECT speech: **{Geldiğ.i.ni/ Geleceğ.i.ni} söyledi.** 'He said {that he had come/that he was going to come}.'

* **der demez** 'as soon as, at exactly, right at, on the dot', lit., 'as soon as one says': **Beni kafeteryada bekle,** * **saat 5 [beş] der demez** * **orada.yım.** 'Wait for me at {the cafeteria/the snack bar}. * I'll be [lit., ** I'm] there * at five on the dot.' **Öğretmen "Ders bitti" der** demez öğrenciler dışarı fırladı. 'As soon as the teacher said that the class was over, the students rushed out.' *829:8*. instantaneousness: ADV. at once.

* **derken** [de- + -[I/A]r + ken 'while' = derken, lit., 'while saying'] (1) 'at that very moment, just then': **Herkes kuraklıktan bahsediyordu. Derken, yağmur başladı.** 'Everyone was talking about the drought. At that very moment it began to rain.' **Öğrenciler öğretmen.in gelmeyeceğ.i.ni sanıyorlardı, derken öğretmen sınıfa girdi.** 'The students thought that the teacher was not going to come. Just then the teacher entered the classroom.' **Derken efendim...** 'And then sir...' *829:8*. instantaneousness: ADV. at once.
(2) 'intending to, thinking, with sth in mind': * **Çocuğu kurtarayım derken az kalsın ben de boğulacaktım.** 'While intending to save the child [lit., While thinking 'let me save the child'], I too almost drowned.' *380:11*. intention: PREP., CONJ. for.

diye [de- + adverbial suf. -[y]A] lit., 'saying', implying also 'saying to oneself' and thus 'thinking, with this in mind'. The various other translations derive from the above. **Diye** often follows direct speech.
(1) θ, i.e., usually not translated:
1.1 It is obligatory between direct speech and ANY verb of verbal expression [i.e., saying, asking, responding, requesting, shouting, warning, etc.] EXCEPT the verb **de-** itself. While it is usually not translated, sometimes 'saying' may be appropriate. The words expressed may often be rendered in English as direct or indirect speech: * **Üst.ün.ü baş.ın.ı kirletme diye sana kaç defa söyledim.** 'How many times have I told you not to [lit., told you SAYING don't] {get yourself dirty!/soil your clothes!}' [üst baş 'clothes, what one has on'] **Arkadaşım.A "Ne zaman {geldin/geleceksin}" diye sordum.** 'I asked θ my friend when {he had come/he was going to come [lit., I asked my friend SAYING "when {did you come/are you going to come}?"].' **"Geliyorum" diye cevap verdi.** 'He answered θ, "I'm coming."' [lit., He answered

SAYING 'I'm coming']. **Annem ban.A "Akşam erken gel" diye rica etti.** 'My mother asked me to come early in the evening [lit., asked me SAYING "Come early in the evening."].' **Ahmet yangını görünce "Aman Allahım!" diye bağırdı.** 'When Ahmet saw the fire, he shouted [saying] "O my God!".' **Denize düşen adam "İmdat! İmdat!" diye haykırıyordu.** 'The man who had fallen into the sea was screaming [saying], "Help! Help!"' **Ninem kedi.si.nE "Minnoş" diye seslenir.** 'My grandmother calls out to her cat saying "Minnoş".' **Annem kızacak DİYE sen.İ uyarmıştım.** 'I had warned you [THAT] my mother would get angry [lit., SAYING my mother will get angry].'

1.2 θ between a name and the verb of naming: **Antrenör, basketbol takımı.nı "Kartallar" diye adlandırdı.** 'The coach called the basketball team θ "The Eagles" [lit., SAYING "The Eagles"].' **Türkiye'nin Avrupa tarafında kalan kısm.ı "Trakya" diye adlandırılır.** 'The part of Turkey [remaining] in Europe is called θ Thrace [lit., is called SAYING "Thrace"].' **Ninem kedisi.nİ "Minnoş" diye çağırıyor.** 'My grandmother calls her cat θ Minnosh [lit., calls her cat SAYING Minnoş].'

(2) expressions of reason 'because': **Ne diye?** 'Why? [lit., ** Saying what?]': S: **Ne diye darıldı?** 'Q: Why was he angry?' C: **Teklifini reddettim diye ban.A darıldı.** 'A: He was angry with me BECAUSE [lit., SAYING] I had rejected his proposal.' **Hakan: Sınıftaki kızlar pembe pantolon giydim diye benimle dalga geçtiler.** 'Hakan: The girls in the class made fun of me BECAUSE [lit., SAYING] I wore pink trousers.' **Hastasın diye sana çorba yaptım.** 'Because [lit., SAYING] you are ill, I made some soup for you.' *887:10.* attribution: CONJ. because.

(3) expressions of purpose:
3.1 when preceded by the imperative or optative:
a) 'so that; lest': **Ne diye?** 'Why?, For what purpose?' S: **Ne diye haritaya baktın?** 'Q: Why did you look at the map?' C: **Kaybolma.YAYIM diye.** 'A: So that I would not get lost [lit., SAYING LET ME not get lost].'

Kaybolma.YALIM diye haritaya baktık. 'So that WE would not get lost, we looked at the map [lit., SAYING LET US not get lost...].' **Çocuk babası görme.SİN diye dolab.A saklandı.** 'The child hid himself IN the closet so that HIS FATHER would not see him [lit., SAYING LET HIS FATHER not...].' *380:11.* intention: PREP, CONJ. for; *896:7.* liability: CONJ. lest.

b) 'in order to, to': S: **Ne diye geldin?** 'Q: Why did you come?' C: **Bu işi bitir.EYİM diye geldim.** 'A: I came in order to finish this job [lit., SAYING LET ME finish...].' **Bu işi bitir.ELİM diye geldik.** 'We came in order to finish this job [lit., SAYING LET US finish...].' **Fırıncıdan ekmek al.SIN diye kendisini gönderdim.** 'I sent him to buy bread from the baker [lit., SAYING {LET/HAVE} HIM buy...].' *380:11.* intention: PREP., CONJ. for.

3.2 'as', i.e., 'for the purpose of, with sth in mind, intending', preceded by a noun: **Bunu şaka diye mi yaptın?** 'Did you do this as [lit., SAYING] a joke?' *380:11.* intention: PREP., CONJ. for.

(4) 'thinking, assuming, with sth in mind': S: **Ne diye o kadar hazırlanmıştın?** 'Q: Why did you prepare so thoroughly?' C: **Akşama misafir gelecek diye o kadar hazırlanmıştım, ama gelmediler.** 'A: I had prepared myself so thoroughly THINKING that guests were going to come in the evening, but they didn't [come].' *950:19.* theory, supposition: CONJ. supposing.

(5) 'named, called, by the name of', when **diye** is preceded by a name, but not followed by a verb of naming, i.e., not as under **1.2** above: S: **Ayla hanım ile konuşabilir miyim?** 'Q: May I please speak with Ayla hanım?' C: **Burada Ayla diye biri yok. Sanırım yanlış numara çevirdiniz.** 'A: There's no one here by that name [lit., There's no one here called [lit., SAYING] Ayla. I'm afraid [lit., I think] you've got [lit., dialed] the wrong number.' *527:14.* nomenclature: ADJ. named. = **adlı**.

(6) 'that can be called, such a thing as, a trace of', stresses the presence or absence of a quality: **İslâm dünyası diye bir dünya var mı?** 'Is there such a world as an Islamic world?' **İnsaf diye bir şey var, değil mi?** 'There is such a thing as fairness, isn't there?' **O adam.da insaf diye bir şey yok.** 'That man doesn't have a trace of fairness in him [lit., ** on that man there is nothing SAYING fairness].' *950:19.* theory, supposition: CONJ. supposing. = **denilen.**

(7) 'as if it were, as, in the capacity of, in place of', preceded by a noun: **Eskiden bazı toplumlar * Tanrı diye güneş.E taparlarmış.** 'In olden times some societies * used to worship θ the sun as [lit., SAYING] a God.' **Tüh, biz.E kazık atmışlar. İpek diye aldığımız bluz polyester çıktı.** 'O damn, they've ripped us off. The blouse [that] we bought {as if it were/thinking it was} [lit., SAYING] silk turned out to be polyester.' *950:19.* theory, supposition: CONJ. supposing.

* **Ne diyorsun?** may indicate surprise: 'Well! What {do you say!/lit., are you saying!}': A: * **Biliyor musun, davayı kazandık.** 'A: Guess what [lit., ** Do you know?], we won the case!' **B: Ne diyorsun? Öyle sevindim ki, anlatamam.** 'B: {Well! What do you say!/You don't say!} That's great! [lit., ** I'm so pleased that I can't say].' **A: Sizin.LE evlenmek istiyorum.** 'A: I want to marry θ you.' **B: * Neler diyorsunuz?** 'B: What are you saying?' *122:19.* wonder: INTERJ. my word!

2 '- think, - think of in a certain way': **Maşallah hâlâ genç görünüyor. Dört çocuk annesi demezsin.** 'God be praised, she still looks young. You wouldn't suspect [lit., say] that she's the mother of four children.' **Saat 10 oldu, hâlâ gelmedi. * Bundan sonra gelir mi dersin?** 'It's ten o'clock, and he still hasn't come. * Do you think he'll still come [lit., after this]?' **Arkadaşıyla ev tutup oturmak istiyormuş. * Bu iş.E herkes ne der?** 'She apparently wants to rent a house with her friend. * What do they [lit., 'everyone', i.e., their friends, family, acquaintances, etc.] say to that?' *** Ne dersin?** '{What do you say?/How about it?}', words commonly used to elicit an opinion. They may come at the beginning or end of the utterance: A: **Ne dersin, bu akşam sinemaya gidelim mi?** 'A: What do you say? How about going to the movies tonight [lit., Shall we go to the movies tonight?]' B: * **Bak, bu çok {iyi/güzel} bir fikir.** 'B: * Now that's a great idea.' * **Yarın pazara gitsek nasıl olur? Ne dersin?** 'How about going to the {bazaar/market} tomorrow? What do you say?' * **Ne yapalım dersiniz?** 'What do you think we should do?' → = **bul- 3,** = **düşün- 4** ['- think, - have an opinion /{about/of}/'].

Diyelim [ki] 'Let's say [that]', i.e., assume, imagine, suppose for the sake of argument that: **Diyelim ki birimiz hastalandık, o zaman ne yapacağız?** 'Let's suppose one of us gets sick, then what will we do?' *950:10.* theory, supposition: - suppose. → = {**farz et-/varsay-**}, = **tut- 9.** *950:19.* theory, supposition: CONJ. supposing; *952:11.* belief: - believe.

3 '- mean; - intend': S: * {**İngilizce.DE/İngilizce.θ**} **'merhaba' ne demek?** 'Q: What is the English {meaning/equivalent} of the word 'merhaba'? C: **'Merhaba' 'hello' demek.** 'A: Merhaba means "hello".' **Bu ne demek?** 'What does this mean?', both in the sense of asking for information and as an expression of indignation. {**Ne demek istediğ.i.ni anlamadım**}. **Ne demek istiyorsun?** '{I don't understand what you mean./I didn't understand what you meant.} What do you mean?' **Hayır, onu demek istemedim.** 'No, I {didn't/don't} mean that.' **A: Fatih yaş günü partine gelmeyecekmiş.** 'A: It seems that Fatih isn't going to come to your birthday party.' **B: * Bu ne demek ya! * Hiç gelmemek olur mu?** 'B: What do you mean? [lit., What does this mean?] * How could he not come [lit., ** Is not coming possible]?!' **S: Merhaba Nermin. Bu saatte seni rahatsız etmek istemezdim ama evde hiç tuz kalmamış, biraz verebilir misin?** 'Q: Hello Nermin. I didn't want to disturb you at this [i.e., inconvenient, late] hour, but we've run out of salt [lit., no salt at all remains at home]. Could you give me a little?' **C: * Ne demek, rahatsızlık olur mu hiç? Elbette veririm.** 'A: What do you mean [i.e., by even hesitating to ask]? It's no inconvenience at all [lit., How could it ever be an inconvenience]?

Of course I'll give you some.' *380:4.*
intention: - intend. → = **kastet- 1.**

Deme ya! 'You don't {say/mean it}!': A: **Duydun mu, Elazığ'da deprem olmuş.** 'A: Have you heard? There's been an earthquake in Elazığ.' B: **Deme ya! Sahi mi? Yapma ya!** 'B: You don't {say/mean it}! Really? Oh go on!' Another alternative: **Ha[y]di ya!** 'You don't say!' *131: * 16.* inexpectation: expressions of inexpectation; *955: * 6.* incredulity: expressions of incredulity.

demek [ki] 'that means, so, thus, therefore, in this case': **Saat altı oldu, Kerem hâlâ görünmedi. {Demek [ki]} gelmeyecek.** 'It's six o'clock. Kerem hasn't appeared yet. {So/It looks like/That means} he's not going to come.' [**Demek** can also go at the end, but then without the **ki**. Thus the following sentence may replace the last one above: **Gelmeyecek, demek.**] * **Demek biz onu okula gidiyor bilirken, o arkadaşlarıyla gezmeye gidiyormuş.** 'So while we were under the impression [lit., ** while knowing, realizing] that he was going to school, he was [actually] going around with his friends.' *518:8.* meaning: - mean.

* **Demek öyle!** 'So that's how things are!' or 'So that's how it is!' *940:11.* discovery: INTERJ. eureka!

4 /A/ '- call /θ/ sb or sth by a certain name': **Anadolu'nun bazı yörelerinde incir.E "yemiş" derler.** 'In some regions of Anatolia they call θ figs yemiş.' **Tanrı.yı inkâr edenler.E kâfir derler.** 'They call θ those who deny [the existence of] θ God kaffirs.' **Kedi erişemediği et.E murdar der. Tilki erişemediği üzüm.E koruk der.** 'A cat calls θ the meat it cannot reach unclean [i.e., canonically unlawful as food]. A fox calls θ the grapes he can't reach unripe [i.e., not edible].' *527:11.* nomenclature: - name. → = {**adlandır-/isimlendir-**}, = {**ad/isim**} **koy-** → **koy- 1,** = {**ad/isim**} **ver-** → **ver-1,** = {**ad/isim**} **tak-**.

dedikodu yap-. → **yap- 3.**

defnedil- [ir] **/A, /{tarafından/CA}/** '- be buried, laid to rest /in, by/, - be

interred /in, by/', for dead bodies only [A. **defin** (deFNi) 'burial, interment' + **et-** = **defnet-** '- bury' + pass. suf. **-Il**]: **Cenazeler vakit geçir.il.meden defnedildi.** 'The corpses were buried without delay [lit., ** without letting time be passed].' * **Nusret amca.nın cenaze.si bugün aile mezarlığı.nA defnedildi.** 'Uncle Nusret [lit., Uncle Nusret's corpse] {was buried/was laid to rest} today in the family {tomb/grave}.' **İstanbul'daki Amerikan Hastanesinde böbrek yetmez-liğ.i.nden yaşam.ı.nı yitiren 63 yaşındaki Amerikalı John Smith, {vasiyeti gereği/vasi-yeti.nE uygun olarak} bugün Hıristiyan Mezarlığı.nA defne-dilldi.** 'The 63-year old American John Smith, who died as a result of kidney failure in the American Hospital in Istanbul, was buried today IN the Christian Cemetery {in accordance with the requirements of his will/in accordance with his will}.' *309:19.* interment: - inter. → = /DA/ **toprağa veril-,** = /A/ **gömül-** [for dead bodies and other objects].

Defol! → **ol- 12.**

1 değ- [er] **1 /A/** 'for sth - touch /θ/, - brush /AGAINST/': The subject is a thing, perhaps part of a person, i.e., a part of his body, his clothing, not usually the whole person himself UNintentionally touching sth: **Elim soba.yA değdi ve yandı.** 'My hand {touched θ/brushed against} the stove and got burned.' **Bahçe kapısı yeni boyanmış; değdiğim.i farketmedim, ceketim boyandı.** 'The garden gate had been newly painted. I didn't notice that I had brushed against it, and my jacket got paint on it.' *223:10.* nearness: - contact. For '- touch' intentionally, on purpose, → = **dokun- 1,** = **el sür-** → **sür- 5.**
2 /A/ 'for sth - reach, - attain /θ/': **Delikanlı öyle uzundu ki, neredeyse başı tavan.A değiyordu.** 'The young man was so tall that his head almost {reached/touched} θ the ceiling.' *158:8.* space: - extend; *186:6.* arrival: - arrive. → = **ulaş- 1,** = **var-**.

nazar değ- /A/ 'for the evil eye - touch /θ/ or - reach /θ/', thus for harm - come /to/ [A. **nazar** 'the malignant look of the evil eye, the evil eye']: **Çocuğ.A nazar değdi, bir haftada eridi.** 'The evil eye touched θ the child. In one week {he/she} wasted away.' **İşlerimiz.E nazar değdi, bir haftadır hiç bir şey satamadık.** 'The evil eye touched θ our business. For one week we've been unable to sell anything.' **Nazar değmesin.** 'May the evil eye not reach it', i.e., May God preserve it. Words used when making a positive statement about or praising sth or sb: **Nazar değmesin, yeni evli çift birbiri.ne çok yakıştı.** 'May the evil eye not reach them. The newly married couple {are a perfect match/lit., are really suited to each other}!' **Nazar değmesin, ne tatlı bir bebek bu, maşallah!** 'May the evil eye not reach him. What a sweet baby [this is]! May God preserve him from evil!' • Pronouncing the Arabic word **Maşallah** 'May God preserve him from evil' alone has the same effect as **Nazar değmesin.** *393:9.* impairment: - impair; *1007:18b.* protection: expressions to protect against misfortune; *1011: * 22.* hindrance: * expressions to prevent unfavorable occurrences.

2 **değ-** [er] 1 /A/ '- be worth /θ/': **Yorulduk ama değdi doğrusu, bu manzarayı hiçbir yerde bulamayız.** 'We got tired [i.e., coming here], but it was really worth it. We won't be able to find a view like this [lit., this view] anywhere.' NON-verbal noun as object: **Bu halı çok kötü, verdiğin para.yA değmez.** 'This rug is of very poor quality. It isn't worth θ the money you paid for it.' VERBAL noun as object: **Bu kitap 12 lira {vermey.E/ödemey.E} değer.** 'This book is worth θ {giving/paying} 12 liras for.' In reference to a process, perhaps a diet: *** Fırsat bu fırsat, denemey.E değer.** 'Here is your chance! [lit., ** The opportunity is this opportunity]. It's worth θ trying.' *** Orası ziyaret etmey.E değer mi?** 'Is that place worth θ visiting?' **Beklediğ.imiz.E değdi, konser çok güzeldi.** 'It was worth θ [our] waiting for. The concert was really beautiful.' **Malatya'ya gitmek istiyorum. Ama bu kadar yol.U * tek baş.IM.a katetmey.E değer mi değmez mi bil.emi.yorum.** 'I want to go to Malatya, but I really wonder [lit., ** I CAN'T know] if it's

worth θ traveling all that distance alone [lit., ** to MY single head].' *998:10.* goodness: - do good. → = **et-** 2.

2 '- hit the spot': **Ohh, * bu yorgunluğ.un üst.ü.ne bu {kahve/çay} değdi doğrusu.** 'Oh, * after I got so tired [lit., ** after this weariness], this {coffee/tea} really hit the spot.' *998:10.* goodness: - do good. → = **iyi gel-** → **gel-** 1, = **[iyi] git-** → **git-** 5.

değerlendir- [ir] [**değer** 'value' + verb-forming suf. **-lAn** = **değerlen-** '- gain in value' + caus. suf. **-DIr**] 1 '- evaluate, - assess, - appraise, - judge, - size up [situation]': **Birbirimizi dış görünüşümüz.e göre değerlendirmemeliyiz.** 'We must not judge each other according to [our outward] appearances.' **Öğrenci.nin başarı.sı.nı değerlendirmek kolay değildir.** 'It isn't easy to evaluate a student's success.' **Bu konuyu kendi çerçevesi içinde değerlendirmek gerekir.** 'One must assess this matter in context [lit., in its own context].' *300:10.* measurement: - measure; *945:9.* judgment: - estimate. → **yorumla-** 1 ['- interpret; - explain'].

2 /I/ '- make good use of, - make the most of, - take advantage of': **Önümüze çıkan fırsatları en iyi şekilde değerlendirmeliyiz.** 'We must make the most [lit., ** We must take advantage in the best way] of the opportunities we have [lit., that appear before us].' → = /DAn/ {**yararlan-/faydalan-/istifade et-**}.

{**vakit/zaman**} **değerlendir-** /ArAk/ '- make good use of time, - make the most of one's time /[by]...ing/' [{A. **vakit** (**vakTİ**)/A. **zaman** (. -)} 'time']: **Hayat çok kısa, vaktimizi iyi değerlendirmeliyiz.** 'Life is very short. We must make good use of our time.' **Otobüs.ün gelme.si.nE daha yarım saat vardı. Vakt.imiz.i alışveriş yap.arak değerlendirdik.** 'There was still half an hour before the bus was due [lit., ** to the coming of the bus]. We made good use of our time shopp.ing.' **Eğer dönem içinde vakt.in.i iyi değerlendirmezsen, {sınav/imtihan} zamanı çok** sıkışırsın. 'If you don't make good use of your time during the {term/semester/quarter} [lit., period], you'll find yourself {in a tight spot/very rushed} at {exam} time.' *330:16.* activity: - make the most of one's time; *387:15.* use: - take advantage of. → ≠ {vakit/zaman} öldür-.

değin- [ir] /A/ '- touch /ON/, - mention /Ө/ a subject': Vaktimiz {kısıtlı/sınırlı} olduğu için her konu.yA değinemeyiz. 'Since our time is {limited}, we can't touch ON every subject.' Yeri gelmişken hava kirliği konu.su.nA da değinmek istiyorum. 'Since this is the appropriate place [lit., ** Since its place, i.e., the place of this topic, has come], I also want to touch ON the issue of air pollution.' Birkaç nokta.yA değinmek istiyorum:... 'I would like to touch ON a few points:...' {İlginç/Önemli} bir konu.yA değindiniz. 'You've touched ON an {interesting/important} issue.' {Kültürel faaliyetlerimiz.E/ Kültürel etkinliklerimiz.E} birazdan değineceğim. 'A little later I will touch {ON our cultural activities}.' Daha önce değindiğimiz bu konu.yu şimdi ayrıntıları.yLA ele alacağız. 'Now we'll take up IN detail this issue which we touched on earlier.' *524:25.* speech: - remark. → = temas et- 2.

değiş- [ir] 1 '[for sth] - change, - vary, - BECOME different' [i.]: Son günlerde hava çok değişti. 'The weather has changed a lot in recent days.' Hava burada çok sık değişir. 'The weather varies a lot here [lit., changes very frequently here].' * Sanki saniye saniye bir şeyler değişiyor gibiydi. 'It was as if things were changing every second.' Aynı ürün.ün fiyat.ı mağaza.dan mağaza.ya değişiyor. * Alırken acele etmemek lâzım. 'The price of the same product varies from store to store. * One must not be in a hurry to buy it [lit., ** when buying one must not hurry].' Ar Sineması'ndaki film değişti mi, biliyor musun? 'Do you know if the movie at the Ar theater has changed?' Burası o kadar değişmiş ki tanıyamadım. 'This place has changed so much that I couldn't recognize it.' * Selim o

eski Selim değil, çok değişmiş. 'Selim isn't his old self [lit., Selim isn't that old Selim]. He's changed a lot.' Proverb: Dert gitmez değişir. '{Trouble/Sorrow} doesn't go away, it [just] changes.' *851:6.* change: - be changed.

2 /lA/ '- exchange, - change sth /with/ sb': * Arkadaşım.la saatler.imiz.i değiştik. 'My friend and I exchanged watches [lit., our watches].' *862:4.* interchange: - interchange.

3 '- change one's clothes': * üstünü değiş- '- change one's clothes' [üst lit., 'clothes, that which is upon sb']: Üst.üm.ü {değiştim/ALSO: değiş.TİR.dim}. 'I changed my clothes.' Değiştir-, not değiş-, is usually used with other nouns denoting items of clothing. *862:4.* interchange: - interchange. → = değiştir- 2.

değiştir- [ir] [değiş- + caus. suf. -DIr] 1 '- change, - alter sth, - make sth change': Sevda saç biçim.i.ni değiştirmiş. 'Sevda has changed her hair style.' {Para/Hastalık} onu çok değiştirdi. '{Money/ Illness} has changed him a lot.' Sistemi {kökü.nDEN} değiştirmek zorundayız. 'We have to change the system {AT its root/fundamentally}.' *851:7.* change: - change, - work or - make a change.

fikrini değiştir- '- change one's mind' [A. fikir (fiKRi) 'idea, mind']: Müzeye gidecektim ama fikr.İM.i değiştirdim ve sinemaya gittim. 'I was going to go to the museum, but I changed MY mind and went to the movies [instead].' Henüz kesin karar vermedim, bu konudaki fikrimi her an değiştirebilirim. 'I haven't decided definitely yet. I may [still] change my mind about this matter at any moment.' Fikrini değiştirirse * haberim olsun. 'If he changes his mind, * let me know [lit., ** let my information be].' *363:6.* changing of mind: - change one's mind. → fikrinden vazgeç- ['- change one's mind, - give up /Ө/ one's idea'], kararından vazgeç- ['- change one's mind, - go back on one's decision'].

2 /lA/ '- exchange sth /FOR/ sth else, - change sth {/FOR/INTO/} sth else, -

replace sth /with/ sth else': In class the teacher to his students: **Lütfen kâğıtlarınızı değiştirin[iz].** 'Please exchange your papers.' {a: **Çarşafları/b: Havluyu/c: Lastiği/d: Yağı} değiştirir misiniz lütfen?** 'Would you please change {a: the sheets/b: the towel/c: the tire/d: the oil}?' {a: **Gömleğ.im/b: İç çamaşır.ım,** i.e., **{fanila/atlet/külot}/c: Elbise.m} kirlenmiş, değiştirmem lâzım.** '{a: My shirt/b: My underwear, i.e., {flannel undershirt/sleeveless undershirt/underpants}/c: My suit} has gotten dirty, I must change it}.' {a: **Çorab.ım.ı/b: Pantalon.um.u} değiştirdim.** 'I changed {a: my socks./b: my {trousers/pants}.}' **Engin eve geldiğinde çok yorgundu. Üzerini değiştirmeden yatağına uzandı.** 'When Engin came home, he was very tired. He stretched out on his bed without changing his clothes.' **Bu {ampul/floresan} yanmış, değiştirelim.** 'This {bulb/fluorescent tube} has burned out. Let's change it.' Proverb: **Kurt köyünü değiştirir, huyunu değiştirmez.** 'A wolf changes his village but does not change his nature.' * **Bu doları Türk lirası.yLA değiştirebilir misiniz?** 'Could you change this dollar bill {FOR/INTO} liras?' → = **boz-** 2. *857:11.* conversion: - convert. **Benimle yer değiştirmek ister misiniz?** 'Would you like to change places with me?' **Dün aldığı gömleği değiştirdi.** 'He exchanged the shirt that he had bought yesterday.' * **Hafta sonunda kardeşim.LE arabalar.ımız.ı değiştirdik.** 'Over the weekend {my brother/my sister} and I exchanged cars [lit., ** '...{my brother/my sister} [we] exchanged our cars].' * **Nur'un İngilizce sözlüğü İLE dolma kalem.im.i değiştirdim.** 'I exchanged my pen FOR Nur's English dictionary.' *862:4.* interchange: - interchange. → = **değiş-** 2.

delir- [ir] '- go crazy, mad, insane, nuts, out of one's mind, - take leave of one's senses, - have a nervous breakdown' [**deli** 'mad, insane' + verb-forming suf. **-r**]: **Zavallı adam kazada bütün ailesini kaybedince delirdi. Şimdi tımarhanede yatıyor.** 'When the poor man lost his whole family in an accident, he had a nervous breakdown. Now he is lying in a mental hospital.' *fig.*: **Delirdin mi sen? Hiç bu havada deniz.e girilir mi?** 'Have you lost your mind? No one goes swimming in weather like this.' [lit., 'Does anyone ever go swimming in this weather?'] * **Altay'la çıkmay.I kabul ettiği.nE göre delirmiş olmalısın.** 'You must be crazy to agree to go out with Altay [lit., Since you agreed to go out with Altay, you must be crazy].' * **Delirecek gibiyim. Ya evden kaçacağım, ya da kendimi öldüreceğim.** 'I'm about to go crazy: either I'll run away from home or I'll kill myself.' *925:21.* insanity, mania: - go mad. → = **aklını {kaybet-/yitir-}, = çıldır-, = {şuurunu/bilincini} kaybet-[or yitir-]** 3 → {kaybet-/yitir-}.

den- [ir] /A/ '- be said, - be called' [**de-** + pass. suf. **-n**]: * **{Türkçe.DE/ Türkçe.θ} bu.nA ne denir?** 'What is this called in Turkish [lit., ** in Turkish TO this what IS said]?' * **{İngilizce.DE/İngilizce.θ} "merhaba" nasıl denir?** 'How is Merhaba {said/expressed} in English?' **Türkiye'nin Asya kıtasındaki toprakları.nA Anadolu denir.** 'Turkey's territories [located] on the continent of Asia are called "Anatolia".' * **Bu yaptığınız.A kabalık denir.** 'What you have done is what they call [lit., what is called] rudeness.' *527:13.* nomenclature: - be called. → = {**adlandırıl-/isimlendiril-**}.

dene- [r] /I/ '- test, - try, - try out, - try on; - attempt, - try /TO/ do sth': **Bu ayakkabı * siz.E olur. Deneyin isterseniz.** 'These shoes * {will fit θ you/are right for you}. {Try them on, if you like./Why don't you try them on?}' **Satıcı: Bu bardaklar kırılmaz, hanımefendi. İsterseniz deneyin. * Deneme.si bedava.** 'Salesman: These [drinking] glasses won't break, ma'am. Try them, if you like. * It doesn't cost anything to try them out [lit., ** its trying is free].' In reference to a process, perhaps a diet: * **Fırsat bu fırsat, deneme.yE değer.** 'Here is your chance! [lit., ** The opportunity is this opportunity]. It's worth θ trying.' NON-verbal noun as object: '- test, - try out an object': **Bütün**

anahtarları denedik, fakat kapıyı açamadık. 'We tried all the keys, but we couldn't open the door.' O mağazadaki pantalonlar.ın hepsi.ni tek tek denedim, {a: * hiç bir.i üzerim.E olmadı./b: Sadece bir tane.si.ni beğendim, * o da defolu çıktı.} 'I tried on all the trousers in that store. {a: * None of them fit [me]./b: I liked only one of them, and * that one too turned out to be imperfect}.' Bu elbise * küçük geldi, {diğer.i.ni/başka biri.ni} deneyebilir miyim? 'This suit * is [lit., ** came] too small. May I try on {the other one/another one}?' * Bu ceketi [üst.ÜN.de] denemek ister misin? 'Do you want to try this jacket on [lit., ** on YOURSELF]?' Bunu deneyebilir miyim? 'Can I try this on?' Üst.ÜM.de deneyebilir miyim? 'May I try it on? [lit., ** on MYSELF].' → = prova et-. # Bu tarif.i ilk defa deniyorum. Umarım yemek iyi olmuştur. 'I'm trying this recipe for the first time. I hope the food has turned out well.' Biz her türlü diplomatik yolu denedik. 'We have tried every diplomatic means.' → = tecrübe et-. Tat- '- taste', not dene- or tecrübe et-, is used in reference to trying, sampling food: Çorbanızı tadayım. 'Let me try [lit., TASTE] your soup.' 941:8. experiment: - experiment.
VERBAL noun as object: '- attempt to, - try out an activity to see if it pleases, is suitable': S: Hiç tenis oynamay.I denedin mi? 'Q: Have you ever tried to play tennis?' C: Hayır, hiç denemedim. 'A: No, I never have.' 941:8. experiment: - experiment.

'- attempt, - try to carry out an activity, see if one can do it': Hırsız oda.yA girmey.İ denemiş ama başar.ama.mış. 'The thief tried to enter θ the room, but he was unsuccessful [lit., he couldn't succeed].' 403:6. endeavor: - attempt. → = /A/ çalış- 2.

denize gir-. → gir-.

denk düş-. → düş- 1.

der demez. → de- 1.

derken. → de- 1.

ders al-. → al- 1.

ders çalış-. → çalış- 1.

ders düzelt-. → düzelt- 2.

ders ver-. → ver- 1.

derse çalış-. → çalış- 1.

dersten kal-. → kal- 1.

dert çek-. → çek- 5.

dert dök-. → dök- 1.

destekle- [r] '- support' [destek 'support' + verb-forming suf. -lA]: * Ailesi Selim'i her zaman {a: her konuda/b: maddî {olarak/yönden/bakımdan}/c: manevî {olarak/yönden/bakımdan}} destekledi. 'Selim's family has always supported him [lit., His family has always supported Selim] {a: in every matter/b: financially [or materially]/c: morally}.' 449:12. aid: - support; 124:10. hope: give hope; 492:16. courage: - encourage. → tut- 10 ['- support a team'].

detaya gir-. → {ayrıntıya/ayrıntılara/detaya/detaylara} gir-. → gir-.

devam et- [eDer] [A. devam (. -) 1 'continuation'. 2 'attendance']: 1 '- last, - continue, - go on': Ders devam ediyor. 'The lesson is {going on/continuing}.' Bütün gece boyunca çatışmalar devam etti. 'The {skirmishes/battles} continued throughout the night.' 811:4b. continuity: for sth - continue; 826:6. durability: - endure. → = sür- 2.

2 /A/ '[for sb] - continue /{θ/WITH}/ sth, - go on /WITH/ sth, - keep [on] doing sth': * Şimdilik bu kadar yeter. Sonra devam ederiz. 'That's enough for now [lit., For now this much suffices]. We'll continue later.' * "Eee" diyerek devam etmemi istedi. 'Saying "{Well/So}?" [i.e., then what?], he asked me to continue [lit., ** my continuing].' NON-verbal noun as object: Ders.E devam edin, durmayın. 'Continue {θ/WITH} the lesson, don't stop.'
VERBAL noun as object: Okumay.A devam edin. 'Continue {TO read/θ reading}.'

Hükümet sözcüsü hiç bir şey olmamış gibi konuşma.sı.nA devam etti. 'The government spokesman continued θ his {speech/remarks} as if nothing had happened.' *267:6.* length: - lengthen; *811:4a.* continuity: - continue sth. → ≠ bırak- 3, ≠ dur- 4.

3 /A/ '- attend /θ/, - go /to/ regularly', for an extended period, e.g., educational institution, school, etc., not for a short term, particular event, such as a concert, soccer game, lecture: Beş sene bu okul.A devam etti. 'He attended θ this school for five years.' *221:8.* presence: - attend. → = git- 4b, = oku- 3. For short-term attendance as in '- attend a concert, soccer game', etc., → git- 4a.

devir- [ir] [A. devir (deVRi) 'turn, revolution' + verb-forming suf. -θ] 1 '- knock over, - overturn': Fırtına koskoca ağacı devirdi. 'The storm knocked over the huge tree.' Kedi süt şişesini devirdi. 'The cat overturned the milk bottle.' *395:19.* destruction: - raze.

2 '- overthrow' regime, government: Ordu hükümeti devirdi ve * yönetim.i el.E aldı. 'The army overthrew the government and * took power [lit., ** took the administration IN hand].' *395:20.* destruction: - overthrow.

dışarı[ya] çık-. → çık- 2.

dışla- [r] /DAn/ [dış- 'the outside, exterior part of anything' + verb-forming suf. -lA] '- exclude, - cast out, - ostracize /from/': Hiç kimse.yi sırf hapse girdiği için toplum.dan dışlamay.a hakkımız yok. 'We have no right to exclude anyone from society simply because he has been in prison.' *772:4.* exclusion: - exclude.

dışlan- [ır] /{tarafından/CA}, DAn/ [dışla- + pass. suf. -n] '- be excluded, cast out, ostracized /by, from/': Toplum tarafından dışlanmak hoş bir duygu olmasa gerek. 'It must not be {pleasant/lit., a pleasant feeling} to be excluded from society.' Bütün arkadaşları tarafından dışlandı. * Kimse yüz.ü.nE bakmıyor. 'He was ostracized by all his friends. * No one looks him IN the face [lit.,

looks IN his face].' *772:4.* exclusion: - exclude.

1 dik- [er] 1 '- sew, - make by sewing', when the object to be created by sewing is specified: Annem ban.A yeni bir elbise dikti. 'My mother made [lit., sewed] me a new dress.'

dikiş dik- '- sew' [dikiş 'sewing'], lit., ** '- sew a sewing', when the object to be created by sewing is not specified: Serpil'in annesi hayatını dikiş dik.erek kazanır. 'Serpil's [f.] mother earns her living by sew.ing.' Proverb: Terzi kendi dikişini dikemez. 'A tailor cannot do his own sewing.', i.e., make his own clothes. *741:4.* sewing: - sew; *891:8.* production: - produce, - create.

2 '- darn': çorap dik- '- darn [nonwoolen] socks': Babaannem delinen çoraplarımı dikti. 'My paternal grandmother darned my socks, which were full of holes.' → = çorap ör- [for woolen socks] → ör- 3. *396:14.* restoration: - repair.

2 dik- [er] 1 /A/ '- plant /IN/', plants, saplings, seedlings, not seeds. The dative case goes on the noun of place designating the destination of the planting: S: Fidanları nere.yE diksinler? 'Q: θ Where should they plant the saplings?' C: Bina.nın {a: arka.sı.nA/b: ön.ü.nE/c: yan.ı.nA/d: çevre.si.nE/e: karşı.sı.nA}. 'A: {a: Behind/b: In front of/c: At the side of/d: Around/e: Facing} the building.' Geçen sene bahçe.yE diktiğimiz fidanlar bu sene * çiçek açtı. 'The saplings that we planted IN the garden last year * bloomed this year.' Proverb: Ağaç dikmek bir evlât yetiştirmek kadar hayırlıdır. 'To plant a tree is as blessed as to raise a child.' → = ek- ['- sow, - plant /IN/', seeds, not plants, seedlings, saplings, trees]. *1067:18.* agriculture: - plant.

2 /A/ '- set up, - erect /{IN/ON}/': Köy.E önce elektrik direklerini diktiler. 'They first set up electric poles IN the village.' *159:16.* location: - establish; *200:9.* verticalness: - erect.

dik dik bak-. → bak- 1.

{dikkat/dikkati}. → çek- 1.

dikkat et- [eDer] [A. dikkat (dikkatİ) 'careful attention'] 1 /A/ '- pay attention /to/, - see /to/; - be careful, - watch out /FOR/': **Dikkat et!** 'Watch out!, Careful!' NON-verbal noun as object: **Caddeyi geçerken arabalar.A dikkat et!** 'When crossing the street, watch out FOR [the] cars!' **Araba kullanırken trafik işaretleri.nE dikkat et!** 'While driving, pay attention to the traffic signs!' * **Adımların.A dikkat et!** 'Watch θ your step [lit., ** stepS].' **Ütü çok kızdı, elin.E dikkat et!** 'The [clothes] iron got very hot. Watch your hand!' VERBAL noun as object: **Aşure yaparken şeker.in iyice karışmış olma.sı.nA dikkat etmek lâzım.** 'When making aşure [a dessert], one must see to it that the sugar is well mixed [lit., ** pay attention TO the sugar's having been well mixed].' *339:7.* carefulness: - be careful; *399: * 9.* warning: expressions of; *982:5.* attention: - attend to. → = **dikkatli ol-** → **ol-** 12.

2 /A/ '- notice /θ/, - observe /θ/, - take note /OF/': **Orhan'ın kapıyı {ne zaman/nasıl} açtığ.ı.nA dikkat etmedim.** 'I didn't notice {when/how} Orhan had opened the door.' **Orhan'ın kapıyı açıp açmadığ.ı.nA dikkat etmedim.** 'I didn't notice θ whether or not Orhan had opened the door.' *940:5.* discovery: - detect; *982:6.* attention: - heed. → = **dikkat çek-** → **çek-** 1, = **farket-** 1, = **gözle-** 1, = **farkına var-** ['- notice, - become aware /OF/, - realize'].

dikkate al-. → **al-** 1.

dikkati çek-. → {**dikkat/dikkati**} **çek-.** → **çek-** 1.

dikkati dağıl-. → **dağıl-** 1.

dikkatini çek-. → **çek-** 1.

dikkatini topla-. → **topla-** 1.

dikkatli ol! → **ol-** 12.

diktir- [ir] /A/ '- have /θ/ sb sew or stitch sth, - have /θ/ sb make sth by sewing' [1 **dik-** + caus. suf. **-DIr**]: {**Bu ceket.İ/Bu elbise.yİ/Bu pantalon.U**} **kim.E diktirdin?** 'θ Who[m] did you have make {this

suit/this jacket/these {trousers/pants}}?' *741:4.* sewing: - sew.

dile- [r] 1 '- wish, - want, - desire' [P. **dil** 'heart' + verb-forming suf. **-A**]: In a letter home or on the phone: **Anneciğim, seni çok özledim, * burada ol.abil.men.i dilerdim.** 'Dear mother, I've missed you a lot. * I wish you {were/lit., could be} here [lit., ** your being able to be here].' * **Dilersen biz.e gidelim.** '{How about going to {my/our} house [lit., ** to us].}/If you want, let's go to my house [lit., ** to us].' **Alaaddin'in lâmbasından çıkan cin "Dile benden ne dilersen" dedi.** 'The genie that came out of Aladdin's lamp said, "Ask of me whatever you desire".' *100:14.* desire: - desire. → = **arzu et-**, = **iste-** 1.

The following express particular wishes: **başarılar dile-** /A/ '- wish /θ/ sb much success, - express wishes for much success /to/ sb' [**başarı** 'success']: **Yeni dekanımızı tebrik edip görevinde başarılar diledik.** 'We congratulated our new dean and wished him much success in his work.' **Yeni bir işe başlamışsın, * hayırlı olsun, başarılar dilerim.** '[I hear that] you've begun a new job. * {Good luck/All the best}, I wish you much success.' **Okul müdürü {sınav/imtihan} haftasından önce tüm öğrenciler.E başarılar diledi.** 'Before {the examination} week, the school director wished θ all the students much success.' *409:7c.* success: - wish success; *504:13.* courtesy: - give one's regards.

başsağlığı dile- /A/ '- offer or - express one's condolences /to/' [**baş**, 'head', here representing the whole person; **sağ** 'healthy, alive', **sağlık** 'health'; **baş.sağlığ.ı** 'condolence', lit., ** 'head health'], lit., ** '- express wishes for head health [i.e., to those remaining alive]': **Annesi vefat eden Nurten hanım.a başsağlığı diledik.** 'We expressed [our] condolences to Nurten hanım, whose mother had passed away.' The actual words we said to her were: **Başınız sağ olsun.** 'My sincere condolences [lit., ** May your head be healthy].' Here again **baş**, 'head', represents the whole person. **Yakın.ları.na başsağlığı diliyorum.** 'I offer my condolences to those close to him.' *121:6.* comfort: - comfort.

* mutlulukLAR dile- /A/ '- wish /θ/ sb MUCH happiness' [mutluluk 'happiness']: Form in a telegram of congratulations to a newly married couple: **Yeni evliler.E mutluluklar dileriz.** 'We wish θ the newly married couple much happiness.' **Her ikiniz.E bir ömür boyu mutluluklar dilerim.** 'I wish θ both of you lifelong happiness.' *** Yeni yıl.ınız.ı kutlar, başarı ve mutluluklar dilerim.** '{Best wishes for the new year and much success and happiness./I congratulate you on the new year [lit., ** I congratulate your new year] and wish you much success and happiness.}' *504:13.* courtesy: - give one's regards; *1009:7.* prosperity: - prosper.

2 /DAn/ '- ask for sth /from/ sb, - request sth /from/ sb, - ask sth /OF/ sb': **Dile ben.DEN ne dilersen. İstediğin her şey.İ alacağım.** 'Ask OF me whatever you desire. I'll give you anything you want.' *440:9.* request: - request. → = **iste- 2,** = **rica et-.**

özür dile- /DAn, için/ '- beg sb's pardon, - apologize /TO [sb], for [sth]/, - make an apology /TO/' [A. özür 'pardon']: *** Vazoyu kırınca annem.DEN özür diledim.** 'When I broke the vase, I apologized TO my mother [lit., ** I requested pardon FROM my mother].' An expression requesting forgiveness: **Özür dilerim.** '{I'm sorry./I apologize.}': **Özür dilerim, {geç kaldım./geciktim.}** 'I'm sorry {I'm late}.' **{Rahatsız ettiğim/Beklettiğim} için özür dilerim.** 'Sorry for {disturbing you/making you wait}.' **Dün olanlar için özür dilerim.** 'I apologize for the things that happened yesterday.' Responses to the apology: **Rica ederim.** '{That's all right./Never mind./No need to apologize.}' **{Önemli/Mühim} değil.** 'It's not {important}.' **{Zararı/Ziyanı} yok.** 'No problem.' *148:3b.* forgiveness: expressions requesting forgiveness; *658:5.* atonement: - apologize. → = **affedersiniz** → affet- 2, = **kusura bakma** → bak- 1.

dilim dilim kes-. → kes- 1.

dilimle- [r] '- cut into slices, - slice' [dilim 'slice' + verb-forming suf. -lA]: **Soğanları soyup ince ince dilimleyin.** 'Peel the onions and slice them into small pieces.' **Domatesin çekirdekli kısmını çıkarıp {a: enine/b: ince ince/c: halka halka} dilimleyin.** 'Remove the portion of the tomatoes with the seeds and cut them [i.e., the tomatoes] {a: vertically/b: into thin slices/c: into rings}.' *792:6.* part: - separate; *801:11.* separation: - sever. → = **dilim dilim kes-** → kes- 1, **doğra-** ['- cut (up) into slices or pieces; - carve, - chop into bits, - mince'].

dilini tut-. → {çenesini/dilini} tut-. → tut- 4.

din- [er] '- cease, - stop, - let up', mostly with certain limited categories of subjects: Nouns of weather: **{a: Rüzgâr/b: Yağmur/c: Kar/d: Dolu/e: Fırtına} dindi. Artık dışarı çıkabiliriz.** '{a: The wind/b: The rain/c: The snow/d: The hail/e: The storm} has stopped. We can go out now.' **Çocuklar parka gitmek için yağmur.un dinme.si.ni bekliyordu.** 'The children were waiting for the rain to stop to go to the park.'
Nouns of physical or mental pain: **Kocası öldüğünden beri {acı.sı/gözyaşlar.ı} dinmiyor.** '{She hasn't stopped grieving [lit, her sorrow hasn't ceased]/She hasn't stopped weeping [lit., her tears haven't stopped]} since her husband died.' *** Beş saattir baş ağrım dinmiyor.** 'My headache hasn't {let up/stopped} for five hours.' **Dün kesilen parmağım.ın acı.sı hâlâ dinmedi.** 'My finger that got cut yesterday still hurts [lit., ** The pain from my finger...still hasn't stopped].'
Some nouns of emotion: *** Adnan'A [olan] öfkem {dindi./dinmedi.}** 'My anger toward Adnan {has stopped./has not stopped.}' *819:6.* end: - come to an end; *856:7.* cessation: for sth - cease. → = **bit- 1,** = **dur- 2,** = **sona er-** → er-, = **kesil- 2.**

1 dinle- [r] 1 /a: I, b: üzerinden, c: DAn/ '- listen /a: TO, b: {ON/over}, c: ON/, - hear': Proverb: **Az söyle, çok dinle.** 'Say little but do a lot of listening.' **Çene.n.i tut da söyleyeceğim.İ dikkatle dinle.**

'Hold your tongue [lit., ** 'jaw, chin'] and listen carefully TO what I'm going to say.' {Konuşmacılar.I/Yurdanur'U} {dikkatle/sessizce} dinledim. 'I listened {attentively/silently} {TO the speakers/TO Yurdanur}. Bu programı internet üzerinden dinleyebilirsiniz. 'You can hear this program {ON/over} the Internet.' Başbakanın konuşmasını bant.TAN dinledim. 'I listened to the President's speech ON the tape.' Bu {kased.İ/CD'yİ [pronounce: si diyi]} dinleyebilir miyim? 'May I listen TO this {cassette/CD}?' S: Ne dinlemek istersin? 'Q: What would you like to {listen TO/hear}?' C: Mozart dinlemek isterim. 'A: I would like to {listen to/hear} [some] Mozart.', that kind of music', his music. S: Mozart mı yoksa Beethoven mi dinlemek istersin? 'Q: Would you like to {listen to/hear} [some] Mozart or [some] Beethoven?' C: Mozart dinlemek isterim. 'A: I want to listen to [some] Mozart.' S: Klâsik müzik mi dinlemek istersiniz, yoksa halk müziği mi? 'Q: Do you want to listen to [some] classical music or [some] folk music?' C: Klâsik müzik dinlemek isterim. 'A: I want to listen TO [some] classical music.' S: Mozart'I mı Beethoven'İ mi dinlemek istersin? 'Q: Would you like to {listen TO/hear} the Mozart or the Beethoven?' C: Mozart'I dinlemek isterim. 'A: I would like to {listen TO/hear} the Mozart.' On the radio at the conclusion of a news cast: Haberleri dinlediniz. 'You have {heard/listened to} the news.' 48:10. hearing: - listen.

2 '- heed, - obey, - listen /to/': Gençler genellikle büyükler.i.nİn dedikler.i.nİ dinlemezler. 'Young people generally don't listen {to their elders/lit., to what their elders say}.' Garson şiş kebap ye.me.MİZ.i tavsiye etti ama biz * tavsiyesi.nİ dinlemedik. * Keşke tavsiyesi.nE uysaydık! 'The waiter recommended that WE eat [lit., ** OUR eating] shish kebab, but * we didn't take [lit., listen to] his recommendation. * If only we had followed θ his advice!' Babası.nI dinlemedi ve evden çıktı gitti. 'He didn't {listen to/obey} his father and left the house.' 'Adam intihar edecek' diye uyardık. * Dinleyen olmadı. 'We warned them that [lit., ** saying] the man would commit suicide. * Nobody listened [lit., there was no one who listened].' Proverb: Gönül ferman dinlemez. 'The heart does not listen to edicts.' • Note carefully the difference between this verb and 1 dinlen- and 2 dinlen-. 326:2. obedience: - obey.

{lâf/söz} dinle- '- obey, - heed what one is told; - act on sb's advice', very common in the negative: '- disobey, not - heed' [{P. lâf/söz} 'word, talk']: Bu çocuk çok yaramaz, hiç lâf dinlemiyor. 'This child is very naughty. He never listens [to what he's been told].' Alper çok uslu çocuktur, * çok lâf dinler. 'Alper is a very well-behaved child. * He does what he is told.' 326:2. obedience: - obey. → = söz tut- → tut- 5, = uy- 6, ≠ sözünden çık- → çık- 1.

söz dinle-. → directly above.

2 dinle- [r] only with certain nouns: * {başını/kafasını} dinle- '- rest, - put one's {mind [lit., ** head]} at ease': S: Tatilde nereye gideceksin? 'Q: θ Where are you going to go on [your] vacation?' C: Hiç bir yere. Evde oturup {baş.IM.ı/kafa.M.ı} dinleyeceğim. 'A: {Nowhere/I'm not going anywhere}. I'm just going to stay at home and rest [{MY head}].' 20:6. rest, repose: - rest. → = 1 dinlen-, = istirahat et-, = yorgunluk çıkar- → çıkar- 3.

1 dinlen- [ir] '- rest': Bugün yazıhanemde çok yoruldum, eve gidip dinleneceğim. 'I got very tired at the office [lit., at my office] today. I'm going to go home and rest.' * {Gücü.M/Takat.IM} tükendi, lütfen biraz dinlenelim. 'I'm tired out [lit., ** {my strength} is used up]. Please let's rest a bit.' {Önce/Evvelâ} biraz dinlenin. Sonra çalışırız. '{First} rest a bit. Then we'll work.' Note carefully the difference between this verb and dinle-. 20:6. rest, repose: - rest. → = {başını/ kafasını} dinle- → 2 dinle-, = istirahat et-, = yorgunluk çıkar- → çıkar- 3, ≠ yorul- ['- get tired'].

109

2 dinlen- [ir] [dinle- + pass. suf. -n]: 1 '- be heeded, - be heard and obeyed': Artık {öğütlerimiz/ nasihatlarımız} dinlenmiyor. '{Our advice} isn't being heeded any more.' Artık {tavsiyelerimiz/ önerilerimiz} dinlenmiyor. 'Our {recommendations/suggestions} aren't being heeded any more.' 326:2. obedience: - obey.

2 '- be listened to': O şarkılar artık dinlenmiyor. 'No one listens to those songs anymore [lit., ** Those songs aren't being listened to anymore].' 48:10. hearing: - listen.

dipnot düş-. → {not/dipnot} düş-. → düş- 6.

diren- [ir] 1 /a: DA, b: diye, c: için/ '- insist /a: {on/UPON}, b: saying, c: ON/, - refuse to' with a preceding negative verb: Niçin hâlâ yalan söylemek.te direniyor, anlamıyorum. 'I don't understand why he still insists on lying.' • Note the three patterns, here with the negative verb:
a) Bizim çocuk hasta ama doktora git.me.mek.te direniyor. 'Our child is ill, but he refuses to go to the doctor [lit., ** he insists on not going to the doctor].'
b) Bizim çocuk hasta ama {doktora git.mem diye direniyor}. 'Our child is sick but he refuses to go to the doctor [lit., ** he insists saying "I won't go to the doctor."]'
c) Bizim çocuk hasta ama doktora git.me.mek için direniyor. 'Our child is sick, but he refuses TO go to the doctor.' Polisler yürü.me.mek.te direnen mahkûmu sürükle.yerek götürdü. 'The police dragged off [lit., ** took by dragg.ing] the convict who refused to walk [by himself] [lit., ** who insisted on not walking].' 361:7. obstinacy: - balk; 421:8. demand: - insist; 442:3. refusal: - refuse. → = inat et- 2, = ısrar et-.
2 /A karşı/ '- resist, - hold out /against/': Göstericiler polisin müdahalesi.ne rağmen hemen dağılmadılar, uzun süre direndiler. 'Despite the intervention of the police, the demonstratiors did not disperse at once but held out for a long time.' Düşman.a karşı uzun süre direndik ama sonunda geri çekilmek zorunda kaldık. 'We held out against the enemy for a long time, but finally we were forced to retreat.' 361:7. obstinacy: - balk; 453:4. resistance: - stand fast.

diret- [ir] /a: DA, b: diye, c: için/ '- insist /a: {on/UPON}, b: saying, c: ON/ [having one's own way]': • Note the three patterns:
a) Öğrenci sadece müdür beyle görüş.mek.te diretti. 'The student insisted on speaking only to the director.'
b) Öğrenci sadece müdür beyle görüş.ür.üm diye diretti. Same. lit., 'The student insisted saying, "I'll speak only to the director."'
c) Öğrenci sadece müdür beyle görüş.mek için diretti. 'The student insisted on speaking only to the director.' 361:7. obstinacy: - balk; 421:8. demand: - insist. → = ısrar et-.

dobra dobra konuş-. → konuş-.

dobra dobra söyle-. → söyle- 1.

doğ- [ur] 1 '- be born': S: {a: Hangi yıl.da [or * Kaç yıl.ı.nda]/b: Hangi ayda/c: Hangi günde/d: Hangi gün/e: Hangi tarihte} doğdunuz? 'Q: {a: In what [lit., which] year/b: In what month/c: On what day/d: What day/e: On what date} were you born?' C: {a: 1961 yıl.ı.nda/b: Mart ay.ı.nda/c: Mart ay.ı.nın yirmidörd.ü.nde/ d: 24 Mart 1961'de} doğdum. 'A: I was born {a: in the year 1961/b: in the month of March/c: on the 24th of March/d: on the 24th of March 1961}.' İzmir'de doğdum ama İstanbul'da büyüdüm. 'I was born in Izmir, but I grew up in Istanbul.' Atatürk, 1881 yılında Selânik'te doğdu. 'Atatürk was born in the year 1881 in Thessalonica.'

• Note also the following common patterns rendering a similar meaning but with the ADJECTIVE doğumlu 'birthed' [doğum 'birth' + adjective-forming suf. -lI]: S: * Kaç doğumlu.sun? 'Q: When were you born?' C: {a: 1961/b: Mart 1961/c: 24 Mart 1961} doğumlu.yum. 'A: I was born [lit., ** I AM birthed] {a: in 1961/b: in March 1961/c: on the 24th of March 1961}.' Atatürk {a: Selânik/b: 1881/c: 1881 Selânik} doğumlu[dur]. 'Atatürk was born

110

{a: in Thessalonica/b: in 1881/c: in 1881 in Thessalonica} [lit., ** Atatürk IS Thessalonica ...birthed].'

Nerede doğdunuz? 'Where were you born?' Proverb: **Doğmaz doğurmaz bir Allah.** 'God alone is the one who {is not born and does not give birth/does not beget and is not begotten}.' A threat: * **Ana.n.DAN doğduğun.A pişman ederim.** 'I'll make you sorry you were ever born [lit., ** born OF your mother]!' *1:2.* birth: - be born. → = **dünyaya gel-** → **gel-** 1, ≠ **öl-** ['- die'], ≠ **hayata göz yum-**, ≠ = **hayatını** {**kaybet-/yitir-**} ['- lose one's life, - die', of unnatural causes], ≠ **vefat et-**; *514:* * 5. threat: INTERJ. specific threats.

2 '- rise, - appear', sun, moon: {**Güneş/Ay**} **erken doğdu.** 'The {sun/moon} rose early.' Proverb: **Gün doğmadan neler doğar.** 'All kinds of things may happen before daybreak [lit., ** (Imagine) what things are born before the sun rises!].' *33:8.* appearance: - appear. → = **ay çık-** → **çık-** 3, = **güneş çık-** → **çık-** 3, ≠ **güneş bat-** → **bat-** 1, ≠ **hava karar-** ['for it - get or - grow dark'], ≠ **ay kaybol-** → **ol-** 12, **yıldız çık-** ['for stars - come out, - appear'] → **çık-** 3.

doğra- [r] '- cut [up] into slices or pieces; - carve, - chop into bits, - mince': **Ispanakları ince ince doğrayın.** 'Chop the spinach up fine.' **Çalı fasulyesini küçük küçük doğrayın.** 'Cut the string beans into small pieces.' **Soğanları yarım halkalar hal.i.nde doğrayın.** 'Cut the onions into [lit., ** into the state of] half rings.' **Patateslerin kabuklarını soyup küp şekl.i.nde doğrayın.** 'Peel the potatoes [lit., the skin of the potatoes] and cut them up into [lit., into the form of] cubes.' Proverb: **Yiyen bilmez, doğrayan bilir.** 'It is not the one who eats [the food] that understands [i.e., what has been involved in producing it], but the one who has cut it up [i.e., prepared it].' *792:6.* part: - separate; *801:13.* separation: - shatter. → = **kıy-** 1, **dilim dilim kes-** ['- slice, - cut into slices'], **dilimle-**. Same.

doğrula- [r] '- verify, - corroborate, - confirm' [**doğru** 'correct, true' + verb-forming suf. -lA]: **Türk Hava Yolları** [THY] **rezervasyonunuzu doğruladı.** 'Turkish airlines has confirmed your reservation.' **Başbakan, işçi ve memur ücretleri.nin artacağ.ı söylentiler.i.ni doğruladı.** 'The prime minister confirmed the rumors that the wages of workers and civil employees would increase.' **Hükümet sözcüsü konu ilgili söylentileri ne doğruladı ne de yalanladı.** 'The government spokesman neither confirmed nor denied the rumors on the subject.' **Arkadaşımın** {**sözlerini/ iddialarını**} **doğruladım.** 'I confirmed [the truth of] my friend's {words/claims}.' *969:12.* certainty: - verify. → = **tasdik et-**, ≠ **yalanla-** for the three last examples above only.

doğrulan- [ır] /{**tarafından/CA**}/ '- be verified, corroborated, confirmed /by/' [**doğrula-** + pass. suf. -n]: **İşçi ve memur ücretleri.nin artacağ.ı söylentileri** [**başbakan tarafından/yetkililer.ce**] **doğrulandı.** 'The rumors that the wages of workers and civil employees would increase were confirmed [by the prime minister/by the authorities].' *969:12.* certainty: - verify. → = **tasdik edil-**, ≠ **yalanlan-**.

doğrusunu yap. → **yap-** 3.

doğruyu söyle-. → {**doğru/doğruyu/ gerçeği/hakikati**} **söyle-** → **söyle-** 1.

doğur- [ur] /I/ [**doğ-** + caus. suf. -Ir]: '- give birth /TO/, - bear': **Annem ben.İ sabah.a karşı doğurmuş.** 'My mother gave birth TO me toward morning.' **Komşumuz Zehra hanım** {a: **sağlıklı bir oğlan** [or **kız**]/b: **ikiz**/c: **üçüz**/d: **dördüz**/e: **beşiz**} **doğurdu.** 'Our neighbor Zehra hanım gave birth TO {a: a healthy boy [or girl]/b: twins/c: triplets/d: quadruplets/e: quintuplets}.' Proverb: **Doğmaz doğurmaz bir Allah.** 'God alone is the one who {is not born and does not give birth/does not beget and is not begotten}.' *1:3.* birth: - give birth. → = **çocuğu ol-** → **ol-** 6, = **dünyaya getir-**.

111

dokun- [ur] 1 /A/ '- touch /θ/'
physically: **Yurdagül CD'leri
konu.su.nda çok titizdir.
CD'ler.i.nE** [pronounce: si
dilerine] **dokunmasak iyi olur.**
'Yurdagül is very finicky about [lit.,
on the subject of] her CDs. It would
be better if we didn't touch θ her
CDs.' **Dokunabilir miyim?** 'May I
touch it?' **Çiçekler.E
dokunmayınız.** 'Don't touch θ the
flowers!' Proverb: **Elin ile
koymadığın şey.E dokunma.**
'Don't touch θ anything that you have
not placed [there yourself] with your
[own] hand.' *73:6.* touch: - touch;
223:10. nearness: - contact. → =
temas et- 1, = **el sür-** → sür- 5, 1
değ- 1 ['for sth - touch /θ/, - brush
against'].

2 /A/ '- upset /θ/ sb, - make sick, -
affect one's health adversely, for food
or weather not - agree /WITH/ one, -
have a bad effect /ON/': **Yağlı
yemekler mide.m.E dokunuyor.**
'Greasy foods {upset θ my
stomach/give me an upset
stomach/disagree WITH me}.' **S:
Tatlı ister misiniz?** 'Q: Would
you like a dessert?' **C: * Tatlı
almayayım, ban.A dokunuyor.**
'A: I'd better not [lit., Let me not take
a {desert/sweet}]. They disagree [lit.,
It disagrees] WITH me.' → =
midesini boz- ['- make
(physically) sick', subj.: food] →
boz- 1, **midesi bulan-** ['- be upset',
stomach]. **Sıcak havalar ban.A
çok dokunur.** 'Hot weather really
has a bad affect ON me.' *96:16a.*
unpleasure: - distress; *393:9.*
impairment: - impair; *809:9.* disorder:
- disorder.

3 /A/ '- move, - touch, - affect /θ/ sb
emotionally; - disturb, - upset /θ/ sb':
**Müdürün veda konuşması ban.A
çok dokundu.** 'The director's
farewell speech moved θ me deeply.'
**Siz.E böyle dokunacağını
bilseydim, kesinlikle o lâfı
söylemezdim.** 'If I had known that
it was going to affect θ you like this, I
would certainly not have made that
remark.' *93:14.* feelings: - affect;
893:7. influence: - influence. → =
tesir et-.

dol- [ur] 1 /lA/ '[for sth] - fill, - fill up
/with/ [of itself], - BECOME full': *
**Bardak ağzı.nA kadar su [ile]
doldu.** 'The glass filled to the brim
[lit., to its mouth] with water.'

**{Sınıf/Sinema} yavaş yavaş
dolmaya başladı.** '{The
classroom/The movie theater} slowly
began to fill up.' **Salon {a:
tamamen/b: ağz.ı.na kadar/c:
tıka başa} dolmuş, iğne atsan
yere düşmeyecek.** 'The
auditorium [or any large room] had
filled {a: completely/b: to the rafters
[i.e., to its limits, lit., up to its
mouth]/c: to its very limits} so that if
you were to drop a pin there would be
no place for it to land [lit., it (i.e., the
pin) would not fall to the ground].' *
**Hınca hınç dolan tiyatroda
ayakta duracak yer kalmadı.** 'In
the packed [lit., ** densely filling]
theater no standing room remained.'
793:7b. completeness: - fill, - become
full. → ≠ **boşal-** 1. Contrast with
doldur- 1 ['- fill, - MAKE full'].

2 '- expire, - be up, - run out', used
with various nouns denoting time:
{süre/vakit/zaman} dol- 'for
time - expire, - be up' [**süre** 'period,
extension', A. **vakit** (vaKTİ) 'time',
A. **zaman** (. -) 'time']: **Öğrenci:
Süre doldu mu?** 'Student: Is the
time [i.e., for the task] up?' = **Vakit
tamam mı?** # **Öğretmen: Beş
dakika.NIZ var.** 'Teacher: YOU
[still] have five minutes.' → =
{vakit/zaman/süre} geç- → geç-
4.

{süresi/vakti/zamanı} dol-
'for the period of time, validity OF
sth - expire, - be no longer valid, for
sth - be overdue, for sb'S time - be
up', lit., ** 'for ITS time - fill':
**{Pasaportum.un/b:
Ehliyetim.in/c: Vizem.in/d:
İkâmet tezkerem.in/e: Kredi
kartım.ın} süre.si doldu.** '{a:
My passport/b: My license/c: My
visa/d: My residence permit/e: My
credit card} has expired [lit., ** My
passport'S...period has been filled].'
At the end of an examination:
**{Süre.NİZ/Zaman.INIZ/
Vakt.İNİZ} doldu.** '{YOUR
time} is up'. Cf. **Vakit tamam.**
'The time is up.' *390:9.* disuse: -
obsolesce; *820:5.* time: - elapse. → =
{vakti/zamanı/ süresi} geç- →
geç- 4.

dolandır- [ır] '- cheat, - swindle, - rip
off, - defraud': **Adam sadece seni,
beni değil, herkesi dolandırmış.**
'The man ripped off everyone, not
just you and me.' **Piyasaları
dolandıran, bankaları hortum-**

layan pek çok kişi pişkin pişkin ortalıkta geziyor, bu ne biçim adalet! 'Those who swindle the markets, those who gouge [lit., siphon (money) off] the banks are walking about {brazenly/shamelessly}. What kind of justice is this?!' *356:14.* deception: - deceive; *356:18.* : - cheat. → = both *very common slang*: **kazık at-** ['- gyp, - rip off, - swindle, - cheat; - sell sb sth at an exorbitant, outrageous price'] → at-1, **kazıkla-**. Same.

dolaş- [ır] 1 /I/ '- go, - walk, - wander, or - stroll about or around, - make one's way through, - cover ground', usually on foot: **Üç saattir ders çalışıyorum, sıkıldım artık, çıkıp biraz dolaşayım.** 'I've been studying for three hours now. I'm bored. [I think] I'll go out and walk around for a bit.' **S: Neredeydiniz?** 'Q: Where were you?' **C: Parkta biraz dolaştık.** 'A: We were walking around in the park a bit.' **Ünlü profesör 50 yıl boyunca Anadolu'yU karış karış dolaştı.** 'For 50 years the famous professor made his way through Anatolia bit by bit [lit., handspan by handspan].' **Odada bir aşağı, bir yukarı dolaşıyordu.** 'He was walking {back and forth/up and down} [lit., ** one down, one up] in the room.' *177:23.* travel: - wander. → **gez-** ['- go or - walk about, - tour, - sightsee, - stroll'], **yürüyüşe çık-** ['- go out /for/ a walk'] → çık- 2.

2 /I/ '- tour': **Bu yaz bütün Amerika'yI dolaştık.** 'This summer we toured the entire United States.' *177:21.* travel: - journey. → = **gez-**.

doldur- [ur] [dol- + caus. suf. -DIr] 1 '- fill' • Note the two patterns:
a) /I, lA/ '- fill sth /with/ sth, - make sth full': **Benzinci: Kaç litre benzin alacaksınız? * Dolduraým mı?** 'Gas station attendant: How many litres [of gas] do you want [lit., are you going to buy]? {You want me to/Shall I} fill'er up?' **Müşteri: * {a: Beş litre/b: Ful/c: Tamamen/d: depoyu} doldurun.** 'Customer: * {a: [Give me] five liters/b, c, d: Fill'er up} [lit., ** fill {a: five liters/b,c: full/d: the tank}].' **Ful olsun.** [lit., ** Let it be full.] is more common than **Ful doldurun. * Benzin doldurdu.** 'He filled it up

WITH gas [lit., ** He filled gas].' *1020:7.* fuel: - fuel. **Bardağ.I su.yLA doldurdu.** 'He filled the glass WITH water.' **Bütün ev.İ balık kokusu doldurdu.** 'The odor of fish filled the whole house.' Proverb: **Yağmur yağarken küpleri doldurmalı.** 'One must fill the [water] jugs while it is raining.', i.e., take advantage of available opportunities. Make hay while the sun shines.
b) /I, A/ '- fill sth /WITH/ sth', lit., ** '- fill sth INTO sth': * **Garson şarab.I bardaklar.A doldurdu.** '{The waiter filled θ the glasses with the wine [lit., ** filled the wine INTO the glasses]/The waiter poured the wine into the glasses}.' **Garson kadehi {* yarı.sı.nA/ağz.ı.nA} kadar doldurdu.** 'The waiter filled the wine glass {* {half full/halfway} [lit., ** to its half]/to {the top/the rim} [lit., ** to its mouth]}.' * **Suyu şişe.den sürahi.yE boşalttı. * İç.i.nE buzları doldurdu.** 'He poured [lit., emptied] the water from the bottle INTO the pitcher. * He filled it with the ice [lit., ** he filled the ice into its (i.e., the pitcher's) inside].' **Otomobili.nE benzin dolduran bir kişi vurul.arak öldürüldü.** 'A person who was filling his car with gasoline was shot dead [lit., ** was killed by be.ing shot].' → ≠ **boşalt-.** *793:7a.* completeness: - fill sth.

* **yaşını {doldur- [ur]/tamamla- [r]}** '- be or - turn a certain age, - {fill/complete} a certain year of one's life' [**yaş** 'age, years of a person's life'; **tamamla-** '- complete, - finish sth']: * **25 yaş.IM.ı doldurdum.** 'I am 25 years old [lit., ** I have filled MY 25 years].' Contrast this with the following, most common way of expressing one's age: * **Yirmi beş yaş.ı.nda.yım.** 'I'm 25 years old. [lit., ** 'I'm IN year 25.'] • Note, however, that in English the seemingly equivalent, 'I am IN my 25th year' means that I'm 24 years old, i.e., 'I have completed 24, not 25 years.']. *303:9.* age: - mature. → = **yaşına {bas-/gir-}** → bas- 1, gir-.

2 '- fill OUT [application, questionnaire], - fill IN [blanks], - complete a form': **Lütfen şu formu doldurun[uz].** 'Please fill OUT this form.' **Kayıt form.u.nu doldurur musunuz?** 'Would you fill OUT the registration form [e.g., at a hotel]?'

Lütfen ş u boşlukları dol-durun[uz]. 'Please fill IN these blanks.' *793:6.* completeness: - complete.

dolgu düş-. → düş- 1.

don- [ar] /DAn/ 1 '- freeze /{from/DUE TO}/, *fig.:* - feel very cold': Kışın {a: göl/b: nehir/c: ırmak/d: sular} dondu. 'In winter {a: the lake/b: the river/c: the river/d: the water[s]} froze.' → ≠ eri-. # Üç dağcı soğuktan {don.arak öldüler/dondular}. 'Three mountaineers froze to death [lit., ** {died by freez.ing/froze}].' *307:24.* death: - die a natural death. Soğuk.tan ayaklarımız dondu. 'Our feet froze from the cold.' *1022:9.* cold: - freeze. → = buz kesil- ['- turn into ice, - freeze'] → kesil- 5.

2 '- freeze, - seize up, - jam': * Hay Allah! Aksiliğ.E bakın. Tam yazdığım e-maili göndermek üzereyken bilgisayar dondu. Şimdi tekrar yazmam lâzım. ' * O dear! What a {nuisance/bummer}! Just as I was about to send off the e-mail I had written the computer froze. Now I have to write it again.' *854:10.* stability: - become firmly fixed.

doy- [ar] /A/ '- have enough /OF/, - be satisfied /WITH/, - eat one's fill, - be full': In reference to food: S: Biraz daha et alır mısınız? 'Q: Will you have a little more meat?' C1: Teşekkür ederim almayayım. 'A1: No thank you [lit., Thank you, let me not take (any)].' C2: Elleriniz.E sağlık, yemekler enfesti, {çok doydum}. 'A2: Congratulations on your cooking [lit., ** Good health to your hands (i.e., for doing such good cooking)]. The food was just delicious, [but] {I'm full./I've really eaten my fill.}' *993:5.* satiety: - have enough. → ≠ acık-. NON-verbal noun as object: * Çocuk bugün dondurma.yA doydu. 'The child {had his fill OF ice cream/had all the ice cream he wanted}.'
In reference to things other than food: Kumarda milyonlarca lira kazandı, * hâlâ para.yA doymuyor. 'He won millions of liras gambling. * He still isn't satisfied WITH the money [he has].', i.e., he can never get enough money. Proverb: Yenilen pehlivan

güreş.E doymaz. 'A defeated wrestler always wants to wrestle some more [lit., never gets enough OF wrestling].', i.e., never tires of a fight in the hope of eventually winning.
VERBAL noun as object: Tatil o kadar kısaydı ki yüzmey.E doyamadım. 'The {vacation/holiday} was so short that I couldn't do all the swimming I wanted.' Sevgilim, gözleri.ne bakmay.A doyamıyorum. 'My darling, I can never get enough OF looking into your eyes.' • Note the different meaning when used with the suffix 1A: Aç, tok.un yüz.ü.ne bakmak.LA doymaz. 'A hungry person is not filled up [i.e., satisfied] BY looking at the face of a well-fed person.', i.e., He needs real food himself.

* **karnı doy-** '- have one's fill, - have had enough food' [karın (karnı) 'stomach'], lit., ** 'for one's stomach - have had its fill'. • Note the different personal suffixes on karın: Karn.IM doydu. 'I've had enough [lit., ** My stomach has had its fill].' Karn.IMIZ doydu. 'WE've had enough.' * Karn.IM doy.madan ders çalışamam. 'I can't study on an empty stomach [lit., ** without eating MY fill].' *993:5.* satiety: - have enough. → ≠ acık-, ≠ karnı acık-.

doyur- [ur] /lA/ '- feed to satiety' [doy- + caus. suf. -Ir]: Önce çocukları doyuralım, sonra biz yeriz. 'First let's feed the children, then we'll eat.' Çocukları sadece ekmek.le doyuramayız, katık da lâzım. 'We can't feed the children only {bread/with bread}. Katık [i.e., food such as cheese or olives eaten with bread] is also needed.' Proverb: Yetimi giydir, açı doyur, kavgacıyı ayır. 'Clothe the orphan, feed the hungry, and separate those who are fighting [lit., the fighter].' *993:4.* satiety: - satiate.

karnını doyur- '- get sth to eat, - have a meal, - eat, - eat one's fill, - fill one's stomach' [karın (kaRNı) 'stomach']: Karn.IM.ı doyurdum. 'I ate MY fill.' Sinemaya gitmeden önce karn.IMIZ.ı doyuralım. 'Before going to the movies, let's get sth to eat.' *993:4.* satiety: - satiate. → = yemek ye- ['- eat'] → ye- 1.

Part 1: Turkish-English Dictionary of Verbs

dök- [er] 1 /DAn, A/ '- pour /from, {to/INTO}/': **Garson şarabı şişe.den bardaklar.A döktü.** 'The waiter poured the wine from the bottle INTO the glasses.' **Kadın vazodaki suyu lavabo.yA döktü.** 'The woman poured the water in the vase INTO the {sink/washbasin}.' *176:17.* transferal, transportation: - ladle. → **koy-** 1 ['- put, - place', sometimes used for liquids to give the sense of '- pour'].

dert dök- /A/ '- pour out one's troubles, - spill out one's woes /to/, - get sth off one's chest' [P. **dert** 'trouble, care, worry']: **Dert dökmek insan.I rahatlatır.** 'Pouring out one's troubles [to sb] puts a person at ease.' * **Seni sıkan birşeyler var, hiç konuşmuyorsun. Gel, {derdini dök}, rahatlarsın.** 'Something's bothering you [lit., ** Some thingS are...]. You're not saying anything. Come on, {get it off your chest/pour out your troubles/unburden yourself}. You'll feel better.' *120:7.* relief: - lighten.

göz yaşı dök- '- cry, - weep, lit., ** - spill tears' [**göz** 'eye', **yaş** 'moisture, tears']: **Kocam öldükten sonra çok göz yaşı döktüm.** 'After my husband died, I cried a lot.' *12:12* excretion: - excrete; *115:12.* lamentation: - weep. → = **ağla-**, ≠ **gül-** 1.

2 /A, {üstüne/üzerine}/ '- spill /ON, on/': * **Çocuk bardaktaki suyu döktü.** 'The child spilled the glass of water [lit., the water in the glass].' **Çocuk yemeği üzerine döktü.** 'The child spilled the food on himself.' *80:15a.* cleanness: - dirty; *238:17a.* stream: - make overflow.

3 /A, {üstüne/üzerine}/ '- throw out, - spill out as waste /{ON/INTO}, on/': *390:7.* disuse: - discard. **çöp dök-** /A/ '- litter, - throw trash /{ON/INTO}/' [**çöp** 'litter, trash']: **Sokaklar.A çöp dökmeyiniz.** 'Don't litter the streets.' **Sokaklar.A çöp dökmek doğru değildir.** 'It's not right to throw trash ON the streets.' **Çöpleri çöp teneke.si.nE dökünüz.** 'Throw the trash INTO the trash can.' *80:15a.* uncleanness: - dirty; *352:7.* publication: poster: * specific signs; *390:7.* disuse: -

discard; *810:2.* disarrangement: - disarrange. → = **çöp at-** → **at-** 2.

çöpe dök- '- throw /{IN/INTO}/ the trash, - discard, - throw out' [**çöp** 'litter, trash']: **O kutunun içindekiler lâzım değil, çöp.E dökebilirsin.** 'The things in that box are not needed. You can throw them IN the trash.' *390:7.* disuse: - discard. → = **çöpe at-**.

su dök- '- take a {pee/piss}, - urinate' [**su** 'water']: **Su dökmey.E gidiyorum.** 'I'm going to take a pee.' **Su döküp geleyim.** 'Just let me take a pee, and I'll be with you [lit., come].' An always appropriate remark for both urination and defecation is **Tuvalete gidiyorum.** 'I'm going to the restroom.' **Bura.yA su dökmek yasaktır.** 'It is forbidden to urinate θ here.' *12:14.* excretion: - urinate; *352:7.* publication: poster: * specific signs. → = **çiş {yap-/et-}** → **yap-** 3, = **işe-**, = **küçük aptes yap-** → yap- 3, **ihtiyacını gör-** ['- defecate, - urinate'] → **gör-** 4, **tuvalet yap-** ['- have a bowel movement *or* BM, - urinate, - do one's business, - use the facilities, the restroom; - make one's toilet, i.e., usually for a woman to dress or to arrange her hair'] → **yap-** 3.

dökül- [ür] [**dök-** + {pass./refl.} suf. - Il] 1 /A, {üstüne/üzerine}/ '- spill /ON, on/' [I.]: **Kedi şişe.yE çarptı ve süt elbisem.in {üst.ü.ne/üzer.i.ne} döküldü.** 'The cat bumped {AGAINST/INTO} the bottle, and the milk spilled {on} my suit.' *190:13.* emergence: - run out; *238:17b.* stream: - overflow.

2 /a: A, b: {üstüne/üzerine}, c: {tarafından/CA}/ '- be poured out, - be spilled /a: ON, b: on, c: by/': **{Fabrikalar.ca/Fabrikalar tarafından} dökülen atık maddeler tertemiz ırmağı bataklığ.a çevirdi.** 'The waste poured out {by the factories} has turned the sparkling clean river into a swamp.' *80:15a.* cleanness: - dirty; *176:17.* transferal, transportation: - ladle; *238:17a.* stream: - make overflow; *390:7.* disuse: - discard; *908:25.* ejection: - disgorge.

3 /A/ '- flow, - run, - pour /INTO/': **Kızılırmak Karadeniz.E**

115

dökülür. 'The Kızılırmak flows INTO the Black Sea.' **Deprem olunca halk sokaklar.A döküldü.** 'When the earthquake occurred, the people poured out INTO the streets.' *189:9.* entrance: - flow in. → = **ak-** .

4 '- fall out': **Saçlarım dökülüyor. Ne yapmam lâzım, * doktor bey?** 'My hair is falling out. What should I do, * doctor?' *194:8.* descent: - tumble.

<u>dön-</u> [er] **1** /etrafında/ '- turn, - revolve, - rotate /around/': **Dünya güneş.in etraf.ı.nda dönüyor.** 'The earth revolves around the sun.' *913:5.* circuitousness: - circle.

başı dön- '- be dizzy, - get dizzy' [**baş** 'head'], lit., 'for one's head - turn': **Baş.IM dönüyor.** 'I'm dizzy [lit., MY head is turning].' **Baş.IM dönünce düşmemek için duvar.A dayandım.** 'When I became dizzy [lit., ** When MY head turned], I leaned AGAINST the wall so as not to fall.' **Gökdele.nin en üst kat.ı.ndan aşağı.ya bakınca baş.I döndü.** 'When SHE looked down from the top floor of the skyscraper, SHE got dizzy [lit., ** HER head turned].' *984:8.* * distraction, confusion: - be dizzy.

2 /DAn, A/ '- return or - come back /from, to/': **S: Amerika'dan ne zaman döndün?** 'Q: When did you get back from the U.S.?' **C: * Birkaç gün oldu geleli.** 'A: {It's been a couple of days./A couple of days ago.}' **Lütfen bekleyin, {hemen/biraz sonra/beş dakika sonra} döneceğim.** 'Please wait, I'll be {right back/back shortly/back IN five minutes}.' **{a: Hemen/b: Bu gece/c: Yarın/d: Gelecek hafta} dönmeliyim.** 'I must return {a: right away/b: tonight/c: tomorrow/d: next week}.' **İstanbul'DAN Ankara'yA dönüyorum.** 'I'm returning FROM İstanbul TO Ankara.' * **Ne zaman döneceğim belli değil.** 'It's not clear when I'll {be back/return}.' Condition as 'destination': **Hayat normal.E dönüyor.** 'Life is returning to normal.' *163:8b.* regression: - turn back, - come back.

* *place name* **dönüşü** '{after/while} returning from, {during/on} the return from' [**dön-** +

verbal-noun suf. **-Iş** + possessed suf. **-I**]: * **Tatil dönüşü trafik canavarı 22 can aldı.** 'Traffic accidents occurring at the end of the holiday weekend claimed 22 lives [lit., ** On the return from the holiday, the traffic monster took 22 lives].' * **İstanbul dönüşü doğrudan doğruya New York'a uçtum.** 'After returning to Istanbul, I flew directly to New York.' *820:14.* time: - during; *834:7.* subsequence: ADV. after which.

geri dön- /DAn, A/ '- come back, - go back, - turn back, - return /from, to/' [**geri** 'back, rear, the space behind']: **Amcam Almanya'dan {çok parayla/yeni bir eşle/bir Mercedesle} geri döndü.** 'My paternal uncle returned from Germany {with a lot of money/with a new spouse/with a Mercedes}.' **Vapuru kaçırınca gitmekten vazgeçip ev.e geri döndük.** 'When we missed the ferry, we gave up the idea of going there and returned θ home.' **Annem çanta.sı.nı unuttuğ.u.nu farkedince * o kadar yol.DAN geri döndük.** 'When my mother noticed that she had forgotten her {purse/handbag}, * we went all the way back [lit., ** went back FROM that much road].' <u>Proverb</u>: **Atılan ok geri dönmez.** 'The arrow that has been shot does not return.', i.e., What has been done cannot be undone. *163:8b.* regression: - turn back, - come back; *845: * 21.* lateness: PHR. it's too late.

3 /A/ '- turn /{to/TOWARD}/' [ADJ. /A/ **dönük** 'turned /toward/, facing']: **S: Acaba postane nerede?** 'Q: I wonder where the post office is?' **C1: * İkinci cadde.DEN {sağ.A/ sol.A} dönün, ilk büyük bina.** 'A1: Turn {[to the] right/[to the] left} AT the second corner [lit., ** FROM the second street]. It's the first big building.' **C2: * Yüz elli metre ileri.DEN sağ.A dönün.** 'A2: Turn θ right θ 150 meters ahead.' **C3: Köprü.DEN geçince sol.A dönün.** 'A3: Turn θ left after crossing [lit., when crossing] θ the bridge.' *279:6.* curve: - curve. → = **sap-** .

4 '- turn sth, - make sth turn': * **{arkasını/sırtını} dön-** /A/ '- turn around, - turn one's back /to/' [**arka** 'back', **sırt** 'the back of a person or animal']: **Beni görünce arkasını döndü ve gitti.** 'When he saw me, he {turned around/turned his back (to me)} and walked off [lit., ** turned around and went].' *914:9.* rotation: - rotate. → = {arkasını/sırtını} çevir- 1 → çevir- 3.

5 '- go back on': **sözünden dön-** '- go back /ON/ one's word' [söz 'word, promise']: **Onu tanırım, dürüst adamdır; merak etme söz.ü.nDEN dönmez.** 'I know him. He's an honest man. Don't worry, he won't go back ON his word.' *435:4.* nonobservance: - violate. → = sözünde durMA- → dur- 6, = sözünü tutMA- → tut- 5, ≠ sözünde dur- → dur- 6, ≠ sözünü tut- 1 → tut- 5.

6 /A/ '- turn /INTO/, - become /θ/': **Akşam.a doğru yağmur dolu.yA döndü.** 'Toward evening the rain turned INTO hail.' **Onu çok seviyorum, başka biriyle birlikte olduğunu öğrenince çılgın.A döndüm.** 'I love her a lot. When I learned that she was with someone else, I {went/became} θ crazy.' *851:6.* change: - be changed. → = çevir- 8, = dönüş-, = kesil- 5 ['- turn into, - become', often suddenly as a result of fear or other strong emotion], = ol- 1.

döndür- [ür] [dön- + caus. suf. -DIr] 1 /A, A doğru/ '- turn sth /to, toward/': **Televizyonu iyi göremiyorum, biraz ban.a doğru döndürür müsün?** 'I can't see the TV well. Please turn it toward me a little.' **Yüzünü ban.a doğru döndürdü ve gülümsedi.** 'He turned his face toward me and smiled.' **Çiçekler yapraklarını güneş.e doğru döndürdü.** 'The plants turned their leaves toward the sun.' *914:9.* rotation: - rotate. → = çevir- 2.

2 /A/ '- turn sth /INTO/ sth else, - convert': **Yazın deniz kenarındaki evimiz.İ motel.E döndürürüz.** 'In the summer we turn our house at the seaside INTO a motel.' *857:11.* conversion: - convert. → = çevir- 9.

dönüş- [ür] /DAn, A/ '- turn, - change, - be transformed /from, INTO/': **Ona karşı duyduğum aşk bir süre sonra nefret.E dönüştü.** 'After a time the love that I had felt for {her/him} turned INTO hate.' **Kar kısa sürede tipi.yE dönüştü.** 'The snow soon turned INTO a snowstorm.' *851:6.* change: - be changed. → = çevir- 8, = dön- 6, = kesil- 5 ['- turn into, - become', often suddenly as a result of fear or other strong emotion], = ol- 1.

dörtgözle bekle-. → bekle- 1.

döşe- [r] /IA, θ/ '- furnish /with [money, objects], IN [a style, material]/': **Zeki bey emeklilik para.sı.yla evini yeniden döşedi.** 'Zeki bey refurnished [lit., ** furnished again] his house with [money from] his retirement pay.' * **Bütün evimi {a: antika eşyalar.la/b: Kalebodur.θ/c: parke.θ/d: fayans. θ/e: mermer.θ} döşemek istiyorum.** 'I want to {do/furnish} my whole house {a: with antiques/b: IN Kalebodur [a particular brand name for a type of ceramic tile used for walls, floors, kitchen counters, bath tile, etc.]/c: IN parquet/d: IN tile/e: IN marble}.' *385:8.* provision, equipment: - equip.

döşen- [ir] /IA, θ/ '- be furnished /with [money, objects], IN [a style, material]/' [döşe- + pass. suf. - n]: **Süleymanlar.ın ev.i.ni gördün mü? Bütün ev {a: antika eşyalar.la/b: Kalebodur.θ/c: parke.θ/d: fayans.θ/e: mermer.θ} döşenmiş.** 'Have you seen the house of Süleyman's family? The whole house is furnished {a: with antiques/b: IN Kalebodur [a particular brand name for a type of ceramic tile used for walls, floors, kitchen counters, bath tile, etc.]/c: IN parquet/d: IN tile/e: IN marble}.' * **Ev baş.tan baş.a halı.yla döşenmiş.** 'The house was covered from one end to the other [lit., ** from head to head] with rugs.' * **Kız tarafı düğünden önce yeni çift.in ev.i.nin döşenme.si.ni şart koştu.** 'Before the marriage the bride's family [lit., ** the girl {side/party}] stipulated that the new couple's house be furnished.' *385:8.* provision, equipment: - equip.

döv- [er] /I/ '- beat, - strike, - spank, - paddle': * **Annesi vazoyu kırdığı için çocuğunu dövdü.** 'The mother spanked her child because he had broken the vase [lit., ** its mother, because it had broken the vase, beat her child].' **Dövmek iyi**

bir ceza değildir. '{Spanking/ Paddling} is not an effective [lit., good] punishment.' *604:13.* punishment: - whip; *901:14.* impulse, impact: - hit. → **vur-** 1 ['- hit, - strike, - knock, - kick, - slap, - bump', depending on the preceding noun], **dayak at-** ['- beat, - give a whipping, beating, - thrash /θ/'] → at-5.

döviz bozdur-. → bozdur-.

dövüş- [ür] /lA/ '- fight, - struggle, - engage in physical combat /with/ one another' [döv- + recip. suf. -Iş]: Üç kişinin sokakta dövüştüğünü görünce hemen polisi aradım. 'When I observed three people fighting with one another in the street, I at once called the police.' **Maçtan sonra seyirciler * kıyasıya dövüştüler.** 'After the game [i.e., soccer, basketball], the spectators * got into a big brawl.' **Orhan'ın Ali ile dövüştüğünü görür görmez yan.lar.ı.na gittim.** 'As soon as I saw Orhan fighting with Ali, I went {over to/up to} them [lit., ** to their sides].' *457:13.* contention: - contend. → **çatış-** 1 ['- quarrel, - clash /with/'], **kavga et-** ['- fight, - quarrel /with/', physical or just verbal].

dua et- [eDer] 1 '- pray': Biz aile.CE her yemekten sonra dua ederiz. 'We pray together AS a family after every meal.' The most common prayer before the meal: **Bismillahirrahmanirrahim.** 'In the name of God, the Merciful, the Compassionate.' The most common prayer after the meal: **Elhamdulillah.** 'Praise be to God.' *696:12.* worship: - pray. → **namaz kıl-** ['- perform the namaz'], **ibadet et-** ['- worship'], **tap-.** Same.

2 /A, için/ '- pray /to [God], for [sth]/, - supplicate': **Sağlığ.ınız.A kavuşmanız için gece gündüz [Allah'a] dua ettim.** 'I prayed [to God] day and night for you to recover [lit., ** for your attaining θ your health].' **Nur'LA evlenebilmek için [Allah'A] çok dua ettim.** 'I often prayed to God [to be able] to marry θ Nur [f.].' In the same meaning, *more eloquent, formal*: **Nur'U ban.A nasip etmesi için [Allah'A] çok dua ettim.** 'I often prayed [to God] for Him to grant me Nur [in marriage].' **Bu iş.E**

girebilmek için [Allah'A] çok dua ettim. 'I often prayed [to God] [to be able] to get this job [lit., ** to be able to enter θ this job].' In the same meaning, *more eloquent, formal*: **Ban.A bu iş.İ nasip etmesi için [Allah.A] çok dua ettim.** 'I often prayed [to God] for Him to grant me this job.' *440:11.* request: - entreat.

duman çık-. → çık- 3.

dur- [UR] 1 /DA/ '- stop, - come to a stop /at/, - become motionless', person, vehicle, instrument: Taksi şoförüne: {a: Müsait [or Uygun] bir yer.de/b: Bura.da/c: Durak.ta/d: Köşe.de/e: Otel.in ön.ü.nde} durun. 'To the taxi driver: Stop {a: at a suitable place/b: here/c: at the stop/d: at the corner/e: in front of the hotel}.' **Otobüs {köşe.de/durak.ta} durdu.** 'The bus stopped {at the corner/at the [bus] stop}.' *856:7.* cessation: for sth - cease. → **devam et-** 1 ['- continue on', i.e., not to stop]. **Duvar saatimiz durmuş, kurmak lâzım.** 'Our wall clock seems to have stopped. It needs to be wound [lit., ** winding is necessary].' *819:6.* end: - come to an end.

2 '- cease, - stop', a process, activity as subject: {a: Yağmur/b: Kar/c: Fırtına/d: Rüzgâr/e: Dolu} nihayet durdu. '{a: The rain/b: The snow/c: The storm/d: The wind/e: The hail} finally stopped.' **Çocuğun ağlaması bir türlü durmadı.** 'The child's crying just {wouldn't/didn't} stop.' **Bu okula geldiğimden beri durmadan çalışıyorum.** 'I've been working {non-stop/lit., without stopping} since coming to this school.' * **Onu görünce o kadar heyecanlandım ki kalbim duracak gibi oldu.** 'When I saw {her/him/it}, I got so excited my heart almost stopped [lit., ** became like it was going to stop].' *819:6.* end: - come to an end; *856:7.* cessation: for sth - cease. → = **bit-** 1, = **din-**, = **kesil-** 2, = **sona er-** → er-.

3 /DA, başında/ '- stand /{on/at}, {AT/BY}/': **Orta yaşlı bir adam masa.nın baş.ı.nda duruyordu.** 'A middle-aged man was standing {BY/at} the table.' **ayakta dur-** '- stand on one's feet' [ayak 'foot']: **Bütün gün ayakta durmak.tan**

bacaklarım ağrıdı. 'My legs hurt from standing on my feet all day.' * Hınca hınç dolan tiyatroda ayakta duracak yer kalmadı. 'In the packed [lit., ** densely filling] theater there was no more standing room [lit., no standing room remained].' *200:7.* verticalness: - stand.

4 '- stop, - quit [an activity]': Someone is hitting you or otherwise annoying you. You say: {Dursana!/Dursanıza!} 'Stop it! [or Knock it off!]' or somewhat coarse: **Dur be kardeşim, şimdi sırası mı!** 'Stop it man! Is this the time for it?' **Durun, yoksa bağırırım!** 'Stop or I'll scream.' *390:4.* disuse: - cease to use; *856:14.* cessation: INTERJ. cease! → = bırak- **4.**

5 '- wait, - hold on': **Dur!** 'Wait!' S: **Bende otobüs bileti yok. Bir bilet verir misin?** 'Q: I don't have a bus ticket. Would you give me one [lit., a ticket]?' C: * **Dur bakayım. Buldum, al.** 'A: Just a second, let me see. Oh, I've found one, here [lit., take it].' *130:8.* expectation: - await. → = bekle- **1.**

6 /DA, {üstünde/üzerinde}/ '- remain, - stay /{in/at}, on/': **Otobüsümüz İzmir'de çok durmadı.** 'Our bus didn't {stay/stop} in Izmir long.' **Aradığın kitaplar masa.nın {üst.ü.nde/üzer.i.nde} duruyor.** 'The books [that] you are looking for are still [lit., remain] {on} the table.' **Haftalardır duran {kar/buz} sonunda eridi.** 'The {snow/ice}, which had stayed around for weeks, finally melted.' Proverbs: **Akacak kan damarda durmaz.** 'The blood that is going to spill will not stay in the vein.' *963:11.* predetermination: PHR. it is fated. **Boş duran.A şeytan iş bulur.** 'Satan finds work FOR the idle [lit., for the one who remains unoccupied].' **Korkulu rüya görmektense uyanık durmak evladır.** 'It is better to lie [lit., remain] awake than to have bad [lit., frightening] dreams.' *256:5.* remainder: - remain. → = kal- **1.**

'- dwell on a topic, subject': You want to stop further discussion of a subject. You say: **N'olur * bu konu üzerinde daha fazla durmayalım.** 'Oh please, * let's

drop the subject [lit., let's not dwell on this subject any more].' *826:9.* duration:- protract.

* **sözünde dur-** '- keep one's promise, word' [söz 'word, promise']: **O.nA güvenmiyorum; sözünde duracağını sanmam.** 'I don't trust θ him. I don't think he'll keep his promise.' *434:2.* observance: - observe. → = sözünü tut- **1** → tut- **5,** ≠ **sözünden dön-** → dön- **5,** ≠ **sözünü tutMA-** → tut- **5.**

7 '- exist, - be existent, - survive': **Eski Türk yazıtları hâlâ duruyor.** 'The old Turkic inscriptions still survive.' *760:8.* existence: - exist.

8 '- remain inactive in the face of a situation that requires action, - do nothing, - stand by without doing anything': * **NE duruyorsun, birşey.LER yapsana! Hırsız çantamı aldı kaçıyor.** '{What are you waiting for?/WHY are you just standing there?} Do something! A thief has taken my {handbag/purse/briefcase} and is running off [with it].' *329:2.* inaction: - do nothing.

9 /{üstünde/üzerinde}/ '- look or - appear /ON [lit., ** on HIS surface, {üst.ü/üzer.i}, i.e., here the body, excluding the head and feet]/, - suit, - fit' • Note the different possessed suffixes on {üstü/üzeri}: S: **Bu {pantolon/şort} üzer.İ.nde nasıl duruyor?** 'Q: How do these {trousers/shorts} look on HIM?' C1: **Çok iyi duruyor.** 'A1: Very good.' C2: **Hiç iyi durmuyor.** 'A2: Not good at all.' S: **Bu {a: etek/b: elbise/c: tişort/d: kazak} üzer.i.M.de nasıl durdu?** 'Q: How {does/did} this {a: skirt/b: suit/c: T-shirt/d: sweater} look on ME?' C1: **Bu etek üzeri.N.de biraz {uzun/kısa/komik} durdu.** 'A: This skirt {seems/seemed} a little {long/short/ funny} on YOU.' C2: * **Hiç yakışmadı.** 'A2: Terrible [lit., ** It didn't suit at all.]' *866:3.* conformity: - conform. → = gel- **2,** = ol- **8,** = otur- **5,** uy- **1** ['- fit /θ/, - be the right size and shape /FOR/'], yakış- **2** ['for sth - look good /ON/, - suit /θ/', clothing].

10 '- stall', engine, motor vehicle: {a: Motor/b: Araba/c: Otobüs/ d: Motosiklet/e: Bot} sürekli duruyor. '{a: The engine/b: The car/c: The bus/d: The motorcycle/e: The motorboat} keeps stalling [lit., stalls continuously].' *856:7.* cessation: for sth - cease.

11 verb stem.Ip dur- '- keep *verb stem*.ing', e.g., '- keep on do.ing, - do sth continuously': **Karşı masada oturan adam kız.A göz kırp.IP DUR.uyor.** 'The man sitting at the table across from us KEEPs wink.ING AT the girl.' **Baban.la tartış.IP DURma, ne diyorsa onu yap.** 'Don't KEEP argu.ING with your father, just do whatever he says.' *811:4a.* continuity: - continue sth; *855:3.* continuance: - continue.

durdur- [ur] '- stop sb, sth' [**dur-** + caus. suf. **-DIr**]: NON-verbal noun as object: **Arabayı durdurdu ve indi.** 'He stopped the car and got out.' **Şu adamı durdurun!** 'Stop that man!' **Odaya girmek üzereyken beni durdurdu.** 'He stopped me as I was about to enter the room.' **Lütfen * şu kardeş kavga.sı.nı durdurun.** 'Please * stop this {fighting/quarreling} between {brothers/sisters} [lit., ** this {brother/sister} fighting]!' **Kaleci.nin sakatlandığı.nı görünce hakem hemen maçı durdurdu.** 'When the referee saw that the goalkeeper had been hurt, he at once stopped the game.' *856:6.* cessation: - cease sth. → ≠ **başlat-** ['- cause sth to begin, - begin sth, - start sth'].
VERBAL noun as object: **Doktorlar hasta.nın kanama.sı.nı durdura-madılar.** 'The doctors couldn't stop the patient's bleeding.' *856:11.* cessation: - put a stop to; *1011:13.* hindrance: - stop. For such cases as 'Stop that crying!', → = **bırak- 3,** = **kes- 4.**

durula- [r] /lA/ '- rinse /{IN/with}/' [**duru 1** 'clear, limpid.' **2** *prov.* 'watery' + verb-forming suf. **-lA**]: **{Tabakları/Bardakları/Çarşaf-ları} yıkadıktan sonra iyice durula, * deterjan.lı kalmasın.** 'After washing {the dishes/the glasses/the sheets}, rinse them thoroughly. * Don't let any detergent remain on them.' **Tabakları soğuk suy.LA duruladım.** 'I rinsed the {plates/dishes} {IN/with} cold water.' *79:19.* cleanness: - wash. **Durula-** is not used for '- rinse one's mouth'. For that AND for '- rinse

dishes, glasses', but NOT 'sheets', → **çalkala-.**

duş al-. → **al- 1.**

duş yap-. → **yap- 3.**

duy- [ur] **1** '- hear': **Hey! Siz.E sesleniyorum. Beni duymuyor musunuz?** 'Hey, I'm calling to you. Don't you hear me?' * **Arkasından çok bağırdık ama duymadı.** 'We shouted loudly * after him [lit., ** from his back], but he didn't hear [us].' **Her duyduğun.A inanma.** 'Don't believe θ everything you hear.' **Görmedim, duymadım, bilmiyorum de.mekle iş.in iç.i.nden çıkabileceğini mi sanıyorsun?** "Do you think that by saying "I didn't see it, I didn't hear it, I don't know" you'll be able to get out of this situation?' * **Anneannemin kulakları iyi duymuyor.** 'My grandmother doesn't hear well [lit., ** My grandmother's EARS don't hear well].' → = **ağır duy-** below. Proverb: **Sağır duymaz, uydurur.** 'A deaf person doesn't hear; he makes up things.', i.e., He fills in with his imagination for what he can't hear. *48:11.* hearing: - hear. → = **işit- 1.**

ağır duy- '- be hard of hearing' [**ağır** 'heavy, hard']: **Anneannem ağır duyuyor, bağır.arak konuş.** 'My grandmother is hard of hearing; you'll have to shout [lit., ** speak shout.ing].' *49:4.* deafness: - be deaf. → = **ağır işit-** → **işit- 1.**

2 /I/ '- hear /{OF/ABOUT}/, - learn /OF/, - get word /OF/': **Duydun mu, Selim kumar.DA 20 bin lira kazanmış.** 'Have you heard? Selim won 20,000 liras θ gambling.' **Baban bu {iş.İ} duyarsa yandık.** 'If your father hears ABOUT this {affair/business/matter}, we've had it.' **A: Dünkü trafik kaza.sı.nI duydun mu?** 'A: Did you hear ABOUT the traffic accident yesterday?' **B: Hayır duymadım.** 'B: No, I didn't.' **A: Tam 42 kişi ölmüş.** 'A: Exactly 42 people perished.' **B: Şimdiye kadar böyle feci kaza duymadım.** 'B: Up to now I've never heard OF such a terrible accident.' **S: Dün olanlar.I duydun mu?** 'Q: Did you hear what happened [lit., THE thingS that happened] yesterday?' **C:

Duymadım. Ne oldu? 'A: [No,] I didn't. What happened?' * **110** [read: yüz on] yaş.ı.nA kadar yaşayan adam duydum. 'I heard OF a man who lived to the age of 110.' *551:15.* information: - know, - be informed. → = işit- 2.

3 '- feel, - sense' *24:6.* sensation: - sense; *93:10.* feeling: - feel: → = hisset- 1, = sez-. # **gurur duy-** [A. gurur (. -) 'pride, excessive pride', mostly negative implication] (1) /{1A/DAn}/ '- be or - feel proud /OF/, - take pride /IN/', positive implication: NON-verbal noun as object: Animate object /1A/: {a: Oğlum.LA/b: Kızım.LA/c: Kocam.LA/d: Karım.LA/e: Sen.İN.LE} gurur duyuyorum. 'I'm proud {a: OF my son/b: OF my daughter/c: OF my husband/d: OF my wife/e: OF you [s.]}.' Inanimate object /{DAn/1A}/: {İşi.nDEN/ İşi.yLE} gurur duyuyor. 'He is proud OF his job [*or* OF his work, OF what he has done].' Öğretmenim. Mesleğim.{DEN/LE} gurur duyuyorum. 'I'm a teacher. I'm proud OF my profession.' Pronoun as object: {Amerikalıyım/ Türküm}, ve {bu.nDAN/ bu.nun.LA} da gurur duyuyorum. 'I'm {an American/a Turk}, and I'm proud OF it.' VERBAL noun as object: Infinitive as object /DAn/ '- be proud /{OF [doING]/TO [do]}/': Sizin şirketiniz.LE iş {yapmak.TAN} gurur duyuyoruz. 'We are proud {OF doING/TO do} business with your company.' DIk participle as object /{DAn/1A}/: Yaptık-larımız.{DAN/LA} gurur duyu-yoruz. 'We are proud OF what we have done.' Sizin şirketiniz.LE iş yaptığımız için gurur duyu-yoruz. 'We are proud {that we did/of having done} business with with your company.' *136:5.* pride: - take pride. → = /1A/ iftihar et-, = kıvanç duy- → duy- 3, = /1A/ {övün-/öğün-} 1, ≠ /DAn/ utan-. (2) /1A/ '- be or - feel arrogantly proud /OF/, - pride oneself [arrogantly] /ON/', negative implication: NON-verbal noun as object: İnsan.ın {a: zengin-liğ.i.yLE/ b: mal.ı.yLA mülk.ü.yLE/ c: yakışık-lığ.ı.yLA/ d: soy.u.yLA sop.u.yLA} gurur duyması oldukça itici. 'It is quite

{disgusting/lit., repulsive} when a person prides himself {a: ON his wealth/b: ON his property/c: ON his good appearance/d: ON his family line} [lit., ** A person's priding himself on...is quite disgusting...].' VERBAL noun as object: **Mal mülk sahibi olmak.LA gurur duymak ne kadar {saçma/anlamsız} bir şey!** 'How foolish it is to pride oneself ON one's possessions [lit., ON being the possessor of property]!' *136:5.* pride: - take pride; *141:8.* arrogance: - give oneself airs. → = /1A/ **gururlan-.**

ilgi duy- /A [karşı]/ '- be interested /IN/, - take an interest /IN/' [ilgi 'interest'], lit., ** '- feel an interest /towards/': Interest in a non-person object: **Metin** {a: uluslararası meseleler.E/b: sosyal bilimler.E/c: fen bilimleri.nE/d: yabancı film-ler.E/e: {Mersedes/ Mercedes} arabalar.A} büyük ilgi duyu-yor. 'Metin takes a great interest {a: IN international affairs/b: IN the social sciences/c: IN the physical sciences/d: IN foreign films/e: IN Mercedes cars}.' Interest in or liking for a person: **Ahmet** {Ayşe'yE/sarışın kadın-lar.A} [karşı] ilgi duyuyor. 'Ahmet is interested {IN Ayşe/IN blonds [lit., ** in blond women]}.' → **beğen-** 1 ['- like']. *980:3b.* curiosity: - be curious. → = ilgilen-1, ilgi çek- ['- appeal to, - interest'] → çek- 1.

kıvanç duy- /{DAn/1A}/ '- be or - feel proud /OF/, - take pride /IN/': NON-verbal noun as object: Animate object /1A/: {a: Oğlum.LA/b: Kızım.LA/c: Kocam.LA/d: Karım.LA} kıvanç duyuyorum. 'I'm proud {a: OF my son/b: OF my daughter/c: OF my husband/d: OF my wife}.' Inanimate object /{DAn/1A}/: {İşi.nDEN/İşi.yLE} kıvanç duyuyor. 'He is proud OF his job [*or* OF his work, OF what he has done].' Öğretmenim. Mesleğim.{DEN/LE} kıvanç duyuyorum. 'I'm a teacher. I'm proud OF my profession.' Pronoun as object: {Amerikalıyım/ Türküm}, ve {bu.nDAN/ bu.nun.LA} da kıvanç duyuyorum. 'I'm {an American/a Turk}, and I'm proud OF it.' VERBAL noun as object: Infinitive as object /DAn/: Sizin şirketiniz-

.LE iş {yapmak.TAN} kıvanç
duyuyoruz. 'We are proud {OF
doing/TO do} business with your
company.' DIk participle as object
/{DAn/IA} / : Yaptık-
larımız.{DAN/LA} kıvanç
duyuyoruz. 'We are proud OF what
we have done.' Sizin
şirketiniz.LE iş yaptığımız için
kıvanç duyuyoruz. 'We are proud
{that we did/of having done}
business with with your company.'
136:5. pride: - take pride. → = **gurur
duy-** 1 → duy- 3, = /IA/ **iftihar et-**,
= /IA/ {**övün-/öğün-**} 1, ≠ /Dan/
utan-.

mutluluk duy- /DAn/ '- feel or -
be happy, pleased /{TO/θ}/'
[mutluluk 'happiness']: İnsanlar.a
yardımcı olmak.TAN mutluluk
duyuyorum. 'I feel happy θ helping
θ people [lit., being helpful to
people].' Burada bulunmak.TAN
ve bugün aranızda olmak.TAN
büyük bir sevinç ve mutluluk
duyuyorum. 'I'm very pleased and
happy TO be here and TO be
{among/with} you today.' *95:11.*
pleasure: - be pleased. → ≠ **üzüntü
duy-**.

üzüntü duy- '- feel sad, - be upset,
distressed, sad, sorry' [üzüntü
'distress, unhappiness, sorrow']: Ali
okuldan atılınca büyük üzüntü
duydum. 'When Ali was expelled
from school, I was very upset.' Seni
sarhoş görünce üzüntü
duyuyorum. 'I get upset when I see
you drunk.' *112:16.* sadness: - lose
heart. → = **üzül-**, ≠ **mutluluk
duy-** → duy- 3.

duygulan- [ır] /DAn/ '- be moved,
touched, emotionally affected /BY/'
[duygu 'feeling' + verb-forming suf.
-lA + pass. suf. -n]: Arkadaşım.ın
doğum günümde çiçek
gönderme.si.nDEN çok duygu-
landım. 'I was very
{moved/touched} when my friend
sent me flowers on my birthday [lit.,
** BY my friend's sending (me)
flowers on my birthday].' *893:7.*
influence: - influence. → = **etkilen-**
2.

duyur- [ur] /A/ '- announce, - declare
/to/' [duy- + caus. suf. -I r]:
Nişanlandık.ları.nı herkes.e
duyurdular. 'They announced
{their engagement/that they had
gotten engaged} to everyone.'

Dışişleri bakanı istifa
edeceğ.i.ni duyurdu. 'The foreign
minister announced that he would
resign.' {Sınav/İmtihan} sonuç-
ları.nı duyurdular mı? 'Have they
announced the {examination}
results?' Ankara uçağ.ı.nın
geldiğ.i.ni duyurdular. 'They
announced that the plane from
Ankara had arrived.' This verb is not
usually used for '- declare at
customs'. *352:12.* publication: -
announce. → = **açıkla-** 2, = **beyan
et-** ['- announce' and '- declare at
customs'].

dünya evine gir-. → **gir-**.

dünyaya gel-. → **gel-** 1.

dünyaya getir-. → **getir-**.

{**düş/rüya**} **gör-**. → **gör-** 3.

düş kırıklığına uğra-. →
{**hayal/düş**} **kırıklığına uğra-**.
→ **uğra-** 2.

düş kırıklığına uğrat-. →
{**hayal/düş**} **kırıklığına uğrat-**.
→ **uğrat-**.

düş- [er] 1 /DAn, A/ '- fall, - drop [of
itself] /from, {to/IN/INTO/ON/
ONTO}/': Uçurtma alçaldı ve
çatı.yA düştü. 'The kite [i.e., the
toy] came down and fell ON the
roof.' Bisiklet.ten düştü; kolu
kırıldı. 'He fell from [his] bicycle
and broke his arm [lit., his arm
broke].' Tabak masa.DAN yer.E
düştü. 'The plate fell FROM the
table TO the floor.' <u>Proverbs:</u> Çocuk
düş.e kalk.a büyür. 'A child
grows up by falling and getting up
[again].', i.e., through experience.
Deniz.E düşen yılan.A sarılır.
'A person who has fallen INTO the
sea will {embrace θ/cling to} [even] a
snake.' Desperate times call for
desperate measures. Köpek suya
{düşmeyince} {yüzmey.İ/
yüzme.si.ni} öğrenmez. 'A dog
won't learn {to swim} {unless it
falls/as long as it does not fall} into
the water.' Necessity is the mother of
invention. Yukarı.yA tükürme
yüzün.E düşer. 'Do not spit
upward. It will fall [back] ON your
face.', i.e., If you insult those in a
position above you, you will
eventually suffer. *194:5.* descent: -
descend.

denk düş- (1) /A/ '- be suitable, right, timely /FOR/' [denk 'suitable, timely']: For an event to occur at a suitable time: Salı günkü Türkçe dersi programım.A denk düşüyor. 'The Turkish class on Tuesday fits θ my schedule.' For an object to meet a need: Bu araba iyi denk düştü. Tam böyle bir araba.ya ihtiyacımız vardı; hem ucuz hem {sağlam}. 'This car is just right. This is exactly the kind of car we needed: it is both cheap and {well-built/in good condition}.' *842:6.* timeliness: - be timely; *866:3.* conformity: - conform. → = uy- 2, = uygun düş-.
(2) /A/ '- occur or - be /AT/ the same time, - fall /ON/ the same {day/hour}, - coincide' [denk 'equal']: İki {toplantı/ders/konser} aynı gün ve aynı saat.E denk düşüyor. Hangisine gidelim? 'The two {meetings/classes/concerts} are at the same time [lit., ** are ON the same day AT the same time]. Which one shall we go to?' * Akşam saatleri.nE denk düşen programları izleyemiyorum. 'I can't watch the [TV] programs that are on IN the evening [hours].' *830:5.* event: - occur; *835:4.* simultaneity: - coincide.

* dolgu düş- '- lose a [tooth] filling, - have a filling fall out': [Diş] dolgu.M düştü. Hemen bir {dişçiye/diş doktoruna} gitmem lâzım. 'I've lost a [tooth] filling [lit., MY (tooth) filling has fallen out]. I must go to a dentist right away.' *85:46b.* disease: - take sick in particular ways; *194:5.* descent: - descend.

* hat düş- 'for a phone line - be or - become available or free, - get through [on the phone], - get a line' [A. hat (haTTı) 'line'], lit., ** 'for a line to fall': Bayram.ın ilk gün.ü ailemi aradım ama * bir türlü hat düşmedi. Bütün gün boyunca hatlar doluydu. 'On the first day of the bairam I tried to call my family, but {I couldn't get through/no lines were available} [lit., ** the line didn't fall] * no matter how hard I tried [lit., ** no way]. The lines were busy [lit., ** full] all day.' *347:18.* communications: - telephone.

uygun düş- → denk düş- 1 and substitute in the examples there.

* yanlış numara düş- '- have the wrong number' on the phone: A: Ayşe ile {görüşebilir/ konuşabilir} miyim? 'A: May I please {speak} {with/to} Ayşe [f.]?' B: * Burada Ayşe DİYE biri yok. 'B: There's no one here {BY THE NAME OF/CALLED} Ayşe.' A: Özür dilerim. Yanlış numara düştü herhalde.' A: Oh pardon me, I must have the wrong number.' *974:12.* error: - misdo. → yanlış numara çevir- ['- dial the wrong number'] → çevir- 7.

2 '- fall from power': O yıl art arda [pronounce: ardarda] gelen ekonomik krizler yüzünden hükümet düştü. 'That year, due to a series of economic crises [lit., economic crises coming one after the other], the government fell.' *194:8.* descent: - tumble.

3 '- fall, - drop, - go down, - decrease': Hastanın ateşi düştü. 'The patient's temperature fell.' → = azal-, = in- 4, ≠ art- 1, ≠ çık- 6, ≠ yüksel- 2. # Bu hafta sebze fiyatları düştü. 'Vegetable prices fell this week.' *252:6.* decrease: - decrease; *633:6b.* cheapness: - become cheaper. → = in- 4, = ucuzla- ['- get cheaper, - go down or - drop in price'], ≠ pahalan- ['- become more expensive, - increase in price'], ≠ çık- 6, ≠ tırman- 2, ≠ yüksel- 2. # * {Dolar/Mark/Sterlin} gün.den gün.e düşüyor. '[The value of] the {dollar/mark/[English] pound} is falling day by day [lit., from day to day].' İki saatte borsa 39 puan düştü. 'The stock market fell 39 points in two hours.'

4 '- come to one by chance, inheritance': Koca hindiden ban.A sadece bu parça mı düştü? 'Is this the only part of the big turkey that was left FOR me?' *186:6.* arrival: - arrive.

* mirastan düş- '- inherit, - come into [property] /THROUGH/ inheritance, - come to one /AS/ inheritance' [A. miras (- -) 'inheritance']: * Babam.ın mira.sı.nDAN benim pay.ım.A bu ev düştü. '{This house came to me AS an inheritance from my father [lit., ** From my father's inheritance this house fell to my share]./I

inherited this house from my father.}'
479:7. receiving: - inherit. → =
miras kal- ['- be left /to [sb],
{from/BY}/', as an inheritance] →
kal- 2.

5 '- crash, - crack up', plane:
**Havalanırken arıza yapan uçak
düştü.** 'The airplane that had a
mechanical failure {on takeoff/while
taking off} crashed.' *184:44.*
aviation: - crash. → = **yere çakıl-**
→ çakıl- 2.

6 '- put, - place': * {not/dipnot}
düş- '- add or - put a footnote, -
footnote': **Bu maddede ne demek
istediğinizi daha açık ifade
etmek için bir dip not düşseniz
iyi olur.** 'To get your meaning
across more clearly in this paragraph
it might be a good idea to add a
footnote [lit., it would be good if you
added a footnote].' **Makalenizde
çok fazla dipnot var, * bu kadar
dipnot düşmeniz gerekli miydi?**
'You have too many footnotes in your
article. * Did you have to use
{so/this} many footnotes?' **Bura.yA
bir dipnot düşmek.TE fayda
var.** 'It would be useful to put a
footnote θ here.' **Kitabı dikkatlice
okuyun. * Yazar pek çok yer.E
dipnot düşmüş.** 'Read the book
carefully. * The author {has very
many footnotes/has put footnotes IN
very many places}.' *341:11.*
interpretation: - comment upon.

düşün- [ür] **1** ' - think, - reflect, -
consider', use one's mind: S: **Ne
yapıyorsun?** 'Q: What are you
doing?' C: **Düşünüyorum.** 'A: I'm
thinking.' **Karar ver.MEDEN
ÖNCE {çok düşündüm/
düşünmeliyim}.** '{I thought a lot/I
must think} BEFORE decid.ING.'
**"Düşünüyorum, o halde varım."
Descartes.** '"I think, therefore I
am." Descartes.' Proverbs:
Düşün.MEDEN söyleme. 'Think
before you speak [lit., Don't speak
WITHOUT think.ING].' **Önce
düşün, sonra söyle.** 'Think first,
then speak.' Think before you speak.
930:8. thought: - think.

{düşün-/düşünüp} **taşın-** '- think
over carefully, - consider at length, -
ponder, - think hard, - think and
think': • Note the two patterns:
a) With the same suffix on both
düşün- and taşın-: **Düşün.dük
taşın.dık ve Bursa'YA**

yerleşmey.e karar verdik. 'We
considered [all the options] carefully
and [finally] decided to settle IN
Bursa.'
b) With the -Ip suffix on düşün-,
the personal suffix on taşın-: *
**Bütün gece düşün.üp taşın.dı,
fakat * iş.in iç.i.nden çıkamadı.**
'He thought and thought the whole
night, but * he couldn't resolve the
problem [lit., ** couldn't come out of
the inside of the matter].' *930:9.*
thought: - think hard.

2 /I/ '- think, - believe that sth was,
is, or will be the case': **Ayşe'nin
beni {sevdiğ.i.ni/seveceğ.i.ni/
sevebileceğini} düşündüm.** 'I
thought that Ayşe {loved/would
love/could love} me.' **Ayşe'nin
beni sevip {sevmediğ.i.ni/
sevmeyeceğ.i.ni} düşündüm.** 'I
thought about whether Ayşe {loved
me or not/would love me or not}.'
952:10. belief: - think.

3 /I/ '- think /{OF/ABOUT}/, for
one's mind - be occupied /with/':
Bugün Emel'İ düşünüyordum. 'I
was just thinking {OF/ABOUT}
Emel [f.] today.' **Hasan bugün
kim.İ düşünüyormuş?** 'Who was
Hasan thinking ABOUT today?' **İki
defa seslendim, duymadın. Ne
düşünüyorsun?** 'I called out to you
twice. You didn't hear [me]. What
are you thinking ABOUT?', i.e.,
Where is your mind, what is
occupying your mind? *930:20.*
thought: - occupy the mind.

4 /{hakkında/için}/ '- think, - have an
opinion /about [or OF]/': **Osman'ın
evlenme teklifi {hakkında/
için} ne düşünüyorsun?** 'What
do you think {about [or OF]}
Osman's proposal of marriage?'
945:8. judgment: - judge; *952:11.*
belief: - think. → = bul- **3**, = de- **2**
['- think, - think of in a certain way'].

5 /I/ '- think /OF/ [doING] sth, of
taking a particular course of action,
consider': S: **Bu akşam ne
yapacaksın?** 'Q: What are you
going to do this evening?' C:
**{Daha/Henüz} karar vermedim.
Sinemaya gitmey.İ düşünü-
yorum. * Sen de gelir misin?**
'A: I haven't decided {yet}. I'm
thinking OF going to the movies. *
Will you come along?' **Yeni
aldığım saat çalışmıyor. İade
etmey.İ düşünüyorum.** 'The

watch I just bought doesn't work. I'm thinking OF returning it.' **Küçükken doktor olmay.I düşünüyordum.** 'When I was a child, I thought {I would become/OF becoming} a doctor.' *930:8.* thought: - think; *930:12.* : - consider.

* *verb stem.*s A.*personal suffix* mI diye düşün- '- wonder whether': **"Yarın Ankara'ya git.SE.M mi?" diye düşünüyorum.** 'I am wondering whether I should go to Ankara tomorrow [lit., ** IF I go to Ankara tomorrow saying I'm thinking].' *930:12.* thought: - consider; *970:9.* uncertainty: - be uncertain. → = {san-/zannet-} ['- think, suppose'].

{düşün-/düşünüp} taşın-. → düşün- 1 above.

{düşünceye/düşüncelere} dal-. → dal- 2.

{düşünceye/fikre/görüşe} katıl-. → katıl- 3.

düşür- [ür] [düş- + caus. suf -Ir] 1 /DAn, A/ '- drop sth /from, {to/ON}/, - cause sth to fall /from, {to/ON}/, - let sth fall': **Ahmet tabağ.I [masa.DAN] yer.E düşürdü, tabak kırıldı.** 'Ahmet {dropped the plate/let the plate drop} [from the table] ON the floor, [and] it broke.' **Dikkat edin, televizyonu sıkı tutun, {düşürmeyin}.** 'Be careful, hold on to the TV tightly, don't {drop it/let it fall}.' *912:7.* depression: - drop sth. → ≠ kaldır- 1.

2 '- reduce, - bring down': **Hükümet enflasyonu düşüremedi.** 'The government couldn't bring down [the] inflation.' *252:7.* decrease: - reduce. → ≠ {artır-/arttır-} 1, ≠ indir- 3.

düzel- [ir] '- get better, - improve, - straighten out, - recover from an illness; - be put in order, - be corrected' [düz 1 'smooth'. 2 'straight'+ verb-forming suf. -Al]: **Üzülmeyin. Her şey düzelecek.** 'Don't worry. Everything {will be OK/will turn out all right/lit., will straighten out}.' **Son iki yılda ülke ekonomisi {oldukça} düzeldi.** 'In the last two years the economy of the country has improved {considerably/greatly}.' **Bayram dolayı.sı.yla otobüs sefer-**

ler.i.nde ** büyük bir aksama vardı, bereket versin şimdi düzeldi. 'Because of the holiday, * bus service was severely disrupted [lit., ** in the bus trips there was a severe disruption]. Fortunately the situation [lit., it] has now been corrected.'

Health: Doktor: **Bu ilaçları alın, yakında düzelirsiniz.** 'Doctor: Take these medicines, and you'll soon get better.' **Bakanın sağlık durumu düzeliyor.** 'The minister's health [lit., ** health condition] is improving.' *392:7.* improvement: - get better; *392:8.* : - rally, - get better; *396:20.* restoration: - recover. → = iyileş-, ≠ fenalaş- 1, hastalan- ['- become ill, - get sick'], ≠ kötüleş-.

arası düzel- /lA/ 'for matters - get straightened out, patched up between people, - be reconciled /with/ one another', i.e., for relations between people - be reestablished after a falling out [ara 'a space between', here 'the relationship between people']: • Note the different possessed suffixes on ara: * **Nilgün'ün kocası ile ara.SI düzeldi. Bugün evine döndü.** '{a: Things [finally] got {straightened out/patched up} between Nilgün and her husband./b: Nilgün got back together with [i.e., was reconciled] with her husband [lit., ** Nilgün's relationship with her husband straightened out].} She returned home today.' **Ara.MIZ düzeldi.** 'WE've {patched things up/straightened things out} between US [lit., ** the relationship between US has straightened out].' **A r a .NIZ düzeldi mi?** 'Have YOU {sorted things out/patched things up} between you? [lit., ** Has the relationship between you straightened out]?' *465:10.* pacification: - make up. → = barış-, ≠ arası {açıl-/bozul-} → açıl- 9, soğu- 2 ['- cool /TOWARD/, - lose one's love, desire, or enthusiasm /FOR/; - cease to care /FOR/ sb, sth'], uzaklaş- 2 ['- become remote, distant /from/ in feeling (toward sb)]'.

hava düzel- 'for weather - clear up, - become pleasant, good, nice': **Bahar geldi, havalar düzeldi.** 'Spring has come. The weather has {gotten nice/cleared up}.' **Yağmur kesildi, hava düzeldi.** 'The rain has stopped. The weather has {gotten nice/cleared up}.' *392:7.* Improvement: - get better. → = **hava aç-** → aç- 7, = **hava açıl-** → açıl- 7 [• **Düzel-** is used both for seasons and for more temporary weather conditions. **Aç-** and **açıl-** are used mostly for temporary weather conditions.], ≠ **hava boz-** → boz- 4, ≠ **hava bozul-**, ≠ **hava kapan-** ['- cloud over, - become cloudy, overcast'] → kapan- 4, ≠ **kötüleş-**.

düzelt- [ir] [**düzel-** '- be put in order, straighten out of itself' + caus. suf. -t]: **1** '- repair, - fix': **İşçiler bozuk yolları düzelttiler.** 'The workers repaired the damaged roads.' *396:14.* restoration: - repair. For '- repair machinery, buildings', etc., → = **onar-**, = **tamir et-**.

2 '- correct an error; - make up for a deficiency': **Öğretmen öğrenci.nin {hatalar.ı.nı/ kâğıd.ı.nı} düzeltmiş.** 'The teacher corrected the student's {errors/paper}.' **Türkçe konuşurken lütfen {hatalarımı/ yanlışlarımı} düzeltin.** 'Please correct {my mistakes} when I speak Turkish.' **Yanlış yaparsam lütfen düzeltin.** 'If I make a mistake, please correct it.' **Eğer bir yanlışlık varsa düzeltirim.** 'If there's a {fault/mistake}, I'll correct it.' In Turkish usually errors rather than persons are corrected, i.e., 'Correct MY ERROR[S]' is preferred to 'Correct ME'. *396:13.* restoration: - remedy.

*** ders düzelt-** '- pull up one's grade [lit., ** - correct (one's) course], - make up for a deficiency in a course' [A. **ders** 'course, lesson']: **Son sınav.DAN 90 aldım ve biyoloji dersimi düzelttim.** 'I got a 90 ON the final exam and pulled up my grade in biology [i.e., so I'm safe, I'll pass].' *396:13.* restoration: - remedy.

*** not düzelt-** '- pull up one's grade [lit., ** - correct (one's) grade], - make up for a deficiency in a course' [**not** 'grade, mark']: **Biyoloji sınavın.DAN aldığım kötü notu düzelttim ve sınıfımı geçtim.** 'I {pulled up/made up for} the low grade I got ON the biology examination and advanced to the next grade.' *396:13.* restoration: - remedy.

3 '- put in order, - straighten up, - tidy up': **Misafirler gelmeden önce odamı düzelttim.** 'I straightened up my room before the guests came.' *807:12.* arrangement: - tidy, - tidy up. → = **çekidüzen ver-** → ver- 1, = **toparla-** 3, = **topla-** 2, ≠ **dağıt-** 3, ≠ **karıştır-** 4.

'- trim': **{Sakalımı/Bıyığımı/ Favorilerimi} düzeltir misiniz?** At the barber shop: 'Would you trim {my beard/my moustache/my sideburns?}' *3:22.* hair: - cut or - dress the hair; *807:12.* arrangement: - tidy, - tidy up.

üstünü başını düzelt- '- tidy [oneself] up, - smarten [oneself] up [lit., ** - adjust one's clothes]' [**üst baş** 'clothes, what one has on']: **Müdür beyin odasına girmeden önce üst.ÜN.ü baş.IN.ı düzelt, kıyafet.İN.e çeki düzen ver.** 'Before entering the director's room, tidy up [lit., ** adjust YOUR clothes, give order to YOUR {clothes/outfit}].' *79:18.* cleanness: - clean; *807:12.* arrangement: - tidy, - tidy up. → = **üstünü başını {toparla-/topla-}** → toparla- 3, topla- 2.

yatağını düzelt- '- make one's bed': **Yatağını düzeltmeden dışarı çıkamazsın, * ona göre!** 'You can't leave without making your bed, * so act accordingly!' → = **yatağını {topla-/yap-}** → topla- 2, yap- 3. *807:12.* arrangement: - tidy, - tidy up.

4 '- set a watch or clock': **Saatim beş dakika {ileri gitmiş/geri kalmış}, düzelttim.** 'My watch was five minutes {fast/slow} [lit., ** My watch {had gone ahead/had remained behind} five minutes]. I set it.' *396:13.* restoration: - remedy; *787:7.* agreement: - make agree. → = **ayarla-** 1.

düzenle- [r] [**düzen** 'order, arrangement' + verb-forming suf. -1A] **1** '- put in order, - arrange, - organize [sth that is in disorder]': **Konferanstan önce notlarını tekrar bir gözden geçirip düzenlesen iyi olur.** 'It would be good if you looked over your notes again and put them in order before the conference.' *807:8.* arrangement: - arrange.

2 '- arrange; - prepare, - organize, - plan [an event]': **Okulumuz gelecek ay Antalya'ya bir gezi düzenliyor.** 'Our school is organizing a trip to Antalya next month.' **Belediye.ce kapatılan iş yerlerinin sahipleri ortak bir basın toplantısı düzenledi.** 'The owners of the work places [that had been] closed by the municipality organized a joint press conference.' **Belediye.nin Gülhane Parkında düzenlediğ.i konseri binlerce kişi izledi.** 'Thousands of people attended the concert [that] the municipality had organized in the Gülhane Park.' *381:8.* plan: - plan; *405:6.* preparation: - prepare. → = **ayarla-** 3.

3 '- regulate, - control': **Bu âlet oda sıcaklığ.ı.nı düzenliyor.** 'This instrument regulates the room temperature.' *573:8.* direction, management: - direct. → = **ayarla-** 1.

- E -

edil- [ir]. [et- + pass. suf. -Il] → **iptal edil-, tasdik edil-, tehir edil-, telâffuz edil-.**

edin- [ir] /DAn/ '- get, - obtain, - acquire /from/, - pick up' [et- + refl. suf. -In]: {Sonunda/Nihayet} **üniversiteden bir Yüksek lisans diploması edindim.** '{Finally} I obtained a master's degree from {the university/the college}.' **Yıllarca çalıştıktan sonra bir ev edindim.** 'After working for many years, I bought [lit., acquired] a house.' **Kötü arkadaşlar edinme, ahlâkını bozarlar.** 'Don't pick up bad friends. They'll lead you astray [lit., corrupt your morals].' *472:8.* acquisition: - acquire. → = **al-** 3, = **elde et-,** = **ol-** 6.

bilgi edin- /DAn/ '- obtain or - receive information /from/, - learn /from/' [bilgi 'knowledge, information']: **Bu konuda danışma bürosundan bilgi edinmek mümkündür.** 'It is possible to obtain information on this subject from the information bureau.' **İyi ki bu dersi almışım, Osmanlı tarihi hakkında çok bilgi edindim.** 'It's a good thing I took this class. I learned a lot about Ottoman history.' **Edindiğimiz bilgi.ye göre, başbakan yarın Ankara'yA hareket edecek.** 'According to the information we have received, the prime minister will set out FOR Ankara tomorrow.' *570:6.* learning: - learn; *927:14.* knowledge: - learn. → = **öğren-** ['- learn'].

evlât edin- '- adopt a child' [A. evlât (. -) 'child, son']: **Güler teyzem Erzincan depreminde öksüz kalan iki {kardeş.İ} evlât edindi.** 'My maternal aunt Güler adopted two {brothers/ sisters/siblings} who had been orphaned in the Erzincan earthquake.' *480:19.* taking: - appropriate.

Efendime söyleyeyim. → **söyle-** 1.

egzersiz yap-. → **yap-** 3.

eğ- [er] 1 '- bow, - bend, - tip': **baş eğ-** '- bow, - bow one's head or - nod as a sign of respect, - hang one's head in shame': **Öğretmen.i.ni görünce başını eğip selâm verdi.** 'When he saw his teacher, he nodded his head in greeting.' *155:6.* respect: - bow. **Öğrenci kopya çekerken yakalanınca utanç.LA başını ön.E eğdi.** 'When the student was caught copying, he hung his head [lit., forward] IN shame.' *137:9b.* humility: gestures of.

2 '- bend, - bow, - make bend': **Fırtına pek çok elektrik direğini eğdi.** 'The storm bent many telephone poles.' *164:5.* deviation: - deflect.

eğil- [ir] [eğ- + refl. suf. -Il. ADJ. **eğik** 'bent'] 1 /A/ '- bend down /to/': **Yer.e eğilip kalemi aldı.** 'Bending down [to the ground], he picked up the pencil.' **Eğilip yerdeki kalemi aldı.** 'Bending down, he picked up the pencil on the ground.' *204:10.* obliquity: - incline; *912:9.* depression: - bow.

2 '- bow, - bow down': **Eğilip selâm verdi.** 'Bowing, he greeted him.' **Nokta kadar menfaat için virgül gibi eğilme!** 'For an {advantage/benefit} of [no more than] {a dot/a period} [i.e., a very small amount] don't bow down like a comma!' Proverb: **Eğilen baş kesilmez.** 'A head that bows is not cut off.', i.e., A person who is humble

and obedient will not be cut down because he threatens no one. *137:9b.* humility: gestures of; *204:10.* obliquity: - incline; *912:9.* depression: - bow.

3 /A kadar/ '- bend down /TO/, - incline, - lean': **Fırtınada ağaçlar yerler.e kadar eğildi.** 'During the storm, the trees bent down to the ground.' *204:10.* obliquity: - incline.

4 /A/ '- concern oneself /WITH/': **Bu konu.yA eğilelim!** 'Let's concern ourselves WITH this subject.' *897:2.* involvement: - involve; *982:5.* attention: - attend to.

eğit- [ir] /konuda/ '- educate sb /on a subject/' [eğ- + caus. suf. -It]: **Bu konuda önce halkımızı eğitmeliyiz.** 'We must first educate our people on this {subject/matter}.' **Kendimizi her alanda eğitmeliyiz.** 'We must educate ourselves in every {area/field}.' *568:10.* teaching: - teach. → **ders ver-** 1 ['- teach /θ/ sb, - give lessons /to/ sb'] → **ver-** 1, **okut-** 3 ['- teach'], **öğret-** ['- teach /θ/ sb sth, - teach sth /to/ sb'].

{**eğitim/öğrenim/tahsil**} **gör-**. → **gör-** 3.

eğlen- [ir] 1 /a: lA, b: ArAk, c: mAklA/ '- have a good time, - enjoy oneself, - have fun /a: with [sb, sth], b: [by]...ing, c: [BY]...ing/': **Eğleniyor musunuz?** 'Are you having a good time?' **A: Bu gece iyi eğleniyorsun sanırım.** 'A: I think you're really enjoying yourself this evening.' **B: Evet,** * **hem de çılgınlar gibi.** 'B: Yes, and how [lit., ** like crazy ones].' * **Eğlenme.niz.e bakın.** 'Enjoy yourself [lit., ** Look to enjoying yourself].' **Tatilde çok eğlendik.** 'We thoroughly enjoyed ourselves during the {vacation/holiday}.' **Resim** {**yap.arak/yap.mak.la**} **çok eğlendik.** 'We had a very good time draw.ING [lit., mak.ING] pictures.' *95:13.* pleasure: - enjoy oneself; *743:22.* amusement: - amuse oneself. → = {**iyi/hoş**} **vakit geçir-** → **geçir-** 3, **neşelen-** ['- get in a happy mood, - become cheerful, - cheer up'].

2 /lA/ '- make fun /OF/, - joke /with/ sb': **Bacak kadar boyun.a bakmadan benim.LE**

eğlenmey.e utanmıyor musun? 'Aren't you ashamed of making fun OF me considering how short you are [yourself] [lit., ** without looking at your (own) short stature]?' **bacak kadar** 'small, very short'. *508:8.* ridicule: - ridicule. → = **alay et-**, = **alaya al-** → **al-** 1, = **dalga geç-** 2 → **geç-** 1, **gül-** 2 ['- laugh /AT/, - make fun /OF/'].

ehemmiyet ver-. → {**önem/ ehemmiyet**} **ver-.** → **ver-** 1.

ek- /er/ /A/ '- sow, - plant /IN/', seeds, not plants, seedlings, saplings, or trees: **Bu yıl Ege bölgesi çiftçileri tarlaları.nA buğday ektiler.** 'This year farmers in the Aegean region {sowed/planted} wheat IN their fields.' **Dedem köydeki bostan.ın yarı.sı.nA karpuz yarı.sı.nA da kavun ekti.** 'My grandfather sowed θ half of the kitchen garden in the village in watermelons and θ half in [other types of] melons.' Proverbs: **Arpa eken buğday biçmez.** 'He who sows barley will not reap wheat.' **Ekmeden biçilmez.** 'Without planting, nothing is reaped.' Nothing ventured, nothing gained. **Ne ekersen onu biçersin.** 'You reap what you sow.' As you sow, so shall you reap. **Rüzgâr eken fırtına biçer.** 'He who sows the wind reaps the storm.' → = 2 **dik-** 1 ['- plant plants, saplings, seedlings', not seeds]. *1067:18.* agriculture: - plant. → ≠ **biç-** 2.

ekle- [r] /A/ '- add, - append, - affix, - attach, - tack one thing /to/ another' [ek 'addition, supplement' + verb-forming suf. -lA]: **Bulguru yıkayıp süzün ve bir çay kaşığı tuz ekleyin.** 'Wash and strain the cracked wheat and add a teaspoon of salt.' **Mektub.u.nun son.u.na bir de şiir ekledi.** 'He also {appended]/added/attached} a poem to the end of his letter.' *253:5.* addition: - add to. → = **ilâve et-**, = **kat-**.

ekmeğinden ol-. → **ol-** 7.

eksik 1 'lacking'. 2 'deficient', often used with verbs to render 'under': → {**az/eksik**} **tahmin et-** '- underestimate' → **tahmin et-** 2.

eksik ol-. → **ol-** 12.

eksil- [ir] [eksik 'lacking, missing', final **k** to **l** + -θ] 1 '- decrease, - drop, - fall, - become less, - diminish, - go down [level]': **Bankadaki param {gün geçtikçe} eksiliyor.** 'The money I have in the bank is decreasing {day by day/with every passing day/lit., as the days pass}.' **Kavanozdaki şeker epeyce eksildi.** 'The [amount of] sugar in the jar has decreased quite a bit.' **Barajdaki su iyice eksildi.** 'The [amount of] water in the dam has decreased considerably.' **Bu yıl okulumuz.A kayıt yaptıranların sayı.sı birden eksildi.** 'The number of students registering IN our school this year has suddenly dropped.' **Birinci Dünya Savaşı {neden.i.yle/ sebeb.i.yle/yüz.ü.nden} birçok ülkenin nüfus.u büyük oranda eksildi.** '{As a result of} the First World War, the population of many countries fell considerably [lit., in large measure].' *252:6.* decrease: - decrease [i.]. → = **azal-**, ≠ **art-** 1, ≠ **çoğal-**.

2 /DAn/ '- be absent /from/, - be without, - be lacking /θ/': * **Bu dağ.dan kar eksilmez.** 'This mountain is never without snow [lit., Snow is never absent from this mountain].' * **Bizim ev.den misafir eksilmez.** 'Our house is never without visitors [lit., Visitors are never absent from our house].' *222:8.* absence: - absent oneself.

el ele ver-. → ver- 1.

el kaldır-. → kaldır- 1.

el salla-. → salla- 1.

el sık-. → sık- 2.

el sür-. → sür- 5.

el uzat-. → uzat- 2.

* **elde et-** [eDer] /DAn/ '- obtain, - acquire, - get /from/' [el 'hand']: **İstediğiniz kitapları nihayet elde edebildim.** 'I was finally able to {get/obtain} the books you wanted.' **Hayatta risk.e girmeden hiçbir şey elde edemezsin.** * **Ne demişler: "Korkak bezirgân ne kâr eder ne ziyan."** 'In life you can't obtain anything without taking [lit., ** entering] some risks. * As

they say: "The timid merchant makes no profit and incurs no loss".' **Kimse her istediğini, [tümüyle birlikte] elde edemez.** 'No one can get all the things [that] he wants [exactly as he wants them].' **İstediğini elde etmek için her şey.İ yapar.** 'He is willing to do [lit., does] {anything/whatever it takes} to get what he wants.' **Millî takımımız maçta çok iyi bir sonuç elde etti.** 'Our national team did very well in the [soccer] game [lit., obtained a very good result...].' **Bu ürünler.in hep.si.ni petrol.den elde ettiler.** 'They obtained all these products from petroleum.' **Yumuşak bir hamur elde edinceye kadar yoğurun.** 'Knead until the dough is soft [lit., ** until obtaining a soft dough].' *472:8.* acquisition: - acquire. → = **al-** 3, = **ele geçir-** 2 → **geçir-** 1.

ele al-. → al- 1.

ele alın-. → alın- 1.

ele geçir-. → geçir- 1.

elektrik süpürgesi ile süpür-. → süpür-.

{**eleştir-** [ir]/**tenkit et-** [eDer]} /a: {DIğI için/DIğInDAn}, b: DAn dolayı, c: yüzünden/ '- criticize /a: because [or for], b: for, c: {for/on account of}/' [A. **tenkit** (. -) 'criticizing, criticism']: Result of an action as object: **Başbakan.ın dünkü konuşma.sı.nı bütün gazeteler eleştirdi.** 'All the newspapers criticized the speech the prime minister gave yesterday [lit., ** the prime minister's yesterday speech].' **Köşe yazarları ünlü yazarın son romanını {olumlu/ olumsuz} yönde eleştirdiler.** 'The columnists gave the famous writer's latest novel a {positive/negative} review [lit., ** criticized the famous writer's last novel in a {positive/negative} respect].' **Yazar "Edebiyat Tarihi" dersi.nin kaldırıl- ma.sı.nı {ağır bir dille} eleştirdi.** 'The writer {harshly/in harsh language} criticized the elimination of "Literary History" classes.'
Person as object: **Beni eleştirmey.e hakkınız yok. Siz kendiniz.E bakın!** 'You have no right to criticize me. Just look AT

yourself!' Öğrenciler dersi kötü {anlattığ.ı için/ anlat-tığ.ı.ndan} öğretmenlerini eleştirdiler. 'The students criticized their teacher {because he had explained the lesson badly [or for having explained the lesson badly]}.' Dünkü konuşma.sı.ndan dolayı bütün gazeteler başbakanı ağır bir dil.LE eleştirdi. 'All the newspapers criticized the prime minister IN strong {terms/lit., language} [lit., ** WITH a heavy language] for his speech yesterday.' Kendisini bu yazı yüzünden eleştirmiştim. 'I had criticized him for this article.' *510:14.* disapproval: - criticize; *945:14.* judgment: - criticize. → yer- [all negative, harsher than the negative of the two verbs above: '- run down, - point out the faults of, - criticize, - speak ill of, - disparage'], ≠ {öv-/methet-} ['- praise'].

{eleştiril- [ir]/tenkit edil- [ir]} /a: {DIğI için/DIğInDAn}, b: DAn dolayı, c: {tarafından/CA}/ '- be criticized /a: because [or for], b: for, c: by/' [eleştir- + pass. suf. -Il]; tenkit e t - + pass. suf. -Il]: Başbakan.ın dünkü konuşma.sı [bütün gazeteler tarafından] eleştirildi. 'The speech the prime minister gave yesterday [lit., ** The prime minister's yesterday speech] was criticized [by all the newspapers].' Ünlü yazarın son romanı köşe yazarları tarafından {olumlu/olumsuz} yönde eleştirildi. 'The famous writer's last novel received a {positive/negative} review from the columnists [lit., ** was criticized in a {positive/negative} respect by the columnists].' "Edebiyat Tarihi" dersi.nin kaldırılma.sı [yazar tarafından] ağır bir dil.LE eleştirildi. 'The elimination of the "Literary History" class was harshly [lit., ** WITH a heavy language] criticized [by the writer].' Öğretmenler dersi kötü {anlattıklar.ı için/ anlattık-lar.ı.ndan} [öğrenciler tarafından] eleştirildi. 'The teachers were criticized [by the students] {because they had explained the lesson badly [or for having explained the lesson badly]}.' *510:14.* disapproval: - criticize; *945:14.* judgment: - criticize.

eli ayağı tutma-. → tut- 2.

elinden gel-. → gel- 1.

elinden geleni yap-. → yap- 3.

elinden öp-. → öp-.

elini öp-. → öp-.

emek sarf et-. → {harca-/sarf et-} 1.

emek ver-. → ver- 1.

emekle- [r] '- crawl, - creep', i.e., - move on all fours, usually for a baby or infirm person [? emek 'work, labor' + verb-forming suf. -1A]: Bebek emeklemey.e başladı. 'The baby has begun to crawl.' Tünel o kadar dardı ki * hepimiz emekle.yerek yürümek zorunda kaldık. 'The tunnel was so narrow that * we were all obliged to walk on all fours [lit., ** were obliged to walk by crawl.ing].' *177:26.* travel: - creep.

emekliye ayrıl-. → ayrıl- 3.

emin ol-. → ol- 12.

emret- [emreDer] /A/ '- order sth, - command, - order /θ/ sb to do sth' [A. emir (eMRi) 'command, order' + et-]: A waiter in a restaurant politely asks you what you would like to order: Ne emredersiniz efendim? 'What would you [like to] order {sir/ma'am}?' Also in the same situation without the verb: Bir emriniz var mı efendim? lit., ** 'Do you have {an order/a command}, {sir/ma'am}?', or just Emriniz? 'Your order?' Emrettiğiniz yazıları yazdım efendim. 'I wrote what [lit., the writings] you requested, {sir/ma'am}.' * Kumandan askerler.E keşf.E çıkmaları.nı emretti. 'The commander ordered θ the soldiers to go ON reconnaissance.' *420:8.* command: - command. → = buyur- 1.

emrivaki. → Oldu bitti. → bit- 1.

emzir- [ir] '- nurse, - suckle, - breast-feed' [irr. caus. of em- '- suck']: Annesi bebeği emziriyordu. 'The mother [lit., Its mother] was nursing the baby.' Bebeğinizi emziriyor musunuz? 'Do you breast-feed your baby?' *8:19.* eating:

- nourish. → = meme ver- → ver-
1.

endişe et- [eDer] /DAn/ '- worry, - be anxious /ABOUT/, - be concerned /{ABOUT/FOR}/, - be afraid or - fear /FOR/' [P. endişe (. - .) 'care, anxiety, worry']: **A: Geceyarısı oldu, * Murat hâlâ ortada yok. Çok endişe ediyorum.** 'A: It's midnight. * Murat still hasn't turned up [lit., isn't anywhere about]. I'm very {worried/concerned}.' **B1: * Endişe etmek.TE haklısın.** 'B1: You're right to be worried.' **B2: Endişe etmey.e gerek yok.** 'B2: There's no need to worry.' * **Siz.E endişe ettiğim bazı sorunlarım.I danışmak istiyorum.** 'I would like to consult θ you ABOUT some problems that are worrying me [lit., that I'm worried about].' NON-verbal noun as object: **Polis üç gündür kayıp olan çocuğ.un hayat.ı.nDAN endişe ediyor.** 'The police {are concerned {ABOUT/FOR}/fear FOR} the life of the child who has been lost for three days.'
VERBAL noun as object: * **Bizim çocuk uzun zamandır ortalıkta yok; bir çılgınlık yapma.sı.nDAN endişe ediyorum.** 'I haven't seen my child in quite a while [lit., Our child hasn't been around...]. I'm worried θ that he may have gotten into some kind of trouble [lit., ABOUT his having done sth foolish].' *126:6.* anxiety: - feel anxious. = **endişelen-**, → = /DAn/ **kaygılan-**, = /I/ **merak et-** 1.

engelle- [r] /I, ArAk/ '- keep, - prevent, - hinder, - block /sth, by...ing/' [**engel** 'hindrance' + verb-forming suf. **-lA**]: NON-verbal noun as object: **Son anda fren.E bas.arak kaza.yı engelledim.** 'By stepp.ing ON the brake at the last moment, I prevented the accident.'
VERBAL noun as object: * **Polisler yukarı çıkma.mız.ı engellediler.** 'The police {kept/ prevented} us FROM going upstairs [lit., ** prevented our going upstairs].' *1011:14.* hindrance: - prevent. → = /A/ **mâni ol-** → **ol-** 12, = /I/ **önle-**, = **önüne geç-** → **geç-** 1.

er- [er] /A/ '- reach /θ/, - attain /θ/': Proverbs: **Ağaç ne kadar uzasa göğ.E ermez.** 'No matter how tall a tree grows, it never reaches θ the sky.', i.e., No one keeps improving

his status forever. **{Bekleyen/ Sabreden} derviş muradı.nA ermiş.** 'The dervish {who waited/who was patient} reached θ his goal.' Everything comes to him who waits. *186:6.* arrival: - arrive. → = **ulaş-**, = **var-**, = **gel-** 1.

sona er- '- come /to/ an end, - conclude, - end, - finish, - be over' [**son** 'end']: **{Ders/Konser} son.A erdi.** '{The lesson/The concert} has ended.' **Toplantımız burada sona erdi beyler!** 'Gentlemen our meeting is now [lit., ** here] concluded.' On television: **Sayın seyirciler programımız burada sona erdi, hoşça kalın.** 'Dear viewers, this concludes our program [lit., ** our program has ended here]. Good-bye.' **Olimpiyat Oyunları dün sona erdi.** 'The Olympic games ended yesterday.' → = **bit-** 1, ≠ **başla-** 1. # **Yağmur sona erdi.** 'The rain has stopped.' → = **din-**, = **dur-** 2, = **kesil-** 2. *819:6.* end: - come to an end.

olgunluğa er- '- reach or - attain /θ/ maturity, - mature, - grow up' [**olgunluk** 'maturity']: **Artık olgunluğ.a erdi, eski hatalarını tekrarlamayacağı.nA eminim.** 'He's finally grown up. I'm sure θ [that] he's not going to repeat his former mistakes.' *303:9.* age: - mature; *407:8.* accomplishment: - ripen.

eri- [r] /DA/ '- melt, - dissolve /in/': **Haftalardır duran {kar/buz} sonunda eridi.** 'The {snow/ice}, which had stayed around for weeks, finally melted.' *1062:5.* liquefaction: - liquefy. → ≠ **don-**. # **Şeker su.da erir.** 'Sugar dissolves in water.' *34:2a.* disappearance: - disappear; *805:3.* disintegration: - disintegrate.

eriş- [ir] [**er-** + recip. suf. **-Iş**] 1 /A/ '- reach /θ/, - arrive /AT/, - get /to/': **Erken yola çıkarsak zamanında {θ/uçağ.a} erişiriz.** 'If we set out early, we'll get {there/to the plane} in time.' *186:6.* arrival: - arrive. → = **gel-** 1, = **var-**, = **ulaş-**, = **yetiş-** 1 ['- catch /θ/ a vehicle, - make it /to/, - get /to/ a place, - arrive in time /FOR/; - be in time /FOR/'], ≠ **yola çık-** → **çık-** 2, ≠ **yola koyul-**, ≠ **hareket et-** 2 [subj.: vehicle or person in vehicle], ≠ **kalk-** 2 [subj.: various vehicles].

2 /A/ '- reach /θ/, - extend one's reach /to/, - get /to/' a place with one's hands: the top shelf: **Kedi erişemediği et.E murdar der. Tilki erişemediği üzüm.E koruk der.** 'A cat calls θ the meat it cannot reach unclean [i.e., canonically unlawful as food]. A fox calls θ the grapes he can't reach unripe [i.e., not edible].' *261:6.* distance, remoteness: - extend to. → = **uzan-** 3, = **yetiş-** 5.

3 /A/ '- attain /θ/ [one's objective], - reach /θ/ [one's goal], - achieve /θ/ [one's purpose], - gain /θ/ [one's end[s]]': **Çok gayret etmeden {a: amac.ı.nA/b: gaye.si.nE/c: hedef.i.nE/d: o makam.A} erişemezdi.** 'Without working very hard, he couldn't have {a: achieved θ his purpose/b: attained θ his objective/c: reached θ his goal}/d: attained θ that {post/position/office}}.' **Yılda 500.000 ton üretim kapasite.si.nE erişmek için ek tesisler.E ihtiyacımız var bu fabrikada.** 'To attain a yearly production capacity of 500,000 tons we need θ additional {units/installations} in this factory.' *407:4.* accomplishment: - accomplish; *409:8.* success: - achieve one's purpose.

4 /A/ '- access /θ/, - gain access /to/, - get /{to [a source of information]/ON [the Internet]}/': **Artık internet saye.si.nde pek çok kaynağ.A hızlı bir şekilde erişmek mümkün.** 'Now, thanks to the Internet, it's possible to access θ many sources rapidly.' **Temsilci-liklerimiz.in web siteler.i.nE erişmek için lütfen simge-ler.i.nİ tıklayınız.** 'To access θ the Web sites of {the representatives of our businesses/our agents}, please click ON the relevant [lit., their] icons.' *186:6.* arrival: - arrive; *189:7.* entrance: - enter; *1041:18.* computer science: - computerize.

erit- [ir] '- melt, - dissolve, - liquefy, - cause to become liquid' [eri- + caus. suf. -t]: **Bir yemek kaşığı tereyağını * hafif ateşte erit.** 'Melt a tablespoon of butter * over low heat.' *1019:21.* heating: - melt; *1062:5.* liquefaction: - liquefy.

{**ertele-** [r]/**tehir et-** [eDer]} /a: A, b: A, c: A kadar/ '- postpone, - put off /a: for, b: to, c: {till/until}/' [erte *archaic* 'the next, the following' + verb-forming suf. -1A; A. **tehir** (- -) 'a postponing, postponement']: **Yağmur.dan dolayı toplantı.yI {a: hafta.yA/b: bir hafta sonra.yA}/c: iki hafta sonra.yA} erteledik.** 'We postponed the meeting {a, b: FOR a week}/c: FOR two weeks} because of [the] rain.' **Yağmur {neden.i.yle/yüz.ü.nden/dola-yı.sı.yla/sebeb.i.yle} ders.i {a: yarın.A/b: gelecek hafta.yA/c: yeni bir açıklama.yA} kadar erteledik.** '{Because of} [the] rain, we postponed the class {a: until tomorrow/b: until next week/c: until further notice}.' **Öğretmen öğleden sonra saat 3'teki sınav.I yarın sabah saat 8'e erteledi.** 'The teacher postponed the examination scheduled for 3 o'clock this afternoon to 8 o'clock tomorrow morning.' **Ev taksidini ödemek için sadece üç günümüz kaldı. Ertelemek için bir çözüm [yolu] bulmalıyız.** 'We have only 3 days to make our house payment [lit., ** pay the house installment]. We must find a way to put it off.' **Vatanî görevlerini daha fazla erteleyemeyecekler.** 'They can't postpone their military [lit., homeland] service any longer.' VERBAL noun as object: **Sağlığımız için yapacak-larımız.ı bile erteliyoruz.** 'For our health we put off even the things we have to do.' **Amcam ev.E dönüş.ü.nü erteledi.** 'My paternal uncle postponed his return θ home.' *845:9.* lateness: - postpone. → = **bırak-** 6, ≠ **öne al-** ['- move up in time, - make earlier than originally planned'] → **al-** 1.

{**ertelen-** [ir]/**tehir edil-** [ir]} /a: A, b: A, c: A kadar, d: {tarafından/CA}/ '- be postponed, delayed, put off /a: for, b: to, c: {till/until}, d: by/': [ertele- + pass. suf. -n; A. **tehir et-** + pass. suf. -Il]: **Yağmur.dan dolayı futbol maçı {a: hafta.yA/b: bir hafta sonra.yA/c: iki hafta sonra.yA} [idare tarafından] ertelendi.** 'Because of rain, the soccer game was postponed {a, b: FOR a week}/c: FOR two weeks} [by the administration].' **Yağmur {neden.i.yle/yüz.ü.nden/dola-yı.sı.yla/sebeb.i.yle} futbol** maçı {a: yarın.A/b: gelecek hafta.yA/c: yeni bir açıkla-ma.yA} kadar ertelendi. '{Because of [*or* due to]} rain, the soccer game was postponed {a: until tomorrow/b: until next week/c: until further notice}.' *845:9.* lateness: - postpone. → = **kal- 4.**

es- [er] 'for wind - blow, - be windy': S: **Hava nasıl?** 'Q: How's the weather?' C1: * **Çok esiyor.** 'A1: It's very windy [lit., ** It's blowing a lot].' C2: **Ilık bir rüzgâr esiyor.** 'A2: A warm wind is blowing.' **Hafif hafif esen rüzgâr çiçeklerin kokusunu taşıyordu.** 'The soft [lit., Lightly blowing] breezes were carrying the scent of the flowers.' Proverbs: **Esmeyince kıpırdamaz.** 'If there is no breeze [lit., As long as it doesn't blow], there is no movement [lit., it doesn't move].', i.e., There is a cause for everything. **Her zaman gemicinin istediği rüzgâr esmez.** 'The breeze that a seafarer wants doesn't always blow.' *318:20.* wind: - blow. → **üfle- 1** [for sb '- blow', on sth hot to cool it, smoke into room].

eski- [r] '[for a non-living thing] - get or - become worn-out, - wear out, - get old' [eski 'old' + verb-forming suf. -θ]: {a: **Takım elbisem**/b: **Arabam**/c: **Koltuklarım**/d: **Çamaşır makinam**} çok eskidi; * **yeni.si.ni almam gerekiyor.** '{a: My suit/b: My car/c: My armchairs/d: My washing machine} has gotten quite worn-out. * I must buy a new one [lit., ** a new one of it].' *393:20.* impairment: - wear, - wear away. → = **yıpran- 1.** For a person as a subject of '- get old, - age', → **ihtiyarla-, yaşı ilerle-** → **ilerle- 3, yaşlan-.**

esne- [r] '- yawn': * **Çocuk uyku saati geldiğinde esnemeye başladı.** 'When it was his bedtime, the child began to yawn.' **Konuşurken o kadar çok esniyordu ki, söylediklerini anlayamadım.** 'While he was speaking, he was yawning so much that I couldn't understand what he was saying.' * **Uykusunu tam alamamış olmalı, hâlâ esniyor.** 'He musn't have been able to get enough sleep. He's still yawning.' *292:16.* opening: - gape.

{**eşlik et-** [eDer]/**refakat et-** [eDer]} /A/ '- accompany /θ/, - go [along] /WITH/' [{eşlik/A. refakat} 'accompaniment']: * **Aldığım davetiye 2 kişilik. Ban.A eşlik eder misin?** 'The invitation I received is for two people [lit., ** is (a) two-person (invitation)]. Will you {come with me/accompany θ me}?' *formal:* **Cumhurbaşkanımız sayın Ahmet Necdet Sezer'E bu ziyaretinde Dışişleri Bakanı sayın Abdullah Gül ile Devlet Bakanı ve Başbakan Yardımcısı sayın Abdüllatif Şener eşlik edeceklerdir.** 'On this visit Foreign Minister Abdullah Gül and Minister without Portfolio and Deputy Prime Minister Abdüllatif Şener will accompany θ our President Ahmet Necdet Sezer.' **Biz.E kim eşlik edecek?** 'Who will accompany θ us?' **Japon şef Komatsu'nun yöneteceğ.i orkestra Copan'ın 1. Piyano Konçertosu'nda {en gözde/ dünyaca tanınmış} piyanistlerimiz.den İdil Biret'E eşlik edecek.** 'The orchestra that the Japanese conductor Komatsu will conduct will accompany θ İdil Biret, one of our {most prominent/world famous} pianists, in Chopin's piano concerto no. 1.' *768:7.* accompaniment: - accompany. → = /lA/ **gel-** ['- come /with/'] → **gel- 1,** = /lA/ **git-** ['- go /with/'] → **git- 1a,** /A/ **katıl- 2** ['- join a group'].

et- [eDer] 1 '- do, - perform'. → = **eyle-,** = **kıl-** [with a limited set of nouns as subject], = **kıy- 3** [with a very limited set of nouns as subject]: Proverbs: * **Eden bulur.** 'He who does sth will suffer the consequences of his action [lit., ** The one who does will find (the consequences)].' **Etme komşun.a gelir baş.ın.a.** 'Don't do it to your neighbor; it [i.e., what you have done to him] will come back to you [lit., ** come to your head].' Do unto others as you would have them do unto you. **Baş** 'head' here stands for the whole body, person. In contrast to the examples above, et-, like **eyle-** and **kıl-,** usually forms a phrasal verb with a preceding, usually Arabic but sometimes Turkish, noun as in **telefon et-.** It is used ALONE without a preceding noun mostly when it refers back to such a phrasal verb: S: **Teoman'A telefon edeyim mi?** 'Q: Shall I [tele]phone θ Teoman?' C: **Evet, ET.** 'A: Yes,

DO.' The verb for '- do' or '- make' when it is not a part of or associated with a phrasal verb is usually yap-. This dictionary has the following *noun* et- verb entries:

A: acele et-, alay et-, aldırış etme-, analiz et-, arzu et-, ateş et-, ayıp et-.

B: bayram et-, beyan et-.

Ç: çiş et-, çocukluk et-.

D: dans et-, dava et-, davet et-, devam et-, dikkat et-.

E: elde et-, endişe et-, eşlik et-.

F: farz et-, flört et-.

G: göç et-, gürültü et-.

H: hakaret et-, hak et-, hareket et-, hata et-, hayret et-, hediye et-, hitap et-, hizmet et-, hücum et-.

I: ısrar et-.

İ: iade et-, ibadet et-, icad et-, icap et-, idare et-, ifade et-, iflâs et-, ihmal et-, ihraç et-, ihtar et-, ikaz et-, ikna et-, ikram et-, ilâve et-, imtihan et-, imza et-, inkâr et-, intihar et-, ispat et-, istifa et-, istirahat et-, işaret et-, ithaf et-, ithal et-, itiraf et-, itiraz et-, iyi et-, iyilik et-, izah et-.

K: kabul et-, kahvaltı et-, kavga et-, kehanet et-, kontrol et-, kopya et-.

M: masraf et-, merak et-, meşgul et-, muayene et-, muhabbet et-, mukayese et-, münakaşa et-, müracaat et-, müsaade et-.

N: nefret et-, niyet et-.

P: park et-, pazarlık et-, protesto et-.

R: rahat et-, rahatsız et-, refakat et-, rica et-.

S: sarf et-, seyahat et-, sohbet et-, sote et-, söz et-, sünnet et-.

Ş: şikâyet et-.

T: tahammül et-, tahlil et-, tahmin et-, tahrik et-, tahsil et-, takdim et-, takdir et-, takip et-, taklit et-, talep et-, tamir et-, tanıklık et-, tarif et-, tasarruf et-, tasdik et-, tavsiye et-, tayin et-, tebrik et-, tecavüz et-, tecrübe et-, tedavi et-, tehdit et-, tehir et-, teklif et-, temas et-, tekrar et-, telâffuz et-, telefon et-, tembih et-, tenkit et-, tercih et-, tercüme et-, tereddüt et-, terk et-, tesadüf et-, tesir et-, teslim et-, teşekkür et-, teşvik et-, tetkik et-.

Ü: ümit et-.

V: var et-, vefat et-.

Y: yardım et-, yasak et-, yemin et-, yok et-, yolcu et-.

Z: zahmet et-, ziyaret et-.

If the nominal form of a noun changes when followed by a vowel, the et- is written together with that noun [e.g., af becomes aff, bahis, becomes bahs before a vowel]. This dictionary has the following *noun* et- entries where et- is written together with the preceding noun: affet-, bahset-, benzet-, emret-, farket-, hallet-, hisset-, kahret-, kastet-, katet-, kaybet-, kaydet-, keşfet-, methet-, reddet-, seyret-, tabettir-, vadet-, yönet-, zannet-.

In the above, the first element of the phrasal verb is a NOUN. This dictionary has the following et-phrasal verb entries in which the first element is an ADJECTIVE: rahatsız et-, meşgul et-. *328:6.* action: - do; *407:4.* accomplishment: - accomplish. → = eyle-, = kıl-.

2 '- be worth', often with words designating amounts: S: Bu çanta {kaç para/kaç lira} eder? 'Q: {How much/How many liras} is this handbag [Also: purse *or* briefcase] worth?' C: Bu çanta 50 lira eder. 'A: This handbag is worth 50 liras.' S: Bu çanta 50 lira eder mi? 'Q: Is this briefcase worth 50 lira?' C: {Evet, eder./Hayır, etmez.} 'A: {Yes, it is./No, it isn't.}' *998:10.* goodness: - do good. → = 2 değ- 1. # beş para etME- 'NOT - be worth a cent': Bu yüzük beş para etmez, sizi kandırmışlar. 'This ring isn't worth a cent. They've cheated you.'

3 '- amount to, - equal, - add up to, - make, - get': Bir artı bir iki eder. 'One {and/plus} one {makes/is} two.' 284'Ü [read: iki yüz seksen dörd.Ü] 2'yE [read: iki.yE] BÖLERSEK, 142 eder. '284 divided by 2 is 142 [lit., If WE DIVIDE 284 INTO 2, 142 remains].' 284 [read: iki yüz seksen dört] 2'yE [read: iki'yE] BÖLÜNÜRSE 142 eder. Same. [lit., If 284 IS DIVIDED INTO 2, one gets 142.]' *789:5.* equality: - equal; *791:8.* whole: - total; *1016:18.* mathematics: - sum up.

etkile- [r] /I/ '- affect, - influence, - have an effect /{ON/UPON}/, - impress' [etki 'effect, influence' + verb-forming suf. -lA]: Bu olaylar seçimler.İ nasıl etkileyecek? 'How will these events affect the elections?' İnsan kopyalamak yaşamımız.I nasıl etkileyecek? 'How will the cloning of human beings affect our lives?' İstifa piyasalar.I etkilemedi. 'The resignation did not affect the markets.' Amerika'nın tutumu karar.I büyük oranda etkileyecek. 'America's policy will greatly affect the decision.' Savaş memleketin ekonomik sistemi.nİ {olumsuz/olumlu} yönde etkileyecektir. 'The war will have a {negative/positive} effect ON the economic system of the country.' Doktorlar kahve.nin kalb.İ etkilediğ.i.ni söylüyorlar. 'Doctors say that coffee affects the heart.' → /A/ dokun- 2 ['- affect one's health negatively']. Çocuğun ağlaması hepimiz.İ etkiledi. 'The child's weeping affected all of us.' → = /A/ dokun- 3. # Başbakan konuşması ile herkes.İ etkiledi. 'The prime minister impressed everyone with his talk.' Mükemmel Türkçesiyle hepimiz.İ etkiledi. 'He impressed us all with his excellent Turkish.' 893:7. influence: - influence. → = /A/ tesir et-.

etkilen- [ir] 1 /DAn/ '- be influenced /BY/, - show the influence /OF/' [etkile- + pass. suf. -n]: Bob'ın söylediği şarkılardan Türk müziğ.i.nDEN etkilenmiş olduğu anlaşılıyor. 'It's clear from the songs [that] Bob sang that he was influenced BY Turkish music.' 893:7. influence: - influence.

2 /DAn/ '- be moved, emotionally affected, impressed /BY/': * Arkadaşım.ın doğum günümde çiçek gönderme.si.nDEN çok etkilendim. 'I was very moved when my friend sent me flowers on my birthday [lit., ** BY my friend's sending (me) flowers on my birthday].' Mükemmel Türkçesi.nDEN hepimiz etkilendik. 'We were all impressed BY his excellent Turkish.' 893:7. influence: - influence. → = duygulan-.

etrafa bak-. → bak- 1.

etrafını sar-. → sar- 3.

evde kal-. → kal- 1.

evlât edin-. → edin-.

evlen- [ir] /lA/ '- get married /TO/, - marry /θ/' [ev 'house' + verb-forming suf. -lAn. ADJ. evli 'married']: Benim.LE evlenir misin Şebnem? 'Will you marry θ me, Şebnem?' Şebnem ile Burak dün evlendiler. 'Şebnem [f.] and Burak got married yesterday.' Nazan Tarık'LA genç yaş.ta evlenmiş, hâlâ onun.LA evli. 'Nazan [f.] married θ Tarık while young [lit., at a young age]. She is still married TO him.' Ailesi yüzünden evlenemiyoruz. 'We can't get married because of his family. Ben.DEN * yaşça hayli {büyük/küçük} bir bey.LE evlendim. 'I married a man considerably {older/younger} THAN me [lit., ** in age].' Proverb: Allah evlenenle ev yapan.A yardım eder. 'God helps θ those who marry {and/or} build a house.' 563:15. marriage: - get married. → = dünya evine gir-, ≠ ayrıl- 1 ['- get or - be divorced /from/, - split up /WITH/'], ≠ boşan-. Same.

evlendir- [ir] /lA/ '- marry, - give sb in marriage /TO/' [evlen- + caus. suf. -DIr]: Kerim bey geçen hafta küçük kızı.nı bir doktor.LA evlendirdi. 'Last week Kerim bey gave his younger daughter in marriage TO a doctor.' 563:14. marriage: - join in marriage. → = kız ver- ['- give a girl in marriage'] → ver- 1; nikâh kıy- ['- perform the civil marriage ceremony, - officially join in marriage, - marry'] → kıy- 3.

eyle- [r] '- do, - perform.' This verb, like et- and kıl-, forms a phrasal verb with a preceding, usually Arabic but sometimes Turkish noun. It is usually used alone without a preceding noun only when it refers back to such a phrasal verb. It commonly occurs in certain fixed expressions. The verb for '- do' or '- make' when it is not a part of a phrasal verb or does not refer back to one is usually yap-. This dictionary has only the following phrasal verb with eyle-: rahmet eyle-. 328:6. action: - do; 407:4. accomplishment: - accomplish. → = et- 1, = kıl- [with a limited set of nouns as subject], = kıy- 3 [with a very limited set of nouns as subject].

ez- [er] '- crush, - mash, - grind, - pulverize': Sarımsakları ayıklayıp havanda ezin. 'Peel the pieces of garlic and {crush/pound} them in a mortar.' O karıncayı bile ezmek.TEN kaçınan çok merhametli bir insandı. 'He was a very compassionate person who wouldn't hurt even a fly [lit., a very compassionate person who would avoid θ stepping on (lit., crushing) even an ant].' *1049:9.* powderiness, crumbliness: - pulverize.

ezbere bil-. → bil- 1.

ezberle- [r] '- memorize, - commit to memory, - learn by heart' [P. ezber 'memorization' + verb-forming suf. -lA]: Ezberlediğin o şiiri şimdi okur musun? 'Would you now recite the poem that you have memorized?' Öğretmenin verdiği şiiri ezberlemek istemiyordu. 'He didn't want to memorize the poem that the teacher had assigned.' Öğretmen bu şiiri * ezber{.E/.DEN} okumamı istedi, fakat ezberleyemedim. 'The teacher asked me to recite this poem * {from} memory, but I wasn't able to memorize it.' *570:8.* learning: - memorize; *988:17.* memory: - memorize.

- F -

faks çek-. → çek- 9.

faks gönder-. → gönder-.

faksla- [r] /A/ '- fax sth /to/' [faks 'fax' + verb-forming suf. -lA]: Bu mektub.U Ankara'ya faksladım. 'I faxed this letter to Ankara.' Bu belgeler.İ hemen fakslamam gerekiyor. 'I must fax these documents at once.' Bu belgeler.İ buradan fakslayabilir miyim? 'Can I {fax/send} these documents from here?' Bu dilekçem.in saat 5'e kadar okula yetişme.si gerekiyor. Hemen fakslayabilir misin? 'This application of mine must get to the school by 5 o'clock. Can you fax it right away?' *347:19.* communications: - telegraph. → faks çek- ['- send a fax /to/'] → çek- 9, faks gönder- ['- send a fax /to/'].

farkedil- [ir] /tarafından/ '- be noticed, observed /by/' [farket- + pass. suf. -Il]: Kız o kadar güzeldi ki, diğer kızların içinde hemen farkediliyordu. 'The girl was so beautiful that she immediately stood out [lit., ** was {distinguished/ noticed}] among the other girls.' "Palet" gerçekten iyi bir lokantadır. İçeri girer girmez kalitesi farkedilir. '"Palet" is really a good restaurant. As soon as one enters, its high quality is apparent [lit., is noticed].' *940:5.* discovery: - detect.

farket- [eDer] [A. fark (faRKı) 'difference, discrimination' + et-]: 1 '- notice, - observe, - perceive, - realize': NON-verbal noun as object: Dikkatle bakınca kafasındaki yarayı farkettim. 'When I looked closely, I noticed the wound on his head.' *940:5.* discovery: - detect. VERBAL noun as object: Otobüs.ün istasyon.DAN {ayrıldığ.ı.nı/ayrılacağ.ı.nı} farketmedim. 'I didn't notice that the bus {had left/was going to leave} θ the station.' Kedi.nin sütü {ne zaman/nasıl} döktüğ.ü.nü farketmedim. 'I didn't notice {when/how} the cat had spilled the milk.' Kedi.nin sütü döküp {dökmediğ.i.ni/dökmeye-ceğ.i.ni} farkedemedim. 'I couldn't determine whether or not the cat {had spilled/was about to spill} the milk.' Yanlış numara çevirdiğini farkedince telefonu hemen kapattı. 'When he realized that he had dialed the wrong number, he hung up right away.' Takip edildiği.ni farkeden genç kız koşmak.tan nefes nefese kalmıştı. 'The young girl, who had noticed that she was being followed, was out of breath from running.' *27:12.* vision: - see; *982:6.* attention: - heed. → = dikkat et- 2, = farkına var-, = gözle- 1.

2 '- make a difference, - matter', often in the negative: Farketmez. 'It doesn't make any difference': Artık doktor gelse de farketmez. Çünkü hasta öldü. 'Now even if the doctor comes, it won't make any difference, because the patient has died.' A: Oda balkonlu mu olsun efendim? 'A: Do you want a room with a balcony, {sir/ma'am} [lit., Should the room be with a balcony]?' B: [Benim için] {hiç

farketmez}. 'B: It doesn't {make any difference at all/matter at all} [to me].' A: * **Kahve mi içersin çay mı?** 'A: What will you have [lit., drink], coffee or tea?' B: * **Farketmez.** 'B: [Whichever.] It doesn't {make any difference/matter}.' A: **Farketmezse çay yapayım.** 'A: If it doesn't make any difference, I'll make tea.' *997:11.* unimportance: - be unimportant; *997:24.* unimportance: PHR. it does not matter. → = **olsa da olur, olmasa da** → ol- 11 → olsa.

3 '- distinguish, - make out': **Karanlıkta {gel.en.i} farkededim.** 'In the darkness I couldn't make out {the person who/the thing that} was approaching.' * **Karanlıkta seni farkedemedim.** 'In the darkness I couldn't {see you/make you out/see who you were}.' *27:12.* vision: - see. → = **seç-** 2.

farkına var-. → var-.

{**farz et-** [eDer]/**varsay-** [ar]} '- assume, - imagine, - suppose sth for the sake of argument' [A. **farz** 'supposition, hypothesis', **var** 'existent', **say-** '- count, - consider']: {**Farzedelim [ki]/Farzet [ki]**} '{Let's suppose [that]/Suppose [that]}': **Biraz para biriktirmemiz lâzım. Farzedelim ki birimiz hastalandı, o zaman ne yapacağız?** 'We must save a little money. Let's suppose that one of us gets sick, then what will we do?' *950:19.* theory, supposition: CONJ. supposing. **Öğretmen: Şimdi bu küçük topu ay, büyük topu da dünya farzedelim.** 'Teacher: Now let's assume that this small ball is the moon and that the large ball is the earth.' **Suçlu olduğu kanıtlanan.a kadar, onu suçsuz farz etmeliyiz.** 'We must {assume/consider} him innocent until proven guilty.' *950:10.* theory, supposition: - suppose. → = **de-** 2, = **tut-** 9.

faydalan- → {**yararlan-**/**faydalan-**/**istifade et-**}.

fazla 'excessive, superfluous', often used with verbs to render 'over', as in **fazla ısın-** '- overheat'. = **çok**, ≠ **az**. See directly below.

fazla ısın-. → ısın- 1.

fazla tahmin et-. → tahmin et- 2.

felâket geçir-. → geçir- 2.

felç ol-. → ol- 10.2.

fena ol-. → ol- 10.2.

fenalaş- [ır] [A. **fena** (. -) 'bad' + verb-forming suf. -lAş] 1 '- get worse, - deteriorate': **Hasta sabah.a karşı fenalaştı.** 'The patient got worse toward morning.' **İşler fenalaştı.** '{Things/Matters} have gotten worse.' *393:16.* impairment: - deteriorate. → = **gerile-** 2, = **kötüleş-**, = **zayıfla-** 2, ≠ **iyileş-**.

2 /DAn/ '- feel faint, - feel suddenly sick, - get sick, - take ill /{from/DUE TO}/': **Dün otobüste bir kadın sıcak.TAN fenalaştı.** 'Yesterday on the bus a woman suddenly got sick {from/DUE TO} the heat.' *85:46a.* disease: - take sick in general. → = **fena ol-** 1 → ol- 10.2, = **hasta ol-** ['- get sick; - be ill'] → ol- 10.2, = **hastalan-** ['- become ill, - get sick'], = **rahatsız ol-** 1 ['- feel or - become indisposed, slightly ill, sick, - be under the weather'] → ol- 10.2, = /A/ **yakalan-** 2 ['- catch /θ/ or - come down /WITH/ an illness'], ≠ **iyileş-**.

fermuar çek-. → çek- 4.

fırçala- [r] /lA/ '- brush /with/, - brush off' [**fırça** 'brush' + verb-forming suf. -lA]: **Banyo yaptıktan sonra saçlarımı fırçaladım.** 'After taking a bath, I brushed my hair.' **Yatmadan önce dişlerimi mutlaka fırçalarım.** 'Without fail, I always brush my teeth before going to bed.' **Sokağ.a çıkmadan önce ayakkabılarımı ve elbisemi fırçaladım.** 'Before going out [lit., to the street], I brushed off my shoes and my suit.' *79:23.* cleanness: - sweep.

fırla- [r] 1 /DAn, A/ '- jump up, - leap up /from, to/, - rush or - dart out, - fly out': PERSON as subject: **Öğretmen "Ders bitti" der demez öğrenciler dışarı fırladı.** 'As soon as the teacher said that the class was over, the students rushed out.' **Önü.m.E bir çocuk fırlayınca aniden fren yap.mak zor.u.nda kaldım.** 'When a child darted out θ in front of me, I suddenly had to hit the brakes.'

yerinden fırla- '- jump up from one's place': **Ahmet yangın haberini duyunca yerinden fırladı.** 'When Ahmet heard the news of the fire, he jumped up [from his place].' Often with the verb **git-**: **Yangın haberini duyunca yerinden fırlayıp gitti.** 'When he heard the news of the fire, he jumped up from his place and went out.' → ≠ **çök-** 2.

THING as subject: **Öğrenci tahtayı silerken silgi elinden fırladı.** 'While the student was erasing the blackboard, the eraser flew out of his hand.' *193:9.* ascent: - shoot up; *200:8.* verticalness: - rise; *366:5.* leap: - leap.

2 /DAn, A/ '- skyrocket, - increase or - rise suddenly, - soar, - jump /from, to/': **Sebze, meyva fiyatları birdenbire fırladı.** 'Vegetable and fruit prices suddenly skyrocketted.' **Domates.in fiyat.ı 25 kuruş.TAN 50 kuruş.A fırladı.** 'The price of tomatoes jumped FROM 25 kurush TO 50 kurush [i.e., per kilo].' *251:6.* increase: - grow, increase [i.]. For '- increase' without the notion of suddenness, → = **art-** 1, = **çık-** 6, = **yüksel-** 2, ≠ **düş-** 3.

fırlat- [ır] /A, A doğru/ '- hurl, - fling, - throw /{AT/to/INTO}, toward/; - launch [rocket, etc.] /INTO/ [space]' [**fırla-** + caus. suf. **-t**]: **Osman kuşlar.A doğru bir taş fırlattı.** 'Osman threw a stone AT the birds.' *903:10.* pushing, throwing: - throw. → = **at-** 1. # **Amerikalılar uza.yA yeni bir {uydu/füze} fırlattılar.** 'The Americans have launched a new {satellite/rocket} INTO space.' *903:10.* pushing, throwing: - throw; *1072:13.* rocketry, missilery: - launch.

fırsat kaçır-. → **kaçır-** 2.

fısılda- [r] /A/ '- whisper /{IN/INTO}/' [**fısıl** the sound of a whisper + verb-forming suf. **-D A**]: **Cemil Serpil'in yan.ı.nA yanaştı ve kulağ.ı.nA bir şey.LER fısıldadı.** 'Cemil came up to Serpil [f.] [lit., ** came up to Serpil's side] and whispered something [lit., ** somethingS] IN her ear.' *52:10.*

faintness of sound: - murmur. → ≠ **bağır-** ['- shout, - scream, - yell'], ≠ **bağırıp çağır-** → **çağır-** 3, ≠ **haykır-**.

fikir al-. → **al-** 1.

fikir paylaş-. → **paylaş-**.

{fikir/görüş} savun-. → **savun-**.

fikir ver-. → **ver-** 1.

fikre katıl-. → **{düşünceye/fikre/görüşe} katıl-.** → **katıl-** 3.

fikrinden vazgeç-. → **vazgeç-**.

fikrine itiraz et-. → **itiraz et-**.

fikrini değiştir-. → **değiştir-** 1.

film bas-. → **bas-** 3.

film {bastır-/tabettir-}. → **{bastır-/tabettir-}.**

film çek-. → **çek-** 7.

film çevir-. → **çevir-** 3.

film tabettir-. → **{bastır-/tabettir-}.**

film yıkat-. → **yıkat-** 2.

filmde oyna-. → **oyna-** 3.

fiyat al-. → **al-** 3.

fiyat koy-. → **koy-** 1.

* **flört et-** [eDer] /lA/ '- go [out] on a date /with/, - go out /with/, - date, - be dating', but with the intention of marriage. NOT the English '- flirt': **Murat ile Nazlı 5 aydan beri flört ediyorlar.** 'Murat and Nazlı [f.] have been {going out with each other/dating} for 5 months.' *562:14.* lovemaking, endearment: - make love; *769:16.* assemblage: - come together. → = **çık-** 10.

fotoğraf çek-. → **{resim/fotoğraf} çek-.** → **çek-** 7.

fotoğraf çektir-. → **{resim/fotoğraf} çektir-.** → **çektir-** 3.

fotokopi çek-. → **çek-** 8.

- G -

garibine git-. → {acayibine/
garibine/tuhafına} git-. → git-
1 b.

gebert- [ir] '- bump off, - wipe out, - rub
out, - do in, - nuke, - zap', all
contemptuous for '- kill' [geber- '-
croak', *contemptuous* for '- die', +
caus. suf. -t]: A threat: **Gebertirim!**
'I'll kill you!' *308:13.* killing: <non-
formal terms> - waste; *514: * 5.*
threat: INTERJ. specific threats.

gecele- [r] '- spend the night
somewhere' [gece 'night' + verb-
forming suf. -l A]: **Arabamız
bozulunca küçük bir motelde
geceledik.** 'When our car broke
down, we spent the night in a small
motel.' **Evi olmadığı için bazen
parklarda, bazen köprü
altlarında gecelerdi.** 'Because he
was homeless [lit., didn't have a
home], he would sometimes spend
the night in parks, sometimes under
bridges.' *820:6.* time: - spend time.
→ **sabahla-** ['- spend the night
somewhere, - stay up all night'],
{vakit/zaman} geçir- ['- spend
time'] → geçir- 3.

geceyi gündüze kat-. → kat-.

gecik- → {geç kal-/gecik-}. → kal-
1.

geç- [er] 1 /DAn, A/ '- pass
/THROUGH, {to/INTO}/, - go past, -
cross /θ/ sth, - trespass' [ADJ. **geçici**
'temporary, passing']: **Tren
tünel.DEN geçti.** 'The train passed
THROUGH the tunel.' **Orman.ın
iç.i.nDEN geçerek köy
yol.u.nA çıktım.** 'Passing
THROUGH [lit., ** the inside of] the
forest, I came out ON the road to the
village.' **İplik iğne.DEN
geçmiyor.** 'The thread won't pass
THROUGH the needle.' **Güreş
millî takımımız olimpiyatlarda
tüm rekorları kır.arak * tarih.E
geçti.** 'By break.ing all the records
at the Olympics, our national
wrestling team * entered the history
books [lit., passed INTO history].'
**Sınır.DAN geçen 80 kaçak,
polis tarafından yakalandı.**
'Eighty fugitives who had crossed θ
the border were seized by the police.'
Askerî bölge. Geçmek yasaktır.
'Military zone. No trespassing.'

352:7 publication: poster: * specific
signs. Proverbs: **Deniz.DEN geçti
çayda boğuldu.** 'He crossed
{θ/OVER} the ocean but drowned in
the brook.', i.e., {From/OUT OF} the
frying pan into the fire. *393:48.*
impairment: ADV. out of the frying
pan into the fire. **Herkesin geçtiği
köprü.DEN sen de geç.** 'You
[should] also cross {θ/OVER} the
bridge that everyone crosses.', i.e.,
Do what most people do, even if it is
not entirely to your liking. *177:20.*
travel: - traverse; *866:10.* conformity:
don't rock the boat.

/I/ '- go beyond, - cross': **Taksi o
kadar hızlı gidiyordu ki,
yoldaki bütün arabaları geçti.**
'The taxi was going so fast that it
passed all the cars on the road.' S: **İş
Bankası nerede biliyor
musunuz?** 'Q: Do you know where
the İş Bank is?' C: * **Hemen
postane.yİ geç.ince.** 'A: Just past
the post office [lit., As soon as one
passes the post office].' **Cadde.yİ
geçerken arabalar.A dikkat
edin.** 'When crossing the street,
watch out FOR [the] cars.' **Bu iş
için çok geç kaldın. Daha önce
başvurmalıydın. 'At.ı alan
Üsküdar.I geçti.'** 'You have
applied for this job too late [lit., You
are too late for this job]. You should
have applied earlier. [As the proverb
says:] "The one who has
{taken/stolen} the horse has already
gone beyond Üsküdar [i.e., a section
of Istanbul]".' *177:20.* travel: -
traverse; *845: * 21.* lateness: PHR.
it's too late; *909:8.* overrunning: -
pass.

'- exceed, - go beyond, - outdo': **Hız
sınırını geçtiniz.** 'You have
exceeded the speed limit.' Proverb:
Kabiliyetli çırak ustayı geçer.
'The capable apprentice outdoes the
master.' *909:4.* overrunning: -
overrun; *992:9.* excess: - exceed.

geç- in telling times past the hour. •
Note the two question patterns and
the use of the accusative case suffix -
I in the responses to both:
a) S: **Saat kaç?** 'Q: {What time is
it?/What's the time?}' C1: [Saat]
5'İ 20 geçiyor. 'A1: It's {five
twenty/20 past five}.' C2: [Saat]
5'İ çeyrek geç.İYOR. 'A2: It's a
quarter {past/after} 5.'
b} S: **Saat kaç.TA?** 'Q: AT what
time?' Note the use of **geçe** [geç- +

the adverbial suffix -[y]A] in the responses: C1: [Saat] 5'İ 20 geçe. 'A1: AT {five twenty/20 past five}.' C2: [Saat] 5'İ çeyrek geç.E. 'A2: AT a quarter {past/after} 5.'

'- pass by, - get through': You are in a crowded place, and you want to get through. You say: Affedersiniz, geçebilir miyim? 'Excuse me, may I {pass/get} by?' or * Müsaadenizle geçeyim. lit., ** 'With your permission, I'll pass by.'

* başından geç- '- happen to, - experience, - go through', lit., ** '- pass through one's head', where 'head', represents the whole person. • Note: This phrase does not mean '- occur to one', which the literal translation suggests. The event experienced is usually interesting, good, exciting, or unusual rather than unfortunate. Thus this phrase is in contrast to başına gel-: Tatilde baş.IM.dan çok ilginç bir olay geçti. 'During the holidays {I had a very interesting experience/a very interesting thing happened to ME}.' Başımdan geçenleri ve tanık olduğum olayları bir bir anlatayım. 'Let me tell you in detail [lit., ** one by one] what happened to me and what I witnessed.' * Filiz'in baş.ı.ndan tam dört evlilik geçti. 'Filiz {has been/was} married altogether four times [lit., ** Altogether four marriages passed through Filiz's head].' 830:5. event: - occur. → = /A/ ol- 2.

* dalga geç- [dalga 1 'wave'. 2 'absentmindedness'] (1) '- let one's mind, attention wander, - be off in the clouds': Öğretmen öğrenciye: Bütün ders dalga geçtin herhalde, sorularım.ın hiç bir.i.ne cevap veremiyorsun. 'The teacher to the student: You've probably been off in the clouds for the whole lesson. You can't answer even one of my questions.' 983:3. inattention: - wander.
(2) /lA, diye/ '- make fun /OF [sb], BECAUSE [lit., saying]/': Hakan: Sınıftaki kızlar pembe pantolon giydim DİYE benim.LE dalga geçtiler. 'Hakan: The girls in the class made fun OF me BECAUSE I wore pink trousers.' 508:8. ridicule: - ridicule. → = alay et-, = alaya al- → al- 1, = eğlen- 2, gül- 2 ['-

laugh /AT/, - mock /θ/, - make fun /OF/'].
(3) /lA/ '- play around, - trifle, - dally /with/', i.e., not - take seriously' [obj.: sb's affections]: Tufan Zeynep'le dalga geçiyor, evlenmey.E hiç niyet.İ yok. 'Tufan is just playing around with Zeynep. He has no intention at all OF marrying her.' 997:14. unimportance: - trifle. → = oyna- 5.

* ırzına geç- '- rape, - violate' [ırz 'chastity, purity, honor']: O adamı kızkardeşim.in ırz.ı.nA geçtiği için vurdum, pişman değilim. 'I shot that man because he had raped my sister. I have no regrets.' 480:15. taking: - possess sexually; 665:20. unchastity: - seduce. → = saldır- 2 ['- rape /θ/, - assault /θ/ sexually', not necessarily rape.], = tecavüz et- 2. Same.

* İş işten geçti. 'It's too late', lit., ** 'the matter has passed from the matter': Ödevlerinizi geçen hafta bana vermeniz gerekiyordu, artık bir şey yapamam, iş iş.TEN geçti, notları idareye teslim ettim bile. 'You should have turned in your homework last week. Now there's nothing I can do [lit., I can't do anything]. It's too late. I've already turned in your grades to the department [lit., administration].' 845: * 21. lateness: PHR. it's too late. → = Olan {oldu/olmuş}. → ol- 11.

karşıya geç- /DAn/ '- pass /to/ the {opposite/other} side, - cross /θ/, - cross over /θ/' [karşı 'the place opposite, facing']: The area crossed is not indicated: You are about to cross a street. You say: Karşı.yA geçelim. 'Let's cross.' The area crossed is indicated: Vatan Caddesi'nDEN karşı.yA geç- tikten sonra doğru ileri yürü. 'After crossing θ Vatan Avenue, go [lit., walk] straight ahead.' 177:20. travel: - traverse; 909:8. overruning: - pass.

* kendinden geç- [kendi 'self'], lit., ** '- pass from, i.e., out of, oneself' (1) '- pass out, - faint, - lose consciousness': Kafasını masa.yA çarpınca, kendi.nDEN geçti. 'When he hit his head ON the table, he passed out.' 25:5. insensibility: - faint. → = bayıl- 1, = kendini kaybet- 1, = {şuurunu/

bilincini} kaybet-[or yitir-] 1 →
{kaybet-/yitir-}, ≠ ayıl- 2 ['- come
to'], ≠ kendine gel- 1 ['- come to']
→ gel- 1.
(2) *fig.* '- be beside oneself with joy,
- be carried away [by joy], - be
ecstatic, in Paradise': **Partide o
kadar eğlendik ki,
kendi.MİZ.den geçtik.** 'At the
party we had such a good time WE
were simply {beside ourselves/carried
away/in paradise}.' *95:11.* pleasure: -
be pleased. → = kendini {kaybet-
/NOT ~~yitir~~-} 2, = **bayram et-**.
(3) '- pass out, - fall asleep': **O
kadar yorgundum ki yatağ.a
yatar yatmaz kendi.M.den
geçmişim.** 'I was so tired that as
soon as I hit {the bed/the sack} I
must have passed out.' *22:16.* sleep: -
go to sleep. → **uykuya dal-** ['- fall
asleep; - doze off, - drop off /to/
sleep'] → **dal-** 2.

* **kontrolden geç-** '- be checked, -
be checked out, examined':
**Havaalanında {a: {yolcular/
ziyaretçiler}/b: herkes}
kontrolden geçiyordu.** 'At the
airport {a: {travelers/visitors} were/b:
everyone was} being checked.'
937:24. inquiry: - examine.

* **muayeneden geç-** '- have a
physical examination, a physical, a
check-up' [A. **muayene** (. - .) 'an
examining, examination'], lit., ** '-
pass THROUGH a physical': **Genel
bir muayene.DEN geçmeniz
gerekiyor.** 'You must have a
{check-up/physical}.' *91:29.* therapy:
- undergo treatment; *937:24.* inquiry:
- examine. → = **muayene ol-** → **ol-**
10.1.

* **önüne geç-** [er] '- prevent' [**ön**
'the front part of anything', lit., '-
pass to {the front of/its front}']:
**Savaş.IN ön.Ü.nE geçmek için
ülkeler elbirliği ile
çalışmalıdır.** 'To prevent war,
nations {must cooperate/lit., work IN
concert}.' *1011:14.* hindrance: -
prevent. → = /I/ **engelle-**, = /A/
mâni ol- → **ol-** 12, = /I/ **önle-**.

sınıfa geç- '- go on or - graduate to
the next grade [e.g., from the fifth
grade to the sixth] or to another class
or section of the same grade' [A.
sınıf 'class, grade']: **Emine ikinci
sınıf.A geçti.** 'Emine [f.] went on
to the second grade.' *409:7b.* success:

- succeed in specific ways. → ≠
sınıfta kal- ['- be held back in
school, - stay behind, - fail or - flunk
a grade, not - go on to the next
grade'] → **kal-** 1.

* **sınıfını geç-** '- go on to the next
grade, lit., ** - pass one's grade [e.g.,
from the fifth grade to the sixth]' [A.
sınıf 'class, grade']: **Biz
sınıf.IMIZ.ı geçtik.** 'We passed to
the next grade [lit., ** passed OUR
grade].' **Mehmet çalışkan bir
öğrenci olsaydı sınıfını
geçerdi.** 'If Mehmet had been a
hardworking student, he would have
passed on to the next grade.' *409:7b.*
success: - succeed in specific ways.
→ ≠ **sınıfta kal-** ['- be held back in
school, - stay behind, - fail or - flunk
a grade, not - go on to the next
grade'] → **kal-** 1.

2 '- pass or - spread from one person
to another', disease: **{Kızamık/Su
çiçeği/Kabakulak} bulaşıcı
hastalıklardır. * On.dan o.na
geçer.** '{Measles/Chicken pox/
Mumps} are contagious diseases. *
They pass from one person to another
[lit., ** from him to him].' *770:4b.*
dispersion: - disperse, - become
dispersed. → = **yayıl-**.

3 '- occur, - happen, - take place',
events: **{Bu hikâyedeki/Bu
romandaki/Bu filmdeki} olaylar nerede geçiyor?** 'Where do
the events {in this story/in this
novel/in this movie} take place?'
**{Bu hikâye/Bu roman/Bu
filim} nerede geçiyor?** 'Where
does {this story/this novel/this
movie} take place?' **Tarih
sahne.si.nDEN nice olaylar
geçti ve geçmeye devam
edecek.** 'Many events have occurred
ON [lit., ** passed THROUGH] the
stage of history and will continue to
occur.' * **Bu okulda geçen
anılarım artık çok uzaklarda
kaldı.** 'My memories of this school
[lit., ** remembered events which
took place in this school] seem very
distant now [lit., ** remained at great
distances].' *830:5.* event: - occur. →
= **ol-** 2.

4 '- pass, - end, - come to an end, -
be over': **İki haftadır nezleydim,
çok şükür geçti.** 'I had a cold for
two weeks. Thank God it's over.'
jocular: **Nezle ilâç kullanırsan**

bir haftada, kullanmazsan 7 günde geçer. 'A cold is over in one week if you take [lit., use] some [lit., a] medicine, in seven days if you don't [lit., don't use one].' **Kolumdaki yara geçmeyince bir doktor.A başvurdum.** 'When the wound on my arm did not heal [lit., ** pass], I consulted θ a doctor.' Someone is in a difficult situation. You comfort him saying: **Üzülme, bu da geçer.** 'Don't worry. This too {will/shall} pass.' *121: * 17.* comfort: words of comfort. You were in a difficult situation which has now thankfully passed. You say: * **Bu da geçti.** 'Now this too is {over/past} [lit., Now this too has passed].' Proverbs: **Bıçak yarası geçer, dil yarası geçmez.** 'A knife wound heals [lit., ** passes], a wound inflicted by the tongue [lit., a tongue wound, i.e., an insult, harsh words, etc.] does not.' • This is the exact opposite of the English proverb 'Sticks and stones will break my bones, but words will never hurt me'. It reflects Turkish sensitivity to harsh words. *524: * 35.* speech: proverbs. * **Sayılı gün[ler] çabuk geçer.** 'Deadlines come to an end before you know it [lit., ** Numbered day(s) pass quickly].' *761:6.* nonexistence: - cease to exist; *820:17.* PHR. time flies; *836:6.* past: - pass. → ol- **9.3** ['for time - have passed, - elapse, - be over'].

Geçmiş olsun. → ol- 11. → olsun.

{vakit/zaman/süre} geç- 'for time - pass; for time - expire, - be up' [A. **vakit** (vaKTİ) 'time', A. **zaman** (. -) 'time', **süre** 'period, extension']: **Sohbet çok güzeldi, * vakit nasıl geçti anlamadım.** 'The chat was very pleasant. * I don't know where the time went [lit., I don't understand how the time passed].' = {süre/vakit/zaman} **dol-** → dol- 2.

{vakti/zamanı/süresi} geç- 'for the period of time, validity OF sth - expire, be no longer valid, for sth - be overdue, for sb'S time - be up'. lit., 'for ITS time - pass': {a: **Pasaportunuz.un/b: Ehliyetiniz.in/c: Vizeniz.in/d: İkâmet izniniz.in/e: Kredi kartınız.ın} vakt.i geçmiş yenilemeniz gerekiyor.** '{a: Your passport/b: Your license/c: Your

visa/d: Your residence permit/e: Your credit card} has expired. You must **renew it.**' **Bu kuponu kullanamazsınız çünkü vakt.i geçmiş.** 'You can't use this coupon any more because it's no longer {valid/any good}.' * **Bu ilâc.ın vakt.i geçmiş, içilmez.** 'This medicine isn't good any more [lit., ** This medicine's time has passed]. It can't be used [lit., ** It isn't to be drunk].' **Bu kitab.ın vakt.i geçmiş kütüphaneye geri vermeliyim.** 'This book is overdue. I must return it to the library.' *390:9.* disuse: - obsolesce; *820:5.* time: - elapse. → = {süresi/vakti/zamanı} **dol-** → dol- 2.

5 '- be valid, legal': **Beş yüz liralık banknotlar tedavül.DEN kalktı. * Artık geçmiyor.** 'Five hundred lira notes have gone OUT OF circulation. * They are no longer {valid/legal tender} [lit., ** are no longer passing].' *673:8.* legality: - legalize.

6 '- go [well or badly]': **S:** {a: **Seyahatiniz/b: Yolculuğunuz/c: Ziyaretiniz/d: Toplantı/e: Ders/f: Parti} nasıl geçti?** 'Q: How did {a, b: your trip/c: your visit/d: the meeting/e: the lesson/f: the party} go?' **C:** {a: **Gayet rahat/b: İyi/c: [Ehh] şöyle böyle/d: Kötü/e: Berbat} geçti.** 'A: It went {a: extremely well [lit., ** very comfortably]/b: well/c: [oh] so so/d: badly/e: terribly}.' **Fena geçmedi.** '{Not bad./It didn't go badly.}' **Önümüzdeki sene daha iyi geçecek.** 'Next year will {be/go} better.' * **Yatılı okul yaşantım çok eğlenceli geçti.** 'My boarding school life was full of amusement [lit., ** passed very amusingly].' Proverb: **Biri yapar biri bozar, dünya böyle geçer.** 'One builds; another ruins it. This is the way of the world [lit., ** Thus the world passes].' *162:2.* progression: - progress. → = **git- 5.**

7 '- be mentioned, written, related, referred to, spoken about, discussed, - occur', in a written work: **Bu kitapta geçen olay ve kişiler.in gerçek.LE alaka.sı yoktur.** A standard English formulation of this statement found in books of fiction: 'The events and persons mentioned in this book are fictitious, and any

resemblance to real events and persons is purely coincidental [lit., ** The events and people mentioned in this book have no relation TO reality].' *551:8.* information: - inform.

8 /DA/ '- occur, - be present, - be found', words in a text: **Parçada geçen yabancı kelimeleri bulunuz.** 'Find the foreign words [that occur] in this {selection/ passage}.' *221:6.* presence: - be present. → = **bulun-** 2, = **ol-** 3.

geç kal-. → **kal-** 1.

geçimini sağla-. → **sağla-.**

geçin- [ir] /lA/ [geç- + refl. suf. -In] 1 '- get along or on /with/', persons with each other: **Amcam çok iyi bir insandı. Herkes.LE iyi geçinir, kimse.yİ kırmazdı.** 'My uncle was a very good person. He got along with everyone. He didn't {offend/hurt} anyone.' {**Karı koca/İki kardeş**} **çok iyi geçiniyorlar.** '{The couple/The two siblings} get on very well.' **Aile ve çevremle iyi geçinen bir insanım.** 'I'm a person who gets on well with my family and my {community/circle}.' **O adam.la * bunca yıl nasıl geçindi, * hayret doğrusu.** 'How did she [ever] get along with that man * for all these years! * It's really surprising!' *409:12.* success: - manage. → = **anlaş-** 1 ['- understand one another, - get along or on with one another'].
2 /lA, ArAk/ '- make one's living /[BY], by...ing/, - subsist /by means of/, - get by, - manage /ON/ [a salary]': S: * **Bu hayat pahalılığ.ı.nda bu maaş.LA nasıl geçiniyorsunuz?** 'Q: With prices being what they are [lit., ** In this life expensiveness] how do you {manage/get by} ON this salary?' C1: * **Geçinip gidiyoruz işte!** 'A1: Well, we manage somehow!' C2: * **Zor geçiniyoruz.** 'A2: {We're having a hard time./It's not easy.}' S: {**Ne.yle/Nasıl**} **geçiniyorsunuz?** 'Q: {How [lit., With what]/How} do you make your living?' C: {a: **Öğretmenlik.le** [or **Öğretmenlik yap.arak**]/b: **Yazarlık.la** [or **Yazarlık yap.arak**]/c: **Kütüphanecilik.le** [or **Kütüphanecilik yap.arak**]}

geçiniyorum. 'A: I make MY living {a: [BY] teaching [or lit., ** by do.ing teach.ing]/b: [BY] writing [or lit., ** by do.ing writing]/c: as a librarian [or lit., ** by do.ing librarianship]}.' Another common question to elicit a person's occupation: **Mesleğiniz nedir?** 'What is your {occupation/ profession}?' *385:11.* provision, equipment: - make a living; *409:12.* success: - manage. → = **geçimini sağla-**, = **hayatını kazan-** → **kazan-** 1, = **iş yap-** 1 ['- do work for a living'] → **yap-** 3.

geçir- [ir] 1 /DAn/ '- cause to pass, - make pass /THROUGH/, - pass' [geç- + caus. suf. -Ir]: **Çamurlu yol.DAN araba.yI zor geçirdim.** 'I drove the car THROUGH the muddy road with difficulty [lit., ** caused the car to pass THROUGH the muddy road...].' *172:5a.* motion: - move sth.

'- pass, - promote': **Öğretmen bütün öğrencilerini geçirdi.** 'The teacher passed all his students [i.e., gave them passing grades].' *446:2.* promotion: - promote. → ≠ **sınıfta bırak-** → **bırak-** 1.

* **ele geçir-** lit., ** '- cause to pass INTO hand' [el 'hand'] (1) '- catch, - capture, - seize': **Polis üç yıldır aradığı katili sonunda ele geçirdi.** 'The police finally caught the murderer they had been looking for for 3 years.' → = **yakala-** 1. # **Askerler ancak üç aylık** {**kuşatma.dan/muhasara.dan**} **sonra** {**şehr.i/kale.yi**} **ele geçirebildiler.** 'The soldiers were able to capture {the city/the fortress} only after a three month {seige}.' *472:8.* acquisition: - acquire; *480:14.* taking: - seize.
(2) '- obtain, - get hold of, - acquire': **İşadamı Nihat Can'ın yolsuz-luklarını gösteren belgeleri ele geçirdik.** 'We obtained documents revealing the improprieties of the businessman Nihat Can.' *472:8.* acquisition: - acquire. → = **al-** 3, = **elde et-**.

* **gözden geçir-** '- go /OVER/, - look /OVER/, - scrutinize, - check, - check out, - have a look /AT/, - examine, - inspect, - review' [göz 'eye'], lit., ** '- cause to pass THROUGH the eye': **Bir plân**

yaptım. Gözden geçirir misiniz? 'I've worked out a plan. Would you please look it over?' Ev ödevimi gözden geçirir misiniz? 'Would you [please] check my homework?' Kitabı almadan önce iyice gözden geçirdim. 'I {looked over/checked out} the book carefully before buying it.' Başbakan aldığı raporu gözden geçiriyordu. 'The prime minister was {looking OVER/considering} the report he had received.' Evlilik kararınızı tekrar gözden geçirmekte fayda var. 'It would be useful for you to {review/reconsider} your decision to get married [lit., ** your marriage decision].' 27:14. vision: - scrutinize. → incele- ['- examine carefully, closely, minutely, - inspect, - investigate, - research'], tetkik et-. Same., kontrol et- ['- check, - inspect, - check on, - check to see whether sth is the case or not'], muayene et- ['- examine', mostly for a doctor and a patient].

* muayeneden geçir- '- examine, - subject /TO/ a physical examination, physical, checkup' [A. muayene (. - . .) 'an examining, examination'], lit., ** '- cause sb to pass THROUGH an examination': Doktor çocuğu sıkı bir muayeneden geçirdi. 'The doctor {examined the child thoroughly/subjected the child TO a thorough [physical] examination}.' 27:14. vision: - scrutinize; 91:24. therapy: - treat; 937:24. inquiry: - examine. → = muayene et- ['- examine', mostly for a doctor and a patient].

2 '- undergo, - experience' 830:8. event: - experience: ameliyat geçir- '- have or - undergo an operation': Geçen yıl ağır bir ameliyat geçirdim, Allah'a şükür şimdi iyiyim. 'Last year I {had/underwent} a serious operation. Thank God I'm well now.' • Note the following pattern when the type of operation is indicated: * Geçen yıl bir mide ameliyat.ı geçirdim. 'Last year {my stomach was operated on./I HAD an operation ON my stomach.}' 91:29. therapy: - undergo treatment. → = ameliyat ol- → ol- 10.1.

bunalım geçir- '- be in a depression, - be or - get depressed' [bunalım 1 'state of depression or

despair'. 2 'crisis']: Kardeşim nişanlısı terkedince ciddî bir bunalım geçirdi, * kendini toparlaması biraz zaman alır. 'When my brother's fiancée left him, he got {severely/really} depressed. * It'll take a little while for him to pull himself together.' Annem ruhsal bir bunalım geçiriyor. 'My mother is going through a depression [lit., a mental crisis].' 112:16. sadness: - lose heart. → bunalıma gir- ['- go /INTO/ a depression, - get depressed'].

felâket geçir- '- experience or - live through a disaster' [A. felâket (. - .) 'disaster, calamity']: Geçen yıl büyük bir felâket geçirdik, evimiz yandı. 'Last year we experienced a great disaster: our house burned down.' 1010:10. adversity: - come to grief.

kaza geçir- '- have an accident, - be in an accident, - get into an accident' [A. kaza (. -) 'accident']: Duydun mu? Orhan'ın annesi geçen hafta {feci/ağır/çok kötü} bir trafik kazası geçirmiş. 'Have you heard? Last week Orhan's mother was in a {terrible/severe/very bad} car accident.' Başbakan uçak kazası geçirdi. 'The prime minister was in a plane accident.' 1010:10. adversity: - come to grief. → kaza yap- ['- have an accident, - get into an accident, - be in an accident, - cause an accident'].

3 '- spend [time]': {vakit/zaman} geçir- /a: lA, b: ArAk, c: mAklA/ '- spend time /a: with [sb, sth], b: [by]...ing, c: [BY]...ing/' [{A. vakit (vaKTİ), A. zaman (. -)} 'time']: {iyi/hoş} vakit geçir- '- have a good time, - enjoy oneself, - have fun' [P. hoş 'pleasant, pleasing']: S: Tatilde nasıl vakit geçirdin? {İyi/Hoş} vakit geçirdin mi? 'Q: How did you spend the holiday? Did you have a {good/pleasant} time?' C: Tatilde çok iyi vakit geçirdim, kitap okudum, yüzdüm, dans ettim. 'A: I had a very good time during the holidays: I read, swam, and danced.' Mine'lerde çok iyi vakit geçirdik. 'We had a good time at Mine's [f.] house.' 95:13. pleasure: - enjoy oneself; 743:22. amusement: - amuse oneself. → = eğlen- 1. # Vakt.İM.i boşa geçirmedim. 'I didn't waste MY time [lit., spend my

time for nothing].' *331:13.* inactivity:
- waste time

Any word of time may be substituted for **vakit**: **Bütün {a: gün.Ü/b: hafta.yI/c: ay.I/d: yıl.I/e: yaz.I} dayımın çiftliğinde geçirdim.** 'I spent the whole {a: day/b: week/c: month/d: year/e: summer} {on/at} my [maternal] uncle's farm.' **Bu hafta.yI {çalış.arak/çalış.makla} geçirdim.** 'I spent this week {work.ing}.' * **Geçen hafta.yI nerede geçirdin?** 'Where did you spend [the] last week?' *820:6.* time: - spend time. → = {**vakit/zaman**} {**harca/sarf et-**} → {**harca/sarf et-**} 2. For other verbs of spending time, → **gecele-** ['- spend the night somewhere'], **sabahla-** ['- spend the night somewhere until morning, - stay up all night'].

Geçmiş olsun. → **ol-** 11. → **olsun.**

gel- [İR] 1 /a: DAn, b: A, c: 1A/ '- come /a: from, b: to, c: with/, - arrive /b: {IN/AT}/': **Mehmet Ankara'DAN İstanbul'A geldi.** 'Mehmet came FROM Ankara TO Istanbul.' * **{Otobüs/Tren/Uçak} kaçta gelecek?** 'At what time is {the bus/the train/the plane} due?' or 'At what time will the bus... {come/arrive}?' → = **var-, ulaş-** 1, = **eriş-** 1, ≠ **git-** 1a, ≠ **kalk-** 2. # **Beklediğiniz mektup geldi.** 'The letter you've been waiting for has arrived.' * **Nasıl oldu da bu nokta.ya geldik?** 'How come we've {reached θ/gotten to} this point?', i.e., this difficult situation, impasse. S: **Aslıhan nerede?** 'Q: Where's Aslıhan?' C: * **Hah, işte geliyor.** 'A: Oh, here she comes.' * **Şimdi geldim.** 'I just got here [lit., ** Now I came].' * **İşte geldik.** 'Here we are': You are coming with a friend to his house for the first time. He says: **Sağdaki ilk ev benim. İşte geldik.** 'The house on the right is mine. Here we are.' **Bura.yA gel!** 'Come here!' **Doktor {bey/hanım}, biraz buraya gelir misiniz?** 'Doctor, could you come here for a minute?', **bey** if the doctor is a man, **hanım** if the doctor is a woman. **Tamirci bugün gelsin mi, gelmesin mi?** '{Do you want the repairman to come today or not? /lit., Should the repairman come today or not?}' * **Bir gün gelecek, çok iyi Türkçe konuşacağım, sen bile şaşıracaksın.** 'One of

these days I'll speak very good Turkish [lit., ** A day will come, and I'll speak very good Turkish]. Even you will be surprised.' A phrase used by a bureaucrat to put off an applicant or by someone describing that situation: **Bugün git, yarın gel.** '{Come back later./[lit., Go (away) today, come (back) tomorrow.]}'
Proverbs: **Kaza geliyorum demez.** 'An accident doesn't announce its coming [lit., doesn't say "I'm coming"].' **Sakla samanı gelir zaman.ı.** 'Save the straw, the time for it will come.'

/1A/ '- come /with/ sb': A: **Akşamleyin tiyatroya gideceğiz.** 'A: In the evening we're going to go to the theater.' B: **Sizinle gelebilir miyim?** 'B: May I come with you?' *582:17.* sociability: - associate with; *768:7.* accompaniment: - accompany. → = /A/ {**eşlik et-/refakat et-**} ['- accompany /θ/, - go [along] /with/'], /A/ **katıl-** 2 ['- join a group'].

/1A/ '- come /{BY/ON}/ a vehicle, /ON/ foot': S: **Nasıl geldiniz?** 'Q: How did you come?' Responses with the name of a vehicle: C1: {**a: Otobüs.LE/b: Dolmuş.LA/c: Taksi.yLE/d: Metro.yLA/e: Araba.yLA/f: Tren.LE/g: Uçak-.LA} geldim.** 'A1: I came {a: BY bus./b: BY shared cab./c: BY taxi./d: BY subway/e: BY car./f: BY train./g: BY plane.} • Note: **Araba.yLA gel-** is ALSO frequently used in the meaning of '- drive [a car] to a place': **Ankara'ya arabayla geldim.** '{I came to Ankara by car./I drove to Ankara.}' → **Arabayla git-** → **git-** 1. *888:5.* operation: - operate sth.
Responses meaning 'on foot': C2: {* **Yürü.yerek/* Yaya [olarak]/* Yayan} geldim.** 'A2: I came {ON foot}.'

S: **Ne.yLE geldiniz?** 'Q: How [lit., ** BY what (means)] did you come?' This question anticipates a VEHICLE as an answer, although it need not, of course, be answered that way. The responses are the same as those under C1 above. *186:6.* arrival: - arrive.

'- come to see or to visit': * **Yarın biz.e gel.** '{Come on over tomorrow./Come to {see/visit} us tomorrow.} [lit., Come to us tomorrow].' *582:19.* sociability: -

visit. For '- go on a visit, - go visiting', → git- 3, misafirliğe git- → git- 3, ziyaret et-, ziyarete git- → git- 3, ziyaretine git- → git- 3.

akla gel- '- occur /to/, - think of, - remember' [A. akıl (aKLı) 'mind']: aklına gel- '- occur /to/ sb [lit., ** - occur to sb's mind]': • Note the different possessed suffixes on akıl: * Akl.IM.a bir şey geldi. 'I just had a thought [lit., ** Something came to MY mind].' * Akl.IM.A ne geldi, biliyor musun? '{Do you know what just occurred to me?/Do you know what I'm thinking?/lit., ** What came to MY mind, do you know?}' Akl.I.na hep kötü {olasılıklar/ihtimaller} geldi. 'All kinds of unpleasant {possibilities} came to HIS mind.' Tam kapı.dan çıkarken pencereleri kapatmadığı akl.I.N.A geldi. 'Just as SHE was going out θ the door {she remembered/it occurred to HER} that SHE had not closed the windows.' Sınavdan çıktıktan sonra kâğıd.A ismimi yazmadığım akl.IM.A geldi. 'After I had left the examination, it occurred to ME that I had not written my name ON the [examination] paper.' Deprem sırasında masa.nın alt.ı.na girmek akl.IM.A gelmedi. 'During the earthquake it didn't occur to ME [lit., ** to MY MIND] to get under the table.' * Nereden akl.IN.a geldi böyle bir soru? 'How [lit., ** From where] did YOU happen to think of such a question?' 930:18. thought: - occur to; 988:10. memory: - remember. → = {hatırla-/anımsa-} ['- remember, - recall, - think of'], = bul- 4 ['- remember, - have it', when one suddenly remembers sth forgotten], ≠ unut- ['- forget'].

aklı başına gel- '- come to one's senses' [A. akıl (aKLı) 'senses, reason, intelligence', baş 'head'], lit., ** 'for one's senses - come to one's head': Hapse girdikten sonra hırsız.IN akl.I baş.ı.na geldi. 'After going to prison, the thief came to his senses.' Bekârken çok para harcardı. Evlendikten sonra aklı başına geldi, para biriktirmeye başladı. 'As long as he was a bachelor, he used to spend a lot of money. After getting married, he came to his senses. He began to

save money.' 570:10. learning: - learn by experience; 924:2. sanity: - come to one's senses. → = akıllan-, adam ol- ['- become morally correct, mature, responsible, - grow up, - amount to sth, - shape up'] → ol- 12.

* aklıma gelmişken 'while it's on my mind, while I'm thinking of it, by the way, speaking of, incidentally [lit., ** while it has come to my mind]': aklıma gelmişken söyleyeyim... 'While it's on my mind, let me just say...' 842:13. timeliness: ADV. incidentally; 930:18. thought: - occur to. The most common expression for a close synonym of this notion is the single word şey lit., 'thing'. → = sırası gelmişken, = yeri gelmişken [below] → gel- 1.

Bana öyle geliyor ki... '{I have {a feeling/a hunch} that.../I get the feeling that.../It seems to me that.../I sense that...}': Bana öyle geliyor ki sen yine BİR {şey.LER/iş.LER} karıştırıyorsun, * ha[y]di hayırlısı. 'I have a feeling that you're {up to sth/stirring {things [lit., matters]} up} again. * Well, I hope it's all for the best.' Bana öyle geliyor ki bu hastalık * beni bitirecek. 'A: It seems to me that this illness * is going to finish me off.' Bana öyle geliyor ki hoca yarın haber vermeden sınav yapacak. * Olur mu olur, o.NDAN her şey beklenir. 'I have a hunch that [our] teacher will give a pop quiz tomorrow [lit., ** will make an exam without giving (advance) notice]. * {[It] Could well be/It's quite possible}. One never knows what he might do [lit., anything can be expected OF him].' 33:10. appearance: - appear to be; 945:8. judgment: - judge; 952:11. belief: - think. → = gibime gel-. → gel- 1 below.

* başına gel- '- happen /to/, - befall', usually a misfortune or something strange [baş 'head', so lit., ** '- come /to/ one's head.' Baş here represents the whole person.] This expression does not mean '- occur to, - come to one's MIND'. To express that idea, → aklına gel- above under akla gel-. • Note the different possessed suffixes on baş when the object is a specific person: Ergin'İN baş.I.na gelen.ler.i duydun mu? Evine hırsızlar girmiş. 'Have you

heard what happened to Engin? Thieves broke INTO [lit., entered θ] his house.' **Dün b a ş .IM.a ne geldi, biliyor musun?** 'Do you know what happened to ME yesterday?' * **Bak şu baş.IM.a gelen.E! Anahtarı içeride unutmuşum, kapıda kaldım.** 'Now just look [at] what happened to me! I seem to have left my key inside, and here I am locked out!' **Böyle acayip şeyler hep benim başıma gelir.** 'Such strange things {only/always} happen to me.' **İlk kez başıma böyle bir şey geliyor.** 'This is the first time that something like this has happened to me.' **Bak bugün baş.IMIZ.a ne geldi!** 'Now just {look/imagine} what happened to US today!' *982:22.* attention: INTERJ. attention! **Korktuğ.UM baş.IM.a geldi.** 'What I had feared happened to ME.' **Bugün inanılmayacak bir şey geldi baş.IM.a.** 'Today an unbelievable thing happened to me.' Proverbs: **Etme komşu.N.a, gelir baş.IN.a.** 'Don't do it to YOUR neighbor; it [i.e., what you have done to him] will come back to you [lit., ** come to YOUR head].' Do unto others as you would have them do unto you. * **Gülme komşu.N.a, gelir baş.IN.a.** 'Don't laugh AT YOUR neighbor [for what happened to him]; it [i.e., the same thing] may happen TO you.' • In the following, note the absence of the possessed suffix on **baş** when the object is not a specific person but people in general: **Aln.A yazılan baş.a gelir.** 'What is written ON the forehead [**alın**, aLNı] will come to pass.', i.e., One can't escape one's fate. **Baş.a gelen çekilir.** 'What happens to a person {will/must} be endured.' *830:5.* event: - occur; *963:11.* predetermination: PHR. it is fated. → = ol- 2.

* **başına gel-** versus **başından geç-**. The subject of the latter is usually sth interesting, good, exciting, or unusual rather than unfortunate. → **başından geç-** → geç- 1.

* **bir araya gel-** /lA/ '- come together, - get together /with/, - meet /with/, - convene' [**ara** 'space'], lit., ** '- come to one space, area, point': **Geçen akşam eski okul arkadaşlarım.la bir ara.yA geldik, hoşça vakit geçirdik.** 'The other night {I/we} got together with my old school friends, and we had a good time.' A: **Çoktandır bir araya gelmedik, anlat bakalım neler yapıyorsun?** A: {Long time no see./We haven't gotten together for a long time.} B: * **Valla nere[sin]den başlasam anlatmaya, bilmiyorum ki.** 'B: * Well really I hardly know where to begin' *769:16.* assemblage: - come together; *769:17.* : - convene. → = **buluş-** [for individuals '- come together, - meet /θ/', usually after a previous agreement to meet], = **toplan-** 3, **karşılaş-** 1 ['- meet one another'], ≠ **dağıl-** 1 [for a group '- scatter, - disperse'].

çişi gel- '- have to go [pee], - have to pee' [**çiş** (nursery language) 'urine, peepee; the NEED to pee'], lit., ** 'for his need to go - come': Usually used by grown-ups for children and by children among themselves: S: **En yakın {a: tuvalet/b: helâ/c: WC** [pronounce: **ve ce**]/**d: 100 numara} nerede acaba? Çiş.İM geldi, bekleyemeyeceğim.** 'Q: Where is the nearest {a: restroom [or toilet]/b: toilet/c: WC/d: toilet [or john]}, I wonder? I really have to go. I can't [lit., won't be able to] wait.' C: **Şu ağacın altında ihtiyac.IN.ı görebilirsin.** 'A: You can do it under that tree [lit., ** You can see (i.e., carry out) YOUR need...].' When a grown-up observes that a child is uncomfortable, he may say: S: **Çiş.İN mi geldi?** 'Q: Do YOU have to go?' C: **Evet, çiş.İM geldi.** 'A: Yes, I {do./have to go.}' Also expressed with **var: Çiş.İN mı var?** 'Do YOU have to go?' * **Çok çişim geldi, altı.m.A kaçırmak.TAN korkuyorum.** 'I have to go real bad, I'm afraid θ [that] I'm going to pee in my pants.' *12:14.* excretion: - urinate. → **tuvaleti gel-** [The expression used by grown-ups among themselves: '- have to use the {bathroom/restroom/toilet}, - have to go'], **tuvaleti var.** Same. → ol- 3, Additional examples. b) 3.6. Issues of necessity.

dünyaya gel- '- be born' [A. **dünya** (. -) 'world'], lit., '- come INTO the world': **Atatürk 1881 {yıl.ı.nda/sene.si.nde} Selânik'te dünya.ya geldi.** 'Atatürk was born {in the year} 1881 in Thessaloniki.' * **Cuma günü kardeşim.in bir oğl.u dünyaya**

geldi. 'On Friday my younger sister had a son.' *1:2.* birth: - be born. → = **doğ-** 1, ≠ **öl-**, ≠ **hayata göz yum-**, ≠ **hayatını {kaybet-/yitir-}** ['- lose one's life, - die', of unnatural causes], ≠ **vefat et-**.

* **elinden gel-** '- be within one's capabilities, - lie in one's power, - be able to do' [**el** 'hand'], lit., ** '- come from one's hand': **Zeynep çok becerikli bir kızdır, el.i.nDEN her iş gelir.** 'Zeynep is a very capable girl. She can do anything.' **Sana gerçekten yardım etmek isterdim ama inan ki el.İM.den hiç bir şey gelmiyor.** 'I would really like to help you, but believe me I simply can't do anything for you.', i.e., It is beyond my ability. **Özür dilerim, bu iş ben.im el.im.den gelmez.** 'I'm sorry but this {task/job} is beyond my abilities.' *18:11.* power, potency: - be able; *19:8.* impotence: cannot.

elinden geleni yap- '- do all one can, - do one's level best' [lit., ** - do what comes from one's hand]: **El.İM.den geleni yapt.IM ama {maalesef beceremedim/* olmadı}.** 'I did MY best, but {unfortunately I failed [lit., wasn't able to succeed]/* things didn't work out}.' **El.İMİZ.den geleni yapmalı.yIZ.** 'WE must do OUR best.' *403:13.* endeavor: - do one's best. → = **çalış[ıp] çabala-** ['- try hard, - do one's best'].

gibime gel- '- seem to me' [**gibi** 'like, as' + first person personal suf. - [I]m + A] This structure is not used with other persons, i.e., is not formed with other personal suffixes on **gibi**: **Annem beni çağırdı gibime geldi, ama emin değilim; belki de kardeşimi çağırmıştır.** 'It seems to me that my mother called me, but I'm not sure. Maybe she called {my brother/my sister}.' → = **Bana öyle geliyor ki...** → above. *33:10.* appearance: - appear to be; *945:8.* judgment: - judge; *952:11.* belief: - think.

gidip gel- /lA/ '- travel back and forth, - commute /BY/ [lit., ** - go and come]': **Babam her gün tren.LE iş.e gidip geliyor.** 'My father commutes to work every day BY train [lit., ...goes to work and comes (home)...].' **Babam her gün**

Silivri'den İstanbul'a gidip geliyor. 'My father commutes to Istanbul from Silivri every day [lit.,...comes from Silivri goes to Istanbul].' *177:18.* travel: - travel.

* **Hoş geldin[iz]!** (1) /A/ 'Welcome /to/' [P. **hoş** 'pleasant, pleasantly']: A: **Hoş geldiniz!** 'A: Welcome! [lit., ** You came pleasantly].' Said to an arriving guest. B: **Hoş bulduk.** 'B: Glad to be here! [lit., We found it pleasant].' **İstanbul'a hoş geldiniz!** 'Welcome to Istanbul!'
(2) Frequently just 'Hello' or 'Hi': Someone arrives home late. Those who were expecting him address the latecomer: **Hoş geldin.** * **Nerede kaldın?** 'Hi. * Where have you BEEN?' *504:* * *20.* courtesy: polite expressions; *585:14.* hospitality, welcome: INTERJ. welcome!

iyi gel- /A/ '- help /θ/, - be beneficial, good /FOR/, - work, - hit the spot' [**iyi** 'good']: * **Ohh, bu yorgunluğ.un üst.ü.ne bu {kahve/çay} iyi geldi.** 'Oh, after getting so tired [lit., ** (coming) after this weariness], this {coffee/tea} really hit the spot.' → = [**iyi**] **git-** → **git-** 5. * **Aspirin baş ağrı.m.A iyi geldi.** 'The aspirin {helped θ/was good FOR} my headache.' *998:10.* goodness: - do good. → = 2 **değ-** 2.

kan gel- /DAn/ '- bleed /from/, for blood - come /from/': **Hasta birden fenalaştı, ağzı.ndan burnu.ndan kan gelmey.e başladı.** 'The patient suddenly became worse. He began to bleed from his mouth and nose.' *12:17.* excretion: - bleed; *190:13.* emergence: - emerge. → = **kan ak-**, = **kana-**.

kendine gel- [**kendi** 'oneself'] (1) '- come to, - regain consciousness, - return to one's usual state' • Note the different possessed suffixes on **kendi**: **Kafasını masa.ya çarpıp bayılan kadın, şimdi kendi.nE geldi.** 'The woman who hit her head on the table and passed out has now regained consciousness.' → = **ayıl-** 2, ≠ **bayıl-** 1, ≠ **kendinden geç-** 1 → **geç-** 1, ≠ **kendini kaybet-** 1, ≠ **{şuurunu/bilincini} kaybet-**[or **yitir-**] 1 → **{kaybet-/yitir-}.** **Bir an nerede ve kim olduğunu bilemedi.** * **Neden sonra**

kendine geldi. 'For a moment he didn't realize [lit., ** couldn't know] where and who he was. * In a little while he came round.' **Yemek yedim,** * **kendi.M.E geldim.** 'I've eaten. * Now I feel more like MYSELF.' **O kadar yorgundum ki ancak iyi bir uykudan sonra kendime gelebildim.** 'I was so tired that I needed a good sleep to recover [lit., that I could only recover after a good sleep].' *306:8.* life: - come to life; *396:20.* restoration: - recover.

(2) '- pull oneself together, - regain self-control, - come to one's senses': **Kendi.N.E gel!** '{Come to YOUR senses!/Pull YOURSELF together!}': **Semra hanım, dansöz olmak isteyen kızına "Saçmalama, kendine gel" diye bağırdı.** 'Semra hanım shouted [saying], "Don't {be silly/talk nonsense}. Come to your senses, [child]" to her daughter who wanted to become a belly dancer.' *428:7.* restraint: - restrain; *570:10.* learning: - learn by experience. → **akıllan-** ['- become wiser through bitter experience, - come to one's senses about a matter, - wise up'], **aklı başına gel-** ['- come to one's senses'] → gel- 1.

kolay gel- '- be easy, - go easily' [**kolay** 'easy']: A: * **Kolay gelsin.** '{a: Good luck with your work./b: ** May it {be easy/go easily/lit., come easy}}', a polite expression one should say to anyone engaged in or about to engage in some usually demanding task. There is no common English equivalent. B: **Sağol.** 'B: Thanks.' *504: * 20.* courtesy: polite expressions; *1013:10.* facility: - go easily.

* **kolayına gel-** '- be easy for' [**kolay** 'easy', here as a noun], lit., ** '- come /to/ one's ease': S: **Niçin bu çorbayı yaptın?** 'Q: Why did you make this soup?' C: **Kolay.IM.a geldi** * **de, ondan.** 'A: It was easy for ME. * That's why.' * **Almanca öğrenmek yerine tercüman tutmak daha kolay.IN.a geliyor.** '{It'll be easier for YOU to hire a translator than to learn German [lit., ** Instead of learning German, it will be easier for YOU to hire a translator].' *1013:10.* facility: - go easily. Also = **kolayına git- 1** → git- 1b, ≠ **zoruna git- 1** → git- 1b.

verb stem.{a: **mAzlIktAn**/b: **mAmAzlIktAn**/c: **mAzdAn**} gel- '- pretend NOT to, - make as if NOT to' [i.e., verb stem {a: **mAz + lIk + DAn**/b: **mA + mAz + lIk + DAn**/c: **mAz + DAn**}]: {a: **Anlamazlıktan**/b: **Bilmezlikten**/c: **Duymazlıktan**/d: **Görmezlikten**/e: **Hatırlamazlıktan**} **gelme!** 'Don't pretend {a: not to have understood/b: not to have known/c: not to have heard/d: not to have seen/e: not to remember}!' We meet, and you act as if you don't know me. I say the following lines of a famous song: * **Eller gibi davranıp görmemezlikten gelme.** 'Don't act like a stranger [lit., strangers], pretending not to have seen me.' *500:12.* affectation: - affect. The affirmative '- pretend' is *verb stem.*{**Ar/mIş**} gibi yap- → yap- 3.

* **sırası gelmişken** 'speaking of, incidentally, by the way, while on the subject, since this is the time for it' [**sıra** 'time'], lit., 'its time having come', i.e., the time for this topic: **Sırası gelmişken söyleyeyim...** 'While on this subject let me just say...' *842:13.* timeliness: ADV. incidentally. The most common closely synonymous expression for this notion is the single word **şey** lit., 'thing'. → = **aklıma gelmişken** above, = **yeri gelmişken** below → gel- 1.

sonuna gel- '- come to the end of' [**son** 'end']: {**Dersler.in/Tatil.in**} **son.u.nA geldik.** 'We've come to the end {of the lessons/of the holiday}.' *819:6.* end: - come to an end [i.].

* **şakaya gel-** 'for sth - be a joking matter', lit., ** '- come to a joke' [**şaka** 'joke']: Perhaps most frequent in the negative: **Ateşle oynamak şaka.ya gelmez.** 'Playing with fire is no joking matter.' **Bu proje.nin şaka.ya gelir taraf.ı yok; bu ay içinde bitmesi lâzım. Yoksa paramızı alamayız.** 'This project is no joking matter [lit., ** has no coming-to-a-joke aspect]. It must be finished within this month, or else we won't be able to collect our money.' *996:12.* importance: - matter; *997:11.* unimportance: - be unimportant.

* **tuvaleti gel-** '- have to use the {bathroom/restroom/toilet}, - have to

go' [F. **tuvalet** 'the NEED to use the toilet'], lit., ** 'for the need to use the toilet - come': **A: En yakın {a: tuvalet/b: helâ/c: WC** [pronounce: **ve ce**]/**d: 100 numara} nerede acaba? Çok tuvalet.IM geldi, bekleye-meyeceğim.** 'Where is the nearest {a: restroom [*or* toilet]/b: toilet/c: WC/d: toilet [*or* john]}, I wonder? I really have to go. I can't [lit., won't be able to] wait.' **B: Şu ağacın altında ihtiyacını görebilirsin.** 'B: You can do it under that tree [lit., ** You can see to your need...].' *12:13*. excretion: - defecate; *12:14*. excretion: - urinate. → = **tuvaleti var.** → ol- 3, Additional examples. b) 3.6. Issues of necessity.

* **uykusu gel-** '- become or - get sleepy' [**uyku** 'sleepiness'], lit., ** 'for one's sleepiness - come': • Note the different possessed suffixes on **uyku: Saat 12 olmuş, çok uyku.M geldi.** 'It's 12 o'clock. I {am/got} very sleepy [lit., ** MY sleepiness has come].' **Uyku.MUZ geldi.** 'WE {are/got} sleepy.' **S: Uyku.N geldi mi kızım?** 'Q: Are YOU sleepy, {dear/child/lit., ** my girl}?' **C1: Evet, * çok uykum geldi.** 'A1: Yes, very.' **C2: Evet, * hem de çok.** 'A2: Yes, * and how!' **Çocuğ.un uyku.su geldi galiba, hemen yatağını yapayım da yatıralım.** 'The child is probably sleepy [lit., ** The child's sleepiness has probably come]. Let me make up his bed right away, and let's put him to bed.' *22:13*. sleep: - sleep. → **uykusu kaç-** ['- be unable to get to sleep'] → kaç- 1.

{vaktinde/zamanında} gel- '- come {in/on} time' [{A. **vakit** (vaKTİ)/A. **zaman** (. -)} 'time'], lit., ** '- come in its time': 'ON time' and 'IN time' are the SAME in Turkish: **Toplantı saat 4'te başladı. Herkes vakti.nde geldi.** 'The meeting began at 4 o'clock. Everyone came ON time.' **Toplantıya herkes vakti.nde geldi.** 'Everyone came to the meeting ON time.' **Treni yakalamak için tam vakti.nde istasyona geldik.** 'We arrived at the station just IN time to catch the train.' *842:6*. timeliness: - be timely. → = **yetiş-** 1 ['- be {in/on} time'], ≠ **{geç kal-/gecik-}** [for a person '- be late'] → kal- 1, ≠ **rötar yap-** ['- be delayed', usually only for public

transportation -- train, bus, ferry, airplane -- not persons] → yap- 3.

* **yanına gel-** '- come up to, over to, lit., - come /to/ the side of' [**yan** 'side']: **Yan.IM.A gel. Beraber kitap okuyalım.** 'Come over here [lit., ** to MY side]. Let's read a book together.' *167:3*. approach: - approach; *223:7*. nearness: - near, - come near. → = **yanaş-** 1, **yaklaş-** ['- approach /Θ/, - draw near /to/, - come close /to/, - come up /to/'].

* **yeri gelmişken** 'speaking of, incidentally, by the way, while on the subject, since this is the place for it' [**yer** 'place'], lit., ** 'its place having come', i.e., the place for this topic: **Yeri gelmişken hava kirliliği konu.su.nA da değinmek istiyorum.** 'Since this is the appropriate place, I also want to touch ON the issue of pollution.' The most common closely synonymous expression for this notion is the single word **şey** lit., ** 'thing'. *842:13*. timeliness: ADV. incidentally. → = **aklıma gelmişken** [above], = **sırası gelmişken** [above] → gel- 1.

zamanında gel-. → **{vaktinde/zamanında} gel-** 1 above.

2 /A/ '- be a certain size /FOR/, - fit': In a shoe store: **Ayakkabı satıcısı: * Nasıl geldi?** 'Shoe salesman: * How {do/did} they fit [lit., ** come]?' **Müşteri: Bu ayakkabı ayağ.ım.A {a: küçük/b: büyük/c: dar/d: * tam} geldi.** 'These shoes are {a: TOO small/b: TOO large/c: TOO narrow/d: * just right} FOR my feet.' • Turkish needs no separate word for 'too' in the above. In a store selling ready-made clothes: **Konfeksiyon satıcısı: Bu {a: elbise/b: ceket/c: etek/d: gömlek} nasıl geldi?** 'Seller of ready-made clothing: How does this {a: suit/b: jacket/c: skirt/d: shirt} fit?' * **Bu pantolon nasıl geldi?** 'How do these trousers fit?' **Müşteri: {a: Kısa/b: Uzun/c: Küçük/d: Büyük/e: Biraz dar/f: Biraz bol/g: Tam/h: İyi} geldi.** 'Customer: It's [*or* They're] {a: TOO short/b: TOO long/c: TOO small/d: TOO large/e: a little narrow/f: a little large/g: just right/h: fine}.' *866:3*. conformity: - conform; *867:4*. nonconformity: not - conform. → = **dur-** 9, = **ol-** 8, = **otur-** 5, **uy-** 1

['- fit /θ/, - be the right size and shape /FOR/'], yakış- 2 ['for sth - look good /ON/, - suit /θ/', clothing].

3 '- come, - climax, - have an orgasm', for both sexes: **Erkeklerin en önemli sorunlarından biri erken gelmeleridir.** 'One of men's most serious problems is premature ejaculation [lit., their coming early].' *75:23.* sex: - climax. → = **boşal-** 3 [more frequently for men but also for women], = **orgazm ol-** [for men and women] → ol- 10.1.

{**gelecek/istikbal**} vadet-. → vadet-.

geliş- [ir] [gel- + recip. suf. -Iş] 1 '- develop, - advance, - evolve; - mature, - fill out [subj.: a person's physique]': In reference to events: **Teknoloji** {**özellikle/bilhassa**} **son on yıl içinde çok gelişti.** 'Technology has really advanced, {especially} in the last ten years.' **Öğrenci olayları beklenmedik şekilde gelişti.** 'The student incidents developed in an unexpected way.' **Olay şöyle gelişti...** 'The event {evolved/unfolded} as follows...' **Durum.un hangi yönde gelişeceğ.i belli değildi.** 'It wasn't clear how [lit., ** in which direction] the situation would develop.' In reference to a person's physique: **Dün komşumun oğlu Hilmi'yi gördüm.** * **Ne kadar gelişmiş!** * **Delikanlı olmuş!** 'I saw my neighbor's son Hilmi yesterday. * My, how he's developed! * He's become quite a young man!' *259:5.* expansion, growth: - become larger; *860:5.* evolution: - evolve. → = **kalkın-** [for a nation '- develop, - advance, - make progress'].

2 '- improve, - get better': **Mary'nin Türkçesi** {a: **gün geçtikçe**/b: **gittikçe**/c: **sürekli/ d: hızla**} **gelişiyor.** 'Mary's Turkish is improving {a: {with every passing day/every day}/b: gradually/c: continually/d: rapidly}.' **Petrol çıktıktan sonra ülkede ekonomik durum birdenbire gelişti.** 'After oil was discovered, the economic situation in the country suddenly improved.' *392:7.* improvement: - get better. → = **ilerle-** 2, ≠ **bozul-**, ≠ **gerile-** 2, ≠ **zayıfla-** 2.

geliştir- [ir] /verb stem-A verb stem-A, ArAk/ [geliş- + caus. suf. -DIr] 1 '- improve, - develop /by *verb stem*.ing/': **Bir yıl içerisinde Mary** {**oku.yarak/oku.ya oku.ya**} **Türkçesi.ni çok geliştirdi.** 'In one year Mary has greatly improved her Turkish {by read.ing/by read.ing a lot}.' *392:9.* improvement: - improve, - make better. → = **ilerlet-** 2.

2 /ArAk/ '- develop, - make larger, - build up /[by]...ing/': **Osman her gün halter çalış.arak vücudunu geliştirdi.** 'By weight lift.ing every day, Osman {developed/built up} his body.' *259:4.* expansion, growth: - make larger.

3 '- develop, - create': **Uzmanlar nüfus artış.ı.nı önlemek için çeşitli metotlar geliştiriyorlar.** 'Experts are developing various methods for preventing population growth.' *891:12.* production: - originate.

gerçeği söyle-. → {**doğru/doğruyu/ gerçeği/hakikati**} **söyle-.** → söyle- 1.

gerçekleş- [ir] '- come true, - be realized, - work out' [gerçek 'reality' + verb-forming suf. -lAş]: **Plânlarım gerçekleşti. Bu yaz tatilimi İtalya'da geçirebileceğim.** 'My plans have {been realized/worked out}. This summer I'm going to be able to spend my {vacation/holiday} in Italy.' {a: **Rüyalarım**/b: **Hayallerim**/c: **İsteklerim**/d: **Arzularım**} **gerçekleşti.** '{a: My dreams/b: My daydreams/c: My wishes/d: My desires} have come true.' **Bu iki** {**olasılık.TAN/ihtimal.DEN**} **bir.i kesinlikle gerçekleşecek.** 'One OF these two {possibilities} will certainly be realized.' *972:12.* truth: - come true.

gereğini yap-. → yap- 3.

gerek- [ir] /için/ '- be necessary, needed, required /{for/IN ORDER TO}/' [gerek 'necessary' + verb-forming. suf. -θ]: **Amerikan Başkonsolosluğuna gidip ne yapmam gerektiğini sordum.** 'I went to the American consulate general and asked what I should do.' NON-verbal noun as subject of gerek-: **Ne gerekiyorsa onu**

yapacağım. 'I'll do whatever is necessary.' **Türkiye için {pasaport/vize} gerekiyor mu?** 'Is a {passaport/visa} required for Turkey?' * **Pasaport işlemler.i için ne gerekiyor?** 'What is required to get a passport [lit., for the passport procedures]?' S: **Türkiye'ye git.mek için ne gerekiyor?** 'Q: What is required to go to Turkey?' C: [Türkiye'ye gitmek için] **para gerekiyor.** 'A: [To go to Turkey] money is required.' **Almanya'ya gidebil.me.SI için para gerekiyor.** 'In order for HIM to be able to go to Germany [lit., ** for HIS being able to...] money is required.'
VERBAL noun as subject. Impersonal necessity: -mAk gerek-: **Her türlü {tehlike.yE/ durum.A} [karşı] {hazır/ hazırlıklı} ol.MAK gerekir.** 'One must be {ready} FOR all kinds of {dangers/situations}.' **{Doğru-.su.nu/Doğru.yu} söyle.MEK gerekirse...** 'To tell the truth [lit., ** If tell.ING {the truth of it/the truth} is necessary]...'
-mAsI gerek-: **Bu dilekçem.in saat 5'e kadar okula yetiş.ME.Sİ gerekiyor.** 'This application of mine must get to the school by 5 o'clock.'
Personal necessity: -mAsI gerek-: **Ne {a: yap.ma.SI/b: yap.ma.M/c: yap.ma.N/d: yap.ma.MIZ/e: yap.ma.NIZ/f: yap.ma.LARI} gerekir?** 'What {a: does HE have to do? [lit., ** His doing what is necessary?]/b: do I have to do?/c: do YOU [s.] have to do]?/d: do WE have to do?/e: do YOU [pl.] have to do?/f: do THEY have to do?}' **Şimdi git.me.M gerekiyor.** 'I have to go now.' **Amerika'dan * bir misafir.im geliyor, haftasonu onunla ilgilenmem gerekiyor.** 'I have a guest coming [lit., A guest of mine is coming] from the U.S. Over the weekend I must {attend to him/look after him/take care of him}.' **Bankadan kredi alabil.me.MIZ için iki kefil bul.ma.MIZ gerekti.** 'For US to get credit from the bank, WE had to find two guarantors.' *962:10.* necessity: - be necessary. → = icap et-, = lâzım ol- → ol- 12.

gerektir- [ir] '- require, - necessitate', non-person subject [gerek- + caus. suf. -DIr]: S: **Bu iş haftada kaç saat çalışma gerektiriyor?** 'Q: How many hours [work] per week does this task require?' C: {a: {Sadece/Yalnız}/b: En az} **3 saat.** 'A: {a: Only/b: At least} 3 hours.' **Bu çalışmalar oldukça yüksek maliyetleri gerektiriyor.** 'These efforts require rather high outlays.' *962:9.* necessity: - require. → = iste- 3.

geri 'back, rear, the space behind' may be used with many verbs to convey the idea of returning, taking back, or remaining behind, etc. as in **geri al-** 1 '- take back [to oneself]'. ≠ **ileri.** See directly below.

geri al-. → al- 1.

geri dön-. → dön- 2.

geri getir-. → getir-.

geri gönder-. → gönder-.

geri kal-. → kal- 1.

geri öde-. → öde-.

geri taşın-. → taşın-.

{geri ver-/iade et-}. → ver- 1.

gerile- [r] [geri 'back, rear, the space behind' + verb-forming suf. -lA] 1 '- move back, - retreat, - fall back': **Polis barikatı karşısında göstericiler geriledi.** 'The demonstrators retreated in the face of the police barricade.' *163:6.* regression: - retreat. → ≠ ilerle- 1.

2 '- get worse, - deteriorate, - worsen': **Ülkenin ekonomik durumu {gün geçtikçe} geriliyor.** 'The nation's economic situation is deteriorating {day by day/with every passing day/lit., as the days pass}.' **Amerika'ya dönünce Türkçem geriledi.** 'When I returned to the U.S., my Turkish got worse.' * **Bir yıldır çalışmadığım için piyano.DA geriledim.** 'Because I had not worked [on it] for a year, my piano playing got worse [lit., ** I got worse IN piano].' *393:16.* impairment: - deteriorate. → = bozul-, = fenalaş- 1, = kötüleş-, = zayıfla- 2, ≠ ilerle- 2, ≠ iyileş-.

gerin- [ir] '- stretch [oneself], - have a stretch' [ger- '- stretch, - tighten sth' + refl. suf. -In]: **Adam yataktan kalktıktan sonra * uzun uzun gerindi.** 'After getting out of bed, the man * had a good stretch [lit., ** stretched long long].' *84:4.* fitness, exercise: - exercise; *2 5 9 : 5.* expansion, growth: - become larger; *725:10.* exertion: - strain.

getir- [ir] /DAn, A/ '- bring, - fetch, - get /from, to/' [irr. caus. of gel-]: **S: Lütfen ban.A bir {a: kalem/b: kültablası/c: bardak/d: çatal/e: kaşık/f: bıçak/g: havlu/h: battaniye} getirir misin?** 'Q: Would you please bring me {a: a pencil/b: an ash tray/c: a [drinking] glass/d: a fork/e: a spoon/f: a knife/g: a towel/h: a blanket}.' **C: Tabii efendim, hemen getiririm.** 'A: Of course, {sir/ma'am}. I'll bring it right away.' **{Kahveci/Çaycı}, iki {kahve/çay} getirir misin?** 'Waiter [lit., ** {coffee man/tea man}], would you please bring 2 {coffees/teas}?' **Gelecek ne getirecek?** 'What will the future bring?' Often used together with the verb **git-** '- go', giving the sense of '- go and {get/fetch}': **İsterseniz gidip getiririm.** 'If you like, I'll go and get it.' Proverb: **Deli ile çıkma yola, başına getirir bela.** 'Don't set out ON a journey with a madman, he will cause you trouble [lit., ** will bring trouble to your head].' **Baş** 'head' here represents the whole person. *176:16.* transferal, transportation: - fetch. → ≠ **götür-** ['- take [away] /from [somewhere], to [somewhere else/'].

* **dünyaya getir-** '- bring /INTO/ the world, - give birth /TO/, - bear' [A. **dünya** (. -) 'world'], the causative of **dünyaya gel-** '- be born', lit., '- COME INTO the world': **Komşumuz Zehra hanım {a: sağlıklı bir oğlan [or kız]/b: ikiz/c: üçüz/d: dördüz/e: beşiz} dünya.yA getirdi.** 'Our neighbor Zehra hanım gave birth to {a: a healthy boy [or girl]/b: twins/c: triplets/d: quadruplets/e: quintuplets].' *1:3.* birth: - give birth. → **çocuğu ol-** → **ol-** 6, = **doğur-**.

geri getir- '- bring sth back [here], - return sth /to/ [this place]' [geri 'back, rear, the space behind']: **S: Kitapları kim geri getirecek?** 'Q: Who will bring the books back?'

C: * **Ben [geri] {getiririm/getireyim}.** 'A: I will [lit., I'll bring them back].' *481:6.* restitution: - recover. → **geri al-** 1 ['- take back'] → **al-** 1, **geri gönder-** ['- send back'], {**geri ver-/iade et-**} ['- give back, - return'] → **ver-** 1.

haber getir- /DAn, A/ '- bring news /from, to/' [A. **haber** 'news']: **Postacı bugün biz.E iyi haberler getirdi.** 'The postman brought us good news today.' *552:11.* news: - report.

hesap getir- /A/ '- bring the check /to/' [A. **hesap** (. -) 'check, bill']: **Müşteri: Lütfen hesabı getirir misiniz?** 'Customer: {Could I have the check please?/lit., Would you please bring the check?}' **Garson: {Hemen getiriyorum/ Baş-üstüne}, efendim.** 'Waiter: {I'll bring it right away/Right away}, {sir/ma'am}.' *478:12.* giving: - give; *630:11.* price, fee: - price.

selâm getir- /DAn/ '- bring greetings /from/' [A. **selâm** (. -) 'greeting, salute']: {a: * **Annem.LER.den/b: Fuat'tan/c: İstanbul'dan/d: Herkesten} selâm getirdim.** 'I've brought greetings {a: * from my mother's family/b: from Fuat/c: from Istanbul/d: from everyone}.' *504:13.* courtesy: - give one's regards. → **selâm söyle-** ['- send, - give or - express one's regards /to, from/', *informal:* '- say "Hi" /to/'] → **söyle-** 1.

uyku getir- '- put to sleep, - make drowsy' [uyku 'sleep']: **Aspirin uyku getiren ilaçlar.dan mı?** 'Is aspirin a medicine that makes one drowsy [lit., ** from the medicines that...]?' * **uykusunu getir-** '- put to sleep', lit., ** '- bring sb's sleep': * **Televizyondaki film çok sıkıcı, uyku.M.u getirdi.** 'The film on television was very boring. It put ME to sleep [lit., ** It brought MY sleep].' *22:20.* sleep: - put to sleep. → ≠ **uykusunu kaçır-** → **kaçır-** 3.

yerine getir- [yer 'place'], lit., ** '- bring to its place' (1) '- carry out a request, wish, order, promise, - execute an order': **Emirlerinizi yerine getirdim, efendim.** 'I have carried out your orders, {sir/ma'am}.' **Vaatlerimi yerine**

getireceğim.E namusum ve şerefim üzerine yemin ederim. 'I swear on my honor and good name [lit., ** on my honor and my honor] that I will carry out my promises.' *434:3.* observance: - perform; *437:9.* compact: - execute. → uy- 5 ['- comply /WITH/, - conform /to/' rules, regulations], çiğne- 3 ['- violate laws, rules, principles'].
(2) '- bring sth back', lit., ** '- bring to its place', i.e., to where it belongs: **Masadan aldığın kitabı hemen yerine getirip koy.** '{Bring/Put} back at once the book that you took from the table.' *481:4.* restitution: - restore.

gez- [er] /a: lA, b: DA, c: lA/ '- go or - walk about, - tour /a: with [sb], b: in [a place], c: IN [a vehicle]/, - sightsee, - stroll': **Mehmet'le * İstanbul'un en güzel yer.ler.i.nİ gezdik.** 'With Mehmet * {I/we} toured the most beautiful places in [lit., of] Istanbul.' • Note the two question patterns:
a) S: * **İstanbul'DA nereler.İ gezdiniz?** 'Q: What places in Istanbul have you seen? [lit., ** IN Istanbul its WHERES have you seen?]'
b) S: * **İstanbul'UN nere.LER.İ.nİ gezdiniz?** 'Q: What places in [lit., OF] Istanbul have you seen? [lit., ** Istanbul'S WHERES have you seen?]' C: **Kapalı Çarşı.yı, Topkapı Saray.ı.nı gezdik.** 'A: We saw the Covered Bazaar and the Topkapı Palace.' **Ankara'da nereleri gezebilirim?** 'What places can I see in Ankara?' **Ha[y]di gezmey.E gidelim.** 'Come on, let's go for a walk.' With particular vehicles: **{Araba.yLA/Fayton.LA} gezmek ister misiniz?** 'Would you like to go for a drive {IN a car/IN a horse drawn-carriage [phaeton]}?' **{Motor.LA/Kayık.LA} gezmek ister misiniz?** 'Would you like to tour about {IN a motorboat/IN a rowboat}?' **Bisiklet.LE birkaç ülke gezdiler.** 'They toured several countries BY bicycle.' Proverbs: **Çok oku.yan değil, çok gez.en bilir.** 'It's not the one who has read a lot, but the one who has traveled {a lot/widely} that knows.' **Çok yaşa.yan bilmez, çok gez.en bilir.** 'It's not the one who has lived long, but the one who has traveled {a lot/widely} that knows [lit., the one who has lived long does not know, the one who has traveled widely knows].' *177:21.* travel: - journey; *177:23.* - wander; *570: * 19.* learning: PHR. experience is the best teacher. → **dolaş-** 1 ['- go, - walk, - wander, or - stroll about or around, - make one's way through, - cover ground', usually on foot. 2 '- tour'], **hava al-** ['- breathe fresh air, - get a breath of fresh air'] → al- 1, **yürüyüşe çık-** ['- go out /for/ a walk'] → çık- 2, **seyahat et-** ['- travel or - take a trip /to/'].

gezdir- [ir] /I/ '- show or - take sb around a place' [gez- + caus. suf. -DIr]: * **Bu şehr.E çok yabancıyım, geleli iki gün oluyor, * ben.i gezdirir misiniz?** '* I'm a total stranger {IN/lit., ** TO} this city. I've been here [only] two days. * Would you show me around?' • Note the different case suffixes on the word **misafirler** 'guests' in the two following sentences: One grammatical object: person as object: **Dün misafirlerimiz.İ gezdirdik.** 'Yesterday we took our guests around.' Two grammatical objects: one person, one place: * **Dün misafirlerimiz.E İstanbul'U gezdirdik.** 'Yesterday we {took/showed} θ our guests around Istanbul.' **Siz.E okul.umuz.U {gezdireyim/gezdirelim}.** '{Let me/Let us} show θ you around our school.' *176:12.* transferal, transportation: - transport; *348:5.* manifestation: - manifest. → **gezmeye çık-** ['- go /θ/ sightseeing'] → çık- 2.

gezin- [ir] [gez- + refl. suf. -In] 1 /DA, arasında/ '- wander, - roam, - walk, or - go about, - stroll, - ramble, - rove /in, among/', usually aimlessly: **Ortalıkta gezinip durma, gel bana yardım et!** 'Don't just keep wandering about aimlessly. Come [over here] and help me!' **Sanat gerçeklikten kopmak ve salt düşler dünyasında gezinmek degildir.** 'Art is not to cut oneself off from reality and to roam about in a world only of dreams.' *177:23.* travel: - wander. → **dolaş-.**

2 /DA, arasında/ '- browse, - surf /on/ [the Internet], - scan, - flip /through/ [TV channels]': **Bilgisayarımı açtım, biraz {a: {internette/ internet üzerinde}/b:**

Web'de/c: siteler arasında} gezindim. 'I turned on my computer and surfed a little {a: on the Internet/b: on the Web/c: through the sites}.' {a: Son haberler/b: Dökümanlar/c: Belgeler/d: Web sayfaları/e: Tablolar/f: Listeler} arasında gezindim. 'I browsed through {a: the latest news items/b, c: the documents/d: the Web pages/e: the tables/f: the lists}.' Eve gelince çok sevdiğim koltuğ.A oturdum ve geç saatler.e kadar televizyon kanallarında gezindim. 'When I came home, I sat down IN my favorite chair and {flipped/browsed} through the television channels until late [hours].' *570:13.* learning: - browse; *1041:18.* computer science: - computerize.

gibime gel-. → gel- 1.

gidil- [ir] /A/ 'for one - get or - go /to/ a place' [git- + pass. suf. -Il, an impersonal passive]: S: * Taksim'e nasıl gidilir? 'Q: How does one get to Taksim [a section of Istanbul]?' Responses with the name of a vehicle: C1: {a: Otobüs.LE/b: Dolmuş.LA/c: Tramvay.LA/d: Taksi.yLE/e: Metro.yLA} gidilir. 'A1: [One goes] {a: BY bus/b: BY shared cab/c: BY streetcar/d: BY taxi/e: BY subway}.' Responses meaning 'on foot': C2: {* Yürü.yerek/* Yaya [olarak]/* Yayan} gidilir. 'A2: [One goes] {ON foot}.'

S: Taksim'e NEYLE gidilir? 'Q: How [lit., ** BY WHAT (means)] does one get to Taksim?' This question anticipates a VEHICLE as an answer, although it need not, of course, be answered that way. The responses are the same as those under C1 above. {Otobüs.LE/ Yürü.yEREK} gidilir mi? 'Can one go {BY bus?/ON foot [lit., ** BY walk.ING]?}' S: Adalet İlkokul.u.na nasıl gidilir? 'Q: How does one get to the Adalet Primary school?' C: Postane.yİ geçin, sağ.a dönün, * hemen orada. 'A: Go past the post office, turn right. * It's right there.' S: Postane.ye * nere.DEN gidilir? 'Q: * How [lit., ** THROUGH where] does one get to the post office?' C: Bu cadde.DEN gidilir. 'A: One goes {THROUGH/B Y WAY OF/ALONG} this street.' • The

impersonal passive form is often used in a report-style narrative given by a member of a group describing a series of actions of that group to one who was not a participant: S: * Fatoş'un doğum günü partisi nasıl geçti, neler yaptınız? 'Q: How was Fatoş's birthday party? What did you do?' C: Önce bir lokanta.ya gidildi ve yemek yenildi. Hediyeler açıldıktan sonra pasta kesildi, sonra da ev.E döndük. 'A: First we went to a restaurant and ate [lit., ** First a restaurant was gone to and food was eaten]. After the presents had been opened, we cut the cake [lit., the cake was cut]. And then we returned θ home.' • Above note the dative case on the SUBJECT of gidil-. # Gidilecek yerler arasında Topkapı Sarayı da var. 'The Topkapı Palace is also one of the places to visit [lit., ** among the places to be gone to].' *177:25.* travel: - go to.

gir- [er] /A, DAn/ '- enter /θ, {THROUGH/BY WAY OF}/, - go /{IN/INTO}, {THROUGH/BY WAY OF}/': Girmeyecek misiniz? 'Aren't you going to {enter θ/go IN}?' Signs: Girmek yasaktır. '{No tresspassing./No admittance.} [lit., To go in is forbidden].' Taşıt giremez. 'No entry [lit., Vehicles cannot enter].' Onsekiz yaşı.nDAN küçükler giremez! 'No one under 18 [is] admitted! [lit., Those younger THAN 18 cannot enter].' *352:7.* publication: poster: * specific signs. * Burası ayakaltı oldu, giren çıkan belli değil. 'This place has become a [regular] thoroughfare. It's not clear who's coming and going [lit., ** The enterers and leavers are not clear].' Proverbs: Güneş giren ev.E doktor girmez. 'A doctor does not enter θ the house that the sun has entered.' Herkes kendi çukur.u.nA girer. 'Everyone enters θ his own pit.', i.e., the pit that he has dug. i.e., Everyone is responsible for his own behavior and will get his just deserts. Rüşvet kapı.DAN girince insaf baca.DAN çıkar. 'When bribery enters THROUGH the door, {justice/fairness} leaves THROUGH the chimney.' *189:7.* entrance: - enter. → ≠ /DAn/ çık- 1.

'- break into': Ev.E hırsız girmiş, bütün {mücevherleri/tabloları} çalmış. 'Thieves {entered θ/broke INTO} the house and stole all {the jewelry/the pictures}.' *189:7.* entrance: - enter; *214:5.* intrusion: - intrude.

'- enter /θ/ a certain period, - become a certain age': İşçilerin grevi onbeşinci gün.ü.ne girdi. 'The workers' strike has entered its 15th day.' *817:7a.* beginning: - begin sth. For some expressions of age of the same pattern but different meaning, see yaşına {bas-/gir-} → bas- 1.

{ayrıntıya/ayrıntılara/detaya/ detaylara} gir- '- go or - enter {INTO detail}' Without the presence of a referent to a specific issue, the English more frequently has the singular 'detail' while the Turkish equivalent may have the singular or the plural: Şu anda vaktimiz {kısıtlı/sınırlı} olduğu için {ayrıntı.yA/ayrıntılar.A} girmek istemiyorum. 'Because at this moment our time is {limited}, I don't want to go INTO {detail/the details}.' İzin verirseniz, biraz daha ayrıntı.yA girelim... 'If you will permit me, let us go INTO a little more detail...' With a referent to a specific issue, the English has two common patterns: one with the word 'detail' in the singular, the other with it in the plural: * Bu iş.İN {ayrıntı.sI.na/ayrıntı.lar.I.na/ detay.I.na/detaylar.I.na} girmeyelim. 'Let's not go INTO {detail on this matter *or* THE detailS OF this matter}.' *765:6.* circumstance: - itemize.

{bahse/iddiaya} gir- /a: 1A, b: A, c: diye/ '- bet /a: θ [sb], b: θ [an amount], c: ON [lit., saying]/, - wager' [A. bahis (baHSi) 'wager, bet'/A. iddia (. . -) 'claim']: Biz hangi takım kazanacak diye bahse giriyoruz. 'We're taking bets ON which team will win [lit., ** We're entering a bet saying...].' * Senin.LE 50 lira.sı.nA bahs.E girerim ki maçı Beşiktaş kazanacak. 'I bet θ you θ 50 liras that Beşiktaş [a soccer team] will win the game [lit., ** I enter a bet WITH you FOR 50 liras that....].' *759:25.* gambling: - bet. → kumar oyna- ['- gamble'] → oyna - 1.

borca gir- /DAn dolayı/ '- go or - get into debt /{because of/due to}/' [borç (borCu) 'debt']: Bu yaz oğlumuzu evlendirdik, düğün masraflar.ı.ndan dolayı * çok borc.A girdik. 'This summer we married off our son. Because of the wedding expenses, * we went deep INTO debt.' *623:6.* debt: - go in debt. → = borçlan-, ≠ borcunu öde- ['- pay up, - pay off an account, one's debts'], ≠ borcunu {kapa-/kapat-}. Same. → {kapa-/kapat-} 8.

bunalıma gir- '- go /INTO/ a depression, - get depressed' [bunalım 1 'state of depression or despair'. 2 'crisis']: Aşk.ı.nA karşılık bulamayan genç bunalım.A girdi. 'The youth whose love was not returned [lit., ** who was unable to find a (positive) response FOR his love] went INTO a depression.' *112:16.* sadness: - lose heart. → bunalım geçir- ['- be in a depression, - be or - get depressed'] → geçir- 2.

* denize gir- '- go swimming /IN/ the {sea/ocean}' [deniz 'sea, ocean'], lit., '- enter θ the sea': Güneş.E aldanıp deniz.E girdim ve hasta oldum. 'Fooled by the sun [i.e., into thinking the water was warm], I went swimming IN the ocean and got sick.' Deniz.E girmek yasaktır. '{Swimming [IN the sea] is forbidden!/No swimming!}' *182:56.* water travel: - swim; *352:7.* publication: poster: * specific signs. → yüz- 1 ['- swim'].

dünya evine gir- /lA/ '- get married, - marry /θ/' [A. dünya (. -) 'world', ev 'house', dünya evi 'the house of (=) the world'], lit., '- enter the house of the world': • Note the two patterns: a) Sonunda Sibel ile Zeki de dünya ev.i.nE girdiler. 'Finally Sibel [f.] and Zeki also got married [i.e., to each other or each one separately to sb else].' b) Sonunda Sibel Zeki ile dünya evine girdi. 'Finally Sibel married Zeki.' * Senin de dünya evine girme zamanın geldi, bak bütün arkadaşların evlendi. 'It's time you too got married. Look, all your friends have gotten married.' *563:15.* marriage: - get married. → = /lA/ evlen- ['- marry sb, - get married to sb'], ≠ ayrıl- 1 ['- get or

- be divorced /from/, - split up /WITH/'], ≠ **boşan-**. Same.

içeri[.yE] gir- '- go /{in/inside}/, - enter /θ/' [**içeri** 'in, inside'], lit., ** '- enter the inside': **İçeri[.yE] girmeyecek misiniz?** 'Aren't you going to go {in/inside}?' Proverb: **Rüşvet kapı.yI vurmadan içeri girer.** 'A bribe will enter without knocking AT the door.' *189:7.* entrance: - enter. → ≠ **dışarı[.yA] çık-** → çık- 2.

* /DAn/ **içeri[.yE] gir-** '- enter /θ/ [a place]', lit., ** '- enter /from/ [the place] /to/ the inside': **Biraz sonra annem elinde çay tepsi.si.yle oda.DAN içeri[.yE] girdi.** 'A little later my mother entered θ the room with a tea tray in her hand.' • Note: the noun designating the place entered has the -DAn suffix. *189:7.* entrance: - enter. → ≠ /DAn/ **dışarı[.yA] çık-** → çık- 1.

imtihana gir-. → {**sınava/ imtihana**} gir- below.

* **işe gir-** '- find work, a job, employment, - become employed' [**iş** 'work, employment'], lit., ** '- enter θ a job': **Üniversite mezunu olma.m.A rağmen hâlâ bir iş.E giremedim.** 'Although I'm a {college/university} graduate, I still haven't been able to find a job.' *724:12.* occupation: - work. → = **iş bul-** → bul- 1.

komaya gir- '- go, - fall, - lapse, or - sink /INTO/ a coma': **Selim geçen hafta kaza geçirmiş, koma.yA girmiş.** 'Selim was in an accident last week and went INTO a coma.' *25:5.* insensibility: - faint. → ≠ **komadan çık-** → çık- 1.

kuyruğa gir-. → {**sıraya/ kuyruğa**} gir- below.

* **masrafa gir-** '- spend a lot of money on sth or to get sth done, - have a lot of expenses, - incur great expense', often with a word such as **çok** 'much, many' indicating a large amount. [A. **masraf** 'expense, outlay'], lit., ** '- enter expenses': **Bu yıl {yeni bir ev.e taşındık/kızımızı evlendirdik}, çok masraf.A girdik.** 'This year {we moved to a new house/gave our

daughter in marriage}. We spent a lot of money.' *626:5.* expenditure: - spend; *729:15.* finance, investment: - finance; *896:4.* liability: - incur. → **para {harca-/sarf et-}** ['- spend money'] → {harca-/sarf et-} 1, **masraf çek-** ['- foot the bill, - pay', *informal, jocular*] → çek- 5, **masraf gör-** ['- meet expenses, - finance, - pay for'] → gör- 4, **masraf karşıla-**. Same, **masraf {et-/yap-}** ['- spend (money) /{ON/FOR}/; - pay out money /FOR/'], **masraftan {kaç-/kaçın-}** ['- avoid /θ/ expense, - economize'] → kaç- 2.

sıkıntıya gir- '- get /INTO/ financial straits, financial difficulty' [**sıkıntı** 1 'distress, trouble'. 2 'financial difficulties, financial straits']: **Mali durumunuz iyi değilse başkası.ndan borç bulabilirim; sıkıntı.yA girmenizi istemem.** 'If your financial position is not good, I can get [lit., find] a loan from sb else. I don't want to put you in financial difficulty [lit., ** I don't want your entering θ financial difficulty].' *1012:12.* difficulty: - get into trouble.

* {**sınava/imtihana**} gir- /DAn/ '- TAKE an examination /IN/' [{**sınav/A. imtihan** (. . -)} 'examination'], lit., ** '- enter θ an examination': **Mehmet Türkçe sınav.ı.na girdi mi?** 'Did Mehmet take {the Turkish examination?/his Turkish examination?}' * **Bugün matematik.TEN sınav.a girdim. Fakat iyi geçmedi, herhalde * matematik.TEN kalacağım.** 'I took an examination IN mathematics today, but I didn't do well [lit., ** it didn't pass well]. * I'll probably fail the course [lit., ** stay FROM mathematics].' **Sen hangi dersler.in sınavlar.ı.na gireceksin?** 'What classes are you going to take your exams in? [lit., ** What class's exams are you going to enter?]' • The LITERAL translation into Turkish of the English '- TAKE an examination', i.e., {**sınav/ imtihan**} al-, is not generally accepted standard Turkish today. *938:4.* answer: - answer. → = {**sınav/imtihan**} ol- → ol- 10.1, **imtihan et-** ['- give an examination, - examine'].

{**sıraya/kuyruğa**} gir- '- get /IN/ [the] line, - line up, - queue up', for a performance, a sports event, a means of transportation [e.g., bus, shared cab], or for a purchase [sıra 'line, order', **kuyruk 1** 'tail'. **2** 'line, queue']: **Sinema biletlerini almak için şu sıra.yA giriniz.** 'To buy your movie tickets get IN that line.' **Taksim dolmuş.u bekliyorsanız, şu sıra.yA girin.** 'If you are waiting for the shared cab to Taksim, get IN this line.' **Müzeye girmeden önce sıra.yA girin.** 'Before entering the museum, {form a line./get in the line.}' **Konser.E bilet al.abil.mek için herkes kuyruğ.A girmiş, sırasını bekliyor.** 'Everyone has lined up and is waiting his turn to buy [lit., to be able to buy] tickets FOR the concert.' *189:7* entrance: - enter; *811:6.* continuity: - line up. → ≠ {sırayı/kuyruğu} **boz-.** → boz- 1.

şoka gir- '- go /INTO/ shock', a medical condition [F. **şok** [Ku] 'shock']: **Trafik kazasından sonra şok.A girince * hemen hastane.ye kaldırıldı.** 'When, after the accident, he went INTO shock, * he was immediately rushed to the hospital.' *85:46b.* disease: - take sick in particular ways. → {şoke/şok} **ol-** ['- be shocked' in the NON-medical sense, i.e., - be astonished] → ol- 10.1.

* tatile gir- '- close or - shut down for vacation [subj.: an institution, school, business], - recess, - go into recess for vacation [subj.: school], - go on vacation [subj.: a person but usually only when considered a member of an institution]' [A. **tatil** (- .) 'vacation, holiday']: {**Orta dereceli okullar/Adlî mahkemeler/Türkiye Büyük Millet Meclisi [TBMM]} tatil.E girdi.** '{The middle schools/The courts/The Turkish Grand National Assembly} have {closed/ recessed} for {vacation/the break}.' For a person considered a member of such an institution but usually not otherwise: **S: Ne zaman tatile gireceksin?** 'Q: When are you going ON vacation?' **C: Otuz bir Mayıs'ta [tatile gireceğim].** 'A: [I'm going ON vacation] May 31.' *20:9.* rest, repose: - vacation; *293:8.* closure: - close shop; *856:8.* cessation: - stop work. When an institution is not involved or a person is not regarded as a member of such an institution, → = **tatile çık-** →

çık- 2, = **tatile git-** → git- 1a, = **tatil yap-** → yap- 3.

yaşına gir-. → **yaşına** {**bas-/gir-**). → bas- 1.

yoluna gir- '- go well, - work or - turn out the way it should, - come out right', lit., ** 'for sth - enter θ its [proper] road': **Merak etmeyin her şey yolu.na girecek.** 'Don't worry. Everything will {work/turn} out all right.' Proverb: **Allah yardım ederse kulu.nA, her iş.i girer yol.u.nA.** 'If God helps θ His servant [i.e., any will-possessing being, mortal], every task [that the servant undertakes] will go well.' *392:7.* improvement: - get better.

* zahmete gir- '- go to trouble' [A. **zahmet** 'trouble, difficulty']: A guest to a host: **A: Yemekler nefisti, * fakat çok zahmet.E girmişsiniz.** 'A: The food was wonderful, * but you really shouldn't have gone to all this trouble [lit., ** you apparently entered θ a lot of trouble]!' **B: * Estağfurullah, hiç zahmet olur mu?** 'B: * What do you mean? It was no trouble at all [lit., How would it be any trouble?]' *995:4.* inexpedience: - inconvenience. → = **zahmet et-, zahmet ol-** ['- be trouble, troublesome, an inconvenience /FOR/'] → ol- 12.

giril- [ir] /DAn/ '- be entered /{THROUGH/BY WAY OF}/', impersonal passive [**gir-** + pass. suf. **-Il**]: **"Girilir" levha.sı.nı görmedin mi? Bu kapı.DAN çıkılmaz, girilir.** 'Didn't you see the "Entrance [lit., ** {It is entered/One enters}]" sign? One doesn't exit THROUGH this door, one enters [THROUGH it].' **Yasak bölge. * Girilmez.** 'Restricted {zone/area}. * No admittance.' *189:7.* entrance: - enter; *352:7.* publication: poster: * specific signs. → ≠ **çıkılır-.**

git- [giDer] **1 a)** /a: DAn, b: A, c: lA, d: 1A/ '- go /a: from, b: to, c: with [a person], d: BY [vehicle]/, - leave, - depart /a: from/': **S:** {**a: Bu adres.e/b: * Ora.yA/c: Tren istasyon.u.na/d: Atatürk havaliman.ı.na/e: Şehir merkez.i.ne} nasıl gidebilirim?** 'How can I {go/get} {a: to this address/b: * there/c: to the train station/d: to the Atatürk Airport/e: to the center of the city}?' Responses with the name of a vehicle: C1: {a: Otobüs.LE/b: Dolmuş.LA/c: Tramvay.LA/d: Taksi.yLE/e: Araba.yLA/f: Vapur.LA/g: Gemi.yLE} gidebilirsiniz. 'A1: You can go {a: BY bus/b: BY shared cab/c: BY streetcar/d: BY taxi/e: BY car/f: BY ferry/g: BY ship}.' • Note: Araba.yLA git- is ALSO frequently used in the meaning of '- drive to a place': Ankara'ya arabayla gittim. '{I went to Ankara by car./I drove to Ankara.}' → Arabayla gel- → gel- 1. 888:5. operation: - operate sth. For responses meaning 'on foot', → below {yürüyerek/yaya [olarak]/ yayan} git-. # Otobüs.LE gidebilir miyim? 'Can I go BY bus?' Elâzığ'dan Ankara'ya 10 saatte gittik. 'We went from Elâzığ to Ankara in ten hours.' Bu yol nere.yE gider? 'θ Where does this road {go/lead}?' Doğru gidiniz. 'Go straight ahead.' Pamukkale'ye gittiniz mi? 'Have you ever {gone to/been to} Pamukkale?' = /DA/ bulun- 2 ['- be /{in/at}/']. Kim.İN.le gittiniz? '{Who did you go with?/With whom did you go?}' → = /A/ {eşlik et-/refakat et-} ['- accompany /θ/, - go [along] /WITH/']. 768:7. accompaniment: - accompany. A phrase used by a bureaucrat to put off an applicant or by someone describing that situation: Bugün git yarın gel. '{Come back later./[lit., Go [away] today, come back tomorrow.]}' Proverbs: Acele giden ecele gider. 'He who goes in haste goes to [his] death.' Dert gitmez değişir. '{Trouble/Sorrow} doesn't go away, it [just] changes.' Gider kılıç yarası, gitmez dil yarası. 'A sword wound will heal [lit., ** go], but a wound inflicted by the tongue [lit., a tongue wound] will not.' This is the exact opposite of the English proverb 'Sticks and stones will break my bones, but words will never hurt me.' It reflects Turkish sensitivity to harsh words. 524: * 35. speech: proverbs. Sel gider, kum kalır. 'The flood waters recede, the sand remains.', i.e., What is weighty remains. 177:25. travel: - go to; 182:13. water travel: - navigate. → ulaş- 1 ['- reach /θ/, - arrive /AT/, - get /to/ a place'], var- ['- reach /θ/, - arrive {IN/AT}, - get /to/'], ≠ gel- 1.

Bas git! → bas- 1.

* başını alıp git- '- take off, - make off, - go away, - leave', in the sense of a permanent departure [baş 'head' here represents the whole person, al- '- take'], lit., ** '- take one's head and go': Yusuf bey.e ne oldu bilmiyoruz. Bir gün başını alıp gitti, * bir daha da ondan haber al.AMA.dık. 'We don't know what happened to Yusuf bey. One day he took off, * and we never heard from him again [lit., ** we COULD NOT get word from him again].' 188:10. departure: - hasten off.

hacca git- [A. hac (haCCı) 'pilgrimage'] '- go /ON/ the Pilgrimage, - make the Pilgrimage [to Mecca]'. İslâm'ın beş şartı; kelime-i şehadet, namaz kılmak, zekât vermek, oruç tutmak ve hacca gitmektir. 'The five pillars [lit., (obligatory) conditions] of Islam are: the Shahadah [lit., the words of affirmation, i.e., to pronounce the words "There is no God but God and Muhammad is his Messenger"], to perform the namaz [i.e., the Islamic prayer ritual], to pay the zakat [i.e., the yearly alms tax required of Muslims, generally regarded as equal to 1/40th of one's property], to [observe the] fast, and to make the Pilgrimage [to Mecca].' Allah nasip ederse ben de bu yıl hacca gideceğim inşallah. 'If God so grants, I too will go ON the Pilgrimage this year, God willing.' 177:21. travel: - journey; 701:14. religious rites: - celebrate.

ileri git- [ileri 'ahead, the space ahead of sth'] (1) '- be fast, ahead': Saatim beş dakika ileri gitmiş, düzelttim. 'My watch was five minutes fast. I set it [lit., ** corrected it, set it right].' 844:5. earliness: - be early. → ≠ geri kal- ['- be slow, behind'] → kal- 1, dur- 1 ['- stop, - come to a stop /at/, - become motionless'].
(2) /{ArAk/mAklA}/ '- go too far, - overstep the limit, - be rude /BY...ing/': Bu kaba sözleri {söyle.yerek/söyle.mekle} çok ileri gittiniz, lütfen * bu konuyu kapatalım. 'By say.ing these rude words you've really gone much too far. * {Let's drop the subject./Let's say no more about

this./lit., ** Let's close this subject.}'
505:3. * *1.* discourtesy: - be
discourteous; *909:9.* overrunning: -
overstep; *992:10.* excess: - overdo. →
= **çok ol-** → **ol-** 12.

* **tatile git-** /A, A/ '- go /to [a
place], {ON/FOR}/ vacation, holiday,
- have a vacation, holiday' [A. **tatil**
(- .) 'vacation, holiday'], lit., ** '- go
to a vacation': * **Üç yıldır tatil.E
gitmedim.** 'I haven't had a vacation
{for/in} 3 years.' S: * **Bu yaz
nere.yE tatil.E gittin?** 'Q: θ
Where did you go {FOR [your]
vacation/ON holiday} this summer?'
C: * **[Bu yaz] İtalya'yA
[tatil.E] gittim.** 'A: [This summer]
I went to Italy [{FOR [my]
vacation/ON holiday}].' **Eğer
işlerimi ayarlayabilirsem bu
yaz** * **Marmaris.E tatil.E
gideceğim.** 'If I can get my affairs
in order, this summer * I'll go TO
Marmaris {FOR [my] vacation/ON
holiday}.' **Mine tatil.E {ne
zaman/kimlerle/neyle}
gideceğ.i.ni plânlıyor.** 'Mine [f.]
is planning {when/with whom [i.e.,
with which people]/how [i.e., by what
vehicle]} she is going to go ON
vacation.' *20:9.* rest, repose: -
vacation. → = **tatile çık-** → **çık-** 1,
= **tatile gir-**, = **tatil yap-** → **yap-**
3.

tuvalete git- '- go to the restroom, -
use the toilet' [F. **tuvalet** 'toilet',
here 'the restroom']: A: **Tuvalete
gitmem gerek, bekler misin?** 'I
have to go to the restroom. Will you
wait?' **Tuvalete gidiyorum.** 'I'm
going to the restroom.' *12:13.*
excretion: - defecate; *12:14.* : urinate.
→ = **ihtiyacını gör-** ['- defecate, -
urinate'] → **gör-** 4, **tuvalet yap-** ['-
have a bowel movement *or* BM, -
urinate, - do one's business, - use the
facilities, the restroom; - make one's
toilet, i.e., usually for a woman to
dress or to arrange her hair'] → **yap-**
3, **çiş {yap-/et-}** ['- urinate, - piss,
- pee'] → **yap-** 3, **küçük aptes yap-**
['- urinate', *formal, polite*] → **yap-** 3,
su dök- ['- take a {pee/piss}, -
urinate'], **büyük aptes yap-** ['-
have a bowel movement *or* BM, -
defecate', *formal, polite*] → **yap-** 3,
dışarı çık-. Same. → **çık-** 2, **işe-**
['- urinate'].

uçakla git- '- fly /to/, - go /to/ BY
plane' [**uçak** 'plane']: **Trabzon'a
uçak.LA gidebilir miyiz?** '{Can
we go to Trabzon BY plane?/Can we
fly to Trabzon?}' Of course **git-** may
be used with the name of any vehicle
to indicate 'going' with that vehicle.
184:36. aviation: - fly. → = **uç-**.

* **üstüne git-** [**üst** 'the top part of
anything'], lit., '- go to the top of' (1)
'- deal strictly, harshly /WITH/, - be
hard /on/': **Yeter artık, çocuğ.un
üst.ü.ne fazla gitme!** 'That's
enough now! Don't be so hard on the
child! [lit., ** Don't go so much to
the top of the child!]' *425:5.*
strictness: - deal hardly or harshly
with.
(2) '- get right down /to/, - attend
/to/': **Dilek çok çalışkandır,
işten kaçmaz; bilâkis iş.in
üst.ü.ne gider.** 'Dilek is very
{hardworking/industrious}. She
doesn't avoid work. On the contrary,
she {gets right down to it/attends to it
right away} [lit., ** goes to the top of
the task].' *724:10.* occupation: -
occupy. → ≠ **kaç-** 2 ['- avoid' a
task].

yol git- '- travel, - cover, - traverse a
distance': **Çok yorucu bir
yolculuk oldu; her gün 300 km.**
[read: **kilometre**] **yol gitmek
zorunda kaldık.** 'It turned out to be
a very tiring journey. We had to
cover 300 kilometers every day.' *
Dört nala bir hayli yol gittik.
'We covered a considerable distance
AT full gallop.' *177:20.* travel: -
traverse. → = **yol yap-** → **yap-** 3, =
katet-.

{**yürüyerek/yaya [olarak]/
yayan} git-** '- walk to a place, - go
somewhere {ON foot}': **Yürü.yerek
gidebilirsiniz.** 'You can {walk
there./go there ON foot [lit., ** by
walk.ing].}' **Okula yürüyerek
gittik.** '{We walked to school./We
went to school on foot.}' **Oraya
yürüyerek gidebilir miyim?**
'Can I {walk there?/go there on
foot?}' • Note the following example
without **git-**: * **Yürüyerek ne
kadar sürer?** 'How long does it take
{to walk there?/to go there on foot?}'
177:27. travel: - walk.

1 b) **Git-** preceded by certain
adjectives and nouns in an **Ahmet'in
kitab.ı** [i.e., possessOR possessED]
structure followed by the dative case
suffix **A** conveys certain states of
feeling, difficulty, ease, etc. • Below

note the different possessed suffixes on the word preceding git-:

* {acayibine/garibine/tuhafına} git- '- find or - think {strange/odd}, - strike one as {strange/odd}, - seem {strange/odd} to' [{A. acaib (. - .)/A. garip (. -)/A. tuhaf} 'strange, odd']. Here as a noun. Lit., ** '- go to one's strange']: **Ahmet'in geceyarısından sonra bize gelme.si anne.m.in garib.i.nE gitti.** '{The fact that Ahmet visited us/lit., Ahmet's visiting us} after midnight struck my mother as strange.' NOT ~~garibine GEL~~. *869:8.* * *1.* abnormality: - find strange. → = yadırga-.

* **hoşuna git-** '- like' [P. **hoş** 'pleasant'. Here as a noun.], lit., ** '- go to one's pleasure']: NON-verbal noun as subject: **Adnan beyin evi Mete'NİN hoş.U.nA gitti mi?** 'Did Mete like Adnan bey's house [lit., ** Did Adnan bey's house go to Mete's pleasure]?' {**Basketbol maçları/Şu çocuk/Yün kazaklar} çok hoş.UM.a gidiyor.** 'I like {basketball games/that child/wool sweaters} a lot [lit., ** (i.e., these items) go much to MY pleasure].' **Hoş.UM.a gitti.** 'I liked it.' **Hoş.UNUZ.A gitti mi?** 'Did YOU [pl.] like it?' VERBAL noun as subject: **Şarkı söyle.MEK hoş.UM.a gidiyor.** 'I like singing [songs].' {**Başkan.IN konuşma.SI} hoş.UM.a gitti.** 'I liked {the prime minister's talk./the way the prime minister talked./the fact that the prime minister talked.}' *95:12.* pleasure: - enjoy. → = beğen-, = hoşlan-, = memnun ol- → ol- 12, = sev- 1, sevin- ['- be glad, pleased'].

* **keyfine git-** '- like, - enjoy' [A. **keyf** 'pleasure'], lit., ** '- go to one's pleasure']: **Eski arkadaşlarıyla oturup konuş.mak dedem.in çok keyf.i.nE gitti.** 'My grandfather really enjoyed sitting and talking with {his old friends/his friends from the old days}.' *95:12.* pleasure: - enjoy.

* **kolayına git-** (1) '- be easy /for/', expresses a preference for an easy alternative. The alternative action, which is not taken, is not, however, more correct or proper. [**kolay** 'easy'. Here as a noun.], lit., ** '- go to one's ease': **Niçin bu çorbayı yaptın?** 'Why did you make this soup?', i.e., as opposed to making some other soup or a dish more diffcult to make. **Kolay.IM.a gitti * de, ondan.** 'It was easy for ME. * That's why.' *1013:10.* facility: - go easily. → = kolayına gel- → gel- 1, ≠ zoruna git- 1.
(2) '- take the easy way out', suggests the alternative action, which is not taken, should have been: **Sana verilen işi doğru dürüst yap, [iş.in] kolay.ı.na gitme!** 'Do the {task/job} [that] you have been given properly! Don't take the easy way out!' *331:15.* inactivity: - take it easy. → = kolayına kaç- → kaç- 1.

* **komiğine git-** '- find funny, amusing, - strike one as funny, - tickle one's funny bone' [**komik** 'comical, funny'. Here as a noun.], lit., ** '- go to one's amusement': **S: Neden gülüyorsun?** 'Q: Why are you laughing?' **C: Komiğ.İM.e gitti * de, ondan!** 'A: It struck ME as funny. * That's why.' *489:13.* wit, humor: - joke.

* **tuhafına git-.** → {acayibine/garibine/tuhafına} git-. above.

* {zoruna/gücüne} git- [{P. zor/güç} 'difficulty'], lit., ** '- go to one's difficulty' (1) '- be difficult, hard for': **Gecenin şu saatinde bulaşık yıkamak zor.UM.a gitti, sabah yıkayacağım.** 'To wash dishes at this time of night is hard for ME. I'll wash them in the morning.' *1012:10.* difficulty: - be difficult. → ≠ kolayına git-.
(2) '- offend /θ/, - hurt /θ/': **Selim'in bana öyle bağırma.sı çok zor.UM.a gitti, artık onunla konuşmayacağım.** 'Selim's shouting at me like this really {offended/hurt} ME. I'm not going to speak to him anymore.' *152:21.* resentment, anger: - offend; *156:5.* disrespect: - offend.

2 '- ride, - go {ON/by} a vehicle'. • **Bin-** versus **git-**. The VERB **bin-** means '- get on a mount or vehicle'. The NOUN form of this verb is usually translated into English by 'riding': {**Bisiklet.E/At.A} bin-mey.I çok severim.** 'I like {bicycle/horse} riding a lot.' The Turkish finite verb that expresses the action of 'going in or by means of a mount or vehicle or riding', however, is not **bin-** but **git-**: **Bisiklet.E**

bindim, şimdi bakkala GİDİYORUM. 'I got on the bike, and now I'm RIDING [lit., going] to the store.' The verb **bin-** is not used for the SECOND verb in the sentence above. *177:33*. travel: - ride.

3 '- go /to/, - visit /θ/': **Dün Ali'ler.E akşam yemeğ.i.nE gittik.** 'Last night we went to Ali's house FOR dinner [lit., the evening meal].' • **Ali** is the first name of a male member of the family. The plural suffix on that FIRST name here denotes the residence of Ali and those people associated with him, e.g., his immediate family or his friends. In English we would say 'Ali's house' or use the LAST name in the plural as in 'the Smiths' house'. In Turkish a person usually uses the first name with the plural suffix to refer to the residence of the family of a person of his own age or younger. When he speaks of the residence of a family of sb specially respected, usually of sb older or sb otherwise held in esteem, or of sb he is not on familiar terms with, he follows the first name with **beyler** for a man, i.e., **Ali beyler**, or with **hanımlar** for a woman, i.e., **Selma hanımlar**. *582:19*. sociability: - visit. → **gel-** 1 [...'- come to see or - visit'], **ziyaret et-**.

* **misafirliğe git-** '- go /ON/ a visit, - go visiting, - pay a visit, - go to visit [a person, not a place], - call on sb', usually a neighbor or friend, not a relative or person of higher station; a casual, not formal, visit [A. **misafir** (. . -) 'guest', **misafirlik** 'a being a guest, visiting, ** guestness']: **Bu akşam misafirliğ.E gidiyoruz.** 'We're going {to call on some people/visiting} tonight.' **S:** * **Anne.N.LER evde mi çocuğum?** 'Q: Are YOUR parents [lit., YOUR motherS, plural, i.e., people associated with your mother] at home, dear [lit., my child]?' • Note that the possessed suffix [i.e., the **N** on **Anne**, a noun of relationship] PRECEDES the plural suffix. This is a frequent feature in such relationship expressions. **C: Hayır, misafirliğe gittiler.** 'A: No, they've gone visiting.' • Note: Although the form **ziyaret.İ.ne git-** is used [see directly below], the parallel structure with **misafirlik**, i.e., ~~misafirliğ.İ.ne git-~~, is NOT. *582:19*. sociability: - visit. For *more*

formal visits, → **gel-** 1, **ziyarete git-, ziyaretine git-, ziyaret et-**.

* **ziyarete git-** '- go to visit or - call on', usually a respected person [i.e., an older person, sb of high station, or perhaps sb requiring special attention such as a sick person], or '- go to visit' a PLACE of reverence associated with such a person [e.g., a cemetery or grave site], or '- go on a visit' in connection with a holiday, bairam. [A. **ziyaret** (. - .) 'visit']: * **Hasta.yI ziyaret.E gittik.** 'We went to visit {the patient/the sick person}.' **Hacı Bayram Veli Hazretlerinin türbe.si.nİ ziyaret.E gittik.** 'We went to visit the tomb of Hacı Bayram Veli Hazretleri [i.e., a Sufi saint].' **Bayramda bütün komşular.I ziyaret.E gittik.** 'During the bairam we went to visit all the neighbors.' *582:19*. sociability: - visit. → = **ziyaretine git-** → directly below, = **ziyaret et-, gel-** 1. For *more casual, informal* visits, → **misafirliğe git-** → above.

* **ziyaretine git-**. Same explanation as above, but not a place unless that place is treated as if it were the person himself. • Note the different grammatical structure. [A. **ziyaret** (. - .) 'visit'], lit., ** '- go to SB'S visit': * **Hasta.NIN ziyaret.i.nE gittik.** 'We went to visit the sick person [lit., ** We went to the sick person's visit].' In the following example, the tomb of a saint is treated as if it were the saint himself since his spirit is thought to reside in the tomb: **Hacı Bayram Veli Hazretleri.NİN ziyaret.i.nE gittik.** 'We went to visit the tomb of Hacı Bayram Veli Hazretleri [lit., ** We went to the visit of Haji Bayram Veli Hazretleri].' **Bayramda bütün komşular.IN ziyaret.i.nE gittik.** 'During the bairam we went to visit all the neighbors.' *582:19*. sociability: - visit. → = **ziyarete git-** above, = **ziyaret et-, gel-** 1, **git-** 3. For *more casual, informal* visits, → **git-** 1a, **misafirliğe git-** → **git-** 3.

4 '- go /to/, - attend /θ/' **a)** For a short period, a particular event: **Dün {sinema.ya/konser.e/futbol maçı.na} gittik.** 'Yesterday we went {to the movies/to a concert/to a soccer game}.'
b) For a long period, educational institution: **S: Hangi okul.a**

gidiyorsun? 'Q: Which school are you {going to/attending}?' C1: {İlkokul.a/Lise.ye/ Üniversite-.ye} gidiyorum. 'A1: I'm going {to primary school/to {high school/lysée}/to college}.' C2: Okumuyorum, çalışıyorum. 'A2: I'm not studying, I work [i.e., at a regular job].' → = devam et- 3, = oku- 3. *221:8.* presence: - attend.

5 '- go or - proceed well, badly': S: İşler nasıl gidiyor? 'Q: How are things going?' C: {a: [Çok] İyi gidiyor./b: Fena değil./c: Şöyle böyle gidiyor./d: Pek iyi gitmiyor./e: [çok] Kötü gidiyor.} 'A: {a: They're going [very] well./b: Not badly./c: They're going so so./d: They're not going so well./e: They're going [very] badly.}' → = İşler nasıl? ['How are things?'] → ol- 3, Additional examples. a) 2. Essential question-word questions: Nasıl? # * Bu iş böyle gitmez. 'Things [lit., this matter] can't go on this way.' *162:2.* progression: - proceed. → = geç- 6.

* boşa git- '- be in vain, of no use, for nothing' [boş 'futile, useless']: Akşama misafir gelecek DİYE o kadar hazırlanmıştım, ama gelmediler. Bütün emeklerim boş.a gitti. 'THINKING that guests were coming {this evening/tonight}, I had made all kinds of preparations, but they [i.e., the guests] didn't come. All my efforts were {in vain/for nothing}.' Bu kadar yıl iyi bir piyanist olabilmen için verdiğim emekler ve paralar boşa gitti. 'For all these years the efforts I made and the money I spent for you to be able to become a good pianist were for nothing.' *391:8.* uselessness: - be useless; *473:6.* loss: - go to waste; *910:3.* shortcoming: - fall through. → boşa çık- ['- come to naught, not - be realized, - be dashed', hopes, expectations, dreams, efforts] → çık- 7.

6 /lA/ '- suit, - go /with/', clothing, food. → = dur- 9 ['- look, - appear /ON/, - suit fit', clothing]: iyi git-/lA/ '- go well /with/' [iyi 'good, well']: S: Ne dersin, bu etek.le bu ceket iyi gitti mi? 'Q: What do you think? Does this jacket go well with this skirt?' C: {Evet, iyi gitti./Hayır, iyi gitmedi.} 'A: {Yes, it does./No, it doesn't.}' • In

the situation depicted above, note the use of the past tense in the Turkish and the present tense in the corresponding English. → = uy- 2. # Ispanak.la yoğurt iyi gider. 'Yogurt goes well with spinach.' *866:3.* conformity: - conform.

giy- [er] /A/ '- put on clothing, - don, - put sth /ON/ [a part of the body]' AND '- BE wearing, - HAVE ON clothing'. Giy- is usually used with larger items of clothing, gloves, and sometimes headgear, but not with accessories or small items such as jewelry, watches, etc.: Paltomu, eldivenlerimi giydim. Sokağ.a çıktım. 'I put on my overcoat and my gloves. I went out [to the street].' Dün partiye giderken annemin elbisesini giydim. 'Yesterday before going to the party, I put on my mother's dress.' Elbisemi dün giydim ve hâlâ giyiyorum. 'I PUT ON my suit yesterday, and I AM STILL WEARING it.' * Baş.ı.nA {şapka/bere} giymişti. 'He had put {on a {hat/beret}./a {hat/beret} ON his head.}' S: * Kaç beden {a: pantolon/b: elbise/c: etek/d: şort} giyiyorsunuz? 'Q: What size {a: {trousers/pants}/b: dress/c: skirt/d: shorts} do you wear?' C: {a: Otuz sekiz beden pantolon/b: Kırk beden elbise/c: Otuz sekiz beden etek/d: Orta beden şort} giyiyorum. 'A: I wear {a: pants size 38/b: dress size 40/c: skirt size 38/d: short size medium}.' Beden refers to the size of garments worn on the main body and legs, with the exception of shirts. Beden is not used for what is worn on the head or feet. The sizes of the latter are indicated with the word numara as follows: S: * Kaç numara {ayakkabı/şapka/gömlek} giyiyorsunuz? 'Q: What size [lit., number] {shoes/hat/shirt} do you wear?' C: {37 numara ayakkabı/2 numara şapka/2 numara gömlek} giyiyorum. 'A: I wear size {37 shoes/2 hat/2 shirt}.' Proverb: * Gün.e göre kürk giymek gerek. 'One must wear the fur appropriate to the day.', i.e., dress as circumstances require. *866:10.* conformity: don't rock the boat. * noun of color.lAr giy- '- dress ALL IN noun of color': Yaşlı hanım siyahlar giymişti. 'The old woman had dressed all in black.' *5:42.* clothing: - don; *5:43.* : - wear, - have on. → ≠ çıkar- 2, tak- ['- put on' small items, accessories such as jewelry, watch, also certain headgear], **sür-** 4 ['- put on perfume'].

giydir- [ir] [giy- + caus. suf. -DIr]: • Note the two patterns:
a) /I [on the noun denoting the person dressed]/ '- dress sb', garment not mentioned: **Üst.ü kirlenince anne.si çocuğ.U yeniden giydirdi.** 'When the child's clothes [üst 'clothes, what one has on'] got dirty, {his/her} mother changed them [lit., ** dressed the child anew].'
Proverb: **Yetimi giydir, açı doyur, kavgacıyı ayır.** 'Clothe the orphan; feed the hungry; separate those who are fighting [lit., the fighter].'
b) /I [on the noun designating the garment if that noun is definite, θ on that noun if it is indefinite], A [on noun designating the person dressed]/ '- dress /θ/ sb /IN/ sth, - have /θ/ sb put sth on or wear sth', person and garment both mentioned: **S: Okula giderken * Yavuz'A ne giydirdin?** 'Q: How did you dress θ Yavuz before he went to school? [lit., What did you have θ Yavuz wear...]' **C: * Yavuz'A {a: bere/b: eldiven/c: palto/d: çizme/e: kazak/f: pantolon} giydirdim.** 'A: I dressed θ Yavuz IN {a: a beret/b: gloves/c: a coat/d: boots/e: a sweater/f: trousers} [lit., I had θ Yavuz wear a beret, etc.].' **Yavuz'A palto.su.nU giydirdim.** 'I had Yavuz (wear/put on) his coat.' *5:38.* clothing: - clothe. → ≠ **soy-** 3.

giyin- [ir] '- dress oneself, - get dressed' [giy- + refl. suf. -In]: **S: Hazír değil misin hâlâ? Daha giyinmedin mi?** 'Q: Aren't you ready yet? Haven't you gotten dressed yet?' **C: Hemen giyinirim.** 'A: I'll get dressed right away.' **Giyindim ve sokağ.A çıktım.** 'I got dressed and went out to the street.' **Faruk'un babası da Başbakan gibi * Ramsey'DEN giyiniyor.** 'Faruk's father, like the prime minister, also * gets his clothing [lit., ** dresses himself] from Ramsey's', a clothing store. Proverb: *** Gün.e göre kürk giyinmek gerek.** 'One must dress oneself in the fur appropriate to the day.', i.e., dress as circumstances require. *5:42.* clothing: - don; *866:10.* conformity: don't rock the boat. → ≠ **soyun-**.

Güle güle giyin[iz]. 'What a nice...!, How nice!' Often used with the name of an item of clothing: e.g., dress, shirt, etc., lit., 'Wear it with pleasure!', a polite expression used when complimenting sb on a new item of clothing [gül- '- laugh' + adv.- forming suf. -[y]A = güle lit., 'laughingly']: **A: Yeni bir elbise aldım.** 'A: I've bought a new suit.' **B: Güle güle giyin[iz].** 'B: Wear it with pleasure.' **A: {Teşekkür ederim./Sağol.}** 'A: {Thank you./Thanks.}' *504: * 20.* courtesy: polite expressions. For other polite expressions of similar meaning and structure → **Güle güle oturun[uz].** → otur-, **Güle güle kullanın[ız].** → kullan-.

gizle- [r] /A/ '- hide, - conceal sth /IN/', i.e., - PUT sth somewhere so it will not be seen: **Yurdaer kardeşin.e aldığı hediye.yİ dolab.ı.nA gizledi. Çünkü o.nA sürpriz yapmak istiyordu.** 'Yurdaer hid the present he had brought for his brother IN his closet because he wanted to surprise him [lit., make a surprise for him].' **Şekeri nere.yE gizleyeceksiniz?** 'θ Where are you going to hide the candy?' **Silâh.ı.nı yatağ.ı.nın altı.nA gizledi.** 'He hid his weapon θ under his bed.' **Teröristleri evi.nDE * gizle.diğ.i iddia.sı.yLA yargılanıyor.** 'He is being tried * ON the allegation that he hid the terrorists in his house.'

/DAn/ '- keep sth secret /from/': **Tunç sınıfta {kaldığ.ı.nı/ kalacağ.ı.nı} babası.nDAN gizledi.** 'Tunç kept from his father [the fact] {that he had been held back in school [lit., ** 'stayed in class', i.e., didn't pass on to the next grade]/that he was going to be held back}.' **Baba.sı.nın öldüğ.ü.nü Canan'DAN gizledik.** 'We kept from Canan the news that his father had died.' *346:6.* concealment: - conceal. → = **sakla-** 1, ≠ **açıkla-** 2.

gizlen- [ir] [gizle- + {pass./refl.} suf. -n]: 1 /DAn, A/ '- hide, - conceal ONESELF /from, IN/': **Çocuk babası görmesin DİYE dolab.A gizlendi.** 'The child hid himself IN the closet SO THAT his father would not see him.' **Hapishaneden çıktıktan sonra * kimse.nin yüz.ü.nE bak.amaz oldu, herkes.ten gizleniyor.** 'After getting out of prison, * he couldn't look anyone IN the face [lit., ** became one who couldn't look INTO anyone's face]. He hid from everyone.' **Teröristler.in gizlendiğ.i ev burasıymış.** 'The house [that] the terrorists {hid in/are hiding in} is here.' *346:8.* concealment: - hide oneself. → = **saklan-** 1.

2 /DAn, tarafından/ '- be hidden /from, by/; - be kept secret /from, by/': **Doğum günü hediyeleri Aslı'dan gizlendi.** 'Her birthday presents were hidden from Aslı.' **Babasının ölüm haberi önce [polis tarafından] gizlendi.** 'The news of his father's death was initially kept secret by the police.' <u>Proverb</u>: **Ağaran baş, ağlayan göz gizlenmez.** 'The head that is turning white, the eye that is weeping cannot be [lit., aren't] hidden.', i.e., Age and sorrow cannot be hidden. *346:6.* concealment: - conceal. → = **saklan-** 2.

göbek at-. → **at-** 1.

göç-. → {**göç et-/göç-**}.

{**göç et-** [eDer]/**göç-** [er]} /DAn, A/ '- migrate /from, to/' [**göç** 'migration']: **Türkler Anadolu'ya Orta Asya'dan göç etmişler.** 'The Turks migrated to Anatolia from Central Asia.' **Köylüler daha iyi işler bul.abil.mek umud.u.yLA büyük şehirler.e göç ediyorlar.** '[The] villagers are migrating to the large cities IN the hope of finding [lit., of being able to find] better jobs.' *177:22.* travel: - migrate.

göm- [er] /A/ '- bury /IN/ [dead bodies and other objects]; - inter /θ/ [usually for dead bodies only]': **Köpek kemiği gömdükten sonra çukuru kapadı.** 'After burying the bone, the dog covered up the hole.' **Büyük dedemin yıllar önce bahçe.yE bir kasa altın gömdüğü söyleniyor ama bulamadık.** 'It is said that my great grandfather many years ago had buried a safe full of gold IN the garden, but we haven't been able to find it.' **A: Komşumuz Cemal bey.i bugün gömdüler.** 'A: They buried our neighbor Cemal bey today.' **B: Allah rahmet eylesin.** 'B: May God have mercy upon his soul.' **Şehit Orhan'ın yer.i.ne başkası.nI gömdüler.** 'They buried someone else in place of the martyr Orhan.' <u>Proverb</u>: **Dün ölen.i dün gömerler.** 'They bury the person who died yesterday yesterday.', i.e., Forget the unpleasant features of the past. *309:19.* interment: - inter. → ≠ **çıkar-**.

gömül- [ür] /A, {tarafından/CA}/ '- be buried /IN, by/ [dead bodies and other objects]; - be interred, laid to rest /IN, by/ [usually for dead bodies only]' [**göm-** + pass. suf. -**Il**]: **Cenazeler vakit geçir.il.meden gömüldü.** 'The corpses were buried without delay [lit., ** without letting time be passed].' * **Nusret amca.nın cenaze.si bugün aile mezarlığ.ı.nA gömüldü.** 'Uncle Nusret [lit., Uncle Nusret's corpse] {was buried/was laid to rest} today IN the family {tomb/grave}.' **İstanbul'daki Amerikan Hastanesinde böbrek yetmez-liğ.i.nden yaşam.ı.nı yitiren 63 yaşındaki Amerikalı John Smith, {vasiyeti gereği/vasiye-ti.nE uygun olarak} bugün Hıristiyan Mezarlığı.nA gömül-dü.** 'The 63-year-old American John Smith, who died as a result of kidney failure in the American Hospital in Istanbul, was buried today IN the Christian Cemetery {in accordance with the requirements of his will/in accordance with his will}.' **Define avcıları hazine.nin gömüldüğ.ü yeri bulmaya çalışıyorlar.** 'The treasure hunters are trying to find the place where the treasure is buried.' *309:19.* interment: - inter. → = /DA/ **toprağa veril-** [dead bodies only], = *formal*: /A, {tarafından/CA}/ **defnedil-** [dead bodies only].

<u>**gönder-**</u> [ir] /A/ '- send sth /to/ sb, - send θ sb sth': **Dün Aydan'A iki gazete, bir de dergi gönderdim.** 'Yesterday I sent θ Aydan [f.] two newspapers and also a magazine.' OR 'Yesterday I sent two newspapers and also a magazine TO Aydan.' **Bavullarımı {yukarı/oda.m.a} gönderir misiniz?** 'Would you please send my baggage {up[stairs]/to my room}?' **Eşyalarımı {istasyon.dan/emniyet.ten/ odam.dan} alacak birini gönderebilir misiniz?** 'Can you send sb to get my things {from the station/from the baggage check/from my room}?' **Bu {paketi/ mektubu} taahhütlü göndermek**

istiyorum. 'I want to send this {package/letter} registered.' *176:15.* transferal, transportation: - send. → = **yolla-, ilet- 1** ['- take or convey /to/, - forward, - pass on /to/'], **postala-** ['- mail, - post, - send off mail /to/'].

'- send sb off /to/': **Dün annemi Bursa'ya gönderdim.** 'I sent my mother off to Bursa yesterday.' *176:15.* transferal, transportation: - send. → **yolcu et-** ['- see off a traveler /to/'], **uğurla-** ['- wish a departing traveler a safe journey, - wish sb Godspeed, - send or - see sb off /to/'].

faks gönder- /A/ '- send a fax /to/': **Bu faksı biz.e kim gönderdi?** 'Who sent us this fax?'. *347:19.* communications: - telegraph. → = **faks çek-** → **çek- 9, faksla-** ['- fax sth /to/'].

geri gönder- '- send back /to/' [geri 'back, rear, the space behind']: **Aldığım bilgisayar bozuk çıktı, geri göndereceğim.** 'The computer I bought turned out to be defective. I'm going to send it back.' **Bu {yoğurt/peynir/süt} bozuk. Bakkala geri göndereceğim.** 'This {yogurt/cheese/milk} is spoiled. I'm going to send it back to the grocery store.' *481:4.* restitution: - restore. → {geri ver-/iade et-} ['- return sth, - give or - take sth back /to/'] → **ver- 1,** ≠ **geri al- 1** ['- take back (here)'] → **al- 1,** ≠ **geri getir-** ['- bring back (here)'].

gör- [ÜR] 1 '- see': S: **Görüyor musun? Benzinci tam köşede.** 'Q: Do you see [it]? The gas station is right [there] on the corner.' C: **Evet, görüyorum.** 'A: Yes, I see it.' • For present time, with verbs of thinking, perception, feeling, etc., Turkish usually has the present continuous tense, i.e., -iyor, while the corresponding English usually has the simple present tense, as above. NON-verbal noun as object: **Asuman'ı sinemada gördüm.** 'I saw Asuman at the movies.' {**Pasaportunuzu/Kimliğinizi** [or **Hüviyetinizi]} görebilir miyim?** 'May I see {your passport/your ID}?' * **Lale'yi gören var mı?** '{Has anyone seen Lale?/lit., Is there anyone who has seen Lale?}' * **Epeydir sizi**

gör.EME.dik. '{I/We} haven't seen [lit., haven't BEEN ABLE to see] you for a long time.' • **a)** The first person plural suffix, here -dik, is frequently used as a polite form for the first person singular. **b)** Turkish uses the inability form, here -EME, in certain situations where the equivalent is not common in English. In this case the inability form is more polite because it suggests a desire that could not be fulfilled. * **Bana yalan söyleme, kitabımı sen aldın,** * **kendi {gözümle/gözlerimle} gördüm.** 'Don't lie to me! It was you who took my book. * I saw you [lit., it, i.e., the event] {with my own eyeS}!' Upon meeting a friend you might say: * **Seni {a: iyi/b: neşesiz} gördüm.** 'It SEEMS to me you're {a: {in good spirits/happy}/b: {unhappy/depressed} [lit., ** I SAW you (in) good spirits...]}' • In reference to a PRESENT condition, certain common Turkish verbs designating a state, i.e., a feeling, emotion, or sensation, often have the simple PAST tense, but the equivalent English has the simple PRESENT tense. * **Neler gördük neler!** 'You can't imagine the things we saw [lit., ** What things we saw, what things]!' **Görmedim, duymadım, bilmiyorum de.mekle iş.in iç.i.nden çıkabileceğini mi sanıyorsun?** 'Do you think that by saying "I didn't see it, I didn't hear it, I don't know" you'll be able to get out of this predicament?' * **Babaannemin gözleri iyi görmüyor.** 'My grandmother [on my father's side] doesn't see well [lit., ** My grandmother's eyes don't see well].'
Proverbs: **Erken süpür, el görsün; akşam süpür er görsün.** 'Sweep [your house] early for others to see [lit., let others see]; sweep it in the evening for your husband to see [lit., let the husband see].' **İşitmek görmek gibi değildir.** 'Hearing is not like [i.e., as effective as] seeing.' Seeing is believing. **Ölüm.Ü gören hastalığ.A razı olur.** 'He who sees θ death will be content WITH illness.'
VERBAL noun as object: **Oya'nın kapıyı açtığ.ı.nı görmedim.** 'I didn't see that Oya [f.] had opened the door.' **Oya'nın kapıyı {ne zaman/nasıl} açtığ.ı.nı görmedim.** 'I didn't see {when/how} Oya had opened the

door.' **Oya'nın kapıyı açıp açmadığ.ı.nı görmedim.** 'I didn't see whether or not Oya had opened the door.' For '- see' in the sense of '- understand' as in 'I see what you mean', → **anla-**. *27:12.* vision: - see.

2 /olarak/ '- regard or - see /θ [sb or sth], AS/, - look /UPON [sb or sth] AS/, - consider /θ [sb, sth]/': **Bu yılın şampiyonu OLARAK Beşiktaş'ı görüyorum.** 'I regard Beşiktaş [i.e., a soccer team] AS this year's champion.' **Herkes başkası.nı {problemler.in/ sorunlar.ın} sorumlu.su OLARAK görüyor.** 'Everyone regards someone else [AS] responsible for the problems.' **Ben kendimi dünya vatandaşı OLARAK görüyorum.** 'I see myself AS a citizen of the world.' *952:11.* belief: - think. → = /A, olarak/ **bak-** → **bak-** 4, = /I/ **say-4**.

3 /DAn/ '- experience, - be the object of sth /from/ sb': Proverb: **Çok yaşayan, çok görür.** 'He who lives long {sees/experiences} much.' *570: * 19.* learning: PHR. experience is the best teacher. **Annem.den büyük {sevgi/iyilik/yakınlık} gördüm.** 'I experienced great {love/goodness/closeness} from my mother.' When sb has sneezed, you say: * **Çok yaşa!** 'Bless you [lit., Live long!]' He responds: **Sen de gör!** or *more formally* * **Siz de görün.** 'Same to you [lit., 'You too {see/experience} it', i.e., a long life]!' *830:8.* event: - experience. → = **uğra-** 2 ['- meet /WITH/, - encounter /θ/, - experience, - be up against', usually a difficult situation], = **karşılaş-** 3 ['- face /θ/, - be confronted /with/, - encounter /θ/, - experience /θ/, - meet /with/, - be up against'], = **ye-** 2.

âdet gör- '- have one's period, - menstruate' [A **âdet** 'menses']: **Âdet gördüğüm için denize girmek istemiyorum.** 'I don't want to go swimming in the ocean today because I'm having my period.' **Düzenli âdet görüyor musunuz?** 'Are you having regular periods?' **Bir süredir âdet görmüyorum.** 'I haven't had a period for some time.' *12:18.* excretion: - menstruate. → = **aybaşı ol-** → **ol-** 10.1.

* {**düş/rüya**} **gör-** (1) '- dream, - HAVE a dream', lit., ** '- {SEE/EXPERIENCE} a dream' [{**düş**/A. **rüya**} 'dream']: A: * **Dün gece {çok ilginç/kötü} bir düş gördüm.** 'A: I had a {very interesting/bad} dream last night.' B: * **Düş.ün.de ne gördün?** 'B: What did you DREAM ABOUT [lit., ** What did you see in your dream]?' Proverb: **Korkulu rüya görmektense uyanık durmak evladır.** 'It is better to lie awake than to have bad [lit., frightening] dreams.' *985:17.* imagination: - dream. → **kâbus gör-** ['- have a nightmare'].
(2) '- imagine, - build up hopes concerning': One sibling to another: **Sen düş görüyorsun.** * **Babam senin Halil ile evlenmen.E izin vermez.** 'You're just dreaming. {Dad/Father} [lit., {My dad/My father}] won't let you marry Halil [lit., ** will not give permission FOR your marrying...].' For '- dream' in the sense of a vision of the future, as in 'I am dreaming about the vacation I'm going to take', → **hayal kur-** → **kur-** 1. *985:17.* imagination: - dream.

{**eğitim/öğrenim/tahsil**} **gör-** '- have an education, - be educated' [**eğitim** 1 'education'. 2 'training', **öğrenim** 'education, schooling', A. **tahsil** (. -) 'education; being educated']: **Yeni başkanımız Amerika Birleşik Devletleri.n'de ekonomi eğitimi görmüş.** 'Our new prime minister studied economics in the United States.' **Hakan oldukça iyi bir eğitim görmüş kıymetli gençlerimiz.den bir.i.dir.** 'Hakan is one of our admirable [lit., valuable] young people who have had quite a good education.' S: **Erdal'ı tanır mısın?** 'Q: Do you know Erdal?' C: **Evet, tanırım. Hiç eğitim görmemiş cahil.in bir.i.dir.** 'A: Yes, I know him. He's an ignoramus who has had no education at all.' *570:11.* learning: - be taught, - receive instruction. → **oku-** 2 ['- study a subject'], **tahsil et-** ['- study a subject', usually as a major field of interest, not as in '- study one's lessons'].

* **kâbus gör-** '- HAVE a nightmare' [A. **kâbus** (- -) 'nightmare']: **Çocuğ.u ter bastı,** * **kâbus mu görüyor ne!** 'The child has broken out in a sweat [lit., ** sweat has

covered the child]. * Is he having a nightmare or what?' *985:17.* imagination: - dream. → {düş/rüya} gör- 1 ['- dream, - HAVE a dream'].

* kurs gör- '- TAKE a course' [F. kurs 'course']: **Bölümümüzde okuyan Amerikalı öğrenciler bir yıl Türkçe kurs.u gördüler.** 'The American students who are studying in our department took a one-year Turkish course.' **Şu anda bir Türkçe kurs.u görüyorum.** 'At present I'm taking a Turkish course.' **Geçen yaz bilgisayar kurs.u gördük.** 'Last summer we took a computer course.' *570:11.* learning: - be taught, - receive instruction.

öğrenim gör-. → {eğitim/öğrenim/tahsil} gör- above.

rüya gör-. → {düş/rüya} gör- above.

tedavi gör- '- receive or - undergo treatment, - be treated' [A. tedavi (. - .) 'treatment']: * **Babam geçen yıl Amerikan Hastanesinde dört ay {kanser tedavi.si/ psikolojik tedavi} gördü.** 'Last year my father was treated {for cancer/for a psychological disorder} for four months at the American Hospital [lit., ** experienced cancer treatment...].' *91:29.* therapy: - undergo treatment.

4 '- carry out, - perform; - furnish, - provide, - see to': **ihtiyacını gör-** '- defecate, - urinate' [A. ihtiyaç (. . -) 'need'], lit., ** '- see (to) one's need': S: **En yakın {a: tuvalet/b: helâ/c: WC [pronounce: ve ce]/d: 100 numara} nerede acaba? Çok tuvalet.İM geldi, bekleyemeyeceğim.** 'Q: Where is the nearest {a: restroom [*or* toilet]/b: toilet/c: WC/d: toilet [*or* john]}, I wonder? I really have to go. I can't wait.' C: **Şu ağacın altında ihtiyacını görebilirsin.** 'A: You can do it under that tree [lit., ** You can see to your need...].' *12:13.* excretion: - defecate; *12:14.* excretion: - urinate. → **tuvalet yap-** ['- have a bowel movement *or* BM, - urinate, - do one's business, - use the facilities, the restroom; - make one's toilet, i.e., usually for a woman to dress or to arrange her hair'] → yap- 3, = **tuvalete git-** ['- go to the restroom, - use the toilet'] → git- 1a,

büyük aptes yap- ['- have a bowel movement, - defecate', *formal, polite*] → yap- 3, **dışarı[.ya] çık-** 2. Same. → çık- 2, **çiş {yap-/et-}** ['- urinate, - piss, - pee'] → yap- 3, **küçük aptes yap-** ['- urinate', *formal, polite*] → yap- 3, **su dök-** ['- take a {pee/piss}, - urinate'] → dök- 3.

iş gör- '- work, - do the job, - serve the purpose' [iş 'job, task, work']: * **Bu {makina/âlet} ne iş görüyor?** '{What does this {machine/instrument} do?/What's this {machine/instrument} used for?}' **Al şunu dene, * belki iş görür.** '{Here, try this./lit., Take this, try it.} * {It may serve the purpose./It may work./It may do the job.}' **Bu bilgisayar fena değil ama ben.İM iş.İM.i görmez, bana daha ileri bir model lâzım.** 'This computer isn't bad, but it doesn't {serve MY purpose/do what I want}. I need a more up-to-date [lit., ** advanced] model.' *407:4.* accomplishment: - accomplish; *994:3.* expedience: - expedite one's affair.

* **masraf gör-** '- meet expenses, - finance, - pay for' [A. masraf 'expense, outlay']: **Üniversite öğrenimim boyunca okul masraflarımı amcam gördü.** 'My [paternal] uncle paid my school expenses throughout my {college/university} education.' **Uluslararası İstanbul Festivali'nin tüm masraflarını İstanbul belediyesi görecek.** 'The municipality of Istanbul will meet all the expenses of the International Istanbul Festival.' *729:15.* finance, investment: - finance. → = **masraf karşıla-** → karşıla- 2, = **para {harca-/sarf et-}** ['- spend money'] → {harca-/sarf et-} 1, = **masraf çek-** ['- foot the bill, - pay', *informal, jocular*] → çek- 5, = **masraf {et-/yap-}, öde-** ['- pay /for/'], **masrafa gir-** ['- spend a lot of money on sth or to get sth done, - have a lot of expenses, - incur great expense'], **masraftan {kaç-/kaçın-}** ['- avoid /θ/ expense, - economize'] → kaç- 2.

görevden al-. → al- 1.

görevlendir- [ir] /lA/ '- charge, - entrust sb /with/, - give sb the task /OF/, - make sb responsible /FOR/, - put sb in charge /OF/' [görev 'task, duty' + verb-forming suf. -lAn = görevlen- '- be assigned' + caus. suf. -DIr]: * **Öğretmen sınıf.ın temizliğ.i İLE beni görevlendirdi.** 'The teacher made me responsible FOR keeping the classroom clean [lit., ** for the cleanliness of the classroom].' *615:11.* commission: - appoint; *641:12.* duty: - obligate. → = {**ata- /tayin et-**}.

görevlendiril- [ir] /lA, {tarafından/CA}/ '- be charged, entrusted /with, by/, - be given the task /OF, by/, - be made responsible /FOR, by/, - be put in charge /OF, by/' [görevlendir- + pass. suf. -Il]: **Bakanlık tarafından {bu iş.le/bu işi yap.mak.la} görevlendirildiniz. Başarılar dilerim!** 'You were charged by the Ministry {with this task/with carry.ing out this task}. I wish you success!' *615:11.* commission: - appoint; *641:12.* duty: - obligate. → = {**atan-/tayin edil-**}, = **tayin ol-** → ol- 12, ≠ **görevden alın-** → alın- 1, ≠ **görevine son veril-** → son veril- → veril-, ≠ **işinden ol-** → ol- 7.

görül- [ür] [gör- + pass. suf. -Il] 1 '- be seen, observed': **Hasta.nın nefes almak.TA güçlük çektiğ.i görüldü.** 'It was observed that the patient was having trouble {θ/in} breathing.' **Şimdiye kadar * böylesi görülmedi ve belki de görülmeyecek.** 'Such a thing has not been seen up to now nor is it likely to be seen [in the future].' *27:12.* vision: - see.

2 /olarak/ '- be regarded, looked UPON, considered /AS/': **Kapkaç olayları hırsızlık OLARAK görülmeli.** 'Purse snatching incidents must be regarded AS {theft/thievery}.' *952:11.* belief: - think.

3 /{tarafından/CA}/ '- be taken care of, attended to, dealt with, handled /by/': * **İşlerimiz nerede görülecek?** 'Where can we get our business [i.e., passport applications, renewals, etc.] taken care of? [lit., Where will our affairs be {dealt with/taken care of}?]' **Pasaport** **işler.i.nin görüldüğ.ü yer burası mı?** 'Is this the place where passport matters are handled?' *982:5.* attention: - attend to.

görün- [ür] [gör- + refl. suf. -In] 1 '- appear, - come into sight; - be seen, - be visible'. • This verb is not used with {tarafından/CA}, i.e., not as in 'She has not been seen BY anybody.' For such usage see görül-: {**Çoktandır/Epeydir**} **görün- medin, * nerelerdeydin?** 'You haven't been seen about {for quite a while}. * Where've you been?' **Ayşe iki gündür görünmüyor.** 'Ayşe hasn't {been seen/appeared} for two days.' **Bu evin bütün odalarından deniz görünüyor. Ne kadar güzel!** 'The ocean {is visible/can be seen} from all the rooms of this house. How nice!' **Kraliçe balkonda göründü ve halkı selâmladı.** 'The queen appeared on the balcony and greeted the people.' **Güneş bugün hiç görünmüyor.** 'The sun hasn't appeared at all today.' Proverb: **Dibi görünmeyen sudan içme.** 'Don't drink from [a source of] water, the bottom of which isn't visible.', i.e., Don't set out to do something for which you lack the necessary information or qualifications. *31:4.* visibility: - show; *33:8.* appearance: - appear.

2 '- seem, - look, - create an impression of': **Bugün çok {a: heyecanlı/b: sevinçli/c: üzgün/ d: kederli/e: düşünceli/f: yorgun} görünüyorsun.** 'You look very {a: thrilled [or excited]/b: happy/c: unhappy [or sad]/d: sad/e: thoughtful/f: tired} today.' A: **Turan, canını sıkan bir şey var mı?** 'A: Is something bothering you, Turan?' B: **Yoo, * neden sordun?** 'B: No, * why do [lit., did] you ask?' A: * **Son günlerde biraz dalgın, biraz durgun görünüyorsun da.** 'A: Well, it's just that you've been looking a little absentminded, a little withdrawn lately.' **Maşallah, annen ne kadar genç görünüyor!** 'My, how young your mother looks!' A: * **Artık geç oldu. Cengiz gelmeyecek herhalde.** 'A: * It's already late. Cengiz probably isn't going to come.' B: * **Öyle görünüyor.** 'B: {It seems so./So it seems.}' *33:10.* appearance: - appear to be.

gibi görün- '- look like' in reference to a condition or type, not a particular person: S: Hava nasıl? 'Q: How's the weather?' C: Yağacak gibi görünüyor. 'A: It looks like it's going to rain.' → = benze- 2. # Makyaj yapınca * kırkında gibi görünüyor. 'When she puts on makeup, * she looks like she's 40 years old [lit., ** in her forty].' 33:10. appearance: - appear to be. Ders almamış gibi görünüyoruz. 'It looks like we haven't learned any lessons.', i.e., from an experience. For '- look like a person' as in '- he looks like his father', → = gibi göster- → göster- 2, = benze- 1.

görüş- [ür] [gör- + recip. suf. -Iş] 1 /lA/ '- see one another; - meet /with/; - talk, - speak, - confer, or - discuss /with/, - see [i.e., confer]': Siz.in.le mutlaka görüşmem lâzım! 'I absolutely must speak with you!' Siz.in.le {hemen/en kısa zamanda/yüzyüze} görüşmem lâzım! 'I must speak with you {right away/as soon as possible/face to face}!' İlk fırsatta görüşelim. 'Let's get together {the first chance we get/lit., at the first opportunity}.' Ne zamandır görüş.EME.dik. Nasılsın? 'We haven't seen [lit., haveN'T BEEN ABLE to see] one another for ages [colloq. 'Long time no see.']. How are you?' S: Kimin.le görüşmek istiyorsunuz? 'Q: Who do you wish to speak with?' C: {a: Nilgün'le/b: Şefiniz.le/c: Menejeriniz.le/d: Patronu-nuz.la/e: Müdürünüz.le/f: Amiriniz.le} görüşmek istiyorum. 'A: I would like to speak {a: with Nilgün/b: with your manager/c: with your boss/d: with your director [of a company]/e: with your superviser [in a bank or factory]/f: with your superior}.' Gidelim, konsolos.la görüşelim. 'Let's go [and] {talk with/discuss it with} the consul.' Talking about sth: * Seninle önemli bir mesele.yi görüşmemiz gerek. '{You and I/We} have to discuss an important matter.' Siyasi diyaloğ.un her iki ülke arasında nasıl geliştiğ.i.ni ve gelişeceğ.i.ni görüştük. 'We discussed how the political dialogue between both countries had developed and would develop.'

On the telephone: S1: Deniz'le görüşmek istiyorum. 'Q1: I'd like to speak with Deniz.' S2: Ahmet'le görüşebilir miyim? 'Q2: Could I speak with Ahmet?' C1: Bir dakika efendim. 'A1: Just a moment please {sir/ma'am}.' C2: Çıkmışlar efendim. 'A2: {He/They} have [just] stepped out {sir/ma'am}.' Again on the telephone: * Kim.in.le görüşüyorum acaba? '{Who am I speaking with?/With whom am I speaking}, may I ask [lit., I wonder]?' = Kim arıyor? 'Who's calling? [lit., ** Who is seeking?]' → ara- 2. * Kendisiyle bazı şeyler görüşmek istiyorum. '{There are some things I'd like to speak to him about./There are some matters I would like to discuss with him.}' 524:20. speech: - speak; 541:11. conversation: - confer.

Leave takings: Görüştüğümüz.E çok memnun oldum! 'Very pleased to meet you [lit., ** AT our having met each other]!' More common in the same situation: Tanıştığımız.A çok memnun oldum! 'Very please to meet you [lit., ** AT our having gotten acquainted with each other!] {Yarın/Sonra} görüşürüz. 'See you {tomorrow/later} [lit., WE'LL see EACH OTHER...]' or {Tekrar/Yine} görüşürüz. 'We'll meet {again}.' Yine görüşmek üzere. 'Till we meet again.' {Bu gece/Yarın/Yakında} görüşmek üzere. 'See you {tonight/tomorrow/soon}.' Arasıra görüşelim. 'Let's get together now and then.' Tekrar ne zaman görüşebiliriz? 'When can we {get together/meet} again?' 188:22. departure: INTERJ. farewell!

2 /lA/ '- make or - place a phone call /TO/': Operatöre: * Türkiye İLE görüşmek istiyorum. 'To the operator: * I'd like to make a call TO Turkey.' * Ödemeli görüşmek istiyorum. 'I'd like to make a collect call.' To the receptionist: * {58'DEN/58 no'lu (read: numaralı) oda.DAN} Kemal Şahin İLE görüşmek istiyorum. 'I'd like to make a call TO Kemal Şahin, {WHOSE [ROOM] NUMBER IS 58/[WHO can be reached AT] room no 58}.' 347:18. communications: - telephone.

görüş savun-. → {fikir/görüş} savun-. → savun-.

görüşe katıl-. → {düşünceye/fikre/ görüşe} katıl-. → katıl- 3.

göster- [ir] /A/ [irr. caus. of gör-] 1 '- show, - demonstrate /to/': NON- verbal noun as object: Suna yeni CD'leri [pronounce: si dileri] san.A gösterdi mi? 'Did Suna [f.] {show θ you the new CDs/show the new CDs TO you}?' Bu pantolonu beğenmedim. * Bir başkası.nI gösterir misiniz? 'I didn't like {these pants/i.e., this pair of pants}. * Would you show me another pair?' To challenge sb you might say: * Ha[y]di göster[in] kendini[zi]! 'Come on, show what you can do [lit., ** show yourself]!' Proverb: Isıracak it dişini göstermez. 'The dog that is going to bite doesn't show its teeth.', i.e., doesn't give a sign that it will attack, i.e., Dangerous people often appear harmless, so beware.
VERBAL noun as object: Satıcı televizyon.un çalıştığ.ı.nI gösterdi. 'The salesman demonstrated that the TV worked.' Satıcı televizyon.un nasıl {çalıştığ.ı.nı/kullanılma.sı gerektiğ.i.ni} gösterdi. 'The salesman showed how the TV {worked/should be used}.' Satıcı televizyon.un çalışma.sı.nı gösterdi. 'The salesman showed how the TV worked [lit., ** the working of the TV].'

'for a timepiece, clock or watch, - show, say the time'. With the main times of the day: The forms below with geçe or kala are apparently not in common use with this verb: • Note the accusative case suffix I: Saat {a: bir.İ/b: bir.İ beş geçe.yİ/c: bir.İ çeyrek geçe.yİ/d: bir buçuğ.U/e: iki.yE yirmi beş kala.yI/f: iki.yE çeyrek kala.yI/g: 12'yİ/h: geceyarı.sı.nI/i: öğle.yİ} gösteriyordu. 'The clock {said/showed} θ {a: 1 o'clock/b: five past 1/c: a quarter past 1/d: one thirty/e: 25 to 2/f: a quarter to 2/g: twelve o'clock [noon or midnight]/h: midnight/i: noon}.' Eve geldiğinde kolundaki saat altı.yI gösteriyordu. 'When he came home, his wristwatch [lit., ** the watch on his arm] {said/showed} six o'clock.' 348:5. manifestation: - manifest.

Allah göstermesin! 'God forbid!': Allah göstermesin, * baş.ı.na bir iş gelse biz ne yaparız? 'God forbid * if something should happen to him [lit., ** come to his head], what would we do?' Baş 'head' above represents the whole person. A: Bana öyle geliyor ki bu hastalık * beni bitirecek. 'A: It seems to me that this illness * is going to finish me off.' B: Allah göstermesin, * o ne biçim söz! 'B: God forbid! * {Don't say such a thing./Don't talk like that./[lit., ** What kind of an utterance is that?]' 1007:18b. protection: expressions to protect against misfortune; 1011: * 22. hindrance: * expressions to prevent unfavorable occurrences.

başarı göster- /DA/ '- be successful /in/', lit., '- demonstrate success /in/' [başarı 'success']: * Dersler.i.nde {büyük bir /üstün} başarı gösteriyordu. 'He was very successful in his lessons [lit., ** He demonstrated {a great/outstanding} success in his lessons].' Öğretmen: Dersler.in.de gösterdiğin başarı.DAN DOLAYI tebrik ederim. 'Teacher: Congratulations on your success in your classes [lit., I congratulate (you) {ON/for} the success you demonstrated in your classes].' Öğrenci: Çok teşekkür ederim efendim. 'Thank you very much, {sir/ma'am}.' * Futbol takımımız final.E çıkma başarı.sı.nı gösterdi. 'Our soccer team succeeded in reaching the finals [lit., ** demonstrated the reaching-finals success].' 409:9. success: - score a success. → = /I/ başar-.

* kolaylık göster- '- make sth easy /FOR/, - facilitate matters /FOR/, - help /θ/, colloq. - give sb a break' [kolaylık 'easement']: Kadın adam.A yalvarıyordu: "Lütfen ban.A biraz kolaylık gösterin. Borcumu yarın ödeyeceğim". 'The woman was pleading WITH the man: "Please help me [colloq., Give me a break., lit., ** 'Show a little easement to me']. Let me pay the money I owe [lit., my debt] tomorrow".' 449:11. aid: - aid; 1013:7. facility: - facilitate. → yardım elini uzat- ['- extend a helping hand /to/, - help out'], yardım et- ['- help /θ/, - assist /θ/'], yardımcı ol- ['- help /θ/, - assist /θ/, - be of assistance /to/, - be helpful /to/'] → ol- 12, yardımda bulun-

[/A/ '- help /θ/, - assist /θ/, - aid /θ/, - provide aid /to/', *formal*], **el ele ver-** ['- help one another'] → ver- 1, ≠ {güçlük/zorluk} çıkar- ['- make or create difficulties /FOR/'] → çıkar- 7.

saygı göster- /A/ '- show respect /{to/FOR}/, - behave respectfully /TOWARD/, - treat with respect, - respect' [s a y g ı 'respect']: {Büyüklerin.E/Başkaları.nın fikirler.i.nE} saygı göster-melisin! 'You must show respect {FOR your elders./FOR the ideas of others.}' *143:10.* kindness, benevolence: - be considerate; *155:5.* respect: - do or - pay hommage to.

* **tepki göster-** /A/ '- react /to/' [tepki 'reaction']: S: Ayrılmak istediğini söylediğin zaman Ayhan nasıl bir tepki gösterdi? 'Q: When you said that you wanted to break up [with him], how did Ayhan react?' [The same idea is frequently expressed as follows: Ayhan'ın tepki.si ne oldu? 'What was Ayhan's reaction?'] C: {a: Şaşırdı./b: Üzüldü./c: Sinir-lendi./d: Kızdı./e: Hiç bir tepki göstermedi.} 'A: {a: He was surprised./b: He was sorry./c: He got {angry/upset}./d: He got angry./e: He didn't react at all.}' Ayrılmak isteme.n.E Ayhan nasıl bir tepki gösterdi? 'How did Ayhan react TO your ask.ING to leave?' *902:5.* reaction: - react. → = karşıla- 3.

yol göster- [yol 'road, way'] (1) /A/ '- show /θ/ sb how to get to a place, - point out the way /to/ sb': Ban.A haritada Isparta'dan Antalya'ya giden yolu gösterir misin? 'On the map would you show θ me the {road/way} from Isparta to Antalya?' *348:5.* manifestation: - manifest.
(2) /A/ '- advise /θ/, - give advice /to/, - guide, - suggest a solution to a problem': Ne yapacağımız.A bir türlü karar veremedik. Biz.E yol gösterir misin? 'We just haven't been able to decide what to do. Would you give us some advice?' Proverb: Tekerlek kırıldıktan sonra yol gösteren çok olur. 'After the wheel [of the cart] has broken, there are many people who will show the way.', i.e., There are always many people ready to offer

advice when it's too late. *422:5.* advice: - advise.

2 '- appear, - appear to be, - look like': S: * Sen.ce şu kadın kaç yaş.ı.nda gösteriyor? 'Q: How old would you say that woman looks? [lit., ** According to you in what year does that woman show?]' C: * Ben.ce 40'ın {alt.ı.nda/ üst.ü.nde} gösteriyor. 'A: I'd say she appears to be {under/over} 40.' Anneniz yaşını hiç göster-miyor. 'Your mother doesn't show her age at all.' * Yaşı 40'ın üst.ü.nde göstermiyor. 'She doesn't {look/appear to be} over 40 [lit., ** Her age doesn't show over forty].' *33:10.* appearance: - appear to be. → **benze-** 2 ['- look like' in the sense of '- resemble'].

* **gibi göster-** '- look like' in reference to a condition or type, not a particular person: * Makyaj yapınca kırkında gibi gösteriyor. 'When she puts on makeup, she looks like she's 40 years old.' *33:10.* appearance: - appear to be. For reference to a person as in '- he looks like his father', → = **gibi görün-** → görün- 2, **benze-** 1 ['- appear, - look like, - seem'].

gösteri yap-. → yap- 3.

gösteriş yap-. → yap- 3.

götür- [ür] /DAn, A/ '- take [away] /from (somewhere), to (somewhere else)/': * Acaba Erenköy.den Taksim'e kaç.A götürürler? 'I wonder how much they'll charge to take sb from Erenköy to Taksim [lit., I wonder FOR how much they'll take sb from Erenköy to Taksim].' Bu çantaları {a: taksi.ye/b: tren.e/c: otobüs.e/d: çıkış.a} götürün. 'Take these bags {a: to the taxi/b: to the train/c: to the bus/d: to the exit}.' Sizi {ev.e/otel.e/havaalanı.na} götüreyim. 'Let me take you {θ home/to the hotel/to the airport}.' Lütfen beni doktor.a götürün. 'Please take me to a doctor.' Mesut kızını okul.a götürdü. 'Mesut took his daughter to school.' Mümkün olduğu kadar az eşya götür! 'Take as few things as possible.' • For '- bring FROM THERE to here', → ≠ **getir-**. You want sb, a waiter, etc., to clear sth away: Lütfen {bunu/bunları} götürün. 'Please take {this/these} away.' → = kaldır- 3. # Hastayı hastane.ye götürdüler. 'They took the patient to the hospital.' → = kaldır- 5. *176:11.* transferal, transportation: - remove. → ilet- 1 ['- take or - convey /to/, - forward, - pass on /to/'], ulaştır- 1 ['- transport, - convey, - bring or - get sth /to/'].

göz at-. → at- 1.

göz kırp-. → kırp-.

göz kulak ol-. → ol- 12.

göz önünde tut-. → tut- 2.

göz yaşı dök-. → dök- 1.

göz yum-. → yum-.

gözden geçir-. → geçir- 1.

gözden kaç-. → kaç- 1.

gözden kaçır-. → kaçır- 2.

gözle- [r] 1 '- notice, - observe' [göz 'eye' + verb-forming suf. -lA]: Türkiye'ye gittiğimde Türk-ler.in çok misafirperver olduğ.u.nu gözledim. 'When I went to Turkey, I observed that the Turks were very hospitable.' *982:6.* attention: - heed. → = dikkat et- 2, = farket- 1, = farkına var-, = dikkatini çek- → çek- 1.

2 '- watch, - observe': Onu çalışırken gözledim, gerçekten çok titiz birisi. 'I observed him {working/while (he was) working}. He is really a very meticulous person.' *27:13.* vision: - look. → = izle- 3, = seyret-.

gözleri yaşar-. → yaşar-.

gözlerine inanaMA-. → inan- 1.

gözlerini yaşart-. → yaşart-.

grip ol-. → ol- 10.2.

gurur duy-. → duy- 3.

gururlan- [ır] /lA/ '- be or - feel arrogantly proud /OF/, - pride oneself arrogantly /ON/', negative implication [A. gurur (. -) 'pride, excessive pride', mostly negative implication] + verb-forming suf. -lAn]: A reprimand that might be addressed to sb exhibiting excessive pride: Gururlanma padişahım, senden büyük Allah var. 'Don't be {so/too} proud of yourself, my Sultan, [remember that] God is greater than you.' VERBAL noun as object: Mal mülk sahibi olmak.LA gururlanmak ne kadar {saçma/anlamsız} bir şey! 'How foolish [a thing] it is to pride oneself ON one's possessions [lit., ON being the possessor of property]!' *136:5.* pride: - take pride; *141:8.* arrogance: - give oneself airs. → = gurur duy- 2 → duy- 3.

{gücü/takatı} tüken-. → tüken-.

gücü yet-. → yet-.

gücüne git-. → {zoruna/gücüne} git-. → git- 1 b).

{güçlük/zorluk} çek-. → çek- 5.

{güçlük/zorluk} çıkar-. → çıkar- 7.

güçlükle karşılaş-. → {zorlukla/güçlükle} karşılaş-. → karşılaş- 3.

gül- [er] 1 /A/ '- laugh /AT/', amusement: S1: {Niye/Neden} gülüyorsun? 'Q1: {Why} are you laughing?' S2: Ne.yE gülüyorsun? 'Q2: What are you laughing AT?' C: Ayşegül'ün anlattığı fıkra.yA gülüyoruz. 'A: We are laughing AT the anecdote [that] Ayşegül [f.] told.' Proverb: Çok gülen çok ağlar. 'He who laughs much weeps much.' → ≠ ağla-, ≠ gözyaşı dök- → dök- 1. *116:8.* rejoicing: - laugh.

Güle güle. [gül- '- laugh' + adv.-forming suf. -[y]A = güle lit., 'laughingly'] (1) 'Goodbye', said by the person REMAINING. = informal: Eyvallah! [The person LEAVING says either 1. Allahaısmarladık. (usually pronounced Alâsmarladık.) 'Goodbye (lit., ** We entrusted you to God).' or 2. Hoşça kal[ın]! 'Goodbye., So long!, Have a good day.'] *188:22.* departure: INTERJ. farewell!
(2) Güle güle 'Bye bye', in the sense of 'Get lost!, Be off!', i.e., not in response to the 2 phrases under (1) above said by a person departing.

908:31. ejection: INTERJ. go away!
→ = **Bas git!** → bas- 1, = **Defol!**
→ ol- 12.
(3) In several widely used polite phrases expressing good wishes. [In the same situations, in place of or together with them, either before or after them, the phrase **Hayırlı olsun!** 'May it be beneficial!' may be used]. The response to all these polite phrases is: {**Teşekkür ederim./Sağol.**} '{Thank you./ Thanks.}'

* **Güle güle giyin[iz].** 'What a nice...!, How nice!' Often used with the name of an item of clothing: e.g., dress, shirt, etc., lit., 'Wear it with pleasure!', a polite expression used when complimenting sb on a new item of clothing. *504: * 20.* courtesy: polite expressions.

* **Güle güle kullanın[ız].** 'What a nice...!, How nice!' Often used with the name of an item for use, lit., 'Use it with pleasure.', a polite expression used to address sb who has acquired a new item for use: **A: Yeni bir {Araba/Televizyon} aldım.** 'A: I've bought a new {car/TV}.' **B: Güle güle kullanın.** 'B: Use it with pleasure.' **A: {Teşekkür ederim./Sağol.}** 'A: {Thank you./Thanks.}' *504: * 20.* courtesy: polite expressions.

* **Güle güle oturun[uz]!** 'What a nice...!, How nice!' Often used with the name of a residence: apartment, house, etc., lit., 'Live [in it] with pleasure!' When visiting people who have moved to a new residence, you say the above or the following: **Yeni evinizde güle güle oturun!** '{My what a nice house!/I hope you enjoy your new house./lit., Live in your new house with pleasure.}' *504: * 20.* courtesy: polite expressions.

kahkaha ile gül- '- laugh loudly, - roar with laughter; - guffaw' [**kahkaha** 'loud laugh; guffaw']: **Şener Şen'in son filmi o kadar komikti ki seyirciler kahkaha ile güldüler.** 'Şener Şen's last film was so funny that the audience [lit., spectators] roared with laughter.' *116:8.* rejoicing: - laugh.

2 /A/ '- laugh /AT/, - mock /θ/, - make fun /OF/': Proverbs: * **Gülme komşun.A, gelir başın.a.** 'Don't

laugh AT your neighbor [for what happened to him], it [i.e., the same thing] may happen to you [lit., ** come to your head.]' **Baş** 'head' here represents the whole person. **Son gülen iyi güler.** 'He who laughs last laughs best [lit., ** laughs well].' *508:8.* ridicule: - ridicule. → /lA/ **alay et-** ['- make fun /OF/, - ridicule /θ/, - mock /θ/'], /lA/ **dalga geç-** 2 ['- make fun /OF/'] → geç- 1, /lA/ **eğlen-** 2 ['- make fun /OF/, - joke /with/ sb'].

* **bıyık altından gül-** '- laugh {UP/IN} one's sleeve, - be secretly amused, - laugh or - smile maliciously [lit., ** laugh FROM under one's moustache]': **Sen konuşurken Ahmet bıyık alt.ı.nDAN gülüyordu.** 'While you were speaking, Ahmet was laughing IN his sleeve.' *508:8.* ridicule: - ridicule.

Güle güle. → gül- above.

gülümse- [r] /A/ '- smile /AT/' [? **gül-** + verb-forming suf. **-ImsA**]: **Ayşe, Ahmet'i görünce gülümsedi.** 'When Ayşe saw Ahmet, she smiled.' **Ayşe Ahmet'E gülümsedi.** 'Ayşe smiled AT Ahmet.' *116:7.* rejoicing: - smile. → ≠ **yüzü buruş-** 1 → buruş-, ≠ **kaş çat-**.

gün al-. → al- 3.

gün ver-. → ver- 1.

güneş aç-. → aç- 8.

güneş banyosu yap-. → yap- 3.

güneş bat-. → bat- 1.

güneş çarp-. → çarp- 1.

güneş çık-. → çık- 3.

güneş doğ-. → doğ- 2.

güneşlen- [ir] '- sunbathe, - sun oneself' [**güneş** 'sun' + verb-forming suf. **-lA** = **güneşle-** '- sunbathe', not in common use, + refl. suf. **-n**]: **Ömer yüzüyor, Aslı da kumsalda güneşleniyor.** 'Ömer is swimming, and Aslı [f.] is sunning herself on the beach.' *1019:19.* heating: - insolate. → = **güneş banyosu yap-** → yap-3.

gürültü {et- [eDer]/yap- [ar]} '- make noise, - be noisy' [gürültü 'noise']: Çocuklar gürültü etmeyin, * başım ağrıyor. 'Children, don't make [so much] noise! * I have a headache [lit., my head aches].' * Gürültü yapmayın. 'Quiet please [lit., Don't make noise].' *53:9.* loudness: - be noisy; *352:7.* publication: poster: * specific signs.

güven- [ir] /A/ '- trust /θ/, - rely /{ON/UPON}/, - depend /ON/, - have confidence /IN/' [güven 'trust' + verb-forming suf. -θ]: Paralarımı Ali'yE bırakabilirim çünkü o.nA güveniyorum. 'I can leave my money WITH Ali because I trust θ him.' Bu iş zor görünür ama yapabilirsin, san.A güveniyorum. 'This task appears difficult, but you can do it, I have confidence IN you.' Proverb: Ablası.nA güvenen kız kocasız kalmış. 'The girl who trusted θ her elder sister remained without a husband.', i.e., Don't rely on those who want the same thing you do. Kendim.E hiç güvenmiyorum. Herhalde bu sınavı geçemeyeceğim. 'I don't have any confidence IN myself at all. I probably won't be able to pass this examination.' Some words of challenge: Kendi.nE güvenen ortaya çıksın! 'Let the person who has confidence IN himself come forward!' "Türk! Övün, çalış, güven!" M.K. Atatürk. '"[O] Turk! Be proud, strive, have confidence!" M[ustafa] K[emal] Atatürk.' *952:15.* belief: - believe in. → = dayan- 2, = inan- 2, emin ol- ['- be or - become sure, certain, convinced /OF/, /θ/ that'] → ol- 12.

güvenini {kaybet-/yitir-}. → {kaybet-/yitir-}.

- H -

haber al-. → al- 3.

haber getir-. → getir-.

haber ver-. → ver- 1.

{haberiniz/bilginiz} olsun. → ol- 11. → olsun.

hacca git-. → git- 1a.

hak et- [eDer] /lA, DIğI için/ '- deserve sth /FOR, because/' [A. hak (haKKı) 1 'right'. 2 'truth']: Takımımız güzel oyun.u.yLA birinciliğ.İ hak etti. 'Our team deserved first place FOR its fine game.' Burçin bu yıl çok çalıştı, iyi bir tatil.İ hak etti. 'Burçin worked very hard this year. He {deserves/deserved} a good vacation.' Burçin bu yıl çok çalış.tığı için iyi bir tatil.İ hak etti. 'Because Burçin worked very hard this year, he {deserves/deserved} a good vacation.' Okulda kavga ettiğin için {a: okuldan uzaklaştırma ceza.sı.nı/b: bu ceza.yı} hak ettin. 'Because you {got into a fight/lit., fought} at school, you deserved {a: to be expelled [lit., deserved the distancing-from-school punishment]/b: this punishment}].' *639:5.* dueness: - deserve.

hak kazan-. → kazan- 1.

hak ver-. → ver- 1.

hakaret et- [eDer] /A/ '- insult /θ/' [A. hakaret (. - .) 'insult']: Cemal bey kendisi.nE hakaret eden komşu.su.nu mahkemeye verdi. 'Cemal bey took the neighbor who had insulted θ him to court.' Sözleri.nE dikkat et, ban.A hakaret ediyorsun. 'Watch your language [lit., your words]! You're insulting θ me.' *156:5.* disrespect: - offend.

hakikati söyle-. → {doğru/doğruyu/gerçeği/hakikati} söyle-. → söyle- 1.

hâkim ol-. → ol- 12.

hakkına tecavüz et-. → tecavüz et- 1.

hal hatır sor-. → hatır sor-. → sor-.

hallet- [halleDer] '- solve, - find a solution /for/, - resolve, - handle, - take care of, - straighten out, - settle', situation, personal problem [A. hall 'a solution, solving' + et-]: Bu mektupların {a: bigisayar.LA/b: bilgisayar.DA} yazılması gerekiyor. Bu işi halleder misiniz? 'These letters must be typed [lit., written] {a: {BY computer/WITH a computer}/b: ON a computer}. Would you {take care of/handle} this matter?' **Bu işi siz.DEN başkası halledemez.** 'No one BUT you can {solve this problem/handle this matter}.' *939:2.* solution: - solve. → **çöz- 2** ['- solve a problem, - figure sth out', usually a puzzle, mathematical problem].

hamile kal-. → **kal- 1.**

haneye tecavüz et-. → **tecavüz et- 1.**

hapı yut-. → **yut-.**

hapşır- [ır] '- sneeze': **Herhalde soğuk aldım, bugün çok sık hapşırdım.** 'I must have caught a cold. I sneezed a lot today.' When sb has sneezed, you say: * **Çok yaşa!** 'Bless you! [lit., ** Live long!]' He responds: **Sen de gör!** or *more formally* * **Siz de görün.** 'Same to you [lit., ** 'You too {see/experience} it', i.e., a long life]!' *57:2.* sibilation: - sibilate; *318:21.* * *1.* wind: - breathe.

{harca- [r]/sarf et- [eDer]} **1** /{A/için}/ '- spend, - expend /{ON [*or* FOR]/ON [*or* for]}/' [A. **harç** 'expenditure' + verb-forming suf. - A, A. **sarf** 'spending, expending']: **{emek/çaba} harca-** /için/ '- expend effort /{for/ON}/ sth, take pains /to/ do sth' [{**emek/çaba**} 'effort']: **Bütün evi {badana yap.mak için/badana yap.arken} çok emek harcadık.** 'We spent a lot of effort {to whitewash/while whitewashing} the whole house.' **Babam öldükten sonra, annem bizleri büyüt.mek için çok emek harcadı.** 'After my father died, my mother took great pains to raise us.' *403:5.* endeavor: - endeavor; *725:9.* exertion: - exert oneself. → = **emek ver-** → **ver- 1, çabala-** ['- strive /to/, - struggle /to/, - do one's best /to/'], **uğraş- 1** ['- strive, - struggle, - endeavor /TO/, - exert oneself, - put forth an effort /for/, - work hard'].

para harca- /{A/için}/ '- spend money /{ON [*or* for]/ON [*or* for]}/': **Fazla para harcamak istemiyorum.** 'I don't want to spend a lot of money.' **Cengiz bugünlerde çok para harcıyor.** 'Cengiz has been spending a lot of money these days.' **Son gezimde {a: {oteller.E/oteller için}/b: {yiyecekler.E/yiyecekler için}} çok para harcadım.** 'On my last

trip I spent a lot of money {a: ON hotels/b: ON food}.' **Bu kitaplar.A {ne kadar/kaç para} harcadınız?** '{How much/How much money} did you spend {FOR/ON} these books?' **Bu ev.in tamir.i için çok para harcadık.** 'We spent a lot of money {ON/for} the repair of this house.' Often {**harca-/sarf et-**} are used without the word **para**: **Bu ceket için elli lira.DAN fazla harcamak istemiyorum.** 'I don't want to spend more THAN 50 liras {for/ON} this jacket.' *626:5.* expenditure: - spend. → = **masraf {et-/yap-}, kazan- 1** ['- earn']. For '- save money', → **para artır-** → {**artır-/arttır-**} **2, para biriktir-** → **biriktir- 2, tasarruf et-.**

2 /için/ '- use, - use up /{to/in order to}/': **Bu pastayı yapmak için iki kilo un harcadık.** 'We used up two kilos of flour to make this cake.' *387:13.* use: - spend; *388:3.* consumption: - consume. → = **bitir- 3.**

{vakit/zaman} harca- /için/ '- spend time /{on/[in order] to}/' [{A. **vakit** (vaKTİ), A. **zaman** (. -)} 'time']: **Bu işi bitirmek için çok vakit harcadım.** 'I spent a lot of time to finish this {task/job}.' **Zaman.I {boşa/boş yere/boşuna} harcamayalım.** 'Let's not waste [the] time [lit., spend [the] time {in vain}].' *820:6.* time: - spend time.

hareket et- [eDer] [A. **hareket** 'motion, movement, activity'] **1** '- move, - stir': **Lütfen hareket etmeyin, ne isterseniz ben getirebilirim.** 'Please don't move, I can bring whatever you want.' **Böyle {kilo almay.a/ şişmanlamay.a} devam edersen, yakında hareket edemeyeceksin.** 'If you continue {to gain weight} like this, you'll soon be unable to move.' *172:5b.* motion: for sth - move. → {**kımılda-/kıpırda-**} ['- move slightly, - budge, - stir, - twitch'], ≠ **dur- 6** ['- remain, - stay /{in/at}, on/'].

2 /A/ '- leave /FOR/, - depart /FOR/', usually by means of a land vehicle, i.e., bus, train, not a boat and not a person on foot: **S: Ankara'yA ne zaman hareket ediyoruz?** 'Q: When do we {leave FOR/set out

FOR} Ankara?' C: {a: Trenimiz/b: Otobüsümüz/c: Uçağımız/d: Arabamız} [Ankara'yA] saat 10'da hareket ediyor. 'A: {a: Our train/b: Our bus/c: Our plane/d: Our car} sets out [FOR Ankara] at 10 o'clock.' Ankara tren.i saat kaçta hareket ediyor? 'At what time does the train leave for Ankara [lit., ...does the Ankara train leave]?' To passengers on a plane: * Uçağımız hareket etmek üzeredir. '{We are about to take off./lit., Our plane is about to take off.}' In the above example, kalk- may be more appropriate. *161:9.* direction: - head for; *188:8.* departure: - set out. → = kalk- 2, ≠ gel- 1, ≠ var-, ≠ ulaş- 1, ≠ eriş- 1.

3 /DAn/ '- leave /θ/, - depart /from/'. As above, usually by means of a land vehicle: S: Tren Ankara'DAN [saat] kaçta hareket etti? 'Q: At what time did the train leave θ Ankara?' C: Ankara'DAN saat 10:00'da hareket etti. 'A: It left θ Ankara at 10 o'clock.' *188:6.* departure: - depart; *188:8.* departure: - set out. → = ayrıl- 3 [also for ships], = kalk- 2 [also for planes], = yola çık- [only for persons as subjects] → çık- 2.

4 /{mAklA/ArAk}/ '- act, - behave, - do /BY...ing [or TO]/' → = davran-. # Her ülke kendi çıkar.ı.nA göre hareket eder. 'Every country acts in accord with its own interests.' *321:4.* behavior: - behave: doğru hareket et- '- do the right thing, act properly': Polis göstericilerin lideriyle {görüş.mekle/ görüş.erek} doğru hareket etti. 'The police did the right thing {by negotiat.ing [or to negotiate]} with the leader of the demonstration.' *637:2.* * 1. right: - do the right thing. → = doğrusunu yap-, = iyi et-, ≠ kötü et-.

{harf harf/harflerini} söyle-. → söyle- 1.

harmanla- [r] '- blend, - combine' [harman 'blending' + verb-forming suf. -lA]: Hazırladığınız sebzelerin hepsini incecik kıyıp salata tabağına alın ve harmanlayın. 'Chop up fine all the vegetables you have prepared, put them in a salad bowel, and blend

them.' *796:10a.* mixture: - mix; *804:3.* combination: - combine.

hasret çek-. → çek- 5.

hasta ol-. → ol- 12.

hastalan- [ır] /DIğI için, DAn/ '- become ill, - get sick, - take sick /because, {AS A RESULT Of/WITH/from}/' [P. hasta 'ill, ill person, patient' + verb-forming suf. -lAn]: Bence bu çocuk çok dondurma ye.diği için hastalandı. '{I'd say/I think} this child has gotten sick because he ate too much ice cream.' Kötü haberi duyunca üzüntü.DEN hastalandı. 'When he heard the bad news, he became ill {WITH/from} sorrow.' *85:46a.* disease: - take sick in general. → = fenalaş- 2 ['- feel faint, - feel suddenly sick, - take ill'], = fena ol- 1. Same. → ol- 10.2, = hasta ol- → ol- 10.2, = rahatsız ol- 1 ['- feel or - become indisposed, slightly ill, sick, - be under the weather'] → ol- 10.2, = /A/ yakalan- 2 ['- catch /θ/ or - come down /WITH/ an illness'], ≠ iyileş-.

haşla- [r] '- boil, - cook sth in boiling water': Öğle yemeğ.i için {yumurta/patates/sebze} haşla- dım. 'I boiled {eggs/potatoes/ vegetables} for lunch [lit., the noon meal].' Ispanağı iyice yıkayıp 5 dakika haşlayın. 'Wash the spinach and boil it for 5 minutes.' *11:4a.* cooking: - cook sth. → kayna- ['- boil' as in 'The water is boiling.'], kaynat- ['- make sth boil'].

haşlan- [ır] [haşla- + {pass./refl.} suf. -n] 1 /tarafından/ '- be boiled, cooked in boiling water /by/': Yumurtalar [bizim aşçı tarafından] haşlandı. 'The eggs have been boiled [by our cook].' Haşlanmış kestane.yİ çok severim. 'I really like boiled chestnuts.' *11:4a.* cooking: - cook sth.

2 /DAn/ '- get scalded /{BY/from}/, - scald or - burn oneself with a hot liquid': Çaydanlıktaki kaynar su üstüm.E döküldü ve haşlandım. 'The boiling water from [lit., in] the teakettle spilled ON me, and I {got scalded/scalded myself}.' Keşke kaplıca havuzuna balıklama atlamasaydım; sıcak su.DAN haşlandım. 'If only I hadn't jumped

177

headlong into the pool of the hot spring! I got scalded {BY/from} the hot water.' *393:13.* impairment: - inflict an injury.

hat düş-. → düş- 1.

hata et- [eDer] /mAklA/ '- make a mistake /BY...ing/; - do wrong /BY...ing/'. This verb is usually preferred when speaking of relatively greater errors in the conduct of one's life rather than of minor errors in matters such as grammar, punctuation. [A. hata (. -) 'mistake, error']: **Bu adamla evlen.MEKLE büyük hata ettim.** 'I made a terrible mistake BY marry.ING this man.' **Avukat ol.MAKLA hata ettim. Keşke öğretmen olsaydım.** 'I made a mistake BY becom.ING a lawyer. If only I had become a teacher!' *974:13.* error: - mistake, - make a mistake. For erring in minor matters → = hata işle- → işle- 2, = hata yap- → yap- 3, = yanıl-, = yanlışlık yap- → yap- 3.

hata işle-. → işle- 2.

hata yap-. → yap- 3.

hatır sor-. → sor-.

{**hatırla-** [r]/**anımsa-** [r]} '- remember, - recall, - think of' [A. hatır (- .) 'memory' + verb-forming suf. -1A, an 'mind' + verb-forming suf. - ImsA]: Thing or person as object: **Bugün liseden bir arkadaşımı gördüm ama ismini hatırlayamadım.** 'Today I saw a friend of mine from {high school/lycée}, but I couldn't remember his name.' **Ne zaman bu şarkıyı dinlesem sen.İ hatırlıyorum.** 'Whenever I hear this song, I think of you.' **Amerika'ya gidince bizi hatırlayacağ.ı.nı zannetmiyorum. Çünkü insan göz.den ırak olunca gönül.den de ırak olur.** 'I don't think he'll remember us when he goes to the U.S., because when a person is out of sight [lit., ** far from the eye] he is also out of mind [lit., ** far from the heart].' **Dedem ben çok küçükken vefat etti, yüzünü {hayal meyal} hatırlıyorum.** 'My grandfather passed away when I was very young. I only remember his face {vaguely/dimly}.'

Event or situation as object: **{Görmüş/Yapmış} olabilirim. Hatırlamıyorum.** 'I may {have seen it/have done it}. I don't remember.' **Buraya daha önce gelseydim hatırlardım.** 'If I had come here earlier, I would {have remembered/remember}.' **Ankara'ya gittim. Hatta oraya birkaç defa gittiğ.im.i hatırlıyorum.** 'I went to Ankara. In fact I remember go.ING there [lit., my having gone there] several times.' **Bunu söylediğ.İM.i hatırlamıyorum ama söylediysem de özür dilerim.** 'I don't remember saying that, but if I did [lit., ** If I said], I apologize.' S: **O zaman çok hastaydın. Hatırlıyor musun?** 'Q: At that time you were very ill, do you remember?' C: * **Hatırlamaz olur muyum?** 'A: How could I ever forget? [lit., ** How could I NOT remember?]' * **Yanlış hatırlamıyorsam sizin.le kardeşimin evinde tanışmıştık.** 'If I remember correctly [lit., ** If I don't remember incorrectly], we met at {my brother's/my sister's} house.'

Note the two following patterns for expressing the same idea:
a) Direct question 'as object': **O filmi {ne zaman/kiminle} gördüm, hatırlamıyorum.** 'I don't remember {when/with whom} I saw that movie [lit., ** {When/With whom} I saw that movie, I don't remember].'
b) Indirect question as object: **O filmi {ne zaman/kiminle} gördüğ.üm.ü hatırlamıyorum.** 'I don't remember {when/with whom} I saw that movie.'

Note the two following patterns for expressing the same idea:
a) Direct question as object: **O filmi gördü mü görmedi mi, hatırlayamıyordu.** 'He couldn't remember whether or not he had seen that movie [lit., ** Did he see that movie, didn't he see that movie, he couldn't remember].'
b) Indirect question as object: **O filmi görüp görmediğ.i.ni hatırlayamıyordu.** 'He couldn't remember whether or not he had seen that movie.' **O dersi almak zorunda olup olmadığ.ı.nı hatırlamıyor.** 'He doesn't remember whether or not he has to take that class.'

For the Turkish of '- remember to...' as in 'Remember to take your keys', the Turkish only permits 'Don't FORGET to...', for which → **unut-**. *988:10.* memory: - remember. → = **akla gel-** ['- occur /to/, - think of, - remember'] → **gel-** 1, = **bul-** 4 ['- remember, - have it', when one suddenly remembers sth forgotten], ≠ **unut-**.

{**hatırlat-** [ır]/**anımsat-** [ır]} [hatırla- and anımsa- + caus. suf. -t] 1 /A/ '- remind /θ/ sb, - cause /θ/ sb to remember a fact or event': İki yıl önce Elif'**LE** tanıştıkları halde, şimdi onun.**LA** tanıştığ.ı.nI hatırlamıyor. O.nA tanıştıklar.ı.nI hatırlattım. 'Although he met θ Elif two years ago, now he doesn't remember meeting θ her [lit., getting acquainted with] her. I reminded θ him that they had met.' Oraya {a: ne zaman/b: niçin/c: nasıl/d: kimlerle} gittiğ.i.ni hatırlattım. 'I reminded him {a: when/b: why/c: how/d: with whom [i.e., with what people]} he had gone there.' *988:20.* memory: - remind.

2 /A/ '- remind sb to do sth': Bakkala gitmey.**İ** unutursam ban.**A** hatırlat. 'If I forget to go to the grocery store, remind θ me.' *988:20.* memory: - remind.

3 /A/ '- remind /θ/ sb of', the features of sb or sth, resemblances, bring a similar person or thing to mind': * Ban.**A** kardeşim.**İ** hatırlatıyorsun. 'You remind θ me OF {my brother/my sister}.' *988:20.* memory: - remind. → **benzet-** 2 ['- compare /to/ AND note the similarity, - liken sth /to/ sth else'].

4 /A/ '- make think of, - bring to mind'. Here associations with places or events rather than similarities bring sb or sth to mind: Bu şarkılar ban.**A** çocukluk ve ilk gençlik yıllarımı hatırlattı. 'These songs reminded θ me of my childhood and the early years of my youth.' Burada her şey ban.**A** sen.**İ** hatırlatıyor. 'Here everything {makes θ me think OF you/reminds θ me OF you}.' *988:20.* memory: - remind.

hava aç-. → aç- 7.

hava açıl-. → açıl- 7.

hava al-. → al- 1.

hava bas-. → bas- 2.

hava boz-. → boz- 4.

hava bozul-. → bozul-.

hava düzel-. → düzel-.

hava kapan-. → kapan- 4.

hava karar-. → karar-.

havadan sudan konuş-. → konuş-.

havalan- [ır] [A. **hava** 'air' + verb-forming suf. -lAn] 1 '- be aired out, - be ventilated': Oda havalandı mı? 'Has the room been aired out?' *317:10.* air, weather.

2 /DAn/ '- take off /from/, - become airborne', airborne vehicles, birds: {Uçak/Helikopter/Kuşlar} havalandı. '{The plane/The helicopter/The birds} took off.' İncirlik üssünden havalanan jetler geri döndü. 'The jets [that took off] from İncirlik airbase have returned.' Havalanırken arıza yapan uçak büyük bir gürültüyle yer.**E** çakılıp ve parçalandı. 'The plane that had a mechanical failure {ON takeoff/while taking off} crashed INTO the ground with a great {roar/noise} and broke into pieces.' *184:38.* aviation: - take off; *188:8.* departure: - set out; *193:10.* ascent: - take off. → = **kalk-** 2, ≠ **in-** 3.

havalandır- [ır] '- air out' [A. havalan- + caus. suf. -DIr]: {a: Ev.in iç.i/b: Araba.nın iç.i/c: Dolap/d: Sınıf} çok kötü kokuyor, havalandıralım. '{a: The house [lit., The inside of the house]/b: The car [lit., the inside of the car]/c: The cupboard/d: The classroom} smells very bad, let's air it out.' Öğrenciler çıkınca pencereleri açıp sınıfları havalandırıyoruz. 'As soon as the students leave, we open the windows and air out the classrooms.' *317:10.* air, weather: - air. → **hava al-** 2 ['- absorb air, - take in air, - get air, (for a place) - air out'] → **al-** 1.

havaya uç-. → uç-.

havaya uçur-. → uçur-.

havla- [r] '- bark' [from **hav** in **hav hav** 'bow wow', + verb-forming suf. -lA]: * {a: Biri/b: Birisi/c: Birileri} geliyor galiba. **Köpekler havlıyor.** '{a, b: Someone/c: Someone [lit., Some people]} must be coming. The dogs are barking.' Proverb: **Havlayan köpek ısırmaz.** 'A barking dog doesn't bite.' *60:2.* animal sounds: - cry.

{hayal/düş} kırıklığına uğra-. → uğra- 2.

{hayal/düş}kırıklığına uğrat-. → uğrat-.

hayal kur-. → kur- 1.

{hayale/hayallere} dal-. → dal- 2.

hayata gözlerini {kapa-/kapat-}. → {kapa-/kapat-} 1.

hayata gözlerini yum-. → göz yum- 2. → yum-.

hayatını {kaybet-/yitir-}. → {kaybet-/yitir-}.

hayatını kazan-. → kazan- 1.

Hayırlı olsun. → ol- 11. → olsun.

haykır- [ır] /A, diye/ '- cry out, - shout, - scream /AT, saying/': **Denize düşen adam "İmdat! İmdat!" DİYE haykırıyordu.** 'The man who had fallen into the sea was screaming θ, "Help! Help!"' *59:6.* cry, call: - cry. → = **bağır-,** = **bağırıp çağır-** → çağır- 3, = **çığlık at-** → at- 1, ≠ **fısılda-** ['- whisper'].

hayret et- [eDer] /A/ [A. hayret 'surprise'] '- be amazed, astonished, surprised /θ [that], AT/': **Serpil herkesin hesabını ödeyince hayret ettim.** 'When Serpil [f.] paid everyone's bill, I was surprised.' PERSON as object: **Herkes.in hesab.ın.ı ödeyince Serpil'E hayret ettim.** 'I was surprised AT Serpil when she paid [i.e., the check] for everyone.' ACTION as object: **Serpil'in bu davranış.ı.nA hayret ettim.** 'I was very surprised AT this behavior of Serpil's.' **Serpil'in, herkesin hesabını ödeme.si.nE hayret ettim.** 'I was surprised θ that Serpil had paid [lit., AT Serpil's paying] everyone's check.' **Akşam yemeğ.i.nE Nurdan'ı çağırma.sı.nA hayret ettim.** 'I was very surprised θ that he had invited [lit., AT his having invited] Nurdan [f.] to dinner.' **Annem benim o konsere Fatma'yla {gittiğ.im.E/gitme.m.E} hayret etti.** 'My mother was surprised θ that I had gone [lit., {AT my having gone/AT my going}] to that concert with Fatma.' **Hayret etme.n.E gerek yok, gayet normal.** 'There is no need FOR you to be surprised [lit., ** FOR your being surprised]. It's quite normal.' *122:5.* wonder: - wonder; *131:7.* inexpectation: - surprise. → = **şaş-,** = **şaşır-** 2.

Hayrola! → ol- 11. → ola.

hazır bulun-. → bulun- 2.

hazır ol-. → ol- 12.

hazırla- [r] /{A/için}/ '- prepare sth, - get sth ready /FOR/' [A. hazır 'ready' + verb-forming suf. -lA]: **Büyük odayı {misafirler.E/ misafirler için} hazırladık.** 'We prepared the large room {FOR the guests}.' S: **Akşam yemeğini [saat] kaçta hazırlayayım?** 'Q: At what time should I prepare dinner [lit., the evening meal]?' C: **Yemeği saat yedide hazırla!** 'A: Prepare the meal at seven o'clock.' **Bu ilâc.ı hazırlayabilir misiniz?** 'Can you prepare this medicine?' **Bu sözlüğü iki yılda hazırladık.** 'We prepared this dictionary in two years.' *405:6.* preparation: - prepare.

bavulunu hazırla- '- pack, - pack up' or just '- prepare one's bags' [It. bavul 'bags, luggage']: **Bu akşam İstanbul'a gitme.N gerekiyor. Lütfen bavul.UN.u hazırla.** 'YOU must go to Istanbul this evening. Please {pack/prepare} YOUR {bags/luggage}.' **Üç saat SONRA uçağ.IM kalkacak ama ben hâlâ bavul.UM.u hazırlayamadım.** 'MY plane leaves IN three hours, but I still haven't been able to {pack/prepare MY bags}.' *212:9.* enclosure: - package. → ≠ **bavulunu aç-** ['- unpack', or just '- open one's bags'] → aç- 1.

kahvaltı hazırla- '- make or - prepare breakfast' • Note: **kahvaltı {et-/yap-}** means '- EAT, HAVE breakfast', NOT '- make or - prepare' it: **Anne: Oğlum senin için kahvaltı hazırladım, neden yemiyorsun?** 'Mother: Son [lit., my son] I PREPARED breakfast for you. Why aren't you eating?' **Oğul: Kahvaltı {yapmay.a/etmey.e} vaktim yok anne, hemen çıkmam lâzım.** 'Son: I don't have time TO EAT breakfast, mom. I have to leave right away.' *405:6.* preparation: - prepare.

reçete hazırla- '- fill or - prepare a prescription', subj.: the pharmacist: **Bu reçete.yi hazırlayabilir misiniz?** 'Can you {fill/prepare} this prescription?' *86:38.* remedy: - remedy; *405:6.* preparation: - prepare.

hazırlan- [ır] [hazırla- + {pass./refl.} suf. -n] 1 /{A/için}/ '- get [oneself] ready, - prepare oneself /FOR/': **Biraz bekleyin. Şimdi hazırlanırım.** 'Just wait a bit. * I'll be ready in a minute [lit., I'll get myself ready right now].' **Bu akşamki konser İÇİN öğleden sonra hazırlanmaya başlayacağım.** 'I'll begin to prepare myself in the afternoon FOR the concert this evening.' **Bir haftadır bu sınav.A hazırlanıyorum.** 'I've been preparing myself FOR this exam for a week.' **Bu sınav.A yeteri kadar hazırlanmadım.** 'I haven't prepared sufficiently FOR this exam.' **Üniversiteye giriş imtihanları.nA hazırlanıyor musunuz?** 'Are you preparing yourself FOR {the college/the university} entrance examinations?' *405:13.* preparation: - prepare oneself.

2 /{tarafından/CA}/ '- be prepared, readied, set up, drawn up /by/': **Düğün salonu [garsonlar tarafından] istediğiniz gibi hazırlandı.** 'The wedding parlor has been set up [by the waiters] as you requested.' **Bu program {hükümet tarafından/hükümet.çe} hazırlandı.** 'This program was drawn up {by the government}.' *405:6.* preparation: - prepare.

hecele- [r] '- syllabify, - say, or - read by syllable', how Turks usually indicate the spelling of a word instead of giving letter names. [hece 'syllable' + verb-forming suf. -lA]: * **Çocuklar hecele.yerek oku-yorlardı: A-me-ri-ka-lı-yım.**

'The children were reading in syllables [lit., by syllabify.ing]: I am an American.' **Soyadınızı heceler misiniz?** 'Would you please spell [lit., ** syllabify] your last name.' *546:7.* letter: - spell. For '- spell', that is, give the names of the letters of the word, which Turks do not usually do, → {harf harf/harflerini} söyle-. → söyle- 1, yazıl- 1 ['- be written'].

hediye et- [eDer] /A/ '- give sth as a gift /to/ sb, - make a present of sth /to/ sb' [A. **hediye** 'present, gift']: * **Yaş gün.ü.nde babam.A kitap hediye ettim.** '{I gave my father a book for his birthday./I gave my father a book as a birthday present [lit., On his birthday, I gave my father a book as a present].' *478:12.* giving: - give; *634:4.* costlessness: - give.

Helâl olsun. → ol- 11. → olsun.

hesap açtır-. → açtır-.

hesap çıkar-. → çıkar- 7.

hesap getir-. → getir-.

hesap {kapa-/kapat-}. → {kapa-/kapat-} 1.

hesapla- [r] '- calculate, - figure up, - add up' [A. **hesap** (. -) 'calculation' + verb-forming suf. -lA]: **Sana olan borcumu hesapladın mı?** 'Did you {figure up how much I owe you/calculate my debt to you}?' **Pazarda ne kadar para harcadığ.ım.ı hesaplıyorum.** 'I'm calculating how much money I spent at the market.' **Geçen ayki yiyecek masraf.ım.ı hesapladım.** 'I calculated my food expenses for last month.' *1016:17.* mathematics: - calculate. → **hesap çıkar-** ['- calculate the bill, - add up the bill'] → çıkar- 7.

heyecanlan- [ır] [A. **heyecan** (. . -) 'excitement' + verb-forming suf. -lAn]: 1 '- get excited, - be enthusiastic, thrilled', positive emotion: **Sevdiği adamı görünce çok heyecanlandı.** 'When she saw the man she loved, she was thrilled.' **New York'a ilk gidişimde çok heyecanlandım.** 'On my first visit [lit., ** going] to New York I was thrilled.' *95:11.* pleasure: - be pleased; *105:18*. excitement: - be excited.

2 '- be or - get upset, nervous, agitated, excited, - panic, - lose one's cool', negative emotion: **Sınavlarda çok heyecanlanırım**. 'I get very {upset/nervous} during examinations.' **A: Eyvah! Treni kaçıracağız**. 'A: O dear! We're going to miss the train!' **B: * Dur, heyecanlanma! Daha tren.in kalkma.sı.na beş dakika var, yetişebiliriz**. 'B: Just hold on now! Don't panic! We've still got five minutes till the train leaves [lit., There are still five minutes to the departure of the train]. We'll be able to {make it/catch it}.' *96:16b*. unpleasure: - be distressed; *128:6*. nervousness: - fidget.

3 '- get turned on sexually': **Denize çıplak giren kadını görünce heyecanlandım**. 'When I saw the woman going into the {sea/ocean} naked, I got turned on.' **Necdet sevgilisinin elini tutunca heyecanlandı**. 'When Necdet took his girlfriend's hand, he got turned on.' *105:12*. excitement: - excite. → = **tahrik ol-** → **ol-** 12. For '- turn on', → **heyecanlandır-** 3, **tahrik et-** 2.

heyecanlandır- [ır] [heyecanlan- + caus. suf. -DIr] 1 '- excite, - thrill, - give a thrill': **Ünlü artisti görmek onu heyecanlandırdı**. 'Seeing the famous {actor/actress/star} gave him a thrill.' *105:12*. excitement: - excite.

2 '- upset, - disturb': **Polis arabası.nın siren çalarak yaklaşma.sı beni çok heyecanlandırdı**. 'The approach of the police car with sirens blasting really upset me.' *96:16a*. unpleasure: - distress; *128:9*. nervousness: - get on one's nerves.

3 '- excite, - turn on sexually', polite: **Mini etekli kızlar beni her zaman heyecanlandırır**. 'Girls in miniskirts always turn me on.' **Güzel bir kadınla dans etmek beni heyecanlandırır**. 'Dancing with an attractive woman turns me on.' *105:12*. excitement: - excite. → = **tahrik et-** 2. For '- GET turned on', → **tahrik ol-** → **ol-** 12, **heyecanlan-** 3.

{hız/sürat} yap-. → **yap-** 3.

hızlan- [ır] [hız 'speed' + verb-forming suf. -lAn] 1 '- gather speed, - speed up, - accelerate, - pick up one's pace': **Uçak önce hızlandı, sonra havalandı**. 'First the plane gathered speed, then it took off.' **Yağmur başlayınca eve gitmek için hızlandım**. 'When it began to rain, I picked up my pace to get home.' *174:10*. swiftness: - accelerate. → ≠ **yavaşla-**.

2 '- get heated, intense, - heat up, - intensify': **Kadın hakları konulu açık oturumda feministler konuşunca tartışma hızlanmaya başladı**. 'When the feminists spoke up during the panel discussion on women's rights, the dispute began to heat up.' *119:3*. aggravation: - worsen.

Hiç belli olmaz. → **ol-** 11 → **olmaz**.

hiç olmazsa. → **ol-** 11 → **olmaz**.

hiçbir şey olmamış gibi. → **ol-** 2.

hisset- [hisseDer] [A. **his** (hiSSi) 'feeling' + et-] 1 '- feel'. * **kendini hisset-** '- feel' well, bad, etc. [kendi 'self'], lit., ** '- feel oneself...': • Note the different personal suffixes on kendi: * **Kendi.ni yaşlı bir insan gibi hissediyor**. 'He feels old [lit., ** He feels HIMself like an old person].' **Bu günlerde kendi.M.i * çok ama çok yalnız hissediyorum**. 'These days I feel * very, very lonely [lit., ** I feel MYself very...].' **Hasta: * Kendi.M.i iyi hissetmiyorum**. 'The patient: I don't feel well [lit., ** I don't feel MYself well].' **Kendi.M.i {a: [çok] {fena/kötü}/b: halsiz/c: zayıf/d: bitkin/e: keyifsiz/f: yorgun} hissediyorum**. 'I feel {a: [very] bad/b: {weak/out of sorts}/c: weak/d: {exhausted/worn out}/e: {depressed/ low/out of sorts}/f: tired}.' **Doktor [hasta ilâç aldıktan sonra]: Şimdi kendi.NİZ.i nasıl hissediyorsunuz?** 'The doctor [after the patient had taken some medicine]: Now how do YOU feel [lit., ** How do you feel YOURself]?' **Hasta: Kendi.M.i {a: daha iyi/b: iyi/c: iyice/d: çok iyi/e: çok daha iyi/f: rahat/g: {güçlü/kuvvetli}/h: zinde/i: formda/j: bomba gibi}**

hissediyorum. 'The patient: I feel {a: better/b: well/c: pretty well/d: very well/e: much better/f: comfortable/g: strong/h: {strong/ vigorous/fit}/i: {in good shape/fit as a fiddle}/j: terrific}.' **Bugün matematik ödevimi teslim ettim. Şimdi kendi.M.i çok {rahat/hafif} hissediyorum.** 'I turned in my math homework today. That's a relief! [lit., Now I feel relieved, lit., {comfortable/** light}].' *24:6.* sensation: - sense; *93:10.* feeling: - feel.

2 '- sense, - feel, - be aware; - notice, - perceive': **O.nun üzgün olduğ.u.nu hissettim.** 'I sensed that he was sad.' **Kendi.M.İ {a: kandırılmış/b: {sorumlu/ mesul}} hissediyorum.** 'I feel {a: [that] I've been cheated/b: responsible}.' **Erdal'ın odaya {a: girdiğ.i.ni/b: gireceğ.i.ni} hissettim.** 'I {felt/sensed} that Erdal {a: had entered/b: {was going to enter/would enter}} the room.' * **Söyleyecekleriniz olduğunu hissediyorum. Çekinmeyin.** 'I can tell [that] you want to say something [lit., that you have sth to say]. Don't hesitate.' * **Öğretmen bir şeyler.in olduğ.u.nu hissediyordu.** 'The teacher sensed that something [lit., ** some thingS] was {going on/up}.'

verb stem.mIş gibi hisset- '- feel {like/as if}': * **Kendi.M.İ daha önce buraya gel.miş gibi hissediyorum.** '{I feel {like/as if} I've been here before./I have a feeling of déjà vu.} [lit., ** I feel MYSELF as if I had come here before].' *24:6.* sensation: - sense; *93:10.* feeling: - feel; *933:4.* intuition, instinct: - intuit. → = sez-, = duy- 3, **farkına var-** ['- notice, - become aware /OF/, - realize'].

hitap et- [eDer] /A/ '- address /θ/ sb', i.e., '- speak /to/ sb, - talk /to/ sb', *formal*. [A. hitap (. -) (hitaBı) 'address']: **Başbakan Manisa'da 30.000 kişi.yE hitap etti.** 'The prime minister addressed θ 30,000 people in Manisa.' **S: Kim.E hitap ediyorsunuz?** 'Q: θ Who[m] are you addressing?' **C: Siz.E hitap ediyorum.** 'A: I'm addressing θ you.' *524:27.* speech: - address. → **söyle-** 3 ['- speak /to/ sb, - talk /to/ sb'], **konuş-** ['- talk, - speak /with,

to/'], **de-** 1, **seslen-** ['- call out /to/, - call'].

hizmet et- [eDer] /A/ '- serve /θ/, - wait /{ON/UPON}/, - attend /to/' [A. hizmet 'service']: **Vatan.A hizmet etmek yurttaşlık görev.i.dir.** 'To serve θ the homeland is the duty of a citizen [lit., citizenship duty].' * **Babam ordu.yA 30 yıl hizmet ettikten sonra geçen yıl {binbaşılık- .TAN/albaylık.TAN} emekli oldu.** 'My father retired {AS a Major [*or* AT the rank of Major/AS a colonel [*or* At the rank of colonel]} [lit., ** from Majorship/from colonelship] last year after serving IN [lit., ** after serving θ] the army for 30 years.' **Aydan hanım kabul gün.ü.nde misafirler.i.ne çok iyi hizmet etti.** 'Aydan hanım was a good hostess [lit., attended to her guests very well] on her visitation [lit., reception] day.', i.e., that special day of the month when a woman receives woman friends at her home. It is usually during the day when the men are at work. *577:13.* servant, employee: - serve.

horla- [r] '- snore': {a: Çok/b: Çok kötü/c: Çok fazla/d: Horul horul} **horluyorsun, uyuya- mıyorum, lütfen bir doktora git, belki * çare.si bulunur.** 'You snore {a: a lot/b: very badly/c: too much/d: loudly}. I can't sleep. Please go to a doctor. Perhaps * there's a cure.' *22:13.* sleep: - sleep; *54:6.* resonance: - resonate; *57:2.* sibilation: - sibilate; *58:3.* stridency: - rasp; *58:9.* : <- sound harshly> - jangle.

Hoş bulduk! → bul- 1.

Hoş geldin[iz]! → gel- 1.

{hoş/iyi} karşıla-. → karşıla- 3.

hoş vakit geçir-. → geçir- 3.

Hoşça kal[ın]! → kal- 1.

hoşlan- [ır] /DAn/ '- like /θ/, - enjoy /θ/, - be pleased /WITH/' [P. hoş 'pleasant, pleasing' + verb-forming suf. -lAn]: NON-verbal noun as object: **Şu kız.DAN çok hoşlanı- yorum.** 'I really like θ that girl.' **Berrin kırmızı elbiseler.DEN hoşlanır.** 'Berrin likes θ red dresses.' **S: Hangi {tür/çeşit)** müzik.TEN hoşlanırsın? 'θ What {kind} of music do you like?' C1: Hepsi.nDEN hoşlanırım. 'A1: I like θ all kinds [lit., all OF them].' C2: Hiçbirisi.nDEN {hoşlan.MIyorum/ hoşlan.MAM}. 'A2: {I doN'T like} θ any of them.' VERBAL noun as object: Araba kullanmak.TAN hoşlanırım. 'I like {θ driving/TO drive} [a car].' *95:12.* pleasure: - enjoy. → = beğen-, = hoşuna git- → git- 1a, = memnun kal- → kal- 1, = memnun ol- → ol- 12, = sev- 1, bayıl- 2 ['- be crazy /ABOUT/'].

'- prefer, - like better'. *noun.DAn mI noun.DAn mI hoşlan-?* '- prefer this or that', a question pattern in which the question particle **mI** is repeated after each alternative object. Other verbs of liking may occur in the same pattern: **S:** * Çin yemekleri.nDEN mi Hint yemekleri.nDEN mi hoşlanırsın? 'Q: Do you prefer θ Chinese or θ Indian food?' **C1:** * İki.si.nDEN de hoşlanırım. 'A1: I like θ {both of them/them both}.' **C2:** İki.si.nDEN de hoşlanmam. 'A2: {I don't like θ either of them./I like θ neither of them.}' *371:17.* choice: - prefer. → = beğen- 2, = {tercih et-/yeğle-} 1.

hoşuna git-. → git- 1b.

hücum et- [eDer] /{A/üzerine}/ [A. hücum (. -) 'attack, assault'] 1 '- attack /θ/, - storm /θ/': * Estergon kale.si.n.E hücum eden düşman.A karşı, kaleyi kahramanca savundular. 'They heroically defended the fortress of Esztergon against the enemy who were attacking θ it [lit., ** Against the enemy who were attacking θ the fortress of Esztergon, they heroically defended the fortress].' Bin beş yüz yirmi altı [1526] Mohaç savaş.ı.nda Macar ve Osmanlı orduları birbirleri.nE hücum etti. 'At the Battle of Mohács [1526], the Hungarian and Ottoman forces attacked θ each other.' * Kuşlar {buğday tarlaları.NA/ buğday tarlaları.NIN ÜZERİNE} hücum etti. 'The birds attacked {θ the wheat fields}.' *459:14.* attack: - attack. → = saldır- 1. # Hücum et- is not used for sexual assault. For that, → tecavüz et- 2, saldır- 2.

2 '- mob /θ/ a place, - rush /to/ a place, - throng /to/': Havalar ısınınca halk plajlar.A hücum etti. 'When the weather got hot, the people thronged to the beaches.' Ekmek bulamayan halk fırınlar.A hücum etti. 'The people who could not find bread mobbed θ the bakery.' *769:16.* assemblage: - come together.

hüzünlen- [ir] '- become or - feel sad, gloomy, melancholy, depressed' [A. hüzün [hüZNü] 'sadness, melancholy' + verb-forming suf. -lAn]: Huzur evindeki bazı ihtiyarlar bayramda ziyaret-ler.i.ne gelen olmadığı için hüzünleniyorlar. 'Some of the old people in the rest home feel sad because no one has come to visit them on the holiday.' Some words of a well-known classical song: Akşam oldu, hüzünlendim ben yine. 'It has become evening, and I have again become melancholy.' *112:16.* sadness: - lose heart.

- I -

ırzına geç-. → geç- 1.

ıslık çal-. → çal- 2.

ısın- [ır] [ısı (today only a noun meaning 'heat' but formerly also a verb '- heat') + refl. suf. -n] 1 '- grow warm, - warm up, - get hot': Babam sobayı yaktı. Ev ısınıyordu. 'My father lit the stove [i.e., one used for heating the house]. The house was warming up.' Havalar gittikçe ısınıyor. 'The weather is gradually becoming warmer.' * Ortalık iyice ısındı. 'The weather around here has really warmed up.' → ≠ soğu- 1. # Yemek ısındı mı? 'Is the food hot yet? [lit., 'Has the food gotten hot yet?]' → ≠ soğu- 1. # Dışarıda çok üşümüştüm ama eve girince ısındım. 'I was very cold outside, but when I entered the house I {got warm/warmed up}.' → ≠ üşü-. *1019:17b.* heating: - get hot.

fazla ısın- '- become overheated, - overheat' [fazla 'too much']: Arabamın motoru {çok/fazla} ısınıyor. 'The engine of my car is {overheating/getting too hot}.' *992:10.* excess: - overdo; *1019:17b.* heating: - get hot. → *vehicle name* su kaynat- ['for a vehicle - overheat (lit., - boil water)'] → kaynat-.

2 '- warm oneself, - warm up': **Ellerini soba.ya uzatmış ısınıyordu.** 'He had held out his hands {toward/over} [lit., to] the stove and was warming himself.' **Sporcular maça başlamadan önce ısındılar.** 'The athletes warmed up before beginning the game [i.e., soccer, basketball].' **Hava soğuktu. Balıkçılar ısınmak için ateş yakmışlardı.** 'The weather was cold. The fishermen had lit a fire [in order] to warm themselves.' *1019:17a.* heating: - heat.

3 /A/ '- come or - grow to like /θ/; - warm {UP TO/to/TOWARDS}': **Nedense o çocuğ.A pek ısınamadım.** 'For some reason or other I just couldn't warm UP TO that {child/fellow/guy}.' *587:10.* friendship: - befriend, - make friends with. → ≠ **soğu- 2**, ≠ **uzaklaş- 2**.

ısır- [ır] '- bite': **Eve giren hırsızı köpek ısırdı.** 'The dog bit the thief who had entered the house.' **Dilimi ısırdım çok acıyor.** 'I bit my tongue. It really hurts.' **Çocuğumuzun dişleri çıktı artık; elmayı ısır.a ısır.a yiyebiliyor.** 'Our child finally got his teeth [lit., Our child's teeth finally appeared]. He can eat an apple bite by bite [lit., ** biting biting].' Proverbs: **Havlayan köpek ısırmaz.** ' A barking dog doesn't bite.' **Isıracak it dişini göstermez.** 'The dog that is going to bite doesn't show its teeth.', i.e., doesn't give a sign that it will attack, i.e., Dangerous people often appear harmless, so beware. **Köpek sahibini ısırmaz.** 'A dog doesn't bite its master.' Don't bite the hand that feeds you. *8:27.* eating: - chew; *26:7.* pain: - inflict pain; *644: * 26.* probity: PHR. one does not cut the hand that gives. → = **sok- 3** ['for a snake - bite'].

ısıt- [ır] 1 /lA/ '- heat sth, - heat up sth /{by means of/with}/, - warm up sth' [ısı (today only a noun meaning 'heat' but formerly also a verb: '- heat') + caus. suf. -t]: **Yemeği ısıtır mısın?** 'Would you [please] heat up the food?' **Fırını 230 dereceye ayarlayıp ısıtın.** 'Heat the oven to a temperature of 230 degrees [lit., ** set the oven to 230 degrees and heat].' S: **Evinizi nasıl ısıtıyorsunuz?** 'Q: How do you heat your house?' C: **Evimizi {soba.yla/kalorifer.le} ısıtıyoruz.** 'A: We heat our house {with stoves/by means of central heating}.' *1019:17a.* heating: - heat. → ≠ **soğut-**.

2 '- warm up' in the field of sports: **Voleybol oynamaya başlamadan önce * adalelerinizi ısıtın.** '* Warm up [lit., ** Warm your muscles] before beginning to play volleyball.' *1019:17a.* heating: - heat.

ıslan- [ır] '- get wet' [ısla- '- wet, - make wet' + refl. suf. -n. ADJ. ıslak 'wet']: **Yağmurda sırılsıklam ıslandık.** 'We got {drenched/soaked} in the rain.' *1063:11.* moisture: - be damp; *1063:13.* : - soak. → ≠ **kuru- 1**, **kurulan- 2** ['- dry oneself'].

ıslat- [ır] '- wet, - make wet, - moisten' [ısla- '- wet, - make wet' + caus. suf. -t. ADJ. ıslak 'wet']: **Çamaşırları yıkamadan bir gün önce ıslatırım.** 'I moisten the laundry the day before I wash it.' **Birbirinizi ıslatmayın, {sonra/ yoksa/aksi taktirde} {üşütüp/üşüyüp} hasta olacaksınız.** 'Don't {get/make} each other wet, {otherwise} you'll {catch a cold/get cold} and get sick.' *1063:12.* moisture: - moisten. → ≠ **kurut-**.

* altını ıslat- '- wet or - soil one's underclothes or bed' [alt 'the underpart of anything'], lit., ** '- wet the area under it': **Çocuk alt.I.nı ıslatmış.** 'The child {wet/soiled} HIMSELF.' Said to a child: * **Yine alt.IN.ı ıslatmışsın!** 'There you've gone and wet YOURSELF again!' *12:13.* excretion: - defecate; *12:14.* : - urinate; *1063:12* moisture: - moisten. → = **altına kaçır-.** → **kaçır- 2**.

ısmarla- [r] 1 /DAn, {A/için}/ '- order sth /from, for/ sb': **O terzi.den {kendim.E/kendim için} yeni bir elbise ısmarlayacağım.** 'I'm going to order a new suit {FOR myself} from that tailor.' In a restaurant: **Garson: Yemeklerinizi ısmarladınız mı efendim?** 'Waiter: Have you ordered [your food], {sir/ma'am}?' **Müşteri: {Evet, ısmarla-**

dım./Hayır, ısmarlamadım.}
'Customer: {Yes, I have./No, I
haven't.}' Müşteri: Garson bey, *
bura.yA bakar mısınız? Ben
bunu ısmarlamadım. 'Customer:
Waiter, * would you come here a
minute [lit., look θ here]. I didn't
order this.' Yemekleri şimdi
ısmarlayabilir miyiz? 'Could we
order [the food] now?'
{Kahvedekiler.E/Kahvedekiler
için} çay ısmarladık. 'We
ordered coffee {FOR those in the
coffee house}.' 440:9. request: -
request. → = söyle- 2 ['- order',
usually only when the order is
spoken, as for example, in a
restaurant, coffee house, etc.], iste-
2 ['- ask for, - request /from/; -
demand sth /from/ sb, - call for sth
/from/'].

2 /A/ * '- put in or - place an order
for sth /WITH/ sb, - order sth
/FROM/ sb [lit., ** order sth TO sb],
- give an order for sth /to/ sb': *
Kahveci.yE kahve ısmarladık.
'{We placed an order FOR coffee
WITH the coffee seller./We ordered
coffee FROM the coffee seller.}'
Another possible translation: 'We
ordered coffee FOR the coffee seller.'
Çarşıya gitmedim. * Alacak-
larım.I Ali'yE ısmarladım. 'I
didn't go to the market. * {I placed an
order WITH Ali FOR the things I was
going to buy./I gave θ Ali an order
FOR the things I was going to buy.}'
440:9. request: - request.

3 /A/ '- entrust sb or sth /to/ sb, -
commit /to/, - commend /to/': Most
frequently found in
Allahaısmarladık. [usually
pronounced Alâsmarladık]
'Goodbye [lit., We entrustED you TO
God].', said by the person
LEAVING. The person
REMAINING says either: 1. Güle
güle. 'Goodbye.' Or 2. informal:
Eyvallah! 188:22. departure:
INTERJ. farewell! = Elveda
'Farewell'. For other departure
formulas, → Hoşça kalın. → kal-
1. Proverb: Bağla atını ısmarla
Hakk'a. 'Tie up your horse [and
then] entrust it to God.' 478:16.
giving: - commit.

ısrar et- [eDer] /a: DA, b: için, c: diye/
'- insist /a: {on/UPON}, b:
{ON/UPON}, c: saying/, - persist /a:
in/' [A. ısrar (. -) 'insistence,
persistence']: Lütfen ısrar etme!

Bu gece burada kalamam.
'Please don't insist. I can't stay here
tonight.' Oğlum, * hiç boşuna
ısrar etme; faydası yok. Bu
saatte dışarı çıkamazsın. 'Son, *
don't waste your breath [lit., ** don't
insist for nothing]. It's no use. You
can't go outside at this hour.' Tuğba
bizimle sinemaya gelmek
istemiyordu ama biz çok ısrar
edince fikrini değiştirdi. 'Tuğba
didn't want to come to the movies
with us, but when we really insisted,
she changed her mind.' Bu akşam
sinemaya gitmek istemiyordum
fakat Tufan çok ısrar edince
karşı çıkamadım. 'I didn't want to
go to the movies this evening, but
when Tufan insisted, I just couldn't
say no [lit., I couldn't oppose her].'
Sen de bizimle gel diye çok
ısrar ettim ama gelmedi. '{I
strongly insisted that she also come
with us/lit., I strongly insisted saying
"you too come with us"}, but she
didn't come.' Satıcı ısrar edince
dayanamadım ve aldım. 'When
the salesman persisted, I couldn't
resist and bought it.' NON-verbal
noun as object: Mahkeme,
karar.ı.nda ısrar ederse bir üst
mahkeme.ye başvuracağım. 'If
the court insists on its decision, I'll
apply to a higher court.'
VERBAL noun as object: Benim
kâğıd.ım.a bak.ma.ma.sı için
{uyardım/ikaz ettim} ama
bak.mak.TA ısrar etti. 'I warned
him not to look at my paper [during a
test, etc.], but he insisted ON looking
[at it].' * Haftasonunda arkadaşlarıyla kampa git.me.si.ne izin
ver.me.si İÇİN annesi.nE ısrar
ediyordu. 'TO his mother he
insisted {θ that she allow him/ON her
allowing him} to go camping with his
friends.' Sınıfa zamanında
gel.me.si İÇİN ısrar ettim. 'I
insisted {θ that he come/ON his
coming} to class on time.'
Ödevler.in.i şimdi
{yap.ma.n.DA/yap.ma.n İÇİN}
ısrar ediyorum. 'I insist {θ that
you do [or ON your doing]} your
homework now.' 361:7. obstinacy: -
balk; 421:8. demand: - insist. → =
diren- 1, = diret-.

- İ -

i- '- be', but only: 1 As a base for the
following tense suffixes. 1.1 For the

past tense suffix **-DI** to give **idi** '{he/she/it} was': **Mehmet hasta idi.** 'Mehmet was ill.' The attached form **-[y]DI** is more common: **Mehmet hasta.ydı.** Same translation. First person singular: **[Ben] hasta idim.** 'I was ill.' The attached form: **Ben hastaydım.**

1.2 For the present AND past inferential tense suffix **-mIş** [the SAME form for both] to give **imiş** 'they say {he/she/it} {is/was}': **Mehmet hasta imiş.** 'They say Mehmet {is/was} ill.' The attached form **-[y]mIş** is more common: **Mehmet hasta.ymış.** Same translation. First person singular: **[Ben] hasta imişim.** 'They say I {am/was} ill.' With the more common attached form: **Ben hastaymışım.** Same translation. For examples of the above and of '- be' in other tenses, see **ol-** 3, Additional examples. a) 3. Selected examples...

2 As a base for the conditional suffix **-sA** to give **ise** 'if {he/she/it} is': **Mehmet hasta ise gelmez.** 'If Mehmet is ill, he won't come.' The attached form **-[y]sA** is more common: **Mehmet {meşgul.sa/ hasta.ysa} gelmez.** 'If Mehmet {is busy/is ill}, he won't come.' First person singular: **[Ben] hasta ise.M gelmem.** 'If I am ill, I won't come.' With the more common attached form: **[Ben] {meşgul.saM/ hasta.ysaM} gelmem** 'If I {am busy/am ill}, I won't come.'

3 As a base for the gerund suffix **-ken** to give **iken** 1. Lit., '{while/when} being'. 2. sometimes 'just before...ing'.
3.1 iken following a noun, an adjective, or an adverb: **Mehmet {çocuk/hasta/burada} iken okumazdı.** 'When Mehmet was {a child/ill/here}, he didn't use to study.' First person: **Ben {çocuk/ hasta/burada} iken okumazdım.** 'When I was {a child/ill/here}, I didn't use to study.' The attached or suffix form, i.e., **-[y]ken**, is more common. Note that the final **e** in it does not change in accord with vowel harmony: **Mehmet {ço cUk.kEn/ hastA.ykEn/buradA.ykEn}...** 'When Mehmet was {a child/ill/here}...'

[• NOTE: 1. {iken/-[y]ken} comes at the END of the dependent Turkish phrase, while the English equivalent, 'when' etc., comes at the BEGINNING of the equivalent English dependent phrase.
2. The Turkish dependent phrase always comes at the BEGINNING of the SENTENCE and is NOT set off with a comma. The English equivalent may come at the BEGINNING OR THE END of the English sentence.
3. The English translation of the verb in the **iken** phrase will depend upon the tense of the main clause.]

3.2 iken may follow the THIRD person SINGULAR OR PLURAL of any tense except the **DI** past. It most frequently follows the aorist:
3.2.1 'when, while': **Postaneye gider iken Ahmet'i gördüm.** 'While going to the post office, I saw Ahmet.' With the much more common attached form: **Postaneye gider.ken Ahmet'i gördüm.** Same translation.
3.2.2 possibly 'just before ...ing', depending on the context: **Cem partiye giderken kolonya sürdü.** 'Cem [m.] put on some cologne before going to the party.'
3.2.3 'BY...ing': **Bunu derken ne kastediyordu?** 'What did he mean by saying this?' *760:8.* existence: - exist; *820:16.* time: CONJ. when.

iade et-. → {**geri ver-/iade et-**}. → **ver-** 1.

ibadet et- [eDer] /A/ '- worship /θ/' [A. **ibadet** (. - .) 'worship']: **Müslümanlar ile Hıristiyanlar farklı ibadet ederler.** 'Moslems and Christians worship differently.' **Bütün gün Allah'a ibadet eder.** 'He worships θ God the whole day long.' **Oğlunu kaybettikten sonra kendi.ni {ibadet.e/ibadet etmey.e} verdi.** 'After the death of his son, he devoted himself {to worship/to worshiping}.' *696:10.* worship: - worship. → = **tap-**.

icap et- [eDer] '- BE necessary, - BE required' [A. **icap** (- -) (icaBı) 'necessity, requirement']: VERBAL noun as subject. Impersonal necessity: **-mAk icap et-**: **Otobüs yoktu. Yürü.MEK icap etti.** 'There were no buses. {One had/It was necessary} to walk [lit., ** walkING was required].'
Personal necessity: **-mAsI icap et-**: **İçeri gir.ebil.mek için para {a:**

öde.me.Sİ/b: öde.me.M/c:
öde.me.N/d: öde.me.MİZ/e:
öde.me.NİZ/f: öde.me.LERİ}
icap etti. 'To enter [lit., to be able to
enter] {a: HE had to pay./b: I had to
pay./c: YOU [s.] had to pay./d:WE
had to pay./e: YOU [pl.] had to
pay./f: THEY had to pay.}' Yolda
araba.mız.ın benzin.i bitti. En
yakın benzin istasyon.u.na
kadar yürü.me.MİZ icap etti.
'We ran out of gas on the way [lit., **
On the way, our car's gasoline ran
out]. WE had to walk as far as the
nearest gas station [lit., ** OUR
walkING to the nearest gas station
was required].' *962:10.* necessity: -
be necessary. → = gerek-, = lâzım
ol- → ol- 12.

icat et- [eDer] '- invent' [A. icat (- -)
(icaDı) 'inventing, invention']:
Ampulü Edison icat etti. 'Edison
invented the light bulb.' *940:2.*
discovery: - discover. → bul- 2 ['-
discover', a place, a truth, a new way
of doing sth, a new invention],
keşfet- ['- discover, - find'].

iç çek-. → çek- 1.

iç- [er] '- take into, inside [one's body]'
[iç 'inside' + -0] 1 '- drink', when
the object of iç- is a drink: Proverb:
Dost ile ye, iç; alışveriş etme.
'Eat and drink with a friend, but don't
do business with him.' S: Ne
içersin[iz]? 'Q: {What would you
like to drink?/What do you
drink?/What will you have to
drink?}' C: {a: Maden su.yu/b:
Meyva su.yu/c: Bira/d: Kırmızı
şarap/e: Kahve/f: Çay/g: Rakı}
içerim. 'A: I'll have [lit., drink] {a:
mineral water/b: fruit juice/c: beer/d:
red wine/e: coffee/f: tea/g: raki}.' •
The possessed form of su 'water' is
irregular: onun su.Yu NOT su.Su:
benim suyum, senin suyun,
bizim suyumuz, etc. S: *
Kahvenizi nasıl içersiniz? 'Q:
How do you take [lit., drink] your
coffee?' [→ Kahvenizi nasıl
seversiniz? 'How do you like your
coffee?' → sev- 1.] C: * {a: Az
şekerli/b: Orta şekerli/c: Çok
şekerli/d: Sade} içerim. 'A: I
take it {a: with little sugar/b: with
medium sugar/c: with a lot of sugar/d:
black}.' Müslümanlar sadece
alkolsüz içkiler içer. '[Good]
Muslims only drink alcohol-free
drinks.' İçecek ne var? 'What is

there to drink?' Often iç-, even
WITHOUT an object designating an
alcoholic drink, may be understood to
mean '- drink alcoholic beverages':
Bahar'ın kocası * çok içiyor.
'Bahar's husband * is a heavy drinker
[lit., drinks * {a lot/too much}].' Bu
gece Umut fazla içti, sarhoş
oldu. 'Umut had too much to drink
this evening. He got drunk.' Proverb:
Dibi görünmeyen sudan içme.
'Don't drink from [a source of] water,
the bottom of which isn't visible.',
i.e., Don't set out to do something for
which you lack the necessary
information or qualifications. *8:29.*
eating: - drink; *88:24.* intoxication: -
tipple; *992:10.* excess: - overdo. → =
içki al- ['- use alcohol habitually']
→ al- 5, = içki kullan- ['- drink
(lit., use) alcoholic beverages'],
yudumlayarak iç- ['- sip, lit., -
drink sipping'] → yudumla-.

2 '- smoke', when the object of iç- is
sth smoked: {a: Sigara/b: Puro/c:
Pipo/d: Esrar/e: Afyon} içiyor.
'He smokes {a: cigarettes/b: cigars/c:
a pipe/d: hashish/e: opium}.' Bir
sigara içmez misiniz? 'Won't
you have [lit., ** smoke] a cigarette?'
Sigara içmek yasaktır. '{No
smoking./Smoking is forbidden.}'
352:7. publication: poster: * specific
signs. Bu akşam çok fazla
[sigara] içtim. 'This evening I
smoked too much.' *992:10.* excess: -
overdo. S: Burada sigara içebilir
miyim? 'Q: {May I smoke here?/Do
you mind if I smoke here?}' C:
Tabii, içebilirsiniz. 'A: Of course
you may smoke.' S: Sigara
içersem rahatsız olur
musun[uz]? 'Q: Will you be
uncomfortable if I smoke?' C: Evet,
olurum. İçmesen[iz] iyi olur.
'A: Yes, I will. It would be better [lit.,
good] if you didn't smoke.' *89:14.*
tobacco: - use tobacco. → = sigara
kullan-. For '- smoke' meaning '-
give off smoke' as in 'The embers are
still smoking', → duman çık- →
çık- 3.

3 '- eat', sometimes when the object
of iç- is a liquid, but not what we
usually consider a drink: Yemekten
önce bir tas çorba içelim.
'Before eating, let's have a bowl of
soup.' Dedem kışın kahvaltıda
çorba içerdi. 'My grandfather used
to eat soup for breakfast in the
winter.' iç- is used even when the

soup is eaten with a spoon, as is usually the case. The verb ye- '- eat' may also be used. → also iç- 4 directly below. *8:20.* eating: - eat.

4 '- take', when the object of iç- is a liquid medicine. İç- is also used for a solid if it is taken with water: **Başın ağrıyordu. {İlâcını/Hapını} içtin mi?** 'You had a headache [lit., Your head was aching]. Have you taken {your medicine/your pills}?' In this situation **al-** '- take' may replace iç-. *8:22.* eating: - devour.

içer- [ir] '- cover, - include, - comprise, - contain' [iç 'inside' + verb-forming suf. -Ar]: {a: **Ara sınav/b: Dönem son.u sınav.ı/c: Final sınav.ı/d: Yıl son.u sınav.ı} bütün kitabı içeriyor mu?** 'Does {a: the midterm examination/b: the quarter [*or* semester] final examination/c: the final examination/d: the year final examination} cover the whole book?' **Öğrenci: Öğretmenim, bu imtihan altıncı dersi de içeriyor mu?** 'Student: Teacher, does this examination also include the 6th lesson?' **Sağlık sigortanız bütün hastalıklar.I içeriyor.** 'Your health insurance covers all illnesses.' **Bir gecelik otel parası kahvaltı.yI da içeriyor mu?** 'Does the hotel rate for one night also include breakfast?' *771:3.* inclusion: - include. → = **içine al-** 1 → al- 1, = **kapsa-, dahil ol-** ['- be included /IN/'] → ol- 12.

içeri[.yE] gir-. → gir-.

içi sıkıl-. → sıkıl- 1.

içil- [ir] '- be taken into, inside [one's body]' [iç- + pass. suf -Il] 1 '- be drunk': **Bu çeşme.nin su.yu {a: içilir mi?/b: içilmez mi?}** 'Is the water from this fountain {a: {drinkable?/safe to drink? [lit., ** is it to be drunk?]/b: not drinkable? [lit., ** is it not to be drunk?]}' • The possessed form of **su** 'water' is irregular: **onun su.Yu** NOT ~~su.Su~~: **ben.im su.yum** 'my water', **sen.in su.yun, biz.im su.yumuz,** etc. *8:29.* eating: - drink.

2 '- be smoked': * **Sigara içilir.** 'Smoking area [lit., ** Cigarettes are smoked].' * **Sigara içilmez.** 'No smoking [lit., ** Cigarettes are not to be smoked].' *89:14.* tobacco: - use tobacco; *352:7.* publication: poster: * specific signs. → also iç- 2.

3 '- be eaten', sometimes when the subject of içil- is a liquid, but not a drink: **Sizin evde çok çorba içilir mi?** 'Do they eat a lot of soup at your house [lit., Is a lot of soup eaten...]?' **Kışın kahvaltıda çorba içilir.** 'Soup is eaten for breakfast in the winter.' İçil- is used even when the soup is eaten with a spoon, as is usually the case. In this situation the verb **yen-** '- be eaten' may replace içil-. *8:20.* eating: - eat.

4 '- be taken', when the subject of içil- is a liquid medicine. İçil- is also used for a solid if it is taken with water: * **Bu haplar {aç/tok} karn.ı.nA içilmez.** 'These pills are not to be taken ON {an empty/a full} stomach [karın, kaRNı].' *8:22.* eating: - devour. → = **alın-** 1.

içi sıkıl-. → sıkıl- 1.

içine al-. → al- 1.

içine çek-. → çek- 1.

idare et- [eDer] 1 '- administer, - direct, - manage, - run, - control, - govern, - rule' [A. idare (. - .) 'management, administration']: **Başbakan ülkeyi çok iyi idare ediyor.** 'The prime minister is running the country very well.' **Kaptan maç boyunca takımı çok güzel idare etti.** 'During the game, the captain {led/coached} the [sports] team very well.' **Bu hükümet ülkeyi dört yıl daha idare edecek.** 'This government is going to run the country for four more years.' **Kaptan fırtınalı havada gemi.si.ni zor idare etti.** 'The captain had difficulty controlling his ship in stormy weather.' *417:13.* authority: - possess or - wield authority; *573:8.* direction, management: - direct; *612:14.* government: - rule. → = **yönet-** 1.

2 /lA, ArAk/ '- economize /BY, by...ing/, - make ends meet /with/; - manage /with/, - manage to get along /with/, - get by /with/': **Babam vefat ettikten sonra çok az bir parayla idare ettik.** 'After my father passed away, we {made ends meet/managed to get along} with very little money.' **S u y u m u z**

tükenince çeşitli bitkiler {ye.mekle/yi.yerek} idare ettik. 'When our water ran out, we managed {by eat.ing} different kinds of plants.' Note a very common *colloq.* response to the following two questions: S1: Nasılsın[ız]? 'Q1: How are you?' or S2: İşler nasıl? 'Q2: How are things [going]?' C: Eh işte, idare ediyoruz. 'A: Well, not bad [lit., We're managing].' *409:12.* success: - manage; *994:4.* expedience: - make shift, - make do. → yetin- 2 ['- make do, - manage /with/, - be able to manage /with/'].

iddiaya gir-. → {bahse/iddiaya} gir-. → gir-.

idman yap-. → yap- 3.

ifade al-. → al- 1.

ifade et- [eDer] [A. ifade (. - .) 1 'expression, statement'. 2 'evidence, deposition'] 1 '- express, - say what one means, - state': * Murat düşüncelerini iyi ifade edemiyor. 'Murat can't express himself well [lit., can't express his thoughts well].' → = düşüncelerini anlat- → anlat- 2. *Formal:* Öncelikle şunu ifade etmek istiyorum:... 'First I would like to state the following:...'

kendini ifade et- '- express oneself': Murat kendi.ni iyi ifade edemiyor. Yabancı bir dilde insan.ın kendi.ni ifade etme.si kolay değil. 'Murat can't express himself well. It's not easy for a person to express himself in a foreign language.' Osman kendini en iyi {şiir.LE/şiir yaz.ARAK} ifade ettiğini düşünüyor. 'Osman thinks [that] he can express himself best {IN verse./BY writ.ING verse.}' *532:4.* diction: - phrase.

2 '- mean, - signify, - express': Bu {a: işaret/b: resim/c: söz/d: yazı} ne ifade ediyor? 'What does this {a: sign/b: picture/c: {remark/ statement/word}/d: piece [of writing]} mean?' *517:17.* signs, indicators: - signify; *518:8.* meaning: - mean. → = de- 3.

3 /için/ *fig.* usually together with a word of quantity: '- be important, of value /{TO/for}/, - mean sth /TO/': * Dostluk benim için çok şey ifade ediyor. 'Friendship {means a lot TO me/is very important TO me}.' *996:12.* importance: - matter.

ifade ver-. → ver- 1.

iflâs et- [eDer] [A. iflâs (. -) 1 'bankruptcy, insolvency'. 2 'failure of a major project or policy']: 1 '- go bankrupt, - go under': {a: Yeşilırmak sineması/b: Bu işyeri/c: Bülent bey/d: Dükkân} iflâs etti. '{a: The Yeşilırmak [lit., Green River] movie house/b: This workplace/c: Bülent bey/d: The shop} has gone bankrupt.' *625:7.* nonpayment: - go bankrupt. → = bat- 2.

2 '- fail completely', a major policy, project, plan, idea, marriage: {Plânımız/Politikamız/Evliliğimiz} iflâs etti. '{Our plan/Our policy/Our marriage} has failed completely.' Son seçimlerde aldığı yenilgiden sonra iktidar parti.si.nin program.ı iflâs etmey.e mahkûmdur. 'After the defeat it sustained in the recent elections, the program of the party in power is doomed to failure.' *410:9a.* failure: - fail.

3 'for sth - become regarded as worthless, - go out of favor, style': Kardeşim, savunduğun ideoloji çoktan iflâs etti, * bırak bu kafayı artık. 'My friend, the ideology [that] you are defending went out of favor a long time ago, * just forget about it now [lit., ** 'leave this head', i.e., mental attitude].' *390:9.* disuse: - obsolesce.

iftihar et- [eDer] /lA/ '- be or - feel proud /OF/, - take pride /IN/' [A. iftihar (. . -) 'pride, a feeling proud']: NON-verbal noun as object: {a: Oğlum.LA/b: Kızım.LA/c: Kocam.LA/d: Karım.LA/e: İşim.LE} iftihar ediyorum. 'I'm proud {a: OF my son/b: OF my daughter/c: OF my husband/d: OF my wife/e: OF my job [or OF my work, OF what I have done]}.' Pronoun as object: {Amerikalıyım/Türküm}, ve * bunun.LA da iftihar ediyorum. 'I'm {an American/a Turk}, and * I'm proud OF it.' VERBAL noun as object: '- be proud /{OF [do]ING/TO [do]}/': Sizin şirketiniz.le iş {yapmak.LA} iftihar ediyoruz. 'We are proud {OF doing/TO do} business with your company.' *136:5.* pride: - take pride. → = /DAn/ **kıvanç duy-** → duy- 3, = /lA/ {**övün-/öğün-**} 1, ≠ /Dan/ **utan-**.

{**iğren-** [ir]/**tiksin-** [ir]} /DAn/ '- feel disgust, horror /AT/, loathing /FOR/; - be disgusted /{BY/WITH}/, revolted /{BY/BECAUSE OF}/': **Yemeğin içinde sinek görünce iğrendim.** 'When I saw a fly in the food, I was disgusted.' → **midesi bulan-** ['- be upset', stomach]. **Odadaki pis koku.DAN iğrendi.** 'He was {revolted/disgusted} BY the stench [lit., bad smell] in the room.' **Yaptığı kötü işleri öğrenince o.nDAN iğrendim.** 'When I learned the despicable things [that] he had done, I was disgusted WITH him.' *64:4.* unsavoriness: - disgust.

ihmal et- '- neglect, - let slide, - slight, not - pay attention to, - fail to do sth, - omit' [A. **ihmal** (. -) 'neglecting']: NON-verbal noun as object: **Derslerin.E iyi çalış, * ödevlerini ihmal etme.** '{Study hard./lit., Study your lessons well.} Don't {fail to do/neglect} your homework.' A more common American English equivalent in this situation: 'Don't forget to do your homework[* NOT ~~homeworkS~~].' **Aman sağlığınızı ihmal etmeyin. * Her şey.in baş.ı sağlık!** 'For goodness sake don't neglect your health. * There's nothing more important than [one's] health! [lit., ** Health is (at) the head of everything!]' **Ailenizi ihmal etmeyin. Sadece telefonla arayıp sormak yetmez, sık sık ziyaret edin.** 'Don't neglect your family. It's not enough just to call them. Visit them often.' VERBAL noun as object: **İstanbul'a gidince adresini verdiğim lokantada imambayıldı ve ayva tatlısı yemeyi sakın ihmal etme!** 'When you go to Istanbul, {be sure/lit., don't fail} to eat **imambayıldı** and quince dessert at the restaurant whose address I gave you!' **İmambayıldı** is the name of a popular dish of stuffed eggplant cooked in olive oil. Written as two words, i.e., **İmam bayıldı**, it means '{The imam was crazy about it./The imam fainted.}' **Tatilde spor yapmayı, bol bol su içmeyi ihmal etmeyin.** 'During the vacation don't forget to do some

sports and to drink lots of water.' <u>Proverb</u>: **Allah imhal eder, ihmal etmez.** 'God may delay [i.e., His punishment or reward], but He never fails to provide {one/it}.' *340:6.* neglect: - neglect.

ihraç et- [eDer] /A/ '- export /to/' [A. **ihraç** (. -) 'export, exportation']: **Türkiye Ortadoğu ülkeleri.ne başlıca buğday, pancar ve tütün ihraç eder.** 'Turkey exports mainly wheat, beets, and tobacco to the countries of the Middle East.' *190:17.* emergence: - export. → ≠ **ithal et-**.

ihtar et-. → {**uyar-/ikaz et-/ ihtar et-**}.

ihtiyaca cevap ver-. → ver- 1.

ihtiyacı karşıla-. → karşıla- 2.

ihtiyacı ol-. → ol- 12.

ihtiyacını gör-. → gör- 4.

ihtiyarla- [r] '- grow old, - age, - get old', for persons, not things [A. **ihtiyar** (. . -) 'old, old person' + verb-forming suf. -lA]: **Babam çok ihtiyarladı. Artık bastonsuz yürüyemiyor.** 'My father has gotten quite old. He can't walk without a cane anymore.' *303:10.* age: - age; *841:9.* oldness: - age. → = **yaşı ilerle-** → ilerle- 3, = **yaşlan-**. For a non-living thing as the subject of '- get old, - become worn-out', → **eski-**.

ikaz et-. → {**uyar-/ikaz et-/ ihtar et-**}.

ikna et- [eDer] /a: A, b: A, c: A dair, d: konusunda/ '- persuade or - convince sb /a: to [do sth], b: θ [that], c: {that/to the effect that}, d: on the subject of/' [A. **ikna** (. -) 'persuasion, persuading']: **Fikr.i.ni herkes.E anlattı fakat kimse.yİ ikna edemedi.** 'He told θ everyone his idea, but he couldn't convince anyone.' **Ayşe'yİ haklı olduğ.um.A [DAİR] ikna ettim.** 'I convinced Ayşe θ that I was right.' **Ayşin'i evlilik konu.su.nda * yanlış düşündüğ.ü.nE ikna ettik.** 'We convinced Ayşin θ * that she was {wrong/mistaken} [lit., thinking incorrectly] about [lit., on the subject of] marriage.' **Turgut'U bu akşam bizimle sinemaya**

gelmey.E ikna ettik. 'We convinced Turgut TO come to the movies with us this evening.' * Mümkün değil, onu ikna edemezsin; * [kendi] gözüyle görse yine inanmaz. 'There's no way you can convince him. * Even if he sees it with his own eyes, he still won't believe it.' *375:23.* motivation, inducement: - persuade; *952:18.* belief: - convince. → = kandır- 2, = inandır-.

ikram et- [eDer] [A. ikram (. -) 'an offering'] 1 /A/ '- serve or - offer /θ/ sb sth, - serve or - offer sth /to/ sb', usually food or drink: Siz.E ne ikram edebilirim? 'What can I offer θ you?' Siz.E bir {kahve/çay/içki} ikram edebilir miyim? '{Can I get you/May I offer you} a {coffee/tea/drink}?' Pazar günü büyükannemlere gittik. {Biz.E ayran ve börek ikram ettiler}. 'On Sunday we went to my grandmother's house. {They offered θ us ayran [i.e., a yogurt and water mixture served as a cold drink] and böreks [i.e., a small, flaky pastry filled with thin layers usually of cheese or cooked ground beef]./They offered ayran and böreks TO us.}' *439:4.* offer: - offer; *478:12.* giving: - give. → = sun- 1, takdim et- 2 ['- present, - submit, - offer sth /to/ sb', report, document rather than food or drink].

2 '- give a discount, - go or - come down in price': A: * Çok pahalı, * biraz ikram edemez misiniz? 'A: That's too {much/expensive}, * won't you come down a bit?' B: Peki, * sizi kırmayalım, madem iki radyo alıyorsunuz, * 10 lira ikramımız olsun. 'B: OK, I don't want to [lit., let me not] {put you off/discourage you}. Since you're buying two radios, * I'll give you 10 liras off [lit., ** let our discount be...].' * Ne kadar ikram edeceksiniz? 'How much of a discount will you give [us]?' *631:2.* discount: - discount. → = in- 5, = indir- 3, ≠ {artır-/arttır-} 1.

ilâve et- [eDer] /A/ '- add sth /to/ sth' [A. ilâve (. -.) 'addition, increase']: Çorba.ya tuz ilâve et. 'Add salt to the soup.' Evimiz.e bir oda ilâve ettik. 'We added a room to our house.' Yağ ile unu kavurun, * iç.i.ne süt ilâve edin. 'Fry oil and flour and * add milk [lit., ** to

its, i.e., the mixture's, inside].' *253:5.* addition: - add to. → = ekle-, = kat-.

ileri al-. → al- 1.

ileri git-. → git- 1a.

ileri kal-. → kal- 1.

ileri sür-. → sür- 1.

ilerle- [r] 1 /DAn, A doğru/ '- advance, - move forward /THROUGH, toward/': Cenaze alay.ı yavaş yavaş ilerliyordu. 'The funeral procession was moving slowly forward.' Askerler ağaçların arası.nDAN hızla ırmağ.A doğru ilerliyordu. 'The soldiers were rapidly advancing THROUGH the trees toward the river.' → ≠ gerile- 1. *fig.*: Her şey plânlandığı gibi ilerliyordu. 'Everything [i.e., plans, projects] was {going forward/proceeding} as planned.' Durum sanıldığının aksine daha farklı bir biçimde ilerliyordu. 'The situation was progressing quite contrary to expectations [lit., to what had been expected].' *162:2.* progression: - progress.

2 '- improve, - get better': Mary'nin Türkçesi ilerliyor. 'Mary's Turkish is improving.' *392:7.* improvement: - get better. → = geliş- 2, ≠ bozul-, ≠ gerile- 2, ≠ kötüleş-.

3 '- pass, - get on', time: {vakit/zaman} ilerle- 'for time - pass, - advance, for it - get late': * Vakit epeyce ilerledi. * Gitsem iyi olur. 'It's gotten quite late [lit., ** time has advanced quite a bit]. * {I'd better go./It would be good if I went.}' *845:7.* lateness: - be late.

* yaşı ilerle- '- get on in years, - grow old, - age, - get old', for people, not things [yaş 'age' of a person]: Hatice'nin yaş.ı ilerliyor * yüzü kırış kırış olmuş. 'Hatice is getting on in years. * Her face has gotten all wrinkled.' *303:10.* age: - age; *841:9.* oldness: - age. → = ihtiyarla-, = yaşlan-.

ilerlet- [ir] [ilerle- + caus. suf. -t] 1 '- advance sth, - move sth forward': Arabanı biraz ilerlet. 'Move your car foward a bit.' *172:5a.* motion: -

move sth; *903:9.* pushing, throwing: - push.

2 /verb stem-A verb stem-A, ArAk/ '- improve, - develop sth /by...ing/': **Mary Türkiye'ye gidince Türkçe'sini çok ilerletti.** 'When Mary went to Turkey, she improved her Turkish a lot.' **Bir yıl içerisinde Mary {oku.ya oku.ya/oku.yarak} Türkçesi.ni çok ilerletti.** 'In one year Mary has greatly improved her Turkish {by read.ing a lot/by read.ing}.' *392:9.* improvement: - improve, - make better. → = **geliştir-** 1.

ilet- [ir] 1 /A/ '- take or - convey /to/, - forward, - pass sth on /to/': **{Mesaj.ın.ı/Haber.in.i/E-mail.in.i} Serkan'a ilettim.** 'I {conveyed your message/passed on your news/forwarded your e-mail} to Serkan.' **S: Lütfen {bayram tebriğimi/başarı dileklerimi/mutluluk dileklerimi} Kemal'ler.e iletir misin?** 'Q: Would you please convey {my best wishes for the holiday/my wishes for success/my wishes for happiness} to Kemal's family?' **C: Tabii efendim, {iletirim/ileteceğim}.** 'A: Of course, {sir/ma'am}, {I'll convey them}.' **Lütfen ev ödevimi öğretmen.e iletir misiniz? Yarın derse gelemeyeceğim.** 'Will you please take my homework to the teacher? I won't be able to come to class tomorrow.' * **Üç {hafta.lığ.ı.nA/ay.lığ.ı.nA} Alanya'ya gidiyorum. Mektuplarımı ban.A iletir misin?** 'I'm going to Alanya FOR three {weeks/months}. Would you forward my mail [lit., letters] to me?' *176:12.* transferal, transportation: - transport; *176:15.* : - send. → = **ulaştır-** 1 ['- transport, - convey, - bring or - get sth /to/'], **gönder-** ['- send sth /to/ sb, - send θ sb sth'], **yolla-**. Same.

2 '- conduct', i.e., - allow to pass through: **Su elektriğ.İ iletir.** 'Water conducts θ electricity.' *239:15.* channel: - channel.

ilgi çek-. → **çek-** 1.

ilgi duy-. → **duy-** 3.

ilgilen- [ir] [ilgi 'interest' + verb-forming suf. -lAn] 1 /lA/ '- be interested /IN/, - take an interest /IN/': **Gençliğimde spor ve müzik.LE ilgilendim.** '{When I was young/lit., In my youth}, I was interested IN sports and music.' **Şimdi spor.LA {fazla/o kadar çok/hiç} ilgilenmiyorum.** 'Now I'm not {very/not that/not at all} interested IN sports.' **Politika.DAN çok, sanat.LA ilgilenirim.** 'I'm more interested IN art THAN in politics.' *980:3b.* curiosity: - be curious. → = **ilgi duy-** → **duy-** 3, **ilgi çek-** ['- appeal to, - interest'] → **çek-** 1.

2 /lA/ '- show concern /FOR/, - be concerned /with/; - attend /TO/, - look /AFTER/': **Her baba.nın çocuklar.ı.yLA ilgilenme.si gerekir.** 'Every father should show concern FOR his children.' **Amerika'dan * bir misafir.im geliyor, haftasonu onun.LA ilgilenmem gerekiyor.** 'I have a guest coming [lit., A guest of mine is coming] from the U.S. Over the weekend I must {attend TO him/look AFTER him/take care OF him}.' **Ev.in bütün alışveriş.i.yLE eşim ilgileniyor, * ben karışmıyorum.** 'My wife attends to all the shopping in the household. * I {don't get involved./don't interfere./stay out of it.}' *339:9.* carefulness: - look after; *982:5.* attention: - attend to. → = /A/ **bak-** 3, = /lA/ **meşgul ol-** 2 → **ol-** 12.

ilgilendir- [ir] [ilgilen- + caus. suf. -DIr] 1 /I/ '- interest, - appeal to, - arouse the interest of, *colloq.* - be into': **Müzik o.nU çok ilgilendiriyor.** 'Music really interests him.' * **Bu konu hepimizi ilgilendiren bir konu.** 'This subject is one [lit., a subject] that {interests/concerns} all of us.' *377:6.* allurement: - attract; *980:3a.* curiosity: - make curious, - interest. → = **ilgi çek-** → **çek-** 1.

2 /I/ '- be one's business, affair, - concern': **Bu konu Füsun'u ilgilendirir. Ben bir şey söyleyemem.** 'This is Füsun's business [lit., ** This subject concerns Füsun]. I can't say anything about it.' **A: Burhan'la tatile çıkmanı istemiyorum.** 'A: I don't want you to go on vacation with Burhan.' **B: Bu sen.İ ilgilendirmez.** 'B: This {does not concern you/is none of your business}.' * **Her ülkenin rejimi**

kendisi.ni ilgilendirir. 'Every regime is [only] its own business.', i.e., is not the business of others on the outside. *897:3.* involvement: - be involved.

ilikle- '- button, - button up' [ilik 'buttonhole; button loop' + verb-forming suf. -lA]: Oğlum ön.ün.ü ilikle, * üşüteceksin. 'Son, button up [lit., ** button your front] [or] you'll * catch a chill.' Pantolon.un.un ön.ü.nü ilikle-mey.i unutmuşsun yine. 'It seems you've forgotten to button {your fly/lit., the front of your pants} again. Pantolon.un.u ilikle. 'Button up {your pants/your fly}.' Dışarıya çıkmadan önce meşin ceketini ilikledi. 'Before going out, he buttoned [up] his leather jacket.' Niçin gömleğ.in.in sadece üç düğme.si.ni ilikledin, hepsi.ni ikilese! 'Why did you button only three buttons on [lit., of] your shirt? Come on, button them all.' Gömleğ.im.i iliklerken iki düğme.si koptu. 'While [I was] buttoning my shirt, two buttons [lit., two of its buttons] popped off.' *293:6.* closure: - close. → ≠ düğmelerini çöz- ['- unbutton'] → çöz- 1.

ilişki kur-. → kur- 1.

imren- [ir] [i m r e n 'envy without malice' + verb-forming suf. -θ] 1 /A/ '- long /FOR/, - feel an appetite /FOR/': Çocuğ.un yediğ.i dondurma.yA imrendim. 'I {AM LONGING/longed} FOR the ice cream [that] the child {is eating/was eating}.' In this sentence if the feeling is understood to continue at present, the present tense translation of imrendim applies; if it is no longer regarded as being in effect, the past tense translation is appropriate. • In reference to a PRESENT condition, certain common Turkish verbs designating a state, i.e., a feeling, emotion, or sensation, often have the simple PAST tense, but the equivalent English has the simple or the continuous PRESENT. *100:15.* desire: - want to. → = özen- 2.

2 /A/ '- long /FOR/ sth unobtainable, - envy without malice': * Yeni eviniz.E imrendim doğrusu, ne kadar güzel! 'I really {envy/envied} you {θ/FOR} your house. How nice it is!' *154:3.* envy: - envy. → = özen- 2, = kıskan- 1.

imtihan et- [eDer] /DAn/ '- test, - give sb an exam /IN/, - examine sb /IN [a subject]/' [A. imtihan (. . -) 'examination']: Mehmet'i bir imtihan et, bakalım çarpım tablo.su.nu öğrenmiş mi? 'Go ahead and test Mehmet. Let's see {if he has learned his multiplication tables./lit., has he learned his multiplication tables?]' Öğretmen: Bugün * öğrenciler.i Türkçe der.si.nDEN imtihan ettim. 'Teacher: Today * I gave the students an exam IN Turkish [lit., ** from the Turkish lesson].' NOT sınav et- or {sınav/imtihan} ver-. *937:21.* inquiry: - interrogate. → ≠ {sınav/ imtihan} ol- ['- take an examination /IN/, - be examined /IN/'] → ol- 10.1, ≠ {sınava/ imtihana} gir- ['- take an examination /IN/'].

imtihan kazan-. → {sınav/imtihan} kazan-. → kazan- 3.

imtihan ol-. → {sınav/imtihan} ol-. → ol- 10.1.

imtihan ver-. → {sınav/imtihan} ver-. → ver- 1.

imtihana gir-. → sınava gir-.

imtihandan kal-. → {sınavdan/imtihandan} kal- 1.

imza at-. → at- 3.

imza et-. → directly below.

{imzala- [r]/imza et- [eDer]} /I/ '- sign' [A. imza (. -) 'signature' + verb-forming suf. -lA]: Benden kalem aldı ve çeki imzaladı. 'She took a pen from me and signed the check.' S: * Nere.yİ imzalamam lâzım? 'Q: Where should I sign?' C1: Lütfen bura.yI imzalayın. 'A: Please sign θ here.' C2: Lütfen çek.in arka.sı.nı imzalayın! 'A2: Please sign the back of the check.' Yazılı belgeler.i okumadan imzala-mam. 'I won't sign [the] documents [lit., written documents] without reading them.' *546:6.* letter: - letter. → = imza at- ['- sign', *perhaps less formal* than the above, *colloq.:* '- put one's John Hancock on (obj.: the check) (lit., - throw (one's) signature ON (the check).'] → at- 3.

in- [er] 1 /DAn, A/ '- go down, - descend /{from/BY WAY OF}, to/': {Yaşlı adam/Dedem} merdivenleri {a: ağır ağır/b: yavaş yavaş/c: dinlene dinlene/d: oflaya puflaya/e: zar zor/f: güçlükle} inmiş. '{The old man/My grandfather} {went down/descended} the stairs {a, b: slowly/c: resting along the way [lit., ** resting resting]/d: huffing and puffing/e, f: with difficulty}.' * Bilge hanım {koşar adımlar.la/koşar adım} merdivenler.DEN indi. 'Bilge hanım ran down θ the stairs.' 174:8. swiftness: - speed; 401:5. haste: - make haste. * Merdivenler.DEN {a: dördüncü kat.tan/b: beşinci kattaki oda.sı.ndan/c: çatı katı.ndan/d: üst kat.tan} indi. 'She went down θ the stairs {a: from the fourth floor/b: from her room on the fifth floor/c: from the roof/d: {from the next floor/from a floor above us/from the top floor}}.' * Altuğ bu merdiven.DEN [aşağı(.ya)] indi. 'Altuğ went down [BY WAY OF] {these stairs/this ladder}.' Altuğ aşağı(.ya) indi. 'Altuğ {came/went} down.', i.e., usually by stairs, ladder. Ben bu merdiven.DEN inemem; çok dik. 'I can't go down θ this ladder. It's too steep.' Proverb: * Her çıkış.ın bir iniş.i var. 'What goes up must come down [lit, Every ascent has a descent].', often in reference to a person's position in society. 194:5. descent: - descend. → ≠ [yukarı(ya)] çık- → çık- 5, ≠ tırman- 1.

* inme in- '- have or - suffer a stroke, - be or - become paralyzed' [inme 'a coming down, stroke']: * Dayı.m.ın sağ taraf.ı.nA inme indi. 'My [maternal] uncle had a stroke that affected his right side [lit., ** a stroke came down ON my uncle's right side].' 85:46b. disease: - take sick in particular ways. → = felç ol- → ol- 10.2.

şehre in- [şehir (şeHRi) 'city'] '- go /θ/ downtown, /INTO/ town, /INTO/ the city', even if the town or city is up a hill: * Dün şehr.E indim. 'I went INTO town yesterday.' 177:18. travel: - travel; 194:5. descent: - descend.

2 /DAn/ '- get down /{from/OFF}/, - get off or out /OF/ a vehicle, - dismount /{θ/from}/ an animal': S: Nerede {inmem lâzım/ inmeliyim}? 'Q: Where {should I get off}?' C: {Gelecek durakta/Son durakta/* İki durak sonra} inin. 'A: Get off {at the next stop./at the last stop./* two stops after this one.}' S: * Kaç durak sonra inmem lâzım? 'Q: How many stops do I still have to go [lit., After how many stops should I get off]?' C: * İki durak sonra inin. 'A: Get off {at the second stop/lit., after two stops}.' Nerede inece ğ.im.i söyleyin lütfen. 'Please tell me where I should get off.' Otobüs.TEN nerede indi? 'Where did he get off θ the bus?' A bus driver may ask you: S: Nerede inmek istiyorsunuz? 'Q: Where do you want to get off?' C1: Gelecek durakta [inmek istiyorum]. 'A1: [I want to get off] at the next stop.' If you are on the bus and want to notify the driver that you want to get off, you may use the complete sentence above, but you are MORE LIKELY just to say: İnecek var. 'I'm getting off', also, but less polite. [lit., ** There is a going-to-get-off (person)].' You use these same words to notify the driver that sb ELSE is trying to get off. When a taxi or shared cab driver asks you where you want to get off, a greater variety of answers is appropriate: C2: {Müsait/Uygun} bir yerde [inmek istiyorum]. 'A2: [I want to get off] at a {suitable} place [i.e., anywhere around here that is suitable].' C3: Köşede. 'A3: At the corner.' C4: Beyaz evin önünde. 'A4: In front of the white house.' 194:7. descent: - get down. → ≠ bin- 1, ≠ atla- 3.

3 /A/ '- land /{AT/IN/ON}/', subj.: plane, but not helicopter: Uçak {saat kaçta/ne zaman} inecek? '{At what time/When} does the plane land?' 2:45'te [iki kırkbeşte] New York'tan kalkan uçak {havaalan.ımız.A/havaliman-.ımız.A} inmek üzeredir. 'The plane that left New York at 2:45 is about to land {AT our airport}.' 184:43. aviation: - land. → = kon- [for a helicopter, bird, not a plane], ≠ havalan- 2, ≠ kalk- 2.

195

4 '- go down, - decrease, - fall', prices, swelling, fever, tire: **Altın fiyatları indi.** 'Gold prices have fallen.' *252:6.* decrease: - decrease; *633:6b.* cheapness: - become cheaper. * **Dolar kaç lira olacak, çıkacak mı, inecek mi?** 'How many liras will there be to a dollar [lit. how many liras will a dollar be], will the number rise or fall [lit., will it, i.e., the dollar, rise or fall]?' → = **fiyatlar düş-** → düş- 3, = **ucuzla-** ['- get cheaper, - go down or - drop in price'], ≠ **fiyatlar yüksel-** → yüksel- 2, ≠ **pahalan-**, ≠ **fiyatlar tırman-** → tırman- 2. **Başımdaki şiş indi.** 'The swelling on my head has gone down.' *252:6.* decrease: - decrease. → ≠ **şiş-** 1. # **Hastanın ateşi indi.** 'The patient's temperature fell.' → = **ateşi azal-**, = **ateşi düş-** → düş- 3, ≠ **ateşi art-** → art- 1, ≠ **ateşi çık-** → çık- 6, ≠ **ateşi yüksel-** → yüksel- 2.

'- go flat, - collapse, - deflate, - lose air [slowly]': {**Lâstikler/Lâstik bot**} **indi.** 'The {tires/rubber boat} went flat.' *260:10.* contraction: - collapse. → = **sön-** [for the items above and **balon** 'balloon'], ≠ **şiş-** 2. For '- get a flat tire [sudden action]', → **lâstik patla-** → patla- 1.

5 '- reduce the price, - go or - come down in price, - give a discount': **Pazarlık SON.U.CU satıcı 5 lira daha indi.** 'AS A RESULT OF bargaining, the salesman went down {another 5 liras/5 liras more}.' *631:2.* discount: - discount. → = **ikram et-** 2, = **indir-** 3.

inan- [ır] [inan 1 'belief'. 2 'faith' + verb-forming suf. -Ө] 1 /A/ '- believe /Ө/ sth, what sb says, sb': * **Onun** {**bütün söyledikler.i.nE/her söylediğ.i.nE**} **inanma.** 'Don't believe {Ө everything he says}.' * **Söyledikler.i.nE mi, yoksa yaptıklar.ı.nA mı inanalım?** 'Shall we believe Ө what he says or Ө what he does [i.e., give greater importance to his words or to his deeds]?' **Küçük çocuk şeker veren adam.ın sözler.i.nE inandı ve onunla gitti.** 'The little child believed Ө the words of the man who had given him candy and went off with him.' → {**aldan-/kan-**} ['- be deceived, fooled, taken in /BY/']. **Doğru.yu söylediğ.in.E inandı.**

'He believed Ө that you had told the truth.' **İddialarını ispat edersen san.A inanırım.** 'If you prove your claims, I'll believe Ө you.' **Bir bilim adamı OLARAK böyle bir iddia.nın doğruluğ.u.nA inanıyor musunuz?** 'AS a {scholar/scientist} do you believe in the truth of such a claim?' * **İster inan ister inanma!** 'Believe it or not!' **Türkçe.yİ o kadar kusursuz konuşuyordu ki birçok kişi Amerikalı olduğu.nA inanmıyordu.** 'He spoke Turkish so {perfectly/lit., faultlessly} that many people didn't believe Ө [that] he was an American.' Proverb: **Yalancının evi yanmış, kimse inanmamış.** 'The liar's house burned down. No one believed him.', i.e., when he said that his house was on fire. *952:10.* belief: - believe. * **İnanın [ki]...** 'Believe me...!': **İnanın [ki] doğru söylüyorum.** 'Believe me, I'm telling the truth.' Another very common phrase used to emphasize the truth of a statement: **Vallahi billahi** '{I swear to God it's true!/So help me God!}' *334:* * *11.* affirmation: INTERJ. I swear! ; *952:10.* belief: - believe.

gözlerine inanaMA- 'NOT to be able - believe Ө one's eyes' [göz 'eye']: **Hediye paket.i.ni açıp da içinden çıkan elmas yüzüğü görünce gözler.i.nE inanamadı.** 'When she opened the gift [lit., gift package] and saw the diamond ring inside [lit., that came out from inside], she couldn't believe Ө her eyes.' **Aman Allahım, gözler.im.E inanamıyorum; şurada oturan bey benim ilkokul arkadaşım Metin değil mi?** 'Oh my God, I can't believe Ө my eyes! Isn't that gentleman sitting there my [old] primary schoolmate Metin?' *954:5.* unbelief: - disbelieve.

2 /A/ '- trust /Ө/, - believe /IN/, - have confidence /IN/': **Ben siz.E inanırım.** 'I {trust Ө you/believe IN you}.' *952:15.* belief: - believe in. → = **güven-**, **emin ol-** ['- be or - become sure, certain, convinced /OF/, /Ө/ that'] → ol- 12.

3 /A/ '- believe /IN/ the truth of, /IN/ the existence of': {**Allah'A/ Tanrı'yA**} **inanırım.** 'I believe {IN God}.' **Allah'ın varlığ.ı.nA inanıyorum.** 'I believe IN the existence of God.' **Öyle bir şey.in**

var olduğ.u.nA inanmıyorum. 'I don't believe {θ that such a thing exists/in the existence of such a thing}.' Proverbs: Allah'A inanmayan.A kul da inanmaz. 'A servant of God [i.e., any will-possessing being, mortal] does not believe θ the person who does not believe IN God.' Fal.A inanma, falsız da kalma. 'Do not believe IN fortune telling, but have a fortune [told] anyway [lit., don't remain without a fortune].' *952:15.* belief: - believe in.

inandır- [ır] /A / '- convince or - persuade sb to believe /θ/ sb or sth, - get sb to believe /θ/ sth, - make sb believe /θ/ sth' [inan- + caus. suf. -DIr]: Turhan olay.ı herkes.E anlattı fakat kimse.yİ inandıramadı. 'Turhan told θ everyone about the event, but he couldn't get anyone to believe [him].' Ali sınıf.ı.nı {geçtiğ.i.nE/geçeceğ.i.nE} anne.si.nİ inandıramadı. 'Ali couldn't convince his mother {θ that he had passed/θ that he was going to pass} on to the next grade [lit., ** pass his grade].' *375:23.* motivation, inducement: - persuade; *952:18.* belief: - convince. → = ikna et-, = kandır- 2.

inat et- [eDer] [A. inat (. -) 'obstinacy, stubbornness']: 1 '- be obstinate, stubborn': * Bırak inat etmey.i de ha[y]di bizimle gel. 'Come on, don't be so stubborn and come with us.' İnat etme, * alırım ayağ.ım.ın alt.ı.nA! 'Don't be stubborn or * I'll give you a whipping [lit., ** take you under my feet].' *361:7.* obstinacy: - balk. → = diren- 1.

2 /DA/ '- persist /IN/, - insist /ON/': Çocuk sütünü iç.me.mek.TE inat ediyor. 'The child insists ON not drinking his milk.' *361:7.* obstinacy: - balk; *421:8.* demand: - insist. → = diren- 1.

fikrinde inat et- '- persist /IN/ or - insist /ON/ one's view, opinion' [A. fikir (fiKRi) 'thought, idea, opinion']: Dediklerimi anlamay.a yanaşmadı, kendi fikr.i.nde inat etti. 'He refused to understand what I had said. He insisted on his own view.' *361:7.* obstinacy: - balk; *421:8.* demand: - insist.

incele- [r] '- examine carefully, closely, minutely, in detail, - study carefully, - inspect, - investigate, - research' [ince 'small, fine' + verb-forming suf. -lA]: Bileziği aldı ve dakikalarca inceledi. 'He took the bracelet and examined it carefully for several minutes.' Başbakan deprem bölgesini inceledi. 'The prime minister inspected the earthquake area.' Araştırmacı, köylüler.in halı dokuma yöntemler.i.ni inceledi. 'The field anthropologist [lit., researcher] investigated methods of rug weaving [in use] among the villagers.' Başvuru {formunuzu/ dilekçenizi} inceledik. {Maalesef işe alınmadınız./ Pazartesi günü işe başlayabilirsiniz.} 'We have considered [lit., examined] {your application}. {Unfortunately you have not been accepted./You may begin work on Monday.}' Her olay.I tek tek inceleyeceğiz. 'We will investigate each {incident/event} one by one.' Bu konuyu üç açıdan inceleyelim. 'Let's examine this issue from 3 {angles/points of view}.' *27:14.* vision: - scrutinize; *937:25.* inquiry: - make a close study of. → = tetkik et-, = muayene et- ['- examine', mostly for a doctor and a patient], araştır- 2 ['- investigate, - explore, - research, - study, - do research on, - try to find out'], kontrol et- ['- check, - inspect, - check on, - check to see whether sth is the case or not'].

indir- [ir] [in- + caus. suf. -DIr] 1 /DAn, A/ '- lower /from, to/, - bring down /from, to/, - take down, - unload, - download': Akşam olunca dükkân.ın {kepenkler.i.ni/panjurlar.ı.nı} indiririz. 'When it is evening, we lower {the [metal rolling] shutters/the [slatted] shutters} of the shop.' Elini önce kaldırdı, sonra indirdi. 'First he raised his hand, then he lowered it.' Taksi şoförü bavulları araba.dan indirdi. 'The taxi driver took the luggage [down] from the car.' → ≠ kaldır- 1. Proverb: Eşeği dam.a çıkaran yine kendi indirir. 'He who takes a donkey up to the roof takes him down again himself.', i.e., The person who creates a difficult situation has to straighten it out himself. → ≠ çıkar- 4. # İnternet.ten bazı faydalı programları indirdim. 'I downloaded some useful programs from the Internet.' *912:4*. depression: - depress; *1041:18*. computer science: - computerize.

2 /DA, DAn/ '- let {off/out}, - drop off, - discharge, - unload /at, from/', passengers: You are in a taxi or shared cab. You want to get out. You say: **Beni {burada/gelecek durakta/köşede} indirin, lütfen.** 'Please {drop/let} me off {here/at the next stop/at the corner}.' On a bus you would usually use the verb **in-**, not **indir-**, and say: **İnecek var. '{**I want to get off [or *informal:* Coming through.]/ Someone wants to get of.} [lit., ** 'There is a going-to-get-off (person).' This could refer to you or to another passenger that you see trying to leave the bus. **Tren yolcuları indirmek için istasyonda durdu.** 'The train stopped at the station to let the passengers off.' *908:23*. ejection: - unload. → = **bırak-** 2, ≠ **al-** 2, ≠ **bindir-**.

3 /DAn, A/ '- lower, - reduce, - decrease, - bring down [prices, rates] /from, to/, - give a discount': **Pek çok mağaza fiyatlarını indirdi.** 'Many stores lowered their prices.' **Çok pahalı! * Biraz indirebilir misiniz?** 'That's {too/very} expensive! * Could you {come down a bit/give us a small discount}?' * **Ne kadar indirebilirsiniz?** 'How much of a discount can you give [us]?' *631:2*. discount: - discount; *633:6a*. cheapness: - lower prices. → = **ikram et-** 2, = **in-** 5, ≠ {**artır-/arttır-**} 1.

4 '- bring down, - knock down': **Boksör ilk rauntta rakibini indirdi.** 'The boxer brought down his opponent in the first round.' *912:5*. depression: - fell. → = **yık-** 2.

indiril- [ir] [indir- + pass. suf. -Il] 1 /a: DAn, b: A, c: {tarafından/CA}/ '- be lowered /a: from, b: to, c: by/': **10 Kasım'da bütün bayraklar * yarı.ya indirilir.** 'On the 10th of November [i.e., the date of Atatürk's death] all flags * are lowered to half {staff/mast}.' *912:4*. depression: - depress.

2 /a: DA, b: DAn, c: tarafından/ '- be let off /a: at [a place], b: from [a vehicle], c: by/': **Son durakta bütün yolcular [sürücü tarafından] indirildi.** 'At the last stop all the passengers were let off [by the driver].' *912:4*. depression: - depress. → ≠ **bindiril-**.

3 /a: DAn, b: A, c: {tarafından/CA}/ '- be lowered, reduced [prices, rates] /a: from, b: to, c: by/': **Dükkân devredileceği için fiyatlar {* yarı yarı.yA/* yüz.de 25 [oranında]} indirildi.** 'Because the shop was going to be sold [lit., 'turned over', i.e., to new owners], prices were lowered {* BY half/* BY 25 %}.' *631:2*. discount: - discount; *633:6a*. cheapness: - lower prices.

inil- [ir] /DAn/ impersonal passive '- be exited, disembarked /{AT, BY WAY OF}/' [in- + pass. suf. -Il]: **Otobüsler.E ön kapı.DAN binilir, arka kapı.DAN inilir.** 'Buses are boarded AT the front [lit., ** FROM the front door] and exited AT the rear [lit., ** FROM the rear door].' • The dative case is required on the SUBJECT of a PASSIVE verb when the ACTIVE form of the SAME verb would require the dative case on the corresponding OBJECT. Thus E is required on **otobüsler**, although that noun is the SUBJECT of the sentence. *194:7*. descent: - get down; *352:7*. publication; poster: * specific signs. → ≠ **binil-**.

inkâr et- [eDer] '- deny, - claim that sth is not true' [A. **inkâr** (. -) 'denial']: VERBAL noun as object: **Adam mahkemede bebeğ.in babası olduğ.u.nu inkâr etti.** 'The man denied in court that he was the father of the baby.' **Çırak paraları aldığ.ı.nı inkâr etti.** 'The apprentice denied that he had taken the money.' **Öğrenci kopya {çektiğ.i.ni/çekeceğ.i.ni} inkâr etti.** 'The student denied {that he had copied/that he was going to copy} [the material].'
NON-verbal noun as object: **Tanrı.yı inkâr edenler.E "kâfir" denir.** 'Those who deny [the existence of] God are called "kafirs".' *335:4*. negation, denial: - deny, not admit. → = **reddet-** 2, ≠ **kabul et-** 3.

inme in-. → **in-** 1.

İnternete bağlan-. → **bağlan-** 3.

İnternetten çık-. → **çık-** 1.

intihar et- [eDer] '- commit suicide, - kill oneself', *formal, legal* [A. intihar (. -) 'suicide']: Havagazını açıp intihar etmiş. * Kimse sebeb.i.ni bilmiyor. 'He turned on the gas and committed suicide. * No one knows why [lit., the reason for it].' *308:21.* killing: - commit suicide. For *less formal, less legal* expressions, → = canına kıy-2 → kıy- 2, = kendini öldür-.

iptal edil- [ir] /{tarafından/CA}, yüzünden/ '- be cancelled, called off /by, {on account of/due to}/' [iptal et- + pass. suf. -Il]: {a: Sınav/b: Konser/c: Maç/d: Toplantı} son dakikada iptal edildi. '{a: The examination/b: The concert/c: The game [i.e., soccer, basketball]/d: The meeting} was cancelled at the last minute.' * İsteğiniz üzerine, rezervasyonunuz iptal edildi. 'At your request, your reservation has been cancelled.' Türk Hava Yolları'nın Londra'ya gidecek olan 241 numaralı {uçuş.u/ sefer.i} hava {şartları/ muhalefeti} yüzünden iptal edildi. 'Turkish Airlines {flight} number 241 to London has been cancelled on account of [the] weather [lit., weather {conditions/** opposition}].' *819:5.* end: - end sth.

iptal et- [eDer] /nedeniyle/ '- cancel, - call off /{for reasons of/on account of}/' [A. iptal (. -) 'cancelling, cancellation']: Bu akşamki yemek rezervasyonumuzu iptal eder misiniz? 'Would you please cancel our dinner reservation for this evening?' Kocam ayağını kırınca haftasonu yapacağımız geziyi iptal ettik. 'When my husband broke his leg, we cancelled our weekend trip [lit., the trip we were going to make over the weekend].' Şarkıcı geçen ay vermesi plânlanan konserini sağlık sorunları nedeniyle iptal etti. 'For reasons of health [lit., Because of health problems], the singer cancelled her concert that had been planned last month.' *819:5.* end: - end sth.

isabet kaydet-. → kaydet- 5.

isim tak-. → {ad/isim} tak-. → tak-.

isimlendir-. → {adlandır-/isimlendir-}.

isimlendiril-. → {adlandırıl-/isimlendiril-}.

ispat et-. → directly below.

{ispatla- [r]/ispat et- [eDer]/kanıtla-[r]} '- prove, - substantiate' [A. ispat (. -) 'proving, proof', kanıt- (Tı) 'evidence, proof' + verb-forming suf. -lA]: Ünlü matematikçi konferansında yeni teoremini ispatladı. 'In his lecture the famous mathematician proved his new theorem.' İddialarını ispatlarsan san.A inanırım. 'If you prove your claims, I will believe θ you.' *956:10.* evidence, proof: - prove.

{kendini/kendisini} ispatla-[or kanıtla-] '- prove oneself, one's worth': Onun kendini ispatlama.sı.nA gerek yok, zaten ne kadar büyük bir sanatçı olduğu.nu herkes biliyor. 'There is no need for him to prove himself [lit., ** FOR his proving himself]. Everybody already knows how great an artist he is.' *956:10.* evidence, proof: - prove.

israf et- [eDer] '- waste, - squander' [A. israf (. -) 'a squandering, wasteful expenditure']: {a: Kâğıd.I/b: Su.yU/c: Elektriğ.İ/d: Para.yI/e: Vakt.İ} israf etme! 'Don't waste {a: [the] paper/b: [the] water/c: [the] electricity/d: [the] money/e: [the] time}!' *486:4.* prodigality: - waste.

iste- [r] 1 '- want, - want to': S: Müzeyi gezmek ister misiniz? 'Q: Would you like to tour the museum?' C: * İstemez olur muyum? '{A: Of course./ Absolutely./lit., ** How could one not want to?}' İstediğiniz kitapları nihayet elde edebildim. 'I was finally able to {get/obtain} the books you wanted.' Kimse her istediğini [tümüyle birlikte] elde edemez. 'No one can get all the things [that] he wants [exactly as he wants them].' İstediğini elde etmek için her şey.İ yapar. 'He is willing to do [lit., does] {anything/whatever it takes} to get what he wants.' İstediğim bu idi. 'That's what I wanted [lit., What I wanted was this].' Yemek salonu istediğiniz gibi hazırlandı. 'The dining room has been set up the way you wanted it.' Proverb: İste.diğ.i.ni söyle-

199

.yen isteme.diğ.i.ni işitir. 'He who says what [ever] he likes [lit., wants] will hear what he doesn't like.' NON-verbal noun as object of iste-: '- want sth'. Satıcı: * Nasıl bir şey istiyorsunuz? 'Salesman: What are you looking for? [lit., What kind of a thing do you want?]' Müşteri: {a: Yün bir ceket/b: Kareli bir gömlek/c: 44 beden bir pantolon/d: Siyah bir kazak} istiyorum. 'Customer: I want {a: a wool jacket/b: a checkered shirt/c: a pair of trousers size 44/d: a black sweater}.' → = bak- 2 [subj.: customer in a store: '- look for, - want', usually for all items EXCEPT food]. Her iki dil.İ de iyi bilen bir tercüman istiyorum. 'I'd like a translator who knows θ both languages well.' Telefon çaldı. * Fatma hanım.ı telefon{.A/.DAN} istiyorlardı. 'The phone rang. * Fatma hanım was wanted [lit., They wanted Fatma hanım] ON the phone.'

VERBAL form as object of iste-. • Note the different patterns:
a) '- want to do sth'. The FULL infinitive as object, where the subject of the first verb ['- want'] is the SAME as the subject of the second verb ['- do']:
  1. -mAk iste-. The verbal object [-mAk] is NOT SEPARATED from the main verb [iste-] and has no suffix: Bir taksi bul.MAK istiyorum. 'I want TO find a taxi.' Here the subject of BOTH verbs, bul- and iste-, is the same, i.e., I, AND the verbal object of iste-, i.e., bulmak, comes NEXT TO the main verb and has no suffix. Siz.e yardımcı olmak isterim fakat elimden bir şey gelmiyor. 'I would like to help θ you [lit., be helpful to you], but there's nothing I can do [lit., ** nothing comes from my hand]}.' Ne de.MEK istiyorsun? 'What do you {mean?/want to say?}' S: Sinemaya gitmek istiyor musun? 'Do you want to go to the movies?' C1: * Çok istiyorum. 'A1: I'd love to.' C2: * Bugün canım istemiyor. 'A2: I'd rather not go today [lit., ** my soul doesn't want to].' * Sinemaya gitmek isteyen var mı? 'Who's up for a movie? [lit., Is there sb who wants to go to a movie?]' Ne yapmak istersin? 'What do you want to do?' Or, when the questioner has a particular event,

such as a movie or concert, in mind: 'What are you up for?'
  2. -mAyI word iste- '- want to'. The verbal object [-mAk] is SEPARATED from the main verb [iste-] and has the accusative case suffix: Bir taksi bulmay.I çok istiyor. 'He wants very much TO FIND a taxi.' Here çok separates bulmak from istiyor and bulmak has the accusative suffix.

b) '- want sb to do sth', where the subject of the first verb ['- want'] is DIFFERENT from the subject of the second ['- do'].
  1. -mAsInı iste- '- want {him/it} to', i.e., the SHORT infinitive [-mA] + the personal suffix, here the third person singular [-sI], + the accusative suffix as object. In all persons: Annesi hemen {a: [benim] gel.mem.i/b: [senin] gel.men.i/c: [onun] gel.mesi.ni/d: [bizim] gel.memiz.i/e: [sizin] gel.meniz.i/f: [onların] gel.meleri.ni} istiyor. 'His mother wants {a: me to come [lit., ** my coming]/b: you [s.] to come/c: him to come/d: us to come/e: you [pl.] to come/f: them to come} at once.' Above the subject of iste-, i.e., Annesi, is different from the subject of gel-, i.e., benim, etc. * Anne.si Kerem'İN derhal buraya gel.ME.Sİ.ni istiyor. 'Kerem's mother wants HIM TO COME here right away [lit., ** his mother wants Kerem's coming...].'
  2. -sIn iste- '- want {him/it} to', i.e., the optative 'as object'. In all persons: Hemen {a: gel.eyim/b: gel.esin/c: gel.sin/d: gel.elim/e: gel.esiniz/f: gel.sinler} istiyor. 'He wants {a: me to come/b: you [s.] to come/c: him to come/d: us to come/e: you [pl.] to come/f: them to come} at once.' With the verb ol-: Baba çocuğuna: Her şey.in olsun istiyorsun ama bu mümkün değil oğlum. * Sabretme.yi bilmen lâzım. 'A father to his child: You want to have everything, but that's not possible. * You have to learn patience [lit., You have to know how to be patient].' 100:14. desire: - desire. → = arzu et-, = dile- 1.

* İstersen[iz] 'What about or How about [** your/our/my] [doing it tomorrow]?, What if [you/we/I] [did it tomorrow]?, Why don't you?, lit.,

If you wish': This form, in addition to its usual uses with its literal translation, frequently appears as a polite introduction to the expression of a preference, proposal, or correction: **Yarın evde olurum.** * **Gel[in] istersen[iz].** 'I'll be at home tomorrow. * {Come on over if you feel like it./Why don't you come on over?}' **Bu ayakkabı * siz.E olur. Deneyin isterseniz.** 'These shoes * {will fit θ you/are right for you}. {Try them on, if you like./Why don't you try them on?}' Your friend wants to go to the movies tonight, but you would rather go tomorrow. You say: **İstersen[iz] yarın gidelim.** '{a: {What/How} about going tomorrow?/b: How about if we went tomorrow?/c: What if we went tomorrow?/d: lit., If you like, let's go tomorrow.}' You have done a task in a certain way. Your teacher or supervisor thinks it should be done somewhat differently. He says: **İstersen[iz] öyle yapalım.** 'How about doing it this way? [lit., If you like, let's do it this way.]' *439:* * *11.* offer: expressions of suggestion; *504:* * *20.* courtesy: polite expressions.

* **canı iste-** '- feel like, - want to' [P. **can** (-) 'soul'], lit., ** 'for one's soul - want': **Bugün can.IM sinemaya gitmek istiyor.** * **Gelir misin?** 'Today I feel like going to the movies. * {Are you coming?/Do you want to come?/Do you want to go with me?/Will you come along?}' {**Canım.ın istediğ.i.ni/Canım ne isterse [onu]**} **yaparım, kimse.den emir almam.** '{I'll do what I like}, I won't take orders from anyone.' *100:14.* desire: - desire. → = **canı çek-** → **çek-** 1.

* **canı isterse** 'I don't care': **A: Tekin senin partine gelmeyecekmiş.** 'A: Tekin isn't going to come to your party.' **B: Canı isterse!** 'B: I don't care [lit., ** 'Whatever HIS soul wants]'. *997:25.* unimportance: no matter.

* **Doğrusunu istersen[iz]** '{To tell the truth/if you want the truth [lit., the truth of it]/to be honest}': **Doğrusunu istersen[iz], bu konu.yU pek de merak etmedim.** 'To tell the truth, I wasn't very curious ABOUT this subject.' *644:22.* probity: ADV. truthfully. → = **Aslına bakarsanız.** ['To tell the

truth', lit., ** 'If you look AT the truth of it'] → **bak-** 1.

2 /DAn/ '- ask for, - request /from/; - demand sth /from/ sb, - call for sth /from/': **Avukat kütüphaneye geldi. Bir kitap istedi.** 'The lawyer came to the library. He asked for a book.' A saying: **Para isteme ben.DEN, buz gibi soğurum senden.** 'Don't ask {me for money/money from me}, or I'll cool toward you like ice.' * **Babam.DAN matematik ödevim.E yardım etme.si.ni istedim.** 'I asked θ my father to help me with my homework [lit., ** asked FROM my father his helping TO my homework].' *440:9.* request: - request. → = **dile-** 2, = **rica et-, ısmarla-** 1 ['- order sth /from, for/']. * **Başbakan gazete.nin kendisi.nden özür dileme.si.ni istedi.** 'The prime minister demanded an apology from the newspaper [lit., ** demanded the newspaper's apologizing from him].' **İşçiler {daha yüksek maaş/daha iyi çalışma şartları} istiyorlar.** 'The workers are demanding {higher wages/better working conditions}.' *421:5.* demand: - demand. → = **talep et-.**

3 '- need, - require', non-person subject: {a: **Patatesler**/b: **Köfteler**/c: **Balıklar**/d: **Patlıcanlar**} **biraz daha kızarmak ister.** '{a: The potatoes/b: The meatballs/c: The fish/d: The eggplants} need to be fried a bit more [lit., need a bit more frying].' *962:9.* necessity: - require. → = **gerektir-.** For a person as the subject of '- need' as in 'I need a new suit', → **ihtiyacı ol-** → **ol-** 12.

istifa et- [eDer] /DAn/ '- resign /from/' [A. **istifa** (. . -) 'resignation']: {a: **Başbakan**/b: **Dekan**/c: **Okul müdürü**/d: **Dışişleri Bakanı**/e: **Rektör**} {a: **özel nedenlerle**/b: **rahatsızlığı nedeniyle**/c: **rüşvet söylentileri nedeniyle**/d: **hakkında çıkan yolsuzluk iddiaları nedeniyle**/e: **basında çıkan haberler nedeniyle**} **dün aniden [görevinden] istifa etti.** '{a: The prime minister/b: The dean/c: The director of the school/d: The foreign minister/e: The chancellor} suddenly resigned yesterday [from his position] {a: for personal reasons/b: due to [** his] illness/c: because of rumors involving bribery/d: because of allegations of {embezzlement/ corruption} [** concerning him] that emerged/e: because of [certain] items that appeared in the press}.' *448:2.* resignation: - resign. → = **görevinden ayrıl-** ['- resign /from/, - leave /θ/ one's position'] → ayrıl- 3, = **işinden ayrıl-** ['- leave or - quit /θ/ one's job'] → ayrıl- 3, = **işinden çık-.** Same. → çık- 1, ≠ **işe gir-** ['- find work, a job, employment, - become employed'], ≠ **iş bul-** ['- find work] → bul- 1.

istifade et-. → {yararlan-/faydalan-/istifade et-}.

istirahat et- [eDer] '- rest' [A. **istirahat** (. . - .) 'rest']: {Önce/Evvelâ} biraz istirahat edin. Sonra çalışırız. '{First} rest a bit. Then we'll work.' *20:6.* rest, repose: - rest. → = {**başını/ kafasını**} **dinle-** → 2 dinle-, = 1 **dinlen-,** = **yorgunluk çıkar-** → çıkar- 3, → **yorul-** ['- get tired'].

istikbal vadet-. → {gelecek/ istikbal} vadet-. → vadet-.

iş bul-. → bul- 1.

iş gör-. → gör- 4.

iş yap-. → yap- 3.

işaret et- [eDer] [A. **işaret** (. - .) 'mark, sign'] 1 /I/ '- point out, - indicate' by means of a gesture: **Kalabalığın içinde yürüyen sarışın kız.I işaret etti.** 'He pointed out the blond girl walking in the crowd.' **Parmağı.yla üç nokta.yI işaret etti.** 'With his finger he pointed out three {points/locations}.' *348:5.* manifestation: - manifest; *982:10.* attention: - call attention to.

2 /A/ '- point out /θ/, - indicate /θ/, - call attention /to/, - note /θ/', a fact: **Başbakan yeni alınan ekonomik tedbirler.in önem.i.nE işaret etti.** 'The prime minister {pointed out/indicated/noted} θ the importance of the new economic measures that had been taken [lit., the importance of the newly taken economic measures].' **Geçen haftaki toplantıda işaret ettiğimiz nokta hâlâ aydınlanmadı.** 'The

point that we called attention to at last week's meeting has still not been clarified.' *348:5.* manifestation: - manifest; *982:10.* attention: - call attention to. → = **dikkat çek-** → çek- 1.

3 /A/ '- make a sign or gesture for sb to do sth': * **Ev sahibi hizmetçiler.E dışarı çıkma.ları.nı işaret etti.** 'The host made a sign for the {help/servants} to go outside [lit., ** indicated their going outside to the servants].' *517:22.* signs, indicators: - signal.

işaret koy-. → koy- 1.

işaretle- [r] /I/ '- mark' [A. **işaret** (. - .) 'mark, sign' + verb-forming suf. - lA]: **Güven Park'a gitmek istiyorum.** * **Nerede olduğ.u.nu haritada işaretler misiniz?** 'I want to go to Güven Park. * Could you mark it [lit., where it is] on the map?' **Kitab.ın bazı yerler.i.nİ işaretledim.** 'I marked several places IN the book [lit., ** several places OF the book].' *348:5.* manifestation: - manifest; *517:19.* signs, indicators: - mark.

işe- [r] /A/ '- urinate, - piss, - pee /ON/': **Bura.yA işemek yasaktır.** 'It is forbidden to urinate θ here.' *12:14.* excretion: - urinate; *352:7.* publication: poster: * specific signs. → = **çiş** {yap-/et-} → yap- 3, = **küçük aptes yap-** → yap- 3, = **su dök-** → dök- 3, **çişi gel-** ['- have to go [pee], - have to pee'] → gel- 1, **ihtiyacını gör-** ['- defecate, - urinate'] → gör- 4.

işe gir-. → gir-.

işin içinden çık-. → çık- 1.

işinden çık-. → çık- 1.

işinden ol-. → ol- 7.

işine son ver-. → son ver-. → ver- 1.

işit- [ir] 1 '- hear': Proverb: **İşitmek görmek gibi değildir.** 'Hearing is not like [i.e., as effective as] seeing.' Seeing is believing. **Ayak seslerini işitmedim.** 'I didn't hear the sound of his footsteps.' **Telefon çalmış, fakat telefon.un çaldığ.ı.nı işitmedim.** 'The phone rang, but I didn't hear it [ringing].' Proverb: İstediğ.i.ni söyle.yen istemediğ.i.ni işitir. 'He who says what[ever] he likes [lit., wants] will hear what he doesn't like.' Zerrin'İ şarkı söylerken işittim, çok beğendim. 'I heard Zerrin [while (she was)] singing. I really enjoyed it.' Zerrin'in şarkı söylediği.nİ işittim, çok beğendim. 'I heard Zerrin singing songs. I really enjoyed it.' Compare the sentence above with the DIk participle as used in the third example under meaning 2 below, where it is used in a 'that' clause equivalent. *48:11.* hearing: - hear. → = duy- 1.

ağır işit- '- be hard of hearing' [ağır 'heavy, hard']: Anneannem ağır işitir, bağır.arak konuş. 'My grandmother is hard of hearing, [you'll have to] shout [lit., ** speak shout.ing].' *49:4.* deafness: - be deaf. → = ağır duy- → duy- 1.

2 /I/ '- hear /{OF/ABOUT}/, - learn /OF/, - get word /OF/': Dün çok feci bir kaza oldu. Sen işitmedin mi? 'Yesterday there was a terrible accident [lit., a terrible accident occurred]. Didn't you hear about it?' Meral'in okuldaki başarılar.ı.nI işitmedin mi? 'Didn't you hear about Meral's successes at school?' Zerrin'in bir klüpte şarkı {a: söyle.diğ.i.ni/b: söyle.yeceğ.i.ni/c: söyle.me.si gerektiğ.i.ni} işittim. 'I heard that Zerrin {a: had sung/b: was going to sing/c: had to sing} songs at a club.' *551:15.* information: - know, - be informed. → = duy- 2.

işle- [r] [iş 'work' + verb-forming suf. -1A] 1 '- function, - work, - operate', for machines running on electricity: Bu alet nasıl işliyor? 'How does this instrument work?' Sistem * tıkır tıkır işliyor. 'The system is working * {like clockwork/ splendidly}.' Tıkır tıkır imitates the sound of the properly working machine. → = çalış- 3. # Bu {a: saat/b: buzdolabı/c: televizyon/d: radyo/e: bilgisayar} işlemiyor. 'This {a: watch [or clock or meter]/b: refrigerator/c: TV/d: radio/e: computer} doesn't work.' For '- work' with a person as subject, as in 'I work in this office', use çalış-1, NOT işle-. *888:7.* operation: - be operative.

2 '- commit, - carry out, - make': cinayet işle- '- commit murder, homicide, - murder' [A. cinayet (. - .) 'murder']: Komiser cinayeti kim.in işlediğ.i.ni meydana çıkardı. 'The police chief disclosed who had committed the murder.' Katl zanlısı cinayeti işlediğ.i.ni itiraf etti. 'The murder suspect admitted that he had comitted the homicide.' Öyle bir karakterim var ki, namus uğru.nA cinayet işleyebilirim. 'I'm the type of person that [lit., I have such a character that I] could commit murder FOR the sake of [my] honor.' *308:15.* killing: - murder.

günah işle- '- commit a sin' [P. günah (. -) 'sin, guilt, crime, fault']: Tanrım! Ne günah işledik? 'O Lord [lit., My God], what sin have we committed?', i.e., so that we are faced with our current troubles. *654:8.* vice: - do wrong.

hata işle- '- make an error or mistake', mostly in minor matters [A. hata (. -) 'mistake, error']: A: Şeytan.A uydum, bir hata işledim, çok pişmanım. 'A: I {followed Satan's orders/did what Satan told me to do}. I made a mistake. I'm very sorry.' B: {İnşallah/Umarım} yine aynı hatayı işlemezsin. 'B: I hope you won't make the same mistake again.' *974:13.* error: - mistake, - make a mistake. → = hata yap-, = yanlışlık yap-, = hata et- [This verb is usually preferred when speaking of relatively greater errors in the conduct of one's life rather than of minor errors in matters such as grammar, punctuation.]

işten at-. → at- 1.

it- [er] /A/ '- push /{to/INTO}/': İtiniz. 'Push.', sign on a door. → ≠ çek- 1. You are on a bus, people are pushing you, you say: İtmeyin [or the causative form İttirmeyin]. 'Don't push!' *352:7.* publication: poster: * specific signs. * Kapıyı itti. İçeri girdi. 'He pushed [OPEN] the door. He entered.' Arabam yolda bozulunca {yolun kenarına/ uygun bir yere} kadar birkaç kişi itti. 'When my car broke down on the {road/way}, several people pushed [it] {to the side of the road/to a convenient place}.' * Sandalyeyi pencere.nin yan.ı.na itti. 'He pushed the chair over to [lit., to the side of] the window.' **Buzdolabını kaldıramayınca it.erek götürdük.** 'When we couldn't lift the refrigerator, we pushed it [lit., took it away by push.ing it].' *901:12.* impulse, impact: - thrust, - push; *903:9.* pushing, throwing: - push.

ithal et- [eDer] /DAn/ '- import /from/' [A. **ithal** (. -) 'importation']: S: **Türkiye {nereden/hangi ülkelerden} petrol ithal ediyor?** 'Q: {From where/From which countries} does Turkey import oil?' C: **Türkiye Suudî Arabistan ve İran'dan petrol ithal ediyor.** 'A: Turkey imports oil from Saudi Arabia and Iran.' *187:14.* reception: - bring in. → ≠ **ihraç et-**.

itiraf et- [eDer] /A/ '- confess, - admit sth /to/ sb, - acknowledge' [A. **itiraf** (. . -) 'confession, admission']: NON-verbal noun as object: **Sanık karakolda suç.u.nu itiraf etmey.e zorlandı.** 'At the police station the {suspect/accused} was forced to confess his guilt.'
VERBAL noun as object: **Hırsız parayı çaldığ.ı.nı {polis.e/ hâkim.e} itiraf etti.** 'The thief admitted {to the police/to the judge} that he had stolen the money.' **Katl zanlısı cinayeti işlediğ.i.ni itiraf etti.** 'The murder suspect admitted that he had comitted the homicide.' **Çocuk kopya çektiğ.i.ni itiraf etti.** 'The child admitted that he had copied it [i.e., cheated].' *351:7.* disclosure: - confess.

itiraz et- [eDer] /A/ '- object /to/, - raise an objection /{to/AGAINST}/' [A **itiraz** (. . -) 'objection']: **Öğrenciler öğretmen.in anlattıklar.ı.nA itiraz ettiler.** 'The students objected to what the teacher had said.' **Fuat ile hiç anlaşamıyoruz. {Her dediğ.im.e} itiraz ediyor.** 'Fuat and I just can't agree on anything. He objects {to whatever I say/to anything I say}.' *333:5.* dissent: - object; *788:5.* disagreement: - disagree. → = **karşı çık-** → **çık-** 3, /I/ **protesto et-** ['- protest /{θ/AGAINST}/'].

fikrine itiraz et- '- object to sb's idea' [A **fikir** (fiKRi) 'thought, idea, opinion']: **Yaz tatilinde dağa çıkma fikr.İM.E arkadaşlar itiraz etti.** '[My] friends objected

TO MY idea of going mountain climbing over summer vacation [lit., ** to my mountain climbing idea].' *333:5.* dissent: - object; *788:5.* disagreement: - disagree. → = **karşı çık-** → **çık-** 3, = **reddet-** 1, **protesto et-** ['- protest /{θ/AGAINST}/'], ≠ **kabul et-** 2.

iyi bil-. → **bil-** 1.

iyi et- [eDer] /mAklA/ '- do the right thing /{to/by...ing}/' [**iyi** 'good, well']: * **Ne iyi ettin de geldin!** '{How nice/What a good thing/How good} that you came!' * **Gel.mek.LE ne [kadar] iyi ettin!** '{What a good thing that you came!/How good that you came!/lit., How well you did {to come./BY coming.}}' *509:22.* approval: bravo!; *637:2.* * *1.* right: - do the right thing. → = **doğru hareket et-** → **hareket et-** 4, = **doğrusunu yap-** → **yap-** 3, ≠ **kötü et-**.

iyi gel-. → **gel-** 1.

iyi git-. → **git-** 6.

iyi karşıla-. → **{hoş/iyi/olumlu} karşıla-.** → **karşıla-** 3.

iyi vakit geçir-. → **vakit geçir-.** → **geçir-** 3.

iyileş- [ir] '- get better, - improve, - get well, - recover from an illness' [**iyi** 'good, well' + verb-forming suf. **-lAş**]: Health: **Kazadan tam dört ay sonra iyileşti.** 'Exactly four months after the accident {he recovered/he got well}.' S: * **Nasıl, biraz iyileştiniz mi?** 'Q: How [are you]? Are you feeling a little better [lit., ** Did you get a little better]?' C1: **Evet, bugün daha iyiyim.** 'A1: Yes, today I'm better.' C2: * **Henüz KENDİM.İ iyi hissetmiyorum.** 'A2: I still don't feel well [lit., ** don't feel MYSELF well].' **Koma halinde hastane.ye kaldırılan asker kısa sürede iyileşti.** 'The soldier who had been brought to the hospital in a coma recovered in a short time.' *396:20.* restoration: - recover. → = **düzel-**, ≠ **fenalaş-** 1, ≠ **kötüleş-**, **hasta ol-** ['- get sick; - be ill'] → **ol-** 10.2, **hastalan-**. Same.

Situations, matters: **İşlerimiz iyileşti.** 'Our affairs [i.e., business

204

matters, deals with money] have improved.' *392:8.* improvement: - rally, - get better; *396:20.* restoration: - recover. → = **düzel-**, ≠ **fenalaş-** 1, ≠ **kötüleş-**.

iyilik et- [eDer] /A/ '- do /θ/ sb a kindness, a good turn, - be good /to/, - treat kindly, - do good' [**iyilik** 'goodness, favor']: **Büyükbabam ban.a çok iyilik etti.** 'My grandfather was very good to me.' **Herkes.e iyilik etmeli.** 'One must treat θ everyone kindly [lit., ** do good to everyone].' <u>Proverb</u>: **İyilik eden iyilik bulur.** 'He who does good will be the recipient of acts of kindness [lit., ** will find goodness].' *143:12.* kindness, benevolence: - do a favor.

izah et- [eDer] /A/ '- explain sth /to/ sb' [A. **izah** (. -) 'explanation']: **A: Neden geç kaldın? İzah et.** 'A: Why {are/were} you late? Explain.' **B: Sabırsızlanma,** * **izah ediyorum işte!** * **Lâf.ın son.u.nU bekle.** 'B: {Just hold on./lit., Don't be impatient.} * I'm explaining it right now! * {Just let me finish./Just wait till I've finished.} [lit., ** Wait for the end of the remark].' **Annem.e** * **neden geç kaldığ.ım.ı izah ettim.** 'I explained to my mother why I was late.' **Annem.e niçin sınıfta kaldığ.ım.ı izah edebilecek miyim acaba?** 'Will I be able to explain to my mother why I was held back in school, I wonder?' **Annem.e sınıfta kaldığ.ım.ı nasıl izah edeceğim?** 'How will I explain to my mother why I was held back in school [lit., ** my having remained in the class]?' * **Annem.e sınıfta kalma.m.ın** {**neden.i.ni/ sebeb.i.ni**} **izah ettim.** 'I explained to my mother why I was held back [lit., ** {the reason of} my remaining in the class].' **Öğretmen sınıfta enflasyon.un** {**neden- ler.i.ni/sebepler.i.ni**} **izah etti.** 'In the class the teacher explained {the reasons for} inflation.' *521:6.* intelligibility: - make clear. → = **açıkla-** 1, = **anlat-** 1.

izin al-. → **al-** 3.

izin ver-. → **ver-** 1.

<u>**izle-**</u> [r] [**iz** 'trace, track' + verb-forming suf. -lA] 1 '- follow, - go behind': **Yolu bilmediğim için Cengiz'i** **izledim.** 'Because I didn't know the {way/road}, I followed Cengiz.' {**Felaketler/Kötü haberler**} **birbirini izliyor.** '{Disasters/ Items of bad news} are following one upon the other.' *166:3.* following: - follow. → = **takip et-** 1, = **kovala-** 2 ['- follow one another in rapid succession, - succeed', events, days].

2 '- observe, - follow, - monitor, - keep abreast of': **Son zamanlarda** {**olup/olan**} **bitenler.i pek izleyemedim, önemli bir haber var mı?** 'I haven't been able to keep abreast of [the] events recently. Is there some important news?' **Hükümetimiz Orta Doğudaki** {**gelişmeler.i/olaylar.ı**} **dikkatle izliyor.** 'Our government is carefully {following/ monitoring/observing} {[the] developments/[the] events} in the Middle East.' * **Suna moda.yI yakından izler.** 'Suna [f.] follows [the] fashions closely.' * **Haberleri hangi kaynaklar.dan izliyor- sunuz?** 'Where do you get your news from? [lit., From which sources do you follow the news?]' *982:5.* attention: - attend to. → = **takip et-** 2.

3 '- watch, - look at, - view': **Balkonda oturup** {**güneşin doğuşunu/güneşin batışını/ gelen geçeni**} **izledim.** 'I sat on the balcony and watched {the sunrise/the sunset/the passersby}.' **S: Sen de oynamak ister misin?** 'Q: Do you want to play, too?' **C: Hayır, ben sadece izleyeceğim.** 'A: No, I'll just watch.' • Note the use of the accusative case in the following: {**Hangi/Ne**} **tür programlar.I izliyorsunuz?** 'What kind of programs do you watch?' **S: Televizyon.U izliyor musunuz?** 'Q: Are you watching TV [i.e., ** the television set]?' **C: Hayır, kapatabilirsiniz.** 'A: No, you may turn it off.' **S: Akşamları televizyon izler misiniz?** 'Q: Do you watch television in the evenings?' **C: Hayır, ben genellikle kitap okurum.** 'A: No, I usually read [books].' **Dün akşam** {**a: televizyon/b: bir film/c: bir oyun** [*or* **piyes**]/**d: bir maç**} **izledim.** 'Last night I watched {a: TV/b: a movie/c: a play/d: a game [i.e., soccer, basketball]}.' **Televizyon.da bir** {**a: film/b: belgesel/c: müzik programı/d:**

konser} izledik. 'We watched a {a: movie/b: documentary/c: music program/d: concert} on TV.' * **Doğru kanaldasınız;** * **lütfen biz.i izlemey.e devam edin!** 'You have the right channel [lit., ** You are on the right channel]. {Please stay tuned./Don't go away!} [lit., Please continue to watch us]', words said before a TV program breaks for a commercial. *27:13.* vision: - look. → = bak- 1, = seyret-.

4 '- attend, - be present at and - follow what is going on': **Sınıfa girip * dersi izledim.** 'I entered the classroom and * {attended the class./followed along [lit., followed the lesson].}' **Sezen Aksu'nun konserini pek çok ünlü isim izledi.** 'Very many well-known {persons/lit., names} attended Sezen Aksu's concert.' **Belediyenin Gülhane Park'ında düzenlediği konseri binlerce kişi izledi.** 'Thousands of people attended the concert [that] the city [lit., municipality] had organized in the Gülhane Park.' *221:8.* presence: - attend.

- J -

jimnastik yap-. → yap- 3.

- K -

kabul et- [eDer] [A. kabul (. -) 'acceptance, receiving'] **1** '- accept, - take': {a: **Çek**/b: **Kredi kartı**/c: **Euro**/d: **Dolar**/e: **Mark**/f: **Sterlin**} **kabul ediyor musunuz?** '{Do/Will} you accept {a: checks/b: credit cards/c: euros/d: dollars/e: marks/f: English pounds}?' * **Sivas'tan ödemeli arıyorlar. Kabul ediyor musunuz?** 'There's a collect call from Sivas [lit., They are calling collect...]. Will you accept [the call]?' **İstifamı Bakan.a sundum ama kabul etmedi.** 'I submitted my resignation to the minister, but he didn't accept it.' *479:6.* receiving: - receive. → ≠ reddet- 1.
2 /I/ '- agree /to/ or - accept a proposal, suggestion, - approve': * **Erol Nermin'e sinema.ya gitmey.İ teklif etti, Nermin de memnuniyetle kabul etti.** 'Erol

suggested to Nermin [f.] that they go to the movies [lit., suggested going to the movies to Nermin], and Nermin {was happy to accept/lit., accepted with pleasure}.' **Topkapı Müzesini gezmey.İ önerdim. Fakat arkadaşlar kabul etmedi.** 'I suggested touring the Topkapı Museum, but [my] friends didn't accept [the suggestion].' **Aslı sinema artisti olmak istiyordu fakat ailesi kabul etmedi.** 'Aslı [f.] wanted to be a movie actress, but her family did not approve.' NON-verbal noun as object: **Nermin Erol'un evlenme teklif.i.ni kabul etti.** 'Nermin [f.] accepted Erol's proposal of marriage.' **Evlenme teklif.i.ni kabul etme.si İÇİN kız.A yalvardı.** 'He begged θ the girl TO accept his proposal of marriage [lit., ** FOR her accepting...].' * {**Ne önerirsem önereyim**} **hiç biri.ni kabul etmiyor, hepsi.ni reddediyor.** 'He rejects whatever I propose [lit., ** {Whatever I propose/No matter what I propose}, he doesn't accept any of them, he rejects them all].' **Konuşmacının yorumlarını {körü körüne/sorgulamadan} kabul etmek zorunda değiliz.** 'We aren't obliged to accept {blindly/without questioning} the speaker's interpretations.' VERBAL noun as object: **Oktay'la çıkmay.I kabul ettiğin.E göre çıldırmış olmalısın.** 'You must be {crazy/nuts} to agree to go out with Oktay [lit., Since you agreed to go out with Oktay you...].' *441:2.* consent: - consent; *509:9.* approval: - approve. → ≠ itiraz et-, ≠ reddet- 1.

3 '- admit, - accept [a fact as true], - acknowledge': **Çırak paraları aldığ.ı.nı kabul etmiyor.** 'The apprentice {denies/lit., does not admit} that he took the money.' **Evlilik konusunda yanlış düşündüğ.ümüz.ü kabul etmiyoruz.** 'We do not accept that we were mistaken [lit., ** thought incorrectly] on the subject of marriage.' *332:8.* assent: - assent. → ≠ inkâr et-, ≠ reddet- 2.

4 '- accept, - regard with tolerance': **İnsanları olduğu gibi kabul etmeliyiz.** 'We must accept people as they are.' *134:5.* patience: - endure; *978:7.* broad-mindedness: - keep an open mind.

kâbus gör-. → gör- 3.

kaç- [ar] 1 /Dan, A/ '- escape, - run away, - flee /from, to/, - get away /from/': * NE duruyorsun, birşey.LER yapsana! Hırsız çantamı aldı kaçıyor. '{What are you waiting for?/WHY are you just standing there?} Do something [lit., ** somethingS]! A thief has taken my {purse/bag/briefcase} and is running off [with it].' Cuma günü {güpegündüz/gece karan-lığında} üç mahkûm cezaevi.nden kaçmış. 'On Friday {in broad daylight/in the dark of night} three convicts escaped from the prison.' Hırsız annesinin evi.ne kaçmış. 'The thief escaped to his mother's house.' Polisler, kaçmaya çalışan hırsızı gözaltına aldı. 'The police took into custody [lit., ** under eye] the thief who was attempting to flee.' Katil olay yer.i.nden {a: yayan/b: yaya olarak/c: * koş.arak/d: arabay.LA/e: metro.yA bin.erek} kaçtı. 'The murderer escaped from the scene [lit., ** the place of the event] {a, b: on foot/c: * {AT a run/by runn.ing}/d: BY car/e: by gett.ing ON a subway}.' Ayyaş babasının kötü muamelesi.nE dayanamayan çocuk evden kaçtı. 'The child who couldn't stand θ his drunk father's cruel treatment ran away from home.' Çocuğun eli.nden kaçan balon hızla yükseldi. 'The balloon that got away from the child [lit., from the child's hand] rose swiftly.' Proverbs: Kaçan balık büyük olur. 'The fish that gets away becomes the big one.', i.e., The thing missed is regarded as better than what it was. Yağmur.dan kaçarken dolu.yA tutuldu. 'While escaping the rain, he got caught IN the hail.' {From/Out of} the frying pan into the fire. 369:6. escape: - escape; 393:48. impairment: ADV. out of the frying pan into the fire.

ağzından [lâf] kaç- 'for words - unintentionally escape /from/ or - pop /OUT OF/ one's mouth' [lâf 'word', ağız (aĞZı) 'mouth']: Aslında bunu san.a söyle.me.mem lâzımdı, [lâf] ağz.IM.dan kaçtı. 'I really shouldn't have said that to you, but it just popped out of MY mouth.' 369:10. escape: - find vent.

çorap kaç- 'for women's stockings - run' [çorap 'stocking']: Eyvah çorabım kaçtı, * üstelik yeni almıştım. * Eskiden çoraplar daha dayanıklıydı, şimdi çok çabuk kaçıyor. 'Oh dear, I've got a run in my stockings, * and I just bought them too! * Stockings used to hold up better [lit., were more durable]. Now they run in no time at all.' Allah kahretsin, çorabım çivi.yE takıldı ve kaçtı. 'Oh darn, my stocking got caught ON a nail and ran.' 393:20. impairment: - wear, - wear away.

gözden kaç- '- be overlooked, not - be noticed, - overlook, - escape one's eye or notice' [göz 'eye']: Impersonal: Bu hata gözden kaçtı. 'This error has {been overlooked/escaped notice}.' Personal: Ödevinde birkaç tane imlâ hatası buldum, her herhalde göz.ÜN.den kaçtı. 'I found several spelling errors in your homework. {You probably overlooked them./They probably escaped YOUR notice.} [lit., ** escaped from YOUR eye].' A: Raporun son sayfasında bazı küçük hatalar buldum. 'A: I found some small errors on the last page of the report.' B: Öyle mi? Göz.ÜM.den kaçmış, farketmedim. 'B: Really? They must have escaped MY notice. I didn't notice them.' 340:6. neglect: - neglect; 983:2. inattention: - be inattentive.

* kolayına kaç- '- take the easy way out' [kolay 'easy'], lit., ** '- flee to its easy': Sana verilen işi doğru dürüst yap, [iş.in] kolay.ı.na kaçma! 'Do the {task/job} [that] you have been given properly! Don't take the easy way out!' 331:15. inactivity: - take it easy. → = kolayına git- 2 → git- 1b.

* uykusu kaç- /a: {DAn}, b: DIğI için, c: yüzünden/ '- be unable to get to sleep /a: {from/BECAUSE OF}, b: because, c: because of/' [uyku 'sleep'], lit., ** 'for one's sleep - escape': S: Gece yarısı mutfakta ne arıyorsun? 'Q: What are you looking for in the kitchen at midnight?' C: Uyku.M kaçtı, bir şeyler yiyorum. 'A: I can't get to sleep [lit., ** MY sleep escaped]. I'm just munching [lit., ** eating somethingS].' * {a: Kahve [or

Çay] içtiğ.imiz için/b: Yarınki sınav.ı düşünmek.ten/c: Televizyondaki korku filmi yüz.ü.nden/d: Gürültü.den} uyku.MUZ kaçtı, uyuya-mıyoruz. 'WE can't get to sleep {a: because we drank coffee [or tea]/b: BECAUSE OF thinking about tomorrow's examination/c: because of the horror film [we saw] on TV/d: BECAUSE OF the noise}.' 23:3. wakefulness: - keep awake. → uykusu gel- ['- become or - get sleepy'] → gel- 1.

2 /DAn/ '- avoid /θ/, - stay away /from/': Mümkün olduğu kadar tatlı ve şekerli gıdalar.DAN kaçın. 'Avoid θ sweet foods as much as possible.' Yasadışı yollar.DAN kaçın. 'Avoid θ illegal {ways/methods}.' Bu iş.TEN kaçmak olmaz. 'It won't do to avoid θ this {job/task/matter}.' Gerçekler.DEN kaçmak, sorunu çözmez daha da derinleştirir. 'To avoid realities doesn't solve the problem, it just makes things worse [lit., ** deepens it].' Dilek çok çalışkan; iş.TEN kaçmaz bilâkis * üstüne gider. 'Dilek is very hardworking. She doesn't avoid θ work. On the contrary * she gets right down to it.' Bilmediğini bilmeyen.DEN kaçın. '{Avoid θ/Stay away /from/} the person who doesn't know that he doesn't know.' 368:6. avoidance: - avoid. → ≠ üstüne git- 2 → git- 1a.

* masraftan {kaç-/kaçın-} '- avoid /θ/ expense, - economize' [A. masraf 'expense, outlay']: Yasemin hanım alışveriş yaparken {gereksiz masraf-.TAN/gereksiz masraf yap-mak.TAN} kaçar. 'Yasemin hanım avoids {θ needless expenses/θ making needless expenditures} while shopping.' Ömer bey.ler masraftan kaçtıkları için oğullarına düğün töreni yapmadılar. 'Because the Ömer family was economizing, they didn't provide a wedding feast for their sons.' 484:5. parsimony: - stint. Often in the negative: masraftan {kaçMA-/kaçınMA-} '- spare /θ/ NO expense': Babam ablamın düğünü.nDE hiçbir masraftan kaçmadı. 'My father spared no expense ON my older sister's wedding.' Bakanlığımız Türkiye'yi tanıtmak için hiç bir

masraftan kaçmayacaktır. 'Our Ministry will spare no expense to make Turkey known to the world.' 626:5. expenditure: - spend. → ≠ masrafa gir- ['- spend a lot of money on sth or to get sth done, - have a lot of expenses, - incur great expense'].

3 * '- seem', strange, inappropriate: Bence bu kelime uygun değil, biraz {tuhaf/acaip} kaçıyor. '{I say/I think} this word is not appropriate. It seems a bit {strange}.' 33:10 appearance: - appear to be.

kaçın- [ır] /DAn/ '- avoid /θ/ sb or sth or /θ/ doing sth; - refrain /from/ sth or /from/ doing sth' [kaç- + refl. suf. -In]: NON-verbal noun as object: Yasadışı yollar.DAN kaçının. '{Avoid θ/Refrain FROM} illegal {ways/methods}.' Bu tür hareketler.DEN kaçınmanız gerekir. 'You must {avoid θ/refrain FROM} such {actions/behavior}.' Bu tür {insanlar.DAN/ kişiler.DEN} kaçınmak lâzım. 'One must avoid such people.' VERBAL noun as object: Genelleme yapmak.TAN kaçın-malıyız. 'We must {avoid θ/refrain from} making [broad] generalizations.' Eski kocasını görünce konuşmak.TAN kaçın-dı ve * yolunu değiştirdi. 'When she saw her former husband, she avoided θ speaking [to him] and * took off in another direction [lit., ** changed her path].' O karıncayı bile ezmek.TEN kaçınan çok merhametli bir insandı. 'He was a very compassionate person who wouldn't hurt even a fly [lit., a very compassionate person who would avoid θ stepping on (lit., crushing) even an ant].' 329:3. inaction: - refrain; 368:6. avoidance: - avoid; 668:7. temperance: - abstain. → = sakın- 1.

* masraftan kaçın- → masraftan {kaç-/kaçın-}. → kaç- 2.

kaçır- [ır] [kaç- + caus. suf. -Ir] 1 '- miss, - be too late for a vehicle, event, or a meeting with a person': Çabuk olmazsan treni kaçıracağız. 'If you don't hurry, we'll miss the train.' → {geç kal-/gecik-} ['- be late /FOR/'] → kal- 1, yetiş- 1 ['- catch /θ/ a vehicle, make it /to/, get /to/ a place, arrive in time /FOR/; - be in time /FOR/']. * Çok uyumak.TAN {dersi/ randevuyu} kaçırdım. 'BECAUSE I overslept [lit., ** from oversleeping], I missed {the class/the appointment}.' Seni kaçırmamak için erken geldim. 'I came early so as not to miss you.' *410:14.* failure: - miss; *843:5.* untimeliness: - miss an opportunity.

'- miss, not - hear or - catch what has been said': Ne söylediğ.iniz.i kaçırdım. Lütfen tekrar eder misiniz? 'I {missed/couldn't catch} what you said. Would you {say that again?/please repeat it?}' *48:11.* hearing: - hear; *843:5.* untimeliness: - miss an opportunity. → = duyMA- ['NOT - hear'] → duy- 1, = işitME- . Same. → işit- 1, ≠ yakala- 2.

2 '- let escape or go by, - let get away, - miss a chance': Dünkü maçta Hakan çok gol kaçırdı. 'In the [soccer] game yesterday, Hakan missed many shots [at the goal].' * Düşmanı elimizden kaçırdık. 'We let the enemy get away [lit., ** escape from our hands].' * Polisiye filmlerini hiç kaçırmam. 'I never miss a detective film [lit., detective films].' *410:14.* failure: - miss.

ağzından [lâf] kaçır- '- let slip, pop out, - blurt out, - let a secret out unintentionally' [lâf 'word', ağız (aĞZı) 'mouth'], lit., '- let words escape from one's mouth': Asuman'a sırlarınızı söyle-meyin. * Ağz.ı.ndan [lâf] kaçırır. 'Don't tell your secrets to Asuman. * She has a big mouth [lit., ** She lets (words) escape from her mouth].' Özür dilerim, sana hakaret etmek istemiyordum. Fakat {bu kötü lâfı} ağz.IM.DAN kaçırdım. 'Pardon me, I didn't mean to insult you, but I just let {this inappropriate remark/these impolite words} pop OUT OF MY mouth.' *351:4.* disclosure: - diclose.

* altına kaçır- '- wet or - soil one's underclothes or bed' [alt 'the underpart of anything']: Çocuk alt.I.na kaçırmış. 'The child {wet/soiled} HIMSELF.' Words to a child: * Yine alt.IN.a kaçır-mışsın! 'There you've gone and wet YOURSELF again!' *12:13.* excretion: - defecate; *12:14.* : - urinate; *1063:12* moisture: - moisten. → = altını ıslat-.

fırsat kaçır- '- miss an opportunity, - let an opportunity slip away or go /by/' [A. fırsat 'opportunity, chance, occasion']: Bu iyi bir fırsat, kaçırmayın! 'This is a good opportunity. Don't miss it!' Bu {olağanüstü/mükemmel/ harika} fırsatı kaçırmayın. 'Don't miss this {extraordinary/ perfect/fantastic [*or* splendid]} opportunity.' Zengin olabilirdim ama hayatım boyunca çok fırsat kaçırdım. 'I could have been rich, but in the course of my life I let many opportunities go by.' Türkçe sınav.ı.n.DAN kalınca Türkiye'ye gitme fırsat.ı.nı kaçırdım. 'When I failed θ the Turkish language examination, I lost the chance to go to Turkey.' Proverb: Eldeki fırsatı kaçırma, bir daha geçmez el.E. 'Don't let the opportunity at hand slip away. It will not return [lit., ** pass INTO hand again].' *843:5.* untimeliness: - miss an opportunity; *410:14.* failure: - miss. → = {şans/fırsat} kaybet- → {kaybet-/yitir-}.

3 '- kidnap, - abduct, - carry off; - hijack': Silahlı iki kişi Ahmet bey.in oğlunu {güpegündüz/ gece karanlığında} kaçırmış. 'Two armed men kidnapped the son of the businessman Ahmet bey {in broad daylight/in the dark of night}.' *482:20.* theft: - abduct.

uçak kaçır- /A/ '- hijack a plane /to/' [uçak 'plane']: Hava korsanları Türk Havayolları uçağ.ı.nı Lübnan'a kaçırdı. 'The highjackers hijacked the Turkish Airlines plane to Lebanon.' *482:20.* theft: - abduct.

* uykusunu kaçır- '- keep awake, - make it impossible to go to sleep' [uyku 'sleep'], lit., '- steal away one's sleep': * {Kahve/Çay/ Televizyondaki korku filmi} uyku.M.u kaçırdı. '{The coffee/The tea/The horror film on television} kept ME awake [lit., ** stole away MY sleep].' *23:3.* wakefulness: - keep awake. → ≠ uykusunu getir-.

kafası karış-. → {kafası/aklı} karış-. → karış- 4.

kafasını boz-. → boz- 1.

kafasını dinle-. → {başını/ kafasını} dinle-. → 2 dinle-.

kahkaha ile gül-. → gül- 1.

kahret- [kahreDer] [A. kahır (kaHRı) 'oppression' + et-] 1 '- distress sb greatly, - drive to distraction': Kız.ım.ın felç olma.sı beni kahretti. 'My daughter's becoming paralyzed distressed me greatly.' Bu kız beni kahrediyor, hiç ders çalışmıyor. 'This girl really drives me to distraction. She just doesn't study.' 96:16a. unpleasure: - distress; 98:14. unpleasantness: - distress.

2 '- crush, - overcome, - destroy, - damn': in the curse: [Allah] kahretsin! 'Oh [God] damn [{him/her/it}]!': [Allah] kahret- sin! Yine sular akmıyor. 'O [God] damn it! The water isn't running again!' 395:10. destruction: - destroy'; 513:11. curse: INTERJ. damn! → Kahrolsun! 1 ['Damn {him/her/it}! To hell with {him/it}! Let {him/it} be damned!'] → kahrol- → ol- 12.

kahrol-. → ol- 12.

kahvaltı {et- [eDer]/yap- [ar]} '- have or - eat breakfast, - breakfast' [kahvaltı 'breakfast']: Kahvaltı ettiniz mi? 'Have you had breakfast?' Saat yedide kahvaltı ettik. 'We had breakfast at 7 o'clock.' Henüz kahvaltı etmedik. 'We haven't had breakfast yet.' Bugün çok erken kahvaltı ettim. 'I had breakfast very early this morning.' NOT ~~kahvaltı ye-~~. 8:21. eating: - dine. • Note: '- MAKE, - PREPARE breakfast' is kahvaltı hazırla-, NOT ~~kahvaltı yap-~~.

kahvaltı hazırla-. → hazırla-.

kahvaltı yap-. → yap- 3.

kal- [IR] 1 /DA/ '- remain, - stay /{at/in/on}/' [ADJ. kalıcı 'permanent']: [Para.nın] Üst.ü [siz.de] kalsın. 'Keep the change [lit., ** Let the rest (of the money) stay (on you)].' Proverb: Sel gider, kum kalır. 'The flood waters recede, the sand remains.', i.e., What is weighty remains. 256:5. remainder: - remain; 386:12. store, supply: - reserve.

Staying at a place: Ankara'da bir ay kaldım. 'I stayed in Ankara [for] one month.' S: {Türkiye'de/ Burada} ne kadar kalacaksınız? 'Q: How long will you be staying {in Turkey/here}?' C1: {a: Yalnız bu gece/b: Dört gece/c: Birkaç gün/d: Bir hafta/e: Beş ay/f: 24 Mart'a kadar/g: Annem gelinceye kadar} [kalacağız]. 'A: [We're going to stay] {a: only tonight/b: four nights/c: a few days/d: one week/e: five months/f: until March 24th/g: until my mother comes}.' C2: Henüz ne kadar kalacağım.ı bilmiyorum. 'A2: I don't know yet how long I'm going to stay.' Daha ne kadar kalacaksınız? 'How much longer are you going to stay?' Gelmişken biraz kal bari. 'Well, since you've come, why don't you stay {a bit/a little}?' S: Nerede kalıyorsunuz? 'Q: Where are you staying?' C: {Hilton Otel.i.nde/Bir pansi- yonda} kalıyorum. 'A: I'm staying {at the Hilton Hotel/in a pension}.' Ankara'ya giderken İstanbul'A da uğrayacağım, ama orada {olsa olsa/en fazla} iki gün kalırım her halde. 'On my way to Ankara [lit., While going to Ankara], I'll stop off IN Istanbul too, but I'll probably stay there {at most} [only] two days.' In class in reference to a place in a lesson or a text: * Nerede kaldık? '{Where did we leave off?/Where did we stop?}' Proverb: Ne ileri koş, ne geride kal. 'Don't run ahead, but don't stay behind either.', i.e., Be moderate.

Staying with people: S1: Kim.İN.le [becoming more common: Kim.le] kalıyorsunuz? 'Q1: {Who are you staying with?/With whom are you staying?}' S2: Kim.LER.le kalıyorsunuz? 'Q: {Who are you staying with?/With whom are you staying?}', i.e., with what PEOPLE. C1, C2, and C3 below are possible answers to both the questions above: C1: Aile.m.in yan.ı.nda kalıyorum. 'A1: I'm staying WITH [lit., ** at the side of] my family.' The above is the most likely response when any place where the family is living is understood, i.e., their permanent residence or a temporary residence. C2: Aile.m.le [birlikte] kalıyorum. 'A2: I'm {staying/living} [together] with my family.' The above is the most likely response when the permanent family residence is understood. C3: * {Yalnız/Tek baş.IM.a} kalıyor.UM. 'A3: I 'm {staying/living} {alone}.' • Note that the possessed suffix on baş agrees with the subject of the sentence. See also **misafir kal-** below. For another dialogue used when discussing what people one is living or staying with, → **otur- 3**. *225:7*. habitation: - inhabit.

In situations involving a late arrival: **Ayşe daha gelmedi. * Nerede kaldı acaba? * Hâlâ ortalarda yok.** 'Ayşe hasn't come yet. * I wonder where she IS [lit., ** where she has STAYED]. * She's nowhere to be seen [lit., She's still not anywhere about].' Someone arrives at a place late. Those who were expecting him address the latecomer: **Hoş geldin. * Nerede kaldın?** 'Hi. * Where have you BEEN?' When considering the past: **O günler geride kaldı.** 'Those days are {behind us/past} [lit., ** remained behind].' *855:3*. continuance: - continue. → = **otur-4**, = **dur- 6**.

'- remain in a certain condition or state': **Sahibi ölünce kedi {aç/evsiz} kaldı.** 'When its master died, the cat was left {hungry/ homeless}.' * **Aç kal.arak zayıflamak olmaz.** 'One shouldn't [lit., It isn't proper to] lose weight by starv.ing oneself [lit., by remaining hungry].' **Bu cinayet {muamma/ sır} OLARAK kalacak.** 'This homicide will remain θ a mystery.' **Bu savaş.a ilgisiz kalamayız.** 'We cannot remain indifferent to this war.' When expressing surprise about the changes, usually negative, that one has lived to see: * **Ne günler.E kaldık.** '{So this is what things have come to!/So things have come to this!/What times [lit., days] we have lived to see!}' *122:19*. wonder: INTERJ. my word! Proverbs: **Abla.sı.nA güvenen kız kocasız kalmış.** 'The girl that trusted θ her elder sister remained without a husband.', i.e., Don't trust those who want the same thing you do. **Fal.A inanma, falsız da kalma.** 'Do not believe IN fortune telling, but have a fortune [told] anyway [lit., don't remain without a fortune].' **Kusursuz dost arayan, dostsuz kalır.** 'He who seeks a friend without faults will remain without friends.'

akılda kal- '- remain or - stick in one's mind, - recall, - remember' [A. akıl (aKLı) 'mind']: Impersonal: **Böyle ufak tefek şeyler akıl.da hiç kalmıyor.** 'Such minor matters just don't stick in one's mind.' Personal: • Note the different possessed suffixes on akıl: akl.I.nda kaldığ.ı.nA göre 'as HE remembers [lit., ** as IT remains in HIS mind]': **{Akl.IM.da/ Akl.IMIZ.da} kaldığ.ı.na göre, saat onda bir otobüs var.** 'As {I/WE} remember it, there's a bus at ten o'clock [lit., ** as it remains {in MY mind/in OUR mind(s)...].' **Aklımda kalanlar şunlardır:...** '{Here's what I remember.../What I remember is this...}' *988:10*. memory: - remember. → = {**hatırla-/anımsa-**}, = **bul- 4** ['- remember, - have it', i.e., 'I have it', when one suddenly remembers sth forgotten], ≠ **akıldan çık-** → **çık- 1**, ≠ **unut-**.

* **Aramızda kalsın.** 'Just between us [lit., Let it remain between us].', when conveying a confidence. *345:20*. secrecy: ADV. confidentially.

* **Arzunuza kalmış.** 'It's up to you., You decide., As you wish.' [P. arzu 'desire, wish'], lit., ** 'It remains TO your desire': S: **Siz.E katılabilir miyim?** 'Q: May I join θ you?' [Also: **Sizinle gelebilir miyim?** 'May I come with you?'] C: **{Tabii, * memnun oluruz./* Arzu.nuz.a kalmış.}** 'A: {Of course, * we'd be delighted./* It's up to you.}' *323:5*. will: ADV. at will.

* **dersten kal-** '- fail /θ/ or - flunk /{θ/IN}/ a course' [A. ders 'lesson']: **Matematik ders.i.nDEN kalmay.ı hiç beklemiyorduk.** 'We certainly didn't expect to fail {θ/IN} mathematics.' *410:9b*. failure: - fail in specific areas.

* **dışarıda kal-** '- be locked out' [dışarı 'outside']: **Bak şu başıma gelene! Anahtarı içeride unutmuşum, dışarıda kaldım.** 'Now just look what happened to me! I left [lit., forgot] my [lit., the] key inside. I'm locked out.' *293:6*. closure: - close. → = **kapıda kal-** ['- be locked out', lit., '- remain at the door'] → **kal- 1**, = **anahtarı içeride**

unut- ['- lock oneself out of a room or building (lit., - forget the key inside)'] → unut-.

* evde kal- '- remain unmarried [for a woman], - be an old maid' [ev 'house'], lit., '- remain at home': Güler'in yaşı 35'e geldi hâlâ evlenmedi; * artık evde kaldı. 'Güler has reached the age of 35. She still hasn't married. * She's an old maid now.' 565:5. celibacy: - be unmarried.

* {geç kal-/gecik- [ir]} /A/ '- be late /FOR/' [geç 'late' + verb-forming suf. -Ik]: Ha[y]di uyan * artık, saat on oldu, iş.E geç kalacaksın. 'Come on, wake up now. * It's 10 o'clock. You'll be late FOR work.' Konser.E geç kalmayalım. 'Let's not be late FOR the concert.' * Az daha geç kalıyorduk. 'We were almost late.' A: * Geç kal.DIM, özür dilerim. 'A: I'm sorry {I'M/I was} late.' B: * {a: Önemli değil./b: Zararı [or Ziyanı] yok.} 'B: No problem. [lit., a: Not important./b: ** There is no harm in it.]' In A if the 'being late' occurred 'just now', then 'I AM late' is the most likely translation. If it occurred at an earlier time, then 'I WAS late' is appropriate. • In reference to a PRESENT condition, certain common Turkish verbs designating a state, i.e., a feeling, emotion, or sensation, often have the simple PAST tense, but the equivalent English has the simple PRESENT tense. S: Niçin geç kaldınız? 'Q: Why {ARE/were} you late?' C: {Yağışlı/Yağmurlu} hava {yüzünden/nedeniyle} geç kaldım. 'A: {I'm/I was} late [or delayed] {because of} the {wet/rainy} weather.' Konser.E geç kalma. 'Don't be late FOR the concert.' * Akşam.A geç kalma! 'Don't stay out too late θ {this evening/tonight}.' Zaman.ı.nda mı geldim, yoksa geç mi kaldım? '{Am/Was} I IN time [lit., Did I come in time for it] or {am/was} I late?' * Randevularım.A daima zamanında giderim. Geç kalmay.ı sevmem. 'I always arrive FOR [lit., ** go TO] my {appointments/engagements/rendez-vous} ON time. I don't like to be late.' * Randevuları.nA beş dakika gecikmişler. 'They were five minutes late FOR their {appointment/engagement/rendez-vous}.' Hiç bu kadar gecik-mezdi, çok merak ediyorum. 'She has never been {so/this} late. I'm really worried.' * Hayırdır, niye bu kadar geciktin? 'Is everything OK? Why {ARE/were} you so late?' {Otobüs/Tren/Uçak} niye bu kadar gecikti, bilmiyorum. 'I don't know why {the bus/the train/the plane} {IS/was} so late.' 845:7. lateness: - be late. → = rötar yap- ['- be delayed', usually only for public transportation: -- train, bus, ferry, airplane -- not persons] → yap-3, kaçır- 1 ['- miss', a vehicle], yetiş- 1 ['- be {in/on} time'], {vaktinde/zamanında} gel- ['- come {in/on} time'] → gel- 1, ≠ erken gel- ['- be early'] → gel- 1.

geri kal- [geri 'back, rear, the space behind'] (1) /DA/ '- get, - stay, - remain, - fall, or - lag behind /in/' some activity, lessons, etc.: Hastalığı.ndan dolayı Arzu bir dönem okula gidemedi ve {dersleri.nDE/arkadaşları.-nDAN} geri kaldı. 'Because of [her] illness, Arzu couldn't go to school for a {term/semester/quarter} [lit., period] and {got behind IN her classes/fell behind her fellow students [lit., friends]}.' İkinci Dünya Savaşından sonra pek çok ülke ekonomik OLARAK geri kaldı. 'After the Second World War many countries remained economical.LY behind.' 166:4. following: - lag; 217:8. rear: - be behind.
(2) '- be slow, behind', clock: Saatim hep geri kalıyor. 'My watch is always slow.' Saatim beş dakika geri kalmıştı ama düzelttim. 'My watch was five minutes slow, but I set it.' 845:7. lateness: - be late. → ≠ ileri git- 1 ['- be fast, ahead'] → git- 1a.

* hamile kal- '- get pregnant' [A. hamile (- . .) 'pregnant']: Cemile hanım 5 yıl evlilikten sonra hamile kaldığını öğrenince çok sevindi. 'When, after 5 years of marriage, Cemile hanım learned that she had become pregnant, she was delighted.' 78:12. reproduction, procreation: - be pregnant.

* Hoşça kal[ın]! 'Have a good day, Goodbye', said by the person leaving [hoşça 'pleasantly']. Responses of the person remaining: 1. Güle güle! 'Goodbye.' 2.

informal: **Eyvallah!** 'So long.' **Hoşça kalın, sizleri çok özleyeceğiz.** 'Goodbye, we'll really miss you.' **Sene.YE görüşmek üzere hoşça kalın.** 'Goodbye UNTIL {next year/a year FROM NOW}.' *188:22.* departure: INTERJ. farewell! For another common formula said by the person leaving, → = **Allahaısmarladık.** → ısmarla- 3.

* **imtihandan kal-**. → {**sınavdan/imtihandan**} **kal-**. → below.

* **kaldı ki** (1) 'moreover, besides, anyhow, anyway': **Saat 6 [altı] oldu, hâlâ gelmedi. Kaldı ki çok daha erken evde olması gerekiyordu.** 'It's now six o'clock, and he still hasn't come. And {anyway/besides}, he should have been home much earlier [lit., ** his being at home was required].' *384:10.* ADV. manner, means: anyhow.
(2) 'let alone, so {how/why} would he': * **Kendine bile kahve almaz, kaldı ki sana alsın.** 'He doesn't even order coffee for himself, so why would he order some for you?' *772:10.* exclusion: PREP. excluding.

* **kalırsa** /A/ 'if it were left up /to/, /in/ one's view, opinion'. Mostly encountered with the first person in **bana kalırsa** '{If it were left up to me/In my opinion/}': **Hakim çocuğun ifadesine inanmadı. Bana kalırsa, çocuk doğru[yu] söylüyordu.** 'The judge did not believe the child's testimony. In my view, the child was telling the truth.' *952:29.* belief: ADV. in one's opinion. = **bence** ['{I say/I think}'].

* **kapıda kal-** '- be locked out' [**kapı** 'door'], lit., '- remain at the door': * **Bak şu başıma gelene! Anahtarı içeride unutmuşum, kapıda kaldım.** 'Now just look what happened to me! I left [lit., forgot] my [lit., the] key inside. I'm locked out.' *293:6.* closure: - close. → = **dışarıda kal-** ['- remain outside'], = **anahtarı içeride unut-** ['- lock oneself out of a room or building (lit., - forget the key inside)'] → **unut-**.

* **memnun kal-** /DAn/ '- be pleased, happy /WITH/' [A. **memnun** (. -) 'pleased']: **Antalya'daki otel.DEN**

memnun kaldım. 'I was pleased WITH the hotel in Antalya.' **Yeni hizmetçi.DEN memnun kaldık.** 'We {are/were} pleased WITH the new help.' *95:12.* pleasure: - enjoy. → = **memnun ol-** → **ol-** 12.

* **misafir kal-** /DA/ '- stay AS a guest /at/' [A. **misafir** (. - .) 'guest']: **Bu yaz İstanbul'a gittiğimde iki hafta amcamlarda misafir kaldım.** 'When I went to Istanbul this summer, I stayed at my [paternal] uncle's house.' *225:8.* habitation: - sojourn.

* **nefes nefese kal-** /DAn/ '- be or - get out of breath, - pant, - huff and puff /from/' [A. **nefes** 'breath'], lit., ** '- remain breath to breath': * {**Yokuş.u/Merdivenler.i**} **çık.an.a kadar nefes nefese kaldım.** 'By the time I got to the top of the {hill/stairs}, I was out of breath.' **Takip edildiği.ni farkedip kaçan genç kız, koşmak.tan nefes nefese kalmıştı.** 'The young girl, who had noticed [that] she was being followed and was running away, was out of breath from running.' *21:5.* fatigue: - burn out; *318:21.* * *1.* wind: - breathe.

* **Nerede kaldı** 'So whatever happened to...?, So where's...?': **Ayşe hanım müslümanlığı ile övünür ama geçen Ramazanda bir gün bile oruç tutmamış. Nerede kaldı bunun müslümanlığı?** 'Ayşe hanım prides herself on her Muslim piety, but during the past Ramadan she didn't fast for even a day. Whatever happened to her Muslim piety?' This notion is frequently expressed with the question word **Hani?** 'So where's...?': **Hani bunun müslümanlığı?** 'So where's her Muslim piety?' *132:* * *7.* disappointment: expressions of.

* **öksüz kal-** '- have lost one's mother', father remains alive or, less accurately, '- have lost both parents, - be orphaned'. Sometimes, but not accurately, '- have lost only one's father' [**ök** *archaic* 'mother' + suf. -**sIz** 'without']: **Nilgün teyzem Erzincan depreminde öksüz kalan iki kardeşi evlât edindi.** 'My maternal aunt Nilgün adopted two {brothers/sisters/siblings} who had been {left motherless/orphaned}

in the Erzincan earthquake.' *256:5.* remainder: - remain. For '- have lost one's father', → **yetim kal-**.

Sağlıcakla kalın. '{Take care./lit., Remain in good health and happiness.}' Said by someone off on a journey to those remaining behind. *188:22.* departure: INTERJ. farewell!; *504: * 20.* courtesy: polite expressions.

* {**sınavdan/imtihandan**} **kal-** '- fail or - flunk /θ/ an examination' [{**sınav**/A. **imtihan** (. . -)} 'e x a m i n a t i o n']: **Biyoloji sınav.ı.nDAN kaldığımı öğrendim, çok üzgünüm.** 'I learned that I had failed θ the biology exam. I'm very depressed.' *410:9b.* failure: - fail in specific areas. → ≠ {**sınav/imtihan**} **kazan-** → kazan- 3, ≠ {**sınav/imtihan**} **ver-** → ver- 1.

* **sınıfta kal-** '- be held back in school, - stay behind, - fail or - flunk a grade, not - go on to the next grade', i.e., a level in school, 5th grade, 6th grade, not a course [A. **sınıf** 'grade']: **Suat {yeteri kadar/düzenli} çalışmadığı için, sınıfta kaldı.** 'Because Suat didn't work {hard enough/systematically}, he was held back in school.' **Sınıfta kalınca okul.DAN iyice soğudu.** 'When he was held back in school [i.e., wasn't passed on to the next grade], he lost all interest IN school.' *410:9b.* failure: - fail in specific areas. → ≠ **sınıfını geç-** ['- go on to the next grade (e.g., from the fifth grade to the sixth)'] → geç- 1, ≠ **sınıfa geç-** ['- go on or - pass to the next grade [e.g., from the fifth grade to the sixth] or to another class or section of the same grade'] → geç- 1.

{**şaşır-/şaşırıp**} **kal-**. → şaşır- 1, 2.

şaştı kal-. → şaş-.

* **yetim kal-** '- have lost one's father', mother remains alive, or, less accurately, '- have lost both parents, - be orphaned', but not have lost only one's mother [A. **yetim** (. -) 'one who has lost his father']: **Araba kazasında babaları ölünce üç kardeş yetim kaldı.** 'When their father died in a car accident, the three {brothers/sisters} were orphaned.'

Their mother may still be alive. *256:5.* remainder: - remain. For '- have lost one's mother', → **öksüz kal-**.

* **yolda kal-** '- be delayed, - be held up on the way, - remain on the way': **Arabamız bozuldu, tam 4 dört saat yolda kaldık.** 'Our car broke down. We were {delayed/held up} exactly 4 hours.' *845:8.* lateness: - delay. → = {**geç kal-/gecik-**} [for a person '- be late, - be delayed'] → above, ≠ **erken gel-** ['- be early'] → gel- 1, {**vaktinde/zamanında**} **gel-** ['- come {in/on} time', persons and vehicles] → gel- 1, **yetiş- 1** ['- be {in/on} time'].

-mAk zorunda kal- '- be obliged /to/, - be forced /to/, - have /to/' [P. **zor** 'compulsion'], lit., ** '- remain in the necessity of': **Önüme bir çocuk fırlayınca aniden fren yap.mak zor.u.nda kaldım.** 'When a child darted out in front of me, I suddenly had to hit the brakes.' **Çok yorucu bir yolculuk oldu; her gün 100 km.** [read: kilometre] **yol yapmak zorunda kaldık.** 'It was a very tiring journey. We had to cover 100 kilometers every day.' *962:10.* necessity: - be necessary.

2 /A/ '- be left over, - remain /to/': S: **Evde pirinç var mı?** 'Q: Is there any rice in the house?' C: {**Pek fazla [pirinç] kalmadı./Hiç pirinç kalmadı.**} 'A: {There isn't much [rice] left./There's no rice left at all.}' **Ekmek kalmadı.** 'There's no bread left.' A more common response to a {**var/yok**} question employs {**var/yok**}: {**Ekmek var./Ekmek yok.**} '{There is some bread./There isn't any bread.}' **Hiç bir şey kalmadı.** 'There's nothing left.' **Ahmet'in hemen hemen hiç para.sı kalmadı.** 'Ahmet {has almost no money left/is almost out of money}.' → = art- 2. # **Dün hastaydım. Doktor ilâç verdi. * Şimdi hiç bir şeyim kalmadı.** 'Yesterday I was ill. The doctor gave [me] some medicine. * Now I'm {just fine/perfectly well} [lit., ** Nothing of mine (i.e., the illness) has remained].' A saying on the inevitability of death: * **Bu dünya [Sultan] Süleyman'A bile kalmadı.** 'Even [Sultan] Süleyman had to leave the world behind [lit., ** This world did not remain even to

214

Süleyman].' *256:5*. remainder: - remain.

'for sth - remain /to/, - come /to/, - be left /to/ sb as inheritance': **Babamın noter.e yazdırdığı vasiyet.e göre bütün mal varlığı ban.a kalıyordu.** 'According to the will my father had the notary draw up, his whole estate comes to me.' **miras kal-** /A, DAn/ '- be left /to [sb], {from/BY}/', as an inheritance [A. **miras** (- -) 'inheritance']: * **Bu ev ban.a babam.DAN [miras] kaldı.** 'This house was left to me [as an inheritance] {from/BY} my father.' *479:7*. receiving: - inherit. → = **mirastan düş-** ['- inherit, - come into [property] /THROUGH/ inheritance, - come to one /AS/ inheritance'] → **düş-** 4.

3 /A/ 'for time - remain /to/': * **Bugün itibariyle 3 hafta kaldı.** '{As of today, we've still got three weeks./Counting from today, three weeks remain.}' NON-verbal noun as object: * **Seçimler.E iki gün kaldı.** '{The elections {are/were} two days off./Two days {remain/remained} to the elections.}' * **Bayram.A az kaldı.** 'The bairam is almost upon us.'
VERBAL noun as object: * **Sözler.im.i bitirmey.e vakit kalmadı.** 'I had no time to finish what I was saying [lit., ** Time to finish my words did not remain].' * **Okul'un bitme.si.ne üç gün kaldı.** '{The end of school is still three days off./There are still three days to the end [lit., ** finishing] of school.}' * **65 yaşım.a girmem.e altı ay kaldı.** 'I'll be 65 years old in six months [lit., ** Six months remained to my entering my 65 year].' *256:5*. remainder: - remain.

* **kala** /A/ [**kal-** + adverbial suf. -[y]A] lit., 'remaining, staying' **(1)** 'AT [a certain time] to or before [the hour]': S: **Saat kaç.TA geldi?** 'Q: AT what time did he come?' * C: **[Saat] beş.E {yirmi/çeyrek/on} kala.** 'A: AT {20 [minutes]/a quarter/ten [minutes]} TO five.' *833:7*. previousness: PREP. prior to.
(2) 'BEFORE, prior to', always following a specific time expression: After a NON-verbal noun followed by a time expression: **Konferans.A birkaç gün kala geldi.** 'He came a few days BEFORE the lecture [lit., ** several days remaining to the

lecture].' After a VERBAL noun followed by a time expression: **Konferans.ın başlama.sı.nA beş gün kala geldi.** 'He came five days BEFORE the beginning of the lecture.' *833:7*. previousness: PREP, prior to.
(3) 'FROM, before reaching a PLACE, at a specific distance from', always following a specific measure of distance: **Okul.A on kilometre kala * benzin bitmiş.** '[At a distance of] ten kilometers FROM [the] school * {the car/we} ran out of gas [lit., ** Ten kilometers remaining TO the school the gas ran out].' *261:14*. distance, remoteness: ADV. at a distance; *833:7*. previousness: prior to. For other examples of a verb stem with the adverbial suf. -(y)A → **diye** → **de-** 1, **Güle güle** → **gül-** 1.

4 /A/ '- be put off /to/ another time'. • This form is not used with an agent noun preceded by {**tarafından/CA**}, i.e., not as in 'The meeting was put off by the administration.' For such usage, see {**ertelen-/tehir edil-**}: **Yargılanma kararı haziran.a kaldı.** 'The decision regarding a [court] hearing has been put off to June [lit., ** remained to June].' * **İstanbul'a git.me.miz cuma'ya kaldı.** 'Our trip [lit., ** Our going] to İstanbul has been put off to Friday.' *845:9*. lateness: - postpone. → = {**ertelen-/tehir edil-**}.

kalabalığa dal-. → **dal-** 3.

kalbinden yarala-. → **yarala-**.

kalbini kır-. → **kır-** 1.

kaldı ki. → **kal-** 1.

kaldır- [ır] [irr. caus. of **kalk-**] **1** /DAn/ '- raise, - lift up, - pick up /from/': **Telefon.un ahize.si.ni kaldır-dıktan sonra 325 15 21'İ tuşlayın.** 'After picking up the receiver, press 325 15 21.' **Düşen çocuğu yer.den kaldırdı.** 'He picked up [from the ground] the child who had fallen down.' **Buzdolabını kaldıramayınca it.erek götür-dük.** 'When we couldn't lift the refrigerator, we pushed it [lit., took it away by push.ing it].' **Misafir gelecek, koltukların üzerinden örtüleri kaldır.ıver.** 'Guests are coming. Please take the drop cloths off the furniture.' • The structure *verb stem*.Iver-, as above, even without **lütfen**, may convey the sense of a polite request. Proverbs: **Allah kimseye kaldıramayacağı yük vermez.** 'God never gives anyone a load [that] he cannot bear.' **Kaldıramayacağın yük.ün alt.ı.nA girme.** 'Don't take on a burden [lit., ** enter under a load] you cannot lift.' Don't bite off more than you can chew. *911:5.* elevation: - elevate. → ≠ **indir-** 1 ['- lower, - bring down, - take down'], **düşür-** 1 ['- drop sth'].

başını kaldır- /DAn/ '- raise one's head /from/, - look up /from/': **Kitaptan başını kaldırdı ve bana bir soru sordu.** 'He looked up [lit., raised his head] from the book and asked me a question.' *911:5.* elevation: - elevate. → ≠ **indir-** 1.

el kaldır- (1) '- raise one's hand', to get permission to talk in various circumstances, to get a teacher's attention at the university level: **Lütfen el kaldır.madan konuşmayınız.** 'Please don't speak without [first] raising your hand.' **Elini önce kaldırdı, sonra indirdi.** 'First he raised his hand, then he lowered it.' **Konuşmak istiyorsanız önce elinizi kaldırın.** 'If you want to speak, first raise your hand.' **Lütfen Türkçe dersini alanlar ellerini kaldırsın!** 'Will [lit., Let] those who are taking the Turkish class raise their hands.' At lower level schools **parmak kaldır-** is more common. See below. *911:5.* elevation: - elevate; *982:10.* attention: - call attention to.
(2) /A/ '- raise one's hand, a hand /AGAINST/', i.e., to strike: **Ablan.A el kaldırmay.A utanmıyor musun!** 'Aren't you ashamed to raise your hand AGAINST your older sister!' *453:3.* resistance: - offer resistance; *911:5.* elevation: - elevate.

* **parmak kaldır-** '- raise one's hand [lit., finger]'. This expression is used like **el kaldır-**, above, but is more common than that expression in schools below the university level. Substitute in the examples above under **el kaldır-**. *911:5.* elevation: - elevate; *982:10.* attention: - call attention to.

* **tahtaya kaldır-** '- SEND to the blackboard' [P. **tahta** 'board, blackboard']: **Bugün matematik dersinde öğretmen beni tahta.ya kaldırdı. Tam üç problem çözdürdü.** 'Today in math class the teacher sent me to the blackboard. He had me solve exactly three problems.' *176:15.* transferal, transportation: - send.

2 '- get sb up from bed': **Beni saat {a: altı.da/b: altı.yI beş geçe/c: * altı.yI çeyrek geçe/d: altı buçuk.ta/e: * yedi.yE yirmi beş kala/f: * yedi.yE çeyrek kala/g: 12'de/h: yarımda} kaldırır mısınız?** 'Will you please {get/wake} me up {a: at 6 o'clock/b: at five minutes past 6/c: * at a quarter past six/d: at six thirty/e: * at 25 minutes to seven/f: * at a quarter to seven/g: at 12 o'clock [at noon or at midnight]/h: at 12:30 [most frequently a.m., but also p.m.].' **Beni {geceyarı.sı/ öğleyin} kaldırır mısınız?** 'Will you please get me up {at or around midnight/at or around noon}?' → **uyandır-** ['- wake sb up, awaken sb'].

3 /DAn/ '- take away, - clear away, - remove /from/': **Lokantada: A: Müşteri: Lütfen {bunu/ tabakları/bardakları} [masa.dan] kaldırın.** 'At a restaurant: A: Customer: Please take {this/the plates/the glasses} away [from the table].' **B: Garson: Başüstüne efendim.** 'B: Waiter: Right away, {sir/ma'am}.' **Keşke yemekleri kaldırmasaydınız! Başka gelenler olabilir.** 'If only you hadn't cleared away the food! Others may still come.' → = **götür-**, ≠ **getir-**. Before an examination: **Öğretmen: Sıralardaki fizik kitaplarını kaldırın.** 'Teacher: Remove your physics books from your desks [lit., your physics books on the desks].' *176:11.* transferal, transportation: - remove.

* **sofra kaldır-** '- clear, after a meal, anything upon which a meal may be placed' [A. **sofra** 'table, wooden or metal tray, mat, spread']: * **Yemek yedikten sonra annem sofrayı kaldırdı.** 'After we had eaten, my mother cleared the table.' *176:11.* transferal, transportation: - remove; *772:5.* exclusion: - eliminate. → ≠ **sofra kur-** → **kur-** 1.

4 '- abolish, - do away with, - lift, - repeal, - eliminate, - eradicate': Hükümet {taşıt vergi.si.ni/ bedelli askerliği} kaldırdı. 'The government has abolished [or repealed] {the transportation tax/payment in place of military service}.' Türk Hükümeti {a: sıkıyönetim.i/b: sokağ.a çıkma yasağ.ı.nı/c: ambargo.yu} kaldırdı. 'The Turkish government has lifted {a: martial law [lit., ** tight administration]/b: the curfew [lit., ** the going-out-to-the-street prohibition]/c: the ambargo}.' Sağlık Bakanlığı artık yavaş yavaş yok olan çiçek hastalığını tamamen kaldırmak için genel bir aşı kampanyası başlatıyor. 'The Ministry of Health is beginning a mass innoculation campaign to completely eradicate smallpox, which is now slowly disappearing.' 445:2. repeal: - repeal; 772:5 exclusion: - eliminate.

5 * /A/ '- take sb /to/ the hospital or morgue': Dün gece * {aşırı halsizlik/dayanılmaz bir baş ağrısı} şikâyet.i ile dedemi hastane.ye kaldırdılar. 'Yesterday they took my grandfather, who was complaining OF {exhaustion/an unbearable headache}, to the hospital [lit., ** they took to the hospital my grandfather with the complaint of...].' Trafik kazasında ölenler.İ hemen morg.a kaldırdılar. 'They immediately took [the bodies of] those who had died in the traffic accident to the morgue.' 176:11. transferal, transportation: - remove. → = götür-, = ilet- 1, = ulaştır- 1.

kalem aç-. → aç- 6.

kalırsa. → kal- 1.

kalk- [ar] 1 /DAn/ '- get up /{from/OUT OF}/, - rise /from/, - stand up': Adam yer.i.nden kalkıp uzaklaştı. 'The man got up [lit., rose from his place] and {left/made off}.' Karda düşünce, yer.den güçlük.le kalktım. 'When I fell in the snow, I had a hard time getting up [lit., I got up from the ground with difficulty].' Proverbs: Çocuk düş.e kalk.a büyür. 'A child grows up by falling and getting up [again].', i.e., through experience. → ≠ düş- 1. # Öfke.yLE kalkan zarar.la

oturur. 'He who rises IN anger sits down with loss', i.e., is acting against his own interests. → ≠ otur- 1. You politely suggest to your companion[s] that it's time to leave a place, i.e., a restaurant or a party: * {İsterseniz/Arzu ederseniz} kalkalım. 'Shall we {leave/go}? [lit., ** If you wish, let's get up].' A more abrupt formulation: {Kalk/Ha[y]di} gidelim! '{Get up/Come on}, let's go!' When you enter the room, everyone is about to rise. Politely you respond: Rica ederim, kalkmayın. 'Please don't get up.' You, a guest, have stood up in preparation to leave. Your host says: Niye kalktınız? * Biraz daha otursaydınız. 'Why are you getting up [lit., Why did you get up]? * Won't you stay a little longer? [lit., If you would only sit a little longer].' 193:8. ascent: - ascend; 200:8. verticalness: - rise.

'- get up, - get out of bed, - arise': Sabahleyin [saat] yedide kalktım. 'I got up at seven [o'clock] in the morning.' Meral hanım daha kalkmadı, hâlâ yatıyor. 'Meral hanım hasn't gotten up yet; she's still in bed.' 23:6. wakefulness: - get up. Proverbs: Erken yat, erken kalk. 'Go to bed early, rise early.' Early to bed, early to rise. Gün ile yatan gün ile kalkar. 'He who goes to bed with the sun gets up with the sun.' Gün is a less common equivalent for güneş 'sun'. 844:17. the early bird gets the worm. Körle yatan şaşı kalkar. 'He who lies down [i.e., keeps company] with a blind person will get up cross-eyed.', i.e., Beware of the company you keep. → uyan- ['- wake up'], ≠ yat- 1, ≠ uyu- 2 ['- go to sleep, - fall asleep, - drop off to sleep']. You have been ill. Now you are better. You ask the doctor: [yatak.TAN] Kalkabilir miyim? 'May I get up [OUT OF bed]?' 193:8. ascent: - ascend; 200:8. verticalness: - rise.

* ayağa kalk- '- stand up, - get /to/ one's feet' [ayak 'foot']: Öğretmen sınıfa girince öğrenciler ayağ.a kalktılar. 'When the teacher entered the classroom, the students got to their feet.' 193:8. ascent: - ascend; 200:8. verticalness: - rise. → fırla- 1 ['- jump to one's feet'], ≠ otur- 1 ['- sit down /IN/', i.e., move INTO a sitting position], ≠ çök- 2 ['-

217

sit down suddenly, heavily /IN/, - collapse /INTO/', chair].

* **tahtaya kalk-** '- go to the blackboard' [P. **tahta** 'board, blackboard']: **Öğretmen, çocuklara "Ha[y]di, tahta.ya kalkın" dedi.** 'The teacher said to the students, "All right, go to the blackboard".'

2 /DAn/ '- leave, - depart, - take off /from/', subj.: various vehicles of public transportation: S: **Tren zaman.ı.nda kalkar mı?** 'Q: Does the train [usually] leave on time?' C: {**Kalkar./Kalkmaz.**} 'A: {It does./It doesn't.}' * **Uçağımız kalkmak üzeredir.** '{We are about to take off./lit., Our plane is about to take off.}' → = **hareket et- 2.**
With place of departure: S: **Eminönü dolmuş.u nere.den kalkıyor?** 'Q: Where does the Eminönü shared cab leave from?' C1: {a: * **Hemen karşı.dan/b: Yan sokak.tan/c: Biraz ileri.den/d: Karşıki durak.tan**} [**kalkıyor**]. 'A1: [It leaves] {a: * from right across the {street/way}/b: from the side street/c: [from] up ahead a bit/d: from the stop across the street}.' C2: **Bura.dan kalkmıyor.** 'A2: It doesn't leave from here.' **Tren hangi peron.dan kalkıyor?** 'From which platform does the train leave?'
With relative times of departure: S: **Bundan sonraki** {a: **otobüs/b: dolmuş/c: tren/d: uçak/e: araba vapuru**} {[**saat**] **kaçta/ne zaman**} **kalkıyor?** 'Q: {At what time/When} does the next {a: bus/b: shared cab/c: train/d: plane/e: ferry boat} leave?' For a plane, → = **havalan- 2.** # C1: **Henüz kalktı.** 'A1: It has already left.' C2: **Bir saat önce kalktı.** 'A2: It left an hour ago.' C3: * **15 dakika SONRA kalkıyor.** 'A3: It leaves IN 15 minutes.'

With hours of departure: C4: {a: [**Saat**] **beş.te/b:** [**Saat**] **beş.İ beş geçe/c:** [**Saat**] **beş.İ çeyrek geçe/d:** [**Saat**] **beş buçuk.ta/e:** [**Saat**] **6'ya çeyrek kala/f:** [**Saat**] **6'ya 5 kala/g:** [**Saat**] **12'de/h:** [**Saat**] **yarım.da**} **kalkıyor.** 'A4: It leaves {a: at 5 o'clock./b: AT five past five./c: AT a quarter past five./d: at five thirty./e: AT a quarter to six./f: AT five minutes to six./g: at 12 o'clock [at

noon or at night]./h: at 12:30 [a.m. or p.m.]}'

With divisions of the day as time of departure: C5: {a: **Sabah** [or **Sabahleyin**]/b: **Öğlen** [or **Öğleyin**]/c: **Akşam** [or **Akşamleyin**]/d: **Gece** [or **Geceleyin**]} **kalkıyor.** 'A5: It leaves {a: in the morning./b: at noon./c: in the evening [from sunset to about 10 p.m.]./d: at night [from about 10 p.m. to sunrise].}'

Divisions of the day plus hours: C6: **Yarın akşam saat 6'da kalkıyor.** 'A6: It leaves tomorrow at 6 o'clock in the evening.'

• **Kalk-** is not used with an object of destination as in '- set off FOR ANKARA', for which → = **hareket et- 2.** *184:38:* aviation: - take off; *188:8.* departure: - set out; *193:10.* ascent: - take off. → = **yola çık-** ['- start off, - set out /ON/ a {trip/journey}, - set out /ON/ the road', person on foot or vehicle] → **çık- 2,** ≠ **var-,** ≠ **eriş- 1.**

3 '- BE repealed, abolished, lifted, struck down, - be no longer valid': **Taşıt vergisi kalktı.** 'The transportation tax has been {repealed/abolished}.' {a: **Sıkıyönetim/b: Sokağ.a çıkma yasağ.ı/c: Ambargo**} **kalktı.** '{a: Martial law [lit., ** Tight administration]/b: The curfew [lit., ** the going-out-to-the-street prohibition]/c: The ambargo} has been lifted.' ≠ **kon-.**

tedavülden kalk- '- go out of circulation', money [A. **tedavül** (. - .) 'circulation']: **Beş yüz liralık banknotlar tedavül.DEN kalktı.** * **Artık geçmiyor.** 'Five hundred lira notes have gone OUT OF circulation. * They are no longer {valid/legal tender} [lit., ** are no longer passing].' *445:2.* repeal: - repeal. ≠ **tedavüle gir-.**

kalkın- [ır] '- develop, - advance, - make progress' [**kalk-** + refl. suf. **-In**]: **Türkiye hızla kalkınmakta olan bir ülkedir.** 'Turkey is a rapidly developing {nation/country}.' **GAP [Güney-Doğu Anadolu Projesi] projesi bu bölge.nin kalkınma.sı.nA yol açacak.** 'The GAP [South-East Anatolia Project] Project will bring about θ the development of this region.' *860:5.* evolution: - evolve. → = **geliş-** 1 [also in reference to technology, events].

kalkış- [ır] /A/ '- try or - attempt /to/ do sth that is beyond one's power or outside one's authority, - dare /to/' [kalk- + recip. suf. -Iş]: **Gemi iskele.ye iyice yanaş.madan binme.ye kalkışma!** 'Don't attempt to board the ship before it has drawn all the way up to the pier!' *352:7.* poster: * specific signs. * **O adam ban.A lâf atmak.la kalmadı, aynı zamanda [ban.A] el.le temas etmey.e de kalkıştı.** 'That man not only assaulted me verbally [lit., ** by throwing remarks AT me], he also {dared/went so far as} to touch θ me.' *403:6.* endeavor: - attempt. → **çalış-** 2 ['- try /to/, - attempt /to/'], **kıy-** 4 ['- bring oneself /to/ or - dare /to/ do sth that would discomfort, harm sb'].

kamp yap-. → **yap-** 3.

kan-. → {aldan-/kan-}.

kan ak-. → **ak-**.

kan gel-. → **gel-** 1.

kana- [r] '- bleed' [**kan** 'blood' + verb-forming suf. -A]: **Oğuz elma keserken elini de kesti. Eli hâlâ kanıyor.** 'While cutting an apple, Oğuz also cut his hand. It [lit., his hand] is still bleeding.' *12:17.* excretion: - bleed; *190:13.* emergence: - run out. → = **kan ak-**, = **kan gel-** → **gel-** 1.

kandır- [ır] [kan- + caus. suf. -DIr] 1 '- deceive, - fool, - take in, - mislead': **Satıcı beni kandırdı, kötü mal.ı.nı sattı.** 'The salesman misled me. He sold me defective goods [lit., his defective goods].' **Bu yüzük * beş para etmez, sizi kandırmışlar.** 'This ring * isn't worth a cent. They've cheated you.' **Yalan söyledin, beni kandırdın.** 'You told a lie, you fooled me.' **Allahaşkına {kendimizi/bir-birimizi} kandırmayalım. Başarısızlığımız.ın neden.i.ni başka yerde aramaya gerek yok. Yeteri kadar çalışmadık. * Hata tamamen bizim.** 'For goodness sake! Let's not fool {ourselves/one another}. There's no need to look elsewhere for the reason for our failure. We didn't study enough. * {It's entirely our fault./The fault is entirely ours.}' *356:14.* deception: - deceive; *356:18.* : - cheat. → = **aldat-** 1.

2 /için/ '- persuade or - convince sb /TO/ do sth, - talk sb /INTO/ doing sth': **Benimle sinema.ya gelme.si İÇİN onu kandırdım.** '{I convinced him TO come [lit., ** FOR his coming] to the movies with me./I talked him INTO coming to the movies with me.}' *375:23.* motivation, inducement: - persuade; *952:18.* belief: - convince. → = **inandır-**, = **ikna et-**, ≠ /DAn/ {vazgeçir-/caydır-}.

kanıtla-. → {ispatla-/ispat et-/kanıtla-}.

{**kapa-** [r]/**kapat-** [ır]} 1 '- close, - shut sth' [ADJ. **kapalı** 'closed, shut']: The teacher wants to do some oral work with the students. She says: * **Kitaplar.I {kapayalım/kapatalım}, lütfen.** 'Close your books, please [lit., Let's close THE books, please].' **Yağmur başladı, pencereyi {kapa/kapat}.** 'It's raining. Close the window.' **Çocuk uyuyor. * Kapıyı yavaş {kapa/kapat}.** 'The child is sleeping. * Close the door {gently/quietly} [i.e., Don't slam the door].' → ≠ **kapıyı çarp-** ['- slam the door'] → **çarp-** 1, ≠ **kapıyı vur-**. Same. → **vur-** 1. * **Tencere.nin kapağ.ı.nı {kapar/kapatır} mısın?** 'Would you please put the cover on the pot [lit., close the cover of the pot]?' **Emre sevgilisine: "Gözlerini {kapa/kapat}, san.A bir sürprizim var" dedi.** 'Emre said to his girlfriend, "Close your eyes, I have a surprise FOR you."' **Saklambaç oyun.u.nda * ebe olan Berrin gözlerini {kapadı/kapattı} ve yirmiye kadar saymaya başladı.** 'In the game of hide and seek, * Berrin, who was it [lit., the midwife], closed her eyes and began to count to 20.' → = **göz yum-** 1 ['- close eyes'] → **yum-**. Proverbs: **Allah gümüş kapıyı kaparsa altın kapıyı açar.** 'If God closes the silver door, He opens the golden door.', i.e., Don't be discouraged: a better opportunity may follow one lost. *130: * 16.* expectation: proverbs. **At çalındıktan sonra ahırın** kapısını kapatmak {boşunadır/ beyhudedir}. 'After the horse has been stolen, it is useless to close the door of the barn.' To lock the barn door after the horse is gone. *845: * 21.* lateness: PHR. it's too late. **Kapını iyi kapa, komşunu hırsız tutma.** 'Close your door tight, and don't consider your neighbor a thief.' *293:6.* closure: - close. → = **ört- 2** [obj.: door, window, cover, curtains], ≠ **aç- 1.**

hayata gözlerini {kapa-/kapat-} '- pass away, - pass on, - die', *formal, respectful* [A. **hayat** (. -) 'life', **göz** 'eye'], lit., ** '- close one's eyes to life': **Atatürk 10 Kasım 1938'de hayat.A gözlerini {kapadı/kapattı}.** 'Atatürk died on the tenth of November 1938.' *307:19.* death: - die. → = **hayata gözlerini yum-**, = **hayatını {kaybet-/yitir-}** ['- lose one's life, - die', of unnatural causes], = **öl-**, = **ömrünü tamamla-** ['- complete one's life, - come to the end of one's life, - die, - pass away'], = **son nefesini ver-** ['- breathe one's last breath, - die'] → **ver- 1**, = **vefat et-**, = **canından ol-** ['- lose one's life, - die', mostly for an unexpected and undeserved death] → **ol- 7**, ≠ **doğ- 1**, ≠ **dünyaya gel-** → **gel- 1.**

hesap {kapat-/kapa-} '- close an account' [A. **hesap** (. -) (hesaBı) 'account, bill']: **Akbank'taki hesabımı kapatmak istiyorum. Lütfen gerekli işlemleri yapar mısınız?** 'I would like to close my {Akbank account/account at the Akbank}. Would you please carry out the necessary procedures?' **O bankadaki hesabımı kapattım.** 'I closed my account at that bank.' *293:6.* closure: - close. → ≠ **hesap açtır-.**

2 '- turn /{off/out}/ or - switch /{off/out}/: {a: Elektriği/b: Işığı/c: Lâmbaları/d: Bilgisayarı/e: Fırını/f: Ocağı/ g: Radyoyu/h: Televizyonu} {kapa/kapat}.** 'Turn off {a: the light[s] [lit., electricity]/b: the light[s]/c: the lamps]/d: the computer/e: the stove/f: the gas burner [i.e., on the stove top, not the stove]/g: the radio/h: the television}.' *856:12.* cessation: - turn off; *1026:11.* darkness, dimness: - turn off the light; *1031:25.* electricity: - electrify. → =

söndür- 2 [for all items above except computer, radio, and TV], ≠ **aç- 2.**

'- turn off', water, the faucet: **Çiçekleri sulamak için {su.yu/musluğ.u/çeşme.yi} açmıştım ama kapa.yıp kapa.ma.dığı.m.ı hatırlamıyorum.** 'To water the flowers I turned on {the water/the faucet/the fountain}, but I don't remember whether I turned it off or not.' *856:12.* cessation: - turn off. → ≠ **aç- 1.**

3 '- cover up': **Köpek kemiği gömdükten sonra çukuru {kapadı/kapattı}.** 'The dog, after burying the bone, covered up the hole.' *346:6.* concealment: - conceal. → = **ört- 1**, ≠ **aç- 1.**

4 /A/ '- close sth up /IN/': **Annem tavukları kümes.E {kapadı/ kapattı}.** 'My mother shut the chickens up IN the coop.' *429:12.* confinement: - confine.

5 '- block, obstruct' [ADJ. **kapalı** 'blocked, obstructed']: **Yolu {kapıyorsunuz/kapatıyorsunuz}, arabanızı çeker misiniz lütfen?** 'You are blocking the road, would you please move [lit., ** pull] your car?' **Kar yolları {kapadı/kapattı}.** 'The snow blocked the roads.' *293:7.* closure: - stop, - stop up; *1011:14.* hindrance: - prevent.

6 '- drop the subject, topic of conversation, - conclude the discussion of a subject': **{konu/bahis} kapa-** [or **kapat-**] [{**konu/bahis** (baHSi)} 'subject, topic']: **N'olur kapat bu {konu.yu/bahs.i}.** 'Oh please, drop the [lit. this] subject.' * **Yeter artık, çok ileri gittiniz. Bu konu.yu {kapasak/kapatsak} iyi olur.** 'That's enough already! You've really gone too far. {Let's drop the subject/lit., It would be good if we dropped this subject}.' **Bu konuyu kapatmadan [önce] son bir soru sormak istiyorum.** 'Before concluding [discussion of] this subject, I would like to ask a final question.' *819:5.* end: - end sth. → ≠ **konu aç-** → **aç- 10.**

7 '- close, - shut down an organization, business, school, - abolish': İşadamı Hasan Gürbüz Yalova'daki dokuma fabrikasını {kapadı/kapattı}. 'The businessman Hasan Gürbüz has shut down his textile factory in Yalova.' Savcılık Yıldız Gazetesini bir hafta {kapadı/ kapattı}. 'The attorney general closed down the Yıldız [lit., 'Star'] Newspaper for one week.' 293:8. closure: - close shop. → ≠ aç- 1.

8 '- pay up, - pay off': * borcunu {kapa-/kapat-} '- pay up, - pay off an account, one's debts, - settle one's debts, one's account' [borç (borCu) 'debt, loan']: Bankaya olan borcumu bu ay {kapadım/kapattım}. 'This month I paid off {my bankloan./my loan from the bank.} [lit., my debt to the bank].' 624:13. payment: - pay in full. → = borcunu öde-, ≠ borca gir- ['- go or - get into debt'], ≠ borçlan-. Same.

9 '- close up', the space between lines on a printed page, etc.: Satırların arası çok geniş olmuş. Biraz {kapayın/kapatın}. 'There is too much space between the lines [lit., The space between the lines has become too great]. Close it up a bit.' 293:6. closure: - close.

kapan- [ır] [kapa- + refl. suf. -n]. The action of this verb is involuntary; an agent is not present. An inanimate cause may be. [Contrast with kapatıl-.] 1 '- close, - shut, i.e., - BECOME closed' [i.]: Geç kaldık, bütün mağazalar kapanmış. 'We were late. All the stores had closed.' Bakkal şimdi kapalı. Çünkü burada dükkânlar akşam sekizde kapanıyor. 'The grocery store is closed now, because [the] shops here close at eight in the evening.' Proverb: Bir kapı kapanırsa bin kapı açılır. 'If one door closes, one thousand doors will open.' 130: * 16. expectation: proverbs. Rüzgâr.dan dolayı kapı [{kendi kendine/kendiliğinden}] sessizce kapandı. 'The door blew shut [lit., Because of the wind the door closed silently (by itself)].' 293:6. closure: - close. → ≠ açıl- 2.

'- close or - end an academic year': Haziran sonunda okullar kapanacak. 'At the end of June the schools will close.' * Okullar ay.ın kaç.ı.nda kapanıyor? '{On what date/On what day of the month} do the schools close?' 293:6. closure: - close. → ≠ açıl- 4.

* telefon kapan- 'for the phone - be hung up': * Yetişemedim, telefon kapandı. 'I couldn't get there in time. They had hung up.' 347:18. communications: - telephone. → hat kesil- ['for phone lines - be cut or - go dead'] → kesil- 3.

2 '- go off': Evin bütün {ışıkları/lâmbaları} kapandı. 'All the {lights/lamps} in the house went off.' 856:12. cessation: - turn off; 1031:25. electricity: - electrify. → ≠ açıl- 6, ≠ yan- 4.

3 '- close, - shut down temporarily or permanently', subj.: organization, business, school: Dükkan {saat kaçta/ne zaman} kapanıyor? '{At what time/When} does the store close?' Yalova'daki demir-çelik fabrikası kapandı. 'The iron and steel factory at Yalova has closed down.' Yıldız gazetesi kapandı. 'The Yıldız [lit., Star] Newspaper has closed down.' 293:8. closure: - close shop. → ≠ açıl- 3.

4 /A, DAn/ '- be blocked, obstructed /to, {DUE TO/BECAUSE OF}/'. • This verb is not used with an agent noun preceded by {tarafından/CA}, i.e., not as in 'The roads were blocked BY the police.' For such usage, see kapatıl- 4: Köprüye giden yollar kar.DAN trafiğ.e kapandı. 'The roads going to the bridge were blocked to traffic BECAUSE OF snow.' 293:7. closure: - stop, - stop up. → ≠ açıl- 8.

hava kapan- '- cloud over, - become cloudy, overcast' [hava 'air, weather'. ADJ. kapalı 'overcast']: Sabahleyin güneş vardı. Şimdi hava {kapanıyor/kapandı}. 'In the morning the sun was shining. Now it [lit., the weather] {is clouding over/has become cloudy [or overcast]}.' 319:6. cloud: - cloud. → hava boz- ['for the weather - turn bad'] → boz- 4, hava bozul-. Same., ≠ hava açıl- → açıl- 7.

5 '- be dropped, closed', an issue, a topic, subject: **Bu konu burada kapandı. Lütfen bir daha açılmasın.** 'This issue is now [lit., here, at this point] closed. We're not going to take it up again [lit., ** Let it not be opened again].' **Bu konu.nun kapanma.sı.nı siz istemiştiniz. Peki, şimdi niye tekrar açmak istiyorsunuz?** 'You had requested that this issue be {dropped/closed}. All right, but then why do you want to open it again now?' *819:6.* end: - come to an end [i.]. → ≠ **açıl- 10.**

kapat- [ır] [kapa- + caus. suf. -t]: Same as **kapa-**, meanings 1-8. See {**kapa-/kapat-**} above. However **kapat-**, rather than **kapa-**, is usually used in the following:

telefonu kapat- '- hang up', on the phone: **Yanlış numara çevirdiğini farkedince telefonu hemen kapattı.** 'When he realized that he had dialed the wrong number, he hung up right away.' For 'Please {DON'T hang up/hold/stay on the line}', use **Ayrılmayın lütfen.** rather than **Kapatmayın.** → **ayrıl- 3,** ≠ **telefon.U aç-** ['- get, - answer, or - pick up the (tele)phone'] → **aç- 5.**

* telefonu yüz.ü.nE kapat- '- hang up ON sb' [lit., ** - close the phone TO sb's face]: **Sevil sözler.İM.den hoşlanmadı ve telefonu yüz.ÜM.E kapattı.** 'Sevil didn't like what I was saying [lit., MY words] and hung up on ME.' *347:18.* communications: - telephone.

kapatıl- [ır] [kapat- + pass. suf. -Il]. The action of this verb is voluntary, done by an animate agent. [Contrast with **kapan-.**] **1** /{tarafından/CA}/ '- be closed, shut /by/': **Bankanın kapısı [bekçi tarafından] kapatıldı.** 'The door to the bank was closed [by the {guard/watchman}].' **Yağmur yağıyor, camlar kapatıldı mı?** 'It's raining. Have the windows been closed?' **Akbank'taki hesabınız kapatıldı.** 'Your account at the Akbank has been closed.' *293:6.* closure: - close. → ≠ **açıl- 1.**

2 /{tarafından/CA}/ '- be turned or switched {off/out} /by/': **Evin bütün {ışıkları/lâmbaları} [ev sahibi tarafından] kapatıldı.** 'All the {lights/lights *or* lamps} in the house were turned off [by the owner (of the house)].' *856:12.* cessation: - turn off; *1026:11.* darkness, dimness: - turn off the light; *1031:25.* electricity: - electrify. → ≠ **açıl- 5.**

3 /{tarafından/CA}/ '- be closed down, shut down permanently /by/', subj.: organization, business, school: **Yıldız gazetesi savcılık tarafından kapatıldı.** 'The Yıldız [lit., Star] Newspaper has been closed down by the attorney general's office.' **Bu işyeri ruhsatsız olduğu {a: gerekçesiyle/b: için} {belediye.ce/belediye tarafından} kapatıldı.** 'This workplace has been closed down {by the municipality} {a: on the grounds that/b: because} it was [operating] without a license.' **Kurallar.A aykırı satış yapan bakkal {belediye memurları tarafından/belediye.ce} kapatıldı.** 'The grocery store that was operating illegally [lit., making sales contrary TO the regulations] was closed down {by the municipal authorities [lit., employees]/by the {city/municipality}}.' **Belediye.ce kapatılan iş yerlerinin sahipleri ortak bir basın toplantısı düzenledi.** 'The owners of the workplaces [that had been] closed by the municipality organized a joint press conference.' *293:8.* closure: - close shop. → ≠ **açıl- 1.**

4 /{tarafından/CA}/ '- be blocked, obstructed /by/': **Köprüye giden yollar [polisler tarafından] kapatıldı.** 'The roads going to the bridge were blocked [by the police].' *293:7.* closure: - stop, - stop up. → ≠ **açıl- 8.**

5 /A, tarafından/ '- be closed or shut up /IN, by/': **Tavuklar [çiftçi tarafından] kümes.E kapatıldı.** 'The chickens were shut up IN the coop [by the farmer].' *429:12.* confinement: - confine.

6 /{tarafından/CA}, lA/ '- be covered [up] /by [sb], with [sth]/': **Çiçek tohumları konduktan sonra çukur [bahçıvanlar tarafından] kapatıldı.** 'After the flower seeds had been placed in it, the furrow was covered [by the gardeners].' **Ceset mezar.A konduktan sonra üst.ü toprak.la [işçiler tarafından] kapatıldı.** 'After the body was placed IN the grave, the grave [lit., **

its top] was covered with earth [by the workers].' *346:6.* concealment: - conceal.

7 '- be paid up or off, - be settled', accounts: **borç kapatıl-** 'for an account - be paid off': **Bankaya olan borcumuz kapatıldı.** 'Our bankloan [lit., our debt to the bank] has been paid off.' *624:13.* payment: - pay in full. → ≠ **borca gir-** ['- go or - get into debt], ≠ **borçlan-**. Same.

kapattır- [ır] /A/ '- have /θ/ sb close sth' [kapat- + caus. suf. - D I r]: **Yerimden kalkamadığım için {kapı.yı/pencere.yi} oğlum.A kapattırdım.** 'Because I couldn't get up from my seat, I had θ my son close {the door/the window}.' *293:6.* closure: - close. → ≠ **açtır-**.

* **hesap kapattır-** '- close an account' [A. **hesap** (. -) 'account'], lit., '- have an account closed': **Müşteri: Akbank'taki hesabımı kapattırmak istiyorum.** 'Customer: I want to close my account at the Akbank [lit., I want to have my account closed].' The causative is used here because the actual closing of the account is going to be done by the bank, not by the person withdrawing the money. *293:6.* closure: - close. → ≠ **hesap açtır-**.

kapı çarp-. → **çarp-** 1.

kapıda kal-. → **kal-** 1.

kapıl- [ır] /A/ '- be seized, grabbed, carried off, away /BY/, - be overcome, captivated /BY/' [kap- 1 '- snatch, seize, catch'. 2 '- carry off' + pass. suf. -Il]: By a physical object, physically: **Irmağ.a girince akıntı.yA kapıldı.** 'When he entered the river, he was carried away BY the current.' *480:14.* taking: - seize.
By an attractive feature, emotionally: **Kızın {güzelliğ.i.nE/para.sı.nA} kapılarak evlenme teklif etti.** 'Carried away BY the girl's {beauty/money}, he proposed marriage.' Proverb: **Güzelliğ.E kapılma, huy.A bak.** 'Don't be {captivated/carried away} BY beauty, look rather AT [a person's] disposition.'
By an emotion, with nouns of emotion: **Evde ışıklar birdenbire sönünce {a: endişe.yE/b:**

heyecan.A/c: korku.yA/d: paniğ.E} kapıldım. 'When the lights suddenly went out in the house, I was overcome {a: BY worry/b: BY [subj.: usually anxiety/c: BY fear/d: BY panic}.'
By a moral weakness, a temptation: **Zaman zaman zaaflarımız.A kapılıyoruz.** 'From time to time we {are overcome BY/give in TO} our {weaknesses/temptations}.' *105:12.* excitement: - excite.

kapıyı çarp-. → **çarp-** 1.

kapsa- [r] '- cover, - include, - comprise, - contain' [kap 'container' + verb-forming suf. -sA]: {a: **Ara sınav/b: Dönem son.u sınav.ı/c: Final sınav.ı/d: Yıl son.u sınav.ı} neleri kapsıyor?** 'What does {a: the midterm examination/b: the quarter [*or* semester] final examination/c: the final examination/d: the year final examination} include?' **Bütün kitabı kapsıyor mu?** 'Does it cover the whole book?' **Sağlık sigortanız bütün hastalıklar.ı kapsıyor mu?** 'Does your health insurance cover everything [lit., all illnesses]?' **Öğrenci: Öğretmen.İM, bu {imtihan/sınav} altıncı dersi de kapsıyor mu?** 'Student: Teacher [lit., ** 'MY teacher', the common Turkish form of address to one's teacher], does this examination also cover Lesson 6?' **Bir gecelik otel parası kahvaltı.yı da kapsıyor.** 'The hotel rate for one night also includes breakfast.' *771:3.* inclusion: - include. → = **içer-**, = **içine al-** 1 → **al-** 1, **dahil ol-** ['- be included /IN/'] → **ol-** 12.

kar yağ-. → **yağ-**.

karala- [r] [kara 'black' + verb-forming suf. -lA] 1 '- deface with drawings, scribblings, grafitti': **Oğlum, * kaç defa söyledim duvarları karalama diye.** 'Son, * how often have I told you not to deface the walls [lit., ** ...how often I told you saying don't deface the walls].' *1003:4.* blemish: - blemish.

2 '- cross out or off, - scratch out, lit., - black out': **Yazdığı şiiri beğenmeyince karalayıp çöp.E attı.** 'When he didn't like the poem he had written, he scratched it out and threw it IN the trash.' *395:16.*

destruction: - obliterate. → = {üstünü/ üzerini} çiz- 2.

3 '- slander': * **Onu bunu karalamay.ı bırak, kendin.E bak!** 'Stop slandering others [lit., ** that one this one], just take a look AT yourself.' *512:11.* disparagement: - slander.

karar- [ır] '- get dark; - turn black' [**kara** 1 'black'. 2 'dark' + verb-forming suf. -r]: * **hava karar-** 'for it - get or grow dark' [A. **hava** 'atmosphere, weather'], lit., ** 'for the weather - get dark': **Ha[y]di çocuğum ev.E gir, hava karardı.** 'Come inside [the house]–[lit., enter θ the house], dear [lit., my child]. {It's/It has} gotten dark.' *1026:12.* darkness, dimness: - grow dark. → **güneş bat-** ['for the sun - sink'] → bat- 1, ≠ **güneş çık-** ['for the sun - appear'] → çık- 3, ≠ **güneş doğ-**. Same. → doğ- 2.

karar al-. → al- 1.

karar ver-. → ver- 1.

kararından vazgeç-. → vazgeç-.

kararını geri al-. → geri al-. → al- 1.

kararlaştır- [ır] /I/ '- decide /to/, - come to a decision'. This verb, being reciprocal, always has as its subject at least two people reaching a decision together. [A. **karar** (. -) 'decision' + recip. suf. -lAş '- be decided' + caus. suf. -DIr]: **Ne yapacağ.ımız.I henüz kararlaştıramadık.** 'We haven't yet been able to decide what to do.' * **Faruk ile bu ay evlenmey.İ kararlaştırdık.** 'Faruk and I decided to get married this month.' *359:7.* resolution: - resolve. → = **karar ver-** [subj.: usually one or more individuals but not a group, organization or society acting in an official capacity] → ver- 1, = **karar al-** [subj.: usually a group or organization acting in an official capacity] → al- 1.

karış- [ır] 1 /A/ 'for one thing - be or - get mixed /{WITH/INTO}/ another' [ADJ. **karışık** 'mixed']: **Nohutla pirinç * birbir.i.nE karışmış.** 'The chickpeas and rice * have gotten {mixed WITH [or INTO] one another/all mixed up}.' **Aşure yaparken şeker.in iyice karışmış olma.sı.na dikkat etmek lâzım.** 'When making aşure [a dessert], one must see to it that the sugar is well mixed [lit., ** pay attention to the sugar's having been well mixed].' *796:10b.* mixture: - mix, - become mixed.

2 /DAn/ '- get mixed up, jumbled /{BECAUSE OF/DUE TO}/' [ADJ. **karışık** 'jumbled, disorganized']: **Rüzgâr.DAN bütün ders notlarım karıştı.** 'BECAUSE OF the breeze, all my class notes have gotten mixed up.' *796:10b.* mixture: - mix, - become mixed.

3 /DAn/ '- get messed or mussed up /{from/BECAUSE OF/DUE TO}/': {**Rüzgâr.DAN/Dans etmek-.TEN**} **Betül'ün saçları karışmış.** 'Betül's [f.] hair got mussed up {BECAUSE OF the wind/from dancing}.' *810:2.* disarrangement: - disarrange. → = dağıl- 3.

4 '- get confused, mixed up' [ADJ. **karışık** 'confused']: * **İşler iyice karıştı.** 'Things have gotten thoroughly confused.' **Durum gittikçe karışıyor.** 'The situation is getting more and more confused.'

{**kafası/aklı**} **karış-** '[for a person] - get confused, mixed up' [A. **kafa** 'head', A. **akıl** (aKLı) 'intelligence, mind'], lit., ** 'for one's {head/mind} - get confused': **S: Üçüncü soruyu neden yapamadın Ali?** 'Q: Why couldn't you do the third question Ali?' **C:** {**Kafam/Aklım**} **karıştı,** * **düşünemedim,** * **o.ndan.** 'A: I got confused and * couldn't think [straight]. * That's why [lit., ** {From that/Because of that}].' *984:7b.* distraction, confusion: - get confused. → = şaşır- 3.

5 /A/ '- interfere /IN/, - meddle /IN/, - get involved /IN/ [negative sense]': * **Sen karışma!** 'You stay out of this!' **Sen benim işlerim.E karışma!** 'Don't interfere IN my business!' * **Karı koca kavga.sı.nA karışma!** 'Don't {get involved/interfere} IN quarrels between husbands and wives [lit., ** IN husband-wife quarrels].' **Böyle** {**pis/çirkin**} **işler.E karışma-yalım.** 'Let's not get involved IN such dirty business.'

Arif de * çok oluyor artık! Bu mesele.yE karışma.ya hiç hakkı yok! 'Arif * has really gone too far this time. He has no right at all to meddle IN this matter.' Bu dönemde yabancı devletler imparatorluğun içişleri.nE karışıyordu. 'In this period, foreign states were interfereing IN the internal affairs of the Empire.' Kimse bizim içişlerimiz.E karışmasın! 'Let no one interfere IN our internal affairs!' Eşim işim.E karışmaz. 'My {spouse/husband/wife} doesn't interfere IN my affairs.' * Her şeyim.E karışıyor. 'She interferes IN all aspects of my life [lit., ** in my everything].' Ev.in bütün alışveriş.i.yLE eşim ilgileniyor, * ben karış- mıyorum. 'My wife attends to all the shopping in the household. * I {don't get involved/don't interfere/stay out of it}.'

6 /A/ '- join /IN/, - get involved /IN/ [not necessarily in a negative sense]': Olaylar.A üniversite öğrenci- leri de karıştı. '{The college/The university} students also got involved IN the events.' Proverbs: Acele iş.E şeytan karışır. 'The devil gets involved IN work hastily done [lit., hasty work].' Haste makes waste. Bilmediğin iş.E karışma, bilmediğin yol.A gitme. 'Don't get involved IN a matter you don't understand, and don't set out ON a path you don't know.' 476:5. participation: - participate. → katıl- 2 ['- participate /IN/, - take part /IN/, - get involved /IN/; - join /θ/ a group'], = burnunu sok- 2.

karışmam (1) 'I'm not going to get involved., I don't want to have anything to do with it., Leave me out of this., I'm staying out of this.': A: Şu iki adam kavga ediyor, ayırsana. 'A: Those two men are fighting. Come on, separate them.' B: * Ben karışmam. 'B: {I'm not going to get involved./I don't want [to have] anything to do with it.}' S: Anne, hafta sonunda arkadaşlarımla futbol maçına gitmek istiyorum. * Ne dersin? 'Q: Mother, I want to go to the soccer game. * What do you think?' C: Ben karışmam, babana sor. 'A: {Leave me out of this./I'm staying out of this.} Ask your father.' 214:5. intrusion: - intrude; 467:5. neutrality:

- remain neutral; 981:2. incuriosity: - take no interest in.
(2) '{I won't be [held] responsible for what happens./Who knows what I might do./Don't blame me if I lose control and lash out.}': {Canımı sıkma/Kafamı bozma}, yoksa * karışmam, [* ona göre]! '{Don't get on my nerves/Don't spoil my mood}, or * who knows what I might do, [* so act accordingly]!' 514: * 5. threat: INTERJ. specific threats.

söze karış- '- join /θ/ a conversation or - break /INTO/ a conversation' [söz 'word, utterance']: O sırada Leylâ hanım söz.e karıştı. 'At that point Leylâ hanım {joined/broke into} the conversation.' 476:5. participation: - participate.

7 /A/ '- disappear or - melt /INTO/': Hırsız kalabalığ.A karış.ıver.di. 'The thief quickly {disappeared/melted} INTO the crowd.' The structure verb stem.Iver- here conveys the sense of 'just, quickly, with ease'. 34:2a. disappearance: - disappear. → = dal- 2, kaybol- ['- be lost, - get lost; - disappear from sight'] → ol- 12.

karıştır- [ır] [karış- + caus. suf. -DIr] 1 /lA/ '- mix, - stir, - blend /with/': Bu pastayı yaparken ilkönce yumurta ile şekeri karıştırdım. 'To make this pastry, I first of all mixed eggs and sugar.' Kaynamakta olan sütü devamlı karıştırarak {şekeri/pirinci} ilâve edin. 'Stirring the boiling milk [lit., the milk that is boiling] continuously, add {the sugar/the rice}.' Tahta kaşık.la yavaş yavaş karıştırarak 5 dakika pişirin. 'Stirring slowly with a wooden spoon, cook it for five minutes.' 796:10a. mixture: - mix sth.

2 /lA, A/ '- confuse or - mix up sb or sth /with/ sb or sth else': Bu kitabı diğeri ile karıştırdım. 'I confused this book with the other one.' Dedem çok ihtiyarladı. Bütün torunlarını birbir[ler]i.yle karıştırıyor. 'My grandfather has gotten quite old. He confuses all his grandchildren with one another.' Roman kahramanı.yla yazarı karıştırmamak gerekir. 'One must not confuse the author with the hero of the novel.' Bu konuları birbiri.nE karıştırmamak lâzım.

'One must not confuse these issues [WITH each other/one WITH the other].' * **Elmalarla armutlar toplanmaz; sap.la samanı karıştırma.** 'Apples and pears aren't gathered together. Don't mix apples and oranges [lit., the straw with the stem].' *8 1 0 : 3.* disarrangement: - confuse; *944:3.* indiscrimination: - confound.

3 /I/ '- rummage or - search /THROUGH/, - leaf, - thumb, or - flip /THROUGH/': * **B i r i s i çekmecelerim.İ karıştırmış.** 'Someone has rummaged THROUGH my drawers.' **Gazeteleri okuyamadım, * şöyle bir karıştırdım.** 'I wasn't able to read the newspapers. * I just flipped through them.' Proverb: **Müflis {tüccar/bezirgân} eski defterlerini karıştırır.** 'The bankrupt merchant leafs through his old account books.', i.e., recalls his past successes. *937:26.* inquiry: - examine cursorily; *937:33.* : - ransack. → **göz at-** ['- glance /AT/, - take a look /AT/'] → **at- 1, şöyle bir bak-** ['- just look around, - browse'] → **bak- 1.**

4 '- mess up, - put into disorder': **Anne: Sakın ortalığ.ı karıştırma, uslu uslu otur, kitabını oku.** 'Mother: Mind you now, don't go and mess up the place [ortalık 'the place round about, the environment']! Just sit there quietly [lit., properly] and read your book.' *810:2.* disarrangement: - disarrange. → = **dağıt- 3,** ≠ **çekidüzen ver-** → **ver- 1,** ≠ **düzelt- 3,** ≠ **topla- 2.**

5 '- be up to sth; - stir things up, - stir up trouble': **Bana öyle geliyor ki sen yine BİR {şey.LER/ iş.LER} karıştırıyorsun, * ha[y]di hayırlısı.** 'It seems to me you're {up to sth [*or* stirring things up]} again. * Well, I hope it's all for the best.' *381:9.* plan: - plot; *1012:14.* difficulty: - cause trouble.

karnı doy-. → **doy-.**

karnı zil çal-. → **çal- 3.**

karnını doyur-. → **doyur-.**

karşı çık-. → **çık- 3.**

karşıla- [r] [**karşı** 'the place opposite, facing' + verb-forming suf. **-lA**] 1 /DA, lA/ '- go to meet, - meet, - welcome, - greet sb /at [a place], with/': **Ahmet bey misafirlerini kapıda karşıladı.** 'Ahmet bey {met/greeted} his guests at the door.' **Bugün annem Malatya'dan gelecek. * Havaalanına gidip o.nU karşılamalıyım.** 'Today my mother is going to arrive from Malatya. * I must go to the airport to meet her.' **Bugün * Turkiye'den misafirim gelecek, havaalanı.nDAN karşılamam ve ilgilenmem gerekiyor.** 'Today I'm having visitors [lit., my visitors are coming] from Turkey. I'll have to meet them AT the airport and {attend to/look after} them.' **Halk yeni başbakanı çoşkun bir sevgi.yle karşıladı.** 'The people {met/greeted} the new president enthusiastically [lit., ** with an enthusiastic love].' *769:16.* assemblage: - come together.

2 '- cover, - pay; - be enough /for/, - meet a need': **ihtiyaç karşıla-** '- meet a need' [A. **ihtiyaç** (. . -) 'need']: **Yeni yapılan baraj, Doğu Anadolu'NUN su ve elektrik ihtiyac.I.nı {büyük ölçüde} karşılayacak.** 'The newly constructed dam will {largely/to a large extent} meet the needs of eastern Anatolia for water and electricity.' **Aşkolsun Mine'ye doğrusu! Aile.nin bütün ihtiyaçlar.ı.nı * tek başına karşılıyor.** 'Well really bravo to Mine! She's providing for all the family's needs * [quite] alone.' *990:4.* sufficiency: - suffice. → = **ihtiyaca cevap ver** → **ver- 1.**

masraf karşıla- '- meet expenses, - finance, - pay for' [A. **masraf** 'expense, outlay']: **Bu masrafları nasıl karşılayacağız?** 'How shall we meet these expenses?' **Üniversite öğrenimim boyunca okul masraflarımı amcam karşıladı.** 'My uncle paid my [school] expenses throughout my {college/university} education.' **Uluslararası İstanbul Festivali'nin tüm masraflarını İstanbul belediyesi karşılayacak.** 'The Istanbul municipality will meet all the expenses of the International Istanbul Festival.' **Aldığım asgarî ücret yemek masrafımı bile karşılamıyor.**

'The minimum wage I {get/receive} doesn't even meet my food expenses.' *729:15.* finance, investment: - finance. → = masraf gör- → gör- 4, = öde- ['- pay /for/'], = masraf {et-/yap-}, = masraf çek- ['- foot the bill, - pay', *informal, jocular*] → çek- 5, masrafa gir- ['- spend a lot of money on sth or to get sth done, - have a lot of expenses, - incur great expense'].

3 /I/ '- respond /TO/, - react /TO/': Patronum işten ayrılma isteğim.i {anlayış.la/şaşkın-lık.la/hayret.le} karşıladı. 'My boss reacted {with understanding/with surprise [*or* consternation]/with amazement} TO my request to {quit/leave the job}.' *902:5.* reaction: - react. → = tepki göster- → göster- 1.

atak karşıla- '- return a serve', in a game: Çok iyi {masa tenisi/pingpong} oynuyor, ataklar.ı.nı karşılamak neredeyse imkânsız. 'He plays {table tennis/ping-pong} very well. It's almost impossible to return his serves.' *748:3.* tennis: - play tennis.

{hoş/iyi/olumlu} karşıla- /I/ '- approve /OF/', most common in the negative [P. hoş 'pleasant, pleasing', iyi 'good, well', olumlu 'positive']: NON-verbal noun as object: * Evlilik öncesi beraberliğ.İ hoş karşılamıyorum. 'I don't approve OF people going about together [lit., togetherness] before marriage.' Öğretmen müzeye gitme öneri.miz.i hoş karşıladı. 'The teacher approved OF our suggestion to go to a museum.' VERBAL noun as object: Baban arkadaşlarının evinde yatma.n.I hoş karşılamıyor. 'Your father doesn't approve OF your sleeping over at your friends' house[s].' *509:9.* approval: - approve. → = onayla-.

karşılaş- [ır] [karşıla- + recip. suf. -ş]: 1 /IA/ '- meet one another': * Sonunda sizin.LE karşılaştık. Oğlum bana siz.DEN çok bahsetti. '[Well,] we've finally met! [lit., ** Finally {I've/we've} met θ you]. My son has often spoken to me {OF/ABOUT} you.' Eminim, istediğin gibi dürüst ve seni anlayabilecek bir genç.LE pek yakında karşılaşacaksın. 'I'm sure that very soon you will meet θ an upright young man of the kind you want who will be able to understand you.' Beş yıldır görüşmeyen arkadaşlar karşılaştıklarında birbirlerini sevinçle kucakla-dılar. 'When the friends who had not seen each other for 5 years met, they embraced [one another].' *769:16.* assemblage: - come together. → = buluş- ['- come together, - meet /θ/', usually after a previous agreement to meet], bir araya gel- ['- come together, - get together /with/, - meet /with/'] → gel- 1.

2 /IA/ '- meet /θ/ sb by chance, - run or - bump /INTO/ sb': İstasyonun önünde karşılaştık. 'We met [one another] by chance in front of the station.' Ayhan ile İstanbul'da karşılaştım. 'I ran INTO Ayhan in Istanbul.' *131:6.* inexpectation: - be unexpected; *223:11.* nearness: - meet. → = /A/ rastla- 1, = /A/ tesadüf et- 1.

3 /IA/ '- face /θ/, - be confronted /with/, - encounter /θ/, - experience /θ/, - meet /with/, - be up against': Odaya girerken olağanüstü bir durum.LA karşılaştım. 'When I entered the room, I {was confronted with/encountered θ} an {extraordinary/unusual} situation.' İleride ne gibi sorunlar.LA karşılaşabilirim? 'θ What kind of problems might I encounter in the future?'

{zorluk.LA/güçlük.LE} karşılaş- '- encounter or - experience /θ/ difficulty, - meet /with/ difficulty': Gümrükte herhangi bir zorluk.LA karşılaşır mıyım? 'Will I encounter θ any difficulty at customs?' *216:8.* front: - confront; *830:8.* event: - experience; *1012:11.* difficulty: - have difficulty. → = /DA/ {güçlük/zorluk} çek- → çek- 5, = /DA/ zorlan- 3, = /A/ uğra- 2 ['- meet /WITH/, - encounter /θ/, - experience, - be up against', usually a difficult situation].

4 '- play one another, - meet, - compete', sports teams: İngiltere ve Türk millî futbol takımları bugün İstanbul'da karşılaşa-caklar. 'The English and Turkish national soccer teams will compete in Istanbul today.' *457:18.* contention: - compete.

{karşılaştır- [ır]/mukayese et-[eDer]} /lA/ '- compare sb or sth /with/ sb or sth else' [karşılaş- + caus. suf. -DIr, A. mukayese (. - . .) 'comparison']: Gezdiğim her ülke.yI kendi ülkem.le karşılaştırırım. 'I compare θ every country I have visited with my own country.' Amerikan basını Saddam'ı Hitler ile karşılaştırdı. 'The U.S. press compared Saddam to Hitler.' İzmir ile Ankara üzümleri.ni karşılaştırırsak, İzmir üzümleri.nin daha iyi olduğ.u.nu görürüz. 'If we compare the grapes from Izmir and Ankara, we'll see that the grapes from İzmir are better.' Lütfen beni başkaları ile karşılaştırmayın. Ben herkes.ten farklıyım. 'Please don't compare me with anyone else. I'm unique [lit., different from everyone].' 942:4. comparison: - compare. → benzet- 2 ['- compare /to/ AND note the similarity, - liken sth /to/ sth else'].

karşılığını ver-. → ver- 1.

karşılık bekle-. → bekle- 2.

karşılık ver- 1. → ver- 1.

karşısına çık-. → çık- 3.

karşıya geç-. → geç- 1.

kastet- [kasteDer] [A. kasıt (kaSDı) 'intention, purpose, evil intent' + et-] 1 /lA, DAn/ '- mean, - have in mind, - intend to say /BY/': Person as object: Alın.ma.nız.a gerek yok, siz.i kastetmedim. 'There is no need for you to get offended. I didn't mean you.'
Thing as object: Onun kitab.ı.nı değil, arkadaşının kitab.ı.nı kastettim. 'I didn't mean his book, I meant his friend's book.' "Kültür" {* der.KEN/de.mekLE} ne.yi kastettiğini anlamıyorum. Lütfen tanımlar mısın? 'I don't know what you mean BY [lit., ** {WHILE saying/BY saying}] "culture". Would you please define it?' Bu.nDAN ne.yi kastettiği.ni bilmiyorum. 'I don't know what he meant BY that.'
Fact as object: A: Yani Ahmet'in yalan söylediğ.i.ni mi ima ediyorsun? 'A: So are you suggesting that Ahmet lied?' B: Hayır, onu kastetmedim. 'B: No,

I didn't mean that.' 380:4. intention: - intend; 519:4. latent meaningfulness: - imply. → = de- 3.

2 /A/ '- have designs /{ON/AGAINST}/, - harbor evil intentions /TOWARD/, - intend to do sb harm': Düşman {can.ımız.A/ mal.ımız.A/ırz.ımız.A} kasdetmişti, * savaş.TAN başka çare kalmamıştı. 'The enemy had designs {ON our lives/ON our property/ON our honor}. * There was no way out BUT war [lit., ** other THAN war no solution had remained].' 381:9. plan: - plot.

kaşı- [r] '- scratch', usually an itch, no harm is inflicted: {Başımı/ Kolumu/Ayağımı} kaşıdım. 'I scratched {my head/my arm/my foot}.' Kafam kaşındı ben de kaşıdım, * ne var bunda? 'My head itched, and I scratched it. * So what of it [lit., ** What is there in this]?' O kadar meşgulüm ki kafamı kaşıyacak vaktim yok. 'I'm so busy I don't even have time to scratch my head.' 290:3. furrow: - furrow. → tırmala- ['- scratch' when pain is inflicted, as in 'My cat scratched me', rather than when an itch is scratched], çiz- 3 ['- scratch', with an instrument as subject, as in 'He scratched my car.']

kaşın- [ır] [kaşı- + refl. suf. -n] 1 '-itch': * Kafam kaşındı ben de kaşıdım, * ne var bunda? '* My head itched, and I scratched it. * So what of it [lit., ** What is there in this]?' * {Başım/Kolum/ Ayağım} kaşın.DI. Kaşıyayım. '{My head/My arm/My foot} ITCHES. Let me scratch it.' In this example it is clear from the second sentence that the PAST tense in the first refers to a state in effect at PRESENT, i.e., the time of speaking, so the translation is PRESENT tense. • In reference to a PRESENT condition, certain common Turkish verbs designating a state, i.e., a feeling, emotion, or sensation, often have the simple PAST tense, but the equivalent English has the simple PRESENT tense. The present continuous tense is used when emphasis is on the present state as opposed to present result: Başım {kaşındı./kaşınıyor.} 'My head itches.' 74:5. sensations of touch: - tingle.

2 '- scratch oneself':
{Köpek/Kedi} kaşınıyor. 'The
{dog/cat} is scratching itself.' 290:3.
furrow: - furrow.

kaşlarını çat-. → çat-.

kat- [ar] /A/ '- add sth /to/ sth, - mix sth
/INTO/ sth': Sütçü süt.E su
katmış. 'The milk seller has added
water to the milk [i.e., adulterated the
milk WITH water].' Çorba.ya
biraz daha tuz kat. 'Add a little
more salt to the soup.' Lütfen bana
kazayı olduğu gibi anlat, *
kendin.den bir şey katma! 'Tell
me about the accident just as it
happened. * Be completely objective
[lit., ** Don't add anything from
yourself].' 253:5. addition: - add to.
→ = ekle-, = ilâve et-. For '- add'
as in mathematics, → topla- 4,
toplan- 5.

* geceyi gündüze kat- '- work
{night and day/day and night}, - work
very hard, - burn the midnight oil'
[gece 'night', gündüz 'daytime'],
lit., ** '- add night to daytime':
Elimdeki projeyi bugün.E
yetiştirebilmek için gece.yi
gündüz.e kattım. '[In order] to be
able to complete my current project
[lit., ** the project in my hand] BY
today, I worked day and night.'
725:13. exertion: - work hard.

katet- [kateDer] '- travel, - cover, -
traverse a distance; - go through, -
pass through a place' [A. kat 'a
cutting, intersecting' + et-]: Çok
yorucu bir yolculuk oldu; her
gün 100 km. [read: kilometre]
{a: katetmek/b: yol yapmak/c:
yol gitmek} zorunda kaldık. 'It
was a very tiring journey. We had {to
cover} 100 kilometers a day.'
Alternatives b and c are more
common than a in speech today.
177:20. travel: - traverse. → = yol
{yap-/git-} → yap- 3, git- 1a.

katıl- [ır] [kat- + {pass./refl.} suf. - Il] 1
/A, tarafından/ '- be added /to/, - be
mixed /WITH, by/': Süt.E [bizim
aşçı tarafından] su katılmış.
'Water was {added to/mixed WITH}
the milk [by our cook].' 253:5.
addition: - add to.

2 /A/ '- participate /IN/, - take part
/IN/, - get involved /IN/; - join /θ/ a
group': S: Dün akşamki
toplantı.yA katıldınız mı? 'Q:

Did you participate IN {last night's
meeting/the meeting last night}?' C:
Hayır * işim vardı,
katılamadım. 'A: No, * I was busy
[lit., I had some {business/work}]. I
couldn't participate.' * Dünya.nın
nere.si.nde olursanız olun, bu
yarışma.yA katılabilirsiniz.
'You may participate IN this
{contest/ competition} anywhere in
the world [lit., {No matter where you
are in the world/Wherever you are in
the world}, you may participate IN
this {contest/competition}].'
Proverbs: Kavga.yA katılma,
bilmediğin iş.E atılma. 'Don't
get involved IN a fight, and don't
venture INTO a matter you don't
understand.' Yol bilen kervan.A
katılmaz. 'The one who knows the
way doesn't join θ the caravan.'
476:5. participation: - participate. →
karış- 6 ['- join /IN/, get involved
/IN/ (not necessarily negative
sense)']. S: Akşamleyin tiyatroya
gidiyoruz. Biz.E katılmak ister
misiniz? 'A: We're going to the
movies this evening. Would you like
to join θ us?' C: Elbette isterim.
'A: Of course I would.' S: Siz.E
katılabilir miyim? 'Q: May I join
θ you?' [Also: Siz.in.le gelebilir
miyim? '{May/Can} I come with
you?'] C: {a: Tabii, memnun
oluruz./b: * Arzunuza
kalmış./c: Nasıl isterseniz./d:
Nasıl arzu ederseniz.} 'A: {a: Of
course, we'd be delighted./b: * It's up
to you./c, d: As you wish.}' 582:17.
sociability: - associate with. → = ile
gel- ['- come with'] → gel- 1, = ile
git- ['- go with'] → git- 1a.

3 /A/ '- share /θ/ [sb's opinions,
views], - agree, - concur /WITH/ sb':
After a view has been expressed one
might ask: Siz ne kadar
katılıyorsunuz? 'To what extent do
you agree?' Person as object: *
Haklısınız, kesinlikle siz.E
katılıyorum. 'You're right. {I agree
entirely WITH you./I'm in total
agreement WITH you.}' B u
noktada diğer konuşmacılar.ın
tüm.ü.nE katılıyorum. 'On this
point I agree WITH all the other
speakers.'
Thought, notion, or words as object:
A rather old but still very appropriate
expression: * İsabet kaydettiniz
azizim, çok doğru, dediğiniz.E
aynen katılıyorum. '{You're right
on the mark/You've hit the nail on
the head}, my friend, quite right. I

entirely agree with you [lit., I entirely concur IN what you have said].' **Bu değerlendirmeler.E Dışişleri Bakanlığı katılıyor mu?** 'Does the Foreign Ministry concur with these {conclusions/views}?'

* **{düşünceye/fikre/görüşe} katıl-** '- agree /WITH/, share /θ/, concur {IN thoughts/IN opinions/IN views}' [düşünce 'thought, idea, opinion', A. fikir (fiKRİ) 'thought, idea, opinion', görüş 'view, opinion']: * **Düşünceler.İNİZ.E {katılıyorum./katılmıyorum.}** 'I {agree [lit., ** participate IN YOUR thoughts]/don't agree [*or* disagree]} WITH YOU.' **Görüşünüz.E bütün kalb.im.le katılıyorum.** 'I concur * whole heartedly [lit., * with {my whole heart/all my heart}] WITH your view.' **İleri sürülen her {görüş.E/fikr.E} katılmak zorunda değilim.** 'I'm not obliged to concur WITH every {view/idea} that is proposed.' *332:9.* assent: - concur. → = **fikir paylaş-**, = **{fikir/görüş} savun-** 2 → **savun-.**

fikre katıl-. → under 3 above.

görüşe katıl-. → under 3 above.

katla- [r] /A/ '- fold /{IN/INTO}/' [kat 'layer, stratum, fold' + verb-forming suf. -lA]: **Öğrenci kâğıdı önce iki.yE sonra dörd.E katladı.** 'The student folded the piece of paper first {IN/INTO} two and then {IN/INTO} four.' *291:5.* fold: - fold.

katlan- [ır] [katla- + {pass./refl.} suf. -n] 1 /A, tarafından/ '- be folded /INTO, by/': **Kâğıt önce iki.yE sonra dörd.E [öğrenci tarafından] katlandı.** 'The paper was first folded INTO two and then INTO four [by the student].' *291:5.* fold: - fold.

2 /A/ '- put up /WITH/, - bear /θ/, - stand /θ/, - tolerate /θ/, - endure /θ/, - suffer /θ/, - take /θ/': **Türk hamamları çok sıcak olur. Onbeş dakikadan fazla katlanamazsınız.** 'Turkish baths get very hot. You can't stand [being in one, i.e., in the hot steam section, for] more than fifteen minutes.' NON-verbal noun as object: **Yazın İzmir'in sıcağı.nA katlanamıyorum.** 'I can't stand θ the heat in Izmir [lit., Izmir's heat] in the

summer.' **Kızım Amerika'ya gidince çok özledim, ayrılığ.ı.nA katlanamadım, ben de * arka.sı.nDAN gittim.** 'When my daughter went off to the United States, I missed her very much. I couldn't bear θ being {away/separated} from her and * followed her [lit., ** went FROM her back].' **Siz de çok oldunuz ama, bu kaba sözleriniz.E katlanmak zorunda değilim, * yeter artık!** 'You've really gone too far, but I don't have to put up with these rude words of yours, * enough already!' **Annem ve babam ölünce her türlü zorluğ.A yalnız başıma katlandım.** 'When my mother and father died, I put up WITH all kinds of difficulties by myself.' **Gemi batınca ıssız bir adada beş gün açlığ.A katlandım.** 'When the boat sank, I endured θ hunger on an {uninhabited/secluded} island for five days.' Proverb: **Gülü seven diken.i.nE katlanır.** 'The one who loves the rose will put up with its thorns.'
VERBAL noun as object: **Bebeğ.in ağlama.sı.nA katlanamadım ve evden ayrıldım.** 'I couldn't stand θ the baby's crying and left θ the house.' *134:5.* patience: - endure; *1047:3.* toughness: - toughen. → = **dayan-** 3, = **tahammül et-**, = **çek-** 5, **uğraş-** 3 ['- put up with a person'].

kavga çıkar-. → **çıkar-** 7.

kavga et- [eDer] /lA/ '- fight, - quarrel /with/', physical or just verbal. [kavga 'fight, quarrel']: **Tufan bugün okulda Fikret ile kavga etti.** 'Tufan fought with Fikret {at/in} school today.' **Çocuklar kavga etmeyin!** 'Children, don't fight!' **Sporcular maçtan sonra kavga ettiler.** 'The athletes fought after the game.' **Çocukken çok kavga eder, annemi üzerdim.** 'When I was a child, I used to {fight a lot/get into a lot of fights} and worry my mother.' *456:11.* disaccord: - quarrel; *457:13.* contention: - contend. → **çatış-** 1 ['- quarrel, - clash /with/'], **dövüş-** ['- fight, - struggle, - engage in combat /with/ one another, in striking one another'].

kavur- [ur] '- fry, - roast': **Soğanları zeytinyağında 5 dakika kadar pembeleşince.ye kadar kavurun.** 'Fry the onions in olive oil

about 5 minutes until they turn pink.'
**Eti [tencere.ye] ilâve edip tahta
kaşıkla karıştırarak rengi
dönen.e kadar kavurun.** 'Add the
meat [to the saucepan] and, stirring
with a wooden spoon, fry it until it
changes color.' **Bir tencerede
sıvıyağı kızdırın. Et, soğan,
domates, tuz ve karabiber
ekleyip kavurun.** 'Heat up some
oil in a saucepan. Add meat,
tomatoes, salt and black pepper and
fry [the mixture].' **Tavada 5 kaşık
sıvıyağı kızdırın. Ciğerlerin
fazla unlarını silkeleyip kızgın
yağ.a atın. Tuz serpip kavurun.**
'Heat up 5 spoon fulls of oil in a
frying pan. Shake the excess flour off
the liver and add it [i.e., the liver] to
the hot oil. Sprinkle on some salt and
fry.' Proverb: **Akşam kavur,
sabah savur.** 'Cook [lit., fry] it at
night, use it up in the morning.', a
reference to sb who uses up all that he
obtains. *11:4a.* cooking: - cook sth.
→ = kızart- 1.

kavuş- [ur] 1 /A/ '- meet /θ/ sb, - come
together, - be reunited /WITH/, -
meet /θ/ sb again after a long
absence': {**Yıllar.dır/Yıllar.ca**}
**görmediğim oğlum.A
kavuştum.** 'I was reunited WITH
my son, whom I hadn't seen {for
years [also: IN years]}.' Proverb:
**Dağ dağ.A kavuşmaz, insan
insan.A kavuşur.** 'Mountains do
not meet [lit., Mountains do not meet
θ mountains] but people do.', i.e.,
Mountains cannot move from their
places to meet one another: **"Dağ
dağ.A kavuşmaz, insan insan.A
kavuşur" derler,** * {**çok doğru**}!
**Geçen gün yıllardır
görmediğim asker arkadaşım
çıkageldi, ne kadar mutlu
oldum, anlatamam. Oturduk,
eski güzel günleri yadettik.**
'They say that "Mountains do not
meet one another but people do." *
{How true!/Right on!} The other day
an old army buddy I hadn't seen for
years suddenly turned up. I can't tell
you how happy I was! We sat down
and recalled those great old days.'
799:11. joining: - be joined. →
buluş- ['- come together, - meet /θ/',
usually after a previous agreement to
meet].

2 /A/ '- succeed in getting or
attaining θ sth sought, - obtain, - get':
**Sağlığ.ınız.A kavuşmanız için
gece gündüz [Allah'a] dua**

ettim. 'I prayed [to God] day and
night for your recovery [lit., ** for
your attaining θ your health].' *409:8.*
success: - achieve one's purpose.

kavuştur- [ur] /A/ '- unite, - reunite
/WITH/, - bring together /WITH/, -
join sb or sth /to/ sb or sth else'
[kavuş- + caus. suf. -DIr]: **Polisler
kaçırılan çocuğ.u üç gün sonra
aile.si.nE kavuşturdu.** 'Three
days later the police reunited WITH
his family the child who had been
kidnapped.' **İstanbul Boğaz
Köprüsü Asya ile Avrupa
kıtaları.nı birbiri.nE kavuşturdu.** 'The Bosphorus bridge in
Istanbul joined the continents of Asia
and Europe [to one another].' *799:5.*
joining: - put together. → =
birleştir-, yaklaştır- ['- bring one
thing /{to/NEAR/UP TO/OVER
TO}/ another, - join'].

* **Allah kavuştursun!** 'May God
{reunite you/bring you together
[again]}', said to those remaining
behind after sb has departed on a
journey: **A: Bugün annemle
babamı İstanbul'a uğurladık.**
'A: Today we saw my {mother and
father/mom and dad} off to Istanbul.'
**B: * Öyle mi! Allah
kavuştursun!** 'B: * Is that so! May
God bring you together again.' *504: *
20.* courtesy: polite expressions. → ≠
ayır- 1.

kay- [ar] 1 /A/ '- slide, - slip, - skid; -
slide over /to/': **Muz kabuğu.nA
basınca {kayıp yere
düştüm/ayağım kaydı}.** 'I slipped
ON a banana peel [lit., when I
stepped ON a banana peel, {I slipped
and fell to the ground/my foot
slipped}].' **Elindeki bardak
parmakları.nın ara.sı.nDAN
kayıp yere düştü.** 'The glass in his
hand slipped THROUGH his fingers
and fell to the ground.' In a theater:
**Biraz kenar.a kayarsanız ben
de filmi görebilirim.** '{Would
you mind moving down a bit so I,
too, can see the movie?/Please
{move/slide} over a bit so I, too, can
see the movie} [lit., If you would
slide over to the side a bit so I, too,
can see the movie].' *177:35.* travel: -
glide; *194:9.* descent: - slide.

2 '- sled': **Çocuklar tepe.den
aşağı.ya doğru kızakları.yla
kayıyorlar.** 'The children are
sledding down the hill [lit., ** sliding

with their sleds from the hill downward].' *177:35*. travel: - glide.

3 '- ski': **Ağabeyim** [usually pronounced: **âbim**] **çok güzel kayıyor.** 'My older brother skis very well.' *177:35*. travel: - glide; *753:4*. skiing: - ski. → = **kayak yap-** → yap- 3.

{**kaybet-** [kaybeDer]/**yitir-** [ir]} '- lose' [**kayıp** (kaYBı) 'loss' + **et-**]: Lose an object: {a: **Pasaportumu/b: Cüzdanımı/c: Eşyalarımı/d: Anahtarımı/e: Kimliğimi**} **kaybettim.** 'I've lost {a: my passport/b: my wallet/c: my luggage/d: my key/e: my identity card}.' **Çantan nerede?** * **Sakın onu kaybetmiş ol.ma.yasın!** 'Where's your {handbag/purse/ briefcase}? * I do hope you haven't lost it!' Proverb: **Hiçbir şey.İ olmayan hiçbir şey kaybetmez.** 'He who has nothing loses nothing.' *473:4*. loss: - lose. → ≠ **bul-** 1. Lose at a game: * **Türk Millî futbol takımı Fransa ile yaptığı maçı kaybetti.** 'The Turkish national soccer team lost to France [lit., ** lost the game it had made with France].' → ≠ 2 **yen-** 2. Proverb: **Kumar.DA kazanan aşk.TA kaybeder.** 'He who wins AT gambling loses IN love.' Lucky at cards, unlucky in love. **Duydun mu, Semra bütün parasını * kumar.DA kaybetmiş.** 'Have you heard? Semra * lost all her money θ gambling.' → ≠ **kazan-** 2.

'- lose [sb to death]': **Annemizi tam üç yıl önce kaybettik.** 'We lost our mother exactly three years ago.' *307:19*. death: - die. → = **hayata gözlerini {kapa-/kapat-}** → {kapa-/kapat-} 1, = **hayata gözlerini yum-** → göz yum- 1, = **öl-,** = **ömrünü tamamla-** ['- complete one's life, come to the end of one's life, - die, pass away'], = **son nefesini ver-** ['- breathe one's last breath, - die'] → ver- 1, = **vefat et-,** = **canından ol-** ['- lose one's life, - die', mostly for an unexpected and undeserved death] → ol- 7, ≠ **doğ-** 1, ≠ **dünyaya gel-** → gel- 1.

aklını {kaybet-/yitir-} '- lose one's mind, - go crazy' [A. **akıl** (aKLı) 'mind']: **Kadın bebeğinin çalındığını öğrenince aklını kaybetti.** 'When the woman learned that her baby had been kidnapped [lit., stolen], she lost her mind.' *925:21*. insanity, mania: - go mad. → = **çıldır-,** = **delir-,** = {**şuurunu/ bilincini**} **kaybet-** [or **yitir-**].

{**bekâretini/kızlığını**} **kaybet-** [or **yitir-**] '- lose one's virginity', only for women. There is no common Turkish equivalent term for men. [{A. **bekâret/kızlık**} 'virginity']: **Süheyla evlenmeden önce bekâretini kaybetmek istemi-yordu.** 'Süheyla didn't want to lose her virginity before getting married.' *75:21*. sex: - copulate; *665:20*. unchastity: - seduce.

bilincini kaybet-. → {**şuurunu/bilincini**} **kaybet-** below.

güvenini {kaybet-/yitir-} /A karşı/ '- lose one's faith /IN/' [**güven** 'faith, belief']: **İnsanlar.A KARŞI güvenimi kaybettim.** 'I've lost my faith IN {people/mankind}.' *132:4*. disappointment: - be disappointed.

hayatını {kaybet-/yitir-} '- lose one's life, - die', usually of unnatural causes: in an accident, through murder, etc. [A. **hayat** (. -) 'life']: **Tren kazasında 53 kişi hayatını kaybetti.** 'Fifty-three people lost their lives in the train accident.' *307:19*. death: - die. → = **hayata gözlerini {kapa-/kapat-}** → {kapa-/kapat-} 1, = **hayata gözlerini yum-** → göz yum- 1, = **öl-,** = **ömrünü tamamla-** ['- complete one's life, - come to the end of one's life, - die, - pass away'], = **son nefesini ver-** ['- breathe one's last breath, - die'] → ver- 1, = **vefat et-,** = **canından ol-** ['- lose one's life, - die', mostly for an unexpected and undeserved death] → ol- 7, ≠ **doğ-** 1, ≠ **dünyaya gel-** → gel- 1.

kendini {kaybet-/NOT yitir-} lit., '- lose oneself' (1) '- lose consciousness, - pass out, - faint' [**kendi** 'self']: **Sıcaktan fenalaşan kadın kendini kaybetti.** 'The woman who had felt faint from the heat passed out.' *25:5*. insensibility: - faint. → = **bayıl-** 1, = **kendinden geç-** 1 → geç- 1, = {**şuurunu/ bilincini**} **kaybet-** [or **yitir-**] 1, ≠ **ayıl-** 2, ≠ **kendine gel-** 1 → gel- 1.

(2) '- be beside oneself with joy, - be carried away [by joy], - be ecstatic, in Paradise': **Partide o kadar eğlendik ki, kendimizi kaybettik.** 'At the party we had such a good time we were simply {carried away/in Paradise}.' *95:11.* pleasure: - be pleased. → = **kendinden geç-** 2 → geç- 1.

(3) '- be beside oneself with anger, - lose control as a result of anger, - lose one's temper, - go into a towering rage': **Öyle sinirlendim ki kendimi kaybettim, ne söylediğimi hatırlamıyorum.** 'I got so angry that I just lost control. I don't remember what I said.' *152:20.* resentment, anger: - fly into a rage. → = **patla-** 2, = {**şuurunu/bilincini**} **kaybet-** 2.

kızlığını kaybet-. → {**bekâretini/kızlığını**} **kaybet-** above.

{**şans/fırsat**} **kaybet-** '- miss or - lose {a chance/an opportunity}': * **Türkçe sınav.ı.nı ver.eme.yince Türkiye'ye gitme {şans.ı.nı/fırsat.ı.nı} kaybettim.** 'When I failed [lit., ** couldn't give] the Turkish language examination, I lost the {chance/opportunity} to go to Turkey.' *410:14.* failure: - miss; *843:5.* untimeliness: - miss an opportunity. → = **fırsat kaçır-** → **kaçır-** 2, ≠ **kazan-** 2 ['- win /{/AT/IN}, IN/'].

{**şuurunu/bilincini**} **kaybet-**[or **yitir-**] [A. **şuur** 'mind, consciousness, intelligence; moral sense, judgment', **bilinç** 'consciousness'] (1) '- lose consciousness, - pass out, - faint [lit., ** - lose one's consciousness]': **Oldukça ciddî bir kaza geçirmiş. O yüzden * şuur.u.nu kaybetmiş, henüz * kendi.nde değil.** 'He was involved in a serious accident. As a result, * he lost consciousness [lit., ** HIS consciousness]. He still * hasn't returned to normal [lit., ** is not in himself].' *25:5.* insensibility: - faint. → = **bayıl-** 1, = **kendinden geç-** 1 → geç- 1, = **kendini kaybet-** 1, ≠ **ayıl-** 2 ['- come to, - regain consciousness'], ≠ **kendine gel-** 1 → gel- 1.

(2) '- lose self-control, - lose one's temper': **Öyle sinirlendim ki şuurumu kaybettim.** 'I got so angry that I just lost my temper.'

152:20. resentment, anger: - fly into a rage. → = **patla-** 2, = **kendini** {**kaybet-**/NOT ~~yitir-~~} 3.

(3) '- go out of one's mind, - go crazy, - be out of one's senses': **Kadın bebeğinin çalındığını öğrenince şuurunu kaybetti.** 'When the woman learned that her baby had been kidnapped [lit., stolen], she went crazy.' *925:21.* insanity, mania: - go mad. → = **aklını** {**kaybet-**/**yitir-**}, = **çıldır-**, = **delir-**.

* {**umudunu/ümidini**} **kaybet-**[or **yitir-**] '- lose [one's] hope, - despair, - give up hope' [{**umut (umuDu)/ümit (ümiDi)**} 'hope']: A: **Bir aydır iş arıyorum, hâlâ bulamadım.** 'A: I've been looking for work for a month now. I still haven't been able to find any.' B: **Umud.UN.u kaybetme, bulursun.** 'B: Don't give up [lit., ** YOUR] hope. You'll find sth.' *125:10.* hopelessness: - despair.

ümidini kaybet-. → directly above.

{**vakit/zaman**} **kaybet-**[or **yitir-**] /mAklA, mAktAn/ '- lose or - waste time /ing, {from/because of}...ing/' [{A. **vakit** (vaKTİ)/A. **zaman** (. -)} 'time']: **Vakit kaybetmemeliyiz.** 'We musn't {lose/waste} [any] time.' * **Kaybedecek zamanımız yok.** 'We have no time to lose.' **Işıl'ı {bekler.KEN/bekle.MEKLE/beklemek.TEN} çok vakit kaybettim.** 'I lost a lot of time {WHILE wait.ING/wait.ING/BECAUSE OF wait.ING} for Işıl.' **Takıldığınız soruları atlayın, vakit kaybetmeyin.** 'Skip the questions you are stuck on. Don't waste time.'

hiç vakit kaybetmeden 'without wasting {lit., any time/a minute/a moment}': **Osman'ın nereye gittiğ.i.ni biliyorum. Ha[y]di hiç vakit kaybetmeden o.nA yetişelim.** 'I know where Osman went. Let's catch up WITH him {without losing any time/right away }.' *331:13.* inactivity: - waste time; *391:8.* uselessness: - be useless. → = {**vakit/zaman**} **öldür-** ['- waste or - kill time'], {**vakit/zaman**} **kazan-** 1 ['- save time', i.e., not - use time] → kazan- 4, ≠ {**vakit/zaman**} **değerlendir-** ['-

233

use time well, efficiently, - make good use of one's time'].

yolunu {**kaybet-/yitir-**} '- lose one's way, - get lost' [yol 'way, road']: * **Burası neresi? Neredeyim? Galiba yol.UM.u kaybettim.** 'What is this place? [lit., ** Its here its where?] Where am I? It seems [that] I've lost MY way.' *473:4*. loss: - lose. → **kaybol-** ['- be lost, - get lost'] → ol- 12.

zaman kaybet-. → {**vakit/zaman**} **kaybet-** above.

kaybol-. → ol- 12.

kaydet- [kaydeDer] 1 /A/ '- register or - enroll sb [not oneself] /IN [a course], {IN/AT} [a school]/' [A. **kayıt** (kaYDı) 'a registering, record' + **et-**]: **Bu sene çocuğum.U** {a: **kurs.A/b: okul.A/c: ilk- okul.A/d: lise.yE/e: üniver- site.yE**} **kaydettim.** 'This year I registered my child {a: IN the course/b: IN the school/c: IN [the] primary school/d: IN {high school/the lycée}/e: AT {the college/the university}}.' *549:15*. record: - record. → = **yazdır-** 2. For '- register ONESELF, NOT sb else, in a course', → /A/ **kaydol-** → ol- 12, /A/ **yazıl-** 2.

2 /A/ '- record sth /IN/, - enter sth /IN/, - write sth down /IN/': **Babam düzenli OLARAK günlük tutmuş,** * **yaşadıklarını sıcağı sıcağına kaydetmiş.** 'My father regular.LY kept a diary and * recorded the events of his life [lit., ** what he had lived (through)] while they were still fresh in his memory.' **Öğretmen öğrencilerin** {a: **Ara sınav/b: Dönem son.u sınav.ı/c: Final sınav.ı/d: Yıl son.u sınav.ı**} **notlar.ı.nı** {**dizüstü bilgisayarı.nA/not defteri.nE**} **kaydetti.** 'The teacher recorded the students' {a: midterm examination/b: quarter [or semester] final examination/c: final examination/d: year final examination} grades {IN her laptop computer/IN her grade book}.' *549:15*. record: - record. → = **yaz-** 1 ['- write, - write down'].

3 /A, lA/ '- record, - tape /ON [a medium], with [an instrument]/': {**Düğün.de/Mezuniyet tören.i.nde**} **dijital kamera.yla**

çektiğimiz resimleri CD'yE kaydettim. 'I recorded the pictures we had taken with a digital camera {at the wedding/at the graduation ceremony} ON a CD.' {**Video.m.u/Vidyo.m.u**} tele- vizyondaki filmi kaydetmesi için programladım. 'I programmed {my VCR} to tape the movie [(showing) on television].' *549:15*. record: - record.

4 '- state, - announce, - declare, - note', *formal, official*: in speech and in writing: **İstanbul Valisi birden bastıran kış nedeniyle sürücülerin daha dikkatli olmaları gerektigini kaydetti.** 'The governor of Istanbul stated that drivers should be more careful {with/lit., because of} the sudden onset of winter.' As an introduction to a following declaration: {**Başbakan/Belediye başkanı**} **şunları kaydetti...** '{The prime minister/The mayor} stated as follows:...' *334:5*. affirmation: - affirm; *524:24*. speech: - state.

5 '- achieve or - make', with nouns indicating progress, development, success: **Ekonomik göstergeler itibariyle ülkemiz son yıllarda büyük bir** {**ilerleme/başarı**} **kaydetti.** 'According to economic indicators, our country has {made great progress/achieved great success} in recent years.' *392:7*. improvement: - get better; *409:7a*. success: - succeed.

isabet kaydet- [A. isabet (. - .) 'a hitting the mark'] (1) '- hit the mark, target': **İyi bir** {a: **okçu/b: atıcı**} **sayılmam, on atış.TAN sadece altısında isabet kaydettim,** * **geri.si karavan.a.** 'I'm not [lit., I'm not considered] a good {a: {archer/bowman}/b: {marks- man/shot}}. OUT OF ten attempts [lit., shots], I hit the target only six times. * The rest missed the target entirely [lit., ** the rest of it to the cauldron].' *223:10* nearness: - contact; *409:7b*. success: - succeed in specific ways.
(2) '- get it right, - be right, - be on target, - be right on the mark': **İsabet kaydettiniz azizim, çok doğru, dediğiniz.E aynen katılıyorum.** '{You're right on the mark/You've hit the nail on the head}, my friend, quite right. I agree with you entirely [lit., I entirely concur IN what you

have said].' *409:7b.* success: - succeed in specific ways; *972:10.* truth: - be right.

sayı kaydet- '- score, - make points in a game, contest' [**say** 'number, point in a game']: **Maça ikinci yarıda girmesine rağmen tam 22 sayı kaydetti.** 'In spite of the fact that he entered the game in the second half, he scored a full 22 points.' *409:9.* success: - score a success.

kaydol-. → **ol-** 12.

kaygılan- [ır] /DAn, diye/ '- worry, - get anxious, worried /ABOUT, {THAT/lit., saying}/' [**kaygı** 'anxiety, worry' + verb-forming suf. -lAn]: **A: Sen dün gece eve gelmeyince kaygılandım.** 'A: When you [s.] didn't come home last night, I got worried.' **B: O konuda kaygılanmay.a gerek yok, çocuk değilim.** 'B: There's no need to worry about that [lit., on that subject]. I'm not a child.' **O dürüst biridir. Borcunu ödemeyecek DİYE kaygılanma.** 'He's an honest {fellow/person}. You needn't worry THAT he won't pay what he owes [lit., Don't worry THAT he won't pay what he owes].' **Bu gibi şeyler.DEN kaygılanma.N.a gerek yok.** 'There is no need for YOU to worry ABOUT such things.' *126:6.* anxiety: - feel anxious. → = /DAn/ **endişe et-,** = /I/ **merak et-** 1.

kayna- [r] '- boil, - come to a boil' [i.]: **Çay suyu kaynadı, demler misin?** 'The water for tea is boiling [lit., has boiled]. Would you please brew [the tea]?' **Ocağ.A koyduğumuz su kaynadı. Hemen makarna yapalım.** 'The water [that] we put ON the stove is boiling. Let's make some macaroni right away.' **Ocağı kapar mısın lütfen, çaydanlıktaki su bir saattir * fokur fokur kaynıyor, neredeyse tamamen buharlaştı.** 'Turn off the stove please, the water in the teapot * has been bubbling away for an hour now. It has almost completely boiled away [lit., turned into steam].' Proverbs: **Herkesin tenceresi kapalı kaynar.** 'Everyone's pot cooks with the lid on.', i.e., Troublesome family matters should stay within the family. **İki baş bir kazanda kaynamaz.** 'Two

[sheep] heads won't boil in one pot.', i.e., Two strong-headed people won't work well together. Too many cooks spoil the soup. *320:4.* bubble: - bubble. For '- boil sth', i.e., '- cook sth in boiling water', → **haşla-.**

kaynaklan- [ır] /DAn/ '- result, - originate, - stem, - emanate, or - spring /from/, - be due /TO/' [**kaynak** 'source, origin' + verb-forming suf. -lAn]: **S: * Bu mesele nere.den kaynaklanıyor, biliyor musunuz?** 'Q: What's the {cause/source} of this problem [lit., ** from where does this problem originate], do you know?' **C1: * Hiç bir fikrim yok.** 'A1: I haven't {the faintest idea/a clue}.' **C2: * Bütün mesele parasızlık.tan kaynaklanıyor.** 'A2: It's all due to a lack of money [lit., ** The whole problem originates from moneylessness].' **Hata teknik bir neden.den kaynaklandı.** 'The error resulted from a technical failure [lit., cause].' **Bütün düzensizlik müdür.ün {vaktinde gelmeme.si.nDEN/olmama.sı.n.DAN} kaynaklanıyor.** 'All the disorder is due TO the fact {that the director doesn't come on time [lit., ** the director's not coming on time]/that there is no director [lit., ** the director's not being]}.' *886:5.* effect: - result from.

kaynat- [ır] '- boil sth, - cause sth to boil' [**kayna-** + caus. suf. -t]: **Biraz su kaynatıp kahve yaptım.** 'I boiled a little water and made some coffee.' *11:4a.* cooking: - cook sth; *320:4.* bubble: - bubble; *1019:17a.* heating: - heat.

vehicle name **su kaynat-** 'for a vehicle - overheat [lit., - boil water]': **Araba sıcak.TAN su kaynattı.** 'The car has overheated [lit., ** boiled water DUE TO the heat].' → **fazla ısın-** ['- become overheated, - overheat'] → **ısın-** 1. *320:4.* bubble: - bubble; *992:10.* excess: - overdo; *1019:17b.* heating: - get hot.

kaz- [ar] '- dig': **Çiftçi derin bir {kuyu/çukur} kazdı.** 'The farmer dug a deep {well/{hole/pit/ditch}}.' **Mezarcı aynı gün tam beş mezar kazdı.** 'The gravedigger dug {a whole/exactly} five graves on the same day.' **Define avcıları, bizim bölgede kazmadık yer bırakmadılar.** 'In our region the treasure hunters didn't leave anyplace untouched [lit., undug].' Words of a song sometimes found as a sign on the back of minibusses: **Boşuna kazma mezarcı, aşkımızı gömemezsin.** 'Don't dig [a grave] in vain, gravedigger. You cannot bury our love', i.e., because it is so great. **Kazdığı kuyu.yA kendisi düştü.** 'He fell INTO the well he himself had dug.' * **Bütün gün {bahçe.yİ/tarla.yI} kazdı.** 'He dug IN {the garden/the field} the whole day long [lit., ** he dug θ {the garden/the field}...].' **İğneyle kuyu kazmak.** 'To dig a well with a needle.', i.e., to attempt sth with inadequate means. <u>Proverb</u>: **Akarsu, çukurunu kendi kazar.** 'Running water cuts its own channel [lit., cuts its channel itself].', i.e., An enterprising person creates his own oppportunities. *284:15.* concavity: - excavate.

kaza geçir-. → **geçir-** 2.

kaza yap-. → **yap-** 3.

<u>kazan-</u> [ır] 1 '- earn': S: * **Ayşe ay.DA ne kadar [para] kazanıyor?** 'Q: How much [money] does Ayşe earn θ a month [lit., ** IN a month]?' C: **Ay.DA 2 bin lira kazanıyor.** 'A: She earns 2,000 liras θ a month.' <u>Proverb</u>: **Kazanmak kolay, saklamak zordur.** 'To earn is easy; to keep [i.e., what one has earned] is difficult.' *624:20.* payment: - be paid. → ≠ **para harca-** → {**harca-/sarf et-**}.

hak kazan- /A/ '- earn or - win the right /to/' [A. **hak** (ha**KK**ı) 'one's right, due']: **Ağabeyim** [usually pronounced: **âbim**] **Hukuk Fakültesi'ni bitir.erek avukat olmay.a hak kazandı.** 'By finish.ing law school [lit., the Law Faculty] my older brother earned the right to be a lawyer.' **Kardeşim Millî takım.A girmey.e hak kazandı.** 'My brother won a place on the National [soccer] team [lit., ** earned the right to enter θ the National team].' *472:8.* acquisition: - acquire.

hayatını kazan- /ArAk/ '- earn one's living, livelihood /by...ing/, - make one's living /by...ing/' [A. **hayat** (. -) 'life']: S: **Hayat.INIZ.ı {neyle/nasıl} kazanıyorsunuz?** 'Q: {How} do

you make YOUR living?' C: **Hayat.IM.ı {a: öğretmenlik/b: doktorluk/c: mühendislik/d: yazarlık/e: boyacılık/f: garsonluk} yap.arak kazanıyorum.** 'A: I make MY living as {a: a teacher/b: a doctor/c: an engineer/d: a writer/e: a shoeshine boy/f: a waiter} [lit., ** by do.ing {a: {teaching/lit., the profession of teaching}/b:....].' *385:11.* provision; equipment: - make a living. → = **geçimini sağla-**, = **geçin-** 2, **iş yap-** 1 ['- do work for a living'] → **yap-** 3.

2 /DA, DAn/ '- win /{AT/IN}, IN/': **Basketbol maç.ı.nı hangi takım kazandı?** 'Which team won the basketball game?' → = 2 **yen-**. # **Sonunda Leylâ {a: boşanma/b: ev/c: miras/d: sigorta} dava.sı.nı kazandı.** 'Finally Leylâ won her {a: divorce/b: house [i.e., She got the house as a result]/c: inheritance/d: insurance} case.' → ≠ **kaybet-**. # **Bir Türkçe sınav.ı.nda başarılı oldu ve onbeş günlük Türkiye gezi.si kazandı.** 'He passed [lit., was successful in] a Turkish examination and won a 15 day tour of Turkey.' **Duydun mu, Selim kumar.DA 5 bin lira kazanmış.** 'Have you heard? Selim won 5,000 liras θ gambling.' <u>Proverb</u>: **Kumar.DA kazanan aşk.TA kaybeder.** 'He who wins AT gambling loses IN love.' Lucky at cards, unlucky in love. **Turhan okulda düzenlenen çekiliş.TE bilgisayar seti kazandı.** 'Turhan won a computer IN a drawing held at the school.' The source of the winnings is indicated by the noun with **DAn**: * **Erhan millî piyango.DAN 5 bin lira kazanınca bayram etti.** 'When Erhan won 5,000 liras IN the national lottery, he {celebrated/was in seventh heaven}.' → = 2 **yen-** 2 [for a team '- win'], ≠ **kaybet-**.

'- win a place in an educational institution or department, - get in': A: **Sizin oğlunuz bu sene üniversite sınav.ı.nA girdi mi?** 'A: Has your son taken [lit., ** entered] θ {the college/the university} [entrance] exams this year?' B: **Evet, girdi.** 'A: Yes, he has.' A: * **Nere.yİ kazandı?** 'A: Where has he gotten in [lit., ** WHERE has he won]?' * **Hangi {a: okul.u/b: üniversite.yi/c: bölüm.ü/d: fakülte.yi}** kazandı?} 'A: {Which/What} {a: school/b: {college/university}/c: department/d: school of a university [e.g., medical, law] *or* department [e.g., literature]} has he gotten into [lit., ** won]?' B: {Boğaziçi Üniversite.si.ni/Edebiyat Fakülte.si.ni} kazandı. 'B: He got into {Boğaziçi University./the department of literature.}' *249:7.* superiority: - best; *411:3.* victory: - triumph.

3 '- pass a test, examination': * {sınav/imtihan} kazan- '- pass a test, examination' [{sınav/A. imtihan} 'examination']: Sınav.ı kazandı ve tıp fakülte.si.nE girdi. 'He passed the examination and entered θ [the] medical school.' *409:7b.* success: - succeed in specific ways. → = {sınavı/imtihan} ver- → ver- 1, ≠ {sınavdan/imtihandan} kal- → kal- 1.

4 /lA/ '- get, - gain /BY/': * Ben.İ patron.A şikâyet etmek.LE ne kazandın? 'What did you gain BY complaining ABOUT me TO the boss?' *472:8.* acquisition: - acquire.

{vakit/zaman} kazan- [{A. vakit (vaKTİ), A. zaman (. -)} 'time'] (1) '- save time', i.e., not - use time: {Vakit/Zaman} kazanmak için hemen bir taksi.yE atladım ama yine de uçağ.A yetişemedim. 'To save time I immediately hopped INTO a taxi, but in spite of that I couldn't catch θ the plane.' *390:5.* disuse: not - use. → ≠ {vakit/zaman} kaybet-[or yitir-] ['- lose or - waste time'], {vakit/zaman} değerlendir- ['- use time well, efficiently, - make good use of one's time']. (2) '- gain time', i.e., obtain extra time to achieve a goal, complete a task: {Vakit/Zaman} kazanmak için beni lüzumsuz sorularla oyalıyordu. 'To gain {time}, he was diverting me with useless questions.' *845:9.* lateness: - postpone.

kazık at-. → at- 1.

kazıkla- [r] /I/ '- gyp, - rip off, - swindle, - cheat; - sell sb sth at an exorbitant, outrageous price', *very common slang* [kazık *slang* 'trick, swindle' + verb-forming suf. -lA]: Tüh, biz.İ kazıklamışlar. * İpek

DİYE aldığımız bluz polyester çıktı. 'O {darn/damn}, they've really ripped us off. * The blouse that we bought THINKING it was silk [lit., ** thinking it θ silk] turned out to be polyester.' Ömer biz.İ öyle bir kazıkladı ki, ömrüm boyunca unutmayacağım. 'Ömer cheated us so {badly/flagrantly} that I shall never forget it as long as I live.' *356:19.* deception: nonformal terms - gyp. → = /A/ kazık at- → at- 1, = *formal*: /I/ dolandır-, /DAn/ fazla para al- ['- overcharge'] → al- 1.

kehanet et- [eDer] /A/ '- make a prediction, - predict /θ/ that...', the subject is a wise man, oracle, fortune-teller, or soothsayer only [A. kehanet (. - .) 'soothsaying, prediction']: Yaşlı adam çok yakında kıyamet.in kopacağ.ı.nA kehanet etti. 'The old man predicted θ that the end of the world [lit., that doomsday] would come very soon.' *961:9.* prediction: - predict. → = kehanette bulun- → bulun- 3. For '- predict' when the subject is an ordinary person or expert, not a wise man or oracle, → önceden bildir-.

kehanette bulun-. → bulun- 3.

kenara çek-. → çek- 1.

kendinden geç-. → geç- 1.

kendine gel-. → gel- 1.

Kendine iyi bak! → bak- 3.

kendini beğen-. → beğen-.

{kendini/kendisini} {ispatla-/kanıtla-}. → {ispatla-/ispat et-/kanıtla-}.

kendini kaybet-. → {kaybet-/yitir-}.

kendini öldür-. → öldür-.

kes- [er] 1 '- cut' [ADJ. kesik]: Akşam yemeği için karpuzla kavunu keser misin? 'Would you cut the watermelon and [the other kind of] melon for the evening meal?' Kızım, bıçakla oynama elini kesebilirsin! '{Dear/Child/lit., ** My girl}, don't play with the knife, you may cut your hand!' Proverbs: Kılıç kınını kesmez. 'A sword doesn't cut its own sheath.' **Veren eli kimse kesmez.** 'One does not cut the hand that gives.' *224:4*. interval: - cleave; *644: * 26*. probity: PHR. one does not cut the hand that gives. At the barber's: **{Berber/Kuaför}: Saçlarınızı nasıl kesme.m.i istersiniz?** '{Barber/{Hairdresser/Barber}}: How would you like me to cut your hair?' **Müşteri: Çok kısa kesmeyin.** 'Customer: Don't cut it too short.' **Müşteri: Lütfen şu model.e göre kesin.** 'Customer: Please cut it according to this style.' In a Turkish barber shop the barber may ask his customer to choose the style he wants from a book illustrating various haircuts. **Bura.DAN biraz [daha] keser misiniz?** 'Could you cut a little [more] {OFF/FROM} here?' **{a: Sakal.ın.ı/b: Saçlar.ın.ı/c: Tırnaklar.ın.ı/d: Bıyıklar.ın.ı} biraz kessene!** 'Won't you trim {a: your beard/b: your hair/c: your fingernails/d: Your moustache}?' *3:22*. hair: - cut or - dress the hair; *268:6*. shortness: - shorten.

'- cut across, - intersect': **Bu sokak Atatürk Cadde.si'ni keser mi?** 'Does this street {cut across/intersect} Atatürk Street?' *170:6*. crossing: - cross.

'- cut down': **Tarla {yapmak/ açmak} için ağaçları kestiler.** 'They cut down the trees [in order] to clear a space for a field [lit., {to make/to open} a field].' *912:5*. depression: - fell. → = **biç-** 1.

dilim dilim kes- '- cut [up] into slices, - slice up' [**dilim** 'slice, piece']: **Her iki karpuz.u da dilim dilim kesip çocuklar.A dağıttım.** 'I sliced up both watermelons and distributed the pieces {among/to} the children.' *792:6*. part: - separate; *801:11*. separation: - sever. → = **dilimle-, doğra-** ['- cut [up] into slices or pieces; - carve, - chop into bits, - mince'].

2 '- kill, - butcher': Proverbs: **Altın yumurtlayan tavuğu kesmezler.** 'One doesn't [lit., they don't] kill the goose that lays the golden egg.' *644: * 26*. probity: PHR. one does not cut the hand that gives. **Vakitsiz öten horozun başını keserler.** 'They cut off the head of the rooster that

crows at the wrong time.' *843:7*. untimeliness: ADV. inopportunely.

kurban kes- '- kill an animal as a sacrifice' [A. **kurban** (. -) 1 'sacrifice; victim.' 2 'ram'] In Islam only the following animals are appropriate for sacrifice: **koyun** 'sheep'; **koç** 'ram'; **keçi** 'goat'; **inek** 'cow'; **deve** 'camel'. The meat is distributed to the poor. **Bu kurban bayramında iki kurban kestik.** 'On this Feast of the Sacrifice we sacrificed two animals.' *308:12*. killing: - kill. → **öldür-** ['- kill'].

3 '- interrupt, - break in': **sözünü kes-** '- interrupt, - break in on, - cut in on [conversation]' [**söz** 'word, utterance']: You have interrupted sb. You say: * **Pardon, söz.ÜNÜZ.ü kestim.** 'Sorry, I interrupted you [lit., ** YOUR utterance].' *504: * 20*. courtesy: polite expressions. **Lütfen konuşurken söz.ÜM.ü kesmeyin, sorularınızı konuş- mamdan sonra sorun.** 'Please don't interrupt me [lit., ** MY utterance] when I'm speaking. Ask your questions after I have spoken.' **Dinleyiciler sık sık alkışlayarak konuşmacı.nın söz.Ü.nü kestiler.** 'The audience [lit., listeners], applauding frequently, interrupted the speaker [lit., ** the speaker's utterance].' **Kes-** may used without **söz-** in the same sense when that meaning is clear from the context: **Kadın durmadan konuşuyordu. Bülent ise kesmeden dinliyordu.** 'The woman spoke incessantly [lit., without stopping]. Bülent, for his part, listened without interrupting.' *214:6*. intrusion: - interrupt; *843:4*. untimeliness: - talk out of turn.

4 '- cut out, - stop, - cease': **Yeter artık, kes {ağlamay.ı/ gürültü.yü}!** 'That's enough now, stop {crying/the noise}!' *856:6*. cessation: - cease sth; *856:11*. cessation: - put a stop to; *1011:13*. hindrance: - stop. → = **bırak-** 3, = **durdur-**.

kısa kes- '- cut short' [**kısa** 'short']: **Arkadaşlar lütfen toplantı.yı kısa kesin, binayı boşaltmak zorundayız.** 'Folks, please cut the meeting short. We have to clear out the building.' *268:6*. shortness: - shorten.

[{lâfı/sözü}] kısa kes- '- cut short one's talk', somewhat impolite when used as a command: **Cemil lütfen [{lâfı/sözü}] kısa kes. Bir saattir seni dinliyoruz * hâlâ konu.ya giremedin.** 'Cemil, please cut it [lit., ** the utterance] short. We've been listening to you for an hour [now], and * you still haven't been able to get [around] to [lit., ** enter θ] the point.' **Kısa kes, çok konuştun!** '[Come on,] {cut it short/knock it off}. You've [really] talked too much.' Somewhat more polite: * **Lütfen keser misin artık!** 'Please, really that's enough now [lit., would you cut it short now].' *268:6.* shortness: - shorten.

* **sesini kes-** '- be quiet, - stop talking, - shut up' [**ses** 'voice, sound'], lit., ** '- cut one's sound': **Biraz ses.İN.i kes de, müziği duyalım.** 'Keep quiet for a moment so we can hear [lit., and let's hear] the music.' The same meaning may be conveyed with **kes-** alone: **Kes artık, yeter!** 'Stop it now, that's enough!' *51:5.* silence: - be silent. →
= **sus-** 2.

5 '- issue, - hand out, - give, or - write', a ticket, receipt: * **ceza kes-** /A/ '- fine /θ/, - give a ticket /to/' [A. **ceza** (. -) 'punishment']: * **Polis kırmızı ışık.TA geçen {arac.A/yaya.yA} ceza kesti.** 'The policeman gave a ticket {to the vehicle which/to the pedestrian who} had gone THROUGH the red light.' *604:10.* punishment: - punish. →
cezalandır- ['- punish'], **ceza ver-**. Same. → **ver-** 1.

makbuz kes- '- issue or - write a receipt': **Makbuz kesmeden yardım toplayanlar hakkında yasal işlem yapılacak.** 'Legal action will be taken concerning those who have collected money [lit., (financial) assistance] without issuing a receipt.' *478:13.* giving: - deliver.

6 '- hinder, - block, - impede': **yolunu kes-** '- block one's way, - waylay, - ambush', often to steal from [**yol** 'way, road'], lit., ** '- cut sb's road': **Dün akşam serseriler yol.UM.u kesti ve cüzdanımı almak istedi.** 'Yesterday night some bums stopped ME [lit., ** cut MY road] and wanted to take my wallet.' *346:10.* concealment: - ambush.

kesil- [ir] [**kes-** + {pass./refl.} suf. -Il] 1 /tarafından/ '- be cut, - get cut, - be cut off /by/': **Fatih Köprü.sü'nün açılış kurdele.si başbakan tarafından kesildi.** 'The ribbon for the opening of the Fatih Bridge was cut by the prime minister.' **Cam kırılınca elim kesildi.** 'When the window broke, my hand got cut.'

baş kesil- 'for one's head - be cut off, - be killed': Proverbs: **Eğilen baş kesilmez.** 'A head that bows is not cut off.', i.e., A person who is humble and obedient will not be cut down because he threatens no one. **Vakitsiz öten horozun başı kesilir.** 'The head of a rooster that crows at the wrong time is cut off.' *224:4.* interval: - cleave; *308:12.* killing: - kill; *843:7.* untimeliness: ADV. inopportunely.

2 '- stop, - cease of itself', with a limited set of noun subjects, most having to do with weather: {a: **Rüzgâr/b: Yağmur/c: Kar/d: Dolu/e: Fırtına} kesildi. Dışarı[ya] çıkalım.** '{a: The wind/b: The rain/c: The snow/d: The hail/e: The storm} has stopped. Let's go outside.' *819:6.* end: - come to an end; *856:7.* cessation: for sth - cease. → = **din-**, = **dur-** 2.

3 /{tarafından/CA}/ '- be cut off, interrupted /by/': {**Elektrikler/ Sular/Hava gazı**} {**belediye tarafından/belediye.ce**} **kesildi.** '{The electricity/The water/The gas} was cut off {by the municipality}.' * **Hatlar kesildi.** '{We've been cut off./lit., The (telephone) lines have been cut.}' On the phone: * **Görüş.memiz kesildi.** 'We {have been/were} cut off [lit., ** Our conversation was cut off].' *856:10.* cessation: - interrupt.

ümit kesil- 'for hope - be given up, abandoned' [A. **ümit** (. -) (ümiDi) 'hope, expectation']: Proverb: **Çıkmayan candan ümit kesilmez.** 'Where there's life there's hope [lit., ** Hope is not cut off from a soul that has not left the body].' *125:10.* hopelessness: - despair.

4 /DAn/ '- be deducted /from/': **Memur maaşların.dan vergi {otomatik.MAN/otomatik OLARAK} kesiliyor.** 'Taxes are {automatical.LY} deducted from

employee salaries.' *255:9.* subtraction: - subtract.

5 /θ/ * '- turn into, - become', often suddenly as a result of fear or other strong emotion. *851:6.* change: - be changed. → = çevir- 8, = dön- 6, = ol- 1, = dönüş-. • Note: The noun preceding kesil- has no case suffix: * buz kesil- '- turn INTO ice, freeze' [buz 'ice']: Bugün hava öyle soğuktu ki, eve gelene kadar elim ayağım buz kesildi. 'The weather was so cold today that by the time I got home my hands and feet were frozen [lit., had become ice].' Hayatımda gördüğüm {en korkunç} filmdi, elim ayağım buz kesildi. 'It was {the scariest/the most frightening} movie I've ever seen [in my life]. My hands and feet froze.' *1022:9.* cold: - freeze. → = don-.

taş kesil- '- turn into stone' [taş 'stone']: Arabanın çocuğa çarptığını görünce taş kesildim; * öylece donakaldım. 'When I saw the car hit the child, * I just froze [lit., turned to stone (in horror)].' *1044:7.* hardness, rigidity: - harden.

kestir- [ir] [kes- + caus. suf. -DIr] 1 /A/ '- have sth cut, - have /θ/ sb cut sth': Saçını {kim.E/hangi berber.E} kestirdin? '{θ Who/θ Which barber} did you have cut your hair?' At the barber's: * Saç kestirmek istiyorum. 'I want a haircut [lit., I want to have (my) hair cut].' • Note the plural object: Müşteri: * Saçlar.ım.ı kestirmek istiyorum. 'Customer: I want to have my hair cut.' {Berber/Kuaför}: Nasıl kestirmek istiyorsunuz? '{Barber/{Hairdresser/Barber}}: How do you want [to have] it cut?' [or Nasıl kesme.M.i istersiniz? 'How would you like me to cut it (lit., ** want MY cutting it)?'] Responses for men or women: Çok kısa kesmeyin. 'Don't cut it too short.' Çok kısa kesin lütfen. 'Cut it very short please.' [or Çok kısa kestirmek istiyorum. 'I want (to have) it cut very short.'] In a barber shop the barber may ask his customer to chose the style he wants from a book illustrating various haircuts: Şu model.e göre kesin. 'Cut it according to this style.' [or Şu model.e göre kestirmek istiyorum. 'I want (to have) it cut according to this style.']

Responses for women only: Sadece kâhküllerimi kestirmek istiyorum. 'I want only my bangs cut.' • Sometimes kestir- with a preceding noun means '- cut INTO a certain form': * Kâhkül kestirmek istiyorum. 'I want [to have my hair cut INTO] bangs.' Responses for men only. [The numbers indicate specific lengths from short to long.]: * Saçlarımı {0/1/2/3} numara kesin. 'Cut my hair length {0/1/2/3}.' [or Saçlarımı {0/1/2/3} numara kestirmek istiyorum. 'I want (to have) my hair cut length {O/1/2/3}.'] *3:22.* hair: - cut or - dress the hair. In a shop selling cloth: * Elbiselik bir kumaş kestirmek istiyorum. 'I want to have enough material for a suit cut.' *224:4.* interval: - cleave; *268:6.* shortness: - shorten.

2 '- predict, - figure out, - know what to do or say': * Roman.ın son.u.nun nasıl biteceğ.i.ni kestiremiyorum. 'I can't figure out how the novel is going to end [lit., ** how the end of the novel is going to finish].' Onu birden karşımda görünce {ne yapacağ.ım.ı/ne söyleyeceğ.im.i} kestiremedim. 'When I suddenly came face to face with him [lit., When I suddenly saw him opposite me], I didn't know {what to do/what to say}.' Şaşkınlık içinde ne söyleyeceğini kestiremiyordu. '{Confused/lit., In confusion}, he didn't know what to say.' {Yarın/Bundan sonra} ne olacağ.ı.nı kimse tam olarak kestiremez. 'No one can predict exactly what will happen {tomorrow/after this}.' Seçim sonuçlarını kestirmek çok zor. 'It's very difficult to predict the results of the election.' *960:6.* foresight: - foreknow; *961:9.* prediction: - predict. → önceden bil- ['- know in advance'] → bil- 1, = tahmin et- 3.

3 '- have killed': kurban kestir- '- have an animal killed as a sacrifice, - let an animal be killed as a sacrifice' [A. kurban (. -) 1 'sacrifice; victim'. 2 'ram'] In Islam only the following animals are appropriate for sacrifice: koyun 'sheep'; koç 'ram'; keçi 'goat'; inek 'cow'; deve 'camel'. The meat is distributed to the poor:

Kocam bu Kurban Bayramı'nda iki tane koyun kesmek istiyordu ama ben ikincisini kestirmedim, "Bir tane yeter" dedim. 'My husband wanted to sacrifice two sheep on this Feast of the Sacrifice, but I didn't LET him sacrifice the second one. I said "One is enough".' *308:12.* killing: - kill.

keşfet- [keşfeDer] '- discover, - find' [A. keşif (keŞFi) 'discovery' + et-]: NON-verbal noun as object: Amerika'yI kim keşfetti? 'Who discovered America?' Define.nin yer.i.ni keşfetti. 'He discovered the location of the buried treasure.' Bilim adamları kanser tedavi.si.nde yeni bir yol keşfetmişler. 'Scientists have discovered a new way of treating cancer [lit., a new way in cancer treatment].' VERBAL noun as object: Altın.ın nerede saklandığ.ı.nı keşfetti. 'He discovered where the gold had been hidden.' *940:2.* discovery: - discover. → = bul- 2, icat et- ['- invent'].

keyfine git-. → git- 1b.

kıl- [ar] '- do, - perform', like et- and eyle-, forms a phrasal verb with a preceding noun. It is, however, used with a much more limited number of usually Arabic or Persian nouns. In this dictionary it occurs only with namaz, → namaz kıl-. The verb for '- do' or '- make' when it is not part of a phrasal verb is usually yap-, → yap- 2. *328:6.* action: - do; *407:4.* accomplishment: - accomplish. → = et- 1, = eyle-, = kıy- 3 [with a very limited set of nouns as subject].

{kımılda- [r]/kıpırda- [r]} '- move slightly, - budge, - stir, - twitch' [{kımıl/kıpır} perhaps onomotopoetic words indicating motion + verb-forming suf. -DA]: Kımıldama yoksa vururum! 'Don't move or I'll shoot!' Kıpırdama! * At elindeki silahı! 'Don't move! * Drop your weapon [lit., the weapon in your hand]!' Bu masa çok ağır, yer.i.nden kımıldamıyor. 'This table is very heavy. It won't budge [from its place].' Komadaki hasta.nın göz kapakları kımıldadı. 'The eyelids of the patient in a coma twitched.' Proverb: * Esmeyince kıpırdamaz. 'If there is no breeze [lit., ** As long as it doesn't blow], there is no movement [lit., it doesn't move].', i.e., There is a cause for everything. *172:5b.* motion: for sth - move. → hareket et- 1 ['- move, - stir'].

kına- [r] /DIğI için/ '- reproach, - condemn, - censure /{for/because}/': Ailenize gerekli ilgiyi göstermediğiniz için sizi şiddetle kınıyorum. 'I'm {bitterly/severely} reproaching you {because you didn't devote/for not devoting} the necessary attention to your family.' Birleşmiş Milletler, insan hakları ihlâller.i.ni {şiddetle/sert bir dille} kınadı. 'The United Nations {strongly/in strong language} condemned the violations of human rights.' *510:13.* disapproval: - censure. → ≠ öv-.

kıpırda-. → {kımılda-/kıpırda-}.

kır- [ar] 1 '- break sth' [ADJ. kırık 'broken']: Gözlüğ.üm.ü kırdım. 'I broke my glasses.' • Note the SINGULAR in the Turkish [gözlük] and the PLURAL in the English [glassES]. Gözlük.LER would indicate more than one PAIR of glasses. Çocuklar top oynarken karşıdaki ev.in camlar.ı.nı kırdılar. 'While the children were playing ball, they broke the windows of the house across the street.' Kardeşim geçen gün top oynarken düşüp {a: ayağ.ı.nı/ b: bacağ.ı.nı/c: kalça.sı.nı/d: kol.u.nu} kırdı. 'The other day, while playing soccer, my brother fell and broke {a: his foot/b: his leg/c: his hip/d: his arm}.' *801:12.* separation: - break.

* kalbini kır- '- hurt sb's feelings' [A. kalp (kalBİ) 'heart'], lit., '- break sb's heart', but this literal translation is too strong for the Turkish sense: Berna'yA öyle bağırmamalıydın, kız.IN kalb.İ.ni kırdın. 'You shouldn't have shouted AT Berna like that. You hurt the girl's feelings.' *112:19.* sadness: - aggrieve; *152:21.* resentment, anger: - offend; *393:13.* impairment: - inflict an injury. For the Turkish of the English '- break one's heart', → kalbinden yarala-, yık- 1.

rekor kır- /DA/ '- break a record /in/': Amerikalı sporcu {a:

halterde/b: jimnastikte/c: yüzmede/d: koşmada/e: uzun atlamada/f: dörtyüz metre engelli koşuda/g: yüksek atlamada} rekor kırdı. 'The American athlete broke the record {a: in weight lifting/b: in gymnastics/c: in swimming/d: in running/e: in the long jump/f: in the 400 meter hurdles/g: in the high jump}.' **Güreş millî takımımız olimpiyatlarda tüm rekorları kırarak tarih.E geçti.** 'By breaking all the records at the Olympics, our national wrestling team passed INTO history.' *249:9.* superiority: - outdo; *411:3.* victory: - triumph; *801:12.* separation: - break.

ümidini kır- '- shatter or - destroy sb's hopes': **Ümidinizi kırmak istemem ama bu iş olacak gibi değil.** 'I don't want to shatter your hopes, but I don't think this {project/matter} is going to work out [lit., but this {project/matter} isn't going to work out].' *125:11.* hopelessness: - shatter one's hopes.

2 '- hurt [not physically], - offend': **Amcam çok iyi bir insandı. Herkesle iyi geçinir, kimse.yİ kırmazdı.** 'My uncle was a very good man. He got along well with everyone; he didn't hurt anyone.' *152:21.* resentment, anger: - offend.

3 /A/ '- turn a steering wheel, rudder, sharply /to/ one side, - swerve /to/': **Önüm.e bir çocuk fırlayınca direksiyonu {sağ.A/sol.A} kırmak zorunda kaldım.** 'When a child suddenly jumped out in front of me, I had to swerve [lit., turn the steering wheel] {to the right/to the left}.' *164:3.* deviation: - deviate; *278:5.* angularity: - angle; *368:8.* avoidance: - dodge.

kırıl- [ır] [kır- + {pass./refl.} suf. -Il]: 1 /{tarafından/CA}/ '- be broken /by/': **Ev.in camlar.ı [çocuklar tarafından] kırıldı.** 'The windows of the house were broken [by the children].' *801:12.* separation: - break.

2 '- break, - get broken, - shatter' [i.]: * {a: Ayağım/b: Parmağım/c: Bacağım/d: Burnum/e: * Gözlüğüm.ün cam.ı} kırıldı. 'I've broken {a: my foot/b: my finger/c: my leg/d: my nose/e: * my glasses [lit., ** the glass of my glasses] [lit., My foot,...got broken].'

Deprem sırasında evin bütün camları kırıldı. 'During the earthquake, all the windows in [lit., of] the house shattered.' <u>Proverbs</u>: **Gönül bir sırça saraydır, kırılırsa bir daha yapılmaz.** 'The heart is a crystal palace. If it is broken, it can't be [lit., it isn't] built again.' **Tekerlek kırıldıktan sonra yol gösteren çok olur.** 'After the wheel [i.e., of the cart] has broken, there are many people who will show the way.', i.e., There are always people ready to offer advice when it's too late. *801:12.* separation: - break.

3 /DIğI için, A/ '- be hurt, offended /because, BY [sb]/': * **Bana mektup yazmadığ.ı için o.nA çok kırıldım.** 'I was very hurt that he didn't write me [letters] [lit., I was very offended BY him because he didn't write me letters].' *152:21.* resentment, anger: - offend. → = alın- 3, = darıl- 2.

kırp- [ar]. * **göz kırp-** [göz 'eye'] 1 '- blink': S: **Niçin gözünü kırpıyorsun?** 'Q: Why are you blinking?' C: * **Toz kaçtı * da, ondan.** 'A: Some dust went into my eye. * That's why.' *28:10.* defective vision: - wink; *902:7.* reaction: - pull or - draw back.

2 /A/ '- wink /AT/ sb': **Karşı masada oturan adam kız.A göz kırp.ıp duruyor.** 'The man sitting at the table across from us keeps winking AT the girl.' • Note: The structure *verb stem*.Ip dur- indicates the continuity of the action, i.e., here 'keeps'. *517:22.* signs, indicators: - signal; *562:20.* lovemaking, endearment: - flirt. For '- wink at' in the sense of '- overlook, - close one's eyes to a fault', → **göz yum-** 2.

kısa kes-. → kes- 4.

kısalt- [ır] [kısal- '- become short' + caus. suf. -t] 1 '- shorten, - make short': {**Pantolon.um.un paça.sı.nı/Saçlar.ım.ı**} biraz **kısaltır mısınız?** 'Would you please shorten {the cuffs of my trousers/my hair} a little?' In regard to hair: * {a: **Arka.DAN**/b: **Ön.DEN**/c: **Üst.TEN**/d: **Yan.DAN**} kısaltın. 'Make it short {a: IN the back/b: IN the front/c: ON top/d: ON the sides}'.

268:6. shortness: - shorten. → ≠ **uzat-** 1.

2 '- abridge, - condense, - cut down': **Yazdığın makaleyi biraz kısaltır mısın? Çok uzun olmuş.** 'Would you please cut the article you wrote down a bit? It's gotten too long.' *268:6*. shortness: - shorten.

kıskan- [ır] **1** /I/ '- be jealous /of/; - envy sb [/for/] sth he possesses' [ADJ. **kıskanç** 'jealous, envious']: **Kimse.yi kıskanmıyorum.** 'I'm not jealous of anyone.' * **Kızım çok kıskanç bir çocuk. Kardeş.i.nİ kıskanıyor.** 'My daughter is a very jealous child. She is jealous of her {brother/sister}.' **Kimse.NİN {hayat.I.nI/yaşam.I.nI/mutluluğ.U.nU} kıskanmıyorum.** 'I don't envy anyone {his life/his way of life/his happiness}.' or 'I'm not envious of anyone for his...' **Seven insan kıskanır, kimseyle paylaşmak istemez sevdiğini.** 'The person who loves is jealous. He doesn't want to share the one he loves with anyone.' **Ne güzel eviniz varmış! * Kıskan.DIM doğrusu!** 'What a lovely house you have! * I'M quite jealous!' In this example the PAST tense **kıskandım** refers to a state in effect at PRESENT, i.e., the time of speaking, so the translation is PRESENT tense. • In reference to a PRESENT condition, certain common Turkish verbs designating a state, i.e., a feeling, emotion, or sensation, often have the simple PAST tense, but the equivalent English has the simple PRESENT tense. *153:3*. jealousy: - suffer pangs of jealousy; *154:3*. envy: - envy. → = **imren-** 2, = **özen-** 2.

2 /I, DAn/ '- resent sb's showing affection to or interest in sb else': **Kızım çok kıskanç bir çocuk. * Kardeş.i.nDEN ben.İ kıskanıyor.** 'My daughter is a very jealous child. * She RESENTS {me FOR showing interest IN her {brother/sister}/θ my showing interest IN her brother}.' *153:3*. jealousy: - suffer pangs of jealousy.

3 /I/ * '- be jealously protective of sb, - guard a woman zealously against any sign of disrespect, especially against the attentions of another male, - love jealously': **Nişanlı.sı.nI deliler gibi kıskanıyor.** 'He is madly protective of his fiancée [lit., ** He is jealously protective of his fiancée like mad people].' **Bu adam ben.i herkes.TEN kıskanıyor ve hiç kimseyle arkadaşlık etmem.e fırsat vermiyor.** 'This man is jealously protective of me and doesn't give me the chance to make friends with anyone.' *153:3*. jealousy: - suffer pangs of jealousy; *1007:18a*. protection: - protect.

kıvanç duy-. → **duy-** 3.

kıy- [ar] **1** '- cut up fine, - chop up fine, - mince, - grind [up]': **Önce soğanları ince ince kıyın, daha sonra yağda hafifçe kızartın.** 'First chop up the onions into small pieces. Then brown them lightly in oil.' **Çiğ köfte yapmak için eti üç kez kıymak gerekir.** 'To make **çiğ köfte** ['raw meatballs'] one must grind the meat three times.' **Soğan, kırmızı lahana ve marul yapraklarını incecik kıyın.** 'Chop the onion, the red cabbage, and the lettuce leaves into very small pieces.' *792:6*. part: - separate; *801:13*. separation: - shatter. → = **doğra-**.

2 /A/ '- kill, - murder': * **canına kıy-** [P. **can** (-) 1 'soul'. 2 'life']
(1) '- kill or murder without mercy': **Ormanda kamp yapan beş kişi.NİN can.I.nA kıymışlar.** 'They mercilessly murdered five people who had been camping in the forest.' **Lütfen hakim bey affedin, can.IM.A kıymayın.** 'Please, judge, pardon me. Don't sentence ME to death.' *308:12*. killing: - kill; *395:10*. destruction: - destroy. → = **cinayet işle-** ['- commit murder, - murder'] → **işle-** 2, **öldür-** ['- kill'].
(2) '- commit suicide, - kill oneself': **Havagazını açıp can.ı.nA kıymış. * Kimse sebeb.i.ni bilmiyor.** 'He turned on the gas and committed suicide. No one knows why [lit., the reason for it].' *308:21*. killing: - commit suicide; *395:10*. destruction: - destroy. → = **kendini öldür-**, *more formal, legal:* = **intihar et-**.

3 '- perform, - carry out', with a very limited set of nouns as subject. *328:6*. action: - do; *407:4*. accomplishment: - accomplish. → = **et-**, = **eyle-**, = **kıl-** [with a limited set of nouns as subject]: **nikâh kıy-** '- perform the civil marriage ceremony, officially join in marriage, marry' [A. nikâh (. -) 'engagement, marriage']: **Nikâh memuru: Bana verilen yetkiler.E dayanarak nikâh.INIZ.ı kıyıyor ve sizleri karı koca ilân ediyorum.** 'Civil marriage official: On the basis of [lit., ** basing ON] the authority vested in me, I join YOU in marriage [lit., ** perform your marriage ceremony] and pronounce [lit., ** announce, i.e., make public] you man and wife.' **Nikâh memuru genç çiftin nikâhlar.ı.nı kıydıktan sonra, damat gelini öptü.** 'After the civil marriage official had performed the marriage ceremony, the bridegroom kissed the bride.' *563:14.* marriage: - join in marriage. → **evlendir-** ['- marry, - give sb in marriage'], **kız ver-** ['- give a girl in marriage'] → ver- 1.

4 /A/ '- bring oneself /to/ or - dare /to/ do sth that would discomfort, harm sb': **Bebek gibi uyuyordun, uyandırmay.a kıyamadım.** 'You were sleeping like a baby. I couldn't bring myself to wake you up.' **O kadar zayıf ki ona ağır iş vermey.e kıyamıyorum.** 'He is so {frail/weak} that I can't bring myself to assign him heavy work.' *98:14.* unpleasantness: - distress; *404:3.* undertaking: - undertake. → **kalkış** ['- try or - attempt /to/ do sth that is beyond one's power or outside one's authority, - dare /to/'].

kız- [ar] 1 /A/ '- get or - be angry, cross /{AT/WITH} [sb], θ [that]/' [**kızgın** 'angry']: **A: Ban.A kızmadın değil mi?** 'A: You aren't angry WITH me, are you?' **B1: * Yooo, ne münasebet?** 'B1: No, why should I be?' **B2: Yooo, niye kızayım ki!** 'B2: No, why should I get angry?' Proverb: **Adam kızmayınca belli olmaz.** 'A man cannot be known [lit., ** become clear] unless he gets angry.' *152: * 34.* anger: proverbs. NON-verbal noun as object: **Öğretmen çalışmayan öğrenciler.E çok kızdı. Hâlâ kızgın.** 'The teacher got very angry AT the students who didn't {study/work}. He is still angry.'
VERBAL noun as object: **Filiz'in buraya gelme.si.nE kızmadım.** 'I wasn't angry θ that Filiz [f.] had come here [lit., ** AT Filiz's coming here].' **Filiz'in buraya {gel-**

diğ.i.nE/geleceğ.i.nE} kızmadım. 'I wasn't angry θ that Filiz {had come/was going to come} here.' *152:17.* resentment, anger: - become angry. → = **öfkelen-**, = **sinirlen-**.

2 '[for sth being heated] - get hot': **Ütü çok kızdı; elin.E dikkat et!** 'The [clothes] iron has gotten very hot, watch θ your hand!' Proverb: **Fırın kızmayınca ekmek pişmez.** 'Bread won't bake {unless the oven is hot/as long as the oven is not hot}.' *1019:17b.* heating: - get hot. → ≠ **soğu-** 1.

kız ver-. → ver- 1.

kızar- [ır] [kız- + verb-forming suf. - Ar] 1 '- turn red, - redden, - blush': **Mete'nin bana baktığ.ı.nı farkedince kulaklarıma kadar kızardım.** 'When I noticed Mete looking at me, I blushed {all the way /right} up to my ears.' → **utan-** ['- be ashamed']. **Sonbaharda ağaçların yaprakları kızarır.** 'In fall the leaves [of the trees] turn red.' *41:5.* redness: - redden; *137:9b.* humility: gestures of.

All the following involve applying heat in cooking.
2 '- fry', i.e., - become fried: * {a: **Patatesler**/b: **Köfteler**/c: **Balıklar**/d: **Patlıcanlar**} **biraz daha kızarmak ister.** '{a: The potatoes/b: The meatballs/c: The fish/d: The eggplants} need to be fried a little more [lit., ** want a little more frying].' *11:4b.* cooking: for sth - cook.

3 '- toast', i.e., - become toast: **S: Tost hazır mı?** 'Q: Is the toast ready?' **C: Hayır. Hâlâ [tost makinasında] kızarıyor.** 'A: No, it is still toasting [in the toaster].' *11:4b.* cooking: for sth - cook.

4 '- roast', i.e., '- become roast meat': **Hindi fırında kızarıyor.** 'The turkey is roasting in the oven.' *11:4b.* cooking: for sth - cook.

kızart- [ır] [kızar- + caus. suf. -t] This verb covers several methods of cooking. 1 '- fry, sauté sth': **Yağda patates kızarttım.** 'I fried some potatoes in butter [*also* other oil or fat].' **Zeytinyağını bir tavada kızdırıp {a: etleri**/b: **mantarları**/c: **soğanları**/d: **biberleri} kızartın.** 'Heat up the olive oil in a frying pan and fry {a: the pieces of meat/b: the mushrooms/c: the onions/d: the peppers}.' *11:4a.* cooking: - cook sth. → = **kavur-**, = **sote et-**.

2 '- toast sth': **Kızarmış ekmek severseniz, kızartayım. Tost makinamız var.** 'If you like toast, I'll [lit., let me] make some. We have a toaster.' *11:4a.* cooking: - cook sth.

3 '- roast sth': **Fırında hindi kızartalım mı?** 'Shall we roast some turkey in the oven?' *11:4a.* cooking: - cook sth.

kızartıl- [ır] /tarafından/ [**kızart-** + pass. suf. -Il] This verb covers several methods of cooking. 1 '- be fried, sautéd /by/': {**Patatesler/ Köfteler/Balıklar**} **usta bir aşçı tarafından kızartıldı.** '{The potatoes/The meatballs/The fish} were fried by a skilled cook.' *11:4a.* cooking: - cook sth.

2 '- be toasted /by/': **Sadece tost makinasının maharetı değil bu. Ekmeklerin usta biri tarafından kızartıldığı belli.** 'This isn't just a matter of the excellence of the toaster. It's clear that the bread was toasted by a master.' *11:4a.* cooking: - cook sth.

3 '- be roasted /by/': **Bu lokantada kızartılan tavuklar pek lezzetli değil.** 'The chickens roasted in this restaurant aren't very tasty.' *11:4a.* cooking: - cook sth.

kızdır- [ır] [**kız-** + caus. suf. -DIr] 1 '- anger, - make angry': * **Çocuklar uslu durun, anneniz.i kızdırmayın,** * **olur mu?** '[Come on] {kids/children}, behave yourselves. Don't make your mother angry, * OK?' **Başbakan.ın dün yaptığ.ı konuşma ben.İ çok kızdırdı.** 'The speech [that] the prime minister delivered yesterday made me very angry.' **Beni çok kızdırdı.** * **Sinir.DEN el.IM ayağ.IM tutmuyordu.** 'He made me very angry. * I began to tremble [lit., ** MY hand (and) MY foot were not holding] WITH anger.' <u>Proverb</u>: **Arı kızdır.an.ı sokar.** 'A bee stings the person who angers it.', i.e., A person will lash out at his tormenter even if he himself will also suffer as a result. *152:22.* resentment,

anger: - anger; *152: * 34.* anger: proverbs → = **sinirlendir-**.

2 '- make red hot, - heat thoroughly': **Fırını iyice kızdırdıktan sonra baklava tepsisini koyarsın.** 'After heating the oven thoroughly, {place/lit., you will place} the tray of baklava in it.' **Zeytinyağını bir tavada kızdırıp ekmekleri kızartın.** 'Heat up the olive oil in a frying pan and fry the pieces of bread.' *1019:17a.* heating: - heat.

kızlığını kaybet-. → {**bekâretini/ kızlığını**} **kaybet-.** → {**kaybet- /yitir-**}.

kilitle- [r] [Gk. **kilit** 'lock, padlock' + verb-forming suf. -lA] 1 '- lock': {a: **Kapıyı/b: Dolabı/c: Çantayı/d: Bavulu**} **kilitledim.** 'I locked {a: the door/b: the drawer/c: the briefcase/d: the suitcase}.' *293:6.* closure: - close; *799:8.* joining: - hook.

2 /A/ '- lock up /IN/': **Çiftçi hayvanlar.I ahır.A kilitledi.** 'The farmer locked the animals up IN the stable.' *429:12.* confinement: - confine.

kilo al-. → **al-** 1.

kilo ver-. → **ver-** 1.

Kim bilir? → **bil-** 1.

kira ver-. → **ver-** 1.

kirala- [r] [A. **kira** (. -) '- rent' + verb-forming suf. -lA]: 1 /DAn, A/ '- rent, - lease, - hire /from, FOR/': Place as object: * **Yazlık evimizi Rıdvan beyden aylık 500 lira.yA kiraladık.** 'We rented our summer house from Rıdvan bey FOR 500 liras a month.' **Ev.in sahib.i.ni bulduk ve "Evinizi kiralamak istiyoruz" dedik.** 'We found the owner of the house and said, "We want to rent your house".' Vehicles, equipment as object: **Nere.DEN araba kiralayabilirim?** 'θ Where can I rent a car?' **Bir araba kiralayıp tüm kenti gezdik.** 'We {hired/rented} a car and toured the whole city.' *615:15.* commission: - rent. → = **tut-** 6 [a. '- hire (vehicle), - rent, - engage (vehicle, place); b. - hire, - engage (a person)'].

2 {kirala-/kiraya ver-} /A, A/ '- rent [out], - lease /to, FOR/, place or equipment: S: * Eviniz.İ kim.E kiraladınız? 'Q: Who did you rent your house [out] TO?' C: * Betül'E kiraladık. 'A: We rented it [out] to Betül [f.].' * Sezer bey yazlık evini biz.e aylık 500 lira.yA kiraladı. 'Sezer bey {rented his summer house [out] to us/rented θ us his summer house} FOR 500 liras a month.' {a: Odaları/b: Televizyonları/c: Bisikletleri/d: Fotoğraf makinelerini/e: Gelinlikleri} kiralıyor musunuz? 'Do you rent [out] {a: rooms/b: television sets/c: bicycles/d: cameras/e: wedding gowns}?' 615:16. - rent out.

kiraya ver-. → directly above.

{kirada/kirayla} otur-. → otur- 3.

kirlen- [ir] '- get or - become dirty, soiled, polluted' [kir 'dirt' + verb-forming suf. -lAn]: Saçlarım çok kirlendi. Yıkamam lâzım. 'My hair has gotten very dirty. I must wash it.' Balkon çok kirlenmiş, süpürsene. 'The balcony has gotten very dirty. Why don't you sweep it?' Denizlerimiz {gün geçtikçe} kirleniyor. 'Our oceans are getting more polluted {day by day./with every passing day./lit., as the days pass.}' 80:15b. uncleanness: - get dirty. → = pislen-.

kirlet- [ir] '- get or - make sth dirty, - soil, - pollute' [kir 'dirt' + verb-forming suffix -lA = kirle-, archaic, + caus. suf. -t]: Ortalığı kirletmeyin, akşam.A misafir gelecek. 'Don't get the place [lit., the area round about] dirty. Guests are coming this evening.' Çevreyi kirletmeyiniz. 'Keep the area clean [lit., Don't dirty the area round about].' 352:7. publication: poster: * specific signs. Fabrikaların atıkları çevreyi kirletiyor. 'The waste from the factories is polluting the environment.' Üst.ün.ü baş.ı.nı kirletme diye sana kaç defa söyledim. 'How many times have I told you not to [lit., told you SAYING don't] {get yourself dirty!/soil your clothes!}' [üst baş 'clothes, what one has on'] 80:15a. uncleanness: - dirty. → = pislet-, ≠ temizle-.

klonla-. → kopyala- 2.

kok- [ar] 1 /θ/ '- smell /OF/ sth, - have a smell, - give off a smell': {Bu çiçek/Bu parfüm} ne güzel kokuyor! 'How nice {this flower/this perfume} smells!' Bu {sabun/çarşaf} * mis gibi kokuyor! 'This {soap/sheet} * smells very clean and fresh!' Ayfer'lere gittiğ.im.de yemek yiyorlardı. * Ev.in iç.i balık kokuyordu. 'When I went to Ayfer's house, they were eating. * The house [lit., ** the inside of the house] smelled OF fish [lit., ** smelled θ fish].' 69:6. odor: - have an odor.

2 '- smell [bad], - stink': Bu {a: et/b: süt/c: yemek/d: yumurta} kokmuş, * yenmez. 'This {a: meat/b: milk/c: food/d: egg} smells [bad]. It can't be eaten.' Bu tuvalet pis kokuyor. 'This {restroom/toilet} stinks [lit., smells bad].' Proverb: Balık baş.tan kokar. 'Fish begins to stink from the head [lit., ** stinks from the head].', i.e., Corruption starts at the top. 71:4. stench: - stink; 393:48. impairment: ADV. out of the frying pan into the fire. → bayatla- ['- spoil, - go bad, - go stale'], bozul- ['- spoil (subj.: food)'], dayan- 4 ['- keep, - stay edible (subj.: food)'].

kokla- [r] '- smell sth, - take in the smell of sth' [kok- + verb-forming suf. -lA; koku 'smell, odor']: Bahçedeki gülleri kokladım. 'I smelled the roses in the garden.' Bu parfümleri satın almadan önce teker teker kokladım. 'Before purchasing these perfumes, I smelled them one by one.' 69:8. odor: - smell sth.

Kolay gelsin. → gel- 1.

kolayına gel-. → gel- 1.

kolayına git-. → git- 1b.

kolayına kaç-. → kaç- 1.

kolaylaş- [ır] '- get or - become easy, easier' [kolay 'easy' + verb-forming suf. -lAş]: Yıl son.u.na doğru {dersler} kolaylaştı. 'Toward the end of the year {the classes/the lessons} became easier.' Kocam.la iş böl.ü.mü yapınca, {ev işleri} kolaylaştı. 'When I {had worked out with my husband who was going to do what/lit., had worked out a division of labor with my husband}, the {housework/household tasks} became easier.' *1013:10.* facility: - go easily. → ≠ **zorlaş**-.

kolaylık göster-. → **göster**- 1.

komadan çık-. → **çık**- 1.

komaya gir-. → **gir**-.

komiğine git-. → **git**- 1b.

kon- [ar] /A/ '- land, - perch, - settle, - alight /{ON/UPON}/', subj.: bird, insect, helicopter, not plane: **Pencere.yE** {kuş/kelebek/uğur böceği} **kondu.** 'The {bird/butterfly/lady bug} settled ON the window.' **Helikopter dağ.ın tepe.si.nE kondu.** 'The helicopter landed ON [the] top of the mountain.' *184:43.* aviation: - land; *194:7.* descent: - get down; *194:10.* : - light upon. → ≠ **kalk**- 2, ≠ **havalan**- 2. For an airplane '- land', → **in**- 3.

kontrat yap-. → **yap**- 3.

kontrol et- [eDer] '- check, - inspect, - check on, - check to see whether sth is the case or not' [F. **kontrol** 'checking']: NON-verbal object: E-maillerimi {sık sık/hergün/iki günde bir} **kontrol ederim.** 'I check my e-mail {often [*or* frequently]/every day/once every two days}.' You have just made a purchase. You say: {Hesabı/Faturayı} **kontrol etmek istiyorum.** 'I'd like to check {the bill/the receipt}.' **Lâstikleri kontrol eder misiniz lütfen?** 'Would you please check the tires?' **Patron her gün gelip işçileri kontrol eder.** 'The boss comes and checks on his workers every day.' * **Sağı solu kontrol etti.** 'He checked right and left [lit., ** he checked the right, the left].' VERBAL object: **Çocuklar.ın uyuyup uyumadığ.ı.nı kontrol ettim.** 'I checked [to see] whether or not the children were sleeping.' **Satın almadan önce televizyon.un çalış.ıp çalışmadığ.ı.nı kontrol ettim.** 'Before buying it, I checked to see whether or not the TV set worked.' **Saat.in nasıl çalıştığ.ı.nı kontrol etti.** 'He checked to see

how the watch was working.' *937:24.* inquiry: - examine. → **gözden geçir**- ['- go /OVER/, - look /OVER/, - scrutinize, - check, - have a look /AT/, - examine, - inspect, - review'] → **geçir**- 1, **incele**- ['- examine carefully, closely, minutely, - study carefully, - inspect, - investigate, - research'], **muayene et**- ['- examine', mostly for a doctor and a patient], **tetkik et**- = **incele**-.

kontrolden geç-. → **geç**- 1.

konuş- [ur] /lA, A/ '- talk, - speak /{with/ON/THROUGH}, to/': S: **Kim.in.le konuştun?** 'Q: Who[m] did you speak with?' C: {Türkçe hoca.sı.yla [or öğretmen.i.yle]/Danışman.ı.yla} **konuştüm.** 'A: I spoke {with her Turkish teacher/with her adviser}.' **İnsanlar her yerde cep telefonlar.ı.yLA konuşuyor.** 'Everywhere people are speaking ON their cellphones.' **Başbakan Türkçe tercüman aracılığ.ı.yLA Hürriyet'e konuştu.** 'The prime minister spoke to [the newspaper] Hürriyet THROUGH [lit., ** through the medium of] a Turkish interpreter.' *524:27.* speech: - address. → = **söyle**- 3, **hitap et**- ['- address']. * **Çok konuşma.** 'Don't talk so much.' Proverbs: * **İnsanlar konuş.A konuş.A, hayvanlar koklaş.A koklaş.A [anlaşır].** 'People [come to understand one another] BY speak.ING, animals BY sniff.ING one another.' **Konuşmak okumak.TAN iyidir.** 'Talking is better THAN {reading/studying}.'

Speaking in a language: **Türkçe konuşun! İngilizce konuşmayın lütfen.** 'Speak Turkish! Please don't speak English!' S: * {Nece konuşuyorlar?/Hangi dil.de konuşuyorlar?} 'Q: {What language/In what language} are they speaking?' C: {Almanca/Fransızca/İspanyolca} **konuşuyorlar.** 'A: They're speaking {German/French/Spanish}.' * **Ne kadar güzel Türkçe konuşuyorsunuz!** 'Your Turkish is {wonderful/great}! [lit., How well you speak Turkish!]'

Speaking about sth: **konuş**- /a: I, b: hakkında, c: A dair, d: üzerine, e: konusunda/ '- speak /a, b: about, c: concerning, d: on, e: on the subject of/': **Bugünlerde herkes** {aynı şey.İ/* bunlar.I} konuşuyor. 'These days everyone is talking {about the same thing/* about these things}.' Sabaha kadar {a: lisedeki günlerimiz.İ/b: lisedeki günlerimiz hakkında/c: lisedeki günlerimiz.E dair} konuştuk. 'We spoke {a, b, c: about our {high school/lycée} days} until morning.' * Nişanlımla {a: geleceğ.İ/b: gelecek hakkında/c: gelecek üzerine/d: geleceğ.E dair} konuştuk. 'My fiancée and I spoke {a, b, c: about the future/d: concerning the future} [lit., ** with my fiancée WE spoke about...].'

Speaking about a person: {Ahmet'İ/Ahmet hakkında/Ahmet'E dair} konuştuk. 'We spoke {about Ahmet}.' *524:20.* speech: - speak. → = /DAn/ bahset-, = /DAn/ söz et-.

Speaking in particular ways: Quality and manner of speech: Lütfen yavaş yavaş konuşunuz. 'Please speak slowly.' Lütfen daha yavaş konuşur musunuz? 'Would you please speak more slowly?' * Yüksek sesle konuşmayınız. 'No loud talking! [lit., ** Don't speak loudly].' *352:7.* publication: poster: * specific signs. • When the name of the language is separated from konuş-, that name takes the accusative case: S: John Türkçe.yİ nasıl konuşuyor? 'Q: How does John speak Turkish?' C1: [Türkçeyİ] {a: Ağır/b: Akıcı/c: Aksanlı/d: Aksansız/e: Alçak sesle/f: * Bülbül gibi/g: Doğru dürüst/h: {Duraklayarak/ Duraksayarak}/i: Hızlı/j: [Çok] iyi/k: Kesik kesik/l: [Çok] kötü/m: * Mükemmel/n: Pürüzsüz/o: Şakır şakır/p: * Yavaş/q: Yavaş yavaş} konuşuyor. 'A1: He speaks [Turkish] {a: slowly/b: fluently/c: with an accent/d: without an accent/e: {softly/in a low voice}/f: * fluently [lit., like a nightingale]/g: {properly/correctly}/h: hesistatingly/i: rapidly/j: [very] well/k: {hesistatingly/in gasps}/l: [very] badly/m: * very well/n: fluently/o: fluently/p: * {slowly/softly}/q: slowly}.' C2: * {Çat pat/Yarım yama-lak/Bozuk} Türkçe konuşuyor. 'A2: He speaks {broken} Turkish.' Uçakta Bakanla uzun uzun

konuştuk. 'In the plane we spoke at great length with the Minister.' Türkçeyi o kadar kusursuz ve akıcı konuşuyordu ki birçok kişi Amerikalı olduğu.nA inanmıyordu. 'He spoke Turkish so perfectly [lit., fautlessly] and fluently that many people didn't believe θ [that] he was an American.' * Ne kadar güzel Türkçe konuşuyorsunuz! 'Your Turkish is {wonderful/great}! [lit., How well you speak Turkish!}' Olur olmaz konuşma! 'Don't just talk whenever you feel like it., Don't talk just to hear yourself talk.'

verb stem.mIş gibi konuş- '-speak as if': Hiç bir şey bilmiyor ama [sanki] konu.nun uzman.ı.ymış gibi konuşuyor. 'He doesn't know anything, but he speaks as if he were an expert ON the subject [lit., ** the subject's expert].' Türkiye'deki bütün şehirleri gezip görmüş gibi konuşuyor. 'He speaks as if he had {visited/toured} all the cities in Turkey.' *524:26.* speech: - utter in a certain way.

References to content of speech: {abuk subuk [or abuk sabuk]/saçma sapan} konuş- '-talk nonsense, hogwash' [abuk subuk 'incoherently, not making sense'; saçma sapan 'nonsensically, absurdly']: Abuk subuk konuşup can.ım.ı sıkma! 'Don't annoy me with such foolish talk [lit., ** press my soul by talking nonsense].' *524:26.* speech: - utter in a certain way; *922:6.* foolishness: - be foolish. → = şacmala-.

{açık/açıkça} konuş- '- speak frankly, openly' = {açık/açıkça} söyle-: {Açık/Açıkça} konuş-mak gerekirse 'To tell the truth, to speak openly, frankly [lit., If it is necessary to speak openly]': Açık konuşmak gerekirse, bu tarz kitaplar.A ilgim yok. 'To tell the truth I'm not much interested IN books of this kind.' *644:23.* probity: ADV. candidly. → = {Açık/Açıkça} söylemek gerekirse. → söyle- 1.

açık açık konuş- '- speak quite frankly, quite openly': Madem ki her şey.İ bugün açık açık konuşuyoruz bir de şu olaydan söz edelim. 'Since we are speaking about everything quite openly today, let's also speak about this {event/matter}.' *524:26.* speech: - utter in a certain way; *644:12.* probity: - be frank. = **açık açık söyle-.**

* **arkasından konuş-** '- speak ill of sb behind his back' [**arka** 'back'], lit., ** '- speak from one's back': **Zerrin odadan çıkar çıkmaz arka.sı.ndan konuşmaya başladılar.** 'As soon as Zerrin had left the room, they began to speak about her behind her back.' *512:11.* disparagement: - slander; *524:26.* speech: - utter in a certain way. → **çene çal** ['- chat, - gossip, - chew the fat /with/'] → **çal- 2, dedikodu yap-** ['- gossip /about/'] → **yap- 3.**

ayrıntılı [olarak] konuş- '- speak in detail': **Ayrıntılı olarak oradaki meselelerimiz.İ konuştuk.** 'We spoke in detail about our problems there.' **Bu konular.I bir hayli ayrıntılı konuştuk.** 'We spoke ABOUT these subjects in great detail.'

dobra dobra konuş- /lA/ '- speak bluntly, frankly /with/' [**dobra dobra** 'bluntly, frankly']: **Hakan hiç kimse.DEN çekinmez, herkes.E karşı dobra dobra konuşur.** 'Hakan isn't afraid OF anyone. He speaks frankly {to/with} everyone.' *524:26.* speech: - utter in a certain way; *644:12.* probity: - be frank. → = **dobra dobra söyle-.** → **söyle- 1.**

havadan sudan konuş- '- speak about this and that', various unimportant subjects at random [A. **hava** 'air', **su** 'water']: **S: Üç saat Hatice ile ne yaptınız Allahaşkına?** 'Q: What were you doing for three hours with Hatice, for goodness sake!' **C: Hiç, hava.DAN su.DAN konuştuk.** 'A: Nothing at all. We just talked ABOUT this and that.' *524:26.* speech: - utter in a certain way. = **şundan bundan konuş-.**

kop- [ar] 1 /DAn/ '- break in two, - break, - break off, - come off; - snap or - pop off' [i.] [ADJ. **kopuk** 'broken, snapped off']: **{İp/Tel} koptu.** 'The {thread/wire} has {broken/snapped off}.' **Gömleğim.in iki düğme.si kopmuş, dikmem lâzım.** 'Two buttons have

come [*or* popped] off my shirt. I must sew them [back on].' **Beyaz gömleğim.DEN iki düğme kopmuş.** 'Two buttons have popped off my white shirt.' *801:9.* separation: - come apart.

bağlar kop- /lA/ 'for relations between people - come to an end or - break off; - have a falling out /with/, - become estranged /FROM/' [**bağ** 'tie, bond']: **Akrabalarımız.la {bağlarımız/aramızdaki bağlar} koptu.** * **Yıllardır görüşmüyoruz.** 'My relatives and I have {had a falling out [*or* become estranged} [lit., ** {Our ties with/The ties between us and} our relatives have broken]. * We haven't seen each other {in/for} years.' *379:4.* dissuasion: - disincline; *456:10.* disaccord: - fall out with. → = **arası {açıl-/bozul-}** → **açıl- 9, arası düzel-** ['[for matters] - get straightened out, patched up, between people'].

* **ödü kop-** [**öd** 'gallbladder'] '- be badly frightened, - be terrified', lit., ** 'for one's gallbladder - snap': **Araba birden karşı.m.a çıkınca ödü.M koptu.** 'When the car suddenly appeared in front of me, I was terrified.' *127:10.* fear: - fear.

2 '- break out, - begin', a noisy or dangerous event: **Biraz sonra büyük bir {fırtına/savaş/kavga} koptu.** 'A little later a great {storm/battle/fight} broke out.' → = **patla- 3,** = **çık- 4.**

kıyamet kop- [A. **kıyamet** (. - .) 1 'doomsday, the end of the world when the dead will be resurrected'. 2 'tumult, uproar, disturbance'] (1) 'for doomsday - be at hand, - occur': **Yaşlı adam çok yakında kıyamet.in kopacağ.ı.nA kehanet etti.** 'The old man predicted θ that the end of the world [lit., that doomsday] would come very soon.'
(2) 'for all hell - break loose; for a great commotion - occur': **Babam ablam.ın eve gelmediğ.i.ni öğrenince kıyamet koptu.** 'When my father learned that my older sister had not come home, all hell broke loose.' *671:13.* violence: - erupt; *817:13.* beginning: - originate.

kopar- [ır] [**kop-** + caus. suf. **-Ar**] 1 /DAn/ '- pick, - pluck /{from/OFF}/':

Çiçekleri koparmayınız. 'Don't pick the flowers.' *352:7.* publication: poster: * specific signs. **Bu elmaları ağaç.TAN biz kopardık.** 'We picked these apples {OFF/from} the tree.' Proverb: **Tut.tuğ.u.nu koparır.** 'He plucks whatever he takes hold of.', i.e., He succeeds in whatever he sets out to do. *1067:19.* agriculture: - harvest.

2 /DAn/ '- tear or - rip /OUT OF/, away /from/': **Defterin.DEN iki sayfa koparıp bana verir misin?** 'Would you please tear two pages OUT OF your notebook and give them to me?' *192:10.* extraction: - extract. → **yırt-** ['- tear up, rip up; - tear or rip /{OUT OF/from}/']. **Çocuğu anne.si.nden koparma.ya hakkınız yok.** 'You have no right to tear the child away from its mother.' *801:8.* separation: - separate.

3 /DAn/ '- manage to get, usually in the face of difficulty, - finagle, - wangle, - wrangle, - get sth /{from/OUT OF}/ sb': **Haftasonu arkadaşlarımla dağa çıkmak için sonunda babam.dan izin koparabildim.** 'I was finally able to wrangle permission from my father to go mountain climbing with my friends this weekend.' *192:10.* extraction: - extract.

kopart- [ır] **1** /DAn/ Same as **kopar- 1**, but less frequent in that sense: '- pick, pluck /{from/OFF}/': **Çiçekleri kopartmayınız.** 'Don't pick the flowers.' *352:7.* publication: poster: * specific signs. **Bu elmaları ağaç.TAN biz koparttık.** 'We picked these apples {from/OFF} the tree.' *1067:19.* agriculture: - harvest.

2 /DAn/ Same as **kopar- 2**: '- tear /OUT OF/': **Defterin.DEN iki sayfa kopartıp bana verir misin?** 'Would you please tear two pages OUT OF your notebook and give them to me?' *192:10.* extraction: - extract; *801:11.* separation: - sever. → = **yırt-**.

3 /DAn/ Same as **kopar- 3**: '- manage to get, usually in the face of difficulty, - finagle, - wangle, - wrangle, - get sth /{from/OUT OF}/ sb': **Haftasonu arkadaşlarımla dağ.a çıkmak için sonunda babam.dan izin kopartabildim.** 'I was finally able to get permission from my father to go mountain climbing with my friends this weekend.' *192:10.* extraction: - extract.

4 [kopar- + caus. suf. -t] '- HAVE or - LET θ sb do' the action of **kopar- 1, 2,** and **3** above: **Elim alçıda olduğu için çiçekleri ben koparamadım. Burcu'ya koparttım.** 'Because my hand was in a cast, I couldn't pick the flowers. I had θ Burcu pick them.'

kopya çek-. → **çek- 8.**

kopya et- [eDer] /DAn, A/ [It. **kopya** 'copy'] '- copy /from, INTO/, - reproduce', cheating is not implied: **Matematik ders.i.nin notlar.ı.nı Deniz'in defter.i.nden kendi defterim.E kopya ettim.** 'I copied the math class notes from Deniz's [m., f.] notebook INTO my own [notebook].' *784:8.* copy: - copy. → = **kopya çek- 1** → **çek- 8, kopya çek- 2** ['- copy', in the sense of '- crib, - cheat'] → **çek- 8.**

kopyala- [r] **1** /DAn, A/ '- copy [documents, files, disks, drives] /from, to/, - make a copy' [It. **kopya** 'copy' + verb-forming suf. -1A]: **Bu {dökümanı/yazıyı} bilgi-sayarınıza kopyalamak için burayı tıklayınız.** 'To copy this document to your computer, click here.' **Disket kopyalamak için hangi komut kullanılır?** 'Which command is used to copy a floppy?' **Yeni bir sabit disk aldım ve eski sabit diskimdeki tüm dosyaları yeni sabit diskim.e kopyaladım.** 'I bought a new hard drive and copied all the files on my old hard drive to my new hard drive.' **İzinsiz kopyalamak kesinlikle yasaktır.** 'It is absolutely forbidden to make a copy without permission.' *784:8.* copy: - copy; *1041:18.* computer science: - computerize.

2 '- clone': **İnsan {kopyalamak/klonlamak} yaşamımızı nasıl etkileyecek?** 'How will the cloning of human beings affect our lives?' **Kim kimler.i {kopyalamak/klonlamak} istiyor?** 'Who wants to clone who[m]?' *784:8.* copy: - copy. = **klonla-.**

kopyasını çek-. → **çek- 8.**

kopyasını çıkar-. → **çıkar- 7.**

from my father to go mountain climbing with my friends this weekend.' *192:10.* extraction: - extract.

kork- [ar] /DAn, A/ '- be afraid or frightened /OF/, - fear /θ/, - be afraid /to/' [ADJ. korkak 'fearful, timid; cowardly']: İyi bir öğrenciyim ama sınav.a girdiğimde çok korkuyorum. 'I'm a good student, but I'm really afraid when I take an exam.' Kork.acak ne var * bunda? 'What is there to be afraid of [* in that]?' Merak etme, korkacak bir şey yok. 'Don't worry, there's nothing to be afraid of.' Kork.tuğ.uM baş.IM.a geldi. 'What I feared happened [to ME] [lit., ** came to MY head].' Here baş 'head' represents the whole person. Less common: Kork.tuğ.uM.A uğradım. '{What I had feared happened./I was up against what I had feared.}' The first line of the Turkish national anthem, lyrics by Mehmet Akif: Korkma, sönmez bu şafaklarda yüzen alsancak. 'Fear not, the crimson flag [i.e., the Turkish flag] waving in the morning twilight will never fade.' NON-verbal noun as object: /DAn/ '- be afraid or frightened /OF/, fear /θ/': Ben dişçi.DEN korkuyorum. {a: * Hem de çok./b: Çok korkuyorum çoook./c: Deli gibi korkuyorum!} 'I'm afraid OF the dentist. {a: * And how!/b: I'm really afraid!/c: ** I'm afraid like crazy!}' • In b: above note the lengthening for emphasis of the o in the second çok. # Ben Allah'TAN başka kimse.DEN korkmam. 'I fear θ no one BUT God.' Allah'TAN korkmuyorsan kul.DAN utan! 'If you don't fear θ God, [at least] fear θ a servant of God [i.e., any will-possessing being, mortal].' Halam {köpek.TEN/böcekler.DEN/ yüksek.TEN} çok korkardı. 'My paternal aunt was very afraid {OF dogs/OF insects/OF heights}.' Karanlık.TAN korktuğum için akşamları * sokağ.a çıkamam. 'Because I'm afraid OF the dark, I can't go out [lit., to the street] in the evening.' Sezen üzerine gelen köpek.TEN korkarak baba.sı.nın el.i.ni tuttu. 'Sezen, fearing θ the dog that was coming toward her, took her father's hand.' Öyle korkak bir adam ki, gölgesi.nDEN bile korkuyor. 'He's such a coward [lit., cowardly man] that he's even afraid OF his shadow.' Hiçbir grup.TAN çekindiğim, korktuğum yok. 'I'm not intimidated BY or afraid OF any group.' Proverbs: Cahil.DEN

kork, aslan.DAN korkma. 'Fear θ the ignorant person, don't fear θ the lion.' Ölmüş eşek kurt.TAN korkmaz. 'A donkey that has died does not fear θ the wolf.' Utan utanmaz.DAN, kork korkmaz.DAN. 'Be ashamed OF a shameless person and fear θ a fearless person.'

VERBAL noun as object: a) Fear of doing sth negative UNINTENTIONALLY, of falling into error or an unpleasant situation: /DAn/: Infinitive as object: {Hata/Yanlış} yapmak.TAN korkma! {Yoksa/Aksi taktirde} bu dili öğrenemezsin. 'Don't be afraid {OF making/to make} {mistakes}, {otherwise} you won't be able to learn this language.' Hasta olmak.TAN değil, [tedavi için] geç kalmak.TAN kork! 'Don't be afraid OF becoming ill, but rather of being late for treatment.' Yanlış anlaşılmak.TAN korkuyorum. 'I'm afraid OF being misunderstood.' Short infinitive plus personal suffix as object: * Babam.ın beni yanlış anlama.sı.nDAN korkuyorum. 'I'm afraid θ [that] my father will misunderstand me [lit., ** OF my father's understanding me incorrectly].' Ben.i babam.a şikâyet etmeniz.DEN korkuyorum. 'I'm afraid θ you're going [lit., ** OF your complaining] to complain about me to my father.' Future participle as object: Bazan yanlış bir şey yapacağım.DAN korkuyorum. 'Sometimes I'm afraid [that] {I'll do something wrong./I'm going to do something wrong.}' Yapacaklarınız.DAN korkuyorum. 'I'm afraid of what you're going to do.'

b) /A/ '- be afraid /to/ [venture to do, undertake], - be afraid or frightened /OF/ [doing]', i.e., fear of UNDERTAKING, PURPOSEFULLY doing, sth because of a possible danger: /A/ Dağ.a çıkmay.A korkuyorum. 'I'm afraid to go mountain climbing.' Annem doktora gitmey.E korkuyor. 'My mother is afraid to go to the doctor.'

diye kork- '- be afraid that, - fear that': Preceded by the future tense: Hep deprem olacak diye korkuyorum. 'I'm always afraid [that] there'll be an earthquake.'

251

Preceded by the aorist tense: {İlişkimiz.E/İşimiz.E} nazar değer diye korkuyor. 'He's afraid [that] the evil eye will affect {θ our relationship/θ our work}.' Sometimes diye comes at the end of the sentence: * Korkuyorum gelip de seni bulamam diye. 'I'm afraid I'll come and not be able to find you.' Preceded by a conditional: Deprem çok şiddetli olursa diye korkuyorum. 'I'm afraid [thinking]: What if the earthquake is very strong?'

/için/ kork- '- be afraid /for/': Böyle durumlarda ben gerçekten {buradaki insanlar/yeni doğacak bebekler.in geleceğ.i} için korkuyorum. 'Under these circumstances, I'm really afraid for {the people here/the future of babies yet to be born [lit., that will be born]}.'

Korkarım [ki]... 'I'm afraid [that]', introduces information the speaker is reluctant to convey: Korkarım siz.E yardım edemeyeceğim. 'I'm afraid [that] I won't be able to help θ you.' On the phone: S: Ayla ile konuşabilir miyim? 'Q: May I please speak with Ayla [f.]?' C: Burada * Ayla DİYE biri yok. Korkarım yanlış numara çevirdiniz. 'A: There's no one here * by that name [lit., There's no one here CALLED Ayla]. I'm afraid you've got [lit., dialed] the wrong number.' Saat 10 oldu. Korkarım gelmeyecek. 'It's ten o'clock. I'm afraid he's not going to come.' More frequently reluctance is expressed with maalesef 'unfortunately': S: Demek benimle sinemaya gitmek istemiyorsun. 'Q: So you don't want to go to the movies with me.' C: * Maalesef öyle. 'A: Unfortunately that's the way it is.' S: Bana biraz borç verebilir misin? 'Q: Could you lend me some money?' C: Maalesef hayır. 'A: Unfortunately no.' *127:10.* fear, frighteningness: - fear. → = ürk- 2; *504: * 20.* courtesy: polite expressions.

korkut- [ur] /I/ '- frighten, - scare' [kork- + caus. suf. -It]: Köpek {kardeşimi} korkuttu. 'The dog frightened {my younger brother/my younger sister}.' Deprem beni çok korkuttu, * yüreğim ağzım.A geldi. 'The earthquake really scared me. * My heart jumped [lit., came] INTO my throat.' *127:15.* fright, frightingness: - frighten.

korna çal-. → çal- 2.

kornaya bas-. → bas- 2.

koru- [r] /DAn, A karşı/ '- protect /from, against/, - defend /against/': Ailesini korumak her baba.nın görev.i.dir. 'It is the duty of every father to protect his family.' → = sakın- 3. # Ormanları koruyalım. 'Let's protect the forests.' *352:7.* publication: poster: * specific signs. Askerler vatanlarını korurlar. 'Soldiers defend their fatherland.' → savun- ['- defend']. Aşı bizi {hastalıklar.dan/hastalıklar.A karşı} korur. 'Vaccinations protect us {from diseases/against diseases}.' Allah korusun. 'May God preserve him [from misfortune].' → = Allah saklasın. → sakla- 4, Allah göstermesin. ['God forbid!', that such a thing should happen] → göster- 1. *460:8.* defense: - defend.; *504: * 20.* courtesy: polite expressions; *1007:18a.* protection: - protect; *1007:18b.*: expressions to protect against misfortune; *1011: * 22.* hindrance: * expressions to prevent unfavorable occurrences.

koş- [ar] /a: DAn, b: A, c: arkasından, d: peşinden/ 1 '- run /a: from, b: {to/AFTER}, c: after, d: after/, - pursue': Ha[y]di çocuklar, otobüs geliyor, koşun, koşun! 'Come on {children/kids}, the bus is coming. Run, run!' Hırsız.ın {arka.sı.nDAN/peş.i.nDEN} koştum ama yakalayamadım. 'I ran {after} the thief, but I couldn't catch him.' Soluk soluğa durağ.a koştum ama otobüs.E yetişemedim. 'I ran to the stop quite out of breath, but I couldn't catch θ the bus.' Çok fazla koşmak.tan yoruldum. 'I got tired from running too much.' Çocuklar koş.a koş.a geldiler. 'The children came running.' Proverbs: Bir iş.İ bitir.meden [başka] bir iş.E koşma. 'Without having finished one task, don't {pursue/run AFTER} another [task].' Ne ileri koş ne geride kal. 'Don't run ahead, but don't stay behind either.', i.e., Be moderate. *174:8.* swiftness: - speed; *401:5.* haste: - make haste.

2 '- lay down, - set, or - establish [a condition]: * **şart koş-** /için/ '- lay down, - set, or - establish a condition or prerequisite /for/, - make a stipulation that, - stipulate that, - state clearly and firmly as a requirement' [A. **şart** 'condition, stipulation']: **Bu bölüm.E kayıt olmak için her hangi bir şart koşmuyorlar.** 'They have set no prerequisites of any kind for registering IN this section [i.e., a department at a university].' **Türkçe profesörü yeni öğrenciler.in dersi almadan önce yeterlilik sınav.ı.na girme.leri.ni şart koştu.** 'The professor of Turkish stipulated that new students must take [lit., ** enter] a qualifying examination before taking the course.' **Kız tarafı düğünden önce yeni çift.in ev.i.nin döşenme.si.ni şart koştu.** 'Before the marriage the bride's family [lit., ** the girl {side/party}] stipulated that the new couple's house be furnished.' *958:4.* qualification: - make conditional.

kov- [ar] 1 /DAn/ '- throw, - chase, or - run sb /OUT OF/, - eject sb /from/': **Müdür kendisine rüşvet teklif eden adama "Defol!" dedi ve odasından kovdu.** 'The director said "Get out!" to the person who had offered him a bribe and threw him out of his room.' Proverb: **Doğru söyle.yen.i dokuz köy.DEN kovarlar.** 'He who tells the truth will be run OUT OF nine villages [lit., They will run the one who tells the truth OUT OF...].' *908:13.* ejection: - eject. → **Bas git!** ['Off with you!, Away with you!, Be off!, Beat it!, Clear out!, Go away!, Scram!'] → **bas-** 1, **Defol!** Same. → **ol-** 12.

2 '- fire, - dismiss, - get rid of': **işten kov-** '- fire, - sack, - can, - dismiss from a job', *informal*, usually implies a misdeed, inappropriate behavior, not simply a need to reduce the work force [**iş** 1 'work'. 2 'job']: **İşten** may be omitted if it can be understood from the context: **Patron çalışmadığ.ı.nı görünce {a: şoförü/b: hizmetçiyi/c: aşçıyı/ d: bahçıvanı/e: kapıcıyı/f: garsonu} * azarlayarak [işten] kovdu.** 'When the boss saw that he was not working, he fired {a: the

driver/b: {the help/the servant}/c: the cook/d: the gardener/e: {the caretaker/the doorman}/f: the waiter}, * giving him a severe dressing down.' *908:20.* <nonformal terms> - fire. → *informal:* = **işten at-** → **at-** 1, *neutral:* = **işten çıkar-** → **çıkar-** 1, *formal:* = **görevden al-** → **al-** 1, *neutral:* = **işine son ver-** → **son ver-** → **ver-** 1, ≠ {**ata-/tayin et-**}, ≠ **görevlendir-**.

kovala- [r] 1 '- chase, - try to catch or get, - pursue': **Polis hırsızı kovaladı.** 'The police chased the thief.' **Eli.nE bir sopa alıp bahçesine giren tavukları kovaladı.** 'She took a stick [IN her hand] and chased away the chickens that had entered her garden.' *382:8.* pursuit: - pursue.

2 '- follow one [upon] another in rapid succession, - succeed': {a: **Günler günler.İ/b: Aylar aylar.I/c: Yıllar yıllar.I**} **kovaladı ve sonunda mezun oldum.** '{a: Days followed days/b: Months followed months/c: Years followed years}, and finally I graduated.' **O yıl {olaylar/ felâketler/başarılar} birbiri.nİ kovaladı.** 'That year {events/ disasters/successes} followed one upon the other.' *814:2.* sequence: - succeed. → = **birbirini izle-** → **izle-** 1, = **birbirini takip et-** → **takip et-** 1.

koy- [ar] 1 /A, üzerine/ '- put, - place /{IN/ON}, {on/upon}/': **Satıcı verdiğ.im paraları saydı ve ceb.i.nE koydu.** 'The salesman counted the money I had given him and put it IN his pocket.' **Çiçekleri vazo.yA koydu.** 'He placed the flowers IN the vase.' *191:3.* insertion: - insert. → = **sok-** 1, ≠ **al-** 1, ≠ **çıkar-** 1. # **Nere.yE koydum gözlüğümü?** 'θ Where have I put my glasses?' **Masayı balkon.A koydu.** 'He placed the table ON the balcony.' **Başını yastığ.A koyar koymaz derin bir uyku.yA daldı.** '{As soon as his head hit the pillow/lit., As soon as he placed his head ON the pillow}, he dropped off INTO a deep sleep.' **Sınavdan önce öğretmen "Kitapları masa.nın {üzer.i.ne/üst.ü.ne} koyun"** **dedi.** 'Before the examination, the teacher said, "Put your books [lit., the books] {on top of} the table".'

Yemeğ.E {a: tuz/b: biber/c: sarımsak/d: soğan/e: şeker} **koymay.I unutma!** 'Don't forget to put {a: salt/b: pepper/c: garlic/d: onions/e: sugar} ON the food!' <u>Proverbs</u>: **Bükemediğin eli öp başın.A koy.** 'Kiss and then place ON your head the hand that you cannot bend back.', as in arm wrestling, i.e., Make peace with those you cannot defeat by force. **Elin ile koymadığ.ın şey.E dokunma.** 'Don't touch θ anything that you have not placed [there yourself] with your [own] hand.' → = bırak- 2, ≠ al- 1. *159:12*. location: - place. → = at- 3.

/DAn, A/ With a liquid often '- pour /from, INTO/': **Garson şarabı bardaklar.A koydu.** 'The waiter poured the wine INTO the glasses.' → = dök- 1. *176:17*. transferal, transportation: - ladle.

{ad/isim} koy- '- name' [{ad/A. isim (iSMi)} 'name']: • Note the two patterns:
a) The noun designating the object named is in the dative case, the name given is in an **Ahmet'in kitab.ı** [i.e., possessOR possessED] structure with the noun {ad/isim}, and this structure takes the accusative case: * **Yeni doğan bebeğ.E babaannesi.nin {ad.ı.nı/ism.i.ni} koydular.** 'They named the newborn baby after her grandmother on her father's side [lit., ** ON the newborn baby they placed its grandmother's name].' **Yeni doğan bebeğ.E Zeynep {ad.ı.nı/ism.i.ni} koydular.** 'They named the newborn baby 'Zeynep' [lit., ** They placed the name Zeynep on the newborn baby].'
b) In the second pattern the noun designating the object named is in an **Ahmet'in kitab.ı** [i.e., possessOR possessED] structure with the noun {ad/isim}, and this structure takes the accusative case; the name given is in the nominative case: * **Yeni doğan bebeğ.in {ad.ı.nı/ism.i.ni} Zeynep koydular.** 'They named the newborn baby "Zeynep" [lit., ** They placed the newborn baby's name "Zeynep"].' * **Kedim.in {ad.ı.nı/ism.i.ni} "Pamuk" koydum.** 'I named my cat "Cotton" [lit., ** I placed my cat's name "Cotton"].' *527:11*. nomenclature: - name. → = {ad/isim} ver- → ver- 1, = {adlandır-/isimlendir-}, = {ad/ isim} tak-

['- name, - call, - dub /θ/', usually with a negative connotation when the object is a person].

fiyat koy- /A/ '- set or - fix a price /ON/' [fiyat 'price']: **Müşteri: Televizyon tamiri için ne kadar [{ücret/para}] alıyorsunuz?** 'Customer: How much [{of a fee/money}] do you charge to repair a TV set [lit., for TV repair]?' **Tamirci: Önce bir bakmam lâzım. Sonra bir fiyat koyarız.** 'Repairman: First I have to take a look. Then we'll set a price.' **Hükümet, Tekel malları.nA yeni fiyat koydu.** 'The government has set new prices ON government monopoly products.' Today the Turkish government produces mostly only tobacco and alcoholic drinks, but since private firms may also produce them, the government in fact no longer holds a monoply, although the word **tekel** 'monoply' is still used for government products. *630:11*. price, fee: - price.

işaret koy- /A/ '- mark, - mark up, - put notations /IN/ [A. işaret (. - .) 'mark, sign']: **Kitab.ın bazı yerler.i.nE işaret koydum.** '{I marked up the book in various places./I put notations in various places in the book.}' *517:19*. signs, indications: - mark.

tarih koy-. → tarih {at-/koy-}. → at- 3.

teşhis koy- '- diagnose, - make a diagnosis, - come up with a diagnosis' [A. teşhis 'a diagnosing, diagnosis']: **Doktor hasta.nın kan.ı.nı analiz etti ve * şeker hastalığ.ı teşhis.i koydu.** 'The doctor analyzed the patient's blood and * {diagnosed [her condition as] diabetes/made a diagnosis of diabetes} [lit., ** placed a sugar disease diagnosis].' **Geçen ay özel bir hastanede çok iyi bir doktor.A muayene oldum. Bir çok film çektirdim, tahliller yaptırdım, ama sağlam bir teşhis koyamadılar.** 'Last month I was examined in a private hospital BY a very good doctor. I had many X-rays taken and tests made, but they couldn't come up with a definite diagnosis.' *341:9*. interpretation: - interpret.

yerine koy- '- put sth IN its place, away [i.e., where it belongs], - put back, - return /to/ its place, - replace' [yer 'place']: **Aldığın kitapları hemen yerine koy.** 'Put back at once the books you took.' *386:10.* store, supply: - store; *390:6.* disuse: - put away; *396:11.* restoration: - restore, - put back.

2 '- put or - place food /ON/ sb's plate, - serve [out] food /to/ sb': * **Ban.A bir dolma daha koyar mısın lütfen?** 'Would you give me another dolma [i.e., stuffed tomatoe, pepper, etc.] please? [lit., Would you serve me one more dolma, please?]' *159:12.* location: - place; *176:17.* transferal, transportation: - ladle; *478:12.* giving: - give. → = ver- 1.
3 /A, için/ '- put sth /θ [somewhere], for/, - set sth aside /for/': **Yaz tatili için {bir kenar.A/banka.yA} bir miktar para koydum.** 'I put a certain amount of money {aside/IN the bank} for summer vacation.' → **para yatır-** 1 ['- deposit money in an account'] → **yatır-** 2. *159:12.* location: - place; *386:12.* store, supply: - reserve. → = **ayır-** 2, **sakla-** 3 ['- save or - keep sth /FOR/, - set sth aside /FOR/'].

koyul- [ur] /A/ '- begin /θ/ sth, - set /ABOUT/, - set /to/, - embark /UPON/' [koy- + refl. suf. -Il, so lit., '- set oneself /to/ [a task]': **Kolları sıvayıp iş.E koyulduk.** 'We rolled up our [lit., the] sleeves and set to work.' *817:7a.* beginning: - begin sth. → = **başla-** 2.

* **yola koyul-** '- start off, - set out or - leave /ON/ a {trip/journey}, - set out /ON/ the road', person on foot or vehicle [yol 'road, way']: **Akşam yemeğini yer yemez yol.A koyulduk.** 'As soon as we had had our {dinner/supper} [lit., the evening meal], we set out [ON the road].' *188:8.* departure: - set out. → = **yola çık-** → **çık-** 2, = **hareket et-** 2, = **kalk-** 2, ≠ **var-**, ≠ **eriş-** 1.

kötüleş- [ir] '- deteriorate, - become bad, - get worse' [kötü 'bad' + verb-forming suf. -lAş]: **Hasta gece kötüleşmişti fakat sabah.A karşı iyileşti.** 'The patient had gotten worse in the evening but improved toward morning.' *393:16.* impairment: - deteriorate. → = **fenalaş-** 1, = **zayıfla-** 2, ≠

iyileş-. # **Havalar kötüleşmeye başladı.** 'The weather has begun to deteriorate.' → = **bozul-**, ≠ **açıl-** 7, ≠ **düzel-**, ≠ **iyileş-**.

kucakla- [r] '- embrace, - take in one's arms; - hug': [kucak 'embrace' + verb-forming suffix -lA]: **Beş yıldır görmediği arkadaşını görünce onu sevinçle kucakladı.** 'When he saw a friend of his that he hadn't seen for five years, he joyfully embraced him.' *562:18.* lovemaking, endearment: - embrace. → /A/ **sarıl-** 1 ['- embrace /θ/, - put or - throw one's arms /AROUND/'].

birbirlerini kucakla- '- embrace or - hug one another': **Beş yıldır görüşmeyen arkadaşlar karşılaştıklarında birbirlerini sevinçle kucakladılar.** 'When the friends who had not seen each other for 5 years met, they embraced [one another].' → = **kucaklaş-**. *562:18.* lovemaking, endearment: - embrace.

kucaklaş- [ır] '- embrace or - hug one another' [kucakla- + recip. suf. -ş]: **Bir süre bakıştıktan sonra, kucaklaştılar.** 'After looking at one another for a moment, they embraced.' *562:18.* lovemaking, endearment: - embrace. → = **birbirlerini kucakla-**, /A/ **sarıl-** 1 ['- embrace /θ/, - put or - throw one's arms /AROUND/'].

kullan- [ır] /olarak, yönde/ '- use, - make use of /AS, in a [certain] way/': S: **{Kalem.iniz.i/Bilgi-sayar.ınız.ı/Telefon.unuz.u} kullanabilir miyim?** 'Q: Could I use {your pencil/your computer/your phone}?' C: **Tabii, buy[u]run.** 'A: Of course, go right ahead.' **Bu ay çok {a: su/b: elektrik/c: kömür/d: gaz/e: benzin} kullanmışız.** 'It seems we've used a lot of {a: water/b: electricity/c: coal/d: gas/e: gasoline} this month.' **Zaman.ı iyi kullanın.** 'Make good use of {[your] time/the time}.' **Enerjinizi yapıcı yönde kullanın.** 'Use your energy creatively [lit., ** in a creative direction].' *jocular:* **Nezle ilâç kullanırsan bir haftada, kullanmazsan 7 günde geçer.** 'A cold is over [lit., ** passes] in one week if you take [lit., use] some medicine, in seven days if you don't.' **Derede yüzen odun parçalarını toplayıp yakacak OLARAK**

kullanıyorduk. 'We collected the pieces of wood floating on the stream and used them AS firewood.' Amcam evin küçük odalarından birini büro OLARAK kullanıyor. 'My [paternal] uncle uses one of the small rooms in the house AS an office.' Yangın ve deprem hal.i.nde asansörü kullanmayınız. 'In case of fire or earthquake don't use the elevator.' *352:7.* publication: poster: * specific signs; *387:10.* use: - use.

vehicle name kullan-. This structure forms various verbs indicating the driving of vehicles: araba kullan- '- drive, - use a car' [araba 'car']: S1: Nasıl bir araba kullanıyorsunuz? 'Q1: What kind of a car do you drive?' C1: * Toyota kullanıyorum. 'A1: I drive a Toyota.' The following are more common equivalent dialogues: S2: Arabanızın {markası/ modeli} nedir? lit., ** 'Q2: What is {the brand/the model} of your car?' or S3: Nasıl bir arabanız var? 'Q3: What kind of a car do you have?' C 2,3: a) Arabamın markası Toyota. 2005 model. lit., ** 'The brand of my car is Toyota, the 2005 model.' b) Benim 2005 model bir Toyota'm var. 'I have a 2005 [model] Toyota.' Benim arabam yok fakat ara sıra babamın arabasını kullanıyorum. 'I don't have a car, but {once in a while/now and then} I use my father's car.' Hızlı araba kullanmay.ı seviyorum. 'I like {to drive/driving} fast.' Şoför.ün içkili araba kullanma.sı, dört kişi.nin ölüm.ü.nE sebep oldu. 'The drunk driver [lit., The driver's drunk driving] caused θ the death of four people.' When you are in a vehicle, without using the name of that vehicle, you might say to the driver: Daha yavaş kullanabilir misiniz? 'Could you drive more slowly?' * Dikkatli kullanın. 'Drive carefully.' *888:5.* operation: - operate sth. → *vehicle name* sür-. → sür- 1.

uçak kullan- '- fly a plane' [uçak 'plane']: Uçak kullanabilir misiniz? 'Can you fly a plane?' S: Uçağı kim kullandı? 'Q: Who flew the plane?' C: {Pilot/ Kendisi} kullandı. 'A: {The pilot/He himself} flew it.' *184:37.* aviation: - pilot. → uç- ['- fly from one place to another'], uçakla git-. Same. → git- 1a.

Güle güle kullanın[ız]. 'What a nice...!, How nice!' Often used with the name of an item for use: e.g., car, TV, etc., lit., ** 'Use it with pleasure', a polite expression used to address sb who has acquired a new item for use. [gül- '- laugh' + adv.-forming suf. -[y]A = güle lit., 'laughingly']: A: Yeni bir {Araba/Televizyon} aldım. 'A: I've bought a new {car/TV}.' B: Güle güle kullanın. 'B: Use it with pleasure.' A: {Teşekkür ederim./Sağol.} 'A: {Thank you./Thanks.}' *504: * 20.* courtesy: polite expressions. For other polite expressions of similar meaning and structure, → Güle güle otur[un]. → otur-, Güle güle giy[in]. → giyin-.

oy kullan- '- vote, - exercise the vote, - cast a vote': S: Son seçimlerde oy kullandın mı? 'Q: Did you vote in the last elections?' C: {Evet, kullandım./Hayır, kullanmadım.} 'A: {Yes, I did./No, I didn't.}' *371:18.* choice: - vote. → = oy ver- ['- vote, - vote /for/, - give the vote /to/'] → ver- 1.

yerine kullan- '- substitute one thing for another, - use sth instead of or in place of sth else' [yer 'place']: Bu tarif.e göre tereyağı yer.i.ne margarin kullanabilirsiniz. 'According to this recipe, you may {substitute margarin for butter/use margarin instead of butter}.' *861:4.* substitute: - substitute.

'- use habitually', usually of certain substances: * doğum kontrol hapı kullan- '- be /on/ the pill, - use birth control pills' [doğum 'birth', hap 'pill']: Doğum kontrol hapı kullanıyorum. 'I'm on the pill.' *1011:10.* hindrance: - hinder.

* içki kullan- '- drink [lit., ** - use alcoholic beverages]' [içki 'drink']: S: İçki kullanır mısınız? 'Q: Do you drink?' C: {Evet, kullanırım./Hayır, kullanmam.} 'A: {Yes, I do [lit., ** I use]./No, I don't.}' *88:24.* intoxication: - tipple. → = iç- 1, = {alkol/içki} al- → al- 5.

256

sigara kullan- '- smoke cigarettes.' Substitute sigara for içki directly above. *89:14*. tobacco: - use tobacco. → = sigara iç- → iç- 2.

kumar oyna-. → oyna- 1.

kur yap-. → yap- 3.

<u>kur-</u> [ar] 1 /A/ '- set up, - assemble /{IN/ON}/; - establish, - found': Yeni aldığımız kitaplığ.ı ve yemek masa.sı takım.ı.nı salon.A kurduk. 'IN the guest room we set up the book case and the dining room set we had just bought.' Çadırımızı {nehir/deniz/göl} kenar.ı.nA kurduk. 'We set up our tent ON the shore of {the river/the sea/the lake}.' Türkiye Cumhuriyetini Atatürk kurdu. 'Atatürk founded the Republic of Turkey.' *159:16*. location: - establish; *200:9*. verticalness: - erect; *817:11*. beginning: - inaugurate; *891:10*. production: - establish.

aile kur- '- start a family, - set up a household': Her şey o kadar pahalı ki aile kurmak DA zor. 'Everything is so expensive, it's EVEN difficult to set up a household.' *817:11*. beginning: - inaugurate; *891:10*. production: - establish.

bağlantı kur- /lA/ '- make contact /with/, - contact /θ/, - get in touch /with/, - establish ties, connections /with/, - connect, - get through /to/' [bağlantı 'connection, tie, link']: Şu sıralar bir takım ticarî bağlantılar kurmak üzereyiz. 'At this time we are about to establish a set of commercial ties.' O şirketin müdürü.yle bağlantı kurabildiniz mi? 'Were you able to contact θ the director of that company?' On the phone: Lütfen hat.TAN ayrılmayın, bağlantı kurmay.a çalışıyorum. 'Please {don't hang up/stay on the line/hold} [lit., ** Please don't leave θ the line]. I'm trying {to connect you/to get through}.' → = bağla- 2. *223:10*. nearness: - contact; *343:8*. communication: - communicate with, - get in touch with. → = temas kur-; *347:18*. communications: - telephone.

hayal kur- /a: hakkında, b: lA ilgili, c: A dair, d: üzerine/ '- dream, - build up fanciful hopes /a: about, b:

concerning, c: {concerning/ regarding}, d: about/' [A. hayal (. -) (hayalî) 1 'imagined thing, image'. 2 'daydream']: • Note a relatively rare use of the plural here on the noun following çok: Evleneceğ.i adam hakkında çok hayal.LER kurmuştu. 'She had built up all kinds of hopes about the man [that] she was going to marry.' Gelecek ile ilgili [also {Gelecek hakkında/Gelecek üzerine/ Geleceğ.E dair}] hayal kurmak.tan ders çalışamıyor. 'He can't study because he is dreaming {about the future}.' *985:17*. imagination: - dream. → = {düş/rüya} gör- 2 → gör- 3. For '- dream' at night, → {düş/rüya} gör- 1 → gör- 3.

ilişki kur- /lA/ '- form or - establish relationships /with/' [ilişki 'connection, relationship']: Erol çok çekingen bir çocuk olduğu için insanlar.la ilişki kurmak.TA zorlanıyor. 'Because Erol is a very shy child, he has trouble θ forming relationships with people.' *774:5*. relation: - relate to; *817:11*. beginning: - inaugurate.

plân kur- '- make, - devise, - draft, - establish, or - formulate a plan': Kurduğum bütün plânlar altüst oldu. 'All the plans I made have {been upset/gone awry}.' *381:8*. plan: - plan; *964:4*. prearrangement: - prearrange. → {plânla-/tasarla-} ['- plan, - envisage'].

sofra kur- /A/ '- lay or - set a table, tray, mat, spread or like object for a meal /IN/ a place' [A. sofra 'anything for setting a meal upon: table, wooden or metal tray, mat, spread']: Anne, * sofrayı kur.ma.N.A yardım edeyim. '{Mom/Mother}, let me help you set the table [lit., ** help TO YOUR setting the table].' Sofra.yı bahçe.yE kurduk. 'We set up the table IN the garden.' Annem sofrayı kurunca yemek yemeğe başladık. 'When my mother had set the table, we began to eat.' Ayşe hanım biz.e en yeni tabak takım.ı.yla sofra kurdu. 'Ayşe hanım set the table for us with her newest dinnerware.' Ali Ağa'nın oğl.u.nun düğün.ü.nde beş bin kişilik muhteşem bir sofra kurdular. 'At the wedding feast for Ali Ağa's son, they set out a magnificent spread for 5,000 people.' *159:16.* location: - establish; *405:6.* preparation: - prepare. → ≠ **sofra kaldır-** → kaldır- 3.

temas kur- /IA/ (1) '- get in contact /with/, - contact /θ/, - establish contact /with/' [A. **temas** (. -) 'contact']: **Ekrem'in Almanya'da o l d u ğ . u . n u d u y d u m. Kendisi.yLE nasıl temas kurabilirim?** 'I've heard that Ekrem is in Germany. How can I {contact θ him/get in contact with him}?' *223:10.* nearness: - contact; *343:8.* communication: - communicate with, - get in touch with. → = **bağlantı kur-**.
(2) '- wind, - set [a watch, clock, meter, toy, or music box]': **Saatim durmuş, kurayım.** 'My watch has stopped. Let me wind it.' **Duvar saatimiz durmuş, kurmak lâzım.** 'Our wall clock has stopped. It needs to be wound [lit., ** Winding is necessary].' *787:7.* agreement: - make agree; *914:9.* rotation: - rotate.

kurban kes-. → kes- 2.

kurban kestir-. → kestir- 3.

kurs gör-. → gör- 3.

kurşun at-. → at- 6.

kurtar- [ır] /DAn/ '- rescue, - save /from/': **Babam deniz.e atladı ve su.ya düşen çocuğu kurtardı.** 'My father jumped INTO the ocean and saved the child who had fallen INTO the water.' **Polis, kadını katil.in el.i.nDEN kurtardı.** 'The police rescued the woman from the hands of the murderer.' * **Canımı zor kurtardım.** 'I was barely able to save my life [lit., ** my soul].' **A: Bizim yan komşumuz geçen hafta haps.E atılmış, çok üzüldüm.** 'A: Last week our next-door neighbor was thrown INTO prison. I'm very upset.' **B: Allah kurtarsın.** 'B: May God save him.' Proverbs: **Dilini tutan başını kurtarır.** 'He who holds his tongue will save his head.' **Elini versen kolunu kurtaramazsın.** 'If you give him a hand, he'll take an arm [lit., If you give your hand, you won't be able to save your arm].' Give him an inch, and he'll take a mile. **Gemisini kurtaran kaptan.** 'It is the captain who saves his ship.', i.e.,

A qualified person will find a way out of a difficult situation. *398:3.* rescue: - rescue.

kurtarıl- [ır] /{tarafından/CA}, DAn/ '- be rescued, saved /by, from/' [**kurtar-** + pass. suf. -Il]: **Deniz.E düşen yolcular {balıkçı- lar/dalgıçlar} tarafından kurtarıldı.** 'The passengers who had fallen INTO the ocean were saved by {the fishermen/the divers}.' **Yolcular yanan {otobüs- .ten/tren.den} kurtarıldı.** 'The passengers were rescued from the burning {bus/train}.' **Hasta hemen ameliyat.A alındı ama maalesef kurtarılamadı.** 'The patient was taken INTO surgery at once, but he couldn't be saved.' *398:3.* rescue: - rescue; *504: * 20.* courtesy: polite expressions.

kurtul- [ur] 1 /DAn/ '- be rescued, saved /from/, - escape /{θ/from}/, - manage to get away /from/, - avoid /θ/, - survive /θ/'. • This verb is not used with an agent noun preceded by {tarafından/CA}, i.e., not as in 'He was saved BY the police.' For such usage see **kurtarıl-**: **Allah [siz.DEN] razı olsun doktor bey, * saye.niz.de kızım kurtuldu.** 'May God be pleased [WITH you], doctor. * Thanks to you, my daughter has survived.' * **Kaza.da ölüm.DEN zor kurtuldular.** 'They barely escaped θ death in the accident.' * **Kaza.DAN zor kurtuldular.** 'They barely {survived/avoided} θ the accident.' **Çarpışan arabalardaki iki kişi yaralan.madan kurtuldu.** 'The two people in the cars that had collided were rescued unharmed [lit., ** without being injured].' **Yangın.DAN kurtulmak için üçüncü kat.tan yer.e atladı.** 'He jumped from the third floor to the ground [in order] to escape θ the fire.' **Alkollü sürücü kaza.DAN {şans eseri/mucize eseri} hafif yaralarla kurtuldu.** 'The drunk driver {luckily/miraculously} survived θ the accident with [only] slight wounds.' **Hırsız * polisler.in el.i.nDEN kurtuldu ve kaçtı.** 'The thief managed to escape from the clutches of the police [lit., managed to get away from the hands of the police and fled].' **Kazada uçakta bulunan 200 yolcu ve 8 mürettebat.TAN kurtulan olmadı.** 'OF the 200 passengers and 8 crew members in the plane at the [time of the] accident none survived.' Proverb: **Azmin elinden hiç bir şey kurtulmaz.** 'Nothing escapes from the hand of determination.', i.e., Determination will inevitably bring success. *369:6*. escape: - escape; *398:3*. rescue: - rescue.

2 /DAn/ '- get or - be rid /OF/ sb or sth unpleasant, - avoid, - shake /OFF/, - manage to get away /from/': **{a: Peşimdeki adam.DAN/b: Fizik ders.i.nDEN/c: Sinekler-.DEN/d: Borçlarım.DAN} kurtulmak istiyorum.** 'I want to {a: shake OFF the man who is following me/b: be rid OF physics classes/c: be rid OF flies/d: be rid OF my debts}.' * **{Ne yapayım da bu herif.TEN kurtulayım?/Ne yapsam da bu herif.TEN kurtulsam?}** 'What can I do to get rid of this fellow?' *368:6*. avoidance: - avoid; *431:8*. liberation: - free oneself from.

kuru- [r] [kuru 'dry' + θ] 1 '- dry, - get dry, - become dry': **Çamaşırlar kurudu.** 'The laundry has dried.' *1064:6b*. dryness: - dry, - become dry. → ≠ ıslan-.

2 '- dry up, - wither': **Susuz kalınca çiçekler kurudu.** 'When the flowers were left unwatered, they withered.' Proverbs: **Adam.A dayanma ölür, ağac.A dayanma kurur, duvar.A dayanma yıkılır. Hakk'A dayan!** 'Don't rely ON a person, he will die; don't lean AGAINST a tree, it will wither; don't lean AGAINST a wall, it will collapse. Rely UPON God!' **Ağaç kökünden kurur.** 'A tree dries up from its roots.', i.e., A thing can't endure if its central core is destroyed. *393:48*. impairment: ADV. out of the frying pan into the fire; *1064:6b*. dryness: - dry, - become dry.

kurul- [ur] [kur- + pass. suf. -Il] 1 /A, {tarafından/CA}/ '- be set up, assembled /{IN/ON}/ by; - be established, founded /by/': **Yeni aldığımız kitaplık ve yemek masa.sı takım.ı salon.A kuruldu.** 'The book case and the dining room set we had bought were set up IN the guest room.' **Çadırımız {nehir/deniz/göl} kenar.ı.nA kuruldu.** 'Our tent was set up ON the shore of {the river/the sea/the lake}.' **Türkiye**

Cumhuriyeti Atatürk tarafından kuruldu. 'The Republic of Turkey was founded by Atatürk.' **Geçen yıl Türkiye'de dört yeni siyasî parti kuruldu.** 'Four new political parties were established in Turkey last year.' **Üniversitelerde öğrenci dernekleri kuruldu.** 'Student associations were established in {the universities/the colleges}.' *159:16*. location: - establish; *200:9*. verticalness: - erect; *817:11*. beginning: - inaugurate; *891:10*. production: - establish.

2 '- be wound, set [a watch, clock, meter, toy, or music box]': **{Saat} kuruldu.** '{The watch/The clock/The meter} has been set.' *787:7*. agreement: - make agree; *914:9*. rotation: - rotate.

kurula- [r] /lA/ '- dry, - wipe dry /with/' [kuru 'dry' + verb-forming suf. - lA]: **Saçımı havlu ile kuruladım.** 'I dried my hair with the towel.' **Yine tabakları kurulamadan bırakmışsın.** 'It seems you've again left the dishes without drying them.' *1064:6a*. dryness: - dry, - make dry. → ≠ ıslat-.

kurulan- [ır] /{tarafından/CA}/ [kurula- + {pass./refl.} suf. -n] 1 '- be dried /by/': **Hatırlıyorum da, küçükken başkası tarafından yıkanmak ve kurulanmak pek hoşuma gitmiyordu.** 'And I remember, when I was a child I didn't much like to be bathed and dried by {anybody/somebody else [i.e., by somebody other than the person who usually performed this service].' *1064:6a*. dryness: - dry, - make dry.

2 /lA/ '- dry oneself /with/': You are in the shower and sb wants to speak to you. You say: **Tamam, hemen kurulanıp çıkıyorum!** 'All right, I'll just dry myself and be right out [lit., ** I'm just drying myself and coming out].' **Ben hamamda yıkandıktan sonra geniş bir havluyla kurulanırım ve giyinmeden önce bir süre dinlenirim.** 'After washing myself in the hamam, I dry myself with a big towel and rest [for] a while before getting dressed.' *1064:6a*. dryness: - dry, - make dry. → ıslan- ['- get wet'].

kurut- [ur] '- dry, - make sth dry' [kuru- + caus. suf. -t]: **Saçlarını kuruttun mu?** 'Have you dried your hair?' **Annem çamaşırları bahçe.yE asarak kurutur.** 'My mother dries the laundry by hanging it up IN the garden.' *1064:6a.* dryness: - dry , - make dry. → ≠ ıslat-.

kus- [ar] '- throw up': **Midem bulanıyor, kusacağım.** 'My stomach is upset. I'm going to throw up.' *908:26.* ejection: - vomit. → = **çıkar- 6** ['- vomit'], ≠ **yut-** ['- swallow (food), - take pills; - gulp down food'].

Kusura bakma. → bak- 1.

kuşkulan-. → {şüphelen-/şüphe et- /kuşkulan-}.

<u>kutla-</u> [r] [kut 'good luck, happiness' + verb-forming suf. -lA] 1 '- celebrate': NON-verbal noun as object: **{Geçen yılbaşı gece.si.ni/Ramazan Bayram- .ı.nı/Kurban Bayram.ı.nı} siz.de kutlamıştık.** 'We celebrated {last New Year's Eve/Ramadan/the Feast of the Sacrifice} at your place [lit., ** at YOU].' **Dedem geçen gün seksen beşinci yaş gün.ü.nü evinde parti ver.erek dostlar.ı.yla [birlikte] kutladı.** 'My grandfather celebrated his eighty-fifth birthday [together] with his friends the other day by giv.ing a party at his home.' VERBAL noun as object: **Ömer'in arkadaşları kafeteryada toplanarak [onun] okulu bitirme.si.ni kutladılar.** 'Ömer's friends, by meeting in {the cafeteria/the snack bar}, celebrated his graduation [lit., ** his finishing his school].' *487:2.* celebration: - celebrate.

2 /a: için, b: DIğI için, c: DAn dolayı, d: DAn ötürü/ '- congratulate sb /a: {for/ON}, b: {because/ {ON/FOR}}, c,d: {ON/FOR}/': **Ömer okul.u.nu bitirdi. Arkadaşları telefon ederek o.nU kutladılar.** 'Ömer graduated [lit., ** finished his school]. His friends called him up and congratulated him.' **S: Ömer'İ ne için kutladın[ız]?** 'Q: What did you congratulate Ömer for?' **C: Okulunu {bitir.DİĞ.İ İÇİN} kutladık.** 'A: We congratulated him {BECAUSE he had finished/ON [his] finishing} school.' **Derslerinde gösterdiğ.in başarı.DAN DOLAYI seni kutlarım.** 'I congratulate you {ON/FOR} the success you have demonstrated in your studies.' **Başbakan Türk medyasını bu girişimleri.nDEN ÖTÜRÜ kutladı.** 'The prime minister congratulated the Turkish media FOR their efforts.' **Ömer'i kutlama.nız.ın sebeb.i nedir?** 'Why are you congratulating Omer? [lit., ** What is the reason for your congratulating Omer?]' *149:2.* congratulate: - congratulate. → = **tebrik et-**.

Kutlu olsun! → ol- 11. → olsun.

kuyruğa gir-. → gir-.

kuyruğu boz-. → {sırayı/kuyruğu}. → boz- 1.

küçük aptes yap-. → yap- 3.

küçümse- [r] [küçük 'small, little' - k + verb-forming suffix -ImsA] 1 '- look down upon, - regard sb or sth as inferior, - treat with disrespect or contempt, - hold sb in contempt, - despise', *nonformal:* '- put sb down', *slang:* '- dis': **Kimse.yi küçümseme,** * **"ummadığın taş baş yarar".** 'Don't {belittle anyone/treat anyone with contempt}. "It is the unexpected stone [lit., the stone (that) you don't expect] that cuts the head".' i.e., You never know what a person treated this way may do. *157:3.* contempt: - disdain. → ≠ **önemse-**.

2 '- underrate, - underestimate, - minimize, - belittle': **{a: Tehditleri/b: Tehlikeleri/c: Zorlukları/d: Engelleri} ne küçümsemek ne de abartmak doğrudur.** 'It's not right either to minimize or to exaggerate {a: [the] threats/b: [the] dangers/c: [the] difficulties/d: [the] obstacles}.' **Ne küçümse insanlar.I. Ne de önemse gereğin.DEN çok.** 'Don't underestimate anyone, but also don't give him more importance THAN necessary.' **Hiçbir rakibi küçümseme lüksümüz yok.** 'We don't have the luxury of underestimating any competitor.' *252:9.* decrease: - minimize. → ≠ **abart-**, ≠ **büyüt- 2**, ≠ **önemse-**, ≠ /A/ {önem/ehemmiyet} ver- → ver- 1.

260

{küfret- [küfreDer]/söv- [er]} /A, DIğI
için/ '- curse /θ/, - swear /AT,
because/' [A. küfür (küFRü)
'swearing, cussing' + et-]: *
Cengiz'in ağzı çok bozuk,
{küfretmeden/sövmeden}
konuşamıyor. 'Cengiz has a very
foul mouth [lit., Cengiz's mouth is
very foul]. He can't speak without
swearing.' Cengiz borcunu
zamanında ödemediğin için
san.A küfretmiş. 'Cengiz swore
AT you because you had not paid him
what you owed him [lit., your debt] in
time.' 513:6. curse: - curse.

küs- [er] /A, DIğI için/ '- be offended or
hurt /BY/; - be mad or angry /AT,
because/, - be put out /WITH,
because/' [ADJ. küskün 'offended,
hurt; mad, put out']: Küsmeyin, bu
akşam sizinle yemeğ.E çıkmam
imkânsız, çünkü annemi ziyaret
etmem lâzım. 'Don't be offended. I
can't go out to eat with you this
evening because I have to visit my
mother.' Mezuniyet törenine
gelmediği için Hülya Nazan'A
küsmüş. 'Hülya [f.] was {put out
WITH/mad AT} Nazan [f.]
BECAUSE she had not come to the
graduation ceremony.' 152:17.
resentment, anger: - become angry;
152:21. : - offend. → = darıl- 1,
kız- ['- get or - be angry, cross /AT
[sb], θ [that]/'].

- L -

{lâf/söz} dinle-. → 1 dinle- 2.

[{lâfı/sözü}] kısa kes-. → kes- 4.

Lânet olsun! → ol- 11. → olsun.

lâstiği patla-. → patla- 1.

lâzım ol-. → ol- 12.

- M -

mahkemeye ver-. → ver- 1.

mahkûm ol-. → ol- 12.

mahzuru ol-. →
{sakıncası/mahzuru} ol-. → ol-
12.

makbuz kes-. → kes- 5.

makyaj yap-. → yap- 3.

mal ol-. → ol- 12.

mâni ol-. → ol- 12.

masraf çek-. → çek- 5.

masraf {et- [eDer]/yap- [ar]}
/{A/için}/ '- spend [money] /{ON [or
FOR]/ON [or for]}/; - pay /FOR/' [A.
masraf 'expense, outlay']: Bu yıl
kızımızı evlendirdik, çok
masraf ettik. 'This year we gave
our daughter in marriage. We spent a
lot of money.' {Yiyeceğ.E/
Yiyecek için} yıl.DA ne kadar
masraf ediyorsunuz? 'How much
do you spend θ a year {ON [or
FOR]} food?' S: Dün markette ne
kadar masraf ettin? 'Q: How
much did you spend at the
supermarket yesterday?' C: 20 lira
masraf ettim. 'A: I spent 20 liras.'
626:5. expenditure: - spend; 729:15.
finance, investment: - finance; 896:4.
liability: - incur. → = masraf çek-
['- foot the bill, pay', informal,
jocular] → çek- 5, = para {harca-
/sarf et-} ['- spend money'] →
{harca-/sarf et-} 1, = masraf gör-
['- meet expenses, - finance, - pay
for'] → gör- 4, = masraf karşıla-.
Same. → karşıla- 2, = masrafa gir-
['- spend a lot of money on sth or to
get sth done, - have a lot of expenses,
- incur great expense'], masraftan
{kaç-/kaçın-} ['- avoid /θ/
expense, - economize'] → kaç- 2.

masraf gör-. → gör- 4.

masraf karşıla-. → karşıla- 2.

masraf yap-. → masraf {et-/yap-}.

masrafa gir-. → gir-.

masraftan {kaç-/kaçın-}. → kaç- 2.

verb stem.{mAzlIktAn/mAmAz-
lIktAn/mAzdAn} gel-. → gel- 1.

meç yap-. → yap- 3.
meç yaptır-. → {meç/röfle} yaptır-.
→ yaptır- 2.

Mekânı cennet olsun. → ol- 11. →
olsun.

261

mektuplaş- [ır] /IA/ '- write letters to one another, - correspond /with/, - be in correspondence /with/ by letter' [A. mektup (. -) (mektuBu) 'letter' + recip. suf. -lAş]: Geçen yaz tanıştığ.ımız arkadaşlar.LA mektuplaşıyoruz. 'We're {corresponding/in correspondence} with the people we got acquainted with this past summer.' *343:6.* communication: - communicate, - be in touch; *553:10.* correspondence: - correspond.

meme ver-. → ver- 1.

memnun kal-. → kal- 1.

memnun ol-. → ol- 12.

merak et- [eDer] [A. merak (. -) 1 'concern, worry'. 2 'curiosity'] 1 /I/ '- worry /ABOUT/, - be concerned /ABOUT/': Merak etme, geç kalmam. 'Don't worry, I won't be late.' Merak etmeyin * her şey yolu.na girecek. 'Don't worry. * Everything will {work/turn} out all right [lit., ** will enter its road].' Babam biraz rahatsız. Merak ediyoruz. 'My father {doesn't feel well/is a bit under the weather}. We're concerned.' NON-verbal noun as object: Oğlum.U merak ediyorum. Acaba nerede şimdi? 'I'm concerned ABOUT my son. I wonder where he is now.' VERBAL noun as object: Oğlum.un eve {ne zaman/ nasıl/kiminle} döneceğ.i.ni merak ettim. 'I was concerned about {when/how/with whom} my son would return home.' Oğlum.un eve dönüp {dönmediğ.i.ni/ dönmeyeceğ.i.ni} merak ettim. 'I was concerned about whether or not my son {had returned/was going to return} home.' *126:6.* anxiety: - feel anxious. → = /DAn/ endişe et-, = /DAn/ kaygılan-.

2 /I/ '- be curious /ABOUT/': Çok merak ediyorum, * acaba Türkçe biliyor mu? 'I'm very curious -- * do you suppose he knows Turkish?' Baba.sı.nI çok merak ediyorum, acaba nasıl bir adam? 'I'm very curious ABOUT his father -- I wonder what kind of a man he is.' En çok ne.yI merak ediyorum biliyor musunuz? '[Do] You know what {I'm most curious ABOUT?/intrigues me most?}' S: Sence başka

gezergenlerde hayat var mı? 'Q: Do you think there is life on other planets?' C: * Doğrusunu istersen[iz] bu konu.yU pek de merak etmedim. 'A: To tell the truth [lit., ** If you want the truth of it], I haven't been very curious ABOUT this subject.' • Note the two patterns: Past time reference:
a) The direct question precedes the main verb: * Zafer dün akşam partiye gitti mi gitmedi mi çok merak ediyorum. 'I'm very curious as to whether or not Zafer went to the party last night [lit., ** Did Zafer go to the party last night, didn't he go I'm very curious].'
b) The direct question becomes an object with the accusative case suffix: Zafer'İN dün akşam partiye gid.İP gitmediğ.İ.nİ çok merak ediyorum. Same translation as above [lit., ** 'I'm very curious about Zafer'S having gone, not having gone to the party last night.']
• The analogous two patterns for future time:
a) The direct question precedes the main verb: Zafer bu akşam partiye gidecek mi, gitmeyecek mi çok merak ediyorum. 'I'm very curious as to whether or not Zafer will go to the party tonight [lit., ** Zafer will he go, won't he go to the party tonight I'm very curious].'
b) The direct question becomes an object with the accusative case suffix: Zafer'İN bu akşam partiye gid.İP gitmeyeceğ.İ.nİ çok merak ediyorum. Same translation as above [lit., ** 'I wonder very much about Zafer'S going to go, not going to go to the the party tonight.'] *980:3b.* curiosity: - be curious.

merhabalaş- [ır] /IA/ '- greet one another' [A. merhaba (. . -) 'hello' + recip. suf. -lAş]: Onu tanımıyorum ama her sabah merhabalaşıyoruz. 'I don't know him, but we greet each other every morning.' * {Yan [or Kapı] komşumuz/Karşı komşumuz}.LA her sabah merhabalaşıyoruz. '{My next-door neighbor and I/My neighbor across the way and I} greet each other every morning.' *585:10.* hospitality, welcome: - greet. → = selâmlaş-, ≠ vedalaş-.

mesaj bırak-. → bırak- 2.

meşgul çık-. → çık- 7.

meşgul et- [eDer] '- occupy; - disturb, - bother, - distract' [A. meşgul (. -) 'busy, occupied'], lit., ** '- make busy': Affedersiniz, siz.İ bir dakika meşgul edebilir miyim? * Aradığım adresi bulamıyorum da! 'Excuse me, could I disturb you for a moment? * It's just that I can't seem to find this address [lit., the address I'm looking for].' Bu duyuruyu size okumak istiyorum. * Siz.İ bir dakika meşgul edeceğim. 'I want to read you this announcement. * It'll take [just] a moment [of your time] [lit., ** I'm going make you busy for a moment].' Another more common way of requesting a person's time: * Bir dakikanızı alabilir miyim? 'May I take a moment of your time?'

Some common signs: İş başındaki memurları meşgul etmeyin. 'Don't disturb those who are working [lit., the employees (who are) at work].' Lütfen tuvalet.i fazla meşgul etmeyin. 'Please don't occupy the restroom too long.' A sign in a bus: Yolculuk sırasında şoförü {a: meşgul/b: rahatsız} etmeyin. 'Don't {a: {distract/disturb}/b: disturb} the driver [during the trip].' 352:7. publication: poster * specific signs; 724:10. occupation: - occupy; 984:6. distraction: - distract. → rahatsız et- ['- bother, disturb'].

meşgul ol-. → ol- 12.

methet-. → {öv-/methet-}.

meydana çık-. → {ortaya/meydana} çık-. → çık- 3.

meydana çıkar-. → {ortaya/meydana} çıkar-. → çıkar- 7.

mezun ol-. → ol- 12.

midesi bulan-. → bulan-.

midesini boz-. → boz- 1.

misafir kal-. → kal- 1.

misafirliğe git-. → git- 3.

misal al-. → {örnek/misal} al-. → al- 1.

misal ver-. → {örnek/misal} ver-. → ver- 1.

miyavla- [r] '- meow' [miyav 'meow' + verb-forming suf. -lA]: Kedi miyavlıyor, herhalde acıktı. 'The cat is meowing. It's probably hungry.' 60:2. animal sounds: - cry.

mola ver-. → ver- 3.

morali bozul-. → bozul-.

moralini boz-. → boz- 1.

muayene et- [eDer] '- examine', mostly for a doctor and a patient [A. muayene (. - . .) 'inspection, examination']: Doktor annemi iyice muayene etti. 'The doctor thoroughly examined my mother.' 27:14. vision: - scrutinize; 91:24. therapy: - treat; 937:24. inquiry: - examine. → = muayeneden geçir- → geçir- 1, = incele- ['- examine carefully, closely, minutely, in detail, - study carefully, - inspect, - investigate, - research', usually not a patient], = tetkik et-. Same., gözden geçir- ['- go /OVER/, - look /OVER/, - scrutinize, - check, - have a look /AT/, - examine, - inspect, - review'] → geçir- 1, kontrol et- ['- check, - inspect, - check on, - check to see whether sth is the case or not'].

muayene ol-. → ol- 10.1.

muayeneden geç-. → geç- 1.

muayeneden geçir-. → geçir- 1.

muhabbet et- [eDer] /lA/ '- chat, - have a [friendly] chat /with/' [A. muhabbet 1 'affection, love'. 2 'friendly conversation, chat']: Eski okul arkadaşlarımla buluşup saatlerce muhabbet ettik. '{I/We} met with some old school friends of mine, and we chatted for hours.' * Akşam biz.e gelsenize, çay içip muhabbet ederiz. 'Why don't you come on over to our house [lit., to us] this evening? We'll have [lit., drink] some tea and chat.' Arkadaşımın babasıyla muhabbet ettik. '{I/We} chatted with my friend's father.' Aile.CE sofra başında muhabbet etmey.i çok severiz. 'We just love to sit at the table AS a family and chat.' 541:10. conversation: - chat. → = sohbet et-.

mukayese et-. → {karşılaştır-/mukayese et-}.

mutluluk duy-. → duy- 3.

mutluluklar dile-. → dile- 1.

Mübarek olsun. → ol- 11. → olsun.

mümkün ol-. → ol- 12.

münakaşa et- [eDer] /a: 1A, b: hakkında, c: konusunda, d: I/ '- debate heatedly; - have an intense discussion; - argue /a: with, b: about, c: on the subject of, d: about/, - dispute', usually confrontational, in a negative sense [A. münakaşa (. - . .) 'argument, dispute']: **Baban.la münakaşa etme, ne diyorsa onu yap.** 'Don't argue with your father, just do whatever he says.' **Fabrika i ş ç i l e r i ü c r e t l e r {hakkında/konusunda/.İ} patron.la münakaşa ettiler.** 'The factory workers argued with the boss {about/on the subject of/about} wages.' *934:16.* reasoning: - argue. → = tartış- 2.

müracaat et-. → {başvur-/müracaat et-}.

müsaade al-. → al- 3.

müsaade et- [eDer] /A/ '- permit, - allow, - let /θ/ sb, - give sb permission /to/' [A. müsaade (. - . .) 'permission']: When attempting to make one's way through a crowd, as when getting off a bus, or going to the head of a line in an emergency: **Müsaade eder misiniz?** '{Excuse me./May I pass by?}' **A: Çabuk olmazsan sinema.yA geç kalacağız.** 'A: If you don't hurry, we'll be late FOR the movies.' **B: * Bir dakika müsaade et, * hemen hazırlanırım.** 'B: * Just give me a minute, I'll be ready [lit., get ready] right away.' **Sinemaya gitmek istiyorum fakat babam ban.A müsaade etmez.** 'I want to go to the movies, but my father won't let /θ/ me.' In a request **müsaade** is frequently used without **et-:** When leaving a gathering: **A: * Geç oldu. * Ban.A müsaade, gitmem lâzım. Randevum var.** 'A: * It's late. Excuse me [lit., ** to me permission], I've got to go. I have an appointment.' **B: * Müsaade sizin.** 'B: {[Please] go ahead, no

problem./You may go.} [lit., Permission is yours].'

'- permit sb to do sth, - let sb do sth': * **Ön.e geç.me.M.E müsaade eder misiniz?** 'Would you permit me to go [lit., ** permit TO MY PASSING] to the front [i.e., of a line]?' * **Babası sinema.ya git.me.Sİ.nE müsaade etmedi.** 'His father did not permit HIM to go to the movies [lit., ** permit TO HIS GOING].' *443:9.* permission: - permit. → = izin ver- → ver- 1, {izin/müsaade} al- ['- get permission /from, to/'] → al- 3, ≠ {yasakla-/yasak et-}.

- N -

nakit öde-. → öde-.

namaz kıl- [ar] '- perform the namaz' [P. **namaz** (. -) 'Islamic prayer ritual']: **İslâm'ın beş şartı; kelime-i şehadet, namaz kılmak, zekât vermek, oruç tutmak ve hacca gitmektir.** 'The five pillars [lit., (obligatory) conditions] of Islam are: the Shahadah [lit., the words of affirmation, i.e., to pronounce the words "There is no God but God and Muhammad is his Messenger"], to perform the namaz, to pay the zakat [i.e., the yearly alms tax required of Muslims, generally regarded as equal to $1/40^{th}$ of one's property], to [observe the] fast, and to make the Pilgrimage [to Mecca].' **Müslümanlar günde beş vakit namaz kılarlar: sabah, öğle, ikindi, akşam, yatsı.** 'Muslims perform the namaz [i.e., the Islamic prayer ritual] five times a day: IN the morning [actually before sunrise], AT noon [actually just after noontime], IN the late afternoon, IN the evening [just after sunset], and about two hours after sunset.' **Kurulta.yA katılan parti yöneticileri * toplu halde namaz kıldı.** 'The party administrators, who were participating IN the general meeting, performed the namaz * as a group.' *696:12.* worship: - pray; *701:14.* religious rites: - celebrate. → dua et-1 ['- pray'], ibadet et- ['- worship'], tap-. Same.

Nasıl ol-...da... → ol- 2.

nazar değ-. → 1 değ- 2.

Ne bileyim ben? → bil- 1.

{Ne olacak?/Ne olmuş?} → ol- 11. → olacak.

Ne olur ne olmaz. → ol- 11. → olur.

Ne olursa olsun. → ol- 11. → olur.

neden ol-. → {sebep/neden} ol-. → ol- 12.

nefes al-. → al- 1.

nefes çek-. → çek- 1.

nefes nefese kal-. → kal- 1.
nefes tut-. → tut- 4.

nefes ver-. → ver- 1.

nefret et- [eDer] /DAn/ '- hate /θ/, - loathe /θ/, - detest /θ/, - abhor /θ/, - feel an aversion /FOR/' [A. nefret 'disgust, loathing, aversion']: {a: Üvey annem.DEN/b: Sekreterlik iş.i.nDEN/c: Bulaşık yıkamak.TAN/d: Trenle seyahat etmek.TEN/e: Babam.ın sürekli nasihat etme.si.nDEN} nefret ediyorum. 'I hate {a: θ my stepmother/b: θ secretarial work/c: θ washing dishes/d: θ traveling by train/e: θ my father's constantly giving advice}.' 103:5. hate: - hate. → /DAn/ {iğren-/tiksin-} ['- feel disgust, horror, loathing /AT/; - be disgusted /WITH/'], ≠ bayıl- ['- be crazy /ABOUT/ sth, - like sth a great deal'], ≠ çok sev- → sev- 1 ['- love, like; - be fond of'].

Nerede kaldı. → kal- 1.

neşelen- [ir] '- get in a happy mood, - become cheerful, - cheer up' [A. neşe 'gaiety, merriment, joy' + verb-forming suf. -lAn]: Ha[y]di neşelen artık! O meseleyi ben hallederim. 'Come on, cheer up now! I'll solve that problem.' 109:20. cheerfulness: PHR. cheer up! * {Sınav.DAN/İmtihan.DAN} çıktığımda moralim çok bozuktu. Fakat soruları doğru yaptığ.ı.m.ı öğrenince neşelendim. 'When I got OUT OF the examination, I was really depressed. But when I learned that I

had done the questions correctly, I cheered up.' Ağlayan çocuk, anne.si.nin geldiğ.i.ni görünce neşelendi ve sustu. 'When he saw his mother coming, the child who had been crying cheered up and calmed down [lit., became quiet].' Partide iyi vakit geçirdik, çok neşelendik. 'We had a good time at the party. We became very cheerful.' 95:11. pleasure: - be pleased. → sevin- ['- be glad, pleased'], eğlen- 1 ['- have a good time, - enjoy oneself, - have fun'].

neşelendir- [ir] '- make sb feel happy, - put sb in good spirits, - cheer sb up, - delight' [neşelen- + caus. suf. -DIr]: Serdar'ın anlat.tığ.ı fıkralar bizi çok neşelendirdi. 'The anecdotes [that] Serdar told put us in a good mood.' Sirkteki palyaço seyircileri çok neşelendirdi. 'The clown at the circus delighted the spectators.' 109:7. cheeerfulness: - cheer.

nezle ol-. → ol- 10.2.

nikâh kıy-. → kıy- 3.

nişanlan- [ır] /lA/ '- get engaged /TO/' [P. nişan 'betrothal, engagement' + verb-forming suf. -lA = nişanla- '- betroth' + refl. suf. -n]: Sevilay ile Kerim dün gece nişanlandılar. 'Sevilay [f.] and Kerim got engaged last night.' * Sevilay dün gece Kerim İLE nişanlandı. 'Sevilay got engaged TO Kerim last night.' 436:6. promise: - be engaged.

nitelendir- [ir] /olarak/ '- characterize, - describe /AS/' [archaic nite 'how?' + verb-forming suf. -lA = nitele- '- characterize' + pass. suf. -n = nitelen- '- be characterized' + cause suf. -DIr]: Fabrika sahibi işçiler.in grev karar.ı.nı delilik OLARAK nitelendirdi. 'The owner of the factory characterized the workers' decision to strike AS madness.' 349:9. representation, description: - describe; 864:10. particularity: - characterize. → = tarif et-.

niyet et- [eDer] /A/ '- intend, - mean, - aim, - plan, or - make up one's mind /to/ do sth': Sabah erkenden yola çıkmay.a niyet ettim fakat uyanamadım. 'I intended to set out early in the morning, but I couldn't wake up.'

'- make a decision to do sth and then to state one's intention to oneself, silently or out loud, to carry out the act'. This meaning applies in reference to certain acts required by the religion of Islam for which such a statement of intention is required before the act is carried out and for that act to be valid: **Yarın oruç tutmay.a niyet ettim.** 'I stated my intention to fast tomorrow.' Just before performing a namaz, in the following case the one performed in the morning before sunrise, the believer would say: * **Niyet ettim sabah namaz.ı.nın farz.ı.nı kılmay.a.** 'I am stating my intention to perform the **fard** [i.e., the obligatory part] of the early morning prayer.' [For other namaz times, see the entry **namaz kıl-**, above.] • Note the use of the PAST tense in the Turkish and the PRESENT tense in the English. In reference to a PRESENT condition or activity, certain common Turkish verbs often have the simple PAST tense, but the equivalent English has the simple PRESENT tense. *359:7.* resolution: - resolve; *380:4.* intention: - intend to. → **karar ver-** ['- decide'] → **ver-** 1.

N'olur[sun]. → **ol-** 11. → **olur.**

{not/dipnot} düş-. → **düş-** 6.

not düzelt-. → **düzelt-** 2.

not ver-. → **ver-** 1.

numarala- [r] /I/ '- number, - assign a number /to/' [**numara** 'number' + verb-forming suf. **-lA**]: **Ödevimi bitirdikten sonra sayfaları numaraladım.** 'After finishing my homework, I numbered the pages.' *1016:16.* mathematics: - number.

- O -

okşa- [r] '- caress, - stroke, - fondle, - pat, - pet': * **Anne.si kız.ı.nın {a: yanağ.ı.nı/b: saçlar.ı.nı/c: baş.ı.nı/d: sırt.ı.nı} okşadı.** 'The mother [lit., her mother] caressed her daughter's {a: cheek/b: hair/c: head/d: back}.' **Çocuk sokaktaki {kediyi/köpeği} okşadı.** 'The child petted {the cat/the dog} [that was] in the street.' *73:8.* touch: - stroke; *1042:6.* friction: - rub. → = **sev-** 2.

oku- [r] 1 '- read', with an object present or implied: **Bu sayfa.yı {a: sesli/b: yüksek sesle/c: alçak sesle/d: * iç.İNİZ.den/e: kendi kendi.NİZ.e} okuyun, lütfen.** 'Please read this page {a: {out loud/aloud}/b: {aloud/in a loud voice}/c: {softly/in a low voice}/d: * silently [lit., ** from YOUR (pl.) inside]/e: to YOURSELF (pl.)}.' {* **İç.İM.den/Kendi kendi.M.e} okudum.** 'I read silently [lit., ** {from MY inside]./to MYself.}]' **Dün yüz sayfalık bir kitabı * baş.ı.ndan son.u.na kadar okudum.** 'Yesterday I read a hundred-page book * from start to finish [lit., ** from its start to its finish].' **Başbakan.ın Amerika'ya {a: gittiğ.i.ni/b: gideceğ.i.ni/c: gitme.si gerektiğ.i.ni} gazetede okudum.** 'I read in the paper that the prime minister {a: had gone/b: was going to go/c: had to go} to the United States.' **Başbakan.ın Amerika'ya {ne zaman/ kimlerle/niçin [or neden]} gittiğ.i.ni gazetede okudum.** 'I read in the paper {when/with whom [i.e., with which people]/why} the prime minister had gone to the United States.' * **Bu kitabı mutlaka okuyun! {a: Çok {yararlı/ faydalı}/b: Çok eğlenceli/c: Çok öğretici/d: Sürükleyici}. * El.iniz.DEN bırakamayacak-sınız.** 'Be sure to read this book! It is {a: very {useful}/b: very entertaining/c: very {educational/ instructive/informative}/d:{absorbing /fascinating/gripping/riveting/en-grossing}}. * You won't be able to put it down [lit., ** release it from your hands].' Proverbs: **Çok okuyan değil, çok gezen bilir.** 'It's not the one who reads a lot, but the one who travels widely that knows [a lot].' *570: * 19.* learning: PHR. experience is the best teacher. * **Deme kış yaz, oku yaz.** 'Regardless of whether it's winter or summer [lit., ** Don't say winter or summer], keep reading and writing [lit.,** read, write].' **Konuşmak okumak.TAN iyidir.** 'Talking is better THAN {reading/studying}.' *570:12.* learning: - study.

2 '- study [somewhere], - study a subject': **Arkadaşımın çocukları özel burs.LA {Amerika'da/yurt dış.ı.nda} okuyor.** 'My friend's children are studying {in the U.S./abroad [*or* outside the country]}

ON a private scholarship.' **Turgut iki yıl Fransızca okudu.** 'Turgut studied French for two years.' **Serpil'in İngilizcesi iyidir, çünkü * öğretim dili İngilizce olan bir okulda bütün dersleri * İngilizce okudu.** 'Serpil's English is good because she studied all her subjects in English at a school where the language of instruction was English.' *570:12.* learning: - study. → = çalış- 1, = tahsil et- [obj.: usually a speciality: economics].

3 '- attend a school, level of school': * {a: **İlkokul.U/b: Lise.yİ/c: Üniversite.yİ} Ankara'da okudum.** 'I attended {a: primary school/b: {high school/lycée}/c: {college/university}} in Ankara.' *221:8.* presence: - attend. → = /A/ **devam et- 3,** = git- **4b.**

4 '- recite', without a text, from memory: **Bu şiiri ezberlemen gerekiyordu. Ezberlediysen, lütfen oku, dinleyeyim.** 'You should have memorized this poem. If you have [memorized it], please recite it [for me] and let me hear it.' **Öğretmen bu şiiri * ezber{.E/.DEN} okumamı istedi, fakat ezberleyemedim.** 'The teacher asked me to recite this poem * {from} memory, but I wasn't able to memorize it.' **Şair en sevilen şiirlerinden birini okudu.** 'The poet recited one of his best loved poems.' **Müezzin ezan okudu, demek ki namaz vakti geldi.** 'The muezzin has recited the call to prayer. That means [that] the time for the namaz [i.e., the Islamic prayer ritual] has come.' * **Merhum.un ARKA.SI.NDAN dua okuduk.** 'We recited a prayer FOR [lit., ** from the back of] the deceased.' **Merhum için dua okuduk.** 'We recited a prayer for the deceased.' **{Yarınki sınavım için/Yarınki sınavım iyi geçsin DİYE} dua okudum.** 'I recited a prayer SO THAT my exam tomorrow would go well [lit., ** {for my exam tomorrow/SAYING let my exam tomorrow go well}].' *543:10.* public speaking: - declaim; *988:17.* memory: - memorize.

5 '- sing': **şarkı oku-** '- sing, - sing songs' [**şarkı** 'song']: **Zeki Müren çok güzel şarkı okurdu.** 'Zeki Müren sang very beautifully.' Contrast the above with the following: {**Bu şarkı.yI/Bu**

şarkılar.I} Zeki Müren çok güzel okurdu. 'Zeki Müren sang {this song/these songs} very well.' **Zeki Müren çok güzel şarkı.LAR okurdu.** 'Zeki Müren sang very beautiful songs.' *708:38.* music: - sing. → = **şarkı söyle-** → **söyle- 4.** *708:38.* music: - sing.

okut- [ur] [oku- + caus. suf. -t] **1** /A/ '- have or - let /θ/ sb read sth': **Bu kitab.I okumadım, başkası.nA okuttum.** 'I didn't read this book, I had θ sb else read it.' **Öğretmen sınıf.A ders kitabından beş sayfa okuttu.** 'The teacher had θ the class read five pages from the textbook.' **Cemile nine okuma yazma bilmediği için mektub.u.nU torun.u.nA okuttu.** 'Because Grandmother Cemile did not know how to read and write, she had her grandson read her letter.' **Ablam nişanlımdan gelen mektubu okumak isteyince okuttum.** 'When my older sister asked to read the letter that had come from my fiancée, I LET her read it.' *570:12.* learning: - study.

2 /I/ '- make it possible for sb to be educated, - have sb educated, - see to sb's education, - educate sb, - send sb to school [i.e., pay his way]': **Bütün öğrenim.im boyunca beni amcam okuttu.** 'Throughout the course of my education my uncle supported me [lit., had me educated, i.e., paid for my education].' *568:10.* teaching: - teach; *570:12.* learning: - study.

3 /A/ '- teach /to/': **Gelecek yıl üniversitede [Amerikalı öğrenciler.E] {a: Türkçe/b: Fransızca/c: matematik/d: tarih} okutacağım.** 'Next year I'm going to teach [American students] {a: Turkish/b: French/c: mathematics/d: history} at {the college/the university}.' For a verbal object as in '- teach sb {to swim/swimming}', → **öğret-.** *568:10.* teaching: - teach. → = **ders ver- 1** → ver- 1, = **eğit-** ['- educate sb /on a subject/'].

ol- [UR]. This entry consists of three sections: 1. Numbers 1-10: Ol- by meaning; 2. Number 11: Certain forms of ol- in alphabetical order;

3. Number 12: {Noun/Adjective} ol- phrases in alphabetical order.

1-10. Ol- by meaning

1 '- become, - be; - turn out, - work out', in all tenses: S: * Büyüyünce ne olacaksın Nihat? 'Q: Nihat, what do you want to be [lit., ** what will you become] when you grow up?' C: {Doktor/Mühendis/Pilot} olacağım. 'A: I'm going to be {a doctor/an engineer/a pilot}.' Fatma doktor olacaktı ama mimar oldu. 'Fatma was planning to become [lit., was going to become] a doctor, but she became an architect.' Avukat ol.MAKLA hata ettim. Keşke öğretmen olsaydım. 'I made a mistake BY becom.ING a lawyer. If only I had become a teacher!' * Arkadaşlarımız ne oldu? 'WHATEVER became OF our friends?' * Ne olacağız? 'What's going to become OF us?' * Ne yaptıysam olmadı. 'No matter what I did, it didn't work out.' Tahmin edildiği gibi olmadı. 'It didn't turn out as [was] {anticipated/foreseen}.' * Bunu yaptığım iyi oldu. 'It's a good thing that I did this [lit., ** My having done this turned out well].' A: * Geç oldu. * Ban.A müsaade, gitmem lâzım. Randevum var. 'A: * It's [{become/gotten}] late. Excuse me [lit., ** to me permission], I've got to go. I have an appointment.' B: * Müsaade sizin. 'B: {[Please] go ahead, no problem./You may go.} [lit., ** Permission is yours].' Ben tarifi aynen uyguladım ama olmadı. 'I followed the recipe {exactly/to the letter}, but it didn't turn out [right].' A sentence that frequently occurs in conversations on politics: * N'olacak [i.e., ne olacak] bu memleket.in hal.i? 'What's going to become of this country? [lit., ** What will this country's condition become?]' Proverbs: Bakarsan bağ olur, bakmazsan dağ olur. 'If you look after it, it will become a vineyard; if you don't, it will become a mountain [i.e., a barren area].' * "Ne oldum" dememeli, "Ne olacağım" demeli. 'One must not say, "This is what I have become", but rather "[Who knows] what I will become"', i.e., One must not boast about one's present state, but keep in mind future uncertainty. 760:12.

existence: - become. → = çevir- 8, = dön- 6, = kesil- 5 ['- turn into, - become,' often suddenly as a result of fear or other strong emotion].

2 '- happen, - occur, - take place, - go on', when preceded by a noun subject designating or implying an event: S: * N'oldu? [= Ne oldu?] 'Q: {What happened?/What's the matter?}' C1: {Kaza/Trafik kaza.sı/Yangın} oldu. 'A1: {An accident/A traffic accident/A fire} occurred.' C2: * Kaza geçirdim. 'A2: I had an accident.', i.e., car, etc. C3: * Neler oldu neler! 'A3: You can't imagine what all happened [lit., ** What things happened, what things]!' C4: Hiç bir şey olmadı. 'A4: Nothing [at all] happened.' → = geç- 3. * N'oluyor [= Ne oluyor] burada? 'What's {happening/going on} here?' Hiç kimse ne.LER olduğunu anlayamıyordu. 'No one could understand what [lit., ** what things] was going on.' * Öğretmen bir şeyler.in olduğ.u.nu hissediyordu. 'The teacher sensed that something [lit., ** some thingS] was {going on/up}.' * Sonunda beklenen oldu. 'What was {anticipated/expected} finally happened.' S: Nasıl oldu? 'Q: How did it happen?' C: Nasıl oldu bilmiyorum. 'A: I don't know how it happened.' Dün olanlar için özür dilerim. 'I apologize for the things that happened yesterday.' Bir daha olmayacak. 'It won't happen again.' S: Ne olacak şimdi? 'Q: What's going to happen now?' C: {* Ne bileyim ben? [or Bilmem ki]./Allah bilir.} 'A: {How should I know?/[Only] God knows.}' {İlginç/İnanılmaz} şeyler oluyor. '{Interesting/Unbelievable} things are happening.' S: {a: Hangi yıl.da [or * Kaç yıl.ı.nda]/b: Hangi ayda/c: Ay.ın kaç.ın.da/d: Hangi {gün/günde}/e: Hangi tarihte} oldu? 'Q: {a: In what [lit., which] year/b: In what month/c: On what date/d: On what day/e: On what date} did it happen?' C: {a: 1961 yıl.ı.nda/b: Mart ay.ı.nda/c: Ay.ın yirmidörd.ü.nde/d: * Pazartesi [günü]/e: 24 Mart 1961'de} oldu. 'A: It happened {a: in the year 1961/b: in the month of March/c: on the 24th of the month/d: * on Monday/e: on the 24th of March 1961}.' Yarın ne olacağ.ı.nı kimse bugün.DEN kestiremez.

'No one can predict θ today what will happen tomorrow.' **Keşke olmasaydı.** '{If only it hadn't happened!/I wish it hadn't happened!}' *113: * 14.* regret: PHR. if only. **Aman, o.nA bir şey olmasın!** 'Oh dear, don't let anything happen to him!' **Kimse.yE bir şey olmadı.** 'Nothing happened to anybody.' **Deprem olunca halk sokaklar.A döküldü.** 'When the earthquake occurred, the people poured out INTO the streets.' Proverb: **Kul.un dediğ.i olmaz, Allah'ın dediğ.i olur.** 'What God's humble servant [i.e., any mortal] says does not happen, what God says, does.'

hiçbir şey olmamış gibi 'as if nothing had happened': **Hiçbir şey olmamış gibi davranamayız.** 'We can't go on [lit., behave] as if nothing had happened.' **Sanki hiç bir şey olmamış gibi yan.ım.a gelip konuşmaya başladı.** 'She came up to me [lit., ** up to my side] and began to speak as if nothing had happened.'

*** Nasıl ol-...da...?** '{How is it that...?/informal: How come...?}': **Nasıl oluyor da...?: Daha geçen sene Türkçe öğrenmeye başlayan Oliver nasıl oluyor da bu kadar güzel Türkçe konuşabiliyor, * hayret doğrusu!** 'How is it that Oliver, who began to study Turkish only last year, can speak such good Turkish? * It's really surprising!' **Nasıl oldu da...?** '{How come...?/How did it happen that...?}': **Nasıl oldu da böyle oldu?** 'How come things turned out {this way/like this}?' **Nasıl oldu da daha önce sizinle tanışmadık?** '{How come/How did it happen} [that] we didn't get acquainted earlier?' **Nasıl oldu da bu noktaya geldik?** 'How come we've {reached θ/gotten to} this point?', i.e., this difficult situation, impasse. *887:8.* attribution: ADV. why?; *950:19.* theory, supposition: CONJ. supposing.

830:5. event: - occur. → = **başından geç-** ['- happen to, - experience, - go through', usually sth interesting, good, exciting, or unusual rather than unfortunate, thus in contrast to **başına gel-**] → geç- 1, = **başına gel-** ['- happen /to/, - befall', usually

a misfortune or something strange]. → gel- 1.

3 '- be, - exist'. *760:8.* existence: - exist. Turkish equivalents of '- be' occur in two main types of sentences: **a)** In sentences such as **Ahmet hasta[dır].** 'Ahmet is ill', where **Ahmet**, the subject, is followed by **hasta** 'ill', the predicate, that is, the part of the sentence that describes the subject. We use the letter 'A' to symbolize the subject, **Ahmet**, and the letter 'B' to symbolize the predicate, **hasta** 'ill', and refer to such sentences as 'A is B'-type sentences, sometimes referred to as equational sentences. In them the predicate is followed by some form of **ol-**.

• In this entry we treat **ol-** as a cover term for all forms expressing '- be, - exist', that is, for θ, i.e., for no verb, in the witnessed present tense [as in the sentence above], for **i-** in the witnessed past tense, i.e., **hastaydı** [less common: **hasta idi**], in the inferential present and past tenses, i.e., **hastaymış** [less common: **hasta imiş**], and in the conditional, i.e., **hastaysa** [less common: **hasta ise**]. **Ol-** itself is used in other cases [for example, in the future tense: **hasta olacak**], etc. The form of **ol-** is then followed by the personal suffixes.

The unstressed emphatic suffix **-DIr**, shown following **hasta** in the first sentence above, is found in writing and in formal speech in the witnessed present tense, third person singular and plural of '- be' sentences. In such sentences it is not common in ordinary speech and is encountered mostly in statements and questions involving a general truth or a definition, which is why it is in brackets. For a comprehensive discussion of the senses this suffix may convey that are not treated here, see a standard Turkish grammar such as Göksel and Kerslake [2005] or Lewis [2000].

[Witnessed tenses, such as in the first sentence above, that is, tenses not ending in **mIş**, convey a sense of certainty: they indicate that the speaker has witnessed the event or state mentioned or that it is generally accepted as fact. In contrast, inferential forms, also sometimes referred to as 'dubitative' or 'unwitnessed' and ending in **mIş**, e.g., **hasta imiş** [see the table below], convey the speaker's uncertainty or distance him from the event or state. This distance may be expressed by such English expressions as 'supposedly, they say that, it seems, I infer that', etc., or by expressions showing that the speaker is now aware of something he did not realize before or did not expect, such as 'I now realize that, It turns out that', etc.]

b) Turkish equivalents of '- be' also occur in sentences such as **Masada kitap var[dır]**. 'There {IS A book/ARE [SOME] books} on the table.', sometimes referred to as 'existential' sentences, where the existence of sth is at issue. We call such sentences 'There is'-type sentences. In them the subject, above **kitap**, is indefinite.

• Note that in the sentence above, with the singular noun, the type of item is important, not its number, and that the singular noun may be translated singular [i.e., A book] or plural [i.e., (SOME) bookS].

The subject is followed in the affirmative by the adjective **var** 'existing, existent.' In the negative, the adjective **yok** 'non-existent' replaces **var**: **Masada kitap yok[tur]**. 'There {AREN'T ANY books/ARE NO books} on the table.'

Both the adjectives **var** and **yok** are then 1. followed by a form of **ol-** [i.e., by θ, i.e., by no verb, in the witnessed present tense, by **i-** in the witnessed past tense **vardı** (less common: **var idi**), in the inferential present and past tenses, i.e., **varmış** (less common: **var imiş**), and in the conditional **varsa** (less common **var ise**)], or are
2. replaced by **ol-** in certain instances, i.e., by {**olur/olmaz**} in the aorist and by {**olacak/ olmayacak**} in the future tense.

A number or other word of quantity may precede the singular noun: **Masada** {**bir/üç/birçok**} **kitap var[dır]**. 'There {is a book/are three books/are many books} on the table.' The subject may be in the plural. In that case the plurality of the subject is

emphasized or the fact that that noun is of different types: **Masada kitaplar var[dır]**. 'There are [some] books on the table.' For other types of {**var/yok**} sentences → {**var/yok**} **ol-** → ol- 12.

The table below shows both types of '- be' sentences, i.e. **a)** and **b)**, under the main tenses, statement forms only, in both the witnessed and the inferential forms. Under 'A is B'-type sentences, each tense is shown with the third person singular subject [**Ahmet**] and, as a representative of the other persons where other personal suffixes are involved, with the first person singular subject [**ben** 'I']. For more complete paradigms, see a grammar such as Lewis 2000. Additional examples of both types of '- be' sentences follow the table.
(+) = affirmative sentence
(-) = negative sentence

TABLE OF MAIN TENSES OF TURKISH '- BE' EQUIVALENTS

PRESENT TENSE
a) 'A is B'-type sentences
Witnessed
Here **ol-** = θ, i.e., **ol-** does not appear. In the negative **değil** means 'not'.

Third person singular subject
(+) **Ahmet hasta[dır]**. 'Ahmet [is] ill.'
(-) **Ahmet hasta değil[dir]**. 'Ahmet [is] not ill.'

Of course the subject, the 'A' in a Turkish 'A is B'-type sentence, may be absent but be understood from a preceding context. It is then represented in English by a pronoun:
(+) **Hasta[dır]**. 'He [is] ill.'
(-) **Hasta değil[dir]**. 'He [is] not ill.'

First person singular subject
(+) [**Ben**] **hasta.yım**. 'I['m] ill.'
(-) [**Ben**] **hasta değil.im**. 'I['m] not ill.'

Inferential
Here **ol-** = **i-** and appears in the independent word **imiş** [i.e., **i+miş**] '{he/she/it} supposedly is' or 'they say that {he/she/it} is', etc., or in the

attached, more common form - [y]mIş:

Third person singular subject
(+) **Ahmet hasta.ymış** [less common: **hasta imiş**]. 'They say Ahmet is ill.'
(-) **Ahmet hasta değil.miş** [less common: **değil imiş**]. 'They say Ahmet isn't ill.'

First person singular subject
(+) **[Ben] hastaymış.ım** [less common: **hasta imiş.im**]. 'They say I'm ill.'
(-) **[Ben] hasta değilmiş.im** [less common: **değil imiş.im**]. 'They say I'm not ill.'

b) 'There is'-type sentences
Witnessed
Here **ol-** = θ, i.e., **ol-** does not appear. **Var** is an adjective meaning 'existent', **yok** is an adjective meaning 'non-existent':

(+) **Masada kitap var[dır]**. 'There {IS A book/ARE SOME books} on the table.'
(-) **Masada kitap yok[tur]**. 'There [ISN'T a book/AREN'T ANY books] on the table.'

[For {**var/yok**} used with the personal suffixes directly attached and with noun or pronoun subjects, e.g., **Ben** {**varım/yokum**}, → {**var/yok**} **ol-** a) → **ol-** 12 below.]

Inferential
Here **ol-** = **i-** and appears in the independent word **imiş** [i.e., **i+miş**] '{he/she/it} supposedly is' or 'they say that {he/she/it} is', etc., or in the attached, more common form - [y]mIş:

(+) **Masada kitap varmış** [less common: **var imiş**]. 'They say there {IS A book/ARE SOME books} on the table.'
(-) **Masada kitap yokmuş** [less common: **yok imiş**]. 'They say there {ISN'T A book/AREN'T ANY books} on the table.'

PAST TENSE
a) 'A is B'-type sentences
Witnessed
Here **ol-** = **i-** and appears in the independent word **idi** [i.e., **i+DI**] '{he/she/it} was' or in the attached, more common form -[y]dI.

Third person singular subject
(+) **Geçen sene Ahmet hasta.ydı**. [less common: **hasta idi**]. 'Ahmet was ill last year.'
(-) **Geçen sene Ahmet hasta değil.di** [less common: **hasta değil idi**]. 'Ahmet wasn't ill last year.'

First person singular subject
(+) **Geçen sene [ben] hasta.ydım**. [less common: **hasta idim**]}. 'I was ill last year.'
(-) **Geçen sene [ben] hasta değil.dim** [less common: **değil idi.m**]. 'I wasn't ill last year.'

Inferential
Here the verb forms are the SAME as the PRESENT tense inferential forms above. Only the context or a time expression, such as **geçen sene** below, will indicate which translation is appropriate: **Geçen sene Ahmet hastaymış** [less common: **hasta imiş**]. 'They say Ahmet was ill last year.' Etc.

b) 'There is'-type sentences
Witnessed
Here **ol-** = **i-** and appears in the independent word **idi** [i.e., **i+DI**] '{he/she/it} was' or in the attached, more common form -[y]dI.

(+) **Dün masada kitap var.dı** [less common: **var idi**]. 'There {was a book/were some books} on the table yesterday.'
(-) **Dün masada kitap yok.tu** [less common: **yok idi**]. 'There {wasn't a book/weren't any books} on the table yesterday.'

Inferential
Here the verb forms are the SAME as the PRESENT tense inferential forms above. Only the context or a time expression, such as **dün** below, will indicate which translation is appropriate: **Dün masada kitap var.mış** [less common: **var imiş**]. 'They say there {was a book/were some books} on the table yesterday.' Etc.

FUTURE TENSE
a) 'A is B'-type sentences
Witnessed
Third person singular subject
(+) **Gelecek sene Ahmet mezun olacak**. 'Ahmet is going to {graduate/be a graduate} next year.'

(-) Gelecek sene Ahmet mezun olmayacak. 'Ahmet isn't going to graduate next year.'

First person singular subject
(+) Gelecek sene [ben] mezun olacağ.ım. 'I'm going to graduate next year.'
(-) Gelecek sene [ben] mezun olmayacağ.ım. 'I'm not going to graduate next year.'

Inferential
Third person singular subject
(+) Gelecek sene Ahmet mezun olacakmış. 'They say Ahmet is going to graduate next year.'
(-) Gelecek sene Ahmet mezun olmayacakmış. 'They say Ahmet isn't going to graduate next year.'

First person singular subject
(+) Gelecek sene [ben] mezun olacakmış.ım. 'They say I'm going to graduate next year.'
(-) Gelecek sene [ben] mezun olmayacakmış.ım. 'They say I'm not going to graduate next year.'

b) 'There is'-type sentences
• Here {ol-/olma-} replace {var/yok}.
Witnessed
(+) Yarın toplantı olacak. 'There {is going to be a meeting/are going to be [some] meetings} tomorrow.'
(-) Yarın toplantı olmayacak. 'There {isn't going to be a meeting/aren't going to be [any] meetings} tomorrow.'

Inferential
(+) Yarın toplantı olacakmış. 'They say there {is going to be a meeting/are going to be [some] meetings} tomorrow.'
(-) Yarın toplantı olmayacakmış. 'They say there {isn't going to be a meeting/aren't going to be [any] meetings} tomorrow.'

• Note, however, that, as in English, the PRESENT tense forms may also be used for FUTURE TIME: Yarın toplantı var. 'There {is a meeting/are some meetings} tomorrow.'

Additional examples

a) Examples of 'A is B'-type sentences

1. Yes-no questions: S: Ahmet çalışkan mı? 'Q: Is Ahmet bey hardworking?' C1: Evet, çalışkan. 'A1: Yes, he's hardworking.' C2: Hayır, çalışkan değil. 'A2: No, he's not hardworking.'

S: Ahmet çalışkan değil mi? 'Q: Isn't Ahmet hardworking?' • Note: Do not pause between çalışkan and değil! C1: Evet, çalışkan. 'A1: Yes, he is [hardworking].' C2: Hayır, çalışkan değil. 'A2: No, he isn't [hardworking].'

S: Ahmet çalışkan, değil mi? 'Q: Ahmet is hardworking, {ISN'T he?/ISN'T that so?/right?}' • Note: Above do pause between çalışkan and değil! C1: Evet, çalışkan. 'A1: Yes, he is [hardworking].' C2: Hayır, çalışkan değil. 'A2: No, he isn't [hardworking].'

When değil mi follows a negative statement, it must be translated affirmative if the less common translation 'isn't that so?' is not used: S: Ahmet çalışkan değil, değil mi? 'Q: Ahmet ISN'T hardworking, {IS he/ISN'T that so [or right]}?' C1: * Evet, değil. 'A1: Yes, that's right[, he isn't].' C2: * Hayır, çalışkan. 'A2: No, that's not right[, he is].'

An 'or' question: Ahmet bey burada mı, değil mi? 'Is Ahmet bey here or not?' C1: Burada. 'A1: He's here.' C2: Burada değil. 'A2: He isn't here.'

Additional examples of the main patterns above: * Hiçbir şey eskisi gibi değil. 'Nothing is like it used to be.' Ne zaman döneceğim belli değil. 'It's not clear when I'll {be back./return.}' Some patterns related to activity: S: Sen bugün boş musun? 'Q: Are you {free/off} today?' C: Bugün hiç boş vaktim yok. Ama yarın boşum. 'A: I don't have any free time at all today, but I'm free tomorrow.' For a meeting or appointment: S: * Bugün {müsait misin?/uygun musun?} 'Q: Are you available today? [or: Is today good for you?, or: Does today work for you?, lit., ** Are you {convenient/suitable} today]?' C: Bugün {müsaitim/uygunum} ama yarın {işim var/ meşgulum}. 'A: {I'm available today/Today is good [*or:* OK]}, but tomorrow {I have something to do/I'm busy}.'

2. Essential question-word questions: With h-beginning question words: Hangi 'Which?': S: Hangi kitap sizin? 'Q: Which book is yours?' C: Bu kitap benim. 'A: This book is mine.'
* Hangi günler? '{What [lit., Which] days?/ON what days?}': S: Türkçe dersiniz hangi günler? 'Q: On what days is your Turkish lesson?' C: [Türkçe dersim] salı günler.i. 'A: My Turkish lesson is on Tuesdays.' → also Ne günleri? below under Ne?
Hangisi? 'Which [one] of them?': S: * Bu kitaplar{.DAN/.ın} hangi.si sizin? 'Q: Which [one] OF these books is yours?' C: {a: Bu/b: Büyüğ.ü/c: Küçüğ.ü/d: Yeşil.i} benim. 'A: {a: This one/b: The big one/c: The small one/d: The green one) is mine.'
Hangileri? 'Which [ones] [of them]?': S: Bu kitaplar{.DAN/.ın} hangi.leri sizin? 'Which OF these books are yours?' C: {a: Bunlar/b: Büyük.leri/c: Küçük.leri/d: Yeşil.leri} 'A: {a: These/b: The large ones./c: The small ones./d: The green ones.}'

With k-beginning question words: Kaç? 'How many?': S: * Saat kaç? 'Q: What time is it?' C: Saat {a: [tam] beş/b: beş.i on geçiyor/c: beş.i çeyrek geçiyor/d: beş buçuk/e: altıya yirmi var/f: altıya çeyrek var/g: yarım}. 'A: It's {a: [exactly] 5 o'clock./b: ten past five./c: a quarter past five./d: five thirty./e: twenty to six./f: a quarter to six./g: twelve thirty [at noon or at night].}' S: Saatiniz kaç? 'Q: What time do you have?' The responses may be the same as those above or less commonly as follows: C: * Saatim beş. 'A: My watch says five o'clock.' S: [Sizin] telefon numaranız {* kaç?/ne?} 'Q: What is your telephone number?' C: [Benim] telefon numaram (212) 325 68 41. 'A: My telephone number is (212) 325 68 41.'

S: * Kaç kişisiniz? 'Q: How many of you are there [in your party]? [lit., How many are you?]', at a restaurant, for example. C: [Biz] beş kişiyiz. 'A: There are {five of us./five in our party.} [lit., We are five.] S: * Kaç kardeşsiniz? 'Q: How many brothers and sisters are you in your family [lit., How many siblings are you?]' C: * Biz dört kardeşiz. {a: * İki.si erkek, iki.si kız./b: İki erkek, iki kız.} 'A: There are four of us [lit., We are four siblings]. {a: Two [of them are] boys, two [of them are] girls./b: Two boys, two girls.}

S: * Kaç yaşındasınız? 'Q: How old are you [lit., ** In how many years are you?]' S: * Yirmi bir yaşındayım. 'A: I'm 21 years old.' [lit., ** 'I'm in 21 years', but the Turkish is today generally regarded as meaning that a person is no longer IN that many years but has actually completed them].

* Kaça? 'lit., For how much [per unit]?': S1: Domates[ler] kaça? 'Q1: How much are tomatoes?' S2: Domates[ler].in kilo.su kaça? 'Q2: {How much is a kilo of tomatoes?/How much are tomatoes a kilo?}' C: [Domates(ler).in] kilo.su bir lira. 'A: [Tomatoes are] one lira a kilo.' S: Karpuz[lar].ın tane.si kaça? 'Q: How much are watermelons apiece?' C: [Karpuz[lar].ın] tane.si beş lira. 'A: [watermelons are] five liras apiece.' → Ne kadar below.

{Kaçı?/Kaç tanesi?} '{How many of them?/How many units of them?}': S: Bunlar{.ın/.DAN} kaç.ı sizin? 'Q: How many {of} these are yours?' C1: Hepsi benim. 'A1: All of them are mine.' C2: Hiç biri benim değil. 'A2: None of them are mine.' C3: Beş.i benim, altı.sı sizin. 'A3: Five [of them] are mine, six [of them] are yours.' S: * {Bugün/Yarın/Öbür gün} ay.ın kaç.ı? 'Q: What is the date {today/tomorrow/the day after tomorrow}?' C: Bugün... ay.ın beş.i. 'A: Today... is the fifth [of the month].'

Kaçıncı? '{What?/Which?}', in numerical sequence [lit., ** 'How manyeth?']: S: Bu kaçıncı ders? 'Q: {What/Which} lesson is this?' C: [Bu] yirmi beşinci ders. 'A: This is the twenty fifth lesson.' **S: Alıştırma kaçıncı sayfada?** 'Q: {What/Which} page is the exercise on?' **C: Beşinci sayfada.** 'A: On page five [lit., On the fifth page].' **S: Mehmet beyin ofisi kaçıncı katta?** 'Q: {What floor is Mehmet bey's office on?/On which floor is Mehmet bey's office?}' **C: Altıncı katta.** 'A: On the sixth floor.'

Kaçta? lit., ** 'At how many?': **Saat kaçta?** 'At what time?': **S: Toplantı saat kaçta?** 'Q: At what time is the meeting?' **C: [Toplantı] saat {a: [tam] üçte/b: * üç.ü on geçe/c: * üç.ü çeyrek geçe/d: üç buçukta/e: * dörd.e yirmi kala/f: * dörd.e çeyrek kala/g: yarımda}.** 'A: The meeting is (a: at [exactly] 3 o'clock/b: at ten past three/c: at a quarter past three/d: at half past three/e: * at twenty to four/f: at a quarter to four/g: at noon}.'
Kaçtan? 'How much per unit, i.e., apiece, per kilo?': **S: Karpuzlar kaçtan?** 'How much are melons apiece?' **C: Tanesi 3 liradan.** 'A: They are 3 liras apiece.'

Kim? 'Who?': **S: Kim o?** 'Q: Who's that?' **S: Bu [kişi] kim?** 'Q: Who is this [person]?' **C: [Bu] Ayşe'nin annesi.** 'A: [This is] Ayşe's mother.' * **S: Siz kimsiniz?** 'Q: Who are you?' **C1: Ahmet'in Türkçe hocası.yım.** 'A1: I am Ahmet's Turkish teacher.' **C2: * Ben Özgür Sezer.** 'A2: I'm Özgür Sezer.' • Note: The first person singular suffix is usually not used when a person identifies himself by name. It may, however, be used for emphasis, as in the following, where a contrast is indicated: **Ben Özgür Sezer'İM, Turhan Şimşek değilim.** 'I am Özgür Sezer, not Turhan Şimşek.'

Kimde? '{Who has?/lit., On [or With] whom?}': **S: Kitap kimde?** 'Q: Who has the book {on/with} {him/her}?' **C: Fatma'da.** 'A: {Fatma {does./has it.}/It is with Fatma.}' **S: * Sıra kimde?** 'Whose turn is it?' **C: [Sıra] bende.** 'A: It's my turn.'

Kimin? 'Whose?': **S: Bu [kitap] kimin?** 'Q: Whose [book] is this?' **C: O [kitap] benim.** 'A: That [book] is mine.' **S: Bu kim.in kitab.ı?** 'Q: Whose book is this?'

C: O benim kitabım. 'A: That is my book.'

Kimler? '{Who?/Which people?}': * **S: Kimler öğrenci.** 'Q: Which ones [i.e., which persons] are students?' **C: Şu hanımlar öğrenci.** 'A: These ladies are students.'

With n-beginning question words: **Nasıl?** 'How?': **S: Nasılsınız?** 'Q: How are you?' **C1: {a: [İyiyim.] Teşekkür ederim/b: Sağol/c: Elhamdülillah}. Siz nasılsınız?** 'A1: {a: {Fine, thank you./Good.}/b: [Fine.] Thanks/c: [Fine.] Thank God}. How are you?' In these exchanges the answer often omits iyiyim 'I'm fine.' **C2: * Hiç iyi değilim. * Dün akşamdan beri dişim ağrıyor.** 'A2: Not well at all. * {I've had a toothache/My tooth has been hurting} since last night.' **S: Hava nasıl?** 'How's the weather?' **C: {a: Çok güzel./b: Fevkalade./c: Hiç güzel değil./d: Çok kötü./e: Berbat./f: Açık./g: Bulutlu./h: Kapalı./i: [Biraz] Rutubetli./j: Nemli./k: Yağmurlu./l: Sıcak./m: Soğuk./n: Rüzgârlı./o: Güneşli./p: Serin.}** '{a: Very nice./b: Splendid./c: Not nice at all./d: Very bad./e: Terrible./f: Clear./g: Cloudy./ h: Overcast./i, j: [A little] Humid./k: Rainy./l: Hot./m: Cold./n: Windy./o: Sunny./p: Cool.}' **S: * Kahveniz nasıl olsun?** 'Q: * How do you want your coffee [lit., ** How should your coffee be]?' **C: {a: Az şekerli/b: Şekerli/c: Orta şekerli/d: Çok şekerli/e: Sade} olsun.** 'A: [** Let it be] {a: With little sugar./b: With sugar./c: With medium sugar./d: Very sweet [lit., with a lot of sugar]./e: * Black [lit., without sugar].}' → **Neli?** Below. **S: İşler nasıl?** 'Q: How are things?' **C: {a: [Çok] İyi./b: Fena değil./c: Şöyle böyle./d: Pek iyi değil./e: [Çok] Kötü.}** 'A: {a: [Very] good./b: Not bad./c: So so./d: Not so good./e: [Very] Bad.}' → = **İşler nasıl gidiyor?** → git- 5.

* **{Nasıl [bir]?/Ne gibi [bir]?}** 'What kind of [a]?': **S: Bu nasıl bir kitap?** 'What kind of [a] book is this?' **C: {a: Çok {yararlı/faydalı}/b: Çok eğlenceli/c: Çok öğretici/d: Sürükleyici}. * El.iniz.DEN bırakamayacaksınız.** 'Be sure to read this book! It

is {a: very useful/b: very entertaining/c: very {educational/instructive/informative}/d: {absorbing/fascinating/gripping/riveting/engrossing}}. * You won't be able to put it down [lit., ** release it FROM your hands].' → also **Ne {tür/çeşit}?** above.

Ne? 'What?': S: {Bu/O} ne[dir]? 'Q: What's {this/that}?', a question requesting identity and also expressing indignation, as in English. C: **Kitap[tır].** 'It's a book.' S: * {Bunlar/Onlar} ne? 'Q: What are {these/those}?' C: {Bunlar/Onlar} kitap. 'A: {These/Those} are bookS.' • Note the singular noun in the Turkish response. S: Tavla nedir? 'Q: What is tavla?' C: Tavla [bir] oyundur. 'A: Tavla is a game.' S: Bu {kelime.nin/cümle.nin} {anlam.ı/mana.sı} nedir? 'Q: What is the {meaning} of this {word/sentence}?' C: Bu {kelime.nin/cümle.nin} {anlam.ı/mana.sı}... 'A: The meaning of this {word/sentence} is...' S: Bu {kelime.nin/cümle.nin} Türkçe.si nedir? 'Q: What is the Turkish of this {word/sentence}?' C: Bu {kelime.nin/cümle.nin} Türkçe.si... 'A: The Turkish of this sentence is...' S: {Bu kelime.nin/"Küçük" kelime.si.nin} {eşanlamlı.sı/zıtanlamlı.sı} nedir? 'Q: What is the {synonym/antonym} {of this word?/of the word "Küçük?"} C: {Bu kelime.nin/"Küçük" kelime.si.nin} {eşanlamlı.sı/zıtanlamlı.sı} "..."[tür]. 'A: The {synonym/antonym} {of this word/of the word "Küçük"} is "...".' S: * {Bugün ne[dir]?/Bugün günlerden nedir?} 'Q: What day is it today?' C: Bugün {a: pazartesi/b: salı/c: çarşamba/d: perşembe/e: cuma/f: cumartesi/g: pazar}. 'A: Today is {a: Monday/b: Tuesday/c: Wednesday/d: Thursday/e: Friday/f: Saturday/g: Sunday}.' → also **Ne günü?** below. [Sizin] adresiniz ne[dir]? 'What is your address?' C: [Adresim] Cumhuriyet Cad. Zambak Apt. No: 26/5, 34400 Sultanahmet, Istanbul. 'A: [My address is] Cumhuriyet Boulevard, No. 26/5, 34400, Sultanahmet, Istanbul.'

Ne biçim? 'What kind of a?': In a derogatory sense: * **Ne biçim adamsın sen yahu!** 'What kind of a {fellow/person} are you anyway?' → {Nasıl [bir]?/Ne gibi [bir]?} above, **Ne {tür/çeşit}?** below.

Ne gibi [bir]? 'What kind of [a]?': → {Nasıl [bir]?/Ne gibi [bir]?} above.

* **Ne günü?** '{What day?/* ON what day?}': S: Bugün ne gün.ü? 'S: What day is it today?' C: Bugün pazar gün.ü. 'A: Today is Sunday.' → also **Bugün ne?** above under **Ne?** # S: Konferans ne günü? 'Q: [On] What day is the conference?' C: [Konferans] * cumartesi günü. 'A: [The conference is] * on Saturday.' * **Ne günler.i?** 'On what days?': S: Türkçe dersiniz ne günleri? 'Q: On what days is your Turkish lesson?' C: Türkçe dersim pazartesi, çarşamba, ve cuma günler.i. 'A: My Turkish lesson is on Mondays, Wednesdays, and Fridays.' → also **Hangi günler?** above under **Hangi?** For other examples of this structure, → **Ne noun.[s]I?** below.

Ne hakkında? 'About what?': S: Bu kitap ne hakkında? 'Q: What is this book about?' C: [Bu kitap] Türkiye hakkında. 'A: This book is about Turkey.'

Ne kadar? 'How much?': → **Kaça** above and substitute **ne kadar** for it there. S: Borcum ne kadar? 'A: What do I owe [you]? [lit., What is my debt?]' C: Borcunuz 100 lira. 'A: {You owe/Your debt is} 100 liras.'

Ne renk? 'What color?': S: Bu kumaş ne renk? 'Q: What color is this cloth?' C: [Bu kumaş] {a: beyaz/b: gri/c: kahverengi/d: kara/e: kırmızı/f: mavi/g: mor/h: pembe/i: sarı/j: siyah/k: yeşil} 'A: This cloth is {a: white/b: gray/c: brown/d: black/e: red/f: blue/g: purple/h: pink/i: yellow/j: black/k: green}.'

* **Rengi ne?** 'What color is it [lit., ** What is its color]?': S: Bu kumaş.ın reng.i ne? 'Q: What is the color of this cloth?' C: [Bu kumaş.ın] reng.i beyaz. 'A: It's

white [lit., ** The color of this cloth is white].'

Ne *noun*.[s]I? 'What kind of *noun*?': S: * O bey ne hoca.sı? 'Q: What does that gentleman teach? [lit., ** What teacher is that gentleman?]' C: {a: Tarih/b: Edebiyat/c: Matematik/d: Dil} hoca.sı. 'A: He's {a: a history/b: a literature/c: a math/d: a language} teacher.' Q: * Bu [kitap] ne kitab.ı? 'Q: What kind of book is this? [lit., ** This (book) is what (kind of) book?]' C1: Bu kitap tarih kitab.ı. 'A1: This book is a history book.' C2: Bu tarih kitab.ı. 'A2: It's a history book.' → also Ne günü? above.

Ne {tür/çeşit}? 'What kind?': S: Bu ne {tür/çeşit} bir kitap? 'Q: What {kind} of [a] book is this? C: Bu {[bir] roman./[bir] hikâye kitab.ı./[bir] şiir kitab.ı.} 'A: This is {a novel./a story book./a book of poetry.}' S: Bu ne {tür/çeşit} bir film? 'What kind of a movie is this?' C: Bu {[bir] aşk film.i/[bir] macera film.i/ [bir] kovboy film.i.} 'A: It's {a love story [lit., love movie]./an adventure movie./a cowboy movie.}' → also {Nasıl [bir]?/Ne gibi [bir]?} above.

* Ne tarafta? 'Which way? [lit., ** On which side?]' S: Posthane ne tarafta? 'Q: Which way is the post office?' For some possible responses, → Nerede? below.

Ne zaman? 'When?': S: Toplantı ne zaman? 'When is the meeting?' C: [Toplantı] {a: Bugün/b: Yarın/c: Öbür gün/d: Bu akşam/e: Saat ikide/f: Bugün saat ikide}. 'A: [The meeting is] {a: Today/b: Tomorrow/c: The day after tomorrow/d: This evening/e: At two o'clock/f: Today at two o'clock}.'

* Neli? 'With what on it?, How? [lit., With what?]' [ne + adj. suf. -lI]: S: * Sandviç neli olsun? 'What do you want on the sandwich [lit., ** With what should the sandwich be?]' C: * {Peynir.li/ Kaşar.lı/Sosis.li} olsun. 'A: I'll have it {with cheese/with kashar cheese/with sausage} [lit., Let it be with ...].' S: Kahve neli olsun? 'How do you want the coffee [lit., ** With what should the coffee be]?' For possible responses, → the more common question Kahveniz nasıl olsun? → Nasıl? above.

Nerede? 'Where [lit., Where at]?': S: Kitap nerede? 'Q: Where's the book?' C1: Masa.nın {a: üst.ü.nde/b: üzeri.nde/c: alt.ı.nda} 'A1: {a, b: on [top of]/c: under} the table.' C2: * Semra'da. 'A2: {Semra has it./It's with Semra.}' C3: Bulamıyorum. * Hah, işte burada! 'A3: I can't find it. Oh, here it is!' S: Postane nerede? 'Where's the post office?' C1: {a: Biraz iler[i]de./b: Köşede./c: Doğru gidin, iki sokak sonra sola dönün, sağ tarafta.} 'A1: {a: It's up ahead a bit./b: At the corner./c: * Go straight ahead two blocks, then turn left. It's on the right [side].}' C2: Bilmiyorum. Soralım. 'A2: I don't know. Let's ask.' S: Çocuk nerede? 'Q: Where's the child?' C: Ev.in {a: ön.ü.nde/b: arka.sı.nda/c: ileri.si.nde/d: geri.si.nde/e: yan.ı.nda/f: sağ.ı.nda/g: sol.u.nda}. 'A: {a: in front of/b: in back of/c: a bit ahead of/d: further behind/e: at the side of/f: at the right [side] of/g: at the left [side] of} the house.' Bir saatten beri bekliyorum. * Neredesin? 'I've been waiting for an hour. * Where have you been? [lit., ** Where are you?]' → Ne tarafta? above, Neresi? and Neresinde? below.

Nerelerde? 'Where?, In what places? [lit., ** In wheres?]': Merhaba Suzan, * nerelerdesin? Çoktan beri görüşemedik. 'Hello Suzan. * Where have you been? {We haven't seen each other for quite a while./colloq.: Long time no see.}'

* Nereli? 'Where is he from?' [nere + adj. suf. -lI]. This question asks for a person's country, city, or province of origin, what he regards as his real home: S: Ayşe nereli? 'Q: Where is Ayşe from?' C: İstanbullu. 'A: She's from Istanbul.' S: Siz nereli.siniz? 'Q: Where are you from?' C: {a: Amerikalı.yım./b: Newyorklu.yum.} 'A: I'm {a: {from the U.S./an American.}/b: {from New York./a New Yorker.}}' Some responses are formed without the -lI suffix, including the following: C: {a: Alman.ım./b:

Fransız.ım./c: Türk.üm./d: * Türkiyeli.yim.} 'I'm {a: {a German./from Germany.}/b: {French./from France.}/c: a Turk./d: from Turkey.}' The last response indicates a native or inhabitant of Turkey, not necessarily a Moslem Turk.

* **Neresi?** 'Where?, What place [lit., ** Its where?]': S: * **Burası neresi?** 'Q: {What place is this?/Where are we? [lit., ** Its here its where?]}' C1: * **[Burası] Taksim.** 'A1: This is Taksim [i.e., a section of Istanbul] [lit. ** Its here is Taksim.]' S: * **Orası neresi?** 'Q: {What place is that [over there]?/What's that place over there?} [lit., ** Its there its where?]' C: **Orası Taksim.** 'A: That's Taksim [lit., ** Its there is Taksim.]' S: **Hastane neresi?** 'Q: Where is the hospital?' C1: **Hastane burası.** 'A1: {The hospital is here./This is the hospital.}' C2: **Burası.** 'A2: {This is it./Here it is./It's here.}' C3: **Hastane orası.** 'A3: {The hospital is over there.}' C4: **Orası.** 'A4: {It's over there./That's it over there.}' C5: The responses under **Nerede?** above that have a place as the explicit or understood subject may also be used in response to questions with **neresi?**, e.g., **Biraz iler[i]de.** 'It's up ahead a bit.', etc. • Unlike **nerede?**, however, **neresi?** is not used in the pattern *Noun* **neresi?** when that noun designates an object or a person, i.e., NOT ~~Kitap neresi?~~ or ~~Ahmet neresi?~~

Neresinde? 'Where in [lit., ** In its where]?, * Where in relation to?', when asking for the location of a place within a larger area or for the relation of a place to surrounding areas: S: **Ankara Türkiye'nin nere.si.nde?** a: **Kuzey.i.nde mi,** b: **güney.i.nde mi,** c: **doğu.su.nda mı,** d: **batı.sı.nda mı,** e: **orta.sı.nda mı?** 'Q: Where in Turkey is Ankara: a: In the north, b: in the south, c: in the east, d: in the west, or e: in the middle? [lit., ** {a: in its north/in the north of it}, b:...]' S: * **Ankara Konya'nın nere.si.nde?** 'Q: Where is Ankara in relation to Konya [i.e., another city in Turkey]?' C: * **Ankara Konya.nın kuzey.i.nde.** 'A: Ankara is {north/to the north} of Konya.'

Nereye? 'Where to?': You meet a friend on the street. You say: **Merhaba Leyla.** * **Nereye böyle?** 'Hi Leyla, * {Where are you off to?/Where to? [lit., ** Where to {like this?/in this way?}]'

* **Nesi?** lit., '{his/its} what?', a question for determining how one person, less commonly a thing, is related to another: S: * **O adam {Selim'in/o.nun} ne.si[dir]?** 'Q: How is that man related to {Selim/him} [lit., ** That man is {Selim's/his} what]?' C: **O adam Selim'in {a: baba.sı/b: büyük-baba.sı/c: dede.si/d: amca.sı/e: dayı.sı/f: enişte.si/g: kardeş.i/h: ağabey.i [usually pronounced: âbi.si]/i: yeğen.i}.** 'A: That man is Selim's {a: father/b, c: grandfather/d: [paternal] uncle/e: [maternal] uncle/f: {uncle by marriage/cousin's husband}/g: brother/h: older brother/i: nephew}.' **O hanım {Serpil'in/o.nun} nesi[dir]?** 'Q: How is that woman related to {Serpil/her} [lit., ** That woman is {Serpil's/her} what]?' C: **O hanım Serpil'in {a: anne.si/b: büyükanne.si/c: anneanne.si/d: hala.sı/e: teyze.si/f: yenge.si/g: kız kardeş.i/h: abla.sı/i: yeğen.i}.** 'A: That woman is Serpil's {a: mother/b, c: grandmother/d: [paternal] aunt/e: [maternal] aunt/f: {aunt by marriage/cousin's wife}/g: sister/h: older sister/i: niece}.' With other possessor pronouns: S: **O adam {a: [benim] ne.yim?/b: [senin] ne.yin?/c: [bizim] ne.yimiz/d: [sizin] ne.yiniz}** 'Q: What is that man {a: to me?/b: to you [s.]?/c: to us?/d: to you [pl.]?}' C: **O adam {a: [benim] baba.m...}** 'A: That man is {a: my father...}'

* **Neymiş, neymiş?** '{What's that?/What was that?/I didn't catch that.}', when you didn't catch some words spoken. In an ordinary conversation, the usual, more polite phrase to elicit a repetition is, however, **Efendim?** 'lit., ** My {sir/ma'am}?'

Niçin? [= **Ne için?**] 'Why?, For what?': **Kitap niçin burada?** 'Why is the book here?'

Niye? Same as above. Substitute for **niçin** in the example.

3. Selected examples with various forms of ol- expressing '- be.' In alphabetical order by form of ol-, usually in the third person. Examples with other persons may appear in the entry.

Where ol- = θ, i.e., is not present: **Öyle bir karakterim var ki, namus uğru.nA cinayet işleyebilirim.** 'I'm the type of person that [lit., I have such a character that I] could commit murder FOR the sake of [my] honor.'

Where ol- = i-: **İstediğim buydu** [= bu idi]. 'That's what I wanted [lit., What I wanted was this].' * **Burası çok güzel yermiş** [= less common: **yer imiş**]. 'What a nice place! [lit., ** This place (** Its here) is a very nice place].' Said when a place turns out to be especially nice or nicer than expected. **Hava ne güzelmiş** [= less common: **güzel imiş**]. '{What beautiful weather!/How nice the weather is!}' Said when one is especially pleased or surprised by the nice weather. **Hastayken** [= **Hasta iken**] **derse gelmiyoruz.** 'When we're ill [lit., When ill], we don't come to class.' = **Hasta** {olduğumuz zaman/olduğumuzda/olunca} **derse gelmiyoruz.** For additional examples, see the entry i-.

olabil- '- be able to be': **Anneciğim, seni çok özledim,** * **burada ol.abil.men.i dilerdim.** 'Dear mother, I've missed you a lot. * I wish you {were/lit., could be} here [lit., ** your being able to be here].'

olacak 'what {is going to/will/would} be': **Hep deprem olacak diye korkuyorum.** 'I'm always afraid [that] there'll be an earthquake.' As an adjective: **16.** [read: **on altıncı**] **yüzyılda yaşayan kâhin Nostradamus, 20.** [read: **yirminci**] **yüzyılda olacak depremler ve önemli olaylar hakkında kehanette bulunmuş.** 'The oracle Nostradamus, who lived in the sixteenth century, predicted θ the earthquakes and important events that would occur in the twentieth century.' As a noun: **Olacak olur.** 'What will be will be.' * **Bu yaz sıcak olacağ.A benziyor.** 'It looks like this summer is going to be hot.'

olacağı 'that {he/it} is {going to/will} be, lit., ** {his/its} going to be': As a noun: As the subject of the sentence: **Hasta olacağı açık.** 'It's clear that he's going to be ill.' As the object of the sentence: **Hasta olacağı.nı biliyorum.** 'I know that he is going to be ill.' * **İş olacağ.ı.nA varır.** 'What will be, will be [lit., ** Matters will get to where they are going to be].' *963:11.* predetermination: PHR. it is fated.

olan '{he who/what/that} {is/was}': As an adjective: **Türkçe.si mükemmel olan öğrenciler Türkiye'ye gitmek için burs alabiliyorlar.** '[The] students with excellent Turkish [lit., (The) students whose Turkish is excellent] may receive scholarships to go to Turkey.' * **Babası hastanede olan çocuk bugün derse gelemedi.** 'The child whose father is in the hospital [lit., ** his father-in-the-hospital-being child] didn't come to class today.' As a noun: As the subject of the sentence: Proverb: **Deli olan hediye.yE sevinir, akıllı olan üzülür.** 'A fool [lit., he who is crazy] is pleased WITH a gift, an intelligent person [lit., he who is intelligent] is sorry.' This is because an intelligent person realizes that the receiver is obliged to reciprocate. **[Asıl] önemli olan...** 'What's [really] important [is]...': A: **Size küçük bir hediye vermek istiyorum,** * **"çam sakızı çoban armağanı."** 'A: I want to give you a small present, * it's just a little something [lit., "A shepherd's gift is pine gum," a phrase said to imply the modest character of the gift.] B: **Çok teşekkür ederim,** * **önemli olan bunu düşünmüş olmanız.** 'B: Thank you very much. * What's important is the thought [lit., ** your having thought of this].' **Bence asıl önemli olan {şu}:...** 'I say {what's important/the important {issue/point}} is {this/as follows}:...'

olduğu 'that {he/it} {is/was}, {his/its} being': As an adjective: **Hasta olduğ.UMUZ zaman derse gelmiyoruz.** 'When WE are ill, we don't come to class.' = **Hasta** {olduğumuzda/olunca/iken} **derse gelmiyoruz.** As a noun: As the subject of the sentence: **Adam.ın bu kadar hasta olduğ.u bilinmiyordu.** 'It was not known [that] the man was so ill.' As the object of the sentence: **Adam.ın bu kadar hasta** <u>olduğ.u.NU</u> **bilmiyordum.** 'I didn't know [that] the man was so ill.' **Adam mahkemede bebeğ.in babası** <u>olduğ.u.nU</u> **inkâr etti.** 'The man denied in court that he was the father of the baby.'

olduğu gibi → ol- 11.

olduğu halde → ol- 11.

olduğu kadar → ol- 11.

{**olduğundan/olduğu için**} 'because {he/it} {is/was}': [**Ben**] **hasta** {**olduğu.Mdan/olduğu.M için**} **derse gidemedim.** 'Because I was ill, I couldn't go to class.' *887:10.* attribution: CONJ. because.

olmak '- be, being': As the subject of the sentence: **Doktor olmak iyi bir şey.** 'It's a good thing to be a doctor.' As the object of the sentence: **Doktor olmak istiyorum.** 'I want to be a doctor.' **Doktor olmay.I çok istiyorum.** 'I want very much to be a doctor.' The pattern above is used when the verb, here **iste-**, is separated from its object. With another case suffix: **Eşim hasta olmak.TAN korkuyor.** 'My {wife/husband} is afraid OF being ill.'

olmak üzere → ol- 11.

olmakla {**beraber/birlikte**} → ol- 11.

olmalı '{he/it} {must/should} be': Necessity: **Saat dokuzda okulda olmalı.yIZ.** 'WE must be at school at nine o'clock.' *962:10.* necessity: - be necessary.

{**olmalı/olsa gerek**} '{he/it} must be': Inference: **Garson bey, bizim hesab.A bir daha bakar mısınız?** * **Bir yanlışlık** {**olmalı/olsa gerek**}. 'Waiter, would you please take a look AT our check again. * There must be some mistake.' **Şu adam.ın kıyafet.i.nE bak, ne tuhaf! Yabancı** {**olmalı/olsa gerek**}. **Bence bu adam kesinlikle Türk olamaz.** 'Just look AT how that guy is dressed [lit., AT that person's attire]. How {weird/strange}! He {must be} a foreigner. * I don't think that man can possibly be a Turk [lit., I think that

man can't possibly be a Turk].' **Toplum tarafından dışlanmak hoş bir duygu ol.MA.sa gerek.** 'It must NOT be {pleasant/lit., a pleasant feeling} to be excluded by society.' **Turan bey bugün işe gelmedi. Hasta olmalı.** 'Turan bey didn't come to work today. He must be ill.'
• Note the same forms used with a main verb other than ol-: **Turhan bey * çok kötü öksürüyor, üşüt.müş** {**olmalı/olsa gerek**}. 'Turhan * has a terrible cough [lit., is coughing terribly], he must have caught a chill.' *967:4.* probability: - be probable.

olması '{his/its} being': As the subject of the sentence: * **Ahmet'in doktor olması iyi bir şey.** 'It's a good thing Ahmet is a doctor [lit., ** Ahmet's being a doctor is a good thing].' As the object of the sentence: **Annem** [**benim**] **doktor olma.M.ı istiyor.** 'My mother wants ME to be [lit., wants MY being] a doctor.'

olmasına {**rağmen/karşın**} → ol- 11.

olmuş 'it seems {he/it} {has been/was}': **Yeni reklam kampanya.sı ürünlerin satışında etkili OL.MUŞ.A benziyor.** 'It appears that the new ad campaign HAS BEEN effective in [increasing] sales [of the products].'

olsa 'if {he/it} were': **Zengin olsa.M bol bol seyahat ederdim.** 'If I were rich, I would travel a lot.' In 'ever' constructions: * **Ne iş olsa yaparım.** 'I'll do whatever work there is.' For other uses of **olsa**, → ol- 11.

olsa gerek → {**olmalı/olsa gerek**} above.

olsaydı 'if {he/it} {were/had been}': **Daha çalışkan olsay.DIM * dersleri.Mİ başarırdım.** 'If I had worked harder [lit., been more hardworking], * I would have succeeded IN MY lessons.'

olsun 'let {him/it} be, may {he/it} be': **Saat kaçta sinemada** {**olayım/olalım/olsun**}? 'At what time {should I be/should we be/should he be} at the movies?'

221:6. presence: - be present. → = **bulun- 2**. # S: * **Çayınız şekerli mi olsun, şekersiz mi?** 'Q: Do you want your tea with sugar or without [lit., Should your tea be...]?' C: **{Şekerli/Şekersiz} olsun.** 'A: {With sugar./Without sugar.}' * **Nasıl arzu edersen öyle olsun.** '{Have it your way./lit., Let it be as you wish.}' At the gas station: * **Ful olsun.** 'Fill'er up [lit., ** Let it be full].' * **O olmasın bu olmasın, peki ne olsun?** 'That won't do and this won't do. Well then, what do you want [lit., ** That shouldn't be, this shouldn't be. OK [then], what should be]?' **Yapacağız.** * **Bu.nDAN hiç kimse.nin şüphe.si olmasın.** 'We'll do it. * Let there be no doubt ABOUT that [lit., ** Let no one's doubt about that be].' **Yanlışlık olmasın.** 'Let there be no mistake': **Elimizdeki son başvuru formu bu. Lütfen dikkatli doldurun, yanlışlık olmasın.** 'This is the final application form. Please fill it out carefully so there's no mistake.' **Askerdeyken {san.a bir şey olmasın}/başın.a bir şey gelmesin} diye annen her gün dua etti. Bakalım * hakkını nasıl ödeyeceksin?** 'Your mother prayed everyday while you were doing your military service that {no harm would come to you}. * I wonder how you can ever repay her [lit., pay (her) her due]?' As 'the object' of the sentence: **Annem doktor olsun istiyor.** 'My mother wants him to become a doctor.' **Allah yardımcımız olsun.** 'May God help us.' *1007:18b.* protection: expressions to protect against misfortune; *1011:* * 22. hindrance: expressions to prevent unfavorable occurrences. → **ol- 3**, Additional examples. a) 3. Selected examples...: olsun. For additional examples with **olsun** in some common expressions, → **ol- 11** → **olsun** below.

olunca 'when {he/it} {is/was}': **Hasta olunca derse gelmiyoruz.** 'When we're ill [lit., When ill], we don't come to class.' = **Hasta {olduğumuz zaman/olduğumuzda/iken} derse gelmiyoruz.** # **İnsan göz.den ırak olunca gönül.den de ırak olur.** 'When a person is out of sight [lit., ** far from the eye] he is also out of mind [lit., ** far from the heart].' **Akşam olunca dükkân.ın {kepenkler.i.ni/panjurlar.ı.nı}**

indiririz. 'When it is evening, we lower {the [metal rolling] shutters/the [slatted] shutters} of the shop.' **Yorgun olunca erken yatar.** 'When she's tired, she goes to bed early.'

olup olma- 'whether or not, lit., - be or not - be': **olup olmadığı** 'lit., whether {he/it} {is/was} or {is/was} not': As the subject of the sentence: **Defter.in masada olup olmadığ.ı belli değil.** 'It isn't clear whether the notebook {is/was} on the table or not.' As the object of the sentence: **Defter.in masada olup olmadığ.ı.NI bilmiyor.** 'He doesn't know if the notebook {is/was} on the table or not.'

olur '{he/it} {will/would} be, is generally or usually of a certain quality': **Yarın evde olur.UM.** * **Gel[in] istersen[iz].** 'I'll be at home tomorrow. * {Come over if you feel like it./Why don't you come over?}' **Şimdi {gitmesem/okumasam} daha iyi olur.** 'It would be better {if I didn't go/if I didn't read} now.' **İzmir'in üzümleri iyi olur.** 'The grapes from İzmir are usually good.'

For more examples of 'A is B'-type statements, → **Proverbs in the Turkish English Dictionary of Verbs.**

---

b) Examples of 'There is'-type, i.e., **{var/yok}**, sentences

1. Yes-no questions: Basic patterns. S: **Masada kitap var mı?** 'Q: {Is there a book on the table?/Are there {some/any} books on the table?}' **C1: [Evet,] Var.** 'A1: Yes, there {is./are.}' **C2: [Hayır,] Yok.** 'A2: No, there {isn't./aren't.}'

S: **Masada kitap yok mu?** 'Q: {Isn't there a book on the table?/Aren't there any books on the table?}' **C1:** * **[Hayır,] Var.** 'A1: There {is./are.}' **C2:** * **[Evet,] Yok.** 'A2: There {isn't./aren't.}'

S: **Masada kitap var, değil mi?** 'Q: {There is a book on the table, isn't there?/There are some books on the table, aren't there?}' **C1: Evet, var.** 'A1: Yes, there {is/are}?' **C2: Hayır, yok.** 'A2: No, there {isn't/aren't}.'

When **değil mi** follows a negative statement, it must be translated affirmative if the less common translation 'isn't that so?' is not used: **S: Masada kitap yok, değil mi?** 'Q: {There isn't a book on the table, is there?/There aren't any books on the table, are there?}' **C1: * Evet, yok.** 'A1: That's right [lit., Yes], there {isn't/aren't}.' **C2: Hayır, var.** 'A2: That's wrong [lit., No], there {is one/are some}.'

An 'or' question: **S: Masada kitap var mı, yok mu?** 'Q: {Is there a book on the table or not?/Are there {some/any} books on the table or not?}' **C1: Masada kitap var.** 'A1: {There is a book on the table./There are some books on the table.}' **C2: Masada kitap yok.** 'A2: {There aren't any books on the table./There are no books on the table./There isn't a book on the table.}'

2. Essential question-word questions: With **h**-beginning question words: **Hangi?** 'Which?' → {**Ne/Hangi**} **tür?** below under **n**-beginning question words.

With **k**-beginning question words: **Kaç?** 'How many?': **S: Sınıfta kaç kişi var?** 'Q: How many people are there in the classroom?' **C: [Sınıfta] On iki kişi var.** 'A: There are twelve people [in the classroom].' **Her sınıfta kaç kişi var?** 'Q: How many people are there in each class?' → **Kaçar?** below. For **var** in telling time before the hour, → above, **Saat kaç?** under **Kaç?** under a) Examples of 'A is B'-type sentences. Essential question-word questions and answers. With **k**-beginning question words.

* Kaçar? 'How many each?': **S: Her sınıfta kaçar öğrenci var?** 'Q: How many students are there in each class?' **C: [Her sınıfta] {a: bir.er öğrenci/b: {iki.şer/ dörd.er/altı.şar/on iki.şer} öğrenci} var.** 'A: [In each class] there {a: is one student/b: are {two/four/six/twelve} students.' → **Kaç?** above.

Kim? 'Who?': For **kim** in questions with {**var/yok**}, → {var/yok} **ol-** → **ol-** 12.

With **n**-beginning question words: **Nasıl?** 'How?': **A: Orada şeker yok.** 'A: There's no sugar there.' **B: * Nasıl yok, daha demin oraya iki kilo şeker koydum!** 'B: * {How's that?/How come there isn't any?} I put two kilos of sugar there just a moment ago!'

Ne? 'What?': **S: Masada ne var?** 'Q: What's on the table?' **C: [Masada] kitap var.** 'A: There {IS A book/ARE SOME books} [on the table].' **S: * Masada neler var?** 'Q: What things are there on the table?' **C1: [Masada] kitap ve kalem var.** 'A1: There {is a book and a pencil [or pen]/are books and pencils [or pens]} on the table.' **C2: Masada kitaplar var.** 'A2: There are [some] books on the table.' **S: Masada başka ne var?** 'Q: What else is [there] on the table?' **C: [Masada] kitap.TAN BAŞKA hiç bir şey yok.** 'A: There's nothing on the table ASIDE FROM {the book/the books}.' **Kafam kaşındı ben de kaşıdım, * ne var bunda?** 'My head itched, and I scratched it. * So what of it [lit., ** What is there in this]?' **Kork.acak ne var * bunda?** 'What is there to be afraid of [in that]?' **Bununla ne alakası var?** 'What does that have to do with this?'

* *noun*.DAn ne var?: '{What do you have in the way of...?/What kind of...do you have?/lit., ** What is there FROM...?}', while shopping: **S: Meyvalardan ne var?** 'Q: What do you have in the way of fruit?'

* *noun of meal*.DA ne var? 'What's FOR *noun of meal*': **S: * {a: Yemek.TE/b: Kahvaltı.DA/ c: Öğle yemeğ.i.nDE/d: Akşam yemeğ.i.nDE} ne var?** 'Q: What's {a: there to eat?, i.e., for a meal but excluding breakfast/b: FOR breakfast/c: FOR lunch/d: FOR {dinner/lit., the evening meal}}?' **C: Yemek.TE mercimek çorbası, kuru fasulye ve pilav var.** 'A: There's lentil soup, navy beans, and rice [FOR dinner].'

* Ne var ne yok? 'Q: {How are things?/What's going on?/What's happening?/What's up?/What's new?}' [lit.,** 'What existent, what non-existent?'] = **Ne haber?** ['What news?']: **S: Merhaba Selim, ne var ne yok?** 'Hi Selim, {What's

281

up?/How are things?}' **C**: İyilik, sağlık. * **Sen.DE[N] ne var ne yok?** 'A: Everything's fine [lit., ** goodness, health]. * How are things WITH you?' * **D e m e k Istanbul'dan yeni geldin.** * **Eee, anlat bakalım, memlekette ne var ne yok?** 'So you've just come from Istanbul. * Well, tell us what's going on {back home./lit., in the country.}' *504: * 20.* courtesy: polite expressions.

{Ne/Hangi} tür [or **çeşit**]? 'What kind of?': **S**: **{Ne/Hangi} tür kitap var burada?** 'Q: What kind of books are there here?' **C1**: **Burada {a: roman/b: şiir/c: hikâye/d: deneme/e: inceleme/ f: ansiklopedi} var.** 'There are {a: novels/b: poetry/c: stories/d: essays/e: studies of different kinds/f: encyclopaedias].' **C2**: **[Burada] {her tür/türlü türlü} kitap var.** 'A2: There are all kinds of books [here].' **C3**: **Burada hiç kitap yok.** 'A3: There aren't any books at all here.'

* **Neli?** 'With what on it?' [ne + adj. suf. -lI]. **A**: **Bir tost istiyorum.** * **Neli var?** 'A: I'd like a toasted sandwich. * What kind do you have [lit., ** With what is there]?' **B**: **{Peynirli/Kaşarlı/ Sosisli} var.** 'B: We have [lit., There's] some {with cheese/with kashar cheese/with sausage}.' **A**: * **Sosisli olsun.** 'A: I'll have sausage [lit., Let it be with sausage].'

Nerede? 'Where [at]?': **S**: **Buralarda {iyi bir lokanta/içme su.yu} var mı?** 'Q: Is there {a good restaurant/any drinking water} around here?' **C**: **Hayır, hiç yok.** 'A: No, there isn't.' **S**: **Nerede var?** 'Q: Where is there {one/any/some}?'

Niçin? [= **Ne için?**] 'Why?, For what?': **Burada niçin kitap var?** 'Why are there books here?' **Burada niçin kitap yok?** 'Why aren't there any books here?'

Niye? Same as above. Substitute for **niçin** in the examples.

3. Additional examples by issue
3.1. Issues of the presence of sth in a place: **Müşteri**: * **Tıraş olmak istiyorum**, * **sıra var mı?** 'Customer I want a '[hair] cut'. * Are there people ahead of me [lit., Is there

a line]?' **Yakınlarda faks çekebileceğim bir yer var mı?** 'Is there a place nearby where I can send a fax?' **Buralarda kamp yapabileceğimiz bir yer var mı?** 'Is there a place around here where we can camp?' **Buralarda park edecek yer var mı?** 'Is there a place to park around here?' **Bu mahallede bakkal yok mu?** 'Isn't there a grocery store in this neighborhood?'

Some examples with the -**An** participle [i.e., *verb stem*.**An** form] as an adjective for a noun subject of the {**var/yok**} sentence: When I expect an affirmative response: **A**: **Turan, canını sık.an bir şey mi var?** 'A: Is something bothering you, Turan?' **B**: **Yoo,** * **neden sordun?** 'B: No, * why do [lit., did] you ask?' **A**: * **Son günlerde biraz {dalgın/durgun} görünüyorsun da.** 'A: Well, it's just that you've been looking a little {absentminded/ withdrawn} lately.' * **Ankara'yI tanıtan bir kitap var mı?** '{Do you know of/lit., Is there} a book about Ankara [i.e., a guide book]? [lit., Is there a book that gives information about Ankara?]' *760:8.* existence: - exist. An example with the -**An** participle as a noun subject of the {**var/yok**} sentence: **Kitaplarda yazılan şeylerin içinde akl.A yatkın olan.ı var, olmayan.ı var; iyi.si var, kötü.sü var.** 'Among the things written in books there are things that are reasonable [lit., in accord WITH reason], things that are not; there are good things, bad things.'

3.2. Issues of the presence or existence of a person in a place: **Burada Ahmet bey {ism.i.nde/ diye} biri var mı?** 'Is there someone {named} Ahmet bey here?' **Bu yer.in sahib.i var mı?** 'Has this seat been taken?/lit., ** 'Does this place have an owner?]' Some examples with a participle [i.e., *verb stem*.**An** form] as a noun subject of the {**var/yok**} sentence: **Bana soru sormak iste.yen var mı?** 'Is there {anyone/someone} who would like to ask me a question?' **Ben gezmey.E çıkıyorum, gelmek isteyen var mı?** 'I'm going {out for a walk/θ sight-seeing}. Does anyone want to come along [lit., Is there anyone who wants to come]?' **S**: * **Bura.da oturan var mı?** 'Q:

{Is anyone sitting here?/Is this place {taken/occupied}?' [= **Bura.nın sahib.i var mı?** lit., ** Does this place have an owner?] **C1: Evet, burada {arkadaşım/birisi} oturuyor.** 'A1: Yes, {my friend/sb} is sitting here.' **C2: * Hayır, yok.** 'A2: {No, it's free./No, it's not taken./No, no one is sitting here.}'

Examples with {**biri/birisi**} 'sb, someone' and **kimse** 'anybody, anyone; nobody, no one': **S: Evde {a: {biri/birisi}/b: kimse} var mı?** 'Is there {a: sb/b: anybody} in the house?' **C1: Evet, evde {biri/birisi} var.** 'A1: Yes, there is sb in the house.' **C2: Hayır, evde [hiç] kimse yok.** 'A2: No, {There isn't anybody [at all]/There's no one [at all]} in the house.'

S: Evde [hiç] kimse yok mu? 'Q: Isn't there anybody [at all] in the house?' **C1: * Evet, [evde] [hiç] kimse yok.** 'A1: Yes, there is no one in the house.' **C2: * Hayır, evde {biri/birisi} var.** 'No, there is sb in the house.' An 'or' question: **S: Evde {a: {biri/birisi}/b: kimse} var mı, yok mu?** 'Q: Is there {a: sb/b: anybody} in the house or not?' **C1: {Biri/Birisi} var.** 'A: There is somebody.' **C2: Kimse yok.** 'A2: {There isn't {anybody/anyone}/There is nobody.}' **Ban.A yardım edecek [hiç bir] kimse yok.** 'There is no one around to help me.' **Sağ.ı.na sol.u.na baktı. Kimse yoktu.** 'He looked to his right; he looked to his left. There was no one there.'

3.3. Issues of source: **Oğuz'DAN haber var mı?** 'Is there any news {OF [i.e., about]/from} Oğuz?'

3.4. Issues of concern over a state of affairs: • Note the word order when the questioner anticipates an affirmative response: **S: * Bir şey mi var?** 'A: Is sth {wrong/the matter}?' **C1: Cüzdanımı kaybettim.** 'A1: I've lost my wallet.' **C2: Hayır, bir şey yok.** 'A2: No, it's nothing.' **Merak etme, korkacak bir şey yok.** 'Don't worry, there's nothing to be afraid of.' **Otobüsü kaçırdık, * yapacak bir şey yok.** 'We've missed the bus. * There's nothing TO BE done.' **Yapabileceğimiz hiçbir şey yok. Çok üzgünüm.** 'There's nothing [that] we can do. I'm very

sorry.' * **Artık dönüş yok!** 'Now there's {no way back!/no turning back!}' Proverbs: **Her derd.in {deva.sı/çare.si} var[dır].** 'There is a remedy for every care.' * **Her {iş.TE/şey.DE} bir hayır var[dır].** 'There is a good side TO every matter.' Every cloud has a silver lining. A proverb that notes the power of women for good or evil: **Kadın var ev yapar, kadın var ev yıkar.** 'Some women make a home; others wreck a home [lit., There are women who make a home; there are women who wreck a home].' A less formal structure with the same meaning: **Ev yapan kadın[lar] da var, ev yıkan kadın[lar] da.**

3.5. Issues of means to a place, person, goal, or solution to a problem: **Bugün Ankara'ya {tren/otobüs/uçak} var mı?** 'Is there {a train/a bus/a plane} to Ankara today?' **Bu sorunu çözme.nin yol.u var mı?** 'Is there a way of solving this problem?' **telefon var** /A/ 'for there - be a phone call /FOR/': **Siz.E telefon var.** 'There's a call FOR you.' *347:18.* communications: - telephone. → = **Sizi telefon.DAN {istiyorlar/arıyorlar}.** ['There's a (telephone) call for you.'] → **ara-** 2.

3.6. Issues of necessity: **çişi var** '- have to go [pee], - have to pee.' Usually used by grown-ups for children and by children among themselves: When a grown-up observes that a child is uncomfortable, he may say: **Çiş.İN mi var?** 'Do YOU have to pee?' The same idea may be expressed with **çişi gel-: Çiş.İN mi geldi?** → **gel-** 1. For the expression used by grown-ups among themselves, → **tuvaleti var** below. *12:14.* excretion: - urinate.

gerek {var/yok} /A/ 'lit., {There's/There isn't} a need {to/FOR}': NON-verbal noun as object: **Ucuz kahramanlığ.A gerek yok. Ölmek değil, onurluca yaşamaktır zor olan.** 'There is no need FOR easy [lit., cheap] heroism. What is difficult is not to die, but to live honorably.' VERBAL noun as object: Impersonal object: **Bu öyle saçma bir iddia ki yalanlamay.A bile gerek yok.** 'This is such an absurd claim that there is even no need to deny it.'

283

Personal object: **Tıraş olma.M.A gerek var mı?** 'Do I have to shave [lit., ** Is there a necessity FOR MY shaving]?' * **Bağırma.N.A gerek yok. Ne dediğin.i anladım.** 'There's no need FOR YOU to shout [lit., ** FOR your shouting]. I understood what you said.' **Bu gibi şeyler.DEN kaygılanma.N.A gerek yok.** 'There is no need FOR YOU to worry ABOUT such things.' **Hocayla konuşup sınavı tekrar almak istediğini söyle, çekinme.N.E gerek yok.** * **Olsa olsa "hayır" der.** 'Talk {to/with} the teacher and tell him [that] you want to retake the exam. {Don't be shy./lit., There's no need FOR YOU to hesitate.} * The worst that can happen is that he'll say "no".' **Alın.ma.NIZ.A gerek yok, siz.i kastetmedim.** 'There's no need FOR YOU to get offended. I didn't mean you.' *962:10.* necessity: - be necessary.

tuvaleti var '- have to use the {restroom/facilities/toilet}, - have to go' [F. **tuvalet** 'the NEED to use the toilet'] Used by grown-ups among themselves: **Tuvalet.İN var mı?** 'Do YOU have to use the {restroom/facilities/toilet}?' → = **tuvaleti gel-** → **gel-** 1. For the expression usually used by grown-ups for children and by children among themselves, → **çişi var** above. *12:13.* excretion: - defecate; *12:14.* : - urinate. → = **tuvaleti gel-** → **gel-** 1.

3.7. Issues of time: * **Daha tren.in kalkma.sı.na beş dakika var, yetişebiliriz.** 'We've still got five minutes till the train leaves [lit., There are still five minutes to the departure of the train]. We'll be able to {make it/catch it}.' **Tren.in kalkma.sı.na az var. Koş!** 'The train will soon leave [lit., There is little time left till the departure of the train]. Run!' * **Saat sekiz.E daha vardı.** 'There was still some time till 8 o'clock.'

4. Miscellaneous additional examples: **-AcAğI {var/yok}** 'he has {something/nothing} - [do]', lit., ** 'his going - (do sth) (is) {existent/non-existent}': **Bu konuda bir {diyeceğ.İM/ söyleye-ceğ.İM} yok.** 'I have nothing to say on this subject.' **Bu konuda {diyeceğ.İN/söyleyeceğ.İN}**

var mı? 'Do YOU have something to say on this subject?'

* **Bir varmış, bir yokmuş** 'Once upon a time [lit., ** Once there was, once there wasn't].'

* **dahası var.** '{[and] that's not all/there's more to come}' [**daha** 'more'], lit., ** 'its more (is) existent': **Lütfen söz.üm.ü kesme de dinle, dahası var.** 'Please don't interrupt me [lit., ** cut my utterance] and listen. That's not all [i.e., I have more to say about it].' *253:14.* addition: PHR. et cetera.

* **-DIğI yok** 'he has never, is never...', lit., ** 'his {doing/having done} (is) not'. This structure calls attention to a general practice or attitude: **Hiç kimse.DEN çekindiğ.İM, korktuğ.UM yok.** '{I have never been/I'm not} intimidated BY or afraid OF anybody.' **John Türkiye'de uzun süre oturması.nA {rağmen/ karşın} hiç Türkçe öğrendiğ.i yok.** 'Although John has lived in Turkey for a long time, he has never learned any Turkish.'

faydası yok. 'it's no use' [**fayda** 'use, profit, advantage'], lit., ** 'its use (is) non-existent': **Oğlum * hiç boşuna ısrar etme; faydası yok. Bu saatte dışarı çıkamazsın.** 'Son, * don't waste your breath [lit., ** don't insist for nothing]. It's no use. You can't go outside at this hour.' **O üniversiteye başvuru yapma.nın fayda.sı yok, * çünkü süresi geçti.** 'It's no use to apply to that {college/university} * because it's too late [lit., ** its time has passed].' Proverb: **Korku.nun ecel.E fayda.sı yok.** 'Fear is of no use AGAINST the final hour of death.', i.e., It will come when it is ordained. *391: * 16.* uselessness: PHR. it's no use.

* **İnecek var.** 'I'm getting off', also, but less polite, 'Coming through [lit., ** There is a going-to-get-off (person)].' You say these words to notify the bus driver that you want to get off. You use the same words to alert him that sb else is trying to get off.

-mAk yok! 'No...ing!', a pattern expressing prohibition: **Çamurla oynamak yok, * {tamam**

mı?/oldu mu?} 'No playing with mud, * is that understood?' **Burada sigara içmek yok.** 'There will be no smoking here.' * **Gevezelik yok!** 'No talking! [lit., ** No {chattering/babbling}!]' **Ağlamak yok!** 'No crying!' *399: * 9.* warning: expressions of. → -mAk olmaz ['it won't do to do sth, one shouldn't, it's not appropriate to do sth'] → ol- 11 → olmaz.

Nedeni yok! '{There's no particular reason/Just because}', lit., ** '{Its reason/Its because} [is] non-existent.' **S: Mehmet, bugün pek keyfin yok, moralin bozuk gibi. Neden?** 'Q: Mehmet, you look kind of out of sorts today, like you are depressed. Why?' **C: Nedeni yok.** 'A: No particular reason.'

* **Öğrenme.nin yaş.ı yok!** '{One can learn at any age./It's never too late to learn./There's no age limit to learning [lit., ** Learning's age (is) non-existent].'

* *noun designating a language*.**s I** var 'He {knows/speaks} *noun designating a language*': {a: **Türkçe.si/b: İngilizce.si/c: Almanca.sı/d: Fransızca.sı**} var. 'He {knows/speaks} {a: Turkish/b: English/c: German/d: French}.' or '{There is a Turkish...version [or translation] of it [i.e., a book, etc.]./A Turkish...version [or translation] of it exists.}' This pattern with **var**, rather than one with the verb **konuş-** '-speak', e.g., **Türkçe konuşur**, is usually used to express 'He SPEAKS' the language. *524:26.* speech: - utter in a certain way.

* {**Zararı/Ziyanı**} yok. 'No problem., It doesn't matter.' [[A. **zarar**/P. **ziyan**] 'harm']: **A: * Geç kal.DIM, özür dilerim.** 'A: I'm sorry {I'M/I was} late.' **B: Zararı yok.** 'B: No problem.' *997:25.* unimportance: PHR. no matter.

4 '- be possible': * **Derman.ı olmayan dert yoktur.** 'There's no such thing as a trouble without a remedy [lit., ** A trouble {whose remedy is not possible/which doesn't have a remedy} does not exist].' **Dönüş.ü olmayan bir yol.a girdim.** 'I have set out {on/upon} [lit., entered] a road from which there is no return.' **Tövbe.si olmayan**

günah var mıdır? 'Is there a sin one cannot repent of?'

Olacak gibi değil 'It's impossible., It won't work out., It's not going to happen., It can't be done [lit., ** It isn't like it will be].': {**Moralinizi bozmak/Ümidinizi kırmak**} **istemem ama bu iş olacak gibi değil.** 'I don't want {to spoil your mood/to shatter your hopes}, but I don't think this {project/matter} is going to work out [lit., but this {project/matter} isn't going to work out].' *966:11.* impossibility: PHR. no can do.

Olacak {iş/şey} değil! 'It's {impossible/absurd}!, It's not going to happen!, It's out of the question!, It's unbelievable!, It's unheard of!, Can you believe it?, [Just] imagine!, Can you imagine?, How could such a thing happen?, How is it possible?': **Güpegündüz dükkanımı soymuşlar, olacak {iş/şey} değil!** 'They robbed my store in broad daylight! {It's unbelievable!/Can you believe it?}' **Bu yol haritası Orta Doğu'ya barış getirecekmiş. Ben bu.nA inanmıyorum; olacak {iş/şey} değil.** 'This road map was supposedly going to bring peace to the Middle East. I don't believe θ it; it's not going to happen.' *122:22.* wonder: INTERJ. imagine!; *966:11.* impossibility: PHR. no can do.

Olur. 'OK., All right., Fine., It's possible., Yes.', always appropriate: **A: * Yarın sinemaya gidelim mi?** 'A: {Do you want to go to the movies tomorrow?/lit., Shall we go to the movies tomorrow?}' **B: Olur, boşum.** 'B: OK. I'm free.' **A: Semra'ya benden çok çok selâm söyleyin.** 'A: Give Semra [f.] my very best regards.' **B: Olur efendim, söylerim.** 'B: OK {sir/ma'am}, I'll tell her.' *332:18.* assent: INTERJ. yes; *965:4* possibility: - be possible. → ≠ **Olmaz** below.

Olur mu? 'OK?, lit., Is that possible?': **A: Yarın sinemaya gidelim. Olur mu?** 'A: Let's go to the movies tomorrow, OK?' **B: Olur, boşum.** 'B: That's fine. I'm free.' **Çocuklar * uslu durun, anneniz.i kızdırmayın, * olur mu?** '[Come on] {kids/children}, * behave yourselves. Don't make your mother angry, * OK?' **Aşkolsun Ebru, * otele gitmek olur mu? Bu gece biz.de kalacaksın.** 'Shame on you Ebru, * how could you think of going to a hotel?! [lit., ** 'Is going to a hotel possible?' The implication being 'of course not.'] Tonight you'll stay at our place [lit., ** at us].'

* Olur mu olur. '{It's quite possible./[It] could well be}': * **Bana öyle geliyor ki hoca yarın haber vermeden sınav yapacak. Olur mu olur, o.nDAN her şey beklenir.** 'It seems to me that [our] teacher will give a pop quiz tomorrow [lit., ** will make an exam without giving (advance) notice]. {[It] Could well be/It's quite possible}, one never knows what he might do [lit., anything can be expected OF him].' *965:4* possibility: - be possible.

Olmaz. 'It's not possible., It's impossible., It can't be done., It won't do., Impossible., No.': **A: Yarın sinemaya gidelim mi?** 'A: {Do you want to go to the movies tomorrow?/lit., Shall we go to the movies tomorrow?}' **B: [Maalesef] Olmaz, ders çalışmam lâzım.** 'B: [Unfortunately,] I can't [lit., It's not possible]. I must study.' **A: * Şu ilaçları alabilir miyim?** 'Could I buy these medicines?}' **B: Tabii, ama * reçetesiz olmaz.** 'Of course, but * not without a prescription [lit., ** without a prescription is not possible].' **S: Bu.nun bizim.LE alaka.sı var mı?** 'Q: {Does that [i.e., matter, issue] concern θ us?/Is that of any concern TO us?}' **C: * Olmaz olur mu?** 'A: {How could it not?/How could it not be?}' *** Olmaz diye bir şey yok.** 'Everything is possible [lit., ** There is nothing called impossible].' Proverbs: * **{a: Hatasız kul/b: Kusursuz güzel} olmaz.** 'There is no such thing as {a: a servant of God [i.e., any will-possessing being, mortal] without faults./b: a beauty without {faults/blemishes}.}' * **"Olmaz! Olmaz!" deme hiç, olmaz olmaz.** 'Don't ever say "{It's impossible, It's impossible/It won't happen, It won't happen}". This expression [lit., 'It's impossible.'] is not correct', i.e., Everything is possible. Never say never. *966:11.* impossibility: PHR. no can do. → ≠ **Olur.**

Olmaz mı? 'OK?, Won't that do?, lit., Isn't that possible?': **Yarın sinemaya gidelim. Olmaz mı?** 'A: Let's go to the movies tomorrow, OK?' In response to an untimely phone call: **Ben de şimdi çıkıyordum, yarın konuşsak * olmaz mı?** 'I was just about to step out. * How about if we talk tomorrow?, OK? [lit., ** If we talk tomorrow, won't that do?]'

5 '- have' is expressed in Turkish in several patterns with **ol-**, all forms of the '- be' structures shown under **ol-** 3 above.
(5.1) '- have' in the sense of ownership AND ALSO presence on or with, i.e., '- have {A/SOME}...', i.e., with the INDEFINITE object in the equivalent ENGLISH, is expressed with the pattern *possessOR noun.[n]In + possessED noun.sI* **ol-**, lit., ** 'for {his/its} sth - be, - exist': **Ahmet'in kitab.ı var[dır].** 'Ahmet has {A book/SOME books}.' • Here the type of item is important, not its number, and the singular noun may be translated singular or plural.

The unstressed emphatic suffix **-DIr**, shown above following **var**, is found in writing and in formal speech in the 'witnessed' present tense, third person singular and plural, of '- have' sentences. [A 'witnessed' tense is one, like in the sentence above, not ending in **mIş**.] In such sentences it is not common in ordinary speech and is encountered mostly in statements and questions involving a general truth or a definition, which is why it is in brackets. For a comprehensive discussion of the senses this suffix may convey that are not treated here, see a standard Turkish grammar such as Lewis [2000].

A number or other word of quantity may precede the singular noun: **Ahmet'in {bir/üç/birçok} kitab.ı var[dır].** 'Ahmet has {a book/three books/many books}.' The possessed noun may be in the plural. Here the plurality of the subject is emphasized or the fact that that noun is of different types: **Ahmet'in kitapları var[dır].** 'Ahmet has some books.' In the witnessed present tense **ol-** = θ.

(5.2) '- have', more precisely '- be the owner of', is expressed with the pattern *possessOr noun + possessOR noun*.[n]In sahib.i ol-. With the DEFINITE object in the equivalent ENGLISH: <u>Ahmet kitab.ın sahib.i[dir].</u> 'Ahmet is THE owner of the book.' With the INDEFINITE object in the equivalent ENGLISH: Ahmet {bir/üç/birçok} ev.in sahibi[dir]. 'Ahmet is the owner of {a house/three houses/many houses}.'

(5.3) '- have {ON/WITH}', more precisely '[for sth] - be {on/with} sb', the usual pattern for indicating the presence or existence of sth in a PLACE is expressed as follows:
(5.3.1) '- have {A/SOME} {on/with}', i.e., with an INDEFINITE object in the equivalent ENGLISH is expressed with the pattern *possessOR noun*.DA + *possessED noun* ol-: <u>Ahmet'TE kitap var[dır].</u> 'Ahmet has {A book/SOME books} {ON/WITH} him [lit., ** ON Ahmet book (is) existent]'. In the witnessed present tense ol- = θ. • Here, as in 5.1 above, the type of item is important, not its number, and the singular noun may be translated singular or plural. Here too, a number or other word of quantity may precede the singular noun: Ahmet'te {bir/üç/birçok} kitap var[dır]. 'Ahmet has {a book/three books/many books} with him.' The possessed noun may be in the plural. Here the plurality of the subject is emphasized or the fact that that noun is of different types: Ahmet'te kitaplar var[dır]. 'Ahmet has some books with him.'
(5.3.2) '- have THE...{on/with}', i.e., with the DEFINITE object in the equivalent ENGLISH:
(5.3.2.1) With the Turkish subject PRECEDING the noun for person: • Note that var is absent in the present tense. *Possessed noun + possessor noun*.DA ol-: <u>Kitap Ahmet'te[dir].</u> 'Ahmet has THE book {on/with} him [lit., ** Book (is) ON Ahmet].' K i t a p l a r Ahmet'te[dir]. 'Ahmet has the books {on/with} him.'
(5.3.2.2) The Turkish subject may FOLLOW the noun for person: • Note that var is present except in the future tense. Presence and also ownership: *Possessor noun*.DA + *possessed noun* ol-: <u>Ahmet'te bu kitap var.</u> 'Ahmet has this book {on/with} him now [lit., ** On Ahmet this book [is] existent].' •

Note: WITHOUT **bu** or some other definite marker such as **benim**, etc., the object would be INDEFINITE in English, i.e., A book, SOME books, etc., and the pattern would be that of 5.3.1 above.

TABLES OF MAIN TENSES OF TURKISH '- HAVE' EQUIVALENTS BY PATTERN

Each pattern above is presented in detail below. The main tenses of each are given and under each tense, in both the witnessed and the inferential forms, are statements with the third person singular subject [**Ahmet**] and, as representative of the other persons, statements with the first person singular subject [**ben** 'I']. [As was noted under ol- 3, witnessed forms, i.e., those NOT ending with **mI ş**, convey a sense of certainty: they indicate that the speaker has witnessed the event or state mentioned or that it is generally accepted as fact. In contrast, inferential forms, i.e., the **mI ş** forms, also sometimes referred to as 'dubitative' or 'unwitnessed', convey the speaker's uncertainty or distance him from the event or state. This distance may be expressed by such English expressions as 'supposedly, they say that, it seems, I infer that', etc., or by expressions showing that the speaker is now aware of something he did not realize before or did not expect, such as 'I now realize that, It turns out that', etc.] For more complete paradigms, see a grammar such as Lewis 2000. Additional examples follow the tables.

(+) = affirmative sentence
(-) = negative sentence

(5.1) Table 1. '- have' in the sense of ownership and also presence or with: '- have {A/SOME}...', i.e., with the INDEFINITE object in ENGLISH

PRESENT TENSE
Witnessed
Third person singular subject
(+) Ahmet'İN kitab.I var[dır]. 'Ahmet has {A book/SOME books}.'
Note: **Ahmet**, the noun denoting the possessOR, has the possessOR suffix -[n]In. **Kitap** 'book', the noun denoting the thing possessED, has the possessED suffix -[s]I

287

'{his/her/its}': **kitab.I** '{his/her/its} book'. This is followed by the adjective **var** 'existent' and the verb **ol-**, which here = θ, i.e., No verb appears in the PRESENT tense witnessed. In the negative the adjective **yok** 'non-existent' replaces **var**.
(-) **Ahmet'İN kitab.I yok[tur].** 'Ahmet doesn't have {A book/ANY books}.' • Note that in all the examples in this entry under the heading 'indefinite object in English', in an affirmative sentence the SINGULAR noun **kitap** may be translated: {A book/SOME bookS}, in a negative sentence, {A book/ANY bookS}.

First person singular subject
(+) **[Ben.İM] kitab.IM var[dır].** 'I have {A book/SOME books}.'
(-) **[Ben.İM] kitab.IM yok[tur].** 'I don't have {A book/ANY books}.'

Inferential: Here ol- = i- and appears in the independent word **imiş** '{he/she/it} is SUPPOSEDLY' or more frequently, as below, in the attached equivalent **-mIş** and follows {**var/yok**}.

Third person singular subject
(+) **Ahmet'in kitabı var.mış.** 'Ahmet supposedly has {A book/SOME books}.'
(-) **Ahmet'in kitabı yok.muş.** 'Ahmet supposedly doesn't have {A book/ANY books}.'

First person singular subject
(+) **[Ben.İM] kitab.IM var.mış.** 'I supposedly have {A book/SOME books}.'
(-) **[Ben.İM] kitab.IM yok.muş.** 'I supposedly don't have {A book/ANY books}.'

PAST TENSE
Witnessed: Here ol- = i- and appears in the past tense in either the independent word **idi** '{he/she/it} was' or more frequently, as below, in the attached equivalent **-DI**.

Third person singular subject
(+) **Dün Ahmet'in kitabı var.dı.** 'Ahmet HAD {A book/SOME books} yesterday.'
(-) **Dün Ahmet'in kitabı yok.tu.** 'Ahmet DIDN'T have {A book/ANY books} yesterday.'

First person singular subject
(+) **Dün [benim] kitabım var.dı.** 'I had {A book/SOME books} yesterday.'
(-) **Dün [benim] kitabım yok.tu.** 'I didn't have {A book/ANY books} yesterday.'

Inferential: The PAST tense inferential forms are the SAME as the PRESENT tense inferential forms above, that is, {**imiş/-mIş**} can ALSO mean '{he/she/it} WAS supposedly'. Only the context, below provided by the word **dün**, will indicate which translation is appropriate: **Dün Ahmet'in kitabı var.mış.** 'Ahmet supposedly had {A book/SOME books} yesterday.' Etc.

In OTHER THAN the present or past tenses, the verb **ol-** occurs WITHOUT {**var/yok**}:

FUTURE TENSE
Witnessed
Third person singular subject
(+) **Yarın Ahmet'in kitabı olacak.** 'Ahmet will have {A book/SOME books} tomorrow [lit., ** Tomorrow Ahmet's book will be].'
(-) **Yarın Ahmet'in kitabı olmayacak.** 'Ahmet won't have {A book/ANY books} tomorrow [lit., ** Tomorrow Ahmet's book won't be].'

First person singular subject
(+) **Yarın [ben.İM] kitab.IM olacak.** 'I will have {A book/SOME books} tomorrow.'
(-) **Yarın [ben.İM] kitab.IM olmayacak.** 'I won't have {A book/ANY books} tomorrow.'

Inferential
Third person singular subject
(+) **Yarın Ahmet'in kitabı olacakmış.** 'Ahmet supposedly will have {A book/SOME books} tomorrow.'
(-) **Yarın Ahmet'in kitabı olmayacakmış.** 'Ahmet supposedly won't have {A book/ANY books} tomorrow.'

First person singular subject
(+) **Yarın [ben.İM] kitab.IM olacakmış.** 'I supposedly will have {A book/SOME books} tomorrow.'
(-) **Yarın [ben.İM] kitab.IM olmayacakmış.** 'I supposedly won't have {A book/ANY books} tomorrow.'

Additional examples

1. Yes-no questions: By the nature of the object possessed: 1.1 Physical objects as grammatical objects: **Gümrük memuru: Beyan edecek bir şeyiniz var mı?** 'Customs official: Do you have anything to declare?' **Yolcu 1: Hayır, beyan edecek bir şeyim yok.** 'Traveler 1: No, I have nothing to declare.' **Yolcu 2: Evet, iki dizüstü bilgisayarım ve bir kameram var.** 'Traveler 2: Yes, I have two laptop computers and a camera.' **S: * Gümrüğ.e tâbi eşyanız var mı?** 'Q: Do you have anything to declare [lit., anything subject to customs]?' **C1: Hayır, [gümrüğ.e tâbi eşyam] yok.** 'A1: No, I have nothing to declare.' **C2: Bu kamera gümrüğ.e tabi[dir].** 'A2: This camera [is subject to customs].' **{a: Banyolu/b: Duşlu/c: Manzaralı/d: Balkonlu/e: Televizyonlu/f: Klimalı} odanız var mı?** 'Do you have a room {a: with a bath?/b: with a shower?/c: with a view?/d: with a balcony?/e: with television?/f: with air-conditioning?} * **Nezle.yE karşı {bir şey/bir ilâcınız} var mı?** 'Do you have {sth/a medicine} for [lit., against] a cold?' **A: Çocuğunuz var mı?** 'A: Do you have any children?' **B: Bir kızım var efendim.** 'B: I have one daughter, {sir/ma'am}.' **A: * Allah bağışlasın.** 'A: May God not separate her from you.' **Üniversitenin hastanesi var mı?** 'Does the university have a hospital?'

1.2 Desires as objects: A waiter in a restaurant: **Bir arzunuz var mı, efendim?** '{What would you like to order, {sir/ma'am} [lit., ** Do you have a wish...]?', or just **Arzunuz?** 'Your order [lit., ** Your wish]?' Another alternative: * **Ne arzu edersiniz efendim?** '{What can I get you?/What would you like to order [lit., ** What do you wish]}, {sir/ma'am}?' * **S: Ben.DEN ricanız var mı?** 'Q: Is there something you would like me to do [lit., ** Do you have a request OF me]?' * **C: Siz.DEN çok acil, çok önemli bir ricam var.** 'A: I have a very urgent, very important request to make OF you.' **S: Türkiye'ye gidiyorum. * Bir isteğiniz var mı?** 'Q: I'm going to Turkey. * Is there sth I can bring back for you [lit., ** Do you have a wish]?' **C: Evet, size küçük bir paket versem götürebilir misiniz acaba?** 'A: Yes, if I gave you a small package, [I wonder] could you take it [with you]?'

1.3 Time as an object: **S: Sen bugün boş musun?** 'Q: Are you {free/off} today?' **C: Bugün hiç boş vaktim yok. Ama yarın boşum.** 'A: I don't have any free time today, but I'm free tomorrow.' * **Kaybedecek zamanımız yok.** 'We have no time to lose.' **Oğul: * Kahvaltı {yapmay.a/etmey.e} vaktim yok anne, hemen çıkmam lâzım.** 'Son: I don't have time * {to EAT} breakfast, mother. I have to {be off/leave} right away.' **Şimdi vaktim yok {öğleden sonra oynayalım./* iki saat sonra oynasak olur mu?}** 'I don't have time right now, {let's play in the afternoon./* How about if we play in two hours? [lit., If we play in two hours, will that be OK?]}'

1.4 Information as an object: **S: Büyük bir {a: trafik kaza.sı/b: yangın/c: deprem/d: zelzele/e: patlama} oldu. * Haberiniz var mı?** 'Q: There was a big {a: traffic accident./b: fire./c, d: earthquake./e: explosion.} * Have you heard [lit., ** Do you have news]?' **C: * Ya!** [often written **Yaa!** (pronounce: **Yâ!**) to reflect the pronunciation of this word when it expresses surprise] * **Hiç haberim yok.** 'A: * Oh really! * I haven't heard a thing about it [lit., ** I don't have any news at all].' **Bu konuda Mehmet beyin bilgisi var mı?** 'Does Mehmet bey have any information on this subject?'

1.5 Other objects: **Sağlık sigortan var mı?** 'Do you have health insurance?'

An 'or' question: **Haritası var mı, yok mu?** 'Does he have a map or not?'

2. Essential question-word questions: With h-beginning question words: **Hangi?** 'Which?': **S: Öğleden sonra Fatma'nın hangi ders.i var?** 'Q: Which class does Fatma have in the afternoon?' **C:**

Fatma'nın matematik ders.i var. 'A: Fatma has a math class.'

Hangisi? 'Which one [** of them]?': **S: Fatma'nın [kalemler.i.nin] hangi.si var?** 'Q: Which one [of the pens] does Fatma have?' [More common in this sense: **Fatma'DA [kalemler.i.nin] hangi.si var?**] **C: Fatma'nın [kalemler.i.nin] {a: yeni.si/b: eski.si/c: büyüğ.ü/d: küçüğ.ü/e: kırmızı.sı} var.** 'A: Fatma has {a: the new one/b: the old one?/c: the big one/d: the small one/e: the red one}.' [More common in this sense: **Fatma'DA [kalemler.i.nin] {a: yeni.si...} var.**]

Hangileri? 'Which ones [of them]?': **S: Fatma'nın [kalemler.i.nin] hangiler.i var?** 'Q: Which ones [of the pencils (or pens)] does Fatma have?' [More common in this sense: **Fatma'DA [kalemler.i.nin] hangiler.i var?**] **C: Fatma'nın [kalemler.i.nin] {a: yeniler.i/b: eskiler.i/c: büyükler.i/d: küçükler.i/e: kırmızılar.ı} var.** 'A: Fatma has {a: the new ones/b: the old ones/c: the big ones/d: the small ones/e: the red ones} [** of the pens].' [More common in this sense: **Fatma'DA [kalemler.i.nin] {a: yeniler.i...} var.**]

With **k**-beginning question words: **Kaç?** 'How many?': **S: Fatma'nın kaç kitab.ı var?** 'Q: How many books does Fatma have?' **S: Çocuklar.ın kaç kitab.ı var?** 'Q: How many books do the children have?' **C: Çocuklar.ın beş kitab.ı var.** 'A: The children have five books.' **Otel.in kaç oda.sı var?** 'How many rooms does the hotel have?'

* **Kaçar?** 'How many each?': **S: Çocuklar.ın kaçar kitab.ı var?** 'Q: How many books do the children {each have/have apiece}?' **C: Çocuklar.ın {a: bir.er kitab.ı/b: {iki.şer/dörd.er/ altı.şar} kitab.ı} var.** 'A: The children have {a: one book each./b: {two/four/six} books each.}' **S: Kaçar kitabınız var?** 'Q: How many books do each of you have?' **C: Birer kitabımız var.** 'A: We each have one book.'

Kim? 'Who?': **Kim.E sorunuz var?** 'Who do you have a question FOR?' **Kim.in para.sı var?** 'Who has some money?' * **Kim.DEN şüphen var?** '{Who do you suspect?/Who are you suspicious OF?}'

With **n**-beginning question words: **Ne?** 'What?': **S: Ne.si var?** 'Q: What does he have?' Also: 'What's {wrong/the matter} with him?' [With other possessor pronouns: {a: **Neyim/b: Neyin/c: Neyimiz/d: Neyiniz/e: Neleri} var?** 'What's wrong {a: with me?/b: with you [s.]?/c: with us?/d: with you [pl.]?/e: with them?}'] **C: {a: Ateş.i/b: Nezle.si/c: Tansiyon.u/d: Şeker.i/e: Kalb.İ} var.** 'A: He has {a: a fever/b: a cold./c: high blood pressure./d: diabetes./e: a heart condition.}' **Doktor bey, geceleri uyuyamıyorum. * Neyim var?** 'Doctor θ, I can't sleep at night. * What's the matter with me? [lit., What do I have?]' 85:45. disease: - ail.

Ne kadar? 'How much?': **S: * Daha ne kadar şeker var?** 'Q: How much sugar is left [lit., How much more sugar is there]?' **C1: Bir kilo kaldı.** 'A1: One kilo is left.' **C2: Hiç şeker yok.** 'A2: There isn't any sugar at all.' **S: * Daha ne kadar zamanım var?** 'Q: How much time do I {still have?/have left?}' **C1: İki saatiniz var.** 'A1: You have two hours.' **C2: Hiç vakit kalmadı.** 'A2: There's no time left [at all].' **C3: Vakit tamam.** 'A3: The time is up.'

3. Selected examples where the structure *noun*.sI ol- [lit., 'for {his/its} sth - be'] expresses '- have.' In alphabetical order by form of ol-, usually in the third person. Examples with other persons may appear in the entry.

Where **ol-** = **i-**: *noun*.sI {a: **varken** [= **var iken**]/b: **yokken** [= **yok iken**]} '{a: {while/since/as long as} {he/it} has/b: {while/since/as long as} {he/it} does not have}': **Para.NIZ varken** [= **Paranız {olduğu zaman/olduğunda/olunca}}] yeni bir araba alın.** 'Since YOU have the money, buy a new car.' **Para.sı yokken yeni bir araba alamaz.** 'As long as he doesn't have the money, he can't buy a new car.'

noun.sI {a: varsa [= var ise]/b: yoksa [= yok ise]} '{a: if {he/it} has/b: if {he/it} does not have}': **Para.sı varsa, yeni bir araba alır.** 'If he has the money, he'll buy a new car.' **Banka hesabım.A bir bakayım, [eğer] yeteri kadar para.M varsa, yeni bir araba alırım.** 'Let me {check/lit., take a look AT} my bank account. If I have enough money, I'll buy a new car.' **Çalınan mücevherlerinizle ilgili olarak herhangi bir kimse.DEN şüpheniz varsa lütfen söyleyin.** 'If there is anyone you suspect in connection with your jewelry that was stolen, please tell [us].'

noun.sI olacağı 'that he {is going to/will} have [lit., ** his sth's going to be]': As the subject of the sentence: **Vakt.i olacağı açık.** 'It's clear that he's going to have time.' As the object of the sentence: **Vakt.İM olacağı.nı biliyorum.** 'I know that I'm going to have time.'

noun.sI olan '{he/the one} who has sth [lit., ** the one whose sth {is/was}], the thing which has sth': As an adjective: **Soru.SU olan öğrenci var mı?** 'Is there a student who has a question?' * **Derman.ı olmayan dert yoktur.** 'There's no such thing as a trouble without a remedy [lit., ** A trouble which doesn't have a remedy does not exist].' As a noun: As the subject of the sentence: **Soru.SU olan var mı?** '{Does anyone have a question?/Is there sb who has a question?} [lit., ** His-question-being-one existent?]' * **Daha iyi bir fikr.İ olan varsa söylesin.** 'If anyone has a better idea, let him speak up.' * **Çocuğ.U olan var, olmayan var, olamayan var.** 'There are those who have children, those who don't have them, those who can't have them.' **Hiçbir şey.İ olmayan hiçbir şey kaybetmez.** 'He who has nothing loses nothing [lit., ** The one whose nothing is not, loses nothing].' As the possessor of another noun: **İş.İ olmayanlar.ın sayı.sı günden güne çoğalıyor.** 'The number of {the unemployed/those without work/lit., those who do not have work} is increasing day by day.' As the object of the sentence: **Soru.SU olan.A baktım.** 'I looked AT the one who had a question.'

noun.sI olduğu 'that {he/it} {has/had}, {his/its} having sth [lit., ** {his/its} sth's being]': As an adjective: **Para.MIZ olduğ.u zaman** [= **Paramız {olduğunda/olunca/varken}**] **bu arabayı aldık.** 'When WE had money, we bought this car.' As a noun: As the subject of the sentence: **Adam.ın bu kadar borc.U olduğ.u bilinmiyordu.** 'It was not known that the man had so much debt.' As the object of the sentence: **Bu kadar borc.U olduğ.u.NU doğrusu hiç ummuyordum.** 'I really never expected that he would have this large a debt [lit., his debt being this much].' **Ben o.NUN evli ve çocuk.larI olduğ.U.nu biliyordum.** 'I knew that he was married and had children [lit., ** know his being married and his children being].' In other constructions: **Evi olmadığı için bazen parklarda, bazen köprü altlarında gecelerdi.** 'Because he was homeless [lit., didn't have a home], he would sometimes spend the night in parks, sometimes under bridges.'

noun. s I olmalı '{he/it} {must/should have} sth [lit., ** {his/its} sth {must/should} be]': Necessity: **Para.M olmalı.** 'I must have some money [lit., ** MY money must be].' *962:10.* necessity: - be necessary.

noun.sI {olmalı/olsa gerek} '{he/it} {must/should have} sth [lit., ** {his/its} sth {must/should} be]' Inference: **Turan beyin her halde çok parası {olmalı/olsa gerek}. Bugünlerde çok para harcıyor.** 'Turan bey {must be very rich./lit., must have a lot of money.} He's been spending a lot [of money] these days.' *967:4.* probability: - be probable.

noun.sI olsa 'if {he/it} had [lit., ** if {his/its} sth were]': **Para.M olsa yeni bir araba alırdım.** 'If I had the money, I would buy a new car.'

noun.sI olsa gerek → *noun*.sI {olmalı/olsa gerek} above.

noun.sI olsaydı 'if [only] {he/it} had [lit., ** if {his/its} sth had been]': **Para.M olsaydı * neler yapardım!** 'If I had money, * you can't imagine what I'd do [lit., what things I'd do]!'

noun.sI olsun 'let {him/it} have it [lit., ** let {his/its} sth be]': As an object: **Baba çocuğuna: Her şey.İN olsun istiyorsun ama bu mümkün değil oğlum. * Sabretmey.i bilmen lâzım.** 'A father to his child: You want to have everything [lit., ** that YOUR everything be], but that's not possible. * You have to learn patience [lit., ** You have to know how to be patient].'

noun.sI olunca 'when {he/it} has [lit., ** when {his/its} sth is]': **Para.MIZ olunca [= Paramız {olduğu zaman/olduğunda/ varken}] yeni bir araba alacağız.** 'When WE have the money, WE'll buy a new car.'

noun.sI olup olma- 'lit., ** '[for] {his/its} sth - be or not - be': *noun*.sI **olup olmayacağı** 'whether {he/it} will have or not [lit., whether {his/its} sth will be or will not be]': As a noun: As the subject of the sentence: **Yarın vakt.İM olup olmayacağı belli değil.** 'It's not clear whether I'll have time tomorrow or not [lit., ** my time's being or not being].' As the object of the sentence: **Yarın vakt.İM olup olmayacağı.nI bilemiyorum.** 'I don't know [lit., can't know] whether I'll have time tomorrow or not.'

noun.sI olursa 'if {he/it} has [lit., ** if {his/its} sth {is/will be}]': **Vakt.İN olursa * biz.e gel.** 'If YOU have [the] time, {drop by/stop by/call on us} [lit., ** come to us].'

4. Miscellaneous examples: A mental state as an object: **Açık konuşmak gerekirse, bu tarz kitaplar.A ilgim yok.** 'To tell the truth {I'm not interested IN such books./lit., I have no interest IN such books.}' **Bu haber hakkında henüz bir yorumum yok.** 'I don't have an opinion about this news story yet.' **S: Haber doğru mu?** 'Q: Is the news correct?' **C: Yorum yok.** 'A: No comment.'

Time as an object: **Dün san.A uğrayacaktım ama vaktim yoktu.** 'I was going to call ON you yesterday, but I had no time.' **O kadar meşgulum ki kafamı kaşıyacak vaktim yok.** 'I'm so busy I don't even have time to scratch my head.'

A right as an object: **Arif de çok oluyor artık! Bu mesele.yE karışmay.a hiç hakkı yok!** 'Arif has really gone too far this time. He has no right at all to meddle IN this matter.' Proverb: **Aşağı.da oturmazsan yukarı.da da yerin yoktur.** 'If you can't sit below, you'll have no place above either.'

A benefit as an object: **Neyse uzatmayalım. * Bu tartışma.nın hiçbir fayda.sı yok.** 'Anyway let's not drag it [i.e., the discussion] out. * There's absolutely no point to this argument [lit., ** This argument has absolutely no use].'

A written document as an object: *name of a type of written document*.sI **var**: This structure is frequently used to indicate authorship rather than possession: *** Meşhur yazar.ın onbeş {a: kitab.ı/b: makale.si/c: yazı.sı} var.** 'The famous author HAS {WRITTEN/AUTHORED} fifteen {a: books/b, c: articles}' [lit., 'The author HAS fifteen {a: books/b, c: articles}.', a translation appropriate in contexts where possession rather than authorship is the issue]. *469:4.* possession: - possess; *547:19.* writing: - write.

(5.2) Table 2. '- have' in the sense of ownership only, lit., '- be the owner of', NOT '- have ON or WITH one'

PRESENT TENSE
Witnessed: Here ol- = θ, i.e., ol- does not appear. In the negative **değil** means 'not'.

Third person singular subject
(+) **Şimdi Ahmet ev.İN sahib.İ[dir].** 'Ahmet is the owner of the house now.'
(-) **Şimdi Ahmet ev.İN sahib.İ değil[dir].** 'Ahmet isn't the owner of the house now.'

First person singular subject
(+) [Ben] şimdi ev.in sahib.i.yİM. 'I'm the owner of the house now.'
(-) [Ben] şimdi ev.in sahib.İ değil.İM. 'I'm not the owner of the house now.'

Inferential: Here ol- = i- and appears in the independent word imiş or, as below, more frequently in the attached equivalent -[y]mIş.

Third person singular subject
(+) Şimdi Ahmet ev.in sahib.i.ymiş. 'Ahmet is supposedly the owner of the house now.'
(-) Şimdi Ahmet ev.in sahib.i değil.miş. 'Ahmet is supposedly not the owner of the house now.'

First person singular subject
(+) [Ben] şimdi ev.in sahib.i.ymişim. 'I'm supposedly the owner of the house now.'
(-) [Ben] şimdi ev.in sahib.i değil.mişim. 'I'm supposedly not the owner of the house now.'

PAST TENSE
Witnessed
Third person singular subject
(+) O zaman Ahmet ev.in sahib.i.ydi. 'Ahmet WAS the owner of the house at that time.'
(-) O zaman Ahmet ev.in sahib.i değil.di. 'Ahmet WASN'T the owner of the house at that time.'

First person singular subject
(+) O zaman [ben] ev.in sahib.i.ydim. 'I WAS the owner of the house at that time.'
(-) O zaman [ben] ev.in sahib.i değil.dim. 'I WASN'T the owner of the house at that time.'

Inferential: Here the verbs are the SAME as the PRESENT tense inferential forms above. Only the context or a time expression, such as o zaman below, will indicate which translation is appropriate: O zaman Ahmet ev.in sahib.i.ymiş. 'Ahmet was supposedly the owner of the house at that time.' Etc.

FUTURE TENSE
Witnessed
Third person singular subject
(+) Yarın Ahmet ev.in sahib.i olacak. 'Ahmet will be the owner of the house tomorrow.'

(-) Yarın Ahmet ev.in sahib.i olmayacak. 'Ahmet won't be the owner of the house tomorrow.'

First person singular subject
(+) Yarın [ben] ev.in sahib.i olacağım. 'I will be the owner of the book tomorrow.'
(-) Yarın [ben] ev.in sahib.i olmayacağım. 'I won't be the owner of the house tomorrow.'

Inferential
Third person singular subject
(+) Yarın Ahmet ev.in sahib.i olacak.mış. 'Ahmet will supposedly be the owner of the house tomorrow.'
(-) Yarın Ahmet ev.in sahib.i olmayacak.mış. 'Ahmet will supposedly not be the owner of the house tomorrow.'

First person singular subject
(+) Yarın ben ev.in sahib.i olacakmış.ım. 'I will supposedly be the owner of the house tomorrow.'
(-) Yarın ben ev.in sahib.i olmayacakmış.ım. 'I will supposedly not be the owner of the house tomorrow.' *469:4.* possession: - possess.

(5.3) '- have ON or WITH' in the sense of presence
(5.3.1) Table 3. '- have {A/SOME} {on/with}', i.e., with an INDEFINITE object in ENGLISH

PRESENT TENSE
Witnessed
Third person singular subject
(+) Şimdi Ahmet'TE kitap var[dır]. 'Now Ahmet has {A book/SOME books} {ON/WITH} him.' lit., ** 'Now ON Ahmet book [is] existent'. Note: **Ahmet**, the noun denoting the location or possessOR, has the locative suffix -DA: **Ahmet'te**. The word **kitap**, the noun denoting the thing present or possessed, follows, has no suffix, and is followed by **var** and **ol-**, which = θ in the present tense. In the negative **yok** replaces **var**:
(-) Şimdi Ahmet'TE kitap yok[tur]. 'Now Ahmet doesn't have {A book/ANY books} {ON/WITH} him.' lit., ** 'Now ON Ahmet book [is] non-existent'.

293

For the other persons substitute the pronouns for Ahmet: (+) Şimdi **benDE** kitap var[dır]. 'Now I have {A book/SOME books} {ON/WITH} me.', etc.

Inferential
Third person singular subject
(+) **Şimdi Ahmet'te kitap var.mış.** 'Ahmet supposedly has {A book/SOME books} {on/with} him now.'
(-) **Şimdi Ahmet'te kitap yok.muş.** 'Ahmet supposedly doesn't have {A book/ANY books} {on/with} him now.'

PAST TENSE
Witnessed
Third person singular subject
(+) **Dün Ahmet'te kitap var.dı.** 'Ahmet HAD {A book/SOME books} {on/with} him yesterday.'
(-) **Dün Ahmet'te kitap yok.tu.** 'Ahmet DIDN'T HAVE {A book/ANY books} {on/with} him yesterday.'

Inferential: Here the verb forms are the SAME as the PRESENT tense inferential forms above. Only the context or a time expression, such as **dün** below, will indicate which translation is appropriate: **Dün Ahmet'te kitap var.mış.** 'Ahmet supposedly had {A book/SOME books} {on/with} him yesterday'. Etc.

* In OTHER THAN present or past time, the verb **ol-** is used without {var/yok}:

FUTURE TENSE
Witnessed
Third person singular subject
(+) **Yarın Ahmet'te gazete olacak.** 'Ahmet will have {A newspaper/SOME newspapers} {on/with} him tomorrow.'
(-) **Yarın Ahmet'te gazete olmayacak.** 'Ahmet won't have {A newspaper/ANY newspapers} {on/with} him tomorrow.'

Inferential
Third person singular subject
(+) **Yarın Ahmet'te gazete olacak.mış.** 'Ahmet supposedly will have {A newspaper /SOME newspapers}{on/with} him tomorrow.'
(-) **Yarın Ahmet'te gazete olmayacak.mış.** 'Ahmet

supposedly won't have {A newspaper/ANY newspapers} {on/with} him tomorrow.' *469:4.* possession: - possess.

Additional examples

1. Yes-no questions: **S: Ahmet'te kitap var mı?** 'Q: Does Ahmet have {a book/any [*or* some] books} {on/with} him?' **C1: Evet, [Ahmet'te kitap] var.** 'A1: Yes, he does [lit., Yes, {there is a book/there are some books} {on/with} Ahmet].' **C2: Hayır, [Ahmet'te kitap] yok.** 'A2: No, he doesn't [lit., No, {there isn't a book/there aren't any books {on/with} Ahmet].'

An 'or' question: **S: Ahmet'te kitap var mı, yok mu?** 'Q: Does Ahmet have {a book/some [*or* any] books} on him or not?' **C1: [Evet,] Ahmet'te kitap var.** 'A1: Yes, he does [lit., ** Yes, {there is a book/there are some books} on Ahmet].' **C2: [Hayır,] Ahmet'te kitap yok.** 'A2: No, he doesn't [lit., ** No, there are no books on Ahmet].'

2. Essential question-word questions: **Kimde?** '{Who has?/lit., On [*or* With] whom?': **S: Kimde kitap var?** 'Q: Who has {a book/some books}? **C: Bende kitap var.** 'A: I do [lit., I have {a book/some books} on me].'

(5.3.2) '- have THE...{on/with}', i.e., with the DEFINITE object in ENGLISH:
(5.3.2.1) Table 4. The Turkish subject precedes the location, the person.
• Note that {var/yok} are absent.

PRESENT TENSE
Witnessed
Third person singular subject
(+) **Şimdi kitap Ahmet'te[dir].** 'Ahmet has THE book {on/with} him now [lit., ** 'Now book [is] ON Ahmet].' • Note the word order: **Kitap**, the subject in the Turkish, precedes **Ahmet**. **Ahmet**, the noun designating the person on whom the book is found, follows and has the locative case suffix: **-DA. Ol-** = θ.
(-) **Şimdi kitap Ahmet'te {değil[dir]/yok[tur]}.** 'Ahmet

doesn't have THE book {on/with} him now.'

Inferential
Third person singular subject
(+) **Şimdi kitap Ahmet'te.ymiş.**
'Ahmet supposedly has the book on him now.'
(-) **Şimdi kitap Ahmet'te {değil.miş/yok.muş}.**
'Supposedly Ahmet does not have the book {on/with} him now.'

PAST TENSE
Witnessed
Third person singular subject
(+) **Dün kitap Ahmet'te.ydi.**
'Ahmet HAD the book {on/with} him yesterday [lit., ** Yesterday the book was ON Ahmet].'
(-) **Dün kitap Ahmet'te {değil.di/yok.tu}.** 'Ahmet DIDN'T HAVE the book {on/with} him yesterday [lit., ** Yesterday book {was ON Ahmet/was not ON Ahmet}].'

Inferential: Here the verb forms are the SAME as the PRESENT tense inferential forms above: **Dün kitap Ahmet'te.ymiş.** 'Ahmet supposedly had the book {on/with} him yesterday.' Etc.

FUTURE TENSE
Witnessed
Third person singular subject
(+) **Yarın kitap Ahmet'te olacak.** 'Ahmet will have the book {on/with} him tomorrow.'
(-) **Yarın kitap Ahmet'te olmayacak.** 'Ahmet won't have the book {on/with} him tomorrow.'

Inferential
Third person singular subject
(+) **Yarın kitap Ahmet'te olacak.mış.** 'Ahmet will supposedly have the book {on/with} him tomorrow.
(-) **Yarın kitap Ahmet'te olmayacak.mış.** 'Ahmet will supposedly not have the book {on/with} him tomorrow.'

Additional examples

1. Yes-no questions: **S: Kitap Ahmet'te mi?** 'Q: Does Ahmet have the book {on/with} him?' **C1: Evet, kitap Ahmet'te.** 'A: Yes, he does [lit., ** Yes, the book is {on/with} Ahmet].' **C2: Hayır,**

kitap Ahmet'te değil. 'A2: No, he doesn't [lit., No, the book isn't {on/with} Ahmet.'

An 'or' question: **S: Kitap Ahmet'te mi, değil mi?** 'Q: Does Ahmet have the book {on/with} him or not?' **C1: Kitap Ahmet'te.** 'A1: Ahmet has the book {on/with} him.' **C2: Kitap Ahmet'te değil.** 'A2: Ahmet doesn't have the book {on/with} him.'

2. Essential question-word questions: With **h**-beginning question words:
Hangi 'Which?': **S: Fatma'da hangi gazete var?** 'Q: Which newspaper does Fatma have {on/with} her?' **C: Fatma'da Hürriyet gazetesi var.** 'A: Fatma has Hürriyet ['Freedom'] {on/with} her.'
Hangisi? 'Which one [of them]?': **S: Fatma'da [kalemler.in] hangi.si var?** 'Q: Which one [of the pens] does Fatma have {on/with} her?' **C: Fatma'da [kalemler.in] {a: yeni.si/b: eski.si/c: büyüğ.ü/d: küçüğ.ü/e: kırmızı.sı} var.** 'A: Fatma has {a: the new one/b: the old one/c: the big one/d: the small one/e: the red one} [of the pens] {on/with} her.'
Hangileri? 'Which ones [of them]?': **S: Fatma'da [kalemler.in] hangiler.i var?** 'Q: Which ones [of the pens] does Fatma have {on/with} her?' **C: Fatma'da [kalemler.in] {a: yeniler.i/b: eskiler.i/c: büyükler.i/d: küçükler.i/e: kırmızılar.ı} var.** 'A: Fatma has {a: the new ones/b: the old ones/c: the big ones/d: the small ones/e: the red ones} [of the pens] {on/with} her.'

With **k**-beginning question words:
Kimde? '{Who has?/lit., On [or With] whom?}': **S: Kitap kimde?** 'Q: Who has the book {on/with} him?' **C: Kitap Fatma'da.** 'A: Fatma has the book {on/with} her.'

(5.3.2.2) Table 5. The Turkish subject MAY FOLLOW the noun designating the person. This pattern conveys both presence and ownership. • Note that {var/yok} are present except in the future tense. Note also: WITHOUT **bu** or some other definite marker such as **benim**, etc., the object would be INDEFINITE in English, i.e., a book, any books, etc., and the pattern would be that of 5.3.1 above.

PRESENT TENSE
Witnessed
Şimdi Ahmet'te bu kitap {var/yok}. 'Ahmet {has/doesn't have} this book {on/with} him now [lit., ** Now on Ahmet this book (is) {existent/non-existent}].' • Note the word order: **Ahmet**, the person on whom the book is found, precedes the Turkish subject, **bu kitap**, and has the locative case suffix: **-DA**.

Inferential
Şimdi Ahmet'te bu kitap {varmış/yokmuş}. 'Ahmet {supposedly has/supposedly doesn't have} this book now.'

PAST TENSE
Witnessed
Dün Ahmet'te bu kitap {vardı/yoktu}. 'Ahmet {had/didn't have} this book {on/with}him yesterday.'

Inferential
Here the verb forms are the SAME as the PRESENT tense inferential forms above.
Dün Ahmet'te bu kitap {varmış/yokmuş}. 'Ahmet {supposedly had/supposedly didn't have} this book {on/with} him yesterday.' Etc.

FUTURE TENSE
Witnessed
Yarın Ahmet'te bu kitap {olacak/olmayacak}. 'Ahmet {will have/won't have} this book {on/with} him tomorrow.'

Inferential
Yarın Ahmet'te bu kitap {olacakmış/olmayacakmış}. 'Ahmet {will supposedly have/will supposedly not have} this book {on/with} him tomorrow.'

6 '- acquire, - get, - obtain {A/SOME}' • Note that the INDEFINITE object, is expressed with the pattern: **[bir]** *noun*.**sI** ol-, lit., ** 'for {its/his} sth - come into being', where **bir** is optional and where, in contrast to *noun*.**sI** ol- for '- have', as above in 5.1, ol- appears in ALL tenses: **Bankanın verdiği ucuz kredi sayesinde beniM de güzel bir araba.M oldu.** 'Thanks to the low rate of credit that the bank offered [lit., gave], I, too, got a fine car.' * **Son bağışlar.la birlikte tam bin kitab.IMIZ oldu.** 'Including [lit., together with] the latest donations, WE have now acquired a total of a thousand books.' *472:8*. acquisition: - acquire. → = **edin-**, = **elde et-**, = **ele geçir-** 2 → **geçir-**, = **sahip ol-** → **ol-** 12.

çocuğu ol- /DAn/ '- have {children/a child} /from/, - give birth to a child': **Birinci kocası.ndan üç çocuğu olmuş.** 'She had three children {from/WITH} her first husband.' * **Bu zavallı kadın.ın çocuğ.u olmuyor.** 'This poor woman can't have {children/a child}.' *1:3*. birth: - give birth. → = **doğur-**, = **dünyaya getir-**.

7 /DAn/ '- lose, - be deprived /OF/': **canından ol-** '- lose one's life, - die', mostly for an unexpected and undeserved death [P. **can** (-) 1 'soul'. 2 'life'], lit., '- be deprived of one's life': **Kavga edenleri ayırmaya çalışırken canından oldu.** 'He lost his life while attempting to separate those who were fighting.' **Hız tutku.su yüzünden canından oldu.** 'He lost his life as a result of his passion for speeding [lit., ** of his speeding passion].' *307:19*. death: - die. → = **hayata gözlerini {kapa-/kapat-}** → **{kapa-/kapat-}** 1, = **hayata gözlerini yum-** → **göz yum-** 1, = **hayatını {kaybet-/yitir-}**, = **öl-**, = **son nefesini ver-** ['- breathe one's last breath, - die'] → **ver-** 1, = **vefat et-**, ≠ **doğ-** 1, ≠ **dünyaya gel-** → **gel-** 1.

ekmeğinden ol- '- be deprived of one's livelihood, - lose one's livelihood' [**ekmek** 'bread'], lit., '- be deprived of one's bread': **Lütfen beni bu grev iş.i.nE karıştırmayın, ekmeğ.İM.den olmak istemem.** 'Please don't get me involved IN this strike business. I don't want to lose MY livelihood.' *473:4*. loss: - lose.

işinden ol- '- be fired, relieved of one's position' [**iş** 1 'work'. 2 'job'], lit., '- be deprived of one's job': *neutral*: **Tembelliğ.i yüzünden iş.İ.nden oldu.** 'He was fired because of [his] laziness.' *908:19*. ejection: - dismiss. → = *formal*: **görevden alın-** → **alın-** 1, = **görevine son veril-** → **son veril-**

→ veril-, ≠ {atan-/tayin edil-}, ≠ görevlendiril-, = tayin ol- → ol-12.

servetinden ol- '- lose one's fortune' [A. servet 'wealth, riches'], lit., '- be deprived of one's wealth': Kumar yüzünden servet.İ.nden oldu. 'He lost HIS fortune by gambling.' 473:4. loss: - lose. → {kaybet-/yitir-} ['- lose'].

8 /A/ '- be suitable, right, appropriate /FOR/, - fit, - be fit /FOR/': Bu ayakkabı siz.E olur. Deneyin isterseniz. 'These shoes will fit you. {Try them on, if you like./Why don't you try them on?}' Bu şapka başım.A olmuyor. '{This hat doesn't fit me./lit., This hat isn't [right] FOR my head.}' O mağazadaki pantolonlar.ın hepsi.ni tek tek denedim, * hiç bir.i [üzerim.E] olmadı. 'I tried on all the trousers in that store. * None of them fit [me].' 866:3. conformity: - conform. → = dur- 9, = gel- 2, = git- 6, = otur- 5, = uy-1, = yakış- 2.

9 '- be completed, finished, over, done, - reach a final stage, - become ready, mature':
(9.1) '- be done, completed, ready': Oğlum tamirciye sor bakalım bizim araba [tamir] oldu mu? 'Son, go ahead and ask the mechanic [lit., repairman] if our car is ready yet.' Eczacıya: Benim ilâçlarım [hazır] oldu mu acaba? 'To the pharmacist: {Is my prescription ready?/Is my medicine ready?/lit., Are my medicines ready}, I wonder?' S: Yemek oldu mu? 'Q: Is the food ready?' C: * Oluyor. 'A: It's on the way [lit., ** becoming].' Çay oldu. 'The tea is ready.' 405:14. preparation: - be prepared. → = hazır ol- → ol- 12.
(9.2) '- ripen, - become ripe': Üzümler daha olmadı. Koparma onları, yiyemezsin. 'The grapes {aren't ripe yet/haven't ripened yet}. Don't pick them. You won't be able to eat them.' 303:9. age: - mature.
(9.3) '- have passed, elapsed, - be over', with time-designating noun subjects: S: {Kaç yıldır/Kaç yıldan beri} burada çalışıyorsunuz? 'Q: {How many years} have you been working here?' C: İki yıl {oldu/oluyor} galiba, * niye sordunuz? 'A: It's probably

been [about] two years. * Why {do/did} you ask?' 836:6. the past: - pass. → = geç- 4.

10 * '- become subject to; - become afflicted with, - catch; - undergo', procedure, state, condition:
(10.1) None illness: * ameliyat ol-/A, not with tarafından/ '- be operated on /BY/, - have or undergo an operation [lit., ** - BE an operation]' [A. ameliyat (. . . -) 'medical operation']: Doktor hasta.nın yaşayabilme.si için ameliyat olma.sı gerektiğ.i.ni söyledi. 'The doctor said that for the patient to live, he would have to have an operation.' * Bu hastalık ameliyat ol.madan geçmez. 'This illness will not be cured [lit., pass] without an operation [lit., without having an operation].' Özel bir hastanede {çok ünlü bir doktor.A/çok ünlü bir cerrah.A} ameliyat oldu ama maalesef kurtarılamadı. 'He was operated on in a private hospital {BY a very famous doctor/BY a very famous surgeon}, but unfortunately he couldn't be saved.'

• Note the two following patterns including the type of operation: a) * Geçen yıl mide ameliyat.ı oldum. 'Last year {my stomach was operated on./I HAD an operation ON my stomach.} [lit., ** I became stomach operation...].'
b) Geçen yıl mide.M.DEN ameliyat oldum. Same [lit., ** I was operated FROM MY stomach...] * {Ameliyat/Mide ameliyat.ı} olmalı mıyım? 'Must I have {an operation?/an operation on my stomach?}' 91:29. therapy: - undergo treatment. → = ameliyat geçir-. → geçir- 2.

* aybaşı ol- '- have one's period, - menstruate' [aybaşı 'menstruation']: Zerrin bugün kendini iyi hissetmiyor, aybaş.ı olmuş. 'Zerrin isn't feeling well today. She's having her period.' 12:18. excretion: - menstruate. → = âdet gör- → gör-4.

* muayene ol- /A, not with tarafından/ '- be examined /BY/' [A. muayene (. - . .) 'an examining, examination']: Geçen ay özel bir hastanede çok iyi bir doktor.A muayene oldum. Bir çok film çektirdim, tahliller

yaptırdım, ama {kesin/net/sağlam} bir teşhis koyamadılar. 'Last month I was examined in a private hospital BY a very good doctor. I had many X-rays taken and tests made, but they couldn't come up with [lit., ** place] a definite diagnosis.' 91:29. therapy: - treat; 937:24. inquiry: - examine. → = muayeneden geç- → geç- 1.

* orgazm ol- '- come, - climax, - have an orgasm', for both sexes: Kadınlar.ın en önemli cinsel sorunlar.ı.ndan bir.i orgazm olamamalarıdır. 'One of the most serious sexual problems of women is that they are unable to have an orgasm.' 75:23. sex: - climax. → = boşal- 2 [more frequently for men but also for women], = gel- 3 [for both sexes].

* {sınav/imtihan} ol- /DAn/ '- take an examination /IN/, - be examined /IN/ [lit., ** - BE an examination]' [{sınav/A. imtihan} 'examination']: Bugün matematik.TEN ve İngilizce.DEN sınav oldum. İkisi de iyi geçti. 'Today I was examined IN mathematics and IN English. Both [exams] went well.' • The LITERAL translation into Turkish of the English '- TAKE an examination', i.e., {sınav/imtihan} al-, is not generally accepted standard Turkish. 938:4. answer: - answer. → = {sınava/imtihana} gir-, ≠ imtihan et- ['- test, - examine sb /IN [a subject]/'].

* sünnet ol- '- be circumcised' [A. sünnet 'ritual circumcision']: Erkek kardeşim bugün sünnet olacak. {Akşam.A} evimizde sünnet {düğün.ü/merasim.i} var. 'My brother is going to be circumcised today. {This evening/Tonight} there is a circumcision {ceremony} at our house.' 701:16. religious rites: - baptize.

* {şoke/şok} ol- /karşısında/ '- be shocked, - go into shock /AT/', non-medical sense [F. şok (Ku) 'shock']: Kimya.DAN kal.dığı.m.ı öğrenince şoke oldum. 'When I learned [that] I had failed {θ/IN} chemistry, I went into shock.' Yıllardır görmediğim arkadaşımı aniden karşımda görünce şoke oldum. 'When I

suddenly saw [standing there] in front of me my friend whom I had not seen {for/in} years, I went into shock.' * Aldığımız cevap KARŞI.SI.NDA şoke olduk. 'We were shocked AT the answer we received.' 131:7. inexpectation: - be startled. → şoka gir- ['- go /INTO/ shock', a medical condition].

* tıraş ol- [P. tıraş 1 'shaving, shave'. 2 'haircut'] (1) '- shave oneself, - shave': Tıraş olma.m {lâzım/gerek}. 'I need a shave [lit., ** My shaving (is) {necessary}].' Şimdi tıraş oluyorum, Davud'a söyle, sonra arasın. 'I'm shaving now, tell Davud to call back later [lit., tell Davud, have him call later].' * Tıraş olma.m.A gerek var mı? 'Do I have to shave [lit., Is there a necessity FOR my shaving]?' 3:22. hair, feathers: - cut or - dress the hair; 255:10. subtraction: - excise; 268:6. shortness: - shorten.
(2) '- get or - have a shave or a haircut': Since the word tıraş can mean 'shave' or 'hair cut', the following dialogue may occur: Müşteri: * Tıraş olmak istiyorum, * sıra var mı? 'Customer I want a 'cut'. * {Is anyone ahead of me?/lit., Is there a line]?' Berber: Saç [tıraşı] mı, sakal [tıraşı] mı? 'Barber: Hair or beard [cut]?' Müşteri 1: * Saç ve sakal tıraş.ı olmak istiyorum. 'Customer 1: I want a shave and a haircut [lit., ** a hair and beard cut].' Müşteri 2: {Saç/Sakal} tıraş.ı olmak istiyorum. 'Customer 2: 'I want {a hair cut/a shave}.' Berbere gittim, saç ve sakal tıraş.ı oldum. 'I went to the barber and had a haircut and a shave.' 3:22. hair, feathers: - cut or - dress the hair; 255:10. subtraction: - excise; 268:6. shortness: - shorten. → sakal tıraşı yap- ['- shave sb, - give sb a shave'] → yap- 3.

(10.2) With nouns designating ill health, an illness: *noun designating an illness* ol- '- catch, - come down with, - get *noun designating an illness*' [lit., ** - become the disease] [For '- have an illness', → ol- 5, (5.1) Table 1, Additional examples. 2. Essential question-word questions. With n-beginning question words: Nesi var?]: * {a: Bronşit/b: Kabakulak/c: Kızamık/d: Verem/e: Kanser} oldu. 'He came down with {a: bronchitis/b: the mumps/c: the measles/d: tuberculosis/e: cancer}.' → /A/ **yakalan-** 2 ['- catch /θ/ or - come down /WITH/, - be struck down /BY/ an illness']. *85:46a* disease: - take sick in general.

Some more examples with the most common conditions and ailments:

* **felç ol-** '- be or - become paralyzed, - have or - suffer a stroke' [A. felç (felCi) 'paralysis']: **Yüksek tansiyon {a: neden.i.yle/b: sebeb.i.yle/c: .dan dolayı/d: netice.si.nde} * dayım.ın sağ taraf.ı.nA inme indi. Hiç bir ilâç fayda etmeyince felç oldu.** '{a, b: Because of/c: Due to/d: As a result of} high blood pressure, * my [maternal] uncle had a stroke that affected his right side. Since no medicine was effective, he became paralyzed.' **Geçirdiği trafik kazasından sonra {dayım/ dayımın bacakları} felç oldu.** 'After a traffic accident [lit., After a traffic accident that he had], {my maternal uncle/the legs of my maternal uncle} became paralyzed.' *85:46b.* disease: - take sick in particular ways. → = **inme in-**.

fena ol- [A. fena (. -) 1 'bad; evil'. 2 'ill, sick'. 3 'terrible, miserable'] (1) '- feel faint, - feel suddenly sick': **Bu otobüs çok havasız, fena oluyorum.** 'This bus is very stuffy. I'm going to faint.' *85:46a.* disease: - take sick in general. → = **fenalaş-** 2, = **hastalan-**, = **hasta ol-** → ol-10.2, = **rahatsız ol-** 1 → ol-10.2, = /A/ **yakalan-** 2 ['- catch /θ/ or - come down /WITH/ an illness'], ≠ **iyileş-** ['- get better, - improve, - get well, - recover from an illness']. (2) '- be upset, - feel terrible, - feel anguish': **Osman'ın karı.sı.ndan boşandığını duyunca çok fena oldum.** 'When I heard that Osman had gotten divorced from his wife, I {was very upset/felt terrible}.' *96:16b.* unpleasure: - be distressed.

* **grip ol-** '- have or - come down with the flu, influenza' [F. **grip** 'influenza, grippe, flu']: * **Nihal grip olmuş, iki gündür okula gelemiyor.** 'Nihal has come down with the flu. For two days she hasn't been able to come to school.' **Havalar birden soğuyunca hepimiz grip olduk.** * **Hâlâ**

grib.iz. 'When the weather suddenly turned cold, all of us came down with the flu. * We still have it.' **İki hafta önce grip oldum ve hâlâ grib.im, oysa doktor bir haftada geçer demişti.** 'I got the flu two weeks ago. I still have it, although the doctor had said [that] it would be over [lit., pass] in a week.' *85:46b.* disease: - take sick in particular ways.

hasta ol- /DAn/ '- get sick /from/; - be ill /from/' [P. **hasta** 'ill']: S: **Dün niye gelmedin?** 'Q: Why didn't you come yesterday?' C: **Hasta oldum, * o yüzden gelemedim.** 'A: I got sick. * That's why I couldn't come.' **İki hafta önce hasta oldum, maalesef hâlâ hastayım, * henüz iyileşemedim.** 'I got sick two weeks ago. Unfortunately I'm still sick. * I haven't been able to get over it [lit., get well] yet.' **Sınıf.ta kalınca üzüntü.den hasta oldu.** 'When he was held back in school [lit., in class, i.e., didn't pass on to the next grade], he was so depressed [that] he got sick [lit., ** he got sick from depression].' *85:45.* disease: - ail; *85:46a.* : - take sick in general. → = **fena ol-** 1 → ol- 10.2, = **fenalaş-** 2 ['- feel faint, - feel suddenly sick, - take ill'], = **hastalan-** ['- become ill, - get sick'], = **rahatsız ol-** 1 → ol-10.2, = /A/ **yakalan-** 2 ['- catch /θ/ or - come down /WITH/ an illness'], ≠ **iyileş-** ['- get better, - improve, - get well, - recover from an illness'].

* **nezle ol-** '- catch or - get a cold' [A. **nezle** 'a cold']: **Sermet nezle oldu, üşütmüş olmalı.** 'Sermet has caught a cold. He must have caught a chill.' **Geçen hafta nezle olmuştum, * hâlâ nezleyim.** 'I caught a cold last week, and * I still have it.' *85:46b.* disease: - take sick in particular ways. → **soğuk al-** ['- get a chill, - catch a chill', the early stage of a cold] → al- 3, **üşüt-** 2. Same.

rahatsız ol- (1) /DAn/ '- feel or - become indisposed, slightly ill, sick, - be under the weather /from/' [**rahatsız** 'uncomfortable, indisposed']: **Dün akşam yediğim yemekler.den rahatsız oldum, hâlâ rahatsızım.** 'Last night I got sick from the food that I ate. I'm still sick.' *85:45.* disease: - ail; *85:46a.* : - take sick in general. → = **fenalaş-** 2

Part 1: Turkish-English Dictionary of Verbs

['- feel faint, - feel suddenly sick, - take ill'], = **fena ol-**. Same. → ol- 10.2, = **hastalan-** ['- become ill, - get sick'], = **hasta ol-**. Same. → ol- 10.2, = /A/ **yakalan- 2** ['- catch /θ/ or - come down /WITH/ an illness'], ≠ **iyileş-** ['- get better, - improve, - get well, - recover from an illness'].
(2) /DAn/ '- feel or - become ill at ease, uncomfortable /from/': **Ankara'dan Antalya'ya yaptığım otobüs yolculuğunda çok rahatsız oldum. Çünkü yanımdaki kadın çok konuşuyordu.** 'On the bus trip that I made from Ankara to Antalya I became very uncomfortable because the woman next to me [lit., at my side] was talking too much.' * **Ses.ten rahatsız olmam.** 'Noise doesn't bother me [lit., ** I don't become uncomfortable from noise].' *96:13.* unpleasure: - annoy. → ≠ **rahat et-**, ≠ **rahatla-**.

11 The meanings of certain forms of **ol-** do not fall clearly or exclusively into any one of the meanings given under numbers 1-10 above. We give these forms here in alphabetical order. Forms without examples below will be found with examples in sections 1-10 of **ol-** above, as indicated after each such item.

ola: * **Hayrola?** 'What's up?, What's going on?, What's the matter?, What's wrong?' [A. **hayır** (haYRı) 'good fortune, well being' + **ola** 'may it be'], lit., 'May it [i.e., whatever has happened] be for the best': **Hayrola, pek {telaşlı} görünüyorsun. {Ne oldu?/Bir şey mi oldu?}** 'What's the matter, you look very {excited/agitated/ *colloq.* uptight}. {What happened?/ Has sth happened?}' **Hayrola, yüzün kıpkırmızı, hasta mısın?** 'What's the matter? Your face is quite red. Are you ill?' **Hayrola! Ne var?** 'Good news, I hope! What's up?' *133:13.* premonition: - promise; *830:* * *14.* event: PHR. what's up? Some other more common expressions for asking 'What's going on?, What's happening?, What's up?': **Ne var ne yok?** lit., ** 'What existent, what not existent?', **N'aber?** = **Ne haber?** 'What news?'

olacak: olacak gibi değil 'it's impossible, it won't work out, it's not

going to happen, it can't be done [lit., ** it isn't like it will be]' → ol- 4.

olacak {iş/şey} değil! 'It's {impossible/absurd}!, It's not going to happen!, It's out of the question!, It's unbelievable!, It's unheard of!, Can you believe it?, [Just] imagine!, Can you imagine?, How could such a thing happen?, How is it possible?' → ol- 4.

* **{Ne olacak?/Ne olmuş?}** 'So what [of it]?', i.e., It doesn't matter: **A: Nevin bugün gelmeyecek.** 'A: Nevin [f.] isn't going to come today.' **B:** * **Ee, {ne olmuş/ne olacak} yani?** * **Gelmezse gelmesin!** 'B: Well, so what? * It's no big deal if she doesn't come [lit., ** If she doesn't come, let her not come].' *221:6.* presence: - be present; *997:26.* unimportance: PHR. what does it matter?

Olan {oldu/olmuş}. 'What's done is done., It's too late now.', i.e., No use crying over spilled milk. **Arabamı çarptığın için artık üzülme, ne yapalım, olan oldu.** 'Stop worrying now [lit., Don't worry] about having hit my car [lit., because you hit my car]. What can we do? What's done is done.' **Olan olmuş, yapılacak bir şey yok.** '{It's over and done with/What's done is done}. There nothing to be done.' *845:* * *21.* lateness: PHR. it's too late. → = **İş işten geçti.** → geç- 1.

* **olarak** lit., 'being'. Various translations. More than one may be appropriate in a single sentence: **(1)** 'being': **Hipokrat yemini etmiş bir doktor OLARAK ayrım yapmadan bütün hastalarımı tedavi etmeye çalışırım.** 'BEING a doctor who had taken the Hippocratic oath, I try to treat all my patients, making no distinction among them.'
(2) 'as', following a noun: **Kendimi başkası OLARAK tanıttım.** 'I passed myself off AS someone else [i.e., as someone I was not].' **Beşiktaş'A bu yılın şampiyonu OLARAK bakıyorum.** 'I regard θ Beşiktaş [i.e., a soccer team] AS this year's champion.' **Bu.nA çare OLARAK ne öneriyorsunuz?** 'What do you recommend AS a solution FOR this [problem]?' **Fabrika sahibi işçiler.in grev**

300

karar.ı.nı delilik OLARAK nitelendirdi. 'The owner of the factory characterized the workers' decision to strike AS madness.' Hemen hemen hiç bir ülke Kıbrıs'I devlet OLARAK tanımadı. 'Almost no country has recognized Cyprus AS a state.' Askerliğ.İM.i {er/çavuş/yedek subay} OLARAK yaptım. 'I did my military service AS {a private/a sergeant/a reserve officer}.' Sadece ders kitaplarını {okumak.la} yetinmedim. Ek OLARAK başka kaynaklar da kullandım. 'I wasn't satisfied {to read/with reading} only the text books, I also used other sources AS supplementary reading [lit., ** as supplement].' Üniversiteyi bitirince Millî Eğitim Bakanlığı tarafından öğretmen OLARAK küçük bir kasaba.yA atandım. 'When I had finished {university/college}, I was appointed by the Ministry of Education AS a teacher TO a small town.' * Herkes başkası.nı {sorunların/problemlerin} sorumlusu OLARAK görüyor. 'Everyone regards someone else [AS] responsible for the problems.' Derede yüzen odun parçalarını toplayıp yakacak OLARAK kullanıyorduk. 'We collected the pieces of wood floating on the stream and used them AS firewood.'
(3) 'ly' adverbs, following an adjective. Aşağıdaki kelimeleri {alfabetik OLARAK/alfabe.yE göre} sıralayın. 'Arrange the words below {alphabetical.LY/in alphabetical order [lit., according to the alphabet]}.' Doktorun verdiği hapları her gün düzenli OLARAK alıyorum. 'Every day I regular.LY take the pills [that] the doctor prescribed [lit., gave].' İkinci Dünya Savaşından sonra pek çok ülke ekonomik OLARAK geri kaldı. 'After the Second World War, many countries remained economical.LY behind.' Memur maaşların.dan vergi {otomatik OLARAK/otomatik.MAN} kesiliyor. 'Taxes are {automatical.LY} deducted from employee salaries.' Bu çok yaygın OLARAK kullanılan bir {a: deyim/b: ifade/c: cümle/d: atasözü}. 'This is a very wide.LY used {a: idiom/b: expression/c: sentence/d: proverb}.'
(4) 'θ', i.e., not translated, meaning in a certain condition: Çıplak OLARAK denize giren kadını görünce tahrik oldum. 'When I saw the woman going into the {ocean/sea} θ naked, I got turned on.' İkinci Dünya Savaş.ı.ndan sonra Almanya, Doğu ve Batı OLARAK iki.yE bölündü. 'After the Second World War, Germany was divided INTO two [parts]: θ East and West.' Kayıp kadın {ölü [olarak]/boğulmuş OLARAK} bulundu. 'The woman who had disappeared was found {θ dead/θ {strangled/drowned}}.' Directions in a cookbook: 20 dakika pişirip sıcak OLARAK servis yapın. 'Cook for 20 minutes and [then] serve θ hot.' Bu cinayet {sır/muamma} OLARAK kalacak. 'This homicide will remain θ a mystery.'
(5) 'in', following different parts of speech: Ayrıntılı OLARAK meselelerimiz.İ konuştuk. 'We spoke IN detail about our problems.' Otele olan borcumu nakit OLARAK ödedim. 'I paid my hotel bill [lit., what I owed θ the hotel] IN cash.' With the names of languages: Biz.E biraz kendiniz.DEN bahseder misiniz? * Türkçe OLARAK lütfen. 'Would you please tell us a little ABOUT yourself? * IN Turkish please.'
(6) 'at' with verbs of estimation following a number: Kalabalığı 6 bin kişi OLARAK tahmin ettik. 'We estimated the crowd {AT/TO BE/AS BEING} 6,000 people.'
(7) other expressions: Şu an için {kesin/kati} [OLARAK] bir şey söyleyemiyorum ama galiba bu dersi geçtim sonunda. 'For the moment I can't say FOR SURE, but I think I have probably finally passed this course.' Enflasyon.u önleyecek tedbirler.LE ilgili OLARAK senin.LE aynı fikirleri paylaşmıyorum. 'I don't share your ideas CONCERNING measures to be taken {in regard to/against} θ inflation.' Dünkü olay.LA ilgili OLARAK polis şüpheli şahısları toplamaya başladı. 'The police began to gather suspicious persons IN CONNECTION WITH yesterday's incident.' *384:11.* manner, means: somehow.

* **Oldu.** 'OK!, All right!, Fine., Agreed.' [= **Tamam.**] *informal, usually not used to a superior:* One friend to another: A: **Saat yedide**

bize gel, oldu mu? 'A: Be at [lit., Come to] our place at seven o'clock, {OK?/agreed?}' **B: Oldu.** 'B: {OK./Agreed.}' A mother to her child: **Çamurla oynamak yok, oldu mu?** 'No playing with mud, is that understood?' *399: * 9.* warning: expressions of. → = **Anlaşıldı mı?** ['Is that understood?'] → **anlaşıl-.** *332:18.* assent: INTERJ. yes.

Oldu bitti. 'It's over and done with [lit., It happened, it's finished].' **Neyse, oldu bitti, * bu mesele.yE takılıp kalmayalım artık, ileri.ye bakalım.** 'Anyway, it's over and done with. * Let's not get hung up ON this problem now. Let's forget about it and {move on/look to the future}.' *819:14.* end: PHR. that's all.

oldubitti 'a done deal, a fait accompli'. An older and today more learned equivalent: **emrivaki: Arkadaşlar, bir {oldubitti/ emrivaki} karşısındayız, bence sonuçlarını iyice düşünmeden bu anlaşmayı imzalamayalım.** '{Guys/Friends}, we are faced with {a done deal/a fait accompli}. I think we shouldn't sign this agreement without considering the consequences carefully [lit., ** According to me, let's not sign this agreement...]' **Oğlumuz biz.E danışmadan o kız.LA evlenmey.e karar vermiş, düğün davetiyelerini bile bastırmışlar. {Oldubitti/ Emrivaki} karşısındayız yani, * ne yapabiliriz ki?** 'Our son decided to marry that girl without consulting us. They even printed the wedding invitations! So we're faced with {a done deal/a fait accompli}, * what can we do?' **Ben bu tür {oldubittileri/emrivakileri} hiç sevmem.** 'I don't like such done deals at all.' *328:3.* action: NOUN act.

Oldu mu? 'Is that understood?' → oldu, above.

oldu olacak 'now that things have {gone so far/reached this point}': **Epey geç oldu ama oldu olacak sabahlayalım da şu işi bitirelim artık, yarına kalmasın.** 'It's quite late, but {now that matters have gone so far/now that we've reached this point}, let's finish this work now so that we don't have to deal with it tomorrow [lit., it isn't

left to tomorrow].' *845: * 21.* lateness: PHR. it's too late.

oldu olmadı 'it's been barely': **Bu işe başlayalı on yıl oldu olmadı.** 'It's been barely ten years since he began this job.' **İşe başlıyalı iki hafta oldu olmadı, * müdürle birbirimiz.e girdik, * iyi mi!** 'I had been on the job [for] barely two weeks [lit., It had been barely two weeks since beginning the job] * when the director and I started going at each other [i.e., fighting]. * {How do you like that!/How's that!/Can you imagine!}' *223:8.* nearness: - be near.

* Nasıl ol-...da...? '{How is it that...?/*informal*: How come...?}' → ol- 2.

olduğu: olduğu gibi (1) 'as it {is/was}': **Maaşını * olduğu gibi karısı.na teslim eder.** 'He turns his whole salary [lit., * 'as it is', i.e., as he received it, without removing any part of it] over to his wife.' **İnsanları olduğu gibi kabul etmeliyiz.** 'We must accept people as they are.' **Amcam eskiden olduğu gibi şimdi de çok sigara içiyor. * Hiç olmazsa biraz azaltsaydı!** 'My [paternal] uncle smokes just as he used to. * If he would at least just cut down a bit!' **Dünyanın her yerinde olduğu gibi {bizde/bizim ülkemizde} de bir takım {üçkâğıtçılar} var.** 'Just as everywhere else [lit., ** in every place of the world], in our country [lit., {among us/in our country}] too there are all kinds of [lit., ** a set of] {swindlers/cheats/crooks}.' *777:9.* sameness: ADV. identically.
(2) 'as it happened': **Lütfen bana kazayı olduğu gibi anlat, * kendin.den bir şey katma!** 'Tell me about the accident just as it happened. * Be completely objective [lit., ** Don't add anything from yourself].' *777:9.* sameness: ADV. identically.
(3) 'besides being; besides having': → **olduğu kadar** below and substitute it in the examples there. *253:11.* addition: ADV. additionally.

olduğu halde 'although, inspite of being, despite being [lit., in the state of {his/its} being]': **Hasta olduğu halde okula geldi.** 'Although he was ill, he came to

302

school.' In other persons: **Hasta olduğ.UM halde, okula geldim.** 'Although I was ill, I came to school.' *338:8.* compensation: ADV., CONJ. notwithstanding. → = **olmakla {beraber/birlikte}** below, = **olmasına {rağmen/karşın}** below.

olduğu kadar 'besides being; besides having': **O kadını çok beğeniyorum; güzel olduğu kadar akıllı da.** 'I like that woman a lot. Besides being beautiful, she's also intelligent.' **Oda küçük olduğu kadar karanlık da.** 'Besides being small, the room is dark.' **İsmail bey çok zengin bir insan. Pek çok {gayri menkul.u/taşınmaz.ı} olduğu kadar {yastık altında/bankada} da epeyce parası var.** 'Ismail bey is a very rich man. In addition to having a lot of property [*or* real estate], he has quite a lot of money {under his pillow/in the bank}.' *253:11.* addition: ADV. additionally. → also **mümkün olduğu kadar** → ol- 12.

oldum olası 'for as long as anyone can remember, from time immemorial, always, never [when followed by a negative verb]'. This is an invariable form used mostly in sentences either with a first-person singular subject or some other first person-singular reference. This is due to the presence of the first-person singular form **oldum**. With a first-person singular subject: **Biliyorsun seni oldum olası çok beğeniyorum, seviyorum. Benim.LE evlenir misin?** 'You know that I have always really liked you, loved you. Will you marry θ me?' **Oldum olası doğayı sevmişimdir.** 'It seems I have always loved nature.' With a non-first person singular subject: **Oldum olası o adamı hiç gözüm tutmadı zaten.** 'I have never {thought much of/had much confidence in} that fellow anyway [lit., ** My eyes have never held that man anyway].' **Biz oldum olası sloganları seven bir ulus olmuşuz.** 'We have always been a country that loves slogans.' **Kızıl saçlı kızlar oldum olası beni çekmişlerdir.** 'Redheads have always attracted me.' *828:11.* perpetuity: ADV. always. Only in reference to the first-person singular:

= **kendimi bildim bileli** [lit., ** 'as long as I have known myself'].

olmadık 'unheard-of, incredible, unprecedented': **Keşke onun.LA hiç tanışmasaydım. * Başıma olmadık işler çıkardı.** 'I wish I had never met θ him. * He caused {me all kinds of incredible trouble/got me in all kinds of incredible trouble}.' *869:10.* abnormality: unusual.

olmak üzere (1) 'θ [lit., (as) being]': *** Sınıfımızda iki.si Alman, dörd.ü Fransız ve altı.sı Amerikalı olmak üzere toplam on iki kişi var.** 'There are altogether 12 people in our class: two Germans, four French [students], and six Americans [lit., two of them being German, four of them French, and six of them American].'
(2) '- be on the point of being, - be almost, - be [just] about to be, - be on the verge of being': **Lütfen hemen kalkmayın, biraz daha kalın; * kahveniz olmak üzere.** 'Please don't get up. Stay {a little/a bit} longer. * Your coffee is almost ready.' *223:8.* nearness: - be near.

olmakla {beraber/birlikte} 'although, inspite of being, despite being [lit., ** together with being]': **İstanbul doğumlu olmakla beraber aslen Gaziantepli.** 'Although he was born in Istanbul, he is really from Gaziantep [i.e., has his home and family there].' **Doğru dürüst bir eğitimi olmamakla beraber ağzı iyi lâf yapıyor.** 'Although he hasn't had a proper education, he speaks a good line [lit., ** his mouth makes good {words/expressions}].' *338:8.* compensation: ADV., CONJ. notwithstanding. → = **olduğu halde** above, = **olmasına {rağmen/karşın}** below.

{olmalı/olsa gerek} → ol- 3, Additional examples, 3. Selected examples...

olmasına {rağmen/karşın} 'although he {is/was}, inspite of the fact that he {is/was}': **Ali hasta olması.nA {rağmen/karşın} okula gitti.** 'Ali went to school although he was ill.' *338:8.* compensation: ADV., CONJ. notwithstanding. → = **olduğu**

303

halde, = olmakla {beraber/bir-
likte} above.

* Olmaz. 'It's not possible., It's
impossible., It can't be done., It won't
do., Impossible., No.' → ol- 4 above.

Hiç belli olmaz. '{It's hard to
say./It's impossible to say./You can
never tell.} [lit., It {won't be/isn't}
clear.]': S: Turhan bey bugün
gelir mi? 'Will Turhan bey come in
today?' C: * Hiç belli olmaz,
{bakarsın/belki} gelir. *
Gelmeyebilir de. '{It's hard to
say./It's impossible to say./You can
never tell.} {Maybe} he will. * He
may even not come.' 970: * 30.
uncertainty: PHR. it's not certain.

hiç olmazsa 'at least':
Biliyorum, pek vaktin yok ama
hiç olmazsa bir gün kal. 'I know,
you don't have much time, but stay at
least one day.' Amcam eskiden
olduğu gibi şimdi de çok sigara
içiyor. * Hiç olmazsa biraz
azaltsaydı! 'My [paternal] uncle
smokes just as he used to. * If he
would {at least/just} cut down a bit!'
248:10. insignificance: ADV. in a
certain or limited degree.

-mAk olmaz 'it won't do to do
sth, one shouldn't, it's not appropriate
to do sth': Bu iş.TEN kaçmak
olmaz. 'It won't do to avoid θ this
{job/task}.' Aç kalarak zayıflamak olmaz. 'One shouldn't [lit., It
isn't proper to] lose weight by
starving oneself [lit., by remaining
hungry].' Proverb: Din.i dinar.A
satmak olmaz. 'One shouldn't sell
one's religion [lit., the religion] FOR
dinars.', i.e., for money [dinar a
monetary unit]. Yaramazlar.A
uymak olmaz. 'It won't do to
emulate θ those who {are
naughty/misbehave}.' 638:2. * 1.
wrong: - do the wrong thing. → -
mak yok ['No...ing!', a pattern
expressing prohibition] → ol- 3,
Additional examples. b) 4.
Miscellaneous additional examples.

olmuş: Ne olmuş? → olacak →
* {Ne olacak?/Ne olmuş?}
above.

olsa: olsa da olur, olmasa
da 'it doesn't make any differencce,
it doesn't matter if it happens or not,
it may happen or not', i.e., it's not
important: Bir araba almak

istiyorum ama çok da önemli
değil, olsa da olur olmasa da,
çünkü aslında metroyla her
yere gitmek mümkün. 'I want to
buy a car, but [actually] that's not so
important. * It really doesn't make
any difference because it's possible to
go everywhere by {subway/metro}.'
997:24. unimportance: PHR. it does
not matter. → = farketmez →
farket- 2.

olsa gerek → {olmalı/olsa}
above.

olsa olsa 'at most, at the [very]
most, the worst that can happen':
Olsa olsa bu karpuz iki kilodur,
* daha fazla değildir. 'This water
melon weighs [lit., is] two kilos at
most, * no more.' Ankara'ya
giderken İstanbul'A da
uğrayacağım, ama orada {olsa
olsa/en fazla} iki gün kalırım
her halde. 'On my way to Ankara
[lit., While going to Ankara], I'll stop
off IN Istanbul too, but I'll probably
stay there {at most} [only] two days.'
Hocayla konuşup sınavı tekrar
almak istediğini söyle,
çekinmen.E gerek yok. Olsa
olsa "hayır" der. 'Talk {to/with}
the teacher and tell him [that] you
want to retake the exam. {Don't be
shy./lit., There's no need for you to
hesitate.} The worst that can happen
is that he'll say "no".' 248:10
insignificance: ADV. in a certain or
limited degree. → = olsun olsun
below.

olsun (1) 'Fine., That's fine.,
That's OK., I don't care., I don't
mind., So be it!, All right., Never
mind.': Çocuk: Anne matematik
ödevimi bugün bitiremeye-
ceğim galiba. 'A child: Mother, I
don't think I'll be able to [lit., I think
I won't be able to] finish my math
homework today.' Anne: Olsun
yavrum, önemli değil, yarın
yaparsın. 'The mother: {Never
mind/That's OK}, dear. That doesn't
matter. You'll do it tomorrow.' A: *
Bence sen o dersi bırak, çok
zor. 'A: * {I say/I think} you should
drop that class. It's too difficult.' B:
Olsun, önemli değil. * Zoru
başarmak bana daha fazla
heyecan verir. 'B: That's OK. It
doesn't matter. * [The challenge of]
succeeding in something difficult is
more exciting.' 332:20. assent: PHR.
so be it.

(2) 'that may be {so/true}, but; OK, but; yes, but; be that as it may': A: * Sigarayı bırak, yoksa genç yaşta ölürsün. 'A: Stop smoking, or you'll die at an early age.' B1: Olsun, * ben zaten bıktım bu hayat.TAN. 'B1: That may be true, but I've about had it with this life anyway.' B2: Proverb: Atın ölümü arpadan olsun. 'B2: Let the horse die from eating barley [lit., Let the death of the horse be from barley].', i.e., from something that provides sustenance, pleasure, i.e., At least I'll die from sth that gives me pleasure. *338:8.* compensation: ADV., CONJ. notwithstanding.
(3) 'at least, if only, even': * Sana çok kırgınım. İki aydır İstanbul'dasın ama {bir kez/bir kere/bir defa} olsun beni aramadın. 'I'm very {offended/hurt}. You've been in Istanbul for two months, but you haven't looked me up even {once}.' *248:10* insignificance: ADV. <in a certain or limited degree>. = hiç olmazsa above, = hiç değilse, = bari.

olsun olsun olsun 'at the very most, at most': A: Olsa olsa oraya yedi saatte gidilir. 'A: It takes at most seven hours to get there.' B: * Bence de. Olsun olsun sekiz saat olsun, haydi * bilemedin dokuz saat [olsun]. * Ne farkeder ki? Sabah erkenden yol.a çıkarsak akşama ora.ya varırız. 'B: * I agree. Let's say it'll take [lit., Let it be] at most eight hours. OK, * let's say we're wrong [lit., ** you couldn't know], and it turns out to be nine hours. What difference does it make anyway? If we set out early in the morning, we'll get θ there by evening.' *248:10.* insignificance: ADV. in a certain or limited degree. → = olsa olsa above.

olsun...olsun 'both...and...; whether...or': Büyük [olsun], küçük [olsun] herkes.e insan olarak saygı göstermeliyiz. 'We must show respect to everyone [as a person], {whether he is young or old/be he young or old/both young and old} [lit., old or young].' Or: İster büyük olsun ister küçük [olsun]... *863:6.* generality: whatever; *872:7.* doubleness: ADJ. both. = ister...ister...

* Afiyet olsun. 'Bon appétit!, Enjoy!' [A. afiyet (- . .) 'health, good health'] A phrase used to address anyone who is about to begin eating, who is eating, or who has just finished eating. • It is used much more frequently than the equivalent English. You see sb eating. You say: Afiyet olsun! 'Bon appétit!' S: * Buyur, beraber yiyelim! 'Q: Will you join me?' [lit., 'Come on, let's eat together.'] C: Teşekkür ederim, ben yedim. San.A afiyet olsun. 'A: Thank you, I've already eaten. [But] you enjoy!' or 'Bon appétit to you!' You praise your hostess for her cooking. You say: A: Dolmalar çok güzel olmuş, * elinize sağlık. 'A: The dolmas [i.e., stuffed tomatoes, peppers, etc.] really turned out {great/splendidly}! * {Congratulations!/Well done!} [lit., ** Health to your hands!]', a standard compliment to a hostess for the food she has prepared. Your hostess responds: B: Afiyet olsun. 'B: I'm glad you {enjoyed it/like it}' or 'Bon appétit.' *8:35.* eating: INTERJ. chow down!; *504: * 20.* courtesy: polite expressions.

Allah yardımcımız olsun. 'May God help us.' → ol- 3, Additional examples. a) 3. Selected examples...: olsun.

Allah [sizden] razı olsun. 'May God be pleased [with you].' → razı ol- 2 → ol- 12.

* Aşkolsun. lit., ** 'Let love be' [A. aşk 'love, passion' + olsun 'let it be']: (1) 'Shame on you!, For shame!': Aşkolsun Oya, * otele gitmek olur mu? Bu gece * biz.de kalacaksın. 'Shame on you, Oya [f.], * how could you think of going to a hotel?! [lit., ** 'going to a hotel will that do?' The implication being 'of course not.'] * Tonight you'll stay {with us/at our place} [lit., ** at us].' *510:27.* disapproval: INTERJ. God forbid!
(2) /A/ 'Good for {him/you}!, Bravo!, Nice going!': When speaking directly to the person being praised: Aşkolsun John, bir yılda Türkçe.yİ ne kadar güzel öğrenmişsin! '{Good for you/Bravo} John, you've really learned a lot of Turkish in just one year! [lit., ** how well you have learned θ Turkish...]' When praising sb to sb else [• Note the dative case]:

Aşkolsun Mine'yE doğrusu! Aile.nin bütün ihtiyac.ı.nı {tek başına} karşılıyor. '{Good FOR Mine!/Bravo to Mine!} She's providing for all the family's needs {all alone/all by herself}.' *149:4.* congratulation: INTERJ. congratulations!; *509:22.* approval: INTERJ. bravo! = **Aferin!**, → = **Çok yaşa!** 2 → **yaşa-** 1, = **Helâl olsun** 2. → **ol-** 11 → **olsun.**

Başınız sağ olsun. → sağ ol- → ol- 12.

* Geçmiş olsun. 'May it pass., May it be past.' a phrase that must be said to a person who has just mentioned a misfortune [illness, accident] that has befallen him [geçmiş 'past']: **A: Hastalandığını duydum, * çok üzül.DÜM. * Geçmiş olsun.** 'A: I heard that you were ill. * {I'M/I was} very sorry. * Get well soon [lit., ** May it be past].' • In reference to a PRESENT condition, certain common Turkish verbs designating a state, i.e., a feeling, emotion, or sensation, such as **üzül-** above, often have the simple PAST tense, but the equivalent English has the simple PRESENT tense. **B: {Teşekkür ederim./Sağol.}** 'B: {Thank you./Thanks.}' *504: * 20.* courtesy: polite expressions.

{Haberiniz/Bilginiz} olsun 'Be {advised/informed/aware} [that], Take note, Just to let you know, Is that understood?, OK?' [A. **haber** 1 'news'. 2 'information'; **bilgi** 1 'knowledge'. 2 'information']: **Adam karısına: Bu akşam eve biraz geç geleceğim, haberin olsun.** 'A man to his wife: I'll be [lit., ** I'll come] a bit late this evening. Just to let you know.' **Sekreter patronuna: Efendim vergi dairesinden aradılar, * bir an önce ilgili evrakları göndermenizi istiyorlar, bilginiz olsun.** 'A secretary to her boss: Sir, Be advised: they called from the tax office. They want you to send the relevant papers * at once.' A warning: **Anne çocuğuna: Ödevlerini yapmadan dışarı çıkamazsın, {haberin olsun/* ona göre}!** 'A mother to her child: You can't go outside until you've done your homework, {is that understood?/* so act accordingly!}'

*399: * 9.* warning: expressions of; *982:22.* attention: INTERJ. attention!

Hayırlı olsun. /A/ 'Good luck., Congratulations., May it go well., May it be beneficial, useful /to/., May it benefit /θ/.' [A. **hayır** (haYRı) 'good fortune, well being' + -**lI** 'having' = **hayırlı** 'beneficial, auspicious']: **A: Dün yeni bir iş.E başvurdum.** 'I applied FOR a new job yesterday.' **B: {Hayırlı olsun./Bol şanslar./Şansınız bol olsun.}** 'Good luck!' *971:22.* chance: INTERJ. break a leg! **A: * Yeni {eviniz/arabanız/işiniz} hayırlı olsun.** 'A: Congratulations ON your new {house/car/job} [lit., ** May your new...be beneficial]!' **B: Teşekkür ederim.** 'B: Thank you.' For another expression used when congratulating sb on a new acquisition, → **Güle güle kullanın.** → **kullan-. Başbakan: "Atatürk Barajı tüm halkımız.A hayırlı olsun".** 'The prime minister: May the Atatürk Dam {be beneficial to/benefit θ} all our people.' *133:13.* premonition: - promise; *387:17.* use: - avail; *504: * 20.* courtesy: polite expressions.

* Helâl olsun. lit., ** 'Let it be canonically lawful (for you).' [A. **helâl** (. -) 'canonically lawful'] (1) 'It's all yours., No need to thank me., Take it with my blessings., I give up all rights to it.' Said to forgive any outstanding obligations, financial or otherwise: **A: * San.A 50 lira borcum kaldı.** 'A: I still owe θ you 50 liras [lit., ** My 50-lira debt to you remains].' **B: Helâl olsun.** 'B: Forget it. Keep it.' A person who is departing or dying and wants to leave in a state of not owing anything to anyone may say: **Hakkınızı helâl edin.** 'Relinquish your rights [i.e., to anything or absolve me of any obligation I may still have to you].' Those remaining say: **Helâl olsun.** 'We do so [lit., ** Let {them/it} be relinquished].' *370: * 9.* abandonment: expressions of.
(2) /A/ 'Bravo /to/!, Good for {him/you}!, Nice going!': * **Helâl olsun adam.A, * tam üç üniversite bitirmiş.** 'Good for him [lit., FOR the man]! * He {has degrees/graduated} from [lit., ** finished] [altogether] 3 {colleges/universities}!' *149:4.* congratulation: INTERJ. congratulations!; *509:22.* approval:

INTERJ. bravo! = **Aferin!**, → = **Aşkolsun.** 2 → above, = **Ç o k yaşa!** 2 → yaşa- 1.

* **Herşey gönlünüzce olsun!** '{I hope everything turns out the way you want it to./May everything turn out as you wish.}' *504: * 20.* courtesy: polite expressions.

Kahrolsun! (1) 'Damn {him/her/it}!, To hell with {him/it}!, Let {him/it} be damned!' (2) 'Down with it!' → kahrol- → ol- 12.

Kutlu olsun! 'May it be blessed [kutlu]', a formula of congratulation on birthdays and religious as well as on other, non-religious, official holidays: **Bayram.INIZ kutlu olsun!** 'Best wishes for the holiday [lit., May YOUR holiday be {blessed/auspicious}]!' **Yeni yıl.ınız kutlu olsun!** 'Happy New Year!' **Noel.iniz kutlu olsun!** 'Merry Christmas!' **Doğum gün.ünüz kutlu olsun.** 'A: Happy birthday!' A suitable response to all the above: **{Teşekkür ederim./Sağolun.}** * **Siz.İN de!** '{Thank you./Thanks.} * The same to you [lit., ** YOURS too].' → **Mübarek olsun.** ['May it be blessed.', a formula of congratulation used exclusively on religious holidays.] *149:4.* congratulations: INTERJ. congratulations!; *504: * 20.* courtesy: polite expressions. → below, **Tebrik ederim.** ['Congratulations', for an accomplishment, success] → tebrik et-.

Lânet olsun! 'Damn {him/her/it}!' [A. **lânet** (- .) 'curse']: **Lânet olsun! Yine sular akmıyor.** 'O damn it! The water isn't running again!' *513:11.* curse: INTERJ. damn! → = **kahretsin!** → kahret- 2.

Mekânı cennet olsun. 'May his [eternal] resting place be paradise.' One of several phrases said upon hearing of a death. The deceased may also be addressed as follows: **Mekânın cennet olsun.** 'May your [eternal] resting place be paradise.' *307: * 39.* death: expressions used upon hearing of a

death; *504: * 20.* courtesy: polite expressions.

Mübarek olsun. 'May it be blessed.' [A. **mübarek** (. - .)], a formula of congratulation used exclusively on religious holidays. A: **{Ramazan Bayramınız/Kurban Bayramınız/Kandiliniz} mübarek olsun.** 'A: May {your Ramadan holiday/your Feast of the Sacrifice/your Kandil Feast} be blessed.' B: * **Siz.İN de.** 'B: The same to you [lit., ** YOURS too].' *149:4.* congratulations: INTERJ. congratulations!; *504: * 20.* courtesy: polite expressions. → **Kutlu olsun.** ['May it be blessed', a formula of congratulation on birthdays and religious as well as on other, non-religious, official holidays] → ol- 11, olsun, above, **Tebrik ederim.** ['Congratulations', for an accomplishment] → tebrik et-.

* **Sağ olsun.** 'Bless {him/her}!' → sağ ol- → ol- 12.

* **Sağlık olsun.** 'Don't worry about it., Never mind.' [sağlık 'health'], lit., ** Let there be health.]': A: **Matematik sınavı.nDAN çok kötü bir not aldım. Bilmiyorum ne yapacağım?** 'A: I got a very bad grade ON the math exam. I don't know what to do [lit., what I will do].' B: * **Boş ver, sağlık olsun! Bir dahaki sınav.A çok daha fazla çalışırsın,** * **olur biter. Dünyanın sonu değil ya!** 'B: Never mind; don't worry about it. You'll study a lot harder FOR the next exam. * And that'll be the end of it. It's not the end of the world, you know!' *121: * 17.* comfort: words of comfort; *504: * 20.* courtesy: polite expressions.

Sıhhatler olsun. [Usually pronounced **sâtler olsun**] 'May you enjoy good health., Good health to you' [A. **sıhhat** 'health'], lit., ** 'May healthS [i.e., much health] be.' A formula used to address sb who has been the object of a personal [bodily] service: The barber uses it after he has cut your hair, the bath attendant uses it when he has just rubbed you down, or sb who has not performed the service notices that such a service has been performed for you or that you have performed it on yourself uses it. * **Sıhhatler olsun! Tıraş**

olmuşsun. 'May you enjoy good health! You've had a shave!' In some circumstances a complimentary English phrase may serve as an approximate equivalent. For example, if sb notices that his friend has had a haircut, he might say: Nice haircut! *504: * 20.* courtesy: polite expressions.

Şansınız {bol/açık} olsun! 'Good luck!' [F. **şans** 'luck, chance, fortune', **bol** 'abundant', **açık** 'open, liberal']: A: **Dün yeni bir iş.E başvurdum.** "I applied FOR a new job yesterday.' B: **{Hayırlı olsun./Bol şanslar./Şansınız {bol/açık} olsun.}** 'Good luck!' *971:22.* chance: INTERJ. break a leg!

Şükürler olsun [ki]... /A/ '{Thanks be /to/ God [that].../Praise be /to/ God [that]...}' 'God' is always implied although a word for God may not appear. [A. **şükür (şüKRü)** 'gratitude, thankfulness']: **Şükürler olsun ki, kazayı birkaç sıyrıkla atlatmış.** 'Thank God he survived the accident with just a few scrapes.' **Şükürler olsun Allah'A, bize bu günleri de gösterdi.** 'Thank θ God that * we have lived to see such days too! [lit., Thanks be to God. ** He has shown us these (good) days too].' *150:6.* gratitude: INTERJ. thanks!; *509:22.* approval: INTERJ. bravo! ≠ **Ne yazık ki...** ['What a pity that...'].

* Toprağı bol olsun. 'May he rest in peace' [**toprak** 'earth, soil'], lit., ** May his earth be abundant.', said upon hearing of the death of a non-Muslim, today sometimes also said of a Muslim. The equivalent expression for a Muslim is **Allah rahmet eylesin.** 'May God have mercy upon him.' → rahmet eyle-. *307: * 39.* death: expressions used upon hearing of a death; *504: * 20.* courtesy: polite expressions.

* Uğurlar olsun. 'Have a good {trip/journey}.' [**uğur** 'good luck']: A: **Nereye gidiyorsun?** 'A: Where are {you going?/you off to?}' B: **Almanya'ya gidiyorum.** 'B: I'm {going to/off to} Germany.' A: **Öyle mi, uğurlar olsun.** 'A: {Really?/Is that so?} Have a good {trip/journey}.' *188:22.* departure: INTERJ. farewell! → = **Yolunuz açık olsun.**, directly below.

Yazıklar olsun! (1) 'What a shame!'
(2) '{Damn/Darn} [it]!', an expression of annoyance. → yazık ol- → ol- 12.

Yolunuz açık olsun. 'Have a good {trip/journey} [yol 'road, way'], lit., ** May your {road/way} be open.]' → **Uğurlar olsun.**, directly above, and substitute there. *188:22.* departure: INTERJ. farewell! Also: = **Hayırlı yolculuklar,** = **İyi yolculuklar.**

Yuh olsun! '{For shame!/Shame on them!}' [**Yuh** '{Boo!/Yuk!/Ugh!}']: **Memleketi soydular, * soğan.A çevirdiler, yuh olsun!** 'They've {robbed/peeled} the nation. They've turned it INTO an onion. Shame on them!' A wordplay since **soy-** means both '- rob' and '- peel'. **Bizim şirketin kâr etmesi.nE rağmen geçen gün 50 işçi.yİ işten çıkardı. Yuh olsun!** 'Although our company made a profit, they fired θ 50 workers the other day. Shame on them!' *510:27.* disapproval: INTERJ. God forbid!

* Ziyade olsun! 'May you always enjoy abundance!', words said to a hostess after a meal or to a person who, when with friends, has paid the bill. [A. **ziyade** (. - .) 'excess, abundance'], lit., ** 'May abundance be': A [The guest to the hostess]: **Ziyade olsun!** 'May you always enjoy abundance!' B [The hostess]: *** Afiyet olsun!** 'I'm glad you {enjoy[ed] it/like[d] it}.' or 'Bon appétit.' *8:35.* eating: INTERJ. chow down!; *504: * 20.* courtesy: polite expressions.

{olup/olan} biten 'what happened, event': **Son zamanlarda {olup/olan} bitenler.i pek izleyemedim, önemli bir haber var mı?** 'I haven't been able to keep {abreast of/up with} [the] events recently. Is there some important news?' **Sen önce bana {olup/olan} biteni bir anlat bakalım, belki bir çare bulurum.** 'First tell me [in detail] what happened. Perhaps I can find a solution.' = **olay** ['event, happening']. *830:2.* event: NOUN event.

* Olur. 'OK., All right., Fine., It's possible., Yes.', always appropriate. → ol- 4 above.

* N'olur[sun]. 'Please., Oh please., Won't you please., Pretty please.', an expression of insistent entreaty. [ne 'what' + olur + -sIn], lit., ** 'What you become': Ne olur bırakma beni. 'Please don't leave me.' N'olur * bu konu üzerinde daha fazla durmayalım. 'Oh please, * let's drop the subject [lit., let's not dwell on this subject any more].' A: Özür dilerim, bu akşam sizinle sinemaya gelemeyeceğim. 'A: I'm sorry, I won't be able to come to the movies with you tonight.' B: N'olursun gel, sensiz sinemaya gitmek istemiyoruz. 'B: {Oh please come/Oh do come, please}. We don't want to go to the movies without you.' The equivalent English often has 'please' at the end of the statement to render the required emphasis. 440:20. request: INTERJ. please.

* Ne olur ne olmaz 'Just in case': Ne olur ne olmaz, * her ihtimal.E karşı sen iki saat önce yol.a çık. 'Just in case, * {just to be safe/lit., against any eventuality}, set out two hours early.' Ne olur ne olmaz, tatil.E çıkarken * yan.ın.A biraz nakit para al. 'Just in case, when you go ON {vacation/holiday} * take a little cash WITH you [lit., ** to your side].' Ne olur ne olmaz [diye] ben sana adresimi vereyim. 'Just in case, let me give you my address.' 965:10. possibility: ADV. by any possibility.

* Ne olursa olsun. 'No matter what, Anyway, In any case, Come what may': Ben kararlı idim. Ne olursa olsun oraya gidecek, onunla konuşacaktım. 'I was determined. No matter what, I was going to go there and speak with him.' 969:26. certainty: ADV. without fail.

olur olmaz (1) 'just any [old], whatever, any...that': * Olur olmaz her şey.İ kafa.n.A takma, * oluruna bırak! 'Don't just let every little thing that happens {get to/bug} you [lit., ** Don't stick everything into your head]. * Just let things be.' Olur olmaz kişilerle arkadaş olma, * baş.ın.ı bela.ya sokarlar. 'Don't make friends with just anybody. They may {bring you trouble/get you into trouble} [lit., ** stick your head into trouble].' Olur olmaz zamanda kapımı çalan şu satıcılar.DAN bıktım artık. 'I've just about had it now WITH these salesmen that keep ringing at my door at just any old time.' 863:15. generality: every.
(2) 'at random, without thinking, purposelessly': Olur olmaz konuşma! '{Don't just talk whenever you feel like it./Don't talk just to hear yourself talk.}' * Ben konuşurken olur olmaz gülmesi.nE canım sıkıldı. 'I was annoyed that, when I was speaking, he was smiling inappropriately [lit., ...I was annoyed AT his smiling inappropriately].' 971:20. chance: ADV. purposelessly.

* oluruna bırak- '- let matters run or take their course without interference, - leave or - let well enough alone, - let nature take its course, - let things be': A: Boş ver, * takma kafana, her şey.İ oluruna bırak. Göreceksin, * her şey yol.u.na girecek. 'A: Never mind, forget about it, don't let it {get to/bug} you. Let things [lit., everything] be. You'll see, everything will turn out OK.' B: * İyi de, oluruna bırakırsam, işler nasıl yürüyecek, * söyler misin lütfen? 'B: Well OK, but if I just let things be [and don't do anything], how are things going to get done? * Just tell me that, will you.' 430:16. freedom: not - interfere.

12 {Noun/Adjective} ol- phrases in alphabetical order. Since most such phrases may be translated with either '- be' or '- become', and sometimes with neither, rather than place these phrases under any one meaning, we give a selection of the most common phrases in alphabetical order below and provide some common meanings of each. Since we treat ol- in the meaning of '- be, - exist' as a cover term for all forms equivalent to '- be, - exist' [that is, for Ø, i.e., for no verb, in the present tense, for i- in the witnessed past tense idi (hasta idi), and in the inferential present and past tenses, i.e., imiş (hasta imiş), and for ol- itself in other cases (hasta olacak)], every entry may not actually contain the form ol-.

adam ol- '- become morally correct, a solid citizen, mature, responsible, - grow up, - amount to sth, - shape up', used for both men and women. The word **adam** [A. 1 'man'. 2 'person'] implies above all a person of solid moral principles and usually one in good standing in Turkish society. This person is usually married, the possessor of a trade or profession, a steady income, and a solid standard of living. **Otuz yaşı.nA geldi hâlâ adam olamadı. * Tek yaptığı arkadaşlarıyla gezip dolaşmak.** 'He's reached the age of thirty, and he still hasn't been able to amount to anything. * All he does [lit., The only thing he does] is hang out with his friends.' Some typical words of self-criticism heard among Turks: **Millet ay.a çıktı, biz hâlâ * yerimizde sayıyoruz. * Biz.DEN adam olmaz abi!** 'People have gone to the moon, but * we're just marking time [i.e., making no progress]. * We're just not going to amount to anything, {pal/colloq. dude/mate}.' **Oku da adam ol!** 'Study and {become an effective person!/shape up!}' **Biz ne zaman adam oluruz biliyor musun? Kendimiz.E güven-diğimiz zaman.** 'Do you know when we will become mature? When we have faith IN ourselves.' Some words of a well-known tale in which a wise father is addressing a son who thinks he has achieved success by attaining a high position in society: **Ben sana "vezir olamazsın" demedim, "adam olamazsın" dedim.** 'I didn't tell you that you couldn't be a vizier but that you couldn't be a man [i.e., in the full sense of that word].' *303:9.* age: - mature. → **akıllan-** ['- become wiser through bitter experience, - come to one's senses about a matter, - wise up'], **aklı başına gel-**. Same. → **gel-** 1.

* Afiyet olsun. → **ol-** 11. → **olsun.**

âşık ol- /A/ '- fall in love /WITH/' [A. **âşık** 'in love, lover']: Person as object: **Kenan Suna'yA âşık oldu, onun.LA evlenmek istiyor.** 'Kenan has fallen in love WITH Suna. He wants to marry θ her.' **Fazıl geçen yaz Zeynep'E aşık oldu, * hâlâ sırılsıklam âşık.** 'Fazıl fell in love WITH Zeynep [f.] last summer. * He's still madly in love [with her].' Thing as

object: **Antalya'ya gidince * tabiat.ın güzelliğ.i.nE âşık oldum.** 'When I went to Antalya, I fell in love WITH its natural beauty [lit., the beauty of nature (there)].' *104:22.* love: - fall in love. → /A/ **çarpıl-** [colloq. '- be swept off one's feet /BY/, fall /FOR/ sb', i.e., fall in love /WITH/].

çabuk ol- '- be quick, - hurry' [çabuk 'quick']: **Çabuk ol, sinema.yA geç kalacağız.** 'Hurry up, we'll be late FOR the movies.' **Çabuk olmazsan treni kaçıracağız.** 'If you don't hurry, we'll miss the train.' *401:5.* haste: - make haste. → = **acele et-**, ≠ **yavaş ol-**.

* çok ol- /{ArAk/mAklA}/ '- go too far, - overstep the limit, - be rude /BY...ing/' [çok 'a lot, much, too much']: **Arif de çok oluyor artık! Bu mesele.yE karışmay.a hiç hakkı yok!** 'Arif has really gone too far this time. He has no right at all to meddle IN this matter.' **Siz de çok oldunuz ama bu kaba sözleriniz.E katlanmak zorunda değilim, * yeter artık!** 'You've really gone too far, but I don't have to put up with these rude words of yours, * enough already!' *505:3.* * 1. discourtesy: - be discourteous; *909:9.* overruning: - overstep; *992:10.* excess: - overdo. → = **ileri git-** 2 → **git-** 1a.

* dahil ol- /A/ '- be included /IN/' [A. **dahil** (- .) 'interior, inside']: **Vergi.si de dahil mi?** 'Is the tax [lit., ** its tax] also included?' **Otel ücret.i.nE kahvaltı da dahil mi?** 'Is breakfast also included IN the price of the hotel?' **{Sınav.A/ İmtihan.A} beşinci ders de dahil mi?** 'Is lesson five also included {IN the examination}?' *771:3.* inclusion: - include. → **içer-** ['- cover, - include, - comprise, - contain'], **içine al-** 1. Same. → **al-** 1, **kapsa-**. Same.

Defol! 'Get lost!, Beat it!, Scram!, Get out!, Go away!, Be off!, Off with you!, Clear out!, Away with you!' [A. **def** 'a repulsion' + **ol-**]: **Artık seni görmek istemiyorum, defol!** 'I don't want to see you anymore. Get out!' **Defol git baş.ım.dan! Artık seni görmek istemiyorum.** 'Get away from me [lit., ** from my head]. I don't want to see you anymore.' **Baş** 'head' here represents the whole body, person. **Müdür kendisine rüşvet teklif eden adam.a "Defol!" dedi ve oda.sı.nDAN kovdu.** 'The director said "Get out!" to the person who had offered him a bribe and threw him OUT OF his room.' *908:31.* ejection: INTERJ. go away! → = **Bas git!** → bas- 1, **kov-** 1 ['- throw, - chase, or - run sb /OUT OF/, - eject sb /from/'].

dikkatli ol- '- be careful' [dikkatli 'careful']: A mother to her child who is about to cross the street: * **Karşı.dan karşı.ya geçerken dikkatli ol.** 'Be careful when crossing [the street] [lit., when passing from (one) side to (the other) side].' **Pazar.DAN domates alırken dikkatli ol,** * **sakın çürükleri alma.** 'When buying tomatoes AT the market be careful. * Mind you, don't buy rotten ones!' *339:7.* carefulness: - be careful; *399: * 9* warning: expressions of. → = **dikkat et-** 1.

eksik ol- /DAn/ '- be absent /from/, - miss' [eksik 1 'lacking'. 2 'deficient']: Often in the negative: **Ertan hiç bir parti.den eksik olmaz.** 'Ertan never misses a party [lit., would never be absent from any party].' Proverb: **Deniz kenarında dalga eksik olmaz.** 'Waves are never absent from the shore.', i.e., Trouble is to be expected in certain places.

* **Eksik olmasın.** 'God bless', an expression of appreciation or gratitude: **Eksik olmasın, annem her hafta beni arar.** 'God bless her [lit., ** May she never be absent], my mother calls me up every week.'

* **Eksik olmayın.** 'Thank you [lit., ** May you not be absent, i.e., May you (always) be around]': **A: Hastasın DİYE sana çorba yaptım.** 'A: BECAUSE you are ill, I made some soup for you.' **B: Eksik olma, sağol.** 'B: Bless you, thanks.' **A1: Annem aniden hastalanıp öldü.** 'A1: My mother suddenly became ill and died.' **B: Baş.ınız sağ olsun.** 'B: My sincere condolences [lit., ** May your head be healthy].' **Baş** 'head' here represents the whole body, person. **A2: Siz de sağolun, eksik olmayın.** 'A2: May you too be healthy! Thank you.' or **A2: Eksik**

olmayın, * **dostlar sağ olsun.** 'A2: Thank you. * May [our] friends be healthy.' *150:6.* gratitude: INTERJ. thanks!; *222:7.* absence: - be absent. → = **Sağolun.** → ol- 11, → **sağ ol-**, = **Teşekkür ederim.** → **teşekkür et-**.

emin ol- /{DAn/A}/ '- be or - become sure, certain, convinced /OF/, /θ/ that': [A. **emin** (. -) 'sure, certain']: **Osman'ın geleceği.nİ sanıyorum, fakat emin değilim.** 'I think [that] Osman is going to come, but I'm not sure.' **Yarın geleceğim, {emin ol!/emin olabilirsin.}** 'I'm going to come tomorrow, {believe me! [lit., be sure!]/you may be sure!}' VERBAL noun as object: * **Sen.in bu iş.İ de başaracağ.ın{.DAN/.A} emin.im.** 'I'm sure θ [that] you'll succeed IN this {job/task} too.' **Yarın geleceğ.im{.DEN/.E} emin olabilirsin.** 'You {can/may} be sure θ [that] I'll come tomorrow.' **Bu iş.TEN para kazanacağ.ımız{.DAN/.A} emin misin?** 'Are you sure θ [that] we're going to earn money IN this business?' **Uçak biletini görünce Murat'ın Paris'e gideceği{.nDEN/.nE} emin oldum.** 'When I saw his plane ticket, I {was sure/was finally convinced} θ [that] Murat was going to go to Paris.'

/DAn/ '- be sure /OF/, - trust /θ/ sb': **Aydan güvenilir bir kızdır ama Sevda'DAN emin değilim.** 'Aydan [f.] is a trustworthy girl, but I'm not sure OF Sevda.' *969:9.* certainty: - be certain. → **iyi bil-** ['- know for sure, certain'] → bil- 1.1, /A/ **güven-** ['- trust /θ/, - rely /{ON/UPON}/, - depend /ON/, - have confidence /IN/'], /A/ **inan-** 2. Same.

göz kulak ol- /A/ '- watch /{θ/OVER}/, - keep an eye /ON/', so that no harm comes to [göz 'eye', kulak 'ear'], lit., ** '- be eye [and] ear': **Tuvalete gidiyorum, eşyalarım.A göz kulak olur musun?** 'I'm going to the restroom. Will you please keep an eye ON my things?' *1007:20.* protection: - watch.

hâkim ol- /A/ '- control /θ/, - get or - keep control /{OF/OVER}/, - keep in line', people or one's emotions, actions: **Öğretmen sınıf.A hâkim olamıyor.** 'The teacher can't control θ the class.' El.in.E, dil.in.E, bel.in.E hâkim ol! 'Control θ your hands, θ your tongue, and your θ loins.' Lütfen öfkelenmeyin Tunç bey! * Sinirleriniz.E hâkim olun. 'Please don't lose your temper Tunç bey. Control yourself! [lit., ** Get control OVER your nerves].' * Kendin.E hâkim ol, "Öfke.yle kalkan zarar.LA oturur." '{Get control OF yourself./Get a hold OF yourself}, [as the proverb says:] "He who rises IN anger sits down with loss."', i.e., at a disadvantage to his own interests. 106:7. inexcitability: - compose oneself; 417:13. authority: - possess or - wield authority; 428:7. restraint: - restrain; 668:6. temperance: - restrain oneself.

hazır ol- '- be ready, prepared' [A. hazır (- .)]: S: Hazır mısın? 'Q: Are you ready?' C1: Hazırım. 'A1: [Yes,] I'm ready.' C2: {Daha/Henüz} hazır değilim. 'A2: [No,] I'm not ready yet.' Müşteri: Yeni elbisem {ne zaman/ne zaman.A} hazır olur? 'Customer: {When/BY when} will my new suit be ready?' Terzi: {a: Yarın.A/b: Üç gün SONRA/c: Bir hafta SONRA/d: Gelecek hafta} [hazır olur]. 'Tailor: [It'll be ready] {a: BY tomorrow/b: IN three days/c: IN a week/d: next week}.' Akşam yemeği ne {vakit/zaman} hazır olur? 'When will the evening meal be ready?' {[Saat] kaçta} hazır olursun? '{At what time} will you be ready?' 405:14. preparation: - be prepared. → = ol- 9.1.

ihtiyacı ol- /A/ '[for sb] - need /θ/, - be in need /OF/, - have need /{OF/FOR}/, - require /θ/' [A. ihtiyaç (. . -) (ihtiyaCı) 'necessity, need'], lit., ** 'for {sth's/sb's} need - exist': • Note the different personal suffixes on ihtiyaç. NON-verbal noun as object: Satıcı: * Yardım.A ihtiyac.INIZ var mı? * Nasıl bir şey istiyorsunuz? 'Salesman: Do you need help [lit., ** Do YOU [pl.] have need FOR help]? * What kind of thing are you looking for [lit., do you want]?' S: Ne.yE ihtiyac.IN var? 'Q: θ What do YOU [s.] need?' C1: Para.yA ihtiyac.IM var. 'A1: I {need θ money/have need OF money}.' C2: Hiç bir şey.E ihtiyac.IM yok. 'A2: I don't need θ anything at all.' Bir şey.E

ihtiyacınız olursa bana söyleyin. 'If you need θ {anything/sth}, tell me.' En fazla ihtiyacım olan şey, sabır. 'What I need most is patience.' VERBAL noun as object: Dinlenmey.E ihtiyac.IMIZ var. 'WE need to rest.' 962:9. necessity: - require. For a THING as the SUBJECT of '- need', as in 'This food needs more cooking', → = iste-3.

kahrol- [ur] /D A n/ '- be deeply grieved or distressed, - be devastated or overcome /{WITH/BY}/ grief' [A. kahır (kaHRı) 1 'grief, deep sorrow; great distress'. 2 'unjust treatment' + ol-]: Kızımı böyle hasta gördükçe kahroluyorum. 'Whenever I see my daughter sick like this, I'm just devastated.' Hanımı ölünce üzüntü.DEN kahroldu. 'When his wife died, he was overcome WITH grief.' 112:17. sadness: - grieve. → = yıkıl- 3 ['- lose one's health and morale; for sb - be broken or ruined by a disaster, - be devastated'], morali bozul- ['- get depressed, discouraged, - lose heart'].

Kahrolsun! (1) 'Damn {him/her/it}!, To hell with {him/it}!, Let {him/it} be damned!': Yurdumuz.A saldıran düşman-lar kahrolsun! 'Damn the enemies who are attacking θ our country!' * Biz.i bu haller.e düşürenler kahrolsun! 'Damn {the/those} people who have brought us to these [distressing] circumstances! [lit., ** who have caused us to fall INTO these conditions].' → [Allah] kahretsin! ['O [God] damn {him/it}!'] → kahret- 2. (2) 'Down with ...!': Kahrolsun {Faşizm!/Komunizm!/Sömürge-cilik!} 'Down with {Fascism!/Communism!/imperialism!}' 513:11. curse: INTERJ. damn!

kaybol- '- be lost, - get lost; - disappear from sight' [A. kayıp (kaYBı) 'loss' + ol-]: Dün aldığım kitap kayboldu. * Bir türlü bulamıyorum. 'The book I bought yesterday {got lost/has disappeared}. * I simply can't find it anywhere [lit., ** (in) any way].' İzmir'e ilk git.tiği.m.de yolları bilmediğim için kayboldum. 'The first time I went to Izmir I got lost because I didn't know the streets.' Amcam geçen yıl kayboldu. * Hâlâ o.nDAN bir haber yok. 'My [paternal] uncle disappeared last year. * We still haven't had any word {OF/from} him [lit., ** from him there is no news].' → yolunu {kaybet-/yitir-} ['- lose one's way, - get lost']. Often with ortadan [orta 'the middle', i.e., the area round about]: Kedim şimdi şuradaydı, * ortadan kayboldu. 'My cat was just here. * It has disappeared.' Proverb: Çıngıraklı deve kaybolmaz. 'A camel that has a bell won't get lost.', i.e., A person who has distinguished himself won't be forgotten. 473:4. loss: - lose. → karış- 7 ['- disappear or - melt /INTO/', thief into a crowd], ≠ çık- 3. # {Ay/Yıldızlar} kayboldu. 'The {moon/stars} have disappeared.' → ≠ ay doğ- → doğ- 2, ≠ yıldızlar çık- → çık- 3. 34:2a. disappearance: - disappear.

kaydol- /A/ '- register or - enroll [oneself], - get oneself registered /FOR [a course], {IN/AT} [a school]/' [A. kayıt (kaYDı) 'a registering, record' + ol-]. Bu sene {a: Türkçe kurs.u.nA/b: okul.A/c: ilkokul.A/d: lise.yE/e: üniversite.yE} kaydolacağım. 'This year I'm going to register {a: FOR the Turkish course/b: IN the school/c: IN [the] primary school/d: IN the {high school/lycée}/e: AT {the college/the university}}.' 549:15. record: - record. → = yazıl- 2. For '- register sb [not oneself] in a course', → kaydet- 1, yazdır- 2.

lâzım ol- /{için/A}/ '- be or - become necessary, needed /FOR/' [A. lâzım (- .) 'necessary']: S: Siz.E ne lâzım? 'Q: What do you need? [lit., ** What is necessary FOR you?]' C: [Ban.A] kâğıt lâzım. 'A: I need some paper.' Siz.E para lâzım olacak mı? 'Are you going to need some money?' Pasta için biraz daha krema lâzım oldu. 'The pastry {needed/needs} a little more frosting.' Soğan lâzım oldu, manav.a gidebilir misin? 'We need onions [lit., onions are needed], can you go to the {fruit and vegetable seller/greengrocer}?' 962:10. necessity: - be necessary. → = gerek-, = icap et-.

mahkûm ol- (1) /A/ '- be sentenced, condemned /to/ a punishment' [A. mahkûm (. -) 'sentenced']: Genç bir kadın.I öldüren katil {15 yıl.a/ömür boy.u haps.e/idam.a} mahkûm oldu. 'The murderer who had killed a young woman was sentenced {to 15 years/to life {in prison/imprisonment}/to death}.' Hırsızlık suç.u.ndan yargılanan adam, mahkeme sonunda 3 yıl hapis ceza.sı.na mahkûm oldu. 'The man tried FOR [the crime of] theft was sentenced to a three-year prison term at the conclusion of the trial.' 602:3. condemnation: - condemn. → = cezalandırıl- 2.

(2) /A/ '- be condemned, doomed /to/': Arkadaşım kazada ölmedi ama tekerlekli sandalye.yE mahkûm oldu. 'My friend didn't die in the accident, but he was condemned to a wheel chair.' 602:3. condemnation: - condemn.

mahzuru ol-. → {sakıncası/mahzuru} ol- below.

* mal ol- /A, A/ '- cost /θ [sb], θ [sth]/' [A. mal 'property']: A: Saatim bozuk. 'A: My watch is broken.' B: Tamir edebilirim. 'B: I can repair it.' A: Ban.A {kaç.A/kaç lira.yA} mal olur? 'A: {θ How much/θ How many liras} will it cost θ me?' B: Siz.E çok pahalı.yA mal olmaz. 'B: It won't cost θ you θ very much.' {Bu ev/Bu araba/Bu eşyalar} Ahmet bey.E 10 bin lira.yA mal oldu. '{This house/This car/These things} cost θ Ahmet bey θ 10,000 liras.' Kendi diktiğim elbise ban.A 15 lira.yA mal oldu. 'The dress that I sewed myself cost θ me θ 15 liras.' Bu tatil biz.E 80 lira.yA mal oldu. 'This vacation cost θ us θ 80.' fig. Ali ile arkadaşlığım ban.A * pahalı.yA mal oldu. 'My friendship with Ali * cost θ me θ a lot.', i.e., caused me a lot of trouble. 630:13. price, fee: - cost. → = tut- 7.

* mâni ol- /A/ '- prevent /θ/, - hinder /θ/, - hold up, - detain /θ/' [A. mâni (- -) 'obstacle, hindrance'], lit., '- be a hindrance /to/': NON-verbal noun as object: Son anda fren.E basarak kaza.yA mâni oldum. 'By stepping ON the brake at the last moment, I prevented θ the accident.' PERSON as object: A: * Tunç bey ban.A müsaade, gitmem lâzım. 'A: Tunç bey, with your permission [lit., ** permission TO me], {I must

be going./I've got to go [*often pronounced*: I've gotta go.]}' **B: O halde san.A mâni olmayayım.** 'B: In that case I won't {hold you up/detain θ you} [lit., ** let me not be a hindrance TO you].' = → /I/ **tut- 3.**
VERBAL noun as object: **Babası bu iş.e gir.me.si.nE mâni olmadı mı?** 'Didn't his father prevent him from undertaking this task? [lit., ** prevent TO his entering θ this work]' * **Arkadaşlarım içeri[ye] girmem.E mâni oldular.** 'My friends prevented me from entering [lit., ** prevented TO my entering inside].' *1011:14* hindrance: - prevent. → = /I/ **engelle-**, = /I/ **önle-**, = **önüne geç-** → **geç- 1.**

memnun ol- '- be pleased, happy, satisfied' [A. **memnun** (. -) 'pleased']: /A/ '- be pleased /θ/ [that]'. VERBAL noun as object: **Seni tanı.dığı.m.A çok memnunum.** 'I'm very pleased {to have met you/θ THAT I met you}.' * **[Çok] memnun ol.DUM.** '[I'M] [Very] pleased to meet you.' • In reference to a PRESENT condition, certain common Turkish verbs designating a state, i.e., a feeling, emotion, or sensation, often have the simple PAST tense, but the equivalent English has the simple PRESENT tense. **Tanıştığımız.A çok memnun oldum!** 'Very pleased to meet you [lit., ** AT our having met each other]!' **Sizin.LE tanış.tığı.m.A memnun oldum.** '{Pleased to meet you./I'm pleased θ THAT I got acquainted with you.}' *504: * 20.* courtesy: polite expressions. **Bunu bana sor.duğ.u.nA memnun olmadım.** 'I wasn't pleased θ THAT he had asked me this.'

/DAn/ '- be pleased, satisfied /WITH/, - like /θ/': NON-verbal noun as object: **Ankara'DAN memnunum.** 'I like θ Ankara.' **Oteliniz.DEN memnun musunuz?** '{Do you like θ/Are you satisfied [*or* happy] WITH} your hotel?'
VERBAL noun as object: **Yeni işçi.nin çalışma.sı.nDAN çok memnunum.** 'I'm very pleased WITH the new worker's work.' *95:12.* pleasure: - enjoy. → = **memnun kal-** → **kal- 1**, = **beğen- 1**, = **hoşuna git-** → **git- 1b**, = **sev-**, **sevin-** ['- be glad, pleased'].

meşgul ol- /lA/ [A. **meşgul** (. -) 'busy'] (1) '- be busy or occupied /with/, - deal /with/': **Geçen hafta siz.i {ziyaret.E gelemedim/ arayamadım}. Çünkü çok meşguldüm.** 'I {couldn't come to visit you/couldn't look you up} last week because I was very busy.' **Bütün gün küçük kızım.la meşgul oldum.** 'I was busy with my little girl the whole day.' **Çocuklar.la meşgul olur musunuz?** 'Will you deal with the children?' *330:10.* activity: - be busy; *724:11.* occupation: - busy oneself with. → = **uğraş- 2.**
(2) '- be concerned /with/, - take an interest /IN/': **Oğlumun ev ödevler.i ile yakından meşgul olurum.** 'I take a keen interest IN my son's homework [lit., ** I'm closely concerned WITH my son's homework].' *982:5.* attention: - attend to. → = **ilgilen- 2.**

mezun ol- /DAn/ '- graduate /from/' [A. **mezun** (- -) 'graduated, a graduate']: {a: **İlkokul.dan/b: Ortaokul.dan/c: Lise.den/d: * Üniversite.den/e: İstanbul Üniversite.si'nden/f: {Hukuk/ Tıp} Fakülte.si'nden/g: Edebiyat Fakülte.si'nden} bu yıl mezun oldum.** 'I graduated {a: from primary school/b: from junior high school/c: from {high school/lycée}/d: from college [*or* university]/e: from Istanbul University/f: from {law/medical} school/g: from the department of literature} this year.' • Note also the following pattern involving a compound: **Meral ve ben Psikoloji bölüm.ü mezun.u.yuz.** 'Meral [f.] and I are graduates of the Psychology Department [lit., are Psychology Department graduates].' * **Fizik.TEN mezun oldum.** 'I got a degree {IN physics./from the department of physics.}' *409:7b.* success: - succeed in specific ways; *793:6.* completeness: - complete. → = **bitir- 4** ['- graduate from, - finish a school or department of a university'].

mümkün ol- '- be possible' [A. **mümkün** 'possible']: **Bu konuda danışma masa.sı.nDAN bilgi edinmek mümkündür.** '{It's possible to/One can} obtain information on this subject {AT/from} the information desk.' **Her gün onlarca mektup**

alıyorum, hepsi.nİ cevaplamam mümkün değil. 'I receive many [lit., ** tens of] letters every day. It isn't possible for me to answer them all [lit., My answering them all is not possible].' {Bu kadar az/350 liralık} bir burs.LA yetinmek mümkün değil. İş bulup çalışmak istiyorum. 'It's not possible to manage {ON/with} {such a small/a 350 lira} scholarship. I want to find a job and work.' Bütün insanlar.I aldatman.ın mümkün olduğ.u.nu mu sanıyorsun? 'Do you think you can deceive all the people? [lit., Do you think deceiving all the people is possible?]' Bu kitabı ciddî bir eser saymak mümkün değil[dir]. 'It's not possible to regard this book as a serious work.' * Mümkün değil, onu ikna edemezsin; * [kendi] gözüyle görse yine inanmaz. 'There's no way you can convince him. * Even if he sees it with his own eyes, he still won't believe it.'

Mümkün [ol-] is often a still more polite alternative to *verb stem*.Abilir miyim? '{May I?/Could I?}' in requesting permission: A student to a teacher: * Sınav.a bir hafta sonra girmem mümkün mü? [= girebilir miyim?] 'Could I take the examination a week from now [lit., ** Is my taking the exam a week from now possible]?' Bura.dan okul.a faks çekmem mümkün mü acaba? 'I wonder if I could send a fax to the school from here?' *965:4.* possibility: - be possible; *966:4.* impossibility: - be impossible.

mümkün olduğu kadar 'as...as possible': Mümkün olduğu kadar tatlı ve şekerli gıdalar.DAN kaçının. 'Avoid θ sweet foods as much as possible.' Başvuru işlemleri.nE mümkün olduğu kadar erken başlamakta yarar var[dır]. 'It would be good [lit., useful] to begin θ the application procedures as early as possible.' Mümkün olduğu kadar {az eşya götür!/yanına az eşya al!} 'Take as few things as possible.' *965:10.* possibility: by any possibility.

pişman ol- /a: DIğInA, b: DIğI için, c: DIğInDAn dolayı/ '- regret, - feel remorse, - be sorry /a: θ [that], b: FOR [having done sth], c: because/' [P. pişman (. -) 'regretful, sorry']:

Film çok güzelmiş. Zeynep seninle sinemaya {a: gitme.diğ.i.nE/b: gitme.diğ.i İÇİN/c: gitme.diğ.i.nDEN DOLAYI} pişman oldu. 'The film was very good. Zeynep was sorry {a: θ [that] SHE didn't go/b: not to have gone [lit., ** for HER not having gone]/c: because SHE didn't go} to the movies with you.' Emine'ye öyle {a: bağır.dığ.IM.A/b: bağırdığ.IM için/c: bağırdığ.IM.dan dolayı} pişmanım. 'I'm sorry {a: θ [that] I shouted/b: for having shouted [lit., ** for MY having shouted]/c: because I shouted} at Emine [f.] like that.' *113:6.* regret: - regret. → üzüntü çek- 2 ['- feel regret, sorrow, - be sorry'] → çek- 5.

bin pişman ol- '- be extremely sorry' [bin 'a thousand']: Füsun ile beraber ev tuttuğum.A bin pişman oldum. Son derece geçimsiz bir kızmış. 'I'm extremely sorry [that] I rented a house together with Füsun. It turns out [that] she is extremely hard to get along with [lit., ** is an extremely hard-to-get-along-with girl].' *113:6.* regret: - regret.

razı ol- (1) /A/ '- agree, - consent, or - be willing /to/, - approve; - be content /WITH/' [A. razı (- .) 'approving, pleased']: Gül sinema artisti olmak istiyordu, fakat ailesi razı olmadı. 'Gül wanted to be a movie actress, but her family didn't {consent/approve}.' Şirketin müdürü sonunda emekli olmay.A razı oldu. 'The director of the company finally agreed to retire.' S: Hikmet Çelik ile evlenmey.E razı mısın? 'Q: Will you consent to marry θ Hikmet Çelik?' C: {Evet, razıyım./Hayır, razı değilim.} 'A: {Yes, I will./No, I won't.}' Proverb: Ölüm.Ü gören hastalığ.A razı olur. 'He who sees θ death will be content WITH illness.' → = yetin- 1. *105:5.* contentment: - be content; *441:2.* consent: - consent; *509:9.* approval: - approve.
(2) /DAn/ '- be pleased /WITH/, approving, - approve': Allah razı olsun. 'May God be pleased [WITH you]', a common formula to express gratitude: Allah [siz.DEN] razı olsun doktor bey, * saye.niz.de kızım kurtuldu. 'May God be

pleased [WITH you], doctor. * Thanks to you, my daughter has been saved.' *95:11.* pleasure: - be pleased; *150:6.* gratitude: INTERJ. thanks!; *509:9.* approval: - approve.

sağ ol- '- be healthy, alive [**sağ**]' *306:7.* life: - live: { **S a ğ o l ! / Sağolun!** } '{Thanks./Thank you.} [lit., ** Be healthy]', an equivalent of **Teşekkür ederim**. It is very common between peers and friends: **S: Nasılsınız?** 'Q: How are you?' **C: Sağolun!** 'A: Fine, thank you.' A response often heard today: 'Good.' Note that in this context, as with **Teşekkür ederim**, the Turkish usually omits **İyiyim**. 'Fine'. **S:** * **Biraz daha kek alır mısınız?** 'Q: Will you have [lit., ** take] a little more cake?' **C: Sağolun,** * **almayayım.** 'A: Thank you, * I've had enough [lit., ** let me not take (any more)].' **Doğum gün.ü hediye.si için sağolun.** 'Thank you for the birthday gift.' *150:6.* gratitude: INTERJ. thanks! → = **Eksik olmayın.** → ol- above, = **Teşekkür ederim.** → teşekkür et-.

* **Sağ olsun.** 'Bless {him/her}!': **Sağ olsun, Nilüfer olmasaydı biz bu işi bitiremezdik.** 'Bless her! Had it not been for Nilüfer [f.], we wouldn't have been able to finish this task.' *509:22.* approval: INTERJ. bravo! For 'Bless you' in response to a sneeze, → **Çok yaşa!** 3. → yaşa- 2.

* **Başın[ız] sağ olsun.** '{My [sincere] condolences./*less formal:* I'm so sorry to hear it.} [lit., ** May your head be healthy]', said to sb telling of a death in his family. **Baş** 'head' here represents the whole body, person: **A: Baba.nız.ın vefat ettiğ.i.ni öğrendim. Başınız sağ olsun.** 'A: I have learned that your father has passed away. {My sincere condolences./I'm so sorry.}' **B: Eksik olmayın, teşekkür ederim. {Sizler sağolun./ Dostlar sağ olsun.}** 'B: Bless you [lit., ** May you never be absent], thank you. {May you [too] be healthy./lit., May friends be healthy.}' An expression used by a member of a circle of friends or acquaintences to other members of that circle upon the death of a member: * **Baş.IMIZ sağ olsun.** [lit., ** May OUR head be healthy]:

İlkokul müdürümüz vefat etmiş. * **En sevdiğimiz öğretmendi. Başımız sağ olsun.** 'Our primary school principle has died. * He was our favorite [lit., most beloved] teacher. *83:6.* health: - enjoy good health; *121:* * 17. comfort: words of comfort; *504:* * 20. courtesy: polite expressions.

* **Canın[ız] sağ olsun.** '{It doesn't matter!/Never mind.}', words of consolation. lit., ** 'May your soul be {strong/well}.' [P. **can** (-) 1 'soul'. 2 'life']: **A: Eyvah, vazoyu kırdım.** 'A: O dear, I've broken the vase.' **B: Üzülme[yin], canın[ız] sağ olsun.** 'B: Don't worry. {It doesn't matter!/Never mind}.' **A: Kazada arabam mahvoldu.** 'A: My car got {totaled/destroyed} in the accident.' **B: Canın sağ olsun,** * **[o.nun] yeni.si.ni alırsın.** 'B: {It doesn't matter!/Never mind}, * you'll buy a new one [lit., ** a new one of it].' When the loss affects closely involved parties, as in the case of a jointly owned car: **Üzülme,** * **can.IMIZ sağ olsun, yeni.si.ni alır.IZ.** 'Don't worry. {It doesn't matter./Never mind.} [lit., ** May OUR soul be {strong/well}]. WE'll buy a new one.' *121:* * 17. comfort: words of comfort; *504:* * 20. courtesy: polite expressions.

* **Sağol[un], varol[un]!** 'Thank you very much!': **A: Mektuplarını postaya verdim.** 'A: I've mailed your letters.' **B: Sağol[un], varol[un]!** 'B: Thank you very much!' = **Çok teşekkür ederim.** → teşekkür et-. *150:6.* gratitude: INTERJ. thanks!

sahip ol- [A. **sahip** (- .) 'possessor, owner'] lit., '- become the owner, possessor /of/ sth, - obtain /Ө/, - acquire /Ө/, - get /Ө/ sth; - be the owner, possessor /of/, - own or - possess sth, - have'. **Sahip ol-**, like the literal English equivalent, is usually a formal expression; '- have' is usually expressed in Turkish in other ways, → ol- 5. • Note the following three patterns: *a) n o u n.*A **sahip ol-: Allah'a şükür, istediğim <u>her şey.E</u> sahip oldum.** 'Thank God I got Ө everything I wanted.' **Türkiye'ye gittiğimde her gün Türkçe konuşma {a: şans.ı.nA/b: fırsat.ı.nA/c: imkân.ı.nA}**

sahip oldum. 'When I went to Turkey, I got {a: θ the chance/b, c: θ the opportunity} to speak Turkish every day.' Bu iş için gerekli bilgi ve tecrübe.yE sahip olduğumu düşünüyorum. 'I think I {possess/have} θ the knowledge and experience necessary for this {job/task}.' Mükemmel bir internet site.si.nE sahip olmak isterseniz bizi arayınız. 'If you want to become the owner OF an excellent Internet site, look us up.' In an advertisement: Herkesin Sahip Olmak İsteyeceği Bir Otomobil! 'A car that everyone wants to {own/have}!' *Very formal*: {a: Bilgisayar sertifika.sı.nA/ b: Ekonomi yüksek lisans.ı.nA/c: B Sınıfı sürücü ehliyet.i.nE/d: 20 yıllık iş tecrübe.si.nE} sahibim. 'I have θ {a: a certificate in computer science/b: a master's degree in economics/c: a class B driver's license/d: 20 years' work experience).' The sentence above is more frequently expressed in the following pattern: Bilgisayar sertifikam var., etc.

b) *noun* sahib.i ol-: Kardeşim çok erken evlendi, genç yaşta çoluk çocuk sahib.i oldu. 'My brother got married very early and had * {children/a family} while still young.' Her konuda bilgi sahib.i olmak güzel bir şey! 'To be informed about every subject is a good thing!' Çok çalıştı, sonunda {* iyi bir meslek sahib.i/* mal mülk sahib.i} oldu. 'He worked {hard/a lot} and finally {* became established in a good profession [or trade]/* became a wealthy person [lit., a man of property, movable and immovable]}.' Bilgi sahib.i olmadan fikir sahib.i olursan böyle saçmalarsın işte! 'If you have an opinion without having the [necessary] knowledge, you'll talk nonsense just like this!', i.e., like you are talking now. Evli ve üç çocuk sahib.i.yim. 'I'm married and have three children.' * Bu şirkette %35 [read: yüzde otuz beş] hisse sahib.i.yim. 'I own a 35 percent share in this company.'

c) *noun*.nIn sahib.i ol-: Yetenekleri ve becerisi sayesinde Türkiye'nin en ünlü pastane.si.nin sahib.i olmuş. 'Thanks to his qualifications and his success, he became the owner of Turkey's most famous pastry shop.' Bu ülke.nin gerçek sahib.i biziz! 'We are the real owners of this nation!' To an attendant in a parking lot: * Bakar mısınız, bu araba.nın sahib.i kim? 'Sir [lit., Will you look here], who is the owner of this car?' * Mal sahib.i, mülk sahib.i, hani bu.nun ilk sahib.i? 'Owner of chattels, owner of real estate, property, but do you know who is the first owner [of this]?', i.e., Just remember that the possessor of all worldly goods is really God, that we are their owners only temporarily. *469:4.* possession: - possess; *472:8.* acquisition: - acquire.

{sakıncası/mahzuru} ol- 'for there - be an objection to, - mind, - object to' [{sakınca/A. mahzur (. -)} 'objection, drawback'], lit., ** 'for sth's objection - exist': S: {Sigara iç.MEM.İN/Camı aç.MAM.IN} bir sakınca.sı var mı? 'Q: Would you mind if {I smoked/I opened the window}? [lit., ** Is MY smoking'S...objection existent?]' C1: Hiç sakınca.sı yok, * buy[u]run. 'A1: {I don't mind./I have no objection.} [lit., ** No objection of it (is) existent]. * Go right ahead.' C2: * Benim için sakınca.sı yok, fakat burada sigara içmek yasak. 'A2: As far as I'm concerned, it's OK [lit., ** For me there is no objection of it], but smoking is forbidden here.' *333:5.* dissent: - object.

sarhoş ol- (1) /DAn, 1A/ '- be, - become, or - get drunk, tipsy, intoxicated, inebriated, high /{from/with}, {ON/with}/' drink [P. sarhoş 'drunk, intoxicated']: Bu gece Umut fazla içti, sarhoş oldu. 'Umut {had too much to drink/drank too much} this evening. He got drunk.' Bu herif yine {a: körkütük/b: zil zurna/c: feci} sarhoş olmuş. 'This fellow has become {a: blind drunk./b: {soused./looped.}/c: terribly drunk.}' /1A/ with drinks: Bir iki kadeh {a: rakı/b: viski/c: bira/d: şarap} ile bile sarhoş olurum. 'I get drunk after only one or two glasses of {a: raki/b: whisky/c: beer/d: wine}.' 3 duble {rakı.dan/votka.dan/ konyak.tan} sonra sarhoş olurum. 'After three doubles {of raki/of vodka/of cognac} I get drunk.' Öyle sarhoş olmuş ki ev.i.nin

yol.u.nu bile bulamamış. 'He got so drunk [that] he couldn't even find his way home [lit. ** couldn't find his home's road].' **Sarhoş olmasaydın böyle yapmazdın.** 'If you hadn't {been drunk/become drunk}, you wouldn't have {acted like that/done that}.' Words of a song: **Öyle sarhoş olsam ki bir daha ayılmasam!** 'Let me get so drunk that I never sober up again!' *88:26.* intoxication, alcoholic drink: - get drunk; *88:27.* : - be drunk. → ≠ **ayıl-** 1 ['- sober up'].
(2) /DAn/ '- be or - become drunk /WITH/ joy, delight, happiness, pleasure': **Mutluluk.TAN sarhoş olmuştum, * sanki bulutlar.ın üst.ü.nde yürüyordum.** 'I had become so drunk WITH happiness * [that] I was walking on clouds [lit., it was as if I were walking on the clouds].' *95:11.* pleasure: - be pleased.

{sebep/neden} ol- /A/ '- bring about /θ/ sth, - cause /θ/ sth, - be the means of' [{A. **sebep** (sebeBi)/**neden**} 'cause, reason']: **Sigara kanser.E sebep oluyor.** 'Cigarette smoking causes [lit., Cigarettes cause] θ cancer.' * **Şoför.ün içkili araba kullanma.sı, dört kişi.nin ölüm.ü.nE sebep oldu.** 'The driver's drunk driving caused θ the death of four people.' *885:10.* cause: - cause. → = **yol aç-** 2 → **aç-** 1.

taburcu ol- /DAn/ '- be discharged, released /from/ a hospital', originally especially in reference to a soldier passed fit for service after an illness. [**tabur** 'batallion', **taburcu** 'a person discharged from a hospital, fit for military service after an illness']: **Annem hastane.den bugün taburcu oluyor.** 'My mother is being discharged from the hospital today.' *431:5.* liberation: - release. ≠ **hastahaneye yatırıl-** ['- check oneself into a hospital'], ≠ **hastahaneye kaldırıl-** ['- be {admitted to/checked into} a hospital'], **tedavi altına alın-** ['- be taken in for treatment'] → **alın-** 1.

tahrik ol- '- get turned on sexually' [A. **tahrik** (. -) 'an inciting, exciting']: **Çıplak OLARAK denize giren kadını görünce tahrik oldum.** 'When I saw the woman going into the {ocean/sea} θ naked [lit., ** {BEING/AS} naked], I

got turned on.' **Ersin abazan.ın bir.i.dir, bir kızla tokalaşsa bile tahrik olur.** 'Ersin is a real horny fellow. When he shakes hands with a girl, he gets turned on.' *105:12.* excitement: - excite. → = **heyecanlan-** 3. For '- turn on sexually', → **tahrik et-** 2, **heyecanlandır-** 3.

* **tayin ol-** /A, olarak/ [A. **tayin** (- -) 'an appointing, appointment']
(1) '- be appointed, assigned, named /to [a position], AS/'. • This verb is not used with an agent noun preceded by {tarafından/CA}, i.e., not as in 'He was appointed by the judge.' For such usage, see {**atan-/tayin edil-**}, **görevlendiril-**: **Babam öğretmen OLARAK küçük bir kasaba.yA tayin oldu.** 'My father was appointed AS a teacher TO a small town.' *615:11.* commission: - appoint. → = {**atan-/tayin edil-**}, = **görevlendiril-**, ≠ **görevden alın-** → **alın-** 1, ≠ **görevine son veril-**.
(2) '[for a person] - be transferred /to/ another post, position': **Ankara'da görev yaparken Turhan bey Hakkari'ye tayin oldu.** 'While serving in Ankara, Turhan bey was transferred to Hakkari.' *271:9.* transference: - transfer. → = {**atan-/tayin edil-**}, ≠ **görevinden alın-** → **alın-** 1.

{var/yok} ol-. At the beginning of entry ol- 3 b) above, {var/yok} without personal suffixes are shown in 'There is-type' sentences [**Masada kitap var.** '{There's a book/There are some books} on the table.']. In entry ol- 5 above, they are shown in different '- have-type' sentences [**Kitabım var.** 'I have a book.'; **Bende kitap var.** 'I have a book on me.', etc.]. In all the patterns above and in all tenses of each, {var/yok} do not have personal suffixes and the form **ol-**, while it appears in some tenses, does not appear in that form TOGETHER WITH {var/yok}. Below we take up two other uses of {var/yok}: a) with the personal suffixes directly attached and followed by **ol-** as θ, i.e., the form **ol-** is not present, and b) without the personal suffixes attached and followed directly by the separate verb **ol-**.

a) {var/yok} with the personal suffixes directly attached and with noun or pronoun subjects [e.g., **Ben {varım/yokum}**]. (1) '{- exist, - be/not - exist, not - be'}, where {existence/non-existence} in general, not in a particular condition and not in the sense of presence or absence in a particular place is at issue. Examples are limited, perhaps mostly to certain fixed expressions. In two Turkish versions of René Descartes's famous phrase **Cogito, ergo sum.** 'I think, therefore I am.': **Düşünüyorum, öyleyse varım.** 'I think, therefore I am.' **Düşünüyorum, o halde varım.** 'I think, therefore [lit., in that case] I am.' In an expression of the transience of human life: **Fani dünya. Bugün varız, yarın yokuz.** 'It's a transitory world. We're here today, gone tomorrow.' Sometimes in the first person singular: **Bugün varım, yarın yokum.** 'I'm here today, gone tomorrow.' *760:8.* existence: - exist; *761:6.* nonexistence: - cease to exist; *827: * 11.* transience: PHR. "all flesh is grass" - Bible.

(2) /DA/ '- be {present/absent} /{in/at}/' some [particular] location, with a definite subject. NOT '- be' with an ADJECTIVE or NOUN as the B in an 'A is B'-type sentence [i.e., NOT ~~Ahmet {hasta/doktor} var. 'Ahmet is {ill/a doctor}.'~~, NOT ~~Ben {hasta/doktor} varım.~~, BOTH INCORRECT]. Present tense: S: **Sınıfta kim var?** 'Q: Who is in the classroom?' C: **Sınıfta {Fatma var/biz varız}.** 'A: {Fatma is/We are} in the classroom.' • Note that the above is not a 'There is-type' sentence because the subject is definite, not indefinite: NOT ** ~~'There is Fatma...in the room.'~~ [Compare the sentence above with the following 'There is-type' sentence, where the subject is indefinite: **Sınıfta kitap var.** 'There {is a book/are some books} on the table.'] With the definite subject in various locations: S: **{Öğrenci listesinde/Resimde} var mı.SIN?** 'Q: Are YOU {on the student list/in the picture}?' C: **{Varım./Yokum.}** 'A: {I am./I'm not.} This structure also conveys the sense of availability: **Bu kitap her kitapçıda var.** '{This book is available at every book dealer./Every bookdealer has this book.}' → = *more formal:* **bulun- 4.**

Past tense: This tense is formed with **idi** [attached form **-ydI**] or **imiş** [attached form **-ymIş**]: **Ben dün toplantıda vardım** [or rarely **var idim**]. 'I was PRESENT at the meeting yesterday.' An approximate equivalent with different emphasis: **Ben dün toplantıdaydım** [or less commonly **toplantıda idim**]. 'I was at the meeting yesterday.' A formal equivalent of the first sentence above: **Ben dün toplantıda HAZIR bulundum.** → **hazır bulun-** → **bulun- 2. Dünkü partide sen de varmışsın.** 'You, too, were apparently present at the party yesterday.' An approximate equivalent with different emphasis: **Sen de dünkü partideymişsin** [or less commonly **partide imişsin**]. 'You, too, were apparently at the party yesterday.' **Anadolu gezisinde sizler yokmuşsunuz.** 'You apparently weren't on the Anatolian tour.' An approximate equivalent with a different emphasis: **Sizler Anadolu gezisinde değilmişsiniz.**

Future tense: The nearest equivalent future tense forms of the above are the same as those of the future tense of '- be' as shown above under **ol- 3** at the beginning of the entry: **Ben yarın toplantıda olacağım.** 'I'll be at the meeting tomorrow.', i.e., **{var/yok}** are UNLIKELY to be used together with the future tense of **ol-** as, for example: ~~Ben yarın toplantıda var olacağım.~~ For instances where **{var/yok}** are used in common expressions together with **ol-**, see **b)** below. *221:6.* presence: - be present. → = **hazır bulun-** → **bulun- 2.**

(3) /DA/ The equivalent of various expressions of willingness or unwillingness to participate /IN/ an activity, such as 'Count {me/us} {in/out}.', 'We're with you.', '{- be a part of, - be on board [i.e., for an activity, not a vehicle], - go along with, - refuse to go along with [i.e., a plan], - have no part of}', or to express a dare, wager, or challenge, such as 'I {dare/challenge} you.' It seems to occur only in the first and second person, singular and plural, and usually only in the present tense: **Ben varım.** 'Count me in.' **Ben yokum.** 'Count me out.' **Biz varız.** 'Count us in.' **Biz yokuz.** 'Count us out.' **Böyle bir şey yapacaksanız {ben de varım/biz de varız}.** 'If you're going to do such a thing, {I'm

with you too/We're with you too}.'
S: {Arkadaş} bu iş.te var
mısın, yok musun; açık söyle.
'Q: {My friend/Pal/Buddy/*slang*:
Dude/Mate}, are you with us in this
[matter/affair] or not, tell us openly.'
C1: Elbette varım. 'A1: Of
course, I am.' C2: Ben bu iş.te
yokum arkadaş, hayatım.ın geri
kalan kısm.ı.nı hapiste
geçirmek istemiyorum. 'A2: No,
I'm not, {My friend...}, I don't want
to spend the rest of my life in jail.'
Bu iş.te biz yokuz. 'Count us out
of this business.' * Kavga.da
yokuz. 'We want no part of [lit., in]
the dispute.'
VERBAL noun as object: /A/
Seneye uzunca bir tatil.e
çıkmay.A, bütün Avrupa.yı
gezmey.E var mısınız? 'Are you
willing to go on a long
{vacation/holiday} next year, to tour
all of Europe?' Bu konuyu
televizyonda seyirciler.in
huzur.u.nda tartışmay.A var
mısın? 'Are you prepared to debate
this subject on television in front of
an audience [lit., in the presence of
viewers]?'
NON-verbal noun as object: Var
mısın [benimle] {yarış.A/bir el
tavla.yA}? '{Will you join me/Are
you with me} {IN the race?/IN a
hand of backgammon?}' *324: * 11.*
willingness: PHR. expressions of
willingness; *771: * 8.* inclusion:
PHR. count me in; *325: * 10.*
unwillingness: PHR. expressions of
unwillingness; *772: * 11.* exclusion:
PHR. count me out.

b) {var/yok} without the personal
suffixes attached and followed
directly by the separate verb ol-, i.e.,
{var/yok} ol- '{- exist, - be/not -
exist, not - be}; {- come into
existence, being, - be created/- go out
of existence, - be destroyed}': [Var]
olmak veya olmamak. 'To be or
not to be.' Evren nasıl var oldu?
'{How did the universe come into
being?/How was the universe
created?}' Kıyâmet gün.ü her şey
yok olur. 'On the Day of Judgment
everything will be destroyed.' Bazı
bilim adamları diyorlar ki "Hiç
bir şey yoktan var olmaz, var
olan bir şey de yok olmaz!"
'Some men of science say, "Nothing
can be created from nothing, and a
thing {that exists/has been created}
cannot be destroyed".' Amacımız
{var olan/mevcut} sorunları

çözmek veya * en az.a
indirmektir. 'Our aim is to solve
{existing} problems or * to minimize
them as much as possible [lit., ** to
lower (them) to the least].'
Etrafımızda hissetmediğimiz
fakat var olan şeyler
bulunabilir. Neden olmasın?
'There may be things around about us
that we cannot sense but that exist.
Why not?' Dünyamızın kuzey ve
güney yarımküresi arasında var
olan sosyal uçurum büyüyor.
'The [existing] social gap between the
northern and southern hemispheres of
our world is increasing.' <u>Proverb</u>: Bir
anda var olan bir anda yok
olur. 'What exists one moment
disappears the next.' Here today,
gone tomorrow. *827: * 11.*
transience: PHR. "all flesh is grass" -
Bible. Yok olan tarihî eserler.
'Historical artifacts that {are
disappearing/have disappeared}.'
Yok olan köyler. 'Extinct
villages.' Zaman'IN var olduğ.U
hangi anlamda söylenebilir? 'In
what sense can it be said that time
exists?' Öyle bir şey.İN var
olduğ.U.nu hiç tahmin
etmemiştim. 'I had never imagined
that such a thing existed.' Öyle bir
şey.in var olduğ.u.nA
inanmıyorum. 'I don't believe {θ
that such a thing exists/in the
existence of such a thing}.' var
olduğu {sürece/*less current*:
müddetçe} 'as long as...exists':
İnsan var olduğu
{sürece/müddetçe} din de var
olacaktır. 'As long as mankind
exists, religion, too, will exist.'
Bugün var olan türlerin yüzde
yirmisin.in gelecek yüzyılda
yok olacağ.ı tahmin ediliyor. 'It
is estimated [lit., being estimated] that
20 % of the species existing today
will disappear in the next century.' *
Bu ülkede demokrasi var
sandım, yanılmışım. 'I thought
there was democracy in this country. I
guess I was {wrong/mistaken}.' In a
fixed expression: * Sağol[un],
varol[un]! 'Thank you very much!'
150:6. gratitude: INTERJ. thanks! →
= Çok teşekkür ederim. →
teşekkür et-. *760:8.* existence: - exist;
761:6. nonexistence: - cease to exist.

yardımcı ol- /A/ '- help /θ/, - assist
/θ/, - be of assistance /to/, - be helpful
/to/' [yardımcı 'helper, helpful'],
lit., '- be a helper, helpful /to/': Siz.E
nasıl yardımcı olabilirim? 'How

can I help θ you?' {Siz.E} yardımcı olabilir miyim? 'Can I help θ you?' İnsanlar.a yardımcı olmak.LA övünme, * Allah bilsin yeter. 'Don't boast ABOUT being helpful to people. * It's enough if God knows [lit., Let God know, that's enough].' Allah yardımcımız olsun. 'May God help us [lit., be our helper].' 449:11. aid: - aid. → = yardım et- ['- help /θ/, - assist /θ/'], yardımda bulun-. Same. *more formal.* → bulun- 3, el ele ver- ['- help one another'] → ver- 1, yardım elini uzat- ['- extend a helping hand /to/, - help out, - extend aid, assistance /to/'] → el uzat-, → uzat- 2, yardımlaş- ['- help one another'].

yazık ol- /A/ '- be a shame, pity /FOR/' [yazık 'a pity, a shame']: /A/ yazık oldu '{What a pity/How sad} /FOR/ [lit., ** It was a pity /FOR/]': Nermin'E yazık oldu. O kadar çalıştığı halde sınıfta kaldı. '{What a pity/How sad} FOR Nermin. Although she worked so hard, she was held back in school [lit., ** 'stayed in the class', i.e., didn't advance to the next grade].' Millî Takım.A yazık oldu. Çok iyi oynadığı halde yenildi. 'What a pity FOR the national team! Although it played very well, it was beaten.' *113: * 13.* regret: INTERJ. what a pity!

        Yazıklar olsun! (1) 'What a shame!': A: Duydun mu, Ahmet rüşvet almış. 'A: Have you heard? Ahmet has supposedly taken a bribe.' B: Tüh, yazıklar olsun! * Hiç beklemezdim. 'B: Oh, what a shame! * I would never have expected [such a thing].' *510:27.* disapproval: INTERJ. God forbid!
(2) '{Damn/Darn} [it]!', an expression of annoyance: Tüh, yazıklar olsun! Biletleri evde unuttum, şimdi tiyatroya nasıl gireceğiz? 'Oh {damn/darn} [it]! I've left [lit., forgotten] the tickets at home. Now how are we going to get into the theater?' *98:31.* unpleasantness: INTERJ. eeyuck!

yok ol-. → {var/yok} ol- above.

zahmet ol- /A/ '- be trouble, troublesome, an inconvenience /FOR/' [A. zahmet 'trouble,

difficulty']: Someone offers to do sth for you: A: Paltonuzu ben getiririm. 'A: I'll get your coat.' B1: * Siz.E zahmet olacak. 'B1: That's going to be troublesome FOR you.' B2: Zahmet olmazsa. 'B2: If it's no trouble for you.' A: * Estağfurullah. 'A: No trouble at all.' Zahmet olmazsa bana bir bardak soğuk su verir misiniz? 'If it's not too much trouble, {would you please get me a glass of cold water?/could I please have a glass of cold water/lit., would you please give me a glass of cold water?}' *96:16a.* unpleasure: - distress; *504: * 20.* courtesy: polite expressions; *995:4.* inexpedience: - inconvenience.

oldu olmadı. → ol- 11.

olgunluğa er-. → er-.

olmadık. → ol- 11.

olmakla {beraber/birlikte}. → ol- 11.

olsa. → ol- 11.

olumlu karşıla-. → {hoş/iyi/ olumlu} karşıla-. → karşıla- 3.

olur olmaz. → ol- 11 → olur.

oluruna bırak-. → bırak- 2, ol- 11 → olur.

oluş- [ur] /DAn/ '- come into being /OUT OF/, - occur; - be formed, composed, made up /OF/, - consist /OF/' [ol- + recip. suf. -Iş]: Mağaralar nasıl oluşur? 'How do caves come into being?' Ay tutulması dünya'nın güneş ile ay ara.sı.na girmesiyle oluşur. 'An eclipse of the moon occurs when the earth comes [lit., ** with the earth's entering] between the sun and the moon.' Su iki hidrojen ve bir oksijen.DEN oluşur. 'Water is composed OF two hydrogen [molecules] and one oxygen [molecule].' Bu alet üç parça.DAN oluşuyor. 'This instrument {consists/is made up} OF three parts.' Grubumuz geçen yıl beş kişi.DEN oluşuyordu. 'Last year our group {consisted/was made up} OF five people.' *795:3.* composition: - compose.

oluştur- [ur] /DAn/ '- form, - create, - make up, - constitute /{from/OUT OF}/' [oluş- + caus. suf. -DIr]: **Öğretmen farklı sınıflardaki kız ve erkek öğrenciler.den bir grup oluşturdu.** 'The teacher formed a group from male and female students of different classes.' *891:8.* production: - produce, - create. → = **var et-,** = **yap-** 1, = **yarat-,** ≠ **yık-** 1, ≠ **yok et-** 1.

onar- [ır] '- repair, - fix, - put in running order, - mend' [o **n-** '- improve' + caus. suf. -**Ar**]: **Saatçi saatimi onardı.** 'The watchmaker repaired my watch.' **Bizim evde, bozulan aletleri hep babam onarır.** 'In our house it's always my father who repairs everything [lit., {the implements/the tools}] that breaks down.' **Anneannem {delinen çorabımı/yırtılan eteğimi/ sökülen kazağımı} onardı.** 'My grandmother mended {my socks which were full of holes/my torn skirt/my sweater which had become unravelled}.' *396:14.* restoration: - repair. → = **tamir et-,** = **düzelt-** 1 ['- repair, - fix', roads], **çorap dik-** ['- darn (non-wollen) socks'] → 1 dik- 2, **çorap ör-** ['- darn (wollen) socks'] → ör- 3.

onayla- [r] /I/ '- approve, - approve /OF/' [onay 'approval' + verb-forming suffix -lA]: NON-verbal noun as object: **Cumhurbaşkanı yeni bakanlar kurul.u üyeler.i.ni hemen onayladı.** 'The President of the Republic at once approved the new members of the Council of Ministers.' **Terörist eylemler.i onaylamıyoruz.** 'We do not approve OF terrorist activities.' **Gülnur hanım birkaç söz söyledi. Odadakiler kendisini başlarını sallayarak onayladılar.** 'Gülnur hanım said a few words. Those in the room, nodding their heads, approved [i.e., of what she had said, but lit., ** of her].' *509:9.* approval: - approve. → = **tasdik et-,** ≠ **reddet-** 1. VERBAL noun as object: **Babam yeni bir araba alma.m.ı onayladı, ama gönülsüzce.** 'My father approved OF my buying a new car, but reluctantly.' * **Bu tür kitaplar.ın yayınlanma.sı.nı {a: elbette/b: kesinlikle/c: pek} onaylamıyoruz.** 'We {a: certainly/b: {definitely/absolutely} do

not approve/c: don't much approve} OF the publication [lit., ** of the BEING published] of such books.' *509:9.* approval: - approve. → = {hoş/iyi} karşıla- → karşıla- 2.

onaylan- [ır] /{tarafından/CA}/ '- be approved /by/' [onayla- + pass. suf. -n]: NON-verbal noun as subject: **Yeni bakanlar kurul.u {hemen/gecikmeksizin} onaylandı.** 'The new Council of Ministers was approved {at once/without delay}.' *509:9.* approval: - approve. → = **doğrulan-,** = **tasdik edil-.** VERBAL noun as subject: **Bu kitaplar.ın gelecek yıl yayınlanma.sı {Kültür Bakanlığı tarafından/Kültür Bakanlığı.nca} onaylandı.** 'The publication of these books next year was approved {by the Ministry of Culture}.'

onur ver-. → {şeref/onur} ver-. → ver- 1.

onurlandır- [ır] /I, {ArAk/mAklA}/ '- honor /by...ing/' [It. **onur** 'honor' + verb-forming suf. -lAn = **onurlan-** '- be honored' + caus. suf. -DIr]: **Evimiz.e {gel.erek/gel.mekle} biz.i onurlandırdınız efendim.** 'You honored us {by com.ing} to our house, {sir/ma'am}.' *646:8.* honor: - honor. → = /A, {ArAk/mAklA}/ {şeref/onur} ver- → ver- 1.

orgazm ol-. → ol- 10.1.

{ortaya/meydana} çık-. → çık- 3.

{ortaya/meydana} çıkar-. → çıkar- 7.

oruç tut-. → tut- 5.

otostop yap-. → yap- 3.

otur- [ur] 1 /A/ '- sit down /IN/', i.e., move INTO a sitting position: **Oturmaz mısınız?** 'Won't you sit down?' **A: Oturunuz lütfen.** 'A: Please sit down.' **B: Nere.yE oturayım?** 'B: θ Where should I sit?' **A: {Şura.yA/Şu koltuğ.A} oturun.** 'A: Sit [down] {over here/IN that armchair}.' **Bura.yA oturabilir miyim?** 'May I sit down θ here?' **A: Nilgün nere.yE otursun?** 'A: θ Where should Nilgün [f.] sit?' **B: Şura.yA**

otursun. 'B: Have her sit θ over there.' * Gel şöyle! * Yan.ım.A otur. 'Come over here! * Sit down beside me [lit., ** TO my side].' * Yan yan.A oturdular. 'They sat down side BY side [lit., ** side TO side].' Televizyon.un karşı.sı.n.daki koltuğ.A oturdu. 'He sat down IN the armchair facing the TV set.' Öğrenciler * ikili gruplar halinde {karşılıklı/yüzyüze} oturdu. 'The students sat down * in groups of two [lit., ** in the state of groups of two] {face to face}.' Proverb: Öfke.yLE kalkan zarar.la oturur. 'He who gets up IN anger sits down with loss', i.e., at a disadvantage to his own interests. *912:10.* depression: - sit down. → yerleş- 1 ['- settle oneself down {IN/INTO}' a chair, armchair, etc.], çök- 2 ['- sit down suddenly, heavily /IN/, - collapse /INTO/', chair], ≠ ayağa kalk- ['- get to one's feet'] → kalk- 1, ≠ fırla- 1 ['- jump to one's feet'].

2 /DA/ '- sit, - be sitting /in/', not motion, but position: S: Nurten nere.DE oturuyor? 'Q: Where is Nurten [f.] sitting?' C: Şu koltuk.TA oturuyor. 'A: She is sitting IN that armchair.' S: Bura.da oturan var mı? 'Q: {Is anyone sitting here?/Is this seat {taken/occupied}?}' = Bura.nın sahib.i var mı? lit., ** 'Does this place have an owner?' C1: Evet, bura.da {arkadaşım/birisi} oturuyor. 'A1: Yes, {my friend/sb} is sitting here.' C2: Hayır, yok. 'A2: No, there isn't.' Proverb: Aşağı.da oturmazsan yukarı.da da yerin yoktur. 'If you can't sit down below, you'll have no place above either.' *173:10.* quiescence: - sit.

3 /DA/ '- live, - reside /{in/at}/, - inhabit /θ/': S: Nere.de oturuyorsunuz? 'Q: Where do you live?' C: Ankara.da [oturuyorum]. 'A: [I live] in Ankara.' S: {* Ankara'NIN nere.Sİ.nde/ Ankara'da nerede} oturuyorsunuz? 'Q: Where in Ankara do you live? [lit., {** In Ankara's where/Where in Ankara}...]' C: {Kızılay'da/Kızılay semt.i.n.de} [outruyorum]. 'A: I live {in Kızılay/in the Kızılay section}.' To ask for a specific part of a larger area, e.g., a city, one may also ask: * Ne taraf.ta oturuyorsun? 'In what part [of the city] do you live?' S: * Bura.yA yakın mı oturuyorsunuz? 'Q: Do you live near θ here?' C1: Evet, yakın oturuyorum. 'A1: Yes, I live nearby.' C2: Hayır, * uzak.ta oturuyorum. 'A2: No, I live far away [lit., * at a distance].' S: Ailenizle [birlikte] mi oturuyorsunuz? 'Q: Do you live [together] with your family?' C: Hayır, {yalnız/tek baş.IM.a} oturuyorum. 'A: No, I live {alone}.' • Note that the possessED suffix on baş agrees with the subject of the sentence. For another dialogue used when discussing the people one is living or staying with, see kal- 1. {Yukar[ı]da/Aşağıda} oturuyorum. 'I live {upstairs [lit., above]/downstairs [lit., below}.' Proverb: Sırça köşkte oturan, komşu.su.nA taş atmamalı. 'A person who lives in a crystal palace shouldn't throw stones AT his neighbor.' People who live in glasshouses shouldn't throw stones. *225:7.* habitation: - inhabit. → = yaşa- 2, hayat sür- ['- lead a (certain kind of) life'] → sür- 6.

Güle güle oturun[uz]. 'What a nice...!, How nice!' Often used with the name of a residence: apartment, house, etc., lit., 'Live [in it] with pleasure!', a polite expression used when visiting people who have moved to a new residence. [gül- '-laugh' + adv.- forming suf. -[y]A = güle lit., 'laughingly']: A: Yeni evinizde güle güle oturun! 'A: My what a nice house! lit., ** Live in your new house with pleasure!' B: {Teşekkür ederim./Sağol.} 'B: {Thank you./Thanks.}' *504: * 20.* courtesy: polite expressions. → Hayırlı olsun. ['May it be beneficial, useful., May it benefit.'] → ol- 11 → olsun.

* {kira.DA/kira.yLA} otur- '-rent' [A. kira (. -) 'rent'], lit., ** '-live {in rent/BY MEANS OF rent}': Evi satın mı aldınız, yoksa {kira.DA/kira.yLA} mı oturuyorsunuz? 'Did you buy the house or {are you renting}?' *615:15.* commission: - rent. → kiraya ver- ['- rent out'] → ver- 1.

4 '- stay, - remain': Kendine bir yer bulana kadar {ben.im.le/*becoming more common:* ben.le} oturabilirsin. 'You may

stay {with me} until you find a place [for yourself].' * **Orhun'lara gittik, iki saat oturduk.** 'We went to Orhun's house [lit., to the Orhuns] and stayed two hours.' • **Orhun** is the first name of a male member of the family. The plural suffix on that FIRST name here denotes the residence of Ali and those people associated with him, e.g., his immediate family or his friends. In English we would say 'Orhun's house' or use the LAST name in the plural as in 'the Smiths' house'. In Turkish a person usually uses the first name with the plural suffix to refer to the residence of the family of a person of his own age or younger. When he speaks of the residence of a family of sb specially respected, usually of sb older or sb otherwise held in esteem, or of sb he is not on familiar terms with, he follows the first name with **beyler** for a man, i.e., **Orhun beyler,** or with **hanımlar** for a woman, i.e., **Selma hanımlar.** *855:3.* continuance: - continue. → = **kal-** 1.

5 /{üzerine/üstüne}/ '- fit /θ/, - suit /θ/': * **Bu elbise {üzer.in.E/ üzer.iniz.E} iyi oturmuş,** * **güle güle kullanın.** 'This suit fits θ {you [s.]/you [pl.]} well. * Wear it happily!' *866:3.* conformity: - conform. → = **dur-** 9, = **gel-** 2, = **ol-** 8, **uy-** 1 ['- fit /θ/, - be the right size and shape /FOR/'], **yakış-** 2 ['for sth - look good /ON/, - suit /θ/', clothing].

oy kullan-. → **kullan-**.

oy ver-. → **ver-** 1.

<u>oyna-</u> [r] [oyun 1 'game'. 2 'play, theatrical presentation'. 3 'dance, folk dance'. 4 'trick, ruse' + verb-forming suf. -A] 1 /lA/ '- play a game /with/': S: **Benim.le {tavla/satranç/ dama} oynar mısın?** 'Q: Will you play {backgammon/ chess/checkers} with me?' C1: **Evet. Oynarım.** 'A1: Yes, sure [lit., I'll play].' C2: **Hayır.** * **Tavla... bilmiyorum.** 'A2: No, I don't know how to play backgammon... [lit., ** I don't know backgammon...].' S: **{a: Masa tenis.i/b: Briç} oynayalım mı?** 'Q: Shall we play {a: {ping pong/table tennis}/b: bridge}?' C1: **{Haydi/Olur,} oynayalım.** 'A1: {Yes [lit., Come on]/OK,} let's [play].' C2: **Şimdi vaktim yok**

{a: öğleden sonra oyna- yalım./b: * iki saat SONRA oynasak olur mu?} 'A2: I don't have time right now, {a: let's play in the afternoon./b: * How about if we play IN two hours? [lit., If we play IN two hours, will that be OK?]}' S: **Ne oynuyorsunuz?** 'Q: What are you playing?' C: **Tavla oynuyoruz.** 'A: We're playing backgammon.' S: * **Spor yapıyor musun?** 'Do you {play/engage in} [lit., ** make] any sports?' C: **Evet,** * **vaktim olursa haftada bir iki saat {basketbol/futbol/tenis} oynu- yorum.** 'A: Yes, when I have time, I play {basketball/ soccer/tennis} one or two hours a week.' *743:23.* amusement: - play; *747:4.* basketball: - play basketball; *748:3.* tennis: - play tennis; *752:4.* soccer: - play soccer. See also **oyun oyna-** below when the game played is not specified.

kumar oyna- /lA/ '- gamble /with/' [A. **kumar** 'gambling']: **Kumar oynadı ve bütün parasını kaybetti.** 'He gambled and lost all his money.' **Kumar oynamam.** 'I {don't/won't} gamble.' **Ben millet.le kumar oynamam.** 'I won't gamble with the nation.', i.e., put the nation at risk. *759:23.* gambling: - gamble. → {**bahse/ iddiaya} gir-** ['- bet, - wager'].

oyun oyna- (1) /lA/ '- play a game /with/' or just '- play', when the game is not specified: **Ne zaman oyun oynayacağız?** 'When are we going to play?' S: **Kışın hangi oyunlar.I oynarsınız?** 'Q: Which games do you play in [the] winter?' C: **Satranç ve tavla oynarım.** 'A: I play chess and backgammon.' **Piknikte hepimiz çocuklar gibi oyun oynadık.** 'At the picnic all of us, like children, played games.' *743:23.* amusement: - play.
(2) /{lA/A}/ '- play a trick /ON/' [oyun 'trick']: **Ben.im.LE oyun oynama!** 'Don't play any tricks {ON me}!' or **Ban.A oyun oynama!** Same. **Bu oyun.u ban.A oynama!** 'Don't play this trick ON me.' *356:15.* deception: - fool.

2 'for a movie or film - play, - show, - be on, - be running, showing': **film oyna-** [F. **film**]: S: **Bu gece {Ar'da/Ar Sinema.sı'nda} hangi film oynuyor?** 'Q: What movie is playing {at the Ar/at the Ar [movie] theater} this evening?' C: *

Şener Şen'in bir film.i oynuyormuş. 'A: A Şener Şen film is playing.' Şener Şen is a movie star. The same structure would be used if he were the director. S: Bu film {ne zamandan beri} {oynuyor/gösteriliyor}? 'Q: {How long/Since when} has this movie {been playing/been showing}?' C: Bu film {altı haftadan beri/geçen haftadan beri} {oynuyor/gösteriliyor}. 'A: This movie {has been playing/has been showing} {for six weeks/since last week}.' S: Bu film ne zamana kadar oynayacak biliyor musun? 'Q: Do you know how long [lit., until when] this movie will be playing?' C: Bu film {gelecek ay.A/haziran.nın onaltı.sı.nA} kadar oynayacak. 'A: This movie will be playing until {θ next month/θ the 16th of June}.' 714:16. photography: - project; 888:7. operation: - be operative.

3 /DA/ '- play a role, - portray a character, - perform, - act /in/ a play or movie' [F. film]: * Bu film.de baş rol.DE kim oynuyor? 'Who plays the lead in this film? [lit., ** In this film who plays IN the lead role?]' * Bu filmde Türkân Şoray kör BİR kız.I oynuyor. 'In this movie Türkân Şoray plays A blind girl.' Yeşilçam'ın meşhur film artisti Türkân Şoray yüz.den fazla filmde oynamış. 'The famous Yeşilçam movie star Türkân Şoray has acted in more than a hundred films.' Yeşilçam [lit., 'Greenpine'], a section of Istanbul, is the Turkish equivalent of Hollywood. 704:29. show business, theater: - act. → = film çevir- 1 → çevir- 3.

4 '- dance, - perform a dance', used with the names of various folk dances: Çok iyi {zeybek/çiftetelli} oynar. 'He dances the {zeybek/çiftetelli} very well.', the names of two Turkish folk dances. Proverb: Aç ayı oynamaz. 'A hungry bear won't dance.' 705:5. dance: - dance. → dans et- ['- dance'], göbek at- ['- belly dance, - perform a belly dance'] → at- 1.

5 /lA/ '- play around, - trifle, - dally /with/', i.e., not take seriously' [obj.: sb's affections]: Words of a song: * Benim.le oynama, söyledim sana. 'I told you not to trifle with me

[lit., ** Don't trifle with me, I told you].' 997:14. unimportance: - trifle. → = dalga geç- 3 → geç- 1.

oynaş- [ır] [oyna- + recip. suf. -ş] 1 '- play with one another': Ev.e gel.diği.m.de çocuklar bahçede oynaşıyordu. 'When I came home, the children were playing with each other in the garden.' Her sabah pencere.nin ön.ü.nde serçeler oynaşır. 'Every morning the sparrows play with each other in front of the window.' 743:23. amusement: - play.

2 /lA/ '- carry on a love affair /with/', slang '- make out /with/': Polis gel.diği.nde aşıklar parkta oynaşıyorlardı. 'When the police came, the lovers were making out in the park.' Baba: Oğlanlar.la oynaş.acağına oturup dersi.nE çalış! 'Father: Instead of fooling around with boys sit down and study θ your lessons!' Kız: Ben kimse.yle oynaşmıyorum. 'Daughter: I'm not fooling around with anyone.' 562:14. lovemaking, endearment: - make love; 562:16. lovemaking, endearment: - caress. → = seviş- 2.

oyun oyna-. → oyna- 1.

- Ö -

öde- [r] /a: A, b: için, c: A/ '- pay /a: θ [sb], b: for [sth], c: for [sth]/': Taksiden inmeden önce şoföre "Ne kadar ödeyeceğim?" diye sordum. 'Before getting out of the taxi, I asked the driver [saying], "How much do I owe? [lit., How much am I going to pay]"' A more common way of expressing the same question: Borcum ne kadar? 'How much do I owe [lit., What is my debt]?' {Elmalar için/Elmalar.A} ne kadar ödeyeceğim? 'How much should I pay [lit., am I going to pay] {FOR the apples}?' Kaç para ödemem lâzım? 'How much do I have to pay?' Ayrı ayrı ödemek istiyoruz. 'We'd like to pay separately [i.e., go dutch].' • Note: In Turkey 'going dutch' is not common. Among a group of friends one person usually pays for everyone, but on following occasions each member of the group is expected to take his turn. Lütfen {ban.A/kasa-

.yA} ödeyin. 'Please pay {θ me/θ the cashier}.' *624:10.* payment: - pay. → = **para ver-** → **ver-** 1, = **masraf çek-** ['- foot the bill, - pay', *informal, jocular*] → **çek-** 5, = **masraf gör-** ['- meet expenses, - finance, - pay for'] → **gör-** 4, = **masraf karşıla-**. Same. → **karşıla-** 2, = **masraf {et-/yap-}, para yatır-** 2 ['- pay money for municipal services (i.e., water, gas)', when the money is paid into a public institution's bank account] → **yatır-** 2, **masrafa gir-** ['- spend a lot of money on sth or to get sth done, - have a lot of expenses, - incur great expense'].

borcunu öde- '- pay up, - pay off an account, - pay one's debts or bills, - settle one's debts or one's account' [**borç** (**borCu**) 'debt']: **Otel.e olan borc.um.u {a: nakit OLARAK/ b: nakt.EN/c: çek.LE/d: kredi kartı.yLA/e: seyahat çeki.yLE} ödedim. * Artık rahatım.** 'I paid what I owed θ the hotel {a: IN cash/b: IN cash/c: BY check/d: BY credit card/e: BY traveler's check}. * {That's a load off my mind./That's a relief.} [lit., ** Now at last I'm at peace.]' **Borc.u.nu kim.e ödeme-si gerekiyor, siz.e mi, yoksa vezne.ye mi?** 'Who[m] should he pay, you or the cashier [lit., ** the cashier's window, at a bank or other financial institution]?' **Alacakları-mı {tahsil edemediğim/alama-dığım} için borçlarımı öde-yemedim.** 'Because I couldn't collect the money [that was] due me, I couldn't pay my debts.' *624:13.* payment: - pay. → = **borcunu {kapa-/kapat-}, ≠ borca gir-** ['- go or - get into debt'], ≠ **borçlan-**. Same.

geri öde- '- pay back money, - repay' [**geri** 'back, rear, the space behind']: **Ev almak için banka.ya 50 bin lira borçlandım. Fakat borcumu geri ödeyemedim.** 'To purchase a home I got 50,000 liras in debt to the bank, but I couldn't repay my debt.' **Banka.ya olan borcu-mu geri ödedim.** 'I paid back to the bank the money I owed.' *624:11.* payment: - repay.

{nakit/nakit olarak/nakten} öde- /A/ '- pay θ sb IN cash, - pay IN cash /to/, - pay cash' [A. **nakit** (**naKDİ**) 'ready money, cash']: **Patron memurlar.A maaşları.nı**

nakit ödedi. 'The boss paid θ the employees their salaries IN cash.' **Bu kadar çok para.yI nakit öde-yemem. Siz.E çek yazacağım.** 'I can't pay [you] θ this much money IN cash. I'll write θ you a check.' *624:17.* payment: - pay cash.

peşin öde- '- pay IN advance' [**peşin** 'IN advance']: **Yeni televizyon.um.un %** [read: **yüzde**] **20'si.ni peşin ödedim.** 'I put a 20% down payment on my television set [lit., ** I paid for 20 percent of my television set IN advance.]' **İlk taksidi peşin mi ödemeliyim? Yoksa gelecek ay mı?** 'Should I pay the first installment IN advance or next month?' **Peşin mi ödeyeceksiniz, * taksit yapalım mı?** 'Are you going to pay in advance, or * shall we arrange for installments?' *624:10.* payment: - pay.

* taksitle öde- '- pay IN installments' [A. **taksit** 'installment']: **[Geri] kalan.ı.nı taksit.LE ödeyeceğim.** 'I'll pay {the balance/the remainder/the rest} [lit., ** (its) remaining part] IN installments.' *624:10.* payment: - pay.

ücret öde- '- pay' [A. **ücret** (**ucreTi**) 'cost, fee'], lit., '- pay the price': **Şu sıralar öyle dalgınım ki! Geçen gün lokantada yemek yedim ama ücret ödemeden çıktım.** 'I'm so absent-minded these days! The other day I ate at a restaurant, but I left without paying.' The salesman in a store: **Beyefendi * bakar mısınız? * Aldığınız ceket.in ücret.i.ni {ödeme-diniz/ödemey.i unuttunuz} galiba.** 'Oh sir, [lit., Sir, ** would you look (here)], * I think {you haven't paid/you've forgotten to pay} for your jacket [lit., ** the cost of the jacket].' *624:10.* payment: - pay.

ödemeli ara-. → **ara-** 2.

ödü kop-. → **kop-** 1.

ödüllendir- [ir] /lA/ '- award sb sth as a prize, - reward sb /with/ sth, - give sb sth as a reward' [**ödül** 'prize, award, reward' + verb-forming suf. -lAn (no such verb in current use) + caus. suf. -DIr]: **Öğretmen başarılı öğren-cileri birer kitap.la ödül-lendirdi.** 'The teacher {awarded each of the successful students a book as a prize./rewarded each of the successful students with a book./gave the successful students each a book as a prize.}' **Çocuklarınızı her zaman ödüllendirmeyin. {Gerektiğinde/Ara sıra} cezalandırın.** 'Don't always reward your children. Punish them {when necessary./once in a while.}' *624:10.* payment: - pay. → ≠ **cezalandır-**, ≠ **ceza ver-** → **ver-** 1.

ödüllendiril- [ir] /lA/ '- be awarded a prize, - be given a reward /of/, - be rewarded /with/' [ödüllendir- + pass. suf. -Il]: **Yılın {a: sinema sanatçıları/b: öğretmenleri/c: anneleri/d: sporcuları} ödüllendirildi.** 'The year's [outstanding] {a: movie stars/b: teachers/c: mothers/d: athletes} were given awards.' **Yılın öğretmeni iki haftalık tatil ile ödüllendirildi.** 'The teacher of the year [i.e., The year's outstanding teacher] was rewarded with a two-week vacation.' *624:10.* payment: - pay. → ≠ **cezalandırıl-**.

ödünç al-. → **al-** 1.

ödünç ver-. → **ver-** 1.

öfkelen- [ir] /A/ '- get angry, enraged, furious /AT/' [öfke 'anger; rage, wrath' + verb-forming suf. -lAn. ADJ. **öfkeli** 'angry']: **Lütfen öfkelenmeyin Tunç bey! Sinirleriniz.E hakim olun.** 'Please don't lose your temper Tunç bey. Control yourself! [lit., Get control OVER your nerves].' PERSON noun as object: **Evden ayrıldığını öğrenince Süleyman'A öfkelendi.** 'He got angry AT Süleyman when he learned that he had left the house.' VERBAL noun as object: * **Süleyman'ın evden ayrılma-.sı.nA öfkelendi.** 'He got angry because Süleyman had left the house [lit., ** AT Süleyman's having left the house].' → = **kız-** 1, = **sinirlen-.** *152:17.* resentment, anger: - become angry.

öğle yemeği ye-. → **ye-** 1.

öğren- [ir] /DAn/ '- learn, - find out /from/': Proverbs: **Bilmemek ayıp değil, öğrenmemek ayıptır.** 'Not knowing is not shameful, but not learning is [shameful].' **Sanatı**

ustadan görmeyen öğrenmez. 'He who doesn't learn [lit., ** see, experience] the {craft/skill} from a master won't learn it.' NON-verbal noun as object: S: **Türkçe.yİ nasıl öğrendin?** 'Q: How did you learn θ Turkish?' C: **{Okulda/* Kendi kendi.m.E/* Konuş.A konuş.A} öğrendim.** 'A: I learned it {At school/* BY myself/* BY speak.ING it a lot}.' **Kendi kendinize Türkçe öğrenin!** 'Learn Turkish by yourself!' **Türkçe öğrendi mi?** 'Did he learn Turkish?' **On senedir Türkiye'de oturduğu halde Türkçe.yİ {hâlâ doğru dürüst/bir türlü} öğrenemedi.** 'Although he has lived in Turkey for ten years, he {still hasn't been able to learn Turkish properly./hasn't been able to learn Turkish at all.}' **Dersinizi öğrendiniz mi?** 'Did you learn your lesson?', not in a moral sense. '- master' is expressed by this verb preceded by an appropriate adverb, e.g., **çok iyi öğren-** lit., '- learn very well': **John Türkçe.yİ çok iyi öğrendi.** 'John {has mastered Turkish./has learned Turkish very well.}' *570:9.* learning: - master.

VERBAL noun as object: Proverb: **Köpek suya düşmeyince {yüzmey.İ/yüzme.si.ni} öğrenmez.** 'A dog won't learn {to swim} unless it falls into the water.' Necessity is the mother of invention. **Türkiye'ye gitmek için nasıl vize al.ın.acağ.ı.nı konsolosluk.tan öğrendim.** 'I found out from the consulate how one gets a visa [lit., how a visa will be obtained] for [lit., to go to] Turkey.' **Postacı.nın ne zaman geleceğ.i.ni öğrenmek istiyorum.** 'I want to find out when the mailman is going to come.' **Sema'nın öğrenim.i.ni {tamamla.dığ.ı.nı/tamamla.yacağ.ı.nı} öğrendim.** 'I learned that Sema {had completed/was going to complete} her education.' **Sema'nın öğrenim.i.ni tamamlayıp {a: tamamlama.dığ.ı.nı/b: tamamlama.yacağ.ı.nı} öğrenemedim.** 'I couldn't find out whether or not Sema {a: had completed/b: was going to complete} her education.' *570:6.* learning: - learn; *927:14.* knowledge: - learn. → **bilgi edin-** ['- obtain information'].

öğrenim gör-. → **{eğitim/öğrenim/tahsil} gör-.** → **gör-** 3.

öğret- [ir] /A/ '- teach /θ/ sb sth, - teach sth /to/ sb' [irr. caus. of **öğren-**]: NON-verbal noun as object: **Dedem ban.A çok şey öğretti.** 'My grandfather taught me a lot of things.' **Bilmeyenler.E Türkçe öğretiriz.** 'We teach Turkish to those who do not know it.' **Ban.A birkaç temel {deyim} öğretir misin?** 'Would you teach me some basic {idioms/phrases/expressions}?' VERBAL noun as object: **S: San.A Osmanlıca {okumay.I/okuma-.sı.nı} kim öğretti?** 'Who taught you {how to read} [lit., ** reading] Ottoman Turkish?' **C: Ahmet bey öğretti.** 'A: Ahmet bey did.' **Kardeşim.e Kuran {okumay.I/ okuma.sı.nı} ben öğrettim.** 'I taught my younger sister [or brother] {how to read} the Qur'an.' **Bankaya nasıl para yatıracağ.ı.nı kızkardeşim.E öğrettim.** 'I taught θ my sister how she should deposit money in the bank.' *568:10.* teaching: - teach. → = **okut-** 3, = **eğit-** ['- educate sb /on a subject/'], = **ders ver-** 1 ['- teach /θ/ sb, - give lessons /to/ sb'] → **ver-** 1.

öğün-. → {**övün-/öğün-**}.

öksür- /ür/ '- cough': **Dün gece ablam hastaydı. Sabaha kadar öksürdü.** 'My older sister was ill last night. She coughed until morning.' **Turhan bey * çok kötü öksürüyor, üşüt.müş {olsa gerek/olmalı}.** 'Turhan * has a terrible cough [lit., is coughing terribly], he must have caught a chill.' *318:21.* * 1. wind: - breathe.

öksüz kal-. → **kal-** 1.

öl- [ÜR] /DAn/ '- die /{OF/AS A RESULT OF}/': **Ankara'daki tren kazasında iki kişi ölmüş.** 'Two people died in the train crash in Ankara.' **Atatürk 10 Kasım 1938'de sabahleyin {dokuz.U beş geçe/9:05'te} Dolmabahçe Saray.ı.nda öldü.** 'Atatürk died on the tenth of November 1938 at 5 minutes past nine in the morning at the Dolmabahçe Palace.' **Doktorlar hasta.nın {a: AIDS'TEN/b: verem.DEN/c: kanser.DEN/d: kalp kriz.i.nDEN/e: * doğal nedenler.LE} öl.düğ.ü.nü açıkladı.** 'The doctors disclosed that the patient had died {a: OF AIDS/b: OF TB/c: OF cancer/d: OF a heart attack/e: * OF natural causes}.'

Açlık.TAN ölüyorum. '{I'm dying OF hunger./I'm famished.}' **Susuzluk.TAN ölüyorum.** '{I'm dying OF thirst./I'm dying FOR a drink.}' *100:19.* desire: - hunger. **Ucuz kahramanlığ.A gerek yok. Ölmek değil, onurluca yaşamaktır zor olan.** 'There is no need for easy [lit., cheap] heroism. What is difficult is not to die, but to live honorably.'

-ArAk öl- lit., ** '- die by...ing': **7 çocuk {a: don.arak/b: yan.arak/c: boğul.arak} öldü.** 'Seven children {a: froze to death/b: {burned to death/lost their lives in the fire}/c: drowned} [lit., ** died {a: by freez.ing/b: by burn.ing/c: by drown.ing].' *307:24.* death: - die a natural death; *1022:9.* cold: - freeze.

Proverbs: **Dün ölen.i dün gömerler.** 'They bury the person who died yesterday.', i.e., Forget the unpleasant features of the past. **Namussuz yaşa.maktansa namuslu ölmek yeğdir.** 'It's better to die honorably than to live dishonorably.' Death before dishonor. **Nasıl yaşarsak öyle ölürüz.** 'However we live, so shall we die.' **Ölmüş eşek kurt.TAN korkmaz.** 'A donkey that has died does not fear θ the wolf.' *307:19.* death: - die. → = **hayata gözlerini {kapa-/kapat-}** → {**kapa-/kapat-**} 1, = **hayata gözlerini yum-** → **göz yum-** 1, = **hayatını {kaybet-/yitir-}** ['- lose one's life, die', of unnatural causes], = **ömrünü tamamla-** ['- complete one's life, come to the end of one's life, - die, pass away'], = **son nefesini ver-** ['- breathe one's last breath, - die'] → **ver-** 1, = **vefat et-**, = **canından ol-** ['- lose one's life, - die', mostly for an unexpected and undeserved death] → **ol-** 7, ≠ **doğ-** 1 ['- be born], ≠ **dünyaya gel-** → **gel-** 1.

ölç- [er] '- measure': **Kız.ım.ın boy.u.nu ölçtüm. * Tam 1 metre geldi.** 'I measured [the height of] my daughter. * She's a whole 1 meter tall [lit., ** It (i.e., her height) came (to) a whole 1 meter].' *300:10.* measurement: - measure.

öldür- [ür] '- kill' [**öl-** + caus. suf. -DIr]: **Katil evdeki üç kişi.yi öldürmüş.** 'The murderer killed {θ/the} three people in the house.'

308:12. killing: - kill. → = **kes-** 2 ['- kill, - butcher'], **canına kıy-** 1 ['- kill or murder without mercy'] → **kıy-** 2, **cinayet işle-** ['- commit murder, - murder'] → **işle-** 2.

kendini öldür- '- kill oneself, - commit suicide': * **Delirecek gibiyim. Ya evden kaçacağım ya da kendimi öldüreceğim.** 'I'm about to go crazy: either I'll run away from home or I'll kill myself.' *308:21.* killing: - commit suicide. → = **canına kıy-** 2, *more formal, legal:* = **intihar et-**.

{**vakit/zaman**} **öldür-** /ArAk/ '- waste or - kill time /[by]...ing/' [{A. **vakit** (vaKTİ)/A. **zaman** (. -)} 'time']: **Erhan'A çok kızıyorum. Bütün gün kahvede oturup vakit öldürüyor.** 'I'm very angry AT Erhan. He sits in the coffee house all day long wasting [his] time.' **Bütün gün kahvede otur.arak vakit öldürüyor.** 'He kills time [by] sitt.ing in the coffee house all day long.' *331:13.* inactivity: - waste time; *391:8.* uselessness: - be useless. → = {**vakit/zaman**} **kaybet-**[or **yitir-**] ['- lose or - waste time'], ≠ {**vakit/zaman**} **değerlendir-** ['- use time well, efficiently, - make good use of one's time'].

öldürül- [ür] /tarafından, ArAk/ '- be killed /by [sb], by...ing/' [**öldür-** + pass. suf. -Il]: **Abisi iki yıl önce bir kavgada öldürüldü.** 'His elder brother was killed in a fight two years ago.' **Yeni evli çift eve giren hırsızlar tarafından öldürülmüş.** 'The newly married couple was murdered by some thieves who had entered the house.' **Kalb.i.nDEN bıçaklan.arak öldürüldü.** 'He was killed by be.ing knifed IN the [lit., ** in his] heart.' *308:12.* killing: - kill.

ömrünü tamamla-. → **tamamla-**.

önceden bil-. → **bil-** 1.

önceden bildir-. → **bildir-**.

öne al-. → **al-** 1.

önem ver-. → {**önem/ehemmiyet**} **ver-.** → **ver-** 1.

önemse- [r] /I/ '- attach, - ascribe, or - give importance /TO/, - consider

important, - value, - think highly /of/' [**önem** 'importance' + verb-forming suf. -sA]: **Biz Türkler dostluğ.U çok önemseriz.** 'We Turks value θ friendship highly.' **Bu dersi hiç önemsemiyorum.** 'I don't attach any importance to this class at all.' **Kenan senin fikirlerin.i çok önemsiyor.** 'Kenan really values your ideas.' **Kenan seni çok önemsiyor.** 'Kenan thinks highly of you.' *996:13.* importance: - value. → = /A/ {**önem/ehemmiyet**} **ver-** → **ver-** 1, ≠ **küçümse-** 2.

{**öner-** [ir]/**teklif et-** [eDer]} /A/ '- propose, - suggest /to/' [**ön** 'the front part of anything' + verb-forming suf. -Ar, A. **teklif** (. -) 'proposal, offer']: NON-verbal noun as direct object: **Ban.a iyi bir lokanta önerir misiniz?** 'Could you suggest a good restaurant [to me]?' **Bu.nA çare OLARAK ne öneriyorsunuz?** 'What do you recommend AS a solution {to/for} this [problem]?' {**Ne önerirsem önereyim**} **hiç biri.ni kabul etmiyor, hepsi.ni reddediyor.** '{Whatever/No matter what} I propose, he rejects [lit., ** doesn't accept any of them], he rejects all my proposals [lit., ** rejects all of them].' → = **tavsiye et-**. # **Yeni açılan fabrika babam.a müdürlük önerdi.** 'The newly opened factory proposed the directorship to my father.' **Halil, Ayşe'ye evlenme önermiş.** 'Halil proposed marriage to Ayşe.' VERBAL noun as direct object: The FULL infinitive [-mAk] as object: **Tez danışman.ım.a yeni bir araştırma yapmay.I önerdim.** 'I suggested to my thesis advisor doing a new research project.' **Arkadaşlarım.a sinemaya git.mey.İ önerdim.** 'I proposed to {the guys/the girls/[lit., my friends] θ that we go [lit., going] to the movies.' The SHORT infinitive [-mA] + the possessED suffix [-sI] as object [-mAsI]: **Patron.A yeni bir ürün** {**yapma.SI.nI/yapma.MIZ.I**} **önerdim.** 'I suggested to the boss {that HE make [lit., ** HIS making]/that WE make [lit., ** OUR making]} a new product.' **Ne yapma.M.I önerirsiniz?** 'What do you recommend [that] I do [lit., ** MY doing]?' **Arkadaşlarım.a sinemaya gitme.MİZ.İ önerdim.** 'I suggested to my friends that WE go [lit., ** OUR going] to the movies.' *439:5.* offer: - propose. → = **ileri**

sür- 1 ['- put forward or - advance an idea, suggestion, or proposal, - propose'] → sür- 1.

önle- [r] /ArAk/ '- prevent /by...ing/' [ön 'front' + verb-forming suf. -lA]: NON-verbal noun as object: **Son anda fren.E bas.arak kaza.yı önledim.** 'By stepp.ing ON the brake at the last moment, I prevented the accident.'
VERBAL noun as object: **Doktorlar {hastalığ.ın ilerleme.si.ni} önlediler.** 'The doctors prevented {the disease from spreading/the spread [lit., advance] of the disease}.' *1011:14* hindrance: - prevent. → = /I/ engelle-, = /A/ mâni ol- → ol- 12, = önüne geç- → geç- 1.

Önüne bak! → bak- 1.

önüne geç-. → geç- 1.

öp- [er] /DAn/ '- kiss /ON/': **Ahmet annesine "Allah'a ısmarladık" dedi. Annesi de o.nU yanak.ları.nDAN öptü.** 'Ahmet said "Goodbye" to his mother. And his mother kissed him ON the [lit., his] cheeks.' **elini öp-** '- kiss the hand of', a gesture of respect when greeting or taking leave of an older man or woman: **Anneanne.si.nin el.i.ni öpüp baş.ı.nA koydu.** 'He kissed his grandmother's hand and placed her hand ON his [fore]head.' Proverbs: **Bükemediğin eli öp başın.A koy.** 'Kiss and then place ON your head the hand that you cannot bend back.', as in arm wrestling, i.e., Make peace with those you cannot defeat by force. **Veren eli herkes öper.** 'Everyone kisses the hand that gives.'

Common letter closings: * **Elleriniz.DEN öperim.** 'Kind regards., Kindest regards [lit., ** I kiss you ON your hands].', a concluding salutation in a letter to a SENIOR. * **Gözlerin[iz].DEN öperim.** 'Kind regards [lit., ** I kiss you ON your eyes].', a concluding salutation in a letter to a JUNIOR. * **Yanakların.DAN öperim.** 'Take care., All the best., Best wishes., Best. [lit., I kiss you ON your cheeks].', a concluding salutation in a letter between close friends of similar age or an older person to one younger, regardless of sex. *155:6* : - bow; *155: * 15.* respect: expressions of respect; *504: * 20.* courtesy: polite expressions; *562:19.* lovemaking, endearment: - kiss.

öpüş- [ür] /lA/ '- kiss one another' [öp- + recip. suf. -Iş]: **Öyle özlemişiz ki birbirimizi, sarılıp öpüştükten sonra hemen oracıkta uzun bir sohbet.E daldık.** 'We had missed each other so much that after embracing and kissing [one another], right there we plunged INTO a long, friendly conversation.' **Dedem, sokak ortasında öpüşmey.E utanmıyor musunuz, diyerek gençleri azarladı.** 'My grandfather scolded the young people saying, "Aren't you ashamed {OF kissing/to kiss} [right] there in the middle of the street!"' *562:19.* lovemaking, endearment: - kiss.

ör- [er] **1** '- knit', when the object knitted is specified: **Kış için kendim.E iki kazak ördüm.** 'For the winter I knitted {myself two sweaters/two sweaters FOR myself}.'

örgü ör- '- knit', lit., ** '- knit a knitting', when the object knitted is not specified: **Sevinç çok güzel örgü örer.** 'Sevinç knits very well.' *740:6.* weaving: - weave; *891:8.* production: - produce, - create.

2 '- braid': **Okula gider.ken saçlarını ördü.** 'Before going to school, she braided her hair.' • The aorist form of a verb of motion followed by **iken** [suffix form **-ken**], usually translated 'while...ing', may designate an action completed SHORTLY BEFORE another action, in which case it may be translated 'before...ing.' *3:22.* hair: - cut or - dress the hair.

3 '- darn': **çorap ör-** '- darn [{woolen/wool}] socks': **Baba-annem delinen yün çoraplarımı ördü.** 'My paternal grandmother darned my woolen socks that were full of holes.' → = **çorap dik-** [for non-woolen socks] → 1 dik- 2. *396:14.* restoration: - repair.

örgü ör-. → ör- 1.

örnek al-. → {örnek/misal} al-. → al- 1.

örnek ver-. → {örnek/misal} ver-. → ver- 1.

ört- [er] **1** '- cover' • Note the two patterns: **a)** /lA/ '- cover, - cover up sth /with/; - veil': **Suudî Arabistan'da kadınlar.ın çoğ.u yüzlerini peçe ile örterler.** 'In Saudi Arabia most women cover their faces with a veil.' **Bebeği yatağ.ı.nA yatırıp üst.ü.nü {yorgan.la/örtü.yle} örttü.** 'She put the baby to bed [lit., in its bed] and covered him [lit., ** his top, upper surface **üst.ü**] up {with a comforter/with a cover}.' **İki kızkardeşim var, biri başını örtüyor, diğeri örtmüyor.** 'I have two sisters. One covers her head [i.e., with the headcovering traditional for a Muslim woman], the other one doesn't.'
* b) /üzerine/ '- cover, - cover up /θ/ sth with [lit., ** - cover sth /{over/ON}/ sth], - spread sth /{over/on}/ sth': *** Polisler cesed.in üzer.i.nE beyaz bir örtü örttüler.** '{The police covered the body [lit., ** the body's top, upper surface, **üzeri**] with a white sheet [lit., white cover]./The police spread a white sheet over the body.}' *295:19.* covering: - cover.

2 '- conceal, - hide, - cover up': **Lütfen suçunuzu örtmeye çalışmayın.** 'Please don't try to hide your {offense/guilt/sin}.' **{Gerçeği/Hakikati} örtmek için elinizden geleni yaptınız ama nafile, adalet.ın pençe.si.nden kurtulamayacaksınız.** 'You've done your best to conceal {the truth} but in vain. You won't be able to save yourself from the arm of the law [lit., from justice].' Underlying the following examples is the Islamic belief that if a believer conceals the weaknesses and faults of others, God will conceal his weaknesses and faults in the hereafter. **Hataları örtmek husus.u.nda, Hz. Peygamber (sas** [i.e., for the Arabic: **sallâllahu aleyhi ve sellem]) müminleri teşvik etmektedir.** 'The Noble Prophet (peace be upon him) encourages the believers to conceal errors [lit., ** on the matter of concealing errors].' **Biri.nin ayıb.ı.nı örtmek o.na atlas elbise giydirmekten daha hayırlıdır.** 'To conceal sb's faults is more blessed than to dress him in a satin garment.' **Hataları örtmekte gece gibi ol!** 'Be like the night in concealing faults!' **Mevlâna**

Celaleddin Rumi. *346:6.* Concealment: - conceal.

3 '- close, - shut sth' door, window, cover, curtains: **Evden çıkmadan önce perdeyi örttün mü?** 'Did you close the curtains before leaving the house?' *293:6.* closure: - close. → = {kapa-/kapat-} 1, ≠ aç- 1.

öt- [er] **1** for various animals to produce a sound: '- sing [of birds], - chirp [of birds or insects], - crow [of roosters]': **Kuşlar sabahleyin erkenden ötmey.E başladılar.** 'The birds began {to sing/θ singing} early in the morning.' Proverbs: **Bahar gel.me.yince bülbül ötmez.** '{Until spring comes/As long as spring hasn't come}, nightingales do not sing.' **Bir çöplükte iki horoz ötmez.** 'Two roosters won't crow on one garbage dump.', i.e., One master in a house is enough. **Vakitsiz öten horozun başını keserler.** 'They cut off the head of the rooster that crows at the wrong time.' *60:5.* animal sounds: [birds] - warble; *842:12.* timeliness: ADV. opportunely; *843:7.* untimeliness: ADV. inopportunely.

2 for various wind instruments to produce a sound: 'for a horn - play, a whistle - make a sound, an alarm - go off, - sound, or - screech': **Bu {düdük/boru} ötmüyor.** 'This {whistle [or pipe (musical instrument)]/horn [or bugle]} won't play.' *708:39b.* music: - play, - make a sound. **Çocuk arabanın kapısını zorlayınca alarm sistemi ötmeye başladı.** 'When the child forced the door of the car, the alarm system went off [lit., ** began to sound].' *58:8.* stridency: - screech.

öttür- [ür] '- blow a whistle' [öt- + caus. suf. -DIr]: *** Kaçan hırsızı görünce bekçi düdüğ.ü.nü uzun uzun öttürdü.** 'When the {guard/watchman} saw the thief running off [lit., the fleeing thief], he blew a long blast on his whistle [lit., ** blew his whistle long long].' *58:8.* stridency: - screech; *708:42.* music: - blow a horn.

{öv- [er]**/methet-** [metheDer]**}** /DAn dolayı, için, **nedeniyle**/ '- praise sb or sth /for/ sth', not usually with God as the object. [A. **medih** (meDHi) 'praise' + et-]: **Eleştiride amaç övmek ya da yermek değil,**

nesnel bir değerlendirme yapmak olmalıdır. 'In criticism the purpose should not be to praise or to find fault, but to make an objective evaluation.' Person as object: {Çalışkanlığımdan dolayı/Çok iyi Türkçe konuştuğum için} bütün öğretmenlerim beni överdi. 'All my teachers used to praise me {for my diligence/because I spoke Turkish very well}.' * Kendimi övmek gibi olmasın... '{I don't mean to boast/I don't want to appear to be boasting [lit., ** Let it not be like to praise myself]}, but...': Kendimi övmek gibi olmasın, * bu konuda oldukça iyiyim diyebilirim. 'I don't mean to boast, * but I may say that on this issue I come out [lit., ** I am] rather well.' → = Övünmek gibi olmasın. → {övün-/öğün-} 1. Thing as object: Eleştirmenler ünlü yazarın son kitabını şiirsel üslûbu nedeniyle övdüler. 'The critics praised the author's lastest book for its poetical style.' 509:12. approval: - praise. → ≠ {eleştir-/tenkit et-} ['- criticize', negatively and positively; negatively not as harsh as yer-], ≠ yer-.

övül- [ür] /{tarafından/CA}, nedeniyle/ '- be praised /by, FOR/' [öv- + pass. suf. -Il]: Ünlü yazarın son kitabı şiirsel uslübu nedeniyle eleştirmenler tarafından övüldü. 'The famous author's latest book was praised by the critics FOR its poetical style.' 509:12. approval: - praise. ≠ yeril-.

{övün- [ür]/öğün- [ür]} [öv- + refl. suf. -In] 1 /lA/ '- be proud /OF/, - take pride /IN/, - pride oneself /ON/': "Türk! Övün, çalış, güven!" M.K. Atatürk. '"[O] Turk! Be proud, strive, have confidence!" M[ustafa] K[emal] Atatürk.' NON-verbal noun as object: Ayşe hanım müslümanlığı.yLA övünür ama geçen Ramazanda bir gün bile oruç tutmamış. 'Ayşe hanım prides herself ON her Muslim piety, but during the past Ramadan she didn't fast for even a day.' VERBAL noun as object: * Amcam çok iyi piyano çalmak.LA övünür. 'My paternal uncle is very proud OF {how well he plays the piano/his excellent piano playing}.' 136:5. pride: - take pride. → = /lA/ gurur duy- 2 → duy- 3, = /lA/

iftihar et-, = /DAn/ kıvanç duy- → duy- 3, ≠ utan-.

2 /lA/ '- praise oneself, - boast, - brag /{OF/ABOUT}/': * Övünmek gibi olmasın... '{I don't mean to boast/I don't want to appear to be boasting [lit., ** Let it not be like to praise myself]}, but...': Övünmek gibi olmasın, sesim güzeldir. 'I don't mean to boast, but I do have a good voice [lit., my voice is good].' → = Kendimi övmek gibi olmasın. → öv-. NON-verbal noun as object: Zenginliğ.in.LE övünme, bir kıvılcım yeter; güzelliğin.LE övünme, bir sivilce yeter. 'Do not boast OF your wealth, one spark is enough [to destroy it]; do not brag OF your beauty, one pimple is enough [to spoil it].' VERBAL noun as object: İnsanlar.a yardımcı olmak.LA övünme, * Allah bilsin yeter. 'Don't boast ABOUT being helpful to people. * It's enough if God knows [lit., Let God know, that's enough].' 502:6. boasting: - boast; 504: * 20. courtesy: polite expressions; 509:12. approval: - praise. → ≠ yer-.

özen- [ir] [özen 'care, careful attention' + verb-forming -θ] 1 /lA/ '- take great pains /to/ do sth well, - go to great pains /to/ do sth well, - take pains /{WITH/OVER}/ sth': Oldukça titiz bir sanatçıdır, son eser.i.nE de çok özenmiş. 'He's quite a meticulous artist. He {went to great pains WITH/took great pains OVER} his most recent work.' 403:11. endeavor: - make a special effort.

2 /A/ '- want badly sth that sb else has; - want to be in the situation that sb else is in': Çocuğun yediği dondurma.yA özendim. 'I longed FOR the ice cream that the child was eating.' * Yeni eviniz.E özendim doğrusu, ne kadar güzel! 'I really {envy/envied} you [for] your house, how nice it is!' • In reference to a PRESENT condition, certain common Turkish verbs designating a state, i.e., a feeling, emotion, or sensation, often have the simple PAST tense, but the equivalent English has the simple PRESENT tense. 100:16. desire: - wish for. → = imren- 1; 154:3. envy: - envy. → = kıskan- 1, = imren- 2 ['- long /FOR/ sth unobtainable, - envy without malice'].

3 /A/ '- try to imitate /θ/ sb': Çocukluğ.um.da bazı artistler.E özenirdim, onlar gibi konuş-may.a çalışırdım. '{When I was a child/lit., In my youth}, I used to try to imitate θ certain movie stars. I would try to speak like them.' *336:5.* imitation: - imitate.

4 /A/ '- have a passing fancy to do sth', usually sth one knows little about: **Bir ara doktor olmay.a özenmiştim, iyi ki olmamışım.** * **Ban.A göre bir iş değilmiş.** 'At one point I wanted to become a doctor. It's a good thing I didn't. * I guess it wasn't the right thing for me [lit., It apparently wasn't a profession appropriate for me].' *364:4.* caprice: - blow hot and cold.

özetle- [r] '- summarize, - sum up' [özet 'summary' + verb-forming suf. -1A]: **Salih derse gelemedi. Fakat Kenan ona öğretmen.in anlattıklar.ı.nı özetledi.** 'Salih couldn't come to class, but Kenan summarized for him what the teacher had said.' **Öğretmen sınıfta {a: yaptık.lar.ı.nı/b: yapacak-.lar.ı.nı/c: yapma.sı gereken-ler.i} özetledi.** 'The teacher summarized {a: what he had done/b: what he was going to do/c: what he should do} in class.' **Edindiğim izlenimi {şöyle/şu şekilde} özetleyeyim...** 'Let me summarize my observations [lit., ** the observations I acquired] {as follows/in the following way}:...' **Özetlemek gerekirse...** 'If it is necessary to summarize...' A summary statement is sometimes introduced simply by **Özet.LE** 'IN summary,...' *268:6.* shortness: - shorten; *557:5.* abridgment: - abridge; *557:7.* : ADV. in brief; *848:8.* repetition: - iterate. → = **toparla- 2.**

özle- [r] /I/ '- miss, - long /FOR/ sb or sth absent' [öz 'self' + verb-forming suf. -1A]: **Tahsin'i bir yıldır görmüyorum. Onu çok özle.DİM.** 'I haven't seen Tahsin for a year. I MISS him very much.' • In reference to a PRESENT condition, as above, certain common Turkish verbs designating a state, i.e., a feeling, emotion, or sensation, often have the simple PAST tense, but the equivalent English has the simple PRESENT tense, or, as below, the PRESENT PERFECT tense. **Anneciğim, seni çok özledim,**

keşke şimdi burada yanımda olsaydın! 'Dear mother, {I MISS/I'VE MISSED} you a lot. If only you were here with me [lit., at my side].' **Seni ne kadar özlediğ.im.i bilemezsin.** 'You have no idea [lit., ** You can't know] how much I miss you!' **{Sevgilim/Anneciğim} seni ne kadar özlediğimi bir bilsen!** '{Dear/Mommy}, if you only knew how much I miss you!' **Türkiye'ye dön.düğü.n.de seni çok özleyeceğiz.** 'When you return to Turkey, we'll miss you a lot.' **Öyle özlemişiz ki birbirimizi, sarılıp öpüştükten sonra hemen oracıkta uzun bir sohbet.E daldık.** 'We had missed each other so much that after embracing and kissing, right [then and] there we plunged INTO a long, friendly conversation.' *100:16.* desire: - wish for; *991:7.* insufficiency: - want. → also = /I/ **ara- 4,** = /A/ **hasret çek-** → **çek- 5.**

özür dile-. → **dile- 2.**

- P -

pahalan- [ır] '- become more expensive, - increase in price' [paha 'price' + verb-forming suf. -1An]: * **Fırıncılar ekmeğ.E zam yaptılar. Böylece ekmek 5 kuruş pahalandı.** 'The bakers increased the price of bread [lit., ** made a price increase TO bread]. Thus the price of bread went up 5 kurush [lit., ** bread became 5 kurush more expensive].' **Son günlerde yumurta çok pahalandı.** 'In recent days eggs have gotten a lot more expensive.' *251:6.* increase: - grow, increase [i.]. → = **fiyatlar art-** → **art- 1,** = **fiyatlar fırla-** → **fırla- 2,** = **fiyatlar çık-** → **çık- 6,** = **fiyatlar tırman-** → **tırman- 2,** = **fiyatlar yüksel-** → **yüksel- 2,** ≠ **fiyatlar düş-** → **düş- 3,** ≠ **fiyatlar in-** → **in- 4,** ≠ **ucuzla-.**

paket yap-. → **yap- 3.**

paketle- [r] '- wrap, - wrap up, - make a package of' [It. paket 'package' + verb-forming suf. -1A]: **Lütfen {şu kitabı/şu bardakları/şu elbise-yi} paketler misiniz?** 'Would you please wrap [up] {this book/these [drinking] glasses/this suit}?' *295:20.* covering: - wrap. → = **paket yap-** → yap- 3, **paket sar-** ['- wrap a package'] → sar- 1, ≠ **paket aç-** → aç- 1.

para al-. → al- 1.

para çek-. → çek- 2.

para {geri ver-/iade et-}. → {geri ver-/iade et-}. → ver- 1.

para harca-. → {harca-/sarf et-} 1.

para sarf et-. → {harca-/sarf et-} 1.

para ver-. → ver- 1.

para yatır-. → yatır- 2.

paraca gücü yet-. → yet-.

parçala- [r] '- cut up, - chop up, - break into pieces, - smash, - tear to pieces' [**parça** 'piece' + verb-forming suf. -lA]: **Şöminede yakacağımız odunları parçaladım.** 'I chopped up the pieces of wood that we're going to burn in the fireplace.' **Kasap tavukları parçaladı ve dolab.A koydu.** 'The butcher cut up the chickens and put them IN the refrigerator.' **Sirkte bir adam aslan kafes.i.nE düşmüş. Aslan adamı herkes.in göz.ü önünde parçalamış.** 'At the circus a man fell INTO the lion's cage. In sight of everyone, the lion tore the man to pieces.' *801:13.* separation: - shatter.

parçalan- [ır] [**parçala-** + {pass./refl.} suf. -n] 1 /{tarafından/CA}/ '- be broken [up], smashed, torn, cut up, chopped up, or pulled to pieces /by/': **Eğer şömineyi yakmak istiyorsanız, bahçedeki odunlar.ın parçalanma.sı gerekiyor.** 'If you want to light the fireplace, some of the firewood in the garden will have to be chopped up.' **Kazada Orhan'ın elleri parçalanmış.** 'Orhan's hands were severely injured [lit., ** broken up] in the accident.' **Koskoca Osmanlı İmparatorluğu I. [read: birinci] Dünya Savaşı sonunda {düşmanlar tarafından/düşmanlar.ca} parçalandı.** 'At the conclusion of World War I the vast Ottoman Empire was broken up {by the

enemy}.' *801:13.* separation: - shatter.

2 '- break into pieces, - shatter', i.e., - come apart: **Havalanırken arıza yapan uçak büyük bir gürültüyle yer.E çakılıp parçalandı.** 'The plane that had a mechanical failure while taking off crashed INTO the ground with {a great noise/a roar} and broke into pieces.' **Elindeki bardak parmaklarının arasından kaydı, yere düşüp parçalandı.** 'The glass in his hand slipped through his fingers, fell to the ground, and shattered.' *801:13.* separation: - shatter.

yüreği parçalan- 'for one's heart - be wrenched upon seeing sth sad, - grieve, - be extremely upset' [**yürek** 'heart'], lit., ** 'for one's heart - be broken into pieces', but without the force this literal translation has in English: **Yaralıları görünce hepimiz.in yüreğ.i parçalandı.** 'When we saw the wounded, all of us were extremely upset.' For '- for one's heart to be broken', → yıkıl- 3. *112:17.* sadness: - grieve. → = acı- 2, = üzül-.

park et- [eDer] /{A/DA}/ '- park a vehicle /{AT/in}/{AT/in}/'. In general, the locative case suffix is on the noun designating the broader area, the dative case suffix on the noun designating a particular place within that broader area, though this distinction may not be strictly observed. S: **Nere{.yE/.DE} park edebilirim?** 'Q: {Where} can I park?' C1: **Apartman.ın {a: ön.ü{.nE/.nDE}/b: arka.sı{.nA/.nDA} park edebilirsiniz.** 'A1: You may park {a: in front of/b: behind} the apartment building.' C2: **Garaj.A park edebilirsiniz.** 'A2: You may park IN the garage.' **Buralarda park edecek yer var mı?** 'Is there a place to park around here?' * **Burada ne kadar süreyle park edebilirim?** 'How long can I park here?' **Bura{.yA/.DA} park etmek yasaktır.** 'It is forbidden to park {here}.' *159:12.* location: - place; *352:7.* publication: poster: * specific signs.

parla- [r] '- shine, - sparkle': **{Güneş/Ay} pırıl pırıl parlıyor.** 'The {sun/moon} is shining brightly.' **Yıldızlar pırıl pırıl parlıyor.**

'The stars are {shining brightly/sparkling}.' {Elmas yüzük/Altın kolye/Ayna} parlıyordu. 'The {diamond ring/gold necklace/mirror} was {shining/sparkling}.' Sevinç.TEN {gözleri/yüzü/gözleri.nin iç.i} parlıyordu. '{His eyes/His face/The pupils of his eyes} were shining WITH pleasure.' 1024:23. light: - shine.

parmak kaldır-. → kaldır- 1.

parti ver-. → ver- 1.

patla- [r] [pat, the sound of an explosion, + verb-forming suf. -lA. ADJ. patlak 'exploded, flat (tire)'] 1 '- burst, - explode': {Balon/Lâstik} patladı. 'The {balloon/tire} burst.' Televizyon patlayınca yangın çıktı. 'When the television set exploded, a fire broke out.' Birdenbire kendi.m.i savaşın ortasında buldum. Yanımda bombalar patlıyordu. 'Suddenly I found myself in the midst of the battle. Bombs were bursting at my side.' 671:14. violence: - explode.

lâstiği patla- '- get a flat [tire]' [lâstik 1 'rubber', the material. 2 'tire'], lit., 'for its tire - burst': {* Yol.un yarı.sı.nda/Yarış sıra.sı.nda} bisikletim.in lastiğ.i patladı. '{* Half way there [lit., ** at the half of the road]/During the race} my bicycle had a flat [lit., the tire of my bicycle burst].' 260:10. contraction: - collapse; 671:14. violence: - explode. For 'a tire - go flat', i.e., - lose air slowly, → in- 4; ≠ şiş- 2 ['- fill up with air'].

2 /DAn/ '- be ready to explode, - feel like screaming /{ON ACCOUNT OF/DUE TO}/, - explode, - fly off the handle, colloq. - lose one's cool': Tatilde okuyacak iyi bir kitap bulamadım. Çok sıkılıyorum. Neredeyse patlayacağım. 'I couldn't find a good book to read over {the vacation/the holidays}. I'm really annoyed. I'm about to explode.' A: Bir saatten beri bekliyorum. * Neredesin? 'A: I've been waiting for an hour. * Where have you been? [lit., ** Where are you?]' B: * Dur! * {Patlama}! * İşte geliyorum. 'B: * {Just hold on!/Just hold your horses!} * {Don't blow your top!/Don't fly off the handle!/Don't lose your cool!} * {I'm

coming./I'm on my way.}' 152:20. resentment, anger: - fly into a rage.

3 'for sth unpleasant - break out': Birden {fırtına/savaş} patladı. 'A {storm/battle} suddenly broke out.' 817:13. beginning: - originate. → = kop- 2, = çık- 4, başla- 1 ['- begin'].

paylaş- [ır] /lA/ '- share sth /with/ sb' [pay 'share' + recip. suf. -lAş]: Masrafları paylaşalım. 'Let's share the costs.' Babam.ın verdiğ.i parayı {kardeşim.le} paylaştım. 'I shared the money that my father had given [me] {with my brother/with my sister}.' Bu önemli haberi sizler.le paylaşmak istedim. 'I wanted to share this important news with you.' Seven insan kıskanır, kimse.yle paylaşmak istemez sevdiğini. 'The person who loves is jealous. He doesn't want to share the one he loves with anyone.' Proverb: İki köpek bir kemiğ.İ paylaşamaz. 'Two dogs can't share θ one bone.' Arkadaşlar, bugün İstanbul'LA ilgili anılarımı sizin.le paylaşmak istiyorum. '{Friends/ Guys}, today I would like to share with you my memories of Istanbul.' Türkiye'de * başınız.dan geçen ilginç olayları bizimle paylaşır mısınız? 'Would you please share with us the interesting events you experienced in Turkey [lit., ** that passed through your head]?' 476:6. participation: - share.

fikir paylaş- /lA/ '- agree, - share opinions, thoughts /with/' [A. fikir (fiKRi) 'thought, idea, opinion']: * {Fikir/Fikirleri} paylaşmak {insan.A} yeni şeyler kazandırır. 'The sharing of {ideas} benefits {θ a person/θ mankind} by bringing forth new things [lit., ** the sharing of ideas wins new things for...].' * Babamla aynı fikirleri paylaşıyoruz. 'My father and I share the same views [agree].' 332:9. assent: - concur. → = {düşünceye/ fikre/görüşe} katıl- → katıl- 3, = {fikir/görüş} savun- 2 → savun-.

With various words denoting feelings: Yakın arkadaşlarımla {a: sevincimi/b: neşemi/c: mutluluğumu/d: üzüntümü/e: acımı/f: kederimi/g: duygularımı} paylaşıyorum. 'I share {a: my pleasure/b: my joy/c: my happiness/d: my sorrow/e: my sorrow/f: my grief [or sorrow]/g: my feelings} with my close friends.' *476:6.* participation: - share.

paylaştır- [ır] /A/ '- serve out, - dish out, - distribute a {serving/share} /{INTO/ONTO}/' [paylaş- + caus. suf. -DIr]: Çorbayı kaseler.E paylaştırıp üzerine kaşar peynir.i serpin. 'Dish the soup [out] INTO the bowels and sprinkle kaşar cheese on top.' Salata malzemelerini ve közlenmiş biberleri dekoratif bir şekilde tabaklar.A paylaştırın. 'Dish out the salad makings and the broiled peppers ONTO the plates in a decorative fashion.' *176:17.* transferal, transportation: - ladle.

pazarlık et- [eDer] /a: için, b: üzerinde, c: lA/ '- bargain, - haggle, - dicker /a: for [sth], b: over [sth], c: with [sb]' [pazar 'market' + noun-forming suf. -lIk = pazarlık 'bargaining']: Bir halı almak istiyorduk. Satıcı fiyat.ı.nın 80 lira olduğ.u.nu söyledi. Yarım saat pazarlık ettikten sonra 80 liralık halı.yI 50 lira.yA aldık. 'We wanted to buy a rug. The salesman said that it cost [lit., its price was] 80 liras. After bargaining for half an hour, we bought the 80-lira rug FOR 50 liras.' Eğer İstanbul'da alışveriş yapacaksanız pazarlık {etmey.i/etmesi.ni} öğrenmeli-siniz. 'If you are going to do shopping in Istanbul, you must learn how to bargain.' Halıcı.yla şu halı {için/üzerinde} yarım saat pazarlık ettik ve sonunda anlaştık. 'We dickered {for/over} that rug for half an hour with the rug dealer, and finally we came to an understanding.' *731:17.* commerce, economics: - bargain.

perhiz yap-. → yap- 3.

perma yaptır-. → yaptır- 2.

peşin öde-. → öde-.

pislen- [ir] '- get or - become dirty, soiled, polluted' [pis 'dirt' + verb-forming suffix -lAn]: Denizlerimiz {gün geçtikçe} pisleniyor. 'Our oceans are getting more polluted {day by day/with every passing day/lit., as the days pass}.' *80:15b.* uncleanness: - get dirty. → = kirlen-.

pislet- [ir] '- get or - make sth dirty, - soil, - pollute' [pis 'dirt' + verb-forming suffix -lA + caus. suf. -t]: * Üst.ün.ü baş.ın.ı pisletme DİYE sana kaç defa söyledim! 'How many times have I told you not to get your clothes [= üst baş] dirty! [lit., ** How many times I told you SAYING, 'Don't get your clothes dirty.']' * Ortalığ.ı pisletmeyin {akşam.A} misafir gelecek. 'Don't make the place [lit., ** the area round about] dirty. Guests are coming {this evening/tonight}.' Fabrikalar.ın atıklar.ı çevre.yi pisletiyor. 'The waste from the factories is polluting the environment.' *80:15a.* uncleanness: - dirty. → = kirlet-, ≠ temizle-.

piş- [ir] 'for sth - cook, - bake': Yemek daha pişmedi mi? 'Hasn't the food cooked yet?' Yemek pişti. Ateşi söndür. 'The food has cooked. Turn off the gas.' Proverb: Fırın kızmayınca ekmek pişmez. 'Bread won't bake {unless the oven is hot/as long as the oven is not hot}.' *11:4b.* cooking: for sth - cook.

pişir- [ir] '- cook, - bake sth' [piş- + caus. suf. -Ir]: * Oya'nın annesi çok güzel yemek pişirir. 'Oya's mother is a very good cook [lit., cooks food very well].' Lütfen bunu biraz daha pişirir misiniz? 'Would you please cook this a little more?' * Önceden ısıtılmış 175 derece.ye ayarlı fırında 35-40 dakika pişirin. 'Cook it for 35 to 40 minutes in a 175-degree oven [lit., ** in an oven that has been set and previously heated to 175 degrees].' At home, not at a restaurant, a mother, father or other person close to a young woman is speaking: Kızım bize iki {a: az şekerli/b: orta şekerli/c: çok şekerli/d: sade} kahve pişir.iver. 'Dear [lit., ** My girl], two coffees please {a: with little sugar/b: with medium sugar/c: with a lot of sugar/d: with no sugar}.' • The structure *verb stem*.Iver-, as above, even without lütfen, may convey the sense of a polite request. Proverb: Ne pişirirsen onu yersin. 'You eat whatever you cook.', i.e., You get what you deserve. *11:4a.* cooking: - cook sth.

pişman ol-. → ol- 12.

plân kur-. → kur- 1.

{plânla- [r]/tasarla- [r]} /I/ '- plan, - envisage' [{F. plân/A. tasar} 'plan' + verb-forming suf. -lA. In modern Turkish the independent noun in use is tasarı rather than tasar]: NON-verbal noun as object: Babam çok düzenli bir adamdı. Yapacağı işi önceden plânlardı. 'My father was a very organized {man/person}. He would plan in advance {what/lit., the task} he was going to do.' Bu araştırma proje.si.ni öğrenciler plânladılar. 'The students planned this research program.' VERBAL noun as object: S: Bugün ne yapmay.I plânladınız? 'Q: What did you plan to do today?' C1: Topkapı müzesini gezmey.İ plânladık. 'A1: We planned to visit the Topkapı museum. C2: Hiçbir şey plânlamadık. 'A2: We didn't plan anything [at all].' Cumhuriyet Bayramı için cumartesi günü saat birde büyük bir konser vermey.İ plânlıyoruz. 'Saturday at 1 o'clock we are planning to give a big concert for the Republic Holiday.' Osman yazın {yapacaklar.ı.nı/ yapma.sı gerekenler.i} plânladı. 'Osman planned {what he was going to do/what things he had to do} in the summer.' Mine tatil.E {ne zaman/kimlerle/neyle} gideceğ.i.ni plânlıyor. 'Mine is planning {when/with whom [i.e., with what people]/how [by what vehicle]} she is going to go ON {vacation/holiday}.' 381:8. plan: - plan; 964:4. prearrangement: - prearrange. → plân kur- ['- make, - devise, - draft, - establish, or - formulate a plan'], programla- 1 ['- schedule'].

postala- [r] /A/ '- mail, - post, - send off, - mail /to/' [It. posta 'mail' + verb-forming suf. -lA]: {Bu mektubu/Bu paketleri} postalayabilir misiniz? 'Could you mail {this letter?/these packages?}' Geçen hafta annem.e yazdığım mektubu ancak bugün postalayabildim. 'Only today was I able to send off the letter that I had written to my mother last week.' 176:15. transferal, transportation: - send; 553:12. correspondence: - mail. → = noun for item of mail at- 4, = noun for item of mail {gönder-/yolla-}.

postalan- [ır] /A, {tarafından/CA}/ '- be mailed, posted, sent off /to, by/' [postala- + pass. suf. -n]: S:

Mektuplar postalandı mı? 'Q: Have the letters been mailed?' C: Bugün postalandı efendim! 'A: They were mailed today, {sir/ma'am}.' Hazırladığınız paketler yeni sekreter tarafından postalandı. 'The packages [that] you prepared were mailed by the new secretary.' Paketler hangi adres.e postalandı? 'To what address were the packages sent?' 176:15. transference: - send; 553:12. correspondence: - mail.

pratik yap-. → yap- 3.

programla- [r] [F. program 'plan, schedule' + verb-forming suf. -lA] 1 '- schedule': Yapacağımız bütün işleri programlayalım. 'Let's schedule all the tasks we're going to do.' Gelecek ay yapacağımız Avrupa seyahatini şimdiden programladık. 'We've already scheduled the trip to Europe that we're going to make next month.' 964:4. prearrangement: - prearrange. → plân kur- ['- make, - devise, - draft, - establish, or - formulate a plan'], {plânla-/tasarla-} ['- plan, - envisage'].

2 /A, için/ '- set an instrument /FOR/, - program a computer /FOR/': Çorbamı ısıtmak için mikrodalga fırını 30 saniye.yE programladım. 'To heat my soup, I set the microwave oven FOR 30 seconds.' {Video.m.u/ Vidyo.m.u} televizyondaki filmi kaydetmesi için programladım. 'I programmed {my VCR} to tape the movie on television.' 964:4. prearrangement: - prearrange; 1041:18. computer science: - computerize.

3 '- develop or - create computer materials or games': Amcam değişik şirketler için bilgisayar oyunlarını programlıyor. 'My paternal uncle is developing computer games for various companies.' 891:12. production: - originate; 1041:18. computer science: - computerize.

protesto et- [eDer] /I/ '- protest sth or against sth' [It. protesto 'protest']: Öğrenciler okul yemekler.i.ni şiddetle protesto ettiler. 'The students strongly protested AGAINST the school food.' Halk başbakan.ın ülke.yi savaş.A sokma karar.ı.nı protesto etti. 'The people protested θ the prime minister's decision to bring the nation into the war [lit., ** the prime minister's bring-the-nation-into-war decision].' 333:5. dissent: - object; 451:3. opposition; - oppose. → /A/ itiraz et- ['- object /to/, - raise an objection /{to/AGAINST}/'], /A/ karşı çık-. Same. → çık- 3.

prova et- [eDer] '- try on', clothing [It. prova 'trial']: Bu elbise * küçük geldi, {diğer.i.ni/başka bir.i.ni} prova edebilir miyim? 'This suit * is [lit., ** came] too small. May I try on {the other one/another one}?' * Bu ceketi [üst.ÜN.de] prova etmek ister misin? 'Do you want to try this jacket on [lit., ** on YOUR (s.) upper surface]?' Üst.ÜM.de prova edebilir miyim? 'May I try it on [lit., ** on MY upper surface]?' Bir prova etmek ister miydiniz? 'Would you like to try it [i.e., a piece of clothing] on?' 941:8. experiment: - experiment. → = dene- 1.

prova yap-. → yap- 3.

- R -

rahat bırak-. → bırak- 4.

* rahat et- [eDer] '- BE, - BECOME comfortable, - feel better, at ease' [A. rahat 'comfort, comfortable']: Burada rahat edeceğiniz.i umarım. 'I hope you'll be comfortable here.' Evlenince biraz rahat edeceğim. 'When I get married, I'll be more comfortable.' Doktor iğne yapınca hasta biraz rahat etti. 'When the doctor had given the injection, the patient felt a little better.' Often used with nouns for parts of the body as subjects: Bu ayakkabıyı giyince ayaklarım rahat etti. 'When I put on these shoes, my feet felt better.' Arkam.A yastık koyunca sırtım rahat etti. 'When I put a pillow behind me [lit., ** TO my back], my back felt better.' Proverb: Evvel zahmet çeken sonra rahat eder. 'He who first endures hardship will later enjoy comfort.' 120:8. relief: - be relieved. → = rahatla-, ≠ rahatsız ol- 2 → ol- 10.2.

rahatını boz-. → boz- 1.

* rahatla- [r] '- feel better, - be relieved', after experiencing sickness, pain, or fatigue, '- become comfortable' [A. rahat 'comfortable' + verb-forming suf. -lA]: Bütün yıl çalıştık. Derslerimiz bitince bir hayli rahatlayacağız. 'We have worked hard all year. We'll feel a lot better when our classes are over.' 120:8. relief: - be relieved. → = rahat et-, ≠ rahatsız ol- 2 → ol- 10.2.

rahatsız et- [eDer] '- bother, - disturb' [rahatsız 'uncomfortable']: On the door of hotel rooms, etc.: Lütfen rahatsız etmeyiniz. 'Please do not disturb.' 352:7. publication: poster: * specific signs. {Ses/Gürültü} beni rahatsız {etmez/etmiyor}. '{Noise} doesn't bother me [or I don't mind {noise}].' Kitap okuyorum, lütfen beni rahatsız etme! 'I'm reading [a book], please don't disturb me!' In this type of situation the English equivalent often is: I'm TRYING TO read [a book], please don't disturb me!' → = rahatı boz- → boz- 1. Rahatsız ettiğim için özür dilerim. '[I'm] Sorry for disturbing you [lit., ** because I disturbed you].' The following words may serve as a polite means of initiating a conversation: * Rahatsız etmiyorum ya? 'I {hope/trust} I'm not disturbing you, but....' 96:13. unpleasure: - annoy; 343:8. * 1. communication: conversation initiators.

rahatsız ol-. → ol- 10.2.

rahmet eyle- [r] /A/ '[for God] - be merciful /to/ or - have mercy /{ON/UPON}/' [A. rahmet 'God's mercy']: Allah rahmet eylesin. 'May God have mercy [UPON him].', said upon hearing of the death of a Muslim, today sometimes also said of a non-Muslim. The equivalent expression for a non-Muslim is Toprağı bol olsun. 'May he rest in peace [lit., ** May his earth be abundant],' although this expression may sometimes also be said for a Muslim. → ol- 11 → olsun. A: Dün gece büyükbabam vefat etti. 'A: My grandfather passed away last night.' B: Allah [o.nA] rahmet eylesin. * Başınız sağ olsun. 'B: May God have mercy UPON him [i.e., on the deceased so that he may go to Paradise]. * May you be healthy [lit., ** May your head be healthy].' The usual English response is 'I'm so sorry to hear it.', or similar words of commiseration. **Baş** 'head' here represents the whole person. *145:4.* pity: - have pity; *307:* * *39.* death: expressions used upon hearing of a death; *504:* * *20.* courtesy: polite expressions; *601:4.* acquital: - acquit.

randevu al-. → **al-** 3.

randevu ver-. → **ver-** 1.

rastla- [r] usually pronounced **rasla-** [P. **rast** (-) 'right, straight' + verb-forming suf. -1A] 1 /A/ '- meet by chance, - run or - bump /INTO/, - encounter /θ/, - come or - chance /UPON/': **Dün limanda Serpil'E rastladım.** 'Yesterday I ran INTO Serpil [f.] at the pier.' * **San.A rastladığım çok iyi oldu. Epeydir seni arıyordum.** '{I'm so glad I ran INTO you./ It's a good thing I ran INTO you./lit., It's very good [that] I ran INTO you.} I've been looking for you for quite a while.' **İzmir'e giderken yolda leylek sürü.sü.nE rastladık.** 'While going to Izmir, on the way we came UPON a flock of storks.' *131:6.* inexpectation: - be unexpected; *223:11.* nearness: - meet. → = /A/ **tesadüf et-** 1, = /lA/ **karşılaş-** 2. * **Sekiz otobüs.ü.nE rastladığım iyi oldu, yoksa okula yürü.yerek gidecektim.** 'It's a good thing [that] I chanced upon the eight o'clock bus, otherwise I would have gone to school ON foot [lit., ** by walk.ing].' → **yetiş-** 1 ['- catch /θ/ a vehicle, - make it /to/, - get /to/ a place, - arrive in time /FOR/; - be in time /FOR/'].

2 /A/ '- hit /θ/ sth by chance, not intention, - collide /WITH/': **Yurdanur'A attığım top cam.A rastladı.** 'The ball I threw to Yurdanur hit θ the window.' *901:13.* impulse, impact: - collide. → = **tesadüf et-** 2, **çarp-** 1 ['- hit /θ/, - strike /θ/, - bump /{AGAINST/INTO/ON}/, - run or - crash /INTO/'], **vur-** 1 ['- hit, - strike'], **çarpış-** [(for vehicles) '- collide, - run into'].

razı ol-. → **ol-** 12.

reçete hazırla-. → **hazırla-**.

reddet- [reddeDer] [A. **r e d** (reDDi) 'rejection' + et-] 1 '- refuse, - reject': **Onu doktora götürmek istedim fakat reddetti.** 'I wanted to take him to the doctor, but he refused [to go].' **Sedat sinema artisti olmak istiyordu fakat ailesi reddetti.** 'Sedat wanted to be a movie actress, but his family {rejected the idea/did not approve}.' → = **karşı çık-** → **çık-** 3. NON-verbal noun as object: **Arkadaşım.ın verdiğ.i parayı reddettim.** 'I refused the money [that] my friend gave [me].' **Müge evlenme teklifimi reddetti. Çok üzgünüm.** 'Müge [f.] refused my proposal of marriage. I'm very depressed.' {**Ne önerirsem önereyim**} **hiç biri.ni kabul etmiyor, hepsi.ni reddediyor.** '{Whatever/No matter what} I propose, he rejects [lit., ** doesn't accept any of them], he rejects all my proposals [lit., ** rejects all of them].'
VERBAL noun as object: **Öğretmen verdiği notu değiştirmey.i reddetti.** 'The teacher refused to change the grade [that] he had given.' *442:3.* refusal: - refuse. → = **karşı çık-** → **çık-** 3, ≠ **razı ol-** → **ol-** 12, ≠ **kabul et-** 1.

2 '- deny, - claim that sth is not true': **Hırsız kolyeyi çaldığ.ı.nı reddetti.** 'The thief denied that he had stolen the necklace.' *335:4.* negation, denial: - deny. → = **inkâr et-**, ≠ **kabul et-** 3.

refakat et-. → {**eşlik et-/refakat et-**}.

rekor kır-. → **kır-** 1.

rendele- [r] '- grate' [P. **rende** 'grater' + verb-forming suf. -1A]: **Havuç ve turpu temizleyip yıkayın ve rendeleyin.** 'Clean and wash the carrots and beets and grate them.' *1049:9.* powderiness, crumbliness: - pulverize.

resim çek-. → {**resim/fotoğraf**} **çek-**. → **çek-** 7.

resim çektir-. → {**resim/fotoğraf**} **çektir-**. → **çektir-** 3.

resim çiz-. → **çiz-** 1.

rezervasyon yaptır-. → **yaptır-** 2.

Rica ederim. → directly below.

rica et- [eDer]. NON-verbal noun as object: /DAn/ '- ask /θ/ sb for sth, - request sth /from/ sb' [A. rica (. -) 'request']: Bir harita rica edebilir miyim? 'May I have a map?' S: * Bir kibrit rica edeceğim. 'Q: May I trouble you for a match? [lit., ** I will {ask for/request} a match.]' • The future tense above conveys a sense of courtesy. A common, polite response to a request: C: Tabii, * buy[u]run. 'A: Of course, * here you are.' Ahmet ben.den kibrit rica etti. 'Ahmet asked θ me for a match.' VERBAL noun as object: /{DAn/A}/ '- ask /θ/ sb to do sth': * Zeki'DEN ban.A yardım etme.si.nİ rica ettim. 'I asked θ Zeki to help [lit., ** his helping] me.' Babam.DAN [bana] bir ayakkabı alma.sı.nI rica ettim. 'I asked θ my father to buy [lit., ** his buying] [me] some shoes.' * Bavulumu taşıma.sı için Engin'E rica ettim. 'I asked θ Engin to carry [lit., ** for his carrying] my bags.' Öğretmen Zehra'nın tahtaya gitme.si.ni rica etti. 'The teacher asked Zehra [f.] to go [lit., ** Zehra's going] to the blackboard.' → = iste- 2. The actual words of the request may precede diye 'saying': * Annem ban.A "Akşam erken gel" DİYE rica etti. 'My mother asked me to come early in the evening [lit., ** asked me SAYING "Come early in the evening."].' → sor- [for '- ask a question', etc.].

Rica ederim. (1) 'Please' a) In a simple request: Rica ederim, konuşmayın. 'Please, don't talk.' = lûtfen. 440:9. request: - request.
b) In expressing an objection: A: Kahvenizi nasıl istersiniz? 'A: How would you like your coffee?' B: Orta şekerli olsun, zahmet olmazsa. 'B: Medium sweet, if it's no trouble.' A: Rica ederim. Hiç zahmet değil. 'A: [Oh] Please, it's no trouble at all.' A: Saliha san.A çok darıldım, Yahya'ya benim için "Çok cimridir" demişsin. 'A: Saliha [f.], I'm very angry AT you. You apparently told Yahya that I am very stingy [lit., ** concerning me you said...].' B: Rica ederim, yanılıyorsun. Ben öyle bir şey demedim. 'B: [Oh] Please, you're mistaken. I said no such thing.' 333:4. dissent: - dissent. The sense of

the following two uses is 'You need not humble yourself to me to thank me or to make the request.'
(2) 'No problem., You're welcome., Don't mention it.': A: Çok teşekkür ederim. 'A: Thank you very much.' B: Rica ederim. 'B: {No problem./You're welcome./Don't mention it.}' In the above Rica ederim may be followed or replaced by Bir şey değil. '{You're welcome./lit., It's nothing.}' 504: * 20. courtesy: polite expressions.
(3) Usually not translated or occasionally by 'Sure' or 'No problem': S: Hoca.M, önemli bir işim var; bugün biraz erken çıkabilir miyim? 'Q: {Professor/Teacher} [lit., ** {MY professor/MY teacher}], the common form of address to a professor or teacher], I have an important matter to attend to today. May I leave a little early?' C: * Rica ederim, tabi [çıkabilirsiniz]. 'A: * Sure. Of course you may [leave (early)].' 504: * 20. courtesy: polite expressions.

röfle yaptır-. → {meç/röfle} yaptır-. → yaptır- 2.

röntgen çektir-. → çektir- 3.

rötar yap-. → yap- 3.

rüya gör-. → {düş/rüya} gör-. → gör- 3.

- S -

saat tut-. → tut- 5.

sabahla- [r] '- spend the night somewhere, - stay up all night' [A. sabah 'morning' + verb-forming suf. -lA]: Bugünkü sınav.A çalışmak için, dün gece sabahladım. 'I stayed up all last night to study FOR today's exam.' Bütün oteller doluydu. Bir parkta sabahladık. 'All the hotels were full. We spent the night in a park.' Deprem.in olduğ.u gece korku.DAN kimse uyuyamadı. Bütün kent sabahladı. 'The night of the earthquake [lit., The night the earthquake occurred] no one could sleep BECAUSE OF fear. The whole city stayed up all night.' * {Ne o/Hayrola} Turhan, çok yorgun ve bitkin görünüyorsun, dün akşam sabahladın * mı yoksa? 'What's {the matter/up}, Turhan? You look very tired, {beat/shot/lit., worn out}. * Could it be that you were up all night [lit., last night]?' *820:6.* time: - spend time. → **gecele-** ['- spend the night somewhere'], {**vakit/zaman**} **geçir-** ['- spend time'] → geçir- 3.

sabırsızlan- [ır] '- get, - become, or - be impatient' [A. **sabır** (saBRı) 'patience' + **sız** 'without' = **sabırsız** 'impatient' + verb-forming suf. -**lAn**]: A: **Neden geç kaldın, söyle!** 'A: Why were you late? Explain.' B: * **Sabırsızlanma, anlatıyorum işte!** * **Lâf.ın son.u.nU bekle.** 'B: Just hold on [lit., ** Don't become impatient]. I'm getting to it [lit., explaining it] right now! * Just wait till I've finished [lit., ** Wait for the end of the remark].' *135:4.* impatience: - be impatient. → = **sabrı tüken-** ['for one's patience - run out or - be exhausted'], ≠ **sabret-** ['- be patient'].

sabret- [sabreDer] '- be patient' [A. **sabır** (saBRı) 'patience' + **et-**. ADJ. **sabırlı** 'patient']: **Ben** {**sabretmey.İ/sabretme.si.ni**} **bilen bir insanım.** 'I'm a person who knows how to be patient.' Proverb: {**Sabreden/Bekleyen**} **derviş murad.ı.nA ermiş.** 'The dervish {who was patient/who waited} reached θ his goal.' Everything comes to him who waits. *134:4.* patience: - be patient. → **sabrı tüken-** ['for one's patience - run out or - be exhausted'], ≠ **sabırsızlan-** ['- get, - become, or - be impatient'].

sabrı tüken-. → tüken-.

saçlarını yaptır-. → yaptır- 2.

saçma sapan konuş-. → {**abuk sabuk/saçma sapan**} **konuş-.** → konuş-.

saçmala- [r] '- talk nonsense, - talk {garbage/rot}, - be silly' [**saçma** 'absurd remark, piece of hogwash' + verb-forming suffix -**lA**]: **Semra hanım, dansöz olmak isteyen kızına "Saçmalama, kendine gel" diye bağırdı.** 'Semra hanım shouted [saying], "Don't {be silly/talk nonsense}. Come to your senses, [child]" to her daughter who wanted to become a belly dancer.'

Bilgi sahib.i olmadan fikir sahib.i olursan böyle saçmalarsın işte! 'If you have an opinion without having the [necessary] knowledge, you'll talk nonsense just like this!', i.e., as you are doing now. *520:5.* meaninglessness: - talk nonsense; *922:6.* foolishness: - be foolish. → = {**abuk sabuk/saçma sapan**} **konuş-** → konuş-.

sağ ol-. → ol- 12.

sağla- [r] /A/ '- provide /to/, - procure, - get, - obtain sth /FOR/' [**sağ** 1 'alive, living'. 2 'healthy, well'. 3 'strong, solid' + verb-forming suf. -**lA**]: **Kızım.ın bir el.i yağda bir el.i balda, eşi o.nA her istediğini sağlıyor.** 'My daughter is well-off [lit., My daughter's one hand is in oil, her other hand is in honey]. Her husband provides θ her with whatever she wants.' **Öncelikli hedefimiz bölge ülkeleri arasında istikrar, barış ve güven sağlamaktır.** 'Our primary aim is to provide stability, peace, and security among the countries of the region.' **Fakirler.e yardım sağlayan kurumların sayısı yeterli değil.** 'There aren't enough organizations providing aid to the poor [lit., The number of organizations providing aid to the poor is not sufficient].' *385:7.* provision, equipment: - provide.

geçimini sağla- /IA, ArAk/ '- make one's living, - provide [a living] for, - support [one's family] /[BY], by...ing/' [**geçim** 'living, getting by']: S: **Geçim.İNİZ.i ne.yle sağlıyorsunuz?** 'Q: How [lit., ** with what] do you make YOUR living?' C: **Geçim.İM.i** {a: **öğretmenlik.le** [or **öğretmenlik yap.arak**]/b: **yazarlık.la** [or **yazarlık yap.arak**]/c: **kütüp-hanecilik.le** [or **kütüphanecilik yap.arak**]} **sağlıyorum.** 'A: I make MY living {a: [BY] teach.ing [or lit., ** by do.ing teaching]/b: [BY] writ.ing [or lit., ** by do.ing writing]/c: as a librarian [or lit., ** by do.ing librarianship]}.' **Sen.in ve çocuklar.ın geçim.i.ni sağla-mak için çalışıyorum.** 'I'm working to provide [a living] for you and the children.' Another common question to elicit a person's occupation is: **Mesleğiniz nedir?** 'What is your {occupation/

profession}?' *385:11.* provision, equipment: - make a living. → = **geçin-** 2, = **hayatını kazan-** → kazan- 1, = **iş yap-** → yap- 3.

Sağlıcakla kalın. → kal- 1.

Sağlık olsun. → ol- 11 → olsun.

{Sağol!/Sağolun[uz]!} → sağ ol-. → ol- 12.

Sağ olsun. → sağ ol- → ol- 12.

Sağol[un], varol[un]! → sağ ol-. → ol- 12.

sahip ol-. → ol- 12.

sakal tıraşı yap-. → yap- 3.

sakatlan- [ır] '- get or - be hurt, - become physically disabled; - become crippled; - become maimed or mutilated'. The injury may be temporary or permanent. [A. **sakat** 'defective, deformed' + verb-forming suffix -1A + refl. suf. -n]: **Buzda kayıp düşünce sakatlandım.** 'When I slipped and fell on the ice, I got hurt.' **İtalya Türkiye millî maçında ünlü futbolcu Hakan sakatlandı.** 'In the Italy-Turkey national soccer game the famous player Hakan was hurt.' *393:13.* impairment: - inflict an injury. → **yaralan-** 1 ['- be wounded, injured'].

sakın- [ır] 1 /DAn/ '- avoid /θ/, - keep [oneself] away /from/, or - steer clear /OF/ sb or sth': **Düşmanların.DAN sakın!** '{Keep away from/Steer clear OF} your enemies!' * **Günah.TAN sakınmak o kadar da kolay değil.** 'It's not so easy to avoid θ sin.' **Taklitler.i.nDEN sakınınız.** 'Avoid θ imitations [lit., ** imitations of it]', reference to a product. *329:3.* inaction: - refrain; *368:6.* avoidance: - avoid; *352:7.* publication: poster: * specific signs; *668:7.* temperance: - abstain. → = **kaçın-**.

2 /DAn/ '- guard /AGAINST/; - watch out /FOR/ sth dangerous': * **Sen düşmanların.DAN değil, asıl dostların.DAN sakın!** 'What is important is not to guard yourself AGAINST your enemies but rather to guard yourself AGAINST your friends.' *339:8.* carefulness: - be vigilant.

3 /DAn/ '- protect /from/': **Çocuğunu sakınmak isterken * kadın.ın kendi.si arabanın altında kalıyordu.** 'While trying [lit., wanting] to protect her child, * the woman herself almost got run over [lit., ** remained under the car].' Proverb: **Yiğit kısmı gözünü budak.tan sakınmaz.** 'Brave young men [lit., The brave young segment (of the population)] do not shrink from danger [lit., do not shield their eyes from a (threatening) branch].' **Gözünü budak.tan sakınmayan bir yiğitti.** 'He was a fearless young man [lit., a young man who did not shield his eyes from a (threatening) branch].' *1007:18a.* protection: - protect. → = **koru-**.

sakıncası ol-. → {sakıncası/ mahzuru} ol-. → ol- 12.

sakla- [r] 1 /A/ '- hide, - conceal sth /IN/', i.e., - put sth somewhere so it will not be seen: **Yurdaer kardeşin.e aldığı hediye.yİ dolab.ı.nA sakladı. Çünkü o.nA sürpriz yapmak istiyordu.** 'Yurdaer hid the present he had brought for his brother IN his closet because he wanted {to surprise him/make a surprise for him}.' **Şekeri nere.yE saklayacak-sınız?** 'θ Where are you going to hide the candy?' **Silâh.ı.nı yatağ.ı.nın alt.ı.nA sakladı.** 'He hid his weapon θ under his bed.' **Teröristleri evi.nDE sakla.dığ.ı iddia.sı.yLA yargılanıyor.** 'He is being tried ON {the charge/the allegation} that he hid the terrorists in his house.'

/DAn/ '- keep sth secret /from/': **Tunç sınıfta {a: kaldığ.ı.nı/b: kalacağ.ı.nı} babası.nDAN sakladı.** 'Tunç did not let his father know [lit., kept from his father (the fact)] {a: that he had been held back in school [lit., ** 'stayed in the class', i.e., didn't pass on to the next grade]/b: that he was going to be held back}.' **Baba.sı.nın öldüğ.ü.nü Canan'DAN sakladık.** 'We kept from Canan the news that his father had died.' Proverb: **Derdini saklayan derman bulamaz.** 'He who keeps his troubles [to himself] won't be able to find a remedy [for them].' *346:6.* concealment: - conceal. → = **gizle-**, ≠ **açıkla-** 2.

2 /DA/ '- keep or - store sth IN a place,' NOT '- put it there': **Annem değerli mücevherlerini banka.DA saklar.** 'My mother keeps her valuable jewelry IN the bank.' **Bozul.ma.ma.sı İÇİN {eti/peyniri/sütü} buzdolabı.nDA sakla.** 'Keep {the meat/the cheese/the milk} IN the refrigerator SO THAT it won't spoil.' *386:12.* store, supply: - reserve; *397:8.* preservation: - preserve; *474:5.* retention: - retain.

3 /A/ '- save, - keep, or - hold sth /FOR/, - set sth aside /FOR/': **Pasta.nın bir kısm.ı.nı {akşam.A/Ahmet'E} sakladı.** 'He set aside some of the pastry {FOR the evening/FOR Ahmet}.' → = ayır- 2. # **Mektuplarımı ben {gel.ince.yE/gel.en.E} kadar saklayın.** 'Keep [or Hold] my letters until I come.' Proverbs: **Kazanmak kolay, saklamak zordur.** 'To earn is easy; to keep [i.e., what one has earned] is difficult.' **Sakla samanı gelir zaman.ı.** 'Save the straw, the time for it will come.' *474:5.* retention: - retain.

4 /DAn/ 'for God - protect, - preserve, - shield sb /from/ [misfortune]': **Allah saklasın.** 'May God preserve him [i.e., from misfortune].': **A: Saat 12 oldu, hâlâ gelmediler. * Başlar.ı.na bir kaza mı geldi acaba?** 'A: It's midnight, and they still haven't come. * I wonder if they've had an accident [lit., ** 'if an accident has come to their heads. **Baş** 'head' here represents the whole person]. **B: Allah saklasın.** 'B: I hope not [lit., May God preserve [them] (from such a misfortune)].' → = **Allah korusun.** → koru-. *504: * 20.* courtesy: polite expressions; *1007:18a.* protection: - protect; *1007:18b.* : expressions to prevent misfortune; *1011: * 22.* hindrance: * expressions to prevent unfavorable occurrences.

saklan- [ır] /DAn, A/ [sakla- + {pass./refl.} suf. -n] 1 '- hide or - conceal oneself /from, IN/': **Çocuk babası görme.SIN DİYE dolab.A saklandı.** 'The child hid himself IN the closet SO THAT his father would not see him.' **Hapishaneden çıktıktan sonra * kimse.nin yüz.ü.nE bak.amaz oldu, herkes.TEN saklanıyor.**

'After getting out of prison, he could not look anyone IN the face [lit., ** became one who could not look IN anyone's face]. He has been hiding from everyone.' * **Teröristler.in saklandığ.ı ev burasıymış.** 'Here is [or This is] the house where the terrorists supposedly {hid/are hiding}.' *346:8.* concealment: - hide oneself. → = **gizlen-** 1.

2 /DAn, tarafından/ '- be hidden /from, by/; - be kept secret /from, by/': **Altın.ın nerede saklandığ.ı.nı keşfetti.** 'He discovered where the gold had been hidden.' * **Doğum günü hediyeleri Aslı'dan [annesi tarafından] saklandı.** 'Aslı's birthday presents were hidden from her [by her mother] [lit., Her birthday presents were hidden from Aslı...].' **Babasının ölüm haberi Canan'dan saklandı.** 'The news of his father's death was kept from Canan.' *346:6.* concealment: - conceal. → = **gizlen-** 2.

3 /DA/ '- be kept, maintained /in/ a place': **Öldüğ.ü.nden beri anneannemin mücevherleri kasa.da saklanıyor.** 'My grandmother's jewelry has been kept in the safe [box] since she passed away.' *397:8.* preservation: - preserve.

4 /için, tarafından/ '- be saved, kept, set aside /FOR, by/': **Abla.sı.nın küçülmüş elbise.leri [annesi tarafından] bebek için saklandı.** 'Her older sister's clothes, which had gotten too small, were set aside for the baby [by her mother].' *386:12.* store, supply: - reserve.

saldır- [ır] [sal- '- let attack, - let loose /ON/' + caus. suf. -DIr] 1 /A/ '- attack /θ/, - light /INTO/': **Düşman dün {sabah.a karşı/gece karanlığ.ı.nda} şehr.E saldırdı.** 'The enemy attacked θ the city [şehir (şeHRi)] yesterday {toward morning/in the dark of night}.' **Kurtuluş Savaşında [1919-1922] topraklarımız.A saldıran düşman.A karşı hep birlikte yurdumuz.U savunduk.** 'During the War for Independence [1919-1922], we all together defended our homeland against the enemy who had attacked our soil.' **Fenerbahçe-Galatasaray maçından sonra iki takım.ın heyecanlı taraftarlar.ı**

birbirleri.nE saldırdı. 'After the Fenerbahçe-Galatasaray soccer game, the enthusiastic supporters of the two teams lit INTO each other.' Sign in a garden: Yaklaşmayın. Köpek var, saldırır! 'Beware the dog! [lit., Don't approach. There is a dog. It will attack.]' Köpekler bahçeye giren yabancı.yA saldırdı. 'The dogs attacked θ the stranger who had entered the garden.' 352:7. publication: poster: * specific signs; 459:14. attack: - attack. → = hücum et- 1.

2 /A/ '- rape /θ/, - assault /θ/ sexually', not necessarily rape: Adam kız.A saldırdı. 'The man attacked θ the girl.' 459:14. attack: - attack; 480:15. taking: - possess sexually; 665:20. unchastity: - seduce. → = ırzına geç- ['- rape, - violate'] → geç- 1, = tecavüz et- 2.

salıver- [ir] '- let go, - set free, - release': Hava korsanları iki saat pazarlıktan sonra yolcular.ın bir kısm.ı.nı salıverdi. 'The hijackers released some of the passengers after two hours of negotiations.' 120:6. relief: - release; 398:3. rescue: - rescue; 431:5. liberation: - release. → = bırak- 5, = serbest bırak- → bırak- 5.

salla- [r] 1 '- wave': Resmî geçit töreninde öğrenciler bayrak ve {filamaları} sallıyorlardı. 'During the parade the students were waving flags and {pennants/ streamers}.' 915:11. oscillation: - wave.

el salla- /A/ '- wave /to/' [el 'hand']: Tren göz.den kaybolan.a kadar el salladı. 'She waved until the train {went out of sight/disappeared} [lit., ** got lost from sight].' Şermin okula giderken annesi.ne el salladı. 'As Şermin was going off to school, she waved to her mother.' 517:22. signs, indicators: - signal; 915:11. oscillation: - wave.

2 '- push [a child in a swing], - rock [a cradle]': A child sitting in a swing to her mother: Daha hızlı sallar mısın? 'Would you push me a little harder?' jocular: Niye uykusuz-sun? Sabaha kadar beşik mi salladın? 'Why are you tired [lit., ** sleepless]? Have you been rocking the cradle all night [lit., till

morning].' 901:12. impulse, impact: - thrust, - push; 903:9. pushing, throwing: - push.

3 '- shake, - rock sth': Deprem bütün şehri salladı. 'The earthquake shook the whole city [şehir (şeHRi)].' 916:10. agitation: - agitate.

başını salla- '- shake one's head' in affirmation, negation, or surprise [baş 'head']: * {Evet/Hayır} anlam.ı.nda [or diye] başını salladı. 'She shook her head {"Yes" [i.e., up and down]/"No" [i.e., from side to side or, less likely, from down to up]} [lit., ** shook her head in the meaning of (or saying) {yes/no}].' "Böyle bir şey olamaz, inanmıyorum" dedi başını sallayarak. '"Such a thing is impossible [lit., cannot be], I don't believe it," she said shaking her head [i.e., from side to side].' * {a: Haklısın/b: Anladım} der gibi başını salladı. 'He shook his head as if to say {a: "You're right"/b: "I {understand/understood}"}.' 131: * 17. inexpectation: gestures of; 441:3. * 1. consent: gestures of; 442:5. * 1. refusal: gestures of; 916:10. agitation: - agitate.

{san- [IR]/zannet- [zanneDer]} '- think, - suppose' [A. zan (zaNNı) 'thought' + et-]: S: Yağmur yağacak mı * sen.ce? 'Q: Do you think it's going to rain [lit., ** Will it rain * in your view]?' {C 1: Sanırım./C2: * Sanmam.} '{A1: I think so./A2: I don't think so [or I doubt it].}' Oğuz'un biz.e {gel.diğ.i.ni/ gel.eceğ.i.ni} sanıyordum. 'I thought that Oğuz {had come/was going to come} to our house [lit., to us].' Aşık olduğ.um.u sanıyorum. 'I think I'm in love.' Gelecek yıl mezun olabileceğ.im.İ sanıyorum. 'I think [that] I'll be able to graduate next year.' Korkulacak bir şey olduğunu sanmıyorum. 'I don't think {there is anything to be afraid of./it is anything to be afraid of.}' → = düşün- 2, = tahmin et- 1. * Bu ülkede demokrasi var sandım, yanılmışım. 'I thought there was democracy in this country. I guess I was {wrong/mistaken}.' Karanlıkta * sen.İ Yasemin sandım. 'In the darkness * I thought [that] you were Yasemin [f.] [lit., ** I thought you Yasemin].' A more formal equivalent: Sen.İN Yasemin olduğ.un.U sandım. 'I thought [that] you were Yasemin [lit., ** I thought YOUR {being/having been} Yasemin].' → /A/ benzet- 1 ['- mistake one thing or person /FOR/ another']. * Sen kendin.İ ne sanıyorsun? 'Just who do you think you are [lit., ** What do you think yourself]?' * Sen.İ kütüphanede sanıyordum. 'I thought [that] you were in the library [lit., ** I thought you in the library].' or Sen.İN kütüphenede olduğ.un.U sanıyordum. 'I thought [that] you were in the library [lit., ** I thought your {being/having been} in the library].' Şaka yapıyorlar sandım. 'I thought they were joking.' * Siz.İ çalışıyor sanıyorlar. 'They think [that] you are working.' • Note the structure of the preceding sentence: The direct object sizi 'you' is followed by the third person singular of the present continuous tense of the verb çalış-. Proverb: Minare.yİ yaptırmayan yerden * bitmiş sanır. 'A person who has [never] had a minaret built * thinks that it has sprung from the ground.', i.e., like a plant. He doesn't realize the difficulties involved in the construction. *500:11.* belief: - think; *952:11.* belief: - think.

sap- [ar] /A/ '- turn /to/, - make a turn /to/; - turn /INTO/ or - enter /θ/ a road; - swerve /to/, - veer /to/': * S: **Postaneye nasıl gidebilirim, tarif eder misiniz?** 'A: Would you tell me how I can get to the post office? [lit., ** How can I get to the post office, would you describe?]' C1: * **İki sokak sonra beyaz binayı geçin, {sağ.A/sol.A} sapın.** 'A1: After [you have gone] two blocks [lit., streets], go past the white building and turn {[to the] right/[to the] left}.' C2: **Her hangi bir taraf.A sapmadan doğru gidin.** 'A2: Go straight ahead without turning off [IN any direction].' *279:6.* curve: - curve. → = dön- 3.

sapta-. → {tespit et-/sapta-}.

sar- [ar] 1 /A, IA/ '- wrap one thing /{IN/AROUND}, with/ another': At the bookstore: **Lütfen bu kitabı sarar mısınız?** 'Would you please wrap this book?' When buying a gift: **Lütfen {bunu/bu paketi} güzel bir kâğıt.LA sarar mısınız,**

hediye olacak. 'Would you please wrap {this/this package} IN some nice paper? * It's for a gift [lit., It's going to be a gift].' More common English for the situation above: 'Would you please gift-wrap this...?' **Eski elbiselerini bir kâğıd.A sararak kapı.nın ön.ü.ne bıraktı.** 'Wrapping his old clothes IN some paper, he left them in front of the door.' *295:20.* covering: - wrap; *769:20.* assemblage: - bundle; *799:9.* joining: - bind. → **paketle-** ['- wrap, - wrap up, - make a package of'], **paket yap-**. Same. → yap- 3, ≠ aç- 1.

2 /IA/ '- bandage, - bind /with/': **Annesi Yıldız'ın yara.sı.nı temiz bir bezle sardı.** 'Yıldız's mother bandaged her [i.e., Yıldız's] wound with a clean piece of cloth [lit., ** Her mother bandaged Yıldız's wound...].' *91:24.* therapy: - treat; *799:9.* joining: - bind.

3 /I/ '- surround, - envelop': **Alevler bütün evi sarmıştı.** 'Flames enveloped the whole house.' *209:6.* environment: - surround; *212:5.* enclosure: - enclose.

çevresini sar- '- surround' [çevre 'the area around, surroundings']: **Mahallenin çocukları hemen simitçi.nin çevre.si.ni sarmışlar.** 'The children of the neighborhood at once surrounded the simit seller.' simit 'a crisp, ring-shaped, sesame-seed covered, salty, pretzel-like pastry usually sold on portable stands by itinerant peddlars.' *209:6.* environment: - surround; *212:5.* enclosure: - enclose.

etrafını sar- '- surround, - envelop' [A. etraf (. -) 'sides, surroundings']: * **Düşman askerleri {etraf.IMIZ.I/etraf.LARI.nı} sarmıştı.** 'The enemy soldiers surrounded {US/THEM} [lit., ** {our sides/their sides}].' *209:6.* environment: - surround; *212:5.* enclosure: - enclose.

sarar- [ır] [ADJ. sarı 'yellow'] 1 '- turn yellow, - yellow': **Sonbaharda ağaçların yaprakları sararır.** 'In the fall, the leaves of the trees turn yellow.' **Eski defterin yaprakları sararmıştı.** 'The pages of the old notebook had turned yellow.' *43:3.* yellowness: - yellow.

2 '- turn or - grow pale, - pale': *
Tuğba hasta mı acaba? * **İyice
sararmış, solmuş, hemen
doktor.a haber verelim!** 'I
wonder whether Tuğba is ill. * She
has become quite pale [lit., **
become yellow (i.e., from healthy
pink, then) pale]. Let's notify the
doctor right away.' * **Hasta.nın
yüz.ü iyice sarardı.** 'The patient
[lit., The face of the patient] had
become quite pale.' **Aniden
polisleri görünce** * **hırsız.ın
yüz.ü sarardı.** 'When the thief
suddenly saw the police, he turned
pale [lit., ** When he suddenly saw
the police, * the thief's face turned
pale].' *36:6.* colorlessness: - lose
color; *127:13.* fear, frighteningness: -
flinch.

sarf et-. → {harca-/sarf et-}.

sarhoş ol-. → ol- 12.

sarıl- [ır] [**sar-** + {pass./refl.} suf. -Il] 1
/A/ '- embrace /Ө/, - put or - throw
one's arms /AROUND/': * **Ekrem
otobüs.E binmeden önce bütün
arkadaşları.nA tek tek sarıldı.**
'Before getting ON the bus, Ekrem
embraced Ө all his friends one by
one.' **Yurtdışından gelen
kocası.nA hasretle sarıldı.** 'She
{ardently/passionately} embraced Ө
her husband, who had come from
abroad.' **Ayrılmadan önce son
bir defa daha birbirleri.nE
sarıldılar.** 'Before {parting/going
their separate ways}, they embraced Ө
one another once more one last time.'
**Annesi.nin boyn.u.nA sarılıp
ağlamağa başladı.** 'She threw her
arms AROUND her mother's neck
[boyun (boYNu)] and began to cry.'
Proverb: **Denize düşen yılan.A
sarılır.** 'A person who has fallen into
the sea will {embrace Ө/cling to}
[even] a snake.' Desperate times call
for desperate measures. *125: * 19.*
hopelessness: proverbs; *562:18.*
lovemaking, endearment: - embrace.
→ /I/ **kucakla-** ['- embrace, - take in
one's arms; - hug'], **kucaklaş-** ['-
embrace or - hug one another'].

2 /a: A, b: 1A, c: tarafından/ '- be
wrapped /a: IN, b: with, c: by [sb]/':
**Kitabınız satıcı tarafından
hediye kâğıdı{.nA/.yLA}
sarıldı.** 'Your book has been gift-
wrapped by the salesperson [lit.,
wrapped {IN/with} gift paper...].'

769:20. assemblage: - bundle; *799:9.*
joining: - bind.

sat- [ar] /a: A, b: A, c: DAn, d: için, e:
1A/ '- sell sth /a: to [sb], b:
{FOR/AT} [a price, in total or per
unit], c: {FOR/AT} [a price, only per
unit], d: for, e: {BY/THROUGH}/': •
Note the three question patterns:
a) S: <u>**Karpuz.U kaç.A** satıyor-</u>
sunuz? 'Q: {What/How much} are
you selling watermelons FOR {IN
TOTAL/PER UNIT, i.e., apiece or
per kilo, etc.}?' C1: **Tane.si.nİ 75
kuruş.A satıyoruz.** 'A1: We're
selling them {FOR/AT} 75 kurush
apiece.'
C2: **Kilo.su.nU 25 kuruş.A
satıyoruz.** 'A2: We're selling them
{FOR/AT} 25 kurush {a/per} kilo.'

b) S: <u>**Karpuz.UN
{tane.Sİ.ni/kilo.SU.nu} kaç.A**</u>
satıyorsunuz? 'Q: {What/How
much} are you selling watermelons
FOR {apiece/per kilo}?' Same
responses as under **a)** above.

c) S: <u>**Karpuz.U kaç.TAN**</u>
satıyorsunuz? 'Q: {What/How
much} are you selling watermelons
FOR [i.e., PER UNIT, i.e.,
{apiece/per kilo}, etc.]?' C1:
**Tane.si.ni 75 kuruş.TAN
satıyoruz.** 'We're selling them
FOR 75 kurush apiece.' C2:
**Kilo.su.nu 25 kuruş.TAN
satıyoruz.** 'A2: We're selling them
FOR 25 kurush {a/per} kilo.'

Helvayı kilo.yLA satıyorlar.
'They sell [the] halvah BY the kilo.'
**Evleri.nİ bir {emlakçı/
komisyoncu} aracılığ.ı.yLA
Ahmet beyler.e sattılar.** 'They
sold their house to the Ahmet bey
family THROUGH [lit., by means of]
{a real estate agent/an agent}.' **{Ateş
pahas.ı.nA/* Yok paha.sı.nA}
sattılar.** 'They sold it {AT an
exorbitant price/* FOR a pittance}.'
Para için kendini dahi satar. 'He
will sell even his soul [lit., himself]
for money.' **Ancak hainler
vatanları.nı düşman.a satarlar.**
'Only traitors sell their country to the
enemy.' Proverb: **Din.i dinar.A
satmak olmaz.** 'One should not sell
one's religion [lit., ** the religion]
FOR money [lit., for dinars, a
monetary unit].' * **Ucuzluk.TA
alır, pahalılık.TA satar.** '{He
buys low and sells high./He buys
when it is cheap [lit., ** IN

cheapness], and he sells when it is expensive [lit., ** IN expensiveness].}' *734:8.* sale: - sell. → ≠ **al-** 4 ['- buy, - purchase'], ≠ **satın al-**. Same. → al- 4, **alışveriş yap-** ['- shop, - do shopping'] → yap- 3, **çarşıya çık-** ['- go /θ/ shopping'] → çık- 2.

satıl- [ır] /a:A, b: A, c: DAn, d: 1A, e: {tarafından/CA}/ '- be sold /a: to [sb], b: {FOR/AT} [a price, in total or per unit], c: {FOR/AT} [a price, only per unit], d: {FOR/BY}, e: by/, - sell /FOR/ [sat- + pass. suf. -Il]: **Bira nerede satılır?** 'Where is beer sold?' **Helva kilo.yLA satılır.** 'Halvah is sold BY the kilo.' Proverb: **Akıl para İLE satılmaz.** 'Wisdom is not [i.e., cannot be] sold FOR money.' • Note the three question patterns: [In the following **kavun** refers to various types of melon, excluding watermelon.]
a) S: Kavun kaç.A satılıyor? 'Q: {What/How much} are melons selling FOR? [i.e., {IN TOTAL/PER UNIT, i.e., {apiece/per kilo, etc.}]?' **C1: Tane.si 75 kuruş.A satılıyor.** 'A1: They're selling FOR 75 kurush apiece.' **C2: Kilo.su 25 kuruş.A satılıyor.** 'A2: They're selling FOR 25 kurush a kilo.'

b) S: Pazarda kavun.un {tane.si/kilo.su} kaç.A satılıyor, biliyor musun? 'Q: Do you know {what/how much} melons are selling FOR {apiece/per kilo} at the market?' **C1: Evet.** 'A1: Yes'. Then the same responses as under **a)** above.

c) S: Kavun kaç.TAN satılıyor? 'Q: {What/How much} are melons selling FOR [i.e., PER UNIT, i.e., {apiece/per kilo}, etc.]?' **C1: Tane.si 75 kuruş.TAN satılıyor.** 'A1: They're selling FOR 75 kurush apiece.' **C2: Kilo.su 25 kuruş.TAN satılıyor.** 'A2: They're selling FOR 25 kurush {a/per} kilo.' *734:12.* sale: - be sold. → ≠ alın- 2.

satın al-. → al- 4.

satışa çık-. → çık- 2.

savaş- [ır] /a: A karşı, b: 1A, c: 1A birlikte [*or* beraber]/ '- fight /a: against [sb or sth], b: with [i.e., against sb], against [sth], c: together with [sb]/, - battle, -

wage war' [**savaş** 'fight, battle, war' + verb-forming suf. -θ]: **Dedem I.** [read: **birinci**] **Dünya Savaşı'nda hemen hemen her cephede savaşmış.** 'In World War I my grandfather fought on almost every front [i.e., front line].' **Almanlar ve Osmanlılar I. Dünya Savaşı'nda aynı tarafta savaştılar.** 'The Germans and the Ottoman Turks fought on the same side in World War I.'
A force or person as the opposing object: **Kurtuluş Savaşı'nda Türkler pek çok {millet.E karşı/millet.LE} kahramanca savaştı.** 'In the War for Independence, the Turks fought valiantly {against/with [i.e., against]} many countries.'
A deficiency or defect as the enemy. Only 'against' in the English: * **Yeni hükümet {yolsuzluklar.A karşı/yolsuzluk.LA} savaşma.yA kararlı.** 'The new government is determined to fight {AGAINST improper use of funds}.'
'Against...with' an enemy: **Türkler Kore Savaşı'nda [komünistlere karşı] Amerikalılar.la {birlikte [or beraber]/omuz omuza} savaştı.** 'The Turks fought [against the Communists] {together/shoulder to shoulder} with the Americans in the Korean war.' *457:13.* contention: - contend.

savun- [ur] /A karşı/ '- defend /against/': **Kurtuluş Savaşı'nda [1919-1922] dedelerimiz, düşman.A karşı yurdumuz.U kahramanca savundu.** 'During the War for Independence [1919-1922], our ancestors heroically defended our country against the enemy.' **Askerlerimiz kanlarının son damlasına kadar şehri savunurlar.** 'Our soldiers will defend the city [şehir (şeHRi)] to the last drop of their blood.' **Avukat sanığı çok iyi savundu.** 'The lawyer defended the accused very well.' **Kardeşim, savunduğun ideoloji çoktan iflâs etti, * bırak bu kafayı artık.** 'My friend [lit., ** my sibling], the ideology [that] you are defending went out of favor a long time ago, * just forget about it now [lit., ** 'leave this head', i.e., mental attitude].' *460:8.* defend: - defend; *1007:18a.* protection: - protect. → **koru-** ['- protect'].

{fikir/görüş} savun- [A. fikir (fiKRi) 'idea, view, opinion', görüş 'view, opinion'] (1) '- defend {opinions/views}': * İnandığı konuda fikr.i.ni savunma.sı, kişi.nin kendi.nE olan güven.i.ni artırır. 'When a person defends his views on a subject that he believes in, he increases his confidence IN himself [lit., ** A person's defending his views...increases...].' Aldığı bütün eleştiriler.E rağmen {fikr.i.ni/fikirler.i.ni} son.u.nA kadar savundu. 'In spite of all the criticisms he received, he defended {his view/his views} to the [lit., {its/their}] [very] end.' 460:8. defend: - defend.
(2) /a: lA, b: konusunda, c: hakkında, d: ile ilgili/ '- agree, - share opinions, thoughts /a: with, b: {on/lit., on the subject of}, c: about, d: concerning/': * Evlilik öncesi ilişki {konusunda/hakkında} senin.LE aynı fikirleri savunuyorum. 'I share your ideas {on/about} sexual relations before marriage [lit., ** I share the same ideas with you...].' Enflasyon.u önleyecek tedbirler {a: konusunda/b: hakkında/c: .LE ilgili OLARAK} senin.LE aynı fikirleri savunmuyorum. 'I don't share your ideas {a: {on/lit., the subject of}/b: about/c: concerning} measures to be taken against θ inflation.' 332:9. assent: - concur. →
= {düşünceye/fikre/görüşe} katıl- → katıl- 3, = fikir paylaş-.

görüş savun-. → {fikir/görüş} savun-. → directly above.

say- [ar] 1 '- count', i.e., - determine or - say the number of: Öğretmen sınıf.A girince önce öğrencileri saydı. 'When the teacher entered θ the classroom, he first counted the students.' Öğretmen Yasemin'e "Bir'DEN on'A kadar say" dedi. 'The teacher said to Yasemin [f.], "Count FROM one TO ten".' Satıcı verdiğ.im paraları saydı ve ceb.i.nE koydu. 'The salesman counted the money I had given him and put it IN his pocket.' 244:4. quantity: - quantify.

2 '- list, - enumerate, - say the names of': Türkiye'nin en büyük 4 şehri.ni sayabilir misiniz? 'Can you tell me the names of Turkey's four largest cities?' Zeki çocuk Avrupa'daki bütün ülkelerin başkentlerini saydı. 'The intelligent child named the capitals of all the countries in Europe.' 870:8. list: - list.

3 '- respect': Müdürümüz Oktay bey.İ hepimiz sever ve sayarız. 'We all like and respect our director Oktay bey.' 155:4. respect: - respect.

4 '- regard, - look upon sb or sth /as/, - consider': Bu kitabı ciddî bir eser saymak mümkün değil[dir]. 'It's not possible to regard this book as a serious work.' Herşey.E rağmen Engin'i arkadaşım sayıyorum. 'In spite of everything, I [still] consider Engin my friend.' 952:11. belief: - think. →
= /I, olarak/ gör- → gör- 2, = /A, olarak/ bak- → bak- 4.

saygı göster-. → göster- 1.

saygılar sun-. → sun- 1.

sayı kaydet-. → kaydet- 5.

sebep ol-. → {sebep/neden} ol-. → ol- 12.

seç- [er] 1 /{A/için}/ '- choose, - select, - pick sb or sth /for/': Yavuz amcam çok güzel karpuz seçer. 'My [paternal] Uncle Yavuz really knows how to choose watermelons [lit., chooses watermelons very well].' Seçtiğim karpuz iyi çıktı. 'The watermelon I chose turned out to be good.' {Senin için/San.A} seçtiğim kitapları beğendin mi? 'Did you like the books I selected {for you}?' → ayır- 2 ['- set aside /for/']. * Biri İngilizce biri Türkçe, iki kitap aldım. Bir.i.nİ seç. 'I've bought two books, one English, the other Turkish. Choose one [of them].' * Bu kitaplar.DAN bir.i.nİ seç! 'Choose one OF these books.' * Teypler.in iki.si de çok güzel. Seçmek çok zor. 'Both tape players are very nice. It's very difficult to choose.' → = {tercih et-/yeğle-} 2, = beğen- 2.

/A/ '- elect sb /to/ a position': * Sizi {başkan/başkan.lığ.A} seçtik. 'We elected you {president [or chairman]/to the presidency [or chairmanship]}.' 371:13. choice: - choose.

2 /I/ '- distinguish, - make out, - see clearly': Gözlüğümü evde unuttuğum için etrafımdaki insanları seçemiyordum. 'Because I left [lit., forgot] my glasses at home, I couldn't make out the people around me.' Önceden hiç görmüyordu. Şimdi iri cisimleri seçebiliyor. 'Previously he couldn't see at all. Now he can make out large objects.' 27:12. vision: - see. → = farket- 3.

seçil- [ir] [seç- + pass. suf. -Il] 1 /{A/için}, {tarafından/CA}/ '- be chosen, selected, picked /for, by/': Yarın TBMM [Türkiye Büyük Millet Meclisi] Başkanı {milletvekilleri tarafından/ milletvekilleri.nce} seçilecek. 'Tomorrow the head of the TGNA [Turkish Grand National Assembly] will be selected {by the deputies}.' Bu gece Türkiye güzellik kraliçesi seçilecek. 'Tonight the beauty queen of Turkey will be chosen.' 371:13. choice: - choose.

/A, {A/için}/ '- be elected /to, for/': Amerika Birleşik Devletleri'nin Başkanlığ.ı.nA kim seçilecek? 'Who will be elected to the office of President of the United States?' Meclis Başkanı o makam.A {* 4 yıllığ.ı.nA/4 yıl için} seçildi. 'The head of parliament was elected to that position {for 4 years}.'

2 '- be seen clearly, - be distinguished, - be made out': Sis yüz.ü.nden * arabalar seç.il.miyor. 'Because of the fog, * one can't make out the cars [lit., ** The cars are not made out].' 27:12. vision: - see. = farkedil-.

selâm getir-. → getir-.

selâm söyle-. → söyle- 1.

selâm ver-. → ver- 1.

selâm yolla-. → yolla-.

selâmla- [r] '- greet, - salute' [A. selâm (. -) 'greeting, salute' + verb-forming suf. -lA]: PERSON as object: Sporcular maçtan sonra seyircileri selâmladılar. 'After the game, the athletes saluted the spectators.' Cumhurbaşkanı köşkün balkonundan halkı selâmladı. 'The president of the republic greeted the people from the balcony of the presidential palace.' 585:10. hospitality, welcome: - greet. → = selâm ver- → ver- 1, selâm söyle- ['- send, - give, or - express one's regards /to, from/', informal: '- say "Hi" /to/'] → söyle- 1.
FLAG as object: bayrağı selâmla- '- salute the flag': Öğrenciler geçit töreninde bayrağı selâmladılar. 'During the parade the students saluted the flag.' Bayram kutlamaları sırasında askerler bayrağı selâmladılar. 'During the holiday celebrations, the soldiers saluted the flag.' 155:5. respect: - do or - pay homage to; 517:22. signs, indicators: - signal.

selâmlaş- [ır] /lA/ '- greet one another' [selâmla- + recip. suf. -ş]: Remzi'yLE her sabah durakta karşılaşır, selâmlaşırız. '{I/We} always meet Remzi at the bus stop, and we {say "Hello"/greet each other}.' • In the above sentence at least two people are involved: Remzi and me. There may be more: Remzi, some friends of ours, and me. {Yan [or Kapı] komşumuz/Karşı komşumuz}.LA konuşmadık, sadece selâmlaştık. 'We didn't speak with {our next-door neighbor /our neighbor across the way}. We only greeted each other.' Arkadaş değiliz, sadece selâmlaşırız. 'We're not friends [i.e., We're only acquaintances]. We only greet each other.' 585:10. hospitality, welcome: - greet. → = merhabalaş-, ≠ vedalaş-.

servetinden ol-. → ol- 7.

servis yap-. → yap- 3.

ses çıkar-. → çıkar- 7.

sesini kes-. → kes- 4.

seslen- [ir] /A/ '- call out /to/, - call' [ses 'voice, sound' + verb-forming suf. -lAn]: Yardım.A ihtiyacın olursa ban.a seslen. * {Hemen gelirim./Hemen yardım.ın.A koşarım.} 'If you need help, call out to me. * {I'll come right away./I'll come running to help you [lit., ** I'll run to your assistance] right away.}' Hey! * Siz.E sesleniyorum. Beni duymuyor musunuz? 'Hey, I'm calling θ you. Don't you hear me?' * Ninem kedi.si.nE "Minnoş" diye seslenir. 'My grandmother calls out to her cat saying "Minnoş".' 59:8. cry, call: - vociferate. → çağır- 1 ['- call, - send for, - summon /to/'].

sev- [er] 1 '- love, - like; - be fond of': NON-verbal noun as object: Kerem Aslı'yı {çok/delicesine} seviyordu. 'Kerem {deeply/madly} loved Aslı [f.].' Vatanımı ve milletimi çok severim. 'I deeply love my homeland and my people.' S: Kahvenizi nasıl seversiniz? 'Q: How do you like your coffee?' [→ Kahvenizi nasıl içersiniz? 'How do you take (lit., drink) your coffee?' → iç- 1.] C: {a: Az şekerli./b: Orta şekerli./c: Çok şekerli./d: Sade.} 'A: {a: With little sugar./b: With medium sugar./c: With a lot of sugar./d: black}.' Ne (tür/çeşit} musiki seversiniz? 'What {kind} of music do you like?' * Kim ne derse desin, ben bu {Maliye Bakanı'nı/sözlüğü/mevsimi} seviyorum. 'No matter what anyone says, I like that {Minister of Finance/dictionary/season}.' Proverbs: Gönül kimi severse güzel odur. 'Whomever the heart loves that is the beauty.' Gülü seven diken.i.nE katlanır. 'The one who loves the rose will put up with its thorns.' Sev beni, seveyim seni. 'Love me, and I'll love you.' You scratch my back, and I'll scratch yours. VERBAL noun as object: S: Boş zamanınızda en çok ne yapmay.I seversiniz? 'Q: What do you like to do best in your spare time?' C: Kitap okumay.I çok severim. 'A: I'm very fond of reading [lit., reading books].' Ablam araba kullanmay.I hiç sevmiyor. 'My older sister doesn't like driving at all.' 95:12. pleasure: - enjoy; 104:19. love: - love. → beğen- 1 ['- like'], hoşuna git ['- like'] → git- 1b, = memnun kal-. Same. → kal- 1, = memnun ol-. Same. → ol- 12, sevin- ['- be glad, pleased'], ≠ /DAn/ nefret et- ['- hate /θ/, - loathe /θ/, - detest /θ/, - abhor /θ/, - feel an aversion /FOR/'].

2 '- fondle, - caress, - pet': Kediyi yavaş sev, sakın can.ı.nı acıtma, seni tırmalayabilir. 'Pet the cat gently. Take care, don't hurt it [lit., ** hurt its soul]. It might scratch

you.' 73:8. touch: - stroke; 1042:6. friction: - rub. → = okşa-.

sevil- [ir] /tarafından/ '- be loved, liked, enjoyed /by/, - be popular /WITH/' [sev- + pass. suf. -Il]: Yeni tarih öğretmeni [çalışkan öğrencileri tarafından] çok sevildi. 'The new history teacher was {very popular [WITH her hardworking students]/ much loved [by her hardworking students]}.' Yeni televizyon dizi.si [halk tarafından] çok sevildi. 'The new television series was {very popular [WITH the public]/much liked [by the public]}.' 95:12. pleasure: - enjoy; 104:19. love: - love. → tutul- 3 ['for sth - catch on, - become popular or fashionable, - win a following'].

sevin- [ir] /a: A, b: DIğI için, c: A/ '- be glad, pleased /a: {ABOUT/AT/WITH}, b: because, c: θ [that]/' [sev- + refl. suf. -In]: • Note how this verb differs in structure and meaning from sev- above. Ban.a yardımcı olursan çok sevineceğim. 'I would be very happy if you would help me [lit., ** be helpful to me].' Teyzem hediyesini görünce çok sevindi. 'When my maternal aunt saw her present, she was very pleased.' NON-verbal noun as object: Bu haber.E çok sevin.DIM. 'I {AM/was} very pleased {ABOUT/AT} this news.' • In reference to a PRESENT condition, certain common Turkish verbs designating a state, i.e., a feeling, emotion, or sensation, often have the simple PAST tense, but the equivalent English has the simple PRESENT tense. Bu haber karşısında ne kadar sevindim * bilemezsiniz. '* You can't imagine [lit., ** know] how pleased I was at this news.' Proverb: Deli olan hediye.yE sevinir, akıllı olan üzülür. 'A fool [lit., he who is crazy] is pleased WITH a gift, an intelligent person [lit., he who is intelligent] is sorry.' This is because an intelligent person realizes that the receiver is obliged to reciprocate. VERBAL noun as object: Seni gördüğ.üm.E çok sevindim. 'I'm very glad θ [that] I saw you.' Beni görmey.e geldiğ.in için çok sevindim. 'I was very pleased that you came to see me.' 95:11. pleasure: - be pleased. → beğen- 1 ['- like'], hoşuna git-. Same. → git- 1b, memnun kal- ['- be pleased

/WITH/'] → kal- 1, **memnun ol-**. Same. → ol- 12, ≠ **üzül-**.

sevindir- [ir] /IA, ArAk/ '- please, - make sb happy, - delight sb /with, by...ing/' [sevin- + caus. suf. -DIr]: **Bu haber beni çok sevindirdi.** 'This news made me very happy.' **Sınavda gösterdiğin başarı.yla beni çok sevindirdin.** 'You made me very happy with your success [lit., with the success you demonstrated] on the exam.' **Ara sıra hediye ver.erek çocukları sevindiririm.** 'I make the children happy by giv.ing them presents now and then.' **Bu hafta buraya gel.erek bizi çok sevindirdin.** 'By com.ing here this week, you made us very happy.' *95:8.* pleasure: - gladden. → ≠ **üz-**.

seviş- /ir/ [sev + recip. suf. -Iş] 1 '- love or - like each other; - be fond of each other': **Çelik ailesi ile Uzel ailesi iyi dosttur. Çok sevişirler.** 'The Çelik family and the Uzel family are good friends. They are very fond of each other.' *104:19.* love: - love.

2 /IA/ '- caress each other, *slang:* - make out /with/; - make love /with/, - have sexual intercourse /with/': **Genç çift kumsalda sevişiyordu.** 'The young couple was making out on the beach.' **O.nun.la seviştin mi?** 'Did you make love with {her/him}?' *75:21.* sex: - copulate; *562:14.* lovemaking, endearment: - make love; *562:16.* lovemaking, endearment: - caress. → = **oynaş- 2** ['- carry on a love affair /with/', *slang:* '- make out /with/'], = **cinsel ilişkide bulun** ['- have sex /with/, - have sexual intercourse /with/', *formal, polite*] → **bulun- 3**, = **yat- 2** ['- go to bed /with/, - sleep /with/', i.e., have sex /with/].

seyahat et- [eDer] /A/ '- travel or - take a trip /to/' [A. **seyahat** (tİ) (. - .) 'journey, trip']: **Siz çok seyahat eder misiniz?** '{Do you travel a lot?/Do you do a lot of traveling?}' **Türkiye'nin güney sahilleri.ne seyahat etmek istiyorum.** 'I'd like to take a trip to the south coast of Turkey.' * **Bir iş için yarın Ankara'ya seyahat ediyorum.** 'I'm traveling to Ankara tomorrow {ON business./ON a business matter.}' **Zengin olsam bol bol seyahat ederdim.** 'If I were rich, I would travel a lot.' {Seyahat etmey.İ/Seyahat.İ} **seviyorum.** 'I like {to travel/traveling}.' **Babam emekli olduktan sonra sık sık seyahat etmey.e başladı.** 'After my father retired, he began to travel a lot.' *177:18.* travel: - travel. → **gez-** ['- go or - walk about, - tour, - sightsee, - stroll'].

seyret- [seyreDer] /I/ '- watch, - look at, - view' [A. **seyir** (seYRi) 'a watching, looking at' + et-]: **Dün akşam** {a: **Televizyon**/b: **film**/c: **oyun** [or **piyes**]/d: **maç**} **seyrettim.** 'Last night I watched {a: TV/b: a movie/c: a play/d: a game [i.e., soccer, basketball]}.' **Televizyon.da bir** {a: **film**/b: **belgesel**/c: **müzik programı**/d: **konser**} **seyrettik.** 'We watched a {a: a movie/b: a documentary/c: a music program/d: a concert} on TV.' **Hangi Televizyon kanalını seyrediyorsunuz?** 'Which [TV] channel do you watch?' → = **izle- 3.** # **Balkonda oturup** {a: **güneş.in doğuş.u.nu**/b: **güneş.in batış.ı.nı**/c: **gelen geçen.i**/d: **etraf.ı**} **seyrettim.** 'I sat on the balcony and watched {a: the sunrise/b: the sunset/c: the passersby/d: the area round about}.' **S: Sen de oynamak ister misin?** 'Q: Do you want to play too?' **C: Hayır, ben sadece seyredeceğim.** 'A: No, I'll just watch.' *27:13.* vision: - look. → = **izle- 3.**

sez- [er] '- understand sth intuitively, - sense, - have a feeling, - feel, - perceive, - discern': **Annem üzgün olduğ.um.u sezdi.** 'My mother sensed [that] I was sad.' **Herkes bir şeyler.in olacağ.ı.nı sezebiliyordu.** 'Everyone could sense that something was going to happen.' **Erdal'ın oda.yA** {**girdiğ.i.ni**/**gir.eceğ.i.ni**} **sezdik.** 'We sensed that Erdal {had entered/was going to enter} θ the room.' **Tehlike.nin yaklaştığ.ı.nı sezdim.** 'I felt that danger was approaching.' **Babam büyük bir** {**fırtına.nın**/**savaş.ın**/**kavga.nın**} **kopacağ.ı.nı seziyordu.** 'My father sensed that a great {storm/battle/fight} was about to break out.' *24:6.* sensation: - sense; *93:10.* feeling: - feel; *933:4.* intuition, instinct: - intuit. → = **hisset- 2.**

Sıhhatler olsun. → **ol- 11.** → **olsun.**

sık- [ar] 1 '- squeeze; - pinch, - be too tight' [ADJ. sıkı 'tight']: {Portakalları/Üzümleri} sıktım. 'I squeezed {the oranges/the grapes} [i.e., to get the juice out].' * Bu kemer belimi çok sıkıyor. 'This belt is too tight [lit., ** pinches my waist {very/too} much].' * {Bu kemer/Bu ayakkabı} çok sıktı. '{This belt is/These shoes are} too tight.' This idea is also commonly expressed as follows: {Bu kemer/Bu ayakkabı} çok sıkı. '{This belt is/These shoes are} very tight.' * Bura.sı sıkıyor. '{It pinches/They pinch} here [lit., ** It's here pinches].' 260:8. contraction: - squeeze.

el sık- /I/ '- shake hands /with/, - shake sb's hand' [el 'hand']: Misafirler.e hoş geldiniz dedim ve ellerini sıktım. 'I welcomed [lit., said 'Welcome' to] the visitors and shook hands with them [lit., shook their hands].' 585:10. hospitality: - greet; 915:14. oscillation: - move up and down. → = tokalaş-.

2 /A/ '- squeeze, - squirt, - spray /ON/': Çorba.n.A limon sıktın mı? 'Did you squeeze some lemon [juice] ON your soup?' {İtfaiyeciler} yangın.A su sıkıyor. '{The firemen are/The fire brigade is} spraying water ON the fire.' 908:25. ejection: - disgorge.

3 '- annoy, - bother': Hay Allah! Anahtarları arabanın içinde unuttum. Şimdi ne yapacağım? * Böyle şeyler de {insan.I} çok sıkıyor. 'O dear! I've left [lit., forgotten] my keys in the car. What'll I do now? * Such things are really irritating [lit., annoy {a person/people} a lot].' • Above the accusative suffix on insan indicates the whole class of human beings, mankind, anyone. Note the possible translations for this generic use. Seni sıkan birşeyler var, hiç konuşmuyorsun. Gel, {derdini dök}, rahatlarsın. '* Something's bothering you [lit., ** some thingS are...]. You're not saying anything. Come on, {get it off your chest/pour out your troubles/unburden yourself}. You'll feel better.' 96:13. unpleasure: - annoy; 98:15. unpleasantness: - vex.

* canını sık- lit., ** '- press or - squeeze one's soul' [P. can (-) 'soul'] (1) '- bore': Senin askerlik hikâyelerin can.IM.ı çok sıkıyor. 'Your stories about your experiences in the military really bore me [lit., ** MY soul].' Ülkü can.ım.ı çok sıkıyor, onunla bir araya gelmek istemiyorum. 'Ülkü really bores me. I don't want to get together with her.' 118:a. tedium: - bore.
(2) '- annoy, - irritate, - bother, - get on sb's nerves': When I expect an affirmative response: A: Turan, canını sıkan bir şey mi var? 'A: Is something bothering you, Turan?' B: Yoo, * neden sordun? 'B: No, * why do [lit., did] you ask?' A: * Son günlerde biraz dalgın biraz durgun görünüyorsun da. 'A: Well, it's just that you've been looking a little absentminded, a little withdrawn lately.' Çocukların bu kaba davranışları çok canımı sıkıyor. 'This rude behavior of the children really annoyed me.' Kaynanam bugün yine imalı imalı konuşarak canımı sıktı. 'My stepmother's accusatory comments again today [lit., my stepmother speaking in a way suggesting (i.e., I was at fault)] really annoyed me.' A threat: Can.IM.ı sıkma, yoksa * karışmam, [* ona göre]! 'Don't get on MY nerves, or * who knows what I might do, [* so act accordingly]!' 96:13. unpleasure: - annoy; 514: * 5. threat: INTERJ. specific threats.

sıkıl- [ır] /DAn/ [sık- + {pass./refl.} suf. -Il], lit., '- be pressed'. 1 '- get tired /OF/, - get or - be bored /WITH/': Dünkü derste çok sıkıldım. Çünkü öğretmen bildiğim konuları anlattı. 'I got very bored in class yesterday [lit., in yesterday's class] because the teacher explained things [lit., {subjects/topics}] I [already] knew.' Üç saattir ders çalışıyorum, sıkıldım artık, * çıkıp biraz dolaşayım. 'I've been studying for three hours now. I'm bored. * [I think] I'll go out and walk around [for] a bit.' NON-verbal noun as object: Yalnızlık.TAN sıkılırsan * biz.e gel, sohbet eder oyun oynarız. 'If you {get bored/get tired OF being alone}, * come on over [lit., come to us]. We'll chat and play games.'
VERBAL noun as object: Aynı müziği dinlemek.TEN sıkıldım, lütfen değiştir şu CD'yi. 'I'm tired OF hearing the same music.

Please change the CD.' *118:7.* tedium: - get bored. → = {bık-/usan-}.

canı sıkıl- [P. can (-) 'soul'] (1) /DAn/ '- be or - get bored /BY/, - be tired /OF/', lit., ** 'for one's soul - be pressed': **Bugün matematik dersinde can.IM çok sıkıldı. Çünkü öğretmen * hep bildiğim konuları anlattı.** 'I got really bored in math class today because the teacher * kept explaining [lit., * always explained] things [lit., {subjects/topics}] I [already] knew.' **Yaz tatilinde kuzenlerim * bize geldi, hiç can.IM sıkılmadı.** 'During the summer holidays my [male] cousins * came over [lit., to us]. I was never bored.' **Bu ev.DEN sıkıldım, başka bir eve taşınmak istiyorum.** 'I'm tired OF this house. I want to move to another one.' *118:7b.* tedium: - get bored. → = {bık-/usan-}, = içi sıkıl-.
(2) /A/ '- be annoyed /AT/, vexed /{BY/BECAUSE OF/FROM}/': **S: Neden * suratını asıyorsun, birşey mi oldu?** 'Q: Why * are you sulking? {Is sth wrong?/lit., Has sth happened?}' NON-verbal noun as object: **C: Müdür bey, haftasonunda da çalışmamı istiyor, bu.nA çok canım sıkıldı.** 'A: The director wants me to work on the weekend too. I'm very annoyed [AT that].' **Cemil bey.E canım sıkıldı; borcunu hâlâ ödemedi.** 'I'm very annoyed AT Cemil bey. He still hasn't paid {what he owes [me]/lit., his debt}.' VERBAL noun as object: * **Ben konuşurken olur olmaz gülmesi.nE canım sıkıldı.** 'I was annoyed that when I was speaking he was smiling inappropriately [lit., AT his smiling inappropriately].' *96:13.* unpleasure: - annoy.
(3) /A/ '- be upset, disturbed, troubled /{BY/AT}/, sorry, distressed /AT/, out of sorts, in a bad mood': **S: * Hayrola, * niye canın sıkıldı?** 'Q: What's the matter? * What's bothering you?' **C: Kardeşim hastalanmış * da, onun için.** 'A: My brother {is sick/has taken ill}. * That's why.' **Verdiğin haber.E canım çok sıkıldı.** 'I was very upset BY your news [lit., ** the news that you gave].' *96:16b.* unpleasure: - be distressed.

* **içi sıkıl-** /mAktAn/ '- get or - be bored /{θ/from}...ing/' [iç 'inside, heart'], lit., ** 'for one's

{inside/heart} - be pressed': **Bütün gün evde oturmak.TAN iç.İM sıkıldı, ha[y]di sinemaya gidelim.** '{I'm/I got} bored {θ/from} sitting at home all day. Come on, let's go to the movies.' *118:7b.* tedium: - get bored. → = canı sıkıl- 1.

2 '- become bashful, - get, - be, or - feel embarrassed' [ADJ. sıkılgan]: **Tanımadığım kişilerle konuşurken sıkılırım.** 'I get embarrassed when I talk {with/to} people I don't know.' *96:15.* unpleasure: - chagrin. → = utan-.

sıkıntı çek-. → çek- 5.

sıkıntıya gir-. → gir-.

sıkış- [ır] [sık- + recip. suf. -Iş] 1 '- get stuck, - become tightly wedged or jammed' [ADJ. sıkışık]: **Resim çekemiyorum. Film sıkıştı.** 'I can't take a picture. The film has jammed.' **Pantolonum.un fermuar.ı sıkıştı, {* açılmıyor/açamıyorum}.** 'The zipper of {my pants/my trousers} has gotten stuck. {It won't open./I can't open it.}' **Bu oda.nın kapı.sı sıkışmış, * açılmıyor.** 'The door to the room has gotten stuck. * It won't open.' *854:10.* stability: - become firmly fixed.

2 /A/ '- get caught /IN/, - be pinched /IN/': **Ceketim kapı.yA sıkıştı.** 'My jacket got caught IN the door.' *854:10.* stability: - become firmly fixed.

3 '- be placed close together, - be squeezed; - be very crowded, cramped, - feel cramped, - be congested; - be or - get {backed/piled} up, - pile up': **Otobüs çok kalabalıktı, * iki kişi bir koltuğ.A sıkıştık.** 'The bus was very crowded. * The two of us got squeezed INTO a single seat [lit., ** Two people we got squeezed...].' In a bus you might say: * **Biraz ileri gider misiniz, çok sıkıştım.** 'Would you please move forward a bit. I really feel {cramped/squeezed}.' *260:8.* Contraction: - squeeze. * **Trafik iyice sıkıştı.** 'The traffic has really {backed/piled} up.' *260:8.* Contraction: - squeeze; *769:19.* assemblage: - pile.

4 * '- get in a jam, - be or - find oneself in a tight spot, under pressure, in difficulty': **Bu hafta tam dört [tane] sınavım var, * iyice sıkıştım.** 'This week I have altogether 4 exams. * I'm under a lot of pressure.' **Eğer dönem içinde vakt.in.i iyi değerlendirmezsen, {sınav} zamanı çok sıkışırsın.** 'If you don't make good use of your time during the {term/semester/ quarter} [lit., period], you'll find yourself {in a tight spot/very rushed} at exam time.' <u>Proverb</u>: **Kul sıkışmayınca Hızır yetişmez.** 'Elias will not come to help unless a servant of God [i.e., any will-possessing being, mortal] is in a tight spot.', i.e., Until the need arises, a person will not find a solution to his problems, said when unexpected assistance reaches a person in difficulty. Necessity is the mother of invention. *297:13.* weight: - burden; *1012:12.* difficulty: - get into trouble.

'- be hard up, short of money': **Beklediğim çek hâlâ gelmedi, gerçekten * çok sıkıştım.** 'The check I've been expecting still hasn't come. * I'm really hard up.' *619:5.* poverty: - be poor; *1012:12.* difficulty: - get into trouble.

5 '- feel the need to relieve oneself, - feel the need to go to the toilet, - be bursting': *** Çok sıkıştım. Hemen tuvalete gitmem lâzım.** '* I'm simply bursting. I have to go to the restroom right away.' *12:12.* excretion: - excrete.

{sınav/imtihan} kazan-. → kazan- 3.

{sınav/imtihan} ol-. → ol- 10.1.

{sınav/imtihan} ver-. → ver- 1.

{sınava/imtihana} gir-. → gir-.

{sınavdan/imtihandan} kal-. → kal- 1.

sınıfa geç-. → geç- 1.

sınıfını geç-. → geç- 1.

sınıfta bırak-. → bırak- 1.

sınıfta kal-. → kal- 1.

Sinirim tepeme çıktı. → çık- 5.

sırala- [r] /a: DAn, b: A, c: A göre, d: olarak/ '- put or - arrange in a row or in a certain order /a: from, b: to, c: {according to/by}, d: -ly/' [sıra 1 'row, line'. 2 'order, sequence' + verb-forming suf. -lA]: **Dosyaları konular.ı.nA göre {özen.le} sıraladı.** 'He arranged the files {with care/carefully} by subject [lit., by their subject].' **Aşağıdaki rakamları küçük.TEN büyüğ.E doğru sıralayın.** 'Arrange the numbers below in order FROM small TO large.' **Aşağıdaki kelimeleri {alfabe.yE göre/alfabetik OLARAK} sıralayın.** 'Arrange the words below {in alphabetical order [lit., according to the alphabet]/ alphabetical.LY}.' *807:8.* arrangement: - arrange.

sırası gelmişken. → gel- 1.

sıraya gir-. → gir-.

{sırayı/kuyruğu} boz-. → boz- 1.

sırtını çevir-. → {arkasını/sırtını} çevir-. → çevir- 3.

sırtını dön-. → {arkasını/sırtını} dön-. → dön- 4.

sigara iç-. → iç- 2.

sigorta yaptır-. → yaptır- 2.

sigortala- [r] /A karşı, DAn/ '- insure /against, WITH/' [It. sigorta 'insurance' + verb-forming suf. -lA]: **{Evimizi/Arabamızı/ Eşya-larımızı} sizin tavsiye ettiğiniz [or önerdiğiniz] şirket.TEN sigortaladık.** 'We insured {our house/our car/our things} WITH the company [that] you recommended.' **Her {çeşit/türlü} kaza.yA karşı kendimizi sigortaladık.** 'We've insured ourselves against all {kinds} of accidents.' *1007:18a.* protection: - protect. → = /A/ sigorta yaptır-.

sil- [er] 1 /lA, A/ '- wipe up, - wipe away, - wipe [usually sth wet] /with, {IN/ON}/; - dry': **Mendil.le gözyaşlarını sildi.** 'She wiped away her tears with the handkerchief.' **Ellerim.İ şu havlu.yA silebilir miyim?** 'May I wipe my hands {ON/IN} this towel?' *** Ameliyat sırasında hemşireler operatör.ün ter.i.ni siliyorlardı.** 'During the operation, the nurses were wiping the perspiration from the [face of the] surgeon [lit., ** were wiping the surgeon's perspiration].' *1064:6a.* dryness: - dry, - make dry.

2 /1A/ '- wipe CLEAN /with/', usually with a wet cloth or mop: **Misafir gelmeden önce annem {a: camları/b: sehpaları/c: kapıları/d: bütün evi} güzelce sildi.** 'Before the guest[s] came, my mother wiped {a: the windows/b: the small tables [i.e., end, coffee, etc.]/c: the doors/d: the whole house} quite clean.' * **Yerleri paspas.la sildi.** 'She mopped the floors [lit., wiped the floors with a mop].' *79:18.* cleanness: - clean. → **temizle-** ['- clean'], **tozunu al-** ['- dust'] → **al-1.**

3 /1A/ '- erase /with/, - delete /with/': **Öğrenciler, öğretmen gelmeden [önce] tahtayı sildiler.** 'The students erased the blackboard before the teacher came in.' **Çocuklar, tahtayı niçin yeni silgi.yle silmiyorsunuz?** 'Children, why don't you erase the board with the new earaser?' **Uzun süredir bakamadığım için epey e-mail birikmiş. Bir kısmını okumadan sildim.** 'Because I hadn't been able to look at it for a long time, quite a lot of e-mail had {piled up/accumulated}. I deleted some [lit., a part of it] without reading it.' *255:12.* subtraction: [written text] - delete.

sinirlen- [ir] /A/ '- get angry, mad /AT/; - get irritated, annoyed /AT/, - get in a state /ABOUT/, upset /θ [that]/'. Not usually '- get nervous' in the sense of '- get anxious, worried' [sinir 'nerve' + verb-forming suf. -lAn. ADJ. sinirli]: **Sinirlenme! "Öfke.yLE kalkan zarar.la oturur."** 'Don't get angry! [i.e., Remember the proverb:] "He who rises IN anger sits down with loss" [i.e., at a disadvantage to his own interests].' **Boşuna tahrik etmey.E çalışma [beni], bugün sinirlen.me.mey.E kararlıyım.** 'Don't waste your time trying to provoke me [lit., ** Don't try in vain to provoke me]. Today I'm determined not to get angry.' **Sinirlenip * ağz.ı.na gelen.i söylemeye başladı.** 'Getting angry, * he began to say just anything that came into his head [lit., ** to his

mouth].' **Babam sınıfta kaldığ.ım.ı duyunca çok sinirlendi.** 'When my father heard that I had been held back in school [lit., ** 'stayed in the class', i.e., didn't pass on to the next grade], he got very angry.' **Otel görevlisi yalan söyle.yince babam sinirlendi.** 'When the hotel employee {lied/told a lie}, my father got angry.'
VERBAL noun as object: * **Otel görevlisi.nin yalan söyleme.si.nE sinirlendi.** 'He got angry when the hotel employee told a lie [lit., ** AT the hotel clerk's telling a lie].' **Kızım.ın Emre'yle sinemaya {a: gitme.si.nE/b: git.tiğ.i.nE/c: gid.eceğ.i.nE} sinirlendim.** 'I was very upset {a: AT my daughter's going/b: θ that my daughter had gone/c: θ that my daughter was going to go} to the movies with Emre.' *96:16b.* unpleasure: - be distressed; *152:17.* resentment, anger: - become angry; *856:16.* unpleasure: - distress. → = **öfkelen-,** = **sinirleri bozul- 1,** = **kız- 1.**

sinirlendir- [ir] /ArAk/ '- make sb angry, mad, - anger; - irritate, - annoy, - get on sb's nerves /by...ing/.' NOT '- make sb nervous, anxious' [sinirlen- + caus. suf. -DIr]: **Çocuklar yaramazlık yap.arak annelerini sinirlendirdiler.** 'The children made their mother angry by being naughty [lit., ** by do.ing naughtiness].' **Millî takımın zayıf bir rakib.E yenilmesi herkesi sinirlendirdi.** 'The defeat of the national team BY a weak rival angered everyone.' *96:14.* unpleasure: - irritate; *96:16a.* distress: - distress; *105:14.* excitement: - agitate; *128:9.* nervousness: - get on one's nerves; *152:22.* resentment, anger: - anger; *916:10.* agitation: - agitate. → = **kızdır- 1.**

sinirleri bozul-. → **bozul-.**

sofra kur-. → **kur- 1.**

soğu- [r] **1** '- get cold; - cool [down]' [ADJ. soğuk 'cold' - k = soğu-]: **Ders çalışmay.I bırak da gel artık, yemek.ler soğuyor.** 'Stop studying and come now. The food [lit., ** 'foods', i.e., dishes] is getting cold.' → ≠ **ısın- 1,** = **kız- 2.** * **Hava.lar iyice soğudu.** 'The weather [lit., ** weatherS] has gotten quite cold.' → ≠ ısın- 1. *1022:9.* cold: - freeze.

2 /DAn/ '- cool /TOWARD/, - lose one's love, desire, or enthusiasm /FOR/; - cease to care /FOR/ sb or sth': NON-verbal as object: **Bakkal Orhan'ın bana kazık attığını anlayınca on.DAN iyice soğudum.** 'When I found out that Orhan the grocer had cheated me, I really cooled TOWARD him.' Proverb: **Para isteme benden, buz gibi soğurum sen.DEN.** 'Don't ask me for money, or I'll become like ice toward you [lit., cool TOWARD you like ice].' → = **uzaklaş- 2** ['- become remote or distant /from/ in feeling'], **arası {açıl-/bozul-}** ['- have a falling out /with/ sb, - get on bad terms /with/'] → **açıl- 9, arası düzel-** ['for things - get straightened out, patched up between people'], ≠ **ısın- 3. #** **Sınıfta kalınca okul.DAN iyice soğudu.** 'When he was held back in school [i.e., wasn't passed on to the next grade], he lost all interest IN school.'
VERBAL noun as object: **Düşüp ayağımı kırınca kayak yapmak.TAN iyice soğudum.** 'After I fell and broke my foot, I lost my enthusiasm FOR skiing completely.' *261:7.* distance, remoteness: - keep one's distance; *379:4.* dissuasion: - disincline; *456:10.* disaccord: - fall out with.

soğuk al-. → **al- 3.**

soğut- [ur] [soğu- + caus. suf. -t] **1** '- cool, - cool sth down, - chill, - make sth cool or cold, - let sth cool, get cold': **Misafirler neredeyse gelecek. İçecekleri soğuttunuz mu?** 'The guests will soon be here [lit., will soon come]. Have you chilled the drinks?' **Suyu buzdolabında soğuttum.** 'I cooled the water in the refrigerator.' **Kenan, yemeğini soğutma, * ha[y]di masaya gel.** 'Kenan, don't let your food get cold. * Come and eat [lit., Come to the table].' *1022:10.* cold: - make cold. → ≠ **ısıt-.**

2 /DAn/ '- cause sb to lose love, desire, or enthusiasm /FOR/ sb or sth, - dampen sb's enthusiasm /FOR/, - put sb /off/ sb or sth, - cool sb /TOWARD/': **Ayağım.ın kırıl-**

ma.sı bile beni kayak yapmak.TAN soğutmadı. 'Even the fact that my leg got broken [lit., ** my leg's getting broken] didn't dampen my enthusiasm FOR skiing.' **Mehmet'in saçma sapan tavırları beni o.nDAN soğuttu.** 'Mehmet's {ridiculous/silly} behavior {put me off/cooled me /TOWARD/him}.' *1011:10.* hindrance: - hinder.

sohbet et- [eDer] /lA/ '- chat, - talk, - have a chat /with/' [A. sohbet 'friendly conversation, chat, or talk']: **Akşam bize gelsenize, çay içip sohbet ederiz.** 'Why don't you come on over to our house this evening? We'll drink tea and chat.' **Aile.CE sofra başında sohbet etmey.i çok severiz.** 'We love to sit around the table AS a family and chat.' **Eski okul arkadaşlarımızla buluşup saatlerce sohbet ettik.** '{I/We} met with some old school friends of {mine/ours}, and we chatted for hours.' **Dün gece babamla sabaha kadar sohbet ettik.** 'Last night {I/we} chatted with my father until morning.' *541:10.* conversation: - chat. → = **muhabbet et-.**

sohbete dal-. → **dal- 4.**

sok- [ar] **1** /A/ '- insert, - thrust, - shove, - stick, - put, - introduce /{IN/INTO}/': **Oğlum, hava çok soğuk, ellerini cebin.E soksana!** 'Son, the weather is very cold, why don't you put your hands IN your pockets?' **Şişe.DEN çıkan bu cini yeniden şişe.yE sokmak kolay olmayacak.** 'It won't be easy to put this genie that has gotten OUT OF the bottle back INTO the bottle again.' **Bazı egzersizleri günlük yaşam.ınız.ın akış.ı içi.nE sokma.ya çalışın.** 'Try to introduce some exercises into your daily routine.' Proverb: **Aç elini kor.A sokar.** 'A hungry person will [even] stick his hands INTO glowing embers.', i.e., A person will go to great lengths to satisfy a pressing need. Desperate times call for desperate measures. *191:3.* insertion: - insert; *125: * 19.* hopelessness: proverbs. → = **koy- 1.**

burnunu sok- [burun (buRNu) 'nose'] (1) /A/ '- stick one's nose /{IN/INTO}/, - interfere /IN/': **Lütfen işlerim.E burnunu**

sokma! '{Don't stick your nose IN my business!/Keep your nose out of my business!}' *214:5*. intruder: - intrude. → = karış- 5.
(2) /A/ *colloq.* '- participate /IN/, - get involved /IN/, - take up', when the activity is sth unexpected, often foreign: **Cüneyt şimdi de golf oynuyormuş, onun da burn.u.nu sokmadığ.ı hiç bir spor kalmadı.** 'It seems that Cüneyt is now also playing golf. There is no sport left that he hasn't gotten involved IN.' → = katıl- 2, = karış- 6. *476:5*. participation: - participate.

* 2 /A/ '- let, - permit, - allow sb /{IN/INTO}/ a place': **Ziyaret saat.i dışında kimse.yİ hastane.yE sokmazlar.** 'They don't allow anyone {IN/INTO} the hospital outside of visiting hours.' * **Üzer.i.ni aramadan kimse.yİ büyükelçi.nin yan.ı.nA sokmam.** 'I won't allow anyone near the ambassador [lit., ** to the ambassador's side] {unless I have searched him [lit., ** his surface] first/without having searched him}.' *189:7* entrance: - enter; *443:9*. permission: - permit.

3 /DAn/ '[for a snake] - bite sb /{ON/IN}/; [for an insect] - sting sb /{ON/IN}/': **A: Cemil'i yılan sokmuş!** 'A: A snake has bitten Cemil.' **B: Nere.si.nDEN sokmuş?** 'B: Where has it bitten him? [lit., ** ON his where has it bitten him?]' **A: * {Kol.u.nDAN/Bacağ.ı.nDAN} [sokmuş].** 'A: [It has bitten him] {ON the [lit., his] arm/ON the [lit., his] leg.}' **Yılan Ahmet'in bacağ.ı.nı sokmuş.** 'The snake bit Ahmet's leg.' **Fatma'yı kol.u.nDAN {arı/böcek/sivrisinek} sokmuş.** '{A bee/An insect/A mosquito} stung Fatma [f.] ON the [lit., her] arm.' <u>Proverb</u>: **Arı kızdıranı sokar.** 'A bee stings the person who angers it.', i.e., A person will lash out at his tormenter even if he himself will also suffer as a result. *8:27*. eating: - chew; *26:7*. pain: - inflict pain. → = ısır- [for an animal (dog, etc.), person '- bite'].

sokağa çık-. → çık- 2.

solla- [r] '[for a driver] - pass a vehicle on its left side' [**sol** 'left' + verb-forming suf. -lA]: **Bu yolda**

sollamak yasaktır. 'No passing [lit., On this street it is forbidden to pass on the left].' *352:7*. publication: poster: * specific signs. **Otobüs sinyal vermeden kamyonu solladı ve geçti.** 'Without making a signal, the bus passed the truck on the left.' A sign sometimes found on the back of a car, warning a driver to avoid an accident: * **Hatalı sollama, eve acı haber yollama!** 'Don't make an illegal left pass [lit., ** Don't pass on the left illegally]. Don't send bad news home.' *220:3*. * *1*. left side: - turn left.

son ver-. → ver- 1.

sona er-. → er-.

sonuna gel-. → gel- 1.

<u>sor-</u> [ar] a) /A/ '- ask /θ/ sb sth': * **Türkçe sorun.** 'Ask IN Turkish.' **Siz.E bir şey sormak istiyorum.** 'I would like to ask θ you sth.' **S: Siz.E bir şey sorabilir miyim?** 'Q: {Could/May} I ask θ you sth?' **C: {a: Tabii./b: Buy[u]run./c: Elbette./d: Hay hay} efendim sorun.** 'A: {a: Of course./b: Go right ahead./c, d: Of course.}, {sir/ma'am}, ask.' **Ne sormak istiyorsunuz?** 'What {would you like/lit., do you want} to ask?' **Sormak istediğiniz şey nedir?** 'What is it [that] you {would like/lit., want} to ask?' **Konsolos bey.E sorar mısınız?** 'Would you [please] ask θ the consul?' **S: İşler nasıl?** 'Q: How are things going?' **C1: Hiç sorma!** 'A1: Don't even ask!' **C2: {İşler.İ} sormasan iyi olur.** 'A2: It would be better if you didn't ask {ABOUT things/how things are}.', i.e., They are terrible. **C3: Ah ah, hiç sorma, * neler oldu neler!** 'A3: Oh, oh, don't ask! * You can't imagine what all happened [lit., ** What things happened, what things]!' * **Kim.E {sor.sanız/sor.arsanız sorun} bilir.** 'Everyone you ask knows [lit., ** θ whomever you ask knows].' **Elindeki adresi sor.a sor.a buldu.** 'She found the address she was looking for [lit., the address in her hand] by asking [lit., ** BY ask.ING and ask.ING, i.e., by persistent questioning].' <u>Proverbs</u>: **Sor.a sor.a Bağdat bulunur.** 'BY ask.ING and ask.ING, one finds Bagdad [lit., Bagdad is found].' Seek and ye shall find. **Üzümü ye de bağ.ı.nı sorma.** 'Eat the grapes, but

357

don't ask about the [lit., its] vineyard.' Don't look a gift horse in the mouth. **Yol sor.MAKLA bulunur.** 'The [right] {road/way} is found BY ask.ING.' *937:20.* inquiry: - inquire.

Indirect questions occur in two main patterns: **1.** The exact words of the question are followed by **diye** 'saying': **Arkadaşım.A "Ne zaman {git.tiniz/gid.ecek-siniz}" diye sordum.** 'I asked my friend when {HE had gone/HE was going to go} [lit., ** I asked my friend saying "when {did YOU go/are YOU going to go}?"].' A 'whether or not' question: **Git.tiniz mi git.me.diniz mi diye sordum.** 'I asked him whether he had gone or not [lit., ** I asked saying {did you go/didn't you go}?]'
2. In the second pattern, the direct question is transformed into a **DIk** or **AcAk** noun clause, which becomes the object of **sor-**: **Arkadaşım.A ne zaman {git.tiğ.i.ni/ gid.eceğ.i.ni} sordum.** 'I asked my friend when {HE had gone/HE was going to go}.' **Amerikan Başkonsolosluğuna gidip ne yapmam gerektiğ.i.ni sordum.** 'I went to the American consulate general and asked what I should do.' A 'whether or not' question: **Gid.ip git.me.diği.ni sordum.** 'I asked him whether he had gone or not.'

Asking for the time: **Orhan'A saat.İN kaç olduğ.U.nu sorun.** 'Ask Orhan what time it is.' *Informal:* * **Orhan'A sor.sana saat kaç?** 'Why don't you ask θ Orhan what time it is? [lit., ** Why don't you ask θ Orhan what time IS IT?]' **Orhan'A sor bakalım saat kaç?** Same. **Orhan'A saat.İN kaç olduğ.U.nu sordum.** 'I asked Orhan what time it was.' **Orhan'A saat kaç diye sordum.** Same [lit., ** I asked Orhan saying 'What time (is it)?'].* * **Yol.DAN geçen bir adam.A saat.İ sordum.** 'I asked θ a man who was passing by [lit., ** passing ALONG the road] the time [lit., the hour].' • Note also the following way of requesting the time: * **Saatiniz kaç?** 'What time do you have?' *937:20.* Inquiry: - inquire.

b) [a) is at the top of the entry] **/DAn/** '- ask sth /OF/ sb or /AT/ an office, - ask /θ/ sb or /AT/ an office for sth', frequently information:

Konsolosluk.TAN, Türkiye'ye gitmek için nasıl vize al.ın.acağı.nİ sorduk. 'We asked AT the Consulate how to get [lit., ** how is gotten] a visa to go to Turkey.' **Üniversitenin Kayıt Kabul İşlerin.DEN bu dönemin ne zaman biteceği.nİ sorduk.** 'We asked AT [the College/the University] Registrar's Office when this semester would end.' Proverb: **Hekim.DEN sorma, çeken.DEN sor.** 'Don't ask θ the doctor, ask θ the one who is suffering', i.e., the one who has experienced the pain. Today the term **doktor** is usually preferred to the older term **hekim.**

c) /I/ '- ask /{FOR/ABOUT}/ sb': * **Birisi geldi, siz.İ sordu.** 'Someone came by and asked {FOR you., i.e., wanted to speak with you/ABOUT you}.' **Bana siz.İ sordu.** 'He asked me ABOUT you.' *440:9.* request: - request. For '- ask for a thing', → **iste-** 2. For '- ask for, - request sth from sb', → **rica et-.**

arayıp sor- '- look sb up': **Yıllardır Suat'tan haber alamıyorum. Hiç arayıp sormuyor.** 'For years now I haven't had any news of Suat. He never looks me up.' When very informally addressing a close male friend of the same age or younger that you haven't seen for a while: **Mehmet n'aber** [i.e., **ne haber**] **ya, ulan hiç arayıp sormuyorsun.** 'Mehmet, what's up, guy? You never look me up.' *937:20.* inquiry: - inquire; *937:30.* inquiry: - seek. For '- look up a fact, - consult for information', → **{başvur-/müracaat et-}** 1.

hatır sor- '- inquire after sb's health, - ask how sb is' [A. **hatır** (-.) '(a person's) feelings, sensitivities']: * **Uzun zamandır annemle konuşama.dık, bu akşam arayıp hatır.ı.nı sorayım.** '{I/We} haven't been able to speak with my mother for a long time, I'll call her up this evening and ask her how she is.' • Two or more people may be involved in the preceding sentence: my mother and me OR my mother, some other people, and me. • Note the different possessED suffixes on **hatır: Yılmaz'ın babası hastaymış, ziyaret.i.ne gidemedik, bari bu akşam telefonla hatır.I.nı**

soralım. 'Ahmet's father is ill. We couldn't visit him. Let's at least call up tonight and ask how he is.' {a: Hatır.IM.ı/b: Hatır.IN.ı/c: Hatır.I.nı/d: Hatır.IMIZ.ı/e: Hatır.INIZ.ı/f: Hatır.LARI.nı} sordu. 'He asked {a: how I was/b: how YOU [s.] were/c: how HE was/d: how WE were/e: how YOU [pl.] were/f: how THEY were}.'

hal hatır sor-. Same as hatır sor- but lit., ** '- ask the state, feeling' [A. hal (-) 'state, condition']: Hal hatır sorduktan sonra annem hemen misafirleri sofraya davet etti. 'After asking them how they were, my mother invited the guests to the table.' Also with the personal suffixes on hatır: Hal hatır.IM.ı sordu. 'He asked how I was.' *83:6.* health: - enjoy good health; *937:20.* inquiry: - inquire.

soru sor- '- ask a question' [soru 'question']: Bir soru sorabilir miyim? 'May I ask a question?' A more common alternative: Bir şey sorabilir miyim? 'May I ask sth?' Bir soru sormak istiyorum. 'I would like to ask a question.' A more common alternative: Bir şey sormak istiyorum. 'I would like to ask sth.' Bana soru sormak isteyen var mı? 'Is there anyone who would like to ask me a question?' Another alternative: Soru.su olan var mı? '{Does anyone have a question?/Is there sb who has a question? [lit., ** His-question-being-one existent?]' *937:20.* inquiry: - inquire. → ≠ {cevap/yanıt} ver- → ver- 1, ≠ /I/   {cevapla-/cevaplandır-/yanıtla-}, ≠ karşılık ver- 1 → ver- 1.

sorguya çek-. → çek- 6.

soru sor-. → sor-.

sote et- [eDer] '- sauté' [F. sauté]: Soğan ve sarımsakları ekleyip pembeleşinceye kadar sote edin. 'Add the onions and garlic and sauté [the mixture] until the onions and garlic become pink.' *11:4a.* cooking: - cook sth. → = kızart- 1.

soy- [ar] 1 '- peel': Aytekin elmayı dilim dilim doğrayıp soydu. 'Aytekin sliced up the apple and peeled the slices.' Domatesleri

yıkayıp * kabuk.ları.nı soyun. 'Wash the tomatoes and * peel them [lit., ** peel its skins].' *6:8.* unclothing: - peel.

2 '- rob, - strip of valuables': Hırsızlar Osman'ın dükkân.ı.nı soymuşlar. 'The thieves robbed Osman's shop.' Proverb: * Bir çıplağ.I bin zırhlı soyamaz. 'One thousand armed soldiers cannot rob a single naked man.' An example combining meanings 1 and 2 of soy- in a word play: Memleketi soydular * soğan.A çevirdiler, yuh olsun! 'They've swindled [or peeled] the nation. They've turned it INTO an onion. Shame on them!' *482:14.* theft: - rob.

3 '- undress, - take sb's clothes off': * Anne.Sİ yıkamak için küçük çocuğu soydu. 'The mother undressed the little child to wash {him/her} [lit., ** {HIS/HER} mother undressed the little child ...].' For '- undress oneself, → soyun- below. *6:7.* unclothing: - undress. → ≠ giydir-.

soyul- [ur] [soy- + pass. suf. -Il] 1 /tarafından/ '- be peeled /by/': Meyvaların hepsi [aşçı tarafından] soyuldu mu? 'Has all the fruit been peeled [by the cook]?' *6:8.* unclothing: - peel.

2 /tarafından/ '- be robbed, stripped of valuables /by/': Soyuldum. 'I've been robbed.' Alış veriş pasajında bulunan dükkan bir ay içinde belirsiz kişiler tarafından iki kez soyuldu. 'The shop located in a mall was robbed twice in one month by unknown persons.' Eski okul müdür.ü.nün Ankara'daki ev.i önceki gün gece 2 sıralarında kendi ve eşi uyuduğu sırada pencere.DEN giren hırsızlar tarafından soyuldu. 'The former school principal's house in Ankara was robbed the night before last around two a.m. by thieves who had entered THROUGH the window while he and his wife slept.' *482:14.* theft: - rob.

soyun- [ur] '- undress oneself, - take off or - remove one's clothes' [soy- + refl. suf. -In]: Doktor hastasına "Şu odaya girin ve soyunun" dedi. 'The doctor said to his patient, "Go into this room and take off your clothes".' Yatağın üstüne soyun-madan uzandı. 'He stretched out on the bed without undressing.' For '-undress sb else', → soy- 3 above. 6:7. unclothing: - undress. → = *word for clothes* çıkar- 2, ≠ giyin-.

sön- [er] 1 /DAn/ '- go out /BECAUSE OF/', fire, lights, candle, lamps [ADJ. sönük 'extinguished', fire, light]: Rüzgâr.DAN mum söndü. 'BECAUSE OF the wind the candle went out.' Işıklar sönünce derslerimiz.E çalışamadık. 'When the lights went out, we couldn't study θ our lessons.' S: Lâmbalar niye söndü? 'Q: Why have the lamps gone out?' C: Elektrik.LER kesildi * de, ondan. 'A: The electricity has been cut off. * That's why.' 1021:8. incombustibility: - burn out; 1026:12. darkness, dimness: - grow dark. → ≠ yan- 4.

2 '- go flat, - collapse, - deflate, - lose air', usually a gradual loss of air pressure [ADJ. sönük 'deflated, flat', balloon, tire]: {Balon/Lâstikler/ Lâstik bot} söndü. '{The balloon/The tires/The rubber boat} collapsed.' 260:10. contraction: - collapse. → patla- 1 ['- burst, - explode', balloon, tire], in- 4 ['- go flat (slowly)', a tire, rubber boat], ≠ şiş- 2 ['- fill up with air'].

3 '- become extinct', volcano: Bu yanardağ yıllar önce sönmüş. 'This volcano became extinct years ago.' 1021:8. incombustibility: - burn out.

söndür- [ür] [sön- + caus. suf. -DIr] 1 '- put out, - extinguish': {Ateşi/Sigaraları} söndürün! 'Put out {the fire/the cigarettes}!' Lütfen emniyet kemerlerinizi takınız ve sigaralarınızı söndürünüz. 'Please fasten [lit., put on] your seat belts and put out your cigarettes.' 352:7. publication: poster: * specific signs. Komşular itfaiye gelmeden yangını söndürdüler. 'The neighbors put out the fire before the firemen came.' 1021:7. incombustibility: - fight fire. → üfle- 2 ['- blow out (candle)'], ≠ yak- 1.

2 '- turn off': {a: Elektriği/b: Fırını/c: Işığı/d: Lâmbaları/e: Ocağı} söndür. 'Turn off {a: the electricity/b: the oven/c: the light/d: the lamps]/e: the stove}.' Kapa- or

kapat-, not söndür-, are used with bilgisayar 'computer', radyo, or TV. 856:12. cessation: - turn off; 1026:11. darkness, dimness: - turn off the light; 1031:25. electricity: - electrify. → ≠ aç- 2.

söv-. → {söv-/küfret-}.

söyle- [r] 1 /A/ '- say, - tell /{to/θ}/': * Türkçe söyleyin. 'Say it IN Turkish.' * Bunu Türkçe nasıl söylersiniz? 'How do you say this IN Turkish?' * Allah rıza.sı için söyleyin...Bu tartışma.nın ne fayda.sı var? 'For God's sake [lit., approval] tell us...What is the use of this {dispute/argument}?' Sizi görmek isteyen adam.a ne söyleyeyim? 'What shall I say to the man who {wants/is asking} to see you?' Polis.E bildiğimiz her şey.İ söyledik. 'We told θ the police θ {everything/all} we knew.' * Ne söyledi ban.A söyle. 'Tell me, what did he say?' * {Bil.en/Daha iyi bir fikr.i ol.an} varsa söylesin. 'If anyone {knows/has a better idea}, let him speak up.' * Söyleyecekleriniz olduğunu hissediyorum. Çekinmeyin. 'I sense that you want to say something [lit., that you have sth to say]. Don't hesitate.' Proverbs: Az söyle, çok dinle. 'Say little but do a lot of listening.' Derdini söylemeyen derman bulamaz. 'He who keeps his troubles to himself [lit., doesn't tell his troubles] will not be able to find a remedy [for them].' Önce düşün sonra söyle. 'Think first, then speak.' Think before you speak. In general, not in reference to a particular project: Söylemek kolay, yapmak {zor/güç}. 'It is easy to talk [i.e., about plans], but {difficult} to get things done.', i.e., Talk is cheap. In reference to a particular project: Söyleme.si kolay, yapma.sı güç. 'It is easy to talk about it but difficult to carry it out [lit., ** Its saying is easy, its doing is difficult].' Easier said than done. Tatlı ye, tatlı söyle. 'Eat sweet things, speak sweetly.' 524: * 35. speech: proverbs. VERBAL noun [i.e., the DIk or AcAk forms] as object: Ne söyle.diğ.i.ni ban.A söyle. 'Tell θ me what he said.' Hikmet'in de burada ol.duğ.u.nu söylemeliydiniz. 'You should have told me that Hikmet, too, was here.' Beni burada gör.düğ.ün.Ü kimse.yE söyleme. 'Don't tell θ anyone that you saw me here.' **Ankara'ya birkaç defa {git.tiğ.i.ni/ gid.eceğ.i.ni} söyledi.** 'He said {that he had gone/that he would go [*or* was going to go]} to Ankara several times.' Proverb: İste.diğ.i.ni söyle.yen isteme-.diğ.i.ni işitir. 'He who says what [ever] he likes [lit., wants] will hear what he doesn't like.' **Şimdi siz.E ne yapma.nız gerek.tiğ.i.nİ söyleyeceğim.** 'Now I'm going to tell θ you what you have to do.' *524:23.* speech: - say.

'- tell sb to do sth': In the following note how direct commands become indirect commands with **söyle-**:
1. The DIRECT command in a statement: **Öğretmen: Orhan gel!** 'The teacher: Orhan, [you (s.)] come!'
2. A person asks what the teacher, above, had said: **Öğretmen ne dedi?** 'What did the teacher say?'
3. The response may appear in two patterns:
a) The short infinitive [i.e., the infinitive without the final **k**] with the possessED suffixes replaces the imperative and is followed by **söyle-**: **Öğretmen Orhan'IN gelme-.Sİ.nİ söyledi.** 'The teacher told Orhan to come [lit., ** told Orhan's coming].' In all persons [The possessor pronouns in brackets are used when emphasis is required.]: **{a: [Benim] Gelme.m.İ/b: [Senin] Gelme.n.İ/c: [Onun] Gelme.si.nİ/d: [Bizim] Gelme-.miz.İ/e: [Sizin] Gelme.niz.İ/f: [Onların] Gelme.leri.nİ} söyledi.** 'He told {a: me to come/b: you [s.] to come/c: him to come/d: us to come/e: you [pl] to come/f: them to come}.'
b) In the second pattern, the words of the DIRECT command precede the word **diye** 'saying', which is followed by the verb **söyle-**: **Öğretmen "Orhan gel" diye söyledi.** [More common: **Öğretmen "Orhan gel" dedi.**] 'The teacher said, "Orhan come".' Another example of this pattern but with the negative command: **Üst.ün.ü baş.ın.ı pisletme diye sana kaç defa söyledim!** 'How many times have I told you not to get your clothes [= üst baş] dirty! [lit., ** How many times I told you saying, 'Don't get your clothes dirty.']' *420:8.* command: - command.

Some common phrases used in conversation to focus attention on a following statement: **{Açık/ Açıkça} söylemek gerekirse** 'To tell the truth [lit., If it is necessary to speak openly]' → = **{Açık/Açıkça} konuşmak gerekirse** → konuş-. *644:23.* probity: ADV. candidly. See also below under **doğru söyle-**. * **{Aklıma gelmişken} söyle-yeyim...** '{Incidentally/While I'm thinking about it} [lit., ** Since it has come to my mind], let me say....' **Hatırımdayken şunu da söyleyeyim:...** 'While it's on my mind, let me also say this:....' **Hemen şunu söyleyeyim ki...** 'Let me say right now that...' * **Ne yalan söyleyeyim.** '{To tell the truth [lit., Why should I lie]./I won't hide it from you.}' *644:22.* probity: ADV. truthfully. **Sana bir şey söyleyeyim:..** 'Let me tell you sth:...' **Sana bir şey söyleyeyim mi?** 'Shall I tell you sth?' **Şimdilik şu kadar.ı.nı söyleyeyim.** 'For now let me just say this much.' **Şu kadar.ı.nı söyleyeyim ki...** 'Let me just say....' * **Unutmadan söyleyeyim...** 'Before I forget [let me just say]...' *524:23.* speech: - say.

• **de- versus söyle-**: De- is the only verb that may DIRECTLY follow a DIRECT quotation: **"Geliyorum" dedi.** 'He said, "I'm coming."' A form of it, **diye** 'saying', MUST come between the ACTUAL WORDS said and any OTHER verb of communicating, i.e., saying, asking, answering, shouting, etc.: * **"Geliyorum" diye cevap verdi.** 'He answered [saying], "I'm coming."' Söyle-, on the other hand, is NOT used DIRECTLY after a direct quotation BUT after the **DIk** or **AcAk** participles in INDIRECT speech: **{Geldiğ.i.ni/Gele-ceğ.i.ni} söyledi.** 'He said {that he had come/that he was going to come}.'

dobra dobra söyle- '- speak bluntly, frankly' [**dobra dobra** 'bluntly, frankly']: **Sibel kimsenin arkasından konuşmaz. Düşün-düklerini dobra dobra söyler.** 'Sibel doesn't speak behind anyone's back. She always expresses her thoughts [quite] bluntly.' *644:12.*

probity: - be frank. → = dobra dobra konuş-.

{doğru/doğru.yu/gerçeğ.i/haki-kat.i} söyle- '- tell {the truth}' [doğru 'true, truly', {doğru.yu/gerçeğ.i/hakikat.i} 'the truth']: Doğru söyle, dün sinemaya gittin, değil mi? 'Tell {the truth}, you went to the movies yesterday, didn't you?' Doğru söylemek gerekirse, bu yaz Ahu ile tatil.E çıkmak istemiyorum. 'To tell the truth [lit., If it is necessary to tell the truth], I don't want to go ON {vacation/holiday} with Ahu [f.] this summer.' The possessed form plus the accusative may also occur: Doğru.SU.nu söylemek gerekirse... 'To tell the truth [lit., ** ITS truth]...', that is, the truth about a certain matter]. 351:7. disclosure: - confess; 644:22. probity: ADV. truthfully. {Doğru/Doğruyu} söyle, yalan söyleme. 'Tell the truth, don't tell lies.' * Gerçeği nasıl söylesem ona? 'How {can/shall} I tell him the truth, I wonder.' Doktor bey, lütfen bana gerçeği söyleyin, babamın durumu çok mu ağır? 'Doctor, tell me the truth. Is my father's condition very serious?' Proverb: Doğru söyleyeni dokuz köy.DEN kovarlar. 'He who tells the truth will be run out of nine villages [lit., They will run the one who tells the truth OUT OF...].' 644:11. probity: - speak or - tell the truth. → ≠ yalan söyle-.

* Efendime söyleyeyim. 'Let's see, let me see, um, ah, er', a filler phrase used when stalling for time. The word Efendim alone more commonly serves the same function: Geçen yaz Avrupa'ya bir seyahat yaptık. Almanya, Fransa ve {efendime söyleyeyim/efendim}, İtalya ve İsviçre'ye de uğradık. 'Last summer we took a trip to Europe. We stopped off in Germany, France, and, {let's see}, also in Italy and in Switzerland.' 362:13. irresolution: ADV. * filler phrases and stallers. For other filler phrases, → Ne bileyim ben. 2 → bil- 1, Nasıl anlatayım? → anlat- 1, Nasıl anlatsam? → anlat- 1.

gerçeği söyle-. → {doğru/doğruyu-/gerçeği/hakikati} söyle- above.

hakikati söyle-. → {doğru/doğruyu-/gerçeği/hakikati} söyle- above.

{harf harf/harfler.i.ni} söyle- '- spell, - say {letter by letter/the letters of [a word]}' [A. harf (harfî) 'letter']. However when indicating how a word is written, Turks usually pronounce the word in syllables rather than give letter names. S: İsminizi anlayamadım. Lütfen harf harf söyler misiniz? 'Q: I didn't catch [lit., ** understand] your [first] name. Would you please spell it [lit., ** say it letter by letter]?' C: Tabii, je-e-a-ne-ne-e. 'A: {Of course./Sure.} J,E,A,N,N,E.' Adınız.ın ve soyadınız.ın harfler.i.ni söyler misiniz? 'Would you please spell [lit., ** say the letters of] your first and last names?' While English speakers usually use well-known first names to clarify the spelling of a word, i.e., j as in James, b as in Bill, etc., Turkish speakers use the names of well-known Turkish cities. 546:7. letter: - spell. → hecele- ['- give the syllables of a word, - syllabify'], yazıl 1 ['- be written', often used in describing the spelling of a word].

selâm söyle- /A, DAn/ '- send, - give, or - express one's regards /to, from/', informal: '- say "Hi" /to/' [A. selâm (. -) 'salutation, greeting']: You'll be seeing some friends of mine. I tell you: * Arkadaşlar.a [ben.den] selâm söyleyin. '{Give my regards/Say "Hi"} to [our] friends [lit., ** say regards (from me) to the friends].' * Gülnur siz.e selâm söyledi. 'Gülnur [f.] {sends [her] regards/says hi} to you.' or 'Gülnur sends θ you [her] regards.' • Note: the past tense in the usual Turkish, the present tense in the usual English. A common equivalent: Gülnur'un selâmları var. lit., ** 'Gülnur has greetings [for you].' Amcam.ın selâm.ı.nı söyle-yince * bana çok yakınlık gösterdiler. 'When I passed on my uncle's regards, * they were very nice to me [lit., ** showed great closeness to me].' 504:13. courtesy: - give one's regards. → selâm yolla- ['- send greetings /to/', informal: '- say "Hi" /to/'], selâm getir- ['- bring greetings /from/'].

yalan söyle- '- lie, - tell lies' [yalan 'lie']: Hakikati söyle, yalan söyleme. 'Tell the truth, don't {lie/tell lies}.' **Yalan söylemek çok ayıptır.** 'It's very shameful to tell lies.' * **Fena halde yalan söylüyor.** 'He's a big liar.' [lit., ** 'He tells lies in a bad state', i.e., to a great extent]. * **Hiç utanmadan sıkılmadan yalan söylüyor.** 'He lies without the slightest shame or regret.' * **Bana yalan söyleme, kitabımı sen aldın,** * **kendi {* gözümle/ gözlerimle} gördüm.** 'Don't lie to me! It was you who took my book. * I saw you [lit., it, i.e., the event] {with my own eyeS}!' * **Lütfen birbirimiz.E yalan söyleme-yelim, ikimiz de biliyoruz babamın evliliğimiz.E neden karşı çıktığını.** 'Please, let's not kid ourselves [lit., tell lies to one another]. We both know why my father opposed θ our marriage.' * **Ne yalan söyleyeyim.** '{To tell the truth [lit., Why should I lie]./I won't hide it from you.}': **Ne yalan söyleyeyim, ilk gördüğümde seni pek sevmemiştim.** 'To tell the truth, when I first saw you I didn't like you very much.' *354:19.* falseness: - lie; *645:11.* improbity: - be dishonest. → ≠ {doğru/ doğruyu/gerçeği/hakikati} söyle-. *644:22.* probity: ADV. truthfully.

2 '- order', usually only when the order is spoken as, for example, in a restaurant or a coffee house: **Lokanta.yA girdi ve bir çorba söyledi.** 'He entered θ the restaurant and ordered a bowl of soup.' *440:9.* request: - request. → = **ısmarla-** [This verb can be used as above but also in almost every other situation involving ordering as, for example, from a catalogue].

3 /A/ '- speak /to/ sb, - talk /to/ sb': **S: Kim.e söylüyorsunuz?** 'Q: Who[m] are you speaking to?' **C: Siz.e söylüyorum.** 'A: I'm speaking to you.' **Baksanıza, siz.e söylüyorum. Bilet almadan geçtiniz.** '{Look here/Hey there}, I'm talking to you. You've gone through without buying a ticket.' **Ban.a mı söylüyorsunuz?** 'Are you speaking to me?' *524:27.* speech: - address. → = **konuş-, hitap et-** ['- address'].

4 '- sing': **Operada bu akşam kim söylüyor?** 'Who is singing at the

opera tonight?' **şarkı söyle-** '- sing' [**şarkı** 'song']: **Sezen Aksu çok güzel şarkı söyler.** 'Sezen Aksu sings beautifully.' Contrast this with: {**Bu şarkı.yı/Bu şarkılar.ı**} **Sezen Aksu çok güzel söyler.** 'Sezen Aksu sings {this song/these songs} very well.' **Sezen Aksu çok güzel şarkı.lar söyler.** 'Sezen Aksu sings beautiful songs.' *708:38.* music: - sing. → = **şarkı oku-** → **oku-** 5.

söz bulAMA-. → **bul-** 1.

söz dinle-. → {**lâf/söz**} **dinle-.** → 1 **dinle-** 2.

söz et- [eDer] /DAn/ '- talk /ABOUT/, - tell /{ABOUT/OF}/, - mention /θ/' [**söz** 'word, utterance']: **Biz.E biraz kendiniz.DEN söz eder misiniz?** 'Would you please tell us a little ABOUT yourself?' **San.A okul.la ilgili plânlarım.DAN söz etmedim galiba.** 'I have probably not {told you {ABOUT/OF}/mentioned θ} my plans {for/regarding} school.' **Bugün siz.E bir başka konu.DAN söz edeceğim.** 'Today I'm going to {talk ABOUT/discuss θ} another subject with you.' *551:8.* information: - inform. → = /DAn/ **bahset-,** = /a: I, b: hakkında../ **konuş-** ['- talk /a, b: about.../'].

sözünü et- '- mention, - make mention of': **Söz.ü.nü ettiğiniz makaleyi yayınladınız mı?** 'Did you publish the article {[[that] you had mentioned?/that you had made mention of?}' *541:12.* conversation: - discuss; *551:8.* information: - inform.

söz tut-. → **tut-** 5.

söz ver-. → **ver-** 1.

söze karış-. → **karış-** 6.

sözü kısa kes-. → [{lâfı/sözü}] kısa **kes-.** → **kes-** 4.

sözünde dur-. → **dur-** 6.

sözünden çık-. → **çık-** 1.

sözünden dön-. → **dön-** 5.

sözünü et-. → **söz et-.**

sözünü kes-. → **kes-** 3.

sözünü tut-. → tut- 5.

spor yap-. → yap- 3.

su dök-. → dök- 3.

su kaynat-. → kaynat-.

su ver-. → ver- 1.

suçla- [r] /a: 1A, b: DAn dolayı, c: konusunda/ '- accuse /a, c: OF/, - blame /b: FOR/' [suç 1 'offense, blameworthy act'. 2 'crime' + verb-forming suf. -1A]: Beni suçlama, bu benim hatam değil. 'Don't blame me. It's not my fault!' NON-verbal noun as indirect object: Başbakan gazeteciler.i yalan-cılık.LA suçladı. 'The prime minister accused the reporters OF lying.' Başarısızlıklar.ın.DAN DOLAYI hep beni suçluyorsun. * Biraz da hatayı kendinde ara! 'You always blame me FOR your failures. * Why don't you look just a little for the fault in yourself?' Amerika Birleşik Devletleri terörizm konu.su.nda Libya'yı suçladı. 'The U.S. accused Libya OF [lit., ** on the subject of] terrorism.'
VERBAL noun as indirect object: Evliliğ.i.nin yıkılma.sı.nDAN DOLAYI kocasını suçladı. 'She blamed her husband FOR the failure of her marriage.' 599:8. accusation: - blame.

sula- [r] /I/ '- water, - give water /to/,' plants, animals [su 'water' + verb-forming suf. -1A]: Çiçekler.İ sulamay.I unutma! 'Don't forget to water the flowers!' Babam öğleden sonra {çim.LER.i} suladı. 'In the afternoon my father watered {the lawn/the grass} [lit., ** the grassES].' Hayvanlar.ı suladın mı? 'Have you watered the animals?' 1063:12. moisture: - moisten; 1068:7. animal husbandry: - tend. → = su ver- → ver- 1.

sun- [ar] 1 /A/ '- offer, - present, - submit /to/': Dilekçe.m.i okul müdür-lüğ.ü.ne sundum. 'I presented my petition to the office of the school principal.' İstifa.m.ı Bakan.a sundum ama kabul etmedi. 'I submitted my resignation to the minister, but he didn't accept it.' Dün {yüksek lisans [or master]/doktora} tez.im.i

jüri.ye sundum. 'Yesterday I submitted my {master's/doctor's} thesis to the [academic] {committee/jury}.' → = takdim et- 2. # Misafirlerim.E mercimekli köfte ve ayran sundum. 'I offered θ my guests lentil meat balls and ayran.' → = ikram et- 1 ['- offer food or drink']. 439:4. offer: - offer.

saygılar sun- '- pay or - offer one's respects, - give or - send one's regards or compliments /to/' [saygı 'respect, esteem']: On a greeting card: * {Sayın hocam/Kıymetli öğretmenim} yeni yıl.ınız.I kutlar, saygılarımı sunarım. '{My dear teacher/My esteemed teacher}, I congratulate you ON the new year [lit., ** congratulate your new year] and offer my respects.' 155:5. respect: - do or - pay hommage to; 504:13. courtesy: - give one's regards.

2 /A/ '- perform, - play, or - sing sth /FOR/ sb': Sayın seyirciler, bu gece siz.E iki şarkı sunuyorum. 'Dear [lit., ** respected] viewers, tonight I'm going to perform [lit., ** I'm presenting] two songs FOR you.' 328:9. action: - perform; 708:39a. music: - play sth. → çal- 2 ['- play a musical instrument, radio, record player, tape recorder; - play, - perform' a piece of music'], yorumla- 2 ['- interpret, - perform', a piece of music].

surat as-. → as- 1.

sus- [ar] 1 '- be silent, - remain silent, not - say anything': Ayşenur dün çok üzgündü. Bütün gün sustu, hiç konuşmadı. 'Ayşenur was very {sad/unhappy} yesterday. She was silent the whole day. She didn't say a word [lit., didn't speak at all].' 51:5. silence: - be silent.

2 '- stop talking, - fall or - become silent': Ömer ile Yavuz, Cansu hakkında konuşuyorlardı. Cansu yanlar.ı.na gelince sustular. 'Ömer and Yavuz were speaking about Cansu. When Cansu came up to them [lit., ** to their sides], they fell silent.' Ağlayan çocuk, anne.si.nin geldiğ.i.ni görünce neşelendi ve sustu. 'The child who was crying, when he saw that his mother had come, became cheerful and quieted down.'

364

* Yeter artık, sus! 'That's about enough now! {Be quiet!/Shut up!}' Sus be! 'Shut up!' *abrupt, impolite*, as in English. *51:7*. silence: - fall silent. → = sesini kes- → kes- 4.

susa- [r] '- get or - be thirsty' [su 'water' + verb-forming suf. -sA]: Dün iş yerimde hiç su yoktu. Çok susadım. 'Yesterday there was no water in the office [lit., in my workplace]. I {got/was} very thirsty.' Plajda çok susadım ama hiç su bulamadım. 'I {got/was} very thirsty on the beach, but I couldn't find any water.' * Çok susa.DIM. * Bir bardak su verir misin? '{I'M/I got} very thirsty. May I please have a glass of water?' In this utterance, in contrast to the first two above, the feeling of thirst is present now, at the time of speaking. • In reference to a PRESENT condition, certain common Turkish verbs designating a state, i.e., a feeling, emotion, or sensation, often have the simple PAST tense, but the equivalent English has the simple PRESENT tense. *100:19*. desire: - hunger. → acık- ['- be hungry'].

sünnet et- [eDer] '- circumcise' [A. sünnet 'ritual circumcision']: Her iki kardeş.im.i aynı sünnetçi sünnet etti. 'The same circumciser circumcised both my younger brothers.' *701:16*. religious rites: - baptize.

sünnet ol-. → ol- 10.1.

süpür- [ür] /lA/ '- sweep /with/': Balkon çok kirlenmiş, süpürsene. 'The balcony has gotten very dirty, why don't you sweep it?' Kapıcı bütün apartmanın merdivenlerini süpürmüş. '{The caretaker/The doorman} has swept the stairs of the whole apartment building.' Proverb: Erken süpür, el görsün; akşam süpür er görsün. 'Sweep [your house] early for others to see [lit., ** let others see]; sweep it in the evening for your husband to see [lit., ** let the husband see].' *79:23*. cleanness: - sweep.

elektrik süpürgesi ile süpür- '- vacuum' [süpürge 'sweeper']: Eve geldiğimde annem elektrik süpürgesi ile halıları süpürüyordu. 'When I got home, my mother was vacuuming the rugs.' *79:23*. cleanness: - sweep.

sür- [er] 1 '- drive a vehicle, - push a vehicle, - push sth forward': *vehicle name* sür-. This structure forms various verbs of driving vehicles. = *vehicle name* kullan-: araba sür- '- drive [a car]': Araba sürmey.İ severim. 'I like θ {driving/to drive}.' Lütfen arabanı dikkatli sür. 'Please drive [your car] carefully.' Ümit araba.sı.nı {a: [çok] hızlı/b: yavaş/c: dikkatli/d: dikkatsiz} sürüyordu. 'Ümit was driving his car {a: [very] fast/b: slowly/c: carefully/d: carelessly}.' *888:5*. operation: - operate sth. For 'What kind of car do you drive?' and various responses, → kullan- = *vehicle name* kullan-.

* ileri sür- [ileri 'further on, forward'] (1) '- put forward or - advance an idea, suggestion, or proposal, - propose': Üniversite gençleri {öğrenim harçları/ müfredat} konusunda yeni fikirler ileri sürdüler. '{The college/The university} students [lit., The college... youth] {came up with/put forward} new ideas on {expenditures for education/ curriculum}.' İleri sürülen {her görüş.E/her fikr.E} katılmak zorunda değilim. 'I'm not obliged to concur {IN every idea} that is proposed.' *439:5*. offer: - propose. → = öner-, = teklif et-.
(2) '- claim, - maintain': Muhalefet partisi iktidar partisi.nin ülkeyi iyi yönetemediğ.i.ni ileri sürdü. 'The opposition party claimed that the party in power was not able to run the country well.' *334:5*. affirmation: - affirm.

2 '- last, - continue, - go on': S: {Sınav/Toplantı/Film} ne kadar sürer? 'Q: How long will {the examination/the meeting/the film} last?' C1: {Aşağı yukarı/En az} 2 saat [sürer]. 'A1: [It will last] {about/at least} two hours.' C2: İki saat.TEN {fazla/az} sürer. 'A2: It'll last {more/less} THAN two hours.' C3: Epey uzun sürer. 'A3: It'll last quite a while.' C4: Fazla sürmez. 'A4: It won't last long.' Uzun süreceğ.i açık. 'It's clear that it's going to last a long time.' Proverb: * Yemeğ.i uzun sür.en.in ömr.ü kısa olur. 'A person who spends a long time eating will have a short life [lit., ** The life of the one whose eating lasts long

will be short].' *811:4b.* continuity: for sth - continue. → = **devam et-** 1.

3 '- take time, - last': Noun of road or journey as subject: **S1: Yolculuk {ne kadar/kaç saat} sürer?** 'Q1: {How long/How many hours} does [*or* will] the trip take?' **S2: * Yol {ne kadar/kaç saat} sürer?** 'Q2: {How long/How many hours} does it take to get there? [lit., ** {How long/How many hours} does the road take?]'

Noun of destination as subject: **S: * Benzinci [bura.dan] {ne kadar/kaç saat} sürer?** 'Q: {How long/How many hours} does it take to get to the gas station [from here]? [lit., ** {How long/How many hours} does the gas station take (from here)?]'

Noun of process as subject: **S: * Oraya gitmek {ne kadar/kaç saat} sürer?** 'Q: {How long/How many hours} does it take to go there [lit., ** {How long/How many hours} does going there take]?' **S: * Araba.nın tamir.i {ne kadar/kaç saat} sürer?** 'Q: {How long/How many hours} will it take to repair the car [lit., ** {How long/How many hours} will the car's repair take]?'

With expressions of manner: **S: {a: * Yürü.yEREK/b: Otobüs.LE/ c: Dolmuş.LA/d: Tramvay.LA/ e: Metro.yLA/f: Taksi.yLE} ne kadar sürer?** 'Q: How long does it take {a: * {to walk [lit., ** BY walk.ING...]?/to go ON foot?}/b: BY bus?/c: BY shared cab?/d: BY streetcar?/e: BY subway?/f: BY taxi?}' **S: Taksi.yLE git.SE.niz kaç dakika sürer?** 'Q: How many minutes would it take IF you went BY cab?'

Destination and manner together: **S: * Bura.dan havaalanı taksi.yLE ne kadar sürer?** 'Q: How long does it take to go to the airport BY taxi? [lit., ** From here how long does the airport take by taxi?]' **C: [Bura.dan] {on dakika/beş saat} sürer.** 'A: It takes {ten minutes/five hours} [from here].' *820:6.* time: - spend time. → = **çek-** 10, = {**vakit/zaman**} **al-** → **al-** 1.

4 /A, {üstüne/üzerine}/ '- apply sth /to, to the surface of/ sth, - spread, - rub, - smear or - put sth /ON/ sth': **Kek.in üst.ü.nE bolca krema sürdü.** 'She spread quite a lot of frosting ON the cake.' **Zehra partiye gider.ken {a: pudra/b: krem/c: ruj/d: parfüm/e: kolonya} sürdü.** 'Zehra [f.] applied {a: powder/b: cold cream/c: lipstick/d: perfume/e: cologne} BEFORE going to the party.' • The aorist form of a verb of motion followed by **iken** [suffix form **-ken**], usually translated 'WHILE...ing', may designate an action completed SHORTLY BEFORE another action, in which case it is translated 'BEFORE...ing'. **Cem partiye giderken {kolonya/tıraş losyonu/briyantin} sürdü.** 'Cem put on some {cologne/aftershave/brilliantine} before going to the party.' *295:19.* covering: - cover.

5 /A/ '- let one thing touch /θ/ another': **el sür-** [er] '- touch /θ/' with the hands [**el** 'hand']: **Müzedeki eserler.E el sürmeyiniz.** 'Don't touch θ the objects in the museum.' **Lütfen çiçekler.E el sürmeyiniz.** 'Please don't touch θ the flowers.' *73:6.* touch: - touch; *223:10.* nearness: - contact; *352:7.* publication: poster: * specific signs. → = **dokun-** 1. For other THINGS as the subject of '- touch, brush against', → 1 **değ-** 1.

6 '- lead, - conduct': **hayat sür-** '- lead a [certain kind of] life': **Adam orada son derece {a: rahat/b: keyifli/c: huzurlu/d: sıkıcı/e: münzevi/f: lüks/g: çalkantılı/ h: macera dolu/i: sakin/j: zor} bir hayat sürüyor.** 'The man is leading an extremely {a: comfortable/b: pleasant/c: {peaceful/tranquil}/d: boring/e: solitary/f: luxurious/g: turbulent/h: adventurous/ i: {calm/tranquil}/j: difficult} life over there.' **{Gurbette} nasıl bir hayat sürdüğ.üm.ü yalnızca ben bilirim.** 'Only I know what kind of a life I'm leading {away from home/in exile}.' *306:7.* life: - live. → **otur-** 3 ['- live, - reside /{in/at}/, - inhabit /θ/', a place], **yaşa-** 1 ['- live', as opposed to die], 2 = **otur-** 3.

sürat yap-. → **yap-** 3.

{**süre/vakit/zaman**} **dol-.** → **dol-** 2.

sürükle- [r] 1 /A/ '- drag sb or sth along the ground /to/' [**sür-** + verb-forming suf. **-[A/I]klA**]: **Kaldırmay.a gücüm yetme.yince {çamaşır makinesini/buzdolabını} sürükle.yerek çıkardım.** 'When I didn't have the strength to lift it, I got {the washing machine/the refrigerator} out by dragg.ing it.' *904:4.* pulling: - pull.

2 /A/ '- drag sb /to/ a place against his will, - drag off': **Polisler yürümemek.TE direnen mahkûmu sürükle.yerek götürdü.** 'The police dragged off the convict who refused to walk [by himself] [lit., ** took away by dragg.ing the convict who insisted ON not walking].' *904:4.* pulling: - pull.

sürün- [ür] [sür- + refl. suf. -In] 1 '- crawl along the ground': **Askerler gece karanlığında sürün.erek sessizce düşman mevziler.i.nE doğru yaklaşıyorlardı.** 'The soldiers, crawl.ing along the ground in the dark of night, were silently approaching θ enemy positions.' *177:26.* travel: - creep.

2 '- live in misery, - live a miserable life, - be just scraping {along/by}, - be barely surviving, getting by, - be just keeping body and soul together, - be living through hard times': **Açlık ve sefalet içinde sürünen milyonlarca insan var.** 'There are millions of people living miserable lives in hunger and poverty.' **S: N'aber** [short for: **Ne haber**]? 'Q: What's up [lit., What news]?' **C: * Ne olsun, sürünüp gidiyoruz işte.** 'A: * Well, what do you expect? We're just barely {getting by/keeping body and soul together}.' * **sürüm sürüm sürün-** '- live a life of great misery, undergo great suffering': A harsh curse: **Sürüm sürüm sürünürsün inşallah.** 'May you suffer the greatest misery!' *96:19.* unpleasure: - suffer; *513:11.* curse: INTERJ. damn!

süsle- [r] /lA/ '- decorate, - adorn /with/' [süs 'ornament' + verb-forming suf. -lA]: **Çocuk bayramında bütün ilkokullar, sınıflarını bayraklarla, çiçeklerle süslemişlerdi.** 'On the Children's holiday all the primary schools had decorated their classrooms with flags and flowers.' *498:8.* ornamentation: - ornament; *1015:15.* beauty: - beautify.

süslen- [ir] [süsle- + {pass./refl.} suf. -n] 1 /lA/ '- deck oneself out /IN/, - adorn oneself /with/, - doll oneself up /IN/': **Zerrin'i gördün mü, * parti için nasıl da süslenmiş.** 'Did you see Zerrin? * Just look how she has dolled herself up for the party!' **İlkbaharda kırlar çiçekler.le süslenir.** 'In the spring the countryside adorns itself with

flowers.' *5:41.* clothing: - dress up; *498:8.* ornamentation: - ornament; *1015:15.* beauty: - beautify.

2 /lA, tarafından/ '- be decorated, adorned, embellished /with, by/': **Bayramda okulumuz [öğrenciler tarafından] çiçekler.le süslendi.** 'For the holiday our school was decorated with flowers [by the students].' *498:8.* ornamentation: - ornament; *1015:15.* beauty: - beautify.

süz- [er] '- strain; - filter out': **{Pirinci/Bulguru} birkaç kez yıkayıp süzün ve kaynar su.ya ekleyin.** 'Wash and strain {the rice/the cracked wheat} several times and add it to the boiling water.' *79:22.* cleanness: - refine.

- Ş -

şaka yap-. → yap- 3.

şakaya gelME-. → gel- 1.

şansını zorla-. → zorla- 2.

Şansınız {bol/açık} olsun! → ol- 11 → olsun.

şarkı oku-. → oku- 5.

şarkı söyle-. → söyle- 1.

şart koş-. → koş-.

şaş- [ar] /A/ '- be amazed, astonished, surprised /θ [that], AT/': **Mine'nin Tayfun'la {evlendiğ.i.nE/ evleneceğ.i.nE} çok şaştım.** 'I was very surprised θ that Mine [f.] {had married/was going to marry} Tayfun.' **Bu davranış.ı.nA çok şaştım.** 'I was very surprised AT this behavior of his.' *122:5.* wonder: - wonder; *131:7.* inexpectation: - surprise. → = hayret et-, = şaşır- 2.

Şaş- is often found together with the verb **kal-** '- remain, - stay' in the form **şaştı kal-** to convey a higher level of amazement: **Müzedeki tarihî eserleri görünce şaş.TIM kal.DIM. Yüzyıllarca önce ne güzel eşyalar yapılmış!** 'When I saw the historical works in the museum, I was amazed: What beautiful works were produced centuries ago!' *122:5.* wonder: - wonder; *131:7.* inexpectation: - surprise. → = {şaşır-/şaşırıp} kal- → şaşır- 2.

şaşır- [ır] **1** /I/ '- be confused, bewildered, at a loss /AS TO/ what to say or do, - be taken aback, bewildered /{AT/in the face of}/ an unexpected situation' [ADJ. **şaşkın**]: **Adamın bütün eşyaları çalınmış.** * **Ne.yE uğradığını şaşırdı.** 'All the man's possessions had been stolen. * He couldn't understand what had happened to him.' **On.un Almanya'da olduğ.u.nu sanıyordum. Birdenbire karşı.M.a çıkınca** * **ne diyeceğim.İ şaşırdım.** 'I thought he was in Germany. When he suddenly appeared in front of me, * I didn't know what to say [i.e., I was confused AS TO what to say].' *970:9.* uncertainty: - be uncertain; *984:7b.* distraction, confusion: - get confused.

Şaşır- often occurs together with the verb **kal-** '- remain, stay' in the forms {şaşır-/şaşırıp} kal-, to convey a higher level of confusion, etc., so the last example above could end as follows: ...**ne diyeceğim.İ {şaşır.dım/şaşırıp} kaldım.**

2 /A, karşısında/ '- be amazed, astonished, surprised /AT, AT [lit., in the face of]/': **Bunu duyunca hiç şaşırmadım.** 'When I heard this, I wasn't {a bit/at all} surprised.' **Öyle şaşırdı ki,** * **söyleyecek söz bulamıyordu.** 'He was so surprised * [that] he {didn't know what to say/was at a loss for words} [lit., ** that he couldn't find words to say].' **Bir yıldır Betül'ü görmüyordum. Dün görünce çok şaşırdım.** * **Ne kadar şişmanlamış!** 'I hadn't seen Betül for a year. When I saw her yesterday, I was {really/very} surprised. {She'd put on so much weight!/She'd gotten so fat!/How fat she had gotten!}' NON-verbal noun as object: **Senin bu enerjin.E şaşırıyorum, doğrusu!** 'I'm really astounded AT this energy of yours!' VERBAL noun as object: {**Bu davranışı.nA/Bu davranışı karşı.sı.nda**} **çok şaşırdım.** 'I was very surprised {AT this behavior of his}.' **Filiz'in Tayfun'la {evlendiğ.i.nE/evleneceğ.i.nE} şaşırdım.** 'I was surprised θ that

Filiz [f.] {had married/was going to marry} Tayfun.' Since **şaşır-** often occurs together with the verb **kal-** '- remain, - stay' in the forms {şaşır-/şaşırıp} kal-, to convey a higher level of amazement, the last two examples above could end as follows: ...{şaşır.dım/şaşırıp} kaldım. *122:5.* wonder: - wonder; *131:7.* inexpectation: - surprise. → = **hayret et-,** = **şaş-.**

3 /I/ '- confuse, - get confused /{about/regarding/as to}/, - lose track of, count of': **Çetin paralar.ı.nı sayarken {şaşırdı}, baştan saymaya başladı.** 'Çetin {got confused/lost count} while counting his money and began to count [again] from the beginning.' * **Bugün.ün hangi gün olduğ.u.nu şaşırdı.** '{He lost track of the days./lit., He got confused about what day it was today.}' **Günleri şaşırmış ve salı pazarına gitmiş. Halbuki** * **daha pazartesi.** 'He got his days mixed up and went to the [place of] the Tuesday Market. However * today is only Monday.' *970:9.* uncertainty: - be uncertain; *984:7b.* distraction, confusion: - get confused. → = {**aklı/kafası**} **karış-** → **karış-.**

* **yolunu şaşır-** '- lose one's way, - get lost, not - know which way to turn' [**yol** 'road, way']: **Dün san.a gelecektim, fakat yol.UM.U şaşırdım, evini bulamadım.** 'I was going to come and visit you yesterday [lit., was going to come to you...], but I lost MY way and couldn't find your house.' **Funda'lara giderken yanlış sokağ.a girince yol.UMUZ.u şaşırdık, evi bulamadık.** 'While going to Funda's [f.] house, we turned INTO the wrong street and lost OUR way. We couldn't find the house.' Proverb: **Eski kurt yolunu şaşırmaz.** 'An old wolf won't lose his way.' *970:9.* uncertainty: - be uncertain. In a moral sense: **A: Çetin bey şimdi de kumar oynamaya başlamış.** 'A: Çetin bey has now also begun to gamble.' **B: Bu adam iyice yolunu şaşırdı artık.** 'B: This man has now really {lost his way/gone astray}.' *473:4.* loss: - lose; *654:9.* vice: - go wrong.

{şaşır-/şaşırıp} kal-. → şaşır- 1, 2.

şaşırt- [ır] [**şaşır-** + caus. suf. -t]: **1** '- surprise, - bewilder, - confuse, - catch off guard': O.nun Almanya'da oldu.ğ.u.nu sanıyordum. * Birdenbire karşı.M.a çıkması, beni şaşırttı. * Ne diyeceğim.I bil.EME.dim. 'I thought he was in Germany. * When he suddenly appeared in front of me, I was surprised [lit., His sudden appearance in front of me surprised me]. * I didn't [lit., ** COULDN'T] know what to say.' 984:7a. distraction, confusion: - confuse.

2 '- surprise, - astonish': Filiz'in Tayfun'LA evlenme.si ben.i çok şaşırttı doğrusu. 'Filiz's marriage TO Tayfun [lit., Filiz's marrying θ Tayfun] really surprised me.' jocular: Beyefendi bu ne kibarlık! Şaşırtıyorsunuz beni. 'Sir, what is this [sudden show of] courtesy!? You really surprise me!' 122:6. wonder: - astonish.

3 '- confuse, - distract, - make sb lose track or count of, - cause sb to lose track or count of': Bak, bu paraları üçüncü kez sayıyorum; lütfen beni şaşırtma! 'Look, I'm counting this money for the third time [now]. Please don't make me lose count!' 984:6. distraction: - distract; 984:7a.: - confuse.

şaştı kal-. → şaş-.

{şeref/onur} ver-. → ver- 1.

şifa ver-. → ver- 1.

şikâyet et- [eDer] [A. şikâyet (. - .) 'complaint']. • Note the two patterns:
a) /DAn, A/ '- complain /{OF/ABOUT}, to [yourself or to a friend, but usually not to an authority]/': Complaining about a situation: Annem {a: gürültü-.DEN/ b : otel.in pisliğ.i.nDEN/c: yemekler.in kötülüğ.ü.nDEN/d: mağaza-lar.ın pahalılığ.ı.nDAN} şikâyet etti. 'My mother complained {a: OF the noise/b: OF the dirty hotel [lit., ** the dirt of the hotel]/c: OF the bad food [lit., the low quality of the food]/d: OF the high prices of the stores}.' {Bu.n.DAN/* Bunlar.DAN} şikâyet etti. 'She complained {OF that/* OF these things}.', i.e., the things mentioned above. Hep durumumuz.DAN şikâyet ederiz. 'We're always complaining

ABOUT our {situation/circum-stances}.' Rahatsız olan şikâyet etsin. 'Let {those who are/the one who is} disturbed [i.e., by a situation] complain.'
Complaining about a person: Farkında mısın bilmiyorum, her karşılaşmamızda Cemil'DEN şikâyet ediyorsun. 'I don't know whether you've noticed, but whenever we meet you complain ABOUT Cemil.' 333:5. dissent: - object. → = yakın-.
b) /a: I, b: A, c: DIğI için/ '- complain /a: {OF/ABOUT}, b: to [an authority], c: because/': Complaining about a situation: Annem otel.in {gürültüsü.nÜ/pisliğ.i.nI/ yemekler.i.nin kötülüğ.ü.nÜ} otel müdürü.nE şikâyet etmiş. 'My mother complained {ABOUT the noise/ABOUT the dirt/ABOUT the bad food} of the hotel TO the hotel manager.' {Bu.nU/* Bunlar.I} şikâyet etmiş. 'She complained {ABOUT that/* ABOUT these things}.', i.e., the things mentioned above.
Complaining about a person: Görevini yapmayan memur.U müdür.E şikâyet ettim. 'I complained TO the director ABOUT the employee who was not doing his work.' S: Adnan'I niçin şikâyet ettin? 'Q: Why did you complain ABOUT Adnan?' C: İşini yapma.dığ.ı için. 'A: because he {didn't do/hadn't done/wasn't doing} his work.' * Kim.İ kim.E şikâyet edeceksiniz? 'TO whom can [lit., will] you complain ABOUT sb?' 333:5. dissent: - object; 599:7. accusation: - accuse.

şiş- [er] 1 /DAn/ '- swell, - swell up, - get puffed up /{from/BECAUSE OF}/': Ağlamak.tan gözlerim şişti. 'My eyes swelled up from crying.' {Böceğ.in/Arı.nın/ Akreb.in} soktuğ.u yer şişti. 'The place {the insect/the bee/the scorpion} stung swelled up.' 259:5. expansion, growth: - become larger; 283:11. convexity, protuberance: - bulge. → ≠ in- 4.

2 '- fill up with air': {Balon/Arabanın lâstikleri/ Lâstik bot} şişti. '{The balloon/The tires of the car/The rubber boat} filled with air.' 259:5. expansion, growth: - become larger; 283:11. convexity, protuberance: - bulge. The two following verbs

Part 1: Turkish-English Dictionary of Verbs

indicate a gradual loss of air pressure: → ≠ **sön-** 2 [balloon, tires, rubber boat]; ≠ **in-** 4 [tires, rubber boat]. The following verb indicates a sudden loss of air pressure: → **patla-** 1 ['- burst, - explode', balloon, tire].

şişmanla- [r] '- get fat, - put on weight' [**şişman** 'fat' + verb-forming suf. -1A]: Bir yıldır Hülya'yı görmüyordum. Dün görünce çok şaşırdım. Ne kadar şişmanlamış! 'I hadn't seen Hülya for a year. When I saw her yesterday, I was {really/very} surprised. {She'd put on so much weight!/She'd gotten so fat!/How fat she had gotten!}' Son günlerde çok şişmanladım. * Biraz kilo vermem lâzım. 'I have gained a lot of weight lately. * I must lose a little [lit., ** give a few kilos].' 259:8. expansion, growth: - fatten. → = kilo al- → al- 1, = topla- 3, = toplan- 4, ≠ kilo ver- → ver- 1, ≠ zayıfla- 1.

şok ol-. → {şoke/şok} ol-. → ol- 10.1.

şoka gir-. → gir-.

{şoke/şok} ol-. → ol- 10.1.

şöyle bir bak-. → bak- 1.

Şuna bak be! → bak- 1.

{şuurunu/bilincini} kaybet-. → {kaybet-/yitir-}.

{şuurunu/bilincini} yitir-. → {kaybet-/yitir-}.

şükret- [şükreDer] /a: A, b: DAn dolayı, c: A/ [A. **şükür** (şüKRü) 'gratitude, thankfulness' + **et-**]: '- give thanks /a: to [God], b: {for/because of}, c: θ [that]/, - praise /a: θ [God], b: {for/because of}, c: θ [that]/, - be thankful [a: to [God], b: FOR/'. Although the word **Allah** 'God' may not always appear with this verb, He is always understood to be the recipient of the thanks: Bize verdiği nimetler.DEN DOLAYI Allah'A şükrederiz. '{We thank θ God/We give thanks to God} FOR the benefits he has bestowed upon us.' * Kaza.yI ucuz atlattığımız.A şükrettik. 'We thanked God θ that we {had not been harmed/had gotten off lightly} in the accident.' * Beter.in beter.i var,

hal.in.E şükret! 'There is always sth worse [lit., ** The worse has a worse]. Be thankful FOR your [present] situation.' Proverb: Bir ye de bin şükret. 'Eat one thing, but be grateful [to God] for a thousand.', i.e., Gratitude to God is always inadequate to His bounty. 150:4. gratitude: - thank; 509:12. approval: - praise. → **Şükürler olsun.** ['{Thanks be /to/ God [that].../Praise be /to/ God [that]...}'] → ol- 11 → olsun.

Şükürler olsun [ki]... → ol- 11. → olsun.

{şüphelen- [ır]/**şüphe et-** [eDer]/**kuşkulan-** [ır]} /D A n/ '- suspect θ sb, - suspect θ sth, - suspect sb /OF/ sth, - suspect sb /OF/ doing sth' [{A. **şüphe/kuşku** 'suspicion, doubt' + verb-forming suf. -1An]: NON-verbal noun as object: Altın kolyem çalınınca hizmetçi.DEN şüphelendim. 'When my gold necklace was stolen, I suspected θ the maid.' Hastalık.TAN şüpheleni-yorsanız bu telefon numaralarını arayın. 'If you suspect {that you have a disease/lit., θ a disease}, call these [i.e., the following] phone numbers.' VERBAL noun as object: {Karım.ın/Kocam.ın} beni aldat.tığ.ı.nDAN şüphelendim. 'I suspected θ that {my wife/my husband} {had deceived/had cheated on} me [lit., ** of {my wife's/my husband's} having cheated...].' {Karım.ın/Kocam.ın} ben.İ aldatma.sı.nDAN şüphelendim. 'I suspected {my wife/my husband} OF {deceiv.ING/cheat.ING on} me [lit., ** I suspected θ my wife's...deceiving me].' 952:11. belief: - think.

- T -

tabettir-. → {bastır-/tabettir-}.

taburcu ol-. → ol- 12.

tadına bak-. → bak- 1.

tahammül et- [eDer] /A/ '- put up /WITH/, - bear /θ/, - stand /θ/, - tolerate /θ/, - endure /θ/, - suffer /θ/, - take /θ/.' More formal, less current than **dayan-** 3 or **katlan-** 2. [A.

370

tahammül 'endurance, patience']: Türk hamamları çok sıcak olur. Onbeş dakikadan fazla tahammül edemezsiniz. 'Turkish baths get very hot. You can't stand being in one [i.e., in the hot steam section] for more than fifteen minutes.'
NON-verbal noun as object: Kızım Amerika'ya gidince çok özledim, ayrılığ.ı.nA tahammül edemedim, * ben de arka.sı.nDAN gittim. 'When my daughter went off to the United States, I missed her very much. I couldn't bear being {away/separated} from her and * followed her [lit., ** went from her back].' {Aptal insanlar.A/Yazın İzmir'in sıcağ.ı.nA} tahammül edemiyorum. 'I can't stand {θ stupid people/θ the heat in Izmir in the summer}.' Artık bu sözlerin.E tahammül edemiyorum, lütfen benimle daha dikkatli konuş. 'I can't take θ these [harsh] words of yours any longer. Please speak more tactfully [lit., carefully] with me.' Annem ve babam ölünce her türlü zorluğ.A yalnız başıma tahammül ettim. 'When my mother and father died, I put up WITH all kinds of difficulties by myself.' Açlığ.A tahammül edebilirim ama susuzluğ.A asla! 'I can bear θ hunger, but never thirst.'
VERBAL noun as object: Bebeğ.in ağlama.sı.nA tahammül edemedim ve ev.DEN ayrıldım. 'I couldn't stand θ the baby's crying and left θ the house.' 134:5. patience: - endure; 1047:3. toughness: - toughen. → = dayan- 3, = katlan- 2, = çek- 5, /lA/ uğraş- 3 ['- put up /with/ a person'].

tahlil et- [eDer] '- analyze' [A. tahlil (. -) 'analysis']: NON-verbal noun as object: Doktor hastanın kanını tahlil etti ve * şeker hastalığ.ı teşhis.i.ni koydu. 'The doctor analyzed the patient's blood and * diagnosed [her condition as] diabetes [lit., ** placed the sugar disease diagnosis].' Tarihteki olayları tahlil edip, onlardan ders almalıyız. 'We must analyze historical events and {learn/lit., take lessons} from them.' Edebiyat dersinde "Küçük Ağa" adlı romanı tahlil edeceğiz. 'In literature class we will analyze the novel entitled "The Little Aga".'

VERBAL noun as object: Sosyologlar, köylüler.in kent.e göç etmeler.i.ni tahlil ediyorlar. 'Sociologists are analyzing the migration of villagers to the city.' 800:6. analysis: - analyze; 934:15. reason: - reason. → = analiz et- ['- analyze blood, historical event'], incele- ['- examine carefully, closely, minutely, in detail, - study carefully, - inspect, - investigate, - research'], tetkik et-. Same.

tahmin et- [eDer] [A. tahmin (. -) 'guess, estimation'] 1 '- guess; - conjecture, - suppose; - surmise': Annem.in İstanbul'A {a: dün döndüğ.ü.nü/b: yarın döne-ceğ.i.ni/c: yakında dönmek zorunda olduğ.u.nu} tahmin ediyorum. 'I guess that my mother {a: returned to Istanbul yesterday/b: will return to Istanbul tomorrow/c: will soon have to return to Istanbul}.' 950:10. supposition: - suppose; 952:11. belief: - think; 967:5. probability: - think likely. → düşün-2 ['- think, - believe that sth was, is, or will be the case'], {san-/zannet-} ['- think, - suppose'].

2 /olarak/ '- estimate /{AT/TO BE/AS BEING}/, - judge, - reckon, - take a guess': S: Kütüphanemizde kaç kitap var, tahmin et. 'Q: How many books are there in our library? Take a guess.' → = Bil bakalım ['Take a guess'] → bil- 4. C: * Vallahi bilmiyorum. 100 bin mi? 'A: * Gosh [lit., ** By God] I really don't know. A hundred thousand?' * Kalabalığı 6 bin kişi OLARAK tahmin ettik. 'We estimated the crowd {AT/TO BE/AS BEING} 6,000 people.' 945:9. judgment: - estimate; 950:11. theory, supposition: - conjecture. → = bil- 4.

{az/eksik} tahmin et- '- underestimate' [az 'little, small amount', eksik 'deficient, lacking']: Davete gelecek misafirler.in sayı.sı.nı az tahmin etmişim, yemekler yetmedi. 'I seem to have underestimated the number of guests that were to come to the party. There wasn't enough food.' Pirinc.in miktar.ı.nı az tahmin etmişim, bir kilo olduğ.u.nu düşünüyordum, oysa üç kilo çıktı. 'I seem to have underestimated the amount of rice. I thought [that] there was one kilo. However it seems that there were 3 kilos [lit., 3 kilos turned up].' *949:2.* underestimation: - underestimate. → ≠ **fazla tahmin et-**.

fazla tahmin et- '- overestimate' [A. **fazla** 'too much, too many']: * **Davet.e gelecek olan misafirler.in sayı.sı.nı fazla tahmin etmişim,** * **yemekler arttı.** 'I seem to have overestimated the number of guests that were to come to the party [lit., ** to the invitation]. * Some food was left over.' **Pirinc.in miktar.ı.nı fazla tahmin etmişim, on kilo olduğ.u.nu düşünüyordum, oysa yalnız üç kilo çıktı.** 'I seem to have overestimated the amount of rice. I thought [that] there were ten kilos. However it seems that only 3 kilos turned up.' *948:2.* overestimation: - overestimate; *992:10.* excess: - overdo. → ≠ **{az/eksik} tahmin et-**.

3 '- forecast, - predict, - figure out': **Meteoroloji {doğru/yanlış} tahmin etti.** 'The weather bureau forecast {correctly/incorrectly}.' **Roman.ın son.u.nun nasıl biteceğ.i.ni tahmin edemiyorum.** 'I can't {predict/figure out} how the novel is going to end [lit., ** how the end of the novel is going to finish].' *960:6.* foresight: - foreknow; *961:9.* prediction: - predict. → = **kestir- 2**, = **önceden bil-** → **bil-** 1.

tahrik et- [eDer] [A. **tahrik** (. -) **1** 'an inciting, provoking'. **2** 'an exciting']: **1** '- incite, - provoke, - instigate, - foment': **Boşuna tahrik etmey.E çalışma [beni], bugün sinirlen.me.mey.E kararlıyım.** 'Don't waste your time trying to provoke me [lit., Don't try in vain to provoke me]. Today I'm determined not to get angry.' **Böyle [hamasî] nutuklar atarak halkı tahrik etmey.E hakkınız yok.** 'You have no right to incite the people by making such [heroic] speeches.' *375:17.* motivation, inducement: - incite.

2 '- turn on sexually, - excite': **Mini etekli kızlar beni her zaman tahrik eder.** 'Girls in miniskirts always turn me on.' **Güzel bir kadınla dans etmek beni tahrik**

eder. 'Dancing with an attractive woman always turns me on.' *105:12.* excitement: - excite. → = **heyecanlandır- 3**. For '- GET turned on', → **tahrik ol-** → **ol-** 12, **heyecanlan- 3**.

tahrik ol-. → **ol-** 12.

* **tahsil et-** [eDer] '- study a subject', usually as a major field of interest. Not '- study one's lessons' [A. **tahsil** (. -) 'education, being educated, learning']: **Amcam Londra'da ekonomi tahsil etmiş.** 'My uncle studied economics in London.' **S: Ne tahsil ediyorsunuz?** 'Q: What are you studying?', i.e., as a major subject. **C: {a: Tıp/b: Fizik/c: Kimya/d: Matematik/e: Fen bilimleri} tahsil ediyorum.** 'A: I'm studying {a: medicine/b: physics/c: chemistry/d: mathematics/ e: the sciences}.' → = **oku- 2**. Note also the following common question without **et-**: **S: Tahsiliniz nedir?** 'Q: What is your education [i.e., the highest level of education you have attained]?' **C1:** * **{İlkokul/Ortaokul} mezun.u.yum.** 'A1: I * finished {primary school/middle or secondary school} [lit., I'm a primary school...graduate].' **C2: {a: Lise/b: Üniversite} mezun.u.yum.** 'A2: I graduated from {a: {high school/lycée}/b: {college/universite}}. [lit., I'm a {high school/lycée}...graduate.]' However, if at this moment I see you studying, and I want to know what you are working on now, I will ask: **Ne çalışıyorsunuz?** 'What are you {studying/working on}?' I will not use **tahsil et-**. *570:12.* learning: - study. → **{eğitim/öğrenim/tahsil} gör-** ['- have an education, - be educated'] → **gör- 3**.

tahsil gör-. → **{eğitim/öğrenim/tahsil} gör-**. → **gör- 3**.

tahtaya kaldır-. → **kaldır-** 1.

tahtaya kalk-. → **kalk-** 1.

tak- [ar] /A/ '- attach, - fasten sth /to/, - wear, - put sth /ON/ [oneself, usually small items, accessories: glasses, jewelry, also certain headgear], - put up [curtains]': **Öğretmen gözlüğünü taktı ve yüksek sesle okumaya başladı.** 'The teacher put on his glasses and in a loud voice began to read.' **Annem evden çıkmadan önce** {a: saat.i.ni/b: yüzüğ.ü.nü/c: toka.sı.nı/d: kolye.si.ni/e: küpe.si.ni/f: bileziğ.i.ni/g: eşarb.ı.nı/h: peruğ.u.nu} **taktı.** 'Before my mother left the house, she put on {a: her watch/b: her ring/c: her barette/d: her necklace/e: her earings/f: bracelet/g: her scarf/h: her wig}.' **Babam toplantıya gitmeden önce** {a: kravat.ı.nı/b: papyon.u.nu/c: şapka.sı.nı/d: bere.si.ni} **taktı.** 'Before going to the meeting, my father put on {a: his tie/b: his bow tie/c: his hat/d: his beret}.' *5:42.* clothing: - don. → ≠ **çıkar-** 2. For '- put on', regular items of clothing, i.e., coat, hat, etc., not accessories → **giy-**. # **Lütfen sigaralarınızı söndürünüz ve emniyet kemerlerinizi takınız.** 'Please put out your cigarettes and fasten [lit., put on] your seat belts [lit., security belts].' *352:7.* publication: poster: * specific signs. → ≠ **aç-** 1. # **Misafirler gelmeden önce yeni perdelerimizi taktık.** 'We put up our new curtains before the guests arrived.' → ≠ **indir-** 1. *202:8.* pendency: - suspend; *799:7.* joining: - fasten.

{ad/isim} **tak-** /A/ '- name, - call, - dub /θ/', usually with a negative connotation when the object is a person [{ad/A. isim (iSMi)} 'name'], lit., ** '- put a name /ON/': **Kedim.E "Tekir" ad.ı.nı taktım.** 'I named θ my cat "Tekir" [lit., ** ON my cat I put the name Tekir].' In the sense of a nickname: **Öğrenciler fizik öğretmen.i.nE "Atom Ali" ad.ı.nı taktılar.** 'The students called θ their physics teacher "Atom Ali".' *527:11.* nomenclature: - name. → = {ad/isim} **koy-** → **koy-** 1, = {ad/isim} **ver-** → **ver-** 1, = {adlandır-/isimlendir-}.

isim tak-. → directly above.

takatı tüken-. → {gücü/takatı} **tüken-.** → **tüken-.**

takdim et- [eDer] /A/ [A. **takdim** (. -) 'introducing'] 1 '- introduce, - present one person /to/ another': **Siz.i misafirler.e takdim edeyim.** 'Let me introduce you to the guests.' **Siz.e** {a: kendim.i/b: nişanlım.ı/c: öğretmenim.i/d: ailem.i/e: arkadaşım.ı} **takdim edeyim.** 'Let me introduce {a: myself/b: my fiancée/c: my teacher/d: my family/e: my friend} to you.' *587:14.* friendship: - introduce. → = **tanıştır-.**

2 '- present, - submit, - offer sth /to/ sb': **Raporum.u müdür bey.e takdim ettim.** 'I presented my report to the director.' *439:4.* offer: - offer. → = **sun-** 1. For '- offer food or drink', → **ikram et-** 1.

takdir et- [eDer] [A. **takdir** (. -) 'an appreciating, appreciation'] 1 '- appreciate, - value, - respect, - admire': **Ev.in bütün iş.i.ni tek başıma yapıyorum, yine de beni takdir etmiyorsun.** 'I do all the housework by myself, and still you don't appreciate me.' **Suzan'ı çok takdir ediyorum, hem üniversitede okuyor hem de çalışıp hasta anne.si.nE bakıyor.** 'I really admire Suzan. She studies at {the college/the university}, works, and also {looks AFTER/takes care OF} her sick mother.' *155:4.* respect: - respect; *996:13.* importance: - value.

2 '- appreciate, - understand sb's situation, difficulties': **Derslerin.in ne kadar zor olduğ.u.nu takdir ediyorum, ancak bir ailen olduğunu da unutmamalısın.** 'I {appreciate/understand} how difficult your classes are, but you must not forget that you have a family too.' **takdir edersiniz ki...** 'you will appreciate that...': **Benim için oldukça zor ama takdir edersiniz ki ikiniz.DEN bir.i.ni tercih etmek zorundayım.** 'It is quite difficult for me [i.e., to choose], but you will appreciate that I'm obliged to choose between you [lit., one OF the two of you].' *521:7.* intelligibility: - understand. → **anla-** ['- understand, - realize', in most circumstances].

takıl- [ır] [**tak-** + refl. suf. **-Il**]: 1 /A/ '- get stuck, snagged, caught /ON/', a physical obstacle prevents further movement: **Ayağım taş.A takıldı, düştüm.** 'My foot got caught ON a rock, and I fell down.' **Allah kahretsin, çorabım çivi.yE takıldı ve kaçtı.** 'Oh darn, my stocking got snagged ON a nail and ran.' *1011:10.* hindrance: - hinder.

2 /A/ '- get stuck, hung up /ON/ a problem': **Beşinci soru.yA takıldım.** 'I got stuck ON the fifth question.' **Takıldığınız soruları atlayın, vakit kaybetmeyin.** 'Skip the questions you get stuck on. Don't waste time.' * **Onun takıldığı noktadairenin fiyatıydı.** 'What he got hung up on was the price of the apartment.' *1011:10.* hindrance: - hinder; *1012:11.* difficulty: - have difficulty.

aklı takıl- /A/ [akıl (aKLı) 'intelligence, mind'] '- be preoccupied, obsessed /WITH/', lit., ** 'for one's mind - get stuck /ON/ a question, problem': * **Bu soru.yA aklı.M takıldı, bir türlü cevab.ı.nı bulamıyorum..** 'I'm preoccupied with this question [lit., ** MY mind got stuck ON this question]. I just can't {think of/lit., find} an answer to it.' *1011:10.* hindrance: - hinder; *1012:11.* difficulty: - have difficulty. **İbrahim'E aklı.M takıldı, iyileşti mi acaba?** 'İbrahim is on my mind [lit., ** MY mind got stuck ON İbrahim]. Has he recovered, I wonder?' **Aklı.N sınav.A takıldı galiba, merak etme, * iyi geçmiştir.** 'A: You're probably preoccupied WITH the examination. Don't worry. * You did well [lit., It went well].' *930:20.* thought: - occupy the mind.

aklına takıl- '- stick in one's mind and bother one, - occupy one's mind': **O soru aklı.M.a takıldı, bir türlü cevab.ı.nı bulamıyorum.** 'That question has stuck in MY mind and is occupying ME. I just can't {think of/lit., find} an answer to it.' **İbrahim aklı.M.a takıldı, iyileşti mi acaba?** 'İbrahim is on MY mind: Has he recovered I wonder?' **Yine aklı.N.a Türkçe sınavı takıldı galiba, merak etme * iyi geçmiştir.** 'The Turkish exam is probably on YOUR mind again. Don't worry, * {I bet you did well./You probably did well.} [lit., ** it probably passed well].' *930:20.* thought: - occupy the mind.

takip et- [eDer] [A. takip (- -) 'a following, pursuing'] 1 '- follow, - go behind': **Hastane.nin nerede olduğ.u.nu biliyorum, beni takip edin.** 'I know where the hospital is, follow me.' **Avcılar yaralı geyiği iki gün takip**

ettiler. 'The hunters followed the wounded deer for two days.' A maxim of murder mysteries: **{Parayı/Kadını} takip et, olayı çöz.** 'Follow {the money/the woman} and {solve the crime/figure out what happened [lit., the event].}' *166:3.* following: - follow. → = izle-1, kovala- 2 ['- follow one another in rapid succession, - succeed', days, weeks].

2 '- observe, - follow, - monitor, - keep abreast of': **Hükümetimiz Orta Doğudaki {gelişmeler.i/ olaylar.ı} dikkatle takip ediyor.** 'Our government carefully monitors {[the] developments/[the] events} in the Middle East.' **Suna moda.yı yakından takip eder.** 'Suna [f.] follows the [latest] fashions closely.' **Televizyon programları.nı {takip ediyor musunuz/takip eder misiniz}?** 'Do {you follow [or keep abreast of]} [the] television programs?' **Son gelişmeleri * dakikası dakikasına internet.TEN takip edebilirsiniz.** 'ON the Internet you can follow * minute by minute the latest developments.' *982:5.* attention: - attend to. → = izle- 2.

taklit et- [eDer] '- imitate, - copy, - ape' [A. taklit (. -) 'an imitating, imitation']: **Küçük kız annesini taklit ediyordu, onun gibi makyaj yapmaya çalışıyordu.** 'The little girl was imitating her mother. She was trying to put on makeup like her.' An older brother might say the following to his younger brother: **Maymun gibi beni taklit edip durma!** 'Don't just keep imitating me like a monkey!' *336:5.* imitation: - imitate.

taksi çevir-. → çevir- 1.

taksitle öde-. → öde-.

talep et- [eDer] /DAn/ '- ask for, - request /from/; - demand sth /from/ sb, - call for sth /from/ [A. talep (taleBi) 1 'an asking, requesting'. 2 'desiring, wishing']: **Bakan gazete.nin kendisi.nden özür dileme.si.ni talep etti.** 'The [government] minister demanded an apology from the newspaper [lit., ** demanded the newspaper's requesting an apology from him].' **İşçiler {daha yüksek maaş/daha iyi çalışma şartları} talep edi-**

yorlar. 'The workers are demanding {higher wages/better working conditions}.' *421:5.* demand: - demand; *440:9.* request: - request. → = iste- 2.

tamamla- [r] '- complete, - finish' [A. tamam (. -) 'complete, finished' + verb-forming suf. -lA]: E v ödevlerimi tamamladım. 'I've finished my homework.' Özkan {öğrenim.i.ni/tahsil.i.ni} tamamladı ve memleketine döndü. 'Özkan completed {his education} and returned to his homeland.' *793:6.* completeness: - complete; *819:7.* end: - complete. → = bitir- 1 ['- finish sth, - bring sth to an end'], = son ver- ['- bring /θ/ sth to an end, - conclude, - finish, - put an end /to/ sth'] → ver- 1, ≠ başla- 2.

ömrünü tamamla- '- complete one's life, - come to the end of one's life, - die, - pass away', person; '- outlive its useful life, usefulness', machine [A. ömür (öMRü) 'life']: Person as subject: Osman efendi ömrünü tamamlamış, Allah rahmet eylesin! 'Osman efendi has passed away. May God have mercy upon his soul!' Doktor.un dediğ.i.n.e göre bu hasta ömrünü tamamlamış, en fazla iki ay yaşarmış. 'According to the doctor [lit., According to what the doctor said], this patient has come to the end of his life. At most he will live for [only] two more months.' *307:19.* death: - die. → = hayata gözlerini {kapa-/kapat-} → {kapa-/kapat-} 1, = hayata gözlerini yum- → göz yum- 1, = hayatını {kaybet-/yitir-} ['- lose one's life, - die', of unnatural causes], = öl-, = son nefesini ver- ['- breathe one's last breath, - die'] → ver- 1, = vefat et-, = canından ol- ['- lose one's life, - die', mostly for an unexpected and undeserved death] → ol- 7, ≠ doğ- 1, ≠ dünyaya gel- → gel- 1.
Machine as subject: Bu makina ömrünü tamamlamış, * yeni.si.ni almamız lâzım. 'This machine has outlived its usefulness. * We must purchase a new one [lit., ** a new one of it].' *393:16.* impairment: - deteriorate.

tamamlan- [ır] /{tarafından/CA}/ '- be completed, finished /by/' [tamamla- + pass. suf. -n]: Ev ödevlerim

tamamlandı. 'My homework is finished.' * Üniversite {öğrenimim/tahsilim} tamamlandı. '{I have graduated from college [or university]./lit., My college...education is completed.}' Geçen yıl ölen ünlü ressamın tamamlanmamış eserleri sergilendi. 'The unfinished works of the famous painter who died last year were exhibited.' Roman, yazarın yakın arkadaşı tarafından tamamlandı. 'The novel was completed by the writer's close friend.' *793:6.* completeness: - complete; *819:7.* end: - complete.

tamir et- [eDer] '- repair, - fix, - put in running order' [A. tamir (. -) 'repair, repairing']: {Radyom/Saatim} bozuldu. Acaba tamir edebilir misiniz? '{My radio/My watch} is broken [lit., ** has broken down]. I wonder if you could repair it?' * Bu ayakkabıları kaç.A tamir edersiniz? 'How much will you charge to repair these shoes? [lit., FOR how much will you repair these shoes?]' *396:14.* restoration: - repair. → = düzelt- 1 [roads, not machinery or shoes], = onar-.

tanı- [r] 1 (1.1) '- know sb, - be acquainted /WITH/ sb': S : Emre'nin babasını tanır mısın? 'Q: Do you know Emre's father?' C: {* Eski.den beri/Uzun yıllar.DIR} tanıyorum. 'A: [Yes,] I've known him {* from way back/FOR many years}.' Figen isim.li biri[si].ni tanıyor musunuz? 'Do you know sb named Figen?' Otuz yıl.DIR birbirimizi {tanırız/tanıyoruz}. 'We've known each other FOR thirty years.' → tanış-.
(1.2) '- know the real nature of sb, what kind of person he is', not in the casual sense of '- be acquainted with': İnsan.ı tanımak zordur. 'It is difficult to [really] know a person.' *587:9.* friendship: - be friends; *927:12.* knowledge: - know. For '- know a THING, FACT', AND a person's real NATURE, i.e., what KIND of a person he is, → bil- 1.2.

2 /DAn/ '- recognize sb or sth /{BY/from}/': Olcay'la üç yıl önce tanışmıştık. Salona girince onu hemen tanıdım. 'I met [lit., had gotten acquainted with] Olcay three years ago. When {I/he} entered the room, I recognized him at

once.' * **Sizi bir yer.den tanıyor gibi.yim.** 'Don't I know you from somewhere? [lit., ** I'm like I know you from a place.]' You and I hear a song. I ask you: * **Bu şarkıyı tanıdın[ız] mı?** '{Do/Did} you recognize this song?' In the sentence above, in this context, **tanıdın[ız]** refers to a current feeling, so it would probably be translated with the PRESENT tense. If the question referred to a past time, i.e., yesterday, to a feeling no longer in effect, it would be translated with the PAST tense. • In reference to a PRESENT condition, certain common Turkish verbs designating a state, i.e., a feeling, emotion, or sensation, often have the simple PAST tense, but the equivalent English has the simple PRESENT tense. **Amcam.ın ses.i.ni tanıdım.** 'I recognized my [paternal] uncle's voice.' **Amcam.ı ses.i.nDEN tanıdım.** 'I recognized my [paternal] uncle {BY/from} his voice.' * **Burası o kadar değişmiş ki tanı.yama-.dım.** 'This place [lit., ** Its here] has changed so much [that] I {can/COULD} [hardly] recognize it.' *988:12.* memory: - recognize.

3 '- get to know sb, - become acquainted /WITH/ sb, - meet sb': **Geçen hafta Ferhat'I bir partide tanımıştık.** 'We met Ferhat at a party last week.' **{Ahmet/Sen.İN} gibi bir insan tanımadım.** 'I have never met a person like {Ahmet/you}.' *587:10.* friendship: - befriend, - make friends with.

4 '- know a subject, area of study': **Eniştem {arabalar.I/kuşlar.I/ eski eserler.İ} {çok iyi/ yakından} tanır.** 'My brother-in-law knows a lot about {θ cars/θ birds/θ antiques} [lit., knows cars...{very well/lit., ** closely}.' *927:12.* knowledge: - know. → = **bil- 1, = anla-.**

5 /A/ '- grant a period of time, a grace period /to/': *noun of time* **tanı-: süre tanı-** /A, için/ '- grant a period of time, a grace period /to, for/': * **Hikmet borcunu ödemesi için kiracısı.nA 3 gün süre tanıdı.** 'Hikmet granted θ his renter three days grace [lit., a 3-day period] {to pay/for paying} his bill [lit., debt].' *478:12.* giving: - give; *845:9.* lateness: - postpone. → =

{zaman/vakit/süre} ver- → **ver-1.**

6 /olarak/ '- recognize a government, - recognize /AS/ [a state]': **Mustafa Kemal Paşa İstanbul hükümetini tanımadı ve Ankara'da yeni bir hükümet kurdu.** 'Mustafa Kemal Pasha did not recognize the Istanbul government and formed a new government in Ankara.' **Hemen hemen hiç bir ülke Kıbrıs'ı [devlet OLARAK] tanımadı.** 'Almost no country has recognized Cyprus [AS a state].' *332:11.* assent: - acknowledge.

tanıklık et- [eDer] /a: için, b: A dair, c: lehine, d: aleyhine/ '- testify /a: {for/on behalf of}, b: {θ [that]/to the effect that}, c: {for/on behalf of}, d: against/, - give evidence, - be a witness in a court case' [**tanıklık** 'testifying, bearing witness']: **Zerrin'in boşanma davasında tanıklık edeceğim.** 'I'll testify in Zerrin's divorce case.' **Bu davada benim için tanıklık eder misin?** 'Would you testify for me in this court case?' **Ayşe, Fatih'i Serdar'ın vurduğ.u.nA dair tanıklık etti.** 'Ayşe testified θ that Serdar had shot Fatih.' **Suat, Mehmet'in {lehine/aleyhine} tanıklık etti.** 'Suat testified {for [or on behalf of]/against} Mehmet.' *956:9.* evidence, proof: - testify. → **ifade ver-** [*law* '- give evidence /to/, - testify, - give testimony, - give or - make a statement'] → **ver-1,** ≠ **ifade al-** ['- examine sb and - record his testimony, - take a deposition /from/'] → **al-1.**

tanımla- [r] '- define' [**tanım** 'definition' + verb-forming suf. -lA]: S: * **"Kültür" {derken/demekle} ne.yi kastettiği.ni anlamıyorum. Lütfen tanımlar mısın?** 'Q: I don't know what you mean by [lit., ** {while saying/by saying}] "culture". Would you please define it?' C: **Olur. Tanımla-yayım. Kültür...demek-tir.** 'A: OK, I'll define it. Culture means...' *341:9.* interpretation: - interpret. → = **karşılığını ver-** ['- give the equivalent of a word, - define'] → **ver-3.**

tanış- [ır] /lA/ '- get to know, - get acquainted /with/ one another, - meet /θ/; - be acquainted with, - know one another' [tanı- + recip. suf. -ş]: * Tanıştığımız.A memnun oldum efendim. 'Pleased to meet you, {sir/ma'am} [lit., I'm pleased θ (that) we got to know each other...].' * Nasıl oldu da daha önce sizin.LE tanışmadık? 'How come we didn't meet earlier?' * Yanlış hatırlamıyorsam sizin.LE kardeşimin evinde tanışmıştık. 'If I remember correctly [lit., If I don't remember incorrectly], we met at my brother's house.' Serpil İLE * öğrencilik yıllarımda tanıştım. 'I {met θ/got to know} Serpil [f.] * while I was a student [lit., in my student years].' S: Fikret sen Osman'LA tanıştın mı? 'Q: Fikret, have you met θ Osman?' C: Keşke onun.LA hiç tanışmasaydım. * Başıma olmadık işler çıkardı. 'A: I wish I had never met θ him. * He caused {me all kinds of incredible trouble/got me in all kinds of incredible trouble}.' * Birbirlerinden 1500 km uzakta yaşıyorlardı. İnternette tanıştılar. 'They lived [at a distance of] 1500 kilometers apart. They {met/got acquainted} on the Internet.' Otuz yıl.DIR tanışıyoruz. 'We've known each other FOR thirty years.' → birbirini tanı- ['- know one another'] → tanı- 1.1. 587:9. friendship: - be friends; 587:10. : - befriend, - make friends with.

tanıştır- [ır] [tanış- + caus. suf. -DIr] '- introduce one person to another.' • Note the three patterns:
a) No case suffix on the noun denoting the person being introduced: A: Tanıştırayım: {a: annem/b: babam/c: kardeşim Nur/d: öğretmenim Aysel hanım [family name: Çelik]/e: eşim Selma/f: patronum Selim bey [family name: Şimşek]}. 'A: Let me introduce: {a: my mother/b: my father/c: my younger brother Nur/d: my teacher Miss [or {Mrs./Ms.}] Çelik/e: my wife Selma/f: my boss Selim Şimşek}.' A very common, not formal response: B1: [Tanıştığımız.A] memnun oldum. 'B1: Pleased TO meet you.' Formal: B2: Siz.i tanımak.TAN şeref duydum. 'B2: I'm honored to know you [lit., ** I have felt honor FROM knowing you].' A very polite response to the above: O şeref ban.a ait. 'C: The honor is mine [lit., That honor belongs to me].'

b) In the second pattern, /I/ on the noun denoting the person introduced, /l A/ on the noun denoting the person he is being introduced TO: '- introduce one person /TO/ another, - make one person known /TO/ another': S: * Ben.İ Özcan'LA tanıştırır mısınız? 'Q: Would you introduce me TO Özcan?' C: Tanıştırayım. 'A: Sure [lit., {Let me introduce [you]./I'll introduce [you].}]'
c) In the third pattern, /I/ on the noun denoting the person introduced, /A/ on the noun denoting the person he is being introduced TO: '- introduce one person /to/ another': Siz.E kardeşim Remzi'yİ tanıştırayım. 'Let me introduce my brother Remzi TO you.' 587:14. friendship: - introduce. → = takdim et- 1.

tanıt- [ır] /A, olarak/ '- introduce sb or sth /to, AS/, - make sb or sth known /to, AS/, - acquaint θ sb with sth, - inform, - tell θ sb about sth.' Here the action is not reciprocal, as was the case with tanıştır- above. [tanı- + caus. suf. -t]: Person as direct object: Kendiniz.i [biz.E] tanıtır mısınız? 'Would you {tell [us] about/lit., introduce} yourself?' Konuşmacı konuşmasına başlamadan önce {kendi.ni/ kendi.si.ni} tanıttı. 'The speaker introduced {himself} before beginning his speech.' * kendisini başkası olarak tanıt- '- pass oneself off as sb else': KendiMİ başkası OLARAK tanıttım. 'I passed MYSELF off AS someone else [i.e., as someone I was not].' 354:22. falseness: - pose as; 587:14. friendship: - introduce.
Thing or topic as direct object: * Ülkemiz.İ tüm dünya.yA tanıtmalıyız. 'We must {inform θ the whole world about our country/make our country known TO the whole world}.' Yeni lokanta Amerikalılar.A Türk mutfağ.ı.nI tanıtıyor. 'The new restaurant introduces Turkish cuisine to Americans.' * Ankara'yI tanıtan bir kitap var mı? '{Do you know of/lit., Is there} a book about Ankara [i.e., a guide book]? [lit., Is there a book that gives information about Ankara?]' Bu kitap adam.ın hiç bilmediğimiz yönler.i.ni tanıtıyor. 'This book tells us about the {sides/aspects} of

the man we didn't know anything about.' *551:8.* information: - inform.

tap- [ar] /A, diye/ '- worship /θ [sb or sth], AS [sb or sth]/': * **Eskiden bazı toplumlar Tanrı DİYE güneş.E taparlarmış.** 'In olden times some societies used to worship θ the sun AS a God.' *696:10.* worship: - worship. → = **ibadet et-**.

tara- [r] **1** '- comb': **Sabahleyin kalktıktan sonra saçlarımı yıkadım ve taradım.** 'In the morning after getting up I washed and combed my hair.' *79:21.* cleanness: - comb.

2 '- comb, - search through': {**Yüksek lisans/Doktora**} **tezim.LE ilgili bütün birinci el kaynakları taradım.** 'I have combed through all the primary [lit., ** first hand] sources relating to my {master's/doctor's} thesis.' **Tara-** together with the verb **ara-** /I/ ['- look /FOR/, search /FOR/'] implies a thorough search: {**ara-/arayıp**} **tara-** '- search thoroughly'. • Note the two patterns:
a) With the same personal suffix on both **ara-** and **tara-**: **Ara.dım tara.dım ama bulamadım.** 'I searched [everywhere] but couldn't find it.'
b) In the second pattern, with the -Ip suffix on **ara-**, the personal suffix on **tara-**: **Polisler bütün uçağ.ı ara.yıp tara.dılar, ama ihbar ed.il.en bombayı bulamadılar.** 'The police thoroughly searched the whole plane, but they couldn't find the bomb they had been warned about [lit., ** the bomb that had been warned about].' **Bütün albümlerimi ara.yıp tara.dım, ama Hasan'ın resm.i.ni bulamadım.** 'I searched through all my photo albums, but I couldn't find Hasan's picture.' *937:31.* inquiry: - search.

3 '- spray or - pepper with fire [i.e., bullets], - blaze away at, - strafe, - rake with shot': **Cinnet geçiren biri otomatik silahıyla duraktaki yolcuları taramış.** 'Someone who had run amuck sprayed those waiting at the [bus or shared cab] stop with [fire from] an automatic rifle.' **Soyguncular kaçarken makinali tüfeklerle bankayı taradı.** 'As the robbers were escaping, they sprayed the bank

with [fire from their] machine guns.' *459:22.* attack: - pull the trigger.

tarif et- [eDer] /A/ '- describe sb or sth /to/' [A. **tarif** (- .) 'description']: Describing a person or thing: **Banka memurları soyguncu.yu polis.e tarif ettiler.** 'The employees of the bank [lit., the bank employees] described the thief to the police.'

Describing directions to a place: • Note the two patterns:
a) The ROAD is the object of the description: **S: Taksim'e gitmek istiyorum. Ban.a** {**yol.u**} **tarif eder misiniz?** 'Q: I want to go to Taksim [i.e., a section of Istanbul]. Would you tell me how to get there [lit., ** Would you describe {the way/the road} to me]?'
b) In another common pattern the DESTINATION is the object: **S:** * **Postane.yİ tarif eder misiniz?** 'Q: Would you please tell me how to get to the post office? [ALSO and lit., Would you please describe THE POST OFFICE?]' A possible response to BOTH Turkish questions above: **C: Buradan doğru gidin,** * **iki sokak sonra,** {**sağ.A/sol.A**} **sapın. Postane köşede.** 'A: Go straight [ahead] two blocks [lit., ** streets] and turn {right [*or* to the right]/left [*or* to the left]} [lit., ** Go straight (ahead) from here. * After two blocks...]. The post office is at the corner.' [Question pattern b) above may be taken in its literal sense and answered accordingly: **S: Kızılay'da yeni yapılan postaneyi tarif eder misin?** 'Q: Would you describe the new post office that has just been built at Kızılay?' **C:** * **İş Bankası'nın yanındaki üç katlı, büyük beyaz bina.** 'A: It's the large, white, three-story building next to the İş Bank (lit., three-story, large white...]'.

Describing a process: **Ağabeyime İzmir'e nasıl gideceğ.i.ni tarif ettim.** 'I explained to my older brother how he should go to Izmir.' **Mühendisler, yeni makinalar.ın** {**nasıl çalıştığ.ı.nı/çalışma- .sı.nı**} **işçiler.e tarif ettiler.** 'The engineers explained to the workers {how the new machines worked/how the new machines work [lit., ** the working of the new machines]}.' **Annem pirinç pilâv.ı.nı nasıl yaptığ.ı.nı tarif etti. 'My mother described how she {makes/made} rice pilaf.' *349:9.* representation, description: - describe; *864:10.* particularity: - characterize. → = nitelendir-.

tarih {at-/koy-}. → at- 3.

tart- [ar] /A/ '- weigh, - weigh out sth /FOR/ sb': **Bana üç kilo {a: un/b: şeker/c: elma/d: kıyma/e: patates} tartar mısınız?** 'Would you please weigh out three kilos of {a: flour/b: sugar/c: apples/d: ground beef/e: potatoes} for me?' **Benim seçtiğim domatesleri tarttınız mı?** * **Kaç kilo geldi?** 'Did you weigh the tomatoes I selected? * How much do they weigh? [lit., ** How many kilos did they come (to)?]' **Oğlumu tarttım.** * **Tam 15 kilo.** 'I weighed my son. * [He weighed] exactly 15 kilos.' *297:10.* weight: - weigh; *300:10.* measurement: - measure.

tartıl- [ır] [tart- + {pass./refl.} suf. -Il] 1 /tarafından/ '- be weighed /by/': **Uçağ.A binmeden önce bütün bavullarım [yer hostesi tarafından] tartıldı.** 'Before I got on the plane, all my baggage was weighed [by the baggage attendant].' *297:10.* weight: - weigh; *300:10.* measurement: - measure.

2 '- weigh oneself': **Dün tartıldım.** * **Tam 75 {kilo geldim./ kiloyum.}** 'I weighed myself yesterday. * I weigh exactly 75 kilos [lit., ** {I came/I am} exactly...].' *297:10.* weight: - weigh; *300:10.* measurement: - measure.

tartış- [ır] [tart- + recip. suf. -Iş] 1 /a: lA, b: hakkında, c: konusunda, d: I/ '- debate, - discuss, or - argue /a: with, b: about, c: on the subject of, d: about/', the pros and cons of an issue, not confrontational in a negative sense: **Eve geldiğimde annem ve babam seçimler.i kim.in kazanacağ.ı.nı tartışıyorlardı.** 'When I came home, my mother and [my] father were arguing about who was going to win the elections.' **Kürtaj.a karşı olanlar.la kürtaj taraftarlar.ı bugün üniversitede tartışacaklar.** 'Those opposed to abortion and abortion-rights advocates will debate today at {the college/the university}.' **Konuyu tartışalım.** * **Sonunda doğruyu buluruz.** 'Let's debate the issue. * In the end we'll arrive at [lit., find] the truth.' * **Bu kişilerin durumu tartışmalı.** '{The status of these people must be discussed./One must discuss the status of these people.}' *934:16.* reasoning: - argue.

2 /a: lA, b: hakkında, c: konusunda, d: I/ '- debate, - discuss, or - argue /a: with, b: about, c: on the subject of, d: about/ '- debate heatedly; - have an intense discussion /a: with, b: about, c: on the subject of, d: about/; - argue, - dispute', usually confrontational: **Baban.la tartış.ıp dur.ma, ne diyorsa onu yap.** 'Don't keep arguing with your father, just do what he says [lit., ** whatever he says, do it].' [The structure **verb stem**.Ip dur- in the above means '- keep (do)ing, keep on (do)ing, do sth continuously'.] **Fabrika işçileri ücretler {hakkında/konusunda} patron.la tartıştı.** 'The factory workers argued with the boss {about/on the subject of} wages.' * **Olmayan bir konu.yU tartışıyorlar.** 'They are arguing about a "non-subject."', i.e., an issue already settled or not worth arguing about. *934:16.* reasoning: - argue. → = münakaşa et-.

tasarla-. → {plânla-/tasarla-}.

tasarruf et- [eDer] /için/ '- save [up] /for/' [A. tasarruf 'saving']: **Geleceğim için tasarruf etmeliyim. Mutlu bir gelecek için tasarruf şart!** 'I must save for my future. For a happy future, saving is absolutely necessary [lit., is an (absolute) condition]!' **Bu yıl 10 bin lira tasarruf ettim.** 'This year I saved 10,000 liras.' **Tasarruf ettiğim paralarla bir araba almay.ı düşünüyorum.** 'With the money I've saved I'm thinking of buying a car.' *635:4.* thrift: - economize. → = **para artır-** → {artır-/arttır-} 2, = **para biriktir-** → biriktir- 2, **masraftan {kaç-/kaçın-}** ['- avoid /θ/ expense, - economize'] → kaç- 2, ≠ **para {harca-/sarf et-}** ['- spend money'] → {harca-/sarf et-} 1, ≠ **masraf çek-** ['- foot the bill, - pay', *informal, jocular*] → çek- 5, ≠ **masraf {et-/yap-}**, ≠ **masrafa gir-** ['- spend a lot of money on sth or to get sth done, - have a lot of expenses, - incur great expense'].

tasdik edil- [ir] /{tarafından/CA}/ '- be confirmed, affirmed, ratified, certified, notarized /by/' [tasdik et- + pass. suf. -Il]: İşçi ve memur ücretler.i.nin artacağ.ı söylentileri {başbakan tarafından/yetkililer.ce} tasdik edildi. 'The rumors that the wages of workers and civil employees would increase were confirmed {by the prime minister/by the authorities}.' Nüfus kâğıtlarımız ve evlilik cüzdanımız İngilizce.yE çevrildi ve [noter tarafından] tasdik edildi. 'Our identification papers and our marriage certificate were translated INTO English and [then] notarized [by the notary public].' 969:12. certainty: - verify. → = doğrulan-, = onaylan-.

tasdik et- [eDer] '- confirm, - affirm, - ratify, - certify, - notarize' [A. tasdik (. -) 'a confirming']: Noter İngilizceye tercüme ettirdiğimiz nüfus kâğıtlarımızı ve evlilik cüzdanımızı tasdik etti. 'The notary public notarized our identification papers and our marriage certificate which we had had translated INTO English.' 969:12. certainty: - verify. → = doğrula-, = onayla-.

taş- [ar] [taş archaic 'outside, exterior' + verb-forming suf. -Ө] 1 '- boil over': Dikkat et! * Kahve taşıyor. 'Watch out! * The coffee is {boiling over/ABOUT TO boil over}.' • The Turkish present continuous tense may indicate an action ABOUT TO take place as well as one in progress.

2 /DAn/ '- overflow, - run over /DUE TO/': Bu nehir ne zaman yağmur yağsa böyle taşıyor. 'Whenever it rains, this river overflows [its banks] like this.' * Aşırı yağmur.DAN baraj taştı. 'The dam overflowed DUE TO excessive rain.'

/A, dışarı/ '- spill out': Daha büyük bir dolab.a ihtiyacım var. Eşyalarım dışarı taşıyor. 'I need Ө a larger closet. My things are spilling out.' * Salonlar doldu taştı. 'The rooms filled up and [then the people] spilled out.' Öğrencilerin boykotu sokağ.A taştı. 'The student boycott [lit., ** students' boycott] spilled out INTO the street.' 238:17b. stream: - overflow. → = boşal- 2.

taşı- [r] /a: DAn, b: A, c: lA arasında/ '- carry, - move, or - transport /a: from, b: to, c: between/' [taş archaic 'outside, exterior' + verb-forming suf. -I]: Lütfen şu bavulu taşır mısınız? 'Would you please carry this suitcase [for me]?' Bavullarınızı taşıyabilir miyim? 'May I carry your bags?' * Bir elinde çanta bir elinde şemsiye taşıyordu. 'In one hand he was carrying a briefcase, in the other, an umbrella.' Bütün kitaplarımı ev.den yazıhanem.e taşıdım. 'I carried all my books from [my] home to my office.' Bu vapurlar Kadıköy ile Karaköy arasında yolcu taşırlar. 'These ferries carry passengers between Kadıköy and Karaköy [i.e., two sections of Istanbul].' Hafif hafif esen rüzgâr çiçeklerin kokusunu taşıyordu. 'The soft [lit., lightly blowing] breezes were carrying the scent of the flowers.' • Note the difference in form and meaning between taşı- and taşın- directly below. 176:12. transferal, transportation: - transport.

taşın- [ır] /DAn, A/ '- move [oneself], - change one's place of residence, business /from, to/' [taşı- + refl. suf. -n]: Ankara'dan İzmir'e taşındık. 'We moved from Ankara to Izmir.' Yalçın * kira.sı daha az bir ev buldu. Yarın o ev.e taşınacak. Eşyalarını Orhan'ın kamyoneti {ILE} taşıyacak. 'Yalçın found * a house with a lower rent [lit., ** its-rent-less a house]. Tomorrow he will move there [lit., to that house]. He'll move his belongings {IN/with} Orhan's pickup truck.' 159:17. location: - settle; 176:12. transferal, transportation: - transport.

In the following examples note the equivalent English phrasal verbs: Yeni evimiz.e taşındık ama henüz tam yerleşemedik. 'We've MOVED INTO our new home, but we haven't been able to settle in completely yet.' Dün yeni bir ev tuttuk; muhtemelen gelecek ay taşınacağız. 'We rented a new house yesterday. We'll probably MOVE IN next month.' S: Cemil bey hâlâ sizin apartmanda mı oturuyor? 'Q: Does Cemil bey still live in your apartment building?' C:

Hayır, geçen yıl taşındı. 'A: No, he MOVED OUT last year.' **buradan taşın-** '- move AWAY [lit., move from here]'. **buradan** is not needed if the notion of 'away' is clear from the context: **Yandaki komşumuz başka bir şehirde iş bulmuş, * o yüzden [bura.dan] taşındı.** 'Our next-door neighbor found work in another city. * That's why he moved away [from here].' *188:6.* departure: - depart.

{düşün-/düşünüp} taşın-. → düşün- 1.

geri taşın- '- move back [to a previously occupied place]' [**geri** 'back, rear, the space behind']: **Üniversitenin yurdunu beğenmeyince önceki kaldığı ev.e geri taşındı.** 'Since he didn't like {the college/the university} dorms, he moved back to the house [that] he had stayed in before.' *163:6.* regression: - retreat.

tat- [taDar] '- taste, - sample, - try the taste of' [**tat** 'taste' + verb-forming suf. -Ø]: **Çin lokanta.sı.nın yemekler.i.ni hiç tattın mı? Çok nefis.** 'Have you ever tasted the food at [lit., ** of] the Chinese restaurant? It's excellent.' **Çorbanızı tadayım.** 'Let me try your soup.' Proverbs: **Acıyı tatmayan tatlıyı anlamaz.** 'He who has not tasted the bitter will not appreciate [lit., ** understand] the sweet.' **Bir bakmak.TAN bir tatmak yeğdir.** 'It is better to taste once THAN to look once.' *62:7.* taste: - taste; *941:8.* experiment: - experiment. → = **tadına bak-** → bak- 1.

tatil yap-. → yap- 3.

tatile çık-. → çık- 2.

tatile gir-. → gir-.

tatile git-. → git- 1a.

tavsiye et- [eDer] /A/ '- recommend, - propose, or - suggest sth /to/ sb, - advise sb to do sth' [A. **tavsiye** 'a recommending, recommendation; advice, suggestion']: NON-verbal noun as direct object: * **Ban.A iyi bir {a: otel/b: motel/c: lokanta/d: gece kulübü/e: kamp yeri/f: doktor} tavsiye edebilir misiniz?** 'Could you recommend me

a good {a: hotel/b: motel/c: restaurant/d: night club/e: camp ground/f: doctor}?' In a restaurant you ask the waiter: **Ne tavsiye edersiniz?** 'What do you recommend?' **Hangi {şarab.I/çorba.yI/kebab.I} tavsiye edersiniz?** 'Which {θ wine/θ soup/θ kebab} do you recommend?' **Alpay bey elbise diktirmek istiyormuş. O.na benim terzi.m.İ tavsiye ettim.** 'Alpay bey wanted to have a suit made. I recommended my tailor to him.' VERBAL noun as direct object: **Garson şiş kebap ye.me.MİZ.i tavsiye etti ama biz * tavsiyesi.nİ dinlemedik. * Keşke tavsiyesi.nE uysaydık!** 'The waiter recommended that WE eat [lit., ** OUR eating] shish kebab, but * we {didn't take/lit., didn't listen to} his recommendation. * If only we had followed θ his advice!' *422:5.* advice: - advise; *439:5.* offer: - propose; *509:11* approval: - commend. → = **öner-, fikir ver-** 2 ['- give advice /to/, - advise /θ/, - suggest a course of action /to/'] → ver- 1.

tayin edil-. → {atan-/tayin edil-}.

tayin et-. → {ata-/tayin et-}.

tayin ol-. → ol- 12.

tebrik et- [eDer] /a: {DAn dolayı}, b: için, c: I, d: IA/ '- congratulate sb /a: {FOR/ON}, b: {for/ON}, c: {FOR/ON}, d: BY/' [A. **tebrik** (. -) 'congratulation, congratulating']: **Tebrik ederiz efendim. 50 bin lira.yI kazanan talihli sizsiniz.** 'Congratulations, {sir/ma'am}. You are the lucky winner of 50,000 liras [lit., the lucky one who has won...].' Person as object: **Başbakan madalya kazanan sporcular.ı tebrik etti.** 'The prime minister congratulated the athletes who had won medals.' **Derslerinde gösterdiğ.in {başarı.dan dolayı/başarı için} sen.i tebrik ederim.** 'I congratulate you {for [or ON] the success} you have demonstrated in your studies.' **Gençlik ve Spor Bakanı dünya şampiyonu olan sporcu.yu {başarı.sı.ndan dolayı/başarı.sı için} tebrik etti.** 'The Minister of Athletics [lit., The Minister of Youth and Sports] congratulated the world-class athlete {for [*or* ON] his success}.'

Occasion, event as object: * **Amcam yeni iş.im.i** {a: e-posta.yLA/b: e-mail.LE/c: telefon.LA} **tebrik etti.** 'My uncle congratulated me {ON/FOR} my new job {a, b: BY e-mail/c: BY phone} [lit., ** congratulated my new job...].' *149:2.* congratulation: - congratulate. → = **kutla- 2.**

Tebrik ederim. 'Congratulations', lit., 'I congratulate [you].' For an accomplishment, success: **A: Geçen ay okulumu bitirdim.** 'A: Last month I graduated [lit., ** finished my school].' **B: Tebrik ederim.** 'B: Congratulations!' **A: Teşekkür ederim.** 'A: Thank you.' Somebody tells you that he has received good news. You respond: * **Gözün[üz] aydın. Tebrik ederim.** 'I'm so happy for you [lit., ** Your eyes bright]. Congratulations.', said to sb whose long-awaited desire has been realized. The plural noun often replaces **Tebrik ederim**: **Tebrikler!** 'Congratulations!' For congratulations on birthdays and religious AND nonreligious official holidays: **A:** * {**Kurban bayram.ınız.ı/Ramazan bayram.ınız.ı/Kandil.iniz.i**} **tebrik ederim.** 'A: Congratulations {ON your Feast of the Sacrifice/ON your Ramadan/ON your **Kandil** Feast.} [lit., ** I congratulate your Feast of the Sacrifice...].' **B:** {**Teşekkür ederim./Allah razı olsun./* Ben de tebrik ederim.**} 'B: {Thank you./May God be pleased with you./* I, for my part, congratulate you.}' *149:4.* INTERJ. congratulations. → **Kutlu olsun.** ['May it be blessed', a formula of congratulation on birthdays and religious as well as on other, non-religious, official holidays] → ol- 11 → olsun, **Mübarek olsun.** ['May it be blessed.', a formula of congratulation used exclusively on religious holidays.] → ol- 11 → olsun.

tecavüz et- [eDer] [A. **tecavüz** (. - .) 'attack']: 1 /A/ '- violate [law], - infringe /ON/, - transgress /ON/': **hakk.ı.nA tecavüz et-** '- infringe /ON/ someone's rights' [A. **hak** (ha**KK**ı) 'one's right, due']: In regard to any group of people waiting in a line at the movies, the theater, a soccer match, a bank, etc.: **Lütfen sırayı bozmayın,** * **birbiriniz.in**

hakk.ı.nA tecavüz etmeyin. 'Please don't cut in [line] [lit., ** spoil the line]. * Don't violate one another's rights.' **Hükümet.in yabancı dil.LE öğrenim.i yasaklama.sı insan haklar.ı.nA tecavüz etmektir.** 'The government's prohibition of instruction IN foreign languages is a violation of [lit., violates] human rights.'

haneye tecavüz et- '- trespass /ON/ sb's property' [P. **hane** 'house']: **Komşu.su.nun hane.si.nE tecavüz ettiği için haps.E girdi.** 'He was imprisoned [lit., entered θ prison] because he had trespassed ON his neighbor's property [i.e., grounds or house].' *214:5.* intrusion: - intrude; *674:5.* illegality: - break or - violate the law.

2 /A/ '- rape /θ/, - assault /θ/ sexually': **Birçok kadın.A tecavüz eden sapık geçen gün yakalandı.** 'The pervert who had raped θ several women was apprehended the other day.' *459:14.* attack: - attack; *480:15.* taking: - possess sexually; *665:20.* unchastity: - seduce. → = **ırzına geç-** ['- rape, - violate'] → geç- 1, = **saldır- 2.**

tecrübe et- [eDer] '- try on [clothing], - try out [equipment], - see how sth or sb works out, - give sb a trial period' [A. **tecrübe** 'experience, trial, test']: Equipment as object: **Bir de bu** {a: **bilgisayar.ı/b: buzdolabı.nı/c: müzik seti.ni/d: fırın.ı/e: televizyon.u**} **tecrübe edelim.** 'Let's also try out this {a: computer/b: refrigerator/c: music console/d: oven/e: television set}.' Clothing as object: **A:** * **Yeni aldığım elbise küçük geldi.** 'A: The suit I just bought is too small [lit., ** came small].' **B: Satın almadan önce tecrübe etmedin mi?** 'B: Didn't you try it on before buying it?' **Tecrübe edebilir miyim?** 'May I try it on?' → = **dene- 1,** = **prova et-.** Person as object: **Yeni** {a: **hizmetçi.yi/b: kapıcı.yı/c: sekreter.i/d: şoför.ü**} **bu hafta bir tecrübe edelim, eğer memnun kalırsak iş.E alırız.** 'Let's see how the new {a: {help/maid}/b: {caretaker/door-man}/c: secretary/d: driver} works out this week. If we're satisfied, we'll hire {him/her} [lit., ** take {him/her}

TO work].' *941:8*. experiment: - experiment. → = dene-. • In regard to food, tat- ['- taste, - sample (food)]', is used rather than tecrübe et- or dene-.

tedavi altına alın-. → alın- 1.

tedavi et- [eDer] 1 '- treat a person, disease, or part of the body' [A. tedavi (. - .) 'treatment']: Since this verb means both '- treat' and '- cure', both meanings may be possible in some examples: A: Amcan.ın iyileştiğ.i.ni duydum, * çok sevindim. * Hangi doktor tedavi etti? 'A: I {hear/lit., heard} that your [paternal] uncle {has recovered/has gotten better}. * I'm so glad. * Which doctor {treated/cured} him?' More likely English in this situation: 'Who {treated/cured} him?' or 'What was the name of the doctor who {treated/cured} him?' B: Ahmet bey [tedavi etti]. 'B: Ahmet bey did [lit., [{treated/cured} him].' Kırılan ayağımı o doktor tedavi etti. 'That doctor treated my broken footl.' Onu burada Devlet Hastanesinde tedavi etmeye başladılar, daha sonra Amerikan Hastane.si.nE sevkettiler. 'They began to treat her here in the State Hospital. Later they took her to the American Hospital.' *91:24*. therapy: - treat.

2 '- cure a person or a disease': O gerçekten çok iyi bir doktor. * Annemin şeker hastalığ.ı.nı {kısa sürede/bir kaç ayda} tedavi etmişti. 'He's really a very good doctor. He cured my mother's diabetes {in a short time/in a few months}.' Doktorlar teyzemi tedavi etmeye çalıştılar ama [tedavi] edemediler. 'Doctors tried to cure my aunt, but they couldn't [cure her].' *86:38*. remedy: - remedy; *396:15*. restoration: - cure. → /A/ şifa ver- ['- restore to health, - cure, - heal'].

tedavi gör-. → gör- 3.

tedavülden kalk-. → kalk- 3.

tehdit et- [eDer] /lA/ '- threaten sb /with/ sth' [A. tehdit (. -) 'threat']: Hırsız ben.i silâh.la tehdit etti. 'The thief threatened me with a weapon.' Uçak korsanları istedikleri yerine getirilmezse bütün yolcuları öldürmek.le

tehdit ettiler. 'The hijackers threatened to kill all the passengers if their demands were not met.' *514:2*. threat: - threaten.

tehir edil-. → {ertelen-/tehir edil-}.

tehir et-. → {ertele-/tehir et-}.

teklif et-. → {öner-/teklif et-}.

tekme {at-/vur-). → at- 5.

tekme ye-. → ye- 2.

{tekrar et- [eDer]/tekrarla- [r]} '- repeat' [A. tekrar (. -) 'repetition, repeating' + verb-forming suf. -lA]: * Anla.YAMA.dım. * Lütfen {tekrar eder misiniz/tekrarlar mısınız}? 'I didn't [lit., COULDN'T] understand. * Would you please repeat what you said?' • In the situation above, the negative potential, i.e., Anla.YAMA.dım, is usually preferred to the simple negative past, i.e., Anla.MADIM. 'I DIDN'T understand.' The former indicates that an effort to understand has been made. • The English verb '- repeat' usually requires an object, i.e., what you said. Söylediklerinizi duy.AMA.dım. Tekrar eder misiniz lütfen? 'I didn't [lit., COULDN'T] hear what you said. Would you please repeat?' * Ne söylediğ.iniz.i kaçırdım. * Lütfen tekrar eder misiniz? 'I {missed/couldn't catch} what you said. Would you please repeat [{it?/what you said?}]' The most common way of requesting a speaker to repeat what he said is to say the sngle word Efendim? 'Pardon?' lit., '{Sir/Ma'am}?' *848:7*. repetition: - repeat.

tekrarla-. → {tekrar et-/tekrarla-} directly above.

tel çek-. → çek- 9.

telâffuz edil- [ir] '- be pronounced' [A. telâffuz et- + pass. suf. -Il]: Bu kelime nasıl telâffuz edilir? 'How is this word pronounced?' *524:23*. speech: - say.

telâffuz et- [eDer] '- pronounce' [A. telâffuz 'a pronouncing, pronunciation']: Bu kelimeyi telâffuz edemiyorum. Nasıl telâffuz edersiniz? 'I can't pronounce this word. How do you pronounce it?' Another way of asking for the pronunciation of a word: * **B u kelime.nin telâffuz.u nasıl?** 'What [lit., ** How] is the pronunciation of this word?' *524:23.* speech: - say.

telefon aç-. → telefon {et-/aç-} directly below.

telefon {et- [eDer]/aç- [ar]} /A, DAn/ '- phone /θ [sb], from/, - call, - call up, - make a phone call /to, from/' [aç '- open']: **Nereden telefon edebilirim?** 'Where can I make a call from?' **Buradan telefon edebilir miyim?** '{Can/May} I call from here?' * **Bir telefon edebilir miyim?** 'May I make a phone call?' **Siz.E yarın telefon edebilir miyim?** 'May I call θ you tomorrow?' **Konsolosluğ.um.A telefon etmek istiyorum.** 'I want to phone θ my consulate.' **Daha sonra yine telefon ederim.** 'I'll call back later.' **Bu gece anne.m.E telefon {etmeliyim/açmalıyım}. Çünkü epeydir o.nA telefon {etmedim/açmadım}.** 'I must phone θ my mother this evening because I haven't phoned θ her for quite a while.' S: * **Hani dün bana telefon edecektin?** 'Q: You were going to call me yesterday. What happened?' C: * **Telefon ettim ama kimse karşılık vermedi.** 'A: I TRIED TO phone [you], but no one answered.' • Note that '- ANSWER the [tele]phone' is not **telefon aç-** but **telefon.U aç-** or **telefon.A {bak-/cevap ver-}** → bak- 3, ver- 1. *347:18.* communications: - telephone. → **telefonla ara-** ['- call up (lit., - search for by phone), - ring up']. → ara- 2.

telefon kapa-. → kapan- 1.

telefona bak-. → bak- 3.

telefona cevap ver-. → cevap ver-. → ver- 1.

telefonla ara-. → ara- 2.

telefonlaş- [ır] /lA/ '- talk /with/ {on/over} the phone, - talk /with/ {by/on the} phone' [telefon + recip. suf. -lAş]: **Betül'le pek görüşemiyoruz. Ama sık sık telefonlaşıyoruz.** '{I/We} can't often get together with Betül [f.], but we frequently talk [with each other] {by/on the} phone.' • In the sentence above there are at least two people: Betül and me. There may be more: Betül, some friends of ours, and me. **Ben Ankara'dan döndüğümden beri iki günde bir telefonlaşıyoruz.** 'Since I've returned from Ankara, we've spoken on the phone every other day [lit., ** once in two days].' *343:6.* communication: - communicate, - be in touch; *347:18.* communications: - telephone.

telefonu aç-. → aç- 5.

telefonu kapat-. → kapat-.

telefonu yüzüne kapat-. → kapat-.

temas et- [eDer] 1 /A/ '- touch /θ/ sb or sth physically': elle temas et- '- touch [with the hands]' [el 'hand']: * **O adam ban.A lâf atmak.la kalmadı, aynı zamanda [ban.A] el.le temas etmey.e de kalkıştı.** 'That man not only assaulted me verbally [lit., ** by throwing remarks AT me], he also {dared/went so far as} to touch θ me.' *73:6.* touch: - touch; *223:10.* nearness: - contact. → = dokun- 1.

/lA/ '- bring into contact /with/': * **Yanıcı maddeler.in ateş.le temas etmeme.si gerekir.** 'One must not bring inflammable materials into contact with fire.' *73:6.* touch: - touch; *223:10.* nearness: - contact. → = dokun- 1.

2 /A/ '- touch /{ON/UPON}/, - mention /θ/ a subject': **Vaktimiz kısıtlı olduğu için her konu.yA temas edemeyiz.** 'Since our time is limited, we can't touch ON every subject.' **Yer.i gelmişken hava kirliliği konu.su.nA da temas etmek istiyorum.** 'Since this is the appropriate place [lit., ** its place having come], I also want to touch ON the issue of air pollution.' *524:25.* speech: - remark. → = değin-.

temas kur-. → kur- 1.

temize çek-. → çek- 8.

temizle- [r] '- clean' [temiz 'clean' + verb-forming suf. -lA]: **Lütfen** {bunu/ön camı/odayı} {iyice/ adamakıllı} temizleyin. 'Please clean {this/the windshield/the room} {well/thoroughly}.' **Yeni hizmetçimiz evi {çok iyi} temizledi.** 'Our new {help/cleaning lady} cleaned the house {very well/thoroughly}.' *79:18.* cleanness: - clean. → sil- 2 ['- wipe clean', usually with a wet cloth or mop], ≠ kirlet-, ≠ pislet-.

temsil et- [eDer] '- represent' [A. **temsil** (. -) 'a representing']: **Öğrenci sorunlar.ı.nın tartışıldığ.ı toplantıda bizim fakülteyi ben temsil ettim.** 'At the meeting where student problems were discussed, I represented our faculty.' **Sayın Mehmet Çevik TBMM'de [= Türkiye Büyük Millet Meclisi'nde] hukuk komisyonlarında Ak Parti'yi temsil eden en dirayetli milletvekilidir.** 'Mr. Mehmet Çevik is the most capable deputy to represent the Ak Party in the legal committees of the Turkish Grand National Assembly.' *576:14.* deputy, agent: - represent.

teneffüs yap-. → yap- 3.

tenkit edil-. → {eleştiril-/tenkit edil-}.

tenkit et-. → {eleştir-/tenkit et-}.

tepki göster-. → göster- 1.

ter bas-. → bas- 4.

{**tercih et-** [eDer]/**yeğle-** [r]} [A. **tercih** (. -) 'preference'; **yeğ** 'better, preferable' + verb-forming suf. -lA] **1** /A/ '- prefer sb or sth /to/ sb or sth else, - like sb or sth better than sb or sth else, - like best': NON-verbal noun as object: **Tülay hep pahalı mağazaları tercih eder.** 'Tülay always prefers expensive stores.' **S: Kiraz.I mı, yoksa muz.U mu tercih edersiniz?** 'Q: Do you prefer cherries or bananas?' or 'THE cherries or THE bananas'. • The accusative suffix [-I] designates BOTH the whole class in general AS WELL AS some particular members of the class. **C: Kiraz.ı tercih ederim.** 'A: I prefer cherries.' or 'THE cherries.' **Kiraz var, muz var. Hangi.si.nİ tercih edersiniz?** 'We have [lit., There are] [both] cherries and bananas. Which do you prefer?'

Meyvalar.DAN hangi.si.nİ tercih edersin? 'Which fruits [lit., OF the fruits which] do you prefer?' VERBAL noun as object: * **Babam Volvo yer.i.ne {Mersedes/ Mercedes} almay.I tercih etti.** 'My father preferred buying a Mercedes TO buying a Volvo [lit., preferred buying a Mercedes in place of a Volvo].' **S:** * **Yarın pikniğ.E gidelim mi?** 'Q: {How about going ON a picnic tomorrow?/Why don't we go ON a picnic tomorrow?/lit., Shall we go ON a picnic tomorrow?}' **C:** * **Yarın ol.ma.ma.sı.nı tercih ederim.** * **Çarşamba.ya ne dersin?** 'A: {Couldn't we do it some other time?/Preferably not tomorrow [lit., ** I would prefer its not being tomorrow]}. * {How about Wednesday?/lit., What would you say to Wednesday?}'
• Compare the following three patterns for expressing preference with verbal noun objects. In the preferred choice, the object always has the accusative case suffix. The ALTERNATIVE, underlined, is expressed with DIFFERENT forms:
a) Sinema.ya git.MEY.İ televizyon seyret.MEY.E **tercih ederim.** 'I prefer going to the movies TO watching television.'
b) Sinema.ya git.MEKTENSE **televizyon seyretmey.İ tercih ederim.** 'I would rather watch television THAN go to the movies.'
c) Sinemaya git.MEK YER.İ.NE **televizyon seyretmey.İ tercih ederim.** 'INSTEAD OF go.ING to the movies, I would rather watch television.' *371:17.* choice: - prefer.

2 * '- choose, - select, - pick', for oneself, not sb else: **Babam "Biri İngilizce biri Türkçe iki kitap aldım. Biri.nİ tercih et" dedi.** * **Ben Türkçe olan.I tercih ettim.** 'My father said, "I have bought two books, one English and one Turkish. Choose one of them".' * I chose THE Turkish one.' **Benim için oldukça zor ama [takdir edersiniz ki] iki.niz.DEN bir.i.ni tercih etmek zorundayım.** 'It is quite difficult for me [to choose], but [you will appreciate that] I'm obliged to choose between you [lit., one OF the two of you].' * **Tam güvenlik için sigortalı yollamay.I tercih edin.** 'To be completely safe, send it insured [lit., For complete safety, choose to send it insured].' *371:13.*

choice: - choose. → = seç- 1, = beğen- 2.

tercüme et- [eDer] /DAn, A/ '- translate /from, INTO/' [A. tercüme 'translation, translating']: **Bu cümle.yİ Türkçe.DEN İngilizce.yE tercüme eder misiniz?** 'Would you please translate this sentence FROM Turkish INTO English?' **Turistler.in söyledikler.i.ni babam.A tercüme ediyorum.** 'I'm translating FOR my father what the tourists {said/are saying}.' *341:12.* interpretation: - translate. → = aktar- 2, = çevir- 6.

tereddüt et- [eDer] /{DA/A}/ '- hesitate /TO/; - waver, - falter' [A. tereddüt 'a hesitating, hesitation']: **Beni {aramak.TA/aramay.A} tereddüt etmeyin!** 'Don't hesitate TO look me up!' **Tereddüt etme.n.E gerek yok, doğru cevap bu.** 'There's no need FOR you to hesitate [lit., ** for your hesitating]. This is the correct answer.' * **Dilim.in uc.u.na geldi ama söyleyip söylememek.TE tereddüt ettim.** 'It was on [lit., ** it came to] the tip of my tongue, but I hesitated whether to say it or not.' **Ben olsam bunu {yapmak.TA/yapmay.A} bir saniye bile tereddüt etmezdim.** 'If it were me, I wouldn't hesitate [for] even a second to do it.' *362:7.* irresolution: - hesitate. → = /{A/DAn}/ çekin-.

terk et- [eDer] '- leave, - abandon', usually permanently. [A. **terk** 'abandonment']: **Erhan işini terk etmiş.** 'Erhan has left his job.' **Atilla evlendikten iki yıl sonra karısını terk etti.** 'Atilla left his wife {after two years of marriage/two years after getting married}.' **Yolcular {batmak.ta olan gemiyi} terk ettiler.** 'The passengers abandoned {the sinking ship/the ship that was sinking}.' **Ya sev ya terk et!** '[Either] love it or leave it.' 'It' here is understood to refer to one's homeland. *370:5.* abandonment: - abandon. → = bırak- 3, = ayrıl- 3.

terle- [r] '- sweat, - perspire' [**ter** 'perspiration' + verb-forming suf. -lA]: **Bugün hava çok sıcaktı.** * **Buram buram terledim.** 'Today the weather was very hot. * I perspired {a lot/profusely}.' Proverb:

Hamama giden terler. 'He who goes to a hamam [i.e., Turkish bath] will sweat.', i.e., A person must bear the consequences of his actions. If you can't stand the heat, get out of the kitchen. *12:16.* excretion: - sweat. → **ter bas-** ['- break out in a sweat, - be covered in sweat'] → bas- 4.

tesadüf et- [eDer] [A. **tesadüf** (. - .) 'chance event, accidental encounter, coincidence'] 1 /A/ '- meet by chance, - run or - bump /INTO/, - encounter /θ/, - come or - chance /UPON/': **Havaalanında bir okul arkadaşım.A tesadüf ettim.** 'I ran INTO a school friend [of mine] at the airport.' *131:6.* inexpectation: - be unexpected; *223:11.* nearness: - meet. → = /lA/ karşılaş- 2, = /A/ rastla- 1, /lA/ buluş- ['- come together, - meet /θ/', usually after a previous agreement to meet].

2 /A/ '- hit /θ/ sth by chance, not intention, - collide /WITH/': **Süheyla'ya attığım top cam.A tesadüf etti.** 'The ball I threw to Süheyla [f.] hit θ the window.' *901:13.* impulse, impact: - collide. → = /A/ rastla- 2, /A/ çarp- 1 ['- hit /θ/, - strike /θ/, - bump /{AGAINST/INTO/ON}/, - run or - crash /INTO/'], vur- 1 ['- hit, - strike /a: θ [sb, sth], b: with, c: ON/, - knock, - kick, - slap, - bump', depending on the preceding noun], çarpış- ['- collide, - run into' in reference to vehicles].

Tesadüfe bakın. → bak- 1.

tesir et- [eDer] /A/ '- affect /θ/, - influence /θ/, - have an effect /{ON/UPON}/, - do good' [A. **tesir** (- -) 'effect, influence']: **Televizyondaki film ban.A çok tesir etti.** 'The films on television have had a great effect ON me.' **Başım çok ağrıyordu. Hiçbir ilâç tesir etmedi.** 'I had a terrible headache. No medicine did any good.' *893:7.* influence: - influence. → = /A/ dokun- 3 ['- move, - touch, - affect /θ/ sb emotionally; - disturb, - upset /θ/ sb'], = /I/ etkile-.

teslim et- [eDer] /A/ '- hand sth over /to/, - turn sth over /to/, - deliver sth /to/, - turn sth in /to/' [A. **teslim** (. -) 'handing over, submission']: **Lütfen {sınav/imtihan} kâğıtlarını teslim edin!** 'Please turn in your {examination} papers.'

Hoca.M, {ödevlerimizi/çalış-malarımızı} ne zaman teslim edeceğiz? '{Professor/ Teacher} [lit., ** '{My professor/My teacher}', the common Turkish form of address to one's teacher], when are we to hand in our {assignments}?' **Kapıcı gönderdiğim paketi yarın siz.e teslim edecek.** 'Tomorrow {the caretaker /the doorman} will turn over to you the package I sent.' **Bu paketi adresim.e teslim eder misiniz?** 'Would you deliver this package to my address?' **Maaşını * olduğu gibi karısı.na teslim eder.** 'He turns his whole salary [lit., * 'as it is', i.e., as he received it, without removing any part of it] over to his wife.' **Dükkân sahibi hırsızı polis.e teslim etti.** 'The shopkeeper turned the thief over to the police.' **Sokak ortasında bulduğu parayı sahib.i.nE teslim etti.** 'He turned over to the [lit., its] owner the money he had found in the middle of the street.' **Bir mobilya reklâmı: Şahin Mobilya'dan aldığınız mobilya-ları eviniz.e teslim ederiz.** 'An advertisement for furniture: We will deliver to your house the furniture you buy from Şahin Furniture.' *478:13.* giving: - deliver. → ≠ **al-** 3 ['- get, - receive /from/'].

{**tespit et-** [eDer]/**sapta-** [r]} 1 '- determine or - establish the existence of, - find, - discover': **Bu kitabı hızlı bir şekilde oku.mam.A rağmen pek çok hata tespit ettim.** 'Although I read this book quickly, I found very many errors [in it].' **Her konuda tam bir görüş birliği içinde olduğ.umuz.u memnuniyet.le tespit ettik.** 'We were pleased to discover [lit., We discovered with pleasure] that we were in complete agreement [lit., ** in complete unity of opinion] on every matter.' *940:2.* discovery: - discover.

2 '- set, - fix the time of': **Düğün tarih.imiz.i daha tespit edemedik.** 'We haven't been able to set the date for our wedding [lit., set our wedding date] yet.' *864:11.* particularity: - specify; *964:4.* prearrangement: - prearrange. = **belirle-**.

teşekkür et- [eDer] /a: A, b: A, c: için/ '- thank /a: θ [sb], b: for, c: for/, - be obliged /a: to [sb], b: for, c: for/' [A.

teşekkür 'thanking']: **Teşekkür ederim!** a) As a response to 'How are you?': S: **Nasılsınız?** 'Q: How are you?' C1: * [**İyiyim.**] **Teşekkür ederim!** * **Siz nasılsınız?** 'A1: * {Fine/Good}, thank you. {How are you?/How about you?}' In this frequent exchange, the answer often omits **iyiyim**, but the English usually has an equivalent, with 'Good' a frequent response. Other frequent responses: C2: {**Sağolun/Sağol**}, [**iyiyim**]. 'A2: {Thank you./Thanks.} [lit., ** Be well], [I'm well.]'
b) When thanking for an object. 1. The object is not mentioned: You are given sth. You say: **Teşekkür ederim.** 'Thank you.' Other frequent responses: **Teşekkür.LER.** 'ThankS.' Or {**Sağolun!/Sağol!**} '{Thank you./Thanks.}', or **Sağol[un], varol[un]!** 'Thank you very much!' Also heard but not so widely accepted because it is from the French: **Mersi.** #
2. The object received is mentioned:
• Note: only **için**, not A for 'for': {**Hediye/Hediyeniz**} **İÇİN teşekkür ederim.** 'Thank you FOR {the gift/your gift}.' Possible responses equivalent to 'You're welcome', etc.: **Bir şey değil.** lit., 'It's nothing.' or **Rica ederim.** lit., ** 'I request.' or **Estağfurullah.** 'Don't mention it.'
c) When thanking for interest or an activity or action not expressed in a verb form. • Note the two possibilities for 'for': **için** and A: At the end of a letter of request: {**İlginiz için/İlginiz.E**} * **şimdiden teşekkür ederim.** 'Thank you * in advance {FOR your attention} [lit., ** your interest] to this matter.' {**Yardımınız için/Yardımınız.A**} **teşekkür ederim.** 'Thank you {FOR your help}.' Possible Turkish responses are the same as indicated under b) above, but a common English equivalent today is 'No problem.'
d) Thanking for an activity expressed as a verbal object. • Note: only **için**, not ~~A~~: **Buraya gel.diğ.İNİZ için teşekkür ederim.** 'Thank you for coming here [lit., ** for YOUR having come here].' Possible responses are the same as under c) above.

• Note also the less common form **Teşekkür ed.İYORUM**, frequently heard on the radio or TV when a correspondent or interviewee is being thanked for his contribution. *150:4.* gratitude: - thank; *150:6.* gratitude: INTERJ. thanks! → = **Eksik olmayın.** → ol- 12, = **Sağol!** → sağ ol- → ol- 12.

teşhis koy-. → koy- 1.

teşvik et- [eDer] /a: konusunda, b: için, c: lA/ '- encourage, - spur sb on /a: to [lit., in the matter of], b: TO, c: with/; - inspire sb; - encourage sb to do or - participate in sth; - promote the development of' [A. **teşvik** (. -) 'encouraging, urging on']: * **Babam yabancı dil öğren.mem.i her zaman teşvik etmiştir.** 'My father always encouraged me to learn [lit., ** encouraged my learning] foreign languages.' * **Öğretmenim Türkçe öğren.mem konu.su.nda beni teşvik etti.** 'My teacher encouraged me to learn Turkish [lit., ** encouraged me in the matter of my learning Turkish].' * **İyi bir balerin ol.ABİL.mem İÇİN annem daima beni teşvik etmiştir.** 'My mother always encouraged me TO become [lit., ** FOR my BEING ABLE to become] a good ballerina.' **Öğrenciler.E okuma alışkanlığ.ı.nı kazandırmak için onları ödüller.le teşvik etmeliyiz.** 'To get θ students into [lit., to acquire] the habit of reading, we must encourage them with prizes.' *375:21.* motivation, inducement: - encourage; *492:16.* courage: - encourage.

tetkik et- [eDer] '- examine carefully, closely, minutely, in detail, - study carefully, - inspect, - investigate, - research' [A. **tetkik** (. -) 'detailed investigation, scrutiny']: **Hakim bütün belgeleri tetkik etti ve kararını verdi.** 'The judge examined all the documents and {handed down/gave} his decision.' **Müfettişler olayı tetkik ediyorlar.** 'The inspectors are investigating the incident.' *27:14.* vision: - scrutinize; *937:25.* inquiry: - make a close study of. → = **incele-, muayene et-** ['- examine', mostly for a doctor and a patient], **araştır-2** ['- investigate, - explore, - research, - study, - do research on, - try to find out'], **kontrol et-** ['- check, - inspect, - check on, - check to see whether sth is the case or not'].

tıkla- [r] /{I/A/üzerine}/ '- click /ON/', computer language [tık 'click', the

sound + verb-forming suf. -lA]: Both the accusative and dative case suffixes occur. The first tends to be preferred. **Sözcük yazım kuralları için soru işareti.nİ tıklayın.** 'For the spelling rules, click ON the question mark.' **İlgili web sayfa.sı.nI tıklayın.** 'Click ON the relevant Web page.' **Daha fazla bilgi için * bura.yI tıklayın[ız].** 'For further information * click θ here.' * **Başlığ.A tıklayın.** 'Click ON the heading.' **Aşağıdan istediğiniz programı seçip üzerine bir kez tıklayınız.** 'From [the choices] below choose the program you want and click on it once.' **Temsilciliklerimiz.in web siteler.i.nE erişmek için lütfen simgeler.i.nİ tıklayınız.** 'To access θ the Web sites of {the respresentatives of our businesses/our agents}, please click ON the [relevant, lit., their] icons.' * **Bura.yA çift tıklayınız.** 'Click θ here twice.' *56:7.* explosive sound: - snap; *297:11.* weight: - weigh on; *1041:18.* computer science: - computerize.

tıraş ol-. → ol- 10.1.

tırmala- [r] '- scratch', harm inflicted, of cats, etc.: S: **Koluna ne oldu?** 'Q: What happened to your arm?' C: **Kedim tırmaladı.** 'A: My cat scratched [me].' *290:3.* furrow: - furrow; *393:13.* impairment: - inflict an injury. → **kaşı-** ['- scratch', when an itch is scratched], **çiz- 3** ['- scratch', as in 'The dust scratched the lens.'].

tırman- [ır] /A/ 1 '- climb /θ/ sth, - climb /to/ a place': * **Dün {a: şu merdiven.E/b: şu direğ.E/c: şu dağ.A/d: şu tepe.yE/e: şu ağac.A} tırmandık.** 'Yesterday we climbed {a: θ that ladder/b: θ that pole/c: θ that mountain/d: θ that hill/e: θ that tree}.' **Dün şu dağ.ın tepe.si.nE tırmandık.** 'Yesterday we climbed TO the top of that mountain.' *193:11.* ascent: - climb. → = **çık- 5,** ≠ **in- 1.**

2 '- climb, - rise, - go up, - increase': **Fiyatlar gün.den gün.e tırmanıyor.** 'Prices are {climbing/rising/going up/increasing} from day to day.' **Enflasyon gün.den gün.e tırmanıyor.** 'Inflation is increasing from day to day.' *251:6.* increase: - grow, increase [I.]. → = **art- 1,** =

388

çık- 6, = çoğal- ['- increase in number'], = yüksel- 2, ≠ düş- 3, ≠ in- 4.

tiksin-. → {iğren-/tiksin-}.

titre- [r] 1 / DAn/ '- shiver /{WITH/from}/': Hasta {soğuk-.TAN/ateş.TEN} tir tir titriyordu. 'The patient was shivering violently {WITH cold [or from the cold]/WITH fever [or from fever]}.' 916:11. agitation: - shake.

2 /DAn/ '- tremble /{WITH/IN}/, - shake /WITH/': Çocuklar {Korku.DAN/Sinir.DEN/Heyecan.DAN} titriyorlardı. 'The children were trembling {WITH [or IN] fear/WITH anger/WITH excitement}.' Ellerim o kadar titriyordu ki anahtarları sokup kapıyı açmay.ı başaramamış-tım. 'My hands were trembling so {much/hard/violently} that I couldn't get the key in the lock and open the door.' 127:14. fear, frighteningness: - tremble; 152:25a. anger: gestures of anger; 916:11. agitation: - shake. → eli ayağı tutMA-. → tut- 2.

tokalaş- [ır] /lA/ '- shake hands /with/' [toka 'a shaking hands' + recip. suf. -lAş]: * Ahmet'le tokalaştık. '{I/We} shook hands with Ahmet.' • In the sentence above at least two people are involved: Ahmet and me. There may be more: Ahmet, some friends of ours, and me. Misafirler.le tek tek tokalaştık. 'We shook hands with the guests one by one.' 585:10. hospitality, welcome: - greet; 915:14: oscillation: - move up and down. → = el sık- → sık- 1.

tokat at-. → at- 5.

tokat ye-. → ye- 2.

toparla- [r] 1 '- gather together, - collect': Çalıştığım konu.yla ilgili toparladığım malzeme.yi sizinle paylaşmak isterim. 'I want to share with you the materials I have collected regarding the topic I'm working on.' 769:18. assemblage: - bring or - gather together. → = topla- 1.

2 '- summarize, - put information in a nutshell': * Konuşma için siz.e ayrılan süre 20 dakika; *

ayrıntı.ya girmeden kısaca toparlarsanız iyi olur. 'You have 20 minutes to speak [lit., ** the time allotted to you for speaking is 20 minutes]. Please [lit., It would be good if you would] summarize concisely without going into detail.' 268:6. shortness: - shorten; 557:5. abridgment: - abridge; 848:8. repetition: - iterate. → = özetle-. # Toparlayacak olursak... 'To summarize, In summary [lit., If we are to summarize]...' 557:7 abridgment: ADV. in brief.

3 '- straighten up, - tidy up, - pick up, - put in order': Misafirler gelmeden önce odamı toparladım. 'I tidied up my room before the guests came.' 807:12. arrangement: - tidy, - tidy up. → = çekidüzen ver- → ver- 1, = topla- 2, = düzelt- 3, ≠ dağıt- 3, ≠ karıştır- 4.

üstünü başını toparla- '- tidy [oneself] up, - smarten [oneself] up' [üst baş 'clothes, what one has on']: Kazadan sonra üst.ÜM.ü baş.IM.ı toparlayıp hemen yola çıktım ve * bir taksi çevirdim. 'After the accident, I tidied MYSELF up, set out at once, and * hailed [lit., ** turned] a {cab/taxi}.' 79:18. cleanness: - clean; 807:12. arrangement: - tidy, - tidy up. → = üstünü başını {düzelt-/topla-} → düzelt- 3, topla- 2.

kendini toparla- '- pull or - get oneself together': Kardeşimi nişanlısı terkedince ciddî bir bunalım geçirdi, hâlâ kendini toparlayamadı. 'When my brother's financée left him, he got {really/severely} depressed. He hasn't been able to pull himself together yet.' 106:7. inexcitability: - compose oneself.

topla- [r] 1 /DAn, A/ '- collect, - gather, - assemble /from, IN/': Bahçe.den biraz çiçek topladım ve vazo.yA koydum. 'I gathered some flowers from the garden and placed them IN a vase.' * Çocukluğ.um.dan beri pul topluyorum. 'I've been collecting stamps since I was a child [lit., ** since my childhood].' Gidip eşyalarımı toplayacağım. 'I'll go and collect my things.' Müdür açılış konuşma.sı yapmak için öğrencileri spor salon.u.nA topladı. 'The principal [i.e., of the school] assembled the students IN the gym in order to make a welcoming [lit., opening] speech.' **Dünkü olay.LA İLGİLİ OLARAK polis şüpheli şahısları toplamaya başladı.** 'The police began to gather suspicious persons IN CONNECTION WITH yesterday's incident.' *769:18.* assemblage: - bring or - gather together. → = **biriktir-**, = **toparla-**, ≠ **dağıt-** 1. # **Kuruduktan sonra çamaşırları toplamay.I unutma!** 'Don't forget θ to take {in/down} the laundry after it has dried!' → ≠ **çamaşır as-** ['- hang up the laundry'] → **as-** 1.

dikkatini topla- /A/ '- concentrate, - focus, or - concentrate one's attention /ON/': **{Yorgunluk-.tan/Uykusuzluk.tan} olsa gerek, sınavda bir türlü dikkat.İM.i toplayamadım.** 'Probably {because I was tired [lit., ** because of tiredness]/because of lack of sleep}, I just couldn't concentrate during the examination.' **Bütün dikkat.İMİZ.i topladık ve dersi dinlemey.e başladık.** 'We concentrated all OUR attention and began to listen to the lesson.' *982:8.* attention: - pay attention. → **dikkati dağıl-** ['- be distracted'] → **dağıl-** 1.

2 '- straighten up, - tidy up, - pick up, - put in order': * **Misafirler gelmeden önce odamı topladım.** 'I {straightened up my room/put my room in order} before the guests came.' *807:12.* arrangement: - tidy, - tidy up. → = **çekidüzen ver-** → **ver-** 1, = **düzelt-** 3, = **toparla-** 3, ≠ **dağıt-** 3, ≠ **karıştır-** 4.

üstünü başını topla- '- tidy [oneself] up, - smarten [oneself] up' [**üst baş** 'clothes, what one has on']: **Kazadan sonra üst.ÜM.ü baş.IM.ı toplayıp hemen yola çıktım ve * bir taksi çevirdim.** 'After the accident, I tidied MYSELF up, set out at once, and * hailed [lit., ** turned] a {cab/taxi}.' *79:18.* cleanness: - clean; *807:12.* arrangement: - tidy, - tidy up. → = **üstünü başını {düzelt-/toparla-}** → **düzelt-** 3, **toparla-** 3.

yatağını topla- '- make one's bed': **Yatağını toplamadan dışarı çıkamazsın, * ona göre!** 'You

can't go out without [first] making your bed, * so act accordingly!' → = **yatağını {düzelt-/yap-}** ['- make one's bed'] → **düzelt-** 3, **yap-** 3. *807:12.* arrangement: - tidy, - tidy up.

3 '- put on weight, - gain weight': **Emel biraz toplamış gibi geldi bana.** 'It seems to me that Emel [f.] has put on a little weight.' *259:8.* expansion, growth: - fatten. → = **kilo al-** → **al-** 1, = **şişmanla-**, = **toplan-** 4, ≠ **kilo ver-** → **ver-** 1, ≠ **zayıfla-** 1.

4 /I/ '- add one number to another': * **85 ile 15'İ toplarsan 100 olur.** 'If you add 85 and 15, you get 100.' [lit., ** '100 becomes,' i.e., results]. *253:5.* addition: - add to; *1016:17.* mathematics: - calculate. ≠ **çıkar-** 5. For '- add sth to sth', → **kat-**, **ekle-**, **ilâve et-**.

toplan- [ır] [**topla-** + {pass./refl.} suf. -n]: **1** /DA, {tarafından/CA}/ '- be collected, gathered, assembled, harvested /{at/in}, by [sb]/': **Saat 10'da dağıtılan {sınav/imtihan} kâğıtları saat 1'de [öğretmen tarafından] toplandı.** 'The {examination} papers that had been distributed at 10 o'clock were collected at 1 o'clock [by the teacher].' **Tarladaki mahsul ay sonuna kadar toplanacak.** 'The crops in the field will be harvested by the end of the month.' *769:18.* assemblage: - bring or - gather together. → ≠ **dağıtıl-**.

2 /tarafından/ '- be straightened up, tidied up, picked up /by/': **Misafirler gelmeden önce bütün ev [ev sahibi tarafından] toplanmıştı.** 'Before the visitors came, the whole house had been tidied up [by the host].' *807:12.* arrangement: - tidy, - tidy up.

3 /DA/ '- get together, - gather, - assemble, - meet, - convene /{in/at}/': **Engin** is a man's first name. • Note the three possible patterns: **Yarın akşam {Engin'in evinde/* Engin'lerin evinde/* Engin'lerde} toplanacağız.** 'Tomorrow night we'll meet {at Engin's house}.' *769:16.* assemblage: - come together. → = **bir araya gel-** → **gel-** 1, ≠ **dağıl-** 1. # **Meclis daha önce kararlaştırıldığı gibi hafta {son.u/son.u.nda}**

toplanacak. 'The parliament will meet at the end of the week as previously planned [lit., decided].' *769:17.* : - convene. → = **bir araya gel-** → gel- 1, ≠ **dağıl-** 1.

4 '- put on weight, - gain weight': **Emel biraz daha toplanmış gibi geldi.** 'It seems [to me] that Emel [f.] has put on a little more weight.' *259:8.* expansion, growth: - fatten. → = **kilo al-** → al- 1, = **şişmanla-**, = **topla-** 3, ≠ **kilo ver-** → ver- 1, ≠ **zayıfla-** 1.

5 '- be added up': **85 ile 15 toplanırsa 100 {olur/çıkar}.** * 'If 85 and 15 are added, you get 100 [lit., ** 100 {will be/comes out}].' *253:5.* addition: - add to; *1016:17.* mathematics: - calculate. → ≠ **çık-** 9.

toprağa veril-. → veril-.

Toprağı bol olsun. → ol- 11. → olsun.

topuz yaptır-. → yaptır- 2.

tozunu al-. → al- 1.

tuhafına git-. → {**acayibine/ garibine/tuhafına**} git-. → git- 1 b.

tuşla- [r] /{I/A}/ '- press a key, - enter or - punch in a PIN or credit card number, - click /ON/' [**tuş** 'key of an instrument', e.g., piano, typewriter, touch telephone, + verb-forming suf. -1A]: Both the accusative and dative case suffixes occur. The first tends to be preferred. **Telefon.un ahize.si.ni kaldırdıktan sonra 325 15 21'İ tuşlayın.** 'After lifting the receiver, press 325 15 21.' **İngilizce için 1'İ, Türkçe için 2'yİ operatör.E bağlanmak için 3'Ü tuşlayın.** 'For English press 1; for Turkish, press 2; to * speak to [lit., be connected to] an operator, press 3.' **Kredi kartınız.ın {numara.sı.nı/ şifre.si.ni} tuşlayın.** 'Enter [*or* Punch in] {your PIN./your credit card number.} *or* Click on {the number/the PIN} of your credit card.' *297:11.* weight: - weigh on; *912:4.* depression: - depress.

tut- [ar] **1** /DAn/ '- grasp, - seize, - catch, - grab, - take hold of /BY/', also '- hold /BY/': **Sezen üzerine gelen köpek.ten korkarak baba.sı.nın el.i.ni tuttu.** 'Sezen, fearing θ the dog that was coming toward her, took her father's hand.' **Murat kardeş.i.nin el.i.nDEN tuttu.** 'Murat took his sister BY the [lit., her] hand.' **Salih on dakika önce yakaladığı kuşu bırakmadı, hâlâ elinde tutuyor.** 'Salih didn't release the bird he had caught ten minutes ago. He is still holding it in his hand.' **Merdiveni {sıkı/şöyle} tut, bırakma.** 'Hold on to the ladder {tightly/like this}. Don't let go.' **{Öyle} tutma, {böyle/şöyle} tut.** 'Don't hold it {like that/that way}, hold it {like this [*or*: this way]}.' Proverbs: **Gençlik bir kuştur,** * **uçtu mu tutamazsın.** 'Youth is a bird: * once it has flown away, you can't catch it [again].' **Tut.tuğ.u.nu koparır.** 'He plucks whatever he takes hold of.', i.e., He succeeds in whatever he sets out to do. *474:6.* retention: - hold, - grip; *480:14.* taking: - seize. → = **yakala-** 1, ≠ **bırak-** 5.

balık tut- '- fish, - catch fish' [**balık** 'fish']: **Geçen yıl burada çok balık tuttuk.** 'We caught a lot of fish here last year.' **Bu sahil{.DE/.DEN} balık tutmak yasaktır.** 'It is forbidden to fish {ON/lit., from} this shore.' • The locative case emphasizes the place where the activity of fishing occurs, the ablative case, the source, the place from which the fish are taken. *382:10.* pursuit: - fish.

2 '- keep, - maintain, - hold in a certain state or condition': **Çay almay.a gidiyorum. Lütfen yerimi tutar mısınız?** 'I'm going to get some tea. Would you please {keep/hold} my place [for me]?' *474:7.* retention: - hold, - keep. → = **sakla-** 3. # {a: **Odanı**/b: **Evini**/c: **Arabanı**/d: **Elbiseni**/e: **Kitaplarını**} **temiz tut.** 'Keep {a: your room/b: your house/c: your car/d: your dress [*or* suit]/e: your books} clean.' Proverb: **Ayağını sıcak tut başını serin.** 'Keep your feet warm, but your head cool.' *397:8.* preservation: - preserve.

* **eli ayağı tutMA-** /DAn/ '- be shaky, unsteady /{WITH/BECAUSE OF}/', a reaction of shock to bad

news or a frightening event or a sign of anger. [el 'hand', ayak 'foot'], lit., ** 'for one's hand and foot NOT - hold': {Kazadan/Depremden} sonra bir müddet el.İM ayağ.IM tutmadı. 'After {the accident/the earthquake}, I was shaky for a while [lit., ** MY hand (and) MY foot did not hold].' Beni çok kızdırdı. * Sinir.DEN elim ayağım tutmuyordu. 'He made me very angry. * I was shaking [lit., ** MY hand (and) MY foot were not holding] WITH anger.' *127:14.* fear, frighteningness: - tremble; *152:25a.* anger: gestures of anger; *916:11.* agitation: - shake. → titre- 2.

* göz önünde tut- '- keep or - bear in mind, - remember, - realize, - consider' [göz 'eye', ön 'the front part of anything']: Başvurunuzu göz önünde tutuyoruz. 'We are considering your application.' Şimdi bütün ihtimalleri göz önünde tutalım. 'Now let's keep all the possibilities in mind.' Önerinizi göz önünde tutacağım. 'I'll keep your proposal in mind.' *930:12.* thought: - consider; *988:10.* memory: - remember.

3 '- detain, - hold up, - keep sb': Randevun var, biliyorum. Sen.İ tutmayayım. 'You have an appointment, I know. Don't let me hold you up.' *1011:14* hindrance: - prevent. → = /A/ mâni ol- → ol- 12.

4 '- restrain, - hold [back], - keep control of' *428:7.* restraint: - restrain: Gözyaşlarını tutamıyordu. 'She couldn't hold back her tears.' * Çişini tutamayınca çocuk altına yaptı. 'When the child couldn't hold it [lit., ** hold his urine back] anymore, he wet himself.'

* {çenesini/dilini} tut- '- hold one's tongue, - keep quiet' [çene 'jaw, chin', dil 'tongue']: Çene.N.i tut da söyleyeceğim.İ dikkatle dinle. 'Hold YOUR [s.] tongue and listen carefully TO what I'm going to say.' Sana kaç defa çene.N.i tutma.n.ı söyledim, yine de Sema'ya her şey.İ anlatmışsın. 'How many times have I told you to hold YOUR [s.] tongue, and yet it seems you've gone and told Sema everything.' Bu sırr.ım.ı * bir tek sana söylüyorum, çeneni tut, sakın kimseye söyleme. 'I'm

telling this secret [of mine] * only to you. Hold your [s.] tongue. Mind you, don't tell anyone.' Proverb: Dilini tutan başını kurtarır. 'He who holds his tongue will save his head.' *51:5.* silence: - be silent; *344:6.* uncommunicativeness: - keep to oneself. → ≠ ses çıkar- → çıkar- 7; *428:7.* restraint: - restrain.

nefes tut- '- hold one's breath' [A. nefes 'breath']: D o k t o r : Nefesinizi tutun. 'Doctor: Hold your breath.' *173:7.* quiescence: - be still. → içine çek- ['- inhale'] → çek- 1, nefes al- ['- breathe, - take a breath; - inhale'] → al- 1, nefes çek- ['- take a wiff, drag (of tobacco)] → çek- 1, nefes ver- ['- breathe out, - exhale, - let out a breath'] → ver- 1.

5 '- observe a ritual, - keep an observance or practice' *434:2.* observance: - observe: oruç tut- '- keep or - observe the fast, - fast' [oruç 'fast']: İslâm'ın beş şartı; kelime-i şehadet, namaz kılmak, zekât vermek, oruç tutmak ve hacca gitmektir. 'The five pillars [lit., (obligatory) conditions] of Islam are: the Shahadah [lit., the words of affirmation, i.e., to pronounce the words "There is no God but God and Muhammad is his Messenger"], to perform the namaz [i.e., the Islamic prayer ritual], to pay the zakat [i.e., the yearly alms tax required of Muslims, generally regarded as equal to 1/40th of one's property], to [observe the] fast, and to make the Pilgrimage [to Mecca].' Ramazanda 0 30 [otuz] gün oruç tuttum. 'During Ramadan I fasted FOR 30 days.' *515:4.* fasting: - fast; *701:14.* religious rites: - celebrate.

saat tut- '- time, - keep time, - watch the time, - keep track of the time' [A. saat 1 'hour; time'. 2 'watch, clock']: Saat tuttum, evden okula tam 25 dakikada geldik. 'I was watching the time. We came home from school in exactly 25 minutes.' Saat tutar mısın, bakalım su.yun alt.ı.nda ne kadar kalabileceğim? 'Will you keep time? Let's see how long I'll be able to stay under the water.' *831:11.* measurement of time: - time.

söz tut- '- take, - follow, - heed, or - listen to advice' [söz 1 'word, utterance'. 2 'promise']: **Bu çocuk çok yaramaz, hiç söz tutmuyor.** 'This child is very {bad/naughty}. He never listens to anyone.' *326:2.* obedience: - obey; *422:7.* advice: - take or - accept advice. → = {**lâf/söz**} **dinle-** → 1 dinle- 2.

sözünü tut- (1) '- keep one's promise, word': **Bu yıl okulumu bitireceğim.E [dair] annem.E söz verdim, söz.ÜM.ü tuttum.** 'I promised θ my mother θ that this year I would graduate [lit., ** finish my school]. I kept MY word.' **Önce söz.ÜN.ü tut, sonra namus.TAN bahset.** 'First keep YOUR [s.] word, then talk ABOUT honor.' *434:2.* observance: - observe. → = **sözünde dur-** → dur- 6, ≠ **sözünden dön-** → dön- 5.
(2) '- take, - follow, - heed, or - listen to the advice of sb, - take sb's advice': **Söz.ÜM.ü tutsaydın bunlar baş.ın.a gelmezdi.** 'If you had taken MY advice, these things would not have happened to you [lit., ** come to your head].' **Baş** 'head' here represents the whole person. **Sana Türkçe ders.i.ni al dedim ama söz.üm.ü tutmadın, şimdi pişmansın değil mi?** 'I told you to take the Turkish class, but you didn't take my advice. Now {you're sorry/you regret it}, don't you?' *326:2.* obedience: - obey; *422:7.* advice: - take or - accept advice. → = {**lâf/söz**} **dinle-** → 1 dinle- 2, = **uy-** 6, ≠ **sözünden çık-** → çık- 1.

* **yas tut-** '- mourn, - be in mourning' [**yas** 'mourning']: **Geçen yıl Fatma hanım.ın kocası vefat etti; hâlâ yas tutuyor.** 'Fatma hanım's husband died last year. She's still in mourning.' *112:17.* sadness: - grieve; *115:10.* lamentation: - lament; *434:2.* observance: - observe.

6 a) /DAn, A/ '- hire, - rent [vehicle, place] /from, FOR/': **Dün bir taksi tutacaklarmış ama paraları yetmemiş.** 'They were going to hire a taxi yesterday, but they didn't have enough money [lit., their money didn't suffice].' **Akdeniz turu için bir aylığ.ı.na 20 bin lira.yA bir yat tuttuk.** 'For a Mediterranean tour we hired a yacht for a month FOR 20,000 liras.' **Dün yeni bir ev tuttuk; muhtemelen gelecek ay taşınacağız.** 'We rented a new house yesterday. We'll probably move in next month.' *615:15.* commission: - rent. → = **kirala-** 1 .

b) /DAn/ '- hire, - engage [a person] /from/': **Komşumuz * yeni bir hizmetçi tuttu.** 'Our neighbor * has hired new help [lit., a new servant].' **Ben yeni bir {a: temizlikçi/b: aşçı/c: şoför/d: kapıcı} tutmak istiyorum.** 'I want to hire a new {a: cleaning woman [lit., ** cleaning person]/b: cook/c: driver/d: {caretaker/ doorman}}.' *615:14.* commission: - employ.

7 '- amount to, - come to, - add up to, - total, - cost, - make': S: **Acaba bura.dan ora.ya kaç.A götürürler?** 'Q: I wonder how much they'll charge to take sb from here to there? [lit., FOR how much they'll take sb from here to there?]' C: * **İyi bilmiyorum ama her halde 30 lira tutar.** 'A: I'm not sure [lit., ** I don't know well], but it will probably {come/amount} to 30 liras.' **Bu ayki yiyecek masrafımız {ne kadar/kaç lira} tuttu?** 'What [lit., {How much/How many liras}] did our food expenses for the month come to?' **Taksiyle Erenköy'e gitmek istiyoruz. * Ücret ne tutar?** 'We want to {take a taxi to Erenköy./lit., go to Erenköy by taxi.} * What's the fare?' * **Tur ne kadar tutar?** 'How much is the tour?' * **Fiyatı ne kadar tutacak?** '{How much will/What'll} it cost?' * **Hepsi {ne kadar/kaç lira} tuttu?** 'What's the total? [lit., {How much/How many liras} did they all (i.e., a series of items) add up to?]' *630:13.* price, fee: - cost; *791:8.* whole: - total; *1016:18.* mathematics: - sum up. → = /A/ **mal ol-** → ol- 12.

8 '- suffer from motion sickness, - get motion sick', i.e., from riding in a vehicle: * **Beni {a: deniz/b: otobüs/c: uçak/d: tren/e: motor/f: gemi} tutar.** 'I get {a: seasick/b: sick on a bus/c: airsick/d: sick on a train/e: sick on a motorboat/f: seasick [i.e., sick on a steamship]} [lit., ** the sea ... holds me.]' *85:46b.* disease: - take sick in particular ways.

9 '- assume, - imagine, - suppose for the sake of argument': {**Tutalım [ki]/Tut ki**} '{Let's suppose [that]/Suppose that}': **Biraz para**

tasarruf etmemiz lâzım. Tutalım ki birimiz hastalandık, o zaman ne yapacağız? 'We must save a little money. Suppose one of us gets sick, then what will we do?' Öğretmen: Tutalım [ki] bu küçük top ay, büyük top da dünya olsun. 'Teacher: Now let's assume [that] this small ball is the moon and that the large ball is the earth.' 950:19. theory, supposition: CONJ. supposing. → = de- 2, = {farz et-/varsay-}.

10 '- support a team': S: Hangi takım.I tutuyorsunuz, Galatasaray'I mı, Beşiktaş'I mı? 'Q: Which [soccer] team do you support, Galatasaray or Beşiktaş?' C1: * Galatasaray.lı.yım. 'A1: {I support Galatasaray./I am a Galatasaray supporter.} lit., ** I'm a Galatasarayan].' C2: Ben hiçbir takım.I tutmuyorum. 'A2: I don't support any team.' 124:10. hope: give hope; 492:16. courage: encourage. → destekle- ['- support financially, morally', not usually a team].

tutukla- [r] '- arrest sb, - put sb under arrest' [tutuk 'sb who is under arrest' + verb-forming suf. -lA]: Polis evimizi soyan hırsızı tutukladı. 'The police arrested the thief who had robbed our house.' 429:15. confinement: - arrest.

tutuklan- [ır] /{tarafından/CA}/ '- be arrested, - be put under arrest /by/' [tutukla- + pass. suf. -n]: Evimizi soyan hırsız dün gece mahallî polis tarafından tutuklandı. 'The thief who robbed our house was arrested by the local police last night.' 429:15. confinement: - arrest.

tutul- [ur] [tut- + {pass./refl.} suf. -Il]: 1 /DAn/ '- be grasped, seized, caught, taken hold of /BY/': Proverbs: El eliyle yılan tutulur. 'A snake is caught with someone else's hand.', i.e., Let someone else do the dirty work. İnsan sözü.nDEN, hayvan yuları.nDAN tutulur. 'A person is taken hold of [i.e., controlled] BY his {words/promises}, an animal BY its reins.' 474:6. retention: - hold, - grip; 480:14. taking: - seize. → = yakalan- 1.

2 '- be taken, occupied, held', for a seat, a place: * Bu yer tutuldu mu? 'Is this seat {taken/free}? [lit.,

Has this place been taken?]' The same idea is also commonly expressed as follows: Bu yer.in sahib.i var mı? lit., ** 'Does this place have an owner?' 474:7. retention: - hold, - keep; 480:14. taking: - seize.

3 /CA, arasında/ 'for sth - catch on, - become popular or fashionable, - win a following /{IN/AMONG}, {IN/among}/': İsmet Özel'in yeni kitabı {edebiyat çevreleri.nCE/ üniversite öğrencileri.nCE} çok tutuldu. 'İsmet Özel's new book has really become popular {IN literary circles/AMONG {college/ university} students}.' Bu şarkı * aramızda çok tutuldu. 'This song * became very popular IN our crowd [lit., among us].' 578:8. fashion: - catch on.

4 '- go into eclipse': {Ay/Güneş} tutuldu. 'The {sun/moon} has gone into eclipse.' Ay tutulması dünya.nın güneş.le ay ara.sı.na girmesiyle oluşur. 'An eclipse of the moon occurs when the earth comes [lit., with the earth's entering] between the sun and the moon.' Güneş tutulması ay.ın güneş.le dünya ara.sı.na girmesiyle oluşur. 'An eclipse of the sun occurs when the moon comes [lit., with the moon's entering] between the sun and the earth.' 1026:9. darkness, dimness: - darken.

5 /DAn/ 'for a part of one's body - get stiff /from/': Bütün gün sandalyede oturmak.tan {a: ensem/b: boynum /c: sırtım/d: belim/e: kolum/f: bacaklarım} tutuldu. 'From sitting in a chair the whole day {a: my neck [i.e., the back part of it]/b: my neck [i.e., the front part of it] [boyun, boynu]/c: my back [i.e., from the shoulders to the waist]/d: my lower back/e: my arm/f: my legs} got stiff.' 393:13. impairment: <- inflict an injury>; 1044:9. hardness, rigidity: - stiffen.

6 /A/ '- be caught /IN/ certain unfavorable weather conditions': Proverb: Yağmur.dan kaçarken dolu.yA tutuldu. 'While escaping from the rain, he got caught IN the hail.' {From/Out of} the frying pan into the fire. 317:10. air, weather: - air; 393:48. impairment: ADV. out of the frying pan into the fire. → = yakalan- 4.

tutuş-. → yanıp tutuş- → yan- 7.

tuvalet yap-. → yap- 3.

tuvalete git-. → git- 1a.

tuvaleti gel-. → gel- 1.

tüken- [ir] '- run out, - give out, - sell out': * {Şeker/Elma/Tereyağı} tükendi. 'We've run out of {sugar/apples/butter} [lit., The sugar...has run out].' * Bütün paramız tükendi. '{We've run out of money/lit., All our money has run out}.' Suyumuz tükenince çeşitli bitkiler {ye.mekle/ yi.yerek} idare ettik. 'When our water ran out, we managed {by eat.ing} different kinds of plants.' Biletler.in {a: hep.si/b: çoğ.u/c: yarı.sı/d: yüzde 75'i [read: yetmiş beş.i]} tükendi. '{a: All of/b: Most of/c: Half of/d: 75 percent of} the tickets have sold out.' Proverb: Kanaat tükenmez hazinedir. 'Contentment [i.e., with what God has granted] is an inexhaustible treasure.' 388:4. consumption: - be consumed. → = bit- 3.

{gücü/takatı} tüken- 'for one's strength - give out, - be exhausted, tired out' [{güç/A. takat} 'strength']: {Güc.ÜM/Takat.IM} tükendi, lütfen biraz dinlenelim. 'I'm tired out [lit., ** MY strength has given out]. Please let's rest a bit.' 21:5. fatigue: - burn out.

sabrı tüken- 'for one's patience - run out or - be exhausted' [A. sabır (saBRı) 'patience']: * Benim de sabrım tükendi artık. Sen.DEN ayrılıyorum. 'I've finally had it, too [lit., My patience, too, has finally run out]. I'm leaving θ you.' 135:5. impatience: - have no patience with. → = sabırsızlan- ['- get, - become, or - be impatient'], ≠ sabret- ['- be patient'].

tükür- [ür] /A/ '- spit /{ON/IN/INTO}/': Lütfen yerler.E tükürmeyiniz. 'Please don't spit ON the ground.' 352:7. publication: poster: * specific signs. Doktor "Tahlil yapmamız gerekiyor, lütfen şu bardağ.A tükürün" dedi. 'The doctor said, "We must {run a test/lit., do an analysis}, please spit INTO this glass".' * Öyle zor durumdayım

ki! [Proverb:] * Aşağı tükürsen sakal, yukarı tükürsen bıyık! 'I'm in a really tight spot [lit., I'm in such a difficult position that]! * I'm between a rock and a hard place [lit., If you spit downwards (you get it in your) beard, if you spit upwards (you get it in your) moustache].' Yukarı.yA tükürme yüzün.E düşer. 'Do not spit upward. It will fall [back] ON your face.', i.e., If you insult those in a position above you, you will eventually suffer. 13:6. secretion: - salivate.

- U -

ucuzla- [r] '- get cheaper, - go down or - drop in price' [ucuz 'cheap' + verb-forming suf. -lA]: Karpuz ucuzladı. Acaba kavun ne zaman ucuzlayacak? 'Watermelons have gotten cheaper. I wonder when [other] melons will drop in price.' 252:6. decrease: - decrease; 633:6b. cheapness: - become cheaper. → = fiyatlar düş- → düş- 3, = fiyatlar in- → in- 4, ≠ fiyatlar fırla- ['for prices - skyrocket, - increase or rise suddenly, - soar, - jump'] → fırla- 2, ≠ fiyatlar tırman- → tırman- 2, ≠ fiyatlar yüksel- → yüksel- 2, ≠ pahalan-.

uç- [ar] /a: A, b: lA, c: üzerinde/ '- fly /a: to, b: IN, c: over/, - fly away': Yarın İstanbul'a uçuyorum. 'I'm flying to Istanbul tomorrow.' * İstanbul dönüşü doğrudan doğruya New York'a uçtum. 'After returning to Istanbul, I flew directly to New York.' → = uçakla git- → git- 1a. Türk Hava Yolları [THY] dünyanın bütün büyük şehirleri.ne uçar. 'Turkish airlines flies to all the world's major cities.' * Devlet Başkanları özel uçakları İLE uçarlar. 'Ministers of state fly IN their private planes.' Uçağımız saat 6 sularında İtalya üzerinde uçuyordu. 'At about six o'clock our plane was flying OVER Italy.' Hangi yükseklik.te uçuyoruz? 'At what altitude are we flying?' Deniz.in üzer.i.nde martılar uçuyordu. 'Gulls were flying OVER the ocean.' Lindbergh, New York'tan Paris'e 33 saat 29,5 [yirmi dokuz buçuk] dakikada uçtu. 'Lindbergh flew from New York to Paris in 33 hours and 29 1/2 minutes.' Proverbs: Allah uçamayan kuşa alçacık dal verir. 'God gives a bird that cannot fly a very low branch.' Gençlik bir kuştur, * uçtu mu tutamazsın. 'Youth is a bird: * once it has flown away, you can't catch it [again].' Kanatsız kuş uçmaz. 'A bird without wings can't [lit., doesn't] fly.', i.e., Qualifications are required for success. Tek kanatla kuş uçmaz. 'A bird with [only] one wing can't [lit., doesn't] fly.', i.e., Limited qualifications are not enough. *184:36.* aviation: - fly. → uçak kullan- ['- fly a plane'].

* havaya uç- '- blow up' [A. hava 'air'], lit., '- fly INTO the air': {Füzenin isabet ettiği bina/Cephaneler} havaya uçtu. '{The building that the missile hit/The amunition} blew up.' *671:14.* violence: - explode.

uçak kaçır-. → kaçır- 3.

uçak kullan-. → kullan-.

uçakla git-. → git- 1a.

uçur- [ur] '- make fly, - blow about, away' [uç- + caus. suf. -Ir]: Rüzgâr Suna'nın {saçlarını/kâğıtlarını} uçuruyordu. 'The wind was blowing Suna's {hair/papers} about.' *318:20.* wind: - blow.

* havaya uçur- '- blow sth up' [A. hava 'air'], lit., ** '- cause to fly INTO the air': Teröristler başkanlık saray.ı.nı havaya uçurdu. 'Terrorists blew up the presidential palace.' *395:18.* destruction: - blow up.

uçurtma uçur- '- fly a kite, kites': Yusuf uçurtma uçurmay.I çok sever. 'Yusuf loves {to fly/flying} kites.' *184:37.* aviation: - pilot; *744:10.* sports: throwing sports.

uğra- [r] 1 /A/ '- stop in /AT/, - drop in /{AT/ON}/, - drop /BY/, - call /{ON/UPON}/, - call in /AT/, - stop off /IN/', person or vehicle as subject: Person as subject: * {Bir ara} biz.E uğrayın. 'Drop in AT our place [lit., ** AT us] {sometime/at some point}.' Buraya kadar yürümüşken, bari bizim ev.E de uğrayalım. 'Since we've walked this far, let's at least drop in AT our house too.' {Vaktim olursa/Vakit bulursam} kütüphane.yE

uğrayacağım. '{If I have [the] time/If I find [the] time}, I'm going to stop in AT the library.' Dün san.A uğrayacaktım ama vaktim {olmadı/yoktu}. 'I was going to call ON you yesterday, but I had no time.' Oktay yarın otele gelebilirse ban.A uğrasın. 'If Oktay can come to the hotel tomorrow, have him drop in ON me.' Tekrar ne zaman uğrayayım? 'When should I drop {BY/IN} again?' Ankara'ya giderken İstanbul'A da uğrayacağım, ama orada {olsa olsa/en fazla} iki gün kalırım her halde. 'On my way to Ankara [lit., While going to Ankara], I'll stop off IN Istanbul too, but I'll probably stay there {at most} [only] two days.' *582:19.* sociability: - visit. Vehicle as subject: Gemi hangi limanlar.A uğrayacak? 'AT which ports will the ship call in?' *189:7* entrance: - enter.

2 /A/ '- meet /WITH/, - encounter /θ/, - experience, - be up against', usually a difficult situation: Adamın bütün eşyaları çalınmış. * Ne.yE uğradığını şaşırdı. 'All the man's possessions had been stolen. * {He couldn't understand what had happened to him./He didn't know what had hit him.}' Korktuğum.A uğradım. '{What I had feared happened./I was up against what I had feared.}' A more common equivalent: Korktuğum baş.IM.a geldi. lit., ** 'What I had feared came to MY head.', where baş 'head' represents the whole person. *830:8.* event: - experience; *1012:11.* difficulty: - have difficulty. → = /DA/ {güçlük/zorluk} çek- → çek- 5, = /DA/ zorlan- 3, = {zorluk.LA/ güçlük.LE} karşılaş- → karşılaş- 3, = ye- 2.

* {hayal/düş} kırıklığına uğra- '- be disappointed' [A. hayal (. -) 'imagined thing', düş 'dream', kırıklık 'brokenness']: Tatil için Antalya'ya gidemeyeceğimizi öğrenince {hayal/düş} kırıklığ.ı.nA uğradım. 'When I learned that we wouldn't be able to go to Antalya for the holidays, I was disappointed.' *132:4.* disappointment: - be disappointed.

uğraş- [ır] 1 /için/ '- strive, - struggle, - endeavor /TO/, - exert oneself, - put forth an effort /for/, - work hard

396

/for/': **Bütün gün matematik ödev.im.i bitirmek için uğraştım.** 'I struggled the whole day TO finish my math homework.' *403:11.* endeavor: - make a special effort. → = **çabala-, çalış- 2** ['- try /to/, - attempt /to/'], {**emek/çaba**} **harca-** ['- expend effort /{for/ON}/ sth, - take pains /to/ do sth'] → {harca-/sarf et-} 1, **emek ver-** ['- put effort /INTO/, - devote effort /to/, - work /AT/, - take pains /WITH/'] → **ver-** 1.

2 /lA/ '- work /ON/, - be engaged /IN/, - be busy or occupied /with/, - devote oneself /TO/ a task': **Hayatı boyunca başkaları.nın dertler.i İLE uğraştı.** 'Throughout his life he {devoted himself TO/was occupied WITH/worked on} other people's problems.' * **Hangi sporlar.LA uğraşıyorsunuz?** 'Which sports do you engage IN?' *724:11.* occupation: - busy oneself with. → = **meşgul ol-** 1 → **ol-** 12.

3 /lA/ *fig.* '- put up /with/ a person': **S: Baba, bugün * pazara gitmesek olmaz mı?** 'Q: Dad, * how about it if we don't go to the market today?' **C: Eee, ha[y]di yürü yahu. Bir de seninle mi uğraşacağız?** 'A: Come on, on with you! Do we have to put up with you too?' *134:5.* patience: - endure.

uğrat- [ır] /A/ '- cause sb - meet /with/ or - encounter /θ/ a difficulty, disaster' [uğra- + caus. suf. -t]: {**hayal/düş**} **kırıklığına uğrat-** '- disappoint': **Senden çok şeyler bekliyorduk, biz.İ hayal kırıklığı.nA uğrattın.** 'We expected a lot from you, but you disappointed us.' **Bu yeni hükümet de seçmen.İ hayal kırıklığı.nA uğrattı.** 'This new government also disappointed the electorate.' *132:2.* disappointment: - disappoint.

uğurla- [r] /A/ '- wish a departing traveler a safe journey, - wish sb Godspeed, - send or - see sb off /to/' [uğur 'good luck' + verb-forming suf. -lA]: **Kardeşim.İ dün Almanya'yA uğurlarken "{a: Yolun açık olsun/b: Sağlıcakla git/c: Uğurlar olsun/d: Hayırlı yolculuklar}" dedik.** 'While sending {my brother/my sister} off /to/ Germany yesterday, we said "{a: Have a good journey/b: Go in good health and happiness/c: Have a safe

trip/d: May your journey go well}!"' * **Görüşme sonra.sı * kapı.ya kadar uğurladı.** 'After the meeting, * he took him as far as the door [i.e., when sending him off].' *188:16.* departure: - say or - bid good-bye; *504:13.* courtesy: - give one's regards. → = **yolcu et-**, *noun of person* **gönder-** ['- send sb off /to/' a place].

Uğurlar olsun. → directly above and under **ol-** 11. → **olsun.**

ulaş- [ır] 1 /A/ '- reach /θ/, - arrive /AT/, - get /to/ a place': **Akşam vakti köy.E ulaştık.** 'We {reached θ/arrived AT} the village in the evening.' **Tren [saat] kaçta Adana'yA ulaşır?** 'At what time will the train reach θ Adana?' **Biz.E toplantının sonuçları hakkında henüz tam ve ayrıntılı bilgi ulaşmadı.** 'Complete and detailed information on the results of the meeting have not yet reached θ us.' **Bu hedef.E ulaş.abilmek için daha zaman.A ihtiyaç var.** 'To reach [lit., To be able to reach] θ this goal, more time is required.' Proverb: **Ağaç ne kadar uzasa göğ.E ulaşmaz.** 'No matter how tall a tree grows, it never reaches θ the sky.', i.e., No one keeps improving his position forever. **Eğer bu formülü uygularsak çözüm.E ulaşabiliriz.** 'If we apply this mathematical formula, we can arrive AT a solution.' **Karantina altına alınanların sayısı 10 bin.E ulaştı.** 'The number of those quarantined [lit., taken under quarantine] reached θ 10,000.' *158:8.* space: - extend; *186:6.* arrival: - arrive. → = **er-**, = **eriş-** 1, = **var-**, = **gel-** 1, ≠ **hareket et-** 2.

2 /A/ '- reach /θ/, - contact /θ/, - get in touch /WITH/': In regard to telephone communication: **S: Siz.E nasıl ulaşabiliriz?** 'Q: How can we reach θ you?' **C: * Ben.İ iş yerim.DEN hafta iç.i saat 9-5 [read: dokuz beş] arası şu telefon numara.sı.nDAN arayabilirsiniz.** 'A: You can reach [lit., ** look for] me AT my place of work weekdays between 9 and 5 AT the following phone number.' * **Ban.A 347 15 00'DAN [read: üç yüz kırk yedi onbeş çift sıfır.DAN] ulaşabilirsiniz.** 'You can reach me AT 347 15 00 [lit., ** pair zero].' **Bu numarayı arayarak biz.E**

ulaşabilirsiniz. 'You can reach us by calling this number.' *343:8*. communication: - communicate with, - get in touch with.

ulaşıl- [ır] /DAn/ '- be reached, contacted /AT/': Ahmet'E bu numara.DAN ulaşılabilir. 'θ Ahmet can be reached AT this [telephone] number.' *343:8*. communication: - communicate with, - get in touch with.

ulaştır- [ır] /A/ '- transport, - convey, - bring, or - get sth /to/' [ulaş- + caus. suf. -DIr]: Tren bizi 6 [altı] saatte bura.yA ulaştırdı. 'The train brought us θ here in six hours.' Saat beşe kadar evraklarını biz.e ulaştırırsan imzalatabilirsin. 'If you can get your documents to us by five o'clock, you can have them signed.' → = getir-. # Bu resimleri annem.e ulaştırabilir misiniz? 'Can you get these pictures to my mother?' *176:12*. transferal, transportation: - transport; *176:15*. : - send. → = ilet-1, gönder- ['- send sth /to/ sb, - send θ sb sth'], yolla-. Same.

um-. → {ümit et-/um-}.

{umudunu/ümidini} kaybet-. → {kaybet-/yitir-}.

{umutlan- [ır]/ümitlen- [ir]} '- become hopeful, - begin to hope, - get one's hopes up' [{umut (umuDu)/ümit (ümiDi)} 'hope' + verb-forming suf. -lAn} 'hope']: * Boşuna umutlanma! Geri dönmeyecek. 'Don't get your hopes up {for nothing/in vain}! He won't {come back/return}.' *124:8*. hope: - be hopeful.

unut- [ur] /DA/ '- forget /at/': a) Forget an object: The literal meaning of the Turkish is '- forget', but the more frequent English equivalent is '- leave': Kitabımı kütüphane.de unuttum. 'I left [lit., forgot] my book at the library.' Çantamı ev.de unuttum. 'I forgot my {handbag/purse/briefcase} at home.'

anahtarı içeride unut- '- lock oneself out of a place' [anahtar 'key', içeride 'inside'], lit., '- forget the key inside': * Bak şu baş.IM.a gelen.e! Anahtarı içeride unutmuşum, * dışarıda kaldım. 'Now just look what happened to me

[lit., ** what came to MY head]! I seem to have left [lit., forgot] my [lit., the] key inside. * I'm locked out [lit., ** I have remained outside].' *293:6*. closure: - close. → = dışarıda kal- ['- be locked out', lit., '- remain outside'] → kal- 1, = kapıda kal- ['- be locked out', lit., ' - remain at the door'] → kal- 1.

b) Forget knowledge: a past occurrence or intention: * Unutmadan söyleyeyim... 'Before I forget let me just say...' Öğrendiklerim.in bir kısm.ı.nı unuttum. Çok unutkanım. 'I forgot some [lit., a part] of what I had learned. I'm very forgetful.' Yaşadığımız kâbusu ömrümüz boyunca unutamayız. 'As long as we live, we'll never be able to forget the nightmare [that] we've lived through.' Hiç unutmam... 'I'll never forget [i.e., the {day/time} when]...': Hiç unutmam, o yaz deniz kenarında küçük bir motelde kalıyorduk. 'I'll never forget: That summer we were staying at the shore in a small motel.' Unutmamak gerekir ki... '{One must not forget.../It must not be forgotten that...}' O filmi daha önce {seyret.tiğ.i.nİ/seyretmiş ol.duğ.u.nU} unutmuştu. 'He had forgotten {that he had seen} that movie before.' O filmi {seyr.edeceğ.i.ni} unutmuştu. 'He had forgotten {that he was going to see} that film.' Şu bilgisayar.A bir türlü alışamıyorum; programlar.A nasıl gir.il.e.ceğini {hep/sürekli} unutuyorum. 'I simply can't get used to that computer. I keep forgetting [or I'm {always} forgetting] how to enter the programs [lit., how the programs are entered].' Proverb: Alim unutmuş, kalem unutmamış. 'The scholar forgot, but the pen did not.', i.e., A fact is preserved only if it is written down.

c) Forget to carry out an action: * Nihal'le sinemaya gidecektik. * Nasıl da unuttum! * Çok ayıp ettim. '{I was/We were} going to go to the movies with Nihal. * How could I {forget/have forgotten}! * I behaved shamefully.' * Haa, bak [az kalsın] unutuyordum. Bu akşam bir iş toplantım var, biraz gecikebilirim, merak etme. 'Oh look, I almost forgot. This evening I have a work-related meeting. I may be a little late. Don't worry.' O filmi seyretmey.İ unuttu. 'He forgot TO SEE that film.' Bakkala gitmey.İ unutursam ban.A hatırlat. 'If I forget to go to the grocery store, remind θ me.' * Bakkala gitmey.İ unutmazsın, değil mi? 'You won't forget to go to the grocery store, will you?' In the following, note that '- REMEMBER to...' is expressed with the Turkish of 'Don't FORGET to...': * Çiçekler.İ sulamay.ı unutma! '{Don't forget/Remember} to water the flowers!' Yarın bakkala gitmelisin. Sakın unutma! 'You must go to the grocery store tomorrow. Mind you, don't forget!' * Sakın unutmuş olmayın. 'I do hope you haven't forgotten [lit., ** Mind you, do not be having forgotten].' 989:5. forgetfulness: - forget. → = aklından çık- → çık- 1, ≠ {hatırla-/anımsa-}, ≠ bul- 4 ['- remember, - have it', when one suddenly remembers sth forgotten].

usan-. → {bık-/usan-}.

utan- [ır] /a: DAn, b: DAn dolayı, c: A/ '- be ashamed /a: OF, b: on account of, c: OF/, - be embarrassed /on account of/': Aydın benden borç isterken çok utandı. 'Aydın was very embarrassed when asking me for a loan.' Baba.sı Adnan'ı sigara içerken gördü. Adnan çok utandı. 'Adnan's father saw Adnan smoking [lit., ** His father saw Adnan smoking]. Adnan was very embarrassed.' * Hiç utanmadan sıkılmadan yalan söylüyor. 'He lies without the slightest shame or regret.' NON-verbal noun as object: Partideki {hoş olmayan davranışları.nDAN/hoş olma-yan davranışları.nDAN DOLAYI} çok utandı. 'He was very ashamed {OF his bad behavior/ON ACCOUNT OF his bad behavior} at the party.' Proverb: Utan utanmaz.DAN, kork korkmaz.DAN. 'Be ashamed OF a shameless person and fear θ a fearless person.' Utan! 'For shame!, Shame on you!' 510:27. disapproval: INTERJ. God forbid! VERBAL noun as object: * Anne.nE böyle davranmay.A utanmıyor musun? 'Aren't you ashamed OF behaving like this TOWARD your mother?' 96:15. unpleasure: - chagrin; 137:9a.

humility: - be humiliated. → = sıkıl- 2, ≠ gurur duy- 1 → duy- 3, ≠ iftihar et-, ≠ kıvanç duy- → duy-3, ≠ övün- 1, kızar- ['- turn red, - redden, - blush', i.e., a sign of embarrassment].

uy- [ar]. All definitions involve the appropriateness or suitability of one item or situation for another. 1 /A/ '- fit /θ/, - be the right size and shape /FOR/': Bu araba verilen tarif.E uyuyor. 'This car fits θ the description provided [lit., given].' Anahtar kilid.E uymuyor. {Anahtarcı çağırmamız lâzım./* Herhalde yanlış anahtarı almışım.} 'The key doesn't fit θ the lock. {We must call the locksmith./* I must have taken the wrong key.}' A person is trying on a suit. He says: S: * Elbise üst.ÜM.E uydu mu? 'Q: Does the suit fit me?' [üst 'the body excluding the head and feet', lit., ** 'Does the suit fit θ MY body?'] In this context uydu refers to a present situation so it is appropriately translated with the present tense. If the same question occurred in past time, i.e., yesterday, the same verb would be translated with the past tense. • In reference to a PRESENT condition, certain common Turkish verbs designating a state, i.e., a feeling, emotion, or sensation, often have the simple PAST tense, but the equivalent English has the simple PRESENT tense. C1: Çok iyi {uydu./uyuyor.} 'A1: It {fits} very well.' or C2: Hiç {uymadı./uymuyor.} 'A2: It {doesn't fit} at all.' * O elbiseyi kendin.E nasıl yakıştırdın, san.A hiç uymadı. 'How could you have imagined that that suit would look good on you! It doesn't fit θ you at all!' 866:3. conformity: - conform. → = ol- 8, = yakış- 2 ['for sth - look good /ON/, - suit /θ/', clothing], dur- 9 ['- look, - appear /ON, - suit, - fit', clothing], gel- 2 ['- be a certain size /FOR/, - fit'].

2 /A/ '- suit /θ/, - be right, suitable /FOR/' [ADJ. uygun 'suitable, appropriate']: Bu fiyat {san.A/ hesabın.A} uyuyor mu? 'Does this price suit {θ you/θ your pocketbook [lit., your account]}?' O dersi almak isterdim ama * saatleri ban.A uymuyor. 'I would like to take that class, but * the time

isn't right FOR me [lit., ** its hours don't suit me].' Proverb: **Evdeki hesap çarşı.yA uymaz.** 'Calculations [i.e., about what things will cost] made at home won't be right FOR the market.', i.e., Plans made may not be realistic. *842:6.* timeliness: - be timely; *866:3.* conformity: - conform.

3 /A/ '- match /θ/, - go [well] /WITH/, - look good /WITH/, - go together': **Yeni perdeler koltuk takım.ı.nA uydu mu?** 'Did the new curtains {match θ/go WITH} the chair set?' **Bu renkler birbiri.nE uymuş.** 'These colors go well together.' *866:3.* conformity: - conform.

4 /A/ '- be compatible /WITH/, - conform /to/': **Bu video kasetini Türkiye'de seyredemeyiz. Çünkü Türk televizyon sistem.i.nE uymuyor.** 'We can't watch this video cassette in Turkey because it isn't compatible WITH the Turkish TV system.' **Bu makinayı Türkiye'de kullanamam, çünkü bizim elektrik sistem.i.nE uymuyor.** 'I can't use this machine in Turkey because it isn't compatible WITH our electrical system.' **İnsanın dedikleriyle davranışları birbiri.nE uymalı, * öz.ü söz.ü bir olmalı.** 'What a person says and what he does [lit., his behavior] must {be in accord [WITH one another]/colloq. jibe}. His essential being [lit., essence] and his words must be one.' **Bu adam hiçbir katil tip.i.ne uymuyor.** 'This man doesn't conform to any of the standard "murderer" types.' *866:3.* conformity: - conform.

5 /A/ '- comply /WITH/, - conform /to/, - follow or - act in accordance /WITH/ rules, regulations': **Eğer bu ülkede yaşamak istiyorsan, {kanunlar.ımız.A/kurallar.ımız.A} uyacaksın.** 'If you want to live in this country, you {must/lit., will} comply {WITH our laws/WITH our rules}.' **Garson şiş kebap ye.me.MİZ.i tavsiye etti ama biz * tavsiyesi.nİ dinlemedik. * Keşke tavsiyesi.nE uysaydık!** 'The waiter recommended that WE eat [lit., OUR eating] shish kebab, but we didn't take [lit., listen to] his recommendation. * If only we had followed θ his advice!' Proverbs: **Zaman san.A uymazsa sen**

zaman.A uy. 'If the time is not suitable FOR you, adapt yourself TO the time.' **Zaman.A uymak gerek.** 'One must conform to the times.' *326:2.* obedience: - obey; *434:2.* observance: - observe; *866:3.* conformity: - conform; *866:10.* : don't rock the boat. → **yerine getir-** 1 ['- carry out, - perform, - execute an order, a wish'], **çiğne-** 3 ['- violate laws, rules, principles'].

6 /A/ '- obey /θ/, - heed /θ/, - listen /to/, - act in accordance with the wishes of': **Şu çocuk kimse.ye uymaz, * hep istediğini yapar.** 'That child doesn't listen to anyone. * He always does just {as he likes/what he wants}.' **Gençler genellikle * büyükler.i.nin dedikler.i.ne uymazlar.** 'Young people generally * don't listen to their elders [lit., to what their elders say].' * **Şeytan.a uydum, bir hata işledim, çok pişmanım.** 'I {followed Satan's orders./did what Satan told me to do./listened to Satan}. I made a mistake. I'm very sorry.' *326:2.* obedience: - obey. → = {lâf/söz} **dinle-** → 1 dinle- 2, = **söz tut-** → tut- 5, ≠ **sözünden çık-** → çık- 1.

7 /A/ '- follow /θ/, - follow the example of, - act in accord /WITH/, - emulate /θ/, - imitate the actions of': **Namazda cemaat imam.A uyar.** 'In the namaz [i.e., the Muslim prayer ritual] the members of the community follow θ [the lead of] the imam.' **Yaramazlar.A uymak olmaz.** 'It won't do {to follow the example of/to emulate} θ those who {are naughty/misbehave}.' *336:7.* imitation: - emulate.

uyan- [ır] '- wake up, - awake' [ADJ. **uyanık** 'awake']: **Dün sabah {[çok] erken/* erken.den/[çok] geç} uyandım.** 'I woke up {[very] early/* early/[very] late} yesterday morning.' **Ha[y]di uyan * artık saat on oldu, iş.E geç kalacaksın.** 'Come on, wake up. * It's already 10 o'clock. You'll be late FOR work.' *23:4.* wakefulness: - awake. → **kalk-** 1 ['- get up, - rise'], ≠ **uyu-** 2, **yat-** 1 ['- go to bed, - lie down, - retire for the night'], ≠ **uykuya dal-** ['- fall asleep; - doze off, - drop off /to/ sleep'] → dal- 2, ≠ **uyukla-** ['- doze, - doze off'].

uyandır- [ır] '- wake sb up, - awaken sb' [uyan- + caus. suf. -DIr]: Lütfen beni yarın sabah saat beşte uyandırın. 'Please wake me up tomorrow morning at five o'clock.' Ev arkadaşını uyandırmamaya çalışarak sessizce kapıyı açtı. 'Trying not to wake up his roommate [lit., his housemate], he quietly opened the door.' Proverb: Uyuyan aslan.ı uyandırma. 'Don't wake up {a/the} sleeping lion.' Let sleeping dogs lie. 23:5. wakefulness: - wake sb up. → kaldır- 2 ['- get sb up from bed'].

{uyar- [ır]/ikaz et- [eDer]/ihtar et- [eDer]} /için, diye/ '- warn sb /{to/about}, THAT [lit., saying]/' [A. ikaz (- -) 'warning']: Warning against an action: Arkadaşının {sınav/imtihan} kâğıdına baktığını görünce öğretmen Tülay'I uyardı. 'When he observed Tülay looking at her friend's {examination} paper, the teacher warned her [lit., ** When he observed her looking at her friend's examination paper, the teacher warned Tülay].' {Onu yap.MA-.ma.N/Oraya git.ME.me.N} için sen.i kaç defa uyardım, ama beni dinlemedin. 'How many times have I warned {YOU NOT to do that/YOU NOT to go there}, but you didn't listen to me.'
Warning, informing about a future possibility: * Annem kızacak DİYE sen.i uyarmıştım. 'I had warned you THAT [lit., ** SAYING] my mother would get angry.' 'Adam intihar edecek' DİYE uyardık. * Dinleyen olmadı. 'We warned them THAT the man would commit suicide. * Nobody listened [lit., ** There was no one who listened].' Cemil borcunu ödemez diye seni uyarmıştım. 'I had warned you that Cemil {doesn't/won't/wouldn't} pay his debts.' Faizlerin düşeceğini biliyordunuz. {Neden beni uyarma-dınız?/Beni uyarabilirdiniz.} 'You knew that interest rates were going to fall. {Why didn't you warn me?/You could have warned me.}' İyi ki bizleri uyardınız. 'It's a good thing you warned us.' 399:5. warning: - warn.

uydur- [ur] [uy- + caus. suf. -DIr] 1 /A/ '- make one thing fit /{θ/INTO}/ another, - improvise, i.e., - fabricate out of what is conveniently on hand

/FOR/': Hırsız kilid.E bir anahtar uydurup kapıyı açmış. 'The thief improvised a key FOR the lock and opened the door.' 866:3. conformity: - conform; 891:12. production: - originate.

2 /I/ '- make up, - invent, - dream up, - concoct, - think up': Hatasını örtmek için türlü türlü {hikâyeler/yalanlar} uydurdu. 'To cover up his mistake, he concocted all kinds of {stories/lies}.' Biliyorsan konuş, uydurma! 'If you know, {out with it/say it}. Don't make things up!' Proverb: Sağır duymaz, uydurur. 'A deaf person doesn't hear; he makes up things.', i.e., He fills in with his imagination for what he can't hear. 354:18. falseness: - fabricate.

3 /I/ '- manage to scrape together or to come up with': Someone has to leave and dress quickly with what is available. He says: Üzeri.m.E bir şeyler uydurup hemen çıkıyorum, * yarım saat SONRA oradayım. 'I managed to scrape together some clothes [lit., ** some things FOR over myself]. I'm leaving right away. * I'll be [lit., ** I am] there IN half an hour.' 769:18. assemblage: - bring or - gather together.

uygula- [r] /A/ '- carry out, - apply /to/, - follow, - put a plan, law, or formula into practice' [uy- + noun-forming suf. -GI + verb-forming suf. -lA]: Doktorunuz.un öneriler.i.ni dikkatle uygulayın. 'Follow your doctors {recommendations/ directions} carefully.' Eğer bu formülü uygularsak çözüm.E ulaşabiliriz. 'If we apply this mathematical formula, we can arrive AT a solution.' Üniversiteler yeni yönetmeliği uygulamaya başla-dılar. '{The universities/The colleges} have begun to {apply/enforce} the new regulations.' Orhan'ın fikirler.i çok güzel ama önce kendi uygulasa iyi olur. 'Orhan's ideas are wonderful [lit., very fine], but he should [lit., it would be good for him to] apply them first himself.' Pasta.nın nasıl yapıldığ.ı.nı öğrendik şimdi uygulayalım. 'We have learned how the cake is made. Now let's apply [that knowledge].' Ben tarifi {a: aynen/b: olduğu gibi/c: titizlikle/d: en ince noktasına kadar} uyguladım ama olmadı. 'I followed the recipe {a: exactly/b: as it was [written]/c: precisely/d: down to the smallest detail}, but it didn't turn out [right].' *387:11.* use: - apply.

uygun düş-. → düş- 1.

uyku getir-. → getir-.

uykusu gel-. → gel- 1.

uykusu kaç-. → kaç- 1.

uykusunu getir-. → getir-.

uykusunu kaçır-. → kaçır- 3.

uykuya dal-. → dal- 2.

<u>uyu</u>- [r] **1** '- sleep': S: **Dün gece iyi uyudunuz mu?** 'Q: Did you sleep well last night?' C: {**Evet, çok iyi uyudum./Maalesef fazla kahve içtiğim için hiç uyuyamadım.**} 'A: {Yes, I slept very well./Unfortunately I couldn't sleep at all because I had [drunk] too much coffee.}' **Dün gece sadece üç saat uyudum.** 'I slept [for] only three hours last night.' **Doktor bey, geceleri uyuyamıyorum.** * **Neyim var?** 'Doctor θ, I can't sleep at night. * What's the matter with me? [lit., What do I have?]' **Telefon çaldığında uyuyordum.** 'I was sleeping when the phone rang.' **Huzur içinde rahat uyusun.** 'May he rest in peace [lit., May he sleep comfortably in peace]', said upon hearing of the death of a Muslim or non-Muslim. *307: * 39.* death: expressions used upon hearing of a death; *504: * 20.* courtesy: polite expressions. <u>Proverbs</u>: **Su uyur, düşman uyumaz.** 'Water sleeps [i.e., becomes motionless], but an enemy does not [sleep].', i.e., Be alert. **Uyuyan aslan.I uyandırma.** 'Don't wake up {a/the} sleeping lion.' Let sleeping dogs lie. **Uyuyan yılanın kuyruğu.nA basma.** 'Don't step ON the tail of a sleeping snake.' *22:13.* sleep: - sleep.

çok uyu- '- sleep a lot, too much, - oversleep': **Çok uyumaktan dersi kaçırdım.** 'Because I overslept, I missed the class.' **Dün geceki parti çok geç bitti, onun için çok uyudum.** 'The party ended very late last night. That's why I

{overslept/slept a lot}.' *22:13.* sleep: - sleep; *992:10.* excess: - overdo.

2 '- go to sleep, - fall asleep, - drop off to sleep': **Dün gece saat 11:30'da** [read: **onbir buçukta**] **uyudum.** 'I went to sleep at 11:30 last night.' **Genellikle saat kaçta uyursunuz?** 'At what time do you usually go to sleep?' **Erken uyu, erken uyan.** 'Go to sleep early and wake up early.' **Yatar yatmaz uyudu.** 'As soon as he {lay down/hit the {sack/bed}}, he fell sleep.' **Başımı yastığ.A koyduğum gibi uyudum.** 'As soon as I placed my head ON the pillow, I dropped off to sleep.' *22:16.* sleep: - go to sleep. → **uykuya dal-** ['- fall asleep; - doze off, - drop off /to/ sleep'] → dal- 2, **uyukla-** ['- doze, - doze off'], **yat-** 1 ['- go to bed, - lie down, - retire for the night'], ≠ **uyan-** ['- wake up'], ≠ **kalk-** 1 ['- get up, - rise'].

uyukla- [r] '- doze, - doze off' [uyu- + verb-forming suf. -[A/I]klA]: **Büyükbabam yemeğini yedikten sonra sırtını duvar.A dayadı ve uyuklamaya başladı.** 'After eating, my grandfather leaned [lit., ** leaned his back] AGAINST the wall and began to doze off.' He is sitting on a backless sofa. **Eve geldiğimde annem televizyon.un karşı-.sı.nda uyukluyordu.** 'When I came home, my mother was dozing in front of [lit., ** facing] the TV.' *22:13.* sleep: - sleep; *22:16.* : - go to sleep. → = **uykuya dal-** ['- fall asleep'; - doze off, - drop off /to/ sleep'], **uyu-** 2 ['- go to sleep, - fall asleep, - drop off to sleep'], ≠ **uyan-** ['- wake up, - awake'].

uza- [r] **1** '- get longer, - grow taller, - grow' [ADJ. uzun 'long', uzak 'far, distant' - k = uza-]: **Hayret, bu {bitki de/çocuk da} ne kadar uzadı!** 'My, but how this {plant/child} has grown!' <u>Proverb</u>: **Ağaç ne kadar uzasa göğ.E ulaşmaz.** 'No matter how tall a tree grows, it never reaches θ the sky.', i.e., No one keeps improving his status forever. *251:6.* increase: - grow, increase [i.]. **boyu uza-** '- grow in height, stature' [boy 'height; stature']: * **Murat'IN boy.U 5 cm.** [read: **santimetre**] **uzadı.** 'Murat [lit., ** Murat's height] has grown 5 centimeters.' *251:6.* increase: - grow, increase [i.].

2 '- drag on, - go on': **Beş yıldır miras meselesini halledemedik, artık bu iş çok uzadı.** 'For five years now we haven't been able to settle the inheritance problem. This matter has [really] dragged on [for] too long now.' *826:7.* durability: - linger on.

uzaklaş- [ır] /DAn/ [uzak 'far' + verb-forming suf. -lAş] 1 '- leave /θ/, - go away /from/, - become distant /from/, - move away /from/, - make off': **Tren istasyon.DAN yavaş yavaş uzaklaştı.** 'The train slowly left θ the station.' **Adam yerinden kalkıp uzaklaştı.** 'The man got up [lit., rose from his place] and {left/took off}.' **Bir kapkaççı yaşlı bir kadının çantasını kapıp olay yerinden hızla uzaklaştı.** 'A pickpocket snatched an old woman's {purse/handbag} and quickly made off [lit., left the place of the event].' *188:6.* departure: - depart. → = git- 1a, = ayrıl- 3 ['- leave, - depart /from/'], ≠ yaklaş-, ≠ gel- 1, ≠ var-. # uzaklaşıp git- '- make off, - be off, - go off': **Tren düdüğünü çalarak uzaklaşıp gitti.** 'The train, blowing its whistle, went off.'

2 '- become remote, distant /from/ in feeling': **Beş yıldır babasını görmediği için o.ndan iyice uzaklaştı.** 'Because he had not seen his father for five years, he felt very {distant/remote} from him.' *261:7.* distance, remoteness: - keep one's distance; *379:4.* dissuasion: - disincline; *456:10.* disaccord: - fall out with. → = soğu- 2 ['- cool /TOWARD/, - lose one's love, desire, or enthusiasm /FOR/; - cease to care /FOR/ sb or sth'], arası {açıl-/bozul-} ['- have a falling out /with/, - get on bad terms /with/'] → açıl- 9, bağlar kop- ['for relations between people - come to an end, - break off, - have a falling out /with/, - become estranged /FROM/'] → kop- 1, ≠ ısın- 3, arası düzel- ['for things - get straightened out, patched up between people'].

uzan- [ır] [uza- + refl. suf. -n] 1 /A/üstüne/ '- lie down /{ON/on}/, - stretch oneself out /{ON/on}/': **Engin eve geldiğinde çok yorgundu. Üzerini değiştirmeden yatağına uzandı. Gözlerini yumdu. * Çok geçmeden derin bir uyku.yA**

daldı. 'When Engin came home, he was very tired. He stretched out on his bed without changing his clothes. He closed his eyes. * Soon [lit., ** without much (time) passing] he fell INTO a deep sleep.' **Doktor: Lütfen şura.yA uzanın.** 'The doctor: Please lie down θ over here.' *201:5.* horizontalness: - lie; *912:11.* depression: - lie down. → yat- 1 ['- go to bed, - lie down, - retire for the night', ALSO '- BE lying down, - be in bed']. Often in the sense of stretching out for a nap: **S: Baban nerede?** 'Q: Where's your father?' **C: Biraz uzandı, dinleniyor.** 'A: He's stretched out for a bit. He's resting.' *22:13.* sleep: - sleep.

2 /DA/ '- extend over, - stretch out /{OVER/on/ALONG}/, - cover': **Yol.un iki taraf.ı.nDA çam ağaçları uzanıyordu.** 'Pine trees stretched ALONG both sides of the road.' *295:30.* covering: - overlie.

3 /A/ '- stretch one's hands out /to/, - reach /θ/ [a place with one's hands: the top shelf]; - reach /θ/, - get /to/, or - go as far as [i.e., a distant destination]': **Şeker kavanozu dolab.ın en üst.ü.nde, [o.nA] uzanamıyorum.** 'The sugar bowl is on the very top shelf of the cupboard. I can't reach θ it.' → = yetiş- 5, = eriş- 2. # **Bu yaz tatil.E güneye gittik. Mersin'E kadar uzandık.** 'This summer FOR {vacation/the holiday} we went {south/to the south}. We got as far as Mersin.' → = var-, = git- 1a. *261:6.* distance, remoteness: - extend to.

uzat- [ır] 1 '- lengthen, - make long, - let out' [uza- + caus. suf. -t]: **Pantolon.um.un paça.sı.nı biraz uzatır mısınız?** 'Would you please lengthen the cuffs of my trousers {a little/a bit}?' *267:6.* length: - lengthen. → ≠ kısalt- 1.

2 /A/ '- hold sth out /to/, - extend, - pass sth /to/ sb': **Ban.A {tuz.u/ biber.i/hardal.ı} uzatabilir misin[iz]?** 'Could you pass me {the salt/the pepper/the mustard}?' **Elindeki hediye.yi arkadaş.ı.na uzattı.** 'He held out the gift in his hand to his friend.' **Burhan yeni tanıştığı müdürle tokalaşmak için elini uzattı.** 'Ahmet held out his hand to shake hands with the director he had just met.' **Ellerini soba.ya uzatmış ısınıyordu.** 'He

held his hands out toward the stove and was warming himself.' <u>Proverb</u>: **Ayağ.ı.nı yorgan.ın.a göre uzat.** 'Stretch out your legs [lit., feet] according to [the length of] your quilt.', i.e., Act within your means, abilities. *261:6.* distance, remoteness: - extend to; *439:4.* offer: - offer.

el uzat- /A/ '- reach out to help' [el 'hand']: * **yardım elini uzat-** /A/ '- extend a helping hand /to/, - help out, - extend aid, assistance /to/' [yardım 'help'], lit., ** '- extend the hand of help': **Fakir çocuklar.a yardım el.İNİZ.i uzatın.** 'Extend a helping hand [lit., ** YOUR hand of help...] to poor children.' **Eğer bütün mahalle yardım elini uzatmasaydı yanan evlerin yerine yeni.si.ni yapmak çok zor olacaktı.** 'If the whole neighborhood had not extended a helping hand, it would have been very hard to build new houses [lit., ** its new one] in place of the ones [lit., houses] that had burned.' *449:11.* aid: - aid. → **el ele ver-** ['- help one another'] → **ver-** 1, **yardım et-** ['- help /θ/, - assist /θ/'], **yardımcı ol-** ['- help /θ/, - assist /θ/, - be of assistance /to/, - be helpful /to/'] → **ol-** 12, **yardımda bulun-** = yardım et-. *more formal.* → **bulun-** 3, **yardımlaş-** ['- help one another'].

3 '- prolong, - drag out, - extend': {a: **Pasaportunuzu**/b: **Vizenizi**/c: {**Oturum İzninizi/ Oturum Belgenizi/İkamet tezkerenizi**}} **uzatabilirsiniz.** 'You can extend {a: your passport/b: your visa/c: your residence permit}.' **Kültür Bakanı müzelerin ziyaret saatini uzattı.** 'The Minister of Culture extended the visiting hours of the museums.' * **Konuşmacı konuşma.sı.nı çok uzattı.** 'The speaker went on too long [lit., ** dragged out his {speech/talking} too much].' * **Lâfı uzatmayalım.** 'Let's not drag the matter [lit., the discussion] out.', i.e., Let's {get/come} to the point. **Neyse uzatmayalım.** * **Bu tartışma.nın hiçbir fayda.sı yok.** 'Anyway, let's not drag it [i.e., the discussion] out. * There's absolutely no point to this argument [lit., ** This argument has absolutely no use].' *267:6.* lengthen: - lengthen.

4 '- LET grow out': {**Saçlarımı/Sakalımı/Tırnak-**

larımı} **uzatmak istiyorum.** 'I want to let {my hair/my beard/my fingernails} grow out.' *267:6.* lengthen: - lengthen.

- Ü -

ücret al-. → **al-** 1.

ücret öde-. → **öde-.**

üfle- [r] [üf, the sound of blowing, + verb-forming suf. -lA] 1 '- blow': **Sigara.sı.nın duman.ı.nı oda.nın iç.i.nE üfledi.** 'He blew the smoke of his cigarette INTO the room [lit., ** into the inside of the room].' <u>Proverb</u>: **Süt.TEN ağzı yanan yoğurdu üfle.yerek yer.** 'A person whose mouth has been burned BY [hot] milk blows on [his] yogurt [before] eating it [lit., eats the yogurt blow.ing on it].' Yogurt is usually eaten cold. Once bitten, twice shy. *318:21.* * 1. wind: - breathe. → **es-** ['for the wind, breeze - blow'].

2 '- blow out': **Turhan, * elektrikler geldi, mumu üfle.yiver.** 'Turhan, * the lights have come back on, please blow out the candle.' • The structure *verb stem*.**Iver-**, as above, even without **lütfen**, may convey the sense of a polite request. *318:21.* * 1. wind: - breathe; *1021:7.* incombustibility: - fight fire. → **söndür-** 1 ['- put out, - extinguish', fire, cigarettes], ≠ **yak-** 1.

ümidini kaybet-. → {umudunu/ ümidini} kaybet-. → {kaybet-/yitir-}.

ümidini kır-. → **kır-** 1.

{**ümit et-** [eDer]/**um-** [ar]} [A. ümit (. -) (ümiDi) 'hope, expectation'] 1 '- hope': **Ümit ederim [ki] tekrar görüşürüz.** 'I hope we'll meet again.' **Burada rahat edeceğinizi ümit ederim.** 'I hope you'll be comfortable here.' **Ümit ederim [ki] yine aynı hatayı işlemezsin.** 'I hope you won't make the same mistake again.' **A:** * **Belma dün bir trafik kazası geçirdi.** 'A: Belma [f.] was in a traffic accident yesterday.' **B: Ümit ederim [ki] ciddî bir şey yoktur.** 'B: I hope [that] she's all right [lit., there's nothing serious].' *

Her şey yolunda ümit ederim. 'I hope everything's going well [lit., ** is on its road, i.e., is proceeding as it should be].' • Note: In most instances where the English speaker uses the verb '- hope' in phrases such as: 'I hope [that]...' or 'I hope so', the Turkish speaker prefers the Arabic-origin phrase İnşallah. '{God willing./If God wills.}' to the verbs {ümit et-/um-}. Thus the first statement above would more commonly occur as follows: İnşallah tekrar görüşürüz. or Tekrar görüşürüz inşallah. Proverb: Misafir umduğunu değil, bulduğunu yer. 'A guest doesn't eat what he hopes for, he eats what he finds.', i.e., He can't be picky. *100:16.* desire: - wish for; *124:7.* hope: - hope.

2 '- expect': İhsan bey.in saat dörtte yazıhaneme geleceğ.i.ni ümit ediyordum, ama gelmedi. 'I expected İhsan bey to come to my office at 4 o'clock, but he didn't {turn up/lit., come}.' * Bu kadar borc.u olduğ.u.nu doğrusu hiç ümit etmiyordum. 'I really never expected that he would get so deeply in debt [lit., have such a debt].' Proverbs: Ummadığın taş baş yarar. 'It is the unexpected stone [lit., the stone (that) you don't expect] that cuts the head.' Ummadığın yer.den yılan çıkar. 'A snake [i.e., evil, treachery] will appear from the place where you least [lit., don't] expect it.' *130:5.* expectation: - expect. → = bekle- 2.

ümit kesil-. → kesil- 3.

ümitlen-. → {umutlan-/ümitlen-}.

üre- [r] /ArAk/ '- increase, - multiply, - proliferate, - reproduce /by...ing/', subj.: almost exclusively living things [i.]: Tavşanlar çok hızlı ürerler. 'Rabbits reproduce very rapidly.' Hücreler bölün.erek ürüyorlar. 'Cells increase [in number] by divid.ing.' *78:7.* reproduction, procreation: - reproduce; *251:6.* increase: - grow, increase [i.]. → = çoğal-.

üret- [ir] [üre- + caus. suf. -t] 1 '- produce, - manufacture': Demir-çelik üreticileri bu yıl daha fazla demir-çelik üretecekleri.ni söylediler. 'The iron-steel producers said that this year they would produce more iron and steel.' Suudi Arabistan petrol üretiyor ve satıyor. 'Saudi Arabia produces and sells petroleum.' *891:8.* production: - produce, - create.

2 '- raise': Amcam çiftliğinde {tavuk/sebze} üretiyor. 'My paternal uncle raises {chickens/vegetables} on his farm.' *891:8.* production: - produce, - create; *1068:6.* animal husbandry: - raise. → = yetiştir- 1 ['- raise', children, animals, plants].

ürk- [er] 1 /DAn/ '- start, - be startled /BY/ [subj.: person or animal]; - shy [subj.: animal only]'. All these English verbs indicate a sudden physical movement in reaction to a fright: At önüne çıkan yılan.DAN ürküp kaçmay.a başladı. 'The horse was startled BY the snake that [suddenly] appeared in front of it and took off [lit., began to run away].' *127:13.* fear, frightingness: - flinch; *131:5.* inexpectation: - be startled.

2 /DAn/ '- take fright, - be seized with sudden fright, - be suddenly afraid /OF/.' All these English verbs indicate fear but not necessarily a sudden physical movement in reaction to that fear: Hırsızın elindeki bıçağı görünce ürktü. 'When he saw the knife in the hand of the thief, he took fright.' Polis.TEN ürkmeniz.E gerek yok, * onlar sizin yardımcınızdır. 'There's no need for you to fear θ the police. * They are there to help you [lit., They are your helpers].' *127:11.* fear, frightingness: - take fright. → = kork-.

üstüne git-. → git- 1a.

üstünü başını toparla-. → toparla- 3.

üstünü başını topla-. → topla- 2.

üşen- [ir] /A/ '- be too lazy, apathetic, or indifferent /to/ do sth, not - bother or - take the trouble /to/ do sth': Üşenme! Ödevini yap! 'Don't be lazy! Do your homework!' O kadar tembel birisi ki {yerinden kalkmay.a/ağzını açmay.a} üşeniyor. 'He's such a lazy person that he doesn't even bother {to get up from his place/to open his mouth}.'

102:4. indifference: not - care; *331:12.* inactivity: - idle.

üşü- [r] '- feel cold, - be cold, - get cold': **Bugün hava çok soğuk. * Üşüyorum.** 'The weather is very cold today. * I'm cold.' **Bugün hava çok soğuktu. Epey üşüdüm.** 'Today the weather was very cold. I {was/got} quite cold.' *1022:9.* cold: - freeze. → ≠ ısın- 1 ['- grow warm, - warm up, - get hot'].

üşüt- [ür] [üşü- + caus. suf. -t] 1 '- give sb a chill': **Karadeniz {hava}.sı beni üşüttü.** 'The Black Sea {air/weather} gave me a chill.' *1022:10.* cold: - make cold.

2 '- get a chill, - catch a chill', the early stage of a cold: **Serdar nezle oldu. Herhalde üşütmüş.** 'Serdar has caught a cold. He must have caught a chill.' **Saçımı kurulamadan çıktığım için biraz üşütmüşüm.** 'Because I left without drying my hair, I got a chill.' **Turhan bey * çok kötü öksürüyor, üşüt.müş {olsa gerek/olmalı}.** 'Turhan * has a terrible cough [lit., is coughing terribly]. He must have caught a chill.' *85:46b.* disease: - take sick in particular ways; *1022.9.* cold: - freeze. → = soğuk al- → al- 3.

ütüle- [r] '- iron, - press' [ütü 'iron' used for ironing clothes + verb-forming suf. -1A]: **İşine gitmeden önce, kocamın pantolonunu ve gömleğini ütüledim.** 'I ironed my husband's trousers and shirt before he went to work.' **Bu gömlekleri ütüler misiniz?** 'Would you please iron these shirts?' *287:6.* smoothness: - press.

üz- [er] '- upset, - distress, - worry; - sadden' [ADJ. üzgün 'unhappy, sad']: **Bu haber beni çok üzdü.** 'This news really upset me.' → ≠ **sevindir-.** # **Çocukken çok kavga eder, annemi üzerdim.** 'When I was a child, I used to fight a lot and worry my mother.' *112:18.* sadness: - sadden; *126:4.* anxiety: - concern; *126:5.* : - make anxious.

üzül- [ür] /A/ '- be upset, distressed /{ABOUT/BY/AT}/, - be concerned, worried /ABOUT/; - be or - feel sad /θ/ that, - be sorry /ABOUT/' [üz- + refl. suf. -Il. ADJ. üzgün 'unhappy, sad']: **Sınıfta kaldığımı**

öğrenince çok üzüldüm. 'When I learned that I had been held back in school [lit., ** 'stayed in the class', i.e., had not advanced to the next grade], I was very upset.' **Bu haber.E çok üzüldüm.** 'I was very sorry ABOUT this news.' Proverb: **Deli olan hediye.yE sevinir, akıllı olan üzülür.** 'A fool [lit., he who is crazy] is pleased WITH a gift, an intelligent person [lit., he who is intelligent] is sorry.' This is because an intelligent person realizes that the receiver is obliged to reciprocate. → ≠ **sevin-.** # A: **Cemile'nin babası hastaymış.** 'A: It seems that Cemile's father is ill.' B: **Yazık! Çok üzül.DÜM.** 'B: That's too bad! I'M {so/awfully} sorry.' In this sentence **üzüldüm** refers to a feeling still felt at the time of speaking so it is appropriately translated with the present tense. • In reference to a PRESENT condition, certain common Turkish verbs designating a state, i.e., a feeling, emotion, or sensation, often have the simple PAST tense, but the equivalent English has the simple PRESENT tense. A: **Yapabileceğimiz hiçbir şey yok. Çok üzgünüm.** 'A: There's nothing we can do. I'm very sorry.' B: * **O kadar üzülecek bir şey yok, üzülme.** 'B: There's nothing to be that concerned about [lit., ** A that-much-to-be-worried-about thing is not]. Don't worry.' **Üzülme, bu da geçer.** 'Don't be upset. This too {will/shall} pass.' *109:20.* cheerfulness: PHR. cheer up!; *112:16.* sadness: - lose heart; *121:* 17.* comfort: words of comfort; *126:4.* anxiety: - concern; *126:6.* : - feel anxious. → = endişe et-. # **Yangında ölen insanlar.A çok üzüldüm.** 'I {AM/was} very sorry FOR the people that perished in the fire.' → = acı- 2. # **Bu.nA çok üzüldünüz, değil mi?** 'You were quite distressed BY this [situation], weren't you?' → = üzüntü duy- → duy- 3, /I/ merak et- 1 ['- worry /ABOUT/, - be concerned /ABOUT/'].

üzüntü çek-. → çek- 5.

üzüntü duy-. → duy- 3.

- V -

vaat et-. → vadet-.

vadet- [vadeDer] /A/ '- promise /θ/ sb
sth', today *less common, more formal*
than **söz ver-** [A. **vaat** (vaad**İ**)
'promise' + **et**-]: **Siz.E
vadediyorum. Mutlaka kızınızı
bulacağım**. '{I promise θ you/You
have my word}: I will certainly find
your daughter.' NON-verbal noun as
object: **Şu an siz.E hiç bir şey
{vadedemem/vadedecek
durum.da değilim}**. '{I can't
promise/I'm not in a position to
promise} θ you anything at this time.'
VERBAL noun as object: **Babam
yaş günümde ban.A bir saat
almay.I vadetti.** 'My father
promised to buy me a watch on my
birthday.' **Ümran [benim] sırrımı
saklayacağ.ı.nı vadetti**. 'Ümran
promised that she would keep my
secret.' **İktidar partisi yeniden
seçilirse ücretleri artıracağ.ı.nı
vadetti**. 'The party in power
promised that, if it is reelected [lit.,
elected again], it would raise wages.'
* **Doğacaktır san.A vadettiği
günler Hakk'ın/Kimbilir belki
yarın, belki yarın.DAN da
yakın**. 'The days that God has
promised θ you will surely
come/Who knows, perhaps
tomorrow, perhaps even sooner
THAN tomorrow.' M. Akif Ersoy.
436:4. promise: - promise. → = **söz
ver-** → ver- 1, **yemin et**- ['- swear
/to [sb], that/'].

{**gelecek/istikbal**} **vadet**- '- be
promising, - have a promising future'
[{**gelecek**/A. **istikbal**} 'future']: *
**Bu genç gelecek vadediyor,
el.İ.nDEN tutmak lâzım**. 'This
young man is very promising [lit., **
promises a future]. One must guide
him [lit., take him BY HIS hand].'
124:10. hope: - give hope; *133:13*.
premonition: - promise.

{**vakit/zaman**} **al**-. → al- 1.

{**vakit/zaman**} **değerlendir**-. →
değerlendir-.

{**vakit/zaman**} **geçir**-. → geçir- 3.

{**vakit/zaman**} **harca**-. → {harca-
/sarf et-} 2.

{**vakit/zaman**} **ilerle**-. → ilerle- 1.

{**vakit/zaman**} **kaybet**-. → {kaybet-
/yitir-}.

{**vakit/zaman**} **kazan**-. → kazan- 4.

{**vakit/zaman**} **öldür**-. → öldür-.

{**vakit/zaman**} **sarf et**-. → {harca-
/sarf et-} 2.

vakit ver-. → {zaman/vakit} ver-.
→ ver- 1.

{**vakti/zamanı**} **geç**-. → geç- 4.

{**vaktinde/zamanında**} **gel**-. → gel-
1.

var is not a verb but an adjective meaning
'existing, existent'. In addition to its
use in the formation of the entries **var
et**- and **varsay**- below, it is used
with the Turkish equivalent of '- be',
which is the verb **ol**-. This dictionary
shows **var** with **ol**- in 'There is' -
type sentences under the entry **ol**- 3
b); in sentences expressing '- have'
under the entry **ol**- 5; and in some
other uses under **ol**- 12 under
{**var/yok**} **ol**-. The negative of **var**
is **yok** 'non-existent'.

var et- [eDer] '- create', only God as
subject [**var** 'existing, existent']:
**Allah dünya.yı [yok.tan] var
etti**. 'God created the universe [from
nothing].' **Yok.tan var etmek
Allah'a mahsustur**. 'To create sth
from nothing is [an attribute]
exclusive to God.' **Hepimiz.İ ve
bütün dünya.yI var eden
Allah'tır**. 'God is the one who
created all of us and the whole
world.' *891:8*. production: - produce,
- create. → = **oluştur**-, = **yarat**-, ≠
yık- 1, ≠ **yok et**- 1.

var- [IR] /A / '- reach /θ/, - arrive
/{IN/AT}/, - get /to/': **Otobüsümüz
Erzurum'A sabah saat beşte
vardı**. 'Our bus arrived IN Erzurum
at 5 o'clock in the morning.'
**Trenimiz Sirkeci istasyon.u.nA
gece yarısı vardı**. 'Our train
arrived AT the Sirkeci station at
midnight.' **Bodrum'A {saat
kaçta/ne zaman} varırız?** '{At
what time/When} will we {get
TO/arrive IN} Bodrum?' Proverbs: *
İş olacağ.ı.nA varır. 'What will
be will be [lit., ** Matters will get to
the place they are going to be].' **Ok
menzil.i.nE varır**. 'The arrow will
reach θ its mark.', i.e., What is
destined will occur. *186:6*. arrival: -

407

arrive. → = er-, = eriş- 1, = gel- 1, = ulaş- 1, yetiş- 1 ['- catch /θ/ a vehicle, - make it /to/, - get /to/ a place, - arrive in time /FOR/; - be in time /FOR/'], ≠ git- 1a, ≠ hareket et- 3, ≠ kalk- 2; *963:11.* predetermination: PHR. it is fated.

* **farkına var-** '- notice, - become aware /OF/, - realize' [A. **fark 1** 'difference'. **2** 'discrimination, awareness'], lit., ** '- reach the awareness of': * **Aylardan beri mektup** {yazmadığ.IN.ın/ yazmadığ.IMIZ.ın} **fark.ı.nA vardım.** 'I realized that {YOU [s.]/WE} hadn't written a letter for months [lit., ** I reached θ the awareness of {YOUR [s.]/OUR} not having written a letter...].' *940:5.* discovery: - detect; *982:6.* attention: - heed. → = dikkat et- 2, = farket- 1, = gözle- 1, hisset- 2 ['- sense, - feel, - be aware; - notice, - perceive'].

varsay-. → {farz et-/varsay-}.

vazgeç- [er] /DAn/ '- give up /θ/, - drop /θ/ a matter': **Almanya'ya gitmek istiyorduk. Fakat vize işleriyle ilgili bir sürü güçlük** {çıkardılar/çıkarttılar}, **vazgeçtik.** 'We wanted to go to Germany, but they created a whole series of difficulties for us related to getting a visa [so] we dropped the matter.' NON-verbal noun as object: Proverb: * **Huylu huyu.nDAN vazgeçmez.** 'A person of a certain disposition doesn't give up θ his disposition.', i.e., Temperament tends to remain as it is. A leopard doesn't change its spots. VERBAL noun as object: **Bu yaz Bodrum'a gitmek.TEN vazgeçtik.** 'We gave up θ [the idea of] going to Bodrum [i.e., a town in south western Anatolia] this summer.' *370:7.* abandonment: - give up. → = /A/ **boş ver-** 2 → ver- 1.

fikrinden vazgeç- '- change one's mind, - give up /θ/ one's idea' [A. **fikir** (fiKRi) 'idea']: **Alanya'ya gitme fikr.i.nDEN vazgeçtik.** 'We gave up θ the idea of going to Alanya.' *363:6.* changing of mind: - change one's mind'; *370:7.* abandonment: - give up. → **fikrini değiştir-** ['- change one's mind'] → değiştir- 1, **kararından vazgeç-** [see the entry directly below].

* **kararından vazgeç-** '- change one's mind, - go back on one's decision' [A. **karar** (. -) 'decision'], lit., ** '- give up FROM one's decision': **Onun.la evlenmek istiyordum ama daha sonra karar.IM.dan vazgeçtim.** 'I wanted to marry θ {her/him}, but later I changed MY mind.' *363:6.* changing of mind: - change one's mind'; *370:7.* abandonment: - give up. → **fikrinden vazgeç-** [see the entry directly above], **fikrini değiştir-** ['- change one's mind'] → değiştir- 1.

{vazgeçir- [ir]/caydır- [ır]} /DAn/ '- talk sb /OUT OF/ sth, - dissuade or - deter sb /from/, - prevent or - keep sb /from/' [vazgeç- + caus. suf. -Ir; cay- '- give up a plan' + caus. suf. -DIr]: **Vazgeçir-** is more common than **caydır-.** **O dersi bırakmay.a karar vermiştim ama {ev arkadaşım} beni vazgeçirdi.** 'I had decided to drop that class, but {my roommate/the person I live with/lit., my housemate} talked me OUT OF it.' **Çok uğraştım ama onu** {istifa.DAN/istifa etmek-.TEN} **vazgeçiremedim.** 'I tried really hard, but I couldn't talk him OUT OF resigning.' **Cinnet geçiren adamcağızı polis iki saatlik bir çabadan sonra intihar etmek.TEN vazgeçirdi.** 'After a two-hour effort, the police finally talked the poor man who had gone crazy OUT OF committing suicide.' **Polis öğrencileri yürüyüş.TEN vazgeçirdi.** 'The police talked the students OUT OF the march.' **Huylu.yu huy.u.nDAN vazgeçiremezsin.** 'You can't talk a person of a certain disposition OUT OF his disposition.' **Hiçbir şey beni bu yaz Türkiye'ye gitmek.TEN vazgeçiremez.** 'Nothing can {keep/prevent/deter} me from going to Turkey this summer.' **Çıkarttıkları bir sürü vize güçlükleri plânladığımız seyahat.ten bizi vazgeçirdi.** 'All the [lit., The whole series of] visa difficulties [that] they created, dissuaded us from the journey we had planned.' *379:3.* dissuasion: - dissuade. → ≠ **kandır-** 2 ['- persuade or - convince sb /TO/ do sth, - talk sb /INTO/ doing sth'].

vedalaş- [ır] /1 A/ '- bid or - say goodbye, farewell /TO/ one another' [A. veda (. -) 'farewell, goodbye' + recip. suf. -lAş]: Partiden ayrılırken herkes.LE tek tek vedalaştım. 'When leaving the party, I said good-bye TO everyone, one by one.' *188:16.* departure: - say or - bid good-bye. → ≠ merhabalaş-, ≠ selâmlaş-, uğurla- ['- wish a departing traveler a safe journey, - wish sb Godspeed, - send or - see sb off'].

vefat et- [eDer] /DAn/ '- pass away, - die /{OF/AS A RESULT OF}/, - pass on', only for persons, not other living things. Always *polite, formal*, the verb used in newspaper obituaries. [A. vefat (. -) 'death']: Ümit'in babası {geçen yıl/beş yıl önce} kanser.DEN vefat etmiş. 'Ümit's father died OF cancer {last year/5 years ago}.' *307:19.* death: - die. → = hayata gözlerini {kapa-/kapat-} → {kapa-/kapat-} 1, = hayata gözlerini yum- → göz yum- 1, = hayatını {kaybet-/yitir-} ['- lose one's life, - die', of unnatural causes], = öl-, = ömrünü tamamla- ['- complete one's life, - come to the end of one's life, - die, - pass away'], = son nefesini ver- ['- breathe one's last breath, - die'] → ver- 1, = canından ol- ['- lose one's life, - die', mostly for an unexpected and undeserved death] → ol- 7, ≠ doğ- 1, ≠ dünyaya gel- → gel- 1.

ver- [İR] 1 /A/ '- give /to/, - donate /to/': Yemek listesi.ni verir misiniz? 'Would you please {give me/pass} the menu?' Kazandığım para.yı babam.a verdim. 'I gave the money [that] I had {earned/won} to my father.' → ilet- 1 ['- take or - convey /to/, - forward, - pass on /to/'], ≠ al- 1. # Fatma hanım bütün mallarını Kızılay'a verdi. 'Fatma hanım {gave/donated} all her property to the Red Crescent [i.e., the Muslim equivalent of the Red Cross].' → = bağışla- 1 ['- donate']. Karım ban.a aslan gibi iki oğul verdi. 'My wife gave me two healthy [lit., ** lion-like] sons.' Proverbs: Aldığını veren aradığını bulur. 'He who returns [lit., gives] what he borrows [lit., what he takes] will find what he seeks.' * Elini versen kolunu kurtaramazsın. 'If you give him a hand, he'll take an arm [lit., ** If you give your hand, you won't be able to save your arm].' Give him an inch, and he'll take a mile. * Veren el alan el.DEN üstündür. 'The hand that gives is {superior TO/better THAN} the hand that takes.' It is better to give than to receive. Veren eli herkes öper. 'Everyone kisses the hand that gives.' Veren eli kimse kesmez. 'One does not cut the hand that gives.' *478:12.* giving: - give; *644: * 26.* probity: PHR. one does not cut the hand that gives.

{ad/isim} ver- /A/ '- give a name /to/, - name /θ/' [{ad/A. isim (iSMi)} 'name']: * Yeni doğan bebeğ.e babaanne.si.nin ad.ı.nı verdiler. 'They named /θ/ the newborn baby after her grandmother on her father's side [lit., ** gave /θ/ the newborn baby his father's mother's name].' * Kedim.e "Pamuk" ad.ı.nı verdim. '{I named θ my cat "Cotton."/I gave θ my cat the name "Cotton."}' *527:11.* nomenclature: - name. → = {ad/isim} koy- → koy- 1, = {adlandır-/isimlendir-}, = {ad/isim} tak-.

akıl ver- /A/ '- give advice /to/, - advise /θ/' [A. akıl (aKLı) 'intelligence']: Yeni bir araba almak istiyoruz. * Nasıl bir şey alalım, biz.e biraz akıl verir misin? 'We want to buy a new car. * What kind of a car [lit., thing] should we buy? Would you give us some [lit., a little] advice?' Ne akıl verdi san.a? 'What advice did he give {you/to you}?' Lütfen bana yardımcı ol, akıl ver. Çok zor durumdayım. 'Please help me [lit., ** be a helper to me]. Give me some advice. I'm in {a real predicament/a very difficult situation}.' A: Lütfen sigara içme Metin, biliyorsun sağlığına zararlı. 'A: Please don't smoke, Metin. You know it's harmful to your health.' B: Sana kaç defa ban.A akıl verme dedim. 'B: How many times have I told you * I don't need your advice [lit., don't give me ({gratuitous/unwanted}) advice]!' *422:5.* advice: - advise. → = fikir ver- 2 below, ≠ fikir al- → al- 1, ≠ akıl al- → al- 1.

Allah belâsını versin. '[May] God damn him! [lit., May God give (him) his misfortune, i.e., his punishment]' [Allah 'God', A. belâ 'misfortune']: **A: Bugün bir kapkaççı ablamın çantasını alıp kaçmış.** 'A: Today a purse-snatcher ran off [lit., ** took and fled] with my older sister's purse.' **B: Allah belâsını versin.** '[May] God damn him!' *513:11.* curse: INTERJ. damn!

Allah kolaylık versin. 'May God make it easy for you', said to sb about to undertake a task. [kolaylık 'ease, easiness']: **A: Gelecek hafta üç tane sınavım var.** 'A: I have three examinations next week.' **B: Allah kolaylık versin.** 'B: May God make it easy for you.' *504: * 20.* courtesy: polite expressions.

A: Allah rahatlık versin. 'A: Good night' [rahatlık 'comfort', lit., 'May God give (you) comfort']. **B: {Teşekkür ederim./Sağol.} Siz.e de.** 'B: {Thank you./Thanks.} The same to you.' • Used before retiring, going to bed, not usually when bidding farewell in the evening, as, for example, when leaving a party. **İyi geceler.** 'Good night.' may be used both when going to bed and also when bidding farewell in the evening. *188:23.* departure: good night!; *504: * 20.* courtesy: polite expressions.
Allah sağlık versin. 'May God grant [you] good health.' [sağlık 'good health']: **A: Hâlâ iş bulamadım, bilmiyorum ne yapacağım.** 'I still haven't been able to find work. I don't know {what I'll do./what to do.}' **B: Boş ver, Allah sağlık versin, * gerisi hallolur.** 'Never mind. * You have your health/lit., Just let God give [you] good health. The other things [lit., the rest, i.e., the problems] will get resolved.' *504: * 20.* courtesy: polite expressions.

bahşiş ver- /A/ '- tip /θ/ sb, - give /θ/ sb a tip, - give a tip /to/ sb' [P. **bahşiş** 'tip', i.e., money, not information]: **Taksiden inin
ce şoför.E bahşiş verdim.** 'When I got out of the taxi, I {tipped θ the driver/gave θ the driver a tip}.' * {a: Garson.A/b: Kapıcı.yA/c: Oda hizmetçi.si.nE} ne kadar bahşiş vereyim?** 'How much should I tip {a: θ the waiter/b: θ {the caretaker/the doorman}/c: θ {the maid/the help/lit., ** the room servant}}?' *624:10.* payment: - pay.

* bereket versin [ki] 'Thank goodness, Fortunately' [A. **bereket**

1 'abundance'. 2 'blessing'. 3 'fortunately']: **Elektrikler kesilince asansörde kaldım. Bereket versin [ki] hemen yardım.ım.a koştular.** 'When the electricity was cut off, I was stuck in the elevator. Thank goodness they at once ran to my aid.' **Bayram dolayı.sı.yla otobüs seferler.i.nde * büyük bir aksama vardı, bereket versin şimdi düzeldi.** 'Because of the holiday, * bus service was severely disrupted [lit., ** In the bus trips there was a severe disruption]. Fortunately the situation [lit., it] has now been corrected.' *1009:16.* prosperity: ADV. fortunately. = **Allahtan [ki]**, = **iyi ki**, ≠ **maalesef**, ≠ **yazık ki**.

bilgi ver- /a: A, b: hakkında, c: ile ilgili/ '- give or - provide information /a: to, b: about, c: concerning/, - inform, - tell /about/' [bilgi 1 'knowledge'. 2 'information']: **Aileniz hakkında biz.e biraz bilgi verir misiniz?** 'Would you {tell us a little/provide us a little information} about your family?' **Spiker yarınki hava durumu hakkında bilgi verdi.** 'The announcer [i.e., on TV or radio] provided information about tomorrow's weather.' **Öğretmen dünya.nın oluşum.u {hakkında/ile ilgili} bilgi verdi.** 'The teacher provided information {about/concerning} the creation of the world.' *551:8.* information: - inform. → = **bildir-**, = **haber ver-** → ver- 1, ≠ **haber al-** → al- 3.

borç ver- /A/ '- lend [money only], - extend a loan /to/' [borç (borCu) 'debt, loan']: **Ban.A biraz borç [para] verir misin?** '{I wonder if I could ask you for a little loan?/lit., Would you please lend me a little money?}' *620:5.* lending: - lend. → = **ödünç ver-** ['- lend money or anything else'] → ver- 1, ≠ **borç al-** ['- take or - accept a loan'] → al- 1, ≠ **ödünç al-** ['- borrow money or anything else /from/'] → al- 1.

boş ver- [boş 'empty'] (1) '- not - bother /about/, - take no notice /of/, - ignore', *informal*: **Boş ver.** 'Never mind, forget it': **A: Oturma odası.nA bir koltuk daha alalım mı?** 'A: {How about buying/lit.,

410

Shall we buy} another [i.e., one more] armchair FOR the living room?' B: Boş ver, almayalım. 'B: Oh don't bother. Let's not [buy one].' A: Dün istediğin kitabı alamadım. 'A: Yesterday I couldn't buy the book you wanted.' B: Boş ver, önemli değil. 'B: Never mind, it isn't important.' A: Bugün size Türkçe bir roman getirecektim, fakat unuttum. 'A: I was going to bring you a novel in Turkish today, but I forgot.' B: Boş ver * {canım}, üzülme. * Yarın getirirsin. 'B: Never mind * {θ/my friend/pal/mate/my dear}, don't worry. * Bring it [lit., You'll bring it] tomorrow.' Boş ver, * sınavın kötü geçti DİYE bu kadar üzülmeye değmez. 'Never mind, * it's not worth getting so upset just BECAUSE your exam went badly.' A: Şu adam hep bana bakıyor. 'A: This man is always looking at me.' B: Boş ver, aldırma. 'B: Never mind, just ignore him.' S: Dün Murat'ı başka bir kızla gördüm, ne yapayım? 'Q: Yesterday I saw Murat with another girl. What should I do?' C: Boş ver, aldırış etme. Nasılsa sana döner. 'A: Never mind, don't pay any attention. He'll come back to you anyway.' 997:25. unimportance: PHR. no matter. → = aldırış etme-, = aldırma- → aldır- 2.
(2) /A/ '- give up /θ/ sth': Nevin evlendikten sonra piyano dersleri.nE boş verdi. 'Nevin [f.] gave up θ [her] piano lessons after getting married.' 370:7. abandonment: - give up. → = /DAn/ vazgeç-.

{cevap/yanıt} ver- /A/ '- answer /θ/, - reply, - respond /to/' [A. cevap (. .-) (cevaBı) 'answer, response', yanıt. Same.]: Bizimle sinemaya geleceksen, saat 6'ya [read: altıya] kadar cevap ver. 'If you're going to come to the movies with us, let us know [lit., respond] by six o'clock.' Ban.A cevap ver. 'Answer θ me.' Aşağıdaki sorular.A cevap veriniz. 'Answer θ the questions below.' { * Anket.E/* Sınav kâğıd.ı.nA} cevap veriniz. 'Answer {θ the questionnaire/* θ the questions on the exam [lit., ** the exam paper]}.' * Kapı.yI {çaldım}, ama kimse cevap vermedi. 'I {knocked/rang} AT the door, but nobody answered.' • The equivalent of the English 'that'

clause may be rendered by the EXACT WORDS of the answer separated from the verb of answering by diye 'saying': "Şimdi geliyorum" DİYE cevap verdi. 'He answered THAT he was coming now [lit., ** "I'm coming now" SAYING he answered].' 938:4. answer: - answer. → = /I/ {cevapla-/cevaplandır-/yanıtla}, = karşılık ver- 1 → ver- 1, = ≠ soru sor-.

ihtiyaca cevap ver- '- meet θ a need' [A. ihtiyaç (. . -) (ihtiyaCı) 'necessity, need'], lit., '- answer θ a need': Yeni yapılan baraj Doğu Anadolu.nun su ve elektrik ihtiyac.ı.nA büyük ölçüde cevap verecek. 'The new [lit., newly constructed] dam will largely meet θ Eastern Anatolia's need for water and electricity.' 990:4. sufficiency: - suffice. → = ihtiyaç karşıla- → karşıla- 2.

telefona cevap ver- '- get, - pickup, or - answer θ the phone': Telefon çalıyor, cevap verir misin lütfen? 'The phone is ringing, would you please {answer/get} it?' Telefon.A cevap verdim. 'I answered θ the phone.' 347:18. communications: - telephone; 982:5. attention: - attend to. → = telefonA bak- → bak- 3, = telefonU aç- → aç- 5, ≠ telefon kapan- ['for the phone - be hung up'] → kapan- 1, ≠ telefon.U kapat- ['- hang up'] → kapat-.

ceza ver- /A/ '- punish' [A. ceza (. -) 'punishment']: * Öğretmen ders.i dinlemeyen öğrenciler.E ceza verdi. 'The teacher punished θ the students who weren't listening to the lesson.' Çocuk vazoyu kırınca * annesi o.nA oda.dan çıkma.ma ceza.sı verdi. 'When the child broke the vase, * his mother punished him by not permitting him to leave the room [lit., ** gave θ him the not-leaving-from-room punishment].' 604:10. punishment: - punish. → = cezalandır-, ceza kes- ['- fine /θ/, - give a ticket /to/'] → kes- 5, ≠ ödüllendir-.

çekidüzen ver- /A/ '- put in order, - straighten up, - tidy up' [çekidüzen 'order, tidiness']: Müdür beyin odasına girmeden önce üst.ÜN.ü baş.IN.ı düzelt, kıyafet.İN.e çeki düzen ver. 'Before entering the director's room, tidy up [lit., ** adjust YOUR clothes, give order to YOUR {clothes/outfit}].' * Ayna.nın karşı.sı.nda kendisine çekidüzen verdi. 'Looking in the mirror [lit., ** {Opposite/Facing} the mirror], she tidied herself up.' *807:12.* arrangement: - tidy, - tidy up. → = düzelt-, = üstünü başını {düzelt-/toparla-/topla-} ['- tidy up, - straighten up, - smarten up (lit., - adjust one's clothes)]' → düzelt- 3, toparla- 3, topla- 2.

ders ver- /A/ [A. ders 'lesson, class'] (1) '- teach /θ/ sb, - give lessons /to/ sb': Gelecek yıl üniversitede ders vereceğim. 'Next year I'm going to teach at {the college/the university}.' → = okut- 3, eğit- ['- educate sb /on a subject/'], öğret- ['- teach /θ/ sb sth, - teach sth /to/ sb']. *noun designating a subject of study* ders.i: Gelecek yıl üniversitede {a: Türkçe/b: Fransızca/c: matematik/d: tarih} ders.İ vereceğim. 'Next year I'm going to teach {a: Turkish/b: French/c: mathematics/d: history} at {the college/the university} [lit., give Turkish...lessons...].' Hasan evinde İngilizce ders.i veriyor. 'Hasan gives English lessons at home [i.e., in his own house].' *568:10.* teaching: - teach. → = öğret-, ≠ ders al- 1 ['- take lessons /from/'] → al- 1.
(2) /A/ '- teach a MORAL lesson /to/': Nergis'in arkamdan konuşma.sı ban.A iyi bir ders verdi. O.nA güven.me.mem gerek.tiğ.i.ni anladım. 'Nergis's speaking behind my back taught me a good lesson. I understood that I mustn't trust θ her.' *568:10.* teaching: - teach. → = öğret-.

ehemmiyet ver-. → {önem/ ehemmiyet} ver- below.

* el ele ver- '- help one another' [el 'hand'], lit., ** '- give hand to hand': Köylüler el el.E ver.erek köy.E yeni bir okul binası yaptılar. 'The villagers, help.ing one another, built a new school [building] FOR the village.' *449:11.* aid: - aid. → = yardımlaş-, el uzat- 2 ['- reach out to help'], yardımcı ol- ['- help /θ/, - assist /θ/,

- be of assistance /to/, - be helpful /to/'] → ol- 12.

emek ver- /A/ '- put effort /INTO/, - devote effort /to/, - work /AT/, - take pains /WITH/' [emek (emeĞi) 1 'work'. 2 'trouble, pains']: Bu ödev.E çok emek verdim. 'I put a lot of effort INTO this homework.' Çocuklarım.A çok emek verdim. 'I devoted a lot of {attention/effort} to my children.' *403:5.* endeavor: - endeavor. → = {emek/çaba} harca- ['- expend effort /{for/ON}/ sth, - take pains /to/ do sth'] → {harca-/sarf et-} 1, çabala- ['- strive /to/, - struggle /to/, - do one's best /to/'], uğraş- 1 ['- strive, - struggle, - endeavor /TO/, - exert oneself, - put forth an effort /for/, - work hard'].

fikir ver- /A, hakkında/ [A fikir (fiKRi) 'thought, idea, opinion'] (1) '- express an opinion /to, about/, - give an opinion, idea, or impression /about/': Bu film biz.e Birinci Dünya Savaş.ı.nın sebepler.i hakkında fikir verdi. 'This movie gave us an idea of the causes of the First World War.' *608:12.* description: - describe; *945:8.* judgment: - judge. → bilgi ver- → ver- 3 above.
(2) '- give advice /to/, - advise /θ/, - suggest a course of action /to/': Yeni bir araba almak istiyoruz. Nasıl bir şey alalım, biz.e biraz fikir verir misin Cengiz? 'We want to buy a new car. What kind of a car [lit., thing] should we buy? Would you give us some [lit., a little] advice, Cengiz?' *422:5.* advice: - advise. → = akıl ver- above, öner- ['- propose, - suggest /to/'], tavsiye et- ['- recommend, - advise, - propose, - suggest sth /to/'].

{geri ver-/iade et- [eDer]} /A/ '- give or - take sth back /to/, - return sth /to/.' The second verb is *more formal.* [geri 'back, rear, the space behind', A. iade (. - .) 'returning, giving back']: Nilüfer'den aldığım 100 lira.yı geri verdim. 'I returned the 100 liras [that] I had borrowed [lit., taken] from Nilüfer.' Yeni aldığım saat bozuk çıktı, çalışmıyor. Saatçi.ye geri vermey.İ düşünüyorum. 'The new watch I just bought turned out to be defective. It doesn't work. I'm thinking OF returning it to the jeweler [lit., ** 'watchman', i.e., maker, seller, or repairer of watches].' **Müşteri: Bu çantayı geri verebilir miyim?** 'Customer: Can I return this {handbag/purse/briefcase}?' **Satıcı 1: Maalesef, geri veremezsiniz efendim.** 'Salesman 1: Unfortunately you can't, {sir/ma'am}.' **Satıcı 2: Tabii, geri verebilirsiniz.** 'Salesman 2: Of course you can [give it back].'

para {geri ver-/iade et-} '- give a refund, - refund money, - give back money': **Müşteri: Paramı geri verir misiniz? * İşte fatura.** 'Customer: I would like a refund [lit., Would you return my money?]. * Here's the receipt.' **Satıcı: Paranızı geri veremeyiz fakat başka bir çanta.yLA değiştirebiliriz.** 'Salesman: We can't refund your money, but we can exchange it [i.e., the handbag] FOR another handbag.' *481:4.* restitution: - restore. → **geri gönder-** ['- send sth back'], ≠ **geri al- 1** ['- take sth back (to oneself)'] → **al- 1**, ≠ **geri getir-** ['- bring sth back'].

gün ver- /A/ '- give a {date/day} for an appointment /to/' [**gün** 'day']: **S: Doktor muayene için gün verdi mi?** 'Q: Did the doctor give you an appointment for an examination?' **C: * Evet, hafta.yA salı gün.ü.nü verdi.** 'A: Yes, he gave me one for Tuesday a week from today [lit., He gave me Tuesday a week (from now)].' *964:4.* prearrangement: - prearrange. → ≠ **gün al-** ['- {make/get} an appointment for a {date/day}, - set a {date/day} /for/'] → **al- 3**, **randevu ver-** below.

haber ver- /A/ '- inform /θ/, - tell, - report /to/' [A. **haber** 'news, information']: **A: Bir mektup geldi.** 'A: A letter has come.' **B: Bir dakika, Figen'E haber vereyim.** 'B: Just a moment, I'll {inform/tell} θ Figen.' **Figen'E haber verdiniz mi?** 'Did you {inform/tell} θ Figen?' **Misafirler gelir gelmez ban.A haber verin.** 'Tell θ me as soon as the guests arrive.' *** Maalesef siz.e acı bir haber vereceğim.** 'Unfortunately I have some bad news for you [lit., ** ...I'll give θ you a (piece of) bad news].' **Elif'ler.E {a: git.tiğ.iniz.i/b: gid.eceğ.iniz.i/c: git.meniz gerektiğ.i.ni} haber verdiniz mi?** 'Did you inform θ [them] {a:

that you had gone/b: that you were going to go/c: that you had to go} to Elif's house?' **Halit'ler.E {a: nasıl/b: ne zaman/c: neden/d: niye/e: niçin/f: kimlerle} gideceğiniz.i haber verdiniz mi?** 'Did you inform θ [them] {a: how/b: when/c, d, e: why/f: with whom [i.e., with what people]} you were going to go to Halit's house?' **Halit'ler.E gidip {gitme-diğiniz.i/gitmeyeceğiniz.i} haber verdiniz mi?** 'Did you inform θ him whether or not {you had gone/you were going to go} to Halit's house?' **Onbir uçağ.ın gel.diğ.i.nİ haber verdiler.** 'They reported that eleven planes had come.' **Onbir uçağ.I.nın geldiğ.i.ni haber verdiler.** 'They reported that the 11 o'clock plane had come.' *** Eskiden annesi.nE her şey.İ haber verirmiş.** 'Formerly she used to report everything TO her mother.' *551:8.* information: - inform. → = **bildir-**, = **bilgi ver-** above, ≠ **haber al-** → **al- 3.**

hak ver- /A, konusunda/ '- acknowledge or - think /θ/ sb or sb's action to be right, correct /on the {issue/matter} of/' [A. **hak** (haKKı) 1 'right'. 2 'truth'], lit., ** '- give right /to, on the {issue/matter} of/': PERSON noun as object: **Kerem'in anlattıklarını dinleyince çevre temizliği konu.su.nda o.nA hak verdim.** 'When I listened to what Kerem had said, I thought [that] he was correct on the matter of the cleanliness of the environment.' VERBAL noun as object: *** Üvey annesi.nin yaptıklar.ı.nı öğrenince zavallı kız.IN evi terketme.Sİ.nE hak verdim.** 'When I found out the things that her stepmother had done, I thought [that] the poor girl was right {to leave/IN leaving} home [lit., ** I gave right TO the poor girl's leaving...].' *332:11.* assent: - acknowledge.

ifade ver- /A/ *law* '- give evidence /to/, - testify, - give testimony, - give or make a statement' [A. **ifade** (. - .) 1 'expression, statement'. 2 'evidence, deposition']: **Trafik kazasını gören annem polis.e {ifade/ifade.si.ni} verdi.** 'My mother, who had witnessed the traffic accident, gave {evidence/her evidence} to the police.' *956:9.* evidence, proof: - testify. → **tanıklık et-** ['- testify, - give evidence, - be a witness in a court case'], ≠ **ifade al-** → al- 1.

imtihanı[nı] ver-. → {sınav/ imtihan} ver- below.

izin ver- /A/ '- give /θ/ sb permission, - give permission /to/ sb, - allow, - let, or - permit /θ/ sb' [A. **izin** (iZNi) 'permission']: PERSON noun as object: **Sinemaya gitmek istiyorum fakat babam ban.A izin vermez.** 'I want to go to the movies, but my father won't {let me/give me permission}.' VERBAL noun as object: * **Öğretmen öğrenciler.İN şarkı söyle.me.Sİ.ne izin verdi.** 'The teacher {a: {allowed/permitted} the students to sing/b: gave the students permission to sing/c: let the students sing} songs [lit., ** gave permission to THE STUDENTS' sing.ING songs].' * **Babam sinemaya git.me.M.E izin vermedi.** 'My father didn't {a: {allow/permit} ME to/b: give ME permission to/c: let ME} go to the movies [lit., ** didn't give permission to MY go.ING].' *443:9.* permission: - permit. → = **müsaade et-**, {izin/müsaade} **al-** ['- get permission /from, to/'] → al-3, ≠ {yasakla-/yasak et-}.

karar ver- /A/ '- decide /to/, - make up one's mind /to/, - make a decision /to/, - resolve /to/' [A. **karar** (. -) 'decision']: S: **Hangi sinemaya gidelim?** 'Which {movie/movie theater} shall we go to?' C: **Siz karar verin.** 'A: You decide.' **Karar vermeden önce {çok düşündüm./düşünmeliyim.}** '{I thought a lot/I must think} before deciding.' Direct statement as 'object': **Bu durumda ne yapmamız gerek, karar veremiyorum.** 'I can't decide what we should do in this situation [lit., ** In this situation what should we do, I can't decide].' * **Akşam yemeği için ne yapayım karar veremedim.** 'I couldn't decide what to make for dinner [lit., ** What shall I make for dinner, I couldn't decide].' VERBAL noun as object: Verbal object implied: S: **Ne.yE karar verdiniz?** 'Q: θ What have you decided?' C: {**Daha/Henüz**} **karar veremedim.** 'A: I haven't {yet} been able to decide.' Verbal object explicit: S: **Bu yaz ne yapacaksın?** 'Q: What are you going to do this summer?' C1: **Bu**

yaz Antalya'ya gitmey.e karar verdim. 'A1: I decided to go to Antalya this summer.' C2: * **N e yapacağ.ım.A** {**daha/henüz**} **karar veremedim.** 'A2: I haven't {yet} been able to decide θ what I'm going to do.' C3: **Ne yapacağ.ım.A** {**bir türlü**} **karar veremedim.** 'A3: I haven't been able to decide {at all} θ what I'm going to do.' **Ne yapacağım.ı, ne.yE karar vereceğimi bilemiyorum.** 'I just don't [lit., ** can't] know what to do, what to decide.' **Ne.yE karar vereceğimi şaşırdım.** 'I {don't/didn't} know what to do [lit., ** I {am/was} confused as to what to decide].' **Onun.LA evlenmey.e karar vermiştim ama sonra vazgeçtim.** 'I had decided to marry θ {him/her}, but then I changed my mind.' **O dersi bırakmay.a karar vermiştim ama** {**ev arkadaşım**} **beni vazgeçirdi.** 'I had decided to drop that class, but {my roommate/the person I live with/lit., my housemate} talked me out of it.' * **Hakim sanığ.ın suçlu olduğ.u.nA karar verdi.** 'The judge decided θ that the suspect was guilty.' * **Hakim tutuklu.nun serbest bırak.ıl.ma.sı.nA karar verdi.** 'The judge decided θ {that the person under arrest should be released/on the release of the person under arrest} [lit., ** decided to the being released of the...].' *359:7.* resolution: - resolve. → = **karar al-** [subj.: usually a group, organization, or society acting in an official capacity] → al- 1, = **kararlaştır-** [subj.: at least two persons reaching a decision together], **kararından vazgeç-** ['- change one's mind'].

karşılık ver- /A/ [**karşılık** 'response'] (1) '- respond /to/, - react /to/ a situation; - answer /θ/, - reply /to/ a question': **Eğer tanımadığın biri yolda san.A gülümserse nasıl karşılık verirsin?** 'If sb you don't know smiles AT you [out] on the street, how will you respond [i.e., behave]?' **Hiç bir mektubum.a karşılık vermedi.** 'He didn't {answer θ/respond to} any of my letters [lit., He responded to none of my letters].' * **Kapı.yI** {**çaldım çaldım**}, **ama kimse karşılık vermedi.** 'I {knocked and knocked/rang and rang} AT the door, but nobody answered.' * **Telefon ettim ama kimse karşılık**

vermedi. 'I TRIED TO phone him [lit., ** I phoned him], but no one answered.' *902:5*. reaction: - react. **Aşağıdaki sorular.A karşılık veriniz.** 'Answer θ the questions below.' *938:4*. answer: - answer. → = {cevap/yanıt} ver- above, = /I/ {cevapla-/cevaplandır-/yanıtla- }, ≠ soru sor-.
(2) '- talk back /to/, - answer back /to/': **Baban.a karşılık verme, * ne diyorsa onu yap!** 'Don't talk back to your father. * Just do what he says [lit., Whatever he says, do it]!' *142:8*. insolence: - sauce.

karşılığını ver- '- give the equivalent of a word, - define' [karşılık 'equivalent']: **Bu kelime.nin İngilizce karşı- lığ.ı.nı kim verebilir?** 'Who can give the English equivalent of this word?' **Aşağıdaki İngilizce kelimeler.in Türkçe karşılık- lar.ı.nı veriniz.** 'Give the Turkish equivalents of the English words below.' *341:9*. interpretation: - interpret. → = tanımla- ['- define'].

kız ver- '- give a girl in marriage /to/' [kız 1 'girl'. 2 'virgin']: **S: Kızınızı kim.e verdiniz?** 'Q: Who did you give your daughter in marriage to?' **C: Süleyman bey.lerin küçük oğlu.na verdik.** 'A: We gave her to the young son of the Süleyman family.' **Süleyman** is the FIRST name of the head of the family. *563:14*. marriage: - join in marriage. → **evlendir-** ['- marry, - give sb in marriage /TO/'], **nikâh kıy-** ['- perform the civil marriage ceremony, - officially join in marriage, - marry'] → kıy- 3.

* kilo ver- '- lose weight': **Bu ay tam dört kilo verdim.** 'I lost exactly 4 kilos this month.' *** Üzüntü.sü.nDEN bir haftada tam beş kilo verdi.** 'BECAUSE OF worry [lit., ** her worry], she lost exactly five kilos in one week.' **Doktor: Sağlığınız için en az 10 kilo vermeniz şart.** 'Doctor: For the sake of your health you must lose at least 10 kilos.' *270:13*. narrowness, thinness: - slenderize. → = zayıfla- 1, ≠ şişmanla-, ≠ kilo al- → al- 1, ≠ topla- 3, ≠ toplan- 4.

kira ver- '- pay rent /to/' [A. kira (. -) 'rent, rent money']: **S: * Kirayı ay.DAN ay.A mı veriyorsunuz?**

'Q: Do you pay the rent {BY the month/monthly} [lit., FROM month TO month]?' **C: Hayır kirayı üç ay.DA bir veriyorum.** 'A: No, I pay [the rent] once θ every three months.' **S: Kirayı kim.e veriyorsunuz?** 'Q: Who do you pay your [lit., the] rent to?' **C1: Kirayı ev sahib.i.nE veriyorum.** 'A1: I pay θ [the rent to] the landlord [lit., the owner of the house].' **C2: Kirayı * ev sahib.i.nin hesab.ı.na banka.ya yatırı- yorum.** 'A2: I deposit the rent * into the landlord's bank account [lit., ** into the landlord's account into the bank].' *624:10*. payment: - pay. → {kirada/kirayla} otur- ['- rent', i.e., - live by (paying) rent] → otur- 3.

kiraya ver-. → kirala- 2.

mahkemeye ver- '- sue, - take to court' [A. mahkeme 'court']: **Cemal bey kendisi.nE hakaret eden komşu.su.nu mahkeme.ye verdi.** 'Cemal bey took the [lit., his] neighbor who had insulted θ him to court.' *598:12*. legal action: - sue. → **dava aç-** ['- bring a suit or charges /against [sb], for [a misdeed]/, - file a complaint /against/ sb, - sue sb'] → aç- 12, **dava et-** ['- bring a suit or charges /AGAINST/, - sue'].

meme ver- '- breast-feed, - nurse, - suckle' [meme 'breast']: **Koltukta oturmuş, bebeğ.e meme veriyordu.** 'She had sat down in the chair and was [breast] feeding the baby.' Proverb: **Ağlamayan çocuğ.a meme vermezler.** 'One doesn't [lit., They don't] {nurse /lit., give the breast to} a child that doesn't cry.' The squeaky wheel gets the oil. → = emzir-. *8:19*. eating: - nourish.

misal ver-. → {örnek/misal} ver- below.

nefes ver- '- breathe out, - exhale, - let out a breath' [A. nefes 'breath']: **Doktor: Derin derin nefes alıp verin.** 'Doctor: Take a deep deep breath, then exhale.' *318:21*. * 1. wind: - breathe. → ≠ içine çek- ['- inhale'] → çek- 1, ≠ nefes al- ['- breathe, - take a breath; - inhale'] → al- 1, ≠ nefes çek- ['- take a wiff, drag (of tobacco)]' → çek- 1, **nefes tut-** ['- hold one's breath'] → tut- 4.

son nefesini ver- '- breathe one's last breath, - die': **Amcam, * sizlere ömür, dün akşam son nefesini verdi.** 'My [paternal] uncle, * [long] life to you [i.e., to the people addressed], breathed his last breath last night.' *307:19.* death: - die; *318:21.* * 1. wind: - breathe. → = **hayata gözlerini {kapa-/kapat-}** → {kapa-/kapat-} 1, = **hayata gözlerini yum-** → göz yum- 1, = **hayatını {kaybet-/yitir-}** ['- lose one's life, - die', of unnatural causes], = **öl-,** = **ömrünü tamamla-** ['- complete one's life, - come to the end of one's life, - die, - pass away'], = **vefat et-,** = **canından ol-** ['- lose one's life, - die', mostly for an unexpected and undeserved death] → ol- 7, ≠ **doğ-** 1, ≠ **dünyaya gel-** → gel- 1.

not ver- /A/ '- give a grade or mark /to/ sb or sth, - give /θ/ sb or sth a grade, - grade /θ/ sb or sth, - mark [an exam]': Person as object: **Öğretmen bu {sefer/kez} kardeşim.E {yüksek/düşük} not vermiş.** 'This {time} the teacher gave θ my brother [*or* my sister] {a high/a low} grade.'
Student production as object: * **Öğretmen kardeşim.in {sınav kâğıd.ı.nA/ödev.i.nE} yüksek not vermiş.** 'The teacher gave my brother a high mark {ON his examination/ON his homework.} [lit., ** gave {θ my brother's examination paper/θ my brother's homework} a high grade].' **Öğretmen verdiği notu değiştirmey.i reddetti.** 'The teacher refused to change the grade [that] he had given.' *945:9.* judgment: - estimate.

onur ver-. → {şeref/onur} ver-. → ver- 1 below.

oy ver- /A/ '- vote, - vote /for/, - give the vote /to/': **Oy.un.u {kim.e/hangi parti.ye} verdin?** '{Who/Which party} did you vote for?' **İnsanlar kim.e oy verecekler.i.ni bilmiyorlar, hatta hiç oy verme.me.yİ bile düşünüyorlar.** 'People don't know who they are going to vote for. In fact they are even considering not voting at all.' *371:18.* choice: - vote. → = **oy kullan-** ['- vote, - exercise the vote, - cast a vote'].

ödünç ver- /A/ '- lend money or an item /to/, - extend a loan /to/' [ödünç 'loan']: * **Ban.a biraz para ödünç verir misin?** 'Would you please lend me a little money?' → = **borç ver-** [money only]. → ≠ **borç al-** ['- take or - accept a loan', money only] → al- 1. * **Bana coğrafya kitabını birkaç günlüğ.ü.nE ödünç verir misin?** 'Would you lend me your geography book FOR a few days?' *620:5.* lending: - lend. → ≠ **ödünç al-** ['- borrow money or anything else /from/'] → al- 1.

{önem/ehemmiyet} ver- /A/ '- attach, - ascribe, or - give importance /to/, - consider important, - value /θ/, - think highly /of/' [{önem/A. ehemmiyet} 'importance']: NON-verbal noun as object: **Başbakan "Dış politika.ya önem veriyoruz" dedi.** 'The prime minister said, "We attach importance to foreign policy."' **Kenan senin fikirleri.nE çok önem veriyor.** 'Kenan values θ your {opinion/ideas} highly.' **Biz dostluğ.A önem veririz.** 'We value θ friendship.' **Doktor OLARAK, kim olursa olsun, hastaların.A önem veririm.** 'BEING a doctor, I value θ my patients, no matter who they are.' **Kenan san.A çok önem veriyor.** 'Kenan really {values/respects} θ you.'
VERBAL noun as object: **Suat, Nur'un partiye gelme.si.nE çok önem verdi.** 'Suat considered it very important that Nur come to the party [lit., ** gave great importance to Nur's coming to the party].' **Suat Nur'un partiye gelip gelme.me.si.nE önem vermez.** 'Suat doesn't care whether Nur comes to the party or not [lit., ** does not give importance to Nur's coming, not coming to the party].' *996:13.* importance: - value. → = /I/ **önemse-,** ≠ **küçümse-** 2.

{örnek/misal} ver- '- give, - cite, or - provide examples /for/' [{örnek/A. misal (. -) (misali)} 'example']: **Ne demek istediğinizi {anla.YAMA.dım}. Lütfen bir örnek verir misiniz?** '{I don't/I didn't/lit., I COULDN'T} understand what you meant. Would you please give me an example?' **Örnek vereyim, * daha iyi anlaşılır.** 'Let me give an example. * It will clear things up [lit., ** It (i.e., the matter) will be better understood].' **Şimdi size bu konu İLE ilgili bir iki örnek vereceğim.** 'Now I'll give you one or two examples ON this topic.' **{Konu.yu} daha iyi açıklamak için bir örnek vermek istiyorum.** 'I'd like to give an example to explain {the issue/the subject} more clearly.' **Anlaşılabilmesi için bir örnek vermek gerekirse...** 'If it is necessary to provide an example to clarify the matter...[lit., in order for (the matter) to be able to be clarified].' **Öğretmen.in anlattıklar.ı.nı anlamamıştık. Ancak * güncel bir örnek verdiği zaman anladık.** 'We didn't understand what the teacher was explaining. We only understood when he gave * an example from daily life.' *956:13.* evidence, proof: - cite.

para ver- /a: A, b: **A**, c: için/ '- pay /a: to, b: FOR, c: for/' [**para** 'money']: **{Bu elbise.yE/Bu elbise için} ne kadar para verdin?** 'How much did you pay {FOR this suit}?' **{Bu.nA/ Bu.nUN için} ne kadar para verdin?** 'How much did you pay {for this}?' **Bu elbise için terzi.yE ne kadar para verdin?** 'How much money did you pay θ the tailor FOR this suit?' **Onun için ne kadar para verdin?** 'How much did you pay for it?' **O.na ne kadar para verdin?** 'How much did you pay {HIM/HER}?' Proverb: **Parayı veren düdüğü çalar.** 'He who pays the money plays the whistle.', i.e., He who pays the piper calls the tune. *624:10.* payment: - pay. → = **öde-**, ≠ **para al-** → **al-** 1.

parti ver- /için/ '- give or - have a party /for/' [F. **parti** 'party']: **Yaş günüm için bir parti vermek istiyorum.** 'I want to have a birthday party [lit., ** I want to give a party for my birthday].' **Üniversiteyi bitirince ailem benim için bir parti verdi.** 'When I finished {college/ university}, my family gave a party for me.' *585:8.* hospitality, welcome: - entertain.

randevu ver- /a: A, b: A, c: için/ '- give or - grant an appointment /a: to [sb], b: FOR [sb], c: for [a time]/, - make an appointment /b: FOR [sb]/' [F. **randevu** 'appointment']: **Bakan bey bugünlerde çok meşgul.**

Sekreteri hiç kimse.yE randevu vermiyor. 'The minister is very busy these days. His secretary isn't making any appointments for anyone.' **Doktor bey 23 Eylül saat 4:15 için ban.a randevu verdi.** 'The doctor gave me an appointment for September 23rd at 4:15.' *478:12.* giving: - give; *964:4.* prearrangement: - prearrange. → **gün ver-** → **ver-** 1 above, ≠ **randevu al-** ['- get an appointment'] → **al-** 3, **gün al-** ['- get a {date/day} for an appointment '] → **al-** 3.

selâm ver- /A/ '- greet, - salute' [A. **selâm** (. -) 'salutation, greeting']: Person, not flag, as object: **Bana baktı ve * başıyla sessizce selâm verdi.** 'He looked at me and nodded {hello/in greeting} [lit., ...greeted (me) silently with (a nod of) his head].' **Asker kumandanını görünce selâm verdi.** 'When the soldier saw his commander, he saluted [him].' *585:10.* hospitality, welcome: - greet. → = **selâmla-** [person or flag as objects].

{sınav/imtihan} ver- (1) '- pass a test, exam[ination].' NOT for a teacher '‐ give an examination': **Öğrenci: {Türkçe sınav.ı.nı/ Türkçe ders.i.nin sınav.ı.nı} verdim ve sınıfımı geçtim.** 'A student: I passed {my Turkish exam/the exam for my Turkish class} and advanced to the next grade [lit., ** passed my class].' **Başka bir öğrenci: Maalesef ben sınav.ı ver.EME.dim ve sınıfta kaldım.** 'Another student: Unfortunately I didn't [lit., COULDN'T] pass the exam and was held back [lit., ** 'stayed in the class', i.e., didn't pass on to the next grade].' *409:7b.* success: - succeed in specific ways. → = **{sınav/ imtihan} kazan-** → **kazan-** 3, ≠ **{sınavdan/imtihandan} kal-** → **kal-** 1.
(2) /A, DAn/ '- GIVE an exam[ination] /to [sb], IN [a subject]/': **Bugün öğretmen öğrenciler.E {Türkçe.DEN/Felsefe.DEN/* Türkçe ders.i.nDEN} {sınav/imtihan} verdi.** 'Today the teacher gave the students an exam {IN Turkish/IN philosophy/* ON [the materials from] the Turkish lesson}.' *937:21.* inquiry: - interrogate. → = **imtihan et-** ['- test, - examine sb /IN [a subject]/'].

son ver- /A/ '- bring /θ/ sth to an end, - conclude, - finish, - put an end /to/ sth' [son 'end, conclusion'] *819:5.* end: - end sth. → = bitir- 1, = tamamla- ['- complete, - finish'], ≠ başla- 2.

işine son ver- '- fire, - relieve sb of his position' [iş 1 'work'. 2 'job'], lit., ** '- give an end /to/ sb's job', *neutral:* * **A n n e m hizmetçi.miz.in iş.i.ne son verdi.** 'My mother fired our servant.' *908:19.* ejection: - dismiss. → *formal:* = görevden al- → al- 1, *informal:* = işten {at-/kov-} → at- 1, kov- 2, *neutral:* = işten çıkar- → çıkar- 1, ≠ {ata-/tayin et-}, ≠ görevlendir-.

söz ver- /a: A, b: A, c: A dair, d: için, e: üzerine/ '- give one's word /a: to [sb], b: θ [that], c: to the effect that, d: that, e: on/, - promise /θ [sb sth], - assure' [söz 'word, utterance']: **Siz.E söz verdiğim kitap işte budur.** 'Here is the book I promised θ you.' **Bu yıl okulumu bitireceğim.E [dair] annem.E söz verdim, söz.üm.ü tutmak istiyorum.** 'I promised θ my mother θ that this year I would graduate [lit., ** finish my school]. I want to keep my promise.' **Kardeşim babam.A bir daha yalan söylemeyeceğ.i.nE [dair] söz verdi.** 'My brother promised θ my father θ that he would not lie again.' **S: Yarın benimle sinemaya geleceksin, değil mi?** 'Q: You'll come to the movies with me tomorrow, won't you?' **C: Evet, geleceğim, söz veriyorum.** 'A: Yes, I'll come. I promise.' * **Ayşe'yE yardım etmek İÇİN söz vermiştim.** 'I had promised θ Ayşe that I would help her [lit., ** I had promised θ Ayşe FOR helping].' * **Sigarayı bırakmak İÇİN kendi kendim.E söz vermiştim.** 'I had promised θ myself [that] I would stop smoking [lit., ** I had promised θ myself FOR leaving cigarettes].' **S: Biraz daha oturmaz mısın? Yemeği beraber yerdik.** 'Q: Won't you stay a little longer? We could eat together.' **C: Çok iyi olurdu, ama şimdi gitmem lâzım. Çünkü akşam yemeği için Aydın'A söz verdim.** 'A: That would have been nice, but I must go now because I promised θ Aydın [that] I would have dinner with him [lit., ** promised Aydın for the evening meal].' {a:

Namusum/b: Şerefim/c: Namusum ve şerefim} üzerine söz veriyorum. 'I {swear/promise} on {a: my honor/b: {my honor/my integrity}/c: lit., my honor and {my honor/my integrity}}.' *436:4.* promise: - promise. → = vadet- [today *less common, more formal* than söz ver-], yemin et- ['- swear /to [sb], that/'], sözünü tut- 1 ['- keep one's word or promise /to/'] → tut- 5.

su ver- /A/ '- give water /to/ [people, plants, animals], - water [plants, animals]': {**Çiçekler.e/ Hayvanlar.a} su verdin mi?** 'Did you water {the flowers?/the animals?}' *1063:12.* moisture: - moisten; *1068:7.* animal husbandry: - tend. → = /I/ sula-.

{şeref/onur} ver- /A, {ArAk/mAklA}/ '- honor /θ, by...ing/' [A. şeref 'honor']: **Evimiz.e {gel.erek/gel.mekle} biz.e şeref verdiniz efendim.** 'You honored us {by coming} to our house, {sir/ma'am}.' *646:8.* honor: - honor. → = /I, {ArAk/mAklA}/ onurlandır-.

şifa ver- /A/ '- restore to health, - cure, - heal' [A. şifa (. -) 'a restoring to health, good health']: **A: Kardeşim hasta, bir haftadır * yatıyor.** 'A: My brother is sick. * He's been in bed [lit., ** been lying down] for a week.' **B: Allah şifa versin!** 'B: May God restore him to health [lit., give him good health].' *86:38.* remedy: - remedy; *396:15.* restoration: - cure; *504:* * 20. courtesy: polite expressions. → tedavi et- 2 ['- cure a person or a disease'].

vakit ver-. → {zaman/ vakit/süre} ver- below.

yanıt ver-. → {cevap/yanıt} ver- above.

yol ver- '- yield, - give way', in traffic [yol 'road, way']: Traffic sign: **Yol ver.** '{Yield./Give way.}' *352:7.* publication: poster: * specific signs; *433:7.* submission: - yield.

zahmet ver- '- inconvenience /θ/, - trouble /θ/, - cause trouble /to/, - put sb to a lot of trouble, - put sb out, - give trouble /to/ sb' [A. **zahmet** 'trouble, difficulty, inconvenience']: Frequent in polite exchanges between a guest and his host: **Misafir: Pasta ve börekler çok nefis olmuş, fakat siz.E çok zahmet verdik.** 'Guest: The pastries and böreks were splendid [lit., very delicious], but we caused θ you a lot of trouble [i.e., by providing the occasion on which you had to prepare them].' **Ev sahibi: Estağfurullah. * Hiç zahmet olur mu?** 'The host [lit., owner of the house]: Please [i.e., don't say such a thing]. * How could it be trouble [for us]?' *995:4.* inexpedience: - inconvenience; *1012:13.* difficulty: - trouble. → **zahmet et-** ['- take trouble, - put oneself to trouble'].

{**zaman/vakit/süre**} **ver-** '- give sb some time [to finish a task]' [**süre** 'period, extension', A. **vakit** (vaKTİ) 'time', A. **zaman** (. -) 'time']: {**Hoca.M**}, **ödevimi henüz bitiremedim, ban.a biraz daha zaman verir misiniz?** '{Professor/Teacher} [lit., ** {MY professor/MY teacher}, the common form of address to a professor or teacher], I haven't been able to finish my homework yet. Would you give me a little more time?' * **Sana bir hafta süre veriyorum.** 'I'm giving you a week [lit., ** a one week period].' *845:9.* lateness: - postpone. → = **süre tanı-** → **tanı-** 5.

zekât ver- '- pay the zakat' [A. **zekât** (. -) 'the yearly alms tax required of Muslims, generally regarded as equal to 1/40th of one's property']: **İslâm'ın beş şartı; kelime-i şehadet, namaz kılmak, zekât vermek, oruç tutmak ve hacca gitmektir.** 'The five pillars [lit., (obligatory) conditions] of Islam are: the Shahadah [lit., the words of affirmation, i.e., to pronounce the words "There is no God but God and Muhammad is his Messenger"], to perform the namaz [i.e., the Islamic prayer ritual], to pay the zakat, to [observe the] fast, and to make the Pilgrimage [to Mecca].' **S: Zekâtını bu yıl {kim.e/* nere.ye} vermey.i düşünüyorsun?** 'Q: {To whom/To what groups [lit., ** To where]} are you considering to pay your zakat this year?' **C: Bu yıl zekâtımı {üniversitedeki fakir öğrenciler.e/Çocuk Esirgeme Kurumu'na} vereceğim.** 'A: This year I'll give my zakat {to poor university students/to the Children's Protective Society}.' **Zekâtını vermeyen mal.ı.nın hayr.ı.nı göremez.** 'The person who has not paid his zakat cannot obtain [lit., ** see, experience] the benefit of his {wealth/goods}.' *624:10.* payment: - pay; *701:14.* religious rites: - celebrate.

2 /A/ '- assign /to/': **Müdür bey bu işi kim.e verdi?** '{Who did the director assign this {task/project/job} to?/To whom did the director assign this {task/project/job}?}' **Öğretmen.in verdiğ.i şiiri ezberlemek istemiyordu.** 'He didn't want to memorize the poem that the teacher had assigned.' *478:12.* giving: - give.

3 /A/ '- take a break', with nouns designating 'break, rest', etc: * **ara ver-** /A/ '- take a break /FROM/, - stop doing sth for a while' [**ara** 'interlude, space'], lit., '- give a break /TO/': **Çok çalıştık biraz ara verebilir miyiz?** 'We've been working hard, can we take a brief break?' **İki saattir çalışıyoruz, yorulduk. Ha[y]di on beş dakika ara verelim.** 'We've been working for two hours. We're tired. Come on, let's take a fifteen minute break.' **Öğretmen: * Ha[y]di ders.E biraz ara verelim.** 'Teacher: Come on, let's take a short break FROM the lesson.' **Tanınmış sinema yıldızı * gönül işler.i.nE bir süreliği.nE ara verdiğini söyledi.** 'The famous movie star said * that she had taken a break FROM affairs of the heart FOR a while.' *20:8.* rest, repose: - take a rest; *224:3.* interval: - interspace. → = **mola ver-** → below, next item, = **teneffüs yap-** → **yap-** 3.

mola ver- '- stop for a rest [while traveling], - take a break [while working], - make a rest stop', for workers or vehicles, not students or professionals except when speaking *very informally* [It. **mola** 'rest, pause, break']: **İşçiler: Sabahtan beri çalışıyoruz, artık mola verelim.** 'Workers: We've been working all morning. Let's finally take a break.' **Ankara'dan İzmir'e giderken otobüsümüz üç defa mola verdi.** 'While going from Ankara to Izmir, our bus made three rest stops.' *20:8.* rest, repose: - take a rest; *224:3.* interval: - interspace. → = **ara ver-**

419

→ preceding subentry, = teneffüs yap- → yap- 3.

4 The structure verb stem.Iver-, i.e., I + ver-, may convey the sense of 'just, quickly, with ease': {a: Saatler/b: Günler/c: Haftalar/ d: Aylar/e: Mevsimler/f: Yıllar} ne çabuk geç.iverdi. 'How quickly {a: the hours/b: the days/c: the weeks/d: the months/e: the seasons/f: the years} have passed!' *174:17.* swiftness: ADV. swiftly.

5 The structure verb stem.Iver-, even without lütfen 'please', may convey the sense of a polite request: Ha[y]di kızım, şu pencereleri sil.iver. 'Come on {dear/child/lit., ** my girl}, [would you] please wipe these windows.' Turhan, * elektrikler geldi, mumu üfle.yiver. 'Turhan, * the lights have come back on. [Would you] please blow out the candle.' *440:20.* request: INTERJ. - please; *504: * 20.* courtesy: polite expressions.

veril- [ir] /A/ '- be given /to/' [ver- + pass. suf. -Il]: Bu görev kim.e verildi? '{θ Who was given this task?/To whom was this task given?}' *478:12.* giving: - give.

son veril- /{tarafından/CA}/ '- be ended, concluded /by/' [son 'end'] *819:5.* end: - end sth: görevine son veril- '- be fired' [görev 1 'duty'. 2 'office, post'], lit., ** 'for an end to be given to his duty': Profesör Bilgin'in görev.i.ne son verildi. 'Professor Bilgin was fired [lit., ** Professor Bilgin's duty was given an end to].' *908:19.* ejection: - dismiss. → = görevden alın- → alın- 1, = işinden ol- → ol- 7, ≠ {atan-/tayin edil-}, ≠ tayin ol- → ol- 12.

toprağa veril- /DA/ '- be buried, laid to rest /in/, - be interred /in/', for dead bodies only [toprak 'earth, ground']: Cenazeler vakit geçir.il.meden toprağ.A verildi. 'The corpses were buried without delay [lit., ** without letting time be passed].' * Nusret amcanın cenaze.si bugün aile mezarlığı.nda toprağ.A verildi. 'Uncle Nusret [lit., Uncle Nusret's corpse] {was buried/was laid to rest} today in the family {tomb/grave}.' İstanbul'daki Amerikan Hastanesinde böbrek yetmez-

liğ.i.nden yaşam.ı.nı yitiren 63 yaşındaki Amerikalı John Smith, {vasiyeti gereği/vasiyeti.nE uygun olarak} bugün Hıristiyan Mezarlığı'nda toprağa verildi. 'The 63-year-old American John Smith, who died as a result of kidney failure in the American Hospital in Istanbul, was buried today IN the Christian cemetery {in accordance with the requirements of his will/in accordance with his will}.' *309:19.* interment: - inter. → = formal: /A/ defnedil-, = /A/ gömül- [for dead bodies and other objects].

vicdan azabı çek-. → çek- 5.

vur- [UR] 1 /a: A, b: lA, c: A/ '- hit, - strike /a: θ [sb, sth], b: with, c: ON/, - knock, - kick, - slap, - bump', depending on the preceding noun: Hedef.E üç kurşun attı ama vuramadı. 'He shot three bullets AT the target, but he {missed/lit., couldn't hit it}.' * Arabam.ı direğ.E vurdum. '{I ran my car INTO a pole./I ran INTO a pole with my car./I struck θ a pole WITH my car.} [lit., ** I struck my car INTO a pole].' → = çarp- 1. # {Başım.ı/ Kolum.u/Ayağım.ı} kapı.yA vurdum. 'I hit [or bumped] {my head/my arm/my foot} ON the door.' *901:14.* impulse, impact: - hit.

eliyle vur- '- slap, - strike with one's hand' [el 'hand']: Nihat * el.i.yLE suratım.A vurdu. 'Nihat * slapped me IN the face [lit., ** hit θ my face WITH his hand].' *604:12.* punishment: - slap; *901:19.* impulse, impact: - hit. → = tokat {at-/vur-) → at- 5, tokat ye- ['- get a slap, - be slapped'] → ye- 2.

* kapıyı vur- (1) '- knock {AT/ON} the door': * Kapı.yI vurdu ve içeri girdi. 'He knocked AT the door and entered.' Proverb: Rüşvet kapı.yI vurmadan içeri girer. 'A bribe enters without knocking AT the door.' *901:16.* impulse, impact: - pound. → = kapıyı çal- → çal- 4. (2) '- slam the door': Genç adam sinirli bir şekilde kapıyı vurup çıkmıştı. 'The young man angrily slammed the door and left.' *53:7.* loudness: - din. → = kapıyı çarp- → çarp- 1, ≠ kapıyı yavaş {kapa-/kapat-} ['- close the door

{gently/quietly}', i.e., Don't slam the door.'] → {kapa-/kapat-} 1.

tekme vur-. → tekme {at-/vur-). → at- 5.

tokat vur-. → tokat {at-/vur-). → at- 5.

yumruk vur-. → yumruk {at-/vur-}. → at- 5.

2 /I/ '- shoot; - shoot dead': **Kan davası yüzünden beş köylü birbirini vurdu.** 'Because of a blood feud, five villagers shot one another.' **O adamı kızkardeşim.in ırz.ı.nA geçtiği için vurdum, pişman değilim.** 'I shot that man because he had raped my sister. I have no regrets.' • Note the difference between **Arif'E vurdu.** 'He {STRUCK/HIT} Arif.' and **Arif'İ vurdu.** 'He SHOT Arif.' *308:17.* killing: - strike dead; *903:12.* pushing, throwing: - shoot.

vurgula- [r] [vurgu 'accent, stress' + verb-forming suf. -lA] 1 '- emphasize, - stress, - lay stress on', often with a word denoting importance or necessity: **Öğretmenimiz {hep/daima} telâffuz.un önem.i.ni vurgulardı.** 'Our teacher {always} used to stress the importance of pronunciation.' **Toplantıda su tasarruf.u.nun {gereklilİğ.i.ni/önem.i.ni} vurguladılar.** 'At the meeting they stressed {the necessity/the importance} of water conservation.' *996:14.* importance: - emphasize. → = altını çiz- 2 ['-underline, - emphasize'].
2 '- accent, - accentuate, - stress, - put the stress on': **İstanbul kelimesinde "tan" hece.si.ni iyi vurgulayın.** 'In the word "Istanbul" put heavy stress on the syllable "tan" [lit., ** stress the syllable "tan" well].' *901:12.* impulse, impact: - thrust, - push; *996:14.* importance: - emphasize.

- Y -

yadırga- [r] '- find strange, odd': **Çocuk nedense bir türlü uyumuyor, herhalde yerini yadırgadı.** 'For some reason the child just isn't going to sleep. He probably finds this place [lit., ** his place, i.e., where he is] strange.' To express disapproval: **Bu kaba davranış.ın.ı gerçekten çok yadırgadım.** 'I really found this {rude/vulgar} behavior of yours very strange.' *869:8.* * *1.* abnormality: - find strange. → = {acayibine/garibine/tuhafına} git- → git- 1b.

yağ- [ar] '- come down', mostly of rain, snow, hail. *194:5.* descent: - descend: **kar yağ-** '- snow' [kar 'snow']: **Sabahleyin pencere.DEN baktım. Çok kar yağmış.** 'I looked {OUT/OUT OF} the window in the morning. It had snowed heavily.' * **Mevsim kıştı, kar yağıyordu.** 'It was winter [lit., ** The season was winter]. It was snowing.' *1022:11.* cold: - hail. For snow '- stop', → din-, dur- 2, kesil- 2.

yağmur yağ- '- rain' [yağmur 'rain']: **Bugün yağmur yağacak mı?** 'Is it going to rain today?' From your own observation [i.e., of clouds, etc.] you say: * **Yağmur yağacak gibi.** 'It looks like it's going to rain.' or **Galiba yağmur yağacak.** Same translation as above or 'It's probably going to rain.' From what you have heard or read you say: **Yağmur yağacakmış.** '{They say/I hear} it's going to rain.' **{Çok fazla/Şiddetli} yağmur yağıyordu.** 'It was raining {a lot/heavily}.' * **Sağanak hal.i.nde yağmur yağıyordu.** 'It was pouring down heavily [lit., ** It was raining in the state of a downpour].' * **Bardak.tan boşanır.casına yağmur yağıyordu.** 'It was {pouring/raining cats and dogs} [lit., ** raining as if a (drinking) glass were being emptied all at once].' Note also the synonym **yağmur yap-** lit., ** '- make rain': **Dün sabah {biraz/çok} yağmur yaptı ama * sonra birden hava açtı.** 'Yesterday morning it rained {a little/a lot}, but * then it suddenly cleared up [lit., ** the weather opened].' **Üç gün aralıksız yağdıktan sonra, sonunda yağmur {dindi/kesildi}.** 'After it had rained continuously for three days, the rain finally {stopped}.' **Üç gündür yağan yağmur dinmiş.** 'The rain that had been coming down for three days stopped.' Proverb: **Yağmur yağarken küpleri doldurmalı.** 'One must fill the [water] jugs while it is raining.', i.e., take advantage of available opportunities. Make hay while the sun shines. *316:9* rain: - rain. For rain '- stop', → din-, dur- 2, kesil- 2.

yağla- [r] '- grease, - oil' [yağ 'oil, grease' + verb-forming suf. -lA]: **Fırın tepsi.si.ni hafifçe yağlayın.** 'Lightly grease the baking pan.' {**Traş makina.sı.nın dişler.i.ni/Bisiklet.in zincir.i.ni**} **en az ayda bir kere yağlarsan iyi olur.** 'It would be good if you oiled {the razor [lit., the teeth, i.e., cutting edge, of the razor]/the bicycle chain} at least once a month.' *1054:8.* oils, lubricants: - oil.

yağmur çisele-. → **çisele-.**

<u>**yak-**</u> [ar] 1 '- light, - ignite, - set /ON/ fire, - set fire /TO/, - burn': {**a: Ocağ.ı/b: Fırın.ı/c: Soba.yı/d: Şömine.yi/e: Mangal.ı**} **yakar mısın?** 'Would you please light {a: the range [only the burners on top of the stove]/b: the oven/c: the stove [used for heating]/d: the fireplace/e: the **mangal** [i.e., a kind of brazier]}.' **Ahmet bey bir** {**sigara/ puro/pipo**} **yaktı. Derin bir nefes** {**çekti/aldı**}. 'Ahmet bey lit up a {cigarette/cigar/pipe}. He took a deep drag [*or* inhaled deeply].' → ≠ **söndür- 1.** # **Bu odunları sobada yakabilirsiniz.** 'You {can/may} burn this wood in the stove.' **Teröristler tiyatro bina.sı.nI yakmışlar.** 'The terrorists {set fire TO the theater [lit., theater building]/set the theater ON fire}.' <u>Proverb:</u> **Ateş düştüğü yeri yakar.** 'A fire burns [only] the place where it falls.', i.e., A calamity really affects only its immediate victims. *1019:22.* heating: - ignite.

ateş yak- '- light a fire' [P. **ateş** 'fire']: **Hava soğuktu. Balıkçılar ısınmak için ateş yakmışlardı.** 'The weather was cold. The fishermen had lit a fire [in order] to warm themselves.' *1019:22.* heating: - ignite. → ≠ **söndür- 1.**

2 '[for a substance or instrument, not a fire] - burn, - make smart, - ache': {**Acı biber/Sıcak çay/Şurup**} **ağzımı yaktı.** '{The hot pepper/The hot tea/The medicine [i.e., as a syrup]} burned my mouth.' **Kızım, süt sıcak.** * **Birden içme, ağzını**

yakarsın. Yavaş yavaş yudumla.yarak iç. '{Dear/Child/lit., ** My girl}, the milk is hot. * Don't [try to] drink it all at once. You'll burn your mouth. * Sip it slowly [lit., ** Drink by sipp.ing it].' *26:7.* pain: - inflict pain.

* **canını yak-** '- hurt' [P. **can** (-) 'soul'], lit., ** '- burn sb's soul': **Dikiş dikerken elime batan iğne can.IM.ı yaktı.** 'While sewing, I pricked myself with a needle and hurt myself [lit., ** the needle that sank into MY hand hurt MY soul].' A threat: **Yakarım can.ın.ı!** 'I'll really make you suffer [lit., ** I'll burn your soul]!' *26:7.* pain: - inflict pain. → = **canını acıt-** ; *514: * 5.* threat: INTERJ. specific threats.

3 '- turn *or* - switch on', electricity, light, lamp, but NOT radio, TV: * **Oda.nın iç.i çok karanlık.** {**Işığ.ı/Lâmba.yı/Elektriğ.i**} **yakar mısın?** 'The room [lit., ** the inside of the room] is very dark. Would you turn on {the light[s]/the lamp/the electricity}?' *1031:25.* electricity: - electrify. → = **aç- 2** [also for radio, TV], ≠ {**kapa-/kapat-**} **2,** ≠ **söndür- 2.**

yakala- [r] /DAn/ 1 '- catch; - collar, - nab; - seize, - grab, - snatch, - get hold of /BY/' [**yaka** 'collar' + verb-forming suf. -lA]: **Sinan topu attı, Emre yakaladı.** 'Sinan threw the ball, and Emre caught it.' → ≠ **at- 1** [' - throw']. **Hırsız.ın** {**arka.sı.nDAN/peş.i.nDEN**} **koştum ama yakalayamadım.** 'I ran {after} the thief, but I couldn't catch him.' **Polis hırsızı * kolu.nDAN yakaladı.** 'The {[police] officer/cop} * caught the thief {BY THE arm/lit., by HIS arm}.' → = **ele geçir- 1** → **geçir- 1. Kaçan balonu yakaladım.** 'I caught the balloon that was flying away [lit., escaping].' *480:14.* taking: - seize. → = **tut- 1,** ≠ **bırak- 5.**

2 '- catch, - be able to hear, understand': **Türkçem hâlâ istediğim düzeyde değil. Bir konuşma dinlerken bazen çok önemli kelimeler.i** {**kaçırı-yorum/yakalayamıyorum**}. 'My Turkish isn't yet at the level I would like it to be. When listening to a conversation, I sometimes {miss/can't catch} [some] important

Part 1: Turkish-English Dictionary of Verbs

words.' *48:11.* hearing: - hear; *521:7.* intelligibility: - understand. → ≠ kaçır- 1.

yakalan- [ır] [yakala- + pass. suf. -n] 1 /{tarafından/CA}/ '- be caught /by/; - be collared, nabbed /by/; - be seized, grabbed, snatched /by/': **Hırsızlar bir saat süren kovalamaca sonunda yakalandılar.** 'The thieves were caught at the end of a one hour chase.' **Bisikletli kapkaççı amansız bir takip sonucu yakalandı.** 'The purse-snatcher on a bicycle was caught as a result of a relentless pursuit.' **Üç bombacı {a: suçüstü/b: kaçarken} yakalandı.** 'Three bombers were caught {a: {red handed/in the act}/b: while fleeing}.' **Polise 3,5 [üç buçuk] kilo eroin satmak * isterken yakalandılar.** 'They were caught * trying to sell 3.5 kilos of heroin to the police.' **Sınır.DAN geçen 80 kaçak, polis tarafından yakalandı.** 'Eighty fugitives who had crossed {θ/over} the border were seized by the police.' **Müzeden kıymetli eserleri çalan hırsız [polis tarafından] yakalandı.** 'The thief who had stolen valuable objects from the museum was caught [by the police].' *480:14.* taking: - seize. → = tutul- 1.

2 /A/ '- catch /θ/, - come down /WITH/, or - be struck down /BY/ an illness': **Arkadaşım ağır bir hastalığ.A yakalandı, inşallah * atlatır.** 'My friend has come down WITH a serious illness, I hope [lit., God willing] * he'll pull through.' **Zavallı çocuk {a: amansız/b: ölümcül/c: öldürücü/d: vahim/e: tedavisi olmayan} bir hastalığ.A yakalandı.** 'The poor child was struck down BY {a: {a cruel/an unsparing}/b, c: a fatal/d: {a serious/a grave}/e: an incurable} disease.' *85:46a.* disease: - take sick in general. **Tatil.e gittiği şehirde {ciddî bir hastalığ.A/ kolera.yA} yakalanarak hastane.ye kaldırıldı.** 'Having come down {WITH a serious illness/WITH cholera} in the city that he had gone to on vacation, he was taken to the hospital.' → = fena ol-1 → ol- 10.2, = fenalaş- 2, = hasta ol- → ol- 10.2, = hastalan-, = rahatsız ol- 1 → ol- 10.2, iyileş- ['- get better, - improve, - get well, - recover from an illness'].

3 /A/ '- be caught /ON/ camera, /BY/ the lens, - be photographed unexpectedly or unawares': **Hırsız kasayı soyarken {kamera.yA/ objektif.E} yakalanmış.** 'The thief was caught {ON camera/BY the lens} as he was robbing the safe.' *714:14.* photography: - photograph.

4 /A/ '- be caught /IN/ certain unfavorable weather conditions': **Yolda {a: yağmur.A/b: kar.A/c: dolu.yA/d: tipi.yE} yakalandık.** 'On the way we were caught {a: IN the rain/b: IN the snow/c: IN the hail/d: IN the {snow-storm/blizzard}}.' Proverb: **Yağmurdan kaçarken dolu.yA yakalandık.** 'While escaping from the rain, we got caught IN the hail', i.e., Out of the frying pan into the fire. *317:10.* air, weather: - air. → = tutul- 6.

yakın- [ır] /D A n, A/ '- complain /ABOUT, to/ yourself or to a friend, but usually not to a responsible authority': **{a: Gürültü.DEN/b: Otel.in pisliğ.i.nDEN/c: Yemekler.in kötülüğ.ü.nDEN/ d: Mağazalar.ın pahalı-lığ.ı.nDAN} yakındı.** She complained {a: ABOUT the noise/b: ABOUT the dirty hotel [lit., ** the dirt of the hotel]/c: ABOUT the bad food [lit., the low quality of the food]/d: ABOUT the high prices of the stores}.' **{Bu.nDAN/* Bunlar.DAN} yakındı.** 'She complained {ABOUT that/* ABOUT these things}.', i.e., the things mentioned above. *333:5.* dissent: - object. → = şikâyet et- a).

* **yakış-** [ır] 1 /A/ '- be suitable, appropriate, right /FOR/, - be suited /to/, - be becoming /to/, - go well /IN/, - become /θ/': NON-verbal noun as subject: **Bu çiçek karşı köşe.yE daha çok yakışır.** 'This plant would {be/go} better IN the facing corner.' **Bu köşe.yE bir abajur yakışır.** 'A lamp would go well IN this corner.' **Ahmet ve Ayşe mükemmel bir çift, birbirleri.nE çok yakışıyorlar.** 'Ahmet and Ayşe are a perfect couple. They are {perfect FOR/perfectly suited TO} each other.' **Kardeş.in.e vurduğ.un.u görünce çok şaşırdım. Bu hareket san.A hiç yakışmıyor.** 'When I saw you hitting your younger brother, I was very surprised.

Such behavior [lit., This action] does not become θ you at all.' Proverb: **Her şey yerinde yakışır.** 'Everything is appropriate in its [own] place.' A place for everything and everything in its place.
VERBAL noun as subject: **Bu yaşta sigara içmek san.A hiç yakışmıyor.** 'It's quite inappropriate [lit., It isn't at all appropriate] for you to smoke at your age [lit., at this (young) age].' *866:3.* conformity: - conform.

2 /A/ 'for sth - look good /ON/, - suit /θ/': **Bu elbise san.A çok yakışıyor!** 'This suit looks very good ON you!' **Bu pantolon o.nA hiç yakışmadı.** 'These trousers {looked terrible ON him/didn't look good ON him at all}.' Proverb: * **Güzel.E ne yakışmaz.** 'Anything will look good ON an attractive person. [lit., What doesn't look good on a beauty?].' *866:3.* conformity: - conform. → = **iyi dur-** → **dur-** 9, = **tam gel-** → **gel-** 2, = **uy-** 1.

* **yakıştır-** [ır] /A/ '- regard sth as suitable /FOR/ sb; - think that sth befits /θ/ sb', often in the negative abilitative form [yakış- + caus. suf. -DIr]: Thing as object: * **O elbise.yi kendi.nE nasıl yakıştırmış, * hayret doğrusu!** 'How could he have imagined that that suit would look good on him! * I'm really surprised [lit., It's really surprising]!'
Behavior as object: * **Bu yaşta sigara içmey.İ san.A hiç yakıştır.AMA.dım.** 'I couldn't imagine that you would be smoking at this [young] age.', i.e., It's unlike you. * **Büyükler.E KARŞI saygısızlık etme.N.i san.A yakıştır.AMI.yorum.** 'I'm surprised at YOUR lack of respect FOR [your] elders [i.e., I CAN'T reconcile your showing disrespect for your elders with what I know about you. This isn't like you at all.].' * **Anne.n.e yalan söyleme.N.i san.A yakıştır.AMA.dım.** 'I was surprised at YOUR {telling lies/lying} to your mother [i.e., I COULDN'T reconcile your lying with what I know about you.].' *866:3.* conformity: - conform; *867:4.* nonconformity: not - conform.

yaklaş- [ır] /A/ '- approach /θ/, - draw near /to/, - come close /to/, up /to/, over /to/': **Çok ciddîyim, * yaklaşma, vururum.** 'I'm quite

serious. * Keep your distance [lit., Don't approach], [or] I'll shoot.' * **Yaklaşmayın. Köpek var, saldırır.** 'Beware of the dog! [lit., Don't approach. There is a dog. It will attack.].' *352:7.* publication: poster: * specific signs. **Vapur yavaş yavaş liman.A yaklaştı.** 'The steamer slowly approached θ the pier.' **Tanımadığım bir adam yan.ım.A yaklaştı.** 'A man I didn't know {came over to/came up to/approached θ} me [lit., ** came to my side].' **Askerler gece karanlığında sürün.erek sessizce düşman mevziler.i.nE doğru yaklaşıyorlardı.** 'The soldiers, crawl.ing along the ground in the dark of night, were silently approaching enemy positions.' → = **gel-** 1, = **ulaş-** 1, = **var-**, = **yanaş-** 1, ≠ **uzaklaş-** 1. * {a: Gitme/b: Dönme/c: Yemek/d: Ders/e: Konser} **zaman.ı yaklaşıyor.** 'The time for {a: departure/b: returning/c: eating/d: the lesson/e: the concert} is approaching.' **Savaş adım adım yaklaşıyor.** 'War is approaching step by step.' **Tehlike.nin yaklaştığ.ı.nı sezdim.** 'I sensed that danger was approaching.' *167:3.* approach: - approach; *223:7.* nearness: - near, - come near. → = **gel-** 1.

yaklaştır- [ır] /A/ '- bring one thing /{to/NEAR/UP TO/OVER TO}/ another, - join' [yaklaş- + caus. suf. -DIr]: **Turgut sandalye.yi masa.yA yaklaştırdı.** 'Turgut brought the chair OVER TO the table.' **Yeni yapılan köprü iki semti birbiri.ne yaklaştırdı.** 'The new [lit., newly built] bridge joined the two districts [to each other].' *223:13.* nearness: - juxtapose; *799:5.* joining: - put together. → **getir-** ['- bring /from, to/, - fetch, - get'], ≠ **uzaklaştır-**.

yalan söyle-. → **söyle-** 1.

yalanla- [r] '- deny, - contradict, - refute, - declare or - show to be false or wrong' [yalan 'lie' + verb-forming suf. -lA]: The information as object: **Basın sözcü.sü {haberi/ iddiaları/söylentileri} yalanladı.** 'The press spokesman denied {the report/the claims [or allegations]/the rumors}.' **Büyükelçi bazı gazetelerde kendisi.ne atfen yayımlanan bazı haberleri yalanladı.** 'The ambassador denied certain published reports attributed to him in certain newspapers.' **Hükümet sözcüsü konu.yLA ilgili söylentileri ne doğruladı ne de yalanladı.** 'The government spokesman {neither confirmed nor denied/did not confirm or deny} the rumors [ON the subject].' **Bu öyle saçma bir iddia ki yalanlamay.a bile gerek duymuyorum.** 'This is such an absurd claim that I don't even feel the need to deny it.'

The act of stating as object: **Fatma bu sözleri söylediğini hemen yalanlamıştı.** 'Fatma at once denied [that] she had said these words.'

The claimer as object: * **Öyle diyorsunuz ama [somut] gerçekler {siz.İ yalanlıyor}.** 'That's what you say, but the facts [lit., (concrete) facts] {contradict you/show that you are wrong}.' *335:4.* negation, denial: - deny; *451:6.* opposition: - contradict; *957:5.* disproof: - refute. → ≠ **doğrula-,** ≠ **tasdik et-.**

yalnız bırak-. → **bırak-** 4.

yalnızlık çek-. → **çek-** 5.

yalvar- [ır] /A, için/ '- plead /with [sb], for/, - beg /θ [sb], {for/TO}/, - beseech /θ [sb], {for/TO}/': **Kadın adam.A yalvarıyordu: "Lütfen ban.A biraz kolaylık gösterin. Borcumu yarın ödeyeceğim".** 'The woman was pleading WITH the man: "Please give me a break [lit., ** Show me a little ease]. I'll pay what I owe you [lit., my debt] tomorrow".' **Evlenme teklif.i.ni kabul etme.si İÇİN kız.A yalvardı.** 'He begged θ the girl TO accept his proposal of marriage [lit., ** FOR her accepting...].' **Günahlar.ı.nı affetme.si İÇİN Allah'A yalvarıyordu.** 'He was beseeching θ God TO forgive his sins [lit., ** FOR His forgiving of his sins].' *440:11.* request: - entreat.

yan- [ar] 1 'for sth - burn, - be on fire, - be burning; - burn up, down' [i.] [ADJ. **yanık** 'burnt']: **Dünkü orman yangınında iki ev yandı.** 'Two houses burned in yesterday's forest fire.' **Üç katlı bina cayır cayır yanıyordu.** 'The three story building was burning fiercely.' **7 çocuk yan.ARAK öldü.** 'Seven children burned to death [lit., ** died BY burn.ING].' *307:24.* death: - die a

natural death. Proverbs: **Herkes kendi günah.ı.na göre yanar.** 'Everyone burns according to his own sins.' **Yalancının evi yanmış, kimse inanmamış.** 'The liar's house burned down. No one believed him.', i.e., when he said that his house was on fire. *1019:24.* heating: - burn.

canı yan- '- feel pain' [P. **can** (-) 'soul'], lit., 'for one's soul to burn': * **Ayağım taş.A çarpınca can.IM çok yandı.** '{When I hit my foot ON a rock/lit., When my foot hit θ the rock}, it really hurt [lit., ** MY soul really burned].' *26:8.* pain: - suffer pain. → = **canı acı-** → **acı-** 1.

2 '- burn out': **Bu {ampul/ floresan} yanmış, değiştirelim.** 'This {bulb/ fluorescent tube} has burned out. Let's change it.' *1021:8.* incombustibility: - burn out.

3 /DAn/ '- get or - be burned, scorched, singed /{BY/from}/; - get a burn, - get scalded; - get sunburned': **Elim kızgın fırın.a değdi ve yandı.** 'My hand touched θ the hot oven and got burned.' **{Acı biber.DEN/Sıcak çay.DAN/ Şurup.TAN} ağzım yandı.** 'My mouth got burned {{BY/from} the hot pepper/{BY/from} the hot tea/{BY/ from} the medicine [i.e., in the form of a syrup]}.' **Güneş.TEN kollarım ve bacaklarım yandı.** 'My arms and legs got burned {BY/from} the sun.' **Bu yaz epey yandım.** 'This summer I got {very/really/quite} sunburned.' Proverb: **Süt.TEN ağzı yanan yoğurdu üfle.yerek yer.** 'A person whose mouth has been burned BY [hot] milk blows on [his] yogurt [before] eating it [lit., eats the yogurt blow.ing on it].' Yogurt is usually served cold. Once bitten, twice shy. *1019:24.* heating: - burn.

4 * '- GO on', a source of light: **{Işık/Lâmba/Ampul} yandı.** '{The light/The lamp/The light bulb} went on.'

'- turn [yellow, red, green. subj.: traffic lights only]': * **Karşıda {sarı/kırmızı/yeşil} ışık yandı.** 'Across the street [lit., On the {opposite/facing} side], the light turned {yellow/red/green} [lit., ** the yellow (traffic)... light went on].' *1024:27.* light: - grow light. → =

425

açıl- 6, ≠ sön- 1, ≠ kapan- 2, ≠ kesil- 3 ['- be cut off, interrupted /by/', electricity, water].
5 '- BE on [light, electricity], - be burning [light]': {Işık/Lâmba} yanıyor. '{The light/The lamp} is on.'

'- be a color', traffic lights only: * Bak kırmızı ışık yanıyor. 'Look, the light is red [lit., ** the red (traffic) light IS burning].' 1024:23. light: - shine.

6 colloq. '- have had it; - be sunk, done for, doomed, in serious trouble': Baban bu {iş.İ} duyarsa yandık. 'If your father hears ABOUT this {affair/business/matter}, we've had it.' 395:11 destruction: - do; 1012:11. difficulty: - have difficulty. → = hapı yut-.

7 /A, için/ '- be consumed with love /for/, - be madly in love /WITH/, - be mad /ABOUT/; - feel a burning [sexual] desire /for/, slang: - have the hots /for/': Aslı için yandı kül oldu Kerem. 'Kerem was madly in love with Aslı [f.] [lit., ** burned for Aslı], he became ashes.' 104:19. love: - love.

yanıp tutuş- /A, için/ '- be consumed with passion /for/, - be mad /about/, slang: - have the hots /for/': Metin Filiz İÇİN yanıp tutuşuyor ama kızın bu.nDAN haberi bile yok. 'Metin is simply mad ABOUT Filiz [f.] [lit., has caught fire and is burning for Filiz], but the girl is completely unaware OF that [lit., doesn't even have any news of that].' 104:19. love: - love.

8 '- get overexposed', photographs: Tatil.de çektiğim fotoğraflar.ın hep.si yanmış. 'All the photographs [that] I took {on/during} my [lit., the] vacation got overexposed.' 714:14. photography: - photograph.

yanaş- [ır] 1 /A/ '- draw near /to/, - approach /θ/; - come up /to/, over /to/, - sidle up /to/' [yan 'side' + verb-forming suf. -Aş] → = yaklaş-: yanına yanaş- '- come up to, over to, - come /to/ the side of, - sidle up to': Cemil {Serpil'E/ Serpil'in yan.ı.nA} yanaştı ve kulağı.nA bir şeyler fısıldadı. 'Cemil {came up to Serpil/over to Serpil [lit., ** came up to Serpil's side]} and

whispered something [lit., ** somethingS] IN her ear.' 167:3. approach: - approach; 223:7. nearness: - near, - come near. → = yanına gel- → gel- 1.

2 /A/ 'for a vehicle - draw or - pull /{UP TO/ALONGSIDE}/': for a ship - dock, a train - draw or - pull up to the platform': Tren peron.A yanaştı. 'The train has {pulled/drawn} UP TO the platform.' Yalova vapur.u iskele.yE yanaşmak üzere. 'The Yalova ferry is about to draw UP TO the pier.' Gemi iskele.yE iyice yanaşmadan binmey.e kalkış-ma! 'Don't attempt to get on the ship before it has drawn all the way UP TO the pier! [lit., ** without it drawing well up to the pier]' 167:3. approach: - approach; 223:7. nearness: - near, - come near; 352:7. publication: poster: * specific signs. → = yaklaş-.

3 /A/ * '- be willing or inclined /to/, - want /to/, - be willing to agree /to/; - go along /WITH/ a plan': Usually used in the negative: Babam dediklerimi anlamay.a yanaş-madı, kendi fikr.i.nde inat etti. 'My father {lit., didn't want to understand/wasn't willing to listen to} what I had said. He insisted on his own opinion.' 324:3. willingness: - be willing; 441:2. consent: - consent.

yanıl- [ır] '- be mistaken, wrong': * Uzaktan gelen adam.ı Yusuf sanıp selâm verdim; ama yanılmışım, değilmiş. 'Thinking the person coming in the distance was Yusuf, I greeted him, but it seems I was mistaken. Apparently it wasn't him.' * Sen.İ dürüst biri bilirdim ama yanılmışım. '[Here] I thought you were an honest person [lit., ** I knew you an honest person], but I guess I was wrong.' * Bu ülkede demokrasi var sandım, yanılmışım. 'I thought {we had a democracy here/this was a democracy [lit., there was democracy in this country]}. I guess I was {wrong/mistaken}.' Yanılmıyor-sam Erdoğan yarın gelecek. 'If I'm not mistaken, Erdoğan will come tomorrow.' A: Saliha san.A çok darıldım, Yahya'ya benim için "Çok cimridir" demişsin. 'A: Saliha [f.], I'm very angry AT you. You apparently told Yahya that I am very stingy [lit., Concerning me you said to Yahya...].' **B: Rica ederim, yanılıyorsun.** * **Ben öyle bir şey demedim.** 'B: Please, you're mistaken. I said no such thing.' * **Yanılıyor olabilirim.** 'I {may/might} be mistaken.' **Ne dersiniz, yanılıyor muyum?** 'What do you think, am I mistaken?' Proverbs: **Akıl yanılır, kalem yanılmaz.** 'The mind may be mistaken, but the pen never is.', i.e., The memory may fail, but what is written down is not forgotten. **Çok bilen çok yanılır.** 'He who knows a lot [also] makes lots of mistakes.' *947:2.* misjudgment: - misjudge; *974:10.* error: - be wrong. In reference to minor matters: → = **hata işle-** → **işle-** 2, = **hata yap-** → **yap-** 3, = **yanlışlık yap-** → **yap-** 3. In reference to relatively greater errors in the conduct of one's life. → = **hata et-**.

yanına gel-. → **gel-** 1.

yanıt ver-. → {**cevap/yanıt**) **ver-**. → **ver-** 1.

yanıtla-. → {**cevapla-/cevaplandır-/yanıtla-**}.

yanlış anla-. → **anla-**.

yanlış anlaşıl-. → **anlaşıl-**.

yanlış numara düş-. → **düş-** 1.

yanlış yap-. → **yap-** 3.

yanlışlık yap-. → **yap-** 3.

yansıt- [ır] [**yansı-** '- be reflected' + caus. suf. -t] 1 /A/ '- reflect /to/', obj.: light, image: **Bu ayna görüntüyü iyi yansıtmıyor.** 'This mirror doesn't reflect [the image] well.' **Gezegenler güneşten aldığı ışığı dünya.ya yansıtırlar.** 'The planets reflect [to the earth] the light [that] they receive from the sun.' *349:11.* representation, description: - image.

2 /I/ '- reflect, - show, - reveal': **Bence, bu makale yazar.ın şu anki** {**düşünceler.i.ni/görüşler.i.ni**} **yansıtmıyor.** 'In my opinion, this article doesn't reflect the writer's current {thoughts/views}.' *336:5.* imitation: - imitate. → = **göster-** 1.

yap- [ar] 1 /DAn/ '- make sth /{from/OUT OF}/, - build': * **Öğrenciler çömlekleri ne.DEN yaptılar?** '{What did the students make the pots OUT OF?/Also: Why did the students make the pots?}' **Öğrenciler çömlekleri çamur-.DAN yaptılar.** 'The students made the pots OUT OF clay.' * **Akşam yemeği için ne yapayım karar veremedim.** 'I couldn't decide what to make for dinner [lit., ** What shall I make for dinner I couldn't decide].' **Orhan bey deniz kenarında güzel bir ev yaptı.** 'Orhan bey built a beautiful house on the seashore.' • In this sentence **Orhan** did the actual construction OR had sb else do it, although in the latter case **yaptır-**, the causative form of **yap-**, is more usual. → **yaptır-** 1. Proverbs: **Biri yapar biri bozar, dünya böyle geçer.** 'One builds, another ruins it, this is the way of the world [lit., ** thus the world passes].' **Ev yap, ev yıkma.** 'Build a house; don't tear down a house.' **Yıkmak kolay, yapmak zordur.** 'To destroy is easy; to create is difficult.' A proverb that notes the power of women for good or evil: * **Kadın var ev yapar, kadın var ev yıkar.** 'Some women make a home, others wreck a home [lit., There are women who make a home. There are women who wreck a home'].' A different structure with essentially the same meaning: **Ev yapan kadın[lar] da var, ev yıkan kadın[lar] da.** *891:8.* production: - produce, - create. → = **oluştur-** ['- form, - create, - make up, - constitute /from/'], = **var et-** ['- create', only God as subject], = **yarat-** ['- create', more frequently used with God as subject], ≠ **yık-** 1 ['- demolish, - wreck; - pull down, - tear down, - knock down; - destroy; - ruin'], ≠ **yok et-** 1 ['- destroy, - do away with, - get rid of'].

2 '- do': **S: Bugün ne yaptınız?** 'Q: What did you do today?' **C:** {**Ev ödev.im.i/Dersler.i.mi/Ödevler.i.mi**} **yaptım.** 'A: I did {my homework [primary school]/my lessons/my assignments}.' * **Doğru olanı yaptı.** 'He did the right thing [lit., the thing that was right].' **Gereğini yapacağım.** 'I'll do what's necessary.' **Ne gerekiyorsa onu yapacağım.** 'I'll do whatever is necessary.' **Yapacağız.** * **Bu.nDAN hiç kimse.nin**

şüphe.si olmasın. 'We'll do it. * Let there not be any doubt ABOUT that [lit., ** Let no one's doubt be...].' <u>Proverb</u>: Hoca.nın dediğ.i.ni yap, yaptığ.ı.nı yapma. 'Do what the teacher says, not what he does.' Don't do as I do, do as I say. Senin yüzünden öğretmenden * azar işittim, * yaptığ.ın.ı beğendin mi? 'Because of you I got an earful [lit., ** heard scolding] from the teacher. * Well, are you proud of yourself now [lit., Do you like what you did]?' * Beğendin mi yaptığın işi? 'Now just look at what you've done! Are you {proud of/pleased with} yourself? [lit., ** Do you like the business you did?]' 510:27. disapproval: INTERJ. God forbid! <u>Proverb</u>: In general, not in reference to a particular project: Söylemek kolay, yapmak {zor/güç}. 'It is easy to talk [i.e., about plans], but {difficult} to get things done.' Talk is cheap. In reference to a particular project: Söyleme.si kolay, yapma.sı güç. 'It is easy to talk about it but difficult to carry it out [lit., ** Its saying is easy, its doing is difficult].' Easier said than done. Şimdi ne {yapalım/yapayım}? 'What {shall we/shall I} do now?' Also 'What CAN {we do/I do} now?' [i.e., There is nothing to be done]. Arabamı çarptığın için artık üzülme, ne yapalım * olan oldu. 'Stop worrying [lit., Don't worry anymore] about having hit my car. What can we do [lit., 'What shall we do?', i.e., There's nothing to be done]? * What's done is done.' S: Neden ekmek almadın? 'Q: Why didn't you buy bread?' C: Vaktim yoktu, fırına gidemedim, ne yapayım? 'A: I didn't have time. I couldn't go to the bakery. Well, what can I do now? [lit., What shall I do?]' Ne yapayım? Elimde değil. 'What can I do? It's out of {my hands/my control}.' * Ne yaptıysam olmadı. 'No matter what I did, it didn't work out.' Otobüsü kaçırdık, * yap.ACAK bir şey yok. 'We've missed the bus. * There's nothing TO BE done.' Yapabileceğimiz hiçbir şey yok. Çok üzüldüm. 'There's nothing we can do. I'm very sorry.' 19:21. impotence: INTERJ. no can do. S: * Mektuplar.I ne yaptınız? 'Q: What did you do WITH the letters?' C: Bütün mektuplar postalandı efendim!

'A: All the letters have been mailed, {sir/ma'am}.' Asking for advice: * Ne yap.sa.m acaba? 'I wonder what I should do?' * Ne diyorsam onu yap lütfen. 'Please do what I say.' * Ne yapalım dersiniz? 'What do you think we should do?' Making a suggestion: Şöyle bir şey yap.sa.k... '{What if/Suppose} we did the following...' 439: * 11. offer: expressions of suggestion. In the negative as a reprimand: A child is playing with the radio. You say: * Yapma * çocuğum, radyo bozulur. 'Hey, {don't do that/stop that}, * dear [lit., my child]. The radio will break.' 407:4. accomplishment: - accomplish.

* Yapma ya! '{You don't say!/You don't mean it!/Don't give me that!/Oh go on!/Well I declare!} [lit., Don't do (that)].', an expression of surprised disbelief: A: İstanbul'dan Ankara'ya dört saatte gelmişler. 'A: They came to Ankara from Istanbul in four hours.' B: Yapma ya! 'B: You don't say!', etc. Some other common expressions of disbelief or surprise: Sahi mi? 'Really?' Deme ya! 'You don't say!' Ha[y]di ya! 'You don't say!' 131: * 16. inexpectation: expressions of inexpectation; 955: * 6. incredulity: expressions of incredulity.

3 In various phrases:
aktarma yap- '- transfer from one vehicle to another, - change vehicles' [aktarma 'change of vehicles: buses, trains']: S: Aktarma yapma.mız gerekiyor mu? 'Q: Do we have to transfer?' C1: Hayır, bu tren doğruca Erzurum'a gider. 'A1: No, this train goes directly to Erzurum.' C2: Evet, * Ankara{'DA/'DAN} aktarma yapacaksınız. 'A2: Yes, * you'll have to change {IN Ankara}.' 861:4. substitution: - substitute.

alıntı yap- /DAn/ '- quote /θ/ sth, - quote /from/ sth, - cite /θ/ sth' [alıntı 'quote, citation']: Konuşmanız gerçekten çok ilginçti. Makalemde siz.DEN alıntı yapabilir miyim? 'Your talk was really very interesting. May I quote θ you in my article?' A teacher to his students: Çocuklar, kitaplar.dan alıntı yaparken lütfen kaynak gösterin! 'Boys and girls [lit., Children], when quoting from books, please cite [your] sources!' **Kaynak göstermeden pek çok kitap.tan alıntı yaptığı için o yazar hakkında soruşturma açıldı.** 'That writer became the subject of an inquiry [lit., ** an inquiry was opened about that writer...] because he had made numerous quotes from books without citing [his] sources.' **İsmet Özel en çok alıntı yaptığım yazarlardandır.** 'İsmet Özel is one of the authors I have quoted most.' *848:7.* repetition: - repeat.

alıştırma yap- '- do exercises, drills', on the blackboard, in a book or workbook, not usually orally [**alıştırma** 'training, exercise']: **Türkçe sınavından önce biraz alıştırma yapalım.** 'Before the Turkish exam let's do some {exercises/drills}.' *328:8.* action: - practice. → = **egzersiz yap-** 3 → yap- 3, **pratik yap-** ['- do usually oral, conversational practice, - practice a foreign language orally'] → yap- 3.

alışveriş yap- '- shop, - do shopping' [**alış** 'buying, taking', **veriş** 'giving', **alışveriş** 'shopping']: **Dün {şehr.E} inip alışveriş yaptım.** 'Yesterday I went {to town/θ downtown} and did some shopping.' *731:16.* commerce, economics: - trade with; *733:8.* purchase: - shop. → = **alışveriş et-**, = **al- 4** ['- buy, - purchase'], **satın al-**. Same. → al- 4, **alışverişe çık-** ['- go /θ/ shopping'] → çık- 2, **çarşıya çık-** ['- go /θ/ shopping', lit., '- go /to/ the market'] → çık- 2, ≠ **sat-** ['- sell'].

verb stem.{Ar/mIş} **gibi yap-** '- pretend, - make as if': **Odaya girdiğimde çocuk uyumuyordu ama uyu.MUŞ gibi yaptı.** 'When I came into the room, the child wasn't sleeping, but he pretended TO BE asleep.' **Odaya girdiğimde uyumuyordu ama uyu.YORMUŞ gibi yaptı.** 'When I came into the room, he wasn't sleeping, but he pretended TO BE [{sleeping/asleep}]'. **Odaya girdiğimde çalışmıyordu ama çalış.IYORMUŞ gibi yaptı.** 'When I came into the room, he wasn't working, but he pretended TO BE [working]'. **Bizim çocuk çalış.IR gibi yapıyor ama hiç çalışmıyor.** 'Our child pretends that

he is working, but he isn't working at all.' *500:12.* affectation: - affect. For '- pretend NOT to...', → *verb stem.*{ a: mAzlIktAn/b: mAmAzlIktAn/c: mAzdAn} **gel-** → gel- 1.

arıza yap- '- break down, - go out of order, - have a mechanical failure', usually for large items run on energy sources such as fuel, batteries, or house current, less frequently for small items such as clocks, radios, videos. [A. **arıza** (- . .) 'breakdown']: **Havalanırken arıza yapan uçak {düştü/yer.E çakıldı}.** 'The airplane that had a mechanical failure {while taking off/on takeoff} crashed [lit., {fell/nose dived INTO the ground}].' {a: **Araba**/b: **Motosiklet**/c: **Teyp**/d: **Televizyon**/e: **Radyo**/f: **Bilgisayar**} **arıza yaptı.** '{a: The car/b: The motorcycle/c: The tape recorder/d: The TV/e: The radio/f: The computer} broke down.' *393:25.* impairment: - get out of order. For '- break down' of almost every kind of mechanical item, including small items such as clocks, radios, → **bozul-**.

askerlik yap- /olarak/ '- do military service /AS/, - serve in the armed forces /AS/' [A. **asker** 'soldier' + abstract noun-forming suf. -lIk = **askerlik** 'soldiering, military service']: * **Mehmet 15 ay askerlik yaptı.** 'Mehmet did 15 months of military service.' Since military service is an important experience in a Turkish man's life, he is often asked about it. • Note the possessed suffixes on **askerlik**: **Askerliğ.İNİZ.i yaptınız mı?** 'Have you done YOUR military service?' S: **Askerliğ.İNİZ.i nerede yaptınız?** 'Q: Where did you do YOUR military service?' C: **Askerliğ.İM.i Denizli'de yaptım.** 'A: I did MY military service in Denizli.' S: * **Askerliğinizi ne OLARAK yaptınız?** 'Q: {What did you do your military service AS?/In what capacity did you serve?} C: **Askerliğ.İM.i {er/çavuş/yedek subay} OLARAK yaptım.** 'A: I did my military service AS {a private/a sergeant/a reserve officer}.' *458:18.* warfare: - serve.

banyo yap- (1) '- take a bath, -bathe' [It. **banyo** 'bath']: **Burada banyo yapabilir miyim?** 'Can I take a bath here?' *79:19.* cleanness: - wash. → **duş yap-** ['- take a shower, - shower'] → yap- 3, **yıkan- 1** ['- wash oneself; - take a bath, - bathe'], **güneş banyosu yap-** ['- sunbathe, - take a sunbath'] → yap- 3.
(2) * '- develop photographic film' [F. **film** (filmi)]: **Bu filmi banyo yapar mısınız?** 'Would you please develop this film?' *714:15.* photography: - process. → **film bas-** ['- develop and print' or only '-print', photographic film] → bas- 3.

büyük aptes yap- '- have a bowel movement *or* BM, - defecate', *formal, polite* [**büyük** 'large, big', P. **abdest** 'the ritual ablution']: **Doktor: Bugün büyük aptes yaptınız mı?** 'Doctor: Have you had a bowel movement today?' *or* **Bugün büyük aptes.İNİZİ yaptınız mı?** lit., 'Have you had YOUR bowel movement today?' **Hasta: Hayır, yapmadım.** 'Patient: No I haven't.' **Çocuk tuvalet bulamayınca büyük aptes.İNİ ağacın altı.nA yaptı.** 'When the child couldn't find a {restroom/toilet}, he did HIS business [i.e., defecated] θ under a tree.' *12:13.* excretion: - defecate. → = **dışarı[.ya] çık- 2** → çık- 2, **ihtiyacını gör-** ['- defecate, - urinate'] → gör- 4, **tuvalet yap-** ['- have a bowel movement *or* BM, - urinate, - do one's business, - use the facilities, the restroom; - make one's toilet, i.e., usually for a woman to dress or to arrange her hair'].

çiş {yap-/et- [eDer]} '- piss, - pee, - take a {piss/pee}' Usually used by grown-ups for children and by children among themselves. [**çiş** 'peepee', i.e., urine']: **Tuvalet bulamayınca çişini ağacın altı.nA yaptı.** 'When he couldn't find a {restroom/toilet}, he took a piss θ under a tree.' *12:14.* excretion: - urinate. → = **işe-,** = **küçük aptes yap-** → yap- 3, = **su dök-** → dök- 3, **ihtiyacını gör-** ['- defecate, - urinate'] → gör- 4, **tuvalet yap-** ['- have a bowel movement *or* BM, - urinate, - do one's business, - use the facilities, the restroom; - make one's toilet, i.e., usually for a woman to

dress or to arrange her hair'] → below.

dedikodu yap- /hakkında/ '- gossip /about/' [**dedikodu** 'gossip']: **Başkaları hakkında dedikodu yapmak hem ayıp hem günahtır.** 'It is both shameful and a sin to speak of others behind their backs.' **bir kimsenin dedikodu-sunu yap-** '- gossip about sb [lit., ** - do sb's gossip': * **Arzu çok dedikoducu bir kızdır,** * **daima başkaları.nın dedikodu.su.nu yapar.** 'Arzu is a terrible gossip [lit., ** a very gossipy girl]. * She always gossips ABOUT others [lit., ** Does the gossip of others].' *552:12.* news: - gossip. → **arkasından konuş-** ['- speak ill of sb behind his back'], **çene çal-** ['- chat, - gossip, - chew the fat'] → çal- 2.

degree name **yap-** '- get or - do a [{master's/Ph.D.} degree] /in/': **1998'de Boğaziçi Üniversite.si Fizik Bölüm.ü.nden mezun oldum. Aynı bölümde master ve doktora yaptım.** 'In 1998 I graduated from the Physics Department of Bosphorus University. I {got/did} my master's and doctor's degrees in the same department.' *570:9.* learning: - master. → **mezun ol-** → ol- 12.

doğrusunu yap- '- do the right thing': **Hükümet doğrusunu yapıyor.** 'The government is doing the right thing.' *637:2.* * *1.* right: - do the right thing. → = **doğru hareket et-** → hareket et- 4, = **iyi et-,** ≠ **kötü et-.**

duş yap- '- take a shower, - shower' [**duş** 'shower' for washing]: **Hava çok sıcak. Çok terliyim. Duş yapmak istiyorum.** 'The weather is very hot. {I'm very sweaty./I'm all covered with sweat.} I want to take a shower.' *79:19.* cleanness: - wash. → = **duş al-** → al- 1, **yıkan- 1** ['- wash oneself; - take a bath, - bathe'].
egzersiz yap- [F. **egzersiz** 'practice, exercise'] (1) '- work out, - do exercises, calisthenics, physical training': **Öğrenciler her gün aynı saatte okul.un bahçe.si.nde egzersiz yapı-yorlar.** 'The students {work out/do calisthenics [*or* exercises]} on the playground [lit., in the garden of the school] every day at the same time

hour.' Her sabah yarım saat egzersiz yapın, ama kendinizi fazla yormayın. 'Work out every morning for half an hour, but don't tire yourself out.' *84:4*. fitness, exercise: - exercise; *328:8*. action: - practice; *725:8*. exertion: - exert. → = idman yap- ['- exercise, - do gymnastics, physical training, - train [oneself physically]'] → yap- 3, jimnastik yap- ['- do gymnastics'] → yap- 3.
(2) '- do exercises as physical therapy': **Kol ameliyat.ım.dan sonra, doktor her gün iki saat egzersiz yapma.m.ı istedi**. 'After the operation on my arm [lit., ** my arm operation], the doctor asked me to do two hours of exercises every day [lit., ** asked my doing...]' *328:8*. action: - practice; *725:8*. exertion: - exert.
(3) '- do drills, exercises on the blackboard or in a workbook': **Türkçe sınavından önce biraz egzersiz yapalım**. 'Before the Turkish examination, let's do some drills.' *328:8*. action: - practice. → = alıştırma yap- → yap- 3.

elinden geleni yap- '- do one's best' [el 'hand', gelen '{that which/what} comes'], lit., • do what comes from one's hand: • Note the personal suffixes on el: **El.İN.den gelen.İ yap**. 'Do YOUR best!' **Öğretmen çocuklar.ın okuma yazmay.ı öğren.ebil.me.si için el.İ.nden geleni yapıyordu**. 'The teacher was doing HER best to get the children to learn to read and write [lit., ** for the children's being able to learn to read and write].' **Bu evliliğ.in devam etme.si için el.İM.den geleni yaptım, fakat başarılı ol.AMA.dım**. 'I did MY best to keep this marriage together [lit., for the continuation of this marriage], but I {failed/was unsuccessful/lit., ** COULDN'T be successful}.' *403:13*. endeavor: - do one's best. → = çalış[ıp] çabala- ['- try hard, - do one's best'].

gereğini yap- '- do what a situation requires, necessitates, - do what has to be done' [gerek 'what is required']: **Polis bey,** * **bu adam.DAN şikâyetçiyim, lütfen gereğini yapın**. 'Officer, * I want to lodge a complaint [lit., I am a complainant] AGAINST this man. Please do what has to be done.' *

Arkadaşlar, lütfen herkes * işini ciddî.yE alsın, yoksa * kimse.nin göz.ü.nün yaş.ı.nA bakmam, gereğini yaparım. 'Come on {people/guys}, * I want everyone to [lit., Let everyone] take his work seriously, or else * I won't give a hoot about anyone's feelings [lit., consider anyone's tears] and do what has to be done.' *962:9*. necessity: - require.

gösteri yap- '- hold a {demonstration/protest}, - demonstrate against' [gösteri 'demonstration']: **Maaş zamm.ı.nı az bulan işçiler fabrika önünde gösteri yapacaklar**. 'The workers who {find/found} the wage increase inadequate will hold a demonstration in front of the factory.' *333:5*. dissent: - object.

gösteriş yap- '- show off, - be a show-off' [gösteriş 'showing off, ostentation']: **Gösteriş yapma!** '{Don't show off./Don't be a show-off.}' **Gürkan daima yeni elbiseleri ile gösteriş yapardı**. 'Gürkan would always show off with his new clothes.' *501:16*. ostentation: - show off. → = hava bas- 2 → bas- 2.

güneş banyosu yap- '- sunbathe, - take a sunbath' [güneş 'sun', banyo 'bath']: **Aslı {deniz kenar.ı.nda/plâjda/sahilde} güneş banyosu yapıyor**. 'Aslı [f.] is taking a sunbath {at the seashore/at the beach/at the shore}.' *1019:19*. heating: - insolate. → = güneşlen-.

gürültü yap-. → gürültü {et-/yap-}.

hata yap- /lA/ '- make a mistake, error', mostly in minor matters such as spelling, calculation, not in the conduct of one's life [A. hata (. -) 'error, mistake']: **Öğretmen: Dikkat et, {a: toplama/b: çıkarma/c: çarpma/d: bölme} işlemler.i.nde hata yapmışsın**. 'Teacher: Be careful! It seems you've made some mistakes in {a: addition/b: subtraction/c: multiplication/d: division} [lit., ** in {a: addition...} operations].' * **Biz nerede hata yaptık?** 'Where did we {go wrong?/make a mistake?}' *974:13*. error: - mistake, - make a mistake. In reference to minor matters → = yanlışlık yap- → yap- 3, =

431

hata işle- → işle- 2, = yanıl-. In reference to relatively greater errors in the conduct of one's life → = hata et-.

{hız/sürat} yap- '- speed, - go too fast' [{hız/A. sürat} 'speed']: Hız yapmayın. '{No speeding./Don't speed.}' {Şehir içinde/Bu caddede} hız yapmak yasaktır. 'It is forbidden to speed {in the city/on this street}.' 352:7. publication: poster: * specific signs. Aşırı hız yapmak.TAN [polis.TEN] * ceza yedik. '* We were fined [lit., ** ate punishment] [BY the police] FOR speeding.' S: Kaza nasıl oldu biliyor musun? 'Q: Do you know how the accident happened?' C: Evet, şoför fazla hız yapıyordu. 'A: Yes, the driver was {speeding/going too fast}.' Polis aşırı hız yapan arabanın şoförüne "Kenar.A çek" diye bağırdı. 'The police shouted at the driver who had been driving too fast [saying], "Pull over [to the side]".' 174:8. swiftness: - speed; 401:5. haste: - make haste.

idman yap- '- exercise, - do gymnastics, physical training, - train [oneself physically]' [A. idman (. -) 'gymnastics, physical exercise or training']: Öğrenciler okulun bahçesinde idman yapıyorlar. 'The students are {exercising/doing gymnastics} in the schoolyard.' 84:4. fitness, exercise: - exercise; 328:8. action: - practice; 725:8. exertion: - exert. → = egzersiz yap- 1 ['- work out, - do exercises, calisthenics, physical training'] → yap- 3, jimnastik yap- ['- do gymnastics'] → yap- 3.

iş yap- [iş 'work'] (1) '- do sth [lit., ** work] for a living': S: Ne iş yapıyorsunuz? 'Q: What do you do for a living [lit., What work are you doing]?' = Ne iş.LE meşgulsünüz? lit., ** 'What work are you occupied WITH?' • Answers often occur in two patterns of similar meaning, the first perhaps more common than the second:
a) C1: {a: Öğretmen.im/b: Doktor.um/c: Mühendis.im/d: Hemşire.yim/e: Subay.ım}. 'A1: {I'm a teacher/b: I'm a doctor/c: I'm an engineer/d: I'm a nurse/e: I'm an officer [i.e., in the military]}.'
b) C2: {a: Öğretmen.lik/b: Doktor.luk/c: Mühendis.lik/d:

Hemşire.lik/e: Subay.lık} yapıyorum. 'A2: The same translations as above, but lit., ** 'I do {a: teaching]/b: doctoring/c: engineering]/d: nursing]/e: the work of an officer}.' 385:11. provision, equipment: - make a living. → = geçimini sağla- ['- make one's living, - provide [a living] for, - support (one's family)'], = geçin- 2 ['- make one's living /[BY]/, - subsist /by means of/, - get by, - manage /ON/ (a salary)'], = hayatını kazan- →kazan- 1.
(2) /lA/ '- do business /with/': Siz.in.le iş yapmak bir zevk! 'It's a pleasure to do business with you!' 731:16. commerce, economics: - trade with. → = /lA/ alışveriş et-.

jimnastik yap- '- do gymnastics': Öğrenciler okulun bahçesinde jimnastik yapıyorlar. 'The students are doing gymnastics in the schoolyard.' 84:4. fitness, exercise: - exercise; 328:8. action: - practice; 725:8. exertion: - exert. → = idman yap- ['- exercise, - do gymnastics, physical training, - train (oneself physically)'] → yap- 3, egzersiz yap- 1 ['- work out, - do exercises, calisthenics, physical training'] → yap- 3.

kahvaltı yap-. → kahvaltı {et/yap-}.

kamp yap- '- camp, - go camping': Buralarda kamp yapabileceğimiz bir yer var mı? 'Is there a place around here where we can camp?' Burada kamp yapabilir miyiz? 'Can we camp here?' 225:11. habitation: - camp.

kayak yap- '- ski' [kayak 'ski, skiing']: Kayak yapmay.A Uludağ'a gittik. Her gün kayak yaptık. 'We went to Uludağ to ski. We skied every day.' 177:35. travel: - glide; 753:4. skiing: - ski. → = kay- 3.

kaza yap- '- have an accident, - get into an accident, - be in an accident, - cause an accident' [A. kaza (. -) 'accident']: Geçen gün otobanda giderken kaza yaptım. * Araba.DA çok fazla hasar var ama ben Allah'a şükür birkaç sıyrıkla kurtuldum. 'The other day while driving [lit., going] along the highway I had an accident. * {The car was badly damaged/lit., There was a lot of damage TO the car}, but thank God I escaped with [only] a few {scratches/scrapes}.' * **Amaan haaa, kaza yapmayın.** 'For goodness sake, don't have an accident!' The final vowels in the first two words, usually written **aman** and **ha**, are stretched out and read long [i.e., **amân, hâ**] for emphasis. *1010:10.* adversity: - come to grief. → **kaza geçir-** ['- have an accident, - be in an accident, - get into an accident'].

kontrat yap- /lA/ '- make a contract, - sign a contract or agreement /with/' [It. **kontrat** 'contract, agreement']: **Ev sahibi ile iki senelik bir kontrat yaptık.** 'We signed a two-year lease [for an apartment] with the owner of the house.' *332:10.* assent: - come to an agreement. → **anlaş-** 2 ['- agree, - come to an agreement, - reach an understanding'].

kur yap- /A/ *formal, polite* '- chase /AFTER/, - court /θ/, - pay court /to/, - try to woo /θ/, i.e., - approach with sexual intent' [F. **kur** 'courtship; flirtation']: **O adam görgüsüz.ün tek.i.dir. Her gördüğü kadın.A kur yapar.** 'That man is a real {playboy/cad} [lit., unmannerly person]. He chases AFTER every woman he sees.' **Partide gördüğü sarışın kız.A kur yapmasına rağmen * tavlayamadı.** 'Although he chased AFTER the blond [girl] he saw at the party, * he couldn't {get anywhere with/lit., snow} her.' *382:8.* pursuit: - pursue; *562:21.* lovemaking, endearment: - court. → = **asıl-** 3 [a *less formal, slang* equivalent: '- come on /to/ sb, - make a play /FOR/ sb, - chase /AFTER/ sb'].

küçük aptes yap- '- urinate', *formal, polite* [**küçük** 'small, little', P. **abdest** 'the ritual ablution']: **Doktor: Bugün küçük aptes yaptınız mı?** 'Doctor: Have you urinated today?' or **Bugün küçük aptes[İNİZİ] yaptınız mı?** lit., ** 'Have you done YOUR urination today?' **Hasta: Hayır, yapmadım.** 'Patient: No I haven't.' **Tuvalet bulamayınca küçük aptes.İNİ ağacın altı.nA yaptı.** 'When he couldn't find a {restroom/toilet}, he urinated [lit., ** did HIS urination] θ

under a tree.' *12:14.* excretion: - urinate. → = **çiş** {yap-/et-} → yap-3, = **işe-**, = **su dök-** → dök- 3, **ihtiyacını gör-** ['- defecate, - urinate'] → gör- 4, **tuvalet yap-** ['- have a bowel movement *or* BM, - urinate, - do one's business, - use the facilities, the restroom; - make one's toilet, i.e., usually for a woman to dress or to arrange her hair'] → yap-3.

makyaj yap- '- put on makeup, - make oneself up' [F. **makyaj** 'a making up, makeup']: * **Lâle çok iyi makyaj yapar.** 'Lâle really knows how to put makeup on.' **Partideki kızlar.ın hep.si makyaj yapmıştı.** 'All of the girls at the party had put on makeup.' **Bu kadar makyaj yapma, baban kızıyor.** 'Don't put on so much makeup. Your father will get angry.' *1015:15.* beauty: - beautify. → = **boya-** 2.

masraf yap-. → masraf {et-/yap-}.

meç yap- '- give sb highlights, - put highlights, streaks of color, in sb's hair' [**meç** 1 'hair's being streaked with artificial color'. 2 'strand or lock of hair']: At the hair salon: **Meç yapar mısınız?** 'Would you give me highlights?' *3:22.* hair: - cut or - dress hair; *35:13.* color: - color; *1015:15.* beauty: - beautify.

otostop yap- '- hitchhike' [**otostop** 'hitchhiking']: * **Ergun geçen yaz otostop yap.ARAK bütün Avrupa'yI dolaştı.** 'Last summer Ergun hitchhiked all through Europe [lit., ** BY hitchhik.ING toured...].' **Mehmet otostop yapan kızları araba.sı.nA aldı.** 'Mehmet picked up [lit., took INTO his car] the girls who were hitchhiking.' *177:31.* travel: - hitchhike.

paket yap- [ar] /I/ '- wrap, - wrap up, - make a package of' [It. **paket** 'package, parcel']: **Lütfen * {şu kitapları/şu bardakları/şu elbiseyi} paket yapar mısınız?** 'Would you please * wrap up {these books/these glasses/this suit} [lit., ** make these books...a package].' *295:20.* covering: - wrap. → = **paketle-, paket sar-** ['- wrap a package'] → sar- 1, ≠ **paket aç-** ['-open a package'] → aç- 1.

perhiz yap- '- diet, - go on a diet', both for losing weight and for the treatment of a medical condition [P. **perhiz** (. -) 'diet']: **Annem zayıflamak için perhiz yapıyor.** 'My mother is dieting to lose weight.' **Doktor kilo ver.me.m gerektiğ.i.ni söyleyince * perhiz yapmay.a karar verdim.** 'When the doctor said that I had to lose weight, * I decided to go on a diet.' **Anneannemde {şeker hastalığı/yüksek tansiyon} çıkınca * perhiz yapmay.a başladı.** 'When my [maternal] grandmother [first] developed {diabetes/high blood pressure} [lit., When {diabetes/high blood pressure} appeared in my (maternal) grandmother], * she went on a diet [lit., began to diet].' *7:17.* nutrition: - diet.

pratik yap- /ArAk/ '- do usually oral, conversational practice, - practice a foreign language orally /by...ing/' [F. **pratik** (ği) 'practice']: **Türkçe sınavından önce biraz pratik yapalım.** 'Before the Turkish examination, let's do some oral practice.' **Arkadaşım İngilizce öğrenmeye başladı ya, * nerde bir turist gör.se pratik yapmak için [o.na] yanaşıyor.** 'Well, as you know, my friend has begun to study English. * Wherever he sees a tourist, he goes up to him to get in some practice.' **Türkçemi turistlerle pratik yap.arak geliştirdim.** 'I improved my Turkish by practic.ing with tourists.' *328:8.* action: - practice.

prova yap- '- rehearse' [It. **prova** 'rehearsal']: **Bugün oynaya-cağımız yeni oyun.un prova.sı.nı yapacağız.** 'Today we'll rehearse the new play that we're going to perform.' *704:32.* show business, theater: - rehearse.

rötar yap- '- be delayed', usually with a subject designating a means of public transportation, i.e., train, bus, ferry, airplane, not a person [F. **rötar** 'delay']: **{a: Uçak/b: Tren/c: Otobüs/d: Vapur/e: Araba vapuru} [yoğun] kar yağışı {nedeniyle/yüzünden} iki saat rötar yaptı.** '{a: The plane/b: The train/c: The bus/d: The steamship/e:

The ferry} was delayed [for] two hours {due to} [heavy] snow.' *845:8.* lateness: - delay. → = {**geç kal-/gecik-**} [for a person '- be late, - be delayed'] → kal- 1, = **yolda kal-** ['- be delayed, held up on the way, - remain on the way (subj.: person or vehicle)]' → kal- 1, ≠ **erken gel-** ['- be early'] → gel- 1, {**vaktinde/zamanında**} **gel-** ['- come {in/on} time', persons and vehicles] → gel- 1, **yetiş-** 1 ['- be {in/on} time'].

* **sakal tıraşı yap-** '- shave sb, - give sb a shave' [sakal 'beard', P. **tıraş** 'shaving, shave']: **Sakal tıraşı yapar mısın?** 'Would you give me a shave?' *3:22.* hair, feathers: - cut or - dress the hair; *255:10.* subtraction: - excise; *268:6.* shortness: - shorten. → **tıraş ol-** 2 ['- get or - have a shave or a haircut'] → ol- 10.1.

servis yap- '- serve [food]': Directions in a cookbook: **20 dakika pişirip sıcak OLARAK servis yapın.** 'Cook for 20 minutes and [then] serve θ hot.' **Hangi yemekleri ve tatlıları soguk servis yapmak gerekir, biliyor musun?** 'Do you know which dishes and desserts should be served cold?' *478:12.* giving: - give.

spor yap- '- do sports, - engage in sports, - take part in sports': S: **Spor yapıyor musun?** 'Do you {play/engage in} any sports?' C1: **Evet, her sabah bir saat koşuyorum.** 'A1: Yes, I run an hour every morning.' C2: **Evet, * vaktim olursa haftada bir iki saat {basketbol/futbol/tenis} oynuyorum.** 'A2: Yes, * when I have time, I play {basketball/soccer/tennis} one or two hours a week.' *84:4.* fitness, exercise: - exercise; *743:23.* amusement: - play; *752:4.* soccer: - play soccer.

sürat yap-. → {**hız/sürat**} **yap-.** → yap- 3.

şaka yap- /A/ [**şaka** 'joke'] (1) '- play a joke or trick /ON/': **Bir Nisanda öğretmenimiz.E şaka yaptık; başka sınıf.la yer değiştirdik.** 'On the first of April [i.e., April Fools Day] we played a trick ON our teacher: We went into a classroom other than our usual one [lit., ** changed places with another classroom].' *489:14.* wit, humor: - trick. → = **oyun oyna- 2** → oyna- 1.

(2) '- be joking, kidding, - make a joke, not - be telling the truth': A: **Tebrik ederiz efendim. 50 bin lira.yI kazanan talihli sizsiniz.** 'A: Congratulations, {sir/ma'am}. You are the lucky winner of 50,000 liras [lit., the lucky one who has won...].' B: **Allah aşkına ban.A böyle şaka yapmayın.** 'B: For goodness sake don't joke WITH me like that.' A: **Şaka yapmıyorum, doğruyu söylüyorum. Siz kazandınız.** 'A: I'm not joking. I'm telling the truth. You have won.' **Ban.A niçin kızdığını anlamıyorum.** * **Sadece şaka yapmıştım.** 'I don't understand why you got angry AT me. * I was only kidding.' * **Şaka yapıyorlar sandım.** 'I thought they were joking [lit., ** They are joking, I thought].' *490:5.* banter: - banter.

* **tatil yap-** '- go on a {vacation/holiday}, - take a {vacation/holiday}' [A. **tatil** (- .) 'holiday, vacation']: S: **Bu yaz tatil yaptınız mı?** 'Q: Did you {take a vacation/go on a holiday} this summer?' C: **Evet, Bodrum'a gittik.** 'A: Yes, we went to Bodrum [i.e., a resort city in southwestern Turkey].' *20:9.* rest, repose: - vacation. → = **tatile çık-** → çık- 2, = **tatile gir-**, = **tatile git-** → git-1a.

teneffüs yap- '- take a break' [A. **teneffüs 1** 'respiration, breathing.' **2** 'recess, break']: **İki saattir çalışıyoruz, yorulduk. Ha[y]di on beş dakika teneffüs yapalım.** 'We've been working for two hours. We're tired [lit., We got tired]. Come on, let's take a fifteen minute break.' *20:8.* rest, repose: - take a rest; *224:3.* interval: - interspace. → = **ara ver-** → ver- 3, = **mola ver-** → ver- 3.

tuvalet yap- '- have a bowel movement *or* BM, - urinate, - do one's business, - use the facilities, the restroom; - make one's toilet, i.e., usually for a woman to dress or to arrange her hair' [F. **tuvalet** 'toilet', here 'the functions carried out in the restroom or, most commonly, by a women in her boudoir or dressing room']: S: * **Çocuğunuz tuvaletini kendi yapabiliyor mu?** 'Q: * {Is your child potty

trained?/Is your child able to do his business by himself?}' C: **Küçük tuvaletini yapıyor ama büyük tuvaletini henüz kendi yapamıyor.** 'A: He can urinate [lit., urinates] by himself, but he can't do his BM yet.' **Bizim çocuk kabız oldu galiba, tuvaletini yaparken zorlanıyor.** 'Our child is constipated. He's probably having trouble doing his BM.' *12:13.* excretion: - defecate; *12:14.* : - urinate. → **tuvalete git-** ['- go to the restroom, - use the toilet'] → git-1 a), **büyük aptes yap-** ['- have a bowel movement *or* BM, - defecate', *formal, polite.*] → yap- 3, **dışarı[.ya] çık-.** [Same.] → çık- 2, **ihtiyacını gör-** ['- defecate, - urinate'] → gör- 4, **çiş {yap-/et-}** ['- urinate, - piss, - pee'] → yap- 3, **küçük aptes yap-** ['- urinate', *formal, polite*] → yap- 3, **su dök-** ['- take a {pee/piss}, - urinate'].

yanlış yap- '- get or - do sth wrong, incorrectly' [**yanlış 1** 'error, mistake'. **2** 'wrong']: **Nerede yanlış yaptım acaba?** 'I wonder where I made a mistake.' **Sınavda dört soru.yU yanlış yaptım.** 'I {got/did} θ four questions on the exam wrong.' *974:12.* error: - misdo.

yanlışlık yap- '- make a mistake', mostly in minor matters rather than in the conduct of one's life [**yanlışlık** 'mistake, error']: **Sınavda ikinci soruda yanlışlık yapmışım.** 'It seems I've made a mistake in the second question on the exam.' *974:13.* error: - mistake, - make a mistake. In reference to minor matters → = **hata işle-** → işle- 2, = **hata yap-** → yap- 3, = **yanıl-** ['- be mistaken, wrong']. For a verb usually preferred in reference to relatively greater errors in the conduct of one's life, → = **hata et-**.

yaramazlık {yap-/et- [eDer]} '- be naughty, - misbehave' [**yaramazlık** 'naughtiness']: **Çocuklar yaramazlık yapmayın!** * **Güzel güzel oynayın.** 'Children, {behave yourselves/lit., don't be naughty}. * Play nicely.' *322:4.* misbehavior: - misbehave.

yatağını yap- (1) '- make up one's bed, - arrange one's bedclothes, bedding' [**yatak** 'bed']: **Yatağını yapmadan dışarı çıkamazsın,** *

435

ona göre! 'You can't leave without making your bed, * so act accordingly!' → = yatağını {topla-/düzelt-} ['- make one's bed'] → topla- 2, düzelt- 3. *807:12.* arrangement: - tidy, - tidy up.
(2) '- make up or - prepare a bed for sb': Çocuğ.un uyku.su geldi galiba, hemen yatağını yapayım da yatıralım. 'The child is probably sleepy [lit., ** The child's sleepiness has probably come]. Let me make up his bed right away, and let's put him to bed.' *405:6.* preparation: - prepare. → = hazırla-.

yatırım yap- /{DA/A}/ '- invest /in/, - make an investment /in/' [yatırım 'investment']: Hangi alanlarda yatırım yapmamızı önerirsiniz? 'Which sectors do you suggest [that] we invest in?' Bugünlerde {iş adamları/yatırımcılar} ekonomi.nin hangi alanlar.ı.nda yatırım yapıyorlar? 'Which areas are {businessmen/investors} investing in these days?' Bir çok alanda yatırım yaptım ama hiç birinde tutunamadım. 'I invested in several sectors, but I couldn't maintain a position in any of them.' Türkiye'de yatırım yapmak bütün A[vrupa]B[irliği] ülke-leri şirketler.i.nin çıkar.ı.nadır. 'Investment in Turkey is in the interest of all E[uropean]U[union] countries.' İyi ki Türkiye'de yatırım yapmışız. 'It seems it's a good thing we invested in Turkey.' Yatırım yaparken iyi niyet yetmez, bilgi şart! 'When investing, good intentions are not enough. [Good] information is absolutely necessary.' *626:5.* expenditure: - spend.

yol yap- '- travel, - cover, or - traverse a distance' [yol 'road, way']: Çok yorucu bir yolculuk oldu; her gün 100 km. [read: kilometre] yol yapmak zorunda kaldık. 'It was a very tiring journey. We had to cover 100 kilometers every day.' • Note also the following where an expression of distance replaces yol: Araban.LA günde kaç kilometre yaptığını hesap ettin mi hiç? 'Have you ever calculated how many kilometers you covered {* BY car/IN your car/lit., ** WITH your car} each day?' *177:20.* travel: - traverse. → = yol git- → git- 1a, = katet-.

yapıştır- [ır] /A/ '- glue, - paste, - tape, or - stick sth /{ON/ONTO/to}/ sth': Kardeşim sevdiği bütün artistler.in resimler.i.ni oda-.sı.nın duvar.ı.nA yapıştırmış. 'My sister pasted the pictures of all the {actors/actresses} that she liked ON the walls of her room.' * İzinsiz ilân yapıştırmak yasaktır. 'Post no bills [lit., To post bills without permission is forbidden].' *352:7.* publication: poster: * specific signs; *799:5.* joining: - put together; *802:9.* cohesion: - stick together.

Yapma ya! → yap- 2.

yaptır- [ır] [yap- + caus. suf. -DIr] 1 /A/ '- have /θ/ sb make or build sth': Terzim.E bayram için yeni bir elbise yaptırdım. 'I had θ my tailor make [me] a new suit for the holiday.' Aşçım.A patlıcanlı kebap yaptırdım. 'I had θ my cook make some eggplant kebab.' A: Antalya'da yazlık ev yaptırdık. 'A: We built a summer house [lit., had a summer house built] in Antalya.' B: Kim.E yaptırdınız? 'B: θ Who[m] did you have build it?' A: Meşhur mimar Erol Çetin'E. 'A: θ The famous architect Erol Çetin.' Proverb: Minare.yİ yaptırmayan yerden bitmiş sanır. 'A person who has [never] had a minaret built thinks that it has sprung from the ground.', i.e., like a plant. He doesn't realize the difficulties involved in the construction. *891:8.* production: - produce, - create.

2 /A/ '- have /θ/ sb do sth': S: [Bu.nu/Evin badanası.nı] kim.E yaptırdın? 'Q: θ Who did you have do {this/the painting of the house}?' C1: Arkadaşım.A yaptırdım. 'A1: I had θ my friend do it.' C2: {Bana tavsiye edilen bir badanacı.yA/Özel bir şirket.E} yaptırdım. 'A2: I had {θ a painter who had been recommended to me/θ a private company} do it.' *328:6.* action: - do; *407:4.* accomplishment: - accomplish.

boya yaptır- /A/ '- have θ sth colored', hair [boya 1 'paint'. 2 'dye'. 3 'color']: * Saçlarım.A boya yaptırmak istiyorum. 'I want to have θ my hair colored [lit., ** have color made TO my hair].' *3:22.* hair: - cut or - dress hair; *35:13.*

color: - color; *1015:15.* beauty: - beautify.

{meç/röfle} yaptır- /A/ '- have one's hair streaked, highlighted, - have highlights, streaks of color, put /IN/ one's hair' [Sl. meç 1 'rapier, a small sword'. 2 'streak (in hair)'; F. röfle 'highlight']: Saçlarım.A meç yaptırmak istiyorum. 'I want to have highlights [put IN my hair].' *3:22.* hair: - cut or - dress hair; *35:13.* color: - color; *1015:15.* beauty: - beautify.

* perma yaptır- /A/ '- have or - get a perm[anent]' [perma 'permanent wave', F. permanente], lit., ** '- have a permanent wave made /IN/': * Saçlarım.A perma yaptırmak istiyorum. 'I want to have a perm[anent] [lit., ** have a permanent wave made IN my hair].' *3:22.* hair: - cut or - dress hair; *1015:15.* beauty: - beautify.

* rezervasyon yaptır- /için, DA/ '- make a reservation /for [sb, a time], at [a hotel, restaurant, casino]/' [rezervasyon, F. réservation], lit., '- have a reservation made.' The guest uses the form yaptır-, rather than the non-causative yap- because the clerk is regarded as making the reservation: Müşteri: Bu akşam için {otelinizde/lokantanızda/gazinonuzda} rezervasyon yaptırmak istiyorum. 'Customer: I want to make a reservation for this evening {at your hotel/at your restaurant/at your casino}.' Otelci: * Kaç kişilik rezervasyon yaptırmak istiyorsunuz? 'Hotel clerk: * How many people do you want to make a reservation for? [lit., ** A how-many-person reservation do you want to have made?]' *477:9.* apportionment: - allot. → = yer ayırt-.

röfle yaptır- → {meç/röfle} yaptır- above.

saçlarını yaptır- /I/ '- have one's hair styled' [saç 'hair']: Saçlarım.I yaptırmak istiyorum. 'I want to have my hair styled.' *3:22.* hair: - cut or - dress hair; *1015:15.* beauty: - beautify.

* sigorta yaptır- /A/ '- insure /θ/, - take out insurance /ON/' [It. sigorta 'insurance']: * Sağlık sigortası yaptırdın mı? 'Have you taken out health insurance?}' {Evin.E/Araban.A/* Eşyaların.A} sigorta yaptırdın mı? '{Have you taken out insurance {ON your house/ON your car/* ON your furniture and household effects}?/Have you insured your...}' *1007:18a.* protection: - protect. → = /I/ sigortala-.

topuz yaptır- /I/ '- have one's hair put in a bun' [topuz 'bun, knot of hair']: * Saçlarım.I topuz yaptırmak istiyorum. 'I want to have my hair put IN a bun.' *3:22.* hair: - cut or - dress hair; *1015:15.* beauty: - beautify.

yarala- [r] /I, DAn/ '- wound sb /IN/, - injure, - hurt' [yara 'wound' + verb-forming suf. -lA]: * Çocuğun attığı taş kafa.m.ı yaraladı. 'The stone the children threw wounded me IN the head [lit., ** wounded my head].' Avcı tavşanı yaraladı. 'The hunter wounded the rabbit.'

{kendini/kendisini/kendi kendini} yarala- '- hurt {oneself}': Makasla oynayan çocuk {kendi.ni/kendisi.ni/kendi kendini} yaraladı. 'The child who was playing with the scissors hurt {himself}.' → = yaralan- 2.

* kalbinden yarala- '- break sb's heart' [A. kalp (kalBİ) 'heart'], i.e., '- wound sb IN [lit., ** from] his heart': Beni kalb.İM.DEN yaraladın. 'You broke my heart [lit., ** You wounded me IN MY heart].', i.e., gravely: You wounded me in the most sensitive place. Stronger than kalbini kır- ['- hurt sb's feelings'] → kır- 1. *112:19.* sadness: - aggrieve; *393:13.* impairment: - inflict an injury. → = yık- 1.

yaralan- [ır] [yarala- + {pass./refl.} suf. -n] 1 /DAn, {tarafından/CA}/ '- be wounded, hurt, injured /IN, by/': Banka.yA yapılan silâhlı soygun sonucu 5 kişi {a: ağır/b: hafif/c: hafif şekilde} yaralandı. 'Five people were {a: seriously/b, c: slightly} injured IN [lit., as a result of] the armed robbery carried out AT [lit., ** (directed) TO] the bank.' Trafik kazalarında 1.550 kişi yaralanırken 39 kişi can verdi. 'While 1,550 people were wounded in traffic accidents, 39 people died.' Çarpışan arabalardaki iki kişi yaralan.madan kurtuldu. 'Two people in the cars that had collided were rescued unharmed [lit., ** without being injured].' Çocuğun attığı taş ile kafam yaralandı. 'My head was injured by the stone [that] the child had thrown.' * Kol.um.DAN yaralandım. 'I was wounded IN the [lit., my] arm.' Düşman {askerler.i.nce/askerler.i tarafından} yaralanan dedem çok geçmeden ölmüş. 'My grandfather, who had been wounded {by enemy soldiers}, * died soon afterwards [lit., ** without much (time) passing].' 393:13. impairment: - inflict an injury. → sakatlan- ['- become physically disabled, - be hurt; - become crippled; - become maimed or mutilated'].

2 '- hurt oneself, - get hurt': * Makasla oynayan çocuk yaralandı. 'The child who was playing with the scissors hurt himself.' → = {kendini/ kendisi-ni/kendi kendini} yarala-. 393:13. impairment: - inflict an injury. → = sakatlan-.

yaramazlık {yap-/et-}. → yap- 3.

{yararlan- [ɪr]/faydalan- [ɪr]/istifade et- [eDer]} /DAn/ '- benefit or - profit /from/, - make good use /OF/, - take advantage /OF/; - utilize /θ/' [{yarar/A. fayda/A. istifade (. . - .} 'use, advantage'. {yarar/fayda} + verb-forming suf. -lAn]: Geçen {dönem} aldığım fizik dersi.nden çok yararlandım. 'I really profited from the physics course I took last {term/semester/quarter/lit., ** period}.' Bilgilenmek için hangi kaynaklar.DAN yararlanır-sınız? 'To get information [lit., To become informed] what sources do you use [lit., make use OF]?' Türkçe öğrenirken {televizyon.dan/ internet.ten} çok yararlandım. 'While learning Turkish, I greatly profited {from television/from the Internet}.' * Biz bu fırsat.TAN yararlanmay.I bilecek miyiz? 'Will we know how to take advantage OF this opportunity?' 387:15. use: - take advantage of. → = değerlendir- 2.

yarat- [ɪr] '- create': Allah ilk önce Adem ile Havva'yı yarattı. 'God first created Adam and Eve.' Her şey.İ yaratan ve yok eden

Allah'tır. 'God is the one who creates θ all that is and destroys it.' Proverb: Allah kulunu kısmeti ile yaratır. 'God creates His servant [i.e., any will-possessing being, mortal] together with his fate.' 963:11. predetermination: PHR. it is fated. Some Turks believe that the verb yarat- should be used only with God as the subject, that this verb means only '- create sth from nothing [i.e., yoktan var etmek]', a creation exclusive to God, but examples with other subjects such as the following also abound in the press and in speech: Dede Efendi'nin yarat.tığ.ı besteler.in benzer.i yoktur. 'There are no compositions like those Dede Efendi created [i.e., composed].' Bu haber sınıfta {neşeli/kötü/sinirli} bir hava yarattı. 'This news created a {cheerful/bad/tense} mood [or atmosphere] in the class.' İbrahim Tatlıses'in konser.i İzmir'de olay yarattı. 'Ibrahim Tatlıses's concert created a sensation [lit., event] in Izmir.' Üniversiteli öğrencilerin yürüyüşü olay yarattı ve bazı öğrenciler yaralandı. 'The march held by {college/university} students created a scene, and several students were wounded.' 891:8. production: - produce, - create. → = oluştur-, = var et-, ≠ yık- 1, ≠ yok et- 1.

yardım elini uzat-. → uzat- 2.

yardım et- [eDer] /A/ '- help /θ/, - assist /θ/' [yardım 'help, assistance']: Noun for a person as grammatical object: Siz.E yardım edebilir miyim? 'Can I help θ you?' {Bavullarım} çok ağır, ban.A yardım eder misiniz? '{My bags are/My luggage is} very heavy. Would you {help θ me/give me a hand}?' Ortalıkta gezinip durma, gel ban.A yardım et! 'Don't just keep wandering about aimlessly. Come [over here] and help me!' * Ban.A yardım edecek [hiç bir] kimse yok. 'There is no one [at all] around to help me.' Proverbs: Allah evlenenle ev yapan.A yardım eder. 'God helps θ those who marry and build a house.' Allah yardım ederse kulu.nA, her iş.i girer yol.u.nA. 'If God helps θ His servant [i.e., any will-possessing being, mortal], every task [that the servant undertakes] will go well [lit., ** will enter θ its path].'

Noun for a task as grammatical object: * {Türkçe.M.E/Türkçe ders.İM.E} yardım eder misiniz? 'Would you please help {ME WITH my Turkish/ME WITH my Turkish lesson}? [lit., ** help TO MY ...?]' * Çantalar.ım.ı taşıma.M.A yardım eder misiniz? 'Would you help ME [to] carry MY bags [lit., ** help TO MY carry.ING my bags]?' * Şu numara.yı bulma.MIZ.A yardım eder misiniz? 'Would you please help US [to] find this number [lit., ** help TO OUR find.ING this number]?' Ağabeyim [usually pronounced: âbim] yeni öğrenciler.in matematik ödevler.i.ni yapma.LAR.I.NA yardım etti. 'My older brother helped THE NEW STUDENTS WITH their math homework [lit., ** helped TO THE NEW STUDENTS' do.ING THEIR math homework].'

• In an emergency, such as a fire, etc., the usual translation of 'Help!' is İmdat! [in comics often written İmdaat! to reflect the pronunciation, i.e., imdât, used in an emergency] rather than Yardım edin. But İmdat! may be followed by yardım edin: İmdat, yardım edin! Perhaps 'Come quick! Help!' Yetişin, imdat! Boğuluyorum. 'Come quick! Help! I'm drowning!' *449:11.* aid: - aid. → = yardımda bulun-. Same, *more formal.* → bulun- 3, = yardımcı ol- ['- help /Θ/, - assist /Θ/, - be of assistance /to/, - be helpful /to/'] → ol- 12, yardım elini uzat- ['- extend a helping hand /to/, - help out, - extend aid, assistance /to/'] → uzat- 2, el ele ver- ['- help one another'] → ver- 1, yardımlaş- ['- help one another'], kolaylık göster- ['- make sth easy /FOR/, - facilitate matters /FOR/, - help /Θ/, *colloq.* - give sb a break'] → göster- 1.

yardımcı ol-. → ol- 12.

yardımda bulun-. → bulun- 3.

yardımlaş- [ır] '- help one another' [yardım 'help, assistance' + recip. suf. -lAş]: * Meslektaşlarımızla pek çok konuda yardımlaşıyoruz. 'My colleagues and I help each other on many issues.' Yardımlaşmak iyidir ama {sınav/imtihan} esna.sı.nda

değil. 'Helping each other is fine, but not during {an examination}.' *449:11.* aid: - aid. → = el ele ver- ['- help one another'] → ver- 1, yardım elini uzat- ['- extend a helping hand /to/, - help out, - extend aid, assistance /to/'], yardım et- ['- help /Θ/, - assist /Θ/'], yardımda bulun-. Same, *more formal.* → bulun- 3, yardımcı ol- ['- help /Θ/, - assist /Θ/, - be of assistance /to/, - be helpful /to/'] → ol- 12.

yargıla- [r] '- hear a case; - try sb, a case; - judge or - adjudicate a case, - pass judgment on' [yargı 1 'lawsuit'. 2 'decision in a court of law' + verb-forming suf. -lA]: Yargıçların görevi yargılamak. 'It is the job of judges to {hear cases/pass judgment}.' Yanlış anlamayın, benim amacım sizi yargılamak değil, sadece gerçeği öğrenmek. 'Don't misunderstand. My purpose is not to {pass judgment/sit in judgment} on you, but to find out the truth.' Lütfen * hemen yargılamayın, iyice [bir] düşünün. 'Please * don't rush to judgment [lit., ** judge right away]. [First] think carefully.' *594:5.* jurisdiction: - administer justice; *598:17.* legal action: - try; *945:8.* judgment: - judge.

yarış- [ır] [yarış 1 'race'. 2 'competition' + Θ] 1 /lA/ '- race /Θ/ sb, - race /with/ sb': Atletimiz bugünkü yarışta çok iyi yarıştı, * ancak ikinci oldu. 'Our athlete performed [lit., raced] very well in today's race, * but he came in only second.' * Şu duvar.A kadar {senin.le/sen.le} yarışalım. 'I'll race Θ you to the wall over there [lit., ** 'LET'S race to the wall over there {with you}']. *457:19.* contention: - race.

2 /lA/ '- compete /with/': Sınıf birincisi olmak için hep arkadaşları ile yarışırdı. '[In order] to be first in the class he would always compete with his friends.' *457:18.* contention: - compete.

yas tut-. → tut- 5.

yasak et-. → {yasakla-/yasak et-}.

{yasakla- [r]/yasak et- [eDer]} '- forbid, - prohibit' [yasak 1 'prohibition'. 2 'forbidden' + verb-forming suf. -lA]: **Okul idaresi sınıflarda sigara iç.İL.me.si.ni yasakladı.** 'The school administration forbade the smoking [lit., ** the BEING smoked...] of cigarettes in the classrooms.' **Annem Rıdvan ile görüş.mem.i yasakladı.** 'My mother forbade me to see [lit., ** my {seeing/meeting with}] Rıdvan.' • Note the use of the ADJECTIVE **yasak** following the full infinitive in common prohibitions: **Sigara içmek yasak[tır].** '{Smoking is forbidden./It is forbidden to smoke.}' *444:3*. prohibition: - prohibit. → ≠ **izin ver-** → **ver-** 1, ≠ **müsaade et-**.

yasaklan- [ır] /{tarafından/CA}/ '- be forbidden, prohibited /by/' [yasakla- + pass. suf. -n]: **Yurd.A giriş ve çıkışlar [yetkililer tarafından] yasaklandı.** 'Passage in and out of the country has been forbidden [by the authorities] [lit., ** Entrances INTO the country and exits have been forbidden...].' **Parklarda alkollü içki içmek yasaklandı.** 'The drinking of alcoholic beverages in the parks has been forbidden.' *444:3*. prohibition: - prohibit.

yasla-. → {daya-/yasla-}.

yaşa- [r] [yaş 'age' + verb-forming suf. -A] 1 '- live': **Yaşa ve öğren.** 'Live and learn.' **Az ye, çok yaşa.** 'Eat little and live a long time.' * **124 yaşına kadar yaşayan [bir] adam duydum.** 'I heard OF a man who lived to the age of 124.' **Yaratıcı insan daha uzun yaşıyor.** 'A creative person lives longer.' **Ucuz kahramanlığ.A gerek yok. Ölmek değil, onurluca yaşamaktır zor olan.** 'There is no need for easy [lit., cheap] heroism. What is difficult is not to die, but to live honorably.' Proverbs: **Çok yaşayan bilmez, çok gezen bilir.** 'It's not the one who has lived long, but the one who has traveled widely that knows [lit., The one who has lived long does not know, the one who has traveled a lot knows].' **Çok yaşayan, çok görür.** 'He who lives long {sees/experiences} much.' *570: * 19*. learning: PHR. experience is the best teacher. **Namussuz yaşa.MAKTANSA namuslu ölmek yeğdir.** 'It's better to die honorably THAN to live dishonorably.' Death before dis-

honor. **Nasıl yaşarsak öyle ölürüz.** 'However we live, so shall we die.' *306:7*. life: - live. → ≠ **öl-**, ≠ **vefat et-**.

Çok yaşa! (1) 'Long Live...!': **Padişahım çok yaşa!** 'Long live my {Sultan/King}!' **Çok yaşa Türkiye!** 'Long live Turkey!' *116:2*. rejoicing: cheer; *509:22*. approval: INTERJ. bravo!
(2) 'Bravo!, Hurray!, Good for you!': A teacher to her students: **Çok yaşayın! Ne güzel çalışıyorsunuz!** 'Bravo! How nicely you are working!' = **Aferin!**, → = **Aşkolsun.** → ol- 11 → olsun, = **Helâl olsun.** → ol- 11 → olsun. The following are the words of a cheer in support of a team. The first part consists of the verb broken down into syllables which are repeated: * **Ya, ya, ya, şa, şa, şa, {bizim takım/Fenerbahçe} çok yaşa!** 'Hurray for {our team/Fenerbahçe [i.e., a famous soccer team]}! [or Rah, rah, rah for...] [lit., Ya, ya, ya, şa, şa, şa, long live {our team/Fenerbahçe}!]' *116:2*. rejoicing: cheer; *149:4*. congratulation: INTERJ. congratulations; *509:22*. approval: INTERJ. bravo!
(3) 'Bless you! [lit., Live long!]', a response to a person who has sneezed [**hapşır-** '- sneeze']. The traditional response of the person who has sneezed: **Sen de gör!** 'Same to you!' [lit., 'You too {see/experience} it', i.e., a long life] *504: * 20*. courtesy: polite expressions. For 'Bless {him/her}', → **sağ olsun** → **sağ ol-** → ol- 12.

2 /DA/ '- live, - reside /{in/at}/, - inhabit /θ/': **Otur-** is more common than **yaşa-** in this meaning: **Büyük amcam {a: 5 yıldır/b: 5 yıldan beri/c: yıllardır/NOT ~~yıllarca~~} Antalya'da yaşıyor.** 'My great [paternal] uncle {has lived/has been living} in Antalya {a, b: for five years/c: for years}.' **Büyük amcam {5 yıl/yıllarca/NOT ~~yıllardır~~} Antalya'da yaşadı.** 'My great uncle lived in Antalya {for five years/for years}.' • Note: **-DIr** and -**DAn beri** 'since, for', as above, are used for action that began in the past and is continuing now; **-lArcA** 'for', preceded by a word designating a period, i.e., years, months, etc., is not used for present continuing action. S: **Ailenizle [birlikte] mi yaşıyor-**

sunuz? 'Q: Do you live [together] with your family?' C: Hayır, {yalnız [başına]/tek başına} yaşıyorum. 'A: No, I live {alone}.' For another dialogue used when discussing the people one is living or staying with, see kal- 1. 225:7. habitation: - inhabit. → = otur- 3, hayat sür- ['- lead a (certain kind of) life'] → sür- 6.

3 '- live through, - experience, - have, - enjoy, or - go through an experience': * Hayatımın en güzel günlerini yaşıyorum. '{a: I'm {living through/experiencing} the best days of my life./b: I'm having the time of my life.}' En {heyecanlı/parlak} günlerimizi yaşıyoruz. 'We are living through our most {exciting/brilliant} days.' Çok önemli, çok mutlu günler yaşıyoruz. 'We are living through very momentous, very happy days.' * Çok şey yaşadık. 'We're gone through a lot.' Fenerbahçe'ye yeni transfer edilen Osman takım arkadaslarıyla * çok güzel bir birliktelik yaşadıklarını söyledi. 'Osman, who has just been tranferred to Fenerbahçe [i.e., a soccer team], said that he and his team members were getting along {great/very well/famously} [lit., ** were living a nice togetherness].' Ülke.miz.in kader.i.ni tayin edecek tarihî bir olay.I yaşıyoruz. 'We are living through a historical event that will determine the fate of our country.' Türk-Amerikan ilişkisi en tehlikeli, en kritik günlerini yaşıyor. 'Turkish-American relations are going through their most dangerous, critical days.' Tarihimizin en {utanç verici/zor} dönemini yaşıyoruz. 'We are living through the most {humiliating/difficult} period in our history.' En yakın arkadaşım şu sıralar sağlık sorunu yaşıyor. 'My closest friend is {having/experiencing} a health problem these days.' Türkiye parasal sorunlar yaşıyor. 'Turkey is {having/experiencing} financial problems.' Yaşadığımız kabusu ömrümüz boyunca unutamayız. 'As long as we live we'll never be able to forget the nightmare [that] we've lived through.' Onunla aynı şeyi yaşamak istemiyorum. 'I don't want to {live through/go through} the same thing with her again.'

Otelimizin barında yoğun bir gün.ün ard.ı.ndan, * canlı müzik eşliğ.i.nDE, en sevdiğiniz içinizi yudumla-yarak romantik bir gece yaşayabilirsiniz. 'After a busy day, you can enjoy a romantic evening in the bar of our hotel, sipping your favorite drink TO [lit., ** IN] the accompaniment of lively music.' 830:8. event: - experience.

yaşar- [ır] [yaş 'tears' + verb-forming suf. -Ar]: gözleri yaşar- 'for one's eyes - fill with tears, for tears - come to one's eyes; for one's eyes - water' [göz 'eye']: Film o kadar acıklıydı ki, gözlerim yaşardı. 'The movie was so sad that tears came to my eyes.' Çok etkilendim, gözlerim yaşardı. '{I'm/I was} deeply moved. Tears came to my eyes.' Also ironically as a response to a trumped-up excuse such as: 'I couldn't come to the exam because my grandmother passed away.' 115:12. lamentation: - weep. Soğan doğrarken gözlerim yaşardı. 'While I was cutting up onions, my eyes watered.' 13:5. secretion: - secrete.

yaşart- [ır] '- bring tears to one's eyes, - make sb's eyes fill with tears, - make cry, weep; - make sb's eyes water' [yaşar- + caus. suf. -t]: gözlerini yaşart- '- bring tears to one's eyes, make one's eyes water' [göz 'eye']: Müdürün veda konuşması hepimiz.in gözler.i.ni yaşarttı. 'The director's farewell speech brought tears to the eyes of all of us.' 115:12. lamentation: - weep. {Soğan/Acı biber} gözlerimiz.i yaşarttı. '{The onion/The hot pepper} made our eyes water.' 13:5. secretion: - secrete.

yaşına bas-. → yaşına {bas-/gir-). → bas- 1.

yaşına gir-. → yaşına {bas-/gir-). → bas- 1.

yaşını {doldur-/tamamla-}. → doldur- 1.

yaşını tamamla-. → yaşını {doldur-/tamamla-}. → doldur- 1.

yaşlan- [ır] '- grow old, - age, - get old', for people, not things [yaş 'age' of a person + verb-forming suf. -lAn]: Babam epeyce yaşlandı. Artık yürüyemez oldu. 'My father has {gotten quite old/aged quite a bit}. He can't walk anymore.' *303:10.* age: - age; *841:9.* oldness: - age. → = ihtiyarla-, = yaşı ilerle- → ilerle-3. For a NON-living thing as a subject of '- get old', → eski-.

yat- [ar] 1 '- go to bed, - lie down, - retire for the night', also '- BE lying down, - be in bed': * Sen daha oturacak mısın? * Uyku.m geldi, yatıyorum. 'Are you going to stay up [lit., ** sit] a while longer? * I'm sleepy [lit., ** my sleepiness has come]. I'm {going [off]/off} to bed.' Babam her zaman erken yatardı. 'My father would always go to bed early.' Her gün {onbir buçukta/11:30'da [read: onbir otuzda or onbir buçukta]} yatarım. 'I go to bed at 11:30 every night [lit., day].' Nazlı daha kalkmadı, hâlâ yatıyor. 'Nazlı hasn't gotten up yet, she's still in bed.' Derler ki burada büyük bir veli yatıyormuş. 'They say that a great [Sufi] saint lies [buried] here.' An address to the deceased: Nur içinde yat. 'May you rest in peace [lit, in light].' A statement about the deceased: Nur içinde yatsın, çok iyi bir insandı rahmetli. 'May he rest in peace. The deceased was a very good person.' *307: * 39.* death: expressions used upon hearing of a death; *504: * 20.* courtesy: polite expressions. Proverbs: Erken yat, erken kalk. 'Go to bed early, rise early.' Early to bed, early to rise. Gün ile yatan gün ile kalkar. 'He who goes to bed with the sun gets up with the sun.' *844:17.* earliness: PHR. the early bird gets the worm. Korkulu rüya görmektense uyanık yatmak hayırlıdır. 'It is better to lie awake than to have bad dreams.' Körle yatan şaşı kalkar. 'He who lies down [i.e., keeps company] with a blind person will get up cross-eyed.', i.e., Beware of the company you keep. *22:17.* sleep: - go to bed; *201:5.* horizontalness: - lie; *912:11.* depression; - lie down. → uyu- 2 ['- go to sleep'], uzan- 1 ['- lie down /ON/, - stretch oneself out /ON/'], ≠ kalk- 1.

2 /lA/ '- go to bed /with/, - sleep /with/', i.e., - have sex /with/: S: Onunla yattın mı? Bana doğruyu söyle! 'Q: Did you sleep with {him/her}? Tell me the truth!' C: Evet, onunla yattım. Çünkü onu seviyorum. 'A: Yes I did, because I love {him/her}.' *75:21.* sex: - copulate; *562:14.* lovemaking, endearment: - make love. → = cinsel ilişkide bulun- ['- have sex /with/, - have sexual intercourse /with/', *formal, polite*] → bulun- 3, = seviş-2 ['- caress each other, *slang:* - make out /with/; - make love /with/, - have sexual intercourse /with/'], = oynaş-2 ['- carry on a love affair /with/', *slang* '- make out /with/'].

yatağını yap-. → yap- 3.

yatır- [ır] /A/ [yat- + caus. suf. -Ir] 1 '- put sb to bed, - have sb lie down /{IN/ON}/': * Annesi bebeği yatağ.ı.nA yatırdı. 'The mother put the baby to bed [lit., ** Its mother put the baby IN its bed].' Çocuğ.un uyku.su geldi galiba, hemen yatağını yapayım da yatıralım. 'The child is probably sleepy [lit., ** The child's sleepiness has probably come]. Let me make up his bed right away, and let's put him to bed.' *22:19.* sleep: - put to bed.

2 '- deposit': para yatır- [para 'money'] A noun designating money may replace the word para. (1) /A/ '- deposit money /IN/ an account': S: Kirayı kim.e veriyorsunuz? 'Q: Who do you pay your [lit., the] rent to?' C: Kirayı * ev sahib.i.nin hesab.ı.na banka.ya yatırıyorum. 'A: I deposit the rent * into my landlord's bank account [lit., ** into the landlord's account into the bank].' {a: Aylığımı/b: Maaşımı/c: Babamdan aldığım parayı} banka.yA yatırdım. 'I deposited {a: my monthly check [lit., salary]/b: my salary [i.e., monthly or otherwise]/c: the money I received from my father} IN the bank.' * Babamdan ban.a miras kalan malları para.ya çevirip özel bir finans kurum.u.nA yatırdım. 'I took the money I got from selling [lit., I converted into money] the property that I inherited [lit., that remained to me] from my father and deposited it IN a private financial institution.' *159:14.* location: - deposit. → ≠ para çek- → çek- 2. (2) /A/ '- pay money for municipal services.' The money is deposited into a public institution's bank account: * Telefon para.sı.nı PTT'yE [pronounce: pe-te-te'yE, i.e., Posta Telgraf Telefon'A] yatırdım. 'I paid my phone bill [lit.,

** paid the phone money to the Post, Telegraph, and Telephone Office].' * {Elektrik/Su/Gaz} fatura.sı.nı banka.yA yatırdım. 'I paid my [lit., the] {electric/water/gas} bill [lit., to the bank].' Dün vergimi yatırdım. 'I paid my taxes yesterday.' *624:10.* payment: - pay. → = öde-, = para ver- → ver- 1.

yatırım yap-. → yap- 3.

yavaşla- [r] '- slow down, - lose speed, - die down [rain]' [yavaş 'slow' + verb-forming suf. -lA]: To a taxi driver: Biraz yavaşla, şimdi {biri.nE/birisi.nE} çarpacaksın. 'Slow down a bit, you're going to hit {θ sb} now.' * En önde koşan atlet bir ara yavaşlayınca arkadan gelen onu geçti. 'When the athlete * in the lead [lit., running in front] slowed down at one point, the one behind him passed him.' Yağmur yavaşladı. Artık dışarı çıkabiliriz. 'The rain has died down. We can go out now.' *175:9.* slowness: - slow. → ≠ acele et-, ≠ çabuk ol- → ol- 12, ≠ hızlan- 1.

yayıl- [ır] /a: DAn, b: A, c: yoluyla/ '- spread /a: from, b: to, c: {through/by means of}/': Disease: Hastalığ.ın yayılma.sı.nı önlemek {için/amac.ı.yla} tüm okulları 6 hafta süreyle kapattılar. '{[In order] to} prevent the spread of the disease, they closed all the schools for six weeks.' S: AIDS nasıl yayılıyor? 'Q: How does AIDS spread?' C: AIDS sadece cinsel ilişki yoluyla değil, kan alışverişi yoluyla da yayılıyor. 'A: AIDS spreads not only through sexual contact, it also spreads through the exchange of blood.'
Fire: Sabah saatlerinde nedeni belirlenemeyen orman yangını hızla civar köyler.e doğru yayıldı, yakın şehirlerden gelen itfaiye ekipleri tarafından ancak akşam.a doğru kontrol altına alınabildi. 'In the morning hours a forest fire of undetermined origins spread rapidly to the surrounding villages. It could be brought under control only toward evening by teams of firefighters coming from nearby cities.'
News: Başbakanın rahatsızlık geçirdiği haberleri kısa sürede televizyon, radyo ve internet yoluyla {memleket.in/dünya.nın} {dört bir yan.ı.na/her

yan.ı.na} yayıldı. 'In a short time, the news that the prime minister was ill spread {to the four corners of/to all parts} {of the country/of the world} by [way of] TV, radio, and the Internet.' * Aslı astarı olmayan bu abuk subuk {dedikodular/söylentiler} * kulak.tan kulağ.a hızla yayılıyor. 'This unfounded, foolish {gossip} is spreading rapidly * through the grapevine [lit., ** from ear to ear].'
Religion: Amerika'da en hızlı yayılan din İslâm'dır. 'Islam is the most rapidly spreading religion in the U.S.'
Empire: Osmanlı Devleti üç kıtada birden hızla yayıldı. 'The Ottoman Empire spread in all of three continents.' *770:4b.* dispersion: - disperse, - become dispersed. → = geç- 2 ['- pass or - spread from one person to another', subj: disease].

yayımla- [r] [yayım 1 'publication'. 2 'broadcast' + verb-forming suf. -lA]: /DA/ 1 '- publish /in/': Profesör makalesini {nerede/hangi dergide} yayımladı? '{Where/In which journal} did the professor publish his article?' Söz.ü.nü ettiğiniz makaleyi yayımladınız mı? 'Did you publish the article [that] you had mentioned?' * Siz.ce yayınevi bu kitabı yayımlar mı? '{Do you think the publishing house will publish this book?/In your view will the publishing house publish this book?}' Birleşmiş Milletler, insan hakları ihlâller.i.ni kınayan yeni bir bildiri yayımladı. 'The United Nations published a new statement condemning human rights violations.' *548:14.* printing: - print.

2 /DAn/ '- broadcast /ON/ radio or television': Bu kanalın yayımladığı programları beğenmiyorum. 'I don't like the programs {on this channel/lit., [that] this channel broadcasts}.' *1033:25.* radio: - broadcast; *1034:14.* television: - televise.

yayımlan- [ır] /DA, {tarafından/CA}/ [yayımla- + pass. suf. -n]: 1 '- be published /in, by/': S: Bu yazı nerede yayımlanacak? 'Q: Where will this article be published?' C: Nokta dergi.si.nin Kasım sayı.sı.nda yayımlanacak. 'A: It will be published in the November issue of the magazine Nokta.' #

443

Bahsettiğiniz kitap geçen yıl Kültür Bakanlığı tarafından yayımlandı. 'The book you mentioned was published last year by the Ministry of Culture.' *548:14.* printing: - print.

2 '- air, - be aired, carried, broadcast, - be on [radio or television]': With the name of the broadcasting instrument /{D A n/DA}/: Kaza haberi dün {radyo.DAN/ televizyon.DAN} yayımlandı. '[The] news of the accident aired {ON the radio/ON TV} yesterday.' With the name of the wave length /DAn, üzerinden/: Selâm FM [pronounce: ef em] otuzbeş nokta iki [35.2] {dalga boy.u.nDAN/ dalga boy.u üzeri.nDEN} yayımlanıyor. 'Selam FM [i.e., a radio station] broadcasts [lit., ** is broadcast] ON 35.2 meters.' With the name of the channel /DA/: * Galatasaray maçı hangi kanal.DA yayımlanacak? '{Which channel will carry the Galatasaray soccer game?/Which channel will the soccer game be on?/lit., On which channel will the Galatasaray soccer game be broadcast?}' With the time of the broadcast /DA/: O film eylül ay.ı.nın ikinci hafta.sı.nda, çarşamba günü saat 21'de [read: yirmi birde] yayımlandı. 'That film {aired/was carried/was broadcast} [in] the second week of September, on Wednesday at 9 pm.' With both the time and the name of the channel /DA/: O belgesel film 15/11/2005 [read: onbeş/onbir/ iki bin beş] tarihi.nDE saat 17:30'da [read: on yedi otuzda] Kanal 7'DE yayımlanacak. 'That documentary will {air/be} on November 15th, 2005 at 5:30 pm on Channel 7.' With the name of a program /DA/: "Güne Başlarken" programı.nDA yayımlananlar hiç ilgimi çekmiyor. 'The items [broadcast] on the "Early Morning [lit., Beginning the Day] Show" don't interest me at all.' *1033:25.* radio: - broadcast; *1034:14.* television: - televise.

yaz- [ar] 1 /a: A, b: A, c: DA, d: lA/ '- write /a: to [sb], b: {ON/IN}, c: {in/on}, d: with/': The dative case [A] is used on the noun designating the destination, the addressee, of the information: Emine kim.E mektup yazmış? 'Who[m] did Emine [f.] write {a letter/letters} TO?' Tebeşiri aldı ve tahta.yA adı.nI yazdı. 'He took the chalk and wrote his name ON the blackboard.' İsmini defteri.nE yazdı. 'He wrote his name {IN/ON} his notebook.' Çiğdem'in telefon numara.sı.nI bura.yA yazın. 'Write Çiğdem's [f.] phone number down θ here.' İsmim.İ nere.yE yazayım? 'θ Where should I write my name?' The locative case [DA] is used on the noun designating the location of the information: Müdür.e gönderdiği mektup.TA ne yazmış? 'What did he write IN the letter that he sent to the director?' Mektup.TA Ankara'ya {a: gittiğ.i.ni/b: gideceğ.i.ni/c: gitme.si gerek- tiğ.i.ni} yazmış. 'IN the letter he wrote {a: that he had gone/b: that he would go/c: that he should go} to Ankara.' Mektup.TA {ne zaman/kiminle/nereye} git- tiğ.i.ni yazmamış. 'IN the letter he didn't write {when/with whom/where} he had gone.' Mektup.TA büyükanne.m.in bize gelip gelmediğ.i.ni yaz- madım. 'IN the letter I didn't indicate [lit., write] whether or not my grandmother had come to visit us [lit., had come to us].' {a: Bu konu.da/b: Bu konu hakkında/ c: Bu konu.yA dair/d: Bu konu {üzerine/üstüne}} ne yazdı? 'What did he write {a: on this subject/b: about this subject/c: concerning this subject/d: on this subject}?' * Bu olay.I daha önce iki üç kez yazmıştı. 'He had written ABOUT this event two or three times before.' • In reference to words on a sign or poster the present continuous tense active is often used where the English might have the passive: Uçaktaki tuvalette * "Lütfen tuvalet.İ fazla meşgul etmeyin" yazıyordu. 'In an airplane restroom were written the words, * "Please don't occupy the restroom too long".' • Note the present continuous tense in the Turkish and the simple present tense in the English in words that introduce a correspondent's report: Ahmet Çelik Ankara'dan yaz.IYOR. 'Ahmet Çelik WRITES from Ankara.' Proverb: * Deme kış yaz, oku yaz. 'Regardless of whether it's winter or summer [lit., ** Don't say winter or summer], keep reading and

Part 1: Turkish-English Dictionary of Verbs

writing [lit., ** read, write].' • Note: To express authorship, the **Ahmet'in kitab.ı** [i.e., possessOR possessED] structure, rather than the verb **yaz-**, is frequently used: **Meşhur yazar.IN beş kitab.I var.** 'The famous author has written five books [lit., HAS five books].' Of course the literal meaning of this Turkish could also apply, depending on the context. **Bil bakalım * bu şiir kimin?** 'Come on, take a guess: * who wrote this poem [lit., whose poem is this]?' *547:19.* writing: - write; *549:15.* record: - record. → = **kaydet-** 2 ['- record, - enter, - write down'].

2 '- say', when referring to a written document or sign. In such cases a continuous tense is frequent in Turkish: * **Bugünkü gazetede neler yazıyor?** '{What does it say [lit., ** is it writing] in today's paper?/What does today's paper say?/What's in today's paper?/What's in the paper today?}' * **O pasta tarif.i.nde ne yazıyor?** 'What does it say on that pastry menu?' *547:19.* writing: - write. For '- say' when a person is the subject, → **de-** 1, **söyle-** 1.

yazdır- [ır] 1 /A/ '- have /Θ/ sb write, - get /Θ/ sb to write, - let /Θ/ sb write' [**yaz-** + caus. suf. **-DIr**]: * **On parmak bilmediğim için tezim.İ başkası.nA yazdırdım.** 'Because I couldn't touch-type [lit., ** I didn't know ten fingers], I had Θ sb else type [lit., write] my thesis.' *547:19.* writing: - write.

2 /A/ '- register or - enroll sb, not oneself, /IN [a course], {IN/AT} [a school]/': **Bu sene çocuğum.U {a: Türkçe kurs.u.nA/b: okul.A/c: ilkokul.A/d: lise.yE/e: üniversite.yE} yazdırdım.** 'This year I registered my child {a: IN the Turkish course/b: IN the school/c: IN [the] primary school/d: IN [the] {high school/lycée}/e: {IN [the] college/AT the university}}.' *549:15.* record: - record. → = **kaydet-** 1. For '- register ONESELF, not sb else in a course, etc.', → /A/ **kaydol-** → **ol-** 12, /A/ **yazıl-** 2.

yazık ol-. → **ol-** 12.

Yazıklar olsun! → **yazık ol-.** → **ol-** 12.

yazıl- [ır] [**yaz-** + {pass./refl.} suf. **-Il**] 1 /a: A, b: A, c: DA, d: lA, e: tarafından/ '- be written /a: to [sb], b: {ON/IN}, c: {in/on}, d: with, e: by/': **Bu mektupların {a: bigisayar.LA/b: bilgisayar.DA} yazılması gerekiyor.** 'These letters must be written {a: {BY computer/WITH a computer}/b: ON a computer}. This verb is often used when asking for the spelling of a word, particularly a foreign one: **S: Cincinnati kelimesi nasıl yazılıyor?** 'Q: How is the word "Cincinnati" written [i.e., spelled]?' **C: Ce-i-ne-ce-i-ne-ne-a-te-i DİYE yazılıyor.** 'A: It is spelled c-i-n-c-i-n-n-a-t-i [lit., ** it is written SAYING...].' Proverb: **Aln.A yazılan başa gelir.** 'What is written ON one's forehead [**alın**, aLNı] will come to pass [lit., ** 'will come to one's head', where **baş** 'head' represents the whole person., i.e., One can't escape one's fate.]. **Bu kütüphanede kimin tarafından yazıldığı belli olmayan pek çok elyazması var.** 'In this library there are very many anonymous manuscripts [lit., ** manuscripts of which it is not clear by whom they were written].' *547:19.* writing: - write. → = {harf harf/harflerini} **söyle-** ['- spell, - say {letter by letter/the letters of [a word]}'] → **söyle-** 1, **hecele-** ['- give the syllables of a word, - syllabify', the most common Turkish way of indicating the spelling of a word].

2 /A/ '- register [oneself], - get oneself registered /IN [a course], {IN/AT} [a school]/': **Bu sene {a: Türkçe kurs.u.nA/b: okul.A/c: ilkokul.A/d: lise.yE/e: üniversite.yE} yazılacağım.** 'This year I'm going to register {a: IN the Turkish course/b: IN the school/c: IN [the] primary school/d: IN the {high school/lycée}/e: AT the university [or college]}.' *549:15.* record: - record. → = **kaydol-** → **ol-** 12. For '- register sb [not oneself] in a course, etc.', → **kaydet-** 1, **yazdır-** 2.

ye- [r] 1 '- eat': **A: Şükran hanım * {buy[u]run}, beraber yiyelim.** 'A: Şükran hanım, * {come over here [i.e., to the food]/help yourself}. {Won't you join me?/lit., Let's eat together.}' **B: Teşekkür ederim, ben biraz önce yedim.** 'B: Thank you, but I ate just a little while ago.' **Dünden beri hiçbir şey**

445

yemedim. * Karnım çok aç. 'I haven't eaten anything since yesterday. I'm {famished/very hungry} [lit., ** my stomach, karın, kaRNı, is very hungry].' * Aç karnı.nA bir kilo incir yedim. 'I ate a kilo of figs ON an empty stomach.' Proverbs: Başaran bal yer, başaramayan yal yer. 'The one who succeeds eats honey; the one who cannot succeed eats mash.' Dost ile ye, iç; alışveriş etme. 'Eat and drink with a friend, but don't do business with him.' Ne pişirirsen onu yersin. 'You eat whatever you cook.', i.e., You get what you deserve. Süt.TEN ağzı yanan yoğurdu üfle.yerek yer. 'A person whose mouth has been burned BY [hot] milk blows on [his] yogurt [before] eating it [lit., eats the yogurt blow.ing on it].' Yogurt is usually eaten cold. Once bitten, twice shy. Tatlı ye, tatlı söyle. 'Eat sweet things, speak sweetly.' Üzümü ye de bağ.ı.nı sorma. 'Eat the grapes, but don't ask about the [lit., its] vineyard.' Don't look a gift horse in the mouth. Yiyen bilmez, doğrayan bilir. 'It is not the one who eats [the food] that understands [i.e., what has been involved in producing it], but the one who has cut it up [i.e., prepared it].'

• The form yemek is ALSO a NON-verbal NOUN meaning 'food'. Thus yemek ye- literally means '- eat FOOD' and is used when the food eaten is not specified: Yemek yedin[iz] mi? 'Have you eaten?' S: Nerede yemek yedin? 'Q: Where did you eat?' C: {a: Evde/b: * Dışarda/c: Lokanta-da/d: Kebapçıda/e: Restoran-da}. 'I ate {a: at home/b: * out/c: at a restaurant/d: at a kebab restaurant/e: at a restaurant}.' Sevda'yı gördüğüm zaman yemek yiyordu. 'When I saw Sevda, she was eating.' Günde yalnız iki öğün yemek yer. 'He eats only two meals a day.' 8:20. eating: - eat. → karnını doyur- ['- get sth to eat, - have a meal, - eat, - eat one's fill, - fill one's stomach'], iç- 3 ['- eat', sometimes when the object of iç- is a liquid, but not a drink (e.g., soup)], kahvaltı {et-/yap-} ['- have or - eat breakfast, - breakfast'].

abur cubur ye- '- have a snack, - snack, - eat food as a casual snack.' The food may include, but is not limited to, junk food, i.e., cookies, candy, candy bars, etc., the kind of food sold in vending machines in the U.S.: Abur cubur yemek sağlığ.A zararlıdır. 'Snacking is bad FOR [your] health.' 8:26. eating: - pick. → atıştır- 2 ['- grab a bite, - have or - eat a snack, - snack'].

akşam yemeği ye- '- have or - eat the evening meal, i.e., - have dinner or supper': Akşam yemeğin.İ yediniz mi? 'Have you had {dinner/lit., your dinner}?' Akşam yemeğin.İ nerede yediniz? 'Where did you have {dinner/lit., your dinner}?' Nerede akşam yemeği yediniz? 'Where did you have dinner?' 8:21. eating: - dine.

[çok] fazla yemek ye- '- overeat, - overindulge': Çok fazla yemek yedim. * Rahatsız oldum. 'I've eaten too much. * I'm stuffed [lit., ** I became uncomfortable].' 992:10. excess: - overdo.

öğle yemeği ye- '- have the noon meal, - have or - eat lunch.' Substitute öğle for akşam in the examples in the entry akşam yemeği ye- above. 8:21. eating: - dine.

2 '- experience, - receive, - be the object of', with certain nouns. 830:8. event: - experience. → = gör- 3, karşılaş- 3 ['- face /θ/, - be confronted /with/, - encounter /θ/, - experience /θ/, - meet /with/, - be up against'], uğra- 2 ['- meet /WITH/, - encounter /θ/, - experience, - be up against', usually a difficult situation].

* ceza ye- /DAn, DAn/ '- be punished or fined /BY [sb], FOR [sth]/' [A. ceza (. -) 'punishment'], lit., ** '- eat punishment /from, for/': Aşırı hız yapmak.TAN [polis.TEN] ceza yedik. 'We were fined [lit., punished] [BY the police] FOR speeding.' {Gaz/Elek-trik} fatura.sı.nı vaktinde ödemey.i unutunca ceza yedik. 'We were fined when we forgot to pay our {gas/electric} bill on time.' Müge bugün gelemeyecek, çünkü odadan çık.ma.ma ceza.sı yedi. 'Müge isn't going to be able to come today because she is being punished by not being permitted to leave her [lit., the] room [lit., ** ate the not-leaving-room punishment].' 603:5. penalty: - fine; 604:20. punishment: - be punished.

→ = ceza al- → al- 3, = cezalandırıl- 1, ≠ ödüllendiril-.

With nouns denoting different kinds of blows: **dayak ye-** /DAn/ '- get a thrashing, beating /from/' [**dayak (ğı)** 'beating']: **Küçükken babamdan epey dayak yedim.** 'When I was young, I got a lot of beatings from my father.' *604:13.* punishment: - whip; *901:16.* impulse, impact: - pound. → **dayak at-** ['- beat, - give a whipping, beating, - thrash /θ/'] → at- 5.

tekme ye- '- get a kick, - receive a blow' [**tekme** 'a kick']. See the example under **yumruk ye-** below. *901:21.* impulse, impact: - kick. → **tekme {at-/vur-)** ['- kick'] → at- 5.

tokat ye- '- get a slap, - be slapped' [**tokat** 'a slap']. See the example under **yumruk ye-** below. *604:12.* punishment: - slap; *901:19.* impulse, impact: - slap. → **tokat {at-/vur-)** ['- slap'] → at- 5.

yumruk ye- '- get a punch, - be punched' [**yumruk** 'punch']: * **Fazla ileri gitme, {tekme.yİ/tokad.I/yumruğ.U} yersin** * **ha!** 'Don't go too far! [lit., ** too far ahead', i.e., don't test my patience]. You'll get {a kick/a slap/a punch}, * I warn you!' • Note the use of the accusative case above but 'a' in the corresponding English. *901:14.* impulse, impact: - hit. → **yumruk {at-/vur-)** ['- punch'] → at- 5.

yeğle-. → {tercih et-/yeğle-}.

yemeğe çık-. → çık- 2.

yemek ye-. → ye- 1.

yemin et- [eDer] /a: A, b: A, c: A dair, d: diye/ '- swear or - vow /a: to [sb], b: θ [that], c: [to the effect] that, d: that [lit., saying]/; - take an oath' [A. **yemin** (. -) 'oath']: **Doğru söylüyorum, yemin ederim.** 'I'm telling the truth, I swear.' **Doğru söylüyorum diye yemin etti.** 'He swore that he was telling the truth [lit., ** He swore saying I'm telling the truth].' **Yemin ederim, siz.İ {yaptıklarınız.A/yaptığınız.A} pişman edeceğim.** 'I swear [that] I'll make you regret {θ the things [that] you've done/θ what you've done}.' {a: **Doğru söyle-**

.diğim.E/b: Yalan söyle.ME-.diğim.E/c: Kolyeyi çal.MA-.diğim.A} yemin ederim. 'I swear {a: θ that I told the truth/b: θ that I did NOT tell a lie/c: θ that I did NOT steal the necklace}.' **Duyduklar.ı.nı kimse.ye söylemeyeceğ.i.nE DAİR yemin etti.** 'He swore that he would never tell anyone the things [that] he had heard.' **San.A yemin ediyorum ki bu sırrını kimse öğrenmeyecek.** 'I swear to you that no one will learn this secret of yours.' **Vaatlerimi yerine getireceğim.E namusum ve şerefim üzerine yemin ederim.** 'I swear on my honor and good name [lit., ** on my honor and my honor] that I will carry out my promises.' *334: * 11.* affirmation: INTERJ. I swear!; *436:4.* promise: - promise. For '- promise', → **söz ver-** → ver- 1, **vadet-.**

1 **yen-** [ir] /tarafından/ '- be eaten /by/' [ye- + pass. suf. -n]: **Dolaptaki bütün meyveler yenmiş.** 'All the fruit in the cupboard had been eaten.' **Bu meyva çürümüş, yenmez.** 'This fruit has spoiled. It can't be eaten.' **Çiğ köfte daha çok Güneydoğu Anadolu'da yenir.** 'Raw meatballs are eaten mostly in Southeast Anatolia.' Proverb: **Çiğnemeden ekmek yenmez.** 'Bread cannot be [lit., is not] eaten without chewing it.' *8:20.* eating: - eat. → = 2 **yenil-.**

2 **yen-** [ir] 1 '- overcome, - conquer, - beat, - defeat': * **Beşiktaş futbol takımı Fenerbahçe'yİ 3-0** [read: **üç sıfır] yendi.** 'The Beşiktaş soccer team defeated Fenerbahçe 3 [TO] 0.' **Selçuklu Türkleri [1071] Malazgirt savaşında Bizanslıları yendi.** 'The Seljuk Turks defeated the Byzantines at the battle of Manzikert [1071].' **Yükseklik korkumu bir türlü yenemiyorum.** 'I just can't overcome my fear of heights.' *412:6.* defeat: - defeat.

2 '- win': {**Hangi takım/Kim} yeniyor?** '{Which team/Who} is winning?' *249:7.* superiority: - best; *411:3.* victory: - triumph. → = **kazan-** 2, ≠ **kaybet-.**

1 **yenil-** [ir] /A, not with **tarafından**/ '- be conquered, beaten, defeated /BY/' [yen- + pass. suf. -Il]: **Masa**

tenis.i.nde çoğu zaman yenilirdi. 'He was usually beaten in table tennis.' **Millî Takım.A yazık oldu. Çok iyi oynadığı halde yenildi.** 'What a pity FOR the national [soccer] team! Although it played very well, it was beaten.' **Fenerbahçe bu hafta da Beşiktaş'A yenildi.** 'This week, too, Fenerbahçe [a soccer team] was defeated BY Beşiktaş [another team].' **Boksörümüz Kübalı rakib.i.nE yenildi.** 'Our boxer was defeated BY his Cuban opponent.' Proverbs: **Bir yiğit ne kadar kahraman olsa da sevdiğ.i.nE yenilir.** '{No matter how strong a brave man may be, he will still be {defeated/ conquered} BY his lover.' **Yenilen pehlivan güreş.E doymaz.** 'A defeated wrestler always wants to wrestle some more [lit., never gets enough OF wrestling].', i.e., in the hope of eventually winning. *412:6.* defeat: - defeat.

2 **yenil-** [ir] '- be eaten' [**yen-** + pass. suf. -**Il**]. This verb in this meaning is common in writing, but less so in speech than 1 **yen-**: **Çiğ köfte daha çok Güneydoğu Anadolu'da yenilir.** 'Raw meatballs are eaten mostly in Southeast Anatolia.' Proverb: **Yenilen değil, hazmedilen besler.** 'It is not what is eaten but what is digested that nourishes [the body].' *8:20.* eating: - eat. → = 1 **yen-**.

yer- [er] '- run down, - point out the faults of, - criticize, - speak ill of, - disparage' [**yer** 'earth, ground' + verb-forming suf. -**θ**]: * **İyi de kardeşim, eleştirmek ayrıdır, yermek ayrı...** 'Well, all right {my friend/pal} [lit., my brother], criticizing sb is one thing, but running sb down is another thing [altogether] [lit., ** to criticize is separate, to run down is separate].' *512:8.* disparagement: - disparage. → {**eleştir-/tenkit et-**} ['- criticize', negatively and positively; negatively not as harsh as **yer-**], ≠ {**öv-/methet-**} ['- praise'].

yer ayırt-. → **ayırt-.**

yeri gelmişken. → **gel-** 1.

yerine getir-. → **getir-.**

yerleş- [ir] /A/ [**yer** 'place' + verb-forming suf. -**lAş**] '- locate, - settle, or - establish oneself /IN/ a place permanently or temporarily': * **Düşündük taşındık ve Bursa'YA yerleşmeye karar verdik.** 'We considered [all the options] carefully and [finally] decided to settle IN Bursa [a city].' **Yeni evimiz.E taşındık ama henüz tam yerleşemedik.** 'We've moved INTO our new home, but we haven't been able to settle in completely yet.' *159:17.* location: - settle.

'- settle [oneself] down /{IN/INTO}/' a chair, armchair, etc.: **Şömine.nin yan.ı.ndaki koltuğ.A** * **şöyle bir yerleşip verdiğin kitabı okumaya başladım.** 'I settled down * comfortably IN the the armchair by the fireplace and began to read the book you had given me.' *159:17.* location: - settle; *912:10.* depression <act of lowering>: - sit down. → **otur-** 1 ['- sit down /IN/'], **çök-** 2 ['- sit down suddenly, heavily /IN/, - collapse /INTO/ (armchair)'], ≠ **ayağa kalk-** ['- get to one's feet'] → **kalk-** 1, ≠ **fırla-** 1 ['- jump to one's feet'].

yet- [er] /A/ '- suffice /FOR/, - be enough /FOR/': **Bu para ban.A yeter.** 'This money is enough FOR me.' **Hepimiz çok acıkmıştık. Aldığım ekmekler yetmedi.** 'All of us were very hungry. I didn't buy enough bread [lit., The bread I bought didn't suffice].' **Dün bir taksi tutacaklarmış ama paraları yetmemiş.** 'They were going to {get/hire} a taxi yesterday, but they didn't have enough money [lit., their money didn't suffice].' **Yatırım yaparken iyi niyet yetmez, bilgi şart!** 'When investing, good intentions are not enough. [Good] information is absolutely necessary.' * **Beğendiğim elbise.yİ alma.m.A param yetmedi.** 'I didn't have enough money to buy [lit., ** My money did not suffice FOR my buying] the suit that I liked.' → = **dayan-** 5 ['- last, - hold out, - be enough /FOR/', supplies], = **yetiş-** 6 ['- be enough /FOR/, - suffice /FOR/']. In reference to a task in progress: **Şimdilik bu kadar yeter. Sonra devam ederiz.** 'That's enough for now [lit., For now this much suffices]. We'll continue later.'

bu yetmiyormuş gibi... '[And] as if this weren't enough...': * Hiç bir iş.E el.i.ni sürmüyor, bu yetmiyormuş gibi bir de emir vermey.e kalkıyor. 'He doesn't do a lick of work [lit., ** put his hand TO any task]. And as if that weren't enough, he {has the nerve/dares} to tell others what to do [lit., to give orders (to others)]!' 990:4. sufficiency: - suffice.

[paraca] gücü yet- '- afford, - have enough money /FOR/' [güç 'strength, force', para 'money' + suf. -CA 'in respect to, -wise'], lit., 'for one's strength [in respect to money, money-wise] - suffice': Sanırım bu evi almay.A [paraca] güc.ÜM {yetmez/yeter}. 'I think I {can't/can} afford to buy this house [lit., ** ...MY strength (money-wise) {won't suffice/will suffice}...].' 618:11. wealth: - have money; 626:7. expenditure: - afford.

yetim kal-. → kal- 1.

yetin- [ir] [yet- + refl. suf. -In] 1 /lA/ '- be content, satisfied /with/, - content oneself /with/': NON-verbal noun as object: Zengin olmak istiyorsan tek bir iş.le yetinmemelisin. 'If you want to become rich, you must not content yourself with [working at] just one job.' Sadece ders kitapları.yla yetinmedim, başka kitaplar da okudum. 'I didn't content myself only with textbooks, I also read other books.' Allah dostları bir lokma, bir hırka ile yetinir. 'Friends of God [i.e., Sufis, those not attached to the things of this world] are content with a piece of bread and a cloak.'
VERBAL noun as object: Sadece ders kitaplarını {okumak.la/ okuma.yla} yetinmedim. Ek OLARAK başka kaynaklar da kullandım. 'I wasn't satisfied only {to read [or with reading]} the text books. I also used other sources AS supplementary reading [lit., ** as supplement].' An introduction to following words: * Şimdilik şu kadar.ı.nı söylemek.le yetineyim. 'For now let me just say this much.' 107:5. contentment: - be content. → = razı ol- 1 → ol- 12.

2 /lA/ '- make do, - manage /with/, - be able to manage /with/': Para biriktirebilmek için tam iki yıl aynı giysiler.le yetindim. '[In order] to be able to save money, I made do with the same clothes for two whole years.' Yaz tatilinde param çabuk bitti. Günde bir öğün yemek ile yetindim. 'During the summer {vacation/ holiday} my money quickly ran out. I made do with one meal a day.' {Bu kadar az/350 liralık} bir burs.la yetinmek mümkün değil. İş bulup çalışmak istiyorum. 'It's not possible to manage with {such a small/a 350 lira} scholarship. I want to find a job and work.' 409:12. success: - manage; 994:4. expedience: - make shift, - make do. → idare et- 2 ['- economize, - make ends meet; - manage /with/, - get by /with/'].

yetiş- [ir] 1 /A/ '- catch /θ/ a vehicle, - make it /to/ a place in time /FOR/, - get /to/ a place in time /FOR/, - arrive in time /FOR/; - be in time /FOR/': Daha tren.in kalkma.sı.na beş dakika var, yetişebiliriz. 'We've still got five minutes {before/till} the train leaves [lit., ** There are still five minutes to the departure of the train]. We'll be able to {make it/catch it}.' * Tren.E güç yetiştik. '{a: We barely {made it to/caught θ} the train [lit., We made it to the train with difficulty]./b: We almost missed the train.}' Tren.E ancak yetiştik. 'We just made it to the train.' Koştuk ama otobüs.E yetişemedik. 'We ran, but we couldn't catch θ the bus.' In reference to a missed phone call: Yetişemedim, * telefon kapandı. 'I couldn't get there in time. * They had [already] hung up [lit., ** the telephone had been hung up].' 174:13. swiftness: - overtake; 186:6. arrival: - arrive; 409:8. success: - achieve one's purpose. → = {vaktinde/zamanında} gel- → gel- 1, = eriş- 1, ≠ kaçır- 1 ['- miss, - be too late for a vehicle, event'], ≠ {geç kal-/gecik-} [for a person '- be late, - be delayed'] → kal- 1, ≠ rötar yap- ['- be delayed', usually for public transportation -- train, bus, ferry, airplane -- not persons] → yap- 3.

2 /A/ '- catch up /WITH/, - overtake /θ/, - go fast enough to join /θ/': Ha[y]di biraz hızlı yürüyelim, öndeki grub.A yetişelim. 'Come on, let's walk a little faster. Let's catch up WITH the group up ahead.' Osman'ın nereye gittiğini

449

biliyorum. Ha[y]di hiç vakit kaybetmeden o.nA yetişelim. 'I know where Osman went. Come on, let's catch up WITH him {right away/lit., without losing any time}.' *174:13.* swiftness: - overtake.

3 /A/ '[for sth] - be ready, finished /BY/ a specified time': **Bir elbise diktirmek istiyorum. Yarın.A yetişir mi?** 'I want to have a suit made [lit., ** sewn]. Will it be ready BY tomorrow?' *405:14.* preparation: - be prepared.

4 '- arrive in time to help sb; - come to sb's aid in time': **{Cankurtaran/Ambülans} tam zamanında yetişti.** 'The ambulance arrived just in time.' * **Yetişin, imdat! Boğuluyorum.** 'Come quick! Help! I'm drowning!' <u>Proverb:</u> **Kul sıkışmayınca Hızır yetişmez.** 'Elias will not come to help unless a servant of God [i.e., any will-possessing being, mortal] is in a tight spot.', i.e., Until the need arises, a person will not find a solution to his problems, said when unexpected assistance reaches a person in difficulty. *186:6.* arrival: - arrive; *409:8.* success: - achieve one's purpose; *449:11.* aid: - aid.

5 /A/ '- reach /θ/, - get up /to/' a place with one's hands: the top shelf: **Şeker kavanozu dolab.ın en üst.ü.nde, yetişemiyorum.** 'The sugar bowl is at the top of the cupboard. I can't reach θ it.' **Üst raflardaki kitaplar.A yetişemiyorum.** 'I can't reach θ the books on the top shelves.' *261:6.* distance, remoteness: - extend to. → = **uzan-** 3, = **eriş-** 2.

6 /A/ '- be enough /FOR/, - suffice /FOR/': **Bu kadar yemeğ.in herkes.E yetişeceğ.i.ni sanmıyorum.** 'I don't think this much food will be enough FOR everyone.' * **Parti çok kalabalıktı.** * **Allah'tan içecekler yetişti.** 'There were a lot of people at the party [lit., the party was very crowded]. * Fortunately there were enough drinks [lit., ** From God the drinks sufficed].' *990:4.* sufficiency: - suffice. → = **dayan-** 5 ['- last, - hold out, - be enough /FOR/', supplies], = **yet-** ['- suffice /FOR/, - be enough /FOR/'].

7 '- be grown [crops], - be raised [crops, animals]', on a farm: S: **Bu çiflikte ne yetişir?** 'Q: What is {grown/raised} on this farm?' C1: **{Mandalina/Portakal} yetişir.** 'A1: {Tangerines/Oranges} [are grown (here)].' C2: **{Tavuk/Hindi} yetişir.** 'A2: {Chickens/Turkeys} [are raised (here)].' *1067:16.* agriculture: - farm; *1068:6.* animal husbandry: - raise. → **besle-** 2 ['- raise (animals, not crops), - keep (animals, pets)'].

8 /A/ '- keep up /WITH/, - keep pace /WITH/': **Hayat pahalılığ.ı.nA para yetişmiyor.** '[People's] Income [lit., money] isn't keeping up WITH the cost of living.' *990:4.* sufficiency: - suffice.

yetiştir- [ir] [yetiş- + caus. suf. -DIr] 1 '- grow [crops], - raise [crops, animals]': **Amcam çiftliğinde {tavuk/sebze} yetiştiriyor.** 'My paternal uncle raises {chickens/ vegetables} on his farm.' *891:8.* production: - produce, - create; *1068:6.* animal husbandry: - raise. → = **üret-** 2 ['- raise', plants, animals on a farm].

2 '- bring up, - rear, - raise, - educate, - train', children: * **Annem ben küçükken ölmüş, beni teyzem yetiştirdi.** 'My mother died when I was a child. My [maternal] aunt raised me.' **Çocuklarınızı ne kadar kibar yetiştirmişsiniz, tebrik ederim.** '{Your children are so well-mannered!/How well-mannered your children are!} [lit., ** How {polite/refined} you have brought up your children], congratulations!' <u>Proverb:</u> **Ağaç dikmek bir evlât yetiştirmek kadar uğurludur [= hayırlıdır].** 'To plant a tree is as blessed as to raise a child.' *568:13.* teaching: - train. → = **büyüt-** 3 ['- raise or bring up a child'].

* 3 '- catch up on, - make up for lost time on', a work, a task: **Vaktinde çalışmadı, {dönem} son.u.nda bütün ödevleri.ni yetiştirmey.E çabalıyor.** 'He didn't do his work on time. At the end of the {term/semester/quarter/lit., period} he's struggling to catch up on all his homework.' **Elimdeki proje.yi bugün.E yetiştirebilmek için * {gece.yİ gündüz.E/gece.m.İ gündüz.üm.E} kattım.** '[In order]

to be able to complete my current project [lit., ** the project in my hand] BY today, * I worked day and night [lit., ** {I added night to daytime/I added my night to my daytime}].' *338:4.* compensation: - compensate.

yık- [ar] 1 /lA/ '- demolish, - wreck; - pull down, - tear down, - knock down /with/; - destroy; - ruin': **Belediye görevlileri buldozerlerle bütün gecekonduları yıktı.** 'With bull-dozers the municipal workers demolished all the squatter houses.' Proverbs: **Yıkmak kolay, yapmak zordur.** 'To destroy is easy; to create is difficult.' *395:17.* destruction: - demolish. A proverb that notes the power of women for good or evil. **Kadın var ev yapar, kadın var ev yıkar.** 'Some women make a home, others wreck a home [lit., There are women who make a home, there are women who wreck a home].' A different structure with essentially the same meaning: **Ev yapan kadın[lar] da var, ev yıkan kadın[lar] da.** → = yok et- ['- destroy, - do away with, - get rid of'], ≠ oluştur- ['- form, - create, - make up, - constitute /from/'], ≠ yap-1 ['- make'], ≠ yarat- ['- create'].

'- break sb's heart': **Çocuğumun uyuşturucu bağımlısı olduğ.u.nA {ilişkin/dair} haber beni yıktı.** 'The news that my child was a drug addict [lit., {concerning} my child's being a...] broke my heart.' *112:19.* sadness: - aggrieve. → = kalbinden yarala-.

2 '- knock down, - fell sb or sth; - send sb sprawling, - lay sb flat; - topple sth, - overthrow': **Fırtına ağaçları ve elektrik direkleri.ni yıktı.** 'The storm knocked down the trees and electric poles.'

yere yık- '- knock to the ground, - topple' [yer 'ground']': **Boksör bir yumruk.TA rakibini yer.e yıktı.** 'WITH one blow, the boxer knocked his rival to the ground.' * **Ağır yük eşeğ.i yer.E yıktı.** 'The heavy load {toppled/brought down} the donkey [lit., brought the donkey to the ground].' *912:5.* depression: - fell. → = indir- 4.

3 /{üstüne/üzerine}/ '- load sb down with sth, - load sth down /upon/ sb, - pile or - dump sth /{on/upon/} sb', so

as to weigh down: **Lütfen ev.in bütün işler.i.ni ben.im {üst.üm.e/üzer.im.e} yıkma.** 'Please don't {load/dump} all the housework {on me}.' *159:15.* location: - load.

yıka- [r] /DA, 1 A/ '- wash sth /in, {IN/with}/': **Ellerimi nerede yıkayabilirim?** 'Where can I wash my hands?' **Ellerini sabun.la yıka.** 'Wash your hands with soap.' **Lütfen çamaşırları yıkamay.A götürün.** 'Please take the laundry {to be washed/lit., FOR washing}.' Washing instructions on clothing: **Bu gömleği {sıcak su.DA/ deterjan.LA/beyazlatıcı ilâç.LA} yıkamayın.** 'Don't wash this shirt {IN hot water/IN detergent/WITH bleach}.' **{Soğuk/ Sıcak/Ilık} su.yLA yıkayın.** 'Wash IN {cold/hot/warm} water.' **{Tabaklari/Bardakları/Çarşafları} yıkadıktan sonra iyice durula,** * **deterjan.lı kalmasın.** 'After washing {the dishes/the glasses/the sheets}, rinse them thoroughly. * Don't let any detergent remain on them.' Proverb: * **Ne kadar yıkarsan yıka, kan kanla temizlenmez.** 'No matter how hard you try [lit., how much you wash], blood cannot be washed away [lit., is not cleansed] with blood.' *79:19.* cleanness: - wash.

yıkan- [ır] [yıka- + {pass./refl.} suf. -n] 1 /lA/ '- wash oneself /with/; - take a bath, - bathe': **Bu sabah sıcak su ve sabunla {a: * bir güzel/b: güzelce/c: tertemiz} yıkandım.** 'This morning I washed myself {a, b: * thoroughly/c: {quite/squeaky} clean} with hot water and soap.' *79:19.* cleanness: - wash. → banyo yap- 1 ['- take a bath, - bathe'] → yap- 3, duş al- ['- take a shower'] → al- 1, duş yap-. Same. → yap- 3.

2 /tarafından/ '- be washed, bathed /by/': **Çamaşırlar yıkandı.** 'The laundry has been washed.' **{Yün kazağım/Gömleğim/Elbisem} yıkandıktan sonra çekti.** '{My wool sweater/My shirt/My suit} shrank after it was washed.' **Küçük bebek {yıkanmay.I} seviyor.** 'The little baby likes {to be bathed/being bathed}.' **Hatırlıyorum da, küçükken başkası tarafından yıkanmak ve kurulanmak pek hoşuma gitmiyordu.** 'And I remember,

when I was a child I didn't much like to be bathed and dried by {anybody/somebody else [i.e., by somebody other than the person who usually performed this service]}.' *79:19.* cleanness: - wash.

yıkat- [ır] **1** /A/ '- have sth washed, - have /θ/ sb wash sth, - get sth washed /BY/' [yıka- + caus. suf. -t]: **Çamaşırlarım.I yıkattım.** 'I had my laundry washed.' **Ben yıkamadım, bir kadın.A yıkattım.** 'I didn't wash it myself, I had θ a woman wash it.' * **Çamaşırlarım.I bir kadın.A yıkatıyorum.** '{I have a woman who washes my laundry./lit., I have θ a woman wash my laundry.}' **Kuaför.de saçlarımı yıkatmak istiyorum.** 'I want to have my hair washed at the hairdresser's.' *79:19.* cleanness: - wash.

2 '- have developed': **film yıkat-** '- have photographic film developed [but not printed]' [F. **film** (filmi)]: **Bu filmleri yıkatmak istiyorum.** 'I want to have these films developed.' *714:15.* photography: - process. → **film bas-** ['- develop and print' or only '- print', photographic film] → bas- 3, **film {bastır-/tabettir-}** ['- have developed and printed' or just '- have printed', photographic film].

yıkıl- [ır] [yık- + {pass./refl.} suf. -Il]: **1** /{tarafından/CA}, lA/ '- be demolished, wrecked /by, with/; - be pulled down, torn down, knocked down; - be destroyed; - be ruined': **Tarihî Berlin Duvarı [halk tarafından] yıkıldı.** 'The historic Berlin wall was demolished [by the people].' {**a: Kaçak/b: Ruhsatsız**} **inşaatlar buldozer.le yıkıldı.** '{a: The unlicensed/b: {The unlicensed/The unauthorized}} buildings were demolished with bulldozers.' *395:17.* destruction: - demolish.

2 /sonucu/ '- collapse, - fall down /as a result of/' [**sonuç** 'result']: **Büyük deprem sonucu şehirdeki evler.in çoğ.u yıkıldı.** 'IN [lit., As a result of] the great earthquake, most of the houses in the city collapsed.' **Fırtına çıkınca kamptaki çadırların hepsi yıkıldı.** 'When the storm broke out, all the tents in the camp collapsed.'

Proverbs: **Adam.A dayanma ölür, ağac.A dayanma kurur, duvar.A dayanma yıkılır. Hakk'A dayan!** 'Don't rely ON a person, he will die; don't lean AGAINST a tree, it will wither; don't lean AGAINST a wall, it will collapse. Rely UPON God!' **Ağaç kökünden yıkılır.** 'A tree {collapses/topples} from its roots.' *393:24.* impairment: - break down; *393:48.* : ADV. out of the frying pan into the fire. → = **çök-** 1.

3 '- lose one's health and morale; for sb - be broken or ruined by a disaster, - be devastated': **Babamın ölümünden sonra annem yıkıldı.** 'After my father's death, my mother was devastated.' *112:17.* sadness: - grieve; *393:24.* impairment: - break down. → = **kahrol-** ['- be deeply grieved or distressed, - be devastated or overcome /{WITH/BY}/ grief'] → ol- 12, **morali bozul-** ['- get depressed, discouraged, - lose heart'].

yıpran- [ır] **1** 'for sth - get worn-out, - wear out': **Herhalde en sık kullandığın sözlük bu, çok yıpranmış.** 'This is probably the dictionary you've used most. It's quite worn-out.' *393:20.* impairment: - wear, - wear away. → = **eski-**.

2 'for sb - lose much of his vigor, energy; - be or - become worn-out, burned-out, or spent': **Çok yıprandım, eski gücüm yok.** 'I'm quite worn-out. I don't have {the strength I used to have/lit., my former strength}.' *16:9.* weakness: - become weak; *21:5.* fatigue: - burn out.

yırt- [ar] /DAn/ '- tear up, - rip up; - tear or - rip /{OUT OF/from}/': **Yazdığı şiiri beğenmeyip yırttı.** 'Not liking the poem he had written, he tore it up.' **Defteriniz.DEN kâğıt yırtmayın.** 'Don't tear pages [lit., paper] {OUT OF/from} your notebook.' *192:10.* extraction: - extract; *801:11.* separation: - sever. → = {**kopar- 2/kopart- 2**} ['- tear, - rip /OUT OF/, away /from/'].

yırtıl- [ır] /DAn, tarafından/ '- be or - get torn, ripped /{OUT OF/from}, by/' [yırt- + pass. suf. -Il]: **Defterim.DEN iki sayfa yırtılmış. Kim yırttı?** 'Two pages have been torn OUT OF my notebook. Who did it [lit., tore (them) out]?' Çivi.yE takılınca eteğim yırtıldı. 'When my skirt got caught ON a nail, it got torn [lit., ** When it got caught ON a nail, my skirt got torn].' *192:10.* extraction: - extract'; *801:11.* separation: - sever.

Yine bekleriz. 'Please come again.' → bekle- 1.

yitir-. → {kaybet-/yitir-}.

yoğur- [ur] '- knead' [yoğ- '- become thick, - thicken' + caus. suf. -Ir]: * Yumuşak bir hamur elde edinceye kadar yoğurun. 'Knead until the dough is soft [lit., ** until obtaining a soft dough].' *1045:6.* softness, pliancy: - soften.

yok is not a verb but an adjective meaning 'not existing, non-existent.' In addition to its use in the formation of the entries yok et- and yokla- below, this dictionary shows yok with the verb ol- ['- be'] in the negative of 'There is'-type sentences under the entry ol- 3 b); in the negative of sentences expressing '- have' under the entry ol- 5; and in some other uses under ol- 12 under {var/yok} ol-. The affirmative of yok is var 'existing, existent'.

yok et- [eDer] [yok 'not existing, nonexistent'] 1 '- destroy, - do away with, - get rid of': Proverb: Her şey.İ yaratan [= var eden] ve yok eden Allah'tır. 'God is the one who creates all that is and destroys it.' Allah isyankâr olan Lût kavmini yok etti. 'God destroyed the rebellious Lot tribe.' • While var et- is usually used only with God as a subject, yok et- is used with other subjects as well: Yangın * her şey.imiz.i yok etti. 'The fire * destroyed all we had [lit., ** our everything].' Kadın koca.sı.nA "Bütün gençliğimi yok ettin" diye bağırıyordu. 'The woman shouted AT her husband [saying], "You have {destroyed/ruined} my whole youth."' *395:10.* destruction: - destroy. → = yık- 1 ['- demolish, - wreck; - pull down, - tear down, - knock down; - destroy; - ruin'], ≠ oluştur- ['- form, - create, - make up, - constitute /from/'], ≠ var et- ['- create', only God as subject], ≠ yap- 1, ≠ yarat- ['- create', more frequently used with God as subject].

2 /A/ '- make disappear /to/': Sihirbaz tavşanı yok etti. 'The magician made the rabbit disappear.' Tren biletleri * şimdi masanın üzerinde duruyordu, * onları nere.yE yok ettin, * çabuk söyle! 'The train tickets were on the table * just now. * What {did you do with them?/have you done with them?} [lit., ** Where have you made them disappear /to/?]' * Out with it [lit., Tell me quickly]!' *34:2b.* disappearance: - make disappear.

yokla- [r] [yok 'non-existent' + verb-forming suf. -lA] The following all involve determining whether sth is so or not, or how it is. 1 '- feel, - examine, or - inspect for sth with one's fingers, - feel around': Yankesici usulca adamın cüzdanını yokladı. 'The pickpocket stealthily felt for the man's wallet.' Karanlık odada elektrik düğmesini bulmak için ellerimle duvarı yokladım. 'In the dark room I felt around [with my hands] to find the electric switch.' *73:6.* touch: - touch; *937:24.* inquiry: - examine.

2 '- check AT a place [lit., check a place] to determine how things are': * Bugün banka.yI yine yokladım. Param hâlâ gelmemiş. 'Today I checked AT the bank again [lit., checked the bank]. It seems my money still hasn't come.' Banka sana paranın geldiğini haber vermez. * Sen sık sık banka.yı yokla. 'The bank won't let you know that the money has arrived. * Check back [lit., ** Check the bank] frequently.' *937:23.* inquiry: - investigate.

3 '- check up on people to determine their situation': Çocukları * bir yokla bakalım ne yapıyorlar. '* Go and check on the kids and let's see what they're up to.' *937:23.* inquiry: - investigate.

yol aç-. → aç- 1.

yol git-. → git- 1a.

yol göster-. → göster- 1.

yol ver-. → ver- 1.

yol yap-. → yap- 3.

yola çık-. → çık- 2.

yola koyul-. → koyul-.

yolcu et- [eDer] /A/ '- see a traveler off /to/' [yolcu 'traveler']: Annemi dün Edirne'ye yolcu ettim. 'I saw my mother off to Edirne yesterday.' *188:16.* departure: - say or - bid good-bye. → = uğurla- ['- wish a departing traveler a safe journey, - wish sb Godspeed, - send or - see sb off /to/'], *noun of person* gönder- ['- send sb off /to/' a place].

yolda kal-. → kal- 1.

yolla- [r] /A/ '- send /to/' [yol 'road, way' + verb-forming suf. -l A]: Mektuplarımı şu adres.e yollayın. 'Send my letters to {this/the following} address.' *176:15.* transferal, transportation: - send; *553:12.* correspondence: - mail. → = gönder-.

selâm yolla- /A/ '- send greetings /to/', *informal:* '- say "Hi" /to/': {Kardeşim}.den mektup aldım, hepiniz.e selâm yolluyor. 'I got a letter from {my brother/my sister}. {He/She} sends greetings to all of you.' *504:13.* courtesy: - give one's regards. → selâm söyle- ['- send, - give, or - express one's regards /to, from/', *informal:* '- say "Hi" /to/'] → söyle- 1, selâm getir- ['- bring greetings /from/'].

yoluna gir-. → gir-.

yolunu {kaybet-/yitir-}. → {kaybet-/yitir-}.

yolunu kes-. → kes- 6.

yolunu şaşır-. → şaşır- 3.

Yolunuz açık olsun. → ol- 11. → olsun. → Uğurlar olsun.

yorgunluk çıkar-. → çıkar- 3.

yor- [ar] '- tire, - make tired': Bu {a: ders/b: ev ödevi/c: {sınav/ imtihan}/d: tartışma/e: oyun} beni çok yordu. * Artık biraz dinleneyim. 'This {a: class/b: homework/c: {examination}/d: discussion/e: game} has made me very tired. * I need to rest a bit [lit., Let me rest a bit] now.' Her sabah yarım saat egzersiz yapın, ama kendinizi fazla yormayın.

'Work out every morning for half an hour, but don't tire yourself out.' *21:4.* fatigue: - fatigue.

yorul- [ur] /DAn/ '- get tired /from/, - be tired /from/, - tire [oneself]' [yor- + pass. suf. -Il]: Dün çok çalıştım. Çok yoruldum. Erken yattım. 'Yesterday I worked {a lot/hard}. I {got/WAS} very tired. I went to bed early.' * Bugün çok çalıştım. Çok yorul.DUM. Şimdi yatıyorum. 'I worked {a lot/hard} today. {I'M/I got} very tired. I'm going to bed now.' Sabah yediden beri ayaktayım. Çok yorul.DUM. 'I've been on my feet since 7 o'clock this morning. {I'M/I got} very tired.' In the last two examples above, the fatigue is understood to continue to the present moment of speaking. • In reference to a PRESENT condition, certain common Turkish verbs designating a state, i.e., a feeling, emotion, or sensation, often have the PAST tense, but the equivalent English has the PRESENT tense. Çalışmak.TAN yorul.DUM. Artık emekli olmak istiyorum. '{I'M/I got} tired OF working. Now I want to retire.' In English, however, this type of result in present time is usually expressed with the ADJECTIVE 'tired' plus a form of the verb '- be'. Turkish has a closely equivalent structure: the ADJECTIVE yorgun 'tired' + -[y]Im 'I am', the present tense suffix of the Turkish '- be' equivalent: Yorgun.um. 'I'm tired.' • Although a literal equivalent of the English, it is less frequently encountered than yoruldum. It appears to be used mostly when the emphasis is on a present state rather than on a present result: Şimdi çok yorgunum; sinemaya yarın gitsek olur mu? 'I'm very tired now. How about going to the movies tomorrow [instead].' Proverb: Rüzgar.ın ön.ü.ne düşmeyen yorulur. 'He who doesn't give way [lit., ** fall down] against the force of [lit., in front of] the wind will tire.', i.e., The person who resists the trends of his society will suffer the consequences. *21:4.* fatigue: - fatigue; *866:10.* conformity: don't rock the boat. → bit- 2 ['- be worn-out, exhausted, tired out /from/']. For '- rest', → 1 dinlen-, istirahat et-, yorgunluk çıkar- → çıkar- 3.

yorumla- [r] [yorum 'interpretation; explanation' + verb-forming suf. -lA] 1 '- interpret; - explain': Olayları hep kendi istediğ.in şekilde yorumluyorsun. 'You always interpret events [just] the way [lit., in the way] you want!' Bizim bilim adamlarımız yeni bulunmuş tarihî yazıtları yorumladılar. 'Our scholars have interpreted the newly discovered historic inscriptions.' Anneannem dün gece * gördüğüm rüyamı çok güzel yorumladı. 'My grandmother * interpreted the dream I had [lit., ** saw] last night very {skillfully/positively}.' 341:9. interpretation: - interpret. → değerlendir- 1 ['- evaluate, - assess, - appraise, - judge, - size up (situation)'].

2 '- interpret, - perform', a piece of music: Piyanistimiz dünkü konser.i.nde Mozart'ı {çok güzel/[çok] kötü} yorumladı. 'Our pianist interpreted Mozart {very well/[very] badly} at his concert yesterday.' 341:9. interpretation: - interpret; 708:39a. music: - play sth. → çal- 2 ['- play a musical instrument, radio, record player, tape recorder; - play or - perform a piece of music'], sun- 2 ['- perform, - play, or - sing sth /FOR/ sb'].

yönet- [yöneDer] [yön 'direction' + et-] 1 '- administer, - direct, - manage, - run, - control, - govern, - rule': Okul.u, müdür.ü ile yardımcıları yönetiyor. 'The principal [lit., its (i.e., the school's) principal] and his assistants run the school.' * Böl, parçala, yönet! 'Divide and rule [lit., ** Divide, break up, and rule].' O sultan devleti yönetecek çap.TA değildi. 'That sultan was not OF [lit., ** IN] a caliber to govern the state.' 417:13. authority: - possess or - wield authority; 573:8. direction, management: - direct; 612:14. government: - rule. → = idare et- 1.

2 '- conduct', an orchestra: Dünkü konserde yeni orkestra şefi orkestrayı çok başarılı yönetti. 'The new [orchestra] conductor conducted the orchestra very successfully in yesterday's concert.' 708:45. music: - conduct.

yudumla- '- sip' [yudum 'sip, swallow, gulp' + verb-forming suf. -lA]: * Keyfine bak, sen kahveni yudumlarken ben valizleri hazırlarım. 'Just {amuse/enjoy} yourself [for a bit]. While you're sipping your coffee, I'll get the baggage ready.'

yudumlayarak iç- '- sip, lit., - drink sipping': * Ben çayı ağır ağır yudumla.yarak içmeyi severim. 'I like to sip my tea very slowly [lit., like to drink tea sipp.ing it very slowly].' Yavrum, çorba çok sıcaksa, üfle.yerek, yudumlayarak iç. 'Dear, if the soup is too hot, blow on it and [then just] sip it [lit., ** sip it blow.ing (on it)].' Kızım, süt sıcak; * birden içme, ağzını yakarsın. Yavaş yavaş yudumlayarak iç. '{Dear/Child/lit., ** My girl}, the milk is hot. * Don't [try to] drink it all at once. You'll burn your mouth. Sip it slowly.' Otelimizin barında yoğun bir gün.ün ard.ı.ndan, * canlı müzik eşliğ.i.nde, en sevdiğiniz içkinizi yudumlayarak romantik bir gece yaşayabilirsiniz. 'After a busy day, you can enjoy a romantic evening in the bar of our hotel, sipping your favorite drink TO [lit., ** IN] the accompaniment of lively music.' 8:29. eating: - drink.

Yuh olsun. → ol- 11. → olsun.

yuhala- [r] '- boo, - jeer' [yuha '{Boo!/Yuk!/Ugh!}' + verb-forming suf. -lA]: Maçtan sonra seyirciler * hakemi yuhaladılar ve ıslık çaldılar. 'After the match, the spectators booed and whistled at the {umpire/referee} [lit., booed the umpire...and whistled].' Konser sıra.sı.nda seyirciler * şarkıcıyı yuhalayıp ıslık çaldılar. 'During the concert, the audience booed and whistled at the singer [lit., boed the singer and whistled].' 508:10. ridicule: - boo. → ıslık çal- ['- whistle', as a sign of disapproval] → çal- 2, ≠ alkışla- ['- applaud /θ/ sb, - applaud or - clap /FOR/ sb'].

yum- [ar] '- close', commonly used with 'eyes' as object: göz yum- [göz 'eye'] (1) '- close one's eyes': Engin eve geldiğinde çok yorgundu. Üzerini değiştirmeden yatağ.ı.nA uzandı. Gözlerini yumdu. * Çok geçmeden derin bir uyku.yA daldı. 'When Engin came home, he was very tired. He stretched out ON his bed without changing his clothes. He closed his eyes. * Soon [lit., ** without much (time) passing] he fell INTO a deep sleep.' 293:6. closure: - close. → = {kapa-/kapat-} 1 ['- close' eyes and other objects], ≠ aç- 1 ['- open' eyes and other objects].

* hayata gözlerini yum- '- pass away, - pass on, - die', formal, used for highly respected persons [A. hayat (. -) 'life', göz 'eye'], lit., ** '- close one's eyes to life': Atatürk 10 Kasım 1938'de hayat.A gözlerini yumdu. 'Atatürk passed away on the tenth of November 1938.' 307:19. death: - die. → = hayata gözlerini {kapa-/kapat-} → {kapa-/kapat-} 1, = hayatını {kaybet-/yitir-} ['- lose one's life, - die', of unnatural causes], = öl-, = ömrünü tamamla- ['- complete one's life, - come to the end of one's life, - die, - pass away'], = son nefesini ver- ['- breathe one's last breath, - die'] → ver- 1, = vefat et-, = canından ol- ['- lose one's life, - die', mostly for an unexpected and undeserved death] → ol- 7, ≠ doğ- 1, ≠ dünyaya gel- → gel- 1.

(2) /A/ '- close one's eyes /to/, - disregard /θ/, - take no notice /OF/, - turn a blind eye /to/, - overlook /θ/, - wink /AT/ a fault': Suat'ın sınavda kopya çekme.si.ne araştırma görevli.si göz yumdu. 'The research assistant closed his eyes to the fact that Suat {had copied/was copying} on the exam.' 148:4. forgiveness: - condone; 983:2. inattention: - be inattentive. → göz kırp- 2 ['- wink' in flirting].

yumruk {at-/vur-). → at- 5.

yumruk ye-. → ye- 2.

yut- [ar] '- swallow [food], - take pills; - gulp down food': * Başım çok ağrıyordu, iki tane aspirin yuttum. 'I had a terrible headache [lit., My head was hurting a lot]. I took two aspirins.' Doktorun verdiği hapları her gün düzenli OLARAK yutuyorum. 'Every day I regular.LY take the pills [that] the doctor prescribed [lit., gave].' Ayvadan bir parça ısırdı fakat yutamadı, boğazında kaldı. 'He took a bite of a quince but couldn't swallow it, and it stuck [lit., remained] in his throat.' Proverb: Büyük balık küçük balığı yutar. 'The big fish swallows the little fish.' 8:22. eating: - devour. → ≠ çıkar- 6 ['- vomit'], ≠ kus- ['- throw up'].

* hapı yut- colloq. '- have had it, - be sunk, done for, doomed, in serious trouble' [hap 'pill'], lit., ** '- swallow the pill': Bu ödevi cuma gün.ü.ne kadar bitiremezsem hapı yuttum [demektir]. 'If I can't finish this homework by Friday, [{then/lit., that means}] I'm done for.' Ev kirasını bu ay da ödeyemezsek hapı yuttuk. Ev sahibi bizi mutlaka çıkarır. 'If we can't pay the rent this month either, we've had it. The landlord will certainly {throw us out/evict us}.' 395:11. destruction: - do; 1012:11. difficulty: - have difficulty. → = yan- 6.

yüksel- [ir] [yüksek 'high', final k to l + -θ] 1 /DAn, A/ '- rise, - go up, - ascend /from, to/', in a vertical plane: Çocuğun elinden kaçan balon hızla yükseldi. 'The balloon that got away from the child [lit., escaped from the child's hand] rose swiftly.' Uçak 3000 metre.ye kadar yükseldi. 'The plane ascended to [an altitude of] 3000 meters.' → ≠ alçal- 1, ≠ in- 1. # Ahmet bey 5 yıl içerisinde memurluk.tan müdürlüğ.e yükseldi. 'Within five years Ahmet bey rose from being an employee [lit., ** from employeeship] to being a director [lit., to the directorship].' 193:8. ascent: - ascend.

2 /DAn, A/ '- increase, - rise, - go up /from, to/', prices, temperature, blood pressure, value: Son günlerde fiyatlar çok yükseldi. 'Prices have risen a lot in recent days.' Hasta.nın ateş.i otuz sekiz.den kırk.a yükselmiş. 'The patient's temperature rose from 38 to 40 degrees.' Hasta.nın tansiyon.u {aniden/yavaş yavaş/çok} yükselmiş. 'The patient's blood pressure rose {suddenly/slowly/a lot}.' * Dolar hızla yükseliyor. 'The [value of the] dollar is rising rapidly.' 251:6. increase: - increase [i.]. → = art- 1, = çık- 6, = fırla- 2 ['- skyrocket, - increase or - rise suddenly, - soar'], = tırman- 2, pahalan- ['- become more

expensive, - increase in price'], ≠
düş- 3, ≠ **in-** 4, **ucuzla-** ['- get
cheaper, - go down or - drop in
price'].

yüreği parçalan-. → **parçalan-**.

yürü- [r] 1 '- walk, - take a walk': **Her
sabah en az iki saat yürürüm.** 'I
walk at least two hours a day.'
**Kızım bir yaşında yürümey.e
başladı.** 'My daughter began to
walk at the age of 1.' **Bu sabah
yürüdünüz mü?** 'Did you
{walk/take a walk} this morning?' →
{**yürüyerek/yaya** [**olarak**]/
yayan} **git-** ['- walk to a place, - go
somewhere on foot'] → **git-** 1a.
177:27. travel: - walk.

2 '- hurry along, - go quickly': *
[**Çabuk**] **yürü! Okula geç
kaldık.** '{Get going!/Get
moving!/On with you!/lit., Walk
[quickly]!} We're late for school.'
**Karanlık basmadan eve
gidelim, [çabuk] yürü!** 'Let's go
home before it gets dark. Come on,
move [lit., Walk (quickly)]!' *401:5.*
haste: - make haste.

yürüyüşe çık-. → **çık-** 2.

yüz- [er] 1 '- swim' [**yüz** 'surface' +
verb-forming suf. **-θ**]: **A:
Yüzmey.E gidelim.** 'A: Let's {go
swimming/go for a swim}.' **B:
Maalesef {yüzme/yüzmey.İ/
yüzme.si.nİ} bilmiyorum.** 'B:
Unfortunately I don't know {how to
swim} [lit., ** don't know
swimming].' **Yüzmey.e gitmek
ister misiniz?** 'Do you want to {go
for a swim/go swimming}?'
Yüzmey.İ çok severim. 'I really
like swimming.' **Buralarda nerede
yüzebiliriz?** 'Where can we swim
around here?' **Yüzmek yasaktır.**
'No swimming [lit., Swimming is
prohibited].' *352:7.* publication:
poster: * specific signs. <u>Proverb</u>:
**Köpek suya {düşmeyince}
{yüzmey.İ/yüzme.si.ni}
öğrenmez.** 'A dog won't learn {to
swim} {unless it falls/as long as it
does not fall} into the water.'
Necessity is the mother of invention.
182:56. water travel: - swim. →
denize gir- ['- go swimming /IN/
the {sea/ocean}'].

2 /{DA/üzerinde}/ '- float /on/':
**Gölün üzerinde yüzen
nilüferleri görüyor musun, ne**

hoş! 'Do you see the water lilies
floating on the lake? How delightful!'
**Derede yüzen odun parçalarını
toplayıp yakacak OLARAK
kullanıyorduk.** 'We collected the
pieces of wood floating on the stream
and used them AS firewood.' *182:54.*
water travel: - float.

yüzü buruş-. → **buruş-**.

yüzünü buruştur-. → **buruştur-**.

- Z -

zahmet et- [eDer] '- take trouble, - put
oneself to trouble' [A. **zahmet**
'trouble, difficulty, inconvenience']:
Someone offers you coffee: **A: *
Kahvenizi nasıl içersiniz?** 'A:
How do you take [lit., drink] your
coffee?' **B: Orta şekerli içerim,
ama zahmet ediyorsunuz.** 'B: I
{take/like} [lit., drink] it medium
sweet, but you're putting yourself to
[a lot of] trouble [i.e., to prepare it for
me].' **A: Rica ederim. Hiç
zahmet değil.** 'A: Please, it's no
trouble at all.' *995:4.* inexpedience: -
inconvenience. → **zahmet ver-** ['-
inconvenience /θ/, - trouble /θ/, -
cause trouble /to/, - put sb to a lot of
trouble'] → **ver-** 1.

zahmet ol-. → **ol-** 12.

zahmet ver-. → **ver-** 1.

zahmete gir-. → **gir-**.

zaman al-. → {**vakit/zaman**} **al-**. →
al- 1.

zaman değerlendir-. → {**vakit/
zaman**} **değerlendir-**. →
değerlendir-.

zaman geçir-. →
{**vakit/zaman**}**geçir-**. → **geçir-**
3.

zaman harca-. → {**vakit/zaman**}
harca-. → {**harca-/sarf et-**} 2.

zaman ilerle-. → {**vakit/zaman**}
ilerle-. → **ilerle-** 1.

zaman kaybet-. → {**vakit/zaman**}
kaybet-. → {**kaybet-/yitir-**}.

zaman öldür-. → {vakit/zaman} öldür-. → öldür-.

zaman sarf et-. → {harca-/sarf et-} 2.

zaman ver-. → {zaman/vakit} ver-. → ver- 1.

zamanı geç-. → {vakit/zaman} geç-. → geç- 4.

zamanında gel-. → {vaktinde/ zamanında} gel-. → gel- 1.

zannet-. → {san-/zannet-}.

zayıfla- [r] [A. zayıf 'light in weight, weak' + verb-forming suf. -lA] 1 '- lose weight': **Zayıflamak istiyorum ama * başara-mıyorum.** 'I want to lose weight, but I can't [lit., ** can't succeed].' **Annem zayıflamak için perhiz yapıyor.** 'My mother is dieting to lose weight.' **Bir haftada 6 kilo zayıflayabilirsiniz.** 'You can lose 6 kilos in one week.' **Ameliyattan sonra babam çok zayıfladı.** 'After the operation, my father lost a lot of weight.' **Aç kalarak zayıflamak olmaz.** 'One shouldn't [lit., It isn't proper to] lose weight by starving oneself [lit., ** by remaining hungry].' *270:13.* narrowness, thinness: - slenderize. → = kilo ver- → ver- 1, ≠ kilo al- → al- 1, ≠ şişmanla-, ≠ topla- 3, ≠ toplan- 4.

2 '- deteriorate, - go downhill, - get worse, - get weak, - decline in quality': **Türkiye'den döndükten sonra Türkçem zayıfladı.** 'After I returned from Turkey, my Turkish deteriorated.' **Bazen en yakın arkadaşlarım.ın bile ism.i.ni hatırlayamıyorum, gitgide hafızam zayıflıyor.** 'Sometimes I can't remember the names of even my closest friends. My memory is gradually {getting worse/failing}.' *393:16.* impairment: - deteriorate. → = fenalaş- 1 , = gerile- 2, = kötüleş-, ≠ geliş- 2, ≠ ilerle- 2, ≠ iyileş-.

zekât ver-. → ver- 1.

Ziyade olsun. → ol- 11. → olsun.

ziyaret et- [eDer] /I/ '- visit, - pay a visit /to/ a person or place, - call on sb' [A. ziyaret (. - .): **Dün eski okul arkadaşlarım.I ziyaret ettim.** 'Yesterday I visited my old school friends.' **Bayramda büyüklerimiz.İ ziyaret ederiz.** 'During the holidays we visit our elders.' **Hacılar önce Mekke'yİ sonra Medine'yİ ziyaret ediyorlar.** 'Hajjis visit first Mecca and then Medina.' **Anıtkabir.İ ziyaret etmek istiyorum.** 'I want to visit Atatürk's tomb.' **İstanbul'un bütün müzeler.i.nİ ziyaret ettik.** 'We visited all the museums in [lit., of] Istanbul.' *582:19.* sociability: - visit. For *more formal* visits, → = ziyarete git- → git- 3, = ziyaretine git- → git- 3. See also gel- 1. For *more casual, informal* visits, → **misafirliğe git-** → git- 3.

ziyarete git-. → git- 3.

ziyaretine git-. → git- 3.

zorla- [r] [P. zor 'force' + verb-forming suf. -lA] 1 /A/ '- force sb /to/ do sth, - make sb /θ/ do sth, - drive sb /to/ do sth': **Çocuk çorba içmek istemeyince annesi onu zorladı.** 'When the child didn't want to eat the soup, her mother made her [eat it].' **Fakirlik o.nU hırsızlık yapmay.A zorladı.** 'Poverty drove him to steal [lit., ** to do thievery].' **Çocuklar.I kitap okumay.A zorlamak gerekir.** 'One must make θ children θ read.' * **Zorlamay.A gerek yok, bu çocuk okumayacak.** 'It's no use resorting to force [lit., ** There's no need for forcing]. This child [just] won't study.' **Nur'U benimle sinemaya gelmey.E zorladım.** 'I forced Nur to come to the movies with me.' The Turkish for a phrase from Qur'an 2:256: **Dinde zorlama yoktur.** 'There is no compulsion in the Religion.', i.e., Islam does not condone forced conversion. *424:4.* compulsion: - compel.

2 '- force or - try to force or - break sth open': **{Kapıyı/Kilidi} zorlama!** 'Don't try to force {the door/the lock}!' **Hırsız kapıyı zorladı ve içeri girdi.** 'The thief forced the door open and entered.' *424:6.* compulsion: - press.

şansını zorla- '- push or - press one's luck' [F. **şans** 'luck']: **Şansını zorlama!** 'Don't push your luck!' *971:12.* chance: - risk.

zorlan- [ır] [zorla- + {pass./refl.} suf. -n] 1 /A, tarafından/ '- be forced, constrained, or compelled /to [do sth], by/; - be coerced /INTO [doing sth], by/': **Sanık karakolda [polis tarafından] suçunu itiraf etmey.e zorlandı.** 'At the police station, the thief was forced [by the police] to admit his guilt.' *424:4.* compulsion: - compel.

2 /{tarafından/CA}/ '- be forced or broken open /by/': **Kapı zorlanmış, hırsız mı girdi acaba?** 'The door was forced open. I wonder if a thief has entered.' **Kapı.nın {hırsızlar.ca/hırsızlar tarafından} zorlandığ.ı belli.** 'It's clear that the door was forced {by thieves}.' *424.6.* compulsion: - press.

3 /DA/ '- have a hard time, difficulty, trouble /{θ/on/in}/, - experience adversity': **Yeteri kadar hazırlanamadığım için Türkçe sınav.ı.nda çok zorlandım.** 'Because I couldn't prepare enough, I had a lot of trouble on the Turkish [language] examination.' **Bu kitabı İngilizceden Türkçe.yE aktaran kişi belli ki çok zorlanmış.** 'It's clear that the person who translated this book from English INTO Turkish had {a very hard time/great difficulty}.' **Erol çok çekingen bir çocuk olduğu için insanlar.la ilişki kurmak.TA zorlanıyor.** 'Because Erol is a very shy child, he has trouble θ forming relationships with people.' *1010:9.* adversity: - have trouble; *1012:11.* difficulty: - have difficulty. → = **{güçlük/zorluk} çek-** → çek- 5, = **{zorlukla/güçlükle} karşılaş-** ['- encounter or - experience /θ/ difficulty, - meet /with/ difficulty'] → karşılaş- 3.

zorlaş- [ır] '- become more difficult, harder' [P. **zor** 'difficult' + verb-forming suf. -lAş]: **Öyle bir durum olursa * işimiz çok zorlaşır.** 'If such a situation arises, * things will get a lot more difficult for us [lit., our affairs will get more difficult].' **Türkçe dersleri başlangıçta kolaydı. Ama {gittikçe zorlaşmay.a/gün geçtikçe zorlaşmay.a} başladı.** 'In the beginning the Turkish lessons were easy, but they have begun {to get more and more difficult/to get more difficult day by day}.' *1012:10.* difficulty: - be difficult. → ≠ **kolaylaş-.**

zorluk çek-. → **{güçlük/zorluk} çek-.** → çek- 5.

zorluk çıkar-. → **{güçlük/zorluk} çıkar-.** → çıkar- 7.

{zorlukla/güçlükle} karşılaş-. → karşılaş- 3.

{zoruna/gücüne} git-. → git- 1 b).

zorunda kal-. → kal- 1.

PART 2.
ENGLISH-TURKISH INDEX

PART 2. ENGLISH-TURKISH INDEX

Below the separate hyphen preceding the English verb represents the word 'to': - abandon = to abandon. The hyphen attached to the Turkish verb stem represents the suffix mAk, i.e., {mak/mek}: bırak- = bırakmak.

Turkish verbs are followed by numbers indicating a meaning only when they occur with more than one meaning in our **Turkish Dictionary of Verbs.**

The symbol θ marks the absence of an element in one language where the other language has a separate corresponding element. Thus in the entry '- abhor /θ/, loathe /θ/, detest /θ/, hate /θ/', below, each English verb is shown as not being followed by an element, here a preposition, where the Turkish equivalent has the ablative case suffix DAn, frequently translated 'from'. The symbol serves as a warning against omitting the Turkish suffix when translating from English to Turkish.

- A -

- ABANDON, - stop, - quit [a lesson, an action]: bırak- 3. 856:6. cessation: - cease sth.
- abandon, - leave [permanently: one's job, wife, ship]: terk et-, bırak- 3. 370:5. abandonment: - abandon.

- ABDUCT, - carry off, - kidnap; hijack: kaçır- 3. 482:20. theft: - abduct.

- ABHOR ./θ/, - loathe /θ/, - detest /θ/, - hate /θ/: /DAn/ nefret et-. 103:5. hate: - hate.

- ABOLISH, - do away with, - repeal [law], - eliminate, - eradicate [disease]: kaldır- 4. 445:2. repeal: - repeal; 772:5 exclusion: - eliminate.
- abolish, - close, or shut down [organization, business, school]: {kapa-/kapat-} 7. 293:8. closure: - close shop.

- ABRIDGE, - cut down, - condense [piece of writing]: kısalt- 2. 268:6. shortness: - shorten.

- ACCELERATE, - gather speed, - speed up [subj.: vehicle, person]: hızlan- 1. 174:10. swiftness: - accelerate [i.].

- ACCENT, - accentuate, - stress [obj.: word, syllable]: vurgula- 2. 901:12. impulse, impact: - thrust, - push.

- ACCEPT or - agree /to/ [a proposal, suggestion]: kabul et- 2. 441:2. consent: - consent.

- accept [a gift, travelers' checks], - take: kabul et- 1. 479:6. receiving: - receive.
- accept or - admit [a fact as true], - acknowledge: kabul et- 3. 332:8. assent: - assent.
- accept, - regard with tolerance [accept people as they are]: kabul et- 4. 134:5. patience: - endure; 978:7. broad-mindedness: - keep an open mind.

- ACCESS /θ/, - gain access /to/, - get /to/ [the Internet, a source of information]: /A/ eriş- 4. 186:6. arrival: - arrive; 189:7. entrance: - enter; 1041:18. computer science: - computerize.

- ACCOMPANY /θ/, - go [along] /WITH/: /A/ {eşlik et-/ refakat et-}, /lA/ gel- ['- come /with/ sb'], /lA/ git- ['- go /with/ sb'] → git- 1a. 768:7. accompaniment: - accompany.

- ACCUSE sb /OF/, - blame sb /FOR/: /a: lA, b: DAn dolayı, c: konusunda/ suçla-. 5 9 9 : 8. accusation: - blame.

- ACHE, - hurt, - throb with pain: acı- 1, ağrı-. 26:8. pain: - suffer pain.

- ACHIEVE, - make [with nouns indicating progress, development, success]: kaydet- 5. 392:7. improvement: - get better; 409:7a. success: - succeed.
- achieve /θ/ [one's purpose], - attain /θ/ [one's objective], - reach /θ/ [one's

463

goal], - gain [one's end[s]]: **eriş-** 3. *407:4.* accomplishment: accomplish; *409:8.* success: - achieve one's purpose.

- ACKNOWLEDGE, - admit, - confess [a misdeed]: /A/ **itiraf et-**. *351:7.* disclosure: - confess.
- acknowledge /θ/ sb or sb's action to be right /on the {issue/matter} of/: /A, **konusunda/ hak ver-** → **ver-** 1. *332:11.* assent: - acknowledge.

- ACQUAINT sb /WITH/ sb or sth, - make sb or sth known /to, AS/ sb, - introduce sb or sth /to/ sb: /A, **olarak/ tanıt-**. *551:8.* information: - inform; *587:14.* friendship: - introduce.

- ACQUIRE /from/, - get /from/, - obtain /from/: /DAn/ **edin-, ele geçir-** 2 → **geçir-** 1, /DAn/ **elde et-**. *472:8.* acquisition: - acquire.
- acquire /θ/, - get /θ/, - obtain /θ/ sth, - become the owner, possessor /OF/ sth: /A/ **sahip ol-** → **ol-** 12. *472:8.* acquisition: - acquire.

- ACT, - behave, - do [well] /BY...ing [*or* TO]/: /{mAklA/ArAk}/ [doğru] **hareket et-** 4. *321:4.* behavior: - behave.
- act, - portray a character, - perform /in/ a play or movie [subj: actor]: /DA/ **oyna-** 3. *704:29.* show business, theater: - act.
- act in a movie or film, - make a movie [subj.: actor]: **film çevir-** 1 → **çevir-** 3. *704:29.* show business, theater: - act.

- ADD one thing /to/ another: /A/ **ekle-** ['- append, affix, attach, tack one thing (on) /to/ another': note to a letter], /A/ **ilâve et-** [salt to soup; room to a house], /A/ **kat-** [salt to soup; - mix sth /into/ sth: water into milk]. *253:5.* addition: - add to.
- add a FOOTNOTE, - footnote: {not/dipnot} **düş-** → **düş-** 6. *341:11.* interpretation: - comment upon.
- add one NUMBER to another: /I/ **topla-** 4. *1016:17.* mathematics: - calculate.
- add UP, - calculate, - figure up: **hesapla-**. *1016:17.* mathematics: - calculate.
- add up THE BILL, - calculate the bill, - figure up the bill [at a restaurant or a hotel: The waiter added up the bill.]: **hesap çıkar-** → **çıkar-** 7. *1016:18.* mathematics: - sum up.

- add up TO, - amount to, - come to, - total, - cost [What did the bill add up to?]: **tut-** 7. *630:13.* price, fee: - cost; *791:8.* whole: - total; *1016:18.* mathematics: - sum up.
- add up to, - amount to, - equal, - make, - get [in mathematical operations]: **et-** 3. *789:5.* equality: - equal; *791:8.* whole: - total; *1016:18.* mathematics: - sum up.

- ADDRESS /θ/ sb [i.e., '- speak /to/ sb, - talk /to/ sb'], *formal*: /A/ **hitap et-**. *524:27.* speech: - address.

- ADMINISTER, - direct, - manage, - run, - govern, - rule, - control: **idare et-** 1, **yönet-** 1. *417:13.* authority: - possess or - wield authority; *573:8.* direction, management: - direct; *612:14.* government: - rule.

- ADMIRE, - appreciate, - value, - respect [obj.: a person, a quality: your diligence]: **takdir et-** 1. *155:4.* respect: - respect; *996:13.* importance: - value.

- ADMIT, - accept [a fact as true], - acknowledge: **kabul et-** 3. *332:8.* assent: - assent.
- admit, - confess /to/, - acknowledge /θ/ [a misdeed]: /A/ **itiraf et-**. *351:7.* disclosure: - confess.

- ADOPT a child: **evlât edin-**. *480:19.* taking: - appropriate.

- ADORE: /A/ **bayıl-** 2, **çok sev-** → **sev-** 1. *101:7.* eagerness: - be enthusiastic; *104:19.* love: - love.

- ADORN oneself /with/, - deck oneself out /IN/, - doll oneself up /IN/: /lA/ **süslen-** 1. *5:41.* clothing: - dress up.
- ADVANCE, - move forward /THROUGH, toward/ [subj.: procession, time]: /DAn, A doğru/ **ilerle-** 1. *162:2.* progression: - progress
- advance, - develop, - evolve [subj.: technology]: **geliş-** 1. *860:5.* evolution: - evolve.
- advance, - develop, - make progress [subj.: a nation]: **kalkın-**. *860:5.* evolution: - evolve.
- advance sth, - move sth forward [Move your car foward a bit.]: **ilerlet-** 1. *172:5a.* motion: - move sth; *903:9.* pushing, throwing: - push.
- advance or - put forward an idea, suggestion, proposal: **ileri sür-** 1 → **sür-** 1. *439:5.* offer: - propose.

- ADVISE /θ/, - give advice /to/: /A/ akıl ver- → ver- 1, /A/ fikir ver- 2 → ver- 1, /A/ yol göster- 2 → göster- 1. *422:5.* advice: - advise.
- advise sb to do sth, - recommend, - propose, or - suggest sth /to/ sb [He advised me to go to Istanbul.]: /A/ tavsiye et-. *422:5.* advice: - advise; *439:5.* offer: - propose; *509:11.* approval: - commend.

- AFFECT /θ/, - influence /θ/, - have an effect /{ON/UPON}/: /I/ etkile-, /A/ tesir et-. *893:7.* influence: - influence.
- affect, - move, or - touch /θ/ sb emotionally [subj.: the director's farewell speech]; - disturb, - upset /θ/ sb [subj.: a person's inappropriate words]: /A/ dokun- 3. *93:14.* feelings: - affect; *893:7.* influence: - influence.
- affect /θ/ one's health adversely, - make /θ/ sb sick [subj.: food], for food or weather not - agree /WITH/ one, - have a bad effect /ON/: /A/ dokun- 2. *96:16a.* unpleasure: - distress; *393:9.* impairment: - impair; *809:9.* disorder: - disorder.

- AFFORD: /A/ [paraca] gücü yet- [I can afford (to buy) this house.]. *618:11.* wealth: - have money; *626:7.* expenditure: - afford.

- AGE, - grow old, - get old [subj.: persons]: ihtiyarla-, yaşı ilerle- → ilerle- 3, yaşlan-. *303:10.* age: - age; *841:9.* oldness: - age.

- AGREE /TO/ or - accept a proposal, suggestion: kabul et- 2. *441:2.* consent: - consent.
- agree, - consent or - be willing /to/ do sth: /A/ razı ol- 1 → ol- 12. *441:2.* consent: - consent.
- agree /WITH/ sb, sb's ideas, - share ideas, views: /A/ katıl- 3 [person as object: I agree with you.], {a: düşünceye/b: fikre/c: görüşe} katıl- 3 ['- share {thoughts/opinions/views}'], /IA/ {fikir/görüş} paylaş- ['- share {thoughts/views} /with/'], {fikir/görüş} savun- 2. Same. *332:9.* assent: - concur.
- agree, - come to an agreement, - reach an understanding /a: with, b: {on/upon}, c: {on/upon}, d: on the subject of, e: {to/in order to}/: /a: 1A, b: DA, c: üzerinde, d: konusunda, e: için/ anlaş- 2. *332:10.* assent: - come to an agreement.

AGREED., OK!, All right!, Fine.: Oldu. → ol- 11 → oldu. *332:18.* assent: INTERJ. yes.

- AIM, - intend, - mean, - plan or - make up one's mind /to/ do sth: /A/ niyet et-. *359:7.* resolution: - resolve; *380:4.* intention: - intend.

- AIR, - be aired, carried, broadcast, - be on [radio or television]: /DAn/ yayımlan- 2. *1033:25.* radio: - broadcast; *1034:14.* television: - televise.

- AIR OUT [obj.: rooms]: havalandır-. *317:10.* air, weather: - air.
- air out, - get some air [subj.: rooms]: hava al- 2 → al- 1. *317:10.* air, weather: - air.

- ALIGHT, - settle, - perch, - land /{ON/UPON}/ [subj.: bird, insect, helicopter, not plane]: /A/ kon-. *194:7.* descent: - get down; *194:10.* : - light upon.

- ALLOW /θ/ sb, - give sb permission /to/, - let /θ/ sb, - permit /θ/ sb: /A/ izin ver- → ver- 1, /A/ müsaade et-. The causative form of any verb [that is, any verb stem with one of the following six causative suffixes: -Ar, -Art, -DIr, -Ir, -It, -t] also expresses permission, as in second part of the following sentence: She wanted to use the phone, and he allowed her to use it. For a list of all causative verbs included in this dictionary, see the **Index of Turkish Verb Suffixes**. [also → - have sth done]. *443:9.* permission: - permit.
- allow or - permit sb /{IN/INTO}/ a place, - let sb enter /θ/ a place: /A/ sok- 2. *189:7.* entrance: - enter; *443:9.* permission: - permit.

ALTHOUGH: olduğu halde, olmakla {beraber/birlikte}, olmasına {rağmen/karşın} → ol- 11. *338:8.* compensation: ADV., CONJ. notwithstanding.

- AMBUSH, - waylay, - block one's way [often to steal from]: yolunu kes- → kes- 6. *346:10.* concealment: - ambush.

- AMOUNT TO, - add up to, - come to, - total, - cost: tut- 7. *630:13.* price, fee: - cost; *791:8.* whole: - total; *1016:18.* mathematics: - sum up.

465

- amount to, - equal, - add up to, - make, - get [in mathematical operations]: **et-** **3**. *789:5.* equality: - equal; *791:8.* whole: - total; *1016:18.* mathematics: - sum up.
- amount to sth, - shape up, - grow up, - become mature, morally correct, responsible [used for both men and women]: **adam ol-** → **ol-** 12. *303:9.* age: - mature.

- ANALYZE: **analiz et-** [blood, historical event], **tahlil et-** [blood, historical event, literary work]. *800:6.* analysis: - analyze; *934:15.* reason: - reason.

{AND that's not all/there's more to come}: **dahası var** → **ol-** 3, Additional examples. b) 4. Miscellaneous additional examples. *253:14.* addition: PHR. et cetera.
and then, sir...: **Derken efendim...** → **de-** 1. *829:8.* instantaneousness: ADV. at once.

- ANGER, - make angry: **kızdır-** **1**. *152:22.* resentment, anger: - anger.
- anger, - make sb angry, mad; - irritate, - annoy /by...ing/: **/ArAk/** **sinirlendir-**. *152:22.* resentment, anger: - anger.

- ANNOUNCE: **beyan et-**, **duyur-**. *352:12.* publication: - announce.
- announce, - declare, - note, - state [*formal, official:* in speech and in writing]: **kaydet-** **4**. *334:5.* affirmation: - affirm; *524:24.* speech: - state.

- ANNOY, - bother, - be annoying to, - get on sb's nerves, - irritate: **canını sık-** **2** → **sık-** 3, **sık-** **3**. *96:13.* unpleasure: - annoy; *98:15.* unpleasantness: - vex.
- annoy, - irritate, - bother, - disturb: **rahatsız et-**. *96:13.* unpleasure: - annoy.

- ANSWER /θ/ a question, - respond or - reply /to/ a question: **soruyA** **{cevap ver-/karşılık ver- 1}** → **ver-** 1, **soruyU {cevapla-/cevaplandır-/yanıtla-}** → **{cevapla-/cevaplandır-/yanıtla-}**. *938:4.* answer: - answer.
- answer /θ/ a person, - give sb an answer: **/A/ {cevap/yanıt} ver-** → **ver-** 1, **/I/ {cevapla-/cevaplandır-/yanıtla-}**. *938:4.* answer: - answer.

- answer BACK /to/, - talk back /to/: **/A/ karşılık ver-** 2 → **ver-** 1. *142:8.* insolence: - sauce.
- answer or - get the DOOR: **kapıya bak-** → **bak-** 3. *982:5.* attention: - attend to.
- answer, - get, or - pick up the PHONE: **telefonU aç-** → **aç-** 5, **telefonA {bak-/cevap ver-}** → **bak-** 3, **cevap ver-** → **ver-** 1. *347:18.* communications: - telephone; *982:5.* attention: - attend to.

ANYHOW, anyway, besides, moreover: **kaldı ki** 1 → **kal-** 1. *384:10.* manner, means: ADV. anyhow.

ANYWAY, In any case, No matter what, Come what may: **Ne olursa olsun** → **ol-** 11 → **olur**. *969:26.* certainty: ADV. without fail.

- APOLOGIZE /TO [sb], for [sth]/, - beg sb's pardon, - make an apology /TO/: **/DAn, için/ özür dile-** → **dile-** 2. *658:5.* atonement: - apologize.

- APPEAL to, - interest, *colloq.:* - be into [This kind of art appeals to me.]: **ilgi çek-** → **çek-** 1, **/I/ ilgilendir-** 1. *377:6.* allurement: - attract; *980:3a* curiosity: - make curious, - interest.
- appeal, - refer, - turn /to, for/ [assistance, money]: **/A, için/ {başvur-/müracaat et-}** 1. *387:14.* use: - avail oneself of; *937:30.* inquiry: - seek.

- APPEAR /θ/, - look like, - seem /θ/: **/A/ benze-** 2. *33:10.* appearance: - appear to be.
- appear, - be seen, - come into view [subj.: sun in the sky]: **görün-** 1. *31:4* visibility: - show; *33:8.* appearance: - appear.
- appear or - emerge /from/, - come out /OF/ [an enclosed place or from behind sth]: **/DAn/ çık-** 3. *190:11.* emergence: - emerge.
- appear, - emerge, - rise: **doğ-** 2 [subj.: sun, moon], **çık-** 3 [subj: sun, moon, stars], **güneş {aç-/çık-}** ['for the sun - come out, appear'] → **aç-** 8, **çık-** 3. *33:8.* appearance: - appear; *190:11.* emergence: - emerge.
- appear, - turn up, - come out, - be revealed [the truth], - come forward [the guilty person]: **{ortaya/meydana} çık-** → **çık-** 3. *351:8.* disclosure: - be revealed.
- appear, - seem [tired, happy], - look like [It appears he isn't going to come.]:

466

görün- 2. *33:10.* appearance: - appear to be.

- appear, - be issued, - come out [article in a newspaper, issue of a publication]: çık- 8. *33:8.* appearance: - appear.
- appear or - seem TO BE, - look [She doesn't appear to be over forty.]: göster- 2 . *33:10.* appearance: - appear to be.

- APPEND /to/, - affix /to/, - attach /to/, - add or tack one thing /to/ another [note to a letter]: /A/ ekle-. *253:5.* addition: - add to.

- APPLAUD /θ/ sb, - applaud or - clap /FOR/ sb [obj.: person, not performance]: alkışla-. *509:10.* approval: - applaud.

- APPLY or - submit an application /to, for/: /A, için/ {başvur-/müracaat et-} 2. *440:10.* request: - petition.
- apply sth /to/, - follow [directions], - carry out a plan, - put a plan, law, or formula into practice: /A/ uygula-. *387:11.* use: - apply.
- apply sth /to, to the surface of/, - spread, - rub, or - smear sth /ON/ [cream to skin]: /A, {üstüne/üzerine}/ sür- 4. *295:19.* covering: - cover.

- APPOINT, - assign, or - name sb /to [a position], AS [a teacher]/: /A, olarak/ {ata-/tayin et-}. *615:11.* commission: - appoint.

- APPRECIATE, - value, - respect, - admire [obj.: a person, a quality: your diligence]: takdir et- 1 . *155:4.* respect: - respect; *996:13.* importance: - value.
- appreciate, - understand a person's situation, difficulties: takdir et- 2. *521:7.* intelligibility: - understand.

- APPROACH /θ/, - draw near /to/, - come close /to/, up /to/, over /to/, - sidle up /to/: /A/ yaklaş-, / A / yanaş- 1, yanına gel- ['- come up to the side of, over to'] → gel- 1. *167:3.* approach: - approach; *223:7.* nearness: - near, - come near.

- APPROVE /OF/: /I/ {hoş/iyi/ olumlu} karşıla- → karşıla- 3, kabul et- 2; /I/ onayla-, /A/ razı ol- 1. → ol- 12. *509:9.* approval: - approve.

ARE THERE [any good restaurants around here?]: [Buralarda iyi lokanta] var mı? → ol- 3, Additional examples. b) 3.1. Issues of

presence... *221:6.* presence: - be present; *760:8.* existence: - exist.

- ARGUE [the pros and cons, not confrontational in a negative sense], - dispute; - debate; - have a discussion /a: with, b: about, c: on the subject of, d: about/: /a: 1A, b: hakkında, c: konusunda, d: I/ tartış- 1. *934:16.* reasoning: - argue.
- argue [confrontational, heated] /a: with, b: about, c: on the subject of, d: about/, dispute, - debate; - have a heated discussion: /a: 1A, b: hakkında, c: konusunda, d: I/ {münakaşa et-/tartış- 2}. *934:16.* reasoning: - argue.

- ARISE, - rise /from/, - get up /{from/OUT OF}/ [bed, chair], - stand up: /DAn/ kalk- 1. *193:8.* ascent: - ascend; *231:8.* verticalness: - rise.

- ARRANGE, - organize, - put in order: ayarla- 2, düzenle- 1. *807:8.* arrangement: - arrange.
- arrange, - put in a row or in a certain order [shoes, files] /a: from, b: to, c: {according to/by}, d: -ly/: /a: DAn, b: A, c: A göre, d: olarak/ sırala-. *807:8.* arrangement: - arrange.
- arrange, - organize, - plan, - prepare [an event: trip, concert]: ayarla- 3, düzenle- 2, {plânla-/tasarla-}. *381:8* plan: - plan; *405:6.* preparation: - prepare.

- ARREST, - put under arrest [thief]: tutukla-. *429:15.* confinement: - arrest.

- ARRIVE /{IN/AT}/, - come /to/, - get /IN/, - get /to/, - reach /θ/: /A/ gel- 1, /A/ ulaş- 1, /A/ var-. *186:6.* arrival: - arrive.
- arrive in TIME /FOR/, - get /to/ a place in time /FOR/, - be in time /FOR/, - catch /θ/ a vehicle, - make it /to/ in time /FOR/: /A/ yetiş- 1. *186:6.* arrival: - arrive; *409:8.* success: - achieve one's purpose.
- arrive in time to help sb; - come to sb's aid in time: yetiş- 4. *186:6.* arrival: - arrive; *409:8.* success: - achieve one's purpose; *449:11.* aid: - aid.

AS, in the capacity of [I did my military service as a pilot.]: olarak 2 → ol- 11. *384:11* manner, means: ADV. somehow.
as, for the purpose of, with sth in mind, intending [I did it as a joke.]: diye-

3.2 → de- 1. *380:11*. intention: PREP., CONJ. for

as, as if it were, in the capacity of, in place of [They worshipped the sun as a God.]: **diye-** 7 → de- 1. *950:19*. theory, supposition: CONJ. supposing.

{as FAR AS HE KNOWS/To the best of his knowledge}: **Bildiği kadarıyla**. → bil- 1. *927:30*. knowledge: ADV. to one's knowledge.

{as far as HE UNDERSTANDS/As far as he can tell/To the best of his understanding}: **Anladığı kadarıyla**. → anla- 1. *927:30*. knowledge: ADV. to one's knowledge.

as IF NOTHING HAD HAPPENED: **hiçbir şey olmamış gibi** → ol- 2. *950:19*. theory, supposition: CONJ. supposing.

as it HAPPENED: **olduğu gibi** 2. → ol- 11 → olduğu. *777:9*. sameness: ADV. identically.

as it {IS/WAS}: **olduğu gibi** 1. → ol- 11 → olduğu. *777:9*. sameness: ADV. identically.

as [MUCH] AS POSSIBLE: **mümkün olduğu kadar**. → mümkün ol- → ol- 12. *965:10*. possibility: by any possibility.

as SOON AS: **der demez** → de- 1. *829:8*. instantaneousness: ADV. at once.

- ASCEND, - climb, - mount or go up /BY WAY OF [stairs], to/: **/DAn, A / çık-** 5. *193:11*. ascent: - climb.
- ascend, - rise, - go up [balloon]: **yüksel-**. *193:8*. ascent: - ascend.

- ASK sb's ADVICE, - take or - get advice /from/, - consult /θ/ sb: **/DAn/ akıl al-** → al- 1. *422:7*. advice: - take or - accept advice.
- ask sb or /AT/ an office FOR INFORMATION, - request information /from/: **/DAn/ sor-**. *937:20*. inquiry: - inquire.
- ask /{FOR/ABOUT}/ sb [Ahmet came and asked {for/about} you.]: **/I/ sor-**. *937:20*. inquiry: - inquire; *440:9*. request: - request.
- ask FOR STH /FROM/ sb [Fatma asked her friend for a book.]: **/DAn/ dile-2, /DAn/ iste-** 2, **/DAn/ rica et-**, **/DAn/ talep et-**. *440:9*. request: - request.
- ask HOW SB IS, - inquire after sb's health: **hatır sor-**. *83:6*. health: - enjoy good health; *937:20*. inquiry: - inquire.

- ask /θ/ sb a QUESTION: **/A/ soru sor-**. *937:20*. inquiry: - inquire.
- ask THE TIME: **{Saatin kaç olduğunu/Saati} sor-** [lit., '- ask {what time it is./the hour.}'] → sor-. *937:20*. inquiry: - inquire.

- ASSAULT /θ/ SB SEXUALLY, - rape /θ/: **ırzına geç-** [' - rape, - violate'] → geç- 1, **/A/ tecavüz et-** 2 ['- rape /θ/, - assault /θ/ sexually (not necessarily rape)]', **/A/ saldır-** 2. Same. *459:14*. attack: - attack; *480:15*. taking: - possess sexually; *665:20*. unchastity: - seduce.

- ASSEMBLE or - set up [machine, furniture] /{IN [the room]/ON [the table]}/: **/A/ kur-** 1. *159:16*. location: - establish; *200:9*. verticalness: - erect.
- assemble, - get together, - gather /{in/at}/ [subj.: a group of people: They assembled {in the living room./at Osman's house.}]: **/DA/ toplan-** 3. *769:16*. assemblage: - come together.

- ASSESS, - evaluate, - appraise, - judge, - size up [situation]: **değerlendir-** 1. *300:10*. measurement: - measure; *945:9*. judgment: - estimate.

- ASSIGN, - appoint, - name sb /to [a position] AS [a teacher]/: **/A, olarak/ {ata-/tayin et-}**. *615:11*. commission: - appoint.
- assign sth /to/ [obj.: homework, a task to sb]: **/A/ ver-** 2. *478:12*. giving: - give.

- ASSIST /θ/, - help /θ/ sb: **/A/ yardım et-**, *formal*: **/A/ yardımda bulun-** → bulun- 3, **/A/ yardım elini uzat-** ['- extend a helping hand to'] → uzat- 2. *449:11*. aid: - aid.
- assist, - help one another, - give one another a hand: **el ele ver-** → ver-1, **yardımlaş-**. *449:11*. aid: - aid.
- assist /θ/, - help /θ/, - be of assistance /to/, - be helpful /to/: **/A/ yardımcı ol-** → ol- 12. *449:11*. aid: - aid.

- ASSUME, - suppose, - imagine for the sake of argument: **de- 2, farz et-, tut- 9, varsay- 1**. *950:10*. theory, supposition: - suppose.

ASSUMING, thinking, with sth in mind: **diye 5** → de- 1. *950:19*. theory, supposition: CONJ. supposing.

- ASSURE, - promise [I assure you that he will come.]: /A/ söz ver- → ver- 1, today *less common, more formal*: /A/ vadet-. *436:4.* promise: - promise.

- ASTONISH, - surprise: şaşırt- 2. *122:6.* wonder: - astonish.

AT [a certain TIME] TO [the hour] [in telling time: at a quarter to five]: /A/ kala 1 → kal- 3. *833:7.* previousness: PREP. prior to.

at a specific DISTANCE FROM [always following a specific measure of distance: at a distance of two kilometers from the school]: /A/ kala 3 → kal- 3. *261:14.* distance, remoteness: ADV. at a distance.

at LEAST: hiç olmazsa → ol- 11 → olmaz, olsun 3 → ol- 11. *248:10.* insignificance: ADV. in a certain or limited degree.

at MOST, at the [very] most: olsa olsa → ol- 11 → olsa. *248:10* insignificance: ADV. in a certain or limited degree.

at RANDOM, without thinking, puposelessly: olur olmaz 2 → ol- 11. *863:15.* generality: every.

at THAT VERY MOMENT, just then: derken 1 → de- 1. *829:8.* instantaneousness: ADV. at once.

- ATTACH or - fasten sth /to/, - put up [curtains]: /A/ tak-. *202:8.* pendency: - suspend; *799:7.* joining: - fasten.
- attach, - affix, - append, - add, - tack one thing /to/ another [note to a letter]: /A/ ekle-. *253:5.* addition: - add to.
- attach importance /to/, - value /θ/, - consider important: /I/ önemse-, /A/ {önem/ehemmiyet} ver- → ver- 1. *996:13.* importance: - value.

- ATTACK /θ/, - storm /θ/ [territory, forces]: /{A/üzerine}/ hücum et- 1, /A/ saldır- 1. *459:14.* attack: - attack.
- attack or - assault /θ/ sb sexually [not necessarily rape], - rape /θ/: /A/ saldır- 2, /A/ tecavüz et- 2. *459:14.* attack: - attack; *480:15.* taking: - possess sexually; *665:20.* unchastity: - seduce.

- ATTAIN /θ/, - reach /θ/ [a goal, God]: /A/ er-. *186:6.* arrival: - arrive.
- attain /θ/ [one's objective], - reach /θ/ [one's goal], - achieve /θ/ [one's purpose], - gain [one's end[s]]: eriş- 3. *407:4.* accomplishment:

accomplish; *409:8.* success: - achieve one's purpose.

- ATTEMPT or - try /to/ do sth: /A/ çalış- 2, /I/ dene-. *403:6.* endeavor: - attempt.
- attempt, - try, or - dare /to/ do sth that is beyond one's power or outside one's authority: /A/ kalkış-. *403:6.* endeavor: - attempt.

- ATTEND /θ/, - go /to/: /A/ devam et- 3 [for a long period (educational institution: school, university), not for a short period or particular event (concert, soccer game, lecture)], /A/ git- 4 [for a long period (school, university) or a short period (concert, soccer game)], /I/ izle- 4 ['- attend, - be present at and follow what is going on (obj.: concert)'], /I/ oku- 3 [an educational institution regularly]. *221:8.* presence: - attend.
- attend /TO/ [guests], - serve /θ/ [one's country, guests], - wait /{ON/ UPON}/ [guests]: /A/ hizmet et-. *577:13.* servant, employee: - serve.
- attend /to/, - look /AFTER/, - take care /OF/ [guests, a matter, the phone]: /A/ bak- 3, /lA/ ilgilen- 2, /lA/ meşgul ol- → ol- 12. *339:9.* carefulness: - look after; *982:5.* attention: - attend to; *1007:19.* protection: - care for.
- attend /to/, - get right down /TO/ [a matter]: üstüne git- 2 → git- 1a. *724:10.* occupation: - occupy.

- ATTRACT ATTENTION, - catch the attention, - strike the eye: {dikkat/dikkati} çek- → çek- 1. *982:11.* attention: - meet with attention.

- AVOID /θ/ [work]: /DAn/ kaç- 2. *368:6.* avoidance: - avoid.
- avoid /θ/ sb or sth, or doing sth; - refrain /from/ sth or /from/ doing sth: /DAn/ kaçın-. *329:3.* inaction: - refrain; *368:6.* avoidance: - avoid; *668:7.* temperance: - abstain.
- avoid, - get out of doing something complicated; - escape from a difficult situation, predicament: işin içinden çık- 1 → çık- 1. *368:7.* avoidance: - evade.
- avoid /θ/, - keep [oneself] away /from/, or - steer clear /OF/ sth or sb: /DAn/ sakın- 1. *329:3.* inaction: - refrain; *368:6.* avoidance: - avoid; *668:7.* temperance: - abstain.
- avoid /θ/, - get or - be rid /OF/, - shake /OFF/ sb or sth unpleasant [an annoying person, classes, debts,

flies]: /DAn/ kurtul- 2. *368:6.*
avoidance: - avoid.
- avoid expense, - economize: masraftan
{kaç-/kaçın-} → kaç- 2. *484:5.*
parsimony: - stint.

- AWAIT /θ/, - wait /FOR/: /I/ bekle- 1.
130:8. expectation: - await.

- AWAKE, - wake up [When did she
awake?]: uyan-. *23:4.* wakefulness: -
awake.

- AWAKEN sb, - wake sb up: uyandır-.
23:5. wakefulness: - wake sb up.

- AWARD sb sth as a prize, - reward sb
/with/ sth, - give sb sth as a reward:
/lA/ ödüllendir-. *624:10.* payment:
- pay.

AWAY with you!: → Beat it!

- B -

- BAKE sth [The baker is baking the
bread.]: pişir-. *11:4a.* cooking: -
cook sth.
- bake [** - become baked: The bread is
baking.]: piş-. *11:4b.* cooking: for
sth - cook.

- BANDAGE, - bind [wound]: /I/ sar- 2.
91:24. therapy: - treat; *799:9.* joining:
- bind.

- BARGAIN, - dicker, - haggle /a: for
[sth], b: over [sth], c: with [sb]/: /a:
için, b: üzerinde, c: lA/ pazarlık
et-. *731:17.* commerce, economics: -
bargain.

- BARK [subj.: dogs]: havla-. *60:2.*
animal sounds: - cry.

- BATHE, - take a bath, - wash oneself
/with/ [soap] /IN/ [warm water]: /lA/
yıkan- 1. *79:19.* cleanness: - wash.

- BE, - exist: ol- 3, 12 → {var/yok}
ol-. *221:6.* presence: - be present;
760:8. existence: - exist.
- be, - become [What do you want to be
when you grow up?]: ol- 1. *760:12.*
existence: - become.
- be [a color. subj.: traffic lights only: The
light is green.]: yan- 5. *1024:23.*
light: - shine.
- be, the passive, as in '- be [done]'. The
passive form of a verb is formed by
adding one of the following three
suffixes to the verb stem: 1. -Il after

all consonants except l: sev- '- love',
sevil- '- be loved'.
2. -In after l: al- '- take', alın- '- be
taken'.
3. -n after any vowel: topla- '-
collect', toplan- '- be collected'. For
a list of all the passive verbs included
in this dictionary, see the Index of
Turkish Verb Suffixes.
The agent of the passive verb follows
two equivalents of the English 'by':
1. the postposition tarafından:
Kapıcı tarafından alındı. 'It was
taken by the doorman.' or
2. the attached suffix -CA:
Hükümet.çe ilân edilmiş. 'It was
announced by the government.'

- be A JOKING MATTER: şakaya gel-
→ gel- 1. *997:11.* unimportance: - be
unimportant.
- be ABANDONED, given up [subj.:
hope]: ümit kesil- → kesil- 3.
125:10. hopelessness: - despair.
- be ABLE to do, - lie in one's power, - be
within one's capabilities: elinden
gel- → gel- 1. *18:11.* power,
potency: - be able.
- be able to manage /with/, - make do or -
manage /with/: /lA/ idare et- 2,
/lA/ yetin- 2. *994:4.* expedience: -
make shift, - make do.
- be ABOLISHED, repealed [law, tax], -
be lifted [martial law], - be struck
down [law]: kalk- 3. *445:2.* repeal: -
repeal.
- be ABSENT /from/, - miss [Ahmet
never misses a party.]: /DAn/ eksik
ol- → ol- 12. *222:7.* absence: - be
absent.
- be absent /from/, lacking /θ/ [children
from home, snow from mountain]:
/DAn/ eksil- 2. *222:8.* absence: -
absent oneself.
- be ACCUSTOMED /TO/, - get used /to/:
/A/ alış- 1. *373:12.* custom, habit: -
be used to.
- be ACQUAINTED /WITH/ sb, - know
sb: /I/ tanı- 1.1, /lA/ tanış- ['- get
to know, - get acquainted /with/ one
another, - meet /θ/; - be acquainted
with, - know one another']. *587:9.*
friendship: - be friends.
- be ADDED /to/ [water to milk], - be
mixed /WITH/ [water WITH milk]:
/A/ katıl- 1. *253:5.* addition: - add
to.
- be added up [numbers]: toplan- 5.
1016:17. mathematics: - calculate.
- be or - become ADDICTED /to/: /A/
alış- 2. *373:11.* custom, habit: -
become a habit.
- be ADORNED, decorated, embellished
/with/: /lA/ süslen- 2. *498:8.*

ornamentation: - ornament; *1015:15.*
beauty: - beautify.

- be ADVISED, informed, aware [that], take note, just to let you know, is that understood?, OK?: {haberiniz/ bilginiz} olsun. → ol- 11 → olsun. *399: * 9.* warning: expressions of; *982:22.* attention: INTERJ. attention!

- be emotionally AFFECTED, moved, touched /BY/: /DAn/ duygulan-, /DAn/ etkilen- 2. *893:7.* influence: - influence.

- be AFRAID or - fear /FOR/, - worry, - be anxious /ABOUT/, - be concerned /{ABOUT/FOR}/: /DAn/ endişe et-. *126:6.* anxiety: - feel anxious.

- be afraid or frightened /OF/, - fear /θ/, - be afraid /to/: /DAn, A/ kork- 1. *127:10.* fear, frighteningness: - fear.

- be AHEAD, fast [clock, watch]: ileri git- 1 → git- 1a. *844:5.* earliness: - be early.

- be AIRED, carried, broadcast, - air /ON/ radio or television: /DAn/ yayımlan- 2. *1033:25.* radio: - broadcast; *1034:14.* television: - televise.

- be AIRED OUT [room, clothes], - be ventilated [room]: havalan- 1. *317:10.* air, weather: - air.

- be ALIVE, healthy: sağ ol- → ol- 12. *83:6.* health: - enjoy good health; *306:7.* life: - live.

- be ALMOST, - be on the point of being, - be [just] about to be, - be on the verge of being: olmak üzere 2. → ol- 11. *223:8.* nearness: - be near.

- be AMAZED: → - be surprised.

- be AN INCONVENIENCE, trouble, troublesome /FOR/: /A/ zahmet ol- → ol- 12. *96:16a.* unpleasure: - distress; *504: * 20.* courtesy: polite expressions; *995:4.* inexpedience: - inconvenience

- be AN OLD MAID, - remain UNMARRIED [for a woman]: evde kal- → kal- 1. *565:5.* celibacy: - be unmarried.

- be ANGRY /{AT/WITH}/, mad /AT/: /A/ kız- 1, /A/ küs-, /A/ darıl- 1. *152:17.* resentment, anger: - become angry.

- be ANNOYED /AT/, vexed /{BY/BECAUSE OF/FROM}/: /A/ canı sıkıl- 2 → sıkıl- 1. *96:13.* unpleasure: - annoy.

- be ANNOYING to, - annoy, - bother, - get on sb's nerves, - irritate: canını sık- 2 → sık- 3, sık- 3. *96:13.* unpleasure: - annoy; *98:15.* unpleasantness: - vex.

- be ANXIOUS /ABOUT/, - worry /ABOUT/: /DAn/ endişe et-. *126:6.* anxiety: - feel anxious.

- be APPOINTED, assigned, named /to [a position], AS [a teacher]/: /A, olarak/ tayin ol- 1. • This verb is not used with an agent noun preceded by {tarafından/CA} 'by', i.e., not as in 'He was appointed by the Ministry.' → ol- 12; - be appointed, assigned, named /a: to [a position], b: AS [a teacher], c: by [the Ministry]/: /a: A, b: olarak, c: {tarafından/ CA}/ {atan-/tayin edil-}. *615:11.* commission: - appoint.

- be APPROPRIATE, suitable, right /FOR/ [subj.: certain behavior for a person]: /A/ yakış- 1. *866:3.* conformity: - conform.

- be APPROVED /by/: /{tarafından/ CA}/ onaylan-. *509:9.* approval: - approve.

- be ARRESTED, - be put under arrest /by/: /{tarafından/CA}/ tutuklan-. *429:15.* confinement: - arrest.

- be or - feel ARROGANTLY PROUD /OF/, - pride oneself arrogantly /ON/: /lA/ gurur duy- 2 → duy- 3, /lA/ gururlan-. *136:5.* pride: - take pride; *141:8.* arrogance: - give oneself airs.

- be ASHAMED /a: OF, b: on account of, c: OF/, embarrassed /on account of/: /a: DAn, b: DAn dolayı, c: A/ utan-. *96:15.* unpleasure: - chagrin; *137:9a.* humility: - be humiliated.

- be ASSEMBLED, gathered, collected, harvested /{at/in}, by [sb]/: /DA, {tarafından/CA}/ toplan- 1. *769:18.* assemblage: - bring or - gather together.

- be ASSIGNED, appointed, named /to [a position], AS [a teacher]/: → - be APPOINTED, assigned, named /to [a position], AS [a teacher]/.

- be ASTONISHED: → - be surprised.

- be ASTOUNDED, dumbfounded, astonished, amazed, surprised: {şaşır-/şaşırıp} kal- → şaşır- 2, şaştı kal- → şaş-. *122:5.* wonder: - wonder; *131:7.* inexpectation: - surprise.

- be AT A LOSS /AS TO/ what to say or do, - be confused, taken aback, bewildered /{AT/in the face of}/ an unexpected situation: /I/ şaşır- 1. *970:9.* uncertainty: - be uncertain.

- be at a loss FOR WORDS, NOT - know what to say: söz bulAMA-. → bul- 1. *51:8.* silence: - silence.

- be at HAND [subj. doomsday]: kıyamet kop- 1. → kop- 2. *671:13.*

violence: - erupt; *817:13.* beginning: - originate.

- be ATTENDED TO [affairs, matters], dealt with, taken care of, handled /by/: /{tarafından/CA}/ görül- 3. *982:5.* attention: - attend to.

- be AVAILABLE, - have an item [at a store: Is this book available?]: /DA/ bulun- 4, /DA/ var → {var/yok} ol- → ol- 12, a) 2. *221:6.* presence: - be present.

- be available, - have time [for a person: Are you available for coffee today?]: {müsait/uygun} ol- → ol- 3, Additional examples. a) 1. Yes-no questions. Additional examples of the main patterns.

- be or - become available or free [phone line], - get through [on the phone], - get a phone line: hat düş- → düş- 1. *347:18.* communications: - telephone.

- be AWARDED a prize, - be given a reward /OF/, - be rewarded /with/: /lA/ ödüllendiril-. *624:10.* payment: - pay.

- be [right] BACK, - return /from/: /DAn/ dön- 2. *163:8b.* regression: - turn back, - come back.

- be BADLY SHAKEN UP, for one's nerves - get shot: sinirleri bozul- 2 → bozul-. *128:7.* nervousness: - lose self-control.

- be BAKED, - bake [The bread is baking.]: piş-. *11:4b.* cooking: for sth - cook.

- be BATHED, washed /{with [soap]/IN [warm water]}, by/: /lA, tarafından/ yıkan- 2. *79:19.* cleanness: - wash.

- be BEATEN, conquered, defeated /BY/: /A, not with tarafından/ 1 yenil-. *412:6.* defeat: - defeat.

- be BECOMING /to/, - become /θ/ [This behavior is not becoming to you.]: /A/ yakış- 1. *866:3.* conformity: - conform.

- be BENEFICIAL, good /FOR/, - help /O/, - work [aspirin for a headache]: /A/ iyi gel- → gel- 1. *998:10.* goodness: - do good.

- be BESIDE ONESELF with anger, - lose control as a result of anger, - go into a towering rage: kendini kaybet- 3. *152:20.* resentment, anger: - fly into a rage.

- be beside oneself with joy, - be carried away [by joy], - be ecstatic: kendinden geç- 2 → geç- 1, kendini kaybet- 2. *95:11.* pleasure: - be pleased.

- be BEYOND ONE'S ABILITIES: elinden gelME- → elinden gel- → gel- 1. *19:8.* impotence: cannot.

- be BLESSED, auspicious: → May it be blessed.

- be BLOCKED, obstructed [roads] /by/ sb: /{tarafından/CA}/ kapatıl- 4. *293:7.* closure: - stop, - stop up.

- be blocked, obstructed [roads] /to [traffic], {DUE TO/BECAUSE OF} sth: snow]/: /A, DAn/ kapan- 4. *293:7.* closure: - stop, - stop up.

- be BOARDED [subj.: person], - be put /ON/ a vehicle or a mount [i.e., horse]: /A/ bindiril-. *159:12.* location: - place; *193:12.* ascent: - mount.

- be boarded [subj.: vehicle], - be mounted [subj.: animal] /{AT/from}/ [the front, the rear]: /DAn/ binil-. *193:12.* ascent: - mount.

- be BOILED, cooked in boiling water /by/ [The eggs have been boiled.]: /tarafından/ haşlan- 1. *11:4a.* cooking: - cook sth.

- be BORED, fed up, disgusted /WITH/, - be or - get tired /OF/: /DAn/ {bık-/usan-}, /DAn/ sıkıl- 1. *118:7b.* tedium: - get bored.

- be BORN: doğ- 1, dünyaya gel- [lit., '- come into the world'] → gel- 1. *1:2.* birth: - be born.

- be BOUGHT, purchased /by, for/: /{tarafından/CA}, A/ alın- 2. *733:7.* purchase: - purchase.

- be BROADCAST, aired, carried, - air /ON/ radio or television: /DAn/ yayımlan- 2. *1033:25.* radio: - broadcast; *1034:14.* television: - televise.

- be BROKEN /by/ [subj.: windows, glasses]: /{tarafından/CA}/ kırıl- 1. *801:12.* separation: - break.

- be broken [up], smashed, torn, cut up, chopped up, or pulled to pieces /by/: /{tarafından/CA}/ parçalan- 1. *801:13.* separation: - shatter.

- be broken, ruined, devastated by a disaster [subj.: a person]; - lose one's health and morale: yıkıl- 3. *112:17.* sadness: - grieve; *393:24.* impairment: - break down.

- be broken or forced open [locked door] /by/: /{tarafından/CA}/ zorlan- 2. *424:6.* compulsion: - press.

- be BURIED /IN, by/: /A, {tarafından/CA}/ gömül- [for dead bodies and other objects], *formal:* /A, {tarafından/CA}/ defnedil- [for dead bodies only], /DA/ toprağa veril- [for dead bodies only]. *309:19.* interment: - inter.

472

- be or - get BURNED, scorched, singed /{BY/from}/; - get a burn, - get scalded; - get sunburned: /DAn/ yan- 3. *1019:24.* heating: - burn.
- be BURNING [light], - be on [light, electricity]: yan- 5. *1024:23.* light: - shine.
- be BUSY or occupied /with/, - deal /with/ [subj.: person]: /lA/ meşgul ol- → ol- 12. *330:10.* activity: - be busy; *724:11.* occupation: - busy oneself with.
- be busy or occupied /with/ a job, - work /ON/ sth, - be engaged /IN/ sth [involving extra effort, struggle], - devote oneself /TO/ a task: /lA/ uğraş- 2. *724:11.* occupation: - busy oneself with.
- be busy [subj.: phone line]: meşgul çık- → çık- 7. *330:10.* activity: - be busy.

- be CALLED, dubbed, named, referred to /AS, by/: /{diye/olarak}, {tarafından/CA}/ {adlandırıl-/isimlendiril-}. *5 2 7 : 1 3.* nomenclature: - be called.
- be called [What is this called?], - be said: /A/ den-. *583:13.* nomenclature: - be called.
- be called OFF, cancelled /by, {on account of/due to}/: /{tarafından/CA}, yüzünden/ iptal edil-. *819:5.* end: - end sth.
- be CAPTIVATED /BY/ [a person, beauty]: /A/ kapıl-. *105:12.* excitement: - excite.
- be CAREFUL, - look out, - watch out /FOR/: dikkat et- 1, dikkatli ol- → ol- 12. *339:7.* carefulness: - be careful; *399: * 9* warning: expressions of.
- be CARRIED, aired, broadcast [subj: program], - air, - be on [radio or television]: /DAn/ yayımlan- 2. *1033:25.* radio: - broadcast; *1034:14.* television: - televise.
- be CARRIED AWAY /BY/, - be crazy /about/, - adore /θ/, - like /θ/ sth a great deal: /A/ bayıl- 2. *101:7.* eagerness: - be enthusiastic.
- be carried away [by joy], - be beside oneself with joy, - be ecstatic: kendinden geç- 2 → geç- 1, kendini kaybet- 2. *95:11.* pleasure: - be pleased.
- be carried away /BY/ [a current of water or an emotion: fear, panic, anxiety]: /A/ kapıl-. *105:12.* excitement: - excite; *480:14.* taking: - seize.
- be CAST OUT, excluded, ostracized /by, from/: /{tarafından/CA}, DAn/ dışlan-. *772:4.* exclusion: - exclude.

- be CAUGHT, seized, grasped, taken hold of /BY/ [body part: the neck]: /DAn/ tutul- 1. *474:6.* retention: - hold, - grip; *480:14.* taking: - seize.
- be caught /by/; - be collared, nabbed /by/; - be seized, grabbed, snatched /by/ [the police]: /{tarafından/CA}/ yakalan- 1. *480:14.* taking: - seize.
- be caught /by/ the lens: → - be caught /ON/ camera.
- be caught /IN/ certain unfavorable weather conditions [rain, snow]: /A/ tutul- 6, /A/ yakalan- 4. *317:10.* air, weather: - air.
- be caught /ON/ camera /BY/ the lens, - be photographed unexpectedly or unawares: /A/ yakalan- 3. *714:14.* photography: - photograph.
- be CHARGED, entrusted /with, by/, - be given the task /OF, by/, - be made responsible /FOR, by/, - be put in charge /OF, by/: /lA, tarafından/ görevlendiril-. *615:11.* commission: - appoint; *641:12.* duty: - obligate.
- be CHEATED, deceived /by/: /{tarafından/CA}/ aldatıl-. *356:14.* deception: - deceive; *356:18.* : - cheat.
- be CHECKED, - be checked out, examined [travelers at the airport]: kontrolden geç- → geç- 1. *937:24.* inquiry: - examine.
- be CHILDISH, - act childishly: çocukluk et-. *921:12.* unintelligence: - be stupid.
- be CHOPPED UP, cut up [hard substance] /by/: /{tarafından/CA}/ parçalan- 1. *801:13.* separation: - shatter.
- be CHOSEN, selected, picked /for, by/: /{A/için}, {tarafından/CA}/ seçil- 1. *371:13.* choice: - choose.
- be CIRCUMCISED: sünnet ol- → ol- 10.1. *701:16.* religious rites: - baptize.
- be or - become CLEAR, - be understood /by/: /{tarafından/CA}/ anlaşıl-. *521:5.* intelligibility: - be understood.
- be CLEARED, opened, unblocked /to/ [roads to traffic]: /A/ açıl- 8. *292:12.* opening: - unclose.
- be CLOSED, dropped [an issue, a topic, subject]: kapan- 5. *819:6.* end: - come to an end [i.].
- be closed, shut /by/: /{tarafından/CA}/ kapatıl- 1. *293:6.* closure: - close.
- be closed up, shut up /IN, by/: /A, {tarafından/CA}/ kapatıl- 5. *429:12.* confinement: - confine.
- be closed, shut DOWN permanently /by/ [subj.: organization, business,

school]: /{tarafından/CA}/ kapatıl- 3. *293:8.* closure: - close shop.

- be, - get, or - feel COLD: üşü-. *1022:9.* cold: - freeze.

- be COLLECTED, gathered, assembled, harvested /{at/in}, by [sb]/: /DA, {tarafından/CA}/ toplan- 1. *769:18.* assemblage: - bring or - gather together.

- be or - become COMFORTABLE, - feel better, relieved: rahat et-, rahatla-. *120:8.* relief: - be relieved.

- be COMPELLED, forced, constrained /to [do sth], by/; - be coerced /INTO [doing sth], by/: / A, tarafından/ zorlan- 1. *424:4.* compulsion: - compel.

- be COMPLETED, finished /by/ sb: /{tarafından/CA}/ tamamlan-. *793:6.* completeness: - complete; *819:7.* end: - complete.

- be COMPOSED /OF/, made up /OF/, formed /OF/, consist /OF/: /DAn/ oluş-. *795:3.* composition: - compose.

- be CONCEITED, stuck, up, stuck on oneself: kendini beğen-. *140:6.* vanity: - be stuck on oneself.

- be CONCERNED /ABOUT/, - worry /ABOUT/: /I/ merak et- 1, /DAn/ endişe et-. *126:6.* anxiety: - feel anxious.

- be concerned, worried /ABOUT/, - be upset, distressed /{ABOUT/BY/AT}/; - be sad that, - feel sad that, - be sorry /ABOUT/: /A/ üzül-. *112:16.* sadness: - lose heart; *126:4.* anxiety: - concern; *126:6.* anxiety: - feel anxious.

- be concerned /with/, - take an interest /IN/: /lA/ meşgul ol- 2 → ol- 12. *982:5.* attention: - attend to.

- be concerned /with/, - show concern /FOR/ [father for his children]; - attend /TO/, - look /AFTER/: /lA/ ilgilen- 2. *339:9.* carefulness: - look after; *982:5.* attention: - attend to.

- be CONCLUDED, ended /by/: /{tarafından/CA}/ son veril-. *819:5.* end: - end sth.

- be CONDEMNED, sentenced /TO/ a punishment: /lA/ cezalandırıl- 2, /A/ mahkûm ol- 1 → ol- 12. *602:3.* condemnation: - condemn.

- be condemned, doomed /to/ [a fate: life in a wheelchair]: /A/ mahkûm ol- 2 → ol- 12. *602:3.* condemnation: - condemn.

- be CONFIRMED, verified, corroborated [fact]: doğrulan-, tasdik edil-. *969:12.* certainty: - verify.

- be CONFRONTED or - meet [/with/ difficulties], - encounter, - face, or -

experience [/Ө/ difficulties]: [{zorluk.la/güçlük.le}] karşılaş- 3. *216:8.* front: - confront; *830:8.* event: - experience; *1012:11.* difficulty: - have difficulty.

- be CONFUSED, at a loss /AS TO/ what to say or do, - be taken aback, - be bewildered /{AT/in the face of}/ an unexpected situation: /I/ şaşır- 1. *970:9.* uncertainty: - be uncertain.

- be CONNECTED /to/, - be put through /to/ [the (telephone) operator]: /A/ bağlan- 2. *799:11.* joining: - be joined.

- be connected, tied up [package], fastened, bound /to, with, by/, - be tied /{to/AROUND}/, with, by/: /A, lA, tarafından/ bağlan- 1. *799:9.* joining: - bind.

- be CONQUERED, defeated, beaten /BY/: /A, not with tarafından/ 1 yenil-. *412:6.* defeat: - defeat.

- be CONSIDERED, taken up [subject, topic]: ele alın- → alın- 1. *404:3.* undertaking: - undertake.

- be considered, regarded, looked UPON /AS/: /olarak/ görül- 2. *952:11.* belief: - think.

- be CONSUMED with passion /for/, - be mad /about/, *slang:* - have the hots /for/: /A, için/ yanıp tutuş- → yan- 7. *104:19.* love: - love.

- be CONTACTED, reached /AT/ [Ahmet can be reached at this (telephone) number.]: /DAn/ ulaşıl-. *343:8.* communication: - communicate with, - get in touch with.

- be CONTENT, satisfied /with/: /A/ razı ol- 1 → ol- 12, /lA/ yetin- 1. *107:5.* contentment: - be content.

- be COOKED, boiled in boiling water /by/ [The eggs have been {cooked/boiled}.]: /tarafından/ haşlan- 1. *11:4a.* cooking: - cook sth.

- be COVERED IN SWEAT, - break out in a sweat /{from/because of}/ [anxiety, fear]: /DAn/ ter bas- → bas- 4. *12:16.* excretion: - sweat; *127:13.* fear, frighteningness: - flinch.

- be COVERED [UP] [seeds, dog bone] /by/: /{tarafından/CA}/ kapatıl- 6. *346:6.* concealment: - conceal.

- be CRAZY /ABOUT/, - adore /Ө/, - like /Ө/ sth or sb a great deal, - be carried away /BY/: /A/ bayıl- 2. *101:7.* eagerness: - be enthusiastic.

- be CRITICIZED /a: because [*or* for], b: for, c: by/: /a: {DIğI için/ DIğInDAn}, b: DAn dolayı, c: {tarafından/CA}/ {eleştiril-/tenkit edil-}. *510:14.* disapproval: - criticize; *945:14.* judgment: - criticize.

474

- be or - get CROSS, angry /{WITH/AT}/: /A/ darıl- 1. *152:17.* resentment, anger: - become angry.
- be CURIOUS /ABOUT/: /I/ merak et- 2. *980:3b.* curiosity: - be curious.
- be or - get CUT [HAND], - be or - get cut off /by/ [head]: /tarafından/ kesil- 1. *224:4.* interval: - cleave.
- be cut OFF, interrupted, stopped [electricity, gas, water, phone conversation] /by/: /{tarafından/ CA}/ kesil- 3. *856:10.* cessation: - interrupt.
- be cut off [subj.: head]: baş kesil- → kesil- 1. *224:4.* interval: - cleave; *308:12.* killing: - kill.
- be cut UP, chopped up /by/: /{tarafından/CA}/ parçalan- 1. *801:13.* separation: - shatter.

- be DASHED, - come to naught, not - be realized [hopes, expectations, dreams]: boşa çık- → çık- 7. *395:23.* destruction: - perish; *473:6.* loss:- go to waste; *9 1 0 : 3.* shortcoming: - fall through.
- be DECEIVED, fooled, taken in /BY [a person or thing]/: /A, not with tarafından/ {aldan-/kan-}. *356:14.* deception: - deceive.
- be deceived, cheated /by [a person or agency, not a thing]/: /{tarafından/CA}, not with A/ aldatıl-. *356:14.* deception: - deceive; *356:18.* : - cheat.
- be DECORATED, adorned, embellished /with/: /lA/ süslen- 2. *498:8.* ornamentation: - ornament; *1015:15.* beauty: - beautify.
- be DEDUCTED /from/ [subj.: taxes]: /DAn/ kesil- 4. *255:9.* subtraction: - subtract.
- be DEFEATED, conquered, beaten /BY/: /A, not with tarafından/ 1 yenil-. *412:6.* defeat: - defeat.
- be DELAYED, held up, - be late /on account of, due to/ [weather, traffic] [subj.: person or vehicle]: [hava, trafik] /yüzünden/ {geç kal- /gecik-} → {geç kal-/gecik-} → kal- 1. *845:7.* lateness: - be late.
- be delayed, postponed /a: for, b: to, c: {till/until}, d: by/ [subj.: event, meeting]: /a: A, b: A, c: A kadar, d: {tarafından/CA}/ {ertelen- /tehir edil-}, /A/ kal- 4 [Kal- is not used with an agent noun, as are the forms above.] *845:9.* lateness: - postpone.
- be delayed, held up: rötar yap- [subj.: usually only for public transportation -- train, bus, ferry, airplane -- not

persons] → yap- 3, yolda kal- [subj.: person or vehicle] → kal- 1. *845:8.* lateness: - delay.
- be DEMOLISHED, wrecked: → - be destroyed.
- be DEPRESSED, sad: üzüntü çek- 1 → çek- 5. *112:16.* sadness: - lose heart.
- be or - get depressed, - be in a depression: bunalım geçir- → geçir- 2. *112:16.* sadness: - lose heart.
- be DEPRIVED OF ONE'S LIVELIHOOD, - lose one's livelihood: ekmeğinden ol-. → ol- 7. *473:4.* loss: - lose.
- be DESTROYED; - be demolished, wrecked /by, with/; - be pulled down, torn down; - be ruined [subj.: building]: /{tarafından/CA}, lA/ yıkıl- 1. *395:17.* destruction: - demolish.
- be DEVASTATED, broken, ruined by a disaster [subj.: a person]; - lose one's health and morale: yıkıl- 3. *112:17.* sadness: - grieve; *393:24.* impairment: - break down [i.].
- be devastated, deeply grieved, distressed, overcome /{WITH/BY}/ grief: /DAn/ kahrol- → ol- 12. *112:17.* sadness: - grieve.
- be DIFFICULT, hard for: zoruna git- 1 → git- 1b. *1012:10.* difficulty: - be difficult.
- be or - become physically DISABLED, - get or - be hurt; - become crippled; - become maimed or mutilated: sakatlan-. *393:13.* impairment: - inflict an injury.
- be DISAPPOINTED: {hayal/düş} kırıklığına uğra- → uğra- 2. *132:4.* disappointment: - be disappointed.
- be {DISCHARGED/RELEASED} /from/ a hospital: /DAn/ taburcu ol- → ol- 12. *431:5.* liberation: - release.
- be DISCUSSED, mentioned, written about, related, referred to, spoken about, - occur [facts in a written work] [Where is this topic discussed?]: geç- 7. *5 5 1 : 8.* information: - inform.
- be DISGUSTED /{BY/WITH}/, revolted /{BY/BECAUSE OF}/, - feel disgust, horror /AT/, loathing /FOR/: /DAn/ {iğren-/tiksin-}. *64:4.* unsavoriness: - disgust.
- be DISTINGUISHED, seen clearly, - be made out: seçil- 2. *27:12.* vision: - see.
- be or - get DISTRACTED: dikkati dağıl- → dağıl- 1. *984:6.* distraction, confusion: - distract.

- be DISTRESSED, sad, sorry, upset [over some event]: **üzüntü duy-** → duy-3. *112:16.* sadness: - lose heart.
- be DISTRIBUTED, handed out /a: by [sb], b: by means of, c: to/: /a: {tarafından/CA}, b: lA, c: A/ **dağıtıl-.** *770:4a.* dispersion: - disperse sth.
- be DIVIDED, split /INTO, by/ [house into rooms by owners]: /A, {tarafından/CA}/ **ayrıl-** 2, /A, {tarafından/CA}/ **bölün-.** *801:8.* separation: - separate.
- be divided /BY/ [mathematical division: 4 by 2]: /A/ **bölün-.** *1016:17.* mathematics: - calculate.
- be or - get DIVORCED /from/, - split up /WITH/: /DAn/ **boşan-,** /DAn/ **ayrıl-** → ayrıl- 1. *566:5.* divorce, widowhood: - divorce.
- be or - get DIZZY: **başı dön-** → dön-1. *914:9.* rotation: - rotate; *984:8* * distraction, confusion: - be dizzy.
- be DONE, completed, ready: **ol-** 9.1. *405:14.* preparation: - be prepared.
- be DONE FOR, sunk, doomed, in serious trouble; - have had it: *colloq.*: **hapı yut-, yan-** 6. *395:11.* destruction: - do; *1012:11.* difficulty: - have difficulty.
- be DOOMED, condemned /to/ [a fate: life in a wheel chair]: /A/ **mahkûm ol-** 2 → ol- 12. *602:3.* condemnation: - condemn.
- be DOWN, - break down, - crash, - fail [subj.: a system, computer]: **çök-** 5. *393:24.* impairment: - break down.
- be DRAWN UP, set up, prepared, readied /by/: /{tarafından/CA}/ **hazırlan-** 2. *405:6.* preparation: - prepare.
- be DRIED /by/: /{tarafından/CA}/ **kurulan-** 1. *1064:6a.* dryness: - dry, - make dry.
- be DRIVEN or hammered /{IN/INTO}, by/ [subj.: nail, peg]; - be pegged, nailed down: /A, {tarafından/CA}/ **çakıl-** 1. *799:8.* joining: - hook.
- be DROPPED, closed [an issue, a topic, subject]: **kapan-** 5. *819:6.* end: - come to an end [i.].
- be DRUNK, *pass.* of - drink [Where is this drink drunk?]: **içil-** 1. *8:29.* eating: - drink.
- be, - become, or - get DRUNK, tipsy, intoxicated, inebriated, high /{from/with}, {ON/with}/ [drink]: /DAn, lA/ **sarhoş ol-** 1 → ol- 12. *88:26.* intoxication, alcoholic drink: - get drunk; *88:27.* : - be drunk.
- be or - become drunk /WITH/ joy, delight, happiness, pleasure: /DAn/

sarhoş ol- 2 → ol- 12. *95:11.* pleasure: - be pleased.
- be DUBBED, called, named, referred to /AS, by/: /{diye/olarak}, {tarafından/CA}/ {**adlandırıl-/isimlendiril-**}. *527:13.* nomenclature: - be called.
- be DUE [When is the plane due?]: **gel-**1. *186:6.* arrival: - arrive.
- be due /TO/, - emanate /from/, - result /from/, - originate /from/, - stem /from/, or - spring /from/: /DAn/ **kaynaklan-.** *886:5.* effect: - result from.

- be EASY, - go easily: **kolay gel-** → gel- 1. *504: * 20.* courtesy: polite expressions; *1013:10.* facility: - go easily.
- be easy for sb: **kolayına gel-** → gel-1, **kolayına git-** 1 → git- 1b. *1013:10.* facility: - go easily.
- be EATEN /BY/: /tarafından/ 1 **yen-** [most common form in speech and writing], 2 **yenil-** [common in writing, less so in speech], **içil-** 3 [for soup]. *8:20.* eating: - eat.
- be ECSTATIC, - be beside oneself with joy, - - be carried away [by joy]: **kendinden geç-** 2 → geç- 1, **kendini kaybet-** 2. *95:11.* pleasure: - be pleased.
- be EDUCATED, - have an education: {**eğitim/öğrenim/tahsil**} **gör-** → gör- 3. *570:11.* learning: - be taught.
- be ELECTED /a: to, b: for, c: by/: /a: A, b: {A/için}, c: {tarafından/CA}/ **seçil-** 1. *371:13.* choice: - choose.
- be EMBARRASSED /on account of/, - be ashamed /OF/: /DAn dolayı/ **utan-.** *96:15.* unpleasure: - chagrin; *137:9a.* humility: - be humiliated.
- be embarrassed, - become bashful, shy: **sıkıl-** 2, **utan-.** *96:15.* unpleasure: - chagrin, * - become chagrined.
- be EMBELLISHED, decorated, adorned /with/: /lA/ **süslen-** 2. *498:8.* ornamentation: - ornament; *1015:15.* beauty: - beautify.
- be ENDED, concluded /by/: /{tarafından/CA}/ **son veril-.** *819:5.* end: - end sth.
- be ENGAGED /IN/, busy /with/ a job, - work /ON/ sth, - devote oneself /TO/ a task [involving extra effort, struggle]: /lA/ **uğraş-** 2. *724:11.* occupation: - busy oneself with.
- be ENOUGH /FOR/, - suffice /FOR/: /A/ **yet-, yetiş-** 6. *990:4.* sufficiency: - suffice.
- be ENTERED /THROUGH, BY WAY OF/ [subj.: place. Impersonal passive: This building is entered through this

door.]: /DAn/ giril-. *189:7.*
entrance: - enter.

- be ENTHUSIASTIC, thrilled, - get excited [positive emotion]: **heyecanlan-** 1. *95:11.* pleasure: - be pleased; *105:18* excitement: - be excited.

- be ENTRUSTED, charged /with, by/, - be given the task /OF, by/, - be made responsible /FOR, by/, - be put in charge /OF, by/: /lA, tarafından/ **görevlendiril-**. *615:11.* commission: - appoint; *641:12.* duty: - obligate.

- be ESTABLISHED, founded /by/ [subj.: organization]: /{tarafından/CA}/ **kurul-**. *891:10.* production: - establish.

- be EXAMINED /IN/, - take an examination /IN/: /DAn/ {sınav/imtihan} **ol-** → ol- 10.1. *938:4.* answer: - answer.

- be examined [physical exam] /BY/: /A, not with tarafından/ **muayene ol-** → ol- 10.1. *91:29.* therapy: - undergo treatment; *937:24.* inquiry: - examine.

- be EXCLUDED, cast out, ostracized /by, from/: /{tarafından/CA}, DAn/ **dışlan-**. *772:4.* exclusion: - exclude.

- be EXCUSED [from class: You may be excused., i.e., leave]: **çık-** 1, **git-** 1a. *443:20* permission: by your leave.

- be EXHAUSTED, worn-out, tired out /from/: /DAn/ **bit-** 2, {gücü/takatı} **tüken-** [for {one's strength} to give out]. *21:5.* fatigue: - burn out.

- be exhausted [subj.: patience], - be impatient, for one's patience - run out: **sabrı tüken-**. *135:5.* impatience: - have no patience with.

- be EXISTENT, - exist, - survive [old inscriptions]: **dur-** 7. *760.8.* existence: - exist.

- be EXITED /{AT/from}/ [the rear] [vehicle]: /DAn/ **inil-**. *194:7.* descent: - get down.

- be EXPIRED, no longer valid, overdue: {vakti/zamanı/süresi} **geç-** → geç- 4. *390:9.* disuse: - obsolesce.

- be FAMISHED, - die of hunger: **açlıktan öl-**. *100:19.* desire: - hunger

- be FAST, ahead [clock, watch]: **ileri git-** 1 → git- 1a. *844:5.* earliness: - be early

- be FED UP, disgusted /WITH/, bored /WITH/, tired /OF/, - get tired /OF/: /DAn/ {bık-/usan-}, /DAn/ **sıkıl-** 1. *118:7b.* tedium: - get bored.

- be FINED or punished /BY [sb], FOR [sth]/: /DAn, DAn/ **ceza ye-** →

ye- 2. *603:5.* penalty: - fine; *604:20.* punishment: - be punished.

- be FINISHED, completed /by/ sb: /{tarafından/CA}/ **tamamlan-**. *793:6.* completeness: - complete; *819:7.* end: - complete.

- be finished, ready /BY/ a specified time [subj.: a thing: an order, a suit]: /A/ **yetiş-** 3. *405:14.* preparation: - be prepared.

- be FIRED, relieved of one's {duties/position}: **görevden alın-** → alın- 1, **görevine son veril-** → son veril- → veril-, **işinden ol-** → ol- 7. *908:19.* ejection: - dismiss.

- be FOLDED /INTO [thirds], by [sb]/: /A, tarafından/ **katlan-** 1. *291:5.* fold: - fold.

- be FOND OF; - love, - like: **sev-** 1. *104:19.* love: - love

- be fond of EACH OTHER; - love or like each other: **seviş-** 1. *104:19.* love: - love.

- be FOOLED, taken in, deceived /BY [a person or thing]/: /A, not with tarafından/ {aldan-/kan-}. *356:14.* deception: - deceive.

- be FOR NOTHING [efforts, money], of no use, in vain: **boşa git-** → git- 5. *391:8.* uselessness: - be useless.

- be FORBIDDEN, prohibited /by/: /{tarafından/CA}/ **yasaklan-**. *444:3.* prohibition: - prohibit.

- be FORCED, constrained, compelled /to [do sth], by/; - be coerced /INTO [doing sth], by/: /A, tarafından/ **zorlan-** 1. *424:4.* compulsion: - compel.

- be forced /to/, - be obliged /to/, - have /to/ [do sth] [not with {tarafından/CA}]: **-mAk zorunda kal-** → kal- 1. *962:10.* necessity: - be necessary.

- be forced or broken open [locked door] /by/: /{tarafından/CA}/ **zorlan-** 2. *424:6.* compulsion: - press.

- be FORMED, composed, or made up /OF/, consist /OF/: /DAn/ **oluş-**. *795:3.* composition: - compose.

- be FOUND, discovered /a: {in/at} [a place], b: by [a person], c: BY...ing/ [Where was this animal {found/discovered}?]: /a: DA, b: {tarafından/CA}, c: mAklA/ **bulun-** 1. *940:2.* discovery: - discover.

- be found, located, - exist /{in/at}/ a place [subj.: sb or sth: Where is this animal found?]: /DA/ **bulun-** 2. *221:6.* presence: - be present; *760:8.* existence: - exist.

- be found, - occur, - be present /in/ [words in a text: How often is this

word found in the document?]: /DA/
geç- 8. *221:6.* presence: - be present.

- be FOUNDED, established /by/ [subj.:
organization]: /{tarafından/CA}/
kurul- 1. *891:10.* production: -
establish.

- be FRIED, sautéd /by/ [The potatoes are
being fried by the cook.]:
/tarafından/ kızartıl- 1. *11:4a.*
cooking: for sth - cook.

- be FRIGHTENED or afraid /OF/, - fear
/θ/: /DAn/ kork-. *127:10.* fear,
frighteningness: - fear.

- be badly frightened, - be terrified: ödü
kop- → kop- 1. *127:10.* fear,
frighteningness: - fear.

- be FULL [I'm full], - eat one's fill, -
have had enough food: doy-, karnı
doy-. *993:5.* satiety: - have enough.

- be FURNISHED /with [money, objects],
IN [a style, material]/ [subj.: house]:
/lA, θ/ döşen-. *385:8.* provision,
equipment: - equip.

- be GATHERED, assembled, collected,
harvested /{at/in}, by [sb]/: /DA,
{tarafından/CA}/ toplan- 1.
769:18. assemblage: - bring or -
gather together.

- be GIVEN /TO/: /A/ veril-. *478:12.*
giving: - give.

- be given A REWARD, - be awarded a
prize: ödüllendiril-. *624:10.*
payment: - pay.

- be given UP, abandoned [subj.: hope]:
ümit kesil- → kesil- 3. *125:10.*
hopelessness: - despair.

- be GLAD, pleased /a:
{ABOUT/AT/WITH}, b: because, c:
θ [that]/: /a: A, b: DIğI için, c:
A/ sevin-. *95:11.* pleasure: - be
pleased.

- be GOOD /TO/, - do /θ/ sb a kindness, a
good turn, - do good, - treat kindly:
/A/ iyilik et-. *143:12.* kindness,
benevolence: - do a favor.

- be GRASPED, seized, caught, taken
hold of /BY/ [body part: the neck]:
/DAn/ tutul- 1. *474:6.* retention: -
hold, - grip.

- be deeply GRIEVED or distressed, - be
devastated or overcome
/{WITH/BY}/ grief: /DAn/ kahrol-
→ ol- 12. *112:17.* sadness: - grieve.

- be GROWN [crops], - be raised [crops,
animals]: yetiş- 7. *1067:16.*
agriculture: - farm.

- be HAMMERED or driven /{IN/INTO},
by/ [subj.: nail, peg]; - be pegged,
nailed down: /A, {tarafından/
CA}/ çakıl- 1. *799:8.* joining: -
hook.

- be HANDED OUT, distributed /a: by
[sb], b: by means of, c: to/: /a:
{tarafından/CA}, b: lA, c: A/
dağıtıl-. *770:4a.* dispersion: -
disperse sth.

- be HANDLED [affairs, matters], taken
care of, attended to, dealt with /by/:
/{tarafından/CA}/ görül- 3.
982:5. attention: - attend to.

- be HANGED /a: {to/ON} [a tree], b:
FOR [a crime], c: by [bandits]/: /a:
A, b: lA, c: {tarafından/CA}/
asıl- 2. *202:8.* pendency: - suspend;
604:19. punishment: - hang.

- be HAPPY, pleased, satisfied /WITH/ [a
situation, a hotel]: /DAn/ memnun
kal- → kal- 1, /DAn/ memnun ol-
→ ol- 12. *95:12.* pleasure: - enjoy.

- be HARD, difficult /FOR/: zoruna git-
1 → git- 1b. *1012:10.* difficulty: - be
difficult.

- be hard OF HEARING: ağır duy- →
duy- 1, ağır işit- → işit- 1. *49:4.*
deafness: - be deaf.

- be hard ON, - deal strictly, harshly
/WITH/: üstüne git- 1 → git- 1a.
425:5. strictness: - deal hardly or
harshly with.

- be hard UP, short of money: sıkış- 4.
619:5. poverty: - be poor; *1012:12.*
difficulty: - get into trouble.

- be HARVESTED, collected, gathered,
assembled, /{at/in}, by [sb]/: /DA,
{tarafından/CA}/ toplan- 1.
769:18. assemblage: - bring or -
gather together.

- be HEALTHY, alive: sağ ol- → ol- 12.
83:6. health: - enjoy good health;
306:7. life: - live.

- be HEARD AND OBEYED, - be
heeded: 2 dinlen- 1. *326:2.*
obedience: - obey.

- be HELD BACK IN SCHOOL, - stay
back, - fail or flunk /θ/ a grade [a
level in a school, not a course: When
he didn't study, he was held back.]:
sınıfta kal- → kal- 1. *410:9b.*
failure: - fail in specific areas.

- be held UP, delayed, - be late /on
account of, due to/ [weather, traffic]
[subj.: person or vehicle]: [hava,
trafik] /yüzünden/ {geç kal-
/gecik-} → {geç kal-/gecik-} →
kal- 1. *845:7.* lateness: - be late.

- be held up, delayed: rötar yap- [subj.:
usually only for public transportation
-- train, bus, ferry, airplane -- not
persons] → yap- 3, yolda kal-
[subj.: person or vehicle] → kal- 1.
845:8. lateness: - delay.

- be HIDDEN /from, by/; - be kept secret
/from, by/: /DAn, tarafından/
saklan- 2, /DAn, tarafından/

gizlen- 2. *346:6.* concealment: - conceal.

- be HUNG /a: {ON/IN}, b: by [sb], c: BY [part of body], d: {on the occasion of/on account of}/: /a: A, b: {tarafından/CA}, c: DAn, d: nedeniyle/ asıl- 1. *202:8.* pendency: - suspend.

- be or - become HUNGRY: acık-, karnı açık-. *100:19.* desire: - hunger.

- be very hungry; for one's stomach - growl from hunger: karnı zil çal- → çal- 3. *100:19.* desire: - hunger.

- be HURT, injured, wounded /IN [the arm]/by [the enemy]/ [physically]: /DAn, {tarafından/CA}/ yaralan- 1. *393:13.* impairment: - inflict an injury.

- be or - get hurt, - become physically disabled; - become crippled; - become maimed or mutilated: sakatlan-. *393:13.* impairment: - inflict an injury.

- be hurt [not physically], offended /because, BY/: /DIğI için, A/ kırıl- 3. *152:21.* resentment, anger: - offend.

- be hurt or offended /BY/; - be mad or angry /AT, because/, - be put out /WITH, because/: /A, DIğI için/ küs-. *152:17.* resentment, anger: - become angry; *152:21.* : - offend.

- be ILL /from/; - get sick /from/: /DAn/ hasta ol- → ol- 10.2. *85:45.* disease: - ail.

- be IMPATIENT, for one's patience - run out or be exhausted: sabrı tüken-. *135:5.* impatience: - have no patience with.

- be, - get, or - become impatient: sabırsızlan-. *135:4.* impatience: - be impatient.

- be IMPORTANT /{to/for}/, - mean sth /to/, - be of value {to/for} [Your friendship is important to me.]: /için/ ifade et- 3. *996:12.* importance: - matter.

- be IMPOSSIBLE: mümkün olMA- → mümkün ol- → ol- 12. *966:4.* impossibility: - be impossible.

- be IMPRESSED, moved, emotionally affected /BY/: /DAn/ etkilen- 2. *893:7.* influence: - influence.

- be or - find oneself IN A TIGHT SPOT, under pressure, in difficulty, - get in a jam: sıkış- 4. *297:13.* weight: - burden; *1012:12.* difficulty: - get into trouble.

- be IN AN ACCIDENT, - have an accident, - get into an accident, [car, plane]: kaza geçir- → geçir- 2. *1010:10.* adversity: - come to grief.

- be in an accident, - have an accident, - get into an accident, - cause an accident: kaza yap- → yap- 3. *1010:10.* adversity: - come to grief.

- be IN BED, - be lying down: yat- 1. *22:17.* sleep: - go to bed; *201:5.* horizontalness: - lie.

- be IN CHARGE OF, - administer, - control an area [The army is in charge of the region.]: idare et- 1, yönet- 1. *417:13.* authority: - possess or - wield authority; *573:8.* direction, management: - direct; *612:14.* government: - rule.

- be IN CONFLICT, - clash [ideas, interests, appointments]: çatış- 2. *779:5.* difference: - differ; *788:5.* disagreement: - disagree.

- be IN CONTRADICTION /with/, - be contradictory, - conflict /with/ [ideas]: /lA/ çeliş-. *788:5.* disagreement: - disagree.

- be IN CORRESPONDENCE /with/, - correspond /with/, - write [letters] to one another: /lA/ mektuplaş-. *343:6.* communication: - communicate, - be in touch; *553:10.* correspondence: - correspond.

- be IN A DEPRESSION, - be or - get depressed: bunalım geçir- → geçir- 2. *112:16.* sadness: - lose heart.

- be IN MOURNING, - mourn: yas tut- → tut- 5. *112:17.* sadness: - grieve; *115:10.* lamentation: - lament; *434:2.* observance: - observe.

- be IN PAIN, - hurt, - feel pain [His hand got cut. It hurts. He's in pain.]: canı acı- → acı- 1. *26:8.* pain: - suffer pain.

- be IN SERIOUS TROUBLE, done for, doomed, sunk; - have had it: *colloq.*: hapı yut-, yan- 6. *395:11.* destruction: - do; *1012:11.* difficulty: - have dificulty.

- be IN SEVENTH HEAVEN, overjoyed, on cloud nine, - have a ball: bayram et-. *95:11.* pleasure: - be pleased.

- be or - find oneself IN A TIGHT SPOT, under pressure, in difficulty, - get in a jam: sıkış- 4. *297:13.* weight: - burden; *1012:12.* difficulty: - get into trouble.

- be IN TIME /FOR/; - arrive in time /FOR/, - catch /θ/ a vehicle, - make it /to/ in time /FOR/: /A/ yetiş- 1. *174:13.* swiftness: - overtake; *409:8.* success: - achieve one's purpose.

- be IN VAIN, of no use, for nothing [efforts, money]: boşa git- → git- 5. *391:8.* uselessness: - be useless; *910:3.* shortcoming: - fall through.

- be INCLINED, willing /to/, - be willing to agree /to/; - go along /WITH/ a plan: /A/ yanaş- 3. *324:3.*

willingness: - be willing; *441:2.* consent: - consent.

- be INCLUDED /IN/: /A/ dahil ol- → ol- 12. *771:3.* inclusion: - include

- be INFLUENCED /BY/, - show the influence /OF/: /DAn/ etkilen- 1. *893:7.* influence: - influence

- be INJURED, hurt, wounded /IN [the arm], by [the enemy]/: /DAn, {tarafından/CA}/ yaralan- 1. *393:13.* impairment: - inflict an injury.

- be INTERESTED /IN/ sth, - take an interest /IN/: /A [karşı]/ ilgi duy- → duy- 3, /lA/ ilgilen- 1. *980:3b.* curiosity: - be curious.

- be INTERRED, buried /IN, by/ [subj.: for dead bodies only]: *formal:* /A, {tarafından/CA}/ defnedil-, /DA/ toprağa veril-, / A, {tarafından/CA}/ gömül- [for dead bodies and other objects]. *309:19.* interment: - inter.

- be INTERRUPTED, cut off, stopped [electricity, water, gas, phone conversation] /by/: /{tarafından/CA}/ kesil- 3. *856:10.* cessation: - interrupt.

- be INTO *colloq.*, - interest, - appeal to [He's really into this type of music.]: ilgi çek- → çek- 1, /I/ ilgilendir- 1. *377:6.* allurement: - attract; *980:3a.* curiosity: - make curious, - interest.

- be ISSUED, - come out, - appear [article in newspaper, issue of periodical]: çık- 8. *33:8.* appearance: - appear.

- be JEALOUS /OF/, - envy sb for sth: /I/ kıskan- 1. *153:3.* jealousy: - suffer the pangs of jealousy; *154:3.* envy: - envy.

- be JEALOUSLY PROTECTIVE OF, - guard a woman zealously against any sign of disrespect, especially against the attentions of another male, - love jealously: kıskan- 3. *153:3.* jealousy: - suffer the pangs of jealousy; *1007:18a.* protection: - protect.

- be JOKING, kidding, not - be telling the truth, - make a joke: şaka yap- 2 → yap- 3. *490:5.* banter: - banter.

- be a joking matter, not serious: şakaya gel- → gel- 1. *997:11.* unimportance: - be unimportant.

- be KEPT, maintained /in/ a place [jewelry in a safe]: /DA/ saklan- 3. *397:8.* preservation: - preserve.

- be kept SECRET /from, by/; - be hidden /from, by/: /DAn, tarafından/ gizlen- 2, /DAn, tarafından/

saklan- 2. *346:6.* concealment: - conceal.

- be KILLED /by [sb], by...ing/: /tarafından, ArAk/ öldürül-. *308:12.* killing: - kill.

lit., ** - be KNOCKED AT [There was a knock at the door.]: kapı çalın- → çalın- 4. *901:16.* impulse, impact: - pound.

- be LATE /FOR/ [subj.: sb for a meeting, appointment; subj.: a vehicle]: /A/ {geç kal-/gecik-} → kal- 1. *845:7.* lateness: - be late.

- be too late for a vehicle, event, or a meeting with a person, - miss: /I/ kaçır- 1. *410:14.* failure: - miss; *843:5.* untimeliness: - miss an opportunity.

- be LAID TO REST, buried, interred /in, by/ [for dead bodies only]: *formal:* /A, {tarafından/CA}/ defnedil-, /DA/ toprağa veril-, / A, {tarafından/CA}/ gömül- [for dead bodies and other objects]. *309:19.* interment: - inter.

- be too LAZY, apathetic, or indifferent to do sth, not - bother or - take the trouble do sth: /A/ üşen-. *102:4.* indifference: not - care; *331:12.* inactivity: - idle.

- be LEFT OVER, - remain: art- 2, kal- 2. *256:5.* remainder: - remain.

- be LEFT, - remain, - come /TO [sb as an inheritance], {from/BY} [sb]/: /A/ kal- 2, /A, DAn/ miras kal- → kal- 2. *479:7.* receiving: - inherit.

- be LEGAL, valid [subj.: money, passport]: geç- 5. *673:8.* legality: - legalize.

- be LET OFF /a: at [a place], b: from [a vehicle], c: by [a driver]/ [passengers]: /a: DA, b: DAn, c: tarafından/ indiril- 2. *912:4.* depression: - depress.

- be LIFTED [martial law], - be repealed, abolished [law, taxes], - be struck down [law]: kalk- 3. *445:2.* repeal: - repeal.

- be LIKED, loved, enjoyed /by/, - be popular /with/: /tarafından/ sevil-. *95:12.* pleasure: - enjoy; *104:19.* love: - love.

- be LISTENED TO [music]: 2 dinlen- 2. *48:10.* hearing: - listen.

- be LOCKED OUT [of house, room]: dışarıda kal-, kapıda kal- → kal- 1. *293:6.* closure: - close.

- be LONELY: yalnızlık çek- → çek- 5. *584:7.* seclusion: - seclude oneself; *871:6.* oneness: - stand alone.

- be LOOKED FOR, sought /by/: /{tarafından/CA}/ aran-. *937:30.* inquiry: - seek.

- be looked UPON, regarded, considered /AS/: /olarak/ görül- 2. *952:11.* belief: - think.
- be or - get LOST: kaybol- → ol- 12. *473:4.* loss: - lose.
- be lost, - lose one's way: yolunu kaybet-. *473:4.* loss: - lose.
- be or - get lost /IN/ thought, for one's mind - wander off, - give oneself up /to/ reverie, - reminisce: {düşünceye/düşüncelere} dal- → dal- 2. *984:9.* distraction, confusion: - muse; ; *988:11.* memory: - reminisce.
- be LOVED: → - be LIKED.
- be LOWERED /a: from, b: to, c: by [a person, agency]/ [subj.: an object]: /a: DAn, b: A, c: {tarafından/CA}/ indiril- 1. *912:4.* depression: - depress.
- be lowered, reduced [prices, rates]: /a: DAn, b: A, c: {tarafından/CA}/ indiril- 3. *631:2.* discount: - discount; *633:6a.* cheapness: - lower prices.
- be LYING DOWN, - be in bed: yat- 1. *22:17.* sleep: - go to bed; *201:5.* horizontalness: - lie.

- be MAD /AT/, angry /{AT/WITH}/: /A/ kız- 1, /A/ küs-, /A/ darıl- 1. *152:17.* resentment, anger: - become angry.
- be MADE OUT, - be seen clearly, - be distinguished: seçil- 2. *27:12.* vision: - see.
- be MADE UP /OF/, composed /OF/, formed /OF/, - consist /OF/: /DAn/ oluş-. *795:3.* composition: - compose.
- be MADLY IN LOVE /WITH/, - be consumed with love /for/, - be mad /ABOUT/; - feel a burning [sexual] desire /for/, *slang:* - have the hots /for/: /A, için/ yan- 7. *104:19.* love:- love.
- be MAILED, posted, sent off [package, letter] /to, by/: /A, tarafından/ postalan-. *176:15.* transferal, transportation: - send; *553:12.* correspondence: - mail.
- be MENTIONED, discussed, written about, related, referred to, spoken about, - occur [facts in a written work] [Where is this topic mentioned?]: geç- 7. *551:8.* information: - inform.
- be MERCIFUL /to/, - have mercy /{ON/UPON}/ [the deceased] [subj.: only God]: /A/ rahmet eyle-. *145:4.* pity: - have pity; *601:4.* acquittal: - acquit.

- be MESSED UP, - get untidy [room, hair]: dağıl- 4. *810:2.* disarrangement: - disarrange.
- be MISTAKEN, wrong: yanıl-. *947:2.* misjudgment: - misjudge; *974:10.* error: - be wrong.
- be MISUNDERSTOOD: yanlış anlaşıl-. *342:2.* misinterpretation: - misinterpret.
- be MIXED, - get mixed /{WITH/INTO}/ [various substances]: /A/ karış- 1. *796:10b.* mixture: - mix, - become mixed.
- be mixed /WITH/ [water with milk], - be added to [water to milk]: /A/ katıl- 1. *253:5.* addition: - add to.
- be MOUNTED [animal], - be boarded [vehicle] /{AT/from}/ [the front, the rear]: /DAn/ binil-. *193:12.* ascent: - mount.
- be MOVED, touched, emotionally affected /BY/: /DAn/ duygulan-, /DAn/ etkilen- 2. *893:7.* influence: - influence.
- be MULTIPLIED /BY/ [5 by 4]: /lA/ çarpıl- 1. *1016:17.* mathematics: - calculate.

- be NAILED, pegged down; - be driven or hammered /{IN/INTO}, by/ [subj.: nail, peg]: /A, {tarafından/CA}/ çakıl- 1. *799:8.* joining: - hook.
- be NAMED, called, dubbed, referred to /AS, by/: /{diye/olarak}, {tarafından/CA}/ {adlandırıl-/isimlendiril-}. *527:13.* nomenclature: - be called.
- be named, appointed, assigned /to [a position], AS [a teacher]/: /A, olarak/ tayin ol- → ol- 12. *615:11.* commission: - appoint.
- be named, appointed, assigned /a: to [a position or a place], b: AS [a teacher], c: by [the Ministry]/: /a: A, b: olarak, c: {tarafından/CA}/ {atan-/tayin edil-}. *615:11.* commission: - appoint.
- be NAUGHTY, - misbehave: yaramazlık {yap-/et-} → yap- 3. *322:4.* misbehavior: - misbehave.
- be NECESSARY, required /{for/in order to}/: /için/ gerek-, /için/ icap et-, /{için/A}/ lâzım ol- → ol- 12. *962:10.* necessity: - be necessary.
- be NERVOUS, agitated, upset, excited, - panic, - lose one's cool [negative emotion]: heyecanlan- 2. *96:16b.* unpleasure: - be distressed; *128:6.* nervousness: - fidget.
- be NO JOKING MATTER, - be serious: şakaya gelME- → şakaya gel- → gel- 1. *996:12.* importance: - matter.
- be NO LONGER VALID, expired, overdue: {vakti/zamanı/süresi}

geç- → geç- 4. *390:9.* disuse: - obsolesce.

- be NOISY, - make noise: **gürültü** {**et-/yap-**}. *53:9.* loudness: - be noisy.
- be NOTICED, observed: **farkedil-**. *940:5.* discovery: - detect.

- be OBEYED and heard, - be heeded: **2 dinlen-** 1. *326:2.* obedience: - obey.
- be OBLIGED /to/, - be forced /to/ [not with {**tarafından/CA**}], - have /to/: **-mAk zorunda kal-** → kal- 1. *962:10.* necessity: - be necessary.
- be OBSERVED, seen: **görül-** 1. *27:12.* vision: - see.
- be OBSESSED, preoccupied /WITH/: /A/ **aklı takıl-** → takıl- 2. *930:20.* thought: - occupy the mind.
- be OBSTINATE, stubborn: **inat et-** 1. *361:7.* obstinacy: - balk.
- be OBSTRUCTED, blocked [roads] /by/ sb: /{**tarafından/CA**}/ **kapatıl-** 4. *293:7.* closure: - stop, - stop up.
- be obstructed, blocked [roads] /to [traffic], {DUE TO/BECAUSE OF} sth: snow]/: /A, DAn/ **kapan-** 4. *293:7.* closure: - stop, - stop up.
- be OCCUPIED, taken, held [place, seat]: **tutul-** 2. *474:7.* retention: - hold, - keep; *480:14.* taking: - seize.
- be occupied or busy /with/, - deal /with/: /lA/ **meşgul ol-** 1 → ol- 12. *330:10.* activity: - be busy; *724:11.* occupation: - busy oneself with.
- be OF ASSISTANCE /TO/, - be helpful /to/, - help /θ/, - assist /θ/: /A/ **yardımcı ol-** → ol- 12. *449:11.* aid: - aid.
- be OF NO USE, in vain, for nothing [efforts, money]: **boşa git-** → git- 5. *391:8.* uselessness: - be useless.

Be OFF!: → Beat it!
- be off IN THE CLOUDS, - let one's mind, attention wander: **dalga geç-** 1 → geç- 1. *983:3.* inattention: - wander.
- be OFFENDED or hurt /BY/; - be mad or angry /AT, because/, - be put out /WITH, because/: /A, DIğI için/ **küs-**. *152:17.* resentment, anger: - become angry; *152:21.* : - offend.
- be offended or hurt /BY, because of/, - take offense /AT/: /A, DAn dolayı/ **alın-** 3. *156:5.* disrespect: - offend.
- be offended, hurt [not physically] /BY/: /A/ **darıl-** 2, /A/ **kırıl-** 3. *152:21.* resentment, anger: - offend.
- be an OLD MAID, - remain UNMARRIED [for a woman]: **evde kal-** → kal- 1. *565:5.* celibacy: - be unmarried.

- be ON [light, electricity], - be burning [light]: **yan-** 5. *1024:23.* light: - shine.
- be on CLOUD NINE, in seventh heaven, - be overjoyed, - have a ball: **bayram et-**. *95:11.* pleasure: - be pleased.
- be on FIRE, - be burning: **yan-** 1. *1019:24.* heating: - burn.
- be on TARGET, - get it right, - be right, - be right on the mark: **isabet kaydet-** 2. → kaydet- 5. *409:7b.* success: - succeed in specific ways; *972:10.* truth: - be right.
- be on THE PILL: **doğum kontrol hapı kullan-**. *1011:10.* hindrance: - hinder.
- be on THE {POINT/VERGE} OF BEING: → - be almost.
- be ONE'S BUSINESS, - concern [This is none of your business. This concerns you.]: /I/ **ilgilendir-** 2. *897:3.* involvement: - be involved.
- be OPENED /by/ [subj.: door, window]: /{**tarafından/CA**}/ **açıl-** 1. *292:11.* opening: - open.
- be opened /to/, cleared, unblocked [roads to traffic]: /A/ **açıl-** 8. *292:12.* opening: - unclose.
- be opened, taken up [topic, subject]: **açıl-** 10. *404:3.* undertaking: - undertake.
- be OPERATED ON, - have or - undergo an operation: **ameliyat geçir-** → geçir- 2, **ameliyat ol-** → ol- 10.1. *91:29.* therapy: - undergo treatment.
- be operated on /BY/: /A, not with **tarafından**/ **ameliyat ol-** → ol- 10.1. *91:29.* therapy: - undergo treatment.
- be ORPHANED, - have lost both parents: **öksüz kal-** [More accurately: - have lost one's mother (father remains alive}. Sometimes, but not accurately: - have lost only one's father] → kal- 1. *256:5.* remainder: - remain.
- be OSTRACIZED, cast out, excluded /by, from/: /{**tarafından/CA**}, DAn/ **dışlan-**. *772:4.* exclusion: - exclude.
- be or - get OUT OF BREATH, - pant, - huff and puff /from/: /DAn/ **nefes nefese kal-** → kal- 1. *21:5.* fatigue: - burn out; *318:21.* * 1. wind: - breathe.
- be OVER, - come to an end, - conclude, - end, - finish: **bit-** 1 [most subjects], **sona er-** [most subjects] → er-, **din-** [weather: wind, rain, snow, hail, storm; pain: headache; tears; emotion: anger]. *819:6.* end: - come to an end.

- be over, - let out, - break up [always with the notion of the dispersion of the participants: subj.: party, meeting, concert, match, film]: **dağıl-** 2. *770:8.* dispersion: - disband.

- be OVERDUE, expired, no longer valid: **{vakti/zamanı/süresi} geç-** → geç- 4. *390:9.* disuse: - obsolesce.

- be OVERJOYED, in seventh heaven, on cloud nine, - have a ball: **bayram et-** . *95:11.* pleasure: - be pleased.

- be OVERLOOKED, - escape one's notice or one's eye [a fact, an error]: **gözden kaç-** → kaç- 1. *340:6.* neglect: - neglect.

- be PAID UP, settled [accounts]: **kapatıl-** 7. *624:13.* payment: - pay in full.

- be PATIENT: **sabret-.** *134:4.* patience: - be patient.

- be PEELED [vegetables: potatoes] /by/: **/tarafından/ soyul-** 1. *6:8.* unclothing: - peel.

- be PEGGED, nailed down; - be driven or hammered /{IN/INTO}, by/ [subj.: nail, peg]: **/A, {tarafından/CA}/ çakıl-** 1. *799:8.* joining: - hook.

- be PHOTOGRAPHED unexpectedly or unawares, - be caught /ON/ camera, /BY/ the lens: **/A/ yakalan-** 3. *714:14.* photography: - photograph.

- be PICKED UP, tidied up, straightened up [messy room] /by/: **/tarafından/ toplan-** 2. *807:12.* arrangement: - tidy, tidy up.

- be or - get {PILED/BACKED} UP, - pile UP [subj.: traffic]: **sıkış-** 3. *260:8.* contraction: - squeeze; *769:19.* assemblage: - pile.

- be a PITY, shame /FOR/: **/A/ yazık ol-** → ol- 12. *113:* * *13.* regret: INTERJ. what a pity!

- be PLAYED [musical instrument, piece of music] /by/: **/{tarafından/CA}/ çalın-** 2. *708:39a.* music: - play sth.

- be PLEASED, happy, satisfied /WITH/: **/DAn/ memnun kal-** → kal- 1, **/DAn/ memnun ol-** → ol- 12. *95:12.* pleasure: - enjoy.

- be pleased, glad /a: {ABOUT/AT/WITH}, b: because, c: θ [that]/: **/a: A, b: DIğI için, c: A/ sevin-.** *95:11.* pleasure: - be pleased.

- be pleased /θ/ [that]: **/A/ memnun ol-.** → ol- 12. *95:12.* pleasure: - enjoy.

- be pleased /WITH/, - like /θ/; - enjoy /θ/: **/DAn/ hoşlan-.** *95:12* pleasure: - enjoy.

- be pleased /WITH/, approving [said of God, describing His reaction to a person's good deed]: **/DAn/ razı**

ol- 2 → ol- 12. *95:11.* pleasure: - be pleased; *150:6.* gratitude: INTERJ. thanks!

- be POPULAR /with/, - be liked, loved, enjoyed /by/: **/tarafından/ sevil-.** *95:12.* pleasure: - enjoy; *104:19.* love: - love.

- be POSSIBLE: **ol- 4, mümkün ol-.** → ol- 12. *965:4* possibility: - be possible.

- be POSTED, mailed, sent off [package, letter] /to, by/: **/A, tarafından/ postalan-.** *176:15.* transferal, transportation: - send; *553:12.* correspondence: - mail.

- be POSTPONED, delayed /a: for, b: to, c: {till/until}, d: by/': /a: A, b: A, c: A kadar, d: {tarafından/CA}/ **{ertelen-/tehir edil-}, /A/ kal-** 4 [**Kal-** is not used with an agent noun, as are the forms above.] *845:9.* lateness: - postpone.

- be POURED OUT or spilled /a: ON, b: on, c: by/': /a: A, b: **{üstüne/üzerine},** c: **{tarafından/CA}/ dökül-** 2. *80:15a.* cleanness: - dirty; *176:17.* transferal, transportation: - ladle; *238:17a.* stream: - make overflow; *390:7.* disuse: - discard; *908:25.* ejection: - disgorge.

- be PRAISED /by, for/: **/{tarafından/CA}, nedeniyle/ övül-.** *509:12.* approval: - praise.

- be PREOCCUPIED, obsessed /WITH/: **/A/ aklı takıl-** → takıl- 2. *930:20.* thought: - occupy the mind.

- be PREPARED, readied, set up, drawn up /by/: **/{tarafından/CA}/ hazırlan-** 2. *405:6.* preparation: - prepare.

- be PRESENT /{at/in}/ [subj.: person or thing]: **/DA/ bulun-** → bulun- 2, **/DA/ ol-** 2. *221:6.* presence: - be present; *760:8.* existence: - exist.

- be present /{at/in}/ [subj.: person]: **/DA/ hazır bulun-** → bulun- 2, **/DA/ var ol-** → **{var/yok} ol-** a) 2 → ol- 12. *221:6.* presence: - be present; *760:8.* existence: - exist.

- be present, - be found, - occur /in/ [words in a text: Is this word present in the document?]: **/DA/ geç-** 8. *221:6.* presence: - be present.

- be PROHIBITED, forbidden /by/: **/{tarafından/CA}/ yasaklan-.** *444:3.* prohibition: - prohibit.

- be PROMISING, - have a promising future: **{gelecek/istikbal} vadet-.** *124:10.* hope: - give hope; *133:13.* premonition: - promise.

- be PRONOUNCED [words]: **telâffuz edil-.** *524:23.* speech: - say.

- be PROUD /OF/, - feel pride /IN/, - take pride /IN/: /lA/ iftihar et-, /lA/ {övün-/öğün-} 1, /{lA/DAn}/ gurur duy- 1 → duy- 3, /DAn/ kıvanç duy- → duy- 3. *136:5*. pride: - take pride.
- be PUBLISHED /in, by/: /DA, {tarafından/CA}/ yayımlan- 1. *548:14*. printing: - print.
- be PULLED down, torn down; - be demolished, wrecked /by, with/; - be destroyed; - be ruined [subj.: building]: /{tarafından/CA}, lA/ yıkıl- 1. *395:17*. destruction: - demolish.
- be PUNCHED, - get a punch: yumruk ye- → ye- 2. *901:14*. impulse, impact: - hit.
- be PUNISHED /BY/, - receive punishment /from/: /DAn/ ceza al- → al- 3. *604:10*. punishment: - punish.
- be punished /with/: /lA/ cezalandırıl- 1. *604:10*. punishment: - punish.
- be punished or fined /BY [sb], FOR [sth]/: /DAn, DAn/ ceza ye- → ye- 2. *603:5*. penalty: - fine; *604:20*. punishment: - be punished.
- be PUT OFF: → - be POSTPONED.
- be put /ON/ a vehicle or mount [horse], - be boarded [subj.: person: He was put ON the train by his teacher.]: /A/ bindiril-. *193:12*. ascent: - mount.
- be put OUT /WITH, because/, - be mad or angry /AT, because/; - be offended or hurt /by/: /A, DIğI için/ küs-. *152:17*. resentment, anger: - become angry; *152:21*. : - offend.
- be put THROUGH /to/, - be connected /to/ [the (telephone) operator]: /A/ bağlan- 3. *799:11*. joining: - be joined.
- be put UNDER ARREST, - be arrested /by/: /{tarafından/CA}/ tutuklan-. *429:15*. confinement: - arrest.

- be QUICK, - hurry: çabuk ol- → ol- 12. *401:5*. haste: - makc hastc.
- be QUIET, - become silent, - stop talking, - shut up: sesini kes- → kes- 4, sus- 2. *51:7*. silence: - fall silent.

- be RAISED [crops, animals], - be grown [crops]: yetiş- 7. *1067:16*. agriculture: - farm; *1068:6*. animal husbandry: - raise.
- be REACHED, contacted /AT/ [Ahmet can be reached AT this (telephone) number.]: /DAn/ ulaşıl-. *343:8*. communication: - communicate with, - get in touch with.

- be READIED, prepared, set up, drawn up /by/: /{tarafından/CA}/ hazırlan- 2. *405:6*. preparation: - prepare.
- be READY, prepared: hazır ol- → ol- 12, ol- 9.1. *405:14*. preparation: - be prepared.
- be ready, finished /BY/ a specified time [subj.: a thing: suit]: /A/ yetiş- 3. *405:14*. preparation: - be prepared.
- be ready TO EXPLODE, - feel like screaming /{ON ACCOUNT OF/DUE TO}/, - blow up, - explode, - fly off the handle, - lose one's temper, one's cool: /DAn/ patla- 2. *152:20*. resentment, anger: - fly into a rage.
- be REALIZED, - come true [plans, dreams, desires, wishes], - work out [subj.: plans]: gerçekleş-. *972:12*. truth: - come true.
- be RECEIVED, taken /from/ [Where was this letter received from?]: /DAn/ alın- 1. *480:21*. taking: - take from.
- be RECONCILED, - come to an understanding, - make up /with/ sb [after a quarrel]: /lA/ arası düzel-, /lA/ barış-. *465:10*. pacification: - make up.
- be REDUCED, lowered [prices, rates]: /a: DAn, b: A, c: {tarafından/CA}/ indiril- 3. *631:2*. discount: - discount; *633:6a*. cheapness: - lower prices.
- be REFERRED TO /AS, by/, - be named, called, dubbed /θ/: /{diye/olarak}, {tarafından/CA}/ {adlandırıl-/isimlendiril-}. *527:13*. nomenclature: - be called.
- be REGARDED, looked UPON, considered /AS/: /olarak/ görül- 2. *952:11*. belief: - think.
- be RELIEVED of one's {duties/position}, - be fired: görevden alın- → alın- 1, görevine son veril- → son veril- → veril-, işinden ol- → ol- 7. *908:19*. ejection: - dismiss.
- be or - feel RELUCTANT, hesitant, embarassed to do sth /in the presence of/, - hesitate /to/, not - dare /to/ do sth: /{A/DAn}/ çekin-. *325:4*. unwillingness: - demur; *362:7*. irresolution: - hesitate.
- be REPEALED, abolished [law, taxes], - be lifted [martial law], - be struck down [law]: kalk- 3. *445:2*. repeal: - repeal.
- be REQUIRED, necessary, needed /{for/in order to}/: /için/ gerek-, /için/ icap et-, /{için/A}/ lâzım

ol- → ol- 12. *962:10.* necessity: - be necessary.

- be RESCUED, saved /by, from/: /{tarafından/CA}, D A n / kurtarıl-. *398:3.* rescue: - rescue.

- be rescued, saved /from/, - escape /{θ/from}/, - manage to get away /from/, - avoid /θ/, - survive /θ/ [accident]: → - be saved, recued /from/.

- be REUNITED /WITH/, - meet again after a long absence, - meet, - come together [persons]: /A/ kavuş- 1. *799:11.* joining: - be joined.

- be REVEALED, - come to light, - come out [the truth], - appear, - turn up, - turn out, - come forward [the guilty person]: {ortaya/meydana} çık- → çık- 3. *351:8.* disclosure: - be revealed.

- be REWARDED /with/, - be awarded a prize, - be given a reward /OF/: /lA/ ödüllendiril-. *624:10.* payment: - pay.

- be or - get RID /OF/, - avoid sb or sth unpleasant, - shake /OFF/ [an annoying person, classes, debts, flies]: /DAn/ kurtul- 2. *368:6.* avoidance: - avoid.

- be RIGHT, suitable, appropriate /FOR/ [subj.: a particular behavior for a person]: /A/ yakış- 1. *866:3.* conformity: - conform.

- be right, suitable, timely /FOR/ [car for need, class for schedule]: /A/ denk düş- 1 → düş- 1, /A/ uygun düş- → düş- 1. *842:6.* timeliness: - be timely; *866:3.* conformity: - conform.

- be right, - be right on the mark, - get it right, - be on target: isabet kaydet- 2. → kaydet- 5. *409:7b.* success: - succeed in specific ways; *972:10.* truth: - be right.

- be RIPPED, torn /{OUT OF/from}, by/ [pages from a book]: /DAn, tarafından/ yırtıl-. *192:10.* extraction: - extract; *801:11.* separation: - sever.

- be ROASTED /by/ [The meat is being roasted by the cook.]: /tarafından/ kızartıl- 3. *11:4a.* cooking: - cook sth.

- be ROBBED, stripped of valuables /by/: /tarafından/ soyul- 2. *482:14.* theft: - rob.

- be RUDE, - go too far, - overstep the limit /BY...ing/: /{ArAk/mAklA}/ çok ol- → ol- 12, /{ArAk/ mAklA}/ ileri git- 2 → git- 1a. *505:3.* * 1. discourtesy: - be discourteous; *909:9.* overrunning: - overstep; *992:10.* excess: - overdo.

- be RUNG [bell]: çalın- 3. *54:8a.* resonance: - ring, - cause to ring.

- be SAD, sorry, distressed: üzül-, üzüntü duy- → duy- 3. *112:16.* sadness: - lose heart.

- be SAID, - be called [How is **merhaba** said in English? What is this called in Turkish.]: /A/ den-. *527:13.* nomenclature: - be called.

- be SATISFIED, content /with/: /A/ razı ol- 1 → ol- 12, /lA/ yetin- 1. *107:5.* contentment: - be content.

- be SAUTÉD, fried /by/ [The pieces of bread are being sautéd by the cook.]: /tarafından/ kızartıl- 1. *11:4a.* cooking: for sth - cook.

- be SAVED, rescued /by, from/: /{tarafından/CA}, D A n / kurtarıl-. *398:3.* rescue: - rescue.

- be saved, rescued /from/, - escape /{θ/from}/, - manage to get away /from/, - avoid /θ/, - survive /θ/ [accident]: /DAn/ kurtul- 1. [This verb is not used with an agent noun preceded by **tarafından** as in 'He was saved by the police.' For such usage, see **kurtarıl-**.] *369:6.* escape: - escape, *398:3.* rescue: - rescue.

- be saved, kept, set aside /FOR, by/: /için, tarafından/ saklan- 4. *386:12.* store, supply: - reserve.

- be SCORCHED, singed /{BY/from}/, burned, - get burned; - get a burn, - get scalded; - get sunburned: /DAn/ yan- 3. *1019:24.* heating: - burn.

- be SEEN, observed: görül- 1. *27:12.* vision: - see.

- be seen, - appear, or - come into view [sun in the sky]: görün- 1. [This verb is not used with {tarafından/CA}, i.e., not as in 'She has not been seen BY anybody', for which → görül- 1.] *31:4* visibility: - show; *33:8.* appearance: - appear.

- be seen CLEARLY, - be distinguished, - be made out: seçil- 2. *27:12.* vision: - see.

- be SEIZED /BY/ [a current of water, a state inspiring an emotion (beauty), an emotion (fear, panic, anxiety), a moral weakness]: /A/ kapıl-. *105:12.* excitement: - excite; *480:14.* taking: - seize.

- be seized, caught, grasped, taken hold of /BY/ [body part: the neck]: /DAn/ tutul- 1. *474:6.* retention: - hold, - grip; *480:14.* taking: - seize.

- be seized, grabbed, snatched /by/; - be caught /by/; - be collared, nabbed /by/ [the police]: /{tarafından/CA}/ yakalan- 1. *480:14.* taking: - seize.

- be SELECTED, chosen, picked /for, by/: /{A/için}, {tarafından/CA}/ seçil- 1. *371:13*. choice: - choose.

- be SENT OFF, mailed, posted [package, letter] /to, by/: /A, tarafından/ postalan-. *176:15*. transferal, transportation: - send; *553:12*. correspondence: - mail.

- be SENTENCED, condemned /TO/ a punishment: /lA/ cezalandırıl- 2, /A/ mahkûm ol- 1 → ol- 12. *602:3*. condemnation: - condemn.

- be SERIOUS, no joking matter: şakaya gelME- → şakaya gel- → gel- 1. *996:12*. importance: - matter.

- be SET, wound [watch, clock, meter, toy, music box]: kurul- 2. *787:7*. agreement: - make agree; *914:9*. rotation: - rotate.

- be set ASIDE /FOR, by/, - be saved, kept /FOR, by/: /A, tarafından/ saklan- 4. *386:12*. store, supply: - reserve.

- be set UP, prepared, readied, drawn up /by/: /{tarafından/CA}/ hazırlan- 2. *405:6*. preparation: - prepare.

- be SETTLED, paid up [accounts]: kapatıl- 7. *624:13*. payment: - pay in full.

- be SHAKY, unsteady /{WITH/ BECAUSE OF} [a reaction of shock to bad news or a frightening event or a sign of anger]: /DAn/ eli ayağı tutMA- → tut- 2. *127:14*. fear, frighteningness: - tremble; *152:25a*. anger: gestures of anger; *916:11*. agitation: - shake.

- be a SHAME, pity /FOR/: /A/ yazık ol- → ol- 12. *98:31*. unpleasantness: INTERJ. eeyuck!

- be SHOCKED, - go into shock /AT/ [non-medical]: /karşısında/ {şoke/ şok} ol- → ol- 10.1. *131:7*. inexpectation: - surprise.

- be SHORT OF MONEY, hard up: sıkış- 4. *619:5*. poverty: - be poor; *1012:12*. difficulty: - get into trouble.

- be a SHOW-OFF, - show off: gösteriş yap- → yap- 3. *501:16*. ostentation: - show off.

- be SHUT, closed down permanently /by/ [subj.: organization, business, school]: /{tarafından/CA}/ kapatıl- 3. *293:8*. closure: - close shop.

- be SHUT UP, closed up /IN, by/: /A, /{tarafından/CA}/ kapatıl- 5. *429:12*. confinement: - confine.

- be SICK /OF/, fed up, disgusted /WITH/, tired /OF/: /DAn/ {bık- /usan-}, /DAn/ sıkıl- 1. *118:7b*. tedium: - get bored.

- be SILENT, remain silent, not to say anything: sus- 1. *51:5*. silence: - be silent.

- be SILLY, - talk nonsense, - talk {garbage/rot}: saçmala-. *520:5*. meaninglessness: - talk nonsense; *922:6*. foolishness: - be foolish.

- be SINGED /{BY/from}/, - get or - be burned, - be scorched; - get a burn, - get scalded; - get sunburned: /DAn/ yan- 3. *1019:24*. heating: - burn.

- be SITTING /in/, - sit /in/ [a chair, position: He is sitting in that chair. Not motion into a sitting position as in: Sit (down) in that chair.]: /DA/ otur- 2. *173:10*. quiescence: - sit.

- be SITUATED, located /{in/at}/: /DA/ bulun- 2, /DA/ ol- 2. *221:6*. presence: - be present; *760:8*. existence: - exist.

- be a certain SIZE [right size, large, small] /FOR/: /A/ gel- 2. *866:3*. conformity: - conform.

- be SLAPPED, - get a slap: tokat ye- → ye- 2. *604:12*. punishment: - slap; *901:19*. impulse, impact: - slap.

- be SLOW, behind, - run late [clock, watch]: geri kal- 2 → kal- 1. *845:7*. lateness: - be late.

- be SMASHED, broken into pieces, - be cut up, chopped up, torn into pieces /by/: /{tarafından/CA}/ parçalan- 1. *801:13*. separation: - shatter.

- be SMOKED: içil- 2. *89:14*. tobacco: - use tobacco.

- be SOLD /a: to [sb], b: {FOR/AT} [in total or per unit], c: {FOR/AT} [only per unit], d: {BY [the kilo]/FOR [money]}, e: by [sb]/, - sell /FOR/: /a: A, b: A, c: DAn, d: lA, e: (tarafından/CA}/ satıl-. *734:12*. sale: - be sold.

- be SORRY [in words of apology: I'm sorry, I can't go tonight.]: özür dile- → dile- 2. *658:5*. atonement: - apologize.

- be sorry, sad, sorry, distressed [about some event]: üzül-, üzüntü duy- → duy- 3. *112:16*. sadness: - lose heart.

- be sorry, - regret [an act one has committed]: /a: DIğInA, b: DIğI için, c: DIğI.nDAn dolayı/ pişman ol- → ol- 12, /DIğI için/ üzüntü çek- 2 → çek- 5. *113:6*. regret: - regret.

- be SOUGHT, looked for /by/ [A child is being sought.]: /{tarafından/CA}/ aran-. *937:30*. inquiry: - seek.

- be SPILLED or poured out /a: ON, b: on, c: by/: /a: A, b: {üstüne/üzerine}, c: {tarafından/CA}/ dökül- 2.

486

80:15a. cleanness: - dirty; *176:17.* transferal, transportation: - ladle; *238:17a.* stream: - make overflow; *390:7.* disuse: - discard; *908:25.* ejection: - disgorge.

- be SPLIT, divided /INTO, by/ [house into rooms by owners]: /A, {tarafından/CA}/ ayrıl- 2, /A, {tarafından/CA}/ bölün-. *801:8.* separation: - separate.
- be STARTLED /BY/, - start [subj.: person or animal], - shy [subj.: animal only] [All these English verbs indicate a sudden physical movement in reaction to a fright.]: /DAn/ ürk- 1. *131:5.* inexpectation: - be startled.
- be STIFLED, suffocated, - suffocate, - smother, - be strangled, - feel faint: boğul- 2. *308:18.* killing: - strangle.
- be STOLEN /from, by/: /DAn, {tarafından/CA}/ çalın- 1. *482:13.* theft: - steal.
- be STOPPED, cut off, interrupted [electricity, water, gas, phone conversation] /by/: /tarafından/ kesil- 3. *856:10.* cessation: - interrupt.
- be STRAIGHTENED UP, tidied up, picked up [messy room] /by/: /tarafından/ toplan- 2. *807:12.* arrangement: - tidy, tidy up.
- be STRANGLED, suffocated, stifled, - suffocate, - feel faint: boğul- 2. *308:18.* killing: - strangle.
- be STRUCK DOWN [law], - be lifted [martial law], - be abolished, repealed [law, tax]: kalk- 3. *445:2.* repeal: - repeal.
- be struck down /BY/, - catch /θ/, - come down /WITH/ an illness: /A/ yakalan- 2. *85:46a.* disease: - take sick in general.
- be STUBBORN, obstinate: inat et- 1. *361:7.* obstinacy: - balk.
- be STUCK UP, STUCK ON ONESELF, conceited: kendini beğen-. *140:6.* vanity: - be stuck on oneself.
- be SUBTRACTED /FROM/: /DAn/ çık- 9. *255:9.* subtraction: - subtract; *1016:17.* mathematics: - calculate.
- be SUCCESSFUL /IN/, - succeed /IN/: /I/ başar-. *409:7a.* success: - succeed.
- be successful /in/, - demonstrate success /in/: /DA/ başarı göster- → göster- 1. *409:9.* success: - score a success.
- be SUFFOCATED: → - be strangled.
- be SUITABLE, right, appropriate /FOR/ [subj.: certain behavior for a person]: /A/ yakış- 1. *866:3.* conformity: - conform.
- be suitable, right, timely /FOR/ [That class fits my schedule.]: /A/ denk

düş- 1 → düş- 1, /A/ uygun düş- → düş- 1. *842:6.* timeliness: - be timely; *866:3.* conformity: - conform.
- be SUNK, done for, in serious trouble; - have had it: *colloq.:* hapı yut-, yan- 6. *395:11.* destruction: - do; *1012:11.* difficulty: - have difficulty.
- be or - become SURE, certain /OF/, - be sure, certain, convinced /θ/ that; - become sure, certain /OF/: /{DAn/A}/ emin ol- → ol- 12. *969:9.* certainty: - be certain.
- be SURPRISED, amazed, astonished /AT/: /A/ hayret et-, /A/ şaş-, /A/ şaşır- 2. *122:5.* wonder: - wonder; *131:7.* inexpectation: - surprise.
- be SWEPT OFF ONE'S FEET, - fall /FOR/ [i.e., - fall in love with]: /A, not with tarafından/ çarpıl- 2. *104:22.* love: - fall in love.
- be SWITCHED or turned OFF /by/ [subj.: lights, electricity, lamps, computer, oven, stove, gas burner, radio, TV]: /{tarafından/CA}/ kapatıl- 2. *856:12.* cessation: - turn off; *1031:25.* electricity: - electrify.
- be switched or turned ON /by/ [subj.: lights, lamps]: /{tarafından/CA}/ açıl- 5. *817:11.* beginning: - inaugurate; *1031:25.* electricity: - electrify.

- be TAKEN, received /from/ [Where was this article taken from?]: /DAn/ alın- 1. *480:21.* taking: - take from.
- be taken [medicine when taken with water, lit., - be drunk]: içil- 4. *8:22.* eating: - devour.
- be taken, occupied, held [place, seat]: tutul- 2. *474:7.* retention: - hold, - keep; *480:14.* taking: - seize.
- be taken CARE OF [affairs, matters], attended to, dealt with, handled /by/: /{tarafından/CA}/ görül- 3. *982:5.* attention: - attend to.
- be taken in FOR TREATMENT: tedavi altına alın- → alın- 1. *91:24.* treatment: - treat.
- be taken HOLD OF /BY/ [body part: the neck], - be seized, caught, grasped /BY/: /DAn/ tutul- 1. *474:6.* retention: - hold, - grip.
- be taken IN, deceived, fooled /BY [a person or thing]/: /A, not with tarafından/ {aldan-/kan-}. *356:14.* deception: - deceive.
- be taken UP, considered, broached [subject, topic]: açıl- 10, ele alın- → alın- 1. *404:3.* undertaking: - undertake.
- be TERRIFIED, badly frightened: ödü kop- → kop- 1. *127:10.* fear, frighteningness: - fear.

- be or - get THIRSTY: **susa-**. *100:19.* desire: - hunger.
- be THRILLED, enthusiastic, - get excited [positive emotion]: **heyecanlan-** 1. *95:11.* pleasure: - be pleased; *105:18.* excitement: - be excited.
- be TIDIED UP, straightened up, picked up [messy room] /by/: **/tarafından/ toplan-** 2. *807:12.* arrangement: - tidy, tidy up.
- be TIED /{to/AROUND}, with, by/, - be connected, tied up, fastened, bound /to, with, by/: **/A, lA, tarafından/ bağlan-** 1. *799:9.* joining: - bind.
- be or - get TIRED /from/ [an activity], - tire [oneself]: **/DAn/ yorul-**. *21:4.* fatigue: - fatigue.
- be or - get tired /OF/, bored /WITH/, fed up, disgusted /WITH/: **/DAn/ {bık-/usan-}, /DAn/ sıkıl-** 1. *118:7b.* tedium: - get bored.
- be tired OUT, exhausted, for one's strength - give out: **{gücü/takatı} tüken-**. *21:5.* fatigue: - burn out.
- be /TO/, - go /to/ [Have you ever been to Ankara?]: **/A/ git-** 1a. *177:25.* travel: - go to.
- be TOASTED /by/ [The bread is being toasted by the cook.]: **/tarafından/ kızartıl-** 2. *11:4a.* cooking: - cook sth.
- be TORN, ripped /{OUT OF/from}, by/ [pages from book]: **/DAn, tarafından/ yırtıl-**. *192:10.* extraction: - extract.
- be torn INTO PIECES, broken, cut up, chopped up, smashed /by/: **/{tarafından/CA}/ parçalan-** 1. *801:13.* separation: - shatter.
- be TOUCHED, moved, emotionally affected /BY/: **/DAn/ duygulan-, /DAn/ etkilen-** 2. *893:7.* influence: - influence.
- be TOWED AWAY /BY/ [car]: **/{tarafından/CA}/ çektiril-**. *904:4.* pulling: - pull.
- be TRANSFERRED /to/ another location [sb in a certain position or post]: **/A/ tayin ol-** 2 → ol- 12. *271:9.* transference: - transfer.
- be TRANSFORMED /from, into/, - turn /from, into/ [love into hate, snow into snowstorm]: **/DAn, A/ dönüş-**. *851:6.* change: - be changed.
- be TREATED [for an illness], - receive or undergo treatment: **tedavi gör-** → gör- 3. *91:29.* therapy: - undergo treatment.
- be TROUBLE, troublesome, an inconvenience /FOR/: **/A/ zahmet ol-** → ol- 12. *96:16a.* unpleasure: - distress; *504: * 20.* courtesy: polite

expressions; *995:4.* inexpedience: - inconvenience.
- be TROUBLED, upset, disturbed /{BY/AT}/, sorry, distressed /AT/, out of sorts, in a bad mood: **/A/ canı sıkıl-** 3 → sıkıl- 1. *96:16b.* unpleasure: - be distressed.
- be TURNED or switched OFF /by/ [subj.: [lights, electricity, lamps, computer, oven, stove, gas burner, radio, TV]: **/{tarafından/CA}/ kapatıl-** 2. *856:12.* cessation: - turn off; *1031:25.* electricity: - electrify.
- be turned or switched ON /by/ [subj.: lights, lamps]: **/{tarafından/CA}/ açıl-** 5. *817:11.* beginning: - inaugurate; *1031:25.* electricity: - electrify.
- be or - get turned on sexually: **tahrik ol-** → ol- 12, **heyecanlan-** 3. *105:12.* excitement: - excite.

- be UNABLE TO GET TO SLEEP /a: {from/BECAUSE OF}, b: because, c: because of/: **/a: DAn, b: DIğI için, c: yüzünden/ uykusu kaç-** → kaç- 1. *23:3.* wakefulness: - keep awake.
- be UNBLOCKED, cleared, opened /to/ [roads to traffic]: **/A/ açıl-** 8. *292:12.* opening: - unclose.
- be or - become UNCOMFORTABLE, - feel ill at ease: **rahatsız ol-** 2 → ol- 10.2. *96:13.* unpleasure: - annoy.
- be or - find oneself UNDER PRESSURE, in a tight spot, in difficulty, - get in a jam: **sıkış-** 4. *297:13.* weight: - burden; *1012:12.* difficulty: - get into trouble.
- be UNDERSTOOD /by/, - be or - become clear, - be determined: **/{tarafından/CA}/ anlaşıl-**. *521:5.* intelligibility: - understand.
- be UNFAITHFUL /TO/, - cheat /ON/ [wife to husband]: **/I/ aldat-** 2. *356:18.* deception: - cheat; *645:12.* improbity: - be unfaithful.
- be UNIMPORTANT, - make NO difference, NOT - matter: **fark etME-** → fark et-. *997:9.* unimportance: - be unimportant.
- be UNSTEADY, shaky [a reaction of shock to bad news or a frightening event]: **/DAn/ eli ayağı tutMA-** → tut- 2. *127:14.* fear, frighteningness: - tremble; *152:25a.* anger: gestures of anger; *916:11.* agitation: - shake.
- be UP [time], - expire, - run out: **{süre/vakit/zaman} dol-** → dol- 2, **{vakit/zaman/süre} geç-** → geç- 4. *390:9.* disuse: - obsolesce; *820:5.* time: - elapse.

- be UP FOR [event: movie, concert]: **iste-** 1 a) 1. *100:14.* desire: - desire.
- be UP TO STH; - stir things up, - stir up trouble: **karıştır-** 5. *381:9.* plan: - plot; *1012:14.* difficulty: - cause trouble.
- be UPSET, distressed, - feel terrible, - feel anguish [at bad news]: **fena ol-** 2 → ol- 10.2. *96:16b.* unpleasure: - be distressed.
- be upset, disturbed, troubled /{BY/AT}/, sorry, distressed /AT/, out of sorts, in a bad mood [not as strong as **fena ol-** 2 above]: /A/ **canı sıkıl-** 3 → **sıkıl-** 1. *96:16b.* unpleasure: - be distressed.
- be upset, distressed, sad, sorry: **üzül-, üzüntü duy-.** *112:16.* sadness: - lose heart.
- be or - get upset, agitated, excited [negative emotion], nervous [at exam time], - panic, - lose one's cool: **heyecanlan-** 2. *96:16b.* unpleasure: - be distressed; *128:6.* nervousness: - fidget.
- be upset [subj.: stomach], - feel sick to one's stomach, - have an upset stomach, - feel nauseated, nauseous, - get queasy: **midesi bulan-.** *85:46b.* disease: - take sick in particular ways.
- be USED TO, accustomed /to/, - get used /to/: /A/ **alış-** 1. *373:12.* custom, habit: - be used to.
- be USED UP, for no more - be left, - run out of [supplies: food, fuel]: **bit-** 3, **tüken-.** *388:4.* consumption: - be consumed.

- be VALID, legal [subj.: money, passport]: **geç-** 5. *673:8.* legality: - legalize.
- be VENTILATED [room], aired out [room, clothes]: **havalan-** 1. *317:10.* air, weather: - air.
- be VERIFIED, confirmed, corroborated /by/ [fact]: /{tarafından/CA}/ **doğrulan-,** /{tarafından/CA}/ **tasdik edil-.** *969:12.* certainty: - verify.

- be WASHED, bathed /{with [soap]/IN [warm water]}, by/: /1A, tarafından/ **yıkan-** 2. *79:19.* cleanness: - wash.
- be WEARING [clothing, size 38], - have on clothing [Also: - don, - PUT on clothing]: **giy-.** *5:43.* clothing: - wear, - have on.
- be WEIGHED /by/: /tarafından/ **tartıl-** 1. *297:10.* weight: - weigh; *300:10.* measurement: - measure.
- be WELCOME /to/: /A/ **hoş gel-** in Hoş geldin[niz]! 1 'Welcome!' →

gel- 1. *585:14.* hospitality, welcome: INTERJ. welcome!
- be WILLING /to/, - consent /to/, - agree /to/ do sth: /A/ **razı ol-** 1 → ol- 12. *441:2.* consent: - consent.
- be willing, inclined /to/, - be willing to agree /to/; - go along /WITH/ a plan: /A/ **yanaş-** 3. *324:3.* willingness: - be willing; *441:2.* consent: - consent.
- be WINDY [It's windy.], - blow [subj.: wind]: **es-.** *318:20.* wind: - blow.
- be WITHIN ONE'S CAPABILITIES, - lie in one's power, - be able to do: **elinden gel-** → gel- 1. *18:11.* power, potency: - be able.
- be WORN-OUT, exhausted, tired out /from/: /DAn/ **bit-** 2. *21:5.* fatigue: - burn out.
- be or - become worn-out, burned-out, or spent [subj.: people]; for sb - lose much of his vigor, energy: **yıpran-** 2. *16:9.* weakness: - become weak; *21:5.* fatigue: - burn out.
- be WORRIED, anxious /{ABOUT/ CONCERNING}/: /DAn/ **endişe et-.** *126:6.* anxiety: - feel anxious.
- be worried, concerned /ABOUT/, upset, distressed /{ABOUT/BY/AT}/; - be sad, sorry /θ/ that, - feel sad /θ/ that: /A/ **üzül-.** *112:16.* sadness: - lose heart; *126:6.* anxiety: - feel anxious.
- be WORTH /θ/: /A/ 2 **değ-** 1, et- 2. *998:10.* goodness: - do good.
- be WOUND, set [watch, clock, meter, toy, music box]: **kurul-** 2. *787:7.* agreement: - make agree; *914:9.* rotation: - rotate.
- be WOUNDED, injured, hurt /IN [the arm], by [the enemy]/: /DAn, {tarafından/CA}/ **yaralan-** 1. *393:13.* impairment: - inflict an injury.
- be WRAPPED /a: IN, b: with, c: by [sb]/: /a: A, b: 1A, c: tarafından/ **sarıl-** 2. *769:20.* assemblage: - bundle; *799:9.* joining: - bind.
- be WRECKED, demolished; - be pulled down, torn down /by, with/; - be destroyed; - be ruined [subj.: building]: /{tarafından/CA}, 1A/ **yıkıl-** 1. *395:17.* destruction: - demolish.
- be WRITTEN /a: to [sb], b: {ON/IN}, c: {in/on}, d: with, e: by [the teacher]/: /a: A, b: A, c: DA, d: 1A, e: tarafından/ **yazıl-** 1. *547:19.* writing: - write.
- be WRONG, mistaken: **yanıl-.** *947:2.* misjudgment: - misjudge; *974:10.* error: - be wrong.

- BEAR /θ/, - endure /θ/, - put up /WITH/, - stand /θ/, - suffer /θ/, - tolerate /θ/, - take /θ/: **çek-** 5, /A/ **dayan-** 3, /A/

489

katlan- 2, *more formal, less current than the above*: /A/ tahammül et-. *134:5*. patience: - endure; *1047:3*. toughness: - toughen.

- bear, - give birth /TO/: /I/ doğur-, /I/ dünyaya getir-. *1:3*. birth: - give birth.

- BEAT, - strike: /I/ döv-. *604:13*. punishment: - slap; *901:14*. impulse, impact: - hit.
- beat [subj.: heart]: at- 7, çarp- 2. *916:12*. agitation: - flutter.
- beat, - defeat, - overcome, - conquer: 2 yen- 1. *412:6*. defeat: - defeat.
- beat, - give a whipping, beating, - thrash /θ/: /A/ dayak at- → at- 5. *604:13*. punishment: - slap; *901:14*. impulse, impact: - hit.
- beat, - whip [food: yogurt and egg whites]: çırp-. *916:10*. agitation: - agitate.

Beat it!, Get lost!, Away with you!, Be off!, Clear out!, Go away!, Scram!: Defol! → ol- 12, Bas git! → bas- 1, Güle güle ['Bye bye', not in response to either Allahaısmarladık. 'Goodbye' or Hoşça kal[ın]. 'Goodbye, Have a good day.'] → Güle güle 2 → gül- 1. *908:31*. ejection: INTERJ. go away!

BECAUSE: diye 2 → de- 1. *887:10*. attribution: CONJ. because.

- BECOME, - be; - turn out, - work out: ol- 1. *760:12*. existence: - become.
- become or - turn /INTO/ [rain into hail]: /A/ çevir- 8, /A/ dön- 6, /A/ dönüş-. *851:6*. change: - be changed.
- become suddenly, suddenly - turn into [subj.: often a person, often as a result of strong emotion: turn to stone]: /θ/ kesil- 5. *851:6*. change: - be changed.
- become /θ/, - be becoming /to/ [This behavior does not become you.]: /A/ yakış- 1. *866:3*. conformity: - conform.

- become or - get ACCUSTOMED /to/ or used /to/: /A/ alış- 1. *373:12*. custom, habit: - be used to.
- become ACQUAINTED /WITH/ sb, - get to know sb, - meet sb: /I/ tanı- 3. *587:10*. friendship: - befriend, - make friends with.
- become or - be ADDICTED /to/: /A/ alış- 2. *373:11*. custom, habit: - become a habit.
- become or - turn a certain AGE: yaşını {doldur-/tamamla-} → doldur- 1, yaşına {bas-/gir-} → bas- 1. *303:9*. age: - mature.

- become AWARE /OF/, - realize, - notice: farkına var-. *940:5*. discovery: - detect; *982:6*. attention: - heed.
- become aware /OF/, - realize, - understand: anla-. *521:7*. intelligibility: - understand.

- become BAD, - deteriorate, - get worse: fenalaş- 1, gerile- 2, kötüleş-, zayıfla- 2. *393:16*. impairment: - deteriorate.
- become BASHFUL, - be embarrassed: sıkıl- 2, utan-. *96:15*. unpleasure: - chagrin.
- become CHEERFUL, - get in a happy mood: neşelen-. *95:11*. pleasure: - be pleased.
- become CLOUDY or overcast [sky], - cloud over: hava kapan- → kapan- 4. *319:6*. cloud: - cloud.
- become or - get COLD [weather]: soğuk bas- → bas- 4. *1022:9*. cold: - freeze.
- become or - be COMFORTABLE, - feel better, relieved: rahat et-, rahatla-. *120:8*. relief: - be relieved.
- become CRIPPLED; - become physically disabled, - get or - be hurt; - become maimed or mutilated: sakatlan-. *393:13*. impairment: - inflict an injury.

- become or - get DIRTY, soiled, polluted: kirlen-, pislen-. *80:15b*. uncleanness: - get dirty.
- become physically DISABLED: → become CRIPPLED.
- become DISTANT or remote /from/ in feeling: /DAn/ uzaklaş- 2. *261:7*. distance, remoteness: - keep one's distance; *379:4*. dissuasion: - disincline; *456:10*. disaccord: - fall out with.
- become DRY, - dry, - dry out [laundry]: kuru- 1. *1064:6b*. dryness: - dry, - become dry.

- become or - get EASY, easier [task, classes, lessons]: kolaylaş-. *1013:10*. facility: - go easily.
- become EMPTY, - empty out; - become vacant: boşal- 1. *190:13*. emergence: - run out.
- become or - get ENGAGED /TO/: /lA/ nişanlan-. *436:6*. promise: - be engaged.
- become EVIDENT; - be revealed, - come to light: {ortaya/meydana} çık- → çık- 3. *351:8*. disclosure: - be revealed.
- become EXTINCT [volcano]: sön- 3. *1021:8*. incombustibility: - burn out.

- become HARDER, more difficult: zorlaş-. *1012:10.* difficulty: - be difficult.
- become or - get HOT [weather]: sıcak bas- → bas- 4. *1018:22.* heat: - be hot.

- become or - get ILL, - take sick /{AS A RESULT OF/WITH/from}/: /DAn/ hastalan-, /DAn/ hasta ol- → ol-10.2, /DAn/ rahatsız ol- 1 → ol-10.2. *85:46a.* disease: - take sick in general.
- become, - get, or - be IMPATIENT: sabırsızlan-. *135:4.* impatience: - be impatient.

- become LESS [in quantity], - decrease, - diminish: azal-, eksil- 1. *252:6.* decrease: - decrease [i.].

- become MATURE, morally correct, responsible, - grow up, - amount to sth, - shape up [used for both men and women]: adam ol- → ol- 12. *303:9.* age: - mature.
- become or - feel MELANCHOLY, sad, gloomy, depressed: hüzünlen-. *112:16.* sadness: - lose heart.
- become MORE EXPENSIVE, - go up in price: fiyatlar {çık-/tırman-/yüksel-} → çık- 6, tırman- 2, yüksel- 2, pahalan-. *251:6.* increase: - grow, increase [i.].

- become OVERCAST, cloudy, - cloud over [sky]: hava kapan- → kapan-4. *319:6.* cloud: - cloud.
- become the OWNER, possessor /OF/ sth, - obtain /θ/, - acquire /θ/, - get /θ/ sth: /A/ sahip ol- → ol- 12. *472:8.* acquisition: - acquire.

- become PARALYZED, - have or - suffer a stroke: felç ol- → ol- 10.2, ime in- → in- 1. *85:46b.* disease: - take sick in particular ways.
- become POPULAR, fashionable, for sth - catch on or - win a following /{IN/AMONG}, {IN/among}/ [subj.: fashion, song, book]: /CA, arasında/ tutul- 3. *578:8.* fashion: - catch on.

- become REMOTE or distant /from/ in feeling: /DAn/ uzaklaş- 2. *261:7.* distance, remoteness: - keep one's distance; *379:4.* dissuasion: - disincline; *456:10.* disaccord: - fall out with.
- become RIPE, - ripen: ol- 9.2. *303:9.* age: - mature.

- become SAD, gloomy, depressed, melancholy: hüzünlen-. *112:16.* sadness: - lose heart.
- become SILENT, - stop talking, - be quiet: sesini kes- → kes- 4; sus- 2. *51:7.* silence: - fall silent.
- become or - get SLEEPY: uykusu gel- → gel- 1. *22:13.* sleep: - sleep.

- become WISER through bitter experience, - come to one's senses about a matter, - wise up: akıllan-, aklı başına gel- → gel- 1. *570:10.* learning: - learn by experience; *924:2.* sanity: - come to one's senses.
- become WORN-OUT, - get old [for things only, not people]: eski-. *393:20.* impairment: - wear, - wear away.
- become or - be worn-out, burned-out, or spent [subj.: people]; for sb - lose much of his vigor, energy: yıpran-2. *16:9.* weakness: - become weak; *21:5.* fatigue: - burn out.
- become or - get WRINKLED: buruş-, yüzü buruş- 2 ['for a person's face - become or - get wrinkled']. *290:3.* furrow: - furrow; *303:10.* age: - age.

BEFORE /θ/, prior /to/ [always following a specific time expression: 'five days before the meeting']: /A/ kala 2 → kal- 3. *833:7.* previousness: PREP. prior to.

- BEG /θ/, - plead /WITH [sb], {for/to}/: /A, için/ yalvar-. *440:11.* request: - entreat.
- beg sb's PARDON, - apologize /TO [sb], for [sth]/, - make an apology /TO/ sb: /DAn, için/ özür dile- → dile- 2. *658:5.* atonement: - apologize.

- BEGIN, - start [The class has begun.]: başla- 1. *817:7b.* beginning: for sth - begin.
- begin or - start /θ/ sth [The teacher began θ the class. The student began {to work/working}.]: /A/ başla- 2. *817:7a.* beginning: - begin sth.
- begin, - open [subj.: schools, season: When does the {academic year/basketball season} begin?]: açıl- 4. *292:11.* opening: - open.
- begin sth, - cause sth to begin, - start sth [The referee began the game.]: /I/ başlat-. *817:7a.* beginning: - begin sth.
- begin SUDDENLY, - plunge into an activity: /A/ dal- 4: sohbete dal- ['- get involved IN, - plunge INTO a friendly conversation']. *541:10.*

conversation: - chat; *817:9.*
beginning: - enter.
- begin a VACATION, - leave FOR
{vacation/the holiday[s]}, - go ON
{vacation/holiday}: **tatile çık-** →
çık- 2. *20:9.* rest, repose: - vacation.

- BEHAVE, - act, or - do [well] /BY...ing
[*or* TO]/: **/{mAklA/ArAk}/**
[doğru] hareket et- 4. *321:4.*
behavior: - behave.
- behave /TOWARD, toward/, - deal
/WITH/, - treat /θ/ [well or badly]:
/A, A karşı/ davran-. *321:6.*
behavior: - treat.
- behave respectfully /toward/, - show
respect /{to/FOR}/, - treat with
respect, - respect [a person, a person's
ideas]: **/A/ saygı göster-** →
göster- 1. *143:10.* kindness,
benevolence: - be considerate; *155:5.*
respect: - do or - pay hommage to.
- behave shamefully /BY...ing/: **/mAklA/**
ayıp et-. *322:4.* misbehavior: -
misbehave.

- BELIEVE /θ/ [sth or sb, what sb says]:
/A/ inan- 1. *952:10.* belief: -
believe.
- believe /IN/, - trust /θ/: **/A/ güven-**,
/A/ inan- 2. *952:15.* belief: -
believe in.
- believe /IN/ the truth of, /IN/ the
existence of [God]: **/A/ inan-** 3.
952:15. belief: - believe in.
Believe me! [its true]: **İnanın [ki]** →
inan- 1. *334: * 11.* affirmation:
INTERJ. I swear!

- BELITTLE, - underrate, - underestimate,
- minimize: **küçümse-** 2. *252:9.*
decrease: - minimize.

- BELLY DANCE, - perform a belly
dance: **göbek at-** → at- 1. *705:5.*
dance: - dance.

- BEND, - bow, - make bend [wind bends
trees]: **eğ-** 2. *164:5.* deviation: -
deflect.
- bend DOWN /to/ [to pick up]: **/A/**
eğil- 1. *204:10.* obliquity: - incline;
912:9. depression: - bow.
- bend down /to/, - incline, - lean [trees to
the ground]: **/A kadar/ eğil-** 3.
204:10. obliquity: - incline.

- BENEFIT or - profit /from/, - make good
use /OF/, - take advantage /OF/; -
utilize /θ/: **/DAn/ {yararlan-**
/faydalan-/istifade et-}. *387:15.*
use: - take advantage of.

- BEQUEATH, - leave sth /to/ sb [obj.:
property]: **/A/ bırak-** 7. *478:18.*
giving: - bequeath.

BESIDES, moreover, anyhow, anyway:
kaldı ki 1 → kal- 1. *384:10.*
manner, means: ADV. anyhow.
Besides being; besides having: **olduğu**
gibi 3, **olduğu kadar.** → ol- 11 →
olduğu. *253:11.* addition: ADV.
additionally.

BEST WISHES: **Mübarek olsun!** [a
formula of congratulation exclusively
for religious holidays] → ol- 11 →
olsun, **Kutlu olsun!** [a formula of
congratulation on religious as well as
on other, non-religious, official
holidays and on birthdays]. → ol- 11
→ olsun. *149:2.* congratulation:
INTERJ. congratulations.

- BET /a: θ [sb], b: θ [an amount], c: ON
[lit., saying]/, wager': **/a: lA, b: A,**
c: diye/ {bahse/iddiaya} gir-.
759:25. gambling: - bet.

- BEWILDER, - surprise, - confuse, -
catch off guard: **şaşırt-** 1. *984:7a.*
distraction, confusion: - confuse.

- BID GOODBYE, farewell /TO/ one
another, - say farewell /TO/ one
another: **/lA/ vedalaş-**. *188:16.*
departure: - say or - bid good-bye.

- BIND or - bandage [wound]: **/I/ sar-** 2.
91:24. therapy: - treat; *799:9.* joining:
- bind.

- BITE /{ON/IN}/ [the leg]: **/DAn/ ısır-**
[subj.: dog], **/DAn/ sok-** 3 [subj.:
snake, insect. Also '- sting': subj.:
insect, bee]. *8:27.* eating: - chew;
26:7. pain: - inflict pain;

- BLAME /FOR/, - accuse /OF/: **/a: lA,**
b: DAn dolayı, c: konusunda/
suçla-. *599:8.* accusation: - blame.

- BLEED [wound]: **/DAn/ kan ak-** [lit.,
'for blood - flow /from/'], **/DAn/**
kan gel- [lit., 'for blood - come
/from/'] → gel- 1, **kana-** ['- bleed'].
12:17. excretion: - bleed; *190:13.*
emergence: - run out.

- BLEND, - mix, - stir [eggs and sugar]:
karıştır- 1. *796:10a.* mixture: - mix
sth.
- blend, - combine [salad ingredients]:
harmanla-. *796:10a.* mixture: - mix;
804:3. combination: - combine.

BLESS {him/her}!: **Sağ olsun.** → sağ ol- → ol- 12. *509:22.* approval: INTERJ. bravo!

Bless you [in response to a sneeze]: **Çok yaşa! 3** → yaşa- 1. *504:20.* courtesy: polite expressions.

- BLINK [eyes]: **göz kırp- 1.** *28:10.* defective vision: - wink; *902:7.* reaction: - pull or - draw back.

- BLOCK, - obstruct [traffic or snow blocks roads]: **{kapa-kapat-} 5.** *293:7.* closure: - stop, - stop up; *1011:14.* hindrance: - prevent.
- block /FROM/, - prevent /θ/, - hinder /θ/: **/I/ engelle-, /A/ mâni ol-** → ol- 12, **/I/ önle-, önüne geç-** → geç- 1. *1011:14.* hindrance: - prevent.
- block ONE'S WAY [often to steal from], - waylay, - ambush: **yolunu kes-** → kes- 6. *346:10.* concealment: - ambush.

- BLOSSOM, - bloom, - flower, - open [flower]: **aç- 9.** *310:32.* plants: - flower.

- BLOW [The wind is blowing.]: **es-.** *318:20.* wind: - blow.
- blow about, away, - make fly [wind blows her hair about, papers away]: **uçur-.** *318:20.* wind: - blow.
- blow [obj.: smoke]: **üfle- 1.** *318:21.* * *1.* wind: - breathe.
- blow or - hit /θ/ the HORN [of a car]: **kornaya bas-** → bas- 2. *58:8.* stridency: - screech; *708:42.* music: - blow a horn; *912:4.* depression: - depress.
- blow OUT [obj.: candle]: **üfle- 2.** *1021:7.* incombustibility: - fight fire.
- blow UP, - explode [The building blew up.]: **havaya uç-.** *671:14.* violence: - explode.
- blow sth up [Terrorists blew up the presidential palace.]: **havaya uçur-.** *395:18.* destruction: - blow up.
- blow up, - lose one's temper /{ON ACCOUNT OF/DUE TO}: **/DAn/ patla- 2.** *152:20.* resentment, anger: - fly into a rage.
- blow a WHISTLE: **öttür-.** *58:8.* stridency: - screech; *708:42.* music: - blow a horn.

- BLURT OUT, - let slip or pop out, - let a secret out unintentionally: **ağzından lâf kaçır-** → kaçır- 2. *351:4.* disclosure: - diclose.

- BLUSH, - turn red: **kızar- 1.** *41:5.* redness: - redden; *137:9b.* humility: gestures of.

- BOARD /θ/ [obj.: vehicle], - mount /θ/ [obj.: animal: horse], - get /ON/, - get on board [obj.: vehicle or animal]: **/A/ bin- 1.** *193:12.* ascent: - mount.

- BOAST /{OF/ABOUT}/, - brag /{OF/ABOUT}/, - praise oneself: **/lA/ {övün-/öğün-} 2.** *502:6.* boasting: - boast.

- BOIL, - BE boiling [The water is boiling.], come to a boil: **kayna-.** *320:4.* bubble: - bubble.
- boil, - cook sth in boiling water [He boiled the vegetables.]: **haşla-.** *11:4a.* cooking: - cook sth.
- boil sth [cause to boil: He boiled the water.]: **kaynat-.** *11:4a.* cooking: - cook sth; *320:4.* bubble: - bubble; *1019:17a.* heating: - heat.

- BOLT DOWN, - gobble up, - gobble down, - wolf down [food]; - gulp down [a drink]: **atıştır- 1.** *8:23.* eating: - gobble.

- BOMB [The terrorists bombed the building.]: **bombala-.** *459:23.* attack: - bomb.

BON appétit!, Enjoy!: **Afiyet olsun.** → ol- 11 → olsun. *8:35.* eating: INTERJ. chow down!; *504:* * *20.* courtesy: polite expressions.

- BOO, - jeer: **yuhala-.** *508:10.* ridicule: - boo.

- BORE [Grandfather's war stories bored us.]: **canını sık- 1** → sık- 3. *118:7a.* tedium: - bore.

- BORROW /from/: **/DAn/ borç al-** [loan, money only] → al- 1, **/DAn/ ödünç al-** [money or anything else] → al- 1. *621:3.* borrowing: - borrow.

BOTH...and...; whether...or: **olsun...olsun** → ol- 11. *863:6.* generality: whatever.

- BOTHER, - disturb, - annoy, - irritate, - get on sb's nerves: **canını sık- 2** → sık- 3, **sık- 3, rahatsız et-.** *96:13.* unpleasure: - annoy.

- BOW, - bow down [in greeting]: **eğil- 2.** *137:9b.* humility: gestures of;

204:10. obliquity: - incline; *912:9.* depression: - bow.
- bow, - bend, - tip: **eğ-** 1. *155:6.* respect: - bow; *204:10.* obliquity: - incline.
- bow ONE'S HEAD, - bow down: **baş eğ-** → **eğ-** 1. *137:9b.* humility: gestures of; *155:6.* respect: - bow.

- BRAG /ABOUT/, - boast /{OF/ ABOUT}/, - praise oneself: /lA/ {övün-/öğün-} 2. *502:6.* boasting: - boast.

- BRAID HAIR: **saç ör-** → **ör-** 2. *3:22.* hair: - braid.

BRAVO!, Good for {him/you}!, Nice going!: **Çok yaşa!** 2 → **yaşa-** 1, **Aşkolsun!** 2 → **ol-** 11 → **olsun, Helâl olsun!** 2 → **ol-** 11 → **olsun.** *149:4.* congratulation: INTERJ. congratulations!; *509:22.* approval: INTERJ. bravo!

- BREAK [obj.: dishes, glasses, arm, leg]: **kır-** 1. *801:12.* separation: - break.
- break, - GET broken [subj.: dishes, glasses, arm, leg]: **kırıl-** 2. *801:12.* separation: - break.
- break [obj.: watch, agreement], - ruin, - spoil, - corrupt [obj.: morals], - violate [rules]: **boz-** 1. *393:10.* impairment: - spoil; *395:10.* destruction: - destroy.
- break a BILL, - make change /for/, - give change /for/: **boz-** 2. *857:11.* conversion: - convert.
- break DOWN, - go out of order: **arıza yap-** [usually for large items run on energy sources such as fuel, batteries or house current, less frequently for small items such as clocks, radios, videos] → **yap-** 3, **bozul-** [for large and small items of all kinds]. *393:25.* impairment: - get out of order.
- break down, - crash, - fail, - be down [subj.: a system, computer]: **çök-** 5. *393:24.* impairment: - break down.
- break sb's HEART: **kalbinden yarala-, yık-** 1. *112:19.* sadness: - aggrieve.
- break IN ON, - interrupt, - cut in on [conversation]: **sözünü kes-** → **kes-** 3. *214:6.* intrusion: - interrupt; *843:4.* untimeliness: - talk out of turn.
- break in TWO [subj.: thread], - break, - break off, - come off [subj.: button]; - snap or - pop off: **kop-** 1. *801:9.* separation: - come apart.
- break INTO [thieves into house]: /A/ **gir-.** *214:5.* intrusion: - intrude.

- break /into/ or - join /θ/ a conversation: **söze karış-** → **karış-** 6. *476:5.* participation: - participate.
- break sth into PIECES, - cut up, - smash, - tear to pieces: **parçala-.** *801:13.* separation: - shatter.
- break into pieces, - shatter [The glass broke into a thousand pieces.]: **parçalan-** 2. *801:13.* separation: - shatter.
- break LOOSE [for all hell to]; for a great commotion - occur: **kıyamet kop-** 2 → **kop-** 2. *671:13.* violence: - erupt; *817:13.* beginning: - originate.
- break OUT, - begin [subj.: a noisy or dangerous event]: **kop-** 2. *671:13.* violence: - erupt; *817:13.* beginning: - originate.
- break out [sth unpleasant: storm, battle]: **çık-** 4, **patla-** 3. *817:13.* beginning: - originate.
- break out IN A SWEAT /{from/because of}/ [anxiety, fear], - be covered in sweat: /DAn/ **ter bas-** → **bas-** 4. *12:16.* excretion: - sweat; *127:13.* fear, frighteningness: - flinch.
- break one's PROMISE: **sözünde durMA-** → **dur-** 6, **sözünden dön-** → **dön-** 5, **sözünü tutMA-.** *435:4.* nonobservance: - violate.
- break a RECORD /in/ [sports]: /DA/ **rekor kır-** → **kır-** 1. *249:9.* superiority: - outdo; *411:3.* victory: - triumph.
- break UP, - disband, - disintegrate, - fall apart [dispersal of members: subj.: household, family, poitical party]: **dağıl-** 3. *805:3.* disintegration: - disintegrate.
- break up, - split up, - part company /WITH/ [The couple broke up.; She broke up WITH her boyfriend.]: /DAn/ **ayrıl-** 1. *801:19.* separation: - part company.

- BREAKFAST, - eat or - have breakfast: **kahvaltı** {**et-/yap-**}. NOT ~~kahvaltı ye-~~. *8:21.* eating: - dine.

- BREAST-FEED, - nurse, - suckle: /I/ **emzir-,** /A/ **meme ver-** → **ver-** 1. *8:19.* eating: - nourish.

- BREATHE, - take a breath: **nefes al-** → **al-** 1. *89:14.* tobacco: - use tobacco; *187:12.* reception: - draw in; *318:21.* * *1.* wind: - breathe.
- breathe FRESH AIR, - get a breath of fresh air: **hava al-** 1 → **al-** 1. *318:21.* * *1.* wind: - breathe.
- breathe ONE'S LAST BREATH: **son nefesini ver-** → **nefes ver-** → **ver-**

1. *307:19*. death: - die; *318:21*. * *1*.
wind: - breathe.
- breathe OUT, - exhale, - let out a breath:
nefes ver- → ver- 1. *318:21*. * *1*.
wind: - breathe.

- BRING /from, to/, - fetch /from/: /DAn,
A/ getir-. *176:16*. transferal,
transportation: - fetch.
- bring ABOUT /θ/ sth, - cause /θ/ sth, -
lead /to/: /A/ {sebep/neden} ol-
→ ol- 12, /A/ yol aç- 2 → aç- 1.
885:10. cause: - cause.
- bring BACK [here], - return sth /to/ [this
place]: /A/ geri getir-. *481:6*.
restitution: - recover.
- bring sth back to its place, i.e., to where
it belongs: yerine getir- 2. *481.4*.
restitution: - restore.
- bring or - file CHARGES /against, for/, -
sue: /aleyhine, için/ dava aç- →
aç- 12, /I/ dava et-. *598:12*. legal
action: - sue.
- bring DOWN, - lower /from, to/, - take
down [obj.: shutters, baggage]:
/DAn, A/ indir- 1. *912:4*.
depression: - depress.
- bring down, - reduce, - decrease, - lower
[prices, rates], - give a discount:
indir- 3. *631:2*. discount: - discount;
633:6a. cheapness: - lower prices.
- bring down, - reduce [inflation]: düşür-
2. *252:7*. decrease: - reduce.
- bring down, - knock down [The boxer
brought down his opponent]: indir-
4. *912:5*. depression: - fell.
- bring FORTH, - create, - cause sth to
come out or appear /from/: /DAn/
çıkar- 7. *891:8*. production: -
produce, - create.
- bring GREETINGS /from/: /DAn/
selâm getir-. *504:13*. courtesy: -
give one's regards.
- bring INTO CONTACT /with/: /lA/
temas et- 1 [inflammable materials
with fire]. *223:10*. nearness: - contact.
- bring /{to/NEAR/UP TO/OVER TO}/:
/A/ yaklaştır-. *223:13*. nearness: -
juxtapose.
- bring NEWS /from, to/: /DAn, A/
haber getir-. *552:11*. news: - report.
- bring ONESELF /TO/ or - dare /to/ do
sth that would discomfort or harm sb:
/A/ kıy- 4. *98:14*. unpleasantness: -
distress; *404:3*. undertaking: -
undertake.
- bring OUT, - issue, - put out a
publication: çıkar- 7. *352:14*.
publication: - issue.
- bring TEARS TO ONE'S EYES, - make
one's eyes water: yaşart-,
gözlerini yaşart-. *13:5*. secretion: -
secrete; *115:12*. lamentation: - weep.

- bring THE CHECK [at a restaurant] /to/:
/A/ hesap getir-. *478:12*. giving: -
give; *630:11*. price, fee: - price.
- bring sth /TO/, - convey /to/, - transport
/to/: /A/ ulaştır- 1. *176:12*.
transferal, transportation: - transport;
176:15. : - send.
- bring TO AN END, - conclude, - finish
sth: /I/ bitir- 1, /A/ son ver- →
ver- 1. *819:5*. end: - end sth.
- bring TO LIGHT; - expose to view, -
disclose, - reveal: {ortaya/
meydana} çıkar- → çıkar- 7.
351:4. disclosure: - disclose.
- bring TO MIND, - make think of
[associations with places or events
rather than similarities bring sb or sth
to mind: That restaurant where we
used to meet makes me think of
you.]: {hatırlat-/anımsat-} 4.
988:20. memory: - remind.
- bring TOGETHER, - join, - unite:
birleştir-, kavuştur-. *799:5*.
joining: - put together.
- bring UP, - rear, - raise, - train, - educate
[children]: yetiştir- 2. *568:13*.
teaching: - train.
- bring up or - raise a subject, - move on
to a new subject, topic: konu aç- →
aç- 10. *817:12*. beginning: - open.

- BROADCAST /ON/ radio or television
[They broadcast the news of the
accident ON the radio.]: /DAn/
yayımla- 2. *1033:25*. radio: -
broadcast; *1034:14*. television: -
televise.

- BROWSE, just - look around [in a
store]: şöyle bir bak- → bak- 1,
sadece bak- → bak- 1. *733:8*.
purchase: - shop; *937:26*. inquiry: -
examine cursorily.
- browse, - surf /on/ [the Internet], - scan,
- flip /through/ [TV channels]: /DA,
arasında/ gezin- 2. *570:13*.
learning: - browse; *1041:18*.
computer science: - computerize.

- BRUSH [teeth, hair], - brush off
[clothing]: fırçala-. *79:23*.
cleanness: - sweep.
- brush AGAINST, for sth - touch /θ/ sth
[physically, usually unintentionally,
by mistake: My hand {brushed
against/touched /θ/} the stove.]: /A/
1 değ- 1. *223:10*. nearness: -
contact.

- BUDGE, - move slightly, - stir:
{kımılda-/kıpırda-}. *172:5b*.
motion: for sth - move.

- BUILD [a house]: **yap-** 1 [usually if the subject is doing the actual construction], **yaptır-** 1 [if the subject is having sb else do the actual construction]. *891:8.* production: - produce, - create.
- build UP FANCIFUL HOPES /{about/con-cerning}/, - dream: {**düş/rüya**} **gör-** 2 → gör- 3, /a: **hakkında**, b: **lA ilgili**, c: **A dair**, d: **üzerine**/ **hayal kur-** → kur- 1. *985:17.* imagination: - dream.

- BUMP, - hit [one's head] /ON/: /**A**/ **vur-** 1. *901:14.* impulse, impact: - hit.
- bump /{AGAINST/INTO/ON}/, - hit /θ/, - strike /θ/, - strike sth /ON/: /**A**/ **çarp-** 1. *901:13.* impulse, impact: - collide.
- bump OFF, - wipe out, - rub out, - do in, - nuke, - zap. *Contemptuous for* - kill: **gebert-**. *308:13.* killing: non-formal terms: - waste; *514: * 5.* threat: INTERJ. specific threats.
- bump or - run /INTO/, - meet by chance, - encounter /θ/, - chance /UPON/: /**lA**/ **karşılaş-** 2, **karşısına çık-** ['- appear suddenly in front of, - bump into'], /**A**/ **rastla-** 1, *formal:* /**A**/ **tesadüf et-** 1. *131:6.* inexpectation: - be unexpected; *223:11.* nearness: - meet.

- BURN, - be on fire, - be burning [The building is burning.]: **yan-** 1. *1019:24.* heating: - burn.
- burn, - ignite, - light, - set /ON/ fire, - set fire /TO/ [He burned the papers in the fireplace.]: **yak-** 1. *1019:22.* heating: - ignite.
- burn, - make smart or ache [Hot pepper burns one's mouth.]: **yak-** 2. *26:7.* pain: - inflict pain.
- burn DOWN or UP [The liar's house burned down.]: **yan-** 1. *1019:24.* heating: - burn.
- burn or - scald ONESELF with a hot liquid, - get scalded /{BY/from}/: /**DAn**/ **haşlan-** 2. *393:13.* impairment: - inflict an injury.
- burn OUT [subj.: light bulb]: **yan-** 2. *1021:8.* incombustibility: - burn out.
- burn TO DEATH: **yanarak öl-.** → yan- 1. *1019:24.* heating: - burn.

- BURST [bomb, tire], - explode: **patla-** 1. *671:14.* violence: - explode.

- BURY SB OR STH /IN/ a place; - inter /θ/: /**A**/ **göm-.** *309:19.* interment: - inter.

- BUTCHER or - kill an animal as a sacrifice, - sacrifice an animal: **kurban kes-.** → kes- 2. *308:12.* killing: - kill.

- BUTTON, - button up: **ilikle-.** *293:6.* closure: - close.

- BUY or - purchase sth /a: AT [a price, total OR per unit], b: AT [a price, PER unit], c: AT [a store], d: from [a person]/: /a: **A**, b: **DAn**, c: **DAn**, d: **DAn**/ [satın] **al-** → al- 4. *733:7.* purchase: - purchase.

BY THE NAME OF, called, named: **diye** 5 → de- 1. *527:14.* nomenclature: ADJ. named.
BY THE WAY, speaking of, incidentally: **aklıma gelmişken** [lit., since it, i.e., the subject, has come to my mind], **sırası gelmişken** [lit., since its time, i.e., the time for this subject, has come], **yeri gelmişken** [lit., since its place, i.e., the place for this topic, has come]. *842:13.* timeliness: ADV. incidentally; *930:18.* thought: - occur to.

- C -

- CALCULATE, - figure up, - add up: **hesapla-.** *1016:17.* mathematics: - calculate.
- calculate, - add up, or - figure up the bill [at a restaurant or a hotel]: **hesap çıkar-** → çıkar- 7. *1016:18.* mathematics: - sum up.

- CALL, - send for, - summon /to/ [obj.: a doctor, an ambulance]: /**A**/ **çağır-** 1. *420:11.* command: - summon.
- call, - call up, - phone /θ/ sb, - make a phone call /to/ sb: /**A**/ **telefon** {**et-**/**aç-**}. *347:18.* communications: - telephone.
  call, - name, - dub, - refer to /AS/: /**diye**/ {**adlandır-**/**isimlendir-**}, /**A**/ **de-** 4. *527:11.* nomenclature: - name.
- call /θ/, - name /θ/, - dub /θ/ [with a negative connotation when the object is a person]: /**A**/ {**ad/isim**} **tak-.** *527:11.* nomenclature: - name.
- call or - draw ATTENTION to, - point out /θ/, - note /θ/ [obj.: a fact]: /**A**/ **dikkat çek-** → çek- 1, /**A**/ **işaret et-** 2. *982:10.* attention: - call attention to.
- call BACK, - phone back, - call again: [**telefonla**] **tekrar ara-** → ara- 2. *347:18.* communications: - telephone.

- call /BY/ a certain name, - refer to /AS/ [i.e., - use a certain name in referring to]: **/diye/ çağır-** 4. *527:11.* nomenclature: - name.
- call COLLECT [telephone], - make a collect call: **ödemeli ara-** → ara- 2. *347:18.* communications: - telephone.
- call FOR, - pick up sb /AT/ [a hotel]: **/DAn/ ara-** 3. *176:16.* transferal, transportation: - fetch.
- call for, - demand [apology, better pay]: **iste- 2, talep et-**. *421:5.* demand: - demand.
- call IN AT [ship at a port]: **/A/ uğra-** 1. *189:7* entrance: - enter.
- call OFF, - cancel /{for reasons of/on account of}/: **/nedeniyle/ iptal et-**. *819:5.* end: - end sth.
- call ON, - visit: **/A/ gel-** 1 ['- come to (sb's house)'], **/A/ git-** 3 ['- go to (sb's house)']. *582:19.* sociability: - visit.
- call on sb, - pay a visit, - go on a visit, - go to visit sb [usually a neighbor or friend, not a relative or sb of higher station, a casual, not formal visit], not a place: **misafirliğe git-** → git- 3. *582:19.* sociability: - visit.
- call on sb, - visit, - pay a visit /to/ a person or a place: **/I/ ziyaret et-**. *582:19.* sociability: - visit.
- call OUT /TO/: **/A/ seslen-**. *59:8.* cry, call: - vociferate.
- call UP, - phone, - ring up: [telefonla] **ara-** → ara- 2. *347:18.* communications: - telephone.
- call UPON: → - call ON.

CALLED, named, by the name of: **diye** 5 → de- 1. *527:14.* nomenclature: ADJ. named.

- CAMP, - go camping: **kamp yap-** → yap- 3. *255:11.* habitation: - camp.

- CANCEL, - call off /{for reasons of/on account of}/: **/nedeniyle/ iptal et-**. *819:5.* end: - end sth.

- CAPTURE, - seize [a place: city, fortress]: **ele geçir-** 1 → geçir- 1. *472:8.* acquisition: - acquire; *480:14.* taking: - seize.
- capture, - catch, - seize [a person], - take prisoner: **ele geçir-** 1 → geçir- 1, **yakala-** 1. *480:14.* taking: - seize.

- CARESS, - stroke, - fondle, - pet, - pat: **okşa-, sev-** 2. *73:8.* touch: - stroke; *1042:6.* friction: - rub.
- caress EACH OTHER, *slang:* - make out /with/; - make love, - have sexual intercourse /with/: **/lA/ seviş-** 2. *562:14.* lovemaking, endearment: - make love; *562:16.* : - caress.

- CARRY, - move, - transport /from, to/: **/DAn, A/ taşı-**. *176:12.* transferal, transportation: - transport.
- carry OFF, - kidnap, - abduct; - hijack: **kaçır-** 3. *482:20.* theft: - abduct.
- carry ON /WITH/ sth, - continue or - go on /WITH/ sth: **/A/ devam et-** 2. *811:4a.* continuity: - continue sth.
- carry on A LOVE AFFAIR /WITH/, *slang:* - make out /with/; - make love /with/: **oynaş-** 2. *562:14.* lovemaking, endearment: - make love; *562:16.* : - caress.
- carry OUT, - put a plan, law, or formula into practice, - apply [our knowledge] /to/ [this project], - follow [directions]: **/A/ uygula-**. *387:11.* use: - apply.
- carry out a request, wish, order, promise, - execute an order: **yerine getir-** 1. *434:3.* observance: - perform; *437:9.* compact: - execute.

- CASH a check, i.e., - have or - get a check cashed [subj.: the CUSTOMER at a bank who gives a check to sb else, i.e., a teller, FOR cashing]: **çek bozdur-** → bozdur- 2. *728:29.* money: - cash.
- cash a check [subj.: the TELLER cashes the check the customer has submitted, i.e., gives the money to the customer]: **çek boz-** → boz- 3. *728:29.* money: - cash.

- CAST OUT, - exclude, - ostracize /from/: **/DAn/ dışla-**. *772:4.* exclusion: - exclude.

- CATCH [a ball, etc.]: **yakala-** 1. *480:14.* taking: - seize.
- catch [thief], - collar, - nab; - capture, - seize, - grab, - snatch; - get hold of [sb who is escaping] /BY/ [body part: the neck]: **ele geçir-** 1 → geçir- 1, **/DAn/ tut-** 1, **/DAn/ yakala-** 1. *480:14.* taking: -seize.
- catch, - be able to hear or understand [words]: **yakala-** 2. *48:11.* hearing: - hear; *521:7.* intelligibility: - understand.
- catch /θ/, - board /θ/ [train, bus, plane]: **/A/ bin-** 1. *193:12.* ascent: - mount.
- catch /θ/ a plane, train; - hop /INTO/ a taxi, car, bus: **/A/ atla-** 3. *193:12.* ascent: - mount.
- catch /θ/ a vehicle, - make it /to/ in time /FOR/, - get /to/ a place in time /FOR/, - arrive in time /FOR/; - be in time /FOR/: **/A/ yetiş-** 1. *174:13.*

swiftness: - overtake; *409:8.* success: - achieve one's purpose.

- catch /θ/ or - come down /WITH/, - be struck down /BY/ an illness: /A/ **yakalan-** 2. *85:46a.* disease: - take sick in general.

- catch or - get a CHILL, - catch a cold: **soğuk al-** → al- 3, **üşüt-** 2 [both verbs indicate early symptoms of a cold, not as serious as **nezle ol-**, the next stage]. *85:46b.* disease: - take sick in particular ways; *1022:9.* cold: - freeze.

- catch or - get a COLD: **nezle ol-** [more serious than **soğuk al-, üşüt-** 2] → ol- 10.2. *85:46b.* disease: - take sick in particular ways.

- catch FISH, - fish: **balık tut-** → tut-1. *382:10.* pursuit: - fish.

- catch OFF GUARD, - surprise, - bewilder, - confuse: **şaşırt-** 1. *984:7a.* distraction, confusion: - confuse.

- catch ON, - become popular or fashionable, - win a following /{IN/AMONG}, {IN/among}/ [subj.: fashion, song, book]: /CA, **arasında/ tutul-** 3. *578:8.* fashion: - catch on.

- catch UP ON, - make up for lost time on [homework after getting behind]: **yetiştir-** 3. *338:4.* compensation: - compensate.

- catch up WITH, - overtake /θ/, - go fast enough to join /θ/: /A/ **yetiş-** 2. *174:13.* swiftness: - overtake.

- CAUSE /θ/ sth, - bring about /θ/ sth, - lead /to/: /A/ {sebep/neden} **ol-** → ol- 12, /A/ **yol aç-** 2 → aç- 1. *885:10.* cause: - cause.

- cause an accident, - have an accident, - get into an accident, - be in an accident: **kaza yap-** → yap- 3. *1010:10.* adversity: - come to grief.

- cause sth to COME OUT or - appear, - create, - bring forth: **çıkar-** 7. *891:8.* production: - produce, - create.

- cause sth to INCREASE, - increase sth [factory increases output]: {**artır-/arttır-**} 1. *251:4.* increase: - increase sth.

- cause sb to LOSE love, desire, or enthusiasm /FOR/, - dampen sb's enthusiasm /FOR/, - put sb /OFF/ sb or sth: /DAn/ **soğut-** 2. *1011:10.* hindrance: - hinder.

- cause sth to PASS /THROUGH/ [car through mud, thread through needle, students to pass a course]: /DAn/ **geçir-** 1. *172:5a.* motion: - move sth; *446:2.* promotion: - promote.

- cause TROUBLE /to/, - inconvenience /θ/, trouble /θ/ sb, - put sb out, - give

trouble /to/: /A/ **zahmet ver-** → ver- 1. *995:4.* inexpedience: - inconvenience; *1012:13.* difficulty: - trouble.

- cause trouble, - stir things up, - stir up trouble: **karıştır-** 5. *381:9.* plan: - plot; *1012:14.* difficulty: - cause trouble.

- CEASE, - come to an end, - let up, - stop: **din-** [subj.: nouns of weather: wind, hail, snow, rain, storm; nouns of physical or mental pain: sorrow, tears; some nouns of emotion: anger], **dur-** 2 [subj.: nouns of weather: wind, hail, snow, rain, storm], **kesil-** 2 [subj.: nouns mostly related to weather: wind, hail, snow, rain, storm]. *744:6.* cessation: - cease [i.]; *819:6.* end: - come to an end.

- cease sth, - MAKE sth stop, - cut sth out [obj.: noise, crying]: **kes-** 4. *856:6.* cessation: - cease sth.

- cease to care /FOR/ sb or sth; - cool /TOWARD/, - lose one's love, desire, or enthusiasm /FOR/: /DAn/ **soğu-** 2. *261:7.* distance, remoteness: - keep one's distance; *379:4.* dissuasion: - disincline.

- CELEBRATE: **kutla-** 1. *487:2.* celebration: - celebrate.

- CENSURE, - condemn, - reproach /{for/because}/: /DIğI için/ **kına-**. *510:13.* disapproval: - censure.

- CHANCE /UPON/, - run or - bump /INTO/, - meet by chance, - come /UPON/, - encounter /θ/: /lA/ **karşılaş-** 2, /A/ **rastla-** 1, *formal:* /A/ **tesadüf et-** 1. *131:6.* inexpectation: - be unexpected; *223:11.* nearness: - meet.

- CHANGE, - become different, - vary [The weather has changed.]: **değiş-** 1. *851:6.* change: - be changed.

- change, - EXCHANGE sth /with/ sb [My friend and I changed seats.]: /lA/ **değiş-** 2. *862:4.* interchange: - interchange.

- change or - exchange sth /{FOR/INTO}/ sth [dollars for liras]: /lA/ **değiştir-** 2. *851:7.* change: - change, - work or - make a change; *862:4.* interchange: - interchange.

- change or - make change /for/, - give change /for/, - break a bill [a specified unit of money into smaller units]: **boz-** 2. *857:11.* conversion: - convert.

- change one's CLOTHES: üstünü
değiş- → değiş- 3. *862:4.*
interchange: - interchange.
- change FOR THE WORSE, - get worse
[weather]: [hava] {boz-/bozul-}
→ boz- 4, bozul-. *393:16.*
impairment: - deteriorate.
- change FOREIGN MONEY into local
currency, - HAVE sb change foreign
money [subj.: the CUSTOMER, who
gives his foreign money to sb, i.e., a
teller, to get the equivalent local
currency]: döviz bozdur- →
bozdur- 2. *857:11.* conversion: -
convert.
- change foreign money into local
currency, - GIVE local currency in
return for foreign currency [subj.: the
TELLER who gives the customer
local currency in return for foreign
currency]: döviz boz-→ boz- 3.
857:11. conversion: - convert.
- change ONE'S MIND: fikrini
değiştir- → değiştir- 1, fikrinden
vazgeç-, kararından vazgeç-.
363:6. changing of mind: - change
one's mind; *370:7.* abandonment: -
give up.
- change VEHICLES, - transfer from one
vehicle to another [Do I have to
change buses?]: aktarma yap- →
yap- 3. *861:4.* substitution: -
substitute.

- CHARACTERIZE, - describe /AS/:
/olarak/ nitelendir-. *349:9.*
representation, description: -
describe; *864:10.* particularity: -
characterize.

- CHARGE [money: How much do you
charge?]: para al- → al- 1, ücret
al- → al- 1. *630:12.* price, fee: -
charge.
- charge sb /with/, - entrust sb /with/, -
give the task /OF/, - assign, - make sb
responsible /FOR/: /1A/
görevlendir-. *615:11.* commission:
- appoint; *641:12.* duty: - obligate.

- CHASE [AFTER], - try to catch or get, -
pursue [police chase thief]: kovala-
1, /a: DAn, b: A, c: arkasına, d:
peşine/ koş- ['- run /a: from, b:
{to/AFTER}, c: after, d: after/,
pursue']. *382:8.* pursuit: - pursue.
- chase /AFTER/ sb, - pursue, i.e., -
approach with sexual intent: *polite,
formal:* /A/ kur yap- ['- court /ө/, -
pay court /to/, - try to woo /ө/'] →
yap- 3, *slang:* /A/ asıl- 3 ['- come
on /to/ sb, - make a play /FOR/ sb'].

382:8. pursuit: - pursue; *562:21.*
love-making, endearment: - court.

- CHAT, - talk, - converse [in a friendly
manner] /1A/: /1A/ muhabbet et-
, /1A/ sohbet et-. *541:10.*
conversation: - converse.
- chat, - make small talk, - gossip, - chew
the fat: çene çal- → çal- 2. *541:10.*
conversation: - chat.

- CHEAT, - deceive [The salesman
cheated the customer.]: aldat- 1,
kandır- 1. *356:18.* deception: -
cheat.
- cheat, - gyp, - rip off, - swindle; - sell
somone sth at an exorbitant,
outrageous price: *formal term:*
dolandır-. *356:18.* deception: -
cheat. The two following verbs are
very common slang: /A/ kazık at-
→ at- 1, /I/ kazıkla-. *356:19.* :
nonformal terms - gyp.
- cheat by exchanging information orally
[in a class]: kopya çek- 2 → çek-
8. *356:18.* deception: - cheat.
- cheat /ON/, - be unfaithful /TO/ [wife to
husband]: /I/ aldat- 2. *356:18.*
deception: - cheat; *645:12.* improbity:
- be unfaithful.

- CHECK, - check out, - look over, - go
over, - examine, - scrutinize, - review
[obj.: report, examination paper]:
gözden geçir- → geçir- 1. *27:14.*
vision: - scrutinize.
- check, - inspect, - check out, - check on
[whether sth is the case or not, a
machine]: kontrol et-. *937:24.*
inquiry: - examine.
- check at a place to determine how things
are [check at the bank to see if a
deposit has been made]: /I/ yokla-
2. *937:23.* inquiry: - investigate.
- check OUT, - inspect: → - check, -
inspect.
- check or - take out BOOKS FROM THE
LIBRARY: kütüphaneden kitap
al- → al- 1. *192:10.* extraction: -
extract.
- check out OF A {HOTEL/MOTEL}:
{otelden/motelden} ayrıl- →
ayrıl- 3. *188:13.* departure: - check
out.
- check UP ON people to determine their
situation: yokla- 3. *937:23.* inquiry:
- investigate.

- CHEER UP sb, - delight sb, - make sb
feel happy, - put sb in good spirits:
neşelendir-. *109:7.* cheerfulness: -
cheer.

Cheer up!: **Neşelen!** → neşelen-, **Üzülme!** [lit., 'Don't worry.'] → üzül-. *109:20.* cheerfulness: PHR. cheer up!

- CHEW: **çiğne-** 1. *8:27.* eating: - chew.
- chew the fat, - chat, - gossip: **çene çal-** → çal- 2. *541:10.* conversation: - chat.

- CHILL, - cool sth down, - make sth cool or cold [He chilled the drinks.], - let sth cool, get cold: **soğut-** 1. *1022:10.* cold: - make cold.

- CHIRP [of birds or insects], - crow [of rooster], - sing [of birds]: **öt-** 1. *60:5.* animal sounds: [birds] - warble.

- CHOOSE, - pick, - select sth or sb /for/: **/{A/için}/ seç-** 1 [for oneself or sb else], **beğen-** 2 [for oneself, not sb else], **{tercih et-/yeğle-}** 2 [for oneself, not sb else]. *371:13.* choice: - choose.

- CHOP INTO BITS, - mince; - cut [up] into slices or pieces: **doğra-**. *792:6.* part: - separate; *801:13.* separation: - shatter.
- chop UP FINE, - cut up fine, - mince, - grind [up] [vegetables, meat]: **kıy-** 1. *792:6.* part: - separate; *801:13.* separation: - shatter.

- CIRCUMCISE: **sünnet et-**. *701:16.* religious rites: - baptize.

- CITE, - give, or - provide an example /FOR/: **/A/ {örnek/misal} ver-** → ver- 1. *956:13.* evidence, proof: - cite.
- cite /θ/ sth, - quote /θ/ sth, - quote /from/ sth: **/DAn/ alıntı yap-** → yap- 3. *848:7.* repetition: - repeat.

- CLAIM, - maintain: **ileri sür-** 2 → sür- 1. *334:5.* affirmation: - affirm.
- claim that sth is not true, - deny: **inkâr et-, reddet-** 2. *335:4.* negation, denial: - deny.

- CLAP or - applaud /FOR/ sb, - applaud /θ/ sb [obj.: person, not performance]: **/I/ alkışla-**. *509:10.* approval: - applaud.

- CLARIFY, - explain sth /to/ sb, - give the reasons for: **/A/ açıkla-** 1, **/A/ anlat-** 1, **/A/ izah et-**. *521:6.* intelligibility: - make clear.

- CLASH, - quarrel /with/: **/lA/ çatış-** 1. *456:11.* disaccord: - quarrel; *457:13.* contention: - contend.
- clash, - be in conflict [subj.: ideas, interests, appointments]: **çatış-** 2. *779:5.* difference: - differ; *788:5.* disagreement: - disagree.

- CLEAN: **temizle-**. *79:18.* cleanness: - clean.

- CLEAR a way /to/, lit., - open a road /to/: **/A/ yol aç-** 1 → aç-1. *292:13.* opening: - make an opening.
- clear AWAY, - take away [dirty dishes] /from/ [table]: **/DAn/ kaldır-** 3. *176:11.* transferal, transportation: - remove.

Clear OUT!: → Beat it!
- clear out [people from building], - empty sth, - empty sth out /INTO/ [They cleared out the building. He emptied the trash into the trash barrel.]: **/A/ boşalt-**. *908:22.* ejection: - evacuate sth.
- clear a TABLE, or anything upon which a meal may be placed, after a meal: **sofra kaldır-** → kaldır- 3. *176:11.* transferal, transportation: - remove; *772:5.* exclusion: - eliminate.
- clear UP, - become pleasant, good, nice [weather]: **hava {aç-/açıl-}** → aç-7, açıl- 7, **hava düzel-**. *392:7.* improvement: - get better.

- CLICK /ON/ [in computer language]: **/{I/A/üzerine}/ tıkla-**. *56:7.* explosive sound: - snap; *297:11.* weight: - weigh on; *1041:18.* computer science: - computerize.
- click /ON/, - press a key, - enter or - punch in [a PIN or credit card number]: **/{I/A}/ tuşla-**. *297:11.* weight: - weigh on; *912:4.* depression: - depress.

- CLIMAX, - come, - have an orgasm: **gel-** 3 [for both sexes], **boşal-** 3 [more frequently for men but also for women, also '- ejaculate'], **orgazm ol-** [for both sexes] → ol- 10.1. *75:23.* sex: - climax.

- CLIMB, - mount, - go up [stairs], - ascend /BY WAY Of [stairs], to/: **/DAn, A/ çık-** 5. *193:11.* ascent: - climb.
- climb: **dağa çık-** [obj.: only mountains] → çık- 5, **tırman-** 1 [obj.: tree, mountain, hill]. *193:11.* ascent: - climb.
- climb or - increase [subj.: prices]: **art-** 1, **çık-** 6, **fırla-** 2 ['- increase suddenly, - rise suddenly, - soar, -

skyrocket, - jump'], **pahalan-, tırman-** 2, **yüksel-** 2. *251:6.* increase: - grow, increase [i.].

- CLONE: **kopyala-** 2, **klonla-** → kopyala- 2. *784:8.* copy: - copy.

- CLOSE, - shut sth: **{kapa-/kapat-}** 1 [obj.: the door, your books], **ört-** 3 [obj.: curtains, door, window, cover]. *293:6.* closure: - close.
- close, - shut [i.e., - become closed: The door closed.]: **kapan-** 1. *293:6.* closure: - close.
- close a BANK ACCOUNT [subj.: bank customer]: **hesap kapattır-.** *293:6.* closure: - close.
- close, - shut DOWN, - abolish [obj.: organization, business, school]: **{kapa-/kapat-}** 7. *293:8.* closure: - shut up shop.
- close or - shut down for vacation, - recess, - go into recess for vacation [subj.: schools]: **tatile gir-.** *20:9.* rest, repose: - vacation; *293:8.* closure: - close shop; *856:8.* cessation: - stop work.
- close one's EYES: **göz yum-** 1. *293:6.* closure: - close.
- close one's eyes /TO/, - disregard /θ/, - take no notice /OF/, - overlook /θ/, - turn a blind eye /to/, - wink /AT/ a fault: /A/ **göz yum-** 2. *148:4.* forgiveness: - condone; *293:6.* closure: - close; *983:2.* inattention: - be inattentive.
- close UP [the space between lines in a text]: **{kapa-/kapat-}** 9. *293:6.* closure: - close.
- close sb or sth up /IN/ a place: /A/ **{kapa-/kapat-}** 4. *429:12.* confinement: - confine.

- CLOTHE: → - DRESS.

- CLOUD OVER, - become cloudy or overcast [sky]: **hava kapan-** → kapan- 4. *319:6.* cloud: - cloud.

- COINCIDE, - occur or - be /AT/ the same time, - fall /ON/ the same {day/hour}: /A/ **denk düş-** 2 → düş- 1. *830:5.* event: - occur; *835:4.* simultaneity: - coincide.

- COLLAPSE, - fall down [subj.: building, tent]: **çök-** 1, **yıkıl-** 2. *393:24.* impairment: - break down.
- collapse, - come to an end, - fall [subj.: empire]: **çök-** 4. *393:24.* impairment: - breakdown.
- collapse, - deflate, - go flat: **sön-** 2 [subj.: balloon, tire, rubber boat], **in-**

4 [subj.: tire, rubber boat]. *260:10.* contraction: - collapse.
- collapse /INTO/, - sit down suddenly, heavily /IN/ [a chair]: /A/ **çök-** 2. *912:10.* depression: - sit down.

- COLLECT [stamps], - gather: **biriktir-** 1, **topla-** 1, **toparla-** 1. *769:18.* assemblage: - bring or - gather together.
- collect ONE'S THOUGHTS or oneself; - pull or - get oneself together: **kendini toparla-** → toparla- 3. *106:7.* inexcitability: - compose oneself.

- COLLIDE, - clash, - run into each other: **çarpış-.** *901:13.* impulse, impact: - collide.
- collide /WITH/, - hit /θ/ [ball hits window by chance, accident]: /A/ **rastla-** 2, /A/ **tesadüf et-** 2. *901:13.* impulse, impact: - collide.

- COLOR, - paint /θ/ a color: /A/ **boya-.** *35:13.* color: - color.

- COMB [hair]: **tara-** 1. *79:21.* cleanness: - comb.
- comb or - search through [plane for bomb, photo album for picture]: the verb **ara-** followed by the verb **tara-** in two patterns: a) the same personal suffix on both verbs: **ara- tara-** [e.g., **aradı taradı**], b) **-Ip** on the first verb, the personal suffix on the second: **arayıp tara-** [e.g., **arayıp taradı**] → tara- 2. *937:31.* inquiry: - search.

- COMBINE, - blend [salad ingredients]: **harmanla-.** *796:10a.* mixture: - mix; *804:3.* combination: - combine.

- COME /from, to/: /DAn, A/ **gel-** 1. *186:6.* arrival: - arrive.
- come or - climax, - have an orgasm: → - climax.
- Please come AGAIN [words to departing guests]: **Yine bekleriz.** → bekle- 1. *504: * 20.* courtesy: polite expressions.
- come BACK, - return /from, to/: /DAn, A/ **dön-** 2, /DAn, A/ **geri dön-** → dön- 2. *163:8b.* regression: - turn back, - come back.
- come CLOSE /to/, up /to/, over /to/, - approach /θ/, - draw near /to/, - sidle up /to/: /A/ **yaklaş-,** /A/ **yanaş-** 1. *167:3.* approach: - approach; *223:7.* nearness: - near, - come near.

- come DOWN, - descend /{from/BY WAY OF}, to/ [person by way of

stairs, off a vehicle]: **/DAn, A/ in-**
1. *194:5.* descent: - descend.

- come down [subj.: rain, snow, hail]:
yağ-. *194:5.* descent: - descend.

- come down, - descend /from, to/ a lower
level [subj.: plane, birds, balloon]:
/DAn, A/ alçal- 1. *194:5.* descent:
- descend.

- come down IN PRICE /FOR/ sb, -
reduce the price /FOR/ sb, - make a
reduction in price /FOR/ sb, - give a
discount /to/ sb: **/A/ ikram et-** 2,
in- 5, **indir-** 3. *631:2.* discount: -
discount.

- come down /UPON/, - settle /on/ [subj.:
fog, smoke]: **/{üstüne/üzerine}/**
çök- 3. *194:10.* descent: - light
upon.

- come down /WITH/, - catch /θ/, - be
struck down /by/ an illness: **/A/**
yakalan- 2. *85:46a.* disease: - take
sick in general.

- come FORWARD [subj.: a guilty
person], - appear, - come out [the
truth]: **{ortaya/meydana} çık-** →
çık- 3. *351:8.* disclosure: - be
revealed.

- come /{IN/ON}/ TIME: **{vaktinde/**
zamanında} gel- → **gel-** 1. *842:6.*
timeliness: - be timely.

- come INTO BEING /OUT OF/, - occur:
/DAn/ oluş-. *795:3.* composition: -
compose.

- come OFF, - break off, - break in two, -
break; - snap or - pop off: **kop-** 1.
801:9. separation: - come apart.

- come ON /TO/ sb, - make a play /FOR/
sb, - chase /AFTER/ sb, i.e., -
approach with sexual intent, *slang:*
/A/ asıl- 3. *382:8.* pursuit: - pursue;
562:21. lovemaking, endearment: -
court.

- come OPEN, - open [The door opened
and the man walked in.]: **açıl-** 2.
292:11. opening: - open.

- come OUT, - appear, - rise: **doğ-** 2
[subj.: sun, moon], **çık-** 3 [subj.: sun,
moon, stars], **güneş {aç-/ çık-}**
['for the sun - come out, appear'] →
aç- 8, **çık-** 3. *33:8.* appearance;
appear; *190:11.* emergence: - emerge.

- come out, - appear, - be issued [article in
newspaper, issue of paper]: **çık-** 8.
33:8. appearance: - appear.

- come out, - turn out [well, badly:
photographs]: **çık-** 7. *830:7.* event: -
turn out; *886:4.* effect: - result.

- come out, - go out [spot, stain]: **çık-** 11.
34:2a. disappearance: - disappear.

- come out /AGAINST/, - object /to/, -
oppose, - say no /to/: **/A/ karşı çık-**

→ **çık-** 3. *451:3.* opposition: -
oppose.

- come /OUT OF/, - emerge /from/ [an
enclosed space: room]: **/DAn/ çık-**
1. *190:11.* emergence: - emerge.

- come /out of/ or - emerge /from/ a coma:
komadan çık-. → **çık-** 1. *190:11.*
emergence: - emerge; *392:8.*
improvement: - rally, - get better.

- come out RIGHT, - work out, - turn out
the way it should, - go well: **yoluna**
gir-. *392:7.* improvement: - get
better.

- come OVER TO: → - come up to the
side of.

- come /to/, - get /to/, - arrive /AT/, - reach
/θ/: **/A/ gel-** 1, **/A/ var-**, **/A/ ulaş-**
1. *186:6.* arrival: - arrive.

- come /to/ one [by chance, inheritance]:
/A/ düş- 4, **/A/ kal-** 2. *186:6.*
arrival: - arrive; *479:7.* receiving: -
inherit.

- come to, - regain consciousness: **ayıl-**,
kendine gel- 1 → **gel-** 1. *306:8.*
life: - come to life; *396:20.*
restoration: - recover.

- come to, - amount to, - add up to, - total,
- cost: **tut-** 7. *630:13.* price, fee: -
cost; *791:8.* whole: - total; *1016:18.*
mathematics: - sum up.

- come to A BOIL, - boil: **kayna-**. *320:4.*
bubble: - bubble.

- come to a STOP, - stop [vehicle: bus,
train]: **dur-** 1. *744:7.* cessation: -
stop, come to a stop.

- come to sb's AID IN TIME; - arrive in
time to help sb: **yetiş-** 4. *186:6.*
arrival: - arrive; *449:11.* aid: - aid. f

- come to AN AGREEMENT, - agree, -
reach an agreement /a: with, b:
{on/upon}, c: {on/upon}, d: on the
subject of, e: {to/in order to}/: **/a:**
1A, b: DA, c: üzerinde, d:
konusunda, e: için/ anlaş- 2.
332:10. assent: - come to an
agreement.

- come to an END, - be over, - conclude, -
end, - finish: **bit-** 1 [subj.: almost
anything], **sona er-** [meeting,
concert, play] → **er-**. *819:6.* end: -
come to an end.

- come to an end, - pass, - end, - be over
[difficult situation, illness]: **geç-** 4.
761:6. nonexistence: - cease to exist;
836:6. past: - pass.

- come to an UNDERSTANDING, - make
up [after a quarrel], - be reconciled, -
make peace /with/: **/1A/ barış-**.
465:10. pacification: - make up.

- come or - grow TO LIKE; - warm /{UP
TO/to/TOWARDS}/: **/A/ ısın-** 3.
587:10. friendship: - befriend, - make
friends with.

- come to NAUGHT, not - be realized, - be dashed [hopes, expectations, dreams]: **boşa çık-** → çık- 7. *395:23.* destruction: - perish; *473:6.* loss:- go to waste; *9 1 0 : 3.* shortcoming: - fall through.

- come to ONE'S SENSES about a matter, - become wiser through bitter experience, - wise up: **akıllan-, aklı başına gel-** → gel- 1. *570:10.* learning: - learn by experience; *924:2.* sanity: - come to one's senses.

- come to one's senses, - pull oneself together, - regain self-control: **kendine gel- 2** → gel- 1. *570:10.* learning: - learn by experience; *924:2.* sanity: - come to one's senses.

- come to SEE or - visit: **/A/ gel-** 1. *582:19.* sociability: - visit.

- come to THE END OF [lesson, holiday]: **sonuna gel-** → gel- 1. *819:6.* end: - come to an end.

- come TOGETHER, - meet /θ/ [individuals]: **/lA/ buluş-** [usually after an arrangement to meet has been made], **/lA/ bir araya gel-** → gel- 1. *769:16.* assemblage: - come together.

- come together, - meet, - convene [groups, societies]: **bir araya gel-** → gel- 1, **toplan- 3.** *769:17.* assemblage: - convene.

- come TRUE, - be realized [plans, dreams, desires, wishes], - work out [subj.: plans]: **gerçekleş-.** *972:12.* truth: - come true.

- come UP, - arise [problem, matter]: **çık- 4.** *830:5.* event: - occur.

- come up /TO/, close /to/, over /to/, - approach /θ/, - draw near /to/: **/A/ yaklaş-, /A/ yanaş- 1.** *167:3.* approach: - approach; *223:7.* nearness: - near, - come near.

- come up to THE SIDE OF, over to, - sidle up /to/: **yanına {gel-/yanaş-}** → gel- 1, → yanaş- 1. *167:3.* approach: - approach .

- come or - chance /UPON/, - meet by chance, - run or - bump /INTO/, - encounter /θ/: **/lA/ karşılaş- 2, /A/ rastla- 1,** *formal:* **/A/ tesadüf et- 1.** *131:6.* inexpectation: - be unexpected; *223:11.* nearness: - meet.

Come WHAT MAY, In any case, No matter what, Anyway: **Ne olursa olsun** → ol- 11 → olur. *969:26.* certainty: ADV. without fail.

- COMMAND, - order, - decree: **buyur-1, emret-.** *420:8.* command: - command.

- COMMEND /TO/: → - commit /to/.

- COMMENT /ON/, - remark /ON/, - note, - point out: **/I/ belirt-, /A/ dikkat çek-** → çek- 1, **/A/ işaret et- 2.** *524:25.* speech: - remark.

- COMMIT /to/, - entrust /to/, - commend /to/: **/A/ ısmarla- 3** [Most frequently found in **Allahaısmarladık.** 'Goodbye (lit., We entrustED you TO God).', said by the person leaving.] *188:22.* departure: INTERJ. farewell!; *478:16.* giving: - commit.

- commit MURDER, homicide, - murder: **cinayet işle-** → işle- 2. *308:15.* killing: - murder.

- commit a SIN: **günah işle-** → işle- 2. *654:8.* vice: - do wrong.

- commit SUICIDE, - kill oneself: **kendini öldür-, canına kıy- 2** → kıy- 2, *more formal, legal:* **intihar et-.** *308:21.* killing: - commit suicide.

- commit TO MEMORY, - learn by heart, - memorize: **ezberle-.** *570:8.* learning: - memorize; *988:17.* memory: - memorize.

- COMMUTE /by/ [a vehicle], - travel back and forth [He commutes to work every day.]: **/lA/ iş ile ev arasında gidip gel-** → gel- 1. *177:18.* travel: - travel.

- COMPARE /{with/to}/: **/lA/ {karşılaştır-/mukayese et-}** [with both verbs no result of the comparison is implied], **/A/ benzet- 2** ['- compare /to/ AND note the similarity, - liken sth /to/ sth else']. *942:4.* comparison: - compare.

- COMPETE /with/: **/lA/ yarış- 2.** *457:18.* contention: - compete.

- compete, - play one another, - meet [sports teams]: **/lA/ karşılaş- 4.** *457:18.* contention: - compete.

- COMPLAIN /{OF/ABOUT}, to [yourself or to a friend, but usually not to a responsible authority]/: **/DAn, A/ şikâyet et- a), /DAn, A/ yakın-.** *333:5.* dissent: - object; *599:7.* accusation: - accuse.

- complain /a: {OF/ABOUT}, b: to [an authority], c: because/: **/a: I, b: A, c: DIğI için/ şikâyet et- b).** *333:5.* dissent: - object.

- COMPLETE, - finish: **tamamla-.** *793:6.* completeness: - complete; *819:7.* end: - complete.

- complete one's life, - come to the end of one's life [both for people and machines], - die, - pass away: **ömrünü tamamla-**. *307:19.* death: - die.
- complete a certain year of one's life, - turn or reach a certain age: **yaşını {doldur-/tamamla-}** → doldur- 1. *303:9.* age: - mature.

- COMPLY /with/, - conform /to/, - follow or - act in accordance /WITH/ [rules, regulations]: **/A/ uy-** **5.** *326:2.* obedience: - obey; *434:2.* observance: - observe; *866:3.* conformity: - conform.

- COMPOSE music /for/: **/için/ bestele-**. *708:46.* music: - compose.

- CONCEAL, - hide sth /IN/ [i.e., - PUT sth somewhere for safekeeping]: **/A/ gizle-** 1, **/A/ sakla-** 1. *346.6* concealment: - conceal.
- conceal, - hide, - cover up [the truth, faults]: **ört-** 2. *346.6* concealment: - conceal.
- conceal, - hide ONESELF /from, IN/: **/DAn, A/ gizlen-** 1, **/DAn, A/ saklan-** 1. *346:8.* concealment: - hide oneself.

- CONCENTRATE [one's mind], - focus one's attention /ON/: **/A/ dikkatini topla-** → topla- 1. *982:8.* attention: - pay attention.

- CONCERN, - be one's business [This concerns you. This is none of your business.]: **/I/ ilgilendir-** 2. *897:3.* involvement: - be involved.
- concern oneself /WITH/ [a subject, topic]: **/A/ eğil-** **4.** *897:2.* involvement: - involve; *982:5.* attention: - attend to.

- CONCLUDE, - come to an end, - be over, - end, - finish [The lesson has concluded.]: **bit-** 1, **sona er-** → er- . *819:6.* end: - come to an end.
- conclude sth, - bring an end /TO/, - finish [We have concluded the lesson.]: **/I/ bitir-** 1, **/A/ son ver-** → ver- 1. *819:5.* end: - end sth.
- conclude, - finish, or - close the discussion of a subject, - drop the subject or topic of conversation: **{kapa-/kapat-}** 6. *819:5.* end: - end sth.

- CONCOCT, - make up, - invent, - dream up, - think up [story, lie]: **uydur-** 2. *354:18.* falseness: - fabricate.

- CONDEMN, - censure, - reproach /{for/because}/: **/DIğI için/ kına-**. *510:13.* disapproval: - censure.

- CONDUCT [obj.: orchestra]: **yönet-** 2. *708:45.* music: - conduct.
- conduct [Water conducts electricity.]: **ilet-** 2. *239:15.* channel: - channel.

- CONFER /with/, - discuss /with/; - meet /with/: **/lA/ görüş-** 1. *524:20.* speech: - speak; *541:11.* conversation: - confer.

- CONFESS /to/, - admit /to/, - acknowledge /θ/ [a misdeed]: **/A/ itiraf et-**. *351:7.* disclosure: - confess.

- CONFIRM [fact, reservation], - verify, - corroborate: **doğrula-, tasdik et-**. *969:12.* certainty: - verify.

- CONFUSE or - mix up sb or sth /with/ sb or sth else: **/lA, A/ karıştır-** 2. *810:3.* disarrangement: - confuse; *944:3.* indiscrimination: - confound.
- confuse, - get confused /{about/ regarding/as to}/, - lose track or count of [what day it is]: **/I/ şaşır-** 3. *984:7a.* distraction, confusion: - confuse.
- confuse, - surprise, - bewilder, - catch off guard: **şaşırt-** 1. *984:7a.* distraction, confusion: - confuse.
- confuse, - distract, - make sb lose track or count of, - cause sb to lose track or count of: **şaşırt-** 3. *984:6.* distraction: - distract; *984. :7:* - confuse.

- CONGRATULATE sb: **/a: için, b: DIğI için, c: DAn dolayı, d: DAn ötürü/ kutla-** 2 ['- congratulate sb /a: {for/ON}, b: {because/{ON/FOR}}, c, d: {ON/ FOR}/ an accomplishment: having passed an examination], **/a: {DAn dolayı}, b: için, c: I, d: lA/ tebrik et-** ['- congratulate /a: {FOR/ON}, b: {for/ON}, c: {FOR/ ON}, d: BY/']. *149:2.* congratulation: - congratulate.
Congratulations!: **Güle güle kullanın!** [said to sb who has just bought sth new] → kullan-, **Hayırlı olsun!** [said to sb who has just moved into a new house] → ol- 11 → olsun, **Kutlu olsun!** [for religious as well as other, non-religious, official holidays, birthdays] → ol- 11 → olsun, **Mübarek olsun!** [exclusively for religious holidays] → ol- 11 → olsun, **Tebrik ederim!** [for successfully

carrying out a task] → tebrik et-. *149:4.* congratulation: INTERJ. congratulations!

- CONNECT /to, with/ [Telephone operator: Let me connect you.]: /A, 1A/ bağla- 2, bağlantı kur- → kur- 1. *799:5.* joining: - put together.
- connect ONESELF /to/, - log on /to/ [the Internet]: /A/ bağlan- 3. *617:14.* association: - join; *1041:18.* computer science: - computerize.

- CONQUER, - overcome, - beat, - defeat: 2 yen- 1. *412:6.* defeat: - defeat.

- CONSENT, - agree, or - be willing /to/ do sth: /A/ razı ol- 1 → ol- 12. *441:2.* consent: - consent.

- CONSIDER [application for a job, views, factors]: dikkate al- ['- take note of, - take into consideration'] → al- 1, {I/hakkında} düşün- ['- think {about}'] → düşün- 5, gözden geçir- [obj.: report] → geçir- 1, göz önünde tut- ['- keep in mind'] → tut- 2, incele- [obj.: application]. *930:12.* thought: - consider; *945:8.* judgment: - judge.
- consider, - take up a matter: ele al- → al- 1. *404:3.* undertaking: - undertake.
- consider /θ [sb or sth], AS/ [He considered his teacher as a model for himself.]: /A, olarak/ bak- 4, /I, olarak/ gör- 2, /I/ say- 4. *952:11.* belief: - think.
- consider AT LENGTH, - ponder, - think over carefully, - think and think: {düşün-/düşünüp} taşın- → düşün- 1. *930:9.* thought: - think hard; *930:11.* - think about.
- consider IMPORTANT, - attach importance /to/, - value /θ/: /A/ {önem/ehemmiyet} ver- → ver- 1, /I/ önemse-. *996:13.* importance: - value.

- CONSIST /OF/, - be made up, composed, or formed /OF/: /DAn/ oluş-. *795:3.* composition: - compose.

- CONSTITUTE, - form, - create /{from/OUT OF}/: /DAn/ oluştur-. *891:8.* production: - produce, - create.

- CONSULT /θ [sb, an office], {about/on the subject of}/, - refer /to [sb], regarding/: /A, {konusunda}/ danış-. *387:14.* use: - avail oneself of; *541:11.* conversation: - confer.

- consult /θ/ sb, - ask sb's advice, - take or - get advice /from/ sb: /DAn/ akıl al- → al- 1, fikrini al- → al- 1. *422:7.* advice: - take or - accept advice.
- consult /θ [sb, an office, a book], for/, - refer, - resort, or - turn /to, for/, - have recourse /to, for/, - look sth up /IN [a reference source: dictionary]/: /A, için/ {başvur-/müracaat et-} 1. *387:14.* use: - avail oneself of; *937:30.* inquiry: - seek.
- consult a person: bilgisine danış- [lit., ** - consult /θ/ sb's knowledge]. *387:14.* use: - avail oneself of; *937:30.* inquiry: - seek.

- CONTACT /θ/, - get in contact /with/: /1A/ bağlantı kur- [obj.: person by phone] → kur- 1, /1A/ temas kur- [obj.: a person] → kur- 1. *223:10.* nearness: - contact; *343:8.* communication: - communicate with, - get in touch with.
- contact /θ/, - reach /θ/, - get in touch /WITH/ [a person]: /A/ ulaş- 2. *343:8.* communication: - communicate with, - get in touch with.

- CONTAIN, - hold [This bottle contains 2 quarts.]: içine al- 2 → al- 1. *771:3.* inclusion: - include.

- CONTINUE, - last, - go on [The lesson is continuing.]: devam et- 1, sür- 2. *811:4b.* continuity: for sth - continue; *826:6.* durability: - endure.
- continue /{θ/WITH}/ sth, - go on /WITH/ sth, - keep [on] doing sth [Continue (with) the lesson.]: /A/ devam et- 2. *267:6.* length: - lengthen; *811:4a.* continuity: - continue sth.

- CONTRADICT, - be in contradiction [ideas, behavior]: çeliş-. *451:6.* opposition: - contradict.
- contradict, - deny, - refute, - declare or - show to be false or wrong: yalanla-. *335:4.* negation, denial: - deny; *451:6.* opposition: - contradict; *957:5.* disproof: - refute.

- CONTROL /θ/, - get or - keep control /{OF/OVER}/, - keep in line [people or one's emotions, actions: The teacher couldn't control {the class/himself}.]: /A/ hâkim ol- → ol- 12. *106:7.* inexcitability: - compose oneself; *417:13.* authority: - possess or - wield authority; *428:7.*

restraint: - restrain; *668:6.*
temperance: - restrain oneself.
- control, - administer, - be in charge of
AN AREA [The army controls the
region.]: **idare et-** 1, **yönet-** 1.
417:13. authority: - possess or - wield
authority; *573:8.* direction,
management: - direct; *612:14.*
government: - rule.
- control, - regulate [This instrument
controls the heat.]: **ayarla-** 1,
düzenle- 3. *573:8.* direction,
management: - direct.

- CONVENE, - come together, - meet
[subj.: groups, societies]: **bir araya
gel-** → gel- 1, **toplan-** 3. *769:17.*
assemblage: - convene.

- CONVERSE [in a friendly manner], -
chat, - talk /with/: /lA/ **muhabbet
et-**, /lA/ **sohbet et-**. *541:10.*
conversation: - converse.

- CONVERT, - turn sth /INTO/ sth else:
/A/ **çevir-** 9, /A/ **döndür-** 2.
857:11. conversion: - convert.

- CONVEY, - take /to/ [message,
congratulations]: /A/ **ilet-** 1, /A/
aktar- 1. *176:10.* transferal,
transportation: - transfer; *176:15.* : -
send.
- convey, - bring, - transport sth /to/: /A/
ulaştır-. *176:12.* transferal,
transportation: - transport.

- CONVINCE or - persuade sb to believe
/θ/ sb or sth: /A/ **inandır-**. *375:23.*
motivation, inducement: - persuade;
952:18. belief: - convince.
- convince or - persuade sb /a: to [do sth],
b: θ [that], c: {that/to the effect that},
d: on the subject of/: /a: A, b: A, c:
A dair, d: **konusunda**/ **ikna et-**.
375:23. motivation, inducement: -
persuade; *952:18.* belief: - convince.
- convince or - persuade sb /TO/ do sth, -
talk sb /INTO/ doing sth: /için/
kandır- 2. *375:23.* motivation,
inducement: - persuade; *952:18.*
belief: - convince.

- COOK sth [The cook is cooking the
food.]: **pişir-**. *11:4a.* cooking: - cook
sth.
- cook [i.e., - become cooked: The food is
cooking.]: **piş-**. *11:4b.* cooking: for
sth - cook.
- cook sth in boiling water, - boil: **haşla-**.
11:4a. cooking: - cook sth.

- COOL [down]; - get cold: **soğu-** 1.
1022:9. cold: - freeze.

- cool sth down, - chill, - make sth cool or
cold [He cooled the drinks.], - let sth
cool or get cold: **soğut-** 1. *1022:10.*
cold: - make cold.
- cool /TOWARD/, - lose one's love,
desire, or enthusiasm /FOR/; - cease
to care /FOR/ sb or sth: /DAn/
soğu- 2. *261:7.* distance,
remoteness: - keep one's distance;
379:4. dissuasion: - disincline.

- COPY [not cheating]: /DAn, A/
kopya et- ['- copy /from, into/'],
kopyasını {**çek-**/**çıkar-**} ['- make
a copy of'] → çek- 8, çıkar- 7. *784:8.*
copy: - copy.
- copy [documents, files, disks, drives]
/from, to/, - make a copy: /DAn, A/
kopyala- 1. *784:8.* copy: - copy;
1041:18. computer science: -
computerize.
- copy illegitimately [cheat]: **kopya çek-**
1 → çek- 8. *356:18.* - cheat.
- copy, - imitate, - ape [The child is
{copying/imitating} her mother.]:
taklit et-. *336:5.* imitation: - imitate.

- CORRECT [an error, less likely with a
person as object, as in: The teacher
corrected him.]: **düzelt-** 2. *396:13.*
restoration: - remedy.

- CORRESPOND /with/, - be in
correspondence /with/, - write
[letters] to one another: /lA/
mektuplaş-. *343:6.* communication:
- communicate, - be in touch; *553:10.*
correspondence: - correspond.

- CORROBORATE, - confirm [fact,
reservation], - verify: **doğrula-**,
tasdik et-. *969:12.* certainty: -
verify.

- CORRUPT ONE'S MORALS, - lead
astray: **ahlâkını boz-** → boz- 1.
393:12. impairment: - corrupt.

- COST /θ [sb], θ [sth]/ [It cost θ him θ
many liras.]: /A, A/ **mal ol-** → ol-
12, **tut-** 7. *630:13.* price, fee: - cost.

- COUGH: **öksür-**. *318:21.* * 1. wind: -
breathe.

- COUNT, i.e., - determine or say the
number of: **say-** 1. *244:4.* quantity -
quantify.
Count {me/us} in: **Ben varım**. '{Count
me in./I'm with you.}', **Biz varız**.
'{Count us in./We're with you.}' →
{var/yok} ol- a) 3 → ol- 12. *771:* *
8. inclusion: PHR. count me in.

Count {me/us} out: **Ben yokum.** '{Count me out./I want no part of it.}', **Biz yokuz.** '{Count us out./We want no part of it.}' → {var/yok} ol- a) 3 → ol- 12. *772: * 11.* exclusion: PHR. count me out.

- COURT /θ/, - pay court /to/, - try to woo /θ/, - chase /AFTER/, i.e., - approach with sexual intent, *polite, formal:* **/A/ kur yap-** → yap- 3. *562:21.* lovemaking, endearment: - court.

- COVER, - cover up /with/ [child with blanket]: **/lA/ ört-** 1. *295:19.* covering: - cover.
- cover [insurance covers illness, check covers amount of bill, examination covers the whole course]: **içine al-** 1 → al- 1, **içer-, kapsa-.** *771:3.* inclusion: - include.
- cover, - pay [a bill]; - be enough /for/, - meet a need: **karşıla-** 2. *990:4.* sufficiency: - suffice.
- cover, - extend /OVER/, - stretch out /{OVER/on/ALONG}/ [trees over both sides of road]: **/DA/ uzan-** 2. *295:30.* covering: - overlie.
- cover, - travel, - traverse a distance [We covered 100 kilometers a day.]: **yol {yap-/git-}** → yap- 3, git- 1a, **katet-.** *177:20.* travel: - traverse.
- cover UP [hole, ditch]: **{kapa-/kapat-}** 3. *346:6.* concealment: - conceal.
- cover up [the truth, faults], - conceal, - hide: **ört-** 2. *346.6* concealment: - conceal.

- COZY UP /to/: → - COURT.

- CRASH, - crack up [The plane crashed on arrival.]: **düş-** 5 ['- crash, - crack up'], **[yere] çakıl-** ['- nose dive /into/ (a place), - crash, - crack up'] → çakıl- 2. *184:44.* aviation: - crash.
- crash, - run INTO [He crashed his car INTO a telephone pole.]: **/A/ çarp-** 1. *901:13.* impulse, impact: - collide.
- crash, - fail, - break down, - be down [subj.: a system, computer]: **çök-** 5. *393:24.* impairment: - break down.

- CRAWL, - creep, i.e., - move on all fours [subj.: usually a baby or infirm person]: **emekle-.** *177:26.* travel: - creep.
- crawl along the ground [soldiers in the dark of night]: **sürün-** 1. *177:26.* travel: - creep.

- CREATE, - constitute, - form /{from/OUT OF}/: **/DAn/ oluştur-.** *891:8.* production: - produce, - create.

- create, - develop: **geliştir-** 3 [new methods], **programla-** 3 [computer materials or games]. *891:12.* production: - originate; *1041:18.* computer science: - computerize.
- create [God created the universe. Although a subject other than God, as in: This news created a sensation, is frequent with this verb, some Turkish Muslims do not approve of such usage.]: **yarat-.** *891:8.* production: - produce, - create.
- create, - bring forth, - cause sth to come out or appear /from/: **/DAn/ çıkar-** 7. *891:8.* production: - produce, - create.
- create or - make DIFFICULTIES /FOR, on account of/: **/A, DAn dolayı/ {güçlük/zorluk} çıkar-** → çıkar- 7. *1012:14.* difficulty: - cause trouble.

- CREEP, - crawl, i.e., - move on all fours: **emekle-.** *177:26.* travel: - creep.

- CRITICIZE /a: because [or for], b: for, c: {for/on account of}/: **/a: {DIğI için/DIğInDAn}, b: DAn dolayı, c: yüzünden/ {eleştir-/tenkit et-}.** *510:14.* disapproval: - criticize; *945:14.* judgment: - criticize.
- criticize, - run down, - point out the faults of, - speak ill of, - disparage [more negative than the verbs in the above entry]: **yer-** 1. *512:8.* disparagement: - disparage.

- CROSS [The object crossed is indicated: He crossed θ the street.]: **/DAn/ geç-** 1. *909:8.* overrunning: - pass.
- cross OUT or off, - scratch out sth written: **{üstünü/üzerini} çiz-** 2, **karala-** 2 ['- black out']. *395:16.* destruction: - obliterate.
- cross-EXAMINE, question, interrogate: **sorguya çek-** → çek- 6. *937:21.* inquiry: - interrogate.
- cross OVER /θ/, - go across, - go /to/ the other side: **/DAn/ karşıya geç-** → geç- 1. *177:20.* travel: - traverse; *909:8.* overrunning: - pass.

- CROW [subj.: rooster], - sing [subj.: birds], - chirp [subj.: birds or insects]: **öt-** 1. *60:5.* animal sounds: [birds] - warble.

- CRUMPLE UP [papers]; - wrinkle, - make sth wrinkled [clothes]: **buruştur-.** *291:6.* fold: - wrinkle.

- CRUSH, - mash, - grind, - pulverize: ez-. *1049:9.* powderiness, crumbliness: - pulverize.
- crush, - overcome, - destroy, - damn: **kahret-** 2 [in the curse [Allah] kahretsin!]. *395:10.* destruction: - destroy; *513:11.* curse: INTERJ. damn!

- CRY, - weep: **ağla-, göz yaşı dök-** → dök- 1. *12:12* excretion: - excrete; *115:12.* lamentation: - weep.
- cry OUT, - shout, - scream /AT, saying/: /A, diye/ **haykır-**. *59:6.* cry, call: - cry.

- CURE a person or a disease: **tedavi et-** 2. *86:38.* remedy: - remedy; *396:15.* restoration: - cure.
- cure, - restore to health, - heal [a person]: /A/ **şifa ver-** [in Allah şifa versin! 'May God restore him to health'] → ver- 1. *86:38.* remedy: - remedy; *396:15.* restoration: - cure.

- CURSE /θ/, - swear /AT, because/: /A, DIğI için/ {**küfret-/söv-**}. *513:6.* curse: - curse.

- CUT [obj.: bread, hair, one's hand]: **kes-** 1. *3:22.* hair: - cut or - dress the hair; *224:4.* interval: - cleave; *268:6.* shortness: - shorten.
- cut ACROSS, - intersect [one street another]: **kes-** 1. *170:6.* crossing: - cross.
- cut DOWN [tree]: **kes-** 1. *912:5.* depression: - fell.
- cut down, - abridge, - condense [article, book]: **kısalt-** 2. *268:6.* shortness: - shorten.
- cut IN [a line at the movies, theater, soccer match, bank]: {**sırayı/ kuyruğu**} **boz-** 1 → boz- 1. *214:5.* intrusion: - intrude.
- cut in ON, - interrupt, - break in on [conversation]: **sözünü kes-** → kes- 3. *214:6.* intrusion: - interrupt; *843:4.* untimeliness: - talk out of turn.
- cut [up] INTO SLICES, - slice up: **dilimle-, dilim dilim kes-** → kes- 1. *792:6.* part: - separate; *801:11.* separation: - sever.
- cut OFF [sb's head]: **kes-** 1. *224:4.* interval: - cleave.
- cut OUT, - stop, - cease [obj.: that crying, the noise]: **kes-** 4. *856:11.* cessation: - put a stop to; *1011:13.* hindrance: - stop.
- cut out [cloth], - cut up [timber], - cut sth to size in accordance with a model or measure: **biç-** 1. *262:7.* form: - form.

- cut SHORT [obj.: meeting, talk]: **kısa kes-** → kes- 4. *268:6.* shortness: - shorten.
- cut UP, - break into pieces, - smash, - tear to pieces: **parçala-**. *801:13.* separation: - shatter.
- cut up [timber], - cut out [cloth], - cut sth to size in accordance with a model or measure: **biç-** 1. *262:7.* form: - form.
- cut up fine, - chop up fine, - mince, - grind [up] [vegetables, meat]: **kıy-** 1. *792:6.* part: - separate; *801:13.* separation: - shatter.
- cut [up] into slices or pieces; - carve, - chop into bits, - mince: **doğra-**. *792:6.* part: - separate; *801:13.* separation: - shatter.

- D -

DAMN {him/her/it}!, To hell with {him/it}!: [Allah] **Kahretsin!** → kahret- 2, **Lânet olsun!** → ol- 11 → olsun, **Kahrolsun!** 1 ['Damn {him/her/it}! To hell with {him/her/it}! Let {him/her/it} be damned!'] → kahrol- → ol- 12. *513:11.* curse: INTERJ. damn!

Damn it! [an expression of annoyance, not as strong as the above]: **Yazıklar olsun.** → → ol- 11 → olsun. *98:31.* unpleasantness: INTERJ. eeyuck!

- DAMPEN sb's enthusiasm /FOR/, - cause sb to lose love, desire, or enthusiasm /FOR/, - put sb /OFF/ sb or sth: /DAn/ **soğut-** 2. *1011:10.* hindrance: - hinder.

- DANCE: **dans et-**. *705:5.* dance: - dance.
- dance [used with the names of various dances: **zeybek**, etc.]: **oyna-** 4. *705:5.* dance: - dance.

- DARE, - attempt, or - try /to/ do sth that is beyond one's power or outside one's authority: /A/ **kalkış-**. *403:6.* endeavor: - attempt.

- DARN socks: **çorap dik-** [non-woolen socks] → 1 dik- 2, **çorap ör-** [woolen socks] → ör- 3. *396:14.* restoration: - repair.

Darn.: → DAMN {him/her/it}!

- DASH, - rush /INTO/ [a place], - enter /θ/ [a place] suddenly: /A/ **dal-** 3. *189:7.* entrance: - enter.

- DATE /θ/ sth [a document], - put the date /{IN/ON}, on/ sth: /A, {üzerine/üstüne}/ tarih at-[or koy-] → tarih {at-/koy-} → at- 3. *831:13.* measurement of time: - date.

- date, - be dating, - go [out] on a date /with/, - go out /with/ [with the intention of marriage]: /lA/ çık- 10, flört et- [Not the English '- flirt']. *562:14.* lovemaking, endearment: - make love; *769:16.* assemblage: - come together.

- DAYDREAM, - start to daydream, - go off /INTO/ daydreams, reverie, - reminisce: {hayale/hayallere} dal- → dal- 2. *984:9.* distraction, confusion: - muse; *988:11.* memory: - reminisce.

- DEAL /WITH/ sb, - behave /TOWARD sb, toward sb/, - treat /θ/ sb [well, badly]: /A, A karşı/ davran-. *321:6.* behavior: - treat.

- deal /with/, - be busy or occupied /with/: /lA/ meşgul ol- 1 → ol- 12. *330:10.* activity: - be busy; *724:11.* occupation: - busy oneself with.

- deal strictly, harshly /WITH/, - be hard /on/: üstüne git- 1 → git- 1a. *425:5.* strictness: - deal hardly or harshly with.

- DEBATE /a: with, b: about, c: on the subject of, d: about/; - have a discussion /with/; - argue or dispute /with/: /a: lA, b: hakkında, c: konusunda, d: I/ tartış- 1 [the pros and cons, not confrontational in a negative sense]. *934:16.* reasoning: - argue.

- DECEIVE, - fool, - take in, - mislead [subj.: salesman; obj.: customer]: aldat- 1 , kandır- 1. *356:14.* deception: - deceive.

- DECIDE, - make a decision, - resolve: /için/ karar al- [subj.: usually a group or organization acting in an official capacity] → al- 1, /A/ karar ver- [subj.: usually an individual rather than a group or organization] → ver- 1, /I/ kararlaştır- [subj.: at least two persons reaching a decision together]. *359:7.* resolution: - resolve.

- DECK ONESELF OUT /IN/, - adorn oneself /with/, - doll oneself up /IN/: /lA/ süslen- 1. *5:41.* clothing: - dress up.

- DECLARE, - announce: beyan et- [at customs and elsewhere], duyur- [not at customs but elsewhere]. *352:12.* publication: - announce.

- declare, - announce, - state, - note [*formal, official*: in speech and in writing]: kaydet- 4. *334:5.* affirmation: - affirm; *524:24.* speech: - state.

- DECLINE in value [money: dollar, mark], - fall [prices, temperature]: düş- 3. *633:6b.* cheapness: - become cheaper.

- decline in quality [an ability, memory], - deteriorate, - go downhill: zayıfla- 2. *393:16.* impairment: - deteriorate.

- DECORATE /with/, - adorn /with/: /lA/ süsle-. *498:8.* ornamentation: - ornament; *1015:15.* beauty: - beautify.

- DECREASE, - diminish, - become less [amount]: azal-, eksil- 1. *252:6.* decrease: - decrease [i.].

- decrease or - drop IN PRICE, for prices - fall, - drop: fiyatlar {düş-/in-} → düş- 3, in- 4; ucuzla-. *252:6.* decrease: - decrease; *633:6b.* cheapness: - become cheaper.

- DECREE, - command, - order: buyur- 1, emret-. *420:8.* command: - command.

- DEFACE with drawings, scribblings, grafitti: karala- 1. *1003:4.* blemish: - blemish.

- DEFEAT, - beat, - overcome, - conquer: 2 yen- 1. *412:6.* defeat: - defeat.

- DEFECATE, - have a bowel movement [*formal, polite*]: büyük aptes yap- → yap- 3, dışarı[.ya] çık- 2 → çık- 2. *12:13.* excretion: - defecate.

- defecate, - urinate: ihtiyacını gör- → gör- 4, tuvalet yap- ['- have a bowel movement *or* BM, - urinate; - make one's toilet, i.e., usually for a woman to dress or to arrange her hair'] → yap- 3. *12:13.* excretion: - defecate; *12:14.* : - urinate.

- DEFEND /against/, - protect /from, against/: /DAn, A karşı/ koru-. *460:8.* defend: - defend; *1007:18a.* protection: - protect.

- defend [country /against/ enemy attack, accused /against/ charges]: /A karşı/ savun-. *460:8.* defend: - defend; *1007:18a.* protection: - protect.

- defend one's {OPINIONS/views}: {fikir/görüş} savun- 1. *460:8.* defend: - defend.

- DEFINE [a word]: **tanımla-, karşılığını ver-** ['- give the equivalent (of a word)'] → ver- 1. *341:9.* interpretation: - interpret.

- DEFLATE, - collapse, - go flat: **sön-** 2 [subj.: balloon, tire, rubber boat], **in-** 4 [subj.: tire, rubber boat]. *260:10.* contraction: - collapse.

- DELETE [e-mail], - erase [error, blackboard] /with/: **/lA/ sil-** 3. *255:12.* subtraction: [written text] - delete.

- DELIGHT SB, - cheer sb up, - put sb in good spirits, - make sb feel happy: **neşelendir-.** *109:7.* cheerfulness: - cheer.

- DELIVER /to/, - hand or - turn over /to/: **/A/ teslim et-.** *478:13.* giving: - deliver.

- DEMAND, - call for [apology, better pay]: **iste-** 2, **talep et-.** *421:5.* demand: - demand.

- DEMEAN ONESELF, - stoop to doing sth despicable, - sink to a low [level in behavior]: **alçal-** 2. *137:7.* humility: - humble oneself.

- DEMOLISH, - wreck; - pull down, - tear down, - knock down /with/; - destroy; - ruin: **/lA/ yık-** 1. *395:17.* destruction: - demolish.

- DEMONSTRATE AGAINST, - hold a {demonstration/protest}: **gösteri yap-** → yap- 3. *333:5.* dissent: - object.
- demonstrate SUCCESS /in/, - be successful /in/: **/DA/ başarı göster-** → göster- 1. *409:9.* success: - score a success.

- DENY, - claim that sth is not true: **inkâr et-, reddet-** 2. *335:4.* negation, denial: - deny.
- deny, - contradict, - refute, - declare or - show to be false or wrong: **yalanla-.** *335:4.* negation, denial: - deny; *451:6.* opposition: - contradict; *957:5.* disproof: - refute.

- DEPART, - leave /from, for/, - go away /from/: **/DAn, A / ayrıl-** 3 [from city, party], **/DAn/ çık-** 1 [from an enclosed place: house, room], **/DAn/ git-** 1a [from anywhere], **/DAn/ uzaklaş-** 1 ['- move away from': train from station]. *188:6.* departure: - depart.

- depart, - leave /from/: **/DAn/ hareket et-** 3 [usually by means of a land vehicle, i.e., bus or train, not a boat, and not a person on foot]. *188:6.* departure: - depart.

- DEPEND or - rely /{ON/UPON}/ for support: **/A/ dayan-** 2, **sırtını {daya-/yasla-}** 2. *952:16.* belief: - rely on.

- DEPOSIT MONEY /IN/ [bank, account]: **/A/ para yatır-** 1 → yatır- 2. *159:14.* location: - deposit.

- DEPRESS SB, - spoil sb's mood: **moralini boz-.** → boz- 1. *112:18.* sadness: - sadden.

- DESCEND, - go down /{from/BY WAY OF}, to/ [person by way of stairs, from a vehicle]: **/DAn, A/ in-** 1. *194:5.* descent: - descend.
- descend or - come down /from, to/ a lower level [subj.: plane, birds, balloon]: **/DAn, A/ alçal-** 1. *194:5.* descent: - descend.

- DESCRIBE sth /to/: **/A/ tarif et-.** *349:9.* representation, description: - describe; *864:10.* particularity: - characterize.
- describe, - characterize /AS/: **/olarak/ nitelendir-.** *349:9.* representation, description: - describe; *864:10.* particularity: - characterize.
- describe, - tell /about/: **/I/ anlat-** 3. *349:9.* representation, description: - describe; *864:10.* particularity: - characterize.

- DESERVE sth /FOR, because/: **/lA, DIğI için/ hak et-.** *639:5.* dueness: - deserve.

- DESIRE, - want: **arzu et-, dile-** 1, **iste-** 1. *100:14.* desire: - desire; *100:15.* : - want to.

- DESPAIR, - lose or - give up hope: **{umudunu/ümidini} kaybet-**[or yitir-] → {kaybet-/yitir-}. *125:10.* hopelessness: - despair.

- DESTROY /with/; - demolish, - wreck /with/; - pull down, - tear down, - knock down /with/; - ruin [building]: **/lA/ yık-** 1. *395:17.* destruction: - demolish.
- destroy, - do away with, - get rid of [God creates and destroys; fire destroys belongings]: **yok et-** 1. *395:10.* destruction: - destroy

- destroy, - exhaust, - kill, - finish off [a person: Drink, gambling, and women destroyed him.]: **bitir-** 2. *395:10.* destruction: - destroy.
- destroy, - crush, - overcome: **kahret-** 2 [in the curse **(Allah) kahretsin!**]. *395:10.* destruction: - destroy; *513:11.* curse: INTERJ. damn!
- destroy or - shatter sb's HOPES: **ümidini kır-.** → kır- 1. *125:11.* hopelessness: - shatter one's hopes.

- DETAIN, - hold up, - keep [I don't want to detain you.]: **/A/ mâni ol-** → ol-12, **/I/ tut-** 3. *1011:14.* hindrance: - prevent.

- DETER or - dissuade sb /from/, - talk sb /OUT OF/ sth: **/DAn/ {vazgeçir-/caydır-}.** *379:3.* dissuasion: - dissuade.

- DETERIORATE, - get worse [patient, economic situation, an ability]: **fenalaş-** 1, **gerile-** 2, **kötüleş-**, **zayıfla-** 2. *393:16.* impairment: - deteriorate.

- DETERMINE or - establish the existence of, - find [errors in a composition]: **{tespit et-/sapta-}** 1. *940:2.* discovery: - discover.

- DETEST /θ/, - loathe /θ/, - hate /θ/, - abhor /θ/: **/DAn/ nefret et-.** *103:5.* hate: - hate.

- DEVELOP, - make larger /[by]...ing/ [one's body by exercising]: **/ArAk/ geliştir-** 2. *259:4.* expansion, growth: - make larger.
- develop, - create: **geliştir-** 3 [obj.: new methods, products], **programla-** 3 [computer materials or games]. *891:12.* production: - originate; *1041:18.* computer science: - computerize.
- develop, - evolve, - unfold [subj.: technology, events]: **geliş-** 1. *860:5.* evolution: - evolve.
- develop, - advance, - make progress [subj.: a nation]: **kalkın-.** *860:5.* evolution: - evolve.
- develop photographic film: **banyo yap-** 2 → yap- 3. *714:15.* photography: - process.
- develop and print or only - print photographic film: **film bas-** → bas- 3. *714:15.* photography: - process.

- DEVOTE EFFORT /to/, - put effort /INTO/, - work /AT/, - take pains /WITH/: **/A/ emek ver-** → ver- 1. *403:5.* endeavor: - endeavor.

- DIAGNOSE, - make a diagnosis [obj.: a disease]: **teşhis koy-** → koy- 1. *341:9.* interpretation: - interpret.

- DIAL [a phone number]: **[numara] çevir-** 7. *347:18.* communications: - telephone; *914:9.* rotation: - rotate.
- dial the wrong number: **yanlış numara çevir-.** → çevir- 7. *347:18.* communications: - telephone; *914:9.* rotation: - rotate.

- DICKER, - haggle, - bargain /a: for [sth], b: over [sth], c: with [sb]/: **/a: için, b: üzerinde, c: lA/ pazarlık et-.** *731:17.* commerce, economics: - bargain.

- DIE /{OF/AS A RESULT OF}/ [hunger, thirst; for any living thing]: **/DAn/ öl-.** *307:19.* death: - die.
- die, - pass away [only for persons]: **hayata gözlerini {kapa-/kapat-/yum-}** → {kapa-/kapat-} 1, göz yum- 1, **hayatını {kaybet-/ yitir-}** ['- lose one's life', usually of unnatural causes: in an accident, through murder, etc.], **ömrünü tamamla-** ['- complete one's life, come to the end of one's life'], **vefat et-.** *307:19.* death: - die.
- die DOWN [rain], - slow down, - lose speed [vehicle, runner]: **yavaşla-.** *175:9.* slowness: - slow.

- DIET, - go on a diet [both for losing weight and for the treatment of a medical condition]: **perhiz yap-** → yap- 3. *7:17.* nutrition: - diet.

- DIFFERENTIATE, - separate, - distinguish [Language differentiates man from animals.]: **ayır-** 4. *864:10.* particularity: - characterize.

- DIG [well, ditch, hole, grave]: **kaz-.** *284:15.* concavity: - excavate.
- dig UP [body, treasure]: **çıkar-** 1. *192:11.* extraction: - disinter.

- DINE OUT, - go out {for/to} dinner: **yemeğe çık-** → çık- 2. *8:21.* eating: - dine.

- DIRECT, - administer, - manage, - run, - control, - govern, - rule: **idare et-** 1, **yönet-** 1. *417:13.* authority: - possess or - wield authority; *573:8.* direction, management: - direct; *612:14.* government: - rule.

Part 2: English-Turkish Index

- DIRTY sth, - get or - make sth dirty, - soil, - pollute: **kirlet-, pislet-.** *80:15a.* uncleanness: - dirty.

- DISAGREE [You and I disagree on this matter.], - disagree /with/ [I disagree with him on this matter.]. The negative of the following: **anlaş-** 2, {düşünceye/fikre/görüşe} **katıl-** → katıl- 3, {fikir/görüş} **paylaş-**, {fikir/görüş} **savun-** 2. *788:5.* disagreement: - disagree.
- disagree /WITH/ sb [This food disagrees WITH me.], - upset /θ/ sb [subj.: food], - affect /θ/ one's health adversely, - make /θ/ sb sick, for food or weather not - agree /WITH/ one, - have a bad effect /ON/: **/A/ dokun-** 2. *96:16a.* unpleasure: - distress; *393:9.* impairment: - impair; *809:9.* disorder: - disorder.

- DISAPPEAR: **kaybol-** → ol- 12. *34:2a.* disappearance: - disappear.
- disappear /into/ a larger body of people [subj.: thief]: **/A/ dal-** 3, **/A/ karış-** 7, **/A/ kaybol-** → ol- 12. *34:2a.* disappearance: - disappear.

- DISAPPOINT [We expected a lot from you, but you disappointed us.]: {hayal/düş} **kırıklığına uğrat-.** *132:2.* disappointment: - disappoint.

- DISAPPROVE /of/ [sb's behavior, actions]: This concept may be covered by the negative of the following verbs: {hoş/iyi} **karşıla-** → karşıla- 3, **kabul et-** 2, **onayla-**, **razı ol-** 1, 2 → ol- 12. *510:10.* disapproval: - disapprove.

- DISBAND, - break up, - fall apart, - disintegrate [dispersal of members: subj.: household, family, political party]: **dağıl-** 3. *805:3.* disintegration: - disintegrate.

- DISCARD, - throw out, - away, - throw /{IN/INTO}/ the trash: **at-** 2, **çöpe** {at-/dök-} → at- 2, dök- 3. *390:7.* discard: - discard.

- DISCHARGE, - let {off/out), - unload [passengers] /at, from/: **/DA, DAn/ indir-** 2. *908:23.* ejection: - unload; *912:4.* depression: - depress.

- DISCLOSE, - reveal /to/, - make public: **/A/ açıkla-** 2. *351:4.* disclosure: - disclose.
- disclose, - reveal, - expose to view; - bring to light: {ortaya/meydana}

çıkar- → çıkar- 7. *351:4.* disclosure: - disclose.

- DISCOVER: **bul-** 2, **keşfet-.** *940:2.* discovery: - discover.

- DISCUSS, - confer /with/; - meet /with/: **/lA/ görüş-** 1. *524:20.* speech: - speak; *541:11.* conversation: - confer.
- discuss /θ/, - talk /ABOUT/, - mention /θ/: **/DAn/ bahset-, /DAn/ söz et-, sözünü et-.** *541:12.* conversation: - discuss; *551:8.* information: - inform.

- DISH OUT, - serve out, - distribute a {serving/share} /{INTO/ONTO}/ [food onto plate]: **/A/ paylaştır-.** *176:17.* transferal, transportation: - ladle.

- DISINTEGRATE, - break up, - disband, - fall apart [dispersal of members: subj.: household, family, political party]: **dağıl-** 3. *805:3.* disintegration: - disintegrate.

- DISMISS: *formal:* **görevden al-** ['- fire, relieve sb of his {duties/position}'] → al- 1, **işine son ver-** ['- fire, - relieve sb of his position'] → ver- 1. *908:19.* ejection: - dismiss. *informal:* **işten** {at-/kov-} ['- fire, - sack, - can'] → at- 1, kov- 2. *908:20.* : <nonformal terms> - fire.

- DISMOUNT /{θ/from}/ an animal, - get down /{from/OFF}/ a vehicle: **/DAn/ in-** 2. *194:7.* descent: - get down.

- DISOBEY: **sözünden çık-** ['- disobey, not - do what sb says'] → çık- 1, **dinleME-** ['NOT - heed, - obey, or - listen /to/'] → 1 dinle- 2, {lâf/söz} **dinleME-** ['NOT - heed what one has been told'] → 1 dinle- 2. *327:6.* disobedience: - disobey.

- DISPARAGE, - run down, - point out the faults of, - criticize, - speak ill of: **yer-** 1. *512:8.* disparagement: - disparage.

- DISPENSE, - distribute, - hand out, - serve [out] /to/ [food to the needy]: **/A/ dağıt-** 2. *770:4a.* dispersion: - disperse sth.

- DISPERSE [The police dispersed the demonstrating students.], - scatter /to/ [The wind scattered the papers.]: **/A/**

dağıt- 1. *770:4a.* dispersion: - disperse sth.

- disperse, - scatter /to/ [i.e., - BECOME dispersed: The students dispersed to their classrooms.]: /A/ dağıl- 1. *770:8.* dispersion: - disband.

- DISPUTE, - argue; - debate heatedly; - have an intense discussion /a: with, b: about, c: on the subject of, d: about/: /a: 1A, b: hakkında, c: konusunda, d: I/ {münakaşa et-/tartış- 2}. *934:16.* reasoning: - argue.

- DISREGARD /θ/, - close one's eyes /to/, - take no notice /OF/, - overlook /θ/, - turn a blind eye /to/, - wink /AT/ a fault: /A/ göz yum- 2. *148:4.* forgiveness: - condone; *983:2.* inattention: - be inattentive.

- DISSOLVE /in/ [subj.: sugar dissolves in water], - melt [subj.: ice, snow]: /DA/ eri-. *34:2a.* disappearance: - disappear; *805:3.* disintegration: - disintegrate; *1062:5.* liquefaction: - liquefy.

- dissolve, - melt, - liquefy, - cause to become liquid [Dissolve some sugar in water.]: erit-. *1019:21.* heating: - melt; *1062:5.* liquefaction: - liquefy.

- DISSUADE or - deter sb /from/, - talk sb /OUT OF/ sth: /DAn/ {vazgeçir-/caydır-}. *379:3.* dissuasion: - dissuade.

- DISTINGUISH, - make out, - see clearly: farket- 3, seç- 2. *27:12.* vision: - see.

- distinguish, - differentiate, - separate [Language distinguishes man from animals.]: ayır- 4. *864:10.* particularity: - characterize.

- DISTRACT, - confuse, - make sb lose track or count of, - cause sb to lose track or count of: şaşırt- 3. *984:6.* distraction: - distract; *984:7a.* : - confuse.

- distract, - disturb, - bother [people at work]; - occupy [restroom too long]: meşgul et-. *724:10.* occupation: - occupy; *984:6.* distraction: - distract.

- DISTRESS, - worry, - upset; - sadden: üz-. *112:18.* sadness: - sadden; *126:4.* anxiety: - concern; *126:5.* : - make anxious.

- distress sb GREATLY, - drive to distraction: kahret- 1. *96:16a.* unpleasure: - distress; *98:14.* unpleasantness: - distress.

- DISTRIBUTE, - hand out, - dispense, - serve [out] /to/ [food to the needy]: /A/ dağıt- 2. *770:4a.* dispersion: - disperse sth.

- DISTURB, - bother, - annoy, - irritate: rahatını boz- → boz- 1, rahatsız et-. *96:13.* unpleasure: - annoy.

- disturb, - upset [subj.: the sound of sirens]: heyecanlandır- 2. *96:16a.* unpleasure: - distress.

- disturb, - bother, - distract [people at work]; - occupy [restroom too long]: meşgul et-. *724:10.* occupation: - occupy; *984:6.* distraction: - distract.

- disturb, - upset /θ/ sb [subj.: a person's inappropriate words]; - affect, - move, or - touch /θ/ sb emotionally [subj.: the director's farewell speech]: /A/ dokun- 3. *93:14.* feelings: - affect; *893:7.* influence: - influence.

- DIVE, - plunge /INTO/ [the ocean], {from/OFF} [the pier]/: /A, DAn/ dal- 1. *367:6.* plunge: - plunge.

- DIVIDE /INTO/: /A/ ayır- 3, /A/ böl-. *801:8.* separation: - separate.

- DIVORCE [husband divorces wife]: boşa-. *566:5.* divorce, widowhood: - divorce.

- DO: yap- 2. *328:6.* action: - do; *407:4.* accomplishment: - accomplish.

- do, - perform: [The following four verbs form phrasal verbs with Arabic and Turkish nouns and are not frequently used alone to express '- do, perform' unless they refer back to such nouns: et- 1, eyle-, kıl- [with a limited set of nouns], kıy- [with a very limited set of nouns]. *328:6.* action: - do; *407:4.* accomplishment: - accomplish.

- do AWAY WITH, - abolish, - repeal [law], - eliminate, - eradicate [disease]: kaldır- 4. *445:2.* repeal: - repeal; *772:5* exclusion: - eliminate.

- do BUSINESS /with/ sb: /1A/ alışveriş et-, /1A/ iş yap- 2. → yap- 3. *731:16.* commerce, economics: - trade with.

- do or - get a DEGREE [master's, doctor's]: *degree name* [e.g., master, doktora] yap-. → yap- 3. *570:9.* learning: - master.

- do DRILLS, exercises [on the blackboard or in a book or workbook]: alıştırma yap- → yap- 3, egzersiz yap- 3 → yap- 3. *328:8.* action: - practice.

- do EXERCISES as physical therapy [as after an operation]: egzersiz yap- 2

→ yap- 3. *84:4.* fitness, exercise: - exercise; *328:8.* action: - practice.

- do sth FOR A LIVING [What do you do for a living?]: **iş yap-** 1 → **yap-** 3. *385:11.* provision, equipment: - make a living.

- do GOOD, - hit the spot [subj.: coffee when you are tired]: **2 değ-** 2. *998:10.* goodness: - do good.

- do GYMNASTICS: **jimnastik yap-** → **yap-** 3. *84:4.* fitness, exercise: - exercise; *725:8.* exertion: - exert.

- do gymnastics, physical training, - train [oneself physically], - exercise: **idman yap-**. → **yap-** 3. *84:4.* fitness, exercise: - exercise; *725:8.* exertion: - exert.

- do IN, - bump off, - wipe out, - rub out, - nuke, - zap. *Contemptuous for* - kill: **gebert-**. *308:13.* killing: non-formal terms: - waste; *514:* * *5.* threat: INTERJ. specific threats.

- do INCORRECTLY, - get or - do sth wrong [questions on an exam]: **yanlış yap-** → **yap-** 3. *974:12.* error: - misdo.

- do /θ/ sb a KINDNESS, a good turn, - be good /to/, - do good, - treat kindly: **/A/ iyilik et-**. *143:12.* kindness, benevolence: - do a favor.

- do NOTHING, - remain inactive in the face of a situation that requires action, - stand there without doing anything: **dur-** 8. *329:2.* inaction: - do nothing.

- do ONE'S BEST: **elinden geleni yap-** → **yap-** 3. *403:13.* endeavor: - do one's best.

- do one's best /to/, - strive /to/, - struggle /to/: **/A/ çabala-**. *403:13.* endeavor: - do one's best.

- do one's MILITARY SERVICE, - serve in the armed forces: **askerlik yap-** → **yap-** 3. *458:18.* warfare: - serve.

- do RESEARCH ON, - research, - explore, - investigate, - study, - try to find out: **araştır-** 2. *937:23.* investigate: - investigate.

- do the RIGHT THING: **iyi et-**, **doğrusunu yap-** → **yap-** 3. *509:22.* approval: bravo!; *637:2.* * *1.* right: - do the right thing.

- do SHOPPING, - shop: **alışveriş yap-** → **yap-** 3, **alışverişe çık-** → **çık-** 2. *733:8.* purchase: - shop.

- do SPORTS, - engage in sports, - take part in sports: **spor yap-** → **yap-** 3. *84:4.* fitness, exercise: - exercise; *743:23.* amusement: - play.

- do THE JOB, - serve the purpose, - work [subj.: machine]: **iş gör-** → **gör-** 4. *387:17.* use: - avail; *407:4.* accomplishment: - accomplish;

994:3. expedience: - expedite one's affair.

- do or - serve TIME, a prison sentence: **ceza çek-** → **çek-** 5, **cezasını çek-** 2 ['- do or - serve time /for/...'] → **çek-** 5. *429:18.* confinement: - be imprisoned; *824:5.* spell: - take one's turn.

- do WELL /BY...ing [*or* TO/ [He did (well) by speaking out (*or* to speak out).]: **/{mAklA/ArAk}/ doğru hareket et-** → **hareket et-** 4, **/mAklA/ iyi et-**. *637:2.* * *1.* right: - do the right thing.

- do WHAT A SITUATION REQUIRES, necessitates, - do what has to be done: **gereğini yap-**. *962:9.* necessity: - require.

- do or - get sth WRONG, - do incorrectly [questions on an exam]: **yanlış yap-** → **yap-** 3. *974:12.* error: - misdo.

- DOCK [subj.: a ship]; - draw, - pull /{UP TO/ALONGSIDE}/ a place [train to platform]: **/A/ yanaş-** 2. *167:3.* approach: - approach.

- DOLL ONESELF UP /IN/, - deck oneself out /IN/, - adorn oneself /with/: **/lA/ süslen-** 1. *5:41.* clothing: - dress up.

- DON, - put on clothing [Also: '- be wearing']: **giy-**. *5:42.* clothing: - don.

- DONATE /to/, - make a donation /to/, - give /to/ [a charity]: **/A/ bağışla-** 1. *478:12.* giving: - give.

DON'T get me wrong: **Yanlış anlaşılmasın.** → **anlaşıl-**. *521:7.* intelligibility: - understand.

Don't give me that!, You don't say!, You don't mean it!, Oh go on!, Well I declare!: **Yapma ya!** [lit., 'Don't do (that).'] *131:* * *16.* inexpectation: expressions of inexpectation; *955:* * *6.* incredulity: expressions of incredulity.

Don't worry! It doesn't matter: **Canın sağ olsun!** → **sağ ol-** → **ol-** 12. *121:* * *17.* comfort: words of comfort; *504:* * *20.* courtesy: polite expressions.

Don't worry., Don't be sad., Cheer up!: **Üzülme!** → **üzül-**. *109:20.* cheerfulness: PHR. cheer up!

Don't worry. This too shall pass.: **Üzülme, bu da geçer.** → **üzül-**. *121:* * *17.* comfort: words of comfort; *504:* * *20.* courtesy: polite expressions.

- DOUBT: [Will she come? I doubt it (i.e., I don't think so)., I doubt that she will come (i.e., I don't think she'll come).]: {sanMA-/zannetME-} → {san-/zannet-}. *500:11*. belief: - think; *952:11*. belief: - think.

DOWN WITH ... [fascism, communism]!: **Kahrolsun ...!** → kahrolsun 2 → ol- 11 → olsun. *513:11*. curse: INTERJ. damn!
- DOWNLOAD /from [the Internet], to/: /DAn, A/ **indir-** 1. *912:4*. depression: - depress; *1041:18*. computer science: - computerize.

- DOZE OFF, - drop off to sleep, - fall asleep: **uykuya dal-** → dal- 2. *22:16*. sleep: - go to sleep.
- doze off, - doze: **uyukla-**. *22:13*. sleep: - sleep; *22:16*. : - go to sleep.

- DRAFT, - make, - devise, - establish, or - formulate a plan: **plan kur-** → kur- 1. *381:8*. plan: - plan; *964:4*. prearrangement: - prearrange.

- DRAG sb or sth ALONG THE GROUND /to/: /A/ **sürükle-** 1. *904:4*. pulling: - pull.
- drag sb /to/ a place against his will, - drag off: /A/ **sürükle-** 2. *904:4*. pulling: - pull.
- drag ON, - go on [subj.: matter, court case]: **uza-** 2. *826:7*. durability: - linger on.
- drag OUT, - prolong [speech], - extend [hours]: **uzat-** 3. *267:6*. lengthen: - lengthen.

- DRAW sth /{ON/IN}, on/ a surface: /A, {üstüne/üzerine}/ **çiz-** 1. *349:9*. representation, description: - describe.
- draw A LINE UNDER, - underline, - underscore /IN [ink], with [a ruler]/: /IA/ **altını çiz-** 1 → çiz- 1. *517:19*. signs, indicators: - mark.
- draw NEAR /to/, - approach /θ/, - come close /to/, up /to/, over /to/: /A/ **yaklaş-**, /A/ **yanaş-** 1. *167:3*. approach: - approach; *223:7*. nearness: - near, - come near.
- draw a PICTURE, pictures: /A/ **resim çiz-** → çiz- 1. *349:9*. representation, description: - describe.
- draw or - pull /{UP TO/ALONGSIDE}/ a place [for a ship - dock, a train - draw up to the platform]: /A/ **yanaş-** 2. *167:3*. approach: - approach.

- DREAM [at night]: {düş/rüya} **gör-** 1 → gör- 3. *985:17*. imagination: - dream.
- dream [not at night], - build up fanciful hopes /{about/concerning}/: {düş/rüya} **gör-** 2 → gör- 3, /a: hakkında, b: 1A ilgili, c: A dair, d: üzerine/ **hayal kur-** → kur- 1. *985:17*. imagination: - dream.

- DRESS oneself, - get dressed: **giyin-**. *5:42*. clothing: - don.
- dress, - clothe sb: **giydir-** a) /I [on the noun designating the person dressed]/ '- dress sb [garment not mentioned]', b) /I [on the noun designating the garment if that noun is definite, /θ/ on that noun if it is indefinite], A [on noun designating the person dressed]/ '- dress /θ/ sb /IN/ sth, have /θ/ sb put sth on or wear sth'. *5:38*. clothing: - clothe.

- DRIFT /IN/ [subj.: smoke, fog]: **bas-** 4.

- DRINK: **iç-** 1. *8:29*. eating: - drink.
- drink [alcoholic beverages]: {alkol/içki} **al-** → al- 5, [içki] **iç-** 1, **içki kullan-**. *88:24*. intoxication: - tipple.

- DRIVE [a vehicle]: *vehicle name* {kullan-/sür-} [e.g., araba {kullan-/sür-} '- drive a car'] → kullan-, sür- 1. *888:5*. operation: - operate sth.
- drive to a place [I drove to San Francisco.]: *vehicle name*.1A **gel-** [e.g., arabayla gel- lit., '- come by car'] → gel- 1, *vehicle name*.1A **git-** [e.g., arabayla git- lit., '- go by car'] → git- 1. *888:5*. operation: - operate sth.
- drive sb to a place [I drove my sister to town.]: *vehicle name*.1A *verb of transportation* [e.g., arabayla bırak-] → bırak- 2. *159:12*. location: - place.

- DRIZZLE, - sprinkle, - rain lightly: **çisele-**. *316:9* rain: - rain.

- DROP, - fall /from, {to/IN/INTO/ON/ONTO}/, fall [The dish dropped from the table ON the floor.]: /DAn, A/ **düş-** 1. *194:5*. descent: - descend.
- drop sth /from, {to/ON}/ [He dropped the dish ON the floor.], - let fall: /DAn, A/ **düşür-** 1. *912:7*. depression: - drop sth.
- drop, - fall [subj.: number of students], - decrease, - get or - run low on

[supplies: sugar, gas]: **azal-, eksil-** 1. *252:6.* decrease: - decrease.

- drop /θ/, - give up /θ/ [idea, plan]: **/DAn/ vazgeç-.** *370:7.* abandonment: - give up.

- drop a CLASS, lessons: **bırak-** 3. *370:5.* abandonment: - abandon.

- drop IN /{AT/ON}/, - drop /BY/, - stop in /AT/, - stop off /IN/ [obj.: person or place]: **/A/ uğra-** 1. *582:19.* sociability: - visit.

- drop in PRICE, - get cheaper, - decrease in price: **fiyatlar {düş-/in-}** → **düş-** 3, **in-** 4; **ucuzla-.** *252:6.* decrease: - decrease; *633:6b.* cheapness: - become cheaper.

- drop [in THE MAIL] [obj.: letter]: **/A/ at-** 4. *553:12.* correspondence: - mail.

- drop OFF [person or thing] /AT/, - leave off /AT/: **/A/ bırak-** 2. *159:12.* location: - place.

- drop off, - let {OFF/out}, - discharge, - unload [passengers] /at, from/: **/DA, DAn/ indir-** 2. *908:23.* ejection: - unload; *912:4.* depression: - depress.

- drop off TO SLEEP, - doze off, - fall asleep: **uykuya dal-** → **dal-** 2. *22:16.* sleep: - go to sleep.

- drop the SUBJECT, - conclude, - finish or - close the discussion of a subject: **{kapa-/kapat-}** 6. *819:5.* end: - end sth.

- DROWN /{BECAUSE OF/DUE TO}/: **/DAn/ boğul-** 1, **boğularak öl-** → **boğul-** 1. *308:18.* killing: - strangle; *367:7.* plunge: - submerge.

- DRY [face ON towel]; - wipe /with, {IN/ON}/: **/lA, A/ sil-** 1. *79:18.* cleanness: - clean; *1064:6a.* dryness: - dry, - make dry.

- dry, - dry out, - get or - become dry [laundry]: **kuru-** 1. *1064:6b.* dryness: - dry, - become dry.

- dry [hair], - wipe dry [dishes]: **kurula-.** *1064:6a.* dryness: - dry, - make dry.

- dry, - make dry: **kurut-.** *1064:6a.* dryness: - dry, - make dry.

- dry ONESELF /with/: **/lA/ kurulan-** 2. *1064:6a.* dryness: - dry, - make dry.

- dry UP, - wither [flowers]: **kuru-** 2. *1064:6b.* dryness: - dry, - become dry.

- DUB, - call, - name, - refer to /AS/: **/diye/ {adlandır-/isimlendir-},** **/A/ de-** 4. *527:11.* nomenclature: - name.

- dub, - name, - call [usually with a negative connotation when the object is a person]: **/A/ {ad/isim} tak-.** *527:11.* nomenclature: - name.

- DUMP or - pile sth /{on/upon}/ sb, - load sb down /with/ sth, - load sth down /upon/ sb [obj.: a task]: **/{üstüne/üzerine}/ yık-** 3. *159:15.* location: - load.

- DUST: **tozunu al-** → **al-** 1. *79:18.* cleanness: - clean.

- DWELL ON A TOPIC, SUBJECT: **{üstünde/üzerinde}/ dur-** → **dur-** 6. *826:9.* duration:- protract.

- E -

- EARN [money]: **kazan-** 1. *624:20.* payment: - be paid.

- earn or - make ONE'S LIVING, livelihood /by...ing/: **/ArAk/ geçimini sağla-, /ArAk/ geçin-** 2, **/ArAk/ hayatını kazan-** → **kazan-** 1. *385:11.* provision, equipment: - make a living; *409:12.* success: - manage.

- earn or - win the right /to/: **/A/ hak kazan-** → **kazan-** 1. *472:8.* acquisition: - acquire.

- EAT: **ye-** [preceded by the name of a food: She was eating kebab.], **yemek ye-** [when the specific food eaten is not indicated: She was eating when I came in.] → **ye-** 1. *8:20.* eating: - eat.

- eat [sometimes when the object is a liquid but not a drink, e.g., soup]: **iç-** 3. *8:20.* eating: - eat.

- eat food as a casual snack, - have a snack, - snack [The food may include, but is not limited to, junk food, i.e., cookies, candy, candy bars, etc., the kind of food sold in vending machines in the U.S.]: **abur cubur ye-** → **ye-** 1. *8:26.* eating: - pick.

- eat or - have BREAKFAST, - breakfast: **kahvaltı {et-/yap-}** → **yap-** 3. NOT ~~kahvaltı ye-~~. *8:21.* eating: - dine.

- eat or - have DINNER or supper, i.e., the evening meal: **akşam yemeği ye-** → **ye-** 1. *8:21.* eating: - dine.

- eat or - have LUNCH, - have the noon meal: **öğle yemeği ye-** → **ye-** 1. *8:21.* eating: - dine.

- eat ONE'S FILL, - have enough, - be full [I'm full.]: **doy-, karnı doy-.** *993:5.* satiety: - have enough.

- eat or - have a SNACK, - snack /ON/ sth, - grab a bite: **atıştır-** 2. *8:26.* eating: - pick.

- ECONOMIZE, - avoid expense: **masraftan {kaç-/kaçın-}** → kaç-2. *484:5.* parsimony: - stint.
- economize /by/, - make ends meet /with/; - manage /with/, - manage to get along /with/, - get by /with/ [little money]: /1A/ **idare et-** 2, /1A/ **yetin-** 2. *409:12.* success: - manage; *994:4.* expedience: - make shift, - make do.

- EDUCATE sb /on a subject/: /konuda/ **eğit-**. *568:10.* teaching: - teach.
- educate, - train, - bring up, - raise, - rear [children]: **yetiştir-** 2. *568:13.* teaching: - train.
- educate, - make it possible for sb to be educated, - have sb educated, - see to sb's education, - send sb to school [i.e., - pay his way]: **okut-** 2. *568:10.* teaching: - teach.

- EJACULATE, - come, - climax, - have an orgasm: **boşal-** 3 [more frequently for men but also for women]. *75:23.* sex: - climax; *908:25.* ejection: - disgorge.

- EJECT or - expel sb /from/, - throw sb /OUT OF/ [person from room]: /DAn/ **kov-** 1. *908:13.* ejection: - eject.

- ELECT sb /to/ [chairmanship, presidency]: /A/ **seç-** 1. *371:13.* choice: - choose.

- ELIMINATE, - eradicate [disease], - repeal, - do away with, - abolish [law]: **kaldır-** 4. *445:2.* repeal: - repeal; *772:5* exclusion: - eliminate.

- EMANATE, - result, - originate, - stem, or spring /from/, - be due /TO/: /DAn/ **kaynaklan-**. *886:5.* effect: - result from.

- EMBRACE, - take in one's arms; - hug: /I/ **kucakla-**. *562:18.* lovemaking, endearment: - embrace.
- embrace /θ/, - put, or - throw one's arms /AROUND/: /A/ **sarıl-** 1. *562:18.* lovemaking, endearment: - embrace.
- embrace or - hug ONE ANOTHER: **kucaklaş-, birbirlerini kucakla-**. *562:18.* lovemaking, endearment: - embrace.

- EMERGE /from/, - appear /from/, - come out /OF/: /DAn/ **çık-** 1 [person, thing from a place]. 3 [sun, moon, stars]. *190:11.* emergence: - emerge.

- emerge /from/ or - come /out of/ a coma: **komadan çık-**. → çık- 1. *190:11.* emergence: - emerge; *392:8.* improvement: - rally, - get better.

- EMPHASIZE, - stress [the importance, necessity of]: **vurgula-** 1, **altını çiz-** 2 ['- underline, - emphasize'] → çiz- 1. *996:14.* importance: - emphasize.

- EMPTY, - become empty, - empty out [The cookie jar emptied out in ten minutes.]: **boşal-** 1. *190:13.* emergence: - run out.
- empty sth, - empty sth out /INTO/ [He emptied the trash into the trash barrel.], - clear out [people from building]: /A/ **boşalt-**. *908:22.* ejection: - evacuate sth.

- EMULATE /θ/, - imitate the actions of, - follow the example of, - act in accord /with/: /A/ **uy-** 7. *336:7.* imitation: - emulate.

- ENCOUNTER /θ/, - meet by chance, - come or - chance /UPON/, - run /INTO/: /1A/ **karşılaş-** 2, /A/ **rastla-** 1, *formal:* /A/ **tesadüf et-** 1. *131:6.* inexpectation: - be unexpected; *223:11.* nearness: - meet.
- encounter, - face, or - experience /θ/ DIFFICULTIES, - meet or - be confronted /with/ difficulties: **{zorlukla/güçlükle} karşılaş-** → karşılaş- 3, /A/ **uğra-** 2. *216:8.* front: - confront; *830:8.* event: - experience; *1012:11.* difficulty: - have difficulty.

- ENCOURAGE or - spur sb on /a: to [lit., in the matter of], b: TO, c: with/; - inspire sb; - encourage sb to do or participate in sth; - promote the development of: /a: **konusunda**, b: **için**, c: 1A/ **teşvik et-**. *375:21.* motivation, inducement: - encourage; *492:16.* courage: - encourage.

- END, - BE over, - come to an end, - conclude, - finish: **bit-** 1 [any subject], **sona er-** [most subjects: concert, meeting] → er-, din- [only a limited number of subjects: most related to weather: hail, rain, storm; some related to emotions: tears, pain, anger]. *819:6.* end: - come to an end.
- end, - come to an end, - be over, - pass [difficult situation, illness]: **geç-** 4. *761:6.* non-existence: - cease to exist; *836:6.* past: - pass.

- ENDEAVOR, - struggle, - strive, - work hard, - try hard /to/: **/için/ uğraş-** 1. *403:11.* endeavor: - make a special effort.

- ENDURE /θ/, - bear /θ/, - put up /WITH/, - stand /θ/, - suffer /θ/, - tolerate /θ/, - take /θ/: **çek-** 5, **/A/ dayan-** 3, **/A/ katlan-** 2, *more formal, less current than the above:* **/A/ tahammül et-.** *134:5.* patience: - endure; *1047:3.* toughness: - toughen.
- endure PAIN, - suffer pain, - be in pain [physical or mental]: **acı çek-** → çek- 5. *26:8.* pain: - suffer pain.
- endure TROUBLES, - suffer [mental anguish rather than direct physical pain, i.e., illness, lack of money, marriage troubles]: **dert çek-** → çek- 5. *26:8.* pain: - suffer pain.

- ENGAGE sb, - hire sb: **tut-** 6b. *615:14.* commission: - employ.
- engage in sports, - take part in sports, - do sports: **spor yap-** → yap- 3. *84:4.* fitness, exercise: - exercise; *743:23.* amusement: - play.

- ENJOY /θ/ sth; - like /θ/, - be pleased /WITH/: **/DAn/ hoşlan-.** *95:12.* pleasure: - enjoy.
- enjoy, - like: **keyfine git-** → git- 1b. *95:12.* pleasure: - enjoy.
- enjoy [fine weather], lit., - live through, - experience, - have [problems], - go through [difficult period]: **yaşa-** 3. *830:8.* event: - experience.
- enjoy oneself, - have a good time, - have fun /a: with [sb or sth], b: [by]...ing, c: [BY]...ing/': /a: 1A, b: ArAk, c: mAklA/ **eğlen-**[or {iyi/hoş} **vakit geçir-**] → eğlen- 1, → geçir- 3. *95:13.* pleasure: - enjoy oneself; *743:22.* amusement: - amuse oneself.
Enjoy!, Bon appétit! [A phrase used to address anyone who is about to begin eating, who is eating, or who has just finished eating.]: **Afiyet olsun.** → ol- 11 → olsun. *8:35.* eating: INTERJ. chow down!; *504: * 20.* courtesy: polite expressions.

- ENLARGE, - make larger [photograph]: **büyüt-** 1. *259:4.* expansion, growth: - <make larger>.

- ENROLL or - register sb [not oneself] /IN [a course], {IN/AT} [a school]/: **/A/ kaydet-** 1, **/A/ yazdır-** 2. *549:15.* record: - record.
- enroll or - register [oneself], - get oneself registered /FOR [a course], {IN/AT}

[a school]/: **/A/ kaydol-** → ol- 12, **/A/ yazıl-** 2. *549:15.* record: - record.

- ENTER /θ, {THROUGH/BY WAY OF}/, - go /INTO, {THROUGH/BY WAY OF}/ [the place entered is indicated: He entered the room through the door.]: **/A, DAn/ gir-.** *189:7.* entrance: - enter.
- enter, - go /{in/inside}/ [the place entered is not indicated: The door opened, and he entered.]: **içeri[.ye] gir-.** *189:7.* entrance: - enter.
- enter /θ/ or - turn /INTO/ a road; - swerve /to/, - veer /to/ - turn /to/, - make a turn /to/: **/A/ sap-.** *279:6.* curve: - curve.
- enter or - go INTO DETAIL: {ayrıntıya/ayrıntılara/detaya/ **detaylara**} **gir-.** *765:6.* circumstance: - itemize.
- enter sth /IN/, - record sth /IN/, - write sth down /IN/: **/A/ kaydet-** 2. *549:15.* record: - record.
- enter or - punch in [a PIN or credit card number], - press a key, - click /ON/: /{I/A}/ **tuşla-.** *297:11.* weight: - weigh on; *912:4.* depression: - depress.

- ENTRUST /to/, - commit /to/, - commend /to/: **/A/ ısmarla-** 3 [Most frequently found in **Allahaısmarladık.** 'Goodbye (lit., We entrustED you TO God).', said by the person leaving.] *188:22.* departure: INTERJ. farewell!; *478:16.* giving: - commit.
- entrust sb /with/, - charge sb /with/ [a task, duty], - give sb the task /OF/, - make sb responsible /FOR/, - put sb in charge /OF/: **/lA/ görevlendir-.** *615:11.* commission: - appoint; *641:12.* duty: - obligate.

- ENUMERATE, - list, - say the names of [the days, capital cities of the world]: **say-** 2. *870:8.* list: - list.

- ENVELOP, - surround: {çevresini/ **etrafını**} **sar-** → sar- 3, /I/ **sar-** 3. *209:6.* environment: - surround; *212:5.* enclosure: - enclose.

- ENVISAGE, - plan: {**plânla-/ tasarla-**}. *964:4.* prearrangement: - prearrange.

- ENVY sb /FOR/ sth he possesses; - be jealous /OF/: **imren-** 2, **kıskan-** 1, **özen-** 2. *154:3.* envy: - envy.

- EQUAL, - add up to, - amount to, - make, - get [in mathematical operations]: et- 3. *789:5.* equality: - equal; *791:8.* whole: - total; *1016:18.* mathematics: - sum up.

- ERADICATE, - eliminate [disease], - repeal, - do away with, - abolish [law]: kaldır- 4. *445:2.* repeal: - repeal; *772:5* exclusion: - eliminate.

- ERASE [error, blackboard] /with/, - delete [e-mail] /with/: /lA/ sil- 3. *255:12.* subtraction: [written text] - delete.

- ERECT, - set up [pole, flag staff] /{IN/ON}/: /A/ 2 dik- 2. *159:16.* location: - establish; *200:9.* verticalness: - erect.

- ESCAPE, - flee, - run away, - get away /from, to/: /DAn, A/ kaç- 1. *369:6.* escape: - escape.
- escape /θ/ [death], - escape or - manage to get away /from/ [the hands of the police], - survive /θ/ [accident]: /DAn/ kurtul- 1. *369:6.* escape: - escape.
- escape FROM A DIFFICULT SITUATION, predicament; - get out of or - avoid doing something complicated: işin içinden çık- → çık- 1. *368:7.* avoidance: - evade.
- escape /FROM/ or - pop /OUT OF/ one's mouth [subj.: words]: ağzından lâf kaç- → kaç- 1. *369:10.* escape: - find vent.
- escape one's NOTICE or one's eye [a fact, an error], - be overlooked: gözden kaç- → kaç- 1. *340:6.* neglect: - neglect.

- ESTABLISH [business, republic]: kur- 1. *159:16.* location: - establish.
- establish or - form relationships /with/: /lA/ ilişki kur- → kur- 1. *774:5.* relation: - relate to; *817:11.* beginning: - inaugurate.
- establish the existence of, - find [errors in a composition]: {tespit et-/sapta-} 1. *940:2.* discovery: discover.
- establish ties, connections /with/, - make contact /with/, - contact /θ/, - get in touch /with/, - connect /with/: /lA/ bağlantı kur- → kur- 1. *223:10.* nearness: - contact; *343:8.* communication: - communicate with, - get in touch with.

- ESTIMATE {AT/TO BE/AS BEING}/, - judge, - reckon, - take a guess [how many]: /olarak/ tahmin et- 2. *945:9.* judgment: - estimate.

- EVALUATE, - assess, - appraise, - judge, - size up [situation]: değerlendir- 1. *300:10.* measurement: - measure; *945:9.* judgment: - estimate.

- EVAPORATE, - turn into steam, - vaporize: buharlaş-. *1065:8.* vapor, gas: - vaporize.

- EVICT, - throw out /of/: /DAn/ çıkar- 1. *908:15.* ejection: - evict.

- EVOLVE, - develop: geliş- 1. *860:5.* evolution: - evolve.

- EXAGGERATE, - overstate, - make too much of: abart-, büyüt- 2. *355:3.* exaggeration: - exaggerate; *992:10.* excess: - overdo.

- EXAMINE [mostly for a doctor and a patient]: muayene et-. *27:14.* vision: - scrutinize; *91:24.* therapy: - treat; *937:24.* inquiry: - examine.
- examine, - subject to a [physical] examination [a doctor and a patient]: /I/ muayeneden geçir- → geçir- 1. *27:14.* vision: - scrutinize; *91:24.* therapy: - treat; *937:24.* inquiry: - examine.
- examine, - feel, or - inspect for sth [with one's fingers], - feel around: yokla- 1. *73:6.* touch: - touch; *937:24.* inquiry: - examine.
- examine, - go /OVER/, - look /OVER/, - scrutinize, or - review [usually a document: article, paper, plan, report]: gözden geçir- → geçir- 1. *27:14.* vision: - scrutinize.
- examine or - study CAREFULLY, closely, minutely, in detail [an object, document, not usually a doctor a patient], - inspect, - research: incele-, tetkik et-. *27:14.* vision: - scrutinize; *937:25.* inquiry: - make a close study of.

- EXCEED, - go beyond [obj.: speed limit]: geç- 1. *909:4.* overrunning: - overrun; *992:9.* excess: - exceed.

- EXCHANGE sth /with/ sb, - change [My friend and I exchanged seats.]: /lA/ değiş- 2. *862:4.* interchange: - interchange.
- exchange sth /FOR/ sth else, - change sth {/FOR/INTO/} sth else [dollars for liras], - replace sth /with/ sth else: /lA/ değiştir- 2. *851:7.* change: -

change, - work or - make a change; *862:4.* interchange: - interchange.

- EXCITE, - thrill, - give a thrill: **heyecanlandır-** 1. *105:12.* excitement: - excite.
- excite, - turn on sexually: **tahrik et-** 2, **heyecanlandır-** 3. *105:12.* excitement: - excite.

- EXCLUDE, - cast out, - ostracize /from/: /DAn/ **dışla-**. *772:4.* exclusion: - exclude.

- EXCUSE, - forgive, or - pardon sb /because of, because/: /DAn **dolayı, DIğI için/ affet-** 2, /I/ **bağışla-** 2. *148:3a.* forgiveness: - forgive.
Excuse me [For getting sb's attention: Excuse me. May I ask you a question?]: **Affedersiniz.** → affet- 2. *148:3b.* forgiveness: expressions requesting forgiveness; *343:8.* * *1.* communication: conversation initiators.
Excuse me. I beg your pardon [for a mistake, for being late]: **Özür dilerim.** → dile- 2, **Kusura bakma.** → bak- 1. *148:3b.* forgiveness: expressions requesting forgiveness.
Excuse me, may I pass by? [when attempting to make one's way through a crowd, when getting off a bus]: **Müsaade eder misiniz?** → müsaade et-. *443:9.* permission: - permit.

- EXECUTE an order, - carry out a request, wish, order, or promise: **yerine getir-** 1. → getir-. *434:3.* observance: - perform; *437:9.* compact: - execute.

- EXERCISE, - do gymnastics, physical training, - train [oneself physically]: **idman yap-** → yap- 3. *84:4.* fitness, exercise: - exercise; *725:8.* exertion: - exert.

- EXHALE, - breathe out, - let out a breath: **nefes ver-** → ver- 1. *318:21.* * *1.* wind: - breathe.

- EXHAUST, - destroy, - kill, or - finish off [a person: Drink, gambling, and women exhausted him.]: **bitir-** 2. *395:10.* destruction: - destroy.

- EXIST, - be: **ol-** 3, 12 → {**var/yok**} **ol-, dur-** 7 [old inscriptions]. *221:6.* presence: - be present; *760:8.* existence: - exist.

- EXPECT: **bekle-** 2, {**ümit et-/um-**} 2. *130:5.* expectation: - expect.
- expect sth in return for sth given or done: **karşılık bekle-** → bekle- 2. *130:8.* expectation: - await.

- EXPEL or - eject sb /from/, - throw sb /OUT OF/ [person from room]: /DAn/ **kov-** 1. *908:13.* ejection: - eject.

- EXPEND EFFORT /{for/ON}/ sth, - take pains /TO/ do sth: /için/ {**emek/çaba**} **harca-** → {harca-/sarf et-} 1. *403:5.* endeavor: - endeavor; *725:9.* exertion: - exert oneself.

- EXPERIENCE, - be the object of [acts of kindness, mother's love]: **gör-** 3. *830:8.* event: - experience.
- experience, - happen to sb, - go through [usually sth interesting, good, exciting, or unusual rather than unfortunate or strange, thus in contrast to **başına gel-**]: **başından geç-** → geç- 1. *830:5.* event: - occur.
- experience, - live through, - have [problems], - enjoy [fine weather], - go through [difficult period]: **yaşa-** 3. *830:8.* event: - experience.
- experience, face, or encounter /θ/ DIFFICULTIES, meet /with/ difficulties: {**zorlukla/güçlükle**} **karşılaş-** → karşılaş- 3, /A/ **uğra-** 2. *216:8.* front: - confront; *830:8.* event: - experience; *1012:11.* difficulty: - have difficulty.
- experience or - live through a DISASTER: **felâket geçir-** → geçir- 2. *1010:10.* adversity: - come to grief.
- experience or - undergo [MISFORTUNE, disaster, accident]: **geçir-** 2. *830:8.* event: - experience.

- EXPIRE, - be up, - run out [time]: {**süre/vakit/zaman**} **dol-** → dol- 2. *390:9.* disuse: - obsolesce; *820:5.* time: - elapse.

- EXPLAIN sth /to/ sb, - give the reasons for: /A/ **açıkla-** 1, /A/ **anlat-** 1, /A/ **izah et-**. *521:6.* intelligibility: - make clear.
- explain or - interpret [the meaning of an event, dream]: **yorumla-** 1. *341:9.* interpretation: - interpret.

- EXPLODE, - burst [subj.: bomb, tire]: **patla-** 1. *671:14.* violence: - explode.

- explode, - blow up [The building exploded.]: **havaya uç-**. *671:14.* violence: - explode.
- explode, - be ready to explode, - feel like screaming /{ON ACCOUNT OF/DUE TO}/, - fly off the handle, - lose one's cool, - blow up: **/DAn/ patla-** 2. *152:20.* resentment, anger: - fly into a rage.

- EXPLORE, - investigate, - research, - do research on, - study, - try to find out: **araştır-** 2. *937:23.* inquiry: - investigate.
- EXPORT /to/: **/A/ ihraç et-**. *190:17.* emergence: - export.

- EXPRESS or - offer one's CONDOLENCES /to/ [upon hearing of sb's death]: **/A/ başsağlığı dile-** → dile- 1. *121:6.* comfort: - comfort.
- express one's FEELINGS, thoughts, ideas; - express oneself: **{duygularını/düşüncelerini/ fikirlerini} anlat-** → anlat- 2, **{duygularını/düşüncelerini/ fikirlerini} ifade et-** → ifade et- 1. *532:4.* diction: - phrase.
- express ONESELF: **kendini ifade et-** → ifade et- 1. See also directly above for another way of expressing this notion. *532:4.* diction: - phrase.
- express or - give an OPINION /ON/, - give an idea or impression /about/ [subj.: person, event, film]: **/hakkında/ fikir ver-** 1 → ver- 1. *608:12.* description: - describe; *945:8.* judgment: - judge.
- express, - send, or - give one's REGARDS /to/, - say 'hi' /to/: **/A/ selâm söyle-** → söyle- 1. *504:13.* courtesy: - give one's regards.
- express WISHES FOR SUCCESS /to/ sb, - wish /θ/ sb success: **/A/ başarılar dile-** → dile- 1. *409:7c.* success: - wish success; *504:13.* courtesy: - give one's regards.

- EXTEND [hours], - prolong [meeting], - drag out [speech]: **uzat-** 3. *267:6.* lengthen: - lengthen.
- extend A HELPING HAND /to/, - help out, - extend aid or assistance /to/: **/A/ yardım elini uzat-** → uzat- 2. *449:11.* aid: - aid.
- extend A LOAN /TO/, - lend money /to/: **/A/ borç ver-** → ver- 1, **/A/ ödünç ver-** [also '- lend an item'] → ver- 1. *620:5.* lending: - lend.
- extend or - hold sth OUT /to/: **/A/ uzat-** 2. *439:4.* offer: - offer.
- extend /OVER/, - stretch out /{OVER/on/ALONG}/, - cover [trees over both sides of road]: **/DA/ uzan-** 2. *295:30.* covering: - overlie.

- EXTINGUISH, - put out [fire, cigarettes, lights]: **söndür-** 1. *1021:7.* incombustibility: - fight fire.

EYES front!: **Önüne bak!** → bak- 1.

- F -

- FACE, - encounter, or - meet /with/ difficulties: **{zorlukla/güçlük-le} karşılaş-** → karşılaş- 3, **/A/ uğra-** 2. *216:8.* front: - confront; *830:8.* event: - experience; *1012:11.* difficulty: - have difficulty.

- FAIL, - come to nothing [The effort failed.]: **boşa çık-** → çık- 7, **boşa git-** → git- 5. *473:6.* loss: - go to waste; *910:3.* shortcoming: - fall through.
- fail, - break down, - crash, - be down [subj.: a system, computer]: **çök-** 5. *393:24.* impairment: - break down.
- fail completely [subj.: a major policy, project, plan, idea, marriage]: **iflâs et-** 2. *410:9a.* failure: - fail.
- fail or - flunk /θ/ a COURSE: **dersten kal-** → kal- 1. *410:9b.* failure: - fail in specific areas.
- fail or - flunk /θ/ an EXAMINATION: **{sınavdan/imtihandan} kal-** → kal- 1. *410:9b.* failure: - fail in specific areas.
- fail, - stay behind, - be held back in school, or - flunk /θ/ a GRADE [a level in a school, not a course: When he didn't study, he failed.]: **sınıfta kal-** → kal- 1. *410:9b.* failure: - fail in specific areas.
- fail or - flunk SB, - leave sb in a grade [The teacher failed the student.]: **sınıfta bırak-** → bırak- 1. *410:17.* failure: - flunk sb.
- fail or - neglect TO DO STH, - omit: **ihmal et-**. *340:6.* neglect: - neglect.

- FAINT, - pass out, - lose consciousness: **bayıl-** 1, **kendinden geç-** 1 → gec- 1, **kendini kaybet-** 1 → {kaybet-/yitir-}, **{şuurunu/ bilincini} kaybet-** [or **yitir-**] 1 → {kaybet-/yitir-}. *25:5.* insensibility: - faint.

- FALL, - drop [of itself] /from, {to/IN/INTO/ON/ONTO}/ [The plate fell ON the floor.]: **/DAn, A/ düş-** 1. *194:5.* descent: - descend.

- fall, - come to an end, - collapse [empire]: **çök-** 4. *3 9 3 : 2 4.* impairment: - break down.
- fall [temperature], - drop [prices], - decline in value [money: dollar, mark]: **düş-** 3. *633:6b.* cheapness: - become cheaper.
- fall, - drop [subj.: number of students], - decrease, - become less, - get or - run low on [supplies: sugar, gas]: **azal-, eksil-** 1. *252:6.* decrease: - decrease.
- fall APART, - break up, - disband, - disintegrate [dispersal of members: subj.: household, family, political party]: **dağıl-** 3. *805:3.* disintegration: - disintegrate.
- fall ASLEEP, - go to sleep, - drop off to sleep: **uyu-** 2. *22:16.* sleep: - go to sleep.
- fall asleep, - doze off, - drop off /to/ sleep: **uykuya dal-** → dal- 2. *22:16.* sleep: - go to sleep.
- fall asleep, - pass out: **kendinden geç-** 3 → geç- 1. *22:16.* sleep: - go to sleep.
- fall BACK, - move back, - retreat: **gerile-** 1. *163:6.* regression: - retreat.
- fall DOWN [building], - collapse: **çök-** 1. *393:24.* impairment: - break down.
- fall /FOR/ sb, - be swept off one's feet /BY/ [i.e., - fall in love with]: /A, not with **tarafından/ çarpıl-** 2. *104:22.* love: - fall in love.
- fall FROM POWER [government]: **düş-** 2. *194:8.* descent: - tumble.
- fall IN LOVE /WITH/: /A/ **âşık ol-** → ol- 12. *104:22.* love: - fall in love.
- fall, - go, - lapse, or - sink INTO A COMA: **komaya gir-**. *25:5.* insensibility: - faint.
- fall /ON/ the same {day/hour}, - occur or - be /AT/ the same time, - coincide: /A/ **denk düş-** 2 → düş- 1. *830:5.* event: - occur; *835:4.* simultaneity: - coincide.
- fall OUT [hair]: **dökül-** 4. *194:8.* descent: - tumble.

- FAST, - keep or - observe the fast: **oruç tut-** → tut- 5. *434:2.* observance: - observe; *515:4.* fasting: - fast; *701:14.* religious rites: - celebrate.

- FASTEN or - attach sth /to/, - put up [curtains]: /A/ **tak-**. *2 0 2 : 8.* pendency: - suspend; *799:7.* joining: - fasten.

- FAX sth /to/: /A/ **faksla-**. *347:19.* communications: - telegraph.

- FEAR /θ/, - be afraid or frightened /OF/, - be afraid /to/: /DAn, A/ **kork-** 1. *127:10.* fear, frighteningness: - fear.
- fear or - be afraid /FOR/, - worry or - be anxious /ABOUT/, - be concerned /{ABOUT/FOR}/: /DAn/ **endişe et-**. *126:6.* anxiety: - feel anxious.

- FEED, - nourish: **besle-** 1. *385:9.* provision, equipment: - provision.
- feed to satiety /with/: /lA/ **doyur-**. *993:4.* satiety: - satiate.

- FEEL [pride, interest, happiness, sorrow, pain], sense: **duy-** 3. *24:6.* sensation: - sense.
- feel [well, ill, weak]: **hisset-** 1. *24:6.* sensation: - sense; *93:10.* feeling: - feel.
- feel or - understand sth intuitively, - sense, - perceive, - discern: **hisset-** 2, **sez-**. *93:10.* feeling: - feel; *933:4.* intuition, instinct: - intuit.
- feel, - examine, or - inspect for sth with one's fingers, - feel around: **yokla-** 1. *73:6.* touch: - touch; *937:24.* inquiry: - examine.
- feel or - be ARROGANTLY PROUD /OF/, - pride oneself arrogantly /ON/: /lA/ **gurur duy-** 2 → duy- 3, /lA/ **gururlan-**. *136:5.* pride: - take pride; *141:8.* arrogance: - give oneself airs.
- feel BETTER, relieved, - be or - become comfortable: **rahat et-, rahatla-**. *120:8.* relief: - be relieved.
- feel or - be COLD, - get cold: **üşü-**. *1022:9.* cold: - freeze.
- feel VERY COLD, - freeze /{from/DUE TO}/: /DAn/ **don-**. *1022:9.* cold: - freeze.
- feel CRAMPED, squeezed [in a crowd of people]: **sıkış-** 3. *260:8.* contraction: - squeeze.
- feel DISGUST /AT/, horror /AT/, loathing /FOR/: /DAn/ {**iğren-/tiksin-**}. *64:4.* unsavoriness: - disgust.
- feel EMBARASSED or reluctant - do sth /in the presence of/ sb: → - feel reluctant.
- feel FAINT, - be suffocated, - suffocate, - be stifled, strangled. [All imply a lack of sufficient air or oxygen.]: **boğul-** 2. *308:18.* killing: - strangle.
- feel faint, suddenly sick: → - feel suddenly sick.
- feel GUILTY, - feel pangs of conscience /{on account of/for}/: /DIğI için/ **vicdan azabı çek-** → çek- 5. *113:6.* regret: - regret.
- feel or - be HAPPY /{TO/θ}/: /DAn/ **mutluluk duy-** → duy- 3. *95:11.* pleasure: - be pleased.

- feel HESITANT /to/ do sth, - hesitate /to/ do sth: → - feel reluctant.
- feel or - become ILL AT EASE: → - feel or become uncomfortable.
- feel or - become INDISPOSED, slightly ill, under the weather: **rahatsız ol-** 1 → ol- 10.2. *85:46a.* disease: - take sick in general.
- feel {LIKE/as if} [I feel like I've met you before.]: *verb stem*.**mIş gibi hisset-** → hisset- 2. *24:6.* sensation: - sense; *93:10.* feeling: - feel; *933:4.* intuition, instinct: - intuit.
- feel like [doING sth]: **canı çek-** → çek- 1, **canı iste-** → iste- 1. *100:14.* desire: - desire.
- feel like SCREAMING /{ON ACCOUNT OF/DUE TO}/, - be ready to explode, - explode, - fly off the handle, - lose one's temper, - lose one's cool, - blow up: **/DAn/ patla-** 2. *152:20.* resentment, anger: - fly into a rage.
- feel NAUSEATED: → - feel sick to one's stomach.
- feel the NEED TO RELIEVE ONESELF, to go to the toilet: **sıkış-** 5, **tuvaleti gel-** → gel- 1. *12:12.* excretion: - excrete.
- feel PAIN, - hurt: **canı acı-** → acı- 1, **canı yan-** → yan- 1. *26:8.* pain: - suffer pain.
- feel PANGS OF CONSCIENCE: → - feel guilty.
- feel PRIDE /IN/, - be proud /OF/, - take pride /IN/: **/lA/ iftihar et-, /lA/ {övün-/öğün-}** 1, **/{lA/ DAn}/ gurur duy-** 1 → duy- 3, **/DAn/ kıvanç duy-** → duy- 3. *136:5.* pride: - take pride.
- feel or - be RELIEVED, - feel better: **rahat et-, rahatla-.** *120:8.* relief: - be relieved.
- feel or - be RELUCTANT, hesitant, embarassed to do sth /in the presence of/, - hesitate /to/, not - dare /to/ do sth: **/{A/DAn}/ çekin-.** *325:4.* unwillingness: - demur; *362:7.* irresolution: - hesitate.
- feel SAD, gloomy, depressed, melancholy: **hüzünlen-.** *112:16.* sadness: - lose heart.
- feel SICK: **rahatsız ol-** 1 ['- feel indisposed, - feel slightly ill, - be under the weather']. → ol- 10.2. *85:46a.* disease: - take sick in general.
- feel sick TO ONE'S STOMACH, - have an upset stomach, - feel nauseated, nauseous, - get queasy, - be upset [stomach]: **midesi bulan-.** *85:46b.* disease: - take sick in particular ways.

- feel that there is a SIMILARITY between, - see or - feel a resemblance, - think that sb or sth is /LIKE/ sb or sth else: **/A/ benzet-** 2. *988:20.* memory: - remind.
- feel SUDDENLY SICK, - feel faint: **fenalaş-** 2, **fena ol-** 1 → ol- 10.2. *85:46a.* disease: - take sick in general.
- feel SORE, - hurt: **acı-** 1, **ağrı-.** *26:8.* pain: - suffer pain.
- feel SORRY /FOR/, - pity /θ/: **/A/ acı-** 2. *145:3.* pity: - pity, - feel sorry for.
- feel TERRIBLE, - be upset, - feel anguish, - be distressed [at bad news]: **fena ol-** 2 → ol- 10.2. *96:16b.* unpleasure: - be distressed.
- feel or - become UNCOMFORTABLE, ill at ease: **rahatsız ol-** 2 → ol- 10.2. *96:13.* unpleasure: - annoy.

- FELL sb or sth; - knock down, - send sb sprawling, - lay sb flat; - topple sth, - overthrow: **yık-** 2. *912:5.* depression: - fell.

- FETCH, - bring /from, to/: **/DAn, A/ getir-.** *176:16.* transferal, transportation: - fetch.

- FIGHT [physical or verbal], - quarrel /with/: **/lA/ kavga et-.** *456:11.* disaccord: - quarrel; *457:13.* contention: - contend.
- fight, - struggle, - engage in physical combat /with/ one another [individuals]: **/lA/ dövüş-.** *457:13.* contention: - contend.
- fight /a: against [sb or sth], b: with [i.e., against sb], against [sth: improper use of funds], c: together with [sb]/, - battle, - wage war: **/a: A karşı, b: lA, c: lA birlikte** [*or* **beraber**]/ **savaş-.** *457:13.* contention: - contend.

- FIGURE OUT, - solve a problem [a puzzle, mathematical problem]: **çöz-** 2. *939:2.* solution: - solve.
- figure out [how the novel is going to end], - predict, - know what to do or say: **kestir-** 2, **tahmin et-** 3. *960:6.* foresight: - foreknow; *961:9.* prediction: - predict.
- figure UP, - calculate, - add up: **hesapla-** [in most situations], **hesap çıkar-** [the bill at a restaurant or a hotel] → çıkar- 7. *1016:17.* mathematics: - calculate; *1016:18.* : - sum up.

- FILE A SUIT or charges /against [sb], for [a misdeed]/, - file a complaint or claim /against/, - sue sb: **/aleyhine,** için/ dava aç- → aç- 12, /I/ dava et-. *598:12.* legal action: - sue.

- FILL sth /with/ sth, - MAKE sth full [He filled the bottle with water.]: /I, 1A/ doldur- 1 a ['- fill sth with sth'], /I, A/ doldur- 1b [lit., ** '- fill sth INTO sth'] → doldur- 1. *793:7a.* completeness: - fill sth; *1020:7.* fuel: - fuel.
- fill, - fill up /with/, - BECOME full [The theater soon filled.]: /lA/ dol- 1. *793:7b.* completeness: - fill, - become full.
- fill IN [the blanks]: [boşlukları] doldur- → doldur- 2. *793:6.* completeness: - make whole, complete.
- fill OUT [application, questionnaire]: doldur- 2. *793:6.* completeness: - make whole, complete.
- fill out [subj.: a person's body], - develop physically, - mature: geliş- 1. *259:5.* expansion, growth: - become larger; *860:5.* evolution: - evolve.
- fill a PRESCRIPTION [subj.: the pharmacist]: reçete hazırla-. *86:38.* remedy: - remedy; *405:6.* preparation: - prepare.
- fill one's STOMACH with food, - fill up /ON/: karnını doyur-. *993:4.* satiety: - satiate.
- fill sth [UP] /WITH/ AIR, - pump up [tires] [Mehmet filled the tires (up) with air.]: /A/ hava bas- 1 → bas- 2. *793:7a.* completeness: - fill sth.
- fill [up] with air, i.e., - become full of air [balloon]: şiş- 2 . *259:5.* expansion, growth: - become larger; *283:11.* convexity, protuberance: - bulge.
- fill WITH TEARS [eyes], for tears - come to one's eyes; for one's eyes - water: gözleri yaşar-. *13:5.* secretion: - secrete; *115:12.* lamentation: - weep.

- FILM, - make a film, movie: film çek- [subj.: both amateur and professional film makers] → çek- 7, film çevir- 2 [subj.: professional film makers] → çevir- 3. *714:14.* photography: - photograph.

- FILTER OUT; - strain [rice from water]: süz-. *79:22.* cleanness: - refine.

- FINAGLE, - wangle, - manage to get [usually in the face of difficulty], - get sth /OUT OF/ sb [permission], - wrest sth /from/ sb: /DAn/ {kopar- 3/kopart- 3}. *192:10.* extraction: - extract.

- FINANCE, - meet expenses, - pay the expenses, - put up [the] money for: masraf gör- → gör- 4, masraf karşıla- → karşıla- 2. *729:15.* finance, investment: - finance.

- FIND: bul- 1. *940:2.* discovery: - discover.
- find, - determine, or - establish the existence of [errors in a composition]: {tespit et-/sapta-} 1. *940:2.* discovery: - discover.
- find, - think of or about in a certain way [How do you find this book?]: bul- 3. *945:11.* judgment: - decide.
- find FUNNY, amusing, - strike one as funny, - tickle one's funny bone: komiğine git- → git- 1b. *489:13.* wit, humor: - joke.
- find a JOB, employment, - become employed: iş bul-, işe gir-. *724:12.* occupation: - work.
- find ONESELF or - be IN A TIGHT SPOT, under pressure, in difficulty, - get in a jam: sıkış- 4. *297:13.* weight: - burden; *1012:12.* difficulty: - get into trouble.
- find OUT: /DAn/ haber al- ['- receive news /{OF/from}/'] → al- 3, /DAn/ bilgi edin- ['- receive information /from/'], /DAn/ öğren- ['- learn /from/']. *570:6.* learning: - learn; *927:14.* knowledge: - learn.
- find a SOLUTION /for/, - handle, - solve, or - resolve [situation, personal problem, matter]: /I/ hallet-. *939:2.* solution: - solve.
- find a solution /{for/to}/ a problem, - find a way of solving a problem, - find a way to do sth: /{için/A}/ çözüm yolu bul- → bul- 1. *939:2.* solution: - solve.
- find sth STRANGE or odd, for sth - strike one as strange: {acayibine/ garibine/tuhafına} git- → git- 1b, yadırga-. *869:8.* * 1. abnormality: - find strange.

- FINE /θ/ sb, - give a ticket /to/ sb or to a vehicle: /A/ ceza kes- → kes- 5. *604:10.* punishment: - punish.

Fine., Agreed., All right!, OK!: Oldu. → ol- 11. *332:18.* assent: INTERJ. yes.

- FINISH, - BE over, - come to an end, - conclude, - end [The lesson is finished.]: bit- 1, sona er- → er-. *819:6.* end: - come to an end.
- finish, - BRING to an end, - conclude [He finished the lesson.]: /I/ bitir- 1, /A/ son ver- → ver- 1. *819:5.* end: - end sth.

- finish, - COMPLETE sth [He finished his homework.]: **tamamla-**. *793:6*. completeness: - complete; *819:7*. end: - complete.
- finish a school, - graduate: **bitir- 4**. *409:7b*. success: - succeed in specific ways; *793:6*. completeness: - complete.
- finish OFF, - exhaust, - destroy, - kill [a person: Drink, gambling, and women finished him off.]: **bitir- 2**. *395:10*. destruction: - destroy.

- FIRE a gun /AT/, - shoot bullets /AT/: **/A/ kurşun at-** → **at- 6**. *903:12*. pushing, throwing: - shoot.
- fire /{ON/UPON}/, - shoot /AT/: **/A/ ateş et-**. *459:22*. attack: - pull the trigger; *903:12*. pushing, throwing: - shoot.
- fire, - dismiss: *formal:* **görevden al-** ['- fire, - relieve sb of his {duties/position}'] → **al- 1, işine son ver-** ['- fire, - relieve sb of his position'] → **ver- 1**. *908:19*. ejection: - dismiss. *informal:* **işten {at-/kov-}** ['- fire, - sack, - can'] → **at- 1, kov- 2**. *908:20*. ; <nonformal terms> - fire.

- FISH, - catch fish: **balık tut-** → **tut- 1**. *382:10*. pursuit: - fish.

- FIT /θ/, - suit /θ/ [subj.: clothes]: **/A/ uy- 1, /A/ gel- 2, /{üzerine/üstüne}/ otur-** → **otur- 5**. *866:3*. conformity: - conform.

- FIX, - repair, - put in running order [obj.: machine]: **onar-, tamir et-**. *396:14*. restoration: - repair.
- fix, - repair [roads]: **düzelt- 1**. *396:14*. restoration: - repair.
- fix a DATE or time /FOR/ an event [They have fixed a date for the wedding.]: **{tespit et-/sapta-} 2**. *864:11*. particularity: - specify; *964:4*. prearrangement: - prearrange.
- fix or - set a PRICE /ON/ [goods or services]: **/A/ fiyat koy-** → **koy- 1**. *630:11*. price, fee: - price.

- FLEE, - run away, - escape /from, to/: **/DAn, A/ kaç- 1**. *369:6*. escape: - escape.

- FLING, - hurl, - throw /{AT/to/INTO}, toward/: **/A/ at- 1, /A, A doğru/ fırlat-**. *903:10*. pushing, throwing: - throw.

- FLIP, - turn over, - turn [page, omelette]: **çevir- 3**. *205:5*. inversion: - invert.

- flip /through/ [TV channels], - browse, - surf /on/ [the Internet], - scan: **/DA, arasında/ gezin- 2**. *570:13*. learning: - browse; *1041:18*. computer science: - computerize.

- FLOAT /on/ [lilies float on water]: **/{DA/üzerinde}/ yüz- 2**. *182:54*. water travel: - float.

- FLOW /from, {to/INTO}/, - pour /from, INTO/ [The water is flowing from the hose.]: **/DAn, A / ak-**. *190:13*. emergence: - run out; *238:16*. stream: - flow.
- flow, - pour, - run /INTO/ [river into the sea, people into the street]: **/A/ dökül- 3**. *189:9*. entrance: - flow in.

- FLOWER, - bloom, - blossom, - open [flower]: **aç- 9**. *310:32*. plants: - flower.

- FLUNK or - fail /θ/ a course: **dersten kal-** → **kal- 1**. *410:9b*. failure: - fail in specific areas.
- flunk, - stay behind, - be held back in school, - fail a grade [a level in a school, not a course: When he didn't study, he was held back.]: **sınıfta kal-** → **kal- 1**. *410:9b*. failure: - fail in specific areas.
- flunk or - fail SB, - leave sb in a grade, not - pass sb [The teacher flunked the student.]: **sınıfta bırak-** → **bırak- 1**. *410:17*. failure: - flunk sb.

- FLY /to/ [a place]: **/A/ uç-, /A/ uçakla git-** → **git- 1a**. *184:36*. aviation: - fly.
- fly /a: to [a place], b: IN [a plane], c: over [the city]/: **/a: A, b: 1A, c: üzerinde/ uç-**. *184:36*. aviation: - fly.
- fly A KITE: **uçurtma uçur-**. *184:37*. aviation: - pilot.
- fly OFF THE HANDLE, - be ready to explode, - feel like screaming /{ON ACCOUNT OF/DUE TO}/, - explode, - lose one's cool, - blow up: **/DAn/ patla- 2**. *152:20*. resentment, anger: - fly into a rage.
- fly OUT of one's hand [subj.: object: eraser], out of one's seat [subj.: person]: **/DAn/ fırla- 1**. *193:9*. ascent: - shoot up; *200:8*. verticalness: - rise; *366:5*. leap: - leap.
- fly A PLANE: **uçak kullan-**. *184:37*. aviation: - pilot.

- FOCUS one's attention /ON/, - concentrate [one's mind] /ON/: **/A/**

Part 2: English-Turkish Index

dikkatini topla- → topla- 1. *982:8.* attention: - pay attention.

- FOLD /{IN/INTO}/ [paper /{in/into}/ thirds, fifths]: /A/ katla-. *291:5.* fold: - fold.

- FOLLOW, - go behind: izle- 1; takip et- 1. *166:3.* following: - follow.
- follow, - observe, - monitor, - keep abreast of [events, trends, fashions, TV]: izle- 2, takip et- 2. *982:5.* attention: - attend to.
- follow, - heed, - take, or - listen to ADVICE: söz tut- → tut- 5, sözünü tut- 2 ['- heed, - take the advice of sb, - take sb's advice'] → tut- 5. *326:2.* obedience: - obey; *422:7.* advice: - take or - accept advice.
- follow [DIRECTIONS], - apply sth /to/, - carry out a plan, - put a plan, law, or formula into practice: /A/ uygula-. *387:11.* use: - apply.
- follow the EXAMPLE OF, - act in accord /WITH/, - emulate /θ/, - imitate the actions of [In the namaz (i.e., the Islamic prayer ritual) the members of the community follow θ (the lead of) the imam.]: /A/ uy- 7. *336:7.* imitation: - emulate.
- follow ONE [UPON] ANOTHER in rapid succession, - succeed [subj.: times: days, months; events: disasters]: kovala- 2. *814:2.* sequence: - succeed.
- follow RULES, regulations, - comply /WITH/, - conform /to/: /A/ uy- 5. *326:2.* obedience: - obey; *434:2.* observance: - observe; *866:3.* conformity: - conform.

- FONDLE, - caress, - stroke, - pat, - pet: okşa-, sev- 2. *73:8.* touch: - stroke; *1042:6.* friction: - rub.

- FOOL, - deceive, - take in, - mislead: kandır- 1. *356:14.* deception: - deceive.

- FOOT the bill, - pay, *informal, jocular*: masraf çek- → çek- 5. *729:15.* finance, investment: - finance.

- FOOTNOTE, - add a footnote: {not/ dipnot} düş- → düş- 6. *341:11.* interpretation: - comment upon.

FOR AS LONG AS ANYONE CAN REMEMBER, from time immemorial, always ['never' when followed by a negative verb]: oldum olası → ol- 11 → oldum. *828:11.* perpetuity: ADV. always.

For SHAME!, Shame on you!: Aşk olsun! 1 → ol- 11 → olsun, Utan! → utan-, /mAklA/ Çok ayıp ettin! ['You behaved very shamefully /BY...ing/!'] → ayıp et-. *510:27.* disapproval: INTERJ. God forbid!

For shame!, Shame on them!: Yuh olsun! → ol- 11 → olsun. *510:27.* disapproval: INTERJ. God forbid!

- FORBID, - prohibit: {yasakla-/yasak et-}. *444:3.* prohibition: - prohibit.

- FORCE sb /to/ do sth, - make sb /θ/ do sth: /A/ zorla- 1. *424:4.* compulsion: - compel.
- force or - try to force or to break sth open [locked door]: zorla- 2. *424:6.* compulsion: - press.

- FORGET: unut-. *989:5.* forgetfulness: - forget.
- forget, - slip one's mind: akıldan çık- → çık- 1. *989:7.* forgetfulness: - be forgotten.
Forget about it!, Never mind!: Boş ver! → boş ver- 1 → ver- 1. *997:25.* unimportance: PHR. no matter.

- FORGIVE, - excuse, or - pardon sb /FOR, because of, because/: /DAn dolayı, DIğI için/ affet- 2, /I/ bağışla- 2. *148:3a.* forgiveness: - forgive.
- forgive, - pardon, or - excuse an act: affet- 1. *148:3a.* forgiveness: - forgive.

- FORM, - create, - constitute /{from/OUT OF}/: /DAn/ oluştur-. *891:8.* production: - produce, - create.
- form A LINE, - line up, - get in [the] line, - queue up: {sıraya/kuyruğa} gir-. *811:6.* continuity: - line up.
- form or - establish RELATIONSHIPS /with/: /lA/ ilişki kur- → kur- 1. *774:5.* relation: - relate to; *817:11.* beginning: - inaugurate.

FORTUNATELY, Thank goodness: Bereket versin [ki] → ver- 1. *1009:16.* prosperity: ADV. fortunately.

- FORWARD [letters, e-mail] /to/: /A/ ilet- 1. *176:15.* transferal, transportation: - send.

- FOUND [business, republic]: kur- 1. *159:16.* location: - establish.

526

- FREE, - set free, - let go, - release, - liberate [hostages, prisoners]: **serbest bırak-** → bırak- 5, **salıver-**. *120:6.* relief: - release; *398:3.* rescue: - rescue; *431:4.* liberation: - liberate; *431:5.* : - release.

- FREEZE /{from/DUE TO}/, - feel very cold: **/DAn/ don- 1.** *1022:9.* cold: - freeze.
- freeze, - seize up, - jam [subj.: computer]: **don- 2.** *854:10.* stability: - become firmly fixed.
- freeze TO DEATH: **donarak öl-.** → don-. *1022:9.* cold: - freeze.

- FRIGHTEN, - scare: **korkut-.** *127:15.* fear, frighteningness: - frighten.

- FROWN, - knit one's brows: **kaşlarını çat-.** *152:25a.* resentment, anger: gestures of; *510:20.* * 1. disapproval: gestures of.

- FRY sth [The cook is frying the potatoes.]: **kavur-, kızart- 1** [Also: sauté]. *11:4a.* cooking: - cook sth.
- fry [i.e., ** - become fried: The potatoes are frying.]: **kızar- 2.** *11:4b.* cooking: for sth - cook.

- FUNCTION, - work [subj.: machine, not a person: How does this machine function?]: **çalış- 3, işle- 1.** *888:7.* operation: - be operative.

- FURNISH a place /with [money, objects], IN [a style, material]/: **/1A, θ/ döşe-.** *385:8.* provision, equipment: - equip.

- G -

- GAIN ACCESS /to/, - access /θ/, - get /{to [a source of information]/ON [the Internet]}/: **/A/ eriş- 4.** *186:6.* arrival: - arrive; *189:7.* entrance: - enter; *1041:18.* computer science: - computerize.
- gain [ONE'S END[S]], - attain /θ/ [one's objective], - reach /θ/ [one's goal], - achieve /θ/ [one's purpose]: **eriş- 3.** *407:4.* accomplishment: accomplish; *409:8.* success: - achieve one's purpose.
- gain TIME [i.e., - obtain extra time to achieve a goal, to complete a task]: **{vakit/zaman} kazan- 2** → kazan- 4. *845:9.* lateness: - postpone.

- gain WEIGHT, - put on weight: **kilo al-** → al- 1, **topla- 3, toplan- 4.** *259:8.* expansion, growth: - fatten.

- GAMBLE: **kumar oyna-** → oyna- 1. *759:23.* gambling: - gamble.

- GATHER, - collect sth: **biriktir- 1, topla- 1, toparla- 1.** *769:18.* assemblage: - bring or - gather together.
- gather, - get together, - assemble [We gathered at Ahmet's house.]: **toplan- 3.** *769:16.* assemblage: - come together; *769.17.* : - convene.
- gather speed, - accelerate, - speed up [subj.: vehicle, person]: **hızlan- 1.** *174:10.* swiftness: - accelerate [i.].

- GET, - acquire, - obtain /from/: **/DAn/ edin-, ele geçir- 2** → geçir- 1, **/DAn/ elde et.** *472:8.* acquisition: - acquire.
- get /θ/, - obtain /θ/, - acquire /θ/ sth, - become the owner or possessor /OF/ sth: **/A/ sahip ol-** → ol- 12. *472:8.* acquisition: - acquire.
- get, - gain /by/ [What will you get by complaining?]: **/1A/ kazan- 4.** *472:8.* acquisition: - acquire.
- get, - receive /from/: **/DAn/ al- 3.** *479:6.* receiving: - receive.
- get, - add up to, - amount to, - equal, - make [in mathematical operations: If 284 is divided BY [lit., INTO] 2, one gets 142.]: **et- 3.** *789:5.* equality: - equal; *791:8.* whole: - total; *1016:18.* mathematics: - sum up.
- get sb to believe /θ/ sth, - persuade or - convince sb to believe /θ/ sb or sth: **/A/ inandır-.** *375:23.* motivation, inducement: - persuade; *952:18.* belief: - convince.

- get A BID, estimate, quote /from/, - receive a price offer /from/ [a company]: **/DAn/ fiyat al-** → al- 3. *630:11.* price, fee: - price.

- get or - catch A CHILL: **soğuk al-** → al- 3, **üşüt- 2.** *85:46b.* disease: - take sick in particular ways; *1022.9.* cold: - freeze.
- get or - catch A COLD: **nezle ol-** → ol- 10.2. *85:46b.* disease: - take sick in particular ways.
- get ACCUSTOMED /TO/, used /to/: **/A/ alış- 1.** *373:12.* custom, habit: - be used to.
- get ACQUAINTED /WITH/ one another, - meet: **/1A/ tanış-.** *587:10.* friendship: - befriend, - make friends with.

- get ADVICE, an idea /a: from, b: about, c: on the subject of/: **/a: DAn, b: hakkında, c: konusunda/ fikir al-** → al- 1. *422:7.* advice: - take or - accept advice.
- get ALONG /with/ sb, - get on /with/ sb: **anlaş-** 1, **/lA/ geçin-** 1. *409:12.* success: - manage.
- get ANGRY, enraged, or furious /{AT/WITH}/: **/A/ kız-** 1, **/A/ öfkelen-**, **/A/ sinirlen-**. *152:17.* resentment, anger: - become angry.
- get or - be angry /{WITH/AT}/, - get mad /AT, BECAUSE/: **/A, diye/ darıl-** 1. *152:17.* resentment, anger: - become angry.
- get ANXIOUS, - worry /about/: **/DAn/ kaygılan-**. *126:6.* anxiety: - feel anxious.
- get an APPOINTMENT /from, for/, - make an appointment /for/: **/DAn, için/ gün al-** [only for a (date/day)] → al- 3, **/DAn, için/ randevu al-** [for any time] → al- 3. *582:19.* sociability: - visit; *964:4.* prearrangement: - prearrange.
- get AWAY, - run away, - escape /from/: **/DAn/ kaç-** 1. *369:6.* escape: - escape.
- get one's money BACK, - get a refund /from/: **/DAn/ parasını geri al-** → geri al- 1 → al- 1. *481:6.* restitution: - recover.
- get back, - move back /from/: **/DAn/ gerile-** 1. *163:6.* regression: - retreat; *168:2.* recession: - recede.
- get or - be {BACKED/PILED} UP, - pile UP [subj.: traffic]: **sıkış-** 3. *260:8.* contraction: - squeeze; *769:19.* assemblage: - pile.
- get BAD or worse [weather, an ability]; - break down, - go out of order, - give out [machine]; - spoil [subj: food]: **bozul-**. *393:16.* impairment: - deteriorate.
- get a BEATING or thrashing /from/: **/DAn/ dayak ye-** → ye- 2. *604:13.* punishment: - whip; *901:16.* impulse, impact: - pound.
- get BEHIND, - fall, - lag, or - stay behind /in/ [some activity, lessons]: **/DA/ geri kal-** 1 → kal- 1. *166:4.* following: - lag; *217:8.* rear: - be behind.
- get BETTER, - improve [subj.: an ability, one's Turkish, not weather or health]: **geliş-** 2, **ilerle-** 2. *392:7.* improvement: - get better.
- get better, - improve, - clear up [weather]: **hava {aç-/açıl-}** → aç- 7, açıl- 7, **hava düzel-**. *392:7.* improvement: - get better.

- get better, - improve, - get well, - recover [from illness]: **düzel-, iyileş-**. *392:8.* improvement: - rally, - get better; *396:20.* restoration: - recover.
- get BORED /WITH/, - grow tired /OF/, - tire /OF/, - get or - be fed up /WITH/: **/DAn/ {bık-/usan-}, /DAn/ sıkıl-** 1, **/DAn/ canı sıkıl-** 1 → sıkıl- 1, **/DAn/ içi sıkıl-** → sıkıl- 1. *118:7b.* tedium: - get bored.
- get a BREATH OF FRESH AIR, - breathe fresh air: **hava al-** 1 → al- 1. *318:21.* * 1. wind: - breathe.
- get BROKEN, - break [subj.: dishes, glasses]: **kırıl-** 2. *801:12.* separation: - break.
- get or - be BURNED, scorched, singed /{BY/from}/; - get a burn, - get scalded; - get sunburned: **/DAn/ yan-** 3. *1019:24.* heating: - burn.
- get BY, - make one's living /by...ing/, - subsist /BY MEANS OF/, - manage /ON/ [a salary] [How do you {get by/make your living}?]: **/lA, ArAk/ geçin-** 2. *385:11.* provision, equipment: - make a living.
- get BY /WITH/, - manage /with/, - manage to get along /with/ [very little money]; - economize /BY/, - make ends meet /with/: **/lA/ idare et-** 2, **/lA/ yetin-** 2. *994:4.* expedience: - make shift, - make do.

- get CAUGHT /IN/, - be pinched /IN/ [jacket in door]: **/A/ sıkış-** 2. *854:10.* stability: - become firmly fixed.
- get caught, snagged, stuck /ON/ [a physical obstacle prevents further movement]: **/A/ takıl-** 1. *1011:10.* hindrance: - hinder.
- get CHANGE /for/, - have sb break a bill [subj.: customer at a bank]: **bozdur-** 1. *857:11.* conversion: - convert.
- get CHEAPER, - go down in price, - drop in price: **fiyatlar {düş-/in-}** → düş- 3, in- 4, **ucuzla-**. *252:6.* decrease - decrease; *633:6b.* cheapness: - become cheaper.
- get or - catch a CHILL: **soğuk al-** → al- 3, **üşüt-** 2. *85:46b.* disease: - take sick in particular ways; *1022.9.* cold: - freeze.
- get or - catch a COLD: **nezle ol-** → ol- 10.2. *85:46b.* disease: - take sick in particular ways.
- get COLD; - cool [subj.: a thing]: **soğu-** 1. *1022:9.* cold: - freeze.
- get or - be cold, - feel cold [subj.: a living being]: **üşü-**. *1022:9.* cold: - freeze.

528

- get or - become cold [subj.: weather]: **soğuk bas-** 4. *1022:9.* cold: - freeze.
- get CONFUSED, mixed up [subj.: a person]: {**kafası/aklı**} **karış-** → karış- 4, **şaşır-** 3. *984:7b.* distraction, confusion: - get confused.
- get or - keep CONTROL /{OF/OVER}/, - control /θ/, - keep in line [people or one's emotions, actions: The teacher couldn't get control over {the class/himself}.]: /A/ **hâkim ol-** → ol- 12. *106:7.* inexcitability: - compose oneself; *417:13.* authority: - possess or - wield authority; *428:7.* restraint: - restrain; *668:6.* temperance: - restrain oneself.
- get or - be CUT [hand]: **kesil-** 1. *224:4.* interval: - cleave.
- get or - be CUT OFF or interrupted [electricity, water, gas, phone conversation] /by/: /**tarafından**/ **kesil-** 3. *856:10.* cessation: - interrupt.

- get or - grow DARK [sky, lit., weather]: **hava karar-**. *1026:12.* darkness, dimness: - grow dark.
- get or - do a DEGREE [master's, doctor's]: *degree name* [e.g., **master, doktora] yap-**. → yap- 3. *570:9.* learning: - master.
- get or - be DEPRESSED, - be in a depression: **bunalım geçir-** → geçir- 2. *112:16.* sadness: - lose heart.
- get depressed, discouraged, - lose heart: **morali bozul-**. *112:16.* sadness: - lose heart.
- get depressed, - go into a depression: **bunalıma gir-**. *112:16.* sadness: - lose heart.
- get one's DESERTS, dues, - suffer for a deed: **cezasını çek-** 1 → çek- 5. *639:6.* dueness: - get one's deserts.
- get or - become DIRTY, soiled: **kirlen-, pislen-**. *80:15b.* uncleanness: - get dirty.
- get or - make sth DIRTY, - dirty sth, - soil, - pollute: **kirlet-, pislet-**. *80:15a.* uncleanness: - dirty.
- get or - be DIVORCED /from/, - split up /WITH/: /**DAn**/ **ayrıl-** 1, /**DAn**/ **boşan-**. *566:5.* divorce, widowhood: - divorce.
- get or - be DIZZY: **başı dön-** → dön- 1. *914:9.* rotation: - rotate; *984:8.* distraction, confusion: * - be dizzy.
- get DOWN /{from/OFF}/, - get off or out /OF/ a vehicle, - dismount /{θ/from}/ an animal: /**DAn**/ **in-** 2. *194:7.* descent: - get down.

- get RIGHT DOWN to, - attend to [a matter]: **üstüne git-** 2 → git- 1a. *724:10.* occupation: - occupy.
- get DRENCHED, soaked [I went out in the rain and got drenched.]: **sırılsıklam ıslan-**. *1063:13.* moisture: - soak.
- get DRESSED, - dress oneself: **giyin-**. *5:42.* clothing: - don.
- get or - become DRY, - dry [subj.: laundry], - dry out: **kuru-** 1. *1064:6b.* dryness: - dry, - become dry.
- get, - become, or - be DRUNK, tipsy, intoxicated, inebriated, high /{from/with}, {ON/with}/: /**DAn, 1A**/ **sarhoş ol-** 1 → ol- 12. *88:26.* intoxication, alcoholic drink: - get drunk; *88:27.* : - be drunk.
- get or - become EASY, easier [classes, lessons]: **kolaylaş-**. *1013:10.* facility: - go easily.
- get or - become ENGAGED /TO/: /**1A**/ **nişanlan-**. *436:6.* promise: - be engaged.
- get EXCITED, - be enthusiastic or thrilled [positive emotion]: **heyecanlan-** 1. *95:11.* pleasure: - be pleased; *105:18.* excitement: - be excited.
- get or - be excited [negative emotion], upset, agitated, nervous, - panic, - lose one's cool: **heyecanlan-** 2. *96:16b.* unpleasure: - be distressed; *128:6.* nervousness: - fidget.

- get FAT, - put on weight: **şişmanla-**. *259:8.* expansion, growth: - fatten.
- get A FLAT [sudden action: subj.: tire]: **lastiği patla-** → patla- 1. *260:10.* contraction: - collapse.
- get, - obtain sth /FOR/, - provide /to/, - procure: /**A**/ **sağla-**. *385:7.* provision, equipment: - provide.
- get or - receive sth /FROM/: /**DAn**/ **al-** 3. *479:6.* receiving: - receive.
- get or - take sth /from/: /**DAn**/ **al-** 1. *480:21.* taking: - take from.

- get or - have a HAIRCUT: **saç kes-** → kes- 1, **saç kestir-** → kestir- 1, **tıraş ol-** 2 ['- get or - have a shave OR a haircut'] → ol- 10.1. *3:22.* hair, feathers: - cut or - dress the hair.
- get HEATED, intense, - heat up, - intensify [subj.: dispute]: **hızlan-** 2. *119:3.* aggravation: - worsen.
- get HOLD /OF/, - obtain, - acquire [documents]: **ele geçir-** 2 → geçir- 1. *472:8.* acquisition: - acquire.
- get one's HOPES UP, - become hopeful, - begin to hope: {**umutlan-**

/ümitlen-}. *124:8.* hope - be hopeful.

- get HOT [sth being heated: clothes iron, stove]: **kız-** 2. *1019:17b.* heating: - get hot.
- get or - become hot [weather]: **sıcak bas-** → bas- 4. *1018:22.* heat: - be hot.
- get HUNG UP, stuck /ON/ a problem: **/A/ takıl-** 2. *1011:10.* hindrance: - hinder; *1012:11.* difficulty: - have difficulty.
- get or - be HURT, - become physically disabled; - become crippled; - become maimed or mutilated: **sakatlan-**. *393:13.* impairment: - inflict an injury.

- get an IDEA or advice /a: from, b: about, c: on the subject of/: **/a: DAn, b: hakkında, c: konusunda/ fikir al-** → al- 1. *422:7.* advice: - take or - accept advice.
- get, - be, or - become IMPATIENT: **sabırsızlan-**. *135:4.* impatience: - be impatient.
- get IN, - arrive /AT/ [When does the train get in?]: **/A/ gel-** 1, **/A/ ulaş-** 1, **/A/ var-**. *186:6.* arrival: - arrive.
- get in or - win a place in an educational institution or department: **kazan-** 2. *249:7.* superiority: - best; *411:3.* victory: - triumph.
- get in A HAPPY MOOD, - become cheerful, - cheer up: **neşelen-**. *95:11.* pleasure: - be pleased.
- get in A HUFF /about/: → - get in a state.
- get in A JAM, - be or - find oneself in a tight spot, under pressure, in difficulty: **sıkış-** 4. *297:13.* weight: - burden; *1012:12.* difficulty: - get into trouble.
- get in A STATE /{ABOUT/ CONCERNING}/, - get angry, mad /AT/, - get upset, tense, irritable /AT/, - get worked up /OVER/: **/A/ sinirlen-, sinirleri bozul-** 1 → bozul-. *96:16b.* unpleasure: - be distressed; *152:17.* resentment, anger: - become angry.
- get in CONTACT /with/, - contact /Ө/, - establish contact /with/: **/lA/ temas kur-** → kur- 1. *223:10.* nearness: - contact; *343:8.* communication: - communicate with, - get in touch with.
- get in [the] LINE, - line up, - queue up: **{sıraya/kuyruğa} gir-**. *811:6.* continuity: - line up.
- get or - put in ORDER, - arrange [affairs, matters]: **ayarla-** 2. *807:8.* arrangement: - arrange.

- get in TOUCH /with/, - reach /Ө/, - contact /Ө/ [a person]: **/A/ ulaş-** 2. *343:8.* communication: - communicate with, - get in touch with.
- get INFORMATION /to/, - inform /Ө/, - report /to/: **/A/ bildir-, /A/ bilgi ver-** → ver- 1, **/A/ haber ver-** → ver- 1. *551:8.* information: - inform.
- get INTO DEBT /{because of/due to}/: **/DAn dolayı/ borca gir-**. *623:6.* debt: - owe.
- get into debt /to [sb], for [an amount]/, - owe /Ө [sb], Ө [an amount]/: **/A, Ө/ borçlan-**. *623:5.* debt: - owe.
- get into FINANCIAL STRAITS, financial difficulty: **sıkıntıya gir-**. *1012:12.* difficulty: - get into trouble.
- get INVOLVED /IN/: **/A/ karış-** 6 [The students got involved in the events.], **/A/ burnunu sok-** 2. [*colloq. Turkish*, when the activity is sth unexpected, often foreign: the game of golf for most Turks] → sok- 1; *476:5.* participation: - participate.
- get involved /IN/, - plunge /INTO/ a friendly conversation: **sohbete dal-** → dal- 4. *476:5.* participation: - participate; *541:10.* conversation: - chat.
- get IRRITABLE, upset, or tense, - get in a state, huff /ABOUT/; - get angry, mad /AT/: **/A/ sinirlen-, sinirleri bozul-** 1 → bozul-. *96:16b.* unpleasure: - be distressed; *152:17.* resentment, anger: - become angry.
- get IT RIGHT, - be right, - be right on the mark, - be on target: **isabet kaydet-** 2. → kaydet- 5. *409:7b.* success: - succeed in specific ways; *972:10.* truth: - be right.

- get JAMMED, stuck, - become tightly wedged or jammed [zipper, door, key in lock]: **sıkış-** 1. *854:10.* stability: - become firmly fixed.

- get a KICK, - receive a blow: **tekme ye-** → ye- 2. *901:21.* impulse, impact: - kick.

- get LATE [It had gotten very late.]: **{vakit/zaman} ilerle-** → ilerle- 3. *845:7.* lateness: - be late.
- get LONGER, - grow taller, - grow: **uza-** 1. *251:6.* increase: - grow, increase [i.].
- get LOST, - be lost: **kaybol-** → ol- 12. *473:4.* loss: - lose.
- get lost, - lose one's way, not - know which way to turn [physically and morally]: **yolunu şaşır-** → şaşır- 3. *473:4.* loss: - lose; *654:9.* vice: - go

wrong; *970:9.* uncertainty: - be uncertain.

Get lost!: → Beat it!

- get, - be, or - become LOST IN THOUGHT, for one's mind - wander off, - give oneself up to reverie, - reminisce: **{düşünceye/ düşüncelere} dal-** → dal- 2. *984:9.* distraction, confusion: - muse; *988:11.* memory: - reminisce.

- get or - run LOW ON [supplies: sugar, gas], - decrease, - become less: **azal-.** *252:6.* decrease: - decrease.

- get MARRIED /TO/, - marry /θ/ [He {married θ/got married /TO/} his girlfriend.]: **/lA/ evlen-, /lA/ dünya evine gir-** → gir-. *563:15.* marriage: - get married.

- get MESSED UP, mussed UP /{from/BECAUSE OF/DUE TO}/ [hair]: **/DAn/ karış-** 3. *810:2.* disarrangement: - disarrange.

- get mixed UP, jumbled [subj.: notes, papers]: **karış-** 2. *796:10b.* mixture: - mix, - become mixed.

- get mixed up, confused [subj.: person]: **{kafası/aklı} karış-** → karış- 4, **şaşır-** 3. *984:7b.* distraction, confusion: - get confused.

- get or - be MIXED /{WITH/INTO}/ [various substances]: **/A/ karış-** 1. *796:10b.* mixture: - mix, - become mixed.

- get NEWS, word /{OF/from}/, - find out /from/: **/DAn/ haber al-** → al- 3. *570:6.* learning: - learn.

- get /OFF, OUT OF/ a vehicle, - get down /{from/OFF}/ a vehicle, - dismount /{θ/from}/ an animal: **/DAn/ in-** 2. *194:7.* descent: - get down.

- get OLD, - age [subj.: persons]: **ihtiyarla-, yaşı ilerle-** → ilerle- 3, **yaşlan-.** *303:10.* age: - age; *841:9.* oldness: - age.

- get old or worn-out, - wear out [subj.: objects, not living things: car, rug]: **eski-.** *393:20.* impairment: - wear, - wear away.

- get /ON/, - get on board, - board /θ/ [vehicle: bus], - mount /θ/ [a mount: horse]: **/A/ bin-** 1. *193:12.* ascent: - mount.

- get ON or along /with/ sb: **anlaş-** 1, **/lA/ geçin-** 1. *409:12.* success: - manage.

- get on sb's nerves /by...ing/, - irritate, - annoy; - make sb angry, mad, - anger sb /by...ing/: **/ArAk/ sinirlendir-.** *96:14.* unpleasure: - irritate; *96:16a.* : - distress; *105:14.* excitement: -

agitate; *128:9.* nervousness: - get on one's nerves; *152:22.* resentment, anger: - anger; *916:10.* agitation: - agitate.

- get /{ON [the Internet]/to [a source of informtion]/}, - gain access /to/, - access /θ/: **/A/ eriş-** 4. *186:6.* arrival: - arrive; *189:7.* entrance: - enter; *1041:18.* computer science: - computerize.

- get ONE'S JUST DESERTS or dues, - suffer for a deed: **cezasını çek-** 1 → çek- 5. *639:6.* dueness: - get one's deserts.

- get one's HOPES UP, - become hopeful, - begin to hope: **{umutlan-/ümitlen-}.** *124:8.* hope - be hopeful.

- get sb's OPINION or view, - consult: **fikrini al-** → al- 1. *422:7.* advice: - take or - accept advice.

- get OUT OF or - avoid doing something complicated; - escape from a difficult situation, predicament: **işin içinden çık-** 1 → çık- 1. *368:7.* avoidance: - evade.

- get or - be out of BREATH, - pant, - huff and puff /from/: **/DAn/ nefes nefese kal-** → kal- 1. *21:5.* fatigue: - burn out; *318:21.* * *1.* wind: - breathe.

- get out of LINE [ticket taker to people lined up: Don't get out of line!]: **{sırayı/kuyruğu} boz-** 2 → boz- 1. *263:3.* formlessness: - deform; *810:2.* disarrangement: - disarrange.

- get out of ORDER, - break down [machine]: **arıza yap-** [usually for large items run on energy sources such as fuel, batteries or house current, less frequently for small items such as clocks, radios, videos] → yap- 3, **bozul-** [for large and small items of all kinds]. *393:25.* impairment: - get out of order.

- get sth /OUT OF/ sb, - wrangle sth /from/ sb, - manage to get, usually in the face of difficulty [obj.: permission]: **/DAn/ {kopar-3/kopart- 3}.** *192:10.* extraction: - extract.

- get OVER or - kick an ILLNESS, - pull through, - overcome or survive a difficulty: **atlat-.** *396:20.* restoration: - recover.

- get OVEREXPOSED [photographs]: **yan-** 8. *714:14.* photography: - photograph.

- get or become PARALYZED, - have or - suffer a stroke: **felç ol-** → ol- 10.2, **inme in-** → in- 1. *85:46b.* disease: - take sick in particular ways.

- get PATCHED UP, for matters - get straightened out between, for people - be reconciled /with/ one another: /lA/ arası düzel-. *465:10*. pacification: - make up.
- get PERMISSION /from, to [do sth]/: /DAn, için/ {izin/müsaade} al- → al- 3. *443:9. * 1*. permission: - get permission.
- get PREGNANT: hamile kal- → kal- 1. *78:12*. reproduction, procreation: - be pregnant.
- get PUFFED UP /{from/BECAUSE OF}/, - swell [up] [eyes from crying, skin from a sting]: /DAn/ şiş- 1. *259:5*. expansion, growth: - become larger; *283:11*. convexity, protuberance: - bulge.
- get a PUNCH, - be punched: yumruk ye- → ye- 2. *901:14*. impulse, impact: - hit.

- get QUEASY [stomach], - feel nauseated, nauseous, for one's stomach - be upset, - have an upset stomach: midesi bulan-. *85:46b*. disease: - take sick in particular ways.

- get sth READY /FOR/, - make ready, - prepare sth [He got the room ready for the guests.]: /{A/için}/ hazırla-. *405:6*. preparation: - prepare.
- get [ONESELF] READY, - prepare oneself /FOR/ [He got (himself) ready for the exam.]: /{A/için}/ hazırlan- 1. *405:13*. preparation: - prepare oneself.
- get a REFUND /from/, - get one's money back: /DAn/ parasını geri al- → geri al- 1 → al- 1. *481:6*. restitution: - recover.
- get RID OF, - throw out, - discard [old newspapers]: at- 2. *390:7*. disuse: - discard.
- get rid of [obj.: a person], - dismiss: *formal:* görevden al- ['- fire, - relieve sb of his {duties/position}'] → al- 1, işine son ver- ['- fire, - relieve sb of his position'] → ver- 1. *908:19*. ejection: - dismiss. *informal:* işten {at-/kov-} ['- fire, sack, can'] → at- 1, kov- 2. *908:20. :* <nonformal terms> - fire.
- get rid /OF/ sb or sth, - be rid /OF/ sb or sth unpleasant, - avoid, - shake /OFF/ [an annoying person, classes, debts, flies]: /DAn/ kurtul- 2. *368:6*. avoidance: - avoid.
- get RIGHT DOWN TO, - attend to [a matter]: üstüne git- 2 → git- 1a. *724:10*. occupation: - occupy.

- get SCALDED /{BY/from}/, - scald or - burn oneself with a hot liquid: /DAn/ haşlan- 2. *393:13*. impairment: - inflict an injury.
- get or - have a SHAVE or a haircut: tıraş ol- 2 → ol- 10.1. *3:22*. hair, feathers: - cut or - dress the hair; *255:10*. subtraction: - excise; *268:6*. shortness: - shorten.
- get PREGNANT: hamile kal- → kal-
- get an electrical SHOCK: /I/ elektrik çarp → çarp- 4. *1031:25*. electricity, magnetism: - electrify.
- get SHOT [subj.: one's nerves], - be badly shaken up: sinirleri bozul- 2 → bozul-. *128:7*. nervousness: - lose self- control.
- get SICK, - take sick, - become ill /{AS A RESULT OF/WITH/from}/: /DAn/ hastalan-, /DAn/ hasta ol- → ol- 10.2. *85:46a*. disease: - take sick in general.
- get sick, - take ill, - feel faint, - feel suddenly sick: fenalaş- 2. *85:46a*. disease: - take sick in general.
- get sick from riding in a vehicle: boat, bus, plane, - suffer from motion sickness: tut- 8. *85:46b*. disease: - take sick in particular ways.
- get a SLAP, - be slapped: tokat ye- → ye- 2. *604:12*. punishment: - slap; *901:19*. impulse, impact: - slap.
- get or - become SLEEPY: uykusu gel- → gel- 1. *22:13*. sleep: - sleep.
- get SNAGGED, caught, stuck /ON/ [a physical obstacle prevents further movement]: /A/ takıl- 1. *1011:10*. hindrance: - hinder.
- get SOAKED, drenched [I went out in the rain and got soaked.]: sırılsıklam ıslan-. *1063:13*. moisture: - soak.
- get SB TO DO STH: → - have /θ/ sb DO sth.
- get STH OFF ONE'S CHEST, - pour out one's troubles, - spill out one's woes /to/: /A/ dert dök- → dök- 1. *120:7*. relief: - lighten.
- get STH TO EAT: karnını doyur-. *993:4*. satiety: - satiate.
- get STIFF /from/ [subj.: part of the body: neck, back]: /DAn/ tutul- 5. *393:13*. impairment: - inflict an injury; *1044:9*. hardness, rigidity: - stiffen. for things
- get STRAIGHTENED OUT, for matters - get patched up between, for people - be reconciled /with/ one another: /lA/ arası düzel-. *465:10*. pacification: - make up.
- get STUCK, - become tightly wedged or jammed [zipper, door, key in lock]: sıkış- 1. *854:10*. stability: - become firmly fixed.

- get stuck /IN/, - sink /INTO/ [car in mud]: /A/ bat- 1. *194:6.* descent: - sink.
- get stuck, snagged, caught /ON/ [a physical obstacle prevents further movement]: /A/ takıl- 1. *1011:10.* hindrance: - hinder.
- get stuck, hung up /ON/ a problem: /A/ takıl- 2. *1011:10.* hindrance: - hinder; *1012:11.* difficulty: - have difficulty.
- get SUNBURNED: yan- 3. *1019:24.* heating: - burn.
- get SUNSTROKE: /A/ güneş çarp- → çarp- 1. *85:46b.* disease: - take sick in particular ways.

- get TENSE, irritable, upset, - get in a state /{ABOUT/CONCERNING}/; - get angry, mad /AT/: /A/ sinirlen-, sinirleri bozul- 1 → bozul-. *96:16b.* unpleasure: - be distressed; *152:17.* resentment, anger: - become angry.
- get or - answer THE DOOR: kapıya bak- → bak- 3. *982:5.* attention: - attend to.
- get, - answer, or - pick up THE PHONE: telefonU aç- → aç- 5, telefonA {bak-/cevap ver-} → bak- 3, → ver- 1. *347:18.* communications: - telephone; *982:5.* attention: - attend to.
- get or - be THIRSTY: susa-. *100:19.* desire: - hunger.
- get a THRASHING, beating /from/: /DAn/ dayak ye- → ye- 2. *604:13.* punishment: - whip; *901:16.* impulse, impact: - pound.
- get THROUGH /TO/, - reach sb or a place [by phone: I couldn't get through {to my parents/to Ankara}.]: /lA/ bağlantı kur- → kur- 1. *343:8.* communication: - communicate with, - get in touch with; *347:18.* communications: - telephone.
- get through [on the phone], - get a phone line, for a phone line - be or - become available or free: hat düş- → düş- 1. *347:18.* communications: - telephone.
- get or - be TIRED /from/, - tire [oneself]: /DAn/ yorul-. *21:4.* fatigue: - fatigue.
- get tired /OF/, - be bored /WITH/, fed up /WITH/, tired /OF/: /DAn/ {bık-/usan-}, /DAn/ sıkıl- 1. *118:7b.* tedium: - get bored.
- get or - go /TO/ [How does ONE get to the airport?]: /A/ gidil-. *177:25.* travel: - go to.
- get /to/, - come /to/, - arrive /{IN/AT}/, - reach /θ/ [a destination]: /A/ gel- 1,

/A/ ulaş- 1, /A/ var-, /A/ eriş- 1. *186:6.* arrival: - arrive.
- get /to/ [a place with one's hands], - reach /θ/ [the top shelf]: /A/ uzan- 3, /A/ yetiş- 5, /A/ eriş- 2. *261:6.* distance, remoteness: - extend to.
- get /to/, - access /θ/, - gain access /to/ [the Internet, a source of information]: /A/ eriş- 4. *186:6.* arrival: - arrive; *189:7.* entrance: - enter; *1041:18.* computer science: - computerize.
- get sb to DO STH: → - have /θ/ sb DO sth.
- get to KNOW sb, - become acquainted /WITH/ sb, - meet: /I/ tanı- 3. *587:10* friendship: - befriend, - make friends with.
- get to know, - get acquainted /with/ ONE ANOTHER, - meet /θ/; - be acquainted with, - know one another': /lA/ tanış-. *587:10.* friendship: - befriend, - make friends with.
- get /to/ ONE'S FEET, - stand up: ayağa kalk- → kalk- 1. *193:8.* ascent: - ascend; *200:8.* verticalness: - rise.
- get TOGETHER, - come together, - assemble, - gather: bir araya gel- → gel- 1, toplan- 3. *769:16.* assemblage: - come together.
- get or - be TORN, ripped /{OUT OF/from}, by/ [pages from a book]: /DAn, tarafından/ yırtıl-. *192:10.* extraction: - extract'; *801:11.* separation: - sever.
- get or - be TURNED ON sexually: tahrik ol- → ol- 12, heyecanlan- 3. *105:12.* excitement: - excite.

- get or - be UNTIDY, messed up [room, hair]: dağıl- 4. *810:2.* disarrangement: - disarrange.
- get UP /{from/OUT OF}/ [chair], - rise /from/, - stand up, - get up, - get out of bed, - arise: /DAn/ kalk- 1. *193:8.* ascent: - ascend; *200:8.* verticalness: - rise.
- get SB UP: uyandır- ['- wake sb up'], kaldır- 2 ['- get sb up (from bed)']. *23:5.* wakefulness: - wake sb up.
- get UPSET, tense, irritable /AT/, - get worked up /OVER/, - get in a state /ABOUT/, - get on edge, - get nervous; - get angry, mad /AT/: /A/ sinirlen-, sinirleri bozul- 1 → bozul-. *96:16b.* unpleasure: - be distressed; *152:17.* resentment, anger: - become angry.
- get USED /TO/, - become accustomed /to/: /A/ alış- 1. *373:12.* custom, habit: - be used to.

- get or - grow WARM, - warm up: ısın- 1. *1019:17b.* heating: - get hot.

- get WELL, better, - improve, - recover [from illness]: **düzel-, iyileş-**. *392:8.* improvement: - rally, - get better; *396:20.* restoration: - recover.

Get WELL SOON.: **Geçmiş olsun!** → ol- 11 → olsun. *504: * 20.* courtesy: polite expressions.

- get WET: **ıslan-**. *1063:11.* moisture: - be damp.

- get WORD, news /{OF/from}/, - find out /from/: **/DAn/ haber al-** → al- 3. *570:6.* learning: - learn.

- get word /OF/, - hear /{OF/ABOUT}/, - learn /OF/: **/I/ duy- 2, /I/ işit- 2.** *551:15.* information: - know, - be informed.

- get word /TO/, - inform /θ/: **/A/ bildir-, /A/ haber ver-** → ver- 1. *551:8.* information: - inform.

- get WORKED UP /OVER/, - get in a state /ABOUT/, - get upset, tense, irritable /AT/; - get angry, mad /AT/: **/A/ sinirlen-, sinirleri bozul- 1** → bozul-. *96:16b.* unpleasure: - be distressed.

- get WORN-OUT, - wear out [subj.: thing, e.g., car, rug, not living thing]: **yıpran- 1.** *393:20.* impairment: - wear, - wear away.

- get worn-out, tired /from/ [subj.: person]: **/DAn/ yorul-.** *2 1 : 4.* fatigue: - fatigue.

- get WORSE, - deteriorate [patient, economic situation, an ability]: **bozul-, fenalaş- 1, kötüleş-, zayıfla- 2.** *393:16.* impairment: - deteriorate.

- get worse, - deteriorate, - worsen, lit., - revert to a previous, less advanced state [economic situation, an ability]: **gerile- 2.** *393:16.* impairment: - deteriorate.

- get worse, - change for the worse [weather]: **[hava] {boz-/bozul-}** → boz- 4, bozul-. *393:16.* impairment: - deteriorate.

- get or - become WRINKLED: **buruş-, yüzü buruş- 2** ['for a person's face - become or - get wrinkled']. *290:3.* furrow: - furrow; *303:10.* age: - age.

- get or - do sth WRONG, - do incorrectly [questions on an exam]: **yanlış yap-** → yap- 3. *974:12.* error: - misdo.

- GIVE /to/: **/A/ ver- 1.** *478:12.* giving: - give.

- give /to/ [a charity], - donate /to/, - make a donation /to/: **/A/ bağışla- 1.** *478:12.* giving: - give.

- give A {LIFT/ride} to, - pick up [by car], - take on [passengers]: **al- 2.**

176:16. transferal, transportation: - fetch.

- give ADVANCE NOTICE, - inform /θ/ sb in advance: **/A/ önceden bildir-**. *961:9.* prediction: - predict.

- give ADVICE /to/, - advise /θ/: **/A/ akıl ver-** → ver- 1, **/A/ fikir ver- 2** → ver- 1, **/A/ yol göster- 2** → göster-1. *422:5.* advice: - advise.

- give or - grant an APPOINTMENT /to/: **/A/ gün ver-** ['- give a {date/day} for an appointment'] → ver- 1, **/A/ randevu ver-** ['- give an appointment'] → ver- 1. *478:12.* giving: - give; *964:4.* prearrangement: - prearrange.

- give AWAY, - donate /to/ [He gave (away) all his old clothes to the Red Crescent.]: **/A/ bağışla- 1, /A/ ver- 1.** *478:12.* giving: - give.

- give or - take sth BACK /to/, - return sth /to/: **/A/ {geri ver-/iade et-}.** The second verb is *more formal.* → ver-1. *481:4.* restitution: - restore.

- give a BEATING: → - give a WHIPPING.

- give BIRTH /TO/, - bear: **/I/ doğur-, /I/ dünyaya getir-**. *1:3.* birth: - give birth.

- give sb a BREAK, - make things easy /FOR/, - facilitate matters /FOR/, - help /θ/: **/A/ kolaylık göster-** → göster- 1. *449:11.* aid: - aid; *1013:7.* facility: - facilitate.

- give or - make CHANGE /for/, - break a bill [larger bill, coin into smaller]: **boz- 2.** *857:11.* conversion: - convert.

- give sb a CHILL [subj.: air, weather]: **üşüt- 1.** *1022:10.* cold: - make cold.

- give COMFORT /to/ [in this vocabulary only in **Allah rahatlık versin** (lit., May God give comfort), a formula meaning 'Good night', used when going to bed, not, for example, simply when leaving a party]: → ver-1. *188:23.* departure: good night!

- give a {DATE/DAY} FOR AN APPOINTMENT /to/: **/A/ gün ver-** → ver- 1. *964:4.* prearrangement: - prearrange.

- give a DISCOUNT /to/, - make a reduction in price /FOR/, - go down in price /FOR/: **/A/ ikram et- 2, in- 5, indir- 3.** *631:2.* discount: - discount.

- give the EQUIVALENT OF A WORD, - define: **karşılığını ver-** → ver- 1. *341:9.* interpretation: - interpret.

- give EVIDENCE /a: {for/on behalf of}, b: {θ [that]/to the effect that}, c: {for/on behalf of}, d: against/, - testify, - be a witness in a court case: /a: için, b: A dair, c: lehine, d: aleyhine/ tanıklık et-. *956:9.* evidence, proof: - testify.
- give evidence /to/, - testify, - give testimony, - give or - make a statement [law]: /A/ ifade ver- → ver- 1. *956:9.* evidence, proof: - testify.
- give an EXAMINATION /to, IN/ [subj.: teacher]: /I, DAn/ {imtihan/NOT s̶ı̶n̶a̶v̶} et-, / A, DAn/ {sınav/imtihan} ver- 2 → ver- 1. *937:21.* inquiry: - interrogate.
- give, - cite, or - provide an EXAMPLE /FOR/: /A/ {örnek/misal} ver- → ver- 1. *956:13.* evidence, proof: - cite.

- give sth as a GIFT /to/ sb, - make a present of sth /to/ sb: /A/ hediye et-. *478:12.* giving: - give; *634:4.* costlessness: - give.
- give a GRADE or mark /to/ sb or sth, - give /θ/ sb or sth a grade, - grade /θ/ sb or sth, - mark [an exam]: /A/ not ver- → ver- 1. *945:9.* judgment: - estimate.

- give a HAND /to/, - help /θ/, - assist /θ/: /A/ yardım et-. *449:11.* aid: - aid.
- give one another a hand, - help one another: el ele ver- → ver- 1, yardımlaş-. *449:11.* aid: - aid.

- give an IDEA or impression /about/, - express or - give an opinion /ON/ [subj.: person or thing such as a film]: /hakkında/ fikir ver- 1 → ver- 1. *608:12.* description: - describe; *945:8.* judgment: - judge.
- give, - ascribe, or - attach IMPORTANCE /to/, - value /θ/, - consider important: /A/ {önem/ ehemmiyet} ver- → ver- 1, /I/ önemse-. *996:13.* importance: - value.
- give sb IN MARRIAGE /TO/: /IA/ evlendir- ['- marry sb /TO/'], /A/ kız ver- ['- give a girl in marriage /to/'] → ver- 1. *563:14.* marriage: - join in marriage.
- give or - provide INFORMATION /to/: /A/ bilgi ver- → ver- 1, /A/ haber ver- → ver- 1. *551:8.* information: - inform.

- give LESSONS /to/ sb, - teach /θ/ sb: /A/ ders ver- → ver- 1. *568:10.* teaching: - teach.

- give a {LIFT/ride} to, - pick up [by car], - take on [passengers]: al- 2. *176:16.* transferal, transportation: - fetch.

- give a NAME /to/, - name /θ/: /A/ {ad/isim} koy- → koy- 1, /A/ {ad/isim} ver- → ver- 1. *527:11.* nomenclature: - name.

- give OFF A SMELL, - smell /OF/, - have a smell: /θ/ kok- 1. *69:6.* odor: - have an odor.
- give ONESELF AIRS, - show off, - act snobbishly: hava bas- 2. *501:16.* ostentation: - show off.
- give an OPINION, idea, or impression /about/, - express an opinion /ON/: /hakkında/ fikir ver- 1→ ver- 1. *608:12.* description: - describe; *945:8.* judgment: - judge.
- give an ORDER for sth /to/ sb, - order [goods], - place or - put an order for sth /WITH/ sb, - order sth /FROM/ sb [lit., ** - order sth TO sb]: /A/ ısmarla- 2. *440:9.* request: - request.
- give OUT, - go out of order, - break down [machines]: arıza yap- [usually for large items run on energy sources such as fuel, batteries or house current, less frequently for small items such as clocks, radios, videos] → yap- 3, bozul- [for large and small items of all kinds]. *393:25.* impairment: - get out of order.
- give out, - run out [subj.: supplies: food, fuel]: bit- 3, tüken-. *388:4.* consumption: - be consumed.

- give or - have a PARTY: parti ver- → ver- 1. *585:8.* hospitality, welcome: - entertain.
- give PERMISSION /to/ sb, - allow /θ/ sb /to/, - let /θ/ sb, - permit /θ/ sb: /A/ izin ver- → ver- 1, /A/ müsaade et-. The causative form of verbs [that is, verb stems with one of the following six causative suffixes: -Ar, -Art, -DIr, -Ir, -It, -t] may also express permission, as in second part of the following sentence: She wanted to use the phone, and he let her. For a list of all causative verbs included in this dictionary, see the Index of Turkish Verb Suffixes [→ also '- have sth done']. *443:9.* permission: - permit.

- give, - send, or - express one's REGARDS /to/, - say 'hi' /to/: /A/ selâm söyle- → söyle- 1. *504:13.* courtesy: - give one's regards.

535

Part 2: English-Turkish Index

- give a REFUND, - refund money, - give back money: **para {geri ver-/iade et-}** → {geri ver-/iade et-} → ver- 1. *481:4.* restitution: - restore.
- give a {RIDE/lift} to, - pick up [i.e., by car], - take on [passengers]: **al- 2.** *176:16.* transferal, transportation: - fetch.

- give sb a SHAVE, - shave sb: **sakal tıraşı yap-** → yap- 3. *255:10.* subtraction: - excise; *268:6.* shortness: - shorten.

- give sb the TASK /of/, - charge sb /with/, - entrust sb /with/, - make sb responsible /FOR/, - put sb in charge /OF/: **/1A/ görevlendir-.** *615:11.* commission: - appoint; *641:12.* duty: - obligate.
- give TESTIMONY, - testify, - give or - make a statement, - give evidence /to/: **/A/ ifade ver-** → ver- 1. *956:9.* evidence, proof: - testify.
- give THANKS /a: to [God], b: {for/because of}, c: θ [that]/, - praise [a: θ [God]/, b: {for/because of}, c: θ [that]/: **/a: A, b: DAn dolayı, c: A/ şükret-.** *150:4.* gratitude: - thank; *509:12.* approval: - praise.
- give a THRILL, - thrill, - excite: **heyecanlandır- 1.** *105:12.* excitement: - excite.
- give a THRASHING: → - give a WHIPPING.
- give a TICKET /to/ sb, to a vehicle, - fine /θ/: **/A/ ceza kes-** → kes- 5. *604:10.* punishment: - punish.
- give some TIME /to/ sb [to complete a task]: **/A/ {zaman/vakit/süre} ver-** → ver- 1. *845:9.* lateness: - postpone.
- give /θ/ sb a TIP, - tip /θ/ sb, - give a tip /to/ sb [money, not information]: **/A/ bahşiş ver-** → ver- 1. *624:10.* payment: - pay.
- give sb a TRIAL PERIOD, - see how sth or sb works out, - try on [clothing], - try out [equipment]: **tecrübe et-.** *941:8.* experiment: - experiment.
- give TROUBLE /to/, - inconvenience /θ/, - trouble /θ/, - cause trouble /to/, - put sb /to/ a lot of trouble, - put sb out: **/A/ zahmet ver-** → ver- 1. *995:4.* inexpedience: - inconvenience; *1012:13.* difficulty: - trouble.

- give UP /θ/, - drop /θ/ [idea, plan]: **/DAn/ vazgeç-.** *370:7.* abandonment: - give up.
- give up /θ/ [piano lessons]: **/A/ boş ver- 2** → ver- 1, **/DAn/ vazgeç-.** *370:7.* abandonment: - give up.

- give up HOPE, - despair, - lose hope: **{umudunu/ümidini} kaybet-**[or yitir-] → {kaybet-/yitir-}. *125:10.* hopelessness: - despair.

- give WATER /TO/: **/A/ su ver-** [obj.: people, plants, animals] → ver- 1, **/I/ sula-** [obj.: plants, animals']. *1063:12.* moisture: - moisten; *1068:7.* animal husbandry: - tend.
- give WAY [in traffic], - yield: **yol ver-** → ver- 1. *352:7.* publication: poster: * specific signs; *433:7.* submission: - yield.
- give a WHIPPING, beating, thrashing, - beat, - thrash: **ayağının altına al-** → al- 1, **/A/ dayak at-** → at- 5. *514: * 5.* threat: INTERJ. specific threats; *604:13.* punishment: - whip; *901:14.* impulse, impact: - hit.
- give one's WORD /to [sb], {about/concerning} [sth]/, - promise /θ/ sb sth: **/A, {A dair/için}/ söz ver-** → ver- 1, today *less common, more formal*: **/A/ vadet-.** *436:4.* promise: - promise.

- GLANCE or - take a look /AT/ [your newspaper]: **/A/ göz at-** → at- 1. *937:26.* inquiry: - examine cursorily.

- GLARE /AT/, - stare angrily /AT/: **/A/ dik dik bak-** → bak- 1. *27:16:* - glare; *152:25a.* resentment, anger: gestures of.

- GLUE, - paste, - tape, or - stick sth /{ON/ONTO/to}/ sth: **/A/ yapıştır-.** *799:5.* joining: - put together; *802:9.* cohesion: - stick together.

- GO or - proceed [well or badly: journey, examination]: **geç- 6, git- 5.** *162:2.* progression: - progress.
- go, - walk, or - stroll ABOUT, - tour [obj.: a place: on foot or in a vehicle], - sightsee: **/I/ gez-.** *177:21.* travel: - journey; *177:23.* : - wander.
- go, - walk, - wander, or - stroll, about, around, - make one's way through [usually on foot]: **/I/ dolaş- 1.** *177:23.* travel: - wander.
- go ACROSS, - go /to/ the other side, - cross /θ/, - cross over /θ/: **/DAn/ karşıya geç-** → geç- 1. *177:20.* travel: - traverse; *909:8.* overrunning: - pass.
- go [ALONG] /WITH/, - accompany /θ/: **/A/ {eşlik et-/refakat et-}, /1A/ gel-** ['- come /with/ sb'], **/1A/ git-** ['- go /with/ sb'] → git- 1a. *768:7.* accompaniment: - accompany.

- go along /WITH/ a plan; - be inclined or willing /to/, - be willing to agree /to/: /A/ yanaş- 3. *324:3.* willingness: - be willing; *441:2.* consent: - consent.
- go AWAY /from/; - leave, - depart, - quit: /DAn/ ayrıl- 3 [from friends, city, party], /DAn/ çık- 1 [from an enclosed place: house, room], /DAn/ git- 1a ['- go from (anywhere)'], /DAn/ uzaklaş- 1 ['- move away from', train from station]. *188:6.* departure: - depart.

Go away!: → Beat it!

- go BACK, - come back, - turn back, - return /from, to/: /DAn, A / g e r i dön- → dön- 2. *163:8b.* regression: - turn back, - come back.
- go back /ON/ one's word: sözünden dön- → dön- 5. *435:4.* nonobservance: - violate.
- go BAD, - spoil [subj.: all kinds of food]: bozul-. *393:22.* impairment: - decay.
- go bad, - go stale, - spoil [subj.: certain foods: bread, fish]: bayatla-. *393:22.* impairment: - decay.
- go BANKRUPT, - go under: bat- 2, iflâs et- 1. *625:7.* nonpayment: - go bankrupt.
- go BEYOND, - exceed [obj.: speed limit]: geç- 1. *909:4.* overrunning: - overrun; *992:9.* excess: - exceed.
- go BY MEANS OF [i.e., car, bus]: *vehicle name*.L A git- [e.g., araba.ylA git-]. → git- 1a. *177:25.* travel: - go to; *182:13.* water travel: - navigate.
- go CAMPING, - camp: kamp yap- → yap- 3. *255:11.* habitation: - camp.
- go CRAZY, mad, insane, nuts, out of one's mind, - take leave of one's senses: aklını {kaybet-/yitir-}, çıldır-, delir-, {şuurunu/bilincini} kaybet-[or yitir-] 3 → {kaybet-/yitir-}. *925:21.* insanity, mania: - go mad.
- go DOWN, - descend /{from/BY WAY OF}, to/: /DAn, A/ in- 1. *194:5.* descent: - descend.
- go down [subj.: swelling, prices]: in- 4. *252:6.* decrease: - decrease.
- go down [subj.: prices]: fiyatlar {düş-/in-} → düş- 3, in- 4. *252:6.* decrease: - decrease; *633:6b.* cheapness: - become cheaper.
- go down IN PRICE, - get cheaper, - drop in price: ucuzla- [subj.: object for sale]. *252:6.* decrease: - decrease; *633:6b.* cheapness: - become cheaper.

- go down in price /FOR/ sb, - give a discount /to/ sb, - make a reduction in price /FOR/ sb: /A/ ikram et- 2, in- 5, indir- 3. *631:2.* discount: - discount.
- go DOWNHILL, - decline in quality, - deteriorate [an ability, memory]: zayıfla- 2. *393:16.* impairment: - deteriorate.
- go /θ/ DOWNTOWN, /INTO/ town, /INTO/ the city: şehre in- → in- 1. *177:18.* travel: - travel; *194:5.* descent: - descend.
- go FLAT, - deflate, - collapse: sön- 2 [subj.: balloon, tire, rubber boat], in- 4 [subj.: tire, rubber boat]. *260:10.* contraction: - collapse.
- go FOR A DRIVE: arabayla gez-. *177:21.* travel: - journey.
- go out /FOR/ A WALK, a stroll: yürüyüşe çık- → çık- 2, gezmeye çık- ['- go {out for a walk/θ sightseeing}'] → çık- 2. *177:29.* travel: - go for a walk.
- go /{IN/INSIDE}/, - enter [The specific place entered is not indicated: The door opened, and he went in.]: /{içeri[.ye]}/ gir-. *189:7.* entrance: - enter.
- go /INTO, {through/by way of}/, - enter /θ, {through/by way of}/ [The place entered may be indicated: He went into the room through the door.]: /A, DAn/ gir-. *189:7.* entrance: - enter.
- go, - lapse, - fall, or - sink into A COMA: komaya gir-. *25:5.* insensibility: - faint.
- go into DEBT: borca gir-. *623:6.* debt: - go in debt.
- go into A DEPRESSION, - get depressed: bunalıma gir-. *112:16.* sadness: - lose heart.
- go or - enter into DETAIL: {ayrıntıya/ayrıntılara/detaya/detaylara} gir-. *765:6.* circumstance: - itemize.
- go into ECLIPSE [sun, moon]: tutul- 4. *1026:9.* darkness, dimness: - darken.
- go into RECESS for vacation, - recess for vacation [subj.: schools], - close or - shut down for vacation [subj.: an institution, school, business]: tatile gir-. *20:9.* rest, repose: - vacation; *293:8.* closure: - close shop; *856:8.* cessation: - stop work.
- go into SHOCK [non-medical], - be shocked /AT/: /karşısında/ {şoke/şok} ol- → ol- 10.1. *131:7.* inexpectation: - surprise.
- go /into/ shock [a medical condition]: şoka gir-. *85:46b.* disease: - take sick in particular ways.

- go ON, - continue, - last [The meeting went on for two hours.]: **devam et-1, sür-** 2. *811:4b.* continuity: for sth - continue; *826:6.* durability: - endure.
- go on, - happen, - occur, - take place [What's going on here?]: **ol-** 4. *830:5.* event: - occur.
- go on, - drag on [matter, court case]: **uza-** 2. *826:7.* durability: - linger on.
- go on [light, lamp]: **açıl-** 6, **yan-** 4. *1024:27.* light: - grow light.
- go on a DATE /with/ sb: → - go out /WITH/.
- go on a DIET, - diet [both for losing weight and for the treatment of a medical condition]: **perhiz yap-** → yap- 3. *7:17.* nutrition: - diet.
- go on a HOLIDAY or a vacation, - take a holiday, vacation: **tatil yap-** → yap- 3, **tatile çık-** ['- go ON {vacation/holiday}, - leave FOR {vacation/the holiday[s]}, - begin a vacation'], **tatile git-** → git- 1a. *20:9.* rest, repose: - vacation; *856:8.* cessation: - stop work.
- go on FOOT: {**yürüyerek/yaya [olarak]/yayan**} **git-** → git- 1a. *177:27.* travel: - walk.
- go on SALE [not necessarily at a reduced price]: **satışa çık-** → çık-2. *734:10.* sale: - put up for sale.
- go on THE PILGRIMAGE, - make the Pilgrimage to Mecca: **hacca git-** → git- 1a. *177:21.* travel: - journey; *701:14.* religious rites: - celebrate.
- go on /TO/ THE NEXT GRADE, - graduate [from the fifth grade to the sixth]: **sınıfa geç-** → geç- 1, **sınıfını geç-** → geç- 1. *409:7b.* success: - succeed in specific ways.
- go ON {vacation/holiday}, - leave FOR {vacation/the holiday[s]}, - begin a vacation [subj.: people]: **tatile çık-** → çık- 2. *20:9.* rest, repose: - vacation.
- go /on/ a VISIT, - pay a visit, - go to visit a person, - call /ON/ sb [usually a neighbor or friend, not a relative or a person of higher station, i.e., a casual, not formal visit]: **misafirliğe git-** → git- 3. *582:19.* sociability: - visit.
- go on /WITH/, - continue /{θ/WITH}/ sth [They went on with the meeting.]: /A/ **devam et-** 2. *267:6.* length: - lengthen; *811:4a.* continuity: - continue sth.
- go or - step {OUT/OUTSIDE}: **dışarı[.ya] çık-** 1 → çık- 2. *190:12.* emergence: - exit.
- go out [fire, lights, candle, lamps]: **sön-** 1. *1021:8.* incombustibility: - burn

out; *1026:12.* darkness, dimness: - grow dark.
- go or - come out [spot, stain]: **çık-** 11. *34:2a.* disappearance: - disappear.
- go [out] /FOR/ a walk: **yürüyüşe çık-** → çık- 2. *177:29.* travel: - go for a walk.
- go out {for/to} DINNER, - dine out: **yemeğe çık-** → çık- 2. *8:21.* eating: - dine.
- go out OF CIRCULATION [money]: **tedavülden kalk-** → kalk- 3. *445:2.* repeal: - repeal.
- go out OF FAVOR, - become regarded as worthless [ideology]: **iflâs et-** 3. *390:9.* disuse: - obsolesce.
- go out OF ORDER, - break down, - give out [machine]: **arıza yap-** [usually for large items run on energy sources such as fuel, batteries or house current, less frequently for small items such as clocks, radios, videos] → yap- 3, **bozul-** [for large and small items of all kinds]. *393:25.* impairment: - get out of order.
- go out /{THROUGH/BY WAY OF}, to/; - go up /to/, - climb /to/ [impersonal passive: ONE does not go out (THROUGH) this door.]: /DAn, A/ **çıkıl-**. *190:12.* emergence: - exit.
- go out /WITH/, - go [out] on a date /with/, - date, - be dating [with the intention of marriage]: /lA/ **çık-** 10, **flört et-** [Not the English '- flirt']. *562:14.* lovemaking, endearment: - make love; *769:16.* assemblage: - come together.
- go /OVER/, - examine, - look /OVER/, - scrutinize, - review [usually a document: article, paper, plan, report]: **gözden geçir-** → geçir- 1. *27:14.* vision: - scrutinize.

- go PAST [obj.: a place], - go beyond: /DAn/ **geç-** 1. *909:8.* overrunning: - pass.

- go /θ/ SHOPPING: **alışverişe çık-** → çık- 2, **çarşıya çık-** → çık- 2. *733:8.* purchase: - shop.
- go SIGHT-SEEING: **gezmeye çık-** → çık- 2. *917:6.* spectator: - sight-see.
- go STALE, - spoil, - go bad [subj.: certain foods: bread, fish]: **bayatla-**. *393:22.* impairment: - decay.
- go SWIMMING in the {sea/ocean}: **denize gir-**. *182:56.* water travel: - swim.
- go THROUGH [a difficult period], - live through, - experience, - have

[problems], - enjoy [fine weather]: **yaşa-** 3. *830:8.* event: - experience.

- go /TO/, - attend /θ/: **/A/ devam et-** 3 [for a long period (educational institution: school, university), not for a short period or particular event (concert, soccer match, lecture)], **/A/ git-** 4 [for a long period (school, university) or a short period (concert, soccer match)], **/I/ oku-** 3 [an educational institution regularly]. *221:8.* presence: - attend.
- go to BED, - lie down, - retire for the night: **yat-** 1. *22:17.* sleep: - go to bed; *201:5.* horizontalness: - lie.
- go to bed /with/, - sleep /with/, i.e., - have sex with: **/lA/ yat-** 2. *75:21.* sex: - copulate; *562:14.* lovemaking, endearment: - make love.
- go to GREAT PAINS /to/ do sth well, - take great pains /to/ do sth well, - take pains /{WITH/OVER}/ sth: **/A/ özen-** 1. *403:11.* endeavor: - make a special effort.
- go /to/ a LOT OF TROUBLE [to do sth for guests, as a favor: prepare a meal]: **zahmete gir-**. *995:4.* inexpedience: -
- go to MEET, - meet, - welcome, - greet sb /at [a place], with/: **/DA, lA/ karşıla-** 1. *769:16.* assemblage: - come together.
- go /to/ a PLACE, - visit /θ/ a place: **/A/ gidil-**, **/A/ git-** 3. *177:25.* travel: - go to.
- go to SEE, - visit /θ/: **/A/ git-** 3. *582:19.* sociability: - visit.
- go to SLEEP, - fall asleep, - drop off to sleep: **uyu-** 2. *22:16.* sleep: - go to sleep.
- go /to/ the BATHROOM, - use the toilet: **tuvalete git-** → git- 1a. *12:13.* excretion: - defecate; *12:14.* : urinate.
- go /to/ the BLACKBOARD: **tahtaya kalk-** → kalk- 1.
- go /to/ the OTHER SIDE, - cross /θ/, - go across: **/DAn/ karşıya geç-** → geç- 1. *177:20.* travel: - traverse; *909:8.* overrunning: - pass.
- go to VISIT: **/I/ ziyarete git-** ['- call upon' usually a respected person, i.e., an older person, a person of high station or perhaps sb requiring special attention such as a sick person or '- go to visit' a place of reverence associated with such a person, such as a cemetery or grave site or '- pay a visit' in connection with a holiday, bairam] → git- 3; **ziyaretine git-** [obj.: person only, not a place] → git- 3. *582:19.* sociability: - visit.
- go TOO FAR - overstep the limit, - be rude /BY...ing/: **/{ArAk/mAklA}/**

çok ol- → ol- 12, **/{ArAk/mAklA}/ ileri git-** 2 → git- 1a. *505:3.* * *1.* discourtesy: - be discourteous; *909:9.* overrunning: - overstep; *992:10.* excess: - overdo.

- go too FAST [vehicle], - speed: **{hız/sürat} yap-** → yap- 3. *174:8.* swiftness: - speed.
- go UNDER, - go bankrupt: **bat-** 2, **iflâs et-** 1. *625:7.* nonpayment: - go bankrupt.
- go UP, - climb: **/DAn, A/ çık-** 5 [/BY WAY OF (stairs), to/], **dağa çık-** ['- climb mountains'] → çık- 5. *193:11.* ascent: - climb.
- go up IN PRICE, - become more expensive: **fiyatlar {çık-/tırman-/yüksel-}** → çık- 6, tırman- 2, yüksel- 2, **pahalan-**. *251:6.* increase: - grow, increase [i.].
- go up /TO/, - rise /to/, - ascend [plane, balloon]: **/A/ yüksel-** 1. *193:8.* ascent: - ascend.

- go WELL OR BADLY: **geç-** 6 [perhaps more common in the past tense: How did the lesson go?], **git-** 5 [perhaps more common in the present continuous tense: How is the lesson going?]. *162:2.* progression: - proceed.
- go well, - work or - turn out the way it should, - come out right: **yoluna gir-**. *392:7.* improvement: - get better.
- go [along] /WITH/, - accompany /θ/: **/A/ {eşlik et-/refakat et-}**, **/lA/ gel-** ['- come /with/ sb'], **/lA/ git-** ['- go /with/ sb'] → git- 1a. *768:7.* accompaniment: - accompany.
- go [well] /WITH/: **/lA/ [iyi] git-** [jacket with skirt, spinach with yogurt] → git- 6, **/A/ uy-** 3 ['- look good /WITH/, - match /θ/', new curtains with furniture]. *866:3.* conformity: - conform.

- GOBBLE UP, - gobble down, - bolt down, - wolf down [food]; - gulp down [a drink]: **atıştır-** 1. *8:23.* eating: - gobble.

[O] GODDAMN [{him/her/it}]!: **[Allah] kahretsin!** → kahret- 2. *513:11.* curse: INTERJ. damn.
God forbid!: **[Allah] göstermesin.** → göster- 1. *1011:* * 22. hindrance: expressions to prevent unfavorable occurrences.

GOODBYE!: **Allahaısmarladık.** [said by the person LEAVING] → ısmarla-

3, Görüşmek üzere. ['Till we meet again.'] → görüş- 1, Güle güle [said by the person remaining behind] → gül- 1, Hoşça kalın! ['Have a {good/nice} day, Goodbye (lit., stay pleasantly)', said by the person leaving] → kal- 1. *188:22.* departure: INTERJ. farewell!

Good FOR {HIM/YOU}!, Nice going!, Bravo!: Çok yaşa! 2 → yaşa- 1, Aşkolsun! 2 → ol- 11 → olsun, Helâl olsun! 2 → ol- 11 → olsun. *149:4.* congratulation: INTERJ. congratulations!; *509:22.* approval: INTERJ. bravo!

Good HEALTH TO YOU, May you enjoy good health [A formula used to address sb after he has had a shave, haircut, bath]: Sıhhatler olsun. → ol- 11 → olsun. *504: * 20.* courtesy: polite expressions.

Good LUCK!: {Hayırlı olsun./Bol şanslar./Şansınız bol olsun.} → ol- 11 → olsun. *971:22.* chance: INTERJ. break a leg!

Good NIGHT. [used before retiring, going to bed, usually not simply when bidding farewell in the evening as, for example, when leaving a party. Then İyi geceler is used]: Allah rahatlık versin. → ver- 1. *188:23.* departure: good night!

- GOSSIP /about/: /hakkında/ dedikodu yap- → yap- 3. *552:12.* news: - gossip.
- gossip, - chat, - chew the fat /with/: /lA/ çene çal- → çal- 2. *541:10.* conversation: - chat.

- GOVERN, - rule, - administer, - direct, - manage, - run, - control: idare et- 1, yönet- 1. *417:13.* authority: - possess or - wield authority; *573:8.* direction, management: - direct; *612:14.* government: - rule.

- GRAB, - grasp, - seize, - take hold of: yakala- 1. *480:14.* taking: - seize.
- grab a bite, - snack /ON/ sth, - have or - eat a snack: atıştır- 2. *8:26.* eating: - pick.

- GRADE /θ/ sb or sth, - mark /θ/ [an exam], - give a grade or mark /to/, - give /θ/ sb or sth a grade: /A/ not ver- → ver- 1. *945:9.* judgment: - estimate.

- GRADUATE /from/ a school: /DAn/ mezun ol- → ol- 12, bitir- 4 ['- graduate from, - finish a school'].

409:7b. success: - succeed in specific ways; *793:6.* completeness: - complete.

- GRANT or - give an APPOINTMENT /to/: /A/ gün ver- ['- give a {date/day} for an appointment'] → ver- 1, /A/ randevu ver- ['- give an appointment'] → ver- 1. *478:12.* giving: - give; *964:4.* prearrangement: - prearrange.
- grant a PERIOD OF TIME, a grace period /to, for/ [making a payment]: /A, için/ süre tanı- → tanı- 5. *478:12.* giving: - give; *845:9.* lateness: - postpone.

- GRASP, - seize, or - take hold of /BY/, - catch, - grab. Also '- hold /BY/ [body part: the neck]': /DAn/ tut- 1. *480:14.* taking: - seize.

- GRATE [vegetables, cheese]: rendele-. *1049:9.* powderiness, crumbliness: - pulverize.

- GREASE, - oil: yağla-. *1054:8.* oils, lubricants: - oil.

- GREET, - salute [person, not flag]: /I/ selâmla-, /A/ selâm ver- → ver- 1. *585:10.* hospitality, welcome: - greet.
- greet, - welcome, - go to meet, - meet sb /at [a place], with/: /DA, lA/ karşıla- 1. *769:16.* assemblage: - come together.
- greet one another: /lA/ merhabalaş-, /lA/ selâmlaş-. *585:10.* hospitality, welcome: - greet.

- GRIEVE, for one's heart - be wrenched upon seeing sth sad: yüreği parçalan- → parçalan- 2. *112:17.* sadness: - grieve.

- GRIMACE, - scowl, - make a face: yüzü buruş- 1 → buruş-, yüzünü buruştur-. *152:25a.* resentment, anger: gestures of; *265:8.* distortion: - grimace; *510:20. * 1.* disapproval: gestures of.

- GRIND [UP], - chop up fine, - mince [vegetables, meat]: kıy- 1. *801:13.* separation: - shatter.
- grind, - crush, - mash, - pulverize: ez-. *1049:9.* powderiness, crumbliness: - pulverize.

- GROW [subj.: almost anything], - grow up [subj.: children]: büyü-. *259:5.* expansion, grow: - become larger; *303:9* age: - mature.

- grow [subj.: crops], - be raised [crops]: What grows on this farm?']: **yetiş-** 7. *1067:16.* agriculture: - farm.
- grow [obj.: crops], - raise [obj.: crops, animals]: **yetiştir-** 1. *891:8.* production: - produce, - create; *1068:6.* animal husbandry: - raise.
- grow, - grow taller, - get longer: **uza-** 1. *251:6.* increase: - grow, increase [i.].
- grow or - get DARK [sky, lit., weather]: **hava karar-.** *1026:12.* darkness, dimness: - grow dark.
- grow IN HEIGHT: **boyu uza-** → uza- 1. *251:6.* increase: - grow, increase [i.].
- grow OLD, - age [subj.: persons]: **ihtiyarla-, yaşı ilerle-** → ilerle- 3, **yaşlan-.** *303:10.* age: - age; *841:9.* oldness: - age.
- grow or - turn PALE, - pale: **sarar-** 2. *36:6.* colorlessness: - lose color; *127:13.* fear, frighteningness: - flinch.
- grow TIRED /OF/, - tire /OF/, - get bored /WITH/: /DAn/ {**bık-/ usan-**}, /DAn/ **sıkıl-** 1, /DAn/ **canı sıkıl-** 1 → sıkıl- 1, **içi sıkıl-** → sıkıl- 1. *118:7b.* tedium: - get bored.
- grow or - come TO LIKE; - warm /{UP TO/to/TOWARDS}/: /A/ **ısın-** 3. *587:10.* friendship: - befriend, - make friends with.
- grow UP [The children have grown up.], - grow [in most contexts]: **büyü-.** *259:5.* expansion, growth: - become larger; *303:9.* age: - mature.
- grow up, - reach or - attain /θ/ maturity, - mature [subj.: person]: **olgunluğa er-** → er-. *303:9.* age: - mature; *407:8.* accomplishment: - ripen.
- grow up, - become mature, morally correct, responsible, - shape up, - amount to sth, [Grow up!]: **adam ol-** → ol- 12. *303:9.* age: - mature.
- grow or - get WARM, - warm up: **ısın-** 1. *1019:17b.* heating: - get hot.

- GROWL from hunger [subj.: one's stomach]; - be very hungry: **karnı zil çal-** → çal- 3. *54:8b.* resonance: - ring, make a ringing sound; *100:19.* desire: - hunger.

- GUARD /AGAINST/; - watch out /FOR/ sth dangerous: /DAn/ **sakın-** 2. *339:8.* carefulness: - be vigilant.

- GUESS, - suppose, - surmise [that he will come]: **tahmin et-** 1. *950:10.* theory, supposition: - suppose; *952:11.* belief: - think; *967:5.* probability: - think likely.
- guess, - take a guess [at how many]: **bil-** 4, **tahmin et-** 2.1. *945:9.* judgment:

- estimate; *950:11.* theory, supposition: - conjecture.
Guess what? [a phrase used to call attention to following words: Guess what?: He won the lottery!]: **Biliyor musun?** [lit., 'Do you know?']. → bil- 1. *982:22.* attention: INTERJ. attention!

- GULP DOWN FOOD, - swallow food, pills: **yut-.** *8:22.* eating: - devour.
- gulp down [a drink]; - gobble down, - gobble up, - bolt down, - wolf down [food]: **atıştır-** 1. *8:23.* eating: - gobble.

- GYP, - rip off, - swindle, - cheat; - sell somone sth at an exorbitant, outrageous price. The two following verbs are *very common slang*: /A/ **kazık at-** → at- 1, /I/ **kazıkla-.** *356:19.* deception: nonformal terms - gyp.

- H -

- HAGGLE, - bargain, - dicker /a: for [sth], b: over [sth], c: with [sb]/: /a: **için,** b: **üzerinde,** c: 1A/ **pazarlık et-.** *731:17.* commerce, economics: - bargain.

- HAIL a cab, taxi: **taksi çevir-** → çevir- 1. *420:11.* command: - summon; *517:21.* signs, indicators: - gesture.

- HAND IN /to/, - turn in /to/ [obj.: test, term paper]: /A/ **teslim et-,** /A/ **ver-** 1. *478:13.* giving: - deliver.

- HAND OUT, - dispense, - distribute, - serve [out] /to/ [food to the needy]: /A/ **dağıt-** 2. *770:4a.* dispersion: - disperse sth.
- hand out, - issue, - give, or - write [a traffic ticket, receipt]: /A/ **kes-** 5. *478:13.* giving: - deliver.

- HAND OVER, - turn over, or - deliver /to/: /A/ **teslim et-.** *478:13.* giving: - deliver.

- HANDLE, - solve, or - find a solution /for/, - resolve [situation, personal problem, matter]: **hallet-.** *939:2.* solution: - solve.

- HANG [up] /{IN/ON}/, - hang sb /BY/ [Hang the laundry up IN the garden. They hung him up BY his feet.]: /A,

DAn/ as- 1. *202:8*. pendency: - suspend.

- hang ON, - wait: **bekle-** 1. *130:8*. expectation: - await.

- hang sb /{to/ON}, FOR [a crime]/ [as a form of execution]: /A, lA/ as- 2. *202:8*. pendency: - suspend; *604:18*. punishment: - hang.

- hang UP [telephone]: **telefon kapan-** ['for the phone - be hung up': They had hung up.] → kapan- 1, **telefonU kapat-** [He had hung up.] → kapat-; in the negative also **AyrılMAyın** [Don't hang up./Stay on the line.] → ayrıl- 3. *347:18*. communications: - telephone.

- hang up /ON/ sb [telephone, impolite action]: **telefonu yüzüne kapat-** → kapat-. *347:18* communications: - telephone.

- hang up [shirt, laundry] /{IN/ON}/: /A/ as- 1. *202:8*. pendency: - suspend.

- HAPPEN, - occur, - take place, - go on: **geç- 3, ol- 4**. *830:5*. event: - occur.
- happen /to/, - befall [a person, subj.: usually a misfortune or sth strange]: **başına gel-** → gel- 1. *830:5*. event: - occur.

- HARBOR evil intentions /TOWARD/, - have designs /{ON/AGAINST}/, - intend to do sb harm: /A/ **kastet-** 2. *381:9*. plan: - plot.

- HARM [subj.: the evil eye], for the evil eye - touch /θ/ or - reach /θ/: /A/ **nazar değ-** → 1 değ- 2. *393:9*. impairment: - impair.

- HATE /θ/, - loathe /θ/, - detest /θ/, - abhor /θ/: /DAn/ **nefret et-**. *103:5*. hate: - hate.

- HAVE: **ol- 5**. *469:4*. possession: - possess.
- have it [as in 'I have it', when one suddenly recalls sth forgotten, or in the sense of 'Oh, I know', when one suddenly discovers the solution to a problem]: **bul- 4**. *988:10*. memory: - remember.

- have an ACCIDENT, - be in an accident, - get into an accident [car, plane]: **kaza geçir-** → geçir- 2. *1010:10*. adversity: - come to grief.
- have an accident, - get into an accident, - be in an accident, - cause an accident: **kaza yap-** → yap- 3. *1010:10*. adversity: - come to grief.

- have a BALL, - be overjoyed, - be in seventh heaven, - be on cloud nine: **bayram et-**. *95:11*. pleasure: - be pleased.

- have a BOWEL MOVEMENT, - defecate [*formal, polite*]: **büyük aptes yap-** → yap- 3, **dışarı[.ya] çık- 2** → çık- 2, **tuvalet yap-** ['- have a bowel movement *or* BM, - urinate; - make one's toilet, i.e., usually for a woman to dress or to arrange her hair'] → yap- 3. *12:13*. excretion: - defecate.

- have or - eat BREAKFAST, - breakfast: **kahvaltı {et-/yap-}** → yap- 3. NOT ~~kahvaltı ye-~~. *8:21*. eating: - dine.

- have /a: θ [sb] BUY, purchase sth, b: AT [a price], c: AT [a store], d: from [sb]/: /a: A, b: A, c: DAn, d: DAn/ **aldır-** 1. *733:7*. purchase: - purchase.

- have a CHECK-UP, a physical, a general physical examination: **muayeneden geç-**. *91:29*. therapy: - undergo treatment; *937:24*. inquiry: - examine.

- have {CHILDREN/A CHILD}: **çocuğu ol-** → ol- 6. *1:3*. birth: - give birth.

- have sth COLORED, painted, or dyed /θ/ [a color]; - have /θ/ sb COLOR, paint, or dye sth /θ/ [a color]: /A/ **boyat-**. *35:13*. color: - color.

- have /θ/ sth colored [obj.: hair]: /A/ **boya yaptır-** → yaptır- 2. *35:13*. color: - color; *1015:15*. beauty: - beautify.

- have CONFIDENCE /IN/, - trust /θ/, - rely /{ON/UPON}/, - depend /ON/: /A/ **güven-**. *952:15*. belief: - believe in.

- have a CRAVING FOR: **canı çek-** → çek- 1. *100:14*. desire: - desire.

- have sth CUT, - have /θ/ sb cut sth: /A/ **kestir-** 1. *224:4*. interval: - cleave; *268:6*. shortness: - shorten.

- have photographic film DEVELOPED [but not printed]: **film yıkat-** → yıkat- 2. *714:15*. photography: - process.

- have photographic film developed and printed or just printed: **film {bastır- /tabettir-}**. *714:15*. photography: - process.

- have DESIGNS /{ON/AGAINST}/, - harbor evil intentions /TOWARD/, - intend to do sb harm: /A/ **kastet-** 2. *381:9*. plan: - plot.

- have DIFFICULTY, a hard time, trouble /{θ/on/in}/: /DA/ **{güçlük/ zorluk} çek-** → çek- 5, /DA/ **zorlan-** 3. *1010:9*. adversity: - have trouble; *1012:11.* difficulty: - have difficulty.

- have difficulties, troubles, - suffer annoyance, inconvenience: **sıkıntı çek-** → **çek-** 5. *1012:11.* difficulty: - have difficulty.

- have DINNER: In the U.S., dinner is the main meal of the day. On weekdays, it is usually in the evening; on Sundays it may be at noon or in the afternoon. In Turkey, no matter what the day, the main meal is in the evening. Thus **akşam yemeği ye-** '- have the evening meal', i.e., dinner or supper. → **ye-** 1. *8:21.* eating: - dine.

- have /θ/ sb DO sth. Also often '- LET /θ/ sb do sth' [I didn't do it myself. I had θ Mehmet do it.]: **/A/ yaptır-** 2 [i.e., **yap-** '- do' + caus. suf. **-DIr** = **yaptır-**] *328:6.* action: - do. When another verb is substituted for 'do' in the above as, for example, in '- have sb READ sth', the Turkish equivalent again has the Turkish causative verb form [**oku-** '- read' + caus. suf. **-t** = **okut-**]. For the formation of Turkish causative verbs, see the **Index of Turkish Verb Suffixes**. *885:10.* cause: - cause.

- have a DREAM, - dream: **{düş/rüya} gör-** 1 → **gör-** 3. *985:17.* imagination: - dream.

- have had an EDUCATION, - be educated: **{eğitim/öğrenim/tahsil} gör-** → **gör-** 3. *570:11.* learning: - be taught.

- have an EFFECT /{ON/UPON}/, - influence /θ/, - affect /θ/: **/I/ etkile-**, **/A/ tesir et-.** *893:7.* influence: - influence.

- have ENOUGH [food], - eat one's fill: **/A/ doy-**, **karnı doy-.** *993:5.* satiety: - have enough.

- have a FALLING OUT /with/, - get on bad terms /with/: **/lA/ arası {açıl-/bozul-}** → **açıl-** 9. *379:4.* dissuasion: - disincline; *456:10.* disaccord: - fall out with.

- have a falling out /with/, - become estranged /FROM/; for relations between people - come to an end, - break off: **/lA/ bağlar kop-** → **kop-** 1. *379:4.* dissuasion: - disincline; *456:10.* disaccord: - fall out with.

- have the FLU, influenza: **grip ol-** → **ol-** 10.2. *85:46b.* disease: - take sick in particular ways.

- have FUN: → - have a GOOD TIME.

Have a GOOD {TRIP/JOURNEY}!: **Uğurlar olsun.** → **ol-** 11 → **olsun, Yolunuz açık olsun.** → **ol-** 11 → **olsun.** *188:22.* departure: INTERJ. farewell!

- have a GOOD TIME, - have fun, - enjoy oneself /a: with [sb, sth], b: [by]...ing, c: [BY]...ing/': **/a: lA, b: ArAk, c: mAklA/ eğlen-**[or **{iyi/hoş} vakit geçir-**] → **eğlen-** 1, **geçir-** 3. *95:13.* pleasure: - enjoy oneself; *743:22.* amusement: - amuse oneself.

- have HAD IT; - be done for, doomed, sunk, in serious trouble: *colloq.:* **hapı yut-, yan-** 6. *395:11.* destruction: - do; *1012:11.* difficulty: - have difficulty.

- have or - get a HAIRCUT: **saç kes-** → **kes-** 1, **saç kestir-** → **kestir-** 1. *3:22.* hair: - cut or - dress the hair.

- have one's HAIR HIGHLIGHTED, streaked, - have highlights, streaks of color, put /IN/ one's hair [hair salon process]: **{meç/röfle} yaptır-** → **yaptır-** 2. *3:22.* hair: - cut or - dress hair; *35:13.* color: - color; *1015:15.* beauty: - beautify.

- have one's HAIR PUT IN A BUN: **topuz yaptır-** → **yaptır-** 2. *3:22.* hair: - cut or - dress hair; *1015:15.* beauty: - beautify.

- have one's HAIR STYLED: **saçlarını yaptır-** → **yaptır-** 2. *3:22.* hair: - cut or - dress hair; *1015:15.* beauty: - beautify.

- have a HARD TIME, difficulty, trouble /{θ/on/in}/: **/DA/ {güçlük/zorluk} çek-** → **çek-** 5, **/DA/ zorlan-** 3. *1010:9.* adversity: - have trouble; *1012:11.* difficulty: - have difficulty.

- have HIGHLIGHTS, streaks of color, put /IN/ one's hair: → - have one's hair highlighted.

- have an ILLNESS: *noun designating an illness.***SI var:** e.g., **Nezle.si var.** 'He has a cold.' → **ol-** 5, (5.1) Table 1. Additional examples. 2. Essential question-word questions. With **n**-beginning question words: **Nesi var?** *85:45.* disease: - ail.

- have IN MIND, - intend to say, - mean /BY/ [I didn't have that in mind.]: **/lA, DAn/ kastet-** 1. *380:4.* intention: - intend; *519:4.* latent meaningfulness: - imply.

- have an INFLUENCE /{ON/UPON}/, - affect /θ/, - influence /θ/: **/I/ etkile-**, **/A/ tesir et-.** *893:7.* influence: - influence.

- have an animal KILLED as a sacrifice, - let an animal be killed as a sacrifice: **kurban kestir-** → kestir- 3. *308:12.* killing: - kill.

- have a LOOK AROUND, - look around: **etrafa bak-** → bak- 1. *27:13.* vision: - look; *937:31.* inquiry: - search.
- have a look /AT/: **/A/ bak-** 1. *27:13.* vision: - look.
- have LOST one's FATHER [mother remains alive]; less accurately: - have lost both parents; - be orphaned [but not have lost only one's mother]: **yetim kal-** → kal- 1. *256:5.* remainder: - remain.
- have lost one's MOTHER [father remains alive]; less accurately: - have lost both parents; - be orphaned; sometimes, but not accurately: - have lost only one's father: **öksüz kal-** → kal- 1. *256:5.* remainder: - remain.
- have a LOT OF EXPENSES, - incur great expense, - spend a lot of money on sth or to get sth done: **masrafa gir-**. *626:5.* expenditure: - spend; *729:15.* finance, investment: - finance; *896:4.* liability: : - incur.
- have or - eat LUNCH, - have the noon meal: **öğle yemeği ye-** → ye- 1. *8:21.* eating: - dine.

- have /θ/ sb MAKE sth. Also often '- LET /θ/ sb make sth' [I didn't make it myself. I had Mehmet make it.]: **/A/ yaptır-** 1. *891:8.* production: - produce, - create.
- have MERCY /{ON/UPON}/, - be merciful /to/ [the deceased] [subj.: only God]: **/A/ rahmet eyle-**. *145:4.* pity: - have pity; *601:4.* acquittal: - acquit.

- have a NIGHTMARE: **kâbus gör-** → gör- 3. *985:17.* imagination: - dream.

- have ON clothing, - be wearing [clothing, size 38]. Also '- don, - PUT on clothing': **giy-**. *5:43.* clothing: - wear, - have on.
- have /θ/ sb OPEN sth, - get sb to open sth: **açtır-**. *292:11* opening: - open.
- have an OPERATION, - be operated on: **ameliyat geçir-** → geçir- 2, **ameliyat ol-** → ol- 10.1. *91:29.* therapy: - undergo treatment.
- have an ORGASM, - climax, - come: **gel-** 3 [for both sexes], **boşal-** 3 [more frequently for men, but also for women, also: '- ejaculate'], **orgazm ol-** [for both sexes] → ol- 10.1. *75:23.* sex: - climax.

- have sth PAINTED, colored, or dyed /θ/ [a color]; - have /θ/ sb paint, color, or dye sth /θ/ [a color]: **/A/ boyat-**. *35:13.* color: - color.
- have or - give a PARTY: **parti ver-** → ver- 1. *585:8.* hospitality, welcome: - entertain.
- have PASSED, - elapsed, - be over [with time-designating noun subjects: two years have passed since...]: **ol-** 9.3. *836:6.* the past: - pass.
- have a PASSING FANCY to do sth [one usually knows little about]: **/A/ özen-** 4. *364:4.* caprice: - blow hot and cold.
- have to PEE, - have to go peepee: **çişi gel-** → gel- 1. *12:14.* excretion: - urinate.
- have one's PERIOD, - menstruate: **âdet gör-** → gör- 3, **aybaşı ol-** → ol- 10.1. *12:18.* excretion: - menstruate.
- have or - get a PERM[ANENT] [hair procedure]: **/A/ perma yaptır-** → yaptır- 2. *3:22.* hair: - cut or - dress hair; *1015:15.* beauty: - beautify.
- have a PHYSICAL, a general physical examination, a check-up: **muayeneden geç-**. *91:29.* therapy: - undergo treatment; *937:24.* inquiry: - examine.
- have {PICTURES/PHOTOGRAPHS} taken, - have /θ/ sb take {pictures/ photographs}: **/A/ {resim/ fotoğraf} çektir-** → çektir- 3. *714:14.* photography: - photograph.
- just have photographic film PRINTED or - have developed and printed: **film {bastır-/tabettir-}**. *714:15.* photography: - process.
- have [PROBLEMS], - live through, - experience [problems], - go through [difficult period], - enjoy [fine weather]: **yaşa-** 3. *830:8.* event: - experience.
- have a PROMISING FUTURE, - be promising: **{gelecek/istikbal} vadet-**. *124:10.* hope: - give hope; *133:13.* premonition: - promise.
- have PULLED [tooth]: **diş çektir-** → çektir- 2. *91:24.* therapy: - treat; *904:4.* pulling: - pull.

- have or - let /θ/ sb READ sth: **/A/ okut-** 1. *570:12.* learning: - study.
- have RECOURSE /to, for/, - refer, - resort, or - turn /to, for/ [person], - look sth up /IN [a reference source: dictionary]/: **/A, için/ {başvur-/müracaat et-}** 1. *387:14.* use: - avail oneself of; *937:30.* inquiry: - seek.

- have SEX, sexual intercourse /with/: *formal, polite:* **/IA/ cinsel ilişkide**

Part 2: English-Turkish Index

bulun- ['- have sex, sexual relations
with'] → bulun- 3, *informal*: /lA/
seviş- 2 ['- make love; - make out, -
caress each other']. *562:16.*
lovemaking, endearment: - caress;
/lA/ yat- 2 ['- go to bed /with/'].
75:21. sex: - copulate; *562:14.*
lovemaking, endearment: - make
love.
- have /θ/ sb SEW or stitch sth, - have /θ/
sb make sth by sewing: /A/ diktir-.
741:4. sewing: - sew.
- have or - get a SHAVE or a haircut:
tıraş ol- 2 → ol- 10.1. *3:22.* hair,
feathers: - cut or - dress the hair;
255:10. subtraction: - excise; *268:6.*
shortness: - shorten.
- have a SNACK, - snack /ON/ sth, - grab
a bite: atıştır- 2. *8:26.* eating: - pick.
- have a snack, - snack, - eat food as a
casual snack [The food may include,
but is not limited to, junk food, i.e.,
cookies, candy, candy bars, etc., the
kind of food sold in vending
machines in the U.S.]: abur cubur
ye- → ye- 1. *8:26.* eating: - pick.
- have STREAKS OF COLOR, highlights,
put /IN/ one's hair, - have one's hair
highlighted, streaked [hair salon
process]: {meç/röfle} yaptır- →
yaptır- 2. *3:22.* hair: - cut or - dress
hair; *35:13.* color: - color; *1015:15.*
beauty: - beautify.
- have a STRETCH, - stretch [oneself
after waking up]: gerin-. *84:4.*
fitness, exercise: - exercise; *259:5.*
expansion, growth: - become larger;
725:10. exertion: - strain.
- have or - suffer a STROKE, - get or -
become paralyzed: felç ol- → ol-
10.2, inme in- → in- 1. *85:46b.*
disease: - take sick in particular ways.
- have SUPPER or dinner, the evening
meal: akşam yemeği ye- → ye- 1.
8:21. eating: - dine.
- have /θ/ sb WRITE sth, - get /θ/ sb to
write sth, - let /θ/ sb write sth: /A/
yazdır- 1. *547:19.* writing: - write.

- have THE WRONG NUMBER [on the
phone]: yanlış numara düş- →
düş- 1. *974:12.* error: - misdo.
- have TO, - be forced or obliged to [do
sth] [not with {tarafından/CA}]: -
mAk zorunda kal- → kal- 1.
962:10. necessity: - be necessary.
- have to GO [PEE], - have to pee: çişi
gel- → gel- 1. *12:14.* excretion: -
urinate.
- have to USE the {bathroom/restroom/
toilet}, - have to go: tuvaleti gel-
→ gel- 1. *12:13.* excretion: - excrete.

- have a TOOTH pulled: diş çektir- →
çektir- 2. *91:24.* therapy: - treat;
904:4. pulling: - pull.
- have [vehicle] TOWED, - have /θ/ sb
tow sth: /A/ çektir- 1. *904:4.*
pulling: - pull.
- have TROUBLES, difficulties, - suffer
annoyance, inconvenience: sıkıntı
çek- → çek- 5. *1012:11.* difficulty: -
have difficulty.

- have an UPSET STOMACH, - feel sick
to one's stomach, - be upset [subj.:
stomach], - feel nauseated, nauseous,
- get queasy: midesi bulan-.
85:46b. disease: - take sick in
particular ways.

- have sth [laundry, rugs] WASHED, -
have /θ/ sb wash sth, - get sth washed
/BY/ sb: /A/ yıkat- 1. *79:19.*
cleanness: - wash.
- have or - make sb WORK, - allow sb -
work, - work sb: /I/ çalıştır- 1 a).
424:4. compulsion: - compel.
- have or - make /θ/ sb WORK ON sth; -
tutor /θ/ sb: /A/ çalıştır- 1 b).
424:4. compulsion: - compel; *568:11.*
teaching: - tutor.
- have or - get /θ/ sb to WRITE sth, - let
/θ/ sb write sth: /A/ yazdır- 1.
547:19. writing: - write.
- have the WRONG NUMBER [on the
phone]: yanlış numara düş- →
düş- 1. *974:12.* error: - misdo.

- have an X-RAY [TAKEN]: röntgen
çektir- → çektir- 3. *714:14.*
photography: - photograph.

- HEAL,- cure [a person], - restore to
health: /A/ şifa ver- [in Allah
şifa versin! 'May God restore him
to health'] → ver- 1. *86:38.* remedy: -
remedy; *396:15.* restoration: - cure.

- HEAR [sense of hearing]: duy- 1, işit-
1. *48:11.* hearing: - hear.
not - HEAR or - catch, i.e., - miss, what sb
has said: kaçır- 1. *48:11.* hearing: -
hear; *410:14.* failure: - miss; *843:5.*
untimeliness: - miss an opportunity.
- hear /{OF/ABOUT}/, - learn /OF/, - get
word /OF/: /I/ duy- 2, /I/ işit- 2.
551:15. information: - know, - be
informed.
- hear a CASE; - try sb, a case; - judge or
adjudicate a case, - pass judgment on:
yargıla-. *594:5.* jurisdiction: -
administer justice; *598:17.* legal
action: - try; *945:8.* judgment: -
judge.

545

- HEAT sth, - heat up sth /{by means of/with}/, - warm up sth [obj.: soup]: /1A/ ısıt-. *1019:17a.* heating: - heat.
- heat up, - get heated, intense, - intensify [subj.: dispute]: hızlan- 2. *119:3.* aggravation: - worsen.

- HEAVE A SIGH, - sigh: iç çek- → çek-1. *52:14.* faintness of sound: - sigh.

- HEED, - listen /TO/, - obey: /I/ 1 dinle- 2. *326:2.* obedience: - obey.
- heed, - take, or - listen to ADVICE: söz tut- → tut- 5, sözünü tut- 2 ['- heed, - take the advice of sb, - take sb's advice'] → tut- 5. *326:2.* obedience: - obey; *422:7.* advice: - take or - accept advice.
HELLO., Hi.: Hoş geldin[iz]! 2. *504: * 20.* courtesy: polite expressions; *585:14.* hospitality, welcome: INTERJ. welcome!

- HELP /θ/, - assist /θ/: /A/ yardım et-, *formal*: /A/ yardımda bulun- → bulun- 3, /A/ yardım elini uzat- ['- extend a helping hand /to/'] → uzat- 2. *449:11.* aid: - aid.
- help /θ/, - assist /θ/, - be of assistance /to/, - be helpful /to/: /A/ yardımcı ol- → ol- 12. *449:11.* aid: - aid.
- help or - assist ONE ANOTHER, - give one another a hand: el ele ver- → ver- 1, yardımlaş-. *449:11.* aid: - aid.
- help /θ/, - make things easy /FOR/, - facilitate matters /FOR/, - give sb a break: /A/ kolaylık göster- → göster- 1. *449:11.* aid: - aid; *1013:7.* facility: - facilitate.
- help /θ/, - be beneficial, good /FOR/, - work [subj.: aspirin for a headache]: /A/ iyi gel- → gel- 1. *998:10.* goodness: - do good.
Help YOURSELF! [said when offering food]: Buy[u]run[uz]. → buyur- 2. *504: * 20.* courtesy: polite expressions.

- HESITATE /to/, - feel or - be hesitant, embarrassed, reluctant /to/ do sth /in the presence of/, not - dare /to/ do sth: /{A/DAn}/ çekin-. *325:4.* unwillingness: - demur; *362:7.* irresolution: - hesitate.
- hesitate /to/; - waver, - falter: /{DA/A}/ tereddüt et-. *362:7.* irresolution: - hesitate.

HEY there! *informal*, Look here!, Say: {Baksana!/Baksanıza!} → bak-

1. *982:22.* attention: INTERJ. attention!

HI., Hello.: Hoş geldin[iz]! 2. *504: * 20.* courtesy: polite expressions; *585:14.* hospitality, welcome: INTERJ. welcome!

- HIDE, - conceal sth /IN/ [i.e., - PUT sth somewhere for safekeeping]: /A/ gizle- 1, /A/ sakla- 1. *346.6* concealment: - conceal.
- hide, - conceal, - cover up [the truth, faults]: ört- 2. *346.6* concealment: - conceal.
- hide or - conceal ONESELF /from, IN/: /DAn, A/ gizlen- 1, /DAn, A/ saklan- 1. *346:8.* concealment: - hide oneself.

- HIJACK a plane /to/: /A/ uçak kaçır- → kaçır- 3. *482:20.* theft: - abduct.

- HINDER, - prevent, - stop sb from doing sth: /I/ engelle-, /A/ mâni ol- → ol- 12, /I/ önle-, önüne geç- → geç- 1. *1011:14.* hindrance: - prevent.

- HIRE [vehicle], - rent [vehicle, place], - lease /from, FOR/: /DAn, A/ kirala- 1, /DAn, A/ tut- 6a. *615:15.* commission: - rent.
- hire sb, - engage sb /from/: /DAn/ tut- 6b. *615:14.* commission: - employ.

- HIT, - bump [one's head] /ON/: /A/ vur- 1. *901:14.* impulse, impact: - hit.
- hit, - strike, or - bump /{AGAINST/ INTO/ON}/: /A/ çarp- 1. *901:13.* impulse, impact: - collide.
- hit /θ/ sth, - collide /WITH/ sth by chance, accident [ball hits window]: /A/ rastla- 2, /A/ tesadüf et- 2.
- hit, - strike, or - knock /a: θ [sb, sth], b: with, c: ON/: /a: A, b: lA, c: A/ vur- 1. *901:14.* impulse, impact: - hit.
- hit /θ/ or - honk /θ/ A CAR HORN: korna çal- → çal- 2, kornaya bas- → bas- 2. *58:8.* stridency: - screech; *708:42.* music: - blow a horn; *912:4.* depression: - depress.
- hit THE MARK, target [subj.: marksman]: isabet kaydet- 1 → kaydet- 5. *223:10* nearness: - contact; *409:7b.* success: - succeed in specific ways.
- hit THE SPOT [subj.: coffee when you're tired], - do good: 2 değ- 2, iyi gel- → gel- 1, iyi git- → git- 5. *998:10.* goodness: - do good.

- HITCHHIKE: otostop yap- → yap- 3. *177:31*. travel: - hitchhike.

- HOLD /BY/, - take hold of /BY/ [body part: the neck]: /DAn/ tut- 1. *474:6*. retention: - hold, - grip.
- hold, - contain [This bottle holds 2 quarts.]: içine al- 2 → al- 1. *771:3*. inclusion: - include.
- hold [on the phone: Will you please hold?]: Ayrılmayın[ız]. ['Don't hang up.'] → ayrıl- 3, Bekleyin[iz]. ['Wait.'] → bekle- 1. *347:18*. communications: - telephone.
- hold BACK [tears], - restrain, - keep control of: tut- 4. *428:7*. restraint: - restrain.
- hold one's BREATH: nefes tut-. *173:7*. quiescence: - be still.
- hold a {DEMONSTRATION/protest}, - demonstrate against: gösteri yap- → yap- 3. *333:5*. dissent: - object.
- hold or - keep /FOR/: tut- 2 [a seat, a place], /A/ sakla- 3 [Hold my letters FOR me until I return.] *474:7*. retention: - hold, - keep.
- hold a HELPING HAND OUT /TO/, - extend a helping hand /to/, - help out: /A/ yardım elini uzat- → uzat- 2. *449:11*. aid: - aid.
Hold ON!, Wait!, Just a second!: Dur! → dur- 5. *130:8*. expectation: - await.
- hold on TO [the ladder], i.e., don't let go: tut- 1. *474:6*. retention: - hold, - grip.
- hold OUT, - last, - be enough /FOR/ [subj.: money, fuel]: /A/ dayan- 5. *990:4*. sufficiency: - suffice.
- hold out /against/, - resist /θ/: /A karşı/ diren- 2. *361:7*. obstinacy: - balk; *453:4*. resistance: - stand fast.
- hold sth out /to/, - extend sth /to/: /A/ uzat- 2. *439:4*. offer: - offer.
- hold one's TONGUE, - keep quiet: {çenesini/dilini} tut- [lit., '- hold {one's jaw or chin/one's tongue}'] → tut- 4. *51:5*. silence: - be silent; *344:6*. uncommunicativeness: - keep to oneself; *428:7*. restraint: - restrain.
- hold UP, - detain, - keep /θ/ [Don't let me hold you up.]: /A/ mâni ol- → ol- 12, /I/ tut- 3. *1011:14*. hindrance: - prevent.

- HONK /θ/ or - hit /θ/ a car horn: korna çal- → çal- 2, kornaya bas- → bas- 2. *58:8*. stridency: - screech; *708:42*. music: - blow a horn; *912:4*. depression: - depress.

- HONOR SB /by...ing/: /I, {ArAk/mAklA}/ onurlandır-, /A, {ArAk/mAklA}/ {şeref/ onur}

ver- → ver- 1. *646:8*. honor: - honor.

- HOP /INTO/ a taxi, car, bus; - catch /θ/ a plane, train: /A/ atla- 3. *193:12*. ascent: - mount.

- HOPE: {ümit et-/um-} 1. *100:16*. desire: - wish for; *124:7*. hope: - hope.

HOW ABOUT or what about [** {your/our/my}] [doing it tomorrow]?, What if [{you/we/I}] [did it tomorrow]?, lit., 'If you wish' [a polite way of introducing the expression of a preference, proposal, or correction]: I'd rather not go today. {WHAT/How} about going tomorrow?]: İsterseniz... → iste- 1. *439: * 11*. offer: expressions of suggestion; *504: * 20*. courtesy: polite expressions.
How CAN [lit., {shall/should}] I {relate/explain} it?: Nasıl anlatayım? → anlat- 1, Nasıl anlatsam? → anlat- 1. *362:13*. irresolution: ADV. * filler phrases and stallers.
{How IS IT THAT...?/informal: How come...?}: Nasıl ol-...da...? → ol- 2. *887:8*. attribution: ADV. why?
{How SAD/What a pity} /FOR/ [the losing team]: /A/ yazık oldu. → yazık ol- → ol- 12. *113: * 13*. regret: INTERJ. what a pity!
How SHOULD I know?: Ne bileyim [ben]? 1. → bil- 1. *929:11*. ignorance: - not know.

- HUG; - embrace, - take in one's arms: kucakla-. *562:18*. lovemaking, endearment: - embrace.
- hug or - embrace ONE ANOTHER: kucaklaş-, birbirlerini kucakla-. *562:18*. lovemaking, endearment: - embrace.

- HURL, - fling, or - throw /{AT/to/INTO}, toward/: /{A}, A doğru/ fırlat-. *903:10*. pushing, throwing: - throw.

- HURRY /in order to/: /için/ acele et-. *401:5*. haste: - make haste.
- hurry, - be quick: çabuk ol- → ol- 12, yürü- 2 ['- walk quickly']. *401:5*. haste: - make haste.

- HURT, - feel sore [My head hurts.]: acı- 1, ağrı-. *26:8*. pain: - suffer pain.

547

- hurt, - feel pain, - be in pain [His hand got cut. It hurts. He's in pain.]: **canı acı-** → acı- 1. *26:8.* pain: - suffer pain.
- hurt sb [physically]: **canını acıt-, canını yak-** → yak- 2. *26:7.* pain: - inflict pain.
- hurt sb [not physically], - offend: **kır-** 2. *152:21.* resentment, anger: - offend.
- hurt sb's FEELINGS: **kalbini kır-** → kır- 1. *112:19.* sadness: - aggrieve; *152:21.* resentment, anger: - offend.
- hurt {ONESELF}: {a: **kendini**/b: **kendisini**/c: **kendi kendini**} **yarala-, yaralan-** 2. *393:13.* impairment: - inflict an injury.

- I -

I'M AFRAID THAT... [introduces information the speaker is reluctant to convey]: **Korkarım [ki]...** → kork-. *504: * 20.* courtesy: polite expressions.
I'm REALLY PISSED OFF.: **Sinirim tepeme çıktı.** → çık- 5. *152:25b.* resentment, anger: expressions of.
I'm [SO] HAPPY FOR YOU. Congratulations: **Gözünüz aydın. Tebrik ederim.** → tebrik et-. *149:4.* congratulation: INTERJ. congratulations!
I'm SO SORRY TO HEAR IT. [said to sb telling of a death in his family]: **Başınız sağ olsun.** → sağ ol- → ol- 12. *83:6.* health: - enjoy good health; *121: * 17.* comfort: words of comfort; *504: * 20.* courtesy: polite expressions.
I DON'T CARE! **Canı isterse!** → canı iste- → iste- 1. *997:25.* unimportance: PHR. no matter.
I don't MEAN TO BOAST, BUT..., *or* ..., if I have to say so myself: **Övünmek gibi olmasın...** → {övün-/öğün-} 2. *502:6.* boasting: - boast; *504: * 20.* courtesy: polite expressions.
I GIVE UP ALL RIGHTS TO IT [lit., 'Let it be canonically lawful (for you)'. Said to forgive any outstanding obligations, financial or otherwise]: **Helâl olsun.** 1 → ol- 11 → olsun. *370: * 9.* abandonment: expressions of abandonment.
{I HAVE {A FEELING/A HUNCH} THAT.../I get the feeling that.../It seems to me that.../I sense that...}: **Bana öyle geliyor ki...** → gel- 1. *33:10.* appearance: - appear to be;

945:8. judgment: - judge; *952:11.* belief: - think.
I have IT [when one suddenly recalls sth forgotten, or in the sense of 'Oh, I know', when one suddenly discovers the solution to a problem]: **bul-** 4. *988:10.* memory: - remember.
I {HOPE/TRUST} I'm not disturbing you[, am I, but...]: **Rahatsız etmiyorum ya?** → rahatsız et-. *343:8. * 1.* communication: conversation initiators.
I hope everything turns out the way you want it to., MAY everything turn out as you wish.: **Herşey gönlünüzce olsun!** → ol- 11 → olsun. *504: * 20.* courtesy: polite expressions.
I SWEAR [I'm telling the truth]: **[Doğru söylüyorum,] yemin ederim.** *334: * 11.* affirmation: INTERJ. I swear!
I WONDER: **Bilmem.** → bil- 1. *929:11.* ignorance: - not know.

If it were left up /to/ sb, in sb's view, opinion: /A/ **kalırsa.** → kal- 1. *952:29.* belief: ADV. in one's opinion.
If you want the truth, To tell the truth: **Doğrusunu istersen[iz].** → iste- 1. *644:22.* probity: ADV. truthfully.

- IGNITE, - light, - set on fire, - set fire to, - burn: **yak-** 1. *1019:22.* heating: - ignite.

- IGNORE , - disregard , NOT - mind, NOT - pay attention to: **aldırış etME-.** *982:6.* attention: - heed.

- ILLUSTRATE with examples, - give, - cite, or - provide examples /FOR/ [He illustrated his point with many excellent examples.]: /A/ {**örnek/misal**} **ver-** → ver- 1. *956:13.* evidence, proof: - cite.

- IMAGINE things, - build up [usually vain] hopes concerning: {**düş/rüya**} **gör-** 2 → gör- 3. *985:17.* imagination: - dream.
- imagine, - assume, or - suppose for the sake of argument: **de-** 2, **farz et-, tut-** 9, **varsay-** 1. *950:10.* theory, supposition: - suppose.
Imagine!, Just look at that, will you!, [Why] the nerve!: **Şuna bak be!** → bak- 1. *152:25b.* resentment, anger: expressions of.

- IMITATE, - copy, - ape [The child is imitating her mother.]: **taklit et-.** *336:5.* imitation: - imitate.

548

- imitate the actions of, - emulate /θ/, or - follow /θ/ the example of, - act in accord /with/ [In the namaz (i.e., the Muslim prayer ritual) the members of the community follow θ (the lead of) the imam.]: /A/ uy- 7. *336:7.* imitation: - emulate.

- IMPORT /from/: /DAn/ ithal et-. *187:14.* reception: - bring in.

IMPOSSIBLE., It's not possible., It's impossible., It can't be done., It won't do., No.: Olmaz. → ol- 4. *966:4.* impossibility: - be impossible.

- IMPRESS, - affect, - influence, - have an effect /{ON/UPON}/: /I/ etkile-. *893:7.* influence: - influence.
- IMPROVE, - get better [an ability, one's Turkish, not weather or health]: geliş- 2, ilerle- 2. *392:7.* improvement: - get better.
- improve, - get better, - get well, - recover from an illness: düzel-, iyileş-. *392:7.* improvement: - get better; *392:8.* : - rally, - get better; *396:20.* restoration: - recover.
- improve, - get better, - clear up [weather]: hava {aç-/açıl-} → aç-7, açıl- 7, hava düzel-. *392:7.* improvement: - get better.
- improve or - develop STH [He is improving his Turkish.]: geliştir- 1, ilerlet- 2. *392:9.* improvement: - improve, - make better.

- IMPROVISE, i.e., - fabricate out of what is conveniently on hand /FOR/ [key FOR a lock], - make one thing FIT /{θ/INTO}/ another: /A/ uydur- 1. *866:3.* conformity: - conform; *891:12.* production: - originate.

IN ANY CASE, No matter what, Anyway, Come what may: Ne olursa olsun → ol- 11 → olur. *969:26.* certainty: ADV. without fail.

IN ORDER TO, to: diye- 3.1b → de- 1. *380:11.* intention: PREP., CONJ. for.

INCIDENTALLY: → by the way.

- INCITE, - provoke, - instigate, - foment: tahrik et- 1 . *375:17.* motivation, inducement: - incite.

- INCLINE, - lean [subj.: trees, telephone poles after a storm]: eğil- 3. *204:10.* obliquity: - incline.

- INCLUDE, - cover [Does the hotel rate for one night include breakfast?], -

encompass: içine al- 1 → al- 1, içer-, kapsa-. *771:3.* inclusion: - include.

- INCONVENIENCE /θ/, - trouble /θ/, - cause trouble /to/, - put sb out, - give trouble /to/: /A/ zahmet ver- → ver- 1. *995:4.* inexpedience: - inconvenience; *1012:13.* difficulty: - trouble.

- INCREASE or - rise suddenly, - skyrocket [subj.: prices, temperature]: fırla- 2. *251:6* increase: - grow, increase [i.].
- increase, - BECOME more [subj.: quantity, amount]: art- 1, çoğal-. *251:6.* increase: - grow, increase [i.].
- increase in price, - become more expensive: fiyatlar {çık-/tırman-/yüksel-} → çık- 6, tırman- 2, yüksel- 2, pahalan-. *251:6.* increase: - grow, increase [i.].
- increase STH, - cause sth to increase: {artır-/arttır-} 1. *251:4.* increase: - increase.

INCREDIBLE, u n h e a r d - o f, unprecedented: olmadık → ol- 11. *869:10.* abnormality: unusual.

- INCUR GREAT EXPENSE, - spend a lot of money on sth or to get sth done, - have a lot of expenses: masrafa gir-. *626:5.* expenditure: - spend; *729:15.* finance, investment: - finance; *896:4.* liability: - incur.

- INDICATE, - point out: /I/ işaret et- 1 [sb or sth, not a fact, by means of a gesture], /A/ işaret et- 2 [- call attention /to/, - note /θ/ (obj.: a fact)]. *348:5.* manifestation: - manifest; *982:10.* attention: - call attention to.

- INDULGE, - give free rein to one's desires: çok or fazla with any verb relating to appetite: fazla iç- '- drink too much' → iç- 1, fazla yemek ye- '- overeat, - overindulge [in food]' → ye- 1. *992:10.* excess: - overdo.

- INFLUENCE /θ/, - have an effect /{ON/UPON}/, - affect /θ/: /I/ etkile-, /A/ tesir et-. *893:7.* influence: - influence.

- INFORM /θ/, - get information /to/, - report /to/: /A/ bildir-, /A/ bilgi ver- → ver- 1, /A/ haber ver- → ver- 1. *551:8.* information: - inform.

549

- INHABIT /θ/, - reside /{in/at}/, - live /{in/at}/: /DA/ otur- 3, /DA/ yaşa- 2. *225:7.* habitation: - inhabit.

- INHALE: içine çek- → çek- 1, nefes al- → al- 1. *89:14.* tobacco: - use tobacco; *187:12.* reception: - draw in; *318:21.* * *1.* wind: - breathe.

- INHERIT, - come into [property] /through/ inheritance: mirastan düş- → düş- 4. *479:7.* receiving: - inherit.

- INJURE, - wound /IN/ [a part of the body], - hurt: /I, DAn/ yarala-. *393:13.* impairment: - inflict an injury.

- INQUIRE after sb's health, - ask how sb is: hatır sor-. *83:6.* health: - enjoy good health; *937:20.* inquiry: - inquire.

- INSERT, - thrust, - shove, - stick, - introduce, - put /{IN/INTO}/ [hands IN pocket]: /A/ sok- 1. *191:3.* insertion: - insert.

- INSIST /{ON/UPON}/, - persist /IN/: /DA/ diret-, /DA/ inat et- 2, /DA, için/ ısrar et-. *361:7.* obstinacy: - balk; *421:8.* demand: - insist.
- insist /{on/UPON}/: /DA/ diren- 1. *361:7.* obstinacy: - balk; *421:8.* demand: - insist.
- insist /ON/ or - persist /IN/ one's own view, opinion: fikrinde inat et- → inat et- 2. *361:7.* obstinacy: - balk.

- INSPECT, - look /OVER/, - examine, - go /OVER/, - have a look /AT/, - check, - check out, - review, - scrutinize [a document]: gözden geçir- ['- look over'] → geçir- 1, muayene et- ['- examine', mostly for a doctor and a patient]. *27:14.* vision: - scrutinize.
- inspect, - examine, or - study carefully, minutely, in detail: incele-, tetkik et-. *27:14.* vision: - scrutinize; *937:25.* inquiry: - make a close study of.
- inspect, - check out, - check [whether sth is the case or not, a machine]: kontrol et-. *937:24.* inquiry: - examine.
- inspect, - examine, or - feel for sth with one's fingers, - feel around: yokla- 1. *73:6.* touch: - touch; *937:24.* inquiry: - examine.

- INSPIRE sb; - encourage sb to do or participate in sth; - promote the development of; - encourage or - spur sb on /a: to [lit., in the matter of], b: TO, c: with/: /a: konusunda, b: için, c: lA/ teşvik et-. *375:21.* motivation, inducement: - encourage; *492:16.* courage: - encourage.

- INSTIGATE, - incite, - provoke, - foment: tahrik et- 1. *375:17.* motivation, inducement: - incite.

- INSULT /θ/: /A/ hakaret et-. *156:5.* disrespect: - offend.

- INSURE /against [sth], WITH [a company]/: /A karşı, DAn/ sigortala-. *1007:18a.* protection: - protect.
- insure /θ/, - take out insurance /ON/: /A/ sigorta yaptır- → yaptır- 2. *1007:18a.* protection: - protect.

- INTEND, - aim, - mean, - plan, or - make up one's mind /to/ do sth: /A/ niyet et-. *359:7.* resolution: - resolve; *380:4.* intention: - intend.
- intend to do sb harm, - harbor evil intentions /TOWARD/, - have designs /{ON/AGAINST}/: /A/ kastet- 2. *381:9.* plan: - plot.

- INTER /θ/; - bury /IN/: /A/ göm-. *309:19.* interment: - inter.

- INTEREST, - appeal to, *colloq.*: - be into [Music really interests him.]: ilgi çek- → çek- 1, /I/ ilgilendir- 1. *377:6.* allurement: - attract; *980:3a.* curiosity: - make curious, - interest.

- INTERFERE /IN/, - meddle /IN/ [sb's business]: /A/ burnunu sok- 1 ['- stick one's nose /{IN/INTO}/'] → sok- 1, /A/ karış- 5. *214:5.* intrusion: - intrude.

- INTERPRET or - explain [the meaning of an event, a dream [Not '- translate from one language into another']: yorumla- 1. *341:9.* interpretation: - interpret.
- interpret or - translate orally or in writing /from [one language], INTO [another]/: /DAn, A/ aktar- 2, /DAn, A/ çevir- 6, /DAn, A/ tercüme et-. *341:12.* interpretation: - translate.
- interpret, - perform [a piece of music]: yorumla- 2. *341:9.* interpretation: - interpret; *708:39a.* music: - play sth.

- INTERROGATE, - question, - cross-examine: **sorguya çek-** → çek- 6. *937:21.* inquiry: - interrogate.

- INTERRUPT, - break in on, - cut in on [conversation]: **sözünü kes-** → kes- 3. *214:6.* intrusion: - interrupt; *843:4.* untimeliness: - talk out of turn.

- INTERSECT, - cut across [one street intersects another]: **kes-** 1. *170:6.* crossing: - cross.

- INTRODUCE or - present one person /to/ another: **/A/ takdim et-** 1, **/{1A/A}/ tanıştır-**. *587:14.* friendship: - introduce.
- introduce sb or sth /to, AS/ sb, - acquaint sb /WITH/ sb or sth, - make sb or sth known /to, AS/: **/A, olarak/ tanıt-**. *551:8.* information: - inform; *587:14.* friendship: - introduce.
- introduce /INTO/ [exercises into daily routine]: **/A/ sok-** 1. *191:3.* insertion: - insert.

- INVENT [new mouse trap]: **icat et-**. *940:2.* discovery: - discover.
- invent, - make up, - dream up, - concoct, - think up [story, lie]: **uydur-** 2. *354:18.* falseness: - fabricate.

- INVEST /in/, - make an investment /in/: **/{DA/A}/ yatırım yap-** → yap- 3. *626:5.* expenditure: - spend.

- INVESTIGATE, - explore, - research, - do research on, - study, - try to find out: **araştır-** 2. *937:23.* inquiry: - investigate.

- INVITE /{to/FOR}/ [They invited us /{to/FOR}/ dinner.]: **/A/ çağır-** 2, *more formal:* **/A/ davet et-**. *440:13.* request: - invite.

- IRON, - press [clothes]: **ütüle-**. *287:6.* smoothness: - press.

- IRRITATE, - annoy sb, - get on sb's nerves; - make sb angry, mad, - anger sb /by...ing/: **/ArAk/ sinirlendir-**. *96:14.* unpleasure: - irritate; *96:16a.* : - distress; *105:14.* excitement: - agitate; *128:9.* nervousness: - get on one's nerves; *152:22.* resentment, anger: - anger; *916:10.* agitation: - agitate.
- irritate, - bother, - annoy, - disturb: **rahatsız et-**. *96:13.* unpleasure: - annoy.

IS THAT UNDERSTOOD?: **Anlaşıldı mı?** → anlaşıl-, **Oldu mu?** → ol- 11

→ **oldu**. *399:* * *9* warning: expressions of.

Is THERE [a good restaurant around here?]: **[Buralarda iyi bir lokanta] var mı?** → ol- 3, Additional examples. b) 3.1. Issues of presence... *221:6.* presence: - be present; *760:8.* existence: - exist.

- ISSUE, - bring out, - put out [a publication]: **çıkar-** 7. *352:14.* publication: - issue.
- issue, - hand out, - give /to/, or - write [a traffic ticket, receipt]: **/A/ kes-** 5. *478:13.* giving: - deliver.
- issue or - write a receipt: **makbuz kes-** → kes- 5. *478:13.* giving: - deliver.

IT DOESN'T MATTER! Don't worry!: **Canın sağ olsun!** → sağ olsun → ol- 12. *121:* * *17.* comfort: words of comfort; *504:* * *20.* courtesy: polite expressions.
It doesn't matter., NO HARM DONE.: **zararı yok** → ol- 3, Additional examples. b) 4. Miscellaneous additional examples. *997:25.* unimportance: PHR. no matter.
It doesn't matter IF IT HAPPENS OR NOT, it may happen or not, it's not so important: **olsa da olur, olmasa da**. → ol- 11. *997:24.* unimportance: PHR. it does not matter.
It's A GOOD THING [that I did this]: **[Bunu yaptığım] iyi oldu.** → ol- 1. *760:12.* existence: - become.
It's ALL YOURS., No need to thank me., Take it with my blessings., I give up all rights to it.: **Helâl olsun.** 1 → ol- 11 → olsun. *370:* * *9.* abandonment: expressions of.
It's BEEN BARELY [two weeks since...]: **oldu olmadı** → ol-11 → oldu. *223:8.* nearness: - be near.
It's IMPOSSIBLE., It can't be done., It won't do., Impossible., No.: **Olmaz.** → ol- 4. *966:11.* impossibility: PHR. no can do.
It's impossible., It won't work out., It's not going to happen., It can't be done.: **Olacak gibi değil** → ol- 4. *966:11.* impossibility: PHR. no can do.
It's {impossible/absurd}!, It's not going to happen!, It's out of the question!, It's unbelievable!: **Olacak {iş/şey} değil!** → ol- 4. *122:22.* wonder: INTERJ. imagine!; *966:11.* impossibility: PHR. no can do.
It's NO USE: **faydası yok.** → ol- 3, Additional examples. b) 4. Miscellaneous additional examples.

*391: * 16.* uselessness*:* PHR. it's no use.

It's OVER AND DONE WITH: **Oldu bitti.** → ol- 11. *819: 14.* end: PHR. that's all.

It's POSSIBLE., OK., All right., Fine., Yes.: **Olur.** → ol- 4. *332:18.* assent: INTERJ. yes; *965:4* possibility: - be possible.

It's QUITE POSSIBLE., [It] could well be.: **Olur mu olur.** → ol- 4. *965:4* possibility: - be possible.

It's TOO LATE NOW., What's done is done., No use crying over spilled milk.: **Olan oldu.** → ol- 11. *845: * 21.* lateness: PHR. it's too late.

It's UP TO YOU., You decide.: **Arzunuza kalmış.** → kal- 1. *323:5.* will: at will.

It WON'T DO TO DO STH, one shouldn't, it's not appropriate to do sth: **mAk olmaz.** *638:2. * 1.* wrong: - do the wrong thing.

- ITCH [My head itches.]: **kaşın-** 1. *74:5.* sensations of touch: - tingle.

- J -

- JAM, - freeze, - seize up [subj.: computer]: **don-** 2. *854:10.* stability: - become firmly fixed.

- JEER, - boo: **yuhala-.** *508:10.* ridicule: - boo.

- JOIN, - unite, - bring together: **birleştir-** [bridge joins Europe and Asia], **kavuştur-** [bridge joins Europe and Asia, police unite lost child with parents]. *799:5.* joining: - put together.
- join /θ/ [sb or a group: May I join θ you?]: **/A/ katıl-** 2. *582:17.* sociability: - associate with.
- join /θ/ a conversation or - break /INTO/ a conversation: **söze karış-** → karış- 6. *476:5.* participation: - participate.
- join IN, - get involved /IN/ [not necessarily in a negative sense] [The students joined in the demonstration.]: **karış-** 6. *476:5.* participation: - participate.
- join officially IN MARRIAGE, - perform the civil marriage ceremony, - marry [t.]: **nikâh kıy-** → kıy- 3. *563:14.* marriage: - join in marriage.

- JUDGE, - estimate /AT/, - take a guess, - reckon [how many]: **/olarak/**

tahmin et- 2.1. *945:9.* judgment: - estimate.
- judge, - assess, - appraise, - evaluate, - size up [situation]: **değerlendir-** 1. *300:10.* measurement: - measure.
- judge or - adjudicate a case, - pass judgment on; - hear a case; - try sb, a case: **yargıla-.** *594:5.* jurisdiction: - administer justice; *598:17.* legal action: - try; *945:8.* judgment: - judge.

- JUMP, - leap /a: from, b: to, c, d: over/: /a: DAn, b: A, c: DAn, d: üzerinden/ **atla-** 1. *366:5.* leap: - leap.
- jump UP, - leap up /from/ [one's place, seat]: /DAn/ **fırla-** 1. *193:9.* ascent: - shoot up; *200:8.* verticalness: - rise; *366:5.* leap: - leap.

JUST any [old], whatever, any...that: **olur olmaz** 1 → ol- 11. *863:15.* generality: every.

Just between us.: **Aramızda kalsın.** → kal- 1. *345:20.* secrecy: ADV. confidentially.

Just look AT that, will you!, Imagine!, [Why] the nerve!: **Şuna bak be!** → bak- 1. *152:25b.* resentment, anger: expressions of.

just, quickly, with ease: *verb stem.***Iver-**. → ver- 4. *174:17.* swiftness: ADV. swiftly.

just in case: **Ne olur ne olmaz** → ol- 11 → olur. *965:10.* possibility: ADV. by any possibility.

just then, at that very moment: **derken** 1 → de- 1. *829:8.* instantaneousness: ADV. at once.

- K -

- KEEP or - hold /FOR/: **tut-** 2 [a seat, a place], /A/ **sakla-** 3 [my letters FOR me until I return]. *474:7.* retention: - hold, - keep.
- keep, - maintain, or - hold sth in a certain state or condition [room clean]: **tut-** 2. *397:8.* preservation: - preserve.
- keep or - continue doing sth, - go on /WITH/ [Keep working, don't stop.]: /A/ **devam et-** 2. *811:4a.* continuity: - continue sth.
- keep [on]...ing, - do sth continuously [He kept arguing with his father.]: *verb stem.***Ip dur-.** → dur- 11. *811:4a.* continuity: - continue sth; *855:3.* continuance: - continue.

- keep, - hold up, - detain [Don't let me keep you.]: /A/ **mâni ol-** → ol- 12, /I/ **tut-** 3. *1011:14.* hindrance: - prevent.
- keep or - store sth IN a place [He keeps the tools in that chest.]: /DA/ **sakla-** 2. *474:5.* retention: - retain.
- keep [i.e., - stay edible. subj.: food]: **dayan-** 4. *826:6.* durability: - endure.
- keep AN EYE /ON/, - watch /{θ/OVER}/ [so that no harm comes to]: /A/ **göz kulak ol-** → ol- 12. *1007:20.* protection: - watch.
- keep AWAKE, - make it impossible to go to sleep [subj.: coffee, tea]: **uykusunu kaçır-** → kaçır- 3. *23:3.* wakefulness: - keep awake.
- keep [oneself] AWAY /FROM/, - steer clear /OF/, or - avoid /θ/ sth or sb: /DAn/ **sakın-** 1. *329:3.* inaction: - refrain; *368:6.* avoidance: - avoid; *668:7.* temperance: - abstain.
- Keep the CHANGE.: **Üstü kalsın.** → kal- 1. *386:12.* store, supply: - reserve.
- keep CONTROL OF or - restrain one's tongue, - keep quiet: {**çenesini/dilini**} **tut-** [lit., '- hold {** one's jaw or chin/one's tongue}'] → tut- 4. *51:5.* silence: - be silent; *344:6.* uncommunicativeness: - keep to oneself; *428:7.* restraint: - restrain.
- keep, - hold, or - save sth /FOR/, - set sth aside /FOR/: /A/ **sakla-** 3. *386:12.* store, supply: - reserve; *474:5.* retention: - retain.
- keep or - observe the FAST, - fast: **oruç tut-** → tut- 5. *434:2.* observance: - observe; *515:4.* fasting: - fast; *701:14.* religious rites: - celebrate.
- keep or - bear IN MIND, - remember, - realize, - consider: **gözönünde tut-** → tut- 2. *930:12.* thought: - consider; *988:10.* memory: - remember.
- keep [PETS, animals], - raise [animals]: **besle-** 2. *1068:6.* animal husbandry: - raise.
- keep QUIET, - remain silent, - be silent, not - say anything: **sus-** 1. *51:5.* silence: - be silent.
- keep quiet, - hold one's tongue: {**çenesini/dilini**} **tut-** [lit., '- hold {** one's jaw or chin/one's tongue}'] → tut- 4. *51:5.* silence: - be silent; *344:6.* uncommunicativeness: - keep to oneself; *428:7.* restraint: - restrain.
- keep quiet, not - say anything, not - speak up: **ses çıkarMA-** 1 → çıkar- 7. *524:22.* speech: - speak up.
- keep SB WAITING, - let or make sb wait: **beklet-**. *845:8.* lateness: - delay.

- keep sth SECRET /from/: /DAn/ **gizle-** 1, /DAn/ **sakla-** 1. *346:6.* concealment: - conceal.
- keep TIME, - time, - watch the time, - keep track of the time: **saat tut-** → tut- 5. *831:11.* measurement of time: - time.
- keep UP /WITH/, - keep pace /WITH/ [income with cost of living]: /A/ **yetiş-** 8. *990:4.* sufficiency: - suffice.
- keep one's WORD or promise: **sözünde dur-** → dur- 6, **sözünü tut-** 1 → tut- 5. *434:2.* observance: - observe.

- KICK /θ/ sb, sth: /A/ **tekme** {at-/vur-}. → at- 5. *901:21.* impulse, impact: - kick.
- kick or - get over an ILLNESS, - pull through, - overcome or - survive a difficulty: **atlat-**. *396:20.* restoration: - recover.

- KIDNAP, - abduct, - carry off; - hijack: **kaçır-** 3. *482:20.* theft: - abduct.

- KILL: **öldür-**. *308:12.* killing: - kill.
- kill or - murder without mercy: **canına kıy-** 1 → kıy- 2. *308:12.* killing: - kill.
- kill, - finish off, - exhaust, - destroy [a person: Drink, gambling, and women killed him.]: **bitir-** 2. *395:10.* destruction: - destroy.
- kill or - butcher an animal as a sacrifice, - sacrifice an animal: **kurban kes-** → kes- 2. *308:12.* killing: - kill.
- kill ONESELF, - commit suicide: **kendini öldür-, canına kıy-** 2 → kıy- 2, *more formal, legal:* **intihar et-**. *308:21.* killing: - commit suicide.
- kill or - waste TIME /[by]...ing/: /ArAk/ {**vakit/zaman**} **öldür-**. *331:13.* inactivity: - waste time; *391:8.* uselessness: - be useless.

- KIND regards: **Ellerinizden öperim.** [lit., 'I kiss you ON your hands', a concluding salutation in a letter to a SENIOR, man or woman] → öp-, **Gözlerinizden öperim.** [lit., 'I kiss you ON your eyes', a concluding salutation in a letter to a JUNIOR, man or woman] → öp-. *155: * 15.* respect: expressions of respect.

- KISS /ON/ [a part of the body: the cheek]: /DAn/ **öp-**. *562:19.* lovemaking, endearment: - kiss.
- kiss one another [Ahmet and Fatma kissed; we kissed]: **öpüş-**. *562:19.* lovemaking, endearment: - kiss.

- KNEAD [dough]: **yoğur-**. *1045:6.* softness, pliancy: - soften.

- KNIT: **ör-** 1 [when the object knitted is specified: She knitted a sweater.], **örgü ör-** [when the object knitted is not specified: She knitted for two hours.] → ör- 1. *740:6.* weaving: - weave; *891:8.* production: - produce, - create.
- knit one's brows, - frown: **kaşlarını çat-**. *152:25a.* resentment, anger: gestures of; *510:20.* * 1. disapproval: gestures of.

- KNOCK, - hit, - strike /a: θ [sb or sth], b: with, c: ON/: **/a: A, b: lA, c: A/ vur-** 1. *901:14.* impulse, impact: - hit.
- knock /{AT/ON}/ the DOOR: **kapı.yI {çal-/vur-}** → çal- 4, vur- 1. *901:16.* impulse, impact: - pound.
- knock DOWN, - pull down, - tear down; - demolish, - wreck /with/; - destroy; - ruin [obj.: building]: **/lA/ yık-** 1. *395:17.* destruction: - demolish.
- knock down, - bring down [The boxer knocked down his opponent.]: **indir-** 4. *912:5.* depression: - fell.
- knock down, - fell; - send sb sprawling, - lay sb flat; - topple sth, - overthrow: **yık-** 2. *912:5.* depression: - fell.
- Knock it off!, Quit it!, Stop it! [when sb is bothering you]: **Bırak!** → bırak- 4, **Rahat bırak!** → bırak- 4, **Dur!** → dur- 4. *390:4.* disuse: - cease to use; *856:6.* cessation: - cease sth.
- knock sth {OFF/from} [He knocked the ashtray {OFF/from} the table.]: **/DAn/ düşür-**. *340:9.* neglect: - do carelessly.
- knock OVER [tree], - overturn [dish]: **devir-** 1. *395:19.* destruction: - raze.
- knock TO THE GROUND, - topple: **yere yık-**. → yık- 2. *912:5.* depression: - fell.

- KNOW /AS/, - think of /AS/: **/θ/ bil-** 3. *952:11.* belief: - think.
- know [a FACT, not a person]: **bil-** 1.1. *927:12.* knowledge: - know.
- know FROM MEMORY, by heart: **ezbere bil-** → bil- 1. *988:17.* memory: - memorize.
- know HOW to do sth: **bil-** 2. *927:12.* knowledge: - know.
- know IN ADVANCE, - predict: **önceden bil-** → bil- 1. *960:6.* foresight: - foreknow.
- know or - speak a LANGUAGE: *noun designating a language*.sI **var**, e.g., **Türkçesi var.** 'He {knows/speaks} Turkish.' Also: 'A

Turkish version [or translation] of it [a book, etc.] exists.' → ol- 3, Additional examples. b) 4. Miscellaneous additional examples. *524:26.* speech: - utter in a certain way.
- know sb, - be acquainted /WITH/ sb: **/I/ tanı-** 1.1, **/lA/ tanış-** ['- get to know, - get acquainted /with/ one another, - meet /θ/; - be acquainted with, - know one another']. *587:9.* friendship: - be friends.
- know sb, i.e., the real nature of sb, what kind of person he is: **bil-** 1.1, **tanı-** 1.2. *927:12.* knowledge: - know.
- know a SUBJECT, area of study [speciality such as cars, birds, not mathematics]: **bil-** 4. *927:12.* knowledge: - know.

- L -

- LABOR, - work: **çalış-** 1. *724:12.* occupation: - work; *725:12.* exertion: - work.

- LAG, - get, - fall, or - stay behind /in/ [some activity, lessons]: **/DA/ geri kal-** 1 → kal- 1. *166:4.* following: - lag; *217:8.* rear: - be behind.

- LAND, - perch, - settle, or - alight /{ON/UPON}/ [subj.: bird, insect, helicopter, not plane]: **/A/ kon-**. *184:43.* aviation: - land; *194:7.* descent: - get down; *194:10.* : - light upon.
- land /{AT/IN/ON}/ [subj.: plane, but not helicopter]: **/A/ in-** 3. *184:43.* aviation: - land; *194:7.* descent: - get down.

- LAPSE, - fall, - go, or - sink /INTO/ a coma: **komaya gir-**. *25:5.* insensibility: - faint.

- LAST, - continue, - go on [The parade lasted for three hours.]: **devam et-** 1, **sür-** 2. *811:4b.* for sth - continue; *826:6.* durability: - endure.
- last, - hold out, - be enough /FOR/ [subj.: supplies, money]: **/A/ dayan-** 5. *990:4.* sufficiency: - suffice.

- LAUGH /AT/ [amusement]: **/A/ gül-** 1. *116:8.* rejoicing: - laugh.
- laugh /AT/ [ridicule], - mock /θ/, - make fun /OF/: **/A/ gül-** 2. *508:8.* ridicule: - ridicule.
- laugh LOUDLY, - roar with laughter; - guffaw: **kahkaha ile gül-** → gül- 1. *116:8.* rejoicing: - laugh.

- laugh /{UP/IN}/ ONE'S SLEEVE, - be secretly amused, - laugh or - smile maliciously: **bıyık altından gül-** → gül- 2. *508:8.* ridicule: - ridicule.

- LAUNCH [rocket, etc.] /INTO/ [space]: **/A/ fırlat-**. *903:10.* pushing, throwing: - throw; *1072:13.* rocketry, missilery: - launch.

- LAY DOWN, - set, or - establish a condition, prerequisite /for/, - make a stipulation that, - stipulate that, - state clearly and firmly as a requirement: **/için/ şart koş-** → koş- 2. *958:4.* qualification: - make conditional.

- lay, - set, or - prepare a TABLE [or other surface for a meal]: **sofra kur-** → kur- 1. *159:16.* location: - establish; *405:6.* preparation: - prepare.

- LEAD /to/, - come out /{AT/ON}/ [Where does this road lead?]: **/A/ çık-** 3. *190:11.* emergence: - emerge.

- lead /to/, - bring about /θ/ sth, - cause /θ/ sth: **/A/ {sebep/neden} ol-** → ol- 12, **/A/ yol aç- 2** → aç- 1. *885:10.* cause: - cause.

- lead sb ASTRAY, - corrupt sb's morals: **ahlâkını boz-** → boz- 1. *393:12.* impairment: - corrupt.

- lead a [certain kind of] LIFE: **hayat sür-** → sür- 6. *306:7.* life: - live.

- LEAF or - thumb /THROUGH/ [book, papers], - rummage or - search /THROUGH/ [drawers, pocketbook]: **/I/ karıştır-** 3. *937:26.* inquiry: - examine cursorily; *937:33.* : - ransack.

- LEAN [oneself] /{AGAINST/ON}/ [He is leaning against the wall.]: **/A/ dayan-** 1, **/A/ sırtını {daya-/yasla-}** 1 [lit., ** '- lean one's back /{AGAINST/ON}/']. *159:14.* location: - deposit; *204:10.* obliquity: - incline; *900:22.* support: - rest on.

- lean [subj.: telephone poles after a storm], - incline: **eğil-** 3. *204:10.* obliquity: - incline.

- lean, - rest, or - prop sth /{AGAINST/ON}/ [He leaned his head against the wall.]: **/A/ {daya-/yasla-}**. *159:14.* location: - deposit; *204:10.* obliquity: - incline.

- LEAP or - jump /a: from, b: to, c, d: over/: **/a: DAn, b: A, c: DAn, d: üzerinden/ atla-** 1. *366:5.* leap: - leap.

- leap UP or - jump up /from/ [one's place, seat]: **/DAn/ fırla-** 1. *193:9.*

ascent: - shoot up; *200:8.* verticalness: - rise.

- LEARN [a subject, lessons]: **öğren-**. *927:14.* knowledge: - learn.

- learn BY HEART, - commit to memory, - memorize: **ezberle-**. *570:8.* learning: - memorize; *988:17.* memory: - memorize.

- learn /from/: **/DAn/ öğren-** ['- learn, - find out /from/'], **/DAn/ bilgi edin-** ['- obtain or - receive information /from/, - learn /from/']. *570:6.* learning: - learn; *927:14.* knowledge: - learn.

- learn a [MORAL] LESSON /from/: **/DAn/ ders al-** 2 → al- 1. *570:6.* learning: - learn.

- LEASE [house, car], - rent /from, FOR/: **/DAn, A/ kirala-** 1, **/DAn, A/ tut-** 6a. *615:15.* commission: - rent.

- lease [OUT], - rent [out] /to, FOR/ [obj.: place, equipment]: **/A, A/ {kirala-/kiraya ver-}** → kirala- 2. *615:16.* commission: - rent out.

- LEAVE [i.e., not - take sth from where it is], - leave sth /{on/in/at}/ [Don't take the books. Leave them on the table.], - leave behind, /in/ a certain condition [Leave the window open.]: **/DA/ bırak-** 1. *256:6.* remainder: - leave; *370:5.* abandonment: - abandon.

- leave sth /{ON/IN/AT}/ [i.e., - PUT sth somewhere: Don't keep holding the books. Leave them on the table.], - drop sth off /AT/: **/A/ bırak-** 2. *159:12.* location: - place.

- leave sth somewhere [lit., - FORGET it there: I left my wallet at home.]: **unut-** a). *989:5.* forgetfulness: - forget.

- leave, - abandon [permanently: one's job, wife, ship]: **bırak-** 3, **terk et-**. *370:5.* abandonment: - abandon.

- leave sb ALONE [Leave me alone! I have to concentrate.]: **yalnız bırak-** → bırak- 4. *390:4.* disuse: - cease to use; *871:6.* oneness: - stand alone.

- leave /FOR/, - depart /FOR/ [usually by means of a land vehicle, i.e., bus, train, not a boat and not a person on foot: **/A/ hareket et-** 2. *161:9.* direction: - head for; *188:8.* departure: - set out.

- leave, - depart, - take off /from/ [subj.: various vehicles of public transportation: shared cab, bus, ferry, train, plane]: **/DAn/ kalk-** 2. *188:8.* departure: - set out.

- leave or - set out, - start off /ON/ a {trip/journey}, - set out /ON/ the road [person on foot or vehicle]: **yola** {çık-/koyul-} → çık- 2, koyul-. *188:8.* departure: - set out; *817:7a.* beginning: - begin sth.

- leave for {vacation/the holiday[s]}, - begin a vacation, - go ON {vacation/holiday}: **tatile çık-** → çık- 2. *20:9.* rest, repose: - vacation.

- leave, - depart /from, for/: **/DAn, A/ ayrıl-** 3 [from city, party], **/DAn/ çık-** 1 [usually from enclosed area: house, room], **/DAn/ git- 1a** [from anywhere], **/DAn/ hareket et-** 3 [usually by means of a land vehicle, i.e., bus, train, not a boat and not a person on foot], **/DAn/ uzaklaş-** 1 ['- move away /from/': train from station]. *188:6.* departure: - depart.

- leave or - quit /θ/ one's JOB [not necessarily retirement]: **işten {ayrıl-/çık-}** → ayrıl- 3, çık- 1. *188:9.* departure: - quit; *448:2.* resignation: - resign.

- leave a MESSAGE /for/: **/için/ mesaj bırak-** → bırak- 2. *159:12.* location: - place.

- leave sb or sth OFF /AT/, - drop off /AT/: **/A/ bırak-** 2. *159:12.* location: - place.

- leave sth /TO/ sb, - bequeath sth /to/ sb [obj.: property]: **/A/ bırak-** 7. *478:18.* giving: - bequeath.

- leave /to/ A LATER TIME, - postpone /{to/TILL/UNTIL}/, - put off /to/, - defer /to/: **/A/ bırak-** 6, **/A, A kadar/ {ertele-/tehir et-}**. *845:9.* lateness: - postpone.

- LEND money, - extend a loan /to/: **/A/ borç ver-** → ver- 1, **/A/ ödünç ver-** → ver- 1. *620:5.* lending: - lend.

- lend money or anything else /to/: **/A/ ödünç ver-** → ver- 1. *620:5.* lending: - lend.

- LENGTHEN, - make long, - let out [dress, trousers]: **uzat-** 1. *267:6.* length: - lengthen.

LEST, for fear that: **diye 3.1a** → de- 1. *896:7.* liability: CONJ. lest.

- LET, - allow /θ/ sb, - give permission /to/, - permit /θ/ sb: **/A/ izin ver-** → ver- 1, **/A/ müsaade et-**. The causative form of any verb [that is, any verb stem with one of the following six causative suffixes: -Ar, -Art, -DIr, -Ir, -It, -t] also expresses permission, as in second part of the sentence: She wanted to use the phone, and he let her. For a list of all the causative verbs included

in this dictionary, see the **Index of Turkish Verb Suffixes.** [→ also - have sth done]. *443:9.* permission: - permit.

- let ALONE, so {how/why} would he: **kaldı ki 2** → kal- 1. *772:10.* exclusion: PREP. excluding.

- let sth COOL, get cold, - cool sth down, - chill, - make sth cool or cold: **soğut-** 1. *1022:10.* cold: - make cold.

- let FALL /from, {to/ON}/, - drop sth, - cause sth to fall: **/DAn, A/ düşür-** 1. *912:7.* depression: - drop sth.

- let GO BY, - miss [chances, opportunities]: **kaçır-** 2. *410:14.* failure: - miss; *843:5.* untimeliness: - miss an opportunity.

- let go OF, - release, - free, - set free, - liberate [a captive animal, hostages, prisoners]: **bırak-** 5, **serbest bırak-** → bırak- 5, **salıver-**. *120:6.* relief: - release; *398:3.* rescue: - rescue; *431:4.* liberation: - liberate; *431:5.* : - release.

- let GROW OUT [hair, fingernails]: **uzat-** 4. *267:6.* lengthen: - lengthen.

- let, - permit, or - allow /{IN/INTO}/ a place: **/A/ sok-** 2. *189:7.* entrance: - enter; *443:9.* permission: - permit.

- let sb KNOW sth, - inform /θ/ sb: **/A/ bildir-**, **/A/ bilgi ver-** → ver- 1, **/A/ haber ver-** → ver- 1. *551:8.* information: - inform.

- let {OFF/out}, - discharge, - unload [passengers] /at, from/: **/DA, DAn/ indir-** 2. *908:23.* ejection: - unload; *912:4.* depression: - depress.

- let ONE'S MIND, attention wander, - be off in the clouds: **dalga geç-** 1 → geç- 1. *983:3.* inattention: - wander.

- let OUT, - break up [subj.: meeting, concert, game, film], - be over [subj.: party]: **dağıl-** 2. *770:8.* dispersion: - disband.

- let out, - lengthen, - make long [dress, trousers]: **uzat-** 1. *267:6.* length: - lengthen.

- let out a breath, - breathe out: **nefes ver-** → ver- 1. *318:21.* * 1. wind: - breathe.

- let SLIP, pop out, - blurt out, - let a secret out unintentionally: **ağzından lâf kaçır-** → kaçır- 2. *351:4.* disclosure: - disclose.

- let or make SB WAIT, - keep sb waiting: **beklet-**. *845:8.* lateness: - delay.

Let's say [that] [i.e., - assume, - suppose for the sake of argument that]: **Diyelim [ki]** → de- 2. *950:19.* theory, supposition: CONJ. supposing.

Let's see, let me see, um, er, ah..: **Efendime söyleyeyim...** → söyle- 1. *362:13.* irresolution: ADV. * filler phrases and stallers.

{Let's suppose [that]/Suppose [that]}: **{Farzedelim [ki]/Farzet [ki]}** → {farz et-/varsay-}, **{Tutalım [ki]/Tut ki}** → tut- 9. *950:19.* theory, supposition: CONJ. supposing.

- let or - leave WELL ENOUGH ALONE, - let matters run or take their course without interference, - let nature take its course, - let things be: **oluruna bırak-** → bırak- 2, ol- 11. *430:16.* freedom: not - interfere.

- LIBERATE, - free, - set free, - let go, - release [hostages, prisoners]: **serbest bırak-** → bırak- 5, **salıver-.** *120:6.* relief: - release; *398:3.* rescue: - rescue; *431:4.* liberation: - liberate; *431:5.* : - release.

- LIE, - tell lies: **yalan söyle-** → söyle- 1. *354:19.* falseness: - lie; *645:11.* improbity: - be dishonest.
- lie DOWN, - go to bed, - retire for the night: **yat-** 1. *22:17.* sleep: - go to bed; *201:5.* horizontalness: - lie; *912:11.* depression: - lie down.
- lie down /{ON/on}/, - stretch oneself out /{ON/on}/ [bed, couch]: /{A/üstüne}/ **uzan-** 1. *201:5.* horizontalness: - lie; *912:11.* depression: - lie down.
- lie IN ONE'S POWER, - be within one's capabilities, - be able to do: **elinden gel-** → gel- 1. *18:11.* power, potency: - be able.

- LIFT UP, - pick up, - raise /from/: /DAn/ **kaldır-** 1. *911:5.* elevation: - elevate.

- LIGHT, - ignite, - set on fire, - set fire to, - burn: /I/ **yak-** 1. *1019:22.* heating: - ignite.
- light a FIRE: **ateş yak-** → yak- 1. *1019:22.* heating: - ignite.
- light UP [{a cigarette/a cigar/a pipe}]: [{sigara/puro/pipo}] **yak-** → yak- 1. *1019:22.* heating: - ignite.

- LIKE, - love; - be fond of: **sev-** 1. *95:12.* pleasure: - enjoy; *104:19.* love: - love.
- like: /I/ **beğen-** 1, /DAn/ **hoşlan-, hoşuna git-** → git- 1b, **keyfine git-** → git- 1b, /DAn/ **memnun ol-** → ol- 12. *95:12.* pleasure: - enjoy.

- like /θ/ sth A GREAT DEAL, - adore /θ/, - be carried away /BY/, - be crazy /ABOUT/: /A/ **bayıl-** 2. *101:7.* eagerness: - be enthusiastic.
- like BEST, - like sb or sth better than sb or sth else, - prefer sb or sth /to/ sb or sth else: /A/ {**tercih et-/yeğle-**} 1, /DAn/ **hoşlan-.** *371:17.* choice: - prefer.
- like or - love EACH OTHER; - be fond of each other: **seviş-** 1. *104:19.* love: - love.

- LIKEN, - note a resemblance between, - think that sb or sth is /LIKE/ sb or sth else: /A/ **benzet-** 2. *942:4.* comparison: - compare; *988:20.* memory: - remind.

- LINE UP, - get in [the] line, - queue up: {**sıraya/kuyruğa**} **gir-.** *811:6.* continuity: - line up.

- LIST, - enumerate, - say the names of [the days, capital cities of the world]: **say-** 2. *870:8.* list: - list.

- LISTEN /a: TO [music], b: {ON/over} [the Internet], c: ON [a tape]/: /a: I, **b: üzerinden, c: DAn/** 1 **dinle-** 1. *48:10.* hearing: - listen.
- listen /TO/, - heed, - obey: /I/ 1 **dinle-** 2. *326:2.* obedience: - obey.

- LITTER [/θ/ the streets], - throw trash [/{ON/INTO}/ the streets]: [**sokaklar.A**] **çöp** {**at-/dök-**} → at- 2, dök- 3. *80:15a.* uncleanness: - dirty; *390:7.* discard: - discard; *810:2.* disarrangement: - disarrange.

- LIVE [as opposed to '- die']: **yaşa-** 1. *306:7.* life: - live.
- live /{in/at}/, - reside /{in/at}/, - inhabit /θ/: /DA/ **otur-** 3, /DA/ **yaşa-** 2. *225:7.* habitation: - inhabit.
- live or - stay with people: **yanında kal-** → kal- 1. *225:7.* habitation: - inhabit.
Live in it with pleasure!: **Güle güle otur[un].** [said to sb who has just moved into a new residence] → otur- 3. *504:* * *20.* courtesy: polite expressions.
- live IN MISERY, - live a miserable life, - be just scraping {along/by}, - be barely surviving, getting by, - be just keeping body and soul together, - be living through hard times: **sürün-** 2. *96:19.* unpleasure: - suffer.
- live THROUGH, - experience, - have [problems], - enjoy [fine weather]: **yaşa-** 3. *830:8.* event: - experience.

- live through or - experience a disaster: **felâket geçir-** → geçir- 2. *1010:10.* adversity: - come to grief.

- LOAD sb down /with/ sth, - load sth down /upon/ sb, - pile or - dump sth /{on/upon/} sb [obj.: a burdensome task]: **/{üstüne/üzerine}/ yık-** 3. *159:15.* location: - load.

- LOATHE /θ/, - detest /θ/, - hate /θ/, - abhor /θ/: **/DAn/ nefret et-**. *103:5.* hate: - hate.

- LOCK [obj.: door]: **kilitle-** 1. *293:6.* closure: - close; *799:8.* joining: - hook.

- lock ONESELF OUT [of a room, building]: **anahtarı içeride unut-** → unut-. *293:6.* closure: - close.

- lock sth UP /IN/: **/A/ kilitle-** 2. *429:12.* confinement: - confine.

- LOG OFF, - get off /θ/ the Internet: **internetten çık-** → çık- 1. *1041:18.* computer science: - computerize.

- log ON /to/, - connect oneself /to/ the Internet: **internete bağlan-**. → bağlan- 3. *617:14.* association: - join; *1041:18.* computer science: - computerize.

- LONG FOR, - miss [sb or sth absent], - yearn for: **/I/ ara-** 4, **/A/ hasret çek-** → çek- 5, **/I/ özle-**. *100:16.* desire: - wish for; *991:7.* insufficiency: - want.

- long /FOR/, - feel an appetite /FOR/: **/A/ imren-** 1. *100:16.* desire: - wish for.

- long /FOR/ sth unobtainable, - envy without malice: **/A/ imren-** 2, **/A/ özen-** 2. *154:3.* envy: - envy.

- LOOK /AFTER/, - take care /OF/, - attend /to/ [guests, a matter, the phone]: **/A/ bak-** 3, **/lA/ ilgilen-** 2, **/lA/ meşgul ol-** → ol- 12. *339:9.* carefulness: - look after; *982:5.* attention: - attend to; *1007:19.* protection: - care for.

- look after, - take care of, - keep [letters until I return from my vacation]: **sakla-** 3. *474:5.* retention: - retain.

- look one's AGE: **yaşını göster-** → göster- 2. *33:10.* appearance: - appear to be.

- look AROUND, - have a look around: **etrafa bak-** → bak- 1. *27:13.* vision: - look at; *937:31.* inquiry: - search.

- [just] look around [in a store], - browse: **şöyle bir bak-** → bak- 1, **sadece bak-** → bak- 1. *733:8.* purchase: - shop; *937:26.* inquiry: - examine cursorily.

- look AT, - watch, - view [TV, play, video]: **izle-** 3, **seyret-**. *27:13.* vision: - look.

- look DOWN UPON, - regard sb or sth as inferior, - treat with disrespect or contempt, - hold sb in contempt, - despise, *informal:* - put sb down, *slang:* - dis: **küçümse-** 1. *157:3.* contempt: - disdain.

- look /FOR/, - search /FOR/: **/I/ ara-** 1, **/A/ bak-** 2. *937:30.* inquiry: - seek.

- look /{from/OUT/THROUGH}, AT/: **/DAn, A/ bak-** → bak- 1. *27:13.* vision: - look at.

- look GOOD /ON/ [This suit looks good on you.]: **/A/ yakış-** 2. *866:3.* conformity: - conform.

- Look HERE!, - Say, *informal:* Hey there!: **{Baksana!/Baksanıza!}** → bak- 1. *982:22.* attention: INTERJ. attention!

- look LIKE, - resemble /θ/ [He looks like his father.]: **/A/ benze-** 1. *783:7.* similarity: - resemble.

- look like /θ/ [It looks like it's going to rain.], - appear, - seem: **/A/ benze-** 2, **gibi görün-** → görün- 2, **gibi göster-** → göster- 2. *33:10.* appearance: - appear to be.

- look like, - appear to be: **göster-** 2. *33:10.* appearance: - appear to be.

- look [good, bad] /ON/, - appear /on/, - suit [How does this jacket look on me?]: **/DA/ dur-** 9. *866:3.* conformity: - conform.

- look OUT, - be careful, - watch out /FOR/: **/A/ dikkat et-** 1, **dikkatli ol-** → ol- 12. *339:7.* carefulness: - be careful; *399: * 9* warning: expressions of.

- look out /OF/ [the window]: **/DAn/ bak-** 1. *27:13.* vision: - look.

- look OVER, - go over, - check, - check out, - examine, - scrutinize, - review: **gözden geçir-** → geçir- 1. *27:14.* vision: - scrutinize.

- look UP, - raise one's head /from/ [one's book]: **/DAn/ başını kaldır-** → kaldır- 1. *911:5.* elevation: - elevate.

- look sb up: **arayıp sor-**. *937:30.* inquiry: - seek.

- look sth up /IN [a reference source: dictionary], for/, - consult /θ [sb or sth], for/: **/A, için/ {başvur-/müracaat et-}** 1. *387:14.* use: - avail oneself of; *937:30.* inquiry: - seek.

- look /UPON [sb or sth], AS/ [He looked upon his teacher as a model for himself.]: /A, olarak/ bak- 4, /I, olarak/ gör- 2, /I/ say- 4. *952:11.* belief: - think.

- LOSE [wallet]: {kaybet-/yitir-}. *473:4.* loss: - lose.
- lose [sb to death: We lost our father last year.]: {kaybet-/yitir-}. *307:19.* death: - die; *473:4.* loss: - lose.
- lose or - miss {a CHANCE/an opportunity}: {şans/fırsat} kaybet-. *410:14.* failure: - miss; *843:5.* untimeliness: - miss an opportunity.
- lose CONSCIOUSNESS, - pass out, - faint: bayıl- 1, kendinden geç- 1 → gec- 1, kendini kaybet- 1 → {kaybet-/yitir-}, {şuurunu/ bilincini} kaybet-[or yitir-] 1 → {kaybet-/yitir-}. *25:5.* insensibility: - faint.
- lose one's COOL: → - lose one's TEMPER.
- lose one's FAITH /IN/ [humanity]: /A karşı/ güvenini {kaybet-/ yitir- } → {kaybet-/yitir-}. *132:4.* disappointment: - be disappointed.
- lose a [tooth] FILLING: dolgu düş- → düş- 1. *85:46b.* disease: - take sick in particular ways; *194:5.* descent: - descend.
- lose a GAME, match: kaybet-. *473:4.* loss: - lose.
- lose one's HEALTH and morale; for sb - be broken, ruined, or devastated by a disaster: yıkıl- 3. *112:17.* sadness: - grieve; *393:24.* impairment: - break down.
- lose HEART, - get depressed, discouraged: morali bozul-. *112:16.* sadness: - lose heart.
- lose HOPE, - despair, - give up hope: {umudunu/ümidini} kaybet-[or yitir-] → {kaybet-/yitir-}. *125:10.* hopelessness: - despair.
- lose ONE'S COOL, - panic, - get or - be excited [negative emotion], upset, agitated, nervous: heyecanlan- 2. *96:16b.* unpleasure: - be distressed; *128:6.* nervousness: - fidget.
- lose one's LIFE [usually of unnatural causes: in an accident, through murder, etc.]: hayatını {kaybet-/yitir-}. *307:19.* death: - die.
- lose one's LIVELIHOOD, - be deprived of one's livelihood: ekmeğinden ol-. → ol- 7. *473:4.* loss: - lose.
- lose one's LOVE, desire, or enthusiasm /FOR/, - cool /TOWARD/; - cease to care /FOR/ sb or sth: /DAn/ soğu- 2. *261:7.* distance, remoteness: - keep

one's distance; *379:4.* dissuasion: - disincline.
- lose one's MIND: aklını {kaybet-/yitir-}, çıldır-, delir-, {şuurunu/bilincini} kaybet-[or yitir-] 3 → {kaybet-/yitir-}. *925:21.* insanity, mania: - go mad.
- lose one's TEMPER, - lose one's cool, - be ready to explode /{ON ACCOUNT OF/DUE TO}/, - explode, - fly off the handle, - blow up: /DAn/ patla- 2, sinirleri bozul- 1 → bozul-, {şuurunu/bilincini} kaybet-[or yitir-] 2 → {kaybet-/yitir-}. *152:20.* resentment, anger: - fly into a rage.
- lose SPEED, - slow down [vehicle, runner], - die down [rain]: yavaşla-. *175:9.* slowness: - slow.
- lose or - waste TIME /ing, {from/because of}...ing/: /mAklA, mAktAn/ {vakit/zaman} kaybet-[or yitir-] → {kaybet-/yitir-}. *331:13.* inactivity: - waste time; *391:8.* uselessness: - be useless.
- lose TRACK OF, - lose count of, - confuse, - get confused /{about/regarding/as to}/: /I/ şaşır- 3. *970:9.* uncertainty: - be uncertain; *984:7b.* distraction, confusion: - get confused.
- lose one's VIRGINITY [for women only. There is no commonly used Turkish equivalent term for men.]: {bekâretini/kızlığını} kaybet-[or yitir-] → {kaybet-/yitir-}. *75:21.* sex: - copulate; *665:20.* unchastity: - seduce.
- lose one's WAY, - be lost: yolunu {kaybet-/yitir-}. *473:4.* loss: - lose.
- lose one's way, - get lost, not - know which way to turn [physically and morally]: yolunu şaşır- → şaşır- 3. *473:4.* loss: - lose; *654:9.* vice: - go wrong; *970:9.* uncertainty: - be uncertain.
- lose WEIGHT: kilo ver- → ver- 1, zayıfla- 1. *270:13.* narrowness, thinness: - slenderize.

- LOVE, - like; - be fond of: sev- 1. *95:12.* pleasure: - enjoy; *104:19.* love: - love.
- love or - like EACH OTHER; - be fond of each other: seviş- 1. *104:19.* love: - love.

- LOWER /from, to/, - bring down /from, to/, - take down [obj.: shutter, baggage]: /DAn, A/ indir- 1. *912:4.* depression: - depress.

- lower, - reduce, - decrease, - bring down [prices, rates], - give a discount: **indir-** 3. *631:2.* discount: - discount; *633:6a.* cheapness: - lower prices.

- M -

- MAIL, - post, - send off mail: **/A/ at-** 4 ['- drop in the mail'], **postala-** ['-mail']. *176:15.* transferal, transportation: - send; *553:12.* correspondence: - mail.

- MAINTAIN, - claim [that sth is true]: **ileri sür-** 2 → **sür-** 1. *334:5.* affirmation: - affirm.
- maintain or - hold sth in a certain state or condition [room clean]: **tut-** 2. *397:8.* preservation: - preserve.
- MAKE: **yap-** 1. *328:6.* action: - do; *891:8.* production: - produce, - create.
- make, - add up to, - amount to, - equal, - get [in mathematical operations: One and one makes two.]: **et-** 3. *789:5.* equality: - equal; *791:8.* whole: - total; *1016:18.* mathematics: - sum up.
- make by sewing, - sew [She sewed herself a dress.]: 1 **dik-**. *741:4.* sewing: - sew; *891:8.* production: - produce, - create.

- make the ACQUAINTANCE OF sb, - meet sb, - become acquainted /WITH/ sb, - get to know sb: **/I/ tanı-** 3. *587:10.* friendship: - befriend, - make friends with.
- make sb ANGRY, - anger: **kızdır-** 1. *152:22.* resentment, anger: - anger.
- make sb angry, mad, - anger; - irritate, - annoy, - get on sb's nerves /by...ing/: **/ArAk/ sinirlendir-**. *96:14.* unpleasure: - irritate; *105:14.* excitement: - agitate; *128:9.* nervousness: - get on one's nerves; *152:22.* resentment, anger: - anger; *916:10.* agitation: - agitate.
- make an APOLOGY /TO/ sb, - beg sb's pardon, - apologize /TO [sb], for [sth]/: **/DAn, için/ özür dile-** → **dile-** 2. *658:5.* atonement: - apologize.
- make an APPOINTMENT /for/, - get an appointment /from, for/: **/DAn, için/ gün al-** [only for a (date/day)] → **al-** 3, **/DAn, için/ randevu al-** [for any time] → **al-** 3. *582:19.* sociability: - visit; *964:4.* prearrangement: - prearrange.

- make [up] one's BED: **yatağını {topla-/düzelt-/yap-}** → **topla-** 2,

düzelt- 3, → **yatağını yap-** 1 → **yap-** 3. *807:12.* arrangement: - tidy, tidy up.
- make or - prepare BREAKFAST: **kahvaltı hazırla-**. *405:6.* preparation: - prepare.

- make a phone CALL /TO/, - place a call /TO/ [To the operator: I would like to make a call {to Ankara./to sb at the following number.}]: **/lA/ görüş-** 3. *347:18.* communications: - telephone.
- make CHANGE /for/, - give change /for/, - break a bill: **boz-** 2. *857:11.* conversion: - convert.
- make a CLEAN COPY of a piece of writing, - recopy, - rewrite: **temize çek-** → **çek-** 8. *784:8.* copy: - copy.
- make CLEAR, - state: **belirt-**. *334:5.* affirmation: - affirm; *524:24.* speech: - state.
- make a COLLECT [telephone] CALL /to/, - call collect: **ödemeli ara-** → **ara-** 2. *347:18.* communications: - telephone.
- make a CONTRACT, - sign a contract or agreement /with/: **/lA/ kontrat yap-** → **yap-** 3. *332:10.* assent: - come to an agreement.
- make a COPY OF: **kopyasını {çek-/çıkar-}** → **çek-** 8, **çıkar-** 7. *784:8.* copy: - copy.

- make a DECISION, - decide, - resolve: **/için/ karar al-** [subj.: usually a group or organization acting in an official capacity] → **al-** 1, **/A/ karar ver-** [subj.: usually an individual rather than a group or organization] → **ver-** 1, **/I/ kararlaştır-** [subj.: at least two persons reaching a decision together], **/A/ niyet et-** Also: '- make a decision to do sth and then to state one's intention to oneself, silently or out loud, to carry out the act decided upon'. This verb is used in reference to certain acts required by the religion of Islam for which such a statement of intention is required before the act is carried out and for that act to be valid. *359:7.* resolution: - resolve; *380:4.* intention: - intend to.
- make a DIAGNOSIS, - diagnose [obj.: a disease]: **teşhis koy-** → **koy-** 1. *341:9.* interpretation: - interpret.
- make no DIFFERENCE, - be UNimportant, NOT - matter: **fark etME-**. *997:9.* unimportance: - be unimportant.
- make or - create DIFFICULTIES, - make trouble /FOR, on account of/: **/A, DAn dolayı/**

{güçlük/zorluk} çıkar- → çıkar- 7. *1012:14.* difficulty: - cause trouble.

- make or - get sth DIRTY, - dirty, - soil, - pollute: **kirlet-, pislet-.** *80:15a.* uncleanness: - dirty.

- make DISAPPEAR: **yok et-** 2 [magician makes rabbit disappear]. *34:2b.* disappearance: - make disappear.

- make sb /θ/ DO sth, - force sb /to/ do sth: **/A/ zorla-** 1. *424:4.* compulsion: - compel.

- make do, - manage /with/, - be able to manage /with/ [very little money]: **/lA/ idare et-** 2, **/lA/ yetin-** 2. *994:4.* expedience: - make shift, - make do.

- make sth EASY /FOR/, - facilitate matters /FOR/, - give sb a break, - help /θ/: **/A/ kolaylık göster-** → göster- 1. *449:11.* aid: - aid; *1013:7.* facility: - facilitate.

- make ENDS MEET /with/, - economize /BY/; - manage /with/, - manage to get along /with/, - get by /with/ [very little money]: **/lA/ idare et-** 2, **/lA/ yetin-** 2. *409:12.* success: - manage; *994:4.* expedience: - make shift, - make do.

- make one's EYES WATER, - bring tears to one's eyes: **gözlerini yaşart-.** *13:5.* secretion: - secrete; *115:12.* lamentation: - weep.

- make a FACE, - grimace, - scowl: **yüzü buruş-** 1 → buruş-, **yüzünü buruştur-.** *152:25a.* resentment, anger: gestures of; *265:8.* distortion: - grimace; *510:20.* * 1. disapproval: gestures of.

- make a FILM, movie, - film: **film çek-** [subj.: both amateur and professional film makers] → çek- 7, **film çevir-** 2 [subj.: professional film makers] → çevir- 3. *714:14.* photography: - photograph.

- make one thing FIT /{θ/INTO}/ another, - improvise, i.e., - fabricate sth out of what is conveniently on hand /FOR/ [key FOR a lock]: **/A/ uydur-** 1. *866:3.* conformity: - conform; *891:12.* production: - originate.

- make FLY, - blow about, away [wind makes papers fly about]: **uçur-.** *318:20.* wind: - blow.

- make FRIENDS /with/: **/I/ tanı-** 3 ['- become acquainted /WITH/ sb, - get to know sb, - meet sb'], **/lA/ tanış-** ['- get acquainted with one another, - meet': I met her while I was a student.] *587:10.* friendship: - befriend, - make friends with.

- make FUN /OF/, - ridicule / θ/, - mock /θ/: **/lA/ alay et-, /I/ alaya al-** → al- 1, **/lA, diye/ dalga geç-** 2 → geç- 1, **/lA/ eğlen-** 2. *508:8.* ridicule: - ridicule.

- make GOOD USE /OF/, - take advantage /OF/, - benefit or - profit /from/; - utilize /θ/: **/DAn/ {yararlan-/faydalan-/istifade et-}.** *387:15.* use: - take advantage of.

- make good use of time, - make the most of one's time /[by]...ing/: **/ArAk/ {vakit/zaman} değerlendir-** → değerlendir- 2. *330:16.* activity: - make the most of one's time.

- make sb HAPPY, - please sb /with, by...ing/: **/lA, ArAk/ sevindir-.** *95:8.* pleasure: - gladden.

- make red HOT [oven]: **kızdır-** 2. *1019:17a.* heating: - heat.

- make an INVESTMENT /in/, - invest /in/: **/{DA/A}/ yatırım yap-** → yap- 3. *626:5.* expenditure: - spend.

- make IT /TO/ IN TIME /FOR/, - get /to/ a place in time /FOR/, - arrive in time /FOR/, - catch /θ/ a vehicle; - be in time /FOR/: **/A/ yetiş-** 1. *174:13.* swiftness: - overtake; *409:8.* success: - achieve one's purpose.

- make a JOKE, - be joking, kidding, not - be telling the truth: **şaka yap-** 2 → yap- 3. *490:5.* banter: - banter.

- make sb or sth KNOWN /to, AS/, - acquaint sb /WITH/ sth, - introduce [a person or a thing] /to/ sb: **/A, olarak/ tanıt-.** *551:8.* information: - inform; *587:14.* friendship: - introduce.

- make or - earn one's LIVING, livelihood /by...ing/: **/ArAk/ geçimini sağla-, /ArAk/ geçin-** 2, **/ArAk/ hayatını kazan-** → kazan- 1. *385:11.* provision, equipment: - make a living; *409:12.* success: - manage.

- make LOVE, - have sexual intercourse /with/; - caress one another; *slang:* - make out /with/: **/lA/ seviş-** 2. *562:14.* lovemaking, endearment: - make love; *562:16.* : - caress.

- make a MISTAKE: **/lA/ hata et-** [usually in reference to relatively greater errors in the conduct of one's life, less frequently in minor matters such as grammar, punctuation], **hata**

işle- [mostly in minor matters] →
işle- 2, /lA/ hata yap- [mostly in
minor matters] → yap- 3, yanıl- ['-
make a mistake, - be mistaken',
mostly in minor matters], yanlışlık
yap- [in minor matters] → yap- 3.
974:13. error: - mistake, - make a
mistake.

- make the MOST OF ONE'S TIME, -
make good use of time /[by]...ing/:
/ArAk/ {vakit/zaman}
değerlendir- → değerlendir- 2.
330:16. activity: - make the most of
one's time.

- make a MOVIE, film, - produce a film:
film çek- [subj.: both amateur or
professional film makers] → çek- 7,
film çevir- 2 [subj.: producer,
professional film makers] → çevir- 3.
704:28. show business, theater: -
dramatize; *714:14.* photography: -
photograph.

- make NO DIFFERENCE, - be
UNimportant, NOT - matter: fark
etME-. *997:9.* unimportance: - be
unimportant.

- make NOISE, - be noisy: gürültü {et-
/yap-}. *53:9.* loudness: - be noisy.

- make OFF, - take off, - go away, - leave
[a permanent departure; subj.:
person]: başını alıp git- → git- 1a.
188:10. departure: - hasten off.

- make ONESELF UP, - put on makeup:
makyaj yap- → yap- 3. *1015:15.*
beauty: - beautify.

- make OUT, - distinguish, - see clearly:
farket- 3, seç- 2. *27:12.* vision: -
see.

- make out /WITH/, - caress one another; -
make love, - have sexual intercourse
/with/: oynaş- 2, /lA/ seviş- 2.
562:14. lovemaking, endearment: -
make love; *562:16.* : - caress.

- make PEACE /with/, - make up /with/, -
come to an understanding /with/:
/lA/ barış-. *465:10.* pacification: -
make up.

- make a PHOTOCOPY OF, - photocopy:
fotokopi çek- → çek- 8. *784:8.*
copy: - copy.

- make the PILGRIMAGE, - go on the
Pilgrimage to Mecca: hacca git- →
git- 1a. *177:21.* travel: - journey;
701:14. religious rites: - celebrate.

- make, - devise, - draft, - establish, or -
formulate a PLAN: plan kur- →
kur- 1. *964:4.* prearrangement: -
prearrange.

- make a PLAY /FOR/ sb, - come on /to/
sb, - chase /AFTER/ sb, i.e., -

approach with sexual intent, *slang:*
/A/ asıl- 3. *382:8.* pursuit: - pursue;
562:21. lovemaking, endearment: -
court.

- make a PREDICTION, - predict: /A/
önceden bildir- [lit., '- inform /θ/
in advance', subj.: ordinary persons
and experts, but not usually persons
divinely inspired or oracles, etc.],
kehanet et-, kehanette bulun-
[subj. of the last two verbs above:
wise men, oracles, fortune-tellers, or
soothsayers only] → bulun- 3. *961:9.*
prediction: - predict.

- make a PRESENT /to/ sb of sth, - give
sth as a gift /to/ sb: /A/ hediye et-.
478:12. giving: - give; *634:4.*
costlessness: - give.

- make or - achieve [with nouns indicating
PROGRESS, development, success]:
kaydet- 5. *392:7.* improvement: -
get better; *409:7a.* success: - succeed.

- make PUBLIC, - reveal, - disclose /to/:
/A/ açıkla- 2. *351:4.* disclosure: -
disclose.

- make sth READY /FOR/, - get sth ready,
- prepare sth /FOR/: /{A/için}/
hazırla-. *405:6.* preparation: -
prepare.

- make RED HOT [oven]: kızdır- 2.
1019:17a. heating: - heat.

- make a REDUCTION IN PRICE /FOR/
SB, - go down in price /FOR/ sb, -
give a discount /to/ sb: /A/ ikram
et- 2, in- 5, indir- 3. *631:2.*
discount: - discount.

- make a RESERVATION /for [sb, a
time], at [a place]/: /için, DA/
rezervasyon yaptır- → yaptır- 2.
477:9. apportionment: - allot.

- make sb RESPONSIBLE /FOR/, -
entrust sb /with/ [a task, duty], -
charge sb /with/, - give sb the task
/of/, - put sb in charge /OF/: /lA/
görevlendir-. *615:11.* commission:
- appoint; *641:12.* duty: - obligate.

- make no SENSE OF, NOT - understand
or - grasp: aklı alMA-. *522:11.*
unintelligibility: not - understand.

- make /θ/ sb SICK, - upset /θ/ sb [subj.:
food], - affect one's health adversely,
for food or weather not - agree
/WITH/ one, - have a bad effect
/ON/: /A/ dokun- 2. *96:16a.*
unpleasure: - distress; *393:9.*
impairment: - impair; *809:9.* disorder:
- disorder.

- make sick, - make sick TO ONE'S
STOMACH [subj.: food]: midesini
boz- → boz- 1. *96:16a.* unpleasure: -
distress; *393:9.* impairment: - impair;
809:9. disorder: - disorder.

- make a SIGN or gesture for sb to do sth: /A/ işaret et- 3. *517:22.* signs, indicators: - signal.
- make a STATEMENT, - testify, - give testimony, evidence /to/ [law]: /A/ ifade ver- → ver- 1. *956:9.* evidence, proof: - testify.
- make /θ/ sb SUFFER: → - make TROUBLE.

- make a [TELE]PHONE CALL /to/, - phone /θ/, - call up, - ring up [Let me make a phone call to my mother.]: /A/ telefon {et-/aç-}. *347:18.* communications: - telephone.
- make a [telephone] call /TO/, - place a call /TO/ [To the operator: I would like to make a call {to Ankara/to Kemâl Şahin, whose number is 512 34 58}].: /lA/ görüş- 2. *347:18.* communications: - telephone.
- make a collect [(TELE)PHONE] CALL /to/, - call collect: ödemeli ara- → ara- 2. *347:18.* communications: - telephone.
- make sth EASY /FOR/, - facilitate matters /FOR/, - give sb a break, - help /θ/: /A/ kolaylık göster- → göster- 1. *449:11.* aid: - aid; *1013:7.* facility: - facilitate.
- make THINK OF, - bring to mind, - remind of [Associations with places or events rather than similarities bring sb or sth to mind: 'That restaurant where we used to meet makes me think of you.']: {hatırlat-/anımsat-} 4. *988:20.* memory: - remind.
- make TIRED, - tire [exam makes student tired]: yor-. *21:4.* fatigue: - fatigue.
- make one's TOILET, i.e., usually for a woman to dress or to arrange her hair; - have a bowel movement *or* BM, - urinate: tuvalet yap- → yap- 3. *12:13.* excretion: - defecate; *12:14.* : - urinate.
- make TROUBLE, - make or - create difficulties /FOR, on account of/: /A, DAn dolayı/ {güçlük/zorluk} çıkar- [authorities create difficulties] → çıkar- 7. *1012:14.* difficulty: - cause trouble.
- make trouble /FOR/, - cause /θ/ sb to suffer, - cause /θ/ sb trouble [This child has made a lot of trouble for me.]: /A/ çektir- 4. *96:16a.* unpleasure: - distress; *98:15.* unpleasantness: - vex.

- make UP, - invent, - dream up, - concoct, - think up [story, lie]: uydur- 2. *354:18.* falseness: - fabricate.

- make oneself up, - put on makeup: makyaj yap- → yap- 3. *1015:15.* beauty: - beautify.
- make up or - prepare a BED for sb: yatağını yap- 2 → yap- 3. *405:6.* preparation: - prepare.
- make [up] one's BED: yatağını {topla-/düzelt-/yap-} → topla- 2, düzelt- 3, → yatağını yap- 1 → yap- 3. *807:12.* arrangement: - tidy, tidy up.
- make up FOR A DEFICIENCY IN A COURSE, - pull up one's grade in a course: ders düzelt- → düzelt- 2, not düzelt- → düzelt- 2. *396:13.* restoration: - remedy.
- make up FOR LOST TIME ON, - catch up on, [homework after getting behind]: yetiştir- 3. *338:4.* compensation: - compensate.
- make up one's MIND /to/, - decide /to/, - make a decision /to/, - resolve /to/: /A/ karar ver- → ver- 1. *359:7.* resolution: - resolve.
- make up WITH sb [after a quarrel], - come to an understanding /with/, - make peace /with/: /lA/ barış-. *465:10.* pacification: - make up.
- make USE OF, - use /AS, in a [certain] way/: /olarak, yönde/ kullan-. *387:10.* use: - use.

- make or let sb WAIT, - keep sb waiting: beklet-. *845:8.* lateness: - delay.
- make WET, - wet, - moisten: ıslat-. *1063:12.* moisture: - moisten.
- make or - have /θ/ sb WORK, - allow sb to work, - work sb: /I/ çalıştır- 1 a). *424:4.* compulsion: - compel.
- make or - have /θ/ sb WORK on sth; - tutor /θ/ sb: /A/ çalıştır- 1 b). *424:4.* compulsion: - compel; *568:11.* teaching: - tutor.

- MANAGE, - administer, - direct, - run, - control, - rule, - govern: idare et- 1, yönet- 1. *573:8.* direction, management: - direct.
- manage TO GET, usually in the face of difficulty, - wrangle, - get sth /OUT OF/ sb [permission]: /DAn/ {kopar- 3/kopart- 3}. *192:10.* extraction: - extract.
- manage to get AWAY /FROM/, - shake off [an annoying person, flies]: /DAn/ kurtul- 1. *431:8.* liberation: - free oneself from.
- manage to SCRAPE TOGETHER or to come up with [some things needed in the last minute: clothes for a party]: /I/ uydur- 3. *769:18.* assemblage: - bring or - gather together.

- manage /WITH/, - manage to get along /with/, - get by /with/; - make ends meet /with/ [very little money], - economize /BY/: /lA/ idare et- 2, /lA/ yetin- 2. *409:12.* success: - manage; *994:4.* expedience: - make shift, - make do.

- MANUFACTURE, - produce [goods]: üret- 1. *891:8.* production: - produce, - create.

- MARK [places in a book]: /I/ işaretle-. *348:5.* manifestation: - manifest; *517:19.* signs, indicators: - mark.
- mark, - mark up, - put notations /IN/ [a book]: /A/ işaret koy- → koy- 1. *517:19.* signs, indicators: - mark.
- mark [an exam], - give a grade or mark /to/ sb or sth, - give /θ/ sb or sth a grade, - grade /θ/ sb, sth: /A/ not ver-. → ver- 1. *945:9.* judgment: - estimate.

- MARRY /θ/ sb, - get married /TO/ [He {married θ/got married /TO/} his girlfriend.]: /lA/ e v l e n-, /lA/ dünya evine gir- → gir-. *563:15.* marriage: - get married.
- marry [The priest married the couple.], - give sb in marriage /TO/ [Kemâl Bey gave his younger daughter in marriage TO a doctor.]: /lA/ evlendir-. *563:14.* marriage: - join in marriage.
- marry, - perform the civil marriage ceremony, - officially join in marriage [subj.: civil official]: nikâh kıy- → kıy- 3. *563:14.* marriage: - join in marriage.

- MASH, - crush, - grind, - pulverize: ez-. *1049:9.* powderiness, crumbliness: - pulverize.

- MASTER a field of knowledge [She has really mastered Turkish.]: çok iyi öğren- [lit., '- learn very well'] → öğren- 1. *570:9.* learning: - master.

- MATCH /θ/, - go [well] /WITH/, - look good /WITH/ [new curtains with furniture]: /lA/ iyi git- → git- 6, /A/ uy- 3. *866:3.* conformity: - conform.

not - MATTER, - be of NO importance /to/: /için/ farketME- → farket- 2. *997:9.* unimportance: - be unimportant.

- MATURE, - develop physically: geliş- 1. *259:5.* expansion, growth: -

become larger; *860:5.* evolution: - evolve.
- mature, - reach, or - attain /θ/ maturity, - grow up [subj.: person]: olgunluğa er- → er-. *303:9.* age: - mature; *407:8.* accomplishment: - ripen.

MAY EVERYTHING TURN OUT AS YOU WISH., I hope everything turns out the way you want it to.: Herşey gönlünüzce olsun! → ol- 11 → olsun. *504: * 20.* courtesy: polite expressions.

May GOD BE PLEASED [WITH YOU]: Allah [sizden] razı olsun. → razı ol- 2 → ol- 12. *95:11.* pleasure: - be pleased; *150:6.* gratitude: INTERJ. thanks!; *509:9.* approval: - approve.

May God DAMN HIM!: Allah belâsını versin. → ver- 1. *513:11.* curse: INTERJ. damn!

May God GRANT [YOU] GOOD HEALTH: Allah sağlık versin. → ver- 1. *504: * 20.* courtesy: polite expressions.

May God HAVE MERCY UPON HIM [i.e., on the deceased so that he may go to Paradise, said upon hearing of the death of a Muslim, today sometimes also of a non-Muslim.]: Allah rahmet eylesin. → rahmet eyle-. *145:4.* pity: - have pity; *307: * 39.* death: expressions used upon hearing of a death; *504: * 20.* courtesy: polite expressions; *601:4.* acquital: - acquit.

May God HELP US: Allah yardımcımız olsun. → ol- 3, Additional examples. a) 3. Selected examples...: olsun. *1007:18b.* protection: expressions to protect against misfortune; *1011: * 22.* hindrance: expressions to prevent unfavorable occurrences.

May God MAKE IT EASY FOR YOU. [A phrase that should be said to sb hard at work]: Allah kolaylık versin! → ver- 1. *504: * 20.* courtesy: polite expressions.

May God PRESERVE HIM [from misfortune].: Allah {korusun/ saklasın}. → koru, sakla- 4. *504: * 20.* courtesy: polite expressions; *1007:18b.* protection: expressions to protect against misfortune; *1011: * 22.* hindrance: expressions to prevent unfavorable occurrences.

May God RESTORE HIM TO HEALTH: Allah şifa versin! → şifa ver- → ver- 1. *86:38.* remedy: - remedy; *396:15.* restoration: - cure; *504: * 20.* courtesy: polite expressions.

May God REUNITE YOU [said to those remaining behind after sb has departed on a journey]: **Allah kavuştursun!** → kavuştur-. *504: * 20.* courtesy: polite expressions.

May God SAVE HIM: **Allah kurtarsın.** → kurtar-. *398:3.* rescue: - rescue.

May HE REST IN PEACE [said of the deceased]: **Huzur içinde rahat uyusun!** → uyu- 1. *22:13.* sleep: - sleep, **Nur içinde yat.** 'May he rest in peace [lit, in light].' → yat- 1, **Toprağı bol olsun.** [lit., 'May his earth be abundant', said upon hearing of the death of a non-Muslim, today sometimes also of a Muslim]. → ol- 11 → olsun. *307: * 39.* death: expressions used upon hearing of a death; *504: * 20.* courtesy: polite expressions.

May HIS [ETERNAL] RESTING PLACE BE PARADISE.: **Mekânı cennet olsun.** → ol- 11 → olsun. *307: * 39.* death: expressions used upon hearing of a death; *504: * 20.* courtesy: polite expressions.

May IT BE BLESSED.: **Kutlu olsun!** a formula of congratulation for religious as well as other, non-religious, official holidays → ol- 11 → olsun, **Mübarek olsun!** a formula of congratulation exclusively for religious holidays → ol- 11 → olsun. *149:4.* congratulation: INTERJ. congratulations!; *504: * 20.* courtesy: polite expressions.

May it PASS., May it be PAST. [A phrase that must be said upon hearing of a person's misfortune (illness, accident, etc.).]: **Geçmiş olsun!** → ol- 11 → olsun. *504: * 20.* courtesy: polite expressions.

May it GO EASILY., May it be easy. [A polite expression one should say to anyone engaged in or about to engage in some usually demanding task.]: **Kolay gelsin!** → gel- 1. *504: * 20.* courtesy: polite expressions; *1013:10.* facility: - go easily.

May it go WELL., May it be beneficial., Congratulations: /A/ **Hayırlı olsun!** → ol- 11 → olsun. *133:13.* premonition: - promise; *149:4.* congratulation: INTERJ. congratulations!; *387:17.* use: - avail; *504: * 20.* courtesy: polite expressions.

May YOU ALWAYS ENJOY ABUNDANCE! [Words said to a hostess after a meal or to a person who, when with friends, has paid the bill]: **Ziyade olsun!** → ol- 11 → olsun. *8:35.* eating: INTERJ. chow down!; *504: * 20.* courtesy: polite expressions.

May you ENJOY GOOD HEALTH., Good health to you. [A formula used to address sb after he has had a shave, haircut, bath]: **Sıhhatler olsun!** → ol- 11 → olsun. *504: * 20.* courtesy: polite expressions.

May you SUFFER THE GREATEST MISERY! [A harsh curse]: **Sürüm sürüm sürünürsün inşallah.** → sürün- 2. *513:11.* curse: INTERJ. damn!

Maybe: **bakarsın[ız]** → bak- 1. *965:9.* possibility: ADV. possibly.

- MEAN [What does this word mean?]: **de- 3, ifade et- 2.** *518:8.* meaning: - mean. 1/13/2005 12:49 AM
- mean, - signify, - express [subj.: sign, picture, word]: **ifade et- 2.** *517:17.* signs, indicators: - signify; *518:8.* meaning: - mean.
- mean, - have in mind, - intend to say /BY/ [That's not what I meant.]: /1A, DAn/ **kastet- 1.** *380:4.* intention: - intend; *519:4.* latent meaningfulness: - imply.
- mean A LOT /TO/, - be valuable /to/ [Your friendship means a lot to me.]: /A/ **ifade et- 3.** *996:12.* importance: - matter.
- mean, - intend, - aim, - plan, or - make up one's mind /TO/ DO sth: /A/ **niyet et-.** *359:7.* resolution: - resolve; *380:4.* intention: - intend to.
- MEASURE: **ölç-.** *300:10.* measurement: - measure.

- MEDDLE /IN/, - interfere /WITH/ [sb's business]: /A/ **burnunu sok- 1** ['- stick one's nose /{IN/INTO}/'] → sok- 1, /A/ **karış- 5.** *214:5.* intrusion: - intrude.

- MEET, - go to meet, - welcome, - greet sb /at [a place], with/: /DA, 1A/ **karşıla- 1.** *769:16.* assemblage: - come together.
- meet, - come together [individuals, usually after an arrangement to meet has been made]: /1A/ **buluş-.** *769:16.* assemblage: - come together.
- meet, - convene, - come together [groups, societies]: **bir araya gel-** → gel- 1, **toplan- 3.** *769:17.* assemblage: - convene.
- meet sb, - become acquainted /WITH/ sb, - get to know sb, - make the acquaintance of sb: /I/ **tanı- 3.** *587:10.* friendship: - befriend, - make friends with.

565

- meet, - get acquainted /with/ ONE ANOTHER: **birbirini tanı-** → tanı- 3, **/lA/ tanış-**. *587:10*. friendship: - befriend, - make friends with.

- meet AGAIN after a long absence, - be reunited /WITH/, - meet, - come together [persons]: **/A/ kavuş-** 1. *799:11*. joining: - be joined.

- meet /θ/ BY CHANCE, - bump or - run /INTO/, - come or - chance /UPON/, - encounter /θ/: **/lA/ karşılaş-** 2, **/A/ rastla-** 1, *formal:* **/A/ tesadüf et-** 1. *131:6*. inexpectation: - be unexpected; *223:11*. nearness: - meet.

- meet EXPENSES, - finance, - pay for: **masraf gör-** → gör- 4, **masraf karşıla-** → karşıla- 2. *729:15*. finance, investment: - finance.

- meet a NEED: **ihtiyaca cevap ver-** → ver- 1, **ihtiyaç karşıla-** → karşıla- 2. *990:4*. sufficiency: - suffice.

- meet ONE ANOTHER: **/lA/ karşılaş-** 1 [people], 4 [sports teams]. *457:18*. contention: - compete; *769:16*. assemblage: - come together.

- meet /WITH/; - confer /with/, - discuss /with/: **/lA/ görüş-** 1. *524:20*. speech: - speak; *541:11*. conversation: - confer.

- meet /with/ difficulties, - encounter, - face, or experience /θ/ difficulties: **{zorlukla/güçlükle} karşılaş-** 3, **/A/ uğra-** 2. *216:8*. front: - confront; *830:8*. event: - experience; *1012:11*. difficulty: - have difficulty.

- MELT [subj.: ice, snow], - dissolve /in/ [subj.: sugar in water]: **/DA/ eri-**. *34:2a*. disappearance: - disappear; *805:3*. disintegration: - disintegrate; *1062:5*. liquefaction: - liquefy.

- melt, - dissolve, - liquefy, - cause to become liquid [Melt some butter.]: **erit-**. *1019:21*. heating: - melt; *1062:5*. liquefaction: - liquefy.

- MEMORIZE, - commit to memory, - learn by heart: **ezberle-**. *988:17*. memory: - memorize.

- MEND [socks, sweater]: **onar-**. *396:14*. restoration: - repair.

- MENSTRUATE, - have one's period: **âdet gör-** → gör- 3, **aybaşı ol-** → ol- 10.1. *12:18*. excretion: - menstruate.

- MENTION /θ/, - talk /ABOUT/, - discuss /θ/: **/DAn/ bahset-, /DAn/ söz et-, sözünü et-**. *541:12*.

conversation: - discuss; *551:8*. information: - inform.

- mention /θ/ a subject, - touch /ON/ a subject: **/A/ değin-, /A/ temas et-** 2. *524:25*. speech: - remark.

- MEOW [cats]: **miyavla-**. *60:2*. animal sounds: - cry.

- MERIT, - deserve: **/I/ hak et-**. *639:5*. dueness: - deserve.

- MESS UP, - put into disorder: **dağıt-** 3 [children mess up house, wind messes up hair], **karıştır-** 4 [child messes up room]. *810:2*. disarrangement: - disarrange.

- MIGRATE /from, to/: **/DAn, A/ {göç et-/göç-}**. *177:22*. travel: - migrate.

- MINCE, - grind [up], - chop up fine, - cut up fine [vegetables, meat]: **kıy-** 1. *792:6*. part: - separate; *801:13*. separation: - shatter.

- mince, - chop into bits; - cut [up] into slices or pieces: **doğra-**. *792:6*. part: - separate; *801:13*. separation: - shatter.

- MIND, - object to [Do you mind if I smoke?], for there - be an objection to: **{sakıncası/mahzuru} ol-** → ol- 12. *333:5*. dissent: - object.

not - MIND, care /ABOUT/, or pay attention /to/: **aldırış etME-, /A/ aldırMA-** 2. *340:6*. neglect: - neglect; *997:9*. unimportance: - be unimportant.

not - mind or care [I don't mind. It doesn't matter to me.]: **/için/ fark etME-**. *997:9*. unimportance: - be unimportant.

not - mind, not - bother one [I don't mind noise.]: **rahatsız etME-** → rahatsız et-, **rahatsız olMA-** → rahatsız ol- 2 → ol- 10.2. *96:13*. unpleasure: - annoy.

- MINIMIZE, - belittle, - underrate, - underestimate: **küçümse-** 2. *252:9*. decrease: - minimize.

- MISBEHAVE, - be naughty: **yaramazlık {yap-/et-}** → yap- 3. *322:4*. misbehavior: - misbehave.

- MISLEAD, - deceive, - fool, - take in: **kandır-** 1. *356:14*. deception: - deceive.

- MISS, - long for [after an absence], - yearn for: **/I/ ara-** 4, **/A/ hasret çek-** → çek- 5, **/I/ özle-**. *100:16*.

desire: - wish for; *991:7*. insufficiency: - want.

- miss, - be too late for a vehicle, event, or a meeting with a person: **kaçır-** 1. *410:14.* failure: - miss; *843:5* untimeliness: - miss an opportunity.
- miss, - be absent /from/ [Ahmet never misses a party.]: **/DAn/ eksik ol-** → ol- 12. *222:7.* absence: - be absent.
- miss an opportunity, - let an opportunity slip away or go by: **fırsat kaçır-** → kaçır- 2. *410:14.* failure: - miss; *843:5.* untimeliness: - miss an opportunity.
- miss, not - hear or - catch what sb has said: **kaçır-** 1. *48:11.* hearing: - hear; *410:14.* failure: - miss; *843:5.* untimeliness: - miss an opportunity.
- miss, - overlook, - escape one's eye or notice [You have missed this error.], - be overlooked, not - be noticed [This error has been overlooked.]: **gözden kaç-** → kaç- 1. *983:2.* inattention: - be inattentive.
- miss out on a news story, - miss a scoop: **atla-** 4. *983:2.* inattention: - be inattentive.

- MISTAKE one thing or one person /FOR/ another: **/A/ benzet-** 1. *974:13.* error: - mistake, - make a mistake.

- MISUNDERSTAND: **yanlış anla-.** *342:2.* misinterpretation: - misinterpret.

- MIX sth /INTO/ sth [water into milk], - add sth /to/ sth [salt to soup]: **/A/ kat-.** *253:5.* addition: - add to.
- mix sth /WITH/ sth else, - stir, - blend [eggs and sugar]: **/lA/ karıştır-** 1. *796:10a.* mixture: - mix sth.
- mix UP or - confuse sb or sth /with/ sb or sth else: **/lA, A/ karıştır-** 2. *810:3.* disarrangement: - confuse; *944:3.* indiscrimination: - confound.

- MOB /θ/ a place, - rush as a group /to/ a place, - throng /to/ [When the weather was hot, the people mobbed θ the beaches.]: **/A/ hücum et-** 2. *769:16.* assemblage: - come together.

- MOCK /θ/, - make fun /OF/ - ridicule /θ/: **/lA/ alay et-, /I/ alaya al-** → al- 1, **/lA, diye/ dalga geç-** 2 → geç- 1. *508:8.* ridicule: - ridicule.
- mock /θ/, - laugh /AT/ [ridicule], - make fun /OF/: **/A/ gül-** 2. *508:8.* ridicule: - ridicule.

- MOISTEN, - wet, - make wet: **ıslat-.** *1063:12.* moisture: - moisten.

MOREOVER, besides, anyhow, anyway: **kaldı ki** 1 → kal- 1. *384:10.* manner, means: ADV. anyhow.

- MOUNT /θ/ [obj.: animal: horse], - get /ON/, - get on board, - board /θ/ [obj.: vehicle: bus]: **/A/ bin-** 1. *193:12.* ascent: - mount.
- mount or - go up /BY WAY OF [stairs], to/, - ascend, - climb: **/DAn, A/ çık-** 5. *193:11.* ascent: - climb.

- MOURN, - be in mourning: **yas tut-** → tut- 5. *112:17.* sadness: - grieve; *115:10.* lamentation: - lament; *434:2.* observance: - observe.

- MOVE, - carry, - transport sth /from, to/: **/DAn, A/ taşı-.** *176:12.* transferal, transportation: - transport.
- move [I'm so tired I can't move.]: **hareket et-** 1. *172:5b.* motion: for sth - move.
- move or - change one's place of residence or business /from, to/: **/DAn, A/ taşın-.** *159:17.* location: - settle; *176:12.* transferal, transportation: - transport.
- move, - touch, - affect /θ/ sb emotionally [subj.: the director's farewell speech]; - disturb, - upset /θ/ sb [subj.: a person's inappropriate words]: **/A/ dokun-** 3. *93:14.* feelings: - affect; *893:7.* influence: - influence.
- move AWAY [to another neighborhood, city: He got a job in another city, so he moved away.]: **[buradan] taşın-**. *188:6.* departure: - depart.
- move BACK, - fall back, - retreat: **gerile-** 1. *163:6.* regression: - retreat.
- move back [return to a previous residence after having moved away]: **geri taşın-.** → taşın-. *163:6.* regression: - retreat.
- move FORWARD, - advance /THROUGH, toward/ [subj.: procession]: **/DAn, A doğru/ ilerle-** 1. *162:2.* progression: - progress.
- move sth forward [Move your car forward a bit.]: **ilerlet-** 1. *172:5a.* motion: - move sth; *903:9.* pushing, throwing: - push.
- move IN [a new residence: She moved in yesterday morning.]: **/A/ taşın-.** *159:17.* location: - settle.
- move ON TO a new subject, - bring up or - raise a subject, topic: **konu aç-** → aç- 10. *817:12.* beginning: - open.
- move OUT [of a residence: After the fight, she moved out.]: **/DAn/ taşın-**. *188:6.* departure: - depart.

- move OVER, - slide over /to/ [Move over a bit so I can see the screen better.]: /A/ kay- 1. *177:35.* travel: - glide; *194:9.* descent: - slide.
- move SLIGHTLY, - budge, - stir: {kımılda-/kıpırda-}. *1 7 2 : 5 b.* motion: for sth - move.
- move UP in time, - make earlier than originally planned [meeting]: öne al- → al- 1. *163:8a.* regression: - turn sth back.

- MOW, - reap /with/: /lA/ biç- 2. *1067:19.* agriculture: - harvest.

- MULTIPLY, - increase, - proliferate /by...ing/ [subj.: almost exclusively living things: Cells multiply by dividing.]: /ArAk/ çoğal-, /ArAk/ üre-. *78:7.* reproduction, procreation: - reproduce; *251:6.* increase: - grow, increase [i.].
- multiply /BY/ [mathematics: 4 x 6]: /lA/ çarp- 3. *1016:17.* mathematics: - calculate.

- MURDER, - commit murder, homicide: cinayet işle- → işle- 2. *308:15.* killing: - murder.

MUST BE [He must be a foreigner.], *inference*: {olsa gerek/olmalı} → ol- 11. *967:4.* probability: - be probable.

- N -

- NAME, - call, - refer to /AS/: /diye/ {adlandır-/isimlendir-}, /A/ de- 4. *527:11.* nomenclature: - name.
- name /θ/, - give a name /to/: /A/ {ad/isim} koy- → koy- 1, /A/ {ad/isim} ver- → ver- 1, /A/ {ad/isim} tak- [usually derogatory, in reference to a person, i.e., - give a nickname or other similar appellation]. *527:11.* nomenclature: - name.
- name, - appoint, - assign sb /to [a position], AS [a teacher]/: /A, olarak/ {ata-/tayin et-}. *615:11.* commission: - appoint.

NAMED, called, by the name of: diye 6 → de- 1. *527:14.* nomenclature: ADJ. named.

- NEED /θ/, - require /θ/, - have need /{OF/FOR}/ [I need θ some money.]: /A/ ihtiyacı ol- → ol- 12. *962:9.* necessity: - require.
- need, - require, - be necessary [non-person subject: This food needs to

cook more.]: gerektir-, iste- 3. *962:9.* necessity: - require.

- NEGLECT, - let slide, - slight, not - pay attention to, - fail to do sth, - omit: ihmal et-. *340:6.* neglect: - neglect.

NEVER mind!, Forget it!: Boş ver. → boş ver- 1 → ver- 1. *997:25.* unimportance: PHR. no matter.

NICE going!, Bravo!, Good for {him/you}!: Çok yaşa! 2 → yaşa- 1, Aşkolsun! 2 → ol- 11 → olsun, Helâl olsun! 2 → ol- 11 → olsun. *116:2.* rejoicing: cheer; *149:4.* congratulation: INTERJ. congratulations!; *509:22.* approval: INTERJ. bravo!
NO harm done., It doesn't matter.: zararı yok →→ ol- 3, Additional examples. b) 4. Miscellaneous additional examples. *997:25.* unimportance: PHR. no matter.
No matter what, In any case, Anyway, Come what may: Ne olursa olsun → ol- 11 → olur. *969:26.* certainty: ADV. without fail.
No...ing! [No smoking!]: -mAk yok! → 3, Additional examples. b) 4. Miscellaneous additional examples. *399: * 9.* warning: expressions of.

- NOSE DIVE /INTO/ the ground, - crash, - crack up [subj.: airplane]: yere çakıl- → çakıl- 2. *184:44.* aviation: - crash.

NOT - be able to believe one's eyes: gözlerine inanaMA- → inan- 1. *954:5.* unbelief: - disbelieve.
not - bother one, not - mind [Noise doesn't bother me.]: rahatsız etME- → rahatsız et-, rahatsız olMA- → rahatsız ol- 2 → ol- 10.2. *96:13.* unpleasure: - annoy.
not - dare /to/ do sth, - be or - feel reluctant, hesitant, embarassed to do sth /in the presence of/, - hesitate /to/: /{A/DAn}/ çekin-. *325:4.* unwillingness: - demur; *362:7.* irresolution: - hesitate.
not - hear or - catch, i.e., - miss what sb has said: kaçır- 1. *48:11.* hearing: - hear; *410:14.* failure: - miss; *843:5.* untimeliness: - miss an opportunity.
not - know what to say, - be at a loss for words: söz bulAMA-. → bul- 1. *51:8.* silence: - silence.
not - matter, - be UNimportant, - make NO difference: fark etME- → farket- 2. *997:9.* unimportance: - be unimportant.

not - mind, not - pay attention to, - disregard, - ignore: **aldırış etME-**. *340:6.* neglect: - neglect; *997:12.* unimportance: - attach little importance to.

not - object, not - raise one's voice /against/: **ses çıkarMA-** → çıkar- 7. *453:3.* resistance:- offer resistance.

not - separate sb from sb else [mother from child], - spare sb's life: **bağışla-** 3. *430:14.* freedom: - exempt; *504: * 20.* courtesy: polite expressions.

not - speak up, not - say anything, - keep quiet: **ses çıkarMA-** 1 → çıkar- 7. *524:22.* speech: - speak up.

not - understand or - grasp, - make NO sense of: **aklı alMA-**. *522:11.* unintelligibility: not - understand.

- NOTE, - remark /on/, - comment /on/, - point out: /I/ **belirt-**, /A/ **dikkat çek-** → çek- 1, /A/ **işaret et-** 2. *524:25.* speech: - remark.

- note, - state, - announce, - declare [*formal, official*: in speech and in writing]: **kaydet-** 4. *334:5.* affirmation: - affirm; *524:24.* speech: - state.

- NOTICE, - observe, - take note /of/: /A/ **dikkat et-** 2, **gözle-** 1. *982:6.* attention: - heed.

- notice, - perceive, - realize: **farket-** 1, **farkına var-**. *27:12.* vision: - see; *940:5.* discovery: - detect; *982:6.* attention: - heed.

- NOURISH, - feed: **besle-** 1. *385:9.* provision, equipment: - provision.

NOW that things have {gone so far/reached this point}: **oldu olacak** → ol- 11. *845: * 21.* lateness: PHR. it's too late.

- NUMBER [obj.: pages, lines], - assign a number /to/: **numarala-**. *1016:16.* mathematics: - number.

- NURSE, - breast-feed, - suckle: /I/ **emzir-**, /A/ **meme ver-** → ver- 1. *8:19.* eating: - nourish.

- O -

[O] God damn [it]!: **Allah kahretsin!** → kahret- 2. *513:11.* curse: INTERJ. damn!

- OBEY, - heed, - listen /TO/: /I/ 1 **dinle-** 2. *326:2.* obedience: - obey.

- obey or - heed what one is told; - act on sb's advice: {lâf/söz} **dinle-** → 1 dinle- 2, **uy-** 6. *326:2.* obedience: - obey.

- OBJECT to, - mind [Do you object if I smoke?], for there - be an objection to: {sakıncası/mahzuru} **ol-** → ol- 12. *152:13.* resentment, anger: - take amiss; *333:5.* dissent: - object.

- object /to/, - raise an objection /{to/AGAINST}/: /A/ **itiraz et-**. *333:5.* dissent: - object; *788:5.* disagreement: - disagree.

- object /to/, - oppose /θ/, - come out /against/, - say no /to/: /A/ **karşı çık-** → çık- 3. *451:3.* opposition: - oppose; *788:5.* disagreement: - disagree.

- OBSERVE, - follow, - monitor, - keep abreast of [events, trends, fashions, TV]: **izle-** 2, **takip et-** 2. *982:5.* attention: - attend to.

- observe or - keep THE FAST, - fast: **oruç tut-** → tut- 5. *434:2.* observance: - observe; *515:4.* fasting: - fast; *701:14.* religious rites: - celebrate.

- OBSTRUCT, - block [The traffic is obstructing the roads.]: {kapa-/kapat-} 5. *293:7.* closure: - stop, - stop up.

- OBTAIN, - acquire, - get /from/: /DAn/ **edin-**, **ele geçir-** 2 → geçir- 1, /DAn/ **elde et-**. *472:8.* acquisition: - acquire.

- obtain /θ/, - acquire /θ/, - get /θ/ sth, - become the owner, possessor /OF/ sth: /A/ **sahip ol-** → ol- 12. *472:8.* acquisition: - acquire.

- obtain, - procure, - get /FOR/, - provide /to/: /A/ **sağla-**. *472:8.* acquisition: - acquire.

- obtain or - receive INFORMATION /from/: /DAn/ **bilgi edin-**. *570:6.* learning: - learn; *927:14.* knowledge: - learn.

- obtain WORD, news /{OF/from}/: /DAn/ **haber al-**. *570:6.* learning: - learn; *927:14.* knowledge: - learn.

- OCCUPY [restroom too long]; - disturb, - bother, - distract [people at work]: **meşgul et-**. *724:10.* occupation: - occupy; *984:6.* distraction: - distract.

- OCCUR, - happen, - take place [event], - go on: **geç-** 3, **ol-** 4. *830:5.* event: - occur.

- occur, - come into being [eclipse]: /DAn/ oluş-. 795:3. composition: - compose.
- occur or - be /AT/ the same time, - fall /ON/ the same {day/hour}, - coincide: /A/ denk düş- 2 → düş- 1. 830:5. event: - occur; 835:4. simultaneity: - coincide.
- occur, - be present, - be found /in/ [words in a text: How often does this word occur in this document?]: /DA/ geç- 8. 221:6. presence: - be present.
- occur, - come up [problem, matter], - break out [battle, war, storm]: çık- 4. 830:5. event: - occur.
- occur /to/ [one's mind], - think of [That didn't occur to me.]: akla gel- → gel- 1. 930:18. thought: - occur to.

OFF with you!: → Beat it!

- OFFEND, - hurt [not physically]: kır- 2. 152:21. resentment, anger: - offend.

- OFFER, - present, or - submit /to/ [obj.: report, petition, thesis]: /A/ sun- 1, /A/ takdim et- 2. 439:4. offer: - offer.
- offer or - serve [food, drink at a party, gathering] /to/ sb, - offer or - serve /θ/ sb sth: /A/ ikram et- 1, /A/ sun- 1. 439:4. offer: - offer; 478:12. giving: - give.
- offer or - express one's CONDOLENCES /to/ [after hearing of sb's death]: /A/ başsağlığı dile- → dile- 1. 121:6. comfort: - comfort.

- OIL, - grease: yağla-. 1054:8. oils, lubricants: - oil.

OK!, Fine., Agreed., All right!: Oldu. → ol- 11. 332:18. assent: INTERJ. yes.
OK., All right., Fine., It's possible., Yes.: Olur. → ol- 4. 332:18. assent: INTERJ. yes; 965:4 possibility: - be possible.

- OMIT, - skip [a lesson, step in a process]: atla- 2. 340:7. neglect: - leave undone.

- OPEN [Open the door.]: aç- 1. 292:11. opening: - open.
- open, - come open [The door opened and the man walked in.]: açıl- 2. 292:11. opening: - open.
- open [When do the schools open?], - begin an academic year, for a [soccer, basketball] season - begin: açıl- 4. 292:11. opening: - open.
- open, - open up [temporarily or permanently; subj.: organization, business]: açıl- 3. 292:11. opening: - open.
- open [subj.: flower], - blossom, - bloom, - flower: aç- 9. 310:32. plants: - flower.
- open a BANK ACCOUNT [subj.: the bank customer]: hesap açtır-. 292:11. opening: - open.
- open a ROAD /to/, - clear a way /to/: /A/ yol aç- 1 → aç- 1. 292:13. opening: - make an opening.

- OPERATE, - work, - run [Can you operate this machine?]: çalıştır- 2. 888:5. operation: - operate sth.
- operate, - run [These buses don't {operate/run} frequently on weekends.]: çalış- 3, işle- 1. 888:7. operation: - be operative.

- OPPOSE /θ/, - come out /against/, - object /to/, - say no /to/: /A/ karşı çık- → çık- 3. 451:3. opposition: - oppose.

- ORDER sth /for/ sb: /{A/için}/ ısmarla- 1. 440:9. request: - request.
- order [goods], - place or - put an order for sth /WITH/ sb: /A/ ısmarla- 2. 440:9. request: - request.
- order, - command, - decree: buyur- 1, emret-. 420:8. command: - command.
- order [usually only when the order is spoken as, for example, in a restaurant or a coffee house]: söyle- 2. 440:9. request: - request.

- ORGANIZE, - plan, - prepare, - arrange [an event: trip, concert]: ayarla- 3, düzenle- 2, {plânla-/tasarla-}. 381:8 plan: - plan; 405:6. preparation: - prepare.
- organize, - put in order, - arrange [sth that is in disorder]: düzenle- 1. 807:8. arrangement: - arrange.

- ORIGINATE, - stem, - emanate, - result, or spring /from/, - be due /TO/: /DAn/ kaynaklan-. 886:5. effect: - result from.

- OSTRACIZE, - cast out, - exclude /from/: /DAn/ dışla-. 772:4. exclusion: - exclude.

- OUTDO [The apprentice outdoes the master.]: geç- 1. 992:9. excess: - exceed.

- OVER + *verb*, as in '- overeat'. Turkish renders the equivalent of many English verbs that begin with 'over' with **daha** 'more', **çok** 'a lot', or **fazla** 'more' plus the Turkish equivalent of the English verb following 'over'. Thus '- overwork' is rendered by **fazla çalış-** lit., '- work a lot' OR '- work TOO MUCH'; '- overeat' is rendered by **fazla yemek ye-** lit., '- eat too much', or '- drink too much' by **fazla iç-**.
An additional degree of intensity may be conveyed by adding **çok** or **pek**: **çok fazla çalış-** lit., '- work much too much'. In this index English verbs that begin with 'over' are listed separately below. The Turkish equivalents will usually be found in the **Turkish-English Dictionary of Verbs** under the Turkish equivalent for the English verb following 'over'. *992:10.* excess: - overdo. → ≠ - underestimate, - underrate.

- OVERCHARGE: **fazla para al-** → para al- → al- 1. *632:7.* expensiveness: - overprice; *992:10.* excess: - overdo.

- OVERCOME, - beat, - defeat: **2 yen-** 1. *412:6.* defeat: - defeat.
- overcome or - survive a difficulty, - get over or - kick an illness, - pull through: **atlat-**. *396:20.* restoration: - recover.

- OVERDO, - overwork: **{çok/fazla} çalış-** 1. *992:10.* excess: - overdo.

- OVEREAT, - eat too much, - overindulge [in food]: **[çok] fazla yemek ye-** → ye- 1. *992:10.* excess: - overdo.

- OVERESTIMATE [the importance, amount, number of]: **fazla tahmin et-** → tahmin et- 2. *948:2.* overestimation: - overestimate; *992:10.* excess: - overdo.

- OVERFLOW, - run over [subj.: water, things in closet]: **taş- 2, boşal-** 2. *238:17b.* stream: - overflow.

- OVERHEAT, - become too hot [car motor]: **fazla ısın-** → ısın- 1, **araba su kaynat-** → kaynat-. *992:10.* excess: - overdo; *1019:17b.* heating: - get hot.

- OVERINDULGE: **fazla yemek ye-** ['- eat too much'] → ye- 1, **fazla iç-** ['- drink or - smoke too much'] → iç- 1, 2. *992:10.* excess: - overdo.

- OVERLOOK, - escape one's eye or notice, - miss [You have overlooked this error.], - be overlooked, not - be noticed [This error has been overlooked.]: **gözden kaç-** → kaç- 1. *983:2.* inattention: - be inattentive.
- overlook /θ/, - disregard /θ/, - close one's eyes /to/, - take no notice /OF/, - turn a blind eye /to/, - wink /AT/ a fault: /A/ **göz yum-** 2. *148:4.* forgiveness: - condone; *983:2.* inattention: - be inattentive.

- OVERSLEEP, - sleep too much, - sleep a lot: **çok uyu-** → uyu- 1. *22:13.* sleep: - sleep; *992:10.* excess: - overdo.

- OVERSTATE, - exaggerate, - make too much of: **abart-, büyüt-** 2. *355:3.* exaggeration: - exaggerate; *992:10.* excess: - overdo.

- OVERTAKE /θ/, - catch up /WITH/, - go fast enough to join /θ/: /A/ **yetiş-** 2. *174:13.* swiftness: - overtake.

- OVERTHROW [REGIME, government]: **devir-** 2. *395:20.* destruction: - overthrow.

- OVERTURN [dish], - knock over [tree]: **devir-** 1. *395:19.* destruction: - raze.

- OVERWORK, - work too much: **{çok/fazla} çalış-** 1. *992:10.* excess: - overdo.
- OWE /θ [sb], θ [an amount]/, - get into debt /to [sb], {θ/for} [an amount]/: /A, θ/ **borçlan-**. *623:5.* debt: - owe.

- P -

- PACK [UP], - prepare one's bags [He packed his suitcase.]: **bavulunu hazırla-**. *212:9.* enclosure: - package.

- PAINT, - color sth /θ/ a color: /A/ **boya-**. *35:13.* color: - paint.

- PALE, - turn or - grow pale: **sarar-** 2. *36:6.* colorlessness: - lose color.

- PALPITATE, - pound, - race [subj.: heart]: **{kalbi/yüreği} hızlı hızlı**

at-[or çarp-] → at- 7, çarp- 2.
916:12. agitation: - flutter.

- PANIC, - lose one's cool, - get or - be
excited [negative emotion], upset,
agitated, nervous: **heyecanlan-** 2.
96:16b. unpleasure: - be distressed;
128:6. nervousness: - fidget.

- PARDON, - excuse, - forgive sb /for,
because of/: **/DAn dolayı, DIğI
için/ affet-** 2, **/I/ bağışla-** 2.
148:3a. forgiveness: - forgive.
Pardon me., Excuse me., I'm sorry.:
Affedersiniz. [for getting sb's
attention and for apologizing] →
affet- 2, **Özür dilerim.** [only for
apologizing] → dile- 2, **Kusura
bakma.** [only for apologizing] →
bak- 1. *148:3b.* forgiveness:
expressions requesting forgiveness.

- PARK /{AT/in}/{AT/in}/ [obj.:
vehicle]: **/{A/DA}/ park et-.**
159:12. location: - place.

- PART company /WITH/, - break up
/WITH/, - separate from one another:
/DAn/ ayrıl- 1. *801:19.* separation:
- part company.

- PARTICIPATE /IN/, - take part /IN/
[meeting]: **/A/ katıl-** 2. *476:5.*
participation: - participate.
- participate /IN/, - get involved /IN/, -
take up [*colloq. Turkish*, when the
activity is sth unexpected, often
foreign: the game of golf for most
Turks]: **/A/ burnunu sok-** 2 →
sok- 1. *476:5.* participation: -
participate.

- PASS [obj.: the salt and pepper]: **ver-
1, uzat-** 2. *478:12.* giving: - give;
478. :13: - deliver.
- pass, - promote [obj.: students in a
course]: **/DAn/ geçir-** 1. *446:2.*
promotion: - promote.
- pass or - spread /from [one person], to
[another]/ [subj.: disease]: **/DAn, A/
geç-** 2. *770:4b.* dispersion: -
disperse, become dispersed.
- pass, - end, - come to an end, - be over
[difficult situation, illness]: **geç-** 4.
761:6. nonexistence: - cease to exist;
836:6. past: - pass.
- pass AWAY, - die [only for persons]: *all
formal*: **hayata gözlerini {kapa-
/kapat-/yum-}** → {kapa-/kapat-}
1, → göz yum- 2, **hayatını
{kaybet-/yitir-}** ['- lose one's
life', usually of unnatural causes: in

an accident, through murder, etc.],
vefat et-. *307:19.* death: - die.
- pass an EXAMINATION: **{sınav/
imtihan} kazan-** → kazan- 3,
{sınav/imtihan} ver- → ver- 1.
409:7b. success: - succeed in specific
ways.
- pass one's GRADE [i.e., from the fifth
grade to the sixth]: **sınıfını geç-** →
geç- 1. *409:7b.* success: - succeed in
specific ways.
- pass ON, - convey [message, warning]
/to/: **/A/ ilet-** 1, **/A/ aktar-** 1.
176:10. transferal, transportation: -
transfer; *176:15.* : - send.
- pass ONESELF OFF AS SB ELSE:
kendisini başkası olarak tanıt-.
→ tanıt- 1. *354:22.* falseness: - pose
as.
- pass OUT, - lose consciousness, - faint:
bayıl- 1, kendinden geç-1 →
gec- 1, **kendini kaybet-** 1 →
{**kaybet-/yitir-**}, {**şuurunu/
bilincini} kaybet-[or yitir-]** 1 →
{kaybet-/yitir-}. *25:5.* insensibility: -
faint.
- pass out, - fall asleep: **kendinden geç-
3** → geç- 1. *22:16.* sleep: - go to
sleep.
- pass /to/ the {opposite/other} side, -
cross, - cross over [the thing crossed
is not indicated: He {crossed
over/went to the other side}.]:
karşıya geç- → geç- 1. *177:20.*
travel: - traverse.
- pass /THROUGH/: **/DAn/ geç-** 1.
177:20. travel: - traverse.
- pass a vehicle on it's left side [subj.:
driver]: **solla-.** *220:3.* * 1. left side: -
turn left.

- PASTE, - glue, - tape, or - stick sth
/{ON/ONTO/to}/ sth: **/A/ yapıştır-
.** *799:5.* joining: - put together; *802:9.*
cohesion: - stick together.

- PAT, - fondle, - caress, - stroke, - pet:
okşa-, sev- 2. *73:8.* touch: - stroke;
1042:6. friction: - rub.

- PATRONIZE /θ/ [a business
establishment], - shop /AT/, - trade
/AT/: **/DAn/ alışveriş et-.** *731:16.*
commerce, economics: - trade with;
733:8. purchase: - shop.

- PAY /to, for/: **/A, için/ öde-, /A,
için/ para ver-** → ver- 1, **ücret
öde-.** *624:10.* payment: - pay.
- pay [for municipal services: telephone,
electricity, water, gas, etc. The money
is deposited in a special bank

account]: /A/ **para yatır-** 2 →
yatır- 2. *624:10.* payment: - pay.
- pay ATTENTION /to/, - see /to/; - be
careful, - watch out /FOR/: /A/
dikkat et- 1. *339:7.* carefulness: -
be careful; *399: * 9.* warning:
expressions of; *982:5.* attention: -
attend to.
- pay BACK [money], - repay: **geri öde-**
. *624:11.* payment: - repay.
- pay COURT /TO/, - court /θ/, - try to
woo /θ/, - chase /AFTER/, i.e., -
approach with sexual intent: *polite,
formal*: /A/ **kur yap-** → yap- 3.
562:21. lovemaking, endearment: -
court.
- pay the EXPENSES, - put up the money,
- finance: Proper in any context:
masraf gör- → gör- 4, **masraf
karşıla-** → karşıla- 2, *informal,
jocular*: **masraf çek-** ['- foot the
bill'] → çek- 5. *729:15.* finance,
investment: - finance.
- pay IN ADVANCE: **peşin öde-**.
624:10. payment: - pay.
- pay in CASH /to/: /A/ **{nakit/nakit
olarak/nakten}** **öde-**. *624:17.*
payment: - pay cash.
- pay in INSTALLMENTS: **taksitle
öde-**. *624:10.* payment: - pay.
- pay OFF ONE'S DEBTS, - pay off an
account, - pay up, - settle one's debts:
**borcunu öde-, borcunu {kapa-
/kapat-}** → {kapa-/kapat-} 8.
624:13. payment: - pay in full.
- pay RENT [for room, house] /to/: /A/
kira ver- → ver- 1. *624:10.*
payment: - pay.
- pay or - offer one's RESPECTS, - give
or - send one's regards or
compliments /to/: /A/ **saygılar sun-**
→ sun- 1. *155:5.* respect: - do or -
pay hommage to; *504:13.* courtesy: -
give one's regards.
- pay UP, - pay off an account, - settle
one's debts: **borcunu öde-,
borcunu {kapa-/kapat-}** →
{kapa-/kapat-} 8. *624:13.* payment: -
pay in full.
- pay a VISIT, - go on a visit, - go to visit
sb, - call on sb [usually a neighbor or
friend, not a relative or sb of higher
station, a casual, not formal visit]:
misafirliğe git- → git- 3. *582:19.*
sociability: - visit.
- pay a visit /to/ a person or place, - visit, -
call on sb: /I/ **ziyaret et-**. *582:19.*
sociability: - visit.
- pay the zakat: **zekât ver-**. → ver- 1.
624:10. payment: - pay; *701:14.*
religious rites: - celebrate.

- PEE, - piss, - take a {pee/piss}, - urinate:
çiş {yap-/et-} → yap- 3, **işe-,
küçük aptes yap-** → yap- 3, **su
dök-** → dök- 3. *12:14.* excretion: -
urinate.

- PEEL [fruit, vegetable]: **soy-** 1. *6:8.*
unclothing: - peel.

- PEPPER or - spray with fire [i.e.,
bullets], - blaze away at, - strafe, -
rake with shot: **tara-** 3. *459:22.*
attack: - pull the trigger.

- PERCEIVE /θ/, - notice /θ/, - take note
/OF/: /A/ **dikkat et-** 2, /I/ **farket-**
1. *27:12.* vision: - see; *940:5.*
discovery: - detect; *982:6.* attention: -
heed.

- PERCH, - land, - settle, - alight
/{ON/UPON}/ [subj.: bird, insect]:
/A/ **kon-**. *194:7.* descent: - get
down; *194:10.* : - light upon.

- PERFORM, do: [The following four
verbs form phrasal verbs with Arabic
and Turkish nouns and are not
frequently used alone to express '-
perform, do' unless they refer back to
such nouns]: **et-** 1, **eyle-, kıl-** [with
a limited set of nouns], **kıy-** [with a
very limited set of nouns]. *328:6.*
action: - do; *407:4.* accomplishment:
- accomplish.
- perform or - act /IN/ A PLAY OR
MOVIE, - portray a character: /DA/
oyna- 3. *704:29.* show business,
theater: - act.
- perform, - play, or - sing sth /FOR/ sb:
/A/ **sun-** 2. *328:9.* action: - perform;
708:39a. music: - play sth.
- perform, - interpret [piece of music]:
yorumla- 2. *708:39a.* music: - play
sth.
- perform the civil MARRIAGE
CEREMONY, - officially join in
marriage, - marry: **nikâh kıy-** →
kıy- 3. *563:14.* marriage: - join in
marriage.
- perform the NAMAZ, i.e., the Islamic
prayer ritual: **namaz kıl-**. *696:12.*
worship: - pray; *701:14.* religious
rites: - celebrate.
- perform the RITUAL ABLUTION:
aptes al-. *79:19.* cleanness: - wash.

- PERMIT: → - let, allow.
- permit, - let, or - allow sb /{IN/INTO}/ a
place: /A/ **sok-** 2. *189:7.* entrance: -
enter; *443:9.* permission: - permit.

- PERSPIRE, - sweat: **terle-**. *12:16.*
excretion: - sweat.

- PERSIST /IN/, - insist /{ON/UPON}/:
/DA/ diren- 1, /DA/ inat et- 2,
/DA, için/ ısrar et-. *361:7.*
obstinacy: - balk; *421:8.* demand: -
insist.

- persist /IN/ or - insist /ON/ one's own
view, opinion: fikrinde inat et- →
inat et- 2. *361:7.* obstinacy: - balk.

- PERSUADE or - convince sb to believe
/θ/ sb or sth, - get sb to believe /θ/
sth: /A/ inandır-. *375:23.*
motivation, inducement: - persuade;
952:18. belief: - convince.

- persuade or - convince sb /a: to [do sth],
b: θ [that], c: {that/to the effect that},
d: on the subject of/: /a: A, b: A, c:
A dair, d: konusunda/ ikna et-.
375:23. motivation, inducement: -
persuade; *952:18.* belief: - convince.

- persuade or - convince sb /to/ do sth, -
talk sb /INTO/ doing sth: /için/
kandır- 2. *375:23.* motivation,
inducement: - persuade; *952:18.*
belief: - convince.

- PET, - fondle, - caress, - stroke, - pat:
okşa-, sev- 2. *73:8.* touch: - stroke;
1042:6. friction: - rub.

- PHONE /θ/ [sb], from/, - call, - call up, -
make a [phone] call /to, from/: /A,
DAn/ telefon {et-/aç-}. *347:18.*
communications: - telephone.

- phone BACK, - call back: [telefonla]
tekrar ara- → [telefonla] ara- →
ara- 2. *347:18.* communications: -
telephone.

- PHOTOCOPY, - make a photocopy of:
fotokopi çek- → çek- 8. *784:8.*
copy: - copy.

- PHOTOGRAPH, - take {pictures/
photographs}: {resim/fotoğraf}
çek- → çek- 7. *714:14.*
photography: - photograph.

- PICK, - choose, - select sth or sb /FOR/:
/{A/için}/ seç- 1 [for oneself or sb
else], {tercih et-/yeğle-} 2 [for
oneself, not sb else], beğen- 2 [for
oneself, not sb else]. *371:13.* choice: -
choose.

- pick, - pluck [flowers, apples]
/{from/OFF}/: /DAn/ kopar- 1, less
frequent in this sense: kopart- 1.
1067:19. agriculture: - harvest.

- pick or - start a FIGHT /with/, - provoke
a quarrel /with/: /lA/ kavga çıkar-
→ çıkar- 7. *375:17.* motivation,
inducement: - incite; *459:14.* attack: -
attack; *817:7a.* beginning: - begin sth.

- pick UP, - lift, - raise /from/: /DAn/
kaldır- 1. *911:5.* elevation: - elevate.

- pick sth up /from/ [the ground], - take
/from, to/: /DAn, A/ al- 1. *480:21.*
taking: - take from.

- pick up /AT/, - collect sth or sb
/{AT/from}/ [a place], - give sb a lift,
- take on [passengers]: /DAn/ al- 2.
176:16. transferal, transportation: -
fetch.

- pick up sb, - call for sb /AT/ [a place]:
/DAn/ ara- 3. *176:16.* transferal,
transportation: - fetch.

- pick up, - straighten up, - tidy up, - put
in order [room]: düzelt- 3, topla-
2, toparla- 3. *807:12.* arrangement:
- tidy, tidy up.

- pick up, - get, or - answer the PHONE:
telefonU aç- → aç- 5, telefonA
{bak-/cevap ver-} → bak- 3,
cevap ver- → ver- 1. *347:18.*
communications: - telephone; *982:5.*
attention: - attend to.

- PILE or - dump sth /{on/upon}/ sb, -
load sb down /with/ sth, - load sth
down /upon/ sb [obj.: a burdensome
task]: /{üstüne/üzerine}/ yık- 3.
159:15. location: - load.

- pile UP, - be or - get {backed/piled} up
[subj.: traffic]: sıkış- 3. *260:8.*
contraction: - squeeze; *769:19.*
assemblage: - pile.

- PILOT or - fly a plane: uçak kullan-.
184:37. aviation: - pilot.

- PINCH with one's fingers: çimdikle-.
26:7. pain: - inflict pain; *260:8.*
contraction: - squeeze.

- pinch, - be too tight [These shoes
pinch.]: sık- 1. *260:8.* contraction: -
squeeze.

- PISS, - pee, - take a {pee/piss}, - urinate:
çiş {yap-/et-} → yap- 3, işe-,
küçük aptes yap- → yap- 3, su
dök- → dök- 3. *12:14.* excretion: -
urinate.

- PITY /θ/, - feel sorry /FOR/: /A/ acı- 2.
145:3. pity: - pity, - feel sorry for.

- PLACE or - put /{IN/ON}, {on/upon}/:
/A, üzerine/ koy- 1. *159:12.*
location: - place; *191:3.* insertion: -
insert.

- place a CALL /to/, - make a phone call
/TO/: /lA/ görüş- → görüş- 2.
347:18. communications: - telephone.

- place or - put in an ORDER for sth
/WITH/ sb: /A/ ısmarla- 2. *440:9.*
request: - request.

- PLAN, - arrange, - organize, - prepare [an event]: **ayarla-** 3, **düzenle-** 2, {**plânla-/tasarla-**}. *381:8* plan: - plan; *964:4.* prearrangement: - prearrange.

- plan, - aim, - intend, - mean, or - make up one's mind /to/ do sth: **/A/ niyet et-**. *359:7.* resolution: - resolve; *380:4.* intention: - intend.

- PLANT /IN/: **/A/ 2 dik-** 1 [obj.: plants, seedlings, saplings, trees, not seeds], **/A/ ek-** [obj.: seeds, not plants, seedlings, saplings, trees. Also '- sow /IN/']. *1067:18.* agriculture: - plant.

- PLAY: **oyna-** 1 [when the game is specified: I'm playing chess.], **oyun oyna-** 1 [when the game is not specified: She was playing when I came in.] → oyna-1. *743:23.* amusement: - play.

- play, - perform, or - sing sth /FOR/ sb: **/A/ sun-** 2. *328:9.* action: - perform; *708:39a.* music: - play sth.

- play, - run, - be on or showing [subj.: movie or theater production: Where is that movie playing?]: **oyna-** 2. *714:16.* photography: - project; *888:7.* operation: - be operative.

- play or - make a sound [subj.: a wind instrument]: **öt-** 2. *708:39b.* music: - play, - make a sound [i.].

- play AROUND /WITH/, - trifle /with/, i.e., not - take seriously [obj.: sb's affections]: **/1A/ dalga geç-** 3 → geç- 1, **oyna-** 5. *997:14.* unimportance: - trifle.

- play BASKETBALL: **basketbol oyna-** → oyna- 1. *747:4.* basketball: - play basketball.

- play a JOKE or trick /ON/: **/A/ şaka yap-** 1 → yap- 3. *489:14.* wit, humor: - trick.

- play a MUSICAL INSTRUMENT: **çal-** 2. *708:39a.* music: - play sth.

- play ONE ANOTHER, - meet, - compete [sports teams]: **/1A/ karşılaş-** 4. *457:18.* contention: - compete.

- play a ROLE, - portray a character, - perform in a play or movie: **oyna-** 3. *704:29.* show business, theater: - act.

- play SOCCER: **futbol oyna-** → oyna- 1. *752:4.* soccer: - play soccer.

- play a TAPE, CD, record: **çal-** 2. *708:39a.* music: - play sth.

- play TENNIS: **tenis oyna-** → oyna- 1. *748:3.* tennis: - play tennis.

- play a TRICK /ON/: **/{1A/A}/ oyun oyna-** 2 → oyna- 1. *356:15.* deception: - fool.

- play or - watch a VIDEO TAPE: → **seyret-**. *27:13.* vision: - look.

- play WITH ONE ANOTHER: **oynaş-** 1. *743:23.* amusement: - play.

- PLEAD /with [sb], {for/TO}/, - beg /θ/ sb: **/A, için/ yalvar-**. *440:11.* request: - entreat.

- PLEASE sb, - make sb happy /with, by...ing/: **/1A, ArAk/ sevindir-**. *95:8.* pleasure: - gladden.

Please: **Rica ederim.** 1a) In a simple request: Please don't talk. → **rica et-**. *440:9.* request: - request. 1b) In expressing an objection: [Oh] Please, you're mistaken. I said no such thing. → **rica et-**. *333:4.* dissent: - dissent.

Please., Won't you please., Pretty please. [a formula of entreaty]: **N'olursun.** → ol- 11 → **olur**. *440:20.* request: INTERJ. please.

Please come again [words to departing guests]: **Yine bekleriz.** → bekle- 1. *504: * 20.* courtesy: polite expressions.

- PLUCK, - pick [flowers, apples] /{from/OFF}/: **/DAn/ kopar-** 1, less frequent in this sense: **kopart-** 1. *1067:19.* agriculture: - harvest.

- PLUMMET, - plunge, - fall [prices]: **düş-** 3. *633:6b.* cheapness: - become cheaper.

- PLUNGE, - dive /INTO [the ocean], {from/OFF} [the pier]/: **/A, DAn/ dal-** 1. *367:6.* plunge: - plunge.

- plunge into, - begin an activity suddenly: **/A/ dal-** 4: **sohbete dal-** ['- get involved IN, - plunge INTO a friendly conversation']. *541:10.* conversation: - chat; *817:9.* beginning: - enter.

- POINT OUT, - indicate [sb or sth, not a fact, by means of a gesture]: **/I/ işaret et-** 1. *348:5.* manifestation: - manifest; *982:10.* attention: - call attention to.

- point out, - note, - remark /ON/, - comment /ON/ [fact]: **/I/ belirt-**, **/A/ dikkat çek-** → çek- 1, **/A/ işaret et-** 2. *524:25.* speech: - remark.

- point out the way /to/, - show sb how to get to a place: **/A/ yol göster-** 1 → göster- 1. *348:5.* manifestation: - manifest.

- POLLUTE, - dirty, - soil, - get or - make sth dirty: **kirlet-, pislet-**. *80:15a.* uncleanness: - dirty.

- POP OFF, - snap off; - break in two [subj.: thread], - break, - break off, - come off [subj.: button]: **kop-** 1. *801:9.* separation: - come apart.
- pop /OUT OF/ or - escape /from/ one's mouth [subj.: words]: **ağzından lâf kaç-** → kaç- 1. *369:10.* escape: - find vent.

- PORTRAY a character, - play a role in a play or movie: **oyna-** 3. *704:29.* show business, theater: - act.

- POST, - mail, - send off [mail]: /A/ **at-** 4 ['- drop in the mailbox'], **postala-** ['- mail']. *176:15.* transferal, transportation: - send; *553:12.* correspondence: - mail.

- POSTPONE, - put off /{to/TILL/ UNTIL}/, - leave /to/ a later time, - defer: /A/ **bırak-** 6, /A, A kadar/ {**ertele-/tehir et-**}. *845:9.* lateness: - postpone.

- POUND, - race, - palpitate [subj.: heart]: {**kalbi/yüreği**} **hızlı hızlı at-**[or **çarp-**] → at- 7, çarp- 2. *916:12.* agitation: - flutter.

- POUR /from, INTO/, - flow /from, {to/INTO}/ [The water is pouring into the lake.]: /DAn, A/ **ak-**. *190:13.* emergence: - run out; *238:16.* stream: - flow.
- pour sth /from (one place or container), INTO (another)/ [The waiter is pouring the water into the glasses.]: /DAn, A/ **dök-** 1, /DAn, A/ **koy-** 1. *176:17.* transferal, transportation: - ladle.
- pour DOWN, - rain hard, - rain cats and dogs: **bardaktan boşanırcasına yağmur yağ-** → yağ-. *316:9.* rain: - rain.
- pour OUT ONE'S TROUBLES, - spill out one's woes /to/, - get sth off one's chest: /A/ **dert dök-** → dök- 1. *120:7.* relief: - lighten.

- POUT; - put on a sour face, - look annoyed, angry or unhappy; - sulk: **surat as-** → as- 1. *110:14.* ill humor: - sulk; *265:8.* distortion: - grimace.

- PRACTICE a musical instrument, a game [Turhan practices the piano five

hours a day.]: **çalış-** 1. *328:8.* action: - practice.
- practice ORALLY the foreign language one is learning; usually - do oral, conversational practice /by...ing/: /ArAk/ **pratik yap-** → yap- 3. *328:8.* action: - practice.

- PRAISE sb or sth /for/ sth [obj.: not usually God]: /DAn dolayı, için, nedeniyle/ {**öv-/methet-**}. *509:12.* approval: - praise.
- praise /a: θ [God], b: {for/because of}, c: θ [that], - give thanks /a: to [God], b: {for/because of}, c: θ [that]/: /a: A, b: DAn dolayı, c: A/ **şükret-**. *150:4.* gratitude: - thank; *509:12.* approval: - praise.
- praise oneself, - boast, - brag /{OF/ABOUT}/: /lA/ {**övün-/ öğün-**} 2. *502:6.* boasting: - boast.

- PRAY /to/ [in general]: /A/ **dua et-** 1. *696:12.* worship: - pray.
- pray, i.e., - perform the namaz, i.e., the Islamic prayer ritual: **namaz kıl-**. *696:12.* worship: - pray; *701:14.* religious rites: - celebrate.
- pray /to [God], for [sth]/, - supplicate: /A, için/ **dua et-** 2. *440:11.* request: - entreat.

- PREDICT, - make a prediction: /A/ **önceden bildir-** [lit., '- inform /θ/ sb in advance', subj.: ordinary persons and experts, but not usually persons divinely inspired or oracles, etc.], **kehanet et-, kehanette bulun-** [subj. of the last two verbs above: wise men, oracles, fortune-tellers, or soothsayers only] → bulun- 3. *961:9.* prediction: - predict.
- predict, - figure out [how the novel is going to end], - know what to do or say: **kestir-** 2, **tahmin et-** 3. *960:6.* foresight: - foreknow; *961:9.* prediction: - predict.

- PREFER sb or sth /to/ sb or sth else, - like best, - like sb or sth better /than/ sb or sth else: /A/ {**tercih et-/yeğle-**} 1. *371:17.* choice: - prefer.

- PREPARE, - make or - get sth ready /FOR/ [He prepared the room for the guests.]: /{A/için}/ **hazırla-**. *405:6.* preparation: - prepare.
- prepare or - make BREAKFAST: **kahvaltı hazırla-**. *405:6.* preparation: - prepare.
- prepare or - get ONESELF ready /FOR/ [He prepared himself for the exam.]: /{A/için}/ **hazırlan-** 1. *405:13.* preparation: - prepare oneself.

576

- PRESENT, - offer, - submit /to/ [obj.: report, petition, thesis]: /A/ sun- 1, /A/ takdim et- 2. *439:4.* offer: - offer.
- present or - introduce one person /to/ another: /A/ takdim et- 1, /{A/lA}/ tanıştır-. *587:14.* friendship: - introduce.

- PRESERVE, - protect, - shield sb /from/ [misfortune] [subj.: God]: /DAn/ sakla- 4. *504: * 20.* courtesy: polite expressions; *1007:18a.* protection: - protect.

- PRESS /{θ/ON}/, - push /θ/ [button, horn]: /A/ bas- 2. *297:11.* weight: - weigh on; *912:4.* depression: - depress.
- press a key, - enter or - punch in [a PIN or credit card number], - click /ON/: /{I/A}/ tuşla-. *297:11.* weight: - weigh on; *912:4.* depression: - depress.
- press [clothes], - iron: ütüle-. *287:6.* smoothness: - press.
- press or - push one's luck: şansını zorla- → zorla- 2. *971:12.* chance: - risk.

- PRETEND TO: *verb stem.{Ar/mIş}* gibi yap- → yap- 3. *500:12.* affectation: - affect.
- pretend NOT TO, - make as if not to [with certain verbs]: *verb stem.{a: mAzlIktAn/b: mAmAzlIktAn/ c: mAzdAn}* gel- → gel- 1. *500:12.* affectation: - affect.

- PREVENT [accidents], - stop, - hinder sb from doing sth: /I/ engelle-, /A/ mâni ol- → ol- 12, /I/ önle-, önüne geç- → geç- 1. *1011:14.* hindrance: - prevent.
- prevent or - keep sb /from/, - talk sb /OUT OF/ sth, - dissuade or - deter sb /from/: /DAn/ {vazgeçir-/ caydır-}. *379:3.* dissuasion: - dissuade.
- PRIDE ONESELF ARROGANTLY /ON/, - be or - feel arrogantly proud /OF/: /lA/ gurur duy- 2 → duy- 3, /lA/ gururlan-. *136:5.* pride: - take pride; *141:8.* arrogance: - give oneself airs.

- PRINT, - publish: bas- 3. *548:14.* printing: - print.
- print only or both - develop and - print photographic film: film bas- → bas- 3. *714:15.* photography: - process.

- PRIOR /TO/, before [always following a specific time expression: five days prior to the meeting]: /A/ kala 2 → kal- 3. *833:7.* previousness: PREP. prior to.

- PROCEED, - go well or badly: geç- 6, git- 5. *162:2.* progression: - progress.

- PRODUCE, - manufacture [goods]: üret- 1. *891:8.* production: - produce, - create.
- produce, - make a MOVIE [subj.: producer, professional film maker]: film çevir- 2 → çevir- 3. *704:28.* show business, theater: - dramatize; *714:14.* photography: - photograph.

- PROFIT or - benefit /from/, - make good use /OF/, - take advantage /OF/; - utilize /θ/: /DAn/ değerlendir- 2, /DAn/ {yararlan-/faydalan- /istifade et-}. *387:15.* use: - take advantage of.

- PROGRAM a computer /FOR/, - set an instrument /FOR/: /A/ programla- 2. *964:4.* prearrangement: - prearrange; *1041:18.* computer science: - computerize.

- PROHIBIT, - forbid: {yasakla-/yasak et-}. *444:3.* prohibition: - prohibit.

- PROLONG [meeting], - drag out [speech], - extend [hours]: uzat- 3. *267:6.* lengthen: - lengthen.

- PROMISE /θ/ sb sth, - promise sth to sb, - give one's word /to [sb], {about/concerning/that}/: /A, {A dair/için}/ söz ver- → ver- 1, today *less common, more formal:* /A/ vadet-. *436:4.* promise: - promise.

- PROMOTE, - pass [obj.: students in a course]: /DAn/ geçir- 1. *446:2.* promotion: - promote.
- promote the development of; - inspire sb; - encourage sb to do sth or to participate in sth; - encourage or - spur sb on /a: to [lit., in the matter of], b: TO, c: with/: /a: konusunda, b: için, c: lA/ teşvik et-. *375:21.* motivation, inducement: - encourage; *492:16.* courage: - encourage.

- PRONOUNCE [words, sentences]: telâffuz et-. *524:23.* speech: - say.

- PROPOSE, - recommend, or - suggest sth /to/ sb, - advise sb to do sth: /A/

tavsiye et-. *439:5.* offer: - propose; *509:11.* approval: - commend.
- propose, - suggest /to/: /A/ {öner-/teklif et-}. *439:5.* offer: - propose.

- PROTECT /{AGAINST/from}/, - defend: /DAn/ koru-. *460:8.* defend: - defend; *1007:18a.* protection: - protect.
- protect, - preserve, - shield sb /from/ [misfortune] [subj.: God]: /DAn/ sakın- 3, /DAn/ sakla- 4. *1007:18a.* protection: - protect.

- PROTEST sth or against sth: /I/ protesto et-. *333:5.* dissent: - object; *451:3.* opposition: - oppose.

- PROVE, - substantiate: {ispatla-/ispat et-/kanıtla-}. *956:10.* evidence, proof: - prove.
- prove ONESELF, one's worth: {kendini/kendisini} ispatla-[or kanıtla-]. *956:10.* evidence, proof: - prove.

- PROVIDE /to/, - procure, - get, - obtain /FOR/: /A/ sağla-. *472:8.* acquisition: - acquire.
- provide or - give information /to/: /A/ bildir-, /A/ bilgi ver- → ver- 1, /A/ haber ver- → ver- 1. *551:8.* information: - inform.
- provide [a living] for, - support [one's family] /by...ing/: /ArAk/ geçimini sağla-. *385:11.* provision, equipment: - make a living.

- PROVOKE, - incite, - instigate, - foment: tahrik et- 1. *375:17.* motivation, inducement: - incite.
- provoke a QUARREL /with/, - pick or - start a fight /with/: /lA/ kavga çıkar- → çıkar- 7. *375:17.* motivation, inducement: - incite; *459:14.* attack: - attack; *817:7a.* beginning: - begin sth.

- PUBLISH, - print: bas- 3. *548:14.* printing: - print.
- publish [book] /in/: /DA/ yayımla- 1. *548:14.* printing: - print.
- PULL, - tow: çek- 1. *904:4.* pulling: - pull.
- pull ASIDE, - pull off to the side [police address to driver]: kenara çek- → çek- 1. *164:6.* deviation: - avoid.
- pull DOWN, - knock down, - tear down; - demolish, - wreck /with/; - destroy; - ruin [obj.: building]: /lA/ yık- 1. *395:17.* destruction: - demolish.
- pull ONESELF TOGETHER, - regain self-control, - come to one's senses:

kendine gel- 2 → gel- 1. *428:7.* restraint: - restrain.
- pull or - get oneself together; - collect one's thoughts, oneself: kendini toparla- → toparla- 3. *106:7.* inexcitability: - compose oneself.
- pull OUT [of a parking spot], - steer one's vehicle to the left: solla- 2. *220:3.* * *1.* left side: - turn left.
- pull SHUT [curtains]: çek- 4. *293:6.* closure: - close.
- pull THROUGH, - get over or - kick an illness, - overcome or - survive a difficulty: atlat-. *396:20.* restoration: - recover.
- pull UP ONE'S GRADE in a course, - make up for a deficiency in a course: ders düzelt- → düzelt- 2, not düzelt- → düzelt- 2. *396:13.* restoration: - remedy.
- pull or - draw /{UP TO/ALONGSIDE}/ a place: for a ship - dock, a train - draw or - pull up /to/ the platform: /A/ yanaş- 2. *167:3.* approach: - approach.

- PULVERIZE, - crush, - mash, - grind: ez-. *1049:9.* powderiness, crumbliness: - pulverize.

- PUMP UP, - fill with air [tires]: /A/ hava bas- 1 → bas- 2. *793:7a.* completeness: - fill sth.

- PUNCH /θ/ sb: /A/ yumruk {at-/vur-} → at- 5. *901:14.* impulse, impact: - hit.
- punch in or - enter [a PIN or credit card number], - press a key, - click /ON/: /{I/A}/ tuşla-. *297:11.* weight: - weigh on; *912:4.* depression: - depress.

- PUNISH: /I/ cezalandır-, /A/ ceza ver- → ver- 1. *604:10.* punishment: - punish.

- PURCHASE or - buy sth /a: AT [a price, total or per unit], b: AT [a price, per unit], c: AT [a store], d: from [a person]}/: /a: A, b: DAn, c: DAn, d: DAn/ [satın] al- → al- 4. *733:7.* purchase: - purchase.

PURPOSELESSLY, at random, without thinking: olur olmaz 2 → ol- 11. *863:15.* generality: every.

- PURSUE, - chase, - try to catch or get [police pursue thief]: kovala- 1, /a: DAn, b: A, c: arkasına, d: peşine/ koş- ['- run /a: from, b: {to/AFTER}, c: after, d: after/,

pursue'] → koş- 1. *382:8.* pursuit: -
pursue.

- PUSH /θ/ or - press /{θ/ON}/ [button,
horn]: /A/ **bas-** 2. *297:11.* weight: -
weigh on; *912:4.* depression: -
depress.
- push [Don't push! Push the door shut.], -
push /to [the side]/: /A/ **it-**. *901:12.*
impulse, impact: - thrust, - push;
903:9. pushing, throwing: - push.
- push [a child in a swing], - rock [a
cradle]: **salla-** 2. *901:12.* impulse,
impact: - thrust, - push; *903:9.*
pushing, throwing: - push.
- push or - press one's luck: **şansını**
zorla- → zorla- 2. *971:12.* chance: -
risk.

- PUT, - place /{IN/ON}, {on/upon}/: /A/
at- 3 [salt on food], /A, **üzerine/**
koy- 1. *159:12.* location: - place;
191:3. insertion: - insert.
- put ON, - turn on [If the instrument is
already on and you want to make a
change], - switch [TV channel, radio
station], - turn /TO/ [page 5, TV
channel]: /I/ **çevir-** 4 . *371:14.*
choice: - select; *914:9.* rotation: -
rotate.
- put on [TV channel, radio station], - turn
/TO/ [page 2, TV channel], - tune
/{TO/INTO}/ [radio station]: /I/ **aç-**
3. *371:14.* choice: - select; *914:9.*
rotation: - rotate.
- put one's ARMS /AROUND/, -
embrace, - hug, - take in one's arms:
/I/ **kucakla-**, /A/ **sarıl-** 1. *562:18.*
lovemaking, endearment: - embrace.
- put one's arms around ONE
ANOTHER: **birbirlerini kucakla-**
, **kucaklaş-**. *562:18.* lovemaking,
endearment: - embrace.
- put or - set ASIDE /FOR/: /A/ **ayır-** 2,
/A, **için/ koy-** 3. *386:12.* store,
supply: - reserve.
- put AWAY, - put back, - return /to/ its
place, - replace: **yerine koy-** →
koy- 1. *386:10.* store, supply: - store;
390:6. disuse: - put away; *396:11.*
restoration: - restore, - put back.
- put the DATE /{IN/ON}, on/ sth, - date
/θ/ sth [a document]: /A,
{**üzerine/üstüne}/ tarih at-**[or
koy-] → tarih {at-/koy-} → at- 3.
831:13. measurement of time: - date.
- put sth DOWN [Don't keep holding it.
Put it down.]: **bırak-** 5. *159:14.*
location: - deposit.
- put sb down, - hold sb in contempt, -
despise *informal, slang*: - dis, *formal*:
- look down upon, - regard sb or sth
as inferior, - treat with disrespect or

contempt: **küçümse-** 1. *157:3.*
contempt: - disdain.
- put EFFORT /INTO/, - devote effort /to/,
- work /AT/, - take pains /WITH/:
/A/ **emek ver-** → ver- 1. *403:5.*
endeavor: - endeavor.
- put an END TO, - bring to an end, -
conclude, - finish: /I/ **bitir-** 1, /A/
son ver- → ver- 1. *819:5.* end: - end
sth.
- put FORWARD or - advance an idea,
suggestion, proposal: **ileri sür-** 1 →
sür- 1. *439:5.* offer: - propose.
- put /{IN/INTO}/, - insert, - thrust, -
shove, - stick /{IN/INTO}/ [hands
into pocket, one's nose into other
people's affairs]: /A/ **sok-** 1. *191:3.*
insertion: - insert.
- put IN or - place AN ORDER for sth
/WITH/ sb: /A/ **ısmarla-** 2. *440:9.*
request: - request.
- put IN ORDER, - straighten up, - tidy up
[room]: **düzelt-** 3, **topla-** 2,
toparla- 3. *807:12.* arrangement: -
tidy, tidy up.
- put or - get in order, - arrange [affairs,
matters]: **ayarla-** 2. *807:8.*
arrangement: - arrange.
- put in order, - organize, - arrange [sth
that is in disorder: papers]: **düzenle-**
1. *807:8.* arrangement: - arrange.
- put or - arrange IN A ROW or in a
certain order [shoes, files, by size] /a:
from, b: to, c: {according to/by}, d: -
ly/: /a: **DAn**, b: **A**, c: **A göre**, d:
olarak/ sırala-. *807:8.*
arrangement: - arrange.
- put IN RUNNING ORDER, - fix, -
repair: **onar-**, **tamir et-**. *396:14.*
restoration: - repair.
- put [a plan, law, or formula] INTO
PRACTICE, - carry out, - apply /to/, -
follow [directions]: /A/ **uygula-**.
387:11. use: - apply.
- put OFF, - postpone /{to/TILL/
UNTIL}/, - leave /to/ a later time, -
defer: /A/ **bırak-** 6, /A, **A kadar/**
{**ertele-/tehir et-}**. *845:9.* lateness:
- postpone.
- put sb /OFF/ sb or sth, - dampen sb's
enthusiasm /FOR/, - cause sb to lose
love, desire, or enthusiasm /FOR/:
/DAn/ **soğut-** 2. *1011:10.*
hindrance: - hinder.
- put ON [oneself, small items: glasses,
jewelry, seat belts, some headgear,
not other major items of clothing]:
/A/ **tak-**. *5:42.* clothing: - don;
202:8. pendency: - suspend; *799:7.*
joining: - fasten.
- put sth /ON/ sth, - apply sth /to, to the
surface of/, - smear or - rub sth /ON/
[put cream ON skin]: /A,

{üstüne/üzerine}/ sür- 4. *295:19.* covering: - cover.

- put on CLOTHING, - don [Also: - BE wearing], - put sth /ON/ [a part of the body: He had put a hat on his head.]: /A/ giy-. *5:42.* clothing: - don.
- put on MAKEUP, - make oneself up: makyaj yap- → yap- 3. *1015:15.* beauty: - beautify.
- put food /ON/ sb's PLATE, - serve [out] food /to/: /A/ koy- 2. *159:12.* location: - place; *176:17.* transferal, transportation: - ladle; *478:12.* giving: - give.
- put on a SOUR FACE, - look annoyed, angry, or unhappy; - sulk; - pout: surat as- → as- 1. *265:8.* distortion: - grimace; *110:14.* ill humor: - sulk.
- put sb /ON/ a VEHICLE [bus, plane] or on a mount [horse]: /A/ bindir-. *159:12.* location: - place; *193:12.* ascent: - mount.
- put on WEIGHT, - gain weight: kilo al- → al- 1, topla- 3, toplan- 4, şişmanla- ['- put on weight, - get fat']. *259:8.* expansion, growth: - fatten.
- put ONESELF OUT, - take trouble: zahmet et-. *995:4.* inexpedience: - inconvenience.
- put OUT, - issue, - bring out a publication: çıkar- 7. *352:14.* publication: - issue.
- put out, - extinguish [fire, cigarettes]: söndür- 1. *1021:7.* incombustibility: - fight fire.
- put sb TO BED, - have sb lie down /{IN/ON}/: /A/ yatır- 1. *22:19.* sleep: - put to bed.
- put to SLEEP [subj.: boring lecture]: uyku getir-. *22:20.* sleep: - put to sleep.
- put THROUGH /TO/, - connect /WITH/: [Telephone operator: Would you please put me through to Mert bey?]: /A/ bağla- 2. *799:5.* joining: - put together.
- put UP [curtains], - attach or - fasten sth /to/ sth: /A/ tak-. *202:8.* pendency: - suspend; *799:7.* joining: - fasten.
- put up /WITH/, - bear /θ/, - endure /θ/, - stand /θ/, - suffer /θ/, - tolerate /θ/, - take /θ/: /A/ dayan- 3, /A/ katlan- 2, *more formal, less current than the above:* /A/ tahammül et-, /lA/ uğraş- 3. *134:5.* patience: - endure; *1047:3.* toughness: - toughen.

- Q -

- QUARREL, - fight /with/: /lA/ kavga et-. *456:11.* disaccord: - quarrel; *457:13.* contention: - contend.
- quarrel, - clash /with/ [subj.: street gangs]: /lA/ çatış- 1. *456:11.* disaccord: - quarrel; *457:13.* contention: - contend.

- QUESTION, - cross-examine, - interrogate: sorguya çek- → çek- 6. *937:21.* inquiry: - interrogate.

- QUEUE UP, - get /IN/ the line [for stamps, a movie]: {sıraya/ kuyruğa} gir- 1. *189:7.* entrance: - enter.

QUICKLY, with ease, just: *verb stem.*Iver- → ver- 4. *174:17.* swiftness: ADV. swiftly.

QUIT it!, Knock it off!, Stop it! [when sb is bothering you]: Bırak! → bırak- 4, Rahat bırak! → bırak- 4, Dur! → dur- 4. *390:4.* disuse: - cease to use; *856:6.* cessation: - cease sth.
- quit or - leave /θ/ ONE'S JOB [not necessarily retirement]: işten {ayrıl-/çık-} → ayrıl- 3, çık- 1. *188:9.* departure: - quit; *448:2.* resignation: - resign.

- QUOTE /θ/ sth, - quote /from/ sth, - cite /θ/ sth: /DAn/ alıntı yap- → yap- 3. *848:7.* repetition: - repeat.

- R -

- RACE /θ/ sb, - race /with/ sb: /lA/ yarış- 1. *457:19.* contention: - race.
- race, - pound, - palpitate [subj.: heart]: {kalbi/yüreği} hızlı hızlı at-[or çarp-] → at- 7, çarp- 2. *916:12.* agitation: - flutter.

- RAIN: yağmur yağ-. *316:9.* rain: - rain.
- rain CATS AND DOGS, - pour down, - rain hard: bardaktan boşanırcasına yağmur yağ- → yağ-. *316:9.* rain: - rain.

- RAISE, - lift up, - pick up /from/: /DAn/ kaldır- 1. *911:5.* elevation: - elevate.
- raise [ANIMALS], - keep [animals, pets]: besle- 2. *1068:6.* animal husbandry: - raise.

- raise [ANIMALS, crops on a farm]: **üret- 2, yetiştir- 1**. *891:8.* production: - produce, - create; *1068:6.* animal husbandry: - raise.
- raise, - rear, - bring up, - educate, - train [CHILDREN]: **büyüt- 1, yetiştir- 2**. *568:13.* teaching: - train.
- raise one's HAND to get the teacher's attention [in a class]: At the university level: **el kaldır- 1** → kaldır- 1; At levels below the university **parmak kaldır-** [lit., '-raise finger'] is more common. → kaldır- 1. *911:5.* elevation: - elevate; *982:10.* attention: - call attention to.
- raise one's hand /AGAINST/ [i.e., - strike]: **/A/ el kaldır- 2** → kaldır- 1. *453:3.* resistance: - offer resistance; *911:5.* elevation: - elevate.
- raise an OBJECTION /{to/AGAINST}/, - object /to/: **/A/ itiraz et-**. *333:5.* dissent: - object; *788:5.* disagreement: - disagree.
- raise or - increase PRICES, rates: **{artır-/arttır-} 1**. *251:4.* increase: - increase.
- raise or - bring up a SUBJECT, topic [Don't raise that subject again.]: **konu aç-** → aç- 10. *817:12.* beginning: - open.
- raise one's VOICE , - speak up: **ses çıkar- 1** → çıkar- 7. *524:26.* speech: - utter in a certain way.
- raise one's voice AGAINST, - say sth against, - object, - voice one's opinions, - say sth: **ses çıkar- 2** → çıkar- 7. *453:3.* resistance:- offer resistance.

- RAPE, - violate: **ırzına geç-** → geç- 1. *459:14.* attack: - attack; *480:15.* taking: - possess sexually; *665:20.* unchastity: - seduce.
- rape /θ/, - assault /θ/ sexually [not necessarily rape]: **/A/ saldır- 2, /A/ tecavüz et- 2**. *459:14.* attack: - attack; *480:15.* taking: - possess sexually; *665:20.* unchastity: - seduce.

- REACH /θ/ a place, - arrive /{IN/AT}/, - come /to/, - get /to/: **/A/ gel- 1, /A/ ulaş- 1, /A/ var-**. *186:6.* arrival: - arrive.
- reach /θ/, - attain /θ/ [a goal, God]: **/A/ er-**. *186:6.* arrival: - arrive.
- reach /θ/ [one's goal], - attain /θ/ [one's objective], - achieve /θ/ [one's purpose], - gain [one's end[s]]: **eriş- 3**. *407:4.* accomplishment: accomplish; *409:8.* success: - achieve one's purpose.

- reach /θ/, - get /to/ [a place with one's hands: I can't reach the top shelf.]: **/A/ uzan- 3, /A/ yetiş- 5, /A/ eriş- 2**. *261:6.* distance, remoteness: - extend to.
- reach /θ/, - contact /θ/, - get in touch /WITH/ [a person]: **/A/ ulaş- 2**. *343:8.* communication: - communicate with, - get in touch with.
- reach /θ/ sb [on the phone], - get THROUGH /TO/ [I couldn't reach my parents.]: **/lA/ bağlantı kur-** → kur- 1. *343:8.* communication: - communicate with, - get in touch with.
- reach as far as, - touch [θ/ [His head {reached/ touched} /θ/ the ceiling.]: **/A/ 1 değ- 2**. *158:8.* space: - extend; *223:10.* nearness: - contact.
- reach or become a certain AGE, - turn a certain age: **yaşını {doldur-/tamamla-}, yaşa {bas-/gir-}** → bas- 1. *303:9.* age: - mature.
- reach or - attain /θ/ MATURITY, - mature, - grow up [subj.: person]: **olgunluğa er-** → er-. *303:9.* age: - mature; *407:8.* accomplishment: - ripen.
- reach OUT TO HELP: **/A/ el uzat-** → uzat- 2. *449:11.* aid: - aid.
- reach an UNDERSTANDING, - come to an agreement, - agree /a: with, b: {on/upon}, c: {on/upon}, d: on the subject of, e: {to/in order to}/: **/a: 1A, b: DA, c: üzerinde, d: konusunda, e: için/ anlaş- 2**. *332:10.* assent: - come to an agreement.

- REACT /to/, - respond /to/: **karşıla- 3** [to a situation, a proposal], **/A/ karşılık ver- 1** [both to a question and a situation] → ver- 1, **/A/ tepki göster-** [to a situation, a proposal] → göster- 1. *902:5.* reaction: - react.

- READ: **oku- 1**. *570:12.* learning: - study.
- read or - say BY SYLLABLE, - syllabify [the common Turkish way of indicating spelling]: **hecele-**. *546:7.* letter: - spell.
- read OUT LOUD [as opposed to reading silently]: **yüksek sesle oku-** → oku- 1. *570:12.* learning: - study.
- read SILENTLY: **içinden oku-** → oku- 1. *570:12.* learning: - study.
For other ways of reading, → oku- 1.

- REALIZE, - understand: **anla-**. *521:7.* intelligibility: - understand.

- realize, - become aware /OF/, - notice: **farket-** 1, **farkına var-**. *940:5.* discovery: - detect; *982:6.* attention: - heed.

- REAP, - mow /with/: **/lA/ biç-** 2. *1067:19.* agriculture: - harvest.

- REBEL, - revolt, - rise up /AGAINST/, - riot: **/A karşı/ ayaklan-, / A / başkaldır-**. *327:7.* disobedience: - revolt.

- REBUKE, - scold, - reprimand /{for/because}/: **/DIğI için/ azarla-**. *510:17.* disapproval: - reprove.

- RECALL, - remember: {**hatırla-** /**anımsa-**}, **akılda kal-** → **kal-** 1, **bul-** 3 [when one suddenly remembers sth forgotten]. *988:10.* memory: - remember.

- RECANT, - take back, - retract, or - rescind one's words: **sözünü geri al-** → **geri al-** 1 → **al-** 1. *445:2.* repeal: - repeal.

- RECEIVE, - get /from/: **/DAn/ al-** 3. *479:6.* receiving: - receive.
- receive or - obtain INFORMATION /from/, - learn /from/: **/DAn/ bilgi edin-**. *570:6.* learning: - learn; *927:14.* knowledge: - learn.
- receive NEWS, word /{OF/from}/, - find out /from]: **/DAn/ haber al-** → **al-** 3. *570:6.* learning: - learn; *927:14.* knowledge: - learn.
- receive or - get PERMISSION /from, to/: **/DAn, için/ {izin/müsaade} al-** → **al-** 3. *443:9.* * 1. permission: - get permission.
- receive a PRICE OFFER /from/ [a company], - get a bid, estimate, quote /from/: **/DAn/ fiyat al-** → **al-** 3. *630:11.* price, fee: - price.
- receive or - undergo TREATMENT, - be treated [for an illness]: **tedavi gör-** → **gör-** 3. *91:29.* therapy: - undergo treatment.

- RECITE [without a text, from memory]: **oku-** 4. *543:10.* public speaking: - declaim; *988:17.* memory: - memorize.

- RECKON, - estimate /{AT/TO BE/AS BEING}/, - take a guess, - judge [how many]: **/olarak/ tahmin et-** 2.1. *945:9.* judgment: - estimate.

- RECOGNIZE sb or sth /{BY/from}/: **/DAn/ tanı-** 2. *988:12.* memory: - recognize.
- recognize a government, - recognize /AS/ [a state]: **/olarak/ tanı-** 6. *332:11.* assent: - acknowledge.

- RECOMMEND, - propose, or - suggest sth /to/ sb, - advise sb to do sth: **/A/ tavsiye et-**. *422:5.* advice: - advise; *439:5.* offer: - propose; *509:11* approval: - commend.

- RECOPY, - rewrite, - make a clean or fresh copy of a piece of writing: **temize çek-** → **çek-** 8. *784:8.* copy: - copy.

- RECORD sth /IN/, - enter sth /IN/, - write sth down /IN/ [a notebook]: **/A/ kaydet-** 2. *549:15.* record: - record.
- record, - tape sth /ON [a medium], with [an instrument]/: **/A, lA/ kaydet-** 3. *549:15.* record: - record.

- RECOVER [from illness], - get better, - improve, - get well: **düzel-, iyileş-**. *392:8.* improvement: - rally, - get better; *396:20.* restoration: - recover.

- REDUCE, - bring down [inflation]: **düşür-** 2. *252:7.* decrease: - reduce.
- reduce, - lower, - decrease, - bring down [prices, rates], - give a discount: **indir-** 3. *633:6a.* cheapness: - lower prices.
- reduce the price, - make a reduction in price /FOR/ sb, - give a discount /to/ sb, - come down in price /FOR/ sb: **/A/ ikram et-** 2, **in-** 5, **indir-** 3. *631:2.* discount: - discount.

- REFER /to/, - consult /θ [a person, office, or book], for/: **/A/ {başvur-** /**müracaat et-}** 1, **/A/ danış-**. *387:14.* use: - avail oneself of; *541:11* conversation: - confer.
- refer to /as/, - call, - dub [i.e., - give a name to]: **/diye/ {adlandır-** /**isimlendir-}, /A/ de-** 4. *527:11.* nomenclature: - name.
- refer to sb /as/, - call sb /by/ a certain name [i.e., - use a certain name in referring to]: **/diye/ çağır-** 4. *527:11.* nomenclature: - name.

- REFLECT [obj.: light, image: This mirror doesn't reflect [the image] well.]: **/A/ yansıt-** 1. *349:11.* representation, description: - image.
- reflect, - reveal, - show [article reflects author's views]: **yansıt-** 2. *336:5.* imitation: - imitate.

- REFRAIN /from/ sth or /from/ doing sth;
- avoid /θ/ sb or sth or /θ/ doing sth:
/DAn/ **kaçın**-. *329:3*. inaction: -
refrain; *368:6*. avoidance: - avoid;
668:7. temperance: - abstain.

- REFUND, - return money, - give back
money, - give a refund: **para** {**geri
ver-/iade et-**} → {geri ver-/iade
et-} → ver- 1. *481:4*. restitution: -
restore.

- REFUSE [to do sth], - reject [an idea, a
proposal]: **diren**- 1 [with a
preceding negative verb], **reddet**- 1.
442:3. refusal: - refuse.

- REFUTE, - deny, - contradict, - declare,
or - show to be false or wrong:
yalanla-. *335:4*. negation, denial: -
deny; *451:6*. opposition: - contradict;
957:5. disproof: - refute.

- REGAIN CONSCIOUSNESS, - come
to: **ayıl**-, **kendine gel**- 1 → gel- 1.
306:8. life: - come to life; *396:20*.
restoration: - recover.
- regain SELF-CONTROL, - pull oneself
together, - come to one's senses:
kendine gel- 2 → gel- 1. *428:7*.
restraint: - restrain.

- REGARD /θ [sb or sth], AS/ [He
regarded his teacher AS a model.]:
/A, olarak/ **bak**- 4, /I, olarak/
gör- 2, /I/ **say**- 4. *952:11*. belief: -
think.
- regard as SUITABLE /FOR/ sb; - think
that sth befits sb: /A/ **yakıştır**-.
867:4. nonconformity: - not conform.
- regard WITH TOLERANCE, - accept
[people as they are]: **kabul et**- 4.
134:5. patience: - endure; *978:7*.
broad-mindedness: - keep an open
mind.

- REGISTER or - enroll sb [not oneself]
/IN [a course], {IN/AT} [a school]/:
/A/ **kaydet**- 1, /A/ **yazdır**- 2.
549:15. record: - record.
- register or - enroll [ONESELF], - get
oneself registered /IN [a course],
{IN/AT} [a school]/: /A/ **kaydol**-
→ ol- 12, /A/ **yazıl**- 2. *549:15*.
record: - record.

- REGRET, - be sorry /that, for/: /a:
DIğInA, b: **DIğI için**, c:
DIğI.nDAn dolayı/ **pişman ol**-
→ ol- 12, /için/ **üzüntü çek**- 2 →
çek- 5. *113:6*. regret: - regret.

- REGULATE, - control [This instrument
regulates the heat.]: **ayarla**- 1,

düzenle- 3. *573:8*. direction,
management: - direct.

- REHEARSE [play, performance]:
prova yap- → yap- 3. *704:32*.
show business, theater: - rehearse.

- REJECT [an idea, a proposal], - refuse
[to do sth]: **reddet**- 1. *442:3*. refusal:
- refuse.

- RELATE sth [a story, event] /to/ sb, -
tell /θ/ sb sth, - tell sth /to/ sb: /A/
anlat- 2. *552:11*. news: - report.

- RELAX, - rest: 1 **dinlen**-, **istirahat
et**-. *20:6*. rest, repose: - rest.
- relax, - unwind, - rest: **yorgunluk
çıkar**- → çıkar- 3. *20:6*. rest, repose:
- rest.

- RELEASE, - let go of, - put down
[object]: **bırak**- 5. *431:5*. liberation:
- release.
- release, - liberate, - free, - set free, - let
go [hostages, prisoners]: **serbest
bırak**- → bırak- 5, **salıver**-. *120:6*.
relief: - release; *398:3*. rescue: -
rescue; *431:4*. liberation: - liberate;
431:5. : - release.

- RELY /{ON/UPON}/, - trust /θ/, - have
confidence /IN/: /A/ **güven**-.
952:15. belief: - believe in.
- rely or - depend /{ON/UPON}/ for
support: /A/ **dayan**- 2, **sırtını
{daya-/yasla-}** 2. *952:16*. belief: -
rely on.

- REMAIN or - stay /{at/in/on}/ a place:
/DA/ **kal**- 1, /DA/ **otur**- 4, /DA/
dur- 6. *256:5*. remainder: - remain;
855:3. continuance: - continue.
- remain, - be left over [no bread left]:
art- 2, **kal**- 2. *256:5*. remainder: -
remain.
- remain BEHIND, - stay, - fall, - lag, or -
get behind /in/ [some activity,
lessons]: **geri kal**- 1 → kal- 1.
166:4. following: - lag; *217:8*. rear: -
be behind.
Remain IN GOOD HEALTH AND
HAPPINESS., Take care. [Said by
someone off on a journey to those
remaining behind.]: **Sağlıcakla
kalın**. → kal- 1. *188:22*. departure:
INTERJ. farewell!; *504: * 20*.
courtesy: polite expressions.
- remain or - be SILENT, not - say
anything, - keep quiet: **sus**- 1. *51:5*.
silence: - be silent.
- remain UNMARRIED [for a woman], -
be an old maid: **evde kal**- → kal- 1.
565:5. celibacy: - be unmarried.

- REMARK /on/, - comment /on/, - note, - point out: /I/ **belirt-**, /A/ **dikkat çek-** → çek- 1, /A/ **işaret et-** 2. *524:25.* speech: - remark.

- REMEMBER, - recall: {**hatırla-/anımsa-**}, **akılda kal-** → kal- 1, **bul- 4** [when one suddenly remembers sth forgotten]. *988:10.* memory: - remember.
- remember, - keep in mind, - bear in mind, - realize, - consider: **gözönünde tut-** → tut- 2. *930:12.* thought: - consider; *988:10.* memory: - remember.
- remember, - occur /to/, - think of, - come to mind: **akla gel-** → gel- 1. *930:18.* thought: - occur to.
- remember to do sth [Remember to take your keys.]: **unutMA-** [lit., '- NOT forget': Don't forget to take your keys.] → unut- c). *989:5.* forgetfullness: - forget.

- REMIND /θ/ sb: /A/ {**hatırlat-/anımsat-**} 1 ['- cause /θ/ sb to remember a fact or event': I reminded him that we had met earlier.]. 2 ['- remind sb to do sth': Remind me to mail that letter.]. *988:20.* memory: - remind.
- remind /θ/ sb /OF/ sb or sth [the features of a person or thing bring a similar person or thing to mind: You remind me of my grandfather.]: /A, I/ {**hatırlat-/anımsat-**} 3, /A/ **benzet-** 2. *988:20.* memory: - remind.

- REMINISCE: {**hayale/hayallere**} **dal-** ['- daydream, - start to daydream, - go off /INTO/ daydreams, reverie'], {**düşünceye/düşüncelere**} **dal-** ['- get, - be, or - become lost in thought, for one's mind - wander off, - give oneself up to reverie'] → dal- 2. *984:9.* distraction, confusion: - muse; *988:11.* memory: - reminisce.

- REMOVE sth /from/, - take sth {OUT OF/from} [money from purse]: /DAn/ **çıkar-** 1. *192:10.* extraction: - extract.
- remove, - take away, - clear away [dirty dishes] /from/ [table]: /DAn/ **kaldır-** 3. *176:11.* transferal, transportation: - remove.
- remove, - take off [clothing: hat, coat]: **çıkar-** 2. *6:6.* unclothing: - take off; *176:11.* transferal, transportation: - remove.
- remove [spots from clothing]: **çıkar-** 2. *192:10.* extraction: - extract.

- RENDER SERVICES /to/, - serve /θ/: /A/ **hizmet et-**. *577:13.* servant, employee: - serve.

- RENT [house, car], - hire [taxi, car] /from, FOR/: /DAn, A/ **kirala-** 1, /DAn, A/ **tut-** 6a. *615:15.* commission: - rent.
- rent [I don't own this house, I rent it., i.e., pay rent to live in it]: {**kirada/kirayla**} **otur-** → otur- 3. *615:15.* commission: - rent.
- rent [OUT], - lease [out] /to, FOR/ [obj.: place, equipment: Mehmet bey rents this house to me.]: /A, A/ {**kirala-/kiraya ver-**} → kirala- 2. *615:16.* commission: - rent out.

- REPAIR, - fix [roads]: **düzelt-** 1. *396:14.* restoration: - repair.
- repair, - fix, - put in running order [machine]: **onar-, tamir et-**. *396:14.* restoration: - repair.

- REPAY, - pay back [money]: **geri öde-**. *624:11.* payment: - repay.

- REPEAL, - do away with, - abolish [law], - eliminate, - eradicate [disease]: **kaldır-** 4. *445:2.* repeal: - repeal; *772:5* exclusion: - eliminate.

- REPEAT: {**tekrar et-/tekrarla-**}. *848:7.* repetition: - repeat.

- REPLACE, - return /to/ its place, - put back, - put away: **yerine koy-** → koy- 1. *386:10.* store, supply: - store; *390:6.* disuse: - put away; *396:11.* restoration: - restore, - put back.

- REPLY or - respond /to/ a question, - answer /θ/ a question: **soruyA** {**cevap ver-/karşılık ver-** 1} → ver- 1, **soruyU** {**cevapla-/cevaplandır-/yanıtla-**}. *938:4.* answer: - answer.

- REPORT /to/, - inform /θ/, - get information /to/: /A/ **bildir-**, /A/ **bilgi ver-** → ver- 1, /A/ **haber ver-** → ver- 1. *551:8.* information: - inform.

- REPRESENT, - be a respresentative of [John represents the students.]: **temsil et-**. *576:14.* deputy, agent: - represent.

- REPROACH, - condemn, - censure /{for/because}/: /DIğI için/ **kına-**. *510:13.* disapproval: - censure.

- REPRODUCE, - multiply /by...ing/ [subj.: almost exclusively living things: Rabbits reproduce very rapidly.]: /ArAk/ çoğal-, /ArAk/ üre-. 78:7. reproduction, procreation: - reproduce; 251:6. increase: - grow [i.].

- REQUEST sth /from/ sb, - ask for sth /from/ sb: /DAn/ iste- 2, /DAn/ rica et-. 440:9. request: - request.

- REQUIRE, - need [non-person subject: This food needs to cook more.]: gerektir-, iste- 3. 962:9. necessity: - require.

- RESCIND or - withdraw one's decision: kararını geri al- → geri al- 1 → al- 1. 363:6. changing of mind: - change one's mind; 370:7. abandonment: - give up.

- RESCUE /from/, - save /from/: /DAn/ kurtar-. 398:3. rescue: - rescue.

- RESEARCH, - do research on, - explore, - investigate, - study, - try to find out: araştır- 2. 937:23. investigate: - investigate.

- RESEMBLE /θ/, - look like [He resembles θ his father.]: /A/ benze- 1. 783:7. similarity: - resemble.

- RESENT sb's showing affection to or interest in sb else: /I, DAn/ kıskan- 2. 153:3. jealousy: - suffer pangs of jealousy.

- RESERVE [a place] /a: for, b: {IN/AT}, c: at, d: in the name of/, - set apart: /a: için, b: DAn, c: DA, d: a d ı n a/ a y ı r t -. 477:9. apportionment: - allot.

- RESIDE /{in/at}/, - live /{in/at}/, - inhabit /θ/: /DA/ otur- 3, /DA/ yaşa- 2. 225:7. habitation: - inhabit.

- RESIGN /from/ or - leave /θ/ a job, post: görevinden ayrıl- → ayrıl- 3, işinden ayrıl- → ayrıl- 3, [görevinden] istifa et-. 448:2. resignation: - resign.

- RESIST, - hold out /against/: /A karşı/ diren- 2. 361:7. obstinacy: - balk; 453:4. resistance: - stand fast.

- RESOLVE, - decide, - make a decision: /için/ karar al- [subj.: usually a group, organization, or society acting in an official capacity] → al- 1, /A/ karar ver- [subj.: individuals or a family rather than another group or organization] → ver- 1, /I/ kararlaştır- [subj.: at least two persons reaching a decision together]. 359:7. resolution: - resolve.

- resolve, - solve, - find a solution /for/, - handle [situation, personal problem, matter]: hallet-, işin içinden çık- 2 ['- resolve a difficult problem, - work out a solution for something complicated'] → çık- 1. 939:2. solution: - solve.

- RESPECT [obj.: a person]: say- 3. 155:4. respect: - respect.

- respect, - admire, - appreciate, - value [obj.: a person, a quality: diligence]: takdir et- 1. 155:4. respect: - respect; 996:13. importance: - value.

- respect, - show respect /{to/FOR}/, - behave respectfully /toward/, - treat with respect [a person, a person's ideas]: /A/ saygı göster- → göster- 1. 143:10. kindness, benevolence: - be considerate; 155:5. respect: - do or - pay hommage to.

- RESPOND, - react /to/: karşıla- 3 [to a situation, a proposal], /A/ karşılık ver- 1 [both to a question and a situation] → ver- 1, /A/ tepki göster- [to a situation, a proposal] → göster- 1. 902:5. reaction: - react.

- respond or - reply /to/ a question, - answer /θ/ a question: soruyA {cevap ver-/karşılık ver- 1} → ver- 1, soruyU {cevapla-/cevaplandır-/yanıtla-}. 938:4. answer: - answer.

- REST, - relax: 1 dinlen-, istirahat et-. 20:6. rest, repose: - rest.

- rest, - unwind, - relax: yorgunluk çıkar- → çıkar- 3. 20:6. rest, repose: - rest.

- rest, - put one's mind at ease: {başını/ kafasını} dinle- → 2 dinle-. 20:6. rest, repose: - rest.

- RESTORE TO HEALTH, - cure, - heal [a person]: /A/ şifa ver- [in Allah şifa versin! 'May God restore him to health'] → ver- 1. 86:38. remedy: - remedy; 396:15. restoration: - cure.

- RESTRAIN, - hold back [tears], - keep control of: tut- 4. 428:7. restraint: - restrain.

- restrain or - control one's tongue, - keep quiet: {çenesini/dilini} tut- [lit., '- hold {** one's jaw or chin/one's tongue}'] → tut- 4. 51:5. silence: - be silent; *344:6*. uncommunicativeness: - keep to oneself; *428:7*. restraint: - restrain.

- RESULT, - originate, - stem, - emanate, or spring /from/, - be due /TO/: **/DAn/ kaynaklan-**. *886:5*. effect: - result from.

- RETIRE for the night, - go to bed, - lie down: **yat-** 1. *22:17*. sleep: - go to bed; *201:5*. horizontalness: - lie.
- retire: **görevinden ayrıl-** ['- retire from one's job, post, duty'] → ayrıl- 3, **emekliye ayrıl-** ['- go into retirement'] → ayrıl- 3. *188:9*. departure: - quit; *448:2*. retirement: - resign.

- RETRACT or - take back one's words, - recant: **sözünü geri al-** → geri al- 1 → al- 1. *445:2*. repeal: - repeal.

- RETREAT, - move back, - fall back: **gerile-** 1. *163:6*. regression: - retreat.

- RETURN /from, to/, - come back /from, to/, - go or - turn back: **/DAn, A/ [geri] dön-** 2. *163:8b*. regression: - turn back, - come back.
- return a SERVE [in tennis, ping-pong]: **atak karşıla-** → karşıla- 3. *748:3*. tennis: - play tennis.
- return STH /to/, - give or - take sth back /to/: **/A/ {geri ver-/iade et-}**. The second verb is *more formal*. → ver- 1. *481:4*. restitution: - restore.

- REUNITE, - unite /WITH/, - bring together /WITH/, - join sb or sth /to/ sb or sth else: **/A/ kavuştur-**. *799:5*. joining: - put together.

- REVEAL, - disclose /to/, - make public: **/A/ açıkla-** 2. *351:4*. disclosure: - disclose.
- reveal, - disclose, - expose to view; - bring to light: **{ortaya/meydana} çıkar-** → çıkar- 7. *351:4*. disclosure: - disclose.

- REVIEW, - go over, - examine, - look over, - scrutinize: **gözden geçir-** → geçir- 1. *27:14*. vision: - scrutinize.

- REVOLT, - rebel, - rise up /AGAINST/, - riot: **/A karşı/ ayaklan-, /A/ başkaldır-**. *327:7*. disobedience: - revolt.

- REWARD sb /with/ sth, - give sb sth as a reward, - award sb sth as a prize:

/lA/ ödüllendir-. *624:10*. payment: - pay.

- REWRITE, - recopy, - make a clean copy of a piece of writing: **temize çek-** → çek- 8. *784:8*. copy: - copy.

- RIDE: **/A/ bin-** 2, **/lA/ git-** 2. *177:33*. travel: - ride.

- RIDICULE /θ/, - make fun /OF/, - mock /θ/: **/lA/ alay et-, /I/ alaya al-** → al- 1, **/lA, diye/ dalga geç-** 2 → geç- 1. *508:8*. ridicule: - ridicule.

RIGHT you are!, *colloq.*: Right on!: **İyi bildin!** → bil- 1. *972:25* truth: PHR. <nonformal terms> right on!

- RING [The doorbell is ringing.]: **çal-** 3. *54:8b*. resonance: - ring, - make a ringing sound.
- ring sth [The man rang the doorbell.]: **zile bas-** → bas- 2. *54:8a*. resonance: - ring, - cause to ring.
- ring UP /θ/, - call up /θ/, - phone /θ/ sb: **/A/ telefon {et-/aç-}**. *347:18*. communications: - telephone.

- RINSE /with/ [a substance], /{with/IN}/ [hot water]: **/lA/ çalkala-** 2 [one's mouth, dishes, glasses], **/lA/ durula-** [dishes, glasses, sheets, not one's mouth]. *79:19*. cleanness: - wash.

- RIOT, - rise up /AGAINST/, - revolt, - rebel: **/A karşı/ ayaklan-, /A/ başkaldır-**. *327:7*. disobedience: - revolt.

- RIP OFF, - gyp, - swindle; - sell somone sth at an exorbitant, outrageous price: *formal term*: **dolandır-**. *356:18*. deception: - cheat. The two following verbs are *very common slang*: **/A/ kazık at-** → at- 1, **/I/ kazıkla-**. *356:19*. : nonformal terms - gyp.
- rip or - tear /{OUT OF/from}/ [pages from notebook]: **/DAn/ {kopar-2/kopart- 2}, /DAn/ yırt-**. *192:10*. extraction: - extract; *801:11*. separation: - sever.
- rip UP, - tear up [obj.: document, paper]: **yırt-**. *801:11*. separation: - sever.

- RIPEN, - become ripe: **ol-** 9.2. *303:9*. age: - mature.

- RISE, - ascend, - go up /to/ [subj.: plane, balloon]: **/A/ yüksel-** 1. *193:8*. ascent: - ascend.
- rise, - appear: **doğ-** 2 [subj.: sun, moon], **çık-** 3 [subj.: sun, moon,

586

stars], **güneş** {**aç-/çık-**} ['for the sun - come out, - appear'] → aç- 8, çık- 3. *33:8.* appearance; - appear; *190:11.* emergence: - emerge.
- rise /from/, - get up /{from/OUT OF}/ [chair], - stand up, - get up, - get out of bed, - arise: **/DAn/ kalk-** 1. *193:8.* ascent: - ascend; *231:8.* verticalness: - rise.
- rise in price, - become more expensive: **fiyatlar** {**çık-/tırman-/yüksel-**} → çık- 6, tırman- 2, yüksel- 2, **pahalan-**. *251:6.* increase: - grow, increase [i.].
- rise or - increase suddenly, - skyrocket, - soar [prices, temperature]: **fırla-** 2. *251:6* increase: - grow, increase [i.].

- ROAM, - wander, - walk, or - go about, - stroll, - ramble, - rove /in, among/ [usually aimlessly]: **/DA, arasında/ gezin-** 1. *177:23.* travel: - wander.

- ROAR with laughter, - laugh loudly; - guffaw: **kahkaha ile gül-** → gül- 1. *116:8.* rejoicing: - laugh.

- ROAST sth [The cook is roasting the chicken.]: **kavur-, kızart-** 3. *11:4a.* cooking: - cook sth.
- roast [i.e., - become roast meat: The meat is roasting.]: **kızar-** 4. *11:4b.* cooking: for sth - cook.

- ROB, - strip of valuables: **soy-** 2. *482:14.* theft: - rob.

- ROCK, - shake [earthquake shakes building]: **salla-** 3. *916:10.* agitation: - agitate.
- rock [a cradle], - push [a child in a swing]: **salla-** 2. *901:12.* impulse, impact: - thrust, - push; *903:9.* pushing, throwing: - push.

- ROTATE, - turn sth [obj.: door handle]: **/I/ çevir-** 1. *914:9.* rotation: - rotate.

- RUB, - spread, or - smear sth /ON/, - apply sth /to, to the surface of/ [rub cream ON skin]: **/A, {üstüne/ üzerine}/ sür-** 4. *295:19.* covering: - cover.
- rub OUT, - bump off, - wipe out, - do in, - nuke, - zap. *Contemptuous for* - kill: **gebert-**. *308:13.* killing: non-formal terms: - waste; *514: * 5.* threat: INTERJ. specific threats.

- RUIN, - spoil, - break, - corrupt [obj: morals], - violate [rules]: **boz-** 1. *393:10.* impairment: - spoil; *395:10.* destruction: - destroy.

- ruin; - pull down, - knock down, - tear down; - demolish, - wreck /with/; - destroy [obj.: building]: **/lA/ yık-** 1. *395:17.* destruction: - demolish.

- RULE: → - run, - administer.

- RUMMAGE, - search /THROUGH/ [drawers, pocketbook], - leaf or thumb /THROUGH/ [book, papers]: **/I/ karıştır-** 3. *937:26.* inquiry: - examine cursorily; *937:33.* : - ransack.

- RUN /a: from, b: {to/AFTER}, c: after, d: after/, pursue/: **/a: DAn, b: A, c: arkasından, d: peşinden/ koş-** → koş- 1. *174:8.* swiftness: - speed; *401:5.* haste: - make haste.
- run, - administer, - direct, - manage, - govern, - rule: **idare et-** 1, **yönet-** 1. *417:13.* authority: - possess or - wield authority; *573:8.* direction, management: - direct; *612:14.* government: - rule.
- run, - operate, - work [Can you run this machine?]: **çalıştır-** 2. *888:5.* operation: - operate sth.
- run, - operate [The buses don't run frequently on weekends.]: **çalış-** 3, **işle-** 1. *888:7.* operation: - be operative.
- run, - be operating, - work [How does this machine run?]: **çalış-** 3. *888:7.* operation: - be operative.
- run, - play, - be on, showing [subj.: film, theater production]: **oyna-** 2. *714:16.* photography: - project; *888:7.* operation: - be operative.
- run [subj.: women's stockings]: **çorap kaç-** → kaç- 1. *393:20.* impairment: - wear, - wear away.
- run AWAY, - escape, - flee /from, to/: **/DAn, A/ kaç-** 1. *369:6.* escape: - escape.
- run DOWN, - point out the faults of, - criticize, - speak ill of, - disparage: **yer-** 1. *512:8.* disparagement: - disparage.
- run down THE STAIRS: {**koşar adımlar.la/koşar adım**} **merdivenler.DEN in-** → in- 1. *174:8.* swiftness: - speed; *401:5.* haste: - make haste.
- run or - bump /INTO/, - meet by chance, - come or - chance /UPON/, - encounter /θ/: **/lA/ karşılaş-** 2, **karşısına çık-** ['- appear suddenly in front of, - bump into'], **/A/ rastla-** 1, *formal:* **/A/ tesadüf et-** 1. *131:6.* inexpectation: - be unexpected; *223:11.* nearness: - meet.

- run or - crash sth INTO [He ran his car into a telephone pole.]: /A/ çarp- 1. *901:13.* impulse, impact: - collide.
- run into each other, - clash, - collide [subj.: vehicles]: çarpış-. *901:13.* impulse, impact: - collide.
- run, - flow, - pour /INTO/ [river into the sea, people into the street]: /A/ dökül- 3. *189:9.* entrance: - flow in.
- run or - get LOW ON [supplies: sugar, gas], - decrease, - become less: azal-. *252:6.* decrease: - decrease.
- run OUT [subj.: patience], - be impatient, for one's patience - be exhausted: sabrı tüken-. *135:5.* impatience: - have no patience with.
- run out [subj.: time], - be up, - expire: {süre/vakit/zaman} dol- → dol- 2. *390:9.* disuse: - obsolesce; *820:5.* time: - elapse.
- run out OF, - be used up, consumed, for no more - be left [supplies: food, fuel]: bit- 3, tüken-. *388:4.* consumption: - be consumed.
- run or - pour /{from/OUT OF}, ONTO/; - overflow [subj.: a liquid]: /DAn, A/ boşal- 2. *190:13.* emergence: - run out.
- run OVER, - overflow [river its banks] /DUE TO/: /DAn/ taş- 2. *238:17b.* stream: - overflow.
- run over sth [He ran over the cat.]: çiğne- 2. *909:7.* overrunning: - run over.
- run UP THE STAIRS: {koşar adımlar.la/koşar adım} merdivenleri çık-. → çık- 5. *174:8.* swiftness: - speed; *401:5.* haste: - make haste.

- RUSH, - hurry [Don't {rush/hurry}.]: acele et-, çabuk ol- → ol- 12. *401:5.* haste: - make haste.
- rush as a group /to/, - mob /θ/ a place, - throng /to/ [When the weather was hot, the people rushed /to/ the beaches.]: /A/ hücum et- 2. *769:16.* assemblage: - come together.
- rush or - dash /INTO/, - enter /θ/ suddenly: /A/ dal- 3. *189:7.* entrance: - enter.

- S -

- SACRIFICE an animal, - kill an animal as a sacrifice: kurban kes- → kes- 2. *308:12.* killing: - kill.

- SADDEN; - upset, - distress, - worry: üz-. *112:18.* sadness: - sadden; *126:4.* anxiety: - concern; *126:5.* : - make anxious.

- SALUTE [obj.: person, not flag], - greet: /I/ selâmla-, /A/ selâm ver- → ver- 1. *585:10.* hospitality, welcome: - greet.
- salute the flag: bayrağı selâmla-. *155:5.* respect: - do or - pay hommage to; *517:22.* signs, indicators: - signal.

- SAMPLE, - taste, - try the taste of: tat-, tadına bak- → bak- 1. *62:7.* taste: - taste; *941:8.* experiment: - experiment.

- SAUTÉ: sote et-, kızart- 1. *11:4a.* cooking: - cook sth.

- SAVE, - keep, or - hold sth /FOR/, - set sth aside /FOR/: /A/ sakla- 3. *386:12.* store, supply: - reserve; *474:5.* retention: - retain.
- save /from/, - rescue /from/: /DAn/ kurtar-. *398:3.* rescue: - rescue.
- save [up] MONEY, - save up /for/: /için/ para {artır- 2/biriktir- 2}, /için/ tasarruf et-. *635:4.* thrift: - economize.
- save TIME [by taking a taxi]: {vakit/zaman} kazan- 1 → kazan- 4. *390:5.* disuse: not - use.
- save UP /for/: → - save [up] MONEY.

- SAY: de- 1 [follows actual words spoken: "I'm coming," he said.], söyle- 1 [follows the DIk, AcAk participles in indirect speech: He said that he had come.] *524:23.* speech: - say.
- say, - tell /{to/θ}/ [in indirect commands]: /A/ söyle- 1 [follows the DIk, AcAk participles in indirect speech; follows the short infinitive plus the possessed suffix [**verb stem.mA.sI**] in indirect commands: He told him to come., He said for him to come.]. *524:23.* speech: - say.
- say [referring to a written document: What does the newspaper say (lit., write)?]: yaz- 2. *547:19.* writing: - write.
- Say., Hey there! [informal], Look here!: {Baksana!/Baksanıza!} → bak- 1. *982:22.* attention: INTERJ. attention!
- say or - bid GOODBYE, farewell /TO/ one another: /lA/ vedalaş-. *188:16.* departure: - say or - bid good-bye.
- say 'HI' /to/, - express, - give, or - send one's regards /to/: /A/ selâm söyle- → söyle- 1. *504:13.* courtesy: - give one's regards.
- say NO /to/, - object /to/, - oppose /θ/, - come out /against/: /A/ karşı çık-

→ çık- 3. *451:3*. opposition: - oppose.
- say, show THE TIME [subj.: a timepiece]: **saat** *hour* **göster-**. → göster- 1. *348:5*. manifestation: - manifest.

- SCALD or - burn oneself with a hot liquid, - get scalded /{BY/from}/: /**DAn**/ **haşlan-** 2. *393:13*. impairment: - inflict an injury.

- SCARE, - frighten: **korkut-**. *127:15*. fear, frighteningness: - frighten.

- SCATTER sth /to/ [The wind scattered the papers.], - disperse /to/ [The police dispersed the demonstrators.]: /**A**/ **dağıt-** 1. *770:4a*. dispersion: - disperse sth.
- scatter, - disperse /to/ [i.e., - BECOME scattered: The {students/clouds} scattered.]: /**A**/ **dağıl-** 1. *770:8*. dispersion: - disband.

- SCHEDULE: **programla-** 1. *964:4*. prearrangement: - prearrange.

- SCOLD, - rebuke, - reprimand /{for/because}/: /**DIğI için**/ **azarla-**. *510:17*. disapproval: - reprove.

- SCORE, - make points in a game or contest: **sayı kaydet-** → kaydet- 5. *409:9*. success: - score a success.

- SCOWL, - make a face, - grimace: **yüzü buruş-** 1 → buruş-, **yüzünü buruştur-**. *152:25a*. resentment, anger: gestures of; *265:8*. distortion: - grimace; *510:20*. * *1*. disapproval: gestures of.

SCRAM!: → Beat it!

- SCRATCH, - scarify [subj.: an instrument on metal]: **çiz-** 3. *290:3*. furrow: - furrow; *393:13*. impairment: - inflict an injury; *517:19*. signs, indicators: - mark.
- scratch [obj.: a place that itches: She scratched her head. No pain is inflicted.]: **kaşı-**. *290:3*. furrow: - furrow.
- scratch [when pain is inflicted rather than when an itch is scratched: My cat scratched me.]: **tırmala-**. *290:3*. furrow: - furrow; *393:13*. impairment: - inflict an injury.
- scratch ONESELF in a place that itches [No pain is inflicted.]: **kaşın-** 2. *290:3*. furrow: - furrow.

- scratch or - cross OUT or off sth written: {**üstünü/üzerini**} **çiz-** 2, **karala-** 2 ['- black out']. *395:16*. destruction: - obliterate.

- SCREAM, - shout, - yell /AT, saying/: /**A, diye**/ **bağır-**, **bağırıp çağır-** → çağır- 3, **çığlık at-** → at- 1. *59:6*. cry, call: - cry.
- scream, - cry out, - shout /AT, saying/: /**A, diye**/ **haykır-**. *59:6*. cry, call: - cry.

- SCREECH [subj.: car horn]: **öt-** 2. *58:8*. stridency: - screech.

- SCRUTINIZE, - go over, - examine, - look over, - review: **gözden geçir-** → geçir- 1. *27:14*. vision: - scrutinize.

- SEARCH /FOR/, - look /FOR/: /**I**/ **ara-** 1, /**A**/ **bak-** 2. *937:30*. inquiry: - seek.
- search THOROUGHLY, - search through: **araştır-** 1. *937:31*. inquiry: - search.
- search or - rummage /THROUGH/ [drawers, pocketbook], - leaf or - thumb /THROUGH/ [book, papers]: /**I**/ **karıştır-** 3. *937:26*. inquiry: - examine cursorily, *937:33*. : - ransack.
- search or - comb THROUGH [plane for bomb, photo album for picture]: **arayıp tara-** → tara- 2. *937:31*. inquiry: - search.

- SEE: **gör-** 1. *27:12*. vision: - see.
- see, - understand ['I see', in response to an explanation]: **anla-**. *521:7*. intelligibility: - understand.
- see CLEARLY, - distinguish, - make out: **farket-** 3, **seç-** 2. *27:12*. vision: - see.
- see HOW STH OR SB WORKS OUT, - give sb a trial period, - try on [clothing], - try out [equipment]: **tecrübe et-**. *941:8*. experiment: - experiment.
- see a traveler OFF /to/: /**A**/ **yolcu et-**. *188:16*. departure: - say or - bid good-bye.
- see or - send sb OFF /to/, - wish a departing traveler a safe journey, - wish sb Godspeed: /**A**/ **uğurla-**. *188:16*. departure: - say or - bid good-bye; *504:13*. courtesy: - give one's regards.
- see ONE ANOTHER, - see sb for the purpose of discussing an issue, - meet /with/; - confer /with/: /**lA**/ **görüş-** 1. *524:20*. speech: - speak; *541:11*. conversation: - confer.

589

- see or - feel a RESEMBLANCE or a similarity between, - think that sb or sth is /LIKE/ sb or sth else: /A/ **benzet-** 2. *988:20.* memory: - remind.
- see TO, - attend to, - take care of [obj.: the arrangements, the tickets]: /A/ **bak-** 3. *982:5.* attention: - attend to.
- See YOU [later].: [**Sonra**] **görüşürüz.** → görüş- 1. *188:22.* departure: INTERJ. farewell!; *504:* * *20.* courtesy: polite expressions.
- See you TOMORROW., lit., We'll see each other tomorrow.: **Yarın görüşürüz.** → görüş- 1. *188:22.* departure: INTERJ. farewell!; *504:* * *20.* courtesy: polite expressions.

- SEEM, - appear, - look /LIKE/: /A/ **benze-** 2, **göster-** 2, **görün-** 2. *33:10.* appearance: - appear to be.
- seem, - appear, - create an impression of: **görün-** 2. *33:10.* appearance: - appear to be.
- seem [strange, inappropriate]: **kaç-** 3. *33:10* appearance: - appear to be.
- seem to me: **gibime gel-** → gel- 1, **Bana öyle geliyor ki...** → gel- 1. *33:10.* appearance: - appear to be; *945:8.* judgment: - judge; *952:11.* belief: - think.

- SEIZE, - grab, - grasp, or - take hold of /BY/ [body part: the neck]: /DAn/ **tut-** 1. *480:14.* taking: - seize.
- seize, - grab, - snatch, or - get hold of [sb who is escaping]; - catch [thief] /BY/ [body part: the neck]; - collar, - nab: /DAn/ **yakala-** 1. *480:14.* taking: - seize.
- seize, - capture [subj.: thief; a place: city, fortress]: **ele geçir-** 1 → geçir- 1. *472:8.* acquisition: - acquire; *480:14.* taking: - seize.
- seize up, - freeze, - jam [subj.: computer]: **don-** 2. *854:10.* stability: - become firmly fixed.

- SELECT, - choose, - pick /FOR/: /{A/için}/ **seç-** 1 [for oneself or sb else], **beğen-** 2 [for oneself, not sb else], {**tercih et-/yeğle-**} 2 [for oneself, not sb else]. *371:13.* choice: - choose.

- SELL sth /a: to [sb], b: FOR [in total or per unit], c: FOR [only per unit], d: for, e: {BY [the kilo]/THROUGH [an agent]}/ [t.]: /a: A, b: A, c: DAn, d: için, e: lA/ **sat-**. *734:8.* sale: - sell.
- sell /for/, - BE sold /a: to [sb], b: {FOR/AT} [in total or per unit], c: {FOR/AT} [only per unit], d: {BY [the kilo]/FOR [money]}/: /a: A, b: A, c: DAn, d: lA/ **satıl-**. *734:12.* sale: - be sold.
- sell sth for money and then buy sth else with that money: **bozdur-** 3. *862:4.* interchange: - interchange.
- sell OUT [so none are left, subj.: tickets]: **tüken-**. *388:4.* consumption: - be consumed.

- SEND sth /to/ sb, - send sb sth: /A/ **gönder-**, /A/ **yolla-**. *176:15.* transferal, transportation: - send.
- send sth BACK /to/: /A/ **geri gönder-**. *481:4.* restitution: - restore.
- send a FAX /to/: /A/ **faks** {**çek-/gönder-**} → çek- 9, gönder-. *347:19.* communications: - telegraph.
- send /FOR/, - call, - summon /to/ [obj.: a doctor, an ambulance]: /A/ **çağır-** 1. *420:11.* command: - summon.
- send MAIL [OFF], - mail, - post: /A/ **at-** 4 ['- drop in the mailbox'], **postala-** ['- mail']. *176:15.* transferal, transportation: - send; *553:12.* correspondence: - mail. style?
- send OFF /to/: → - SEND sth /to/ sb.
- send or - see sb off /to/, - wish a departing traveler a safe journey, - wish sb Godspeed: /A/ **uğurla-**. *188:16.* departure: - say or - bid good-bye; *504:13.* courtesy: - give one's regards.
- send or - give REGARDS /to/, - express one's regards /to/, - say 'Hi' /to/: /A/ **selâm söyle-** → söyle- 1. *504:13.* courtesy: - give one's regards.
- send one's regards or compliments /to/, - pay or - give one's respects /to/: *quite formal:* /A/ **saygılar sun-** → sun- 1. *155:5.* respect: - do or - pay hommage to; *504:13.* courtesy: - give one's regards.
- send a {TELEGRAM/wire} /to/, - wire /Ø/: /A/ **telgraf çek-** → çek- 9. *347:19.* communications: - telegraph.
- send TO THE BLACKBOARD [teacher sends student]: **tahtaya kaldır-** → kaldır- 1. *176:15.* transferal, transportation: - send.

- SENSE, - feel [pride, interest, happiness, sorrow, pain]: **duy-** 3. *24:6.* sensation: - sense.
- sense, - understand sth intuitively, - feel, - perceive, - discern [I sensed that she was bored.]: **hisset-** 2, **sez-**. *24:6.* sensation: - sense; *93:10.* feeling: - feel; *933:4.* intuition, instinct: - intuit.

- SEPARATE, - take away /from/: /DAn/ **ayır-** 1. *801:8.* separation: - separate.

- separate, - distinguish, - differentiate [Language separates man from animals.]: **ayır- 4** . *864:10.* particularity: - characterize.

- SERVE /θ/ [one's country, guests], - wait /{ON/UPON}/ [guests], - attend /to/ [guests]: **/A/ hizmet et-**. *577:13.* servant, employee: - serve.

- serve [food] [Cook for 20 minutes and then serve hot.]: **servis yap-** → yap- 3. *478:12.* giving: - give.

- serve or - offer [food or drink at a party, gathering] /to/ sb, - serve or - offer /θ/ sb sth: **/A/ ikram et-** 1. *439:4.* offer: - offer; *478:12.* giving: - give.

- serve [(out) food to the needy], - distribute [anything], - hand out, - dispense /to/: **/A/ dağıt- 2.** *770:4a.* dispersion: - disperse sth.

- serve IN THE ARMED FORCES, - do one's military service: **askerliğini yap-** → yap- 3. *458:18.* warfare: - serve.

- serve [OUT] food /to/, - put food /ON/ sb's plate: **/A/ koy- 2.** *159:12.* location: - place; *176:17.* transferal, transportation: - ladle; *478:12.* giving: - give.

- serve out, - dish out, - distribute a {serving/share} /{INTO/ONTO}/ [food onto plate]: **/A/ paylaştır-**. *176:17.* transferal, transportation: - ladle.

- serve a prison SENTENCE, - serve or - do time: **ceza çek-** → çek- 5, **cezasını çek- 2** ['- serve a prison sentence /for/...'] → çek- 5. *429:18.* confinement: - be imprisoned; *824:5.* spell: - take one's turn.

- serve THE PURPOSE, - do the job, - work [subj.: machine]: **iş gör-** → gör- 4. *387:17.* use: - avail; *407:4.* accomplishment: - accomplish; *994:3.* expedience: - expedite one's affair.

- SET, - go down [The sun has set.]: **bat- 1.** *194:6.* descent: - sink; *1026:12.* darkness, dimness: - grow dark.

- set [a watch or clock to the correct time]: **saat düzelt-** → düzelt- 4, **kur- 2.** *396:13.* restoration: - remedy; *787:7.* agreement: - make agree.

- set /{BY/ACCORDING TO}/ [watch according to the radio]: **/A göre/ ayarla- 1.** *787:7.* agreement: - make agree.

- set ABOUT /θ/, - set /to/, - start /θ/, - begin /θ/, - embark /UPON/: **/A/ koyul-**. *817:7a.* beginning: - begin sth.

- set AHEAD, - turn ahead [clocks]: **[saatleri] ileri al-** → al- 1. *162:2.* progression: - progress.

- set sth ASIDE /FOR/, - save sth /FOR/: **/A/ ayır- 2, /A/ koy- 3, /A/ sakla- 3.** *386:12.* store, supply: - reserve; *474:5.* retention: - retain.

- set or - turn BACK [clocks]: **[saatleri] geri al- 2** → al- 1. *163:8a.* regression: - turn sth back.

- set, - lay down, or - establish a CONDITION, prerequisite /for/: **/için/ şart koş-** → koş- 2. *958:4.* qualification: - make conditional.

- set or - fix a DATE, time /FOR/ an event [They have set a date for the wedding.]: **{tespit et-/sapta-}** 2. *864:11.* particularity: - specify; *964:4.* prearrangement: - prearrange.

- set FIRE to, - set on fire, - light, - ignite, - burn: **yak- 1.** *1019:22.* heating: - ignite.

- set FOOT /ON/: **/A/ ayak bas-** → bas- 1. *177:27.* travel: - walk.

- set an INSTRUMENT /FOR/, - program a computer /FOR/: **/A/ programla- 2.** *964:4.* prearrangement: - prearrange; *1041:18.* computer science: - computerize.

- set IN [subj.: darkness, fog]: **bas- 4.** *817:7b.* beginning: for sth - begin.

- set OFF or - start {off/out} /from/ [subj.: vehicle; destination is not indicated]: **/DAn/ kalk- 2.** *188:8.* departure: - set out.

- set ON FIRE, - set fire to, - light, - ignite, - burn: **yak- 1.** *1019:22.* heating: - ignite.

- set OUT, - start off or - leave /ON/ a journey, - set out /ON/ the road [person on foot or vehicle]: **yola {çık-/koyul-}** → çık- 2, koyul-. *188:8.* departure: - set out; *817:7a.* beginning: - begin sth.

- set {out/off} /FOR/, - leave /FOR/ [usually by means of a land vehicle, i.e., bus, train, not a boat and not a person on foot]: **/A/ hareket et- 2.** *161:9.* direction: - head for; *188:8.* departure: - set forth.

- set out /from/, - start out /from/; - depart /from/: **/DAn/ hareket et- 3** [usually by means of a land vehicle, i.e., bus, train, not a boat and not a person on foot]. *188:6.* departure: - depart.

- set or - fix a PRICE /ON/ [goods or services]: **/A/ fiyat koy-** → koy- 1. *630:11.* price, fee: - price.

- set, - lay, or - prepare a TABLE [or other surface for a meal]: **sofra kur-** → kur- 1. *159:16.* location: - establish; *405:6.* preparation: - prepare.

- set or - fix a TIME, date /for/ an event [They have set a time for the wedding.]: {tespit et-/sapta-} 2. *964:6.* prearrangement: - schedule.
- set or - tune /TO/ [TV to the music channel]: /A/ ayarla- 1. *787:7.* agreement: - make agree.
- set UP or - erect [pole, flag staff] /{IN/ON}/: /A/ 2 dik- 2. *159:16.* location: - establish; *200:9.* verticalness: - erect.
- set up /{IN/ON}/, - assemble [machine, furniture] /{IN/ON}/: /A/ kur- 1. *159:16.* location: - establish; *200:9.* verticalness: - erect.
- set up a household, - start a family: aile kur- → kur- 1. *817:11.* beginning: - inaugurate; *891:10.* production: - establish.

- SETTLE one's DEBTS or bills, - pay off an account, - pay up: borcunu öde-, borcunu {kapa-/kapat-} → {kapa-/kapat-} 8. *624:13.* payment: - pay in full.
- settle [oneself] DOWN /{IN/INTO}/ [a chair]: /A/ yerleş-. *159:17.* location: - settle; *912:10.* depression <act of lowering>: - sit down.
- settle, - establish oneself, or - make one's home /IN/ a place permanently or temporarily: /A/ yerleş-. *159:17.* location: - settle.
- settle, - decide, or - resolve a MATTER, problem: hallet-. *939:2.* solution: - solve.
- settle, - alight, - perch, or - land /{ON/UPON}/ [subj.: bird, insect, helicopter, not plane]: /A/ kon-. *194:7.* descent: - get down; *194:10.* : - light upon.
- settle /{ON/UPON}/, - come down /upon/ [subj.: fog, smoke]: /{üstüne/üzerine}/ çök- 3. *194:10.* descent: - light upon.

- SEW, - make by sewing: 1 dik- 1 [when the object to be created by sewing is specified: She sewed herself a dress.], dikiş dik- [when the specific object to be created by sewing is not specified: She sewed for two hours.]. → 1 dik- 1. *741:4.* sewing: - sew; *891:8.* production: - produce, - create.

- SHAKE, - rock [The earthquake shook the whole city.]: salla- 3. *916:10.* agitation: - agitate.
- shake [obj.: liquid: Shake the medicine before using.]: çalkala- 1. *916:10.* agitation: - agitate.
- shake sb's HAND, - shake hands /with/ sb: /I/ el sık- → sık- 1. *585:10.*

hospitality, welcome: - greet; *915:14.* oscillation: - move up and down.
- shake HANDS /WITH/: /lA/ tokalaş-. *585:10.* hospitality, welcome: - greet; *915:14.* oscillation: - move up and down.
- shake one's HEAD [in negation, affirmation, or surprise]: başını salla- → salla- 3. *131: * 17.* inexpectation: gestures of; *441:3. * 1.* consent: gestures of; *442:5. * 1.* refusal: gestures of; *916:10.* agitation: - agitate.
- shake /OFF/ or - manage to get away /from/ [an annoying person, flies]: /DAn/ kurtul- 1. *431:8.* liberation: - free oneself from.
- shake /WITH/ [fear, anger], - tremble /{WITH/IN}/ [fear]: /DAn/ titre- 2. *127:14.* fear, frighteningness: - tremble; *152:25a.* anger: gestures of anger; *916:11.* agitation: - shake.

SHAME on you!, For shame!: Aşk olsun! 1 → ol- 11 → olsun, Utan! → utan-, /mAklA/ Çok ayıp ettin! [You behaved very shamefully /BY...ing/!] → ayıp et-. *510:27.* disapproval: INTERJ. God forbid!
Shame on them!, For shame!: Yuh olsun! → ol- 11 → olsun. *510:27.* disapproval: INTERJ. God forbid!

- SHAPE UP, - amount to sth, - grow up, - become mature, morally correct, responsible [used for both men and women]: adam ol- → ol- 12. *303:9.* age: - mature.

- SHARE sth [money, goods, expenses] /with/ sb: /lA/ paylaş-. *476:6.* participation: - share.
- share IDEAS, views /with/ sb: {a: düşünceye/b: fikre/c: görüşe} katıl- 3 ['- share /θ/ {a: thoughts/b: opinions/c: views}'], /lA/ fikir paylaş- ['- share ideas /with/'], /lA/ {fikir/görüş} savun- 2 ['- share {opinions/views} /with/, - agree, - concur /with/'], /A/ katıl- 3 [obj: person: I agree /WITH/ you.]. *332:9.* assent: - concur.

- SHARPEN: bile- [knife or other blades but not pencil], kalem aç- [pencil, not knife] → aç- 6. *285:7.* sharpness: - sharpen.

- SHATTER [The glass shattered.], - break into pieces: parçalan- 2. *801:13.* separation: - shatter.

- shatter or - destroy sb's HOPES: **ümidini kır-**. → kır- 1. *125:11.* hopelessness: - shatter one's hopes.

- SHAVE: **sakal tıraşı yap-** ['- shave sb, - give sb a shave'] → yap- 3, **tıraş ol-** 1 ['- shave oneself'] → ol-10.1. *3:22.* hair: - cut or - dress the hair; *255:10.* subtraction: - excise; *268:6.* shortness: - shorten.

- SHIELD, - preserve, - protect sb /from/ [misfortune] [subj.: God]: **/DAn/ sakla-** 4. *504: * 20.* courtesy: polite expressions; *1007:18a.* protection: - protect.

- SHINE, - sparkle [subj.: sun, moon, stars, diamond ring, face]: **parla-**. *1024:23.* light: - shine.

- SHIVER /from/ [cold, fever]: **/DAn/ titre-** 1. *916:11.* agitation: - shake.

- SHOOT, - shoot dead: **/I/ vur-** 2. *308:17.* killing: - strike dead; *903:12.* pushing, throwing: - shoot.
- shoot /AT/, - fire /{ON/UPON}/: **/A/ ateş et-**. *459:22.* attack: - pull the trigger; *903:12.* pushing, throwing: - shoot.
- shoot bullets /AT/, - fire a gun /AT/: **/A/ kurşun at-** → at- 6. *903:12.* pushing, throwing: - shoot.
- shoot or - make a FILM, movie: **film çek-** [for both amateur and professional film makers] → çek- 7, **film çevir** 1- ['- act in a movie or film, - make a movie'] → çevir- 3, **film çevir** 2 ['- produce, - make a movie', professional film maker] → çevir- 3. *714:14.* photography: - photograph.

- SHOP, - do shopping: **alışveriş yap-** → yap- 3. *731:16.* commerce, economics: - trade with; *733:8.* purchase: - shop.
- shop /AT/, - trade /AT/, - patronize /θ/ [a business establishment]: **/DAn/ alışveriş et-**. *731:16.* commerce, economics: - trade with; *733:8.* purchase: - shop.

- SHORTEN [cuffs, hair], - make short: **kısalt-** 1. *268:6.* shortness: - shorten.

- SHOUT, - scream, or - yell /AT, saying/ [anger]: **/A, diye/ bağır-, bağırıp çağır-** → çağır- 3, **/A, diye/ haykır-**. *59:6.* cry, call: - cry.

- shout FOR HELP or because of fear, excitement: **çığlık at-** → at- 1, **haykır-**. *59:6.* cry, call: - cry.

- SHOW /θ/ sb sth, - show sth /to/ sb, - demonstrate /to/: **/A/ göster-** 1. *348:5.* manifestation: - manifest.
- show, - play, or - be on [subj.: movie or theater production: Where is that movie showing?]: **oyna-** 2. *714:16.* photography: - project.
- show one's AGE: **yaşını göster-** → göster- 2. *33:10.* appearance: - appear to be.
- show or - take sb AROUND [a place: city]: **/I/ gezdir-**. *176:12.* transferal, transportation: - transport; *348:5.* manifestation: - manifest.
- show CONCERN /FOR/, - be concerned /with/; - attend /TO/, - look /AFTER/: **/lA/ ilgilen-** 2. *339:9.* carefulness: - look after; *982:5.* attention: - attend to.
- show sb HOW TO GET TO a place, - point out the way /to/: **/A/ yol göster-** 1 → göster- 1. *348:5.* manifestation: - manifest.
- show the INFLUENCE /OF/, - be influenced /BY/: **/DAn/ etkilen-** 1. *893:7.* influence: - influence.
- show OFF, - be a show-off: **gösteriş yap-** → yap- 3. *501:16.* ostentation: - show off.
- show off, - act snobbishly, - give oneself airs: **hava bas-** 2. *501:16.* ostentation: - show off.
- show RESPECT /{to/ FOR}/, - behave respectfully /toward/, - treat with respect, - respect [a person, a person's ideas]: **/A/ saygı göster-** → göster- 1. *143:10.* kindness, benevolence: - be considerate; *155:5.* respect: - do or - pay hommage to.
- show, say THE TIME [subj.: a timepiece]: **saat** *hour* **göster-**. → göster- 1. *348:5.* manifestation: - manifest.

- SHOWER, - take a shower: **duş {al-/yap-}** → al- 1, yap- 3. *79:19.* cleanness: - wash.

- SHRINK, - become smaller [subj.: clothing]: **çek-** 1 1. *260:9.* contraction: - shrink.

- SHUT, - close sth: **{kapa-/kapat-}** 1 [obj.: the door/your books], **ört-** 3 [obj.: curtains, door, window, cover]. *293:6.* closure: - close.
- shut, - close [i.e., - become shut: The door shut.]: **kapan-** 1. *293:6.* closure: - close.

593

- shut DOWN, - close, or - abolish [obj.: institution, organization, business, school]: {kapa-/kapat-} 7. *293:8.* closure: - close shop.
- shut down or - close for vacation [subj.: an institution, school, business], - recess, - go into recess for vacation [subj.: schools]: tatile gir-. *20:9.* rest, repose: - vacation; *293:8.* closure: - close shop; *856:8.* cessation: - stop work.
- shut UP, - stop talking, - be quiet: sesini kes- → kes- 4. *51:5.* silence: - be silent.

- SHY [subj.: animal only], - start or - be startled /BY/ [subj.: person or animal] [All these Engish verbs indicate a sudden physical movement in reaction to a fright.]: /DAn/ ürk- 1. *131:5.* inexpectation: - be startled.

- SIDLE UP /TO/, - come up /to/ the side of, over to: yanına {gel-/ yanaş-} → gel- 1, → yanaş- 1. *167:3.* approach: - approach .

- SIGH, - heave a sigh: iç çek- → çek- 1. *52:14.* faintness of sound: - sigh.

- SIGHTSEE, - tour [on foot or in a vehicle], - go about, - walk about, - stroll: /I/ gez-. *177:21.* travel: - journey; *177:23.* : - wander.

- SIGN, - write one's name /ON/ [obj.: letter, document]: /I/ {imzala-/imza et-}, /A/ imza at- '- put one's John Hancock ON [the check] [lit., '- throw {one's} signature ON (the check)'], *perhaps less formal than the above.* → at- 3. *546:6.* letter: - letter.
- sign an AGREEMENT or contract /with/, - make a contract /with/: /lA kontrat yap- → yap- 3. *332:10.* assent: - come to an agreement.

- SIGNIFY, - mean, - express [subj.: sign, picture, word]: ifade et- 2. *517:17.* signs, indicators: - signify; *518:8.* meaning: - mean.

- SING [subj.: person]: söyle- 4. *708:38.* music: - sing.
- sing songs, - sing [subj.: person]: şarkı {oku-/söyle-} → oku- 5, söyle- 4. *708:38.* music: - sing.
- sing [of birds], - chirp [of birds or insects], - crow [of rooster]: öt- 1. *60:5.* animal sounds: [birds] - warble.
- sing, - perform, or - play sth /FOR/ sb: /A/ sun- 2. *328:9.* action: - perform; *708:39a.* music: - play sth.

- SINK, - set [sun]: [güneş] bat-. *194:6.* descent: - sink; *1026:12.* darkness, dimness: - grow dark.
- sink /{IN/INTO}/ [subj.: sun, ship]: /A/ bat- 1. *194:6.* descent: - sink; *1026:12.* darkness, dimness: - grow dark.
- sink, - fall, - go, or - lapse into A COMA: komaya gir-. *25:5.* insensibility: - faint.
- sink TO a low level in behavior, - stoop to doing sth despicable, - demean oneself: alçal- 2. *137:7.* humility: - humble oneself.

- SIP: yudumla-. *8:29.* eating: - drink.

- SIT, - be sitting /in/ [He is sitting in that chair.]: /DA/ otur- 2. *173:10.* quiescence: - sit.
- sit or - sit down /IN/ [i.e., - move /INTO/ a sitting postion: Sit down IN that chair.]: /A/ otur- 1. *912:10.* depression: - sit down.
- sit down suddenly, heavily /IN/, - collapse /INTO/ [a chair]: /A/ çök- 2. *912:10.* depression: - sit down.

- SIZE UP, - assess, - appraise, - evaluate [situation]: değerlendir- 1. *300:10.* measurement: - measure; *945:9.* judgment: - estimate.

- SKI: kay- 3, kayak yap- → yap- 3. *177:35.* travel: - glide; *753:4.* skiing: - ski.

- SKID, - slide, - slip; - slide over /to/ [the side so I can see the screen better]: /A/ kay- 1. *177:35.* travel: - glide; *194:9.* descent: - slide.

- SKIP or - omit [a lesson, a step in a process]: atla- 2. *340:7.* neglect: - leave undone.

- SKYROCKET, - increase suddenly, - soar, or - rise suddenly [prices]: fırla- 2. *251:6.* increase: - grow, increase [i.].

- SLAM [obj.: a door: She slammed the door behind her.]: kapıyı {çarp-/vur-} → çarp- 1, kapıyı vur- 2 → vur- 1. *53:7.* loudness: - din; *293:6.* closure: - close.
- slam [shut] [subj.: a door: The door slammed (shut) behind her.]: kapı çarp- → çarp- 1. *53:7.* loudness: - din; *293:6.* closure: - close; *352:7.* publication: poster: * specific signs.

- SLANDER: karala- 3. *512:11.* disparagement: - slander.

- SLAP /θ/: **eliyle vur-** → vur- 1, /A/ **tokat {at-/vur-}** → at- 5. *604:12.* punishment: - slap; *901:19.* impulse, impact: - slap.

- SLED [winter sport]: **kay-** 2. *177:35.* travel: - glide.

- SLEEP: **uyu-** 1. *22:13.* sleep: - sleep.
- sleep WITH, - go to bed with, i.e., - have sex with: /lA/ **yat-** 2. *75:21.* sex: - copulate; *562:14.* lovemaking, endearment: - make love.

- SLICE UP, - cut up into slices: **dilimle-** , **dilim dilim kes-** → kes- 1. *792:6.* part: - separate; *801:11.* separation: - sever.

- SLIDE, - slip, - skid; - slide over /to/ [the side so I can see the screen better]: /A/ **kay-** 1. *177:35.* travel: - glide; *194:9.* descent: - slide.

- SLIP ONE'S MIND, - forget: **akıldan çık-** → çık- 1. *989:7.* forgetfulness: - be forgotten.

- SLOW DOWN or - lose speed [vehicle, runner], - die down [rain]: **yavaşla-**. *175:9.* slowness: - slow.

- SMARTEN [ONESELF] UP, - tidy [oneself] up [before entering the director's room]: **üstünü başını {düzelt-/toparla-/topla-}** → düzelt- 3, toparla- 3, topla- 2. *79:18.* cleanness: - clean; *807:12.* arrangement: - tidy, tidy up.

- SMASH, - break into pieces, - cut up, - tear to pieces: **parçala-**. *801:13.* separation: - shatter.

- SMEAR, - spread, or - rub sth /ON/, - apply /to, to the surface of/ [smear cream ON skin]: /A, {üstüne/ üzerine}/ **sür-** 4. *295:19.* covering: - cover.

- SMELL sth, - take in the smell of sth [She smelled the roses.]: **kokla-**. *69:8.* odor: - smell.
- smell /OF/ sth, - give off a smell [The room smelled OF fish.]: /θ/ **kok-** 1. *69:6.* odor: - have an odor.
- smell bad, - stink: **kok-** 2. *71:4.* stench: - stink.

- SMILE /AT/: /A/ **gülümse-**. *116:7.* rejoicing: - smile.

- SMOKE [obj.: tobacco, cigarette, pipe]: **iç-** 2. *89:14.* tobacco: - use tobacco.

- smoke cigarettes: **sigara iç-** → iç- 2, **sigara kullan-**. *89:14.* tobacco: - use tobacco.
- smoke, for smoke - rise /from/ [The embers are smoking.]: /DAn/ **duman çık-** → çık- 3. *1018:23.* heat: - smoke, - fume.

- SMOTHER, - suffocate, - be stifled, suffocated, - be strangled, - feel faint: **boğul-** 2. *308:18.* killing: - strangle.

- SNACK /ON/ sth, - have or - eat a snack, - grab a bite: **atıştır-** 2. *8:26.* eating: - pick.
- snack, - have a snack, - eat food as a casual snack [The food may include, but is not limited to, junk food, i.e., cookies, candy, candy bars, etc., the kind of food sold in vending machines in the U.S.]: **abur cubur ye-** → ye- 1. *8:26.* eating: - pick.

- SNAP, - pop off; - break in two [subj.: thread], - break, - break off, - come off [subj.: button]: **kop-** 1. *801:9.* separation: - come apart.

- SNEEZE: **hapşır-**. *57:2.* sibilation: - sibilate; *318:21.* * 1. wind: - breathe.

- SNORE: **horla-**. *22:13.* sleep: - sleep; *54:6.* resonance: - resonate; *57:2.* sibilation: - sibilate; *58:3.* stridency: - rasp; *58:9.* : <sound harshly> - jangle.

- SNOW: **kar yağ-**. *1022:11.* cold: - hail.

So THAT: **diye 3.1a** → de- 1. *380:11.* intention: PREP., CONJ. for.
So THIS IS WHAT THINGS HAVE COME TO!, So things have come to this!, What times [lit., days] we have lived to see!: **Ne günler.E kaldık.** → kal- 1. *122:19.* wonder: INTERJ. my word!
So WHAT?, So what of it?: {**Ne olacak?/Ne olmuş?**} → ol- 11 → olacak. *997:26.* unimportance: PHR. what does it matter?
So WHERE'S...?, So whatever happened to...? [the book you promised me]: **Nerede kaldı?** → kal- 1. *132: * 7.* disappointment: expressions of.

- SOAR, - increase suddenly, - rise suddenly, - skyrocket, or - jump [prices]: **fırla-** 2. *251:6.* increase: - grow, increase [i.].

- SOBER UP: **ayıl-** 1. *516:2.* sobriety: - sober up.

- SOIL, - dirty, - get or - make sth dirty, - pollute: **kirlet-**, **pislet-**. *80:15a.* uncleanness: - dirty.
- soil or - wet one's underclothes or bed: **altına kaçır-** → kaçır- 2, **altını ıslat-**. *12:13.* excretion: - defecate; *12:14.* : - urinate; *1063:12.* moisture: - moisten.

- SOLVE a problem, - figure sth out [puzzle, mathematical problem]: **çöz-** 2. *939:2.* solution: - solve.
- solve, - find a solution /for/, - handle, - resolve [situation, personal problem, matter]: **hallet-**. *939:2.* solution: - solve.

- SOW or - plant /IN/ [obj.: seeds, not plants, seedlings, saplings, trees]: /A/ **ek-**. *1067:18.* agriculture: - plant.

- SPARE sb's LIFE, not - separate sb from sb else [mother from child]: **bağışla-** 3. *430:14.* freedom: - exempt; *504: * 20.* courtesy: polite expressions.
- spare NO EXPENSE: **masraftan {kaçMA-/kaçınMA-}** → kaç- 2. *626:5.* expenditure: - spend.

- SPARKLE, - shine: [subj.: sun, moon, stars, diamond ring, face]: **parla-**. *1024:23.* light: - shine.

- SPEAK /to/ sb, - talk /to/ sb: /A/ **söyle-** 3, /A/ **konuş-**. *524:27.* speech: - address.
- speak or - talk /a, b: about, c: concerning, d: on, e: on the subject of/, - speak a language: /a: I, b: **hakkında**, c: A **dair**, d: **üzerine**, e: **konusunda**/ **konuş-**. *524:20.* speech: - speak.
- speak ABOUT THIS AND THAT, about various subjects at random: **{havadan sudan/şundan bundan} konuş-**. *524:26.* speech: - utter in a certain way.
- speak AS IF [he were an expert]: *verb stem*.**mIş gibi konuş-**. *524:26.* speech: - utter in a certain way.
- speak BLUNTLY, frankly: **dobra dobra {konuş-/söyle-}** → konuş-, söyle- 1. *524:26.* speech: - utter in a certain way; *644:12.* probity: - be frank.
- speak BROKEN [obj.: Turkish, English, etc.], - speak a little of a language: **çat pat konuş-**. *524:26.* speech: - utter in a certain way.
- speak FRANKLY, openly: **{açık/açıkça} konuş-[or söyle]** → konuş-, söyle- 1. *524:26.* speech: -

utter in a certain way; *644:12.* probity: - be frank.
- speak ILL OF sb behind his back: **arkasından konuş-**. *512:11.* disparagement: - slander; *524:26.* speech: - utter in a certain way.
- speak or - know a LANGUAGE: *noun designating a language*.**sI var**, e.g., **Türkçesi var**. 'He {knows/speaks} Turkish.' Also: 'A Turkish version [or translation] of it [a book, etc.] exists.' → ol- 3, Additional examples. b) 4. Miscellaneous additional examples. *524:26.* speech: - utter in a certain way.
- speak UP, - raise one's voice: **ses çıkar- 1** → çıkar- 7. *524:26.* speech: - utter in a certain way.
- speak up AGAINST sth, - say sth against, - raise one's voice against, - object, - voice one's opinions, - say sth: **ses çıkar- 2** → çıkar- 7. *453:3.* resistance:- offer resistance.

SPEAKING OF, incidentally: → by the way.

- SPEED, - go too fast [vehicle]: **{hız/sürat} yap-** → yap- 3. *174:8.* swiftness: - speed.
- speed UP, - accelerate, - gather speed [subj.: vehicle, person]: **hızlan- 1**. *174:10.* swiftness: - accelerate [i.].

- SPELL [say the names of the letters of a word]: **{harf harf/harflerini} söyle-** → söyle- 1. Turks, however, usually pronounce the syllables of a word to indicate spelling. → - syllabify. *546:7.* letter: - spell.

- SPEND MONEY /{ON [or FOR]/ON [or for]}/: /{A/için}/ **para harca-** → {harca-/sarf et-} 1, /{A/için}/ **masraf {et-/yap-}**. *626:5.* expenditure: - spend; *729:15.* finance, investment: - finance; *896:4.* liability: - incur.
- spend a lot of money on sth or to get sth done, - have a lot of expenses, - incur great expense: **masrafa gir-**. *626:5.* expenditure: - spend; *729:15.* finance, investment: - finance; *896:4.* liability: - incur.
- spend THE WHOLE NIGHT somewhere until morning, - stay up all night: **gecele-**, **sabahla-**. *820:6.* time: - spend time.
- spend TIME /a: with [sb or sth], b: [by]...ing, c: [BY]...ing/: /a: IA, b: **ArAk**, c: **mAklA**/ **{vakit/**

zaman} geçir- → geçir- 3. *820:6.*
time: - spend time.
- spend time /{on/[in order] to}/: /için/
{vakit/zaman} harca- → {harca-
/sarf et-} 2. *820:6.* time: - spend time.

- SPILL sth /ON, on/ [He spilled the milk
on the floor.]: /A, {üstüne/
üzerine}/ dök- 2. *238:17a.* stream:
- make overflow.
- spill /ON, on/ [The milk spilled on the
floor.]: /A, {üstüne/üzerine}/
dökül- 1. *190:13.* emergence: - run
out; *238:17b.* stream: - overflow.
- spill OUT as waste, - throw out
/{ON/INTO}/ [obj.: garbage]: /A/
dök- 3. *390:7.* discard: - discard.
- spill out [subj.: things from closet,
people from room]: /A, dışarı/ taş-
2. *238:17b.* stream: - overflow.

- SPIT /{ON/IN/INTO}/: /A/ tükür-.
13:6. secretion: - salivate.

- SPLIT UP, - break up, - part company
/WITH/ [The couple broke up. She
split up WITH her boyfriend.]:
/DAn/ ayrıl- 1. *801:19.* separation:
- part company.
- split up /WITH/, - be or - get
DIVORCED /from/: /DAn/ boşan-
, /DAn/ ayrıl- → ayrıl- 1. *566:5.*
divorce, widowhood: - divorce.

- SPOIL, - go bad [subj.: all kinds of
food]: bozul-. *393:22.* impairment: -
decay.
- spoil, - go bad, - go stale [subj.: certain
foods: bread, fish]: bayatla-. *393:22.*
impairment: - decay.
- spoil sth, - ruin, - break, - corrupt [obj.:
morals], - violate [rules]: boz- 1.
393:10. impairment: - spoil; *395:10.*
destruction: - destroy.
- spoil sb's MOOD, - put or - get sb out of
sorts: kafasını boz-. → boz- 1.
96:13. unpleasure: - annoy.
- spoil sb's mood, - depress sb: moralini
boz-. → boz- 1. *112:18.* sadness: -
sadden.

- SPOT, - notice: farket- 1, farkına
var-. *27:12.* vision: - see; *940:5.*
discovery: - detect; *982:6.* attention: -
heed.

- SPRAIN, - twist [obj.: ankle]: burk-.
393:13. impairment: - inflict an
injury.

- SPRAY or - pepper with fire [i.e.,
bullets], - blaze away at, - strafe, -
rake with shot: tara- 3. *459:22.*
attack: - pull the trigger.

- SPREAD, - rub, or - smear sth /ON/, -
apply sth /to, to the surface of/
[spread cream ON skin]: /A,
{üstüne/üzerine}/ sür- 4. *295:19.*
covering: - cover.
- spread or - pass /from [one person], to
[another]/ [subj.: disease]: /DAn, A/
geç- 2. *770:4b.* dispersion: -
disperse, - become dispersed.
- spread /a: from, b: to, c: {through/by
means of}/ [subj.: fire, disease,
religion, empires, rumor]: /a: DAn,
b: A, c: yoluyla/ yayıl-. *770:4b.*
dispersion: - disperse, - become
dispersed.

- SPRINKLE, - drizzle, - rain lightly:
çisele-. *316:9* rain: - rain.

- SQUEEZE [obj.: oranges to extract the
juice]; - pinch, - be too tight [subj.:
belt]: sık- 1. *260:8.* contraction: -
squeeze.
- squeeze, - squirt, - spray /ON/ [juice on
soup, water on fire]: /A/ sık- 2.
908:25. ejection: - disgorge.

- STALL [subj.: engine, vehicle]: dur-
10. *856:7.* cessation: for sth - cease.

- STAND /θ/, - put up /WITH/, - bear /θ/,
- endure /θ/, - suffer /θ/, - tolerate /θ/,
- take /θ/: /A/ dayan- 3, /A/
katlan- 2, *more formal, less current
than the above:* /A/ tahammül et-.
134:5. patience: - endure; *1047:3.*
toughness: - toughen.
- stand /{on/at/in}, {AT/BY}/: /DA,
başında/ dur- 3. *200:7.*
verticalness: - stand.
- stand ON ONE'S FEET, - be standing:
ayakta dur- → dur- 3. *200:7.*
verticalness: - stand.
- stand UP, - rise /from/, - get up
/{from/OUT OF}/ [bed, chair]:
/DAn/ kalk- 1, ayağa kalk- ['-
get /to/ one's feet'] → kalk- 1. *193:8.*
ascent: - ascend; *200:8.* verticalness: -
rise.

- STARE angrily /AT/, - glare /AT/: /A/
dik dik bak- → bak- 3. *27:16:* -
glare; *152:25a.* resentment, anger:
gestures of.

- START, - begin, - commence [The class
has started.]: başla- 1. *817:7b.*
beginning: for sth - begin.
- start or - begin /θ/ sth [He started θ the
class. He started {to work/working).]:
/A/ başla- 2. *817:7a.* beginning: -
begin sth.
- start sth, - cause sth to begin, - begin sth
[The referee started the game.]: /I/

başlat-. *817:7a.* beginning: - begin sth.

- start, - found, or - establish [organization, republic]; - set up or - assemble [tent, table] /{IN/ON}/: **/A/ kur-** 1. *159:16.* location: - establish; *200:9.* verticalness: - erect; *817:11.* beginning: - inaugurate; *891:10.* production: - establish.

- start, - be startled /BY/ [subj.: person or animal], - shy [subj.: animal only] [All these English verbs indicate a sudden physical movement in reaction to a fright.]: **/DAn/ ürk-** 1. *131:5.* inexpectation: - be startled.

- start a FAMILY, - set up a household: **aile kur-** → kur- 1. *817:11.* beginning: - inaugurate; *891:10.* production: - establish.

- start or - pick a FIGHT /with/, - provoke a quarrel /with/: **/lA/ kavga çıkar-** → çıkar- 7. *375:17.* motivation, inducement: - incite; *459:14.* attack: - attack; *817:7a.* beginning: - begin sth.

- start OFF, - set out, or - leave /ON/ a {trip/journey}, - set out /ON/ the road [person on foot or vehicle]: **yola {çık-/koyul-}** → çık- 2, koyul-. *188:8.* departure: - set out; *817:7a.* beginning: - begin sth.

- start TO DAYDREAM, - daydream, - go off /INTO/ daydreams, reverie, - reminisce: **{hayale/hayallere} dal-** → dal- 2. *984:9.* distraction, confusion: - muse; *988:11.* memory: - reminisce.

- STATE, - make clear: **belirt-**. *334:5.* affirmation: - affirm; *524:24.* speech: - state.

- state, - express, - say what one means: **ifade et-** → ifade et- 1. *532:4.* diction: - phrase.

- state, - note, - announce, - declare [*formal, official*: in speech and in writing]: **kaydet- 4.** *334:5.* affirmation: - affirm; *524:24.* speech: - state.

- STAY or - remain /{at/in/on}/ a place: **/DA/ kal-** 1, **/DA/ dur-** 6, **/DA/ otur-** 4. *256:5.* remainder: - remain; *855:3.* continuance: - continue.

- stay or - live with people: **yanında kal-** → kal- 1. *225:7.* habitation: - inhabit.

- stay AS A GUEST /at/: **/DA/ misafir kal-** → kal- 1. *225:8.* habitation: - sojourn.

- stay BACK IN SCHOOL, - be held back, - fail or flunk /θ/ a grade [a level in a school, not a course: When he didn't study, he stayed back.]:

sınıfta kal- → kal- 1. *410:9b.* failure: - fail in specific areas.

- stay BEHIND, - remain, - get, or - lag behind /in/ [some activity, lessons]: **/DA/ geri kal-** 1 → kal- 1. *166:4.* following: - lag; *217:8.* rear: - be behind.

- stay ON THE LINE, i.e., not - hang up on the phone: **ayrılMA-** → ayrıl- 3. *347:18.* communications: - telephone.

- stay UP all night, - spend the night somewhere until morning: **gecele-, sabahla-.** *820:6.* time: - spend time.

- STEAL /from/: **/DAn/ çal-** 1. *482:13.* theft: - steal.

- STEER CLEAR /OF/, - keep away /from/, or - avoid /θ/ sth or sb: **/DAn/ sakın-** 1. *329:3.* inaction: - refrain; *368:6.* avoidance: - avoid; *668:7.* temperance: - abstain.

- STEM, - result, - originate, - emanate, or - spring /from/, - be due /TO/: **/DAn/ kaynaklan-.** *886:5.* effect: - result from.

- STEP /ON/, - trample /{ON/θ}/ [grass]: **/A/ bas-** 1. *177:27.* travel: - walk.

- step {OUT/OUTSIDE}, - go {out/ outside}: **dışarı[.ya] çık-** 1 → çık- 2. *190:12.* emergence: - exit.

- STICK, - paste, - glue, or - tape sth /{ON/ONTO/to}/ sth: **/A/ yapıştır-**. *799:5.* joining: - put together; *802:9.* cohesion: - stick together.

- stick IN ONE'S MIND, - recall, - remember: **akılda kal-** → kal- 1. *988:10.* memory: - remember.

- stick in one's mind AND BOTHER ONE, - occupy one's mind: **aklına takıl-** → takıl- 2. *930:20.* thought: - occupy the mind.

- stick one's NOSE /INTO/, - interfere /IN/: **/A/ burnunu sok-** 1 → sok- 1. *214:5.* intruder: - intrude.

- STING /{ON/IN}/ [a part of the body] [subj.: bee, insect]: **/DAn/ sok-** 3. *8:27.* eating: - chew; *26:7.* pain: - inflict pain.

- STINK, - smell bad: **kok-** 2. *71:4.* stench: - stink.

- STIPULATE or - lay down a condition or prerequisite /for/, - make a stipulation, - state clearly and firmly as a requirement /for/: **/için/ şart koş-** → koş- 2. *958:4.* qualification: - make conditional.

- STIR, - mix, - blend [obj.: eggs and sugar]: **karıştır-** 1. *796:10a.* mixture: - mix sth.
- stir, - budge, - move slightly: {**kımılda-/kıpırda-**}. *172:5b.* motion: for sth - move.
- stir THINGS UP, - stir up trouble: **karıştır-** 5. *381:9.* plan: - plot; *1012:14.* difficulty: - cause trouble.

- STOOP to doing sth despicable, - sink to a low level in behavior, - demean oneself: **alçal-** 2. *137:7.* humility: - humble oneself.

- STOP [moving], - come to a stop /at/, - become motionless [subj.: person, vehicle]: /DA/ **dur-** 1. *856:7.* cessation: for sth - cease.
- stop, - cease [i]: **din-** [subj.: nouns of weather: wind, hail, snow, rain, storm; nouns of physical or mental pain: sorrow, tears; some nouns of emotion: anger], **dur-** 2 [subj.: a process, activity: weeping; weather: rain, storm], **kesil-** 2 [subj.: nouns mostly of weather: wind, hail, snow, rain, storm]. *744:6.* cessation: - cease [i.]; *819:6.* end: - come to an end; *856:7.* cessation: for sth - cease.
- stop, - cease, or - cut out sth [obj.: noise, crying]: **bırak-** 3, **kes-** 4. *856:6.* cessation: - cease sth.
- stop or - quit sth [when sb is bothering you: Stop it!]: **bırak-** 4, **rahat bırak-** → bırak- 4, **dur-** 4. *390:4.* disuse: - cease to use; *856:6.* cessation: - cease sth.
- stop, - prevent, - hinder sb from doing sth: /I/ **engelle-**, /A/ **mâni ol-** → ol- 12, /I/ **önle-**, **önüne geç-** → geç- 1. *1011:14.* hindrance: - prevent.
- stop FOR A REST [while traveling], - take a break while working, - make a rest stop [subj.: workers or vehicles, not students or professionals except when speaking very informally]: **mola ver-** → ver- 3. *20:8.* rest, repose: - take a rest.
- stop IN /AT/, - drop in /{AT/ON}/, - drop /BY/, - call /{ON/UPON}/, - stop off /IN/: /A/ **uğra-** 1. *582:19.* sociability: - visit.
- stop SB [thief], STH [bleeding, game]: **durdur-**. *856:11.* cessation: - put a stop to; *1011:13.* hindrance: - stop.
- stop TALKING, - be quiet, - become silent: **sus-** 2, **sesini kes-** → kes- 4. *51:7.* silence: - fall silent.
- stop talking, - be quiet, - shut up: **sesini kes-** → kes- 4. *51:5.* silence: - be silent.

- STORE or - keep sth /IN/ a place [He stores the tools in that chest.]: /DA/ **sakla-** 2. *474:5.* retention: - retain.
- STORM /θ/, - attack /θ/: /{A/ **üzerine}/ hücum et-** 1, /A/ **saldır-** 1. *459:14.* attack: - attack.
- STRAIN; - filter out [rice from water]: **süz-**. *79:22.* cleanness: - refine.
- STRAIGHTEN UP, - tidy up, - pick up, - put in order [room]: **düzelt-** 3, **topla-** 2, **toparla-** 3. *807:12.* arrangement: - tidy, tidy up.
- STRESS [the importance, necessity of], - emphasize: **vurgula-** 1, **altını çiz-** 2 ['- underline, - emphasize'] → çiz- 1. *996:14.* importance: - emphasize.
- stress, - accent, - accentuate, - put the stress on [obj.: word, syllable]: **vurgula-** 2. *901:12.* impulse, impact: - thrust, - push; *996:14.* importance: - emphasize.
- STREAM /OUT OF/ [subj.: a liquid or people]: /DAn/ **boşal-** 2. *190:13.* emergence: - run out.
- STRETCH [oneself after waking up], - have a stretch: **gerin-**. *84:4.* fitness, exercise: - exercise; *259:5.* expansion, growth: - become larger; *725:10.* exertion: - strain.
- stretch OUT /{ON/on}/ [bed, couch], - lie down /{ON/on}/: /{A/**üstüne}/ uzan-** 1. *22:13.* sleep: - sleep; *201:5.* horizontalness: - lie; *912:11.* depression: - lie down.
- stretch [one's hands] out to reach /θ/, - reach /θ/, - get /to/ [a place with one's hands: I can't reach the top shelf.]: /A/ **uzan-** 3, /A/ **yetiş-** 5, /A/ **eriş-** 2. *261:6.* distance, remoteness: - extend to.
- STRIKE, - beat: /I/ **döv-**. *604:13.* punishment: - slap; *901:14.* impulse, impact: - hit.
- strike /θ/, - hit /θ/, - bump /{AGAINST/INTO/ON}/: /A/ **çarp-** 1, /A/ **rastla-** 2. *901:13.* impulse, impact: - collide.
- strike [subj.: lightning]: **yıldırım çarp-** → çarp- 1. *901:14.* impulse, impact: - hit.
- strike one AS FUNNY, - find funny, amusing, - tickle one's funny bone: **komiğine git-** → git- 1b. *489:13.* wit, humor: - joke.
- strike one AS STRANGE, - find strange, - think strange: {**acayibine/**

599

garibine/tuhafına} git- → git-
1b, yadırga-. *869:8. * 1.*
abnormality: - find strange.

- STRIP, - rob of valuables: **soy- 2**.
482:14. theft: - rob.

- STRIVE, - struggle, - endeavor, - work
hard, - try hard /to/: **/için/ uğraş- 1**.
403:11. endeavor: - make a special
effort.
- strive /to/, - struggle /to/, - do one's best
/to/: **/A/ çabala-**. *403:13.* endeavor:
- do one's best.

- STROKE, - caress, - fondle, - pat, - pet:
okşa-, sev- 2. *73:8.* touch: - stroke;
1042:6. friction: - rub.

- STROLL, - walk, - wander, or - go about
[usually on foot]: **/I/ dolaş- 1**.
177:21. travel: - journey; *177:23.* : -
wander.
- stroll, - go, or - walk about, - tour [obj.:
place: on foot or in a vehicle], -
sightsee: **/I/ gez-**. *177:21.* travel: -
journey; *177:23.* : - wander.

- STRUGGLE /to/, - strive /to/, - do one's
best /to/: **/A/ çabala-**. *403:13.*
endeavor: - do one's best.
- struggle, - strive, - endeavor, - work
hard, - try hard /to/: **/için/ uğraş- 1**.
403:11. endeavor: - make a special
effort.
- struggle, - fight, - engage in physical
combat /with/ one another: **/lA/
dövüş-**. *457:13.* contention: -
contend.

- STUDY [a topic, not lessons], - explore,
- research, - do research on, -
investigate, - try to find out: **araştır-
2**. *937:23.* investigate: - investigate.
- study [somewhere: in Turkey], - study [a
subject area, not a particular lesson:
Turkish, economics]: **oku- 2**.
570:12. learning: - study.
- study [as a major subject, specialization:
economics, music, not lessons]:
tahsil et-. *570:12.* learning: - study.
- study, - work, - work /ON/ [Where do
you {study/work}?], - practice sth
[piano]: **çalış- 1**. *570:12.* learning: -
study; *725:12.* exertion: - work.
- study [LESSONS] [I'm studying.]: **ders
çalış-** → çalış- 1. *570:12.* learning: -
study.
- study or - work on a particular LESSON
[What lesson are you studying?]:
dersE çalış- → çalış- 1. *570:12.*
learning: - study.
- study or - examine CAREFULLY,
closely, minutely, in detail [an object,

document, not usually a doctor a
patient], - inspect, - research:
incele-, tetkik et-. *27:14.* vision: -
scrutinize; *937:25.* inquiry: - make a
close study of.

- SUBJECT, - expose /to/: **çek-** in:
sorguya çek- ['- cross-examine, -
question, - interrogate, - grill, -
subject to interrogation']. → çek- 6.
643:4. imposition: - impose.

- SUBMIT, - offer, or - present /to/ [obj.:
report, petition, thesis]: **/A/ sun- 1,
/A/ takdim et- 2**. *439:4.* offer: -
offer.
- submit an application or - apply /to, for/
[work, scholarship]: **/A, için/
{başvur-/müracaat et-} 2**.
440:10. request: - petition.

- SUBSIST, - earn, or - make one's living,
livelihood /by...ing/: **/ArAk/
geçimini sağla-, /ArAk/ geçin-
2, /ArAk/ hayatını kazan-** →
kazan- 1. *385:11.* provision,
equipment: - make a living.

- SUBSTANTIATE, - prove: **{ispatla-
/ispat et-/kanıtla-}**. *956:10.*
evidence, proof: - prove.

- SUBSTITUTE ONE THING FOR
ANOTHER, - use sth for or in place
of sth else: **yerine kullan-**. *861:4.*
substitute: - substitute.

- SUBTRACT one number /from/ another:
/DAn/ çıkar- 5. *255:9.* subtraction:
- subtract; *1016:17.* mathematics: -
calculate.

- SUCCEED /IN/, - be successful /IN/: **/I/
başar-**. *409:7a.* success: - succeed.
- succeed in getting or attaining /θ/ sth
sought, - obtain, - get: **/A/ kavuş- 2**.
409:8. success: - achieve one's
purpose.

- SUCKLE, - nurse, - breast-feed: **/I/
emzir-, /A/ meme ver-** → ver- 1.
8:19. eating: - nourish.

- SUE, - bring charges /against, for/:
/aleyhine, için/ dava aç- → aç-
12, **/I/ dava et-**. *598:12.* legal
action: - sue.
- sue, - take to court: **mahkemeye ver-**
→ ver- 1. *598:12.* legal action: - sue.

- SUFFER /θ/, - bear /θ/, - endure /θ/, -
put up /WITH/, - stand /θ/, - tolerate
/θ/, - take /θ/: **çek- 5, /A/ dayan- 3,
/A/ katlan- 2**, *more formal, less*

current than the above: /A/
tahammül et-. *134:5.* patience: -
endure; *1047:3.* toughness: - toughen.
- suffer, - endure pain, - be in pain
[physical or mental]: **acı çek-** →
çek- 5. *26:8.* pain: - suffer pain.
- suffer, - endure or - put up with troubles
[mental rather than physical pain]:
dert çek- → **çek-** 5. *26:8.* pain: -
suffer pain; *830:8.* event: -
experience.
- suffer for a deed, - get one's deserts or
dues: **cezasını çek-** 1 → **çek-** 5.
639:6. dueness: - get one's deserts.
- suffer from motion sickness, - get
motion sick [from riding in a vehicle:
boat, bus, plane]: **tut-** 8. *85:46b.*
disease: - take sick in particular ways.

- SUFFICE /FOR/, - be enough /FOR/:
/A/ **y e t -**, /A/ **yetiş-** 6. *990:4.*
sufficiency: - suffice.

- SUFFOCATE, - be suffocated, -
smother, - be stifled, strangled, - feel
faint: **boğul-** 2. *308:18.* killing: -
strangle.

- SUGGEST, - propose, or - recommend
sth /to/ sb, - advise sb to do sth: /A/
tavsiye et-. *439:5.* offer: - propose;
509:11. approval: - commend.
- suggest, - propose /to/: /A/ {**öner-**
/**teklif et-**}. *439:5.* offer: - propose.
- suggest a solution to a problem, - guide,
- advise /θ/, - give advice /to/: /A/
yol göster- 2. *422:5.* advice: -
advise.

- SUIT, - look good /ON/ [subj.: clothing]:
/A/ **yakış-** 2. *866:3.* conformity: -
conform.
- suit, - fit /θ/ [subj.: clothing]: /A/ **uy-** 1,
/A/ **gel-** 2, /{**üzerine**/ **üstüne**}/
otur- → **otur-** 5. *866:3.* conformity:
- conform.
- suit /θ/, - be right, suitable, convenient
/FOR/: /A/ **uy-** 2. *842:6.* timeliness:
- be timely; *866:3.* conformity: -
conform.

- SULK; - pout; - put on a sour face, -
look annoyed, angry, or unhappy:
surat as- → **as-** 1. *110:14.* ill
humor: - sulk; *265:8.* distortion: -
grimace.

- SUMMARIZE, - sum up: **özetle-**,
toparla- 2. *268:6.* shortness: -
shorten; *557:5.* abridgment: - abridge;
848:8. repetition: - iterate.

- SUMMON /to/, - call or - send /for/
[obj.: a doctor, an ambulance]: /A/

çağır- 1. *420:11.* command: -
summon.

- SUNBATHE: **güneşlen-** ['- sun
oneself'], **güneş banyosu yap-** ['-
take a sunbath'] → **yap-** 3. *1019:19.*
heating: - insolate.

- SUPPLICATE, - pray /to [God], FOR
[sth]/: /A, için/ **dua et-** 2. *440:11.*
request: - entreat.

- SUPPORT [financially, morally]:
destekle-. *124:10.* hope: give hope;
449:12. aid: - support; *492:16.*
courage: - encourage.
- support, - provide [a living] /for/ [one's
family] /by...ing/: /ArAk/ **geçimini**
sağla-. *3 8 5 : 1 1 .* provision,
equipment: - make a living.
- support a team: **tut-** 10. *124:10.* hope:
give hope; *492:16.* courage:
encourage.

- SUPPOSE, - guess, - surmise [that he
will come]: **tahmin et-** 1. *950:10.*
theory, supposition: - suppose;
952:11. belief: - think; *967:5.*
probability: - think likely.
- suppose, - think: {**san-**/**zannet-**}.
952:11. belief: - think.
- suppose, - imagine, - assume for the sake
of argument: **de-** 2, **farz et-**, **tut-** 9,
varsay- 1. *950:10.* theory,
supposition: - suppose.

- SURF or - browse /on/ [the Internet], -
scan, - flip /through/ [TV channels]:
/DA, arasında/ **gezin-** 2. *570:13.*
learning: - browse; *1041:18.*
computer science: - computerize.

- SURMISE, - guess: → - suppose, guess.

- SURPRISE, - astonish [That fact really
surprised me.]: **şaşırt-** 2. *122:6.*
wonder: - astonish.
- surprise, - bewilder, - confuse, - catch
off guard: **şaşırt-** 1. *984:7a.*
distraction, confusion: - confuse.

- SURROUND /with/, - place sth around
sth else: /lA/ **çevir-** 5. *209:6.*
environment: - surround.
- surround, - envelop: {**çevresini**/
etrafını} **sar-** → **sar-** 3, /I/ **sar-** 3.
209:6. environment: - surround;
212:5. enclosure: - enclose.

- SURVIVE /θ/ [obj.: an illness, accident]:
/DAn/ **kurtul-** 1. *369:6.* escape: -
escape, *398:3.* rescue: - rescue.

- survive [subj.: old inscriptions], - exist, - be existent: **dur-** 7. *760:8.* existence: - exist.

- SUSPECT θ sb, - suspect θ sth, - suspect sb /OF/ sth, - suspect sb /OF/ doing sth: /DAn/ {**şüphelen-/şüphe et-/ kuşkulan-**}. *952:11.* belief: - think.

- SWALLOW [food], - take pills; - gulp down food: **yut-**. *8:22.* eating: - devour.

- SWAP, - exchange sth for sth else: /lA/ **değiştir-** 2. *862:4.* interchange: - interchange.

- SWEAR, - vow /a: to [sb], b: θ [that], c: to the effect that, d: that [lit., saying]/; - take an oath: /a: **A**, b: **A**, c: **A dair**, d: **diye/ yemin et-**. *436:4.* promise: - promise.
- swear /AT/, - curse /θ/: /A/ {**küfret- /söv-**}. *513:6.* curse: - curse.

- SWEAT, - perspire: **terle-**. *12:16.* excretion: - sweat.

- SWEEP /with/ [a broom]: /lA/ **süpür-**. *79:23.* cleanness: - sweep.

- SWELL, - swell up, - get puffed up /{from/BECAUSE OF}/ [eyes from crying, skin from sting]: /DAn/ **şiş-** 1. *259:5.* expansion, growth: - become larger; *283:11.* convexity, protuberance: - bulge.

- SWERVE, - turn [a steering wheel, rudder, sharply] /to/ one side: /A/ [**direksiyonu hızla**] **kır-** → **kır-** 3. *164:3.* deviation: - deviate; *278:5.* angularity: - angle; *368:8.* avoidance: - dodge.

- SWIM: **yüz-** 1. *182:56.* water travel: - swim.

- SWINDLE, - gyp, - rip off, - cheat; - sell sb sth at an exorbitant, outrageous price: *formal term:* **dolandır-**. *356:18.* deception: - cheat. The two following verbs are *very common slang:* /A/ **kazık at-** → **at-** 1; /I/ **kazıkla-**. *356:19.* : nonformal terms - gyp.

- SWITCH or - turn /{OFF/out}/: {**kapa- /kapat-**} 2 [obj.: electricity, lights, lamps, computer, oven, stove, gas burner, radio, TV], **söndür-** 2 [obj.: same items as under {**kapa-/kapat-**} 2 above except computer, radio, or TV]. *856:12.* cessation: - turn off;

1026:11. darkness, dimness: - turn off the light; *1031:25.* electricity: - electrify.

- switch or - turn ON: **aç-** 2 [electricity, lights, lamps, radio, TV], **yak-** 3 [electricity, lights, lamps, but not radio, TV]. *1031:25.* electricity: - electrify.

- switch /TO/ [Channel 5], - put on [Channel 5. If the instrument is already on and you want to make a change], - turn /TO/ [page 5]: /I/ **çevir-** 4. *371:14.* choice: - select; *914:9.* rotation: - rotate.

- SYLLABIFY, - say or - read by syllable [Turks prefer this to spelling, that is, to giving the names of the letters of a word.]: **hecele-**. *546:7.* letter: - spell.

- T -

- TAKE /from, to/, - pick sth up /from/: /DAn, A/ **al-** 1. *480:21.* taking: - take from.
- take, - buy [in a store: I'll take the blue one.]: **al-** 4. *733:7.* purchase: - purchase.
- take, - accept [obj.: travelers' checks]: **kabul et-** 1. *479:6.* receiving: - receive.
- take /θ/, - tolerate /θ/, - put up /with/, - bear /θ/, - stand /θ/, - suffer /θ/, - endure /θ/: **çek-** 5, /A/ **dayan-** 3, /A/ **katlan-** 2, *more formal, less current than the above:* /A/ **tahammül et-**. *134:5.* patience: - endure; *1047:3.* toughness: - toughen.

- take ADVANTAGE /OF/ [an offer, opportunity]: /I/ **değerlendir-** 2, /DAn/ {**yararlan-/faydalan- /istifade et-**}. *387:15.* use: - take advantage of.
- take or - get ADVICE /from/, - consult /θ/ sb, - ask sb's advice: /DAn/ **akıl al-** → **al-** 1, **fikrini al-** → **al-** 1. *422:7.* advice: - take or - accept advice.
- take, - heed, or - listen to ADVICE: **söz tut-** → **tut-** 5, **sözünü tut-** 2 ['- heed, - take the advice of sb, - take sb's advice'] → **tut-** 5. *326:2.* obedience: - obey; *422:7.* advice: - take or - accept advice.
- take or - show sb AROUND [a place: city]: /I/ **gezdir-**. *176:12.* transferal, transportation: - transport; *348:5.* manifestation: - manifest.
- take AS AN EXAMPLE, role model /FOR/: /A/ {**örnek/misal**} **al-** → **al-** 1. *956:13.* evidence, proof: - cite.

602

- take AWAY or - separate /from/ [child from its mother]: /DAn/ ayır- 1. *801:8.* separation: - separate.
- take away, - clear away, - remove [dirty dishes] /from/ [table]: /DAn/ kaldır- 2. *176:11.* transferal, transportation: - remove.

- take or - give sth BACK /to/, - return sth /to/ [books to library]: /A/ {geri ver-/iade et-}. The second verb is *more formal.* → ver- 1. *481:4.* restitution: - restore.
- take back [to oneself] /from/: /DAn/ geri al- 1 → al- 1. *481:6.* restitution: - recover.
- take back or - retract one's WORDS, - recant, - rescind: sözünü geri al- → geri al- 1 → al- 1. *445:2.* repeal: - repeal.
- take a BATH, - bathe: banyo yap- → yap- 3. *79:19.* cleanness: - bathe.
- take a bath, - bathe, - wash oneself /with/ [soap] /IN/ [warm water]: /lA/ yıkan- 1. *79:19.* cleanness: - wash.
- take a BREAK [from work]: ara ver- [in most circumstances] → ver- 3, mola ver- [while traveling, for workers or vehicles, not students or professionals except when speaking very informally] → ver- 3, *formal, always appropriate:* teneffüs yap- → yap- 3. *20:8.* rest, repose: - take a rest.
- take a BREATH, - breathe; - inhale: nefes al- → al- 1. *89:14.* tobacco: - use tobacco; *187:12.* reception: - draw in; *318:21. * 1.* wind: - breathe.

Take CARE., lit., Remain IN GOOD HEALTH AND HAPPINESS. [Said by someone off on a journey to those remaining behind.]: Sağlıcakla kalın. → kal- 1. *188:22.* departure: INTERJ. farewell!; *504: * 20.* courtesy: polite expressions.
- take CARE /OF/, - look /AFTER/, - attend /to/ [guests, a matter, the phone]: /A/ bak- 3, /lA/ ilgilen- 2, /lA/ meşgul ol- → ol- 12. *339:9.* carefulness: - look after; *982:5.* attention: - attend to; *1007:19.* protection: - care for.
- take, - accept a {CHECK/CREDIT CARD}: {çek/kredi kartı} kabul et- → kabul et- 1. *479:6.* receiving: - receive.
- take a COURSE: kurs gör- → gör- 3. *570:11.* learning: - be taught.

- take great DELIGHT IN, - delight /IN/: /A/ bayıl- 2. *101:7.* eagerness: - be enthusiastic.

- take a DEPOSITION, - examine sb and record his testimony [law]: ifade al- → al- 1. *956:9.* evidence, proof: - testify.
- take DOWN, - lower, - bring down /from, to/: /DAn, A/ indir- 1. *912:4.* depression: - depress.
- take down [obj.: laundry from clothes line]: topla- 1. *769:18.* assemblage: - bring or - gather together.
- take down IN WRITING, - record, - write /IN/: /A/ yaz- 1. *549:15.* record: - record.
- take a DRAG or puff [on a cigarette]: → - take a puff.
- take the EASY WAY OUT: kolayına git- 2 → git- 1b, kolayına kaç- → kaç- 1. *331:15.* inactivity: - take it easy.
- take an EXAMINATION /IN/, - be examined /IN/: /DAn/ {sınav/imtihan} ol- → ol- 10.1. *938:4.* answer: - answer.
- take an examination /IN/: /DAn/ {sınava/imtihana} gir-. *938:4.* answer: - answer.
- take and pass an examination: {sınav/imtihan} ver- → ver- 1. *409:7b.* success: - succeed in specific ways; *938:4.* answer: - answer.

- take FRIGHT, - be seized with fright: ürk- 2. *127:11.* fear, frightingness: - take fright.
- take [away] /FROM [somewhere]/, to [somewhere else]/: /DAn, A/ götür-. *176:11.* transferal, transportation: - remove.

Take GOOD CARE of yourself! [A common farewell to a person departing for an extended period]: Kendine iye bak! → bak- 3. *188:22.* departure: INTERJ. farewell!; *339:9.* carefulness: - look after; *1007:19.* protection: - care for.
- take GREAT PAINS /to/ do sth well, - go to great pains /to/ do sth well, - take pains /{WITH/OVER}/ sth: /A/ özen- 1. *403:11.* endeavor: - make a special effort.
- take a GUESS, - guess [how many]: bil- 4, tahmin et- 2.1. *945:9.* judgment: - estimate; *950:11.* theory, supposition: - conjecture.

- take HOLD OF, - grab, - grasp, or - seize /BY/ [body part: the neck]: /DAn/ tut- 1, /DAn/ yakala- 1. *480:14.* taking: - seize.
- take a HOLIDAY, vacation, - go on a holiday, vacation: tatil yap- → yap-

3, **tatile git-** → git- 1a. *20:9.* rest, repose: - vacation.

- take ILL, - get sick, - feel faint, - feel suddenly sick: **fenalaş-** 2. *85:46a.* disease: - take sick in general.
- take IN, - deceive, - fool, - mislead: **aldat-** 1, **kandır-** 1. *356:14.* deception: - deceive.
- take IN ONE'S ARMS, - embrace; - hug: **kucakla-**. *562:18.* lovemaking, endearment: - embrace.
- take an INTEREST /IN/, - be interested /IN/: **/A [karşı]/ ilgi duy-** → duy- 3, **/lA/ ilgilen-** 1. *980:3b.* curiosity: - be curious.
- take an interest /IN/, - be concerned /with/, - be occupied /with/: **/lA/ meşgul ol-** 2 → ol- 12. *982:5.* attention: - attend to.
- take LESSONS /from/: **/DAn/ ders al-** 1 → al- 1. *570:11.* learning: - be taught.
- take a LOAN /from/, - borrow /from/: **/DAn/ borç al-** [money only] → al- 1, **/DAn/ ödünç al-** [money or anything else] → al- 1. *621:3.* borrowing: - borrow.
- take a LOOK AT, - glance /AT/ [May I take a look at your newspaper?]: **/A/ göz at-** → at- 1. *937:26.* inquiry: - examine cursorily.

- take MEDICINE: **al-** 1 [in most cases], **iç-** 4 [if the medicine is a liquid or if it is a solid but taken with water]. *8:22.* eating: - devour.
- take MONEY /{OUTOF/from}/, - withdraw money /from/ [bank, account]: **/DAn/ para çek-** → çek- 2. *192:10.* extraction: - extract.

- take NO NOTICE /OF/, - overlook /θ/, - disregard /θ/, - close one's eyes /to/, or - wink /AT/ a fault, - turn a blind eye /to/: **/A/ göz yum-** 2. *148:4.* forgiveness: - condone; *983:2.* inattention: - be inattentive.
- take NOTE /OF/, - notice, - observe: **/A/ dikkat et-** 2, **/I/ gözle-** 1. *982:6.* attention: - heed.
take note, be {advised/informed/aware} [that], just to let you know, is that understood?, OK?: **{haberiniz/ bilginiz} olsun.** → ol- 11 → olsun. *399: * 9.* warning: expressions of; *982:22.* attention: INTERJ. attention!

- take OFF /FOR/, - go away /to/: **/A/ git-** 1a. *177:25.* travel: - go to.
- take off /FROM/, i.e., - become airborne [subj.: plane, helicopter, bird]: **/DAn/ havalan-** 2. *184:38.*

aviation: - take off; *188:8.* departure: - set out; *193:10.* ascent: - take off.
- take off, - make off, - go away, - leave [a permanent departure; subj.: person]: **başını alıp git-** → git- 1a. *188:10.* departure: - hasten off.
- take off or - remove clothing [object indicated: I took off my coat.]: **çıkar-** 2. *6:6.* unclothing: - take off.
- take off one's clothes, - undress oneself [object not indicated: I undressed.]: **soyun-**. *6:7.* unclothing: - undress.
- take OFFENSE /AT/, - be offended or hurt /BY, because of/: **/A, DAn dolayı/ alın-** 3. *156:5.* disrespect: - offend.
- take ON [passengers], - pick up [by car], - give a lift to: **al-** 2. *176:16.* transferal, transportation: - fetch.
- take or - check OUT BOOKS FROM THE LIBRARY: **kütüphaneden kitap al-** → al- 1. *192:10.* extraction: - extract.
- take OUT INSURANCE /ON/, - insure /θ/: **/A/ sigorta yaptır-** → yaptır- 2. *1007:18a.* protection: - protect.
- take sth /{OUT OF/from}/, - remove sth /from/: **/DAn/ çıkar-** 1. *192:10.* extraction: - extract.
- take money /{out of/from}/ or - withdraw money /from/ [bank, account]: **/DAn/ para çek-** → çek- 2. *192:10.* extraction: - extract.

- take PAINS /TO/ do sth, - expend effort /{for/ON}/ sth: **/için/ {emek/ çaba} harca et-** → {harca-/sarf et-} 1. *403:5.* endeavor: - endeavor; *725:9.* exertion: - exert oneself.
- take pains /WITH/, - put effort /INTO/, - devote effort /to/, - work /AT/: **/A/ emek ver-** → ver- 1. *403:5.* endeavor: - endeavor.
- take pains /{WITH/OVER}/ sth, - take great pains /to/ do sth well: **/A/ özen-** 1. *403:11.* endeavor: - make a special effort.
- take PART /IN/, - participate /IN/: **/A/ katıl-** 2. *476:5.* participation: - participate.
- take part in sports, - engage in sports, - do sports: **spor yap-** → yap- 3. *84:4.* fitness, exercise: - exercise; *743:23.* amusement: - play.
- take a {PEE/PISS}, - urinate, - piss, - pee: **çiş {yap-/et-}** → yap- 3, **işe-**, **küçük aptes yap-** → yap- 3, **su dök-** → dök- 3. *12:14.* excretion: - urinate.
- take {PICTURES/PHOTOGRAPHS}, photograph: **{resim/fotoğraf} çek-** → çek- 7. *714:14.* photography: - photograph.

- take PLACE, - happen, - occur: **geç-** 3, **ol-** 2. *830:5.* event: - occur.
- take PRIDE /IN/, - be proud /OF/, - feel pride /IN/: /lA/ **iftihar et-**, /lA/ {**övün-/öğün-**} 1, /{lA/DAn}/ **gurur duy-** 1 → **duy-** 3, /DAn/ **kıvanç duy-** → **duy-** 3. *136:5.* pride: - take pride.
- take a PUFF or drag [on a cigarette], - inhale [cigarette smoke]: **nefes çek-**. → **çek-** 1, **sigaranın dumanını içine çek-** → **içine çek-** → **çek-** 1. *89:14.* tobacco: - use tobacco; *187:12.* reception: - draw in; *318:21.* * *1.* wind: - breathe.

- take a SHOWER, - shower: **duş** {**al-/yap-**} → **al-** 1, **yap-** 3. *79:19.* cleanness: - wash.
- take or - get SICK, - become ill /because, {AS A RESULT OF/WITH/from}/: /DIğI **için**, **DAn/ hastalan-**, /DAn/ **hasta ol-** → **ol-** 10.2. *85:46a.* disease: - take sick in general.
- take a SUNBATH, - sunbathe: **güneş banyosu yap-**. *1019:19.* heating: - insolate.

- take TIME [How long will this take?]: **çek-** 10 [subj.: journey], **sür-** 3 [subj.: meeting, journey], {**vakit/zaman**} **al-** [subj.: meeting, journey] → **al-** 1. *811:4b.* continuity: for sth - continue; *820:6.* time: - spend time.
- take /TO/, - convey /to/: /A/ **götür-**, /A/ **ilet-** 1 [message, congratulations], /A/ **kaldır-** 5 [to hospital, morgue]. *176:12.* transferal, transportation: - transport; *176:15.* : - send.
- take to COURT, - sue: **mahkemeye ver-** → **ver-** 1. *598:12.* legal action: - sue.
- take TROUBLE, - put oneself to trouble: **zahmet et-**. *995:4.* inexpedience: - inconvenience.

- take UP, - consider a matter: **ele al-** → **al-** 1. *404:3.* undertaking: - undertake.
- take sb or sth UP /TO/ [the tenth floor]: /A/ **çıkar-** 4. *911:8.* elevation: - pick up.

- take a WALK, - walk: **yürü-** 1. *177:27.* travel: - walk.
- take a WIFF or puff [of tobacco], - take a drag [on a cigarette]: **nefes çek-**. → **çek-** 1, **sigaranın dumanını içine çek-** → **içine çek-** → **çek-** 1. *89:14.* tobacco: - use tobacco;

187:12. reception: - draw in; *318:21.* * *1.* wind: - breathe.

Take YOUR HANDS OFF ME!: **Ellerini üzerimden çek!** → **çek-** 3. *176:11.* transferal, transportation: - remove.

- TALK or - converse [in a friendly manner] /with/, - chat /with/: /lA/ **muhabbet et-**, /lA/ **sohbet et-**. *541:10.* conversation: - converse.
- talk /a: ABOUT, b: about, c: concerning, d: on, e: on the subject of/, - talk or - speak a language: /a: I, b: **hakkında**, c: A **dair**, d: **üzerine**, e: **konusunda**/ **konuş-**. *524:20.* speech: - speak.
- talk /ABOUT/, - tell /{ABOUT/OF}/, - mention /θ/, - discuss /θ/: /DAn/ **bahset-**, /DAn/ **söz et-**, **sözünü et-**. *541:12.* conversation: - discuss; *551:8.* information: - inform.
- talk or - answer BACK /TO/: /A/ **karşılık ver-** 2 → **ver-** 1. *142:8.* insolence: - sauce.
- talk sb /INTO/ doing sth, - persuade or - convince sb /to/ do sth: /için/ **kandır-** 2. *375:23.* motivation, inducement: - persuade; *952:18.* belief: - convince.
- talk NONSENSE, garbage, hogwash: {**abuk sabuk/saçma sapan**} **konuş-**, **saçmala-**. *520:5.* meaninglessness: - talk nonsense; *922:6.* foolishness: - be foolish.
- talk sb /OUT OF/ sth, - dissuade or - deter sb /from/: /DAn/ {**vazgeçir-/caydır-**}. *379:3.* dissuasion: - dissuade.
- talk /TO/ sb, - speak /to/ sb: /A/ **söyle-** 3, /A/ **konuş-**. *524:27.* speech: - address.
- talk, - confer, - discuss, or - meet /WITH/, - see one another: /lA/ **görüş-** 1. *524:20.* speech: - speak; *541:11.* conversation: - confer.
- talk /with/ {on/over} the phone, - talk /with/ {by/on the} phone: /lA/ **telefonlaş-**. *343:6.* communication: - communicate, - be in touch; *347:18.* communications: - telephone.

- TAPE, - paste, - glue, or - stick sth /{ON/ONTO/to}/ sth: /A/ **yapıştır-**. *799:5.* joining: - put together; *802:9.* cohesion: - stick together.
- tape, - record sth /ON [a medium], with [an instrument]/: /A, lA/ **kaydet-** 3. *549:15.* record: - record.

- TASTE, - try the taste of, - sample: **tat-**, **tadına bak-** → **bak-** 1. *62:7.* taste:

- taste; *941:8.* experiment: - experiment.

- TEACH /θ/ sb sth, - teach sth /to/ sb: /A/ öğret-, /A/ okut- 3. *568:10.* teaching: - teach.
- teach /θ/ sb, - give lessons /to/ sb: /A/ ders ver- → ver- 1. *568:10.* teaching: - teach.
- teach a MORAL LESSON /to/ sb: /A/ ders ver- 2 → ver- 1. *568:10.* teaching: - teach.

- TEAR: yırt-. *801:11.* separation: - sever.
- tear AWAY /from/ [child from its mother]: /DAn/ kopar- 2. *801:8.* separation: - separate.
- tear DOWN, - pull down, - knock down, - demolish, - wreck /with/: /lA/ yık-1. *395:17.* destruction: - demolish.
- tear or - rip /{OUT OF/from}/ [pages from notebook]: /DAn/ {kopar-2/kopart- 2}, /DAn/ yırt-. *192:10.* extraction: - extract; *801:11.* separation: - sever.
- tear TO PIECES, - cut up [meat, flesh], - break into pieces, - smash [vase]: parçala-. *801:13.* separation: - shatter.
- tear UP, - rip up [obj.: document, paper]: yırt-. *192:10.* extraction: - extract; *801:11.* separation: - sever.

- [TELE]PHONE /θ [sb], from/, - call, - call up, - make a [phone] call /to, from/: /A, DAn/ telefon {et-/aç-}. *347:18.* communications: - telephone.

- TELL /θ/ sb sth, - tell sth /to/ sb, - say [obj.: Tell him what happened.]: /A/ söyle- 1. *524:23.* speech: - say.
- tell /θ/ sb sth, - tell sth /to/ sb, - relate sth /to/ sb [obj.: event, story]: /A/ anlat-2. *552:11.* news: - report.
- tell /ABOUT/, - talk /ABOUT/, - mention /θ/: /DAn/ bahset-, /DAn/ söz et-, sözünü et-. *541:12.* conversation: - discuss; *551:8.* information: - inform.
- tell about, - describe: /I/ anlat- 3. *349:9.* representation, description: - describe; *864:10.* particularity: - characterize.
- tell about, - inform /θ/ sb about, - report /to/: /A/ bildir-, /A/ bilgi ver- → ver- 1, /A/ haber ver- → ver- 1. *551:8.* information: - inform.
- tell LIES, - lie: yalan söyle- → söyle-1. *354:19.* falseness: - lie; *645:11.* improbity: - be dishonest.
- tell THE TRUTH: {doğru/doğruyu/ gerçeği/hakikati} söyle- →

söyle- 1. *351:7.* disclosure: - confess; *644:11.* probity: - speak or - tell the truth.
- tell sb TO DO sth: biri.nin *verb stem*.mAsInI söyle- [e.g., Orhan'nın çalışma.sı.nı söyledi. 'He told Orhan to work (lit., ** He told Orhan's working)].' → söyle- 1. *420:8.* command: - command.

- TEST, - give sb a test, an examination: imtihan et-. NOT {sınav/imtihan} ver-. *937:21.* inquiry: - interrogate.
- test, - try, - try out, - try on; - attempt or - try /TO/ do sth: dene-. *403:6.* endeavor: - attempt; *941:8.* experiment: - experiment.

- TESTIFY /a: {for/on behalf of}, b: {θ [that] /to the effect that}, c: {for/on behalf of}, d: against/, - give evidence, - be a witness in a court case: /a: için, b: A dair, c: lehine, d: aleyhine/ tanıklık et-. *956:9.* evidence, proof: - testify.

- THANK /a: θ [sb], b: FOR, c: for/, - be obliged /a: to [sb], b: FOR, c: for/: /a: A, b: A, c: için/ teşekkür et-. *150:4.* gratitude: - thank.
- thank /a: θ [God], b: {for/because of}, c: θ [that]/, - give thanks /a: to [God], b: {for, because of}, c: θ [that]/, - praise [a: God], b: {for/because of}, c: θ [that]/: /a: A, b: DAn dolayı, c: A/ şükret-. *150:4.* gratitude: - thank; *509:12.* approval: - praise.

Thank goodness, Fortunately: Bereket versin [ki] → ver- 1. *1009:16.* prosperity: ADV. fortunately.

Thank you!, Thanks.: Teşekkür ederim. → teşekkür et-, Sağol! → sağ ol- → ol- 12, Eksik olmayın. → eksik ol- → ol- 12. *150:6.* gratitude: INTERJ. thanks!

Thanks be to God that: /A/ Şükürler olsun [ki] → ol- 11 → olsun. *150:6.* gratitude: INTERJ. Thanks!; *509:22.* approval: INTERJ. bravo!

THERE {IS/ARE}: var → ol- 3, Additional examples. b) 3.1. Issues of presence... *221:6.* presence: - be present; *760:8.* existence: - exist.

- THINK, - reflect, - consider, - use one's mind [I'm thinking.]: düşün- 1. *930:8.* thought: - think.
- think, - suppose [I think so.]: {san-/zannet-}. *952:11.* belief: - think.

- think HIGHLY OF, - attach importance /to/, - consider important, - value /θ/: **/A/ {önem/ehemmiyet} ver-** → ver- 1; **/I/ önemse-.** *996:13.* importance: - value.
- think OF, - occur /to/, - remember [I didn't think of that.]: **akla gel-** → gel- 1. *930:18.* thought: - occur to.
- think /{OF/ABOUT}/, for one's mind - be occupied with [I was thinking about Fatma today.]: **/I/ düşün- 3.** *930:20.* thought: - occupy the mind.
- think of in a certain way [What do you {think of/say to} that?]: **de- 2.** *950:10.* theory, supposition: - suppose; *952:11.* belief: - believe.
- think /{of/about}/, - have an opinion /about/ sb, sth: **/hakkında/ düşün- 4.** *952:11.* belief: - think.
- think /of/ [doING] sth, of taking a particular course of action, - consider [I'm thinking of going to the movies.]: **/I/ düşün- 5.** *930:8.* thought: - think; *930:12.* : - consider.
- think OVER carefully, - consider at length, - ponder, - think and think: **{düşün-/düşünüp} taşın-** → düşün- 1. *930:9.* thought: - think hard.
- think or - find sth STRANGE, for sth - strike one as strange: **{acayibine/ garibine/tuhafına} git-** → git- 1b, **yadırga-.** *869:8.* * *1.* abnormality: - find strange.
- think that sb or sth is /LIKE/ sb or sth else, - think that there is a similarity between, - liken: **/A/ benzet- 2.** *942:4.* comparison: - compare; *988:20.* memory: - remind.
- think or - believe that sth was, is, or will be the case: **/I/ düşün- 2.** *952:10.* belief: - think.
- think UP, - make up, - invent, - dream up, - concoct [story, lie]: **uydur- 2.** *354:18.* falseness: - fabricate.

THINKING, assuming, with sth in mind: **diye 4** → de- 1. *950:19.* theory, supposition: CONJ. supposing.

- THRASH, - beat /θ/, - give a whipping, beating: **ayağının altına al-** → al- 1, **/A/ dayak at-** → at- 5. *604:13.* punishment: - slap; *901:14.* impulse, impact: - hit.

- THREATEN /with/: **/lA/ tehdit et-.** *514:2.* threat: - threaten.

- THRILL, - give a thrill, - excite: **heyecanlandır- 1.** *105:12.* excitement: - excite.

- THROB with pain, - ache, - hurt: **ağrı-.** *26:8.* pain: - suffer pain.

- THRONG /to/, - mob /θ/ a place, - rush as a group /to/ a place: **/A/ hücum et- 2.** *769:16.* assemblage: - come together.

- THROW /{AT/ON/IN/INTO}/: **/A/ at- 1.** *903:10.* pushing, throwing: - throw.
- throw, - hurl, or - fling /{AT/to/INTO}, toward/: **/A, A doğru/ fırlat-.** *903:10.* pushing, throwing: - throw.
- throw AWAY, out, - discard [useless things, trash]: **at- 2.** *390:7.* discard: - discard.
- throw /{IN/INTO}/ THE TRASH, - discard, - throw out, away: **çöpe {at-/dök-}** → at- 2, dök- 3. *390:7.* discard: - discard.
- throw or - put ONE'S ARMS /AROUND/, - embrace /θ/: **/A/ sarıl- 1.** *562:18.* lovemaking, endearment: - embrace.
- throw OUT, - spill out as waste /{ON/INTO}/: **/A/ dök- 3.** *390:7.* discard: - discard.
- throw sb /OUT OF/, - eject or - expel sb /from/ [person out of room]: **/DAn/ kov- 1.** *908:13.* ejection: - eject.
- throw out /of/, - evict: **/DAn/ çıkar- 1.** *908:15.* ejection: - evict.
- throw TRASH [/{ON/INTO}/ the streets], - litter [/θ/ the streets]: **[sokaklar.A] çöp {at-/dök-}** → at- 2, dök- 3. *80:15a.* uncleanness: - dirty; *390:7.* discard: - discard; *810:2.* disarrangement: - disarrange.
- throw UP: **kus-.** *908:26.* ejection: - vomit.

- THUMB or - leaf /THROUGH/ [book, papers], - rummage or - search /THROUGH/ [drawers, pocketbook]: **/I/ karıştır- 3.** *937:26.* inquiry: - examine cursorily; *937:33.* : - ransack.

- TICKLE one's funny bone, - strike one as funny, - find funny, amusing: **komiğine git-** → git- 1b. *489:13.* wit, humor: - joke.

- TIDY up, - straighten up, - pick up, - put in order [room]: **düzelt- 3, toparla- 3, topla- 2.** *807:12.* arrangement: - tidy, tidy up.
- tidy [oneself] up, - smarten [oneself] up [before entering the director's room]: **üstünü başını {düzelt-/toparla-/topla-}.** → düzelt- 3, toparla- 3, topla- 2. *79:18.* cleanness: - clean; *807:12.* arrangement: - tidy, tidy up.

- TIE /{to/around}, with/, - tie up, - connect /to/, - fasten /to/: /A, lA/ **bağla**- 1. *799:9.* joining: - bind.

Till we meet again.: **Yine görüşmek üzere.** → görüş- 1. *188:16.* departure: - say or - bid good-bye.

- TIME, - keep time, - watch the time, - keep track of the time: **saat tut**- → tut- 5. *831:11.* measurement of time: - time.

- TIP /θ/ sb, - give /θ/ sb a tip, - give a tip /to/ sb [money, not information]: /A/ **bahşiş ver**- → ver- 1. *624:10.* payment: - pay.

- TIRE /OF/, - get bored, fed up /WITH/, - grow tired /OF/, - be fed up /WITH/: /DAn/ {bık-/usan-}, /DAn/ sıkıl- 1. *118:7b.* tedium: - get bored.
- tire [oneself], - get or - be tired /from/ [an activity]: /DAn/ **yorul**-. *21:4.* fatigue: - fatigue.
- tire, - make tired [exam tires student]: **yor**-. *21:4.* fatigue: - fatigue.

TO hell with {him/it}!, Damn {him/it}!: **Kahrolsun!** → kahrol- → ol- 12. *513:11.* curse: INTERJ. damn!
To tell the truth: **Aslına bakarsanız** [lit., 'If you look at the truth of it'] → bak- 1, **Doğrusunu istersen[iz]** [lit., 'If you want the truth of it.'] → iste- 1; **Ne yalan söyleyeyim.** ['{lit., Why should I lie]./I won't hide it from you.}'] → söyle- 1. *644:22.* probity: ADV. truthfully.
To tell the truth., lit., If it is necessary to speak openly: **{Açık/Açıkça} söylemek gerekirse** → söyle- 1, **{Açık/Açıkça} konuşmak gerekirse** → konuş-. *644:23.* probity: ADV. candidly.

- TOAST sth [The cook is toasting the bread.]: **kızart**- 2. *11:4a.* cooking: - cook sth.
- toast [i.e., - become toast: The bread is toasting.]: **kızar**- 3. *11:4b.* cooking: for sth - cook.

- TOLERATE /θ/, - put up /WITH/, - bear /θ/, - stand /θ/, - suffer /θ/, - endure /θ/, - take /θ/: /A/ **dayan**- 3, /A/ **katlan**- 2, *more formal, less current than the above:* /A/ **tahammül et**-. *134:5.* patience: - endure; *1047:3.* toughness: - toughen.

- TOPPLE, - knock to the ground: **yere yık**-. *912:5.* depression: - fell.

- TOTAL, - amount to, - add up to, - come to, - cost [subj.: item, a bill]: **tut**- 7. *630:13.* price, fee: - cost; *791:8.* whole: - total; *1016:18.* mathematics: - sum up.

- TOUCH /θ/ [with one's hands: Don't touch her CDs!]: /A/ **dokun**- 1, /A/ **el sür**- → sür- 5, /A/ **temas et**- 1. *73:6.* touch: - touch; *223:10.* nearness: - contact.
- touch /θ/ [physically, often unintentionally, by mistake], - brush against [My hand {touched/brushed against} the stove.]: /A/ 1 **değ**- 1. *223:10.* nearness: - contact.
- touch /θ/, - reach as far as [His head {touched/reached} /θ/ the ceiling.]: /A/ 1 **değ**- 2. *158:8.* space: - extend; *223:10.* nearness: - contact.
- touch, - affect, - move /θ/ sb emotionally [subj.: the director's farewell speech]; - disturb, - upset /θ/ sb [subj.: a person's inappropriate words]: /A/ **dokun**- 3. *93:14.* feelings: - affect; *893:7.* influence: - influence.
- touch /ON/, - mention /θ/ a subject: /A/ **değin**-, /A/ **temas et**- 2. *524:25.* speech: - remark.

- TOUR [a place]: /I/ **dolaş**- 2, /I/ **gez**-. *177:21.* travel: - journey.

- TOW, - pull: **çek**- 1. *904:4.* pulling: - pull.

- TRADE /AT/, - shop /AT/, - patronize /θ/ [a business establishment]: /DAn/ **alışveriş et**-. *731:16.* commerce, economics: - trade with; *733:8.* purchase: - shop.

- TRAIN [oneself physically], - exercise, - do gymnastics, physical training: **idman yap**- → yap- 3. *84:4.* fitness, exercise: - exercise; *725:8.* exertion: - exert.
- train, - educate, - bring up, - rear, - raise [children]: **yetiştir**- 2. *568:13.* teaching: - train.

- TRAMPLE /{ON/θ}/, - step /ON/ [grass]: /A/ **bas**- 1. *177:27.* travel: - walk.

- TRANSFER /from [one place], to [another]/, - move /from [one container], to [another]/, - pass on, - convey: /DAn, A/ **aktar**- 1. *176:10.* transferal, transportation: - transfer.
- transfer, - change vehicles [e.g., busses: Do we have to transfer?]: **aktarma**

yap- → yap- 3. *861:4*. substitution: - substitute.

- TRANSLATE orally or in writing /from [one language], INTO [another]/: /DAn, A/ **çevir-** 6, /DAn, A/ **tercüme et-**, /DAn, A/ **aktar-** 2. *341:12*. interpretation: - translate.

- TRANSPORT, - carry, or - move /from, to/: /DAn, A/ **taşı-**. *176:12*. transferal, transportation: - transport.
- transport, - convey, - bring sth /to/: /A/ **ulaştır-** 1. *176:12*. transferal, transportation: - transport.

- TRAVEL or - take a trip /to/: /A/ **seyahat et-**. *177:18*. travel: - travel.
- travel, - cover, or - traverse a distance; - go through or - pass through a place [We traveled 100 kilometeres a day.]: **yol** {yap-/git-} → yap- 3, git- 1a, **katet-**. *177:20*. travel: - traverse.
- travel back and forth, - commute /BY/ [a vehicle]: /lA/ **gidip gel-** → gel- 1. *177:18*. travel: - travel.

- TRAVERSE: → - travel, cover.

- TREAT /θ/, - behave /toward, toward/, - deal /WITH/: /A, A karşı/ **davran-**. *321:6*. behavior: - treat.
- treat a person, disease, or part of the body: **tedavi et-** 1. *91:24*. therapy: - treat.
- treat KINDLY, - be good /to/, - do /θ/ sb a kindness, a good turn, - do good: /A/ **iyilik et-**. *143:12*. kindness, benevolence: - do a favor.
- treat WITH DISRESPECT or contempt, - hold in contempt, - despise, - look down upon, - regard sb or sth as inferior, *informal:* - put sb down, *slang:* - dis: **küçümse-** 1. *157:3*. contempt: - disdain.
- treat WITH RESPECT, - show respect /{to/FOR}/, - behave respectfully /toward/, - respect [a person, a person's ideas]: /A/ **saygı göster-** → göster- 1. *143:10*. kindness, benevolence: - be considerate; *155:5*. respect: - do or - pay hommage to.

- TREMBLE /{WITH/IN}/ [fear], - shake /WITH/ [fear, anger]: /DAn/ **titre-** 2. *127:14*. fear, frighteningness: - tremble; *152:25a*. anger: gestures of anger; *916:11*. agitation: - shake.

- TRESPASS /ON/ sb's property: **haneye tecavüz et-** → tecavüz et- 1. *214:5*. intrusion: - intrude; *674:5*. illegality: - break or - violate the law.

- TRIFLE or - play around /with/, not - take seriously [obj.: sb's affections]: /lA/ **dalga geç-** 3 → geç- 1, **oyna-** 5. *997:14*. unimportance: - trifle.

- TRIM [hair, beard]: **düzelt-** 3. *3:22*. hair: - cut or - dress the hair; *807:12*. arrangement: - tidy, tidy up.

- TROUBLE /θ/ sb, - cause trouble /to/, - inconvenience /θ/, - put sb out, - give trouble /to/: /A/ **zahmet ver-** → ver- 1. *995:4*. inexpedience: - inconvenience; *1012:13*. difficulty: - trouble.

- TRUST /θ/, - believe /IN/: /A/ **güven-**, /A/ **inan-** 2. *952:15*. belief: - believe in.

- TRY or - attempt /to/ [do sth]: /A/ **çalış-** 2, /I/ **dene-**. *403:6*. endeavor: - attempt.
- try or - attempt /to/ do sth that is beyond one's power or outside one's authority, - dare /to/: /A/ **kalkış-**. *403:6*. endeavor: - attempt.
- try [FOOD], - taste, - sample: **tat-**, **tadına bak-** → bak- 1. *62:7*. taste: - taste; *941:8*. experiment: - experiment.
- try HARD, - endeavor, - struggle, - strive, - work hard /to/: /için/ **uğraş-** 1. *403:11*. endeavor: - make a special effort.
- try /ON/ [clothing]: **dene-**, **prova et-**, **tecrübe et-**. *941:8*. experiment: - experiment.
- try OUT, - test [equipment: keys]: **dene-**, **tecrübe et-**. *941:8*. experiment: - experiment.
- try SB, a case; - hear a case; - judge or adjudicate a case, - pass judgment on: **yargıla-**. *594:5*. jurisdiction: - administer justice; *598:17*. legal action: - try; *945:8*. judgment: - judge.
- try TO FIND OUT, - study [a topic, not lessons], - explore, - do research on, - research, - investigate: **araştır-** 2. *937:23*. investigate: - investigate.
- try to FORCE or - break sth open, - force [locked door]: **zorla-** 2. *424:6*. compulsion: - press.
- try to IMITATE /θ/ sb: /A/ **özen-** 3. *336:5*. imitation: - imitate.

- TUNE /{TO/INTO}/ [radio station], - turn /TO/ [obj.: page 5, TV channel]: /I/ **aç-** 3. *371:14*. choice: - select; *914:9*. rotation: - rotate.

- tune /to/, - set /to/ [subj.: radio to the music station]: **/A/ ayarla-** 1. *787:7.* agreement: - make agree.

- TURN, - rotate sth [obj.: door handle]: **/I/ çevir-** 1. *914:9.* rotation: - rotate.
- turn [page, omelette]: **/I/ çevir-** 3. *205:5.* inversion: - invert; *914:9.* rotation: - rotate.
- turn /from, into/, - be transformed [love into hate, snow into snowstorm]: **/DAn, A/ dönüş-**. *851:6.* change: - be changed.
- turn [yellow, red, green. subj.: traffic lights only: The light turned green.]: **yan-** 4. *1024:27.* light: - grow light.

- turn AROUND, - revolve [subj.: wheels]: **dön-** 1. *914:9.* rotation: - rotate.
- turn around, - turn one's BACK /to/: **{arkasını/sırtını} çevir-**[or **dön-**] → **çevir-** 3, **dön-** 4. *914:9.* rotation: - rotate.

- turn BACK or - set back [the clocks]: **[saatleri] geri al-** 2 → **al-** 1. *163:8a.* regression: - turn sth back.
- turn back, - go back, - come back, - return /from, to/: **/DAn, A/ geri dön-** → **dön-** 2. *163:8b.* regression: - turn back, - come back.
- turn one's BACK /TO/: → turn around.
- turn BAD, - change for the worse [weather]: **[hava] {boz-/bozul-}** → **boz-** 4, **bozul-**. *393:16.* impairment: - deteriorate.
- turn a BLIND EYE TO, - close one's eyes /to/, - wink /AT/ a fault: **/A/ göz yum-** 2. *148:4.* forgiveness: - condone; *983:2.* inattention: - be inattentive.

- turn or - become a CERTAIN AGE [He turned 5 last year.], - complete a certain year of one's life: **yaşını {doldur-/tamamla-}** → **doldur-** 1, **yaşa {bas-/gir-}** → **bas-** 1. *303:9.* age: - mature.

- turn sth IN /to/, - hand sth in /to/ [obj.: test, term paper]: **/A/ teslim et-**, **/A/ ver-** 1. *478:13.* giving: - deliver.
- turn /INTO/ or - enter /Ø/ a road; - swerve /to/, veer /to/, - turn /to/, - make a turn /to/: **/A/ sap-**. *279:6.* curve: - curve.
- turn or - convert sth /INTO/ sth else: **/A/ çevir-** 9, **/A/ döndür-** 2. *857:11.* conversion: - convert.
- turn /INTO/, - become /Ø/: **/A/ çevir-** 8, **/A/ dön-** 6, **/A/ dönüş-**. *851:6.* change: - be changed.

- turn /into/, - become [often of a person, suddenly as a result of fear or other strong emotion: When I saw the accident, I turned into stone.]: **/Ø/ kesil-** 5. *851:6.* change: - be changed.
- turn into ICE, - freeze [often of a person, suddenly as a result of fear or other strong emotion]: **buz kesil-** → **kesil-** 5. *1022:9.* cold: - freeze.
- turn into STEAM, - vaporize, - evaporate: **buharlaş-**. *1065:8.* vapor, gas: - vaporize.
- turn into STONE [often of a person, suddenly as a result of fear or other strong emotion]: **taş kesil-** → **kesil-** 5. *1044:7.* hardness, rigidity: - harden.

- turn OFF [a road]: **/DAn/ sap-**. *279:6.* curve: - curve.
- turn or - switch /{off/out}/: **{kapa-/kapat-}** 2 [obj.: electricity, lights, lamps, computer, oven, stove, gas burner, radio, TV], **söndür-** 2 [obj.: same items as under **{kapa-/kapat-}** 2 above EXCEPT computer, radio, or TV]. *856:12.* cessation: - turn off; *1026:11.* darkness, dimness: - turn off the light; *1031:25.* electricity: - electrify.
- turn off [water, the faucet]: **{kapa-/kapat-}** 2. *856:12.* cessation: - turn off.
- turn or - switch ON: **aç-** 2 [radio, lights, lamps, TV], **yak-** 3 [electricity, lights, lamps, but not radio, TV]. *1031:25.* electricity: - electrify.
- turn on sexually, - excite: **tahrik et-** 2, **heyecanlandır-** 3. *105:12.* excitement: - excite.
- turn ONE'S BACK /TO/: → turn around.
- turn OUT, - work out; - become: **ol-** 1. *760:12.* existence: - become.
- turn out [to be true], - be revealed, - come to light, - come out [the truth], - appear, - turn up, - come forward [the guilty person]: **{ortaya/ meydana} çık-** → **çık-** 3. *351:8.* disclosure: - be revealed.
- turn or - work out the way it should, - go well, - come out right: **yoluna gir-**. *392:7.* improvement: - get better.
- turn out, - come out [well, badly: photographs]: **çık-** 7. *830:7.* event: - turn out; *886:4.* effect: - result.
- turn or - switch {out/off}: → - turn or - switch {off/out}.
- turn OVER /to/, - deliver /to/, - hand over /to/: **/A/ teslim et-**. *478:13.* giving: - deliver.

- turn over, i.e., on its back [page, piece of paper]: **arkasını çevir-** 2 → çevir- 3. *205:5.* inversion: - invert.

- turn or - grow PALE, - pale: **sarar-** 2. *36:6.* colorlessness: - lose color.

- turn RED, - blush, - redden: **kızar-** 1. *41:5.* redness: - redden; *137:9b.* humility: gestures of.

- turn [a STEERING WHEEL, rudder, sharply] /to/ one side, - swerve: /A/ **[direksiyonu hızla] kır-** → kır- 3. *164:3.* deviation: - deviate; *278:5.* angularity: - angle; *368:8.* avoidance: - dodge.

- turn /TO/ [page 2, TV channel], - tune /{TO/INTO}/ [radio station], - put on [TV channel, radio station]: /I/ **aç-** 3. *371:14.* choice: - select; *914:9.* rotation: - rotate.
- turn /TO/ [page 2], - switch /to/, - put on [TV channel. If the instrument is already on and you want to make a change]: /I/ **çevir-** 4 . *371:14.* choice: - select; *914:9.* rotation: - rotate.
- turn /to/ [direction: left, right: At the corner turn (to the) right.]: /A/ **dön-** 3, /A/ **sap-**. *279:6.* curvature: - curve.
- turn sth /to, toward/ [obj.: one's face]: /A, A doğru/ **{çevir-/döndür-}** → çevir- 2, döndür- 1. *914:9.* rotation: - rotate.
- turn /to, for/ [information, assistance]: /A, için/ **{başvur-/müracaat et-}** 1 ['- consult dictionary, person'], /DAn/ **yardım iste-** ['- ask help /from/'] → iste- 2. *387:14.* use: - avail oneself of.

- turn UP, - appear, - come out, - be revealed [the truth], - come forward [the guilty person]: **{ortaya/ meydana} çık-** → çık- 3. *351:8.* disclosure: - be revealed.

- turn YELLOW, - yellow [leaves]: **sarar-** 1. *43:3.* yellowness: - yellow.

- TUTOR /θ/ sb; - make or - have / θ/ sb work on sth: /A/ **çalıştır-** 1 b). *424:4.* compulsion: - compel; *568:11.* teaching: - tutor.

- TWIST, - sprain [obj.: ankle]: **burk-**. *393:13.* impairment: - inflict an injury.

- TWITCH, - budge, - stir, - move slightly: **{kımılda-/kıpırda-}**. *172:5b.* motion: for sth - move.

- U -

- UNBUTTON, - untie, - unfasten, - undo: **çöz-** 1. *801:10.* separation: - detach.

- UNDERESTIMATE: **{az/eksik} tahmin et-** → tahmin et- 2. *949:2.* underestimation: - underestimate.

- UNDERGO, - experience [disaster, accident]: **geçir-** 2. *830:8.* event: - experience.
- undergo or - have an operation, - be operated on: **ameliyat geçir-** → geçir- 2, **ameliyat ol-** → ol- 10.1. *91:29.* therapy: - undergo treatment.

- UNDERLINE, - underscore, - draw a line under /IN [ink], with [a ruler]/: /lA/ **altını çiz-** 1 → çiz- 1. *517:19.* signs, indicators: - mark.
- underline, - emphasize: **altını çiz-** 2 → çiz- 1. *996:14.* importance: - emphasize.

- UNDERRATE, - underestimate, - minimize, - belittle: **küçümse-** 2. *252:9.* decrease: - minimize.

- UNDERSTAND: **anla-**. *521:7.* intelligibility: - understand.
- understand sth INTUITIVELY, - sense, - have a feeling, - feel, - perceive, - discern: **sez-**. *93:10.* feeling: - feel; *933:4.* intuition, instinct: - intuit.
- understand ONE ANOTHER: **anlaş-** 1. *521:7.* intelligibility: - understand.
- understand, - appreciate sb's SITUATION, difficulties: **takdir et-** 2. *521:7.* intelligibility: - understand.

- UNDO, - unfasten, - untie, - unbutton: **çöz-** 1. *801:10.* separation: - detach.

- UNDRESS oneself, - take off one's clothes: **soyun-**. *6:7.* unclothing: - undress.
- undress sb [The mother undressed the child.]: **soy-** 3. *6:7.* unclothing: - undress.

- UNFASTEN, - undo, - untie, - unbutton: **çöz-** 1. *801:10.* separation: - detach.

UNHEARD-OF, incredible, unprecedented: **olmadık** → ol- 11. *869:10.* abnormality: unusual.

- UNITE, - join, - bring together: **birleştir-, kavuştur-.** *799:5.* joining: - put together.

- UNLOAD [luggage], - download [computer programs from the Internet], - lower [shutters], - bring down /from, to/, - take down: /**DA, DAn**/ **indir-** 1. *912:4.* depression: - depress; *1041:18.* computer science: - computerize.
- unload, - let {off/out}, - discharge [passengers] /at, from/: /**DA, DAn**/ **indir-** 2. *908:23.* ejection: - unload; *912:4.* depression: - depress.

- UNPACK [suitcase]: **bavulunu aç-** [lit., '- open one's suitcase'] → aç- 1, **bavuldan çıkar-** [lit., '- remove from the suitcase'] → çıkar- 1. *908:23.* ejection: - unload.

- UNTIE: → - UNFASTEN.

- UNWIND, - relax, - rest: **yorgunluk çıkar-** → çıkar- 3. *20:6.* rest, repose: - rest.

- UNWRAP, - open [package]: **aç-** 1. *292:11.* opening: - open.

- UPSET sb, - make sb upset, irritable, tense, angry, - irritate, - put sb in a state, - get sb on edge: **sinirlendir-, heyecanlandır-** 2. *96:14.* unpleasure: - irritate; *96:16a.* : - distress; *105:14.* excitement: - agitate; *128:9.* nervousness: - get on one's nerves; *152:22.* resentment, anger: - anger; *916:10.* agitation: - agitate.
- upset, - disturb /θ/ sb [subj.: a person's inappropriate words]; - touch, - affect, - move /θ/ sb emotionally [subj.: the director's farewell speech]: /**A**/ **dokun-** 3. *93:14.* feelings: - affect; *893:7.* influence: - influence.
- upset, - distress, - worry; - sadden: **üz-.** *112:18.* sadness: - sadden; *126:4.* anxiety: - concern; *126:5.* : - make anxious.

- URINATE, - piss, - pee, - take a {pee/piss}: **çiş {yap-/et-}** → yap- 3, **işe-, küçük aptes yap-** → yap- 3, **su dök-** → dök- 3. *12:14.* excretion: - urinate.
- urinate, - defecate: **ihtiyacını gör-** → gör- 4, **tuvalet yap-** ['- have a bowel movement *or* BM, - urinate; - make one's toilet, i.e., usually for a woman to dress or to arrange her hair'] → yap- 3. *12:13.* excretion: - defecate; *12:14.* : - urinate.

- USE, - make use of /AS, in a [certain] way/: /**olarak, yönde**/ **kullan-.** *387:10.* use: - use.
- use TOBACCO, - smoke [obj.: tobacco, cigarette, pipe]: **iç-** 2. *89:14.* tobacco: - use tobacco.
- use the TOILET, - go to the bathroom: **tuvalete git-** → git- 1a. *12:13.* excretion: - defecate; *12:14.* : - urinate.
- use, - use UP, - consume [money, materials]: **bitir-** 3, {**harca-/sarf et-**} 2. *387:13.* use: - spend; *388:3.* consumption: - consume.

- UTILIZE /θ/; - make good use /OF/, - take advantage /OF/, - benefit or - profit /from/: /**I**/ **değerlendir-** 2, /**DAn**/ {**yararlan-/faydalan-/istifade et-**}. *387:15.* use: - take advantage of.

- V -

- VACUUM: **elektrik süpürgesi ile süpür-** → süpür-. *79:23.* cleanness: - sweep.

- VALUE /θ/, - attach importance /to/, - consider important: /**A**/ {**önem/ ehemmiyet**} **ver-** → ver- 1, /**I**/ **önemse-.** *996:13.* importance: - value.
- value, - respect, - admire, - appreciate [obj.: a person, a quality: your diligence]: **takdir et-** 1. *155:4.* respect: - respect; *996:13.* importance: - value.

- VAPORIZE, - turn into steam, - evaporate: **buharlaş-.** *1065:8.* vapor, gas: - vaporize.

- VARY, - become different, - change: **değiş-** 1. *851:6.* change: - be changed.

- VEIL, - cover one's face with a veil: /**lA**/ **ört-** 1. *295:19.* covering: - cover.

- VERIFY, - corroborate, - confirm [fact, reservation]: **doğrula-, tasdik et-.** *969:12.* certainty: - verify.

- VIEW, - look at, - watch [TV, play, video]: **izle-** 3, **seyret-.** *27:13.* vision: - look.

- VIOLATE laws, rules, principles: **çiğne-** 3. *327:6.* disobedience: - disobey; *435:4.* nonobservance: -

violate; *674:5.* illegality: - break or - violate the law.
- violate [exceptions violate rules], - break [obj.: watch, agreement], - ruin, - spoil, - corrupt [obj.: morals]: **boz-** **1**. *393:10.* impairment: - spoil; *395:10.* destruction: - destroy.
- violate, - rape: **ırzına geç-** → **geç- 1**, **tecavüz et- 2**. *459:14.* attack: - attack; *480:15.* taking: - possess sexually; *665:20.* unchastity: - seduce.

- VISIT: **/A/ gel- 1** ['- come /to/ (sb's place)'], **/A/ git- 3** ['- go /to/ (sb's place)'], **misafirliğe git-** ['- go /ON/ a visit, - go visiting, - pay a visit, - go to visit (a person, not a place), - call on sb', usually a neighbor or friend, not a relative or person of higher station, thus a casual, not formal visit] → **git- 3**, **/I/ ziyaret et-** ['- visit, - pay a visit /to/ a person or place, - call on sb'], **/I/ ziyarete git-** ['- go to visit or - call on', usually a respected PERSON (i.e., an older person, sb of high station), or perhaps sb requiring special attention such as a sick person, or '- go to visit', a PLACE of reverence associated with such a person (e.g., a cemetery or grave site), or '- go on a visit' in connection with a holiday, bairam] → **git- 3**, **ziyaretine git-** [Same explanation as just above, but not a place unless that place is treated as if it were the person himself.] → **git- 3**. *177:25.* travel: - go to; *582:19.* sociability: - visit.

- VOICE one's opinions, - say sth, - speak up against sth, - say sth against, - raise one's voice against, - object: **ses çıkar- 2** → **çıkar- 7**. *453:3.* resistance:- offer resistance.

- VOMIT: **çıkar- 6**. *908:26.* ejection: - vomit.

- VOTE, - exercise the vote, - cast a vote [Did you vote today?]: **oy kullan-**. *371:18.* choice: - vote.
- vote, - vote /for/, - give the vote /to/ [Who did you vote for?]: **/A/ oy ver-**. *371:18.* choice: - vote.

- W -

- WAGE WAR, - fight, - battle [All countries are against waging a nuclear war.]: **savaş-**. *457:13.* contention: - contend.

- WAGER, - bet /a: θ [sb], b: θ [an amount], c: ON/: **/a: 1A, b: A, c: diye/ {bahse/iddiaya} gir-**. *759:25.* gambling: - bet.
- WAIT /FOR/, - await /θ/: **/I/ bekle- 1**. *130:8.* expectation: - await.
- wait, - be patient, - hold on [just a second]: **dur- 5**. *130:8.* expectation: - await.
- wait /{ON/UPON}/ [guests], - attend /to/ [guests], - serve /θ/ [one's country, guests]: **/A/ hizmet et-**. *577:13.* servant, employee: - serve.
- WAKE UP [I woke up at 5 o'clock.], - awake: **uyan-**. *23:4.* wakefulness: - awake.
- wake SB UP [Wake me up at 5 o'clock.], - awaken sb: **uyandır-**. *23:5.* wakefulness: - wake sb up.
- WALK, - take a walk: **yürü- 1**. *177:27.* travel: - walk.
- walk, - stroll, - wander, or - go ABOUT, around, - make one's way through [usually on foot]: **/I/ dolaş- 1**. *177:23.* - wander.
- walk, - go, or - stroll ABOUT, - tour [obj.: a place: Istanbul, on foot or in a vehicle], sightsee: **/I/ gez-**. *177:21.* travel: - journey; *177:23.* : - wander.

- WANDER, - roam, - walk or - go about, - stroll, - ramble, - rove /in, among/ [usually aimlessly]: **/DA, arasında/ gezin- 1**. *177:23.* travel: - wander.
- wander [subj.: one's mind, attention], - be off in the clouds: **dalga geç- 1** → **geç- 1**. *983:3.* inattention: - wander.

- WANGLE, - wrangle, - finagle, - manage to get, usually in the face of difficulty, - get sth out of sb [permission], - wrest sth /from/: **/DAn/ {kopar- 3/kopart- 3}**. *192:10.* extraction: - extract.

- WANT, - want to: **iste- 1**. *100:15.* desire: - want to.
- want, - wish: **dile- 1**. *100:14.* desire: - desire.
- want, - desire: **arzu et-, dile- 1, iste- 1**. *100:14.* desire: - desire; *100:15.* : - want to.
- want badly sth that sb else has; - want to be in the situation that sb else is in: **özen- 2**. *100:16.* desire: - wish for; *154:3.* envy: - envy.

- want NO PART OF, - count {me/us} out: **Ben yokum.** '{Count me out./I want no part of it.}', **Biz yokuz.** '{Count us out./We want no part of it.}' → {var/yok} ol- a) 3 → ol- 12. *772: * 11.* exclusion: PHR. count me out.

- WARM ONESELF [subj.: anyone: by drinking hot tea], - warm up [subj.: athletes before the game]: **ısın-** 2. *1019:17a.* heating: - heat.
- warm UP, - become, - grow, or - get warm [weather]: **ısın-** 1. *1019:17b.* heating: - get hot.
- warm sth up, - heat, - heat up /BY MEANS OF/ [obj.: food, one's house]: /lA/ **ısıt-** 1. *1019:17a.* heating: - heat.
- warm up [obj.: one's muscles]: /lA/ **ısıt-** 2. *1019:17a.* heating: - heat.

- WARN sb /{to/about}, THAT/: **/için, diye/ {uyar-/ikaz et-/ihtar et-}.** *399:5.* warning: - warn.

- WASH sth /in [hot water], {IN [detergent]/with [bleach]}/: /DA, lA/ **yıka-.** *79:19.* cleanness: - wash.
- wash ONESELF /with/ [soap], - take a bath, - bathe /IN/ [warm water]: /lA/ **yıkan-** 1. *79:19.* cleanness: - wash.

- WASTE, - squander [obj.: paper, water, time]: **israf et-.** *486:4.* prodigality: - waste.
- waste or - lose TIME /ing, {from/because of}...ing/: **/mAklA, mAktAn/ {vakit/zaman} kaybet-**[or **yitir-**]. *331:13.* inactivity: - waste time; *391:8.* uselessness: - be useless.
- waste or - kill time /[by]...ing/: /ArAk/ **{vakit/zaman} öldür-.** *331:13.* inactivity: - waste time; *391:8.* uselessness: - be useless.

- WATCH, - look at, - view [TV, play, video]: /I/ **izle-** 3, /I/ **seyret-.** *27:13.* vision: - look.
- watch, - observe [a person, a process]: **gözle-** 2. *982:6.* attention: - heed.
- watch /{θ/OVER}/, - keep an eye /ON/ [so that no harm comes to]: /A/ **göz kulak ol-** → ol- 12. *1007:20.* protection: - watch.
- watch OUT /FOR/, - be careful, - pay attention /to/: /A/ **dikkat et-** 1, **dikkatli ol-** → ol- 12. *339:7.* carefulness: - be careful; *399: * 9.* warning: expressions of.
- watch out /FOR/ sth dangerous; - guard /AGAINST/: /DAn/ **sakın-** 2. *339:8.* carefulness: - be vigilant.

- WATER, - give water /to/ [plants, animals]: /I/ **sula-.** *1063:12.* moisture: - moisten; *1068:7.* animal husbandry: - tend.
- water [subj.: eyes], - fill with tears [subj.: eyes], for tears - come to one's eyes: **gözleri yaşar-.** *13:5.* secretion: - secrete; *115:12.* lamentation: - weep.

- WAVE [hand] /to/: /A/ **el salla-** → salla- 1. *517:22.* signs, indicators: - signal; *915:11.* oscillation: - wave.
- wave [subj.: flags, banners]: **salla-** 1. *517:22.* signs, indicators: - signal; *915:11.* oscillation: - wave.

- WAYLAY, - ambush, - block one's way [often to steal from]: **yolunu kes-** → kes- 6. *346:10.* concealment: - ambush.

- WEAR, - have on, - be wearing: **giy-.** *5:43.* clothing: - wear, - have on.
- wear OUT, - get worn-out [car, rug, not living thing]: **yıpran-** 1. *393:20.* impairment: - wear, - wear away.
Wear it with pleasure!, What a nice!: A polite expression used to address sb who has just acquired a new item of clothing. English speakers usually just express admiration: **Güle güle giyin!** → giyin-. *504: * 20.* courtesy: polite expressions.

- WEEP, - cry: **ağla-, göz yaşı dök-** → dök- 1. *12:12.* excretion: - excrete; *115:12.* lamentation: - weep.

- WEIGH, - weigh out STH /for/ sb: /A/ **tart-.** *297:10.* weight: - weigh; *300:10.* measurement: - measure.
- weigh ONESELF: **tartıl-** 2. *297:10.* weight: - weigh; *300:10.* measurement: - measure.

- WELCOME, - greet, - go to meet, - meet sb /at [a place], with/: /DA, lA/ **karşıla-** 1. *769:16.* assemblage: - come together.
Welcome /to/ [a place]: /A/ **Hoş geldin[iz]!** 1. *504: * 20.* courtesy: polite expressions; *585:14.* hospitality, welcome: INTERJ. welcome!

We'll MEET {again}.: **{Tekrar/Yine} görüşürüz.** → görüş- 1. *188:16.* departure: - say or - bid good-bye; *504:13.* courtesy: - give one's regards. See also: Till we meet again.
We'll SEE each other tomorrow., See you tomorrow.: **Yarın görüşürüz.** →

görüş- 1. *188:22.* departure: INTERJ. farewell!; *504:* * *20.* courtesy: polite expressions.

WELL, LET'S SEE...: The two most common expressions with this meaning, neither formed from a verb, are: **Efendim** and **Şey.** Another is formed from a verb: **Ne bileyim ben?** 2 → bil- 1. For other filler phrases, see **Turkish Verbs by Theme:** *362:13.* irresolution: ADV. * filler phrases and stallers.

Well! What {do you say!/[lit.,] are you saying!} [said in surprise]: **Ne diyorsun?** → de- 1. *122:19.* wonder: INTERJ. my word!

- WET, - make wet, - moisten: **ıslat-.** *1063:12.* moisture: - moisten.
- wet or - soil one's UNDERCLOTHES, bed: **altına kaçır-** → kaçır- 2, **altını ıslat-.** *12:13.* excretion: - defecate; *12:14.* : - urinate; *1063:12.* moisture: - moisten.

WHAT ABOUT or how about [** your/our/my] [doing it tomorrow]?, What if [you/we/I] [did it tomorrow]?, lit., 'If you wish' [a polite way of introducing the expression of a preference, proposal, or correction]: I'd rather not go today. {WHAT/How} about going tomorrow?]: **İstersen[iz]...** → iste- 1. *439:* * *11.* offer: expressions of suggestion; *504:* * *20.* courtesy: polite expressions.

WHAT a COINCIDENCE!: **Tesadüfe bakın.** → bak- 1. *131:15.* inexpectation: ADV. surprisingly; *835:7.* simultaneity: simultaneously.

What a NICE [coat, car, house]!, What a great...!, What a beautiful...!: Whereas English speakers usually just express admiration, Turkish speakers use a variety of expresssions to fit the circumstances: **Güle güle giyin!** 'Wear it with pleasure.' [said to sb who has just bought a new item of clothing] → giyin-, **Güle güle kullanın[ız].** 'Use it with pleasure.' [said to sb who has bought a new item for use: TV] → kullan-, **Güle güle oturunuz.** 'Live in it with pleasure.' [said to sb who has just moved into a new residence] → otur- 3. *504:* * *20.* courtesy: polite expressions.
{What a PITY/How sad} /FOR/ [the losing team]: /A/ **yazık oldu.** →

yazık ol- → ol- 12. *113:* * *13.* regret: INTERJ. what a pity!
What a SHAME!: **Yazıklar olsun!** 1 → yazık ol- → ol- 12. *510:27.* disapproval: INTERJ. God forbid!

What CAN I do? It's out of my control.: **Ne yapayım? Elimde değil.** → yap- 2. *19:21.* impotence: - INTERJ. no can do.
What's DONE is done., It's too late now., No use crying over spilled milk.: **Olan oldu.** → ol- 11. *845:* * *21.* lateness: PHR. it's too late.
What's UP?, What's going on?, What's the matter?, What's wrong?: **Hayrola?** → ol- 11 → ola. *133:13.* premonition: - promise; *387:17.* use: - avail; *830:* * *14.* event: PHR. what's up?
What TIMES [lit., days] we have lived to see!, So this is what things have come to!, So things have come to this!: **Ne günler.E kaldık.** → kal- 1. *122:19.* wonder: INTERJ. my word!

WHATEVER happened to...?, So where's...? [the book you promised me]: **Nerede kaldı?** → kal- 1. *132:* * *7.* disappointment: expressions of.

WHETHER...or; both...and...: **olsun...olsun** → ol- 11. *863:6.* generality: whatever.

WHILE: **iken.** → i- 3. *820:16.* time: CONJ. when.
while it's on my mind, while I'm thinking of it, by the way, speaking of, incidentally: **aklıma gelmişken.** *842:13.* timeliness: ADV. incidentally; *930:18.* thought: - occur to.

- WHIP, - beat [food: yogurt and egg whites]: **çırp-.** *916:10.* agitation: - agitate.

- WHISPER /{IN/INTO}/ [sb's ear]: /A/ **fısılda-.** *52:10.* faintness of sound: - murmur.

- WHISTLE: **ıslık çal-** → çal- 2. *508:10.* ridicule: - boo; *509:10.* approval: - applaud; *708:38.* music: - sing; *708:42.* : - blow a horn.

WHO knows? [rhetorical: i.e., no one knows]: **Kim bilir?** → bil- 1. *929:11.* ignorance: - not know.

- WIN [game, prize, a place on a team or in an educational institution or

615

department] /{AT/IN} [game], IN [source: lottery]/: /DA, DAn/ kazan- 2. *249:7.* superiority: - best; *411:3.* victory: - triumph.
- win [Which team is winning?]: **2 yen-** 2. *249:7.* superiority: - best; *411:3.* victory: - triumph.
- win or - earn the right /to/: /A/ **hak kazan-** → kazan- 1. *472:8.* acquisition: - acquire.
- win a FOLLOWING, - become popular or fashionable, for sth - catch on /{IN/AMONG}, {IN/among}/ [subj.: fashion, song, book]: /CA, **arasında/ tutul-** 3. *578:8.* fashion: - catch on.

- WIND, - set [a watch, clock, toy, music box]: **kur-** 2. *787:7.* agreement: - make agree; *914:9.* rotation: - rotate.
- WINK /AT/ [student at a friend]: /A/ **göz kırp-** 2. *517:22.* signs, indicators: - signal; *562:20.* lovemaking, endearment: - flirt.
- wink /AT/, - take no notice /OF/, - overlook /θ/, - turn a blind eye /to/, - disregard /θ/, or - close one's eyes /to/ a fault: /A/ **göz yum-** 2. *148:4.* forgiveness: - condone; *983:2.* inattention: - be inattentive.

- WIPE /with, {IN/ON}/; - dry [sth wet with sth dry: face on towel]: /lA, A/ **sil-** 1. *79:18.* cleanness: - clean; *1064:6a.* dryness: - dry, - make dry.
- wipe CLEAN /with/ [usually with a wet cloth. obj.: floors, windows, doors]: /lA/ **sil-** 2. *79:18.* cleanness: - clean.
- wipe DRY [dishes], - dry [hair]: **kurula-.** *1064:6a.* dryness: - dry, - make dry.
- wipe OUT, - bump off, - rub out, - do in, - nuke, - zap. *Contemptuous for* - kill: **gebert-.** *308:13.* killing: non-formal terms: - waste; *514: * 5.* threat: INTERJ. specific threats.

- WIRE /θ/, - send a telegram or wire /to/: /A/ **telgraf çek-** → çek- 9. *347:19.* communications: - telegraph.

- WISE UP, - become wiser through bitter experience, - come to one's senses about a matter: **akıllan-, aklı başına gel-** → gel- 1. *570:10.* learning: - learn by experience; *924:2.* sanity: - come to one's senses.

- WISH, - want: **dile-** 1. *100:14.* desire: - desire.
- wish /θ/ sb much HAPPINESS: /A/ **mutluluklar dile-** → dile- 1. *504:13.* courtesy: - give one's regards; *1009:7.* prosperity: - prosper.

- wish a departing traveler a SAFE JOURNEY, - wish sb Godspeed, - send or - see sb off /to/: /A/ **uğurla-.** *188:16.* departure: - say or - bid good-bye; *504:13.* courtesy: - give one's regards.
- wish /θ/ sb much SUCCESS, - express wishes for much success /to/: /A/ **başarılar dile-** → dile- 1. *409:7c.* success: - wish success; *504:13.* courtesy: - give one's regards.

- WITHDRAW or - rescind one's DECISION: **kararını geri al-** → geri al- 1 → al- 1. *363:6.* changing of mind: - change one's mind; *370:7.* abandonment: - give up.
- withdraw MONEY /from/, - take money /{OUT OF/from}/ [bank, account]: /DAn/ **para çek-** → çek- 2. *192:10.* extraction: - extract.

- WITHER, - dry up [leaves, tree]: **kuru-** 2. *1064:6b.* dryness: - dry, - become dry.

- WONDER whether: **bilmem** → bil- 1, ***verb stem.se personal suffix* mI diye düşün-** [e.g., **Gitsem mi diye düşündüm.** 'Should I go, I wonder.'] → düşün- 5. *970:9.* uncertainty: - be uncertain.

WON'T you please?, Please., Pretty please. [a formula of entreaty]: **N'olursun.** → ol- 11 → olsun. *440:20.* request: INTERJ. please.

- WORK, - labor [I'm working.]: **çalış-** 1. *724:12.* occupation: - work; *725:12.* exertion: - work.
- work, - work /ON/, - study [lessons], - practice sth [piano]: **çalış-** 1. *570:12.* learning: - study; *725:12.* exertion: - work.
- work, - function [subj.: machine, not a person: How does this machine work?]: **çalış-** 3, **işle-** 1. *888:7.* operation: - be operative.
- work, - do the job, - serve the purpose [subj.: machine]: **iş gör-** → gör- 4. *387:17.* use: - avail; *407:4.* accomplishment: - accomplish; *994:3.* expedience: - expedite one's affair.
- work HARD, - struggle, - strive, - endeavor /to/: /için/ **uğraş-** 1. *403:11.* endeavor: - make a special effort.
- work NIGHT AND DAY, - work very hard: **geceyi gündüze kat-.** *725:13.* exertion: - work hard.

- work /ON/ sth, - be engaged /IN/ some work, - be busy or occupied /with/ a job [involving extra effort, struggle], - devote oneself /TO/ a task: /lA/ uğraş- 2. *724:11.* occupation: - busy oneself with.
- work OUT, - do exercises, calisthenics, physical training: **egzersiz yap-** 1 → yap- 3, **idman yap-** → yap- 3. *84:4.* fitness, exercise: - exercise; *328:8.* action: - practice.
- work out [subj.: plans], - be realized, - come true [plans, dreams, desires, wishes]: **gerçekleş, ol-** 1. *760:12.* existence: - become; *972:12.* truth: - come true.
- work out, - turn out the way it should, - go well, - come out right: **yoluna gir-.** *392:7.* improvement: - get better.
- work out A SOLUTION for a difficult problem: **işin içinden çık-** 2 → çık- 1. *939:2.* solution: - solve.

- WORRY /ABOUT/, - be concerned /ABOUT/ [obj.: person, illness]: /DAn/ **endişe et-,** /I/ **merak et-** 1. *126:6.* anxiety: - feel anxious.
- worry, - get anxious /about/: /DAn/ **kaygılan-.** *126:6.* anxiety: - feel anxious.
- worry sb, - distress, - upset; - sadden [His behavior worries me.]: **üz-.** *112:18.* sadness: - sadden; *126:4.* anxiety: - concern; *126:5.* : - make anxious.

- WORSHIP /θ/: /A/ **ibadet et-,** /A/ **tap-.** *696:10.* worship: - worship.

- WOUND sb /IN/ [a body part: IN the leg], - hurt, - injure: /I, DAn/ **yarala-.** *393:13.* impairment: - inflict an injury.

- WRANGLE, - finagle, - wangle, - manage to get, usually in the face of difficulty, - get sth /OUT OF/ sb [permission], - wrest /from/: /DAn/ {**kopar- 3/kopart- 3**}. *192:10.* extraction: - extract.

- WRAP one thing /{IN/AROUND}, with/ another: /A, lA/ **sar-** 1. *295:20.* covering: - wrap; *769:20.* assemblage: - bundle; *799:9.* joining: - bind.
- wrap, - wrap up, - make a package of: **paketle-, paket yap-** → yap- 3. *295:20.* covering: - wrap.

- WRECK, - demolish; - ruin; - pull down, - tear down, - knock down /with/; -

destroy [obj.: building]: /lA/ **yık-** 1. *395:17.* destruction: - demolish.

- WREST /from/, - finagle, - wrangle, - manage to get, usually in the face of difficulty, - get sth /OUT OF/ sb [permission]: /DAn/ {**kopar- 3/kopart- 3**}. *192:10.* extraction: - extract.

- WRINKLE, - make sth wrinkled [clothes]; - crumple up [papers]: **buruştur-.** *291:6.* fold: - wrinkle.

- WRITE /a: to [sb], b: {ON/IN}, c: {in/on}, d: with/: /a: A, b: A, c: DA, d: lA/ **yaz-** 1. The Ahmet'in kitabı var structure [i.e., *possessOR noun.[n]In + possessED noun.sI var*] is frequently used to indicate authorship rather than possession: **Yazarın beş kitabı var.** 'The author HAS {WRITTEN/AUTHORED} five books [lit., 'The author HAS five books.', a translation appropriate in contexts where possession rather than authorship is at issue]. *547:19.* writing: - write. → ol- 5, (5.1) Table 1. Additional examples. 3. Selected examples...
- write [letters] to ONE ANOTHER, - correspond /with/, - be in correspondence /with/ by letter: /lA/ **mektuplaş-.** *343:6.* communication: - communicate, - be in touch; *553:10.* correspondence: - correspond.
- write or - issue a receipt: **makbuz kes-** → kes- 5. *478:13.* giving: - deliver.
- write sth DOWN /IN/, - record sth /IN/, - enter sth /IN/ [a notebook]: /A/ **kaydet-** 2. *549:15.* record: - record.

- X -

- Y -

- YAWN: **esne-.** *292:16.* opening: - gape.

- YELL, - scream, or - shout /AT, saying/: /A, diye/ **bağır-, bağırıp çağır-** → çağır- 3, **çığlık at-** → at- 1. *59:6.* cry, call: - cry.

- YELLOW, - turn yellow [leaves]: **sarar-** 1. *43:3.* yellowness: - yellow.

- YIELD, - give way [in traffic]: **yol ver-** → ver- 1. *352:7.* publication: poster * specific signs; *433:7.* submission: - yield.

YOU decide., It's up to you., As you wish.: **Arzunuza kalmış.** → kal- 1. *323:5.* will: ADV. at will.

You don't say!: **Deme ya!** → de- 3. *131: * 16.* inexpectation: expressions of inexpectation; *955: * 6.* incredulity: expressions of incredulity.

You don't say!, You don't mean it!, Don't give me that!, Oh, go on!, Well I declare!: **Yapma ya!** [lit., Don't do (that)]. → yap- 2. *131: * 16.* inexpectation: expressions of inexpectation; *955: * 6.* incredulity: expressions of incredulity.

- Z -

- zip up: **fermuar çek-.** → çek- 4. *293:6.* closure: - close.

PART 3.
TURKISH VERBS BY THEME
[THESAURUS]

Part 3. Turkish Verbs by Theme [Thesaurus]

3.1 Theme Names in Alphabetical Order

To find a theme, locate its name below in alphabetical order. Then find the number following that name in **3.3 Turkish Verbs Classified by Theme**.

To understand how a particular theme fits into the scheme applied in **3.3 Turkish Verbs Classified by Theme**, look up that same number in the **3.2 Bird's Eye View of Themes as Organized in 3.3.**

Two-element category names are alphabetized by both elements. An asterisk * marks two-element category names in which the order of the names as they appear in *Roget's International Thesaurus*, Fifth edition, HarperCollins, 1992, has been reversed to permit alphabetical access to the second element.

- A -

ABANDONMENT 370
ABNORMALITY 869
ABRIDGMENT 557
ABSENCE 222
ACCOMPANIMENT 768
ACCOMPLISHMENT 407
ACCUSATION 599
ACQUISITION 472
ACQUITTAL 601
ACTION 328
ACTIVITY 330
ADDITION 253
ADVERSITY 1010
ADVICE 422
AFFECTATION 500
AFFIRMATION 334
AGE 303
AGGRAVATION 119
AGITATION 916
AGREEMENT 787
AGRICULTURE 1067
AID 449
AIR, WEATHER 317
ALCOHOLIC DRINK, INTOXICATION * 88
ALLUREMENT 377
AMUSEMENT 743
ANALYSIS 800
ANGER, RESENTMENT * 152
ANGULARITY 278
ANIMAL HUSBANDRY 1068
ANIMAL SOUNDS 60
ANSWER 938
ANXIETY 126
APPEARANCE 33
APPORTIONMENT 477
APPROACH 167
APPROVAL 509
ARRANGEMENT 807

ARROGANCE 141
ARRIVAL 186
ASCENT 193
ASSEMBLAGE 769
ASSENT 332
ASSOCIATION 617
ATONEMENT 658
ATTACK 459
ATTENTION 982
ATTRIBUTION 887
AVIATION 184
AVOIDANCE 368

- B -

BANTER 490
BASKETBALL 747
BEAUTY 1015
BEGINNING 817
BEHAVIOR 321
BELIEF 952
BENEVOLENCE, KINDNESS * 143
BIRTH 1
BLEMISH 1003
BOASTING 502
BORROWING 621
BROAD-MINDEDNESS 978
BUBBLE 320

- C -

CAPRICE 364
CAREFULNESS 339
CAUSE 885
CELEBRATION 487
CELIBACY 565
CERTAINTY 969
CESSATION 856
CHANCE 971
CHANGE 851
CHANGING OF MIND 363

CHANNEL 239
CHEAPNESS 633
CHEERFULNESS 109
CHOICE 371
CIRCUITOUSNESS 913
CIRCUMSTANCE 765
CLEANNESS 79
CLOSURE 293
CLOTHING 5
CLOUD 319
COLD 1022
COLOR 35
COLORLESSNESS 36
COMBINATION 804
COMFORT 121
COMMAND 420
COMMERCE, ECONOMICS 731
COMMISSION 615
COMMUNICATION 343
COMMUNICATIONS 347
COMPACT 437
COMPARISON 942
COMPLETENESS 793
COMPENSATION 338
COMPOSITION 795
COMPULSION 424
COMPUTER SCIENCE 1041
CONCAVITY 284
CONCEALMENT 346
CONDEMNATION 602
CONFINEMENT 429
CONFORMITY 866
CONFUSION, DISTRACTION * 984
CONGRATULATION 149
CONSENT 441
CONSUMPTION 388
CONTEMPT 157
CONTENTION 457
CONTENTMENT 107
CONTINUANCE 855
CONTINUITY 811
CONTRACTION 260
CONVERSATION 541
CONVERSION 857
CONVEXITY, PROTUBERANCE 283
COOKING 11
COPY 784
CORRESPONDENCE 553
COSTLESSNESS 634
COURAGE 492
COURTESY 504
COVERING 295
CROSSING 170
CRUMBLINESS, POWDERINESS * 1049
CRY, CALL 59
CURIOSITY 980
CURSE 513
CURVATURE 279
CUSTOM, HABIT 373

- D -

DANCE 705
DARKNESS, DIMNESS 1026

DEAFNESS 49
DEATH 307
DEBT 623
DECEPTION 356
DEFEAT 412
DEFECTIVE VISION 28
DEFENSE 460
DEMAND 421
DENIAL, NEGATION * 335
DEPARTURE 188
DEPRESSION <ACT OF LOWERING> 912
DESCENT 194
DECREASE 252
DESCRIPTION, REPRESENTATION * 349
DESIRE 100
DESTRUCTION 395
DEVIATION 164
DICTION 532
DIFFERENCE 779
DIFFICULTY 1012
DIRECTION [PLACE] 161
DIRECTION, MANAGEMENT 573
DISACCORD 456
DISAGREEMENT 788
DISAPPEARANCE 34
DISAPPOINTMENT 132
DISAPPROVAL 510
DISARRANGEMENT 810
DISCLOSURE 351
DISCOUNT 631
DISCOURTESY 505
DISCOVERY 940
DISEASE 85
DISINTEGRATION 805
DISOBEDIENCE 327
DISORDER 809
DISPARAGEMENT 512
DISPERSION 770
DISPROOF 957
DISRESPECT 156
DISSENT 333
DISSUASION 379
DISTANCE, REMOTENESS 261
DISTORTION 265
DISTRACTION, CONFUSION 984
DISUSE 390
DIVORCE, WIDOWHOOD 566
DOUBLENESS 872
DRYNESS 1064
DUENESS 639
DUPLICATION 873
DURATION 826
DUTY 641

- E -

EAGERNESS 101
EARLINESS 844
EATING 8
ECONOMICS, COMMERCE * 731
EFFECT 886
EJECTION 908

ELECTRICITY, MAGNETISM 1031
ELEVATION 911
EMERGENCE 190
EMPLOYEE, SERVANT * 577
ENCLOSURE 212
END 819
ENDEARMENT, LOVEMAKING * 562
ENDEAVOR 403
ENTRANCE 189
ENVIRONMENT 209
ENVY 154
EQUALITY 789
EQUIPMENT, PROVISION * 385
ERROR 974
ESCAPE 369
EVENT 830
EVIDENCE, PROOF 956
EVOLUTION 860
EXAGGERATION 355
EXCESS 992
EXCITEMENT 105
EXCLUSION 772
EXCRETION 12
EXERCISE, FITNESS * 84
EXERTION 725
EXISTENCE 760
EXPANSION, GROWTH 259
EXPECTATION 130
EXPEDIENCE 994
EXPENDITURE 626
EXPENSIVENESS 632
EXPERIMENT 941
EXPLOSIVE NOISE 56
EXTRACTION 192

- F -

FACILITY 1013
FAILURE 410
FAINTNESS OF SOUND 52
FALSENESS 354
FASHION 578
FASTING 515
FATIGUE 21
FEAR, FRIGHTENINGNESS 127
FEE, PRICE * 630
FEELING 93
FINANCE, INVESTMENT 729
FITNESS, EXERCISE 84
FOLD 291
FOLLOWING 166
FOOLISHNESS 922
FORESIGHT 960
FORGETFULNESS 989
FORGIVENESS 148
FORM 262
FORMLESSNESS 263
FREEDOM 430
FRICTION 1042
FRIENDSHIP 587
FRONT 216
FUEL 1020
FURROW 290

- G -

GAMBLING 759
GAS, VAPOR * 1065
GENERALITY 863
GIVING 478
GOODNESS 998
GOVERNMENT 612
GRATITUDE 150
GROWTH, EXPANSION * 259

- H -

HABIT, CUSTOM * 373
HABITATION 225
HAIR 3
HARDNESS, RIGIDITY 1044
HASTE 401
HATE 103
HEALTH 83
HEARING 48
HEAT 1018
HEATING 1019
HINDRANCE 1011
HONOR 646
HOPE 124
HOPELESSNESS 125
HORIZONTALNESS 201
HOSPITALITY, WELCOME 585
HUMILITY 137
HUMOR, WIT * 489
HUSBANDRY, ANIMAL * 1068

- I -

IGNORANCE 929
ILL HUMOR 110
ILLEGALITY 674
IMAGINATION 985
IMITATION 336
IMPAIRMENT 393
IMPATIENCE 135
IMPORTANCE 996
IMPOSITION 643
IMPOSSIBILITY 966
IMPOTENCE 19
IMPROBITY 645
IMPROVEMENT 392
IMPULSE, IMPACT 901
INACTION 329
INACTIVITY 331
INATTENTION 983
INCLUSION 771
INCOMBUSTIBILITY 1021
INCREASE 251
INCREDULITY 955
INCURIOSITY 981
INDICATORS, SIGNS * 517
INDIFFERENCE 102
INDISCRIMINATION 944
INDUCEMENT, MOTIVATION * 375
INEXCITABILITY 106
INEXPECTATION 131

INEXPEDIENCE 995
INFLUENCE 893
INFORMATION 551
INQUIRY 937
INSANITY, MANIA 925
INSENSIBILITY 25
INSERTION 191
INSIGNIFICANCE 248
INSOLENCE 142
INSTANTANEOUSNESS 829
INSUFFICIENCY 991
INTELLIGIBILITY 521
INTENTION 380
INTERCHANGE 862
INTERMENT 309
INTERPRETATION 341
INTERVAL 224
INTOXICATION, ALCOHOLIC DRINK 88
INTRUSION 214
INTUITION, INSTINCT 933
INVERSION 205
INVESTMENT, FINANCE * 729
INVOLVEMENT 897
IRRESOLUTION 362

- J -

JEALOUSY 153
JOINING 799
JUDGMENT 945

- K -

KILLING 308
KINDNESS, BENEVOLENCE 143
KNOWLEDGE 927

- L -

LAMENTATION 115
LATENESS 845
LEAP 366
LEARNING 570
LEFT SIDE 220
LEGAL ACTION 598
LEGALITY 673
LENDING 620
LENGTH 267
LETTER 546
LIABILITY 896
LIBERATION 431
LIFE 306
LIGHT 1024
LIQUEFACTION 1062
LIST 870
LOCATION 159
LOSS 473
LOUDNESS 53
LOVE 104
LOVEMAKING, ENDEARMENT 562
LUBRICANTS, OILS * 1054

- M -

MAGNETISM, ELECTRICITY * 1031
MANAGEMENT, DIRECTION * 573
MANIA, INSANITY * 925
MANIFESTATION 348
MANNER, MEANS 384
MARRIAGE 563
MATHEMATICS 1016
MEANING 518
MEANINGLESSNESS 520
MEASUREMENT 300
MEASUREMENT OF TIME 831
MEDICAL TREATMENT, THERAPY *
 91
MEMORY 988
MISBEHAVIOR 322
MISINTERPRETATION 342
MISJUDGMENT 947
MISSILERY, ROCKETRY * 1072
MIXTURE 796
MOISTURE 1063
MONEY 728
MOTION 172
MOTIVATION, INDUCEMENT 375
MUSIC 708

- N -

NARROWNESS, THINNESS 270
NEARNESS 223
NECESSITY 962
NEGATION, DENIAL 335
NEGLECT 340
NERVOUSNESS 128
NEUTRALITY 467
NEWS 552
NOMENCLATURE 527
NONCONFORMITY 867
NONEXISTENCE 761
NONOBSERVANCE 435
NONPAYMENT 625
NUTRITION 7

- O -

OBEDIENCE 326
OBLIQUITY 204
OBSERVANCE 434
OCCUPATION 724
ODOR 69
OFFER 439
OILS, LUBRICANTS 1054
OLDNESS 841
ONENESS 871
OPENING 292
OPERATION 888
OPPOSITION 451
ORDER 806
ORNAMENTATION 498
OSCILLATION 915
OSTENTATION 501
OVERESTIMATION 948

OVERRUNNING 909

- P -

PACIFICATION 465
PAIN 26
PARSIMONY 484
PART 792
PARTICIPATION 476
PARTICULARITY 864
PAST, THE 836
PATIENCE 134
PAYMENT 624
PENALTY 603
PENDENCY 202
PERMISSION 443
PERPETUITY 828
PHOTOGRAPHY 714
PITY 145
PLAN 381
PLANTS 310
PLEASURE 95
PLIANCY, SOFTNESS * 1045
PLUNGE 367
POSSESSION 469
POSSIBILITY 965
POVERTY 619
POWER, POTENCY 18
POWDERINESS, CRUMBLINESS 1049
PREARRANGEMENT 964
PREDETERMINATION 963
PREDICTION 961
PREMONITION 133
PREPARATION 405
PRESENCE 221
PRESERVATION 397
PREVIOUSNESS 833
PRICE, FEE 630
PRIDE 136
PRINTING 548
PROBABILITY 967
PROBITY 644
PROCREATION, REPRODUCTION * 78
PRODIGALITY 486
PRODUCTION 891
PROGRESSION 162
PROHIBITION 444
PROMISE 436
PROMOTION 446
PROOF, EVIDENCE * 956
PROSPERITY 1009
PROTECTION 1007
PROTUBERANCE, CONVEXITY * 283
PROVISION, EQUIPMENT 385
PUBLIC SPEAKING 543
PUBLICATION 352
PULLING 904
PUNISHMENT 604
PURCHASE 733
PURSUIT 382
PUSHING, THROWING 903

- Q -

QUALIFICATION 958
QUANTITY 244
QUIESCENCE 173

- R -

RADIO 1033
RAIN 316
REACTION 902
REAR 217
REASONING 934
RECEIVING 479
RECEPTION 187
RECORD 549
REDNESS 41
REFUSAL 442
REGRESSION 163
REGRET 113
REJOICING 116
RELATION 74
RELIEF 120
RELIGIOUS RITES 701
REMAINDER 256
REMEDY 86
REMOTENESS, DISTANCE * 261
REPEAL 445
REPETITION 848
REPRESENTATION, DESCRIPTION 349
REPRODUCTION, PROCREATION 78
REQUEST 440
RESCUE 398
RESENTMENT, ANGER 152
RESIGNATION, RETIREMENT 448
RESISTANCE 453
RESOLUTION 359
RESONANCE 54
RESPECT 155
REST, REPOSE 20
RESTITUTION 481
RESTORATION 396
RESTRAINT 428
RETENTION 474
RETIREMENT, RESIGNATION * 448
RIDICULE 508
RIGHT [IDEALS] 637
RIGIDITY, HARDNESS * 1044
ROCKETRY, MISSILERY 1072
ROTATION 914

- S -

SADNESS 112
SALE 734
SAMENESS 777
SANITY 924
SATIETY 993
SECRECY 345
SECRETION 13
SENSATION 24
SENSATIONS OF TOUCH 74
SEPARATION 801

WORSHIP 696
WRITING 547
WRONG 638

- X -

- Y -

YELLOWNESS 43

- Z -

3.2 BIRD'S EYE VIEW OF THEMES AS ORGANIZED IN 3.3

Below, in numerical sequence, is a list of all the major categories, without the constituent verbs, that appear in section **3.3 Turkish Verbs Classified by Theme**. Gaps in the numerical sequence are due to the fact that section 3.3 does not include all the categories in *Roget's International Thesaurus*, Fifth edition, HarperCollins, 1992, on which it is based. A line between sets of names marks off groups of themes.

CLASS 1: THE BODY AND THE
SENSES

1 BIRTH
3 HAIR
5 CLOTHING
6 UNCLOTHING

7 NUTRITION
8 EATING
11 COOKING

12 EXCRETION
13 SECRETION

16 WEAKNESS
18 POWER, POTENCY
19 IMPOTENCE

20 REST, REPOSE
21 FATIGUE
22 SLEEP
23 WAKEFULNESS

24 SENSATION
25 INSENSIBILITY
26 PAIN

27 VISION
28 DEFECTIVE VISION
31 VISIBILITY
33 APPEARANCE
34 DISAPPEARANCE
35 COLOR
36 COLORLESSNESS
41 REDNESS
43 YELLOWNESS

48 HEARING
49 DEAFNESS
51 SILENCE
52 FAINTNESS OF SOUND
53 LOUDNESS
54 RESONANCE
56 EXPLOSIVE NOISE
57 SIBILATION <HISSING SOUNDS>

58 STRIDENCY <HARSH AND SHRILL
SOUNDS>
59 CRY, CALL
60 ANIMAL SOUNDS

62 TASTE
64 UNSAVORINESS
69 ODOR
71 STENCH

73 TOUCH
74 SENSATIONS OF TOUCH

75 SEX
78 REPRODUCTION, PROCREATION

79 CLEANNESS
80 UNCLEANNESS

83 HEALTH
84 FITNESS, EXERCISE
85 DISEASE
86 REMEDY
88 INTOXICATION, ALCOHOLIC
DRINK
89 TOBACCO
91 THERAPY, MEDICAL TREATMENT

CLASS 2: FEELINGS

93 FEELING
95 PLEASURE
96 UNPLEASURE
98 UNPLEASANTNESS
100 DESIRE
101 EAGERNESS
102 INDIFFERENCE
103 HATE
104 LOVE
105 EXCITEMENT
106 INEXCITABILITY
107 CONTENTMENT
109 CHEERFULNESS
110 ILL HUMOR
112 SADNESS
113 REGRET
115 LAMENTATION
116 REJOICING

118 TEDIUM
119 AGGRAVATION
120 RELIEF
121 COMFORT
122 WONDER
124 HOPE
125 HOPELESSNESS
126 ANXIETY
127 FEAR, FRIGHTENINGNESS
128 NERVOUSNESS
130 EXPECTATION
131 INEXPECTATION
132 DISAPPOINTMENT
133 PREMONITION
134 PATIENCE
135 IMPATIENCE
136 PRIDE
137 HUMILITY
140 VANITY
141 ARROGANCE
142 INSOLENCE
143 KINDNESS, BENEVOLENCE
145 PITY
148 FORGIVENESS
149 CONGRATULATION
150 GRATITUDE
152 RESENTMENT, ANGER
153 JEALOUSY
154 ENVY
155 RESPECT
156 DISRESPECT
157 CONTEMPT

CLASS 3: PLACE AND CHANGE OF PLACE

158 SPACE
159 LOCATION
161 DIRECTION
162 PROGRESSION
163 REGRESSION
164 DEVIATION
166 FOLLOWING
167 APPROACH
170 CROSSING

172 MOTION
173 QUIESCENCE
174 SWIFTNESS
175 SLOWNESS
176 TRANSFERAL, TRANSPORTATION
177 TRAVEL
182 WATER TRAVEL
184 AVIATION
186 ARRIVAL
187 RECEPTION
188 DEPARTURE
189 ENTRANCE
190 EMERGENCE
191 INSERTION
192 EXTRACTION
193 ASCENT

194 DESCENT

200 VERTICALNESS
201 HORIZONTALNESS
202 PENDENCY
204 OBLIQUITY
205 INVERSION

209 ENVIRONMENT
212 ENCLOSURE
214 INTRUSION
216 FRONT
217 REAR
220 LEFT SIDE

221 PRESENCE
222 ABSENCE
223 NEARNESS
224 INTERVAL

225 HABITATION

238 STREAM
239 CHANNEL

CLASS 4: MEASURE AND SHAPE

244 QUANTITY
248 INSIGNIFICANCE
249 SUPERIORITY
251 INCREASE
252 DECREASE
253 ADDITION
255 SUBTRACTION
256 REMAINDER

259 EXPANSION, GROWTH
260 CONTRACTION

261 DISTANCE, REMOTENESS

262 FORM
263 FORMLESSNESS
265 DISTORTION
267 LENGTH
268 SHORTNESS
270 NARROWNESS, THINNESS
278 ANGULARITY
279 CURVATURE
283 CONVEXITY, PROTUBERANCE
284 CONCAVITY
285 SHARPNESS

287 SMOOTHNESS

409 SUCCESS
410 FAILURE
411 VICTORY
412 DEFEAT

420 COMMAND
421 DEMAND
422 ADVICE
424 COMPULSION
425 STRICTNESS
428 RESTRAINT
429 CONFINEMENT
430 FREEDOM
431 LIBERATION
433 SUBMISSION
434 OBSERVANCE
435 NONOBSERVANCE
436 PROMISE
437 COMPACT
439 OFFER

440 REQUEST
441 CONSENT
442 REFUSAL
443 PERMISSION
444 PROHIBITION
445 REPEAL
446 PROMOTION
448 RESIGNATION, RETIREMENT

449 AID
451 OPPOSITION
453 RESISTANCE
456 DISACCORD
457 CONTENTION
458 WARFARE
459 ATTACK
460 DEFENSE
465 PACIFICATION
467 NEUTRALITY

469 POSSESSION
472 ACQUISITION
473 LOSS
474 RETENTION
476 PARTICIPATION
477 APPORTIONMENT
478 GIVING
479 RECEIVING
480 TAKING
481 RESTITUTION
482 THEFT
484 PARSIMONY
486 PRODIGALITY

487 CELEBRATION
489 WIT, HUMOR
490 BANTER

492 COURAGE

498 ORNAMENTATION
500 AFFECTATION
501 OSTENTATION
502 BOASTING
504 COURTESY
505 DISCOURTESY

508 RIDICULE
509 APPROVAL
510 DISAPPROVAL
512 DISPARAGEMENT
513 CURSE
514 THREAT

515 FASTING

CLASS 8: LANGUAGE

517 SIGNS, INDICATORS
518 MEANING
520 MEANINGLESSNESS
521 INTELLIGIBILITY
522 UNINTELLIGIBILITY
524 SPEECH
527 NOMENCLATURE

532 DICTION

541 CONVERSATION
543 PUBLIC SPEAKING

546 LETTER
547 WRITING
548 PRINTING
549 RECORD
551 INFORMATION
552 NEWS
553 CORRESPONDENCE
557 ABRIDGMENT

CLASS 9: HUMAN SOCIETY AND INSTITUTIONS

562 LOVEMAKING, ENDEARMENT
563 MARRIAGE
565 CELIBACY
566 DIVORCE, WIDOWHOOD

568 TEACHING
570 LEARNING

573 DIRECTION, MANAGEMENT

631

577 SERVANT, EMPLOYEE

578 FASHION
582 SOCIABILITY
584 SECLUSION
585 HOSPITALITY, WELCOME

587 FRIENDSHIP
598 LEGAL ACTION
599 ACCUSATION
601 ACQUITTAL
602 CONDEMNATION
603 PENALTY
604 PUNISHMENT

612 GOVERNMENT
615 COMMISSION

617 ASSOCIATION

618 WEALTH
619 POVERTY
620 LENDING
621 BORROWING
623 DEBT
624 PAYMENT
625 NONPAYMENT
626 EXPENDITURE
630 PRICE, FEE
631 DISCOUNT
632 EXPENSIVENESS
633 CHEAPNESS
634 COSTLESSNESS
635 THRIFT

CLASS 10: VALUES AND IDEALS

637 RIGHT
638 WRONG
639 DUENESS
641 DUTY
643 IMPOSITION
644 PROBITY
645 IMPROBITY
646 HONOR

654 VICE
658 ATONEMENT
665 UNCHASTITY
668 TEMPERANCE
671 VIOLENCE
673 LEGALITY
674 ILLEGALITY

696 WORSHIP
701 RELIGIOUS RITES

CLASS 11: ARTS

704 SHOW BUSINESS, THEATER
705 DANCE
708 MUSIC

714 PHOTOGRAPHY

CLASS 12: OCCUPATIONS AND CRAFTS

724 OCCUPATION
725 EXERTION

728 MONEY
729 FINANCE, INVESTMENT
731 COMMERCE, ECONOMICS
733 PURCHASE
734 SALE

740 WEAVING
741 SEWING

CLASS 13: SPORTS AND AMUSEMENTS

743 AMUSEMENT
744 SPORTS
747 BASKETBALL
748 TENNIS
752 SOCCER
753 SKIING
759 GAMBLING

CLASS 14: THE MIND AND IDEAS

760 EXISTENCE
761 NONEXISTENCE
765 CIRCUMSTANCE

768 ACCOMPANIMENT
769 ASSEMBLAGE
770 DISPERSION
771 INCLUSION
772 EXCLUSION

774 RELATION
777 SAMENESS
779 DIFFERENCE
783 SIMILARITY
784 COPY

787 AGREEMENT

788 DISAGREEMENT
789 EQUALITY
791 WHOLE
792 PART
793 COMPLETENESS

795 COMPOSITION
796 MIXTURE
799 JOINING
800 ANALYSIS
801 SEPARATION
804 COMBINATION
805 DISINTEGRATION

806 ORDER
807 ARRANGEMENT <PUTTING IN ORDER>
809 DISORDER
810 DISARRANGEMENT
811 CONTINUITY <UNINTERRUPTED SEQUENCE>
814 SEQUENCE
817 BEGINNING
819 END

820 TIME
824 SPELL <PERIOD OF DUTY, ETC.>
826 DURATION
827 TRANSIENCE
828 PERPETUITY
829 INSTANTANEOUSNESS
830 EVENT
831 MEASUREMENT OF TIME
833 PREVIOUSNESS
834 SUBSEQUENCE
835 SIMULTANEITY
836 THE PAST
841 OLDNESS
842 TIMELINESS
843 UNTIMELINESS
844 EARLINESS
845 LATENESS
848 REPETITION

851 CHANGE
854 STABILITY
855 CONTINUANCE <CONTINUANCE IN ACTION>
856 CESSATION
857 CONVERSION
860 EVOLUTION
861 SUBSTITUTION
862 INTERCHANGE

863 GENERALITY
864 PARTICULARITY
866 CONFORMITY
867 NONCONFORMITY
869 ABNORMALITY

870 LIST
871 ONENESS
872 DOUBLENESS
873 DUPLICATION

885 CAUSE
886 EFFECT
887 ATTRIBUTION
888 OPERATION
891 PRODUCTION
893 INFLUENCE
896 LIABILITY
897 INVOLVEMENT
900 SUPPORT

901 IMPULSE, IMPACT
902 REACTION
903 PUSHING, THROWING
904 PULLING
908 EJECTION
909 OVERRUNNING
910 SHORTCOMING
911 ELEVATION
912 DEPRESSION <ACT OF LOWERING>
913 CIRCUITOUSNESS
914 ROTATION
915 OSCILLATION
916 AGITATION

917 SPECTATOR
921 UNINTELLIGENCE
922 FOOLISHNESS
924 SANITY
925 INSANITY, MANIA

927 KNOWLEDGE
929 IGNORANCE
930 THOUGHT
933 INTUITION, INSTINCT
934 REASONING
937 INQUIRY
938 ANSWER
939 SOLUTION
940 DISCOVERY
941 EXPERIMENT

942 COMPARISON
944 INDISCRIMINATION
945 JUDGMENT
947 MISJUDGMENT
948 OVERESTIMATION
949 UNDERESTIMATION
950 THEORY, SUPPOSITION

952 BELIEF

3.3 TURKISH VERBS CLASSIFIED BY THEME

Note: Below the meanings of a verb are numbered as they are in the **Turkish-English Dictionary of Verbs**.

CLASS 1: THE BODY AND THE SENSES

0-100

1 BIRTH
1:2 - be born | doğ- 1 '- be born'; dünyaya gel- '- be born', lit., '- come /INTO/ the world' → gel- 1.

1:3 - give birth | /DAn/ çocuğu ol- '- have {children/a child} /from/, - give birth to a child' → ol- 6; doğur- '- give birth /TO/, - bear'; dünyaya getir- '- bring /INTO/ the world, - give birth /TO/, - bear'.

3 HAIR
3:22 - cut or - dress the hair | /A/ boya yaptır- '- have sth /θ/ colored [obj.: hair]' → yaptır- 2; düzelt- 3 '- trim [obj: hair, beard]'; meç yap- '- give sb highlights, - put highlights, streaks of color, in sb's hair [hair salon process]' → yap- 3; /A/ {meç/röfle} yaptır- '- have one's hair streaked, highlighted, - have highlights, streaks of color, put /IN/ one's hair [hair salon process]' → yaptır- 2; /A/ perma yaptır- '- have or - get a perm[anent]' → yaptır- 2; /A/ röfle yaptır- = meç yaptır-; saç ör- '- braid hair' → ör- 2; saç kes- '- cut hair' → kes- 1; saç kestir- '- have hair cut' → kestir- 1; saçlarını yaptır- '- have one's hair styled' → yaptır- 2; sakal tıraşı yap- '- shave sb, - give sb a shave' → yap- 3; tıraş ol- 1 '- shave oneself, - shave'. 2 '- get or - have a shave or a haircut' → ol- 10.1; /I/ topuz yaptır- '- have one's hair put in a bun' → yaptır- 2.

5 CLOTHING
5:38 - clothe | giydir- a) /I [on the noun designating the person dressed]/ '- dress sb [garment not mentioned]', b) /I [on the noun designating the garment if that noun is definite, /θ/ on that noun if it is indefinite], A [on noun designating the person dressed]/ '- dress /θ/ sb /IN/ sth, - have /θ/ sb put sth on or wear sth'.

5:41 - dress up | /lA/ süslen- 1 '- deck oneself out /IN/, - adorn oneself /with/, - doll oneself up /IN/'.

5:42 - don, - put on | giy- '- put on clothing, - don, - put sth /ON/ [a part of the body]', also '- be wearing, - have on clothing'. Giy- is usually used with larger items of clothing, gloves, and sometimes headgear, but not with accessories or small items such as jewelry, watches, etc.; giyin- '- dress oneself, - get dressed'; /A/ tak- '- attach, - fasten sth /to/, - wear, - put sth /ON/ [oneself, usually small items, accessories: glasses, jewelry, also some headgear], - put up [curtains]'.

5:43 - wear, - have on | giy- '- be wearing [clothing, size 38], - have on clothing'. Also '- don, - put on clothing'.

6 UNCLOTHING
6:6 - take off | çıkar- 2 '- take off, - remove [clothing: hat, coat]'.

6:7 - undress | soy- 3 '- undress sb, - take sb's clothes off [mother undresses child]'; soyun- '- undress oneself, - take off one's clothes'.

6:8 - peel | soy- 1 '- peel [fruit]'; /tarafından/ soyul- 1 '- be peeled /by/'.

7 NUTRITION
7:17 - diet | perhiz yap- '- diet, - go on a diet' → yap- 3.

8 EATING
8:19 - nourish | /I/ emzir- '- nurse, - suckle, - breast-feed'; /A/ meme ver-. Same, lit., '- give breast /to/' → ver- 1.

8:20 - eat | iç- 3 usually '- drink', but sometimes '- eat', when the object is a liquid but not a drink, e.g., soup; içil- 3 '- be eaten [soup]'; ye- 1 '- eat', when preceded by a noun specifying the thing eaten, e.g., balık ye- '- eat fish'; yemek ye- '- eat [lit., - eat food]', when the specific food is not mentioned: Where are you going to eat? → ye- 1; /tarafından/ **1 yen-** '- be eaten /by/', most common form in speech and in writing; **2 yenil-** '- be eaten', common in writing, less so than 1 **yen-** in speech.

8:21 - dine **akşam yemeği ye-** '- have or - eat the evening meal, i.e., - have dinner or supper' → ye- 1; **kahvaltı {et-/yap-}** '- have or - eat breakfast, - breakfast.' Note: '- make or - prepare breakfast' is **kahvaltı hazırla-**; **öğle yemeği ye-** '- have the noon meal, - have or - eat lunch' → ye- 1; **yemeğe çık-** '- go out {for/to} dinner, - dine out.' For çık- with specific meals, için is used instead of the dative case: **Ahmet bey {kahvaltı/öğle yemeği/ akşam yemeği} için çıktı.** 'Ahmet bey has gone out for {breakfast/lunch/dinner [lit., the evening meal]}.' → çık- 2.

8:22 - devour **iç- 4** '- take', when the object of **iç-** is a liquid medicine. It is also used for a solid if it is taken with water; **içil- 4** '- be taken', when the subject of **içil-** is a liquid medicine. It is also used for a solid if it is taken with water; **yut-** '- swallow [food], - take pills; - gulp down food'.

8:23 - gobble **atıştır- 1** '- bolt down, - gobble up, - gobble down, - wolf down [food]; - gulp down [a drink]'.

8:26 - pick **abur cubur ye-** '- have a snack, - snack, - eat food as a casual snack'. The food may include, but is not limited to, junk food, e.g., cookies, candy, candy bars, etc., the kind of food sold in vending machines in the U.S. → ye- 1; **atıştır- 2** '- grab a bite, - have or - eat a snack, - snack'.

8:27 - chew **çiğne- 1** '- chew'; **ısır-** '- bite [subj.: almost anything]'; /DAn/ **sok- 3** '- bite sb /{ON/IN}/ [a part of the body] [subj.: snake]; - sting sb /{ON/IN}/ [subj.: insect]'.

8:29 - drink **iç- 1** '- drink'; **içil- 1** '- be drunk'; **yudumla-** '- sip'.

8:35 INTERJ. chow down! **Afiyet olsun.** 'Bon appétit!, Enjoy!' → ol-

11 → olsun; **Ziyade olsun!** 'May you always enjoy abundance!', words said to a hostess after a meal or to a person who, when with friends, has paid the bill. → ol- 11 → olsun.

11 COOKING
11:4a - cook sth **haşla-** '- boil, - cook sth in boiling water'; /tarafından/ **haşlan- 1** '- be boiled, cooked in boiling water /by/'; **kaynat-** '- boil, - cause sth to boil'; **kavur-** '- fry, - roast'; **kızart- 1** '- fry, sauté sth'. **2** '- toast sth'. **3** '- roast sth'; /tarafından/ **kızartıl- 1** '- be fried, sautéd /by/'. **2** '- be toasted /by/'. **3** '- be roasted /by/'; **pişir-** '- cook, - bake sth'; **sote et-** '- sauté'.

11:4b for sth - cook **kızar- 2** '- fry', i.e., - become fried: The potatoes are frying. **3** '- toast,' i.e., - become toast: The bread is toasting. **4** '- roast', i.e., - become roast meat: The meat is roasting.; **piş-** 'for sth - cook, - bake'.

12 EXCRETION
12:12 - excrete **ağla-** '- cry, - weep'; **göz yaşı dök-** '- cry, - weep, - spill tears' → dök- 1; **sıkış- 5** '- feel the need to relieve oneself, - feel the need to go to the toilet, - be bursting'; **tuvaleti gel-** '- have to use the {bathroom/restroom/toilet}, - have to go' → gel- 1.

12:13 - defecate **altına kaçır-** '- wet or - soil one's underclothes or bed' → kaçır- 2; **altını ıslat-**. Same; **büyük aptes yap-** '- have a bowel movement or BM, - defecate', *formal, polite.* → yap- 3; **dışarı[.ya] çık-**. Same. → çık- 2; **ihtiyacını gör-** '- defecate, - urinate' → gör- 4; **tuvalet yap-** '- have a bowel movement or BM, - urinate, - do one's business, - use the facilities, the restroom; - make one's toilet, i.e., usually for a woman to dress or to arrange her hair' → yap- 3; **tuvalete git-** '- go to the bathroom, - use the toilet' → git- 1a; **tuvaleti gel-** '- have to use the {bathroom/restroom/toilet}, - have to go.' Used by grown-ups among themselves. → gel- 1; **tuvaleti var**. Same. → ol- 3, Additional examples. b) 3.6. Issues of necessity.

12:14 - urinate | **altına kaçır-** '- wet or - soil one's underclothes or bed' → kaçır- 2; **altını ıslat-**. Same; **çiş {yap-/et-}** '- piss, - pee, - take a {piss/pee}.' Usually used by grown-ups for children and by children among themselves. → yap- 3; **çişi gel-** '- have to go [pee], - have to pee.' Usually used by grown-ups for children and by children among themselves. → gel- 1; **çişi var**. Same. → ol- 3, Additional examples. b) 3.6. Issues of necessity; **ihtiyacını gör-** '- defecate, - urinate' → gör- 4; /A/ **işe-** '- urinate, - piss, - pee /ON/'; **küçük aptes yap-** '- urinate', *formal, polite*; **su dök-** '- take a {pee/piss}, - urinate' → dök- 3; **tuvalet yap-** '- have a bowel movement *or* BM, - urinate, - do one's business, - use the facilities, the restroom; - make one's toilet, i.e., usually for a woman to dress or to arrange her hair' → yap- 3; **tuvalete git-** '- go to the bathroom, - use the toilet' → git- 1a; **tuvaleti gel-** '- have to use the {bathroom/restroom/toilet}, - have to go.' Used by grown-ups among themselves. → gel- 1; **tuvaleti var**. Same. → ol- 3, Additional examples. b) 3.6. Issues of necessity.

12:16 - sweat | /DAn/ **ter bas-** '- break out in a sweat, - be covered in sweat /{from, BECAUSE OF}/' → bas- 4; **terle-** '- sweat, perspire'.

12:17 - bleed | **kana-** '- bleed'; /DAn/ **kan ak-** '- bleed /from/'; /DAn/ **kan gel-** '- bleed /from/, for blood - come /from/' → gel- 1.

12:18 - menstruate | **âdet gör-** '- have one's period, - menstruate' → gör- 3; **aybaşı ol-**. Same. → ol- 10.1.

13 SECRETION

13:5 - secrete | **gözleri yaşar-** 'for one's eyes - fill with tears, for tears - come to one's eyes; for one's eyes - water'; **gözlerini yaşart-** 'for sth - bring tears to one's eyes, - make one's eyes water'.

13:6 - salivate | /A/ **tükür-** '- spit /{ON/IN/INTO}/'.

16 WEAKNESS

16:9 - become weak | **yıpran-** 2 'for sb - lose much of his vigor, energy; - be or - become worn-out, burned-out, or spent'.

18 POWER, POTENCY

18:11 - be able | This concept is usually expressed with the suffix **-[y]Abil** on the verb stem. The i is invariable, i.e., always i not ı: gel- '- come', gel.ebil- '- be able to come', yap- '- do', yap.abil- '- be able to do.' The various tense and personal suffixes follow: gel.ebil.ir.im 'I {can/am able to/may} come.', gel.ebil.di.m 'I was able to come', etc. For the complete paradigm, see a grammar book. For the corresponding negative forms, see 19:8 IMPOTENCE: cannot; **elinden gel-** '- be within one's capabilities, - lie in one's power, - be able to do' → gel- 1.

19 IMPOTENCE

19:8 cannot | This concept is usually expressed with the suffix **-[y]AmA** on a verb stem to form the INability stem of that verb: gel- '- come', gel.eme- '- be UNable to come'. The various tense and personal suffixes follow: gel.eme.m 'I {can'T/am UNable to} come.', gel.eme.di.m 'I {couldN'T/wasN'T able to} come', etc. With the inability form of the verb bil-, an English translation including the expected notion of inability will often seem awkward or over emphatic: **bileme-** '- have no idea, not - be able to figure out, [just] not - know, lit., ** - be unable to know, not - be able to know' → bil- 1.1. For the complete inability paradigm, see a grammar book. For the corresponding affirmative forms, see 18:11 POWER, POTENCY: - be able; **elinden gelME-** '- be beyond one's abilities' → gel- 1.

19:21 INTERJ. no can do! | **Ne yapayım? Elimde değil.** 'What can I do? It's out of my control.' → yap- 2; **Yapabileceğimiz hiçbir şey yok.** 'There's nothing we can do.' → yap- 2; **Yapacak bir şey yok.** 'There's nothing to be done.' → yap- 2.

20 REST, REPOSE

20:6 - rest | **{başını/kafasını} dinle-** '- rest, - put one's mind at ease' → 2 dinle-; 1 **dinlen-** '- rest [oneself]'; <u>istirahat et-</u>. Same; <u>yorgunluk çıkar-</u> '- relax, - unwind, - rest' → çıkar- 3.

20:8 - take a rest <u>ara ver-</u> '- take a break from, - stop doing sth for a while', *always appropriate*. → ver- 3; <u>mola ver-</u> '- stop for a rest [while traveling], - take a break [while working], - make a rest stop [subj.: workers or vehicles, not students or professionals except when speaking *very informally*]' → ver- 3; <u>teneffüs yap-</u> '- take a break', *formal, always appropriate*. → yap- 3.

20:9 - vacation <u>tatil yap-</u> '- go on a {vacation/holiday}, - take a {vacation/holiday} [subj.: a person, not an institution]' → yap- 3; <u>tatile çık-</u> '- go ON {vacation/holiday}, - leave FOR {vacation/the holiday[s]}, - begin a vacation [subj.: a person, not an institution]'; <u>tatile gir-</u> '- close or - shut down for vacation [subj.: an institution, school, business], - recess, - go into recess for vacation [subj.: school], - go on vacation [subj.: a person but usually only when considered as a member of an institution]'; /A, A/ <u>tatile git-</u> '- go /to [a place], {ON/FOR}/ vacation, holiday, - have a vacation, holiday [subj.: a person, not an institution]' → git- 1a.

21 FATIGUE
21:4 - fatigue <u>yor-</u> '- tire, - make tired'; /DAn/ <u>yorul-</u> '- get tired /from/, - be tired /from/, - tire [oneself]'.

21:5 - burn out /DAn/ <u>bit-</u> 2 '- be worn-out, exhausted, tired out /from/'; {gücü/takatı} <u>tüken-</u> 'for {one's strength} - give out, - be exhausted, tired out'; /DAn/ <u>nefes nefese kal-</u> '- be or - get out of breath, - pant, - huff and puff /from/' → kal- 1; <u>yıpran-</u> 2 'for sb - lose much of his vigor, energy; - be or - become worn-out, burned-out, or spent'.

22 SLEEP
22:13 - sleep <u>çok uyu-</u> '- sleep a lot, too much, - oversleep' → uyu- 1; <u>horla-</u> '- snore'; <u>uykusu gel-</u> '- become or - get sleepy' → gel- 1; <u>uyu-</u> 1 '- sleep'; <u>uyukla-</u> '- doze, - doze off'; /{A/üstüne}/ <u>uzan-</u> 1 '-

lie down /{ON/on}/, - stretch oneself out /{ON/on}/ [bed for a nap]'.

22:16 - go to sleep <u>kendinden geç-</u> 3 '- pass out, - fall asleep' → geç- 1; <u>uykuya dal-</u> '- fall asleep; - doze off, - drop off /to/ sleep' → dal- 2; <u>uyu-</u> 2 '- go to sleep, - fall asleep, - drop off to sleep'; <u>uyukla-</u> '- doze, - doze off'.

22:17 - go to bed <u>yat-</u> 1 '- go to bed, - lie down, - retire for the night'. Also '- be lying down, - be in bed'.

22:19 - put to bed /A/ <u>yatır-</u> 1 '- put sb to bed, - have sb lie down /{IN/ON}/'.

22:20 - put to sleep <u>uyku getir-</u> '- put to sleep [subj.: dull TV program]'.

23 WAKEFULNESS
23:3 - keep awake /a: DAn, b: DIĞI için, c: yüzünden/ <u>uykusu kaç-</u> '- be unable to go to sleep /a: {from/BECAUSE OF}, b: because, c: because of/' → kaç- 1; <u>uykusunu kaçır-</u> '- keep awake, - make it impossible to go to sleep [subj.: coffee]' → kaçır- 3.

23:4 - awake <u>uyan-</u> '- wake up, - awake'.

23:5 - wake sb up <u>uyandır-</u> '- wake sb up, - awaken sb'.

24 SENSATION
24:6 - sense <u>duy-</u> 3 '- feel [pride, interest, happiness, sorrow, pain], - sense'; <u>hisset-</u> 1 '- feel, - sense [one's own state: well, bad]'. 2 '- sense, - feel, - be aware; - notice, - perceive'; *verb stem*.<u>mIş gibi hisset-</u> '- feel {like/as if}' → hisset- 2; <u>sez-</u> '- understand sth intuitively, - sense, - have a feeling, - feel, - perceive, - discern'. Same as 93:10. FEELING: - feel.

25 INSENSIBILITY
25:5 - faint <u>bayıl-</u> 1 '- faint, - pass out'; <u>kendinden geç-</u> 1 '- pass out, - faint, - lose consciousness' → geç- 1; <u>kendini kaybet-</u> 1. '- lose consciousness, - pass out, - faint' → {kaybet-/yitir-}; <u>komaya gir-</u> '- go, - fall, - lapse, or - sink /INTO/ a coma'; {şuurunu/bilincini}

kaybet-[or yitir-] 1 = kendini kaybet- 1.

26 PAIN
26:7 - inflict pain | canını acıt- '- hurt sb [physically]'; canını yak-. Same. → yak- 2; çimdikle- '- pinch with one's fingers'; ısır- '- bite [subj.: almost anything]'; /DAn/ sok- 3 '- bite sb /{ON/IN}/ [a part of the body] [subj.: snake]; - sting sb /{ON/IN}/ [subj.: insect]'; yak- 2 '- burn, - make smart [subj.: instrument, substance: pepper]'.

26:8 - suffer pain | acı- 1 '- hurt, - feel sore'; acı çek- '- suffer, - endure pain, - be in pain [physical or mental]' → çek- 5; ağrı- '- ache, - hurt, - throb with pain'; canı acı- '- hurt, - feel pain' → acı- 1; canı yan- '- feel pain' → yan- 1; dert çek- '- suffer, - endure, - put up with troubles [mental pain]' → çek- 5.

27 VISION
27:12 - see | farket- 1 '- notice, - observe, - perceive, - realize'. 3 '- distinguish, - make out'; gör- 1 '- see'; görül- 1 '- be seen, observed'; seç- 2 = farket- 3; seçil- 2 '- be seen clearly, - be distinguished, - be made out'.

27:13 - look at | /DAn, A/ bak- 1 '- look /{from/THROUGH/OUT}, AT/'; etrafa bak- '- look around, - have a look around' → bak- 1; gözle- 2 '- watch, - observe [sb while he is at work]'; /I/ izle- 3 '- watch, - look at, - view' [sunrise, games, TV programs]'; /I/ seyret-. Same.

27:14 - scrutinize | gözden geçir- '- go /OVER/, - look /OVER/, - scrutinize, - check, - check out, - have a look /AT/, - examine, - inspect, - review [homework, a report]' → geçir- 1; incele- '- examine carefully, closely, minutely, in detail, - study carefully, - inspect, - investigate, - research'; muayene et- '- examine [mostly for a doctor and a patient]'; muayeneden geçir- '- examine, - subject /TO/ a physical examination, physical, checkup' → geçir- 1; tetkik et- = incele-.

27:16 - glare | /A/ dik dik bak- '- stare angrily /AT/, - glare /AT/' → bak- 1.

28 DEFECTIVE VISION
28:10 - wink | göz kırp- 1 '- blink' → kırp- .

31 VISIBILITY
31:4 - show | görün- 1 '- appear, - come into sight; - be seen, - be visible'. This verb is not used with {tarafından/CA}, i.e., not as in 'She has not been seen by anybody', for which → görül- 1.

33 APPEARANCE
33:8 - appear | çık- 3 /DAn/ '- appear /from/, - come out /OF/, - emerge /from/ [subj.: stars]'. 8 '- come out, - appear, - be issued [subj.: news, newspaper]'; doğ- 2 '- rise, - appear [subj.: sun, moon]'; görün- 1 '- appear, - come into sight; - be seen, - be visible'. This verb is not used with {tarafından/CA}, i.e., not as in 'She has not been seen by anybody', for which → görül- 1; güneş {aç-/çık-} 'for the sun - come out, appear' → aç- 8, çık- 3.

33:10 - appear to be | /A/ benze- 2 '- appear, - look like, - seem'; gel- as in Bana öyle geliyor ki... '{a: I have {a feeling/a hunch} that.../b: I get the feeling that.../c: It seems to me that.../d: I sense that...}' → gel- 1; gibime gel- '- seem to me' → gel- 1; görün- 2 '- seem, - look, - create an impression of'; göster- 2 '- appear to be, - look like'; kaç- 3 '- seem [strange, inappropriate]'.

34 DISAPPEARANCE
34:2a - disappear | çık- 11 '- go out, - come out [spot, stain]'; /DA/ eri- '- melt, - dissolve /in/ [sugar in water]'; kalabalığa dal- '- plunge or - disappear /INTO/ a crowd [subj.: thief]' → dal- 3; /A/ karış- 7 '- disappear or - melt /INTO/ a larger body of people [subj.: thief]'; kaybol- '- be lost, - get lost; - disappear from sight' → ol- 12.

34:2b - make disappear | /A/ yok et- 2 '- make disappear /to/ [magician makes rabbit disappear]'.

35 COLOR
35:13 - color | /A/ boya- '- paint, - color /θ/ [a color]'; /A/ boya

yaptır- '- have /θ/ sth colored [obj.: hair]' → yaptır- 2; /A/ boyat- '- have sth painted, colored, or dyed /θ/ [a color]; - have /θ/ sb paint, color, or dye sth /θ/ [a color]'; meç yap- '- give sb hightlights, - put highlights, streaks of color, in sb's hair [hair salon process]' → yap- 3; /A/ {meç/röfle} yaptır- '- have one's hair streaked, highlighted, - have highlights, streaks of color, put /IN/ one's hair [hair salon process]' → yaptır- 2; /A/ röfle yaptır- = meç yaptır-.

36 COLORLESSNESS
36:6 - lose color | sarar- 2 '- turn or - grow pale, pale'.

41 REDNESS
41:5 - redden | kızar- 1 '- turn red, - redden, blush'.

43 YELLOWNESS
43:3 - yellow | sarar- 1 '- turn yellow, - yellow'.

48 HEARING
48:10 - listen | /a: I, b: üzerinden, c: DAn/ 1 dinle- 1 '- listen /a: TO [music], b: {ON/over} [the Internet], c: ON [a tape]/, - hear [music]'; 2 dinlen- 2 '- be listened to'.

48:11 - hear | duy- 1 '- hear'; işit- 1. Same; kaçır- 1 '- miss, not - catch [i.e., not - hear what has been said]'; yakala- 2 '- catch, - be able to hear, understand [words]'.

49 DEAFNESS
49:4 - be deaf | ağır {duy-/işit-} '- be hard of hearing' → duy- 1, işit- 1.

51 SILENCE
51:5 - be silent {çenesini/dilini} tut- '- hold one's tongue [lit., {** one's jaw or chin/one's tongue}], - keep quiet' → tut- 4; kes- 4 = sesini kes-; sesini kes- '- be quiet, - stop talking, - shut up' → kes- 4; sus- 1 '- be silent, - remain silent, not - say anything'.

51:7 - fall silent | sus- 2 '- stop talking, - fall or - become silent'.

51:8 - silence | söz bulAMA- '- be at a loss for words, not - know what to say' → bul- 1.

52 FAINTNESS OF SOUND
52:10 - murmur | /A/ fısılda- '- whisper /{IN/INTO}/ [sb's ear]'.

52:14 - sigh | iç çek- '- sigh, - heave a sigh' → çek- 1.

53 LOUDNESS
53:7 - din | kapı çarp- 'for a door - slam shut' → çarp- 1; kapıyı {çarp-/vur-} '- slam the door' → çarp- 1, → kapıyı vur- 2 → vur- 1.

53:9 - be noisy | gürültü {et-/yap-} '- make noise, - be noisy'.

54 RESONANCE
54:6 - resonate | horla- '- snore'.

54:8a - ring, - cause to ring | çal- 4 '- ring [obj.: a bell]'; çalın- 3 '- be rung [subj.: bell]'; zile bas- '- ring a bell' → bas- 2.

54:8b - ring, - make a ringing sound | çal- 3 '- ring, - strike [subj.: bell]'. 4 'for a clock, etc. - ring the hour'; karnı zil çal- 'for one's stomach - growl [lit., - ring] from hunger; - be very hungry' → çal- 3; saat saati çal- 'for the clock - ring the hour' → çal- 4.

56 EXPLOSIVE NOISE
56:7 - snap | /{I/A/üzerine}/ tıkla- '- click /ON/ [in computer language]'.

57 SIBILATION <hissing sounds>
57:2 - sibilate | hapşır- '- sneeze'; horla- '- snore'.

58 STRIDENCY <harsh and shrill sounds>
58:3 - rasp | horla- '- snore'.

58:8 - screech | korna çal- '- hit /θ/ or - honk /θ/ a car horn' → çal- 2; kornaya bas-. Same. → bas- 2; öt- 2 for various wind instruments to produce a sound: 'for a horn - play, a whistle - make a sound, an alarm - go off, - sound, or - screech'; öttür- '- blow a whistle'.

58:9 <- sound harshly> | horla- '- snore'.

59 CRY, CALL

59:6 - cry /A, diye/ **bağır-** '- shout, - scream, - yell /AT, saying/'; **bağırıp çağır-** '- scream and shout, - make a big racket' → çağır- 3; /1A, DAn/ **çığlık at-** '- scream /{with/IN} [fear], WITH [pleasure]/' → at- 1; /A, diye/ **haykır-** '- cry out, - shout, - scream /AT, saying/'.

59:8 - vociferate /A/ **seslen-** '- call out /to/, - call'.

60 ANIMAL SOUNDS

60:2 - cry **havla-** '- bark [dog]'; **miyavla-** '- meow [cat]'.

60:5 [birds] - warble **öt-** 1 '- sing [of birds], - chirp [of birds or insects], - crow [of roosters]'.

62 TASTE

62:7 - taste **tadına bak-** '- taste, - have a taste, - sample a food' → bak- 1; **tat-** '- taste, - sample, - try the taste of a food'.

64 UNSAVORINESS

64:4 - disgust /DAn/ **{iğren-/tiksin-}** '- feel disgust, horror /AT/, loathing /FOR/; - be disgusted /{BY/WITH}/, revolted /{BY/BECAUSE OF}/'.

69 ODOR

69:6 - have an odor /θ/ **kok-** 1 '- smell /OF/ sth, - have a smell, - give off a smell [The room smelled OF fish.]'. See also 71:4. STENCH: - stink.

69:8 - smell sth **kokla-** '- smell sth, - take in the smell of sth [She smelled the roses.]'.

71 STENCH

71:4 - stink **kok-** 2 '- smell [bad], - stink'.

73 TOUCH

73:6 - touch /A/ **dokun-** 1 '- touch /θ/ [physically, subj.: person, not thing,]'; /A/ **el sür-** '- touch /θ/ sth [with the hands]' → sur- 5; /A/ **temas et-** 1 '- touch /θ/ sb or sth physically'; **yokla-** 1 '- feel, - examine, or - inspect for sth with one's fingers, - feel around'.

73:8 - stroke **okşa-** '- caress, - stroke, - fondle, - pat, - pet'; **sev-** 2 '- fondle, - caress, - pet'. Same as 1042:6. FRICTION: - rub.

74 SENSATIONS OF TOUCH

74:5 - tingle **kaşın-** 1 '- itch [My head itches.]'.

75 SEX

75:21 - copulate **{bekâretini/kızlığını} kaybet- [or yitir-]** '- lose one's virginity', only for women. There is no commonly used Turkish equivalent term for men. → {kaybet-/yitir-}; /1A/ **cinsel ilişkide bulun-** '- have sex /with/, - have sexual intercourse /with/', *formal, polite.* → bulun- 3; /1A/ **seviş-** 2 '- caress each other, *slang:* - make out /with/; - make love /with/, - have sexual intercourse /with/'; /1A/ **yat-** 2 '- go to bed /with/, - sleep /with/ [i.e., - have sex /with/]'.

75:23 - climax **boşal-** 3 '- come, - ejaculate, - climax, - have an orgasm', more frequently for men but also for women; **gel-** '- come, - climax, - have an orgasm', for both sexes → gel- 3; **orgazm ol-**. Same. → ol- 10.1.

78 REPRODUCTION, PROCREATION

78:7 - reproduce /ArAk/ **çoğal-** '...- multiply, - grow, - proliferate, - reproduce /by...ing/ [subj.: almost exclusively living things: cells' [i.]; /ArAk/ **üre-** '- increase, - multiply, - proliferate, - reproduce /by...ing/ [subj.: almost exclusively living things]' [i.].

78:12 - be pregnant **hamile kal-** '- get pregnant' → kal- 1.

79 CLEANNESS

79:18 - clean **sil-** 1 /1A, A/ '- wipe up, - wipe away, - wipe /with, {IN/ON}/; - dry [sth wet with sth dry: hands /ON/ [towel]. 2 /1A/ '- wipe clean', usually /with/ a wet cloth [obj.: floors, windows]. 3 /1A/ '- erase, - wipe [blackboard] /with/'; **temizle-** '- clean'; **üstünü başını {düzelt-/toparla-/topla-}** '- tidy [oneself] up, - smarten [oneself] up [lit., ** - adjust one's clothes]' → düzelt- 3, toparla- 4, topla- 2; **tozunu al-** '- dust' → al- 1.

79:19 - wash | aptes al- '- perform the ritual ablution' → al- 1; **banyo yap-** 1 '- take a bath, - bathe' → yap- 3; /lA/ **çalkala-** 2 '- rinse [one's mouth] /with/, [dishes, glasses, but not sheets] /IN/ [hot water]'; /1A/ **durula-** '- rinse [dishes, glasses, sheets, not one's mouth] /{IN/with}/ [cold water]'; **duş {al-/yap-}** '- take a shower, - shower' → al- 1, yap- 3; /DA, 1A/ **yıka-** '- wash sth /in [hot water], {IN [detergent]/with [bleach]}/'; **yıkan-** 1 /1A/ '- wash oneself /with/ [soap]; - take a bath, - bathe /IN/ [warm water]'. 2 /1A, tarafından/ '- be washed, bathed /{with [soap]/IN [warm water]}, by/'; /A/ **yıkat-** 1 '- have sth [laundry, rugs] washed, - have /θ/ sb wash sth, - get sth washed /BY/ sb'.

79:21 - comb | **tara-** 1 '- comb [hair]'.

79:22 - refine | **süz-** '- strain; - filter out [rice from water] '.

79:23 - sweep | **elektrik süpürgesi ile süpür-** '- vacuum' → süpür-; **fırçala-** '- brush [teeth, hair], - brush off [shoes, suit]'; /1A/ **süpür-** '- sweep /with/ [a broom, vacuum cleaner]'.

80 UNCLEANNESS

80:15a - dirty | [sokaklara] çöp **{at-/dök-}** '- litter [/θ/ the streets], - throw trash [/{ON/INTO}/ the streets]' → at- 2, dök- 3; /A, üzerine/ **dök-** 2 '- spill /ON, on/'; /a: A, b: {üstüne/üzerine}, c: {tarafından/CA}/ **dökül-** 2 '- be poured out, - be spilled /a: ON, b: on, c: by/'; **kirlet-** '- get dirty or - make sth dirty, - soil, - pollute'; **pislet-**. Same.

80:15b - get dirty | **kirlen-** '- get or - become dirty, soiled, polluted'; **pislen-**. Same.

83 HEALTH

83:6 - enjoy good health | **hal hatır sor-** '- ask how sb is, - inquire after sb's health' → sor-; **hatır sor-**. Same. → sor-; **sağ ol-** '- be healthy, alive' → ol- 12.

84 FITNESS, EXERCISE

84:4 - exercise | **egzersiz yap-** 1 '- work out, - do exercises, calisthenics, physical training'. 2 '- do exercises as physical therapy' → yap- 3; **gerin-** '- stretch [oneself], - have a stretch'; **idman yap-** '- exercise, - do gymnastics, physical training, - train [oneself physically]' → yap- 3; **jimnastik yap-** '- do gymnastics' → yap- 3; **spor yap-** '- do sports, - engage in sports, - take part in sports' → yap- 3. Same as 725:8. EXERTION: - exert.

85 DISEASE

85:45 - ail | /DAn/ **hasta ol-** '- get sick; - be ill /from/' → ol- 10.2; **rahatsız ol-** 1 '- feel or - become indisposed, slightly ill, sick, - be under the weather' → ol- 10.2; *noun designating an illness*.SI var '- have an illness': Nezle.si var. 'He has a cold.' → ol- 5, (5.1) Table 1. Additional examples. 2. Essential question-word questions. With n-beginning question words: Nesi var?

85:46a - take sick in general | **fena ol-** 1 '- feel faint, - feel suddenly sick' → ol- 10.2; /DAn/ **fenalaş-** 2 '- feel faint, - feel suddenly sick, - get sick, - take ill /{from/due to}/'; /DAn/ **hasta ol-** '- get sick /from/; - be ill /from/' → ol- 10.2; /DIğI için, DAn/ **hastalan-** '- become ill, - get sick, - take sick /because, {as a result of/with/from}/'; **rahatsız ol-** 1 '- feel or - become indisposed, slightly ill, sick, - be under the weather' → ol- 10.2; /A/ **yakalan-** 2 '- catch /θ/ or - come down /with/, - be struck down /BY/ an illness'; *noun designating an illness* **ol-** '- catch, - come down with, - get an illness': Bronşit oldu. 'He came down with bronchitis.' → ol- 10.2.

85:46b - take sick in particular ways | **dolgu düş-** '- lose a [tooth] filling, - have a filling fall out'; **felç ol-** '- be or - become paralyzed, - have or - suffer a stroke' → ol- 10.2; **grip ol-** '- have or - come down with the flu, influenza' → ol- 10.2; **güneş çarp-** '- get sunstroke' → çarp- 1; **inme in-** '- have or - suffer a stroke, - be or - become paralyzed' → in- 1; **midesi bulan-** '- for one's stomach - be upset, - feel sick to one's stomach, - have an upset stomach, - feel nauseated, nauseous, - get queasy'; **nezle ol-** '- catch or - get a cold' → ol- 10.2; **soğuk al-** '- get a chill, - catch a chill', the early stage

642

of a cold. → al- 3; **şoka gir-** '- go /into/ shock [a medical condition]'; **tut-** 8 '- suffer from motion sickness, - get motion sick', i.e., from riding in a vehicle: seasick; **üşüt-** = soğuk al-.

86 REMEDY
86:38 - remedy | **reçete hazırla-** '- fill or - prepare a prescription', subj.: the pharmacist. → hazırla-; **şifa ver-** '- restore to health, - cure, - heal' → ver- 1; **tedavi et-** 2 '- cure a person or a disease'.

88 INTOXICATION, ALCO- HOLIC DRINK
88:24 - tipple | **{alkol/içki} al-** '- drink {alcohol/alcoholic drinks}' → al- 5; [**içki**] **iç-** '- drink alcoholic beverages' → iç- 1. Often **iç-**, even without an object designating an alcoholic drink, may be understood to mean '- drink alcoholic beverages'; **içki kullan-** '- drink [lit., ** - use alcoholic beverages]'.

88:26 - get drunk | /DAn/ **sarhoş ol-** 1 '- be, - become, or - get drunk, tipsy, intoxicated, inebriated, high /{from/with}, {ON/with}/' → ol- 12.

88:27 - be drunk | Same as directly above.

89 TOBACCO
89:14 - use tobacco, - smoke | **iç-** 2 '- smoke'; **içil-** 2 '- be smoked'; **nefes al-** '- breathe, - take a breath; - inhale' → al- 1; **nefes çek-** '- take a wiff, drag, puff [of tobacco]' → çek- 1; **sigara kullan-** '- smoke cigarettes'.

91 THERAPY, MEDICAL TREATMENT
91:24 - treat | **diş çektir-** '- have teeth pulled' → çektir- 2; **muayene et-** '- examine [mostly for a doctor and a patient]'; **muayeneden geçir-** '- examine, - subject /TO/ a physical examination, physical, checkup' → geçir- 1; **sar-** 2 '- bandage, - bind [wound]'; **tedavi altına alın-** '- be taken in for treatment' → alın- 1; **tedavi et-** 1 '- treat a person, disease, or part of the body'. 2 '- cure a person or a disease'.

91:29 - undergo treatment | **ameliyat geçir-** '- have or - undergo an operation' → geçir- 2;

/A, not with **tarafından**/ **ameliyat ol-** '- be operated on /BY/, - have or - undergo an operation' → ol- 10.1; /A, not with **tarafından**/ **muayene ol-** '- be examined /BY/ [physical exam]' → ol- 10.1; **muayeneden geç-** '- have a general physical examination, a physical, a check-up' → geç- 1; **tedavi gör-** '- receive or - undergo treatment, - be treated [for an illness]' → gör- 3.

CLASS 2: FEELINGS

93 FEELING
93:10 - feel | **duy-** 3 '- feel [pride, interest, happiness, sorrow, pain], - sense'; **hisset-** 1 '- feel, sense [one's own state: well, bad]'. 2 '- sense, - feel, - be aware; - notice, - perceive'; *verb stem.*mIş **gibi hisset-** '- feel {like/as if}' → hisset- 2; **sez-** '- understand sth intuitively, - sense, - have a feeling, - feel, - perceive, - discern'. Same as 24:6. SENSATION: - sense.

93:14 - affect | /A/ **dokun-** 3 '- move, - touch, - affect /θ/ sb emotionally; - disturb, - upset /θ/ sb'.

95 PLEASURE
95:8 - gladden | /lA, ArAk/ **sevindir-** '- please, - make sb happy /with, by...ing/'.

95:11 - be pleased | **bayram et-** '- be overjoyed, - be in seventh heaven, - be on cloud nine, - have a ball'; **heyecanlan-** 1 '- get excited, - be enthusiastic, thrilled'; **kendinden geç** 2 '- be beside oneself with joy, - be carried away [by joy], - be ecstatic, in Paradise' → geç- 1; **kendini kaybet-** 2. Same. → {kaybet-/yitir-}; /DAn/ **mutluluk duy-** '- feel or - be happy, pleased /{TO/θ}/' → duy- 3; **neşelen-** '- get in a happy mood, - become cheerful, - cheer up'; /DAn/ **razı ol-** 2 '- be pleased /WITH/, approving, - approve', said of God in response to a good deed. → ol- 12; /DAn/ **sarhoş ol-** 2 '- be or - become drunk /WITH/ joy, delight, happiness, pleasure' → ol- 12; /a: A, b: DIğI için, c: A/ **sevin-** '- be glad, pleased /a: {ABOUT/AT/WITH}, b: because, c: θ [that]/'.

95:12 - enjoy | **beğen-** 1 '- like' [The *verb stem.*mAk structure is not usually used as the object of this verb: NOT ~~Yüzmey.i beğeniyorum.~~]; /DAn/ **hoşlan-** '- be pleased /WITH/, - like /θ/; - enjoy /θ/'; **hoşuna git-** '- like' → git- 1b; **keyfine git-** '- like, - enjoy' → git-1b; /DAn/ **memnun kal-** '- be pleased, happy /WITH/' → kal- 1; **memnun ol-** '- be pleased, happy, satisfied; /A/ '- be pleased /θ/ /that/; /DAn/ '- be pleased, satisfied /WITH/, - like /θ/' → ol- 12; **sev-** 1 '- love, - like; - be fond of'; /tarafından/ **sevil-** '- be loved, liked, enjoyed /by/, - be popular /WITH/'.

95:13 - enjoy oneself /a: 1A, b: ArAk, c: mAklA/ **eğlen-**[or {iyi/hoş} vakit geçir-] '- have a good time, - enjoy oneself, - have fun /a: with [sb or sth], b: [by]...ing, c: [BY]...ing/' → eğlen- 1, geçir- 3.

96 UNPLEASURE
96:13 - annoy **canını sık-** 2 '- annoy, - irritate, - bother' → sık- 3; /A/ **canı sıkıl-** 2 '- be annoyed /AT/, vexed /{BY/BECAUSE OF/FROM}/' → sıkıl- 1; **kafasını boz-** '- spoil sb's mood, - put or - get sb out of sorts' → boz- 1; **rahatını boz-** '- disturb, - annoy' → boz- 1; **rahatsız et-** '- bother, - disturb'; **rahatsız ol-** 2 '- feel or - become ill at ease, uncomfortable' → ol- 10.2; **sık-** 3 '- annoy, - bother'.

96:14 - irritate /ArAk/ **sinirlendir-** '- make sb angry, mad, - anger; - irritate, - annoy, - get on sb's nerves /by...ing/'.

96:15 - chagrin **sıkıl-** 2 '- become bashful, - be or - get embarrassed, - feel embarrassed' /a: DAn, b: DAn dolayı, c: A/ **utan-** '- be ashamed /a: OF, b: on account of, c: OF/, - be embarrassed /on account of/'.

96:16a - distress /A/ **çektir-** 4 '- make /θ/ sb suffer, - cause /θ/ sb to suffer, - cause /θ/ sb trouble, - make trouble /FOR/'; /A/ **dokun-** 2 '- upset /θ/ sb [subj.: food], - make sick, - affect one's health adversely, for food or weather not - agree /WITH/ one, - have a bad effect /ON/'; **heyecanlandır-** 2 '- upset, - disturb'; **kahret-** 1 '- distress sb greatly, - drive to distraction';

midesini boz- '- make [physically] sick, sick to one's stomach [subj.: food]' → boz- 1; /ArAk/ **sinirlendir-** '- make sb angry, mad, - anger; - irritate, - annoy, - get on sb's nerves /by...ing/'; /A/ **zahmet ol-** '- be trouble, troublesome, an inconvenience /FOR/' → ol- 12.

96:16b - be distressed /A/ **canı sıkıl-** 3 '- be upset, disturbed, troubled /{BY/AT}/, sorry, distressed /AT/, out of sorts, in a bad mood' → sıkıl- 1; **fena ol-** 2 '- be upset, - feel terrible, - feel anguish' → ol- 10.2; **heyecanlan-** 2 '- be or - get upset, nervous, agitated, excited, - panic, - lose one's cool', negative emotion; /A/ **sinirlen-** '- get angry, mad /AT/; - get irritated, annoyed /AT/, - get in a state /ABOUT/, upset /θ [that]/'; **sinirleri bozul-** 1 '- get upset, angry, - lose one's cool, temper, composure' → bozul-.

96:19 - suffer **sürün-** 2 '- live in misery, - live a miserable life, - be just scraping {along/by}, - be barely surviving, getting by, - be just keeping body and soul together, - be living through hard times'.

98 UNPLEASANTNESS
98:14 - distress **kahret-** 1 '- distress sb greatly, - drive to distraction'; /A/ **kıy-** 4 '- bring oneself /to/ or - dare /to/ do sth that would discomfort, harm sb'.

98:15 - vex **canını sık-** 2 '- annoy, - irritate, - bother' → sık- 3; /A/ **çektir-** 4 '- make /θ/ sb suffer, - cause /θ/ sb to suffer, - cause /θ/ sb trouble, - make trouble /FOR/'; **sık-** 3 '- annoy, - bother'.

98:31 INTERJ. eeyuck! **Aksiliğa bakın.** '{What a nuisance!/colloq: What a bummer!/What a mess!}' → bak- 1; **Yazıklar olsun.** 1 'What a shame!' 2 '{Damn/Darn} [it]!', an expression of annoyance. → yazık ol- → ol- 12.

100-200

100 DESIRE
100:14 - desire **arzu et-** '- want, - desire'; **canı çek-** '- feel like doing sth, - have a craving for', frequent in the negative. → çek- 1; **canı iste-** '- feel like, - want to' → iste- 1; **dile-** 1

'- wish, - want'; <u>iste-</u> 1 '- want, - want to'.

<u>100:15 - want to</u> <u>iste-</u> 1 '- want, - want to'.

<u>100:16 - wish for, - hope for</u> /I/ <u>ara-</u> 4 '- miss, - long /FOR/ sb or sth absent'; /A/ <u>hasret çek-</u> '- long for, - yearn for, - miss /θ/ sb or sth absent' → çek- 5; /A/ <u>imren-</u> 1 '- long /FOR/, - feel an appetite /for/'; /A/ <u>özen-</u> 2 '- want badly sth that sb else has; - want to be in the situation that sb else is in'; /I/ <u>özle-</u> = ara- 4; {ümit et-/um-} 1 '- hope'.

<u>100:19 - hunger</u> <u>acık-</u> '- be or - become hungry'; <u>açlıktan öl-</u> '- die /OF/ hunger, - be famished'; <u>karnı acık-</u> = acık-; <u>karnı zil çal-</u> 'for one's stomach - growl from hunger; - be very hungry' → çal- 3; <u>susa-</u> '- get or - be thirsty'; <u>susuzluktan öl-</u> '- die /OF/ thirst; - be dying for a drink'.

101 EAGERNESS
<u>101:7 - be enthusiastic</u> /A/ <u>bayıl-</u> 2 '- be crazy /ABOUT/, - adore /θ/, - like sth a great deal, - be carried away /BY/'.

102 INDIFFERENCE
<u>102:4 not - care</u> /A/ <u>üşen-</u> '- be too lazy, apathetic, or indifferent to do sth, not - bother or - take the trouble to do sth'. Also under 331:12. INACTIVITY: - idle.

103 HATE
<u>103:5 - hate</u> /DAn/ <u>nefret et-</u> '- hate /θ/, - loathe /θ/, - detest /θ/, - abhor /θ/, - feel an aversion /FOR/'.

104 LOVE
<u>104:19 - love</u> <u>sev-</u> 1 '- love, - like; - be fond of'; /tarafından/ <u>sevil-</u> '- be loved, liked, enjoyed /by/, - be popular /WITH/'; <u>seviş-</u> 1 '- love or - like each other; - be fond of each other'; /A, için/ <u>yan-</u> 7 '- be consumed with love /for/, - be madly in love /WITH/, - be mad /ABOUT/; - feel a burning [sexual] desire /for/, *slang:* - have the hots /for/'; /A, için/ <u>yanıp tutuş-</u> '- be consumed with passion /for/, - be mad /about/, *slang:* - have the hots for' → yan- 7.

<u>104:22 - fall in love</u> /A/ <u>âşık ol-</u> '- fall in love /WITH/' → ol- 12; /A,

not with **tarafından/** <u>çarpıl-</u> 2 '- be swept off one's feet /BY/, - fall /FOR/ sb', *colloq.*

105 EXCITEMENT
<u>105:12 - excite</u> <u>heyecanlan-</u> 3 '- get turned on sexually'; <u>heyecanlandır-</u> 1 '- excite, - thrill, - give a thrill'. 3 *polite* '- excite, - turn on sexually'; /A/ <u>kapıl-</u> '- be carried off, away /BY/, - be overcome /BY/ [various emotions], - be captivated /BY/ [a person, her beauty]'; <u>tahrik et-</u> = heyecanlandır- 3; <u>tahrik ol-</u> = heyecanlan- 3 → ol- 12.

<u>105:14 - agitate</u> /ArAk/ <u>sinirlendir-</u> '- make sb angry, mad, - anger; - irritate, - annoy, - get on sb's nerves /by...ing/'.

<u>105:18 - be excited</u> <u>heyecanlan-</u> 1 '- get excited, - be enthusiastic, thrilled', positive emotion.

106 INEXCITABILITY
<u>106:7 - compose oneself</u> /A/ <u>hâkim ol-</u> '- control /θ/, - get or keep control /{OF/OVER}/, - keep in line [people or one's emotions, actions]' → ol- 12; <u>kendini toparla-</u> '- pull or - get oneself together' → toparla- 3.

107 CONTENTMENT
<u>107:5 - be content</u> /A/ <u>razı ol-</u> 1 '- agree, - consent, or - be willing /to/, - approve; - be content /WITH/' → ol- 12; /lA/ <u>yetin-</u> 1 '- be content, satisfied /with/, - content oneself /with/'.

109 CHEERFULNESS
<u>109:7 - cheer</u> <u>neşelendir-</u> '- make sb feel happy, - put sb in good spirits, - cheer sb up, - delight sb'.

<u>109:20 PHR. cheer up!</u> <u>Neşelen!</u> 'Cheer up!' → neşelen-; <u>ÜzülME!</u> 'DoN'T be sad., DoN'T worry., Cheer up!' → üzül-.

110 ILL HUMOR
<u>110:14 - sulk</u> <u>surat as-</u> '- put on a sour face, - look annoyed, angry, or unhappy; - sulk; - pout' → as- 1.

112 SADNESS
<u>112:16 - lose heart</u> <u>bunalım geçir-</u> '- be in a depression, - be or get depressed' → geçir- 2; <u>bunalıma</u>

gir- '- go /INTO/ a depression, - get depressed'; **hüzünlen-** '- become or - feel sad, gloomy, melancholy, depressed'; **morali bozul-** '- get depressed, discouraged, - lose heart'; **/A/ üzül-** '- be upset, distressed /{ABOUT/BY/AT}/, - be concerned, worried /ABOUT/; - be or - feel sad /θ/ that, - be sorry /ABOUT/'; **üzüntü çek-** '- endure sorrow, sadness, - be depressed, sad' → çek-5; **üzüntü duy-** '- feel sad, - be upset, distressed, sad, sorry' → duy-3.

112:17 - grieve /DAn/ **kahrol-** '- be deeply grieved or distressed, - be devastated or overcome /{WITH/BY}/ grief' → ol- 12; **yas tut-** '- mourn, - be in mourning [for the dead]' → tut- 5; **yıkıl- 3** '- lose one's health and morale; for sb - be broken or ruined by a disaster, - be devastated'; **yüreği parçalan-** 'for one's heart - be wrenched upon seeing sth sad, - grieve, - be extremely upset' → parçalan- 2.

112:18 - sadden **moralini boz-** '- spoil sb's mood, - depress sb' → boz- 1; **üz-** '- upset, - distress, - worry; - sadden'.

112:19 - aggrieve **kalbinden yarala-** '- break sb's heart'; **kalbini kır-** '- hurt sb's feelings', lit., '- break sb's heart', but this literal translation is too strong for the Turkish sense. → kır- 1; **yık- 1** = kalbinden yarala-.

113 REGRET
113:6 - regret **bin pişman ol-** '- be extremely sorry' → pişman ol- → ol- 12; /a: DIğInA, b: DIğI için, c: DIğInDAn dolayı/ **pişman ol-** '- regret, - feel remorse, - be sorry /a: θ [that], b: FOR [having done sth], c: because/' → ol- 12; /DIğI için/ **üzüntü çek-** 2 '- feel regret, sorrow, - be sorry /{that/on account of/because/for}/ [a past action]' → çek- 5; /DIğI için/ **vicdan azabı çek-** '- feel pangs of conscience, - feel guilty /{on account of/for}/' → çek- 5.

113: * 13 INTERJ. what a pity! /A/ **yazık oldu** '{What a pity/How sad} /FOR/ [the losing team] [lit., It was a pity /FOR/]' → yazık ol- → ol- 12.

113: * 14 PHR. if only **Keşke olmasaydı.** 'If only it hadn't happened!, I wish it hadn't happened!' → ol- 2.

115 LAMENTATION
115:10 - lament **yas tut-** '- mourn, - be in mourning [for the dead]' → tut- 5.

115:12 - weep **ağla-** '- cry, - weep'; **göz yaşı dök-** '- cry, - weep, - spill tears' → dök- 1; **gözleri yaşar-** 'for one's eyes - fill with tears, for tears - come to one's eyes; for one's eyes - water'; **gözlerini yaşart-** '- bring tears to one's eyes [subj.: event, sad film], - make one's eyes water'; **yaşart-** '- bring tears to one's eyes, - make sb's eyes fill with tears, - make cry, weep; - make sb's eyes water'.

116 REJOICING
116:2 cheer **Çok yaşa!** 1 'Long Live..!' 2 'Bravo!, Hurray!' → yaşa- 1.

116:7 - smile /A/ **gülümse-** '- smile /AT/'.

116:8 - laugh /A/ **gül-** 1 '- laugh /AT/ [amusement: a joke]'; **kahkaha ile gül-** '- laugh loudly, - roar with laughter; - guffaw' → gül- 1.

118 TEDIUM
118:7a - bore **canını sık-** 1 '- bore' → sık- 3.

118:7b - get bored /DAn/ **{bık-/usan-}** '- be, - get, or - grow tired /OF/, - tire /OF/, - get bored, fed up /WITH/, - be fed up, disgusted /WITH/'; /DAn/ **canı sıkıl-** 1 '- be or - get bored /BY/, - be tired /OF/' → sıkıl- 1; /mAktAn/ **içi sıkıl-** '- get or - be bored /{θ/from}...ing/' → sıkıl- 1; /DAn/ **sıkıl-** 1 '- get tired /OF/, - be bored /WITH/'.

119 AGGRAVATION
119:3 - worsen **hızlan-** 2 '- get heated, intense, - heat up, intensify [subj.: dispute]'.

120 RELIEF
120:6 - release **bırak-** 5 '- let go of, - release, - put down'; **serbest bırak-** '- release, - free, - set free, - liberate, - let go [prisoners, hostages]' → bırak- 5; **salıver-** = serbest bırak-.

120:7 - lighten /A/ **dert dök-** '- pour out one's troubles, - spill out one's woes /to/, - get sth off one's chest' → dök- 1.

120:8 - be relieved **rahat et-** '- BE, BECOME comfortable, - feel better, at ease'; **rahatla-** '- feel better, - be relieved', after experiencing sickness, pain, or fatigue, '- become comfortable'.

121 COMFORT
121:6 - comfort /A/ **başsağlığı dile-** '- offer or - express one's condolences /to/' → dile- 1.

121: * 17 words of comfort **Başınız sağ olsun.** '{My [sincere] condolences./less formal: I'm so sorry to hear it.}', said to sb telling of a death in his family. → sağ ol- → ol- 12; **Canın sağ olsun!** 'Don't worry! It doesn't matter.' → sağ ol- → ol- 12; **Sağlık olsun.** 'Don't worry about it., Never mind.' → ol- 11 → olsun; **Üzülme.** 'Don't worry.' → üzül-; **Üzülme, bu da geçer.** 'Don't worry. This too shall pass.' → üzül-.

122 WONDER
122:5 - wonder /A/ **hayret et-** '- be amazed, astonished, surprised /θ [that], AT/'; /A/ **şaş-** = hayret et-; **{şaşır-/şaşırıp} kal-** '- be amazed, astonished, astounded, dumbfounded' → şaşır- 2; /A, karşısında/ **şaşır- 2** '- be amazed, astonished, surprised /AT, AT [lit., in the face of]/'; **şaştı kal-** = {şaşır-/şaşırıp} kal- → şaş-.

122:6 - astonish **şaşırt- 2** '- surprise, - astonish'.

122:19 INTERJ. my word! **Ne diyorsun?** 'Well! What {do you say!/lit., are you saying!}'; **Ne günler.E kaldık.** 'So this is what things have come to!, So things have come to this!, What times [lit., days] we have lived to see!' → kal- 1.

122:22 INTERJ. imagine! **olacak {iş/şey} değil!** 'It's {impossible/absurd}!, It's not going to happen!, It's out of the question!, It's unbelievable!, It's unheard of!, Can you believe it?, [Just] imagine!, Can you imagine?, How could such a thing happen?, How is it possible?' → ol- 4.

124 HOPE
124:7 - hope {ümit et-/um-} 1 '- hope'.

124:8 - be hopeful {umutlan-/ümitlen-} '- become hopeful, - begin to hope, - get one's hopes up'.

124:10 - give hope **destekle-** '- support [financially, morally, not usually a team]'; {gelecek/istikbal} vadet- '- be promising, - have a promising future'; **tut- 10** '- support a team'.

125 HOPELESSNESS
125:10 - despair **ümit kesil-** 'for hope - be given up, abandoned' → kesil- 3; {umudunu/ümidini} kaybet-[or yitir-] '- lose one's hope, - despair, - give up hope' → {kaybet-/yitir-}.

125:11 - shatter one's hopes **ümidini kır-** '- shatter or - destroy sb's hopes' → kır- 1.

125: * 19 proverbs **Aç elini kora sokar.** 'A hungry person will [even] stick his hands into glowing embers.', i.e., A person will go to great lengths to satisfy a pressing need. Desperate times call for desperate measures. → sok- 1; **Denize düşen yılana sarılır.** 'A person who has fallen into the sea will {embrace/cling to} [even] a snake.' Desperate times call for desperate measures. → düş-, sarıl-.

126 ANXIETY
126:4 - concern **üz-** '- upset, - distress, - worry; - sadden'; /A/ **üzül-** '- be upset, distressed /{ABOUT/BY/AT}/, - be concerned, worried /ABOUT/; - be or - feel sad /θ/ that, - be sorry /ABOUT/'.

126:5 - make anxious **üz-** '- upset, - distress, - worry, - concern; - sadden'.

126:6 - feel anxious /DAn/ **endişe et-** '- worry, - be anxious /ABOUT/, - be concerned /{ABOUT/FOR}/, - be afraid or - fear /FOR/'; /Dan/ **kaygılan-** '- worry, - get anxious, worried /ABOUT/'; /I/ **merak et- 1** '- worry /ABOUT/, -

be concerned /ABOUT/'; /A/ <u>üzül-</u> '- be upset, distressed /{ABOUT/BY/AT}/, - be concerned, worried /ABOUT/; - be or - feel sad /θ/ that, - be sorry /ABOUT/'.

127 FEAR, FRIGHTENING-NESS

127:10 - fear /DAn, A/ <u>kork-</u> '- be afraid or frightened /OF/, - fear /θ/, - be afraid /to/'; <u>ödü kop-</u> '- be badly frightened, - be terrified' → kop- 1.

127:11 - take fright /DAn/ <u>ürk-</u> 2 '- take fright, - be seized with sudden fright, - be suddenly afraid /OF/'.

127:13 - flinch <u>sarar-</u> 2 '- turn or - grow pale, - pale'; /DAn/ <u>ter bas-</u> '- break out in a sweat, - be covered in sweat /{from, BECAUSE OF}/' → bas- 4; /DAn/ <u>ürk-</u> 1 '- start, - be startled /BY/ [subj.: person or animal]; - shy [subj.: animal]'.

127:14 - tremble /DAn/ <u>eli ayağı tutMA-</u> '- be shaky, unsteady /{WITH/BECAUSE OF}/' [a reaction of shock to bad news or a frightening event or a sign of anger]. → tut- 2; /DAn/ <u>titre-</u> 2 '- tremble /{WITH/IN}/ [fear], - shake /WITH/ [fear, anger]'.

127:15 - frighten <u>korkut-</u> '- frighten, - scare'.

128 NERVOUSNESS

128:6 - fidget <u>heyecanlan-</u> 2 '- be or - get upset, nervous, agitated, excited, - panic, - lose one's cool', negative emotion.

128:7 - lose self-control <u>sinirleri bozul-</u> 2 '- be badly shaken up, for one's nerves - get shot [as result of car accident]'.

128:9 - get on one's nerves <u>heyecanlandır-</u> 2 '- upset, - disturb'; /ArAk/ <u>sinirlendir-</u> '- make sb angry, mad, - anger; - irritate, - annoy, - get on sb's nerves /by...ing/'.

130 EXPECTATION

130:5 - expect <u>bekle-</u> 2 '- expect'; <u>karşılık bekle-</u> '- expect sth in return for sth given or done' →

bekle- 2; {<u>ümit et-/um-</u>} 2 = bekle- 2.

130:8 - await /I/ <u>bekle-</u> 1 '- wait /FOR/, - await'; /I/ <u>dörtgözle bekle-</u> '- wait eagerly /FOR/' → bekle- 1; <u>dur-</u> 5 '- wait, - hold on [just a second]'.

130: * 16 proverbs <u>Allah gümüş kapıyı kaparsa altın kapıyı açar.</u> 'If God closes the silver door, He opens the golden door.', i.e., Don't be discouraged: a better opportunity may follow one lost. → aç- 1, {kapa-/kapat-} 1; <u>Bir kapı kapanırsa bin kapı açılır.</u> 'If one door closes, one thousand doors will open.' → açıl- 2, kapan- 1.

131 INEXPECTATION

131:5 - be startled /DAn/ <u>ürk-</u> 1 '- start, - be startled /BY/ [subj.: person or animal]; - shy [subj.: animal only]', all these English verbs indicate a sudden physical movement in reaction to a fright.

131:6 - be unexpected /lA/ <u>karşılaş-</u> 2 '- meet sb by chance, - run or - bump /INTO/ sb'; <u>karşısına çık-</u> '- appear suddenly in front of, - bump into'; /A/ <u>rastla-</u> 1 '- meet by chance, - run or - bump /INTO/, - encounter /θ/, - come or - chance /UPON/'; /A/ <u>tesadüf et-</u> 1. Same, *more formal*. Same as 223:11. NEARNESS: - meet.

131:7 - surprise /A/ <u>hayret et-</u> '- be amazed, astonished, surprised /θ [that], AT/'; /A/ <u>şaş-</u> = hayret et-; {<u>şaşır-/şaşırıp</u>} <u>kal-</u> '- be amazed, astonished, astounded, dumbfounded' → şaşır- 2; /A, karşısında/ <u>şaşır-</u> 2 '- be amazed, astonished, surprised /AT, AT [lit., in the face of]/'; <u>şaştı kal-</u> = {şaşır-/şaşırıp} kal- → şaş-; /karşısında/ {<u>şoke/şok</u>} <u>ol-</u> '- be shocked, - go into shock /AT/ [non-medical sense]' → ol- 10.1.

131:15 ADV. surprisingly <u>Tesadüfe bakın.</u> 'What a coincidence!' → bak- 1.

131: * 16 expressions of inexpectation <u>Deme ya!</u> 'You don't say!' → de- 3; <u>Yapma ya!</u> 'You don't say!, You don't mean it!, Don't give me that!, Oh go on!, Well

I declare! [lit., Don't do (that)].' →
yap- 2. Same as 955: * 6.
INCREDULITY: expressions of
incredulity.

131: * 17 gestures of inexpectation
başını salla- '- shake one's head',
from side to side in surprise. → salla-
3.

132 DISAPPOINTMENT
132:2 - disappoint {hayal/düş}
kırıklığına uğrat- '- disappoint' →
uğrat-.

132:4 - be disappointed /A karşı/
güvenini {kaybet-/yitir-} '- lose
one's faith /IN/' → {kaybet-/yitir-};
{hayal/düş} kırıklığına uğra- '-
be disappointed' → uğra- 2.

132: * 7 expressions of
disappointment Nerede kaldı?
'So whatever happened to..?, So
where's...?' → kal- 1.

133 PREMONITION
133:13 - promise
{gelecek/istikbal} vadet- '- be
promising, - have a promising future';
Hayırlı olsun. 'Good luck.,
Congratulations., May it go well.,
May it be beneficial, useful /to/., May
it benefit /θ/.' → ol- 11 → olsun;
Hayrola? 'What's going on?,
What's up?, What's the matter?,
What's wrong?' → ol- 11 → ola.

134 PATIENCE
134:4 - be patient sabret- '-
be patient'.

134:5 - endure çek- 5 '- endure, -
suffer, - put up with, - go through
[often with nouns indicating
difficulty, trouble]'; /A/ {dayan-
/katlan-} '- put up /WITH/, - bear
/θ/, - stand /θ/, - tolerate /θ/, - endure
/θ/, - suffer /θ/, - take /θ/' → dayan-
3, katlan- 2; kabul et- 4 '- accept, -
regard with tolerance [accept people
as they are]'; /A/ tahammül et-.
Same as {dayan-/katlan-}, but
more formal, less current; /lA/
uğraş- 3 '- put up /with/ [a person]'.

135 IMPATIENCE
135:4 - be impatient sabırsızlan-
'- get, - become, or - be impatient'.

135:5 - have no patience with
sabrı tüken- 'for one's patience -
run out or - be exhausted'.

136 PRIDE
136:5 - take pride, - pride oneself
gurur duy- 1 /{lA/DAn}/ '- be or
- feel proud /OF/, - take pride /IN/',
positive implication. 2 /lA/ '- be or -
feel arrogantly proud /OF/, - pride
oneself arrogantly /ON/', negative
implication. → duy- 3; /lA/
gururlan- '- be or - feel arrogantly
proud /OF/', negative implication;
/lA/ iftihar et- '- be or - feel proud
/OF/, - take pride /IN/'; /DAn/
kıvanç duy- '- be or - feel proud
/OF/, - take pride /IN/' → duy- 3;
/lA/ {övün-/öğün-} 1 '- be proud
/OF/, - take pride /IN/, - pride oneself
/ON/'.

137 HUMILITY
137.7 - humble oneself alçal- 2 '-
demean oneself, - stoop to doing sth
despicable, - sink to a low level in
behavior'.

137:9a - be humiliated /a: DAn,
b: DAn dolayı, c: A/ utan- '- be
ashamed /a: OF, b: on account of, c:
OF/, - be embarrassed /on account
of/'.

137:9b gestures of humility baş
eğ- '- bow, - bow one's head or - nod
as a sign of respect, - hang one's head
in shame' → eğ- 1; eğil- 2 '- bow, -
bow down'; kızar- 1 '- turn red, -
redden, - blush'.

140 VANITY
140:6 - be stuck on oneself
kendini beğen- '- be conceited,
stuck up, stuck on oneself' → beğen-
1.

141 ARROGANCE
141:8 - give oneself airs /lA/
gurur duy- 2 '- be or - feel
arrogantly proud /OF/, - pride oneself
arrogantly /ON/' → duy- 3; /lA/
gururlan-. Same.

142 INSOLENCE
142:8 - sauce /A/ karşılık ver-
2 '- talk back /to/, - answer back /to/'
→ ver- 1.

143 KINDNESS, BENEVOLENCE

143:10 - be considerate /A/ **saygı göster-** '- show respect /{to/FOR}/, - behave respectfully /TOWARD/, - treat with respect, - respect' → göster- 1.

143:12 - do a favor /A/ **iyilik et-** '- do /θ/ sb a kindness, a good turn, - be good /to/, - treat /θ/ sb kindly, - do good'.

145 PITY

145:3 - pity, - feel sorry for /A/ **acı-** 2 '- pity /θ/, - feel sorry /FOR/'.

145:4 - have pity /A/ **rahmet eyle-** 'for God - be merciful /to/, for God - have mercy /{ON/UPON}/'.

148 FORGIVENESS

148:3a - forgive **affet-** 1 '- forgive an act'. 2 /DAn dolayı, DIğI için/ '- excuse, - forgive, - pardon sb /because of, because/'; /I/ **bağışla-** 2 '- forgive, - pardon sb'.

148:3b expressions requesting forgiveness **Affedersiniz.** 'I beg your pardon.' → affet- 2; **Affet beni.** 'Excuse me., Pardon me., Forgive me., Sorry.' → affet- 2; **Bağışlayın beni.** Same. → bağışla- 2; **Özür dilerim.** 'I'm sorry.' → dile- 2; **Kusura bakma[yın].** = Affet beni. → bak- 1.

148:4 - condone /A/ **göz yum-** 2 '- close one's eyes /to/, - disregard /θ/, - take no notice /OF/, - turn a blind eye /to/, - overlook /θ/, - wink /AT/ a fault' → yum-.

149 CONGRATULATION

149:2 - congratulate /a: için, b: DIğI için, c: DAn dolayı, d: DAn ötürü/ **kutla-** 2 '- congratulate sb /a: {for/ON}, b: {because/{ON/FOR}}, c, d: {ON/FOR}/'; /a: DAn dolayı, b: için, c: I, d: lA/ **tebrik et-** '- congratulate /a: {FOR/ON}, b: {for/ON}, c: {FOR/ON}, d: BY [letter]/'.

149:4 INTERJ. congratulations **Aşkolsun!** 2 'Bravo!' → ol- 11 → olsun; **Çok yaşa!** 2 'Bravo!, Hurray!, Good for you!' → yaşa- 1; **Gözünüz aydın. Tebrik ederim.** 'I'm [so] happy for you.

Congratulations', said to sb whose long-awaited desire has been realized. → tebrik et-; /A/ **Helâl olsun.** 2 'Bravo /to/!, Good for {him/you}!, Nice going!' → ol- 11 → olsun; **Kutlu olsun!** 'May it be blessed!', a formula of congratulation on religious as well as on other, non-religious, official holidays and on birthdays. → ol- 11 → olsun; **Mübarek olsun!** 'May it be blessed!', a formula of congratulation exclusively for religious holidays. → ol- 11 → olsun; **Tebrik ederim.** 'Congratulations.' → tebrik et-, **Tebrikler!** 'Congratulations!'

150 GRATITUDE

150:4 - thank /a: A, b: DAn dolayı, c: A/ **şükret-** '- give thanks /a: to [God], b: {for/because of}, c: θ [that]/, - praise /a: θ [God], b: {for/because of}, c: θ [that]/, - be thankful [a: to [God]/b: FOR'; /a: A, b: A, c: için/ **teşekkür et-** '- thank /a: θ [sb], b: FOR, c: for/, - be obliged /a: to [sb], b: for, c: for/'.

150:6 INTERJ. thanks! **Allah [sizden] razı olsun.** 'May God be pleased [with you].' → razı ol- → ol- 12; **Eksik {olma./olmayın[ız].}** 'Thank you.' → eksik ol- → ol- 12; **Sağol.** 'Thanks.' → sağ ol- → ol- 12; **Sağolun.** 'Thank you.' → sağ ol- → ol- 12; **Sağol[un], varol[un]!** 'Thank you very much!' → sağ ol- → ol- 12; **Sağ olsun!** 'Bless {him/her}!' → sağ ol- → ol- 12; /A/ **Şükürler olsun [ki]...** /A/ 'Thanks be /to/ God [that]...' or 'Praise be /to/ God [that]...' 'God' is always implied although a word for God may not appear. → ol- 11 → olsun; **Teşekkür ederim.** 'Thank you.', *formal*, always appropriate. → teşekkür et-.

152 RESENTMENT, ANGER

152:17 - become angry /A, diye/ **darıl-** 1 '- be or - get mad /AT/, angry /{WITH/AT}, BECAUSE/'; /A/ **kız-** 1 '- get or - be angry, cross /{AT/WITH} [sb], θ [that]/'; /A, DIğI için/ **küs-** '- be offended or hurt /BY/; - be mad or angry /AT, because/, - be put out /WITH, because/'; /A/ **öfkelen-** '- get angry, enraged, furious /AT/'; /A/ **sinirlen-** '- get angry, mad /AT/; - get irritated, annoyed /AT/, - get in a state /ABOUT/, upset /θ [that]/';

650

sinirleri bozul- 1 '- get upset, angry, - lose one's cool, temper, composure'.

☐ **152:20 - fly into a rage** **kendini kaybet-** 3 '- be beside oneself with anger, - lose control as a result of anger, - lose one's temper, - go into a towering rage' → {kaybet-/yitir-}; /DAn/ **patla-** 2 '- be ready to explode, - feel like screaming /{ON ACCOUNT OF/DUE TO}/, - explode, - fly off the handle', *colloq.* '- lose one's cool'; **sinirleri bozul-** 1 '- get upset, angry, - lose one's cool, temper, composure'; {**şuurunu/ bilincini} kaybet-**[or **yitir-**] 2 '- lose self-control, - lose one's temper'.

☐ **152:21 - offend** /A, DAn dolayı/ **alın-** 3 '- be offended /BY, because of/, - take offense /AT/, - be hurt'; /A/ **darıl-** 2 '- be or - get hurt or offended /BY/; - take offense /AT/'; **kalbini kır-** '- hurt sb's feelings [lit., - break sb's heart, but without this strength of feeling in Turkish.]' → kır- 1; **kır-** 2 '- hurt [not physically], - offend'; /DIğI için, A/ **kırıl-** 3 '- be hurt [not physically], offended /because, BY [sb]/'; /A, DIğI için/ **küs-** '- be offended or hurt /BY/; - be mad or angry /AT, because/, - be put out /WITH, because/'; {**zoruna/ gücüne} git-** 2 '- offend /θ/, - hurt /θ/' → git- 1 b).

☐ **152:22 - anger** **kızdır-** 1 '- anger, - make angry'; /ArAk/ **sinirlendir-** '- make sb angry, mad, - anger; - irritate, - annoy, - get on sb's nerves /by...ing/'.

☐ **152:25a gestures of anger** /A/ **dik dik bak-** '- stare angrily /AT/, - glare /AT/' → bak- 1; /DAn/ **eli ayağı tutMA-** '- be shaky, unsteady /{WITH/BECAUSE OF}/' [a reaction of shock to bad news or a frightening event or a sign of anger]. → tut- 2; **kaşlarını çat-** '- knit one's brows, - frown'; /DAn/ **titre-** 2 '- tremble /{WITH/IN}/ [fear], - shake /WITH/ [fear, anger]'; **yüzü buruş-** 1 '- grimace, - scowl, - make a face [lit., for one's face - wrinkle]'; **yüzünü buruştur-.** Same. [lit., ** - wrinkle one's face]'.

☐ **152:25b expressions of anger** **Sinirim tepeme çıktı.** 'I'm really

pissed off' → çık- 5; **Şuna bak be!** 'Just look AT that, will you!, Imagine!, [Why] the nerve!' → bak- 1.

☐ **152: * 34 proverbs** **Adam kızmayınca belli olmaz.** 'A man cannot be known [lit., ** become clear] unless he gets angry.' → kız- 1; **Arı kızdıranı sokar.** 'A bee stings the person who angers it.', i.e., A person will lash out at his tormenter even if he himself will also suffer as a result. → kızdır- 1.

153 JEALOUSY

☐ **153:3 - suffer pangs of jealousy** **kıskan-** 1 /I/ '- be jealous /OF/; - envy sb /FOR/ sth he possesses'. 2 /I, DAn/ '- resent sb's showing affection to or interest IN sb else'. 3 /I/ '- be jealously protective of sb, - guard a woman zealously against any sign of disrespect, especially against the attentions of another male, - love jealously'.

154 ENVY

☐ **154:3 - envy** /A/ **imren-** 2 '- long /FOR/ sth unobtainable, - envy without malice'; /I/ **kıskan-** 1 '- be jealous /OF/; - envy sb for sth he possesses'; /A/ **özen-** 2 '- want badly sth that sb else has; - want to be in the situation that sb else is in'.

155 RESPECT

☐ **155:4 - respect** **say-** 3 '- respect [a person]'; **takdir et-** 1 '- appreciate, - value, - respect, - admire [sb's efforts]'.

☐ **155:5 - do or - pay hommage to** **bayrağı selâmla-** '- salute the flag'; /A/ **saygı göster-** '- show respect /{to/FOR}/, - behave respectfully /TOWARD/, - treat with respect, - respect'; /A/ **saygılar sun-** '- pay or - offer one's respects, - give or - send one's regards or compliments /to/' → sun- 1.

☐ **155:6 - bow** **baş eğ-** '- bow, - bow one's head [as a sign of respect], - hang one's head in shame' → eğ- 1; **eğ-** 1 '- bow, - bend, - tip'; **elini öp-** '- kiss the hand of', a gesture of respect when greeting or taking leave of an older man or woman. → öp-.

☐ **155: * 15 expressions of respect** **Ellerinizden öperim.** 'Kind regards [lit., I kiss you ON your hands]', a concluding salutation in a letter to a SENIOR, man or woman. → öp-; <u>Gözlerinizden öperim.</u> 'Kind regards [lit., I kiss you ON your eyes]', a concluding salutation in a letter to a JUNIOR, man or woman. → öp-.

156 DISRESPECT
156:5 - offend /A, DAn dolayı/ <u>alın-</u> 3 '- be offended or hurt /BY, because of/, - take offense /AT/'; /A/ <u>hakaret et-</u> '- insult /θ/'; {zoruna/gücüne} <u>git-</u> 2 '- offend /θ/, - hurt /θ/' → git- 1 b).

157 CONTEMPT
157:3 - disdain <u>küçümse-</u> 1 '- look down upon, - regard sb or sth as inferior, - treat with disrespect or contempt, - hold sb in contempt, - despise', *informal*: '- put sb down', *slang*: '- dis'.

158 SPACE
158:8 - extend /A/ 1 <u>değ-</u> 2 'for sth - reach, - attain /θ/ [His head almost reached /θ/ the ceiling]'; /A/ <u>ulaş-</u> 1 '- reach /θ/, - arrive /AT/ [A tree will never reach θ the sky.]'.

CLASS 3: PLACE AND CHANGE OF PLACE

159 LOCATION
159:12 - place /A/ <u>at-</u> 3 '- put /ON/ [salt on food]'; /A/ <u>bırak-</u> 2 '- leave /{ON/IN/AT}/ [i.e., - PUT sth somewhere: Don't keep holding the books. Leave them on the table.], - leave or - drop off /AT/'; /A/ <u>bindir-</u> '- put sb /ON/ a vehicle [train, plane] or a mount [animal: horse]'; /A/ <u>bindiril-</u> '- be boarded, - be put /ON/ a vehicle or mount [animal: horse] [subj.: person]'; <u>koy-</u> 1 /A, üzerine/ '- put, - place /{IN/ON}, {on/upon}/'. 2 /A, üzerine/ '- put or - place food /ON/ sb's plate, - serve [out] food /to/ sb'. 3 /A, için/ '- put sth /θ [somewhere], for/, - set sth aside /for/'; /{A/DA}/ <u>park et-</u> '- park [vehicle] /{AT/in}/{AT/in}/'.

159:14 - deposit <u>bırak-</u> 5 '- let go, - release, - put down [Don't keep holding it, put it down.]'; /A/ {daya-/yasla-} '- lean, - prop, - rest sth /{AGAINST/ON}/'; /A/ <u>para yatır-</u> 1 '- deposit money /IN/ [bank, account]' → yatır- 2; /A/

sırtını {daya-/yasla-} 1 '- lean [i.e., oneself, lit., one's back] /AGAINST/'; <u>yasla-</u> = {daya-/ yasla-}.

159:15 - load /{üstüne/üzerine}/ <u>yık-</u> 3 '- load sb down with sth, - load sth down /upon/ sb, - pile or - dump sth /{on/upon/} sb [obj.: a burdensome task]'.

159:16 - establish /A/ 2 <u>dik-</u> 2 '- set up, - erect /IN/ [subj.: electric poles]'; /A/ <u>kur-</u> 1 '- set up, - assemble [machine, furniture] /{IN/ON}/; - establish, - found [business, republic]'; /A, tarafından/ <u>kurul-</u> 1 '- be set up, assembled /{IN/ON}, by/ [subj.: dining room set]; - be established, founded /by/ [subj.: state, association]'; /A/ <u>sofra kur-</u> '- lay or - set a table, tray, mat, spread or like object for a meal /IN/ a place' → kur- 1.

159:17 - settle /DAn, A/ <u>taşın-</u> '- move oneself, - change one's place of residence, business /from, to/'; /A/ <u>yerleş-</u> '- locate, - settle, or - establish oneself /IN/ a place permanently or temporarily; - settle [oneself] down /{IN/INTO}/ [a chair]'.

161 DIRECTION
161:9 - head for /A/ <u>hareket et-</u> 2 '- leave /FOR/, - depart /FOR/', usually by means of a land vehicle, i.e., bus, train, not a boat and not a person on foot.

162 PROGRESSION
162:2 - progress <u>geç-</u> 6 '- go well or badly', perhaps more common in the past tense: How did the lesson go?; <u>git-</u> 5 '- go or - proceed well or badly', perhaps more common in the present continuous tense: How is the lesson going?; /DAn, A doğru/ <u>ilerle-</u> 1 '- advance, - move forward /THROUGH, toward/ [subj.: procession]'; [saatleri] ileri al- '- set or - turn [clocks] ahead, forward' → al- 1.

163 REGRESSION
163:6 - retreat <u>geri taşın-</u> '- move [one's residence] back [to a previously occupied place]'; <u>gerile-</u> 1 '- move back, - retreat, - fall back'.

163:8a - turn sth back öne al- '- move up in time, - make earlier than originally planned [date of departure, examination]' → al- 1; [saatleri] geri al- '- set or - turn back [clocks]' → geri al- 2 → al- 1.

163:8b - turn back, - come back /DAn, A/ dön- 2 '- return or - come back /from, to/'; *noun of place* dönüşü 'returning, upon returning, after returning {to/from}'; /DAn, A/ geri dön- '- come back, - go back, - turn back, - return /from, to/'.

164 DEVIATION
164:3 - deviate /A/ [direksiyonu hızla] kır- '- turn [a steering wheel, rudder, sharply] /to/ one side, - swerve /to/ [the left, right]' → kır- 3.

164:5 - deflect eğ- 2 '- bend, - bow, - make bend [wind bends telephone poles]'.

164:6 - avoid kenara çek- '- pull aside, - pull off /to/ the side [police address to driver]' → çek- 1.

166 FOLLOWING
166:3 - follow izle- 1 '- follow, - go behind'; takip et- 1. Same.

166:4 - lag geri kal- 1 '- get, - stay, - remain, - fall, or - lag behind /in/ [some activity, lessons]' → kal- 1. Same as 217:8. REAR: - be behind.

167 APPROACH
167:3 - approach /A/ yaklaş- '- approach /θ/, - draw near /to/, - come close /to/, up /to/, over /to/'; /A/ yanaş- 1 '- draw near /to/, - approach /θ/; - sidle up /to/'. 2 'for a vehicle - draw or - pull /{UP TO/ ALONGSIDE}/: for a ship - dock, a train - draw or - pull up /to/ the platform'; yanına gel- '- come up to, over to, - come /to/ the side of, - sidle up to' → gel- 1; yanına yanaş- = yanına gel- → yanaş- 1. Same as 223:7. NEARNESS: - near, come near.

170 CROSSING
170:6 - cross kes- 1 '- cut across, - intersect [one street another]'.

172 MOTION
172:5a - move sth /DAn/ geçir- 1 '- cause to pass, - make pass /THROUGH/ [car through mud, thread through needle], - pass, - promote [students]'; ilerlet- 1 '- advance sth, - move sth forward'.

172:5b for sth - move hareket et- 1 '- move, - stir' [i.]; {kımılda-/kıpırda-} '- move slightly, - budge, - stir, - twitch [The table won't budge.]'.

173 QUIESCENCE
173:7 - be still nefes tut- '- hold one's breath' → tut- 4.

173:10 - sit /DA/ otur- 2 '- sit, - be sitting /in/ [a chair]', not '- sit down [i.e., not '- move INTO a sitting position]', for which see /A/ otur- 1. 912:10. DEPRESSION: - sit down.

174 SWIFTNESS
174:8 - speed {hız/sürat} yap- '- speed, - go too fast [vehicle]' → yap- 3; /a: DAn, b: A, c: arkasından, d: peşinden/ koş- 1 '- run /a: from, b: {to/AFTER}, c: after, d: after/, - pursue'; {koşar adımlar.la/koşar adım} merdivenleri çık- '- run up the stairs' → çık- 5; { koşar adımlar.la/koşar adım} merdivenler.DEN in- '- run down the stairs' → in- 1. See also 401:5. HASTE: - make haste.

174:10 - accelerate [i.] hızlan- 1 '- gather speed, - speed up, - accelerate, - pick up one's pace'.

174:13 - overtake /A/ yetiş- 1 '- catch /θ/ a vehicle, - make it /to/ in time /FOR/, - get /to/ a place in time /FOR/, - arrive in time /FOR/; - be in time /FOR/'. 2 '- catch up /WITH/, - overtake /θ/, - go fast enough to join /θ/'.

174:17 ADV. swiftly The structure *verb stem*.Iver-, i.e., I + ver-, may convey the sense of 'just, quickly, with ease': Yap.ıver! 'Just do it!' → ver- 4. See also 440:20. REQUEST: INTERJ. please.

175 SLOWNESS
175:9 - slow yavaşla- '- slow down, - lose speed [vehicle, runner], - die down [rain].'

176 TRANSFERAL, TRANS-PORTATION

| 176:10 - transfer | /Dan, A/ **aktar-** 1 '- transfer /from [one place], to [another]/, - move /from [one container], to [another]/, - pass on, - convey'.

| 176:11 - remove | /DAn/ **çek-** 3 '- take [hands] off'; **çıkar-** 2 '- take off, - remove [clothing]'; /DAn, A/ **götür-** '- take [away] /from [somewhere], to [somewhere else]/'; **kaldır-** 3 '- take away, - clear away, - remove [dirty dishes]'. 5 /A/ '- take sb /to/ the hospital or morgue'; **sofra kaldır-** '- clear, after a meal, anything upon which a meal may be placed' → kaldır- 3.

| 176:12 - transport | /I/ **gezdir-** '- show or - take sb around [a place, city]'; /A/ **ilet-** 1 '- take or - convey /to/, - forward, - pass sth on /to/'; /a: DAn, b: A, c: 1A arasında/ **taşı-** '- carry, - move, or - transport /a: from, b: to, c: between/'; /DAn, A/ **taşın-** '- move oneself, - change one's place of residence, business /from, to/'; /A/ **ulaştır-** '- transport, - convey, - bring, or - get sth /to/'.

| 176:15 - send | /A/ **at-** 4 '- mail, - post, - send off [mail]', *informal*, more like '- drop it /IN/ the mailbox'; /A/ **gönder-** '- send sth /to/ sb, - send θ sb sth; - send sb off /to/'; /A/ **ilet-** 1 '- take or - convey /to/, - forward, - pass on /to/'; /A/ **postala-** '- mail, - post, - send off, - mail /to/', *more formal* than at- 4; /A, {tarafından/CA}/ **postalan-** '- be mailed, posted, sent off /to, by/'; **tahtaya kaldır-** '- send to the blackboard [obj.: student]' → kaldır- 1; /A/ **ulaştır-** '- transport, - convey, - bring, or - get sth /to/'; /A/ **yolla-** = gönder-.

| 176:16 - fetch | /DAn/ **al-** 2 '- pick up /from/, - take on [passengers], - give a {ride/lift}'; /DAn/ **ara-** 3 '- call for or - pick up /AT/ [obj.: person AT a hotel]'; /DAn, A/ **getir-** '- bring, - fetch, - get sth /from, to/'.

| 176:17 - ladle | /DAn, A/ **dök-** 1 '- pour /from, {to/INTO}/'; /a: A, b: {üstüne/üzerine}, c: {tarafın-dan/CA}/ **dökül-** 2 '- be poured out, - be spilled /a: ON, b: on, c: by/'; /DAn, A/ **koy-** 1 With a liquid often '- pour /from, INTO/' otherwise '- put, - place /{IN/ON}, {on/upon}/'. 2 '- put or - place food /ON/ sb's plate, - serve [out] food /to/ sb'; /A/ **paylaştır-** '- serve out, - dish out, - distribute a {serving/share} /{INTO/ONTO}/ [food onto plates]'.

177 TRAVEL

| 177:18 - travel | /1A/ **gidip gel-** '- travel back and forth, - commute /BY/ [vehicle]' → gel- 1; /A/ **seyahat et-** '- travel or - take a trip /to/'; **şehre in-** '- go /θ/ downtown, /INTO/ town, /INTO/ the city', even if the town or city is up a hill → in- 1.

| 177:20 - traverse | **geç-** 1 /DAn, A/ '- pass /THROUGH, {to/INTO}/, - go past, - cross /θ/ sth, - trespass', /I/ '- go beyond, - cross [street, etc.]', the thing crossed is indicated: He crossed the street.; /DAn/ **karşıya geç-** '- pass /to/ the {opposite/other} side, - cross /θ/, - cross over /θ/' → geç- 1; **katet-** '- travel, - cover, - traverse a distance; - go through, - pass through a place'; **yol {yap-/git-}** '- travel, - cover, - traverse a distance' → git- 1a, yap- 3.

| 177:21 - journey | *vehicle name.*1A **gez-**: arabayla gez- '- go for a drive'; /I/ **dolaş-** 2 '- tour'; /a: 1A, b: DA, c: 1A/ **gez-** '- go about, - walk about, - tour /a: with [sb], b: in [a place], c: IN [a vehicle]/, - sightsee, - stroll'; **gezmeye çık-** '- go {out for a walk/θ sight-seeing}' → çık- 2; **hacca git-** '- go /ON/ the Pilgrimage, - make the Pilgrimage to Mecca'. → git- 1a.

| 177:22 - migrate | /DAn, A/ **{göç et-/göç-}** '- migrate /from, to/'.

| 177:23 - wander | /I/ **dolaş-** 1 '- go, - walk, - wander, or - stroll about or around, - make one's way through, - cover ground [usually on foot]'; /a: 1A, b: DA, c: 1A/ **gez** '- go or - walk about, - tour /a: with [sb], b: in [a place], c: IN [a vehicle]/, - sightsee [on foot or in a vehicle], - stroll'; /DA, arasında/ **gezin-** 1 '- wander, roam, - walk or - go about, - stroll, - ramble, - rove /in, among/ [usually aimlessly]'.

| 177:25 - go to | /A/ **gidil-** 'for one - get or - go /to/ a place [How does one get to the airport?]'; /a: DAn, b: A, c: 1A/ **git-** 1a '- go /a: from, b: to, c: BY/, - leave, - depart /from/'.

177:26 - creep | emekle- '- crawl, - creep [i.e., - move on all fours: subj.: usually a baby or infirm person]'; sürün- 1 '- crawl along the ground [soldiers in the dark of night]'.

177:27 - walk | /A/ ayak bas- '- set foot /ON/' → bas- 1; /A/ bas- 1 '- step /ON/, - trample /{ON/θ}/'; yürü- 1 '- walk, - take a walk'; /A/ {yürüyerek/yaya [olarak]/ yayan} git- '- walk /to/ [a place], - go [somewhere] {on foot}' → git- 1a.

177:29 - go for a walk | yürüyüşe çık- '- go out /FOR/ a walk' → çık- 2.

177:31 - hitchhike | otostop yap- '- hitchhike' → yap- 3.

177:33 - ride | bin- 2 '- ride [I like horseback riding.]'; /lA/ git- 2 '- ride, go /{ON/by}/ a vehicle [[I'm going to the grocery store by bicycle./I'm riding my bicycle to the grocery store.}]'.

177:35 - glide | /A/ kay- 1 '- slide, - slip, - skid; - slide over /to/'. 2 '- sled [winter sport]'. 3 '- ski'; kayak yap- '- ski' → yap- 3.

182 WATER TRAVEL
182:13: - navigate {vapur.lA/gemi.ylE) git- '- go ... ferry/BY ship}' → git- 1a.

182:54: - float /{DA/üzerinde}/ yüz- 2 '- float /on/'.

182:56 - swim | yüz- 1 '- swim'; denize gir- '- go swimming /IN/ the {sea/ocean}'.

184 AVIATION
184:36 - fly | /a: A, b: lA, c: üzerinde/ uç- '- fly /a: to, b: IN, c: over/, - fly away'; /A/ uçakla git- '- fly /to/, - go /to/ by plane' → git- 1a.

184:37 - pilot | uçak kullan- '- fly a plane'; uçurtma uçur- '- fly a kite'.

184:38 - take off | /DAn/ havalan- 2 '- take off /from/ [subj.: plane, helicopter]'; /DAn/ kalk- 2. Same as above. Same as 193:10. ASCENT: - take off.

184:43 - land | /A/ in- 3 '- land /{AT/IN/ON}/ [subj.: plane, but not helicopter]'; /A/ kon- '- land, - perch, - settle, - alight /{ON/UPON}/ [subj.: bird, insect, helicopter, but not plane]'.

184:44 - crash | /A/ çakıl- 2 '- crash, - nose dive /INTO/ [subj.: plane]'; düş- 5 '- crash, - crack up [plane]'; yere çakıl- '- nose dive /INTO/ the ground, - crash, - crack up [subj.: plane]' → çakıl- 2.

186 ARRIVAL
186:6 - arrive | düş- 4 '- come to one by chance, inheritance, etc.'; /A/ er- '- reach /θ/, - attain /θ/ [goal, God]'; /A/ eriş- 1 '- reach /θ/, - arrive /AT/, - get /to/'. 4 '- access /θ/, - gain access /to/, - get /{to [a source of informtion]/ON [the Internet]}/'; /a: DAn, b: A, c: lA/ gel- 1 '- come /a: from, b: to, c: with/, - arrive /b: {IN/AT}/'; /A/ ulaş- 1 '- reach /θ/, - arrive /AT/'; /A/ var- '- reach /θ/, - arrive /{IN/AT}/, - get /to/'; /A/ yetiş- 1 '- catch /θ/ a vehicle, - make it /to/ in time /FOR/, - get /to/ a place in time /FOR/, - arrive in time /FOR/; - be in time /FOR/'. 4 '- arrive in time to help sb; - come to sb's aid in time'.

187 RECEPTION
187:12 - draw in | içine çek- '- inhale' → çek- 1; nefes al- '- breathe, - take a breath; - inhale' → al- 1; nefes çek- '- take a wiff, drag, puff [of tobacco]' → çek- 1.

187:14 - bring in | /DAn/ ithal et- '- import /from/'.

188 DEPARTURE
188:6 - depart | /DAn/ ayrıl- 3 '- leave /θ/, - depart /from/ [train from city, person from party]; - check /out of/ a hotel or motel'; /DAn/ çık- 1 '- come out /OF/, - leave [usually from an enclosed place: house, room], - get /OFF/ [train]'; /a: DAn, b: A, c: lA/ git- 1a '- go /a: from, b: to, c: BY/, - leave, - depart /from/'; /DAn/ hareket et- 3 '- leave /θ/, - depart /from/, usually by means of a land vehicle, i.e., bus, train, not a boat and not a person on foot; /DAn, buradan/ taşın- '- move /from, from here [i.e., away]/'; /DAn/ uzaklaş- 1 '- leave /θ/, - go away /from/, - become distant /from/, -

move away /from/ [train from station], - make off'.

188:8 - set out | hareket et- 2 /A/ '- leave /FOR/, - depart /FOR/', usually by means of a land vehicle, i.e., bus, train, not a boat and not a person on foot. 3 /DAn/ '- leave /θ/, - depart /from/'. As above, usually by means of a land vehicle; /DAn/ havalan- 2 '- take off /from/, - become airborne [subj.: airborne vehicles, birds]'; /DAn/ kalk- 2 '- set off, - start off, - leave, - depart, - take off /from/ [subj.: various vehicles]'; yola {çık-/koyul-} '- start off, - set out or - leave /ON/ a {trip/journey}, - set out /ON/ the road [person on foot or vehicle]'. → çık- 2, koyul-.

188:9 - quit | /DAn/ emekliye ayrıl- '- retire /from/, - go into retirement' → ayrıl- 3; görevinden ayrıl- '- resign /from/, - leave /θ/ one's post' → ayrıl- 3; işten {ayrıl-/çık-} '- leave or - quit /θ/ one's job', not necessarily retirement. → ayrıl- 3, çık- 1.

188:10 - hasten off | başını alıp git- '- take off, - make off, - go away, - leave', in the sense of a permanent departure. → git- 1a.

188:13 - check out | {otelden/motelden} ayrıl- '- check out {OF a hotel/OF a motel}' → ayrıl- 3.

188:16 - say or - bid good-bye | /A/ uğurla- '- wish a departing traveler a safe journey, - wish sb Godspeed, - send or - see sb off /to/'; /lA/ vedalaş- '- bid or - say goodbye, farewell /TO/ one another'; /A/ yolcu et- '- see a traveler off /to/'.

188:22 INTERJ. farewell! | Allaha ısmarladık. 'Goodbye.', said by the person departing. → ısmarla- 3; Eyvallah! 'So long.', said by the person remaining, informal; Güle güle. 'Goodbye.', said by the person remaining. → gül- 1; Hoşça kal[ın]! 'Goodbye., So long!, Have a good day.', said by the person departing. → kal- 1; Kendine iyi bak! 'Take good care OF yourself!', a common farewell to a person departing for an extended period. → bak- 3; Sağlıcakla kalın. 'Take

care.', lit., 'Remain in good health and happiness.', said by someone off on a journey to those remaining behind. → kal- 1; [Sonra] görüşürüz. 'See you [later].' → görüş- 1; {Tekrar/Yine} görüşürüz. 'We'll meet {again}.' → görüş- 1; Uğurlar olsun. 'Have a good {trip/journey}.' → ol- 11 → olsun; Yarın görüşürüz. 'See you tomorrow., WE'll see EACH OTHER tomorrow.' → görüş- 1; Yine görüşmek üzere. 'Till we meet again.' → görüş- 1; Yolunuz açık olsun. 'Have a good {trip/journey}' → ol- 11 → olsun. Also = Hayırlı yolcuklar., = İyi yolculuklar.

188:23 good night! | Allah rahatlık versin. 'Good night.', used before retiring, going to bed, usually not simply when bidding farewell in the evening, as, for example, when leaving a party. In that case İyi geceler is used. → ver- 1.

189 ENTRANCE

189:7 - enter | /A, DAn içeri/ dal- 3 '- enter suddenly, - dash, - rush /INTO [the room], IN THROUGH [the door]/'; /A/ eriş- 4 '- access /θ/, - gain access /to/, - get /{to [a source of informtion]/ON [the Internet]}/'; /A, DAn/ gir- '- enter /θ, {THROUGH/BY WAY OF}/, go /{IN/INTO}, {THROUGH/BY WAY OF}/ [the place entered may be indicated]; - break into'; /DAn/ giril- '- be entered /{THROUGH/BY WAY OF}/'; içeri[.ye] gir- '- go {in [or inside]}, - enter', the place entered is not indicated [She {entered/went in}.]; {sıraya/kuyruğa} gir- '- get /IN/ [the] line, - line up, - queue up', for a performance, a sports event, a means of transportation [bus, shared cab], or for a purchase; /A/ sok- 2 '- let, - permit, - allow sb /{IN/INTO}/ a place'; /A/ uğra- 1 '- stop in /AT/, - drop in /{AT/ON}/, - drop /BY/, - call /{ON/UPON}/, - call in /AT/, - stop off /IN/'.

189:9 - flow in | /A/ dökül- 3 '- flow, - run, - pour /INTO/ [river into the sea, people into the street]'.

190 EMERGENCE

190:11 - emerge | çık- 1 /DAn, DAn/ '- come out /OF [room], {THROUGH/BY WAY OF}/, - leave [the room], - get /OFF/ [train]'. **3** /DAn/ '- appear /from/, - come out, - emerge /from/ [subj.: sun, moon, disease], /A/ '- lead /to/, - come out /{AT/ON}/ [subj.: road]'; <u>güneş aç-</u> 'for the sun - come out, - appear' → aç- 8; <u>komadan çık-</u> '- come out of or - emerge from a coma' → çık- 1.

___190:12 - exit___ /DAn, A/ <u>çıkıl-</u> 'for sb or sth - go out /{THROUGH/BY WAY OF}, to/; - go up /to/, - climb /to/', impersonal passive: ONE does not go out THROUGH this door.; <u>dışarı[ya] çık-</u> 1 '- go or - step {out/outside}' → çık- 2.

___190:13 - run out___ /DAn, A/ <u>ak-</u> '- flow /from, {to/INTO}/, - pour /from, INTO/'; <u>boşal-</u> 1 '- become empty, - empty out; - become vacant'. **2** /DAn, A/ 'for a liquid - run, - pour, - stream /{from/OUT OF}, ONTO/; - overflow'; /A, {üstüne/üzerine}/ <u>dökül-</u> 1 '- spill /ON, on/' [i.]; /DAn/ <u>kan ak-</u> '- bleed /from/'; /DAn/ <u>kan gel-</u> '- bleed /from/, for blood - come /from/' → gel- 1; <u>kana-</u> '- bleed'.

___190:17 - export___ /A/ <u>ihraç et-</u> '- export /to/'.

191 INSERTION
___191:3 - insert___ /A/ <u>burnunu sok-</u> 1 '- stick one's nose /INTO/, - interfere /IN/' → sok- 1; /A, üzerine/ <u>koy-</u> 1 '- put, - place /{IN/ON}, {on/upon}/'; /A/ <u>sok-</u> 1 '- insert, - thrust, - shove, - stick, - put, - introduce /{IN/INTO}/'.

192 EXTRACTION
___192:10 - extract___ /DAn/ <u>al-</u> 1 '- take out /from/ [books from library]'; /DAn/ <u>çek-</u> 2 '- take /out of/, - withdraw [money from bank], - remove /from/, - extract [tooth]'; /DAn/ <u>çıkar-</u> 1 '- take sth /{OUT OF/from}/, - remove sth /from/ [things from pocket, luggage]'. **2** ... '- remove a spot /from/ [clothing]'; /DAn/ <u>kopar-</u> 2 '- tear, - rip /OUT OF/ [pages out of notebook], - tear away /from/ [mother from child]'. **3** '- manage to get, usually in the face of difficulty, - finagle, - wangle, - wrangle, - get sth [permission] /{from/OUT OF}/ sb'; <u>kopart-</u> 2 and **3**. Same as **kopar-** 2 and 3; /DAn/ <u>para çek-</u> '- take money /{OUT OF/from}/, - withdraw money

/from/ [bank]' → çek- 2; /DAn/ <u>yırt-</u> '- tear up, - rip up; - tear or - rip /{OUT OF/from}/ [page out of notebook]'; /DAn, tarafından/ <u>yırtıl-</u> '- be or - get torn, ripped /{OUT OF/from}, by/'.

___192:11 - disinter___ <u>çıkar-</u> 1 '- dig up [body, treasure]'.

193 ASCENT
___193:8 - ascend___ <u>ayağa kalk-</u> '- stand up, - get /to/ one's feet' → kalk- 1; /DAn/ <u>kalk-</u> 1 '- get up /{from/OUT OF}/ [chair], - rise /from/, - stand up, - get up, - get out of bed, - arise'; /DAn, A/ <u>yüksel-</u> 1 '- rise, - go up, - ascend /from, to/ [in a vertical plane: balloon]'.

___193:9 - shoot up___ /DAn, A/ <u>fırla-</u> 1 '- jump up, - leap up /from, to/, - rush or - dart out, - fly out'.

___193:10 - take off___ /DAn/ <u>havalan-</u> 2 '- take off /from/ [subj.: plane, helicopter]'; /DAn/ <u>kalk-</u> 2. Same. Same as 184:38. AVIATION: - take off.

___193:11 - climb, - climb up___ /DAn, A/ <u>çık-</u> 5 '- go up, - ascend, - climb, - mount /BY WAY OF [stairs], to/'; <u>dağa çık-</u> '- climb mountains, - go mountain climbing' → çık- 5; /A/ <u>tırman-</u> 1 '- climb /Ø/ sth [tree, mountain, hill], - climb /to/ a place [the to˙ of the mountain]'.

___193:12 - mount___ /A/ <u>atla-</u> 3 '- hop /INTO/ a taxi, car, bus; - catch /Ø/ a plane, train'; /A/ <u>bin-</u> 1 '- get /ON/, - get on board, - board /Ø/, - catch /Ø/, - take /Ø/ [a vehicle: bus, train, plane], - mount /Ø/ [an animal: horse]'; /A/ <u>bindir-</u> '- put sb /ON/ a vehicle or a mount [animal: horse]'; /A/ <u>bindiril-</u> '- be boarded, - be put /ON/ a vehicle or mount [animal: horse] [subj.: person]'; /DA/ <u>binil-</u> '- be boarded [subj.: vehicle], - be mounted [subj.: animal] /{AT/from}/ [the front, the rear]'.

194 DESCENT
___194:5 - descend___ /DAn, A/ <u>alçal-</u> 1 '- come down, - descend /from, to/ [subj.: plane, birds, balloon]'; <u>dolgu düş-</u> '- lose a [tooth] filling, - have a filling fall out'; /DAn, A/ <u>düş-</u> 1 '- fall, - drop [of itself] /from, {to/IN/INTO/ON/ONTO}/'; /DAn, A/ <u>in-</u> 1 '- descend, - go down

/{from/BY WAY OF}, to/'; /A/ <u>kon-</u> '- land, - perch, - settle, - alight /{ON/UPON}/ [subj.: bird, insect, helicopter, not plane]'; <u>şehre in-</u> '- go /θ/ downtown, /INTO/ town, /INTO/ the city', even if the town or city is up a hill. → in- 1; <u>yağ-</u> '- come down [subj.: weather elements: rain, snow, hail]'.

| 194:6 - sink | /A/ <u>bat-</u> 1 '- sink /{IN/INTO}/ [subj.: sun, ship], - set [subj.: sun, moon]'.

| 194:7 - get down | /A/ <u>in-</u> 3 '- land /{AT/IN/ON}/' [subj.: plane, but not helicopter]'; /DAn/ <u>in-</u> 2 '- get down /{from/OFF}/, - get off or out /OF/ a vehicle, - dismount /{θ/from}/ an animal'; /DAn/ <u>inil-</u> '- be exited, disembarked /{AT, BY WAY OF}/ [vehicle]'; /A/ <u>kon-</u> '- land, - perch, - settle, - alight /{ON/UPON}/ [subj.: bird, insect, helicopter, not plane]'.

| 194:8 - tumble | <u>dökül-</u> 4 '- fall out [hair]'; <u>düş-</u> 2 '- fall from power [government]'.

| 194:9 - slide | <u>kay-</u> 1 /A/ '- slide, - slip, - skid; - slide over /to/ [the side]'. 2 '- sled [winter sport]'. 3 '- ski'.

| 194:10 - light upon | /{üstüne/üzerine}/ <u>çök-</u> 3 '- come down /upon/, - settle /on/ [subj.: fog, smoke]'; /A/ <u>kon-</u> '- land, - perch, - settle, - alight /{ON/UPON}/ [subj.: bird, insect, helicopter, not plane]'.

200-300

200 VERTICALNESS

| 200:7 - stand | <u>ayakta dur-</u> '- stand on one's feet' → dur- 3; /DA, başında/ <u>dur-</u> 3 '- stand /{on/at}, {AT/BY}/ [the table]'.

| 200:8 - rise | <u>ayağa kalk-</u> '- stand up, - get /to/ one's feet' → kalk- 1; /DAn, A/ <u>fırla-</u> 1 '- jump up, - leap up /from, to/, - rush or - dart out, - fly out'; /DAn/ <u>kalk-</u> 1 '- get up /{from/OUT OF}/, - rise /from/ [chair, bed], stand up'.

| 200:9 - erect | /A/ 2 <u>dik-</u> 2 '- set up, - erect [electric poles] /{IN/ON}/'; /A/ <u>kur-</u> 1 '- set up, - assemble [machine, furniture] /{IN/ON}/; - establish, - found [state,

association]'; /A, tarafından/ <u>kurul-</u> 1 '- be set up, assembled /{IN/ON}, by/ [subj.: dining room set]; - be established, founded /by/ [subj.: state, association]'.

201 HORIZONTALNESS

| 201:5 - lie | /{A/üstüne}/ <u>uzan-</u> 1 '- lie down /{ON/on}/, - stretch oneself out /{ON/on}/ [bed for a nap]'; <u>yat-</u> 1 '- go to bed, - lie down, - retire for the night', also '- be lying down, - be in bed'.

202 PENDENCY

| 202:8 - suspend | <u>as-</u> 1 /a: A, b: DAn, c: 1A/ '- hang [up] /a: {IN/ON} [a wall], b: BY [his feet], c: with [thumbtacks]/'. 2 / A, 1A/ '- hang /{to/ON}, FOR [a crime]/ [as a form of execution]'; <u>asıl-</u> 1 /a: A, b: tarafından, c: DAn, d: nedeniyle/ '- be hung /a: {ON/IN}, b: by [sb], c: BY [part of body], d: {on the occasion of/on account of}/'. 2 /a: A, b: 1A, c: {tarafından/CA}/ '- be hanged /a: {to/ON} [a tree], b: FOR [a crime], c: by [bandits]/', as a form of execution.; /A/ <u>tak-</u> '- attach, - fasten sth /to/, - wear, - put sth /ON/ [oneself, usually small items, accessories: glasses, jewelry, also certain headgear], - put up [curtains]'.

204 OBLIQUITY

| 204:10 - incline | /A/ {daya-/yasla-} '- lean, - prop, - rest sth /{AGAINST/ON}/'; /A/ <u>dayan-</u> 1 '- lean [oneself] /{AGAINST/ON}/'; <u>eğil-</u> 1 /A/ '- bend down /to/'. 2 '- bow, - bow down'. 3 /A kadar/ '- bend down /TO/, - incline, - lean [subj.: trees]'; /A/ <u>sırtını {daya-/yasla-)</u> 1 '- lean /AGAINST/', lit., '- lean one's back against'; <u>yasla-</u> = daya-.

205 INVERSION

| 205:5 - invert | <u>arkasını çevir-</u> 2 '- turn over [i.e., on its back: obj.: document]' → çevir- 3; <u>çevir-</u> 3 '- turn over, - turn, - flip'.

209 ENVIRONMENT

| 209:6 - surround | /1A/ <u>çevir-</u> 5 '- surround /with/, - place sth /around/ sth else [He surrounded the garden /with/ a wall.]'; <u>çevresini sar-</u> '- surround [The children surrounded him.]' → sar- 3; <u>etrafını sar-</u> '- surround, - envelop [lit., - surround the area around: Enemy soldiers

surrounded him.]' → sar- 3; /I/ <u>sar-</u> 3 '- surround, - envelop' [Flames enveloped the house.]'.

212 ENCLOSURE
212:5 - enclose Same as 209:6.

212:9 - package <u>bavulunu hazırla-</u> '- pack, - pack up' or just '- prepare one's bags'.

214 INTRUSION
214:5 - intrude /A/ <u>burnunu sok-</u> 1 '- stick one's nose /{IN/INTO}/, - interfere /IN/' → sok- 1; /A/ <u>gir-</u> '...- break /INTO/ [thieves into house]'; <u>haneye tecavüz et-</u> '- trespass /ON/ sb's property' → tecavüz et- 1; /A/ <u>karış-</u> 5 '- interfere /IN/, - meddle /IN/, - get involved /IN/ [sb's business]'; <u>{sırayı/kuyruğu} boz-</u> 1 '- cut in a line [at the movies, bank]' → boz- 1.

214:6 - interrupt <u>sözünü kes-</u> '- interrupt, - break in on, - cut in on [conversation]' → kes- 3; <u>kes-</u> without <u>sözünü</u> is also used in the same meaning if the context permits.

216 FRONT
216:8 - confront [{zorlukla/güçlükle}] <u>karşılaş-</u> '- face /θ/, - be confronted /with/, - encounter /θ/, - experience /θ/, - meet /with/, - be up against [{difficulties}]' → karşılaş- 3.

217 REAR
217:8 - be behind /DA/ <u>geri kal-</u> 1 '- get, - stay, - remain, - fall, or - lag behind /in/ [some activity, lessons]' → kal- 1. Same as 166:4 FOLLOWING: - lag.

220 LEFT SIDE
220:3. * 1 - turn left <u>solla-</u> '[for a driver] - pass a vehicle on its left side'.

221 PRESENCE
221:6 - be present θ '- be', in the present tense attested only. For '- be' in other tenses, see bulun- 2, i-, and ol- 2 below; /DA/ <u>bulun-</u> 2 '- be, - exist, - find oneself /{in/at}/, - be situated /{in/at}/ [a place]'. 4 '- have, - be available' in a place such as in a store or a library, *formal, educated usage* [Do you have this book?]; /DA/ <u>geç-</u> 8 '- occur, - be present, -

be found /in/ [words in a text]'; /DA/ <u>hazır bulun-</u> '- be present /{at/in}/ [subj.: person]' → bulun- 2; /DA/ <u>i-</u> '- be /{in/at}/', but only: 1 As a base for the following tense and personal suffixes: 1.1 the -DI past tense: idi '{he/she/it} was'. 1.2 the -mIş present AND past presumptive tenses [one form for both]: imiş '{he/she/it} supposedly {is/was}'. 2 As a base for the present and past conditional, real: ise 'if {he/she/it} is', idiyse 'if {he/she/it} was'. 3 As a base for the gerund suffix -ken: iken 'while being'; /DA/ <u>ol-</u> 3 '- be /{at/in}/', in all tenses except in the present, where ol- = θ, i.e., no verb is used, and in the past, where {idi/.[y]DI} or {imiş/.[y]mIş} is used; /DA/ <u>{var/yok} ol-</u> '- be {present/absent} /{in/at}/ some [particular] location' → ol- 12, a) 2.

221:8 - attend /A/ <u>devam et-</u> 3 '- attend /θ/, - go /to/ regularly for a long period [educational institution: school, university]', not for a short term, particular event, such as a concert, soccer match, lecture; /A/ <u>git-</u> 4 '- go /to/, - attend /θ/' a) for a short period, particular event [movie, concert, soccer game] or b) for a long period [educational institution]; /I/ <u>izle-</u> 4 '- attend, - be present at and follow what is going on [obj.: concert]'; /I/ <u>oku-</u> 3 '- attend [an educational institution, level of school]'.

222 ABSENCE
222:7 - be absent /DAn/ <u>eksik ol-</u> '- be absent /from/, - miss [event: party]' → ol- 12.

222:8 - absent oneself /DAn/ <u>eksil-</u> 2 '- be absent /from/, - be without, - be lacking /θ/'.

223 NEARNESS
223:7 - near, - come near /A/ <u>yaklaş-</u> '- approach /θ/, - draw near /to/, - come close /to/, up /to/, over /to/'; /A/ <u>yanaş-</u> 1 '- draw near /to/, - approach /θ/; - sidle up /to/'. 2 'for a vehicle - draw or - pull /{UP TO/ALONGSIDE}/: for a ship - dock, a train - draw or - pull up /to/ the platform'; <u>yanına gel-</u> '- come up to, over to, - come /to/ the side of, - sidle up to' → gel- 1; <u>yanına yanaş-</u> = yanına gel- → yanaş- 1. Same as 167:3. APPROACH: - approach.

223:8 - be near | oldu olmadı 'it's been barely [two weeks since...]' → ol- 11; olmak üzere 2 '- be on the point of being, - be almost, - be [just] about to be, - be on the verge of being' → ol- 11.

223:10 - contact | /1A/ bağlantı kur- '- make contact /with/, - contact /θ/, - get in touch /with/, - establish ties, connections /with/, - connect, - get through /TO/ [telephone]' → kur- 1; /A/ 1 değ- 1 'for sth - touch /θ/, - brush /AGAINST/': The subject is a thing, perhaps part of a person, i.e., a part of his body, his clothing, not usually the person himself intentionally touching sth. 2 'for sth - reach, - attain' [His head almost reached the ceiling.]; /A/ dokun- 1 '- touch /θ/ physically [subj.: person, not thing]'; /A/ el sür- '- touch /θ/ sth [with the hands]' → sür- 5; isabet kaydet- 1 '- hit the mark, target' → kaydet- 5; /1A/ temas et- 1 '- touch /θ/ sb or sth physically; - bring into contact /with/ [inflammable materials with fire]'; /1A/ temas kur- '- get in contact /with/, - contact /θ/, - establish contact /with/' → kur- 1.

223:11 - meet | /1A/ karşılaş- 2 '- meet sb by chance, - run or - bump /INTO/ sb'; karşısına çık- '- appear suddenly in front of, - bump into'; /A/ rastla- 1 '- meet by chance, - run or - bump /INTO/, - encounter /θ/, - come or - chance /UPON/'; /A/ tesadüf et- 1. Same, *more formal*. Same as 131:6. INEXPECTATION: - be unexpected.

223:13 - juxtapose | /A/ yaklaştır- '- bring one thing /{to/NEAR/UP TO/OVER TO}/ another, - join'.

224 INTERVAL
224:3 - interspace | ara ver- '- take a break from, - stop doing sth for a while', *always appropriate*. → ver- 3; mola ver- '- stop for a rest [while traveling], - take a break [while working], - make a rest stop [subj.: workers or vehicles, not students or professionals except when speaking *very informally*]' → ver- 3; teneffüs yap- '- take a break', *formal, always appropriate*. → yap- 3.

224:4 - cleave | baş kesil- 'for one's head - be cut off, - be killed' → kesil- 1; kes- 1 '- cut [bread, hair, one's hand]'; /tarafından/ kesil- 1 '- be cut, - get cut, - be cut off /by/'; /A/ kestir- 1 '- have sth cut, - have /θ/ sb cut sth'.

225 HABITATION
225:7 - inhabit | /DA/ otur- 3 '- live /{in/at}/, - reside /{in/at}/, - inhabit /θ/'; yanında kal- '- stay, - live with sb' → kal- 1; /DA/ yaşa- 2 = otur- 3.

225:8 - sojourn | /DA/ misafir kal- '- stay as a guest /at/' → kal- 1.

225:11 - camp | kamp yap- '- camp, - go camping' → yap- 3.

238 STREAM
238:16. - flow | /DAn, A/ ak- '- flow /from, {to/INTO}/, - pour /from, INTO/'.

238:17a - make overflow | / A, {üstüne/üzerine}/ dök- 2 '- spill /ON, on/' → dök- 2; /a: A, b: {üstüne/üzerine}, c: {tarafından/CA}/ dökül- 2 '- be poured out, - be spilled /a: ON, b: on, c: by/'.

238:17b - overflow | /DAn, A/ boşal- 2 '- run, - pour, - stream /{from/OUT OF}, ONTO/ [subj.: a liquid]; - overflow'; /A, {üstüne/üzerine}/ dökül- 1 '- spill /ON, on/'; taş- 1 '- boil over'. 2 /DAn/ '- overflow, - run over /DUE TO/', /A, dışarı/ '- spill out'.

239 CHANNEL
239:15 - channel | ilet- 2 '- conduct [water conducts electricity]'.

CLASS 4: MEASURE AND SHAPE

244 QUANTITY
244:4 - quantify | say- 1 '- count', i.e., - determine or - say the number of.

248 INSIGNIFICANCE
248:10 ADV. <in a certain or limited degree> | hiç olmazsa 'at least' → ol- 11 → olmaz; olsa olsa 'at the [very] most, at most' → ol- 11; olsun 3 'at least, if only' → ol- 11.

249 SUPERIORITY

249:7 - best /DA, DAn/ kazan-
2 '- win [match] /{AT/IN} [game],
IN [source: lottery]'; 2 yen- 1 '-
overcome, - conquer, - beat, - defeat'.
2 '- win'.

249:9 - outdo /DA/ rekor kır- '-
break a record /in/ [a sports event]' →
kır- 1.

251 INCREASE

251:4 - increase sth {artır-
/arttır-} 1 '- increase sth, - cause
sth to increase'.

251:6 - grow, increase [i.] art- 1
'- increase, - go up [subj.: prices,
heat, output, risk]'; boyu uza- '-
grow in height, stature [subj.:
person]' → uza- 1; /A/ çık- '- rise, -
go up, - increase /to/ [subj.: prices,
fever]' → çık- 6; /ArAk/ çoğal- '-
increase in number [subj.: population,
students], - multiply, - grow, -
proliferate, - reproduce /by...ing/
[subj.: almost exclusively living
things: cells]' [i.]; /DAn, A/ fırla-
2 '- skyrocket, - increase or - rise
suddenly, - soar, - jump /from, to/
[subj.: prices]'; pahalan- '- become
more expensive, - increase in price
[subj.: goods]'; tırman- 2 '- climb, -
rise, - go up, - increase [subj.: prices,
inflation]'; uza- 1 '- get longer, -
grow taller, - grow [subj.: living
plant]'; /ArAk/ üre- '- increase, -
multiply, - proliferate, - reproduce
/by...ing/ [subj.: almost exclusively
living things: rabbits]'; /DAn, A/
yüksel- 2 '- increase, - rise, - go up
/from, to/ [subj.: prices, temperature,
blood pressure, value]'.

252 DECREASE

252:6 - decrease [i.] azal- '-
decrease, - become less, - get or - run
low on, - drop, - fall [number of
students, gasoline, money in bank
account, patient's temperature]';
düş- 3 '- fall, - drop, - go down, -
decrease [temperature, prices]';
eksil- 1 = azal-; in- 4 '- go down, -
decrease, - fall [prices, swelling,
fever]'; ucuzla- '- get cheaper, - go
down or - drop in price'.

252:7 - reduce düşür-
2 '- reduce, - bring down [inflation]'.

252:9 - minimize küçümse- 2 '-
underrate, - underestimate, -
minimize [threats, dangers], -
belittle'.

253 ADDITION

253:5 - add to /A/ ekle- '- add, -
append, - affix, - attach, - tack one
thing /to/ another'; /A/ ilâve et- '-
add sth /to/ sth'; /A/ kat- '- add sth
/to/ sth, - mix sth /INTO/ sth'; /A/
katıl- 1 '- be added /to/, - be mixed
/WITH/'; /I/ topla- 4 '- add one
number to another'; toplan- 5 '- be
added up [math: if one is added to
two]'.

253:11 ADV. additionally olduğu
gibi 3 'besides being; besides
having' → ol- 11; olduğu kadar.
Same. → ol- 11.

253:14 PHR. et cetera dahası var
'{[and] that's not all/there's more to
come}' → ol- 3, Additional
examples. b) 3.4. Miscellaneous
additional examples.

255 SUBTRACTION

255:9 - subtract /DAn/ çık- 9 '-
be subtracted /from/'; /DAn/ çıkar-
5 '- subtract one number /from/
another'; /DAn/ kesil- 4 '- be
deducted /from/ [taxes from salary]'.

255:10 - excise sakal tıraşı
yap- '- shave sb, - give sb a shave'
→ yap- 3; tıraş ol- 1 '- shave
oneself, - shave'. 2 '- get or - have a
shave or a haircut' → ol- 10.1.

255:12 (written text) - delete /lA/
sil- 3 '- erase [error, blackboard]
/with/, - delete [e-mail] /with/'.

256 REMAINDER

256:5 - remain art- 2 '- be left
over, - remain [food after a dinner]';
/DA, {üstünde/üzerinde}/ dur-
6 '- remain, - stay /{in/at}, on/ [a
place: train at the station]'; kal- 1
/DA/ '- remain, - stay /{at/in/on}/'. 2
/A/ '- be left over [There is no bread
left.], - remain /to/'. 3 /A/ 'for time -
remain /to/'; öksüz kal- '- have lost
one's mother', father remains alive
or, less accurately, '- have lost both
parents, - be orphaned'. Sometimes,
but not accurately, '- have lost only
one's father' → kal- 1; yetim kal- '-
have lost one's father', mother
remains alive or, less accurately, '-
have lost both parents, - be

orphaned', but not have lost only one's mother. → kal- 1.

256:6 - leave /DA/ bırak- 1 '- leave [i.e., not - take sth from where it is], - leave sth /{on/in/at}/ [Don't take the books. Leave them on the table.], - leave behind /in/ a certain condition [Leave the window open.]'.

259 EXPANSION, GROWTH

259:4 - make larger büyüt- 1 '- enlarge [pictures]'; /ArAk/ geliştir- 2 '- develop, - make larger /[by]...ing/ [body by exercising]'.

259:5 - become larger büyü- '- grow, - become larger [subj.: almost anything], - grow up [subj.: children]'; geliş- 1 '- develop, - advance, - evolve; - mature, fill out [subj.: a person's physique]'; gerin- '- stretch [oneself], - have a stretch'; şiş- 1 /DAn/ '- swell, - swell up, - get puffed up /{from/BECAUSE OF}/ [eyes from weeping, skin from a sting]'. 2 '- fill up with air [balloon, tires]'.

259:8 - fatten kilo al- '- put on weight, - gain weight' → al- 1; şişmanla- '- get fat, - put on weight'; topla- 3 = kilo al-; toplan- 4. Same.

260 CONTRACTION

260:8 - squeeze çimdikle- '- pinch with one's fingers'; sık- 1 '- squeeze [oranges to extract the juice]; - pinch, - be too tight [belt]'; sıkış- 3 '- be placed close together, squeezed; - be very crowded, cramped [people in a bus], - feel cramped, - be congested; - be or - get {backed/piled} up, - pile up [traffic]'.

260:9 - shrink çek- 11 '- shrink, - become smaller [clothing]'.

260:10 - collapse in- 4 ... '- go flat, - collapse, - deflate, - lose air [slowly: tire, rubber boat]'; lastiği patla- '- get a flat [tire] [sudden action]' → patla- 1; sön- 2 '- go flat, - collapse, - deflate, - lose air [slowly: balloon, tire, rubber boat]'.

261 DISTANCE, REMOTENESS

261:6 - extend to /A/ eriş- 2 '- reach /θ/, - extend one's reach /to/, - get /to/ [a place with one's hands: the top shelf]'; /A/ uzan- 3 '- stretch

one's hands out /to/, - reach /θ/ [a place with one's hands: the top shelf]; - reach /θ/, - get /to/, or - go as far as [a distant destination]'; /A/ uzat- 2 '- hold sth out /to/, - extend, - pass sth /to/ sb'; /A/ yetiş- 5 '- reach /θ/, - get up /to/ [a place with one's hands: the top shelf]'.

261:7 - keep one's distance /DAn/ soğu- 2 '- cool /TOWARD/, - lose one's love, desire, or enthusiasm /FOR/; - cease to care /FOR/ sb or sth'; /DAn/ uzaklaş- 2 '- become remote, distant /from/ in feeling'.

261:14 ADV. at a distance /A/ kala 3 'from, before reaching a place, at a specific distance from', always following a specific measure of distance: at a distance of ten kilometers from the school. → kal- 3.

262 FORM

262:7 - form biç- 1 '- cut up [timber], - cut out [cloth], - cut sth to size in accordance with a model or measure'.

263 FORMLESSNESS

263:3 - deform {sırayı/kuyruğu} boz- 2 '- get out of line [people waiting for tickets]' → boz- 1.

265 DISTORTION

265:8 - grimace surat as- '- put on a sour face, - look annoyed, angry, or unhappy; - sulk; - pout' → as- 1; yüzü buruş- 1 '- grimace, - scowl, - make a face [lit., ** for one's face - wrinkle]'; yüzünü buruştur- '- grimace, - scowl, - make a face [lit., ** - wrinkle one's face]'.

267 LENGTH

267:6 - lengthen /A/ devam et- 2 '[for sb] - continue /{θ/WITH}/ sth, - go on /WITH/ sth, - keep [on] doing sth'; uzat- 1 '- lengthen, - make long, - let out [dress, trousers]. 3 '- prolong, - drag out [speech].' 4 '- let grow out [hair, fingernails]'.

268 SHORTNESS

268:6 - shorten kes- 1 '- cut [bread, hair, one's hand]'; /A/ kestir- 1 '- have sth cut, - have /θ/ sb cut sth'; kısa kes- '- cut short [obj.: meeting, talk]' → kes- 4; kısalt- 1 '- shorten [cuffs, hair], - make short'. 2 '- abridge, - condense, - cut down [text]'; {lâfı/sözü} kısa kes- '- cut short one's talk' → kes-4; **özetle-** '- summarize, - sum up'; **sakal tıraşı yap-** '- shave sb, - give sb a shave' → yap- 3; **tıraş ol-** 1 '- shave oneself, - shave'. 2 '- get or - have a shave or a haircut' → ol- 10.1; **toparla-** 2 '- summarize, - put information in a nutshell'.

270   NARROWNESS, THINNESS

270:13 - slenderize **kilo ver-** '- lose weight' → ver- 1; **zayıfla-** 1. Same.

278   ANGULARITY

278:5 - angle /A/ **[direksiyonu hızla] kır-** '- turn [a steering wheel, rudder, sharply] /to/ one side, - swerve /to/ [the left, right]' → kır- 3.

279   CURVATURE

279:6 - curve /A/ **dön-** 3 '- turn /{to/TOWARD}/ [the left, right]'; /A/ **sap-** '- turn /to/, - make a turn /to/; - turn /INTO/ or - enter /θ/ a road; - swerve /to/, - veer /to/'.

283   CONVEXITY, PROTUBERANCE

283:11 - bulge **şiş-** 1 /DAn/ '- swell, - swell up, - get puffed up /{from/BECAUSE OF}/ [subj.: eyes from weeping, skin from a sting]'. 2 '- fill up with air [subj.: balloon, tires]'.

284   CONCAVITY

284:15 - excavate **kaz-** '- dig [well, ditch, hole, grave]'.

285   SHARPNESS

285:7 - sharpen **bile-** '- sharpen [knife or other blades but not pencil]'; **kalem aç-** '- sharpen a pencil' → aç- 6.

287   SMOOTHNESS

287:6 - press **ütüle-** '- iron, - press [clothes]'.

290   FURROW

290:3 - furrow /DAn/ **buruş-** '- get wrinkled [clothes /from/ sitting]'; **çiz-** 3 '- scratch, - scarify [subj.: an instrument on metal]'; **kaşı-** '- scratch [obj.: usually an itch, no harm is inflicted]'; **kaşın-** 2 '- scratch oneself [obj.: usually an itch, no harm is inflicted]'; **tırmala-** '- scratch [subj.: cat, harm is inflicted]'; **yüzü**

buruş- 2 'for a person's face - become or - get wrinkled' → buruş-.

291   FOLD

291:5 - fold /A/ **katla-** '- fold [paper] /{IN/INTO}/ [thirds, fifths]'; /A, tarafından/ **katlan-** 1 '- be folded /INTO, by [sb]/'.

291:6 - wrinkle **buruştur-** '- crumple up [papers]; - wrinkle, - make sth wrinkled [clothes]'.

292   OPENING

292:11 - open **aç-** 1 '- open sth'. 2 '- turn or - switch on [electricity, light, radio, TV], - turn on [water, the faucet]'; **açıl-** 1 /{tarafından/ CA}/ '- be opened /by/'. 2 '- come open, - open of its own accord, by itself'. 3 '- open, - open up [temporarily or permanently, subj.: organization, business]. 4 '- open, - begin an academic year, for a season - begin'; /A/ **açtır-** '- have /θ/ sb open sth, - get /θ/ sb to open sth'; **bavulunu aç-** '- unpack', or just '- open one's bags'; **hesap açtır-** '- open an account', lit., '- have an account opened [subj.: a customer at a bank]'.

292:12 - unclose /A/ **açıl-** 8 '- be unblocked, cleared, opened /to/ [roads to traffic]'.

292:13 - make an opening /A/ **yol aç-** 1 '- clear a way /to/, - open a road /to/' → aç- 1.

292:16 - gape **esne-** '- yawn'.

293   CLOSURE

293:6 - close **anahtarı içeride unut-** '- lock oneself out [lit., - forget the key inside]'; **çek-** 4 '- pull shut [obj.: curtains]'; **dışarıda kal-** '- be locked out', of a house, room as a result of leaving one's key inside. → kal- 1; **fermuar çek-** '- zip up [coat]' → çek- 4; **göz yum-** 1 '- close one's eyes'. 2 /A/ '- close one's eyes /to/ sth, - disregard /θ/, - take no notice /OF/, - turn a blind eye /to/, - overlook /θ/, - wink /AT/ a fault'; **hesap kapattır-** '- close an account [at a bank, subj.: the bank customer]'; **ilikle-** '- button, - button up'; **{kapa-/kapat-}** 1 '- close, - shut [obj.: door, window, books]'. 9 '- close up [obj.: the space between lines on a printed page]'; **kapan-** 1 '- close, - shut [i.e., - become closed:

subj.: stores, schools for the academic year]'. **3** '- close, - shut down temporarily or permanently [organization, business]'; /{tarafından/CA}/ **kapatıl-** 1 '- be closed, shut /by/'; **kapattır-** '- have /θ/ sb close sth'; **kapı çarp-** 'for a door - slam shut' → çarp- 1; **kapıda kal-** '- be locked out [of house, room] [lit., - remain at the door]' → kal- 1; **kapıyı {çarp-/vur-}** '- slam the door' → çarp- 1, kapıyı vur- 2 → vur- 2; **kilitle-** 1 '- lock [obj.: door]'; **ört-** 3 '- close, - shut sth [door, window, cover, curtains]'.

293:7 - stop, - stop up {kapa-/kapat-} **5** '- block, - obstruct [subj.: traffic or snow on roads]'; /A, DAn/ **kapan-** 4 '- be blocked, obstructed /to, {DUE TO/BECAUSE OF}/ [subj.: roads to traffic due to snow]'. This verb is not used with an agent noun preceded by /{tarafından/CA}/; /{tarafından/ CA}/ **kapatıl-** 4 '- be blocked, obstructed [roads] /by/ sb'.

293:8 - close shop {kapa-/kapat-} **7** '- close, - shut down [obj.: organization, business, school], - abolish'; **kapan-** 3 '- close, - shut down temporarily or permanently [subj.: organization, business, school: The business closed.]'; /{tarafından/CA}/ **kapatıl-** 3 '- be closed down, shut down permanently /by/ [subj.: organization, business, school]'; **tatile gir-** '- close or - shut down for vacation [subj.: an institution, school, business], - recess, - go into recess for vacation [subj.: school], - go on vacation [subj.: a person but usually only when considered as a member of an institution]'.

295 COVERING
295:19 - cover /lA/ **ört-** 1 '- cover, - cover up sth /with/ [child with blanket]; - veil'; /A, {üstüne/üzerine}/ **sür-** 4 '- apply sth /to/ sth, - spread, - rub, - smear, or - put sth /ON/ sth [frosting on cake]'.

295:20 - wrap **paket yap-** '- wrap, - wrap up, - make a package of' → yap- 3; **paketle-**. Same; /A, 1A/ **sar-** 1 '- wrap one thing /{IN/ AROUND}, with/ another'.

295:30 - overlie /DA/ **uzan-** 2 '- extend over, - stretch out /{OVER/on/ALONG}/ [subj.: trees on both sides of road], - cover'.

297 WEIGHT
297:10 - weigh /A/ **tart-** '- weigh, - weigh out sth /FOR/ sb'; **tartıl-** 1 /tarafından/ '- be weighed /by/ sb'. **2** '- weigh oneself.'

297:11 - weigh on /A/ **bas-** 2 '- press /{θ/ON}/, - push /θ/ [button, horn]'; /{I/A/üzerine}/ **tıkla-** '- click /ON/ [in computer language]'; /{I/A}/ **tuşla-** '- press a key, - enter or - punch in a PIN or credit card number, - click /ON/'.

297:13 - burden: figurative sense **sıkış-** 4 '- get in a jam, - be or - find oneself in a tight spot, under pressure, in difficulty'.

300-400

300 MEASUREMENT
300:10. - measure **değerlendir-** 1 '- evaluate, - assess, - appraise, - judge, - size up [situation]'; **ölç-** '- measure'; /A/ **tart-** '- weigh, - weigh out sth /FOR/ sb'; **tartıl-** 1 /tarafından/ '- be weighed /by/'. **2** '- weigh oneself.'

CLASS 5: LIVING THINGS

303 AGE
303:9 - mature **adam ol-** '- become morally correct, mature, responsible, - grow up, - amount to sth, - shape up', used for both men and women. → ol- 12; **büyü-** '- grow, - become larger [subj.: almost anything], - grow up [subj.: children]'; **ol-** 9.2 '- ripen, - become ripe'; **olgunluğa er-** '- reach or - attain /θ/ maturity, - mature, - grow up' → er-; **yaşına {bas-/gir-}** '- turn a certain age' → bas- 1; **yaşını {doldur-/tamamla-}** '- be or - turn a certain age, - {fill/complete} a certain year of one's life' → doldur-1.

303:10 - age, - grow old **ihtiyarla-** '- grow old, - age, - get old [subj.: persons]'; **yaşı ilerle-** '- get on in years, - grow old, - age, - get old [subj.: persons]' → ilerle- 3; **yaşlan-** = ihtiyarla-; **yüzü buruş-** 2 'for a person's face - become or - get wrinkled' → buruş-. Same as 841:9. OLDNESS: - age, - grow old.

306 LIFE

306:7 - live **hayat sur-** '- lead a [certain kind of] life' → sür- 6; **sağ ol-** '- be healthy, alive' → ol- 12; **yaşa- 1** '- live [as opposed to '- die']'.

306:8 - come to life **ayıl- 2** '- come to, - regain consciousness'; **kendine gel- 1** '- come to, - regain consciousness, - return to one's usual state' → gel- 1.

307 DEATH

307:19 - die **canından ol-** '- lose one's life, - die', mostly for an unexpected and undeserved death. → ol- 7; **hayata gözlerini {kapa-/kapat-}** '- pass away, - pass on, - die', *formal*. → {kapa-/kapat-} 1; **hayata gözlerini yum-**. Same. → yum-; **hayatını {kaybet-/yitir-}** '- lose one's life, - die', usually of unnatural causes: in an accident, through murder, etc. → {kaybet-/yitir-}; **{kaybet-/yitir-}** '- lose [sb to death: We lost our mother last year.]'; **/DAn/ öl-** '- die /{OF/AS A RESULT OF}/', for any living thing; **ömrünü tamamla-** '- complete one's life, - come to the end of one's life, - die, - pass away'; **son nefesini ver-** '- breathe one's last breath, - die' → nefes ver- → ver- 1; **/DAn/ vefat et-** '- pass away, - die /{OF/AS A RESULT OF}/, - pass on', only for persons, not other living things. Always *polite, formal,* the verb used in newspaper obituaries; **yitir-** = {kaybet-/yitir-}.

307:24 - die a natural death **/DAn/ boğul- 1** '- drown /{BECAUSE OF/DUE TO}/'; **boğularak öl-** '- drown' → boğul-1; **donarak öl-** '- freeze to death' → don- 1; **/ArAk/ öl-** '- die /by...ing/' → öl-; **yanarak öl-** '- burn to death' → öl-.

307: * 39 expressions used upon hearing of a death **Allah rahmet eylesin.** 'May God have mercy [UPON him].', said upon hearing of the death of a Muslim, today sometimes also of a non-Muslim → rahmet eyle-; **Huzur içinde rahat uyusun.** 'May {he/she} rest in peace', said upon hearing of the death

of a Muslim or non-Muslim. → uyu-1; **Mekânı cennet olsun.** 'May his [eternal] resting place be paradise.' One of several phrases said upon hearing of a death. The deceased may also be addressed as follows: **Mekânın cennet olsun.** 'May your [eternal] resting place be paradise.' → ol- 11 → olsun; An address to the deceased, Muslim or non-Muslim: **Nur içinde yat.** '[May you] rest in peace [lit, in light].' A statement about the deceased, Muslim or non-Muslim: **Nur içinde yatsın.** 'May he rest in peace.' → yat- 1; **Toprağı bol olsun.** 'May he rest in peace [lit., May his earth be abundant].', said upon hearing of the death of a non-Muslim, today sometimes also of a Muslim. → ol- 11 → olsun.

308 KILLING

308:12 - kill **baş kesil-** 'for one's head - be cut off, - be killed' → kesil-3; **canına kıy- 1** '- kill or - murder without mercy' → kıy- 2; **kes- 2** '- kill, - butcher'; **kestir- 3** '- have killed'; **kıy- 2** '- kill, - murder'; **kurban kes-** '- kill an animal as a sacrifice' → kes- 2; **kurban kestir-** '- have an animal killed as a sacrifice, - let an animal be killed as a sacrifice' → kestir- 3; **öldür-** '- kill'; **/tarafından, ArAk/ öldürül-** '- be killed /by [sb], by...ing/'.

308:13 non-formal terms: - waste **gebert-** '- bump off, - wipe out, - rub out, - do in, - nuke, - zap'. *Contemptuous* for '- kill'.

308:15 - murder **cinayet işle-** '- commit murder, homicide, - murder' → işle- 2.

308:17 - strike dead **/I/ vur- 2** '- shoot; - shoot dead'.

308:18 - strangle [i.] **/DAn/ boğul- 1** '- drown /{BECAUSE OF/DUE TO}/'. **2** '- be suffocated, - suffocate, - smother, - be stifled, - be strangled, - feel faint /{from/ BECAUSE OF/DUE TO}/'.

308:21 - commit suicide **canına kıy- 2** '- commit suicide, - kill oneself' → kıy- 2; **intihar et-**. Same but *more formal, legal*; **kendini öldür-** '- kill oneself, - commit suicide'.

309 INTERMENT

309:19 - inter *formal:* /A, {tarafından/CA}/ **defnedil-** '- be buried, laid to rest /IN, by/, - be interred /IN, by/ [subj.: dead bodies only]'; /A/ **göm-** '- bury /IN/ [obj.: dead bodies and other objects]; - inter /θ/ [obj.: usually for dead bodies only]'; /A, {tarafından/CA}/ **gömül-** '- be buried /IN, by/ [subj.: dead bodies and other objects]; - be interred, laid to rest /IN, by/ [subj.: usually for dead bodies only]'; /DA/ **toprağa veril-** = defnedil- → veril-.

310 PLANTS

310:32 - flower | **aç-** 9 '- open [subj.: flower], - blossom, - bloom, - flower'.

CLASS 6: NATURAL PHENOMENA

316 RAIN

316:9 - rain | **bardaktan boşanırcasına yağmur yağ-** '- pour down, - rain hard, - rain cats and dogs' → yağ-; **çisele-** '- drizzle, - sprinkle, - rain lightly'; **yağmur yağ-** '- rain' → yağ-.

317 AIR, WEATHER

317:10 - air | **hava al-** 2 '- absorb air, - take in air, - get air, - air out [subj.: room]' → al- 1; **havalan-** 1 '- be aired out [room, clothes], - be ventilated [room]'; **havalandır-** '- air out [obj.: clothes, room]'; /A/ **tutul-** 6 '- be caught /IN/ certain unfavorable weather conditions [rain, snow]'. Same as the following; {a: yağmur.A/b: kar.A/c: dolu.yA/ d: tipi.yE} **yakalan-** 4 '- be caught {a: IN the rain/b: IN the snow/c: IN the hail/d: IN the {snowstorm/blizzard}}'.

318 WIND

318:20 - blow | **es-** '- blow [The wind is blowing.], - be windy'; **uçur-** '- make fly, - blow about, away'.

318:21. * 1 - breathe | **hapşır-** '- sneeze'; **hava al-** '- breathe fresh air, - get a breath of fresh air' → al- 1; **içine çek-** '- inhale' → çek- 1; **nefes al-** '- breathe, - take a breath; - inhale' → al- 1; **nefes çek-** '- take a wiff, drag, puff [of tobacco]' → çek- 1; /DAn/ **nefes nefese kal-** '- be or - get out of breath, - pant, - huff and puff /from/' → kal- 1; **nefes**

ver- '- breathe out, - exhale, - let out a breath' → ver- 1; **öksür-** '- cough'; **son nefesini ver-** '- breathe one's last breath, - die' → nefes ver- → ver- 1; **üfle-** 1 '- blow [He blew smoke into the room.]'. 2 '- blow out [candle]'.

319 CLOUD

319:6 - cloud | **hava kapan-** '- cloud over, - become cloudy, overcast [subj.: sky]' → kapan- 4.

320 BUBBLE

320:4 - bubble | **kayna-** '- boil [The water is boiling.], - come to a boil'; **kaynat-** '- boil sth, - cause sth to boil [He boiled the water.]'.

CLASS 7: BEHAVIOR AND THE WILL

321 BEHAVIOR

321:4 - behave /{mAklA/ArAk}/ **hareket et-** 4 '- act, - behave, - do /BY...ing [or TO]/ [He did well {by speaking out/to speak out}]'.

321:6 - treat | /A, A karşı/ **davran-** '- behave /TOWARD, toward/, - deal /WITH/, - treat /θ/'.

322 MISBEHAVIOR

322:4 - misbehave /mAklA/ **ayıp et-** '- behave shamefully /BY...ing/'; **yaramazlık {yap-/et-}** '- be naughty, - misbehave' → yap- 3.

323 WILL

323:5 ADV. at will | **Arzunuza kalmış.** 'It's up to you., You decide., As you wish.' → kal- 1.

324 WILLINGNESS

324:3 - be willing | /A/ **yanaş-** 3 '- be willing or inclined /to/, - be willing to agree /to/; - go along /WITH/ a plan'.

324: * 11 PHR. expressions of willingness | **Ben varım.** '{Count me in./I'm with you.}', **Biz varız.** '{Count us in./We're with you.}' → {var/yok} ol- a) 3 → ol- 12. Same as 771: * 8. INCLUSION: PHR. count me in.

325 UNWILLINGNESS

325:4 - demure | /{A/DAn}/ **çekin-** '- hesitate /to/, - feel, or - be hesitant, reluctant, embarrassed /to/ do sth, not - dare /to/ do sth, *less frequently* - fear'.

325: * 10 PHR. expressions of unwillingness **Ben yokum.** '{Count me out./I want no part of it.}', **Biz yokuz.** '{Count us out./We want no part of it.}' → {var/yok} ol- a) 3 → ol- 12. Same as 772: * 11. EXCLUSION: PHR. count me out.

326 OBEDIENCE
326:2 - obey /I/ 1 **dinle-** 2 '- heed, - obey, - listen /to/'; 2 **dinlen-** 1 '- be heeded, - be heard and obeyed'; **{lâf/söz} dinle-** '- obey, - heed what one is told; - act on sb's advice' → 1 dinle- 2; **söz tut-** '- take, - follow, - heed, or - listen to advice' → tut- 5; **sözünü tut-** 2 '- take, - follow, - heed, or - listen to the advice of sb, - take sb's advice' → tut- 5; /A/ **uy-** 5 '- comply /WITH/, - conform /to/, - follow or - act in accordance /WITH/ rules, regulations'. 6 '- obey /θ/, - heed /θ/, - listen /to/, - act in accordance with the wishes of'.

327 DISOBEDIENCE
327:6 - disobey **çiğne-** 3 '- violate laws, rules, principles'; **sözünden çık-** '- disobey, not - do what sb says' → çık- 1. This category may also be covered by the negative of the verbs under 326:2. OBEDIENCE: - obey.

327:7 - revolt /A karşı/ **ayaklan-** '- rebel, - revolt, - rise up /against/, - riot'; /A/ **başkaldır-** '- rebel, - revolt, - rise up /AGAINST/, - riot'.

328 ACTION
328:3 NOUN act **oldubitti** ' a done deal, fait accompli'. An older and today more learned equivalent: **emrivaki.** → bit- 1, ol- 11.

328:6 - do **et-** 1 '- do, - perform.' Et- forms phrasal verbs with Arabic, Persian, and Turkish nouns and is not frequently used alone to express '- do' unless such a noun is understood. In this dictionary, all phrasal verbs with et- appear as separate entries alphabetized by the first letter of the phrasal verb [i.e., teşekkür et- appears under t]. They are also listed alphabetically, but without definitions or examples, under the entry et-. '- Do' is usually expressed with yap- 2; **eyle-** = et-. In this dictionary, it occurs only with rahmet, → rahmet eyle-; **kıl-.** Same, but used with a much more limited number of usually Arabic or Persian nouns. In this dictionary it occurs only with **namaz,** → namaz kıl-; **kıy-** 3 '- perform, - carry out', with a very limited set of nouns. In this dictionary it occurs only with **nikâh,** → nikâh kıy-; **yap-** 2 '- do'; /A/ **yaptır-** 2 '- have /θ/ sb do sth'.

328:8 - practice **alıştırma yap-** '- do exercises, drills', on the blackboard, in a book or workbook, not usually orally. → yap- 3; **çalış-** 1 '- practice, - work on [piano, tennis]'; **egzersiz yap-** 1 '- work out, - do exercises, calisthenics, physical training'. 2 '- do exercises as physical therapy'. 3 '- do drills, exercises on the blackboard or in a workbook' → yap- 3; **idman yap-** '- exercise, - do gymnastics, physical training, - train [oneself physically]' → yap- 3; **jimnastik yap-** '- do gymnastics' → yap- 3; /ArAk/ **pratik yap-** '- do usually oral, conversational practice, - practice a foreign language orally /by...ing/' → yap- 3.

328:9 - perform /A/ **sun-** 2 '- perform, - play, or - sing sth /FOR/ sb [lit., - present]'. See also 708:39a. MUSIC: - play sth.

329 INACTION
329:2 - do nothing **dur-** 8 '- remain inactive in the face of a situation that requires action, - do nothing, - stand there without doing anything'.

329:3 - refrain /DAn/ **kaçın-** '- avoid /θ/ sb or sth or /θ/ doing sth; - refrain /from/ sth or /from/ doing sth'; /DAn/ **sakın-** 1 '- avoid /θ/, - keep [oneself] away /from/, or - steer clear /OF/ sb or sth'. Same as 668:7. TEMPERANCE: - abstain.

330 ACTIVITY
330:10 - be busy **meşgul çık-** 'for the phone - be busy' → çık- 7; /lA/ **meşgul ol-** 1 '- be busy or occupied /with/, - deal /with/' → ol- 12.

330:16 - make the most of one's time /ArAk/ {vakit/zaman} değerlendir- '- make good use of time, - make the most of one's time /[by]...ing/' → değerlendir- 2.

331 INACTIVITY

331:12 - idle /A/ üşen- '- be too lazy, apathetic, or indifferent to do sth, not - bother or - take the trouble to do sth'. Also under 102:4. INDIFFERENCE: not - care.

331:13 - waste time /mAklA, mAktAn/ {vakit/zaman} kaybet-[or yitir-] '- lose or - waste time /ing, {from/because of}...ing/'; /ArAk/ {vakit/zaman} öldür- '- waste or - kill time /[by]...ing/'. Also under 391:8. USELESSNESS: - be useless.

331:15 - take it easy kolayına git- 2 '- take the easy way out' → git- 1b; kolayına kaç-. Same. → kaç- 1.

332 ASSENT

332:8 - assent kabul et- 3 '- admit, - accept [a fact as true], - acknowledge'.

332:9 - concur {a: düşünceye/b: fikre/c: görüşe} katıl- '- agree /WITH/, - share /θ/, or - concur /IN/ {a: thoughts/b: opinions/c: views}' → katıl- 3; /IA/ fikir paylaş- '- agree, - share opinions, thoughts /with/'; /{a: IA/b: konusunda/c: hakkında/d: ile ilgili}/ {fikir/görüş} savun- 2 '- agree, - share {opinions/thoughts} /{a: with/b: on the subject of/c: about/d: concerning}/' → savun-; /A/ katıl- 3 '- share /θ/ [sb's opinions, views], - agree, - concur /WITH/ sb [I agree with you.]'.

332:10 - come to an agreement /a: 1A, b: DA, c: üzerinde, d: konusunda, e: için/ anlaş- 2 '- agree, - come to an agreement, - reach an understanding /a: with, b: {on/upon}, c: {on/upon}, d: on the subject of, e: {to/in order to}/'; /IA/ kontrat yap- '- make a contract, - sign a contract or agreement /with/' → yap- 3.

332:11 - acknowledge /A, konusunda/ hak ver- '- acknowledge or - think /θ/ sb or sb's

action to be right, correct /on the {issue/matter} of/' → ver- 1; /olarak/ tanı- 6 '- recognize a government, - recognize /AS/ [a state]'.

332:18 INTERJ. yes Oldu. 'OK!, All right!, Fine., Agreed.', informal, not used to a superior. → ol- 11; Olur. 'OK., All right., Fine., It's possible., Yes.', always appropriate. → ol- 4.

332:20 PHR. so be it Olsun 1 'That's OK., I don't care., I don't mind., So be it!, All right., Never mind.' → ol- 1, 11.

333 DISSENT

333:4 - dissent Rica ederim. 1b 'Please', in expressing an objection, as in '[Oh] Please, you're mistaken. I said no such thing.' → rica et-.

333:5 - object fikrine itiraz et- '- object to sb's idea'; gösteri yap- '- hold a {demonstration/protest}, - demonstrate against'; /A/ itiraz et- '- object /to/, - raise an objection /{to/AGAINST}/'; /A/ karşı çık- '- oppose /θ/, - come out /AGAINST/, - object /to/, - say no /to/' → çık- 3; /I/ protesto et- '- protest sth or against sth'; {sakıncası/mahzuru} ol- 'for there - be an objection to, - mind, - object to' → ol- 12; şikâyet et- a) /DAn, A/ '- complain /{OF/ABOUT}, to [yourself or to a friend, but usually not to a responsible authority]/'. b) /a: I, b: A, c: DIğI için/ '- complain /a: {OF/ABOUT} [sth], b: to [an authority], c: because/'; /DAn, A/ yakın- = şikâyet et- a).

334 AFFIRMATION

334:5 - affirm belirt- '- state, - make clear'; ileri sür- 2 '- claim, - maintain'; kaydet- 4 '- state, - announce, - declare, - note', formal, official: in speech and in writing.

334: * 11 INTERJ. I swear! Bak 'Now, Look' [That's a great idea.], an emphatic, a word expressing emphasis. → bak- 1; İnanın [ki] 'Believe me!' → inan- 1; [Doğru söylüyorum,] yemin ederim. '[I'm telling the truth,] I swear.' → yemin et-.

335 NEGATION, DENIAL
335:4 - deny **inkâr et-** '- deny, - claim that sth is not true'; **reddet-** 2. Same; **yalanla-** '- deny, - contradict, - refute, - declare or - show to be false or wrong'.

336 IMITATION
336:5 - imitate /A/ **özen-** 3 '- try to imitate /θ/ sb'; **taklit et-** '- imitate, - copy, - ape'; **yansıt** 2 '- reflect, - show, - reveal [article reflects author's earlier views]'.

336:7 - emulate /A/ **uy-** 7 '- follow /θ/, - follow the example of, - act in accord /WITH/, - emulate /θ/, - imitate the actions of'.

338 COMPENSATION
338:8 ADV., CONJ. notwithstanding **-DIğI halde** in **olduğu halde** 'although, inspite of being, despite being' → ol- 11; **olmakla {beraber/birlikte}** 'although, inspite of being, despite being' → ol- 11; **-mAsınA {rağmen/karşın}** in **olmasına {rağmen/karşın}** 'although {he/it} {is/was}, inspite of the fact that {he/it} {is/was}' → ol- 11; **olsun** 2 'that may be {so/true}, but; OK, but; yes, but; be that as it may' → ol- 11.

339 CAREFULNESS
339:6 - care /A/ **aldır-** 2 '- mind, - care /ABOUT/, - pay attention /to/', usually in the negative: **aldırMA-** '- ignore, NOT - pay attention /to/, NOT - care /ABOUT/'. See 340:6. NEGLECT: - neglect.

339:7 - be careful /A/ **dikkat et-** 1 '- pay attention /to/, - see /to/; - be careful, - watch out /FOR/'; **dikkatli ol-** '- be careful' → ol- 12.

339:8 - be vigilant /DAn/ **sakın-** 2 '- guard /AGAINST/; - watch out /FOR/ sth dangerous'.

339:9 - look after /A/ **bak-** 3 '- look /AFTER/, - take care /OF/, - attend /to/'; /lA/ **ilgilen-** '- show concern /FOR/, - be concerned /with/; - attend /TO/, - look /AFTER/'; **kapıya bak-** '- get or - answer /θ/ the door' → bak- 3; **Kendine iyi bak!** 'Take good care of yourself!' a common farewell to a person departing for an extended period. →

bak- 3; **telefona bak-** '- get or - answer /θ/ the phone' → bak- 3.

340 NEGLECT
340:6 - neglect **aldırış etME-** 'NOT - mind, NOT - pay attention to, - disregard, - ignore'; **aldırMA-** '- ignore, NOT - pay attention /to/, NOT - care /ABOUT/' → aldır- 2; **gözden kaç-** '- be overlooked, not - be noticed, - overlook, - escape one's eye or notice' → kaç- 1; **ihmal et-** '- neglect, - let slide, - slight, not - pay attention to, - fail to do sth, - omit'.

340:7 - leave undone **atla-** 2 '- omit, - skip'.

341 INTERPRETATION
341:9 - interpret **karşılığını ver-** '- give the equivalent of a word, - define' → ver- 1; **tanımla-** '- define [a word]'; **teşhis koy-** '- diagnose, - make a diagnosis, - come up with a diagnosis [of a disease]' → koy- 1; **yorumla-** 1 '- interpret; - explain [an event, situation]'. 2 '- interpret, - perform [a piece of music]'.

341:11 - comment upon {not/dipnot} düş- '- add a footnote, - footnote' → düş- 6.

341:12 - translate /DAn, A/ **aktar-** 2 '- translate /from, INTO/', in written form or orally. Less common than the two following.; /DAn, A/ **çevir-** 6. Same; /DAn, A/ **tercüme et-**. Same.

342 MISINTERPRETATION
342:2 - misinterpret **yanlış anla-** '- misunderstand' → anla-; **yanlış anlaşıl-** '- be misunderstood' → anlaşıl-.

343 COMMUNICATION
343:6 - communicate, - be in touch /lA/ **mektuplaş-** '- write letters to one another, - correspond /with/, - be in correspondence /with/ by letter'; /lA/ **telefonlaş-** '- talk /with/ {on/over} the phone, - talk with {by/on the} phone'.

343:8 - communicate with, - get in touch with /lA/ **bağlantı kur-** '- make contact /with/, - contact /θ/, - get in touch /with/, - establish ties, connections /with/, - connect, - get through /to/ [on the phone]' → kur- 1.

/1A/ <u>temas kur-</u> '- get in contact /with/, - contact /θ/, - establish contact /with/' → kur- 1; /A/ <u>ulaş-</u> 2 '- reach /θ/, - contact /θ/, - get in touch /WITH/'; /DAn/ <u>ulaşıl-</u> '- be reached, contacted /AT/ [a phone number]'.

343:8. * 1 conversation initiators
<u>Affedersiniz.</u> 'Excuse me.' → affet- 2; Pardon. A common non-verb alternative to Affedersiniz.; <u>Rahatsız etmiyorum ya?</u> 'I {hope/trust} I'm not disturbing you [, am I, but...]' → rahatsız et-.

344 UNCOMMUNICATIVE-NESS
344:6 - keep to oneself
<u>{çenesini/dilini} tut-</u> '- hold one's tongue [lit., {** one's jaw or chin/one's tongue}], - keep quiet' → tut- 4.

345 SECRECY
345:20 ADV. confidentially
<u>Aramızda kalsın.</u> 'Just between us [lit., Let it remain between us].', when conveying a confidence. → kal- 1.

346 CONCEALMENT
346:6 - conceal <u>gizle-</u> 1 /A/ '- hide, - conceal sth /IN/ [i.e., - PUT sth somewhere so it will not be seen]', /DAn/ '- keep sth secret /from/'; /DAn, tarafından/ <u>gizlen-</u> 2 '- be hidden /from, by/; - be kept secret /from, by/'; <u>{kapa-/kapat-}</u> 3 '- cover up [hole, ditch]'; /{tarafından/CA}, 1A/ <u>kapatıl-</u> 6 '- be covered [up] /by [sb], with [sth]/'; <u>ört-</u> 2 '- conceaal, - hide, - cover up [the truth, faults]'; <u>sakla-</u> 1 = gizle- 1; <u>saklan-</u> 2 = gizlen- 2.

346:8 - hide oneself /DAn, A/ <u>gizlen-</u> 1 '- hide, - conceal oneself /from, IN/'; /DAn, A/ <u>saklan-</u> 1. Same.

346:10 - ambush <u>yolunu kes-</u> '- block one's way, - waylay, - ambush', often to steal from. → kes- 6.

347 COMMUNICATIONS
347:18 - telephone <u>ayrılMA-</u> 'NOT - hang up [on the phone, as in 'Don't hang up.']' → ayrıl- 3; /1A/ <u>bağlantı kur-</u> '- make contact /with/, - contact /θ/, - get in touch

/with/, - establish ties, connections /with/, - connect, - get through /to/ [on the phone]' → kur- 1; <u>bekle-</u> 1 '- wait, - hold the line [on the phone]'; /I/ <u>çevir-</u> 7 '- dial [a phone number]'; /1A/ <u>görüş-</u> 2 '- make or - place a phone call /TO/ [a place]'; <u>hat düş-</u> 'for a phone line - be or - become available or free, - get through [on the phone], - get a line' → düş- 1; <u>ödemeli ara-</u> '- call collect, - make a collect [phone] call' → ara- 2; <u>ödemeli görüş-</u> '- call collect [by phone], - make a collect call' → görüş- 2; /A, DAn/ <u>telefon {et-/aç-}</u> '- phone /θ [sb], from/, - call, - call up, - make a [phone] call /to, from/'; <u>telefon kapan-</u> 'for the phone - be hung up' → kapan- 1; /A/ <u>telefon var</u> 'for there - be a phone call /FOR/' → ol- 3, Additional examples. b) 3.5. Issues of means to a place; <u>telefona {bak-/cevap ver-}</u> '- get, - pick up, or - answer θ the phone' → bak- 3, ver- 1; /I/ <u>telefondan ara-</u> '- call on the phone' → ara- 2; /I/ <u>[telefonla] ara-</u> '- call up [by phone], - ring up sb' → ara- 2; <u>[telefonla] tekrar ara-</u> '- call back, - call again' → ara- 2; /1A/ <u>telefonlaş-</u> '- talk /with/ {on/over} the phone, - talk /with/ {by/on the} phone'; <u>telefonu aç-</u> = telefona {bak-/cevap ver-}; <u>telefon.U kapat-</u> '- hang up' → kapat-; <u>telefonu yüzüne kapat-</u> '- hang up /ON/ sb' → kapat-.

347:19 - telegraph /A/ <u>faks {çek-/gönder-}</u> '- send a fax /to/' → çek- 9, gönder-; /A/ <u>faksla-</u> '- fax sth /to/'; /A/ <u>telgraf çek-</u> '- send a {telegram/wire} /to/, - wire /θ/' → çek- 9.

348 MANIFESTATION
348:5 - manifest /I/ <u>gezdir-</u> '- show or - take sb around [a place]'; /A/ <u>göster-</u> 1 '- show, - demonstrate /to/'; <u>işaret et-</u> 1 /I/ '- point out, - indicate [sb or sth, not a fact, by means of a gesture]'. 2 /A/ '- point out /θ/, - indicate /θ/, - call attention /to/, - note /θ/ [a fact]'; /I/ <u>işaretle-</u> '- mark [places in a book]'; /I/ <u>saat *hour* göster-</u> 'for a timepiece, clock or watch, - show, say the time' → göster- 1; /A/ <u>yol göster-</u> 1 '- show /θ/ sb how to get to a place, - point out the way /to/ sb' → göster- 1.

670

348:14 ADV. manifestly
anlaşılan 'it is clear that [lit., what is clear, understood], evidently'.

349 REPRESENTATION, DESCRIPTION
349:9 - describe /I/ anlat- 3 '- tell /ABOUT/, - describe /θ/'; /A, {üstüne/üzerine}/ çiz- 1 '- draw /{ON/IN}, on/ [a surface]'; /olarak/ nitelendir- '- characterize, - describe /AS/'; resim çiz- '- draw a picture, pictures' → çiz- 1; /A/ tarif et- '- describe sb or sth /to/'.

349:11 - image /A/ yansıt- 1 '- reflect [light] /to/'.

351 DISCLOSURE
351:4 - disclose açıkla- 2 '- disclose, - make public, - reveal /to/ sb'; ağzından [lâf] kaçır- '- let slip, pop out, - blurt out, - let a secret out unintentionally' → kaçır- 2; {ortaya/meydana} çıkar- '- bring to light; - expose to view, - disclose, - reveal' → çıkar- 7.

351:7 - confess {doğru/doğruyu/gerçeği/hakikati} söyle- '- tell {the truth}' → söyle- 1; /A/ itiraf et- '- confess, - admit sth /to/ sb, - acknowledge /θ/'. For various expressions of confession, → 644:22. PROBITY: ADV. truthfully.

351:8 - be revealed {ortaya/meydana} çık- '- appear, - turn up, - come out, - turn out, - be revealed [the truth], - come forward [subj.: the guilty person]' → çık- 3.

352 PUBLICATION
352:7 poster: * specific signs arranged alphabetically by the first word in the phrase:
A: Askerî bölge. Geçmek yasaktır. 'Military zone. No trespassing.' → geç- 1.

B: Bu yolda sollamak yasaktır. 'No passing [lit., On this street it is forbidden to pass on the left].' → solla-; Burası özel oto parktır. Yabancı araçlar çektirilecektir. 'This is a private parking area. Unauthorized vehicles will be towed away.' → çektiril-; Buraya {işemek/su dökmek} yasaktır. 'It is forbidden {to urinate} here.' → işe-; Buraya park etmek

yasaktır. '{No parking./It is forbidden to park here.}' → park et-.

Ç: Çevreyi kirletmeyiniz. 'Keep the area clean [lit., Don't dirty the area round about].'; Çıkılır. [or Çıkış] 'Exit' → çıkıl-; Çıkmaz yol. '{Dead end./No through road.}' → çık- 3; Çiçekleri koparmayınız. 'Don't pick the flowers.' → kopar- 1; Çimenlere basmayınız. 'Don't step on the grass.' → bas- 1; Çöpleri çöp tenekesine dökünüz. 'Throw the trash into the trash can.' → dök- 3.

D: Denize girmek yasaktır. '{Swimming [in the sea] is forbidden!/No swimming!}' → gir-; Düğmeye basınız. 'Press θ the button.' → bas- 2.

E: Emniyet kemerlerinizi bağlayınız. 'Fasten your seat belts.' → bağla- 1.

G: Gemi iskeleye iyice yanaşmadan binmeye kalkışma! 'Don't attempt to board the ship before it has drawn all the way up to the pier!' → kalkış-; Girilir. [or Giriş] 'Entrance' → giril-; Girmek yasaktır. '{No trespassing./No admittance.}' → gir-; Gürültü yapmayınız. 'Quiet please.' → gürültü {et-/yap-}.

İ: İş başındaki memurları meşgul etmeyin. 'Don't disturb those who are working [lit., ...the employees (who are) at work].' → meşgul et-; İtiniz. 'Push.', sign on door. → it-; İtmeyin. [or the causative form İttirmeyin]. 'Don't push!' → it-; İzinsiz ilân yapıştırmak yasaktır. 'Post no bills [lit., To post bills without permission is forbidden].' → yapıştır-.

K: Kapıya dayanmak yasak ve tehlikelidir. 'To lean {ON/ AGAINST} the door is forbidden and dangerous.', on the inside of a bus door. → dayan- 1; Kemerlerinizi bağlayınız. 'Fasten your seat belts.' → bağla- 1.

L: Lütfen çiçeklere el sürmeyiniz. 'Please don't touch the flowers.' → sür- 5; Lütfen emniyet kemerlerinizi takınız ve

sigaralarınızı söndürünüz.
'Please fasten [lit., put on] your seat
belts and put out your cigarettes.' →
söndür- 1; **Lütfen kapıya
dayanmayın, otomatik kapı
çarpar.** 'Please don't lean ON the
door. The automatic door will slam
shut.' On the inside of a bus door. →
dayan- 1; **Lütfen sigaralarınızı
söndürünüz ve emniyet
kemerlerinizi takınız.** 'Please put
out your cigarettes and fasten [lit., put
on] your seat belts [lit., security
belts].' → tak-; **Lütfen tuvaleti
fazla meşgul etmeyin.** 'Please
don't occupy the restroom too long.'
→ meşgul et-; **Lütfen yerlere
tükürmeyiniz.** 'Please don't spit
ON the ground.' → tükür-.

M: **Müzedeki eserlere el
sürmeyiniz.** 'Please don't touch θ
the items in the museum.' → sür- 5.

O: **Onsekiz yaşından küçükler
giremez!** 'No one under 18 [is]
admitted! [lit., Those younger than 18
cannot enter].' → gir-; **Ormanları
koruyalım.** 'Let's protect the
forests.' → koru-; **Otobüslere ön
kapıdan binilir, arka kapıdan
inilir.** 'Buses are boarded at the
front [lit., from the front door] and
exited at the rear [lit., from the rear
door].' → binil-, → inil-.

R: **Rahatsız etmeyiniz.** 'Do not
disturb.' → rahatsız et-.

S: **Sigara içilir.** 'Smoking area
[lit., ** Cigarettes are smoked.]' →
içil- 2; **Sigara içilmez.** 'No
smoking [lit., ** Cigarettes are not to
be smoked]'. → içil- 2; **Sigara
içmek yasak.** 'No smoking [lit., To
smoke is forbidden].' → iç- 2;
Sokaklara çöp dökmeyiniz.
'Don't {litter θ/throw trash ON} the
streets.' → dök- 3.

Ş: **{Şehir içinde/Bu caddede}
sürat yapmak yasaktır.** 'It is
forbidden to speed {within the city/on
this street}.' → sürat yap- → yap- 3.

T: **Taklitlerinden sakınınız.**
'Avoid θ imitations [lit., imitations of
it]', reference to a product. → sakın-
1; **Taşıt giremez.** 'No entry [lit.,
Vehicles cannot enter].' → gir-.

Y: [**Burası özel oto parktır.**]
Yabancı araçlar çektirilecektir.
'[This is a private parking area.]
Unauthorized vehicles will be towed
away.' → çektiril-; **Yaklaşmayın.
Köpek var, saldırır.** 'Beware of
the dog! [lit., Don't approach. There
is a dog. It will attack.]' → saldır- 1,
→ yaklaş-; **Yangın ve deprem
halinde asansörü
kullanmayınız.** 'In case of fire or
earthquake don't use the elevator.' →
kullan-; **Yasak bölge. Girilmez.**
'Restricted zone. No admittance.' →
giril-; **Yedi yaşından küçükler
binemez.** 'Children under the age of
7 are not allowed to ride! [lit., cannot
{ride/get on}].' → bin- 2; **Yerlere
tükürmeyiniz.** 'Don't spit ON the
ground.' → tükür-; **Yol ver.** Traffic
sign: '{Yield./Give way.}' → ver- 1;
**Yolculuk sırasında şoförü {a:
meşgul/b: rahatsız} etmeyin.**
'Don't {a: {distract/disturb}/b:
disturb} the driver [during the trip].'
A sign in a bus. → meşgul et-;
Yüksek sesle konuşmayınız.
'No loud talking [lit., Don't speak in
a loud voice].' → konuş-; **Yüzmek
yasaktır.** 'No swimming [lit.,
Swimming prohibited].' → yüz- 1.

352:12 - announce /A/ **açıkla-** 2
'- disclose, - make public, - reveal
/to/'; **beyan et-** '- declare, -
announce [at customs, elsewhere]';
/A/ **duyur-** '- announce, - declare
/to/', in most circumstances but not '-
declare' at customs'.

352:14 - issue **çıkar-** 7 '- put out,
- bring out, - issue a publication'.

354 FALSENESS
354:18 - fabricate /I/ **uydur-** 2 '-
make up, - invent, - dream up, -
concoct, - think up [story, lie]'.

354:19 - lie **yalan söyle-** '- lie, -
tell lies' → söyle- 1. See also 645:11.
IMPROBITY: - be dishonest.

354:22 - pose as **kendisini
başkası olarak tanıt-** '- pass
oneself off as sb else' → tanıt- 1.

355 EXAGGERATION
355:3 - exaggerate **abart-** '-
exaggerate, - overstate, - make too
much of'; **büyüt-** 2. Same.

356 DECEPTION

356:14 - deceive / A, not with tarafından/ {aldan-/kan-} '- be deceived, fooled, taken in /BY/ sb, sth'; aldat- 1 '- cheat, - deceive'; /{tarafından/CA}, not with A/ aldatıl- '- be cheated, deceived /by/'. The noun preceding {tarafından/CA} designates a person or agency, not a thing.; dolandır- '- cheat, - swindle, - rip off, - defraud'; /A/ kan- = {aldan-/kan-}; kandır- 1 '- deceive, - fool, - take in, - mislead'.

356:15 - fool /{lA/A}/ oyun oyna- 2 '- play a trick /ON/' → oyna- 1.

356:18 - cheat / A, not with tarafından/ {aldan-/kan-} '- be deceived, fooled, taken in /BY/ sb, sth'; aldat- 1 '- cheat, - deceive'. 2 /I/ '- be unfaithful /TO/, - cheat /ON/'; /{tarafından/CA}, not with A/ aldatıl- '- be cheated, deceived /by/'. The noun preceding {tarafından/CA} designates a person or agency, not a thing.; dolandır- '- cheat, - swindle, - rip off, - defraud'; /A/ kan- = {aldan-/kan-}; kandır- 1 '- deceive, - fool, - take in, - mislead'; kopya çek- 1 '- copy illegitimately [i.e., - cheat, crib]'. 2 '- cheat by exchanging information orally [e.g., during an exam]' → çek- 8.

356:19 nonformal terms - gyp /A/ kazık at- '- gyp, - rip off, - swindle, - cheat; - sell sb sth at an exorbitant, outrageous price', very common slang → at- 1; /I/ kazıkla-. Same.

359 RESOLUTION

359:7 - resolve /için/ karar al- '- make a decision /TO/, - decide /{TO/ON}/, - resolve /TO/ [subj.: usually a group, organization, or society acting in an official capacity]' → al- 1; /A/ karar ver- '- decide /to/, - make up one's mind /to/, - make a decision /to/, - resolve /to/ [subj.: usually one or more individuals but not a group, organization or society acting in an official capacity]' → ver- 1; /I/ kararlaştır- '- decide /to/, - come to a decision [subj.: at least two persons reaching a decision together]'; /A/ niyet et- '- intend, - mean, - aim, - plan, or - make up one's mind /to/ do sth; - make a decision to do sth and

then to state one's intention to oneself, silently or out loud, to carry out the act'. The latter meaning applies in reference to certain acts required by the religion of Islam for which such a statement of intention is required before the act is carried out and for that act to be valid. See also 380:4. INTENTION: - intend s to.

361 OBSTINACY

361:7 - balk diren- 1 /DA/ '- insist /{on/UPON}/, - refuse to [with a preceding negative verb]'. 2 / A karşı '- resist, - hold out /against/'; /DA/ diret- '- insist /{ON/UPON}/ [having one's own way]'; fikrinde inat et- '- persist /IN/ or - insist /ON/ one's view, opinion' → inat et- 2; inat et- 1 '- be obstinate, stubborn'. 2 /DA/ '- persist /IN/, - insist /ON/'; /a: DA, b: için, c: diye/ ısrar et- '- insist /a: {on/UPON}, b: {ON/UPON}, c: saying/, - persist /a: in/'.

362 IRRESOLUTION

362:7 - hesitate /{A/DAn}/ çekin- '- hesitate /to/, - feel, or - be hesitant, reluctant, embarrassed /to/ do sth, not - dare /to/ do sth, less frequently - fear'; /{DA/A}/ tereddüt et- '- hesitate /to/; - waver, - falter'.

362:13 ADV. * filler phrases and stallers The most common are efendim and şey, neither involving verbs. Others formed with verbs are: Efendime söyleyeyim... 'Let's see, let me see, um, ah, er...' → söyle- 1; Nasıl anlatayım? '{How shall I put it?/How can [lit., shall] I explain it?}' → anlat- 1; Nasıl anlatsam? Same. → anlat- 1; Ne bileyim ben? 2 'Well, let's see [lit., ** How should I know?]' → bil- 1.

363 CHANGING OF MIND

363:6 - change one's mind fikrinden vazgeç- '- change one's mind, - give up /θ/ one's idea'; fikrini değiştir- '- change one's mind' → değiştir- 1; kararından vazgeç- '- change one's mind, - go back on one's decision'; kararını geri al- '- withdraw or - rescind one's decision' → geri al- 1 → al- 1.

364 CAPRICE

364:4 - blow hot and cold /A/
özen- 4 '- have a passing fancy to
do sth', usually sth one knows little
about.

366 LEAP
366:5 - leap /a: DAn, b: A, c:
DAn, d: üzerinden/ **atla-** 1 '-
jump, - leap /a: from, b: to, c, d:
over/'; /Dan, A/ **fırla-** 1 '- jump
up, - leap up /from, to/, - rush or -
dart out, - fly out [subj.: person,
object from hand: eraser]'; **yerinden
fırla-** '- jump up from one's place'
→ fırla- 1.

367 PLUNGE
367:6 - plunge /A, DAn/ **dal-** 1
'- dive, - plunge /INTO [the water],
{from/OFF} [the pier]/'.

367:7 - submerge /DAn/ **boğul-**
1 '- drown /{BECAUSE OF/DUE
TO}/'.

368 AVOIDANCE
368:6 - avoid /DAn/ **kaç-** 2 '-
avoid /θ/ [work, expenses], - stay
away /from/ [certain people]'; /DAn/
kaçın- '- avoid /θ/ sb or sth or /θ/
doing sth; - refrain /from/ sth or
/from/ doing sth'; **kurtul-** 2 '- get or
- be rid /OF/ sb or sth unpleasant, -
avoid, - shake /OFF/, - manage to get
away /from/'; /DAn/ **sakın-** 1 '-
avoid /θ/, - keep [oneself] away
/from/, or - steer clear /OF/ sb or sth'.

368:7 - evade **işin içinden çık-**
1 '- escape from a difficult situation,
predicament; - get out of or - avoid
doing something complicated' → çık-
1.

368:8 - dodge /A/ **[direksiyonu
hızla] kır-** '- turn [a steering wheel,
rudder, sharply] /to/ one side, -
swerve /to/ [the left, right]' → kır- 3.

369 ESCAPE
369:6 - escape /Dan, A/ **kaç-** 1
'- escape, - run away, - flee /from, to/,
- get away /from/ [prison, a
policeman]'; /DAn/ **kurtul-** 1 '- be
rescued, saved /from/, - escape
/{θ/from}/, - manage to get away
/from/, - avoid /θ/, - survive /θ/
[accident]'.

369:10 - find vent **ağzından
[lâf] kaç-** 'for words -

unintentionally escape /from/ or - pop
/OUT OF/ one's mouth' → kaç- 1.

370 ABANDONMENT
370:5 - abandon /DA/ **bırak-** 1 '-
leave [i.e., not - take sth from where
it is], - leave sth /{on/in/at}/ [Don't
take the books. Leave them on the
table.], - leave behind, /in/ a certain
condition [Leave the window open.]'.
3 '- stop, - quit an activity, - give up a
habit; - leave, - abandon a person';
/I/ **terk et-** '- leave, - abandon
[usually permanently: one's job,
spouse, ship]'.

370:7 - give up /A/ **boş ver-** 2 '-
give up /θ/ sth [piano lessons]' →
ver- 1; **fikrinden vazgeç-** '-
change one's mind, - give up /θ/
one's idea' → vazgeç-; **kararından
vazgeç-** '- change one's mind' →
vazgeç-; **kararını geri al-** '-
withdraw or - rescind one's decision'
→ geri al- 1 → al- 1; /DAn/
vazgeç- '- give up /θ/, - drop /θ/ a
matter [idea, plan]'.

370: * 9 expressions of
abandonment **Helâl olsun.** 1 'It's
all yours., No need to thank me.,
Take it with my blessings., I give up
all rights to it [lit., Let it be
canonically lawful (for you)].' Said to
forgive any outstanding obligations,
financial or otherwise. → ol- 11 →
olsun.

371 CHOICE
371:13 - choose **beğen-** 2 '-
choose [for oneself, not sb else]';
seç- 1 /{A/için}/ '- choose, -
select, - pick sb or sth /FOR/ [oneself
or sb else], /A/ - elect sb /to/ a
position'; **seçil-** 1 /{A/için},
{tarafından/ CA}/ '- be chosen,
selected, picked /for, by/, /A,
{A/için}/ '- be elected /to, for/';
{tercih et-/yeğle-} 2 '- choose, -
select, - pick sb or sth [for oneself,
not sb else]'.

371:14 - select /I/ **aç-** 3 '- turn
/TO/ [page 5, TV channel], - open
/TO/ [page 5], - tune /{TO/INTO}/
[radio station], - put on or - turn on
[TV channel, radio station]'; /I/
çevir- 4 '- turn /TO/ [page 5, TV
channel], - switch /TO/.' If the
instrument is already on and you want
to make a change: '- put on, - turn on
[TV channel, radio station]'.

371:17 - prefer /A/ {tercih et-/yeğle-} 1 '- prefer sb or sth /to/ sb or sth else, - like sb or sth better than sb or sth else, - like best'. Verbs expressing liking, such as /DAn/ hoşlan- '- like /θ/, enjoy /θ/, be pleased /WITH/', may be used in the sense of '- prefer' in the question pattern *noun*.DAn mI *noun*.DAn mI hoşlan- ? '- prefer this or that?', a question pattern in which the question particle mI is repeated after each alternative object: e.g., Çin yemekleri.nDEN mi Hint yemekleri.nDEN m i hoşlanırsın? 'Q: Do you prefer θ Chinese or θ Indian food?'

371:18 - vote oy kullan- '- vote, - exercise the vote, - cast a vote'; /A/ oy ver- '- vote, - vote /for/, - give the vote /to/' → ver- 1.

373 CUSTOM, HABIT
373:11 - become a habit /A/ alış- 2 '- get, - become, or - be addicted /to/'.

373:12 - be used to /A/ alış- 1 '- get, - become, or - be accustomed /to/; - get, - become, or - be used /to/'.

375 MOTIVATION, INDUCEMENT
375:17 - incite /1A/ kavga çıkar- '- provoke a quarrel, - pick or - start a fight /with/' → çıkar- 7; tahrik et- 1 '- incite, provoke, - instigate, - foment'.

375:21 - encourage /a: konusunda, b: için, c: 1A/ teşvik et- '- encourage or - spur sb on /a: to [lit., in the matter of], b: TO, c: with/; - inspire sb; - encourage sb to do or participate in sth; - promote the development of'.

375:23 - persuade /a: A, b: A, c: A dair, d: konusunda/ ikna et- '- persuade or - convince sb /a: to [do sth], b: θ [that], c: {that/to the effect that}, d: on the subject of/'; /I, A/ inandır- '- convince or - persuade sb to believe /θ/ sb or sth, - get sb to believe /θ/ sth, - make sb believe /θ/ sth'; /için/ kandır- 2 '- persuade or - convince sb /TO/ do sth, - talk sb /INTO/ doing sth'.

377 ALLUREMENT
377:6 - attract ilgi çek- '- appeal to, - interest [This music doesn't appeal to me.]', *colloq.*: '- be into' → çek- 1; /I/ ilgilendir- 1 '- interest, - appeal to, - arouse the interest of', *colloq.*: '- be into'.

379 DISSUASION
379:3: - dissuade /DAn/ {vazgeçir-/caydır-} '- talk sb /OUT OF/ sth, - dissuade or - deter sb /from/, - prevent or - keep sb /from/'.

379:4 - disincline /1A/ arası {açıl-/bozul-} '- have a falling out /with/, - get on bad terms /with/' → açıl- 9; /1A/ bağlar kop- 'for relations between people - come to an end, - break off; - have a falling out /with/, - become estranged /FROM/' → kop- 1; /DAn/ soğu- 2 '- cool /TOWARD/, - lose one's love, desire, or enthusiasm /FOR/; - cease to care /FOR/ sb or sth'; /DAn/ uzaklaş- 2 '- become remote or distant /from/ in feeling'.

380 INTENTION
380:4 - intend to de- 3 '- mean; - intend'; /1A, DAn/ kastet- 1 '- mean, - have in mind, - intend to say /BY/'; /A/ niyet et- '- intend, - mean, - aim, - plan, or - make up one's mind /to/ do sth; - make a decision to do sth and then to state one's intention to oneself, silently or out loud, to carry out the act'. The latter meaning applies in reference to certain acts required by the religion of Islam for which such a statement of intention is required before the act is carried out and for that act to be valid. See also 359:7. RESOLUTION: - resolve.

380:11 PREP., CONJ. for derken 2 'intending to, thinking, with sth in mind' → de- 1; diye 3.1a 'so that; lest'. 3.1b 'in order to, to'. 3.2 'as', i.e., 'for the purpose of, with sth in mind, intending', preceded by a noun. → de- 1.

381 PLAN
381:8 - plan ayarla- 3 '- arrange, - plan [picnic, meeting]'; düzenle- 2 '- arrange; - prepare, - organize, - plan [an event]'; plan kur- '- make, - devise, - draft, - establish, or - formulate a plan' → kur- 1; {plânla-/tasarla-} '- plan, - envisage'.

381:9 - plot karıştır- 5 '- be up to sth; - stir things up, - stir up trouble'; /A/ kastet- 2 '- have

675

designs /{ON/AGAINST}/, - harbor evil intentions /TOWARD/, - intend to do sb harm'.

382 PURSUIT

382:8 - pursue /A/ **asıl-** 3 '- come on /to/ sb, - make a play /FOR/ sb, - chase /AFTER/ sb [i.e., - approach with sexual intent]', *slang*; **kovala-** 1 '- chase, - try to catch or get, - pursue [police chase thief]'; /A/ **kur yap-** '- chase /AFTER/, - court /θ/, - pay court /to/, - try to woo /θ/ [i.e., - approach with sexual intent]', *formal, polite*.

382:10 - fish **balık tut-** '- fish, - catch fish' → tut- 1.

384. MANNER, MEANS

384:10 ADV. anyhow **kaldı ki** 1 'moreover, besides, anyhow, anyway' → kal- 1.

384:11 ADV. somehow **olarak** 1 'being'. 2 'as'. 3 'ly' adverbs. 4 'θ'. 5 'in'. 6 'at', with verbs of estimation following a number. 7 in other expressions. → ol- 11.

385 PROVISION, EQUIP-MENT

385:7 - provide /A/ **sağla-** '- provide /to/, - procure, - get, - obtain sth /FOR/'.

385:8 - equip /1A, θ/ **döşe-** '- furnish /with [money, objects], IN [a style, material]/'; /1A, θ/ **döşen-** '- be furnished /with [money, objects], IN [a style, material]/'.

385:9 - provision **besle-** 1 '- feed, - nourish'.

385:11 - make a living /ArAk/ **geçimini sağla-** '- make one's living, - provide [a living] for, - support [one's family] /by...ing/'; /1A, ArAk/ **geçin-** 2 '- make one's living /by...ing/, - subsist /by means of/, - get by, - manage /ON/ [a salary]'; /ArAk/ **hayatını kazan-** '- earn one's living, livelihood /by...ing/, - make one's living /by...ing/' → kazan- 1; **iş yap-** 1 '- do sth [lit., ** work] for a living [What do you do for a living?]' → yap- 3.

386 STORE, SUPPLY

386:10 - store **yerine koy-** '- put sth IN its place, away [i.e., where it belongs], - put back, - return /to/ its place, - replace' → koy- 1.

386:12 - reserve /için, A/ **ayır-** 2 '- set aside /for, FOR/'; /A, için/ **koy-** 3 '- put sth /θ [somewhere], for/, - set sth aside /for/'; **sakla-** 2 /DA/ '- keep or - store sth IN a place,' not - put it there. 3 /A/ '- save or - keep sth /FOR/, - set sth aside /FOR/'; /için, tarafından/ **saklan-** 4 '- be saved, kept, set aside /FOR, by/'; /DA/ **üstü kal-** '- keep the change', lit., ** 'for the change [money] - remain /on/ [a person]' → kal- 1.

387 USE

387:10 - use /olarak, yönde/ **kullan-** '- use, - make use of /AS, in a [certain] way/'.

387:11 - apply /A/ **uygula-** '- carry out, - apply /to/, - follow, - put a plan, law, or formula into practice'.

387:13 - spend **bitir-** 3 '- use up, - finish [sugar]'; /için/ {**harca-**/**sarf et-**} 2 '- use, - use up /{to/in order to}/'. For '- spend money', → 626:5. EXPENDITURE: - spend; for '- spend time', → 820:6. TIME: - spend time.

387:14 - avail oneself of /A, için/ {**başvur-**/**müracaat et-**} 1 '- consult /θ [sb or sth], for/, - refer, - resort, - turn, or - appeal /to, for/, - have recourse /to, for/, - look sth up /IN/'; **bilgisine danış-** '- consult a person', lit., ** '- consult /θ/ sb's knowledge'; /a: A, b: I, c: konusunda/ **danış-** '- consult /a: θ [sb, an office], b: {about/on}, c: {about/on the subject of}/, - refer /to [sb], regarding/'.

387:15 - take advantage of /I/ **değerlendir-** 2 '- make good use of, - make the most of, - take advantage of'; /ArAk/ {**vakit/zaman**} **değerlendir-** '- make good use of time, - make the most of one's time /[by]...ing/' → değerlendir- 2; /DAn/ {**yararlan-**/**faydalan-**/**istifade et-**} '- benefit or - profit /from/, - make good use /OF/, - take advantage /OF/; - utilize /θ/'.

387:17 - avail / A / <u>Hayırlı olsun.</u> 'Good luck., Congratulations., May it go well., May it be beneficial, useful., May it benefit.' → ol- 11 → olsun; <u>iş gör-</u> '- work, - do the job, - serve the purpose' → gör- 4.

388 CONSUMPTION

388:3 - consume <u>bitir-</u> 3 '- use up, - finish [sugar]'; /için/ {<u>harca-/sarf et-</u>} 2 '- use, - use up /{to/in order to}/'.

388:4 - be consumed <u>bit-</u> 3 '- be used up, for no more - be left, - be all gone, used up, - run out of [sugar]'; <u>tüken-</u>. Same. Also '- sell out [subj.: tickets]'.

390 DISUSE

390:4 - cease to use <u>bırak-</u> 4 '- leave sb alone, - stop bothering sb'; <u>dur-</u> 4. Same; <u>rahat bırak-</u> '- leave in peace, - leave alone' → bırak- 4; <u>yalnız bırak-</u> '- leave sb alone' → bırak- 4.

390:5 not - use {<u>vakit/zaman</u>} <u>kazan-</u> 1 '- save time [i.e., by taking a taxi]' → kazan- 4.

390:6 - put away <u>yerine koy-</u> '- put sth IN its place, away [i.e., where it belongs], - put back, - return /to/ its place, - replace' → koy- 1.

390:7 - discard <u>at-</u> 2 '- throw out, away, - discard, - get rid of'; /A/ <u>çöp</u> {<u>at-/dök-</u>} '- litter, - throw trash /{ON/INTO}/ [the streets]' → at- 2, dök- 3; <u>çöpe</u> {<u>at-/dök-</u>} '- throw /{IN/INTO}/ the trash, - discard, - throw out, away' → at- 2, dök- 3; /A/ <u>dök-</u> 3 '- throw out, - spill out as waste /{ON/INTO}/'; /a: A, b: {üstüne/üzerine}, c: {tarafından/CA}/ <u>dökül-</u> 2 '- be poured out, - be spilled /a: ON, b: on, c: by/'.

390:9 - obsolesce <u>iflâs et-</u> 3 'for sth [ideology] - become regarded as worthless, - go out of favor, style'; {<u>süre/vakit/zaman</u>} <u>dol-</u> 'for time - expire, - be up' → dol- 2; {<u>süresi/vakti/zamanı</u>} <u>dol-</u> 'for the period of time, validity OF sth - expire, - be no longer valid, for sth - be overdue, for sb's time - be up' → dol- 2; {<u>vakit/zaman/süre</u>} <u>geç-</u> 'for time - pass; for time - expire, - be up' → geç- 4; {<u>vakti/zamanı/süresi</u>} <u>geç-</u> 'for the period of time, validity OF sth - expire, - be no longer valid, for sth - be overdue, for sb's time - be up' → geç- 4.

391 USELESSNESS

391:8 - be useless <u>boşa git-</u> '- be in vain, of no use, for nothing' → git- 5; /mAklA, mAktAn/ {<u>vakit/zaman</u>} <u>kaybet-</u>[or <u>yitir-</u>] '- lose or - waste time /ing, {from/because of}...ing/'; /ArAk/ {<u>vakit/zaman</u>} <u>öldür-</u> '- waste or - kill time /[by]...ing/'.

391: * 16 PHR. it's no use <u>faydası yok</u> 'it's no use' → ol- 3, Additional examples. b) 4. Miscellaneous additional examples.

392 IMPROVEMENT

392:7 - get better <u>düzel-</u> '- get better, - improve [lessons, weather, patient, schedule]'; <u>geliş-</u> 2 '- improve, - get better [economy, one's Turkish, not weather or health]'; <u>hava</u> {<u>aç-/açıl-</u>} 'for weather - clear up, - become pleasant, good, nice' → aç- 7, açıl- 7; <u>hava düzel-</u>. Same; <u>ilerle-</u> 2 '- improve, - get better [one's Turkish, not weather or health]'; <u>kaydet-</u> 5 '- achieve or - make [with nouns indicating progress, development, success]'; <u>yoluna gir-</u> '- go well, - work or - turn out the way it should, - come out right'.

392:8 - rally, - get better <u>düzel-</u> '- get better, - improve, - straighten out, - recover from an illness;...'; <u>iyileş-</u> '- get better, - improve, - get well, - recover from an illness'; <u>komadan çık-</u> '- come out of or - emerge from a coma' → çık- 1.

392:9 - improve, - make better /verb stem-A verb stem-A, ArAk/ {<u>geliştir-</u> 1/<u>ilerlet-</u> 2} '- improve, - develop [one's Turkish] /by...ing/'.

393 IMPAIRMENT

393:9 - impair /A/ <u>dokun-</u> 2 '- upset /θ/ sb [subj.: food], - make sick, - affect one's health adversely, for food or weather not - agree /WITH/ one, - have a bad effect /ON/'; <u>midesini boz-</u> '- make [physically] sick, sick to one's stomach [subj.: food]' → boz- 1; /A/ <u>nazar değ-</u>

'for the evil eye - touch /θ/ or - reach /θ/' → 1 değ- 2.

393:10 - spoil boz- 1 '- ruin, - spoil, - break, - corrupt, - violate'.

393:12 - corrupt ahlâkını boz- '- lead sb astray, - corrupt sb's morals' → boz- 1.

393:13 - inflict an injury burk- '- twist, - sprain [obj.: ankle]'; çiz- 3 '- scratch, - scarify [subj.: instrument on metal]'; /DAn/ haşlan- 2 '- get scalded /{BY/from}/, - scald or - burn oneself with a hot liquid'; kalbinden yarala- '- break sb's heart'; kalbini kır- '- hurt sb's feelings' → kır- 1; {a: kendini, b: kendisini, c: kendi kendini} yarala- '- hurt {oneself}'; sakatlan- '- get or - be hurt, - become physically disabled; - become crippled; - become maimed or mutilated'; tırmala- '- scratch', harm inflicted [subj.: cat]; /DAn/ tutul- 5 'for a part of one's body [neck, back] - get stiff /from/ [sitting]'; /I, DAn/ yarala- '- wound sb /IN/ [the arm], - injure, - hurt'; yaralan- 1 /DAn, {tarafından/CA}/ '- be wounded, hurt, injured /IN [the arm], by [the enemy]/'. 2 '- hurt oneself'.

393:16 - deteriorate bozul- '- break down, - go out of order, - give out [machines]; - spoil, - get {bad/worse}, - deteriorate [an ability, weather]'; fenalaş- 1 '- get worse, - deteriorate [patient, economic situation, an ability]'; gerile- 2 '- get worse, - deteriorate, - worsen [economic situation, an ability]'; hava {boz-/bozul-} 'for weather - change for the worse, - turn bad' → boz- 4, bozul-; kötüleş- '- deteriorate, - become bad, - get worse'; ömrünü tamamla- '...- outlive its useful life, usefulness [machine]'. → tamamla-; zayıfla- 2 '- deteriorate, - go downhill, - get worse, - get weak, - decline in quality [an ability, memory]'.

393:20 - wear, - wear away çorap kaç- 'for women's stockings - run' → kaç- 1; eski- '- get or - become worn-out, - wear out, - get old [car, rug, not living thing]'; yıpran- 1 'for sth - get worn-out, - wear out'.

393:22 - decay bayatla- '- spoil, - go bad, - go stale [subj.: certain

foods: bread, fish]'; bozul- '- spoil, - go bad [subj.: all kinds of food]'.

393:24 - break down [i.] çök- 1 '- collapse, - fall down [subj.: buildings]'. 4 '- fall, - come to an end, - collapse [subj.: empire]'. 5 'for a system - fail, - crash, - break down, - be down [computer]'; morali bozul- '- get depressed, discouraged, - lose heart'; /sonucu/ yıkıl- 2 '- collapse, - fall down [subj.: buildings, people] /as a result of/'. 3 '- lose one's health and morale; for sb - be broken or ruined by a disaster, - be devastated'.

393:25 - get out of order arıza yap- '- break down, - go out of order, - have a mechanical failure [usually for large items run on energy sources such as fuel, batteries or house current, less frequently for small items such as clocks, radios, videos]' → yap- 3; bozul- '- break down, - get or - go out of order, - give out [for large and small items of all kinds]'.

393:48 ADV. out of the frying pan into the fire Proverb: Ağaç kökünden {kurur/yıkılır}. 'A tree {dries up/{collapses/topples}} from its roots.', i.e., A thing can't endure if its central core is destroyed. → kuru- 2, yıkıl- 2; Proverb: Balık baştan kokar. 'Fish begins to stink from the head [lit., stinks from the head].', i.e., Corruption starts at the top. → kok- 2; Proverb: Denizden geçti çayda boğuldu. 'He crossed {θ/OVER} the ocean but drowned in the brook.', i.e., {From/Out of} the frying pan into the fire. → geç- 1, boğul- 1; Proverb: Yağmurdan kaçarken doluya tutuldu. 'While escaping from the rain, he got caught in the hail.' {From/Out of} the frying pan into the fire. → kaç- 1, tutul- 6.

395 DESTRUCTION

395:10 - destroy bitir- 2 '- exhaust, - destroy, - kill, - finish off sb [subj.: drinking, gambling, women]'; boz- 1 '- ruin, - spoil, - break, - corrupt, - violate'; canına kıy- 1 '- kill or - murder without mercy'. 2 '- commit suicide, - kill oneself' → kıy- 2; kahret- 2 '- crush, - overcome, - destroy, - damn' in the curse [Allah] kahretsin! 'O [God] damn {him/her/it}!'; yok et- 1 '- destroy, - do away with, - get rid of [God creates and destroys; fire destroy's belongings]'.

395:11 - do for **hapı yut-** '- have had it; - be sunk, done for, doomed, in serious trouble', *colloq.*; **yan-** 6. Same.

395:16 - obliterate /{üstünü/üzerini}/ **çiz-** 2 '- cross out or off, - scratch out [sth written]'; **karala-** 2 '- cross out or off, - scratch out', lit., '- black out [sth written]'.

395:17 - demolish /1A/ **yık-** 1 '- demolish, - wreck; - pull down, - tear down, - knock down /with/; - destroy; - ruin'; /{tarafından/CA}, 1A/ **yıkıl-** 1 '- be demolished, wrecked /by, with/; - be pulled down, torn down, knocked down; - be destroyed; - be ruined'.

395:18 - blow up **havaya uçur-** '- blow sth up [Terrorists blew up the presidential palace.]'.

395:19 - raze **devir-** 1 '- knock over [tree], - overturn [dish]'.

395:20 - overthrow **devir-** 2 '- overthrow [regime, government]'.

395:23 - perish **boşa çık-** '- come to naught, not - be realized, - be dashed [hopes, expectations, dreams, efforts]' → çık- 7.

396 RESTORATION

396:11 - restore, - put back **yerine koy-** '- put sth IN its place, away [i.e., where it belongs], - put back, - return /to/ its place, - replace' → koy- 1.

396:13 - remedy **ders düzelt-** '- pull up one's grade [lit., ** correct (one's) course], - make up for a deficiency in a course' → düzelt- 2; **{hatalar/yanlışlar} düzelt-** '- correct {errors}' → düzelt- 2; **not düzelt-** '- pull up one's grade [lit., ** correct (one's) grade], - make up for a deficiency in a course' → düzelt- 2; **saat düzelt-** '- set a watch or clock' → düzelt- 4.

396:14 - repair **çorap dik-** '- darn [non-woolen] socks' → 1 dik- 2; **çorap ör-** '- darn [woolen] socks' → ör- 3; **düzelt-** 1 '- repair, - fix

[roads, not machines or appliances]'; **onar-** '- repair, - fix, - put in running order [machine], - mend [socks]'; **tamir et-** '- repair [shoes], - fix, - put in running order [machine]'.

396:15 - cure **şifa ver-** '- restore to health, - cure, - heal' → ver- 1; **tedavi et-** 2 '- cure a person or a disease'.

396:20 - recover **atlat-** '- pull through, - get over or - kick an illness, - overcome or - survive a difficulty'; **ayıl-** 2 '- come to, - regain consciousness'; **düzel-** '- get better, - improve, - straighten out, - recover from an illness'; **iyileş-** '- get better, - improve, - get well, - recover from an illness'; **kendine gel-** 1 '- come to, - regain consciousness, - return to one's usual state' → gel- 1.

397 PRESERVATION

397:8 - preserve /DA/ **sakla-** 2 '- keep or - store sth IN a place,' not - put it there; /DA/ **saklan-** 3 '- be kept, maintained /in/ a place [jewelry in a safe]'; **tut-** 2 '- keep [seat for me], - maintain, or - hold in a certain state or condition [room clean]'.

398 RESCUE

398:3 - rescue /DAn/ **kurtar-** '- rescue, - save /from/'; /{tarafından/CA}, DAn/ **kurtarıl-** '- be rescued, saved /by, from/'; /DAn/ **kurtul-** 1 '- be rescued, saved /from/, - escape /{θ/from}/, - manage to get away /from/, - avoid /θ/, - survive /θ/ [accident]'; **salıver-** '- let go, - set free, - release [captive bird, prisoners, hostages]'; **serbest bırak-** '- release, - free, - set free, - liberate, - let go [prisoners, hostages]' → bırak- 5.

399 WARNING

399:5 - warn /için, diye/ {**uyar-** /ikaz et-/ihtar et-} '- warn sb /{to/about}, THAT/'.

399: * 9. expressions of warning **Anlaşıldı mı?** 'Is that {understood/clear}?' → anlaşıl-; **Dikkat et!** 'Be careful., Watch out!' → dikkat et- 1; **Dikkatli ol!** 'Be careful!' → dikkatli ol- → ol- 12; {**Haberiniz/Bilginiz} olsun** 'Be {advised/informed/aware} [that], Take note, Just to let you know, Is that understood?, OK?' → ol- 11 →

olsun; -mAk yok! 'No...ing!': Çamurla oynamak yok oldu mu? 'No playing with mud, is that understood?' → ol- 3, Additional examples. b) 4. Miscellaneous additional examples; Oldu mu? 'Is that {understood/ clear}?' → ol- 12.

400-500

401 HASTE

| 401:5 - make haste | /için/ acele et- '- hurry /in order to/'; çabuk ol- '- be quick, - hurry' → ol- 12; {hız/sürat} yap- '- speed, - go too fast [in vehicle]' → yap- 3; /a: DAn, b: A, c: arkasından, d: peşinden/ koş- 1 '- run /a: from, b: {to/AFTER}, c: after, d: after/, - pursue'; {koşar adımlar.la/koşar adım} merdivenleri çık- '- run up the stairs' → çık- 5; {koşar adımlar.la/koşar adım} merdivenler.DEN in- '- run down the stairs' → in- 1; yürü- 2 '- hurry along, - go quickly'. See also 174:8. SWIFTNESS: - speed.

403 ENDEAVOR

| 403:5 - endeavor | /için/ {emek/çaba} harca- '- expend effort /{for/ON}/ sth, - take pains /TO/ do sth' → {harca-/sarf et-} 1; /A/ emek ver- '- put effort /INTO/, - devote effort /to/, - work /AT/, - take pains /WITH/' → ver- 1.

| 403:6 - attempt | /A/ çalış- 2 '- try /to/, - attempt /to/'; /I/ dene- '- test, - try, - try out, - try on; - attempt, - try /TO/ do sth'; /A/ kalkış- '- try or - attempt /to/ do sth that is beyond one's power or outside one's authority, - dare /to/'.

| 403:11 - make a special effort | /A/ özen- 1 '- take great pains /to/ do sth well, - go to great pains /to/ do sth well, - take pains /{WITH/OVER}/ sth'; /için/ uğraş- 1 '- strive, - struggle, - endeavor /to/, - exert oneself, - put forth an effort /for/, - work hard'.

| 403:13 - do one's best | /A/ çabala- '- strive /to/, - struggle /to/, - do one's best /to/'; çalış[ıp] çabala- '- try hard, - do one's best'; elinden geleni yap- '- do all one can, - do one's level best' → yap- 3.

404 UNDERTAKING

| 404:3 - undertake | açıl- 10 '- be opened, taken up [a topic, subject]'; ele al- '- take up, - consider a matter' → al- 1; ele alın- 'for a matter - be taken up, considered' → alın- 1; /A/ kıy- 4 '- bring oneself /to/ or - dare /to/ do sth that would discomfort, harm sb'.

405 PREPARATION

| 405:6 - prepare sth | ayarla- 3 '- plan, - arrange [an event, appointment]'; düzenle- 2 '- arrange; - prepare, - organize, - plan [an event]'; /{A/için}/ hazırla- '- prepare sth, - get sth ready /FOR/'; /{tarafından/CA}/ hazırlan- 2 '- be prepared, readied, set up, drawn up /by/'; kahvaltı hazırla- '- make or - prepare breakfast'. Note: '- HAVE breakfast, - EAT breakfast, or - breakfast' is kahvaltı {et-/yap-}; reçete hazırla- '- {fill/prepare} a prescription', subj.: the pharmacist. → hazırla-; /A/ sofra kur- '- lay or - set a table, tray, mat, spread or like object for a meal /IN/ a place' → kur- 1; yatağını yap- 2 '- make up or - prepare a bed for sb' → yap- 3.

| 405:13 - prepare oneself | /{A/için}/ hazırlan- 1 '- get [oneself] ready, - prepare oneself /FOR/'.

| 405:14 - be prepared | hazır ol- '- be ready, prepared' → ol- 12; ol- 9.1 '- be done, completed, ready'; /A/ yetiş- 3 '[for sth] - be ready, finished /BY/ a specified time [subj.: a thing: an order, a suit]'.

407 ACCOMPLISHMENT

| 407:4 - accomplish | /A/ eriş- 3 '- attain /θ/ [one's objective], - reach /θ/ [one's goal], - achieve /θ/ [one's purpose], - gain [one's end[s]]'; et- 1 '- do, - perform'. Et- forms phrasal verbs with Arabic, Persian, and Turkish nouns and is not frequently used alone to express '- do' unless such a noun is understood. In this dictionary, all phrasal verbs with et- appear as separate entries alphabetized by the first letter of the phrasal verb [i.e., teşekkür et- appears under t]. They are also listed alphabetically, but without definitions or examples, under the entry et-. '- Do' is usually expressed with yap- 2; eyle- = et-. In this dictionary, it occurs only with rahmet, → rahmet

680

eyle-; **iş gör-** '- work, - do the job, - serve the purpose [subj.: machine]' → gör- 4; **kıl-**. Same as **eyle-**, but used with a much more limited number of usually Arabic or Persian noun objects. In this dictionary, it occurs only with **namaz**, → namaz kıl-; **kıy-** 3 '- perform, - carry out', with a very limited set of nouns. In this dictionary, it occurs only with **nikâh**, → nikâh kıy-; **yap-** 2 '- do'; /A/ **yaptır-** 2 '- have /θ/ sb do sth.'

| 407:8 - ripen | **olgunluğa er-** '- reach or - attain /θ/ maturity, - mature, - grow up' → er-.

409 SUCCESS

| 409:7a - succeed | /I/ **başar-** '- succeed /IN/, - be successful /IN/'; **kaydet-** 5 '- achieve or - make', with nouns indicating progress, development, success.

| 409:7b - succeed in specific ways
bitir- 4 '- graduate from, - finish a school or department of a university'; **isabet kaydet-** 1 '- hit the mark, target [subj.: marksman]'. 2 '- get it right, - be right, - be on target, - be right on the mark' → kaydet- 5; /DAn/ **mezun ol-** '- graduate /from/' → ol- 12; {sınav/imtihan} **kazan-** '- pass a test, examination' → kazan- 3; {sınav/imtihan} **ver-** 1. Same. → ver- 1; **sınıfa geç-** '- go on or - graduate to the next grade [e.g., from the fifth grade to the sixth] or to another class or section of the same grade' → geç- 1; **sınıfını geç-** '- go on to the next grade', lit., ** '- pass one's grade', e.g., from the fifth grade to the sixth. → geç- 1.

| 409:7c - wish success | /A/ **başarılar dile-** '- wish /θ/ sb much success, - express wishes for much success /to/ sb' → dile- 1.

| 409:8 - achieve one's purpose | /A/ **eriş-** 3 '- attain /θ/ [one's objective], - reach /θ/ [one's goal], - achieve /θ/ [one's purpose], - gain [one's end[s]]'; /A/ **kavuş-** 2 '- succeed in getting or attaining /θ/ sth sought, - obtain, - get'; /A/ **yetiş-** 1 '- catch /θ/ a vehicle, - make it /to/ a place in time /FOR/, - get /to/ a place in time /FOR/, - arrive in time /FOR/; - be in time /FOR/'. 4 '- arrive in time to help sb; - come to sb's aid in time'.

| 409:9 - score a success | /DA/ **başarı göster-** '- be successful /in/', lit., '- demonstrate success /in/' → göster- 1; **sayı kaydet-** '- score, - make points in a game, contest' → kaydet- 5.

| 409:12 - manage | **anlaş-** 1 '- understand one another, - get along, on with one another'; **geçin-** 1 /lA/ '- get along /with/, - get on /with/ sb'. 2 /lA, ArAk/ '- make one's living /BY, by...ing/, - subsist /by means of/, - get by, - manage /ON/ [a salary]'; /lA, ArAk/ **idare et-** 2 '- economize /BY, by...ing/, - make ends meet /with/; - manage /with/, - manage to get along /with/, - get by /with/'; /lA/ **yetin-** 2 '- make do, - manage /with/, - be able to manage /with/'.

410 FAILURE

| 410:9a - fail | **iflâs et-** 2 '- fail completely [subj.: a major policy, project, plan, idea, marriage]'.

| 410:9b - fail in specific areas
dersten kal- '- fail /θ/ or - flunk /{θ/IN}/ a course' → kal- 1; {sınavdan/imtihandan} **kal-** '- fail or - flunk /θ/ an examination' → kal- 1; **sınıfta kal-** '- be held back in school, - stay behind, - fail or - flunk a grade, not - go on to the next grade', i.e., a level in school, 5ᵗʰ grade, 6ᵗʰ grade, not a course' → kal- 1.

| 410:14 - miss | **fırsat kaçır-** '- miss an opportunity, - let an opportunity slip away or go by' → kaçır- 2; **kaçır-** 1 '- miss, - be too late for a vehicle, event, or a meeting with a person; - miss, - not to hear or - catch what has been said'. 2 '- let escape or - go by, - let get away, - miss a chance'; {şans/fırsat} **kaybet-** '- miss or - lose {a chance/an opportunity}'. Same as 843:5. UNTIMELINESS: - miss an opportunity.

| 410:17 - flunk sb | **sınıfta bırak-** '- fail, - flunk sb [in a grade]' → bırak- 1.

411 VICTORY

| 411:3 - triumph | /DA, DAn/ **kazan-** 2 '- win /{AT/IN}, IN/ [game, prize], - win a place in an educational institution or department,

- get in [a school]'; /DA/ <u>rekor kır-</u> '- break a record /in/ [a sports event]' → kır- 1; 2 <u>yen-</u> 2 '- win ['Which team won?']'.

412 DEFEAT
412:6 - defeat /I/ 2 <u>yen-</u> 1 '- overcome, - conquer, - beat, - defeat'; /A, not with **tarafından**/ 1 <u>yenil-</u> '- be conquered, beaten, defeated /BY/'.

417 AUTHORITY
417:13 - possess or - wield authority /A/ <u>hâkim ol-</u> '- control /θ/, - get or - keep control /{Of/OVER}/, - keep in line [people or one's emotions, actions]' → ol- 12; <u>idare et-</u> 1 '- administer, - direct, - manage, - run, - control, - govern, - rule'; <u>yönet-</u> 1 = idare et-.

420 COMMAND
420:8 - command <u>buyur-</u> 1 '- order to be done, - command, - decree'; /A/ <u>emret-</u> '- order sth, - command, - order /θ/ sb to do sth'; <u>söyle-</u> 1 '- tell sb to do sth'.

420:11 - summon /A/ <u>çağır-</u> 1 '- call, - send for, - summon /to/, - call sb or sth /FOR/ sb'; <u>taksi çevir-</u> '- hail a cab, taxi' → çevir- 1.

421 DEMAND
421:5 - demand /DAn/ <u>iste-</u> 2 '- ask for, - request /from/; - demand sth /from/ sb, - call for sth [higher wages] /from/'; /DAn/ <u>talep et-</u>. Same, *more formal*.

421:8 - insist /DA/ <u>diren-</u> 1 '- insist /{on/UPON}/, - refuse to [with a preceding negative verb]'; /DA/ <u>diret-</u> '- insist /{on/UPON}/ [having one's own way]'; <u>fikrinde inat et-</u> '- persist /IN/ or - insist /ON/ one's view, opinion' → inat et- 2; /a: DA, b: için, c: diye/ <u>ısrar et-</u> '- insist /a: {on/UPON}, b: {ON/UPON}, c: saying/, - persist /a: in/'; /DA/ <u>inat et-</u> 2 '- persist /IN/, - insist /ON/'.

422 ADVICE
422:5 - advise /A/ <u>akıl ver-</u> '- give advice /to/, - advise /θ/' → ver- 1; /A/ <u>fikir ver-</u> 2 '- give advice /to/, - advise /θ/, - suggest a course of action /to/' → ver- 1; /A/ <u>tavsiye et-</u> '- recommend, - propose, or - suggest sth /to/ sb, - advise sb to do sth'; /A/ <u>yol göster-</u> 2 '- advise /θ/,

- give advice /to/, - guide, - suggest a solution to a problem' → göster- 1.

422:7 - take or - accept advice /DAn/ <u>akıl al-</u> '- ask sb's advice, - take or - get advice /from/ sb, - consult /θ/ sb' → al- 1; /a: DAn, b: hakkında, c: konusunda/ <u>fikir al-</u> '- get an idea or advice /a: from, b: about, c: on the subject of/' → al- 1; <u>fikrini al-</u> '- get sb's opinion or view, - take sb's advice, - consult' → al- 1; <u>söz tut-</u> '- take, - follow, - heed, or - listen to advice' → tut- 5; <u>sözünü tut-</u> 2 '- take, - follow, - heed, or - listen to the advice of sb, - take sb's advice' → tut- 5.

424 COMPULSION
424:4 - compel <u>çalıştır-</u> 1 a) /I/ '- have or - make sb work, - work sb, - allow sb - work'. b) /A/ '- have or - make /θ/ sb work on sth; - tutor sb'; /A/ <u>zorla-</u> 1 '- force sb /to/ do sth, - make sb /to/ do sth, - drive sb /to/ do sth'; /A, tarafından/ <u>zorlan-</u> 1 '- be forced, constrained, or compelled /to [do sth], by/; - be coerced /INTO [doing sth], by/'.

424:6 - press <u>zorla-</u> 2 '- force or - try to force or - break sth open [locked door]'; /{tarafından/CA}/ <u>zorlan-</u> 2 '- be forced or broken open [locked door] /by/'.

425 STRICTNESS
425:5 - deal hardly or harshly with <u>üstüne git-</u> 1 '- deal strictly, harshly /WITH/, - be hard /on/' → git- 1a.

428 RESTRAINT
428:7 - restrain {çenesini/dilini} <u>tut-</u> '- hold one's tongue [lit., {** one's jaw or chin/one's tongue}], - keep quiet' → tut- 4; /A/ <u>hâkim ol-</u> '- control /θ/, - get or - keep control /{OF/OVER}/, - keep in line [people or one's emotions, actions]' → ol- 12; <u>kendine gel-</u> 2 '- pull oneself together, - regain self-control, - come to one's senses' → gel- 1; <u>tut-</u> 4 '- restrain, - hold back [tears], - keep control of [one's tongue]'.

429 CONFINEMENT
429:12 - confine /A/ {<u>kapa-/kapat-</u>} 4 '- close sth up /IN/ [chickens in a coop]'; /A, {tarafından/CA}/ <u>kapatıl-</u> 5 '- be

682

closed up or shut up /IN, by/ [subj.: chickens in a coop]'; /A/ **kilitle-** 2 '- lock up /IN/ [animals in stable]'.

⬜ 429:15 - arrest ⬜ **tutukla-** '- arrest sb, - put sb under arrest'; /{tarafından/CA}/ **tutuklan-** '- be arrested, - be put under arrest /by/'.

⬜ 429:18 - be imprisoned ⬜ **ceza çek-** '- serve a prison sentence, - serve or - do time' → çek- 5; **cezasını çek-** 2 '- serve a prison sentence /for/, - serve or - do time /for/' → çek- 5.

430 FREEDOM
⬜ 430:14 - exempt ⬜ **bağışla-** 3 '- spare sb's life, not - separate sb from sb else'.

⬜ 430:16 not - interfere ⬜ **oluruna bırak-** '- let matters run or - take their course without interference, - leave or - let well enough alone, - let nature take its course, - let things be' → bırak- 2, ol- 11.

431 LIBERATION
⬜ 431:5 - release ⬜ **bırak-** 5 '- let go of, - release, - put down [object, person]'; **salıver-** '- let go, - set free, - release [captive bird, prisoners, hostages]'; **serbest bırak-** '- release, - free, - set free, - liberate, - let go [prisoners, hostages, captive bird]' → bırak- 5; /DAn/ **taburcu ol-** '- be {discharged/released} /from/ a hospital', originally especially a soldier passed fit for service after an illness → ol- 12.

⬜ 431:8 - free oneself from ⬜ /DAn/ **kurtul-** 2 '- get or - be rid /OF/ sb or sth unpleasant, - avoid, - shake /OFF/, - manage to get away /from/'.

433 SUBMISSION
⬜ 433:7 - yield ⬜ **yol ver-** '- yield, - give way', in traffic. → ver- 1.

434 OBSERVANCE
⬜ 434:2 - observe ⬜ **oruç tut-** '- keep or - observe the fast, - fast' → tut- 5; **sözünde dur-** '- keep one's promise, word' → dur- 6; /A/ **sözünü tut-** 1. Same. → tut- 5; **tut-** 5 '- observe a ritual, - keep an observance or practice'; /A/ **uy-** 5 '- comply /WITH/, - conform /to/, - follow or - act in accordance /WITH/

rules, regulations'; **yas tut-** '- mourn, - be in mourning' → tut- 5.

⬜ 434:3 - perform ⬜ **yerine getir-** 1 '- carry out a request, wish, order, promise, - execute an order' → getir-.

435 NONOBSERVANCE
⬜ 435:4 - violate ⬜ **çiğne-** 3 '- violate laws, rules, principles'; **sözünde durMA-** '- break one's promise' → sözünde dur- → dur- 6; **sözünden dön-** '- go back /ON/ one's word' → dön- 5; **sözünü tutMA-** = sözünde durMA- → sözünü tut- 1 → tut- 5.

436 PROMISE
⬜ 436:4 - promise ⬜ /a: A, b: A, c: A dair, d: için, e: üzerine/ **söz ver-** '- give one's word /a: to [sb], b: θ [that], c: to the effect that, d: that, e: that/, - promise /θ/ sb sth' → ver- 1; /A/ **vadet-.** Same. Today *less common, more formal* than söz ver-; /a: A, b: A, c: A dair, d: diye/ **yemin et-** '- swear or - vow /a: to [sb], b: θ [that], c: to the effect that, d: that [lit., saying]/; - take an oath'.

⬜ 436:6 - be engaged ⬜ /1A/ **nişanlan-** '- get engaged /TO/', i.e., preparation for marriage.

437 COMPACT
⬜ 437:9 - execute ⬜ **yerine getir-** 1 '- carry out a request, wish, order, promise, - execute an order' → getir-.

439 OFFER
⬜ 439:4 - offer ⬜ /A/ **ikram et-** 1 '- serve, offer /θ/ sb sth, - serve, - offer sth /to/ sb [obj.: usually food or drink]'; /A/ **sun-** 1 '- offer, - present, - submit /to/ [obj.: a petition, thesis, food]'; /A/ **takdim et-** 2 '- present, - submit, - offer sth /to/ sb [obj.: report, petition, thesis]'; /A/ **uzat-** 2 '- hold sth out /to/, - extend, - pass sth /to/ sb'.

⬜ 439:5 - propose ⬜ **ileri sür-** 1 '- put forward or - advance an idea, suggestion, proposal' → sür- 1; /A/ **{öner-/teklif et-}** '- propose, - suggest /to/'; /A/ **tavsiye et-** '- recommend, - advise, - propose, - suggest /to/'.

⬜ 439: * 11 expressions of suggestion ⬜ **İstersen[iz]** 'What about or how about [** {your/our/my} doing it tomorrow]?,

What if [{you/we/I} did it tomorrow]?, Why don't you?', lit., 'If you wish': This form, in addition to its usual uses with its literal translation, frequently appears as a polite introduction to the expression of a preference, proposal, or correction: I'd rather not go today. How about going tomorrow? → iste-1; **Şöyle bir şey yapsak...** '{What if/Suppose} we did the following...' → yap- 2.

440 REQUEST

440:9 - request /DAn/ dile- 2 '- ask for sth /from/ sb, - request sth /from/ sb, - ask sth /OF/ sb'; ısmarla- 1 /DAn, {A/için}/ '- order sth /from, for/ sb'. 2 /A/ '- put in or - place an order for sth /WITH/ sb, - order sth /FROM/ sb [lit., ** order sth TO sb], - give an order for sth /to/ sb'; /DAn/ iste- 2 '- ask for, - request, - demand sth /from/ sb, - call for sth'; rica et- a) Non-verbal noun as object: /DAn/ '- ask /θ/ sb for sth, - request sth /from/ sb'. b) Verbal noun as object: /{DAn/A}/ '- ask /θ/ sb to do sth'. c) The actual words of the request precede **diye** 'saying': '- ask sb saying "...'''; sor-b) /DAn/ '- ask sth /OF/ sb or /AT/ an office, - ask /θ/ sb or /AT/ an office for sth', frequently information. c) /I/ '- ask /{FOR/ABOUT}/ sb'; söyle- 2 '- order', usually only when the order is spoken as, for example, in a restaurant or a coffee house; /DAn/ talep et- '- want, - require, - demand, - request /from/'.

440:10 - petition /A, için/ {başvur-/müracaat et-} 2 '- apply or - submit an application /to, for/'.

440:11 - entreat /A, için/ dua et- 2 '- pray /to [God], for [sth]/, - supplicate'; /A, için/ yalvar- '- plead /with [sb], for/, - beg /θ [sb], {for/TO}/, - beseech /θ [sb], {for/TO}/'.

440:13 - invite /A/ çağır- 2 '- invite /{to/FOR}/'; /A/ davet et-. Same.

440:20 INTERJ. please The structure **verb stem.Iver-**, i.e., I + ver-, even without **lütfen** 'please', may convey the sense of a polite request: **Ha[y]di kızım, şu pencereleri sil.iver.** 'Come on dear, [would you] please wipe these windows.' → ver- 5. See also 174:17. SWIFTNESS: ADV. swiftly; **N'olur[sun].** 'Please., Oh please., Won't you please., Pretty please.', an expression of insistent entreaty. → ol- 11 → olsun.

441 CONSENT

441:2 - consent kabul et- 2 '- agree /to/ or - accept a proposal, suggestion, - approve /θ/'; /A/ razı ol- 1 '- agree, - consent, or - be willing /to/, - be content /WITH/' → ol- 12; /A/ yanaş- 3 '- be willing or inclined /to/, - be willing to agree /to/; - go along /WITH/ a plan'.

441:3. * 1 gestures of consent başını salla- '- shake one's head [up and down for consent]' → salla-3.

442 REFUSAL

442:3 - refuse diren- 1 '- refuse to [with a preceding negative verb]'; reddet- 1 '- refuse [to do something], - reject [an idea, a proposal]'.

442:5. * 1 gestures of refusal başını salla- '- shake one's head [from side to side for refusal]' → salla- 3.

443 PERMISSION

443:9 - permit /A/ izin ver- '- give /θ/ sb permission, - give permission /to/ sb, - allow, - let, or - permit /θ/ sb' → ver- 1; /A/ müsaade et-. Same; /A/ sok- 2 '- let, - permit, - allow sb /{IN/INTO}/ a place'; In addition to the above, the causative form of any verb [i.e., **verb stem.{Ar-/Dir-/t-/Ir-/It-}**] may indicate permission, i.e., '- let sb do sth', as in the second part of the following sentence: She wanted to use the phone, and he let her.

443:9. * 1 - get permission /DAn, için/ {izin/müsaade} al- '- get permission /from, to/' → al- 3.

444 PROHIBITION

444:3 - prohibit {yasakla-/yasak et-} '- forbid, - prohibit'; /{tarafından/CA}/ yasaklan- '- be forbidden, prohibited /by/'.

445 REPEAL

445:2 - repeal **kaldır-** 4 '- abolish, - do away with, - lift, - repeal [law], - eliminate, - eradicate [disease]'; **kalk-** 3 '- be repealed [law, tax], abolished [law, tax], lifted [martial law], struck down [law]'; **sözünü geri al-** '- take back or - retract one's words, - recant' → geri al- 1 → al- 1.

446 PROMOTION

446:2 - promote /DAn/ **geçir-** '- pass, - promote students /IN/ [a course. Subj.: teacher]'.

448 RESIGNATION, RETIREMENT

448:2 - resign /DAn/ **emekliye ayrıl-** '- retire /from/, - go into retirement' → ayrıl- 3; **görevinden ayrıl-** '- resign /from/, - leave /θ/ one's post' → ayrıl- 3; /DAn/ **istifa et-** '- resign /from/'; **işten {ayrıl-/çık-}** '- leave or - quit /θ/ one's job', not necessarily retirement. → ayrıl- 3, çık- 1.

449 AID

449:11 - aid **el ele ver-** '- help one another' → ver- 1; /A/ **el uzat-** '- reach out to help' → uzat- 2; /A/ **kolaylık göster-** '- make sth easy /FOR/, - facilitate matters /FOR/, - help /θ/, colloq. '- give sb a break' → göster- 1; /A/ **yardım elini uzat-** '- extend a helping hand /to/, - help out, - extend aid, assistance /to/' → uzat- 2; /A/ **yardım et-** '- help /θ/, - assist /θ/'; /A/ **yardımcı ol-** '- help /θ/, - assist /θ/, - be of assistance /to/, - be helpful /to/' → ol- 12; /A/ **yardımda bulun-** = yardım et- more formal. → bulun- 3; **yardımlaş-** '- help one another'; **yetiş-** 4 '- arrive in time to help sb; come to sb's aid in time'.

449:12 - support **destekle-** '- support', financially, morally.

451 OPPOSITION

451:3 - oppose /A/ **karşı çık-** '- oppose /θ/, - come out /AGAINST/, - object /to/, - say no /to/' → çık- 3; /I/ **protesto et-** '- protest sth or against sth'.

451:6 - contradict /lA/ **çeliş-** '- contradict one another [ideas, behavior], - be in conflict, - be contradictory, in contradiction /with/'; **yalanla-** '- deny, -

contradict, - refute, - declare, or - show to be false or wrong'.

453 RESISTANCE

453:3 - offer resistance /A/ **el kaldır-** 2 '- raise one's hand, a hand /AGAINST/ [i.e., - strike]' → kaldır- 1; **ses çıkar-** 2 '- voice one's opinions, - say sth or - speak up against sth, - say sth against, - raise one's voice against, - object' → çıkar- 7.

453:4 - stand fast /A karşı/ **diren-** 2 '- resist, - hold out /against/ [demonstrators against police]'.

456 DISACCORD

456:10 - fall out with /lA/ **arası {açıl-/bozul-}** '- have a falling out /with/ sb, - get on bad terms /with/' → açıl- 9; /lA/ **bağlar kop-** 'for relations between people - come to an end or - break off; - have a falling out /with/, - become estranged /FROM/' → kop- 1; /DAn/ **soğu-** 2 '- cool /TOWARD/, - lose one's love, desire, or enthusiasm /FOR/; - cease to care /FOR/ sb or sth'; /DAn/ **uzaklaş-** 2 '- become remote, distant /from/ in feeling'.

456:11 - quarrel /lA/ **çatış-** 1 '- quarrel, - clash /with/'; /lA/ **kavga et-** '- fight, - quarrel /with/'.

457 CONTENTION

457:13 - contend /lA/ **çatış-** 1 '- quarrel, - clash /with/'; /lA/ **dövüş-** '- fight, - struggle, - engage in physical combat /with/ one another'; /lA/ **kavga et-** '- fight, - quarrel /with/'; /a: A karşı, b: lA, c: lA birlikte [or beraber]/ **savaş-** '- fight /a: against [sb or sth], b: with [i.e., against sb], against [sth], c: together with [sb]/, - battle, - wage war'.

457:18 - compete /lA/ **karşılaş-** 4 '- play one another, - meet, - compete [sports teams]'; /lA/ **yarış-** 2 '- compete /with/'.

457:19 - race /lA/ **yarış-** 1 '- race /θ/ sb, - race /with/ sb'.

458 WARFARE

458:18 - serve /olarak/ **askerlik yap-** '- do military service /AS [a private]/, - serve in the armed forces /AS/' → yap- 3.

459 ATTACK

459:14 - attack /{A/üzerine}/
hücum et- 1 '- attack /θ/, - storm /θ/
[territory, forces]'; /IA/ **kavga
çıkar-** '- provoke a quarrel, - pick or
- start a fight /with/' → çıkar- 7; /A/
saldır- 1 '- attack /θ/, - light /INTO/
[obj.: armies, fortress]'. 2 '- rape /θ/,
- assault /θ/ sexually'; /A/ **tecavüz
et-** 2 = saldır- 2.

459:22 - pull the trigger /A/ **ateş
et-** '- fire /{ON/UPON}/, - shoot
/AT/'; /A/ **kurşun at-** '- shoot
[bullets] /AT/, - fire a gun /AT/' →
at- 6; /I/ **tara-** 3 '- spray or - pepper
with fire [i.e., bullets], - blaze away
at, - strafe - rake with shot'.

459:23 - bomb **bombala-** '-
bomb'.

460 DEFENSE

460:8 - defend {fikir/görüş}
savun- 1 '- defend
{opinions/views}' → savun-; /DAn,
A karşı/ **koru-** '- protect /from,
against/, - defend /against/'; /A
karşı/ **savun-** '- defend [the country
/against/ enemy attack, the accused
/against/ charges]'.

465 PACIFICATION

465:10 - make up /IA/ **arası
düzel-** 'for matters - get straightened
out, patched up between people, - be
reconciled /with/ one another', i.e.,
for relations between people - be
reestablished after a falling out; /IA/
barış- '- make up /with/, - come to
an understanding /with/, - make peace
/with/'.

467 NEUTRALITY

467:5 - remain neutral **karışmam**
1 'I'm not going to get involved., I
don't want to have anything to do
with it., Leave me out of this., I'm
staying out of this.' → karış- 6.

469 POSSESSION

469:4 - possess **sahip ol-** '-
become the owner, possessor /of/ sth,
- obtain /θ/, - acquire /θ/, - get /θ/ sth;
- be the owner, possessor /of/, - own
or - possess sth, - have'. → ol- 5,
(5.2) Table 2. Also: ol- 12.

472 ACQUISITION

472:8 - acquire /DAn/ **al-** 3 '-
get, - receive /from/'; /DAn/ **edin-**
'- get, - obtain, - acquire /from/';

/DAn/ **elde et-** '- obtain, - acquire,
- get /from/'; **ele geçir-** 1 '- catch, -
capture, - seize'. 2 '- obtain, - get
hold of, - acquire' → geçir- 1; /A/
hak kazan- '- earn or - win the right
/to/' → kazan- 1; /IA/ **kazan-** 4 '-
get, - gain /by/'; **noun.sI ol-** 6 '-
acquire, - get, - obtain {A/SOME}',
note the indefinite object; /A/ **sahip
ol-** '- become the owner, possessor
/OF/ sth, - obtain /θ/, - acquire /θ/, -
get /θ/ sth...' → ol- 12; **noun sahibi
ol-**. Same. → ol- 12; **noun.nIn
sahibi ol-.** Same → ol- 12.

473 LOSS

473:4 - lose **ekmeğinden ol-** '-
be deprived of one's livelihood, - lose
one's livelihood' → ol- 7; {**kaybet-
/yitir-**} '- lose [wallet], - lose [sb to
death: We lost our father last year.]';
kaybol- '- be lost, - get lost' → ol-
12; /DAn/ **ol-** 7 '- lose, - be
deprived /OF/'; **servetinden ol-** '-
lose one's fortune' → ol- 7; **yolunu
{kaybet-/yitir-}** '- lose one's way,
- get lost'; **yolunu şaşır-** '- lose
one's way, - get lost, not - know
which way to turn' → şaşır- 3.

473:6 - go to waste **boşa çık-** '-
come to naught, not - realized, - be
dashed [hopes, expectations, dreams,
efforts]' → çık- 7; **boşa git-** '- be in
vain, of no use, for nothing' → git- 5.

474 RETENTION

474:5 - retain **sakla-** 2 /DA/ '-
keep or - store sth /IN/ a place [He
keeps the tools in that chest.]'. 3 /A/
'- save or - keep sth /FOR/, - set sth
aside /FOR/'.

474:6 - hold, - grip /DAn/ **tut-** 1
'- grasp, - seize, - take hold of /BY/, -
catch, - grab, - hold'. Also '- be
holding /BY/'; /DAn/ **tutul-** 1 '- be
grasped, seized, caught, taken hold of
/BY/ [body part: the neck]'.

474:7 - hold, - keep **tut-** 2 '- keep
[obj.: place, seat], - maintain, - hold
in a certain state or condition'; **tutul-**
2 '- be taken, occupied, held [subj.:
place, seat]'.

476 PARTICIPATION

476:5 - participate /A/ **burnunu
sok-** 2 '- participate /IN/, - get
involved /IN/, - take up', *colloq.*
when the activity is sth unexpected,
often foreign: the game of golf for

most Turks. → sok- 1; /A/ **karış-** 6 '- join /IN/, - get involved /IN/ [not necessarily negative sense]'; /A/ **katıl-** 2 '- participate /IN/, - take part /IN/, - get involved /IN/; - join /θ/ [obj.: a person or group for some activity: Let me join θ you.]'; **sohbete dal-** '- get involved /IN/ or - plunge /INTO/ a friendly conversation' → dal- 4; **söze karış-** '- join /θ/ a conversation, - break /INTO/ a conversation' → karış- 6.

476:6 - share | /lA/ **paylaş-** '- share sth /with/ sb'.

477. APPORTIONMENT

477:9 - allot | /a: için, b: DAn, c: DA, d: adına/ **ayırt-** '- reserve [a place] /a: for, b: {IN/AT}, c: at, d: in the name of/, - set apart'; /için, DA/ **rezervasyon yaptır-** '- make a reservation /for [sb, a time], at [a hotel, restaurant, casino]/ [subj.: the guest or person desiring the reservation, not the hotel clerk]' → yaptır- 2.

478 GIVING

478:12 - give | /A/ **bağışla-** 1 '- give /to/, - donate /to/, - make a donation /to/'; /A/ **hediye et-** '- give sth as a gift /to/ sb, - make a present of sth /to/ sb'; **hesap getir-** '- bring the check'; /A/ **ikram et-** '- serve or - offer /θ/ sb sth, - serve or - offer sth /to/ sb [obj.: usually food or drink]'; /A/ **koy-** 2 '- put or - place food /ON/ sb's plate, - serve [out] food /to/ sb'; /a: A, b: A, c: için/ **randevu ver-** '- give or - grant an appointment /a: to [sb], b: for [sb], c: for [a time]/, - make an appointment /b: for [sb]/' → ver- 1; **servis yap-** '- serve [food] [hot, cold]' → yap- 3; /A, için/ **süre tanı-** '- grant a period of time, a grace period /to [sb], for [the payment of a debt]/' → tanı- 5; /A/ **ver-** 1 '- give /to/, - donate /to/'. 2 '- assign /to/'; /A/ **veril-** '- be given /to/'.

478:13 - deliver | /A/ **kes-** 5 '- issue, - hand out, - give, - write [a ticket, receipt]'; /A/ **teslim et-** '- hand sth over /to/, - turn sth over /to/, - deliver sth /to/, - turn sth in /to/'.

478:16 - commit | /A/ **ısmarla-** 3 '- entrust sb or sth /to/ sb, - commit /to/, - commend /to/'. Most frequently found in **Allahaısmarladık.**

'Goodbye [lit., We entrusted you TO God].', said by the person leaving.

478:18 - bequeath | /A/ **bırak-** 7 '- leave sth /to/ sb, - bequeath sth /to/ sb'.

479 RECEIVING

479:6 - receive | /DAn/ **al-** 3 '- get, - receive /from/'; **kabul et-** 1 '- accept, - take [travelers' checks]'.

479:7 - inherit | /A/ **kal-** 2 '- remain, - come /to/, - be left /to/ sb as inheritance'; /A, DAn/ **miras kal-** '- be left /to [sb], {from/BY}/', as an inheritance. → kal- 2; **mirastan düş-** '- inherit, - come into [property] /through/ inheritance' → düş- 4.

480 TAKING

480:14 - seize | **ele geçir-** 1 '- catch, - capture, - seize [obj.: person, city]'; /A/ **kapıl-** '- be seized, grabbed, carried off, away /BY/, - be overcome /BY/, - be captivated /BY/ [subj.: a current of water, a feeling]'; /DAn/ **tut-** 1 '- grasp, - seize, - catch, - grab, - take hold of /BY/', also '- hold /BY/'; /DAn/ **tutul-** 1 '- be grasped, seized, caught, taken hold of /BY/ [body part: the neck]'. 2 '- be taken, occupied, held [subj.: place, seat]'; /DAn/ **yakala-** 1 '- catch; - collar, - nab; - seize, - grab, - snatch, - get hold of /BY/'; /{tarafından/ CA}/ **yakalan-** 1 '- be caught /by/; - be collared, nabbed /by/; - be seized, grabbed, snatched /by/ [police]'.

480:15 - possess sexually | **ırzına geç-** '- rape, - violate' → geç- 1; /A/ **saldır-** 2 '- rape /θ/, - assault /θ/ sexually [not necessarily rape]'; /A/ **tecavüz et-** 2. Same.

480:19 - appropriate | **evlât edin-** '- adopt a child'.

480:21 - take from | /DAn, A/ **al-** 1 '- take /from, to/, - pick sth up /from/'; /DAn/ **alın-** 1 '- be taken, received /from/'.

481 RESTITUTION

481:4 - restore | /A/ **geri gönder-** '- send sth back /to/'; /A/ {**geri ver-/iade et-**} '- give or - take sth back /to/, - return sth /to/'. The second verb is *more formal.* → ver- 1; **para {geri ver-/iade et-}** '- give a refund, - refund money, - give back

money' → {geri ver-/iade et-} → ver-
1; **yerine getir-** 2 '- bring sth back
[lit., - bring to its place, i.e., to where
it belongs]'.

481:6 - recover /DAn/ **geri al-** 1
'- take back [to oneself] /from/' → al-
1; /A/ **geri getir-** '- bring sth back
[here], - return sth /to/ [this place]';
/DAn/ **parasını geri al-** '- get
one's money back, - get a refund
/from/' → geri al- 1→ al- 1.

482 THEFT
482:13 - steal /DAn/ **çal-** 1 '-
steal /from/'; /DAn, {tarafından/
CA}/ **çalın-** 1 '- be stolen /from,
by/'.

482:14 - rob **soy-** 2 '- rob, - strip
of valuables'; /tarafından/ **soyul-**
2 '- be robbed, stripped of valuables
/by/'.

482:20 - abduct **kaçır-** 3 '-
kidnap, - abduct, - carry off; - hijack';
/A/ **uçak kaçır-** '- hijack a plane
/to/' → kaçır- 3.

484 PARSIMONY
484:5 - stint **masraftan {kaç-
/kaçın-}** '- avoid /θ/ expense, -
economize' → kaç- 2.

486 PRODIGALITY
486:4 - waste **israf et-** '- waste, -
squander'.

487 CELEBRATION
487:2 - celebrate **kutla-** 1 '-
celebrate'.

489 WIT, HUMOR
489:13 - joke **komiğine git-** '-
find funny, amusing, - strike one as
funny, - tickle one's funny bone' →
git- 1b.

489:14 - trick /A/ **şaka yap-** 1
'- play a joke or trick /ON/' → yap-
3.

490 BANTER
490:5 - banter /A/ **şaka yap-** 2 '-
be joking, kidding, - make a joke, not
- be telling the truth' → yap- 3.

492 COURAGE
492:16 - encourage **destekle-** '-
support [financially, morally, not
usually a team]'; /a: konusunda, b:
için, c: 1A/ **teşvik et-** '-
encourage, - spur sb on /a: to [lit., in

the matter of], b: TO, c: with/; -
inspire sb; - encourage sb to do or
participate in sth; - promote the
development of'; **tut-** 10 '- support a
team'.

498 ORNAMENTATION
498:8 - ornament /1A/ **süsle-** '-
decorate, - adorn /with/'; **süslen-** 1
/1A/ '- deck oneself out /IN/, - adorn
oneself /with/, - doll oneself up /IN/'.
2 /1A, tarafından/ '- be decorated,
adorned, embellished /with, by/'.
Also 1015:15. BEAUTY: - beautify.

500-600

500 AFFECTATION
500:12 - affect *verb
stem.*{Ar/mIş} **gibi yap-** '-
pretend, - make as if' → yap- 3; *verb
stem.*{a: mAzlIktAn/b:
mAmAzlIktAn/c: mAzdAn}
gel- '- pretend not to, - make as if
not to [e.g., have seen the accident]'
→ gel- 1.

501 OSTENTATION
501:16 - show off **gösteriş yap-**
'- show off, - be a show-off' → yap-
3; **hava bas-** 2 '- show off, - act
snobbishly, - give oneself airs' →
bas- 2.

502 BOASTING
502:6 - boast /1A/ {**övün-/öğün-**
} 2 '- praise oneself, - boast, - brag
/{OF/ABOUT}/'.

504 COURTESY
504:13 - give one's regards /A/
başarılar dile- '- wish /θ/ sb much
success, - express wishes for much
success /to/ sb' → dile- 1; /A/
mutluluklar dile- '- wish /θ/ sb
much happiness' → dile- 1; /A/
saygılar sun- '- pay or - offer one's
respects, - give or - send one's
regards or compliments /to/' → sun-
1; /DAn/ **selâm getir-** '- bring
greetings /from/'; /A, DAn/ **selâm
söyle-** '- send, - give or - express
one's regards /to, from/', *informal:* '-
say "Hi" /to/' → söyle- 1; /A/ **selâm
yolla-** '- send greetings /to/',
informal: '- say "Hi" /to/'; /A/
uğurla- '- wish a departing traveler
a safe journey, - wish sb Godspeed, -
send or - see sb off /to/'.

504: * 20 polite expressions arranged alphabetically by the first word in the phrase:

A: **Afiyet olsun.** 'Bon appétit!, Enjoy!', a phrase used to address anyone who is about to begin eating, who is eating, or who has just finished eating. → ol- 11 → olsun; **Allah bağışlasın.** 'May God not separate {them/her/him} from you.', said to a mother who has just said how many children she has. → bağışla- 3; **Allah göstermesin.** 'God forbid!' → göster- 1; **Allah kavuştursun!** 'May God {reunite you/bring you together [again]}!', said to those remaining behind when sb has departed on a journey. → kavuştur-; **Allah kolaylık versin.** 'May God make it easy for you.', said to sb about to undertake a task. → ver- 1; **Allah korusun.** 'May God preserve him [from misfortune].' → koru-; **Allah kurtarsın.** 'May God save him.', when sb is faced with a misfortune. → kurtar-; **Allah rahatlık versin.** 'Good night [lit., May God give (you) comfort].', said before retiring, going to bed, not usually when bidding farewell in the evening as, for example, when leaving a party. → ver- 1; **Allah [ona] rahmet eylesin. Başınız sağ olsun.** 'May God have mercy upon him. May you be healthy.', said upon hearing of the death of a Muslim. → rahmet eyle-, ol- 12. The equivalent for a non-Muslim is **Toprağı bol olsun.** → ol- 11 → olsun; **Allah sağlık versin.** 'May God grant [you] good health.' → ver- 1; **Allah saklasın.** 'May God preserve him [from misfortune].' → sakla- 4; **Allah şifa versin!** 'May God restore him to health [lit., give him good health].' → ver- 1.

B: **Başınız sağ olsun.** '{My [sincere] condolences./*less formal:* I'm so sorry to hear it.}', said to sb telling of a death in his family. → sağ ol- → ol- 12; **Buy[u]run[uz].** 1 'Please come in.' 2 'Go ahead, you go first [at an entrance].' 3 'Help yourself., Here you are., Won't you have [{a cigarette/candy}]?' 4 'Please do so, go ahead', in response to a request: May I use the phone? 5 /A/ 'Please come /to/ [a place: the table, our house].' → buyur- 2.

C: **Canın sağ olsun!** 'Don't worry! It doesn't matter!', words of consolation. → sağ ol- → ol- 12; **Çok yaşa!** 3 'Bless you! [lit., Live long!]', said when sb has sneezed. The response: **Sen de gör!** 'Same to you [lit., You too {see/experience} it., i.e., a long life].' → yaşa- 1.

E: **Ellerinizden öperim.** 'Kind regards [lit., I kiss you ON your hands].', a concluding salutation in a letter to a senior. → öp-.

G: **Geçmiş olsun.** 'May it pass., May it be passed.', a phrase that must be said to a person who has just mentioned a misfortune [illness, accident] that has befallen him. → ol- 11 → olsun; **Görüştüğümüze çok memnun oldum.** 'Very pleased to meet you.' → memnun ol- → ol- 12; **Gözlerinizden öperim.** 'Kind regards [lit., I kiss you ON your eyes].', a concluding salutation in a letter to a junior. → öp-; **Güle güle giyin[iz].** 'What a nice...!, How nice!' Often used with the name of an item of clothing: e.g., dress, shirt, etc., lit., 'Wear it with pleasure!', a polite expression used when complimenting sb on a new item of clothing. → giyin-; **Güle güle kullanın[ız].** 'What a nice...!, How nice!' Often used with the name of an item for use: e.g., car, TV, etc., lit., 'Use it with pleasure.', a polite expression used to address sb who has acquired a new item for use. → kullan-; **Güle güle oturun[uz].** 'What a nice...!, How nice!' Often used with the name of a residence: apartment, house, etc., lit., 'Live [in it] with pleasure!', a polite expression used when visiting people who have moved to a new residence. → otur- 3.

H: **Hayırlı olsun!** 'Good luck., Congratulations., May it go well., May it be beneficial, useful., May it benefit.' → ol- 11 → olsun; **Herşey gönlünüzce olsun!** '{I hope everything turns out the way you want it to./May everything turn out as you wish.}' → ol- 11 → olsun; /A/ **Hoş geldin[iz]!** 1 'Welcome /to/'. 2 'Hello., Hi.' → gel- 1; **Hoşça kalın!** 'Good-bye!', said by the person leaving. The response: **Güle güle.** → kal- 1; **Huzur içinde rahat uyusun.** 'May he rest in peace [lit., May he sleep comfortably

689

in peace]', said of the deceased. →
uyu- 1.

İ: **İçeri buyurmaz mısınız?**
'Won't you come in?'; **İstersen[iz]**
'What about or how about [**
{your/our/my} doing it tomorrow]?,
What if [{you/we/I} did it
tomorrow]?, Why don't you?', lit., 'If
you wish'. This form, in addition to
its usual uses with its literal
translation, frequently appears as a
polite introduction to the expression
of a preference, proposal, or
correction: I'd rather not go today.
How about going tomorrow? → iste-
1.

I: Iver, i.e., I + ver-. The structure
verb stem.**Iver-**, even without
lütfen 'please', may convey the
sense of a polite request: Ha[y]di
kızım, şu pencereleri sil.iver.
'Come on dear, [would you] please
wipe these windows.' → ver- 5.

K: **Kendimi övmek gibi
olmasın...** '{I don't mean to boast/I
don't want to appear to be boasting
[lit., ** Let it not be like to praise
myself]}, but...' → öv-; **Kolay
gelsin.** '{Good luck with your
work./May it {be easy/go easily/lit.,
** come easy}', a polite expression
one should say to anyone engaged in
or about to engage in some usually
demanding task. There is no common
English equivalent. → gel- 1;
Korkarım [ki]... 'I'm afraid
[that]...', introduces information the
speaker is reluctant to convey. →
kork-; **Kutlu olsun!** 'May it be
blessed!', a formula of congratulation
on birthdays and religious as well as
on other, non-religious, official
holidays. → ol- 11 → olsun.

M: **Mekânı cennet olsun.** 'May
his [eternal] resting place be
paradise.' One of several phrases said
upon hearing of a death. The
deceased may also be addressed as
follows: **Mekânın cennet olsun.**
'May your [eternal] resting place be
paradise.' → ol- 11 → olsun;
Memnun oldum. 'Pleased to meet
you.': **Görüştüğümüze çok
memnun oldum.** 'Very pleased to
meet you [lit., I'm very pleased [that]
we {met/saw each other}].', **Sizinle
tanıştığıma memnun oldum.**
'{Pleased to meet you./I'm pleased θ
that I got acquainted with you.}' →

memnun ol- → ol- 12; **Mübarek
olsun!** 'May it be blessed!', a
formula of congratulation used
exclusively on religious holidays. →
ol- 11 → olsun.

N: **Ne var ne yok?** 'Q: {How are
things?/What's going on?/What's
happening?/What's up?/What's
new?}' → ol- 3, Additional
examples. b) 2. Essential question-
word questions; An address to the
deceased, Muslim or non-Muslim:
Nur içinde yat. 'May you rest in
peace [lit, in light].' A statement
about the deceased, Muslim or non-
Muslim: **Nur içinde yatsın.** 'May
he rest in peace.' → yat- 1.

Ö: **Övünmek gibi olmasın...** '{I
don't mean to boast/I don't want to
appear to be boasting [lit., ** Let it
not be like to praise myself]}, but...'
→ {övün-/öğün-} 2.

P: **Pardon, sözünüzü kestim.**
'Sorry, I have interrupted you.' →
kes- 3.

R: **Rica ederim.** 1 'Please.': a) In a
simple request. b) In expressing an
objection. 2 '{No problem./You're
welcome./Don't mention it.}' 3 in
response to a request. Usually not
translated or occasionally by 'Sure'
or 'No problem' → rica et-.

S: **Sağlıcakla kalın.** 'Take care.',
lit., 'Remain in good health and
happiness.', said by someone off on a
journey to those remaining behind. →
kal- 1; **Sağlık olsun.** 'Don't worry
about it., Never mind.' → ol- 11 →
olsun; **Sıhhatler olsun.** [Usually
pronounced saatler olsun] 'Good
health to you!' A formula used to
address sb who has been the subject
of a personal [bodily] service: The
barber uses it after he has cut your
hair, the bath attendant uses it when
he has just rubbed you down, or sb
who has not performed a service uses
it when he notices that such a service
has been performed for you or that
you have performed it on yourself. →
ol- 11 → olsun; **Size zahmet
olacak.** 'That's going to be
troublesome for you.', said to sb who
has offered to do sth for you. →
zahmet ol- → ol- 12; **Sizinle
tanıştığıma memnun oldum.**
'{Pleased to meet you./I'm pleased θ

that I got acquainted with you.}' →
memnun ol- → ol- 12; [Sonra]
görüşürüz. 'See you [later].' →
görüş- 1. See also 585:14.
HOSPITALITY: INTERJ. welcome!

T: Toprağı bol olsun. 'May he
rest in peace [lit., May his earth be
abundant].', said upon hearing of the
death of a non-Muslim. → ol- 11 →
olsun. The equivalent for a Muslim is
Allah rahmet eylesin. → rahmet
eyle-.

Y: Yarın görüşürüz. 'See you
tomorrow., WE'll see EACH OTHER
tomorrow.' → görüş- 1; Yine
bekleriz. 'Please come again.', a
formula said to departing guests. →
bekle- 1.

Z: Ziyade olsun! 'May you always
enjoy abundance!', words said to a
hostess after a meal or to a person
who, when with friends, has paid the
bill. → ol- 11 → olsun.

505 DISCOURTESY
505:3. * 1 - be discourteous
/{ArAk/mAklA}/ {çok ol-/ileri
git- 2} '- go too far, - overstep the
limit, - be rude /BY...ing/' → ol- 12,
git- 1a.

508 RIDICULE
508:8 - ridicule /1A/ alay et- '-
make fun /OF/, - ridicule /θ/, - mock
/θ/'; /I/ alaya al- '- make fun of, -
ridicule, - laugh at' → al- 8; bıyık
altından gül- '- laugh {up/in}
one's sleeve, - be secretly amused, -
laugh or - smile maliciously' → gül-
2; /1A, diye/ dalga geç- 2 '- make
fun /OF [sb], BECAUSE/' → geç- 1;
/1A/ eğlen- 2 '- make fun /OF/, -
joke /with/ sb'; /A/ gül- 2 '- laugh
/AT/, - mock /θ/, - make fun /OF/'.

508:10 - boo ıslık çal- '- whistle'
→ çal- 2; yuhala- '- boo, - jeer'.

509 APPROVAL
509:9 - approve /I/
{hoş/iyi/olumlu} karşıla- '-
approve /OF/' → karşıla- 3; kabul
et- 2 '- agree /to/ or - accept a
proposal, suggestion, - approve'; /I/
onayla- '- approve sth, - approve
/OF/ sth'; /{tarafından/CA}/
onaylan- '- be approved /by/'; razı
ol- 1 /A/ '- agree, - consent, or - be
willing /to/, - approve; - be content

/WITH/'. 2 /DAn/ '- be pleased
/WITH/, approving, - approve' → ol-
12.

509:10 - applaud /I/ alkışla- '-
applaud /θ/ sb, - applaud or - clap
/FOR/ sb [not for a performance]';
ıslık çal- '- whistle', as a sign of
approval [man at a girl]. → çal- 2.

509:11 - commend /A/ tavsiye
et- '- recommend, - advise, -
propose, - suggest sth /to/'.

509:12 - praise /DAn dolayı,
için, nedeniyle/ {öv-/methet-}
'- praise sb or sth /for/ sth', not
usually with God as the object;
/{tarafından/CA}, nedeniyle/
övül- '- be praised /by, for/'; /a: A,
b: DAn dolayı, c: A/ şükret- '-
give thanks /a: to [God], b:
{for/because of}, c: θ [that]/, - praise
/a: θ [God], b: {for/because of}, c: θ
[that]/, - be thankful /a: to [God], b:
FOR/'.

509:22 INTERJ. bravo! /A/
Aşkolsun. 2 'Good for {him/you}!,
Bravo!, Nice going!' → ol- 11 →
olsun; Çok yaşa! 1 'Long Live..!' 2
'Bravo!, Hurray!, Good for you!' →
yaşa- 1; /A/ Helâl olsun. 2 'Bravo
/to/!, Good for {him/you}!, Nice
going!' → ol- 11 → olsun; Ne iyi
ettin de [geldin]! '{It's good/How
nice/What a good thing/How good}
that [you came]!' → iyi et-; Sağ
olsun. 'Bless {him/her}!' → sağ ol-
→ ol- 12; /A/ Şükürler olsun
[ki]... '{Thanks be /to/ God
[that].../Praise be /to/ God [that]...}'.
'God' is always implied although a
word for God may not appear. → ol-
11 → olsun.

510 DISAPPROVAL
510:10 - disapprove This category
may be covered by the negative of the
verbs under 509:9. APPROVAL: -
approve.

510:13. - censure /DIğI için/
kına- '- reproach, - condemn, -
censure /{for/because}/'.

510:14 - criticize /a: {DIğI
için/DIğInDAn}, b: DAn
dolayı, c: yüzünden/ {eleştir-
/tenkit et-} '- criticize /a: because
[or for], b: for, c: {for/on account
of}/'; /a: {DIğI için/DIğInDAn},

b: DAn dolayı, c: {tarafından/CA}/ {eleştiril-/tenkit edil-} '- be criticized /a: because [or for], b: for, c: by/'. Same as 945:14. JUDGMENT: - criticize.

510:17 - reprove /DIğI için/ azarla- '- scold, - reprimand, - rebuke /{for/because}/'.

510:20. * 1 gestures of disappproval kaşlarını çat- '- knit one's brows, - frown'; yüzü buruş- 1 '- grimace, - scowl, - make a face [lit., for one's face - wrinkle]'; yüzünü buruştur- '- grimace, - scowl, - make a face [lit., - wrinkle one's face]'.

510:27 INTERJ. God forbid! You scold sb for sth he has done. You say: Beğendin mi yaptığın işi? 'Now just look at what you've done! Are you {proud of/pleased with} yourself?' → beğen- 1; /mAklA/ Çok ayıp ettin! 'You behaved very shamefully /BY...ing/!' → ayıp et-; Aşkolsun! 1 'Shame on you!, For shame!' → ol- 11 → olsun; Utan! Same. → utan-; Yazıklar olsun! 1 'What a shame!' → yazık ol- → ol- 12; Yuh olsun! '{For shame!/Shame on them!}' → ol- 11 → olsun.

512 DISPARAGEMENT
512:8 - disparage yer- '- run down, - point out the faults of, - criticize, - speak ill of, - disparage'.

512:11 - slander arkasından konuş- '- speak ill of sb behind his back'; karala- 3 '- slander'.

513 CURSE
513:6 - curse /A, DIğI için/ {küfret-/söv-} '- curse /θ/, - swear /AT, because/'.

513:11 INTERJ. damn! Allah belâsını versin. '[May] God damn {him/her/it}!' → ver- 1; [Allah] kahretsin! '[God] damn {him/her/it}!' → kahret- 2; Kahrolsun! 1 'Damn {him/her/it}!, To hell with {him/her/it}!' 2 'Down with ... [fascism, communism]!' → kahrol- → ol- 12; Lânet olsun! 'Damn {him/her/it}!' → ol- 11 → olsun; Sürüm sürüm sürünürsün

inşallah. 'May you suffer the greatest misery.' → sürün- 2.

514 THREAT
514:2 - threaten /lA/ tehdit et- '- threaten sb /with/ sth'.

514: * 5 INTERJ. specific threats Alırım ayağımın altına! 'I'll give you a whipping!' → al- 1; Anandan doğduğuna pişman ederim. 'I'll make you sorry you were ever born [lit., born OF your mother]!' → doğ- 1; {Canımı sıkma/Kafamı bozma}, yoksa karışmam, [ona göre]! '{Don't get on my nerves/Don't spoil my mood}, or who knows what I might do, [so watch out]!' → canını sık- 2 → sık- 3, kafasını boz- → boz- 1; Gebertirim! 'I'll kill you!' contemptuous. → gebert-; Seni ayağından {tavana/ağaca} asarım! 'I'll hang you {ON the ceiling/ON the tree} BY your feet!' → as- 1; Yakarım canını! 'I'll really make you suffer [lit., ** I'll burn your soul]!' → canını yak- → yak- 2.

515 FASTING
515:4 - fast oruç tut- '- keep or - observe the fast, - fast' → tut- 5.

516 SOBRIETY
516:5 - sober up ayıl- 1 '- sober up'.

CLASS 8: LANGUAGE

517 SIGNS, INDICATORS
517:17 - signify ifade et- 2 '- mean, - signify, - express [subj.: sign, picture, word]'.

517:19 - mark /lA/ altını çiz- 1 '- underline, - underscore, - draw a line under /IN [ink], with [a ruler]/' → çiz- 1; çiz- 3 '- scratch, - scarify [subj.: an instrument on metal]'; /I/ işaret et- '- mark [places in a book]'; /A/ işaret koy- '- mark, - mark up, - put notations /IN/ [places in a book]' → koy- 1; /I/ işaretle- '- mark'.

517:21 - gesture taksi çevir- '- hail a cab, taxi' → çevir- 1.

517:22 - signal /A/ işaret et- 3 '- make a sign or gesture for sb to do sth'; <u>bayrağı selâmla-</u> '- salute the flag'; /A/ <u>el salla-</u> '- wave [hand] /to/', in goodbye or greeting. → salla- 1; /A/ <u>göz kırp-</u> 2 '- wink /AT/ [man at a girl]' → kırp-; <u>salla-</u> 1 '- wave [obj.: flags, banners]'.

518 MEANING
518:8 - mean | <u>de-</u> 3 '- mean [subj.: a word, sentence]; - intend'; <u>ifade et-</u> 2 '- mean, - signify, - express [subj.: sign, picture, word]'.

519 LATENT MEANING-FULNESS
519:4 - imply | /1A, DAn/ <u>kastet-</u> 1 '- mean, - have in mind, - intend to say /BY/'.

520 MEANINGLESSNESS
520:5 - talk nonsense | {abuk sabuk/saçma sapan} <u>konuş-</u> '- talk nonsense, hogwash'; <u>saçmala-</u> '- talk nonsense, - talk {garbage/rot}, - be silly'.

521 INTELLIGIBILITY
521:5 - be understood | /{tarafından/CA}/ <u>anlaşıl-</u> '- be understood /by/, - be or - become clear, - be determined'.

521:6 - make clear | /A/ <u>açıkla-</u> 1 '- explain sth /to/ sb, - clarify sth /FOR/ sb'; /A/ <u>anlat-</u> 1. Same; /A/ <u>izah et-</u>. Same.

521:7 - understand | <u>anla-</u> '- understand, - realize'; /DAn/ <u>anla-</u> '- understand a lot /ABOUT/, - know sth /ABOUT/', usually a field of knowledge, implies expertise'; <u>anlaş-</u> 1 '- understand one another'; <u>takdir et-</u> 2 '- appreciate, - understand sb's situation, difficulties'; <u>yakala-</u> 2 '- catch, - be able to hear, understand [words]'.

522 UNINTELLIGIBILITY
522:11 not - understand | <u>aklı alMA-</u> 'NOT - understand, grasp, figure out, - make NO sense of' → al- 1. This category may also be covered by the negative of verbs under 521:7. INTELLIGIBILITY.

524 SPEECH
524:20 - speak | /1A/ <u>görüş-</u> 1 '- see one another; - meet /with/; - talk, - speak, - confer, or - discuss /with/, - see [i.e., - confer]'; <u>havadan sudan konuş-</u> '- speak {OF/ABOUT} this and that [i.e., various unimportant

subjects at random]'; /a: I, b: hakkında, c: A dair, d: üzerine, e: konusunda/ <u>konuş-</u> '- speak /a, b: about, c: concerning, d: on, e: on the subject of/'; <u>şundan bundan konuş-</u> '- speak ABOUT this and that [i.e., various subjects at random]'; [Türkçe/İngilizce] <u>konuş-</u> '- speak [Turkish/English]'.

524:22 - speak up | <u>ses çıkarMA-</u> 1 '- keep quiet, NOT - say anything, NOT - speak up' → çıkar- 7.

524:23 - say | <u>de-</u> 1 '- say'; <u>söyle-</u> 1 '- say, - tell /{to/θ}/'; <u>telâffuz et-</u> '- pronounce'; <u>telâffuz edil-</u> '- be pronounced'.

524:24 - state | <u>belirt-</u> '- state, - make clear'; <u>kaydet-</u> 4 '- state, - announce, - declare, - note', *formal, official*: used in speech and in writing.

524:25 - remark | <u>belirt-</u> '- state, - make clear'; /A/ <u>değin-</u> '- touch /ON/, - mention /θ/ a subject'; /A/ <u>dikkat çek-</u> '- call or - draw attention /to/, - point out /θ/, - note /θ/' → çek- 1; /A/ <u>işaret et-</u> 2 '- point out, - indicate a fact, - call attention /to/'; /A/ <u>temas et-</u> 2 = /A/ değin-.

524:26 - utter in a certain way | *verb stem*.mIş gibi <u>konuş-</u> '- speak as if [he were an expert]'; <u>ses çıkar-</u> 1 '- raise one's voice, - speak up' → çıkar- 7; *noun designating a language*.sI var. 'He {knows/speaks} *noun designating a language*': Türkçesi var. 'He {knows/speaks} Turkish' or 'A Turkish version [or translation] of it [a book, etc.] exists.' This pattern, rather than Türkçe konuşur, is usually used for expressing 'He speaks' a language. → ol- 3, Additional examples. b) 4. Miscellaneous additional examples. For numerous additional examples of particular ways of speaking, → konuş- and söyle- in the Turkish-English Dictionary of Verbs.

524:27 - address | /A/ <u>hitap et-</u> '- address /θ/ sb', i.e., '- speak /to/ sb, - talk /to/ sb', *formal*; /A/ <u>konuş-</u> '- speak /to/'; /A/ <u>söyle-</u> 3 '- speak /to/ sb, - talk /to/ sb'.

524: * 35 proverbs __Az söyle,__ __çok dinle.__ 'Say little but do a lot of listening.' → söyle- 1; __Bıçak yarası__ __geçer, dil yarası geçmez.__ 'A knife wound heals [lit., passes], a wound inflicted by the tongue [lit., a tongue wound, i.e., an insult, harsh words, etc.] does not.' → geç- 4; __Düşünmeden söyleme.__ 'Think before you speak [lit., Don't speak without thinking].' → düşün- 1; __Gider kılıç yarası, gitmez dil yarası.__ 'A sword wound will heal [lit., go], but a wound inflicted by the tongue [lit., a tongue wound] will not.' This is the exact opposite of the English proverb 'Sticks and stones will break my bones, but words will never hurt me.' It reflects Turkish sensitivity to harsh words. → git- 1; __Önce düşün sonra söyle.__ 'Think first, then speak.' Think before you speak. → söyle- 1; In general, not in reference to a particular project: __Söylemek kolay, yapmak güç.__ 'It is easy to talk [i.e., about plans], but difficult to get things done.', i.e., Talk is cheap. In reference to a particular project: __Söyleme.si kolay, yapma.sı güç.__ 'It is easy to talk about it but difficult to carry it out [lit., ** Its saying is easy, its doing is difficult].' Put your money where your mouth is. → söyle- 1; __Tatlı dil bin kapı açar.__ 'A sweet tongue opens a thousand doors.' → aç- 1; __Tatlı dil yılanı deliğinden çıkarır.__ 'A sweet tongue will get a snake to come out of its hole.' → çıkar- 1; __Tatlı ye, tatlı söyle.__ 'Eat sweet things, speak sweetly.' → söyle- 1.

527 NOMENCLATURE

527:11 - name /A/ {ad/isim} __koy-__ '- name' → koy- 1; /A/ __{ad/isim} tak-__ '- name, - call, - dub /θ/', usually with a negative connotation when the object is a person; /A/ {ad/isim} __ver-__ '- give a name /to/, - name /θ/' → ver- 1; /diye/ __{adlandır-/isimlendir-}__ '- call, - name, - dub, - refer to /AS/'; /diye/ __çağır-__ 4 '- call, - refer to /AS/'; /A/ __de-__ 4 '- call /θ/ sb or sth by a certain name'.

527:13 - be called /{diye/olarak}, {tarafından/CA}/ __{adlandırıl-/isimlendiril-}__ '- be called, named, referred to /AS, by/'; /A/ __den-__ '- be said, - be called ['What is this called in Turkish?'].'

527:14 ADJ. named __diye__ 5 'named, called, by the name of', when diye is preceded by a name, but not followed by a verb of naming. → de- 1.

532 DICTION

532:4 - phrase {a: duygularını/b: düşüncelerini/c: fikirlerini} __anlat-__ '- express or - relate {a: one's feelings/b: one's thoughts/c: one's ideas}; - express oneself' → anlat- 2; __ifade et-__ 1 '- express, - say what one means, - state'; __kendini ifade et-__ '- express oneself' → ifade et- 1.

541 CONVERSATION

541:10 - chat /1A/ __çene çal-__ '- chat, - gossip, - chew the fat /with/' → çal- 2; /1A/ __muhabbet et-__ '- chat, - have a [friendly] chat /with/'; /1A/ __sohbet et-__ '- chat, - talk, - have a chat /with/'; __sohbete dal-__ '- get involved /IN/ or - plunge /INTO/ a friendly conversation' → dal- 4.

541:11 - confer __bilgisine danış-__ '- consult a person', lit., ** '- consult /θ/ sb's knowledge'; /A, konusunda/ __danış-__ '- consult /θ [sb, an office], {about/on the subject of}/, - refer /to [sb], regarding/ [person or reference source: dictionary]'; /1A/ __görüş-__ '- see one another; - meet /with/; - talk, - speak, - confer, - discuss /with/, - see [i.e., - confer]'.

541:12 - discuss /DAn/ __bahset-__ '- talk /ABOUT/ sth, - mention /θ/ sth, - discuss /θ/ sth'; /DAn/ __söz et-__ '- talk /ABOUT/, - tell /{ABOUT/OF}/, - mention /θ/'; __sözünü et-__ '- mention sth, - make mention of sth' → söz et-.

543 PUBLIC SPEAKING

543:10 - declaim __oku-__ 4 '- recite [without a text, from memory]'.

546 LETTER

546:6 - letter /A/ __imza at-__ '- sign /θ/', colloq.: '- put one's John Hancock /ON/ [obj.: check] [lit., ** throw (one's) signature /ON/ the check].' → at- 3. Perhaps less formal than the following: /I/ __{imzala-/imza et-}__ '- sign'.

546:7 - spell {harf harf/harflerini} söyle- '- spell, - say {letter by letter/the letters of [a word]}' → söyle- 1; hecele- '- syllabify, - say or - read by syllable', how Turks usually indicate the spelling of a word instead of giving letter names.

547 WRITING

547:19 - write /a: A, b: A, c: DA, d: lA/ yaz- 1 '- write /a: to [sb], b: {ON/IN}, c: {in/on}, d: with [a pencil]/'. 2 '- say', when referring to a written document or sign, as in: What does today's paper say?; /A/ yazdır- 1 '- have /θ/ sb write, - get /θ/ sb to write, - let /θ/ sb write'; /a: A, b: A, c: DA, d: lA, e: tarafından/ yazıl- 1 '- be written /a: to [sb], b: {ON/IN}, c: {in/on}, d: with [a pencil], e: by [the teacher]/'; The Ahmet'in kitabı var structure [i.e., *possessOR noun*.[n]In + *possessED noun*.sI var] is frequently used to indicate authorship rather than possession: Yazarın beş kitabı var. 'The author HAS {WRITTEN/AUTHORED} five books [lit., 'The author HAS five books.', a translation appropriate in contexts where possession rather than authorship is at issue]. → ol- 5, (5.1) Table 1. Additional examples. 4. Miscellaneous examples.

548 PRINTING

548:14 - print bas- 3 '- print, - publish'; film bas- '- develop and print' or only '- print [photographic film]' → bas- 3; /DA/ yayımla- 1 '- publish /in/'; /DA, {tarafından/CA}/ yayımlan- 1 '- be published /in, by/'.

549 RECORD

549:15 - record kaydet- 1 /A/ '- register or - enroll sb [not oneself] /IN [a course], {IN/AT} [a school]/'. 2 /A/ '- record sth /IN/, - enter sth /IN/, - write sth down /IN/'. 3 /A, lA/ '- record, - tape /ON [a medium], with [an instrument]/'; /A/ kaydol- '- register or - enroll [oneself], - get oneself registered /IN [a course], {IN/AT} [a school]/' → ol- 12; /a: A, b: A, c: DA, d: lA/ yaz- 1 '- write /a: to [sb], b: {ON/IN}, c: {in/on}, d: with [a pencil]/'; /A/ yazdır- 2 '- register or - enroll sb /IN [a course], {IN/AT} [a school]/'; /A/ yazıl- 2 = kaydol-.

551 INFORMATION

551:8 - inform /DAn/ bahset- '- talk /ABOUT/, - mention /θ/, - discuss /θ/'; /A/ bildir- '- inform /θ/, - get information /to/, - report /to/'; /a: A, b: hakkında, c: ile ilgili/ bilgi ver- '- give or - provide information /a: to, b: about, c: concerning/, - inform, - tell /about/' → ver- 1; geç- 7 '- be mentioned, written, related, referred to, spoken about, discussed, - occur [facts in a written work]'; /A/ haber ver- = bildir- → ver- 1; /DAn/ söz et- '- talk /ABOUT/, - tell /{ABOUT/OF}/, - mention /θ/'; sözünü et- '- mention, - make mention of' → söz et-; /A, olarak/ tanıt- '- introduce sb or sth /to, AS/, - make sb or sth known /to, AS/, - acquaint sb /with/ sth, - inform, - tell /θ/ sb about sth'.

551:15 - know, - be informed /I/ duy- 2 '- hear /{OF/ABOUT}/, - learn /OF/, - get word /OF/'; /I/ işit- 2. Same.

552 NEWS

552:11 - report /A/ anlat- 2 '- relate sth /to/ sb, - tell /θ/ sb sth, - tell sth /to/ sb'; /DAn, A/ haber getir- '- bring news /from, to/'.

552:12 - gossip /hakkında/ dedikodu yap- '- gossip /about/' → yap- 3.

553 CORRESPONDENCE

553:10 - correspond /lA/ mektuplaş- '- write [letters] to one another, - correspond /with/, - be in correspondence /with/ sb by letter'.

553:12 - mail /A/ at- 4 '- mail, - post, - send off [mail]', *informal*, perhaps more like '- drop in the mailbox'; postala- '- mail, - post, - send off, - mail /to/', *more formal* than at- 4; /A, {tarafından/CA}/ postalan- '- be mailed, posted, sent off /to, by/ [letter, package]'.

557 ABRIDGMENT

557:5 - abridge özetle- '- summarize, - sum up'; toparla- 2 '- summarize, - put information in a nutshell'.

557:7   ADV.   in   brief Özetleyeyim... 'Let me summarize...' → özetle-;

<u>Toparlayacak olursak...</u> 'To summarize, In summary [lit., If we are to summarize]...' → toparla- 2.

CLASS 9: HUMAN SOCIETY AND INSTITUTIONS

562 LOVEMAKING, ENDEARMENT

562:14 - make love /lA/ <u>çık-</u> 10 '- go [out] on a date /with/, - go out /with/, - date, - be dating', but with the intention of marriage; /lA/ <u>flört et-</u>. Same. Not the English '- flirt'; /lA/ <u>oynaş-</u> 2 '- carry on a love affair /with/, *slang:* - make out /with/'; /lA/ <u>seviş-</u> 2 '- caress each other, *slang:* - make out /with/; - make love /with/, - have sexual intercourse /with/'; /lA/ <u>yat-</u> 2 '- go to bed /with/, - sleep /with/ [i.e., - have sex /with/]'.

562:16 - caress /lA/ <u>oynaş-</u> 2 '- carry on a love affair /with/, *slang:* - make out /with/'; /lA/ <u>seviş-</u> 2 '- caress each other, *slang:* - make out /with/; - make love /with/, - have sexual intercourse /with/'.

562:18 - embrace <u>birbirlerini kucakla-</u> '- embrace or - hug one another'; /I/ <u>kucakla-</u> '- embrace, - take in one's arms; - hug'; <u>kucaklaş-</u> = birbirlerini kucakla-; /A/ <u>sarıl-</u> 1 '- embrace /θ/, - put or - throw one's arms /AROUND/'.

562:19 - kiss /DAn/ <u>öp-</u> '- kiss /ON/ [a part of the body: the eyes]'; <u>öpüş-</u> '- kiss one another'.

562:20 - flirt /A/ <u>göz kırp-</u> 2 '- wink /AT/ [man at a girl]' → kırp-.

562:21 - court i.e., - approach with sexual intent: /A/ <u>asıl-</u> 3 '- come on /to/ sb, - make a play /FOR/ sb, - chase /AFTER/ sb', *slang*; /A/ <u>kur yap-</u> '- chase /AFTER/, - court /θ/, - pay court /to/, - try to woo /θ/', *formal, polite.* → yap- 3.

563 MARRIAGE

563:14 - join in marriage /lA/ <u>evlendir-</u> '- marry, - give sb in marriage /TO/'; /A/ <u>kız ver-</u> '- give a girl in marriage /to/' → ver- 1; <u>nikâh kıy-</u> '- perform the marriage ceremony, - officially join in marriage, - marry' → kıy- 3.

563:15 - get married /lA/ <u>dünya evine gir-</u> '- get married, - marry /θ/ [lit., - enter the house of the world /with/]'; *more common:* /lA/ <u>evlen-</u> '- get married /TO/, - marry /θ/'.

565 CELIBACY

565:5 - be unmarried <u>evde kal-</u> '- remain unmarried [for a woman], - be an old maid [lit., - remain at home]' → kal- 1.

566 DIVORCE, WIDOWHOOD

566:5 - divorce /DAn/ <u>ayrıl-</u> 1 '- get or - be divorced /from/, - split up /WITH/'; /I/ <u>boşa-</u> '- divorce sb'; /DAn/ <u>boşan-</u> '- get divorced /from/, - split up /WITH/'; <u>eşinden ayrıl-</u> '- get or - be divorced /from/ one's spouse, - split up /WITH/ one's spouse' → ayrıl- 1.

568 TEACHING

568:10 - teach /A/ <u>ders ver-</u> 1 '- teach /θ/ sb, - give lessons /to/ sb'. 2 '- teach a moral lesson /to/' → ver- 1; /konuda/ <u>eğit-</u> '- educate sb /on a subject/'; <u>okut-</u> 2 /I/ '- make it possible for sb to be educated, - have sb educated, - see to sb's education, - educate sb, - send sb to school [i.e., pay his way]'. 3 /A/ '- teach sth /to/ sb'; /A/ <u>öğret-</u> '- teach /θ/ sb sth, - teach sth /to/ sb'.

568:11 - tutor <u>çalıştır-</u> 1 b) /A/ '- have or - make /θ/ sb work on sth; - tutor /θ/ sb'.

568:13 - train <u>büyüt-</u> 3 '- raise or - bring up a child'; <u>yetiştir-</u> 2 '- bring up, - rear, - raise, - educate, - train [children]'.

570 LEARNING

570:6 - learn /DAn/ <u>bilgi edin-</u> '- obtain or - receive information /from/, - learn /from/'; /DAn/ <u>ders al-</u> 2 '- learn a [moral] lesson /from/' → al- 1; /DAn/ <u>haber al-</u> '- get word, news /{OF/from}/, - find out /from/' → al- 3; /DAn/ <u>öğren-</u> '- learn, - find out /from/'.

570:8 - memorize <u>ezberle-</u> '- memorize, - commit to memory, - learn by heart'. See also 988:17. MEMORY: - memorize.

570:9 - master <u>çok iyi öğren-</u> '- learn very well, - master' → öğren- 1;

/DA/ *degree name* [e.g., master, doktora] yap- '- get or - do a [{master's/Ph.D.} degree] /IN/' → yap- 3.

570:10 - learn by experience
akıllan- '- become wiser through bitter experience, - come to one's senses about a matter, - wise up'; aklı başına gel- '- come to one's senses' → gel- 1; kendine gel- 2 '- pull oneself together, - regain self-control, - come to one's senses' → gel- 1.

570:11 - be taught, - receive instruction /DAn/ ders al- 1 '- take lessons /from/'; {eğitim/ öğrenim/tahsil} gör- '- have an education, - be educated' → gör- 3; kurs gör- '- take a course' → gör- 3.

570:12 - study çalış- 1 '- work, - study [lessons], - work /ON/, - practice sth [piano]'; ders çalış- '- study ['I'm studying.']' → çalış- 1; derse çalış- '- study, - work on a particular lesson [What lesson are you studying?]' → çalış- 1; oku- 1 '- read'. 2 '- study [somewhere], - study a subject', a subject area, not a particular lesson: Turkish, economics, but not necessarily a major field of interest; okut- 1 /A/ '- have or - let /θ/ sb read sth'. 2 /I/ '- make it possible for sb to be educated; - get sb educated, - educate sb, - send sb to school [pay his way]'; tahsil et- '- study a subject', usually as a major field of interest, specialization: economics, music, not '- study one's lessons'.

570:13 - browse /DA, arasında/ gezin- 2 '- browse, - surf /on/ [the Internet], - scan, - flip /through/ [TV channels]'; şöyle bir bak- '- just look around, - browse [in a store]' → bak- 1.

570: * 19 PHR. experience is the best teacher Proverb: Çok okuyan değil çok gezen bilir. 'It's not the one who has read a lot, but the one who has traveled {a lot/widely} that knows.' → bil- 1.1, gez-, oku- 1. Proverb: Çok yaşayan bilmez, çok gezen bilir. 'It's not the one who has lived long, but the one who has traveled widely that knows [lit., The one who has lived long does not know, the one who has traveled a lot

knows].' → bil- 1.1, gez-, yaşa- 1. Proverb: Çok yaşayan, çok görür. 'He who lives long {sees/experiences} much.' → gör- 3, yaşa- 1.

573 DIRECTION, MANAGE-MENT
573:8 - direct ayarla- 1 '- regulate, - fix, - set, - adjust [guage regulates room temperature]'; düzenle- 3 '- regulate, - control [guage regulates room temperature]'; idare et- 1 '- administer, - direct, - manage, - run, - control, - govern, - rule [person runs school, team, business]'; yönet- 1. Same.

576 DEPUTY, AGENT
576:14 - represent temsil et- '- represent'.

577 SERVANT, EMPLOYEE
577:13 - serve /A/ hizmet et- '- serve /θ/ [one's country, guests], - wait /{ON/UPON}/ [guests], - attend /to/ [guests]'.

578 FASHION
578:8 - catch on /CA, arasında/ tutul- 3 'for [a fashion, song, book] - catch on, - become popular or fashionable, - win a following /{IN/AMONG}, {IN/among}/'.

582 SOCIABILITY
582:17 - associate with /IA/ gel- '- come /with/ [you to the movies]' → gel- 1; /A/ katıl- 2 '- participate /IN/, - take part /IN/, - get involved /IN/; - join /θ/ [obj.: a person or group for some activity: Let me join θ you.]'.

582:19 - visit /A/ gel- 1 '- come to see or - visit'; /A/ git- 3 '- go /to/, - visit /θ/ [a person or a place]'; misafirliğe git- '- go /ON/ a visit, - go visiting, - pay a visit to sb, - go to visit [a person, not a place], - call on sb', usually a neighbor or friend, not a relative or person of higher station; a casual, not formal, visit. → git- 3; /DAn, için/ randevu al- '- make an appointment /for/, - get an appointment /from [sb], for/' → al- 3; /A/ uğra- 1 '- stop in /AT/, - drop in /{AT/ON}/, - drop /BY/, - call /{ON/UPON}/ [a person or a place]'; /I/ ziyaret et- '- visit, - pay a visit /to/ a person or place, - call on sb'; /I/ ziyarete git- '- go to visit or - call on', usually a respected person

697

[i.e., an older person, sb of high station], or perhaps sb requiring special attention such as a sick person, or '- go to visit', a place of reverence associated with such a person [e.g., a cemetery or grave site], or '- go on a visit' in connection with a holiday, bairam → git- 3; **ziyaretine git-**. Same explanation as above, but not a place unless that place is treated as if it were the person himself → git- 3.

584 SECLUSION
584:7 - seclude oneself | **yalnızlık çek-** '- be lonely' → çek- 5.

585 HOSPITALITY, WELCOME
585:8 - entertain | **parti ver-** '- give or - have a party' → ver- 1.

585:10 - greet | /I/ **el sık-** '- shake hands /WITH/ sb, - shake sb's hand' → sık- 1; /IA/ **merhabalaş-** '- greet one another'; /A/ **selâm ver-** = **selâmla-** → ver- 1; /I/ **selâmla-** '- greet [person], - salute [person and flag]'; /IA/ **selâmlaş-** = merhabalaş-; /IA/ **tokalaş-** '- shake hands /with/'.

585:14 INTERJ. welcome! | **Hoş geldin[iz]!** 1 'Welcome!', words of the host. 2 'Hello., Hi.' → gel- 1. The response: **Hoş bulduk!** 'Glad to be here!' → bul- 1.

587 FRIENDSHIP
587:9 - be friends | **tanı-** 1.1 '- know sb, - be acquainted /WITH/ sb'. 1.2 '- know the real nature of sb, what kind of person he is', not in the casual sense of '- be acquainted with'; /IA/ **tanış-** '- get to know, - get acquainted /with/ one another, - meet /θ/; - be acquainted with, - know one another'.

587:10 - befriend, - make friends with | /A/ **ısın-** 3 '- come or - grow to like; - warm {UP TO/to/TOWARDS}/'; /I/ **tanı-** 3 '- get to know sb, - become acquainted /WITH/ sb, - meet sb'; /IA/ **tanış-** '- get to know, - get acquainted /with/ one another, - meet /θ/; - be acquainted with, - know one another'.

587:14 - introduce | /A/ **takdim et-** 1 '- introduce, - present one person /to/ another'; **tanıştır-** /IA/

'- introduce one person /TO/ another', /A/ '- introduce one person /to/ another'; /A, olarak/ **tanıt-** '- introduce sb or sth /to, AS/, - make sb or sth known /to, AS/, - acquaint sb /with/ sth, - inform, - tell /θ/ sb about sth'.

594 JURISDICTION
594:5 - administer justice | **yargıla-** '- hear a case; - try sb, a case; - judge or - adjudicate a case, - pass judgment on'.

598 LEGAL ACTION
598:12 - sue | /aleyhine, için/ **dava aç-** '- bring or - file a suit or charges /against [sb], for [a misdeed]/, - file a complaint or claim /against/ sb, - sue sb' → aç- 12; /I/ **dava et-** '- bring a suit or charges /AGAINST/, - sue'; **mahkemeye ver-** '- sue, - take to court' → ver- 1.

598:17 - try | **yargıla-** '- hear a case; - try sb, a case; - judge or - adjudicate a case, - pass judgment on'.

599 ACCUSATION
599:7 - accuse | **şikâyet et-** a) /DAn, A/ '- complain /{OF/ABOUT} [sth], to [yourself or to a friend, but usually not to a responsible authority]/', b) /a: I, b: A, c: DIğI için/ '- complain /a: {OF/ABOUT} [sth], b: to [an authority], c: because/'.

599:8 - blame | /a: IA, b: DAn dolayı, c: konusunda/ **suçla-** '- accuse /a, c: OF/, - blame /b: FOR/'.

600-700

601 ACQUITTAL
601:4 - acquit | /A/ **rahmet eyle-** 'for God - be merciful /to/, for God - have mercy /{ON/UPON}/'.

602 CONDEMNATION
602:3 - condemn | /IA/ **cezalandırıl-** 2 '- be sentenced /TO/ a punishment [for a crime]'; /A/ **mahkûm ol-** 1 '- be sentenced, condemned /to/ a punishment'. 2 '- be condemned, doomed /to/ [a fate: life in a wheelchair]' → ol- 12.

603 PENALTY

603:5 - fine /DAn, DAn/ <u>ceza ye-</u> '- be punished or fined /BY [sb], FOR [sth]/' → ye- 2.

604 PUNISHMENT

604:10 - punish /DAn/ <u>ceza al-</u> '- receive punishment /from/ sb, - be punished /by/ sb' → al- 3; /A/ <u>ceza kes-</u> '- fine /θ/ sb, - give a ticket /to/ sb, a vehicle' → kes- 5; /A/ <u>ceza ver-</u> '- punish' → ver- 1; /DAn, DAn/ <u>ceza ye-</u> '- be punished or fined /BY [sb], FOR [sth]/' → ye- 2; <u>cezalandır-</u> = ceza ver-; /lA/ <u>cezalandırıl-</u> 1 '- be punished /with/'.

604:12 - slap <u>eliyle vur-</u> '- slap, - strike with one's hand' → vur- 1; /A/ <u>tokat {at-/vur-}</u> '- slap /θ/ sb' → at- 5; <u>tokat ye-</u> '- get a slap, - be slapped' → ye- 2. Same as 901:19. IMPULSE, IMPACT: - slap.

604:13 - whip <u>ayağının altına al-</u> '- give a whipping, beating, thrashing, - beat, - thrash' → al- 1; /A/ <u>dayak at-</u> '- beat, - give a whipping, beating, - thrash /θ/' → at- 5; /DAn/ <u>dayak ye-</u> '- get a thrashing, beating /from/' → ye- 2; <u>döv-</u> '- beat, - strike'.

604:18 - hang /A, DAn, yüzünden/ <u>as-</u> 2 '- hang /to, FOR, for/', as a form of execution.

604:19 - be hanged /a: A, b: lA, c: {tarafından/CA}/ <u>asıl-</u> 2 '- be hanged /a: {to/ON} [a tree], b: FOR [a crime], c: by [bandits]/', as a form of execution.

612 GOVERNMENT

612:14 - rule <u>idare et-</u> 1 '- administer, - direct, - manage, - run, - control, - govern, - rule'; <u>yönet-</u> 1. Same.

615 COMMISSION

615:11 - appoint /A, olarak/ {<u>ata-/tayin et-</u>} '- appoint, - assign, - name sb /to [a position], AS [a teacher]/'; /a: A, b: olarak, c: {tarafından/CA}/ {<u>atan-/tayin edil-</u>} '- be appointed, assigned, named /a: to [a position], b: AS [a teacher], c: by/'; /lA/ <u>görevlendir-</u> '- charge, - entrust sb /with/ [a task, duty], - give sb the task /OF/, - make sb responsible /FOR/, - put sb in charge /OF/'; /lA, tarafından/ <u>görevlendiril-</u> '- be charged, entrusted /with, by/, - be given the task /OF, by/, - be made responsible /FOR, by/, - be put in charge /OF, by/'; <u>tayin edil-</u> → {atan-/tayin edil-}; <u>tayin et-</u> → {ata-/tayin et-}; /A, olarak/ <u>tayin ol-</u> '- be appointed, assigned, named /to [a position], AS [a teacher]' → ol- 12. This verb is not used with an agent noun preceded by {tarafından/CA}. For such usage, see **atan-, görevlendiril-**.

615:14 - employ /DAn/ <u>tut-</u> 6b '- hire sb, - engage sb /from/'.

615:15 - rent /DAn, A/ <u>kirala-</u> 1 '- rent, - lease, - hire /from, FOR/'; {kirada/kirayla} <u>otur-</u> '- rent [I don't own this house, I rent it., i.e., pay rent to live in it] → otur- 3; /Dan, A/ <u>tut-</u> 6a '- hire, - rent [vehicle, place] /from, FOR/'.

615:16 - rent out /A, A/ {<u>kirala-/kiraya ver-</u>} '- rent [out], - lease /to, FOR/ [obj.: place, equipment: Mehmet bey rents this house to me.]' → kirala- 2.

617 ASSOCIATION

617:14 - join /A/ <u>bağlan-</u> 3 '- connect oneself /to/, - log on /to/ [the Internet]'.

618 WEALTH

618:11 - have money [paraca] <u>gücü yet-</u> '- afford, - have enough money /FOR/ [lit., 'for one's strength (in respect to money) - suffice]'.

619 POVERTY

619:5 - be poor <u>sıkış-</u> 4 '- be hard up, short of money'.

620 LENDING

620:5 - lend /A/ <u>borç ver-</u> '- lend [money only], - extend a loan /to/' → ver- 1; /A/ <u>ödünç ver-</u> '- lend money or anything else /to/, - extend a loan /to/' → ver- 1 .

621 BORROWING

621:3 - borrow /DAn/ <u>borç al-</u> '- borrow [money only], - take a loan /from/' → al- 1; /DAn/ <u>ödünç al-</u> '- borrow [money or anything else] /from/' → al- 1.

623 DEBT

623:5 - owe /A, θ/ borçlan- '-
get into debt /to [sb], {θ/for} [an
amount]/, - owe /θ [sb], θ [an
amount]/'.

623:6 - go in debt /DAn dolayı/
borca gir- '- go or - get into debt
/{because of/due to}/'; / A, θ/
borçlan- '- get into debt /to [sb],
{θ/for} [an amount]/, - owe /θ [sb], θ
[an amount]/'.

624 PAYMENT

624:10 - pay /A/ bahşiş ver- '-
tip /θ/ sb, - give /θ/ sb a tip, - give a
tip /to/ sb' → ver- 1; /A/ kira ver-
'- pay rent [for room, house] /to/' →
ver- 1; /a: A, b: için, c: A/ öde- '-
pay /a: θ [sb], b: for [sth], c: for
[sth]'; /lA/ ödüllendir- '- award sb
sth as a prize, - reward sb /with/ sth, -
give sb sth as a reward'; /lA/
ödüllendiril- '- be awarded a prize,
- be given a reward /OF/, - be
rewarded /with/'; /a: A, b: A, c:
için/ para ver- '- pay /a: to, b:
FOR, c: for/' → ver- 1; /A/ para
yatır- 2 '- pay [for municipal
services]'. The money is deposited
into the bank account of the public
institution [e.g., post office, phone
company]. → yatır- 2; peşin öde- '-
pay in advance'; taksitle öde- '-
pay /IN/ installments'; ücret öde- '-
pay'; zekât ver- '- pay the zakat
[i.e., the alms tax]' → ver- 1.

624:11 - repay geri öde- '- pay
back money, - repay'.

624:13 - pay in full borcunu
öde- '- pay up, - pay off an account,
- pay one's debts or bills, - settle
one's debts or one's account';
borcunu {kapa-/kapat-}. Same.
→ {kapa-/kapat-} 8; [borç]
kapatıl- 7 '- be paid up, settled
[account]'.

624:17 - pay cash /A/
{nakit/nakit olarak/nakten}
öde- '- pay /θ/ sb in cash, - pay in
cash /to/, - pay cash'.

624:20 - be paid kazan- 1 '- earn
[money]'.

625 NONPAYMENT

625:7 - go bankrupt bat- 2 '- go
bankrupt, - go under'; iflâs et- 1.
Same.

626 EXPENDITURE

626:5 - spend /{A/için}/
{harca-/sarf et-} 1 '- spend, -
expend /{ON [or FOR]}/{ON [or
for]}/'; masraf çek- '- foot the bill,
- pay', informal, jocular. → çek- 5;
/{A/için}/ masraf {et-/yap-} '-
spend [money] /{ON [or FOR]}/{ON
[or for]}/, - pay /FOR/'; masrafa
gir- '- spend a lot of money on sth or
to get sth done, - have a lot of
expenses, - incur great expense';
masraftan {kaçMA-/kaçınMA-}
'- spare /θ/ NO expense' → kaç- 2;
/{A/için}/ para harca- '- spend
money /{ON [or FOR]/ON [or for]}'
→ {harca-/sarf et-} 1; /{DA/A}
yatırım yap- '- invest /in/, - make
an investment /in/' → yap- 3. For '-
spend time', → 820:6. TIME: - spend
time.

626:7 - afford [paraca] gücü
yet- '- afford, - have enough money
/FOR/ [lit., 'for one's strength (in
respect to money) - suffice]'.

630 PRICE, FEE

630:11 - price /DAn/ fiyat al- '-
receive a price offer /from/, - get a
bid, estimate, quote /from/ [a
company]' → al- 3; /A/ fiyat koy-
'- set or - fix a price /ON/ [goods or
services]' → koy- 1; /A/ hesap
getir- '- bring the check /to/'.

630:12 - charge /A, için/ para
al- '- charge /FOR/, - take money
/FOR/' → al- 1; /için/ ücret al- '-
charge /for/, - take a fee /for/' → al-
1.

630:13 - cost /A, A/ mal ol- '-
cost /θ [sb], θ [sth]/' → ol- 12; tut- 7
'- amount /to/, - come /to/, - add up
/to/, - total, - cost, - make'.

631 DISCOUNT

631:2 - discount /DAn, A /
[fiyatlar] indir- 3 '- lower, -
reduce, - decrease, - bring down
[prices, rates] /from, to/, - give a
discount'; /a: DAn, b : A , c:
{tarafından/CA}/ [fiyatlar]
indiril- 3 '- be lowered, reduced
[prices, rates] /a: from, b: to, c: by
[the owner]/'; ikram et- 2 '- give a
discount, - go or - come down in
price'; in- 5 '- reduce the price, - go
or - come down in price, - give a
discount'. See also 633:6a.
CHEAPNESS: - lower prices.

632 EXPENSIVENESS

632:7 - overprice fazla para al-
'- overcharge' → para al- → al- 1.

633 CHEAPNESS

633:6a - lower prices /DAn, A/
[fiyatlar] indir- 3 '- lower, -
reduce, - decrease, - bring down
[prices, rates] /from, to/, - give a
discount'; /a: DAn, b : A , c:
{tarafından/CA}/ [fiyatlar]
indiril- 3 '- be lowered, reduced
[prices, rates] /a: from, b: to, c: by
[the owner]/'. See also 631:2.
DISCOUNT: - discount.

633:6b - become cheaper fiyatlar
{düş-/in-} 'for prices - fall, - drop'
→ düş- 3, in- 4; ucuzla- '- get
cheaper, - go down or - drop in price'.

634. COSTLESSNESS

634:4 - give /A/ hediye et- '-
give sth as a gift /to/ sb, - make a
present of sth /to/ sb'.

635 THRIFT

635:4 - economize /için/ para
artır- '- save money [up] /for/' →
{artır-/arttır-} 2; /için/ para
biriktir-. Same. → biriktir- 2; /için/
tasarruf et-. Same.

CLASS 10: VALUES AND IDEALS

637 RIGHT

637:2. * 1 - do the right thing
/{mAklA/ArAk}/ doğru hareket
et- '- do the right thing, - act
properly /BY...ing/'; doğrusunu
yap- '- do the right thing';
/mAklA/ iyi et-. Same.

638 WRONG

638:2. * 1 - do the wrong thing -
mAk olmaz 'it won't do to do sth,
one shouldn't, it's not appropriate to
do sth' → ol- 11 → olmaz.

639 DUENESS

639:5 - deserve /1A, DIğI için/
hak et- '- deserve sth /FOR,
because/'.

639:6 - get one's deserts cezasını
çek- 1 '- suffer for a deed, - get
one's just deserts or dues for a deed'
→ çek- 5.

641 DUTY

641:12 - obligate /1A/
görevlendir- '- charge, - entrust sb
/with/ [a task, duty], - give sb the task
/OF/, - make sb responsible /FOR/, -
put sb in charge /OF/'; /1A,
tarafından/ görevlendiril- '- be
charged, entrusted /with, by/, - be
given the task /OF, by/, - be made
responsible /FOR, by/, - be put in
charge /OF, by/'.

643 IMPOSITION

643:4 - impose /A/ çek- 6 '-
subject, - expose /to/'; sorguya çek-
'- cross-examine, - question, -
interrogate, - grill, - subject to
interrogation' → çek- 6.

644 PROBITY

644:11 - speak or - tell the truth
{doğru/doğruyu/gerçeği/haki-
kati} söyle- '- tell the truth' →
söyle- 1.

644:12 - be frank açık açık
konuş-[or söyle-] '- speak quite
frankly, quite openly' → konuş-,
söyle- 1; {açık/açıkça} konuş-[or
söyle-] '- speak frankly, openly' →
konuş-, söyle- 1; dobra dobra
{konuş-/söyle-} '- speak bluntly,
frankly' → konuş-, söyle- 1.

644:22 ADV. truthfully Aslına
bakarsanız 'To tell the truth [lit., If
you look at the truth of it]' → bak- 1;
Doğrusunu istersen[iz] '{To tell
the truth/if you want the truth [lit., the
truth of it]/to be honest}' → iste- 1;
Doğrusunu söylemek gerekirse
'To tell the truth [lit., ITS truth]...',
that is, the truth about a certain
matter. → söyle- 1; Ne yalan
söyleyeyim. '{To tell the truth [lit.,
Why should I lie]./I won't hide it
from you.}' → söyle- 1. See also
351:7. DISCLOSURE: - confess.

644:23 ADV. candidly
{Açık/Açıkça} konuşmak
gerekirse 'To tell the truth, to speak
openly, frankly [lit., If it is necessary
to speak openly]' → konuş-;
{Açık/Açıkça} söylemek
gerekirse Same. → söyle- 1;

644: * 26 PHR. one does not cut
the hand that gives Proverb: Altın
yumurtlayan tavuğu kesmezler.
'One doesn't [lit., they don't] kill the
goose that lays the golden egg.' →

kes- 2; Proverb: **Kılıç kınını kesmez.** 'A sword doesn't cut its own sheath.' → kes- 1; Proverb: **Köpek sahibini ısırmaz.** 'A dog doesn't bite its master.' Don't bite the hand that feeds you. → ısır- 1; Proverb: **Veren eli kimse kesmez.** 'One does not cut the hand that gives.' → kes- 1, ver- 1.

645 IMPROBITY
645:11 - be dishonest | **yalan söyle-** '- lie, - tell lies' → söyle- 1. See also 354:19. FALSENESS: - lie.

645:12 - be unfaithful | /I/ **aldat-** 2 '- be unfaithful /TO/ sb, - cheat /ON/ sb'.

646 HONOR
646:8 - honor | /I, {ArAk/mAklA}/ **onurlandır-** [ır] '- honor /by...ing/'; /A, {ArAk/mAklA}/ **{şeref/onur} ver-** '- honor /θ, by...ing/'. Same. → ver- 1.

654 VICE
654:8 - do wrong | **günah işle-** '- commit a sin'.

654:9 - go wrong | **yolunu şaşır-** '- lose one's way, - get lost, not know which way to turn', here in a moral sense. → şaşır- 3.

658 ATONEMENT
658:5 - apologize | /DAn, için/ **özür dile-** '- beg sb's pardon, - apologize /TO [sb], for [sth]/, - make an apology /TO/' → dile- 2.

665 UNCHASTITY
665:20 - seduce | {bekâretini/kızlığını} **kaybet- [or yitir-]** '- lose one's virginity', only for women. There is no commonly used Turkish equivalent term for men. → {kaybet-/yitir-}; **ırzına geç-** '- rape, - violate' → gec- 1; /A/ **saldır-** 2 '- rape /θ/, - assault /θ/ sexually'; /A/ **tecavüz et-** 2. Same.

668 TEMPERANCE
668:6 - restrain oneself | /A/ **hâkim ol-** '- control /θ/, - get or - keep control /{OF/OVER}/, - keep in line [people or one's emotions, actions]' → ol- 12.

668:7 - abstain | /DAn/ **kaçın-** '- avoid /θ/ sb or sth or /θ/ doing sth; - refrain /from/ sth or /from/ doing sth'; /DAn/ **sakın-** 1 '- avoid /θ/; - keep [oneself] away /from/, - steer clear /OF/ sb'. Same as 329:3. INACTION: - refrain.

671 VIOLENCE
671:13 - erupt | **kıyamet kop-** 1 'for doomsday - be at hand, - occur'. 2 'for all hell - break loose; for a great commotion - occur' → kop- 2; **kop-** 2 '- break out, - begin', a noisy or dangerous event.

671:14 - explode | **havaya uç-** '- blow up [subj.: building hit by missile]'; **lastiği patla-** '- get a flat [tire]' → patla- 1; **patla-** 1 '- burst, - explode'.

673 LEGALITY
673:8 - legalize | **geç-** 5 '- be valid, legal [subj.: particular run of currency]'.

674 ILLEGALITY
674:5 - break or - violate the law | **çiğne-** 3 '- violate laws, rules, principles'; **haneye tecavüz et-** '- trespass /ON/ [sb's property]' → tecavüz et- 1.

696 WORSHIP
696:10 - worship | /A/ **ibadet et-** '- worship /θ/'; /A, diye/ **tap-** '- worship /θ [sb or sth], AS [sb or sth]/'.

696:12 - pray | **dua et-** 1 '- pray'; **namaz kıl-** '- perform the namaz'.

700-800

701 RELIGIOUS RITES
701:14 - celebrate | **aptes al-** '- perform the ritual ablution' → al- 1; **hacca git-** '- go /ON/ the Pilgrimage, - make the Pilgrimage to Mecca' → git- 1a; **namaz kıl-** '- perform the namaz'; **oruç tut-** '- keep or - observe the fast, - fast' → tut- 5; **zekât ver-** '- pay the zakat [i.e., the alms tax]' → ver- 1.

701:16 - baptize | **sünnet et-** '- circumcise'; **sünnet ol-** '- be circumcised' → ol- 10.1.

CLASS 11: ARTS

704   SHOW BUSINESS, THEATER

704:28 - dramatize | film çek- '- make a movie, - film [subj.: both amateur or professional film makers]' → çek- 7; film çevir- 2 '- produce or - make a movie [subj.: producer, professional film maker]' → çevir- 3.

704:29 - act | film çevir- 1 '- act in a movie or film, - make a movie [subj.: actor]' → çevir- 3; oyna- 3 '- play a role, - portray a character, - perform or - act /in/ a play or movie'.

704:32 - rehearse | prova yap- '- rehearse [a play, performance]' → yap- 3.

705 DANCE

705:5 - dance | dans et- '- dance'; göbek at- '- belly dance, - perform a belly dance' → at- 1; oyna- 4 '- dance, - perform a dance', used with the names of various dances: e.g., zeybek.

708 MUSIC

708:38 - sing | ıslık çal- '- whistle' → çal- 2; söyle- 4 '- sing'; şarkı {oku-/söyle-} '- sing, - sing songs' → oku- 5, söyle- 4.

708:39a - play sth | çal- 2 '- play a musical instrument, radio, record player, tape recorder; - play or - perform a piece of music'; /{tarafından/CA}/ çalın- 2 '- be played [musical instrument] /by/; - be played, performed [a piece of music] /by/'; /A/ sun- 2 '- perform, - play, or - sing sth /FOR/ sb'; yorumla- 2 '- interpret, - perform [a piece of music]'.

708:39b - play, - make a sound | öt- 2 For various wind instruments to produce a sound: 'for a horn - play, a whistle - make a sound'. Also '[for an alarm] - go off, - sound, or - screech'.

708:42 - blow a horn | ıslık çal- '- whistle' → çal- 2; korna çal- '- hit /θ/ or - honk /θ/ a car horn' → çal- 2; kornaya bas-. Same. → bas- 2; öttür- '- blow a whistle'.

708:45 - conduct | yönet- 2 '- conduct [orchestra]'.

708:46 - compose music | /için/ bestele- '- compose music /for/'.

714 PHOTOGRAPHY

714:14 - photograph | film çek- '- make a movie, - film [subj.: both amateur and professional film makers]' → çek- 7; film çevir- 2 '- produce, - make a movie [subj.: producer, professional film maker]' → çevir- 3; {resim/fotoğraf} çek- '- take {pictures/photographs} /of/, - photograph' → çek- 7; {resim/fotoğraf} çektir- /A/ '- have {pictures/photographs} taken, - {have/let} /θ/ sb take {pictures/photographs}' → çektir- 3; röntgen çektir- '- have an X-ray [taken]' → çektir- 3; /A/ yakalan- 3 '- be caught /ON/ camera, /BY/ the lens, - be photographed unexpectedly or unawares'; yan- 8 '- get overexposed [photographs]'.

714:15 - process | banyo yap- 2 '- develop photographic film' → yap- 3; film bas- '- develop and print' or only '- print [photographic film]' → bas- 3; film {bastır-/tabettir-} '- have photographic film developed and printed or only printed' → {bastır-/tabettir-}; film yıkat- '- have photographic film developed [but not printed]'.

714:16 - project | oyna- 2 '- play, - show, - be running [subj.: film, theater production]'.

CLASS 12: OCCUPATIONS AND CRAFTS

724 OCCUPATION

724:10 - occupy | meşgul et- '- occupy [restroom]; - disturb, - bother, - distract [people at work]'; üstüne git- 2 '- get right down /to/, - attend /to/ [a matter]' → git- 1a.

724:11 - busy oneself with | /lA/ meşgul ol- 1 '- be busy or occupied /with/, - deal /with/' → ol- 12; /lA/ uğraş- 2 '- work /ON/, - be engaged /IN/, - be busy or occupied /with/, - devote oneself /TO/ [a job, task involving extra effort, struggle]'.

724:12 - work | çalış- 1 '- work, - study, - work /ON/, - practice sth'; iş bul- '- find work, a job, employment, - become employed' → bul- 1; işe gir-. Same.

725 EXERTION

725:8 - exert egzersiz yap- 1 '-work out, - do exercises, calisthenics, physical training'. 2 '- do exercises as physical therapy' → yap- 3; gerin- '- stretch [oneself], - have a stretch'; idman yap- '- exercise, - do gymnastics, physical training, - train [oneself physically]' → yap- 3; jimnastik yap- '- do gymnastics' → yap- 3; spor yap- '- do sports, - engage in sports, - take part in sports' → yap- 3. Same as 84:4. FITNESS, EXERCISE: - exercise.

725:9 - exert oneself /için/ {emek/çaba} harca- '- expend effort /{for/ON}/ sth, - take pains /TO/ do sth' → {harca-/sarf et-} 1.

725:10 - strain gerin- '- stretch [oneself], - have a stretch'.

725:12 - work çalış- 1 '- work, - study, - work /ON/, - practice sth'.

725:13 - work hard geceyi gündüze kat- '- work {night and day/day and night}, - work very hard, - burn the midnight oil [lit., - add night to daytime]'.

728 MONEY

728:29 - cash çek boz- '- cash a check [subj.: the teller at a bank]' → boz- 3; çek bozdur- '- cash a check, - get a check cashed [subj.: the customer at a bank]' → bozdur- 2. For additional types of conversions involving money, → 857:11 CONVERSION: - convert.

729 FINANCE, INVESTMENT

729:15 - finance masraf çek- '- foot the bill, - pay', *informal, jocular.* → çek- 5; /{A/için}/ masraf {et-/yap-} '- spend [money] /{ON [*or* FOR]}/{ON [*or* for]}/, - pay /FOR/'; masraf gör- '- meet expenses, - finance, - pay for' → gör- 4; masraf karşıla-. Same. → karşıla- 2; masrafa gir- '- spend a lot of money on sth or to get sth done, - have a lot of expenses, - incur great expense'.

731 COMMERCE, ECONOMICS

731:16 - trade with alışveriş et- /DAn/ '- shop, - trade /AT/, - patronize /θ/ [a place of business]',

/lA/ '- do business /with/ sb'; alışveriş yap- '- shop, - do shopping' → yap- 3; /lA/ iş yap- 2 '- do business /with/' → yap- 3.

731:17 - bargain /a: için, b: üzerinde, c: lA/ pazarlık et- '- bargain, - haggle, - dicker /a: for [sth], b: over [sth], c: with [sb]/'.

733 PURCHASE

733:7 - purchase /a: A, b: DAn, c: DAn, d: DAn/ [satın] al- 4 '- buy, - purchase sth /a: AT [a price, total OR per unit], b: AT [a price, PER unit], c: AT [a store], d: from [a person]/'; /a: A, b: A, c: DAn, d: DAn/ aldır- 1 '- have /a: θ [sb buy, purchase sth], b: AT [a price], c: AT [a store], d: from [a person]/'; /{tarafından/CA}, A/ alın- 2 '- be bought, purchased /by, FOR/'.

733:8 - shop alışveriş et- /DAn/ '- shop, - trade /AT/, - patronize /θ/ [a place of business], /lA/ '- do business /with/ sb'; alışveriş yap- '- shop, - do shopping' → yap- 3; alışverişe çık- '- go /θ/ shopping' → çık- 2; çarşıya çık- '- go /θ/ shopping', lit., '- go /to/ the market' → çık- 2; sadece bak- '- just look around, - browse [in a store]' → şöyle bir bak- → bak- 1; şöyle bir bak-. Same. → bak- 1.

734 SALE

734:8 - sell /a: A, b: A, c: DAn, d: için, e: lA/ sat- '- sell sth /a: to [sb], b: {FOR/AT} [a price, in total or per unit], c: {FOR/AT} [a price, only per unit], d: for, e: {BY [the kilo]/THROUGH [an agent]}/'.

734:10 - put up for sale satışa çık- '- go /ON/ sale', i.e., - become available for purchase, not necessarily at a reduced price. → çık- 2.

734:12 - be sold /a: A, b: A, c: DAn, d: lA, e: {tarafından/CA} / satıl- '- be sold /a: to [sb], b: {FOR/AT} [a price, in total or per unit], c: {FOR/AT} [a price, only per unit], d: {BY [the kilo]/FOR [money]}, e: by [sb]/, - sell /for/'.

740 WEAVING

740:6 - weave ör- 1 '- knit', when the object knitted is specified: She knitted a sweater.; örgü ör- '- knit', lit., ** '- knit a knitting', when the object knitted is not specified: She knitted θ for two hours. → ör- 1.

741 SEWING

741:4 - sew 1 dik- '- sew, - make by sewing', when the object to be created by sewing is specified: She sewed a dress.; dikiş dik- '- sew', lit., ** '- sew a sewing', when the object to be created by sewing is not specified: She sewed θ for two hours. → 1 dik-; /A/ diktir- '- have /θ/ sb sew or stitch sth, - have /θ/ sb make sth by sewing'.

CLASS 13: SPORTS AND AMUSEMENTS

743 AMUSEMENT

743:22 - amuse oneself /a: 1A, b: ArAk, c: mAklA/ eğlen- 1 '- have a good time, - enjoy oneself, - have fun /a: with [sb or sth], b: [by]...ing, c: [BY]...ing/'; /a: 1A, b: ArAk, c: mAklA/ {iyi/hoş} vakit geçir-. Same. → geçir- 3; *noun of pleasure* bak- '- {amuse/enjoy} onself': Eğlenmenize bakın. 'Enjoy yourself.' Keyfine bak. Same. → bak- 3.

743:23 - play /1A/ oyna- 1 '- play /with/', when the game is specified: I'm playing chess.; oynaş- 1 '- play with one another'; /1A/ oyun oyna- 1 '- play a game /with/' or just '- play', when the game is not specified: She was playing when I came in. → oyna- 1; spor yap- '- do sports, - engage in sports, - take part in sports' → yap- 3.

744 SPORTS

744:10 throwing sports uçurtma uçur- '- fly a kite, kites'.

747 BASKETBALL

747:4 - play basketball /1A/ basketbol oyna- '- play basketball /with/' → oyna- 1.

748 TENNIS

748:3 - play tennis atak karşıla- '- return a serve [in tennis, ping-pong]' → karşıla- 3; /1A/ tenis oyna- '- play tennis' → oyna- 1.

752 SOCCER

752:4 - play soccer /1A/ futbol oyna- '- play soccer' → oyna- 1.

753 SKIING

753:4 - ski kay- 3 '- ski'; kayak yap-. Same. → yap- 3.

759 GAMBLING

759:23 - gamble /1A/ kumar oyna- '- gamble /with/' → oyna- 1.

759:25 - bet /a: 1A, b: A, c: diye/ {bahse/iddiaya} gir- '- bet /a: θ [sb], b: θ [an amount], c: ON [lit., saying]/, - wager'.

CLASS 14: THE MIND AND IDEAS

760 EXISTENCE

760:8 - exist /DA/ bulun- 2 '- be, - exist, - find oneself, - be situated /{in/at}/ [a place]'; dur- 7 '- exist, - be existent, - survive [old manuscripts]'; /DA/ hazır bulun- '- be present /{at/in}/ [subj.: person]' → bulun- 2; ol- 3 '- be' [ol- here is treated as a cover term including θ in the present tense and i- in certain circumstances]; var ol- '{- exist, - be}; {- come into existence, being, - be created}' → {var/yok} ol- b) → ol- 12.

760:12 - become ol- 1 '- become, - be; - turn out, - work out'. See also 851:6. CHANGE: - be changed.

761 NONEXISTENCE

761:6 - cease to exist geç- 4 '- pass, - end, - come to an end, - be over [difficult situation, illness]'; yok ol- '{not - exist, not - be}; {- go out of existence, - be destroyed}' → {var/yok} ol- b) → ol- 12.

765 CIRCUMSTANCE

765:6 - itemize {ayrıntıya/ayrıntılara/detaya/detaylara} gir- '- go or - enter {INTO detail}'.

768 ACCOMPANIMENT

768:7 - accompany /A/ {eşlik et-/refakat et-} '- accompany /θ/, - go [along] /WITH/'; /1A/ gel- 1 '- come /with/ sb'; /1A/ git- '- go /with/ sb' → git- 1a.

769 ASSEMBLAGE

769:16 - come together /1A/ bir araya gel- '- come together, - get together /with/, - meet /with/, - convene' → gel- 1; /1A/ buluş- '- come together, - meet /θ/', usually after a previous agreement to meet; /lA/ <u>çık-</u> 10 '- go [out] on a date /with/, - go out /with/, - date, - be dating'; /lA/ <u>flört et-</u> '- go out /with/, - go on a date with, - date', but with the intention of marriage. Not the English '- flirt'; /{A/üzerine}/ <u>hücum et-</u> 2 '- mob /θ/ a place, - rush /to/ a place, - throng /to/'; /DA, 1A/ <u>karşıla-</u> 1 '- go to meet, - meet, - welcome, - greet sb /at [a place: train station, airport], with/'; /lA/ <u>karşılaş-</u> 1 '- meet one another'. 2 '- meet /θ/ sb by chance, - run /INTO/ sb'. 4 '- play one another, - meet [sports teams]'; /DA/ <u>toplan-</u> 3 '- get together, - gather, - assemble, - convene /{in/at}/'.

<u>769:17 - convene</u> /lA/ <u>bir araya gel-</u> '- come together, - get together /with/, - meet /with/' → gel- 1; <u>toplan-</u> 3 '- get together, - gather, - assemble, - convene'.

<u>769:18 - bring or - gather together</u> <u>biriktir-</u> 1 '- collect [stamps, dolls]'; <u>toparla-</u> 1 '- gather together, - collect'; /DAn, A/ <u>topla-</u> 1 '- collect, - gather, - assemble /from, IN/ [obj.: my things, flowers]'; /DA, {tarafından/CA}/ <u>toplan-</u> 1 '- be collected, gathered, assembled [examination papers], harvested /{at/in}, by [sb]/'; /I/ <u>uydur-</u> 3 '- manage to scrape together or to come up with [some needed things in the last minute: clothes for a party]'.

<u>769:19 - pile</u> <u>sıkış-</u> 3 '- be placed close together, squeezed; - be very crowded, cramped [people in a bus], - feel cramped, - be congested; - be or - get {backed/piled} up, - pile up [traffic]'.

<u>769:20 - bundle</u> /A, 1A/ <u>sar-</u> 1 '- wrap one thing /{IN/AROUND}, with/ another'; /a: A, b: 1A, c: tarafından/ <u>sarıl-</u> 2 '- be wrapped /a: IN, b: with, c: by [sb]/'.

770 DISPERSION
<u>770:4a - disperse sth</u> /A/ <u>dağıt-</u> 1 '- scatter, - disperse sth /to/'. 2 '- distribute /to/, - hand out /to/, - serve [out] /to/, - dispense /to/'; /a: {tarafından/CA}, b: 1A, c: A/ <u>dağıtıl-</u> '- be distributed, handed out /a: by [sb], b: by means of, c: to/'.

<u>770:4b - disperse, - become dispersed</u> /DAn, A/ <u>geç-</u> 2 '- pass

or - spread /from [one person], to [another]/ [subj.: disease]'; /a: DAn, b: A, c: yoluyla/ <u>yayıl-</u> '- spread /a: from, b: to, c: {through/by means of} [subj.: fire, disease, religion, empires, rumor]'.

<u>770:8 - disband</u> <u>dağıl-</u> 1 /A/ '- scatter, - disperse /to/ [subj.: crowd]'. 2 '- let out, - be over, - break up [subj.: concert, match, movie]', always with the notion of the dispersion of the participants. 3 '- break up, - fall apart, - disintegrate, - disband [dispersal of members: subj.: household, family, political party]'.

771 INCLUSION
<u>771:3 - include</u> /A/ <u>dahil ol-</u> '- be included /IN/' → ol- 12; <u>içer-</u> '- cover, - include, - comprise, - contain'; <u>içine al-</u> 1 '- include, - cover [examination covers the whole course], - encompass'. 2 '- hold, - contain [bottle holds 2 quarts]' → al- 1; <u>kapsa-</u> '- cover, - include, - comprise, - contain [insurance covers illness, check covers amount of bill, examination covers the whole course]'.

<u>771: * 8 PHR. count me in</u> <u>Ben varım.</u> '{Count me in./I'm with you.}', <u>Biz varız.</u> '{Count us in./We're with you.}' → {var/yok} ol- a) 3 → ol- 12. Same as 324: * 11. WILLINGNESS: PHR. expressions of willingness.

772 EXCLUSION
<u>772.4 - exclude</u> /DAn/ <u>dışla-</u> '- exclude, - cast out, - ostracize /from/ [person from society]'; /{tarafından/ CA}, DAn/ <u>dışlan-</u> '- be excluded, cast out, ostracized /by, from/'.

<u>772:5 - eliminate</u> <u>kaldır-</u> 4 '- abolish, - do away with, - lift, - repeal [law], - eliminate, - eradicate [disease]'; <u>sofra kaldır-</u> '- clear, after a meal, anything upon which a meal may be placed' → kaldır- 3.

<u>772:10 PREP. excluding</u> <u>kaldı ki</u> 2 'let alone, so {how/why} would he' → kal- 1.

<u>772: * 11 PHR. count me out</u> <u>Ben yokum.</u> '{Count me out./I want no part of it.}', <u>Biz yokuz.</u> '{Count us out./We want no part of it.}' →

{var/yok} ol- a) 3 → ol- 12. Same as 325: * 10. UNWILLINGNESS: PHR. expressions of unwillingness.

774 RELATION
774:5 - relate /1A/ <u>ilişki kur-</u> '- form or - establish relationships /with/' → kur- 1.

777 SAMENESS
777:9 ADV. identically <u>olduğu gibi</u> 1 'as it is'. 2 'as it happened' → ol- 11.

779 DIFFERENCE
779:5 - differ <u>çatış-</u> 2 '- be in conflict, - clash [ideas, interests, appointments]'.

783 SIMILARITY
783:7 - resemble /A/ <u>benze-</u> 1 '- resemble /θ/, - look like'.

784 COPY
784:8 - copy <u>fotokopi çek-</u> '- make a photocopy of, - photocopy' → çek- 8; <u>klonla-</u> '- clone' → kopyala- 2; <u>kopya çek-</u> 1 '- copy illegitimately [i.e., - cheat, crib]'. 2 '- cheat by exchanging information orally [e.g., during an exam]' → çek- 8; /DAn, A/ <u>kopya et-</u> '- copy /from, INTO/, - reproduce', cheating is not implied; <u>kopyala-</u> 1 /DAn, A/ '- copy [documents, files, disks, drives] /from, to/, - make a copy'. 2 '- clone'; <u>kopyasını {çek-/çıkar-}</u> '- make a copy of', cheating is not implied. → çek- 8, çıkar- 7; <u>temize çek-</u> '- recopy, - rewrite, - make a clean or fresh copy of a piece of writing' → çek- 8.

787 AGREEMENT
787:7 - make agree <u>ayarla-</u> 1 /A göre/ '- set /{BY/according to}/ [watch by the radio]', /I, A/ '- set to, - tune to [radio to the music station]'; <u>düzelt-</u> 4 '- set a watch or clock'; <u>kur-</u> 2 '- wind, - set [watch, clock, meter, toy, or music box]'; <u>kurul-</u> 2 '- be wound, set [watch, clock, meter, toy or music box]'.

788 DISAGREEMENT
788:5 - disagree <u>çatış-</u> 2 '- be in conflict, - clash [ideas, interests, appointments]'; /1A/ <u>çeliş-</u> '- contradict one another [ideas, behavior], - be in conflict, - be contradictory, in contradiction /with/'; <u>fikrine itiraz et-</u> '- object

to sb's idea'; /A/ <u>itiraz et-</u> '- object /to/, - raise an objection /{to/AGAINST}/'; /A/ <u>karşı çık-</u> '- oppose /θ/, - come out /AGAINST/, - object /to/, - say no /to/'. This category may also be covered by the negative of verbs under 332:9. ASSENT: - concur.

789 EQUALITY
789:5 - equal <u>et-</u> 3 '- amount to, - equal, - add up to, - make, - get', in mathematical operations.

791 WHOLE
791:8 - total <u>et-</u> 3 '- amount to, - equal, - add up to, - make, - get', in mathematical operations; <u>tut-</u> 7 '- amount to, - come to, - add up to, - total, - cost, - make'.

792 PART
792:6 - separate <u>dilim dilim kes-</u> '- cut [up] into slices, - slice up'; <u>dilimle-</u>. Same; <u>doğra-</u> '- cut [up] into slices or pieces; - carve, - chop into bits, - mince'; <u>kıy-</u> 1 '- cut up fine, - chop up fine, - mince, - grind [up] [vegetables, meat]'. See also 801:11. SEPARATION: - sever.

793 COMPLETENESS
793:6 - complete <u>bitir-</u> 1 '- finish sth, - bring sth to an end'. 4 '- graduate from, - finish a school or department of a university'; <u>doldur-</u> 2 '- fill OUT [application, questionaire], - fill IN [blanks], - complete a form'; /DAn/ <u>mezun ol-</u> '- graduate /from/' → ol- 12; <u>tamamla-</u> '- complete, - finish sth'; /{tarafından/CA}/ <u>tamamlan-</u> '- be completed, finished /by/ sb'.

793:7a - fill sth <u>doldur-</u> 1 '- fill' a) /I, 1A/ '- fill sth /with/ sth, - make sth full'. b) /I, A/ '- fill sth /WITH/ sth [lit., ** - fill sth /INTO/ sth]'; /A/ <u>hava bas-</u> 1 '- fill /WITH/ air, - pump up [obj.: tires]' → bas- 2.

793:7b - fill, - become full /1A/ <u>dol-</u> 1 '[for a container, room] - fill up /with/ sth'.

795 COMPOSITION
795:3 - compose /DAn/ <u>oluş-</u> '- come into being /OUT OF/, - occur; - be formed, composed, made up /OF/, - consist /OF/'.

796 MIXTURE

796:10a - mix sth | harmanla- '-blend, - combine [salad ingredients] '; karıştır- 1 '- mix, - stir, - blend [eggs and sugar]'.

796:10b - mix, - become mixed karış- 1 /A/ 'for one thing - be or - get mixed /{WITH/INTO}/ another [subj.: various substances]'. 2 /DAn/ '- get mixed up, jumbled /{BECAUSE OF/DUE TO}/ [subj.: notes, papers]'.

799 JOINING

799:5 - put together | /A, 1A/ bağla- 1 '- tie /{to/AROUND}, with/, - connect /to/, - tie up /with/, - fasten, - bind. 2 '- put through /to/, - connect sb /with/ [the operator]'; birleştir- '- join, - unite, - bring together'; /A/ kavuştur- '- unite, - reunite /WITH/, - bring together /WITH/, - join sb or sth /to/ sb or sth else'; /A/ yaklaştır- '- bring one thing /{to/NEAR/UP TO/OVER TO}/ another, - join'; /A/ yapıştır- '- glue, - paste, - tape, or - stick sth /{ON/ONTO/to}/ sth'.

799:7 - fasten | /A/ tak- '- attach, - fasten sth /to/, - put sth /ON/ [oneself, usually small items: glasses, jewelry, seat belts, not major items of clothing], - put up [curtains, etc.]'.

799:8 - hook | /A, {tarafından/CA}/ çakıl- 1 '- be driven or hammered /{IN/INTO}, by/ [subj.: nail, peg]; - be pegged, nailed down'; kilitle- 1 '- lock [door]'.

799:9 - bind | /A, 1A/ bağla- 1 '- tie /{to/AROUND}, with/, - connect /to/, - tie up /with/, - fasten, - bind. 2 '- put through /to/, - connect sb /with/ [on the phone]'; bağlan- 1 /A, 1A, tarafından/ '- be tied /{to/AROUND}, with, by/, - be connected, tied up, fastened, bound /to, with, by/'; sar- 1 /A, 1A/ '- wrap one thing /{IN/AROUND}, with/ another'. 2 /I, 1A/ '- bandage, - bind [wound] /with/'; /a: A, b: 1A, c: tarafından/ sarıl- 2 '- be wrapped /a: IN, b: with, c: by [sb]/'.

799:11 - be joined | /A/ bağlan- 2 '- be connected /to/, - be put through /to/ [the phone operator]'; /A/ kavuş- 1 '- meet /θ/ sb, - come together, - be reunited /WITH/, - meet /θ/ sb again after a long absence'.

800-900

800 ANALYSIS

800:6 - analyze | analiz et- '-analyze [blood, historical event]'; tahlil et- '- analyze [blood, historical event, literary work]'.

801 SEPARATION

801:8 - separate | ayır- 1 /DAn/ '-separate, - take away /from/'. 3 /A/ '- divide /INTO/'. 4 '- separate, - distinguish, - differentiate [Language separates man from animals.]'; /A, {tarafından/CA}/ ayrıl- 2 '- be divided, split /INTO, by/'; /A/ böl- = ayır- 3; /A, {tarafından/CA}/ bölün- = ayrıl- 2; /DAn/ kopar- 2 '- tear, - rip /OUT OF/, away /from/'.

801:9 - come apart | kop- 1 '-break in two, - break, - break off, - come off; - snap off, - pop off'.

801:10 - detach | çöz- 1 '- untie, - unfasten, - undo, - unbutton'.

801:11 - sever | dilim dilim kes- '- cut [up] into slices, - slice up' → kes- 1; dilimle-. Same; /DAn/ {kopar- 2/kopart- 2} '- tear, - rip /OUT OF/, away /from/'; /DAn/ yırt- '- tear up, - rip up; - tear or - rip /{OUT OF/from}/ [page out of notebook]'; /DAn, tarafından/ yırtıl- '- be or - get torn, ripped /{OUT OF/from}, by/'. See also 792:6. PART: - separate.

801:12 - break | kır- 1 '- break [He broke the dish.]'; /{tarafından/CA}/ kırıl- 1 '- be broken /by/ [The windows were broken by the children.]'. 2 '- break, - get broken, - shatter [The dish broke.]'; /DA/ rekor kır- '- break a record /in/ [a sports event]' → kır- 1.

801:13 - shatter | kıy- 1 '- cut up fine, - chop up fine, - mince, - grind [up] [vegetables, meat]'; parçala- '- cut up, - chop up, - break into pieces, - smash, - tear to pieces'; parçalan- 1 /{tarafından/CA}/ '- be broken [up], smashed, torn, cut up, chopped up, or pulled to pieces /by/'. 2 '- break into pieces, - shatter [The glass broke.]'.

801:19 - part company | /DAn/ ayrıl- 1 '- part, - part company, - break or - split up /WITH/, - separate

/from/ one another; - get or - be divorced /from/'.

802 COHESION

802:9 - stick together /A/ yapıştır- '- glue, - paste, - tape, or - stick sth /{ON/ONTO/to}/ sth'.

804 COMBINATION

804:3 - combine harmanla- '- blend, - combine [salad ingredients]'.

805 DISINTEGRATION

805:3 - disintegrate dağıl- 3 '- break up, - fall apart, - disintegrate, - disband [dispersal of members: subj.: household, family, political party]'; /DA/ eri- '- melt [subj.: ice], - dissolve /in/ [sugar in water]'.

807 ARRANGEMENT <putting in order>

807:8 - arrange ayarla- 2 '- put or - get in order, - arrange [affairs, matters]'; düzenle- 1 '- put in order, - arrange, - organize [sth that is in disorder]'; /a: DAn, b: A, c: A göre, d: olarak/ sırala- '- put or - arrange in a row or in a certain order /a: from, b: to, c: {according to/by}, d: -ly/ [shoes, files]'.

807:12 - tidy, - tidy up /A/ çekidüzen ver- '- put in order, - straighten up, - tidy up' → ver- 1; düzelt- 3 '- put in order, - straighten up, - tidy up [messy room]; - trim [hair, beard]'; toparla- 3 '- straighten up, - tidy up, - pick up, - put in order [messy room]. 4 '- smarten oneself up, - tidy oneself up'; topla- 2 = düzelt- 3, = toparla- 3; /tarafından/ toplan- 2 '- be straightened up, tidied up, picked up [messy room] /by/'; üstünü başını {düzelt-/toparla-/topla-} '- tidy [oneself] up, - smarten [oneself] up [lit., ** - adjust one's clothes]' → düzelt- 3, toparla- 3, topla- 2; yatağını {topla-/düzelt-/yap-} '- make one's bed' → topla- 2, düzelt- 3, → yatağını yap- 1 → yap- 3.

809 DISORDER

809:9 - disorder /A/ dokun- 2 '- upset /θ/ sb [subj.: food], - make sick, - affect one's health adversely, for food or weather not - agree /WITH/ one, - have a bad effect /ON/'; midesini boz- '- make [physically] sick, - make sick to one's stomach [subj.: food]' → boz- 1.

810 DISARRANGEMENT

810:2 - disarrange [sokaklara] çöp {at-/dök-} '- litter [/θ/ the streets], - throw trash [/{ON/INTO}/ the streets]' → at- 2, → dök- 3; dağıl- 4 '- get untidy, - be messed up [room, hair]'; dağıt- 3 '- mess up, - put into disorder [hair, house]'; /DAn/ karış- 3 '- get messed or mussed up /{from/BECAUSE OF/DUE TO}/ [subj.: hair]'; karıştır- 4 = dağıt- 3; {sırayı/ kuyruğu} boz- 2 '- get out of line [subj.: people waiting for tickets]' → boz- 1.

810:3 - confuse /IA, A/ karıştır- 2 '- confuse or - mix up sb or sth /with/ sb or sth else'.

811 CONTINUITY <uninterrupted sequence>

811:4a - continue sth /A/ devam et- 2 '[for sb] - continue /{θ/WITH}/ sth, - go on /WITH/ sth, - keep [on] doing sth'. With a NON-verbal noun object: We continued /{θ/WITH}/ the lesson. With a VERBAL noun object: We continued {TO read/readING}.; verb stem.Ip dur- '- keep [on] verb stem.ing, e.g., '- keep [on] do.ING, - do sth continuously' → dur- 11.

811:4b for sth - continue çek- 10 '- take, - last so much time [The journey took ten hours.]'; devam et- 1 '- last, - continue, - go on [subj.: examination, meeting]'; sür- 2 = devam et- 1. 3 '- take time'; {vakit/zaman} al- '- take time [subj.: meeting, journey]' → al- 1.

811:6 - line up {sıraya/kuyruğa} gir- '- get /IN/ [the] line, - line up, - queue up', for a performance, a sports event, a means of transportation [bus, shared cab], or for a purchase.

814 SEQUENCE

814:2 - succeed kovala- 2 '- follow one [upon] another in rapid succession, - succeed [subj.: times: days, months; events; disasters]'.

817 BEGINNING

817:7a - begin sth /A/ başla- 2 'for sb - begin or - start /θ/ sth'. With a NON-verbal noun object: We began /θ/ the sixth lesson. With a VERBAL noun object: We began {TO read/readING} the novel.; /I/ başlat- '- cause sth to begin, - begin sth, - start sth [The referee began the game.]'; /A/ **gir-** '- enter /θ/ a certain period, - become a certain age'; /1A/ **kavga çıkar-** '- provoke a quarrel, - pick a fight, - start a fight /with/' → çıkar- 7; /A/ **koyul-** '- begin /θ/ sth, - set /ABOUT/, - set /to/, - embark /UPON/ [a task]'; **yaşına {bas-/gir-}** '- turn a certain age' → bas- 1; **yola {çık-/koyul-}** '- start off, - set out or - leave /ON/ a {trip/journey}, - set out /ON/ the road [person on foot or vehicle].' → çık- 2, koyul-.

817:7b for sth - begin **bas-** 4 '- set in, for a certain state [darkness, fog] - come upon'; **başla-** 1 '- begin, - start [subj.: concert]'.

817:9 - enter /A/ **dal-** 4 '- begin suddenly, - plunge /INTO/ an activity'; **sohbete dal-** '- get involved /IN/ or - plunge /INTO/ a friendly conversation' → dal- 4.

817:11 - inaugurate **aç-** 2 '- turn or - switch on [electricity, light, radio, TV], - turn on [water, the faucet]'. 11 '- establish, - found, - open [school]'; /{tarafından/CA}/ **açıl-** 5 '- be turned or switched on /by/ [subj.: lights, lamps]'; **aile kur-** '- start a family, - set up a household' → kur- 1; /1A/ **ilişki kur-** '- form or - establish relationships /with/' → kur- 1; /A/ **kur-** 1 '- set up, - assemble [machine, furniture] /{IN/ON}/; - establish, - found [business, republic]'; /A, tarafından/ **kurul-** 1 '- be set up, assembled /{IN/ON}, by/ [subj.: dining room set]; - be established, founded /by/ [subj.: state, association]'.

817:12 - open **konu aç-** '- bring up or - raise a subject, - move on to a new subject, topic' → aç- 10.

817:13 - originate **kıyamet kop-** 1 'for doomsday - be at hand,- occur'. 2 'for all hell - break loose; for a great commotion - occur' → kop- 2; **kop-** 2 '- break out, - begin', a noisy or dangerous event; **patla-** 3 'for sth unpleasant [storm, war] - break out'.

819 END
819:5 - end sth **bitir-** 1 '- finish sth, - bring sth to an end [project]'; /nedeniyle/ **iptal et-** '- cancel, -

call off /{for reasons of/on account of}/'; /{tarafından/CA}, yüzünden/ **iptal edil-** '- be cancelled, called off /by, {on account of/due to}/'; {**kapa-/kapat-**} 6 '- drop the subject, topic of conversation, - conclude the discussion of a subject'; /A/ **son ver-** '- bring /θ/ sth to an end, - conclude, - finish, - put an end /to/ sth' → ver- 1; /{tarafından/CA}/ **son veril-** '- be ended, concluded /by [sb]/' → veril-.

819:6 - come to an end **bit-** 1 '- come to an end, - finish, - be over, finished, completed'; **dağıl-** 2 '- let out, - be over, - break up [subj.: party, concert, show, entertainment]', always with the notion of the dispersion of the participants; **din-** '- cease, - stop, - let up [subj.: nouns of weather: rain, storm; nouns of physical or mental pain: tears, headache; nouns of emotion: anger]'; /DA/ **dur-** 1 '- stop, - come to a stop /at/, - become motionless [person, vehicle, instrument]'. 2 '- cease, - stop [subj.: a process: rain, hail]'; **kapan-** 5 '- be dropped, closed [subject, topic]'; **kesil-** 2 '- stop, - cease of itself [subj.: a limited set of nouns most related to weather: wind, hail, snow, rain, storm]'; **sona er-** '- come /to/ an end, - conclude, - end, - finish, - be over' → er-; **sonuna gel-** '- come to the end of' → gel- 1.

819:7 - complete **tamamla-** '- complete, - finish sth'; /{tarafından/CA}/ **tamamlan-** '- be completed, finished /by/'.

819:14 PHR. that's all **Oldu bitti.** 'It's over and done with' → bit- 1, ol- 11.

820 TIME
820:5 - elapse {**süre/vakit/zaman**} **dol-** 'for time - expire, - be up' → dol- 2; {**süresi/ vakti/zamanı**} **dol-** 'for the period of time, validity OF sth - expire, - be no longer valid, for sth - be overdue, for sb's time - be up' → dol- 2; {**vakit/zaman/süre**} **geç-** 'for time - pass; for time - expire, - be up' → geç- 4; {**vakti/zamanı/süresi**} **geç-** 'for the period of time, validity OF sth - expire, - be no longer valid, for sth - be overdue, for sb's time - be up' → geç- 4.

820:6 - spend time | çek- 10 '- take, - last [How long does the trip take?]'; gecele- '- spend the night somewhere'; sabahla- '- spend the night somewhere, - stay up all night'; sür- 3 '- take time [It takes 2 hours to get to the station from here.], - last [subj.: meeting, trip]'; {vakit/zaman} al- '- take time' → al- 1; /a: 1A, b: ArAk, c: mAklA/ {vakit/zaman} geçir- '- spend time /a: with [sb, sth], b: [by]...ing, c: [BY]...ing/' → geçir- 3; /için/ {vakit/zaman} harca- '- spend time /{on/[in order] to}/' → {harca- /sarf et-} 2. See also 330:16. ACTIVITY: - make the most of one's time.

820:14 PREP. during | place name dönüşü '{after/while} returning from, {during/on} the return from' → dön- 2.

820:16 CONJ. when | iken lit., 'while being' → i- 3.

820:17 PHR. time flies | Sayılı gün[ler] çabuk geçer. 'Deadlines come to an end before you know it [lit., ** Numbered day(s) pass quickly].' → geç- 4.

824 SPELL <period of duty, etc.>
824:5 - take one's turn | ceza çek- '- serve a prison sentence, - serve or - do time' → çek- 5; cezasını çek- 2 '- serve a prison sentence, - serve or - do time for' → çek- 5.

826 DURATION
826:6 - endure | dayan- 4 '- keep [subj.: food], - stay edible'; devam et- 1 '- last, - continue, - go on [meeting, process]'; sür- 2 = devam et- 1. 3 '- take time [It takes 2 hours to get to the station from here.]'.

826:7 - linger on | uza- 2 '- drag on, - go on [matter, court case]'.

826:9 - protract | /{üstünde/üzerinde}/ dur- '- dwell /on/ a topic, subject' → dur- 6.

827 TRANSIENCE
827:11 PHR. "all flesh is grass" | Bible | Proverb: Bir anda var olan bir anda yok olur. 'What exists one moment disappears the next.' Bugün varım, yarın yokum. 'I'm here today, gone tomorrow.' Bugün varız, yarın yokuz. 'We're here today, gone tomorrow.' → {var/yok} ol- a) 3 → ol- 12.

828 PERPETUITY
828:11 ADV. always | oldum olası 'for as long as anyone can remember, from time immemorial, always, never [when followed by a negative verb]'. This is an invariable form used mostly in sentences either with a first-person singular subject or some other first person-singular reference. → ol- 11 → oldu.

829 INSTANTANEOUSNESS
829:8 ADV. at once | der demez 'as soon as, at exactly, right at, on the dot [lit., as soon as one says]', a phrase ender. → de- 1; derken 1 'at that very moment, just then [lit., while saying]' → de- 1.

830 EVENT
830:2 NOUN event | {olup/olan} biten 'what happened, event' → bit-1, ol- 11.

830:5 - occur | başına gel- '- happen /to/, - befall [a person, subj.: usually a misfortune or sth strange]' → gel- 1; başından geç- '- happen to, - experience, - go through.' The event experienced is usually interesting, good, exciting, or unusual rather than unfortunate. → geç- 1; çık- 4 '- come up [problem, matter], - occur, - break out [battle, storm]'; /A/ denk düş- 2 '- occur or - be /AT/ the same time, - fall /ON/ the same {day/hour}, - coincide' → düş- 1; geç- 3 '- occur, - happen, - take place [events]'; ol- 2. Same, also '- go on [What's going on?]'.

830:7 - turn out | çık- 7 '- turn out [well, badly]'.

830:8 - experience | çek- 5 '- endure, - suffer, - put up with, - go through', often with nouns indicating difficulty, trouble; geçir- 2 '- undergo [examination], - experience [disaster, accident]'; /DAn/ gör- 3 '- experience, - be the object of sth [acts of kindness, mother's love] /from/ sb' → gör- 3; /1A/ karşılaş- 3 '- face /θ/, - be confronted /with/, - encounter /θ/, - experience /θ/, - meet /with/, - be up against'; /A/ uğra- 2 '- meet /WITH/, - encounter /θ/, -

711

experience [usually a difficult situation]'; **yaşa-** **3** '- live through, - experience, - have [problems], - enjoy [fine weather], - go through [difficult period]'; **ye-** **2** '- experience, - be the object of [with certain nouns: punishment, blows of various kinds]'.

830: * **14 PHR. what's up?**
Hayrola! 'What's up?, What's going on?, What's the matter?, What's wrong?' → ol- 11 → ola; **Hayırola! Ne var?** 'Good news, I hope! What's up?' → → ol- 11 → ola.

831   MEASUREMENT OF TIME

831:11 - time **saat tut-** '- time, - keep time, - watch the time, - keep track of the time' → tut- 5.

831:13 - date **/A, {üzerine/üstüne}/ tarih {at-/koy-}** '- date /θ/ sth, - put the date /{IN/ON}, on/ sth [a document]' → at- 3.

833 PREVIOUSNESS

833:7 PREP. prior to **/A/ kala 1** in telling time: 'AT [a certain time] to or before [the hour]': 'at a quarter to five'. **2** 'before, prior to', always following a specific time expression: five days before the meeting. **3** 'from, before reaching a PLACE, at a specific distance from', always following a specific measure of distance: at a distance of two kilometers from the school. → kal- 3.

834 SUBSEQUENCE

834:7 ADV. after which *place name*__ **dönüşü** '{after/while} returning from, {during/on} the return from' → dön- 2.

835 SIMULTANEITY

835:4 - coincide **/A/ denk düş-** **2** '- occur or - be /AT/ the same time, - fall /ON/ the same {day/hour}, - coincide' → düş- 1.

835:7 ADV. simultaneously
Tesadüfe bakın. 'What a coincidence!' → bak- 1.

836 THE PAST

836:6 - pass **geç- 4** '- pass, - end, - come to an end, - be over [illness, cold]'; **ol-** **9.3** '- have passed, -

elapsed, - be over [subj: nouns of time]'.

841 OLDNESS

841:9 - age, - grow old **ihtiyarla-** '- grow old, - age, - get old [subj.: persons]'; **yaşı ilerle-** '- get on in years, - grow old, - age, - get old [subj.: persons]' → ilerle- 3; **yaşlan-** = **ihtiyarla-**; **yüzü buruş-** **2** 'for a person's face - become or - get wrinkled' → buruş-. Same as 303:10. AGE: - age, grow old.

842 TIMELINESS

842:6 - be timely **/A/ denk düş-** **1** '- be suitable, right, timely /FOR/' → düş- 1; **{vaktinde/zamanında} gel-** '- come {in/on} time' → gel- 1; **/A/ uy-** **2** '- suit /θ/, - be right, suitable, convenient /FOR/ [class hours for schedule]'; **/A/ uygun düş-** = denk düş- 1.

842:12 ADV. opportunely
Proverb: **Bahar gelmeyince bülbül ötmez.** '{Until spring comes/As long as spring hasn't come}, nightingales do not sing.' → öt- 1.

842:13 ADV. incidentally
aklıma gelmişken 'while it's on my mind, while I'm thinking of it, by the way, speaking of, incidentally [lit., while it has come to my mind]' → gel- 1; **sırası gelmişken** 'speaking of, incidentally, by the way, while on the subject [lit., its time having come, i.e., the time for this topic]' → gel- 1; **yeri gelmişken** 'speaking of, incidentally, by the way, while on the subject, since this is the place for it [lit., its place having come, i.e., the place for this topic]' → gel- 1.

843 UNTIMELINESS

843:4 - talk out of turn **sözünü kes-** '- interrupt, - break in on, - cut in on [conversation]' → kes- 3; **kes-** without **sözünü** is also used in the same meaning when that meaning is clear from the context.

843:5 - miss an opportunity **fırsat kaçır-** '- miss an opportunity, - let an opportunity slip away or go /by/' → kaçır- 2; **kaçır- 1** '- miss, - be too late for a vehicle, event, or a meeting with a person; - miss, not - hear or - catch what has been said'. **2** '- let escape or go by, get away, - miss a chance'; {şans/fırsat} kaybet- '- miss or - lose {a chance/an opportunity}'. Same as 410:14. FAILURE: - miss.

843:7 ADV. inopportunely
Proverb: **Vakitsiz öten horuzun başını keserler.** 'They cut off the head of the rooster that crows at the wrong time.' → kes- 2, öt- 1; Proverb: **Vakitsiz öten horozun başı kesilir.** 'The head of a rooster that crows at the wrong time is cut off.' → baş kesil- → kesil- 1, öt- 1.

844 EARLINESS
844:5 - be early **ileri git-** 1 '- be fast, ahead [clock, watch]' → git- 1a.

844:17 PHR. the early bird gets the worm **Erken yat, erken kalk.** 'Go to bed early, rise early.' Early to bed, early to rise. → kalk- 1, yat- 1; **Gün ile yatan gün ile kalkar.** 'He who goes to bed with the sun gets up with the sun.' → kalk- 1, yat- 1.

845 LATENESS
845:7 - be late /A/ {**geç kal-/gecik-**} '- be late /FOR/ [meeting]' → kal- 1; **geri kal-** 2 '- be slow, behind [clock, watch]' → kal- 1; {**vakit/zaman**} **ilerle-** 'for time - pass, - advance, for it - get late [It had gotten very late.]' → ilerle- 3.

845:8 - delay **beklet-** '- let or make sb wait, - keep sb waiting'; **rötar yap-** '- be delayed [subj.: usually a noun designating a means of public transportation, i.e., train, bus, ferry, airplane, not a person]' → yap- 3; **yolda kal-** '- be delayed, held up on the way, - remain on the way [subj.: person or vehicle]' → kal- 1.

845:9 - postpone /A/ **bırak-** 6 '- leave /to/ a later time, - postpone /to/, - put off /to/'; /a: A, b: A, c: A kadar/ {**ertele-/tehir et-**} '- postpone, - put off /a: for, b: to, c: {till/until}/'; /a: A, b: A, c: A kadar, d: {**tarafından/CA**}/ {**ertelen-/tehir edil-**} '- be postponed, delayed, put off /a: for, b: to, c: {till/until}, d: by/'; /A/ **kal-** 4 '- be put off /to/ [another time]'. Kal- is not used with an agent noun preceded by {tarafından/CA}, i.e., not as in 'The meeting was postponed by the administration.'; /A, için/

tanı- 5 '- grant a period of time, a grace period /to [sb], for [the payment of a debt]/', preceded by various nouns of time: /A, için/ süre tanı- '- grant a period of time, a grace period /to, for/'; {**vakit/zaman**} **kazan-** 2 '- gain time [i.e., - obtain extra time to achieve a goal, complete a task]' → kazan- 4; /A/ {**zaman/vakit/süre**} **ver-** '- give /θ/ sb some time [to finish a task]' → ver- 1.

845: * 21 PHR. it's too late
Proverb: **At çalındıktan sonra ahırın kapısını kapatmak** {**boşunadır/beyhudedir**}. 'After the horse has been stolen, it is useless to close the door of the barn.' To lock the barn door after the horse is gone. → çalın- 1; Proverb: **Atı alan Üsküdarı geçti.** 'The one who has {taken/stolen} the horse has already gone beyond Üsküdar (i.e., a section of Istanbul).' → geç- 1; Proverb: **Atılan ok geri dönmez.** 'The arrow that has been shot does not return.', i.e., What has been done cannot be undone. → dön- 2; **İş işten geçti.** 'It's too late'; Proverb: **Kırkından sonra saza başlayan kıyamette çalar.** 'He who begins the [study of the] saz after [the age of] forty, will play it on doomsday.', i.e., Don't waste time on frivolous things; life is short. → başla- 2, çal- 2; Proverb: **Ok yaydan çıktı.** 'The arrow has left θ the bow', i.e., It's too late to solve the problem. → çık- 1; **Olan** {**oldu/olmuş**}. 'What's done is done.', It's too late now.', i.e., No use crying over spilled milk. → ol- 11; Proverb: **Tekerlek kırıldıktan sonra yol gösteren çok olur.** 'After the wheel [of the cart] has broken, there are many people who will show the way.', i.e., There are always many people ready to offer advice when it's too late. → kırıl- 2, yol göster- 2.

848 REPETITION
848:7 - repeat /Dan/ **alıntı yap-** '- quote /θ/ sth, - quote /from/ sth, - cite /θ/ sth' → yap- 3; {**tekrar et-/tekrarla-**} '- repeat'.

848:8 - iterate **özetle-** '- summarize, - sum up'; **toparla-** 2 '- summarize, - put information in a nutshell'.

851 CHANGE

851:6 - be changed /A/ **çevir-** 8 '- turn /INTO/, - become /θ/ [rain into hail]'; **değiş-** 1 '[for sth] - change, - vary, - become different'; /A/ **dön-** 6 '- turn /INTO/, - become /θ/ [rain into hail]'; /Dan, A/ **dönüş-** '- turn, - change, or - be transformed /from, INTO/ [love into hate, snow into snowstorm]'; /θ/ **kesil-** 5 '- turn /INTO/, - become', often suddenly as a result of fear or other strong emotion: person into stone.

851:7 - change, - work or - make a change **değiştir-** 1 '- change, - alter sth, - make sth change'. See also: 363:6. CHANGING OF MIND: - change one's mind.

854 STABILITY

854:10 - become firmly fixed **don-** 2 '- freeze, - seize up, - jam [subj.: computer]'; **sıkış-** 1 '- get stuck, - become tightly wedged or jammed [zipper; door; key in lock]'. 2 /A/ '- get caught /IN/, - be pinched /IN/ [jacket in door]'.

855 CONTINUANCE <continuance in action>

855:3 - continue /DA, {üstünde/üzerinde}/ **dur-** 6 '- remain, - stay /{in/at}, on/'; *verb stem*.**Ip dur-** '- keep [on] *verb stem*.ing, e.g., '- keep [on] do.ing, - do sth continuously' → dur- 11; /DA/ **kal-** 1 '- remain, - stay /{at/in/on}/ [a place]'; /DA, lA/ **otur-** 4 '- stay, - remain /{at/in} [a place], with [sb]/'.

856 CESSATION

856:6 - cease sth **bırak-** 3 '- stop, - drop, or - quit an activity, - give up a habit; - leave, - abandon a person'. 4 '- leave sb alone, - stop bothering sb'; **dur-** 4 '- stop, - quit [an activity]'; **durdur-** '- stop sb [thief], sth [fighting, bleeding, game]'; **kes-** 4 '- cut out, - stop, - cease [obj.: noise, crying]'; **rahat bırak-** '- leave in peace, - leave alone' → bırak- 4; **yalnız bırak-** '- leave sb alone' → bırak- 4.

856:7 for sth - cease **din-** '- cease, - stop, - let up [with certain limited subjects: elements of weather: rain, storm; nouns of physical or mental pain: tears, headache; nouns of emotion: anger]'; **dur-** 1 /DA/ '- stop, - come to a stop /at/, - become

motionless [subj.: person, vehicle, instrument]'. 2 '- cease, - stop [subj.: a process, activity: weeping; weather: rain, storm]'. 10 '- stall [subj.: engine, motor vehicle]'; **kesil-** 2 '- stop, - cease of itself [subj.: mostly nouns related to weather: wind, hail, snow, rain, storm]'.

856:8 - stop work **tatile gir-** '- close or - shut down for vacation [subj.: an institution, school, business], - recess, - go into recess for vacation [subj.: school], - go on vacation [subj.: a person but usually only when considered a member of an institution]'.

856:10 - interrupt /{tarafından/CA}/ **kesil-** 3 '- be cut off, interrupted [electricity, water, gas, phone conversation] /by/'.

856:11 - put a stop to **durdur-** '- stop sb [thief], sth [fight, bleeding, game]'; **kes-** 4 '- cut out, - stop, - cease [crying, noise]'.

856:12 - turn off {**kapa-/kapat-**} 2 '- turn /{off/out}/ or - switch /{off/out} [lights, electricity, lamps, computer, oven, stove, gas burner, radio, TV]; - turn off [water, the faucet]'; **kapan-** 2 '- go off [lights, lamps]'; /{tarafından/CA}/ **kapatıl-** 2 '- be turned or switched {off/out} /by/ [subj.: same items as under {kapa-/kapat-} 2 above]'; **söndür-** 2 '- turn off [obj.: same items as under {kapa-/kapat-} 2 above except computer, radio, or television]'.

857 CONVERSION

857:11 - convert /I/ **boz-** 2 '- change, - make change /for/, - give change /for/, - break a bill', a specified amount of money into smaller units. 3 '- cash [a check], - change money from one form into another, - exchange foreign money into local currency, - give one form of money for another'; /I, A/ **bozdur-** 1 '- get change /for/, - have sb break a bill, a specified unit of money, into smaller units'. 2 '- cash, - have sb cash [a check], - change, - have sb change money from one form into another [check, foreign exchange into local currency]'. 3 '- sell sth for money and then buy sth else with that money'; /A/ **çevir-** 9 '- turn sth /INTO/ sth else, - convert sth /INTO/ sth else [house into motel]'; /lA/

714

değiştir- 2 '- exchange sth /FOR/ sth else, - change sth {/FOR/INTO/} sth else [dollars into liras], - replace sth /with/ sth else'; /A/ **döndür-** 2 = çevir- 9; **döviz boz-** '- change foreign money into local currency, - exchange, - give local currency for foreign currency' → boz- 3; **döviz bozdur-** '- change, - have sb change foreign money into local currency, - exchange' → bozdur- 2.

860 EVOLUTION
860:5 - evolve | **geliş-** 1 '- develop, - advance, - evolve [subj.: events, technology]; - mature, - fill out [subj.: a person's physique]'; **kalkın-** '- develop, - advance, - make progress [subj.: a nation]'.

861 SUBSTITUTION
861:4 - substitute | **aktarma yap-** '- transfer from one vehicle to another, - change vehicles' → yap- 3; **yerine kullan-** '- substitute one thing for another, - use sth instead of or in place of sth else'.

862 INTERCHANGE
862:4 - interchange | **bozdur-** 3 '- sell sth for money and then buy sth else with that money'; /1A/ **değiş-** 2 '- exchange, - change sth /with/ sb'. 3 '- change one's clothes', only in üstünü değiş-; /1A/ **değiştir-** 2 '- exchange sth /FOR/ sth else, - change sth {/FOR/INTO/} sth else [dollars into liras], - replace sth /with/ sth else'; **üstünü değiş-** '- change one's clothes' → değiş- 3.

863 GENERALITY
863:6 whatever | **olsun...olsun** 'both...and...; whether...or' → ol- 11.

863:15 every | **olur olmaz** 1 'just any [old], whatever, any...that' → ol- 11.

864 PARTICULARITY
864:10 - characterize | /I/ **anlat-** 3 '- tell /ABOUT/, - describe /θ/'; **ayır-** 4 '- separate, - distinguish, - differentiate [Language separates man from animals.]'; /olarak/ **nitelendir-** '- characterize, - describe /AS/'; /A/ **tarif et-** '- describe sth /to/ sb'.

864:11 - specify | {tespit et- /sapta-} 2 '- set or - fix the time of'.

866 CONFORMITY
866:3 - conform | /A/ **denk düş-** 1 '- be suitable, right, timely /FOR/' → düş- 1; /{üstünde/üzerinde}/ **dur-** 9 '- look, - appear /ON/ sb, - suit [subj.: clothing]'; /A/ **gel-** 2 '- be a certain size /FOR/, - fit [subj.: clothing]'; /1A/ **git-** 6 '- go /with/ [subj.: clothing, food]'; /A/ **ol-** 8 '- be suitable, right, appropriate /FOR/, - fit, - be fit /FOR/'; /{üzerine/üstüne}/ **otur-** 5 '- fit /θ/, - suit /θ/ [subj.: clothing]'; /A/ **uy-** 1 '- fit /θ/, - be the right size and shape /FOR/ [subj.: clothes]'. 2 '- suit /θ/, - be right, suitable /FOR/ [class hours for person, money for budget]'. 3 '- match /θ/, - go /WITH/, - look good /WITH/, - go together [color of curtains with walls]'. 4 '- be compatible /WITH/ [video cassette with TV system], - conform /to/.' 5 '- comply /WITH/, - conform /to/, - follow or - act in accordance /WITH/ rules, regulations'; /A/ **uydur-** 1 '- make one thing fit /{θ/INTO}/ another, - improvise, i.e., - fabricate out of what is conveniently on hand /FOR/ [key to lock]'; /A/ **uygun düş-** = denk düş- 1; /A/ **yakış-** 1 '- be suitable, appropriate, right /FOR/, - be suited /to/, - be becoming /to/, - go well /IN/, - become /θ/ [flowers for room]'. 2 'for sth - look good /ON/, - suit /θ/ [subj.: clothing]'; /A/ **yakıştır-** '- regard sth as suitable /FOR/ sb; - think that sth befits /θ/ sb', usually in the negative abilitative form yakıştırAMA- in the sense of '- be UNABLE to reconcile sb's behavior on a particular occasion with what one knows of him', as in: This isn't like you at all. It is out of character.

866:10 PHR. don't rock the boat Proverb: **Güne göre kürk giyinmek gerek.** 'One must dress oneself in the fur appropriate to the day.', i.e., dress as circumstances require. → giyin-; Proverb: **Güne göre kürk giymek gerek.** 'One must wear the fur appropriate to the day.', i.e., dress as circumstances require. → giy-; Proverb: **Herkesin geçtiği köprüden sen de geç.** 'You [should] also cross {θ/OVER} the bridge that everyone crosses.', i.e., Do what most people do, even if it is not entirely to your liking. → geç- 1; Proverb: **Zaman sana uymazsa sen zamana uy.** 'If the time is not suitable for you, adapt

yourself to the time.' → uy- 5;
Proverb: **Rüzgarın önüne
düşmeyen yorulur.** 'He who
doesn't give way [lit., fall down]
against the force of [lit., in front of]
the wind will tire.', i.e., The person
who resists the trends of his society
will suffer the consequences. →
yorul-.

867 NONCONFORMITY

867:4 not - conform /A/ {a:
küçük/b: büyük/c: dar} gel- '-
be too {a: small/b: large/c: narrow}
/FOR/ sb [subj.: clothing: shoes]' →
gel- 2; /A/ **yakıştır-** '- regard sth as
suitable /FOR/ sb; - think that sth
befits /θ/ sb', usually in the negative
abilitative form **yakıştırAMA-** in
the sense of '- be UNABLE to
reconcile sb's behavior on a
particular occasion with what one
knows of him', as in: This isn't like
you at all. It is out of character.

869 ABNORMALITY

869:8. * 1 - find strange
{acayibine/garibine/tuhafına}
git- '- find or - think {strange/odd}, -
strike as {strange/odd}, - seem
{strange/odd} /to/' → git- 1b;
yadırga-. Same.

869:10 ADJ. unusual **olmadık**
'unheard-of, incredible,
unprecedented' → ol- 11.

870 LIST

870:8 - list **say-** 2 '- list, -
enumerate, - say the names of [the
days, capital cities of the world]'.

871 ONENESS

871:6 - stand alone **yalnız bırak-**
'- leave sb alone' → bırak- 4;
yalnızlık çek- '- be lonely' → çek-
5.

872 DOUBLENESS

872:7 ADJ. both **olsun...olsun**
'both...and...; whether...or' → ol- 11.

885 CAUSE

885:10 - cause /A/
{sebep/neden} ol- '- bring about
/θ/ sth, - cause /θ/ sth, - be the means
of' → ol- 12; /A/ **yol aç-** 2 '- cause
/θ/, - bring about /θ/, - lead /to/' →
aç- 1. For an explanation of the
causative form of verbs, → '- have
sth done, - have sb do sth' in the
English-Turkish Index.

886 EFFECT

886:4 - result **çık-** 7 '- turn out, -
come out [well, badly: photographs]'.

886:5 - result from /DAn/
kaynaklan- '- result, - originate, -
stem, - emanate, or - spring /from/, -
be due /TO/'.

887 ATTRIBUTION

887:8 ADV. why? **Nasıl ol-
...da...?** '{How is it
that...?/informal: How come...?}' →
ol- 2.

887:10 CONJ. because -DIğI
için and -DIğIndAn →
{olduğundan/olduğu için}
'because {he/it} {is/was}' → ol- 3,
Additional examples. a) 3. Selected
examples...; **diye** 2 'because' → de-
1.

888 OPERATION

888:5 - operate sth **çalıştır-** 2 '-
work, - run, or - operate a machine';
vehicle name {kullan-/sür-} →
kullan-, sür- 1. This structure is used
to indicate the operation of various
vehicles: **araba kullan-** '- drive a
car', **araba sür-.** Same, **uçak
kullan-** '- fly a plane'.

888:7 - be operative **çalış-** 3 '-
function, - work, - run [subj.:
instrument: computer]'; **işle-** 1 '-
function, - work, - operate [subj.:
usually machines running on
electricity]'; **oyna-** 2 '- play, - show,
- be on, - be running, showing [subj.:
film, movie]'.

891 PRODUCTION

891:8 - produce, - create /DAn/
çıkar- 7 '- cause sth to come out or
appear, - create, - produce, - bring
forth /from/'; 1 **dik-** '- sew, - make
by sewing', when the object to be
created by sewing is specified: She
sewed a dress.; **dikiş dik-** '- sew',
lit., ** '- sew a sewing', when the
object being sewed is not specified:
She sewed θ for two hours. → 1 dik-;
/DAn/ **oluştur-** '- form, - create, -
make up, - constitute /{from/OUT
OF}/'; **ör-** 1 '- knit', when the object
knitted is specified: She knitted a
sweater.; **örgü ör-** '- knit', lit., ** '-
knit a knitting', when the object
knitted is not specified: She knitted
for two hours.; **üret-** 1 '- produce, -
manufacture [goods]'. 2 '- raise
[crops, animals on farm]'; **var et-** '-

create [only God as subject]'; /DAn/ **yap-** 1 '- make sth /{from/OUT OF}/, - build'; /A/ **yaptır-** 1 '- have /θ/ sb make sth, build sth'; **yarat-** '- create [God created the universe.]'. Although a subject other than God, as in 'This news created a sensation', is frequent with this verb, some Muslims do not approve of such usage.; **yetiştir-** 1 '- grow [obj.: crops], - raise [obj.: crops, animals]'.

891:10 - establish | **aç-** 11 '- establish, - found, - open [school]'; **aile kur-** '- start a family, - set up a household' → kur- 1; /A/ **kur-** 1 '- set up, - assemble [machine, furniture] /{IN/ON}/; - establish, - found [business, republic]'; /A, tarafından/ **kurul-** 1 '- be set up, assembled /{IN/ON}, by/ [subj.: dining room set]; - be established, founded /by/ [subj.: state, association]'.

891:12 - originate | **geliştir-** 3 '- create, - develop [new methods]'; **programla-** 3 '- develop or - create computer materials or games'; /A/ **uydur-** 1 '- make one thing fit /θ/ another, - improvise, i.e., - fabricate out of what is conveniently on hand [key for lock]'.

893 INFLUENCE

893:7 - influence | /A/ **dokun-** 3 '- move, - touch, - affect /θ/ sb emotionally; - disturb, - upset /θ/ sb'; /DAn/ **duygulan-** '- be moved, touched, emotionally affected /BY/'; /I/ **etkile-** '- affect, - influence, - have an effect /{ON/UPON}/, - impress'; /DAn/ **etkilen-** 1 '- be influenced /BY/, - show the influence /OF/'. 2 '- be moved, emotionally affected, impressed /BY/'; /A/ **tesir et-** '- affect /θ/, - influence /θ/, - have an effect /{ON/UPON}/, - do good [medicine]'.

896 LIABILITY

896:4 - incur | **masraf çek-** '- foot the bill, - pay', *informal, jocular.* → çek- 5; /{A/için}/ **masraf {et-/yap-}** '- spend [money] /{ON [*or* FOR]}/{ON [*or* for]}/; - pay /FOR/'; **masrafa gir-** '- spend a lot of money on sth or to get sth done, - have a lot of expenses, - incur great expense'.

896:7 CONJ. lest | **diye** 3.1a) 'so that; lest' → de- 1.

897 INVOLVEMENT

897:2 - involve | /A/ **eğil-** 4 '- concern oneself /WITH/ [a subject, topic]'.

897:3 - be involved in | /I/ **ilgilendir-** 2 '- be one's business, affair, - concern [This matter concerns you.].'

900-1000

900 SUPPORT

900:22 - rest on | /A/ **{daya-/yasla-}** '- lean, - prop, - rest sth /{AGAINST/ON}/'; /A/ **dayan-** 1 '- lean [oneself] /{AGAINST/ON}/'; /A/ **sırtını {daya-/yasla-}** 1 '- lean /{AGAINST/ON}/ [lit., - lean one's back /{AGAINST/ON}/]' → {daya-/yasla-}.

901 IMPULSE, IMPACT

901:12 - thrust, - push | /A/ **it-** '- push /{to/INTO}/'; **salla-** 2 '- push [a child in a swing], - rock [a cradle]'; **vurgula-** 2 '- accent, - accentuate, - stress, - put the stress on [a syllable, word]'.

901:13 - collide | /A/ **çarp-** 1 '- hit /θ/, - strike /θ/, - bump /{AGAINST/INTO/ON}/, - run or - crash /INTO/'; /IA/ **çarpıl-** '- be struck /by/'; **çarpış-** '- collide, - run into each other'; /A/ **rastla-** 2 '- hit /θ/ sth by chance, not intention, - collide /WITH/ [thrown ball goes astray and hits /θ/ window]'; /A/ **tesadüf et-** 2. Same.

901:14 - hit | **ayağının altına al-** '- give a whipping, beating, thrashing, - beat, - thrash' → al- 1; /A/ **dayak at-** '- beat, - give a whipping, beating, - thrash /θ/' → at- 5; /I/ **döv-** '- beat, - strike'; /a: A, b: IA, c: A/ **vur-** 1 '- hit, - strike /a: θ [sb, sth], b: with, c: ON/, - knock, - kick, - slap, - bump', depending on the preceding noun; /I/ **yıldırım çarp-** 'for lightning - strike' → çarp- 1; /A/ **yumruk {at-/vur-}** '- punch /θ/' → at- 5; **yumruk ye-** '- get a punch, - be punched' → ye- 2.

901:16 - pound | /I/ **çal-** 5 '- knock /{AT/ON}/ [door]'; **çalın-** 4 'lit., ** - be knocked at'; /DAn/ **dayak ye-** '- get a thrashing, beating /from/' → ye- 2; **kapı çalın-** 'lit., ** - be knocked at [door: There was a knock

717

at the door.].' → çalın- 4; **kapıyı {çal-/vur-}** '- knock {AT/ON} the door' → çal- 5, vur- 1.

901:19 - slap **eliyle vur-** '- slap, - strike with one's hand' → vur- 1; /A/ **tokat {at-/vur-}** '- slap /θ/ sb' → at- 5; **tokat ye-** '- get a slap, - be slapped' → ye- 2. Same as 604:12. PUNISHMENT: - slap.

901:21 - kick /A/ **tekme {at-/vur-}** '- kick /θ/' → at- 5; **tekme ye-** '- get a kick, - receive a blow' → ye- 2.

902 REACTION
902:5 - react /I/ **karşıla-** 3 '- respond /TO/, - react /TO/ [a situation, a proposal]'; /A/ **karşılık ver-** 1 '- respond /to/, - react /to/ a situation; - answer /θ/, - reply /to/ a question' → ver- 1; /A/ **tepki göster-** '- react /to/ [a situation]' → göster- 1.

902:7 - pull or - draw back **göz kırp-** 1 '- blink' → kırp- .

903 PUSHING, THROWING
903:9 - push **ilerlet-** '- advance sth, - move sth forward'; /A/ **it-** '- push /{to/INTO}/'; **salla-** 2 '- push [a child in a swing], - rock [a cradle]'.

903:10 - throw /A/ **at-** 1 '- throw /{AT/ON/IN/INTO}/'; /A, A doğru/ **fırlat-** '- hurl, - fling, - throw /{AT/to/INTO}, toward/; - launch [rocket] /INTO/ [space]'.

903:12 - shoot /A/ **ateş et-** '- fire /{ON/UPON}/, - shoot /AT/'; /A/ **kurşun at-** '- shoot [bullets] /AT/, - fire a gun /AT/' → at- 6; /I/ **vur-** 2 '- shoot; - shoot dead'.

904 PULLING
904:4 - pull **çek-** 1 '- pull, - tow, - draw; - attract'; **çektir-** 1 /A/ '- have sth towed, - have /θ/ sb tow sth'. 2 /A/ '- have sth pulled, extracted, - have /θ/ sb pull, extract sth [teeth]'; /{tarafından/CA}/ **çektiril-** '- be towed away [car] /by/'; /A/ **sürükle-** 1 '- drag sb or sth along the ground /to/'. 2 '- drag sb /to/ a place against his will, - drag off'.

908 EJECTION
908:13 - eject /DAn/ **kov-** '- throw, - chase, or - run sb /OUT OF/, - eject sb /from/ [room]'.

908:15 - evict /DAn/ **çıkar-** 1 '- evict, - throw out /of/'.

908:19 - dismiss **görevden al-** '- fire, - relieve sb of his {duties/position}', *formal*. → al- 1; **görevden alın-** '- be fired, relieved of one's {duties/position}' → alın- 1; **görevine son veril-**. Same. → son veril- → veril-; **işinden ol-**. Same. *neutral* → ol- 7; **işine son ver-** '- fire, - relieve sb of his position', *neutral* → son ver- → ver- 1; **işten çıkar-** '- dismiss, - fire [from a job]', *neutral*. → çıkar- 1.

908:20 <nonformal terms> - fire **işten {at-/kov-}** '- fire, - sack, - can, - dismiss from a job', *informal*. → at- 1, kov- 2.

908:22 - evacuate sth /A/ **boşalt-** '- empty sth, - empty sth out /INTO/ [He emptied the trash into the trash barrel.], - clear out [people from building]'.

908:23 - unload **bavulunu aç-** '- unpack', or just '- open one's bags' → aç- 1; /DAn/ **çıkar-** 1 '- take sth /OUT OF/, - remove sth /from/ [things from pocket, luggage]'; /DA, DAn/ **indir-** 2 '- let {off/out}, - drop off, - discharge, - unload /at, from/ [passengers]'.

908:25 - disgorge **boşal-** 3 '- come, - ejaculate, - climax, - have an orgasm,' more frequently for men but also for women; /a: A, b: {üstüne/üzerine}, c: {tarafından/CA}/ **dökül-** 2 '- be poured out, - be spilled /a: ON, b: on, c: by/'; /A/ **sık-** 2 '- squeeze [juice on soup], - squirt, - spray /ON/ [water on fire].'

908:26 - vomit **çıkar-** 6 '- vomit', *formal, polite*; **kus-** '- throw up', as in English, *less formal, less polite*.

908:31 INTERJ. go away! **Bas git!** 'Get lost!, Beat it!, Scram!, Get out!, Go away!, Be off!, Off with you!, Clear out!, Away with you!' → bas- 1; **Defol!** Same. → ol- 12; **Güle güle.** 2 'Bye bye' in the sense

718

of 'Get lost!, Be off!' [i.e., not in response to either 1. **Allaha ısmarladık**. 'Good-bye.' or 2. **Hoşça kal[ın]**! 'Good-bye., Have a good day.', where it means 'Good-bye.'] → gül- 1.

909 OVERRUNNING

909:4 - overrun | **geç-** 1 '- exceed, - go beyond, - outdo [obj.: speed limit]...'.

909:7 - run over | **çiğne-** 2 '- run over sth [The car ran over a cat.]'.

909:8 - pass | **geç-** 1 /DAn, A/ '- pass /THROUGH, {to/INTO}/, - go past, - cross /θ/ sth, - trespass', /I/ '- go beyond, - cross', the thing crossed is indicated: He crossed θ the street.; /DAn/ **karşıya geç-** '- pass /to/ the {opposite/other} side, - cross /θ/, - cross over /θ/' → geç- 1.

909:9 - overstep | /{ArAk/mAklA}/ {**çok ol-/ ileri git-** 2} '- go too far, - overstep the limit, - be rude /BY...ing/' → ol- 12, git- 1a.

910 SHORTCOMING

910:3 - fall through | **boşa çık-** '- come to naught, not - be realized, - be dashed [hopes, expectations, dreams, efforts]' → çık- 7; **boşa git-** '- be in vain, of no use, for nothing' → git- 5.

911 ELEVATION

911:5 - elevate | /DAn/ **başını kaldır-** '- raise one's head /from/, - look up /from/ [one's book]'; **el kaldır-** 1 '- raise one's hand', to get permission to talk in various circumstances, to get a teacher's attention at the university level. 2 /A/ '- raise one's hand, a hand /AGAINST/ [i.e., - strike]' → kaldır- 1; /DAn/ **kaldır-** 1 '- raise, - lift up, - pick up /from/'; **parmak kaldır-** '- raise one's HAND [lit., finger, **parmak**]'. This expression is used like **el kaldır-** above, but is more common than that expression in schools below the university level. → kaldır- 1.

911:8 - pick up | /A/ **çıkar-** 4 '- take sb or sth up /to/, - have sb go up /to/ [the tenth floor]'.

912 DEPRESSION <act of lowering>

912:4 - depress | /A/ **bas-** 2 '- press /{θ/ON}/, - push /θ/ [button, horn]'; **indir-** 1 /DAn, A/ '- lower /from, to/, - bring down /from, to/, - take down, - unload, - download [computer programs from the Internet]'. 2 /DA, DAn/ '- let {off/out}, - drop off, - discharge, - unload /at, from/ [passengers]'; **indiril-** 1 /a: DAn, b: A, c: {tarafından/CA}/ '- be lowered /a: from, b: to, c: by/ [subj.: flags]'. 2 /a: DA, b: DAn, c: tarafından/ '- be let off /a: at [a place], b: from [a vehicle], c: by [the driver]/ [subj.: passengers]'; **korna çal-** '- hit /θ/ or - honk /θ/ a car horn' → çal- 2; **kornaya bas-**. Same. → bas- 2; /{I/A}/ **tuşla-** '- press a key, - enter or - punch in a PIN or credit card number, - click /ON/'.

912:5 - fell | **indir-** 4 '- bring down, - knock down [boxer knocks down opponent]'; **kes-** 1 '- cut down [tree]'; **yere yık-** '- knock to the ground, - topple' → yık- 2; **yık-** 1 '- demolish, - wreck; - pull down, - knock down; - destroy; - ruin; - break sb's heart'. 2 '- knock down, - fell sb or sth; - send sb sprawling, - lay sb flat; - topple sth, - overthrow'.

912:7 - drop sth | /DAn, A/ **düşür-** 1 '- drop sth /from, {to/ON}/, - cause sth to fall /from, {to/ON}/, - let sth fall'.

912:9 - bow | **eğil-** 1 /A/ '- bend down /to/ [to pick up]'. 2 '- bow, - bow down'.

912:10 - sit down | /A/ **çök-** 2 '- sit down suddenly, heavily /IN/, - collapse /INTO/ [a chair]'; /A/ **otur-** 1 '- sit down /IN/ [i.e., - move INTO a sitting postion]'; /A/ **yerleş-** '- settle [oneself] down /{IN/INTO}/ [a chair]'.

912:11 - lie down | /{A/üstüne}/ **uzan-** 1 '- lie down /{ON/on}/, - stretch oneself out /{ON/on}/ [bed for a nap]'; **yat-** 1 '- go to bed, - lie down, - retire for the night'. Also '- be lying down'.

913 CIRCUITOUSNESS

913:5 - circle | /etrafında/ **dön-** 1 '- turn, - revolve, - rotate /around/ [earth around the sun]'.

914 ROTATION

914:9 - rotate | /I/ **aç-** 3 '- turn /TO/ [page 5, TV channel], - open /TO/ [page 5], - tune /{TO/INTO}/ [radio station], - put on or - turn on [TV channel, radio station]'; /A/ {**arkasını/sırtını**} **çevir-**[or **dön-**] '- turn around, - turn one's back /to/' → çevir- 3, dön- 4; **başı dön-** '- be dizzy, - get dizzy [lit., for one's head - turn]' → dön- 1; **çevir-** 1 /I/ '- turn, - rotate [obj.: door handle]'. 2 /A, A doğru/ '- turn sth /to, toward/ [obj.: steering wheel]'. 3 '- turn over, - turn, - flip [page, omelette]'. 4 /I/ '- turn /TO/ [page 5, TV channel], - switch /TO/.' If the instrument is already on and you want to make a change: '- put on, - turn on [TV channel, radio station]'. 7 '- dial [a phone number]'; /etrafında/ **dön-** 1 '- turn, - revolve, - rotate /around/'. 4 '- turn sth, - make sth turn'; /A doğru/ **döndür-** 1 = çevir- 2; **kur-** 2 '- wind, - set [watch, clock, meter, toy, or music box]'; **kurul-** 2 '- be wound, set [watch, clock, meter, toy, or music box]'.

915 OSCILLATION

915:11 - wave | /A/ **el salla-** '- wave [hand] /to/ [in good-bye]' → salla- 1; **salla-** 1 '- wave [obj.: flags, banners]'.

915:14 - move up and down | /I/ **el sık-** '- shake hands /with/, - shake sb's hand' → sık- 1; /lA/ **tokalaş-** '- shake hands /with/'.

916 AGITATION

916:10 - agitate sth | **başını salla-** '- shake one's head' in affirmation, negation, or surprise. → salla- 3; **çalkala-** 1 '- shake [the medicine before using]'; **çırp-** '- beat, - whip [food: yogurt and egg whites]'; **salla-** 3 '- shake, - rock [The earthquake shook the whole city.]'; /ArAk/ **sinirlendir-** '- make sb angry, mad, - anger; - irritate, - annoy, - get on sb's nerves /by...ing/'.

916:11 - shake | /DAn/ **eli ayağı tutMA-** '- be shaky, unsteady /{WITH/BECAUSE OF}/' [a reaction of shock to bad news or a frightening event or a sign of anger]. → tut- 2; /DAn/ **titre-** 1 '- shiver /{WITH/ from}/ [cold, fever]'. 2 '- tremble /{WITH/IN}/ [fear], - shake /with/ [fear, anger, excitement]'.

916:12 - flutter | **at-** 7 '- beat, - palpitate, - pound, - race [subj.: heart]'; **çarp-** 2. Same; {**kalbi/yüreği**} **at-**[or **çarp-**] 'for one's heart - beat' → at- 7, çarp- 2; /DAn/ {**kalbi/yüreği**} **hızlı hızlı at-**[or **çarp-**] 'for one's heart - palpitate, - pound, - race /{BECAUSE OF/IN/WITH/from}/' → at- 7, çarp- 2.

917 SPECTATOR

917:6 - sightsee | **gezmeye çık-** '- go {out for a walk/θ sight-seeing}' → çık- 2.

921 UNINTELLIGENCE

921:12 - be stupid | **çocukluk et-** '- be childish, - act childishly'.

922 FOOLISHNESS

922:6 - be foolish | {**abuk subuk/saçma sapan**} **konuş-** '- talk nonsense, hogwash'; **saçmala-** '- talk nonsense, - talk {garbage/rot}, - be silly'.

924 SANITY

924:2. - come to one's senses | **akıllan-** '- become wiser through bitter experience, - come to one's senses about a matter, - wise up'; **aklı başına gel-** '- come to one's senses' → gel- 1.

925 INSANITY, MANIA

925:21 - go mad | **aklını** {**kaybet-/yitir-**} '- lose one's mind, - go crazy'; **çıldır-** '- go crazy, mad, insane, nuts, out of one's mind, - take leave of one's senses, - lose one's mind, - have a nervous breakdown'; **delir-**. Same; {**şuurunu/ bilincini**} **kaybet-**[or **yitir-**] 3 '- go out of one's mind, - be out of one's senses' → {kaybet-/yitir-}.

927 KNOWLEDGE

927:12 - know | **bil-** 1.1 '- know sth [a fact, a thing, not a person]'. 1.2 '- know the real nature of sb, what kind of person he is, what can be expected of him', not in the more casual sense of '- be acquainted with'. 2 '- know how to do sth [She knows how to swim.]'; **tanı-** 1.1 '- know, - be acquainted /WITH/ sb'. 1.2 '- know the real nature of a person, what kind of person he is', not in the casual sense of '- be acquainted with'. 4 '- know a subject, area of study [speciality such as cars, birds, not mathematics].'

927:14 - learn /DAn/ **bilgi edin-** '- obtain or - receive information /from/, - learn /from/'; /DAn/ **haber al-** '- get word, news /{OF/from}/, - find out /from/' → al-3; /DAn/ **öğren-** '- learn, - find out /from/'.

927:30 ADV. to one's knowledge **Anladığı kadarıyla** '{As far as he understands/As far as he can tell/To the best of his understanding}' → anla-; **Bildiği kadarıyla** '{As far as he knows/To the best of his knowledge}' → bil- 1.

929 IGNORANCE
929:11 not - know **Allah bilir.** 'God knows.', said when one professes ignorance. → bil- 1; **Bilmem.** 'I don't know.' Also 'I wonder' → bil- 1; **Kim bilir?** 'Who knows? [i.e., nobody knows]' → bil-1; **Ne bileyim [ben]?** 1 'How should I know?' → bil- 1.

930 THOUGHT
930:8 - think **düşün-** 1 '- think, - reflect, - consider [i.e., - use one's mind]'. 5 '- think /of/ [doING] sth, of taking a particular course of action, - consider [I'm thinking of going to the movies.]'.

930:9 - think hard **{düşün-/düşünüp} taşın-** '- think over carefully, - consider at length, - ponder, - think hard, - think and think' → düşün- 1.

930:12 - consider **dikkate al-** '- take note /OF/, - take /INTO/ consideration, - consider' → al- 1; **verb stem.sA.personal suffix mI diye düşün-** '- wonder whether': **Git.se.m mi diye düşünüyorum.** 'I wonder whether I should go.' → düşün- 5; /I/ **düşün-** 5 '- think /OF/ [doING] sth, of taking a particular course of action, - consider'; **göz önünde tut-** '- keep or - bear in mind, - remember, - realize, - consider' → tut- 2.

930:18 - occur to **akla gel-** '- occur /to/ [one's mind], - think of, - remember' → gel- 1; **aklıma gelmişken** 'while it's on my mind, while I'm thinking of it, by the way,

speaking of, incidentally [lit., while it has come to my mind]' → gel- 1. The most common non-verbal expression for this notion is the single word **şey** lit., 'thing'.

930:20 - occupy the mind /A/ **aklı takıl-** '- be preoccupied, obsessed /WITH/' → takıl- 2; **aklına takıl-** '- stick in one's mind and bother one, - occupy one's mind' → takıl- 2; /I/ **düşün-** 3 '- think /{OF/ABOUT}/, for one's mind - be occupied /WITH/'.

933 INTUITION, INSTINCT
933:4 - intuit **hisset-** 2 '- sense, - feel, - be aware; - notice, - perceive'; **verb stem.mIş gibi hisset-** '- feel {like/as if}' → hisset- 2; **sez-** '- understand sth intuitively, - sense, - have a feeling, - feel, - perceive, - discern'.

934 REASONING
934:15 - reason **analiz et-** '- analyze [blood, historical event]'; **tahlil et-** '- analyze [blood, historical event, literary work]'.

934:16 - argue /a: 1A, b: hakkında, c: konusunda, d: I/ **münakaşa et-** '- debate heatedly; - have an intense discussion; - argue /a: with, b: about, c: on the subject of, d: about/, - dispute', usually confrontational, heated; /a: 1A, b: hakkında, c: konusunda, d: I/ **tartış-** 1 '- debate, - discuss, or - argue /a: with, b: about, c: on the subject of, d: about/', i.e., the pros and cons of an issue, not confrontational in a negative sense. 2 = münakaşa et-.

937 INQUIRY
937:20 - inquire **arayıp sor-** '- look up [mostly a person rather than a fact]'; **hal hatır sor-** '- ask how sb is, - inquire after sb's health' → sor-; **hatır sor-**. Same. → sor-; **{Saatin kaç olduğunu/Saati} sor-** '- ask {what time it is./the hour.}'; **sor-** a) /A/ '- ask /θ/ sb sth'. b) /DAn/ '- ask sth /OF/ sb or /AT/ an office, - ask /θ/ sb or /AT/ an office for sth [frequently information]'. c) /I/ '- ask {FOR/ABOUT} sb'; **soru sor-** '- ask a question'.

937:21 - interrogate /DAn/ **imtihan et-** '- test, - give sb an exam /IN/, - examine sb /IN [a subject]/', NOT ~~sınav et-~~; /A, DAn/ {sınav/imtihan} ver- 2 '- give an examination /to [sb], IN/ a subject' → ver- 1; **sorguya çek-** '- cross-examine, - question, - interrogate, - grill, - subject /to/ interrogation' → çek- 6.

937:23 - investigate | **araştır-** 2 '- investigate, - explore, - research, - study, - do research on, - try to find out'; **yokla-** 2 '- check at a place to determine how things are [Check at the bank to see if a deposit has been made]'. 3 '- check up on people to determine their situation'.

937:24 - examine | **kontrol et-** '- check, - inspect, - check on, - check to see whether sth is the case or not'; **kontrolden geç-** '- be checked, - be checked out, examined [travelers at the airport]' → geç- 1; **muayene et-** '- examine [mostly for a doctor and a patient]'; /A, not with **tarafından**/ **muayene ol-** '- be examined /BY/ [for a physical examination]' → ol- 10.1; **muayeneden geç-** '- have a general physical examination, a physical, a check-up' → geç- 1; **muayeneden geçir-** '- examine, - subject /TO/ a physical examination, physical, checkup' → gecir- 1; **yokla-** 1 '- feel, - examine, or - inspect sth with one's fingers for [obj.: texture, flesh], - feel around'.

937:25 - make a close study of **incele-** '- examine carefully, closely, minutely, in detail, - study carefully, - inspect, - investigate, - research'; **tetkik et-.** Same.

937:26 - examine cursorily | /A/ **göz at-** '- glance /AT/, - take a look /AT/' → at- 1; /I/ **karıştır-** 3 '- rummage or - search /THROUGH/ [drawers, pocketbook], - leaf, - thumb, or - flip /THROUGH/ [book, papers]'; **şöyle bir bak-** '- just look around, - browse [at a store]' → bak- 1.

937:30 - seek | /I/ **ara-** 1 '- look /FOR/, - search /FOR/'; /{tarafından/CA}/ **aran-** '- be sought, looked for /by/'; **arayıp sor-** '- look sb up'; /A/ **bak-** 2 '- look /{FOR/IN}/, - search /FOR/ [in a book for an article, in a store for all items except food]'; /A, için/ {**başvur-/müracaat et-**} 1 '-

consult /θ [sb or sth], for/, - refer, - resort, - turn, or - appeal /to, for/, - have recourse /to, for/, - look sth up /IN/'. 2 '- apply or - submit an application /to, for/'; **bilgisine danış-** '- consult a person', lit., ** '- consult /θ/ sb's knowledge'; /a: A, b: I, c: konusunda/ **danış-** '- consult /a: θ [sb, an office], b: {about/on}, c: {about/on the subject of}/, - refer /to [sb]/, regarding/'.

937:31 - search | {**ara-/arayıp**} **tara-** '- search [through] thoroughly' → tara- 2; **araştır-** 1 '- search thoroughly, - search through'; **etrafa bak-** '- look /θ/ around, - have a look /θ/ around' → bak- 1.

937:33 - ransack | /I/ **karıştır-** 3 '- rummage or - search /THROUGH/ [drawers, pocketbook], - leaf, - thumb, or - flip /THROUGH/ [book, papers]'.

938 ANSWER

938:4 - answer | /A/ {**cevap/yanıt**) **ver-** '- answer, - reply, - respond /to/ [a person, question, questionnaire]' → ver- 1; /I/ {**cevapla-/cevaplandır- /yanıtla-**} '- answer, - reply, - respond to [a question, a questionnaire, a person]'; /A/ **karşılık ver-** 1 '- respond /to/, - react /to/ a situation; - answer /θ/, - reply /to/ a question' → ver- 1; /DAn/ {**sınava/imtihana**} **gir-** '- take an examination /IN/'; /DAn/ {**sınav/imtihan**} **ol-** '- take an examination /IN/, - be examined /IN/' → ol- 10.1; **soruya cevap ver-** '- answer /θ/ {a/the} question' → ver- 1; **soruyu cevapla-** '- answer the question, - repond TO the question' → {**cevapla-/cevaplandır-/yanıtla-**}; **telefona cevap ver-** '- answer /θ/ the phone' → ver- 1; /I/ **yanıtla-** → {**cevapla-/cevaplandır-/yanıtla-**}.

939 SOLUTION

939:2 - solve | **çöz-** 2 '- solve a problem, - figure sth out [usually a puzzle, mathematical problem]'; /{için/A}/ **çözüm [yolu] bul-** '- find a way of solving a problem, - find a solution /{for/to}/ a problem, - find a way to do sth' → bul- 1; **hallet-** '- solve, - find a solution /for/, - resolve, - handle, - take care of, - straighten out, - settle [situation, personal problem]'; **işin içinden çık-** 2 '- work out a solution for something complicated, - resolve a difficult problem, - figure sth out' → çık- 1.

940 DISCOVERY

940:2 - discover | bul- 1 '- find'. 2 '- discover'; /a: DA, b: {tarafından/CA}, c: mAklA/ bulun- 1 '- be found, discovered /a: {in/at} [a place], b: by [a person], c: BY...ing/'; icad et- '- invent'; keşfet- '- discover'; {tespit et-/sapta-} 1 '- determine or - establish the existence of, - find [errors in a composition]'.

940:5 - detect | /A/ dikkat et- 2 '- notice /θ/, - observe /θ/, - take note /OF/'; farkedil- '- be noticed, observed'; farket- 1 '- notice, - observe, - perceive, - realize'; farkına var- '- notice, - become aware /OF/, - realize'.

940:11.INTERJ. eureka! | Demek öyle! 'So that's how things are!' or 'So that's how it is!' → de- 3.

941 EXPERIMENT

941:8 - experiment | /I/ dene- '- test, - try, - try out, - try on; - attempt, - try /TO/ do sth'; prova et- '- try on [clothing]'; tadına bak- '- taste, - have a taste, - sample a food' → bak- 1; tat- '- taste, - sample, - try the taste of a food'; tecrübe et- '- try on [clothing], - try out [equipment], - see how sth or sb works out, - give sb a trial period'.

942 COMPARISON

942:4 - compare | /A/ benzet- 2 '- liken sb or sth /to/ sb or sth else, - note, - indicate, - see or - feel a resemblance between, - think that sb or sth is /LIKE/ sb or sth else; - compare sb or sth /to/ sb or sth else and note the similarity; for sb or sth - remind sb of sb or sth else; - remind /OF/ [one thing or person brings another to mind]'; With the two following verbs no particular result of the comparison is implied: /1A/ {karşılaştır-/mukayese et-} '- compare sb or sth /with/ sb or sth else'.

944 INDISCRIMINATION

944:3 - confound | /1A, A/ karıştır- 2 '- confuse or - mix up sb or sth /with/ sb or sth else'.

945 JUDGMENT

945:8 - judge | Bana öyle geliyor ki... '{I have {a feeling/a hunch} that.../I get the feeling that.../It seems to me that.../I sense that...}' → gel- 1; /I, hakkında/ düşün- 4 '- think, - have an opinion /{about/of}/'; /hakkında/ fikir ver- 1 '- express an opinion /ON/ sth, - give an opinion, idea, or impression /about/' → ver- 1; gibime gel- '- seem to me' → gel- 1; yargıla- '- hear a case; - try sb, a case; - judge or - adjudicate a case, - pass judgment on'.

945:9 - estimate | bil- 4 '- guess, - take a guess'; değerlendir- 1 '- evaluate, - assess, - appraise, - judge, - size up [situation]'; /A/ not ver- '- give a grade or mark /to/ sb or sth, - give /θ/ sb or sth a grade, - grade /θ/ sb or sth, - mark [an exam]' → ver- 1; /olarak/ tahmin et- 2 '- estimate /{AT/TO BE/AS BEING}/, - judge, - reckon, - take a guess'.

945:11 - decide | bul- 3 '- think of, about in a certain way, - find [How do you find this book?]'.

945:14 - criticize | /a: {DIğI için/DIğInDAn}, b: DAn dolayı, c: yüzünden/ {eleştir-/tenkit et-} '- criticize /a: because [or for], b: for, c: {for/on account of}/'; /a: {DIğI için/DIğInDAn}, b: DAn dolayı, c: {tarafından/CA}/ {eleştiril-/tenkit edil-} '- be criticized /a: because [or for], b: for, c: by/'. Same as 510:14. DISAPPROVAL: - criticize.

947 MISJUDGMENT

947:2 - misjudge | yanıl- '- be mistaken, wrong'.

948 OVERESTIMATION

948:2 - overestimate | fazla tahmin et- '- overestimate [the importance, amount, number of]' → tahmin et- 2.

949 UNDERESTIMATION

949:2 - underestimate | {az/eksik} tahmin et- '- underestimate [the importance, amount, number of]' → tahmin et- 2.

950 THEORY, SUPPOSITION

950:10 - suppose | <u>de-</u> 2 '- think, - think of in a certain way'; {<u>farz et-/varsay-</u>} '- assume, - imagine, - suppose sth for the sake of argument'; <u>tahmin et-</u> 1 '- guess; - conjecture, - suppose; - surmise'; <u>tut-</u> 9 '- assume, - imagine, - suppose for the sake of argument'.

950:11 - conjecture | <u>bil-</u> 4 '- guess, - take a guess'; /olarak/ <u>tahmin et-</u> 2 '- estimate /{AT/TO BE/AS BEING}/, - judge, - reckon, - take a guess'.

950:19. CONJ. supposing | <u>diye</u> 4 'thinking, assuming, with sth in mind'. 7 'as if it were, as, in the capacity of, in place of', preceded by a noun: They used to worship the sun as a God. → de- 1; <u>Diyelim [ki]</u> 'Let's say [that] [i.e., - assume, imagine, suppose for the sake of argument that]' → de- 2; {<u>Farzedelim [ki]/Farzet [ki]</u>} '{Let's suppose [that]/Suppose [that]}' → {farz et-/varsay-}; <u>hiçbir şey olmamış gibi</u> 'as if nothing had happened' → ol- 2; {<u>Tutalım [ki]/Tut ki</u>} '{Let's suppose [that]/Suppose that}' → tut- 9.

952 BELIEF

952:10 - believe | /I/ <u>düşün-</u> 2 '- think, - believe that sth was, is, or will be the case'; /A/ <u>inan-</u> 1 '- believe /θ/ sth, what sb says, sb'.

952:11 - think | /A, olarak/ <u>bak-</u> '- regard /θ [sb or sth], AS/, - look /UPON [sb or sth], AS/, - consider /θ [sb or sth]/' → bak- 4; <u>Bana öyle geliyor ki...</u> '{I have {a feeling/a hunch} that.../I get the feeling that.../It seems to me that.../I sense that...}' → gel- 1; /θ/ <u>bil-</u> 3 '- think of /as/, - know /as/'; <u>de-</u> 2 '- think, - think of in a certain way'; /hakkında/ <u>düşün-</u> 4 '- think, - have an opinion /{about/of}/'; <u>gibime gel-</u> '- seem to me' → gel- 1; /I, olarak/ <u>gör-</u>. = /A, olarak/ bak-. → gör- 2; /olarak/ <u>görül-</u> '- be regarded, looked UPON, considered /AS/'; {<u>san-/zannet-</u>} '- think, - suppose'; /I/ <u>say-</u> 4 '- regard, - look upon sb or sth /as/, - consider'; /DAn/ {<u>şüphelen-/şüphe et-/kuşkulan-</u>} '- suspect θ sb, - suspect θ sth, - suspect sb /OF/

sth, - suspect sb /OF/ doing sth'; <u>tahmin et-</u> 1 '- guess; - conjecture, - suppose; - surmise'.

952:15 - believe in | /A/ <u>güven-</u> '- trust /θ/, - rely /{ON/UPON}/, - depend /ON/, - have confidence /IN/'; /A/ <u>inan-</u> 2 '- trust /θ/, - believe /IN/, - have confidence /IN/'. 3 '- believe /IN/ the truth of /IN/ the existence of [God]'.

952:16 - rely on | /A/ <u>dayan-</u> 2 '- rely or - depend /{ON/UPON}/ for support'; /A/ <u>sırtını {daya-/yasla-}</u> 2. Same, lit., '- lean one's back, sırt, /{AGAINST/ON}/' → {daya-/yasla-}.

952:18 - convince | /a: A, b: A, c: A dair, d: konusunda/ <u>ikna et-</u> '- persuade or - convince sb /a: to [do sth], b: that, c: {that/to the effect that}, d: on the subject of/'; /A/ <u>inandır-</u> '- convince or - persuade sb to believe /θ/ sb or sth, - get, - cause, or - make sb believe /θ/ sth'; /için/ <u>kandır-</u> 2 '- persuade or - convince sb /TO/ do sth, - talk sb /INTO/ doing sth'.

952:29 ADV. in one's opinion | /A/ <u>kalırsa</u> 'if it were left up /to/ sb, in sb's view, opinion.' → kal- 1.

954 UNBELIEF

954:5 - disbelieve | <u>gözlerine inanaMA-</u> 'NOT - be able - believe /θ/ one's eyes' → inan- 1.

955 INCREDULITY

955: * 6 expressions of incredulity | <u>Deme ya!</u> 'You don't say!' → de- 3; <u>Yapma ya!</u> 'You don't say!, You don't mean it!, Don't give me that!, Oh go on!, Well I declare! [lit., Don't do (that)].' → yap- 2. Same as 131: * 16. INEXPECTATION: expressions of inexpectation.

956 EVIDENCE, PROOF

956:9 - testify | /DAn/ <u>ifade al-</u> '- examine sb and to record his testimony, - take a deposition /from/' → al- 1; /A/ <u>ifade ver-</u> *law* '- give evidence /to/, - testify, - give testimony, - give or - make a statement' → ver- 1; /a: için, b: A dair, c: lehine, d: aleyhine/ <u>tanıklık et-</u> '- testify /a: {for/on behalf of}, b: {θ [that]/to the effect that}, c: {for/on behalf of}, d:

724

against/, - give evidence, - be a witness in a court case'.

956:10 - prove {ispatla-/ispat et-/kanıtla-} '- prove, - substantiate'; {kendini/kendisini} ispatla-[or kanıtla-] '- prove oneself, one's worth' → {ispatla-/ispat et-/kanıtla-}.

956:13 - cite /A/ {örnek/misal} al- '- take as an example, role model /FOR/' → al- 1; /A/ {örnek/misal} ver- '- give, - cite, or - provide examples /FOR/' → ver- 1.

957 DISPROOF
957:5 - refute yalanla- '- deny, - contradict, - refute, - declare or - show to be false or wrong'.

958 QUALIFICATION
958:4 - make conditional /için/ şart koş- '- lay down, - set, or - establish a condition or prerequisite /for/, - make a stipulation that, - stipulate that, - state clearly and firmly as a requirement' → koş- 2.

960 FORESIGHT
960:6 - foreknow kestir- 2 '- predict, - figure out [how the novel is going to end], - know what to do or say'; önceden bil- '- know in advance' → bil- 1; tahmin et- 3 = kestir- 2.

961 PREDICTION
961:9 - predict /A/ kehanet et- '- make a prediction, - predict /θ/ that... [subj.: a wise man, oracle, fortune-teller, or soothsayer only]'; /{hakkında/A dair}/ kehanette bulun- '- make a prediction /about or concerning/, - predict /θ/ [subj.: a wise man, oracle, fortune-teller, or soothsayer only]' → bulun- 3; kestir- 2 '- predict, - figure out [how the novel is going to end], - know what to do or say'; /I/ önceden bildir- '- give advance notice /OF/, - predict [subj.: usually ordinary persons or experts, but not particularly persons divinely inspired, oracles, etc.]'; tahmin et- 3 = kestir- 2.

962 NECESSITY
962:9 - require gereğini yap- '- do what a situation requires, necessitates, - do what has to be done' → yap- 3; gerektir- '- require,

- necessitate [How much {time/money} does this process require?]'; /A/ ihtiyacı ol- '- need /θ/, - be in need /OF/, - have need /{OF/FOR}/, - require /θ/ [subj.: a person: I need θ money.]' → ol- 12; /I/ iste- 3 '- need, - require [subj.: non-person: This food needs to cook more.]'.

962:10 - be necessary /için/ gerek- '- be necessary, needed, required /{for/in order to}/'; /için/ icap et-. Same; /A/ gerek {var/yok} {There's/There isn't} a need {to/FOR}' → ol- 3, Additional examples. b) 3.6. Issues of necessity; /{için/A}/ lâzım ol- '- be or - become necessary, needed /FOR/' → ol- 12; -mAk zorunda kal- '- be obliged /to/, - be forced /to/, - have /to/' → kal- 1; - mAlI in olmalı '{he/it} {must/should} be' → ol- 3, Additional examples. a) 3. Selected examples..., and in noun.sI olmalı 'he {must/should have} sth [lit., his sth {must/should} be]' → ol- 5, (5.1) Table 1. Additional examples. 3. Selected examples...

963 PREDETERMINATION
963:11 PHR. it is fated Proverb: Akacak kan damarda durmaz. 'The blood that is going to flow will not stay in the vein.' → kan ak- → ak-, dur- 6; Proverb: Allah kulunu kısmeti ile yaratır. 'God creates His servant [i.e., any will-possessing being, mortal] together with his fate.' → yarat-; Proverb: Alna yazılan başa gelir. 'What is written on the forehead [alın, aLNı] will come to pass.', i.e., One can't escape one's fate. → başına gel- → gel- 1; Proverb: İş olacağına varır. 'What will be will be [lit., Matters will get to the place they are going to be].' → var-; Proverb: Ok menziline varır. 'The arrow will reach its mark.', i.e., What is destined will occur. → var-.

964 PREARRANGEMENT
964:4 - prearrange ayarla- 3 '- arrange, - plan [picnic, meeting]'; /a: DAn, b: için, c: A/ gün al- '- {make/get} an appointment [for a {date/day}] /a: from [sb], b: for [sth], c: FOR [a time]/, - set a date /b: for/' → al- 3; /A/ gün ver- '- give a {date/day} for an appointment /to/' → ver- 1; plan kur- '- make, -

devise, - draft, - establish, or - formulate a plan' → kur- 1; **programla-** 1 '- schedule [tasks]'. 2 /A, için/ '- set an instrument /FOR/, - program a computer /FOR/'; /DAn, için/ **randevu al-** '- get or - make an appointment /from [sb], for [sth]/' → al- 3; /a: A, b: A, c: için/ **randevu ver-** '- give or - grant an appointment /a: to [sb], b: for [sb], c: for [a time]/, - make an appointment /b: for [sb]/' → ver- 1; {**plânla-/tasarla-**} '- plan, - envisage'; {**tespit et-/sapta-**} 2 '- set, - fix the time of'.

965 POSSIBILITY
| 965:4 - be possible | **mümkün ol-** '- be possible' → ol- 12; **ol-** 4; **Olur.** 'OK., All right., Fine., It's possible., Yes.' → ol- 4; **Olur mu olur.** '{It's quite possible./[It] could well be.}' → ol- 4.

| 965:9 ADV. possibly | **bakarsın** 'it might just happen that, possibly, maybe [lit., ** you'll see]' = **belki**. → bak- 1.

| 965:10 ADV. by any possibility | **mümkün olduğu kadar** 'as...as possible [as much as possible]' → mümkün ol- → ol- 12; **Ne olur ne olmaz** 'Just in case' → ol- 11 → olur.

966 IMPOSSIBILITY
| 966:4 - be impossible | **mümkün olMA-** '- be impossible' → mümkün ol- → ol- 12; **olMA-** → ol- 4.

| 966:11 PHR. no can do | **Olacak gibi değil** 'It's impossible., It won't work out., It's not going to happen., It can't be done [lit., ** It isn't like it will be].' → ol- 4; **Olacak {iş/şey} değil!** 'It's {impossible/absurd}!, It's not going to happen!, It's out of the question!, It's unbelievable!, It's undheard of!, Can you believe it?, [Just] imagine!, Can you imagine?, How could such a thing happen?, How is it possible?' → ol- 4; **Olmaz.** 'It's not possible., It's impossible., It can't be done., It won't do., Impossible., No.' → ol- 4.

967 PROBABILITY
| 967:4 - be probable | {**olmalı/olsa gerek**} '{he/she/it} must be' → ol- 3, Additional examples. a) 3. Selected examples ...; **noun.sI** {**olmalı/olsa gerek**} 'he {must/should have} sth [lit., his sth {must/should} be]' → ol- 5, (5.1) Table 1. Additional examples. 3. Selected examples...

| 967:5 - think likely | **tahmin et-** 1 '- guess; - conjecture, - suppose; - surmise'.

969 CERTAINTY
| 969:9 - be certain | /{DAn/A}/ **emin ol-** '- be or - become sure, certain, convinced /OF/, /θ/ that; - be sure /of/, - trust /θ/ sb' → ol- 12; **iyi bil-** '- know for sure, certain' → bil- 1.1.

| 969:12 - verify | **doğrula-** '- verify, - corroborate, - confirm'; /{tarafından/CA}/ **doğrulan-** '- be verified, corroborated, confirmed /by/'; /{tarafından/CA}/ **tasdik edil-** '- be confirmed, affirmed, ratified, certified, notarized /by/'; **tasdik et-** '- confirm, - affirm, - ratify, - certify, - notarize'.

| 969:26 ADV. without fail | **Ne olursa olsun** 'No matter what, Anyway, In any case, Come what may' → ol- 11 → olur.

970 UNCERTAINTY
| 970:9 - be uncertain | **bilmem** 'I don't know.' Also: 'I wonder [whether]' → bil- 1; **verb stem.sA.personal suffix mI diye düşün-** '- wonder whether': **Git.se.m mi diye düşünüyorum.** 'I wonder whether I should go.' → düşün- 5; **şaşır-** 1 /A/ '- be confused, bewildered, at a loss /AS TO/ what to say or do, - be taken aback, bewildered /{AT/in the face of}/ an unexpected situation'. 3 /I/ '- confuse, - get confused /{about/regarding/as to}/, - lose track of, count of'; **yolunu şaşır-** '- lose one's way, - get lost, not - know which way to turn' → şaşır- 3.

| 970: * 30 PHR. it's not certain| **Hiç belli olmaz.** '{It's hard to say./It's impossible to say./You can never tell.} [lit., It {won't be/isn't} clear.]' → ol- 11 → olmaz.

971 CHANCE
971:12 - risk şansını zorla- '- push or - press one's luck' → zorla- 2.

971:20 ADV. purposelessly olur olmaz 2 'at random, without thinking, purposelessly' → ol- 11.

971:22 INTERJ. break a leg! Hayırlı olsun. 'Good luck., Congratulations., May it go well., May it be beneficial, useful., May it benefit.' → ol- 11 → olsun.

972 TRUTH
972:10 - be right isabet kaydet- 2 '- get it right, - be right, - be on target, - be right on the mark' → kaydet- 5.

972:12 - come true gerçekleş- '- come true, - be realized, - work out [plans, dreams, desires, wishes]'.

972:25 PHR. <nonformal terms> right on! İyi bildin! 'Right you are!', colloq.: 'Right on!' → bil- 1.

974 ERROR
974:10 - be wrong yanıl- '- be mistaken, wrong'.

974:12 - misdo yanlış numara çevir- '- dial the wrong number' → çevir- 7; yanlış numara düş- '- have the wrong number [on the phone]' → düş- 1; yanlış yap- '- get or - do sth wrong, incorrectly [questions on an exam]' → yap- 3.

974:13 - mistake, - make a mistake /A/ benzet- 1 '- mistake one thing or person /FOR/ another'; /mAklA/ hata et- '- make a mistake /BY...ing/; - do wrong /BY...ing/'. This verb is usually preferred when speaking of relatively greater errors in life rather than of minor errors in matters such as grammar, punctuation.; /lA/ hata işle- '- make an error or mistake [mostly in minor matters]' → işle- 2; /lA/ hata yap- '- make a mistake, error [mostly in minor matters]' → yap- 3; yanıl- '- be mistaken, wrong [mostly in minor matters]'; yanlışlık yap- '- make a mistake [mostly in minor matters]' → yap- 3.

978 BROAD-MINDEDNESS
978:7 - keep an open mind kabul et- 4 '- accept, - regard with tolerance [accept people as they are]'.

980 CURIOSITY
980:3a - make curious, - interest ilgi çek- '- appeal to, - interest' → çek- 1; /I/ ilgilendir- 1 '- interest, - appeal to, - arouse the interest of'.

980:3b - be curious /A [karşı]/ ilgi duy- '- be interested /IN/, - take an interest /IN/' → duy- 3; /1A/ ilgilen- 1 '- be interested /IN/, - take an interest /IN/'; /I/ merak et- 2 '- be curious /ABOUT/'.

981 INCURIOSITY
981:2 - take no interest in karışmam 1 'I'm not going to get involved., I don't want to have anything to do with it., Leave me out of this., I'm staying out of this.' → karış- 6.

982 ATTENTION
982:5 - attend to /A/ bak- 3 '- look /AFTER/, - take care /OF/, - attend /to/'; /A/ dikkat et- 1 '- pay attention /to/, - see /to/; - be careful, - watch out /FOR/'; /A/ eğil- 4 '- concern oneself /WITH/ [a subject, topic]'; /{tarafından/CA}/ görül- 3 '- be taken care of, attended to, dealt with, handled [affairs, matters] /by/'; /1A/ ilgilen- 2 '- show concern /FOR/ sth, - be concerned /with/; - attend /TO/, - look /AFTER/'; izle- 2 '- observe, - follow, - monitor, - keep abreast of [developments, events, fashions]'; kapıya bak- '- get or - answer θ the door' → bak- 3; /1A/ meşgul ol- 2 '- be concerned /with/, - take an interest /IN/' → ol- 12; takip et- 2 '- observe, - follow, - monitor, - keep abreast of [developments, events, fashions]'; telefona {bak-/cevap ver-} '- get, - pick up, or - answer θ the phone' → bak- 3, ver- 1; telefonu aç-. Same. → aç- 5.

982:6 - heed /A/ dikkat et- 2 '- notice /θ/, - observe /θ/, - take note /OF/'; farket- 1 '- notice, - observe, - perceive, - realize'; farkına var- '- notice, - become aware /OF/, - realize'; gözle- 1 '- notice, - observe [that sth is true]'.

727

982:8 - pay attention /A/ **dikkatini topla-** '- concentrate, - focus or - concentrate one's attention /ON/' → topla- 1.

982:10 - call attention to /A/ **dikkat çek-** '- call or - draw attention /to/, - refer /to/, - point out /Ө/, - note /Ө/ [obj.: a fact]' → çek- 1; **el kaldır-** 1 '- raise one's hand', to get permission to talk in various circumstances, to get a teacher's attention at the university level. → kaldır- 1; **işaret et-** 1 /I/ '- point out, - indicate [sb or sth, not a fact, by means of a gesture]'. 2 /A/ '- point out /Ө/, - indicate /Ө/, - call attention /to/, - note /Ө/ [a fact]'; **parmak kaldır-** '- raise one's HAND [lit., finger, **parmak**]'. This expression is used like **el kaldır-** above, but is more common than that expression in schools below the university level. → kaldır- 1.

982:11 - meet with attention /lA/ **{dikkat/dikkati} çek-** '- attract attention, - catch the attention, - strike the eye /with/ [subj.: a resemblance]' → çek- 1; **dikkatini çek-** '- call sb's attention to sth, for sth - attract sb's attention' → çek- 1.

982:22 INTERJ. attention! {Baksana!/Baksanıza!} 'Look here!, Say', *informal:* 'Hey there!' → bak- 1; **Bana bak!** '[Now] look here! [lit., Look AT me]', an attention-getting formula frequent in warnings. → bak- 1; **Biliyor musun?** 'Guess what [lit., do you know?]', a phrase used to call attention to following words: **Başıma ne geldi, biliyor musun?** '{Guess what happened to me./Do you know what happened to me?}' → bil- 1; **{Haberiniz/ Bilginiz} olsun** 'Be {advised/ informed/aware} [that], Take note, Just to let you know, Is that understood?, OK?' → ol- 11 → olsun.

983 INATTENTION

983:2 - be inattentive atla- 4 '- miss out on news story, - miss a scoop'; /A/ **göz yum-** 2 '- close one's eyes /to/, - disregard /Ө/, - take no notice /OF/, - turn a blind eye to, - overlook /Ө/, - wink /AT/ a fault' → yum-; **gözden kaç-** '- be overlooked, not - be noticed, -

overlook, - escape one's eye or notice'.

983:3 - wander **dalga geç-** 1 '- let one's mind, attention wander, - be off in the clouds' → geç- 1.

984 DISTRACTION, CON-FUSION

984:6 - distract **dikkati dağıl-** '- be or - get distracted' → dağıl- 1; **meşgul et-** '...- disturb, - bother, - distract [people at work]'; **şaşırt-** 3 '- confuse, - distract, - make sb lose track or count of, - cause sb to lose track or count of'.

984:7a - confuse **şaşırt-** 1 '- surprise, - bewilder, - confuse, - catch off guard'. 3 '- confuse, - distract, - make sb lose track or count of, - cause sb to lose track or count of'.

984:7b - get confused {kafası/aklı} karış- '- get confused, mixed up [subj.: person]' → karış- 4; **şaşır-** 1 /I/ '- be confused, bewildered, at a loss /AS TO/ what to say or do, - be taken aback, bewildered /{AT/in the face of}/ an unexpected situation'. 3 /I/ '- confuse, - get confused /{about/regarding/as to}/, - lose track of, count of'.

984:8 * - be dizzy **başı dön-** '- be dizzy, - get dizzy' → dön- 1.

984:9 - muse {düşünceye/düşüncelere} dal- '- get or - be lost /IN/ thought, for one's mind - wander off, - give oneself up /to/ reverie, - reminisce' → dal- 2; **{hayale/hayallere} dal-** '- daydream, - start to daydream, - go off /INTO/ daydreams, reverie, - reminisce' → dal- 2. Same as 988:11. MEMORY: - reminisce.

985 IMAGINATION

985:17 - dream {düş/rüya} gör- 1 '- dream, - have a dream'. 2 '- imagine, - build up [usually vain] hopes concerning' → gör- 3; /a: hakkında, b: lA ilgili, c: A dair, d: üzerine/ **hayal kur-** '- dream, - build up fanciful hopes /a: about, b: concerning, c: {concerning/ regarding}, d: about/' → kur- 1; **kâbus gör-** '- have a nightmare' → gör- 3.

988 MEMORY

988:10 - remember | akılda kal- '- remain or - stick in one's mind, - recall, - remember' → kal- 1; akla gel- '- occur /to/, - think of, - remember' → gel- 1; bul- 4 '- remember, - have it' as in 'I have it', when one suddenly recalls sth forgotten, or in the sense of 'Oh, I know', when one suddenly discovers the solution to a problem; göz önünde tut- '- keep or - bear in mind, - remember, - realize, - consider' → tut- 2; {hatırla-/anımsa-} '- remember, - recall, - think of'.

988:11 - reminisce {düşünceye/düşüncelere} dal- '- get or - be lost /IN/ thought, for one's mind - wander off, - give oneself up /to/ reverie, - reminisce' → dal- 2; {hayale/hayallere} dal- '- daydream, - start to daydream, - go off /INTO/ daydreams, reverie, - reminisce' → dal- 2. Same as 984:9. DISTRACTION, CONFUSION: - muse.

988:12 - recognize | /DAn/ tanı- 2 '- recognize sb or sth /{BY/from}/'.

988:17 - memorize | ezbere bil- '- know from memory, by heart'; ezberle- '- memorize, - commit to memory, - learn by heart'; oku- 4 '- recite [without a text, from memory]'. See also 570:8. LEARNING: - memorize

988:20 - remind | /A/ benzet- 2 'for sb or sth - remind sb of sb or sth else; - remind /OF/ [i.e., one thing or person brings another to mind]'; /A/ {hatırlat-/anımsat-} 1 '- remind /θ/ sb, - cause /θ/ sb to remember a fact or event [I reminded him that we had met earlier.]'. 2 '- remind sb to do sth [Remind me to mail that letter.]'. 3 '- remind /θ/ sb of', the features of sb or sth bring a similar person or thing to mind: You remind me of my brother. 4 '- make think of, - bring to mind.' Here associations with places or events rather than similarities bring sb or sth to mind: That restaurant where we used to meet makes me think of you.

989 FORGETFULNESS

989:5 - forget | unut- '- forget'.

989:7 - be forgotten | akıldan çık- '- slip /θ/ one's mind, - forget' → çık- 1.

990 SUFFICIENCY

990:4 - suffice | /A/ dayan- 5 '- last, - hold out, - be enough /FOR/ [subj.: supplies, money]'; ihtiyaca cevap ver- '- meet a need' → ver- 1; ihtiyaç karşıla- '- meet a need' → karşıla- 2; karşıla- 2 '- cover, - pay; - be enough /for/, - meet a need'; /A/ yet- '- suffice /FOR/, - be enough /FOR/'; /A/ yetiş- 6 '- be enough /FOR/, - suffice /FOR/'. 8 '- keep up /WITH/, - keep pace /WITH/'.

991 INSUFFICIENCY

991:7 - want | /I/ ara- 4 '- miss, - long /FOR/ sb or sth absent'; /A/ hasret çek- '- long for, - yearn for, - miss /θ/ sb or sth absent' → çek- 5; /I/ özle- = ara- 4.

992 EXCESS

992:9 - exceed | geç- 1 '- exceed, - go beyond [obj.: speed limit], - outdo [The apprentice outdoes the master.]'.

992:10 - overdo | abart- '- exaggerate, - overstate, - make too much of'; büyüt- 2 = abart-. The words çok and fazla are used with many verbs to indicate a high degree. Çok '[too] much, [too] many, a lot' indicates both a large amount and excess: çok çalış- '- work {a lot/hard}' or '- work {TOO much/TOO hard}' → çalış- 1. Fazla 'too; too much; too many' usually indicates excess rather than simply a large amount: fazla çalış- 'work {TOO much/TOO hard}' → çalış- 1. Fazla, however, even for excess, is less common than çok. Both words may be used together in the form çok fazla to indicate even greater excess: çok fazla çalış- '- work {much too much/much too hard}'. Any one of the three choices above, i.e., çok, fazla, or çok fazla, may precede many verbs, but not all may be suitable with every verb. This dictionary, in addition to the examples above, has the following with these words as entries or as examples within entries: çok iç- '- drink too much, - be a heavy drinker'; {çok/fazla} iç- '- drink too much, - smoke too much, - overindulge [in drinking (ordinary liquid or alcoholic beverage) or in smoking]' → iç- 1, 2;

/{ArAk/ mAklA}/ <u>çok ol-</u> '- go too far, - overstep the limit, - be rude /BY...ing/' → ol- 12; <u>çok uyu-</u> '- sleep a lot, too much, - oversleep' → uyu- 1; <u>fazla ısın-</u> '- become overheated, - overheat [subj.: motor]' → ısın- 1; /için/ <u>fazla para al-</u> '- overcharge /for/' → para al- → al- 1; <u>fazla tahmin et-</u> '- overestimate [the importance, amount, number of]' → tahmin et- 2; <u>fazla yemek ye-</u> '- overeat, - overindulge [in food]' → ye- 1. Other verbs of excess without **çok** or **fazla**: /{ArAk/mAklA}/ <u>ileri git-</u> 2 = çok ol- → git- 1a; <u>su kaynat-</u> '- overheat [subj.: car]'.

993 SATIETY

993:4 - satiate /1A/ <u>doyur-</u> '- feed to satiety'; <u>karnını doyur-</u> '- get sth to eat, - have a meal, - eat, - eat one's fill, - fill one's stomach'.

993:5 - have enough /A/ <u>doy-</u> '- have enough /OF/, - be satisfied /WITH/ [mostly food but also other item or activity], - eat one's fill, - be full'; <u>karnı doy-</u> '- have one's fill, - have had enough [food]'.

994 EXPEDIENCE

994:3 - expedite one's affair **iş gör-** '- work, - do the job, - serve the purpose [subj.: machine]' → gör- 4.

994:4 - make shift, - make do /1A/ <u>idare et-</u> 2 '- economize /BY/, - make ends meet /with/; - manage /with/, - manage to get along /with/, - get by /with/ [very little money]'; /1A/ <u>yetin-</u> 2 '- make do, - manage /with/, - be able to manage /with/ [very little money]'.

995 INEXPEDIENCE

995:4 - inconvenience **zahmet et-** '- take trouble, - put oneself to trouble'; /A/ **zahmet ol-** '- be trouble, troublesome, an inconvenience /FOR/' → ol- 12; /A/ <u>zahmet ver-</u> '- inconvenience /θ/, - trouble /θ/ sb, - cause trouble /to/ sb, - put /θ/ sb out, - give trouble /to/ sb' → ver- 1; <u>zahmete gir-</u> '- go to trouble'.

996 IMPORTANCE

996:12 - matter /için/ <u>ifade et-</u> 3 '- be important, of value /{TO/for}/, - mean sth /TO/ sb', usually with a word of quantity such as **çok** 'a lot'; <u>şakaya gelME-</u> 'for

sth - be NO joking matter, - be serious' → şakaya gel- → gel- 1.

996:13 - value /A/ {önem/ehemmiyet} <u>ver-</u> '- attach, - ascribe, or - give importance /to/, - consider important, - value /θ/, - think highly /OF/' → ver- 1; /I/ <u>önemse-</u>. Same; <u>takdir et-</u> 1 '- appreciate, - value, - respect, - admire [sb's efforts]'.

996:14 - emphasize <u>altını çiz-</u> 2 '- underline, - emphasize' → çiz- 1; <u>vurgula-</u> 1 '- emphasize, - stress, - lay stress on', often with a noun object denoting importance or necessity. 2 '- accent, - accentuate, - stress, - put the stress on [a syllable, word]'.

997 UNIMPORTANCE

997:11 - be unimportant **farketME-** '- be UNimportant, make NO difference, NOT to matter' → farket- 2; <u>şakaya gel-</u> 'for sth - be a joking matter' → gel- 1.

997:12 - attach little importance to **aldırış etME-** 'NOT - mind, NOT - pay attention to, - disregard, - ignore'; **aldırMA-** '- ignore, NOT - pay attention /to/, NOT - care /ABOUT/'.

997:14 - trifle /1A/ <u>dalga geç-</u> 3 '- play around, - trifle, - dally /with/, i.e., not - take seriously [obj.: sb's affections]' → geç- 1; /1A/ <u>oyna-</u> 5. Same.

997:24 PHR. it does not matter **Farketmez.** 'It doesn't make any difference' → farket- 2; <u>olsa da olur, olmasa da</u> 'it doesn't make any differencce, it doesn't matter if it happens or not, it may happen or not', i.e., it's not important. → ol- 11.

997:25 PHR. no matter **Boş ver!** 'Forget about it!, Never mind.' → boş ver- 1 → ver- 1; <u>Canı isterse!</u> 'I don't care.' → canı iste- → iste- 1; {<u>Zararı/Ziyanı</u>} yok. 'No problem., It doesn't matter.' → ol- 3, Additional examples. b) 4. Miscellaneous additional examples.

997:26 PHR. what does it matter? {<u>Ne olacak?/Ne olmuş?</u>} 'So what [of it]?', i.e., It doesn't matter. → ol- 2.

998 GOODNESS

| 998:10 - do good | 2 **değ-** 1 /A/ '- be worth /θ/ [This rug isn't worth θ that much money.]'. 2 '- hit the spot [subj.: coffee when you are tired], - do good'; **et-** 2 '- be worth', often with words designating amounts [How much is this coin worth?]'; /A/ **iyi gel-** '- help /θ/, - be beneficial, good /FOR/, - work, - hit the spot [aspirin for a headache]' → gel- 1; /A/ **iyi git-**. Same. → git- 5.

1000-2000

1003 BLEMISH

| 1003:4 - blemish | **karala-** 1 '- deface with drawings, scribblings, graffiti'.

1007 PROTECTION

| 1007:18a - protect | /I/ **kıskan-** 3 '- be jealously protective of sb, - guard a woman zealously against any sign of disrespect, - guard especially against the attentions of another male, - love jealously'; /DAn, A karşı/ **koru-** '- protect /from, against/, - defend /against/'; /DAn/ **sakın-** 3 '- protect /from/'; /DAn/ **sakla-** 4 'for God - protect, - preserve, - shield sb /from/ [misfortune]'; /A karşı/ **savun-** '- defend /against/'; /A/ **sigorta yaptır-** '- insure /θ/, - take out insurance /ON/' → yaptır- 2; /A karşı, DAn/ **sigortala-** '- insure /against [sth], WITH [a company]/'.

| 1007:18b expressions to protect against misfortune | **Allah göstermesin.** 'God forbid!' → göster- 1; **Allah {korusun/ saklasın}.** 'May God preserve him [from misfortune].' → koru-, sakla- 4; **Allah yardımcımız olsun.** 'May God help us.' → ol- 3, Additional examples. a) 3. Selected examples...: olsun.; **Nazar değmesin.** 'May the evil eye not reach it', i.e., May God preserve it. Words used when making a positive statement about or praising sth or sb. → 1 değ- 2. Same as 1011: * 22. HINDRANCE: expressions to prevent misfortune.

| 1007:19 - care for | /A/ **bak-** 3 '- look /AFTER/, - take care /OF/, - attend /to/'; **Kendine iyi bak!** 'Take good care OF yourself!', a common farewell to a person departing for an extended period. → bak- 3.

| 1007:20 - watch | /A/ **göz kulak ol-** '- watch /{θ/OVER}/, - keep an eye /ON/', so that no harm comes to. → ol- 12.

1009 PROSPERITY

| 1009:7 - prosper | **mutluluklar dile-** '- wish /θ/ sb much happiness' → dile- 1.

| 1009:16 ADV. fortunately | **Bereket versin [ki]** 'Thank goodness, Fortunately' → ver- 1.

1010 ADVERSITY

| 1010:9 - have trouble | /DA/ **{güçlük/zorluk} çek-** '- have a hard time, difficulty, trouble /{θ/on/in}/, - experience adversity' → çek- 5; /DA/ **zorlan-** 3. Same.

| 1010:10 - come to grief | **felâket geçir-** '- experience or - live through a disaster' → gecir- 2; **kaza geçir-** '- have an accident, - be in an accident, - get into an accident [car, plane]' → gecir- 2; **kaza yap-** '- have an accident, - be in an accident, - get into an accident, - cause an accident' → yap- 3.

1011 HINDRANCE

| 1011:10 - hinder | /A/ **aklı takıl-** '- be preoccupied, obsessed /WITH/, lit., 'for one's mind - get stuck /ON/ a question, problem' → takıl- 2; **doğum kontrol hapı kullan-** '- be /on/ the pill, - use birth control pills'; /DAn/ **soğut-** 2 '- cause sb to lose love, desire, or enthusiasm /FOR/ sb or sth, - dampen sb's enthusiasm /FOR/, - put sb /off/ sb or sth, - cool sb /TOWARD/'; /A/ **takıl-** 1 '- get stuck, snagged, caught /ON/', a physical obstacle prevents further movement. 2 '- get stuck, hung up /ON/ a problem'.

| 1011:13 - stop sth | **bırak-** 4 '- leave sb alone, - stop bothering sb'; **durdur-** '- stop sb [thief], sth [fight, bleeding, game]'; **kes-** 4 '- cut out, - stop, - cease [obj.: noise, crying]'.

| 1011:14 - prevent | /I/ **engelle-** '- keep, - prevent, - hinder, - block'; **{kapa-kapat-}** 5 '- block, - obstruct [road]'; /A/ **mâni ol-** '- prevent, - hinder /θ/, - hold up, - detain' → ol-

12; /I/ **önle-**. Same; **önüne geç-**. Same. → geç- 1; **tut-** 3 '- detain, - hold up, - keep sb'.

1011: * 22. expressions to prevent unfavorable occurrences **Allah göstermesin.** 'God forbid!' → göster- 1; **Allah {korusun/ saklasın}.** 'May God preserve him [from misfortune].' → koru-, sakla- 4; **Allah yardımcımız olsun.** 'May God help us.' → ol- 3, Additional examples. a) 3. Selected examples...: olsun.; **Nazar değmesin.** 'May the evil eye not reach it', i.e., May God preserve it. Words used when making a positive statement about or praising sth or sb. → 1 değ- 2. Same as 1007:18b. PROTECTION: expressions to protect against misfortune.

1012 DIFFICULTY
1012:10 - be difficult **zorlaş-** '- become more difficult, harder'; **zoruna git-** 1 '- be difficult, hard for' → git- 1b.

1012:11 - have difficulty /A/ **aklı takıl-** '- be preoccupied, obsessed /WITH/', lit., 'for one's mind - get stuck /ON/ a question, problem' → takıl- 2; /DA/ **{güçlük/zorluk} çek-** '- have a hard time, difficulty, trouble /{θ/on/in}/, - experience adversity' → çek- 5; **hapı yut-** '- have had it; - be sunk, done for, doomed, in serious trouble', colloq.; **sıkıntı çek-** '- have difficulties, troubles, - suffer annoyance, inconvenience' → çek- 5; /A/ **takıl-** 2 '- get stuck, hung up, snagged /ON/ a problem'; /A/ **uğra-** 2 '- meet /WITH/, - encounter /θ/, - experience [usually a difficult situation]'; **yan-** 6 = hapı yut-; /DA/ **zorlan-** 3 = {güçlük/zorluk} çek-; **{zorlukla/güçlükle} karşılaş-** '- encounter or - experience /θ/ difficulty, - meet /with/ difficulty' → karşılaş- 3.

1012:12 - get into trouble **sıkıntıya gir-** '- get /INTO/ financial straits, financial difficulty'; **sıkış-** 4 '- get in a jam, - be or - find oneself in a tight spot, under pressure, in difficulty; - be hard up, short of money'.

1012:13 - trouble /A/ **zahmet ver-** '- inconvenience /θ/, - trouble /θ/, - cause trouble /to/, - put sb to a lot of trouble, - put sb out, - give trouble /to/ sb' → ver- 1.

1012:14 - cause trouble /A, DAn dolayı/ **{güçlük/zorluk} çıkar-** '- make or - create difficulties /FOR, on account of/, - make trouble /FOR, because of/' → çıkar- 7; **karıştır-** 5 '- be up to sth; - stir things up, - stir up trouble'.

1013 FACILITY
1013:7 - facilitate /A/ **kolaylık göster-** '- make sth easy /FOR/, - facilitate matters /FOR/, - help /θ/, colloq.: - give sb a break' → göster- 1.

1013:10 - go easily **kolay gel-** '- be easy, - go easily' in **Kolay gelsin.** '{Good luck with your work./May it {be easy/go easily/lit., ** come easy}', a polite expression one should say to anyone engaged in or about to engage in some usually demanding task. There is no common English equivalent. → gel- 1; **kolayına gel-** '- be easy for' → gel- 1; **kolayına git-** 1. Same. → git- 1b; **kolaylaş-** '- get or - become easy, easier [classes, lessons]'.

1015 BEAUTY
1015:15 - beautify /A/ **boya yaptır-** '- have /θ/ sth colored [obj.: hair]' → yaptır- 2; **makyaj yap-** '- put on makeup, - make oneself up' → yap- 3; **meç yap-** '- give sb hightlights, - put highlights, streaks of color, in sb's hair [hair salon process]' → yap- 3; / A / **{meç/röfle} yaptır-** '- have one's hair streaked, highlighted, - have highlights, streaks of color, put /IN/ one's hair [hair salon process]' → yaptır- 2; /A/ **perma yaptır-** '- have or - get a perm[anent] [wave IN one's hair]' → yaptır- 2; /A/ **röfle yaptır-** = meç yaptır-; **saçlarını yaptır-** '- have one's hair styled' → yaptır- 2; /IA/ **süsle-** '- decorate, - adorn /with/'; **süslen-** 1 /IA/ '- deck oneself out /IN/, - adorn oneself /with/, - doll oneself up /IN/'. 2 /IA, tarafından/ '- be decorated, adorned, embellished /with, by/'; /I/ **topuz yaptır-** '- have one's hair put in a bun' → yaptır- 2.

CLASS 15: SCIENCE AND TECHNOLOGY

1016 MATHEMATICS
1016:16 - number /I/ numarala- '- number, - assign a number /to/'.

1016:17 - calculate /A/ böl- '- divide one number /BY/ another'; /A/ bölün- '- be divided /BY/'; /1A/ çarp- 3 '- multiply /BY/'; /1A/ çarpıl- 1 '- be multiplied /BY/'; /DAn/ çık- 9 '- be subtracted /from/'; /DAn/ çıkar- 5 '- subtract one number /from/ another'; hesapla- '- calculate, - figure up, - add up [expenses]'; /I/ topla- 4 '- add one number to another'; toplan- 5 '- be added up [numbers]'.

1016:18 - sum up et- 3 '- amount to, - equal, - add up to, - make, - get', in mathematical operations; hesap çıkar- '- calculate the bill, - add up the bill, - figure up the bill [at a hotel or in a restaurant]' → çıkar- 7; tut- 7 '- amount /to/ [expenses, fare], - come to, - add up /to/, - total, - cost, - make'.

1018 HEAT
1018:22 - be hot sıcak bas- '- get or - become hot [weather]' → bas- 4.

1018:23 - smoke, - fume /DAn/ duman çık- 'for smoke - rise /from/, for embers or ruins - smoke' → çık- 3.

1019 HEATING
1019:17a - heat ısın- 2 '- warm oneself, - warm up [subj.: athletes]'; ısıt- 1 /1A/ '- heat sth, - heat up sth /{by means of/with}/, - warm up sth [obj.: food, house]'. 2 '- warm up' in the field of sports: obj.: one's muscles; kaynat- '- boil sth, - cause sth to boil'; kızdır- 2 '- make red hot [obj.: stove], - heat thoroughly'.

1019:17b - get hot araba sıcaktan su kaynat- '- for a car - overheat' → kaynat-; fazla ısın- '- become overheated, - overheat [subj.: motor]' → ısın- 1; ısın- 1 '- grow warm, - warm up, - get hot [subj.: weather, food, person]'; kız- 2 '- get hot [subj.: clothes iron, stove]'.

1019:19 - insolate güneş banyosu yap- '- sunbathe, - take a sunbath' → yap- 3; güneşlen- '- sunbathe, - sun oneself'.

1019:21 - melt /DA/ eri- '- melt [subj.: ice, snow], - dissolve /in/ [sugar in water]'; erit- '- melt, - dissolve, - liquefy [i.e., - cause to become liquid: obj.: Melt some butter.]'. Same as 1062:5. LIQUEFACTION: - liquefy.

1019:22 - ignite ateş yak- '- light a fire' → yak- 1; [{sigara/puro/pipo}] yak- '- light UP [{a cigarette/a cigar/a pipe}]' → yak- 1; yak- 1 '- light, - ignite, - set /ON/ fire, - set fire /TO/, - burn'.

1019:24 - burn yan- 1 'for sth - burn, - be on fire, - be burning; - burn up, down'. 3 /DAn/ '- get or - be burned, scorched, singed /{BY/from}/; - get a burn, - get scalded; - get sunburned'; yanarak öl- '- burn to death' → yan- 1.

1020 FUEL
1020:7 - fuel doldur- 1a) /I, 1A/ '- fill sth /with/ sth, - make sth full'. 1b) /I, A/ '- fill sth /WITH/ sth [lit., ** - fill sth /INTO/ sth]'.

1021 INCOMBUSTIBILITY
1021:7 - fight fire söndür- 1 '- put out, - extinguish [fire, cigarettes, oven, candle, lamps, stove, burners on top of stove]'; üfle- 2 '- blow out [candle]'.

1021:8 - burn out sön- 1 /DAn/ '- go out [fire, lights, candle, lamps] /because of/'. 3 '- become extinct [volcano]'; yan- 2 '- burn out [subj.: light bulb]'.

1022 COLD
1022:9 - freeze, - be cold buz kesil- '- turn INTO ice, - freeze', often suddenly as a result of fear or other strong emotion. → kesil- 5; /DAn/ don- '- freeze /{from/DUE TO}/, fig.: - feel very cold'; donarak öl- '- freeze to death' → don- 1; soğu- 1 '- get cold; - cool [down] [subj.: food on table]'; soğuk al- '- get a chill, - catch a chill', the early stage of a cold. → al- 3; soğuk bas- '- get or - become cold [weather]' → bas- 4; üşü- '- feel cold, - be cold, - get cold [subj.: person]'; üşüt- 2 '- get a chill, - catch a chill [subj.: person]', the early stage of a cold.

733

1022:10 - make cold | soğut- 1 '-cool sth down, - chill, - make sth cool or cold, - let sth cool, get cold'; üşüt-1 '- give sb a chill [subj.: air, weather]'.

1022:11 - hail | kar yağ- '- snow'.

1024 LIGHT
1024:23 - shine | parla- '- shine, - sparkle [subj.: sun, moon, stars, diamond ring, face]'; yan- 5 '- be on [light, electricity], - be burning [light]; - be a color [traffic lights only: The light is green]'.

1024:27 - grow light | açıl- 6 '- go on [lights$ lamps]'; yan- 4 '- go on [lights, lamps, bulb]; - turn [yellow, red, green. subj.: traffic lights only: The light turned yellow.]'.

1026 DARKNESS, DIM-NESS
1026:9 - darken | tutul- 4 '- go into eclipse [sun, moon]'.

1026:11 - turn off the light | {kapa-/kapat-} 2 '- turn /{off/out}/ or - switch /{off/out} [lights, electricity, lamps, computer, oven, stove, gas burner, radio, TV]'; /{tarafından/CA}/ kapatıl- 2 '-be turned or switched {off/out} /by/ [subj.: lights, lamps]'; söndür- 2 '-turn off [the light]'.

1026:12 - grow dark | güneş bat- 'for the sun - sink' → bat- 1; hava karar- 'for it [lit., the weather] - get or - grow dark'; /DAn/ sön- 1 '- go out [fire, lights, candle, lamps] /because of/'.

1031 ELECTRICITY, MAG-NETISM
1031:25 - electrify | aç- 2 '- turn or - switch on [electricity, light, radio, TV]'; /{tarafından/CA}/ açıl- 5 '- be turned or switched on /by/ [subj.: lights, lamps]'. 6 '- go on [subj.: lights, lamps]'; /I/ elektrik çarp- '- get an electrical shock [lit., for electricity - strike]' → çarp- 4; {kapa/kapat} 2 '- turn /{off/out}/ or - switch /{off/out} [lights, electricity, lamps, computer, oven, stove, gas burner, radio, TV]'; kapan- 2 '- go off [subj.: lights, lamps]'; /{tarafından/CA}/ kapatıl- 2 '- be turned or switched /{off/out}/ /by/ [subj.: lights, lamps]'; söndür- 2 '- turn off [obj.: electricity, oven, the lights, the lamps,

the stove, not radio, television]'; yak- 3 '- turn or - switch on [obj.: electricity, light, lamp, but not radio, TV]'.

1033 RADIO
1033:25 - broadcast | /DAn/ yayımla- 2 '- broadcast /ON/ radio or television'; /DAn/ yayımlan- 2 '- air, - be aired, carried, broadcast, - be on [radio or television]'.

1034 TELEVISION
1034:14 - televise | Same as 1033:25. RADIO: - broadcast.

1041 COMPUTER SCIENCE
1041:18 - computerize | /A/ bağlan- 3 '- connect oneself /to/, - log on /to/ [the Internet]'; çök- 5 '[for a system] - fail, - crash, - break down, - be down [computer]'; /A/ eriş- 4 '- access /θ/, - gain access /to/, - get /{to [a source of informtion]/ON [the Internet]}/'; /DA, arasında/ gezin- 2 '-browse, - surf [/on/ the Internet], - scan, - flip /through/ [TV channels]'; /DAn, A/ indir- 1 '...- download /from, to/'; internete bağlan- '- log on /to/ the Internet' → bağlan- 3; internetten çık- '- log off, - get off /θ/ the Internet' → çık- 1; /DAn, A/ kopyala- '- copy [documents, files, disks, drives] /from, to/...'; /A, için/ programla- 2 '- set an instrument /FOR/, - program a computer /FOR/'. 3 '- develop or - create computer materials or games'; /{I/A/ üzerine}/ tıkla- '- click /ON/'. Both the accusative and dative case suffixes occur. The accusative tends to be preferred.

1042 FRICTION
1042:6 - rub | okşa- '- caress, - stroke, - fondle, - pat, - pet'; sev- 2 '- fondle, - caress, - pet'. Same as 73:8. TOUCH: - stroke.

1044 HARDNESS, RIGIDITY
1044:7 - harden | taş kesil- '- turn into stone', often of a person, suddenly as a result of fear or other strong emotion. → kesil- 5.

1044:9 - stiffen | /DAn/ tutul- 5 'for a part of one's body [neck, back] - get stiff /from/ [sitting too long]'.

1045 SOFTNESS, PLIANCY

1045:6 - soften yoğur- '- knead [dough]'.

1047 TOUGHNESS

1047:3 - toughen /I/ çek- 5 '- endure, - suffer, - put up with, - go through', often with nouns indicating difficulty, trouble; /A/ {dayan-/katlan-} '- put up /WITH/, - bear /θ/, - stand /θ/, - tolerate /θ/, - endure /θ/, - suffer /θ/, - take /θ/ [heat]' → dayan- 3, katlan- 2; /A/ tahammül et-. Same, *more formal, less current*.

1049 POWDERINESS, CRUMBLNESS

1049:9 - pulverize ez- '- crush, - mash, - grind, - pulverize'; rendele- '- grate [vegetables, cheese]'.

1054 OILS, LUBRICANTS

1054:8 - oil yağla- '- grease, - oil'.

1062 LIQUEFACTION

1062:5 - liquefy /DA/ eri- '- melt [subj.: ice, snow], - dissolve /in/ [sugar in water]'; erit- '- melt, - dissolve, - liquefy [i.e., - cause to become liquid: Melt some butter.]'. Same as 1019:21. HEATING: - melt.

1063 MOISTURE

1063:11 - be damp ıslan- '- get wet'.

1063:12 - moisten altına kaçır- '- wet or - soil one's underclothes or bed' → kaçır- 2; altını ıslat-. Same; ıslat- '- wet, - make wet, - moisten'; /A/ su ver- '- give water /to/ [people, plants, animals], - water [plants, animals]' → ver- 1; /I/ sula- '- water, - give water /to/ [plants, animals]'.

1063:13 - soak sırılsıklam ıslan- '- get {drenched/soaked} [person in rain]'.

1064 DRYNESS

1064:6a - dry, - make dry /lA/ kurula- '- dry, - wipe dry /with/'; kurulan- 1 /{tarafından/CA}/ '- be dried /by/'. 2 /lA/ '- dry oneself /with/'; kurut- '- dry, - make dry [hair, laundry]'; /lA, A/ sil- 1 '- wipe up, - wipe away, - wipe /with, {IN/ON}/; - dry [sth wet with sth dry: hands /ON/ [towel]'.

1064:6b - dry, - become dry kuru- 1 '- dry, - get dry, - become dry [The laundry has dried.]'. 2 '- dry up, - wither'.

1065 VAPOR, GAS

1065:8 - vaporize buharlaş- '- turn into steam, - vaporize, - evaporate'.

1067 AGRICULTURE

1067:16 - farm yetiş- 7 '- be grown [crops], - be raised [crops, animals]', on a farm.

1067:18 - plant /A/ 2 dik- 1 '- plant [plants, saplings, seedlings, not seeds] /IN/ [garden]'; /A/ ek- '- sow, - plant [seeds, not plants, seedlings, saplings, trees] /IN/ [fields]'.

1067:19 - harvest /lA/ biç- 2 '- reap, - mow /with/'; /DAn/ {kopar-/kopart-} 1 '- pick, - pluck [fruit] /{from/OFF}/ [trees]'.

1068 ANIMAL HUSBANDRY

1068:6 - raise besle- 2 '- raise [animals], - keep [animals, pets]'; üret- 2 '- raise [animals, vegetables on a farm]'; yetiş- 7 '- be grown [crops], - be raised [crops, animals]', on a farm; yetiştir- 1 '- grow [crops], - raise [crops, animals]'.

1068:7 - tend /A/ su ver- '- give water /to/ [people, plants, animals], - water [plants, animals]' → ver- 1; /I/ sula- '- water, - give water /to/ [plants, animals]'.

1072 ROCKETRY, MISSILERY

1072:13 - launch /A, A doğru/ fırlat- '- hurl, - fling, - throw /{AT/to/INTO}, toward/; - launch [rocket] /INTO/ [space]'.

PART 4.
PROVERBS IN
THE TURKISH-ENGLISH
DICTIONARY OF VERBS

PART 4. PROVERBS IN THE TURKISH-ENGLISH DICTIONARY OF VERBS

The approximately 250 proverbs in our dictionary are listed below alphabetically by first word. With this list you can determine if our dictionary includes a particular proverb and find other useful examples of the verbs in it. In each proverb below the stems of the verbs under which it appears in our dictionary are underlined. For example, the first proverb below is found under the verbs **güven-** and **kal-**.

All the verbs in a proverb may not be underlined since all the verbs in a given proverb may not appear as entries in our dictionary at all or may not appear in all the entries where they could appear. If a proverb appears under a meaning other than the first in our dictionary, that verb and the number of that meaning of that verb follow the proverb. For example, the third proverb below appears under the sixth meaning of **karış-**.

Many proverbs are cross-referenced to other proverbs of related meaning also in our dictionary.

- A -

Ablasına güvenen kız kocasız kalmış. 'The girl that trusted her elder sister remained without a husband.', i.e., Don't rely on those who want the same thing you do.

Acele giden ecele gider. 'He who goes in haste goes to [his] death.' → the following item.

Acele işe şeytan karışır. 'The devil gets involved in work hastily done [lit., hasty work].' Haste makes waste. → karış- 6. → the preceding item.

Acıyı tatmayan tatlıyı anlamaz. 'He who has not tasted the bitter will not appreciate [lit., understand] the sweet.'

Aç ayı oynamaz. 'A hungry bear won't dance.' → oyna- 4.

Aç elini kora sokar. 'A hungry person will [even] stick his hands into glowing embers.', i.e., A person will go to great lengths to satisfy a pressing need. Desperate times call for desperate measures. → Denize düşen yılana sarılır.

Adam kızmayınca belli olmaz. 'A man cannot be known [lit., ** become clear] unless he gets angry.'

Adama dayanma ölür, ağaca dayanma kurur, duvara dayanma yıkılır. Hakk'a dayan! 'Don't rely on a person, he will die; don't lean against a tree, it will wither; don't lean against a wall, it will collapse. Rely upon God!' → dayan- 2, yıkıl- 2.

Ağaç dikmek bir evlât yetiştirmek kadar hayırlıdır. 'To plant a tree is as blessed as to raise a child.' → 2 dik- 1, yetiştir- 2.

Ağaç kökünden {kurur/yıkılır}. 'A tree {dries up/{collapses/topples}} from its roots.', i.e., A thing can't endure if its central core is destroyed. → kuru- 2, yıkıl- 2. → Balık baştan kokar.

Ağaç ne kadar uzasa göğe {ermez./ulaşmaz.} 'No matter how tall a tree grows, it never reaches the sky.', i.e., No one keeps improving his status forever.

Ağaran baş, ağlayan göz gizlenmez. 'The head that is turning white, the eye that is weeping cannot be [lit., aren't] hidden.', i.e., Age and sorrow cannot be hidden. → gizlen- 2.

Ağlamayan çocuğa meme vermezler. 'One doesn't [lit., They don't] {nurse /lit., give the breast to} a child that doesn't cry.' The squeaky wheel gets the oil. → meme ver- → ver- 1.

Akacak kan damarda durmaz. 'The blood that is going to spill will not stay in the vein.' → dur- 6. → Allah

739

kulunu kısmeti ile yaratır., Alna yazılan başa gelir.

Akarsu çukurunu kendi kazar. 'Running water cuts its own channel [lit., cuts its channel itself].', i.e., An enterprising person creates his own oppportunities.

Akıl para ile satılmaz. 'Wisdom is not [i.e., cannot be] sold for money.'

Akıl yanılır, kalem yanılmaz. 'The mind may be mistaken, but the pen never is.', i.e., The memory may fail, but what is written down is not forgotten. → Alim unutmuş, kalem unutmamış.

Akıllı bildiğini söyler, deli söylediğini bilmez. 'An intelligent person says what he knows, but a fool doesn't know what he [himself] says.' → bil- 1.1.

Akılsız başın cezasını ayaklar çeker. 'The feet will suffer punishment for an empty [i.e., brainless] head.', i.e., The feet will be forced to do unnecessary walking. → cezasını çek- → çek- 5.

Akşam kavur, sabah savur. 'Cook [lit., fry] it at night, use it up in the morning.', a reference to sb who uses up all that he obtains.

Alçacık eşeğe herkes biner. 'Everyone can ride [lit., rides] a very low donkey.', i.e., Everyone takes advantage of a timid person. → bin- 2.

Aldatayım diyen aldanır. 'He who intends to deceive is deceived [lit., The one who says let me deceive is deceived].'

Aldığını veren aradığını bulur. 'He who returns what he borrows [lit., what he takes] will find what he seeks.'

Alim unutmuş, kalem unutmamış. 'The scholar forgot, but the pen did not.', i.e., A fact is preserved only if it is written down. → unut- b). → Akıl yanılır, kalem yanılmaz.

Allah doğru yoldan ayırmasın. 'May God not lead us astray [lit., ** separate (us) from the true path].'

Allah evlenenle ev yapana yardım eder. 'God helps those who marry and build a house.'

→ yardım et-.

Allah gümüş kapıyı kaparsa altın kapıyı açar. 'If God closes the silver door, He opens the golden door.', i.e., Don't be discouraged: a better opportunity may follow one lost. → {kapa-/kapat-}. → Bir kapı kapanırsa bin kapı açılır.

Allah imhal eder, ihmal etmez. 'God may delay [i.e., His punishment or reward], but He never fails to provide {one/it}.'

Allah kimseye kaldıramayacağı yük vermez. 'God never gives anyone a load [that] he cannot bear.' → Allah uçamayan kuşa alçacık dal verir.

Allah kulunu kısmeti ile yaratır. 'God creates His servant [i.e., any will-possessing being, mortal] together with his fate.' → Akacak kan damarda durmaz., Alna yazılan başa gelir.

Allah uçamayan kuşa alçacık dal verir. 'God gives a bird that cannot fly a very low branch.' → Allah kimseye kaldıramayacağı yük vermez.

Allah yardım ederse kuluna, her işi girer yoluna. 'If God helps His servant [i.e., any will-possessing being, mortal], every task [that the servant undertakes] will go well [lit., ** will enter its path].' → yoluna gir-.

Allah'a inanmayana kul da inanmaz. 'A servant of God [i.e., any will-possessing being, mortal] does not believe the person who does not believe IN God.' → inan- 3.

Alna yazılan başa gelir. 'What is written on the forehead will come to pass.', i.e., One can't escape one's fate. → başına gel- → gel- 1. → Akacak kan damarda durmaz., Allah kulunu kısmeti ile yaratır.

Altın yumurtlayan tavuğu kesmezler. 'One doesn't [lit., they don't] kill the goose that lays the golden egg.' → kes- 2. → Kılıç kınını kesmez., Köpek sahibini ısırmaz., Veren eli kimse kesmez.

Arayan Mevlâsını da bulur, belâsını da. 'He who seeks will find either his Lord or his calamity.', i.e., A person will find whatever he seeks.

Arı kızdıranı sokar. 'A bee stings the person who angers it.', i.e., A person will lash out at his tormenter even if he himself will also suffer as a result. → kızdır- 1, sok- 3.

Arpa eken buğday biçmez. 'He who sows barley will not reap wheat.' → biç- 2.

Aşağı tükürsen sakal, yukarı tükürsen bıyık. '{I'm between a rock and a hard place./Damned if you do; damned if you don't.} [lit., If you spit downwards (you get it in your) beard, if you spit upwards (you get it in your) moustache].'

Aşağıda oturmazsan yukarıda da yerin yoktur. 'If you can't sit down below, you'll have no place above either.' → otur- 2.

At çalındıktan sonra ahırın kapısını kapatmak {boşunadır/beyhudedir}. 'After the horse has been stolen, it is useless to close the door of the barn.' To lock the barn door after the horse is gone. → Atı alan Üsküdarı geçti., Atılan ok geri dönmez., Ok yaydan çıktı.

Ateş düştüğü yeri yakar. 'A fire burns [only] the place where it falls.', i.e., A calamity really affects only its immediate victims.

Ateş olmayan yerden duman çıkmaz. 'Smoke does not appear from a place where there is no fire.' Where there's smoke there's fire. → çık- 3.

Atı alan Üsküdarı geçti. 'The one who has {taken/stolen} the horse has already gone beyond Üsküdar [i.e., a section of Istanbul].', i.e., It's too late. → At çalındıktan sonra ahırın kapısını kapatmak {boşunadır/beyhudedir}., Atılan ok geri dönmez., Ok yaydan çıktı.

Atılan ok geri dönmez. 'The arrow that has been shot does not return.', i.e., What has been done cannot be undone. → dön- 2. → At çalındıktan sonra ahırın kapısını kapatmak {boşunadır/beyhudedir}., Atı alan Üsküdarı geçti., Ok yaydan çıktı.

Atın ölümü arpadan olsun. 'Let the horse die from eating barley [lit., Let the death of the horse be from barley].', i.e., from something that provides sustenance, pleasure. → ol- 11 → olsun 2.

Ayağını sıcak tut başını serin. 'Keep your feet warm, but your head cool.' → tut- 2.

Ayağını yorganına göre uzat. 'Stretch out your legs [lit., feet] according to [the length of] your quilt.', i.e., Act within your means, abilities. → uzat- 2. → Kaldıramayacağın yükün altına girme.

Az söyle, çok dinle. 'Say little but do a lot of listening.' → 1 dinle- 1.

Azmin elinden hiç bir şey kurtulmaz. 'Nothing escapes from the hand of determination.', i.e., Determination inevitably will bring success.

- B -

Bağla atını ısmarla Hakka. 'Tie up your horse [and then] entrust it to God.' → ısmarla- 3. → Deveni sağlam kazığa bağla, ondan sonra Allah'a tevekkül et.

Bahar gelmeyince bülbül ötmez. '{Until spring comes/As long as spring hasn't come}, nightingales do not sing.'

Bakarsan bağ olur, bakmazsan dağ olur. 'If you look after it, it will become a vineyard; if you don't, it will become a mountain [i.e., a barren area].' → bak- 3.

Balık baştan kokar. 'Fish begins to stink from the head [lit., stinks from the head].', i.e., Corruption starts at the top. → kok- 2. → Ağaç kökünden {kurur/yıkılır}.

Başa gelen çekilir. 'What happens to a person {will/must} be endured.' → başına gel-.

Başaran bal yer, başaramayan yal yer. 'The one who succeeds eats honey; the one who cannot succeed eats mash.'

{Bekleyen/Sabreden} derviş muradına ermiş. 'The dervish {who waited/who was patient} reached his goal.' Everything comes to him who waits.

Bıçak yarası geçer, dil yarası geçmez. 'A knife wound heals [lit., passes], a wound inflicted by the tongue [lit., a tongue wound, i.e., an insult, harsh words, etc.] does not.' → geç- 4. → Gider kılıç yarası, gitmez dil yarası., Gönül bir sırça saraydır, kırılırsa bir daha yapılmaz.

Bilmediğin işe karışma, bilmediğin yola gitme. 'Don't get involved in a matter you don't understand, and don't set out on a path you don't know.' → karış- 6.

Bilmemek ayıp değil, öğrenmemek ayıptır. 'Not knowing is not shameful, but not learning is [shameful].'

Bin bilsen de bir bilene danış. 'Even if you know a thousand [things], still consult an expert [lit., sb who knows (more)].'

Bir anda var olan bir anda yok olur. 'What exists one moment disappears the next.' Here today, gone tomorrow. → ol- 12 → {var/yok} ol- → b).

Bir bakmaktan, bir tatmak yeğdir. 'It is better to taste once than to look once.'

Bir çıplağı bin zırhlı soyamaz. 'One thousand armed soldiers cannot rob a single naked man.' → soy- 2. → Hiçbir şeyi olmayan hiçbir şey kaybetmez.

Bir çöplükte iki horoz ötmez. 'Two roosters won't crow on one garbage dump.', i.e., One master in a house is enough. → İki baş bir kazanda kaynamaz.

Bir işi bitirmeden başka işe başlama. 'Without having finished one task, don't begin another [task].' → the following item.

Bir işi bitirmeden [başka] bir işe koşma. 'Without having finished one task, don't {pursue/run after} another [task].' → the preceding item.

Bir kapı kapanırsa bin kapı açılır. 'If one door closes, one thousand doors will open.' → açıl- 2. → **Allah gümüş kapıyı kaparsa altın kapıyı açar.**

Bir ye de bin şükret. 'Eat one thing, but be grateful [to God] for a thousand.'

Bir yiğit ne kadar kahraman olsa da sevdiğine yenilir. 'No matter how strong a brave man may be, he will still be {defeated/conquered} BY his lover.' → 1 yenil-.

Biri yapar biri bozar, dünya böyle geçer. 'One builds; another ruins it. This is the way of the world [lit., ** thus the world passes].'

Boş durana şeytan iş bulur. 'Satan finds work for the idle [lit., for the one who remains unoccupied].' → dur- 6.

Boşanıp kocana varma, sevişip dostuna varma. 'Don't remarry the man you divorced, and don't marry the lover for whom you abandoned your husband.'

{Bugünkü işi/Bugünün işini} yarına bırakma. 'Don't put off to tomorrow what you can do today [lit., ** Don't leave {today's work} to tomorrow].'

Bükemediğin eli öp başına koy. 'Kiss and then place on your head the hand that you cannot bend back [i.e., as in arm wrestling].', i.e., Make peace with those you cannot defeat by force.

Büyük balık küçük balığı yutar. 'The big fish swallows the little fish.'

- C -

Cahilden kork, aslandan korkma. 'Fear θ the ignorant person, don't fear θ the lion.'

Can cefadan da usanır, sefadan da. 'One [lit., ** the soul] grows weary of suffering as well as of pleasure.' → {bık-/usan-}.

- Ç -

Çalışmakla her iş biter. 'With effort [lit., by working] every task is completed.', i.e., Success is achieved.

Çıkmayan candan ümit kesilmez. 'Where there's life there's hope [lit., ** Hope is not cut off from a soul that has not left the body].' → kesil- 3.

Çıngıraklı deve kaybolmaz. 'A camel that has a bell won't get lost.', i.e., A person who has distinguished himself won't be forgotten. → ol- 12.

Çiğnemeden ekmek yenmez. 'Bread cannot be [lit., is not] eaten without chewing it.' → 1 yen-.

Çocuk düşe kalka büyür. 'A child grows up by falling and getting up [again].', i.e., through experience.

Çok bilen çok yanılır. 'He who knows a lot [also] makes lots of mistakes.'

Çok gülen çok ağlar. 'He who laughs much weeps much.'

Çok okuyan değil, çok gezen bilir. 'It's not the one who has read a lot, but the one who has traveled {a lot/widely} that knows.'

Çok yaşayan bilmez, çok gezen bilir. 'It's not the one who has lived long, but the one who has traveled {a lot/widely} that knows [lit., The one who has lived long does not know; the one who has traveled widely knows].'

Çok yaşayan, çok görür. 'He who lives long {sees/experiences} much.' → gör- 3.

- D -

Dağ dağa kavuşmaz, insan insana kavuşur. 'Mountains do not meet but people do.', i.e., Mountains cannot move from their places to meet one another.

Deli ile çıkma yola, başına getirir bela. 'Don't set out on a journey with a madman, he will cause you trouble [lit., will bring trouble to your head].' → yola çık- → çık- 2.

Deli olan hediyeye sevinir, akıllı olan üzülür. 'A fool is pleased with a gift, an intelligent person is sorry.' This is because an intelligent person realizes that the receiver is obliged to reciprocate.

Delinin biri kuyuya bir taş atmış, kırk akıllı çıkaramamış. 'A certain fool threw a stone into the well. Forty wise men couldn't get it out.'

Deme kış yaz, oku yaz. 'Regardless of whether it's winter or summer [lit., ** Don't say winter or summer], keep reading and writing [lit., read, write].' → oku- 1.

Deniz kenarında dalga eksik olmaz. 'Waves are never absent from the shore.', i.e., Trouble is to be expected in certain places. → ol- 12.

Denizden geçti çayda boğuldu. 'He crossed the ocean but drowned in the brook.', i.e., {From/Out of} the frying pan into the fire. → **Yağmurdan kaçarken doluya tutuldu.**

Denize düşen yılana sarılır. 'A person who has fallen into the sea will {embrace Ø/cling to} [even] a snake.' Desperate times call for desperate measures. → Aç elini kora sokar.

Derdi çeken derman arar. 'He who has troubles seeks a remedy [for them].' → dert çek- → çek- 3.

Derdini saklayan derman bulamaz. 'He who keeps his troubles [to himself] won't be able to find a remedy [for them].' → the following item.

Derdini söylemeyen derman bulamaz. 'He who keeps his troubles to himself [lit., doesn't tell his troubles] won't be able to find a remedy [for them].' → the preceding item.

Dert derde benzemez. 'One {trouble/sorrow} does not resemble another.'

Dert gitmez değişir. '{Trouble/Sorrow} doesn't go away, it [just] changes.'

Deveni sağlam kazığa bağla, ondan sonra Allah'a tevekkül et. 'Tie your camel securely to a stake. Then entrust it to God.' → **Bağla** atını ısmarla Hakka.

Dibi görünmeyen sudan içme. 'Don't drink from [a source of] water, the bottom of which isn't visible.', i.e., Don't set out to do something for which you lack the necessary information or qualifications.

Dilini tutan başını kurtarır. 'He who holds his tongue will save his head.' → {çenesini/dilini} tut- → tut- 4.

Dini dinara satmak olmaz. 'One shouldn't sell one's religion [lit., the religion] for dinars.' [**dinar** a monetary unit]. → ol- 11 → olmaz.

Doğmaz doğurmaz bir Allah. 'God alone is the one who {is not born and does not give birth/does not beget and is not begotten}.'

Doğru söyleyeni dokuz köyden kovarlar. 'He who tells the truth will be run out of nine villages [lit., They will run the one who tells the truth out of...].'

Dost başa düşman ayağa bakar. 'A friend looks at [one's] head, an enemy at [one's] feet.' i.e., Always dress as well as possible because both those who know you and those who don't will judge you from your appearance. Or: A friend looks at the real nature of a person, while a person with evil intentions looks at one's shoes, the superficial aspects. Or: A friend looks one in the eye, while one's enemy averts his gaze and looks at one's feet. Or: A friend wants us to succeed, rise in the world, an enemy wants us to slip and fail.

Dost ile ye, iç; alışveriş etme. 'Eat and drink with a friend, but don't do business with him.', i.e., Don't mix business and friendship.

Dün öleni dün gömerler. 'They bury the person who died yesterday.', i.e., Forget the unpleasant features of the past.

Düşünmeden söyleme. 'Think before you speak [lit., Don't speak without thinking].' → Önce düşün sonra söyle.

- E -

Eden bulur. 'He who does sth will suffer the consequences of his action [lit., ** The one who does will find (the consequences)].' → et-.

Eğilen baş kesilmez. 'A head that bows is not cut off.', i.e., A person who is humble and obedient will not be cut down because he threatens no one. → eğil- 2.

Ekmeden biçilmez. 'Without planting, nothing is reaped.' Nothing ventured nothing gained.

El eliyle yılan tutulur. 'A snake is caught with someone else's hand.', i.e., Let someone else do the dirty work.

Eldeki fırsatı kaçırma, bir daha geçmez ele. 'Don't let the opportunity at hand slip away. It will not return [lit., ** pass INTO hand again].' → fırsat kaçır- → kaçır- 2.

Elin ile koymadığın şeye dokunma. 'Don't touch anything that you have not placed [there yourself] with your [own] hand.'

Elini versen kolunu kurtaramazsın. 'If you give him a hand, he'll take an arm [lit., If you give your hand, you won't be able to save your arm].' Give him an inch, and he'll take a mile.

Erken süpür, el görsün; akşam süpür er görsün. 'Sweep [your house] early for others to see [lit., let others see]; sweep it in the evening for your husband to see [lit., let the husband see].'

Erken yat, erken kalk. 'Go to bed early, rise early.' Early to bed, early to rise. → Gün ile yatan gün ile kalkar.

Eski kurt yolunu şaşırmaz. 'An old wolf will not lose his way.' → şaşır- 3.

Esmeyince kıpırdamaz. 'If there is no breeze [lit., ** As long as it doesn't blow], there is no movement [lit., it doesn't move].', i.e., There is a cause for everything.

Eşeği dama çıkaran yine kendi indirir. 'He who takes a donkey up to the roof takes him down again himself.', i.e., The person who creates a difficult situation has to straighten it out himself. → çıkar- 4.

Etme komşuna gelir başına. 'Don't do it to your neighbor; it [i.e., what you have done to him] will come back to you [lit., come to your head].'

Do unto others as you would have them do unto you. → başına gel- → gel-.

Ev yap, ev yıkma. 'Build a house; don't tear down a house.'

Ev yapan kadın[lar] da var, ev yıkan kadın[lar] da. 'There are women who make a home, there are women who wreck a home.' → Kadın var ev yapar, kadın var ev yıkar.

Evdeki hesap çarşıya uymaz. 'Calculations [i.e., about what things will cost] made at home won't be right for the market.', i.e., Plans made may not be realistic. → uy- 2.

Evvel zahmet çeken sonra rahat eder. 'He who first endures hardship will later enjoy comfort.'

- F -

Fala inanma, falsız da kalma. 'Do not believe in fortune telling, but have a fortune [told] anyway [lit., don't remain without a fortune].' → inan- 3.

Fırın kızmayınca ekmek pişmez. 'Bread won't bake {unless the oven is hot/as long as the oven is not hot}.' → kız- 2.

- G -

Gemisini kurtaran kaptan. 'It is the captain who saves his ship.', i.e., A qualified person will find a way out of a difficult situation.

Gençlik bir kuştur, uçtu mu tutamazsın. 'Youth is a bird: once it has flown away, you can't catch it [again].'

Gider kılıç yarası, gitmez dil yarası. 'A sword wound will heal [lit., go], but a wound inflicted by the tongue [lit., a tongue wound] will not.' This is the exact opposite of the English proverb 'Sticks and stones will break my bones, but words will never hurt me.' It reflects Turkish sensitivity to harsh words. → Bıçak yarası geçer, dil yarası geçmez. → also the following item.

Gönül bir sırça saraydır, kırılırsa bir daha yapılmaz. 'The heart is a crystal palace. If it is broken, it can't be [lit., it isn't] built again.' → kırıl- 2. → the preceding item.

Gönül ferman dinlemez. 'The heart does not listen to edicts.' → 1 dinle- 2.

Gönül kimi severse güzel odur. 'Whomever the heart loves that is the beauty.'

Gözünü budaktan sakınmayan bir yiğitti. 'He was a fearless young man [lit., a young man who did not shield his eyes from a (threatening) branch].' → sakın- 3. → Yiğit kısmı gözünü budaktan sakınmaz.

Gülme komşuna, gelir başına. 'Don't laugh at your neighbor [for what happened to him], it [i.e., the same thing] may happen to you [lit., ** come to your head].' → başına gel-, gül- 2.

Gülü seven dikenine katlanır. 'The one who loves the rose will put up with its thorns.' → katlan- 2.

Gün doğmadan neler doğar. 'All kinds of things may happen before daybreak [lit., (Imagine) what things are born before the sun rises!].' → doğ- 2.

Gün ile yatan gün ile kalkar. 'He who goes to bed with the sun gets up with the sun.' Gün is a less common equivalent for güneş 'sun'. → Erken yat, erken kalk.

Gün.e göre kürk giyinmek gerek. 'One must dress oneself in the fur appropriate to the day.', i.e., dress as circumstances require. → the following entry. Also: Zaman sana uymazsa sen zamana uy., Zamana uymak gerek.

Güne göre kürk giymek gerek. 'One must wear the fur appropriate to the day.', i.e., dress as circumstances require. → the preceding item.

Güneş giren eve doktor girmez. 'A doctor does not enter the house that the sun has entered.'

Güzele ne yakışmaz. 'Anything will look good on an attractive person [lit., What doesn't look good on a beauty].' → yakış- 2.

Güzelliğe kapılma, huya bak. 'Don't be {captivated/carried away} by

745

beauty, look rather at [a person's] disposition.'

- H -

Hamama giden ter<u>le</u>r. 'He who goes to a hamam [i.e., Turkish bath] will sweat.', i.e., A person must bear the consequences of his actions. If you can't stand the heat, get out of the kitchen.

{a: Hatasız kul/b: Kusursuz güzel} ol<u>maz.</u> 'There is no such thing as {a: a servant of God [i.e., any will-possessing being, mortal] without faults./b: a beauty without {faults/blemishes}.}' → ol- 4 → olmaz.

<u>Havlayan</u> köpek ısır<u>maz</u>. 'A barking dog doesn't bite.'

Hekimden <u>sorma</u>, <u>çek</u>enden sor. 'Don't ask the doctor, ask the one who is suffering.', i.e., the one who has experienced the pain. → çek- 5, → sor-b).

Her <u>çık</u>ışın bir <u>iniş</u>i var. 'What goes up must come down [lit., Every ascent has a descent].', often said in reference to a person's position in society. → çık- 5, in- 1.

Her derdin {devası/çaresi} vardır. 'There is a remedy for every care.' → ol- 3 → Additional examples. b), 3.4.

Her {işte/şeyde} bir hayır vardır. 'There is a good side to every matter.' Every cloud has a silver lining. → ol- 3 → Additional examples. b), 3.4.

Her koyun kendi bacağından <u>asıl</u>ır. 'Every sheep is hung by its own leg.', i.e., Everyone is held responsible for his own misdeeds. → **Herkes kendi çukuruna <u>gir</u>er.**, **Herkes kendi günahına göre <u>yan</u>ar.**

Her şey yerinde yak<u>ış</u>ır. 'Everything is appropriate in its [own] place.' A place for everythng and everything in its place.

Her şeyi <u>yaratan</u> ve <u>yok ed</u>en Allah'tır. 'God is the one who creates all that is and destroys it.'

Her zaman gemicinin istediği rüzgâr <u>es</u>mez. 'The breeze that a seafarer wants doesn't always blow.'

Herkes kendi aklını <u>beğen</u>ir. 'Everyone values [lit., likes] his own opinion.'

Herkes kendi çukuruna <u>gir</u>er. 'Everyone enters θ his own pit.', i.e., the pit that he has dug. i.e., Everyone is responsible for his own behavior and will get his just deserts. → **Her koyun kendi bacağından <u>asıl</u>ır.** → the following item.

Herkes kendi günahına göre <u>yan</u>ar. 'Everyone burns according to his own sins.' → the preceding item.

Herkesin geçtiği köprüden sen de <u>geç</u>. 'You [should] also cross {θ/OVER} the bridge that everyone crosses.', i.e., Do what most people do, even if it is not entirely to your liking. → **Rüzgarın önüne düşmeyen <u>yorul</u>ur.**, **Zaman sana <u>uy</u>mazsa sen zamana uy.**, **Zamana <u>uy</u>mak gerek.**

Herkesin tenceresi kapalı <u>kayn</u>ar. 'Everyone's pot cooks with the lid on.', i.e., Troublesome family matters should stay within the family.

Hırsızlık bir yumurtadan <u>baş</u>lar. 'Thievery begins with [the theft of] a single egg.'

Hiçbir şeyi olmayan hiçbir şey <u>kaybet</u>mez. 'He who has nothing loses nothing.' → **Bir çıplağı bin zırhlı <u>soy</u>amaz.**

Hocanın <u>dediğ</u>ini <u>yap</u>, yaptığını yapma. 'Do what the teacher says, not what he does.' Don't do as I do, do as I say. → yap- 2.

Huylu huyundan <u>vazgeç</u>mez. 'A person of a certain disposition doesn't give up his disposition.', i.e., Temperament tends to remain as it is. A leopard doesn't change its spots. → **Kurt köyünü <u>değiştir</u>ir, huyunu değiştirmez.**

- I -

Isıracak it dişini <u>göster</u>mez. 'The dog that is going to bite doesn't show its teeth.', i.e., doesn't give a sign that it will attack. Dangerous people often appear harmless, so beware.

- İ -

İki baş bir kazanda kaynamaz. 'Two [sheep] heads won't boil in one pot.', i.e., Two strong-headed people won't work well together. Too many cooks spoil the soup. → **Bir çöplükte iki horoz ötmez.**

İki köpek bir kemiği paylaşamaz. 'Two dogs can't share one bone.'

İnsan sözünden hayvan yularından tutulur. 'A person is taken hold of [i.e., controlled] by his {words/promises}, an animal by its reins.'

İnsanlar konuşa konuşa, hayvanlar koklaşa koklaşa [anlaşır]. 'People [come to understand one another] by speaking, animals by sniffing one another.' → anlaş- 2.

İs karası çıkar, yüz karası çıkmaz. 'The blackness of soot will come out; the blackness of face [i.e., dishonor] will not [come out].' → çık-11.

İstediğini söyleyen istemediğini işitir. 'He who says what[ever] he likes [lit., wants] will hear what he doesn't like.'

İş olacağına varır. 'What will be will be [lit., Matters will get to the place they are going to be].' → **Ok menziline varır.**

İşitmek görmek gibi değildir. 'Hearing is not like [i.e., as effective as] seeing.' Seeing is believing.

İyilik eden iyilik bulur. 'He who does good will be the recipient of acts of kindness [lit., will find goodness].'

- K -

Kabiliyetli çırak ustayı geçer. 'The capable apprentice outdoes the master.'

Kaçan balık büyük olur. 'The fish that gets away becomes the big one.', i.e., The thing missed is regarded as better than what it was.

Kadın var ev yapar, kadın var ev yıkar. 'Some women make a home, others wreck a home [lit., There are women who make a home, there are women who wreck a home'].', a proverb that notes the power of women for good or evil. → **Ev yapan kadın[lar] da var, ev yıkan kadın[lar] da.**

Kaldıramayacağın yükün altına girme. 'Don't take on a burden [lit., ** enter under a load] you cannot lift.' Don't bite off more than you can chew. → Ayağını yorganına göre uzat.

Kanaat tükenmez hazinedir. 'Contentment [with what God has granted] is an inexhaustible treasure.'

Kanatsız kuş uçmaz. 'A bird without wings can't [lit., doesn't] fly.', i.e., Qualifications are required for success.

Kapını iyi kapa, komşunu hırsız tutma. 'Close your door tight, and don't consider your neighbor a thief.'

Kavgaya katılma, bilmediğin işe atılma. 'Don't get involved in a fight, and don't venture into a matter you don't understand.' → katıl- 2.

Kaza geliyorum demez. 'An accident doesn't announce its coming [lit., doesn't say "I'm coming"].'

Kazanmak kolay, saklamak zordur. 'To earn is easy; to keep [i.e., what one has earned] is difficult.' → sakla- 3.

Kılıç kınını kesmez. 'A sword doesn't cut its own sheath.' → Altın yumurtlayan tavuğu kesmezler., Köpek sahibini ısırmaz., Veren eli kimse kesmez.

Kırkından sonra saza başlayan kıyamette çalar. 'He who begins the [study of the] saz after [the age of] forty, will play it on doomsday.', i.e., Don't waste time on frivolous things; life is short. → başla- 2, çal- 2.

Konuşmak okumaktan iyidir. 'Talking is better than {reading/studying}.'

Korkulu rüya görmektense uyanık durmak evladır. 'It is better to lie [lit., remain] awake than to have bad [lit., frightening] dreams.' → gör-3.

Korkunun ecele faydası yok. 'Fear is of no use against the final hour of death.', i.e., It will come when it is ordained. → ol- 3 → Additional examples. b), 4. faydası yok.

Köpek sahibini ısırmaz. 'A dog doesn't bite its master.' Don't bite the hand that feeds you. → **Altın yumurtlayan tavuğu kesmezler.**, **Kılıç kınını kesmez.**, **Veren eli kimse kesmez.**

Köpek suya {düşmeyince} {yüzmeyi/yüzmesini} öğrenmez. 'A dog won't learn {to swim} {unless it falls/as long as it does not fall} into the water.' Necessity is the mother of invention.

Körle yatan şaşı kalkar. 'He who lies down [i.e., keeps company] with a blind person will get up cross-eyed.', i.e., Beware of the company you keep.

Kul sıkışmayınca Hızır yetişmez. 'Elias will not come to help unless a servant of God [i.e., any will-possessing being, mortal] is in a tight spot.', i.e., Until the need arises, a person will not find a solution to his problems, said when unexpected assistance reaches a person in difficulty. Necessity is the mother of invention. → sıkış- 4, yetiş-4.

Kulun dediği olmaz, Allah'ın dediği olur. 'What God's humble servant [i.e., any mortal] says does not happen, what God says, does.' → ol- 2.

Kumarda kazanan aşkta kaybeder. 'He who wins at gambling loses in love.' Lucky at cards, unlucky in love. → kazan- 2.

Kurt köyünü değiştirir, huyunu değiştirmez. 'A wolf changes his village but does not change his nature.' A leopard doesn't change its spots. → değiştir- 2. → **Huylu huyundan vazgeçmez.**

Kusursuz dost arayan, dostsuz kalır. 'He who seeks a friend without faults will remain without friends.'

Kusursuz güzel olmaz.: → {a: Hatasız kul/b: Kusursuz güzel} olmaz.

- L -

- M -

Minareyi yaptırmayan yerden bitmiş sanır. 'A person who has [never] had a minaret built thinks that it has sprung from the ground.', i.e., like a plant. He doesn't realize the difficulties involved in the construction.

Misafir umduğunu değil, bulduğunu yer. 'A guest doesn't eat what he hopes for, he eats what he finds.', i.e., He can't be choosy. → {ümit et-/um-}.

Müflis {tüccar/bezirgân} eski defterlerini karıştırır. 'The bankrupt merchant leafs through his old account books.', i.e., recalls his past successes. → karıştır- 3.

- N -

Namussuz yaşamaktansa namuslu ölmek yeğdir. 'It's better to die honorably than to live dishonorably.' Death before dishonor.

Nasıl yaşarsak öyle ölürüz. 'However we live, so shall we die.'

Ne ekersen onu biçersin. 'You reap what you sow.' As you sow, so shall you reap. → biç- 2. → **Ne pişirirsen onu yersin.**

Ne ileri koş, ne geride kal. 'Don't run ahead, but don't stay behind either.', i.e., Be moderate.

Ne kadar yıkarsan yıka, kan kanla temizlenmez. 'No matter how hard you try [lit., how much you wash], blood cannot be washed away [lit., is not cleansed] with blood.'

"Ne oldum" dememeli, "Ne olacağım" demeli. 'One must not say, "This is what I have become", but rather "[Who knows] what I will become?"', i.e., One must not boast about one's present fortunate state, but keep in mind the possibility of future uncertainty. → ol- 1.

Ne pişirirsen onu yersin. 'You eat whatever you cook.', i.e., You get what you deserve. → **Ne ekersen onu biçersin.**

- O -

Ok menziline varır. 'The arrow will reach θ its mark.', i.e., What is destined will occur. → İş olacağına varır.

Ok yaydan çıktı. 'The arrow has left θ the bow.', i.e., It's too late to solve the problem. → At çalındıktan sonra ahırın kapısını kapatmak {boşunadır/beyhudedir}., Atı alan Üsküdarı geçti., Atılan ok geri dönmez.

"Olmaz! Olmaz!" deme hiç, olmaz olmaz. 'Don't ever say "{It's impossible, It's impossible/It won't happen, It won't happen}". This expression [lit., 'It's impossible.'] is not correct', i.e., Everything is possible. Never say never. → ol- 4 → olmaz.

- Ö -

Öfkeyle kalkan zararla oturur. 'He who rises in anger sits down with loss.', i.e., at a disadvantage to his own interests.

Ölmüş eşek kurttan korkmaz. 'A donkey that has died does not fear the wolf.'

Ölümü gören hastalığa razı olur. 'He who sees death will be content with illness.' → ol- 12.

Önce düşün sonra söyle. 'Think first, then speak.' Think before you speak. → Düşünmeden söyleme.

- P -

Para isteme benden, buz gibi soğurum senden. 'Don't ask {me for money/money from me} or I'll cool toward you like ice.' → iste- 2, soğur- 2.

Para parayı çeker. 'Money attracts θ money.'

Parayı veren düdüğü çalar. 'He who pays the money plays the whistle.', i.e., He who pays the piper calls the tune. → çal- 2, para ver- → ver- 1.

- R -

Rüşvet kapıdan girince insaf bacadan çıkar. 'When bribery enters through the door, {justice/fairness} leaves through the chimney.'

Rüşvet kapıyı vurmadan içeri girer. 'A bribe will enter without knocking at the door.' → içeri[.yE] gir-, kapıyı vur-.

Rüzgâr eken fırtına biçer. 'He who sows the wind reaps the storm.' → biç- 2.

Rüzgarın önüne düşmeyen yorulur. 'He who doesn't give way [lit., ** fall down] against the force of [lit., in front of] the wind will tire.', i.e., The person who resists the trends of his society will suffer the consequences. → Herkesin geçtiği köprüden sen de geç., Zaman sana uymazsa sen zamana uy., Zamana uymak gerek.

- S -

{Sabreden/Bekleyen} derviş muradına ermiş. 'The dervish {who was patient/who waited} reached his goal.' Everything comes to him who waits.

Sağır duymaz, uydurur. 'A deaf person doesn't hear; he makes up things.', i.e., He fills in with his imagination for what he can't hear. → uydur- 2.

Sakla samanı gelir zamanı. 'Save the straw, the time for it will come.' → sakla- 3.

Sanatı ustadan görmeyen öğrenmez. 'He who doesn't learn [lit., see, experience] the {craft/skill} from a master won't learn it.'

Sayılı gün[ler] çabuk geçer. 'Deadlines come to an end before you know it [lit., ** Numbered day(s) pass quickly].' → geç- 4.

Sel gider, kum kalır. 'The flood waters recede, the sand remains.', i.e., What is weighty remains.

Sev beni, seveyim seni. 'Love me, and I'll love you.' You scratch my back and I'll scratch yours.

Sırça köşkte oturan, komşusuna taş atmamalı. 'A person who lives in a crystal palace shouldn't throw stones at his neighbor.' People who live in glass houses shouldn't throw stones. → otur- 3.

Son gülen iyi güler. 'He who laughs last laughs best [lit., ** laughs well].' → gül- 2.

Sora sora Bağdat bulunur. 'By asking and asking, one finds Bagdad [lit., Bagdad is found].' Seek and ye shall find.

Söylemek kolay, yapmak {zor/güç}. 'It is easy to talk [i.e., about plans], but {difficult} to get things done.', i.e., Talk is cheap.

Söylemesi kolay, yapması güç. 'It is easy to talk about it but difficult to carry it out [lit., ** Its saying is easy, its doing is difficult].' Easier said than done. → yap- 2.

Su uyur, düşman uyumaz. 'Water sleeps [i.e., becomes motionless], but an enemy does not [sleep].', i.e., Be alert.

Sütten ağzı yanan yoğurdu üfleyerek yer. 'A person whose mouth has been burned BY [hot] milk blows on [his] yogurt [before] eating it [lit., eats the yogurt blow.ing on it].' Yogurt is usually eaten cold. Once bitten, twice shy. → yan- 3.

- Ş -

- T -

Tatlı dil bin kapı açar. 'A sweet tongue opens a thousand doors.' → the following item.

Tatlı dil yılanı deliğinden çıkarır. 'A sweet tongue will get a snake to come out of its hole.' → the preceding item.

Tatlı ye, tatlı söyle. 'Eat sweet things, speak sweetly.'

Tek kanatla kuş uçmaz. 'A bird with [only] one wing can't [lit., doesn't] fly.', i.e., Limited qualifications are not enough.

Tekerlek kırıldıktan sonra yol gösteren çok olur. 'After the wheel [of the cart] has broken, there are many people who will show the way.', i.e., There are always many people ready to offer advice when it's too late. → kırıl- 2, yol göster- 2.

Terzi kendi dikişini dikemez. 'A tailor cannot do his own sewing.', i.e., make his own clothes. → dikiş dik- → 1 dik-.

Tuttuğunu koparır. 'He plucks whatever he takes hold of.', i.e., He succeeds in whatever he sets out to do.

- U -

Ucuz alan pahalı alır. 'He who buys at a low price buys at a high price.', i.e., pays too much for what he gets. → al- 4.

Ucuzlukta alır, pahalılıkta satar. '{a: He buys low and sells high./b: He buys when it is cheap [lit., ** IN cheapness], and he sells when it is expensive [lit., ** IN expensiveness].}' → al- 4.

Ummadığın yer.den yılan çıkar. 'A snake [i.e., evil, treachery] will appear from the place where you least [lit., don't] expect it.' → çık- 3, → {ümit et-/um-} 2.

Ummadığın taş baş yarar. 'It is the unexpected stone [lit., the stone (that) you don't expect] that cuts the head.' → {ümit et-/um-} 2.

Utan utanmazdan, kork korkmazdan. 'Be ashamed of a shameless person and fear θ a fearless person.'

Uyuyan aslanı uyandırma. 'Don't wake up {a/the} sleeping lion.' Let sleeping dogs lie. → the following item.

Uyuyan yılanın kuyruğuna basma. 'Don't step ON the tail of a sleeping snake.' → the preceding item.

- Ü -

Üzümü ye de bağını sorma. 'Eat the grapes, but don't ask about the [lit., its] vineyard.' Don't look a gift horse in the mouth.

- V -

Vakitsiz öten horozun başını keserler. 'They cut off the head of the rooster that crows at the wrong time.' → kes- 2. → the following item.

Vakitsiz öten horozun başı kesilir. 'The head of a rooster that crows at the wrong time is cut off.' → baş kesil- → kesil- 1. → the preceding item.

Veren el alan elden üstündür. 'The hand that gives is {superior to/better than} the hand that takes.' It is better to give than to receive.

Veren eli herkes öper. 'Everyone kisses the hand that gives.'

Veren eli kimse kesmez. 'One does not cut the hand that gives.' → Altın yumurtlayan tavuğu kesmezler., Kılıç kınını kesmez., Köpek sahibini ısırmaz.

- Y -

Yağmur yağarken küpleri doldurmalı. 'One must fill the [water] jugs while it is raining.', i.e., take advantage of available opportunities. Make hay while the sun shines. → doldur- 1 a).

Yağmurdan kaçarken doluya tutuldu. 'While escaping from the rain, he got caught in the hail.' {From/Out of} the frying pan into the fire. → tutul- 6. → Denizden geçti çayda boğuldu.

Yalancının evi yanmış, kimse inanmamış. 'The liar's house burned down, but no one believed him.'

Yemeği uzun sürenin ömrü kısa olur. 'A person who spends a long time eating will have a short life [lit., ** The life of the one whose eating lasts long will be short].' → sür- 2.

Yenilen değil, hazmedilen besler. 'It is not what is eaten but what is digested that nourishes [the body].' → 2 yenil-.

Yenilen pehlivan güreşe doymaz. 'A defeated wrestler always wants to wrestle some more [lit., never gets enough of wrestling], i.e., never tires of a fight in the hope of eventually winning. → 1 yenil-.

Yetimi giydir, açı doyur, kavgacıyı ayır. 'Clothe the orphan; feed the hungry; separate those who are fighting [lit., the fighter].'

Yıkmak kolay, yapmak zordur. 'To destroy is easy; to create is difficult.'

Yiğit kısmı gözünü budaktan sakınmaz. 'Brave young men [lit., the brave young segment (of the population)] do not shrink from danger [lit., do not shield their eyes from a (threatening) branch].' → sakın- 3. → Gözünü budaktan sakınmayan bir yiğitti.

Yiyen bilmez, doğrayan bilir. 'It is not the one who eats [the food] that understands [i.e., what has been involved in producing it], but the one who has cut it up [i.e., prepared it].' → ye- 1.

Yol bilen kervana katılmaz. 'The one who knows the way doesn't join the caravan.' → katıl- 2.

Yol sormakla bulunur. 'The [right] {road/way} is found by asking.'

Yukarıya tükürme yüzüne düşer. 'Do not spit upward. It will fall [back] on your face.', i.e., If you insult those in a position above you, you will eventually suffer.

- Z -

Zaman sana uymazsa sen zamana uy. 'If the time is not suitable for you, adapt yourself to the time.' → uy- 5. → Güne göre kürk giymek gerek., Güne göre kürk giyinmek gerek., Herkesin geçtiği köprüden sen de geç., Rüzgarın önüne düşmeyen yorulur. → the following item.

Zamana uymak gerek. 'One must conform to the times.' → uy- 5. → the preceding item.

751

PART 5.
TURKISH VERB-FORMING SUFFIXES

PART 5. TURKISH VERB-FORMING SUFFIXES

Many entry verbs in the **Turkish-English Dictionary of Verbs** are followed by brackets enclosing the suffixes involved in their composition. This index groups these suffixes by the element that precedes them. Under A below are the suffixes that form verbs from parts of speech other than verbs. Under B are the suffixes that form verbs from existing verbs. Each suffix is followed by a list of the verbs containing that suffix, and most verbs are shown with the suffix separated from the root. In our dictionary we indicate the composition of an entry verb only when we regard the root of the verb as meaningful for the average linguistically untrained Turk. Thus this index does not include all verb-forming suffixes or all the verbs in our dictionary.

Below, verbs in brackets listed under a suffix are not included in our dictionary as entry verbs, but forms derived from the bracketed verbs are and will be found, without brackets, under the appropriate suffix. Thus [bir.le-] appears under A, under the suffix -lA and [birle.ş-] appears under B, under the suffix -Iş, indicating that neither of these bracketed forms appears as an entry headword in our dictionary, but the related form birleş.tir-, which is an entry headword in our dictionary, appears without brackets under B under -DIr.

A. SUFFIXES THAT FORM VERB STEMS FROM PARTS OF SPEECH OTHER THAN VERBS [ADJECTIVES OR NOUNS]

1. -θ. Verb stems formed without the addition of any verb-forming suffix: acı-, ağrı-, boya-, devir-, eski-, gerek-, göç-, güven-, iç-, imren-, inan-, kuru-, özen-, savaş-, taş-, tat-, yarış-, yer-, yüz-.

Verb stems formed by the addition of a suffix to the root word. The suffixes are listed alphabetically.

2. -A. A suffix no longer productive, i.e., no longer used to form new verbs. The related {adjectives/nouns} appear in parentheses if they are not the same as the root: boş.a-, dil.e-, harc.a- (harç), kan.a-, oyn.a- (oyun), yaş.a-.

3. -[A]l. A suffix that forms verbs relating to quantity or elevation. The related adjectives appear in parentheses: alçal- (alçak, k to l); ayrıl- (ayrı); azal- (az); boşal- (boş); çoğal- (çok, k to ğ); düzel- (düz); eksil- (eksik, k to l); kısal- (kısa); yüksel- (yüksek, k to l).

4. -[A]r. A suffix mostly added to adjectives denoting color. The resulting verb indicates the action or state of becoming or taking on that color. The related adjectives appear in prarentheses: kara.r- (kara), kız.ar- (kırmızı), sarar- (sarı).

Some verbs with this suffix do not refer to color: baş.ar-, deli.r-, iç.er-, ön.er-, yaş.ar-.

5. -[A]ş. A suffix added to nouns: yan.aş-.

6. -DA. A suffix added to words of onomatopoetic origin ending in r or l: fısıl.da-, kımıl.da-, kıpır.da-.

7. -I. In only a very few verbs: taş.ı-.

8. -[I]k. The related adjectives or nouns appear in parentheses: ac.ık- (aç), [bir.ik- (bir)], gec.ik- (geç).

9. -[I]msA. This suffix means '- regard, - consider, or - think of in a certain way': an.ımsa-, küçü.mse- (i.e., küçük- -k + -[I]msA). Another verb in our dictionary with the same suffix, gül.üm.se-, may not belong with the others above and within the

category of verbs formed from parts of speech other than verbs if it is formed from the verb gül-. In regard to it, Lewis [2000, 229] writes: "This -imse- may have been formed on the analogy of benim-se- and mühim-se- but is more likely related to the adjectival suffix -imsi..."

10. -[I]ştır. Intensifying suffix. [This is the reciprocal suffix -[I]ş + the causative suffix -DIr: ara.ştır-, at.ıştır-. For other examples with -DIr, see below: **B. Suffixes that Form Verb Stems from Verbs.**]

11. -lA. The most productive verb-forming suffix.

A: açık.la-, alkış.la-, an.la-, ayar.la-, azar.la-.
B: bağış.la-, bağ.la-, baş.la-, bayat.la-, bek.le-, beste.le-, [bir.le-], bomba.la-.
C: cevap.la-.
Ç: çaba.la-, çimdik.le-, çise.le-.
D: destek.le-, dış.la-, dilim.le-, doğru.la-, duru.la-, [duygu.la-], düzen.le-.
E: ek.le-, emek.le-, engel.le-, erte.le-, etki.le-, ezber.le-.
F: faks.la-, fırça.la-.
G: gece.le-, geri.le-, göz.le-, [güneş.le-].
H: harman.la-, hatır.la-, hav.la-, hazır.la-, hece.le-, hesap.la-.
İ: ihtiyar.la-, iler.le-, ilike.le-, imza.la-, ince.le-, ispat.la-, işaret.le-, iş.le-, iz.le-.
K: kara.la-, karşı.la-, kat.la-, kilit.le-, kira.la-, [kir.le-], kok.la-, kopya.la-, kucak.la-, [kuru.la-], kut.la-.
M: miyav.la-.
N: [nişan.la-], [nite.le-], numara.la-.
O: onay.la-.
Ö: ön.le-, özet.le-, öz.le-.
P: paket.le-, parça.la-, pat.la-, pis.le-, plân.la-, posta.la-, program.la-.
R: rahat.la-, rast.la-, rende.le-, resim.le-.
S: sabah.la-, sağ.la-, [sakat.la-], selâm.la-, sıra.la-, sigorta.la-, sol.la-, suç.la-, su.la-, süs.le-.
Ş: şişman.la-.
T: tamam.la-, tanım.la-, tasar.la-, tekrar.la-, temiz.le-, ter.le-, tık.lA-, tuş.la-, tutuk.la-.
U: ucuz.la-, uğur.la-, uygu.la-.
Ü: üf.le-, ütü.le-.
V: vurgu.la-.
Y: yağ.la-, yaka.la-, yalan.la-, yara.la-, yasak.la-, yavaş-la-, yayım.la-, yok.la-, yol.la-, yorum.la-, yudum.la-, yuha.la-.
Z: zayıf.la-, zor.la-.

12. -lAn. The reflexive AND passive of -lA. Listed below are only those verbs whose -lA form is no longer in use so that it would not be found above. That is, in such cases we are treating -lAn as a separate verb-forming suffix rather than as one formed from -lA. [The reflexive and passive of those verbs whose -lA form is still in use are found below under **B Suffixes that form verb stems from verbs, -[I]n, -n**]. The meaning of the verbs below is often '- become' or '- get into a certain state'.

A: [ad.lan-], akıl.lan-, ayak.lan-.
B: borç.lan-.
C: [ceza.lan-].
D: [değer.len-].
E: ev.len-.
F: fayda.lan-.
G: [görev.len-], gurur.lan-.
H: hasta.lan-, hava.lan-, heyecan.lan-, hız.lan-, hoş.lan-, hüzün.len-.
İ: ilgi.len-.
K: kaygı.lan-, kaynak.lan-, kir.len-, kuşku.lan-.
N: neşe.len-.
O: [onur.lan-].

Ö: öfke.len-.
P: paha.lan-.
S: sabırsız.lan-, ses.len-, sinir.len-.
Ş: şüphe.len-.
U: umut.lan-.
Ü: ümit.len-.
Y: yarar.lan-, yaş.lan-.

13. -lAndIr. The causative of -lAn. The forms listed here are those the -lAn forms of which are not in use and are thus not directly above. That is, in such cases we treat -lAndIr as a separate verb-forming suffix rather than as one formed from -lAn: cevap.landır-, ödül.lendir-, resim.lendir-.

14. -lAş. Originally the reciprocal of -lA, i.e., -lA + -[I]ş. The forms listed here are those the -lA forms of which are not in current use and are thus not found above. That is, in such cases we treat -lAş as a separate verb-forming suffix rather than as one formed from -lA.

14.1 Verbs in which -lAş means '- become, - take on the character of': buhar.laş-, fena.laş-, gerçek.leş-, iyi.leş-, kolay.laş-, kötü.leş-, uzak.laş-.

14.2 Verbs involving reciprocal action: [karar.laş-], mektup.laş-, merhaba.laş-, pay.laş-, telefon.laş-, toka.laş-, veda.laş-, yardım.laş-.

See also -[I]ş below under B. Suffixes that form verb stems from verbs, 3 Reciprocal verbs.

15. -sA: kap.sa-, önem.se-, su.sa-.

B. Suffixes That Form Verb Stems from Verbs

-[A/I]klA. A suffix that indicates repetitive or intermittent action: sür.ükle-, uyu.kla-.

The suffixes below appear in order under the following categories: {passive/reflexive}, reciprocal, and causative.

{Passive/Reflexive} suffixes

In sentences with a passive verb, that is, one with a passive suffix on the verb, the direct object of the corresponding active sentence becomes the subject of the passive sentence. The active verb: aç- '- open sth': Kapıcı kapıyı açtı. 'The doorman opened the door.' Aç- + pass. suf. -ıl = the passive verb aç.ıl- '- be opened': Kapı [kapıcı tarafından] açıldı. 'The door was opened [by the doorman].' The agent, here the doorman, is commonly omitted, but if present and a person, it occurs before the postposition tarafından 'by'. If the agent is an official body or group, it is more frequently followed by the suffix -CA: hükümet.çe 'by the government'.

Verbs with a reflexive suffix indicate an action done to or for the subject of the sentence and thus are often translated with a reflexive pronoun ending in 'self': himself, herself, itself: yıka- '- wash sth' + refl. suf. -n = yıkan- '- wash [oneself]'; giy- '- dress sb' + refl. suf. -in = giy.in- '- dress oneself, - get dressed', et- + refl. suf. -in = edin- '- acquire', i.e., '- get sth for oneself'.

The suffixes below may be both passive and reflexive. Each suffix is followed by the verbs in our dictionary that are formed with it. Each verb is preceded by an abbreviation indicating how that verb is treated there. The verb tartıl- appears below as '{pass./refl.} tart.ıl-', indicating that this verb occurs in our dictionary in the passive with the meaning '- be weighed', as in 'The child was weighed by the nurse', and that it also occurs in the reflexive with the meaning '- weigh oneself', as in 'The boy weighed himself'. Similarly, the verb hazırlan- appears below as '{pass./refl.} hazırla.n-', indicating that this verb occurs in our dictionary in the passive with the meaning '- be

757

prepared', as in 'The lesson has been prepared', and that it also occurs in the reflexive with the meaning '- prepare oneself' as in 'She prepared [herself] to go out'.

The {passive/reflexive} suffixes can also make a verb intransitive in another way. For example, açıl-, which appears below as '{pass./refl.} aç.ıl', occurs in our dictionary in the passive with the meaning '- be opened' as in 'The door was opened by the watchman', but it also occurs in another intransitive in the sense of '- become open', where the agent is not important as in 'The door opened and the man walked out.' Here one may also think of the door as opening itself or by itself.

-Il. After a consonant other than l.

A: {pass./refl.} aç.ıl-, pass. adlandır.ıl-, pass. aldat.ıl-, pass. as.ıl-,
    {pass./refl.} ayr.ıl- [ayır- + {pass./refl.} suf. -Il].
B: pass. bindir.il-, pass. bin.il-, refl. boz.ul-.
C: pass. cezalandır.ıl-.
Ç: {pass./refl.} çak.ıl-, pass. çarp.ıl-, pass. çektir.il-, pass. çık.ıl-.
D: pass. dağıt.ıl-, pass. defned.il-, {pass./refl.} dök.ül-.
E: pass. ed.il [iptal edil-, refl. eğ.il-, tasdik edil-, tehir edil-,
    telâffuz edil-], pass. eleştir.il-.
G: pass. gid.il-, pass. gir.il-, pass. göm.ül-, pass. görevlendir.il-,
    pass. gör.ül-.
İ: pass. iç.il-, pass. indir.il-, pass. in.il-, pass. isimlendir.il-.
K: pass. kapat.ıl-, pass. kap.ıl-, {pass./refl.} kat.ıl-, {pass./refl.} kes.il-,
    {pass./refl.} kır.ıl-,   pass. kızart.ıl-, refl. koy.ul-, pass. kurtar.ıl-,
    pass. kur.ul-.
Ö: pass. ödüllendir.il-, pass. öv.ül-.
R: pass. resimlendir.il-.
S: {pass./refl.} sarıl-, pass. sat.ıl-, pass. seç.il-, pass. sev.il-,
    {pass./refl.} sık.ıl-, pass. soy.ul-.
T: refl. tak.ıl-, {pass./refl.} tart.ıl-, pass. tasdik ed.il-,
    pass. tehir ed.il-, {pass./refl.} tut.ul-.
Ü: refl. üz.ül-.
V: pass. ver.il- [son ver.il-, toprağa veril-].
Y: {pass./refl.} yaz.ıl-, pass. 1 yen.il-, pass. 2 yen.il-, {pass./refl.} yık.ıl-,
    pass. yırt.ıl-, refl. yor.ul-.

An irregular passive: anlaşıl- [passive of anla-].

- [I]n, i.e.,

-n. After a vowel:

A: pass. ara.n-, pass. ata.n-.
B: {pass./refl.} bağla.n-, refl. boşa.n-.
D: pass. de.n-, pass. dışla.n-, pass. dinle.n-, pass. doğrula.n-, pass. döşe.n-,
    pass. duygula.n-.
E: pass. ertele.n-, pass. etkile.n-.
G: {pass./refl.} gizle.n-, refl. güneşle.n-.
H: {pass./refl.} haşla.n-, {pass./refl.} hazırla.n-.
I: refl. ısı.n-, refl. ısla.n-.
K: refl. kapa.n-, refl. kaşı.n-, {pass./refl.} katla.n-, {pass./refl.} kurula.n-,
    refl. nişanla.n-.
O: pass. onayla.n-.
P: {pass./refl.} parçala.n-, pass. postala.n-.
S: refl. sakatla.n-, {pass./refl.} sakla.n-, {pass./refl.} süsle.n-.
T: pass. tamamla.n-, {pass./refl.} topla.n-, refl. taşı.n-, pass. tutakla.n-.
U: refl. uza.n-.
Y: {pass./refl.} yarala.n-, refl. yararla.n, pass. yasakla.n-, {pass./refl.} yıka.n-,
    pass. 1 ye.n-.

-In. After an l: pass. al.ın-, pass. böl.ün-, {pass./refl.} bul.un-, pass. çal.ın-, [pass. nitele.n-].

After a consonant OTHER THAN l. Here the result is DIFFERENT from the passive: refl. çek.in-, refl. ed.in-, refl. geç.in-, refl. ger.in-, refl. gez.in-, refl. giy.in-, refl. gör.ün-, refl. ısın-, refl. kaç.ın-, refl. kalk.ın-, refl. sev.in-, refl. soy.un-, refl. sür.ün-, refl. yet.in-.

Reciprocal suffixes

Most Turkish verbs with a reciprocal suffix denote action "done by more than one subject, one with another or one to another" [Lewis 2000, 146] and are thus frequently translated with reciprocal pronouns such as 'one another, each other'. Some verbs with such suffixes, however, have other functions, as will be clear from the dictionary entries.

-[I]ş, i.e.,

-ş. after a vowel: anla.ş-, [birle.ş-], karşıla.ş-, kucakla.ş-, oyna.ş-, selâmla.ş-, zorla.ş-, tanı.ş-.

-Iş. after a consonant: bul.uş-, çarp.ış-, çat.ış-, döv.üş-, er.iş-, gel.iş-, gör.üş-, kalk.ış-, ol.uş-, öp.üş-, sev.iş-, sık.ış-, tart.ış-.

See also -lAş above under A. Suffixes that form verb stems from parts of speech other than verbs.

Causative suffixes

A causative suffix makes an intransitive verb transitive: değiş- '- change', i.e., '- become different' + caus. suf. -DIr = değiş.tir- '- change sth, - make something different.' It also forms a causative verb from a transitive verb, that is, it forms a verb that means '- cause or - allow sb to do sth, - have, - make, or - let sb do sth', etc.: çalış- '- work' + -DIr = çalıştır- '- have or - make sb work, - work sb, - allow sb to work', etc.

1 Regular causative suffixes

-Ar. Very limited use: çık.ar-, kız.ar-, kop.ar-, on.ar-.

-Art. This dictionary has no examples of a verb with this suffix.

-DIr. After a consonant. The most common causative suffix. After monosyllabic and polysyllabic stems, EXCLUDING polysyllabic stems ending in a vowel, l, or r:

A: aç.tır-, adlan.dır-, al.dır-, art.tır-.
B: bil.dir-, bin.dir-, birik.tir-, birleş.tir-, boz.dur-, buruş.tur-.
C: cay.dır-, cevaplan.dır-, cezalan.dır-.
Ç: çalış.tır-, çek.tir-.
D: değerlen.dir-, değiş.tir-, dik.tir-, dol.dur-, dön.dür-, dur.dur-.
E: evlen.dir-.
G: geliş.tir-, gerek.tir-, gez.dir-, giy.dir-, görevlen.dir-.
H: havalan.dır-, heyecanlan.dır-.
İ: ilgilen.dir-, inan.dır-, in.dir-, isimlen.dir-.
K: kan.dır-, kapat.tır-, kararlaş.tır-, karış.tır-, karşılaş.tır-,
      kavuş.tur-, kes.tir-, kız.dır-.
N: neşelen.dir-, nitelen.dir-.
O: oluş.tur-, onurlan.dır-.
Ö: ödüllen.dir-, öl.dür-, öt.tür-.
P: paylaş.tır-.
R: resimlen.dir-.
S: sal.dır-, sev.in.dir-, sinirlen.dir-, sön.dür-.
T: tabet.tir-, tanış.tır-.
U: ulaş.tır-, uyan.dır-, uy dur-.
Y: yakış.tır-, yaklaş.tır-, yap.tır-, yaz.dır-, yetiş.tir-.

-Ir. After a consonant. After twenty monosyllabic stems, of which our dictionary has thirteen: art.ır-, bit.ir-, doğ.ur-, doy.ur-, duy.ur-, düş.ür-, geç.ir-, kaç.ır-, piş.ir-, uç.ur-, vazgeç.ir-, yat.ır-, yoğ.ur-.

-It. After a few monosyllabic stems, most ending in **k**, of which our dictionary has the following: **kork.ut-, eğ.it-.**

-t. After polysyllabic stems ending in a vowel, **r**, or **l**:

A: acı.t-, anımsa.t-, anla.t-, atla.t-, ayır.t-.
B: başla.t-, belir.t-, bekle.t-, benze.t-, boşal.t-, boya.t-, büyü.t-.
D: düzel.t-.
E: eri.t-.
F: fırla.t-.
G: geber.t-.
H: hatırla.t-.
I: ısı.t-, ısla.t-.
İ: ilerle.t-.
K: kapa.t-, kayna.t-, kısal.t-, kızar.t-, kirle.t-, kopar.t-, kuru.t-.
O: oku.t-.
P: pisle.t-.
S: soğu.t-.
T: tanı.t-.
U: uza.t-.
Ü: üre.t-, üşü.t-.
Y: yansı.t-, yaşar.t-, yıka.t-.

2 Irregular causative forms

The corresponding NON-causative forms are in brackets: **dağıt-** [dağıl-], **emzir-** [em-], **getir-** [gel-], **göster-** [gör-], **kaldır-** [kalk-], **öğret-** [öğren-].